University Casebook Series

March, 1991

ACCOUNTING AND THE LAW, Fourth Edition (1978), with Problems Pamphlet (Successor to Dohr, Phillips, Thompson & Warren)

George C. Thompson, Professor, Columbia University Graduate School of Business.
Robert Whitman, Professor of Law, University of Connecticut.
Ellis L. Phillips, Jr., Member of the New York Bar.
William C. Warren, Professor of Law Emeritus, Columbia University.

ACCOUNTING FOR LAWYERS, MATERIALS ON (1980)

David R. Herwitz, Professor of Law, Harvard University.

ADMINISTRATIVE LAW, Eighth Edition (1987), with 1989 Case Supplement and 1983 Problems Supplement (Supplement edited in association with Paul R. Verkuil, Dean and Professor of Law, Tulane University)

Walter Gellhorn, University Professor Emeritus, Columbia University.
Clark Byse, Professor of Law, Harvard University.
Peter L. Strauss, Professor of Law, Columbia University.
Todd D. Rakoff, Professor of Law, Harvard University.
Roy A. Schotland, Professor of Law, Georgetown University.

ADMIRALTY, Third Edition (1987), with Statute and Rule Supplement

Jo Desha Lucas, Professor of Law, University of Chicago.

ADVOCACY, see also Lawyering Process

AGENCY, see also Enterprise Organization

AGENCY—PARTNERSHIPS, Fourth Edition (1987)

Abridgement from Conard, Knauss & Siegel's Enterprise Organization, Fourth Edition.

AGENCY AND PARTNERSHIPS (1987)

Melvin A. Eisenberg, Professor of Law, University of California, Berkeley.

ANTITRUST: FREE ENTERPRISE AND ECONOMIC ORGANIZATION, Sixth Edition (1983), with 1983 Problems in Antitrust Supplement and 1990 Case Supplement

Louis B. Schwartz, Professor of Law, University of Pennsylvania.
John J. Flynn, Professor of Law, University of Utah.
Harry First, Professor of Law, New York University.

BANKRUPTCY, Second Edition (1989), with 1990 Case Supplement

Robert L. Jordan, Professor of Law, University of California, Los Angeles.
William D. Warren, Professor of Law, University of California, Los Angeles.

BANKRUPTCY AND DEBTOR–CREDITOR LAW, Second Edition (1988)

Theodore Eisenberg, Professor of Law, Cornell University.

UNIVERSITY CASEBOOK SERIES—Continued

BUSINESS CRIME (1990)

Harry First, Professor of Law, New York University.

BUSINESS ORGANIZATION, see also Enterprise Organization

BUSINESS PLANNING, Temporary Second Edition (1984)

David R. Herwitz, Professor of Law, Harvard University.

BUSINESS TORTS (1972)

Milton Handler, Professor of Law Emeritus, Columbia University.

CHILDREN IN THE LEGAL SYSTEM (1983) with 1990 Supplement (Supplement edited in association with Elizabeth S. Scott, Professor of Law, University of Virginia)

Walter Wadlington, Professor of Law, University of Virginia.
Charles H. Whitebread, Professor of Law, University of Southern California.
Samuel Davis, Professor of Law, University of Georgia.

CIVIL PROCEDURE, see Procedure

CIVIL RIGHTS ACTIONS (1988), with 1990 Supplement

Peter W. Low, Professor of Law, University of Virginia.
John C. Jeffries, Jr., Professor of Law, University of Virginia.

CLINIC, see also Lawyering Process

COMMERCIAL AND DEBTOR–CREDITOR LAW: SELECTED STATUTES, 1990 EDITION

COMMERCIAL LAW, Second Edition (1987)

Robert L. Jordan, Professor of Law, University of California, Los Angeles.
William D. Warren, Professor of Law, University of California, Los Angeles.

COMMERCIAL LAW, Fourth Edition (1985), with 1990 Case Supplement

E. Allan Farnsworth, Professor of Law, Columbia University.
John Honnold, Professor of Law, University of Pennsylvania.

COMMERCIAL PAPER, Third Edition (1984), with 1990 Case Supplement

E. Allan Farnsworth, Professor of Law, Columbia University.

COMMERCIAL PAPER, Second Edition (1987) (Reprinted from COMMERCIAL LAW, Second Edition (1987))

Robert L. Jordan, Professor of Law, University of California, Los Angeles.
William D. Warren, Professor of Law, University of California, Los Angeles.

COMMERCIAL PAPER AND BANK DEPOSITS AND COLLECTIONS (1967), with Statutory Supplement

William D. Hawkland, Professor of Law, University of Illinois.

COMMERCIAL TRANSACTIONS—Principles and Policies, Second Edition (1991)

Alan Schwartz, Professor of Law, Yale University.
Robert E. Scott, Professor of Law, University of Virginia.

COMPARATIVE LAW, Fifth Edition (1988)

Rudolf B. Schlesinger, Professor of Law, Hastings College of the Law.
Hans W. Baade, Professor of Law, University of Texas.
Mirjan P. Damaska, Professor of Law, Yale Law School.
Peter E. Herzog, Professor of Law, Syracuse University.

UNIVERSITY CASEBOOK SERIES—Continued

COMPETITIVE PROCESS, LEGAL REGULATION OF THE, Fourth Edition (1990), with 1989 Selected Statutes Supplement

Edmund W. Kitch, Professor of Law, University of Virginia.
Harvey S. Perlman, Dean of the Law School, University of Nebraska.

CONFLICT OF LAWS, Ninth Edition (1990)

Willis L. M. Reese, Professor of Law, Columbia University.
Maurice Rosenberg, Professor of Law, Columbia University.
Peter Hay, Professor of Law, University of Illinois.

CONSTITUTIONAL LAW, Eighth Edition (1989), with 1990 Case Supplement

Edward L. Barrett, Jr., Professor of Law, University of California, Davis.
William Cohen, Professor of Law, Stanford University.
Jonathan D. Varat, Professor of Law, University of California, Los Angeles.

CONSTITUTIONAL LAW, CIVIL LIBERTY AND INDIVIDUAL RIGHTS, Second Edition (1982), with 1989 Supplement

William Cohen, Professor of Law, Stanford University.
John Kaplan, Professor of Law, Stanford University.

CONSTITUTIONAL LAW, Eleventh Edition (1985), with 1990 Supplement (Supplement edited in association with Frederick F. Schauer, Professor, Harvard University)

Gerald Gunther, Professor of Law, Stanford University.

CONSTITUTIONAL LAW, INDIVIDUAL RIGHTS IN, Fourth Edition (1986), (Reprinted from CONSTITUTIONAL LAW, Eleventh Edition), with 1990 Supplement (Supplement edited in association with Frederick F. Schauer, Professor, Harvard University)

Gerald Gunther, Professor of Law, Stanford University.

CONSUMER TRANSACTIONS, Second Edition (1991), with Selected Statutes and Regulations Supplement

Michael M. Greenfield, Professor of Law, Washington University.

CONTRACT LAW AND ITS APPLICATION, Fourth Edition (1988)

Arthur Rosett, Professor of Law, University of California, Los Angeles.

CONTRACT LAW, STUDIES IN, Third Edition (1984)

Edward J. Murphy, Professor of Law, University of Notre Dame.
Richard E. Speidel, Professor of Law, Northwestern University.

CONTRACTS, Fifth Edition (1987)

John P. Dawson, late Professor of Law, Harvard University.
William Burnett Harvey, Professor of Law and Political Science, Boston University.
Stanley D. Henderson, Professor of Law, University of Virginia.

CONTRACTS, Fourth Edition (1988)

E. Allan Farnsworth, Professor of Law, Columbia University.
William F. Young, Professor of Law, Columbia University.

CONTRACTS, Selections on (statutory materials) (1988)

CONTRACTS, Second Edition (1978), with Statutory and Administrative Law Supplement (1978)

Ian R. Macneil, Professor of Law, Cornell University.

UNIVERSITY CASEBOOK SERIES—Continued

COPYRIGHT, PATENTS AND TRADEMARKS, see also Competitive Process; see also Selected Statutes and International Agreements

COPYRIGHT, PATENT, TRADEMARK AND RELATED STATE DOCTRINES, Third Edition (1990), with 1989 Selected Statutes Supplement and 1981 Problem Supplement

Paul Goldstein, Professor of Law, Stanford University.

COPYRIGHT, Unfair Competition, and Other Topics Bearing on the Protection of Literary, Musical, and Artistic Works, Fifth Edition (1990), with 1990 Statutory Supplement

Ralph S. Brown, Jr., Professor of Law, Yale University.
Robert C. Denicola, Professor of Law, University of Nebraska.

CORPORATE ACQUISITIONS, The Law and Finance of (1986), with 1990 Supplement

Ronald J. Gilson, Professor of Law, Stanford University.

CORPORATE FINANCE, Third Edition (1987)

Victor Brudney, Professor of Law, Harvard University.
Marvin A. Chirelstein, Professor of Law, Columbia University.

CORPORATION LAW, BASIC, Third Edition (1989), with Documentary Supplement

Detlev F. Vagts, Professor of Law, Harvard University.

CORPORATIONS, see also Enterprise Organization

CORPORATIONS, Sixth Edition—Concise (1988), with 1990 Case Supplement and 1990 Statutory Supplement

William L. Cary, late Professor of Law, Columbia University.
Melvin Aron Eisenberg, Professor of Law, University of California, Berkeley.

CORPORATIONS, Sixth Edition—Unabridged (1988), with 1990 Case Supplement and 1990 Statutory Supplement

William L. Cary, late Professor of Law, Columbia University.
Melvin Aron Eisenberg, Professor of Law, University of California, Berkeley.

CORPORATIONS AND BUSINESS ASSOCIATIONS—STATUTES, RULES, AND FORMS (1990)

CORRECTIONS, SEE SENTENCING

CREDITORS' RIGHTS, see also Debtor-Creditor Law

CRIMINAL JUSTICE ADMINISTRATION, Fourth Edition (1991)

Frank W. Miller, Professor of Law, Washington University.
Robert O. Dawson, Professor of Law, University of Texas.
George E. Dix, Professor of Law, University of Texas.
Raymond I. Parnas, Professor of Law, University of California, Davis.

CRIMINAL LAW, Fourth Edition (1987)

Fred E. Inbau, Professor of Law Emeritus, Northwestern University.
Andre A. Moenssens, Professor of Law, University of Richmond.
James R. Thompson, Professor of Law Emeritus, Northwestern University.

CRIMINAL LAW AND APPROACHES TO THE STUDY OF LAW Second Edition (1991)

John M. Brumbaugh, Professor of Law, University of Maryland.

CRIMINAL LAW, Second Edition (1986)

Peter W. Low, Professor of Law, University of Virginia.
John C. Jeffries, Jr., Professor of Law, University of Virginia.
Richard C. Bonnie, Professor of Law, University of Virginia.

CRIMINAL LAW, Fourth Edition (1986)

Lloyd L. Weinreb, Professor of Law, Harvard University.

CRIMINAL LAW AND PROCEDURE, Seventh Edition (1989)

Ronald N. Boyce, Professor of Law, University of Utah.
Rollin M. Perkins, Professor of Law Emeritus, University of California, Hastings College of the Law.

CRIMINAL PROCEDURE, Third Edition (1987), with 1990 Supplement

James B. Haddad, Professor of Law, Northwestern University.
James B. Zagel, Chief, Criminal Justice Division, Office of Attorney General of Illinois.
Gary L. Starkman, Assistant U. S. Attorney, Northern District of Illinois.
William J. Bauer, Chief Judge of the U.S. Court of Appeals, Seventh Circuit.

CRIMINAL PROCESS, Fourth Edition (1987), with 1990 Supplement

Lloyd L. Weinreb, Professor of Law, Harvard University.

DAMAGES, Second Edition (1952)

Charles T. McCormick, late Professor of Law, University of Texas.
William F. Fritz, late Professor of Law, University of Texas.

DECEDENTS' ESTATES AND TRUSTS, Seventh Edition (1988)

John Ritchie, late Professor of Law, University of Virginia.
Neill H. Alford, Jr., Professor of Law, University of Virginia.
Richard W. Effland, late Professor of Law, Arizona State University.

DISPUTE RESOLUTION, Processes of (1989)

John S. Murray, President and Executive Director of The Conflict Clinic, Inc., George Mason University.
Alan Scott Rau, Professor of Law, University of Texas.
Edward F. Sherman, Professor of Law, University of Texas.

DOMESTIC RELATIONS, see also Family Law

DOMESTIC RELATIONS, Second Edition (1990)

Walter Wadlington, Professor of Law, University of Virginia.

EMPLOYMENT DISCRIMINATION, Second Edition (1987), with 1990 Supplement

Joel W. Friedman, Professor of Law, Tulane University.
George M. Strickler, Professor of Law, Tulane University.

EMPLOYMENT LAW, Second Edition (1991), with Statutory Supplement

Mark A. Rothstein, Professor of Law, University of Houston.
Andria S. Knapp, Visiting Professor of Law, Golden Gate University.
Lance Liebman, Professor of Law, Harvard University.

ENERGY LAW (1983) with 1986 Case Supplement

Donald N. Zillman, Professor of Law, University of Utah.
Laurence Lattman, Dean of Mines and Engineering, University of Utah.

ENTERPRISE ORGANIZATION, Fourth Edition (1987), with 1987 Corporation and Partnership Statutes, Rules and Forms Supplement

Alfred F. Conard, Professor of Law, University of Michigan.
Robert L. Knauss, Dean of the Law School, University of Houston.
Stanley Siegel, Professor of Law, University of California, Los Angeles.

ENVIRONMENTAL POLICY LAW 1985 Edition, with 1985 Problems Supplement (Supplement in association with Ronald H. Rosenberg, Professor of Law, College of William and Mary)

Thomas J. Schoenbaum, Professor of Law, University of Georgia.

EQUITY, see also Remedies

EQUITY, RESTITUTION AND DAMAGES, Second Edition (1974)

Robert Childres, late Professor of Law, Northwestern University.
William F. Johnson, Jr., Professor of Law, New York University.

ESTATE PLANNING, Second Edition (1982), with 1985 Case, Text and Documentary Supplement

David Westfall, Professor of Law, Harvard University.

ETHICS, see Legal Profession, Professional Responsibility, and Social Responsibilities

ETHICS OF LAWYERING, THE LAW AND (1990)

Geoffrey C. Hazard, Jr., Professor of Law, Yale University.
Susan P. Koniak, Professor of Law, University of Pittsburgh.

ETHICS AND PROFESSIONAL RESPONSIBILITY (1981) (Reprinted from THE LAWYERING PROCESS)

Gary Bellow, Professor of Law, Harvard University.
Bea Moulton, Legal Services Corporation.

EVIDENCE, Sixth Edition (1988 Reprint), with 1990 Case Supplement (Supplement edited in association with Roger C. Park, Professor of Law, University of Minnesota)

John Kaplan, Professor of Law, Stanford University.
Jon R. Waltz, Professor of Law, Northwestern University.

EVIDENCE, Eighth Edition (1988), with Rules, Statute and Case Supplement (1990)

Jack B. Weinstein, Chief Judge, United States District Court.
John H. Mansfield, Professor of Law, Harvard University.
Norman Abrams, Professor of Law, University of California, Los Angeles.
Margaret Berger, Professor of Law, Brooklyn Law School.

FAMILY LAW, see also Domestic Relations

FAMILY LAW Second Edition (1985), with 1991 Supplement

Judith C. Areen, Professor of Law, Georgetown University.

FAMILY LAW AND CHILDREN IN THE LEGAL SYSTEM, STATUTORY MATERIALS (1981)

Walter Wadlington, Professor of Law, University of Virginia.

FEDERAL COURTS, Eighth Edition (1988), with 1990 Supplement

Charles T. McCormick, late Professor of Law, University of Texas.
James H. Chadbourn, late Professor of Law, Harvard University.
Charles Alan Wright, Professor of Law, University of Texas, Austin.

UNIVERSITY CASEBOOK SERIES—Continued

FEDERAL COURTS AND THE FEDERAL SYSTEM, Hart and Wechsler's Third Edition (1988), with 1989 Case Supplement, and the Judicial Code and Rules of Procedure in the Federal Courts (1989)

Paul M. Bator, Professor of Law, University of Chicago.
Daniel J. Meltzer, Professor of Law, Harvard University.
Paul J. Mishkin, Professor of Law, University of California, Berkeley.
David L. Shapiro, Professor of Law, Harvard University.

FEDERAL COURTS AND THE LAW OF FEDERAL–STATE RELATIONS, Second Edition (1989), with 1990 Supplement

Peter W. Low, Professor of Law, University of Virginia.
John C. Jeffries, Jr., Professor of Law, University of Virginia.

FEDERAL PUBLIC LAND AND RESOURCES LAW, Second Edition (1987), with 1990 Case Supplement and 1990 Statutory Supplement

George C. Coggins, Professor of Law, University of Kansas.
Charles F. Wilkinson, Professor of Law, University of Oregon.

FEDERAL RULES OF CIVIL PROCEDURE and Selected Other Procedural Provisions, 1990 Edition

FEDERAL TAXATION, see Taxation

FOOD AND DRUG LAW (1980), with Statutory Supplement

Richard A. Merrill, Dean of the School of Law, University of Virginia.
Peter Barton Hutt, Esq.

FUTURE INTERESTS (1970)

Howard R. Williams, Professor of Law, Stanford University.

FUTURE INTERESTS AND ESTATE PLANNING (1961), with 1962 Supplement

W. Barton Leach, late Professor of Law, Harvard University.
James K. Logan, formerly Dean of the Law School, University of Kansas.

GOVERNMENT CONTRACTS, FEDERAL, Successor Edition (1985), with 1989 Supplement

John W. Whelan, Professor of Law, Hastings College of the Law.

GOVERNMENT REGULATION: FREE ENTERPRISE AND ECONOMIC ORGANIZATION, Sixth Edition (1985)

Louis B. Schwartz, Professor of Law, Hastings College of the Law.
John J. Flynn, Professor of Law, University of Utah.
Harry First, Professor of Law, New York University.

HEALTH CARE LAW AND POLICY (1988)

Clark C. Havighurst, Professor of Law, Duke University.

HINCKLEY, JOHN W., JR., TRIAL OF: A Case Study of the Insanity Defense (1986)

Peter W. Low, Professor of Law, University of Virginia.
John C. Jeffries, Jr., Professor of Law, University of Virginia.
Richard C. Bonnie, Professor of Law, University of Virginia.

INJUNCTIONS, Second Edition (1984)

Owen M. Fiss, Professor of Law, Yale University.
Doug Rendleman, Professor of Law, College of William and Mary.

INSTITUTIONAL INVESTORS, (1978)

David L. Ratner, Professor of Law, Cornell University.

LAND FINANCING, Third Edition (1985)

The late Norman Penney, Professor of Law, Cornell University.
Richard F. Broude, Member of the California Bar.
Roger Cunningham, Professor of Law, University of Michigan.

LAW AND MEDICINE (1980)

Walter Wadlington, Professor of Law and Professor of Legal Medicine, University of Virginia.
Jon R. Waltz, Professor of Law, Northwestern University.
Roger B. Dworkin, Professor of Law, Indiana University, and Professor of Biomedical History, University of Washington.

LAW, LANGUAGE AND ETHICS (1972)

William R. Bishin, Professor of Law, University of Southern California.
Christopher D. Stone, Professor of Law, University of Southern California.

LAW, SCIENCE AND MEDICINE (1984), with 1989 Supplement

Judith C. Areen, Professor of Law, Georgetown University.
Patricia A. King, Professor of Law, Georgetown University.
Steven P. Goldberg, Professor of Law, Georgetown University.
Alexander M. Capron, Professor of Law, University of Southern California.

LAWYERING PROCESS (1978), with Civil Problem Supplement and Criminal Problem Supplement

Gary Bellow, Professor of Law, Harvard University.
Bea Moulton, Professor of Law, Arizona State University.

LEGAL METHOD (1980)

Harry W. Jones, Professor of Law Emeritus, Columbia University.
John M. Kernochan, Professor of Law, Columbia University.
Arthur W. Murphy, Professor of Law, Columbia University.

LEGAL METHODS (1969)

Robert N. Covington, Professor of Law, Vanderbilt University.
E. Blythe Stason, late Professor of Law, Vanderbilt University.
John W. Wade, Professor of Law, Vanderbilt University.
Elliott E. Cheatham, late Professor of Law, Vanderbilt University.
Theodore A. Smedley, Professor of Law, Vanderbilt University.

LEGAL PROFESSION, THE, Responsibility and Regulation, Second Edition (1988)

Geoffrey C. Hazard, Jr., Professor of Law, Yale University.
Deborah L. Rhode, Professor of Law, Stanford University.

LEGISLATION, Fourth Edition (1982) (by Fordham)

Horace E. Read, late Vice President, Dalhousie University.
John W. MacDonald, Professor of Law Emeritus, Cornell Law School.
Jefferson B. Fordham, Professor of Law, University of Utah.
William J. Pierce, Professor of Law, University of Michigan.

LEGISLATIVE AND ADMINISTRATIVE PROCESSES, Second Edition (1981)

Hans A. Linde, Judge, Supreme Court of Oregon.
George Bunn, Professor of Law, University of Wisconsin.
Fredericka Paff, Professor of Law, University of Wisconsin.
W. Lawrence Church, Professor of Law, University of Wisconsin.

LOCAL GOVERNMENT LAW, Second Revised Edition (1986)

Jefferson B. Fordham, Professor of Law, University of Utah.

UNIVERSITY CASEBOOK SERIES—Continued

MASS MEDIA LAW, Fourth Edition (1990)

Marc A. Franklin, Professor of Law, Stanford University.
David A. Anderson, Professor of Law, University of Texas.

MUNICIPAL CORPORATIONS, see Local Government Law

NEGOTIABLE INSTRUMENTS, see Commercial Paper

NEGOTIATION (1981) (Reprinted from THE LAWYERING PROCESS)

Gary Bellow, Professor of Law, Harvard Law School.
Bea Moulton, Legal Services Corporation.

NEW YORK PRACTICE, Fourth Edition (1978)

Herbert Peterfreund, Professor of Law, New York University.
Joseph M. McLaughlin, Dean of the Law School, Fordham University.

OIL AND GAS, Fifth Edition (1987)

Howard R. Williams, Professor of Law, Stanford University.
Richard C. Maxwell, Professor of Law, University of California, Los Angeles.
Charles J. Meyers, late Dean of the Law School, Stanford University.
Stephen F. Williams, Judge of the United States Court of Appeals.

ON LAW IN COURTS (1965)

Paul J. Mishkin, Professor of Law, University of California, Berkeley.
Clarence Morris, Professor of Law Emeritus, University of Pennsylvania.

PENSION AND EMPLOYEE BENEFIT LAW (1990)

John H. Langbein, Professor of Law, University of Chicago.
Bruce A. Wolk, Professor of Law, University of California, Davis.

PLEADING AND PROCEDURE, see Procedure, Civil

POLICE FUNCTION, Fifth Edition (1991)

Reprint of Chapters 1–10 of Miller, Dawson, Dix and Parnas's CRIMINAL JUSTICE ADMINISTRATION, Fourth Edition.

PREPARING AND PRESENTING THE CASE (1981) (Reprinted from THE LAW-YERING PROCESS)

Gary Bellow, Professor of Law, Harvard Law School.
Bea Moulton, Legal Services Corporation.

PROCEDURE (1988), with Procedure Supplement (1989)

Robert M. Cover, late Professor of Law, Yale Law School.
Owen M. Fiss, Professor of Law, Yale Law School.
Judith Resnik, Professor of Law, University of Southern California Law Center.

PROCEDURE—CIVIL PROCEDURE, Second Edition (1974), with 1979 Supplement

The late James H. Chadbourn, Professor of Law, Harvard University.
A. Leo Levin, Professor of Law, University of Pennsylvania.
Philip Shuchman, Professor of Law, Cornell University.

PROCEDURE—CIVIL PROCEDURE, Sixth Edition (1990)

Richard H. Field, late Professor of Law, Harvard University.
Benjamin Kaplan, Professor of Law Emeritus, Harvard University.
Kevin M. Clermont, Professor of Law, Cornell University.

PROCEDURE—CIVIL PROCEDURE, Fifth Edition (1990)

Maurice Rosenberg, Professor of Law, Columbia University.
Hans Smit, Professor of Law, Columbia University.
Rochelle C. Dreyfuss, Professor of Law, New York University.

PROCEDURE—PLEADING AND PROCEDURE: State and Federal, Sixth Edition (1989), with 1990 Case Supplement

David W. Louisell, late Professor of Law, University of California, Berkeley.
Geoffrey C. Hazard, Jr., Professor of Law, Yale University.
Colin C. Tait, Professor of Law, University of Connecticut.

PROCEDURE—FEDERAL RULES OF CIVIL PROCEDURE, 1990 Edition

PRODUCTS LIABILITY AND SAFETY, Second Edition, (1989), with 1989 Statutory Supplement

W. Page Keeton, Professor of Law, University of Texas.
David G. Owen, Professor of Law, University of South Carolina.
John E. Montgomery, Professor of Law, University of South Carolina.
Michael D. Green, Professor of Law, University of Iowa

PROFESSIONAL RESPONSIBILITY, Fifth Edition (1991), with 1991 Selected Standards on Professional Responsibility Supplement

Thomas D. Morgan, Professor of Law, George Washington University.
Ronald D. Rotunda, Professor of Law, University of Illinois.

PROPERTY, Sixth Edition (1990)

John E. Cribbet, Professor of Law, University of Illinois.
Corwin W. Johnson, Professor of Law, University of Texas.
Roger W. Findley, Professor of Law, University of Illinois.
Ernest E. Smith, Professor of Law, University of Texas.

PROPERTY—PERSONAL (1953)

S. Kenneth Skolfield, late Professor of Law Emeritus, Boston University.

PROPERTY—PERSONAL, Third Edition (1954)

Everett Fraser, late Dean of the Law School Emeritus, University of Minnesota.
Third Edition by Charles W. Taintor, late Professor of Law, University of Pittsburgh.

PROPERTY—INTRODUCTION, TO REAL PROPERTY, Third Edition (1954)

Everett Fraser, late Dean of the Law School Emeritus, University of Minnesota.

PROPERTY—FUNDAMENTALS OF MODERN REAL PROPERTY, Second Edition (1982), with 1985 Supplement

Edward H. Rabin, Professor of Law, University of California, Davis.

PROPERTY, REAL (1984), with 1988 Supplement

Paul Goldstein, Professor of Law, Stanford University.

PROSECUTION AND ADJUDICATION, Fourth Edition (1991)

Reprint of Chapters 11–26 of Miller, Dawson, Dix and Parnas's CRIMINAL JUSTICE ADMINISTRATION, Fourth Edition.

PSYCHIATRY AND LAW, see Mental Health, see also Hinckley, Trial of

PUBLIC UTILITY LAW, see Free Enterprise, also Regulated Industries

REAL ESTATE PLANNING, Third Edition (1989), with Revised Problem and Statutory Supplement (1991)

Norton L. Steuben, Professor of Law, University of Colorado.

REAL ESTATE TRANSACTIONS, Revised Second Edition (1988), with Statute, Form and Problem Supplement (1988)

Paul Goldstein, Professor of Law, Stanford University.

RECEIVERSHIP AND CORPORATE REORGANIZATION, see Creditors' Rights

REGULATED INDUSTRIES, Second Edition, (1976)

William K. Jones, Professor of Law, Columbia University.

REMEDIES, Second Edition (1987)

Edward D. Re, Chief Judge, U. S. Court of International Trade.

REMEDIES, (1989)

Elaine W. Shoben, Professor of Law, University of Illinois.
Wm. Murray Tabb, Professor of Law, Baylor University.

SALES, Second Edition (1986)

Marion W. Benfield, Jr., Professor of Law, University of Illinois.
William D. Hawkland, Chancellor, Louisiana State Law Center.

SALES AND SALES FINANCING, Fifth Edition (1984)

John Honnold, Professor of Law, University of Pennsylvania.

SALES LAW AND THE CONTRACTING PROCESS, Second Edition (1991)

(Reprinted from Commercial Transactions, Second Edition (1991)
Alan Schwartz, Professor of Law, Yale University.
Robert E. Scott, Professor of Law, University of Virginia.

SECURED TRANSACTIONS IN PERSONAL PROPERTY, Second Edition (1987) (Reprinted from COMMERCIAL LAW, Second Edition (1987))

Robert L. Jordan, Professor of Law, University of California, Los Angeles.
William D. Warren, Professor of Law, University of California, Los Angeles.

SECURITIES REGULATION, Sixth Edition (1987), with 1990 Selected Statutes, Rules and Forms Supplement and 1990 Cases and Releases Supplement

Richard W. Jennings, Professor of Law, University of California, Berkeley.
Harold Marsh, Jr., Member of California Bar.

SECURITIES REGULATION, Second Edition (1988), with Statute, Rule and Form Supplement (1988)

Larry D. Soderquist, Professor of Law, Vanderbilt University.

SECURITY INTERESTS IN PERSONAL PROPERTY, Second Edition (1987)

Douglas G. Baird, Professor of Law, University of Chicago.
Thomas H. Jackson, Dean of the Law School, University of Virginia.

SECURITY INTERESTS IN PERSONAL PROPERTY (1985) (Reprinted from Sales and Sales Financing, Fifth Edition)

John Honnold, Professor of Law, University of Pennsylvania.

SELECTED STANDARDS ON PROFESSIONAL RESPONSIBILITY, 1991 Edition

SELECTED STATUTES AND INTERNATIONAL AGREEMENTS ON UNFAIR COMPETITION, TRADEMARK, COPYRIGHT AND PATENT, 1989 Edition

SELECTED STATUTES ON TRUSTS AND ESTATES, 1991 Edition

SOCIAL RESPONSIBILITIES OF LAWYERS, Case Studies (1988)

Philip B. Heymann, Professor of Law, Harvard University.
Lance Liebman, Professor of Law, Harvard University.

SOCIAL SCIENCE IN LAW, Second Edition (1990)

John Monahan, Professor of Law, University of Virginia.
Laurens Walker, Professor of Law, University of Virginia.

TAXATION, FEDERAL INCOME (1989)

Stephen B. Cohen, Professor of Law, Georgetown University

TAXATION, FEDERAL INCOME, Second Edition (1988), with 1990 Supplement (Supplement edited in association with Deborah H. Schenk, Professor of Law, New York University)

Michael J. Graetz, Professor of Law, Yale University.

TAXATION, FEDERAL INCOME, Sixth Edition (1987)

James J. Freeland, Professor of Law, University of Florida.
Stephen A. Lind, Professor of Law, University of Florida and University of California, Hastings.
Richard B. Stephens, late Professor of Law Emeritus, University of Florida.

TAXATION, FEDERAL INCOME, Successor Edition (1986), with 1990 Legislative Supplement

Stanley S. Surrey, late Professor of Law, Harvard University.
Paul R. McDaniel, Professor of Law, Boston College.
Hugh J. Ault, Professor of Law, Boston College.
Stanley A. Koppelman, Professor of Law, Boston University.

TAXATION, FEDERAL INCOME, OF BUSINESS ORGANIZATIONS (1991)

Paul R. McDaniel, Professor of Law, Boston College.
Hugh J. Ault, Professor of Law, Boston College.
Martin J. McMahon, Jr., Professor of Law, University of Kentucky.
Daniel L. Simmons, Professor of Law, University of California, Davis.

TAXATION, FEDERAL INCOME, OF PARTNERSHIPS AND S CORPORATIONS (1991)

Paul R. McDaniel, Professor of Law, Boston College.
Hugh J. Ault, Professor of Law, Boston College.
Martin J. McMahon, Jr., Professor of Law, University of Kentucky.
Daniel L. Simmons, Professor of Law, University of California, Davis.

TAXATION, FEDERAL INCOME, OIL AND GAS, NATURAL RESOURCES TRANSACTIONS (1990)

Peter C. Maxfield, Professor of Law, University of Wyoming.
James L. Houghton, CPA, Partner, Ernst and Young.
James R. Gaar, CPA, Partner, Ernst and Young.

TAXATION, FEDERAL WEALTH TRANSFER, Successor Edition (1987)

Stanley S. Surrey, late Professor of Law, Harvard University.
Paul R. McDaniel, Professor of Law, Boston College.
Harry L. Gutman, Professor of Law, University of Pennsylvania.

TAXATION, FUNDAMENTALS OF CORPORATE, Second Edition (1987), with 1989 Supplement

Stephen A. Lind, Professor of Law, University of Florida and University of California, Hastings.
Stephen Schwarz, Professor of Law, University of California, Hastings.
Daniel J. Lathrope, Professor of Law, University of California, Hastings.
Joshua Rosenberg, Professor of Law, University of San Francisco.

TAXATION, FUNDAMENTALS OF PARTNERSHIP, Second Edition (1988)

Stephen A. Lind, Professor of Law, University of Florida and University of California, Hastings.
Stephen Schwarz, Professor of Law, University of California, Hastings.
Daniel J. Lathrope, Professor of Law, University of California, Hastings.
Joshua Rosenberg, Professor of Law, University of San Francisco.

TAXATION, PROBLEMS IN THE FEDERAL INCOME TAXATION OF PARTNERSHIPS AND CORPORATIONS, Second Edition (1986)

Norton L. Steuben, Professor of Law, University of Colorado.
William J. Turnier, Professor of Law, University of North Carolina.

TAXATION, PROBLEMS IN THE FUNDAMENTALS OF FEDERAL INCOME, Second Edition (1985)

Norton L. Steuben, Professor of Law, University of Colorado.
William J. Turnier, Professor of Law, University of North Carolina.

TORT LAW AND ALTERNATIVES, Fourth Edition (1987)

Marc A. Franklin, Professor of Law, Stanford University.
Robert L. Rabin, Professor of Law, Stanford University.

TORTS, Eighth Edition (1988)

William L. Prosser, late Professor of Law, University of California, Hastings.
John W. Wade, Professor of Law, Vanderbilt University.
Victor E. Schwartz, Adjunct Professor of Law, Georgetown University.

TORTS, Third Edition (1976)

Harry Shulman, late Dean of the Law School, Yale University.
Fleming James, Jr., Professor of Law Emeritus, Yale University.
Oscar S. Gray, Professor of Law, University of Maryland.

TRADE REGULATION, Third Edition (1990)

Milton Handler, Professor of Law Emeritus, Columbia University.
Harlan M. Blake, Professor of Law, Columbia University.
Robert Pitofsky, Professor of Law, Georgetown University.
Harvey J. Goldschmid, Professor of Law, Columbia University.

TRADE REGULATION, see Antitrust

TRANSNATIONAL BUSINESS PROBLEMS (1986)

Detlev F. Vagts, Professor of Law, Harvard University.

TRANSNATIONAL LEGAL PROBLEMS, Third Edition (1986) with 1991 Revised Edition of Documentary Supplement

Henry J. Steiner, Professor of Law, Harvard University.
Detlev F. Vagts, Professor of Law, Harvard University.

TRIAL, see also Evidence, Making the Record, Lawyering Process and Preparing and Presenting the Case

UNIVERSITY CASEBOOK SERIES—Continued

TRUSTS, Fifth Edition (1978)

George G. Bogert, late Professor of Law Emeritus, University of Chicago.
Dallin H. Oaks, President, Brigham Young University.

TRUSTS AND ESTATES, SELECTED STATUTES ON, 1991 Edition

TRUSTS AND SUCCESSION (Palmer's), Fourth Edition (1983)

Richard V. Wellman, Professor of Law, University of Georgia.
Lawrence W. Waggoner, Professor of Law, University of Michigan.
Olin L. Browder, Jr., Professor of Law, University of Michigan.

UNFAIR COMPETITION, see Competitive Process and Business Torts

WATER RESOURCE MANAGEMENT, Third Edition (1988)

The late Charles J. Meyers, formerly Dean, Stanford University Law School.
A. Dan Tarlock, Professor of Law, IIT Chicago-Kent College of Law.
James N. Corbridge, Jr., Chancellor, University of Colorado at Boulder, and
    Professor of Law, University of Colorado.
David H. Getches, Professor of Law, University of Colorado.

WILLS AND ADMINISTRATION, Fifth Edition (1961)

Philip Mechem, late Professor of Law, University of Pennsylvania.
Thomas E. Atkinson, late Professor of Law, New York University.

WRITING AND ANALYSIS IN THE LAW, Second Edition (1991)

Helene S. Shapo, Professor of Law, Northwestern University
Marilyn R. Walter, Professor of Law, Brooklyn Law School
Elizabeth Fajans, Writing Specialist, Brooklyn Law School

CASES AND MATERIALS

ON

PLEADING AND PROCEDURE

STATE AND FEDERAL

By

DAVID W. LOUISELL
Late Elizabeth Josselyn Boalt Professor of Law,
University of California, Berkeley

GEOFFREY C. HAZARD, JR.
Sterling Professor of Law, Yale Law School

and

COLIN C. TAIT
Professor of Law, University of Connecticut

SIXTH EDITION

Westbury, New York
THE FOUNDATION PRESS, INC.
1989

Library of Congress Cataloging-in-Publication Data

Louisell, David W.
    Cases and materials on pleading and procedure : state and federal
/ by David W. Louisell, Geoffrey C. Hazard, Jr., and Colin C. Tait.
— 6th ed.
        p.   cm. — (University casebook series)
    Includes index.
    ISBN 0–88277–721–1
    1. Civil procedure—United States—Cases. I. Hazard, Geoffrey C.
II. Tait, Colin C. III. Title. IV. Series
KF8839.L6 1989
347.73′5—dc20
[347.3075]

                                                    89–7945
                                                      CIP

L., H. & T.—Cs. Plead. & Proc. 6th Ed. UCB
1st Reprint—1991

PREFACE TO SIXTH EDITION

The basic approach of the book remains the same—looking at procedure chiefly from the lawyer's viewpoint, examining cases as instances of fundamental procedural problems, and presenting material for what is going on as well as for what is being said. As with previous editions, this one continues to give emphasis to the special problems of modern litigation, including "complex" litigation, discovery abuses and use of sanctions, the pretrial conference, and case management. We have expanded coverage of court costs and attorneys fees. The references have been comprehensively updated. Aside from these changes, this edition involves several rearrangements, some of which, based on teaching experience, revert to the order found in earlier editions. We express our special thanks for the research assistance of Stephen D. Sowle, who has provided absolutely superb help.

G.C.H., Jr.
C.C.T.

April, 1989

*

PREFACE TO FIRST EDITION

The predecessors of these materials have been used for some years in mimeograph form, at the University of Minnesota and the University of California, Berkeley.

A principal goal we have sought to achieve in them is connoted by the title: "Pleading and Procedure: State and Federal." For in our treatment of all major problems we have tried to juxtapose State Code and Federal Rules doctrine. This we have done not only for practical purposes of coverage, though that is of course a significant end in itself. Despite the increasing acceptance of the Federal Rules of Civil Procedure a number of states, including California and New York, still pursue the "Code road." Students preparing for Code practice cannot be ignored; as Cleveland put it, "It is a condition, not a theory, that confronts us." Moreover some problems of procedure, by reason of the nature of our federal system, are primarily of concern in state courts. But beyond these pragmatic considerations, experience in teaching has dictated our method. For we have found that there is no other technique in procedural teaching as effective as comparison between the methods of the two on-going systems of American adjudication, Code practice and the Federal Rules. And profound though our admiration is for the achievements of the latter, we of course do not regard present federal practice as the last possible word. The continuing revision of the Federal Rules is perhaps the greatest vindication of the judicial states-manship that engendered them in the first place; the Federal Rules, like all living institutions, constantly can profit by comparison. And surely the recommendations of the New York Temporary Commission on the Courts, retaining as they do many features of Code practice, caution against accepting the Federal Rules as a procedural monotype. Indeed, in pursuance of our conviction of the values of comparison we have not hesitated to invoke light also from non-common law sources.

But if the juxtaposition of State and Federal pleading and procedure is valuable for comparative purposes, perhaps it is even more meaningful to demonstrate the universality, continuity and persistency of the hard problems of procedure, whatever the forum. Perhaps it is simultaneous study of both systems that offers best the promise of a distillate that may yet provide a universal norm for American procedure—to the extent that one is feasible in a federal system.

We have selected our cases primarily as exemplars of the recurrent problems rather than as sources of doctrine. This necessitates more supplementation by textual notes than perhaps has been customary in other pleading and procedure casebooks. Perhaps some may criticize this method on the ground that it attempts to make things too easy for the student, a bootless and deceptive effort with subject matter as tough as that of pleading and procedure. Such critics we would attempt to disarm by thorough agreement that this subject matter is tough; that superficial glances at hard problems can only be deceptive; that he who would master these problems, must first discipline himself to effort. If then we are asked, why so much textual explanation, our answer is that by clearing away some of the rubbish we hope to lead the students through the tailings to the mines that invite—indeed demand—deep digging. We rather expect the criticism that some of our cases and problems are just too tough, at least for first year students. But we have been teaching them to first year students with the satisfying conviction—unless we are deluded—that when really challenged, the student will respond with the necessary effort. Hence we have not hesitated to draw upon hard cases, provided they are good teaching tools, and to present the tough problems.

Naturally for the Code side of the picture we have drawn heavily upon California cases not only as the jurisdiction of our immediate contact but because the richness of its procedural law, compounded by an intermediate system of appellate review, produced an almost inexhaustible source for intelligent reflection on today's procedural problems. But the similarity of California's Code of Civil Procedure to the other Codes, e.g., New York's, reduces the problem of case selection largely to one of choosing the best teaching tool, regardless of the jurisdiction of origin of the case involved. Of course those using the book in states which have adopted the Federal Rules can for the most part pursue the Federal Rules materials herein. We teach Pleading and Procedure three hours a week for both semesters; but we think the book adaptable, according to need, to various combinations of semester hours. For example, it might be used for either two or three hour courses in (1) Pleading and Joinder, and (2) Jurisdiction and Trials.

This book reflects our attempts while teaching Pleading and Procedure to hold in focus the following different, if sometimes overlapping, viewpoints: (1) That of the law student, as he struggles to master, for example, the many-faceted concept of jurisdiction, or to balance in the scales the "rights" of a pleader with the tactical limitations implicit in the process of "educating" an opponent; (2) That of the lawyer as an advocate in an adversary system, whose objective is to win for his client and for whom outcome is largely the function of judgment and wisdom in marshalling the resources of his cause; (3) That of the judge, interested in effective, efficient, economical and fair determination of controversy, according to prescribed rules; (4) That of the intelligent legislature and lay public, who view procedure as a means of effectuating desired substantive objectives, and therefore as the handmaiden of justice; and (5) That of the jurisprudent, who sees today's procedure in the historical context of the continuum of human conflict. Our emphases shift from problem to problem—when we consider selecting the jury, it may be primarily tactical; when we deal with instructing the jury, it may be principally that of judicial administration—but we hope that all of these viewpoints always remain at least implicit.

Lastly, this book reflects our philosophy, the product perhaps as much of our experience as practitioners as of our reflection as teachers, that procedure is but a phase in the process of settling human controversy, and that the most effective "pleader" and "trial lawyer" is often he who by wise negotiation obviates the necessity of pleading and going to trial. Because of this thinking we give perhaps unusual attention, for a book of this type, to the problem of settling cases.

For whatever success our efforts may achieve, we owe much to our colleagues because of their generosity in making available the learning of all of their disciplines with which pleading and procedure are so inextricably interwoven. In particular, we thank Edward L. Barrett, Jr., who by a scholarly and perceptive selection of California cases on pleading prior to our arrival on the scene at Berkeley paved the way for the assimilation of that phase into our integrated treatment, and who generously bequeathed his work to us; Albert Ehrenzweig, who has always made available his penetrating thinking in the area of jurisdiction; and our new colleague in procedure here, Preble Stolz, who has read much of the manuscript.

D. W. L.
G. C. H., Jr.

April, 1962

*

SUMMARY OF CONTENTS

PART VI. THE PRETRIAL STAGE

PART VII. TRIAL

PART VIII. SPECIAL PROBLEMS OF MODERN LITIGATION

PART IX. REVIEW OF THE DISPOSITION

TABLE OF CONTENTS

PART III. REMEDIES

PART IV. THE PROPER COURT

TABLE OF CONTENTS

TABLE OF CONTENTS

PART IX. REVIEW OF THE DISPOSITION

TABLE OF CASES

Principal cases are in italic type. Non-principal cases are in roman type. References are to Pages.

TABLE OF CASES

TABLE OF CASES

TABLE OF ABBREVIATIONS

In the interests of brevity, we have adopted short form citations for sources frequently cited herein, as follows:

Statutory Materials

C.C. — California Civil Code

C.C.P. — California Code of Civil Procedure

F.R.C.P. — Federal Rules of Civil Procedure

Ill.C.C.P. — Illinois Code of Civil Procedure

N.Y.C.P.L.R. — New York Civil Practice Law and Rules

Secondary Materials

Hart & Wechsler — Hart and Wechsler, The Federal Courts and the Federal System (3d ed. 1988, Bator, Meltzer, Mishkin and Shapiro).

James & Hazard — James and Hazard, Civil Procedure (3d ed. 1985).

Moore — Moore, Moore's Federal Practice (2d ed.).

Weinstein, Korn & Miller — Weinstein, Korn and Miller, New York Civil Practice, 8 vols.

Witkin — Witkin, California Procedure, 10 vols. (3d ed. 1985).

Wright — Wright, Federal Courts (4th ed. 1983).

Wright & Miller — Wright and Miller, Federal Practice and Procedure.

In editing the cases and other materials reprinted herein, we have used asterisks (* * *) to indicate where we have deleted text from the original, and dots (. . .) to indicate where portions of quoted text were deleted by the author of the original.

*

TABLE OF SECONDARY AUTHORITIES

This table includes the following secondary authorities appearing in this book: (a) texts and treatises, except those so frequently cited as to justify including them in the Table of Abbreviations, p. lv; (b) all law review articles (unsigned Notes and Comments are listed at the end of the Table); and (c) other secondary materials that are cited or quoted from herein.

---

*

TABLE OF STATUTES AND RULES

CASES AND MATERIALS

ON

PLEADING AND PROCEDURE

STATE AND FEDERAL

*

Part I

INTRODUCTION

A. AN OVERVIEW OF THE SYSTEM

NOTE ON THE STRUCTURE OF A LAW SUIT

A lawsuit is a process by which a court resolves a controversy between people over some matter. For example, if two drivers have a collision, there may be a dispute over who is to pay for the ensuing losses and how much he is to pay. Conceivably, the two drivers could simply walk into court, tell their story to a judge, and have her give them a decision. Such a procedure would require very simple rules. Unhappily, the procedure for conducting lawsuits cannot be—or at least never has been—that simple.

The procedure problems of lawsuits are, on the contrary, often very complex. Much time will be spent on these complexities. But the student of a complex problem may easily lose his bearings in the maze of complications. It may be helpful, therefore, to describe in rough outline how a relatively simple lawsuit is conducted and to define some of the terms frequently encountered. What follows is an over-simplification and should be treated as such. Furthermore, in points of detail, the procedure and the names of the procedural devices vary somewhat from one jurisdiction to another.

Suppose that Bill Smith, who resides in Oakland, California, buys a hunting rifle at an Oakland sporting goods store operated by Janet Jones. The rifle was manufactured by Automatic Arms Co., a Massachusetts corporation, whose plant and offices are in Worcester, Mass. While Smith is out hunting not long after the purchase, he shoots the gun and the barrel explodes. Smith believes the explosion resulted from a metallurgical defect in the gun barrel. Smith is badly injured and incurs heavy hospital expenses. He is unable to obtain a satisfactory settlement from Jones and Automatic. How does he go about bringing a lawsuit to recover for these expenses?

1. Preliminaries, Jurisdiction and Venue

Probably, the first thing Smith does is to get a lawyer. Once he has a lawyer, the lawyer will handle all the steps in the litigation. For convenience in discussing the litigation, we ordinarily refer to the various steps as being made by Smith. In fact, however, the steps are taken by his lawyer. One point to be borne in mind is that the consequences of any errors in the lawyer's judgment will be visited on Smith himself. Another is that a litigant who cannot retain a lawyer, whether for a fee or through legal aid, can prosecute a lawsuit *in propria persona* (representing himself) only with great difficulty.

The first thing Smith's lawyer will do is to make as thorough an investigation of the facts as he can. This will certainly involve an interview with Smith, inspection of Smith's medical records, interviews with witnesses and with an expert gunsmith. Fact investigation will continue as the case progresses, but

1

when Smith's lawyer has an adequate preliminary grasp of the facts, he will turn to the legal problems confronting him.

The initial legal problem is whether Jones, or Automatic, or anyone else he can think of, has a legal responsibility to pay Smith for his injuries. To find this out, Smith (and here, of course, and from now on when we refer to Smith, we mean his lawyer) will have to study the *substantive law* —the law of torts and of contracts. Smith bought the gun from Jones, so there was a contract of sale between them. Was it breached by reason of the defect in the gun barrel? If it was, what are the damages for breach—the price of the gun, or can more than this be recovered? The gun was made by Automatic. Did it have a duty to make the gun carefully?

Suppose that Smith reaches the following conclusions regarding substantive law:

1. Jones had a contractual duty to provide Smith with a gun that was free from defects, even if the defects were not due to Jones' fault.

2. If Jones breached a contractual duty to Smith, then she is obligated to repay Smith the cost of the gun and to compensate Smith for his injuries.

3. Under the law of torts, Automatic had a duty to provide Smith with a gun free from defects.

4. If Automatic breached a duty to Smith, then it is obligated to repay Smith the cost of the gun and to compensate him for his injuries.

Smith suspects that Jones may not have very much money and may not have insurance to cover her liability to Smith. Since Smith doesn't want an empty victory, and since he assumes that Automatic does have enough money to pay his claim if he wins, Smith concludes the best thing to do is to sue both Jones and Automatic.

The first problem he will encounter is whether *territorial jurisdiction* can be obtained over the defendants. In general, any person who is presently within the state is subject to the jurisdiction of its courts—that is, the person can be compelled to answer claims against her or else have a default judgment rendered against her. Jurisdiction therefore can be obtained over Janet Jones, for she lives in California. What about Automatic? Automatic is in Massachusetts and as far as Smith can tell Automatic has no office in California. May California courts compel Automatic to answer claims against it with respect to transactions in California? The answer is yes. Most states, including California, have statutes that authorize service of process on an out-of-state business enterprise in such circumstances. Hence, Smith concludes that the California courts may obtain territorial jurisdiction over both Jones and Automatic.

The second problem for Smith is to decide what court in California has *jurisdiction over the subject matter* of the proposed lawsuit. California, like most states, has two principal sets of trial courts: (1) The courts of limited jurisdiction. In California, these consist of the Municipal Court, which has authority to handle cases involving amounts up to $25,000, and the Justice Court, also with authority over cases up to $25,000. (2) The court of general jurisdiction, which has authority to handle cases not cognizable in some other court. In California this would be the Superior Court, which hears all cases involving amounts over $25,000. Assume that Smith's injuries cost him $30,000 in hospital bills and, in addition, he wants to recover damages for the permanent disfigurement of his face. This being so, he should file his action in the Superior Court, for it is the court having jurisdiction of the subject matter of the case.

What does Smith do next? He will have to draw up a statement of his claim against the defendants. This statement is designed to tell the defendants what it is, according to Smith, that entitles him to recover a judgment against them. The statement will also help guide the court as it proceeds with the case. This statement, a document drawn in formal language, is the *complaint*—also known in some states as the petition or declaration. In his complaint, Smith will describe who he is, who defendants are, what happened to him, and so on. These assertions are called the *allegations* of the complaint. The rules governing the form and content of the complaint and other pleadings are the rules of *pleading*. We shall discuss the complaint in more detail later on.

Smith has one other preliminary decision to make. There is a Superior Court in each county in California. In which county should he bring the suit? This is a question of *venue,* i.e., the proper place within the state in which to bring the action. Generally speaking, the proper venue is the county where one or all of the defendants reside. Jones lives in Oakland, so proper venue would be there. Hence, Smith will bring his action in the Superior Court in and for the County of Alameda, where Oakland is situated.

Smith has not yet gone to court; everything so far has been done in his lawyer's office. It is now time to advise the defendants and the court of the suit. Accordingly, Smith takes his complaint down to the courthouse and *files* it with the clerk of the Superior Court. By this filing, the suit is officially *commenced.* (In some states, including New York, a suit is not deemed commenced until summons is served on the defendant, a procedure to be described in a moment.) The court now is advised of the suit, but the defendants are not. The device by which the defendants are advised of the suit is the *summons.* At the same time that Smith files his complaint, he hands the clerk a form of summons, containing the names of the parties and a notice to the defendants that they must come in and defend themselves. The clerk puts the court's seal on the summons, thus making it official notice. Because there are two defendants, Smith obtains a summons for each.

Smith now hires a process-server. The sheriff is authorized by law to serve process and in an earlier day, and in many states today, he is the one who customarily serves process. In California, there are private process-serving agencies and in some parts of the state it is customary to use their services. Smith gives the process-server a copy of the summons and a copy of the complaint for each defendant and asks the process-server to make *service* on them. The process-server serves defendant Jones by going to Jones' store and handing her a copy of the summons and complaint. Jones is thus *personally served.* The process-server now endorses on the back of the original summons the fact that service was made. This is the *return of service.* By means of this service, assuming it is in proper form, the court acquires jurisdiction over Jones. Jones is now regarded as before the court and she had better see *her* lawyer about making a defense to the action.

The problem of serving Automatic is more complicated. Automatic doesn't have an office in California and has never formally appointed a local manager or agent, so personal service cannot be made on it. Automatic is a foreign corporation and there are special statutes prescribing the method of serving such corporations. In many states, the statute simply requires that copies of the summons and complaint be delivered to the state Secretary of State, with directions that he send on a copy of each to the foreign corporation's headquarters office. In some states this step must be preceded by obtaining a court order directing that this *substituted service* (i.e., service otherwise than by personal delivery) be made on the foreign corporation. (The papers involved, here as in most instances in litigation, are all prepared by the party and not by the officials, for they are busy.) When the Secretary of State has properly forwarded the summons and complaint, Automatic is subject to the jurisdiction of the court, assuming that it is not improper under the U. S. Constitution to hale Automatic into a California court on this matter.

Smith now awaits the defendants' response. The defendants may think that they have some preliminary objections to the suit. For example, Automatic may think that it is a denial of due process for California to try to assume jurisdiction over Automatic. Automatic doesn't want to litigate in California; it would prefer to compel Smith to come to Massachusetts to make his claim. Automatic also knows that if it *consents* to the jurisdiction of the California court, it will have no ground to complain about a denial of due process. If Automatic, upon receiving the summons in the mail, immediately entered a denial of Smith's claim, it will have made a *general appearance* (i.e., one in which it raised any point on the merits of the case). A general appearance will be treated as equivalent to consent. Therefore, Automatic wants to make what is called a *special appearance,* that is, to appear in the California court for the sole and limited purpose of objecting to California's jurisdiction over it.

Automatic would make its objection by a *motion to quash,* i.e., nullify, the summons. If the motion is granted, the effect will be the same as if Automatic had never been served at all and Smith will have to proceed against Jones alone. If the motion is denied, however, Automatic will be before the court for the purpose of this action just as though it had been personally served. Very likely, its motion would be denied and we will so assume. Automatic must now get down to the business of developing its defenses.

2. Pleadings

In order to consider the defenses the defendants may raise, it is first necessary to consider in more detail the contents of the complaint. There are almost limitless possible problems that may be involved in preparing and defending against a complaint. We shall only consider a few major points.

The first problem is whether, as against each of the defendants considered separately, the complaint states a claim which, if proved, would entitle Smith to recover damages. (Note that at this stage, Smith is not trying to prove anything; he is merely *asserting* what he hopes and expects can be proved at trial.) If his complaint does state such a claim, his complaint is *sufficient in point of substantive law* (in common legal parlance, his complaint *states a cause of action*); if not, his complaint is *insufficient* in that respect. This problem can be easily illustrated.

For example, as to Automatic, the law of torts recognizes that a manufacturer of goods is liable in damages to any person whom the manufacturer could foresee would be injured by a defect in the goods. But though in most jurisdictions the law has now changed in this regard, a manufacturer previously was liable for injury caused by an article made by him *only* if he was negligent in the way he manufactured it. This is a matter of *substantive law.*

Now, the procedural rule is that Smith's complaint must state a claim that is sufficient under the substantive law, that is, the complaint must describe a particular situation that falls within the general class of situations to which the substantive law rule refers.   Suppose that Smith's complaint alleged that Automatic manufactured the gun, that the barrel was defective, that the gun exploded when used, that the explosion was the proximate result of the defect in the barrel and that Smith was thereby injured.   Is Smith's complaint sufficient as a matter of substantive law?   If negligence on Automatic's part is required under the substantive law then Smith's complaint is *not* sufficient, for he has not alleged that Automatic was negligent in the way it manufactured the gun.   But if a manufacturer is liable simply when its product is defective, then Smith's complaint does state a cause of action.

Apart from the requirement that the complaint be sufficient in its substance, the rules of procedure require that the complaint comply with certain rules of form.   The following are examples of rules of form: a complaint based on a contract must state the terms of the contract; a complaint must be signed by the plaintiff or, in certain circumstances, by his attorney; it must describe the claim with sufficient specificity so that the defendants have a fairly clear idea of the nature of the claim being asserted against them.   Smith's complaint must comply with these rules, lest it be found *insufficient in point of form.*   As we shall see, the rules of form are less important than the rule that a complaint must be sufficient in point of substance.

Smith will have drawn up his complaint in the light of these pleading rules.   He will have done the best he can to comply with the rules.   However, he may not have complied with the rules in one or more respects.   The reasons why he did not do so may be: he didn't pay attention to a particular rule; he may have interpreted a certain rule in a way different from the way that the defendants or (more importantly) the judge interpret it; he may have deliberately ignored a rule, hoping the defendants would not object.   Whatever the reasons, Smith has filed his complaint and we may now consider defendants' attacks on the complaint.

Defendants can object, first of all, to errors of form.   In procedural systems known as Code pleading, such as exists in California, the procedural device used for raising many objections to form is called the *special demurrer.*   The term "special demurrer" is a name given by long custom and convenience to a demurrer that raises points of form.   It is to be distinguished from the *general demurrer,* which is the procedural device used for objecting to the sufficiency of the complaint in point of substance.   We will see more of the general demurrer in a moment.   Under the Federal Rules of Civil Procedure, the analogue of the special demurrer is the *motion to make more definite and certain,* which is what its name implies.

Defendants know that if they wish to raise any objections to form, they must do so at the very beginning.   This is so because formal pleading errors are recognized as relatively unimportant and are *waived* if not taken immediately.

Defendants may also have objections in point of substance.   For example, Automatic may believe that it cannot be held liable unless it be established that it was negligent in the way it made the gun.   The complaint, it will be recalled, did not allege that Automatic was negligent.   Most likely, Smith did not so allege because *he* believed that under the substantive law a manufacturer of a dangerous instrumentality is liable for injuries resulting from defects in the instrumentality even though the manufacturer was *not* negligent.   Automatic

may raise its point by means of a *general demurrer*. (The Federal Rules equivalent is a *motion to dismiss for failure to state a claim on which relief may be granted*.) The effect is to say: "Even if what you say is true, you are not entitled to recover under the substantive law." Put another way, the general demurrer says, "So what?"

Observe that so far neither Jones nor Automatic has contested the truth of the allegations on Smith's complaint. All the arguments in support of or against the demurrers interposed by defendants, whether special or general demurrers, will proceed on the assumption that what Smith says is true. A demurrer challenges a pleading's *sufficiency in point of law, not its veracity in point of fact.*

Suppose that Jones and Automatic interpose demurrers on various grounds. The trial judge concludes that Smith's complaint in some particulars is unduly vague, so he *sustains* the special demurrer raising that objection. He decides, however, that the complaint is sufficient in point of substantive law. Hence, he *overrules* the general demurrer. He allows Smith to *amend* his complaint to cure the defect of vagueness. Smith does this by drafting a new complaint, in which he spells out the details more fully. He files the original, called his *amended complaint*, and serves (delivers or mails) copies of it to the attorneys for Jones and Automatic. He does not need to make new service on the defendants themselves, for since the time of their original service they are regarded as present before the court until the litigation is finally disposed of.

The defendants now consider their defenses in point of fact. Doubtless they will expressly *admit* some of the matters alleged by Smith, such as the fact that he bought the gun. They know that they will be *deemed to admit* allegations that they don't deny, so they are careful to deny allegations which they wish to contest. For example, they may deny that the gun barrel was defective and that Smith was injured. They are pretty sure that Smith was injured in some degree, but they are not sure how much. To be on the safe side, they deny that he was injured at all.

These denials will be set forth in their *answer*. The answer is the pleading by which the defendant joins issue with plaintiff on the factual matters presented by the plaintiff's claim. The denials constitute *negative defenses*. But defendants may also have *affirmative defenses*—contentions that there are other factual circumstances which, if proven, would exonerate defendants even if the facts alleged by plaintiff are established. For example, suppose that Automatic suspects that Smith did not use the right type of ammunition in the gun and that this contributed to the explosion. In its answer, Automatic, in addition to denying Smith's allegations, would allege that Smith used the wrong kind of ammunition, that this was a proximate contributing cause of the explosion and hence that Smith was contributorily negligent. Automatic thus contends that even if it turns out that it was liable, there are additional facts which, under the substantive law, result in Smith's being unable to recover or which reduce the amount of his recovery. Affirmative defenses are often spoken of as matters in *avoidance*, rather than denial, of the plaintiff's claim.

Smith might have objections to the defendants' answers very similar to those discussed in connection with the complaint: Smith might think the allegations of the affirmative defense are too vague or that they are not sufficient in point of substantive law. If so, he could *demur*, specially or generally as the case may be, to defendants' answers—or, under the Federal Rules, make an equivalent motion against the answer.

Suppose, however, that Smith does not so demur. One might suppose that Smith should controvert the allegations of contributory negligence. In many jurisdictions, this would indeed be proper, by a pleading known as a *reply*. In most procedural systems, including California's and in the Federal Rules, however, allegations in the answer are *deemed denied*. Hence, Smith need not file any additional pleading.

At this point, therefore, the *pleadings are closed*. So far as the pleadings are concerned, the case is ready for trial.

3. Discovery, Pre-Trial, Summary Judgment

More or less at the same time as the parties are going through the process of formulating the issues to be tried (pleading), they are going through the process of probing the merits of each other's case. This is called *discovery*. The means of discovery are several.

The most useful and most used is the *deposition on oral examination,* or, as it is more simply referred to, the *deposition*. This is a device by which one party may require the other to appear before a court reporter and answer questions put to her by the opposing lawyer. A deposition may be taken not only of a *party* to the action, such as Smith or Jones, but also of witnesses who are not parties, such as Smith's hunting companion. When the lawyer asks questions of the *deponent,* he is said to be *taking* the witness' deposition. The lawyer will try to find out the other side's version of the facts, seeking to find weaknesses and to pin down the testimony. For example, Automatic will take Smith's deposition. Normally, the lawyers for Smith and Automatic will agree on a time mutually satisfactory, Automatic will arrange to have a court reporter on hand, and the deposition will be taken at the office of Automatic's lawyer. There Smith will be asked to identify himself, to give in detail his account of buying the gun, using it and how it exploded. He will be asked about his injuries. He will be asked if there was anyone with him at the time the gun exploded and, if so, to give his companion's name. Probably, Automatic's lawyer will later on take the deposition of the companion, if there was one.

Similarly, Smith will be using discovery against the defendants. Smith will take Jones' deposition. As against Automatic, Smith is not sure whom to interrogate. You can't take the deposition of a witness unless you know his name or can otherwise adequately identify him; Smith doesn't know who is in charge of Automatic's manufacturing operations. He may therefore use, at least in the first instance, *interrogatories to a party*. These are *written* questions addressed to Automatic. Automatic must dig up the information demanded, if it has the information. For example, Smith's interrogatories to Automatic would ask the date on which the gun was made, the information it provided concerning proper ammunition, and so on. On the basis of the answers, Smith may take the depositions of some of Automatic's key personnel.

There are other discovery devices, but they are essentially variations of deposition and written interrogatories. The discovery process serves to let parties know in detail what the litigation is all about. It may result in eliminating some of the issues raised by the pleadings. For example, Smith's testimony may make it quite clear that he was injured by the gun's exploding. Hence, the defendants probably will no longer wish to contest that point. On the other hand, the discovery process may open up new issues, for example, the possibility that Smith was firing the gun at such a rapid rate of fire as to overheat the gun barrel. Automatic therefore would want to amend its answer to assert this additional basis of defense.

It will be helpful if, prior to trial, the parties agree as to what should actually be tried. This can be done at the *pre-trial conference,* a meeting, held either in the courtroom or in the judge's chambers, between the lawyers for the various parties. Sometimes, but usually not, the parties themselves will be present. At this time, the judge will determine whether there are any required amendments to the pleadings, adding issues or eliminating them. She will also inquire about the possibilities of settlement, for the parties may now be close together in their appraisal of the case. She may take care of routine matters which would be time-consuming at the trial, such as the formal identification of documentary evidence (medical records and so on). Finally, the judge may try to ascertain whether there are any points of law that will probably come up at trial which can be decided beforehand. In short, the purpose of the pre-trial conference is to put the case in final shape for trial.

One procedural device we have not discussed must now be mentioned. This is *summary judgment.* It is always possible that there is some fact crucial to the lawsuit that can be established as true beyond real dispute. For example, suppose that Jones sold Smith the gun under a contract which expressly provided that Jones would in no event be liable to the purchaser for any amount beyond the cost of the gun. Assume that the contract was drafted with such care that it clearly bars Smith's claim for injuries against Jones. If this is true, it is obvious that there is no point in proceeding very far against Jones; it would involve only needless expense. Smith, it will be recalled, alleged that Jones breached the contract of sale and Jones denied this, so the issue is in dispute according to the pleadings. But if Jones could produce the contract before the judge, establish by *affidavit*—a sworn written statement of facts—that it was the contract in question, she could then urge that the contract's legal effect was to bar any liability on her part. She could, therefore, move for *summary judgment*—judgment summarily and without a plenary trial.

The motion for summary judgment could be made at any time after the complaint is filed. Indeed, Jones might present this motion before demurring or answering or taking any other procedural step. She would do so by filing a motion asking for judgment in her favor, attaching to the motion her affidavit setting out the facts concerning the sale and including a copy of the sale contract signed by Smith. If Smith did not file a counter affidavit, it would be pretty clear that there was *no genuine issue of fact* as to whether this was the contract under which the gun was sold. Hence, if the judge concluded that the terms of the contract clearly relieved Jones of liability (a matter of substantive law, involving interpretation of the contract), she would grant the motion. If Smith denied that he signed the contract attached to Jones' affidavit, there would be a genuine issue of fact as to whether that was the contract and summary judgment would be denied. The truth would have to be decided at the trial.

4. Trial

Suppose that the case is not disposed of prior to trial and a trial date is therefore set. On the appointed day, the lawyers and parties would convene in court and the trial would commence.

A threshold question will be whether the case should be tried to a jury or not. This being an action *at law,* since it is for damages, it would be triable to a jury on demand of either party. (In contrast, a suit for an injunction is in *equity* and normally is triable to the judge sitting without a jury.) Let us assume that one of the parties has made a timely demand for jury trial; failure to make such a demand would constitute a waiver of the jury trial right.

At the trial the first task is the selection of the jury. In most state courts, a jury in a civil case consists of 12 persons; in many Federal districts, a six person jury is used in civil cases. A court official will have herded a group of prospective jurors into the courtroom. The lawyers proceed to interrogate them, to find out if they are qualified and fair minded and what they are like as people. This is called the *voir dire examination.* Sometimes the primary questioning is done by the judge, but the lawyers in most states are given a chance to ask questions if they wish. A juror revealing bias or some other disqualification will be *challenged for cause.* If a juror has no such disqualification, but one party doesn't like the looks of him, the party normally may excuse the juror by using one of his limited number of *peremptory challenges.* When this process is completed, the jury is sworn by the clerk of the court. It is thereby *impaneled.*

The lawyers now make their *opening statements.* The plaintiff goes first. His lawyer tells the jury what the case is about and what he expects to prove. The defendant may make an opening statement at this time or postpone doing so until after the plaintiff has put in his evidence. Either way, the next thing that happens is that the plaintiff puts in his *case in chief.* Plaintiff has the burden of proof of the matters alleged in his complaint (as to most matters at any rate). He must prove these matters by evidence which is strong enough so that the judge will allow the jury to consider the case and which, plaintiff hopes, is strong enough so that the jury will believe the facts to be as plaintiff claims. Smith himself will testify and his doctor will testify about Smith's injuries. Smith might have an expert metallurgist as a witness concerning the condition of the gun barrel. The testimony which Smith, and the other witnesses put on by him, give in response to questions by Smith's attorney is known as *direct examination* of the witness. When the direct examination of each of Smith's witnesses is concluded, defendants' attorneys may ask him questions, seeking to bring out uncertainties, weaknesses and mistakes. This is *cross-examination.*

After plaintiff has put in his case, he *rests.* By resting, plaintiff says that he has proved enough so that, if the jury believes his evidence, a verdict may be rendered in his favor. Defendants may not think so. For example, suppose that Smith offered no evidence from which it could be concluded that the gun was defective. Automatic could raise the objection by asking for a *non-suit,* called a *dismissal* under the Federal Rules, or for a *directed verdict* (requesting the judge to instruct the jury that they must return a verdict for Automatic), on the ground that plaintiff's proofs as a matter of law fail to make out the elements of a valid claim.

These motions resemble a delayed general demurrer but focus on the plaintiff's proofs rather than his pleading. The motion, that is, contends that even assuming the facts shown by plaintiff's evidence are true, plaintiff is not entitled to recover under the substantive law. In ruling on the motion, the judge will not attempt to decide whether plaintiff's evidence should be believed; she is only deciding the legal question that is presented *assuming* the jury were to believe the evidence.

Suppose that the judge denies the defendant's motion. She may do so either because she disagrees with Automatic's argument as to what the substantive law is, or because she prefers to see what evidence Automatic develops prior to making her ruling. Accordingly, *defendants* would proceed with their *case in chief.* If defendants had not previously made their opening statements, the presentation of their case would be preceded by those statements.

In her case in chief, defendant introduces evidence tending to disprove plaintiff's case. For example, defendants very likely would have their own medical testimony, tending to show that Smith wasn't as badly injured as Smith's evidence seems to indicate. Defendants would also put in evidence to support affirmative defenses they might have, such as contributory negligence. For this purpose, they probably would call plaintiff himself as an *adverse witness.* They might also call other witnesses, such as Smith's hunting companion. Each witness will be directly examined by defendants and may be cross-examined by plaintiff.

At the end of the case, defendants might again move for dismissal or directed verdict. Plaintiff himself might move for a directed verdict, claiming that no evidence offered by defendants in any substantial way tends to disprove the claim. In the case supposed, doubtless both motions would be denied. The case must be put in the hands of the jury.

The plaintiff now *opens his concluding argument.* He reviews the evidence, stressing the points most favorable to him and playing down the defendants' evidence. He will urge the jury to find for Smith and, within limits, encourage the jury to see the evidence in a sympathetic light. Then the *defendants* will make their *concluding arguments,* stressing the evidence favorable to them and trying to discount considerations of sympathy. When defendants are done with this argument, Smith returns with his *closing argument.* Finally, the judge will *instruct the jury.* In her instructions, submitted to her beforehand for approval and amendment by the lawyers for both sides, the judge will tell the jury what the issues are according to the substantive law. She will also tell them who has the burden of proof, and what they must find in order to render a verdict for one side or the other.

The jury then retires for *deliberation.* In closed session, the jury first elects a foreman (spokesman) and then proceeds to decide what they think the facts are. Usually, they will be required to render a *general verdict.* This is a verdict in which they state simply the name of the party for whom they find and, if for plaintiff, the damages he should recover. The lawyers may have requested the judge to require a *special verdict* from the jury. If the judge grants the request, the jury will be given a series of specific questions they must answer. For example, the questions might be: Did Automatic make a proper inspection of the guns it manufactured? Did plaintiff use proper ammunition? And so on.

The jury must reach a decision. In some states and in the Federal courts, they must reach unanimity, although some of these states, and the Federal Rules of Civil Procedure, permit the parties to stipulate otherwise. In California and many other states, 9 out of 12 must agree in favor of one party or the other. If the jury doesn't reach a decision by the necessary majority, and the judge thinks further deliberation will be useless, she may discharge the jury and order a new trial.

If the jury does reach a verdict, it returns to the courtroom, the foreman gives the verdict to the clerk or judge, and the judge then reads it. The parties may ask the jury to be *polled,* i.e., that each juror be individually asked whether he concurs in the verdict. Assuming the necessary majority does concur the verdict will be accepted by the court and the jury will be *discharged.*

The clerk is now called upon to enter the *judgment.* This is the formal order disposing of the case. If in favor of plaintiff, it would say: "Judgment is hereby entered in favor of Smith, and against Jones and Automatic, and each of them, in the amount of \$ (amount found by jury)." Just before or just after entry of judgment, however, the trial judge may have to decide some post-trial motions.

5. Post-trial Motions

Post-trial motions are concerned with two principal problems: First, consideration of the substantive legal sufficiency of plaintiff's claim (or defendant's defense). This point could be raised by a motion by one side or the other for *judgment notwithstanding the verdict.* (The Latin term for this is judgment *non obstante veredicto,* from which is derived the commonly used name for this motion, *judgment n.o.v.*) Such a motion would raise the same point as a motion for directed verdict and, again, resembles a general demurrer.

Second, the parties might assert errors that occurred in the trial itself—errors in the admission of evidence, in the conduct of attorneys, litigants, jurors or judge, and, perhaps most frequently, errors in the instructions to the jury. The appropriate motion in such circumstances is one for a *new trial,* seeking a redetermination that (hopefully) will be free of contaminating procedural errors.

Mention here should be made of procedural devices for relieving a party who is in default. Suppose, to return to our hypothetical case, that Jones, after being served with summons, failed to do anything. After due notice to Jones, Smith would instruct the clerk of the court to note the fact that Jones was *in default* and would apply to the court for a *default judgment.* The judge would conduct a brief ex parte hearing (a hearing at which only Smith is present) on the question of the amount of damages Smith has sustained and would enter a judgment against Jones for the amount that she finds should be awarded.

Perhaps Jones fell seriously ill the day after she was served. She recovers her health after the default judgment has been entered against her. What can she do? She can move the court to *set aside the judgment* and permit her to make her defense.

6. Appeal

After a final judgment has been rendered in the trial court, the losing party may feel that injustice has been done. If so, he may *appeal.* It is beyond the scope of this discussion to consider appeals in any length. But several points should be kept in mind.

First, in general an appeal may be taken only after *final judgment.* We have seen that as the trial progresses, the judge will be called on to make all kinds of rulings—on demurrers, motions, evidence, instructions and post-trial motions. At any point, the judge may make a mistake that will confuse or render erroneous all the subsequent stages of the proceeding. The litigants would hope that such a serious error could be corrected by immediate appeal. However, except in limited situations, no appeal may be taken until the final judgment, for better or worse, has been rendered.

This "final judgment rule" creates a good deal of difficulty. Sometimes a trial judge will make an error at the threshold of litigation which is so important that the rest of the proceedings become pointless. For example, suppose that the trial judge overruled Automatic's motion to quash summons. Under the "final judgment rule," this means that Automatic will have to go through the whole trial before it can appeal the ruling on the motion to quash. This seems too bad, and we find that sometimes statutes and case law provide special remedies for such situations. In the Federal courts and many state courts, certain kinds of orders can be appealed before final judgment; this is called *interlocutory appeal.* Another procedure is the use of the "extraordinary writs," chiefly *mandamus* (or mandate, to use the name in California) and *prohibition.* The first writ commands the trial judge to do something; the second prohibits her from doing something. For example, in the case supposed, Automatic might well seek a *writ of prohibition* from the appellate court, directing the trial judge to desist from entertaining the case as against Automatic.

A second point to be remembered about appeals is that an appellate court is supposed to correct errors, not to render what it thinks is a more just result in the particular case. If the trial judge made a mistake of law and it seems that the mistake affected the outcome, then the appellate court will do something about it—usually, reverse the judgment and order a new trial. This is *reversible error* on the part of the trial court. If the trial judge made a mistake but it didn't seem to have affected the result below, the appellate court will not do anything about it. This is *harmless error* on the part of the trial court. If, however, the trial judge didn't commit any mistakes, and the only objection is that the result doesn't seem just, the appellate court will *not* do anything about it.

A third important point is that appellate courts in general do not review lower court decisions on matters of *fact;* review is ordinarily limited to questions of *law.* This general rule is subject to the important qualification that a fact determination may be reversed on appeal if the appellate court thinks there is no substantial evidence to support the determination in question. Obviously this leaves some latitude to the appellate courts, for "substantial" is a pretty vague criterion. But with this and other qualifications, the generalization holds.

Lastly, the appellate court will not ordinarily consider objections that were not first presented to the trial court. This is simply a catch-all notion of estoppel: a litigant must ordinarily raise his objections at the first opportunity and not be permitted afterthoughts. A corollary of this proposition is that the appellate court will not consider anything not contained in the record presented to it. Thus, the appellate court won't consider an objection, even if made in the court below, unless the appellant puts before the appellate court a record showing that the objection was timely and properly made. Put another way, a case can go all the way to the Supreme Court only if it has been made in the trial court first.

———

NOTE ON THE STRUCTURE OF THE COURT SYSTEM

The court system may be described, again in a simplified way, as follows:

Courts in the American system are of two principal types: trial courts and appellate courts. Trial courts are those tribunals in which proceedings are initiated, the disputed issues framed, the proofs taken and the initial decision handed down. Unless timely application for appellate review is made, the disposition of the trial court is final. And even when appellate review is obtained, the function of the appellate court, speaking generally, is solely that of inquiring whether the trial court properly disposed of the case as presented to it. An appellate court is a court for reviewing what was done at trial and not for reconsidering what might have been done.

1. State Courts

The state courts, as distinguished from the federal courts, are the courts in which disputes are ordinarily heard. The federal courts will be described presently, but the point should be noted immediately that only special classes of cases are cognizable in them.

a. Trial Courts. (1) Courts of Limited Jurisdiction. Most states have courts of limited jurisdiction, i.e., courts that are authorized to hear and determine cases involving a relatively small amount in controversy and (ordinarily) simple issues. The historic prototypes of the courts of limited jurisdiction are the justice court, presided over by a justice of the peace, and city courts, presided over by a city magistrate. The justice court historically had authority to hear civil cases involving claims for money in a small amount, typically $20, and criminal cases involving minor offenses, typically misdemeanors. The municipal court had a similarly limited jurisdiction. See Skoler, Monetary Limitations on Civil Jurisdiction of Minor Courts, 36 So.Calif.L.Rev. 55 (1962).

In a few states the historic pattern still prevails. In most, the court systems have been reorganized, in the following directions: The justice courts have been reduced in number, professionalized (i.e., the justice is required to have legal training), and their maximum monetary jurisdiction increased. The municipal courts have been made uniform in their jurisdiction (so that the authority of municipal courts is the same throughout the particular state), professionalized, and have had their monetary jurisdiction increased. Thus, the Municipal Court in California has jurisdiction of controversies up to $25,000, full-time judges who are law trained, and procedure similar to the Superior Court. In a few states, all trial proceedings are in a single trial court.

The names and authority of courts of limited jurisdiction vary from state to state. Most states still have courts known as justice courts, some have a court analogous to the municipal court, and many have a court of limited jurisdiction known as the "county" court. See Department of Justice, National Criminal Justice Information and Statistics Service, National Survey of Court Organization (1973).

A word should be said about "small claims courts." A "small claims court" is not a separate court at all. Rather, the term refers to a simplified form of procedure available in courts of limited jurisdiction, such as the justice or municipal court, for the trial of cases involving a relatively small amount, $250 to $2,500 or so according to the particular state. See, e.g., C.C.P. 116 et seq. See also Small Cases, infra p. 1249.

(2) Courts of General Jurisdiction. All states have courts, usually organized along county lines, for hearing cases of all types, unlimited by subject matter or amount in controversy. Such a court is referred to as the trial court of general jurisdiction. The court of general jurisdiction is known by different names in different states: in California it is the Superior Court; in New York, it is the Supreme Court; in many states it is the Circuit Court; in other states

it is known as the District Court, the County Court, the Court of Common Pleas, or by other names. Whatever its name this is the court in which are heard all cases that are not channelled elsewhere, i.e., either to an administrative agency or to a court of limited jurisdiction. It is in this court that are applied the state rules of procedure considered in these materials, though in many jurisdictions the same rules also apply in the inferior courts.

In some states, the jurisdiction of the court of general jurisdiction is concurrent with that of the courts of limited jurisdiction so that a case of a size and kind cognizable in a court of limited jurisdiction may nevertheless be brought at plaintiff's option in the court of general jurisdiction. In other states the jurisdiction of the court of general jurisdiction is exclusive of that of the inferior courts: if a case is within the authority of an inferior court it must be brought there and not in the court of general jurisdiction. See, e.g., Calif.Const. Art. VI §§ 10–11.

Reference must be made to certain other specialized types of "courts," such as the "probate" court, the "domestic relations" court and others. In some states, these are indeed separate courts staffed by separate judges. Thus, in New York there is a separate tribunal known as the Surrogate's Court which has probate jurisdiction, i.e., authority to hear matters pertaining to decedents' estates. In many states, however, the terms "probate court" or "domestic relations court" do not refer to separate courts but to specialized procedures applied in the court of general jurisdiction to the particular types of cases referred to.

b. Appellate Courts. (1) Appeals from Inferior Courts. Most states permit appeal of the determinations made by courts of limited jurisdiction. In some states, the mode of appeal is by trial de novo in the court of general jurisdiction, so that a litigant dissatisfied with the result of the disposition by the inferior court may by appropriate procedure request that the case be retried in the court of general jurisdiction. Retrial is usually limited to the issues framed in the lower court, but additional evidence as well as additional argument may be presented. In other states, the mode of appeal is strictly review. That is, the record of the proceedings in the inferior court is presented to the court of general jurisdiction for consideration of the correctness of the disposition of the case as it was presented below. In some states, the appeal to the court of general jurisdiction is the final appeal and no further review may be obtained. In others, under some circumstances, the disposition of the court of general jurisdiction may itself be reviewed by further appeal. See, e.g., C.C.P. 911.

The hearing of cases in trial courts, whether of limited or general jurisdiction, is ordinarily conducted by a single judge. The trial bench in urban areas usually has more than one judge, of course, and in such courts different judges may be called upon to hear various phases of a particular case. Thus, one judge may pass upon preliminary pleading questions, another on questions arising in discovery matters, and yet another preside at trial. But at any hearing only one judge ordinarily sits and decides. This is to be contrasted with the practice in continental civil procedure, where many hearings (at least in trial courts of general jurisdiction) are before a panel of three judges.

(2) Appeals from Courts of General Jurisdiction. All states permit appellate review of the disposition of cases in courts of general jurisdiction. Historically, the procedural devices by which appellate review was obtained were: (1) at common law, by the writ of error or, in certain circumstances, by a special procedural device known as the writ of certiorari; (2) in equity, by an appeal.

See generally Pound, Appellate Procedure in Civil Cases (1941). Today, the procedure for obtaining appellate review is usually referred to as an appeal, though a few states retain the historical terminology and distinctions.

In a few states there is but one appellate court for appeals from the trial courts of general jurisdiction. Such an appellate court is usually known as the Supreme Court of the state, but in some jurisdictions it is known as the Court of Appeals or by some other name.

Most states have intermediate appellate courts as well. Their organization varies from state to state, as do their names, but the usual title is Court of Appeals. In New York, the intermediate appellate court is the Appellate Division of the Supreme Court; in California, it is the Court of Appeal. The intermediate appellate courts in almost all states are several in number, organized along geographical lines by groups of counties.

The subject matter jurisdiction of intermediate appellate courts also varies from state to state. See the historical analysis in Louis, Allocating Adjudicative Decision Making Authority Between the Trial and Appellate Levels: A Unified View of the Scope of Review, the Judge-Jury Question, and Procedural Discretion, 64 N.C.L.Rev. 993 (1986); cf. Project, The Appellate Division of the Supreme Court of New York: An Empirical Study of Its Powers and Functions as an Intermediate State Appellate Court, 47 Ford.L.Rev. 929 (1979). The typical pattern is that all types of appeals from the trial courts are taken to the intermediate appellate court; further appellate review in the state supreme court is obtainable only in the discretion of the supreme court or upon special request of the intermediate appellate court. The procedural device for such further review may be simply an "appeal"; more often it is known as certiorari. In California, review by the Supreme Court of a decision of the Court of Appeal is obtained by "application for hearing," which if granted is followed by a "transfer" of the case from the Court of Appeal to the Supreme Court.

The highest appellate court of a state consists of several judges, the number varying from state to state but typically consisting of seven, as in California, Illinois and New York. The intermediate appellate courts usually consist of a number of judges who sit in panels of three. In the New York Appellate Division five judges sit in any particular appeal.

2. The Federal Courts

The federal court system parallels the court systems of the states except that the authority of federal courts is at all levels special and limited in the kind of cases cognizable.

a. Trial Courts. The principal trial court of the federal system is the district court. Originally, the federal system had two types of trial court, the district courts and the circuit courts. As the result of a series of statutory changes since 1789, the district court has become the only ordinary trial court in the federal system and the circuit court has become exclusively an appellate court.

The district courts are organized along territorial lines called districts. Each district comprises a state or a portion of a state consisting of several counties. Thus, the territory of the Federal District Court for the District of Oregon consists of the State of Oregon. Florida is divided into three—Northern, Middle and Southern; California and New York are divided into four. Some of these districts are divided for administrative purposes into divisions, each of which has a headquarters in a different place within the district. See

28 U.S.C.A. §§ 81 et seq. Each district has one or more judges who, like judges of the state trial courts, normally sit individually in the hearing of any particular case.

The federal district courts have jurisdiction over several types of cases. A principal type includes actions between citizens of different states where the amount in controversy exceeds $50,000. This is known as the "diversity jurisdiction" of the federal courts and it extends, generally speaking, without regard to the subject matter of the controversy. The diversity jurisdiction of the federal courts is concurrent with that of the state courts. A second principal type includes actions by private individuals "arising under" (that is to say, based upon) federal law, known as the "federal question" jurisdiction of the federal courts. For a few types of federal question jurisdiction, a minimum amount in controversy is required; in others the federal district courts have jurisdiction without regard to the amount in controversy. Again in some types of federal question jurisdiction, for example patent infringement suits, the jurisdiction of the federal district courts is exclusive of the states; in others, the state courts have concurrent jurisdiction. A third principal type of federal jurisdiction is actions by or against the Federal Government and its agencies.

In these and other types of actions heard on the "civil" side of the federal district court, the procedure is governed by the Federal Rules of Civil Procedure, considered in detail in these materials. Since 1966 these Rules, with certain supplemental ones, also govern admiralty cases. The federal district courts also have jurisdiction of bankruptcy proceedings, governed by special rules.

In addition to the federal district courts, the United States Claims Court serves as a trial court in certain types of actions against the Government. Its jurisdiction and procedure and the procedure of other specialized federal tribunals are beyond the scope of the present discussion.

b. Appellate Courts. Determinations made in the federal district courts are ordinarily appealable to the Courts of Appeals, the intermediate appellate courts of the federal system. The Courts of Appeals, formerly known as the Circuit Courts, principally are organized territorially by groups of states, the groups being known as circuits. For example, the Court of Appeals for the Second Circuit hears appeals from federal district courts located in the states of New York, Connecticut and Vermont. There are thirteen circuits, eleven bearing numbers (First Circuit, Second Circuit, etc.) with the twelfth being the Court of Appeals for the District of Columbia and the thirteenth being the Court of Appeals for the Federal Circuit. The jurisdiction of the first twelve circuits is based on geography while the Federal Circuit's jurisdiction is based on subject matter. Each Court of Appeals consists of several judges who ordinarily sit in panels of three judges each, but who occasionally hear cases en banc, i.e., with the entire membership sitting. The Courts of Appeals also have important appellate jurisdiction of cases originating in the federal administrative agencies.

The highest court in the federal system is of course the Supreme Court of the United States. The Supreme Court has *original* jurisdiction of a very limited class of cases, chiefly actions between States. Otherwise, the Supreme Court's jurisdiction is appellate. It has appellate jurisdiction not only of cases originating in the lower federal courts but also of certain types of cases originating in the courts of the states. Potentially, any case originating in a federal district court may be taken to the Supreme Court. Most such cases must be appealed initially to the courts of appeals and may be thereafter taken to the Supreme Court only with the latter's permission, although in some circumstances a court of appeals may request an opinion from the Supreme Court on a question presented in a case being considered in the court of appeals.

Of cases originating in the courts of the states, only those presenting questions of federal law—statutory, constitutional or otherwise—may be considered by the Supreme Court. Its consideration of such a case is limited to the federal issues involved. The Supreme Court therefore has but a limited, though vitally important, appellate supervision over decisions of state courts. The court of the state from which an appeal to the Supreme Court may be taken is the highest state court authorized to hear the case. Ordinarily, this means that an appeal to the Supreme Court of the United States will be from the state's supreme court. If, however, the state court system is so organized that appellate review by the state's supreme court is not available in a particular case, then an appeal to the United States Supreme Court may be taken from the lower state court.

The procedure for court of appeals review of district court decisions is by appeal or, in unusual cases, by extraordinary writ. The procedure for appellate review by the Supreme Court is either by appeal or by writ of certiorari, depending on the nature of the case. In practice, both latter types of review are substantially similar.

3. Rulemaking Authority

The rules of civil procedure are found in statutes, case law, and rules of court. The third category requires further explanation because of certain features unique to it. Rules adopted by a court have the force of law and control the conduct of parties, attorneys, and judges. Like other legislation, they are subject to judicial interpretation, so that a body of case law develops around them. Of more than theoretical concern, however, are two fundamental issues: (1) the authority of a court to adopt rules, and (2) the permissible scope of such rules.

The constitutional authority for courts to enact rules of procedure is in a zone of concurrent authority between the separated powers of the judicial and legislative branches of government. Four basic approaches have been employed in allocating the rulemaking authority between courts and legislatures. The first and most common source of judicial rulemaking authority is an explicit legislative delegation of that power to the judiciary under which the legislature has either an express or implied power to review and invalidate rules adopted by the courts. Such is the case with the Federal Rules Enabling Act, 28 U.S.C.A. § 2072. See Burbank, The Rules Enabling Act of 1934, 130 U.Pa.L.Rev. 1015 (1982); Spaniol, Making Federal Rules: The Inside Story, 69 A.B.A.J. 1645 (1983). The second most common system is a constitutional provision granting rulemaking power to the courts and veto power over such rules to the legislature. Third, several state constitutions grant rulemaking authority to the courts without providing any oversight by the legislature. Finally, in a few states the courts have asserted rulemaking authority on the basis of general constitutional provisions concerning the judiciary or based on the historical development of their court systems. See, e.g., Kay, The Rule–Making Authority and Separation of Powers in Connecticut, 8 Conn.L.Rev. 1 (1975).

Judicial rulemaking authority, whatever its basis, is limited to procedural matters, and substantive rules remain the sole province of the legislature. Although the line between substance and procedure is shadowy, a procedural rule that encroaches on substantive rights may violate the constitutional principle of separation of powers. See the discussion in Hanna v. Plumer, infra p. 586. See also Burbank, Sanctions in the Proposed Amendments to the Federal Rules of Civil Procedure: Some Questions About Power, 11 Hofstra L.Rev. 997 (1983).

Unlike the legislative process, which is open to the public, the process used in adopting rules of court is, in many jurisdictions, not open to the public at large. Courts commonly use advisory committees when adopting rules, but public notice, public hearings, and procedures for oral presentation of opposing views are uncommon, and a court's deliberations and votes on the adoption of rules generally are not made available to the public. However, the Federal Rules Enabling Act, 28 U.S.C.A. § 2073, now provides that hearings on the promulgation of federal rules shall be open to the public and minutes of such hearings shall be made available to the public, unless the advisory committee deems it in the public interest to hold a closed meeting, and provides for public notice of hearings and for the publication of reports on proposed rules. The Supreme Court has been criticized for not adequately supervising its advisory committee and for adopting uncritically its recommendations. See Friedenthal, The Rulemaking Power of the Supreme Court: A Contemporary Crisis, 27 Stan. L.Rev. 673 (1975).

4. Judicial Administration

In the past several decades problems of organization of court systems and of judicial administration have received concentrated attention from courts, legislatures, and legal scholars. See generally A.B.A. Standards of Judicial Administration (1977); A.B.A. Standards Relating to Trial Courts (1987); A.B.A. Standards Relating to Appellate Courts (1977); Cecil, Administration of Justice in a Large Appellate Court: The Ninth Circuit Innovations Project (1985); Swanson and Talarico, Court Administration: Issues and Responses (1987). See also the materials on Case Management, infra p. 1223.

HISTORICAL NOTE ON PROCEDURE

1. The Early Evolution of the Writ System

William's conquest of England in 1066 and the years following witnessed the superimposition of Norman feudal institutions on Anglo-Saxon royal and communal institutions and the subsequent emergence of a royal administrative and judicial system that was stronger than either of its predecessors. For present purposes, the significant Anglo-Saxon institutions at the time of the conquest were the crown and the local tribunals. The English crown, theoretically at least, had a responsibility to see that justice was done throughout the realm, i.e., had a direct legitimate interest in all legal disputes. Of English local tribunals there were two principal kinds, the hundred courts (village courts) and the shire courts (analogous to the county court). Communal forums, these courts by the time of the conquest had assumed a territorial jurisdiction in the sense that they were recognized as the appropriate tribunals for disposition of controversies arising in the territory in which they were located. Both acted under a nominal supervision of the crown, thus representing in theory the implementation of the royal interest in justice. The principal shortcoming of the local tribunals was that they were slow and uncertain in operation.

On top of this indigenous English institutional structure the invaders of 1066 erected a para-military governing system. The hierarchy was a pyramid of power built on land grants descending in the first instance from William to his tenants in chief, from the tenants in chief to their feudal subordinates, and from these subordinates to the petty lords of the manor. The lord's authority and responsibility included the power and duty to hold court and to render justice for his tenants. This was the Norman "feudal" court. With the invasion, the Norman court system was transplanted to England and functioned side by side with the English local courts.

As suggested above, the exercise of royal authority in a dispute between man and man could be justified under the Anglo-Saxon theory of the crown. William and his successors held that crown. But such an exercise would also constitute an intrusion into the feudal courts—an invasion of established jurisdiction in derogation of constituted authority. Hence, assertion of royal jurisdiction was impeded both by theoretical limitations imposed by feudalism and by practical objections raised by the barons. Furthermore, the process of royal intrusion, like most constitutional developments, was a series of ad hoc reactions which only in retrospect could be seen as following a pattern.

The earliest forms of royal intervention were not strictly speaking judicial but executive or administrative. The occasion for these early interventions was a wrong, typically involving a breach of the peace, committed somewhere in the realm and unredressed by the local or feudal courts. The instrument of royal intervention was the writ. The writ was nothing more than a written directive from the king to a royal official or to an individual or group of individuals, ordering the addressees to do or refrain from doing a designated act. An example of such a writ, from the reign of Stephen (1135–54), reprinted and translated in Van Caenegem, Royal Writs in England from the Conquest to Glanvill 453–54 (Seld.Soc.1959), is as follows:

> Stephen, king of the English to the bishop of Norwich, greeting. I order to reseise the monks of St. Edmunds of their church of Caistor as fully and justly as they were seised on the day when their abbot left for Rome. And if anything has since been taken away there, let it be justly restored. And let them keep it in peace that no injury is done to them thereof. Witness: Aubrey de Ver. At Westminster.

This method of executive intervention afforded a swift and effective remedy. But it also was easily abused. The writ issued upon the complaint of the alleged injured party: if he had misrepresented the facts, royal intervention would work not justice but injustice. The crown's desire to provide swift redress for wrong was tempered by its desire to be assured that wrong in fact had been done, an age-old dilemma in the administration of justice. In the 12th century, this dilemma was solved in two different ways, both of which, however, resulted in bringing the case before royal officials for hearing. One method directed the sheriff or some other official to advise himself of the facts before proceeding to act. At first, the writs were silent on how the sheriff was to advise himself, but reliance came to be placed on recognition by men of the vicinage, i.e., a jury. By the other method, the alleged wrongdoer was ordered to right the wrong or to appear before the king or his justices and show cause why he had not done so. At the show-cause hearing the merits of the case would be determined. This form of writ was known as a "praecipe," from the Latin word for "order" appearing first after the greeting in the writ. An example, from Van Caenegem, supra at 437, is as follows:

> The king to the sheriff, greeting. Order N. to give back justly and without delay to R. a hundred marks which he owes him, so he says, and of which he complains that he deforces him unjustly. And if he does not do it, summon him by good summoners that he be before me or my justices at Westminster a fortnight after the octave of Easter to show why he has not done it. And have there with you the summoners and this writ. Witness: N. At M.

By this development, a writ that was originally an extraordinary executive interference with the normal course of feudal or local procedure became the triggering device of an ordinary judicial function of the crown.

The procedural steps by which each writ was prosecuted were not uniform but varied from writ to writ. Partly these differences were the consequence of differences in the origin of the various writs. Thus, the *praecipe* type of writ originated as an executive command made without inquiry; when judicialized, it still took the form of a command, the judicial inquiry being made when the defendant appeared in court to "show cause" why he had not obeyed the command. In contrast, the writ of novel disseisin derived from a procedure in which a judicial inquest of complaints was heard first and then executive action followed. This writ is of the *querela* (complaint) type. Other differences in the writs were the products of clerical variation in the Chancery (the royal secretariat from which the writs issued), while still others were the consequence of the age in which the writ was developed. But the point holds that each writ had its own procedure.

The earliest writs concerned controversies over land tenure and its incidents: the writ of novel disseisin was available to remedy a tenant's recent ("novel") ouster from his lands; the writ of mort d'ancestor enabled an heir to recover estates to which he was entitled on the death of a predecessor in interest who died seised in demesne and of right; the writs of debt, detinue, covenant and account, all writs developed in the 12th and 13th centuries, were used chiefly as vehicles for determining controversies over feudal dues between holders of landed estates and those claiming adversely to them. The extent to which new royal writs were fashioned was determined by the felt necessities of the time and the prevailing balance of power between the king on the one hand and the keepers of the feudal courts—the barons—on the other. The resistance of the barons to royal incursions was expressed most dramatically, but only illustratively, in Magna Carta. By the middle of the 13th century or thereabouts, the barons' resistance was strong enough to stem the flow of new common law writs. Further evolution of the writs awaited the appearance of stronger kings and stronger calls for effective justice.

In the meantime, the feudal courts, the local courts, and the borough courts (tribunals of the emergent municipalities) disposed of most of the daily grist of litigation.

See generally Warren, The Governance of Norman and Angevin England (1987); Turner, The English Judiciary in the Age of Glanvill and Bracton (1985); Richardson and Sayles, The Governance of Medieval England from the Conquest to Magna Carta (1963); Stenton, English Justice Between the Norman Conquest and the Great Charter (1964); Milsom, Historical Foundations of the

Common Law (2d ed. 1981).   Compare Watkin, The Significance of 'In Consimili Casu,' 23 Am.J.Legal Hist. 283 (1979).

Another line of royal intervention also had great significance, both contemporaneous and modern. This was the king's direct entertainment of complaints of his subjects. Proceedings before the king and his councillors regarding the complaints—or petitions or "bills" of complaint as they came to be called—start at an early date and are directly related to the Anglo-Saxon theory of kingship as implemented by Norman monarchical vigor. They continue in the 12th and 13th centuries in the form of proceedings by petition or bill (rather than by writ) before the king's justices; they continue in the 13th, 14th and 15th centuries in the form of proceedings by bill before the King's Council or special branches of it known in the 15th and 16th centuries as the Star Chamber and the Court of Requests; they continue in the 15th and subsequent centuries in the form of proceedings by bill before the Chancellor (the pre-eminent member of the King's Council) in what came to be the Court of Chancery. Compare Richardson and Sayles, Introduction, in Select Cases of Procedure Without Writ Under Henry III (Seld.Soc.1941); Sayles, Introduction, in Select Cases in the Court of King's Bench Under Edward III, Vol. V (Seld.Soc.1958); Leadam and Baldwin, Introduction, in Select Cases Before the King's Council 1243–1482 (Seld.Soc.1918); Bayne, Introduction, in Select Cases in the Council of Henry VII (Seld.Soc.1958).

In medieval times, invocation of royal justice by means of writ and by means of petition or bill were overlapping and at times alternative methods of procedure. In later times, procedure by writ became distinctively associated with then-evolved separate royal tribunals, referred to loosely as the common law courts and including the Court of Exchequer, the Court of Common Bench or Court of Common Pleas and the Court of King's Bench; procedure by bill became chiefly associated with the then-evolved Court of Chancery. This difference in procedure is felt even today, particularly in regard to the right to jury trial.

The formalization of procedure during this period was accompanied by the emergence of procedural specialists who understood how the system worked. These specialists were the professional ancestors of modern litigation lawyers. See Symposium, Origins of the English Legal Profession, 5 Law & Hist.Rev. 1 (1987).

2. The Early Evolution of the Royal Courts

The medieval central government was the King's court or *curia regis.* The *curia regis* consisted of a more or less regularly constituted group of chief lords, advisers, retainers and auxiliaries who traveled with the king, giving him counsel, taking care of administrative detail and executing his orders. The chief secretary of the *curia* was the Chancellor; his administrative corps, the Chancery, was principally responsible for the preparation of documents embodying the directives of the king—diplomatic messages, grants of land or privilege, and so on, including the common law writs. So it was that the writs of the common law issued out of Chancery, a practice that continued into the 19th century. Several circumstances conspired, however, to produce specialization of functions within the *curia,* in the form of separate branches of the *curia* that came in time to be referred to as separate courts.

The first of these circumstances was the administrative necessity for orderly record keeping. When the keeping of royal records simply in chronological order became intolerably burdensome, certain types of records were collected not in the "general file" (to use a modern analogue), but in special collections dealing with particular subject matter and, in time, placed in the charge of a particular clerk. Thus, the records dealing with the king's own financial affairs were at an early date consigned to special clerical treatment in the counting house or "exchequer." This was the antecedent of what soon developed into the Court of Exchequer. But in the 12th and early 13th centuries, the chief personnel of the *curia* continued to participate in the administration of most all matters concerning the crown, so that it is not possible to speak of special judges of the Court of Exchequer during this period. Separation of aspects of the king's business was manifested not by the assignment of certain tasks to particular *curiae* but by the maintenance of separate records by particular clerks in the *curia*. The notion that the judges were occupants of independent tribunals, rather than simply a particular group of functionaries in the service of the Crown, did not gain full recognition in legal doctrine until about the time of James I in the early 17th century.

The second principal circumstance that led to the differentiation of the *curia's* functions into separate courts was the historical fact that the early Plantagenet kings had domains in France that were more important to them than England and which required their presence on the continent for long periods of time. In the king's absence, an official known as the Justiciar served in his name and stead. During the long absences of the king abroad, Englishmen became accustomed to the convenience of coming to a royal court stationary at Westminster, rather than trying to catch up with its perambulations over the countryside. This was the origin of the Court of Common Pleas, or Common Bench as it was also known. That branch of the *curia* which still traveled with the king came to be known as the King's Bench, retaining that name and gradually achieving separate organization, even though the royal household had by the 15th century become customarily stationary. The jurisdiction of Common Pleas and King's Bench was not sharply differentiated in the 13th and 14th centuries. By and large, choice between the courts was largely a matter of convenience to the litigants.

This, in radically brief form, is the evolution of the three common law courts—Exchequer, Common Pleas, and King's Bench. Before considering the evolution of the Court of Chancery, it is necessary to touch briefly on the procedure of the common law.

3. Common Law Procedure

In the medieval period, common law procedure for hearing cases was relatively simple and flexible. In proceedings by writ, the terms of the writ disclosed the general nature of plaintiff's complaint. Upon the defendant's appearance, plaintiff stated his complaint orally and in greater detail, the statement being known as plaintiff's declaration. It was required that the claim made in the declaration come within the bounds of the writ. For example, a plaintiff who had obtained a writ of novel disseisin could not "count" (as the making of the declaration came to be known) on some other kind of claim. This requirement was conformable to the principle that the writ alone authorized the hearing of the case, so that a departure from the writ would lead the court beyond its authority. (The requirement of conformity was later administered in a highly technical spirit and made for the procedural casuistries for which common law pleading later came to be justly notorious.)

Defendant responded, also orally, perhaps by denying one of plaintiff's factual contentions, perhaps by arguing that his conduct was not wrongful by the law of the land (i.e., the common law), perhaps by alleging that he was justified in his conduct by reason of certain circumstances which he proceeded to allege. It must be borne in mind that in the background of all medieval litigation was the hope of bringing the parties to some sort of voluntary accord. Hence, judicial responses at all stages of litigation might be more or less tentative suggestions designed to induce one party or the other to yield, rather than flat pronouncements directing a party to do so. Indeed, in the 12th and early 13th centuries, and perhaps even later, the function of the "jurors" was not so much to decide the case as to indicate what they thought to be the facts of the matter. In this early period, if these suggestions were not taken by the parties as a basis for settlement, there would have to be a trial. Only later was the jury's response taken as dispositive of the issues raised.

Jury trial in the middle ages remains a largely unexplored chapter in procedural history. Nevertheless, some points seem clear. The basic theory of medieval jury trial was that the jurors made a finding not so much on evidence presented to them as on the strength of their own knowledge of the facts—personal or by common neighborhood account. One application of this principle was that the jury was to be composed of veniremen from the place where the disputed transaction occurred; another was that special juries would be summoned where the facts of the matter were known to a peculiar group. In effect, the jury would be made up of the known witnesses to the transaction. See, e.g., Sayles, Introduction, in Select Cases in the Court of King's Bench Under Edward III (Seld.Soc.1958). Nevertheless, it appears that even at an early date evidence was presented to juries. Between 1300 and 1700 the rule evolved that juries were to give their verdict solely on evidence presented in open court, though it may well be supposed that verdicts always were importantly influenced by the litigants' standing and repute in the vicinity. More importantly, jury trial came to be the distinctive method of determining facts in the common law courts. See generally Moore, The Jury: Tool of Kings, Palladium of Liberty (2d ed. 1988); Groot, The Jury of Presentment Before 1215, 26 Am.J. Legal Hist. 1 (1982).

As noted above, in early common law procedure all pleadings were oral. No doubt as a means of saving time in routine cases, written pleadings came into use. By the 15th century, written pleadings were the norm and, in time, the requirement. While written pleadings saved time they also invited technicality and delay. Beyond this, from the 14th century onward there was an intermittent but continuing effort by the common law courts to extend the scope of their writs to include types of controversies which previously were outside their bounds. These extensions were not made directly by the frank creation of new writs but indirectly by various linguistic and procedural strategems: Plaintiffs were allowed to allege certain facts that were known to be false (such as the fact that defendant used force in committing the act in question); fictitious parties were allowed to be charged with conduct that was then attributed to the defendant; etc.

By reason of its technicality and its fictions, common law pleading as it stood in the early 19th century could be mastered only by long years of diligent application. Its mysteries sheltered the bar inside a shroud of arcana that was finally pierced only by the assault of Bentham and Dickens and those who took up their demands for reform. On the state of the English courts in the early 19th century, see Christopher (Baron Bowen), Progress in the Administration of

Justice During the Victorian Period, in 1 Select Essays in Anglo-American Legal History at 516 (1907).

In the sea of technicality there emerged islands of simplicity. One of these was the development, under the action of assumpsit, of the so-called "common counts." See Lucke, Slade's Case and the Origin of the Common Counts, 81 Law Q.Rev. 422, 539 (1965), 82 Law Q.Rev. 81 (1966). For example, plaintiff would simply aver that he had at defendant's special instance and request furnished defendant with goods or services at an agreed price and that defendant promised to pay therefor but despite plaintiff's demand had failed to do so, to plaintiff's damage in the stated amount. This was the "indebitatus" count. Similar counts could be made in quantum meruit for the reasonable value of services rendered where no price for them had been expressly agreed upon; in quantum valebat for the reasonable value of goods sold and delivered where no price had been agreed to; and account, which alleged that there was an account owing to plaintiff from defendant (arising out of the sale of goods or rendition of services) and that despite demand it remained unpaid. Taken together—and they were often pleaded together—these constituted the "common counts" and represented an uncomplicated and reasonably certain method of pleading informal contractual claims. So attractive were the "common counts" in simple contract actions that they survived the general reform of common law pleading in the Field Code, considered below. Compare F.R.C.P. Appendix of Forms, Forms 5, 7 and 8.

4. The Emergence of the Court of Chancery

It will be recalled that the basis of royal justice was the complaint of subject to king, praying that justice be done. Subjects continued to appeal to the king not alone by reason of failures of justice in the local and baronial courts, but also by reason of failures of justice in the king's own courts. A principal ground was the application of a plaintiff to have the advantage of his ordinary common law rights notwithstanding the existence of some special privilege, such as a royal grant of immunity to the defendant that prevented enforcement of those rights. Another ground was the inability of plaintiff to prove his right because the transaction had occurred out of the presence of witnesses (who could give the facts to or as a part of a jury), or because the evidence of the transaction belied the truth, as where execution of a document had been induced by fraud or duress.

In the 13th, 14th and 15th centuries these petitions were addressed to and acted upon by the King's Council, the effective successor of the old *curia regis.* In the early years all petitions were passed on by the Council and into the reign of the Stuarts this was so of many petitions touching important matters. Even as late as the early 17th century, the Council *qua* Council retained in its own hands some judicial matters, usually those laden with extraordinary political implications. Apparently matters of a relatively routine, non-criminal nature were referred to the Chancellor, at first with instructions directing him how to proceed, and later simply with the view that he proceed appropriately with the matter. Again, administrative routine was the genesis of jurisdiction. Just when the Chancellor can be identified as a judicial officer is not clear. It was no earlier than 1340 and no later than 1487. In the 16th century, Chancery emerged unmistakably as a court, in the sense of a tribunal with distinct officials, procedure and jurisdiction.

In the pre-Renaissance period, Chancery administered the common law and not the mysterious and supposedly subtler body of doctrine known as "equity" that in later years was said to be its chief characteristic. Indeed, taken as a whole, Chancery proceedings involved not so much a peculiar body of doctrine as a procedure and remedy that were importantly different from the common law. The pleadings in Chancery consisted of the petition or bill, the answer and, if further statements of position were required, plaintiff's replication to the answer and defendant's rejoinder to the replication. All this was similar to bill procedure in the common law courts and, it may be added, substantially identical with procedure in the Star Chamber. See Jones, The Elizabethan Court of Chancery (1967). The features of Chancery procedure that distinguished it from the common law courts were the subpoena and interrogatories, by which the defendant (and the plaintiff as well) could be compelled to testify. Whereas at common law litigants could not be compelled to testify and in later years were not even permitted to do so, the Chancery inquiry permitted the plaintiff to obtain admissions of facts for which he would otherwise be at a loss for proof. This is apparently the true basis for characterizing Chancery as a "court of conscience"—not the Chancellor acting on the basis of his "conscience," but the Chancellor presiding in a court in which defendant's "conscience" was examined. And it would seem that this is the reason why Chancery seemed to be administering a body of doctrine apparently different from the common law courts: A court in which one can get proof of fraud, mistake and breach of trust would seem to be more "equitable" than courts in which, because of barriers to party testimony, evidence of such chicanery was ordinarily not available. At all events, Chancery became associated with "equitable" doctrines, a term still used to refer generally to rules originally applied and developed in that court and including generally problems of fraud, mistake and breach of fiduciary duty. By way of remedies, Chancery typically issued orders commanding restoration of the rightful situation. The common law courts, which had originally granted redress of this character, by the 14th century had come ordinarily to give only damages. The Chancellor's remedial order or injunction remains the distinctive feature of "equity."

The other distinguishing characteristic of modern "equity" is the mode of trial: the determinations of fact are made by the judge and not by a jury. How this developed has not been explored. Certainly at an early stage the Chancellor, when in doubt as to the facts, referred the matter to the common law courts. And there is reason to believe that this was often if not invariably done down through the 18th century.

At the turn of the 18th century in England there were, then, three common law courts—Exchequer, King's Bench and Common Pleas—and the Court of Chancery. A peculiar consequence of the side-by-side evolution of the common law courts and the Court of Chancery was that claims and defenses relating to the same transaction might have to be put forth in two different courts. Thus, if plaintiff purchased a quantity of goods on the basis of false representations, he could sue either in the common law courts for damages for deceit or in equity to rescind the contract and have the money he paid restored to him. But he could not assert these claims in the alternative in one proceeding. This procedural separation of legal and equitable rights and remedies added to the cumbersomeness of early 19th century litigation.

5. The Early Evolution of Procedure in the United States

In America, after initial development of courts modeled on the more informal pattern of English local and borough courts, the procedural trappings of the common law were imported. The importation was limited, however, in two respects. First, *separate* common law courts were not created; rather, the jurisdiction of all the common law courts was vested in a single court. Cf. Matter of Steinway, 159 N.Y. 250, 53 N.E. 1103 (1899). This went a long way to simplifying common law procedure in this country, for the peculiar procedures of the three English courts were blended into one (at times irregular) "common law" procedure. Second, the Court of Chancery very nearly missed being transplanted. In some states, notably Pennsylvania, no court of "equity" was established before 1800; in New York, the powers of a court of equity were assumed by the Supreme Court, which in that state was (and still is) the trial court of general common law jurisdiction; in other states a separate Court of Chancery was created, perpetuating in virgin soil the bifurcation of jurisdiction that had its roots in ancient English history. See Wilson, Courts of Chancery in the American Colonies, in 2 Select Essays in Anglo-American Legal History 779 (1908); Surrency, The Courts in the American Colonies, 11 Am.J.Legal Hist. 253 (1967); Smith and Hershkowitz, Courts of Equity in the Province of New York: The Cosby Controversy, 1732–1736, 16 Am.J.Legal Hist. 1 (1972).

There survived in the England of 1800 some specialized courts. Notable among these were the Court of Admiralty, having jurisdiction of maritime controversies, and the Ecclesiastical Courts, having jurisdiction of certain matrimonial and testamentary matters. By Article III of the United States Constitution, the jurisdiction exercised in England by the Court of Admiralty was conferred on the courts of the new federal government (and remains one of the heads of federal jurisdiction). The disestablishment of religion in this country left the matter of ecclesiastical jurisdiction in limbo for a time; ultimately, jurisdiction of matrimonial causes was conferred on the trial courts of general jurisdiction, while the administration of decedents' estates was vested in "probate" courts.

6. Legislative Reform

By the early decades of the 19th century the English courts had become a public scandal. The common law courts were entangled in procedural subtleties from which they had seemingly little chance and certainly little inclination to extricate themselves. Chancery procedure was in almost equal degree preoccupied with niceties and was hopelessly delayed: suits took decades and more to reach finality. Parliament initiated investigations of Chancery in the 1820's, but little came of it immediately. The obtuse response of the common lawyers to the criticisms of common law pleading was a revision of common law pleading rules, known as the Hilary Rules because adopted in Hilary Term, 1834, which accentuated pleading technicality beyond even the traditional extremes. See Holdsworth, The New Rules of Pleading of the Hilary Term, 1834, 1 Camb.L.J. 261 (1923).

The impulse to reform continued. A series of changes ensued: parties were made competent as witnesses, common law procedure was simplified and made more uniform, Chancery procedure was streamlined and the court authorized to take testimony *viva voce.* In 1873, all the old English central courts were consolidated into one Supreme Court of Judicature and a single body of procedural rules adopted for all controversies without regard to their character as "legal" or "equitable." See Sunderland, The English Struggle for Procedural Reform, 39 Harv.L.Rev. 725 (1926).

In this country the state legislatures even prior to the Revolution had shown a disposition to amend away some of the common law's technicalities, a trend that continued into the 19th century. See Millar, Civil Procedure of the

Trial Court in Historical Perspective 39–42, 176 (1952). Cf. Brown, Frontier Justice: Wayne County 1796–1836, 16 Am.J.Legal Hist. 126 (1972); Wunder, Inferior Courts, Superior Justice: A History of the Justices of the Peace on the Northwest Frontier (1979). The capital event, however, was the sweeping reform embodied in the Field Code of 1848. The Code, known after its chief architect, David Dudley Field of the New York Bar, was a comprehensive reconstitution of rules of procedure, embodying the following chief features:

1. The forms of action, i.e., the writ system, were abolished. In their stead, a single mode of procedure was made applicable alike to all kinds of civil actions, legal and equitable.

2. The pleading stage of litigation was sharply curtailed by reducing the allowable pleadings to the complaint, the answer and (in some states) a reply.

3. Law and equity (in some states) were "merged," in that types of claims and defenses previously cognizable only in courts of law or in courts of equity could now be asserted in the new unitary proceeding, the "one form" of action.

4. An attempt was made to rationalize and restate the rules governing the joinder of claims and of parties.

The Field Code was enacted in New York in 1848. The California legislature of 1849 adopted a version of the Field Code substantially similar to that of New York. From New York, the Field Code was carried westward into most of the states of the Old Northwest and the Great Plains; from California, it was carried eastward into the mountain states. Within 30 years, 28 states had adopted the code, typically devising local minor variations. See Clark on Code Pleading 23 et seq. (2d ed. 1947). That Code remains, much amended, the procedural system of California and is the principal antecedent of the Federal Rules of Civil Procedure and the New York Civil Practice Act.

The most recent major procedural reform was the adoption of the Federal Rules of Civil Procedure. After a long period of agitation, Congress in 1934 adopted the Federal Rules Enabling Act, which conferred on the Supreme Court the power to adopt rules of procedure for the federal district courts. The Supreme Court appointed an Advisory Committee, for which Dean (later Judge) Charles E. Clark was chief draftsman. The Advisory Committee's draft, after minor changes, was put into effect in 1938.

The background of the Federal Rules was this: Prior to 1938 the Federal courts had two "sides"—law and equity. Different rules of procedure governed the respective sides. On the equity side, the procedure was uniform throughout the country and followed in main contours the procedure of the English Court of Chancery. That procedure, as modified by decisional law developed over the years in the Federal courts sitting in equity, was supplemented and in part superseded by rules promulgated from time to time by the United States Supreme Court, most notable of which were the relatively comprehensive Equity Rules of 1912. On the "law" side of the federal district courts, however, the procedure was that of the state in which the federal district court sat. But this general policy of conformity to state procedure, set forth in the Conformity Acts (part of the Judiciary Act of 1789 and subsequent amendatory provisions), was subject to exceptions laid down by statute and developed by case law. The number and uncertainty of the exceptions were substantial. The resulting confusion was an important consideration behind the drive for uniform Federal rules.

On the history of procedure in the Federal courts, see the concise treatment in Hart & Wechsler 749–765; cf. Kerameus, A Civilian Lawyer Looks at Common Law Procedure, 47 La.L.Rev. 493 (1987). For the history of the movement leading up to the Federal Rules, see Burbank, The Rules Enabling Act of 1934, 130 U.Pa.L.Rev. 1015 (1982); Subrin, How Equity Conquered Common Law: The Federal Rules of Civil Procedure in Historical Perspective, 135 U.Pa.L.Rev. 909 (1987); Spaniol, Making Federal Rules: The Inside Story, 69 A.B.A.J. 1645 (1983); Wright 399–408.

The principal features of the Federal Rules were these:

1. A greatly simplified method of pleading was adopted, requiring little more than broad and vague statements of claim and defense.

2. Law and equity were "merged" in that the same procedural rules governed proceedings both "legal" and "equitable," and in that both "legal" and "equitable" claims and defenses might be asserted in the same action.

3. Comprehensive discovery procedures were adopted.

4. There was provision for pre-trial conference, intended to supplant the pleadings as the principal means of defining the controverted issues.

5. Broad rules of permissive joinder of parties and claims were adopted.

Since the promulgation of the Federal Rules of Civil Procedure, a number of states have adopted their provisions substantially intact and many others have taken over substantial portions of them. See Oakley and Coon, The Federal Rules in State Courts: A Survey of State Court Systems of Civil Procedure, 61 Wash.L.Rev. 1367 (1986).

7. Modern Litigation

In the last thirty years or so great change has occurred in the nature of much civil litigation, particularly in the federal district courts. The change has been propelled in part by amendment of the Federal Rules of Civil Procedure, notably in Rule 23 governing class actions. But the primary impetus has been political and social forces that have involved the courts in the resolution of claims to entitlement that previously were resolved in the legislature or in administrative agencies, or that were simply ignored. The principal example is the anti-segregation litigation beginning with Brown v. Board of Education, 347 U.S. 483, 74 S.Ct. 686, 98 L.Ed. 873 (1954) and continuing with comprehensive decrees concerning pupil assignment in the public schools. See Fiss, The Civil Rights Injunction (1978); Metcalf, From Little Rock to Boston: The History of School Desegregation (1983). Other examples include the cases involving "one-man one-vote" beginning with Baker v. Carr, 369 U.S. 186, 82 S.Ct. 691, 7 L.Ed. 2d 663 (1962), reform of prisons and hospitals, e.g., Wyatt v. Stickney, 344 F.Supp. 373 (M.D.Ala.1972), reform of public finance, e.g., Serrano v. Priest, 5 Cal.3d 584, 96 Cal.Rptr. 601, 487 P.2d 1241 (1971), a broad array of consumer protection claims, e.g., United States v. Students Challenging Regulatory Agency Procedures (SCRAP), 412 U.S. 669, 93 S.Ct. 2405, 37 L.Ed.2d 254 (1973), civil and personal rights, e.g., Bivens v. Six Unknown Named Agents, 403 U.S. 388, 91 S.Ct. 1999, 29 L.Ed.2d 619 (1971), and government regulatory matters, e.g., Abbott Laboratories, Inc. v. Gardner, 387 U.S. 136, 87 S.Ct. 1507, 18 L.Ed.2d 681 (1967) (drug regulation). These cases characteristically involve complex factual and legal issues, intense public controversy, and direct or secondary involvement of many different parties and interests. See generally Chayes, The Role of the Judge in Public Law Litigation, infra p. 1203, and Levi, The Business of the Courts: A Summary and a Sense of Perspective, infra p. 1208.

Yet this kind of litigation for the most part is conducted in tribunals and according to procedure conceived for the adjudication of more routine legal controversies, such as the product liability case hypothesized in the Note on the Structure of a Law Suit, supra. What is happening, therefore, is that a single set of procedural rules and traditions nominally governs varieties of civil adjudications that, certainly at the extremes, are radically different from each other. As a result there is not only political controversy over the proper degree of judicial "activism," but also a more specific concern whether contemporary civil procedure and practice is doing what might justly be expected of it. This concern manifests itself at several levels—concern about delay in bringing litigation to conclusion, about undue haste in decision of cases, about excessive pressures to settle, about subordination of "ordinary" litigation to the "big" cases, and about the vitality of the judicial system itself. In response, all kinds of reform proposals are being made, many of them either trivial or so radical as to be unlikely of adoption. Underlying any discussion of specific procedural problems, however, are fundamental issues concerning not only the forms of civil adjudication but the function of law itself.

B. THE ADVERSARY SYSTEM

INTRODUCTORY NOTE ON THE ADVERSARY SYSTEM

Anglo-American judicial procedure is conducted by means of the "adversary" system. As Professor Morgan has said, "The theory of our adversary system of litigation is that each litigant is most interested and will be most effective in seeking, discovering, and presenting the materials which will reveal the strength of his own case and the weakness of his adversary's case so that the truth will emerge to the impartial tribunal that makes the decision." Morgan, Some Problems of Proof Under the Anglo-American System of Litigation 3 (1956). The scope of the lawyer's power and responsibility is wide: "It is the lawyer who makes the initial and usually final decision as to choice of court, size of claim, nature of claim stated, parties, extent and kind of pre-trial investigation, mode of trial (whether jury or non-jury), settlement offers, extent and kind of proofs, style of presentation and argument and, within limits, speed and vigor of prosecution. The courts are called on to intervene only occasionally and then briefly and, compared to the attention given the cause by the lawyers, summarily." Hazard, Research in Civil Procedure 111–112 (1963). The following are some comments of a trial judge:

"Judges do not control the input of cases into the court system, their progress through it or their output out of it. The input of criminal cases is determined by police, who decide who shall be arrested, and by prosecutors, who decide who shall be prosecuted. The supply of civil cases is provided by the attorneys, who file complaints in court.

"The progress of the cases through the system is likewise determined by the lawyers and court clerks. Lawyers close the pleadings and claim the cases for trial, and clerks, aided by computers, place them on the calendar. Occasionally, after a case gets on the trial calendar, judges may do some prodding to get the case heard. However, while judges may sternly direct and order, seldom will they actually dismiss a case because of delay, and lawyers are marvelously adept at finding excuses for adjournments until they are good and ready to try their cases.

"Judges play an important role in presiding over trials by assuring that all the procedural safeguards of due process are met and essential fairness is achieved. However, trials themselves are largely produced and directed by the lawyers. They supply the actors and the script, through the witnesses called and the testimony elicited by direct and cross-examination. Judges, of course, rule on the admissibility of evidence, but this is a negative function of keeping out unreliable evidence rather than an affirmative one of providing the facts upon which a case is determined." Satter, Observations on the Limitations of Judicial Power, 53 Conn.B.J. 439, 439–440 (1979).

The rules of procedure are to the litigating lawyer regulatory and enabling legislation: They tell him or her, or attempt to do so, what the lawyer may and may not do, and they afford the means by which the lawyer can bring about, or attempt to bring about, the results sought.

Such being the case, litigation should be approached by the apprentice lawyer in corresponding fashion. The lawyer should inquire:

(1) In respect to any procedural rule:

     a. Does the rule give an intelligible guide in conducting litigation?

     b. To the extent that the rule is ambiguous, what is the range of its potential application?

     c. Does the rule allow a fair opportunity for achieving proper procedural objectives?

     d. Does the rule adequately protect the other side from unfair maneuver?

(2) In respect to any procedural problem:

     a. What position or course of action might be taken?

        1. Is this the best course under the circumstances?

        2. What arguments can be made in support of the correctness of the position?

     b. What objection is or might be made by the adverse party?

        1. Will it be expedient to make the objection?

        2. What arguments might be made in support of the objection?

     c. What is or will be the court's response, and the reasons assigned for decision?

The lawyer should also ask whether the rules adequately safeguard the client from consequences of the lawyer's incompetence and overreaching, and safeguard the "public interest."

The adversary system is to be contrasted with the systems, sometimes called inquisitorial, prevailing in parts of Europe. Compare Kaplan, Civil Procedure—Reflections on the Comparison of Systems, 9 Buff.L.Rev. 409 (1960), excerpted infra p. 975; David, English Law and French Law: A Comparison in Substance 57–64 (1980). That many American litigants, especially those representing themselves in small claims actions, expect the court to operate in an inquisitorial manner and are unprepared to take the initiative on their own behalf was the conclusion of one study:

"The unifying theme in the interview data is an overestimation of the power and initiative of the civil court. Litigants often see the court as an inquisitorial authority that will recognize the justice of their position and find and punish the wrongdoer, rather than as a largely passive tribunal that renders judgment on the basis of the facts brought before it. Many litigants thus come to the civil court with a model of justice that better fits the criminal system. Understandably, the one plaintiff who had experience with the criminal system had such a model; however, each of the litigants we considered—and numerous other litigants that they represent—shared similar misunderstandings to some extent, irrespective of legal experience or business background." O'Barr and Conley, Lay Expectations of the Civil Justice System, 22 Law & Soc'y Rev. 137 (1988).

Should small claims courts, at least, work on some model other than the adversary one? See Small Cases, infra p. 1249.

There is a vast body of literature on effective advocacy. See, e.g., Packel and Spina, Trial Advocacy: A Systematic Approach (1984); Masterson, Civil Trial Practice: Strategies and Techniques (P.L.I. 1986); Baldwin, Trial Strategies, 23 Trial 120 (Dec. 1987); Markus, A Theory of Trial Advocacy, 56 Tul.L. Rev. 95 (1981); Symposium, Trial Techniques, 8 Litigation 7 (Spring 1982); Symposium, Appellate Advocacy, 4 Litigation 7 (Winter 1978); Godbold, Twenty Pages and Twenty Minutes—Effective Advocacy on Appeal, 30 Sw.L.J. 801 (1976); Thibaut and Walker, Procedural Justice: A Psychological Analysis (1975); Federal Judicial Center, The Quality of Advocacy in the Federal Courts (1978); and Maddi, Improving Trial Advocacy: The Views of Trial Attorneys, 1981 A.B.F.Res.J. 1049, 1075, indicating that trial lawyers believe effective advocacy depends mostly on "preparation, experience and hard work." Cf. Frankel, Partisan Justice (1980).

HAZARD, THE ADVERSARY SYSTEM

Ethics in the Practice of Law, c. 9 (1978).*

The adversary system is a procedure for trial of civil and criminal cases, and is the characteristic form of trial procedure in common law countries. Its essential feature is that a decision is made by judge, or judge with jury, who finds the facts and determines the law from submissions made by partisan advocates on behalf of the parties. The system contrasts with what is generally called the inquisitorial system, used in countries of the civil law tradition such as France and Germany. In this system of trial, which might less invidiously be called the interrogative system, the judge determines the law and finds the facts by his own active investigation and inquiries at trial.

There is probably no "pure" form of either system. Even the most passive judge in an adversary system sometimes asks questions and even the most passive litigant in an interrogative system is something of an advocate when he gives his responses. Furthermore, there are different forms of adversary procedures that vary in the contentiousness of their mood, as interrogative procedures also vary in the intensity with which inquiry is pursued. Nevertheless, the adversary system is distinctive for the fact that the parties, through their lawyers, investigate the facts, frame the legal issues, and present the evidence to a passive tribunal that then reaches decision.

* © 1978, Seven Springs Center, Inc.
Reprinted with permission.

The adversary system has deep roots in the Anglo-American legal tradition. Its antecedent is often said to be the Norman trial by battle, wherein issues in doubt were resolved by the outcome of a duel. Perhaps more relevant is the fact that the key elements of the adversary system—the right to present evidence and the right to assistance of counsel—evolved as legal controls on government absolutism in seventeenth-century England. Thus, the adversary system is not only a theory of adjudication but a constituent of our history of political liberty.

The theory of adjudication in the adversary system, as usually stated, has two linked components. One is that party presentation will result in the best presentation, because each party is propelled into maximum effort in investigation and presentation by the prospect of victory; in contrast, a judge-interrogator is only interested in getting through the day and through his caseload. The other component of the theory is more complex and has to do with the psychology of decision making. It runs essentially as follows: Proof through evidence requires hypothesis; hypothesis requires a preliminary mind-set; if an active judge-interrogator develops the proof, his preliminary mind-set too easily can become his final decision; therefore, it is better to have conflicting preliminary hypotheses and supporting proofs presented by the parties so that the judge's mind can be kept open until all the evidence is at hand.

In this version of the adversary theory, the role of the advocate is central to adjudication, because the advocate is a necessary orchestrator of the proof to be offered by a party. The prominence of the advocate in the adversary system explains in part why the legal profession as a whole strongly supports it. There are other interpretations of the adversary system, however, that attach much less significance to the role of the advocate as an instrument for developing the proofs. One of these interpretations emphasizes the importance of party participation, the idea being that a party's presentation of the case on his behalf gives him a sense of involvement and control in the decision procedure. In this conception of the adversary system, counsel is and should be relegated to the role of coach rather than protagonist, because if the lawyer is protagonist, his client's role is secondary and passive. This form of the adversary system appears to have actually existed in English procedure of about the thirteenth century, but it is found today only in cases, such as in small claims court, where the amount involved is too little to justify hiring a lawyer to present them. These days, if litigation is taken to a lawyer, he takes it over.

There is still another and more radical theory of the adversary system. On this view, trials are not quests for truth in a serious objective or empirical sense, and cannot be. This is because truth is unknowable in any objective sense, or at least because the controversies in which the issues can rationally be resolved by the evidence rarely go to trial, for parties concede what can really be proved. By exclusion, therefore, in the cases that go to trial the evidence is hopelessly ambiguous according to any concept of rational proof, and decision necessarily involves important elements of intuition, predisposition, and bias. On this analysis, a trial is necessarily theatre or ritual to an important extent.

The adversary system has a strange status in the American legal tradition. As noted earlier, it is one derivative of fundamental theories of political liberty. Great cases in the adversary tradition are part of our constitutional folklore—Andrew Hamilton's defense of John Peter Zenger, John Adams's defense of the British soldiers in the Boston Massacre, the Scottsboro case, etc. In recent years, the Supreme Court has substantially equated adversarial trial with due process in the determination of legal rights. Furthermore, the notion that adjudication should proceed by means of competitive presentation has a strong philosophical affinity with the idea of freedom in science, letters, and the arts. As freedom in those domains inheres in open competition in the "marketplace of ideas," so there is freedom in adjudication when it consists of open competition in presentation of evidence and argument. In these respects, the adversary system stands with freedom of speech and the right of assembly as a pillar of our constitutional system. On the other hand, the adversary system in practice is known by its practitioners often to be anything but the truth-revealing process that it pretends to be. When brought forward for discussion [at a seminar of lawyers in 1976], it was thoroughly savaged.

The discussion was initiated by consideration of a thesis previously developed by one of the participants, Judge Marvin Frankel.[1] In essence, the thesis is that an advocate should have a responsibility not merely to present evidence favorable to his client, and to counter unfavorable evidence, but also should share with the judge the responsibility for getting at the truth. As this thesis was explored in the discussion, the following observations were made about the adversary system as it currently exists:

— It is expensive and unwieldy. Its use would be abandoned but for the fact that most cases are not actually tried, the civil cases being mostly settled and the criminal cases being mostly disposed of by bargained plea.

— It involves systematic distortion of the truth. Perjured evidence is commonplace in criminal cases and more than occasional in civil cases, and reconstruction of witness recollection is standard technique. Questioning is conducted not to enlighten but to entrap. Procedural technicality is routinely exploited to impose delay and expense on opposing parties. The procedure for pretrial discovery of evidence is an engine of harassment, having in effect put blank search warrants at the litigants' disposal.

— In cases having public policy significance, the courtroom often is converted into an adjunct political forum in which judicial procedure is used as a device of interest-group warfare. Major antitrust, environmental, civil rights, and some kinds of criminal cases frequently undergo this transformation.

— In criminal cases, the procedure is often a complete charade. For example, a guilty defendant can suppress evidence on the ground that it was obtained in violation of the rules governing police investigations, only to be found guilty on the basis of police agent testimony fabricated to offset the effects of the suppression.

— The public views the whole process with cynical abhorrence.

— Lawyers, at least ones not specialists in trial work, regard a trial as an unmitigated evil, to be avoided if possible but otherwise to be fought according to the prevailing conventions.

1. Frankel, "The Search for Truth: An Umperial View," 123 U.Penna.L.Rev. 1031 (1975).

As the discussion developed, a pall descended on the participants. Some hopeful suggestions were advanced, but desultorily or with irony:

— Maybe arbitration is better; it is cheaper, faster, more private, and less arbitrary. But there was not much optimism about it. The bar at large would be against arbitration as a substitute for adjudication, and would fly the flag and play the national anthem to sustain a successful opposition. Lawyers with experience in arbitration thought that arbitrators were inclined to split the difference between parties, whatever it was, and would not be tough with an obstructionist party.

— Maybe the adversary system would be satisfactory if there were no jury. But abolishing the jury system would require constitutional change that is practically impossible. Furthermore, in the participants' view many of the judges are not much better; at least with a jury there is always a chance of getting someone who is reasonably concerned, intelligent, and disinterested.

— There are good versions of the adversary system. A trial before a capable federal judge presented by competent counsel is a fair trial. But this doesn't happen very often.

— Just results can often be achieved when the judges are simply terrible. Litigants confronted by the ordeal of trial before a judge who is an idiot or bigot will quickly compose their differences—the Quasimodo technique of justice.

— Perhaps all advocates should be governed by the standards applicable to prosecutors. A prosecutor is supposed to be not only a partisan advocate but also a minister of justice, responsible for seeing that unjustified prosecutions are not brought and unjustified convictions not obtained. Why should not all attorneys have such a responsibility?

At this point, the following discussion ensued:

— The prosecutor is unique because he does not have a specific client to and for whom he is responsible. If you have a client, you have to represent him and not "justice" in some abstract sense.

— Well then, why must the advocate in an adversary system be responsible to his client in the way to which we have become accustomed? Why could the advocate not, at least in criminal cases, be a member of the court's staff, responsible to the court for investigating and presenting the side to which he is assigned? Wouldn't that reproduce the functional elements of the present adversary system without its redundancies and excesses?

— There is much to be said for such a system. Indeed, it embodies substantially the theory and practice of the system of adjudication used in the countries that describe themselves as socialist, meaning not only the Soviet Union but also such less patently autocratic regimes as that in Yugoslavia. That, of course, is not a reason for rejecting a reformation in favor of such a system, but it is perhaps a reason for carefully reflecting upon the desirability of doing so.

— The suggestion seems to be that, although the attachment of advocate to client begets the perversions we have been talking about, the detachment of advocate from client might beget worse.

On that note of resignation, the discussion died out. * * *

LLEWELLYN, THE CRAFTS OF LAW RE–VALUED *
28 A.B.A.J. 801 (1942).

Our order establishes itself at your school of law at a time and in an atmosphere which offer to men of the law more of challenge than of comfort. With the fate of the nation in the balance there is call for business men and call for medical men and call for men of the physical sciences. There is call for architects and engineers and for the clergy. There is little call for lawyers. I find no pervading appreciation that law-skills can be mobilized to serve. I find no competitive demand in the armed services for law trained men. I find no fear among civilians that if the law men go or are drafted the community must settle down to suffer for the lack of them.

* * *

I suggest to you that we can settle on at least two reasons why men of the law are invited into cold storage or the scrap heap when their country needs them most. I suggest to you first that we have confused ourselves and so have confused the layman, about the essence of our craftsmanship. We have fooled ourselves, we have fooled our law professors, we have fooled the whole bewildered public, into the idea that the essence of our craft lies in our knowledge of the law. And knowledge of the law we do have, and we do need, but such knowledge is but the precondition of our work. Yet the idea that the essence lies in this peculiar knowledge of the law, that idea gives us a sort of standing, the standing of monopolists in a secret lore; and it may be we have discovered that the priests of any black art can make the uninitiate pay well for mystic service.

But the idea comes at a price. It comes at a price, for instance, of turning out of law school prospective lawyers who know nothing but the law, and have no simplest smattering of how to *lawyer*. It comes indeed at a price of blinding our own eyes to our own daily job, so that in the very process of counselling or of briefing a case we study chiefly *what* courts have decided, and forget *how* they go about deciding cases, and *how* they use the authorities with which they work, and how and why those authorities themselves came into existence. * * * Had lawyers consciously been viewing their work as a *craft of doing and getting things done with* the law, instead of as a mere monopoly of knowledge of the law, * * * they would have been studying that key-craft and its methods, as well as its particular results; they would have been ready. Let me say it again: the essence of our craftsmanship lies in skills, and wisdoms; in practical, effective, persuasive, inventive skills for getting things done, any kind of thing in any field; in wisdom and judgment in selecting the things to get done; in skills for moving men into desired action, any kind of man, in any field; and then in skills for *regularizing* the results, for building into controlled large-scale action such doing of things and such moving of men. Our game is essentially the game of planning and organizing management (not of running it), except that we concentrate on the areas of conflict, tension, friction, trouble, doubt—and in those areas we have the skills for working out results. We are the trouble-shooters.

* * *

HAND, THE DEFICIENCIES OF TRIALS TO REACH THE HEART OF THE MATTER *

3 A.B.C.N.Y. Lectures on Legal Topics 87 (1926).

I have no doubt that if the records of the time of that ancient and apparently earliest of law-givers, Hammurabi, could be completely restored, we should learn that in the third millennium before Christ men were complaining about the inefficiency of legal procedure, and I fancy that if any of you are destined in the year 7000 A.D. to revisit the glimpses of the moon to examine and write a monograph for the celestial choirs upon the condition of human law courts, you will be obliged to report to some Seraphic Commission that mankind still exhibits the same discontentment with its methods of adjusting human differences that you know to-day. I must therefore ask you to believe that in the course of a half hour I do not hope to lay my finger on the cure for a condition which is probably so inherent in our human imperfections as to be persistent as long as the need for litigation itself endures. We shall, I fear, be scarcely satisfied with our settlement of disputes until we have so purged and purified our natures as to bring down the dove of domestic peace to be a permanent sojourner amid the haunts of homo sapiens.

And yet, like other such problems, while we may not hope for a solution, we can, and indeed we must, press toward at least some understanding of our difficulties, for a sound diagnosis is a necessary condition not only to a cure but also to any palliation of our social diseases. And if we cannot hope to reach a formula which will prove the key to the lawyer's paradise, at least it will serve us to know in what directions we can best move and for what success we can hope.

Now a law-suit is an undertaking designed to settle a dispute. * * * Let us at the outset disabuse ourselves of the notion that we are engaged in an impartial and disinterested inquiry into objective truth. We have no right to the fine detachment of spirit of the scientist. Our inquiry must stop as soon as the litigants are, or under the rules must be, satisfied on their differences. Our results have no general significance whatever, we merely reach a passing accommodation which may be altogether foreign to any permanent answer.

* * *

* * * The truth is that no rules [of procedure] in the end will help us. We shall succeed in making our results conform with our professions only by a change of heart in ourselves. It is hard to expect lawyers who are half litigants to forego the advantages which come from obscuring the case and supporting contentions which they know to be false. I do not mean to say that we should abandon the right of the lawyer to make his fee vary with his success, even to the extent of an aliquot share of the recovery. That is a question far beyond the outline of what I have here to say, and I have myself no clear ideas about it. It is important nevertheless that we should realize the price we pay for it, the atmosphere of contention over the trifles, the unwillingness to concede what ought to be conceded, and to proceed to the things which matter. Courts have fallen out of repute; many of you avoid them whenever you can, and rightly. About trials hang a suspicion of trickery and a sense of a result depending upon cajolery or worse. I wish I could say that it was all unmerited. After now

---

* An Address by Learned Hand before the Association of the Bar of the City of New York, Nov. 17, 1921. Copyright 1926 by Ass'n of the Bar of the City of New York.

some dozen years of experience I must say that as a litigant I should dread a lawsuit beyond almost anything else short of sickness and death. You may very properly rejoin that my conclusion is a comment upon my fellows and myself, and I must in part acknowledge the truth of your charge if you do. But I will not acknowledge it all; you cannot, if you will forgive me, make a silk purse out of a sow's ear, and while I am willing to admit that we upon the bench are lacking in firmness, in learning, in industry, and in acumen, you cannot lay it all to us. The administration of justice is a good test of the civilization of the people where it exists; it shows their interest in equity, their freedom to adapt themselves to new conditions and their courage in protecting the weak and controlling the rapacious. It measures the point they have reached in education and in virtue, and how far they are serious in the formal expression of their will. Because, gentlemen, it is not merely in the making of laws that law resides. You can have the wisdom of a Solon and there will be anarchy no less, if you rule a people in whose hearts there is no regard for the laws they make. Among the Banderlog I have no doubt there is an admirable code of laws, but they forget to-day what they said yesterday, and they never really mean what they say at all.

Success in these matters is as mathematicians would say, a function of the advance we have made in civilization. Without a bar which is willing to co-operate, a bench more virtuous and wise than any we are ever to get would do very little. We must not expect too much from formal changes; we may put our finger on this or on that which may be amended, and if it is done, it may help, but the fundamentals lie elsewhere. You get out of a community what there is in it, out of a bar, which now at any rate is nearly a cross-section of that community, what the character and capacity of that bar contains, and neither laws nor principalities nor powers will in the end help you one jot or tittle.

And so I must finish with very little tangible to suggest to you. I did not promise you an answer, for I knew very well at the outset I had none to give. But we must in one way or another live by faith, and perhaps the highest test of it is when it is stricken by a doubt that after all it may be mistaken. We build our visions as we have spiritual strength to hold fast to them and we stand or falter as our constancy rises and falls. And still at times I can have the hope that in America time may at length mitigate our fierce individualism, may teach us the knowledge we so sorely lack that each of us must learn to realize himself more in our communal life whose formal expression is and as I believe will continue to be the law. If through some such conversion we can be taught to abate the intensity of our own wills, to subject our desires to what has been laid down for us, even when we dislike and distrust it, then in this which seems so trivial and minor a detail, the management of our private disputes, we may succeed. But not, I fear, short of something like that; we are made all of a piece, and the cloven hoof will show however well the bestial heart be covered.

NOTE ON ALTERNATIVES TO FORMAL ADJUDICATION

Although the courts through adversarial litigation are the ultimate decision-makers in our system of justice, many alternative forums and procedures exist. Alternative forums may be publicly or privately sponsored, and the procedures followed may be either adversarial or non-adversarial.

Administrative agency hearings constitute a major parallel decision-making system. Federal agencies such as the National Labor Relations Board and the Federal Trade Commission, state agencies such as Utilities Rate Commissions and Worker's Compensation Boards, and local agencies such as Planning and Zoning Commissions all conduct contested adversarial hearings where opposing parties publicly present evidence and argue their cases. At least at the state and local level, these proceedings are generally less formal than courtroom proceedings. The decisions of such governmental agencies in adjudicative proceedings are appealable to the court system.

Other alternatives to formal adjudication have been gaining widespread acceptance in recent years. Such "Alternative Dispute Resolution" ("ADR") procedures cover a wide range of public and private alternatives. Publicly sponsored ADR procedures include court-annexed arbitration and advisory-verdict jury trials, for example. These procedures are authorized by statute or rule. They usually do not provide for a binding determination; rather, the ruling of the factfinder is advisory and is intended to facilitate settlement between the parties. These procedures force the parties to focus at an early point on the merits of the case instead of postponing an analysis of the issues until the end of pretrial procedural jousting. Settlement negotiations that follow a neutral third party's advisory ruling, be it by an arbitrator or a jury, are frequently productive and entail limited expense. If the ADR techniques fail to achieve a settlement, the parties are free to litigate fully in court. In some cases, if a party rejects such an advisory determination, and fails to obtain a better result at trial, that party can be charged the opposition's subsequent attorneys fees and costs.

Private ADR has also gained acceptance. Private ADR is founded on contract, which specifies the procedure to be employed and whether or not the parties will be bound by the result. Binding arbitration involves a neutral factfinder, an adversarial hearing, and a binding result. Other private ADR methods, such as nonbinding arbitration and mini-trials, may be adversarial proceedings, but the factfinder's decision serves simply as a catalyst for settlement.

Most legal controversies are settled by informal negotiation and mediation. Negotiation may take place on several levels: between the parties themselves; between their lawyers; or between the representatives of various interest groups involved. In mediation, a mutually selected neutral party seeks to promote a dialogue by focusing on the parties' underlying mutual interests rather than their incompatible legal rights. A mediator is purely a facilitator and makes no determination of the issues, binding or nonbinding.

Only a small percent of claims filed in court actually go to trial, the vast majority being settled or simply dropped. A much greater number of disputes never reach the court system at all. This high rate of settlement indicates that most parties are capable of agreeing on a result; hence, in many cases formal ADR techniques may only accelerate inevitable settlements.

However, there remain many cases that cannot be settled out of court. If one or both parties insists on a public determination of his or her rights, or seeks a new interpretation of the law, or refuses to acknowledge or respond to the other party's claims, then there is no alternative to formal adjudication.

There is a vast literature on ADR. See generally Goldberg, Green and Sander, Dispute Resolution (1985). See also Arbitration, infra p. 1255.

———

AN ADVERSARY DIALECTIC: REYNOLDS v. BANK OF AMERICA

Litigation by the adversary method has been termed the "dialectic of advocacy." See Adlow, The Dialectic of Advocacy, 36 B.U.L.Rev. 579 (1956). An illustration of that dialectic follows. Reynolds v. Bank of America was an action in the Superior Court of San Mateo County, California, to recover damages for destruction of an airplane. There was a $30,000 verdict and judgment for plaintiff. Defendant appealed, contending no recovery at all should have been allowed. Plaintiff cross-appealed, contending the amount awarded was insufficient. The appeal was taken to the California District Court of Appeal (now Court of Appeal), First Appellate District.

Observe how the dialectic proceeds:

1. Plaintiff's question to the witness and defendant's objection.

2. Plaintiff's offer of proof and defendant's objection.

3. Plaintiff's request for instruction to the jury and defendant's objection.

4. On appeal, plaintiff's argument and defendant's counter-argument.

Notice, too, the response of the court at each point.

1 Civil No. 17,966
In the

DISTRICT COURT OF APPEAL
State of California

————

FIRST APPELLATE DISTRICT

————

Division One

WESLEY REYNOLDS,
      Plaintiff, Respondent and
             Cross-Appellant,
          vs.
BANK OF AMERICA NATION-
AL TRUST AND SAVINGS AS-
SOCIATION, as Executor of the
Last Will and Testament of Rob-
ert Donald Duncan, deceased,
      Defendant, Appellant and
            Cross-Respondent.

CROSS–APPELLANT'S OPENING BRIEF

Appeal from the Judgment of the Superior Court of
the State of California, in and for the
County of San Mateo
Honorable Louis B. Dematteis, Judge

PRELIMINARY STATEMENT

The above captioned case was tried in the Superior Court of San Mateo County before the Honorable Louis B. Dematteis sitting with a jury and resulted in a verdict in favor of plaintiff in the amount of $30,000.00 (Cl.Tr.* p. 16), and judgment on the verdict was duly entered and recorded (Cl.Tr. p. 17).

The Bank of America National Trust and Savings Association, as executor of the Last Will of Robert Donald Duncan (hereafter called cross-respondent), filed a notice of appeal (Cl.Tr. p. 23) and thereafter Wesley C. Reynolds (hereafter referred to as cross-appellant) cross-appealed from the portion of judgment denying recovery for loss of profits (Cl.Tr. p. 25) and by request to prepare reporter's and clerk's transcripts requested "the pleadings" etc., be filed (Cl.Tr. p. 30, line 6). The clerk's transcript includes the complaint (Cl.Tr. pp. 1–5). The subject of appeal involves paragraph 6 of the First Count ** and paragraph 3 of the Second Count (Cl.Tr. p. 2, lines 13–18; Cl.Tr. p. 3, lines 23–25). The appeal of the cross-respondent, Bank of America National Trust and Savings Association, was dismissed with prejudice and said dismissal was duly filed on April 4, 1958, with the Clerk of this Honorable Court. The only appeal remaining is that of Wesley C. Reynolds.

FACTS

The cross-appellant was the owner of a Piper PA–23 Supercustom Apache airplane, registration No. N–1005 (Rep.Tr.† p. 4, line 10) on November 12, 1955, at the City of San Carlos, County of San Mateo; at the request of decedent, Robert Donald Duncan, cross-appellant delivered said airplane to Duncan. Thereafter at 17:15 Pacific Standard Time on November 13, 1955, seven miles 200° true from Cape San Martin, said aircraft was ditched in the Pacific Ocean (Rep.Tr. p. 3, lines 12–17). As a result of said ditching, the aircraft was totally destroyed (Rep.Tr. p. 4, line 21). It would appear that cross-respondent's decedent proceeded northward in inclement weather in low ceilings and poor visibility (Rep.Tr. p. 5, lines 12–13; p. 28, lines 7–10)

[* Clerk's Transcript. This is a reproduced extract from the file in the trial court, prepared by the clerk of the trial court for the purpose of presenting the record to the appellate court.]

[** The first "count" or statement of claim in plaintiff's complaint.]

[† Reporter's Transcript. This is the transcript of the verbatim stenographic notes of the oral proceedings at trial taken by the court reporter.]

when the pilot decided to ditch (Rep.Tr. p. 5, line 19). The pilot was not licensed for instrument flying (Rep.Tr. p. 6, lines 4–6). The aircraft had sufficient fuel for 5 hours, 30 minutes (Rep.Tr. p. 9, line 15) and when ditched had only consumed 2 hours, 45 minutes of fuel (Rep.Tr. p. 10, lines 9–10). Plaintiff and cross-appellant produced the sole survivor of the ill-fated flight (Rep.Tr. p. 42, line 26; p. 58, line 18; p. 88, line 17; p. 119, line 2) who described what transpired. In addition, weather conditions were testified to on the date in question. (Rep.Tr. p. 59, line 8; p. 88, line 4; p. 120, line 7 to p. 150, line 10; Plaintiff's Exhibits 10, 12, 13, 9, 10A–10B). An eyewitness to the weather conditions along the path of flight was called, world famous flyer Peter Gluckman (Rep.Tr. p. 150, line 22; p. 166, line 20), and expert testimony was introduced to show the negligent judgment of cross-respondent's decedent (Rep.Tr. p. 166, lines 8–9; line 26; p. 222, line 17). Expert testimony was introduced on the value of the plane (Rep.Tr. p. 231, line 23). At this point, counsel for cross-appellant asked of witness E. C. Watson, "Do you know what the fair market value of the use of that plane was on November 13, 1955?" Answer: "Yes". (Rep.Tr. p. 231, lines 24–26). Then argument ensued regarding the question (Rep.Tr. pp. 232–248) at which time the Court sustained [cross-]respondent's objection, and so advised the jury (Rep.Tr. p. 248, lines 17–18).

Delivery of a new plane of like make lagged from 13 months to 4½ months (Rep.Tr. p. 260, lines 5–15). When the court excluded testimony regarding loss of profits or loss of use, counsel for cross-appellant made an offer of proof (Rep.Tr. p. 273, line 11; p. 274, line 19) and the Court renewed its ruling precluding introduction of such evidence (Rep. Tr. p. 274, lines 24–26). The offer of proof consisted of the following:

    (a) Offer to prove reasonable rental value of destroyed aircraft $1,200.00 per month;

    (b) Other aircraft of like make and model were not available;

    (c) Reasonable period of replacement using due diligence was 4 or 5 months; and

    (d) Reasonable business worth of $5,000.00 for loss of profits.

The matter was argued and instructions by appellant on loss of use and business profits were barred by the ruling on Rep.Tr. p. 221, lines 24–26. The jury returned a verdict as indicated in the preliminary statement in favor of cross-appellant.

ISSUES

(1) Did the Court err in refusing cross-appellant the right to introduce evidence of loss of use?

(2) Did the Court err in refusing to allow evidence of loss of business profits?

(3) Was the cross-appellant entitled under the circumstances outlined in the offer of proof to recover for loss of use and/or business profits?

THE LAW APPLICABLE

I

LOSS OF USE

The general rule is that loss of use is allowed where the injured property is capable of being repaired, for the time that the owner is deprived of its use while it is being repaired. [citation omitted]

A. Where property is totally destroyed, loss of use is generally not awarded because of the supposition that the injured party will get the total value of the lost property and acquire a replacement immediately. Where, however, the injured person is financially unable to secure a replacement immediately, or where because of the peculiar nature of the property it cannot be readily replaced, that general rule should have no application.

Valencia v. Shell Oil Co. (1944), 23 Cal.2d 840, 844, 147 P.2d 558 (Loss of use allowed amounting to more than $4,000 where owner financially unable to pay the garage bill to get his truck out of hock after the defendant, whose agent had negligently injured the truck, had told the garage man it would pay for the repairs.)

169 A.L.R. at 1094. "If however, an owner is entitled to compensation for loss of use during the time his vehicle is being repaired it is difficult to see why he should be denied any recovery for damages for his loss of use during the time he is unable to replace a destroyed automobile."

B. Where property is totally destroyed there is necessarily a time lapse before a replacement can be acquired. This is especially so in the case of property of the type involved here. Where the property was actually in use at the time it was destroyed, the injured party should recover compensation for the damage caused by the loss of it up to the time when he could replace it.

Louisville & I. Ry. Co. v. Schuester, 183 Ky. 504, 209 S.W. 542, 544, 4 A.L.R. 1344.

II

THE *NORMAL* MEASURE OF DAMAGES FOR THE DESTRUCTION OF PERSONAL PROPERTY IS THE MARKET VALUE IMMEDIATELY PRECEDING THE DESTRUCTION. SPECIAL DAMAGES MAY BE PLEADED IN APPROPRIATE CASES. LOSS OF USE AND/OR LOSS OF PROFITS IS SUCH AN ITEM OF SPECIAL DAMAGES

[citation omitted]

Restatement of the Law of Torts, Vol. IV.

Section 927—Conversion or Destruction of a Thing or of a Legally Protected Interest Therein.

Where a person is entitled to a judgment for the conversion of a chattel or the destruction of any legally protected interest in land or other thing the damages include,

(a) The exchange value of the subject matter or the plaintiff's interest therein at the time and place of the conversion or destruction, or a different value where that is necessary to give just compensation, and

(b) The amount of any further loss suffered as a result of the deprivation, and

(c) Interest from the time at which the value is fixed or compensation for the loss of use.

A. Just as the owner of a building which is destroyed by the negligence of another is entitled to recover as part of his damages the loss of rents up to the time when, with reasonable diligence, it could have been restored, whether it was in fact restored or not, so should the owner of an aircraft which is destroyed by reason of the negligence of another be entitled to recover for the loss of its use for the time until with reasonable diligence he could have replaced it.

Higgins v. L. A. Gas & Elect. Co., 159 Cal. 651, 663, 115 P. 313 (involving a rental building negligently destroyed, the owner being allowed as part of his damages his loss of rent for the time within which the building could with reasonable diligence have been rebuilt).

Calif.Civil Code, Section 3333—For the breach of an obligation not arising from contract, the measure of damages * * * is the amount which will compensate for all the detriment proximately caused thereby, whether it could have been anticipated or not.

* * *

III

LOSS OF PROFITS

As a natural and probable consequence of the negligence established in this case the appellant suffered a loss of profits of a definite and ascertainable amount as a consequence of being deprived of the lost aircraft immediately after its destruction and for a period of time thereafter during which the appellant was unable to secure an adequate replacement, both because of the appellant's financial inability to make such a capital outlay, and because of the unavailability at that time of an aircraft of similar make and design on the market.

A. Loss of profits, specially pleaded, is a proper element of damages in a suit for the negligent destruction of personal property. [citation omitted]

B. The rule governing the recovery of damages for loss of use and/or loss of profits in the case of personal property destroyed through the fault of another, is, or should be, that the injured party may recover for such loss of use or profits from the time of the destruction of the property until such time as he could with reasonable diligence have replaced it.

To deny appellant a recovery for the loss of profits which he sustained as a result of the negligent loss of his aircraft would be to deny him damages which were the direct and proximate result of the negligence established in this case, and which damages are clearly within the wording and contemplation of *Cal.Civil Code*, Section 3333. [citation omitted]

CONCLUSION

In summary, it is cross-appellant's contention that the proper rule when personal property is destroyed under the language of Section 3333 of the *Civil Code* allows recovery for loss of use and/or business profits. The trial Court erred in denying cross-appellant's offer of proof and refusing the right to prove the additional element of damages as alleged in his claim and complaint.

Dated, San Mateo, California

May 12, 1958.

Respectfully submitted,
Nagle & Vale,
By William Nagle, Jr.,
Attorneys for Cross-Appellant.

---

1 Civil No. 17,966
In the
DISTRICT COURT OF APPEAL
State of California

FIRST APPELLATE [DISTRICT]

Division One

WESLEY REYNOLDS,
 Plaintiff, Respondent and
  Cross-Appellant,
vs.
BANK OF AMERICA N. T. & S. A., as Executor of the Last Will and Testament of Robert Donald Duncan, deceased,
 Defendant, Appellant and
  Cross-Respondent.

CROSS–RESPONDENT'S ANSWERING BRIEF

Appeal from the Judgment of the Superior Court of
the State of California, in and for the
County of San Mateo

Honorable Louis B. Dematteis, Judge

FACTS

For purposes of this cross-appeal, the facts can be stated more simply than they appear in cross-appellant's opening brief. The details of the accident are not material.

An airplane was bailed by plaintiff (cross-appellant here) to the decedent of defendant bank (cross-respondent). The plane was ditched at sea. Defendant was unable to satisfy the jury that the loss of the plane was due to no fault of decedent, hence, judgment was awarded on the verdict to plaintiff.

Plaintiff's judgment was for $30,000.00, which, under the court's instructions, was determined by the jury to be the reasonable value of the plane at the time of its loss. At the trial plaintiff offered to prove that he could not replace the plane within 4 or 5 months; that the reasonable rental value of his destroyed plane was $1,200.00 per month; and that "its reasonable business worth during the period that it would require in due diligence to replace said aircraft would be at least the sum of—reasonable sum of $5,000.00, and that the loss of business profits for that period would be at least the sum of $5,000.00. * * *" (R.T. 273:17–274:10.) The court refused to admit such evidence. (R.T. 248:1–10; 274:19–26.)

ISSUES ON CROSS–APPEAL

Plaintiff on this cross-appeal seeks to recover additional sums represented by loss of use "and/or" profits. Although he states three issues in his opening brief (p. 5), the question of law is, simply stated, whether the plaintiff who has recovered the full value of his destroyed plane can, in the circumstances of this case, recover either for loss of use of that plane or for loss of profits from the time of the destruction to the time of replacement.

ARGUMENT

I. PLAINTIFF IS NOT ENTITLED TO LOSS OF USE IN ADDITION TO COMPLETE VALUE OF PLANE AS OF TIME OF DESTRUCTION

A sharp distinction is drawn by the authorities between cases where the bailed goods are damaged and cases where the goods are destroyed. Where the goods are damaged but are capable of being repaired, the owner is entitled to damages for the loss of use during the time that he is deprived of their use. That rule does not obtain, however, where there is a destruction of the bailment, and the owner recovers the full value of his goods. [citation omitted]

Plaintiff * * * cites Valencia v. Shell Oil Co., 23 Cal.2d 840, 147 P.2d 558, and Louisville & I. Ry. Co. v. Schuester, 183 Ky. 504, 209 S.W. 542, 4 A.L.R. 1344. The *Valencia* case involved a damaged truck, not a destroyed one. * * * [citation omitted]

* * * At the pre-trial conference, the damages contended for by plaintiff were the cost of a like plane. (C.T. 12.) In his requested instruction 16, he asked for the value of the destroyed plane. (R.T. 321.) In his requested instruction 21, he asked for the same measure. (R.T. 327.) See also his requested instruction 19. (R.T. 326.) Only in his requested instruction 22 (R.T. 327) did plaintiff suggest other damages; and plaintiff therein asked for damages for inability to replace damaged property, and gave no authority for the application of such a charge to the facts of this case. In view of the foregoing circumstances, plaintiff should not now be permitted to charge error in the refusal to consider damages for loss of use in addition to the full value of the plane.

II. PLAINTIFF IS NOT ENTITLED TO LOSS OF PROFITS IN ADDITION TO COMPLETE VALUE OF PLANE AS OF TIME OF DESTRUCTION

In seeking damages for loss of profits, plaintiff cites four California cases (pp. 12–14 opening brief), all of which are distinguishable. Johnson v. Central Aviation Corp., 103 Cal.App.2d 102, 229 P.2d 114; Tremeroli v. Austin Trailer Equipment Co., 102 Cal.App.2d 464, 227 P.2d 923; and Valencia v. Shell Oil Co., 23 Cal.2d 840, 147 P.2d 558, involved equipment that was damaged and not destroyed. The fourth case, Skupen v. Imperial Irrigation District, 33 Cal.App.2d 392, 91 P.2d 910, involved the flooding of plaintiff's land.

The rule governing the case on appeal is succinctly stated in 25 C.J.S. Damages, section 44:

"Where loss of anticipated profits results from injury to personal property, recovery is limited to the period of time reasonably necessary to restore the property to its condition immediately prior to the injury. Where there has been an entire loss of the property involved in the action, the full value of the property is the measure of damages, and there can be no recovery for anticipated profits. One deprived of his property in a retail establishment cannot recover both lost profits and the value of the use of the premises and equipment."

If plaintiff is seeking such damages in the alternative, he cannot succeed as to the loss of use because the law of California, and almost universally, is contrary to such suggestion. Further, plaintiff's offer of proof was deficient; and finally, if the court committed any error, such error was invited by plaintiff. He cannot recover for loss of profits in addition to the full value of the plane, for such recovery would be contrary to the law of California.

Cross-respondent therefore asks that the judgment be affirmed.

Dated, August 8, 1958.

> Dodd McRae,
> Kirkbride, Wilson, Harzfeld & Wallace,
>   Attorneys for Cross-Respondent.

————

Plaintiff and Cross-Appellant Reynolds filed a closing brief. Oral argument was held. The District Court of Appeals reversed in an opinion by Peters, J., with instructions to the trial court to retry the issue of damages for loss of use and profits. 168 A.C.A. 265, 335 P.2d 741, February 26, 1959. Defendant petitioned the District Court of Appeals for a rehearing, reiterating that plaintiff had failed properly to present in the trial court his contention that he was entitled to recover damages for loss of use and loss of profits. Evidently concluding plaintiff had sufficiently done so in the trial court, the District Court of Appeals denied rehearing. Thereupon, defendant sought a hearing from the Supreme Court of California.

————

1 Civil No. 17,966
In the

DISTRICT COURT OF APPEAL
State of California

————

WESLEY REYNOLDS,
        Plaintiff, Respondent and
                Cross-Appellant,
            vs.
BANK OF AMERICA N. T. & S.
A., as Executor of the Last Will
and Testament of Robert Donald
Duncan, deceased,
        Defendant, Appellant and
                Cross-Respondent

APPELLANT AND CROSS–RESPONDENT'S
PETITION FOR A HEARING BY THE SUPREME COURT

After Decision by the District Court of Appeal, State of
California, First Appellate District, Division One, and
Numbered Therein 1 Civil No. 17,966

County of San Mateo
Honorable Louis B. Dematteis, Judge

*To the Honorable Phil S. Gibson, Chief Justice, and to the
Honorable Associate Justices of the Supreme Court of the State
of California:*

Appellant and Cross-Respondent respectfully petitions the Honorable Supreme Court of the State of California for a hearing herein.

I

QUESTION FOR DECISION

Is plaintiff, owner of an airplane, bailed to defendant, entitled to recover on its total destruction the fair market value of the plane and, in addition thereto, the value of the loss of use thereof, for a period subsequent to such destruction?

II

FACTS

An airplane was bailed by plaintiff (cross-appellant here) to the decedent of defendant bank (appellant and cross-respondent). The plane was ditched at sea. Judgment was awarded on the verdict to plaintiff for $30,000.00, which, under the court's instructions, was determined by the jury to be the reasonable value of the plane at the time of its loss. At the trial plaintiff offered to prove that he could not replace the plane within 4 or 5 months; that the reasonable rental value of his destroyed plane was $1,200.00 per month; and that "its reasonable business worth during the period that it would require in due diligence to replace said aircraft would be at least the sum of— reasonable sum of $5,000.00, and that the loss of business profits for that period would be at least the sum of $5,000.00 * * *" (R.T. 273:17–274:10.) The court refused to admit such evidence. (R.T. 248:1– 10; 274:19–26.)

The District Court of Appeal reversed and directed the trial court to "retry only the issues as to whether the plane was readily replaceable, and, if it is found that it was not, to fix the value of the loss of use for the period reasonably required to replace it."

III

REASONS WHY A HEARING SHOULD BE GRANTED

A hearing should be granted by this Honorable Court to secure uniformity of decision on important questions of law. The decision of the District Court of Appeal is:

1. In conflict with a decision of this Honorable Court namely the case of Butler, et al. v. Collins, 12 Cal. 457, 466.

2. In conflict with its own prior decision and decisions of other District Courts of Appeal namely Griffith v. Bucknam (1st Dist., Div. 2) 81 Cal.App.2d 454, 459–460, 184 P.2d 179; and Bedell v. Mashburn (3rd Dist.) 87 Cal.App.2d 417, 423, 197 P.2d 98.

IV

STATEMENT

The law of California is, and since 1859 has been, that one may not recover the full value of personal property destroyed and, in addition thereto, damages for loss of use. Butler, et al. v. Collins, 12 Cal. 457, 466.[1]

The rule is one of almost universal application. It is stated, with a host of supporting authority, in 25 C.J.S. Damages, Sec. 83, p. 596, as follows:

"The measure of damages for the loss or destruction of personal property is, as a general rule, the reasonable value at the time of the loss."

It was recognized, as such, by the Honorable Court in the relatively recent case of Pfingsten v. Westenhaver, 39 Cal.2d 12, 22, as follows:

"Pfingsten does not dispute the general legal proposition that there cannot be recovery for both total loss of automobile equipment and loss of use of the same equipment."[2]

The general rule has been enunciated by practically every District Court of Appeal in the State. Lane v. Spurgeon, 100 Cal.App.2d 460; Bedell v. Mashburn, 87 Cal.App.2d 417, 423; Shook v. Beals, 96 Cal. App.2d 963; Tatone v. Chin Bing, 12 Cal.App.2d 543. Indeed the decision in the District Court of Appeal below is contrary to an earlier case decided by the same District Court of Appeal but arising out of Division Two thereof, namely, Griffith v. Bucknam, 81 Cal.App.2d 454.

* * *

1. The *Butler* case refused to give damages for loss of profits in addition to the market value of the destroyed personalty. Loss of profits is merely one measure of the value of loss of use, the other is fair rental value during the period of deprivation. Tremeroli v. Austin Trailer Equipment Co., 102 Cal.App.2d 464, 483, 227 P.2d 923.

2. This case, it is true, involved application of the law of the State of Iowa, but the court was obviously stating what it considered to be a rule of general application.

V

CONCLUSION

Before the decision in the District Court of Appeal, the law of California, and almost universally, was contrary to the allowance of loss of use in the circumstances. It is most respectfully urged that the decision should not be permitted to stand, and that a hearing be granted in this Court.

DODD MCRAE,

KIRKBRIDE, WILSON, HARZFELD & WALLACE,

Attorneys for Appellant, Cross-Respondent and Petitioner.

The petition for hearing was granted and the case heard in the Supreme Court of California on the briefs previously submitted to the District Court of Appeal. On November 13, 1959, the Supreme Court delivered its opinion:

REYNOLDS v. BANK OF AMERICA NATIONAL TRUST AND SAVINGS ASSOCIATION

Supreme Court of California, 1959.
53 Cal.2d 49, 345 P.2d 926.

GIBSON, CHIEF JUSTICE. The sole question presented on this appeal is whether the owner of personal property which has been wrongfully destroyed is limited in damages to the value of the property at the time of destruction or may also recover for loss of use during the period reasonably required for replacement.

Plaintiff's airplane was abandoned at sea and destroyed as the result of its negligent operation by defendant's testator. In addition to general damages, plaintiff sought special damages for loss of use of the plane until it could be replaced, and he offered to prove that new or used equivalent aircraft were not immediately available, that it would require four or five months to replace the aircraft, that its reasonable rental value was $1,200 per month, and that the loss of business profits for the period reasonably required for replacement was $5,000. The offer of proof was rejected on the ground that such evidence was not admissible. A judgment was rendered for plaintiff in the amount of $30,000, representing the value of the airplane, and he has appealed, claiming that he should have been allowed to prove additional damages for loss of use.

Section 3333 of the Civil Code provides: "For the breach of an obligation not arising from contract, the measure of damages, except where otherwise expressly provided by this Code, is the amount which will compensate for all the detriment proximately caused thereby, whether it could have been anticipated or not." It is established, under this section, that where a vehicle is injured by the wrongful act of another, the owner is entitled to recover for the damage done to the vehicle and also for the loss sustained by being deprived of its use during the time reasonably required for the making of repairs. Valencia v. Shell Oil Co., 23 Cal.2d 840, 844, 147 P.2d 558; Johnson v. Central Aviation Corp., 103 Cal.App.2d

102, 107–108, 229 P.2d 114 [airplane]; Tremeroli v. Austin Trailer Equipment Co., 102 Cal.App.2d 464, 480, 482, 227 P.2d 923; Marshall v. Golden State Milk Products Co., 113 Cal.App. 43, 45, 297 P. 109. There appears to be no logical or practical reason why a distinction should be drawn between cases in which the property is totally destroyed and those in which it has been injured but is repairable, and we have concluded that when the owner of a negligently destroyed commercial vehicle has suffered injury by being deprived of the use of the vehicle during the period required for replacement, he is entitled, upon proper pleading and proof, to recover for loss of use in order to "compensate for all the detriment proximately caused" by the wrongful destruction.

Our conclusion is supported by decisions in several jurisdictions and by the Restatement of Torts. Louisville & N. R. Co. v. Blanton, 304 Ky. 127, 200 S.W.2d 133, 138; Louisville & I. R. Co. v. Schuester, 183 Ky. 504, 209 S.W. 542, 543–545, 4 A.L.R. 1344; Paguio v. Evening Journal Ass'n, 127 N.J.L. 144, 21 A.2d 667, 668; Park v. Moorman Mfg. Co., 121 Utah 339, 241 P.2d 914, 920–921, 40 A.L.R.2d 273; Guido v. Hudson Transit Lines, 3 Cir., 178 F.2d 740, 742–743; Buchanan v. Leonard, D.C., 127 F.Supp. 120, 122; see Rest., Torts, § 927. The refusal in some jurisdictions to allow damages for loss of use of a totally destroyed vehicle appears to be the result of historical limitations upon the action of trover at common law. (See 1 Sedgwick on Damages (9th ed. 1913), § 178, pp. 336–338; Note 35 Cornell L.Q. (1950) 862, 864–867; Note 19 Fordham L.Rev. (1950) 223, 224–225.)

The early case of Butler v. Collins, 12 Cal. 457, 466, relied upon by defendant, is not in point since it did not involve the measure of damages where destroyed chattels are not immediately replaceable. Moreover, the case was decided before the enactment of section 3333 of the Civil Code. Nor is Pfingsten v. Westenhaver, 39 Cal.2d 12, 21–22, 244 P.2d 395, controlling because the court, under conflict of laws principles, was dealing with the law of Iowa. Griffith v. Bucknam, 81 Cal.App.2d 454, 459–460, 184 P.2d 179, is distinguishable. There the plaintiff gave the defendant an option to purchase a stallion at a certain price, and it was held that plaintiff's damages for the wrongful destruction of the horse were limited to the amount she had agreed to accept for the horse. The dictum in Bedell v. Mashburn, 87 Cal.App.2d 417, 423, 197 P.2d 98, that damages for the destruction or conversion of personal property are limited to the actual value of the article, is disapproved.

The rejection of plaintiff's offer to prove special damages for loss of use requires a limited reversal of the judgment to permit trial of the issues raised by the offer of proof. Insofar as the judgment awards plaintiff the value of the airplane, the determination need not be disturbed, and, if additional special damages are found, they may be added to the amount already awarded by the jury.

The judgment is reversed with directions to try the issues raised by plaintiff's claim of loss of use.

TRAYNOR, SCHAUER, SPENCE, McCOMB and WHITE, JJ., and PEEK, J. pro tem., concur.

Part II

CLAIMS AND DEFENSES

A. THE VALIDITY OF THE CLAIM

INTRODUCTORY NOTE ON ASSERTING CLAIMS AND DEFENSES

The rules of substantive law take the form of what Professors Michael and Adler have characterized as "conditional imperatives." Thus, the law of negligence is the statement of the following general conditional imperative: *If* a person does an act, and *if* that act creates an unreasonable risk of injury to another, and *if* the act is done without reasonable care to avoid injury to that other person, and *if* injury proximately results to that other person, *then* the actor is liable in damages to the person injured. Again, the law of contract is the statement of the following conditional imperative: *If* two persons make an agreement that is definite in its terms, and *if* by the terms of the agreement each person is to perform a stated service valuable to the other, and *if* one of the persons fails to perform within the time and in the manner agreed upon, *then* that person is liable in damages to the other person. These are, to be sure, gross oversimplifications of the law of negligence and contract, but in form they truly represent those bodies of law and all bodies of substantive law.

In every case in which it is claimed that a person is entitled to a legal remedy, two questions at least must be considered. First, is there a rule of law, that is, a general conditional imperative, which provides that upon the occurrence of the kind of event (or sequence of events) said to have occurred in the case before the court, the person seeking a remedy is entitled to a remedy? This presents a question of law. Second, what is the event or sequence of events that did occur in the particular case before the court? This is a question of fact. See Michael and Adler, The Trial of an Issue of Fact, 34 Colum.L.Rev. 1224, 1462, at 1241–51 (1934).

Beyond giving answers to these questions, the fair and orderly disposition of a case will or may require that certain other tasks be performed in connection with the case. These include: (1) Notice to the parties of the pendency of the case so that they may be given an opportunity to appear; (2) Notice of the contentions, in point of law and fact, that are made so that the parties will have opportunity to prepare and present matters in rebuttal or by way of excuse; (3) Allocation as between the respective parties and the court of the task of raising the contentions of law and fact that may be relevant to the case; (4) Ascertainment at a conveniently early time of the contentions, in point of law or fact, that are not in dispute so that attention may be directed to the disputed contentions; (5) Recordation of what was decided.

These subsidiary problems of pleading will be considered presently. First, however, we shall focus on the problem of the substantive sufficiency of the complaint, for formulation of a substantively valid legal claim is where a lawsuit must begin.

————

GEOFFREY C. HAZARD, JR., ESQ.
University of California
School of Law (Boalt Hall)
Berkeley 4, California
TH 5–6000, Ext. 2276
[Firm Name Deleted]
——— Building
Oakland 12, California
TEL. ———
Attorneys for Plaintiffs

IN THE MUNICIPAL COURT FOR THE BERKELEY— ALBANY JUDICIAL DISTRICT IN AND FOR THE COUNTY OF ALAMEDA, STATE OF CALIFORNIA

EUGENE M. SWANN, CHERIE A. SWANN, Plaintiffs, vs. EUGENE H. BURKETT, ALINE B. BURKETT and ROBERT H. BURKETT, Defendants.	NO. 12243 AMENDED COMPLAINT FOR DAMAGES

Plaintiff Eugene M. Swann for cause of action alleges:

I

At all times herein mentioned, plaintiffs Eugene M. Swann and Cherie A. Swann were husband and wife. At all times herein mentioned, plaintiff Eugene M. Swann was and is a citizen of the United States and a resident of the State of California. Plaintiff Eugene M. Swann is a Negro.

II

At all times herein mentioned, plaintiff Cherie A. Swann acted on behalf of plaintiffs and each of them.

III

Plaintiff is informed and believes, and on such information and belief alleges that defendants own and operate for profit apartment buildings.

IV

Plaintiff is informed and believes, and on such information and belief alleges that among the apartment buildings owned and operated by defendants is a certain establishment consisting of an apartment building and adjoining cottage located at 2709 Benvenue Avenue in the City of Berkeley, County of Alameda, California. Said apartment building and cottage contains four apartments.

V

Plaintiff is informed and believes, and on such information and belief alleges that at all times herein mentioned defendant Eugene H. Burkett was the agent of defendants Aline B. Burkett and Robert H. Burkett in connection with the management of the apartment building mentioned in Paragraph IV above.

VI

Plaintiff is informed and believes, and on such information and belief alleges that at all times herein mentioned defendant Aline B. Burkett was the agent of defendants Eugene H. Burkett and Robert H. Burkett in connection with the management of the apartment building mentioned in Paragraph IV above.

VII

Immediately prior to August 3, 1960, defendants advertised to the public an apartment for rent.

VIII

On or about August 3, 1960, plaintiffs were informed by defendant Eugene H. Burkett that said apartment was located at 2709 Benvenue Avenue, Berkeley, that it was available and that the rent for said apartment was $100.00 per month.

IX

On or about August 4, 1960, plaintiffs inspected the apartment mentioned in Paragraph VIII. Plaintiffs disclosed to defendant Eugene H. Burkett that they were satisfied with said apartment and desired to rent it. Defendant Eugene H. Burkett informed plaintiffs that in addition to the rent there was a charge for utilities of $20.00 per month. At all times herein mentioned, plaintiffs were ready, willing and able to rent the apartment for a rental of $100.00 per month plus a utilities charge of $20.00 per month.

X

Notwithstanding the readiness, willingness and ability of plaintiffs to rent the apartment, defendants refused to rent the apartment to plaintiffs. Said refusal was on account of plaintiffs' race and color.

XI

As the proximate result of defendants' refusal to rent the apartment, as alleged in Paragraph X above, plaintiff Eugene M. Swann suffered humiliation, shock and indignities, to his damage of $500.00.

Plaintiff Cherie A. Swann for cause of action alleges:

I

At all times herein mentioned, plaintiffs Eugene M. Swann and Cherie A. Swann were husband and wife. At all times herein mentioned, plaintiff Cherie A. Swann was and is a citizen of the United States and a resident of the State of California. Plaintiff Cherie A. Swann is a Negro.

II

At all times herein mentioned, plaintiff Eugene A. Swann acted on behalf of plaintiffs and each of them.

III

Plaintiff Cherie A. Swann alleges all the matters alleged in Paragraphs III, IV, V, VI, VII, VIII, IX and X of the cause of action of plaintiff Eugene M. Swann.

IV

As the proximate result of defendants' refusal to rent the apartment, as alleged in Paragraph III above, plaintiff Cherie A. Swann suffered humiliation, shock and indignities, to her damage of $500.00.

WHEREFORE, plaintiffs pray judgment against defendants and each of them as follows:

In favor of plaintiff Eugene M. Swann for:

1. Damages in the sum of $500.00;

2. For $250.00 in addition to plaintiff's damages;

3. For costs of suit; and

4. For such other and further relief as the Court deems proper.

In favor of plaintiff Cherie A. Swann for:

1. Damages in the sum of $500.00;

2. For $250.00 in addition to plaintiff's damages;

3. For costs of suit; and

4. For such other and further relief as the Court deems proper.

GEOFFREY C. HAZARD, JR.
[Firm Name Deleted]

By *Geoffrey C. Hazard, Jr.*
_____
Geoffrey C. Hazard, Jr.
Attorneys for Plaintiffs

We, Eugene M. Swann and Cherie A. Swann, declare under the penalty of perjury that we are the plaintiffs in the above-entitled action; that we have read the foregoing Complaint, and know the contents thereof; that the same is true of our own knowledge except as to matters which are therein stated on information and belief, and as to those matters we believe them to be true.

Eugene M. Swann
_____
Eugene M. Swann

Cherie A. Swann
_____
Cherie A. Swann

_____

HOWARD W. W_____
_____ Building
Berkeley 4, California
Tel. # _____
Attorney for Defendants

IN THE MUNICIPAL COURT FOR THE BERKELEY-
ALBANY JUDICIAL DISTRICT IN AND FOR THE COUNTY
OF ALAMEDA, STATE OF CALIFORNIA

EUGENE M. SWANN, CHERIE A. SWANN, Plaintiffs, vs. EUGENE H. BURKETT, ALINE B. BURKETT and ROBERT H. BURKETT, Defendants.	NO. 12243 DEMURRER TO AMENDED COMPLAINT

Come now defendants above named and, demurring to the Amended Complaint on file herein, respectfully show to the Court:

I

That the First Cause of Action of said Amended Complaint does not state facts sufficient to constitute a cause of action against the defendants or any of them.

II

That the Second Cause of Action of said Amended Complaint does not state facts sufficient to constitute a cause of action against the defendants or any of them.

WHEREFORE, defendants pray that they be hence dismissed with their costs of suit.

Howard W. W _____
Attorney for Defendants

_____

HOWARD W. W _____
_____ Building
Berkeley 4, California
Tel. # _____
Attorney for Defendants

IN THE MUNICIPAL COURT FOR THE BERKELEY–
ALBANY JUDICIAL DISTRICT IN AND FOR THE COUNTY
OF ALAMEDA, STATE OF CALIFORNIA

EUGENE M. SWANN, CHERIE A. SWANN, Plaintiffs, vs. EUGENE H. BURKETT, ALINE B. BURKETT and ROBERT H. BURKETT, Defendants.	NO. 12243 MOTION TO STRIKE

TO: Plaintiffs above named and to GEOFFREY C. HAZARD, JR., and [Firm Name Deleted], their attorneys:

YOU AND EACH OF YOU ARE HEREBY NOTIFIED that the defendants will move the above Court, located 2120 Grove Street, Berkeley, California, on the 6th day of December, 1960, at 9:00 o'clock A.M. of said day, to strike the following portions of the Amended Complaint on file herein:

I

All of paragraph XI of the First Cause of Action.

II

All of paragraph IV of the Second Cause of Action.

Said motion will be made upon all the records on file herein, upon the Points and Authorities attached hereto, and such other and further authorities as may be produced at said hearing.

Howard W. W_____
Attorney for Defendants

___

NOTE ON SWANN v. BURKETT

1. When the action of Swann v. Burkett * was filed, § 51 of the California Civil Code in relevant part provided:

> "All citizens within the jurisdiction of this State are free and equal, and no matter what their race, color, religion, ancestry or national origin are entitled to the full and equal accommodations, advantages, facilities, privileges, or services in all business establishments of every kind whatsoever."

Section 52 of the Civil Code provided that any person who "makes any discrimination * * * contrary to the provisions of Section 51 * * * is liable * * * for the actual damages, and two hundred fifty dollars * * * in addition thereto, suffered by any person denied the rights provided in Section 51 * * *." Sections 51 and 52 reflected 1959 amendments to a provision that previously had only covered "inns, restaurants, hotels, eating-houses, barbershops, bath-houses, theaters, skating rinks, and all other places of public accommodation or amusement." Moreover, as observed in Swann v. Burkett, 209 Cal.App.2d 685, 691–92, 26 Cal.Rptr. 286, 290 (1962):

> "At the same time that the Legislature adopted the 1959 amendments to sections 51 and 52 * * * it enacted the Hawkins Act (Health & Saf. Code, §§ 35700–35741). Section 35720 makes it unlawful for the owner of 'any publicly assisted housing accommodation * * * to refuse to sell, rent or lease * * * such housing accommodation because of the race, color, religion, national origin, or ancestry of such person or persons.' Section 35730 provides a right of action for restraint of a violation of section 35720 and for damages in a sum not less than $500. Section 35740 provides that the provisions of the act shall not apply to privately owned housing accommodations which are not 'publicly assisted'."

What argument might be made in support of the defendants' demurrer? What argument might be made by plaintiff in opposition to it?

2. Under the Federal Rules what procedural device would defendants appropriately have used instead of the demurrer?

3. In support of their Motion to Strike, defendants filed a Memorandum of Points and Authorities, as follows:

___

* Since Swann v. Burkett there has of course been significant legal development, including federal protection, against racial discrimination in housing. See e.g. Reitman v. Mulkey, 387 U.S. 369, 87 S.Ct. 1627, 18 L.Ed.2d 830 (1967); Jones v. Alfred H. Mayer Co., 392 U.S. 409, 88 S.Ct. 2186, 20 L.Ed.2d 1189 (1968); Trafficante v. Metropolitan Life Ins. Co., 409 U.S. 205, 93 S.Ct. 364, 34 L.Ed.2d 415 (1972).

POINTS AND AUTHORITIES

Code of Civil Procedure, Section 453.

While the trend of the cases may point toward the eventual adoption of a rule which would permit the granting of damages for "mental anguish" without the presence of physical injury, at the present time the contrary is still the rule, and no damages for "mental anguish" can be recovered in the absence of physical injury.

> Espinosa v. Beverly Hospital,
> 114 C.A.2d 232

"Mental suffering alone, or mere fright, unaccompanied by physical injury, will not ordinarily entitle a plaintiff to an allowance of compensatory damages."

> 14 Cal.Jur.2d "Damages",
> Section 47 (pages 674–675)

> Respectfully submitted,

> *Howard W. W* _____
> Attorney for Defendants

Defendants filed a companion memorandum in support of their demurrer. A Memorandum of Points and Authorities is, of course, in substance a brief; it resembles a brief submitted in an appellate court, except that it is typed rather than printed, on legal-size paper rather than printed-brief size, and is usually less elaborate. Compare the briefs in Reynolds v. Bank of America, supra. Under the rules of court in many jurisdictions, and by practice in most, a demurrer or motion that is not accompanied by a statement of legal points and authorities may be treated as lacking merit. See, e.g., California Rules of Court, Superior Court Rules 313(a) and 203. In any event the judges hearing motions appreciate some sort of brief from the parties but, especially in busy metropolitan courts, do not like long-winded ones. It is either required or common practice, and ordinarily prudent, for the party against whom a motion has been made to submit his own countering memorandum of law.

In preparing such a memorandum on behalf of plaintiffs in *Swann,* would it be valuable to know that Restatement Second of Torts says the following:

"§ 46. (1) One who by extreme and outrageous conduct intentionally or recklessly causes severe emotional distress to another is subject to liability for such emotional distress ∗ ∗ ∗."

"§ 48. Comment e. A possessor of land who holds his premises open to the public for business or other purposes may be liable, as in the case of any other person, for the intentional infliction of emotional disturbance by conduct which is extreme and outrageous, under the rule stated in § 46."

What argument could be made with this as authority in opposition to the motion to strike?

4. Suppose that plaintiffs' complaint in Swann v. Burkett had alleged as follows:

I

Defendants own an apartment building. On or about August 4, 1960, they refused to rent an apartment therein to plaintiffs. Said refusal was on account of plaintiffs' race.

II

As a proximate result plaintiffs suffered mental distress to his and her damage of $500 each.

Wherefore, plaintiffs each pray for judgment for $500, for $250 in addition thereto and for costs.

———

a. Would a complaint so drafted be less sufficient as a matter of substantive law than the one actually filed?

b. Would a complaint so drafted comply with the California rules of specificity in pleading? Compare Dino, Inc. v. Boreta Enterprises, infra p. 102. Would it comply with F.R.C.P. 8 in this respect? Compare American Nurses' Ass'n v. Illinois, infra p. 95.

c. As a tactical matter was it desirable for plaintiff to spell out the claim in detail even if the pleading rules might not have so required?

NOTE ON THE COMPLAINT AS AN IMPLICIT CONTENTION ABOUT SUBSTANTIVE LAW

A statement of a "cause of action," in one sense of that over-used term, is the statement that there occurred in fact certain events in the out-of-court world which prima facie show that the complainant is entitled to a remedy. To determine whether the complaint does "state a cause of action," it is necessary to make reference, first, to the applicable substantive law and, second, to the rules of pleading.

The applicable substantive law prescribes the conditions under which a remedy will be granted or denied. While the rules of pleading require that the complaint describe out-of-court events which the plaintiff contends prima facie entitle him to relief, the complaint is not required, and traditionally was not permitted, to state explicitly the substantive law on which it is based. These rules are merely implied. See Clark on Code Pleading 237 n. 88 (2d ed. 1947): "The comparison of an action to a syllogism is a favorite one. It is said that the major premise is a rule of law, not to be pleaded; the minor premise, the facts of the case making the rule of law applicable (these alone are to be pleaded); and the conclusion is the judgment of the court."

This convention is no longer strictly adhered to in the practice of some jurisdictions. For practical reasons, the federal courts have largely abandoned it. Since the federal courts have a restricted jurisdiction, the basis of jurisdiction for a complaint in federal court must be established and it is convenient that this be done by preliminary allegations in the complaint. See F.R.C.P. Form 2. When the basis of jurisdiction is a federal claim, as distinct from diversity, the allegation of the jurisdictional basis is also a reference to the federal legal theory on which the complaint is founded. Such references in turn have proven useful notice to the court and to the defendant of what the plaintiff's legal contentions are, and it is perhaps for this reason that the practice to some extent has been absorbed in state practice.

MOLASKY v. GARFINKLE

United States District Court, Southern District of New York, 1974.
380 F.Supp. 549.

EDWARD WEINFELD, DISTRICT JUDGE. Plaintiffs, individually and in a representative capacity (hereafter "Molaskys"), have, for more then ten years, owned and continue to own shares of common stock in Ancorp National Services, Inc. ("Ancorp"), purchased at an average price of $15 per share. On March 15, 1973, trading in Ancorp common shares was halted on the New York Stock Exchange, and on March 20, 1973, Ancorp filed a petition for arrangement under Chapter XI of the Bankruptcy Act. Plaintiffs allege that as a result they have been unable to sell their shares, since there is no real or active market for them. The first cause of action in general alleges that from January 1970 until trading was halted, all the defendants, except Peat, Marwick, Mitchell & Co., conspired to and did fraudulently manipulate the market in Ancorp common and induced the Molaskys "to refrain from effectuating their announced intention to sell" their shares in the open market, in violation of sections 10(b)[1] and 13(e)(1)[2] of the Securities Exchange Act, and rule 10b–5[3] promulgated thereunder.

1. [Ed. Note:

15 U.S.C.A. § 78j(b):

It shall be unlawful for any person, directly or indirectly, by the use of any means or instrumentality of interstate commerce or of the mails, or of any facility of any national securities exchange—

* * *

(b) To use or employ, in connection with the purchase or sale of any security registered on a national securities exchange or any security not so registered, any manipulative or deceptive device or contrivance in contravention of such rules and regulations as the Commission may prescribe as necessary or appropriate in the public interest or for the protection of investors.]

2. [Ed. Note:

15 U.S.C.A. § 78m(e)(1):

(1) It shall be unlawful for an issuer which has a class of equity securities registered pursuant to section 78*l* of this title, or which is a closed-end investment company registered under the Investment Company Act of 1940 [15 U.S.C. 80a–1 et seq.], to purchase any equity security issued by it if such purchase is in contravention of such rules and regulations as the Commission, in the public interest or for the protection of investors, may adopt (A) to define acts and practices which are fraudulent, deceptive, or manipulative, and (B) to prescribe means reasonably designed to prevent such acts and practices. Such rules and regulations may require such issuer to provide holders of equity securities of such class with such information relating to the reasons for such purchase, the source of funds, the number of shares to be purchased, the price to be paid for such securities, the method of purchase, and such additional information, as the Commission deems necessary or appropriate in the public interest or for the protection of investors, or which the Commission deems to be material to a determination whether such security should be sold.]

3. [Ed. Note:

17 C.F.R. § 240.10b–5. Employment of manipulative and deceptive devices.

It shall be unlawful for any person, directly or indirectly, by the use of any means or instrumentality of interstate

Count II, wherein Peat, Marwick, Mitchell & Co., a partnership ("Peat, Marwick"), is named with the other defendants, charges that it joined the conspiracy alleged in the first count; specifically, that its partners having held themselves out as independent public accountants and auditors, it prepared or reviewed certain financial statements and interim reports of Ancorp that were materially misleading and upon which the Molaskys relied "in evaluating their investment decision to refrain from selling their Ancorp common stock in the open market, or otherwise." Plaintiffs charge that such conduct violated section 17(a) of the Securities Act of 1933,[4] section 10(b) of the 1934 Act, and Rule 10b–5.

Count III, directed only against Peat, Marwick, asserts a common law claim, charging it with gross negligence and alleging that had the Molaskys known the facts which Peat, Marwick failed and omitted to disclose, they would not have refrained from carrying out their announced intention of selling their shares in the open market. This third count is grounded on diversity jurisdiction and pendent jurisdiction.

Peat, Marwick now moves pursuant to Rule 12(b)(6) of the Federal Rules of Civil Procedure to dismiss count II for failure to state a claim upon which relief can be granted. What sticks out clearly is that the Molaskys have not sold their shares, which they acquired more than ten years ago. Thus, at the threshold they face Birnbaum v. Newport Steel Co.[5] and its progeny, which hold that a cause of action under section 10(b) of the 1934 Act or rule 10b–5 requires that a plaintiff be either a defrauded purchaser or a defrauded seller of securities.

While the continued vitality of Birnbaum has been questioned[6] and its holding criticized,[7] and indeed the Seventh Circuit Court of Appeals has looked the other way,[8] our Court of Appeals, despite repeated urgings to overrule Birnbaum, adheres to its holding, and it remains the rule in this circuit.[9] The court has explained its adherence

commerce, or of the mails or of any facility of any national securities exchange,

(a) To employ any device, scheme, or artifice to defraud,

(b) To make any untrue statement of a material fact or to omit to state a material fact necessary in order to make the statements made, in the light of the circumstances under which they were made, not misleading, or

(c) To engage in any act, practice, or course of business which operates or would operate as a fraud or deceit upon any person,

in connection with the purchase or sale of any security.]

4. 15 U.S.C.A. § 77q(a).

5. 193 F.2d 461 (2d Cir.), cert. denied, 343 U.S. 956, 72 S.Ct. 1051, 93 L.Ed. 1356 (1952).

6. Entel v. Allen, 270 F.Supp. 60, 69–70 (S.D.N.Y.1967).

7. See, e.g., Leech, Transactions in Corporate Control, 104 U.Pa.L.Rev. 725, 832–35 (1956); Lowenfels, The Demise of the Birnbaum Doctrine: A New Era for Rule 10b–5, 54 Va.L.Rev. 268, 275–77 (1968).

8. Eason v. General Motors Acceptance Corp., 490 F.2d 654 (7th Cir. 1973).

9. See Haberman v. Murchison, 468 F.2d 1305, 1311–1313 (2d Cir. 1972); GAF Corp. v. Milstein, 453 F.2d 709, 721 (2d Cir. 1971), cert. denied, 406 U.S. 910, 92 S.Ct. 1610, 31 L.Ed.2d 821 (1972); Iroquois Industries, Inc. v. Syracuse China Corp., 417 F.2d 963, 967–970 (2d Cir. 1969), cert. denied 399 U.S. 909, 90 S.Ct. 2199, 26 L.Ed.2d

thereto as reflecting both congressional policy in enacting section 10(b) and that of the SEC in adopting rule 10b–5, and has emphasized that it is not the court's function to extend section 10(b) to transactions not intended to be covered by Congress.[10]

Plaintiffs, recognizing the continuing force of *Birnbaum*, seek to defeat the motion to dismiss by reliance upon such cases as Vine v. Beneficial Finance Co.[11] and A. T. Brod & Co. v. Perlow,[12] which purportedly "relaxed" the *Birnbaum* rule. But those cases are inapplicable and give no support to plaintiffs' position, since in the former it was found that the plaintiff was a "forced" seller, and in the latter a broker who was defrauded was the purchaser of the shares. Thus in each instance plaintiff was either a purchaser or a seller of securities in connection with which fraud was practiced, and therefore came within the terms of the *Birnbaum* holding.

P's arg

So, too, plaintiffs' reliance upon Stockwell v. Reynolds & Co.[13] is misplaced. In that case, plaintiffs alleged that they had intended to sell their shares in a certain company, but were persuaded not to by representations made by the defendant; when, however, they subsequently learned of the falsity of the representations, they sold their stock at a loss. The court held that *Birnbaum* was not a bar, as plaintiffs were sellers of stock. The only issue was whether the sales were "in connection with" the alleged fraud, and the court, reading that requirement liberally, held they were and that plaintiffs were entitled to maintain the action under rule 10b–5. Assuming arguendo that the *Stockwell* decision is correct, it does not aid plaintiffs here, since even after the discovery of the alleged fraud they have retained their stock; they are not sellers, as were the plaintiffs in *Stockwell*.

Plaintiffs' contention that they have not been able to sell since learning of the fraud because trading in Ancorp common stock has been halted on the New York Stock Exchange and a Chapter XI arrangement has been filed, does not change their situation. Essentially, they argue that the very fraud of the defendants which has damaged them at the same time has destroyed the marketability of their shares, thereby preventing them from being sellers, even "forced" sellers. Yet in Iroquois Industries, Inc. v. Syracuse China Corp.,[14] where our Court

P's args

561 (1970); Greenstein v. Paul, 400 F.2d 580, 581 (2d Cir. 1968); cf. International Controls Corp. v. Vesco, 490 F.2d 1334, 1346 n. 16 (2d Cir. 1974); Mutual Shares Corp. v. Genesco, Inc., 384 F.2d 540, 546 (2d Cir. 1967). See also Sargent v. Genesco, Inc., 492 F.2d 750, 762–764 (5th Cir. 1974); VI L. Loss, Securities Regulation 3617–18 (1969).

10. See Iroquois Industries, Inc. v. Syracuse China Corp., 417 F.2d 963, 969 (2d Cir. 1969), cert. denied, 399 U.S. 909, 90 S.Ct. 2199, 26 L.Ed.2d 561 (1970).

11. 374 F.2d 627 (2d Cir.), cert. denied, 389 U.S. 970, 88 S.Ct. 463, 19 L.Ed.2d 460

(1967); see Dudley v. Southeastern Factor & Finance Corp., 446 F.2d 303 (5th Cir.), cert. denied, 404 U.S. 858, 92 S.Ct. 109, 30 L.Ed.2d 101 (1971); Crane Co. v. Westinghouse Air Brake Co., 419 F.2d 787, 798 (2d Cir. 1969), cert. denied, 400 U.S. 822, 91 S.Ct. 41, 27 L.Ed.2d 50 (1970); Feldberg v. O'Connell, 338 F.Supp. 744 (D.Mass.1972).

12. 375 F.2d 393 (2d Cir. 1967).

13. 252 F.Supp. 215 (S.D.N.Y.1965).

14. 417 F.2d 963 (2d Cir. 1969), cert. denied, 399 U.S. 909, 90 S.Ct. 2199, 26 L.Ed.2d 561 (1970).

of Appeals reaffirmed the *Birnbaum* rule and found no 10b–5 liability, the plaintiff was prevented from becoming a purchaser by the fraudulent acts of the defendant. As the court there noted:

> "That the conduct averred in any given case may be reprehensible does not mean that a federal remedy must be furnished by judges. The remedy in many cases may be found in the state courts. . . ." [15]

Moreover, the fact that the company is in Chapter XI does not mean that the shares are not marketable. An arrangement thereunder does not affect the equity owner's interest.[16] The fact that the value of the shares may be depreciated or that they are not immediately marketable does not give the plaintiffs status as buyers or sellers of the shares.

Similarly, section 17(a) protects only defrauded purchasers of securities,[17] which none of the plaintiffs were during any relevant period. Indeed, plaintiffs do not appear to challenge Peat, Marwick on this point. The motion to dismiss the second cause of action is granted.

The foregoing disposition necessarily requires granting the defendant's further motion to dismiss for lack of subject matter jurisdiction the third count of the complaint, which alleges common law claims of negligence and is grounded on both "pendent" [18] and diversity jurisdiction. Dismissal of count II removes pendent jurisdiction under the rule announced by the Supreme Court in United Mine Workers v. Gibbs.[19] Further, it is undisputed that a number of Peat, Marwick partners are citizens of Missouri, as are the plaintiffs, which defeats diversity jurisdiction since the citizenship of the partnership for diversity purposes is that of each partner.[20] However, plaintiffs request that they "be granted leave to add as parties defendant those partners of PMM [Peat, Marwick] involved in the preparation of the reports alleged, who are domiciled outside the State of Missouri. . . ." Plaintiffs have not articulated how adding partners "who are domiciled outside the State of Missouri" would solve their diversity jurisdiction dilemma, since diversity must be complete.[21] If they intend, as they intimate, to name as defendants only those individual partners allegedly involved in the

---

15. Id. at 969.

16. See 11 U.S.C.A. § 706(1); SEC v. United States Realty & Improvement Co., 310 U.S. 434, 60 S.Ct. 1044, 84 L.Ed. 1293 (1940). See also 11 U.S.C.A. § 575.

17. See Iroquois Industries, Inc. v. Syracuse China Corp., 417 F.2d 963, 966 (2d Cir. 1969), cert. denied, 399 U.S. 909, 90 S.Ct. 2199, 26 L.Ed.2d 561 (1970); Superintendent of Insurance v. Bankers Life & Cas. Co., 430 F.2d 355, 359 (2d Cir. 1970), rev'd on other grounds, 404 U.S. 6, 92 S.Ct. 165, 30 L.Ed.2d 128 (1971); Birnbaum v. Newport Steel Corp., 193 F.2d 461, 463 (2d Cir.), cert. denied, 343 U.S. 956, 72 S.Ct. 1051, 93 L.Ed. 1356 (1952); Emco Porcelain Enamel Co. v. Wolfe, [1970–1971 Transfer Binder] CCH Fed.Sec.L.Rep. ¶ 93,143 (1971).

18. See Hurn v. Oursler, 289 U.S. 238, 53 S.Ct. 586, 77 L.Ed. 1148 (1933).

19. 383 U.S. 715, 726, 86 S.Ct. 1130, 16 L.Ed.2d 218 (1966); see Kavit v. A. L. Stamm & Co., 491 F.2d 1176, 1179 (2d Cir. 1974).

20. Great Southern Fire Proof Hotel Co. v. Jones, 177 U.S. 449, 20 S.Ct. 690, 44 L.Ed. 842 (1900); Woodward v. D. H. Overmyer Co., 428 F.2d 880, 883 (2d Cir. 1970), cert. denied, 400 U.S. 993, 91 S.Ct. 460, 27 L.Ed.2d 441 (1971); Eastern Metals Corp. v. Martin, 191 F.Supp. 245, 249–250 (S.D.N.Y.1960).

21. Strawbridge v. Curtiss, 7 U.S. (3 Cranch) 267, 2 L.Ed. 435 (1806).

preparation of the reports, whose citizenship differs from plaintiffs, and to omit the Missouri partners, they are free to do so in an appropriate action. There is no reason to allow the third count to be used as a vehicle for that purpose, since the action was commenced against and names the partnership as the defendant that allegedly committed the acts upon which the claim is predicated. The motion to dismiss count III is also granted.*

NOTE ON THE RELATION BETWEEN THE SUFFICIENCY OF THE COMPLAINT AND JURISDICTION IN FEDERAL COURT

1. The federal courts have limited jurisdiction. The most commonly invoked bases of jurisdiction are 28 U.S.C.A. §§ 1331 ("general" federal question), 1332 (diversity), 1337 (actions arising under Acts regulating commerce), and 1343 (civil rights actions). See generally Introductory Note on Jurisdiction of the Federal Courts, infra p. 523. Which of these provisions were involved in Molasky v. Garfinkle?

2. A federal claim may "arise" under federal law either when a federal statute creating a substantive right expressly provides that it is actionable by an injured party or when Congress is found to have intended that there be an "implied" right of action. The doctrine on implied causes of action is stated in Cort v. Ash, 422 U.S. 66, 95 S.Ct. 2080, 45 L.Ed.2d 26 (1975). See also, e.g., Thompson v. Thompson, 484 U.S. 174, 108 S.Ct. 513, 98 L.Ed.2d 512 (1988). Was this the basis of plaintiffs' contention in Molasky v. Garfinkle that the statute not only protected persons in their situation, but gave them a federal cause of action? Could a state court hold that violation of the Federal Securities Acts may not be actionable by a "nonpurchaser" as a matter of federal law but that it is actionable as a matter of *state* law? Compare Note, State Incorporation of Federal Law: A Response to the Demise of Implied Federal Rights of Action, 94 Yale L.J. 1144 (1985).

3. If an action is brought in federal court on the jurisdictional basis that the claim asserted arises under federal law, what is the situation if defendant disputes the substantive sufficiency of the complaint? The problem is that the question of the validity of plaintiff's claim and the question of the court's jurisdiction coincide. Hence, if the court concludes that the claim is substantively insufficient it might therefore be required to dismiss the action for lack of jurisdiction. Such an approach, while logically coherent, has practical drawbacks. For one thing, the dismissal might not be regarded as res judicata if the plaintiff sought to bring a subsequent state court action based on state law, the rule being that a termination of an action for lack of jurisdiction is not "on the merits" so as to preclude a subsequent action. Equally important, the court might consider that, if it lacked jurisdiction according to the complaint, it could not allow plaintiff to get into the discovery stage in order to bolster the factual basis of his claim. In light of these difficulties, therefore, the rule is established that a federal court has jurisdiction if the complaint has an arguable or "colorable" federal claim. Wheeldin v. Wheeler, 373 U.S. 647, 83 S.Ct. 1441, 10 L.Ed.2d 605 (1963). Did the complaint in Molasky v. Garfinkle meet this test?

4. If a federal court has jurisdiction of an action by reason of one of the claims asserted in it, the court may also have jurisdiction of other related claims. This is the concept of "pendent" jurisdiction, which has two branches.

---

* [Ed. Note: This result is consistent with Blue Chip Stamps v. Manor Drug   Stores, 421 U.S. 723, 95 S.Ct. 1917, 44 L.Ed. 2d 539 (1975).]

Pendent Claim Jx

When the court's jurisdiction is based on a federal claim, it may also adjudicate claims between the parties based on state law that arise out of the same transaction. See United Mine Workers v. Gibbs, 383 U.S. 715, 86 S.Ct. 1130, 16 L.Ed.2d 218 (1966); Carnegie-Mellon Univ. v. Cohill, infra p. 538. This is called pendent *claim* jurisdiction. And, when the court has jurisdiction over one set of parties (whether jurisdiction is based on a federal claim or upon diversity), it may under some circumstances exercise jurisdiction over other parties. See Aldinger v. Howard, infra p. 528, and the Note following. This is called pendent *party* jurisdiction. In either case, the federal court has discretion to refuse to adjudicate the pendent claim. Which of these situations was involved in Molasky v. Garfinkle?

Pendent party Jx

B. PLEADINGS

1. THE ELEMENTS OF A SUFFICIENT COMPLAINT

INTRODUCTORY NOTE ON SUFFICIENCY

The substantive law determines, as we have seen, whether the factual conditions in a dispute are such as to give rise to a valid claim for redress. But the substantive law does not say which of the conditions must be asserted by *plaintiff*, initially by pleading or subsequently by proof, before redress can justifiably be given to him. At a minimum, we might suppose, a plaintiff could be expected to state that he had been injured and that defendant was in some way associated with the doing of the injury. Some such minimum would be required for public convenience and economy, so that courts need not dissipate their energies on those manifesting only malaise. But beyond this minimum, it appears neither *a priori* nor even obviously what should be expected of plaintiff. The question thus presented can be sorted analytically into two problems: What set of factual elements should be regarded as sufficient indication that plaintiff has a grievance justifying judicial consideration, and how should plaintiff be required to assert the facts on which his grievance is based? The classic device for answering these requirements has been pleadings, i.e., written statements of claim and defense made by each side at the beginning of the action.

CLEARY, PRESUMING AND PLEADING: AN ESSAY ON JURISTIC IMMATURITY *
12 Stan.L.Rev. 5 (1959).†

*   *   *

The Substantive Law

Since all are agreed that procedure exists only for the purpose of putting the substantive law effectively to work, a preliminary look at the nature of substantive law, as viewed procedurally, is appropriate.

* The author's footnotes have been omitted.   † Copyright © 1959.

Every dog, said the common law, is entitled to one bite. This result was reached from reasoning that man's best friend was not in general dangerous, and hence the owner should not be liable when the dog departed from his normally peaceable pursuits and inflicted injury. Liability should follow only when the owner had reason to know of the dangerous proclivities of his dog, and the one bite afforded notice of those proclivities. So the formula for holding a dog owner liable at common law is + *ownership* + *notice of dangerous character* + *biting*.

This rule of law becomes monotonous to postmen. Hence the postmen cause to be introduced in the legislature a bill making owners of dogs absolutely liable, i.e., eliminating notice from the formula for liability. At the hearing on the bill, however, the dog lovers appear and, while admitting the justness of the postmen's complaint, point out that a dog ought at least to be entitled to defend himself against human aggression. Then the home owners' lobby points out the usefulness of dogs in guarding premises against prowlers. Balancing these factors, there emerges a statute making dog owners liable for bites inflicted except upon persons tormenting the dog or unlawfully on the owner's premises. The formula for liability now becomes: + *ownership* + *biting* − *being tormented* − *unlawful presence on the premises.*

So in any given situation, the law recognizes certain elements as material to the case, and the presence or absence of each of them is properly to be considered in deciding the case. Or, to rephrase in somewhat more involved language, rules of substantive law are "statements of the specific factual conditions upon which specific legal consequences depend. . . .   Rules of substantive law are conditional imperatives, having the form: *If* such and such *and* so and so, *etc.* is the case, *and unless* such and such *or unless* so and so, *etc.* is the case, *then* the defendant is liable. . . ." Now obviously the weighing and balancing required to determine what elements ought to be considered material cannot be accomplished by any of the methodologies of procedure. The result is purely a matter of substantive law, to be decided according to those imponderables which travel under the name of jurisprudence.

This view of the substantive law may seem unduly Euclidean, yet some system of analysis and classification is necessary if the law is to possess a measure of continuity and to be accessible and usable.

Prima Facie Case and Defense

Under our adversary method of litigation a trial is essentially not an inquest or investigation but rather a demonstration conducted by the parties.

Since plaintiff is the party seeking to disturb the existing situation by inducing the court to take some measure in his favor, it seems reasonable to require him to demonstrate his right to relief. How extensive must this demonstration be? Should it include every substantive element, which either by its existence or non-existence may condition his right to relief? If the answer is "yes," then plaintiff under our dog statute would be required to demonstrate each of the elements in the formula: + *ownership* + *biting* − *tormenting* − *illegal presence on the premises.*

In the ordinary dog case this would not be unduly burdensome, but if the suit is on a contract and we require plaintiff to establish the existence or nonexistence, as may be appropriate, of every concept treated in Corbin and Williston, then the responsibility of plaintiff becomes burdensome indeed and the lawsuit itself may include a large amount of unnecessary territory. Actually, of course, the responsibility for dealing with every element is not placed on plaintiff. Instead we settle for a "prima facie case" or "cause of action," consisting of certain selected elements which are regarded as sufficient to entitle plaintiff to recover, *if* he proves them and *unless* defendant in turn establishes other elements which would offset them. Thus in a simple contract case, by establishing + *offer* + *acceptance* + *consideration* + *breach,* plaintiff is entitled to recover, unless defendant establishes + *accord and satisfaction* or + *failure of consideration* or + *illegality* or − *capacity to contract,* and so on.

Observe that the plus and minus signs change, in accord with proper mathematical rules, when we shift elements to the defendant's side of the equation as "defenses." For example, if plaintiff were required to deal with capacity to contract, it would become + *capacity to contract* as a part of his case, rather than the − *capacity to contract* of defendant's case.

Defenses, too, may be prima facie only and subject to being offset by further matters produced by plaintiff, as in the case of the defense of release, offset by the further fact of fraud in the inducement for the release. The entire process is the familiar confessing and avoiding of the common law.

Allocating the Elements

The next step to be taken is the determination whether a particular material element is a part of plaintiff's prima facie case or a defense. Or, referring back to the statement that rules of substantive law are "conditional imperatives, having the form: *If* such and such *and* so and so, *etc.,* is the case . . . *then* the defendant is liable," should the element in question be listed as an *if* or as an *unless?*

In some types of situations, the test has been purely mechanical, with the mechanics in turn likely to be accidental and casual. Thus, in causes of action based on statute, if an exception appears in the enacting clause, i.e., the clause creating the right of action, then the party relying on the statute must show that the case is not within the exception; otherwise the responsibility for bringing the case within an exception falls upon the opposite party. The principle is widely recognized, but the vagaries of statutory draftsmanship detract largely from its certainty of application. Returning to our dogs, two statutes will serve as illustrations.

> "If any dog shall do any damage to either the body or property of any person, the owner . . . shall be liable for such damage, unless such damage shall have been occasioned to the body or property of a person who, at the time such damage was sustained, was committing a trespass or other tort, or was teasing, tormenting or abusing such dog." Mass.Ann.Laws ch. 140, § 155 (1950).

> "Every person owning or harboring a dog shall be liable to the party injured for all damages done by such dog; but no recovery shall be had for personal injuries to any person when they [sic] are upon the premises of the owner of the dog after night, or upon the owner's premises engaged in some unlawful act in the day time." Ky.Laws 1906, ch. 10, at 25, Ky.Stats.1936, § 68a–5.

The Massachusetts statute was construed as imposing on a two and one quarter year old plaintiff the burden of establishing that he was not teasing, tormenting or abusing the dog, while under the Kentucky statute a plaintiff was held to have stated a prima facie case by alleging only that he was bitten by a dog owned by defendant, leaving questions of presence on the premises at night or unlawful activities in the day time to be brought in as defenses. The difference in result can scarcely be regarded as calculated but is typical. Unfortunately, the statute which states in so many words the procedural effects of its terms is a rarity.

Exceptions in contracts receive similar treatment. If the words of promising are broad, followed by exceptions, the general disposition is to place on defendant the responsibility of invoking the exception. Of course, many of the cases involve insurance policies, with all that implies. In Munro, Brice & Co. v. War Risks Ass'n, during World War I one underwriter insured plaintiffs' ship against loss due to hostilities and another underwriter insured it against perils of the sea except consequences of hostilities. The ship was lost, and plaintiffs sued on both policies. The King's Bench Division held that as regards the first policy plaintiffs must show the loss to have been due to hostilities, but that under the second policy merely establishing the loss was sufficient, leaving it to the underwriter to bring in loss by hostilities as a defense. Since evidence of the cause of loss was wholly lacking, the loss fell on the second underwriter.

Julius Stone commented as follows:

"Every qualification of a class can equally be stated without any change of meaning as an exception to a class not so qualified. Thus the proposition 'All animals have four legs except gorillas', and the proposition 'all animals which are not gorillas have four legs', are so far as their meanings are concerned, identical. . . .

"If the distinction between an element of the rule and an exception to it does not represent any distinction in meaning, it may still remain a valid distinction for legal purposes. In that case, however, it must turn upon something other than the meaning of the propositions involved. It may turn, for instance, merely upon their relative form or order."

So in a few kinds of cases the answer to the question of allocation is found in the structure of a statute or contract, perhaps with some tenuous reference to intent, either of the legislature or of the contracting parties. But what of the great bulk of the cases, involving neither exception in a statute nor limitation upon words of promising? What general considerations should govern the allocation of responsibility for the elements of the case between the parties?

Precedent may settle the manner in a particular jurisdiction, but precedent as such does nothing for the inquiring mind. Thayer was of the view that questions of allocation were to be referred to the principles of pleading, or perhaps to analysis of the substantive law, and "one has no right to look to the law of evidence for a solution of such questions as these. . . ." Books about pleading, however, have not been numerous in recent years, except for the local practice works; and aside from a brief but provocative treatment by Judge Clark they offer slight assistance. The substantive law texts, when they deal with the matter at all, tend to describe results rather than reasons.

Despite Thayer's strictures, his descendants in the field of writing about evidence, by assuming to deal with problems of burden of proof as an aspect of the law of evidence, have found themselves inevitably enmeshed in the problems of allocation and have contributed most of the literature on the subject, although in an introductory and incidental fashion.

Before trying to establish some bench marks for allocation, let us note, though only for the purpose of rejecting them, two which are sometimes suggested. (a) That the burden is on the party having the affirmative; or, conversely stated, that a party is not required to prove a negative. This is no more than a play on words, since practically any proposition may be stated in either affirmative or negative form. Thus a plaintiff's exercise of ordinary care equals absence of contributory negligence, in the minority jurisdictions which place this element in plaintiff's case. In any event, the proposition seems simply not to be so. (b) That the burden is on the party to whose case the element is essential. This does no more than restate the question.

Actually the reported decisions involving problems of allocation rarely contain any satisfying disclosure of the *ratio decidendi*. Implicit, however, seem to be considerations of policy, fairness and probability. None affords a complete working rule. Much overlap is apparent, as sound policy implies not too great a departure from fairness, and probability may constitute an aspect of both policy and fairness. But despite the vagueness of their generality, it is possible to pour enough content into these concepts to give them some real meaning.

(1) *Policy.* As Judge Clark remarks, "One who must bear the risk of getting the matter properly set before the court, if it is to be considered at all, has to that extent the dice loaded against him." While policy more obviously predominates at the stage of determining what elements are material, its influence may nevertheless extend into the stage of allocating those elements by way of favoring one or the other party to a particular kind of litigation. Thus a court which is willing to permit a recovery for negligence may still choose to exercise restraints by imposing on plaintiff the burden of freedom from contributory negligence, as a theoretical, though perhaps not a practical, handicap. Or the bringing of actions for defamation may in some measure be discouraged by allocating untruth to plaintiff as an element of his prima facie case, rather than by treating truth as an affirmative defense. And it must be apparent that a complete lack of proof as to a particular element moves allocation out of the class of a mere handicap and makes it decisive as to the element, and perhaps as to the case itself. In Summers v. Tice plaintiff was hunting with two defendants and was shot in the eye when both fired simultaneously at the same bird. The court placed on each defendant the burden of proving that his shot did not cause the injury. To discharge this burden was impossible, since each gun was loaded with identical shot. In Munro, Brice & Co. v. War Risks Ass'n the absence of proof of the cause of the ship's loss meant that the party on whom that burden was cast lost the case. In these cases the admonition of Julius Stone is particularly apt: "the Courts should not essay the impossible task of making the bricks of judge-made law without handling the straw of policy."

(2) *Fairness.* The nature of a particular element may indicate that evidence relating to it lies more within the control of one party, which suggests the fairness of allocating that element to him. Examples are payment, discharge in bankruptcy, and license, all of which are commonly treated as affirmative defenses. However, caution in making any extensive generalization is indicated by the classification of contributory negligence, illegality, and failure of consideration also as affirmative defenses, despite the fact that knowledge more probably lies with plaintiff. Certainly in the usual tort cases, knowledge of his own wrongdoing rests more intimately in defendant, though the accepted general pattern imposes this burden on plaintiff.

(3) *Probability.* A further factor which seems to enter into many decisions as to allocation is a judicial, i.e., wholly nonstatistical, estimate of the probabili-

ties of the situation, with the burden being put on the party who will be benefited by a departure from the supposed norm.

The probabilities may relate to the type of situation out of which the litigation arises or they may relate to the type of litigation itself. The standards are quite different and may produce differences in result. To illustrate: If it be assumed that most people pay their bills, the probabilities are that any bill selected at random has been paid; therefore, a plaintiff suing to collect a bill would be responsible for nonpayment as an element of his prima facie case. If, however, attention is limited to bills upon which suit is brought, a contrary conclusion is reached. Plaintiffs are not prone to sue for paid bills, and the probabilities are that the bill is unpaid. Hence payment would be an affirmative defense. Or again, "guest" statutes prohibit nonpaying passengers from recovering for the negligence of the driver. If most passengers are nonpaying, then the element of compensation for the ride would belong in the prima facie case of the passenger-plaintiff. If, however, most passengers in the litigated cases ride for compensation, then absence of compensation would be an affirmative defense. In the payment-of-a-bill situation the probabilities are estimated with regard to the litigated situation, payment being regarded generally as an affirmative defense, while in the guest situation they are estimated with regard to such situations generally and not limited to those which are litigated, status as a nonguest being a part of plaintiff's prima facie case. No reason for the shift is apparent, and it may be unconscious. The litigated cases would seem to furnish the more appropriate basis for estimating probabilities.

Matters occurring after the accrual of the plaintiff's right are almost always placed in the category of affirmative defenses. Examples are payment, release, accord and satisfaction, discharge in bankruptcy, and limitations. A plausible explanation is that a condition once established is likely to continue; hence the burden ought to fall on the party benefited by a change.

In the cases of complete absence of proof, a proper application of the probability factor is calculated to produce a minimum of unjust results, and the same is true, though less impressively, even if proof is available.

The Role of Pleading

Determining what elements are relevant to a case and allocating them between the parties does not of necessity have to be done at any particular stage of litigation. These questions can be left suspended in mid-air like Mohammed's coffin until the very end of the case, when it can be decided what are the responsibilities of each party and whether he has discharged them. This is the practice followed in small claims cases. However, decision prior to trial helps to eliminate uncertainties and lends direction and assurance to preparation and presentation. This is one of the useful functions of pleadings. Unhappily, certain characteristics of the legal mind at times enter in to divorce the pleadings from the realities.

*   *   *

On the whole, however, the pleadings can and do constitute reasonably accurate blueprints of the trial which is to follow.   *   *   *

GOMEZ v. TOLEDO

Supreme Court of the United States, 1980.
446 U.S. 635, 100 S.Ct. 1920, 64 L.Ed.2d 572.*

MR. JUSTICE MARSHALL delivered the opinion of the Court.

The question presented is whether, in an action brought under 42 U.S.C. § 1983 against a public official whose position might entitle him to qualified immunity, a plaintiff must allege that the official has acted in bad faith in order to state a claim for relief or, alternatively, whether the defendant must plead good faith as an affirmative defense.

I

Petitioner Carlos Rivera Gomez brought this action against respondent, the Superintendent of the Police of the Commonwealth of Puerto Rico, contending that respondent had violated his right to procedural due process by discharging him from employment with the Police Department's Bureau of Criminal Investigation. Basing jurisdiction on 28 U.S.C. § 1343(3),[2] petitioner alleged the following facts in his complaint.[3] Petitioner had been employed as an agent with the Puerto Rican police since 1968. In April 1975, he submitted a sworn statement to his supervisor in which he asserted that two other agents had offered false evidence for use in a criminal case under their investigation. As a result of this statement, petitioner was immediately transferred from the Criminal Investigation Corps for the Southern Area to Police Headquarters in San Juan, and a few weeks later to the Police Academy in Gurabo, where he was given no investigative authority. In the meantime respondent ordered an investigation of petitioner's claims, and the Legal Division of the Police Department concluded that all of petitioner's factual allegations were true.

In April 1976, while still stationed at the Police Academy, petitioner was subpoenaed to give testimony in a criminal case arising out of the evidence that petitioner had alleged to be false. At the trial petitioner, appearing as a defense witness, testified that the evidence was in fact false. As a result of this testimony, criminal charges, filed on the basis of information furnished by respondent, were brought against petitioner for the allegedly unlawful wiretapping of the agents' telephones. Respondent suspended petitioner in May 1976 and discharged him without a hearing in July. In October, the District Court of Puerto Rico found no probable cause to believe that petitioner was guilty of the allegedly unlawful wiretapping and, upon appeal by the

---

* Some of the Court's footnotes are omitted.

2. That section grants the federal district courts jurisdiction "[t]o redress the deprivation, under color of any State law, statute, ordinance, regulation, custom or usage, of any right, privilege or immunity secured by the Constitution of the United States or by any Act of Congress providing for equal rights of citizens or of all persons within the jurisdiction of the United States."

3. At this stage of the proceedings, of course, all allegations of the complaint must be accepted as true.

prosecution, the Superior Court affirmed. Petitioner in turn sought review of his discharge before the Investigation, Prosecution, and Appeals Commission of Puerto Rico, which, after a hearing, revoked the discharge order rendered by respondent and ordered that petitioner be reinstated with back pay.

Based on the foregoing factual allegations, petitioner brought this suit for damages, contending that his discharge violated his right to procedural due process, and that it had caused him anxiety, embarrassment, and injury to his reputation in the community. In his answer, respondent denied a number of petitioner's allegations of fact and asserted several affirmative defenses. Respondent then moved to dismiss the complaint for failure to state a cause of action, see Fed.Rule Civ.Proc. 12(b)(6), and the District Court granted the motion. Observing that respondent was entitled to qualified immunity for acts done in good faith within the scope of his official duties, it concluded that petitioner was required to plead as part of his claim for relief that, in committing the actions alleged, respondent was motivated by bad faith. The absence of any such allegation, it held, required dismissal of the complaint. The United States Court of Appeals for the First Circuit affirmed. 602 F.2d 1018 (1979).

       *   *   *

II

Section 1983 provides a cause of action for "the deprivation of any rights, privileges, or immunities secured by the Constitution and laws" by any person acting "under color of any statute, ordinance, regulation, custom, or usage, or any State or Territory." 42 U.S.C. § 1983.[6] This statute, enacted to aid in "'the preservation of human liberty and human rights,'" Owen v. City of Independence, 445 U.S. 622, 636, 100 S.Ct. 1398, 1408, 63 L.Ed.2d 673 (1980), quoting Cong.Globe, 42d Cong., 1st Sess., App. 68 (1871) (Rep. Shallebarger), reflects a congressional judgment that a "damages remedy against the offending party is a vital component of any scheme for vindicating cherished constitutional guarantees," 445 U.S., at 651, 100 S.Ct., at 1415. As remedial legislation, § 1983 is to be construed generously to further its primary purpose. See 445 U.S., at 636, 100 S.Ct., at 1407–08.

In certain limited situations, we have held that public officers are entitled to a qualified immunity from damages liability under § 1983. This conclusion has been based on an unwillingness to infer from legislative silence a congressional intention to abrogate immunities that were both "well-established at common law" and "compatible with the purposes of the Civil Rights Act." 445 U.S., at 638, 100 S.Ct., at

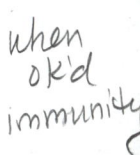

---

6. Section 1983 provides in full: "Every person who, under color of any statute, ordinance, regulation, custom, or usage, of any State or Territory, subjects, or causes to be subjected, any citizen of the United States or other person within the jurisdic-tion thereof to the deprivation of any rights, privileges, or immunities secured by the Constitution and laws, shall be liable to the person injured in an action at law, suit in equity, or other proper proceeding for redress."

1409. Findings of immunity have thus been "predicated upon a considered inquiry into the immunity historically accorded the relevant official at common law and the intentions behind it." Imbler v. Pachtman, 424 U.S. 409, 421, 96 S.Ct. 984, 990, 47 L.Ed.2d 128 (1976). In Pierson v. Ray, 386 U.S. 547, 555, 87 S.Ct. 1213, 1218, 18 L.Ed.2d 288 (1967), for example, we concluded that a police officer would be "excus[ed] from liability for acting under a statute that he reasonably believed to be valid but that was later held unconstitutional, on its face or as applied." And in other contexts we have held, on the basis of "[c]ommon-law tradition . . . and strong public-policy reasons," Wood v. Strickland, 420 U.S. 308, 318, 95 S.Ct. 992, 999, 43 L.Ed.2d 214 (1975), that certain categories of executive officers should be allowed qualified immunity from liability for acts done on the basis of an objectively reasonable belief that those acts were lawful. * * *

Nothing in the language or legislative history of § 1983, however, suggests that in an action brought against a public official whose position might entitle him to immunity if he acted in good faith, a plaintiff must allege bad faith in order to state a claim for relief. By the plain terms of § 1983, two—and only two—allegations are required in order to state a cause of action under that statute. First, the plaintiff must allege that some person has deprived him of a federal right. Second, he must allege that the person who has deprived him of that right acted under color of state or territorial law. See Monroe v. Pape, 365 U.S. 167, 171, 81 S.Ct. 473, 475, 5 L.Ed.2d 492 (1961). Petitioner has made both of the required allegations. He alleged that his discharge by respondent violated his right to procedural due process, see Board of Regents v. Roth, 408 U.S. 564, 92 S.Ct. 2701, 33 L.Ed. 2d 548 (1972), and that respondent acted under color of Puerto Rican law. See Monroe v. Pape, supra, at 172–187, 81 S.Ct., at 476–484.

Moreover, this Court has never indicated that qualified immunity is relevant to the existence of the plaintiff's cause of action; instead we have described it as a defense available to the official in question. See Procunier v. Navarette, supra, 434 U.S., at 562, 98 S.Ct., at 859; Pierson v. Ray, supra, 386 U.S., at 556, 557, 87 S.Ct., at 1219; Butz v. Economou, 438 U.S. 478, 508, 98 S.Ct. 2894, 2911, 57 L.Ed.2d 895 (1978). Since qualified immunity is a defense, the burden of pleading it rests with the defendant. See Fed.Rule Civ.Proc. 8(c) (defendant must plead any "matter constituting an avoidance or affirmative defense"); 5 C. Wright & A. Miller, Federal Practice and Procedure § 1271 (1969). It is for the official to claim that his conduct was justified by an objectively reasonable belief that it was lawful. We see no basis for imposing on the plaintiff an obligation to anticipate such a defense by stating in his complaint that the defendant acted in bad faith.

Our conclusion as to the allocation of the burden of pleading is supported by the nature of the qualified immunity defense. As our decisions make clear, whether such immunity has been established depends on facts peculiarly within the knowledge and control of the defendant. Thus we have stated that "[i]t is the existence of reasonable grounds for the belief formed at the time and in light of all the circumstances, coupled with good-faith belief, that affords a basis for qualified immunity of executive officers for acts performed in the course of official conduct." Scheuer v. Rhodes, supra, 416 U.S., at 247–248, 94 S.Ct., at 1692. The applicable test focuses not only on whether the official has an objectively reasonable basis for that belief, but also on whether "[t]he official himself [is] acting sincerely and with a belief that he is doing right," Wood v. Strickland, supra, 420 U.S., at 321, 95 S.Ct., at 1000. There may be no way for a plaintiff to know in advance whether the official has such a belief or, indeed, whether he will even claim that he does. The existence of a subjective belief will frequently turn on factors which a plaintiff cannot reasonably be expected to know. For example, the official's belief may be based on state or local law, advice of counsel, administrative practice, or some other factor of which the official alone is aware. To impose the pleading burden on the plaintiff would ignore this elementary fact and be contrary to the established practice in analogous areas of the law.[8]

The decision of the Court of Appeals is reversed, and the case is remanded to that court for further proceedings consistent with this opinion.

It is so ordered.

MR. JUSTICE REHNQUIST joins the opinion of the Court, reading it as he does to leave open the issue of the burden of persuasion, as opposed to the burden of pleading, with respect to a defense of qualified immunity.

TEXAS DEPARTMENT OF COMMUNITY AFFAIRS v. BURDINE

Supreme Court of the United States, 1981.
450 U.S. 248, 101 S.Ct. 1089, 67 L.Ed.2d 207.[*]

JUSTICE POWELL delivered the opinion of the Court.

This case requires us to address again the nature of the evidentiary burden placed upon the defendant in an employment discrimination suit brought under Title VII of the Civil Rights Act of 1964, 42 U.S.C. § 2000e et seq. The narrow question presented is whether, after the plaintiff has proved a prima facie case of discriminatory treatment, the

---

8. As then-Dean Charles Clark stated over forty years ago, "It seems to be considered only fair that certain types of things which in common law pleading were matters in confession and avoidance—i.e., matters which seemed more or less to admit the general complaint and yet to suggest some other reason why there was no right—must be specifically pleaded in the answer, and that has been a general rule." ABA Proceedings, Institute at Washington and Symposium at New York City on the Federal Rules of Civil Procedure 49 (1939).

See also 5 C. Wright & A. Miller, Federal Practice and Procedure §§ 1270–1271 (1969). Cf. FTC v. A.E. Staley Mfg. Co., 324 U.S. 746, 759, 65 S.Ct. 971, 977, 89 L.Ed. 1338 (1945) (good-faith defense under Robinson-Patman Act); Barcellona v. Tiffany English Pub. Inc., 597 F.2d 464, 468 (CA5 1979); Cohen v. Ayers, 596 F.2d 733, 739–740 (CA7 1979); United States v. Kroll, 547 F.2d 393 (CA7 1977).

* Some of the Court's footnotes are omitted.

burden shifts to the defendant to persuade the court by a preponderance of the evidence that legitimate, nondiscriminatory reasons for the challenged employment action existed.

I

Petitioner, the Texas Department of Community Affairs (TDCA), hired respondent, a female, in January 1972, for the position of accounting clerk in the Public Service Careers Division (PSC). PSC provided training and employment opportunities in the public sector for unskilled workers. When hired, respondent possessed several years' experience in employment training. She was promoted to Field Services Coordinator in July 1972. Her supervisor resigned in November of that year, and respondent was assigned additional duties. Although she applied for the supervisor's position of Project Director, the position remained vacant for six months.

PSC was funded completely by the United States Department of Labor. The Department was seriously concerned about inefficiencies at PSC. In February, 1973, the Department notified the Executive Director of TDCA, B. R. Fuller, that it would terminate PSC the following month. TDCA officials, assisted by respondent, persuaded the Department to continue funding the program, conditioned upon PSC reforming its operations. Among the agreed conditions were the appointment of a permanent Project Director and a complete reorganization of the PSC staff.

After consulting with personnel within TDCA, Fuller hired a male from another division of the agency as Project Director. In reducing the PSC staff, he fired respondent along with two other employees, and retained another male, Walz, as the only professional employee in the division. It is undisputed that respondent had maintained her application for the position of Project Director and had requested to remain with TDCA. Respondent soon was rehired by TDCA and assigned to another division of the agency. She received the exact salary paid to the Project Director at PSC, and the subsequent promotions she has received have kept her salary and responsibility commensurate with what she would have received had she been appointed Project Director.

Respondent filed this suit in the United States District Court for the Western District of Texas. She alleged that the failure to promote and the subsequent decision to terminate her had been predicated on gender discrimination in violation of Title VII. After a bench trial, the District Court held that neither decision was based on gender discrimination. The court relied on testimony of Fuller that the employment decisions necessitated by the commands of the Department of Labor were based on consultation among trusted advisors and a nondiscriminatory evaluation of the relative qualifications of the individuals involved. He testified that the three individuals terminated did not work well together, and that TDCA thought that eliminating this problem would improve PSC's efficiency. The court accepted this explanation as rational and, in effect, found no evidence that the decisions not to promote and to terminate respondent were prompted by gender discrimination.

The Court of Appeals for the Fifth Circuit reversed in part. 608 F.2d 563 (1979). The court held that the District Court's "implicit evidentiary finding" that the male hired as Project Director was better qualified for that position than respondent was not clearly erroneous. Accordingly, the court affirmed the District Court's finding that respondent was not discriminated against when she was not promoted. The Court of Appeals, however, reversed the District Court's finding that Fuller's testimony sufficiently had rebutted respondent's prima facie case of gender discrimination in the decision to terminate her employment at PSC. The court reaffirmed its previously announced views that the defendant in a Title VII case bears the burden of proving by a preponderance of the evidence the existence of legitimate nondiscriminatory reasons for the employment action and that the defendant also must prove by objective evidence that those hired or promoted were better qualified than the plaintiff. The court found that Fuller's testimony did not carry either of these evidentiary burdens. It, therefore, reversed the judgment of the District Court and remanded the case for computation of backpay. Because the decision of the Court of Appeals as to the burden of proof borne by the defendant conflicts with interpretations of our precedents adopted by other Courts of Appeals, we granted certiorari. 447 U.S. 920, 100 S.Ct. 3009, 65 L.Ed.2d 1112 (1980). We now vacate the Fifth Circuit's decision and remand for application of the correct standard.

II

In McDonnell Douglas Corp. v. Green, 411 U.S. 792, 93 S.Ct. 1817, 36 L.Ed.2d 668 (1973), we set forth the basic allocation of burdens and order of presentation of proof in a Title VII case alleging discriminatory treatment. First, the plaintiff has the burden of proving by the preponderance of the evidence a prima facie case of discrimination. Second, if the plaintiff succeeds in proving the prima facie case, the burden shifts to the defendant "to articulate some legitimate, nondiscriminatory reason for the employee's rejection." Id., at 802, 93 S.Ct., at 1824. Third, should the defendant carry this burden, the plaintiff must then have an opportunity to prove by a preponderance of the evidence that the legitimate reasons offered by the defendant were not its true reasons, but were a pretext for discrimination. Id., at 804, 93 S.Ct., at 1825.

The nature of the burden that shifts to the defendant should be understood in light of the plaintiff's ultimate and intermediate burdens. The ultimate burden of persuading the trier of fact that the defendant intentionally discriminated against the plaintiff remains at all time with the plaintiff. See Board of Trustees of Keene State College v. Sweeney, 439 U.S. 24, 25, n. 2, 99 S.Ct. 295, 296, n. 2, 58 L.Ed.2d 216

(1978); id., at 29, 99 S.Ct., at 297 (Stevens, J., dissenting). See generally 9 Wigmore, Evidence § 2489 (3d ed. 1940) (the burden of persuasion "never shifts"). The *McDonnell Douglas* division of intermediate evidentiary burdens serves to bring the litigants and the court expeditiously and fairly to this ultimate question.

The burden of establishing a prima facie case of disparate treatment is not onerous. The plaintiff must prove by a preponderance of the evidence that she applied for an available position, for which she was qualified, but was rejected under circumstances which give rise to an inference of unlawful discrimination.[6] The prima facie case serves an important function in the litigation: it eliminates the most common nondiscriminatory reasons for the plaintiff's rejection. See Teamsters v. United States, 431 U.S. 324, 358, and n. 44, 97 S.Ct. 1843, 1866, n. 44, 52 L.Ed.2d 396 (1977). As the Court explained in Furnco Construction Corp. v. Waters, 438 U.S. 567, 577, 98 S.Ct. 2943, 2949, 57 L.Ed.2d 957 (1978), the prima facie case "raises an inference of discrimination only because we presume these acts, if otherwise unexplained, are more likely than not based on the consideration of impermissible factors." Establishment of the prima facie case in effect creates a presumption that the employer unlawfully discriminated against the employee. If the trier of fact believes the plaintiff's evidence, and if the employer is silent in the face of the presumption, the court must enter judgment for the plaintiff because no issue of fact remains in the case.[7]

The burden that shifts to the defendant, therefore, is to rebut the presumption of discrimination by producing evidence that the plaintiff was rejected, or someone else was preferred, for a legitimate, nondiscriminatory reason. The defendant need not persuade the court that it was actually motivated by the proffered reasons. See *Sweeney,* supra, at 25, 99 S.Ct., at 296. It is sufficient if the defendant's evidence raises a genuine issue of fact as to whether it discriminated against the

---

6. In *McDonnell Douglas,* supra, we described an appropriate model for a prima facie case of racial discrimination. The plaintiff must show:

"(i) that he belongs to a racial minority; (ii) that he applied and was qualified for a job for which the employer was seeking applicants; (iii) that, despite his qualification, he was rejected; and (iv) that, after his rejection, the position remained open and the employer continued to seek applicants from persons of complainant's qualifications." 411 U.S., at 802, 93 S.Ct., at 1824.

We added, however, that this standard is not inflexible, as "[t]he facts necessarily will vary in Title VII cases, and the specification above of the prima facie proof required from respondent is not necessarily applicable in every respect in differing factual situations." Id., at 802, n. 13, 93 S.Ct., at 1824 n. 13.

In the instant case, it is not seriously contested that respondent has proved a prima facie case. She showed that she was a qualified woman who sought an available position, but the position was left open for several months before she finally was rejected in favor of a male, Walz, who had been under her supervision.

7. The phrase "prima facie case" may denote not only the establishment of a legally mandatory, rebuttable presumption, but also may be used by courts to describe the plaintiff's burden of producing enough evidence to permit the trier of fact to infer the fact at issue. 9 Wigmore, Evidence § 2494 (3d ed. 1940). *McDonnell Douglas* should have made it apparent that in the Title VII context we use "prima facie case" in the former sense.

plaintiff.[8] To accomplish this, the defendant must clearly set forth, through the introduction of admissible evidence, the reasons for the plaintiff's rejection.[9] The explanation provided must be legally sufficient to justify a judgment for the defendant. If the defendant carries this burden of production, the presumption raised by the prima facie case is rebutted,[10] and the factual inquiry proceeds to a new level of specificity. Placing this burden of production on the defendant thus serves simultaneously to meet the plaintiff's prima facie case by presenting a legitimate reason for the action and to frame the factual issue with sufficient clarity so that the plaintiff will have a full and fair opportunity to demonstrate pretext. The sufficiency of the defendant's evidence should be evaluated by the extent to which it fulfills these functions.

The plaintiff retains the burden of persuasion. She now must have the opportunity to demonstrate that the proffered reason was not the true reason for the employment decision. This burden now merges with the ultimate burden of persuading the court that she has been the victim of intentional discrimination. She may succeed in this either directly by persuading the court that a discriminatory reason more likely motivated the employer or indirectly by showing that the employer's proffered explanation is unworthy of credence. See *McDonnell Douglas*, 411 U.S., at 804–805, 93 S.Ct., at 1825–1826.

III

In reversing the judgment of the District Court that the discharge of respondent from PSC was unrelated to her sex, the Court of Appeals adhered to two rules it had developed to elaborate the defendant's burden of proof. First, the defendant must prove by a preponderance of

8. This evidentiary relationship between the presumption created by a prima facie case and the consequential burden of production placed on the defendant is a traditional feature of the common law. "The word 'presumption' properly used refers only to a device for allocating the production burden." F. James & G. Hazard, Civil Procedure § 7.9, at 255 (2d ed. 1977) (footnote omitted). See Fed.Rule Evid. 301. See generally 9 Wigmore, Evidence § 2491 (3d ed. 1940). Cf. J. Maguire, Evidence, Common Sense and Common Law, 185–186 (1947). Usually, assessing the burden of production helps the judge determine whether the litigants have created an issue of fact to be decided by the jury. In a Title VII case, the allocation of burdens and the creation of a presumption by the establishment of a prima facie case is intended progressively to sharpen the inquiry into the elusive factual question of intentional discrimination.

9. An articulation not admitted into evidence will not suffice. Thus, the defendant cannot meet its burden merely through an answer to the complaint or by argument of counsel.

10. See generally J. Thayer, Preliminary Treatise on Evidence 346 (1898). In saying that the presumption drops from the case, we do not imply that the trier of fact no longer may consider evidence previously introduced by the plaintiff to establish a prima facie case. A satisfactory explanation by the defendant destroys the legally mandatory inference of discrimination arising from the plaintiff's initial evidence. Nonetheless, this evidence and inferences properly drawn therefrom may be considered by the trier of fact on the issue of whether the defendant's explanation is pretextual. Indeed, there may be some cases where the plaintiff's initial evidence, combined with effective cross-examination of the defendant, will suffice to discredit the defendant's explanation.

the evidence that legitimate, nondiscriminatory reasons for the discharge existed. 608 F.2d at 567. See Turner v. Texas Instruments, Inc., 555 F.2d 1251, 1255 (CA5 1977). Second, to satisfy this burden, the defendant "must prove that those he hired . . . were somehow *better* qualified than was plaintiff; in other words, comparative evidence is needed." 608 F.2d, at 567 (emphasis in original). See East v. Romine, Inc., 518 F.2d 332, 339–340 (CA5 1975).

A

The Court of Appeals has misconstrued the nature of the burden that *McDonnell Douglas* and its progeny place on the defendant. See Part II, supra. We stated in *Sweeney* that "the employer's burden is satisfied if he simply 'explains what he has done' or 'produc[es] evidence of legitimate nondiscriminatory reasons.' " 439 U.S., at 25, n. 2, 99 S.Ct., at 296 n. 2, quoting id., at 28, 29, 99 S.Ct., at 297–298 (Stevens, J., dissenting). It is plain that the Court of Appeals required much more: it placed on the defendant the burden of persuading the court that it had convincing, objective reasons for preferring the chosen applicant above the plaintiff.[11]

The Court of Appeals distinguished *Sweeney* on the ground that the case held only that the defendant did not have the burden of proving the absence of discriminatory intent. But this distinction slights the rationale of *Sweeney* and of our other cases. We have stated consistently that the employee's prima facie case of discrimination will be rebutted if the employer articulates lawful reasons for the action; that is, to satisfy this intermediate burden, the employer need only produce admissible evidence which would allow the trier of fact rationally to conclude that the employment decision had not been motivated by discriminatory animus. The Court of Appeals would require the defendant to introduce evidence which, in the absence of any evidence of pretext, would *persuade* the trier of fact that the employment action was lawful. This exceeds what properly can be demanded to satisfy a burden of production.

The court placed the burden of persuasion on the defendant apparently because it feared that "[i]f an employer need only *articulate*—not prove—a legitimate, nondiscriminatory reason for his action, he may compose fictitious, but legitimate, reasons for his actions." Turner v.

---

11. The court reviewed the defendant's evidence and explained its deficiency:

"Defendant failed to introduce comparative factual data concerning Burdine and Walz. Fuller merely testified that he discharged and retained personnel in the spring shakeup at TDCA primarily on the recommendations of subordinates and that he considered Walz qualified for the position he was retained to do. Fuller failed to specify any objective criteria on which he based the decision to discharge Burdine and retain Walz. He stated only that the action was in the best interest of the program and that there had been some friction within the department that might be alleviated by Burdine's discharge. Nothing in the record indicates whether he examined Walz' ability to work well with others. This court in *East* found such unsubstantiated assertions of "qualification" and "prior work record" insufficient absent data that will allow a true *comparison* of the individuals hired and rejected." 608 F.2d, at 568.

Texas Instruments, Inc., supra, at 1255 (emphasis in original). We do not believe, however, that limiting the defendant's evidentiary obligation to a burden of production will unduly hinder the plaintiff. First, as noted above, the defendant's explanation of its legitimate reasons must be clear and reasonably specific. * * * See Loeb v. Textron, Inc., 600 F.2d 1003, 1011–1012, n. 5 (CA1 1979). This obligation arises both from the necessity of rebutting the inference of discrimination arising from the prima facie case and from the requirement that the plaintiff be afforded "a full and fair opportunity" to demonstrate pretext. Second, although the defendant does not bear a formal burden of persuasion, the defendant nevertheless retains an incentive to persuade the trier of fact that the employment decision was lawful. Thus, the defendant normally will attempt to prove the factual basis for its explanation. Third, the liberal discovery rules applicable to any civil suit in federal court are supplemented in a Title VII suit by the plaintiff's access to the Equal Employment Opportunity Commission's investigatory files concerning her complaint. See EEOC v. Associated Dry Goods Corp., 449 U.S. 590, 101 S.Ct. 817, 66 L.Ed.2d 762 (1981). Given these factors, we are unpersuaded that the plaintiff will find it particularly difficult to prove that a proffered explanation lacking a factual basis is a pretext. We remain confident that the *McDonnell Douglas* framework permits the plaintiff meriting relief to demonstrate intentional discrimination.

B

The Court of Appeals also erred in requiring the defendant to prove by objective evidence that the person hired or promoted was more qualified than the plaintiff. *McDonnell Douglas* teaches that it is the plaintiff's task to demonstate that similarly situated employees were not treated equally. 411 U.S., at 804, 93 S.Ct., at 1825. The Court of Appeals' rule would require the employer to show that the plaintiff's objective qualifications were inferior to those of the person selected. If it cannot, a court would, in effect, conclude that it has discriminated.

The court's procedural rule harbors a substantive error. Title VII prohibits all discrimination in employment based upon race, sex and national origin. "The broad, overriding interest, shared by employer, employee, and consumer, is efficient and trustworthy workmanship assured through fair and . . . neutral employment and personnel decisions." *McDonnell Douglas,* supra, at 801, 93 S.Ct., at 1823. Title VII, however, does not demand that an employer give preferential treatment to minorities or women. 42 U.S.C. § 2000e–2(j). See Steelworkers v. Weber, 443 U.S. 193, 205–206, 99 S.Ct. 2721, 2728–2729, 61 L.Ed.2d 480 (1979). The statute was not intended to "diminish traditional management prerogatives." Id., at 207, 99 S.Ct., at 2729. It does not require the employer to restructure his employment practices to maximize the number of minorities and women hired. Furnco Construction Co. v. Waters, 438 U.S., at 577–578, 98 S.Ct., at 2949–2950.

The views of the Court of Appeals can be read, we think, as requiring the employer to hire the minority or female applicant whenever that person's objective qualifications were equal to those of a white male applicant. But Title VII does not obligate an employer to accord this preference. Rather, the employer has discretion to choose among equally qualified candidates, provided the decision is not based upon unlawful criteria. The fact that a court may think that the employer misjudged the qualifications of the applicants does not in itself expose him to Title VII liability, although this may be probative of whether the employer's reasons are pretexts for discrimination. Loeb v. Textron, Inc., supra, at 1012, n. 6; see Lieberman v. Gant, 630 F.2d 60, 65 (CA2 1980).

IV

In summary, the Court of Appeals erred by requiring the defendant to prove by a preponderance of the evidence the existence of nondiscriminatory reasons for terminating the respondent and that the person retained in her stead had superior objective qualifications for the position. When the plaintiff has proved a prima facie case of discrimination, the defendant bears only the burden of explaining clearly the nondiscriminatory reasons for its actions. The judgment of the Court of Appeals is vacated and the case is remanded for further proceedings consistent with this opinion.

It is so ordered.

NOTE ON ALLOCATING THE ELEMENTS OF CLAIM AND DEFENSE

1. Could a plausible argument have been advanced in favor of a different allocation in Gomez v. Toledo? Compare the lower court decision, 602 F.2d 1018 (1st Cir. 1979). See also Epstein, Pleadings and Presumptions, 40 U.Chi.L. Rev. 556 (1973).

2. What difference could it make whether plaintiff rather than defendant had the burden of allegation with respect to a given factual element? Consider the question of introduction of evidence on the issue at trial, and the question of burden of proof.

3. The elements essential to a sufficient complaint are pretty well established for most recurrent types of claims. See James & Hazard, c. 3. In any given jurisdiction, cases can usually be found that recite them. For example:

Swaw v. Ortell, 137 Ill.App.3d 60, 92 Ill.Dec. 49, 484 N.E.2d 780 (1984): "A complaint in fraud must allege (1) that a false statement of material fact was made as opposed to an opinion; (2) that the party making the representation knew or believed the representation to be untrue; (3) that the party to whom the representation was made had a right to rely on it and in fact did so; (4) that the representation was made for the purpose of inducing the other party to act, or refrain from acting upon it; and (5) reliance by the person to whom the statement was made led to his injury."

Ferguson v. Alfred Schroeder Development Co., 658 S.W.2d 62 (Mo. App.1983): "The allegations of the petition included * * *: Defendant is engaged in the development and building of subdivisions and residences. On July 23, 1975, plaintiffs, as buyers, and defendant, as seller, entered into a written contract for the sale of a 'single family residence.' The contract, entitled 'Construction Contract' and incorporated in the petition, described defendant as 'builder.' It provided for the sale of 'certain real estate and property' situated on a certain lot in a subdivision in St. Charles, Missouri, 'being a three-bedroom brick veneer dwelling with an attached two-car brick veneer garage, being or to be erected on said lot. . . .'

"On September 5, 1975, plaintiffs paid defendant the purchase price and received the deed. Defendant knew that plaintiffs would use the premises as a family residence and defendant impliedly warranted that the residence was constructed in a skillful and workmanlike manner and was free from defects in workmanship and materials. Plaintiffs relied upon defendant's skill and judgment and on the implied warranty. The residence was not suitable or fit for such purpose in that the foundation was so constructed as to allow water to enter the basement and accumulate on the basement floor, two doors were improperly installed so as to allow water to enter the residence, the garage floor cracked and settled and allowed water to collect and interfered with plaintiffs' use of the garage, and the driveway and front walk cracked and settled.

"Plaintiffs on numerous occasions, within a reasonable time after discovery of the breach of warranty, notified defendant of the defects. The conditions have worsened and the residence is unfit to live in. The value of the residence in its defective condition was $25,000 less than its value as impliedly warranted. The prayer was for judgment in the amount of $25,000."

Indeed, for mine run types of litigation, from one jurisdiction to another there is relatively minor variation in the formulae. Historically, the one variation worth special notice was the different treatment accorced contributory negligence in negligence actions. While most states held the negligence of plaintiff to be an affirmative defense, Illinois and a few other jurisdictions required plaintiff to allege her freedom from contributory negligence. See, e.g., Williams v. Rock River Sav. & Loan Ass'n, 51 Ill.App.2d 5, 200 N.E.2d 848 (1964). All jurisdictions now hold that the burden of pleading and proof of contributory negligence is on the defendant. See Prosser and Keeton, Torts § 65 (5th ed. 1984). See also F.R.C.P. 8(c). In some states formerly holding to the contrary rule, the change came about through the adoption of comparative negligence regimes. See, e.g., Alvis v. Ribar, 85 Ill.2d 1, 52 Ill.Dec. 23, 421 N.E.2d 886 (1981). See also Note on the Answer, infra p. 121.

4. Where the claim is of less common type, plaintiff has the task in the first instance of deciding what elements she should undertake to allege. Consider Swann v. Burkett, supra p. 53 in this connection. What was involved in the decision to allege not only that defendants refused to rent the apartment to plaintiffs, but that they did so on account of plaintiffs' race? Could a plausible argument be made that explanation of the grounds of refusal was for defendants to allege and prove?

5. In Price Waterhouse v. Hopkins, ___ U.S. ___, ___ S.Ct. ___, ___ L.Ed.2d ___, 57 U.S.L.W. 4469 (1989), the burden rules laid out in *Burdine* were modified as applied to "mixed motive" Title VII cases, i.e., cases where the proof indicates that the employer's decision was premised on both legitimate and impermissible factors. Under *Price Waterhouse,* the employer in such a

case must prove that the same decision would have been made in the absence of the impermissible factor.

NOTE ON DEVICES FOR QUESTIONING THE SUFFICIENCY OF THE COMPLAINT

1. The General Demurrer and Analogous Devices

a. The Common Law Demurrer. At common law a "demurrer" was an objection by the defendant, based on one ground or another, that the plaintiff's statement of claim was deficient and for that reason the case should not proceed against him. As stated in 1 Chitty, Pleading *660–662 (10th Am. ed. 1847):

> "When the declaration, plea, or replication, &c. appears on *the face of it* and without reference to *extrinsic* matter, to be defective, either in substance or form, the opposite party may * * * *demur*. A demurrer has been defined to be a declaration that the party demurring will 'go no further,' because the other has not shown sufficient matter against him that he is bound to answer. * * *

> "It should, however, be remembered that a demurrer admits the *facts* pleaded, and merely refers the question of their *legal* sufficiency to the decision of the Court."

The common law demurrer could be grounded on either of two types of objections: First, that the facts alleged were insufficient in point of substantive law; and, second, that the complaint was defective in form in some respect. A demurrer raising objections of the second type had to state specially the ground of demurrer, while a demurrer raising the first type of objection need not state the ground. This rule is stated in Chitty, supra at *663, as follows:

> "Demurrers are either *general* or *special*; *general*, when no particular cause is alleged; *special*, when the particular imperfection is pointed out, and insisted upon, as the ground of demurrer; the former will suffice when the pleading is defective in *substance* and the latter is requisite where the objection is only to the *form* of pleading."

It is from this distinction that the terminological difference between "general" and "special" demurrers is derived. Cf. 5 Witkin 339–343. In modern usage, a general demurrer is a demurrer challenging the substantive sufficiency of the pleading to which it is addressed; a special demurrer is a demurrer raising some other sort of objection which is permitted to be raised by demurrer (as distinct from some other sort of procedural device, such as motion or answer). The special demurrer is considered further in Note on Requiring a More Specific Statement of Claim, infra p. 105.

The demurrer was the original common law scheme to reduce a legal controversy to a single issue of law or fact and to dispose of the controversy by deciding that issue. The corollary in respect to the use of demurrers was that a pleader could either demur—admitting the facts but disputing their legal sufficiency or the regularity of their allegation—or he could answer, and thereby dispute one or more factual allegations. This corollary made the general demurrer a very effective device for disposing of litigation, for a decision overruling the demurrer would result in final judgment for plaintiff, while a decision sustaining it would result in final judgment for defendant. As more fully described below, the general demurrer no longer has this consequence. But it retains its principal common law characteristics:

(1) It admits, arguendo, the matters alleged in the pleading to which it is addressed.

(2) It poses the question, and theoretically only the question, whether the pleading states propositions of fact which, if proved, would entitle the pleader to the relief he seeks.

(3) In deciding the question posed by the demurrer, generally speaking, reference is made only to the pleading to which it refers and not to any other matter (such as affidavits or statements of counsel).

b. The Code Demurrer. The Field Code retained the demurrer but did not expressly perpetuate the terminological difference between the "general" and the "special" demurrer. Instead, the demurrer was authorized for use in certain enumerated circumstances, it being required that the particular ground of demurrer be stated. See First Report of the Commissioners on Practice and Pleadings 148 (1848):

"§ 122. The defendant may demur to the complaint, when it shall appear upon the face thereof, either:

"1. That the court has no jurisdiction of the person of the defendant, or the subject of the action; or

"2. That the plaintiff has not legal capacity to sue; or

"3. That there is another action pending between the same parties, for the same cause; or

"4. That there is a defect of parties, plaintiff or defendant; or

"5. That several causes of action have been improperly united; or

"6. That the complaint does not state facts sufficient to constitute a cause of action.

"§ 123. The demurrer shall distinctly specify the grounds of objection to the complaint. Unless it does so, it may be disregarded."

With certain additions and modifications this language still appears in the statutes of the code pleading states, e.g. C.C.P. 430.10. See James & Hazard § 4.1; Clark on Code Pleading 504 et seq. (2d ed. 1947). It will be observed that of the several grounds for demurrer mentioned, only that in subdivision 6 deals with the substantive sufficiency of the complaint. A demurrer interposed in a code state and raising this question is conventionally called a general demurrer. The effect of such a demurrer in most code pleading states is the same as it was at common law. Typical statements referring to the rules regarding the function and effect of a general demurrer are the following:

Ritter v. Schultz, 211 Iowa 106, 108, 232 N.W. 830, 831 (1930): "A demurrer can apply only as to the matters alleged in, and appearing on the face of, the petition; it concedes that the averments of fact well pleaded in the petition are true; nothing else is considered by the court in the determination of a demurrer to the petition, other than the averments of the petition and the demurrer."

Raneri v. Depolo, 65 Pa.Cmwlth. 183, 441 A.2d 1373 (1982): "A demurrer, which tests a complaint's legal sufficiency, is an assertion that the pleading does not set forth a cause of action upon which relief can be granted * * * and admits every well-pleaded material fact plus all reasonable inferences therefrom. * * * [Plaintiff] is not required here to prove his cause of action; the only issue now before us is whether or not the allegations, if proved, are sufficient to entitle the plaintiff to relief."

See also 5 Witkin 333–337. However, in California the court is permitted, in ruling on a demurrer, to go outside the complaint to the extent of considering matters that may be judicially noticed under the Evidence Code. C.C.P. 430.30. An important practical effect of this provision is that the court in passing on an amended pleading may refer to previous pleadings and take account of facts previously disclosed but now omitted, e.g., expiration of the period of the statute of limitations or the fact that a contract was oral rather than in writing. See, e.g., Neighborhood Action Group v. Calaveras County, 156 Cal.App.3d 1176, 203 Cal.Rptr. 401 (1984).

c. *The Motion to Dismiss.* The Federal Rules of Civil Procedure and the rules in many states have abolished the general demurrer as such. Its function is performed by the motion to dismiss for failure to "state a cause of action," e.g., N.Y.C.P.L.R. 3211(a)(7), or for "failure to state a claim upon which relief can be granted," F.R.C.P. 12(b)(6). Cf. 5 Witkin 385–395.

d. *The Motion to Strike.* Some states by statute, e.g., C.C.P. 435 et seq.; Ill.C.C.P. § 2–615, others by nonstatutory practice, authorize a "motion to strike" a pleading, in whole or in part. When the motion is to strike a complaint in its entirety for failure to state a cause of action, it performs the function of and is treated as a general demurrer. More frequently the motion is employed to strike some part of the allegations of a pleading. See F.R.C.P. 12(f). Typically, such a motion will be used where, although the pleading is substantively sufficient in some measure, the allegations attacked do not afford a ground for the additional relief sought thereby. This was the case in Swann v. Burkett, supra. Under C.C.P. 472a(d), when a motion to strike is granted, the court may allow the party who filed the offending pleading to file an amended pleading. If the motion to strike is denied, the court must allow the party who filed the motion to file an answer. See generally 5 Witkin 395–400.

For an historical and comparative treatment of the demurrer, see Millar, The Fortunes of the Demurrer, 31 Ill.L.Rev. 429, 596, esp. 627–630 (1936). For a general discussion of its use in code pleading states, see Clark on Code Pleading c. 8 (2d ed. 1947); James & Hazard c. 4. For California practice, see C.E.B., 1 Calif.Civ.Pro. Before Trial, c. 9 (1977); 5 Witkin 333–384.

2. The Efficacy of the General Demurrer

As noted above, under the common law system the demurrer was an effective device for disposing of litigation, for decision of the demurrer decided the case. While this was the principal virtue of the demurrer, it was also its principal vice, for it often meant that a case went off on matters of pleading form and style. Starting with a statute in the late 16th century, 27 Eliz. c. 5, the direction of development has been to reduce the risk that decision on demurrer would be based solely on irregularities in pleading. In the modern history of Anglo-American procedure, a fundamental conflict of policy has been whether pleadings should be detailed in their statement of claim: It is argued that they should be detailed enough so that non-meritorious claims can quickly and cheaply be exposed and the litigation terminated at an early stage; it is contended on the other hand that a litigant with an arguably meritorious claim should not be summarily swept out of court on account of a bumbling lawyer or a squinting judge. We now turn to this problem.

2. THE PROBLEM OF SPECIFICITY

COOK, "FACTS" AND "STATEMENTS OF FACT"
4 U.Chi.L.Rev. 233 (1937).*

* * * What, for example, is the meaning of the word "facts," and what of the words "statements of fact"? Our problem thus reduces itself to this: What do the words "facts" and "statements of fact" mean? Let us begin with "facts". "Facts," we are told, are just what they are, they exist. Here it will be useful to recall to mind a well-known statement found in a leading text-book on code pleading. This writer tells us:

> "The issuable facts [in an action or suit] should not only be stated to complete exclusion of the law and the evidence, but they should be alleged *as they actually existed or occurred*. . . .   The allegations must be of dry, naked, actual facts."

Note that underlying this passage are two assumptions: (a) the "facts" existed or occurred; (b) they can be "alleged," i.e., "stated" in language which will describe them "as they actually existed or occurred." The eminent author of the passage quoted is not alone in this belief; it is shared by men in other walks of life, even by scientists of reputation. Thus we find a professor of chemistry in one of our large universities telling us that

> "the fundamental facts of chemistry will still be valid at the end of the next half century. Of course that must be, for facts, defined as 'the direct result of observation, unmodified by any act of reason,' are external."

If we ask how much sense and how much non-sense such statements make, we shall discover first of all that all those who make such statements are assuming—as indeed do all scientists the present writer happens to know—that there is an external world of "fact," and that we must take due account of these external "facts" if we wish to continue to exist and be more or less comfortable. On this much all are agreed. It is in this sense of the word "facts" that we can say that "facts" are coercive; that they exist independently of our will; that they are "compelling elements of common-sense experience, a careful adjustment to which is the necessary condition of successful, or even continued living."

Suppose now that we wish to make some "statement" about these "facts": can we describe them as they "actually exist or occur," that is, "dry, naked, actual facts"? The writers quoted, pleader and scientist alike, obviously assume that we can. And that, the present writer is convinced, is not only an erroneous assumption; it is philosophical and scientific non-sense which ignores the difficulties involved in the use of language and in the determination of what you are going to say the "facts" are. Upon another occasion, when discussing the problem orally before a bar association, I ventured to suggest that had the framers of the Code, had the judges who construed it, had the legal profession generally, realized this, much useless litigation might have been avoided and large sums of money saved both for clients and for the community.

Let us examine into the matter. When we look at this "external world" of coercive "facts," with what are we presented? Here it is difficult to talk at all

* Copyright 1937 by the University of Chicago Press. Footnotes omitted.

without saying more, and also less, than one is justified in doing, and so one runs the risk of serious misinterpretation. Nevertheless the risk must be taken. Without attempting precise analysis—that is unnecessary for our present purposes—we can at least say that what is "out there" in the external world presents itself to us as a shifting varying series of changing patterns of color, sound, odor, and what not. We may with C. I. Lewis call this the "given," meaning thereby the element in all experience which we are aware we do not create by thinking and can not in general displace and alter. Or, as the present writer expressed the matter upon another occasion, we may call this the "brute fact element" in experience, or perhaps "brute, raw events." If we try to describe this "given," these "brute, raw events," we discover first of all that there are an infinite number of aspects in any "situation," and that in order to talk about it at all we have to select from among these infinitely varied aspects those which for some reason or other we are going to talk about. In the second place we discover that in talking about the selected aspects we have to relate them in such a way as to put them under some category, some class, for which we have (or perhaps create) a verbal symbol or name. If for example I say that I have in my hand a fountain pen, I have selected from the variety of colors, shapes, etc. now presented to me a particular combination, and I have related these selected aspects so as to place them into the class of "objects" represented by the verbal symbol "fountain pen."

In other words, in making a "statement of fact" about the "given" situation (series of events), so as to state "what it is," I have in every case necessarily selected certain aspects, thereby neglecting all the other possible aspects which I might have observed, and then have interpreted the selected "data"—to use a scientific term—so as to bring them under some category. Then and only then can I say "what it is," that is, make a "statement of fact." * * *

* * * [I]n order to state the "facts" of a given situation a pleader must first select from the infinite number of aspects of the "given"—the "crude, raw events"—those which he deems to be of importance, that is to say, "relevant" to the purpose in hand, which is to inform the court and the other party of the grounds upon which he claims the court ought to intervene in his behalf. Having made his selection he must relate the selected "data," i.e., interpret them, by putting them into categories, i.e., under certain verbal symbols. As he is a lawyer, it will not be surprising if before he is through he uses verbal symbols which have for lawyers acquired a technical significance. Here he proceeds exactly as would a chemist or a physician or the member of any learned profession. Ignoring for the moment this latter aspect of the lawyer's attempt to state to the court and the other party the grounds of his claim, let us note another source of difficulty. To see just what this is it may be helpful once again to leave the field of law and discuss a simple situation in everyday life.

Suppose I am looking out of the window of the room in which you and I are and you ask me: "What do you see?" Any reply I make, assuming I see "something," will be a "statement of fact." Suppose my reply is: "I see an object": this tells you something but not much; nevertheless it is a "statement of fact." Perhaps you ask for a more detailed statement. I reply: "I see an inorganic object." You now know more than before, but perhaps you are still not satisfied, and my next reply may be: "I see a vehicle." This is equally a "statement of fact," as will be a statement that "I see an automobile." I may under your urging go on to more and more detailed statements, such as: "I see a five passenger sedan"; "I see a 1935 Ford four-door sedan, with blue body and black wheels"; and so on. Each statement becomes more and more detailed, tells you more and more about what you could see if you were to look.

Suppose now the only directions you were to give me when you asked me to look out of the window and tell you what I saw were that I was to "state in plain and concise language the facts" of the situation outside the window, or at least of that part of it in which I was interested; or suppose, to adopt language like that of the Illinois Civil Practice Act, you told me to "state what you see in plain and concise language." Is it not clear that any one of the answers given above would prima facie comply with these directions, and that none of these answers would be an adequate guide to me as to what you wished to know? There seems only one answer to this, namely, that I would be completely at a loss as to how general or how specific you desired my statement to be.

In other words, a direction to "state the facts" of a situation or to "describe the situation" is an inadequate guide without more. The matter will, to be sure, be helped if I know for what purpose my answer is to be used, and of course that is the case in pleading: the pleader's statement is for the purpose of informing the court and the other party of the grounds upon which the pleader asks action in favor of his client. Even so our difficulties are not over. How much of the "concrete particularity" of the given situation shall the pleader tell the court and the other party? The language of the English order, of the New York Civil Practice Act, and of the Illinois Civil Practice Act are silent on the point. If we say by way of explanation: "Tell enough fairly to apprise the court and the other party of the issues," there is still plenty of opportunity for doubt as to what is required.

At this point we may with profit refer to the fact that a lawyer—as distinguished, let us say, from a chemist—will use lawyer's words in stating his "facts," that is, in interpreting the selected "data" by putting them into categories. His categories will be legal categories, not chemical. An examination of any pleading ever drawn will show that this is precisely what every pleader does. Consider the following approved forms found in the official Connecticut form book. They read:

"FOR CONVERSION OF GOODS

"1. On October 1st, 1878, the defendant had in his possession ten barrels of flour, worth six dollars a barrel, belonging to the plaintiff.

"2. On said day the defendant sold the said flour, without authority from the plaintiff, and thereby converted the same to his own use.

"The plaintiff claims $80 damages."

"ORDINARY TRESPASS DE BONIS

"1. On May 20th, 1879, the plaintiff was lawfully possessed of ten chairs.

"2. On said day the defendant forcibly took said chairs from the possession of the plaintiff and carried them away.

"The plaintiff claims $10 damages."

Note the techical legal terms: "Possession"; "belonging to the plaintiff"; "authority"; "sold"; "converted"; "lawfully possessed"; "forcibly took"; "carried away." Obviously only a legally trained person can tell what is meant. It may be asked: "Are these statements which are proper in Connecticut 'statements of fact' or are they merely 'conclusions of law'?" The answer obviously is that they are both. The statement that the plaintiff was "lawfully possessed" of the goods in question is very properly interpreted as an assertion that some one of a large number of shifting and varying groups of factual events had taken place, the net legal consequence of which was that the plaintiff was "lawfully possessed" of the goods. Any one of a large number of combinations of events will, of course, result in conferring "possession"—as distinguished from mere physical custody—upon a person. Proof of any such combination of events will be proof of the "possession." The approved form of statement thus leaves out much of the "concrete particularity" of the events "as they occurred." Any statement will necessarily do that. The only question is, has the statement left out so much that it is not sufficient fairly to apprise court and counsel on the other side of what the plaintiff expects to rely upon?

At this point we come to the crux of the matter. How much is enough? Obviously, the codes as formulated, either in New York or Illinois, give no answer to that: as many answers might be given as there are persons who attempt an answer, were it not for one thing, namely, past habits and practices of the legal profession, in Illinois and in other states. Small wonder that in England, in New York, and other code states chaos reigned after the adoption of the "simplified procedure." The ancient landmarks had been swept away and no new ones had been put in their place. Connecticut, be it noted, escaped this confusion and chaos by a very simple expedient: it offered the profession along with the vague provisions of the code a set of officially approved but not required forms for all the ordinary actions. It thus erected new landmarks in place of the old and the Connecticut practitioner did not lose his way in a war of words over what was and what was not a "statement of fact" and what a "mere conclusion of law," one being permitted and the other not.

If the foregoing analysis is accepted, we must conclude that the time-honored distinction between "statements of fact" and "conclusions of law" is merely one of degree, comparable to the difference between saying: "I see an object" and "I see a sedan" in the example given above.

    * * *

Although the Connecticut forms discussed by Professor Cook are now outdated, the problems he addresses are not, and presumably never will be no matter how simplified the pleading rules become. The year after Professor Cook's article appeared, the Federal Rules were formally adopted and incorporated the "notice pleading" approach whereby a complaint need only contain "a short and plain statement of the claim showing that the pleader is entitled to relief." F.R.C.P. 8(a). While this certainly represented an advance over the code pleading rules which previously reigned, described by Weinstein and Distler, infra, problems of specificity remain. See American Nurses' Ass'n v. State of Illinois, infra p. 95, and Dino, Inc. v. Boreta Enterprises, infra p. 102. Consider also the following official forms from the Appendix of Forms to the Federal Rules, which were adopted following Connecticut's lead. Do they escape the problems identified by Professor Cook?

FORM 9

COMPLAINT FOR NEGLIGENCE

1. Allegation of jurisdiction.

2. On June 1, 1936, in a public highway called Boylston Street in Boston, Massachusetts, defendant negligently drove a motor vehicle against plaintiff who was then crossing said highway.

3. As a result plaintiff was thrown down and had his leg broken and was otherwise injured, was prevented from transacting his business, suffered great pain of body and mind, and incurred expenses for medical attention and hospitalization in the sum of one thousand dollars.

Wherefore plaintiff demands judgment against defendant in the sum of _____ dollars and costs.

FORM 11

COMPLAINT FOR CONVERSION

1. Allegation of jurisdiction.

2. On or about December 1, 1936, defendant converted to his own use ten bonds of the _____ Company * * * of the value of _____ dollars, the property of plaintiff.

Wherefore plaintiff demands judgment against defendant in the sum of _____ dollars, interest, and costs.

WEINSTEIN AND DISTLER, COMMENTS ON PROCEDURAL REFORM: DRAFTING PLEADING RULES
57 Colum.L.Rev. 518 (1957).*

I. The Drafter's Dilemma

* * * [E]nforcement of high and strict standards of pleading has been demonstrated to be a practical impossibility. Adept pleaders are reluctant to reveal their position in too precise a form early in the litigation—often because it is not then clear what evidence will be produced at the trial—and inept pleaders may be unable to do so. It is generally conceded that the outcome of a case ought not to depend upon technical deficiencies in draftsmanship, whether or not intended. Thus, amendments are freely granted and leave to replead has become the routine disposition of motions to compel pleadings to measure up to rigid standards. Such repeated motions do little more than waste the efforts of both the court and the litigants. As a practical matter the moving party is usually well aware of the substance of the amendment that will result from a motion. Since a motion will serve to educate his opponent, when courts do not penalize merely technical deficiency, a prudent attorney will only attack a pleading to gain delay or to test his belief that his opponent's technical deficiency reflects a substantive lack that will dispose of the case. The former motive cannot be condoned; the latter is a disguised attack on the merits and

creates an artificial distinction in procedure between pleading an essential, but untrue, allegation and wholly failing to plead it.

If a strict rule of pleading is thus unworkable, a flexible rule has equally serious objections. Since flexible pleadings—in the sense both of general rules and of non-technical enforcement—cannot precisely define and limit issues, other pre-trial procedures must be relied upon. Yet, flexibility itself creates problems in the utilization of such procedures. For example, free discovery may be unnecessarily costly—indeed, it is subject to abuse as an instrument of harassment and bad faith—unless the court is able to determine the relevancy of proposed inquiry. The minimal standard for pleadings would seem to be determined by this limitation and by considerations of fairness in facilitating preparation for trial or serious settlement negotiations by the parties to the dispute.

In short, the draftsman of a rule of pleading is faced with a dilemma. On the one hand, a rule which sets strict standards, emphasizing the importance of pleadings, does not achieve the expected results and is difficult to enforce and wasteful of court energy. On the other hand, a rule which provides flexible standards, minimizing written pleadings, places burdens upon pretrial procedures but may inadequately control them and is wasteful of litigants' energy in preparation for trial. Neither extreme represents an acceptable solution, although each has advantages. A reexamination of the pleading problem, made in historical perspective, indicates that each new reform to a large extent reflects a shift from one horn of the dilemma to the other.

II. Pleading in Historical Perspective

A. The Common Law

Written pleadings as we know them today were evolved through resort to both logic and experience. Issues were originally formulated at an oral and informal consultation so that they could be tried at nisi prius where they involved an issue of fact or en banc at London where they turned on an issue of law. The logic of the common law and the pressure on the judges' time gave rise to a system of using successive stages of written pleadings to boil down a controversy to a single issue of law or fact. The forms of action were limited and rigid, and controversies that would not easily fit into the molds were forced into them. This necessitated legal fictions and artificial devices and led to use of noninformative multiple and common counts and the general issue. The results were pleadings that conformed to the rules but frustrated their functions.

Pressure for change culminated in such reforms as the Hilary Rules of 1834 which required extensive detail and strict standards. Thereafter, none but the special pleaders had the skill to draft pleadings which conformed to the new requirements. The Hilary Rules were intended to revitalize common law pleading, to return to issues easily formulated and expeditiously resolved. Their effect was nothing short of disastrous: as a result of the technicality of the Rules an intolerable burden of procedural litigation clogged the courts. The conclusion of the common law experience was clear—it was neither possible nor wise to utilize written pleadings to reduce an entire controversy to one defined issue.

B. Code Pleading

The theory persisted that pleadings should, and could, effectively isolate and precisely formulate the issues. In 1848 David Dudley Field and his fellow reformers tried a different approach. Their New York Code of 1848 sought only simple truthful statements of the facts showing that there was a cause of action. The number of pleadings was severely curtailed. It was hoped that all issues of fact in an action could be thus quickly and simultaneously developed so that they could be tried together. The Field Code was widely adopted as a step in the direction of flexibility, but strict enforcement soon hampered its implementation. For, in order to formulate precise factual issues, a pleader had to state "facts," not "conclusions"; and in order that the issues be material according to the substantive law, the stating of "evidence" was condemned.

It is now generally conceded that it is virtually impossible logically to distinguish among "ultimate facts," "evidence," and "conclusions." Essentially any allegation in a pleading must be an assertion that certain occurrences took place. The pleading spectrum, passing from evidence through ultimate facts to conclusions, is largely a continuum varying only in the degree of particularity with which the occurrences are described.

Although giving lip-service to the code requirements, courts soon developed exceptions and characterizations to avoid either technical dispositions regardless of merits or virtually impossible drafting standards. "Evidence" was not only permitted, it was sometimes required in order to give adequate notice of the pleader's intentions. On the other hand, "conclusions" were permitted to avoid unnecessary prolixity. Special pleading rules were promulgated for the pleading of particular matters and for certain types of actions. In some, general allegations are expressly permitted in exception to the rule prohibiting conclusions. In others, specific details are required, details which otherwise would be considered "evidence." Thus, there developed by statutory and judicial pronouncement a gradual whittling away of the theoretical requirements of pleading.

But the trend away from a strict enforcement of the code requirement was costly. When particular language was judicially tagged acceptable in particular situations as the allegation of a material fact, the procedural litigation shifted to other language. Requirements of pleading were strict in one area, flexible in another, and undefined in a third. Lengthy disputes were had over the meaning of such phrases as "facts constituting a cause of action." The procedural structure was again overly technical and complex, and pleadings were still not effectively isolating and formulating issues. Some measure of relief was effected by discovery devices, developed to take over these functions, and by liberal interpretation clauses and provisions for free amendment and joinder.

C. The English Experience Under the Judicature Acts

A procedural revolution came about in England as a result of the Judicature Acts of 1873–75. Although the first years of the unfamiliar procedure were marked by confusion and expense, the broad powers in the courts to draft rules soon brought forth bold and imaginative suggestions for reform.

Among the proposals seriously considered was one for the total abolition of written pleadings. It had become apparent that in limited classes of action, pleadings were wholly unnecessary, for the issues were always the same and were simple and well understood. Moreover, the "summons for directions," and concomitant transfer of control of the litigation from the parties to a master, were more effective at issue formulation and isolation than pleadings had ever been. The proposal for abolition of pleadings was widely debated, and, although it was adopted only in limited areas, the value and function of pleading were brought into sharp focus. The result was an approach to pleading that has helped stamp English procedure as a modern prototype for about three-quarters of a century.

The English solution to the rule-drafting problem was not astonishing: it comprised a general admonition to pleaders in much the same language as the codes combined with illustrative forms of greatly simplified pleading. Although the strict pleaders protested and critics assailed the forms as not complying with the rule (as indeed was the case), the curious formula was successful. As a result, it has been a powerful influence on subsequent pleading reform, most notably in the federal rules, adopted in 1938.

Of course, not all of the credit for the English success belongs to the use of illustrative forms. The "summons for directions," the consolidation of objections to a pleading and their reservation until a later stage, the supervision of the master, all were large factors in de-emphasizing the technicalities of English pleading; the forms were only a small part of the structure. The existence of a specialized English bar of trial lawyers also undoubtedly played a part in the success of these reforms. Nevertheless it seems worthwhile to point out that the Connecticut Practice Book, in existence for as long as the new English practice, contains a multitude of simple forms and has contributed largely to the lack of technicality of pleading in that state.

D. The Federal Rules

When the Federal Rules of Civil Procedure were overhauled in 1938, the drafters were faced with thousands of decisions construing the code requirements of pleading which were phrased in terms of "ultimate facts," "material facts," and "cause of action." A study of these decisions led to the conclusion that the terms had acquired shades of meaning—and of obscurity—wholly unwarranted by the purposes of the rules in which they were contained. Consequently, a new terminology was adopted and these code terms were entirely abandoned. This change swept away all of the interpretations that had caused so much difficulty. A complaint under the new federal rules was only required to contain "a short and plain statement of the claim showing that the pleader is entitled to relief." Illustrative forms indicated the simplicity of the new requirement.

Despite the hostility that the new terminology engendered, this de-emphasis of pleading discouraged procedural hair-splitting. The terminology and forms have been adopted with apparent success in many jurisdictions. Others, in adopting the federal rules generally, have altered the federal formulation of the pleading requirement to include the terms "facts" or "cause of action," while retaining the identical forms. Proposals for similar amendment of the federal rule itself, however, have been rejected.

* * *†

---

† At the end of the foregoing article, Professors Weinstein and Distler appended a useful select bibliography on the pleading problem, 57 Colum.L.Rev. 524–25.

AMERICAN NURSES' ASSOCIATION v. STATE OF ILLINOIS

United States Court of Appeals for the Seventh Circuit, 1986.
783 F.2d 716.

POSNER, CIRCUIT JUDGE.

This class action charges the State of Illinois with sex discrimination in employment, in violation of Title VII of the Civil Rights Act of 1964, 42 U.S.C. § 2000e, and the equal protection clause of the Fourteenth Amendment. The named plaintiffs are two associations of nurses plus 21 individuals, mostly but not entirely female, who work for the state in jobs such as nursing and typing that are filled primarily by women. The suit is on behalf of all state employees in these job classifications. The precise allegations of the complaint will require our careful attention later, but for now it is enough to note that they include as an essential element the charge that the state pays workers in predominantly male job classifications a higher wage not justified by any difference in the relative worth of the predominantly male and the predominantly female jobs in the state's roster.

The complaint was filed in May 1984, and before the state answered, an amended complaint was filed early in July. Less than a month later the state moved to dismiss the complaint or, in the alternative, for summary judgment. In November the plaintiffs filed a memorandum in opposition to the state's motion, to which they attached exhibits not obtained in the course of pretrial discovery—for there had been no discovery. In April 1985 the district judge dismissed the complaint under Fed.R.Civ.P. 12(b)(6) but without ruling on the state's alternative request for summary judgment, 606 F.Supp. 1313. The ground for dismissal was that the complaint pleaded a comparable worth case and that a failure to pay employees in accordance with comparable worth does not violate federal antidiscrimination law. The plaintiffs appeal. They argue that their case is not (or perhaps not just) a comparable worth case and that in characterizing the complaint as he did the district judge terminated the lawsuit by a semantic manipulation. * * *

* * *

* * * [A]s we understand the plaintiffs' position it is not that a mere failure to rectify traditional wage disparities between predominantly male and predominantly female jobs violates federal law. The circuits that have considered this contention have rejected it, see Spaulding v. University of Washington, 740 F.2d 686, 706–07 (9th Cir. 1984). * * *

The next question is whether a failure to achieve comparable worth—granted that it would not itself be a violation of law—might permit an inference of deliberate and therefore unlawful discrimination, as distinct from passive acceptance of a market–determined disparity in wages. * * *

*   *   *

*   *   * The relevance of a comparable worth study in proving sex discrimination is that it may provide the occasion on which the employer is forced to declare his intentions toward his female employees. *   *   *

     *   *   *

Knowledge of a disparity is not the same thing as an intent to cause or maintain it; if for example the state's intention was to pay market wages, its knowledge that the consequence would be that men got higher wages on average than women and that the difference might exceed any premium attributable to a difference in relative worth would not make it guilty of intentionally discriminating against women. Similarly, even if the failure to act on the comparable worth study could be regarded as "reaffirming" the state's commitment to pay market wages, this would not be enough to demonstrate discriminatory purpose. To demonstrate such a purpose the failure to act would have to be motivated at least in part by a desire to benefit men at the expense of women.

     *   *   *

Another point is that the Bennett Amendment to Title VII (the last sentence in 42 U.S.C. § 2000e–2(h)) authorizes employers to pay different wages to men and women provided that the difference would be lawful under the Equal Pay Act, which allows unequal pay for equal work if the inequality results from "any . . . factor other than sex," 29 U.S.C. § 206(d)(1)(iv). The Supreme Court in [County of Washington v. Gunther, 452 U.S. 161, 101 S.Ct. 2242 (1981)] assumed without quite deciding that the Bennett Amendment allows an employer charged (necessarily under Title VII rather than the Equal Pay Act) with paying unequal wages for unequal work to defend by showing that the inequality is based on something other than sex, even if the result is a disparate impact. See 452 U.S. at 171, 101 S.Ct. at 2249. This reading would confine the scope of Title VII in a case such as the present to intentional discrimination.

So if all that the plaintiffs in this case are complaining about is the State of Illinois' failure to implement a comparable worth study, they have no case and it was properly dismissed. We must therefore consider what precisely they are complaining about. Our task would be easier if the complaint had been drafted with the brevity that the Federal Rules of Civil Procedure envisage though do not require. Before the era of modern pleading ushered in by the promulgation of the rules in 1938, a plaintiff to survive a motion to dismiss the complaint had to plead facts which if true showed that his legal rights had been invaded. The problem was that without pretrial discovery, which ordinarily could not be conducted before the complaint was filed, the plaintiff might not know enough facts to be able to make the required showing. For fact pleading the federal rules substituted notice pleading. The complaint would have to indicate the nature of the plaintiff's claim with only enough specificity to enable the parties to determine the preclusive effect of a judgment disposing of the claim ("a short and plain statement of the claim showing that the pleader is entitled to relief," Rule 8(a)(2)). The Appendix of Forms to the federal rules illustrates with a complaint for negligence that, so far as the invasion of the plaintiff's legal rights are concerned, says only: "On June 1, 1936, in a public highway called Boylston Street in Boston, Massachusetts, defendant negligently drove a motor vehicle against plaintiff who was then crossing said highway." Form 9, ¶ 2; and see Rule 84 ("the forms contained in the Appendix of Forms are sufficient under the rules and are intended to indicate the simplicity and brevity of statement which the rules contemplate"). The plaintiff was expected to use pretrial discovery to gather the facts showing the defendant's negligence and the defendant could serve contention interrogatories on the plaintiff to learn the theory behind the claim. See Rule 33(b), and Note of Advisory Committee to the 1970 amendment thereto. When discovery was complete, a pretrial order would be issued formulating the issues for trial; this order would perform many of the functions of the complaint in a system of fact pleading. See Rule 16. See generally Wright, The Law of Federal Courts § 68 (4th ed. 1983).

The idea of "a plain and short statement of the claim" has not caught on. Few complaints follow the models in the Appendix of Forms. Plaintiff's lawyers, knowing that some judges read a complaint as soon as it is filed in order to get a sense of the suit, hope by pleading facts to "educate" (that is to say, influence) the judge with regard to the nature and probable merits of the case, and also hope to set the stage for an advantageous settlement by showing the defendant what a powerful case they intend to prove. The pleading of facts is well illustrated by the present case. The complaint is twenty pages long and has a hundred page appendix (the comparable worth study).

A plaintiff who files a long and detailed complaint may plead himself out of court by including factual allegations which if true show that his legal rights were not invaded. Kaiser Aluminum & Chemical Sales, Inc. v. Avondale Shipyards, Inc., 677 F.2d 1045, 1050 (5th Cir. 1982); Associated Builders, Inc. v. Alabama Power Co., 505 F.2d 97, 100 (5th Cir.1974); Orthmann v. Apple River Campground, Inc., 757 F.2d 909, 915 (7th Cir.1985) (dictum); 5 Wright & Miller, Federal Practice and Procedure § 1357, at p. 604 (1969). The district judge thought the plaintiffs had done that here. Let us see.

The key paragraph of the complaint is paragraph 9, which reads as follows:

> Defendants State of Illinois, its Departments and other Agencies subject to the State Personnel Code, and State Officials, have intentionally discriminated and continue to intentionally discriminate against female state employees in the terms and conditions of their employment because of their sex and because of their employment in historically female-dominated sex-segregated job classifications. Defendants have intentionally discriminated and continue

to discriminate against male state employees because of their employment in historically female-dominated sex-segregated job classifications. The acts, practices and policies of discrimination for which defendants are responsible include, but are not limited to, the following:

(a) Use of a sex-biased system of pay and classification which results in and perpetuates discrimination in compensation against women employed in historically female-dominated sex-segregated job classifications;

(b) Use of a sex-biased system of pay and classification which, because it results in and perpetuates discrimination in compensation against women employed in historically female-dominated sex-segregated job classifications, adversely affects males employed in such historically female-dominated sex-segregated job classifications;

(c) Compensation at lower rates of pay of female employees in historically female-dominated sex-segregated job classifications which are or have been evaluated as being of comparable, equal, or greater worth than historically male-dominated sex-segregated job classifications which receive higher rates of pay;

(d) Compensation at lower rates of pay of male employees in historically female-dominated sex-segregated job classifications which are or have been evaluated as being of comparable, equal, or greater worth than historically male sex-segregated job classifications which receive higher rates of pay;

(e) Compensation at lower rates of pay of female employees than male employees performing work of equal skill, effort and responsibility under similar working conditions;

(f) More favorable treatment in compensation of male state employees than of similarly situated female employees;

(g) Discrimination in classification.

If this were the entire charging part of the complaint, there would be no question of dismissing it for failure to state a claim. The paragraph initially charges the state with intentional discrimination against its female employees, because of their sex; and this, standing alone, would be quite enough to state a claim under Title VII. It continues, "and because of their employment in historically female-dominated sex-segregated job classifications," and then adds a claim on behalf of male employees in those classifications. The continuation could be interpreted as an allegation that the state's failure to adopt a wage scale based on the principle of comparable worth violates Title VII, and if so fails to state a claim. But the mention of "sex-segregated" blurs the picture. If the state has deliberately segregated jobs by sex, it has violated Title VII. Anyway a complaint cannot be dismissed merely because it includes invalid claims along with a valid one.

* * *

Subparagraphs (a) through (g) present a list of particular discriminatory practices; and since they are merely illustrative ("not limited to"), the complaint would not fail even if none of them were actionable. Some are, some aren't. If (a), the "use of a sex-biased system for pay and classification which results in and perpetuates discrimination in compensation against women employed in historically female-dominated sex-segregated job classifications," just means that the state is paying wages determined by the market rather than by the principle of comparable worth, it states no claim. But if it means to allege that the state has departed from the market measure on grounds of sex—not only paying higher than market wages in predominantly male job classifications and only market wages in predominantly female classifications, but keeping women from entering the predominantly male jobs ("sex-segregated")—it states a claim. Subparagraph (b) adds nothing. If the state is discriminating against women by maintaining unwarranted wage differentials between predominantly male and predominantly female jobs, any men who happen to find themselves in predominantly female jobs will be, as it were, dragged down with the women—will be incidental victims of a discrimination targeted against others.

Subparagraph (c) is an effort to fit the case to the mold of *Gunther.* * * * But as we said earlier, the failure to accept the recommendations in a comparable worth study is not actionable. Paragraph 9(c) thus fails to state a claim—as does (d), which is the same as (c) except that it, like subparagraph (b), complains on behalf of male occupants of predominantly female jobs.

Subparagraphs (e) and (f) are inscrutable. If they complained about payment of unequal pay for the same work they would state a claim under the Equal Pay Act. But that Act is not cited in the complaint, perhaps deliberately, and the substitution of "work of equal skill" etc. for "equal work . . . of equal skill" etc. may also be deliberate. The intention may be to claim that different pay for different *but comparable* work violates Title VII—and if so this is a comparable worth claim by a different name, and fails. However, when a defendant is unclear about the meaning of a particular allegation in the complaint, the proper course is not to move to dismiss but to move for a more definite statement. See Fed.R.Civ.P. 12(e); United States v. Employing Plasterers Ass'n, 347 U.S. 186, 189, 74 S.Ct. 452, 454, 98 L.Ed. 618 (1954).

That leaves subparagraph (g)—"Discrimination in classification." This could be a reprise of the comparable worth allegations or it could mean that in classifying jobs for pay purposes the responsible state officials had used the fraction of men in each job as a factor in deciding how high a wage to pay—which would be intentional discrimination.

Maybe the allegations in paragraph 9 are illuminated by subsequent paragraphs of the complaint. Paragraph 10, after summarizing the comparable worth study, says, "Defendants knew or should have known of the historical and continuing existence of patterns and practices of discrimination in compensation and classification, as documented at least in part by the State of Illinois Study." All that the study "documents," however, is that 28 percent of the employees subject to the state's personnel code are employed in 24 job classifications, in each of which at least 80 percent of the employees are of the same sex, and that based on the principles of comparable worth the 12 predominantly female job classifications are underpaid by between 29 and 56 percent. For example, an electrician whose job is rated in the study at only 274 points in skill, responsibility, etc. has an average monthly salary of $2,826, compared to $2,104 for a nurse whose job is rated at 480 points. These disparities are consistent, however, with the state's paying market wages, and of course the fact that the state knew that market wages do not always compare with the principles of comparable worth would not make a refusal to abandon the market actionable under Title VII. But at the very end of paragraph 10 we read, "Moreover, defendants have knowingly and *willfully* failed to take any action to correct such discrimination" (emphasis added), and in the word "willfully" can perhaps be seen the glimmerings of another theory of violation that could survive a motion to dismiss. Suppose the state has declined to act on the results of the comparable worth study not because it prefers to pay (perhaps is forced by labor-market or fiscal constraints to pay) market wages but because it thinks men deserve to be paid more than women. Cf. Crawford v. Board of Education, 458 U.S. 527, 539 n. 21, 102 S.Ct. 3211, 3218 n. 21, 73 L.Ed.2d 948 (1982). This would be the kind of deliberate sex discrimination that Title VII forbids, once the statute is understood to allow wage disparities between dissimilar jobs to be challenged (*Gunther*).

"Willfully" is, however, a classic legal weasel word. Sometimes it means with wrongful intent but often it just means with knowledge of something or other. Willful evasion of taxes means not paying when you know you owe tax. After reading the comparable worth study the responsible state officials knew that the state's compensation system might not be consistent with the principles of comparable worth ("might" because there has been no determination that the comparable worth study is valid even on its own terms—maybe it's a lousy comparable worth study). But it would not follow that their failure to implement the study was willful in a sense relevant to liability under Title VII. They may have decided not to implement it because implementation would cost too much or lead to excess demand for some jobs and insufficient demand for others. The only thing that would make the failure a form of intentional and therefore actionable sex discrimination would be if the motivation for not implementing the study was the sex of the employees—if for example the officials thought that men ought to be paid more than women even if there is no difference in skill or effort or in the conditions of work.

*   *   *

We have said that a plaintiff can plead himself right out of court. But the court is not to pounce on the plaintiff and by a crabbed and literal reading of the complaint strain to find that he has pleaded facts which show that his claim is not actionable, and then dismiss the complaint on the merits so that the plaintiff cannot replead. (The dismissal would preclude another suit based on any theory that the plaintiff could have advanced on the basis of the facts giving rise to the first suit. Alexander v. Chicago Park District, 773 F.2d 850, 854 (7th Cir.1985); Bunker Ramo Corp. v. United Business Forms, Inc., 713 F.2d 1272, 1277 (7th Cir.1983).) The district judge did not quite do that here, because this complaint can easily be read to allege a departure from the principles of comparable worth, and no more. But that reading is not inevitable, and the fact that it is logical and unstrained is not enough to warrant dismissal. In the system created by the Federal Rules of Civil Procedure a complaint "should not be dismissed for failure to state a claim unless it appears beyond doubt that the plaintiff can prove no set of facts in support of his claim which would entitle him to relief." Conley v. Gibson, 355 U.S. 41, 45–46, 78 S.Ct. 99, 102, 2 L.Ed.2d 80 (1957). This language, repeated though it has been in countless later cases (see, e.g., Hishon v. King & Spaulding, 467 U.S. 69, 104 S.Ct. 2229, 2233, 81 L.Ed.2d 59 (1984)), should not be taken literally; for taken literally it would permit dismissal only in frivolous cases. As we said earlier, if the plaintiff, though not required to do so, pleads facts, and the facts show that he is entitled to no relief, the complaint should be dismissed. There would be no point in allowing such a lawsuit to go any further; its doom is foretold. But this is not such a case. * * *

Furthermore, a complaint is not required to allege all, or any, of the facts logically entailed by the claim. If Illinois is overpaying men relative to women, this must mean—unless the market model is entirely inapplicable to labor markets—that it is paying women at least their market wage (and therefore men more), for women wouldn't work for less than they could get in the market; and if so the state must also be refusing to hire women in the men's jobs, for above-market wages in those jobs would be a magnet drawing the women from their lower-paying jobs. Maybe the references in the complaint to the segregation of jobs by sex are meant to allege such refusals but if not this pleading omission would not be critical. A plaintiff does not have to plead evidence. If these plaintiffs admitted or the defendants proved that there was no steering or other method of segregating jobs by sex, the plaintiffs' theory of discrimination might be incoherent, and fail. But a complaint does not fail to state a claim merely because it does not set forth a complete and convincing picture of the alleged wrongdoing. So the plaintiffs do not have to allege steering even if it is in some sense implicit in their claim.

     * * *

     * * * It is premature to conclude that there is *no* worthwhile remedy for the intentional discrimination that consists of overpaying workers in predominantly male jobs because most of those workers are male. We emphasize, however, that proof of this causality is essential and is not to be inferred merely from the results of a comparable worth

study and from the refusal of the employer to implement the study's recommendations. * * * But the plaintiffs are entitled to make additional efforts to prove a case of intentional discrimination within the boundaries sketched in this opinion.

Reversed and Remanded.

DINO, INC. v. BORETA ENTERPRISES, INC.

District Court of Appeal of California, 1964.
226 Cal.App.2d 336, 38 Cal.Rptr. 167.

SALSMAN, JUSTICE. Appellant filed a complaint against respondent seeking an injunction and damages for alleged unfair competition. Respondent's general demurrer to the complaint was sustained without leave to amend and appellant appeals from the judgment thereafter entered.

These allegations appear in the complaint: "V. Ever since on or about June 19, 1962, plaintiff has been and now is engaged in the business of putting on stage productions and serving refreshments under the name 'ON BROADWAY' at 435 Broadway, San Francisco, California. VI. The name 'ON BROADWAY' has acquired a secondary meaning in the entertainment field through its continuous use by plaintiff. VII. On or about October 15, 1962, defendants began to operate a similar business under the name 'OFF BROADWAY' at 1024 Kearny Street, San Francisco, California, which address is in the same city block as plaintiff's said place of business * * * X. In choosing the name 'OFF BROADWAY' and said location defendants intended to and did deceive the prospective customers of plaintiff and the general public. Such action has actually misled, and still misleads many customers into patronizing defendants' said establishment in the belief that they are patronizing plaintiff, to the detriment and damage of plaintiff's profit and business. XI. Defendants threaten to and will continue to use the name 'OFF BROADWAY' unless restrained from so doing by this Court, and defendants will proceed to carry on a business under said name with the express purpose of deceiving plaintiff's customers and the public in general into believing that defendants' said business is plaintiff's said business. XII. The actions of defendants above pleaded were wrongful and are calculated to unfairly compete with plaintiff and to injure plaintiff's business, and such actions have resulted, and if allowed to continue, will continue to result, in irreparable harm and injury to plaintiff's business and business profits; and plaintiff has no adequate legal remedy."

The complaint states a cause of action for unfair competition. That cause of action is codified in Civil Code section 3369. Subsections 2 and 3 of that section read: "2. Any person performing or proposing to perform an act of unfair competition within this State may be enjoined in any court of competent jurisdiction. 3. As used in this section, unfair competition shall mean and include unlawful, unfair or fraudulent business practice. . . ." To state a cause of action for unfair competition here, appellant need only allege that its name has acquired a secondary meaning; that respondent's name, later adopted and used, has deceived or is likely to deceive or confuse the public, and that appellant has been or is likely to be damaged by respondent's conduct. (Academy of Motion Picture Arts and Sciences v. Benson, 15 Cal.2d 685, 104 P.2d 650; Family Record Plan, Inc. v. Mitchell, 172 Cal. App.2d 235, 342 P.2d 10.) Appellant's complaint clearly makes such allegations, because appellant has plainly stated that its name has acquired a secondary meaning in the entertainment field, and that respondent's use of a similar name has actually misled the public into patronizing respondent's place of business in the belief they were patronizing appellant's place of business. These allegations raise issues of fact. Whether appellant's name has in fact achieved the status of secondary meaning can only be determined after an inquiry into the facts. It cannot be determined at the demurrer stage of the proceedings.

Respondent argues, however, that use of a common trade name that does not deceive the average person may not be enjoined and cites Fidelity etc. Co. v. Federal etc. Co., 217 Cal. 307, 18 P.2d 950; Sunlite Bakery v. Homekraft Baking Co., 119 Cal.App.2d 148, 259 P.2d 711 and Beverly Hills Hotel Corp. v. Hilton Hotels, 134 Cal.App.2d 345, 285 P.2d 1012. In the cited cases however, the court entered its judgment only after trial on the merits, and the judgment in each case was based upon the facts found by the court. Here the court had before it only the complaint and demurrer. The demurrer of course admitted all facts well pleaded and it must necessarily follow that if appellant properly pleaded that its name had achieved a secondary meaning, the demurrer should have been overruled.

This brings us to the principal question involved in the appeal, namely, has appellant properly pleaded that its name has acquired a secondary meaning? The complaint merely states that "The name 'ON BROADWAY' has acquired a secondary meaning in the entertainment field through its continuous use by plaintiff." While respondent's demurrer admits all facts well pleaded, however improbable the allegations may be (Woodroof v. Howes, 88 Cal. 184, 189, 26 P. 111), matters improperly pleaded such as conclusions of law are not admitted by the demurrer. (Faulkner v. Cal. Toll Bridge Authority, 40 Cal.2d 317, 329, 253 P.2d 659; 2 Witkin, California Procedure, p. 1471.) Thus there is some merit in respondent's charge that the complaint pleads only legal conclusions and is therefore insufficient. It is, of course, the rule that ultimate facts must be pleaded, rather than legal conclusions, yet the distinction between ultimate facts and conclusions of law is not always clear or easy to state. In Burks v. Poppy Construction Co., 57 Cal.2d 463, 473–474, 20 Cal.Rptr. 609, 615, 370 P.2d 313, 319, the court said: "The distinction between conclusions of law and ultimate facts is not at all clear and involves at most a matter of degree. (Estate of Bixler, 194 Cal. 585, 589, 229 P. 704; see Clark on Code Pleading (2d ed. 1947) 231; Chadbourn, Grossman, Van Alstyne, California Pleading (1961) 812 et seq.; 2 Witkin, California Procedure (1954) 1140.) For example, the courts have permitted allegations which obviously included conclusions of law and have termed them 'ultimate facts' or 'conclusions of fact.' (See Peninsula, etc. [Properties] Co. v. County of Santa Cruz, 34 Cal.2d 626, 629, 213 P.2d 489 [one is the 'owner' of property]; Rannard v. Lockheed Aircraft Corp., 26 Cal.2d 149, 154, 157 P.2d 1 [act was 'negligently' done]; May v. Farrell, 94 Cal.App. 703, 707, 271 P. 789 [employee was 'acting within the scope of his employment'].) In permitting allegations to be made in general terms the courts have said that the particularity of pleading required depends upon the extent to which the defendant in fairness needs detailed information that can be conveniently provided by the plaintiff, and that less particularity is required where the defendant may be assumed to possess knowledge of the facts at least equal, if not superior, to that possessed by the plaintiff. . . ." Here appellant has merely stated that its name has acquired a secondary meaning which is obviously a conclusion of law. Nevertheless, other allegations of the complaint make clear the length of time appellant has used its name, the manner and method of its use, and allege that both appellant and respondent operate the same general type of business establishment, in close proximity to each other. Under these allegations we think the pleading adequately gives notice to respondent that the public has come to associate appellant's name with the kind of business enterprise conducted by both parties, namely stage productions and entertainment in conjunction with the serving of refreshments, and that respondent's use of a similar name confuses and misleads the public to appellant's damage.

Finally, respondent contends that no secondary meaning could possibly attach to appellant's name because the complaint shows on its face that appellant's name was in use less than four months before respondent opened its business. Here respondent relies heavily upon Beverly Hills Hotel v. Hilton Hotels, supra, where use of a name for more than 40 years did not establish any secondary meaning. We think Beverly Hills Hotel v. Hilton Hotels, supra, is not helpful to appellant and that it is readily distinguishable from the case we now consider. In Beverly Hills Hotel v. Hilton Hotels, supra, it appears that two hotels had used the same or similar names for at least 27 years, and the general confusion caused by the long continued use of similar names prevented the plaintiff in that case from achieving a secondary meaning for its name. On the other hand, in Family Record Plan Inc. v. Mitchell, supra, secondary meaning attached to a name in less than five months' time. These cases clearly demonstrate that the length of time a name has been used by a party is only one factor to be considered in determining whether secondary meaning has attached to a name and that all relevant facts must be considered in passing upon this issue. For this purpose, trial is required.

The judgment is reversed.

DRAPER, P.J., and DEVINE, J., concur.

NOTE ON REQUIRING A MORE SPECIFIC STATEMENT OF CLAIM

1. The Alternative to Notice Pleading

In the late common law and in most code pleading states through the 1930's, the requirement that the complaint plead "facts" reduced itself in administration to a style that can only be called baroque. The baroque style did not merely require the pleader to make a rather detailed disclosure of his case. It required him to state his case in grandiloquent and orotund language. The courts adhering to the style refused to countenance, in Holmes' memorable phrase, "a pleading that did not exclude every misinterpretation capable of occurring to intelligence fired with a desire to pervert." Paraiso v. United States, 207 U.S. 368, 372, 28 S.Ct. 127, 52 L.Ed. 249 (1907). Furthermore, if the pleading's allegations were not "facts well pleaded," under the traditional doctrine they were ignored, so that the complaint was read as though they were absent. The argument in support of the demurrer, as often implicit as not, then runs like this:

(1) If the complaint does not state facts sufficient to constitute a cause of action, it is subject to general demurrer.

(a) A complaint states facts when, but only when, its allegations are of "well pleaded facts."

(b) Allegations of "evidentiary matter" or "conclusions" "by recital" or "made indirectly" are not "well pleaded facts."

(2) Therefore, a complaint which alleges "evidentiary matter" or "conclusions," etc., is subject to general demurrer.

Thus, the general demurrer, though supposedly a device for challenging the substantive sufficiency of the complaint, could be used to object to the lack of sufficient specificity in the complaint. Was that the situation in Dino, Inc. v. Boreta Enterprises?

2. The Special Demurrer and Analogous Devices

At common law the device by which a defendant could compel the plaintiff to make his statement of claim more specific was the special demurrer specifying the points of vagueness complained of. See Shipman, Common Law Pleading 278–79 (3d ed. 1923). The Field Code of 1848 did not include uncertainty as a ground of demurrer, a deficiency cured in New York by an 1849 amendment providing for a motion to make more definite and certain. See N.Y.Laws 1849 c. 438, § 160. Although for a time afterwards there was confusion in New York as to whether the proper device was the demurrer, Fry v. Bennett, 1 Code Rep. (N.S.) 238 (N.Y.1851), or the motion, Howell v. Fraser, 1 Code Rep. (N.S.) 270 (N.Y.1851), it was soon settled that uncertainty should be attacked by the motion to make more definite and certain. See People ex rel. Crane v. Ryder, 12 N.Y. 433 (1855). Most states thereafter adopting the Field Code adopted the motion device, see Clark on Code Pleading 548 (2d ed. 1947), as have the Federal Rules of Civil Procedure, Rule 12(e).

A second device for eliciting specificity from the pleader is the bill of particulars, deriving from the practice in courts of equity. See N.Y.C.P.L.R. §§ 3041 et seq. Some states recognize both a bill of particulars and a motion to make more definite and certain. See Ill.C.C.P. §§ 2–607 and 2–615. F.R.C.P. 12(e) originally provided for a bill of particulars, but experience with its use led the Advisory Committee to conclude that it was being too often employed to require unnecessarily and unfairly detailed statements of claim. In consequence, on recommendation of the Advisory Committee the bill of particulars was dropped from Rule 12(e) in 1948. See 2A Moore ¶ 12.17.

The rules of a few jurisdictions have special requirements of specificity in actions turning on written instruments. Ill.C.C.P. § 2–606, for example, provides that "[i]f a claim or defense is founded upon a written instrument, a copy thereof * * * must be attached to the pleading as an exhibit or recited therein * * *." Similarly, C.C.P. 430.20(c) makes a complaint in a contract action specially demurrable if it fails to disclose whether the contract sued on is written or oral. One function of such a requirement is to permit speedier access to such problems as the Statute of Frauds, which makes certain types of contracts unenforceable unless in writing, and the statute of limitations, which in California, for example, is two years for an oral contract, C.C.P. 339, but four years for a written one, C.C.P. 337.

3. The Efficacy of Specific Pleading

Although the special demurrer or analogous motion is still theoretically available to demand pleading specificity in all jurisdictions, it has been rendered largely an anachronism. In the first place, the degree of specificity presently required of pleading has been greatly reduced. Jurisdictions having the Federal Rules interpret Rule 8 as requiring only general statements of claim. See, e.g., Weaver v. American Nat. Bank, 452 So.2d 469 (Ala.1984); cf. F.R.C.P. Appendix of Forms, Forms 3–11. Even in states retaining the code "facts constituting a cause of action" formula, the specificity requirement in many of them has been reduced to a comparable point. Dino, Inc. v. Boreta Enterprises is illustrative; see also Committee on Children's Television, Inc. v. General Foods Corp., 35 Cal.3d 197, 197 Cal.Rptr. 783, 673 P.2d 660 (1983). Secondly, the present rules afford the pleader almost unlimited opportunity to amend after a special demurrer is sustained and render it an abuse of the trial judge's discretion not to permit amendment. Finally, the function of the special demurrer has been largely supplanted by discovery devices. See, e.g., Lynch v. Patterson, 701 P.2d 1126 (Wyo. 1985); Semole v. Sansoucie, 28 Cal.App.3d 714, 719, 104 Cal.Rptr. 897, 900 (1972) ("modern discovery procedures necessarily affect the amount of detail that should be required in a pleading"). Compare Mitchell v. E–Z Way Towers, Inc., infra p. 110.

Even under the Federal Rules, however, allegations of fraud or mistake must still be pleaded with particularity. See F.R.C.P. 9(b); Semegen v. Weidner, 780 F.2d 727 (9th Cir.1985). Does this exception serve any purpose? See Richman, Lively, and Mell, The Pleading of Fraud: Rhymes Without Reason, 60 So.Calif.L.Rev. 959 (1987). In certain situations, the court may on its own motion require a more particular statement of claim under Rule 12(e); see Elliott v. Perez, 751 F.2d 1472 (5th Cir.1985), holding that in an action against a government official the court should require plaintiff to allege with particularity all material facts negating circumstances that would result in immunity.

Theoretically at least, the function of the special demurrer and its analogues is to require the pleader to state her contentions with sufficient particularity to afford fair notice to her opponent. A question often obscured is, "Fair notice for what purpose?" The minimal purpose is to enable the opponent to prepare his own responsive pleadings and this is as far as Federal Rule 12(e) now goes in allowing the motion to make more definite and certain. It is doubtful, however, that this is really a very serious problem. The response to a vague pleading can be, and typically is, as vague as the pleading itself. For example, Boreta Enterprises could have responded to the complaint by admitting that it was a corporation and denying everything else. Of course, this would leave the issues in the case obscure, but that obscurity, while it might leave the case at large, would not seriously impair the defendant's ability to *plead*: defendant simply opposes plaintiff's fog with fog of his own. The question remains, therefore, as to the function of pleadings and the degree of specificity that can and should be required.

Consider the following:

a.   In the American system of procedure, the decisional function is divided between judge and jury, the former deciding questions of "law" and the latter questions of "fact." But in deciding questions of "fact," the jury frequently has to make a complex appraisal of the rightness or wrongness of particular conduct. This is typically the case in negligence actions, which constitute the largest single type of civil litigation in trial courts of general jurisdiction. Consider, e.g., the analysis that the jury was called on to make concerning the pilot's conduct in Reynolds v. Bank of America, supra. Given the fact that these decisions must be postponed for the jury, and that they are at the crux of the litigated cases, can anything really be served by requiring a particularized statement of claim in the pleadings? Does this circumstance help explain the rule, which obtains in most jurisdictions, that a negligence complaint need only describe the general course of conduct in which the defendant was engaged, e.g., operating a motor vehicle, and state that defendant did so "negligently"? See, e.g., Rannard v. Lockheed Aircraft Corp., 26 Cal.2d 149, 157 P.2d 1 (1945); but cf. Hancock v. Luetgert, 40 Ill.App.3d 808, 353 N.E.2d 165 (1976). See also F.R.C.P. Appendix of Forms, Form 9; James & Hazard § 3.15 et seq.

b.   Some types of cases present substantive legal questions calling for wide-range canvassing of behavior. Thus, an antitrust case, because of the broad and amorphous command of the Sherman Act, 15 U.S.C.A. § 1 (' Every contract, combination * * * or conspiracy, in restraint of trade * * * is * * * illegal"), involves, or at least often involves, a study in modern economic history. The contest of a will for "undue influence" involves a study, by circumstantial evidence, of the psychological world of the decedent. In this connection, consider what would be the lines of proof and the questions for decision on the basis of such proofs in Dino, Inc. v. Boreta Enterprises. If the rules of substantive law cast the case in broad terms, can the procedural rules successfully and properly do so in more precise ones?

The pleading rules may also reflect substantive policy preferences. See, e.g., Hospital Building Co. v. Trustees of Rex Hospital, 425 U.S. 738, 746, 96 S.Ct. 1848, 1853, 48 L.Ed.2d 338, 345 (1976):

> "We have held that 'a complaint should not be dismissed for failure to state a claim unless it appears beyond doubt that the plaintiff can prove no set of facts in support of his claim which would entitle him to relief.' Conley v. Gibson, 355 U.S. 41 * * * (1957). * * * And in antitrust cases, where 'the proof is largely in the hands of the alleged conspirators,' * * * dismissals prior to giving the plaintiff ample opportunity for discovery should be granted very sparingly."

Compare the reading of Conley v. Gibson in *American Nurses*, supra p. 95. See also Harlow v. Fitzgerald, 457 U.S. 800, 102 S.Ct. 2727, 73 L.Ed.2d 396 (1982) (no discovery until immunity issue resolved); Wingate, A Special Plead-

ing Rule for Civil Rights Complaints: A Step Forward or a Step Back?, 49 Mo.L.
Rev. 677 (1984).

4. Revival of Pleading

In recent years, disillusionment has set in about discovery as a means of
clarifying the issues. Although discovery can be effective for this purpose in
relatively simple cases, in such cases the issues are already pretty obvious. Did
anyone have difficulty figuring out the issues in Dino, Inc. v. Boreta Enterprises, for example? Moreover, discovery adds a round of papers and hence
expense in smaller cases. In "big" cases, discovery without guidelines is very
expensive. Hence there could be a revival of pleading.

In Papasan v. Allain, 478 U.S. 265, 106 S.Ct. 2932, 92 L.Ed.2d 209 (1986),
the complaint asserted:

> "By their aforesaid past, present and future deprivations of and to
> Plaintiffs and the Plaintiff class of the use and benefits of their Sixteenth
> Section Lands, while at the same time granting to and securing to all other
> school districts and school children in the State of Mississippi in perpetuity
> the use and benefit of their Sixteenth Section Lands, the State Defendants
> have deliberately, intentionally, purposefully, and with design denied to
> Plaintiffs and the Plaintiff class the equal protection of the laws in
> violation of their rights secured by the Fourteenth Amendment to the
> Constitution of the United States." 478 U.S. at 281–82, 106 S.Ct. at 2942,
> 92 L.Ed.2d at 229.

The complaint also alleged that these actions denied plaintiffs "their rights to
an interest in a minimally adequate level of education, or reasonable opportunity therefor." In reviewing the trial court's dismissal of the complaint, the
Supreme Court made these comments:

> "Although for the purposes of this motion to dismiss we must take all
> the factual allegations in the complaint as true, we are not bound to accept
> as true a legal conclusion couched as a factual allegation. See, e.g., Briscoe
> v. LaHue, 663 F.2d 713, 723 (CA7 1981), aff'd on other grounds, 460 U.S.
> 325, 103 S.Ct. 1108, 75 L.Ed.2d 96 (1983). See generally 2A J. Moore & J.
> Lucas, Moore's Federal Practice ¶ 12.07, p. 12–64, and n. 6 (1985). Petition-
> ers' allegation that, by reason of the funding disparities relating to the
> Sixteenth Section Lands, they have been deprived of a minimally adequate
> education is just such an allegation. Petitioners do not allege that school-
> children in the Chickasaw Counties are not taught to read or write; they
> do not allege that they receive no instruction on even the educational
> basics; they allege no actual facts in support of their assertion that they
> have been deprived of a minimally adequate education. As we see it, we
> are not bound to credit and may disregard the allegation that petitioners
> have been denied a minimally adequate education." 478 U.S. at 286, 106
> S.Ct. at 2944–45, 92 L.Ed.2d at 232.

See also Marcus, The Revival of Fact Pleading Under the Federal Rules of
Civil Procedure, 86 Colum.L.Rev. 433 (1986).

NOTE ON FORM AND STYLE OF PLEADINGS

1. Caption and Body of Pleadings

The rules on the format of pleadings and other papers submitted in
litigation are prescribed in part by statute, in part by general or local rules of

court and in part by custom. See, e.g., C.C.P. 422.30, 422.40, 425.10, 425.12, 425.13, 431.30; California Rules of Court, Superior Court Rule 201; F.R.C.P. 10. See Fed.Rules Serv. for compilations of local rules of Federal District Courts. See also 4 Witkin 56–58; C.E.B., 1 Calif.Civ.Pro. Before Trial c. 22 (1977); C.E.B., California Civil Litigation Forms Manual (1981); West's California Judicial Council Forms.

In general, the rules require that pleadings and other papers have a caption containing the name of the court; the title of the action; the name, address and telephone number of the attorney presenting the paper; and a brief designation of what the paper is (e.g., "Complaint", "Motion to Dismiss"). Papers are ordinarily required to be typed on numbered pages, double-spaced with generous margins.

2. Body of Pleadings and Other Papers

In pleadings it is obligatory or customary to set forth the statements of allegation in separate numbered paragraphs. The organization of paragraphs in pleadings, as in all English usage, is a matter largely up to the author, subject to three considerations. First, "separate" causes of action must be stated separately, i.e., in separate series of consecutively numbered paragraphs. Second, rule or custom dictates that each paragraph deal with a limited subject. Third, the pleader will facilitate securing admissions from his opponent if he puts those allegations which he believes will be uncontroverted (e.g., allegation of ownership of the car in an automobile negligence action) into paragraphs that are separate from those containing allegations which he believes will be controverted (e.g., allegations of negligence). In papers other than pleadings, organization depends on the character of the paper, but the conventions are well established. See, e.g., C.E.B., California Civil Litigation Forms Manual (1981); West's California Judicial Council Forms.

3. Designation of Parties

Where a party is a person other than a natural person suing in his own right, it is customary and usually required that the party's capacity be specially designated. A corporation is not only named, but its state of incorporation is given and it is alleged that the corporation was at all relevant times "duly existing" under the laws of that state. A natural person suing or being sued in a special capacity, such as executor, trustee, receiver, or public officer, is named in that capacity and her capacity is alleged in the body of the complaint. Although older doctrine had it that a failure to designate the capacity of a person suing or being sued in a special capacity was a fatal error, today such an error is generally regarded as a harmless one correctable by amendment.

4. Prayer

At the conclusion of the allegations of the complaint, plaintiff states the relief he seeks. See, e.g., C.C.P. 425.10(b); F.R.C.P. 8(a)(3). Foundation for the prayer must be laid by appropriate allegations in the complaint that describe the nature and extent of the damage suffered. Compare Note, The Definition and Pleading of Special Damage Under the Federal Rules of Civil Procedure, 55 Va.L.Rev. 542 (1969). If the case is contested the relief that may be accorded the plaintiff is not limited to the amount or kind requested. Where the defendant defaults, the relief granted may not exceed that demanded. C.C.P. 580; F.R.C.P. 54(c).

5. Subscription and Verification

Statutes or rules require that all pleadings be subscribed by the party presenting it or by his attorney. See, e.g., C.C.P. 446. In practice, the attorney subscribes them. By statute or rule in many states, and by custom in all states, all papers other than pleadings are also subscribed by the attorney. See 6 Witkin 334. F.R.C.P. 11 requires that all pleadings, which for this purpose includes all papers, F.R.C.P. 7(b)(2), shall be subscribed by the attorney of a party represented by an attorney or by the party if he appears *in propria persona.*

Rule 11 now provides, in relevant part: "The signature of an attorney or party constitutes a certificate by the signer that the signer has read the pleading, motion, or other paper; that to the best of the signer's knowledge * * * formed after reasonable inquiry it is well grounded in fact and is warranted by existing law or a good faith argument for extension, modification, or reversal of existing law, and that it is not interposed for any improper purpose, such as to harass or to cause unnecessary delay or needless increase in the cost of litigation."

A verification is an affidavit appended to a pleading to the effect that the person making it knows, or to the extent stated is informed and believes, that the matters contained therein are true. Verification is made by a party, by an officer of a corporate party or by the attorney in special circumstances, e.g., under C.C.P. 446 when the party is absent from the county in which the attorney has his office. In some jurisdictions, verification is required of most all pleadings. In California, verification is optional except in a limited number of specified types of actions, but if the plaintiff elects to verify his complaint then the defendant normally must verify his answer. C.C.P. 446. In federal court, verification is not required as a general rule, F.R.C.P. 11, and where it is required apparently implies only a good faith belief in the fact alleged. See Surowitz v. Hilton Hotels Corp., 383 U.S. 363, 86 S.Ct. 845, 15 L.Ed.2d 807 (1966); cf. Nemeroff v. Abelson, 620 F.2d 339 (2d Cir. 1980).

Rule 11 and verification of pleadings are considered further in the section on Rule 11 Certification, infra p. 135.

3. THE CONSEQUENCES OF THE COMPLAINT'S INSUFFICIENCY

MITCHELL v. E–Z WAY TOWERS, INC.

United States Court of Appeals for the Fifth Circuit, 1959.
269 F.2d 126.

JOHN R. BROWN, CIRCUIT JUDGE. These cases raise questions limited to the sufficiency of pleadings.

E–Z Way [1] is a Tampa, Florida organization engaged in the production, sale and installation of radio and television towers for use in transmitting and receiving broadcasts. The [Secretary of Labor's] complaint for injunction charged E–Z Way with failing to pay the minimum

---

1. [This appeal involves two actions heard together in the trial court, one against E–Z Way Towers, Inc. (No. 17551), the other against E–Z Way Erectors, Inc. (No. 17552).] Both appellees are referred to jointly as E–Z Way. Clarence Jax, a joint appellee in both Nos. 17551 and 17552, is President and Treasurer of both corporations.

statutory wage for regular and overtime hours, failing to keep records of their employees' wages and hours, and for selling goods manufactured under such conditions in interstate commerce.[2] Fair Labor Standards Act §§ 7, 15(a)(1), 15(a)(2), 15(a)(5), 17, 29 U.S.C.A. § 201 et seq.

To this E–Z Way replied with a "Motion for More Definite Statement"[3] requesting particulars as to the employees, weeks, and records

2. The Complaint in No. 17551 contained these paragraphs:

"V.

"At all times hereinafter mentioned, defendants employed, and are employing approximately twenty-one (21) employees in and about their said place of business in Tampa, Florida, in the production, sale and distribution of radio and television towers. A substantial portion of the radio and television towers so produced has been, and is being, shipped, delivered, transported, offered for transportation and sold in commerce, and shipped, delivered or sold with knowledge that shipment, delivery or sale thereof in commerce is intended from defendants' said place of business to other states, and thus said employees have been, and are, engaged in the production of goods for commerce within the meaning of the Act.

"VI.

"During the period since July 27, 1956, the defendants repeatedly have violated, and are violating the provisions of Sections 7 and 15(a)(2) of the Act by employing some of their employees in the production of goods for commerce, as aforesaid, for workweeks longer than forty (40) hours without compensating the said employees for their employment in excess of forty (40) hours in said workweeks at rates of pay not less than one and one-half times the regular rates at which they were employed."

The Complaint in No. 17552 contained these paragraphs:

"V.

"At all times hereinafter mentioned, defendants employed, and are employing, approximately sixteen (16) employees at various points in Florida and in other states in the assembling and erecting of radio and television towers, which towers are used in transmitting and receiving interstate radio and television broadcasts and constitute integral parts of existing and essential instrumentalities of interstate transmission

and communication. Thus said employees have been, and are, engaged in commerce within the meaning of the Act.

"VI.

"During the period since November 3, 1956, the defendants repeatedly have violated, and are violating, the provisions of Sections 6 and 15(a)(2) of the Act by employing some of their employees in commerce, as aforesaid, at rates of pay less than one dollar ($1.00) an hour."

Both contain an identical paragraph VIII, except for dates, as follows:

"VIII.

"Defendants, being subject to the Act and record-keeping requirements thereof, have violated, and are violating, the provisions of Sections 11(c) and 15(a)(5) of the Act in that since July 27, 1956 [November 3, 1956 in No. 17552], they have failed to make, keep and preserve adequate and accurate records of their employees and the wages, hours and other conditions and practices of employment maintained by them, as prescribed by the said regulations, in that they failed to show adequately and accurately the hours worked each workday and each workweek by many of their employees."

3. That in No. 17552, the shorter of the nearly identical two, is typical.

"The Defendants . . . move this Court to require Plaintiff to furnish them a more definite statement, and allege:

"1. The Complaint is so vague and ambiguous that Defendants cannot reasonably be required to frame a responsive pleading.

"2. The Complaint contains the following defects:

"a) The Complaint fails to allege the specific weeks during which Defendants violated the provisions of the Act.

"b) The Complaint fails to allege the names of the employees concerning whom it is alleged the Defendants failed to keep adequate records.

involved, and a "Motion to Dismiss" based thereon.[4] This Motion contained two theories: that the Complaint (1) "fails to state a claim" and that it (2) "fails to allege in reasonable detail" the violations charged.

While it appears that both motions were before the Court, it is certain that the Court granted only the Motion to Dismiss for failure to state a claim.[5] Any doubt on that score is eradicated by the Court's action following the Secretary's formal election to stand on the Complaint rather than amend as permitted under the initial order, note 5, supra. As a consequence of this the Court entered a final order of dismissal.[6] This was expressly "on the ground that the Complaint fails to allege in reasonable detail and in specific terms and specific acts the manner in which the defendants have violated the provisions of the

"c) The Complaint fails to allege in what respect the records of Defendants were inadequate.

"d) The Complaint fails to allege the class of workers concerning whom the Defendants failed to keep adequate records.

"Wherefore, Defendants pray that Plaintiff be required to furnish to Defendants the following details:

"a. the specific weeks during which Defendants are alleged to have violated the provisions of the Act.

"b. the names and addresses of each employee of the Defendants . . . concerning whom it is alleged that Defendants failed to keep adequate records.

"c. the description of the particular records which Plaintiff alleges are inadequate, and in what respect said records are inadequate.

"d. the class of workers and the nature of work performed by the employees of the Defendants concerning whom it is alleged Defendants failed to keep adequate records."

4. The motions to dismiss were identical in both cases:

"The defendants, E–Z Way Towers, Inc., a corporation, and Clarence Jax, move this court to dismiss the Complaint, and allege as follows:

"1. The Complaint fails to state a claim against the Defendants on which relief can be granted.

"2. The Complaint fails to allege in reasonable detail, and in specific terms and by specific acts the manner in which Defendants have violated the Sections of the Act and promulgated regulations, as alleged in the Complaint."

5. "This matter came on for hearing on defendants' motion for more definite statement and motion to dismiss, the parties appearing by their respective counsel, and the court having heard the arguments of counsel and being otherwise sufficiently advised, finds that the complaint fails to allege in reasonable detail and in specific terms and by specific acts the manner in which the defendants have violated the provisions of the Fair Labor Standards Act as alleged in the complaint and thus fails to state a claim against the defendants on which relief can be granted. It is therefore

"Ordered that plaintiff's complaint be, and the same is hereby, dismissed.

"It is further Ordered that plaintiff have sixty (60) days from the date hereof within which to file an amended complaint."

6. "It being made to appear to the court that on the 22nd day of August, 1958, an order was made and entered dismissing plaintiff's complaint with leave to amend, said dismissal being on the ground that the complaint fails to allege in reasonable detail and in specific terms and specific acts the manner in which the defendants have violated the provisions of the Fair Labor Standards Act and thus fails to state a claim on which relief can be granted, and it appearing to the court that plaintiff has given notice to this court and the attorneys for the defendant of his election to stand on the allegations of his original complaint and thereupon refusing to file an amended complaint or to otherwise amend his complaint now on file in said cause, and the court being fully advised, it is hereby

"Ordered, Adjudged and Decreed that this cause be and the same is hereby finally dismissed."

12B6

Fair Labor Standards Act and thus fails to state a claim on which relief can be granted . . . ." This was, in turn, the exact language of paragraph 2 of the Motion to Dismiss, note [4], supra.

As an order of dismissal for failure to state a claim it cannot stand. Testing the complaint—as filed and on which the Secretary with propriety claimed a right to stand—it meets the standard so frequently repeated by us and now so recently reiterated in the most positive terms. "In appraising the sufficiency of the complaint we follow, of course, the accepted rule that a complaint should not be dismissed for failure to state a claim unless it appears beyond doubt that the plaintiff can prove no set of facts in support of his claim which would entitle him to relief." Conley v. Gibson, 1957, 355 U.S. 41, 45–46, 78 S.Ct. 99, 102, 2 L.Ed.2d 80.

In this light the complaint charges that (a) defendants have employees who are engaged in interstate commerce, (b) that some employees are required to work in excess of 40 hours per week without being paid statutory overtime, (c) others are paid less than the statutory minimum, and that (d) records are not kept with sufficient accuracy to reflect these facts concerning the employees. If evidence is brought forward showing (a) plus (b), (c), (d), or any one of them, the Fair Labor Standards Act would compel a finding and decree for the Secretary leaving to the Court's informed discretion the scope and nature of the precise relief to be granted. Mitchell v. Hodges Contracting Co., 5 Cir., 1956, 238 F.2d 380.

The defendants, and apparently the Trial Court, have confused the proper function of the motion to dismiss for failure to state a claim, F.R.Civ.P. 12(b), 28 U.S.C.A., and the motion for more definite statement under Rule 12(e). The former allows of no discretion in the usual sense. The complaint is either good or not good. The motion for more definite statement, on the other hand, involves, within the applicable standards of that rule, the exercise of that sound and considered discretion committed unavoidably and properly to the Trial Judge as he presides over the continuous process of adjudication from commencement of the litigation through pleadings, pretrial discovery, trial, submission and decision.

Under 12(e) the Court must determine whether the complaint is such that "a party cannot reasonably be required to frame a responsive pleading." But the fact that a careful Judge, in the exercise of that wise discretion controlled by the prescribed principles of that rule, might so conclude does not permit him to dismiss the complaint for failure to state a claim. "It may well be that petitioner's complaint as now drawn is too vague, but that is no ground for dismissing his action . . . ." Glus v. Brooklyn Eastern District Terminal, 1959, 359 U.S. 231, 79 S.Ct. 760, 763, 3 L.Ed.2d 770, 774.

*   *   *

There is more than a mere procedural distinction between the motion to dismiss for failure to state a claim and the motion for more definite statement. The difference is fundamental as this case testifies. If the claim is dismissed because it is too vague or because the plaintiff is unable to supply the details, none of the machinery of discovery whose function it is to ferret out facts and delineate issues before trial can be utilized. On the other hand, with the complaint declared sufficient against a motion to dismiss, the parties, both plaintiff and defendant, are assured both the right fully to exploit the flexible rules of discovery which will disclose in advance of trial what the case is all about and, more important, the full protection of a careful District Judge in the exercise of his wise and considered discretion as the case progresses toward the climax of trial and judgment. And, except for brief periods of 10 or 20 days following the commencement of an action when leave of Court is required, discovery mechanisms of interrogatories, requests for admissions, motions to produce and oral depositions are not contingent upon the state of the pleadings or any necessity for the case to be at formal issue. F.R.Civ.P. 26–37, 28 U.S.C.A.

* * *

If an employer is thought by the Secretary of Labor to be violating the wage and hour provisions of the Fair Labor Standards Act, the most effective way in which the employee can be protected is by the obtaining of an injunction; Mitchell v. Lublin McGaughy & Assoc., 1959, 358 U.S. 207, 215, 79 S.Ct. 260, 3 L.Ed.2d 243, quoted by us in Mitchell v. Strickland Transportation Co., Inc., 5 Cir., 1959, 267 F.2d 821, or an early declaration of the question of coverage, records, compliance, etc.

Upon the filing of a suit seeking an injunction, of course, the filing of defensive pleadings is essential to the Trial Court's fair consideration of the motion for preliminary injunction. Moreover, there are doubtless many cases in which, because of its possession of the records of employment and payrolls and knowledge of its own operations, the defendant in the good faith required by the signing and filing of pleadings, F.R.Civ.P. 11, must admit coverage or violations or both. Upon such admission, of course, the likelihood of the issuing of a preliminary injunction or suitable declaratory order is greatly enhanced. If the time for filing defensive pleadings can be put off, as follows from the filing of a motion for more definite statement, any violations, if such exist, can continue without any effective protection for the employee so much the longer. And in any case, the time of likely trial will be postponed since most trial courts fix dockets on the basis of the case being at issue.

In such a situation it becomes important that great care must be used in passing on a motion for definite statement. In view of the great liberality of F.R.Civ.P. 8, permitting notice pleading, it is clearly the policy of the Rules that Rule 12(e) should not be used to frustrate this policy by lightly requiring a plaintiff to amend his complaint which under Rule 8 is sufficient to withstand a motion to dismiss. It is to be noted that a motion for more definite statement is *not* to be used to assist in getting the facts in preparation for trial as such. Other rules relating to discovery, interrogatories and the like exist for this purpose. Of course, the filing of defensive pleadings is not postponed by proceeding under these other rules.

The Rule provides simply, "If a pleading to which a responsive pleading is permitted is so *vague* or *ambiguous* that a party *cannot reasonably be required to frame a responsive* pleading, he may move . . . ." (Emphasis added.) Before the 1948 amendment the Rule was broader in form. It read that a party might "move for a more definite statement or for a bill of particulars of any matter which is not averred with sufficient *definiteness* or *particularity* to enable him properly to prepare his responsive pleading *or to prepare for trial.*" (Emphasis added.)

Reference to the "bill of particulars" and the preparation for trial was left out of the amended Rule. Moreover the words "definiteness" and "particularity" were changed. This was because these matters could be better handled under the discovery rule. As much had been decided by substantially all of the trial courts that had passed on the matter, even before the Rule was amended. See discussion of the history of the Rule and its application in 2 Moore, Federal Practice No. 12.01, p. 2215, and No. 12.17, p. 2278 et seq. (1948), and see 1 Barron & Holtzoff, Federal Practice and Procedure, § 255 (1950, and 1958 Wright Supplement).

There is, of course, a paucity of appellate court cases dealing with this matter because unless a plaintiff stands on his refusal to comply with an order to make a more definite statement and the complaint is thereupon dismissed, no appealable order results. On the other hand, the error in ordering it becomes immaterial after it has been complied with. There are numerous cases in the district courts in which the policy requiring the restricted application of this rule is made clear. See cases cited in the two texts above referred to and see Millsap v. Lotz, D.C.W.D.Mo., 1950, 10 F.R.D. 612; Blane v. Young, D.C.N.D.Ohio, 1950, 10 F.R.D. 524; Granger v. Shouse, D.C.W.D.Mo., 1950, 10 F.R.D. 439.

Now, as to the application of the Rule to the case before us. We have the complete records; we have the complaints, the essential features of which are set out in this opinion; we find no statement or testimony adduced on the hearing on the motion to indicate why the defendants, from their knowledge of their own records and payrolls as well as their operations, would be unable to either admit or deny the allegations concerning coverage and violations. On the record, there is nothing for the Trial Court's discretion to operate on. It is too plain to require elaboration that if the defendants did not in good faith believe that they had violated the act, or that their operations were subject, in whole or in part to the Act, they could say so by denying the allegations in the complaint, and an issue would be drawn. The same would be true if they entertained a genuine doubt whether from uncertainty in the interpretation of the law or the underlying facts as to coverage of one or more employees, or compliance either with record keeping or payment of requisite wages. More especially if they believed they had violated the Act they could say so, and they should be required to do so. As to any specific cases as to which the Secretary contended there was coverage and had been violations which the defendants wished to get further information about, they would have ample opportunity to follow Rules 26–37 for discovery. It was just such detailed evidentiary information which defendants sought in their motions, see note 3, supra (especially par. 2(a), (b) and par. (a)(b) of the prayer). This evidentiary detail was neither a proper part of the complaint under F.R.Civ.P. 8 nor was it needed to frame a response under Rule 12(a).

As a consequence the cause must be reversed and remanded for further and not inconsistent proceedings.

Reversed and remanded.

HUTCHESON, CHIEF JUDGE (dissenting). [The dissenting opinion is omitted.]

NOTE ON THE EFFECT OF A DECISION OF INSUFFICIENCY

1. Leave to Amend

After a demurrer or motion has been sustained on the ground of the complaint's insufficiency, whether in point of substance or in point of form, the plaintiff is routinely given leave to amend. Failure to grant leave to amend at least once is almost invariably held an abuse of discretion, certainly so if the defect is one of form. Compare F.R.C.P. 15(a). Ordinarily the pleader will be given several opportunities to remedy defects of substance as well as of form. While the measure of indulgence varies from jurisdiction to jurisdiction, it is today on the whole rather generous. See, e.g., State of California ex rel. State Lands Comm'n v. County of Orange, 134 Cal.App.3d 20, 26, 184 Cal.Rptr. 423, 426 (1982) ("if there is any reasonable possibility the plaintiff can state a good cause of action, it is error and an abuse of discretion to sustain the demurrer without leave to amend"); Friedman v. Stadum, 171 Cal.App.3d 775, 217 Cal.Rptr. 585 (1985). On the mechanics, timing and allowable scope of amendments, see Amending the Pleadings, infra p. 125.

Generally speaking, a pleader is required to avail himself of the opportunity to amend, if such an opportunity is extended. This rule is an expression of the general procedural principle that all reasonable efforts to obtain redress must be made in the trial court before resort may be made to an appeal.

2. The Scope of Permissible Amendment

When amendment is sought to be made at the pleading stage, following the sustaining of a demurrer or analogous motion, in most jurisdictions the plaintiff is permitted to amend to expand or shift the basis of his claim so long as the amended complaint continues to refer to the same out-of-court controversy that was the predicate of the original complaint. As stated in, e.g., Trusthouse Forte Management, Inc. v. Garden City Hotel, Inc., 106 A.D.2d 271, 483 N.Y.S.2d 216 (1984), the requirement is that the complaint as amended relate to the "same general set of facts." See also, e.g., Guardianship of Hurley, 394 Mass. 554, 476 N.E.2d 941 (1985).

On avoidance of statutes of limitation by "relation back" amendments, see Amendment and the Statute of Limitations, infra p. 130.

3. Plaintiff's Decision Whether to Amend

Where the objection to the pleading is explicitly on substantive grounds, plaintiff ordinarily refuses to amend, suffers a dismissal of the action and carries the fight over the validity of her claim to the appellate court. She often has no alternative, for her complaint says about all that can be said—if plaintiff is correct in her contention regarding the substantive law.

Where the objection to the pleading is explicitly on formal grounds, plaintiff ordinarily exercises the leave given to amend; the formal defects are cleared up, and the matter proceeds along to the next stage in the trial court. Indeed, plaintiff can often do so where the objection to the pleading is ostensibly one of substance. That was the situation in Mitchell v. E–Z Way, was it not?

Where the objection to the pleading is ambiguously one of substance and one of form, the problem becomes more difficult. The difficulty stems from the juxtaposition of three rules:

   a. Relief should be sought, if available, in the trial court before resort to appeal may be had. This rule requires affirmance on appeal if the plaintiff could have maintained her action on the merits by complying with the trial judge's ruling on matters of form, even if that ruling was wrong.

   b. No action should be concluded by reason of shortcomings in the pleadings, even serious ones. This rule requires reversal on appeal even if the trial judge seemed eminently right in concluding that the complaint was so confused as to make it impossible to get at the substantive legal questions involved. See, e.g., Dioguardi v. Durning, 139 F.2d 774 (2d Cir. 1944); Dussouy v. Gulf Coast Investment Corp., 660 F.2d 594 (5th Cir. 1981).

   c. Resort to an appellate court may be had, in most jurisdictions, only from a final judgment. The only way to obtain a final judgment in the face of a ruling that the complaint is insufficient is to refuse to plead further and suffer dismissal of the action.

Given the third of these rules, is it possible to reconcile the first two? What should the appellate court have done in Mitchell v. E–Z Way if it had concluded, in accord with the trial judge, that the complaint was indeed indefinite and uncertain? Inasmuch as the bother and expense to plaintiff in taking the appeal in Mitchell v. E–Z Way were undoubtedly greater than deferring to the trial judge's conception of proper specificity, why did plaintiff refuse to exercise the opportunity to amend? Did the appellate court come to grips with the problem posed by this refusal?

4. PLEADING INCONSISTENT THEORIES

NOTE ON THE PROBLEM OF CONSISTENCY

Common law pleading rules required that the pleader's allegations be consistent. Consistency was required even where the allegations referred to an out-of-court event which under the substantive law was difficult to classify, or where the pleader, by reason of limited access to the facts, was in a difficult or impossible position to know the true state of affairs. Wigton v. McKinley, 122 Colo. 14, 221 P.2d 383 (1950) is illustrative. This was a quiet title proceeding in which the pleader claimed title, first, as owner under an unrecorded deed from his wife delivered to him prior to her death and, second, as devisee under his wife's will. The court pointed out that if the deed was valid and delivered, the wife would have had nothing to devise, while if the devise was valid it was because the deed was not. Held: "A party to an action may not base his cause upon inconsistent and self-destructive grounds." 122 Colo. at 18, 221 P.2d at 385.

This requirement of consistency put the pleader in a very difficult situation. If plaintiff elected scenario *A*, defendant could defend on the ground that the truth was actually scenario *B*. If the trier of the issue found for defendant, plaintiff might then try to proceed on scenario *B*, incurring the additional cost and also the risk that defendant might then defend on the ground that the real situation was scenario *A*.

To eliminate this kind of dilemma in asserting a claim or an affirmative defense, the Codes typically permit alternative or "hypothetical" statements of claim or defense. See, e.g., C.C.P. 379; F.R.C.P. 8(e)(2). As a corollary, plaintiff is also allowed to present proof at trial without having to "elect" which scenario is true and to have the jury instructed to consider and decide the evidence on the basis of the alternative hypotheses. See 4 Witkin 411–419.

See, e.g., Chirelstein v. Chirelstein, 8 N.J.Super. 504, 73 A.2d 628 (1950): Prior to the present action, the plaintiff wife had sued defendant for divorce in a Florida court. A decree of divorce had been entered. In the present action, plaintiff alleged, first, that the Florida divorce decree was valid and that she was therefore entitled to alimony as a divorcee; and, second, that the Florida decree was invalid because it had been procured through fraudulent allegations of Florida domicile, so that the parties were still married, and that she was entitled now to a divorce and alimony. Defendant objected that plaintiff should not be allowed to take inconsistent positions on the validity of the Florida decree. The court overruled the objection, saying, 8 N.J.Super. at 511, 73 A.2d at 632:

> "I see no basis for requiring an election. Where the interplay of the facts and the law is such that the legal soundness of the respective legal positions is debatable, alternative or hypothetical claims should be permitted. I can perceive no reason for requiring a litigant in these circumstances to make a conclusive anticipation of the views of the court. * * * Where the judicial treatment of the facts is in doubt, justice demands that the litigant be permitted to assert alternative positions which depend upon the successive determinations of the issues raised by the facts."

Compare the problem of asserting alternative claims against multiple defendants, e.g., Lambert v. Southern Counties Gas Co., infra p. 719.

5. THE ANSWER

HOWARD W. W _____
_____ Building
Berkeley 4, California
Tel. # _____
Attorney for Defendants

IN THE MUNICIPAL COURT FOR THE BERKELEY-ALBANY JUDICIAL DISTRICT IN AND FOR THE COUNTY OF ALAMEDA, STATE OF CALIFORNIA

EUGENE M. SWANN, CHERIE A. SWANN,
 	
        Plaintiffs,
 	
      vs.
 	
EUGENE H. BURKETT, ALINE B. BURKETT and ROBERT H. BURKETT,
 	
        Defendants.
	NO. 12243
	
	ANSWER *

Come now defendants above named and answering the alleged First Cause of Action admit, deny and allege as follows:

I

Answering paragraphs I and II of said First Cause of Action, defendants allege that they have insufficient information or knowledge upon which to form a belief, and relying on said ground, and for said reason, deny each and every allegation contained in said paragraphs I and II.

II

Answering paragraph III of said First Cause of Action, defendants deny each and every allegation contained therein; further answering said paragraph III, defendants allege and admit that they own a triplex located at and commonly known as 2709 Benvenue Street, Berkeley.

III

Answering paragraph IV of said First Cause of Action, defendants admit that they own a parcel of real property commonly known as 2709 Benvenue Street in the City of Berkeley, County of Alameda, State of California, and that there is located thereon a triplex and an additional cottage in the rear; except insofar as specifically admitted in this paragraph, defendants deny each and every allegation contained in said paragraph IV.

* For the complaint to which this is the answer, see p. 53 supra.

IV

Answering paragraphs V and VI of said First Cause of Action, defendants admit that any act any of them have undertaken in connection with the renting of any unit of 2709 Benvenue Street, Berkeley, California, was undertaken on behalf of the owners of said real property; except insofar as specifically herein admitted, defendants deny each and every allegation contained in paragraphs V and VI of said First Cause of Action.

V

Answering paragraphs VIII, IX, X and XI of said First Cause of Action, defendants deny each and every allegation therein contained.

WHEREFORE, defendants pray judgment.

Answering the alleged Second Cause of Action of said Complaint, defendants admit, deny and allege as follows:

I

Answering paragraphs I and II of said Second Cause of Action, defendants allege that they have no information or knowledge upon which to form a belief, and for said reason, and relying on said ground, defendants deny each and every allegation contained in said paragraphs.

II

Defendants replead, as though fully set forth, their answers to paragraphs III, IV, V, VI, VIII and X of the First Cause of Action of said Complaint.

III

Answering paragraph IV of said Second Cause of Action, defendants deny each and every allegation therein contained.

WHEREFORE, defendants pray judgment.

As a second and separate and distinct defense to each of the causes of action, defendants allege that neither cause of action of said Amended Complaint states facts sufficient to constitute a cause of action against these defendants, or any of them.

WHEREFORE, defendants pray that plaintiffs take nothing by their Complaint and that defendants be hence dismissed with their costs of suit.

HOWARD W. W_____

Attorney for Defendants

I, EUGENE H. BURKETT, say:

I am one of the defendants in the above entitled matter; the foregoing Answer is true of my own knowledge, except as to the matters which are therein stated on my information or belief, and as to those matters I believe it to be true.

I declare under penalty of perjury that the foregoing is true and correct.

Executed on January 17, 1961 at Berkeley, California.

EUGENE H. BURKETT

NOTE ON THE ANSWER

1. Admission or Denial

The defendant's Answer must respond to the plaintiff's allegations. Conventionally it tracks the complaint paragraph by paragraph. The response to an allegation can be a denial, an admission, or neither, i.e., the Answer may ignore the particular allegation. A *denial* puts the allegation in issue and thereby creates an issue of fact as to the allegation. An *admission* establishes the allegation as true for purposes of the case. A *failure to deny* has the same effect as an admission; see, e.g., C.C.P. 431.20(a), F.R.C.P. 8(d). An admission made in a pleading may also be introduced in other litigation, but it is treated as evidence of the fact in question, which the party may explain away, and not as a concession that is conclusive in the other litigation. See Cleary et al., McCormick on Evidence § 265 (3d ed. 1984).

One of the functions of pleadings is to limit the issues. If facts alleged in the complaint are admitted, they are not in issue, and no evidence is needed to prove their existence. See 9 Wigmore on Evidence § 2591 (Chadbourn ed. 1981). Not only is evidence unneeded, but evidence that is not relevant to an issue raised by the pleadings is immaterial and should not be admitted. Consider Fuentes v. Tucker, 31 Cal.2d 1, 187 P.2d 752 (1947): Plaintiffs sued defendant for the wrongful death of their minor children in an automobile accident. The defendant admitted liability but contested the amount of damages. At trial the plaintiffs offered proof of the force of the impact and of the fact that the defendant was drunk. The court held that the evidence should have been excluded:

"It follows, therefore, if an issue has been removed from a case by an admission in the answer, that it is error to receive evidence which is material solely to the excluded matter. This, of course, does not mean that an admission of liability precludes a plaintiff from showing how an accident happened if such evidence is material to the issue of damages. In an action for personal injuries, where liability is admitted and the only issue to be tried is the amount of damage, the force of the impact and the surrounding circumstances may be relevant and material to indicate the extent of plaintiff's injuries. * * *

"The defendant here by an unqualified statement in his answer admitted liability for the deaths of the children, and the sole remaining question in issue was the amount of damages suffered by the parents. In an action for wrongful death of a minor child the damages consist of the pecuniary loss to the parents in being deprived of the services, earnings, society, comfort and protection of the child. Bond v. United Railroads, 159 Cal. 270, 285, 113 P. 366, 48 L.R.A., N.S., 687, Ann.Cas.1912C, 50. The manner in which the accident occurred, the force of the impact, or defendant's intoxication could have no bearing on these elements of damage. The evidence, therefore, was not material to any issue before the jury, and its admission was error." 31 Cal.2d at 5, 187 P.2d at 755.

2. Denial as Putting in Issue the Material Allegations of the Complaint

a. The Logical Form of a Denial. An allegation of fact is a statement in the form: X is true. A denial of an allegation is a statement in the form: Not (X is true). Accordingly, when a denial is interposed an issue of fact is presented. An issue of fact could likewise be presented if the complaint alleged "X is true" and the answer took the form "Y is true," when both X and Y cannot be true. Thus, suppose:

(1) P alleges: Ownership in P.

(2) D alleges: Ownership in D.

(3) It is not possible for ownership to be in both P and D.

(4) Therefore, ownership in P is in effect denied.

While the defendant could thus raise the issue of fact either by denial of plaintiff's allegations (i.e., propounding a contradictory) or by alleging statements which could not be true if plaintiff's allegations were true (i.e., propounding an inconsistency), the rules of pleading by and large prohibit the latter, characterizing them as "argumentative denials." See Michael and Adler, The Trial of an Issue of Fact: I, 34 Colum.L.Rev. 1224, 1244–47 (1934). Indeed, the traditional rule was that an argumentative denial was not merely bad in form but would be regarded as not denying, and therefore admitting, the allegations of the complaint. See Clark on Code Pleading 591–92 (2d ed. 1947); James & Hazard § 4.7.

A less serious consequence of an argumentative denial is that defendant by alleging the inconsistent proposition, rather than simply denying the plaintiff's allegation, may be required to assume the burden of proof of the inconsistent proposition. See Comment, Effect of Unnecessary Affirmative Pleading Upon the Burden of Proof, 39 Yale L.J. 117 (1929); James & Hazard § 4.7. Is it possible coherently to say that plaintiff has the burden of proving X and defendant the burden of proving Y, when both X and Y cannot be true?

b. The Consequences of a Denial. Generally speaking, a denial has two consequences. First, it imposes on the plaintiff the burden of proving the allegation denied and, second, it permits the defendant to introduce evidence that would tend to disprove the allegation. See Clark on Code Pleading 606–610 (2d ed. 1947); James & Hazard § 4.4. To this generalization there are, however, a number of exceptions of uncertain dimension.

(1) The Effect of Presumptions. Certain types of facts are by statute or case law presumed to have occurred. Sometimes the presumption is made conclusive or "indisputable," so that the fact presumed will be taken as having occurred no matter what evidence might be offered to the contrary; more frequently, the presumption is disputable, so that the fact will be taken as having occurred unless and until evidence is offered suggesting otherwise. See Cleary et al., McCormick on Evidence §§ 342 et seq. (3d ed. 1984). In either case, when an allegation is made of a fact presumed to be true, then a denial of that allegation ordinarily does *not* have the consequence that plaintiff must

undertake to prove it. On the contrary, the defendant will have the burden of introducing evidence to disprove it. See Texas Dept. of Community Affairs v. Burdine, supra p. 75. If the presumption is conclusive, the defendant will not even be permitted to do that. In effect, the application of a presumption works a "reallocation" of the burden of calling the attention of the court to potentially relevant factual circumstances of the case. See generally Cleary, Presuming and Pleading: An Essay on Juristic Immaturity, supra p. 66.

(2) Rules Permitting Certain Matters to be Alleged Generally. Most jurisdictions have rules that permit the plaintiff to allege generally that a certain group of potentially relevant facts have occurred. Most common is that found in, e.g., C.C.P. 457, providing that in contract actions "it may be stated generally that the party duly performed all the conditions on his part." See also C.C.P. 459; F.R.C.P. 9(c)–(e). While a denial of such an allegation will usually suffice to permit defendant to offer proof on the question, the denial does not require plaintiff to offer proof of performance of the conditions unless defendant by affirmative allegation or other notice identifies the condition which he claims was not performed. See Roscoe Moss Co. v. Jenkins, 55 Cal. App.2d 369, 130 P.2d 477 (1942); Clark on Code Pleading 619 (2d ed. 1947).

(3) Rules Requiring that Contentions Inconsistent with the Complaint's Allegations be Affirmatively Alleged. Ordinarily a denial is a sufficient basis for defendant to introduce evidence tending to disprove plaintiff's allegation by proving the truth of a proposition inconsistent with that allegation. At times, however, the courts have held that proof of such an inconsistency is permitted only if, in addition to denying plaintiff's allegation, defendant alleges the inconsistent proposition. Consider, e.g., Jetty v. Craco, 123 Cal.App.2d 876, 267 P.2d 1055 (1954):

Plaintiff sued defendant to recover $4,000 which plaintiff alleged she had loaned to defendant to buy merchandise. Defendant denied this allegation. At trial, defendant sought to show that the plaintiff and he had formed a partnership and that the money was risk capital advanced to the enterprise, and hence not a loan. This evidence was held properly excluded, the court saying, 123 Cal.App.2d at 879–80, 267 P.2d at 1057:

"In order to prove her case plaintiff was not required to prove more than the making of the loan. Defendant under his denials could prove that he did not borrow the money. But the pleadings did not create an issue whether there was some special contract or relationship between the parties that would have constituted a defense to the action. The claim of a partnership and the receipt of the money as a contribution to the partnership was new matter, which, not having been pleaded was not available as a defense to the action. If this were not true a defendant, under mere denials in an action for money loaned, could come up with all manner of claims of special agreements to defeat the action."

Should the availability of broad discovery devices affect the application of the pleading rules regarding defenses? What if plaintiff in Jetty v. Craco had opportunity to take defendant's deposition and thereby obtain his story of the transaction?

What risks does a defendant have to consider when he wishes to make a contention of fact that is not clearly established by the precedents to be admissible in support of a denial?

For a catalogue of the matters regarded as affirmative defenses under the Federal Rules of Civil Procedure, at least for the purposes of pleading, see Rule

8(c) and 2A Moore ¶ 8.27. Many state procedure rules explicitly specify commonly recurring matters that are to be treated as affirmative defenses. See, e.g., Ill.C.C.P. § 2–613(d); N.Y.C.P.L.R. § 3018(b). For the California rules, see 5 Witkin 430–460. The more frequently recurring affirmative defenses are release, see, e.g., Ottenheimer Publishers, Inc. v. Regal Publishers, Inc., 626 S.W.2d 276 (Tenn.App.1981); contributory negligence, see, e.g., Addair v. Bryant, 168 W.Va. 306, 284 S.E.2d 374 (1981); and the statute of limitations, see, e.g., County of San Mateo v. Booth, 135 Cal.App.3d 388, 185 Cal.Rptr. 349 (1982). See also James & Hazard §§ 4.5 et seq.

3. Denials for Lack of Information and Belief

The pleading rules contemplate that the denial of an allegation in a pleading shall be made according to the knowledge of the person responding thereto, so that allegations will be admitted unless known to be false. However, it is recognized that a defendant, at least at the time when required to answer, may not know whether a particular allegation is true or not. Accordingly, the rules permit the defendant to aver that he has no information or belief sufficient to answer and on that basis to deny the allegation. See C.C.P. 431.30(e); F.R.C.P. 8(b).

4. Verification

On verification of answers, see Note on Form and Style of Pleadings, supra p. 108. In addition, C.C.P. 446 requires verification of an answer to a complaint brought by a public agency whether or not the complaint is verified. See generally 4 Witkin 466–467.

NOTE ON THE REPLY

The original Field Code provided for a reply by the plaintiff to any "new matter" raised in defendant's answer. The provision for a reply is found in many of the versions of the Field Code patterned after that adopted in New York. Compare, e.g., Ill.C.C.P. § 2–602. The Federal Rules require a reply only to a counterclaim denominated as such or when the court directs the plaintiff to reply to new matter in an answer. F.R.C.P. 7(a). In jurisdictions where no reply by the plaintiff is required, the matters of affirmative defense may be controverted or avoided without any foundational pleading. See, e.g., Neeff v. Emery Transp. Co., 284 F.2d 432 (2d Cir. 1960); C.C.P. 431.20(b); F.R.C.P. 8(d).

A special problem is presented when the allegations essential to the plaintiff's statement of a cause of action themselves disclose what appears prima facie to be a defense to the claim. This can occur, for example, where plaintiff seeks to enforce an oral agreement of a kind normally rendered unenforceable by the Statute of Frauds unless in writing. To state a claim on such a contract, plaintiff will ordinarily have to reveal its oral character, and must do so in California. C.C.P. 430(10)(g). So stated, the claim is demurrable for failure to state a cause of action, e.g., Loper v. Flynn, 72 Cal.App.2d 619, 165 P.2d 256 (1946). Since she cannot meet the defense by reply, plaintiff is permitted to anticipate the defense and allege facts, such as those disclosing an estoppel to assert the Statute, which avoid it.

C. AMENDED AND SUPPLEMENTAL PLEADINGS

1. AMENDING THE PLEADINGS

MATARAZZO v. FRIENDLY ICE CREAM CORP.

United States District Court, Eastern District of New York, 1976.
70 F.R.D. 556.

BARTELS, DISTRICT JUDGE.

MEMORANDUM—DECISION AND ORDER

This is a motion pursuant to Rule 15 Fed.R.Civ.P. for leave to file an amended complaint in order to (1) allege facts with greater specificity with respect to claims against the defendant, and at the same time to (2) add a pendent common law claim arising out of the same acts, practices and course of conduct. The essence of the original complaint is set forth in the class action determination decided on February 14, 1974, Matarazzo v. Friendly Ice Cream Corp., 62 F.R.D. 65 (E.D.N.Y. 1974).

Defendant Friendly Ice Cream Corp. (Friendly) is a food processor and distributor of ice cream, beverages and food products, operating stores in many states. Plaintiff claims the defendant violated the federal antitrust laws by reason of the manner in which it conducted its business with the plaintiff and those he represents as former store managers. In particular, plaintiff in his original complaint alleges that the contracts with the store managers were not employment contracts but were, in fact, standardized franchise agreements requiring the store managers to purchase all their requirements from Friendly at fixed prices and to charge fixed prices for the same as a condition for the use by them of Friendly's trademark and trade name. These contracts plaintiff claims constitute illegal "tying" arrangements, price fixing and resale price maintenance in violation of the Sherman and Clayton Acts. Defendant contends that the agreement between it and the store managers was not a franchise arrangement, but clearly created the relationship of employer and employee.

While the plaintiff claims that its first proposed amendment (Count I) simply alleges facts with more specificity, the amendment does more than that insofar as it no longer describes the store managers as "franchisees" but eliminates that description which he had used thirteen times in his original complaint.[1] In lieu thereof, the amendment substitutes the words "store manager" and at the same time claims

---

1. The Court finds no infirmity in the present complaint which requires more specific allegations. See Fed.R.Civ.P. 8(a) & (e)(1). This was also true at the time the class status was granted.

that each store was operated as "a separate and independent business entity" and that the managers were in fact "independent contractors operating through restrictive provisions thus constituting a separate and distinct market for the products named" in Friendly's contracts, instructions, rules and regulations, which plaintiff described as "contracts" with independent business contractors.

The second proposed amendment (Count II) sets forth an alleged pendent claim. It states that during the class period defendant, in the course of its contact with class members committed fraud, breach of contract, breach of duty and planned "economic entrapment" with store managers which began with the recruitment of manager trainees and continued through the termination of the relationship with the defendant. The substance of this wrongful conduct, plaintiff claims, was caused by misleading advertisements and false and misleading representations to the store managers by unfair charges and secret rebates from suppliers and unilateral manipulation and diminution of the net profits of the store for a period of ninety days after the termination of the relationship between the parties. * * *

COUNT I

There is no doubt that leave to amend under Fed.R.Civ.P. 15 "shall be freely given when justice so requires," and there is equally no doubt that the court will abuse its discretion by denying leave without a justifying reason, Foman v. Davis, 371 U.S. 178, 182, 83 S.Ct. 227, 230, 9 L.Ed.2d 222 (1962). However, where claims are set forth in the proposed amendment which might materially alter the nature of the action years after the action has been instituted and also after substantial discovery has been conducted, the court should scrutinize the amendment to ascertain if any new issues are actually injected into the case. In the context of Count I of this amendment the issue presented is whether there is a material difference between the allegation that a franchise relationship existed and the allegation that an independent contractor relationship existed. The relationship between the plaintiff and the defendant in both cases must derive initially from the good name and trademark of Friendly.

* * *

The Court finds that the plaintiff can not be charged with bad faith in seeking the amendment and that there has been no showing that the delay per se will be unduly prejudicial. Indeed discovery often justifies a subsequent amendment to the complaint. Even though it is predicated upon a different theory, an amendment should be permitted in the absence of the injection of any new issues requiring new and extensive preparation detrimental to the speedy resolution of the case and prejudicial to the defendant. Middle Atlantic Utilities Co. v. S.M.W. Development Corp., 392 F.2d 380, 385–86 (2d Cir. 1968); Izaak Walton League v. St. Clair, 497 F.2d 849, 854 (8th Cir.), cert. denied, 419 U.S. 1009, 95 S.Ct. 329, 42 L.Ed.2d 284 (1974).

* * * As has been stated before, the real issue in this case is whether the plaintiff was an employee, a franchisee or an independent contractor. If he is an employee and no more, then the plaintiff has no case. If he is not an employee but a franchisee or an independent contractor under a franchise agreement, it does not follow that the terms of the franchise agreement will violate the Sherman and Clayton Acts. See Susser v. Carvel Corp., 332 F.2d 505 (2d Cir.), cert. granted, 379 U.S. 885, 85 S.Ct. 158, 13 L.Ed.2d 91 (1964), cert. dismissed, 381 U.S. 125, 85 S.Ct. 1364, 14 L.Ed.2d 284 (1965); 84 Harv.L.Rev. 1717, 1722 & n. 24 (1971). The purport of the proposed amendment is not easily discoverable unless the plaintiff wishes to escape his original description of the store managers as franchisees for the reason that he believes he will have a better chance of success under the independent contractor theory. In granting class action status on behalf of former store managers, we stated that "[if it is determined that the agreement was a franchise agreement, the sequential issue of violation of antitrust laws would involve predominantly questions of law or fact typical and common to all terminated store managers." Matarazzo v. Friendly Ice Cream Corp., supra, at 70. The difficulty with the plaintiff's position at the present time arises from the fact that the legal notice to the class dated April 1974, informed the members that the complaint stated that the store managers were franchisees of Friendly and that Friendly's defense was that the agreement between store managers and Friendly was "one of employer and employee and not one of franchisor and franchisee" and made no mention of independent contractors. Thus, those who became members of the class did so upon the theory that the issues were whether store managers were franchisees or employees, and not whether store managers were independent contractors and not employees.

Without more, the Court cannot determine whether an independent contractor under the circumstances of this case would assume greater rights as well as greater liabilities to third-parties than a franchisee. This may only be a matter of semantics. See 1 Glickman, Franchising § 4.02 at 4–3 to 4–4 (1975). However, if there are additional burdens to be assumed as independent contractors, members of the class must receive a new notice and have the privilege to opt out. See Fed.R.Civ.P. 23(c)(2). This would delay further the speedy expedition of the trial and might prejudice both parties. If at the trial, evidence indicates that the distinction between a franchisee and an independent contractor injects no new issues into the case, adds no further burdens to the members of the class, nor catches the defendant unprepared, the plaintiff may, under Rule 15, move to amend the pleadings to conform to the evidence. With the above reservation, the Court denies plaintiff's motion to amend the complaint as to Count I.

COUNT II

Plaintiff's application to amend the complaint to add an alleged pendent claim (Count II) raises an entirely different problem. Federal courts have power to assume jurisdiction over state claims in the interest of judicial economy and fairness to the litigants. United Mine Workers v. Gibbs, 383 U.S. 715, 726, 86 S.Ct. 1130, 16 L.Ed.2d 218 (1966). If the claim is derived from a common nucleus of operative facts, then "[t]hat power need not be exercised in every case in which it is found to exist. It has consistently been recognized that pendent jurisdiction is a doctrine of discretion, not of plaintiff's right." Id. at 726, 86 S.Ct. at 1139.

Plaintiff seeks to add a claim of fraud, breach of contract and fiduciary obligations predicated upon defendant's conduct that occurred before, during and after the parties' relationship crystallized. An objective analysis of this cause of action reveals that it does not rise out of the common nucleus of operative facts but covers a much broader spectrum of conduct. * * * In addition, there is great doubt whether there could be class action certification for this type of misrepresentation and fraud. See Ungar v. Dunkin' Donuts of America, Inc., 68 F.R.D. 65, 144–45 (E.D.Pa.1975). Moreover, the nature of this new claim was certainly not made known to the members of the class when the original notice was published, and it is difficult to see how they could be bound one way or the other by a resolution of this issue without a new notice assuming the claim is a proper subject for class action jurisdiction. See Fed.R.Civ.P. 23(b)(3). The proper remedy for this claim under the circumstances is an action in the state court where it could be tried on its own merits without obfuscating the antitrust violations set forth in the present case. To permit such a state claim to be tried together with the federal claim would require this Court to exercise its discretion twice, first with respect to the amendment, and second with respect to pendent jurisdiction. To do so would only becloud the antitrust issue and would confuse the jury in resolving the same.

Accordingly, the motion to amend is denied as to both Counts. So ordered.

NOTE ON CHALLENGING AND AMENDING PLEADINGS AFTER THE PLEADING STAGE

1. Delayed Challenges to the Claim or Defense

The sufficiency in point of substantive law of a claim or defense may be challenged at any time prior to entry of final judgment and, in some circumstances of default judgment, even after judgment. This rule is embodied in provisions of statute and rule, e.g., C.C.P. 430.80; F.R.C.P. 12(h). Thus, the objection may be taken not only by demurrer or analogous motion but by motion for judgment on the pleadings after the pleadings are closed; by motion to strike the pleading, at pretrial conference; by oral demurrer, motion to dismiss or motion for judgment on the pleadings at the opening of trial; by motion at trial objecting to the introduction of any evidence; after presentation of the evidence, by motion for directed verdict or nonsuit; and on appeal. However, under C.C.P. 430.80, a party failing to answer or demur to a complaint or cross-complaint, or failing to demur to an answer, waives all later objections except those concerning a lack of subject matter jurisdiction or failure to state a claim upon which relief may be granted or, in the case of an answer, failure to state sufficient facts to constitute a defense.

2. Delayed Challenges to the Pleadings

The common law and traditional code pleading rule was that objection on the ground of substantive insufficiency could be leveled at any time not only at the claim as made by the *evidence* but also, notwithstanding the evidence, at the *pleading* in which the substantive issue was required to be raised. Thus, even though a litigant might establish by evidence the elements required under the substantive law, if he had not also alleged those elements in his pleading his case was subject to fatal attack. The theory was that a judgment could not be entered unless a "foundation" for it had been laid in the pleadings. See generally Morgan, The Variance Problem, 32 Neb.L.Rev. 357 (1953).

The view in most code pleading states today is less technical. In the first place, the later the challenge to the pleading, the greater the liberality with which the pleading is construed. In the second place, the challenger of the pleading ordinarily must show not only the insufficiency of the pleading but also that the insufficiency worked material hardship to the preparation of the challenger's case. Anno., 20 A.L.R.Fed. 448. And when the challenge is made after the introduction of evidence, if the evidence discloses a tenable case then almost any deficiency in the pleading ordinarily will be deemed supplied by the proof. See, e.g., Ades v. Brush, 66 Cal.App.2d 436, 152 P.2d 519 (1944):

> "Where the parties at the trial treat a certain issue as being involved, and the judgment is based on that issue, it is not a prejudicial error that the complaint defectively alleges, or fails to allege at all, that issue."

See also Stearns v. Fair Employment Practice Comm'n, 6 Cal.3d 205, 98 Cal. Rptr. 467, 490 P.2d 1155 (1971); People v. Toomey, 157 Cal.App.3d 1, 203 Cal.Rptr. 642 (1984).

The Federal Rules of Civil Procedure have abolished the rule that the substantive sufficiency of a claim or defense is determined by the pleadings as distinct from the evidence. F.R.C.P. 15(b). Hence, however deficient a pleading, if evidence is adduced which is sufficient to establish the existence of the elements of the claim or defense referred to in the applicable rule of substantive law, then the litigant is treated as having adequately presented that claim or defense. Cf. General Credit Corp. v. Pichel, 44 Cal.App.3d 844, 118 Cal.Rptr. 913 (1975).

3. Mechanical Problems of Amendment

a. Motion to Amend. In a limited class of circumstances, a pleader may amend her pleading without leave of court. Otherwise, leave of court is required. F.R.C.P. 15(a); C.C.P. 472, 473. When an objection to a pleading is sustained in the stages of litigation prior to trial, leave to amend is usually granted in the order sustaining the objection, or by rules providing that leave shall be deemed granted in such circumstances unless the order otherwise provides. See, e.g., California Rules of Court, Civil Law and Motion Rules, Rule 325(e). Absent such leave, the pleader must make a motion for leave to amend, a motion ordinarily required to be in writing with the proposed amendment attached to it. The amendment is customarily made by tendering a fresh rescript of the pleading as amended. Cf. California Rules of Court, Civil Law and Motion Rules, Rule 327(b). When an amendment is made at pre-trial conference, the amendment may simply be set forth in the pre-trial order or the pre-trial order may direct or permit that an amended rescript of the pleading be prepared. When amendment is made at trial it is normally done by the trial judge's interlineation of the pleading amended or, occasionally, by preparation of a rescript containing the amendment.

On leave to amend, scope of permissible amendment, and considerations affecting the decision whether to amend, see also Note on the Effect of a Decision of Insufficiency, supra p. 116.

b. Service and Filing. An amended pleading offered prior to trial, like any other litigation paper presented prior to trial, is served on the opposing parties by delivering a copy to their attorneys. The original with proof of service is then filed. See, e.g., F.R.C.P. 5. An amendment made at pre-trial or trial is submitted, orally or in writing as the case may be, to opposing counsel before being formally tendered to the court. In either case, properly the amendment itself must be presented to counsel and the court; an order allowing an amendment, even if it contains the terms of the amendment, is technically not the amendment itself. 5 Witkin 526–529. As a matter of practice most mechanical aspects of amendment are handled by stipulation.

c. Effect of Amended Pleading on Prior Pleadings. For most purposes, an amended pleading displaces the pleading originally set up. Thus, for example, when a complaint is amended the amended complaint must be served on opposing parties before the case may progress to further stages of the litigation, e.g., entry of default judgment against the defendant. See, e.g., Engebretson & Co., Inc. v. Harrison, 125 Cal.App.3d 436, 178 Cal.Rptr. 77 (1981). Compare F.R.C.P. Rule 5(a). Furthermore, for most purposes the acceptance of leave to amend is treated as an acquiescence in the trial court's ruling on the original pleading and error may not later be predicated on such a ruling.

4. Amendment and the Statute of Limitations

The problem of most practical significance in amending of pleadings arises when the amendment is made after the statute of limitations has run on the claim stated in the amendment. If the claim stated in the amendment has nothing whatever to do with the transaction referred to in the original complaint, the claim asserted in the amendment is treated as filed at the time of the amendment, and hence will be barred if the statute has run at that time. However, if the claim relates to the same transaction, but is based on a different legal theory or on somewhat different factual aspects of that transaction, then the amendment "relates back" to the date of the original complaint. See F.R.C.P. Rule 15(c). The leading case is Tiller v. Atlantic Coast Line R. Co., 323 U.S. 574, 65 S.Ct. 421, 89 L.Ed. 465 (1945). Compare Grudt v. City of Los Angeles, 2 Cal.3d 575, 86 Cal.Rptr. 465, 468 P.2d 825 (1970): "The prevailing rule * * * is that, if an amendment is sought after the statute of limitations has run, the amended complaint will be deemed filed as of the date of the original complaint provided recovery is sought in both pleadings on the same general set of facts." See Smyser, Rule 15(c) Relation Back of Amendments: A Workable Test, 23 S.D.L.Rev. 55 (1978); Louisell and Anderson, The Safety Appliance Act and the FELA: A Plea for Clarification, 18 Law & Contemp. Probs. 281 (1953); Lewis, The Excessive History of Federal Rule 15(c) and Its Lessons for Civil Rules Revision, 85 Mich.L.Rev. 1507 (1987).

Obviously, there can be dispute as to what constitutes the same "transaction" or "general set of facts."

There are additional difficulties if in the amendment the defendant is differently denominated. See Notice and the Statute of Limitations, infra p. 461, on this problem generally and on the unique California device of "Doe Defendants," and Schiavone v. Fortune, infra p. 452.

On problems of amendment generally, see James & Hazard c. 4; 3 Moore ¶ 15.01 et seq.; 5 Witkin 525–588. On statutes of limitations generally, see Foreclosure of Remedy, infra p. 225.

2. SUPPLEMENTAL PLEADINGS

MANNING v. HYLAND

Supreme Court of New York, Appellate Division, Second Department, 1963.
19 A.D.2d 652, 241 N.Y.S.2d 908.

MEMORANDUM BY THE COURT.

In an action to recover damages for personal injury sustained by plaintiff, a passenger in defendant's automobile, as the result of an accident on the Garden State Parkway in New Jersey, the defendant appeals from an order of the Supreme Court, Queens County, dated August 1, 1962, which denied his motion to serve a supplemental answer pleading as a defense that the action is barred under the law of the State of New Jersey by reason of the fact that after joinder of issue therein, the plaintiff and defendant intermarried.

Order reversed without costs and motion granted. Defendant's time to serve the supplemental answer is extended until 20 days after entry of the order hereon.

The action was commenced on September 24, 1959 and issue was joined on January 8, 1960. Subsequently (on September 9, 1961) the parties were married in Delaware Township, New Jersey. Under the law of that State, a married woman may not sue her husband for personal injuries resulting from her husband's negligence, irrespective of whether the negligence occurred before or after the marriage (New Jersey Statutes Annotated 37:2–5; Koplik v. C. P. Trucking Corp., 27 N.J. 1, 141 A.2d 34).

Plaintiff contends that defendant is guilty of laches; that negotiations for the settlement of her case resulted in an offer by the insurance carrier in the sum of $10,000 which was rejected by a counteroffer on her part; and that on the strength of such negotiations plaintiff committed herself to "extensive debts and a mortgage amounting to several thousand dollars."

The court may, and in a proper case must, on application and upon such terms as are just permit a party to serve a supplemental pleading "alleging material facts which occurred after his former pleading" (Civil Practice Act, § 245). If there has been a delay in moving for leave to serve such a pleading, the facts showing good reason therefor must be stated in order to meet the objection of laches (Plitt v. Illinois Surety Company, 165 App.Div. 973, 150 N.Y.S. 756). Laches cannot be imputed to one who has been justifiably ignorant of the facts giving rise

to a cause of action or defense and who therefore failed to assert it
(C.J.S. Equity § 128). While here it is true that the defendant himself
was aware of the marriage, it would be unrealistic to predicate laches
on his knowledge. The real party in interest, defendant's insurance
carrier, according to the sworn statement of its local claims manager,
first learned on May 16, 1962 of the marriage of plaintiff and defendant
and thereupon without delay notified defendant's attorney. Defendant's attorney swears that he had no prior knowledge of the marriage;
and, by notice dated June 15, 1962, he promptly made the motion for
leave to serve the supplemental pleading.

Whatever prejudice may have resulted from plaintiff's assumption
of an eventual settlement of her claim was not the result of any laches
on defendant's part. The settlement negotiations occurred prior to the
time the insurance carrier had evidence of the marriage. While it is
usually unnecessary to consider the merits of the proposed pleading,
yet, where (as here) the question has been raised on the motion, we are
constrained to do so. In our opinion, the proposed pleading is meritorious (Coster v. Coster, 289 N.Y. 438, 46 N.E.2d 509, 146 A.L.R. 702;
Lauterbach v. Fleischer, 16 A.D.2d 701, 227 N.Y.S.2d 726).

NOTE ON SUPPLEMENTAL PLEADINGS

1. Uses of Supplemental Pleadings

Supplemental pleadings are those referring to "events which have happened since the date of the pleading sought to be supplemented." F.R.C.P.
15(d). They often find use where the defendant, if he has an obligation at all,
has an obligation to render a continuing service of some sort, such as the
obligation to make periodic payments. See, e.g., Perkins v. Benguet Consol.
Mining Co., 55 Cal.App.2d 720, 132 P.2d 70 (1942) (corporate dividends); Brix v.
People's Mutual Life Ins. Co., 2 Cal.2d 446, 41 P.2d 537 (1935) (monthly
installments on a disability insurance policy); Nickerson v. Candler Bldg., Inc.,
156 Ga.App. 396, 274 S.E.2d 582 (1980). Less frequently encountered are
situations where some further conduct of the defendant has aggravated the
earlier claimed injury, e.g., Taylor v. Marine Cooks & Stewards Ass'n, 117 Cal.
App.2d 556, 256 P.2d 595 (1953) (original action for injunction against union
disciplinary proceedings; supplemental complaint for injunction to expunge
expulsion from union); cf. Rexroad v. Kansas Power & Light Co., 192 Kan. 343,
388 P.2d 832 (1964) (claim for indemnity added to original claim for plaintiff's
own injuries). When the original claim fairly implies additional claims, such as
a suit on obligation to make serial payments, the courts at times have been less
insistent on the requirement of a supplemental pleading. See, e.g., Minor v.
Minor, 184 Cal.App.2d 118, 7 Cal.Rptr. 455 (1960) (installments coming due
under support agreement).

2. Restrictions on Supplemental Pleadings

Assertion of a supplemental claim or defense is permitted only with leave
of court, the leave to be granted or denied in the trial judge's "sound discretion." The limits of that discretion are vague, see C.C.P. 464; F.R.C.P. 15(d),
though it is held that the supplemental pleading must be "in furtherance of
and consistent with the original action." Gonzales v. Arbelbide, 155 Cal.App.2d

721, 726, 318 P.2d 746, 750 (1957). Cf. Galler v. Slurzberg, 22 N.J.Super. 477, 484, 92 A.2d 89, 92 (1952) ("Interpretation of the rule [regarding supplemental pleadings] should be influenced by the general principle that all controversies between the parties may be determined in a single action"); Foy v. Foy, 57 N.C.App. 128, 290 S.E.2d 748 (1982); Republic Ins. Co. v. Northern Aire Development, Inc., 94 A.D.2d 764, 463 N.Y.S.2d 23 (1983).

A further restriction is that a supplemental complaint may not be used to cure defects in the original complaint. Normally, of course, an amended as distinct from a supplemental pleading is the proper therapy for a deficient pleading. Resort is sometimes made to a supplemental complaint, however, where the original action was filed prematurely. A typical case is Walton v. County of Kern, 39 Cal.App.2d 32, 102 P.2d 531 (1940):

> "This is an action for damages for a death which, it is claimed, resulted from the improper manner in which a road was maintained by the defendant.

> "The accident and death in question occurred on December 24, 1937. A claim was filed with the defendant county on February 1, 1938, and it is conceded that no order was ever made by the supervisors with respect to rejecting or allowing the claim.

> "The complaint was filed on March 7, 1938, and an answer was filed in April 1938, the exact date not being disclosed by the record. On April 4, 1939, the defendant filed notice of motion for a judgment on the pleadings on the ground that the action was prematurely filed since the supervisors had had ninety days in which to allow or reject the claim. On April 6, 1939, the plaintiff filed notice of motion for permission to file a supplemental complaint, which was attached thereto, and which included an allegation that the claim had been rejected by the failure of the board of supervisors to act upon it within ninety days after it was filed. The two motions were heard together, the motion for leave to file a supplemental complaint being denied and the motion for judgment on the pleadings being granted. The plaintiff has appealed from the judgment.

> "The general rule is that where an action is prematurely brought, and the original complaint must fall, a supplemental complaint has no place as a pleading. Morse v. Steele, 132 Cal. 456, 64 Pac. 690; Lewis v. Fox, 122 Cal. 244, 54 Pac. 823. Ordinarily, a plaintiff's cause of action must have arisen before the filing of the complaint and he may not recover in a cause of action arising after the suit is filed. Kirk v. Culley, 202 Cal. 501, 261 Pac. 994. In Bank of Italy etc. Ass'n v. Bentley, 217 Cal. 644, 20 P.2d 940, 945, the court said: 'Every complaint is predicated upon the theory that the plaintiff therein is entitled to judgment at the time of its filing.'"

Compare Radar v. Rogers, 49 Cal.2d 243, 317 P.2d 17 (1957) (claim against decedent's estate).

F.R.C.P. 15(d), as amended in 1963, seeks to overcome these difficulties. See Advisory Committee on Civil Rules, Proposed Amendments to Rules of Civil Procedure, 31 F.R.D. 621, 637 (1962). See also William Inglis & Sons Baking Co. v. ITT Continental Baking Co., 668 F.2d 1014 (9th Cir.1981); 5 Witkin 588–597.

On the procedure under C.C.P. 464, see Earp v. Nobmann, 122 Cal.App.3d 270, 175 Cal.Rptr. 767 (1981).

D. SUBSTANTIALITY OF CLAIMS AND DEFENSES

INTRODUCTORY NOTE ON THE SUBSTANTIALITY OF PLEADINGS

The traditional rule, that pleadings must be verified, was an attempt to preclude assertions of claims lacking factual merit. See Note on Form and Style of Pleadings, supra p. 108. The requirement had little if any effect toward this end, although from time to time a litigant has been seriously embarrassed on the witness stand by impeaching cross-examination based on a discrepancy between the allegations in his complaint and his testimony. Moreover, courts tend to be somewhat more stringent on inconsistency of allegation in verified complaints. See, e.g., Payne v. Bennion, 178 Cal.App.2d 595, 3 Cal. Rptr. 14 (1960); Premier Electrical Constr. Co. v. LaSalle Nat. Bank, 132 Ill. App.3d 485, 87 Ill.Dec. 721, 477 N.E.2d 1249 (1984). Generally speaking, however, verification is not helpful in preventing sham pleading. In most jurisdictions that require verification, a pleader is permitted to make allegations "upon information and belief," e.g., C.C.P. 446. Furthermore, the veracity of the verification is usually not subject to direct challenge and can be questioned only if it appears from the face of the pleading that the person verifying it was not one of those authorized to do so or that she could not know whereof she spoke, see, e.g., French v. Smith Booth Usher Co., 56 Cal.App.2d 23, 131 P.2d 863 (1942), and even this kind of requirement will not be enforced where plaintiff apparently has a supportable claim but lacks personal knowledge of the facts on which it is based. See Surowitz v. Hilton Hotels Corp., 383 U.S. 363, 86 S.Ct. 845, 15 L.Ed.2d 807 (1966), rehearing denied 384 U.S. 915, 86 S.Ct. 1333, 16 L.Ed.2d 367 (1966); Nemeroff v. Abelson, 620 F.2d 339 (2d Cir. 1980). F.R.C.P. 11 has dispensed with the requirement entirely, except as particularly required by rule or statute. On verification generally see Anno., 68 A.L.R.3d 209.

The modern devices for testing the substantiality of claims are dismissal via summary judgment and sanctions via Rule 11 or its state counterparts. Both refer to the legal sufficiency of the claim. Summary judgment does so directly, by addressing the merits of the claim in light of proffered evidence. Rule 11 does so less directly, by authorizing sanctions where the court finds that a pleading is not "well grounded in fact" or "warranted by existing law or a good faith argument for the extension, modification, or reversal of existing law." Note that the drafters of Rule 11 did not integrate its terminology with that of Rule 56, which requires summary judgment where there is "no genuine issue as to any material fact." It seems clear that any case that can pass factual muster under summary judgment meets the standard of Rule 11. But the converse is not necessarily true: A lawyer might have good grounds following investigation for asserting a factual allegation, but the opposing party's proffered evidence may so refute it that no genuine issue of fact remains. Consider in the materials that follow whether the standards governing summary judgments and those governing Rule 11 sanctions could be better integrated.

1. RULE 11 CERTIFICATION

UNIOIL, INC. v. E.F. HUTTON & CO.
United States Court of Appeals for the Ninth Circuit, 1986.
809 F.2d 548.

WALLACE, CIRCUIT JUDGE:

* * * Alioto appeals from the district court's order imposing sanctions against him for violations of rule 11, Fed.R.Civ.P., in the amount of $294,141.10. * * *

I

Unioil, Inc. (Unioil) is a company engaged in oil and gas exploration and production. During 1983, the price of Unioil's publicly traded stock soared from $1.25 per share early in the year to $13.75 per share in mid-December. At the beginning of February 1984, the stock was trading around $10 per share.

In early February 1984, Unioil's stock sharply declined. On February 7 the *Wall Street Journal* published an article reporting that several professional investors were selling Unioil stock "short" (i.e., were selling for future delivery stock that they did not yet own) in the belief that it was overvalued. The article stated that some of Unioil's public announcements had proven to be too optimistic. It also disclosed that Unioil's chairman of the board of directors, Richards, had twice previously been cited by the Securities and Exchange Commission for making false and misleading statements. In the days following publication of this article, Unioil stock further plummeted to $2.625 per share.

On March 21, 1984, Unioil, Richards, the Heck companies and Zelezny, filed a complaint in district court. The Heck companies owned large blocks of Unioil shares. Zelezny, a stockbroker, also owned Unioil shares. In addition, the named plaintiffs purported to be representatives of a class of all other Unioil shareholders. Alioto and Barton acted jointly as counsel for all plaintiffs. They sued several brokerage houses and individuals (the defendants), alleging a concerted scheme to sell Unioil stock short in violation of federal antitrust and securities laws, RICO, and various California laws. The complaint further alleged that the defendants had defamed Unioil and Richards.

The role of Zelezny in this purported class action litigation merits special focus. Since the Heck companies were major shareholders of Unioil and appeared to be closely aligned with Unioil management including Richards, Zelezny was the only named plaintiff with the appearance of independence from Unioil leadership. Zelezny had his first contact with this litigation when Barton, the referring co-counsel, approached him in February 1984 about the alleged market manipulation of Unioil stock. Barton, not Zelezny, first raised the subject of Zelezny's becoming a named plaintiff in the case.

Zelezny had not yet agreed to become a named plaintiff when Unioil announced in late February 1984 that it and a group of its shareholders had retained Alioto to institute a class action alleging market manipulation of Unioil stock. Alioto never spoke with Zelezny prior to filing the complaint, nor did he inquire whether Barton had investigated Zelezny's suitability as a named plaintiff in the purported class action. Alioto learned from Barton only that Zelezny had sold Unioil stock the day after the *Wall Street Journal* article appeared.

On May 3, 1984, the defendants commenced a deposition of Zelezny. The following day, Zelezny failed to appear for the continuation of his deposition. Instead, Barton announced that Zelezny had decided to withdraw as a named plaintiff and would not appear for further deposition questioning. The defendants then obtained a magistrate's order requiring Zelezny to complete his deposition. Zelezny appeared for three more days of testimony. Zelezny's deposition testimony was, in the judgment of the district court, "in many critical respects contrary to the allegations of the complaint": (1) whereas the complaint alleged that defendants' short selling and fraudulent misrepresentations drove the price of Unioil stock down and caused shareholders to sell at a loss, Zelezny testified that, aware that short selling was occurring, he purchased rather than sold Unioil shares in the belief that the price of the shares would eventually be driven up when the short sellers had to cover; (2) whereas the complaint alleged that plaintiffs sold Unioil shares at artificially depressed prices between December 1, 1983 and February 29, 1984, Zelezny testified that he thought that Unioil was selling at a fair price until February 7, 1984; and (3) whereas the complaint alleged that plaintiffs engaged in stock transactions based on false statements by defendants, Zelezny testified that he never bought or sold Unioil stock in reliance on anything said by any of the defendants.

On May 14, one day before Zelezny's deposition was to resume again, Barton announced that Zelezny would not appear, that neither plaintiffs nor their attorneys would appear for any further depositions, and that plaintiffs would voluntarily dismiss their complaint. On May 15, 1984, plaintiffs filed a notice purporting to dismiss their entire action without prejudice pursuant to Fed.R.Civ.P. 41(a)(1). One defendant objected to the notice on the ground that dismissal of an alleged class action requires court approval under rules 23(e) and 41(a)(1), Fed. R.Civ.P. Plaintiffs then moved pursuant to rule 41(a)(2), Fed.R.Civ.P., for a court order approving the dismissal of their action without prejudice. In support of their motion, plaintiffs cited three Unioil shareholder class actions that had been filed against Unioil and Richards in mid-April 1984. These actions named Unioil and Richards as defendants and alleged that mismanagement was the cause of the decline in the price of Unioil stock. Perceiving that Alioto and Barton would face a conflict of interest in representing both Unioil and the class of Unioil shareholders, plaintiffs stated their desire not to assert claims on behalf of the shareholder class.

In response to plaintiffs' rule 41(a)(2) motion, defendants asked the district court to require, as a condition of any dismissal without prejudice, that plaintiffs and their counsel pay defendants' attorneys' fees and costs incurred in the action. Pursuant to Fed.R.Civ.P. 11, defendants further sought sanctions of attorneys' fees and costs against plaintiffs' counsel on the grounds that plaintiffs' counsel undertook representation of plaintiffs with conflicting interests and failed to conduct a reasonable inquiry into the factual basis of the complaint. At this juncture, Unioil and Richards, through newly retained counsel, withdrew their motion for court approval of dismissal of their claims.

In November 1984, the district court entered an order granting the motion of the Heck companies and Zelezny for dismissal without prejudice of their individual and class claims *on condition that* these plaintiffs and/or their counsel—Alioto and Barton—"reimburse defendants for their costs and expenses, including attorneys' fees, reasonably incurred in defending against the class action claims." The district court imposed another condition that is not at issue on this appeal.

The district court also imposed rule 11 sanctions of attorneys' fees and costs against Alioto. The court held that Alioto's conduct had violated rule 11 in three respects: (1) Alioto did not conduct a reasonable investigation into the facts upon which the class allegations were made or into the potential conflict of interest that was inherent in undertaking representation of the class of Unioil shareholders in an action in which Unioil was one of the named plaintiffs; (2) Alioto tried to disengage from class discovery without cause and from the class action suit without court approval; (3) Alioto submitted declarations, in opposition to defendants' motions, that plainly did not comport with the requirements for statements under oath.

* * *

The district court referred the determination of the amount of attorneys' fees and costs on the rule 41(a)(2) condition and under the rule 11 sanctions to a magistrate. In an order entered in June 1985, the district court confirmed the magistrate's recommendation that plaintiffs' voluntary dismissal without prejudice of their class action claims be conditioned on the payment by the Heck companies, Zelezny, Alioto, or Barton of $165,774.84 to defendants. The court further confirmed that the rule 11 sanctions required Alioto to pay to defendants within thirty days $294,141.10, such amount to be reduced by any reimbursement received by defendants during that period under the rule 41(a)(2) condition.

* * *

* * * [A] plaintiff who knows or has reason to know that he may withdraw his motion for dismissal will be deemed to have consented to the conditions attached to the voluntary dismissal unless he withdraws his motion within a reasonable time. The Heck companies and Zelezny have not withdrawn their motions within a reasonable time, but have instead pursued an appeal. It follows that they must be deemed to have accepted the district court's conditional voluntary dismissal.

Therefore, the rule 41(a)(2) order from which they and counsel appeal is a final order.

That the order granting the conditional voluntary dismissal is final, however, does not alone mean that we have jurisdiction. To be appealable, an order must be adverse to the appealing party. As a general rule, a plaintiff may not appeal a voluntary dismissal because it is not an involuntary adverse judgment against him. Wickland Oil Terminals v. Asarco, Inc., 792 F.2d 887, 893 (9th Cir.1986); Seidman v. City of Beverly Hills, 785 F.2d 1447, 1448 (9th Cir.1986) (per curiam).

The circuits have provided a range of answers to the question whether this general rule applies to a conditional voluntary dismissal. The Sixth Circuit has held that conditional voluntary dismissals are not appealable, since the plaintiff has agreed to the order, even if with reluctance. Scholl v. Felmont Oil Corp., 327 F.2d 697, 700 (6th Cir. 1964); see also 9 C. Wright & A. Miller, Federal Practice & Procedure § 2376, at 247.

* * *

We spoke on the issue in Coursen v. A.H. Robins Co., 764 F.2d 1329 (9th Cir.) (Coursen), corrected, 773 F.2d 1049 (9th Cir.1985), where we held that a dismissal with prejudice was appealable, whether voluntary or involuntary. 764 F.2d at 1342–43, corrected, 773 F.2d at 1049.

* * *

* * * [W]e hold that a condition of costs and attorney's fees does not involve legal prejudice and therefore does not render a conditional voluntary dismissal adverse and appealable. In so holding, we in no way intend to suggest that we find the amount of costs and fees in this case clearly unreasonable. Nor do we foreclose the possibility that review of clearly unreasonable conditions could be obtained through a writ of mandamus.

Because the condition of costs and attorneys' fees that plaintiffs and counsel challenge does not involve legal prejudice, it is not adverse, and we have no jurisdiction over this appeal. We therefore dismiss the appeal of the rule 41(a)(2) order.

III

Alioto challenges on several grounds the district court's imposition of rule 11 sanctions against him. The jurisdictional defect that precludes our review of the district court's rule 41(a)(2) order does not apply to Alioto's rule 11 appeal, since the court's imposition of sanctions is plainly adverse to him. An order imposing sanctions solely upon counsel, a non-party to the underlying action, is immediately appealable as a final order. Optyl Eyewear Fashion International Corp. v. Style Companies, Ltd., 760 F.2d 1045, 1047 n. 1 (9th Cir.1985); Kordich v. Marine Clerks Association, 715 F.2d 1392, 1393 (9th Cir. 1983).

Rule 11, as amended in 1983, states in part:

> Every pleading, motion, and other paper of a party represented by an attorney shall be signed by at least one attorney of record in his individual name. . . . The signature of an attorney . . . constitutes a certificate by him that he has read the pleading, motion, or other paper; that to the best of his knowledge, information, and belief formed after reasonable inquiry it is well grounded in fact and is warranted by existing law or a good faith argument for the extension, modification, or reversal of existing law, and that it is not interposed for any improper purpose, such as to harass or to cause unnecessary delay or needless increase in the cost of litigation. . . . If a pleading, motion, or other paper is signed in violation of this rule, the court, upon motion or upon its own initiative, shall impose upon the person who signed it, a represented party, or both, an appropriate sanction, which may include an order to pay to the other party or parties the amount of the reasonable expenses incurred because of the filing of the pleading, motion, or other paper, including a reasonable attorney's fee.

Fed.R.Civ.P. 11. A violation of rule 11 need not be premised on a finding of subjective bad faith. Zaldivar v. City of Los Angeles, 780 F.2d 823, 829 (9th Cir.1986) (Zaldivar). Rather, an attorney violates rule 11 whenever he signs a pleading, motion, or other paper without having conducted a *reasonable inquiry* into whether his paper is frivolous, legally unreasonable, or without factual foundation. Id. at 830–31. An attorney also violates rule 11 whenever he signs a paper that is filed for a purpose that is improper under an objective standard. Id. at 831 & n. 9.

In *Zaldivar,* we set forth the following standards of review for orders imposing rule 11 sanctions:

> If the facts relied upon by the district court to establish a violation of the Rule are disputed on appeal, we review the factual determinations of the district court under a clearly erroneous standard. If the legal conclusion of the district court that the facts constitute a violation of the Rule is disputed, we review that legal conclusion *de novo.* Finally, if the appropriateness of the sanction imposed is challenged, we review the sanction under an abuse of discretion standard.

Id. at 828 (footnote omitted).

A.

The primary ground—indeed, according to Alioto's reply brief, the sole ground—upon which the district judge imposed rule 11 sanctions in her November 1984 order was that Alioto had failed to conduct a reasonable inquiry into the facts upon which the class allegations in the complaint were based and into the potential conflict of interest inherent in representing a class of Unioil shareholders while at the same time representing Unioil and Richards.

Whether Alioto's inquiry was reasonable must be determined in light of the circumstances in which he acted. See Fed.R.Civ.P. 11 advisory committee note ("The standard is one of reasonableness under the circumstances.") From factual findings of the district court that Alioto has not shown to be clearly erroneous, we conclude that the relevant circumstances include (1) that Alioto had reason to know that Zelezny was the only named plaintiff with the appearance of independence from Unioil and its management; (2) that Alioto had never previously worked with Barton and knew virtually nothing about him, his experience, or his inquiry into Zelezny's suitability as a class plaintiff; and (3) that the Alioto firm is, and represented itself as, experienced and specialized in complex business litigation. There was a substantial retainer paid to Alioto and there was ample time for investigation and, therefore, there were no severe constraints of time or money that impeded Alioto's inquiry. Finally, we consider it significant that the class allegations filed by Alioto threatened defendants with massive liability and foreseeably aroused a vigorous and costly defense. Just as the gravity of foreseeable injury is relevant to determining a party's standard of care in a negligence case, so should the cost of a foreseeable response by opposing parties be relevant to determining an attorney's standard of reasonable inquiry.

We now consider whether Alioto conducted a reasonable inquiry into the facts upon which the class allegations were based. Alioto does not dispute the district court's findings that he never spoke with Zelezny prior to filing the complaint and that he never asked of, or learned from, Barton information bearing on whether Zelezny was a sophisticated investor, whether Zelezny had relied upon any of the defendants' representations, and whether Zelezny would fairly and adequately represent the class. According to a finding of fact that we do not find clearly erroneous, Alioto knew only that Zelezny had sold Unioil stock the day after the *Wall Street Journal* article was published. We agree with the district court that, aware of this fact alone, Alioto had no reasonable basis for determining that Zelezny's "claims or defenses [were] typical of the claims or defenses of the class," Fed.R. Civ.P. 23(a)(3), or that Zelezny would "fairly and adequately protect the interests of the class," Fed.R.Civ.P. 23(a)(4).

Alioto offers three basic arguments to support his contention that he did not violate rule 11. First, he argues that his reliance on Barton satisfied the requirement of reasonable inquiry. We agree that reliance on forwarding co-counsel may in certain circumstances satisfy an attorney's duty of reasonable inquiry. See Fed.R.Civ.P. 11 advisory committee note. In relying on another lawyer, however, counsel must "acquire[ ] knowledge of facts sufficient to enable him to certify that the paper is well-grounded in fact." Schwarzer, Sanctions Under the New Federal Rule 11—A Closer Look, 104 F.R.D. 181, 187 (1985). An attorney who signs the pleading cannot simply delegate to forwarding co-counsel his duty of reasonable inquiry. Id.

*   *   *

* * * For similar reasons, we affirm the district court's conclusion that Alioto failed to conduct a reasonable inquiry into the potential conflict of interest inherent in representing a class of Unioil shareholders together with Unioil and Richards. As we just stated, the district court properly found that a reasonably competent business attorney should have recognized from the beginning the clear likelihood that Unioil shareholders would bring suit against Unioil management. We focus only on the duty Alioto had to conduct a reasonable inquiry into whether he should bring the class claims in the face of the potential conflict of interest. The record indicates that Alioto made no reasonable inquiry into the potential conflict of interest prior to filing the complaint. The district court properly determined that Alioto thereby violated rule 11. * * *

C.

Once a court finds that an attorney has violated rule 11, it *must* impose sanctions. *Zaldivar,* 780 F.2d at 831; accord Albright v. Upjohn Co., 788 F.2d 1217, 1221–22 (6th Cir.1986); Westmoreland v. CBS, Inc., 770 F.2d 1168, 1174–75 (D.C.Cir.1985) (Westmoreland). Rule 11 authorizes a court to impose "an appropriate sanction, which may include an order to pay to the other party or parties the amount of the reasonable expenses incurred because of the filing of the pleading, motion, or other paper, including a reasonable attorney's fee." Fed.R.Civ.P. 11. "The selection of the type of sanction to be imposed lies of course within the district court's sound exercise of discretion." *Westmoreland,* 770 F.2d at 1175.

In its November 1984 and January 1985 orders, the district court ordered sanctions against Alioto in the amount of reasonable expenses, including attorneys' fees, incurred because of the papers filed in violation of rule 11. This type of sanction plainly comports with rule 11, and we find no abuse of discretion.

Alioto further challenges the amount of the rule 11 sanctions—$294,141.10, to be offset by any reimbursement received by defendants within thirty days pursuant to the rule 41(a)(2) conditional voluntary dismissal. Assisted by a magistrate, the district court determined this amount after careful proceedings in which Alioto fully participated. Alioto's arguments on appeal amount to nothing more than a blanket charge that the amount of the sanctions is patently unreasonable. We agree that the expenses and attorneys' fees determined to have been incurred by the defendants were substantial. But we cannot find them patently unreasonable in light of the massive liability that the complaint filed by Alioto threatened to impose upon multiple defendants. * * *

NOTE ON "REASONABLENESS" IN PLEADINGS UNDER FEDERAL RULE 11

Federal Rule 11 requires a "reasonable inquiry" into the facts and a reasonable argument on the law. Unioil v. E.F. Hutton concerned the reasonableness of the factual inquiry. See also Albright v. Upjohn Co., 788 F.2d 1217

(6th Cir.1986) (5 of 8 defendants never identified as having manufactured drug taken by plaintiff).

As to the legal basis, the pleading must be based on "existing law or a good faith argument for the extension, modification, or reversal of existing law." F.R.C.P. 11. In the case of In re TCI Ltd., 769 F.2d 441 (7th Cir.1985), the court approved sanctions where the plaintiff's lawyer framed the complaint "without any effort to ascertain whether it had a basis in law." However, the distinction between a "good faith argument for the extension, modification, or reversal of existing law" and indifference to existing law is not self-evident, particularly if legal creativity is not to be stifled. Did the legal argument in Molasky v. Garfinkle, supra p. 61, meet the standard established under Rule 11?

There is a vast literature on Rule 11. See, e.g., Note, Plausible Pleadings: Developing Standards for Rule 11 Sanctions, 100 Harv.L.Rev. 630 (1987); Kassin, An Empirical Study of Rule 11 Sanctions (Federal Judicial Center, 1985); Parness, Groundless Pleadings and Certifying Attorneys in the Federal Courts, 1985 Utah L.Rev. 325; Grosberg, Illusion and Reality in Regulating Lawyer Performance: Rethinking Rule 11, 32 Vill.L.Rev. 575 (1987); Johnson and Cassady, Frivolous Lawsuits and Defensive Responses to Them—What Relief is Available?, 36 Ala.L.Rev. 927 (1985) (reviewing state law provisions); Nelken, Sanctions Under Amended Federal Rule 11—Some "Chilling" Problems in the Struggle Between Compensation and Punishment, 74 Geo.L.J. 1313 (1986).

Imposition of costs in federal courts is also authorized by statute where an attorney "multiplies the proceedings * * * unreasonably and vexatiously." 28 U.S.C.A. § 1927. Courts have generally found the conduct proscribed under this section to be the same as that sanctionable under Rule 11. See In re TCI Ltd., supra.

Another issue under Rule 11 concerns the procedure in imposing sanctions. Due process requires notice of the misconduct and opportunity to be heard in defense. An order imposing sanctions should state reasons and the manner in which the sanctions were calculated, such as itemization of hours, rates, and other relevant factors. Brown v. Federation of State Medical Boards, 830 F.2d 1429 (7th Cir.1987). However, although misconduct under Rule 11 resembles criminal contempt, the procedural safeguards of Rule 42(b) of the Federal Rules of Criminal Procedure apparently are not required. See Donaldson v. Clark, 819 F.2d 1551 (11th Cir.1987).

The lower courts are divided whether they have jurisdiction to sanction a plaintiff under Rule 11 when the suit is voluntarily dismissed under F.R.C.P. 41. In addition to *Unioil*, see Szabo Food Service, Inc. v. Canteen Corp., 823 F.2d 1073 (7th Cir.1987) (jurisdiction), with which compare Santiago v. Victim Services Agency, 753 F.2d 219 (2d Cir.1985) (no jurisdiction).

On state law counterparts of Rule 11, see, e.g., C.C.P. 128.5, applied in Lesser v. Huntington Harbor Corp., 173 Cal.App.3d 922, 219 Cal.Rptr. 562 (1985); Note, Sanctions Under California Code of Civil Procedure Section 128.5, 13 Pepperdine L.Rev. 1083 (1986); Note, Divining an Approach to Attorney Sanctions and Iowa Rule 80(a) Through an Analysis of Federal and State Civil Procedure Rules, 72 Iowa L.Rev. 701 (1987). For similar provisions concerning frivolous appeals, see, e.g., C.C.P. 907, interpreted in In re Marriage of Flaherty, 31 Cal.3d 637, 183 Cal.Rptr. 508, 646 P.2d 179 (1982).

Another possible remedy for groundless pleadings and actions is the tort of malicious prosecution, discussed in Further Note on Litigation Expenses, infra p. 274.

2. SUMMARY JUDGMENT

ADICKES v. S. H. KRESS & CO.
Supreme Court of the United States, 1970.
398 U.S. 144, 90 S.Ct. 1598, 26 L.Ed.2d 142.*

MR. JUSTICE HARLAN delivered the opinion of the Court.

Petitioner, Sandra Adickes, a white school teacher from New York, brought this suit in the United States District Court for the Southern District of New York against respondent S. H. Kress & Co. ("Kress") to recover damages under 42 U.S.C.A. § 1983 [1] for an alleged violation of her constitutional rights under the Equal Protection Clause of the Fourteenth Amendment. The suit arises out of Kress' refusal to serve lunch to Miss Adickes at its restaurant facilities in its Hattiesburg, Mississippi, store on August 14, 1964, and Miss Adickes' subsequent arrest upon her departure from the store by the Hattiesburg police on a charge of vagrancy. At the time of both the refusal to serve and the arrest, Miss Adickes was with six young people, all Negroes, who were her students in a Mississippi "Freedom School" where she was teaching that summer. Unlike Miss Adickes, the students were offered service, and were not arrested.

Petitioner's complaint had two counts,[2] each bottomed on § 1983 and each alleging that Kress had deprived her of the right under the Equal Protection Clause of the Fourteenth Amendment not to be discriminated against on the basis of race. The first count charged that Miss Adickes had been refused service by Kress because she was a "Caucasian in the company of Negroes." Petitioner sought, *inter alia,* to prove that the refusal to serve her was pursuant to a "custom of the

* Some of the Court's footnotes are omitted.

1. Rev.Stat. § 1979, 42 U.S.C.A. § 1983 provides:

"Every person who, under color of any statute, ordinance, regulation, custom, or usage, of any State or Territory, subjects, or causes to be subjected, any citizen of the United States or other person within the jurisdiction thereof to the deprivation of any rights, privileges, or immunities secured by the Constitution and laws, shall be liable to the party injured in an action at law, suit in equity, or other proper proceeding for redress."

2. The District Court denied petitioner's request to amend her complaint to include a third count seeking liquidated damages under §§ 1 and 2 of the Civil Rights Act of 1875, 18 Stat. 335. Although

in her certiorari petition, petitioner challenged this ruling, and asked this Court to revive this statute by overruling the holding in the Civil Rights Cases, 109 U.S. 3 (1883), examination of the record shows that petitioner never raised any issue concerning the 1875 statute before the Court of Appeals. Accordingly, the Second Circuit did not rule on these contentions. Where issues are neither raised before nor considered by the Court of Appeals, this Court will not ordinarily consider them. Lawn v. United States, 355 U.S. 339, 362–363, 78 S.Ct. 311, 324–325, 2 L.Ed.2d 321, n. 16 (1958); Husty v. United States, 282 U.S. 694, 701–702, 51 S.Ct. 240, 241–242, 75 L.Ed. 629 (1931); Duignan v. United States, 274 U.S. 195, 200, 47 S.Ct. 566, 568, 71 L.Ed. 996 (1927). We decline to do so here.

community to segregate the races in public eating places." However, in a pretrial decision, 252 F.Supp. 140 (1966), the District Court ruled that to recover under this count, Miss Adickes would have to prove that at the time she was refused service, there was a specific "custom . . . of refusing service to whites in the company of Negroes" and that this custom was "enforced by the State" under Mississippi's criminal trespass statute.[3] Because petitioner was unable to prove at the trial that there were other instances in Hattiesburg of a white person having been refused service while in the company of Negroes, the District Court directed a verdict in favor of respondent. A divided panel of the Court of Appeals affirmed on this ground, also holding that § 1983 "requires that the discriminatory custom or usage be proved to exist in the locale where the discrimination took place, and in the State generally," and that petitioner's "proof on both points was deficient," 409 F.2d 121, 124 (1968).

The second count of her complaint, alleging that both the refusal of service and her subsequent arrest were the product of a conspiracy between Kress and the Hattiesburg police, was dismissed before trial on a motion for summary judgment. The District Court ruled that petitioner had "failed to allege any facts from which a conspiracy might be inferred." 252 F.Supp., at 144. This determination was unanimously affirmed by the Court of Appeals, 409 F.2d, at 126–127.

Miss Adickes, in seeking review here, claims that the District Court erred both in directing a verdict on the substantive count, and in granting summary judgment on the conspiracy count. Last Term we granted certiorari, 394 U.S. 1011, 89 S.Ct. 1635, 23 L.Ed.2d 38 (1969), and we now reverse and remand for further proceedings on each of the two counts.

As explained in Part I, because the respondent failed to show the absence of any disputed material fact, we think the District Court erred in granting summary judgment. With respect to the substantive count, for reasons explained in Part II, we think petitioner will have made out a claim under § 1983 for violation of her equal protection rights if she proves that she was refused service by Kress because of a state-enforced custom requiring racial segregation in Hattiesburg restaurants. We think the courts below erred (1) in assuming that the only proof relevant to showing that a custom was state-enforced related to the Mississippi criminal trespass statute; (2) in defining the relevant state-enforced custom as requiring proof of a practice both in Hattiesburg and throughout Mississippi, of refusing to serve white persons in the company of Negroes rather than simply proof of state-enforced segregation of the races in Hattiesburg restaurants.

---

3. The statute, Miss.Code Ann. § 2046.5 (1956), *inter alia*, gives the owners, managers, or employees of business establish- ments the right to choose customers by refusing service.

I

Briefly stated, the conspiracy count of petitioner's complaint made the following allegations: While serving as a volunteer teacher at a "Freedom School" for Negro children in Hattiesburg, Mississippi, petitioner went with six of her students to the Hattiesburg Public Library at about noon on August 14, 1964. The librarian refused to allow the Negro students to use the library, and asked them to leave. Because they did not leave, the librarian called the Hattiesburg chief of police who told petitioner and her students that the library was closed, and ordered them to leave. From the library, petitioner and the students proceeded to respondent's store where they wished to eat lunch. According to the complaint, after the group sat down to eat, a policeman came into the store "and observed [Miss Adickes] in the company of the Negro students." A waitress then came to the booth where petitioner was sitting, took the orders of the Negro students, but refused to serve petitioner because she was a white person "in the company of Negroes." The complaint goes on to allege that after this refusal of service, petitioner and her students left the Kress store. When the group reached the sidewalk outside the store, "the Officer of the Law who had previously entered [the] store" arrested petitioner on a groundless charge of vagrancy and took her into custody.

On the basis of these underlying facts petitioner alleged that Kress and the Hattiesburg police had conspired (1) "to deprive [her] of her right to enjoy equal treatment and service in a place of public accommodation"; and (2) to cause her arrest "on the false charge of vagrancy."

A. CONSPIRACIES BETWEEN PUBLIC OFFICIALS AND PRIVATE PERSONS—GOVERNING PRINCIPLES

The terms of § 1983 make plain two elements that are necessary for recovery. First, the plaintiff must prove that the defendant has deprived him of a right secured by the "Constitution and laws" of the United States. Second, the plaintiff must show that the defendant deprived him of this constitutional right "under color of any statute, ordinance, regulation, custom, or usage, of any State or Territory." This second element requires that the plaintiff show that the defendant acted "under color of law." [4]

As noted earlier we read both counts of petitioner's complaint to allege discrimination based on race in violation of petitioner's equal protection rights.[5] Few principles of law are more firmly stitched into

4. See, e.g., Monroe v. Pape, 365 U.S. 167, 184, 187, 81 S.Ct. 473, 482, 484, 5 L.Ed. 2d 492 (1961); United States v. Price, 383 U.S. 787, 793, 794, 86 S.Ct. 1152, 1156, 1157, 16 L.Ed.2d 267 (1966).

5. The first count of petitioner's complaint alleges that Kress' refusal to serve

petitioner "deprived [her] of the privilege of equal enjoyment of a place of public accommodation by reason of her association with Negroes and [she] was *thereby discriminated against because of race in violation of the Constitution* of the United States and of Title 42 United States Code,

our constitutional fabric than the proposition that a State must not discriminate against a person because of his race or the race of his companions, or in any way act to compel or encourage racial segregation.[6] Although this is a lawsuit against a private party, not the State or one of its officials, our cases make clear that petitioner will have made out a violation of her Fourteenth Amendment rights and will be entitled to relief under § 1983 if she can prove that a Kress employee, in the course of employment, and a Hattiesburg policeman somehow reached an understanding to deny Miss Adickes service in the Kress store, or to cause her subsequent arrest because she was a white person in the company of Negroes.

The involvement of a state official in such a conspiracy plainly provides the state action essential to show a direct violation of petitioner's Fourteenth Amendment equal protection rights, whether or not the

Section 1983." (App. 4). (Emphasis added.) The conspiracy count alleges, *inter alia*, that Kress and the Hattiesburg police "conspired together to deprive plaintiff of her right to enjoy equal treatment and service in a place of public accommodation."

The language of the complaint might, if read generously, support the contention that petitioner was alleging a violation of Title II, the Public Accommodations provisions, of the 1964 Civil Rights Act, 78 Stat. 243, 42 U.S.C.A. § 2000a et seq. It is clear, and respondent seemingly concedes, that its refusal to serve petitioner was a violation of § 201 of the 1964 Act, 42 U.S.C.A. § 2000a. It is very doubtful, however, that Kress' violation of Miss Adickes' rights under the Public Accommodations Title could properly serve as a basis for recovery under § 1983. Congress deliberately provided no damages remedy in the Public Accommodations Act itself, and § 207(b) provides that the injunction remedy of § 206 was the "exclusive means of enforcing the rights based on this title." Moreover, the legislative history makes quite plain that Congress did not intend that violations of the Public Accommodations Title be enforced through the damages provisions of § 1983. See 110 Cong.Rec. 9767 (remark of floor manager that the language of 207(b) "is necessary because otherwise it . . . would result . . . in civil liability for damages under 42 U.S.C.A. § 1983"); see also 110 Cong.Rec. 7384, 7405.

In United States v. Johnson, 390 U.S. 563, 88 S.Ct. 1231, 20 L.Ed.2d 132 (1968), the Court held that violations of § 203(b) of the Public Accommodations Title could serve as the basis for criminal prosecution under 18 U.S.C.A. § 241 (another civil rights statute) against "outsiders," having

no relation to owners and proprietors of places of public accommodations, notwithstanding the "exclusive" remedy provision of § 207(b). It is doubtful whether the *Johnson* reasoning would allow recovery under § 1983 for Kress' alleged violation of § 201, and indeed the petitioner does not otherwise contend. The Court, in *Johnson*, in holding that the § 207(b) limitation did not apply to violations of § 203, stated: "[T]he exclusive-remedy provision of § 207(b) was inserted *only to make clear that the substantive rights to public accommodation defined in § 201 and § 202 are to be enforced exclusively by injunction.*" 390 U.S., at 567, 88 S.Ct., at 1234.

In any event, we think it clear that there can be recovery under § 1983 for conduct that violates the Fourteenth Amendment, even though the same conduct might also violate the Public Accommodations Title which itself neither provides a damages remedy nor can be the basis of a § 1983 action. Section 207(b) of the Public Accommodations Title expressly provides that nothing in that title "shall preclude any individual . . . from asserting any right based on any other Federal or State law not inconsistent with this title . . . or from pursuing any remedy, civil or criminal, which may be available for the vindication or enforcement of such right." Therefore, quite apart from whether § 207 precludes enforcement of one's rights under the Public Accommodations Title through a damages action under 42 U.S.C.A. § 1983, we think it evident that enforcement of one's constitutional rights under § 1983 is not "inconsistent" with the Public Accommodations Act.

6. E.g., Brown v. Board of Education, 347 U.S. 483, 74 S.Ct. 686, 98 L.Ed. 873 (1954); cf. Barrows v. Jackson, 346 U.S. 249, 73 S.Ct. 1031, 97 L.Ed. 1586 (1953).

actions of the police were officially authorized, or lawful; Monroe v. Pape, 365 U.S. 167, 81 S.Ct. 473, 5 L.Ed.2d 492 (1961); see United States v. Classic, 313 U.S. 299, 326, 61 S.Ct. 1031, 1043, 85 L.Ed. 1368 (1941); Screws v. United States, 325 U.S. 91, 107–111, 65 S.Ct. 1031, 1038–1040, 89 L.Ed. 1495 (1945); Williams v. United States, 341 U.S. 97, 99–100, 71 S.Ct. 576, 578–579, 95 L.Ed. 774 (1951). Moreover, a private party involved in such a conspiracy, even though not an official of the State, can be liable under § 1983. "Private persons, jointly engaged with state officials in the prohibited action, are acting 'under color' of law for purposes of the statute. To act 'under color' of law does not require that the accused be an officer of the State. It is enough that he is a willful participant in joint acitivty with the State or its agents," United States v. Price, 383 U.S. 787, 794, 86 S.Ct. 1152, 1157 (1966).[7]

B. SUMMARY JUDGMENT

We now proceed to consider whether the District Court erred in granting summary judgment on the conspiracy count. In granting respondent's motion, the District Court simply stated that there was "no evidence in the complaint or in the affidavits and other papers from which a 'reasonably-minded person' might draw an inference of conspiracy," 252 F.Supp., at 144, aff'd, 409 F.2d, at 126–127. Our own scrutiny of the factual allegations of petitioner's complaint, as well as the material found in the affidavits and depositions presented by Kress to the District Court, however, convinces us that summary judgment was improper here, for we think respondent failed to carry its burden of showing the absence of any genuine issue of fact. Before explaining why this is so, it is useful to state the factual arguments, made by the parties concerning summary judgment, and the reasoning of the courts below.

In moving for summary judgment, Kress argued that "uncontested facts" established that no conspiracy existed between any Kress employee and the police. To support this assertion, Kress pointed first to the statements in the deposition of the store manager (Mr. Powell) that (a) he had not communicated with the police,[8] and that (b) he had, by a prearranged tacit signal,[9] ordered the food counter supervisor to see

---

7. Although Price concerned a criminal prosecution involving 18 U.S.C.A. § 242, we have previously held that "under color of law" means the same thing for § 1983. Monroe v. Pape, supra, 365 U.S., at 185, 81 S.Ct., at 483 (majority opinion), 212, 81 S.Ct. at 497 (opinion of Frankfurter, J.); United States v. Price, supra, 383 U.S., at 794, 86 S.Ct., at 1157 n. 7.

8. In his deposition, Powell admitted knowing Hugh Herring, chief of police of Hattiesburg, and said that he had seen and talked to him on two occasions in 1964 prior to the incident with Miss Adickes. (App. 123–126). When asked how often the arresting officer, Ralph Hillman, came into

the store, Powell stated that he didn't know precisely but "Maybe every day." However, Powell said that on August 14 he didn't recall seeing any policemen either inside or outside the store (App. 136), and he denied (1) that he had called the police, (2) that he had agreed with any public official to deny Miss Adickes the use of the library, (3) that he had agreed with any public official to refuse Miss Adickes service in the Kress store on the day in question, or (4) that he had asked any public official to have Miss Adickes arrested. App. 154–155.

9. The signal, according to Powell, was a nod of his head. Powell claimed that at

that Miss Adickes was refused service only because he was fearful of a riot in the store by customers angered at seeing a "mixed group" of whites and blacks eating together.[10] Kress also relied on affidavits from the Hattiesburg chief of police,[11] and the two arresting officers,[12] to the effect that store manager Powell had not requested that petition-

a meeting about a month earlier with Miss Baggett, the food counter supervisor, he "told her not to serve the white person in the group if I . . . shook my head no. But, if I didn't give her any sign, to go ahead and serve anybody." App. 135.

Powell stated that he had prearranged this tacit signal with Miss Baggett because "there was quite a lot of violence . . . in Hattiesburg" directed towards whites "with colored people, in what you call a mixed group." App. 131.

10. Powell described the circumstances of his refusal as follows:

"On this particular day, just shortly after 12 o'clock, I estimate there was 75 to 100 people in the store and the lunch counter was pretty—was pretty well to capacity there, full and I was going up towards the front of the store in one of the aisles, and looking towards the front of the store, and there was a group of colored girls, and a white woman who came into the north door, which was next to the lunch counter.

"And the one thing that really stopped me and called my attention to this group, was the fact that they were dressed alike. They all had on, what looked like a light blue denim skirt. And the best I can remember is that they were—they were almost identical, all of them. And they came into the door, and people coming in stopped to look, and they went on to the booths. And there happened to be two empty there. And one group of them and the white woman sat down in one, and the rest of them sat in the second group.

"And, almost immediately there—I mean this, it didn't take just a few seconds from the time they came into the door to sit down, but, already the people began to mill around the store and started coming over towards the lunch counter. And, by that time I was up close to the candy counter, and I had a wide open view there. And the people had real sour looks on their faces, nobody was joking, or being corny, or carrying on. They looked like a frightened mob. They really did. I have seen mobs before. I was in Korea during the riots in 1954 and 1955. And I know what they are. And this actually got me.

"I looked out towards the front, and we have what they call see-through windows. There is no backs to them. You can look out of the store right into the street. And the north window, it looks right into the lunch counter. 25 or 30 people were standing there looking in, and across the street even, in a jewelry store, people were standing there, and it looked really bad to me. It looked like one person could have yelled 'let's get them,' which has happened before, and cause this group to turn into a mob. And, so, quickly I just made up my mind to avoid the riot, and protect the people that were in the store, and my employees, as far as the people in the mob who were going to get hurt themselves. I just knew that something was going to break loose there." App. 133–134.

11. The affidavit of the chief of police, who it appears was not present at the arrest, states in relevant part:

"Mr. Powell had made no request of me to arrest Miss Sandra Adickes or any other person, in fact, I did not know Mr. Powell personally until the day of this statement. [But cf. Powell's statement at his deposition, n. 8, supra.] Mr. Powell and I had not discussed the arrest of this person until the day of this statement and we had never previously discussed her in any way." (App. 107.)

12. The affidavits of Sergeant Boone and Officer Hillman each state, in identical language:

"I was contacted on this date by Mr. John H. Williams, Jr., a representative of Genesco, owners of S. H. Kress and Company, who requested that I make a statement concerning alleged conspiracy in connection with the aforesaid arrest.

"This arrest was made on the public streets of Hattiesburg, Mississippi, and was an officers discretion arrest. I had not consulted with Mr. G. T. Powell, Manager of S. H. Kress and Company in Hattiesburg, and did not know his name until this date. No one at the Kress store asked that the arrest be made and I did not consult with anyone prior to the arrest." (App. 110, 112.)

er be arrested. Finally, Kress pointed to the statements in petitioner's own deposition that she had no knowledge of any communication between any Kress employee and any member of the Hattiesburg police, and was relying on circumstantial evidence to support her contention that there was an arrangement between Kress and the police.

Petitioner, in opposing summary judgment, pointed out that respondent had failed in its moving papers to dispute the allegation in petitioner's complaint, a statement at her deposition,[13] and an unsworn statement by a Kress employee,[14] all to the effect that there was a policeman in the store at the time of the refusal to serve her, and that this was the policeman who subsequently arrested her. Petitioner argued that although she had no knowledge of an agreement between Kress and the police, the sequence of events created a substantial enough possibility of a conspiracy to allow her to proceed to trial, especially given the fact that the noncircumstantial evidence of the conspiracy could only come from adverse witnesses. Further, she submitted an affidavit specifically disputing the manager's assertion that the situation in the store at the time of the refusal was "explosive," thus creating an issue of fact as to what his motives might have been in ordering the refusal of service.

We think that on the basis of this record, it was error to grant summary judgment. As the moving party, respondent had the burden of showing the absence of a genuine issue as to any material fact, and for these purposes the material it lodged must be viewed in the light most favorable to the opposing party.[15] Respondent here did not carry its burden because of its failure to foreclose the possibility that there

13. When asked whether she saw any policeman in the store up to the time of the refusal of service, Miss Adickes answered: "My back was to the door, but one of my students saw a policeman come in." (App. 75.) She went on to identify the student as "Carolyn." At the trial, Carolyn Moncure, one of the students who was with petitioner, testified that "about five minutes" after the group had sat down and while they were still waiting for service, she saw a policeman come in the store. She stated: "[H]e came in the store, my face was facing the front of the store, and he came in the store and he passed, and he stopped right at the end of our booth, and he stood up and he looked around and he smiled, and he went to the back of the store, he came right back and he left out." (App. 302.) This testimony was corroborated by that of Dianne Moncure, Carolyn's sister, who was also part of the group. She testified that while the group was waiting for service, a policeman entered the store, stood "for awhile" looking at the group, and then "walked to the back of the store." (App. 291.)

14. During discovery, respondent gave to petitioner an unsworn statement by Miss Irene Sullivan, a check-out girl. In this statement Miss Sullivan said that she had seen Patrolman Hillman come into the store "[s]hortly after 12:00 noon," while petitioner's group was in the store. She said that he had traded a "hello greeting" with her, and then walked past her check-out counter toward the back of the store "out of [her] line of vision." She went on: "A few minutes later Patrolman Hillman left our store by the northerly front door just slightly ahead of a group composed of several Negroes accompanied by a white woman. As Hillman stepped onto the sidewalk outside our store the police car pulled across the street and into an alley that is alongside our store. The police car stopped and Patrolman Hillman escorted the white woman away from the Negroes and into the police car." (App. 178.)

15. See, e.g., United States v. Diebold, 369 U.S. 654, 655, 82 S.Ct. 993, 994, 8 L.Ed. 2d 176 (1962); 6 V. Moore, Federal Practice ¶ 56.15[3] (2d ed. 1966).

was a policeman in the Kress store while petitioner was awaiting service, and that this policeman reached an understanding with some Kress employee that petitioner not be served.

It is true that Mr. Powell, the store manager, claimed in his deposition that he had not seen or communicated with a policeman prior to his tacit signal to Miss Baggett, the supervisor of the food counter. But respondent did not submit any affidavits from Miss Baggett,[16] or from Miss Freeman,[17] the waitress who actually refused petitioner service, either of whom might well have seen and communicated with a policeman in the store. Further, we find it particularly noteworthy that the two officers involved in the arrest each failed in his affidavit to foreclose the possibility (1) that he was in the store while petitioner was there; and (2) that, upon seeing petitioner with Negroes, he communicated his disapproval to a Kress employee, thereby influencing the decision not to serve petitioner.

Given these unexplained gaps in the materials submitted by respondent, we conclude that respondent failed to fulfill its initial burden of demonstrating what is a critical element in this aspect of the case— that there was no policeman in the store. If a policeman were present, we think it would be open to a jury, in light of the sequence that followed, to infer from the circumstances that the policeman and a Kress employee had a "meeting of the minds" and thus reached an understanding that petitioner should be refused service. Because "[o]n summary judgment the inferences to be drawn from the underlying facts contained in [the moving party's] materials must be viewed in the light most favorable to the party opposing the motion," United States v. Diebold, Inc., 369 U.S. 654, 655, 82 S.Ct. 993, 994, (1962), we think respondent's failure to show there was no policeman in the store requires reversal.

Pointing to Rule 56(e), as amended in 1963,[18] respondent argues that it was incumbent on petitioner to come forward with an affidavit

16. In a supplemental brief filed in this Court respondent lodged a copy of an unsworn statement by Miss Baggett denying any contact with the police on the day in question. Apart from the fact that the statement is unsworn, see Fed.Rules Civ. Proc. 56(e), the statement itself is not in the record of the proceedings below and therefore could not have been considered by the trial court. Manifestly, it cannot be properly considered by us in the disposition of the case.

During discovery, petitioner attempted to depose Miss Baggett. However, Kress successfully resisted this by convincing the District Court that Miss Baggett was not a "managing agent," and "was without power to make managerial decisions."

17. The record does contain an unsworn statement by Miss Freeman in which she states that she "did not contact the police

or ask anyone else to contact the police *to make the arrest which subsequently occurred.*" (App. 177.) (Emphasis added.) This statement, being unsworn, does not meet the requirements of Fed.Rules Civ. Proc. 56(e), and was not relied on by respondent in moving for summary judgment. Moreover, it does not foreclose the possibility that Miss Freeman was influenced in her refusal to serve Miss Adickes by some contact with a policeman present in the store.

18. The amendment added the following to Rule 56(e):

"When a motion for summary judgment is made and supported as provided in this rule, an adverse party may not rest upon the mere allegations or denials of his pleading, but his response, by affidavits or as otherwise provided in this rule, must set forth specific facts show-

properly asserting the presence of the policeman in the store, if she were to rely on that fact to avoid summary judgment. Respondent notes in this regard that none of the materials upon which petitioner relied met the requirements of Rule 56(e).[19]

This argument does not withstand scrutiny, however, for both the commentary on and background of the 1963 amendment conclusively show that it was not intended to modify the burden of the moving party under Rule 56(c) to show initially the absence of a genuine issue concerning any material fact.[20] The Advisory Committee note on the amendment states that the changes were not designed to "affect the ordinary standards applicable to the summary judgment." And, in a comment directed specifically to a contention like respondent's, the Committee stated that "[w]here the evidentiary matter in support of the motion does not establish the absence of a genuine issue, summary judgment must be denied *even if no opposing evidentiary matter is presented.*" [21] Because respondent did not meet its initial burden of establishing the absence of a policeman in the store, petitioner here was not required to come forward with suitable opposing affidavits.[22]

If respondent had met its initial burden by, for example, submitting affidavits from the policemen denying their presence in the store at the time in question, Rule 56(e) would then have required petitioner to have done more than simply rely on the contrary allegation in her complaint. To have avoided conceding this fact for purposes of summary judgment, petitioner would have had to come forward with either (1) the affidavit of someone who saw the policeman in the store or (2) an affidavit under Rule 56(f) explaining why at that time it was impractical to do so. Even though not essential here to defeat respondent's motion, the submission of such an affidavit would have been the

ing that there is a genuine issue for trial. If he does not so respond, summary judgment, if appropriate, shall be entered against him."

19. Petitioner's statement at her deposition, see n. 13, supra, was, of course, hearsay; and the statement of Miss Sullivan, see n. 14, supra, was unsworn. And, the rule specifies that reliance on allegations in the complaint is not sufficient. See Fed.Rule Civ.Proc. 56(e).

20. The purpose of the 1963 amendment was to overturn a line of cases, primarily in the Third Circuit, that had held that a party opposing summary judgment could successfully create a dispute as to a material fact asserted in an affidavit by the moving party simply by relying on a contrary allegation in a well-pleaded complaint. E.g., Frederick Hart & Co. v. Recordgraph Corp., 169 F.2d 580 (1948); United States ex rel. Kolton v. Halpern, 260 F.2d 590 (1958). See Advisory Committee Note on 1963 Amendment to subdivision (e) of Rule 56.

21. Ibid. (emphasis added).

22. In First National Bank of Ariz. v. Cities Service, 391 U.S. 253, 88 S.Ct. 1575, 20 L.Ed.2d 569 (1968), the petitioner claimed that the lower courts had misapplied Rule 56(e) to shift the burden imposed by Rule 56(c). In rejecting this contention we said: "Essentially all that the lower courts held in this case was that Rule 56(e) placed upon [petitioner] the burden of producing evidence of the conspiracy he alleged only *after respondent . . . conclusively showed that the facts upon which he relied to support his allegation were not susceptible of the interpretation which he sought to give them.*" Id., at 289, 88 S.Ct., at 1593. (Emphasis added.) In this case, on the other hand, we hold that respondent failed to show conclusively that a fact alleged by petitioner was "not susceptible" of an interpretation that might give rise to an inference of conspiracy.

preferable course for petitioner's counsel to have followed. As one commentator has said:

> "It has always been perilous for the opposing party neither to proffer any countering evidentiary materials nor file a 56(f) affidavit. And the peril rightly continues [after the amendment to Rule 56(e)]. Yet the party moving for summary judgment has the burden to show that he is entitled to judgment under established principles; and if he does not discharge that burden then he is not entitled to judgment. No defense to an insufficient showing is required." 6 J. Moore, Federal Practice ¶ 56.22[2], pp. 2824–2825 (2d ed. 1966).

II

There remains to be discussed the substantive count of petitioner's complaint, and the showing necessary for petitioner to prove that respondent refused her service "under color of any . . . custom, or usage, of [the] State" in violation of her rights under the Equal Protection Clause of the Fourteenth Amendment.

* * *

The judgment of the Court of Appeals is reversed, and the case remanded to that court for further proceedings consistent with this opinion.†

CELOTEX CORP. v. CATRETT
Supreme Court of the United States, 1986.
477 U.S. 317, 106 S.Ct. 2548, 91 L.Ed.2d 265.*

JUSTICE REHNQUIST delivered the opinion of the Court.

The United States District Court for the District of Columbia granted the motion of petitioner Celotex Corporation for summary judgment against respondent Catrett because the latter was unable to produce evidence in support of her allegation in her wrongful death complaint that the decedent had been exposed to petitioner's asbestos products. A divided panel of the Court of Appeals for the District of Columbia Circuit reversed, however, holding that petitioner's failure to support its motion with evidence tending to *negate* such exposure precluded the entry of summary judgment in its favor. 244 U.S.App. D.C. 160, 756 F.2d 181 (1985). * * *

Respondent commenced this lawsuit in September 1980, alleging that the death in 1979 of her husband, Louis H. Catrett, resulted from his exposure to products containing asbestos manufactured or distributed by 15 named corporations. Respondent's complaint sounded in negligence, breach of warranty, and strict liability. Two of the defen-

---

† The separate opinions of Black, J., concurring in the judgment, Douglas, J., dissenting in part, and Brennan, J., concurring in part and dissenting in part, are omitted. Marshall, J., did not participate.

* Some of the Court's footnotes are omitted.

dants filed motions challenging the District Court's *in personam* jurisdiction, and the remaining 13, including petitioner, filed motions for summary judgment. Petitioner's motion, which was first filed in September 1981, argued that summary judgment was proper because respondent had "failed to produce evidence that any [Celotex] product . . . was the proximate cause of the injuries alleged within the jurisdictional limits of [the District] Court." In particular, petitioner noted that respondent had failed to identify, in answering interrogatories specifically requesting such information, any witnesses who could testify about the decedent's exposure to petitioner's asbestos products. In response to petitioner's summary judgment motion, respondent then produced three documents which she claimed "demonstrate that there is a genuine material factual dispute" as to whether the decedent had ever been exposed to petitioner's asbestos products. The three documents included a transcript of a deposition of the decedent, a letter from an official of one of the decedent's former employers whom petitioner planned to call as a trial witness, and a letter from an insurance company to respondent's attorney, all tending to establish that the decedent had been exposed to petitioner's asbestos products in Chicago during 1970–1971. Petitioner, in turn, argued that the three documents were inadmissible hearsay and thus could not be considered in opposition to the summary judgment motion.

In July 1982, almost two years after the commencement of the lawsuit, the District Court granted all of the motions filed by the various defendants. The court explained that it was granting petitioner's summary judgment motion because "there [was] no showing that the plaintiff was exposed to the defendant Celotex's product in the District of Columbia or elsewhere within the statutory period." Joint App. 217. Respondent appealed only the grant of summary judgment in favor of petitioner, and a divided panel of the District of Columbia Circuit reversed. The majority of the Court of Appeals held that petitioner's summary judgment motion was rendered "fatally defective" by the fact that petitioner "made no effort to adduce *any* evidence, in the form of affidavits or otherwise, to support its motion." 244 U.S. App.D.C., at 163, 756 F.2d, at 184 (emphasis in original). According to the majority, Rule 56(e) of the Federal Rules of Civil Procedure,[3] and this Court's decision in Adickes v. S.H. Kress & Co., 398 U.S. 144, 159, 90 S.Ct. 1598, 1609, 26 L.Ed.2d 142 (1970), establish that "the party

3. Rule 56(e) provides:

"Supporting and opposing affidavits shall be made on personal knowledge, shall set forth such facts as would be admissible in evidence, and shall show affirmatively that the affiant is competent to testify to the matters stated therein. Sworn or certified copies of all papers or parts thereof referred to in an affidavit shall be attached thereto or served therewith. The court may permit affidavits to be supplemented or opposed by depositions, answers to interrogatories, or further affidavits. When a motion for summary judgment is made and supported as provided in this rule, an adverse party may not rest upon the mere allegations or denials of his pleading, but his response, by affidavits or as otherwise provided in this rule, must set forth specific facts showing that there is a genuine issue for trial. If he does not so respond, summary judgment, if appropriate, shall be entered against him."

opposing the motion for summary judgment bears the burden of responding *only after* the moving party has met its burden of coming forward with proof of the absence of any genuine issues of material fact." 244 U.S.App.D.C., at 163, 756 F.2d, at 184 (emphasis in original; footnote omitted). The majority therefore declined to consider petitioner's argument that none of the evidence produced by respondent in opposition to the motion for summary judgment would have been admissible at trial. Ibid. The dissenting judge argued that "[t]he majority errs in supposing that a party seeking summary judgment must always make an affirmative evidentiary showing, even in cases where there is not a triable, factual dispute." Id., at 167, 756 F.2d, at 188 (Bork, J., dissenting). According to the dissenting judge, the majority's decision "undermines the traditional authority of trial judges to grant summary judgment in meritless cases." Id., at 166, 756 F.2d, at 187.

We think that the position taken by the majority of the Court of Appeals is inconsistent with the standard for summary judgment set forth in Rule 56(c) of the Federal Rules of Civil Procedure.[4] Under Rule 56(c), summary judgment is proper "if the pleadings, depositions, answers to interrogatories, and admissions on file, together with the affidavits, if any, show that there is no genuine issue as to any material fact and that the moving party is entitled to a judgment as a matter of law." In our view, the plain language of Rule 56(c) mandates the entry of summary judgment, after adequate time for discovery and upon motion, against a party who fails to make a showing sufficient to establish the existence of an element essential to that party's case, and on which that party will bear the burden of proof at trial. In such a situation, there can be "no genuine issue as to any material fact," since a complete failure of proof concerning an essential element of the nonmoving party's case necessarily renders all other facts immaterial. The moving party is "entitled to judgment as a matter of law" because the nonmoving party has failed to make a sufficient showing on an essential element of her case with respect to which she has the burden of proof. "[T]h[e] standard [for granting summary judgment] mirrors the standard for a directed verdict under Federal Rule of Civil Procedure 50(a). . . ." Anderson v. Liberty Lobby, Inc., 477 U.S. 242, 250, 106 S.Ct. 2505, 2511, 91 L.Ed.2d 202 (1986).

Of course, a party seeking summary judgment always bears the initial responsibility of informing the district court of the basis for its motion, and identifying those portions of "the pleadings, depositions,

---

4. Rule 56(c) provides:

"The motion shall be served at least 10 days before the time fixed for the hearing. The adverse party prior to the day of hearing may serve opposing affidavits. The judgment sought shall be rendered forthwith if the pleadings, depositions, answers to interrogatories, and admissions on file, together with the affidavits, if any, show that there is no genuine issue as to any material fact and that the moving party is entitled to a judgment as a matter of law. A summary judgment, interlocutory in character, may be rendered on the issue of liability alone although there is a genuine issue as to the amount of damages."

answers to interrogatories, and admissions on file, together with the affidavits, if any," which it believes demonstrate the absence of a genuine issue of material fact. But unlike the Court of Appeals, we find no express or implied requirement in Rule 56 that the moving party support its motion with affidavits or other similar materials *negating* the opponent's claim. On the contrary, Rule 56(c), which refers to "the affidavits, *if any* " (emphasis added), suggests the absence of such a requirement. And if there were any doubt about the meaning of Rule 56(c) in this regard, such doubt is clearly removed by Rules 56(a) and (b), which provide that claimants and defendants, respectively, may move for summary judgment *"with or without supporting affidavits* " (emphasis added). The import of these subsections is that, regardless of whether the moving party accompanies its summary judgment motion with affidavits, the motion may, and should, be granted so long as whatever is before the district court demonstrates that the standard for the entry of summary judgment, as set forth in Rule 56(c), is satisfied. One of the principal purposes of the summary judgment rule is to isolate and dispose of factually unsupported claims or defenses, and we think it should be interpreted in a way that allows it to accomplish this purpose.[5]

Respondent argues, however, that Rule 56(e), by its terms, places on the nonmoving party the burden of coming forward with rebuttal affidavits, or other specified kinds of materials, only in response to a motion for summary judgment "made and supported as provided in this rule." According to respondent's argument, since petitioner did not "support" its motion with affidavits, summary judgment was improper in this case. But as we have already explained, a motion for summary judgment may be made pursuant to Rule 56 "with or without supporting affidavits." In cases like the instant one, where the nonmoving party will bear the burden of proof at trial on a dispositive issue, a summary judgment motion may properly be made in reliance solely on the "pleadings, depositions, answers to interrogatories, and admissions on file." Such a motion, whether or not accompanied by affidavits, will be "made and supported as provided in this rule," and Rule 56(e) therefore requires the nonmoving party to go beyond the pleadings and by her own affidavits, or by the "depositions, answers to interrogatories, and admissions on file," designate "specific facts showing that there is a genuine issue for trial."

We do not mean that the nonmoving party must produce evidence in a form that would be admissible at trial in order to avoid summary judgment. Obviously, Rule 56 does not require the nonmoving party to depose her own witnesses. Rule 56(e) permits a proper summary judgment motion to be opposed by any of the kinds of evidentiary materials listed in Rule 56(c), except the mere pleadings themselves,

---

5. See Louis, Federal Summary Judgment Doctrine: A Critical Analysis, 83 Yale L.J. 745, 752 (1974); Currie, Thoughts on Directed Verdicts and Summary Judgments, 45 U.Chi.L.Rev. 72, 79 (1977).

and it is from this list that one would normally expect the nonmoving party to make the showing to which we have referred.

The Court of Appeals in this case felt itself constrained, however, by language in our decision in Adickes v. S.H. Kress & Co., 398 U.S. 144, 90 S.Ct. 1598, 26 L.Ed.2d 142 (1970). There we held that summary judgment had been improperly entered in favor of the defendant restaurant in an action brought under 42 U.S.C. § 1983. In the course of its opinion, the *Adickes* Court said that "both the commentary on and the background of the 1963 Amendment conclusively show that it was not intended to modify the burden of the moving party . . . to show initially the absence of a genuine issue concerning any material fact." Id., at 159, 90 S.Ct., at 1609. We think that this statement is accurate in a literal sense, since we fully agree with the *Adickes* Court that the 1963 Amendment to Rule 56(e) was not designed to modify the burden of making the showing generally required by Rule 56(c). It also appears to us that, on the basis of the showing before the Court in *Adickes,* the motion for summary judgment in that case should have been denied. But we do not think the *Adickes* language quoted above should be construed to mean that the burden is on the party moving for summary judgment to produce evidence showing the absence of a genuine issue of material fact, even with respect to an issue on which the nonmoving party bears the burden of proof. Instead, as we have explained, the burden on the moving party may be discharged by "showing"—that is, pointing out to the District Court—that there is an absence of evidence to support the nonmoving party's case.

The last two sentences of Rule 56(e) were added, as this Court indicated in *Adickes,* to disapprove a line of cases allowing a party opposing summary judgment to resist a properly made motion by reference only to its pleadings. While the *Adickes* Court was undoubtedly correct in concluding that these two sentences were not intended to *reduce* the burden of the moving party, it is also obvious that they were not adopted to *add to* that burden. Yet that is exactly the result which the reasoning of the Court of Appeals would produce; in effect, an amendment to Rule 56(e) designed to *facilitate* the granting of motions for summary judgment would be interpreted to make it *more difficult* to grant such motions. Nothing in the two sentences themselves requires this result, for the reasons we have previously indicated, and we now put to rest any inference that they do so.

Our conclusion is bolstered by the fact that district courts are widely acknowledged to possess the power to enter summary judgments *sua sponte,* so long as the losing party was on notice that she had to come forward with all of her evidence. See 244 U.S.App.D.C., at 167–168, 756 F.2d, at 189 (Bork, J., dissenting); 10A C. Wright, A. Miller & M. Kane, Federal Practice and Procedure § 2720, pp. 28–29 (1983). It would surely defy common sense to hold that the District Court could have entered summary judgment *sua sponte* in favor of petitioner in the instant case, but that petitioner's filing of a motion requesting such a disposition precluded the District Court from ordering it.

Respondent commenced this action in September 1980, and petitioner's motion was filed in September 1981. The parties had conducted discovery, and no serious claim can be made that respondent was in any sense "railroaded" by a premature motion for summary judgment. Any potential problem with such premature motions can be adequately dealt with under Rule 56(f),[6] which allows a summary judgment motion to be denied, or the hearing on the motion to be continued, if the nonmoving party has not had an opportunity to make full discovery.

In this Court, respondent's brief and oral argument have been devoted as much to the proposition that an adequate showing of exposure to petitioner's asbestos products was made as to the proposition that no such showing should have been required. But the Court of Appeals declined to address either the adequacy of the showing made by respondent in opposition to petitioner's motion for summary judgment, or the question whether such a showing, if reduced to admissible evidence, would be sufficient to carry respondent's burden of proof at trial. We think the Court of Appeals with its superior knowledge of local law is better suited than we are to make these determinations in the first instance.

The Federal Rules of Civil Procedure have for more than 50 years authorized motions for summary judgment upon proper showings of the lack of a genuine, triable issue of material fact. Summary judgment procedure is properly regarded not as a disfavored procedural shortcut, but rather as an integral part of the Federal Rules as a whole, which are designed "to secure the just, speedy and inexpensive determination of every action." Fed.Rule Civ.Proc. 1; see Schwarzer, Summary Judgment Under the Federal Rules: Defining Genuine Issues of Material Fact, 99 F.R.D. 465, 467 (1984). Before the shift to "notice pleading" accomplished by the Federal Rules, motions to dismiss a complaint or to strike a defense were the principal tools by which factually insufficient claims or defenses could be isolated and prevented from going to trial with the attendant unwarranted consumption of public and private resources. But with the advent of "notice pleading," the motion to dismiss seldom fulfills this function any more, and its place has been taken by the motion for summary judgment. Rule 56 must be construed with due regard not only for the rights of persons asserting claims and defenses that are adequately based in fact to have those claims and defenses tried to a jury, but also for the rights of persons opposing such claims and defenses to demonstrate in the manner provided by the Rule, prior to trial, that the claims and defenses have no factual basis.

6. Rule 56(f) provides:

"Should it appear from the affidavits of a party opposing the motion that he cannot for reasons stated present by affidavit facts essential to justify his opposition, the court may refuse the application for judgment or may order a continuance to permit affidavits to be obtained or depositions to be taken or discovery to be had or may make such other order as is just."

The judgment of the Court of Appeals is accordingly reversed, and the case is remanded for further proceedings consistent with this opinion.

It is so ordered.

JUSTICE WHITE, concurring in the Court's opinion and judgment.*

JUSTICE BRENNAN, with whom THE CHIEF JUSTICE and JUSTICE BLACK-MUN join, dissenting.

* * * [C]ourts must routinely decide summary judgment motions, and the Court's opinion will very likely create confusion. For this reason, even if I agreed with the Court's result, I would have written separately to explain more clearly the law in this area. However, because I believe that Celotex did not meet its burden of production under Federal Rule of Civil Procedure 56, I respectfully dissent from the Court's judgment.

I

Summary judgment is appropriate where the Court is satisfied "that there is no genuine issue as to any material fact and that the moving party is entitled to a judgment as a matter of law." Fed.Rule Civ.Proc. 56(c). The burden of establishing the nonexistence of a "genuine issue" is on the party moving for summary judgment. 10A C. Wright, A. Miller & M. Kane, Federal Practice and Procedure § 2727, p. 121 (2d ed. 1983) (hereinafter Wright) (citing cases); 6 J. Moore, W. Taggart & J. Wicker, Moore's Federal Practice ¶ 56.15[3] (2d ed. 1985) (hereinafter Moore) (citing cases). * * * This burden has two distinct components: an initial burden of production, which shifts to the non-moving party if satisfied by the moving party; and an ultimate burden of persuasion, which always remains on the moving party. See 10A Wright, Miller & Kane § 2727. The court need not decide whether the moving party has satisfied its ultimate burden of persuasion [2] unless and until the Court finds that the moving party has discharged its initial burden of production. Adickes v. S.H. Kress & Co., 398 U.S. 144,

---

* Justice White's opinion is omitted.

2. The burden of persuasion imposed on a moving party by Rule 56 is a stringent one. 6 Moore ¶ 56.15[3], pp. 56–466; 10A Wright, Miller & Kane § 2727, p. 124. Summary judgment should not be granted unless it is clear that a trial is unnecessary, Anderson v. Liberty Lobby, Inc., 477 U.S. 242, 255, 106 S.Ct. 2505, 2513–14, 91 L.Ed.2d 202 (1986), and any doubt as to the existence of a genuine issue for trial should be resolved against the moving party, Adickes v. S.H. Kress & Co., 398 U.S. 144, 158–159, 90 S.Ct. 1598, 1608–09, 26 L.Ed.2d 142 (1970). In determining whether a moving party has met its burden of persuasion, the court is obliged to take account of the entire setting of the case and must consider all papers of record as well as any materials prepared for the motion. 10A Wright, Miller & Kane § 2721, p. 44; see, e.g., Stepanischen v. Merchants Despatch Transportation Corp., 722 F.2d 922, 930 (CA1 1983); Higgenbotham v. Ochsner Foundation Hosp., 607 F.2d 653, 656 (CA5 1979). As explained by the Court of Appeals for the Third Circuit in In re Japanese Electronic Products Antitrust Litigation, 723 F.2d 238 (1983), rev'd on other grounds sub nom. Matsushita Electric Industrial Co. v. Zenith Radio Corp., 475 U.S. 1002, 105 S.Ct. 1863, 85 L.Ed.2d 157 (1986), "[i]f . . . there is any evidence in the record from any source from which a reasonable inference in the [nonmoving party's] favor may be drawn, the moving party simply cannot obtain a summary judgment. . . ." 723 F.2d, at 258.

157–161, 90 S.Ct. 1598, 1608–10, 26 L.Ed.2d 142 (1970); 1963 Advisory Committee's Notes on Fed.Rule Civ.Proc. 56(e), 28 U.S.C.App., p. 626.

The burden of production imposed by Rule 56 requires the moving party to make a prima facie showing that it is entitled to summary judgment. 10A Wright, Miller & Kane § 2727. The manner in which this showing can be made depends upon which party will bear the burden of persuasion on the challenged claim at trial. If the *moving* party will bear the burden of persuasion at trial, that party must support its motion with credible evidence—using any of the materials specified in Rule 56(c)—that would entitle it to a directed verdict if not controverted at trial. Ibid. Such an affirmative showing shifts the burden of production to the party opposing the motion and requires that party either to produce evidentiary materials that demonstrate the existence of a "genuine issue" for trial or to submit an affidavit requesting additional time for discovery. Ibid.; Fed.Rule Civ.Proc. 56(e), (f).

If the burden of persuasion at trial would be on the *nonmoving* party, the party moving for summary judgment may satisfy Rule 56's burden of production in either of two ways. First, the moving party may submit affirmative evidence that negates an essential element of the nonmoving party's claim. Second, the moving party may demonstrate to the Court that the nonmoving party's evidence is insufficient to establish an essential element of the nonmoving party's claim. See 10A Wright, Miller & Kane § 2727, pp. 130–131; Louis, Federal Summary Judgment Doctrine: A Critical Analysis, 83 Yale L.J. 745, 750 (1974) (hereinafter Louis). If the nonmoving party cannot muster sufficient evidence to make out its claim, a trial would be useless and the moving party is entitled to summary judgment as a matter of law. Anderson v. Liberty Lobby, Inc., 477 U.S. 242, 249, 106 S.Ct. 2505, 2511, 91 L.Ed.2d 202 (1986).

Where the moving party adopts this second option and seeks summary judgment on the ground that the nonmoving party—who will bear the burden of persuasion at trial—has no evidence, the mechanics of discharging Rule 56's burden of production are somewhat trickier. Plainly, a conclusory assertion that the nonmoving party has no evidence is insufficient. * * * Such a "burden" of production is no burden at all and would simply permit summary judgment procedure to be converted into a tool for harassment. See Louis 750–751. Rather, as the Court confirms, a party who moves for summary judgment on the ground that the nonmoving party has no evidence must affirmatively show the absence of evidence in the record. * * * This may require the moving party to depose the nonmoving party's witnesses or to establish the inadequacy of documentary evidence. If there is literally no evidence in the record, the moving party may demonstrate this by reviewing for the court the admissions, interrogatories and other exchanges between the parties that are in the record. Either way, however, the moving party must affirmatively demonstrate that there is no evidence in the record to support a judgment for the nonmoving party.

If the moving party has not fully discharged this initial burden of production, its motion for summary judgment must be denied, and the Court need not consider whether the moving party has met its ultimate burden of persuasion. Accordingly, the nonmoving party may defeat a motion for summary judgment that asserts that the nonmoving party has no evidence by calling the Court's attention to supporting evidence already in the record that was overlooked or ignored by the moving party. In that event, the moving party must respond by making an attempt to demonstrate the inadequacy of this evidence, for it is only by attacking all the record evidence allegedly supporting the nonmoving party that a party seeking summary judgment satisfies Rule 56's burden of production.[3] Thus, if the record disclosed that the moving party had overlooked a witness who would provide relevant testimony for the nonmoving party at trial, the Court could not find that the moving party had discharged its initial burden of production unless the moving party sought to demonstrate the inadequacy of this witness' testimony. Absent such a demonstration, summary judgment would have to be denied on the ground that the moving party had failed to meet its burden of production under Rule 56.

*   *   *

The opinion of the Court in *Adickes* has sometimes been read to hold that summary judgment was inappropriate because the respondent had not submitted affirmative evidence to negate the possibility that there was a policeman in the store. See Brief for Respondent 20, n. 30 (citing cases). The Court of Appeals apparently read *Adickes* this way and therefore required Celotex to submit evidence establishing that plaintiff's decedent had not been exposed to Celotex asbestos. I agree with the Court that this reading of *Adickes* was erroneous and that Celotex could seek summary judgment on the ground that plaintiff could not prove exposure to Celotex asbestos at trial. However, Celotex was still required to satisfy its initial burden of production.

II

I do not read the Court's opinion to say anything inconsistent with or different than the preceding discussion. My disagreement with the

---

3. Once the moving party has attacked whatever record evidence—if any—the nonmoving party purports to rely upon, the burden of production shifts to the nonmoving party, who must either (1) rehabilitate the evidence attacked in the moving party's papers, (2) produce additional evidence showing the existence of a genuine issue for trial as provided in Rule 56(e), or (3) submit an affidavit explaining why further discovery is necessary as provided in Rule 56(f). See 10A Wright, Miller & Kane § 2727, pp. 138–143. Summary judgment should be granted if the nonmoving party fails to respond in one or more of these ways, or if, after the nonmoving party responds, the court determines that the moving party has met its ultimate burden of persuading the court that there is no genuine issue of material fact for trial. See, e.g., First National Bank of Arizona v. Cities Services Co., 391 U.S. 253, 289, 88 S.Ct. 1575, 1592, 20 L.Ed.2d 569 (1968).

Court concerns the application of these principles to the facts of this case.

Defendant Celotex sought summary judgment on the ground that plaintiff had "failed to produce" any evidence that her decedent had ever been exposed to Celotex asbestos. App. 170. Celotex supported this motion with a 2–page "Statement of Material Facts as to Which There is No Genuine Issue" and a 3–page "Memorandum of Points and Authorities" which asserted that the plaintiff had failed to identify any evidence in responding to two sets of interrogatories propounded by Celotex and that therefore the record was "totally devoid" of evidence to support plaintiff's claim. See id., at 171–176.

Approximately three months earlier, Celotex had filed an essentially identical motion. Plaintiff responded to this earlier motion by producing three pieces of evidence which she claimed "[a]t the very least . . . demonstrate that there is a genuine factual dispute for trial," id., at 143: (1) a letter from an insurance representative of another defendant describing asbestos products to which plaintiff's decedent had been exposed, id., at 160; (2) a letter from T.R. Hoff, a former supervisor of decedent, describing asbestos products to which decedent had been exposed, id., at 162; and (3) a copy of decedent's deposition from earlier workmen's compensation proceedings, id., at 164. Plaintiff also apparently indicated at that time that she intended to call Mr. Hoff as a witness at trial. Tr. of Oral Arg. 6–7, 27–29.

Celotex subsequently withdrew its first motion for summary judgment. See App. 167.[5] However, as a result of this motion, when Celotex filed its second summary judgment motion, the record *did* contain evidence—including at least one witness—supporting plaintiff's claim. Indeed, counsel for Celotex admitted to this Court at oral argument that Celotex was aware of this evidence and of plaintiff's intention to call Mr. Hoff as a witness at trial when the second summary judgment motion was filed. Tr. of Oral Arg. 5–7. Moreover, plaintiff's response to Celotex' second motion pointed to this evidence— noting that it had already been provided to counsel for Celotex in connection with the first motion—and argued that Celotex had failed to "meet its burden of proving that there is no genuine factual dispute for trial." App. 188.

On these facts, there is simply no question that Celotex failed to discharge its initial burden of production. Having chosen to base its motion on the argument that there was no evidence in the record to support plaintiff's claim, Celotex was not free to ignore supporting evidence that the record clearly contained. Rather, Celotex was required, as an initial matter, to attack the adequacy of this evidence. Celotex' failure to fulfill this simple requirement constituted a failure

5. Celotex apparently withdrew this motion because, contrary to the assertion made in the first summary judgment motion, its second set of interrogatories had not been served on the plaintiff.

to discharge its initial burden of production under Rule 56, and thereby rendered summary judgment improper.[6]

* * *

Justice Stevens, dissenting.*

ANDERSON v. LIBERTY LOBBY, INC.

Supreme Court of the United States, 1986.
477 U.S. 242, 106 S.Ct. 2505, 91 L.Ed.2d 202. †

Justice White delivered the opinion of the Court.

In New York Times Co. v. Sullivan, 376 U.S. 254, 279–280, 84 S.Ct. 710, 725–726, 11 L.Ed.2d 686 (1964), we held that, in a libel suit brought by a public official, the First Amendment requires the plaintiff to show that in publishing the defamatory statement the defendant acted with actual malice—"with knowledge that it was false or with reckless disregard of whether it was false or not." We held further that such actual malice must be shown with "convincing clarity." Id., at 285–286, 84 S.Ct., at 728–729. See also Gertz v. Robert Welch, Inc., 418 U.S. 323, 342, 94 S.Ct. 2997, 3008, 41 L.Ed.2d 789 (1974). These *New York Times* requirements we have since extended to libel suits brought by public figures as well. See, e.g., Curtis Publishing Co. v. Butts, 388 U.S. 130, 87 S.Ct. 1975, 18 L.Ed.2d 1094 (1967).

This case presents the question whether the clear-and-convincing-evidence requirement must be considered by a court ruling on a motion for summary judgment under Rule 56 of the Federal Rules of Civil Procedure in a case to which *New York Times* applies. * * *

I

Respondent Liberty Lobby, Inc., is a not-for-profit corporation and self-described "citizens' lobby." Respondent Willis Carto is its founder and treasurer. In October 1981, The Investigator magazine published two articles: "The Private World of Willis Carto" and "Yockey: Profile of an American Hitler." These articles were introduced by a third, shorter article entitled "America's Neo–Nazi Underground: Did *Mein Kampf* Spawn Yockey's *Imperium,* a Book Revived by Carto's Liberty Lobby?" These articles portrayed the respondents as neo-Nazi, anti-Semitic, racist, and fascist.

The respondents filed this diversity libel action in the United States District Court for the District of Columbia, alleging that some 28 statements and 2 illustrations in the three articles were false and

---

6. If the plaintiff had answered Celotex' second set of interrogatories with the evidence in her response to the first summary judgment motion, and Celotex had ignored those interrogatories and based its second summary judgment motion on the first set of interrogatories only, Celotex obviously could not claim to have discharged its Rule 56 burden of production. This result should not be different simply because the evidence plaintiff relied upon to support her claim was acquired by Celotex other than in plaintiff's answers to interrogatories.

* Justice Stevens' opinion is omitted.

† Some of the Court's footnotes are omitted.

derogatory. Named as defendants in the action were petitioner Jack Anderson, the publisher of The Investigator, petitioner Bill Adkins, president and chief executive officer of the Investigator Publishing Co., and petitioner Investigator Publishing Co. itself.

Following discovery, the petitioners moved for summary judgment pursuant to Rule 56. In their motion, the petitioners asserted that because the respondents are public figures they were required to prove their case under the standards set forth in *New York Times*. The petitioners also asserted that summary judgment was proper because actual malice was absent as a matter of law. In support of this latter assertion, the petitioners submitted the affidavit of Charles Bermant, an employee of the petitioners and the author of the two longer articles. In this affidavit, Bermant stated that he had spent a substantial amount of time researching and writing the articles and that his facts were obtained from a wide variety of sources. He also stated that he had at all times believed and still believed that the facts contained in the articles were truthful and accurate. Attached to this affidavit was an appendix in which Bermant detailed the sources for each of the statements alleged by the respondents to be libelous.

The respondents opposed the motion for summary judgment, asserting that there were numerous inaccuracies in the articles and claiming that an issue of actual malice was presented by virtue of the fact that in preparing the articles Bermant had relied on several sources that the respondents asserted were patently unreliable. Generally, the respondents charged that the petitioners had failed adequately to verify their information before publishing. The respondents also presented evidence that William McGaw, an editor of The Investigator, had told petitioner Adkins before publication that the articles were "terrible" and "ridiculous."

In ruling on the motion for summary judgment, the District Court first held that the respondents were limited-purpose public figures and that *New York Times* therefore applied. The District Court then held that Bermant's thorough investigation and research and his reliance on numerous sources precluded a finding of actual malice. Thus, the District Court granted the motion and entered judgment in favor of the petitioners.

On appeal, the Court of Appeals affirmed as to 21 and reversed as to 9 of the allegedly defamatory statements. Although it noted that the respondents did not challenge the District Court's ruling that they were limited-purpose public figures and that they were thus required to prove their case under *New York Times,* the Court of Appeals nevertheless held that for the purposes of summary judgment the requirement that actual malice be proved by clear and convincing evidence, rather than by a preponderance of the evidence, was irrelevant: To defeat summary judgment the respondents did not have to show that a jury could find actual malice with "convincing clarity." The court based this conclusion on a perception that to impose the greater evidentiary burden at summary judgment "would change the threshold summary judgment inquiry from a search for a minimum of facts supporting the plaintiff's case to an evaluation of the weight of those facts and (it would seem) of the weight of at least the defendant's uncontroverted facts as well." 241 U.S.App.D.C., at 253, 746 F.2d, at 1570. The court then held, with respect to nine of the statements, that summary judgment had been improperly granted because "a jury could reasonably conclude that the . . . allegations were defamatory, false, and made with actual malice." Id., at 260, 746 F.2d at 1577.

II

A

Our inquiry is whether the Court of Appeals erred in holding that the heightened evidentiary requirements that apply to proof of actual malice in this *New York Times* case need not be considered for the purposes of a motion for summary judgment. Rule 56(c) of the Federal Rules of Civil Procedure provides that summary judgment "shall be rendered forthwith if the pleadings, depositions, answers to interrogatories, and admissions on file, together with the affidavits, if any, show that there is no genuine issue as to any material fact and that the moving party is entitled to a judgment as a matter of law." By its very terms, this standard provides that the mere existence of *some* alleged factual dispute between the parties will not defeat an otherwise properly supported motion for summary judgment; the requirement is that there be no *genuine* issue of *material* fact.

As to materiality, the substantive law will identify which facts are material. * * * Rule 56(e) provides that, when a properly supported motion for summary judgment is made,[4] the adverse party "must set forth specific facts showing that there is a genuine issue for trial." [5] And, as we noted above, Rule 56(c) provides that the trial judge shall then grant summary judgment if there is no genuine issue as to any material fact and if the moving party is entitled to judgment as a matter of law. There is no requirement that the trial judge make findings of fact.[6] The inquiry performed is the threshold inquiry of determining whether there is the need for a trial—whether, in other words, there are any genuine factual issues that properly can be resolved only by a finder of fact because they may reasonably be resolved in favor of either party.

4. Our analysis here does not address the question of the initial burden of production of evidence placed by Rule 56 on the party moving for summary judgment. See Celotex Corp. v. Catrett, 477 U.S. 317, 106 S.Ct. 2548, 91 L.Ed.2d 265 (1986). Respondents have not raised this issue here, and for the purposes of our discussion we assume that the moving party has met initially the requisite evidentiary burden.

5. This requirement in turn is qualified by Rule 56(f)'s provision that summary judgment be refused where the nonmoving party has not had the opportunity to discover information that is essential to his opposition. In our analysis here, we assume that both parties have had ample opportunity for discovery.

6. In many cases, however, findings are extremely helpful to a reviewing court.

The petitioners suggest, and we agree, that this standard mirrors the standard for a directed verdict under Federal Rule of Civil Procedure 50(a), which is that the trial judge must direct a verdict if, under the governing law, there can be but one reasonable conclusion as to the verdict. Brady v. Southern R. Co., 320 U.S. 476, 479–480, 64 S.Ct. 232, 234, 88 L.Ed. 239 (1943). If reasonable minds could differ as to the import of the evidence, however, a verdict should not be directed. Wilkerson v. McCarthy, 336 U.S. 53, 62, 69 S.Ct. 413, 417, 93 L.Ed. 497 (1949). As the Court long ago said in Improvement Co. v. Munson, 14 Wall. 442, 448, 20 L.Ed. 867 (1872), and has several times repeated:

> "Nor are judges any longer required to submit a question to a jury merely because some evidence has been introduced by the party having the burden of proof, unless the evidence be of such a character that it would warrant the jury in finding a verdict in favor of that party. Formerly it was held that if there was what is called a *scintilla* of evidence in support of a case the judge was bound to leave it to the jury, but recent decisions of high authority have established a more reasonable rule, that in every case, before the evidence is left to the jury, there is a preliminary question for the judge, not whether there is literally no evidence, but whether there is any upon which a jury could properly proceed to find a verdict for the party producing it, upon whom the *onus* of proof is imposed." (Footnotes omitted.)

* * *

The Court has said that summary judgment should be granted where the evidence is such that it "would require a directed verdict for the moving party." Sartor v. Arkansas Gas Corp., 321 U.S. 620, 624, 64 S.Ct. 724, 727, 88 L.Ed. 967 (1944). And we have noted that the "genuine issue" summary judgment standard is "very close" to the "reasonable jury" directed verdict standard: "The primary difference between the two motions is procedural; summary judgment motions are usually made before trial and decided on documentary evidence, while directed verdict motions are made at trial and decided on the evidence that has been admitted." Bill Johnson's Restaurants, Inc. v. NLRB, 461 U.S. 731, 745, n. 11, 103 S.Ct. 2161, 2171, n. 11, 76 L.Ed.2d 277 (1983). In essence, though, the inquiry under each is the same: whether the evidence presents a sufficient disagreement to require submission to a jury or whether it is so one-sided that one party must prevail as a matter of law.

B

Progressing to the specific issue in this case, we are convinced that the inquiry involved in a ruling on a motion for summary judgment or for a directed verdict necessarily implicates the substantive evidentiary standard of proof that would apply at the trial on the merits. If the defendant in a run-of-the-mill civil case moves for summary judgment or for a directed verdict based on the lack of proof of a material fact, the judge must ask himself not whether he thinks the evidence unmistakably favors one side or the other but whether a fair-minded jury could return a verdict for the plaintiff on the evidence presented. The mere existence of a scintilla of evidence in support of the plaintiff's position will be insufficient; there must be evidence on which the jury could reasonably find for the plaintiff. The judge's inquiry, therefore, unavoidably asks whether reasonable jurors could find by a preponderance of the evidence that the plaintiff is entitled to a verdict—"whether there is [evidence] upon which a jury can properly proceed to find a verdict for the party producing it, upon whom the *onus* of proof is imposed." *Munson,* supra, 14 Wall., at 448.

In terms of the nature of the inquiry, this is no different from the consideration of a motion for acquittal in a criminal case, where the beyond-a-reasonable-doubt standard applies and where the trial judge asks whether a reasonable jury could find guilt beyond a reasonable doubt. See Jackson v. Virginia, 443 U.S. 307, 318–319, 99 S.Ct. 2781, 2788–2789, 61 L.Ed.2d 560 (1979). Similarly, where the First Amendment mandates a "clear and convincing" standard, the trial judge in disposing of a directed verdict motion should consider whether a reasonable factfinder could conclude, for example, that the plaintiff had shown actual malice with convincing clarity.

* * *

Just as the "convincing clarity" requirement is relevant in ruling on a motion for directed verdict, it is relevant in ruling on a motion for summary judgment. When determining if a genuine factual issue as to actual malice exists in a libel suit brought by a public figure, a trial judge must bear in mind the actual quantum and quality of proof necessary to support liability under *New York Times.* For example, there is no genuine issue if the evidence presented in the opposing affidavits is of insufficient caliber or quantity to allow a rational finder of fact to find actual malice by clear and convincing evidence.

Thus, in ruling on a motion for summary judgment, the judge must view the evidence presented through the prism of the substantive evidentiary burden. This conclusion is mandated by the nature of this determination. The question here is whether a jury could reasonably find *either* that the plaintiff proved his case by the quality and quantity of evidence required by the governing law *or* that he did not. Whether a jury could reasonably find for either party, however, cannot be defined except by the criteria governing what evidence would enable the jury to find for either the plaintiff or the defendant: It makes no sense to say that a jury could reasonably find for either party without some benchmark as to what standards govern its deliberations and within what boundaries its ultimate decision must fall, and these standards and boundaries are in fact provided by the applicable evidentiary standards.

Our holding that the clear-and-convincing standard of proof should be taken into account in ruling on summary judgment motions does not denigrate the role of the jury. It by no means authorizes trial on affidavits. Credibility determinations, the weighing of the evidence, and the drawing of legitimate inferences from the facts are jury functions, not those of a judge, whether he is ruling on a motion for summary judgment or for a directed verdict. The evidence of the non-movant is to be believed, and all justifiable inferences are to be drawn in his favor. *Adickes,* 398 U.S., at 158–159, 90 S.Ct., at 1608–1609. Neither do we suggest that the trial courts should act other than with caution in granting summary judgment or that the trial court may not deny summary judgment in a case where there is reason to believe that the better course would be to proceed to a full trial. Kennedy v. Silas Mason Co., 334 U.S. 249, 68 S.Ct. 1031, 92 L.Ed. 1347 (1948).

* * *

* * * Because the Court of Appeals did not apply the correct standard in reviewing the District Court's grant of summary judgment, we vacate its decision and remand the case for further proceedings consistent with this opinion.

It is so ordered.

JUSTICE BRENNAN, dissenting.

* * *

In my view, if a plaintiff presents evidence which either directly or by permissible inference (and these inferences are a product of the substantive law of the underlying claim) supports all of the elements he needs to prove in order to prevail on his legal claim, the plaintiff has made out a *prima facie* case and a defendant's motion for summary judgment must fail regardless of the burden of proof that the plaintiff must meet. In other words, whether evidence is "clear and convincing," or proves a point by a mere preponderance, is for the factfinder to determine. As I read the case law, this is how it has been, and because of my concern that today's decision may erode the constitutionally enshrined role of the jury, and also undermine the usefulness of summary judgment procedure, this is how I believe it should remain.

JUSTICE REHNQUIST, with whom THE CHIEF JUSTICE joins, dissenting.

The Court, apparently moved by concerns for intellectual tidiness, mistakenly decides that the "clear and convincing evidence" standard governing finders of fact in libel cases must be applied by trial courts in deciding a motion for summary judgment in such a case. The Court refers to this as a "substantive standard," but I think it is actually a procedural requirement engrafted onto Rule 56, contrary to our statement in Calder v. Jones, 465 U.S. 783, 104 S.Ct. 1482, 79 L.Ed.2d 804 (1984), that

> "[w]e have already declined in other contexts to grant special procedural protections to defendants in libel and defamation actions in addition to the constitutional protections embodied in the substantive laws." Id., at 790–791, 104 S.Ct., at 1487–1488.

The Court, I believe, makes an even greater mistake in failing to apply its newly announced rule to the facts of this case. Instead of thus illustrating how the rule works, it contents itself with abstractions and paraphrases of abstractions, so that its opinion sounds much like a treatise about cooking by someone who has never cooked before and has no intention of starting now.

There is a large class of cases in which the higher standard imposed by the Court today would seem to have no effect at all. Suppose, for example, on motion for summary judgment in a hypothetical libel case, the plaintiff concedes that his only proof of malice is the testimony of witness A. Witness A testifies at his deposition that the reporter who wrote the story in question told him that she, the reporter, had done absolutely no checking on the story and had real doubts about whether or not it was correct as to the plaintiff. The defendant's examination of witness A brings out that he has a prior conviction for perjury.

May the Court grant the defendant's motion for summary judgment on the ground that the plaintiff has failed to produce sufficient proof of malice? Surely not, if the Court means what it says, when it states: "Credibility determinations . . . are jury functions, not those of a judge, whether he is ruling on a motion for summary judgment or for a directed verdict. The evidence of the nonmovant is to be believed, and all justifiable inferences are to be drawn in his favor." * * *

The case proceeds to trial, and at the close of the plaintiff's evidence the defendant moves for a directed verdict on the ground that the plaintiff has failed to produce sufficient evidence of malice. The only evidence of malice produced by the plaintiff is the same testimony of witness A, who is duly impeached by the defendant for the prior perjury conviction. In addition, the trial judge has now had an opportunity to observe the demeanor of witness A, and has noticed that he fidgets when answering critical questions, his eyes shift from the floor to the ceiling, and he manifests all other indicia traditionally attributed to perjurers.

May the trial court at this stage grant a directed verdict? Again, surely not; we are still dealing with "credibility determinations."

The defendant now puts on its testimony, and produces three witnesses who were present at the time when witness A alleges that the reporter said she had not checked the story and had grave doubts about its accuracy as to plaintiff. Witness A concedes that these three people were present at the meeting, and that the statement of the reporter took place in the presence of all these witnesses. Each witness categorically denies that the reporter made the claimed statement to witness A.

May the trial court now grant a directed verdict at the close of all the evidence? Certainly the plaintiff's case is appreciably weakened by the testimony of three disinterested witnesses, and one would hope that a properly charged jury would quickly return a verdict for the defendant. But as long as credibility is exclusively for the jury, it seems the Court's analysis would still require this case to be decided by that body.

Thus, in the case that I have posed, it would seem to make no difference whether the standard of proof which the plaintiff had to meet in order to prevail was the preponderance of the evidence, clear and convincing evidence, or proof beyond a reasonable doubt. But if the application of the standards makes no difference in the case that I hypothesize, one may fairly ask in what sort of case *does* the difference in standards make a difference in outcome? Cases may be posed dealing with evidence that is essentially documentary, rather than testimonial; but the Court has held in a related context involving Federal Rule of Civil Procedure 52(a) that inferences from documentary evidence are as much the prerogative of the finder of fact as inferences as to the credibility of witnesses. Anderson v. Bessemer City, 470 U.S. 564, 574, 105 S.Ct. 1504, 1512, 84 L.Ed.2d 518 (1985). The Court affords the lower courts no guidance whatsoever as to what, if any, difference the abstract standards that it propounds would make in a particular case.

* * *

More important for purposes of analyzing the present case, there is no exact analog in the criminal process to the motion for summary judgment in a civil case. Perhaps the closest comparable device for screening out unmeritorious cases in the criminal area is the grand jury proceeding, though the comparison is obviously not on all fours. The standard for allowing a criminal case to proceed to trial is not whether the government has produced prima facie evidence of guilt beyond a reasonable doubt for every element of the offense, but only whether it has established probable cause. See United States v. Mechanik, 475 U.S. 66, 70, 106 S.Ct. 938, 941, 89 L.Ed.2d 50 (1986). Thus, in a criminal case the standard used prior to trial is much more lenient than the "clear beyond a reasonable doubt" standard which must be employed by the finder of fact.

The three differentiated burdens of proof in civil and criminal cases, vague and impressionistic though they necessarily are, probably do make some difference when considered by the finder of fact, whether it be a jury or a judge in a bench trial. Yet it is not a logical or analytical message that the terms convey, but instead almost a state of mind; we have previously said:

"Candor suggests that, to a degree, efforts to analyze what lay jurors understand concerning the differences among these three tests . . . may well be largely an academic exercise. . . . Indeed, the ultimate truth as to how the standards of proof affect decisionmaking may well be *unknowable*, given that factfinding is a process shared by countless thousands of individuals throughout the country. We probably can assume no more than that the difference between a preponderance of the evidence and proof beyond a reasonable doubt probably is better understood than either of them in relation to the intermediate standard of clear and convincing evidence." Addington v. Texas, 441 U.S. 418, 424–425, 99 S.Ct. 1804, 1808, 60 L.Ed.2d 323 (1979) (emphasis added).

The Court's decision to engraft the standard of proof applicable to a factfinder onto the law governing the procedural motion for a summary judgment (a motion that has always been regarded as raising a question of law rather than a question of fact, see, e.g., La Riviere v. EEOC, 682 F.2d 1275, 1277–1278 (CA9 1982) (Wallace, J.)) will do great mischief with little corresponding benefit. The primary effect of the Court's opinion today will likely be to cause the decisions of trial judges on summary judgment motions in libel cases to be more erratic and inconsistent than before. This is largely because the Court has created a standard that is different from the standard traditionally applied in summary judgment motions without even hinting as to how its new standard will be applied to particular cases.

NOTE ON SUMMARY JUDGMENT

1. In virtually all jurisdictions, the motion for judgment on the pleadings is recognized either by rule, e.g., F.R.C.P. 12(c); Ill.C.C.P. § 2–615, or by established practice, as in California. See generally N.Y.Temp.Comm'n, First Preliminary Report 315 (1957) (Statutes and Rules Regulating Summary Judgment, Judgment on the Pleadings and Related Procedures Prior to Trial). The motion is available when the pleadings are closed and raises the same questions as a general demurrer or analogous motion. What is the essential difference between a general demurrer, motion to dismiss, and motion for judgment on the pleadings, on the one hand, and a motion for summary judgment on the other?

2. The motion for summary judgment was an English procedural innovation of the mid-19th century and was initially restricted to actions on commercial paper. Its expansion to other types of actions was halting and hedged by technical restrictions excited by fears of its abuse. Cf. Clark on Code Pleading 557–59 (2d ed. 1947). One persistent problem is whether the pleading of the party moved against, particularly a pleading that is verified, is sufficient controversion of the evidence in support of the motion so as to preclude sustaining the motion. Although this view is still held in some jurisdictions, e.g., Feinman v. City of Jacksonville, 356 So.2d 50 (Fla.App. 1978), in most it is established that the pleadings cannot be relied on as evidence in resistance to the motion, e.g., Coppinger v. Superior Court, 134 Cal.App.3d 883, 185 Cal.Rptr. 24 (1982); Lloyd v. Holland, 659 S.W.2d 103 (Tex.App.1983), a point made explicit in F.R.C.P. 56(e). As Cardozo, J., said in Richard v. Credit Suisse, 242 N.Y. 346, 350, 152 N.E. 110, 111 (1926):

> "The very object of a motion for summary judgment is to separate what is formal or pretended in denial or averment from what is genuine and substantial, so that only the latter may subject a suitor to the burden of a trial."

However, as the Court stated in *Celotex*, the nonmoving party does not necessarily have to produce evidence in a form that would be admissible at trial. And, as the *Adickes* Court said, the nonmoving party does not have to adduce evidence at all until the moving party satisfies its initial burden of showing the absence of a genuine issue of fact.

The formula for administration of summary judgment is essentially the same in most all jurisdictions. As reiterated in Corwin v. Los Angeles Newspaper Serv. Bur., Inc., 4 Cal.3d 842, 851–52, 94 Cal.Rptr. 785, 790–91, 484 P.2d 953, 958 (1971), it is:

> "The matter to be determined by the trial court in considering such a motion is whether the defendant (or plaintiff) has presented any facts which give rise to a triable issue. The court may not pass upon the issue itself. Summary judgment is proper only if the affidavits in support of the moving party would be sufficient to sustain a judgment in his favor and his opponent does not by affidavit show such facts as may be deemed by the judge hearing the motion sufficient to present a triable issue. The aim of the procedure is to discover, through the media of affidavits, whether the parties possess evidence requiring the weighing procedures of a trial. In examining the sufficiency of affidavits filed in connection with the motion, the affidavits of the moving party are strictly construed and those of his opponent liberally construed, and doubts as to the propriety of granting the motion should be resolved in favor of the party opposing the motion. Such summary procedure is drastic and should be used with caution so that it does not become a substitute for the open trial method of determining facts."

The evidence offered in support of and opposition to a motion for summary judgment must be competent in the sense that it consists of documents properly authenticated, and testimony that is on oath and by affiants or deponents who speak from personal knowledge, and material in the sense that it is not merely conclusory. See F.R.C.P. 56(e); C.C.P. 437c. Within these boundaries, the matter offered in support of or opposition to the motion may take the form of affidavits or such items as depositions and other products of the discovery process. F.R.C.P. 56(c) so provides and the same result has been reached in California and most other jurisdictions whose procedure embraces the summary judgment motion. See, e.g., Gordon v. Superior Court, 161 Cal.App.3d 157, 207 Cal.Rptr. 327 (1984) (answers to interrogatories); Schultz v. Regents of Univ. of California, 160 Cal.App.3d 768, 206 Cal.Rptr. 910 (1984) (requests for admissions and admissions in response thereto); Stewart v. United States Leasing Corp., 702 S.W.2d 288 (Tex.App.1985) (depositions). See also Anno., 8 A.L.R.4th 728; Collins, Summary Judgment and Circumstantial Evidence, 40 Stan.L.Rev. 491 (1988). Indeed, development of evidence with an eye to summary judgment is a principal use of discovery.

A crucial issue, of course, is whether the moving party needs to adduce evidence at all, or may merely make a "showing" that the nonmoving party has failed to establish a genuine issue of fact. Are you satisfied with the Court's answer to this question in *Celotex?* Is *Celotex* consistent with *Adickes,* as the Court asserts? Does the Court's allocation of burdens between the moving and nonmoving parties in *Celotex* satisfy you? See Kennedy, Federal Summary Judgment: Reconciling Celotex v. Catrett with Adickes v. Kress and the Evidentiary Problems Under Rule 56, 6 Rev. of Litigation 227 (1987).

In Matsushita Elec. Indus. Co. v. Zenith Radio Corp., 475 U.S. 574, 106 S.Ct. 1348, 89 L.Ed.2d 538 (1986), the Supreme Court held that in order to survive a motion for summary judgment the plaintiff must establish that there is a genuine issue of material fact and that if the factual context renders the claim "implausible," the plaintiff must offer more persuasive evidence to support the claim than would otherwise be necessary.

A motion for summary judgment may be made by defendant with or before the filing of his answer, e.g., Hubicki v. ACF Industries, Inc., 484 F.2d 519 (3d

Cir. 1973), and by plaintiff after a time interval that in most jurisdictions is related to the time allowed defendant to answer. Compare F.R.C.P. 56(a) with F.R.C.P. 12(a). In California and a few other jurisdictions no such interval is specifically prescribed, but presumably a motion would be denied or its hearing postponed if defendant could show embarrassment in trying to meet the motion in haste. See also F.R.C.P. 56(f); Anno., 85 A.L.R.2d 825.

In most jurisdictions summary judgment may be given for or against a part of plaintiff's claim or in favor of plaintiff on the question of liability, leaving for trial the question of damages. See F.R.C.P. 56(d); C.C.P. 437c; N.Y.C.P.L.R. 3212.

In a few jurisdictions there are provisions for what amounts to summary judgment in that special demurrers or analogous motions in certain circumstances are permitted to "speak"—i.e., adduce matter outside the pleadings. See C.C.P. 430.10(c) (another action pending between the parties on the same cause). Under modern rules, a motion to dismiss or for judgment on the pleadings that "speaks" is treated as a motion for summary judgment. F.R.C.P. 12(b), (c). Compare, e.g., Ill.C.C.P. §§ 2–619 and 2–1005; N.Y.C.P.L.R. 3211 and 3212. See also Pianka v. State of California, 46 Cal.2d 208, 293 P.2d 458 (1956); Mancina v. Hoar, 129 Cal.App.3d 796, 181 Cal.Rptr. 347 (1982).

3. C.C.P. 437c contains a number of requirements governing summary judgment procedure. First, a party must notify all other parties to the action of a motion for summary judgment at least 28 days before the hearing date. Second, the hearing on a motion for summary judgment must be held at least 30 days prior to trial. Third, the moving party is required to provide a separate statement setting forth all material facts believed to be undisputed, with reference to the submitted evidence supporting that contention; failure to provide the statement may be grounds for denial of the motion. Fourth, the opposing party must provide a separate statement agreeing or disagreeing with the moving party's contentions and setting forth additional material facts believed to be disputed; failure to comply may be grounds for granting the motion. Finally, the court, in denying a motion for summary judgment, must specify at least one material fact establishing a triable controversy.

4. For illuminating analysis of recurrent problems in administering the summary judgment procedure, see Zack, California Summary Judgment: The Need for Legislative Reform, 59 Calif.L.Rev. 439 (1971); Mullenix, Summary Judgment: Taming the Beast of Burdens, 10 Am.J. Trial Advoc. 433 (1987); Louis, Federal Summary Judgment Doctrine: A Critical Analysis, 83 Yale L.J. 745 (1974); 2 C.E.B., Calif.Civ.Pro. Before Trial, c. 29 (1978).

See also McLauchlan, An Empirical Study of the Federal Summary Judgment Rule, 6 J.Legal Studies 427 (1977), concluding, p. 458:

"First, the summary judgment rule does not dispose of a very large proportion of cases filed in the federal district courts. * * * Second, the success rate of the motion, when used, is fairly high; around 50 per cent of the attempts to use summary judgment are successful at the trial court level."

5. In Nunez v. Superior Oil Co., 572 F.2d 1119, 1123–1124 (5th Cir. 1978), Judge Rubin said:

"There is no litmus that infallibly distinguishes those issues that are 'factual' from those that are 'legal' or 'mixed.' When all those material facts susceptible of objective determination are known, there may be inferences or conclusions to be drawn from them. Many observations that may appear superficially to be factual are the result of inference, viewpoint, and judgment. At ends of the spectrum, it may be relatively easy to separate fact and law, but, as we approach the point where facts and the application of legal rule to them blend, appraising evidentiary facts in terms of their legal consequences and 'applying' law to fact become inseparable processes. In some instances where facts may assume infinite variety, legal rules are deliberately stated in a fashion calling for the application of judgment. Thus, in a suit for personal injury from an automobile accident, it might be ascertained, or even stipulated, that the defendant was driving at 50 miles per hour on a certain road at 6:00 p.m. on a rainy January day. The trier of fact must still decide whether this is 'negligence.' Therefore, the availability of summary judgment depends upon more than an abstract denomination of disputed material issues as 'factual' or 'legal' or 'mixed;' it may turn on whether the application of legal criteria necessarily require judgmental evaluation by the trier of fact, or, to put it another way, whether the trial will require a judge/jury separation of issues.

"If decision is to be reached by the court, and there are no issues of witness credibility, the court may conclude on the basis of the affidavits, depositions, and stipulations before it, that there are no genuine issues of material fact, even though decision may depend on inferences to be drawn from what has been incontrovertibly proved. Under those circumstances, which may be rare, the judge who is also the trier of fact may be warranted in concluding that there was or was not negligence, or that someone acted reasonably or unreasonably, or, as is the case here, that delay under the circumstances proved is justified or unjustified, even if that conclusion is deemed 'factual' or involves a 'mixed question of fact and law.' A trial on the merits would reveal no additional data. Hearing and viewing the witnesses subject to cross-examination would not aid the determination if there are neither issues of credibility nor controversies with respect to the substance of the proposed testimony. The judge, as trier of fact, is in a position to and ought to draw his inferences without resort to the expense of trial. * * *

"But, where a jury is called for, the litigants are entitled to have the jury draw those inferences or conclusions that are appropriate grist for juries. Summary judgment 'was not intended to . . . deprive a litigant of, or at all encroach upon, his right to a jury trial. Judges in giving its flexible provisions effect must do so with this essential limitation constantly in mind.' * * *

"Juries must consider not only 'questions of fact in dispute, [but] questions of conflicting inferences from undisputed facts.' Buffalo Insurance Co. v. Spach, 5 Cir. 1960, 277 F.2d 529, 531. 'Evidentiary facts, though undisputed, do not always conclusively establish the ultimate fact at issue. When the ultimate fact is to be inferred from evidentiary facts, the choice between permissible inferences is for the trier of facts.' Walker v. U. S. Gypsum Co., 5 Cir. 1959, 270 F.2d 857, 862, cert. denied 1960, 363 U.S. 805, 80 S.Ct. 1240, 4 L.Ed.2d 1148. Of course, if there is 'a *complete absence* of probative facts' to support a particular inference, Planters Manufacturing Co. v. Protection Mut. Ins. Co., 5 Cir. 1967, 380 F.2d 869, 874, cert. denied 1967, 389 U.S. 930, 88 S.Ct. 293, 19 L.Ed.2d 282 (emphasis original), or, if 'the facts and inferences point so strongly and overwhelmingly in favor of one party that the Court believes that reasonable men could not arrive at [but one] verdict,' Boeing v. Shipman, 5 Cir. 1969, 411 F.2d 365, 374, the court may bypass the jury.

"Thus, where, as here, the evidentiary facts are not disputed, a court in a non-jury case may grant summary judgment if trial would not enhance its ability to draw inferences and conclusions. But summary judgment is not appropriate if the same case is to be tried to a jury, and the inferences and conclusions to be drawn are genuinely disputed. To put it in another fashion, whether disputed issues are issues of 'fact' for purposes of Rule 56 depends not only on the state of the evidence and the nature of the issue but hinges also on whether the litigants have a right to a jury determination. * * *"

Part III

REMEDIES

A. PLENARY JUDICIAL REMEDIES

NOTE ON LITIGATION AS A LAST RESORT

Litigation is the last resort, short of violence, in the resolution of disputes. It is important to recall the reasons why: a lawsuit is risky and during its pendency leaves the parties in a state of unsettled expectation; it is time-consuming; it is expensive; it is acrimonious. Perhaps most important for a free society, it represents the substitution of compulsion for consensual arrangement. A folk saying sums it up well: "He who goes to court has a wolf by the ears." "Abraham Lincoln once said: 'Discourage litigation. Persuade your neighbors to compromise whenever you can. Point out to them how the nominal winner is often a real loser—in fees, expenses, and waste of time.' In the same vein Judge Learned Hand commented: 'I must say that, as a litigant, I should dread a lawsuit beyond almost anything else short of sickness and death.'" Burger, Isn't There a Better Way?, 68 A.B.A.J. 274, 275 (1982). Eminent jurists have expressed similar sentiments. From the litigants' viewpoint, it is ordinarily an altogether disagreeable process, less disagreeable perhaps only than the violence for which it is the civilized substitute. (This may indeed explain why, despite judicial adjurations to the contrary, lawyers persist in thinking of litigation, and often treating it, as a "game." If they did not so regard it, could they maintain both civility and sanity in defeat?) Despite these admonitions, however, Americans remain litigation prone. See Andrews, Suing as a First Resort: A Review of Mark's The Suing of America and Lieberman's The Litigious Society, 1981 A.B.F.Res.J. 851; but cf. Galanter, Reading the Landscape of Disputes: What We Know and Don't Know (And Think We Know) About Our Allegedly Contentious and Litigious Society, 31 U.C.L.A.L.Rev. 4 (1983).

The rules and conventions of law recognize litigation as an extremity. They permit forms of self-help in a wide variety of circumstances, so long as breach of the peace is avoided. And, self-help failing or being peaceably impracticable, the rules of law encourage and sometimes require that all efforts short of litigation be pursued before the courts' intervention is invoked.

1. Self-Help

The form of self-help most commonly resorted to is the alteration of the financial status quo. A purchaser of goods who claims that he is entitled to a refund from the seller may undertake to help himself to a "refund" by buying additional goods and not paying for them. A shipper of goods on a common carrier claiming compensation for their damage in transit may undertake to "compensate" herself by shipping additional goods and refusing to pay the freight bill. Observe that the effect of these and other kinds of self-help, if they are successful, is to reverse the strategic legal positions of the parties: He who previously was in a position where he would have to assume the offensive to obtain judicial redress now is in a defensive position from which the other party will have to dislodge him by legal action. How should maneuvers of this sort be regarded? As unprincipled wrong-doing, akin to the use of force? Or as justifiable means of adjusting disputes without resort to the courts? What limits should be imposed on the privilege of self-help? Doesn't the answer to this question depend, in part at least, on how inexpensive, speedy, effective and just are the legal processes for adjusting disputes?

On self-help generally see Prosser, Torts 108–145 (5th ed. 1984).

2. Demand Rules

Often the injured party must demand redress from the wrongdoer before proceeding to court. By way of illustration: A person claiming the right to return of chattels wrongfully taken from him ordinarily must demand their return prior to bringing action, cf. Anno., 145 A.L.R. 743; a vendor of real property seeking to enforce a contract for its sale must demand performance by the purchaser prior to bringing action against him, cf. Anno., 94 A.L.R. 1239; a buyer of goods must give prompt notice of any claimed breach of warranty, Uniform Commercial Code § 2–607(3)(a); Anno., 71 A.L.R. 1149; the dishonor of a check must be protested before action can be brought on it, Farnsworth, Negotiable Instruments 78 et seq. (2d ed. 1965). See generally C.E.B., 1 Calif. Civ.Pro. Before Trial, c. 4 (1977).

3. Exhaustion of Remedies Rules

Where the person asserting a wrong has available to her non-judicial machinery for vindication of her rights, she is ordinarily required to invoke that machinery before resorting to the courts. By way of illustration: a stockholder who claims mismanagement of her corporation must make demand on the directors, and sometimes the other shareholders, for rectification of the alleged wrongdoing prior to bringing action in courts, Henn and Alexander, Laws of Corporations §§ 364–366 (3d ed. 1983); Anno., 99 A.L.R.3d 1034; Comment, The Demand and Standing Requirements in Stockholder Derivative Actions, 44 U.Chi.L.Rev. 168 (1976); a member of an unincorporated association, such as a club or a union, who claims to have been wronged in his membership rights by the association must seek redress within the organization before he can seek redress in the courts, Comment, Exhaustion of Remedies in Private, Voluntary Associations, 64 Yale L.J. 369 (1956); a person claiming reparation from a public agency or its employees usually must file a claim for reparation promptly after the transaction and before filing suit, Calif.L.Rev. Comm'n, The Presentation of Claims Against Public Entities (1959); Fredrichsen v. City of Lakewood, 6 Cal.3d 353, 99 Cal.Rptr. 13, 491 P.2d 805 (1971); Soloff v. Board of Education, 90 A.D.2d 829, 455 N.Y.S.2d 832 (1982); cf. Calif.L. Rev.Comm'n, The Presentation of Claims Against Public Officers and Employees (1960); but see Felder v. Casey, ___ U.S. ___, 108 S.Ct. 2302, 101 L.Ed.2d 123 (1988) (state notice-of-claim statute preempted by federal law in civil rights damages suit); a person seeking redress for an injury for which there is or may be a remedy in an administrative agency is usually required to proceed through the agency before coming to the courts, e.g., Ricci v. Chicago Mercantile Exchange, 409 U.S. 289, 93 S.Ct. 573, 34 L.Ed.2d 525 (1973); cf. Rosewell v. LaSalle Nat. Bank, 450 U.S. 503, 101 S.Ct. 1221, 67 L.Ed.2d 464 (1981); Sea and Sage Audubon Society, Inc. v. Planning Commission, 34 Cal.3d 412, 194 Cal.Rptr. 357, 668 P.2d 664 (1983); but cf. Patsy v. Board of Regents, 457 U.S.

496, 102 S.Ct. 2557, 73 L.Ed.2d 172 (1982) (exhaustion not required under Civil Rights Act).

4. Arbitration

If the parties to a transaction or contractual relationship agree that disputes arising out of the transaction or relationship shall be determined by arbitration, such an agreement generally precludes initial resort to the courts. In most jurisdictions, moreover, the courts will specifically enforce such agreements, thus compelling the recalcitrant party to submit to arbitration. See Wilmer, Domke on Commercial Arbitration (rev. ed. 1984); Goldberg, Green and Sander, Dispute Resolution (1985). See also Arbitration, infra p. 1255.

5. Damages

Traditionally, the "primary" legal remedy is damages, i.e., other forms of relief such as an injunction are awarded only under unusual circumstances. Damages at any rate are the only remedy for most forms of serious personal injury and probably the most efficient form of relief to give in cases of economic loss that has already transpired. The chief problems in the damages remedy are how to measure it and how to collect it. A "measure of damages" problem follows.

1. DAMAGES

HELFEND v. SOUTHERN CALIFORNIA RAPID TRANSIT DISTRICT

Supreme Court of California, 1970.
2 Cal.3d 1, 84 Cal.Rptr. 173, 465 P.2d 61.*

TOBRINER, ACTING C. J.

Defendants appeal from a judgment of the Los Angeles Superior Court entered on a verdict in favor of plaintiff, Julius J. Helfend, for $16,400 in general and special damages for injuries sustained in a bus-auto collision that occurred on July 19, 1965, in the City of Los Angeles.

We have concluded that the judgment for plaintiff in this tort action against the defendant governmental entity should be affirmed. The trial court properly followed the collateral source rule in excluding evidence that a portion of plaintiff's medical bills had been paid through a medical insurance plan that requires the refund of benefits from tort recoveries.

1. *The facts.*

[Plaintiff was injured in a collision between his automobile and defendant's bus.]

An ambulance took plaintiff to Central Receiving Hospital for emergency first aid treatment. Upon release from the hospital plaintiff proceeded to consult Dr. Saxon, an orthopedic specialist,

---

* Some of the court's footnotes are omitted.

who sent plaintiff immediately to the Sherman Oaks Community Hospital where he received treatment for about a week. Plaintiff underwent physical therapy for about six months in order to regain normal use of his left arm and hand. He acquired some permanent discomfort but no permanent disability from the injuries sustained in the accident. At the time of the injury plaintiff was 67 years of age and had a life expectancy of about 11 years. He owned the Jewel Homes Investment Company which possessed and maintained small rental properties. Prior to the accident plaintiff had performed much of the minor maintenance on his properties including some painting and minor plumbing. For the six-month healing period he hired a man to do all the work he had formerly performed and at the time of the trial still employed him for such work as he himself could not undertake.

Plaintiff filed a tort action against the Southern California Rapid Transit District, a public entity, and Mitchell, an employee of the transit district. At trial plaintiff claimed slightly more than $2,700 in special damages, including $921 in doctor's bills, a $336.99 hospital bill, and about $45 for medicines.[1] Defendant requested permission to show that about 80 percent of the plaintiff's hospital bill had been paid by plaintiff's Blue Cross insurance carrier and that some of his other medical expenses may have been paid by other insurance. The superior court thoroughly considered the then very recent case of City of Salinas v. Souza & McCue Constr. Co. (1967) 66 Cal.2d 217, 57 Cal.Rptr. 337, 424 P.2d 921, distinguished the *Souza* case on the ground that *Souza* involved a contract setting, and concluded that the judgment should not be reduced to the extent of the amount of insurance payments which plaintiff received. The court ruled that defendants should not be permitted to show that plaintiff had received medical coverage from any collateral source.

After the jury verdict in favor of plaintiff in the sum of $16,300, defendants appealed, raising only two contentions: (1) The trial court committed prejudicial error in refusing to allow the introduction of evidence to the effect that a portion of the plaintiff's medical bills had been paid from a collateral source. (2) The trial court erred in denying defendant the opportunity to determine if plaintiff had been compensated from more than one collateral source for damages sustained in the accident.

We must decide whether the collateral source rule applies to tort actions involving public entities and public employees in which the plaintiff has received benefits from his medical insurance coverage.

1. The plaintiff claimed special damages of $2,737.99 of which $1,302.99 represented medical expenses, $35 repair of plaintiff's watch, about $1,350 expenses and costs incurred as a result of hiring another man to do the work plaintiff normally performed, and $50 plaintiff's share of the automobile repair costs.

2. *The collateral source rule.*

The Supreme Court of California has long adhered to the doctrine that if an injured party receives some compensation for his injuries from a source wholly independent of the tortfeasor, such payment should not be deducted from the damages which the plaintiff would otherwise collect from the tortfeasor. (See, e.g., Peri v. Los Angeles Junction Ry. Co. (1943) 22 Cal.2d 111, 131, 137 P.2d 441.)[2] * * *

Although the collateral source rule remains generally accepted in the United States,[3] nevertheless many other jurisdictions[4] have restricted[5] or repealed it. In this country most commentators have

2. In Peri v. Los Angeles Junction Ry. Co., supra, 22 Cal.2d 111, 131, a case involving a negligently caused automobile accident, this court said, "While it is true that he [plaintiff] received $2 per day compensation while he was unable to work, that sum may not be deducted from his loss of earnings, because it was received from an insurance company under a policy owned and held by him. 'Damages recoverable for a wrong are not diminished by the fact that the party injured has been wholly or partly indemnified for his loss by insurance effected by him, and to the procurement of which the wrongdoer did not contribute; . . .' [citations]."

3. See West, The Collateral Source Rule Sans Subrogation: A Plaintiff's Windfall (1963) 16 Okla.L.Rev. 395, 397–410; see also Fleming, The Collateral Source Rule and Loss Allocation in Tort Law (1966) 54 Cal.L.Rev. 1478, 1482–1483 and fn. 10; 2 Harper & James, The Law of Torts (1968 Supp.) § 25.22, at p. 152. There are many sorts of collateral sources and a great variety of contexts in which the "rule" might be applied. We expressly do not consider or determine the appropriateness of the rule's application in the myriad of possible situations which we have not discussed or which are not presented by the facts of this case.

4. After a period in which it appeared that the courts of the United Kingdom, the country of the rule's origin, would disavow it (see Browning v. War Office (1963) 1 Q.B. 750), the House of Lords in Parry v. Cleaver (1969) 2 W.L.R. 821, has recently reaffirmed the rule and applied it to a case of a tort victim who, following the automobile accident in which he was disabled, received a pension. (See Bradburn v. Great Western Ry. (1874) L.R. 10 Ex. 1; Atiyah, Collateral Benefits Again (1969) 32 Mod.L.Rev. 397.) Most other western European nations have repudiated the rule. (See Fleming, The Collateral Source Rule and Loss Allocation in Tort Law, supra, 54 Cal.L.Rev. 1478, 1480–1484, 1516–1523, 1535–1540.)

5. The New York Court of Appeals has, for example, quite reasonably held that an injured physician may not recover from a tortfeasor for the value of medical and nursing care rendered gratuitously as a matter of professional courtesy. (See Coyne v. Campbell (1962) 11 N.Y.2d 372, 230 N.Y.S.2d 1, 183 N.E.2d 891.) The doctor owed at least a moral obligation to render gratuitous services in return, if ever required; but he had neither paid premiums for the services under some form of insurance coverage nor manifested any indication that he would endeavor to repay those who had given him assistance. Thus this situation differs from that in which friends and relatives render assistance to the injured plaintiff with the expectation of repayment out of any tort recovery; in that case, the rule has been applied. (Kimball v. Northern Elec. Co. (1911) 159 Cal. 225, 231, 113 P. 156; Sykes v. Lawlor (1874) 49 Cal. 236.) On the other hand, New York has joined most states in holding that a tortfeasor may not mitigate damages by showing that an injured plaintiff would receive a disability pension. (Healy v. Rennert (1961) 9 N.Y.2d 202, 213 N.Y.S.2d 44, 173 N.E.2d 777; see Hume v. Lacey (1952) 112 Cal.App.2d 147, 151–152, 245 P.2d 672 (pension does not reduce recovery); Bencich v. Market Street Ry. Co. (1938) 29 Cal.App.2d 641, 647–648, 85 P.2d 556; cf. Groat v. Walkup Drayage & Warehouse Co. (1936) 14 Cal.App.2d 350, 358–359, 58 P.2d 200.) In these cases the plaintiff had actually or constructively paid for the pension by having received lower wages or by having contributed directly to the pension plan.

criticized the rule and called for its early demise.[6]   In *Souza* we took
note of the academic criticism of the rule, characterized the rule as
"punitive," and held it inapplicable to the governmental entity involved
in that case.

We must, however, review the particular facts of *Souza* in order
to determine whether it applies to the present case.   The City of
Salinas brought suit against Souza & McCue Construction Company,
a public works contractor, and its pipe supplier for breach of a
contract to construct a sewer pipe line.   Souza cross-complained
against the city, alleging fraudulent misrepresentation and breach
of implied warranty of site conditions; and against the pipe supplier, alleging a guarantee of performance of the piping and a promise
to indemnify Souza for any losses.   The trial court found that the
city materially misrepresented soil conditions by failing to inform
Souza of unstable conditions known to the city, that with the city's
knowledge Souza relied upon the misrepresentations in bidding, and
that Souza should recover damages proximately caused by the city's
fraudulent breach.

We held that the trial court improperly determined damages
against the city by refusing to allow the city to show that the supplier
had recompensed Souza for some of the damages caused by the city's
breach.   In this contract setting in which the supplier did not constitute
a wholly independent collateral source,[7] we held that the collateral
source rule cannot be applied against public entities because the collat-

6. In recent years commentators have
generally opposed the rule. (2 Harper &
James, The Law of Torts (1968 Supp.)
§ 25.22, at p. 152; see, e.g., Fleming, The
Collateral Source Rule and Loss Allocation in Tort Law, supra, 54 Cal.L.Rev.
1478; James, Social Insurance and Tort
Liability: The Problem of Alternative
Remedies (1952) 27 N.Y.U.L.Rev. 537;
Schwartz, The Collateral Source Rule
(1961) 41 B.U.L.Rev. 348; West, The Collateral Source Rule Sans Subrogation: A
Plaintiff's Windfall, supra, 16 Okla.L.Rev.
395; Note, Unreason in the Law of Damages: The Collateral Source Rule (1964)
77 Harv.L.Rev. 741.)   Of course, the rule
constitutes a valuable weapon in the
plaintiff attorney's arsenal.   (Averbach,
The Collateral Source Rule (1960) 21 Ohio
St.L.J. 231.)   One commentator has noted
the criticism of the rule, but concludes:
"For the present system, however, the
rule seems to perform a needed function.
At the very least, it removes some complex issues from the trial scene.   At its
best, in some cases, it operates as an
instrument of what most of us would be
willing to call justice." (Maxwell, The
Collateral Source Rule in The American
Law of Damages (1962) 46 Minn.L.Rev.
669, 695.)

7. In Laurenzi v. Varnzian (1945) 25
Cal.2d 806, 813, 155 P.2d 633, this court
held that "payments by one tortfeasor on
account of a harm for which he and another are each liable, diminish the amount of
the claim against the other whether or not
it was so agreed at the time of payment
and whether the payment was made before
or after judgment.   Since the plaintiff can
have but one satisfaction, evidence of such
payments is admissible for the purpose of
reducing *pro tanto* the amount of the damages he may be entitled to recover."
Hence, the rule applies only to payments
that come from a source entirely independent of the tortfeasor and does not apply to
payments by joint tortfeasors or to benefits
the plaintiff receives from a tortfeasor's
insurance coverage.   (See De Cruz v. Reid,
supra, 69 Cal.2d 217, 225–226; Witt v.
Jackson (1961) 57 Cal.2d 57, 71–72, 17 Cal.
Rptr. 369, 366 P.2d 641; Turner v. Mannon
(1965) 236 Cal.App.2d 134, 138–139, 45 Cal.
Rptr. 831; Dodds v. Bucknum (1963) 214
Cal.App.2d 206, 212–213, 29 Cal.Rptr. 393;
see 2 Harper & James, The Law of Torts
(1968 Supp.) § 25.22, fns. 5–6, at pp. 153–
154.)

eral source rule appears punitive in nature [8] and punitive damages cannot be imposed on public entities.[9]

Although *Souza's* reasoning as to punitive damages might appear to apply to private tortfeasors [10] as well as public entities and to torts as well as contract actions,[11] we did not there consider the collateral

8. For the proposition that the collateral source rule is punitive, *Souza* cited United Protective Workers v. Ford Motor Co. (7th Cir. 1955) 223 F.2d 49, 54, 48 A.L.R.2d 1285, which is clearly distinguishable from the present tort case because it involved the construction and application of a collective bargaining contract in which the court found neither bad faith nor wilful misconduct sufficient to justify a measure of damages other than the compensation the discharged employee would have received, punitive damages, or prejudgment interest on damages. *Souza* also cited Harper & James, The Law of Torts (1956), section 25.22, pages 1343–1354, which concluded: "If therefore a feeling of revenge and resentment has any place in the law at all, it should certainly be banished as far as possible from the law of civil recovery, practically as well as theoretically. In spite of this, we suggest, it has played a large—though unrecognized—part in justifying plaintiff's double recovery." Although we recognize that in the past a primitive moralism may have engendered the collateral source rule to serve punitive ends, we suggest below that the rule today still serves not mere punitive purposes, but legitimate objectives that may or may not survive the spread of a philosophy of social insurance. *Souza* also cites Fleming, The Collateral Source Rule and Loss Allocation in Tort Law, supra, 54 Cal.L.Rev. 1478, 1482–1484. Professor Fleming seems concerned with the punitive nature of the collateral source rule in cases in which the plaintiff receives a double, treble, or multiple recovery. He notes, however, that "The theory of subrogation offers a neat and well-tried device for at once vindicating the principle of indemnity and reallocating the burden of the loss to the tortfeasor without, however, involving him in multiple liability." (Id. at p. 1498.) Professor Fleming also observes that arrangements for the refund of benefits, such as the one found in the present case, serve to avoid double recovery and reallocate risk from plaintiff's insurer to the tortfeasor or his insurer, and possesses certain advantages over subrogation. (Id. at p. 1526.) The plaintiff's Blue Cross coverage does not present a danger of double recovery because of its refund of benefits provision and thus does not fall within Professor

Fleming's concern about the punitive nature of double recovery.

9. See Government Code section 818. On the issue of whether liability recompensed by a collateral source can be imposed upon a public entity, plaintiff cogently points out that such liability is not imposed upon the innocent taxpayers as *Souza* assumes (see City of Salinas v. Souza & McCue Constr. Co., supra, 66 Cal.2d 217, 227), but upon the entity's insurer. Of course the entity does pay the insurance premiums or the tort recovery, if it is a self-insurer. But such premiums or recoveries are the normal cost of maintaining an enterprise and represent no grievous injury to taxpayers since the entity and its insurer are in an excellent position to spread the risk of loss and to take precautionary measures to prevent injuries.

10. See California Recognizes Collateral Source Rule Exception (Oct. 1969) 10 For the Defense, pp. 61, 69.

11. See Note (1967) The Supreme Court of California, 55 Cal.L.Rev. 1059, 1163–1165. Section 342 of the Restatement of the Law of Contracts (1932) provides that: "Punitive damages are not recoverable for breach of contract. Comment: a. Damages are punitive when they are assessed by way of punishment to the wrongdoer or example to others and not as the money equivalent of harm done. All damages are in some degree punitive and preventative; but they are not so called unless they exceed just compensation measured by the harm suffered." We do not decide whether the collateral source rule should apply in hybrid actions involving both tort and contract claims, because the present case involves only a negligent tort. (See Patent Scaffolding Co. v. William Simpson Constr. Co. (1967) 256 Cal.App.2d 506, 510–511, 64 Cal.Rptr. 187; Greenberg v. Hastie (1962) 202 Cal.App.2d 159, 176–178, 20 Cal.Rptr. 747; Tremeroli v. Austin Trailer Equipment Co. (1951) 102 Cal.App.2d 464, 480–483, 227 P.2d 923; American Alliance Ins. Co. v. Capital Nat. Bank (1946) 75 Cal.App. 2d 787, 791–795, 171 P.2d 449; Clark v. Burns Hamman Baths (1925) 71 Cal.App. 571, 575, 236 P. 152; cf. City of Salinas v. Souza & McCue Constr. Co., supra, 66 Cal. 2d 217, 226–227; Anheuser-Busch, Inc. v.

source rule in contexts different from the specific contractual setting and particular relationship of the parties involved. We distinguish the present case from *Souza* on the ground that in *Souza* the plaintiff received payments from his subcontractor which, in the contractual setting of that case, did not constitute a truly independent source. Obviously, such a "source" differs entirely from the instant one, which derives from plaintiff's payment of insurance premiums. Here plaintiff received benefits from his medical insurance coverage only because he had long paid premiums to obtain them. Such an origin does constitute a completely independent source. Hence, although we reaffirm the holding in *Souza*, we do not believe that its reasoning either compels the abolition of the collateral source rule in all cases or requires an unwarranted exemption from the rule of public entities and their employees involved in tort actions.[12] *Souza* does not even suggest that public employees should be charged with the extra liability which an exemption for public entities might imply.[13]

The collateral source rule as applied here embodies the venerable concept that a person who has invested years of insurance premiums to assure his medical care should receive the benefits of his thrift.[14] The tortfeasor should not garner the benefits of his victim's providence.

The collateral source rule expresses a policy judgment in favor of encouraging citizens to purchase and maintain insurance for personal injuries and for other eventualities. Courts consider insurance a form of investment, the benefits of which become payable without respect to any other possible source of funds. If we were to permit a tortfeasor to mitigate damages with payments from plaintiff's insurance, plaintiff would be in a position inferior to that of having bought no insurance, because his payment of premiums would have earned no benefit. Defendant should not be able to avoid payment of full compensation for the injury inflicted merely because the victim has had the foresight to provide himself with insurance.

Starley (1946) 28 Cal.2d 347, 349–350, 170 P.2d 448, 166 A.L.R. 198.)

12. Cf. Nellis, California Governmental Tort Liability and the Collateral Source Rule (1969) 9 Santa Clara Law. 227.

13. Cf. Note (1967) 55 Cal.L.Rev. 1059, 1165.

14. See Thompson v. Mattucci (1963) 223 Cal.App.2d 208, 209–210, 35 Cal.Rptr. 741 (Blue Cross payment for hospital bills does not reduce plaintiff's recovery); Gersick v. Shilling (1950) 97 Cal.App.2d 641, 649–650, 218 P.2d 583 (error to have admitted testimony that plaintiff's medical bills had been paid by Blue Cross or that plaintiff had received United States Employment Service disability payments). In Lewis v. County of Contra Costa (1955) 130 Cal.App.2d 176, 278 P.2d 756, the court held that the collateral source rule prohibited the trial court from admitting evidence that at the time of the accident plaintiff had accumulated sufficient sick leave to cover the period of his disablement. The court reasoned that "In a very real sense of the term it is as if he had drawn upon his savings account in an amount equal to his salary during the period of his disablement." (130 Cal.App.2d at pp. 178–179.) See also Purcell v. Goldberg (1939) 34 Cal.App.2d 344, 350, 93 P.2d 578 (association which provided in contract that members were liable for medical services only in case they recovered damages); Reichle v. Hazie (1937) 22 Cal.App.2d 543, 547–548, 71 P.2d 849 (collateral source rule applies only insofar as public hospital would receive reimbursement for its gratuitous services from the tort recovery).

Some commentators object that the above approach to the collateral source rule provides plaintiff with a "double recovery," rewards him for the injury, and defeats the principle that damages should compensate the victim but not punish the tortfeasor. We agree with Professor Fleming's observation, however, that "double recovery is justified only in the face of some exceptional, supervening reason, as in the case of accident or life insurance, where it is felt unjust that the tortfeasor should take advantage of the thrift and prescience of the victim in having paid the premium." (Fleming, Introduction to the Law of Torts (1967) p. 131.) As we point out infra, recovery in a wrongful death action is not defeated by the payment of the benefit on a life insurance policy.

Furthermore, insurance policies increasingly provide for either subrogation or refund of benefits upon a tort recovery, and such refund is indeed called for in the present case. (See Fleming, The Collateral Source Rule and Loss Allocation in Tort Law, supra, 54 Cal.L.Rev. 1478, 1479.) Hence, the plaintiff receives no double recovery; [15] the collateral source rule simply serves as a means of by-passing the antiquated doctrine of nonassignment of tortious actions and permits a proper transfer of risk from the plaintiff's insurer to the tortfeasor by way of the victim's tort recovery. The double shift from the tortfeasor to the victim and then from the victim to his insurance carrier can normally occur with little cost in that the insurance carrier is often intimately involved in the initial litigation and quite automatically receives its part of the tort settlement or verdict.[16]

Even in cases in which the contract or the law precludes subrogation or refund of benefits,[17] or in situations in which the collateral

15. In reaffirming our adherence to the collateral source rule in this tort case involving a plaintiff with collateral payments from his insurance coverage, we do not suggest that the tortfeasor be required to pay doubly for his wrong—once to the injured party and again to reimburse the plaintiff's collateral source—as Smith v. City of Los Angeles (1969) 276 Cal.App.2d 156, 81 Cal.Rptr. 120, appears to require.

16. In personal injury cases in which the tort victim is unwilling to sue, subrogation subjects the tort victim to additional trouble and incurs further cost. A provision for refund of benefits, such as in the present case, avoids these difficulties by permitting the tort victim to decide whether to undertake litigation against the tortfeasor. (See Fleming, The Collateral Source Rule and Loss Allocation in Tort Law, supra, 54 Cal.L.Rev. 1478, 1526, 1536–1537.)

17. "Certain insurance benefits are regarded as the proceeds of an investment rather than as an indemnity for damages. Thus it has been held that the proceeds of a life insurance contract made for a fixed sum rather than for the damages caused by the death of the insured are proceeds of an investment and can be received independently of the claim for damages against the person who caused the death of the insured. The same rule has been held applicable to accident insurance contracts. As to both kinds of insurance it has been stated: 'Such a policy is an investment contract, giving the owner or beneficiary an absolute right, independent of the right against any third person responsible for the injury covered by the policy.' [Citations.] . . . An insurer who fully compensates the insured, however, is subrogated to the rights of the insured against [or may receive a refund of benefits from] one who insured his property if the insurance was for the protection of the property of the insured, and was therefore an indemnity contract. [Citation.] In such cases subrogation [or refund of benefits] is the means by which double recovery by the owner is prevented and the ultimate burden shifted to the wrongdoer where it belongs. . . ."

source waives such subrogation or refund, the rule performs entirely necessary functions in the computation of damages. For example, the cost of medical care often provides both attorneys and juries in tort cases with an important measure for assessing the plaintiff's general damages. (Cf., e.g., Rose v. Melody Lane (1952) 39 Cal.2d 481, 489, 247 P.2d 335.) To permit the defendant to tell the jury that the plaintiff has been recompensed by a collateral source for his medical costs might irretrievably upset the complex, delicate, and somewhat indefinable calculations which result in the normal jury verdict. (See Hoffman v. Brandt (1966) 65 Cal.2d 549, 554–555, 55 Cal.Rptr. 417, 421 P.2d 425; Garfield v. Russell (1967) 251 Cal.App.2d 275, 279, 59 Cal.Rptr. 379.)

We also note that generally the jury is not informed that plaintiff's attorney will receive a large portion of the plaintiff's recovery in contingent fees or that personal injury damages are not taxable to the plaintiff and are normally deductible by the defendant.[18] Hence, the plaintiff rarely actually receives full compensation for his injuries as computed by the jury. The collateral source rule partially serves to compensate for the attorney's share and does not actually render "double recovery" for the plaintiff. Indeed, many jurisdictions that have abolished or limited the collateral source rule have also established a means for assessing the plaintiff's costs for counsel directly against the defendant rather than imposing the contingent fee system.[19]

(Anheuser-Busch, Inc. v. Starley, supra, 28 Cal.2d 347, 355 (dissenting opn. of Traynor, J.).)

One Court of Appeal has, however, upheld the refund of benefits provision in a Blue Shield medical insurance contract similar to the one at issue here. (Block v. California Physicians' Service (1966) 244 Cal.App.2d 266, 53 Cal.Rptr. 51.)

18. Section 104(a)(2) of the Internal Revenue Code of 1954 (26 U.S.C.A. § 22(b) (5)) permits the tort victim to exclude from his gross income the amount of damages he receives from a tort verdict or settlement on account of his personal injuries or illness. (See generally, as to the tax consequences of tort cases, Guardino, Tax Aspects of Recoveries and Damages in Lawsuits (April–May 1969) 5 Trial 34.) The plaintiff who had been in a high tax bracket and who recovers for loss of earnings on a pretax basis is placed in a better position than if he had earned the same income. (See Note (1964) 77 Harv.L.Rev. 741, 747.) The United States Court of Appeals for the Second Circuit recently observed that: "in 'the great mass of litigation at the lower or middle reach of the income scale, where future income is fairly predictable, added exemptions or deductions drastically affect the tax and . . . the plaintiff is almost certain to be undercompensated for loss of earning power in

any event.' The under compensation would arise from the erosion of the recovery due to the failure to award attorneys' fees, almost always high in this type of litigation because of their contingent nature, and to continuing inflation; . . . [I]n cases 'at the opposite end of the income spectrum,' failure to deduct for taxes would result in an award that 'would be plainly excessive even after taking full account of the countervailing factors we have mentioned.' " (Petition of Marina Mercante Nicaraguense, S.A. (2d Cir. 1966) (Friendly, C.J.) 364 F.2d 118, 125; see McWeeney v. New York, N. H. & H. R. R. Co. (2d Cir. 1960) 282 F.2d 34, 38–39; O'Connor v. United States (2d Cir. 1959) 269 F.2d 578, 584–586; Leming v. Oilfields Trucking Co. (1955) 44 Cal.2d 343, 358, 282 P.2d 23, 51 A.L.R.2d 107.) Of course, since the issue has been neither briefed nor argued by the parties in this case, we leave open the proper treatment of the tax consequences of tort verdicts.

19. Under workmen's compensation subrogation normally prevents double recovery by shifting the loss to the tortfeasor. (See Lab.Code, §§ 3852–3854, 3856; De Cruz v. Reid, supra, 69 Cal.2d 217, 221–227; Cal. Workmen's Compensation Practice (Cont.Ed.Bar 1963) §§ 19.1–19.37, at pp. 593–622.) In actions to recover against a tortfeasor, the court sets a reasonable at-

In sum, the plaintiff's recovery for his medical expenses from both the tortfeasor and his medical insurance program will not usually give him "double recovery," but partially provides a somewhat closer approximation to full compensation for his injuries.[20]

If we consider the collateral source rule as applied here in the context of the entire American approach to the law of torts and damages, we find that the rule presently performs a number of legitimate and even indispensable functions. Without a thorough revolution in the American approach to torts and the consequent damages, the rule at least with respect to medical insurance benefits has become so integrated within our present system that its precipitous judicial nullification would work hardship. In this case the collateral source rule lies between two systems for the compensation of accident victims: the traditional tort recovery based on fault and the increasingly prevalent coverage based on non-fault insurance. Neither system possesses such universality of coverage or completeness of compensation that we can easily dispense with the collateral source rule's approach to meshing the two systems. (Cf., e.g., Bilyeu v. State Employees' Retirement System (1962) 58 Cal.2d 618, 629, 25 Cal.Rptr. 562, 375 P.2d 442 (concurring opn. of Peters, J.).) The reforms which many academicians propose cannot easily be achieved through piecemeal common law development; the proposed changes, if desirable, would be more effectively accomplished through legislative reform. In any case, we cannot believe that the judicial repeal of the collateral source rule, as applied in the present case would be the place to begin the needed changes.

Although in the special circumstances of *Souza* we characterized the collateral source rule as "punitive" in nature, we have pointed out the several legitimate and fully justified compensatory functions of the rule. In fact, if the collateral source rule were actually punitive, it could apply only in cases of oppression, fraud, or malice and would be inapplicable to most tort, and almost all negligence, cases regardless of whether a governmental entity were involved. (See Civ.Code, § 3294); Note (1967) 55 Cal.L.Rev. 1059, 1165. We therefore reaffirm our adherence to the collateral source rule in tort cases in which the plaintiff has been compensated by an independent collateral source— such as insurance, pension, continued wages, or disability payments—

torney's fee. (See Lab.Code, §§ 3856, 4903; Cal. Workmen's Compensation Practice, supra, § 19.31, at pp. 617–619.) As to the practice of several European countries in which a master assesses attorney's fees directly against the tortfeasor, see generally Abel-Smith & Stevens, Lawyers and the Courts (1967) pp. 377–405; Goodhart, Costs (1929) 38 Yale L.J. 849; Quint, Attorney's Fees—An Item of Damage (1966) 41 Los Angeles Bar Bull. 367; Stoebuck, Counsel Fees Included in Costs; A Logical Development (1966) 38 U.Colo.L.Rev. 202, 206–207.

20. Of course, only in cases in which the tort victim has received payments or services from a collateral source will he be able to mitigate attorney's fees by means of the collateral source rule. Thus the rule provides at best only an incomplete and haphazard solution to providing all tort victims with full compensation. Depriving some tort victims of the salutary protections of the collateral source rule will, short of a thorough reform of our tort system, only decrease the available compensation for injuries. (See McWeeney v. New York, N. H. & H. R. R. Co., supra, 282 F.2d 34, 38; but cf. Schwartz, The Collateral Source Rule, supra, 41 B.U.L.Rev. 348, 351–352.)

for which he had actually or constructively (see fns. 5 and 14, supra) paid or in cases in which the collateral source would be recompensed from the tort recovery through subrogation, refund of benefits, or some other arrangement. Hence, we conclude that in a case in which a tort victim has received partial compensation from medical insurance coverage entirely independent of the tortfeasor the trial court properly followed the collateral source rule and foreclosed defendant from mitigating damages by means of the collateral payments.

3. *The collateral source rule, public entities, and public employees.*

Having concluded that the collateral source rule is not simply punitive in nature, we hold, for the reasons set out infra, that the rule as delineated here applies to governmental entities as well as to all other tortfeasors. We must therefore disapprove of any indications to the contrary in City of Salinas v. Souza & McCue Constr. Co., supra, 66 Cal.2d 217, 226–228.

* * *

The judgment is affirmed.

McComb, J., Peters, J., Mosk, J., Burke, J., and Sullivan, J., concurred.

NOTE ON DAMAGES

1. Damages in Personal Injury Cases

The recitation of facts concerning the injury involved in *Helfend* suggests the items of damage allowed in personal injury actions: Medical expenses, economic losses attributable to the interruption of normal life on account of the injury, lost income during the period required for recovery, and economic loss attributable to any permanency of injury. In addition, plaintiff can recover the monetary amount that the trier of fact assigns for "pain and suffering" endured by plaintiff, temporarily during recovery and permanently as a result of incomplete recovery. Calculation of the amount to be awarded for pain and suffering is highly subjective and has quite elastic possibilities. One procedure used by plaintiffs to give more definite content to this element of damage is the so-called "per diem argument": A money amount for pain each day is suggested to the jury (for example, $50 per day), with the further suggestion that the jury then multiply the plaintiff's period of life expectancy by that rate. The effect is to indicate very substantial recovery for this element of damage. See Beagle v. Vasold, 65 Cal.2d 166, 53 Cal.Rptr. 129, 417 P.2d 673 (1966), where the court held it was an abuse of discretion for the trial judge not to permit this method of argument. See also Tucker v. Union Oil Co., 100 Idaho 590, 603 P.2d 156 (1979). On calculating personal injury damages generally, see C.E.B., Damages: Evaluation and Proof in Personal Injury and Wrongful Death Cases (1977).

Were the criteria used to measure the damages for loss of the plane in Reynolds v. Bank of America, supra p. 39, more meaningful? What is meant by "adequate compensation" in a personal injury case? See Dobbs, Remedies c. 8 (1973); compare Rabin, Dealing with Disasters: Some Thoughts on the Adequacy of the Legal System, 30 Stan.L.Rev. 281 (1978) (discussing the Buffalo Creek disaster, where a dam burst, wiping out a village and killing 125 people).

In response to the perceived explosion in the size of awards for pain and suffering, there is growing interest in placing statutory caps on such noneconomic damages. See, e.g., Gavin, The Constitutionality of Florida's Cap on Noneconomic Damages in the Tort Reform and Insurance Act of 1986, 39 U.Fla.L.Rev. 157 (1987). In 1986, California voters enacted Proposition 51 (codified at C.C. 1431 et seq.), which limits an individual joint tortfeasor's liability for noneconomic damages to the proportion equal to the tortfeasor's share of fault. The California Supreme Court upheld the constitutionality of Proposition 51 in Evangelatos v. Superior Court, 44 Cal.3d 1188, 246 Cal.Rptr. 629, 753 P.2d 585 (1988).

For more on the collateral source rule, discussed in *Helfend,* see Dobbs, Remedies §§ 3.6, 8.10 (1973); Branton, The Collateral Source Rule, 18 St. Mary's L.J. 883 (1987).

2. "Special" and "General" Damages

In the parlance of personal injury litigation, medical and hospital expenses and other outlays for treatment are called "special damages." Damages for income lost in the period of hospitalization and recuperation are also usually included in the reference to "special damages," although in some legal communities they are referred to as part of the "general damages." Damages for reduction in plaintiff's future earning capacity and for his pain and suffering are called "general damages."

The terms "special damages" and "general damages" are also applied in cases other than personal injury litigation. In years past there was much talk in the reports about the supposed difference between them. The distinction was attempted to be maintained for the purpose of limiting recoverable damages in certain types of cases, notably actions for breaches of contract. The distinction was never very satisfactory and today is largely an historical curiosity. The principal contemporary significance of the terms "special" and "general" damages is their use as terms of art in settlement negotiations concerning personal injury cases. The problem of determining the appropriate measure of damages of course remains. See Note, The Definition and Pleading of Special Damage Under the Federal Rules of Civil Procedure, 55 Va.L.Rev. 542 (1969); James & Hazard § 3.22; Brookshire, Economic Damages: Handbook for Plaintiff and Defense Attorneys (1987).

Was there a rational basis for valuation of the indignity claimed to have been suffered in Swann v. Burkett, supra p. 53? Or was that claim a masked form of punitive damages?

3. Damages in Contract Actions

The measure of damages in contract actions generally limits the recovery to the difference between the value of the performance received and the value of the performance promised, less any avoidance of cost the injured party enjoyed because the contract was incomplete. See Dobbs, Remedies c. 12 (1973). This leaves out "disruption" expenses, the various costs to the injured party resulting from the fact that the contract was not performed as and when promised. To avoid this limitation, contracts sometimes specify a formula of damages, called liquidated damages provisions. The courts will not enforce these formulae unless they are "reasonable," which often leads back to the standard measure of contract damages. See Dobbs, supra, § 12.5; Goetz and Scott, Liquidated Damages, Penalties and the Just Compensation Principle: Some Notes on an Enforcement Model and a Theory of Efficient Breach, 77

Colum.L.Rev. 554 (1977); Dunn, Recovery of Damages for Lost Profits (3d ed. 1987); Pettit, Private Advantage and Public Power: Reexamining the Expectation and Reliance Interests in Contract Damages, 38 Hastings L.J. 417 (1987).

For the difference between the measure of damages in contract and tort actions, see, e.g., Egan v. Mutual of Omaha Ins. Co., 63 Cal.App.3d 659, 133 Cal. Rptr. 899 (1976). This difference is often blurred, and has become increasingly so in jurisdictions that permit an action for "bad faith" breach of contract, where consequential and punitive damages may be recovered. See, e.g., Seaman's Direct Buying Serv., Inc. v. Standard Oil Co., 36 Cal.3d 752, 206 Cal.Rptr. 354, 686 P.2d 1158 (1984). But cf. Moradi-Shalal v. Fireman's Fund Ins. Co., 46 Cal.3d 287, 250 Cal.Rptr. 116, 758 P.2d 58 (1988) (no third party damages action against liability insurer for wrongful refusal to settle). On the measure of damages in commercial fraud, cf. Jacobs, The Measure of Damages in Rule 10b–5 Cases, 65 Georgetown L.J. 1093 (1977); Comment, The Measure of Damages Under Section 10(b) and Rule 10b–5, 46 Md.L.Rev. 1266 (1987); Dunn, Recovery of Damages for Fraud (1988).

4. Interest

Interest from the date of accrual of the cause of action to the date of judgment is allowed in some types of actions, such as actions for the recovery of money due under a contract obligation, but ordinarily is not recoverable in actions for injury to person or property. See Comment, Prejudgment Interest: Survey and Suggestion, 77 Nw.U.L.Rev. 192 (1982); Carroll, Jury Awards and Prejudgment Interest in Tort Cases (1983); Wilson, Bosco and Malone, Prejudgment Interest in Personal Injury, Wrongful Death and Other Actions, 30 Trial Law.Guide 105 (1986). Interest accrues on the judgment after its rendition and until it is paid or otherwise satisfied, e.g., Comment, Interest on Judgments in the Federal Courts, 64 Yale L.J. 1019 (1955). The Federal Government is not liable for interest under the doctrine of sovereign immunity, but this bar does not apply to suits based on statutes or contracts that expressly provide for interest or for claims under the takings clause of the Fifth Amendment. See Note, Interest in Judgments Against the Federal Government: The Need for Full Compensation, 91 Yale L.J. 297 (1981). The Supreme Court has held that the Federal Government is not liable for interest where it is a defendant in a civil rights case. See Library of Congress v. Shaw, 478 U.S. 310, 106 S.Ct. 2957, 92 L.Ed.2d 250 (1986).

The rate of interest on judgments is generally governed by statute unless otherwise specified by contract. Because the statutory rates generally are not indexed to inflation or market rates and are not frequently adjusted, the rate often lags behind the prevailing rate of interest. See, e.g., C.C.P. 685.010 (10 percent). Thus, defendants can retain their money and accumulate interest at market rates, creating a disincentive to settle or pay claims or judgments promptly and a positive incentive to delay payment by appeal or otherwise. To eliminate any post-judgment incentive to delay, the federal interest statute was amended in 1982 to tie the legal rate to the market rate. 28 U.S.C.A. § 1961. To eliminate pre-judgment incentives to delay, some states provide for interest from date of injury or suit, or give the trial court discretion to assess interest where a defendant has been deliberately dilatory. Busik v. Levine, 63 N.J. 351, 307 A.2d 571 (1973); Mich.Comp. Laws Ann. § 600.6013. See also Note, Denham v. Bedford: Statutory Prejudgment Interest and Its Effect on Third Party Insurers, 1979 Detroit Col.L.Rev. 345.

5. Punitive Damages

Punitive damages, as the term implies, are amounts awarded against a defendant as punishment for deliberately wrongful conduct and as a deterrent against such conduct by others. See Gertz v. Robert Welch, Inc., 418 U.S. 323, 350, 94 S.Ct. 2997, 41 L.Ed.2d 789 (1974). Traditionally punitive damages were associated with deliberate wrongs against the person, such as assault and defamation; intentional invasions of property, such as wilful trespass; and intentional interference with certain kinds of economic relationships. See Dobbs, Remedies § 3.9 (1973). In recent years there has been a dramatic expansion in the scope and magnitude of punitive damages claims in products liability, insurance, and some other contractual relationships. See, e.g., Tameny v. Atlantic Richfield Co., 27 Cal.3d 167, 164 Cal.Rptr. 839, 610 P.2d 1330 (1980); Photovest Corp. v. Fotomat Corp., 606 F.2d 704 (7th Cir. 1979); McDermott v. Kansas Public Serv. Co., 238 Kan. 462, 712 P.2d 1199 (1986). See also Owen, Problems in Assessing Punitive Damages Against Manufacturers of Defective Products, 49 U.Chi.L.Rev. 1 (1982); Symposium on Punitive Damages, 56 So.Calif.L.Rev. 1 (1982); Comment, Formulating Standards for Awards of Punitive Damages in the Borderland of Contract and Tort, 74 Calif.L.Rev. 2033 (1986). C.C.P. 3294 provides that a plaintiff may recover punitive damages for breach of an obligation not arising from a contract if the defendant is guilty of fraud, oppression, or malice and requires that plaintiff prove the right to such damages by clear and convincing evidence. Plaintiff is also barred under the statute from pleading a specific amount in punitive damages. See also Note, Punitive Damages in California Under the Malice Standard: Defining Conscious Disregard, 57 So.Calif.L.Rev. 1065 (1984).

Partly as a result of the increase in the scope and magnitude of punitive damages liability, there has been growing attention in recent years to whether the Constitution places limits on such damages. The Supreme Court was asked to rule on this question in Bankers Life & Casualty Co. v. Crenshaw, infra p. 1320, but felt that the question was not adequately presented. As that opinion shows, the issues are chiefly whether punitive damages have a "chilling effect" on a litigant's right of access to the courts or impose essentially criminal sanctions in violation of due process, and whether the excessive fines clause of the Eighth Amendment should apply to civil punitive damages awards. In the absence of guidance from the federal courts, some state courts have begun to address these questions. See, e.g., Colonial Pipeline Co. v. Brown, 258 Ga. 115, 365 S.E.2d 827 (1988) (invalidating a $5,000,000 punitive damages award as an excessive fine under state constitution); Ace Truck & Equipment Rentals, Inc. v. Kahn, 103 Nev. 503, 746 P.2d 132 (1987) (overturning a $800,000 punitive damages award as excessive on nonconstitutional grounds). See also Jeffries, A Comment on the Constitutionality of Punitive Damages, 72 Va.L.Rev. 139 (1986); Massey, The Excessive Fines Clause and Punitive Damages: Some Lessons From History, 40 Vand.L.Rev. 1234 (1987). The Supreme Court may finally address the constitutional issues in Kelco Disposal, Inc. v. Browning–Ferris Indust. of Vermont, Inc., 845 F.2d 404 (2d Cir.1988), cert. granted ___ U.S. ___, 109 S.Ct. 527, 102 L.Ed.2d 559 (1988), where the Second Circuit held that an award of $6 million in punitive damages, amounting to more than 100 times plaintiff's actual damages, did not violate the Eighth Amendment.

2. SPECIFIC RELIEF: INJUNCTIONS AND DECLARATORY RELIEF

INTRODUCTORY NOTE ON SPECIFIC RELIEF

The remedy of damages gives plaintiff money (more exactly, the right to collect money through the procedures for executing a judgment). In contrast, under some circumstances he may obtain "specific" relief, by which is meant a court order directing the defendant to do an act, or refrain from doing an act, with the consequence that the plaintiff's position is made better, or its worsening averted. In modern procedure, the injunction is the usual means by which specific relief is provided. This has some important consequences. First, because the injunction derives from equity, the tradition is that whether and on what terms an injunction may issue is a matter of "discretion" of the court. Second, also because the injunction derives from equity, the determination of fact issues going to the remedy is for the judge and not a jury; in most states and to an uncertain degree in the federal courts, the issue of whether the defendant's conduct was wrongful is, in an injunction case, also tried to the court rather than a jury. See Right to Jury Trial, infra p. 997.

The association between the injunction and equity is historical. Simply put, the common law awarded only the remedy of damages in most situations, so that if a party sought specific relief he had to go to equity. See Historical Note on Procedure, supra p. 18. But the common law awarded specific relief in a few situations, of which there are remnants in modern procedure. The most significant of these is replevin, an action to recover possession of personal property. The modern version is referred to as "claim and delivery" in some states. See C.C.P. 511.010 et seq.; 6 Witkin 183 et seq. Compare N.Y.C.P.L.R. § 7101 et seq. However, even here the judgment may only create a liability in the defendant if she does not return the property, and hence in effect is a damages remedy. If plaintiff wishes the very goods, and can show them to be unique, his remedy is an injunction, essentially similar to specific performance. See Note on Injunctions and Declaratory Relief, infra p. 198.

The remedy of injunction is distinct from the damages remedy in yet another way. A judgment for damages does not of itself obligate the defendant to be forthcoming to pay it; it is up to plaintiff to discover defendant's assets through supplementary proceedings. See, e.g., Campbell and Lynn, Creditors' Rights Handbook c. 7 (1985); 8 Witkin 61 et seq.; cf. Olsan v. Comora, 73 Cal. App.3d 642, 140 Cal.Rptr. 835 (1977), and C.E.B., 1 Calif.Civ.Pro. Before Trial, c. 18 (1977) (appointment of receiver). This may culminate in an order directing defendant to place his property at disposal for sale. Such an order is an injunction and as such creates a "personal" obligation to obey. This means the power of contempt of court may be brought to bear. See Rendleman, Compensatory Contempt: Plaintiff's Remedy When a Defendant Violates an Injunction, 1980 U.Ill.L.F. 971.

WEINBERGER v. ROMERO–BARCELO

Supreme Court of the United States, 1982.
456 U.S. 305, 102 S.Ct. 1798, 72 L.Ed.2d 91.*

WHITE, JUSTICE.

The issue in this case is whether the Federal Water Pollution Control Act (FWPCA or Act), 86 Stat. 816, as amended, 33 U.S.C. § 1251 et seq. (1976 ed. and Supp. IV), requires a district court to enjoin immediately all discharges of pollutants that do not comply with the Act's permit requirements or whether the district court retains discretion to order other relief to achieve compliance. The Court of Appeals for the First Circuit held that the Act withdrew the courts' equitable discretion. Romero–Barcelo v. Brown, 643 F.2d 835 (1981). We reverse.

I

For many years, the Navy has used Vieques Island, a small island off the Puerto Rico coast, for weapons training. Currently all Atlantic Fleet vessels assigned to the Mediterranean and the Indian Ocean are required to complete their training at Vieques because it permits a full range of exercises under conditions similar to combat. During air-to-ground training, however, pilots sometimes miss land-based targets, and ordnance falls into the sea. That is, accidental bombings of the navigable waters and, occasionally, intentional bombings of water targets occur. The District Court found that these discharges have not harmed the quality of the water.

In 1978, respondents, who include the Governor of Puerto Rico and residents of the island, sued to enjoin the Navy's operations on the island. Their complaint alleged violations of numerous federal environmental statutes and various other acts.[1] After an extensive hearing, the District Court found that under the explicit terms of the Act, the Navy had violated the Act by discharging ordnance into the waters surrounding the island without first obtaining a permit from the Environmental Protection Agency (EPA).[2] Romero–Barcelo v. Brown, 478 F.Supp. 646 (D.P.R.1979).

* Some of the Court's footnotes are omitted.

1. The complaint charged the Navy with violations of the National Environmental Policy Act of 1969, 42 U.S.C. § 4321 et seq.; the Federal Water Pollution Act, 33 U.S.C. § 1251 et seq.; the Clean Air Act Amendments of 1977, 42 U.S.C. § 7401 et seq.; the Noise Control Act of 1972, 42 U.S.C. § 4901 et seq.; the Resource Conservation and Recovery Act of 1976, 42 U.S.C. § 6901 et seq.; the Endangered Species Act of 1973, 16 U.S.C. § 1531 et seq.; the National Historic Preservation Act of 1966, 16 U.S.C. § 470 et seq.; the Coastal Zone Management Act of 1972, 16 U.S.C. § 1451 et seq.; the Marine Mammal Protection Act of 1972, 16 U.S.C. § 1361 et seq.; the Rivers and Harbors Appropriation Act of 1899, 33 U.S.C. § 401 et seq.; various amendments to the United States Constitution, congressional and presidential directives concerning cessation of Navy operations on the neighboring island of Culebra, and violations of Puerto Rico law.

2. The district court also found that the Navy had violated the National Environmental Protection Act (NEPA) by failing to file an Environmental Impact Statement (EIS) or a reviewable environmental record to support a decision not to file such a

192 PLENARY JUDICIAL REMEDIES Pt. 3

Under the FWPCA, the "discharge of any pollutant" requires a National Pollutant Discharge Elimination System (NPDES) permit. 33 U.S.C. § 1311(a), § 1323(a) (1976 ed. and Supp. IV). The term "discharge of any pollutant" is defined as

"any addition of any *pollutant* to the waters of the contiguous zone or the ocean from any *point source* other than a vessel or other floating craft." 33 U.S.C. § 1362(12) (emphasis added).

Pollutant, in turn, means,

"dredged spoil, solid wastes, incinerator residue, sewage, garbage, sewage sludge, *munitions,* chemical wastes, biological materials, radioactive materials, heat, wrecked or discarded equipment, rock, sand, cellar dirt and industrial, municipal and agricultural waste discharged into water. . . ." 33 U.S.C. § 1362(6) (emphasis added).

And, under the Act, a "point source" is

"any discernible, confined and discrete *conveyance,* including but not limited to any pipe, ditch, channel, tunnel, conduit, well, discrete fissure, container rolling stock, concentrated animal feeding operation, or *vessel* or other *floating craft from which pollutants are or may be discharged.* . . ." 33 U.S.C. § 1362(14) (emphasis added).

Under the FWPCA, the EPA may not issue an NPDES without state certification that the permit conforms to state water quality standards. A state has the authority to deny certification of the permit application or attach conditions to the final permit. 33 U.S.C. § 1341.

As the District Court construed the FWPCA, the release of ordnance from aircraft or from ships into navigable waters is a discharge of pollutants, even though the Environmental Protection Agency, which administers the Act, had not promulgated any regulations setting effluent levels or providing for the issuance of an NPDES permit for this category of pollutants.[3] Recognizing that violations of the Act "must be cured," 478 F.Supp., at 707, the District Court ordered the Navy to apply for an NPDES permit. It refused, however, to enjoin Navy operations pending consideration of the permit application. It

statement, Romero–Barcelo v. Brown, 478 F.Supp. 646, 705 (D.P.R.1979), and had failed to nominate historic sites to the National Register as required under the National Historic Preservation Act. Ibid. It ordered the Navy to nominate such sites and to file an EIS. Id., at 708. The Court of Appeals remanded issues under the Endangered Species Act and the National Historic Preservation Act to the district court for further consideration. Romero–Barcelo v. Brown, 643 F.2d 835, 858, 860, 862 (1981). It vacated the order involving NEPA and remanded with orders to dismiss because the Navy had filed an EIS in the interim. Id., at 862. Only the issue involving the FWPCA is before this Court.

3. The EPA issues effluent limitations for categories and classes of point sources. See generally E. I. du Pont de Nemours & Co. v. Train, 430 U.S. 112, 97 S.Ct. 965, 51 L.Ed.2d 204 (1977); 40 CFR part 400 et seq. In a situation somewhat similar to that before us, the Secretary of Interior has, under the Migratory Bird Treaty Act, 16 U.S.C. § 703 et seq., regulated deposit of shot into water by duck hunters who miss their targets. National Rifle Ass'n v. Kleppe, 425 F.Supp. 1101 (D.D.C.1976), aff'd., 571 F.2d 674 (CADC 1978) (table).

explained that the Navy's "technical violations" were not causing any "appreciable harm" to the environment.[4] Id., at 706. Moreover, because of the importance of the island as a training center, "the granting of the injunctive relief sought would cause grievous, and perhaps irreparable harm, not only to Defendant Navy, but to the general welfare of this Nation."[5] Id., at 707. The District Court concluded that an injunction was not necessary to ensure suitably prompt compliance by the Navy. To support this conclusion, it emphasized an equity court's traditionally broad discretion in deciding appropriate relief and quoted from the classic description of injunctive relief in Hecht Co. v. Bowles, 321 U.S. 321, 329–330, 64 S.Ct. 587, 591–592, 88 L.Ed. 754 (1944): "The historic injunctive process was designed to deter, not to punish."

The Court of Appeals for the First Circuit vacated the District Court's order and remanded with instructions that the court order the Navy to cease the violation until it obtained a permit. 643 F.2d 835 (1981). Relying on TVA v. Hill, 437 U.S. 153, 98 S.Ct. 2279, 57 L.Ed.2d 117 (1978), in which this Court held that an imminent violation of the Endangered Species Act required injunctive relief, the Court of Appeals concluded that the District Court erred in undertaking a traditional balancing of the parties' competing interests. "Whether or not the Navy's activities in fact harm the coastal waters, it has an absolute statutory obligation to stop any discharges of pollutant until the permit procedure has been followed and the Administrator of the Environmental Protection Agency, upon review of the evidence, has granted a permit." 643 F.2d, at 861. The court suggested that if the order would interfere significantly with military preparedness, the Navy should request that the President grant it an exemption from the requirements in the interest of national security.[6]

4. The District Court wrote:

"In fact, if anything, these waters are as aesthetically acceptable as any to be found anywhere, and Plaintiff's witnesses unanimously testified as to their being the best fishing grounds in Vieques . . . . [I]f truth be said, the control of large areas of Vieques [by the Navy] probably constitutes a positive factor in its over all ecology. The very fact that there are in the Navy zones modest numbers of various marine species which are practically nonexistent in the civilian sector of Vieques or in the main island of Puerto Rico, is an eloquent example of *res ipsa loquitur*." 478 F.Supp., at 667, 682.

5. The District Court also took into consideration the delay by plaintiffs in asserting their claims. It concluded that although laches should not totally bar the claims, it did strongly militate against the granting of injunctive relief. 478 F.Supp., at 707.

6. 33 U.S.C. § 1323(a) (1976 ed., Supp. IV) provides, in relevant part:

"The President may exempt any effluent source of any department, agency, or instrumentality in the executive branch from compliance with any such a requirement if he determines it to be in the paramount interest of the United States to do so. . . . No such exemptions shall be granted due to lack of appropriation unless the President shall have specifically requested such appropriation as part of the budgetary process and the Congress shall have failed to make available such requested appropriation. Any exemption shall be for a period not in excess of one year, but additional exemptions may be granted for periods of not to exceed one year upon the President's making a new determination. The President shall report each January to the Congress all exemptions from the requirements of this section granted during the preceding calen-

Because this case posed an important question regarding the power of the federal courts to grant or withhold equitable relief for violations of the FWPCA, we granted certiorari, 454 U.S. 813, 102 S.Ct. 88, 70 L.Ed.2d 81 (1981). We now reverse.

II

It goes without saying that an injunction is an equitable remedy. It "is not a remedy which issues as of course," Harrisonville v. W. S. Dickey Clay Mfg. Co., 289 U.S. 334, 338, 53 S.Ct. 602, 603, 77 L.Ed. 1208 (1933), or "to restrain an act the injurious consequences of which are merely trifling." Consolidated Canal Co. v. Mesa Canal Co., 177 U.S. 296, 302, 20 S.Ct. 628, 630, 44 L.Ed. 777 (1900). An injunction should issue only where the intervention of a court of equity "is essential in order effectually to protect property rights against injuries otherwise irremediable." Cavanaugh v. Looney, 248 U.S. 453, 456, 39 S.Ct. 142, 143, 63 L.Ed. 354 (1919). The Court has repeatedly held that the basis for injunctive relief in the federal courts has always been irreparable injury and the inadequacy of legal remedies. Rondeau v. Mosinee Paper Corp., 422 U.S. 49, 61, 95 S.Ct. 2069, 2077, 45 L.Ed.2d 12 (1975); Sampson v. Murray, 415 U.S. 61, 88, 94 S.Ct. 937, 951, 39 L.Ed.2d 166 (1974); Beacon Theaters, Inc. v. Westover, 359 U.S. 500, 506–507, 79 S.Ct. 948, 954–955, 3 L.Ed.2d 988 (1959); Hecht Co. v. Bowles, supra, at 329, 64 S.Ct., at 591.

Where plaintiff and defendant present competing claims of injury, the traditional function of equity has been to arrive at a "nice adjustment and reconciliation" between the competing claims, Hecht Co. v. Bowles, supra, at 329, 64 S.Ct., at 592. In such cases, the court "balances the conveniences of the parties and possible injuries to them according as they may be affected by the granting or withholding of the injunction." Yakus v. United States, 321 U.S. 414, 440, 64 S.Ct. 660, 675, 88 L.Ed. 834 (1944). "The essence of equity has been the power of the chancellor to do equity and to mold each decree to the necessities of the particular case. Flexibility rather than rigidity has distinguished it." Hecht Co. v. Bowles, supra, 321 U.S., at 329, 64 S.Ct., at 592.

In exercising their sound discretion, courts of equity should pay particular regard for the public consequences in employing the extraordinary remedy of injunction. Railroad Comm'n. v. Pullman Co., 312 U.S. 496, 500, 61 S.Ct. 643, 645, 85 L.Ed. 971 (1941). Thus, the Court has noted that "[t]he award of an interlocutory injunction by courts of equity has never been regarded as strictly a matter of right, even though irreparable injury may otherwise result to the plaintiff," and that "where an injunction is asked which will adversely affect a public interest for whose impairment, even temporarily, an injunction bond cannot compensate, the court may in the public interest withhold relief until a final determination of the rights of the parties, though

dar year, together with his reason for granting such exemption."

postponement may be burdensome to the plaintiff." Yakus v. United States, supra, 321 U.S., at 440, 64 S.Ct., at 675 (footnote omitted).
* * *

In TVA v. Hill, we held that Congress had foreclosed the exercise of the usual discretion possessed by a court of equity. There, we thought that "[o]ne would be hard pressed to find a statutory provision whose terms were any plainer" than that before us. 437 U.S., at 173, 98 S.Ct., at 2291. The statute involved, the Endangered Species Act, 87 Stat. 884, 16 U.S.C. § 1531 et seq., required the District Court to enjoin completion of the Tellico Dam in order to preserve the snail darter, a species of perch. The purpose and language of the statute under consideration in *Hill*, not the bare fact of a statutory violation, compelled that conclusion. Section 7 of the Act, 16 U.S.C. § 1536, requires federal agencies to "insure that actions authorized, funded, or carried out by them do not jeopardize the continued existence of [any] endangered species . . . or result in the destruction or habitat of such species which is determined . . . to be critical." The statute thus contains a flat ban on the destruction of critical habitats. * * *[7]

Other aspects of the statutory scheme also suggest that Congress did not intend to deny courts the discretion to rely on remedies other than an immediate prohibitory injunction. Although the ultimate objective of the FWPCA is to eliminate all discharges of pollutants into the navigable waters by 1985, the statute sets forth a scheme of phased compliance. As enacted, it called for the achievement of the "best practicable control technology currently available" by July 1, 1977 and the "best available technology economically achievable" by July 1, 1983. 33 U.S.C. § 1311(b). This scheme of phased compliance further suggests that this is a statute in which Congress envisioned, rather than curtailed, the exercise of discretion.[11]

The FWPCA directs the Administrator of the EPA to seek an injunction to restrain immediately discharges of pollutants he finds to be presenting "an imminent and substantial endangerment of the health of persons or to the welfare of persons." 33 U.S.C. § 1364(a)

7. The objective of this statute is in some respects similar to that sought in nuisance suits, where courts have fully exercised their equitable discretion and ingenuity in ordering remedies. E.g., Spur Ind. Inc. v. Del E. Webb Development Co., 108 Ariz. 178, 494 P.2d 700 (1972); Boomer v. Atlantic Cement Co., 26 N.Y.2d 219, 309 N.Y.S.2d 312, 257 N.E.2d 870 (1970).

11. We have, however, held some standards related to phased compliance to be absolute. See EPA v. National Crushed Stone Association, 449 U.S. 64, 101 S.Ct. 295, 66 L.Ed.2d 268 (1980). In Middlesex County Sewerage Authority v. National Sea Clammers Ass'n., 453 U.S. 1, 101 S.Ct. 2615, 69 L.Ed.2d 435 (1981), we concluded that the federal common law of nuisance

was preempted by the FWPCA and other similar acts: "In the absence of strong indicia of a contrary congressional intent, we are compelled to conclude that Congress provided precisely the remedies it considered appropriate." Id., at 15, 101 S.Ct., at 2623; see Milwaukee v. Illinois, 451 U.S. 304, 101 S.Ct. 1784, 68 L.Ed.2d 114 (1981). But, as we have also observed in construing this Act: "The question . . . is not what a court thinks is generally appropriate to the regulatory process, it is what Congress intended. . . ." E. I. Du Pont de Nemours & Co. v. Train, 430 U.S. 112, 138, 97 S.Ct. 965, 980, 51 L.Ed.2d 204 (1977). Here we do not read the FWPCA as intending to abolish the courts' equitable discretion in ordering remedies.

(1976 ed., Supp. IV). This rule of immediate cessation, however, is limited to the indicated class of violations. For other kinds of violations, the FWPCA authorizes the Administrator of the EPA "to commence a civil action for appropriate relief, including a permanent or temporary injunction, for any violation for which he is authorized to issue a compliance order. . . ." 33 U.S.C. § 1319(b). The provision makes clear that Congress did not anticipate that all discharges would be immediately enjoined. Consistent with this view, the administrative practice has not been to request immediate cessation orders. "Rather, enforcement actions typically result, by consent or otherwise, in a remedial order setting out a detailed schedule of compliance designed to cure the identified violation of the Act." Brief for Petitioners 17. See Milwaukee v. Illinois, 451 U.S. 304, 320–322, 101 S.Ct. 1784, 1794–1795, 68 L.Ed.2d 114 (1981). Here, again, the statutory scheme contemplates equitable consideration.

Both the Court of Appeals and respondents attach particular weight to the provision of the FWPCA permitting the President to exempt Federal facilities from compliance with the permit requirements. 33 U.S.C. § 1323(a) (1976 ed., Supp. IV). They suggest that this provision indicates Congressional intent to limit the court's discretion. According to respondents, the exemption provision evidences Congress' determination that only paramount national interests justify failure to comply and that only the President should make this judgment.

We do not construe the provision so broadly. We read the FWPCA as permitting the exercise of a court's equitable discretion, whether the source of pollution is a private party or a federal agency, to order relief that will achieve *compliance* with the Act. The exemption serves a different and complementary purpose, that of permitting *noncompliance* by federal agencies in extraordinary circumstances. Exec. Order No. 12088, 3 CFR 243 (1979), which implements the exemption authority, requires the federal agency requesting such an exemption to certify that it cannot meet the applicable pollution standards. "Exemptions are granted by the President only if the conflict between pollution control standards and crucial federal activities cannot be resolved through the development of a practicable remedial program." Brief for Petitioners 26, n. 30.

* * *

III

This Court explained in Hecht Co. v. Bowles, 321 U.S. 321, 64 S.Ct. 587, 88 L.Ed. 754 (1944), that a major departure from the long tradition of equity practice should not be lightly implied. As we did there, we construe the statute at issue "in favor of that interpretation which affords a full opportunity for equity courts to treat enforcement proceedings . . . in accordance with their traditional practices, as conditioned by the necessities of the public interest which Congress has sought to protect." Id., at 330, 64 S.Ct., at 592. * * *

Because Congress, in enacting the FWPCA, has not foreclosed the exercise of equitable discretion, the proper standard for appellate review is whether the district court abused its discretion in denying an immediate cessation order while the Navy applied for a permit. We reverse and remand to the Court of Appeals for proceedings consistent with this opinion.[*]

STEVENS, JUSTICE, dissenting.

The appropriate remedy for the violation of a federal statute depends primarily on the terms of the statute and the character of the violation. Unless Congress specifically commands a particular form of relief, the question of remedy remains subject to a court's equitable discretion.[1] Because the Federal Water Pollution Control Act does not specifically command the federal courts to issue an injunction every time an unpermitted discharge of a pollutant occurs, the Court today is obviously correct in asserting that such injunctions should not issue "automatically" or "mechanically" in every case. It is nevertheless equally clear that by enacting the 1972 amendments to the FWPCA Congress channeled the discretion of the federal judiciary much more narrowly than the Court's rather glib opinion suggests. Indeed, although there may well be situations in which the failure to obtain an NPDES permit would not require immediate cessation of all discharges, I am convinced that Congress has circumscribed the district courts' discretion on the question of remedy so narrowly that a general rule of immediate cessation must be applied in all but a narrow category of cases. The Court of Appeals was quite correct in holding that this case does not present the kind of exceptional situation that justifies a departure from the general rule.

* * *

Our cases concerning equitable remedies have repeatedly identified two critical distinctions that the Court simply ignores today. The first is the distinction between cases in which only private interests are involved and those in which a requested injunction will implicate a public interest. Second, within the category of public interest cases, those cases in which there is no danger that a past violation of law will recur have always been treated differently from those in which an existing violation is certain to continue.

Yakus v. United States, 321 U.S. 414, 441, 64 S.Ct. 660, 675, 88 L.Ed. 834, illustrates the first distinction. The Court there held that Congress constitutionally could preclude a private party from obtaining an injunction against enforcement of federal price control regulations

---

[*] The concurring opinion of Justice Powell is omitted.

[1] Cf. Steelworkers v. United States, 361 U.S. 39, 54–59, 80 S.Ct. 1, 177, 182–185, 4 L.Ed.2d 12 (Frankfurter and Harlan, JJ., concurring).

pending an adjudication of their validity. In any balancing process, the Court explained, special deference must be given to the public interest:

"Even in suits in which only private interests are involved the award is a matter of sound judicial discretion, in the exercise of which the court balances the conveniences of the parties and possible injuries to them according as they may be affected by the granting or withholding of the injunction. . . .

"But where an injunction is asked which will adversely affect a public interest for whose impairment, even temporarily, an injunction bond cannot compensate, the court may in the public interest withhold relief until a final determination of the rights of the parties, though the postponement may be burdensome to the plaintiff." Id., at 440, 64 S.Ct., at 675.

* * *

Hecht Co. v. Bowles, 321 U.S. 321, 64 S.Ct. 587, 88 L.Ed. 754, which the Court repeatedly cites, did involve an attempt to obtain an injunction against future violations of a federal statute. That case fell into the category of cases in which a past violation of law had been found and the question was whether an injunction should issue to prevent future violations. Cf. United States v. W. T. Grant Co., 345 U.S. 629, 633–636, 73 S.Ct. 894, 897–899, 97 L.Ed. 1303; United States v. Oregon Medical Society, 343 U.S. 326, 332–334, 72 S.Ct. 690, 695–696, 96 L.Ed. 978. Because the record established that the past violations were inadvertent, that they had been promptly terminated, and that the defendant had taken vigorous and adequate steps to prevent any recurrence, the Court held that the District Court had discretion to deny injunctive relief. * * *

In contrast to the decision in *Hecht,* today the Court pays mere lip service to the statutory mandate and attaches no weight to the fact that the Navy's violation of law has not been corrected.[8] The Court cites no precedent for its holding that an ongoing deliberate violation of a federal statute should be treated like any garden-variety private nuisance action in which the chancellor has the widest discretion in fashioning relief.[9]

* * *

NOTE ON INJUNCTIONS AND DECLARATORY RELIEF

1. Injunction as an "Extraordinary" Remedy

The tradition was, and to some extent still is, that relief by injunction rather than damages could be obtained only in "extraordinary" circumstances, when the legal remedy (usually damages) was "inadequate." On the early

8. The Navy has been in continuous violation of the statute during the entire decade since its enactment.

9. Indeed, I am unaware of any case in which the Court has permitted a statutory violation to continue.

development of injunction as a remedy, see Raack, A History of Injunctions in England Before 1700, 61 Ind.L.J. 539 (1986). In private litigation, "inadequacy" is found readily, even routinely, in a suit by a purchaser of real property to whom the seller has refused to convey, the remedy being specific performance. See, e.g., Converse v. Fong, 159 Cal.App.3d 86, 205 Cal.Rptr. 242 (1984); cf. Restatement Second of Contracts § 360, Comment e. The same remedy is generally available to enforce a contract for the sale of stock in a corporation whose shares are closely held. Calamari and Perillo, Contracts § 16–3 (3d ed. 1987). For an economic analysis of the concept, see Kronman, Specific Performance, 45 U.Chi.L.Rev. 351 (1978). Compare Schwartz, The Case for Specific Performance, 89 Yale L.J. 271 (1979), and Ulen, The Efficiency of Specific Performance: Toward a Unified Theory of Contract Remedies, 83 Mich.L.Rev. 341 (1984), arguing that specific performance should be routinely available, with Yorio, In Defense of Money Damages for Breach of Contract, 82 Colum.L.Rev. 1365 (1982). Injunctions are also given though not so routinely to restrain nuisances, i.e., activities resulting in continuing intrusion on the plaintiff's property. See, e.g., Scott v. Jordon, 99 N.M. 567, 661 P.2d 59 (1983); Christopher v. Jones, 231 Cal.App.2d 408, 41 Cal.Rptr. 828 (1964). Aside from these situations, the injunction remedy requires a showing of good cause in private litigation. See generally C.E.B., 1 Calif.Civ.Pro. Before Trial, c. 15 (1977). And there is good authority that an injunction should not issue if the threat of harm has ended. See Rondeau v. Mosinee Paper Corp., 422 U.S. 49, 95 S.Ct. 2069, 45 L.Ed.2d 12 (1975).

2. Other "Equitable" Remedies

a. Constructive Trust. One of the historic remedies in equity is the imposition of a "constructive trust." The trust is "imposed" on property which is in the hands of defendant but which in justice belongs or ought to be restored to plaintiff. See Restatement of Restitution § 160 et seq.; Restatement of Trusts § 44 et seq. What is the difference between imposing a constructive trust and awarding a damages remedy?

b. Rescission or Cancellation of Contract. When because of mistake, fraud or other recognized ground, one party is privileged to withdraw from a contract which he has made, he may obtain judicial authorization to do so by seeking rescission of the contract. The resulting decree customarily speaks in terms of "canceling" the contract and provides for restoration of payments made or other measures necessary to restore the status quo ante the contract. See, e.g., Williams v. Marshall, 37 Cal.2d 445, 235 P.2d 372 (1951); Star Pacific Investments, Inc. v. Oro Hills Ranch, Inc., 121 Cal.App.3d 447, 176 Cal.Rptr. 546 (1981).

c. Reorganization of Financial Affairs. Equity also affords remedies to straighten out entangled business transactions, among them: accounting between parties to a complex financial arrangement, e.g., Nat. Bank of Alaska v. J.B.L. & K. of Alaska, Inc., 546 P.2d 579 (Alaska 1976); and receivership for business ventures that are in financial difficulty, see C.E.B., Calif.Civ.Pro. Before Trial, c. 18 (1977).

d. Quiet Title. The suit to quiet title originated as the remedy of a land occupant to put to rest the repeated assertion of ejectment actions against him. In time, it was enlarged so as to afford a remedy to settle and protect interests in land that could not be determined in ejectment. That is to say, it could be used to determine rights in easements and rights based on "equitable" title. It was the precursor of the modern statutory remedy for determination of title.

The history of quiet title and the genesis of the statutory remedy is explained in Wehrman v. Conklin, 155 U.S. 314, 321–22, 15 S.Ct. 129, 131–132, 39 L.Ed. 167, 172 (1894):

> "The general principles of equity jurisprudence, as administered both in this country and in England, permit a bill to quiet title to be filed only by a party in possession against a defendant, who has been ineffectually seeking to establish a legal title by repeated actions of ejectment, and as a prerequisite to such bill it was necessary that the title of the plaintiff should have been established by at least one successful trial at law. Pomeroy's Equity Jurisprudence, sections 253, 1394, and 1396. At common law a party might by successive fictitious demises bring as many actions of ejectment as he chose, and a bill to quiet title was only permitted for the purpose of preventing the party in possession being annoyed by repeated and vexatious actions. The jurisdiction was in fact only another exercise of the familiar power of a court of equity to prevent a multiplicity of suits by bills of peace. A statement of the underlying principles of such bills is found in the opinion of this court in Holland v. Challen, 110 U.S. 15, 19, 3 S.Ct. 495, in which it is said: 'To entitle the plaintiff to relief in such cases the concurrence of three particulars was essential: He must have been in possession of the property; he must have been disturbed in its possession by repeated actions at law; and he must have established his right by successive judgments in his favor. Upon these facts appearing, the court would interpose and grant a perpetual injunction to quiet the possession of the plaintiff against any further litigation from the same source. It was only in this way that adequate relief could be afforded against vexatious litigation and the irreparable mischief which it entailed.'
>
> "This method of adjusting titles by bill in equity proved so convenient, that in many of the States statutes have been passed extending the jurisdiction of a court of equity to all cases where a party in possession, and sometimes out of possession, seeks to clear up his title and remove any cloud caused by an outstanding deed or lien which he claims to be invalid, and the existence of which is a threat against his peaceable occupation of the land, and an obstacle to its sale."

e. Suit to Remove Clouds. At the beginning of the 19th century the courts of equity developed yet another remedy for clearing title to land. This was the bill to remove a cloud. It was a form of *quia timet* ("because he fears") relief, granted to a plaintiff whose possession was as yet undisturbed but who feared that the existence of a document purporting to vest in another title or interest in the land would lead to later disturbance of plaintiff's possession. Its history is described in Howard, Bills to Remove Cloud from Title, 25 W.Va.L.Q. 4 (1917). Compare Leubsdorf, Remedies for Uncertainty, 61 B.U.L.Rev. 132 (1981).

3. Injunction as an "Ordinary" Remedy

In a wide variety of "public law" litigation, the remedy of injunction is the normal mode of relief, although damages for past injury are also awarded in employment discrimination cases and other situations in which a monetary loss can be determined with relative precision. See, e.g., Fiss, The Civil Rights Injunction (1978); Rendleman, The Inadequate Remedy at Law Prerequisite for an Injunction, 33 U.Fla.L.Rev. 346 (1981); Leubsdorf, Completing the Desegregation Remedy, 57 B.U.L.Rev. 39 (1977); Bacigal and Bacigal, A Case Study of the Federal Judiciary's Role in Court-Ordered Busing, 3 J.Law & Pol. 693

(1987); Nagel, Controlling the Structural Injunction, 7 Harv.J.L. & Pub.Pol'y 395 (1984); Note, Implementation Problems in Institutional Reform Litigation, 91 Harv.L.Rev. 428 (1977); cf. Note, Updating the Injunction to Protect Human Health and Safety, 11 Suffolk U.L.Rev. 114 (1976). It has apparently been considered inappropriate, perhaps unthinkable, to award damages relief in cases involving school segregation, prison and hospital mistreatment, and ecological injury. But the idea of putting a monetary value on such injuries is certainly not unthinkable, see Swann v. Burkett, supra p. 53, and it is not unthinkable to do so for large groups of plaintiffs through the class suit device, see Vasquez v. Superior Court, infra p. 842. Furthermore, on principles of economic efficiency and ease of administration, the damages remedy might have some utility, allowing the courts to offer inducements to a defendant's compliance with a "public law" duty instead of trying to direct compliance through an injunction.

In any event, no one can be wholly sanguine about the legitimacy and efficacy of "public law" decrees. There is, of course, the question of "activism" by the judicial branch of government. There is also the question of distribution of authority between the trial court and the appellate court. The tradition is that the scope of appellate review is limited to whether the trial court was guilty of an "abuse of discretion," which leaves a lot of power in one person. See Hinkle, Appellate Supervision of Remedies in Public Law Adjudication, 4 Fla.State U.L.Rev. 411 (1976). More deeply, there is the "realist" question about whether the decrees work out the way they are intended. There is a considerable "impact" literature in political science dealing with this question. See, e.g., Dolbeare and Hammond, The School Prayer Decisions: From Court Policy to Local Practice (1971). For a thoughtful analysis of "structural" decrees, see Handler, The Conditions of Discretion: Autonomy, Community, Bureaucracy (1986); see also Anderson, Implementation of Consent Decrees in Structural Reform Litigation, 1986 U.Ill.L.Rev. 725. See also Complex Litigation, Introduction, infra p. 1203, and Decree, infra p. 1243.

4. Declaratory Relief

Quia timet relief, i.e., granting plaintiff a judicial determination of the legal relationship between himself and another "because he fears" that his out-of-court situation may be prejudiced if he is forced to act without official advice, has a long history in equity. A part of that history is the suit to quiet title or to remove clouds on title, discussed above. Analytically similar is the equitable remedy of interpleader, by which a person holding property claimed by two or more others may commence an action against the claimants and compel them to fight out their competing claims between themselves. In this way, the stakeholder insures against the possibility that the claimants may each later sue her (resulting in multiple litigation) and perhaps may each recover (resulting in multiple liability). See State Farm Fire & Casualty Co. v. Tashire, infra p. 770, and the Note following. Also analytically similar is the petition by a trustee, or other fiduciary charged with managing property, for an examination and approval of his accounts or for directions as to how to proceed in his management, to the end that those claiming an interest in the property or estate in his care may not later assert claims of mismanagement against him. Compare Mullane v. Central Hanover Bank & Trust Co., infra p. 303. For a discussion of these and other historically established procedures of the *quia timet* type, see Borchard, Declaratory Judgments c. IV (2d ed. 1941).

During the 19th century there was little or no expansion in the range of *quia timet* relief beyond the confines of the historic equitable mold. The declaratory judgment, though well known in continental civil procedure, was practically unheard of—and when heard of, regarded with great suspicion—in Anglo-American jurisprudence. By stages, England adopted the declaratory remedy; by legislation, most American jurisdictions have now done so, typically by adoption of a statute patterned after the Uniform Declaratory Judgments Act, 12 U.L.A. 111 (Master ed. 1975); see, e.g., C.C.P. 1060 et seq. See also the Federal Declaratory Judgment Act, 28 U.S.C.A. §§ 2201–2202; F.R.C.P. 57; Restatement Second of Judgments § 33.

The chief difficulty which the declaratory remedy encountered, aside from its supposed novelty, was the fear that it might open the doors to applications for gratuitous judicial advice on problems troublesome but not critical. See Liberty Warehouse Co. v. Grannis, 273 U.S. 70, 47 S.Ct. 282, 71 L.Ed. 541 (1927); cf. Willing v. Chicago Auditorium Ass'n, 277 U.S. 274, 48 S.Ct. 507, 72 L.Ed. 880 (1928) (suggesting that declaratory judgments were beyond the authority of the federal courts under the "cases and controversies" provision of U. S. Const. Art. III). The declaratory remedy is now generally available if the applicant for a declaration can show that he confronts real risk if he proceeds with the course of conduct which he seeks to follow. Compare Gilliland v. County of Los Angeles, 126 Cal.App.3d 610, 179 Cal.Rptr. 73 (1981) (dispute not ripe for adjudication). See also Berkeley v. Alameda County Bd. Supervisors, 40 Cal. App.3d 961, 115 Cal.Rptr. 540 (1974) (where plaintiff alleged a real situation of uncertainty, but defendant's position was legally valid, court should declare for defendant and not dismiss the action); C.E.B., 2 Calif.Civ.Pro. Before Trial, c. 24 (1978). Nevertheless, courts remain wary of permitting declaratory judgment suits when issues are not "ripe" for adjudication, compare Pacific Gas & Elec. Co. v. State Energy Resources Conservation & Development Comm'n, 461 U.S. 190, 103 S.Ct. 1713, 75 L.Ed.2d 752 (1983) (review of statute regulating nuclear plants), with Arizona v. Atchison, T. & S. F. R. Co., 656 F.2d 398 (9th Cir. 1981) (suit before effective date of statute), or when the issues have become "moot," ITT Rayonier Inc. v. United States, 651 F.2d 343 (5th Cir. 1981); McKinnon v. County of Talladega, 745 F.2d 1360 (11th Cir. 1984). See also Standing to Sue, infra p. 779.

Is there anything mysterious about a declaratory judgment? Doesn't every judgment carry with it an implied declaration of rights?

B. PROVISIONAL REMEDIES

1. ATTACHMENT

INTRODUCTORY NOTE ON ATTACHMENT

A "provisional remedy" is a judicial order, obtained at the initial stage of litigation, designed to stabilize the situation pending the final disposition of the case or to provide security to plaintiff that if she succeeds in obtaining judgment she will be able to realize its enforcement. The traditional types of provisional remedy include the seizure of property, which is called attachment, the temporary injunction and analogous remedies.

Neither the common law nor equity had devices for securing plaintiff in her recovery in advance of final judgment. The concern of the old common law and equity courts was rather to work out ways of coercing the defendant to appear for trial, since the established tradition until the 18th century was that a judgment could not be entered in default of an appearance by the defendant. The coercive device used, both in common law and in equity, was the seizure of the defendant's property, called distraint at common law and sequestration in equity.

a. Arrest. In the common law courts there developed the provisional remedy of civil arrest. Originally arrest was available only in a limited number of cases, of which the most significant was the action of trespass, an action which involved actually or theoretically a breach of the king's peace and therefore was quasi-criminal. By the early 19th century it had been made available in a wide variety of actions. It is now abolished in some states, e.g., C.C.P. 501; 11 Calif.L.Rev.Comm'n, Study Relating to Civil Arrest (1970), and narrowly confined in others, e.g., N.Y.C.P.L.R. § 6101, examined in Morris and Wiener, Civil Arrest: A Medieval Anachronism, 43 Brook.L.Rev. 383 (1976) (New York law). Compare the use of arrest in enforcement of contempt of court, e.g., Allison v. County of Ventura, 68 Cal.App.3d 689, 137 Cal.Rptr. 542 (1977). In Kinsey v. Preeson, 746 P.2d 542 (Colo. 1987), it was held that a "body execution" statute, authorizing imprisonment for willful failure to pay a civil judgment, denied due process when applied to an indigent.

b. Attachment. As indicated above, seizure of defendant's property at common law was for the purpose of compelling his appearance, not securing plaintiff's claim. As Professor Millar has observed in his valuable treatment of the subject, Millar, Civil Procedure of the Trial Court in Historical Perspective, c. XXVI (1952), it seems never to have occurred to the common lawyers to use the seized property for the purpose of satisfying plaintiff's demand. The use of attachment for this purpose was, however, an established local custom in some English towns, notably London, and it may have been this example which prompted its American development. In any case, in this country attachment developed initially as "foreign attachment," i.e., as a means of satisfying a claim against a debtor who was absent or incapable of being found but who had property that could be found. The remedy was, however, early extended in the New England states as a provisional remedy in all kinds of actions. See Comment, Attachment Statutes, 38 Yale L.J. 376 (1929).

Other states tended to follow the New York model, which authorized "foreign attachment," i.e., "against a defendant who is not a resident of this State, or * * * who has absconded or concealed himself," in actions for "the recovery of money," N. Y. Laws 1849 c. 438 § 227, or the California model, which authorized attachment in actions "upon contract express or implied," whether or not the defendant was absent, Cal.Civ.Prac.Act of 1853 § 120.

c. Modern Attachment Procedures. Typical statutes permitted attachment against nonresidents and against resident defendants in actions to recover "debts" or in actions predicated on fraud, or both. The use of attachment for the purpose of obtaining jurisdiction over a nonresident was sharply curtailed by the Supreme Court on due process grounds in Shaffer v. Heitner, infra p. 315. In a series of cases beginning with Sniadach v. Family Finance Corp., 395 U.S. 337, 89 S.Ct. 1820, 23 L.Ed.2d 349 (1969), the Supreme Court also imposed due process restrictions on the use of attachment where, as had been usual, property of individuals was attached without a preliminary showing of the validity of the claim being enforced and of the need to prevent defendant from absconding with the property. In Fuentes v. Shevin, 407 U.S. 67, 92 S.Ct. 1983, 32 L.Ed.2d 556 (1972), the Supreme Court held invalid an attachment procedure that permitted "issuance of writs ordering state agents to seize a person's possessions, simply upon the *ex parte* application of any other person who claims a right to them and posts a security bond."

States responded to these decisions by revising their statutes. The California provisions permit attachment in actions "based upon contract, express or implied," if the amount is "readily ascertainable" and is not less than $500 and if, when against an individual, the claim arises out of "trade, business, or profession." C.C.P. 483.010. When defendant is a nonresident, attachment is permitted for any type of claim. C.C.P. 492.010. See Calif.Law Revision Comm'n, Recommendation Relating to Creditors' Remedies, 16 Calif.L.Rev. Comm'n Rpts. 2175 (1982); Comment, Abuse of Process and Attachment: Toward a Balance of Power, 30 U.C.L.A.L.Rev. 1218 (1983).

In North Georgia Finishing, Inc. v. Di-Chem, Inc., 419 U.S. 601, 95 S.Ct. 719, 42 L.Ed.2d 751 (1975), the Court considered the application of Georgia's attachment statute to seizure of business property to enforce a commerical claim. The Court's summation of the deficiencies of the statute noted that it failed to provide for (1) a factual showing based on the affiant's own knowledge, (2) a consideration of that showing by a judge instead of a clerk, and (3) opportunity for early hearing on the questions whether the plaintiff's claim was apparently valid and whether there was risk of dissipation of the property.

Apparently there are situations in which some of these requirements can be dispensed with. See Calero-Toledo v. Pearson Yacht Leasing Co., 416 U.S. 663, 94 S.Ct. 2080, 40 L.Ed.2d 452 (1974) (confiscation by police officials of yacht carrying illegal drugs); Hodel v. Virginia Surface Mining & Reclamation Ass'n, 452 U.S. 264, 101 S.Ct. 2352, 69 L.Ed.2d 1 (1981) (immediate cessation of mining practice deemed by mining inspector to present "reasonable expectation of death or serious injury"). And in Flagg Bros., Inc. v. Brooks, 436 U.S. 149, 98 S.Ct. 1729, 56 L.Ed.2d 185 (1978), it was held that the prior notice requirement is inapplicable to the self-help remedy of sale by a warehouseman. Compare Comment, Creditors' Remedies as State Action, 89 Yale L.J. 538 (1980). State constitutions, however, may impose stricter limitations on self-help procedures. See Sharrock v. Dell Buick-Cadillac, Inc., 45 N.Y.2d 152, 408 N.Y.S.2d 39, 379 N.E.2d 1169 (1978); Svendsen v. Smith's Moving & Trucking Co., 54 N.Y.2d 865, 444 N.Y.S.2d 904, 429 N.E.2d 411 (1981). *Flagg Brothers* was distinguished in Lugar v. Edmondson Oil Co., Inc., 457 U.S. 922, 102 S.Ct. 2744, 73 L.Ed.2d 482 (1982), which held that a prejudgment attachment procedure wherein state officers acted jointly with a private creditor constituted state action and thus was subject to due process requirements.

It is worth noting that the requirements impliedly suggested by the Court in *Di-Chem* are essentially identical to those established for issuance of a temporary restraining order.

d. Lis Pendens Statutes. Lis pendens statutes, which authorize filing notice of a lawsuit affecting real estate on the land records, have also been challenged on due process grounds with varying success. Compare Kukanskis v. Griffith, 180 Conn. 501, 430 A.2d 21 (1980) (procedures unconstitutional where no provision was made for a hearing before or promptly following filing of lis pendens notice), with Chrysler Corp. v. Fedders Corp., 670 F.2d 1316 (3d Cir. 1982) (similar procedures held constitutional). For the Connecticut act as amended after *Kukanskis*, see Conn.G.S. § 52–325. The new act, which provides for a hearing after the filing of a lis pendens notice, was upheld in Williams v. Bartlett, 189 Conn. 471, 457 A.2d 290 (1983). See also Note, A Proposal for the Reformation of the Iowa Lis Pendens Statute, 67 Iowa L.Rev. 289 (1982); Comment, The Use of Lis Pendens in Actions Alleging Constructive Trusts or Equitable Liens: Due Process Considerations, 24 Santa Clara L.Rev. 137 (1984). Compare Patterson v. Cronin, 650 P.2d 531 (Colo.1982) (wheel "boot" placed on car parked overtime violates due process unless a prompt remedy is provided to question "booting").

UNITED STATES v. MIZRAHIE

United States Court of International Trade, 1985.
606 F.Supp. 703.

RE, CHIEF JUDGE:

The question presented in this case is whether a surety seeking indemnification on an import bond, pursuant to 28 U.S.C. § 1583 (1982), may obtain a writ of attachment against an indemnitor's real property located in California. This Court holds that it is empowered to issue a writ of attachment affecting property located in California, and that the requirements of California law, for the issuance of the writ, have been met.

On March 6, 1985, defendant-third-party plaintiff, Safeco Insurance Company of America (Safeco), sought an *ex parte* right to attach order, and the issuance of a writ of attachment affecting real property, located in the State of California, owned by third-party defendant, Rebecca Mizrahie. Upon due consideration and examination of Safeco's application and supporting affidavits, on March 8, 1985, this Court ordered that the Clerk of the Court issue a writ of attachment.

* * *

FACTS

* * * In each of these actions, the United States seeks to recover liquidated damage penalties against Saul Mizrahie for his alleged violations of 19 C.F.R. § 12.80, which governs the importation of vehicles that do not conform to federal motor vehicle safety standards, and against Saul Mizrahie and Safeco for breach of three Immediate Delivery and Consumption Bonds (bonds or consumption bonds).[1] The relief sought by the United States is the recovery of $43,811 in liquidated damage penalties, plus pre-judgment interest from the date of each liquidated damage assessment made by the Customs Service.

The imported merchandise consisted of various models of Mercedez Benz automobiles (vehicles) which were entered, on separate occasions,

1. Pursuant to 19 C.F.R. § 12.80(e), vehicles that do not conform to federal motor vehicle safety standards may not be released unless a surety bond, equal to the value of the vehicle plus estimated duties and taxes, is posted with the Customs Service. The release of the bond is conditioned upon obtaining a statement from the National Highway Traffic Safety Administration, stating that the vehicle has been brought into conformity with all applicable safety standards. Id. If the statement is not obtained and the vehicle not redelivered, liquidated damages in the amount of the bond shall be assessed. Id. See also 19 C.F.R. § 113.14.

at the port of Long Beach, California. On each occasion, the vehicles, which did not conform to federal motor vehicle safety standards, were conditionally released to Saul Mizrahie. As a condition of each vehicle's release, Mizrahie was obligated, within ninety days, either to provide a satisfactory statement that the vehicles had been altered to conform to federal safety standards, or to redeliver the non-conforming vehicles. As security for any liquidated damage penalties that might be incurred for failure to perform his obligations, Mizrahie executed, jointly with Safeco as surety, the three consumption bonds that form the basis of Safeco's cross and third-party claims.

Alleging that Saul Mizrahie neither provided satisfactory statements of conformity, nor redelivered the vehicles within ninety days after their respective releases, the Customs Service, on June 2, 1978 and March 30, 1979, assessed liquidated damages against him. Saul Mizrahie then petitioned for, and was denied, mitigation of the assessment of liquidated damage penalties. Plaintiff, the United States, subsequently brought the three actions against Saul Mizrahie and Safeco.

In each of the three actions Safeco interposed an answer, and cross-claimed for judgment against Saul Mizrahie based upon the common law right of a surety to indemnification from its principal, and upon a written General Agreement of Indemnity, dated June 26, 1977 (Indemnity Agreement). The Indemnity Agreement was executed by Saul and Rebecca Mizrahie, in favor of Safeco.

Pursuant to Rule 4(d) of the Rules of this Court, Rebecca Mizrahie was personally served with a third-party summons and complaint on December 13, 1983 and November 9, 1984. To date, Saul Mizrahie, who has appeared and answered in these actions, has not served an answer to the cross-claims of Safeco as required by Rule 7(a) of the Rules of this Court. Rebecca Mizrahie has neither appeared, nor served an answer to Safeco's third-party complaint.

On January 31, 1985, the United States moved for summary judgment against Saul Mizrahie and Safeco.[2] On March 6, 1985, Safeco moved *ex parte,* pursuant to Rule 64, for a "right to attach order" and for the issuance of a writ of attachment, contending that, since Saul and Rebecca Mizrahie are in default as to Safeco's claims against them, they are liable to Safeco for any judgment which may be obtained by the United States against Safeco.

The following questions were presented by Safeco's application for the issuance of a writ of attachment:

1. Whether this Court is empowered to order the issuance of an *ex parte* writ of attachment affecting property located in the State of California; and

2. Since defendants Saul Mizrahie and Safeco requested and were granted an extension of time until March 21, 1985, to respond to the United States' motions for summary judgment, the motions for summary judgment are still pending.

2. Whether Safeco has satisfied the requirements, under California law, for the issuance of an *ex parte* writ of attachment.

For the reasons that follow, the court has granted Safeco's *ex parte* application for a right to attach order and a writ of attachment.

Jurisdiction

With the enactment of the Customs Courts Act of 1980, Pub.L. No. 96–417, 94 Stat. 1727 (1980), Congress expanded and clarified the jurisdiction of this Court to create "a comprehensive system for judicial review of civil actions arising out of import transactions and federal statutes affecting international trade." Statement of President Carter, 16 Weekly Comp. of Pres.Doc. 2183 (Oct. 11, 1980). See H.R.Rep. No. 96–1235, 96th Cong., 2d Sess. 18–20 (1980), U.S.Code Cong. & Admin. News 1980, p. 3729.

Pursuant to 28 U.S.C. § 1582, this Court was granted exclusive subject-matter jurisdiction over civil penalty actions under sections 592, 704(i)(2), and 734(i)(2) of the Tariff Act of 1930, and over actions "to recover upon a bond relating to the importation of merchandise" required by federal law or Treasury regulations. 28 U.S.C. 1582. In addition, pursuant to 28 U.S.C. § 1583, the Court of International Trade has exclusive jurisdiction over any counterclaim, cross-claim, or third-party action of any party to recover on a bond related to the importation of merchandise that is the subject of the civil action. Id. § 1583.

* * *

Since Safeco's cross-claim and third party action seek indemnification on a bond required by Treasury regulations, this action falls squarely within section 1583. * * *

The Court's Equitable Powers

Of equal significance to the Court's expanded jurisdiction in the 1980 Act was Congress' explicit conferral upon the Court of International Trade of "all the powers in law and equity of, or as conferred by statute upon, a district court of the United States." 28 U.S.C. § 1585 (1982). Thus, the Act granted this Court "remedial powers co-extensive with those of a federal district court." H.R.Rep. No. 96–1235, 96th Cong., 2nd Sess. 61 (1980), U.S.Code Cong. & Admin.News 1980, p. 3773. See also Budd Co. Ry. Div. v. United States, 1 CIT 175, 176–78 (1981). With certain limited exceptions, not relevant here, Congress authorized the Court "to order *any form of relief that is appropriate in a civil action,* including, *but not limited to,* declaratory judgments, orders of remand, injunctions, and writs of mandamus and prohibition." 28 U.S.C. § 2643(c) (emphasis added). See also 28 U.S.C. § 1651 (1982).

* * *

* * *

Federal Rule of Civil Procedure 64, which governs the district courts, provides that provisional remedies, including attachment, "for the purpose of securing satisfaction of the judgment ultimately to be entered in the action are available under the circumstances and in the manner provided by the law of the state in which the district court is held, existing at the time the remedy was sought. . . ." Fed.R.Civ.P. 64.

The language of Rule 64 of the Rules of this Court, which implements this Court's statutory authority under 28 U.S.C. § 1585 and § 2643(c)(1), is substantially similar to Fed.R.Civ.P. 64. Rule 64 of this Court provides that provisional remedies, such as attachment, are available in accordance with "appropriate state law existing at the time the remedy is sought." Although the Federal Rules of Civil Procedure expressly apply only to the federal district courts, it has been held that, where substantially similar, they provide guidance in the interpretation of the rules of this Court. See United States v. Porter, 68 C.C.P.A. 15, 20, C.A.D. 1259, 645 F.2d 52, 57 (1981). Thus, in support of this Court's jurisdiction and to effectuate its judgment, the Rules of this Court permit the attachment of property, prior to judgment, in accordance with, and to the extent permitted by state law. In considering the application for attachment, since the property sought to be attached is real property located in the State of California, the applicable law is the law of California.

* * *

It is well to note that, although the "offices" of this Court are located in the State of New York, trials and other proceedings may be held at "any place within the jurisdiction of the United States." 28 U.S.C. § 256 (1982). See U.S.C.I.T. Rule 77(c)(2). See generally Re, Litigation Before the Court of International Trade, 19 U.S.C.A. vii, x (Supp.1984). It is also noteworthy that the effective reach of the court's process extends throughout the entire United States. See U.S.C.I.T. Rule 4. * * *

* * *

* * * Pursuant to section 1963A, a final judgment entered by the Court of International Trade may be registered in any judicial district, and shall have the same effect and be enforced in the same manner as a judgment of the district court. 28 U.S.C. § 1963A (1982).

Since this Court's jurisdiction under 28 U.S.C. § 1583 is exclusive, a surety seeking indemnification from the principal for breach of the terms of a consumption bond must seek redress before the Court of International Trade. If the preliminary relief sought by Safeco were not available in this Court, it is likely that it would not be available in any other, since all other courts are barred from entertaining Safeco's claims. Id. In providing for exclusive jurisdiction over cross-claims and third-party actions on import bonds, the Congress intended to foster judicial economy, and afford the parties an effective and complete remedy. See, e.g., H.R.Rep. No. 96–1235, 96th Cong., 2d Sess. 61 (1980). Therefore, it is clear that, with the passage of the 1980 Act, Congress provided this Court with the full legal and equitable power to grant complete relief to all parties to an action properly before it, regardless of where the action arose.

* * *

The Issuance of a Writ of Attachment Under California Law

* * *

Under California law, the provisional remedy of prejudgment attachment is statutory, and is designed to ensure the collectability of a judgment by limiting the defendant's control of his assets until plaintiff obtains judgment. Pursuant to Section 483.010 of the California Code of Civil Procedure (C.C.P.), a writ of attachment may be issued:

> [O]nly in an action on a claim or claims for money, each of which is based upon a contract, express or implied, where the total amount of the claim or claims is a fixed or readily ascertainable amount not less than five hundred dollars ($500) exclusive of costs, interest, and attorney's fees.

C.C.P. § 483.010(a). Under the prior version of C.C.P. § 483.010, it has been held that an attachment could properly issue in an action brought by a surety against its indemnitors. See General Insurance Co. of America v. Howard Hampton, Inc., 185 Cal.App.2d 426, 8 Cal.Rptr. 353 (1960).

Clearly, since Safeco's claim against the Mizrahies is based upon a contract of indemnity, seeks money only, and is in an amount that exceeds five hundred dollars, Safeco's application meets the requirements of C.C.P. § 483.010(a).

Under the present California statute, no right to attach order or writ of attachment may be obtained *ex parte* "unless it appears from the facts shown by affidavit that great or irreparable injury would result . . . if issuance of the order were delayed until the matter could be heard on notice." C.C.P. § 485.010(a). This statutory language was the result of the California Supreme Court's decision in Randone v. Appellate Dept. of Sup.Ct. of Sacramento County, 5 Cal.3d 536, 96 Cal. Rptr. 709, 488 P.2d 13 (1971), cert. denied, 407 U.S. 924, 92 S.Ct. 2452, 32 L.Ed.2d 811 (1972), in which California's prior attachment statute was declared unconstitutional.

In *Randone,* a collection agency, without notice, attached the checking account of the petitioners. The collection agency was the assignee of a law firm, to which the petitioners owed $490 for services rendered, plus $130 in accumulated interest. The California Supreme Court found that the statute, permitting attachment of any property of a debtor, including necessities of life, without prior hearing or notice, violated the constitutional guarantee of due process. The court held that notice could be dispensed with only in "extraordinary circumstances," otherwise the statute would be unconstitutional on its face. Id. at 563, 96 Cal.Rptr. at 728, 488 P.2d at 32.

The *Randone* court relied on the United States Supreme Court's decision in Sniadach v. Family Finance Corp., 395 U.S. 337, 89 S.Ct.

1820, 23 L.Ed.2d 349 (1969), which voided a Wisconsin prejudgment wage garnishment statute, and held that the statute, since it sanctioned the taking of property without prior notice, violated procedural due process. The California Supreme Court found that *Sniadach* "returned the entire domain of prejudgement remedies to the long standing procedural due process principle which dictates that, *except in extraordinary circumstances,* an individual may not be deprived of his life, liberty or property without notice and hearing." 5 Cal.3d at 547, 96 Cal.Rptr. at 715, 488 P.2d at 19 (emphasis added). Thus, since the California statute in *Randone* was not sufficiently limited, it was held to be invalid.

The *Randone* court also noted that *Sniadach* referred to only three circumstances that would be sufficient to satisfy the requirement of "extraordinary circumstances." These circumstances were stated to be (1) summary procedures permitting specialized governmental officers to react to financial difficulties at a particular bank by seizing operational control of its assets; (2) summary seizure of misbranded drugs; and (3) prejudgment attachment of property of a non-resident by a resident creditor. 5 Cal.3d at 553–54, 96 Cal.Rptr. 720–21, 488 P.2d at 24–25; see Ewing v. Mytinger and Casselberry, Inc., 339 U.S. 594, 70 S.Ct. 870, 94 L.Ed. 1088 (1950); Fahey v. Malonee, 332 U.S. 245, 67 S.Ct. 1552, 91 L.Ed. 2030 (1947); Coffin Bros. v. Bennett, 277 U.S. 29, 48 S.Ct. 422, 72 L.Ed. 768 (1928); Ownbey v. Morgan, 256 U.S. 94, 41 S.Ct. 433, 65 L.Ed. 837 (1921). The *Randone* court further stated that a constitutionally valid statute could be drafted "to permit attachment before notice in exceptional cases where, for example, the creditor can additionally demonstrate . . . that an actual risk has arisen that assets will be concealed or that the debtor will abscond." Id., 5 Cal.3d at 563, 96 Cal. Rptr. at 727, 488 P.2d at 31 (citations omitted); see also People v. Allstate Leasing Corp., 24 Cal.App.3d 973, 101 Cal.Rptr. 470 (1972).

As a result, and in response to the *Randone* decision, section 485.010(b) now provides that the requirement of showing great or irreparable injury is satisfied only if it is established that:

> (1) Under the circumstances of the case, it may be inferred that there is a danger that the property sought to be attached would be concealed, substantially impaired in value, or otherwise made unavailable to levy if issuance of the order were delayed until the matter could be heard on notice.

C.C.P. § 485.010(b)(1).

In Johnson v. Alexander, 63 Cal.App.3d 806, 134 Cal.Rptr. 101 (1976), the Second District Court of Appeal reviewed C.C.P. § 585.5, the predecessor of section 485.010, and found that the grounds on which an original pre-notice attachment had been based remained valid, and affirmed a lower court decision denying dissolution of the attachment. The court also noted that there remained "a substantial danger that the defendants would transfer, other than in the ordinary course of business, remove or conceal the property sought to be attached." Id. at 814, 134 Cal.Rep. at 106.

Hence, a court must examine the application for a right to attach order and supporting affidavit to determine whether it complies with the following requirements of section 485.220(a):

[A] right to attach order, which shall state the amount to be secured by the attachment, and order a writ of attachment to be issued upon the filing of an undertaking . . . if it finds all of the following:

(1) The claim upon which the attachment is based is one upon which an attachment may be issued.

(2) The plaintiff has established the probable validity of the claim upon which the attachment is based.

(3) The attachment is not sought for a purpose other than the recovery upon the claim upon which the attachment is based.

(4) The affidavit accompanying the application shows that the property sought to be attached, or the portion thereof to be specified in the writ, is not exempt from attachment.

(5) The plaintiff will suffer great or irreparable injury (within the meaning of Section 485.010) if issuance of the order is delayed until the matter can be heard on notice.

Id.

In this case, Safeco moved *ex parte* for a right to attach order, and alleged in its application and supporting papers that there was a danger that the property sought to be attached "would be concealed, impaired in value or made unavailable to levy if issuance of the order were delayed until the matter could be heard on notice."

In support of Safeco's allegation of irreparable injury, the court was furnished with several documents which indicated a potential for "great or irreparable injury" to Safeco. The first document was Saul and Rebecca Mizrahies' statement of financial condition as of July 11, 1977, given to Safeco by the Mizrahies in connection with the issuance of the bonds and indemnity contract at issue. This statement reflects a net worth exceeding three million dollars ($3,000,000), and includes a list of real and other property held by the Mizrahies at that time. Since the dates of the assessments for which the United States brought suit, the Mizrahies have transferred or liquidated their interest in all the property listed in their statement except for the real property located at 6130 Warner Drive, Los Angeles, California. A copy of an Individual Quitclaim Deed from the Los Angeles County Recorder's office reveals that on January 13, 1981, subsequent to the assessment of the liquidated damage penalties underlying this action, Saul Mizrahie transferred record ownership of that property to his wife, Rebecca. It is alleged by Safeco that Rebecca Mizrahie is still record owner of that property, and that it is apparently the Mizrahies' present residence.

The court was also furnished with a copy of an indictment dated January 23, 1985 in "U.S. v. Saul Mizrahie," Criminal Case No. 8500586, currently pending in the United States District Court, Southern District of California. The indictment charges Saul Mizrahie with three counts of concealing merchandise imported contrary to law, in violation of 18 U.S.C. § 545 (1982). The merchandise which is the basis of the indictment is unrelated to the subject matter of this action. Safeco also states that Saul Mizrahie has petitioned the district court for permission to proceed *in forma pauperis* in that criminal action, and that he claims to have no assets.

In light of these overwhelming indications of the Mizrahies' severe financial and legal distress, and their failure to answer Safeco's cross and third-party claims, there is a substantial likelihood that Rebecca Mizrahie would transfer their last significant remaining asset, the Los Angeles house. A grand jury has found sufficient evidence to indict Saul Mizrahie for knowingly and willfully concealing merchandise that he knew was imported contrary to law. All other assets of the Mizrahies have disappeared. If title to the Los Angeles house is transferred, Safeco will suffer "irreparable injury" in that it will be unable to collect a judgment against the Mizrahies. In view of the foregoing, it is the determination of the Court that the statutory requirements of section 485.010, as well as the constitutional requirement of "extraordinary circumstances" for issuance of the writ, have been met. See Johnson v. Alexander, 63 Cal.App.3d 806, 814, 134 Cal. Rptr. 101, 106 (1976); Randone v. Appellate Dept. of Sup.Ct. of Sacramento, 5 Cal.3d 536, 96 Cal.Rptr. 709, 488 P.2d 13 (1971), cert. denied, 407 U.S. 924, 92 S.Ct. 2452, 32 L.Ed.2d 811 (1972).

As for the validity of Safeco's claim, the Mizrahies have defaulted on Safeco's cross and third-party claims. Assuming, therefore, that the government succeeds on the merits, it appears likely that Safeco will be found liable to the government on the consumption bonds. Under California law a written agreement of indemnity is fully enforceable, and may entitle the indemnitor to costs and attorney's fees incurred in prosecuting the indemnification claim. See, e.g., DeWitt v. Western Pacific R.R. Co., 719 F.2d 1448, 1453 (9th Cir.1983); Schackman v. Universal Pictures Co., 255 Cal.App.2d 857, 863, 63 Cal.Rptr. 607 (1967). Since the indemnity agreement in this case was executed in California, and is governed by California law, the Court in issuing the writ determined that Safeco's probability of success on the merits was considerable.

It should be noted that the effect of the writ issued against the Mizrahies' Los Angeles property is only to prevent its transfer prior to judgment, and does not affect their right to possession. In addition, in accordance with the provisions of C.C.P. §§ 489.210 and 489.230, Safeco posted an undertaking in the amount of one hundred thousand dollars ($100,000) to secure payment of any judgment the Mizrahies might recover for the wrongful attachment of their property by Safeco.

Thus, the Court [has] determined that the requirements mandated by California law for the issuance of an *ex parte* writ of attachment were met by Safeco's application in that:

    1. Safeco's claim upon which the attachment is based is for money only and more than five hundred dollars;

    2. Safeco established the probable validity of its claim;

    3. Safeco's attachment was not sought for a purpose other than securing Safeco's recovery on its claims;

    4. Safeco's affidavit showed that the property sought to be attached was not exempt from attachment under C.C.P. § 487.020, and is subject to attachment under C.C.P. § 487.010; and

    5. Safeco showed that it would have suffered great or irreparable injury, within the meaning of C.C.P. § 485.010, if issuance of the order was delayed until the matter could have been heard on notice.

*   *   *

2. PRELIMINARY INJUNCTIONS

INTRODUCTORY NOTE ON TEMPORARY RESTRAINING ORDERS AND PRELIMINARY INJUNCTIONS

A temporary restraining order is the initial step of relief *pendente lite* ("immediately") in a suit for an injunction. The "TRO" may be issued immediately and ex parte upon application of plaintiff if he makes an adequate showing of the apparent necessity for immediate relief. See C.C.P. 527. A bond to indemnify the defendant against loss and expense by reason of the order is ordinarily required. The order is made "returnable" as soon as possible, see C.C.P. 527 ("not later than 15 days or, if good cause appears to the court, 20 days from the date of such order"), by which is meant that defendant is to be served and given an opportunity to appear to show cause why the order should not be permitted to stand. At the hearing on the return, the order may be replaced by a preliminary injunction, issuable only upon bond and upon proof by plaintiff that an injunction is necessary pending plenary trial. See generally 6 Witkin 208–284. The federal procedure is essentially similar, see F.R.C.P. 65. See Granny Goose Foods, Inc. v. Brotherhood of Teamsters, 415 U.S. 423, 94 S.Ct. 1113, 39 L.Ed.2d 435 (1974); 11 Wright & Miller §§ 2941 et seq. See also Urquhart, The Most Extraordinary Remedy: The Injunction, 45 Tex.B.J. 358 (1982); Dorr and Traphagen, Federal Ex Parte Temporary Relief, 61 Denver L.J. 767 (1984); Black, A New Look at Preliminary Injunctions, 36 Ala.L.R. 1 (1984).

LAWSON PRODUCTS, INC. v. AVNET, INC.

United States Court of Appeals for the Seventh Circuit, 1986.
782 F.2d 1429.

FLAUM, CIRCUIT JUDGE.

Lawson Products, Inc. ("Lawson") appeals from the district court's denial of its motion for a preliminary injunction against its competitor, Avnet, Inc. ("Avnet"). This dispute arose out of an alleged scheme by

Avnet to lure customers and sales people away from Lawson in a manner that tortiously interfered with the business and contracts of Lawson. This case, arising in the wake of Roland Machinery Co. v. Dresser Industries, 749 F.2d 380 (7th Cir.1984) and American Hospital Supply Corp. v. Hospital Products Ltd., 780 F.2d 589 (7th Cir.1986), requires us to examine the status of the preliminary injunction remedy in this circuit. Finding that, despite possible contrary readings of recent precedent, the granting of injunctive relief remains a discretionary equitable remedy and one to which we will give the district court's decision great deference, we affirm the denial of the preliminary injunction in this case.

I.

Lawson and the Mechanic's Choice division of Avnet are competitors in the business of developing and distributing industrial and automotive supplies. Both companies' primary method of selling their products is through a sizable number of sales representatives who deal directly with customers. These sales representatives appear to be the key to success in the industry since, according to the evidence adduced before the district court, customer loyalty tends to attach to the sales person rather than the products of any individual company. According to Lawson, Avnet commenced a "raid" on Lawson's sales staff in January of 1983. During the course of the alleged raid at least fifty-seven of the eight hundred sales representatives employed by Lawson were contacted and seven of these individuals left Lawson for employment with Avnet.

This activity led to the filing of this diversity action in August, 1983, Lawson having voluntarily dismissed a similar action brought in Arkansas a few months earlier. Lawson's complaint alleged tortious interference with business and contractual relations, various acts of unfair competition, and a pendent state action under Illinois law for deceptive trade practices and unfair competition. Both parties inundated Judge Kocoras with affidavits resulting in a mass of often conflicting evidence. By stipulation of the parties the case was submitted to the court solely on the basis of this documentary evidence.

Lawson's affidavits portray Avnet's scheme not as a pro-competitive attempt to "out-bid" a rival for valuable talent, but as a many-pronged plot to co-opt the extensive technical training Lawson provides its sales representatives, to acquire confidential information, and to destroy the financial stability of Lawson by encouraging manufacturers, customers, and sales people to breach their contractual, or at least quasi-contractual, obligations to Lawson. This was allegedly accomplished through a series of deceptive practices including misstatements and fabrications about the activities of Lawson's management, as well as at least one instance of commercial bribery and one instance of passing off a Lawson product as that of Avnet. As a result of Avnet's alleged activity seven employees, two of whom eventually returned, left

Lawson. No manufacturers abandoned Lawson, however, and Lawson continued to be a highly profitable enterprise. Nevertheless, Lawson claims that it is suffering an ongoing injury as a result of the competitive disadvantage caused by its competitor's access to confidential information, the decreased morale among its employees, and the continuing threat of further corporate "raids."

The essential facts according to Lawson are that Avnet's Mechanic's Choice division had suffered from a depleted staff of sales representatives which caused Avnet to embark on the plan to co-opt its competitors' sales staff and, consequently, their customers. Lawson's sales representatives are independent contractors rather than employees and only a fraction of these actually signed contracts with the company. Of the seven people Avnet succeeded in luring away only two had written contracts. Conceding this, Lawson still claims that a contractual employment relationship existed and that the company had a legitimate expectancy in the continuation of the relationship.

Before being sent out to the field each representative was given what Lawson claims is the most extensive training in the industry. Upon completion of the training program the sales person was assigned a territory and given a core group of customers as a base for expansion of the individual's business. Also supplied were a price book, a display book, product and operations manuals, and computer printouts that regularly updated customer purchasing patterns. These materials all contained a warning prohibiting unauthorized duplicating, and Lawson produced affidavits indicating that 92 percent of its sales staff viewed these materials as "confidential." The evidence also indicated that none of the documents were marked "confidential" and that the information contained therein was frequently shared with customers. It is the information contained in these materials that Lawson claims was one of the primary aims of the Avnet raid. According to Lawson, Avnet now has access to its price information, customer tendencies, and product specifications, thus allowing the rival to have a competitive advantage in soliciting Lawson customers and the ability to duplicate Lawson products in derogation of Lawson's exclusive manufacturing contracts. Lawson also claims that its technical staff is increasingly unwilling to share information with the sales people in light of Avnet's activities.

Lawson's affidavits catalogue a number of alleged unsavory practices utilized by Avnet. First, Lawson claims that Avnet engaged in an active campaign of misrepresentations concerning Lawson's management, product quality, and prices, which was designed to encourage Lawson's customers, suppliers, and sales representatives to switch to Avnet. Second, Avnet is alleged to have "covertly" used the Lawson people it did recruit to encourage further defections while they were still in the employ of Lawson. Third, Lawson claims that one of its employees was offered a twenty-five dollar bribe to agree to speak with an Avnet recruiter. Finally, the affidavits claim that on two separate occasions Avnet employees attempted to "pass off" Lawson products as those of Avnet; one instance involved a demonstration, the other a shipment. In both cases the product itself had Lawson's name printed upon it.

These activities, according to Lawson's argument, establish a continuing malicious scheme designed to irreparably injure Lawson by seizing a competitive advantage, by destroying the company's "good will" with its customers, and by injuring employee morale through misrepresentations. In an effort to bolster the argument for a continuing operation, Lawson detailed an earlier consent decree entered into by the parties in New Jersey whereby Avnet would refrain from attempting to recruit Lawson sales people who were under contract. Avnet violated the agreement and successful enforcement proceedings were eventually brought.

Avnet countered the evidence and arguments presented by Lawson with its own collection of affidavits that conflict with those of Lawson on practically every matter. The picture Avnet paints is one of normal competition for sales talent where Lawson failed to protect its interests through binding employment contracts. Based on the documentary evidence before him Judge Kocoras concluded that "[p]laintiffs have presented evidence on each required element of the action and defendant has presented equally credible evidence in response." Faced with this morass of evidence, the district judge extensively discussed each element of the requirements for a preliminary injunction under Roland Machinery Co. v. Dresser Industries, 749 F.2d 380 (7th Cir.1984) and concluded that Lawson had failed to meet any single element.

The court first analyzed the likelihood of success on the merits and held that the affidavits failed to establish the commercial malice required for the tort of interference with business relations, the actual breach of contract necessary to the tort of interference with contract, and the confidential nature of the Lawson material that was the key element to the claim for unfair competition. Second, the court concluded that there was no irreparable harm to Lawson and that an adequate remedy at law existed. This was based on the ability of Lawson to actively carry on its business activity and sue for any damages caused by the defendant's activities. The judge also evaluated the harm to the defendant and public policy considerations entailed by the scope of the injunctive relief proposed. The requested injunction required more than a restraint on Avnet from illegal activity; it essentially mandated that Avnet maintain a complete "hands-off" policy with respect to Lawson. The court deemed this to be contrary to the legitimate public interest in competition and unnecessarily injurious to Avnet.

    *   *   *

II.

In two recent opinions this circuit has engaged in an exhaustive and scholarly examination of the law of preliminary injunctions. See Roland Machinery Co. v. Dresser Industries, Inc., 749 F.2d 380 (7th Cir.

1984) ("*Roland* ") and American Hospital Supply Corp. v. Hospital Products Ltd., 780 F.2d 589 (7th Cir.1986) ("*American Hospital* ").

* * *

* * *

1. The Role of the District Judge

The constant theme that permeates both *Roland* and *American Hospital* is that while preliminary injunctions are an equitable, interlocutory form of relief, they are an "exercise of very far-reaching power" (Warner Bros. Pictures, Inc. v. Gittone, 110 F.2d 292, 293 (3d Cir.1940) (per curiam)) and one in which the stakes are sufficiently high to make mistakes very costly.

> The idea underlying these equivalent approaches is that the task for the district judge in deciding whether to grant or deny a motion for preliminary injunction is to minimize errors: the error of denying an injunction to one who will in fact (though no one can know this for sure) go on to win the case on the merits, and the error of granting an injunction to one who will go on to lose. The judge must try to avoid the error that is more costly in the circumstances.

Roland, 749 F.2d at 388. * * *

After an exhaustive discussion of the inability of courts of appeals to arrive at a consensus about how to review the granting or denial of a motion for a preliminary injunction, the court in *Roland* detailed the classic hornbook elements of a proper preliminary injunction. As a threshold matter the movant must establish that there is "no adequate remedy at law," a danger of "irreparable harm," and some "likelihood of success on the merits." As is well-documented in *Roland,* these are all terms that in the context of preliminary injunctions have acquired their own special meaning. See 746 F.2d at 386–88. Having gotten past these threshold inquiries the district court must somehow balance the nature and degree of the plaintiff's injury, the likelihood of prevailing at trial, the possible injury to the defendant if the injunction is granted, and the wild card that is the "public interest." See, e.g., Yakus v. United States, 321 U.S. 414, 440, 64 S.Ct. 660, 674, 88 L.Ed.2d 834 (1944). It is at this point of balancing that the approach of *Roland* and *American Hospital* first suggests a more explicit formula and discusses the role of the district judge in balancing the equities.

a. The Roland and American Hospital Approach

Roland and *American Hospital* adopted a "sliding scale" approach where the possibility of mistake would be minimized by weighing the costs of injunctive relief against the benefits. The benefit of injunctive relief can be determined by combining the probability of success on the merits with the magnitude of the harm to the plaintiff. "The more likely the plaintiff is to win, the less heavily need the balance of harms weigh in his favor; the less likely he is to win, the more need it weigh in his favor." *Roland,* 749 F.2d at 387. See also Maxim's Ltd. v. Badonsky, 772 F.2d 388, 391 (7th Cir.1985). This principle was stated in mathematical terms, cf. Judge Learned Hand's opinion in United States v. Carroll Towing Co., 159 F.2d 169, 173 (2d Cir.1947), in *American Hospital,* at 593. "Grant the preliminary injunction if but only if:

$$P \times H_p > (1-P) \times H_d.$$"

The left hand of the equation is the magnitude of erroneously denying the injunction, arrived at by multiplying the probability that plaintiff will prevail at trial (P) by the harm to the plaintiff caused by the denial of the injunction (H_p). The right hand represents the magnitude of an erroneously granted injunction measured by multiplying the probability that the defendants will prevail at trial (1-P, the inverse of the plaintiff's probability of success) by the harm to the defendant caused by the granting of the motion (H_d). Id. at 593–94.

* * *

First, the concern with the economic cost associated with an erroneously granted injunction is well-placed. The use of the traditional elements coupled with the weighing of interests and harms serves to make the decision-making more principled and thus, hopefully, more accurate. We are convinced that the system, despite its real and semantic shortcomings, see *Roland,* 749 F.2d at 385–86, has acceptably performed its function over the years and is not in need of a drastic overhaul. Nevertheless, the formula, like Judge Hand's negligence standard, does provide an effective shorthand method of expressing the important relationship between the likelihood of success on the merits and the degree of the harm to the non-prevailing party. Comparing the magnitude of potential errors involved in the grant or denial of the motion is an important element of the equitable balance, as the opinions in *Roland* and *American Hospital* correctly emphasize.

However, as those opinions also emphasize, a formula is not a substitute for, but an aid to, judgment. A mathematical formula can create a false impression that the elements of the formula, the magnitudes and probabilities, can be accurately quantified and that through a specified type of mental calculus the singularly "correct" result can be arrived at with some exactitude. The obvious problem with this is that the impression is false; a figure representing the probability of success can be arrived at only through a subjective estimate by the court and the magnitudes of harm are rarely susceptible to quantification because of the subjective values, externalities, and effects on the public interest that may be involved in an injunction case. See, e.g., United States Steel Corp. v. Fraternal Association of Steelhaulers, 431 F.2d 1046, 1048 (3d Cir.1970). In fact, it is the inability to measure damage that often is the reason the plaintiff is seeking the injunction. Thus the equation relies on the same type of subjective, impressionistic weighing that has been part of the traditional preliminary injunction determination. * * * As Judge Bazelon stated over thirty years ago:

When a motion for preliminary injunction is presented to a court in advance of hearing on the merits, it is called upon to exercise its discretion "upon the basis of a series of estimates: the relative importance of the rights asserted and the acts sought to be enjoined, the irreparable nature of the injury allegedly flowing from denial of preliminary relief, the probability of the ultimate success or failure of the suit, the balancing of damage and convenience generally. A mere listing of the guiding considerations demonstrates their intangible nature especially when no attempt is made at this stage to decide finally the questions raised."

Perry v. Perry, 190 F.2d 601, 602 (D.C.Cir.1951). See also National Organization for Women v. Social Security Administration, 736 F.2d 727, 742 (D.C.Cir.1984) (quoting *Perry*).

While the use of an equation has no impact upon the nature of the district court's inquiry, the implication that a "correct" answer can be achieved would represent a change in the law and is thus of greater concern. It must be remembered that preliminary injunctions have the dual characteristic of being equitable, such that there is no "right" to obtain one, Weinberger v. Romero–Barcelo, 456 U.S. 305, 311–13, 102 S.Ct. 1798, 1802–03, 72 L.Ed.2d 91 (1982), and being "by [their] very nature, interlocutory, tentative, provisional, ad interim, impermanent, mutable, not fixed or final or conclusive, characterized by its for-the-time-beingness." Hamilton Watch Co. v. Benrus Watch Co., 206 F.2d 738, 739, 742 (2d Cir.1953). See also United States v. White County Bridge Commission, 275 F.2d 529, 534 (7th Cir.1960). The temporary nature of the remedy mitigates, without eliminating, the concern with the possibility of mistake and need for the "correct" answer. See United States Steel Corp. v. Fraternal Association of Steelhaulers, 431 F.2d at 1048; Miss Universe, Inc. v. Flesher, 605 F.2d 1130, 1133 (9th Cir.1979). More significantly, the equitable personality of injunctive relief requires the result to be a "just" or "fair" result rather than a "correct" result. * * * The district judge, sitting as a chancellor in equity considering a preliminary injunction, endeavors to achieve a rough justice between the parties that will maintain the status quo pending trial. Moore's Federal Practice at ¶ 65.04[1]. The remedy itself can be flexibly crafted to achieve this "rough justice" in the particular case before the court. * * * Thus it is impossible to think in terms of a single correct result. In each case there exist a number of fair accommodations. If a rigid formulaic approach is used, where the motion is granted only if $X > Y$ or so many stated criteria are met, one of the central questions, what kind or degree of relief is appropriate, is not answered. As the type of relief varies the parameters of the injunction equation will also change, making it very difficult to achieve the accurate, cost-minimizing result. Implicit in equity's connection to the vague concept of fairness is a need for flexibility. A.L.K. Corp. v. Columbia Pictures Industries, 440 F.2d 761, 763 (3d Cir.1971) ("In applying these criteria, a district court must have considerable discretion because of the infinite variety of situations which may confront it.

Nevertheless, its discretion is not unlimited and must be *guided by the traditional principles of equity.*") (emphasis added). See also 1 Pomroy's Equity Jurisprudence at §§ 59–60. *Roland* and *American Hospital* do not limit in any way the ability of the district courts to flexibly weigh the competing considerations and mold appropriate relief in preliminary injunction cases.

b. *The Discretion of District Judges*

Besides our concern with the possible misinterpretation of the *American Hospital* equation, the second major area where there is a potential for distortion of our precedent is in the discretion of the district court, a concept intractably interwoven with the scope of appellate review. * * *

During the course of deciding whether to grant the motion the district court must take a number of non-discretionary actions: (1) it must evaluate the traditional factors enunciated in the case law; (2) it must make factual determinations on the basis of a fair interpretation of the evidence before the court; and (3) it must draw legal conclusions in accord with a principled application of the law. See, e.g., Zepeda v. INS, 753 F.2d 719, 724–25 (9th Cir.1983). Once all the equitable factors are before the judge, however, a classic discretionary decision must be made involving how much weight to give individual components of the calculus and to what direction the balance of equity tips. See United States Steel v. Fraternal Association of Steelhaulers, 431 F.2d at 1048. The ultimate decision of whether or not to grant the motion is in a real sense intuitive. * * *

2. *Standard of Review*

* * *

As was stated in the discussion of the discretion of the trial court, the preliminary injunction decision involves the resolution of a number of different issues, some of which are non-discretionary; others, like the final weighing and balancing of the equities, are classically left to the discretion of the district judge. Appellate review therefore must vary with the nature of the lower court decision. When a court of appeals considers a preliminary injunction order, which should set forth the judge's reasoning under Fed.R.Civ.P. 65(d), the factual determinations are reviewed under a clearly erroneous standard and the necessary legal conclusions are given *de novo* review. SEC v. Suter, 732 F.2d 1294, 1300 (7th Cir.1984); E. Remy Martin & Co. v. Shaw–Ross International Imports, 756 F.2d 1525, 1529 (11th Cir.1985). However, the ultimate evaluation and balancing of the equitable factors is a highly discretionary decision and one to which this court must give substantial deference. The variance in the standard of review expressed in *Roland* may, in part, be attributed to the existence of errors of law or fact. Clearly, a factual or legal error may alone be sufficient to establish that the court "abused its discretion" in making its final determination.

See Zepeda v. INS, 753 F.2d 719, 724 (9th Cir.1983) ("A district judge may abuse his discretion in any of three ways: (1) he may apply incorrect substantive law or an incorrect preliminary injunction standard; (2) he may rest his decision to grant or deny a preliminary injunction on a clearly erroneous finding of fact that is material to the decision to grant or deny the injunction; or (3) he may apply an acceptable preliminary injunction standard in a manner that results in an abuse of discretion."). See also Buchanan v. United States Postal Service, 508 F.2d 259, 267 n. 24 (5th Cir.1975); Unicon Management Corp. v. Koppers Co., 366 F.2d 199, 203 (2d Cir.1966). However, in the absence of such an error the district judge's weighing and balancing of the equities should be disturbed on appeal only in the rarest of cases. Thus, the nature of what exactly is being reviewed should not be used to obfuscate the fact that the standard of review of the grant or denial of a preliminary injunction is the deferential "abuse of discretion" standard.

The traditional deferential review is in harmony with the stress in *Roland* and *American Hospital* on mistake minimization. The depth of appellate scrutiny varies with the degree to which the appellate court's perspective approximates the district court's first-hand experience. For example, a court of appeals is in a better position to review legal conclusions than findings of fact, which may have been based on intangibles, like the demeanor of a witness. When it comes to reviewing the weighing and balancing of equities in a preliminary injunction case an appellate court lacks a complete perspective since a cold record cannot totally reflect the district judge's sense of the equities or the merits of a case. Cf. Cone v. West Virginia Pulp & Paper Co., 330 U.S. 212, 216, 67 S.Ct. 752, 755, 91 L.Ed. 849 (1947) (In the context of Rule 50(b) motions, the Court stated the motion "calls for the judgment in the first instance of the judge who saw and heard the witnesses and *has the feel of the case which no appellate printed transcript can impart.*") (emphasis added). And while it is true that the district judge may have to act with some dispatch based on a record that is not fully developed, it is hard to imagine why an appellate judge, relying on a distillation of what was before the lower court, is less likely to "inappropriately" balance the equities involved. * * *

Finally, there is [the] question of how to describe the traditional deferential standard. At one level the issue is somewhat unimportant because regardless of whether the standard is framed in terms of "abuse of discretion" or "bounds of permissible choice," reviewing courts have never appeared to be stymied in reaching results in preliminary injunction cases. * * *

    * * *

The term "abuse of discretion," despite its many shortcomings, still accurately reflects the need for deference to the judgment of the district judge. Attempts at further definition have tended to "produce complication and corresponding confusion." In the absence of a compelling and precise articulation of a standard of review we find no reason in the context of preliminary injunctions to reject the abuse of discretion standard or require an all-encompassing definition of that standard. This approach may be intellectually and theoretically unsatisfying, but it does have the virtue of avoiding unnecessary tinkering with at least one aspect of the judicial system that seems to be functioning smoothly.

3. *The Documentary Evidence*

Lawson contends that because the motion was submitted solely on affidavits this court should engage in a *de novo* review. * * *
* * *

Rule 52(a) of the Federal Rules of Civil Procedure provides, in part, that "[f]indings of fact shall not be set aside unless clearly erroneous and due regard shall be given to the opportunity of the trial court to judge of the credibility of witnesses." In Anderson v. City of Bessemer City, 470 U.S. 564, 105 S.Ct. 1504, 1511–13, 84 L.Ed.2d 518 (1985), the Supreme Court held that the rule should be read literally. It contains no distinctions between types of factual findings and none will be implied. The "clear error" standard applies "even when the district court's findings do not rest on credibility determinations, but are based on physical *or documentary evidence*. . . ." 105 S.Ct. at 1512 (emphasis added). * * * Axiomatically, if there is no effect on our review of the underlying factual determinations there is no impact on the deferential standard of review this court has traditionally required in preliminary injunction appeals.

It must be stressed that while an appellate court need not sit as a court of first impression with respect to the record there is an obligation under Rule 52(a) to engage in a comprehensive review of the documentary evidence to determine if clear error has been committed. *Anderson*, 105 S.Ct. at 1515 (Powell, J. concurring). Thus the appellate role is not to rubber stamp the lower court's determination. But the parties should keep in mind that their opportunity before the district court is "the 'main event' . . . rather than a 'tryout for the road.' " *Anderson*, 105 S.Ct. at 1512 (quoting Wainwright v. Sykes, 433 U.S. 72, 90, 97 S.Ct. 2497, 2508, 53 L.Ed.2d 594 (1977)). The situation is no different if there is a live performance or just a mountain of paper.

III.

Turning to the merits of Lawson's appeal we find no reason to overturn the district court's denial of the preliminary injunction motion. For purposes of reviewing the denial of the preliminary injunction Lawson's claims can be separated into: (1) the past injury and future threat resulting from Avnet's solicitation of Lawson's sales force and acts of commercial disparagement; (2) the competitive advantage given Avnet when it appropriated for its own use Lawson's "confidential" information; and (3) the loss of goodwill resulting from the raid.
* * *

With respect to the injury resulting from the loss of its seven employees the affidavit of Lawson's president established the possibility of money damages reflecting the profits actually lost as a result of the raid. While the difficulty in calculating future profits can often justify the finding of an irreparable injury with no adequate remedy at law, *Roland,* 749 F.2d at 386, there is no *per se* rule that claims of lost profits are invariably uncalculable. See Buckingham Corp. v. Karp, 762 F.2d 257, 262 (2d Cir.1985). Where the president of the plaintiff corporation can propose a figure entitled "Business lost projected for 12 months based on business done since representative's departure" the district court is within its discretion in finding an adequate remedy at law.

Likewise the threat that future raids will irreparably injure the plaintiff before a full trial is held is insufficient to justify a preliminary injunction. Two rationales expressed by the district judge establish the lack of necessity for interlocutory injunctive relief. First, Lawson had at its disposal the ability to take self-protective measures without judicial intervention. In his opinion Judge Kocoras stated:

> In the absence of the proposed order, plaintiffs will likely continue to operate their business. They may continue their efforts to sign their own sales force to written contracts which include restrictive covenants and specifically provide for the confidentiality of company materials such as price lists, customer lists, and display or promotional materials. Plaintiffs are free to sign outside, new [personnel] to similar contracts. Plaintiffs are free to regain any old customers by competing lawfully against Avnet and others. The plaintiffs may sue and recover from these seven salesmen and any others for breach of their fiduciary duties to a former employer and enjoin them as individuals from revealing information which plaintiffs allege is confidential.

Second, the relative degree of past injury does not indicate that Avnet's activities can result in a serious undermining of Lawson's sales force, at least not during the period between the denial of the motion and trial. Avnet contacted fifty-seven of the eight hundred Lawson salespeople, seven of whom actually left. Under the theories of liability presented by Lawson, tortious interference with contractual and business relationships, there is no actionable wrong in the absence of an actual breach, see Ancraft Products Co. v. Universal Oil Products Co., 84 Ill. App.3d 836, 40 Ill.Dec. 70, 405 N.E.2d 1162 (1980). Thus the extent of Lawson's injury from the raid, apart from such intangibles as trade secrets or goodwill, is the loss of seven salespeople. While it may be that Lawson can ultimately establish the wrongfulness of Avnet's actions and Lawson's entitlement to an injunction, where the past injury indicates a very limited threat of future harm during the pretrial period *and* the record is ambivalent as to the merits of the dispute the district court is within its discretion to deny the preliminary injunction.

Thus Lawson's primary claims lie in the areas of loss of goodwill and confidential information because of the potential for future harm and the difficulty of measuring damages. Our review of the record, however, finds ample support for the district court's conclusion that Lawson did not suffer a loss of goodwill or confidential information. First, the affidavits support the court's ruling that "goodwill" attached to the relationship between salesperson and customer rather than the relationship between corporation and customer. Under these circumstances any interest Lawson had in the salesperson's "goodwill" would be adequately compensated in lost profit damages since any injury would presumably not extend beyond the insular salesperson-customer relationship to the corporation in general.

Second, Judge Kocoras correctly found that the customer lists and information, the display books, and price lists were not trade secrets, and thus not confidential information, under Illinois law. Given the evidence that (1) all Lawson's sales force and customers had access to the information; (2) much of the information served to supplement data compiled by the salesperson for his or her own use; (3) the information could be acquired by other means such as phone calls or visits to customers or suppliers whose names could be found in the yellow pages; (4) the information became outdated rapidly; and (5) no formal confidential arrangements were made, this case is indistinguishable from a well-established line of cases in Illinois denying protection where the information is not kept under "lock and key." * * *

    * * *

FURTHER NOTE ON PRELIMINARY INJUNCTIONS

On the circumstances under which a temporary restraining order may be issued without notice, see United Farm Workers v. Superior Court, 14 Cal.3d 902, 122 Cal.Rptr. 877, 537 P.2d 1237 (1975); Dorr and Traphagen, Federal Ex Parte Temporary Relief, 61 Denver L.J. 767 (1984). On the basis and scope of liability on the bond issued in connection with a temporary restraining order, compare Tracy v. Capozzi, 98 Nev. 120, 642 P.2d 591 (1982), with Marshall Durbin & Co. v. Jasper Utilities Bd., 437 So.2d 1014 (Ala.1983). See also Dobbs, Should Security Be Required as a Pre-Condition to Provisional Injunctive Relief?, 52 N.C.L.Rev. 1091 (1974); Note, Recovery for Wrongful Interlocutory Injunctions Under Rule 65(c), 99 Harv.L.Rev. 828 (1986). For an historical and analytic treatment of the conditions under which a preliminary injunction may issue, see Leubsdorf, The Standard for Preliminary Injunctions, 91 Harv.L.Rev. 525 (1978). For a practical guideline, see C.E.B., 1 Calif.Civ.Proc. Before Trial § 15.28 et seq. (1977). A critical practical issue is the availability of appellate review. See 28 U.S.C.A. § 1292(a)(1); Anno., 19 A.L.R.3d 403. See also Mullenix, Burying (With Kindness) the Felicific Calculus of Civil Procedure, 40 Vand.L.Rev. 541 (1987).

C. FORECLOSURE OF REMEDY

UNITED STATES v. KUBRICK

Supreme Court of the United States, 1979.
444 U.S. 111, 100 S.Ct. 352, 62 L.Ed.2d 259.*

MR. JUSTICE WHITE delivered the opinion of the Court.

Under the Federal Tort Claims Act (Act),[1] 28 U.S.C. § 2401(b), a tort claim against the United States is barred unless it is presented in writing to the appropriate federal agency "within two years after such claim accrues." The issue in this case is whether the claim "accrues" within the meaning of the Act when the plaintiff knows both the existence and the cause of his injury or at a later time when he also knows that the acts inflicting the injury may constitute medical malpractice.

I

Respondent Kubrick, a veteran, was admitted to the Veterans Administration (VA) hospital in Wilkes-Barre, Pa., in April 1968, for treatment of an infection of the right femur. Following surgery, the infected area was irrigated with neomycin, an antibiotic, until the infection cleared. Approximately six weeks after discharge, Kubrick noticed a ringing sensation in his ears and some loss of hearing. An ear specialist in Scranton, Pa., Dr. Soma, diagnosed the condition as bilateral nerve deafness. His diagnosis was confirmed by other specialists. One of them, Dr. Sataloff, secured Kubrick's VA hospital records and in January 1969, informed Kubrick that it was highly possible that the hearing loss was the result of the neomycin treatment administered at the hospital. Kubrick, who was already receiving disability benefits for a service-connected back injury, filed an application for an increase

---

* Some of the Court's footnotes are omitted.

[1]. Title 28 U.S.C. § 2674 provides in part:

"The United States shall be liable, respecting the provisions of this title relating to tort claims, in the same manner and to the same extent as a private individual under like circumstances, but shall not be liable for interest prior to judgment or for punitive damages."

Title 28 U.S.C. § 1346(b) provides that the District Courts "shall have exclusive jurisdiction of civil actions on claims against the United States, for money damages, accruing on and after January 1, 1945, for injury or loss of property, or personal injury or death caused by the negligent or wrongful act or omission of any employee of the Government while acting within the scope of his office or employment, under circumstances where the United States, if a private person, would be liable to the claimant in accordance with the law of the place where the act or omission occurred."

Title 28 U.S.C. § 2401(b), the limitations provision applicable to tort claims against the United States, provides:

"A tort claim against the United States shall be forever barred unless it is presented in writing to the appropriate Federal agency within two years after such claim accrues or unless action is begun within six months after the date of mailing, by certified or registered mail, of notice of final denial of the claim by the agency to which it was presented."

in benefits pursuant to 38 U.S.C. § 351,[2] alleging that the neomycin treatment had caused his deafness. The VA denied the claim in September 1969, and on resubmission again denied the claim, on the grounds that no causal relationship existed between the neomycin treatment and the hearing loss and that there was no evidence of "carelessness, accident, negligence, lack of proper skill, error in judgment, or any other fault on the part of the Government."

In the course of pursuing his administrative appeal, Kubrick was informed by the VA that Dr. Soma had suggested a connection between Kubrick's loss of hearing and his prior occupation as a machinist. When questioned by Kubrick on June 2, 1971, Dr. Soma not only denied making the statement attributed to him but also told respondent that the neomycin had caused his injury and should not have been administered. On Dr. Sataloff's advice, respondent then consulted an attorney and employed him to help with his appeal. In rendering its decision in August 1972, the VA Board of Appeals recognized that Kubrick's hearing loss "may have been caused by neomycin irrigation" but rejected the appeal on the ground that the treatment was in accordance with acceptable medical practices and procedures and that the Government was therefore faultless.[3]

Kubrick then filed suit under the Act, alleging that he had been injured by negligent treatment in the VA hospital. After trial, the District Court rendered judgment for Kubrick, rejecting, among other defenses, the assertion by the United States that Kubrick's claim was barred by the two-year statute of limitations because the claim had accrued in January 1969, when he learned from Dr. Sataloff that his hearing loss had probably resulted from the neomycin. The District Court conceded that the lower federal courts had held with considerable uniformity that a claim accrues within the meaning of the Act when "the claimant has discovered, or in the exercise of reasonable diligence, should have discovered, the acts constituting the alleged malpractice," 435 F.Supp. 166, 180 (ED Pa.1977), and that notice of the injury and its cause normally were sufficient to trigger the limitations period. Id., at 184. As the District Court read the authorities, however, a plaintiff could avoid the usual rule by showing that he had exercised reasonable diligence and had no "reasonable suspicion" that there was negligence in his treatment. Id., at 185. "[W]e do not believe it reasonable to

---

2. Title 38 U.S.C. § 351 provides that a veteran who suffers "an injury, or an aggravation of an injury, as the result of hospitalization, medical or surgical treatment" administered by the VA shall be awarded disability benefits "in the same manner as if such disability . . . were service-connected." The regulations require the applicant for benefits to show that "the disability proximately resulted through carelessness, accident, negligence, lack of proper skill, error in judgment, or similar instances of indicated fault on the part of the Veterans Administration." 39 CFR § 3.358(c)(3) (1978).

3. In 1975, upon reconsideration of its decision, the VA Board of Appeals not only found, as it had before, that Kubrick's hearing loss may have been caused by neomycin irrigation but also concluded that there was fault on the part of the VA in administering that drug by irrigation. In the present litigation, the Government contested the allegation of malpractice despite the administrative finding of fault.

start the statute running until the plaintiff had reason at least to suspect that a legal duty to him had been breached." Ibid. Here, the District Court found, Kubrick had no reason to suspect negligence until his conversation with Dr. Soma in June 1971, less than two years prior to presentation of his tort claim.

The District Court went on to hold, based on the expert testimony before it, that a reasonably competent orthopedic surgeon in the Wilkes-Barre community, which the VA doctor held himself out to be, should have known that irrigating Kubrick's wound with neomycin would cause deafness. It was therefore negligent to use that drug in that manner. Damages were determined and awarded.

Except for remanding to resolve a setoff claimed by the United States,[5] the Court of Appeals for the Third Circuit affirmed. 581 F.2d 1092 (1978). It ruled that even though a plaintiff is aware of his injury and of the defendant's responsibility for it, the statute of limitations does not run where the plaintiff shows that "in the exercise of due diligence he did not know, nor should he have known, facts which would have alerted a reasonable person to the possibility that the treatment was improper." Id., at 1097. We granted certiorari to resolve this important question of the administration of the statute, 440 U.S. 906, 99 S.Ct. 1211, 59 L.Ed.2d 453 (1979), and we now reverse.

II

Statutes of limitation, which "are found and approved in all systems of enlightened jurisprudence," Wood v. Carpenter, 101 U.S. 135, 139, 25 L.Ed. 807 (1879), represent a pervasive legislative judgment that it is unjust to fail to put the adversary on notice to defend within a specified period of time and that "the right to be free from stale claims in time comes to prevail over the right to prosecute them." Railway Telegraphers v. Railway Express Agency, 321 U.S. 342, 349, 64 S.Ct. 582, 586, 88 L.Ed. 788 (1944). These enactments are statutes of repose; and although affording plaintiffs what the legislature deems a reasonable time to present their claims, they protect defendants and the courts from having to deal with cases in which the search for truth may be seriously impaired by the loss of evidence, whether by death or disappearance of witnesses, fading memories, disappearance of documents, or otherwise. United States v. Marion, 404 U.S. 307, 322, n. 14, 92 S.Ct. 455, 464, n. 14, 30 L.Ed.2d 468 (1971); Burnett v. New York Central R. Co., 380 U.S. 424, 428, 85 S.Ct. 1050, 1054, 13 L.Ed.2d 941 (1965); Chase Securities Corp. v. Donaldson, 325 U.S. 304, 314, 65 S.Ct. 1137, 1142, 89 L.Ed. 1628 (1945); Missouri K. & T. R. Co. v. Harriman, 227 U.S. 657,

---

5. The VA Board of Appeals' reconsideration of Kubrick's case in 1975 entitled him to an increase in his disability rating as a result of the use of neomycin. By the time of the Court of Appeals' decision, respondent had received over $50,000 in augmented disability benefits. Under 38 U.S.C. § 351, the benefits payments must be set off against the damages awarded in tort; and the increment in future monthly benefits is not paid until the aggregate amount of the benefits withheld equals the damages awarded.

672, 33 S.Ct. 397, 401, 57 L.Ed. 690 (1913); Bell v. Morrison, 1 Pet. 351, 360, 7 L.Ed. 174 (1828).

Section 2401(b), the limitations provision involved here, is the balance struck by Congress in the context of tort claims against the Government; and we are not free to construe it so as to defeat its obvious purpose, which is to encourage the prompt presentation of claims. Campbell v. Haverhill, 155 U.S. 610, 617, 39 L.Ed. 280 (1895); Bell v. Morrison, supra, at 360. We should regard the plea of limitations as a "meritorious defense, in itself serving a public interest." Guaranty Trust Co. v. United States, 304 U.S. 126, 136, 58 S.Ct. 785, 790, 82 L.Ed. 1224 (1938).

We should also have in mind that the Act waives the immunity of the United States and that in construing the statute of limitations, which is a condition of that waiver, we should not take it upon ourselves to extend the waiver beyond that which Congress intended. See Soriano v. United States, 352 U.S. 270, 276, 77 S.Ct. 269, 273, 1 L.Ed.2d 306 (1957); cf. Indian Towing Co. v. United States, 350 U.S. 61, 68–69, 76 S.Ct. 122, 126, 100 L.Ed. 48 (1955). Neither, however, should we assume the authority to narrow the waiver that Congress intended. Indian Towing Co. v. United States, supra.

It is in the light of these considerations that we review the judgment of the Court of Appeals.

III

It is undisputed in this case that in January 1969, Kubrick was aware of his injury and its probable cause. Despite this factual predicate for a claim against the VA at that time, the Court of Appeals held that Kubrick's claim had not yet accrued and did not accrue until he knew or could reasonably be expected to know that in the eyes of the law, the neomycin treatment constituted medical malpractice. The Court of Appeals thought that in "most" cases knowledge of the causal connection between treatment and injury, without more, will or should alert a reasonable person that there has been an actionable wrong. 581 F.2d, at 1096. But it is apparent, particularly in light of the facts in this record, that the Court of Appeals' rule would reach any case where an untutored plaintiff, without benefit of medical or legal advice and because of the "technical complexity" of the case, id., at 1097, would not himself suspect that his doctors had negligently treated him. As we understand the Court of Appeals, the plaintiff in such cases need not initiate a prompt inquiry and would be free to sue at any time within two years from the time he receives or perhaps forms for himself a reasonable opinion that he has been wronged. In this case, for example, Kubrick would have been free to sue if Dr. Soma had not told him until 1975, or even 1980, instead of 1972, that the neomycin treatment had been a negligent act.

There is nothing in the language or the legislative history of the Act that provides substantial basis for the Court of Appeals' construction of the accrual language of § 2401(b). Nor did the prevailing case law at the time the Act was passed lend support for the notion that tort claims in general or malpractice claims in particular do not accrue until a plaintiff learns that his injury was negligently inflicted. Indeed, the Court of Appeals recognized that the general rule under the Act has been that a tort claim accrues at the time of the plaintiff's injury, although it thought that in medical malpractice cases the rule had come to be that the two-year period did not begin to run until the plaintiff has discovered both his injury and its cause.[7] But even so—and the United States was prepared to concede as much for present purposes—the latter rule would not save Kubrick's action since he was aware of these essential facts in January 1969. Reasoning, however, that if a claim does not accrue until a plaintiff is aware of his injury and its cause, neither should it accrue until he knows or should suspect that the doctor who caused his injury was legally blameworthy, the Court of Appeals went on to hold that the limitations period was not triggered until Dr. Soma indicated in June 1971 that the neomycin irrigation treatment had been improper.[8]

7. In Urie v. Thompson, 337 U.S. 163, 69 S.Ct. 1018, 93 L.Ed. 1282 (1949), the Court held that a claim under the Federal Employers' Liability Act did not accrue until the plaintiff's injury manifested itself. In that case, plaintiff Urie contracted silicosis from his work as a fireman on a steam locomotive. His condition was diagnosed only in the weeks after he became too ill to work. The Court was reluctant to charge Urie with the "unknown or inherently unknowable" and held that because of his "blameless ignorance" of the fact of his injury, his claim did not accrue under the Federal Employers' Liability Act until his disease manifested itself. 337 U.S., at 169–170, 69 S.Ct., at 1024–1025. Quinton v. United States, 304 F.2d 234 (CA5 1962), applied the *Urie* approach to medical malpractice claims under the Federal Tort Claims Act. Other circuits have followed suit. Hungerford v. United States, 307 F.2d 99 (CA9 1962); Toal v. United States, 438 F.2d 222 (CA2 1971); Tyminski v. United States, 481 F.2d 257 (CA3 1973); Portis v. United States, 483 F.2d 670 (CA4 1973); Reilly v. United States, 513 F.2d 147 (CA8 1975); Casias v. United States, 532 F.2d 1339 (CA10 1976).

Restatement (Second) of Torts § 899, Comment *e*, pp. 444–445 (1979), reflects these developments:

"One group of cases in which there has been extensive departure from the earlier rule that the statute of limitations runs although the plaintiff has no knowledge of the injury has involved actions for medical malpractice. Two reasons can be suggested as to why there has been a change in the rule in many jurisdictions in this area. One is the fact that in most instances the statutory period within which the action must be initiated is short—one year, or at most two, being the common time limit. This is for the purpose of protecting physi-

cians against unjustified claims; but since many of the consequences of medical malpractice often do not become known or apparent for a period longer than that of the statute, the injured plaintiff is left without a remedy. The second reason is that the nature of the tort itself and the character of the injury will frequently prevent knowledge of what is wrong, so that the plaintiff is forced to rely upon what he is told by the physician or surgeon.

"There are still courts that proceed to apply the rule that the action is barred by the statute even though there has been no knowledge that it could be brought. . . .

"In a wave of recent decisions these various devices have been replaced by decisions meeting the issue directly and holding that the statute must be construed as not intended to start to run until the plaintiff has in fact discovered the fact that he has suffered injury or by the exercise of reasonable diligence should have discovered it. There have also been a number of instances in which a similar rule has been applied to other professional malpractice, such as that of attorneys or accountants and the rule may thus become a general one."

8. The Court of Appeals relied on three federal cases, all decided within the past five years, that held or indicated in dictum that a malpractice plaintiff under the federal act must know the legal implications of the facts, as well as the facts themselves, before the limitations period will begin to run. Exnicious v. United States, 563 F.2d 418, 420, 424 (CA10 1977); Bridgford v. United States, 550 F.2d 978, 981–982 (CA4 1977); Jordan v. United States, 503 F.2d 620 (CA6 1974). Since the holding below, another Circuit has endorsed these views.

We disagree. We are unconvinced that for statute of limitation purposes, a plaintiff's ignorance of his legal rights and his ignorance of the fact of his injury or its cause should receive identical treatment. That he has been injured in fact may be unknown or unknowable until the injury manifests itself; and the facts about causation may be in the control of the putative defendant, unavailable to the plaintiff or at least very difficult to obtain. The prospect is not so bleak for a plaintiff in possession of the critical facts that he has been hurt and who has inflicted the injury. He is no longer at the mercy of the latter. There are others who can tell him if he has been wronged, and he need only ask. If he does ask and if the defendant has failed to live up to minimum standards of medical proficiency, the odds are that a competent doctor will so inform the plaintiff.

In this case, the trial court found, and the United States did not appeal its finding, that the treating physician at the VA hospital had failed to observe the standard of care governing doctors of his specialty in Wilkes-Barre, Pa., and that reasonably competent doctors in this branch of medicine would have known that Kubrick should not have been treated with neomycin. Crediting this finding, as we must, Kubrick need only have made inquiry among doctors with average training and experience in such matters to have discovered that he probably had a good cause of action. The difficulty is that it does not appear that Kubrick ever made any inquiry, although meanwhile he had consulted several specialists about his loss of hearing and had been in possession of all the facts about the cause of his injury since January 1969. Furthermore, there is no reason to doubt that Dr. Soma, who in 1971 volunteered his opinion that Kubrick's treatment had been improper, would have had the same opinion had the plaintiff sought his judgment in 1969.

We thus cannot hold that Congress intended that "accrual" of a claim must await awareness by the plaintiff that his injury was negligently inflicted. A plaintiff such as Kubrick, armed with the facts about the harm done to him, can protect himself by seeking advice in the medical and legal community. To excuse him from promptly doing so by postponing the accrual of his claim would undermine the purpose of the limitations statute, which is to require the reasonably diligent presentation of tort claims against the Government.[10] If there exists in

DeWitt v. United States, 593 F.2d 276 (CA7 1979).

The dissent, like the respondent, relies on *Urie* and *Quinton,* but neither case controls this one. Both dealt with the discovery of the factual predicate for a malpractice claim, but neither addressed the question of plaintiff's awareness of negligence on defendant's part. Contrary to the implications of the dissent, the prevailing rule under the Act has not been to postpone the running of the limitations period in malpractice cases until the plaintiff is aware that he has been legally wronged.

Holdings such as the one before us now are departures from the general rule and, as indicated above, are of quite recent vintage.

10. As the dissent suggests, * * * we are thus in partial disagreement with the conclusion of the lower courts that Kubrick exercised all reasonable diligence. Although he diligently ascertained the cause of his injury, he sought no advice within two years thereafter as to whether he had been legally wronged. The dissent would excuse the omission. For statute of limitations purposes, we would not.

the community a generally applicable standard of care with respect to the treatment of his ailment, we see no reason to suppose that competent advice would not be available to the plaintiff as to whether his treatment conformed to that standard. If advised that he has been wronged, he may promptly bring suit. If competently advised to the contrary, he may be dissuaded, as he should be, from pressing a baseless claim. Of course, he may be incompetently advised or the medical community may be divided on the crucial issue of negligence, as the experts proved to be on the trial of this case. But however or even whether he is advised, the putative malpractice plaintiff must determine within the period of limitations whether to sue or not, which is precisely the judgment that other tort claimants must make. If he fails to bring suit because he is incompetently or mistakenly told that he does not have a case, we discern no sound reason for visiting the consequences of such error on the defendant by delaying the accrual of the claim until the plaintiff is otherwise informed or himself determines to bring suit, even though more than two years have passed from the plaintiff's discovery of the relevant facts about injury.

The District Court, 435 F.Supp., at 185, and apparently the Court of Appeals, thought its ruling justified because of the "technical complexity," 581 F.2d, at 1097, of the negligence question in this case. But determining negligence or not is often complicated and hotly disputed, so much so that judge or jury must decide the issue after listening to a barrage of conflicting expert testimony. And if in this complicated malpractice case, the statute is not to run until the plaintiff is led to suspect negligence, it would be difficult indeed not to apply the same accrual rule to medical and health claims arising under other statutes and to a whole range of other negligence cases arising under the Act and other federal statutes, where the legal implications or complicated facts makes it unreasonable to expect the injured plaintiff, who does not seek legal or other appropriate advice, to realize that his legal rights may have been invaded.

We also have difficulty ascertaining the precise standard proposed by the District Court and the Court of Appeals. On the one hand, the Court of Appeals seemed to hold that a Tort Claims Act malpractice claim would not accrue until the plaintiff knew or could reasonably be expected to know of the Government's breach of duty. Ibid. On the other hand, it seemed to hold that the claim would accrue only when the plaintiff had reason to suspect or was aware of facts that would have alerted a reasonable person to the possibility that a legal duty to him had been breached. Ibid. In any event, either of these standards would go far to eliminate the statute of limitations as a defense separate from the denial of breach of duty.

IV

It goes without saying that statutes of limitation often make it impossible to enforce what were otherwise perfectly valid claims. But that is their very purpose, and they remain as ubiquitous as the statutory rights or other rights to which they are attached or are applicable. We should give them effect in accordance with what we can ascertain the legislative intent to have been. We doubt that here we have misconceived the intent of Congress when § 2401(b) was first adopted or when it was amended to extend the limitations period to two years. But if we have, or even if we have not but Congress desires a different result, it may exercise its prerogative to amend the statute so as to effect its legislative will.

The judgment of the Court of Appeals is reversed.

MR. JUSTICE STEVENS, with whom MR. JUSTICE BRENNAN and MR. JUSTICE MARSHALL join, dissenting.

Normally a tort claim accrues at the time of the plaintiff's injury. In most cases that event provides adequate notice to the plaintiff of the possibility that his legal rights have been invaded. It is well settled, however, that the normal rule does not apply to medical malpractice claims under the Federal Tort Claims Act. The reason for this exception is essentially the same as the reason for the general rule itself. The victim of medical malpractice frequently has no reason to believe that his legal rights have been invaded simply because some misfortune has followed medical treatment. Sometimes he may not even be aware of the actual injury until years have passed; at other times, he may recognize the harm but not know its cause; or, as in this case, he may have knowledge of the injury and its cause, but have no reason to suspect that a physician has been guilty of any malpractice. In such cases—until today—the rule that has been applied in the federal courts is that the statute of limitations does not begin to run until after fair notice of the invasion of the plaintiff's legal rights.

Essentially, there are two possible approaches to construction of the word "accrues" in statutes of limitations: (1) a claim might be deemed to "accrue" at the moment of injury without regard to the potentially harsh consequence of barring a meritorious claim before the plaintiff has a reasonable chance to assert his legal rights, or (2) it might "accrue" when a diligent plaintiff has knowledge of facts sufficient to put him on notice of an invasion of his legal rights. The benefits that flow from certainty in the administration of our affairs favor the former approach in most commercial situations.[1] But in medical malpractice cases the harsh consequences of that approach have generally been considered unacceptable.[2] In all events, this Court adopted the latter approach over 30 years ago when it endorsed the principle that "blameless ignorance" should not cause the loss of a valid

1. See Gates Rubber Co. v. U. S. M. Corp., 508 F.2d 603, 611 (CA7 1975).

2. One should note not only the cases cited by the Court in its footnote 7, ante, but also the reference to "a wave of recent decisions" in the quotation from the Restatement (Second) of Torts in that footnote.

claim for medical injuries. Writing for the Court, Mr. Justice Rutledge expressed the point simply:

> "We do not think the humane legislative plan [Federal Employers Liability Act] intended such consequences to attach to blameless ignorance. Nor do we think those consequences can be reconciled with the traditional purposes of statutes of limitations, which conventionally require the assertion of claims within a specified period of time after notice of the invasion of legal rights." Urie v. Thompson, 337 U.S. 163, 170, 69 S.Ct. 1018, 1025.

This rule has been consistently applied by the Courts of Appeals in the intervening decades without any suggestion of complaint from Congress.

In my judgment, a fair application of this rule forecloses the Court's attempt to distinguish between a plaintiff's knowledge of the cause of his injury on the one hand and his knowledge of the doctor's failure to meet acceptable medical standards on the other. For in both situations the typical plaintiff will, and normally should, rely on his doctor's explanation of the situation.[3]

The *Urie* rule would not, of course, prevent the statute from commencing to run if the plaintiff's knowledge of an injury, or its cause, would place a reasonably diligent person on notice that a doctor had been guilty of misconduct. But if he neither suspects, nor has any reason to suspect, malpractice, I see no reason to treat his claim differently than if he were not aware of the cause of the harm or, indeed, of the harm itself. In this case the District Court expressly found that "plaintiff's belief that there was no malpractice was reasonable in view of the technical complexity of the question whether his neomycin treatment involved excessive risks, the failure of any of his doctors to suggest prior to June 1971 the possibility of negligence, and the repeated unequivocal assertions by the Veterans Administration that there was no negligence on the part of the government." 435 F.Supp. 166, 174.

The Court is certainly correct in stating that one purpose of the statute of limitations is to require the "reasonably diligent presentation of tort claims against the government." * * * A plaintiff who remains ignorant through lack of diligence cannot be characterized as "blameless." But unless the Court is prepared to reverse the Court of Appeals' judgment that the District Court's findings were adequately supported by the evidence, the principle of requiring diligence does not justify the result the Court reaches today. The District Court found that "plaintiff exercised all kinds of reasonable diligence in attempting to establish a medical basis for increased disability benefits." 435

---

3. In its discussion of the reasons why most jurisdictions have adopted a special rule for medical malpractice cases, the Restatement (Second) of Torts notes "that the nature of the tort itself and the character of the injury will frequently prevent knowledge of what is wrong, so that the plaintiff is forced to rely upon what he is told by the physician or surgeon." Restatement (Second) of Torts § 899, Comment *e,* p. 444 (1979).

F.Supp., at 185. That diligence produced not only the Government's denials, but, worse, what may have been a fabrication. It was only after the Government told plaintiff that Dr. Soma had suggested that plaintiff's occupation as a machinist had caused his deafness that plaintiff, by confronting Dr. Soma, first became aware that neomycin irrigation may not have been an acceptable medical practice. Plaintiff was unquestionably diligent; moreover, his diligence ultimately bore fruit. There is no basis for assuming, as this Court holds, that plaintiff could have been more diligent and discovered his cause of action sooner.

The issue of diligence in a negligence case should be resolved by the factfinder—not by the Supreme Court of the United States—and its resolution should depend on the evidence in the record, rather than on speculation about what might constitute diligence in various other circumstances.[4] Since a large number of circuit judges have reached the same conclusion, and since I find nothing in the Court's opinion that lessens my respect for their collective wisdom, I would simply affirm the unanimous holding of the Court of Appeals for the Third Circuit affirming the judgment of the District Court which merely applied well-settled law to the somewhat unusual facts of this case.

NOTE ON STATUTES OF LIMITATIONS AND LACHES

1. Nature and effect

Although there were no definite time periods at common law within which one had to sue, today all jurisdictions have enacted statutes of limitation fixing precise time periods for the commencement of different types of actions. Kyle v. Green Acres at Verona, Inc., 44 N.J. 100, 207 A.2d 513 (1965). For a survey of California's various limitation provisions, see Special Project, California Statutes of Limitations, 16 Sw.U.L.Rev. 1 (1986). Statutes typically provide a longer time period for contract actions than for tort actions. What is the rationale behind such a distinction? What is the appropriate time period for an action for personal injuries by a breach of warranty—is such a claim one in tort or in contract? Is a malpractice suit against a physician or a lawyer based on tort or contract? What consequences, in addition to the application of the statutes of limitations, might flow from a characterization of an action as a tort or breach of contract? See Alter v. Michael, 64 Cal.2d 480, 50 Cal.Rptr. 553, 413 P.2d 153 (1966).

The nature and purpose of statutes of limitation are well stated in *Kubrick*. See also Board of Regents v. Tomanio, 446 U.S. 478, 100 S.Ct. 1790, 64 L.Ed.2d 440 (1980). In theory statutes of limitation merely suspend the remedy and do not extinguish the substantive right, although barring the remedy has the same

---

4. The factual predicate for the Court's speculation is its assumption that if a patient who has been mistreated by one doctor should ask another if the first "failed to live up to minimum standards of medical proficiency, the odds are that a competent doctor will so inform the plaintiff." * * * I am not at all sure about those odds. See W. Prosser, Law of Torts (4th ed. 1971), p. 164; Markus, Conspiracy of Silence, 14 Clev.-Mar.L.Rev. 520 (1965); Seidelson, Medical Malpractice Cases and the Reluctant Expert, 16 Cath.U.L.Rev. 158 (1966). But whatever the odds are generally, I would prefer to have the issue of the diligence in exploring the reason for the unfortunate condition of this deaf plaintiff decided on the basis of evidence relevant to his particular injury.

practical effect in most instances as barring the right. See Osmundsen v. Todd Pacific Shipyard, 755 F.2d 730 (9th Cir.1985). While early judicial attitudes were somewhat hostile to statutes of limitations, the opinion in *Kubrick* represents the modern judicial attitude that the plea of limitation is a "meritorious defense, in itself serving a public interest." Guaranty Trust Co. v. United States, 304 U.S. 126, 58 S.Ct. 785, 82 L.Ed. 1224 (1938).

2. Applicability

Because statutes of limitation are deemed to affect only the remedy and not the substantive right, they are deemed procedural for choice of law purposes. As a result, the governing statute is usually that of the forum where the remedy is sought and not the statute of the place where the action arose. As a further consequence the statute of the forum may bar a remedy even though the action is not barred in the jurisdiction where it arose; conversely, in concept an action barred in the state where it arose may still be brought in a jurisdiction whose own statute does not bar it. Compare Santana v. Holiday Inns, Inc., 686 F.2d 736 (9th Cir.1982), with Dart Industries, Inc. v. Adell Plastics, Inc., 517 F.Supp. 9 (S.D.Ind.1980). See also Comment, Choice of Law: Statutes of Limitation in the Multistate Products Liability Case, 48 Tul.L.Rev. 1130 (1974); Martin, Statutes of Limitations and Rationality in the Conflict of Laws, 19 Washburn L.J. 405 (1980). Two principal exceptions should be noted. First, where a statute creates a right unknown at common law and establishes its own time period for suit, the right is a conditional one and its time condition will be enforced wherever the action is commenced. See, e.g., Price v. Litton Systems, Inc., 784 F.2d 600 (5th Cir.1986) (wrongful death act); Sokolowski v. Flanzer, 769 F.2d 975 (4th Cir.1985) (tort). Second, many jurisdictions have "borrowing" statutes. These statutes typically provide that an action arising in another jurisdiction or affecting a nonresident, and barred in that jurisdiction, is also barred in the forum state. See, e.g., Stafford v. International Harvester Co., 668 F.2d 142 (2d Cir. 1981). Federal law may, in certain cases, preempt state rules, as in Felder v. Casey, __ U.S. __, 108 S.Ct. 2302, 101 L.Ed.2d 123 (1988), where it was held that a state notice-of-claim statute, under which plaintiff's civil rights damages suit was dismissed as time barred, was preempted by federal law.

There are no general federal statutes of limitation. Where a federal claim or statute does not contain its own limitation period, a federal court will borrow the most analogous federal statute or state statute from the state in which it sits, Goodman v. Lukens Steel Co., 482 U.S. 656, 107 S.Ct. 2617, 96 L.Ed.2d 572 (1987), or may sometimes apply the doctrine of laches. Occidental Life Ins. Co. v. E.E.O.C., 432 U.S. 355, 97 S.Ct. 2447, 53 L.Ed.2d 402 (1977). What disadvantages are created by borrowing local state statutes in determining federal rights? Can a federal court judicially create a limitation period for a federal claim? See International Union v. Hoosier Cardinal Corp., 383 U.S. 696, 86 S.Ct. 1107, 16 L.Ed.2d 192 (1966). See also Special Project, Time Bars in Specialized Federal Common Law: Federal Rights of Action and State Statutes of Limitations, 65 Corn.L.Rev. 1011 (1980); Comment, Limitation Borrowing in Federal Courts, 77 Mich.L.Rev. 1127 (1979). On which state statute of limitation to borrow regarding a RICO claim, see Agency Holding Corp. v. Malley-Duff & Assoc., Inc., 483 U.S. 143, 107 S.Ct. 2759, 97 L.Ed.2d 121 (1987); on which to borrow regarding a claim under 42 U.S.C.A. § 1983, see Owens v. Okure, __ U.S. __, 109 S.Ct. 573, 102 L.Ed.2d 594 (1989).

In addition, parties are generally free to contract for limitation periods which differ from the general statutes, and these provisions periods will be enforced unless unreasonable or precluded by statute. Ashburn v. SAFECO Ins. Co., 42 Wash.App. 692, 713 P.2d 742 (1986). Such clauses are typically found in insurance policies, and in that context are construed strictly against the party invoking the shorter period. Backus v. Nationwide Mut. Ins. Co., 56 A.D.2d 724, 392 N.Y.S.2d 765 (1977); Severs v. Country Mut. Ins. Co., 89 Ill.2d 515, 61 Ill.Dec. 137, 434 N.E.2d 290 (1982) (policy period invalid as applied to minor).

Sovereign governments may take advantage of the statute of limitations, but they are not generally subject to the statute except where the sovereign is merely a nominal party or the statute otherwise provides. United States v. City of Palm Beach Gardens, 635 F.2d 337 (5th Cir. 1981). In some jurisdictions the sovereign is subject to the statute when it is suing on a proprietary right as contrasted with a public or governmental right. Board of County Comm'rs of Woodward County v. Willett, 49 Okl. 254, 152 P. 365 (1915). What is the justification for exempting governmental entities from the statute? See Block v. North Dakota ex rel. Board of University and School Lands, 461 U.S. 273, 103 S.Ct. 1811, 75 L.Ed.2d 840 (1983). Should municipal or local governments enjoy the same exemption? See City of Buffalo v. Watkins, 102 Misc.2d 17, 422 N.Y.S.2d 563 (1979); Kelley v. Metropolitan County Bd. of Education, 615 F.Supp. 1139 (M.D.Tenn. 1985).

For a critical analysis of *Kubrick* and its progeny, see Abney, For Whom the Statute Tolls: Medical Malpractice Under the Federal Tort Claims Act, 61 Notre Dame L.Rev. 696 (1986).

3. Computation of Time Periods

The time period is computed from the day on which the plaintiff could have commenced suit, viz., the date the action "accrued," to the day on which he actually commenced suit. In computing the period the law disregards fractions of a day and generally excludes the day on which the action accrued. Camalier & Buckley-Madison, Inc. v. Madison Hotel, Inc., 513 F.2d 407 (D.C.Cir. 1975); SCT (U.S.A.), Inc. v. Mitsui Mfrs. Bank, 155 Cal.App.3d 1059, 202 Cal.Rptr. 547 (1984); F.R.C.P. 6(a). Suit must be "commenced" on or before the last day of the period, but jurisdictions are divided on the question whether the last day should be excluded when it falls on a Sunday or a holiday. See, e.g., Deleon v. Bay Area Rapid Transit Dist., 33 Cal.3d 456, 189 Cal.Rptr. 181, 658 P.2d 108 (1983); Bedard v. Gonzales, 120 Ariz. 19, 583 P.2d 906 (1978).

The concepts of "accrual" and "commencement" are not self-defining and jurisdictions differ on their meaning and effect. Generally speaking, accrual means the time when the plaintiff could have first maintained a suit, i.e., the date when the action was legally complete and the right to sue matured. See Agency Holding Corp. v. Malley-Duff & Assoc., 483 U.S. 143, 107 S.Ct. 2759, 97 L.Ed.2d 121 (1987); Santos v. District Council of New York City, 619 F.2d 963 (2d Cir. 1980). If a condition precedent to suit exists, such as a demand, notice or other act, the action does not accrue until the condition is satisfied. An action for indemnity does not accrue until the indemnitee has suffered a loss through payment of a judgment. See Valley Circle Estates v. VTN Consolidated, Inc., 33 Cal.3d 604, 189 Cal.Rptr. 871, 659 P.2d 1160 (1983). Because plaintiffs may sometimes be ignorant of their right to sue, some statutes, particularly those pertaining to personal injuries from torts, are interpreted to defer the start of the period until the injured person discovered or should have discovered the existence of her cause of action. See Neel v. Magana, Olney, Levy, Cathcart & Gelfand, 6 Cal.3d 176, 98 Cal.Rptr. 837, 491 P.2d 421 (1971). Just how much a plaintiff must discover about her cause of action before the period starts to run is not always clear, as *Kubrick* suggests. See also Gutierrez v. Mofid, 39 Cal.3d 892, 218 Cal.Rptr. 313, 705 P.2d 886 (1985) (one-year limitations period begins to run no later than the time when plaintiff, suspicious of medical malpractice, decided to consult an attorney; plaintiff's remedy was a suit for legal malpractice against her attorney); Comment, Accrual of Statutes of Limitations: California's Discovery Exceptions Swallow the Rule, 68 Calif.L.Rev. 106 (1980); Andre, California Personal Injury Statutes of Limitations: The Modern Tort and the Judicial Abandonment of an Archaic Doctrine, 27 Santa Clara L.Rev. 657 (1987). The discovery rule is frequently coupled with a requirement that the plaintiff use due diligence in ascertaining her rights. Taylor v. Tukanowicz, 290 Pa.Super. 581, 435 A.2d 181 (1981). Did the plaintiff in *Kubrick* exercise reasonable diligence? New York has adopted the "continuous treatment" doctrine in professional malpractice suits, under which a patient or client's cause of action accrues when the professional relationship terminates and not when the negligence or unprofessional conduct occurs. Greene v. Greene, 56 N.Y.2d 86, 451 N.Y.S.2d 46, 436 N.E.2d 496 (1982).

The statute is tolled when the action is "commenced," but jurisdictions differ on what act is deemed to commence an action for purposes of the statute. Under the Federal Rules of Civil Procedure the filing of the complaint in the clerk's office starts the action and tolls the statute in an action based on federal law. F.R.C.P. 3; see United States v. Wahl, 583 F.2d 285 (6th Cir. 1978); Hobson v. Wilson, 737 F.2d 1 (D.C.Cir. 1984); Note, Commencement Rules and Tolling Statutes of Limitations in Federal Court, 66 Cornell L.Rev. 842 (1981). Actions in federal court based on state law are controlled by the applicable state statute. Walker v. Armco Steel Corp., reprinted infra p. 597. In some states an action is commenced on issuance of process while in other states it starts only on service of process. Ibid. See also Collins v. Edwards, 54 N.C. App. 180, 282 S.E.2d 559 (1981). When actual service of process on the defendant is required, statutes frequently establish a further grace period by providing that if process is delivered to a proper officer for service within the statutory period, and if actual service is completed within a fixed time thereafter, the action is deemed timely even though the defendant is served after the expiration of the statute. N.Y.C.P.L.R. § 203(b)(5); Conn.Gen.Stat. § 52–593a. What is the rationale behind such a provision? While actual notice, albeit irregular or informal, will not render the notice inadequate so as to invalidate a judgment, it may not obviate statute of limitation problems. Restatement Second of Judgments § 3, Comment c.

A federal statute, the Soldiers' and Sailors' Civil Relief Act, 50 App.U.S. C.A. § 525, excludes from computation the period of military service in any action by or against any person in the military service or his heirs, personal representatives or assigns, whether such cause of action accrued prior to or during such period of military service. See Bickford v. United States, 656 F.2d 636 (Ct.Cl.1981); Campbell v. Rockefeller, 134 Conn. 585, 59 A.2d 524 (1948).

4. Avoidance of the Statute

Application of the statute of limitations is not a matter of discretion and courts say they will not "balance the equities" or create or expand exceptions so as to avoid hardship or prevent unjust enrichment. See, e.g., Jefferson v. H.K. Porter Co., 648 F.2d 337 (5th Cir. 1981); Aldrich v. McCulloch Properties, Inc.,

627 F.2d 1036 (10th Cir. 1980); but cf. Hosogai v. Kadota, 145 Ariz. 227, 700 P.2d 1327 (1985). Exceptions generally focus on the status of the plaintiff or the conduct of the defendant.

a. Status of the Plaintiff

The plaintiff's personal disability or incapacity to sue, such as infancy or mental incapacity, usually tolls the statute. See Hernandez v. County of Los Angeles, 42 Cal.3d 1020, 232 Cal.Rptr. 519, 728 P.2d 1154 (1986) (extension of period for filing claim by minor). Where a plaintiff has died before the expiration of the period, his personal representative is generally granted a specified period of time after death within which to sue. Such provisions extend the time to sue when necessary but do not operate to shorten the period. N.Y.C.P.L.R. 210(a); Gordon v. Gordon, 110 A.D.2d 623, 487 N.Y.S.2d 574 (1985). Should imprisonment toll the statute? See Anno., 77 A.L.R.3d 735.

b. Conduct of the Defendant

Absence of the defendant from the jurisdiction typically suspends the statute, subject sometimes to a maximum period of years. See, e.g., C.C.P. 351; Conn.G.S. § 52–590; Anno., 55 A.L.R.3d 1158. Should such absence toll the statute where the defendant is subject to personal jurisdiction of the forum without being personally served in the forum state? Compare Dew v. Appleberry, 23 Cal.2d 630, 153 Cal.Rptr. 219, 591 P.2d 509 (1979), with Schmidt v. Polish People's Republic, 742 F.2d 67 (2d Cir. 1984). See also Note, Defendant's Absence May Not Toll Statute of Limitations, 49 U.M.K.C.L.Rev. 88 (1980). A state may constitutionally toll the statute for actions against a foreign corporation that is not represented within the state by a person upon whom process can be served. See G.D. Searle & Co. v. Cohn, 455 U.S. 404, 102 S.Ct. 1137, 71 L.Ed.2d 250 (1982). Fraudulent concealment of a cause of action will defer the statute until discovery or reasonable opportunity for discovery of the cause of action. See Bailey v. Glover, 88 U.S. (21 Wall.) 342, 22 L.Ed. 636 (1874); Richards v. Mileski, 662 F.2d 65 (D.C.Cir.1981); Young v. Haines, 41 Cal.3d 883, 226 Cal.Rptr. 547, 718 P.2d 909 (1986). In a few cases the defendant's behavior may estop him from invoking the statute if his actions have reasonably induced the plaintiff to forgo suit until after the statute had run. See Muraoka v. Budget Rent A Car, Inc., 160 Cal.App.3d 107, 206 Cal.Rptr. 476 (1984); Annos., 39 A.L.R.3d 127, 44 A.L.R.3d 482. A cause of action can be revived and the statute restarted by the defendant's unqualified acknowledgment or new promise to pay a debt, or part payment of a debt, whether such actions occur before or after the statute has run. Brooklyn Bank v. Barnaby, 197 N.Y. 210, 90 N.E. 834 (1910). Where the statute conditions the right itself, however, lapse of time is said to extinguish the right and neither estoppel nor revival usually apply. See Koehler v. Pulvers, 606 F.Supp. 164 (S.D.Cal.1985); Diamond National Corp. v. Dwelle, 164 Conn. 540, 325 A.2d 259 (1973). See also Note, Tolling of Substantive Statutes of Limitation, 32 Rutgers L.Rev. 95 (1979).

c. Savings Statutes

In the absence of statute, an action which is dismissed or fails after the statute of limitations has run cannot be recommenced, even if the original suit was brought within the time period. Because of the harshness of this result when the initial failure or dismissal was not on the merits, most jurisdictions have "savings" statutes that permit a new suit within a specified time period. Being "remedial," such savings statutes are generally "liberally" construed. See Allen v. Greyhound Lines, Inc., 656 F.2d 418 (9th Cir. 1981). Where dismissal is covered by a savings statute, the case may be restarted within the savings period or the general statute of limitations if it has not yet run, i.e., the savings statutes extend but do not shorten the statutory period. United States Fidelity & Guaranty Co. v. E.W. Smith Co., 46 N.Y.2d 498, 414 N.Y.S.2d 672, 387 N.E.2d 604 (1979). Without a federal savings statute, what should a federal court do if faced with a case, started in a state court within the period but dismissed for procedural reasons after the period, which is then refiled in federal court? See Burnett v. New York Central R. R. Co., 380 U.S. 424, 85 S.Ct. 1050, 13 L.Ed.2d 941 (1965). If a state does not have a savings statute, what should a federal court do with a case premised on both federal and state claims which is started in state court within the period and then removed to federal court, where plaintiff later drops the federal claim after the statute has run on the state claims? See Carnegie-Mellon Univ. v. Cohill, infra p. 538. Should a state which has a savings statute apply it to save an action dismissed in another state? See Allen v. Greyhound Lines, Inc., supra.

On avoidance of statutes of limitations by "relation back" amendments, see Amendment and the Statute of Limitations, supra p. 130. On the problems caused by misnomers and by amendments which denominate the defendant differently than in the original complaint, see Notice and the Statute of Limitations, infra p. 461, and Schiavone v. Fortune, infra p. 452.

5. Pleading and Procedure

A plea of limitation, being in the nature of confession and avoidance, is generally deemed an affirmative defense to be pleaded and proved by the party asserting it. F.R.C.P. 8(c); N.Y.C.P.L.R. § 3018(b). See Brush v. Olivo, 81 A.D.2d 852, 438 N.Y.S.2d 857 (1981). Failure to plead the statute waives the defense, Baltimore & Ohio R.R. Co. v. Genesee, 112 A.D.2d 725, 492 N.Y.S.2d 215 (1985), except where the statute conditions the substantive right. See Colyar v. Atlantic States Motor Lines, Inc., 231 N.C. 318, 56 S.E.2d 647 (1949). When the statute is raised as an affirmative defense, the plaintiff must then reply and raise whatever exceptions exist. Smith v. Knight, 608 S.W.2d 165 (Tex.1980). A general denial generally is not sufficient to raise the defense. However, where the right sued on is a statutory right containing its own limitation period, many jurisdictions permit the defendant to raise the defense by a general denial. County v. Pacific Coast Borax Co., 67 N.J.L. 48, 50 A. 906 (1902). While the general rule is that the statute should be raised by answer or plea, when it appears from the face of the complaint that the action is barred by the statute many jurisdictions permit the issue to be raised by demurrer or the equivalent. See Lopez v. Dean Witter Reynolds, Inc., 591 F.Supp. 581 (N.D.Cal.1984).

6. Laches

Laches is to suits in equity what the statute of limitations is to suits at law. Unlike statutes of limitation, however, the theoretical basis for laches is injustice, not just the passage of time. See Brown v. Continental Can Co., 765 F.2d 810 (9th Cir.1985). Thus, for laches to bar an equitable remedy the defendant must prove not merely lapse of time but also that the delay would cause injury, prejudice or disadvantage to the pleader's defense. See Smith v. City of Chicago, 769 F.2d 408 (7th Cir. 1985). While the period of delay for laches is not fixed by the statute of limitations, most courts use the statute by analogy to establish an appropriate period for laches. See Gruca v. United States Steel Corp., 495 F.2d 1252 (3d Cir. 1974). See also Note, Laches in

Federal Substantive Law: Relation To Statutes of Limitations, 56 B.U.L.Rev. 970 (1976).

With the merger of law and equity, should prejudice or detriment be a prerequisite to a defense based on the statute of limitations as well as for laches? For application of the doctrine of laches compare Holt v. County of Monterey, 128 Cal.App.2d 797, 180 Cal.Rptr. 514 (1982), with Miller v. Eisenhower Medical Center, 27 Cal.3d 614, 166 Cal.Rptr. 826, 614 P.2d 258 (1980).

D. COSTS OF LITIGATION

1. COURT COSTS

UNITED STATES v. KRAS

Supreme Court of the United States, 1973.
409 U.S. 434, 93 S.Ct. 631, 34 L.Ed.2d 626.*

MR. JUSTICE BLACKMUN delivered the opinion of the Court.

The Bankruptcy Act and one of this Court's complementary Orders in Bankruptcy impose fees and make the payment of those fees a condition to a discharge in voluntary bankruptcy.

Appellee Kras, an indigent petitioner in bankruptcy, challenged the fees on Fifth Amendment grounds. Upon receiving notice of the constitutional issue in the District Court, the Government moved to intervene as of right under 28 U.S.C. § 2403 and Rule 24(a) of the Federal Rules of Civil Procedure. Leave to intervene was granted. The District Court held the fee provisions to be unconstitutional as applied to Kras. 331 F.Supp. 1207 (EDNY, 1971). It reached this conclusion in the face of an earlier contrary holding by a unanimous First Circuit. In re Garland, 428 F.2d 1185 (1 Cir. 1970), cert. denied, 402 U.S. 966, 91 S.Ct. 1624, 29 L.Ed.2d 130 (1971). Pursuant to 28 U.S.C. § 1252, the Government appealed. * * *

I

Section 14(b)(2) of the Bankruptcy Act, 11 U.S.C. § 32(b)(2), provides that, upon the expiration of the time fixed by the court for filing of objections, "the court shall discharge the bankrupt if no objection has been filed and if the filing fees required to be paid by this title have been paid in full." Section 14(c), 11 U.S.C. § 32(c), similarly provides that the court "shall grant the discharge unless satisfied that the bankrupt . . . (8) has failed to pay the filing fees required to be paid by this title in full." Section 59(g), 11 U.S.C. § 95(g), relates to the dismissal of a petition in bankruptcy and states that "in the case of a dismissal for failure to pay the costs," notice to creditors shall not be

---

* Some of the Court's footnotes are omitted.

required. Three separate sections of the Act thus contemplate the imposition of fees and condition a discharge upon payment of those fees.

Three charges are imposed: $37 for the referee's salary and expense fund, $10 for compensation of the trustee, and $3 for the clerk's services. Sections 40(c)(1), 48(c), and 52(a), 11 U.S.C. §§ 68(c)(1), 76(c) and 80(a). These total $50. The fees are payable upon the filing of the petition. Section 40(c)(1), however, contains a proviso that in cases of voluntary bankruptcy, all the fees "may be paid in installments, if so authorized by General Order of the Supreme Court of the United States."

The Court's General Order in Bankruptcy No. 35(4), as amended June 23, 1947, 331 U.S. 873, 876–877, 11 U.S.C.App., p. 2210, complements § 40(c)(1) and provides that, upon a proper showing by the bankrupt, the fees may be paid in installments within a six-month period, which may be extended not to exceed three months.

II

Robert William Kras presented his voluntary petition in bankruptcy to the United States District Court for the Eastern District of New York on May 28, 1971. The petition was accompanied by Kras' motion for leave to file and proceed in bankruptcy without payment of any of the filing fees as a condition precedent to discharge. The motion was supported by Kras' affidavit containing the following allegations that have not been controverted by the Government:

1. Kras resides in a 2½ room apartment with his wife, two children, ages 5 years and 8 months, his mother, and his mother's 6-year-old daughter. His younger child suffers from cystic fibrosis and is undergoing treatment in a medical center.

2. Kras has been unemployed since May 1969 except for odd jobs producing about $300 in 1969 and a like amount in 1970. His last steady job was as an insurance agent with Metropolitan Life Insurance Company. He was discharged by Metropolitan in 1969 when premiums he had collected were stolen from his home and he was unable to make up the amount to his employer. Metropolitan's claim against him has increased to over $1,000 and is one of the debts listed in his bankruptcy petition. He has diligently sought steady employment in New York City, but because of unfavorable references from Metropolitan, he has been unsuccessful. Mrs. Kras was employed until March 1970, when she was forced to stop because of pregnancy. All her attention now will be devoted to caring for the younger child who is coming out of the hospital soon.

3. The Kras household subsists entirely on $210 per month public assistance received for Kras' own family and $156 per month public assistance received for his mother and her daughter. These benefits are all expended for rent and day-to-day necessities. The rent is $102 per month. Kras owns no automobile and no asset that is non-exempt under the bankruptcy law. He receives no unemployment or disability

benefit. His sole assets are wearing apparel and $50 worth of essential household goods that are exempt under § 6 of the Act, 11 U.S.C. § 24, and under New York Civil Practice Laws and Rules § 5205 (1963). He has a couch of negligible value in storage on which a $6 payment is due monthly.

4. Because of his poverty, Kras is wholly unable to pay or promise to pay the bankruptcy fees, even in small installments. He has been unable to borrow money. The New York City Department of Social Services refuses to allot money for payment of the fees. He has no prospect of immediate employment.

5. Kras seeks a discharge in bankruptcy of $6,428.69 in total indebtedness in order to relieve himself and his family of the distress of financial insolvency and creditor harassment and in order to make a new start in life. It is especially important that he obtain a discharge of his debt to Metropolitan soon "because until that is cleared up Metropolitan will continue to falsely charge me with fraud and give me bad references which prevent my getting employment."

The District Court's opinion contains an order, 331 F.Supp., at 1215, granting Kras' motion for leave to file his petition in bankruptcy without prepayment of fees. He was adjudged a bankrupt on September 13, 1971. Later, the referee, upon consent of the parties, entered an order allowing Kras to conduct all necessary proceedings in bankruptcy up to but not including discharge. The referee stayed the discharge pending disposition of this appeal.

III

In the District Court Kras first presented a statutory argument—and, alternatively, one based in common law—that he was entitled to relief from payment of the bankruptcy charges because of the provisions of 28 U.S.C. § 1915(a).[4] This is the *in forma pauperis* statute that has its origin in the Act of July 20, 1892, c. 209, 27 Stat. 252. See also 28 U.S.C. §§ 832–836 (1940).

* * * In any event, we agree, for the reasons stated by the District Court * * * that § 1915(a) is not now available in bankruptcy. See 2 Collier on Bankruptcy, ¶ 51.01, at 1873–1874 (14th ed. 1971). Neither do we perceive any common law right to proceed without payment of fees. Congress, of course, sometime might conclude that § 1915(a) should be made applicable to bankruptcy and legislate accordingly.

The District Court went on to hold, however, 331 F.Supp., at 1210–1215, that the prescribed fees, payment of which was required as a

---

4. "Any court of the United States may authorize the commencement, prosecution or defense of any suit, action or proceeding, civil or criminal, or appeal therein, without prepayment of fees and costs or security therefor, by a person who makes affida- vit that he is unable to pay such costs or give security therefor. Such affidavit shall state the nature of the action, defense or appeal and affiant's belief that he is enti- tled to redress."

condition precedent to discharge, served to deny Kras "his Fifth Amendment right of due process, including equal protection." Id., at 1212. It held that a discharge in bankruptcy was a "fundamental interest" that could be denied only when a "compelling government interest" was demonstrated. It noted, id., at 1213, that provision should be made by the referee for the survival, beyond bankruptcy, of the bankrupt's obligation to pay the fees. The court rested its decision primarily upon Boddie v. Connecticut, 401 U.S. 371, 91 S.Ct. 780, 28 L.Ed.2d 113 (1971) * * *.

Kras contends that his case falls squarely within *Boddie*. The Government, on the other hand, stresses the differences between divorce (with which *Boddie* was concerned) and bankruptcy, and claims that *Boddie* is not controlling and that the fee requirements constitute a reasonable exercise of Congress' plenary power over bankruptcy.

IV

Boddie was a challenge by welfare recipients to certain Connecticut procedures, including the payment of court fees and costs, that allegedly restricted their access to the courts for divorce. The plaintiffs, simply by reason of their indigency, were unable to bring their actions. The Court reversed a district court judgment that a State could limit access to its courts by fees "which effectively bar persons on relief from commencing actions therein." 286 F.Supp. 968, 972. Mr. Justice Harlan, writing for the Court, stressed state monopolization of the means for legally dissolving marriage and identified the would-be indigent divorce plaintiff with any other action's impoverished defendant forced into court by the institution of a law suit against him. He declared that "a meaningful opportunity to be heard" was firmly imbedded in our due process jurisprudence, 401 U.S., at 377, 91 S.Ct., at 785, and that this was to be protected against denial by laws that operate to jeopardize it for particular individuals, id., at 379–380, 91 S.Ct., at 786–787. The Court then concluded that Connecticut's refusal to admit these good-faith divorce plaintiffs to its courts equated with the denial of an opportunity to be heard and, in the absence of a sufficient countervailing justification for the State's action, a denial of due process, id., at 380–381, 91 S.Ct., at 787.

But the Court emphasized that "we go no further than necessary to dispose of the case before us." Id., at 382, 91 S.Ct. at 788.

"We do not decide that access for all individuals to the courts is a right that is, in all circumstances, guaranteed by the Due Process Clause of the Fourteenth Amendment so that its exercise may not be placed beyond the reach of any individual, for, as we have already noted, in the case before us this right is the exclusive precondition to the adjustment of a fundamental human relationship. The requirement that these appellants resort to the judicial process is entirely a state-created matter. Thus we hold only that a State may not, consistent with the obligations imposed on it by the Due Process Clause of the Fourteenth Amendment, pre-empt the right to dissolve this legal relationship without affording all citizens access to the means it has prescribed for doing so." Id., at 382–383, 91 S.Ct., at 788–789.

Mr. Justice Douglas, concurring in the result, rested his conclusion on equal protection rather than due process. "I do not see the length of the road we must follow if we accept my Brother Harlan's invitation." Id., at 383, 385, 91 S.Ct., at 790. Mr. Justice Brennan concurred in part, for he discerned no distinction between divorce and "any other right arising under federal or state law" and he, also, found a denial of equal protection. Id., at 386, 387, 91 S.Ct., at 791. Mr. Justice Black dissented, id., at 389, 91 S.Ct., at 792, feeling that the Connecticut court costs were barred by neither the Due Process Clause nor the Equal Protection Clause of the Fourteenth Amendment.

V

We agree with the Government that our decision in *Boddie* does not control the disposition of this case and that the District Court's reliance upon *Boddie* is misplaced.

A. *Boddie* was based on the notion that a State cannot deny access, simply because of one's poverty, to a "judicial proceeding [that is] the only effective means of resolving the dispute at hand." 401 U.S., at 376, 91 S.Ct., at 785. Throughout the opinion there is constant and recurring reference to Connecticut's exclusive control over the establishment, enforcement and dissolution of the marital relationship. The Court emphasized that "marriage involves interests of basic importance in our society," ibid., and spoke of "state monopolization of the means for legally dissolving this relationship," id., at 374, 91 S.Ct., at 784. "[R]esort to the state courts [was] the only avenue to dissolution of . . . marriages," id., at 376, 91 S.Ct., at 785, which was "not only the paramount dispute-settlement technique, but, in fact, the only available one," id., at 377, 91 S.Ct., at 785. The Court acknowledged that it knew "of no instance where two consenting adults may divorce and mutually liberate themselves from the constraints of legal obligations that go with marriage, and more fundamentally the prohibition against remarriage, without invoking the State's judicial machinery," id., at 376, 91 S.Ct., at 785. In the light of all this, we concluded that resort to the judicial process was "no more voluntary in a realistic sense than that of the defendant called upon to defend his interests in court" and we resolved the case "in light of the principles enunciated in our due process decisions that delimit rights of defendants compelled to litigate their differences in the judicial forum," id., at 376–377, 91 S.Ct. at 785.

B. The appellants in *Boddie,* on the one hand, and Robert Kras, on the other, stand in materially different postures. The denial of access to the judicial forum in *Boddie* touched directly, as has been noted, on the marital relationship and on the associational interests that surround the establishment and dissolution of that relationship.

On many occasions we have recognized the fundamental importance of these interests under our Constitution. [Citations omitted.] The *Boddie* appellants' inability to dissolve their marriages seriously impaired their freedom to pursue other protected associational activities. Kras' alleged interest in the elimination of his debt burden, and in obtaining his desired new start in life, although important and so recognized by the enactment of the Bankruptcy Act, does not rise to the same constitutional level. [Citations omitted.] If Kras is not discharged in bankruptcy, his position will not be materially altered in any constitutional sense. Gaining or not gaining a discharge will effect no change with respect to basic necessities. We see no fundamental interest that is gained or lost depending on the availability of a discharge in bankruptcy.

C. Nor is the Government's control over the establishment, enforcement, or dissolution of debts nearly so exclusive as Connecticut's control over the marriage relationship in *Boddie*. In contrast with divorce, bankruptcy is not the only method available to a debtor for the adjustment of his legal relationship with his creditors. The utter exclusiveness of court access and court remedy, as has been noted, was a potent factor in *Boddie*. But "[w]ithout a prior judicial imprimatur, individuals may freely enter into and rescind commercial contracts. . . ." 401 U.S., at 376, 91 S.Ct., at 785.

However unrealistic the remedy may be in a particular situation, a debtor, in theory, and often in actuality, may adjust his debts by negotiated agreement with his creditors. At times the happy passage of the applicable limitation period, or other acceptable creditor arrangement, will provide the answer. Government's role with respect to the private commercial relationship is qualitatively and quantitatively different than its role in the establishment, enforcement, and dissolution of marriage.

Resort to the court, therefore, is not Kras' sole path to relief. *Boddie's* emphasis on exclusivity finds no counterpart in the bankrupt's situation. See Cohen v. Beneficial Industrial Loan Corp., 337 U.S. 541, 547–555, 69 S.Ct. 1221, 1226–1229, 93 L.Ed. 1528 (1949).

D. We are also of the opinion that the filing fee requirement does not deny Kras the equal protection of the laws. Bankruptcy is hardly akin to free speech or marriage or to those other rights, so many of which are imbedded in the First Amendment, that the Court has come to regard as fundamental and that demand the lofty requirement of a compelling governmental interest before they may be significantly regulated. [Citations omitted.] Neither does it touch upon what has been said to be the suspect criteria of race, nationality or alienage. [Citations omitted.] Instead, bankruptcy legislation is in the area of economics and social welfare. [Citations omitted.] This being so, the applicable standard, in measuring the propriety of Congress' classification, is that of rational justification. [Citations omitted.]

E. There is no constitutional right to obtain a discharge of one's debts in bankruptcy. The Constitution, Art. I, § 8, cl. 4, merely authorizes the Congress to "establish . . . uniform Laws on the subject of Bankruptcies throughout the United States." Although the first bankruptcy law in England was enacted in 1542, 34 & 35 Henry 8, c. 4, and a discharge provision first appeared in 1705, 4 Anne, c. 17, primarily as a reward for cooperating debtors, J. MacLachlan, Bankruptcy 20–21 (1956), voluntary bankruptcy was not known in this country at the adoption of the Constitution. Indeed, for the entire period prior to the present Act of 1898, the Nation was without a federal bankruptcy law except for three short periods aggregating about 15½ years. * * * Professor MacLachlan has said that the development of the discharge "represents an independent . . . public policy in favor of extricating an insolvent debtor from what would otherwise be a financial impasse" (footnote omitted). J. MacLachlan, Bankruptcy 88. But this obviously is a legislatively created benefit, not a constitutional one, and, as noted, it was a benefit withheld, save for three short periods, during the first 110 years of the Nation's life. * * *

F. The rational basis for the fee requirement is readily apparent. Congressional power over bankruptcy, of course, is plenary and exclusive. Kalb v. Feuerstein, 308 U.S. 433, 438–439, 60 S.Ct. 343, 345–346, 84 L.Ed. 370 (1940). By the 1946 Amendment, 60 Stat. 326, Congress, as has been noted, abolished the theretofore existing practices of the pauper petition and of compensating the referee from the fees he collected. It replaced that system with one for salaried referees and for fixed fees for every petition filed and a specified percentage of distributable assets. It sought to make the system self-sustaining and paid for by those who use it rather than by tax revenues drawn from the public at large. H.R.Rep. No. 1037, 79th Cong., 1st Sess., 4–6 (1945); S.Rep. No. 959, 79th Cong., 2d Sess., 2, 5–6 (1946). The propriety of the requirement that the fees be paid ultimately has been recognized even by those district courts that have held the payment of the fee as a precondition to a discharge to be unconstitutional, for those courts would make the payments survive the bankruptcy as a continuing obligation of the bankrupt. [Citations omitted.]

Further, the reasonableness of the structure Congress produced, and congressional concern for the debtor, are apparent from the provisions permitting the debtor to file his petition without payment of any fee, with consequent freedom of subsequent earnings and of after-acquired assets (with the rare exception specified in § 70(a) of the Act, 11 U.S.C. § 110(a)) from the claims of then existing obligations. These provisions, coupled with the bankrupt's ability to obtain a stay of all debt enforcement actions pending at the filing of the petition or thereafter commenced, §§ 11(a) and 2(a)(15), 11 U.S.C. §§ 29(a) and 11(a)(15); 1A Collier on Bankruptcy ¶ 11.03 (14th ed. 1971); 1 Collier on Bankruptcy ¶ 2.62[4] (14th ed. 1971), enable a bankrupt to terminate his harassment by creditors, to protect his future earnings and property, and to have his new start with a minimum of effort and financial obligation. It serves also, as an incidental effect, to promote and not to defeat the purpose of making the bankruptcy system financially self-sufficient. Cf. Lindsey v. Normet, 405 U.S., at 74–79, 92 S.Ct., at 874–877.

G. If the $50 filing fees are paid in installments over six months as General Order No. 35(4) permits on a proper showing, the required average weekly payment is $1.92. If the payment period is extended for the additional three months as the Order permits, the average weekly payment is lowered to $1.28.[8] This is a sum less than the payments Kras makes on his couch of negligible value in storage, and less than the price of a movie and little more than the cost of a pack or two of cigarettes. If, as Kras alleges in his affidavit, a discharge in bankruptcy will afford him that new start he so desires, and the Metropolitan then no longer will charge him with fraud and give him bad references,[9] and if he really needs and desires that discharge, this much available revenue should be within his able-bodied reach when the adjudication in bankruptcy has stayed collection and has brought to a halt whatever harassment, if any, he may have sustained from creditors.

VI

Mr. Justice Harlan, in his opinion for the Court in *Boddie,* meticulously pointed out, as we have noted above, that the Court went "no further than necessary to dispose of the case before us" and did "not decide that access for all individuals to the courts is a right that is, in all circumstances, guaranteed by the Due Process Clause of the Fourteenth Amendment so that its exercise may not be placed beyond the reach of any individual." 401 U.S., at 382–383, 91 S.Ct., at 788. The Court obviously stopped short of an unlimited rule that an indigent at all times and in all cases has the right to relief without the payment of fees.

We decline to extend the principle of *Boddie* to the no-asset bankruptcy proceeding. That relief, if it is to be forthcoming, should originate with Congress. See Shaeffer, Proceedings in Bankruptcy In Forma Pauperis, 69 Col.L.Rev. 1203 (1969).

Reversed.

Mr. Chief Justice Burger, concurring.

I concur fully in the Court's opinion. The painstaking and precise delineation by Mr. Justice Harlan of the interests involved in *Boddie* ought not to be ignored as the dissenting opinions would do. Moreover, the exclusivity of a State's control of marriage and divorce is a far cry

---

8. If the fees total $40, as they may under General Order No. 15, 305 U.S. 687 (1939), 11 U.S.C.App., p. 2203, these average weekly figures are reduced to $1.54 and $1.03 respectively.

9. We fail to see how a discharge in bankruptcy in itself will prevent the Metropolitan from issuing an unfavorable reference letter about Kras.

from the degree of government control over relations between debtor and creditor, as Mr. Justice Blackmun has pointed out. In a bankruptcy proceeding the government, through the court, is no more than the overseer and the administrator of the process; it is not the absolute and exclusive controller as with the dissolution of marriage. Like the descent and distribution of property for which all States have provided statutes and probate courts, the bankruptcy court is but one mode of orderly adjustment with creditors; it is not the only one since many debtors work out binding private adjustments with creditors.

Surely there are strong arguments, as a matter of policy, for the result the dissenting view asserts. But Congress has not yet seen fit to declare the policy that the dissenters now find in the Constitution. In 1970 Congress authorized a tri-partite commission to review the bankruptcy laws. The Commission has been engaged in its task for more than two years and it is hardly likely that this problem will escape its consideration. The Constitution is not the exclusive source of law reform, even needed reform, in our system.

MR. JUSTICE STEWART, with whom MR. JUSTICE DOUGLAS, MR. JUSTICE BRENNAN, and MR. JUSTICE MARSHALL join, dissenting.

     * * *

Boddie held that a Connecticut statute requiring the payment of an average $60 fee as a prerequisite to a divorce action was unconstitutional under the Due Process Clause of the Fourteenth Amendment, as applied to indigents unable to pay the fee. The Court reasoned that due process protections are traditionally viewed as safeguards for a defendant, because at the point when a plaintiff invokes the governmental power of a court, the judicial proceeding is "the only effective means of resolving the dispute at hand and denial of a defendant's full access to that process raises grave problems for its legitimacy." 401 U.S., at 376, 91 S.Ct., at 785. But a party to a marriage remains under serious and continuing obligation imposed by the State, which cannot be removed except by judicial dissolution of the marital bond. * * *

The violation of due process seems to me equally clear in the present case. It is undisputed that Kras is making a good-faith attempt to obtain a discharge in bankruptcy, and that he is in fact indigent. As was true in *Boddie,* the "welfare income . . . barely suffices to meet the costs of the daily essentials of life and includes no allotment that could be budgeted for the expense to gain access to the courts. . . ." Id., at 372–373, 91 S.Ct., at 783.

Similarly, the debtor, like the married plaintiffs in *Boddie,* originally entered into his contract freely and voluntarily. But it is the government nevertheless that continues to enforce that obligation, and under our "legal system" that debt is effective only because the judicial machinery is there to collect it. The bankrupt is bankrupt precisely for the reason that the State stands ready to exact all of his debts through garnishment, attachment, and the panoply of other creditor remedies.

The appellee can be pursued and harassed by his creditors since they hold his legally enforceable debts.

And in the unique situation of the indigent bankrupt, the Government provides the only effective means of his ever being free of these Government-imposed obligations. As in *Boddie,* there are no "recognized, effective alternatives," id., at 376, 91 S.Ct., at 785. While the creditors of a bankrupt with assets might well desire to reach a compromise settlement, that possibility is foreclosed to the truly indigent bankrupt. With no funds and not even a sufficient prospect of income to be able to promise the payment of a $50 fee in weekly installments of $1.28, the assetless bankrupt has absolutely nothing to offer his creditors. And his creditors have nothing to gain by allowing him to escape or reduce his debts; their only hope is that eventually he might make enough income for them to attach. Unless the Government provides him access to the bankruptcy court, Kras will remain in the totally hopeless situation he now finds himself. The Government has thus truly pre-empted the only means for the indigent bankrupt to get out from under a lifetime burden of debt.

The Government contends that the filing fee is justified by the congressional decision to make the bankruptcy system self-supporting. But in *Boddie* we rejected this same "pay as you go" argument, finding it an insufficient justification for excluding the poor from the only available process to dissolve a marriage. 401 U.S., at 382, 91 S.Ct., at 788. The argument is no more persuasive here. The Constitution cannot tolerate achievement of the goal of self-support for a bankruptcy system, any more than for a domestic relations court, at the price of denying due process of law to the poor. In re Naron, 334 F.Supp. 1150, 1151; In re Smith, 323 F.Supp. 1082, 1088.[9]

In my view, this case, like *Boddie,* does not require us to decide "that access for all individuals to the courts is a right that is, in all circumstances, guaranteed by the Due Process Clause . . . so that its exercise may not be placed beyond the reach of any individual. . . ." 401 U.S., at 382–383, 91 S.Ct., at 788. It is sufficient to hold, as *Boddie* did, that "a State may not, consistent with the obligations imposed on it by the Due Process Clause . . ., pre-empt the right to dissolve this legal relationship without affording all citizens access to the means it has prescribed for doing so." Id., at 383, 91 S.Ct., at 789.

The Bankruptcy Act relieves "the honest debtor from the weight of oppressive indebtedness, and [permits] him to start afresh, free from the obligations and responsibilities consequent upon business misfortunes," Williams v. United States Fidelity & Guaranty Co., 236 U.S.

---

9. See Fuentes v. Shevin, 407 U.S. 67, 90 n. 22, 92 S.Ct. 1983, 1999, 32 L.Ed.2d 556; Bell v. Burson, 402 U.S. 535, 540–541, 91 S.Ct. 1586, 1589–1590, 29 L.Ed.2d 90; Goldberg v. Kelly, 397 U.S. 254, 261, 90 S.Ct. 1011, 1016, 25 L.Ed.2d 287; Cf. Griffin v. Illinois, 351 U.S. 12, 76 S.Ct. 585, 100 L.Ed. 891.

Moreover, there is no evidence that a substantial amount of revenue would be lost by allowing assetless indigents with no present prospects of paying the fee to file without prepayment. Any loss in fees which did result could be partially recouped by allowing the filing fee debt to survive bankruptcy.

549, 554–555, 35 S.Ct. 289, 290, 59 L.Ed. 713. It holds out a promise to the debtor of "a new opportunity in life and a clear field for future effort, unhampered by the pressure and discouragement of pre-existing debt." Local Loan Co. v. Hunt, 292 U.S. 234, 244, 54 S.Ct. 695, 699, 78 L.Ed. 1230. Yet the Court today denies that promise to those who need it most, to those who every day must live face-to-face with abject poverty—who cannot spare even $1.28 a week.

The Court today holds that Congress may say that some of the poor are too poor even to go bankrupt. I cannot agree.*

NOTE ON COURT COSTS

The general American rule is that the successful litigant, whether plaintiff or defendant, recovers "costs." It is roughly accurate to say that "costs" means the incidental expenses of court proceedings, excluding preparation expenses and attorneys fees. The precise limits of the term "costs" vary from jurisdiction to jurisdiction, being governed in part by vague statutory provisions for allowance of costs, see, e.g., 28 U.S.C.A. § 1920; F.R.C.P. 54(d); C.C.P. 1021 et seq., by special statutory provisions dealing with specific items, see, e.g., C.C.P. 1033.5 (list of specific items allowable as costs), and by case law. See Walsh, Taxing Costs in a Civil Case in the United States District Court, 64 Ill.B.J. 294 (1976); Peck, Taxation of Costs in United States District Courts, 42 Neb.L.Rev. 788 (1963). Costs are taxable against the United States, 28 U.S.C.A. § 2412(a), but the taxability of costs against a state or municipality varies with the jurisdiction. Compare C.C.P. 1028 et seq. with N.Y.C.P.L.R. § 8109.

All courts have filing fees, usually modest but sometimes a real barrier to the indigent. See Michelman, The Supreme Court and Litigation Access Fees: The Right to Protect One's Rights, 1973 Duke L.J. 1153, 1974 Duke L.J. 527. If that hurdle can be surmounted, the fees are ordinarily recovered by the judgment winner as part of "costs." The *Boddie* and *Kras* cases appear to distinguish between fundamental rights and merely economic rights, applying equal protection coverage to the former but not the latter. Compare Lindsey v. Normet, 405 U.S. 56, 92 S.Ct. 862, 31 L.Ed.2d 36 (1972) (invalidating requirement that tenant who wished to contest eviction post bond for twice the rent), with Ortwein v. Schwab, 410 U.S. 656, 93 S.Ct. 1172, 35 L.Ed.2d 572 (1973), rehearing denied 411 U.S. 922, 93 S.Ct. 1551, 36 L.Ed.2d 315 (upholding filing fee to appeal reduction in social benefits). Filing fees are typically low but the direct costs of preparing and trying a case, even excluding attorneys fees, are substantial. Major expenses include conducting and responding to discovery devices such as depositions, documents, inspections; expert witness fees; and, for an appeal, sums for transcripts and printing. Whether such costs are recoverable varies with the jurisdiction. See, e.g., 28 U.S.C.A. § 1920; C.C.P. 1033.5. See also Farmer v. Arabian American Oil Co., 379 U.S. 227, 85 S.Ct. 411, 13 L.Ed.2d 248 (1964).

Costs are sometimes recoverable as sanctions for abusing rules or process, e.g., F.R.C.P. 37(a), discussed infra p. 963, or for filing groundless or frivolous pleadings, e.g., F.R.C.P. 11, discussed supra p. 135. Excess costs of a proceeding, including expenses and attorney's fees, may be taxed against a lawyer "who so multiplies the proceeding * * * as to increase costs unreasonably and

---

* The dissenting opinions of Justice Marshall and Justice Douglas are omitted.

vexatiously," 28 U.S.C.A. § 1927. See also C.C.P. 128.5, authorizing award of reasonable expenses, including attorney's fees, for frivolous proceedings. See also Litton Systems, Inc. v. Am. Tel. & Tel. Co., 700 F.2d 785 (2d Cir. 1983), denying plaintiff costs and attorney's fees, ordinarily recoverable of right in an antitrust case, for fraud in pretrial discovery.

To overcome the expense of expert witnesses, can a party subpoena an expert but only pay him the statutory witness fee? See Porterfield, The Right to Subpoena Expert Testimony and the Fees Required to be Paid Therefor, 5 Hastings L.J. 50 (1953). May a party pay a witness a contingent fee? If so, is it wise to do so? See Person v. Association of Bar of City of New York, 554 F.2d 534 (2d Cir. 1977); Barnes v. Boatmen's Nat. Bank of St. Louis, 348 Mo. 1032, 156 S.W.2d 597 (1941). Crawford Fitting Co. v. J.T. Gibbons, Inc., 482 U.S. 437, 107 S.Ct. 2494, 96 L.Ed.2d 385 (1987), held that a trial court had no discretion to award the prevailing party expert witness fees in excess of the $30 per day limit fixed in 28 U.S.C.A. § 1821.

What can be said of a system of court costs that imposes the actual costs of the court system on the users? If justice is to be subsidized, should costs be assessed on a sliding scale according to the financial condition of the litigants or the amount in controversy? See Spector, Financing the Courts Through Fees: Incentives and Equity in Civil Litigation, 58 Judicature 330 (1975); Kakalik and Pace, Costs and Compensation Paid in Tort Litigation (Rand Institute for Civil Justice 1986); Lee, The American Courts as Public Goods: Who Should Pay the Costs of Litigation?, 34 Cath.U.L.Rev. 267 (1985) (recommending that the actual costs to the public of trying a case be allocated to the parties); Trubek, Sarat, Felstiner, Kritzer and Grossman, The Costs of Ordinary Litigation, 31 U.C.L.A.L.Rev. 72 (1983) (arguing that ordinary litigation is cost-effective for the average plaintiff).

The principal sanction for a substantively invalid claim is, of course, to dismiss the claim. See, e.g., Molasky v. Garfinkle, supra p. 61. The principal sanction against a defendant who refuses to defend, or who interposes a meritless defense, is entry of default judgment. See Default Judgments, infra p. 984. There is much greater difficulty in devising noncost sanctions for failure to comply with procedural requirements and orders. Ultimately, the court can dismiss a plaintiff's action or preclude a defendant from relying on a defense improperly interposed. On the former, see Mitchell v. E–Z Way Towers, Inc., supra p. 110. On refusal to permit a defendant to rely on a defense not asserted in compliance with procedural rules, see Taylor v. Illinois, 484 U.S. 400, 108 S.Ct. 646, 98 L.Ed.2d 798 (1988).

2. ATTORNEYS FEES

INTRODUCTORY NOTE ON ATTORNEYS FEES

Attorneys fees are not ordinarily recoverable in American courts. See, e.g., Fleischmann Distilling Corp. v. Maier Brewing Co., 386 U.S. 714, 87 S.Ct. 1404, 18 L.Ed.2d 475 (1967). On the effects of fee shifting on incentives to litigate, see Rowe, The Legal Theory of Attorney Fee Shifting, 1982 Duke L.J. 651; Symposium, Attorney Fee Shifting, 47 Law & Contemp.Probs. 1 (Winter 1984). Exceptions to the general rule include actions in which provision for attorneys fees is made by statute, e.g., C.C.P. 874.010 (partition suits), 836, 1021.5 et seq.; C.C. 4370–71 (dissolution of marriage action); see Berger, Court Awarded Attorneys' Fees: What is "Reasonable"?, 126 U.Pa.L.Rev. 281, 303 n. 104

(1977) (listing federal statutes providing for attorneys' fees); A.B.C.N.Y., Committee on Legal Assistance, Report on Counsel Fees in Public Interest Litigation, 39 The Record 300 (1984). Another exception is recovery of attorneys fees in prior litigation where defendant's out-of-court wrongful conduct brought on litigation by a third party against the plaintiff. See Comment, Recovery of Attorney Fees from Third Party Tortfeasors, 66 Calif.L.Rev. 94 (1978); Leubsdorf, Recovering Attorney Fees as Damages, 38 Rutgers L.Rev. 439 (1986); Anno., 45 A.L.R.2d 1183. See also Brandt v. Superior Court, 37 Cal.3d 813, 210 Cal.Rptr. 211, 693 P.2d 792 (1985) (when an insurer tortiously withholds benefits under an insurance policy, attorneys fees reasonably incurred to compel payment of the benefits are recoverable as an element of damages).

In recent years efforts have been made not only in the legislature but before the courts to modify the prevailing American rule, as in the following case.

SERRANO v. PRIEST
Supreme Court of California, 1977.
20 Cal.3d 25, 141 Cal.Rptr. 315, 569 P.2d 1303.*

SULLIVAN, JUSTICE.

In Serrano v. Priest (1976) 18 Cal.3d 728, 135 Cal.Rptr. 345, 557 P.2d 929 (hereafter cited as *Serrano II*) we affirmed a judgment of the Los Angeles County Superior Court, entered on September 3, 1974, which held essentially (1) that the then-existing California public school financing system was invalid as in violation of state constitutional provisions guaranteeing equal protection of the laws, and (2) that the said system must be brought into constitutional compliance within a period of six years from the date of entry of judgment, the trial court retaining jurisdiction for the purpose of granting any necessary future relief. That judgment is now final.

Within a month after the entry of the foregoing judgment and prior to the filing of defendants' appeals, plaintiffs' attorneys (Public Advocates, Inc. and Western Center on Law and Poverty) made separate motions for an award of reasonable attorneys fees "against defendants Priest [then the state Treasurer], Riles [then and presently the state Superintendent of Public Instruction] and Flournoy [then the state Controller] in their official capacities as officials of the State of California." The motions were not based upon statute but were instead addressed to the equitable powers of the court. Three theories, to be examined in detail by us below, were advanced in support of the award: the so-called "common fund" theory, the "substantial benefit" theory, and the "private attorney general" theory.

A hearing on the issue of entitlement to fees was held * * *. At the conclusion of this hearing the court announced its intention to award $400,000 as reasonable attorneys fees to Public Advocates, Inc. and $400,000 as reasonable attorneys fees to Western Center on Law and Poverty. * * *

---

* Some of the court's footnotes are omitted.

On January 28, 1977, after the rendition of our decision in *Serrano II* but prior to the issuance of the remittitur, a motion was filed in this court for reasonable attorneys' fees in connection with the appeal of this cause. * * * Prior to issuance of the *Serrano II* remittitur we modified our judgment to reserve jurisdiction for the purpose of passing upon this motion in conjunction with the instant appeal.

I

We summarize the contentions advanced in the briefs of the parties:

Defendants contend that the award of attorneys fees was improper on any of the grounds considered. * * * Additionally they argue that even if such an award based on any of these theories were proper in a case in which the prevailing litigant had incurred an obligation to pay for legal services, it could not be justified in a case in which, as here, the plaintiffs had incurred no obligation for such services which were provided without charge by organizations receiving public or tax-exempt charitable funding.[4] In any event, defendants urge, the award in this case is excessive. Finally, defendants also oppose the granting of the motion for attorneys fees on appeal.

Plaintiffs and their attorneys, while agreeing with the trial court's award of fees on the private attorney general theory, contend that the court erred in refusing to base its award additionally on the common fund and substantial benefit theories. * * *

II

Recently in D'Amico v. Board of Medical Examiners (1974) 11 Cal. 3d 1, 112 Cal.Rptr. 786, 520 P.2d 10, we had occasion to point out: "Section 1021 of the Code of Civil Procedure provides in relevant part: 'Except as attorney's fees are specifically provided for by statute, the measure and mode of compensation of attorneys and counselors at law is left to the agreement, express or implied, of the parties. . . .' No state statute provides for the award of attorney's fees in a case of this nature, and there has been no express or implied agreement concerning attorneys fees in this case. However, appellate decisions in this state have created two nonstatutory exceptions to the general rule of section 1021, each of which is based upon inherent equitable powers of the court. The first of these is the well-established 'common fund' principle: when a number of persons are entitled in common to a specific fund, and an action brought by a plaintiff or plaintiffs for the benefit of all results in the creation or preservation of that fund, such plaintiff or plaintiffs may be awarded attorneys fees out of the fund. * * * The second principle, of a more recent development, is the so-called 'sub-

---

4. Public Advocates, Inc. is a nonprofit legal corporation supported by tax-exempt charitable funds. Western Center on Law and Poverty is a public interest law center funded by the Legal Services Corporation. (See 42 U.S.C.A. § 2996 et seq.) Neither may accept fees from clients.

stantial benefit' rule: when a class action or corporate derivative action results in the conferral of substantial benefits, whether of a pecuniary or nonpecuniary nature, upon the defendant in such an action, that defendant may, in the exercise of the court's equitable discretion, be required to yield some of those benefits in the form of an award of attorneys fees. (See, e.g., Knoff v. City, etc., of San Francisco (1969) 1 Cal.App.3d 184, 203–204, 81 Cal.Rptr. 683; Fletcher v. A.J. Industries, Inc. (1968) 266 Cal.App.2d 313, 318–325, 72 Cal.Rptr. 146; see also Sprague v. Ticonic Bank (1939) 307 U.S. 161, 59 S.Ct. 777, 83 L.Ed. 1184; see generally 4 Witkin, Cal.Procedure, supra, Judgment, § 134, pp. 3283–3284.)" (Id. at p. 25, 112 Cal.Rptr. at p. 803, 520 P.2d at p. 27.) Mindful of these observations, we proceed first to determine whether the trial court was correct in concluding that an award of reasonable attorneys fees could not be supported in the instant case under either of the aforementioned exceptions to the rule of section 1021.

(a) The Common Fund Theory

"Although American courts, in contrast to those of England, have never awarded counsels' fees as a routine component of costs, at least one exception to this rule has become as well established as the rule itself: that one who expends attorneys' fees in winning a suit which creates a fund from which others derive benefits, may require those passive beneficiaries to bear a fair share of the litigation costs." (Quinn v. State of California (1975) 15 Cal.3d 162, 167, 124 Cal.Rptr. 1, 4, 539 P.2d 761, 764; fns. omitted.) This, the so-called "common fund" exception to the American rule regarding the award of attorneys fees (i.e., the rule set forth in section 1021 of our Code of Civil Procedure), is grounded in "the historic power of equity to permit the trustee of a fund or property, or a party preserving or recovering a fund for the benefit of others in addition to himself, to recover his costs, including his attorneys' fees, from the fund or property itself or directly from the other parties enjoying the benefit." (Alyeska Pipeline Co. v. Wilderness Society (1975) 421 U.S. 240, 257, 95 S.Ct. 1612, 1621, 44 L.Ed.2d 141; fn. omitted.)

First approved by this court in the early case of Fox v. Hale & Norcross S. M. Co. (1895) 108 Cal. 475, 41 P. 328, the "common fund" exception has since been applied by the courts of this state in numerous cases. (See, e.g., Glendale City Employees' Assn., Inc. v. City of Glendale (1975) 15 Cal.3d 328, 341, fn. 19, 124 Cal.Rptr. 513, 540 P.2d 609; * * * see generally Dawson, Lawyers and Involuntary Clients: Attorney Fees from Funds (1974) 87 Harv.L.Rev. 1597.) In all of these cases, however, the activities of the party awarded fees have resulted in the preservation or recovery of a certain or easily calculable sum of money—out of which sum or "fund" the fees are to be paid.[5] We can find no such "fund" in this case.

---

5. "Fees are awarded under this rationale out of a fund recovered or maintained by the plaintiff, on the theory that all who will participate in the fund should pay the cost of its creation or protection and that this is best achieved by taxing the fund itself for attorney's fees." (Comment, Court Awarded Attorney's Fees and Equal

In relevant findings of fact the trial court found that plaintiffs "have proven that the sum of money available for public education in California is not being spent in accordance with the California Constitution" and "have protected the sum of money available for public education" in the state. Plaintiff urges that these findings are tantamount to a determination that a fund of money for educational use was created by their efforts. The trial court, however, concluded otherwise, reasoning that whatever additional monies are made available for public education as a result of the *Serrano* judgment will flow from legislative implementation of the judgment, not from the judgment itself. That judgment requires substantial equality in educational opportunity for the school children of this state without regard to the taxable wealth per student in the particular district in which a student lives. It does not require any particular level of expenditure. Accordingly, it cannot be said that the efforts of plaintiffs have created or preserved any "fund" of money to which they should be allowed recourse for their fees.

* * *

Finally, even if it were determined that the monies to become available for education in the wake of *Serrano* should be considered a "fund" for these purposes, plaintiffs and their attorneys nowhere suggest that payment should be made to them out of such monies.[7] Instead they seem to indicate, with perhaps intentional vagueness, that their fees should be paid by "the State." * * *

* * * We hold that here, where plaintiffs' efforts have not effected the creation or preservation of an identifiable "fund" of money out of which they seek to recover their attorneys fees, the "common fund" exception is inapplicable. The trial court was correct in so concluding.

(b) *The Substantial Benefit Theory*

* * * This exception, which may be viewed as an outgrowth of the "common fund" doctrine, permits the award of fees when the litigant, proceeding in a representative capacity, obtains a decision resulting in the conferral of a "substantial benefit" of a pecuniary or nonpecuniary nature. In such circumstance, the court, in the exercise of its equitable discretion, thereupon may decree that under dictates of justice those receiving the benefit should contribute to the costs of its production. Although of fairly recent development in California, this exception to the general rule is now well established in our law.

Access to the Courts (1974) 122 U.Pa.L.Rev. 636, 694–695 [cited hereafter as Comment, Equal Access].)

7. Such an award, of course, would necessarily bring about a diminution in educational funding, a result which plaintiffs and their attorneys might be presumed to oppose. Moreover, an award of this kind would essentially constitute the acceptance of a fee from a client, and thus could not be accepted by either of the law firms representing plaintiffs. (See fn. 4, ante; see also Comment, Equal Access, supra, 122 U.Pa. L.Rev. 636, 695; cf. Sanders v. City of Los Angeles (1970) 3 Cal.3d 252, 263, 90 Cal. Rptr. 169, 475 P.2d 201; National Coun. of Com. Mental H.C., Inc. v. Weinberger (D.D.C.1974) 387 F.Supp. 991, 994–995.)

Although the seminal California case on this subject, Fletcher v. A.J. Industries, supra, 266 Cal.App.2d 313, 72 Cal.Rptr. 146, arose in the context of corporate litigation,[8] more recent decisions have applied the "substantial benefit" theory in a wide variety of circumstances, including those involving governmental defendants. Thus in Knoff v. City, etc., of San Francisco, supra, 1 Cal.App.3d 184, 81 Cal.Rptr. 683, a class action, the plaintiffs had secured the issuance of a writ of mandate requiring the board of supervisors to order a full investigation into the loss of property taxes during certain previous years, including the identification of taxable property which had escaped taxation for any reason, and to take appropriate action to recover the taxes due. The Court of Appeal affirmed a judgment awarding the plaintiffs their attorneys fees out of tax revenues to be collected "in consequence of . . . compliance" with the writ of mandate (id. at p. 203, 81 Cal.Rptr. 683), citing Fletcher for the proposition that the award was proper even in the absence of an existing "fund."

In the more recent case of Mandel v. Hodges (1976) 54 Cal.App.3d 596, 127 Cal.Rptr. 244, the plaintiff, a state employee, had successfully challenged the state's practice of giving its employees time off with pay on Good Friday as a violation of constitutional prohibitions against the establishment of religion. The Court of Appeal, affirming an award of attorneys fees against the state, held that a substantial benefit had accrued to the state in the form of the future saving of funds formerly expended for work not performed, and that the trial court, exercising its equitable powers in a suit brought in a representative capacity, had properly shifted the cost burden of producing that benefit to the party enjoying it.

Finally, in Card v. Community Redevelopment Agency (1976) 61 Cal.App.3d 570, 131 Cal.Rptr. 153, the plaintiff taxpayers had secured a judgment declaring invalid a city ordinance purporting to amend an existing redevelopment plan by including areas not covered by the original plan. As a result, certain property tax increment revenues otherwise payable to the redevelopment agency under the amending ordinance became available to various city and county taxing agencies. The Court of Appeal approved a portion of the judgment awarding attorneys fees to be paid by the various taxing agencies in proportion to their respective shares in the tax increment funds, holding that "[t]his

---

8. In Fletcher, a stockholders derivative action, the plaintiffs had obtained an order approving a settlement guaranteeing a beneficial change in corporate management and procedures as well as the arbitration of certain claims of managerial misconduct, with the possibility of future monetary awards. The Court of Appeal, affirming a trial court order awarding attorneys fees and costs to the plaintiffs, held that although no specific "fund" had been created out of which such fees could be awarded on the "common fund" theory, the benefit conferred on the corporation and shareholders justified a shifting of the monetary burden of producing that benefit to all those who would enjoy it. The court placed significant reliance upon certain dicta in the United States Supreme Court's decision in Sprague v. Ticonic Nat. Bank, supra, 307 U.S. 161, 166–167, 59 S.Ct. 777, 83 L.Ed. 1184. (See generally Dawson, Lawyers and Involuntary Clients: Attorney Fees from Funds, supra, 87 Harv.L. Rev. 1597, 1609–1611.)

result substantially benefits the affected taxing agencies, named in the judgment (and through them their taxpayers), since it reduces both the occasion for the [redevelopment agency's] expenditure of such funds and the [agency's] source of such funds as well." (61 Cal.App.3d at p. 583, 131 Cal.Rptr. at pp. 164–65.)

Relying on these and other [9] cases, plaintiffs and their attorneys urge that the award in this case was justified on the "substantial benefit" rationale and that the trial court erred in concluding otherwise. In urging that such a benefit was conferred upon the state as a result of this litigation, they make reference to various factual findings of the trial court on the general subject * * *. To the extent, however, that the subject findings are susceptible of the reading that substantial benefits in the form of increased educational opportunities have been bestowed upon the school children of this state as a necessary result of the *Serrano* decision—or that benefits in the form of tax savings have been bestowed upon the taxpayers—they are without support. The fundamental holding of *Serrano*—i.e., that the existing school finance system, insofar as it operates to deny equality of educational opportunity to the school children of this state, is thereby violative of state equal-protection guarantees—does nothing in and of itself to assure that concrete "benefits" will accrue to anyone. Only in the event that implementing legislation, in establishing the equality of educational opportunity required by *Serrano,* does so at a level higher than that presently enjoyed by the *least* favored student under the present system will concrete "benefits" accrue to *any* school child * * *. In short, concrete "benefits" can accrue to the state or its citizens in the wake of *Serrano* only insofar as the Legislature, in its

9. Among the federal decisions relied upon by plaintiffs and their attorneys are Hall v. Cole (1973) 412 U.S. 1, 93 S.Ct. 1943, 36 L.Ed.2d 702, and Newman v. State of Alabama (M.D.Ala.1972) 349 F.Supp. 278. In *Hall* the United States Supreme Court held that a former union member whose legal action had had the effect of establishing certain rights of free speech within the union was entitled to attorneys fees on the "substantial benefit" theory because the plaintiff, "by vindicating his own right of free speech . . . [had] necessarily rendered a substantial service to his union as an institution and to all of its members . . . [and] reimbursement of [his] attorneys' fees out of the union treasury simply shifts the costs of litigation to 'the class that has benefited from them and that would have had to pay them had it brought the suit.'" (412 U.S. at pp. 8–9, 93 S.Ct. at p. 1948, fn. omitted). In *Newman,* where a class action brought by state prisoners had resulted in a holding that inadequate medical treatment afforded them constituted cruel and unusual punishment within the meaning of the Eighth and Fourteenth Amendments, fees were awarded *against the state* on this theory "because of the positive benefit resulting to the *plaintiffs* and the members of *plaintiffs'* class." (349 F.Supp. at p. 286, italics added.) However the judgment as it related to attorneys fees was subsequently vacated and remanded for reconsideration in light of the intervening decisions in Alyeska Pipeline Co. v. Wilderness Society, supra, 421 U.S. 240, 95 S.Ct. 1612, 44 L.Ed.2d 141 (to be discussed infra) and Edelman v. Jordan (1974) 415 U.S. 651, 94 S.Ct. 1347, 39 L.Ed.2d 662. In *Alyeska* the high court, choosing to treat the "substantial benefit" rule as a part of the "common fund" exception, had clearly indicated that fees could be awarded under this rationale only "from the fund or property itself or directly from *the other parties enjoying the benefit*" (421 U.S. at p. 257, 95 S.Ct. at p. 1621, italics added, fn. omitted), thus suggesting that the approach adopted in *Newman* was erroneous under the federal rule.

implementation of the command of equality which that case represents, chooses to bestow them.

It is also urged, however, that while *Serrano* may not have had the direct effect of producing increased educational opportunity or tax savings, it did produce benefits of a conceptual or doctrinal character which are shared by the state as a whole. Certain findings of the trial court * * * support this contention. Common sense as well speaks in favor of the proposition that plaintiffs and their attorneys, as a result of the *Serrano* litigation, have rendered an enormous service to the state and all of its citizens by insuring that the state educational financing system shall be brought into conformity with the equal protection provisions of our state Constitution so that the degree of educational opportunity available to the school children of this state will no longer be dependent upon the taxable wealth of the district in which each student lives. We have concluded, however, that to award fees on the "substantial benefit" theory on the basis of considerations of this nature—separate and apart from any consideration of actual and concrete benefits bestowed—would be to extend that theory beyond its rational underpinnings. If the effectuation of constitutional or statutory policy, without more, is to serve as a sufficient basis for the award of attorneys fees in this state, the rationale for such awards must be found in a theory more directly concerned with considerations of this nature. It is to such a theory that we now turn.

III

In D'Amico v. Board of Medical Examiners, supra, 11 Cal.3d 1, 112 Cal.Rptr. 786, 520 P.2d 10, plaintiffs had sought an award of fees not only on the "common fund" and "substantial benefit" theories *but also* on two additional theories, both of which were grounded largely on federal case law. The first of these, involving awards against an opponent who has maintained an unfounded action or defense " 'in bad faith, vexatiously, wantonly or for oppressive reasons' " (11 Cal.3d at p. 26, 112 Cal.Rptr. at p. 804, 520 P.2d at p. 28), is not involved in the instant case and we do not address ourselves to it. However, the second, the so-called "private attorney general" concept, was adopted by the trial court as the basis for its award, and we are now called upon to determine its applicability in this jurisdiction.

* * *

* * * In Alyeska Pipeline Co. v. Wilderness Society, supra, 421 U.S. 240, 95 S.Ct. 1612, 44 L.Ed.2d 141, a five to two opinion authored by Justice White, the Supreme Court held that the awarding of attorneys fees on a "private attorney general" theory, in the absence of express statutory authorization, did not lie within the equitable jurisdiction of the federal courts. Such awards, the court held, "would make major inroads on a policy matter that Congress has reserved for itself." (421 U.S. at p. 269, 95 S.Ct. at p. 1627.)

The high court rested its conclusion on two bases. The first, involving the interpretation of an 1853 court costs act, need not long concern us here, for the act in question (presently 28 U.S.C. §§ 1920, 1923) bears little resemblance to the governing statute in this state, section 1021 of the Code of Civil Procedure. In any event the fashioning of equitable exceptions to the statutory rule to be applied in California is a matter within the sole competence of this court. The second basis on which the Supreme Court grounded its decision, however, dealing with the manageability and fairness of such awards in the absence of legislative guidance, goes directly to the heart of the determination here before us. The making of such awards in the absence of statutory authorization, the high court indicated, would leave the courts "free to fashion drastic new rules with respect to the allowance of attorneys' fees to the prevailing party . . . or to pick and choose among plaintiffs and the statutes under which they sue and to award fees in some cases but not in others, depending upon the courts' assessment of the importance of the public policies involved in particular cases." (421 U.S. at p. 269, 95 S.Ct. at p. 1627.) This, the court suggested, would represent an unacceptable and unwise intrusion of the judicial branch of government into the domain of the Legislature.

It is with this consideration foremost in mind that we must assess the arguments advanced by plaintiffs and amici curiae in support of our adoption of the "private attorney general" concept in our state. Those arguments may be briefly summarized as follows: In the complex society in which we live it frequently occurs that citizens in great numbers and across a broad spectrum have interests in common. These, while of enormous significance to the society as a whole, do not involve the fortunes of a single individual to the extent necessary to encourage their private vindication in the courts. Although there are within the executive branch of the government offices and institutions (exemplified by the Attorney General) whose function it is to represent the general public in such matters and to ensure proper enforcement, for various reasons the burden of enforcement is not always adequately carried by those offices and institutions, rendering some sort of private action imperative. Because the issues involved in such litigation are often extremely complex and their presentation time-consuming and costly, the availability of representation of such public interests by private attorneys acting *pro bono publico* is limited. Only through the appearance of "public interest" law firms funded by public and foundation monies, argue plaintiffs and amici, has it been possible to secure representation on any large scale. The firms in question, however, are not funded to the extent necessary for the representation of all such deserving interests, and as a result many worthy causes of this nature are without adequate representation under present circumstances. One solution, so the argument goes, within the equitable powers of the judiciary to provide, is the award of substantial attorneys fees to those public-interest litigants and their attorneys (whether private attorneys acting *pro bono publico* or members of "public interest" law firms) who are successful in such cases, to the end that support may be provided for the representation of interests of similar character in future litigation.

In the several cases in which the courts, persuaded by these and similar arguments, have granted fees on the "private attorney general" theory, various formulations of the rule have appeared. In spite of variations in emphasis, all of these formulations seem to suggest that there are three basic factors to be considered in awarding fees on this theory. These are in general: (1) the strength or societal importance of the public policy vindicated by the litigation, (2) the necessity for private enforcement and the magnitude of the resultant burden on the plaintiff, (3) the number of people standing to benefit from the decision. (See generally, Comment, Equal Access, supra, 122 U.Pa.L.Rev. 636, 666–674.) [16] Thus it seems to be contemplated that if a trial court, in ruling [on] a motion for fees upon this theory, determines that the litigation has resulted in the vindication of a strong or societally important public policy, that the necessary costs of securing this result transcend the individual plaintiff's pecuniary interest to an extent requiring subsidization, and that a substantial number of persons stand to benefit from the decision, the court may exercise its equitable powers to award attorney fees on this theory.

It is at once apparent that a consideration of the first factor may in instances present difficulties since it is couched in generic terms, contains no specific objective standards and nevertheless calls for a subjective evaluation by the judge hearing the motion as to whether the litigation before the court has vindicated a public policy sufficiently strong or important to warrant an award of fees. We are aware of the apprehension voiced in some critiques that trial courts, whose function it is to apply existing law, will be thrust into the role of making assessments of the relative strength or weakness of public policies furthered by their decisions and of determining at the same time which public policy should be encouraged by an award of fees, and which not—a role closely approaching that of the legislative function. (See generally, Comment, Equal Access, supra, 122 U.Pa.L.Rev. 636, 670–

---

16. A fourth factor, suggested by Justice Marshall in his dissenting opinion in *Alyeska*, was the extent to which "shifting [the cost of litigation] to the defendant would effectively place it on a class that benefits from the litigation." (421 U.S. at p. 285, 95 S.Ct. at p. 1635.) The majority, however, in responding to this suggestion, point out that to impose this limitation would result in an expanded version of the "substantial benefit" rule rather than a true "private attorney general" rationale. "When Congress has provided for allowance of attorneys' fees for the private attorney general," the majority stated, "it has imposed no such common-fund conditions upon the award. The dissenting opinion not only errs in finding authority in the courts to award attorneys' fees, without legislative guidance, to those plaintiffs the courts are willing to recognize as private attorneys general, but also disserves that basis for fee shifting by imposing a limiting condition characteristic of other justifications." (421 U.S. at p. 265, fn. 39, 95 S.Ct. at p. 1625.) We find this reasoning persuasive. The "private attorney general" theory must be accepted or rejected on its own merits—i.e., as a theory rewarding the effectuation of significant policy—rather than as a policy-oriented extension of the "substantial benefit" theory burdened with the limitations of that rationale.

671; Comment, The Supreme Court, 1974 Term (1975) 89 Harv.L.Rev. 1, 178–180.)[17] Since generally speaking the enactment of a statute entails in a sense the declaration of a public policy, it is arguable that, where it contains no provision for the awarding of attorney fees, the Legislature was of the view that the public policy involved did not warrant such encouragement. A judicial evaluation, then, of the strength or importance of such statutorily based policy presents difficult and sensitive problems whose resolution by the courts may be of questionable propriety.

Such difficulties, however, are not present in the instant case. The trial court, in awarding fees to plaintiffs, found that the public policy advanced by this litigation was not one grounded in statute but one grounded in the *state Constitution*. Thus, the trial court concluded as a matter of law: "If as a result of the efforts of plaintiffs' attorneys rights created or protected by *the State Constitution* are protected to the benefit of a large number of people, plaintiffs' attorneys are entitled to reasonable attorney's fees from the defendants under the private attorney general equitable doctrine." (Italics added.) Its factual findings, which are not here challenged, establish that the interests here furthered were *constitutional* in stature.[18] Its findings also make clear that the benefits flowing from this adjudication are to be widely enjoyed among the citizens of this state [19] and that the nature of the litigation was such that subsidization of the plaintiffs is justified in the event of their victory.[20] In these circumstances we conclude that an

17. Thus in rejecting the private attorney general theory in *Alyeska*, the high court declared that such a rule "would make major inroads on a policy matter that Congress has reserved for itself" and that federal courts "are not free to fashion drastic new rules with respect to the allowance of attorneys' fees to the prevailing party in federal litigation or to pick and choose among plaintiffs and the statutes under which they sue and to award fees in some cases but not in others, depending upon the courts' assessment of the importance of the public policies involved in particular cases." (Alyeska Pipeline Co. v. Wilderness Society, supra, 421 U.S. 240, 269, 95 S.Ct. 1612, 1627, 40 L.Ed.2d 476.)

18. The trial court found, inter alia, that "[t]he plaintiffs . . . have proven that the sum of money available for public education in California is not being spent in accordance with the California Constitution" and that "[t]he efforts of plaintiffs' attorneys . . . have assured that the billions of dollars spent every year in California on education will be spent in accordance with the California Constitution."

The determination that the public policy vindicated is one of constitutional stature will not, of course, be in itself sufficient to support an award of fees on the theory here considered. Such a determination simply establishes the first of the three elements requisite to the award (i.e., the relative societal importance of the public policy vindicated). (See test accompanying fn. 16, ante.) Only if it is also shown (2) that the necessity for private enforcement in the circumstances has placed upon the plaintiff a burden out of proportion to his individual stake in the matter, and (3) that the benefits flowing from such enforcement are to be widely enjoyed among the state's citizens—only then will an award on the "private attorney general" theory be justified.

19. The trial court found, for example, that "*Serrano* protects the right of every California child to receive a quality of education not dependent on the wealth of the school district in which he or she lives," and that "*Serrano* guarantees that the correlation between tax effort and educational quality will be equal for all children and taxpayers throughout the State of California."

20. The trial court found, for example, that "[t]he plaintiffs in *Serrano* individually did not have the resources to retain counsel to vindicate their rights to equitable educational and taxation systems," and that "[b]ecause of the nature of the consti-

award of attorneys fees to plaintiffs and their attorneys was proper under the theory posited by the trial court.

So holding, we need not, and do not, address the question as to whether courts may award attorney fees under the "private attorney general" theory, where the litigation at hand has vindicated a public policy having a statutory, as opposed to, a constitutional basis. The resolution of this question must be left for an appropriate case.

In sum, we hold that in the light of the circumstance of the instant case, the trial court acted within the proper limits of its inherent equitable powers when it concluded that reasonable attorneys fees should be awarded to plaintiffs' attorneys [21] on the "private attorney general" theory.

IV

It should be clear from what we have said above that the eligibility of plaintiffs' attorneys for the award of fees granted in this case is not affected under the "private attorney general" theory by the fact that plaintiffs are under no obligation to pay fees to their attorneys, or the further fact that plaintiffs' attorneys receive funding from charitable or public sources. Because the basic rationale underlying the "private attorney general" theory which we here adopt seeks to encourage the presentation of meritorious constitutional claims affecting large numbers of people, and because in many cases the only attorneys equipped to present such claims are those in funded "public interest" law firms, a denial of the benefits of the rule to such attorneys would be essentially inconsistent with the rule itself. (See generally Comment, Awards of Attorney's Fees to Legal Aid Offices, supra, 87 Harv.L.Rev. 411.) The propriety of such awards under statutory provisions is already well-established in this state (see Horn v. Swoap, supra, 41 Cal.App.3d 375, 383–384, 116 Cal.Rptr. 113; Trout v. Carleson (1974) 37 Cal.App.3d 337, 342–343, 112 Cal.Rptr. 282), and similar considerations are applicable when the award is made under the court's equitable powers.

tutional rights involved in this case, neither the California Attorney General nor any other public or governmental counsel could reasonably have been expected to institute litigation to vindicate the rights asserted by the plaintiffs in this case."

21. The propriety of a direct award to the plaintiffs' attorney, rather than to plaintiffs themselves, in the exercise of the court's equitable powers, is no longer questioned in the federal courts. (See Central R.R. & Banking Co. v. Pettus (1885) 113 U.S. 116, 124–125, 5 S.Ct. 387, 28 L.Ed. 915;

Brandenberger v. Thompson (9th Cir. 1974) 494 F.2d 885, 889; Miller v. Amusement Enterprises, Inc. (5th Cir. 1970) 426 F.2d 534, 539; Townsend v. Edelman (7th Cir. 1975) 518 F.2d 116, 122–123; see Comment, Awards of Attorney's Fees to Legal Aid Offices (1973) 87 Harv.L.Rev. 411, 422.) The equity powers of California courts are no less expansive in this respect. (See Knoff v. City and County of San Francisco, supra, 1 Cal.App.3d 184, 203–204, 81 Cal. Rptr. 683; Horn v. Swoap (1974) 41 Cal. App.3d 375, 383–384, 116 Cal.Rptr. 113.)

V

We reject the contention of Public Advocates, Inc.[22] that the fee awarded it was inadequate in light of all the circumstances. It is urged that the trial court, in limiting its award to Public Advocates to the admittedly substantial amount of $400,000, failed to take adequate account of the novelty and extreme difficulty of this litigation, its extremely contingent character, the significance of the issues determined, and the standard which the award in this case will set for similar awards in future cases. However, the record clearly indicates that the court considered all of these factors, among many others, in making its determination. Fundamental to its determination—and properly so [23]—was a careful compilation of the time spent and reasonable hourly compensation of each attorney and certified law student involved in the presentation of the case. That compilation yielded a total dollar figure of $571,172.50, of which $225,662.50 was applicable to Public Advocates, Inc., $320,710 to Western Center on Law and Poverty, and $24,800 to time spent by certified law students. Using these figures as a touchstone, the court then took into consideration various relevant factors, of which some militated in favor of augmentation and some in favor of diminution. Among these factors were: (1) the novelty and difficulty of the questions involved, and the skill displayed in presenting them; (2) the extent to which the nature of the litigation precluded other employment by the attorneys; (3) the contingent nature of the fee award, both from the point of view of eventual victory on the merits and the point of view of establishing eligibility for an award; (4) the fact that an award against the state would ultimately fall upon the taxpayers; (5) the fact that the attorneys in question received public and charitable funding for the purpose of bringing law suits of the character here involved; [24] (6) the fact that the monies awarded would inure not to the individual benefit of the attorneys involved but the organizations by which they are employed; and (7) the fact that in the court's view the two law firms involved had approximately an equal share in the success of the litigation. Taking all of these factors into consideration, the court proceeded to make a total award in the amount

22. As indicated above, Western Center on Law and Poverty does not join in this contention.

23. We are of the view that the following sentiments of the United States Court of Appeals for the Second Circuit, although uttered in the context of an antitrust class action, are wholly apposite here: "The starting point of every fee award, once it is recognized that the court's role in equity is to provide just compensation for the attorney, must be a calculation of the attorney's services in terms of the time he has expended on the case. Anchoring the analysis to this concept is the only way of approaching the problem that can claim objectivity, a claim which is obviously vital to the prestige of the bar and the courts." (City of Detroit v. Grinnell Corp. (2d Cir. 1974) 495 F.2d 448, 470; see also Lindy Bros. Bldrs., Inc. v. American R. & S. San. Corp. (3d Cir. 1973) 487 F.2d 161, 167–169; see generally Dawson, Lawyers and Involuntary Clients in Public Interest Litigation, supra, 88 Harv.L.Rev. 849, especially pp. 925–929.)

24. While as we have indicated the fact of public or foundational support should not have any relevance to the question of eligibility for an award, we believe that it may properly be considered in determining the size of the award.

of $800,000 to be shared equally by each of the two law firms representing plaintiffs.

The "experienced trial judge is the best judge of the value of professional services rendered in his court, and while his judgment is of course subject to review, it will not be disturbed unless the appellate court is convinced that it is clearly wrong." (Harrison v. Bloomfield Building Industries, Inc. (6th Cir. 1970) 435 F.2d 1192, 1196; see Mandel v. Hodges, supra, 54 Cal.App.3d 596, 624, 127 Cal.Rptr. 244.) We find no abuse of discretion here.

VI

* * *

The order concerning attorneys' fees filed August 1, 1975 is affirmed. The cause is remanded to the trial court with directions to hear and determine plaintiffs' motions for attorneys' fees [for services rendered on appeal and in opposing defendants' petition for writ of certiorari], in conformity with the views herein expressed and to make and enter all necessary and appropriate orders.*

EVANS v. JEFF D.

Supreme Court of the United States, 1986.
475 U.S. 717, 106 S.Ct. 1531, 89 L.Ed.2d 747.†

JUSTICE STEVENS delivered the opinion of the Court.

The Civil Rights Attorney's Fees Awards Act of 1976 (Fees Act), provides that "the court, in its discretion, may allow the prevailing party . . . a reasonable attorney's fee" in enumerated civil rights actions. 90 Stat. 2641, 42 U.S.C. § 1988. In Maher v. Gagne, 448 U.S. 122, 100 S.Ct. 2570, 65 L.Ed.2d 653 (1980), we held that fees *may* be assessed against state officials after a case has been settled by the entry of a consent decree. In this case, we consider the question whether attorney's fees *must* be assessed when the case has been settled by a consent decree granting prospective relief to the plaintiff class but providing that the defendants shall not pay any part of the prevailing party's fees or costs. We hold that the District Court has the power, in its sound discretion, to refuse to award fees.

I

The petitioners are the Governor and other public officials of the State of Idaho responsible for the education and treatment of children who suffer from emotional and mental handicaps. Respondents are a class of such children who have been or will be placed in petitioners' care.

* The dissenting opinions are omitted.

† Some of the Court's footnotes are omitted.

On August 4, 1980, respondents commenced this action by filing a complaint against petitioners in the United States District Court for the District of Idaho. The factual allegations in the complaint described deficiencies in both the educational programs and the health care services provided respondents. These deficiencies allegedly violated the United States Constitution, the Idaho Constitution, four federal statutes, and certain provisions of the Idaho Code. The complaint prayed for injunctive relief and for an award of costs and attorney's fees, but it did not seek damages.

On the day the complaint was filed, the District Court entered two orders, one granting the respondents leave to proceed *in forma pauperis,* and a second appointing Charles Johnson as their next friend for the sole purpose of instituting and prosecuting the action. At that time Johnson was employed by the Idaho Legal Aid Society, Inc., a private, non-profit corporation that provides free legal services to qualified low-income persons. * * *

* * *

In March 1983, one week before trial, petitioners presented respondents with a new settlement proposal. As respondents themselves characterize it, the proposal "offered virtually all of the injunctive relief [they] had sought in their complaint." Brief for Respondents 5. * * * As was true of the earlier partial settlement, however, petitioners' offer included a provision for a waiver by respondents of any claim to fees or costs. Originally, this waiver was unacceptable to the Idaho Legal Aid Society, which had instructed Johnson to reject any settlement offer conditioned upon a waiver of fees, but Johnson ultimately determined that his ethical obligation to his clients mandated acceptance of the proposal. The parties conditioned the waiver on approval by the District Court.[5]

After the stipulation was signed, Johnson filed a written motion requesting the District Court to approve the settlement "except for the provision on costs and attorney's fees," and to allow the respondents to present a bill of costs and fees for consideration by the court. App. 87. At the oral argument on that motion, Johnson contended that petitioners' offer had exploited his ethical duty to his clients—that he was "forced," by an offer giving his clients "the best result [they] could have gotten in this court or any other court," to waive his attorney's fees. The District Court, however, evaluated the waiver in the context of the entire settlement and rejected the ethical underpinnings of Johnson's argument. * * * Accordingly, the District Court approved the settlement and denied the motion to submit a costs bill.

* * *

5. Paragraph 25 of the Settlement Agreement provides:

"Plaintiffs and defendants shall each bear their own costs and attorney's fees thus far incurred, if so approved by the Court." App. 104.

In addition, the entire settlement agreement was conditioned on the District Court's approval of the waiver provision under Rule 23(e). * * *

II

The disagreement between the parties and *amici* as to what exactly is at issue in this case makes it appropriate to put certain aspects of the case to one side in order to state precisely the question that the case does present.

* * * Rule 23(e) wisely requires court approval of the terms of any settlement of a class action, but the power to approve or reject a settlement negotiated by the parties before trial does not authorize the court to require the parties to accept a settlement to which they have not agreed. Although changed circumstances may justify a court-ordered modification of a consent decree over the objections of a party after the decree has been entered, and the District Court might have advised petitioners and respondents that it would not approve their proposal unless one or more of its provisions was deleted or modified, Rule 23(e) does not give the court the power, in advance of trial, to modify a proposed consent decree and order its acceptance over either party's objection. * * * The question we must decide, therefore, is whether the District Court had a duty to reject the proposed settlement because it included a waiver of statutorily authorized attorney's fees.

That duty, whether it takes the form of a general prophylactic rule or arises out of the special circumstances of this case, derives ultimately from the Fees Act rather than from the strictures of professional ethics. Although respondents contend that Johnson, as counsel for the class, was faced with an "ethical dilemma" when petitioners offered him relief greater than that which he could reasonably have expected to obtain for his clients at trial (if only he would stipulate to a waiver of the statutory fee award), and although we recognize Johnson's conflicting interests between pursuing relief for the class and a fee for the Idaho Legal Aid Society, we do not believe that the "dilemma" was an "ethical" one in the sense that Johnson had to choose between conflicting duties under the prevailing norms of professional conduct. Plainly, Johnson had no *ethical* obligation to seek a statutory fee award. His ethical duty was to serve his clients loyally and competently.[14] Once the proposal to settle the merits was more favorable than the probable outcome of the trial, Johnson's decision to recommend acceptance was consistent with the highest standards of our profession. The District Court, therefore, correctly concluded that approval of the settlement involved no breach of ethics in this case.

---

14. Generally speaking, a lawyer is under an ethical obligation to exercise independent professional judgment on behalf of his client; he must not allow his own interests, financial or otherwise, to influence his professional advice. ABA, Model Code of Professional Responsibility EC 5–1, 5–2 (as amended 1980); ABA, Model Rules of Professional Conduct 1.7(b), 2.1 (as amended 1984). Accordingly, it is argued that an attorney is required to evaluate a settlement offer on the basis of his client's interest, without considering his own interest in obtaining a fee; upon recommending settlement, he must abide by the client's decision whether or not to accept the offer, see Model Code of Professional Responsibility EC 7–7 to EC 7–9; Model Rules of Professional Conduct 1.2(a).

The defect, if any, in the negotiated fee waiver must be traced not to the rules of ethics but to the Fees Act.[15] Following this tack, respondents argue that the statute must be construed to forbid a fee waiver that is the product of "coercion." They submit that a "coercive waiver" results when the defendant in a civil rights action (1) offers a settlement on the merits of equal or greater value than that which plaintiffs could reasonably expect to achieve at trial but (2) conditions the offer on a waiver of plaintiffs' statutory eligibility for attorney's fees. Such an offer, they claim, exploits the ethical obligation of plaintiffs' counsel to recommend settlement in order to avoid defendant's statutory liability for its opponents' fees and costs.[16]

The question this case presents, then, is whether the Fees Act requires a district court to disapprove a stipulation seeking to settle a civil rights class action under Rule 23 when the offered relief equals or exceeds the probable outcome at trial but is expressly conditioned on waiver of statutory eligibility for attorney's fees. For reasons set out below, we are not persuaded that Congress has commanded that all such settlements must be rejected by the District Court. Moreover, on the facts of record in this case, we are satisfied that the District Court did not abuse its discretion by approving the fee waiver.

III

The text of the Fees Act provides no support for the proposition that Congress intended to ban all fee waivers offered in connection with substantial relief on the merits.[17] On the contrary, the language of the Act, as well as its legislative history, indicates that Congress bestowed on the "prevailing *party*" (generally plaintiffs[18]) a statutory eligibility

15. Even state bar opinions holding it unethical for defendants to request fee waivers in exchange for relief on the merits of plaintiffs' claims are bottomed ultimately on § 1988. See District of Columbia Bar Legal Ethics Committee, Op. No. 147, reprinted in 113 Daily Wash.L.Rep. 389, 394–395 (1985); Committee on Professional and Judicial Ethics of the New York City Bar Association, Op. No. 82–80, p. 1 (1985); id., at 4–5 (dissenting opinion); Committee on Professional and Judicial Ethics of the New York City Bar Association, Op. No. 80–94, reprinted in 36 Record of N.Y.C.B.A. 507, 508–511 (1981) * * *.

16. See Committee on Professional Ethics of the New York City Bar Association, Op. No. 80–94, reprinted in 36 Record of N.Y.C.B.A., at 508 ("Defense counsel thus are in a uniquely favorable position when they condition settlement on the waiver of the statutory fee: they make a demand for a benefit which the plaintiff's lawyer cannot resist as a matter of ethics and which the plaintiff will not resist due to lack of interest."). Accord, District of Columbia

Bar Legal Ethics Committee, Op. No. 147, reprinted in 113 Daily Wash.L.Rep. 389, 394 (1985).

17. The operative language of the Fees Act provides, in its entirety:

"In any action or proceeding to enforce a provision of sections 1977, 1978, 1979, 1980, and 1981 of the Revised Statutes, title IX of Public Law 92–318, or in any civil action or proceeding, by or on behalf of the United States of America, to enforce, or charging a violation of, a provision of the United States Internal Revenue Code, or title VI of the Civil Rights Act of 1964, the court, in its discretion, may allow the prevailing party, other than the United States, a reasonable attorney's fee as part of the costs." 90 Stat. 2641, 42 U.S.C. § 1988.

18. See H.R.Rep. No. 94–1558, pp. 6–7 (1976); S.Rep. No. 94–1011, pp. 4–5, and n. 4 (1976); 122 Cong.Rec. 35122–35123 (1976) (remarks of Rep. Drinan); id., at 35125 (remarks of Rep. Kastenmeier).

for a discretionary award of attorney's fees in specified civil rights actions. It did not prevent the party from waiving this eligibility any more than it legislated against assignment of this right to an attorney, such as effectively occurred here. Instead, Congress enacted the fee-shifting provision as "an integral part of the remedies necessary to obtain" compliance with civil rights laws, S.Rep. No. 94–1011, p. 5 (1976), U.S.Code Cong. & Admin.News 1976, p. 5912, to further the same general purpose—promotion of respect for civil rights—that led it to provide damages and injunctive relief. The statute and its legislative history nowhere suggest that Congress intended to forbid *all* waivers of attorney's fees—even those insisted upon by a civil rights plaintiff in exchange for some other relief to which he is indisputably not entitled [20]—any more than it intended to bar a concession on damages to secure broader injunctive relief. Thus, while it is undoubtedly true that Congress expected fee-shifting to attract competent counsel to represent citizens deprived of their civil rights,[21] it neither bestowed fee awards upon attorneys nor rendered them nonwaivable or nonnegotiable; instead, it added them to the arsenal of remedies available to combat violations of civil rights, a goal not invariably inconsistent with conditioning settlement on the merits on a waiver of statutory attorney's fees.[22]

In fact, we believe that a general proscription against negotiated waiver of attorney's fees in exchange for a settlement on the merits

20. Judge Wald has described the use of attorney's fees as a "bargaining chip" useful to plaintiffs as well as defendants. In her opinion concurring in the judgment in *Moore v. National Assn. of Security Dealers, Inc.*, she wrote:

"On the other hand, the *Jeff D.* approach probably means that a defendant who is willing to grant immediate prospective relief to a plaintiff case, but would rather gamble on the outcome at trial than pay attorneys' fees and costs up front, will never settle. In short, removing attorneys' fees as a 'bargaining chip' cuts both ways. It prevents defendants, who in Title VII cases are likely to have greater economic power than plaintiffs, from exploiting that power in a particularly objectionable way; but it also deprives plaintiffs of the use of that chip, even when without it settlement may be impossible and the prospect of winning at trial may be very doubtful." 246 U.S. App.D.C., at 133, 762 F.2d at 1112.

21. See H.R.Rep. No. 94–1558, supra, at 1, 9; S.Rep. No. 94–1011, supra, at 2, 6; 122 Cong.Rec. 33313–33314 (1976) (remarks of Sen. Tunney); id., at 33314–33315 (remarks of Sen. Kennedy); id., at 35128 (remarks of Rep. Seiberling).

22. Indeed, Congress specifically rejected a mandatory fee-shifting provision,

see H.R.Rep. No. 94–1558, supra, at 3, 5, 8; 122 Cong.Rec. 35123 (1976) (remarks of Rep. Drinan), a proposal which the dissent would virtually reinstate under the guise of carrying out the legislative will. Even proponents of nonwaivable fee awards under § 1988 concede that "one would have to strain principles of statutory interpretation to conclude that Congress intended to utilize fee non-negotiability to achieve the purposes of section 1988." Calhoun, Attorney–Client Conflicts of Interest and the Concept of Non–Negotiable Fee Awards under 42 U.S.C. § 1988, 55 U.Colo.L.Rev. 341, 385 (1984). This conclusion is buttressed by Congress' decision to emulate the "over fifty" fee-shifting provisions that had been successful in enlisting the aid of "private attorneys general" in the prosecution of other federal statutes that had been on the books for decades. H.R.Rep. No. 94–1558, supra, at 3, 5. Accord, S.Rep. No. 94–1011, supra, at 3. See also 122 Cong. Rec., supra, at 35123 (appendix to remarks of Rep. Drinan) (listing more than 50 fee-shifting statutes). No one has suggested that the purpose of any of those fee-shifting provisions has been frustrated by the absence of a prohibition against fee waivers.

would itself impede vindication of civil rights, at least in some cases, by reducing the attractiveness of settlement. Of particular relevance in this regard is our recent decision in Marek v. Chesny, 473 U.S. 1, 105 S.Ct. 3012, 87 L.Ed.2d 1 (1985). * * * To promote both settlement and civil rights, we implicitly acknowledged in Marek v. Chesny the possibility of a tradeoff between merits relief and attorney's fees when we upheld the defendant's lump-sum offer to settle the entire civil rights action, including any liability for fees and costs.

In approving the package offer in Marek v. Chesny we recognized that a rule prohibiting the comprehensive negotiation of all outstanding issues in a pending case might well preclude the settlement of a substantial number of cases:

> "If defendants are not allowed to make lump-sum offers that would, if accepted, represent their total liability, they would understandably be reluctant to make settlement offers. As the Court of Appeals observed, 'many a defendant would be unwilling to make a binding settlement offer on terms that left it exposed to liability for attorney's fees in whatever amount the court might fix on motion of the plaintiff.' 720 F.2d [474], at 477 [(CA7 1983)]." 473 U.S., at 6–7, 105 S.Ct., at 3016.

See White v. New Hampshire Department of Employment Security, 455 U.S. 445, 454, n. 15, 102 S.Ct. 1162, 1167, n. 15, 71 L.Ed.2d 325 (1982) ("In considering whether to enter a negotiated settlement, a defendant may have good reason to demand to know his total liability from both damages and fees").

Most defendants are unlikely to settle unless the cost of the predicted judgment, discounted by its probability, plus the transaction costs of further litigation, are greater than the cost of the settlement package. If fee waivers cannot be negotiated, the settlement package must either contain an attorney's fee component of potentially large and typically uncertain magnitude, or else the parties must agree to have the fee fixed by the court. Although either of these alternatives may well be acceptable in many cases, there surely is a significant number in which neither alternative will be as satisfactory as a decision to try the entire case.[23]

The adverse impact of removing attorney's fees and costs from bargaining might be tolerable if the uncertainty introduced into settlement negotiations were small. But it is not. The defendants' potential

---

23. It is unrealistic to assume that the defendant's offer on the merits would be unchanged by redaction of the provision waiving fees. If it were, the defendant's incentive to settle would be diminished because of the risk that attorney's fees, when added to the original merits offer, will exceed the discounted value of the expected judgment plus litigation costs. If, as is more likely, the defendant lowered the value of its offer on the merits to provide a cushion against the possibility of a large fee award, the defendant's offer on the merits will in many cases be less than the amount to which the plaintiff feels himself entitled, thereby inclining him to reject the settlement. Of course, to the extent that the merits offer is somewhere between these two extremes the incentive of both sides to settle is dampened, albeit to a lesser degree with respect to each party.

liability for fees in this kind of litigation can be as significant as, and sometimes even more significant than, their potential liability on the merits. This proposition is most dramatically illustrated by the fee awards of district courts in actions seeking only monetary relief.[24] Although it is more difficult to compare fee awards with the cost of injunctive relief, in part because the cost of such relief is seldom reported in written opinions, here too attorney's fees awarded by district courts have "frequently outrun the economic benefits ultimately obtained by successful litigants." 122 Cong.Rec. 31472 (1976) (remarks of Sen. Kennedy).[25] Indeed, in this very case "[c]ounsel for defendants view[ed] the risk of an attorney's fees award as the most significant liability in the case." Brief of Defendants in Support of Approval of Compromise in Jeff D. v. Evans, No. 80–4091 (D.Idaho), p. 5. Undoubtedly there are many other civil rights actions in which potential liability for attorney's fees may overshadow the potential cost of relief on the merits and darken prospects for settlement if fees cannot be negotiated.

The unpredictability of attorney's fees may be just as important as their magnitude when a defendant is striving to fix its liability. Unlike a determination of costs, which ordinarily involve smaller outlays and are more susceptible of calculation, see Marek v. Chesny, 473 U.S., at 7, 105 S.Ct., at 3016, "[t]here is no precise rule or formula" for determining attorney's fees, Hensley v. Eckerhart, 461 U.S. 424, 436, 103 S.Ct. 1933, 1941, 76 L.Ed.2d 40 (1983).[26] Among other considerations, the district court must determine what hours were reasonably expended on what claims, whether that expenditure was reasonable in light of the success obtained, see id., at 436, 440, 103 S.Ct., at 1941, 1943, and what

---

24. See, e.g., Rivera v. City of Riverside, 763 F.2d 1580, 1581–1583 (CA9 1985) (City ordered to pay victorious civil rights plaintiffs $245,456.25 following a trial in which they recovered a total of $33,350 in damages), cert. granted, 474 U.S. 917, 106 S.Ct. 244, 88 L.Ed.2d 253 (1985); Cunningham v. City of McKeesport, 753 F.2d 262, 269 (CA3 1985) (City ordered to pay some $35,000 in attorney's fees in a case in which judgment for the plaintiff was entered in the amount of $17,000); Copeland v. Marshall, 641 F.2d 880, 891 (CADC 1980) (en banc) ($160,000 attorney's fees awarded for obtaining $33,000 judgment); Skoda v. Fontani, 646 F.2d 1193, 1194 (CA7), on remand, 519 F.Supp. 309, 310 (N.D.Ill.1981) ($6,086.12 attorney's fees awarded to obtain $1 recovery). Cf. Marek v. Chesny, 473 U.S., at 7, 105 S.Ct., at 3016 ($171,692.47 in claimed attorney's fees and costs to obtain $60,000 damages judgment).

25. See, e.g., Grendel's Den, Inc. v. Larkin, 749 F.2d 945, 960 (CA1 1984) (awarding $113,640.85 in fees and expenses for successful challenge to law zoning liquor establishments in Larkin v. Grendel's Den, 459 U.S. 116, 103 S.Ct. 505, 74 L.Ed. 2d 297 (1982)).

26. While this Court has identified "the number of hours reasonably expended on the litigation multiplied by a reasonable hourly rate" as "[t]he most useful starting point for determining the amount of a reasonable fee," Hensley v. Eckerhart, 461 U.S. 424, 433, 103 S.Ct. 1933, 1939, 76 L.Ed.2d 40 (1983), the "product of reasonable hours times a reasonable rate does not end the inquiry," id., at 434, 103 S.Ct., at 1940, for "there may be circumstances in which the basic standard of reasonable rates multiplied by reasonably expended hours results in a fee that is either unreasonably low or unreasonably high." Blum v. Stenson, 465 U.S. 886, 897, 104 S.Ct. 1541, 1548, 79 L.Ed.2d 891 (1984). "A district court is expressly empowered to exercise discretion in determining whether an award is to be made and if so its reasonableness." Id., at 902, n. 19, 104 S.Ct., at 1550, n. 19. See Hensley v. Eckerhart, 461 U.S., at 437, 103 S.Ct., at 1941. The district court's calculation is thus anything but an arithmetical exercise.

is an appropriate hourly rate for the services rendered. Some district courts have also considered whether a "multiplier" or other adjustment is appropriate. The consequence of this succession of necessarily judgmental decisions for the ultimate fee award is inescapable: a defendant's liability for his opponent's attorney's fees in a civil rights action cannot be fixed with a sufficient degree of confidence to make defendants indifferent to their exclusion from negotiation.[27] It is therefore not implausible to anticipate that parties to a significant number of civil rights cases will refuse to settle if liability for attorney's fees remains open,[28] thereby forcing more cases to trial, unnecessarily burdening the judicial system, and disserving civil rights litigants. Respondents' own waiver of attorney's fees and costs to obtain settlement of their educational claims is eloquent testimony to the utility of fee waivers in vindicating civil rights claims. We conclude, therefore, that it is not necessary to construe the Fees Act as embodying a general rule prohibiting settlements conditioned on the waiver of fees in order to be faithful to the purposes of that Act.

IV

The question remains whether the District Court abused its discretion in this case by approving a settlement which included a complete fee waiver.   *   *   *

　　*   *   *

In light of the record, respondents must—to sustain the judgment in their favor—confront the District Court's finding that the extensive structural relief they obtained constituted an adequate *quid pro quo* for their waiver of attorney's fees. The Court of Appeals did not overturn this finding. Indeed, even that court did not suggest that the option of rejecting the entire settlement and requiring the parties either to try the case or to attempt to negotiate a different settlement would have served the interests of justice. Only by making the unsupported assumption that the respondent class was entitled to retain the favorable portions of the settlement while rejecting the fee waiver could

---

27. The variability in fee awards is discussed in, for example, Berger, Court Awarded Attorneys' Fees: What is "Reasonable"?, 126 U.Pa.L.Rev. 281, 283–84 (1977); Diamond, The Firestorm over Attorney Fee Awards, 69 A.B.A.J. 1420 (1983); and National Association of Attorneys General, Report to Congress: Civil Rights Attorney's Fees Awards Act of 1976 (Feb. 3, 1984), reprinted in Hearing on The Legal Fee Equity Act (S. 2802) before the Subcommittee on the Constitution of the Senate Committee on the Judiciary, 98th Cong., 2d Sess., 280–293 (1984).

28. This is the experience of every judge and a majority of the members of a Third Circuit Task Force which concluded that that Circuit's ban on fee negotiations "tends to discourage settlement in some cases and, on occasion, makes it impossible." Report of the Third Circuit Task Force: Court Awarded Fees 38 (1985) (footnotes omitted). The Task Force reasoned:

> "[P]reventing agreement on fees at the time settlement of the merits is discussed . . . makes it difficult for the defendant to ascertain precisely what its liability will be, thereby eliminating the very certainty that makes settlement attractive to the defendant. The net effect . . . may be more trials, thus raising the question whether that cost is justifiable inasmuch as the conflict between settling the merits and discussing fees may be more hypothetical than real." Ibid. (footnotes omitted).

the Court of Appeals conclude that the District Court had acted unwisely.

* * * Unless it issues such a command, we shall rely primarily on the sound discretion of the district courts to appraise the reasonableness of particular class-action settlements on a case-by-case basis, in the light of all the relevant circumstances. * * *

JUSTICE BRENNAN, with whom JUSTICE MARSHALL and JUSTICE BLACKMUN join, dissenting.

Ultimately, enforcement of the laws is what really counts. It was with this in mind that Congress enacted the Civil Rights Attorney's Fees Awards Act of 1976, 42 U.S.C. § 1988 (the Act or Fees Act). Congress authorized fee-shifting to improve enforcement of civil rights legislation by making it easier for victims of civil rights violations to find lawyers willing to take their cases. Because today's decision will make it more difficult for civil rights plaintiffs to obtain legal assistance, a result plainly contrary to Congress' purpose, I dissent.

The Court begins its analysis by emphasizing that neither the language nor the legislative history of the Fees Act supports "the proposition that Congress intended to ban all fee waivers offered in connection with substantial relief on the merits." * * * I agree. There is no evidence that Congress gave the question of fee waivers any thought at all. However, the Court mistakenly assumes that this omission somehow supports the conclusion that fee waivers are permissible. On the contrary, that Congress did not specifically consider the issue of fee waivers tells us absolutely nothing about whether such waivers ought to be permitted. It is black-letter law that "[i]n the absence of specific evidence of Congressional intent, it becomes necessary to resort to a broader consideration of the legislative policy behind th[e] provision. . . ." * * *

* * *

It seems obvious that allowing defendants in civil rights cases to condition settlement of the merits on a waiver of statutory attorney's fees will diminish lawyers' expectations of receiving fees and decrease the willingness of lawyers to accept civil rights cases. * * *

* * * Assume that a civil rights defendant makes a settlement offer that includes a demand for waiver of statutory attorney's fees. The decision whether to accept or reject the offer is the plaintiff's alone, and the lawyer must abide by the plaintiff's decision. See, e.g., ABA, Model Rules of Professional Conduct 1.2(a) (1984); ABA, Model Code of Professional Responsibility EC 7–7 to EC 7–9 (1982). As a formal matter, of course, the statutory fee belongs to the plaintiff, * * * and thus technically the decision to waive entails a sacrifice only by the plaintiff. As a practical matter, however, waiver affects only the lawyer. Because "a vast majority of the victims of civil rights violations" have no resources to pay attorney's fees, H.R.Rep. 1, lawyers cannot hope to recover fees from the plaintiff and must depend entirely on the Fees Act for compensation.[10] The plaintiff thus has no real stake in the statutory fee and is unaffected by its waiver. See Lipscomb v. Wise, 643 F.2d 319, 320 (CA5 1981) (per curiam). Consequently, plaintiffs will readily agree to waive fees if this will help them to obtain other relief they desire.[11] As summed up by the Legal Ethics Committee of the District of Columbia Bar:

> "Defense counsel . . . are in a uniquely favorable position when they condition settlement on the waiver of the statutory fee: They make a demand for a benefit that the plaintiff's lawyer cannot resist as a matter of ethics and one in which the plaintiff has no interest and therefore will not resist." Op. No. 147, reprinted in 113 Daily Washington Reporter, supra, n. 8, at 394.

* * *

And, of course, once fee waivers are permitted, defendants will seek them as a matter of course, since this is a logical way to minimize liability. Indeed, defense counsel would be remiss *not* to demand that the plaintiff waive statutory attorney's fees. A lawyer who proposes to have his client pay more than is necessary to end litigation has failed to fulfill his fundamental duty zealously to represent the best interests of his client. Because waiver of fees does not affect the plaintiff, a settlement offer is not made less attractive to the plaintiff if it includes a demand that statutory fees be waived. Thus, in the future, we must expect settlement offers routinely to contain demands for waivers of statutory fees.

The cumulative effect this practice will have on the civil rights bar is evident. It does not denigrate the high ideals that motivate many civil rights practitioners to recognize that lawyers are in the business of practicing law, and that, like other business people, they are and must be concerned with earning a living.[13] The conclusion that permitting

---

10. Nor can attorneys protect themselves by requiring plaintiffs to sign contingency agreements or retainers at the outset of the representation. *Amici* legal aid societies inform us that they are prohibited by statute, court rule, or Internal Revenue Service regulation from entering into fee agreements with their clients. Brief for NAACP Legal Defense and Educational Fund, Inc., et al. as *Amici Curiae* 10–11; Brief for Committee on Legal Assistance of the Association of the Bar of the City of New York as *Amicus Curiae* 12–13. Moreover, even if such agreements could be negotiated, the possibility of obtaining protection through contingency fee arrangements is unavailable in the very large proportion of civil rights cases which, like this case, seek only injunctive relief. * * *

11. This result is virtually inevitable in class action suits where, even if the class representative feels sympathy for the law-yer's plight, the obligation to represent the interests of absent class members precludes altruistic sacrifice. In class action suits on behalf of incompetents, like this one, it is the lawyer himself who must agree to sacrifice his own interests for those of the class he represents. See, e.g., Model Code of Professional Responsibility EC 7–12 (1982).

13. See Johnson, Lawyers' Choice: A Theoretical Appraisal of Litigation Investment Decisions, 15 Law & Soc.Rev. 567 (1980–1981) (concluding that "fee for service" lawyers will withdraw resources from a given case when total expected costs exceed total expected benefits); Kraus, 29 Vill.L.Rev., at 637 ("No matter how sophisticated the analysis of attorney responses becomes, the conclusion remains that the more we decrease the reasonable expectation of Fees Act awards, the less likely it is that Fees Act cases will be initiated").

fee waivers will seriously impair the ability of civil rights plaintiffs to obtain legal assistance is embarrassingly obvious.

Because making it more difficult for civil rights plaintiffs to obtain legal assistance is precisely the opposite of what Congress sought to achieve by enacting the Fees Act, fee waivers should be prohibited. We have on numerous prior occasions held that "a statutory right conferred on a private party, but affecting the public interest, may not be waived or released if such waiver or release contravenes the statutory policy." Brooklyn Savings Bank v. O'Neil, 324 U.S., at 704, 65 S.Ct., at 900 (holding right to liquidated damages under Fair Labor Standards Act nonwaivable). See also, e.g., Boyd v. Grand Trunk Western R. Co., 338 U.S. 263, 266, 70 S.Ct. 26, 27, 94 L.Ed. 55 (1949) (holding venue provision of Federal Employers' Liability Act nonwaivable); Wilko v. Swan, 346 U.S. 427, 434–438, 74 S.Ct. 182, 186–189, 98 L.Ed. 168 (1953) (holding void an agreement to arbitrate in lieu of judicial remedy provided by Securities Exchange Act); cf. James v. Home Construction Co. of Mobile, Inc., 689 F.2d 1357, 1359 (CA11 1982) (implying a right of action for attorneys to seek fees under Truth-in-Lending Act to further congressional policies). This is simply straightforward application of the well-established principle that an agreement which is contrary to public policy is void and unenforceable. See Restatement (Second) of Contracts § 178 (1981) * * *.

* * *

FURTHER NOTE ON LITIGATION EXPENSES

1. The Contingent Fee

Many plaintiffs' cases, not only personal injury but others as well, are prosecuted on the basis of a contingent fee. In the contingent fee, which is regarded as unethical in most other countries, the plaintiff's lawyer gets nothing if he loses. Indeed, he may suffer out of pocket loss of litigation expenses, for he usually puts them up as "front money." The A.B.A. Code of Professional Responsibility DR 5–103(B) provides: "While representing a client in connection with * * * litigation, a lawyer shall not advance or guarantee financial assistance to his client, except that a lawyer may advance or guarantee the expenses of litigation * * * provided the client remains ultimately liable for such expenses." This does not say the lawyer must enforce that liability, or even make an effort to do so, and the understanding with the client is that he will not. Cf. Anno., 8 A.L.R.3d 1155. If plaintiff wins, the agreement is that the lawyer will get a share, usually receiving one-fourth to one-half of recovery or settlement, the fraction determined by custom, the size and difficulty of the case, and whether the case is tried or settled. See MacKinnon, Contingent Fees for Legal Services (1964); Schwartz and Mitchell, An Economic Analysis of the Contingent Fee in Personal-Injury Litigation, 22 Stan.L.Rev. 1125 (1970); See, An Alternative to the Contingent Fee, 1984 Utah L.Rev. 485. Are there valid reasons to prohibit contingent fee arrangements in divorce or medical malpractice cases, or where an attorney is hired to prosecute criminal statutes? See Note, Contingent Fee Contracts: Contract Related Divorce Action Upheld, 56 Minn.L.Rev. 979 (1972); People ex rel. Clancy v. Superior Court, 39 Cal.3d 740, 218 Cal.Rptr. 24, 705 P.2d 347 (1985) (city's hiring of an attorney on a contingent fee basis to prosecute pornography abatement ordinance gave attorney a financial stake in the outcome of the action and thus created risk of impairing the neutrality required of him as a representative of the government).

2. Determination of Fee

When, as in Serrano v. Priest, the lawyer's fee is fixed by the court rather than by contract with her client, the problem arises of determining the fee. The rule is that the fee must be "reasonable." On what that means, see Berger, Court Awarded Attorneys' Fees: What is "Reasonable"?, 126 U.Pa.L. Rev. 281 (1977); Smith, Standards for Judicial Approval of Attorneys' Fees in Class Action and Complex Litigation, 20 How.L.J. 20 (1977). On the factors to be considered in determining the amount of an attorneys fee award, see Hensley v. Eckerhart, 461 U.S. 424, 103 S.Ct. 1933, 76 L.Ed.2d 40 (1983); Ruckelshaus v. Sierra Club, 463 U.S. 680, 103 S.Ct. 3274, 77 L.Ed.2d 938 (1983). See also Johnson v. Georgia Highway Express, Inc., 488 F.2d 714 (5th Cr. 1974); Derfner and Wolf, Court Awarded Attorney Fees (1984). There is a special reporting service on the subject, the Attorney Fee Awards Reporter. Except in the context of class suits, the problem of conflict of interest between client and attorney in such matters has only recently begun to receive judicial attention. The decision in Evans v. Jeff D. resolved a conflict among the circuits as to whether litigants may settle the issues of both substantive relief and attorneys fees in the same agreement, rejecting arguments that allowing such simultaneous settlements creates a conflict between pursuing relief for the plaintiffs and a fee for the attorney. Are you satisfied with the Court's resolution of the question? What other kinds of conflicts do you think might arise in such situations?

3. Equal Access to Justice Act

The *Alyeska* decision, referred to in Serrano v. Priest, has been partially vitiated by the Equal Access to Justice Act, 28 U.S.C.A. § 2412(b), which makes the United States liable for reasonable fees and expenses of attorneys to the same extent that any other party would be liable under the common law or under the terms of any statute that specifically provides for such an award. That Act also provides for an award of fees and expenses to the prevailing party (other than the United States) incurred by that party in any action other than a tort action brought by or against the United States, unless the court finds that the position of the United States was substantially justified or that special circumstances make an award unjust. 28 U.S.C.A. § 2412(d)(1). Fees and other expenses are defined to include reasonable expenses of expert witnesses, the cost of any study, analysis, engineering report, test or project which is found to be reasonably necessary for the preparation of the party's case, and reasonable attorneys' fees. 28 U.S.C.A. § 2412(d)(2). The use of the word "unless" places the burden on the government to justify its position. F.R.C.P. Rule 37(f) was repealed so as to conform with the Act. For a detailed analysis of the Act, see Robertson and Fowler, Recovering Attorneys' Fees From the Government Under the Equal Access to Justice Act, 56 Tulane L.Rev. 903 (1982). See also Pierce v. Underwood, ___ U.S. ___, 108 S.Ct. 2541, 101 L.Ed.2d 490 (1988) (construing the Act's $75 an hour limit on attorneys fees); Hermann and Hoffmann, Financing Public Interest Litigation in State Court: A Proposal for Legislative Action, 63 Corn.L.Rev. 173 (1978); Note, Reenacting the Equal

Access to Justice Act: A Proposal for Automatic Attorney's Fee Awards, 94 Yale L.J. 1207 (1985).

4. Civil Rights Attorney's Fees Awards Act

The *Alyeska* decision also prompted Congress to enact the Civil Rights Attorney's Fees Awards Act of 1976, 42 U.S.C.A. § 1988, which allows recovery of attorneys fees in a wide range of civil rights cases. The Act generalized an earlier provision permitting recovery of fees in employment discrimination actions based on Title VII of the Civil Rights Act of 1964. 42 U.S.C.A. § 2000e–5(k). Both statutes provide that the court "may award" a reasonable attorneys fee to the "prevailing party." In Christiansburg Garment Co. v. EEOC, 434 U.S. 412, 98 S.Ct. 694, 54 L.Ed.2d 648 (1978), the Supreme Court held that a prevailing defendant in a Title VII suit could be awarded an attorneys fee, but only if plaintiff's action was found to be "unreasonable, frivolous, or vexatious." A prevailing plaintiff, on the other hand, "should ordinarily recover an attorney's fee unless special circumstances would render such an award unjust." These standards were made applicable to fees awarded under the 1976 Act in Hughes v. Rowe, 449 U.S. 5, 101 S.Ct. 173, 66 L.Ed.2d 163 (1980). See also Doe v. Busbee, 684 F.2d 1375 (11th Cir.1982). Is *Christiansburg* consistent with *Jeff D.,* or did the latter case merely make explicit an implied right to waive fees in the interest of achieving substantive relief? For a criticism of the *Jeff D.* decision and an argument that fee waivers should be disallowed where the settlement was coercive, see Comment, Giving Substance to the Bad Faith Exception of Evans v. Jeff D.: A Reconciliation of Evans with the Civil Rights Attorney's Fees Awards Act of 1976, 136 U.Pa.L.Rev. 553 (1987). On Marek v. Chesny, discussed in *Jeff D.,* see infra p. 983. See also Folsom v. Butte County Ass'n of Governments, 32 Cal.3d 668, 186 Cal.Rptr. 589, 652 P.2d 437 (1982), where the California Supreme Court upheld the awarding of attorneys fees under C.C.P. 1021.5, which codified the "private attorney general" doctrine discussed in Serrano v. Priest, over objections that a settlement agreement which was silent on costs precluded a fee award.

Copeland v. Marshall, 641 F.2d 880 (D.C.Cir.1980), established guidelines governing fee awards in civil rights cases and required the setting of a "lodestar" figure, i.e., the number of hours reasonably expended multiplied by a reasonable hourly rate. That figure is then adjusted to reflect the risk that the suit might be unsuccessful, any delay in payment, and unusually good or bad representation. See also National Ass'n of Concerned Veterans v. Secretary of Defense, 675 F.2d 1319 (D.C.Cir.1982); Leubsdorf, The Contingency Factor in Attorney Fee Awards, 90 Yale L.J. 473 (1981). Should fees be awarded to public interest or legal services lawyers who do not charge their clients a fee? Evans v. Jeff D. seems to assume that they should, absent a waiver, and the circuits agree. See, e.g., Oldham v. Ehrlich, 617 F.2d 163 (8th Cir.1980). If fees are sought by a public interest or legal services attorney, should the hourly rate be based on the going community rate for private lawyers or a rate reflecting the real costs to the public interest lawyer in providing the service? See Hamilton v. Daley, 777 F.2d 1207 (7th Cir.1985).

5. Court Appointed Counsel

An indigent's right to appointed counsel under the Due Process Clause of the U.S. Constitution has been recognized where the litigant's physical liberty is in jeopardy. In Lassiter v. Dept. of Social Services, 452 U.S. 18, 101 S.Ct. 2153, 68 L.Ed.2d 640 (1981), the court refused to extend the right to counsel to indigent parents in a parental rights termination case. New York has recognized the right to free counsel in such termination proceedings, In the Matter of Ella R.B., 30 N.Y.2d 352, 334 N.Y.S.2d 133, 285 N.E.2d 288 (1972), but has denied it in divorce proceedings. In re Smiley, 36 N.Y.2d 433, 369 N.Y.S.2d 87, 330 N.E.2d 53 (1975). Cf. Yarbrough v. Superior Court, 39 Cal.3d 197, 216 Cal.Rptr. 425, 702 P.2d 583 (1985) (discretion to appoint counsel for indigent prisoner sued in wrongful death action arising from death of a murder victim); Note, Denial of a Pro Se Litigant's Motion to Appoint Counsel, 50 Ford.L.Rev. 1399 (1982); Shapiro, The Enigma of the Lawyer's Duty to Serve, 55 N.Y.U.L. Rev. 735 (1980); Comment, The Indigent's Right to Counsel in Civil Actions, 12 S.U.L.Rev. 85 (1985).

6. Pro Se Representation

In the United States a civil litigant has the right to represent herself or himself without retaining a lawyer. While this may effect a savings and expand access to the courts, pro se representation has obvious drawbacks particularly for the indigent and poorly educated. In most other countries litigants do not have the right of self-representation and a party must retain a lawyer. Should a pro se litigant be entitled to attorneys fees to the same extent as a party retaining counsel? If so, should the fees be based on community legal rates or the litigant's lost opportunity costs? See Note, Pro Se Can You Sue?: Attorney Fees for Pro Se Litigants, 34 Stan.L.Rev. 659 (1982).

7. Malicious Prosecution

The cost burden that litigation throws on defendants, which under the American rule normally goes uncompensated, has stimulated new interest in the old tort of malicious prosecution. See Birnbaum, Physicians Counterattack: Liability of Lawyers for Instituting Unjustified Medical Malpractice Actions, 45 Ford.L.Rev. 1003 (1977). So far, the definition of liability is very narrowly drawn. See, e.g., Bertero v. National General Corp., 13 Cal.3d 43, 118 Cal.Rptr. 184, 529 P.2d 608 (1974), stating the essential elements as follows: "the prior action (1) was commenced by or at the direction of the defendant and was pursued to a legal determination in * * * plaintiff's favor * * * ; (2) was brought without probable cause * * * ; and (3) was initiated with malice * * * ." See also Prosser and Keeton, Torts § 120 (5th ed. 1984); Anno., 84 A.L.R.3d 555. However, suppose a case in which defendant is basing his defense on a constitutional claim, for example, the right of free speech. Would the analysis in Serrano v. Priest suggest that such a defendant ought to be able to claim attorneys' fees according to a more liberal standard? See also Aragon, Favorable Termination in Malicious Prosecution of Civil Proceedings, 15 Sw.U.L.Rev. 65 (1984); Note, Groundless Litigation and the Malicious Prosecution Debate: A Historical Analysis, 88 Yale L.J. 1218 (1979); Note, Attorneys Fees and the Federal Bad Faith Exception, 29 Hast.L.J. 319 (1977).

On bad faith prosecution of appeals, see Coleman v. Gulf Ins. Group, 41 Cal. 3d 782, 226 Cal.Rptr. 90, 718 P.2d 77 (1986) (disallowing a tort action and holding that the proper remedy is to seek sanctions under C.C.P. 907); In re Marriage of Flaherty, 31 Cal.3d 637, 183 Cal.Rptr. 508, 646 P.2d 179 (1982); Bankers Life & Casualty Co. v. Crenshaw, ___ U.S. ___, 108 S.Ct. 1645, 100 L.Ed.2d 62 (1988) (upholding state law imposing a penalty on unsuccessful appellants as a reasonable means of discouraging frivolous appeals).

Unlike malicious prosecution, there is no recognized tort action for the malicious assertion of false or baseless defenses, though some have argued for the recognition of such an action. See Van Patten and Willard, The Limits of Advocacy: A Proposal for the Tort of Malicious Defense in Civil Litigation, 35 Hastings L.J. 891 (1984).

8. Sanctions Under Rule 11

Under certain circumstances, attorneys fees may be recoverable as sanctions under F.R.C.P. 11 and similar state statutes for the unreasonable or frivolous filing of actions or pleadings. See Rule 11 Certification, supra p. 135.

9. Limitations on Attorneys Fees

Attorneys fees frequently are regulated by statute or court rule in such areas as workers' compensation, probate, and government benefits. Some states have maximum contingent fees schedules for all personal injury litigation. More recently, statutes have been passed that limit contingent fees in medical malpractice litigation in an attempt to reduce the cost of malpractice insurance. Unless such limits are unreasonably low, they are not unconstitutional. See Roa v. Lodi Medical Group, Inc., 37 Cal.3d 920, 211 Cal.Rptr. 77, 695 P.2d 164 (1985) (sliding scale limitation in medical malpractice); American Trial Lawyers Ass'n v. New Jersey Supreme Court, 66 N.J. 258, 330 A.2d 350 (1974) (personal injury contingent fee schedule). See also Calhoun v. Massie, 253 U.S. 170, 40 S.Ct. 474, 64 L.Ed. 843 (1920).

10. Legal Aid

See generally, Cappelletti, Gordley and Johnson, Toward Equal Justice: A Comparative Study of Legal Aid in Modern Societies (1975); Cooper, Public Legal Services: A Comparative Study of Policy, Politics and Practice (1983); Kessler, Legal Services for the Poor (1987).

Part IV

THE PROPER COURT

INTRODUCTORY NOTE ON THE PROPER COURT

There are three basic requirements affecting the validity of a proceeding: (1) that there be adequate notice to the defendant of the proceedings instituted against him; (2) that the court have territorial jurisdiction over the parties; and (3) that the court have subject matter jurisdiction over the action. See generally Hazard, Requisites of a Valid Judgment, 24 Prac.Law. 35 (April 1978). In addition, there is a requirement of proper venue, i.e., the action must be filed in a proper county or district within the court system. See Introductory Note on Venue, infra p. 514. These requirements intersect in various ways.

Subject matter jurisdiction refers to the body of rules used by a state to coordinate the allocation of cases among tribunals within that state. Territorial jurisdiction refers to the body of rules operating as between states to coordinate the zones of adjudicative authority of the respective states. Notice refers to the principle of due process requiring that, generally speaking, prior notice must be given before a party's rights may be determined in a judicial proceeding. Where a lawsuit is wholly centered in one state, the problem of territorial jurisdiction does not arise, although notice and venue requirements still must be met.

From the beginning of our federal system, courts have had to grapple with the problem of the authority of a state to assert jurisdiction over defendants in cases involving transactions not occurring entirely within the boundaries of the state. This is the central problem addressed by the doctrine of territorial jurisdiction. As will be seen presently, the requirements of adequate notice have been historically intertwined with the requirement that a court have territorial jurisdiction. See Mullane v. Central Hanover Bank & Trust Co., infra p. 303. Many of the cases involving challenges to the assertion of territorial jurisdiction arise in the context of a challenge to service of process, which is the normal procedure for effecting notice. In addition, the question of whether a court has territorial jurisdiction over the parties can sometimes depend on the subject matter of the dispute, as where jurisdiction is premised on the "presence" of "property" rather than of the person.

The Restatement Second of Judgments § 4, Comment a, provides the following introduction to the problem of territorial jurisdiction:

"The relevance of territorial boundaries to the exercise of jurisdiction by states within the federal union, and by courts of this country within the international community, arises from the fact that the states and nations are defined as political and legal entities in terms of their geographical boundaries. Since these entities are legally defined in terms of geographical place, the geographical location of a transaction is significant in determining whether a court of such an entity may properly exercise jurisdiction in a particular controversy. At one time, this relationship was expressed in terms of 'power,' referring to the authority of a state's or nation's executive officials to use direct coercion to enforce legal obligations. Under prevailing law, such executive authority could be exercised

279

only in the state or nation in which there was physically present the person or thing to which coercion was to be applied. Accordingly, territorial jurisdiction was defined in terms of presence of the person or thing involved in the litigation, and also voluntary submission to the authority of the court. 'Power' in this sense remains significant at least as a residual basis of jurisdiction."

Broadly speaking, the development of territorial jurisdiction doctrine proceeded from this early focus on physical presence to the modern concept of "minimum contacts" between the forum and the place where the transaction occurred or the parties are located. In the cases that follow, note particularly the changing conceptions of the proper role and authority of states within the federal system.

Beginning with the Judiciary Act of 1789, which created the federal court system, the territorial authority of federal courts has been tied to the governing rules in the respective states where the federal courts sit. In form, the limitation is on the reach of process issuing from the federal courts. See F.R. C.P. 4(e) and (f). Under modern doctrine, this means that a federal court may exercise jurisdiction over a nonresident defendant only if the defendant can be reached under the state's "long arm" statute, which may or may not extend to the full reach of the constitutional "minimum contacts" standard. It is important to note that this limitation on the territorial scope of federal courts is legislative in origin; the territorial jurisdiction of federal courts is restricted because the constitutional and statutory restrictions on state court jurisdiction have been incorporated by reference in the legislation governing the federal courts. In certain types of actions, Congress has created exceptions to this self-imposed limitation and provided for nationwide service of process. See Further Note on Long Arm Statutes, infra p. 414.

Subject matter jurisdiction refers to the rules by which a jurisdiction distributes various types of cases among the courts within that jurisdiction. Although questions of subject matter jurisdiction normally do not involve territorial issues, under state law they may sometimes be defined in geographical terms. For example, actions concerning land title ordinarily must be brought in the county where the land is located, and such a requirement may be construed as "jurisdictional" rather than as a matter of venue. Probably the most vexing problem of subject matter jurisdiction involves the validity of a judgment rendered by a court lacking subject matter jurisdiction where neither the court nor the parties raised the issue during the proceedings. The starting place is that, unlike territorial jurisdiction, a court cannot obtain subject matter jurisdiction over an action by consent (express or implied) of the parties; the rules of subject matter jurisdiction speak to the power of the court to hear a particular type of case and an objection to jurisdiction may be raised at any time, even on appeal, by any party or by the court. These matters are considered further in the Note on Challenging Subject Matter Jurisdiction, infra p. 510.

A. TERRITORIAL JURISDICTION

1. THE LEGAL FORMULAE

a. THE HISTORICAL FORMULA

BARRELL v. BENJAMIN

Supreme Judicial Court of Massachusetts, 1819.
15 Mass. 354.

This was an action of *assumpsit;* and while on trial before the jury, the question arose whether this Court had jurisdiction of the suit. In order to have this question settled by the whole Court, the parties agreed on the following statement of facts:—

Barrell, the plaintiff, is a native citizen of the *United States,* having been born within this commonwealth: but at the time when this action was commenced, and long before, he lived in the town of *Norwich,* in the state of *Connecticut.*

The defendant, *Benjamin,* is a native citizen of the state of *Connecticut;* but more than twenty years past has had, and still has, his domicile in *Demerara;* although, when this action was commenced, he was in *Boston,* on his way to *Demerara;* and the plaintiff's writ was served by arresting his body.

The plaintiff and defendant were partners in a house in *Demerara,* jointly carrying on commerce there as partners for many years before the year 1807, when their copartnership was dissolved. This action was commenced and prosecuted to recover the balance supposed to be due, from the defendant to the plaintiff, on settlement of their accounts. When the *British* took possession of the colony of *Demerara,* in the year 1803, the said *Benjamin* took an oath of allegiance to that government.

If the Court should be of opinion that they ought to hold jurisdiction of the action, it was agreed that the defendant should be holden to render his account, and that auditors should be appointed to audit the same. But if the Court should be of a different opinion, the plaintiff was to become nonsuit, and the defendant recover his costs.

* * *

Parker, C.J. delivered the opinion of the Court. Upon the facts agreed in this case, the defendant's counsel has argued against the jurisdiction of this Court, both from the nature of the contract, and the situation of the parties; and has cited some authorities in support of his argument. Upon examining them, however, and such others as can be found bearing upon the question, it does not appear that any direct decision has been had upon this subject. Indeed, it would seem, from the entire want of authorities in the *English* books, that the question has never been raised there; and the presumption is violent, that the jurisdiction of the common-law courts in such a case would not be doubted.

In the case of Melan vs. Duke de Fitzjames, [1 B. & P. 138] the point was not started. Both the parties were *French* subjects. The defendant had been arrested and held to special bail, on a contract made in *France,* and to be performed at his house there. All that was moved for was, that his bail bond might be discharged, and he permitted to enter a common appearance; because, by the laws of *France,* he was not liable to arrest upon such a contract. Both court and counsel take the ground that the action was maintainable in the *English* courts; and one of the judges was against discharging the bond, because, the contract being personal, and sued in *England,* the creditor was entitled to the remedies afforded by the *English* law.

In the case of Robinson vs. Kerr, printed in a note to the case of Rea vs. Hayden, 3 Mass.Rep. 25, both parties were alien friends, and the contract was made in the country where they both lived. The court would not sustain the action. But it does not appear that either the plaintiff or defendant was within this state when the action was brought. On the contrary, it is to be inferred from the report that both were absent, and that the action was brought because some property of the defendant was found here. It cannot be inferred, from this decision, that, if the defendant had been found within the jurisdiction of the court, and arrested, the suit would have been dismissed. It might well have been thought, that the mere circumstance of property being found here did not give the court jurisdiction over the person of a foreigner, in a suit of another foreigner against him; or perhaps that the court might entertain jurisdiction or not, at their discretion; as seems to have been the opinion of the Supreme Court of the United States in the case of Mason & Al. vs. Ship Blaireau, [2 Cranch, 264] cited in the argument by *Mr. Ward.*

With respect to the two cases which occurred in the Circuit Court of the *United States,* contained in the note before referred to, the report states it as probable that the court refused to sustain the actions, on account of its limited and special jurisdiction, as given to it by the constitution and laws of the *United States.* And there is no doubt that the decision was correct; for it will be found, upon examining the constitution of the *United States,* that a controversy between two foreigners, who are private subjects, is not enumerated as within the judicial power of the *United States.*

But the jurisdiction of this Court, as a court of common law, is unlimited; and all cases, cognizable by any of the courts of common law in *England,* are cognizable here.

Personal contracts are said to have no *situs* or locality, but follow the person of the debtor, wherever he may go; and there seems to be no good reason why courts of any country may not lend their aid to enforce such contracts; especially since it is a well-known principle that, in construing such contracts, the law of the place where they are made will be administered. So that the objection made in this case, of the possible difference between the laws of *Demerara* and this commonwealth, can have no influence on the question.

It is true that the debtor may be put to inconvenience by being obliged to answer in a foreign country. But the creditor may also be put to inconvenience if he should be denied the privilege of suing in a foreign court; for the debtor may withdraw his person and effects from the place of his business; and if he cannot be pursued, may defraud his creditor of his due.

It seems, however, to be admitted in the argument, that if the defendant resided here, there would be no objection to the action; the complaint being that he was arrested within this state, when here only for the purpose of embarking for *Demerara*. But we see no way of upholding the distinction, and there is nothing to be found in the books to support it. A debtor coming here merely for the purpose of embarking may be detained several months before he procures a passage; he may have all his effects about him; and he may never return to the place where he transacted his business. If the creditor cannot take him here, he may lose his chance of securing his debt. On the score of inconvenience, there is nothing in favor of the defendant's argument.

But, for the decision of this particular case, we need not go into any general reasoning. The plaintiff is a citizen of the *United States,* having his domicile in *Connecticut.* By the second section of the fourth article of the constitution of the *United States,* it is provided that "the citizens of each state shall be entitled to all privileges and immunities of citizens in the several states." Since the adoption of the constitution, the citizens of *Connecticut,* or any other state in the *Union,* cannot be considered as foreigners; and indeed are not so considered practically in any courts of law. Citizens of different states may change their domicile from one state to another, and enjoy all the privileges of citizenship wherever they may go.

It will be admitted that a citizen of *Massachusetts* has the privilege to sue any foreigner who may come within this state, whether he come to embark for a foreign country, or to reside here for the purposes of business. If so, a citizen of *Connecticut* has the same privilege secured to him by the constitution; and arguments, which might be plausible if used against a foreigner, cannot avail against a plaintiff who has none of the disabilities of a foreigner attending him.

According to the agreement of the parties, there must be judgment that the defendant account; and auditors must be appointed.

PENNOYER v. NEFF

Supreme Court of the United States, 1877.
95 U.S. (5 Otto) 714, 24 L.Ed. 565.

[Error to the Circuit Court of the United States for the District of Oregon.]

Mr. Justice Field delivered the opinion of the Court.

This is an action to recover the possession of a tract of land, of the alleged value of $15,000, situated in the State of Oregon. The plaintiff asserts title to the premises by a patent of the United States issued to him in 1866, under the act of Congress of Sept. 27, 1850, usually known as the Donation Law of Oregon. The defendant claims to have acquired the premises under a sheriff's deed, made upon a sale of the property on execution issued upon a judgment recovered against the plaintiff in one of the circuit courts of the State. The case turns upon the validity of this judgment.

It appears from the record that the judgment was rendered in February, 1866, in favor of J.H. Mitchell, for less than $300, including costs, in an action brought by him upon a demand for services as an attorney; that, at the time the action was commenced and the judgment rendered, the defendant therein, the plaintiff here, was a non-resident of the State; that he was not personally served with process, and did not appear therein; and that the judgment was entered upon his default in not answering the complaint, upon a constructive service of summons by publication.

The Code of Oregon provides for such service when an action is brought against a non-resident and absent defendant, who has property within the State. It also provides, where the action is for the recovery of money or damages, for the attachment of the property of the non-resident. And it also declares that no natural person is subject to the jurisdiction of a court of the State, "unless he appear in the court, or be found within the State, or be a resident thereof, or have property therein; and, in the last case, only to the extent of such property at the time the jurisdiction attached." Construing this latter provision to mean, that, in an action for money or damages where a defendant does not appear in the court, and is not found within the State, and is not a resident thereof, but has property therein, the jurisdiction of the court extends only over such property, the declaration expresses a principle of general, if not universal, law. The authority of every tribunal is necessarily restricted by the territorial limits of the State in which it is established. Any attempt to exercise authority beyond those limits would be deemed in every other forum, as has been said by this court, an illegitimate assumption of power, and be resisted as mere abuse. D'Arcy v. Ketchum et al., 11 How. 165. In the case against the plaintiff, the property here in controversy sold under the judgment rendered was not attached, nor in any way brought under the jurisdiction of the court. Its first connection with the case was caused by a levy of the execution. It was not, therefore, disposed of pursuant to any adjudication, but only in enforcement of a personal judgment, having no relation to the property, rendered against a non-resident without service of process upon him in the action, or his appearance therein. The court below did not consider that an attachment of the property was essential to its jurisdiction or to the validity of the sale, but held that the judgment was invalid from defects in the affidavit upon which the order of publication was obtained, and in the affidavit by which the publication was proved.

There is some difference of opinion among the members of this court as to the rulings upon these alleged defects.   *   *   *

If, therefore, we were confined to the rulings of the court below upon the defects in the affidavits mentioned, we should be unable to uphold its decision. But it was also contended in that court, and is insisted upon here, that the judgment in the State court against the plaintiff was void for want of personal service of process on him, or of his appearance in the action in which it was rendered, and that the premises in controversy could not be subjected to the payment of the demand of a resident creditor except by a proceeding *in rem;* that is, by a direct proceeding against the property for that purpose. If these positions are sound, the ruling of the Circuit Court as to the invalidity of that judgment must be sustained, notwithstanding our dissent from the reasons upon which it was made. And that they are sound would seem to follow from two well-established principles of public law respecting the jurisdiction of an independent State over persons and property. The several States of the Union are not, it is true, in every respect independent, many of the rights and powers which originally belonged to them being now vested in the government created by the Constitution. But, except as restrained and limited by that instrument, they possess and exercise the authority of independent States, and the principles of public law to which we have referred are applicable to them. One of these principles is, that every State possesses exclusive jurisdiction and sovereignty over persons and property within its territory. As a consequence, every State has the power to determine for itself the civil *status* and capacities of its inhabitants; to prescribe the subjects upon which they may contract, the forms and solemnities with which their contracts shall be executed, the rights and obligations arising from them, and the mode in which their validity shall be determined and their obligations enforced; and also to regulate the manner and conditions upon which property situated within such territory, both personal and real, may be acquired, enjoyed, and transferred. The other principle of public law referred to follows from the one mentioned; that is, that no State can exercise direct jurisdiction and authority over persons or property without its territory. Story, Confl.Laws, c. 2; Wheat.Int.Law, pt. 2, c. 2. The several States are of equal dignity and authority, and the independence of one implies that exclusion of power from all others. And so it is laid down by jurists, as an elementary principle, that the laws of one State have no operation outside of its territory, except so far as is allowed by comity; and that no tribunal established by it can extend its process beyond that territory so as to subject either persons or property to its decisions. "Any exertion of authority of this sort beyond this limit," says Story, "is a mere nullity, and incapable of binding such persons or property in any other tribunals." Story, Confl.Laws, sect. 539.

But as contracts made in one State may be enforceable only in another State, and property may be held by non-residents, the exercise of the jurisdiction which every State is admitted to possess over persons and property within its own territory will often affect persons and property without it. To any influence exerted in this way by a State affecting persons resident or property situated elsewhere, no objection can be justly taken; whilst any direct exertion of authority upon them, in an attempt to give ex-territorial operation to its laws, or to enforce an ex-territorial jurisdiction by its tribunals, would be deemed an encroachment upon the independence of the State in which the persons are domiciled or the property is situated, and be resisted as usurpation.

* * *

So the State, through its tribunals, may subject property situated within its limits owned by non-residents to the payment of the demand of its own citizens against them; and the exercise of this jurisdiction in no respect infringes upon the sovereignty of the State where the owners are domiciled. Every State owes protection to its own citizens; and, when non-residents deal with them, it is a legitimate and just exercise of authority to hold and appropriate any property owned by such non-residents to satisfy the claims of its citizens. It is in virtue of the State's jurisdiction over the property of the non-resident situated within its limits that its tribunals can inquire into that non-resident's obligations to its own citizens, and the inquiry can then be carried only to the extent necessary to control the disposition of the property. If the non-resident have no property in the State, there is nothing upon which the tribunals can adjudicate.

These views are not new. They have been frequently expressed, with more or less distinctness, in opinions of eminent judges, and have been carried into adjudications in numerous cases. * * *

* * * It is the only doctrine consistent with proper protection to citizens of other States. If, without personal service, judgments *in personam,* obtained *ex parte* against non-residents and absent parties, upon mere publication of process, which, in the great majority of cases, would never be seen by the parties interested, could be upheld and enforced, they would be the constant instruments of fraud and oppression. Judgments for all sorts of claims upon contracts and for torts, real or pretended, would be thus obtained, under which property would be seized, when the evidence of the transactions upon which they were founded, if they ever had any existence, had perished.

Substituted service by publication, or in any other authorized form, may be sufficient to inform parties of the object of proceedings taken where property is once brought under the control of the court by seizure or some equivalent act. The law assumes that property is always in the possession of its owner, in person or by agent; and it proceeds upon the theory that its seizure will inform him, not only that it is taken into the custody of the court, but that he must look to any proceedings authorized by law upon such seizure for its condemnation and sale. Such service may also be sufficient in cases where the object of the action is to reach and dispose of property in the State, or of some interest therein, by enforcing a contract or a lien respecting the same, or to partition it among different owners, or, when the public is a party, to condemn and appropriate it for a public purpose. In other words, such service may answer in all actions which are substantially proceedings *in rem.* But where the entire object of the action is to determine the personal rights and obligations of the defendants, that is, where the suit is merely *in personam,* constructive service in this form upon a non-resident is ineffectual for any purpose. Process from the tribunals of one State cannot run into another State, and summon parties there domiciled to leave its territory and respond to proceedings against them. Publication of process or notice within the State where the tribunal sits cannot create any greater obligation upon the non-resident to appear. Process sent to him out of the State, and process published within it, are equally unavailing in proceedings to establish his personal liability.

The want of authority of the tribunals of a State to adjudicate upon the obligations of non-residents, where they have no property within its limits, is not denied by the court below; but the position is assumed, that, where they have property within the State, it is immaterial whether the property is in the first instance brought under the control of the court by attachment or some other equivalent act, and afterwards applied by its judgment to the satisfaction of demands against its owner; or such demands be first established in a personal action, and the property of the non-resident be afterwards seized and sold on execution. But the answer to this position has already been given in the statement, that the jurisdiction of the court to inquire into and determine his obligations at all is only incidental to its jurisdiction over the property. Its jurisdiction in that respect cannot be made to depend upon facts to be ascertained after it has tried the cause and rendered the judgment. If the judgment be previously void, it will not become valid by the subsequent discovery of property of the defendant, or by his subsequent acquisition of it. The judgment, if void when rendered, will always remain void: it cannot occupy the doubtful position of being valid if property be found, and void if there be none. Even if the position assumed were confined to cases where the non-resident defendant possessed property in the State at the commencement of the action, it would still make the validity of the proceedings and judgment depend upon the question whether, before the levy of the execution, the defendant had or had not disposed of the property. If before the levy the property should be sold, then, according to this position, the judgment would not be binding. This doctrine would introduce a new element of uncertainty in judicial proceedings. The contrary is the law: the validity of every judgment depends upon the jurisdiction of the court before it is rendered, not upon what may occur subsequently.

* * *

The force and effect of judgments rendered against non-residents without personal service of process upon them, or their voluntary appearance, have been the subject of frequent consideration in the courts of the United States and of the several States, as attempts have been made to enforce such judgments in States other than those in which they were rendered, under the provision of the Constitution requiring that "full faith and credit shall be given in each State to the public acts, records, and judicial proceedings of every other State;" and the act of Congress providing for the mode of authenticating such acts, records, and proceedings, and declaring that, when thus authenticated, "they shall have such faith and credit given to them in every court within the United States as they have by law or usage in the courts of the State from which they are or shall be taken." In the earlier cases, it was supposed that the act gave to all judgments the same effect in other States which they had by law in the State where rendered. But this view was afterwards qualified so as to make the act applicable only when the court rendering the judgment had jurisdiction of the parties and of the subject-matter, and not to preclude an inquiry into the jurisdiction of the court in which the judgment was rendered, or the right of the State itself to exercise authority over the person or the subject-matter. * * *

* * * In several of the cases, the decision has been accompanied with the observation that a personal judgment thus recovered has no binding force without the State in which it is rendered, implying that in such State it may be valid and binding. But if the court has no jurisdiction over the person of the defendant by reason of his non-residence, and, consequently, no authority to pass upon his personal rights and obligations; if the whole proceeding, without service upon him or his appearance, is *coram non judice* and void; if to hold a defendant bound by such a judgment is contrary to the first principles of justice,—it is difficult to see how the judgment can legitimately have any force within the State. The language used can be justified only on the ground that there was no mode of directly reviewing such judgment or impeaching its validity within the State where rendered; and that, therefore, it could be called in question only when its enforcement was elsewhere attempted. In later cases, this language is repeated with less frequency than formerly, it beginning to be considered, as it always ought to have been, that a judgment which can be treated in any State of this Union as contrary to the first principles of justice, and as an absolute nullity, because rendered without any jurisdiction of the tribunal over the party, is not entitled to any respect in the State where rendered. Smith v. McCutchen, 38 Mo. 415; Darrance v. Preston, 18 Iowa 396; Hakes v. Shupe, 27 id. 465; Mitchell's Administrator v. Gray, 18 Ind. 123.

Be that as it may, the courts of the United States are not required to give effect to judgments of this character when any right is claimed under them. Whilst they are not foreign tribunals in their relations to the State courts, they are tribunals of a different sovereignty, exercising a distinct and independent jurisdiction, and are bound to give to the judgments of the State courts only the same faith and credit which the courts of another State are bound to give to them.

Since the adoption of the Fourteenth Amendment to the Federal Constitution, the validity of such judgments may be directly questioned, and their enforcement in the State resisted, on the ground that proceedings in a court of justice to determine the personal rights and obligations of parties over whom that court has no jurisdiction do not constitute due process of law. Whatever difficulty may be experienced in giving to those terms a definition which will embrace every permissible exertion of power affecting private rights, and exclude such as is forbidden, there can be no doubt of their meaning when applied to judicial proceedings. They then mean a course of legal proceedings according to those rules and principles which have been established in our systems of jurisprudence for the protection and enforcement of private rights. To give such proceedings any validity, there must be a tribunal competent by its constitution—that is, by the law of its creation—to pass upon the subject-matter of the suit; and, if that involves merely a determination of the personal liability of the defendant, he must be brought within its jurisdiction by service of process within the State, or his voluntary appearance.

Except in cases affecting the personal *status* of the plaintiff, and cases in which that mode of service may be considered to have been assented to in advance, as hereinafter mentioned, the substituted service of process by publication, allowed by the law of Oregon and by similar laws in other States, where actions are brought against nonresidents, is effectual only where, in connection with process against the person for commencing the action, property in the State is brought under the control of the court, and subjected to its disposition by process adapted to that purpose, or where the judgment is sought as a means of reaching such property or affecting some interest therein; in other words, where the action is in the nature of a proceeding *in rem*. As stated by Cooley in his Treatise on Constitutional Limitations, 405, for any other purpose than to subject the property of a non-resident to valid claims against him in the State, "due process of law would require appearance or personal service before the defendant could be personally bound by any judgment rendered."

It is true that, in a strict sense, a proceeding *in rem* is one taken directly against property, and has for its object the disposition of the property, without reference to the title of individual claimants; but, in a larger and more general sense, the terms are applied to actions between parties, where the direct object is to reach and dispose of property owned by them, or of some interest therein. Such are cases commenced by attachment against the property of debtors, or instituted to partition real estate, foreclose a mortgage, or enforce a lien. So far as they affect property in the State, they are substantially proceedings *in rem* in the broader sense which we have mentioned.

* * *

It follows from the views expressed that the personal judgment recovered in the State Court of Oregon against the plaintiff herein, then a non-resident of the State, was without any validity, and did not authorize a sale of the property in controversy.

To prevent any misapplication of the views expressed in this opinion, it is proper to observe that we do not mean to assert, by anything we have said, that a State may not authorize proceedings to determine the *status* of one of its citizens towards a non-resident, which would be binding within the State, though made without service of process or personal notice to the non-resident. The jurisdiction which every State possesses to determine the civil *status* and capacities of all its inhabitants involves authority to prescribe the conditions on which proceedings affecting them may be commenced and carried on within its territory. The State, for example, has absolute right to prescribe the conditions upon which the marriage relation between its own citizens shall be created, and the causes for which it may be dissolved. One of the parties guilty of acts for which, by the law of the State, a dissolution may be granted, may have removed to a State where no dissolution is permitted. The complaining party would, therefore, fail if a divorce were sought in the State of the defendant; and if application could not be made to the tribunals of the complainant's domicile in such case, and proceedings be there instituted without personal service of process or personal notice to the offending party, the injured citizen would be without redress. Bish.Marr. and Div., sect. 156.

Neither do we mean to assert that a State may not require a nonresident entering into a partnership or association within its limits, or making contracts enforceable there, to appoint an agent or representative in the State to receive service of process and notice in legal proceedings instituted with respect to such partnership, association, or contracts, or to designate a place where such service may be made and notice given, and provide, upon their failure, to make such appointment or to designate such place that service may be made upon a public officer designated for that purpose, or in some other prescribed way, and that judgments rendered upon such service may not be binding upon the non-residents both within and without the State. * * * The Lafayette Insurance Co. v. French et al., 18 How. 404. * * * Nor do we doubt that a State, on creating corporations or other institutions for pecuniary or charitable purposes, may provide a mode in which their conduct may be investigated, their obligations enforced, or their charters revoked, which shall require other than personal service upon their officers or members. Parties becoming members of such corporations or institutions would hold their interest subject to the conditions prescribed by law. Copin v. Adamson, Law Rep. 9 Ex. 345.

In the present case, there is no feature of this kind, and, consequently, no consideration of what would be the effect of such legislation in enforcing the contract of a non-resident can arise. The question here respects only the validity of a money judgment rendered in one State, in an action upon a simple contract against the resident of

another, without service of process upon him, or his appearance therein.

Judgment affirmed.

[The dissenting opinion of Justice Hunt is omitted.]

NOTE ON THE HISTORICAL DEVELOPMENT OF TERRITORIAL JURISDICTION DOCTRINE

1. The Constitutionalization of Jurisdiction

As indicated by Barrell v. Benjamin, prior to the decision in Pennoyer v. Neff the states of the Union recognized, under legal concepts emanating from international law, that there were limitations on their authority to exercise jurisdiction in cases involving persons or property outside their boundaries. Federal constitutional law, particularly the Full Faith and Credit Clause, was implicated when a judgment of one state was sought to be enforced in another state. The decisions in these recognition-of-judgment cases were the foundation of the analysis in Pennoyer v. Neff. That decision subsumed these jurisdictional concepts under the Due Process Clause of the Fourteenth Amendment, which had only recently been adopted when the Court decided *Pennoyer*. The result was to convert what theretofore was primarily a body of state law rules of self-restraint into a corpus of federal law obligatory upon the states under the Supremacy Clause, U.S. Const. Art. VI. As summarized in Restatement Second of Conflict of Laws § 24, Comment e:

> "In the United States, the due process clause of the Fourteenth Amendment * * * prohibits the States from acting through their courts when they have no judicial jurisdiction * * *. A judgment rendered in this country without judicial jurisdiction is void, even in the State where rendered, and is not entitled to full faith and credit in sister States. Since the extent of the judicial jurisdiction of the * * * individual States is a constitutional question, the decisions of the Supreme Court of the United States are controlling."

Can this result be squared with the premise, also advanced in *Pennoyer*, that the states are independent entities possessing "exclusive jurisdiction and sovereignty over persons and property within [their] territory"? The history of jurisdictional doctrine since *Pennoyer* is in an important sense the effort of courts to construe the principles of territorial jurisdiction in the context of the progressive economic and social integration of the states of the Union. For a review of *Pennoyer* in historical perspective, and a critique of its analysis, see Hazard, A General Theory of State–Court Jurisdiction, 1965 Sup.Ct.Rev. 241.

[handwritten margin note: yes → until non-res enters picture]

2. The Doctrine of Pennoyer v. Neff

Observe that three related ideas weave in and out of the discussion in Pennoyer v. Neff:

> (1) The authority, or "power," of a state to adjudicate a controversy is limited by a territorial dimension. The Court asserts that the relevant territorial dimension is *presence* of the person who is to be subjected to liability or *presence* of the property that is to be the subject of the judgment. The question for the future was whether some other connection besides presence might be sufficient. Observe that, toward the end of the opinion, the Court takes note of "consent" by corporations and other associations as a sufficient connection.

(2) The presence (or other connection) can be either of the person to be held liable or of the property or some other "thing." If it is the person that is present, in conventional terminology the authority being exercised is that of *in personam* jurisdiction; if it is property that is present, the authority is *in rem* or *quasi in rem* jurisdiction. It might make a difference, might it not, whether a particular exercise of jurisdiction were characterized as "in personam" or "in rem"? Suppose the person was present but the property was not, or vice versa. Note also that the opinion refers to "status" (specifically, the marriage relationship) as having a location within a state's territory. What if other kinds of legal relationships were conceived as "things" located in a state's territory?

(3) Notice may be given in an *in rem* proceeding by seizing the thing that is the subject of the action. This makes actual notice in such proceedings rather precarious, doesn't it? Why should substituted service (service otherwise than by personal service of summons on the defendant) be adequate in *in rem* proceedings but not in *in personam* proceedings?

3. Jurisdiction in *In Rem* Proceedings

In the years following Pennoyer v. Neff the Supreme Court clarified the authority of a court to exercise jurisdiction in cases classifiable as *in rem* proceedings. In Arndt v. Griggs, 134 U.S. 316, 10 S.Ct. 557, 33 L.Ed. 918 (1890), the Court was confronted with the question whether a state had authority to adjudicate title to real property within the state where the defendant was a nonresident and where the only notice was by publication. In upholding the assertion of jurisdiction, the Court held such notice sufficient. It expressed particular concern that states not be hindered in settling issues of title to property within their jurisdiction merely because a putative owner or claimant is beyond reach of personal service. Jurisdiction over the property, the Court reasoned, implied jurisdiction to decide rights in the property. Might the Court's particular concern explain why it chose to characterize the proceeding as an *in rem* action concerning the property, as opposed to an *in personam* proceeding concerning the parties' interests in the property? If it had been characterized as an *in personam* proceeding, would publication notice have been sufficient? If it had been so characterized, would there have been territorial jurisdiction under *Pennoyer*?

Another difficult issue is determining where the situs of movable or intangible property is located. One solution was to say that the situs of such property was the place where the owner was domiciled. But other theories were applied as well. In Harris v. Balk, 198 U.S. 215, 25 S.Ct. 625, 49 L.Ed. 1023 (1905), the Court held that a debt owed to a person could be regarded as having situs not where the owner of the debt (i.e., the creditor) was domiciled, but where the debtor was located, and that as the debtor moved, so moved the situs of the debt. Compare the discussion in Barrell v. Benjamin, supra. The Court thus upheld a judgment in favor of a creditor who filed suit against a nonresident debtor and obtained jurisdiction by serving, as garnishee of the debt owed to him, a person who was himself in debt to the debtor and who happened to be temporarily present in the state. As with Arndt v. Griggs, the question arises of why the Court chose not to characterize the underlying relationships in *in personam* terms. That characterization would have precluded the plaintiff from "attaching" the debt owed to his debtor by the third party. Would it be fair to say that courts could pack the result into the premise by either focusing on the persons involved and calling the jurisdiction "in personam" or focusing on the relationships and calling it "in rem"? *[handwritten: yes]*

The disputed claim in the proceeding in Arndt v. Griggs concerned owner- *[handwritten: QIR #1]* ship in the very property over which *in rem* jurisdiction was asserted. That is, the property constituting the *res* was the matter in controversy between the *[handwritten: thing]* parties. In contrast, the proceeding in Harris v. Balk sought to determine a claim unrelated to the property and to use the property as a basis of jurisdic- *[handwritten: QIR #2]* tion and as a means of paying the claim. Both types of proceedings were included in the category of *in rem* proceedings. Within this category, however, distinctions were drawn as follows:

> (1) "True" in rem proceedings. These were proceedings in which the court sought to determine disputed claims in the property and to resolve the claims of all persons—"all the world"—in that property. The prime illustration is a probate proceeding in which claims to the decedent's property are conclusively resolved so that the property may pass to creditors or by inheritance.

> (2) "Quasi in rem" proceedings. These in turn were subclassified into "Type I," proceedings to determine disputed claims in property but aiming to resolve the claims only of specified persons, and "Type II," actions begun through attachment where the claim is unrelated to the property. *[handwritten: i.e. probate / i.e. Mitchell vs. Neff]*

See Restatement of Judgments § 32 (1942). Harris v. Balk was clearly a "Type II" *quasi in rem* action, but Arndt v. Griggs could be classified as either "true" *in rem* (if all claimants were to be concluded) or "Type I" *quasi in rem* (if only the named claimants were to be concluded). In Pennoyer v. Neff, what might the plaintiff in the underlying action have done differently to win a valid judgment? *[handwritten: Quasi in Rem #2 (In Rem)]*

4. Validity and Recognition of Judgments

Observe that in *Pennoyer* the plaintiff obtained judgment by default and the question of jurisdiction arose in subsequent litigation in which the validity of the judgment was challenged. The question of validity thus arose in the context of *recognition* of the judgment. The question of validity can also arise in a threshold objection in the original action. See, e.g., International Shoe Co. v. State of Washington, reprinted just below. See also Restatement Second of Judgments § 10, Comments b and f; Note on Special Appearance and Its Consequences, infra p. 420.

5. The Rules of Pennoyer and Its Progeny

The decisions in *Pennoyer, Arndt, Harris,* and related cases established territorial jurisdiction rules essentially as follows:

> (1) Jurisdiction can be exercised *in personam* over a person who is present within the state. Jurisdiction can be exercised *in rem* over property within the state or "deemed" within the state, whatever that might be.

> (2) When jurisdiction is exercised *in personam,* notice must be given by service of summons or something much like it. When jurisdiction is exercised *in rem,* the property must be seized and notice by publication or the like must be given.

For an emphatic affirmation that presence of the defendant, without any other connection to the forum, is still a sufficient basis for *in personam* jurisdiction, see Humphrey v. Langford, 246 Ga. 732, 273 S.E.2d 22 (1980).

Compare MacLeod v. MacLeod, 383 A.2d 39 (Me.1978), sustaining jurisdiction over a transient American citizen who had no residence in the United States in an action to collect past due spousal support payments, but stating that the action would be dismissed on forum non conveniens grounds if defendant submitted to jurisdiction in a more convenient sister state. On the doctrine of forum non conveniens, see Refusals to Take Jurisdiction, infra p. 427.

[handwritten margin note: OK ct to refuse to hear case even if correct venue for convenience litigants + interest of justice, action should be elsewhere]

6. Subsequent Developments

From about 1900 to 1945, the most significant development in the law of territorial jurisdiction was the enlargement of *in personam* jurisdiction. This began with the notion, referred to in *Pennoyer*, that a business association might be compelled by a state to "consent" to being served with process. This proposition was first stated in Lafayette Ins. Co. v. French, 59 U.S. (18 How.) 404, 407–408, 15 L.Ed. 451 (1855):

> "A corporation created by Indiana can transact business in Ohio only with the consent, express or implied, of the latter State * * *. This consent may be accompanied by such conditions as Ohio may think fit to impose * * *.

> "In this instance, one of the conditions imposed by Ohio was, in effect, that the agent who should reside in Ohio and enter into contracts of insurance there in behalf of the foreign Corporation, should also be deemed its agent to receive service of process in suits founded on such contracts. * * *

> "Nor do we think the means adopted * * * are open to the objection that it is an attempt improperly to extend the jurisdiction of the State beyond its own limits to a person in another State. * * * The process was served within the limits and jurisdiction of Ohio, upon a person qualified by law to represent the Corporation there in respect to such service * * *."

With the sanction given in *Pennoyer* to the "consent" basis of jurisdiction, the states enacted statutes requiring foreign corporations to appoint a local agent for service of process and providing that, should they fail to do so, a state official such as the Secretary of State would be deemed so appointed by corporations engaging in local business transactions. See Smolik v. Philadelphia & Reading Coal & Iron Co., 222 Fed. 148 (S.D.N.Y.1915), approved in Pennsylvania Fire Ins. Co. v. Gold Issue Mining & Milling Co., 243 U.S. 93, 37 S.Ct. 344, 61 L.Ed. 610 (1917).

The consent theory was also instrumental in the expansion of state court jurisdiction in another direction, against nonresident motorists sued for automobile accidents occurring locally. In Hess v. Pawloski, 274 U.S. 352, 47 S.Ct. 632, 71 L.Ed. 1091 (1927), jurisdiction over such a defendant was sustained where service of process was effected under a Massachusetts statute declaring that the use of the state's highways was deemed equivalent to appointing the State Registrar as agent for service of process in actions growing out of accidents on the highways. The statute required not only that summons be served on the Registrar, but also that a copy of it be sent to the defendant by registered mail. The Court held that "the state may declare that the use of the highway by the nonresident is the equivalent of the appointment of the registrar as agent on whom process may be served. * * * Lafayette Ins. Co. v. French."

Along with these expansions of *in personam* jurisdiction, the Court occasionally dealt with the problem of adequate notice. Here, its responses were seemingly contradictory. On the one hand, in Wuchter v. Pizzutti, 276 U.S. 13, 48 S.Ct. 259, 72 L.Ed. 446 (1928), involving a nonresident motorist, the Court said that serving summons on the state's Secretary of State (as the motorist's "agent") was not enough; "due process"—presumably meaning fundamental procedural fairness and not territorial jurisdiction—required a procedure of notice to defendant that would make it "reasonably probable" that he would receive "actual notice." On the other hand, in State of Washington ex rel. Bond & Goodwin & Tucker, Inc. v. Superior Court, 289 U.S. 361, 53 S.Ct. 624, 77 L.Ed. 1256 (1933), the Court sustained "constructive" service on a foreign corporation through service on the Secretary of State. Furthermore, in the *in rem* cases the Court adhered to the proposition that seizure and publication were sufficient as notice.

Then came *International Shoe* and *Mullane*.

b. THE MODERN FORMULA

INTERNATIONAL SHOE CO. v. STATE OF WASHINGTON

Supreme Court of the United States, 1945.
326 U.S. 310, 66 S.Ct. 154, 90 L.Ed. 95.

MR. CHIEF JUSTICE STONE delivered the opinion of the Court.

The questions for decision are (1) whether, within the limitations of the due process clause of the Fourteenth Amendment, appellant, a Delaware corporation, has by its activities in the State of Washington rendered itself amenable to proceedings in the courts of that state to recover unpaid contributions to the state unemployment compensation fund exacted by state statutes, Washington Unemployment Compensation Act, Washington Revised Statutes, § 9998–103a through § 9998–123a, 1941 Supp., and (2) whether the state can exact those contributions consistently with the due process clause of the Fourteenth Amendment.

The statutes in question set up a comprehensive scheme of unemployment compensation, the costs of which are defrayed by contributions required to be made by employers to a state unemployment compensation fund. The contributions are a specified percentage of the wages payable annually by each employer for his employees' services in the state. The assessment and collection of the contributions and the fund are administered by respondents. Section 14(c) of the Act, Wash. Rev.Stat.1941 Supp., § 9998–114c, authorizes respondent Commissioner to issue an order and notice of assessment of delinquent contributions upon prescribed personal service of the notice upon the employer if found within the state, or, if not so found, by mailing the notice to the employer by registered mail at his last known address. That section also authorizes the Commissioner to collect the assessment by distraint if it is not paid within ten days after service of the notice. By §§ 14(e) and 6(b) the order of assessment may be administratively reviewed by an appeal tribunal within the office of unemployment upon petition of the employer, and this determination is by § 6(i) made subject to judicial review on questions of law by the state Superior Court, with further right of appeal in the state Supreme Court as in other civil cases.

In this case notice of assessment for the years in question was personally served upon a sales solicitor employed by appellant in the State of Washington, and a copy of the notice was mailed by registered mail to appellant at its address in St. Louis, Missouri. Appellant appeared specially before the office of unemployment and moved to set aside the order and notice of assessment on the ground that the service upon appellant's salesman was not proper service upon appellant; that appellant was not a corporation of the State of Washington and was not doing business within the state; that it had no agent within the state upon whom service could be made; and that appellant is not an employer and does not furnish employment within the meaning of the statute.

The motion was heard on evidence and a stipulation of facts by the appeal tribunal which denied the motion and ruled that respondent Commissioner was entitled to recover the unpaid contributions. That action was affirmed by the Commissioner; both the Superior Court and the Supreme Court affirmed. 154 P.2d 801. Appellant in each of these courts assailed the statute as applied, as a violation of the due process clause of the Fourteenth Amendment, and as imposing a constitutionally prohibited burden on interstate commerce. * * *

The facts as found by the appeal tribunal and accepted by the state Superior Court and Supreme Court, are not in dispute. Appellant is a Delaware corporation, having its principal place of business in St. Louis, Missouri, and is engaged in the manufacture and sale of shoes and other footwear. It maintains places of business in several states, other than Washington, at which its manufacturing is carried on and from which its merchandise is distributed interstate through several sales units or branches located outside the State of Washington.

Appellant has no office in Washington and makes no contracts either for sale or purchase of merchandise there. It maintains no stock of merchandise in that state and makes no deliveries of goods in intrastate commerce. During the years from 1937 to 1940, now in question, appellant employed eleven to thirteen salesmen under direct supervision and control of sales managers located in St. Louis. These salesmen resided in Washington; their principal activities were confined to that state; and they were compensated by commissions based upon the amount of their sales. The commissions for each year totaled more than $31,000. Appellant supplies its salesmen with a line of samples, each consisting of one shoe of a pair, which they display to prospective purchasers. On occasion they rent permanent sample rooms, for exhibiting samples, in business buildings, or rent rooms in hotels or business buildings temporarily for that purpose. The cost of such rentals is reimbursed by appellant.

The authority of the salesmen is limited to exhibiting their samples and soliciting orders from prospective buyers, at prices and on terms fixed by appellant. The salesmen transmit the orders to appellant's office in St. Louis for acceptance or rejection, and when accepted the merchandise for filling the orders is shipped f.o.b. from points outside Washington to the purchasers within the state. All the merchandise shipped into Washington is invoiced at the place of shipment from which collections are made. No salesman has authority to enter into contracts or to make collections.

The Supreme Court of Washington was of opinion that the regular and systematic solicitation of orders in the state by appellant's salesmen, resulting in a continuous flow of appellant's product into the state, was sufficient to constitute doing business in the state so as to make appellant amenable to suit in its courts. But it was also of opinion that there were sufficient additional activities shown to bring the case within the rule frequently stated, that solicitation within a state by the agents of a foreign corporation plus some additional activities there are sufficient to render the corporation amenable to suit brought in the courts of the state to enforce an obligation arising out of its activities there. International Harvester Co. v. Kentucky, 234 U.S. 579, 587, 34 S.Ct. 944, 946, 58 L.Ed. 1479; People's Tobacco Co. v. American Tobacco Co., 246 U.S. 79, 87, 38 S.Ct. 233, 235, 62 L.Ed. 587, Ann.Cas.1918C, 537; Frene v. Louisville Cement Co., 77 U.S.App.D.C. 129, 134 F.2d 511, 516, 146 A.L.R. 926. The court found such additional activities in the salesmen's display of samples sometimes in permanent display rooms, and the salesmen's residence within the state, continued over a period of years, all resulting in a substantial volume of merchandise regularly shipped by appellant to purchasers within the state. The court also held that the statute as applied did not invade the constitutional power of Congress to regulate interstate commerce and did not impose a prohibited burden on such commerce.

Appellant's argument, renewed here, that the statute imposes an unconstitutional burden on interstate commerce need not detain us. For 53 Stat. 1391, 26 U.S.C. § 1606(a), 26 U.S.C.A. Int.Rev.Code, § 1606(a), provides that "No person required under a State law to make payments to an unemployment fund shall be relieved from compliance therewith on the ground that he is engaged in interstate or foreign commerce, or that the State law does not distinguish between employees engaged in interstate or foreign commerce and those engaged in intrastate commerce." It is no longer debatable that Congress, in the exercise of the commerce power, may authorize the states, in specified ways, to regulate interstate commerce or impose burdens upon it. [Citations omitted.]

Appellant also insists that its activities within the state were not sufficient to manifest its "presence" there and that in its absence the state courts were without jurisdiction, [and] that consequently it was a denial of due process for the state to subject appellant to suit. It refers to those cases in which it was said that the mere solicitation of orders for the purchase of goods within a state, to be accepted without the state and filled by shipment of the purchased goods interstate, does not render the corporation seller amenable to suit within the state. See Green v. Chicago, Burlington & Quincy R. Co., 205 U.S. 530, 533, 27 S.Ct. 595, 596, 51 L.Ed. 916; International Harvester Co. v. Kentucky, supra, 234 U.S. 586, 587, 34 S.Ct. 946, 58 L.Ed. 1479; Philadelphia & Reading R. Co. v. McKibbin, 243 U.S. 264, 268, 37 S.Ct. 280, 61 L.Ed. 710; People's Tobacco Co. v. American Tobacco Co., supra, 246 U.S. 87, 38 S.Ct. 235, 62 L.Ed. 587, Ann.Cas.1918C, 537. And appellant further argues that since it was not present within the state, it is a denial of due process to subject it to taxation or other money exaction. It thus denies the power of the state to lay the tax or to subject appellant to a suit for its collection.

Historically the jurisdiction of courts to render judgment in personam is grounded on their de facto power over the defendant's person. Hence his presence within the territorial jurisdiction of a court was prerequisite to its rendition of a judgment personally binding him. Pennoyer v. Neff, 95 U.S. 714, 733, 24 L.Ed. 565. But now that the capias ad respondendum has given way to personal service of summons or other form of notice, due process requires only that in order to subject a defendant to a judgment in personam, if he be not present within the territory of the forum, he have certain minimum contacts with it such that the maintenance of the suit does not offend "traditional notions of fair play and substantial justice." Milliken v. Meyer, 311 U.S. 457, 463, 61 S.Ct. 339, 343, 85 L.Ed. 278, 132 A.L.R. 1357. See Holmes, J., in McDonald v. Mabee, 243 U.S. 90, 91, 37 S.Ct. 343, 61 L.Ed. 608, L.R.A.1917F, 458. [Citations omitted.]

Since the corporate personality is a fiction, although a fiction intended to be acted upon as though it were a fact, Klein v. Board of Tax Supervisors, 282 U.S. 19, 24, 51 S.Ct. 15, 16, 75 L.Ed. 140, 73 A.L.R. 679, it is clear that unlike an individual its "presence" without, as well as within, the state of its origin can be manifested only by activities carried on in its behalf by those who are authorized to act for it. To say that the corporation is so far "present" there as to satisfy due process requirements, for purposes of taxation or the maintenance of suits against it in the courts of the state, is to beg the question to be decided. For the terms "present" or "presence" are used merely to symbolize those activities of the corporation's agent within the state which courts will deem to be sufficient to satisfy the demands of due process. L. Hand, J., in Hutchinson v. Chase & Gilbert, 2 Cir., 45 F.2d 139, 141. Those demands may be met by such contacts of the corporation with the state of the forum as make it reasonable, in the context of our federal system of government, to require the corporation to defend the particular suit which is brought there. An "estimate of the inconveniences" which would result to the corporation from a trial away from its "home" or principal place of business is relevant in this connection. Hutchinson v. Chase & Gilbert, supra, 45 F.2d 141.

"Presence" in the state in this sense, has never been doubted when the activities of the corporation there have not only been continuous and systematic, but also give rise to the liabilities sued on, even though no consent to be sued or authorization to an agent to accept service of process has been given. [Citations omitted.] Conversely it has been generally recognized that the casual presence of the corporate agent or even his conduct of single or isolated items of activities in a state in the corporation's behalf are not enough to subject it to suit on causes of action unconnected with the activities there. [Citations omitted.] To require the corporation in such circumstances to defend the suit away from its home or other jurisdiction where it carries on more substantial activities has been thought to lay too great and unreasonable a burden on the corporation to comport with due process.

While it has been held in cases on which appellant relies that continuous activity of some sorts within a state is not enough to support the demand that the corporation be amenable to suits unrelated to that activity, [citations omitted] there have been instances in which the continuous corporate operations within a state were thought so substantial and of such a nature as to justify suit against it on causes of action arising from dealings entirely distinct from those activities. [Citations omitted.]

Finally, although the commission of some single or occasional acts of the corporate agent in a state sufficient to impose an obligation or liability on the corporation has not been thought to confer upon the state authority to enforce it, Rosenberg Bros. & Co. v. Curtis Brown Co., 260 U.S. 516, 43 S.Ct. 170, 67 L.Ed. 372, other such acts, because of their nature and quality and the circumstances of their commission, may be deemed sufficient to render the corporation liable to suit. Cf. Kane v. New Jersey, 242 U.S. 160, 37 S.Ct. 30, 61 L.Ed. 222; Hess v. Pawloski, supra; Young v. Masci, supra. True, some of the decisions holding the corporation amenable to suit have been supported by resort to the legal fiction that it has given its consent to service and suit, consent being implied from its presence in the state through the acts of its authorized agents. Lafayette Insurance Co. v. French, 18 How. 404, 407, 15 L.Ed. 451; [citations omitted]. But more realistically it may be said that those authorized acts were of such a nature as to justify the fiction. Smolik v. Philadelphia & R. C. & I. Co., D.C., 222 F. 148, 151. Henderson, The Position of Foreign Corporations in American Constitutional Law, 94, 95.

It is evident that the criteria by which we mark the boundary line between those activities which justify the subjection of a corporation to suit, and those which do not, cannot be simply mechanical or quantitative. The test is not merely, as has sometimes been suggested, whether the activity, which the corporation has seen fit to procure through its agents in another state, is a little more or a little less. St. Louis S. W. R. Co. v. Alexander, supra, 227 U.S. 228, 33 S.Ct. 248, 57 L.Ed. 486, Ann.Cas.1915B, 77; International Harvester Co. v. Kentucky, supra, 234 U.S. 587, 34 S.Ct. 946, 58 L.Ed. 1479. Whether due process is satisfied must depend rather upon the quality and nature of the activity in relation to the fair and orderly administration of the laws which it was the purpose of the due process clause to insure. That clause does not contemplate that a state may make binding a judgment in personam against an individual or corporate defendant with which the state has no contacts, ties, or relations. Cf. Pennoyer v. Neff, supra; Minnesota Commercial Men's Ass'n v. Benn, 261 U.S. 140, 43 S.Ct. 293, 67 L.Ed. 573.

But to the extent that a corporation exercises the privilege of conducting activities within a state, it enjoys the benefits and protection of the laws of that state. The exercise of that privilege may give rise to obligations; and, so far as those obligations arise out of or are connected with the activities within the state, a procedure which requires the corporation to respond to a suit brought to enforce them can, in most instances, hardly be said to be undue. [Citations omitted.]

Applying these standards, the activities carried on in behalf of appellant in the State of Washington were neither irregular nor casual. They were systematic and continuous throughout the years in question. They resulted in a large volume of interstate business, in the course of which appellant received the benefits and protection of the laws of the state, including the right to resort to the courts for the enforcement of its rights. The obligation which is here sued upon arose out of those very activities. It is evident that these operations establish sufficient contacts or ties with the state of the forum to make it reasonable and just according to our traditional conception of fair play and substantial justice to permit the state to enforce the obligations which appellant has incurred there. Hence we cannot say that the maintenance of the present suit in the State of Washington involves an unreasonable or undue procedure.

We are likewise unable to conclude that the service of the process within the state upon an agent whose activities establish appellant's "presence" there was not sufficient notice of the suit, or that the suit was so unrelated to those activities as to make the agent an inappropriate vehicle for communicating the notice. It is enough that appellant has established such contacts with the state that the particular form of substituted service adopted there gives reasonable assurance that the notice will be actual [citations omitted]; McDonald v. Mabee, supra; Milliken v. Meyer, supra. Nor can we say that the mailing of the notice of suit to appellant by registered mail at its home office was not reasonably calculated to apprise appellant of the suit. Compare Hess v. Pawloski, supra, with McDonald v. Mabee, supra, 243 U.S. 92, 37 S.Ct. 344, 61 L.Ed. 608, L.R.A.1917F, 458, and Wuchter v. Pizzutti, 276 U.S. 13, 19, 24, 48 S.Ct. 259, 260, 262, 72 L.Ed. 446, 57 A.L.R. 1230; [citations omitted].

* * *

Appellant having rendered itself amenable to suit upon obligations arising out of the activities of its salesmen in Washington, the state *authorized agent to accept*

may maintain the present suit in personam to collect the tax laid upon the exercise of the privilege of employing appellant's salesmen within the state. For Washington has made one of those activities, which taken together establish appellant's "presence" there for purposes of suit, the taxable event by which the state brings appellant within the reach of its taxing power. The state thus has constitutional power to lay the tax and to subject appellant to a suit to recover it. The activities which establish its "presence" subject it alike to taxation by the state and to suit to recover the tax. [Citations omitted.]

Affirmed.

MR. JUSTICE JACKSON took no part in the consideration or decision of this case.

MR. JUSTICE BLACK delivered the following opinion.

* * *

Certainly appellant can not in the light of our past decisions meritoriously claim that notice by registered mail and by personal service on its sales solicitors in Washington did not meet the requirements of procedural due process. And the due process clause is not brought in issue any more by appellant's further conceptualistic contention that Washington could not levy a tax or bring suit against the corporation because it did not honor that State with its mystical "presence." For it is unthinkable that the vague due process clause was ever intended to prohibit a State from regulating or taxing a business carried on within its boundaries simply because this is done by agents of a corporation organized and having its headquarters elsewhere. To read this into the due process clause would in fact result in depriving a State's citizens of due process by taking from the State the power to protect them in their business dealings within its boundaries with representatives of a foreign corporation. Nothing could be more irrational or more designed to defeat the function of our federative system of government. Certainly a State, at the very least, has power to tax and sue those dealing with its citizens within its boundaries, as we have held before. Hoopeston Canning Co. v. Cullen, 318 U.S. 313, 63 S.Ct. 602, 87 L.Ed. 1722, 145 A.L.R. 1113. Were the Court to follow this principle, it would provide a workable standard for cases where, as here, no other questions are involved. The Court has not chosen to do so, but instead has engaged in an unnecessary discussion in the course of which it has announced vague Constitutional criteria applied for the first time to the issue before us. It has thus introduced uncertain elements confusing the simple pattern and tending to curtail the exercise of State powers to an extent not justified by the Constitution.

The criteria adopted insofar as they can be identified read as follows: Due process does permit State courts to "enforce the obligations which appellant has incurred" if it be found "reasonable and just according to our traditional conception of fair play and substantial justice." And this in turn means that we will "permit" the State to act if upon "an 'estimate of the inconveniences' which would result to the corporation from a trial away from its 'home' or principal place of business," we conclude that it is "reasonable" to subject it to suit in a State where it is doing business.

It is true that this Court did use the terms "fair play" and "substantial justice" in explaining the philosophy underlying the holding that it could not be "due process of law" to render a personal judgment against a defendant without notice to and an opportunity to be heard by him. Milliken v. Meyer, 311 U.S. 457, 61 S.Ct. 339, 85 L.Ed. 278, 132 A.L.R. 1357. In McDonald v. Mabee, 243 U.S. 90, 91, 37 S.Ct. 343, 61 L.Ed. 608, L.R.A.1917F, 458, cited in the Milliken case, Mr. Justice Holmes speaking for the Court warned against judicial curtailment of this opportunity to be heard and referred to such a curtailment as a denial of "fair play," which even the common law would have deemed "contrary to natural justice." And previous cases had indicated that the ancient rule against judgments without notice had stemmed from "natural justice" concepts. These cases, while giving additional reasons why notice under particular circumstances is inadequate, did not mean thereby that all legislative enactments which this Court might deem to be contrary to natural justice ought to be held invalid under the due process clause. None of the cases purport to support or could support a holding that a State can tax and sue corporations only if its action comports with this Court's notions of "natural justice." I should have thought the Tenth Amendment settled that.

I believe that the Federal Constitution leaves to each State, without any "ifs" or "buts," a power to tax and to open the doors of its courts for its citizens to sue corporations whose agents do business in those States. Believing that the Constitution gave the States that power, I think it a judicial deprivation to condition its exercise upon this Court's notion of "fair play," however appealing that term may be. Nor can I stretch the meaning of due process so far as to authorize this Court to deprive a State of the right to afford judicial protection to its citizens on the ground that it would be more "convenient" for the corporation to be sued somewhere else.

There is a strong emotional appeal in the words "fair play," "justice," and "reasonableness." But they were not chosen by those who wrote the original Constitution or the Fourteenth Amendment as a measuring rod for this Court to use in invalidating State or Federal laws passed by elected legislative representatives. No one, not even those who most feared a democratic government, ever formally proposed that courts should be given power to invalidate legislation under any such elastic standards. Express prohibitions against certain types of legislation are found in the Constitution, and under the long settled practice, courts invalidate laws found to conflict with them. This requires interpretation, and interpretation, it is true, may result in extension of the Constitution's purpose. But that is no reason for reading the due process clause so as to restrict a State's power to tax and sue those whose activities affect persons and businesses within the State, provided proper service can be had. Superimposing the natural justice concept on the Constitution's specific prohibitions could operate as a drastic abridgment of democratic safeguards they embody, such as freedom of speech, press and religion, and the right to counsel. This has already happened. Betts v. Brady, 316 U.S. 455, 62 S.Ct. 1252, 86 L.Ed. 1595. Compare Feldman v. United States, 322 U.S. 487, 494–503, 64 S.Ct. 1082, 1085–1089, 88 L.Ed. 1408, 154 A.L.R. 982. For application of this natural law concept, whether under the terms "reasonableness," "justice," or "fair play," makes judges the supreme arbiters of the country's laws and practices. [Citations omitted.] This result, I believe, alters the form of government our Constitution provides. I cannot agree.

True, the State's power is here upheld. But the rule announced means that tomorrow's judgment may strike down a State or Federal enactment on the ground that it does not conform to this Court's idea of natural justice. I therefore find myself moved by the same fears that caused Mr. Justice Holmes to say in 1930:

"I have not yet adequately expressed the more than anxiety that I feel at the ever increasing scope given to the Fourteenth Amendment in cutting down what I believe to be the constitutional rights of the States. As the decisions now stand, I see hardly any limit but the sky to the invalidating of those rights if they happen to strike a majority of this Court as for any reason undesirable." Baldwin v. Missouri, 281 U.S. 586, 595, 50 S.Ct. 436, 439, 74 L.Ed. 1056, 72 A.L.R. 1303.

MULLANE v. CENTRAL HANOVER BANK & TRUST CO.

Supreme Court of the United States, 1950.
339 U.S. 306, 70 S.Ct. 652, 94 L.Ed. 865.

Mr. Justice Jackson delivered the opinion of the Court.

This controversy questions the constitutional sufficiency of notice to beneficiaries on judicial settlement of accounts by the trustee of a common trust fund established under the New York Banking Law, Consol.Laws, c. 2. The New York Court of Appeals considered and overruled objections that the statutory notice contravenes requirements of the Fourteenth Amendment and that by allowance of the account beneficiaries were deprived of property without due process of law. 299 N.Y. 697, 87 N.E.2d 73. The case is here on appeal under 28 U.S.C. § 1257, 28 U.S.C.A. § 1257.

Common trust fund legislation is addressed to a problem appropriate for state action. Mounting overheads have made administration of small trusts undesirable to corporate trustees. In order that donors and testators of moderately sized trusts may not be denied the service of corporate fiduciaries, the District of Columbia and some thirty states other than New York have permitted pooling small trust estates into one fund for investment administration.* The income, capital gains,

---

* Ala.Code Ann., 1940, Cum.Supp.1947, tit. 58, §§ 88 to 103, as amended, Laws 1949, Act 262; Ariz.Code Ann., 1939, Cum. Supp.1949, §§ 51–1101 to 51–1104; Ark. Stat.Ann.1947, §§ 58–110 to 58–112; Cal. Bank.Code Ann., Deering 1949, § 1564;

losses and expenses of the collective trust are shared by the constituent trusts in proportion to their contribution. By this plan, diversification of risk and economy of management can be extended to those whose capital standing alone would not obtain such advantage.

Statutory authorization for the establishment of such common trust funds is provided in the New York Banking Law, § 100–c, c. 687, L.1937, as amended by c. 602, L.1943, and c. 158, L.1944. Under this Act a trust company may, with approval of the State Banking Board, establish a common fund and, within prescribed limits, invest therein the assets of an unlimited number of estates, trusts or other funds of which it is trustee. Each participating trust shares ratably in the common fund, but exclusive management and control is in the trust company as trustee, and neither a fiduciary nor any beneficiary of a participating trust is deemed to have ownership in any particular asset or investment of this common fund. The trust company must keep fund assets separate from its own, and in its fiduciary capacity may not deal with itself or any affiliate. Provisions are made for accountings twelve to fifteen months after the establishment of a fund and triennially thereafter. The decree in each such judicial settlement of accounts is made binding and conclusive as to any matter set forth in the account upon everyone having any interest in the common fund or in any participating estate, trust or fund.

In January, 1946, Central Hanover Bank and Trust Company established a common trust fund in accordance with these provisions, and in March, 1947, it petitioned the Surrogate's Court for settlement of its first account as common trustee. During the accounting period a total of 113 trusts, approximately half *inter vivos* and half testamentary, participated in the common trust fund, the gross capital of which was nearly three million dollars. The record does not show the number or residence of the beneficiaries, but they were many and it is clear that some of them were not residents of the State of New York.

The only notice given beneficiaries of this specific application was by publication in a local newspaper in strict compliance with the

Colo.Stat.Ann., 1935, Cum.Supp. 1947, c. 18, §§ 173 to 178; Conn.Gen.Stat.1949 Rev., § 5805; Del.Rev.Code, 1935, § 4401, as amended, Laws 1943, c. 171, Laws 1947, c. 268; (D.C.) Pub.Law No. 416, 81st Cong., 1st Sess., c. 767, Oct. 27, 1949, 63 Stat. 938; Fla.Stat., 1941, §§ 655.29 to 655.34, F.S.A.; Ga.Code Ann., 1937, Cum.Supp.1947, §§ 109–601 to 109–622; Idaho Code Ann., 1949, Cum.Supp.1949, §§ 68–701 to 68–703; Ill.Rev.Stat.1949, c. 16½, §§ 57 to 63; Ind. Stat.Ann., Burns 1950, §§ 18–2009 to 18–2014; Ky.Rev.Stat., 1948, § 287.230; La. Gen.Stat.Ann., 1939, § 9850.64, Act No. 81 of 1938, § 64; Md.Ann.Code Gen.Laws, 1939, Cum.Supp.1947, art. 11, § 62A; Mass.Ann.Laws, 1933, Cum.Supp.1949, c. 203A; Mich.Stat.Ann.1943, Cum.Supp. 1949, §§ 23.1141 to 23.1153, Comp.Laws 1948, §§ 555.101–555.113; Minn.Stat., 1945, § 48.84, as amended, Laws 1947, c. 234, M.S.A.; N.J.S.A., 1939, Cum.Supp. 1949, §§ 17:9A–36 to 17:9A–46; N.C.Gen. Stat., 1943, §§ 36–47 to 36–52; Ohio Gen. Code Ann. (Page's 1946), Cum.Supp.1949, §§ 715 to 720, 722; Okla.Stat.1941, Cum. Supp.1949, tit. 60, § 162; Pa.Stat.Ann., 1939, Cum.Supp.1949, tit. 7, §§ 819–1109 to 819–1109d; So.Dak.Laws 1941, c. 20; Vernon's Tex.Rev.Civ.Stat.Ann., 1939, Cum. Supp.1949, art. 7425b–48; Vt.Stat., 1947 Rev., § 8873; Va.Code Ann., 1950, §§ 6–569 to 6–576; Wash.Rev.Stat.Ann., Supp. 1943, §§ 3388 to 3388–6; W.Va.Code Ann., 1949, § 4219(1) et seq.; Wisc.Stat.1947, § 223.055.

minimum requirements of N. Y. Banking Law § 100–c(12): "After filing such petition [for judicial settlement of its account] the petitioner shall cause to be issued by the court in which the petition is filed and shall publish not less than once in each week for four successive weeks in a newspaper to be designated by the court a notice or citation addressed generally without naming them to all parties interested in such common trust fund and in such estates, trusts or funds mentioned in the petition, all of which may be described in the notice or citation only in the manner set forth in said petition and without setting forth the residence of any such decedent or donor of any such estate, trust or fund." Thus the only notice required, and the only one given, was by newspaper publication setting forth merely the name and address of the trust company, the name and the date of establishment of the common trust fund, and a list of all participating estates, trusts or funds.

At the time the first investment in the common fund was made on behalf of each participating estate, however, the trust company, pursuant to the requirements of § 100–c(9), had notified by mail each person of full age and sound mind whose name and address was then known to it and who was "entitled to share in the income therefrom . . . [or] . . . who would be entitled to share in the principal if the event upon which such estate, trust or fund will become distributable should have occurred at the time of sending such notice." Included in the notice was a copy of those provisions of the Act relating to the sending of the notice itself and to the judicial settlement of common trust fund accounts.

Upon the filing of the petition for the settlement of accounts, appellant was, by order of the court pursuant to § 100–c(12), appointed special guardian and attorney for all persons known or unknown not otherwise appearing who had or might thereafter have any interests in the income of the common trust fund; and appellee Vaughan was appointed to represent those similarly interested in the principal. There were no other appearances on behalf of any one interested in either interest or principal.

Appellant appeared specially, objecting that notice and the statutory provisions for notice to beneficiaries were inadequate to afford due process under the Fourteenth Amendment, and therefore that the court was without jurisdiction to render a final and binding decree. Appellant's objections were entertained and overruled, the Surrogate holding that the notice required and given was sufficient. 75 N.Y.S.2d 397. A final decree accepting the accounts has been entered, affirmed by the Appellate Division of the Supreme Court, In re Central Hanover Bank & Trust Co., 275 App.Div. 769, 88 N.Y.S.2d 907, and by the Court of Appeals of the State of New York, 299 N.Y. 697, 87 N.E.2d 73.

The effect of this decree, as held below, is to settle "all questions respecting the management of the common fund." We understand that every right which beneficiaries would otherwise have against the trust company, either as trustee of the common fund or as trustee of any individual trust, for improper management of the common trust fund during the period covered by the accounting is sealed and wholly terminated by the decree. See Matter of Hoaglund's Estate, 194 Misc. 803, 811–812, 74 N.Y.S.2d 156, 164, affirmed 272 App.Div. 1040, 74 N.Y.S.2d 911, affirmed 297 N.Y. 920, 79 N.E.2d 746; Matter of Bank of New York, 189 Misc. 459, 470, 67 N.Y.S.2d 444, 453; Matter of Security Trust Co. of Rochester, 189 Misc. 748, 760, 70 N.Y.S.2d 260, 271; Matter of Continental Bank & Trust Co., 189 Misc. 795, 797, 67 N.Y.S.2d 806, 807–808.

We are met at the outset with a challenge to the power of the State—the right of its courts to adjudicate at all as against those beneficiaries who reside without the State of New York. It is contended that the proceeding is one *in personam* in that the decree affects neither title to nor possession of any *res*, but adjudges only personal rights of the beneficiaries to surcharge their trustee for negligence or breach of trust. Accordingly, it is said, under the strict doctrine of Pennoyer v. Neff, 95 U.S. 714, 24 L.Ed. 565, the Surrogate is without jurisdiction as to nonresidents upon whom personal service of process was not made.

Distinctions between actions *in rem* and those *in personam* are ancient and originally expressed in procedural terms what seems really to have been a distinction in the substantive law of property under a system quite unlike our own. Buckland and McNair, Roman Law and Common Law, 66; Burdick, Principles of Roman Law and Their Relation to Modern Law, 298. The legal recognition and rise in economic importance of incorporeal or intangible forms of property have upset the ancient simplicity of property law and the clarity of its distinctions, while new forms of proceedings have confused the old procedural classification. American courts have sometimes classed certain actions as *in rem* because personal service of process was not required, and at other times have held personal service of process not required because the action was *in rem*. See cases collected in Freeman on Judgments, §§ 1517 et seq. (5th ed.).

Judicial proceedings to settle fiduciary accounts have been sometimes termed *in rem*, or more indefinitely *quasi in rem*, or more vaguely still, "in the nature of a proceeding *in rem*." It is not readily apparent how the courts of New York did or would classify the present proceeding, which has some characteristics and is wanting in some features of proceedings both *in rem* and *in personam*. But in any event we think that the requirements of the Fourteenth Amendment to the Federal Constitution do not depend upon a classification for which the standards are so elusive and confused generally and which, being primarily for state courts to define, may and do vary from state to state. Without disparaging the usefulness of distinctions between actions *in rem* and those *in personam* in many branches of law, or on other issues, or the reasoning which underlies them, we do not rest the power of the State to resort to constructive service in this proceeding upon how its courts or this Court may regard this historic antithesis. It is sufficient to observe that, whatever the technical definition of its chosen procedure, the interest of each state in providing means to close trusts that exist by the grace of its laws and are administered under the supervision of its courts is so insistent and rooted in custom as to establish beyond doubt the right of its courts to determine the interests of all claimants, resident or nonresident, provided its procedure accords full opportunity to appear and be heard.

Quite different from the question of a state's power to discharge trustees is that of the opportunity it must give beneficiaries to contest. Many controversies have raged about the cryptic and abstract words of the Due Process Clause but there can be no doubt that at a minimum they require that deprivation of life, liberty or property by adjudication be preceded by notice and opportunity for hearing appropriate to the nature of the case.

In two ways this proceeding does or may deprive beneficiaries of property. It may cut off their rights to have the trustee answer for negligent or illegal impairments of their interests. Also, their interests are presumably subject to diminution in the proceeding by allowance of fees and expenses to one who, in their names but without their knowledge, may conduct a fruitless or uncompensatory contest. Certainly the proceeding is one in which they may be deprived of property rights and hence notice and hearing must measure up to the standards of due process.

Personal service of written notice within the jurisdiction is the classic form of notice always adequate in any type of proceeding. But the vital interest of the State in bringing any issues as to its fiduciaries to a final settlement can be served only if interests or claims of individuals who are outside of the State can somehow be determined. A construction of the Due Process Clause which would place impossible or impractical obstacles in the way could not be justified.

Against this interest of the State we must balance the individual interest sought to be protected by the Fourteenth Amendment. This is defined by our holding that "The fundamental requisite of due process of law is the opportunity to be heard." Grannis v. Ordean, 234 U.S. 385, 394, 34 S.Ct. 779, 783, 58 L.Ed. 1363. This right to be heard has little reality or worth unless one is informed that the matter is pending and can choose for himself whether to appear or default, acquiesce or contest.

The Court has not committed itself to any formula achieving a balance between these interests in a particular proceeding or determining when constructive notice may be utilized or what test it must meet. Personal service has not in all circumstances been regarded as indispensable to the process due to residents, and it has more often been held unnecessary as to nonresidents. We disturb none of the established rules on these subjects. No decision constitutes a controlling or even a very illuminating precedent for the case before us. But a few general principles stand out in the books.

An elementary and fundamental requirement of due process in any proceeding which is to be accorded finality is notice reasonably calculated, under all the circumstances, to apprise interested parties of the pendency of the action and afford them an opportunity to present their objections. Milliken v. Meyer, 311 U.S. 457, 61 S.Ct. 339, 85 L.Ed. 278, 132 A.L.R. 1357; Grannis v. Ordean, 234 U.S. 385, 34 S.Ct. 779, 58 L.Ed. 1363; Priest v. Board of Trustees of Town of Las Vegas, 232 U.S. 604, 34 S.Ct. 443, 58 L.Ed. 751; Roller v. Holly, 176 U.S. 398, 20 S.Ct. 410, 44 L.Ed. 520. The notice must be of such nature as reasonably to convey the required information, Grannis v. Ordean, supra, and it must afford a reasonable time for those interested to make their appearance, Roller v. Holly, supra, and cf. Goodrich v. Ferris, 214 U.S. 71, 29 S.Ct. 580, 53 L.Ed. 914. But if with due regard for the practicalities and peculiarities of the case these conditions are reasonably met the constitutional requirements are satisfied. "The criterion is not the possibility of conceivable injury, but the just and reasonable character of the requirements, having reference to the subject with which the statute deals." American Land Co. v. Zeiss, 219 U.S. 47, 67, 31 S.Ct. 200, 207, 55 L.Ed. 82, and see Blinn v. Nelson, 222 U.S. 1, 7, 32 S.Ct. 1, 2, 56 L.Ed. 65, Ann.Cas.1913B, 555.

But when notice is a person's due, process which is a mere gesture is not due process. The means employed must be such as one desirous of actually informing the absentee might reasonably adopt to accomplish it. The reasonableness and hence the constitutional validity of any chosen method may be defended on the ground that it is in itself reasonably certain to inform those affected, compare Hess v. Pawloski, 274 U.S. 352, 47 S.Ct. 632, 71 L.Ed. 1091, with Wuchter v. Pizzutti, 276 U.S. 13, 48 S.Ct. 259, 72 L.Ed. 446, 57 A.L.R. 1230, or, where conditions do not reasonably permit such notice, that the form chosen is not substantially less likely to bring home notice than other of the feasible and customary substitutes.

It would be idle to pretend that publication alone as prescribed here, is a reliable means of acquainting interested parties of the fact that their rights are before the courts. It is not an accident that the greater number of cases reaching this Court on the question of adequacy of notice have been concerned with actions founded on process constructively served through local newspapers. Chance alone brings to the attention of even a local resident an advertisement in small type inserted in the back pages of a newspaper, and if he makes his home outside the area of the newspaper's normal circulation the odds that the information will never reach him are large indeed. The chance of actual notice is further reduced when as here the notice required does not even name those whose attention it is supposed to attract, and does not inform acquaintances who might call it to attention. In weighing its sufficiency on the basis of equivalence with actual notice we are unable to regard this as more than a feint.

Nor is publication here reinforced by steps likely to attract the parties' attention to the proceeding. It is true that publication traditionally has been acceptable as notification supplemental to other action which in itself may reasonably be expected to convey a warning. The ways of an owner with tangible property are such that he usually arranges means to learn of any direct attack upon his possessory or proprietary rights. Hence, libel of a ship, attachment of a chattel or entry upon real estate in the name of law may reasonably be expected to come promptly to the owner's attention. When the state within which the owner has located such property seizes it for some reason, publication or posting affords an additional measure of notification. A state may indulge the assumption that one who has left tangible property in the state either has abandoned it, in which case proceedings against it deprive him of nothing, cf. Anderson National Bank v. Luckett, 321 U.S. 233, 64 S.Ct. 599, 88 L.Ed. 692, 151 A.L.R. 824; Security Savings Bank v. California, 263 U.S. 282, 44 S.Ct. 108, 68 L.Ed. 301, 31 A.L.R. 391, or that he has left some caretaker under a duty to let him know that it is being jeopardized. Ballard v. Hunter, 204 U.S. 241, 27 S.Ct. 261, 51 L.Ed. 461; Huling v. Kaw Valley Ry. & Imp. Co., 130 U.S. 559, 9 S.Ct. 603, 32 L.Ed. 1045. As phrased long ago by Chief Justice Marshall in The Mary, 9 Cranch 126, 144, 3 L.Ed. 678, "It is the part of common prudence for all those who have any interest in [a thing], to guard that interest by persons who are in a situation to protect it."

In the case before us there is, of course, no abandonment. On the other hand these beneficiaries do have a resident fiduciary as caretaker of their interest in this property. But it is their caretaker who in the accounting becomes their adversary. Their trustee is released from giving notice of jeopardy, and no one else is expected to do so. Not even the special guardian is required or apparently expected to communicate with his ward and client, and, of course, if such a duty were merely transferred from the trustee to the guardian, economy would not be served and more likely the cost would be increased.

This Court has not hesitated to approve of resort to publication as a customary substitute in another class of cases where it is not reasonably possible or practicable to give more adequate warning. Thus it has been recognized that, in the case of persons missing or unknown, employment of an indirect and even a probably futile means of notification is all that the situation permits and creates no constitutional bar to a final decree foreclosing their rights. Cunnius v. Reading School District, 198 U.S. 458, 25 S.Ct. 721, 49 L.Ed. 1125, 3 Ann.Cas. 1121; Blinn v. Nelson, 222 U.S. 1, 32 S.Ct. 1, 56 L.Ed. 65, Ann.Cas.1913B, 555; and see Jacob v. Roberts, 223 U.S. 261, 32 S.Ct. 303, 56 L.Ed. 429.

Those beneficiaries represented by appellant whose interests or whereabouts could not with due diligence be ascertained come clearly within this category. As to them the statutory notice is sufficient. However great the odds that publication will never reach the eyes of such unknown parties, it is not in the typical case much more likely to fail than any of the choices open to legislators endeavoring to prescribe the best notice practicable.

Nor do we consider it unreasonable for the State to dispense with more certain notice to those beneficiaries whose interests are either conjectural or future or, although they could be discovered upon investigation, do not in due course of business come to knowledge of the common trustee. Whatever searches might be required in another situation under ordinary standards of diligence, in view of the character of the proceedings and the nature of the interests here involved we think them unnecessary. We recognize the practical difficulties and costs that would be attendant on frequent investigations into the status of great numbers of beneficiaries, many of whose interests in the common fund are so remote as to be ephemeral; and we have no doubt that such impracticable and extended searches are not required in the name of due process. The expense of keeping informed from day to day of substitutions among even current income beneficiaries and presumptive remaindermen, to say nothing of the far greater number of contingent beneficiaries, would impose a severe burden on the plan, and would likely dissipate its advantages. These are practical matters in which we should be reluctant to disturb the judgment of the state authorities.

Accordingly we overrule appellant's constitutional objections to published notice insofar as they are urged on behalf of any beneficiaries whose interests or addresses are unknown to the trustee.

As to known present beneficiaries of known place of residence, however, notice by publication stands on a different footing. Exceptions in the name of necessity do not sweep away the rule that within the limits of practicability notice must be such as is reasonably calculated to reach interested parties. Where the names and post office addresses of those affected by a proceeding are at hand, the reasons disappear for resort to means less likely than the mails to apprise them of its pendency.

The trustee has on its books the names and addresses of the income beneficiaries represented by appellant, and we find no tenable ground for dispensing with a serious effort to inform them personally of the accounting, at least by ordinary mail to the record addresses. Cf. *Wuchter v. Pizzutti,* supra. Certainly sending them a copy of the statute months and perhaps years in advance does not answer this purpose. The trustee periodically remits their income to them, and we think that they might reasonably expect that with or apart from their remittances word might come to them personally that steps were being taken affecting their interests.

We need not weigh contentions that a requirement of personal service of citation on even the large number of known resident or nonresident beneficiaries would, by reasons of delay if not of expense, seriously interfere with the proper administration of the fund. Of course personal service even without the jurisdiction of the issuing authority serves the end of actual and personal notice, whatever power of compulsion it might lack. However, no such service is required under the circumstances. This type of trust presupposes a large number of small interests. The individual interest does not stand alone but is identical with that of a class. The rights of each in the integrity of the fund and the fidelity of the trustee are shared by many other beneficiaries. Therefore notice reasonably certain to reach most of those interested in objecting is likely to safeguard the interests of all, since any objections sustained would inure to the benefit of all. We think that under such circumstances reasonable risks that notice might not actually reach every beneficiary are justifiable. "Now and then an extraordinary case may turn up, but constitutional law, like other mortal contrivances, has to take some chances, and in the great majority of instances, no doubt, justice will be done." Blinn v. Nelson, supra, 222 U.S. at page 7, 32 S.Ct. at page 2, 56 L.Ed. 65, Ann.Cas. 1913B, 555.

pers. svc not nec,

The statutory notice to known beneficiaries is inadequate, not because in fact it fails to reach everyone, but because under the circumstances it is not reasonably calculated to reach those who could easily be informed by other means at hand. However it may have been in former times, the mails today are recognized as an efficient and inexpensive means of communication. Moreover, the fact that the trust company has been able to give mailed notice to known beneficiaries at the time the common trust fund was established is persuasive that postal notification at the time of accounting would not seriously burden the plan.

R

In some situations the law requires greater precautions in its proceedings than the business world accepts for its own purposes. In few, if any, will it be satisfied with less. Certainly it is instructive, in determining the reasonableness of the impersonal broadcast notification here used, to ask whether it would satisfy a prudent man of business, counting his pennies but finding it in his interest to convey information to many persons whose names and addresses are in his files. We are not satisfied that it would. Publication may theoretically be available for all the world to see, but it is too much in our day to suppose that each or any individual beneficiary does or could examine all that is published to see if something may be tucked away in it that affects his property interests. We have before indicated in reference to notice by publication that, "Great caution should be used not to let fiction deny the fair play that can be secured only by a pretty close adhesion to fact." McDonald v. Mabee, 243 U.S. 90, 91, 37 S.Ct. 343, 61 L.Ed. 608, L.R.A.1917F, 458.

why pub. generally not o.k.

We hold the notice of judicial settlement of accounts required by the New York Banking Law § 100–c(12) is incompatible with the requirements of the Fourteenth Amendment as a basis for adjudication depriving known persons whose whereabouts are also known of substantial property rights. Accordingly the judgment is reversed and the

H

cause remanded for further proceedings not inconsistent with this opinion.

Reversed.

MR. JUSTICE DOUGLAS took no part in the consideration or decision of this case.

MR. JUSTICE BURTON, dissenting.

These common trusts are available only when the instruments creating the participating trusts permit participation in the common fund. Whether or not further notice to beneficiaries should supplement the notice and representation here provided is properly within the discretion of the State. The Federal Constitution does not require it here.

NOTE ON *MULLANE* AND *INTERNATIONAL SHOE*

1. Notice

The significance of *Mullane* so far as notice in *in rem* proceedings took some time to be appreciated. In several subsequent cases, e.g., Walker v. City of Hutchinson, 352 U.S. 112, 77 S.Ct. 200, 1 L.Ed.2d 178 (1956); Schroeder v. City of New York, 371 U.S. 208, 83 S.Ct. 279, 9 L.Ed.2d 255 (1962); Bank of Marin v. England, 385 U.S. 99, 87 S.Ct. 274, 17 L.Ed.2d 197 (1966), the Court reiterated the *Mullane* notice requirement. Compare Karl Senner, Inc. v. M/V Acadian Valor, 485 F.Supp. 287 (E.D.La.1980), holding invalid Rule C of the Federal Admiralty Rules, which permits initiation of an admiralty *in rem* proceeding by seizure of a vessel without notice. Compare Restatement Second of Judgments § 2, Comment a: "Under the Due Process Clause of the Constitution, the requirement of adequate notice applies to all types of proceedings, whether in personam, in rem, or quasi in rem," with id., Comment g:

> "The rule in Mullane v. Central Hanover Bank & Trust Co. recognizes that persons can be bound even if they cannot be found through reasonably diligent search. Assuming that such a search has been made, the fiction is indulged that publication notifies the absentee. 339 U.S. at 317. The underlying rationale, however, is that the interests of a person so remotely situated may justly be sacrificed to those of persons having need to go forward in the practical affairs that the absentee could otherwise subsequently disrupt. It is the search for the absentee that gives expression to the concern for protection of his opportunity to be heard."

2. "Minimum Contacts"

The problem after *International Shoe* has been what connection between a state and a transaction or the people involved in it is sufficient to meet the test of fairness.

Perkins v. Benguet Consol. Mining Co., 342 U.S. 437, 72 S.Ct. 413, 96 L.Ed. 485 (1952): An action was brought in Ohio against a foreign corporation having an office in that state on a cause of action that arose *outside* Ohio. The court found that the corporation's contacts with Ohio were sufficiently substantial— indeed the Ohio office appeared to be its managerial headquarters—as to justify jurisdiction over it without regard to the connection of the cause of action to the forum state. Decision was placed not on the "presence" of the corporation, but on the "minimum contacts" approach of *International Shoe,* the opinion suggesting that while greater "contacts" were required to hold a foreign corporation on a non-forum cause of action, the question was one of degree and not one of "kind" as would be implied by the "presence" formula.

McGee v. International Life Ins. Co., 355 U.S. 220, 78 S.Ct. 199, 2 L.Ed.2d 223 (1957): *X,* a resident of California, purchased a policy of insurance on his life from defendant, an out-of-state insurance company having no office or employees in California and conducting its California business solely by mail. After the mail delivery of the policy to him in California, *X* regularly received premium notices from defendant and made regular responsive remittances. Apparently defendant had never solicited or done any insurance business in California apart from the policy involved in this case. Upon *X*'s death, his named beneficiary sued in a California court to collect the proceeds, serving process on the California Insurance Commissioner and sending a copy thereof by registered mail to defendant's Texas office, pursuant to Calif.Ins.Code §§ 1610–1620, providing that solicitation of insurance "constitutes" the appointment of the commissioner as agent for service of process in suits on insurance so solicited. Default judgment was entered for plaintiff. Plaintiff thereafter sued on the judgment in a Texas court, which refused to recognize the judgment, believing it to have been rendered without jurisdiction. The Supreme Court reversed. In referring to the service made under the California statute, the Court, significantly it would seem, said, 355 U.S. at 221: "[Defendant] was not served with process in California but by registered mail at its principal place of business in Texas." It then went on to say, 355 U.S. at 222–24: "Today many commercial transactions touch two or more States and may involve parties separated by the full continent. * * * It cannot be denied that California has a manifest interest in providing effective means of redress for its residents when their insurers refuse to pay claims. These residents would be at a severe disadvantage if they were forced to follow the insurance company to a distant State in order to hold it legally accountable. When claims were small or moderate individual claimants frequently could not afford the cost of bringing an action in a foreign forum—thus in effect making the company judgment proof. * * * Of course there may be inconvenience to the insurer * * * but certainly nothing which amounts to a denial of due process."

Hanson v. Denckla, 357 U.S. 235, 78 S.Ct. 1228, 2 L.Ed.2d 1283 (1958): A woman created a trust in Delaware and later moved to Florida, where she executed a will and exercised a power of appointment that had been reserved in the Delaware trust. After she died, certain of her heirs who were legatees under the will sued in Florida to have the trust and appointment declared invalid and to have the trust funds flow to them residually under the will. Other heirs, beneficiaries under the trust, then sued in Delaware to have the trust and power of appointment declared valid. The Florida court determined that it had jurisdiction over the Delaware trustee (a bank) and ruled that the trust and appointment were invalid under Florida law. The Delaware court ruled that the trust and appointment were valid and refused to recognize the Florida judgment, holding that Florida had no jurisdiction over the Delaware trustee. The Supreme Court upheld the Delaware judgment and reversed the Florida judgment. It held that the Florida court lacked *in rem* jurisdiction over the trust assets because the assets apparently were located in Delaware, and lacked *in personam* jurisdiction over the Delaware bank because the bank had not "purposely availed" itself of the privilege of conducting activities in Florida.

The Court distinguished *McGee,* stating that the trend toward expanding personal jurisdiction over nonresidents referred to there did not herald "the eventual demise of all restrictions on the personal jurisdiction of state courts." The Court continued: "Those restrictions are more than a guarantee of immunity from inconvenient or distant litigation. They are a consequence of territorial limitations on the power of the respective States." Is this emphasis on sovereignty as opposed to convenience consistent with *International Shoe* and cases following it? Keep in mind the *Hanson* Court's comments as you read Shaffer v. Heitner, reprinted just below, and the cases reprinted in the next section. Despite what the Court held, it seems difficult to distinguish the contacts of the Delaware trustee with Florida, involved in *Hanson,* from the Texas insurer's contacts with California, involved in *McGee.* Furthermore, there seems to be no basis for the Court to have "assumed" the trust assets were located in Delaware. It seems equally plausible to say that the decedent's interest in the trust constituted property in Florida because the decedent was domiciled there.

Many commentators and some courts thought Hanson v. Denckla represented a retreat from the "minimum contacts" principle. Others thought it was an application of that principle. And still others thought it was an aberration explained by its peculiar facts. The Restatement Second of Conflict of Laws, § 27, did not regard the case as undercutting its formulation of the rule of territorial jurisdiction as it then stood:

"(1) A state has power to exercise judicial jurisdiction over an individual on one or more of the following bases:

(a) presence

(b) domicil

(c) residence

(d) nationality or citizenship

(e) consent

(f) appearance in an action

(g) doing business in the state

(h) an act done in the state

(i) causing an effect in the state by an act done elsewhere

(j) ownership, use or possession of a thing in the state

(k) other relationships to the state which make the exercise of judicial jurisdiction reasonable."

A substantially identical formulation is stated regarding corporations. Id., §§ 41 et seq. See also Restatement Second of Judgments § 5. Many of these bases for asserting jurisdiction are considered further in the sections which follow.

———

@IR#2

SHAFFER v. HEITNER

Supreme Court of the United States, 1977.
433 U.S. 186, 97 S.Ct. 2569, 53 L.Ed.2d 683.*

MR. JUSTICE MARSHALL delivered the opinion of the Court.

I

The controversy in this case concerns the constitutionality of a Delaware statute that allows a court of that State to take jurisdiction of a lawsuit by sequestering any property of the defendant that happens to be located in Delaware. Appellants contend that the sequestration statute as applied in this case violates the Due Process Clause of the Fourteenth Amendment both because it permits the state courts to exercise jurisdiction despite the absence of sufficient contacts among the defendants, the litigation, and the State of Delaware and because it authorizes the deprivation of defendants' property without providing adequate procedural safeguards. We find it necessary to consider only the first of these contentions.

I

Appellee Heitner, a nonresident of Delaware, is the owner of one share of stock in the Greyhound Corp., a business incorporated under the laws of Delaware with its principal place of business in Phoenix, Ariz. On May 22, 1974, he filed a shareholder's derivative suit in the Court of Chancery for New Castle County, Del., in which he named as defendants Greyhound, its wholly owned subsidiary Greyhound Lines, Inc.,[1] and 28 present or former officers or directors of one or both of the corporations. In essence, Heitner alleged that the individual defendants had violated their duties to Greyhound by causing it and its subsidiary to engage in actions that resulted in the corporations being held liable for substantial damages in a private antitrust suit[2] and a large fine in a criminal contempt action.[3] The activities which led to these penalties took place in Oregon.

Simultaneously with his complaint, Heitner filed a motion for an order of sequestration of the Delaware property of the individual defendants pursuant to Del.Code Ann., Tit. 10, § 366 (1975).[4] This

---

* Some of the Court's footnotes are omitted.

1. Greyhound Lines, Inc., is incorporated in California and has its principal place of business in Phoenix, Ariz.

2. A judgment of $13,146,090 plus attorneys fees was entered against Greyhound in Mt. Hood Stages, Inc. v. Greyhound Corp., 1972–3 Trade Cas. ¶ 74,824, aff'd 555 F.2d 687 (CA9 1977). App. 10.

3. See United States v. Greyhound Corp., 363 F.Supp. 525 (ND Ill.1973), 370 F.Supp. 881 (ND Ill.), aff'd 508 F.2d 529 (CA7 1974). Greyhound was fined $100,000 and Greyhound Lines $500,000.

4. § 366 provides:

"(a) If it appears in any complaint filed in the Court of Chancery that the defendant or any one or more of the defendants is a nonresident of the State, the Court may make an order directing such nonresident defendant or defendants to appear by a day certain to be designated. Such order shall be served on such nonresident defendant or defendants by mail or otherwise, if practicable, and shall be published in such manner as the Court directs, not less than once a week for 3 consecutive weeks. The Court may compel the appearance of the defen-

motion was accompanied by a supporting affidavit of counsel which stated that the individual defendants were nonresidents of Delaware. The affidavit identified the property to be sequestered as

"common stock, 3% Second Cumulative Preferred Stock and stock unit credits of the Defendant Greyhound Corporation, a Delaware corporation, as well as all options and all warrants to purchase said stock issued to said individual Defendants and all contractural [sic] obligations, all rights, debts or credits due or accrued to or for the benefit of any of the said Defendants under any type of written agreement, contract or other legal instrument of any kind whatever between any of the individual Defendants and said corporation."

The requested sequestration order was signed the day the motion was filed. Pursuant to that order, the sequestrator "seized" approximately 82,000 shares of Greyhound common stock belonging to 19 of the defendants, and options belonging to another two defendants. These seizures were accomplished by placing "stop transfer" orders or their equivalents on the books of the Greyhound Corporation. So far as the record shows, none of the certificates representing the seized property was physically present in Delaware. The stock was considered to be in Delaware, and so subject to seizure, by virtue of Del.Code Ann., Tit. 8, § 169 (1975), which makes Delaware the situs of ownership of all stock in Delaware corporations.

All 28 defendants were notified of the initiation of the suit by certified mail directed to their last known addresses and by publication in a New Castle County newspaper. The 21 defendants whose property was seized (hereafter referred to as appellants) responded by entering a special appearance for the purpose of moving to quash service of process and to vacate the sequestration order. They contended that the *ex parte* sequestration procedure did not accord them due process of law and that the property seized was not capable of attachment in Delaware. In addition, appellants asserted that under the rule of International Shoe Co. v. Washington, 326 U.S. 310, 66 S.Ct. 154, 90 L.Ed. 95 (1945), they did not have sufficient contacts with Delaware to sustain the jurisdiction of that State's courts.

dant by the seizure of all or any part of his property, which property may be sold under the order of the Court to pay the demand of the plaintiff, if the defendant does not appear, or otherwise defaults. Any defendant whose property shall have been so seized and who shall have entered a general appearance in the cause may, upon notice to the plaintiff, petition the Court for an order releasing such property or any part thereof from the seizure. The Court shall release such property unless the plaintiff shall satisfy the Court that because of other circumstances there is a reasonable possibility that such release may render it substantially less likely that plaintiff will obtain satisfaction of any judgment secured. If such petition shall not be granted, or if no such petition shall be filed, such property shall remain subject to seizure and may be sold to satisfy any judgment entered in the cause. The Court may at any time release such property or any part thereof upon the giving of sufficient security."

* * *

The Court of Chancery rejected these arguments in a letter opinion which emphasized the purpose of the Delaware sequestration procedure:

"The primary purpose of 'sequestration' as authorized by 10 Del.C. § 366 is not to secure possession of property pending a trial between resident debtors and creditors on the issue of who has the right to retain it. On the contrary, as here employed, 'sequestration' is a process used to compel the personal appearance of a nonresident defendant to answer and defend a suit brought against him in a court of equity. Sands v. Lefcourt Realty Corp., Del.Supr., 35 Del.Ch. 340, 117 A.2d 365 (1955). It is accomplished by the appointment of a sequestrator by this Court to seize and hold property of the nonresident located in this State subject to further Court order. If the defendant enters a general appearance, the sequestered property is routinely released, unless the plaintiff makes special application to continue its seizure, in which event the plaintiff has the burden of proof and persuasion." App. 75–76.

This limitation on the purpose and length of time for which sequestered property is held, the court concluded, rendered inapplicable the due process requirements enunciated in Sniadach v. Family Finance Corp., 395 U.S. 337, 89 S.Ct. 1820, 23 L.Ed.2d 349 (1969); Fuentes v. Shevin, 407 U.S. 67, 92 S.Ct. 1983, 32 L.Ed.2d 556 (1972); and Mitchell v. W. T. Grant Co., 416 U.S. 600, 94 S.Ct. 1895, 40 L.Ed.2d 406 (1974). App. 75–76, 80, 83–85. The court also found no state law or federal constitutional barrier to the sequestrator's reliance on Del.Code Ann., Tit. 8, § 169 (1975). App. 76–79. Finally, the court held that the statutory Delaware situs of the stock provided a sufficient basis for the exercise of *quasi in rem* jurisdiction by a Delaware court. App. 85–87.

On appeal, the Delaware Supreme Court affirmed the judgment of the Court of Chancery. Greyhound Corp. v. Heitner, 361 A.2d 225 (1976). Most of the Supreme Court's opinion was devoted to rejecting appellants' contention that the sequestration procedure is inconsistent with the due process analysis developed in the *Sniadach* line of cases. The court based its rejection of that argument in part on its agreement with the Court of Chancery that the purpose of the sequestration procedure is to compel the appearance of the defendant, a purpose not involved in the *Sniadach* cases. The court also relied on what it considered the ancient origins of the sequestration procedure and approval of that procedure in the opinions of this Court,[10] Delaware's

---

10. The court relied, 361 A.2d at 228, 230–231, on our decision in Ownbey v. Morgan, 256 U.S. 94, 41 S.Ct. 433, 65 L.Ed. 837 (1921), and references to that decision in North Georgia Finishing, Inc. v. Di-Chem, Inc., 419 U.S. 601, 610, 95 S.Ct. 719, 724, 42 L.Ed.2d 751 (1975) (Powell, J., concurring); Calero-Toledo v. Pearson Yacht Leasing Co., 416 U.S. 663, 679 n. 14, 94 S.Ct. 2080, 2090, 40 L.Ed.2d 452 (1974); Mitchell v. W. T. Grant Co., 416 U.S. 600, 613, 94 S.Ct. 1895, 1903, 40 L.Ed.2d 406 (1974); Fuentes v. Shevin, 407 U.S. 67, 91 n. 23, 92 S.Ct. 1983, 32 L.Ed.2d 556 (1972); Sniadach v. Family Finance Corp., 395 U.S. 337, 339, 89 S.Ct. 1820, 1821, 23 L.Ed.2d 349 (1969). The only question before the Court in *Ownbey* was the constitutionality of a requirement that a defendant whose property has been attached file a bond before entering an appearance. We do not read the recent references to *Ownbey* as neces-

interest in asserting jurisdiction to adjudicate claims of mismanagement of a Delaware corporation, and the safeguards for defendants that it found in the Delaware statute. 361 A.2d, at 230–236.

Appellants' claim that the Delaware courts did not have jurisdiction to adjudicate this action received much more cursory treatment. The court's analysis of the jurisdictional issue is contained in two paragraphs:

Appellate decision

"There are significant constitutional questions at issue here but we say at once that we do not deem the rule of *International Shoe* to be one of them. . . . The reason of course, is that jurisdiction under § 366 remains . . . *quasi in rem* founded on the presence of capital stock here, not on prior contact by defendants with this forum. Under 8 Del.C. § 169 the 'situs of the ownership of the capital stock of all corporations existing under the laws of this State . . . [is] in this State,' and that provides the initial basis for jurisdiction. Delaware may constitutionally establish situs of such shares here, . . . it has done so and the presence thereof provides the foundation for § 366 in this case. . . . On this issue we agree with the analysis made and the conclusion reached by Judge Stapleton in U.S. Industries, Inc. v. Gregg, D.Del., 348 F.Supp. 1004 (1972).[11]

"We hold that seizure of the Greyhound shares is not invalid because plaintiff has failed to meet the prior contacts tests of *International Shoe.*" Id., at 229.

* * * We reverse.

II

The Delaware courts rejected appellants' jurisdictional challenge by noting that this suit was brought as a *quasi in rem* proceeding. Since *quasi in rem* jurisdiction is traditionally based on attachment or seizure of property present in the jurisdiction, not on contacts between the defendant and the State, the courts considered appellants' claimed lack of contacts with Delaware to be unimportant. This categorical analysis assumes the continued soundness of the conceptual structure founded on the century-old case of Pennoyer v. Neff, 95 U.S. 714, 24 L.Ed. 565 (1877).

sarily suggesting that *Ownbey* is consistent with more recent decisions interpreting the Due Process Clause.

Sequestration is the equity counterpart of the process of foreign attachment in suits at law considered in *Ownbey*. Delaware's sequestration statute was modeled after its attachment statute. See Sands v. Lefcourt Realty Corp., 35 Del.Ch. 340, 344–345, 117 A.2d 365, 367 (Sup.Ct.1955); Folk & Moyer, Sequestration in Delaware: A

Constitutional Analysis, 73 Colum.L.Rev. 749, 751–754 (1973).

11. The District Court judgment in *U.S. Industries* was reversed by the Court of Appeals for the Third Circuit, 540 F.2d 142 (1976), cert. pending, No. 76–359. The Court of Appeals characterized the passage from the Delaware Supreme Court's opinion quoted in text as "cryptic conclusions." Id., at 149.

Pennoyer was an ejectment action brought in federal court under the diversity jurisdiction. Pennoyer, the defendant in that action, held the land under a deed purchased in a sheriff's sale conducted to realize on a judgment for attorney's fees obtained against Neff in a previous action by one Mitchell. At the time of Mitchell's suit in an Oregon State court, Neff was a nonresident of Oregon. An Oregon statute allowed service by publication on nonresidents who had property in the State,[13] and Mitchell had used that procedure to bring Neff before the Court. The United States Circuit Court for the District of Oregon, in which Neff brought his ejectment action, refused to recognize the validity of the judgment against Neff in Mitchell's suit, and accordingly awarded the land to Neff. This Court affirmed.

Mr. Justice Field's opinion for the Court focused on the territorial limits of the States' judicial powers. Although recognizing that the States are not truly independent sovereigns, Mr. Justice Field found that their jurisdiction was defined by the "principles of public law" that regulate the relationships among independent nations. The first of those principles was "that every State possesses exclusive jurisdiction and sovereignty over persons and property within its territory." The second was "that no State can exercise direct jurisdiction and authority over persons or property without its territory." Id., at 722. Thus, "in virtue of the State's jurisdiction over the property of the non-resident situated within its limits," the state courts "can inquire into that non-resident's obligations to its own citizens . . . to the extent necessary to control the disposition of the property." Id., at 723. The Court recognized that if the conclusions of that inquiry were adverse to the non-resident property owner, his interest in the property would be affected. Ibid. Similarly, if the defendant consented to the jurisdiction of the state courts or was personally served within the State, a judgment could affect his interest in property outside the State. But any attempt "directly" to assert extraterritorial jurisdiction over persons or property would offend sister States and exceed the inherent limits of the State's power. A judgment resulting from such an attempt, Mr. Justice Field concluded, was not only unenforceable in other States,[15] but was also void in the rendering State because it had been obtained in violation of the Due Process Clause of the Fourteenth Amendment. Id., at 732–733. See also, e.g., Freeman v. Alderson, 119 U.S. 185, 187–188, 7 S.Ct. 165, 166–167, 30 L.Ed. 372 (1886).

This analysis led to the conclusion that Mitchell's judgment against Neff could not be validly based on the State's power over persons within

---

13. The statute also required that a copy of the summons and complaint be mailed to the defendant if his place of residence was known to the plaintiff or could be determined with reasonable diligence. 95 U.S., at 718. Mitchell had averred that he did not know and could not determine Neff's address, so that the publication was the only "notice" given. 95 U.S., at 717.

15. The doctrine that one State does not have to recognize the judgment of another State's courts if the latter did not have jurisdiction was firmly established at the time of *Pennoyer*. See e.g., D'Arcy v. Ketchum, 11 How. 165, 13 L.Ed. 648 (1851); Boswell's Lessee v. Otis, 9 How. 336, 13 L.Ed. 164 (1850); Kibbe v. Kibbe, 1 Kirby 119 (Conn.Super.1786).

its borders, because Neff had not been personally served in Oregon, nor had he consensually appeared before the Oregon court. The Court reasoned that even if Neff had received personal notice of the action, service of process outside the State would have been ineffectual since the State's power was limited by its territorial boundaries. Moreover, the Court held, the action could not be sustained on the basis of the State's power over property within its borders because that property had not been brought before the court by attachment or any other procedure prior to judgment.[16] Since the judgment which authorized the sheriff's sale was therefore invalid, the sale transferred no title. Neff regained his land.

From our perspective, the importance of *Pennoyer* is not its result, but the fact that its principles and corollaries derived from them became the basic elements of the constitutional doctrine governing state court jurisdiction. See, e.g., Hazard, A General Theory of State-Court Jurisdiction, 1965 Sup.Ct.Rev. 241 (hereafter Hazard). As we have noted, under *Pennoyer* state authority to adjudicate was based on the jurisdiction's power over either persons or property. This fundamental concept is embodied in the very vocabulary which we use to describe judgments. If a court's jurisdiction is based on its authority over the defendant's person, the action and judgment are denominated "in personam" and can impose a personal obligation on the defendant in favor of the plaintiff. If jurisdiction is based on the court's power over property within its territory, the action is called "in rem" or "quasi in rem." The effect of a judgment in such a case is limited to the property that supports jurisdiction and does not impose a personal liability on the property owner, since he is not before the court.[17] In *Pennoyer's* terms, the owner is affected only "indirectly" by an *in rem* judgment adverse to his interest in the property subject to the court's disposition.

By concluding that "[t]he authority of every tribunal is necessarily restricted by the territorial limits of the State in which it is established," 95 U.S., at 720, *Pennoyer* sharply limited the availability of *in*

---

16. Attachment was considered essential to the state court's jurisdiction for two reasons. First, attachment combined with substituted service would provide greater assurance that the defendant would actually receive notice of the action than would publication alone. Second, since the court's jurisdiction depended on the defendant's ownership of property in the State and could be defeated if the defendant disposed of that property, attachment was necessary to assure that the court had jurisdiction when the proceedings began and continued to have jurisdiction when it entered judgment. 95 U.S., at 727–728.

17. "A judgment *in rem* affects the interests of all persons in designated property. A judgment *quasi in rem* affects the interests of particular persons in designated property. The latter is of two types. In one the plaintiff is seeking to secure a preexisting claim in the subject property and to extinguish or establish the nonexistence of similar interests of particular persons. In the other the plaintiff seeks to apply what he concedes to be the property of the defendant to the satisfaction of a claim against him. Restatement, Judgments, 5–9." Hanson v. Denckla, 357 U.S. 235, 246 n. 12, 78 S.Ct. 1228, 1235, 2 L.Ed.2d 1283 (1958).

As did the Court in *Hanson*, we will for convenience generally use the term "in rem" in place of "in rem and quasi in rem."

personam jurisdiction over defendants not resident in the forum State. If a nonresident defendant could not be found in a State, he could not be sued there. On the other hand, since the State in which property was located was considered to have exclusive sovereignty over that property, *in rem* actions could proceed regardless of the owner's location. Indeed, since a State's process could not reach beyond its borders, this Court held after *Pennoyer* that due process did not require any effort to give a property owner personal notice that his property was involved in an *in rem* proceeding. See, e.g., Ballard v. Hunter, 204 U.S. 241, 27 S.Ct. 261, 51 L.Ed. 461 (1907); Arndt v. Griggs, 134 U.S. 316, 10 S.Ct. 557, 33 L.Ed. 918 (1890); Huling v. Kaw Valley R. Co., 130 U.S. 559, 9 S.Ct. 603, 32 L.Ed. 1045 (1889).

The *Pennoyer* rules generally favored nonresident defendants by making them harder to sue. This advantage was reduced, however, by the ability of a resident plaintiff to satisfy a claim against a nonresident defendant by bringing into court any property of the defendant located in the plaintiff's State. See, e.g., Zammit, Quasi-In-Rem Jurisdiction: Outmoded and Unconstitutional?, 49 St. John's L.Rev. 668, 670 (1975). For example, in the well-known case of Harris v. Balk, 198 U.S. 215, 25 S.Ct. 625, 49 L.Ed. 1023 (1905), Epstein, a resident of Maryland, had a claim against Balk, a resident of North Carolina. Harris, another North Carolina resident, owed money to Balk. When Harris happened to visit Maryland, Epstein garnished his debt to Balk. Harris did not contest the debt to Balk and paid it to Epstein's North Carolina attorney. When Balk later sued Harris in North Carolina, this Court held that the Full Faith and Credit Clause, U.S.Const., Art IV, § 1, required that Harris' payment to Epstein be treated as a discharge of his debt to Balk. This Court reasoned that the debt Harris owed Balk was an intangible form of property belonging to Balk, and that the location of that property traveled with the debtor. By obtaining personal jurisdiction over Harris, Epstein had "arrested" his debt to Balk, 198 U.S., at 223, 25 S.Ct., at 627, and brought it into the Maryland court. Under the structure established by *Pennoyer,* Epstein was then entitled to proceed against that debt to vindicate his claim against Balk, even though Balk himself was not subject to the jurisdiction of a Maryland tribunal.[18] See also, e.g., Louisville & N.R. Co. v.

---

18. The Court in *Harris* limited its holding to States in which the principal defendant (Balk) could have sued the garnishee (Harris) if he had obtained personal jurisdiction over the garnishee in that State. 198 U.S., at 222–223, 226, 25 S.Ct., at 626, 627, 628. The Court explained:

"The importance of the fact of the right of the original creditor to sue his debtor in the foreign State, as affecting the right of the creditor of that creditor to sue the debtor or garnishee, lies in the nature of the attachment proceeding. The plaintiff, in such proceeding in the foreign State is able to sue out the attachment and attach the debt due from the garnishee to his (the garnishee's) creditor, because of the fact that the plaintiff is really in such proceeding a representative of the creditor of the garnishee, and therefore if such creditor himself had the right to commence suit to recover the debt in the foreign State his representative has the same right, as representing him, and may garnish or attach the debt, provided the municipal law of the State where the attachment was sued out permits it." Id., at 226, 25 S.Ct., at 628.

Deer, 200 U.S. 176, 26 S.Ct. 207, 50 L.Ed. 426 (1906); Steele v. G.D. Searle & Co., 483 F.2d 339 (CA5 1973), cert. denied 415 U.S. 958, 94 S.Ct. 1486, 39 L.Ed.2d 572 (1974).

Pennoyer itself recognized that its rigid categories, even as blurred by the kind of action typified by *Harris,* could not accommodate some necessary litigation. Accordingly, Mr. Justice Field's opinion carefully noted that cases involving the personal status of the plaintiff, such as divorce actions, could be adjudicated in the plaintiff's home State even though the defendant could not be served within that State. 95 U.S., at 733–735. Similarly, the opinion approved the practice of considering a foreign corporation doing business in a State to have consented to being sued in that State. Id., at 735-736; see Lafayette Ins. Co. v. French, 18 How. 404, 15 L.Ed. 451 (1856). This basis for *in personam* jurisdiction over foreign corporations was later supplemented by the doctrine that a corporation doing business in a State could be deemed "present" in the State, and so subject to service of process under the rule of *Pennoyer.* See, e.g., International Harvester Co. v. Kentucky, 234 U.S. 579, 34 S.Ct. 944, 58 L.Ed. 1479 (1914); Philadelphia & R.R. Co. v. McKibbin, 243 U.S. 264, 37 S.Ct. 280, 61 L.Ed. 710 (1917). See generally Note, Developments in the Law, State-Court Jurisdiction, 73 Harv.L.Rev. 909, 919–923 (1960) (hereinafter Developments).

The advent of automobiles, with the concomitant increase in the incidence of individuals causing injury in States where they were not subject to *in personam* actions under *Pennoyer,* required further moderation of the territorial limits on jurisdictional power. This modification, like the accommodation to the realities of interstate corporate activities, was accomplished by use of a legal fiction that left the conceptual structure established in *Pennoyer* theoretically unaltered. Cf. Olberding v. Illinois Central R. Co., 346 U.S. 338, 340–341, 74 S.Ct. 83, 85–86, 98 L.Ed. 39 (1953). The fiction used was that the out-of-state motorist, who it was assumed could be excluded altogether from the State's highways, had by using those highways appointed a designated state official as his agent to accept process. See Hess v. Pawloski, 274 U.S. 352, 47 S.Ct. 632, 71 L.Ed. 1091 (1927). Since the motorist's "agent" could be personally served within the State, the state courts could obtain *in personam* jurisdiction over the nonresident driver.

The motorists' consent theory was easy to administer since it required only a finding that the out-of-state driver had used the State's roads. By contrast, both the fictions of implied consent to service on the part of a foreign corporation and of corporate presence required a finding that the corporation was "doing business" in the forum State. Defining the criteria for making that finding and deciding whether

The problem with this reasoning is that unless the plaintiff has obtained a judgment establishing his claim against the principal defendant, see, e.g., Baltimore & O.R. Co. v. Hostetter, 240 U.S. 620, 36 S.Ct. 475, 60 L.Ed. 829 (1916), his right to "represent" the principal defendant in an action against the garnishee is at issue. See Beale, The Exercise of Jurisdiction *In Rem* to Compel Payment of a Debt, 27 Harv.L. Rev. 107, 118–120 (1913).

they were met absorbed much judicial energy. See, e.g., International Shoe Co. v. Washington, 326 U.S., at 317–319, 66 S.Ct., at 158–160. While the essentially quantitative tests which emerged from these cases purported simply to identify circumstances under which presence or consent could be attributed to the corporation, it became clear that they were in fact attempting to ascertain "what dealings make it just to subject a foreign corporation to local suit". Hutchinson v. Chase & Gilbert, 45 F.2d 139, 141 (CA2 1930) (L. Hand, J.). In *International Shoe* we acknowledged that fact.

The question in *International Shoe* was whether the corporation was subject to the judicial and taxing jurisdiction of Washington. Mr. Chief Justice Stone's opinion for the Court began its analysis of that question by noting that the historical basis of *in personam* jurisdiction was a court's power over the defendant's person. That power, however, was no longer the central concern;

> "But now that the *capias ad respondendum* [*you take to respond*] has given way to personal service of summons or other form of notice, due process requires only that in order to subject a defendant to a judgment *in personam*, if he be not present within the territory of the forum, he have certain minimum contacts with it such that the maintenance of the suit does not offend 'traditional notions of fair play and substantial justice.' Milliken v. Meyer, 311 U.S. 457, 463, 61 S.Ct. 339, 343, 85 L.Ed. 278." 326 U.S., at 316, 66 S.Ct., at 158.

Thus, the inquiry into the State's jurisdiction over a foreign corporation appropriately focused not on whether the corporation was "present" but on whether there have been

> "such contacts of the corporation with the state of the forum as make it reasonable, in the context of our federal system of government, to require the corporation to defend the particular suit which is brought there." Id., at 317, 66 S.Ct., at 158.

Mechanical or quantitative evaluations of the defendant's activities in the forum could not resolve the question of reasonableness:

> "Whether due process is satisfied must depend rather upon the quality and nature of the activity in relation to the fair and orderly administration of the laws which it was the purpose of the due process clause to insure. That clause does not contemplate that a state may make binding a judgment *in personam* against an individual or corporate defendant with which the state has no contacts, ties, or relations." Id., at 319, 66 S.Ct., at 160.[19]

[margin note: Int'l Shoe]

---

19. As the language quoted indicates, the *International Shoe* Court believed that the standard it was setting forth governed actions against natural persons as well as corporations, and we see no reason to disagree. See also McGee v. International Life Ins. Co., 355 U.S. 220, 222, 78 S.Ct. 199, 200, 2 L.Ed.2d 223 (1957) (*International Shoe* culmination of trend toward expanding state jurisdiction over "foreign corporations and other nonresidents"). The differences between individuals and corporations may, of course, lead to the conclusion that a given set of circumstances establishes State jurisdiction over one type of defendant but not over the other.

Thus, the relationship among the defendant, the forum, and the litigation, rather than the mutually exclusive sovereignty of the States on which the rules of *Pennoyer* rest, became the central concern of the inquiry into personal jurisdiction.[20] The immediate effect of this departure from *Pennoyer's* conceptual apparatus was to increase the ability of the state courts to obtain personal jurisdiction over nonresident defendants. See, e.g., Green, Jurisdictional Reform in California, 21 Hastings L.J. 1219, 1231–1233 (1970); Currie, The Growth of the Long Arm: Eight Years of Extended Jurisdiction in Illinois, 1963 U.Ill.L.F. 533; Developments at 1000–1008.

No equally dramatic change has occurred in the law governing jurisdiction *in rem*. There have, however, been intimations that the collapse of the *in personam* wing of *Pennoyer* has not left that decision unweakened as a foundation for *in rem* jurisdiction. Well-reasoned lower court opinions have questioned the proposition that the presence of property in a State gives that State jurisdiction to adjudicate rights to the property regardless of the relationship of the underlying dispute and the property owner to the forum. See e.g., U.S. Industries, Inc. v. Gregg, 540 F.2d 142 (CA3 1976), cert. pending, No. 76–359; Jonnet v. Dollar Savings Bank, 530 F.2d 1123, 1130–1143 (CA3 1976) (Gibbons, J., concurring); Camire v. Scieszka, 116 N.H. 281, 358 A.2d 397 (1976); Bekins v. Huish, 1 Ariz.App. 258, 401 P.2d 743 (1965); Atkinson v. Superior Court, 49 Cal.2d 338, 316 P.2d 960 (1957), appeal dismissed and cert. denied sub nom. Columbia Broadcasting Sys. v. Atkinson, 357 U.S. 569, 78 S.Ct. 1381, 2 L.Ed.2d 1546 (1958). The overwhelming majority of commentators have also rejected *Pennoyer's* premise that a proceeding "against" property is not a proceeding against the owners of that property. Accordingly, they urge that the "traditional notions of fair play and substantial justice" that govern a State's power to adjudicate *in personam* should also govern its power to adjudicate personal rights to property located in the State. See, e.g., Hazard; Von Mehren & Trautman, Jurisdiction to Adjudicate: A Suggested Analysis, 79 Harv.L.Rev. 1121 (1966); Traynor, Is This Conflict Really Necessary?, 37 Tex.L.Rev. 657 (1959) (hereafter Traynor); Ehrenzweig, The Transient Rule of Personal Jurisdiction: The "Power" Myth and Forum Conveniens, 65 Yale L.J. 289 (1956); Developments.

Although this Court has not addressed this argument directly, we have held that property cannot be subjected to a court's judgment unless reasonable and appropriate efforts have been made to give the property owners actual notice of the action. Schroeder v. City of New York, 371 U.S. 208, 83 S.Ct. 279, 9 L.Ed.2d 255 (1962); Walker v. City of

---

20. Nothing in Hanson v. Denckla, supra, is to the contrary. The *Hanson* Court's statement that restrictions on state jurisdiction "are a consequence of territorial limitations on the power of the respective States," id., 357 U.S. at 251, 78 S.Ct., at 1238, simply makes the point that the States are defined by their geographical territory. After making this point, the Court in *Hanson* determined that the defendant over which personal jurisdiction was claimed had not committed any acts sufficiently connected to the State to justify jurisdiction under the *International Shoe* standard.

Hutchinson, 352 U.S. 112, 77 S.Ct. 200, 1 L.Ed.2d 178 (1956); Mullane v. Central Hanover Bank & Trust Co., 339 U.S. 306, 70 S.Ct. 652, 94 L.Ed. 865 (1950). This conclusion recognizes, contrary to *Pennoyer*, that an adverse judgment *in rem* directly affects the property owner by divesting him of his rights in the property before the court. Schroeder v. City of New York, supra, 371 U.S. at 213, 83 S.Ct., at 282; cf. Continental Grain Co. v. Barge FBL–585, 364 U.S. 19, 80 S.Ct. 1470, 4 L.Ed.2d 1540 (1960) (separate actions against barge and barge owner are one "civil action" for purpose of transfer under 28 U.S.C.A. § 1404(a)). Moreover, in *Mullane* we held that Fourteenth Amendment rights cannot depend on the classification of an action as *in rem* or *in personam*, since that is

> "a classification for which the standards are so elusive and confused generally and which, being primarily for state courts to define, may and do vary from state to state." 339 U.S., at 312, 70 S.Ct., at 656.

It is clear, therefore, that the law of state-court jurisdiction no longer stands securely on the foundation established in *Pennoyer*.[21] We think that the time is ripe to consider whether the standard of fairness and substantial justice set forth in *International Shoe* should be held to govern actions *in rem* as well as *in personam*.

III

The case for applying to jurisdiction *in rem* the same test of "fair play and substantial justice" as governs assertions of jurisdiction *in personam* is simple and straightforward. It is premised on recognition that "[t]he phrase, 'judicial jurisdiction over a thing', is a customary elliptical way of referring to jurisdiction over the interests of persons in a thing." Restatement (Second) of Conflict of Laws § 56, Introductory Note (1971) (hereafter Restatement).[22] This recognition leads to the conclusion that in order to justify an exercise of jurisdiction *in rem*, the basis for jurisdiction must be sufficient to justify exercising "jurisdiction over the interests of persons in a thing."[23] The standard for determining whether an exercise of jurisdiction over the interests of persons is consistent with the Due Process Clause is the minimum-contacts standard elucidated in *International Shoe*.

21. Cf. Restatement (Second) of Conflict of Laws § 59, Comment a (possible inconsistency between principle of reasonableness which underlies field of judicial jurisdiction and traditional rule of *in rem* jurisdiction based solely on land in State); § 60, Comment a (same as to jurisdiction based solely on chattel in State); § 68, Comment c (rule of Harris v. Balk "might be thought inconsistent with the basic principle of reasonableness").

22. "All proceedings, like all rights, are really against persons. Whether they are proceedings or rights *in rem* depends on the number of persons affected." Tyler v. Court of Registration, 175 Mass. 71, 76, 55 N.E. 812, 814 (Holmes, C.J.), appeal dismissed, 179 U.S. 405, 21 S.Ct. 206, 45 L.Ed. 252 (1900).

23. It is true that the potential liability of a defendant in an *in rem* action is limited by the value of the property, but that limitation does not affect the argument. The fairness of subjecting a defendant to state-court jurisdiction does not depend on the size of the claim being litigated. Cf. Fuentes v. Shevin, 407 U.S., at 88–90, 92 S.Ct., at 1998–1999 (1972); n. 32, infra.

This argument, of course, does not ignore the fact that the presence of property in a State may bear on the existence of jurisdiction by providing contacts among the forum State, the defendant, and the litigation. For example, when claims to the property itself are the source of the underlying controversy between the plaintiff and the defendant,[24] it would be unusual for the State where the property is located not to have jurisdiction. In such cases, the defendant's claim to property located in the State would normally[25] indicate that he expected to benefit from the State's protection of his interest.[26] The State's strong interests in assuring the marketability of property within its borders[27] and in providing a procedure for peaceful resolution of disputes about the possession of that property would also support jurisdiction, as would the likelihood that important records and witnesses will be found in the State.[28] The presence of property may also favor jurisdiction in cases such as suits for injury suffered on the land of an absentee owner, where the defendant's ownership of the property is conceded but the cause of action is otherwise related to rights and duties growing out of that ownership.[29]

It appears, therefore, that jurisdiction over many types of actions which now are or might be brought *in rem* would not be affected by a holding that any assertion of state-court jurisdiction must satisfy the *International Shoe* standard.[30] For the type of *quasi in rem* action typified by Harris v. Balk and the present case, however, accepting the proposed analysis would result in significant change. These are cases where the property which now serves as the basis for state court jurisdiction is completely unrelated to the plaintiff's cause of action. Thus, although the presence of the defendant's property in a State might suggest the existence of other ties among the defendant, the State, and the litigation, the presence of the property alone would not support the State's jurisdiction. If those other ties did not exist, cases over which the State is now thought to have jurisdiction could not be brought in that forum.

Since acceptance of the *International Shoe* test would most affect this class of cases, we examine the arguments against adopting that

24. This category includes true *in rem* actions and the first type of *quasi in rem* proceedings. See n. 17, supra.

25. In some circumstances the presence of property in the forum State will not support the inference suggested in text. Cf., e.g., Restatement § 60, Comments c, d; Traynor 672–673; Note, The Power of a State to Affect Title in a Chattel Atypically Removed to It, 47 Colum.L.Rev. 767 (1947).

26. Cf. Hanson v. Denckla, 357 U.S., at 253, 78 S.Ct., at 1239.

27. See, e.g., Tyler v. Court of Registration, supra, n. 22.

28. We do not suggest that these illustrations include all the factors that may affect the decision, nor that the factors we have mentioned are necessarily decisive.

29. Cf. Dubin v. City of Philadelphia, 34 Pa.D. & C. 61 (1938). If such an action were brought under the *in rem* jurisdiction rather than under a long arm statute, it would be a *quasi in rem* action of the second type. See n. 17, supra.

30. Cf. Smit, The Enduring Utility of In Rem Rules: A Lasting Legacy of Pennoyer v. Neff, 43 Brooklyn L.Rev. 600 (1977). We do not suggest that jurisdictional doctrines other than those discussed in text, such as the particularized rules governing adjudications of status, are inconsistent with the standard of fairness. See, e.g., Traynor 660–661.

standard as they relate to this category of litigation.[31] Before doing so, however, we note that this type of case also presents the clearest illustration of the argument in favor of assessing assertions of jurisdiction by a single standard. For in cases such as *Harris* and this one, the only role played by the property is to provide the basis for bringing the defendant into court.[32] Indeed, the express purpose of the Delaware sequestration procedure is to compel the defendant to enter a personal appearance.[33] In such cases, if a direct assertion of personal jurisdiction over the defendant would violate the Constitution, it would seem that an indirect assertion of that jurisdiction should be equally impermissible.

The primary rationale for treating the presence of property as a sufficient basis for jurisdiction to adjudicate claims over which the State would not have jurisdiction if *International Shoe* applied is that a wrongdoer

> "should not be able to avoid payment of his obligations by the expedient of removing his assets to a place where he is not subject to an in personam suit." Restatement § 66, Comment a.

Accord, Developments 955. This justification, however, does not explain why jurisdiction should be recognized without regard to whether the property is present in the State because of an effort to avoid the owner's obligations. Nor does it support jurisdiction to adjudicate the underlying claim. At most, it suggests that a State in which property is located should have jurisdiction to attach that property, by use of proper procedures,[34] as security for a judgment being sought in a forum where the litigation can be maintained consistently with *International Shoe*. See, e.g., Von Mehren & Trautman 1178; Hazard 284–285; Beale, supra, n. 18, at 123–124. Moreover, we know of nothing to justify the assumption that a debtor can avoid paying his obligations by removing his property to a State in which his creditor cannot obtain personal jurisdiction over him.[35] The Full Faith and Credit Clause, after all, makes the valid *in personam* judgment of one State enforceable in all other States.[36]

31. Concentrating on this category of cases is also appropriate because in the other categories, to the extent that presence of property in the State indicates the existence of sufficient contacts under *International Shoe,* there is no need to rely on the property as justifying jurisdiction regardless of the existence of those contacts.

32. The value of the property seized does serve to limit the extent of possible liability, but that limitation does not provide support for the assertion of jurisdiction. See n. 23, supra. In this case, appellants' potential liability under the *in rem* jurisdiction exceeds one million dollars. * * *

33. * * * This purpose is emphasized by Delaware's refusal to allow any defense

on the merits unless the defendant enters a general appearance, thus submitting to full *in personam* liability. See n. 12 supra.

34. See North Georgia Finishing, Inc. v. Di-Chem, Inc., supra; Mitchell v. W.T. Grant Co., supra; Fuentes v. Shevin, supra; Sniadach v. Family Finance Corp., supra.

35. The role of *in rem* jurisdiction as a means of preventing the evasion of obligations, like the usefulness of that jurisdiction to mitigate the limitations *Pennoyer* placed on *in personam* jurisdiction, may once have been more significant. Von Mehren & Trautman, 1178.

36. Once it has been determined by a court of competent jurisdiction that the

It might also be suggested that allowing *in rem* jurisdiction avoids the uncertainty inherent in the *International Shoe* standard and assures a plaintiff of a forum.[37] See Folk & Moyer, supra, n. 10, at 749, 767. We believe, however, that the fairness standard of *International Shoe* can be easily applied in the vast majority of cases. Moreover, when the existence of jurisdiction in a particular forum under *International Shoe* is unclear, the cost of simplifying the litigation by avoiding the jurisdictional question may be the sacrifice of "fair play and substantial justice." That cost is too high.

We are left, then, to consider the significance of the long history of jurisdiction based solely on the presence of property in a State. Although the theory that territorial power is both essential to and sufficient for jurisdiction has been undermined, we have never held that the presence of property in a State does not automatically confer jurisdiction over the owner's interest in that property.[38] This history must be considered as supporting the proposition that jurisdiction based solely on the presence of property satisfies the demands of due process, cf. Ownbey v. Morgan, supra, 256 U.S., at 111, 41 S.Ct., at 438 (1921), but it is not decisive. "[T]raditional notions of fair play and substantial justice" can be as readily offended by the perpetuation of ancient forms that are no longer justified as by the adoption of new procedures that

defendant is a debtor of the plaintiff, there would seem to be no unfairness in allowing an action to realize on that debt in a State where the defendant has property, whether or not that State would have jurisdiction to determine the existence of the debt as an original matter. Cf. n. 18, supra.

37. This case does not raise, and we therefore do not consider, the question whether the presence of a defendant's property in a State is a sufficient basis for jurisdiction when no other forum is available to the plaintiff.

38. To the contrary, in Pennington v. Fourth National Bank, 243 U.S. 269, 271, 37 S.Ct. 282, 61 L.Ed. 713 (1917), we said: "The Fourteenth Amendment did not, in guaranteeing due process of law, abridge the jurisdiction which a State possessed over property within its borders, regardless of the residence or presence of the owner. That jurisdiction extends alike to tangible and to intangible property. Indebtedness due from a resident to a non-resident—of which bank deposits are an example—is property within the State. Chicago, Rock Island & Pacific Ry. Co. v. Sturm, 174 U.S. 710, 19 S.Ct. 797, 43 L.Ed. 1144. It is, indeed, the species of property which courts of the several States have most frequently applied in satisfaction of the obligations of absent debtors. Harris v. Balk, 198 U.S. 215, 25 S.Ct. 625, 49 L.Ed. 1023. Substituted service on a non-resident by

publication furnishes no legal basis for a judgment *in personam*. Pennoyer v. Neff, 95 U.S. 714, 24 L.Ed. 565. But garnishment or foreign attachment is a proceeding *quasi in rem*. Freeman v. Alderson, 119 U.S. 185, 187, 7 S.Ct. 165, 30 L.Ed. 372, 373. The thing belonging to the absent defendant is seized and applied to the satisfaction of his obligation. The Federal Constitution presents no obstacle to the full exercise of this power."

See also Huron Holding Corp. v. Lincoln Mine Operating Co., 312 U.S. 183, 193, 61 S.Ct. 513, 517, 85 L.Ed. 725 (1941).

More recent decisions, however, contain no similar sweeping endorsements of jurisdiction based on property. In Hanson v. Denckla, 357 U.S., at 246, 78 S.Ct., at 1236, we noted that a State court's *in rem* jurisdiction is "[f]ounded on physical power" and that "[t]he basis of the jurisdiction is the presence of the subject property within the territorial jurisdiction of the forum State." We found in that case, however, that the property which was the basis for the assertion of *in rem* jurisdiction was not present in the State. We therefore did not have to consider whether the presence of property in the State was sufficient to justify jurisdiction. We also held that the defendant did not have sufficient contact with the State to justify *in personam* jurisdiction.

are inconsistent with the basic values of our constitutional heritage. Cf. Sniadach v. Family Finance Corp., 395 U.S., at 340, 89 S.Ct., at 1822; Wolf v. Colorado, 338 U.S. 25, 27, 69 S.Ct. 1359, 1361, 93 L.Ed. 1782 (1949). The fiction that an assertion of jurisdiction over property is anything but an assertion of jurisdiction over the owner of the property supports an ancient form without substantial modern justification. Its continued acceptance would serve only to allow state court jurisdiction that is fundamentally unfair to the defendant.

We therefore conclude that all assertions of state court jurisdiction must be evaluated according to the standards set forth in *International Shoe* and its progeny.[39]

IV

The Delaware courts based their assertion of jurisdiction in this case solely on the statutory presence of appellants' property in Delaware. Yet that property is not the subject matter of this litigation, nor is the underlying cause of action related to the property. Appellants' holdings in Greyhound do not, therefore, provide contacts with Delaware sufficient to support the jurisdiction of that State's courts over appellants. If it exists, that jurisdiction must have some other foundation.[40]

Appellee Heitner did not allege and does not now claim that appellants have ever set foot in Delaware. Nor does he identify any act related to his cause of action as having taken place in Delaware. Nevertheless, he contends that appellants' positions as directors and officers of a corporation chartered in Delaware[41] provide sufficient "contacts, ties, or relations", International Shoe Co. v. Washington, 326 U.S., at 319, 66 S.Ct., at 160, with that State to give its courts jurisdiction over appellants in this stockholder's derivative action. This argument is based primarily on what Heitner asserts to be the strong interest of Delaware in supervising the management of a Dela-

---

39. It would not be fruitful for us to re-examine the facts of cases decided on the rationales of *Pennoyer* and *Harris* to determine whether jurisdiction might have been sustained under the standard we adopt today. To the extent that prior decisions are inconsistent with this standard, they are overruled.

40. Appellants argue that our determination that the minimum contacts standard of *International Shoe* governs jurisdiction here makes unnecessary any consideration of the existence of such contacts. Brief, at 27; Reply Brief, at 9. They point out that they were never personally served with a summons, that Delaware has no long arm statute which would authorize such service, and that the Delaware Supreme Court has authoritatively held that the existence of contacts is irrelevant to jurisdiction under 10 Del.C. § 366.

As part of its sequestration order, however, the Court of Chancery directed its clerk to send each appellant a copy of the summons and complaint by certified mail. The record indicates that those mailings were made and contains return receipts from at least 19 of the appellants. None of the appellants has suggested that he did not actually receive the summons which was directed to him in compliance with a Delaware statute designed to provide jurisdiction over nonresidents. In these circumstances, we will assume that the procedures followed would be sufficient to bring appellants before the Delaware courts, if minimum contacts existed.

41. On the view we take of the case, we need not consider the significance, if any, of the fact that some appellants hold positions only with a subsidiary of Greyhound which is incorporated in California.

ware corporation. That interest is said to derive from the role of Delaware law in establishing the corporation and defining the obligations owed to it by its officers and directors. In order to protect this interest, appellee concludes, Delaware's courts must have jurisdiction over corporate fiduciaries such as appellants.

This argument is undercut by the failure of the Delaware Legislature to assert the state interest appellee finds so compelling. Delaware law bases jurisdiction not on appellants' status as corporate fiduciaries, but rather on the presence of their property in the State. Although the sequestration procedure used here may be most frequently used in derivative suits against officers and directors, Hughes Tool Co. v. Fawcett Publications, Inc., 290 A.2d 693, 695 (Del.Ch.1972), the authorizing statute evinces no specific concern with such actions. Sequestration can be used in any suit against a nonresident, see e.g., U.S. Industries v. Gregg, supra (breach of contract); Hughes Tool Co. v. Fawcett Publications, Inc., supra (same), and reaches corporate fiduciaries only if they happen to own interests in a Delaware corporation, or other property in the State. But as Heitner's failure to secure jurisdiction over seven of the defendants named in his complaint demonstrates, there is no necessary relationship between holding a position as a corporate fiduciary and owning stock or other interests in the corporation.[43] If Delaware perceived its interest in securing jurisdiction over corporate fiduciaries to be as great as Heitner suggests, we would expect it to have enacted a statute more clearly designed to protect that interest.

Moreover, even if Heitner's assessment of the importance of Delaware's interest is accepted, his argument fails to demonstrate that Delaware is a fair forum for this litigation. The interest appellee has identified may support the application of Delaware law to resolve any controversy over appellants' actions in their capacities as officers and directors.[44] But we have rejected the argument that if a State's law can properly be applied to a dispute, its courts necessarily have jurisdiction over the parties to that dispute.

> "[The State] does not acquire . . . jurisdiction by being the 'center of gravity' of the controversy, or the most convenient location for litigation. The issue is personal jurisdiction, not choice of law. It is resolved in this case by considering the acts of the [appellants]." Hanson v. Denckla, supra, 357 U.S., at 254, 78 S.Ct., at 1240.[45]

43. Delaware does not require directors to own stock. 8 Del.C. § 141(b).

44. In general, the law of the State of incorporation is held to govern the liabilities of officers or directors to the corporation and its stockholders. See Restatement § 309. But see Cal.Corp.Code § 2115 (West Supp.1977). The rationale for the general rule appears to be based more on the need for a uniform and certain standard to govern the internal affairs of a corporation than on the perceived interest of the state of incorporation. Cf. Koster v. Lumbermens Mutual Casualty Co., 330 U.S. 518, 527–528, 67 S.Ct. 828, 833–834, 91 L.Ed. 1067 (1947).

45. Justice Black, although dissenting in *Hanson,* agreed with the majority that "the question whether the law of a State can be applied to a transaction is different

Appellee suggests that by accepting positions as officers or directors of a Delaware corporation, appellants performed the acts required by Hanson v. Denckla. He notes that Delaware law provides substantial benefits to corporate officers and directors,[46] and that these benefits were at least in part the incentive for appellants to assume their positions. It is, he says, "only fair and just" to require appellants, in return for these benefits, to respond in the State of Delaware when they are accused of misusing their powers. Brief for Appellee 15.

But like Heitner's first argument, this line of reasoning establishes only that it is appropriate for Delaware law to govern the obligations of appellants to Greyhound and its stockholders. It does not demonstrate that appellants have "purposefully avail[ed themselves] of the privilege of conducting activities within the forum State," Hanson v. Denckla, supra, at 253, 78 S.Ct., at 1240, in a way that would justify bringing them before a Delaware tribunal. Appellants have simply had nothing to do with the State of Delaware. Moreover, appellants had no reason to expect to be haled before a Delaware court. Delaware, unlike some States,[47] has not enacted a statute that treats acceptance of a directorship as consent to jurisdiction in the State. And "[i]t strains reason . . . . to suggest that anyone buying securities in a corporation formed in Delaware 'impliedly consents' to subject himself to Delaware's . . . jurisdiction on any cause of action." Folk & Moyer, supra, n. 10, at 785. Appellants, who were not required to acquire interests in Greyhound in order to hold their positions, did not by acquiring those interests surrender their right to be brought to judgment only in States with which they had had "minimum contacts."

The Due Process Clause

"does not contemplate that a state may make binding a judgment . . . against an individual or corporate defendant with which the state has no contacts, ties, or relations." International Shoe Co. v. Washington, 326 U.S., at 319, 66 S.Ct., at 160.

Delaware's assertion of jurisdiction over appellants in this case is inconsistent with that constitutional limitation on state power. The judgment of the Delaware Supreme Court must, therefore, be reversed.

It is so ordered.

MR. JUSTICE REHNQUIST took no part in the consideration or decision of this case.

MR. JUSTICE POWELL, concurring.

I agree that the principles of International Shoe Co. v. Washington, 326 U.S. 310, 66 S.Ct. 154, 90 L.Ed. 95 (1945), should be extended to govern assertions of *in rem* as well as *in personam* jurisdiction in state

---

from the question whether the courts of that State have jurisdiction to enter a judgment. . . ." 357 U.S., at 258, 78 S.Ct., at 1242.

46. See, e.g., 8 Del.C. §§ 143, 145.

47. See, e.g., Conn.Gen.Stat. § 33–322; N.C.Gen.Stat. § 55–33; S.C.Code § 33–5–70.

court. I also agree that neither the statutory presence of appellants' stock in Delaware nor their positions as directors and officers of a Delaware corporation can provide sufficient contacts to support the Delaware courts' assertion of jurisdiction in this case.

I would explicitly reserve judgment, however, on whether the ownership of some forms of property whose situs is indisputably and permanently located within a State may, without more, provide the contacts necessary to subject a defendant to jurisdiction within the State to the extent of the value of the property. In the case of real property, in particular, preservation of the common-law concept of *quasi in rem* jurisdiction arguably would avoid the uncertainty of the general *International Shoe* standard without significant cost to " 'traditional notions of fair play and substantial justice.' " Id., at 316, 66 S.Ct., at 158, quoting Milliken v. Meyer, 311 U.S. 457, 463, 61 S.Ct. 339, 343, 85 L.Ed. 278 (1940).

Subject to that reservation, I join the opinion of the Court.

MR. JUSTICE STEVENS, concurring in the judgment.

The Due Process Clause affords protection against "judgments without notice." International Shoe Co. v. Washington, 326 U.S. 310, 324, 66 S.Ct. 154, 162, 90 L.Ed. 95 (opinion of Black, J.). Throughout our history the acceptable exercise of *in rem* and *quasi in rem* jurisdiction has included a procedure giving reasonable assurance that actual notice of the particular claim will be conveyed to the defendant.* Thus, publication, notice by registered mail, or extraterritorial personal service has been an essential ingredient of any procedure that serves as a substitute for personal service within the jurisdiction.

The requirement of fair notice also, I believe, includes fair warning that a particular activity may subject a person to the jurisdiction of a foreign sovereign. If I visit another state, or acquire real estate or open a bank account in it, I knowingly assume some risk that the state will exercise its power over my property or my person while there. My contact with the state, though minimal, gives rise to predictable risks.

Perhaps the same consequences should flow from the purchase of stock of a corporation organized under the laws of a foreign nation, because to some limited extent one's property and affairs then become subject to the laws of the nation of domicile of the corporation. As a matter of international law, that suggestion might be acceptable because a foreign investment is sufficiently unusual to make it appropriate to require the investor to study the ramifications of his decision. But a purchase of securities in the domestic market is an entirely different matter.

One who purchases shares of stock on the open market can hardly be expected to know that he has thereby become subject to suit in a

---

* "To dispense with personal service the substitute that is most likely to reach the defendant is the least that ought to be required if substantial justice is to be done." McDonald v. Mabee, 243 U.S. 90, 92, 37 S.Ct. 343, 344, 61 L.Ed. 608.

forum remote from his residence and unrelated to the transaction. As a practical matter, the Delaware sequestration statute creates an unacceptable risk of judgment without notice. Unlike the 49 other States, Delaware treats the place of incorporation as the situs of the stock, even though both the owner and the custodian of the shares are elsewhere. Moreover, Delaware denies the defendant the opportunity to defend the merits of the suit unless he subjects himself to the unlimited jurisdiction of the court. Thus, it coerces a defendant either to submit to personal jurisdiction in a forum which could not otherwise obtain such jurisdiction or to lose the securities which have been attached. If its procedure were upheld, Delaware would, in effect, impose a duty of inquiry on every purchaser of securities in the national market. For unless the purchaser ascertains both the State of incorporation of the company whose shares he is buying, and also the idiosyncrasies of its law, he may be assuming an unknown risk of litigation. I therefore agree with the Court that on the record before us no adequate basis for jurisdiction exists and that the Delaware statute is unconstitutional on its face.

How the Court's opinion may be applied in other contexts is not entirely clear to me. I agree with Mr. Justice Powell that it should not be read to invalidate *in rem* jurisdiction where real estate is involved. I would also not read it as invalidating other long-accepted methods of acquiring jurisdiction over persons with adequate notice of both the particular controversy and also that their local activities might subject them to suit. My uncertainty as to the reach of the opinion, and my fear that it purports to decide a great deal more than is necessary to dispose of this case, persuade me merely to concur in the judgment.

MR. JUSTICE BRENNAN, concurring in part and dissenting in part.

I join Parts I–III of the Court's opinion. I fully agree that the minimum-contacts analysis developed in International Shoe Co. v. Washington, 326 U.S. 310, 66 S.Ct. 154, 90 L.Ed. 95 (1945), represents a far more sensible construct for the exercise of state-court jurisdiction than the patchwork of legal and factual fictions that has been generated from the decision in Pennoyer v. Neff, 95 U.S. 714, 24 L.Ed. 565 (1877). It is precisely because the inquiry into minimum contacts is now of such overriding importance, however, that I must respectfully dissent from Part IV of the Court's opinion.

I

The primary teaching of Parts I–III of today's decision is that a State, in seeking to assert jurisdiction over a person located outside its borders, may only do so on the basis of minimum contacts among the parties, the contested transaction, and the forum state. The Delaware Supreme Court could not have made plainer, however, that its sequestration statute, Del.Code Ann., Tit. 10, § 366 (1975), does not operate on this basis, but instead is strictly an embodiment of *quasi in rem* jurisdiction, a jurisdictional predicate no longer constitutionally viable:

> "[J]urisdiction under § 366 remains . . . *quasi in rem* founded on the presence of capital stock here, not on prior contact by defendants with this forum." 361 A.2d 225, 229 (1976).

This state-court ruling obviously comports with the understanding of the parties, for the issue of the existence of minimum contacts was never pleaded by appellee, made the subject of discovery, or ruled upon by the Delaware courts.   These facts notwithstanding, the Court in Part IV reaches the minimum-contacts question and finds such contacts lacking as applied to appellants.   Succinctly stated, once having properly and persuasively decided that the *quasi in rem* statute that Delaware admits to having enacted is invalid, the Court then proceeds to find that a minimum-contacts law that Delaware expressly *denies* having enacted also could not be constitutionally applied in this case.

In my view, a purer example of an advisory opinion is not to be found.   True, appellants do not deny having received actual notice of the action in question.   Ante, at n. 40.   But notice is but one ingredient of a proper assertion of state-court jurisdiction.   The other is a statute authorizing the exercise of the State's judicial power along constitutionally permissible grounds—which henceforth means minimum contacts. As of today, § 366 is not such a law.   Recognizing that today's decision fundamentally alters the relevant jurisdictional ground rules, I certainly would not want to rule out the possibility that Delaware's courts might decide that the legislature's overriding purpose of securing the personal appearance in state courts of defendants would best be served by reinterpreting its statute to permit state jurisdiction on the basis of constitutionally permissible contacts rather than stock ownership. Were the state courts to take this step, it would then become necessary to address the question of whether minimum contacts exist here.   But in the present posture of this case, the Court's decision of this important issue is purely an abstract ruling.

     * * *

NOTE ON CLASSIFICATION AS AFFECTING JURISDICTION AFTER SHAFFER v. HEITNER

1. The Implications of Shaffer v. Heitner

After the *Shaffer* decision, Delaware amended its corporation statutes to provide that a nonresident director is deemed to have consented to the appointment of a registered agent for service of process in actions for violation of his duty as a director.   The Delaware Supreme Court upheld the constitutionality of the provision.   Armstrong v. Pomerance, 423 A.2d 174 (Del.1980).   Do you think this is consistent with *Shaffer*?   Consider the text of the Court's opinion at fns. 44–47.   Is the doctrine expressed by cases like Lafayette Ins. Co. v. French and Hess v. Pawloski, discussed supra p. 294, applicable to this question?

good; but doesn't change min. contacts

For a careful analysis of *Shaffer,* see Casad, Shaffer v. Heitner: An End to Ambivalence in Jurisdiction Theory?, 26 Kan.L.Rev. 61 (1977). Among other points made by Professor Casad is that the rule in *Shaffer* could raise serious difficulties for title to property seized by attachment if the owner does not appear at the threshold of the action to contest the court's jurisdiction. Suppose the owner contests the sufficiency of contacts later, thus upsetting the title passed through a default judgment. Professor Casad suggests, 26 Kan.L. Rev. at 80: "While presence of property in the state may be insufficient to force a defendant to adjudicate a claim unrelated to that property, it may provide a sufficient basis for forcing a defendant to present any objection he may have on *International Shoe* grounds in that forum." See also the useful review in Silberman, Shaffer v. Heitner: The End of an Era, 53 N.Y.U.L.Rev. 33 (1978).

Note that the concurring opinions of Justices Powell and Stevens in *Shaffer* urge that the decision not be read to alter the traditional rules governing *quasi in rem* jurisdiction where real estate is involved, at least up to the value of the property. Is this consistent with the rationale of the majority opinion?

Shaffer v. Heitner appears to abolish the distinction between *in rem* and *in personam* proceedings, applying the "minimum contacts" standard of *International Shoe* to both alike. However, the Court's opinion indicates that there may yet be a future for attachment jurisdiction, e.g., in the case of an elusive obligor. See fn. 37. Following on this, there has been a trickle of cases upholding attachment jurisdiction against a defendant lacking "minimum contacts" where there appeared "good reason" to assert jurisdiction. See, e.g., Carolina Power & Light Co. v. Uranex, 451 F.Supp. 1044 (N.D.Cal.1977) (attachment in California in suit by North Carolina company against French company); Louring v. Kuwait Boulder Shipping Co., 455 F.Supp. 630 (D.Conn.1977) (garnishment in Connecticut in suit to collect a debt against a Kuwait corporation that was outside the territorial jurisdiction of all 50 states); Note, The Use of Maritime Attachment as a Jurisdictional Device, 12 Cornell Int'l L.J. 329 (1979) (reviewing two cases sustaining maritime attachment of property located within the district). See also Banco Ambrosiano, S.P.A. v. Artoc Bank & Trust Ltd., infra p. 411. The Supreme Court has yet to recognize such "jurisdiction by necessity," however, and in dicta has expressed a reluctance to do so. See Helicopteros Nacionales de Columbia, S.A. v. Hall, infra p. 384, fn. 13.

In Rush v. Savchuk, 444 U.S. 320, 100 S.Ct. 571, 62 L.Ed.2d 516 (1980), the Court revisited the issue of *in rem* jurisdiction. In that case a Minnesota court asserted jurisdiction over an Indiana defendant whose liability insurer did business in Minnesota. Plaintiff garnished the liability policy obligation, and the Minnesota court held this a basis for adjudicating the motorist's liability up to the limits of the policy. The Minnesota court relied on a latter-day version of the doctrine of Harris v. Balk, discussed supra p. 292, that the presence of a "debt" owed to the defendant is sufficient to support *quasi in rem* jurisdiction. Rejecting this argument, the Court reiterated its holding in *Shaffer* that the mere presence of property is insufficient to support jurisdiction over an unrelated cause of action and that the focus must be on the relationships among the defendant, the forum, and the litigation. It said that relying on the "debt" argument would, in effect, subject defendant to suit in any state where his insurer did business, a consequence which the Court said was unsupportable under any reasonable interpretation of the "minimum contacts" doctrine.

2. Classification and Jurisdiction

Mullane seems to mean that the "reasonable notice" requirement applies to all types of actions, whether classified as *in rem* or *in personam* or relating to "status." *Shaffer* seems to mean that the "minimum contacts" requirement applies, with some qualifications, to both *in rem* and *in personam* proceedings. The question then arises whether it makes a difference any more how a proceeding is classified.

a. Status. It clearly makes a difference today when a suit involves a matter of family status—divorce, separation, custody, adoption, etc. This is because in status proceedings the Supreme Court has applied neither the *Pennoyer* "presence" principle nor the *International Shoe* "minimum contacts" principle, but has instead developed doctrines peculiar to domestic relations law. One of these is the rule of "divisible divorce," under which a state where only one of the spouses resides has authority to award a divorce, effectively permitting remarriage, but not to determine the support obligation or division of property. With the general liberalization of the substantive grounds of divorce, this problem is largely obsolete. Another doctrine is that a state where a child is located has authority to determine custody of the child, but that such a determination may be reconsidered in a state to which the child is later removed—even if the removal is in violation of the custody decree. This problem has largely been resolved by the Federal Parental Kidnapping Prevention Act, 28 U.S.C.A. § 1738A. See Thompson v. Thompson, 484 U.S. 174, 108 S.Ct. 513, 98 L.Ed.2d 512 (1988) (Parental Kidnapping Prevention Act extended full faith and credit requirements to state custody determinations); Note, Federal Jurisdiction Under the Parental Kidnapping Prevention Act, 57 U.Colo.L.Rev. 117 (1985).

b. In Personam versus In Rem. The sovereignty theory, and the attendant distinction between proceedings *in rem* and *in personam,* dies hard. The distinction was central to the Court's reasoning in Hanson v. Denckla, discussed supra p. 313. Assuming *Hanson* is still good law after *Shaffer,* and the Court certainly implies that it is (see fn. 20), does this mean that courts must still examine possible *in rem* and *in personam* bases of jurisdiction as if these involved separable inquiries? If so, what standards could be applied to each after *Shaffer?* In *Hanson,* the Court implied that the *in rem* question depended upon where the trust was deemed "present," while the *in personam* question depended upon the nature of the trustee's relationship with the forum state. Under the principles of *Shaffer* and Rush v. Savchuk, supra, should the Court instead have considered all of the contacts, however denominated, together to determine whether the assertion of jurisdiction was reasonable? For example, by framing the *in rem* question as narrowly as it did, the Court in *Hanson* rejected the argument that the decedent's beneficial interest in the trust constituted a "contact" with the forum state. This factor likewise was not considered in the Court's *in personam* analysis, which focused exclusively on the trustee.

The *Shaffer* rule also raises the question whether simple presence of a defendant remains a sufficient basis for the exercise of *in personam* jurisdiction, or whether there must be some "good reason" to assert jurisdiction if minimum contacts are lacking. The "mere presence" rule of transient jurisdiction is picturesquely displayed in Grace v. MacArthur, 170 F.Supp. 442 (E.D.Ark.1959) (service on passenger in an airplane flying over Arkansas) and retains a continued vitality in the courts. See, e.g., O'Brien v. Eubanks, 701 P.2d 614 (Colo.App.1984) (presence of individual defendant sufficient for personal jurisdiction without regard to minimum contacts). Many commentators do not share this enthusiasm. Compare Humphrey v. Langford, 246 Ga. 732, 273 S.E.2d 22 (1980), with Clermont, Restating Territorial Jurisdiction and Venue for State and Federal Courts, 66 Cornell L.Rev. 411, 425 n. 74 (1981). What role should the *plaintiff's* contacts with the forum play in the jurisdictional inquiry? Compare Keeton v. Hustler Magazine, Inc., 465 U.S. 770, 104 S.Ct. 1473, 79 L.Ed.2d 790 (1984) (lack of plaintiff's contacts irrelevant), with Phillips Petroleum Co. v. Shutts, infra p. 476.

Domicile and citizenship have traditionally been accepted as proper bases for personal jurisdiction. See, e.g., Milliken v. Meyer, 311 U.S. 457, 61 S.Ct. 339, 85 L.Ed. 278 (1940) (Wyoming domicilary served while residing in Colorado); Blackmer v. United States, 284 U.S. 421, 52 S.Ct. 252, 76 L.Ed. 375 (1932) (U.S. citizen residing in France); Restatement Second of Conflict of Laws § 27. Are such bases of jurisdiction consistent with *Shaffer*'s more pragmatic approach to minimum contacts?

The reasoning in *Shaffer* would appear to have undermined the rule in Pennoyer v. Neff that prior attachment of property is a prerequisite for the assumption of *quasi in rem* jurisdiction. See Hodge v. Hodge, 178 Conn. 308, 422 A.2d 280 (1979); Amoco Overseas Oil Co. v. Compagnie Nationale Algerienne de Navigation, 605 F.2d 648 (2d Cir.1979).

For a review and evaluation of the history of the *in rem* and *in personam* doctrines of jurisdiction, see Kalo, Jurisdiction as an Evolutionary Process: The Development of Quasi in Rem and In Personam Principles, 1978 Duke L.J. 1147. For other general analyses of the problems of territorial jurisdiction, see Stein, Styles of Argument and Interstate Federalism in the Law of Personal Jurisdiction, 65 Tex.L.Rev. 689 (1987); Brilmayer and Paisley, Personal Jurisdiction and Substantive Legal Relations: Corporations, Conspiracies, and Agency, 74 Calif.L.Rev. 1 (1986); Sonenshein, The Error of a Balancing Approach to the Due Process Determination of Jurisdiction Over the Person, 59 Temp.L.Q. 47 (1986); von Mehren and Trautman, Jurisdiction to Adjudicate: A Suggested Analysis, 79 Harv.L.Rev. 1121 (1966); Kurland, The Supreme Court, the Due Process Clause and the In Personam Jurisdiction of State Courts, 25 U.Chi.L. Rev. 569 (1958); Note, Developments in the Law—State Court Jurisdiction, 73 Harv.L.Rev. 909 (1960). See also Scoles and Hay, Conflict of Laws cc. 5–8 (Lawyers Ed.1984).

---

2. CONVENIENCE VERSUS SOVEREIGNTY

INTRODUCTORY NOTE ON CONVENIENCE AND SOVEREIGNTY

International Shoe Co. v. State of Washington refers to both "convenience" and the nature of "our federal system" as standards governing the application of the "minimum contacts" formula. The reference to "our federal system" implies that there are limitations on territorial jurisdiction arising from the legal structure of federalism as distinct from the litigant's personal freedom from inconvenience. See also Hanson v. Denckla, discussed supra p. 313. Both of these themes appear and reappear in the cases reprinted below.

WORLD–WIDE VOLKSWAGEN CORP. v. WOODSON

Supreme Court of the United States, 1980.
444 U.S. 286, 100 S.Ct. 559, 62 L.Ed.2d 490.*

MR. JUSTICE WHITE delivered the opinion of the Court.

The issue before us is whether, consistently with the Due Process Clause of the Fourteenth Amendment, an Oklahoma court may exercise *in personam* jurisdiction over a nonresident automobile retailer and its wholesale distributor in a products liability action, when the defendants' only connection with Oklahoma is the fact that an automobile sold in New York to New York residents became involved in an accident in Oklahoma.

I

Respondents Harry and Kay Robinson purchased a new Audi automobile from petitioner Seaway Volkswagen, Inc. (Seaway) in Massena, N.Y., in 1976. The following year the Robinson family, who resided in New York, left that State for a new home in Arizona. As they passed through the State of Oklahoma, another car struck their Audi in the rear, causing a fire which severely burned Kay Robinson and her two children.[1]

The Robinsons [2] subsequently brought a products-liability action in the District Court for Creek County, Okla., claiming that their injuries resulted from defective design and placement of the Audi's gas tank and fuel system. They joined as defendants the automobile's manufacturer, Audi NSU Auto Union Aktiengesellschaft (Audi); its importer Volkswagen of America, Inc. (Volkswagen); its regional distributor, petitioner World-Wide Volkswagen Corporation (World-Wide); and its retail dealer, petitioner Seaway. Seaway and World-Wide entered special appearances,[3] claiming that Oklahoma's exercise of jurisdiction over them would offend the limitations on the State's jurisdiction imposed by the Due Process Clause of the Fourteenth Amendment.[4]

The facts presented to the District Court showed that World-Wide is incorporated and has its business office in New York. It distributes vehicles, parts and accessories, under contract with Volkswagen, to retail dealers in New York, New Jersey, and Connecticut. Seaway, one of these retail dealers, is incorporated and has its place of business in New York. Insofar as the record reveals, Seaway and World-Wide are

---

* Some of the Court's footnotes are omitted.

1. The driver of the other automobile does not figure in the present litigation.

2. Kay Robinson sued on her own behalf. The two children sued through Harry Robinson as their father and next friend.

3. Volkswagen also entered a special appearance in the District Court, but unlike World-Wide and Seaway did not seek review in the Supreme Court of Oklahoma and is not a petitioner here. Both Volkswagen and Audi remain as defendants in the litigation pending before the District Court in Oklahoma.

4. The papers filed by the petitioners also claimed that the District Court lacked "venue of the subject matter," App. 9, or "venue over the subject matter," id., at 11.

fully independent corporations whose relations with each other and with Volkswagen and Audi are contractual only. Respondents adduced no evidence that either World-Wide or Seaway does any business in Oklahoma, ships or sells any products to or in that State, has an agent to receive process there, or purchases advertisements in any media calculated to reach Oklahoma. In fact, as respondents' counsel conceded at oral argument, Tr. of Oral Arg. 32, there was no showing that any automobile sold by World-Wide or Seaway has ever entered Oklahoma with the single exception of the vehicle involved in the present case.

no minimum contacts except Robinsons

Despite the apparent paucity of contacts between petitioners and Oklahoma, the District Court rejected their constitutional claim and reaffirmed that ruling in denying petitioners' motion for reconsideration. * * *

II

The Due Process Clause of the Fourteenth Amendment limits the power of a state court to render a valid personal judgment against a nonresident defendant. Kulko v. Superior Court, 436 U.S. 84, 91, 98 S.Ct. 1690, 1696, 56 L.Ed.2d 132 (1978). A judgment rendered in violation of due process is void in the rendering State and is not entitled to full faith and credit elsewhere. Pennoyer v. Neff, 95 U.S. 714, 732–733, 24 L.Ed. 565 (1878). Due process requires that the defendant be given adequate notice of the suit, Mullane v. Central Hanover Trust Co., 339 U.S. 306, 313–314, 70 S.Ct. 652, 657, 94 L.Ed. 865 (1950), and be subject to the personal jurisdiction of the court, International Shoe Co. v. Washington, 326 U.S. 310, 66 S.Ct. 154, 90 L.Ed. 95 (1945). In the present case, it is not contended that notice was inadequate; the only question is whether these particular petitioners were subject to the jurisdiction of the Oklahoma courts.

As has long been settled, and as we reaffirm today, a state court may exercise personal jurisdiction over a nonresident defendant only so long as there exist "minimum contacts" between the defendant and the forum State. International Shoe Co. v. Washington, supra, at 316, 66 S.Ct., at 158. The concept of minimum contacts, in turn, can be seen to perform two related, but distinguishable, functions. ① It protects the defendant against the burdens of litigating in a distant or inconvenient forum. And it ② acts to ensure that the States through their courts, do not reach out beyond the limits imposed on them by their status as coequal sovereigns in a federal system.

min. contacts reqr'd

① reasonable or Fair

The protection against inconvenient litigation is typically described in terms of "reasonableness" or "fairness." We have said that the defendant's contacts with the forum State must be such that maintenance of the suit "does not offend 'traditional notions of fair play and substantial justice.'" International Shoe Co. v. Washington, supra, at 316, 66 S.Ct., at 158, quoting Milliken v. Meyer, 311 U.S. 457, 463, 61 S.Ct. 339, 342, 85 L.Ed. 278 (1940). The relationship between the defendant and the forum must be such that it is "reasonable . . . to require the corporation to defend the particular suit which is brought there." 326 U.S., at 317, 66 S.Ct., at 158. Implicit in this emphasis on reasonableness is the understanding that the burden on the defendant, while always a primary concern, will in an appropriate case be considered in light of other relevant factors, including the forum State's interest in adjudicating the dispute, see McGee v. International Life Ins. Co., 355 U.S. 220, 223, 78 S.Ct. 199, 201, 2 L.Ed.2d 223 (1957); the plaintiff's interest in obtaining convenient and effective relief, see Kulko v. Superior Court, supra, 436 U.S., at 92, 98 S.Ct., at 1697, at least when that interest is not adequately protected by the plaintiff's power to choose the forum, cf. Shaffer v. Heitner, 433 U.S. 186, 211, n. 37, 97 S.Ct. 2569, 2583, n. 37, 53 L.Ed.2d 683 (1977); the interstate judicial system's interest in obtaining the most efficient resolution of controversies; and the shared interest of the several States in furthering fundamental substantive social policies, see Kulko v. Superior Court, supra, 436 U.S., at 93, 98, 98 S.Ct., at 1697, 1700.

The limits imposed on state jurisdiction by the Due Process Clause, in its role as a guarantor against inconvenient litigation, have been substantially relaxed over the years. As we noted in McGee v. International Life Ins. Co., supra, 355 U.S., at 222–223, 78 S.Ct., at 201, this trend is largely attributable to a fundamental transformation in the American economy:

> "Today many commercial transactions touch two or more States and may involve parties separated by the full continent. With this increasing nationalization of commerce has come a great increase in the amount of business conducted by mail across state lines. At the same time modern transportation and communication have made it much less burdensome for a party sued to defend himself in a State where he engages in economic activity."

The historical developments noted in *McGee*, of course, have only accelerated in the generation since that case was decided.

Nevertheless, we have never accepted the proposition that state lines are irrelevant for jurisdictional purposes, nor could we and remain faithful to the principles of interstate federalism embodied in the Constitution. The economic interdependence of the States was foreseen and desired by the Framers. In the Commerce Clause, they provided that the Nation was to be a common market, a "free trade unit" in which the States are debarred from acting as separable economic entities. H.P. Hood & Sons, Inc. v. Du Mond, 336 U.S. 525, 538, 69 S.Ct. 657, 665, 93 L.Ed. 865 (1949). But the Framers also intended that the States retain many essential attributes of sovereignty, including in particular, the sovereign power to try causes in their courts. The sovereignty of each State, in turn, implied a limitation on the sovereignty of all of its sister States—a limitation express or implicit in both the original scheme of the Constitution and the Fourteenth Amendment.

peculiarity

Hence, even while abandoning the shibboleth that "[t]he authority of every tribunal is necessarily restricted by the territorial limits of the State in which it is established," Pennoyer v. Neff, supra, 95 U.S., at 720, we emphasized that the reasonableness of asserting jurisdiction over the defendant must be assessed "in the context of our federal system of government," International Shoe Co. v. Washington, supra, 326 U.S., at 317, 66 S.Ct., at 158, and stressed that the Due Process Clause ensures, not only fairness, but also the "orderly administration of the laws," id., at 319, 66 S.Ct., at 159. As we noted in Hanson v. Denckla, 357 U.S. 235, 250–251, 78 S.Ct. 1228, 2 L.Ed.2d 1283 (1958):

> "As technological progress has increased the flow of commerce between the States, the need for jurisdiction over nonresidents has undergone a similar increase. At the same time, progress in communications and transportation has made the defense of a suit in a foreign tribunal less burdensome. In response to these changes, the requirements for personal jurisdiction over nonresidents have evolved from the rigid rule of Pennoyer v. Neff, 95 U.S. 714, 24 L.Ed. 565, to the flexible standard of International Shoe Co. v. Washington, 326 U.S. 310, 66 S.Ct. 154, 90 L.Ed. 95. But it is a mistake to assume that this trend heralds the eventual demise of all restrictions on the personal jurisdiction of state courts. [Citation omitted.] Those restrictions are more than a guarantee of immunity from inconvenient or distant litigation. They are a consequence of territorial limitations on the power of the respective States."

Thus, the Due Process Clause "does not contemplate that a state may make binding a judgment *in personam* against an individual or corporate defendant with which the state has no contacts, ties, or relations." International Shoe Co. v. Washington, 326 U.S., at 319, 66 S.Ct., at 159. Even if the defendant would suffer minimal or no inconvenience from being forced to litigate before the tribunals of another State; even if the forum State has a strong interest in applying its law to the controversy; even if the forum State is the most convenient location for litigation, the Due Process Clause, acting as an instrument of interstate federalism, may sometimes act to divest the State of its power to render a valid judgment. Hanson v. Denckla, supra, 357 U.S., at 251, 254, 78 S.Ct., at 1238, 1240.

no IP ju. if no min. contacts even if

← b/c

III

Applying these principles to the case at hand,[10] we find in the record before us a total absence of those affiliating circumstances that are a

min. contacts absent here

---

10. Respondents argue, as a threshold matter, that petitioners waived any objections to personal jurisdiction by (1) joining with their special appearances a challenge to the District Court's subject-matter jurisdiction, see n. 4, supra, and (2) taking depositions on the merits of the case in Oklahoma. The trial court, however, characterized the appearances as "special," and the Oklahoma Supreme Court, rather than finding jurisdiction waived, reached and decided the statutory and constitutional questions. Compare Kulko v. Superior Court, supra, 436 U.S., at 91, n. 5, 98 S.Ct., at 1696, n. 5.

necessary predicate to any exercise of state-court jurisdiction. Petitioners carry on no activity whatsoever in Oklahoma. They close no sales and perform no services there. They avail themselves of none of the privileges and benefits of Oklahoma law. They solicit no business there either through salespersons or through advertising reasonably calculated to reach the State. Nor does the record show that they regularly sell cars at wholesale or retail to Oklahoma customers or residents or that they indirectly, through others, serve or seek to serve the Oklahoma market. In short, respondents seek to base jurisdiction on one, isolated occurrence and whatever inferences can be drawn therefrom: the fortuitous circumstance that a single Audi automobile, sold in New York to New York residents, happened to suffer an accident while passing through Oklahoma.

It is argued, however, that because an automobile is mobile by its very design and purpose it was "foreseeable" that the Robinsons' Audi would cause injury in Oklahoma. Yet "foreseeability" alone has never been a sufficient benchmark for personal jurisdiction under the Due Process Clause. In Hanson v. Denckla, supra, it was no doubt foreseeable that the settlor of a Delaware trust would subsequently move to Florida and seek to exercise a power of appointment there; yet we held that Florida courts could not constitutionally exercise jurisdiction over a Delaware trustee that had no other contacts with the forum State. In Kulko v. Superior Court, 436 U.S. 84, 98 S.Ct. 1690, 56 L.Ed.2d 132 (1978), it was surely "foreseeable" that a divorced wife would move to California from New York, the domicile of the marriage, and that a minor daughter would live with the mother. Yet we held that California could not exercise jurisdiction in a child-support action over the former husband who had remained in New York.

If foreseeability were the criterion, a local California tire retailer could be forced to defend in Pennsylvnia when a blowout occurs there, see Erlanger Mills, Inc. v. Cohoes Fibre Mills, Inc., 239 F.2d 502, 507 (CA4 1956); a Wisconsin seller of a defective automobile jack could be haled before a distant court for damage caused in New Jersey, Reilly v. Phil Tolkan Pontiac, Inc., 372 F.Supp. 1205 (N.J. 1974); or a Florida soft-drink concessionaire could be summoned to Alaska to account for injuries happening there, see Uppgren v. Executive Aviation Services, Inc., 304 F.Supp. 165, 170–171 (Minn.1969). Every seller of chattels would in effect appoint the chattel his agent for service of process. His amenability to suit would travel with the chattel. We recently abandoned the outworn rule of Harris v. Balk, 198 U.S. 215, 25 S.Ct. 625, 49 L.Ed. 1023 (1905), that the interest of a creditor in a debt could be extinguished or otherwise affected by any State having transitory jurisdiction over the debtor. Shaffer v. Heitner, 433 U.S. 186, 97 S.Ct. 2569, 53 L.Ed.2d 683 (1977). Having interred the mechanical rule that a creditor's amenability to a *quasi in rem* action travels with his debtor, we are unwilling to endorse an analogous principle in the present case.[11]

11. Respondents' counsel, at oral argument, see Tr. of Oral Arg. 19–22, 29, sought to limit the reach of the foreseeability standard by suggesting that there is something

This is not to say, of course, that foreseeability is wholly irrelevant. But the foreseeability that is critical to due process analysis is not the mere likelihood that a product will find its way into the forum State. Rather, it is that the defendant's conduct and connection with the forum State are such that he should reasonably anticipate being haled into court there. See Kulko v. Superior Court, supra, 436 U.S., at 97–98, 98 S.Ct., at 1699–1700; Shaffer v. Heitner, 433 U.S., at 216, 97 S.Ct., at 2586, and see id., at 217–219, 97 S.Ct., at 2586–2587 (Stevens, J., concurring in the judgment). The Due Process Clause, by ensuring the "orderly administration of the laws," International Shoe Co. v. Washington, 326 U.S., at 319, 66 S.Ct., at 159, gives a degree of predictability to the legal system that allows potential defendants to structure their primary conduct with some minimum assurance as to where that conduct will and will not render them liable to suit.

When a corporation "purposefully avails itself of the privilege of conducting activities within the forum State," Hanson v. Denckla, supra, at 253, 78 S.Ct., at 1240, it has clear notice that it is subject to suit there, and can act to alleviate the risk of burdensome litigation by procuring insurance, passing the expected costs on to customers, or, if the risks are too great, severing its connection with the State. Hence if the sale of a product of a manufacturer or distributor such as Audi or Volkswagen is not simply an isolated occurrence, but arises from the efforts of the manufacturer or distributor to serve directly or indirectly, the market for its product in other States, it is not unreasonable to subject it to suit in one of those States if its allegedly defective merchandise has there been the source of injury to its owner or to others. The forum State does not exceed its powers under the Due Process Clause if it asserts personal jurisdiction over a corporation that delivers its products into the stream of commerce with the expectation that they will be purchased by consumers in the forum State. Compare Gray v. American Radiator & Standard Sanitary Corp., 22 Ill.2d 432, 176 N.E.2d 761 (1961).

But there is no such or similar basis for Oklahoma jurisdiction over World-Wide or Seaway in this case. Seaway's sales are made in Massena, N.Y. World-Wide's market, although substantially larger, is limited to dealers in New York, New Jersey, and Connecticut. There is no evidence of record that any automobiles distributed by World-Wide are sold to retail customers outside this tristate area. It is foreseeable that the purchasers of automobiles sold by World-Wide and Seaway may take them to Oklahoma. But the mere "unilateral activity of

unique about automobiles. It is true that automobiles are uniquely mobile, see Tyson v. Whitaker & Son, Inc., 407 A.2d 1, 6, and n. 11 (Me.1979) (McKusick, C. J.), that they did play a crucial role in the expansion of personal jurisdiction through the fiction of implied consent, e.g., Hess v. Pawloski, 274 U.S. 352, 47 S.Ct. 632, 71 L.Ed. 1091 (1927), and that some of the cases have treated the automobile as a "dangerous instrumentality."

But today, under the regime of *International Shoe*, we see no difference for jurisdictional purposes between an automobile and any other chattel. The "dangerous instrumentality" concept apparently was never used to support personal jurisdiction; and to the extent it has relevance today it bears not on jurisdiction but on the possible desirability of imposing substantive principles of tort law such as strict liability.

those who claim some relationship with a nonresident defendant cannot satisfy the requirement of contact with the forum State." Hanson v. Denckla, supra, at 253, 78 S.Ct., at 1239–1240.

In a variant on the previous argument, it is contended that jurisdiction can be supported by the fact that petitioners earn substantial revenue from goods used in Oklahoma. The Oklahoma Supreme Court so found, 585 P.2d, at 354–355, drawing the inference that because one automobile sold by petitioners had been used in Oklahoma, others might have been used there also. While this inference seems less than compelling on the facts of the instant case, we need not question the Court's factual findings in order to reject its reasoning.

This argument seems to make the point that the purchase of automobiles in New York, from which the petitioners earn substantial revenue, would not occur *but for* the fact that the automobiles are capable of use in distant States like Oklahoma. Respondents observe that the very purpose of an automobile is to travel, and that travel of automobiles sold by petitioners is facilitated by an extensive chain of Volkswagen service centers throughout the country, including some in Oklahoma. However, financial benefits accruing to the defendant from a collateral relation to the forum State will not support jurisdiction if they do not stem from a constitutionally cognizable contact with that State. See Kulko v. Superior Court, 436 U.S., at 94–95, 98 S.Ct., at 1698–1699. In our view, whatever marginal revenues petitioners may receive by virtue of the fact that their products are capable of use in Oklahoma is far too attenuated a contact to justify that State's exercise of *in personam* jurisdiction over them.

Because we find that petitioners have no "contacts, ties, or relations" with the State of Oklahoma, International Shoe Co. v. Washington, supra, 326 U.S., at 319, 66 S.Ct., at 159, the judgment of the Supreme Court of Oklahoma is reversed.

Mr. Justice Marshall, with whom Mr. Justice Blackmun joins, dissenting.

*   *   *

*   *   *   The majority asserts that "respondents seek to base jurisdiction on one, isolated occurrence and whatever inferences can be drawn therefrom: the fortuitous circumstance that a single Audi automobile, sold in New York to New York residents, happened to suffer an accident while passing through Oklahoma." *   *   *   If that were the case, I would readily agree that the minimum contacts necessary to sustain jurisdiction are not present. But the basis for the assertion of jurisdiction is not the happenstance that an individual over whom petitioner had no control made a unilateral decision to take a chattel with him to a distant State. Rather, jurisdiction is premised on the deliberate and purposeful actions of the defendants themselves in choosing to become part of a nationwide, indeed a global, network for marketing and servicing automobiles.

Petitioners are sellers of a product whose utility derives from its mobility. * * * Petitioners know that their customers buy cars not only to make short trips, but also to travel long distances. In fact, the nationwide service network with which they are affiliated was designed to facilitate and encourage such travel. Seaway would be unlikely to sell many cars if authorized service were available only in Massena, N.Y. Moreover, local dealers normally derive a substantial portion of their revenues from their service operations and thereby obtain a further economic benefit from the opportunity to service cars which were sold in other States. It is apparent that petitioners have not attempted to minimize the chance that their activities will have effects in other States; on the contrary, they have chosen to do business in a way that increases that chance, because it is to their economic advantage to do so.

To be sure, petitioners could not know in advance that this particular automobile would be driven to Oklahoma. They must have anticipated, however, that a substantial portion of the cars they sold would travel out of New York. Seaway, a local dealer in the second most populous State, and World-Wide, one of only seven regional Audi distributors in the entire country, see Brief for Respondents 2, would scarcely have been surprised to learn that a car sold by them had been driven in Oklahoma on Interstate 44, a heavily traveled transcontinental highway. In the case of the distributor, in particular, the probability that some of the cars it sells will be driven in every one of the contiguous States must amount to a virtual certainty. This knowledge should alert a reasonable businessman to the likelihood that a defect in the product might manifest itself in the forum State—not because of some unpredictable, aberrant, unilateral action by a single buyer, but in the normal course of the operation of the vehicles for their intended purpose.

It is misleading for the majority to characterize the argument in favor of jurisdiction as one of " 'foreseeability' alone." * * * As economic entities petitioners reach out from New York, knowingly causing effects in other States and receiving economic advantage both from the ability to cause such effects themselves and from the activities of dealers and distributors in other States. While they did not receive revenue from making direct sales in Oklahoma, they intentionally became part of an interstate economic network, which included dealerships in Oklahoma, for pecuniary gain. In light of this purposeful conduct I do not believe it can be said that petitioners "had no reason to expect to be haled before a[n Oklahoma] court." Shaffer v. Heitner, supra, 433 U.S., at 216, 97 S.Ct., at 2586; * * * Kulko v. California Superior Court, 436 U.S. 84, 97–98, 98 S.Ct. 1690, 1699–1700, 94 L.Ed.2d 132 (1977).

* * *

INSURANCE CORP. OF IRELAND, LTD. v. COMPAGNIE des BAUXITES de GUINEE

Supreme Court of the United States, 1982.
456 U.S. 694, 102 S.Ct. 2099, 72 L.Ed.2d 492.*

JUSTICE WHITE delivered the opinion of the Court.

Rule 37(b), Federal Rules of Civil Procedure, provides that a district court may impose sanctions for failure to comply with discovery orders. Included among the available sanctions is:

"An order that the matters regarding which the order was made or any other designated facts shall be taken to be established for the purposes of the action in accordance with the claim of the party obtaining the order." Rule 37(b)(2)(A).

The question presented by this case is whether this rule is applicable to facts that form the basis for personal jurisdiction over a defendant. May a district court, as a sanction for failure to comply with a discovery order directed at establishing jurisdictional facts, proceed on the basis that personal jurisdiction over the recalcitrant party has been established? Petitioners urge that such an application of the Rule would violate due process: If a court does not have jurisdiction over a party, then it may not create that jurisdiction by judicial fiat.[1] They contend also that until a court has jurisdiction over a party, that party need not comply with orders of the court; failure to comply, therefore, cannot provide the ground for a sanction. In our view, petitioners are attempting to create a logical conundrum out of a fairly straightforward matter.

I

Respondent Compagnie des Bauxites de Guinee (CBG) is a Delaware Corporation, 49% of which is owned by the Republic of Guinea and 51% is owned by Halco (Mining) Inc. CBG's principal place of business is in the Republic of Guinea, where it operates bauxite mines and processing facilities. Halco, which operates in Pennsylvania, has contracted to perform certain administrative services for CBG. These include the procurement of insurance.

In 1973, Halco instructed an insurance broker, Marsh & McLennan, to obtain $20 million worth of business interruption insurance to cover CBG's operations in Guinea. The first half of this coverage was provided by the Insurance Company of North America (INA). The second half, or what is referred to as the "excess" insurance, was

---

* Some of the Court's footnotes are omitted.

1. The petition with which we deal in this case was filed as a cross-petition in response to the petition for certiorari filed in No. 81–290 * * *. We granted the cross-petition, limiting the grant to the question of the validity of the Rule 37(b)(2) sanction. 454 U.S. 963, 102 S.Ct. 502, 71 L.Ed.2d 377 (1981). We shall refer to the cross-petitioners as "petitioners" and to the cross-respondent as "respondent."

provided by a group of 21 foreign insurance companies,[2] 14 of which are petitioners in this action (the excess insurers).

*   *   *

Sometime after February 12, [1974] CBG allegedly experienced mechanical problems in its Guinea operation, resulting in a business interruption loss in excess of $10 million. * * *

In December 1975, CBG filed a two count suit in the Western District of Pennsylvania, asserting jurisdiction based on diversity of citizenship. The first count was against INA; the second against the excess insurers. INA did not challenge personal or subject matter jurisdiction of the District Court. The answer of the excess insurers, however, raised a number of defenses, including lack of *in personam* jurisdiction. Subsequently, this alleged lack of personal jurisdiction became the basis of a motion for summary judgment filed by the excess insurers. The issue in this case requires an account of respondent's attempt to use discovery in order to demonstrate the court's personal jurisdiction over the excess insurers.

Respondent's first discovery request—asking for "[c]opies of all business interruption insurance policies issued by defendant during the period from January 1, 1972 to December 31, 1975"—was served on each defendant in August 1976. In January 1977, the excess insurers objected, on grounds of burdensomeness, to producing such policies. Several months later, respondent filed a motion to compel petitioners to produce the requested documents. In June, 1978, the court orally overruled petitioners' objections. This was followed by a second discovery request in which respondent narrowed the files it was seeking to policies which "were delivered in . . . Pennsylvania . . . or covered a risk located in . . . Pennsylvania." Petitioners now objected that these documents were not in their custody or control; rather, they were kept by the brokers in London. The court ordered petitioners to request the information from the brokers, limiting the request to policies covering the period from 1971 to date. That was in July 1978; petitioners were given 90 days to produce the information. On November 8, petitioners were given an additional 30 days to complete discovery. On November 24, petitioners filed an affidavit offering to make their records, allegedly some 4 million files, available at their offices in London for inspection by respondent. Respondent countered with a motion to compel production of the previously requested documents. On December 21, 1978, the court, noting that no conscientious effort had yet been made to produce the requested information and that no

---

2. The district court described these excess insurers as follows:

"Of the 21 Excess Insurers, 5 are English companies representing English domestic interests but insuring risks throughout the world, particularly in Pennsylvania. Seven are English companies which represent non English parents, or affiliates. The United States, Japan, and Israel are the nationalities of two each of the Excess Insurer Defendants. Switzerland and the Republic of Ireland are the nationalities of one each of the Excess Insurer Defendants. The remaining Excess Insurer Defendant is a Belgium Company which represents the United States parent." 1 App. 196a.

objection had been entered to the discovery order in July, gave petitioners 60 more days to produce the requested information. He also issued the following warning:

> "[I]f you don't get it to him in 60 days, I am going to enter an order saying that because you failed to give the information as requested, that I am going to assume, under rule of Civil Procedure 37B, subsection 2(A), that there is jurisdiction." 1 App. 115a.

A few moments later he restated the warning as follows: "I will assume that jurisdiction is here with this court unless you produce statistics and other information in that regard that would indicate otherwise." Id., at 116a.

On April 19, 1979, the court, after concluding that the requested material had not been produced, imposed the threatened sanction, finding that "for the purpose of this litigation the Excess Insurers are subject to the *in personam* jurisdiction of this Court because of their business contacts with Pennsylvania." * * *

II

* * *

The validity of an order of a federal court depends upon that court's having jurisdiction over both the subject matter and the parties. Stoll v. Gottlieb, 305 U.S. 165, 171–172, 59 S.Ct. 134, 137, 138, 83 L.Ed. 104 (1938); Thompson v. Whitman, 18 Wall. 457, 465, 21 L.Ed. 897 (1874). The concepts of subject matter and personal jurisdiction, however, serve different purposes, and these different purposes affect the legal character of the two requirements. * * *

Federal courts are courts of limited jurisdiction. The character of the controversies over which federal judicial authority may extend are delineated in Article III, § 2, cl. 1. Jurisdiction of the lower federal courts is further limited to those subjects encompassed within a statutory grant of jurisdiction. Again, this reflects the constitutional source of federal judicial power: Apart from this Court, that power only exists "in such inferior Courts as the Congress may from time to time ordain and establish." Art. III, § 1.

Subject matter jurisdiction, then, is an Article III as well as a statutory requirement; it functions as a restriction on federal power, and contributes to the characterization of the federal sovereign. Certain legal consequences directly follow from this. For example, no action of the parties can confer subject matter jurisdiction upon a federal court. Thus, the consent of the parties is irrelevant, California v. La Rue, 409 U.S. 109, 93 S.Ct. 390, 34 L.Ed.2d 342 (1972), principles of estoppel do not apply, American Fire & Casualty Co. v. Finn, 341 U.S. 6, 17–18, 71 S.Ct. 534, 541–542, 95 L.Ed. 702 (1951), and a party does not waive the requirement by failing to challenge jurisdiction early in the proceedings. Similarly, a court, including an appellate court, will raise lack of subject matter jurisdiction on its own motion. * * *

None of this is true with respect to personal jurisdiction. The requirement that a court have personal jurisdiction flows not from Art. III, but from the Due Process Clause. The personal jurisdiction requirement recognizes and protects an individual liberty interest. It represents a restriction on judicial power not as a matter of sovereignty, but as a matter of individual liberty.[10] Thus, the test for personal jurisdiction requires that "the maintenance of the suit . . . not offend 'traditional notions of fair play and substantial justice.'" International Shoe v. Washington, 326 U.S. 310, 316, 66 S.Ct. 154, 158, 90 L.Ed. 95 (1945), quoting Milliken v. Meyer, 311 U.S. 457, 463, 61 S.Ct. 339, 342, 85 L.Ed. 278 (1940).

Because the requirement of personal jurisdiction represents first of all an individual right, it can, like other such rights, be waived. In McDonald v. Mabee, supra, the Court indicated that regardless of the power of the state to serve process, an individual may submit to the jurisdiction of the Court by appearance. A variety of legal arrangements have been taken to represent express or implied consent to the personal jurisdiction of the court. In National Equipment Rental v. Szukhent, 375 U.S. 311, 316, 84 S.Ct. 411, 414, 11 L.Ed.2d 354 (1964), we stated that "parties to a contract may agree in advance to submit to the jurisdiction of a given court," and in Petrowski v. Hawkeye–Security Co., 350 U.S. 495, 76 S.Ct. 490, 100 L.Ed. 639 (1956), the Court upheld the personal jurisdiction of a district court on the basis of a stipulation entered into by the defendant. In addition, lower federal courts have found such consent implicit in agreements to arbitrate.   *   *   *

In sum, the requirement of personal jurisdiction may be intentionally waived, or for various reasons a defendant may be estopped from raising the issue. These characteristics portray it for what it is—a

---

10. It is true that we have stated that the requirement of personal jurisdiction, as applied to state courts, reflects an element of federalism and the character of state sovereignty vis-a-vis other states. For example, in World–Wide Volkswagen Corp. v. Woodson, 444 U.S. 286, 291–292, 100 S.Ct. 559, 564, 62 L.Ed.2d 490 (1980), we stated:

"[A] state court may exercise personal jurisdiction over a nonresident defendant only so long as there exist 'minimum contacts' between the defendant and the forum State. The concept of minimum contacts, in turn, can be seen to perform two related, but distinguishable, functions. It protects the defendant against the burdens of litigating in a distant or inconvenient forum. And it acts to ensure that the States, through their courts, do not reach out beyond the limits imposed on them by their status as coequal sovereigns in a federal system." (Citations omitted.)

Contrary to the suggestion of Justice Powell, post, * * * our holding today does not alter the requirement that there be "minimum contacts" between the nonresident defendant and the forum state. Rather, our holding deals with how the facts needed to show those "minimum contacts" can be established when a defendant fails to comply with court-ordered discovery. The restriction on state sovereign power described in *World–Wide Volkswagen Corp.*, however, must be seen as ultimately a function of the individual liberty interest preserved by the Due Process Clause. That clause is the only source of the personal jurisdiction requirement and the clause itself makes no mention of federalism concerns. Furthermore, if the federalism concept operated as an independent restriction on the sovereign power of the court, it would not be possible to waive the personal jurisdiction requirement: Individual actions cannot change the powers of sovereignty, although the individual can subject himself to powers from which he may otherwise be protected.

legal right protecting the individual. The plaintiff's demonstration of certain historical facts may make clear to the court that it has personal jurisdiction over the defendant as a matter of law—i.e., certain factual showings will have legal consequences—but this is not the only way in which the personal jurisdiction of the court may arise. The actions of the defendant may amount to a legal submission to the jurisdiction of the court, whether voluntary or not.

The expression of legal rights is often subject to certain procedural rules: The failure to follow those rules may well result in a curtailment of the rights. Thus, the failure to enter a timely objection to personal jurisdiction constitutes, under Rule 12(h)(1), a waiver of the objection. A sanction under Rule 37(b)(2)(A) consisting of a finding of personal jurisdiction has precisely the same effect. As a general proposition, the Rule 37 sanction applied to a finding of personal jurisdiction creates no more of a due process problem than the Rule 12 waiver. Although "a court cannot conclude all persons interested by its mere assertion of its own power," Chicago Life Ins. Co. v. Cherry, supra, at 29, 37 S.Ct., at 493, not all rules that establish legal consequences to a party's own behavior are "mere assertions" of power.

Rule 37(b)(2)(A) itself embodies the standard established in Hammond Packing Co. v. Arkansas, 212 U.S. 322, 29 S.Ct. 370, 53 L.Ed. 530 (1909), for the due process limits on such rules.[11] There the Court held that it did not violate due process for a state court to strike the answer and render a default judgment against a defendant who failed to comply with a pretrial discovery order. Such a rule was permissible as an expression of "the undoubted right of the lawmaking power to create a presumption of fact as to the bad faith and untruth of an answer begotten from the suppression or failure to produce the proof ordered. . . . [T]he preservation of due process was secured by the presumption that the refusal to produce evidence material to the administration of due process was but an admission of the want of merit in the asserted defense." Id., at 350–351, 29 S.Ct., at 380.

*   *   *

Petitioners argue that a sanction consisting of a finding of personal jurisdiction differs from all other instances in which a sanction is imposed, including the default judgment in *Hammond Packing*, because a party need not obey the orders of a court until it is established that the court has personal jurisdiction over that party. If there is no obligation to obey a judicial order, a sanction cannot be applied for the failure to comply. Until the court has established personal jurisdiction, moreover, any assertion of judicial power over the party violates due process.

This argument again assumes that there is something unique about the requirement of personal jurisdiction, which prevents it from being

11. The Advisory Committee Notes to the Rule specifically stated that "the provisions of the rule find support in [Hammond Packing Co. v. Arkansas, 212 U.S. 322 [29 S.Ct. 370, 53 L.Ed. 530] (1909)]." * * * See also Societe Internationale v. Rogers, 357 U.S. 197, 209, 78 S.Ct. 1087, 1094, 2 L.Ed.2d 1255 (1958).

established or waived like other rights. A defendant is always free to ignore the judicial proceedings, risk a default judgment and then challenge that judgment on jurisdictional grounds in a collateral proceeding. See Baldwin v. Traveling Men's Ass'n, 283 U.S. 522, 525, 51 S.Ct. 517, 75 L.Ed. 1244 (1931). By submitting to the jurisdiction of the court for the limited purpose of challenging jurisdiction, the defendant agrees to abide by that court's determination on the issue of jurisdiction. That decision will be *res judicata* on that issue in any further proceedings. Id., at 524, 51 S.Ct., at 517. American Surety Co. v. Baldwin, 287 U.S. 156, 166, 53 S.Ct. 98, 101, 77 L.Ed. 234 (1932). As demonstrated above, the manner in which the court determines whether it has personal jurisdiction may include a variety of legal rules and presumptions, as well as straight forward fact-finding. A particular rule may offend the due process standard of *Hammond Packing,* but the mere use of procedural rules does not in itself violate the defendants due process rights.

III

Even if Rule 37(b)(2) may be applied to support a finding of personal jurisdiction, the question remains as to whether it was properly applied under the circumstances of this case.   *   *   *

*   *   * [P]etitioners had ample warning that a continued failure to comply with the discovery orders would lead to the imposition of this sanction. Furthermore, the proposed sanction made it clear that even if there was not compliance with the discovery order, this sanction would not be applied if petitioners were to "produce statistics and other information" that would indicate an absence of personal jurisdiction. 1 App. 116a. In effect, the district court simply placed the burden of proof upon petitioners on the issue of personal jurisdiction.[12] Petitioners failed to comply with the discovery order; they also failed to make any attempt to meet this burden of proof. This course of behavior coupled with the ample warnings demonstrate the "justice" of the trial court's order.

*   *   *

JUSTICE POWELL, concurring in the judgment.

*   *   *

In my view the Court's broadly theoretical decision misapprehends the issues actually presented for decision. Federal courts are courts of limited jurisdiction. Their personal jurisdiction, no less than their subject matter jurisdiction, is subject both to constitutional and to statutory definition. When the applicable limitations on federal jurisdiction are identified, it becomes apparent that the Court's theory could require a sweeping but largely unexplicated revision of jurisdictional doctrine. This revision could encompass not only the personal jurisdiction of federal courts but "sovereign" limitations on state jurisdiction as

---

12. Counsel for petitioners agreed to this characterization of the sanction at oral argument. Trans. of Oral Arg. 47–48.

identified in World–Wide Volkswagen Corp. v. Woodson, 444 U.S. 286, 291–293, 100 S.Ct. 559, 564–565, 62 L.Ed.2d 490 (1980). * * *

I

This lawsuit began when the respondent Compagnie des Bauxites brought a contract action against the petitioner insurance companies in the United States District Court for the Western District of Pennsylvania. Alleging diversity jurisdiction, respondent averred that the District Court had personal jurisdiction of the petitioners, all foreign corporations, under the long-arm statute of the State of Pennsylvania. See Compagnie des Bauxites de Guinea v. Insurance Co. of North America, 651 F.2d 877, 880, 881 (CA3 1981). Petitioners, however, denied that they were subject to the court's personal jurisdiction under that or any other statute. Viewing the question largely as one of fact, the court ordered discovery to resolve the dispute.

* * *

Rule 37(b) is not, however, a jurisdictional provision. As recognized by the Court of Appeals, the governing jurisdictional statute remains the long-arm statute of the State of Pennsylvania. See 651 F.2d, at 881. In my view the Court fails to make clear the implications of this central fact: that the District Court in this case relied on state law to obtain personal jurisdiction.

* * *

As a result of the District Court's dependence on the law of Pennsylvania to establish personal jurisdiction—a dependence mandated by Congress under 28 U.S.C. § 1652—its jurisdiction in this case normally would be subject to the same due process limitations as a state court. See, e.g., Forsythe v. Overmyer, supra, at 782; Washington v. Norton Mfg., Inc., 588 F.2d 441, 445 (CA5 1975); Fisons Ltd. v. United States, 458 F.2d 1241, 1250 (CA7 1972). * * *

* * *

A

Under traditional principles, the due process question in this case is whether "minimum contacts" exist between petitioners and the forum State that would justify the State in exercising personal jurisdiction. See, e.g., World–Wide Volkswagen Corp. v. Woodson, supra, 444 U.S., at 291–293, 100 S.Ct., at 564–565; Shaffer v. Heitner, 433 U.S. 186, 216, 97 S.Ct. 2569, 2586, 53 L.Ed.2d 683 (1977); Hanson v. Denckla, supra, 357 U.S., at 251, 78 S.Ct., at 1238. By finding that the establishment of minimum contacts is not a prerequisite to the exercise of jurisdiction to impose sanctions under Fed.Rule Civ.Proc. 37, the Court may be understood as finding that "minimum contacts" no longer is a constitutional requirement for the exercise by a state court of personal jurisdiction over an unconsenting defendant.[5] Whenever the Court's

---

5. The Court refers to the respondent's prima facie showing of "minimum contacts" only as one factor indicating that the District Court did not abuse its discretion in entering a finding of personal jurisdiction as a sanction under Rule 37(b).

notions of fairness are not offended, jurisdiction apparently may be upheld.

Before today, of course, our cases had linked minimum contacts and fair play as *jointly* defining the "sovereign" limits on state assertions of personal jurisdiction over unconsenting defendants. See World–Wide Volkswagen Corp. v. Woodson, supra, 444 U.S., at 292–293, 100 S.Ct., at 564–565; see Hanson v. Denckla, supra, 357 U.S., at 251, 78 S.Ct., at 1238. The Court appears to abandon the rationale of these cases in a footnote. See ante, * * * n. 10. But it does not address the implications of its action. By eschewing reliance on the concept of minimum contacts as a "sovereign" limitation on the power of States— for, again, it is the State's long-arm statute that is invoked to obtain personal jurisdiction in the District Court—the Court today effects a potentially substantial change of law. For the first time it defines personal jurisdiction solely by reference to abstract notions of fair play. And, astonishingly to me, it does so in a case in which this rationale for decision was neither argued nor briefed by the parties.

B

Alternatively, it is possible to read the Court opinion, not as affecting state jurisdiction, but simply as asserting that Rule 37 of the Federal Rules of Civil Procedure represents a congressionally approved basis for the exercise of personal jurisdiction by a federal district court. On this view Rule 37 vests the federal district courts with authority to take jurisdiction over persons not in compliance with discovery orders. * * *

* * * A plaintiff is not entitled to discovery to establish essentially speculative allegations necessary to personal jurisdiction. Nor would the use of Rule 37 sanctions to enforce discovery orders constitute a mere abuse of discretion in such a case. For me at least, such a use of discovery would raise serious questions as to the constitutional as well as the statutory authority of a federal court—in a diversity case—to exercise personal jurisdiction absent some showing of minimum contacts between the unconsenting defendant and the forum State.

II

In this case the facts alone—unaided by broad jurisdictional theories—more than amply demonstrate that the District Court possessed personal jurisdiction to impose sanctions under Rule 37 and otherwise to adjudicate this case. I would decide the case on this narrow basis.

As recognized both by the District Court and the Court of Appeals, the respondent adduced substantial support for its jurisdictional assertions. By affidavit and other evidence, it made a prima facie showing of "minimum contacts." See 651 F.2d, at 881–882, 886 and n. 9. In the view of the District Court, the evidence adduced actually was sufficient

* * * Generally it views the requirement of personal jurisdiction as a right that may be "established or waived like other rights." * * *

to sustain a finding of personal jurisdiction independently of the Rule 37 sanction. App. to Pet. for Cert. 51a, 53a.

Where the plaintiff has made a prima facie showing of minimum contacts, I have little difficulty in holding that its showing was sufficient to warrant the District Court's entry of discovery orders. And where a defendant then fails to comply with those orders, I agree that the prima facie showing may be held adequate to sustain the court's finding that minimum contacts exist, either under Rule 37 or under a theory of "presumption" or "waiver." * * *

BURGER KING CORP. v. RUDZEWICZ

Supreme Court of the United States, 1985.
471 U.S. 462, 105 S.Ct. 2174, 85 L.Ed.2d 528.*

JUSTICE BRENNAN delivered the opinion of the Court.

The State of Florida's long-arm statute extends jurisdiction to "[a]ny person, whether or not a citizen or resident of this state," who, inter alia, "[b]reach[es] a contract in this state by failing to perform acts required by the contract to be performed in this state," so long as the cause of action arises from the alleged contractual breach. Fla.Stat. § 48.193(1)(g) (Supp.1984). The United States District Court for the Southern District of Florida, sitting in diversity, relied on this provision in exercising personal jurisdiction over a Michigan resident who allegedly had breached a franchise agreement with a Florida corporation by failing to make required payments in Florida. The question presented is whether this exercise of long-arm jurisdiction offended "traditional conception[s] of fair play and substantial justice" embodied in the Due Process Clause of the Fourteenth Amendment. International Shoe Co. v. Washington, 326 U.S. 310, 320, 66 S.Ct. 154, 160, 90 L.Ed. 95 (1945).

I

A

Burger King Corporation is a Florida corporation whose principal offices are in Miami. It is one of the world's largest restaurant organizations, with over 3,000 outlets in the 50 States, the Commonwealth of Puerto Rico, and 8 foreign nations. Burger King conducts approximately 80% of its business through a franchise operation that the company styles the "Burger King System"—"a comprehensive restaurant format and operating system for the sale of uniform and quality food products." * * * Burger King licenses its franchisees to use its trademarks and service marks for a period of 20 years and leases standardized restaurant facilities to them for the same term. In addition, franchisees acquire a variety of proprietary information concerning the "standards, specifications, procedures and methods for operating a Burger King Restaurant." * * * They also receive

* Some of the Court's footnotes are omitted.

market research and advertising assistance; ongoing training in restaurant management;[2] and accounting, cost-control, and inventory-control guidance. By permitting franchisees to tap into Burger King's established national reputation and to benefit from proven procedures for dispensing standardized fare, this system enables them to go into the restaurant business with significantly lowered barriers to entry.

In exchange for these benefits, franchisees pay Burger King an initial $40,000 franchise fee and commit themselves to payment of monthly royalties, advertising and sales promotion fees, and rent computed in part from monthly gross sales. Franchisees also agree to submit to the national organization's exacting regulation of virtually every conceivable aspect of their operations. Burger King imposes these standards and undertakes its rigid regulation out of conviction that "[u]niformity of service, appearance, and quality of product is essential to the preservation of the Burger King image and the benefits accruing therefrom to both Franchisee and Franchisor."   *   *   *

Burger King oversees its franchise system through a two-tiered administrative structure. The governing contracts provide that the franchise relationship is established in Miami and governed by Florida law, and call for payment of all required fees and forwarding of all relevant notices to the Miami headquarters. The Miami headquarters sets policy and works directly with its franchisees in attempting to resolve major problems.   *   *   * Day-to-day monitoring of franchisees, however, is conducted through a network of 10 district offices which in turn report to the Miami headquarters.

The instant litigation grows out of Burger King's termination of one of its franchisees, and is aptly described by the franchisee as "a divorce proceeding among commercial partners."   *   *   * The appellee John Rudzewicz, a Michigan citizen and resident, is the senior partner in a Detroit accounting firm. In 1978, he was approached by Brian MacShara, the son of a business acquaintance, who suggested that they jointly apply to Burger King for a franchise in the Detroit area. MacShara proposed to serve as the manager of the restaurant if Rudzewicz would put up the investment capital; in exchange, the two would evenly share the profits. Believing that MacShara's idea offered attractive investment and tax-deferral opportunities, Rudzewicz agreed to the venture.   *   *   *

Rudzewicz and MacShara jointly applied for a franchise to Burger King's Birmingham, Michigan district office in the autumn of 1978. Their application was forwarded to Burger King's Miami headquarters, which entered into a preliminary agreement with them in February 1979. During the ensuing four months it was agreed that Rudzewicz and MacShara would assume operation of an existing facility in Drayton Plains, Michigan. MacShara attended the prescribed management

2. Mandatory training seminars are conducted at Burger King University in Miami and at Whopper College Regional Training Centers around the country.   *   *   *

courses in Miami during this period, see n. 2, supra, and the franchisees purchased $165,000 worth of restaurant equipment from Burger King's Davmor Industries division in Miami. Even before the final agreements were signed, however, the parties began to disagree over site-development fees, building design, computation of monthly rent, and whether the franchisees would be able to assign their liabilities to a corporation they had formed.[6] During these disputes Rudzewicz and MacShara negotiated both with the Birmingham district office and with the Miami headquarters.[7] With some misgivings, Rudzewicz and Mac-Shara finally obtained limited concessions from the Miami headquarters,[8] signed the final agreements, and commenced operations in June 1979. By signing the final agreements, Rudzewicz obligated himself personally to payments exceeding $1 million over the 20–year franchise relationship.

The Drayton Plains facility apparently enjoyed steady business during the summer of 1979, but patronage declined after a recession began later that year. Rudzewicz and MacShara soon fell far behind in their monthly payments to Miami. Headquarters sent notices of default, and an extended period of negotiations began among the franchisees, the Birmingham district office, and the Miami headquarters. After several Burger King officials in Miami had engaged in prolonged but ultimately unsuccessful negotiations with the franchisees by mail and by telephone,[9] headquarters terminated the franchise and ordered Rudzewicz and MacShara to vacate the premises. They refused and

6. The latter two matters were the major areas of disagreement. Notwithstanding that Burger King's franchise offering advised that minimum rent would be based on a percentage of "approximated capitalized site acquisition and construction costs," * * * Rudzewicz assumed that rent would be a function solely of renovation costs, and he thereby underestimated the minimum monthly rent by more than $2,000. The District Court found Rudzewicz's interpretation "incredible." * * *

With respect to assignment, Rudzewicz and MacShara had formed RMBK Corp. with the intent of assigning to it all of their interest and liabilities in the franchise. Consistent with the contract documents, however, Burger King insisted that the two remain personally liable for their franchise obligations. * * * Although the franchisees contended that Burger King officials had given them oral assurances concerning assignment, the District Court found that pursuant to the parol evidence rule any such assurances "even if they had been made and were misleading were joined and merged" into the final agreement. * * *

7. Although Rudzewicz and MacShara dealt with the Birmingham district office on a regular basis, they communicated directly with the Miami headquarters in forming the contracts; moreover, they learned that the district office had "very little" decisionmaking authority and accordingly turned directly to headquarters in seeking to resolve their disputes. * * *

8. They were able to secure a $10,439 reduction in rent for the third year. * * *

9. Miami's policy was to "deal directly" with franchisees when they began to encounter financial difficulties, and to involve district office personnel only when necessary. * * * In the instant case, for example, the Miami office handled all credit problems, ordered cost-cutting measures, negotiated for a partial refinancing of the franchisees' debts, communicated directly with the franchisees in attempting to resolve the dispute, and was responsible for all termination matters. * * *

continued to occupy and operate the facility as a Burger King restaurant.

B   (P. C.)

Burger King commenced the instant action in the United States District Court for the Southern District of Florida in May 1981, invoking that court's diversity jurisdiction pursuant to 28 U.S.C. § 1332(a) and its original jurisdiction over federal trademark disputes pursuant to § 1338(a). Burger King alleged that Rudzewicz and MacShara had breached their franchise obligations "within [the jurisdiction of] this district court" by failing to make the required payments "at plaintiff's place of business in Miami, Dade County, Florida," * * * and also charged that they were tortiously infringing its trademarks and service marks through their continued, unauthorized operation as a Burger King restaurant * * *. Burger King sought damages, injunctive relief, and costs and attorney's fees. Rudzewicz and MacShara entered special appearances and argued, inter alia, that because they were Michigan residents and because Burger King's claim did not "arise" within the Southern District of Florida, the District Court lacked personal jurisdiction over them. The District Court denied their motions after a hearing, holding that, pursuant to Florida's long-arm statute, "a nonresident Burger King franchisee is subject to the personal jurisdiction of this Court in actions arising out of its franchise agreements." * * * Rudzewicz and MacShara then filed an answer and a counterclaim seeking damages for alleged violations by Burger King of Michigan's Franchise Investment Law, Mich.Comp.Laws § 445.1501 et seq. (1979).

After a 3–day bench trial, the court again concluded that it had "jurisdiction over the subject matter and the parties to this cause." App. 159. Finding that Rudzewicz and MacShara had breached their franchise agreements with Burger King and had infringed Burger King's trademarks and service marks, the court entered judgment against them, jointly and severally, for $228,875 in contract damages. The court also ordered them "to immediately close Burger King Restaurant Number 775 from continued operation or to immediately give the keys and possession of said restaurant to Burger King Corporation," * * * found that they had failed to prove any of the required elements of their counterclaim, and awarded costs and attorney's fees to Burger King.

Rudzewicz appealed to the Court of Appeals for the Eleventh Circuit.[11] A divided panel of that Circuit reversed the judgment,

11. MacShara did not appeal his judgment. See Burger King Corp. v. MacShara, 724 F.2d 1505, 1506, n. 1 (CA11 1984). In addition, Rudzewicz entered into a compromise with Burger King and waived his right to appeal the District Court's finding of trademark infringement and its entry of injunctive relief. * * *

Accordingly, we need not address the extent to which the tortious act provisions of Florida's long-arm statute, see Fla.Stat. § 48.193(1)(b) (Supp.1984), may constitutionally extend to out-of-state trademark infringement. Compare Calder v. Jones, 465 U.S. 783, 788–789, 104 S.Ct. 1482, 1486–1487, 79 L.Ed.2d 804 (1984) (tortious

concluding that the District Court could not properly exercise personal jurisdiction over Rudzewicz pursuant to Fla.Stat. § 48.193(1)(g) (Supp. 1984) because "the circumstances of the Drayton Plains franchise and the negotiations which led to it left Rudzewicz bereft of reasonable notice and financially unprepared for the prospect of franchise litigation in Florida." Burger King Corp. v. MacShara, 724 F.2d 1505, 1513 (1984). Accordingly, the panel majority concluded that "[j]urisdiction under these circumstances would offend the fundamental fairness which is the touchstone of due process." Ibid.

* * *

II

A

The Due Process Clause protects an individual's liberty interest in not being subject to the binding judgments of a forum with which he has established no meaningful "contacts, ties, or relations." International Shoe Co. v. Washington, 326 U.S., at 319, 66 S.Ct., at 160.[13] By requiring that individuals have "fair warning that a particular activity may subject [them] to the jurisdiction of a foreign sovereign," Shaffer v. Heitner, 433 U.S. 186, 218, 97 S.Ct. 2569, 2587, 53 L.Ed.2d 683 (1977) (STEVENS, J., concurring in judgment), the Due Process Clause "gives a degree of predictability to the legal system that allows potential defendants to structure their primary conduct with some minimum assurance as to where that conduct will and will not render them liable to suit," World–Wide Volkswagen Corp. v. Woodson, 444 U.S. 286, 297, 100 S.Ct. 559, 567, 62 L.Ed.2d 490 (1980).

Where a forum seeks to assert specific jurisdiction over an out-of-state defendant who has not consented to suit there,[14] this "fair warning" requirement is satisfied if the defendant has "purposefully directed" his activities at residents of the forum, Keeton v. Hustler Magazine, Inc., 465 U.S. 770, 774, 104 S.Ct. 1473, 1478, 79 L.Ed.2d 790 (1984), and the litigation results from alleged injuries that "arise out of or relate to" those activities, Helicopteros Nacionales de Colombia, S.A. v. Hall,

---

out-of-state conduct); Keeton v. Hustler Magazine, Inc., 465 U.S. 770, 776, 104 S.Ct. 1473, 1479, 79 L.Ed.2d 790 (1984) (same).

13. Although this protection operates to restrict state power, it "must be seen as ultimately a function of the individual liberty interest preserved by the Due Process Clause" rather than as a function "of federalism concerns." Insurance Corp. of Ireland, Ltd. v. Compagnie des Bauxites de Guinee, 456 U.S. 694, 702–703, n. 10, 102 S.Ct. 2099, 2104–2105, n. 10, 72 L.Ed.2d 492 (1982).

14. We have noted that, because the personal jurisdiction requirement is a waivable right, there are a "variety of legal arrangements" by which a litigant may give "express or implied consent to the personal jurisdiction of the court." Insurance Corp. of Ireland, Ltd. v. Compagnie des Bauxites de Guinee, supra, at 703, 102 S.Ct., at 2105. For example, particularly in the commercial context, parties frequently stipulate in advance to submit their controversies for resolution within a particular jurisdiction. See National Equipment Rental, Ltd. v. Szukhent, 375 U.S. 311, 84 S.Ct. 411, 11 L.Ed.2d 354 (1964). Where such forum-selection provisions have been obtained through "freely negotiated" agreements and are not "unreasonable and unjust," The Bremen v. Zapata Off-Shore Co., 407 U.S. 1, 15, 92 S.Ct. 1907, 1916, 32 L.Ed.2d 513 (1972), their enforcement does not offend due process.

466 U.S. 408, 414, 104 S.Ct. 1868, 1872, 80 L.Ed.2d 404 (1984).[15] Thus "[t]he forum State does not exceed its powers under the Due Process Clause if it asserts personal jurisdiction over a corporation that delivers its products into the stream of commerce with the expectation that they will be purchased by consumers in the forum State" and those products subsequently injure forum consumers. World–Wide Volkswagen Corp. v. Woodson, supra, 444 U.S., at 297–298, 100 S.Ct., at 567–568. Similarly, a publisher who distributes magazines in a distant State may fairly be held accountable in that forum for damages resulting there from an allegedly defamatory story. Keeton v. Hustler Magazine, Inc., supra; see also Calder v. Jones, 465 U.S. 783, 104 S.Ct. 1482, 79 L.Ed.2d 804 (1984) (suit against author and editor). And with respect to interstate contractual obligations, we have emphasized that parties who "reach out beyond one state and create continuing relationships and obligations with citizens of another state" are subject to regulation and sanctions in the other State for the consequences of their activities. Travelers Health Assn. v. Virginia, 339 U.S. 643, 647, 70 S.Ct. 927, 929, 94 L.Ed. 1154 (1950). See also McGee v. International Life Insurance Co., 355 U.S. 220, 222–223, 78 S.Ct. 199, 200–201, 2 L.Ed.2d 223 (1957).

We have noted several reasons why a forum legitimately may exercise personal jurisdiction over a nonresident who "purposefully directs" his activities toward forum residents. A State generally has a "manifest interest" in providing its residents with a convenient forum for redressing injuries inflicted by out-of-state actors. Id., at 223, 78 S.Ct., at 201; see also Keeton v. Hustler Magazine, Inc., supra, 465 U.S., at 776, 104 S.Ct., at 1479. Moreover, where individuals "purposefully derive benefit" from their interstate activities, Kulko v. California Superior Court, 436 U.S. 84, 96, 98 S.Ct. 1690, 1699, 56 L.Ed.2d 132 (1978), it may well be unfair to allow them to escape having to account in other States for consequences that arise proximately from such activities; the Due Process Clause may not readily be wielded as a territorial shield to avoid interstate obligations that have been voluntarily assumed. And because "modern transportation and communications have made it much less burdensome for a party sued to defend himself in a State where he engages in economic activity," it usually will not be unfair to subject him to the burdens of litigating in another forum for disputes relating to such activity. McGee v. International Life Insurance Co., supra, 355 U.S., at 223, 78 S.Ct., at 201.

Notwithstanding these considerations, the constitutional touchstone remains whether the defendant purposefully established "minimum contacts" in the forum State. International Shoe Co. v. Washington, supra, 326 U.S., at 316, 66 S.Ct., at 158. Although it has been argued that foreseeability of causing *injury* in another State should be

---

15. "Specific" jurisdiction contrasts with "general" jurisdiction, pursuant to which "a State exercises personal jurisdiction over a defendant in a suit not arising out of or related to the defendant's contacts with the forum." Helicopteros Nacionales de Colombia, S.A. v. Hall, 466 U.S., at 414, n. 9, 104 S.Ct. 1868, 1872, n. 9, 80 L.Ed.2d 404 (1984); see also Perkins v. Benguet Consolidated Mining Co., 342 U.S. 437, 72 S.Ct. 413, 96 L.Ed. 485 (1952).

sufficient to establish such contacts there when policy considerations so require,[16] the Court has consistently held that this kind of foreseeability is not a "sufficient benchmark" for exercising personal jurisdiction. World–Wide Volkswagen Corp. v. Woodson, 444 U.S., at 295, 100 S.Ct., at 566. Instead, "the foreseeability that is critical to due process analysis . . . is that the defendant's conduct and connection with the forum State are such that he should reasonably anticipate being haled into court there." Id., at 297, 100 S.Ct., at 567. In defining when it is that a potential defendant should "reasonably anticipate" out-of-state litigation, the Court frequently has drawn from the reasoning of Hanson v. Denckla, 357 U.S. 235, 253, 78 S.Ct. 1228, 1239–1240, 2 L.Ed.2d 1283 (1958):

> "The unilateral activity of those who claim some relationship with a nonresident defendant cannot satisfy the requirement of contact with the forum State. The application of that rule will vary with the quality and nature of the defendant's activity, but it is essential in each case that there be some act by which the defendant purposefully avails itself of the privilege of conducting activities within the forum State, thus invoking the benefits and protections of its laws."

This "purposeful availment" requirement ensures that a defendant will not be haled into a jurisdiction solely as a result of "random," "fortuitous," or "attenuated" contacts, Keeton v. Hustler Magazine, Inc., 465 U.S., at 774, 104 S.Ct., at 1478; World–Wide Volkswagen Corp. v. Woodson, 444 U.S., at 299, 100 S.Ct., at 568, or of the "unilateral activity of another party or a third person," Helicopteros Nacionales de Colombia, S.A. v. Hall, supra, 466 U.S., at 417, 104 S.Ct., at 1873.[17] Jurisdiction is proper, however, where the contacts proximately result from actions by the defendant *himself* that create a "substantial connection" with the forum State. McGee v. International Life Insurance Co., supra, 355 U.S., at 223, 78 S.Ct., at 201; see also Kulko v. California Superior Court, supra, 436 U.S., at 94, n. 7, 98 S.Ct., at 1698, n. 7.[18] Thus where the defendant "deliberately" has engaged in signifi-

---

16. See, e.g., World–Wide Volkswagen Corp. v. Woodson, 444 U.S. 286, 299, 100 S.Ct. 559, 568, 62 L.Ed.2d 490 (1980) (Brennan, J., dissenting); Shaffer v. Heitner, 433 U.S. 186, 219, 97 S.Ct. 2569, 2588, 53 L.Ed. 2d 683 (1977) (Brennan, J., concurring in part and dissenting in part).

17. Applying this principle, the Court has held that the Due Process Clause forbids the exercise of personal jurisdiction over an out-of-state automobile distributor whose only tie to the forum resulted from a customer's decision to drive there, World–Wide Volkswagen Corp. v. Woodson, supra; over a divorced husband sued for child-support payments whose only affiliation with the forum was created by his former spouse's decision to settle there, Kulko v. California Superior Court, supra; and over

a trustee whose only connection with the forum resulted from the settlor's decision to exercise her power of appointment there, Hanson v. Denckla, 357 U.S. 235, 78 S.Ct. 1228, 2 L.Ed.2d 1283 (1958). In such instances, the defendant has had no "clear notice that it is subject to suit" in the forum and thus no opportunity to "alleviate the risk of burdensome litigation" there. World–Wide Volkswagen Corp. v. Woodson, supra, 444 U.S., at 297, 100 S.Ct., at 567.

18. So long as it creates a "substantial connection" with the forum, even a single act can support jurisdiction. McGee v. International Life Insurance Co., 355 U.S. 220, 223, 78 S.Ct. 199, 201, 2 L.Ed.2d 223 (1957). The Court has noted, however, that "some single or occasional acts" relat-

cant activities within a State, Keeton v. Hustler Magazine, Inc., 465 U.S., at 781, 104 S.Ct., at 1481, or has created "continuing obligations" between himself and residents of the forum, Travelers Health Assn. v. Virginia, 339 U.S., at 648, 70 S.Ct., at 929, he manifestly has availed himself of the privilege of conducting business there, and because his activities are shielded by "the benefits and protections" of the forum's laws it is presumptively not unreasonable to require him to submit to the burdens of litigation in that forum as well.

delib.

protection
&
bene's

Jurisdiction in these circumstances may not be avoided merely because the defendant did not *physically* enter the forum State. Although territorial presence frequently will enhance a potential defendant's affiliation with a State and reinforce the reasonable foreseeability of suit there, it is an inescapable fact of modern commercial life that a substantial amount of business is transacted solely by mail and wire communications across state lines, thus obviating the need for physical presence within a State in which business is conducted. So long as a commercial actor's efforts are "purposefully directed" toward residents of another State, we have consistently rejected the notion that an absence of physical contacts can defeat personal jurisdiction there. Keeton v. Hustler Magazine, Inc., supra, 465 U.S., at 774–775, 104 S.Ct., at 1478; see also Calder v. Jones, 465 U.S., at 778–790, 104 S.Ct., at 1486–1487; McGee v. International Life Insurance Co., 355 U.S., at 222–223, 78 S.Ct., at 200–201. Cf. Hoopeston Canning Co. v. Cullen, 318 U.S. 313, 317, 63 S.Ct. 602, 605, 87 L.Ed. 777 (1943).

Once it has been decided that a defendant purposefully established minimum contacts within the forum State, these contacts may be considered in light of other factors to determine whether the assertion of personal jurisdiction would comport with "fair play and substantial justice." International Shoe Co. v. Washington, 326 U.S., at 320, 66 S.Ct., at 160. Thus courts in "appropriate case[s]" may evaluate "the burden on the defendant," "the forum State's interest in adjudicating the dispute," "the plaintiff's interest in obtaining convenient and effective relief," "the interstate judicial system's interest in obtaining the most efficient resolution of controversies," and the "shared interest of the several States in furthering fundamental substantive social policies." World–Wide Volkswagen Corp. v. Woodson, supra, 444 U.S., at 292, 100 S.Ct., at 564. These considerations sometimes serve to establish the reasonableness of jurisdiction upon a lesser showing of minimum contacts than would otherwise be required. See, e.g., Keeton v. Hustler Magazine, Inc., supra, 465 U.S., at 780, 104 S.Ct., at 1481; Calder v. Jones, supra, 465 U.S., at 788–789, 104 S.Ct., at 1486–1487; McGee v. International Life Insurance Co., supra, 355 U.S., at 223–224,

---

ed to the forum may not be sufficient to establish jurisdiction if "their nature and quality and the circumstances of their commission" create only an "attenuated" affiliation with the forum. International Shoe Co. v. Washington, 326 U.S. 310, 318, 66 S.Ct. 154, 159, 90 L.Ed. 95 (1945); World– Wide Volkswagen Corp. v. Woodson, 444 U.S., at 299, 100 S.Ct., at 568. This distinction derives from the belief that, with respect to this category of "isolated" acts, id., at 297, 100 S.Ct., at 567, the reasonable foreseeability of litigation in the forum is substantially diminished.

78 S.Ct., at 201–202. On the other hand, where a defendant who purposefully has directed his activities at forum residents seeks to defeat jurisdiction, he must present a compelling case that the presence of some other considerations would render jurisdiction unreasonable. Most such considerations usually may be accommodated through means short of finding jurisdiction unconstitutional. For example, the potential clash of the forum's law with the "fundamental substantive social policies" of another State may be accommodated through application of the forum's choice-of-law rules.[19] Similarly, a defendant claiming substantial inconvenience may seek a change of venue.[20] Nevertheless, minimum requirements inherent in the concept of "fair play and substantial justice" may defeat the reasonableness of jurisdiction even if the defendant has purposefully engaged in forum activities. World–Wide Volkswagen Corp. v. Woodson, 444 U.S., at 292, 100 S.Ct., at 564; see also Restatement (Second) of Conflict of Laws §§ 36–37 (1971). As we previously have noted, jurisdictional rules may not be employed in such a way as to make litigation "so gravely difficult and inconvenient" that a party unfairly is at a "severe disadvantage" in comparison to his opponent. The Bremen v. Zapata Off–Shore Co., 407 U.S. 1, 18, 92 S.Ct. 1907, 1917, 32 L.Ed.2d 513 (1972) (re forum-selection provisions); McGee v. International Life Insurance Co., supra, 355 U.S., at 223–224, 78 S.Ct., at 201–202.

B

(1)

Applying these principles to the case at hand, we believe there is substantial record evidence supporting the District Court's conclusion that the assertion of personal jurisdiction over Rudzewicz in Florida for the alleged breach of his franchise agreement did not offend due process. At the outset, we note a continued division among lower courts respecting whether and to what extent a contract can constitute a "contact" for purposes of due process analysis. If the question is whether an individual's contract with an out-of-state party *alone* can automatically establish sufficient minimum contacts in the other party's home forum, we believe the answer clearly is that it cannot. The Court long ago rejected the notion that personal jurisdiction might turn on "mechanical" tests, International Shoe Co. v. Washington, 326 U.S., at 319, 66 S.Ct., at 159, or on "conceptualistic . . . theories of the

---

19. See Allstate Insurance Co. v. Hague, 449 U.S. 302, 307–313, 101 S.Ct. 633, 637–640, 66 L.Ed.2d 521 (1981) (opinion of Brennan, J.). See generally Restatement (Second) of Conflict of Laws §§ 6, 9 (1971).

20. See, e.g., 28 U.S.C. § 1404(a) ("For the convenience of parties and witnesses, in the interest of justice, a district court may transfer any civil action to any other district or division where it might have been brought"). This provision embodies in an expanded version the common law doctrine of forum non conveniens, under which a court in appropriate circumstances may decline to exercise its jurisdiction in the interest of the "easy, expeditious and inexpensive" resolution of a controversy in another forum. See Gulf Oil Corp. v. Gilbert, 330 U.S. 501, 508–509, 67 S.Ct. 839, 843, 91 L.Ed. 1055 (1947).

place of contracting or of performance," Hoopeston Canning Co. v. Cullen, 318 U.S., at 316, 63 S.Ct., at 604. Instead, we have emphasized the need for a "highly realistic" approach that recognizes that a "contract" is "ordinarily but an intermediate step serving to tie up prior business negotiations with future consequences which themselves are the real object of the business transaction." Id., at 316–317, 63 S.Ct., at 604–605. It is these factors—prior negotiations and contemplated future consequences, along with the terms of the contract and the parties' actual course of dealing—that must be evaluated in determining whether the defendant purposefully established minimum contacts within the forum.

In this case, no physical ties to Florida can be attributed to Rudzewicz other than MacShara's brief training course in Miami.[22] Rudzewicz did not maintain offices in Florida and, for all that appears from the record, has never even visited there. Yet this franchise dispute grew directly out of "a contract which had a *substantial* connection with that State." McGee v. International Life Insurance Co., 355 U.S., at 223, 78 S.Ct., at 201 (emphasis added). Eschewing the option of operating an independent local enterprise, Rudzewicz deliberately "reach[ed] out beyond" Michigan and negotiated with a Florida corporation for the purchase of a long-term franchise and the manifold benefits that would derive from affiliation with a nationwide organization. Travelers Health Assn. v. Virginia, 339 U.S., at 647, 70 S.Ct., at 929. Upon approval, he entered into a carefully structured 20–year relationship that envisioned continuing and wide-reaching contacts with Burger King in Florida. In light of Rudzewicz's voluntary acceptance of the long-term and exacting regulation of his business from Burger King's Miami headquarters, the "quality and nature" of his relationship to the company in Florida can in no sense be viewed as "random," "fortuitous," or "attenuated." Hanson v. Denckla, 357 U.S., at 253, 78 S.Ct., at 1239; Keeton v. Hustler Magazine, Inc., 465 U.S., at 774, 104 S.Ct., at 1478; World–Wide Volkswagen Corp. v. Woodson, 444 U.S., at 299, 100 S.Ct., at 568. Rudzewicz's refusal to make the contractually required payments in Miami, and his continued use of Burger King's trademarks and confidential business information after

---

22. The Eleventh Circuit held that MacShara's presence in Florida was irrelevant to the question of Rudzewicz's minimum contacts with that forum, reasoning that "Rudzewicz and MacShara never formed a partnership" and "signed the agreements in their individual capacities." 724 F.2d, at 1513, n. 14. The two did jointly form a corporation through which they were seeking to conduct the franchise, however. See n. 6, supra. They were required to decide which one of them would travel to Florida to satisfy the training requirements so that they could commence business, and Rudzewicz participated in the decision that MacShara would go there. We have previously noted that when commercial activities are "carried on in behalf of" an out-of-state party those activities may sometimes be ascribed to the party, International Shoe Co. v. Washington, 326 U.S. 310, 320, 66 S.Ct. 154, 160, 90 L.Ed. 95 (1945), at least where he is a "primary participan[t]" in the enterprise and has acted purposefully in directing those activities, Calder v. Jones, 465 U.S., at 790, 104 S.Ct., at 1487. Because MacShara's matriculation at Burger King University is not pivotal to the disposition of this case, we need not resolve the permissible bounds of such attribution.

his termination, caused foreseeable injuries to the corporation in Florida. For these reasons it was, at the very least, presumptively reasonable for Rudzewicz to be called to account there for such injuries.

The Court of Appeals concluded, however, that in light of the supervision emanating from Burger King's district office in Birmingham, Rudzewicz reasonably believed that "the Michigan office was for all intents and purposes the embodiment of Burger King" and that he therefore had no "reason to anticipate a Burger King suit outside of Michigan." 724 F.2d, at 1511. * * * This reasoning overlooks substantial record evidence indicating that Rudzewicz most certainly knew that he was affiliating himself with an enterprise based primarily in Florida. The contract documents themselves emphasize that Burger King's operations are conducted and supervised from the Miami headquarters, that all relevant notices and payments must be sent there, and that the agreements were made in and enforced from Miami. Moreover, the parties' actual course of dealing repeatedly confirmed that decisionmaking authority was vested in the Miami headquarters and that the district office served largely as an intermediate link between the headquarters and the franchisees. When problems arose over building design, site-development fees, rent computation, and the defaulted payments, Rudzewicz and MacShara learned that the Michigan office was powerless to resolve their disputes and could only channel their communications to Miami. Throughout these disputes, the Miami headquarters and the Michigan franchisees carried on a continuous course of direct communications by mail and by telephone, and it was the Miami headquarters that made the key negotiating decisions out of which the instant litigation arose. See nn. 7, 9, supra.

Moreover, we believe the Court of Appeals gave insufficient weight to provisions in the various franchise documents providing that all disputes would be governed by Florida law. The franchise agreement, for example, stated:

> "This Agreement shall become valid when executed and accepted by BKC at Miami, Florida; it shall be deemed made and entered into in the State of Florida and shall be governed and construed under and in accordance with the laws of the State of Florida. The choice of law designation does not require that all suits concerning this Agreement be filed in Florida." * * *

See also n. 5, supra. The Court of Appeals reasoned that choice-of-law provisions are irrelevant to the question of personal jurisdiction, relying on Hanson v. Denckla for the proposition that "the center of gravity for choice-of-law purposes does not necessarily confer the sovereign prerogative to assert jurisdiction." 724 F.2d, at 1511–1512, n. 10, citing 357 U.S., at 254, 78 S.Ct., at 1240. This reasoning misperceives the import of the quoted proposition. The Court in *Hanson* and subsequent cases has emphasized that choice-of-law *analysis* —which focuses on all elements of a transaction, and not simply on the defendant's conduct— is distinct from minimum-contacts jurisdictional analysis—which focuses at the threshold solely on the defendant's purposeful connection to the forum.[23] Nothing in our cases, however, suggests that a choice-of-law *provision* should be ignored in considering whether a defendant has "purposefully invoked the benefits and protections of a State's laws" for jurisdictional purposes. Although such a provision standing alone would be insufficient to confer jurisdiction, we believe that, when combined with the 20–year interdependent relationship Rudzewicz established with Burger King's Miami headquarters, it reinforced his deliberate affiliation with the forum State and the reasonable foreseeability of possible litigation there. As Judge Johnson argued in his dissent below, Rudzewicz "purposefully availed himself of the benefits and protections of Florida's laws" by entering into contracts expressly providing that those laws would govern franchise disputes. 724 F.2d, at 1513.[24]

(2)

Nor has Rudzewicz pointed to other factors that can be said persuasively to outweigh the considerations discussed above and to establish the *unconstitutionality* of Florida's assertion of jurisdiction. We cannot conclude that Florida had no "legitimate interest in holding [Rudzewicz] answerable on a claim related to" the contacts he had established in that State. Keeton v. Hustler Magazine, Inc., 465 U.S., at 776, 104 S.Ct., at 1479; see also McGee v. International Life Insurance Co., 355 U.S., at 223, 78 S.Ct., at 201 (noting that State frequently will have a "manifest interest in providing effective means of redress for its residents").[25] Moreover, although Rudzewicz has argued at some length that Michigan's Franchise Investment Law, Mich.Comp.Laws § 445.1501 et seq. (1979), governs many aspects of this franchise relationship, he has not demonstrated how Michigan's acknowledged inter-

---

23. Hanson v. Denckla, 357 U.S., at 253–254, 78 S.Ct., at 1239–1240. See also Keeton v. Hustler Magazine, Inc., 465 U.S., at 778, 104 S.Ct., at 1480; Kulko v. California Superior Court, 436 U.S., at 98, 98 S.Ct., at 1700; Shaffer v. Heitner, 433 U.S., at 215, 97 S.Ct., at 2585.

24. In addition, the franchise agreement's disclaimer that the "choice of law designation does not *require* that all suits concerning this Agreement be filed in Florida," * * * (emphasis added), reasonably should have suggested to Rudzewicz that by negative implication such suits *could* be filed there.

The lease also provided for binding arbitration in Miami of certain condemnation disputes, * * * and Rudzewicz conceded the validity of this provision at oral argument. * * * Although it does not govern the instant dispute, this provision also should have made it apparent to the fran-

chisees that they were dealing directly with the Miami headquarters and that the Birmingham district office was *not* "for all intents and purposes the embodiment of Burger King." 724 F.2d, at 1511.

25. Complaining that "when Burger King is the plaintiff, you won't 'have it your way' because it sues all franchisees in Miami," Brief for Appellee 19, Rudzewicz contends that Florida's interest in providing a convenient forum is negligible given the company's size and ability to conduct litigation anywhere in the country. We disagree. Absent compelling considerations, cf. McGee v. International Life Insurance Co., 355 U.S., at 223, 78 S.Ct., at 201, a defendant who has purposefully derived commercial benefit from his affiliations in a forum may not defeat jurisdiction there simply because of his adversary's greater net wealth.

est might possibly render jurisdiction in Florida *unconstitutional.*[26] Finally, the Court of Appeals' assertion that the Florida litigation "severely impaired [Rudzewicz's] ability to call Michigan witnesses who might be essential to his defense and counterclaim," 724 F.2d, at 1512–1513, is wholly without support in the record. And even to the extent that it is inconvenient for a party who has minimum contacts with a forum to litigate there, such considerations most frequently can be accommodated through a change of venue. See n. 20, supra. Although the Court has suggested that inconvenience may at some point become so substantial as to achieve *constitutional* magnitude, McGee v. International Life Insurance Co., supra, 355 U.S., at 223, 78 S.Ct., at 201, this is not such a case.

The Court of Appeals also concluded, however, that the parties' dealings involved "a characteristic disparity of bargaining power" and "elements of surprise," and that Rudzewicz "lacked fair notice" of the potential for litigation in Florida because the contractual provisions suggesting to the contrary were merely "boilerplate declarations in a lengthy printed contract." 724 F.2d, at 1511–1512, and n. 10. See also post * * * (STEVENS, J., dissenting). Rudzewicz presented many of these arguments to the District Court, contending that Burger King was guilty of misrepresentation, fraud, and duress; that it gave insufficient notice in its dealings with him; and that the contract was one of adhesion. * * * After a 3–day bench trial, the District Court found that Burger King had made no misrepresentations, that Rudzewicz and MacShara "were and are experienced and sophisticated businessmen," and that "at no time" did they "ac[t] under economic duress or disadvantage imposed by" Burger King. * * * Federal Rule of Civil Procedure 52(a) requires that "[f]indings of fact shall not be set aside unless clearly erroneous," and neither Rudzewicz nor the Court of Appeals have pointed to record evidence that would support a "definite and firm conviction" that the District Court's findings are mistaken. United States v. United States Gypsum Co., 333 U.S. 364, 395, 68 S.Ct. 525, 542, 92 L.Ed. 746 (1948). See also Anderson v. Bessemer City, 470 U.S. 564, 573–576, 105 S.Ct. 1504, 1511–1513, 84 L.Ed.2d 518 (1985). To the contrary, Rudzewicz was represented by counsel throughout these complex transactions and, as Judge Johnson observed in dissent below, was himself an experienced accountant "who for five months conducted negotiations with Burger King over the terms of the franchise and lease agreements, and who obligated himself personally to contracts requir-

---

26. Rudzewicz has failed to show how the District Court's exercise of jurisdiction in this case might have been at all inconsistent with Michigan's interests. To the contrary, the court found that Burger King had fully complied with Michigan law, * * * and there is nothing in Michigan's franchise act suggesting that Michigan would attempt to assert exclusive jurisdiction to resolve franchise disputes affecting its residents. In any event, minimum-contacts analysis presupposes that two or more States may be interested in the outcome of a dispute, and the process of resolving potentially conflicting "fundamental substantive social policies," World-Wide Volkswagen Corp. v. Woodson, 444 U.S., at 292, 100 S.Ct., at 564, can usually be accommodated through choice-of-law rules rather than through outright preclusion of jurisdiction in one forum. See n. 19, supra.

ing over time payments that exceeded $1 million." 724 F.2d, at 1514. Rudzewicz was able to secure a modest reduction in rent and other concessions from Miami headquarters, see nn. 8–9, supra; moreover, to the extent that Burger King's terms were inflexible, Rudzewicz presumably decided that the advantages of affiliating with a national organization provided sufficient commercial benefits as to offset the detriments.[28]

III

Notwithstanding these considerations, the Court of Appeals apparently believed that it was necessary to reject jurisdiction in this case as a prophylactic measure, reasoning that an affirmance of the District Court's judgment would result in the exercise of jurisdiction over "out-of-state consumers to collect payments due on modest personal purchases" and would "sow the seeds of default judgments against franchisees owing smaller debts." 724 F.2d, at 1511. We share the Court of Appeals' broader concerns and therefore reject any talismanic jurisdictional formulas; "the facts of each case must [always] be weighed" in determining whether personal jurisdiction would comport with "fair play and substantial justice." Kulko v. California Superior Court, 436 U.S., at 92, 98 S.Ct., at 1696–1697.[29] The "quality and nature" of an interstate transaction may sometimes be so "random," "fortuitous," or "attenuated" [30] that it cannot fairly be said that the potential defendant "should reasonably anticipate being haled into court" in another jurisdiction. World–Wide Volkswagen Corp. v. Woodson, 444 U.S., at 297, 100 S.Ct., at 567; see also n. 18, supra. We also have emphasized that jurisdiction may not be grounded on a contract whose terms have been obtained through "fraud, undue influence, or overweening bargaining power" and whose application would render litigation "so gravely difficult and inconvenient that [a party] will for all practical purposes be deprived of his day in court." The Bremen v. Zapata Off–Shore Co., 407 U.S., at 12, 18, 92 S.Ct., at 1914, 1917. Cf. Fuentes v. Shevin, 407 U.S. 67, 94–96, 92 S.Ct. 1983, 2001–2002, 32

---

28. We do not mean to suggest that the jurisdictional outcome will always be the same in franchise cases. Some franchises may be primarily intrastate in character or involve different decisionmaking structures, such that a franchisee should not reasonably anticipate out-of-state litigation. Moreover, commentators have argued that franchise relationships may sometimes involve unfair business practices in their inception and operation. See H. Brown, Franchising Realities and Remedies 4–5 (2d ed. 1978). For these reasons, we reject Burger King's suggestion for "a general rule, or at least a presumption, that participation in an interstate franchise relationship" represents consent to the jurisdiction of the franchisor's principal place of business. * * *

29. This approach does, of course, preclude clear-cut jurisdictional rules. But any inquiry into "fair play and substantial justice" necessarily requires determinations "in which few answers will be written 'in black and white. The greys are dominant and even among them the shades are innumerable.' " Kulko v. California Superior Court, 436 U.S., at 92, 98 S.Ct., at 1697.

30. Hanson v. Denckla, 357 U.S., at 253, 78 S.Ct., at 1239; Keeton v. Hustler Magazine, Inc., 465 U.S., at 774, 104 S.Ct., at 1478; World–Wide Volkswagen Corp. v. Woodson, 444 U.S., at 299, 100 S.Ct., at 568.

L.Ed.2d 556 (1972); National Equipment Rental Ltd. v. Szukhent, 375 U.S. 311, 329, 84 S.Ct. 411, 421, 11 L.Ed.2d 354 (1964) (BLACK, J., dissenting) (jurisdictional rules may not be employed against small consumers so as to "crippl[e] their defense"). Just as the Due Process Clause allows flexibility in ensuring that commercial actors are not effectively "judgment proof" for the consequences of obligations they voluntarily assume in other States, McGee v. International Life Insurance Co., 355 U.S., at 223, 78 S.Ct., at 201, so too does it prevent rules that would unfairly enable them to obtain default judgments against unwitting customers. Cf. United States v. Rumely, 345 U.S. 41, 44, 73 S.Ct. 543, 545, 97 L.Ed. 770 (1953) (courts must not be " 'blind' " to what " '[a]ll others can see and understand' ").

For the reasons set forth above, however, these dangers are not present in the instant case. Because Rudzewicz established a substantial and continuing relationship with Burger King's Miami headquarters, received fair notice from the contract documents and the course of dealing that he might be subject to suit in Florida, and has failed to demonstrate how jurisdiction in that forum would otherwise be fundamentally unfair, we conclude that the District Court's exercise of jurisdiction pursuant to Florida Stat. § 48.193(1)(g) (Supp.1984) did not offend due process. The judgment of the Court of Appeals is accordingly reversed, and the case is remanded for further proceedings consistent with this opinion.

It is so ordered.

JUSTICE POWELL took no part in the consideration or decision of this case.

JUSTICE STEVENS, with whom JUSTICE WHITE joins, dissenting.

In my opinion there is a significant element of unfairness in requiring a franchisee to defend a case of this kind in the forum chosen by the franchisor. It is undisputed that respondent maintained no place of business in Florida, that he had no employees in that State, and that he was not licensed to do business there. Respondent did not prepare his french fries, shakes, and hamburgers in Michigan, and then deliver them into the stream of commerce "with the expectation that they [would] be purchased by consumers in" Florida. * * * To the contrary, respondent did business only in Michigan, his business, property, and payroll taxes were payable in that state, and he sold all of his products there.

Throughout the business relationship, respondent's principal contacts with petitioner were with its Michigan office. Notwithstanding its disclaimer, * * * the Court seems ultimately to rely on nothing more than standard boilerplate language contained in various documents * * * to establish that respondent " 'purposefully availed himself of the benefits and protections of Florida's laws.' " * * * Such superficial analysis creates a potential for unfairness not only in negotiations between franchisors and their franchisees but, more significantly, in the resolution of the disputes that inevitably arise from time to time in such relationships.

Judge Vance's opinion for the Court of Appeals for the Eleventh Circuit adequately explains why I would affirm the judgment of that court. I particularly find the following more persuasive than what this Court has written today:

* * *

"Just as Rudzewicz lacked notice of the possibility of suit in Florida, he was financially unprepared to meet its added costs. The franchise relationship in particular is fraught with potential for financial surprise. The device of the franchise gives local retailers the access to national trademark recognition which enables them to compete with better-financed, more efficient chain stores. This national affiliation, however, does not alter the fact that the typical franchise store is a local concern serving at best a neighborhood or community. Neither the revenues of a local business nor the geographical range of its market prepares the average franchise owner for the cost of distant litigation. . . .

"The particular distribution of bargaining power in the franchise relationship further impairs the franchisee's financial preparedness. In a franchise contract, 'the franchisor normally occupies [the] dominant role'. . . ."

* * *

Accordingly, I respectfully dissent.

FURTHER NOTE ON PERSONAL LIBERTY AND SOVEREIGNTY

The scope of "sovereignty" is determined in functional terms and not strictly physical territorial terms, isn't it? If this is so, doesn't the functional approach necessarily include a factor of convenience of defendant? Isn't "freedom from undue inconvenience" a component of personal liberty? If so, how does it help analysis to include the factor in a functional definition of sovereignty and then treat it as a separate factor beyond sovereignty?

Correlatively, personal liberty is constrained by legal obligations to others, and responsibility to answer for such obligations in an appropriate court. Doesn't such a constrained concept of personal liberty necessarily include a factor of amenability to process at places where the person's acts have consequences? Hence, constrained personal liberty would seem to be the counterpart of the sovereignty of the state where those consequences occur. If so, how does it help analysis to include the factor in a constrained definition of personal liberty and then treat it as a separate factor beyond such personal liberty?

In the old days, the court had the complementary doctrines of *in personam* jurisdiction and *in rem* jurisdiction, along with "status" and "consent," on which to draw to decide specific cases one way or the other. Recall, e.g., Pennoyer v. Neff, Harris v. Balk, Hanson v. Denckla, and Rush v. Savchuk. Does the new duality of "personal liberty" and "sovereignty" perform a comparable rhetorical function? Thus, if the state's reach is "too far" in a particular case, the "personal liberty" formula is a basis for nullifying the exercise of territorial jurisdiction. If the state's reach is not "too far," the "sovereignty" formula is a basis for sustaining the exercise of jurisdiction. How might the

Court's recognition in Burger King Corp. v. Rudzewicz of a distinction between "general" and "specific" jurisdiction intersect with this rhetorical strategy? On this distinction, see Brilmayer et al., A General Look at General Jurisdiction, 66 Tex.L.Rev. 721 (1988); Twitchell, The Myth of General Jurisdiction, 101 Harv.L.Rev. 610 (1988). See also Drobak, The Federalism Theme in Personal Jurisdiction, 68 Iowa L.Rev. 1015 (1983); Note, Bauxite's "Individual Liberty Interest" and the Right to Control Amenability to Suit in Personal Jurisdiction Analysis, 51 Fordham L.Rev. 1278 (1983).

In World–Wide Volkswagen Corp. v. Woodson, the Court suggests that the ultimate determinant is the litigant's reasonable expectation as to being haled into court. But the litigant's expectation has to come from his lawyer, and the lawyer's expectation comes from what the Court says. Where does that lead?

---

3. CONSENT

M/S BREMEN AND UNTERWESER REEDEREI v. ZAPATA OFF–SHORE CO.

Supreme Court of the United States, 1972.
407 U.S. 1, 92 S.Ct. 1907, 32 L.Ed.2d 513.

MR. CHIEF JUSTICE BURGER delivered the opinion of the Court.

We granted certiorari to review a judgment of the United States Court of Appeals for the Fifth Circuit declining to enforce a forum selection clause governing disputes arising under an international towage contract between petitioner and respondent. The Circuits have differed in their approach to such clauses.[1] For the reasons stated hereafter, we vacate the judgment of the Court of Appeals.

In November 1967, respondent Zapata, a Houston-based American corporation, contracted with petitioner Unterweser, a German corporation, to tow Zapata's ocean-going, self-elevating drilling rig *Chaparral* from Louisiana to a point off Ravenna, Italy, in the Adriatic Sea where Zapata had agreed to drill certain wells.

Zapata had solicited bids for the towage, and several companies including Unterweser had responded. Unterweser was the low bidder and Zapata requested it to submit a contract, which it did. The contract submitted by Unterweser contained the following provision which is at issue in this case:

> "Any dispute arising must be treated before the London Court of Justice."

---

1. Compare, e.g., Central Contracting Co. v. Maryland Casualty Co., 367 F.2d 341 (C.A.3 1966), and Wm. H. Muller & Co. v. Swedish American Line Ltd., 224 F.2d 806 (C.A.2), cert. denied, 350 U.S. 903 (1955), with Carbon Black Export, Inc. v. The Monrosa, 254 F.2d 297 (C.A.5 1958), cert. dismissed 359 U.S. 180 (1959).

In addition the contract contained two clauses purporting to exculpate Unterweser from liability for damages to the towed barge.[2]

After reviewing the contract and making several changes, but without any alteration in the forum-selection or exculpatory clauses, a Zapata vice president executed the contract and forwarded it to Unterweser in Germany, where Unterweser accepted the changes and the contract became effective.

On January 5, 1968, Unterweser's deep sea tug *Bremen* departed Venice, Louisiana, with the *Chaparral* in tow bound for Italy. On January 9, while the flotilla was in international waters in the middle of the Gulf of Mexico, a severe storm arose. The sharp roll of the *Chaparral* in Gulf waters caused its elevator legs, which had been raised for the voyage, to break off and fall into the sea, seriously damaging the *Chaparral*. In this emergency situation Zapata instructed the *Bremen* to tow its damaged rig to Tampa, Florida, the nearest port of refuge.

On January 12, Zapata, ignoring its contract promise to litigate "any dispute arising" in the English courts, commenced a suit in admiralty in the United States District Court at Tampa, seeking $3,500,000 damages against Unterweser *in personam* and the *Bremen in rem*, alleging negligent towage and breach of contract.[3] Unterweser responded by invoking the forum clause of the towage contract, and moved to dismiss for lack of jurisdiction or on *forum non conveniens* grounds, or in the alternative to stay the action pending submission of the dispute to the "London Court of Justice." Shortly thereafter, in February, before the District Court had ruled on its motion to stay or dismiss the United States action, Unterweser commenced an action against Zapata seeking damages for breach of the towage contract in the High Court of Justice in London, as the contract provided. Zapata appeared in that court to contest jurisdiction, but its challenge was rejected, the English courts holding that the contractual forum provision conferred jurisdiction.[4]

2. The General Towage Conditions of the contract included the following:

"1. . . . [Unterweser and its] masters and crews are not responsible for defaults and/or errors in the navigation of the tow.

"2. . . .

"(b) Damages suffered by the towed object are in any case for account of its Owners."

In addition, the contract provided that any insurance of the *Chaparral* was to be "for account of" Zapata. Unterweser's initial telegraphic bid had also offered to "arrange insurance covering towage risk for rig if desired." As Zapata had chosen to be self-insured on all its rigs, the loss in this case was not compensated by insurance.

3. The *Bremen* was arrested by a United States Marshal acting pursuant to Zapata's complaint immediately upon her arrival in Tampa. The tug was subsequently released when Unterweser furnished security in the amount of $3,500,000.

4. Zapata appeared specially and moved to set aside service of process outside the country. Justice Karminski of the High Court of Justice denied the motion on the ground the contractual choice of forum provision conferred jurisdiction and would be enforced absent a factual showing it would not be "fair and right" to do so. He did not believe Zapata had made such a showing, and held that it should be required to "stick to [its] bargain." The Court of Appeal dismissed an appeal on the

In the meantime, Unterweser was faced with a dilemma in the pending action in the United States court at Tampa. The six-month period for filing action to limit its liability to Zapata and other potential claimants was about to expire,[5] but the United States District Court in Tampa had not yet ruled on Unterweser's motion to dismiss or stay Zapata's action. On July 2, 1968, confronted with difficult alternatives, Unterweser filed an action to limit its liability in the District Court in Tampa. That court entered the customary injunction against proceedings outside the limitation court, and Zapata refiled its initial claim in the limitation action.[6]

It was only at this juncture, on July 29, after the six-month period for filing the limitation action had run, that the District Court denied Unterweser's January motion to dismiss or stay Zapata's initial action. In denying the motion, that court relied on the prior decision of the Court of Appeals in Carbon Black Export, Inc. v. The Monrosa, 254 F.2d 297 (C.A.5 1958), cert. dismissed, 359 U.S. 180 (1959). In that case the Court of Appeals had held a forum selection clause unenforceable, reiterating the traditional views of many American courts that "agreements in advance of controversy whose object is to oust the jurisdiction of the courts are contrary to public policy and will not be enforced." 254 F.2d, at 300–301.[7] Apparently concluding that it was bound by the *Carbon Black* case, the District Court gave the forum selection clause little, if any, weight. Instead, the court treated the motion to dismiss under normal *forum non conveniens* doctrine applicable in the absence

---

ground that Justice Karminski had properly applied the English rule. Lord Justice Willmer stated that rule as follows:

"The law on the subject, I think, is not open to doubt. . . . It is always open to parties to stipulate . . . that a particular Court shall have jurisdiction over any dispute arising out of their contract. Here the parties chose to stipulate that disputes were to be referred to the 'London Court,' which I take as meaning the High Court in this country. *Prima facie* it is the policy of the Court to hold parties to the bargain into which they have entered. . . . But that is not an inflexible rule, as shown, for instance, by the case of *The Fehmarn*, [1957] 1 Lloyd's Rep. 511; C.A. [1957] 2 Lloyd's Rep. 551. . . . I approach the matter, therefore, in this way, that the Court has a discretion, but it is a discretion which, in the ordinary way and in the absence of strong reason to the contrary, will be exercised in favour of holding parties to their bargain. The question is whether sufficient circumstances have been shown to exist in this case to make it desirable on the grounds of balance of convenience, that proceedings should not take place in this country. . . ."

[1968] 2 Lloyd's Rep. 158, 162–163.

5.   46 U.S.C.A. §§ 183, 185. See generally G. Gilmore & C. Black, Admiralty §§ 10–15 (1957).

6.   In its limitation complaint, Unterweser stated it "reserve[d] all rights" under its previous motion to dismiss or stay Zapata's action, and reasserted that the High Court of Justice was the proper forum for determining the entire controversy, including its own right to limited liability, in accord with the contractual forum clause. Unterweser later counterclaimed, setting forth the same contractual cause of action as in its English action and a further cause of action for salvage arising out of the *Bremen's* services following the casualty. In its counterclaim, Unterweser again asserted that the High Court of Justice in London was the proper forum for determining all aspects of the controversy, including its counterclaim.

7.   The *Carbon Black* court went on to say that it was, in any event, unnecessary for it to reject the more liberal position taken in Wm. H. Muller & Co. v. Swedish American Line, Ltd., 224 F.2d 806 (CA2), cert. denied 350 U.S. 903 (1955), because the case before it had a greater nexus with the United States than that in *Muller*.

of such a clause, citing Gulf Oil Corp. v. Gilbert, 330 U.S. 501 (1947). Under that doctrine "unless the balance is strongly in favor of the defendant, the plaintiff's choice of forum should rarely be disturbed." Id., at 508. The District Court concluded: "The balance of convenience here is not strongly in favor of [Unterweser] and [Zapata's] choice of forum should not be disturbed."

Thereafter, on January 21, 1969, the District Court denied another motion by Unterweser to stay the limitation action pending determination of the controversy in the High Court of Justice in London and granted Zapata's motion to restrain Unterweser from litigating further in the London court. The District Judge ruled that, having taken jurisdiction in the limitation proceeding, he had jurisdiction to determine all matters relating to the controversy. He ruled that Unterweser should be required to "do equity" by refraining from also litigating the controversy in the London court, not only for the reasons he had previously stated for denying Unterweser's first motion to stay Zapata's action, but also because Unterweser had invoked the United States court's jurisdiction to obtain the benefit of the Limitation Act.

On appeal, a divided panel of the Court of Appeals affirmed, and on rehearing *en banc* the panel opinion was adopted, with six of the 14 *en banc* judges dissenting. As had the District Court, the majority holding rested on the *Carbon Black* decision, concluding that "'at the very least'" that case stood for the proposition that a forum selection clause "'will not be enforced unless the selected state would provide a more convenient forum than the state in which suit is brought.'" From that premise the Court of Appeals proceeded to conclude that, apart from the forum selection clause, the District Court did not abuse its discretion in refusing to decline jurisdiction on the basis of *forum non conveniens.* It noted that (1) the flotilla never "escaped the Fifth Circuit's mare nostrum, and the casualty occurred in close proximity to the district court"; (2) a considerable number of potential witnesses, including Zapata crewmen, resided in the Gulf Coast area; (3) preparation for the voyage and inspection and repair work had been performed in the Gulf area; (4) the testimony of the *Bremen* crew was available by way of deposition; (5) England had no interest in or contact with the controversy other than the forum selection clause. The Court of Appeals majority further noted that Zapata was a United States citizen and "[t]he discretion of the District Court to remand the case to a foreign forum was consequently limited"—especially since it appeared likely that the English courts would enforce the exculpatory clauses.[8] In the Court of Appeals' view, enforcement of such clauses would be contrary to public policy in American courts under Bisso v. Inland

---

8. The record contains an undisputed affidavit of a British solicitor stating an opinion that the exculpatory clauses of the contract would be held "prima facie valid and enforceable" against Zapata in any action maintained in England in which Zapata alleged that defaults or errors in Unterweser's tow caused the casualty and damage to the *Chaparral.*

In addition, it is not disputed that while the limitation fund in the District Court in Tampa amounts to $1,390,000, the limitation fund in England would be only slightly in excess of $80,000 under English law.

Waterways Corp., 349 U.S. 85 (1955), and Dixilyn Drilling Corp. v. Crescent Towing & Salvage Co., 372 U.S. 697 (1963). Therefore, "[t]he district court was entitled to consider that remanding Zapata to a foreign forum, with little or no practical contact with the controversy, could raise a bar to recovery by a United States citizen which its own convenient courts would not countenance." [9]

We hold, with the six dissenting members of the Court of Appeals, that far too little weight and effect was given to the forum clause in resolving this controversy. For at least two decades we have witnessed an expansion of overseas commercial activities by business enterprises based in the United States. The barrier of distance that once tended to confine a business concern to a modest territory no longer does so. Here we see an American company with special expertise contracting with a foreign company to tow a complex machine thousands of miles across seas and oceans. The expansion of American business and industry will hardly be encouraged if, notwithstanding solemn contracts, we insist on a parochial concept that all disputes must be resolved under our laws and in our courts. Absent a contract forum, the considerations relied on by the Court of Appeals would be persuasive reasons for holding an American forum convenient in the traditional sense, but in an era of expanding world trade and commerce, the absolute aspects of the doctrine of the *Carbon Black* case have little place and would be a heavy hand indeed on the future development of international commercial dealings by Americans. We cannot have trade and commerce in world markets and international waters exclusively on our terms, governed by our laws and resolved in our courts.

Forum selection clauses have historically not been favored by American courts. Many courts, federal and state, have declined to enforce such clauses on the ground that they were "contrary to public policy," or that their effect was to "oust the jurisdiction" of the court. [10]

9. The Court of Appeals also indicated in passing that even if it took the view that choice of forum clauses were enforceable unless "unreasonable" it was "doubtful" that enforcement would be proper here because the exculpatory clauses would deny Zapata relief to which it was "entitled" and because England was "seriously inconvenient" for trial of the action.

10. Many decisions reflecting this view are collected in Annot., 56 A.L.R.2d 300, 306–320 (1957), and Later Case Service (1967).

For leading early cases, see, e.g., Nute v. Hamilton Mutual Ins. Co., 72 Mass. (6 Gray) 174 (1856); Nashua River Paper Co. v. Hammermill Paper Co., 223 Mass. 8, 111 N.E. 678 (1916); Benson v. Eastern Bldg. & Loan Assn., 174 N.Y. 83, 66 N.E. 627 (1903).

The early admiralty cases were in accord. See, e.g., Wood & Selick, Inc. v.

Compagnie Generale Transatlantique, 43 F.2d 941 (C.A.2 1930); The Ciano, 58 F.Supp. 65 (E.D.Pa.1944); Kuhnhold v. Compagnie Generale Transatlantique, 251 Fed. 387 (S.D.N.Y.1918); Prince Steam Shipping Co. v. Lehman, 39 Fed. 704 (S.D. N.Y.1889).

In Insurance Company v. Morse, 20 Wall. 445 (1874), this Court broadly stated that "agreements in advance to oust the courts of jurisdiction conferred by law are illegal and void." Id., at 451. But the holding of that case was only that the State of Wisconsin could not by statute force a foreign corporation to "agree" to surrender its federal statutory right to remove a state court action to the federal courts as a condition of doing business in Wisconsin. Thus, the case is properly understood as one in which a state statutory requirement was viewed as imposing an unconstitutional condition on the exercise

Although this view apparently still has considerable acceptance, other courts are tending to adopt a more hospitable attitude toward forum-selection clauses. This view, advanced in the well-reasoned dissenting opinion in the instant case, is that such clauses are prima facie valid and should be enforced unless enforcement is shown by the resisting party to be "unreasonable" under the circumstances.[11] We believe this is the correct doctrine to be followed by federal district courts sitting in admiralty. It is merely the other side of the proposition recognized by this Court in National Equipment Rental, Ltd. v. Szukhent, 375 U.S. 311 (1964), holding that in federal courts a party may validly consent to be sued in a jurisdiction where he cannot be found for service of process through contractual designation of an "agent" for receipt of process in that jurisdiction. In so holding, the Court stated:

> "[I]t is settled . . . that parties to a contract may agree in advance to submit to the jurisdiction of a given court, to permit notice to be served by the opposing party, or even to waive notice altogether." Id., at 315–316.

This approach is substantially that followed in other common-law countries including England.[12] It is the view advanced by noted scholars and that adopted by the Restatement of the Conflict of Laws.[13] It

of the federal right of removal. See, e.g., Wisconsin v. Philadelphia & Reading Coal Co., 241 U.S. 329 (1916).

As Judge Hand noted in Krenger v. Pennsylvania R. Co., 174 F.2d 556 (C.A.2 1949), even at that date there was in fact no "absolute taboo" against such clauses. See, e.g., Mittenthal v. Mascagni, 183 Mass. 19, 66 N.E. 425 (1903); Daley v. People's Bldg., Loan & Sav. Assn., 178 Mass. 13, 59 N.E. 452 (1901) (Holmes, J.). See also Cerro de Pasco Copper Corp. v. Knut Knutsen, O.A.S., 187 F.2d 990 (C.A.2 1951).

11. E.g., Central Contracting Co. v. Maryland Casualty Co., 367 F.2d 341 (C.A.3 1966); Anastasiadis v. SS Little John, 346 F.2d 281 (C.A.5 1965) (by implication); Wm. H. Muller & Co. v. Swedish American Line Ltd., 224 F.2d 806 (C.A.2), cert. denied 350 U.S. 903 (1955); Cerro de Pasco Copper Corp. v. Knutsen, O.A.S., 187 F.2d 990 (C.A.2 1951); Central Contracting Co. v. C. E. Youngdahl & Co., 418 Pa. 122, 209 A.2d 810 (1965).

The *Muller* case was overruled in Indussa Corp. v. SS Ranborg, 377 F.2d 200 (C.A.2 1967), insofar as it held that the forum clause was not inconsistent with the "lessening of liability" provision of the Carriage of Goods by Sea Act, 46 U.S.C.A. § 1303(8), which was applicable to the transactions in *Muller, Indussa,* and *Carbon Black.* That Act is not applicable in this case.

12. In addition to the decision of the Court of Appeal in the instant case, Unterweser Reederei G. m. b. H. v. Zapata Off-Shore Co. (The Chaparral) [1968] 2 Lloyd's Rep. 158 (C.A.), see, e.g., Mackender v. Feldia A. G. [1967] 2 Q.B. 590 (C.A.); The Fehmarn [1958] 1 W.L.R. 159 (C.A.); Law v. Garrett [1878] 8 Ch.D. 26 (C.A.); The Eleftheria. [1970] P. 94. As indicated by the clear statements in *The Eleftheria* and of Lord Justice Willmer in this case, supra, n. 4, the decision of the trial court calls for an exercise of discretion. See generally Dicey & Morris, The Conflict of Laws 979–980, 1087–1088 (8th ed. 1967); Cowen & Mendes da Costa, The Contractual Forum: Situation in England and the British Commonwealth, 13 Am.J. Comp.Law 179 (1964); Reese, The Contractual Forum: Situation in the United States, id., at 187, 190 n. 3; Graupner, Contractual Stipulations Conferring Exclusive Jurisdiction Upon Foreign Courts in the Law of England and Scotland, 59 L.Q. Rev. 227 (1943).

13. Restatement (Second) of the Conflict of Laws § 80 (1971); Reese, The Contractual Forum: Situation in the United States, 13 Am.J.Comp.Law 187 (1964); Ehrenzweig, Conflict of Laws § 41 (1962). See also Model Choice of Forum Act (Uniform Law Commissioners 1968).

accords with ancient concepts of freedom of contract and reflects an appreciation of the expanding horizons of American contractors who seek business in all parts of the world. Not surprisingly foreign businessmen prefer, as do we, to have disputes resolved in their own courts, but if that choice is not available, then a neutral forum with expertise in the subject matter. Plainly the courts of England meet the standards of neutrality and long experience in admiralty litigation. The choice of that forum was made in an arm's-length negotiation by experienced and sophisticated businessmen, and absent some compelling and countervailing reason it should be honored by the parties and enforced by the courts.

The argument that such clauses are improper because they tend to "oust" a court of jurisdiction is hardly more than a vestigial legal fiction. It appears to rest at core on historical judicial resistance to any attempt to reduce the power and business of a particular court and has little place in an era when all courts are overloaded and when businesses once essentially local now operate in world markets. It reflects something of a provincial attitude regarding the fairness of other tribunals. No one seriously contends in this case that the forum-selection clause "ousted" the District Court of jurisdiction over Zapata's action. The threshold question is whether that court should have exercised its jurisdiction to do more than give effect to the legitimate expectations of the parties, manifested in their freely negotiated agreement, by specifically enforcing the forum clause.

There are compelling reasons why a freely negotiated private international agreement, unaffected by fraud, undue influence, or overweening bargaining power,[14] such as that involved here, should be given full effect. In this case, for example, we are concerned with a far from routine transaction between companies of two different nations contemplating the tow of an extremely costly piece of equipment from Louisiana across the Gulf of Mexico, and the Atlantic Ocean, through the Mediterranean Sea to its final destination in the Adriatic Sea. In the course of its voyage, it was to traverse the waters of many jurisdictions. The *Chapparal* could have been damaged at any point along the route, and there were countless possible ports of refuge. That the accident occurred in the Gulf of Mexico and the barge was towed to Tampa in an emergency were mere fortuities. It cannot be doubted for a moment

---

14. The record here refutes any notion of overweening bargaining power. Judge Wisdom in the Court of Appeals noted:

"Zapata has neither presented evidence of nor alleged fraud or undue bargaining power in the agreement. Unterweser was only one of several companies bidding on the project. No evidence contradicts its Managing Director's affidavit that it specified English courts 'in an effort to meet Zapata Off-Shore Company half way.' Zapata's Vice President has declared by affidavit

that no specific negotiations concerning the forum clause took place. But this was not simply a form contract with boilerplate language that Zapata had no power to alter. The towing of an oil rig across the Atlantic was a new business. Zapata did make alterations to the contract submitted by Unterweser. The forum clause could hardly be ignored. It is the final sentence of the agreement, immediately preceding the date and the parties' signatures. . . ." 428 F.2d 888, 907.

that the parties sought to provide for a neutral forum for the resolution of any disputes arising during the tow. Manifestly much uncertainty and possibly great inconvenience to both parties could arise if a suit could be maintained in any jurisdiction in which an accident might occur or if jurisdiction were left to any place where the *Bremen* or Unterweser might happen to be found.[15] The elimination of all such uncertainties by agreeing in advance on a forum acceptable to both parties is an indispensable element in international trade, commerce, and contracting. There is strong evidence that the forum clause was a vital part of the agreement,[16] and it would be unrealistic to think that the parties did not conduct their negotiations, including fixing the monetary terms, with the consequences of the forum clause figuring prominently in their calculations. Under these circumstances, as Justice Karminski reasoned in sustaining jurisdiction over Zapata in the High Court of Justice, "[t]he force of an agreement for litigation in this country, freely entered into between two competent parties, seems to me to be very powerful."

Thus, in the light of present day commercial realities and expanding international trade we conclude that the forum clause should control absent a strong showing that it should be set aside. Although their opinions are not altogether explicit, it seems reasonably clear that the District Court and the Court of Appeals placed the burden on Unterweser to show that London would be a more convenient forum

15. At the very least, the clause was an effort to eliminate all uncertainty as to the nature, location, and outlook of the forum in which these companies of differing nationalities might find themselves. Moreover, while the contract here did not specifically provide that the substantive law of England should be applied, it is the general rule in English courts that the parties are assumed, absent contrary indication, to have designated the forum with the view that it should apply its own law. See, e.g., Tzortzis v. Monark Line A/B [1968] 1 W.L.R. 406 (C.A.); see generally 1 Carver, Carriage by Sea 496–497 (12th ed. 1971); Cheshire, Private International Law 193 (7th ed. 1965); Dicey & Morris, The Conflict of Laws 705, 1046 (8th ed. 1967); Collins, Arbitration Clauses and Forum Selecting Clauses in the Conflict of Laws: Some Recent Developments in England, 2 J.Mar.L. & Comm. 363, 365–370 and n. 7 (1971). It is therefore reasonable to conclude that the forum clause was also an effort to obtain certainty as to the applicable substantive law.

The record contains an affidavit of a Managing Director of Unterweser stating that Unterweser considered the choice of forum provision to be of "overriding importance" to the transaction. He stated that Unterweser towage contracts ordinarily provide for exclusive German jurisdiction and application of German law, but that "[i]n this instance, in an effort to meet [Zapata] halfway, [Unterweser] proposed the London Court of Justice. Had this provision not been accepted by [Zapata], [Unterweser] would not have entered into the towage contract. . . ." He also stated that the parties intended, by designating the London forum, that English law would be applied. A responsive affidavit by Hoyt Taylor, a Vice President of Zapata, denied that there were any discussions between Zapata and Unterweser concerning the forum clause or the question of the applicable law.

16. See nn. 14–15, supra. Zapata has denied specifically discussing the forum clause with Unterweser, but, as Judge Wisdom pointed out, Zapata made numerous changes in the contract without altering the forum clause, which could hardly have escaped its attention. Zapata is clearly not unsophisticated in such matters. The contract of its wholly owned subsidiary with an Italian corporation covering the contemplated drilling operations in the Adriatic Sea provided that all disputes were to be settled by arbitration in London under English law, and contained broad exculpatory clauses. App. 306–311.

than Tampa, although the contract expressly resolved that issue. The correct approach would have been to enforce the forum clause specifically unless Zapata could clearly show that enforcement would be unreasonable and unjust, or that the clause was invalid for such reasons as fraud or overreaching. Accordingly, the case must be remanded for reconsideration.

We note, however, that there is nothing in the record presently before us that would support a refusal to enforce the forum clause. The Court of Appeals suggested that enforcement would be contrary to the public policy of the forum under Bisso v. Inland Waterways Corp., 349 U.S. 85 (1955), because of the prospect that the English courts would enforce the clauses of the towage contract purporting to exculpate Unterweser from liability for damages to the *Chaparral*. A contractual choice of forum clause should be held unenforceable if enforcement would contravene a strong public policy of the forum in which suit is brought, whether declared by statute or by judicial decision. See, e.g., Boyd v. Grand Trunk W. R. R., 338 U.S. 263 (1949). It is clear, however, that whatever the proper reach of the policy expressed in *Bisso*,[17] it does not reach this case. *Bisso* rested on considerations with respect to the towage business strictly in American waters, and those considerations are not controlling in an international commercial agreement. Speaking for the dissenting judges in the Court of Appeals, Judge Wisdom pointed out:

> "[W]e should be careful not to over-emphasize the strength of the *[Bisso]* policy. . . . [T]wo concerns underlie the rejection of exculpatory agreements: that they may be produced by overweening bargaining power; and that they do not sufficiently discourage negligence. . . . Here the conduct in question is that of a foreign party occurring in international waters outside our jurisdiction. The evidence disputes any notion of overreaching in the contractual agreement. And for all we know, the uncertainties and dangers in the new field of transoceanic towage of oil rigs were so great that the tower was unwilling to take financial responsibility for the risks and the parties thus allocated responsibility for the voyage to the tow. It is equally possible that the contract price took this factor into account. I conclude that we should not invalidate the forum selection clause here unless we are firmly convinced that we would thereby significantly encourage negligent conduct within the boundaries of the United States." 428 F.2d, at 907–908. (Footnotes omitted.)

Courts have also suggested that a forum clause, even though it is freely bargained for and contravenes no important public policy of the forum, may nevertheless be "unreasonable" and unenforceable if the chosen forum is *seriously* inconvenient for the trial of the action. Of

17. Dixilyn Drilling Corp. v. Crescent Towing & Salvage Co., 372 U.S. 697 (1963) *(per curiam),* merely followed *Bisso* and declined to subject its rule governing towage contracts in American waters to "indeterminate exceptions" based on delicate analysis of the facts of each case. See 372 U.S., at 698 (Harlan, J., concurring).

course, where it can be said with reasonable assurance that at the time they entered the contract, the parties to a freely negotiated private international commercial agreement contemplated the claimed inconvenience, it is difficult to see why any such claim of inconvenience should be heard to render the forum clause unenforceable. We are not here dealing with an agreement between two Americans to resolve their essentially local disputes in a remote alien forum. In such a case, the serious inconvenience of the contractual forum to one or both of the parties might carry greater weight in determining the reasonableness of the forum clause. The remoteness of the forum might suggest that the agreement was an adhesive one, or that the parties did not have the particular controversy in mind when they made their agreement; yet even there the party claiming should bear a heavy burden of proof.[18] Similarly, selection of a remote forum to apply differing foreign law to an essentially American controversy might contravene an important public policy of the forum. For example, so long as *Bisso* governs American courts with respect to the towage business in American waters, it would quite arguably be improper to permit an American tower to avoid that policy by providing a foreign forum for resolution of his disputes with an American towee.

This case, however, involves a freely negotiated international commercial transaction between a German and an American corporation for towage of a vessel from the Gulf of Mexico to the Adriatic Sea. As noted, selection of a London forum was clearly a reasonable effort to bring vital certainty to this international transaction and to provide a neutral forum experienced and capable in the resolution of admiralty litigation. Whatever "inconvenience" Zapata would suffer by being forced to litigate in the contractual forum as it agreed to do was clearly foreseeable at the time of contracting. In such circumstances it should be incumbent on the party seeking to escape his contract to show that trial in the contractual forum will be so gravely difficult and inconvenient that he will for all practical purposes be deprived of his day in court. Absent that there is no basis for concluding that it would be unfair, unjust, or unreasonable to hold that party to his bargain.

In the course of his ruling on Unterweser's second motion to stay the proceedings in Tampa, the District Court did make a conclusory finding that the balance of convenience was "strongly" in favor of litigation in Tampa. However, as previously noted, in making that finding the court erroneously placed the burden of proof on Unterweser to show that the balance of convenience was strongly in its favor.[19]

---

18. See, e.g., Model Choice of Forum Act § 3(3) (Uniform Law Commissioners 1968), comment: "On rare occasions, the state of the forum may be a substantially more convenient place for the trial of a particular controversy than the chosen State. If so, the present clause would permit the action to proceed. This result will presumably be in accord with the desires of the parties. It can be assumed that they did not have the particular controversy in mind when they made the choice-of-forum agreement since they would not consciously have agreed to have the action brought in an inconvenient place."

19. Applying the proper burden of proof, Justice Karminski in the High Court of Justice at London made the following

Moreover, the finding falls far short of a conclusion that Zapata would be effectively deprived its day in court should it be forced to litigate in London. Indeed, it cannot even be assumed that it would be placed to the expense of transporting its witnesses to London. It is not unusual for important issues in international admiralty cases to be dealt with by deposition. Both the District Court and the Court of Appeals majority appeared satisfied that Unterweser could receive a fair hearing in Tampa by using deposition testimony of its witnesses from distant places, and there is no reason to conclude that Zapata could not use deposition testimony to equal advantage if forced to litigate in London as it bound itself to do. Nevertheless, to allow Zapata opportunity to carry its heavy burden of showing not only that the balance of convenience is strongly in favor of trial in Tampa (that is, that it will be far more inconvenient for Zapata to litigate in London than it will be for Unterweser to litigate in Tampa), but also that a London trial will be so manifestly and gravely inconvenient to Zapata that it will be effectively deprived of a meaningful day in court, we remand for further proceedings.

Zapata's remaining contentions do not require extended treatment. It is clear that Unterweser's action in filing its limitation complaint in the District Court in Tampa was, so far as Zapata was concerned, solely a defensive measure made necessary as a response to Zapata's breach of the forum clause of the contract. When the six-month statutory period for filing an action to limit its liability had almost run without the District Court having ruled on Unterweser's initial motion to dismiss or stay Zapata's action pursuant to the forum clause, Unterweser had no other prudent alternative but to protect itself by filing for limitation of its liability.[20] Its action in so doing was a direct consequence of

findings, which appear to have substantial support in the record:

"[Zapata] pointed out that in this case the balance of convenience so far as witnesses were concerned pointed in the direction of having the case heard and tried in the United States District Court at Tampa in Florida because the probability is that most, but not necessarily all, of the witnesses will be American. The answer, as it seems to me, is that a substantial minority at least of witnesses are likely to be German. The tug was a German vessel and was, as far as I know, manned by a German crew. . . . Where they all are now or are likely to be when this matter is litigated I do not know, because the experience of the Admiralty Court here strongly points out that maritime witnesses in the course of their duties move about freely. The homes of the German crew presumably are in Germany. There is probably a balance of numbers in favor of the Americans, but not, as I am in-

clined to think, a very heavy balance." App. 212.

It should also be noted that if the exculpatory clause is enforced in the English courts, many of Zapata's witnesses on the questions of negligence and damage may be completely unnecessary.

20. Zapata has suggested that Unterweser was not in any way required to file its "affirmative" limitation complaint because it could just as easily have pleaded limitation of liability by way of defense in Zapata's initial action, either before or after the six-month period. That course of action was not without risk, however, that Unterweser's attempt to limit its liability by answer would be held invalid. See G. Gilmore and C. Black, Admiralty § 10–15 (1957). We do not believe this hazardous option in any way deprived Unterweser's limitation complaint of its essentially defensive character so far as Zapata was concerned.

Zapata's failure to abide by the forum clause of the towage contract. There is no basis on which to conclude that this purely necessary defensive action by Unterweser should preclude it from relying on the forum clause it bargained for.

For the first time in this litigation, Zapata has suggested to this Court that the forum clause should not be construed to provide for an exclusive forum or to include *in rem* actions. However, the language of the clause is clearly mandatory and all-encompassing; the language of the clause in the *Carbon Black* case was far different.

The judgment of the Court of Appeals is vacated and the case is remanded for further proceedings consistent with this opinion.*

PHILLIPS PETROLEUM CO. v. SHUTTS

Supreme Court of the United States, 1985.
472 U.S. 797, 105 S.Ct. 2965, 86 L.Ed.2d 628.

[This case appears, infra, p. 476]

NOTE ON CONSENT

"Consent" is a legitimate, but often seductive, alternative to compulsion as a basis of jurisdiction. While consent can clearly be of the "express" variety, as in *M/S Bremen*, and can be "implied" from, e.g., the failure of a class member to opt out after receiving notice, as in *Phillips Petroleum*, it can also be employed as a concept to justify what are obviously exercises of nonconsensual jurisdiction. See, e.g., Lafayette Ins. Co. v. French and Hess v. Pawloski, discussed supra p. 294. Note, however, that consent operates only in the area of territorial jurisdiction; standard doctrine holds that subject matter jurisdiction may not be conferred on a court by consent of the parties. See Insurance Corp. of Ireland v. Compagnie des Bauxites de Guinee, supra p. 346; Note on Challenging Subject Matter Jurisdiction, infra p. 510.

1. Express Consent

M/S Bremen seems to say that when the consent is express, as in a forum selection clause, the specified forum generally should uphold its jurisdiction over the action even if it has no contacts with the transaction. Moreover, another forum generally should respect the agreement even if the latter forum would be a more convenient place for trial. However, *M/S Bremen* involved an international contract made between companies organized and headquartered in different countries, and the specified forum had a reputation for disinterestedness and expertise in the type of controversy involved. How much did these factors influence the Court's decision? What different considerations might have been relevant if the contract had not had this international aspect? Compare Stewart Org., Inc. v. Ricoh Corp., ___ U.S. ___, 108 S.Ct. 2239, 101 L.Ed.2d 22 (1988), holding that 28 U.S.C.A. § 1404(a), the federal venue statute governing transfers on *forum non conveniens* grounds, preempts state rules that deny effect to forum selection clauses. The case further holds that a forum selection clause should be considered in ruling on a motion under § 1404(a) but

_____
* The concurring opinion of White, J., and the dissenting opinion of Douglas, J., are omitted.

should not necessarily be dispositive. See also McRae v. J.D./M.D., Inc., 511 So. 2d 540 (Fla.1987), where a forum selection clause specifying Florida was held ineffective to confer jurisdiction where the transaction had no Florida connection. C.C.P. 410.40 provides that in cases involving transactions exceeding $1 million where the parties have chosen California law to govern their contractual relationship, any person may bring an action in California based on the transaction against a nonresident as long as the nonresident expressly submitted in the contract to the jurisdiction of the California courts.

In National Equipment Rental, Ltd. v. Szukhent, 375 U.S. 311, 84 S.Ct. 411, 11 L.Ed.2d 354 (1964), discussed in *M/S Bremen,* the Supreme Court upheld jurisdiction in New York federal court of a suit filed by a New York corporation against Michigan residents. The defendants had rented farm equipment from plaintiff and signed a form lease by which they appointed a New York resident (whom they did not know) as their agent for service of process. Process was served on that agent in New York and a copy forwarded to defendants in Michigan. The Court held that, so long as defendants receive actual notice, such agency arrangements should not be disturbed by courts. In determining the validity of the arrangement, is it significant that the federal venue provisions permit a diversity action to be brought in the district where the plaintiff resides? See 28 U.S.C.A. § 1391(a). Is it significant that, apart from the agency device, the defendants would probably have been held to have constitutional "minimum contacts" with New York, but that the New York "long arm" statute would not have reached defendants? Compare American Eutectic Welding v. Dytron Alloys Corp., infra p. 403. Justice Black, dissenting in *Szukhent,* suggested that it might be a denial of due process to force the defendants to litigate far from home. What about forcing plaintiffs to do so? Is the point that plaintiff was a big corporation? What if it was a small one and defendants were agribusinessmen? Compare Spiegel, Inc. v. F.T.C., 540 F.2d 287 (7th Cir.1976), where the F.T.C. issued a cease and desist order against the practice of defendant, a mail-order merchandiser, of bringing actions against nonresident customers to collect unpaid accounts in Illinois using the Illinois "long arm" statute, on the ground that it was an unfair business practice.

After a long period of hostility, courts today generally will apply the principles of consent to arbitration agreements, compelling an unwilling party to participate in arbitration under penalty of the risk that the award will go against it by default. See Shearson/American Express, Inc. v. McMahon, infra p. 1259, and the Note following.

Observe that the agreement concerning jurisdiction in *M/S Bremen* called for a "neutral" forum, while that in *Szukhent* called for a "home court" advantage. Would the agreement in *M/S Bremen* have been enforced if it called for adjudication in Hamburg? In *Szukhent,* would an action have been maintainable in New York if the agreement had contained a stipulation that actions on the contract should be brought in a New York court, but had not contained the provision for service of process? How could service have been accomplished in such a case?

2. Implied Consent

The implication of consent in a case like *Phillips Petroleum,* where the class members received notice and were given the chance to opt out of the class, seems relatively straightforward. Other forms of "implied" consent are more problematic and sometimes stretch the natural meaning of the term pretty far.

In Adam v. Saenger, 303 U.S. 59, 58 S.Ct. 454, 82 L.Ed. 649 (1938), a Texas corporation sued a California resident in California state court, to which defendant filed a cross-complaint. Plaintiff did nothing more, whereupon defendant received a default judgment on its cross-complaint and plaintiff's original action was dismissed for want of prosecution. In a later suit brought in Texas on the California judgment, the Texas state court refused to recognize the judgment. The Supreme Court reversed, holding that a nonresident plaintiff who voluntarily avails itself of another state's courts "consents" to the jurisdiction of those courts "for all purposes for which justice to the defendant requires his presence." Suppose defendant had brought in a third party by way of impleader (see infra p. 740) and that third party had asserted a claim against the plaintiff. Would plaintiff be deemed to have consented to that, too? Should it make a difference that the added claims arose out of the same transaction as that sued on by plaintiff?

See Restatement Second of Judgments § 9: "A court may exercise jurisdiction over a person who is a party to a pending action in that or another court of the state in which the court is located when the claim involved arose out of the transaction that is the subject of the pending action or is one that may in fairness be determined concurrently with that action." Compare Insurance Corp. of Ireland v. Compagnie des Bauxites de Guinee, supra p. 346, where defendants were held to have "consented" to jurisdiction when they refused to comply with discovery orders aimed at determining whether jurisdiction existed. Note especially the Court's discussion of the due process interests involved and the defendants' "waiver" of them. See also Threlkeld v. Tucker, 496 F.2d 1101 (9th Cir.1974); Liston v. Butler, 4 Ariz.App. 460, 421 P.2d 542 (1966).

Another form of implied consent is the entrance by defendant of a "general" as opposed to "special" appearance in the litigation. This issue is addressed in Challenging Territorial Jurisdiction, infra p. 416.

3. Jurisdiction Over Class Members Outside the Territory

Phillips Petroleum settled the constitutionality of asserting jurisdiction over out-of-state plaintiff class members where they have a chance to opt out of the suit. Because the decision was based on an implied consent theory, it casts doubt on the constitutionality of asserting jurisdiction over class members outside the territory where such members do not have the choice to opt out. Absent consent or waiver, due process requires jurisdiction based on "minimum contacts." Could this requirement be satisfied by a *Mullane*-type analysis of jurisdiction? Does *Phillips Petroleum* apply to class actions in federal court? See Miller and Crump, Jurisdiction and Choice of Law in Multistate Class Actions After Phillips Petroleum Co. v. Shutts, 96 Yale L.J. 1 (1986). For a critique of the opinion in *Phillips Petroleum*, see Kennedy, The Supreme Court Meets the Bride of Frankenstein: Phillips Petroleum Co. v. Shutts and the State Multistate Class Action, 34 U.Kan.L.Rev. 255 (1985).

As hinted in the *Phillips Petroleum* opinion, significant due process questions are also raised in asserting jurisdiction over absent defendants in a defendant class action. See Note, Defendant Class Actions and Federal Civil Rights Litigation, 33 U.C.L.A.L.Rev. 283 (1985); Note, Personal Jurisdiction and Rule 23 Defendant Class Actions, 53 Ind.L.J. 841 (1978). Compare the discussion in Henson v. East Lincoln Township, infra p. 875.

4. INTERNATIONAL LITIGATION

INTRODUCTORY NOTE ON INTERNATIONAL TERRITORIAL JURISDICTION

The Supreme Court's decisions can be interpreted as recognizing a distinction between territorial jurisdiction as between states within the United States and territorial jurisdiction as between the United States and other countries. However, the Court has not yet worked out an adequate theory of territorial jurisdiction in the international setting. This is primarily because the Court has applied the distinction between convenience and sovereignty in both the interstate and international settings. The distinction, which is difficult to maintain where the territorial problem is as between the states within the United States, is more coherent in the international context but becomes confused when decisional language is brought over from cases involving the interstate context. The differences in context become clearer when account is taken of the fact that interstate choice of forum involves far fewer differences than international choice of forum when it comes substantive rules of liability (compare Asahi Metal Industry Co. v. Superior Court, infra p. 390, with Piper Aircraft Co. v. Reyno, infra p. 427), measures of damages (see M/S Bremen and Unterweser Reederei v. Zapata Off–Shore Co., supra p. 370), and scope of discovery (see Societe Nationale Industrielle Aerospatiale v. United States District Court, 482 U.S. 522, 107 S.Ct. 2542, 96 L.Ed.2d 461 (1987)).

HELICOPTEROS NACIONALES de COLOMBIA, S.A. v. HALL

Supreme Court of the United States, 1984.
466 U.S. 408, 104 S.Ct. 1868, 80 L.Ed.2d 404.*

JUSTICE BLACKMUN delivered the opinion of the Court.

* * *

I

Petitioner Helicopteros Nacionales de Colombia, S.A. (Helicol) is a Colombian corporation with its principal place of business in the city of Bogota in that country. It is engaged in the business of providing helicopter transportation for oil and construction companies in South America. On January 26, 1976, a helicopter owned by Helicol crashed in Peru. Four United States citizens were among those who lost their lives in the accident. Respondents are the survivors and representatives of the four decedents.

At the time of the crash, respondents' decedents were employed by Consorcio, a Peruvian consortium, and were working on a pipeline in Peru. Consorcio is the alter-ego of a joint venture named Williams–Sedco–Horn (WSH).[1] The venture had its headquarters in Houston, Tex. Consorcio had been formed to enable the venturers to enter into a

---

* Some of the Court's footnotes are omitted.

1. The participants in the joint venture were Williams International Sudameri-

cana, Ltd., a Delaware corporation; Sedco Construction Corporation, a Texas corporation; and Horn International, Inc., a Texas corporation.

contract with Petro Peru, the Peruvian state-owned oil company. Consorcio was to construct a pipeline for Petro Peru running from the interior of Peru westward to the Pacific Ocean. Peruvian law forbade construction of the pipeline by any non-Peruvian entity.

Consorcio/WSH [2] needed helicopters to move personnel, materials, and equipment into and out of the construction area. In 1974, upon request of Consorcio/WSH, the chief executive officer of Helicol, Francisco Restrepo, flew to the United States and conferred in Houston with representatives of the three joint venturers. At that meeting, there was a discussion of prices, availability, working conditions, fuel, supplies, and housing. Restrepo represented that Helicol could have the first helicopter on the job in 15 days. The Consorcio/WSH representatives decided to accept the contract proposed by Restrepo. Helicol began performing before the agreement was formally signed in Peru on November 11, 1974.[3] The contract was written in Spanish on official government stationery and provided that the residence of all the parties would be Lima, Peru. It further stated that controversies arising out of the contract would be submitted to the jurisdiction of Peruvian courts. In addition, it provided that Consorcio/WSH would make payments to Helicol's account with the Bank of America in New York City. App. 12a.

Aside from the negotiation session in Houston between Restrepo and the representatives of Consorcio/WSH, Helicol had other contacts with Texas. During the years 1970–1977, it purchased helicopters (approximately 80% of its fleet), spare parts, and accessories for more than $4 million from Bell Helicopter Company in Fort Worth. In that period, Helicol sent prospective pilots to Forth Worth for training and to ferry the aircraft to South America. It also sent management and maintenance personnel to visit Bell Helicopter in Fort Worth during the same period in order to receive "plant familiarization" and for technical consultation. Helicol received into its New York City and Panama City, Fla., bank accounts over $5 million in payments from Consorcio/WSH drawn upon First City National Bank of Houston.

Beyond the foregoing, there have been no other business contacts between Helicol and the State of Texas. Helicol never has been authorized to do business in Texas and never has had an agent for the service of process within the State. It never has performed helicopter operations in Texas or sold any product that reached Texas, never solicited business in Texas, never signed any contract in Texas, never had any employee based there, and never recruited an employee in Texas. In addition, Helicol never has owned real or personal property in Texas and never has maintained an office or establishment there. Helicol has maintained no records in Texas and has no shareholders in

---

2. Throughout the record in this case the entity is referred to both as Consorcio and as WSH. We refer to it hereinafter as Consorcio/WSH.

3. Respondents acknowledge that the contract was executed in Peru and not in the United States. Tr. of Oral Arg. 22–23. See App. 79a; Brief for Respondents 3.

that State.[4] None of the respondents or their decedents were domiciled in Texas, Tr. of Oral Arg. 17, 18,[5] but all of the decedents were hired in Houston by Consorcio/WSH to work on the Petro Peru pipeline project.

Respondents instituted wrongful death actions in the District Court of Harris County, Tex., against Consorcio/WSH, Bell Helicopter Company, and Helicol. Helicol filed special appearances and moved to dismiss the actions for lack of *in personam* jurisdiction over it. The motion was denied. After a consolidated jury trial, judgment was entered against Helicol on a jury verdict of $1,141,200 in favor of respondents.[6] App. 174a.

P.C.

The Texas Court of Civil Appeals, Houston, First District, reversed the judgment of the District Court, holding that *in personam* jurisdiction over Helicol was lacking. 616 S.W.2d 247 (Tex.1981). The Supreme Court of Texas, with three Justices dissenting, initially affirmed the judgment of the Court of Civil Appeals. App. to Pet. for Cert. 46a–62a. Seven months later, however, on motion for rehearing, the court withdrew its prior opinions and, again with three Justices dissenting, reversed the judgment of the intermediate court. 638 S.W.2d 870 (Tex. 1982). In ruling that the Texas courts had *in personam* jurisdiction, the Texas Supreme Court first held that the State's long-arm statute reaches as far as the Due Process Clause of the Fourteenth Amendment permits. Id., at 872.[7] Thus, the only question remaining for the court

---

4. The Colombian national airline, Aerovias Nacionales de Colombia, owns approximately 94% of Helicol's capital stock. The remainder is held by Aerovias Corporacion de Viajes and four South American individuals. See Brief for Petitioner 2, n. 2.

5. Respondents' lack of residential or other contacts with Texas of itself does not defeat otherwise proper jurisdiction. Keeton v. Hustler Magazine, Inc., 465 U.S. 770, 780, 104 S.Ct. 1473, 1481, 79 L.Ed.2d 790 (1984); Calder v. Jones, 465 U.S. 783, 788, 104 S.Ct. 1482, 1486, 79 L.Ed.2d 804 (1984). We mention respondents' lack of contacts merely to show that nothing in the nature of the relationship between respondents and Helicol could possibly enhance Helicol's contacts with Texas. The harm suffered by respondents did not occur in Texas. Nor is it alleged that any negligence on the part of Helicol took place in Texas.

6. Defendants Consorcio/WSH and Bell Helicopter Company were granted directed verdicts with respect to respondents' claims against them. Bell Helicopter was granted a directed verdict on Helicol's cross-claim against it. App. 167a. Consorcio/WSH, as cross-plaintiff in a claim against Helicol, obtained a judgment in the amount of $70,000. Id., at 174a.

7. The State's long-arm statute is Tex. Rev.Civ.Stat.Ann., Art. 2031b (Vernon 1964 & Supp. 1982–1983). It reads in relevant part:

"Sec. 3. Any foreign corporation . . . that engages in business in this State, irrespective of any Statute or law respecting designation or maintenance of resident agents, and does not maintain a place of regular business in this State or a designated agent upon whom service may be made upon causes of action arising out of such business done in this State, the act or acts of engaging in such business within this State shall be deemed equivalent to an appointment by such foreign corporation . . . of the Secretary of State of Texas as agent upon whom service of process may be made in any action, suit or proceedings arising out of such business done in this State, wherein such corporation . . . is a party or is to be made a party."

"Sec. 4. For the purposes of this Act, and without including other acts that may constitute doing business, any foreign corporation . . . shall be deemed doing business in this State by entering into contract by mail or otherwise with a resident of Texas to be performed in whole or in part by either party in this State, or the committing of any tort in

doing business

to decide was whether it was consistent with the Due Process Clause for Texas courts to assert *in personam* jurisdiction over Helicol. Ibid.

II

* * * When a controversy is related to or "arises out of" a defendant's contacts with the forum, the Court has said that a "relationship among the defendant, the forum, and the litigation" is the essential foundation of *in personam* jurisdiction. Shaffer v. Heitner, 433 U.S. 186, 204, 97 S.Ct. 2569, 2579, 53 L.Ed.2d 683 (1977).[8]

Even when the cause of action does not arise out of or relate to the foreign corporation's activities in the forum State,[9] due process is not offended by a State's subjecting the corporation to its *in personam* jurisdiction when there are sufficient contacts between the State and the foreign corporation. Perkins v. Benguet Consolidated Mining Co., 342 U.S. 437, 72 S.Ct. 413, 96 L.Ed. 485 (1952); see Keeton v. Hustler Magazine, Inc., 465 U.S., at 779–780, 104 S.Ct., at 1480–1481. * * *

All parties to the present case concede that respondents' claims against Helicol did not "arise out of," and are not related to, Helicol's activities within Texas.[10] We thus must explore the nature of Helicol's contacts with the State of Texas to determine whether they constitute

whole or in part in this State. The act of recruiting Texas residents, directly or through an intermediary located in Texas, for employment inside or outside of Texas shall be deemed doing business in this State."

The last sentence of § 4 was added by 1979 Tex.Gen.Laws, ch. 245, § 1, and became effective Aug. 27, 1979.

The Supreme Court of Texas in its principal opinion relied upon rulings in U–Anchor Advertising, Inc. v. Burt, 553 S.W.2d 760 (Tex.1977); Hoppenfeld v. Crook, 498 S.W.2d 52 (Tex.Civ.App.1973); and O'Brien v. Lanpar Co., 399 S.W.2d 340 (Tex.1966). It is not within our province, of course, to determine whether the Texas Supreme Court correctly interpreted the State's long-arm statute. We therefore accept that court's holding that the limits of the Texas statute are coextensive with those of the Due Process Clause.

8. It has been said that when a State exercises personal jurisdiction over a defendant in a suit arising out of or related to the defendant's contacts with the forum, the State is exercising "specific jurisdiction" over the defendant. See von Mehren & Trautman, Jurisdiction to Adjudicate: A Suggested Analysis, 79 Harv.L.Rev. 1121, 1144–1164 (1966).

9. When a State exercises personal jurisdiction over a defendant in a suit not

arising out of or related to the defendant's contacts with the forum, the State has been said to be exercising "general jurisdiction" over the defendant. See Brilmayer, How Contacts Count: Due Process Limitations on State Court Jurisdiction, 1900 S.Ct.Rev. 77, 80–81; von Mehren & Trautman, 79 Harv.L.Rev., at 1136–1144; Calder v. Jones, 465 U.S., at 786, 104 S.Ct. at 1485.

10. See Brief for Respondents 14; Tr. of Oral Arg. 26–27, 30–31. Because the parties have not argued any relationship between the cause of action and Helicol's contacts with the State of Texas, we, contrary to the dissent's implication, * * * assert no "view" with respect to that issue.

The dissent suggests that we have erred in drawing no distinction between controversies that "relate to" a defendant's contacts with a forum and those that "arise out of" such contacts. * * * This criticism is somewhat puzzling, for the dissent goes on to urge that, for purposes of determining the constitutional validity of an assertion of specific jurisdiction, there really should be no distinction between the two. * * *

We do not address the validity or consequences of such a distinction because the issue has not been presented in this case. Respondents have made no argument that their cause of action either arose out of or is related to Helicol's contacts with the State of Texas. * * *

the kind of continuous and systematic general business contacts the Court found to exist in *Perkins*. We hold that they do not.

It is undisputed that Helicol does not have a place of business in Texas and never has been licensed to do business in the State. Basically, Helicol's contacts with Texas consisted of sending its chief executive officer to Houston for a contract-negotiation session; accepting into its New York bank account checks drawn on a Houston bank; purchasing helicopters, equipment, and training services from Bell Helicopter for substantial sums; and sending personnel to Bell's facilities in Fort Worth for training.

The one trip to Houston by Helicol's chief executive officer for the purpose of negotiating the transportation-services contract with Consorcio/WSH cannot be described or regarded as a contact of a "continuous and systematic" nature, as Perkins described it, see also International Shoe Co. v. Washington, 326 U.S., at 320, 66 S.Ct., at 160, and thus cannot support an assertion of in personam jurisdiction over Helicol by a Texas court. Similarly, Helicol's acceptance from Consorcio/WSH of checks drawn on a Texas bank is of negligible significance for purposes of determining whether Helicol had sufficient contacts in Texas. There is no indication that Helicol ever requested that the checks be drawn on a Texas bank or that there was any negotiation between Helicol and Consorcio/WSH with respect to the location or identity of the bank on which checks would be drawn. Common sense and everyday experience suggest that, absent unusual circumstances,[11] the bank on which a check is drawn is generally of little consequence to the payee and is a matter left to the discretion of the drawer. Such unilateral activity of another party or a third person is not an appropriate consideration when determining whether a defendant has sufficient contacts with a forum State to justify an assertion of jurisdiction. See Kulko v. California Superior Court, 436 U.S. 84, 93, 98 S.Ct. 1690, 1697, 56 L.Ed.2d 132 (1978) (arbitrary to subject one parent to suit in any State where other parent chooses to spend time while having custody of child pursuant to separation agreement); Hanson v. Denckla, 357 U.S. 235, 253, 78 S.Ct. 1228, 1239, 2 L.Ed.2d 1283 (1958) ("The unilateral activity of those who claim some relationship with a nonresident defendant cannot satisfy the requirement of contact with the forum State"); see also Lilly, Jurisdiction Over Domestic and Alien Defendants, 69 Va.L.Rev. 85, 99 (1983).

The Texas Supreme Court focused on the purchases and the related training trips in finding contacts sufficient to support an assertion of jurisdiction. We do not agree with that assessment, for the Court's opinion in Rosenberg Bros. & Co. v. Curtis Brown Co., 260 U.S. 516, 43 S.Ct. 170, 67 L.Ed. 372 (1923) (Brandeis, J., for a unanimous tribunal),

---

11. For example, if the financial health and continued ability of the bank to honor the draft are questionable, the payee might request that the check be drawn on an account at some other institution.

makes clear that purchases and related trips, standing alone, are not a sufficient basis for a State's assertion of jurisdiction.

*   *   *

III

We hold that Helicol's contacts with the State of Texas were insufficient to satisfy the requirements of the Due Process Clause of the Fourteenth Amendment.[13] Accordingly, we reverse the judgment of the Supreme Court of Texas.

It is so ordered.

JUSTICE BRENNAN, dissenting.

Decisions applying the Due Process Clause of the Fourteenth Amendment to determine whether a State may constitutionally assert *in personam* jurisdiction over a particular defendant for a particular cause of action most often turn on a weighing of facts. *   *   *

What is troubling about the Court's opinion, however, are the implications that might be drawn from the way in which the Court approaches the constitutional issue it addresses. First, the Court limits its discussion to an assertion of general jurisdiction of the Texas courts because, in its view, the underlying cause of action does "not aris[e] out of or relat[e] to the corporation's activities within the State." *   *   * Then, the Court relies on a 1923 decision in Rosenberg Bros. & Co. v. Curtis Brown Co., 260 U.S. 516, 43 S.Ct. 170, 67 L.Ed. 372, without considering whether that case retains any validity after our more recent pronouncements concerning the permissible reach of a State's jurisdiction. By posing and deciding the question presented in this manner, I fear that the Court is saying more than it realizes about constitutional limitations on the potential reach of *in personam* jurisdiction. In particular, by relying on a precedent whose premises have long been discarded, and by refusing to consider any distinction between controversies that "relate to" a defendant's contacts with the forum and causes of action that "arise out of" such contacts, the Court may be placing severe limitations on the type and amount of contacts that will satisfy the constitutional minimum.

In contrast, I believe that the undisputed contacts in this case between petitioner Helicol and the State of Texas are sufficiently important, and sufficiently related to the underlying cause of action, to make it fair and reasonable for the State to assert personal jurisdiction over Helicol for the wrongful death actions filed by the respondents.

---

13. As an alternative to traditional minimum-contacts analysis, respondents suggest that the Court hold that the State of Texas had personal jurisdiction over Helicol under a doctrine of "jurisdiction by necessity." See Shaffer v. Heitner, 433 U.S. 186, 211, n. 37, 97 S.Ct. 2569, 2583, n. 37, 53 L.Ed.2d 683 (1977). We conclude, however, that respondents failed to carry their burden of showing that all three defendants could not be sued together in a single forum. It is not clear from the record, for example, whether suit could have been brought against all three defendants in either Colombia or Peru. We decline to consider adoption of a doctrine of jurisdiction by necessity—a potentially far-reaching modification of existing law—in the absence of a more complete record.

Given that Helicol has purposefully availed itself of the benefits and obligations of the forum, and given the direct relationship between the underlying cause of action and Helicol's contacts with the forum, maintenance of this suit in the Texas courts "does not offend [the] 'traditional notions of fair play and substantial justice,'" International Shoe Co. v. Washington, 326 U.S. 310, 316, 66 S.Ct. 154, 90 L.Ed. 95 (1945) (quoting Milliken v. Meyer, 311 U.S. 457, 463, 61 S.Ct. 339, 342, 85 L.Ed. 278 (1940)), that are the touchstone of jurisdictional analysis under the Due Process Clause. I therefore dissent.

* * *

ASAHI METAL INDUSTRY CO. v. SUPERIOR COURT

Supreme Court of the United States, 1987.
480 U.S. 102, 107 S.Ct. 1026, 94 L.Ed.2d 92.*

JUSTICE O'CONNOR announced the judgment of the Court and delivered the unanimous opinion of the Court with respect to Part I, the opinion of the Court with respect to Part II–B, in which THE CHIEF JUSTICE, JUSTICE BRENNAN, JUSTICE WHITE, JUSTICE MARSHALL, JUSTICE BLACKMUN, JUSTICE POWELL, and JUSTICE STEVENS join, and an opinion with respect to Parts II–A and III, in which THE CHIEF JUSTICE, JUSTICE POWELL, and JUSTICE SCALIA join.

This case presents the question whether the mere awareness on the part of a foreign defendant that the components it manufactured, sold, and delivered outside the United States would reach the forum state in the stream of commerce constitutes "minimum contacts" between the defendant and the forum state such that the exercise of jurisdiction "does not offend 'traditional notions of fair play and substantial justice.'" International Shoe Co. v. Washington, 326 U.S. 310, 316, 66 S.Ct. 154, 158, 90 L.Ed. 95 (1945), quoting Milliken v. Meyer, 311 U.S. 457, 463, 61 S.Ct. 339, 342, 85 L.Ed. 278 (1940).

I

On September 23, 1978, on Interstate Highway 80 in Solano County, California, Gary Zurcher lost control of his Honda motorcycle and collided with a tractor. Zurcher was severely injured, and his passenger and wife, Ruth Ann Moreno, was killed. In September 1979, Zurcher filed a product liability action in the Superior Court of the State of California in and for the County of Solano. Zurcher alleged that the 1978 accident was caused by a sudden loss of air and an explosion in the rear tire of the motorcycle, and alleged that the motorcycle tire, tube, and sealant were defective. Zurcher's complaint named, *inter alia*, Cheng Shin Rubber Industrial Co., Ltd. (Cheng Shin), the Taiwanese manufacturer of the tube. Cheng Shin in turn filed a cross-complaint seeking indemnification from its codefendants and from petitioner, Asahi Metal Industry Co., Ltd. (Asahi), the manufacturer of

---

* Some of the Court's footnotes are omitted.

the tube's valve assembly. Zurcher's claims against Cheng Shin and the other defendants were eventually settled and dismissed, leaving only Cheng Shin's indemnity action against Asahi.

California's long-arm statute authorizes the exercise of jurisdiction "on any basis not inconsistent with the Constitution of this state or of the United States." Cal.Code Civ.Proc.Ann. § 410.10 (West 1973). Asahi moved to quash Cheng Shin's service of summons, arguing the State could not exert jurisdiction over it consistent with the Due Process Clause of the Fourteenth Amendment.

In relation to the motion, the following information was submitted by Asahi and Cheng Shin. Asahi is a Japanese corporation. It manufactures tire valve assemblies in Japan and sells the assemblies to Cheng Shin, and to several other tire manufacturers, for use as components in finished tire tubes. Asahi's sales to Cheng Shin took place in Taiwan. The shipments from Asahi to Cheng Shin were sent from Japan to Taiwan. Cheng Shin bought and incorporated into its tire tubes 150,000 Asahi valve assemblies in 1978; 500,000 in 1979; 500,000 in 1980; 100,000 in 1981; and 100,000 in 1982. Sales to Cheng Shin accounted for 1.24 percent of Asahi's income in 1981 and 0.44 percent in 1982. Cheng Shin alleged that approximately 20 percent of its sales in the United States are in California. Cheng Shin purchases valve assemblies from other suppliers as well, and sells finished tubes throughout the world.

In 1983 an attorney for Cheng Shin conducted an informal examination of the valve stems of the tire tubes sold in one cyclery in Solano County. The attorney declared that of the approximately 115 tire tubes in the store, 97 were purportedly manufactured in Japan or Taiwan, and of those 97, 21 valve stems were marked with the circled letter "A", apparently Asahi's trademark. Of the 21 Asahi valve stems, 12 were incorporated into Cheng Shin tire tubes. The store contained 41 other Cheng Shin tubes that incorporated the valve assemblies of other manufacturers. Declaration of Kenneth B. Shepard in Opposition to Motion to Quash Subpoena, App. to Brief for Respondent 5–6. An affidavit of a manager of Cheng Shin whose duties included the purchasing of component parts stated: "'In discussions with Asahi regarding the purchase of valve stem assemblies the fact that my Company sells tubes throughout the world and specifically the United States has been discussed. I am informed and believe that Asahi was fully aware that valve stem assemblies sold to my Company and to others would end up throughout the United States and in California.'" 39 Cal.3d 35, 48, n. 4, 216 Cal.Rptr. 385, 392, n. 4, 702 P.2d 543, 549–550, n. 4 (1985). An affidavit of the president of Asahi, on the other hand, declared that Asahi "has never contemplated that its limited sales of tire valves to Cheng Shin in Taiwan would subject it to lawsuits in California.'" Ibid. * * *

Primarily on the basis of the above information, the Superior Court denied the motion to quash summons, stating that "Asahi obviously does business on an international scale. It is not unreasonable that they defend claims of defect in their product on an international scale." Order Denying Motion to Quash Summons, Zurcher v. Dunlop Tire & Rubber Co., No. 76180 (Super.Ct., Solano County, Cal., Apr. 20, 1983).

The Court of Appeal of the State of California issued a peremptory writ of mandate commanding the Superior Court to quash service of summons. The court concluded that "it would be unreasonable to require Asahi to respond in California solely on the basis of ultimately realized foreseeability that the product into which its component was embodied would be sold all over the world including California." App. to Pet. for cert. B5–B6.

The Supreme Court of the State of California reversed and discharged the writ issued by the Court of Appeal. 39 Cal.3d 35, 216 Cal. Rptr. 385, 702 P.2d 543 (1985). The court observed that "Asahi has no offices, property or agents in California. It solicits no business in California and has made no direct sales [in California]." Id., at 48, 216 Cal.Rptr., at 392, 702 P.2d, at 549. Moreover, "Asahi did not design or control the system of distribution that carried its valve assemblies into California." Id., at 49, 216 Cal.Rptr., at 392, 702 P.2d, at 549. Nevertheless, the court found the exercise of jurisdiction over Asahi to be consistent with the Due Process Clause. It concluded that Asahi knew that some of the valve assemblies sold to Cheng Shin would be incorporated into tire tubes sold in California, and that Asahi benefited indirectly from the sale in California of products incorporating its components. The court considered Asahi's intentional act of placing its components into the stream of commerce—that is, by delivering the components to Cheng Shin in Taiwan—coupled with Asahi's awareness that some of the components would eventually find their way into California, sufficient to form the basis for state court jurisdiction under the Due Process Clause.

We granted certiorari, 475 U.S. 1044, 106 S.Ct. 1258, 89 L.Ed.2d 569 (1986), and now reverse.

II

A

The Due Process Clause of the Fourteenth Amendment limits the power of a state court to exert personal jurisdiction over a nonresident defendant. "[T]he constitutional touchstone" of the determination whether an exercise of personal jurisdiction comports with due process "remains whether the defendant purposefully established 'minimum contacts' in the forum State." Burger King Corp. v. Rudzewicz, 471 U.S. 462, 474, 105 S.Ct. 2174, 2183, 85 L.Ed.2d 528 (1985), quoting International Shoe Co. v. Washington, 326 U.S. 310, 316, 66 S.Ct. 154, 158, 90 L.Ed. 95 (1945). Most recently we have reaffirmed the oft-quoted reasoning of Hanson v. Denckla, 357 U.S. 235, 253, 78 S.Ct. 1228, 1239, 2 L.Ed.2d 1283 (1958), that minimum contacts must have a basis in "some act by which the defendant purposefully avails itself of the privilege of conducting activities within the forum State, thus invoking the benefits and protections of its laws." *Burger King,* 471 U.S., at 475, 105 S.Ct., at 2183. "Jurisdiction is proper . . . where the contacts proximately result from actions by the defendant *himself* that create a 'substantial connection' with the forum State." Ibid., quoting McGee v. International Life Insurance Co., 355 U.S. 220, 223, 78 S.Ct. 199, 201, 2 L.Ed.2d 223 (1957) (emphasis in original).

Applying the principle that minimum contacts must be based on an act of the defendant, the Court in World–Wide Volkswagen Corp. v. Woodson, 444 U.S. 286, 100 S.Ct. 559, 62 L.Ed.2d 490 (1980), rejected the assertion that a *consumer's* unilateral act of bringing the defendant's product into the forum State was a sufficient constitutional basis for personal jurisdiction over the defendant. It had been argued in *World– Wide Volkswagen* that because an automobile retailer and its wholesale distributor sold a product mobile by design and purpose, they could foresee being haled into court in the distant States into which their customers might drive. The Court rejected this concept of foreseeability as an insufficient basis for jurisdiction under the Due Process Clause. Id., at 295–296, 100 S.Ct., at 566. The Court disclaimed, however, the idea that "foreseeability is wholly irrelevant" to personal jurisdiction, concluding that "[t]he forum State does not exceed its powers under the Due Process Clause if it asserts personal jurisdiction over a corporation that delivers its products into the stream of commerce with the expectation that they will be purchased by consumers in the forum State." Id., at 297–298, 100 S.Ct., at 567 (citation omitted). The Court reasoned:

> "When a corporation 'purposefully avails itself of the privilege of conducting activities within the forum State,' Hanson v. Denckla, 357 U.S. [235,] 253, [78 S.Ct. 1228, 1239, 2 L.Ed.2d 1283 (1958)], it has clear notice that it is subject to suit there, and can act to alleviate the risk of burdensome litigation by procuring insurance, passing the expected costs on to customers, or, if the risks are too great, severing its connection with the State. Hence if the sale of a product of a manufacturer or distributor . . . is not simply an isolated occurrence, but arises from the efforts of the manufacturer or distributor to serve, directly or indirectly, the market for its product in other States, it is not unreasonable to subject it to suit in one of those States if its allegedly defective merchandise has there been the source of injury to its owners or to others." Id., at 297, 100 S.Ct., at 567.

In *World–Wide Volkswagen* itself, the state court sought to base jurisdiction not on any act of the defendant, but on the foreseeable unilateral actions of the consumer. Since *World–Wide Volkswagen,* lower courts have been confronted with cases in which the defendant acted by placing a product in the stream of commerce, and the stream eventually swept defendant's product into the forum State, but the defendant did nothing else to purposefully avail itself of the market in the forum state. Some courts have understood the Due Process Clause, as interpreted in *World–Wide Volkswagen,* to allow an exercise of personal jurisdiction to be based on no more than the defendant's act of placing the product in the stream of commerce. Other courts have understood the Due Process Clause and the above-quoted language in *World–Wide Volkswagen* to require the action of the defendant to be more purposefully directed at the forum State than the mere act of placing a product in the stream of commerce.

The reasoning of the Supreme Court of California in the present case illustrates the former interpretation of *World–Wide Volkswagen.* The Supreme Court of California held that, because the stream of commerce eventually brought some valves Asahi sold Cheng Shin into California, Asahi's awareness that its valves would be sold in California was sufficient to permit California to exercise jurisdiction over Asahi consistent with the requirements of the Due Process Clause. The Supreme Court of California's position was consistent with those courts that have held that mere foreseeability or awareness was a constitutionally sufficient basis for personal jurisdiction if the defendant's product made its way into the forum State while still in the stream of commerce. See Bean Dredging Corp. v. Dredge Technology Corp., 744 F.2d 1081 (CA5 1984); Hendrick v. Daiko Shoji Co., 715 F.2d 1355 (CA9 1983).

Other courts, however, have understood the Due Process Clause to require something more than that the defendant was aware of its product's entry into the forum State through the stream of commerce in order for the state to exert jurisdiction over the defendant. In the present case, for example, the State Court of Appeal did not read the Due Process Clause, as interpreted by *World–Wide Volkswagen,* to allow "mere foreseeability that the product will enter the forum state [to] be enough by itself to establish jurisdiction over the distributor and retailer." App. to Pet. for Cert. B5. In Humble v. Toyota Motor Co., Ltd., 727 F.2d 709 (CA8 1984), an injured car passenger brought suit against Arakawa Auto Body Company, a Japanese corporation that manufactured car seats for Toyota. Arakawa did no business in the United States; it had no office, affiliate, subsidiary, or agent in the United States; it manufactured its component parts outside the United States and delivered them to Toyota Motor Company in Japan. The Court of Appeals, adopting the reasoning of the District Court in that case, noted that although it "does not doubt that Arakawa could have foreseen that its product would find its way into the United States," it would be "manifestly unjust" to require Arakawa to defend itself in the United States. Id., at 710–711, quoting 578 F.Supp. 530, 533 (ND Iowa 1982). See also Hutson v. Fehr Bros., Inc., 584 F.2d 833 (CA8 1978); see generally Max Daetwyler Corp. v. R. Meyer, 762 F.2d 290, 299 (CA3 1985) (collecting "stream of commerce" cases in which the "manufacturers involved had made deliberate decisions to market their products in the forum state").

We now find this latter position to be consonant with the requirements of due process. The "substantial connection," *Burger King,* 471 U.S., at 475, 105 S.Ct., at 2184; *McGee,* 355 U.S., at 223, 78 S.Ct., at 201, between the defendant and the forum State necessary for a finding of minimum contacts must come about by *an action of the defendant purposefully directed toward the forum State.* Burger King, supra, 471 U.S., at 476, 105 S.Ct., at 2184; Keeton v. Hustler Magazine, Inc., 465 U.S. 770, 774, 104 S.Ct. 1473, 1478, 79 L.Ed.2d 790 (1984). The placement of a product into the stream of commerce, without more, is not an act of the defendant purposefully directed toward the forum State. Additional conduct of the defendant may indicate an intent or purpose to serve the market in the forum State, for example, designing the product for the market in the forum State, advertising in the forum State, establishing channels for providing regular advice to customers in the forum State, or marketing the product through a distributor who has agreed to serve as the sales agent in the forum State. But a defendant's awareness that the stream of commerce may or will sweep the product into the forum State does not convert the mere act of placing the product into the stream into an act purposefully directed toward the forum State.

Assuming, *arguendo,* that respondents have established Asahi's awareness that some of the valves sold to Cheng Shin would be incorporated into tire tubes sold in California, respondents have not demonstrated any action by Asahi to purposefully avail itself of the California market. Asahi does not do business in California. It has no office, agents, employees, or property in California. It does not advertise or otherwise solicit business in California. It did not create, control, or employ the distribution system that brought its valves to California. Cf. Hicks v. Kawasaki Heavy Industries, 452 F.Supp. 130 (MD Pa.1978). There is no evidence that Asahi designed its product in anticipation of sales in California. Cf. Rockwell International Corp. v. Costruzioni Aeronautiche Giovanni Agusta, 553 F.Supp. 328 (ED Pa. 1982). On the basis of these facts, the exertion of personal jurisdiction over Asahi by the Superior Court of California* exceeds the limits of due process.

B

The strictures of the Due Process Clause forbid a state court from exercising personal jurisdiction over Asahi under circumstances that would offend "traditional notions of fair play and substantial justice." International Shoe Co. v. Washington, 326 U.S., at 316, 66 S.Ct., at 158; quoting Milliken v. Meyer, 311 U.S., at 463, 61 S.Ct., at 342.

---

* We have no occasion here to determine whether Congress could, consistent with the Due Process Clause of the Fifth Amendment, authorize federal court personal jurisdiction over alien defendants based on the aggregate of *national* contacts, rather than on the contacts between the defendant and the State in which the federal court sits. See Max Daetwyler Corp. v. R. Meyer, 762 F.2d 290, 293–295 (CA3 1985); DeJames v. Magnificence Carriers, Inc., 654 F.2d 280, 283 (CA3 1981); see also Born, Reflections on Judicial Jurisdiction in International Cases, to be published in 17 Ga.J.Int'l & Comp.L. 1 (1987); Lilly, Jurisdiction Over Domestic and Alien Defendants, 69 Va.L.Rev. 85, 127–145 (1983).

We have previously explained that the determination of the reasonableness of the exercise of jurisdiction in each case will depend on an evaluation of several factors. A court must consider the burden on the defendant, the interests of the forum state, and the plaintiff's interest in obtaining relief. It must also weigh in its determination "the interstate judicial system's interest in obtaining the most efficient resolution of controversies; and the shared interest of the several States in furthering fundamental substantive social policies." *World–Wide Volkswagen*, 444 U.S., at 292, 100 S.Ct., at 564 (citations omitted).

A consideration of these factors in the present case clearly reveals the unreasonableness of the assertion of jurisdiction over Asahi, even apart from the question of the placement of goods in the stream of commerce.

Certainly, the burden on the defendant in this case is severe. Asahi has been commanded by the Supreme Court of California not only to traverse the distance between Asahi's headquarters in Japan and the Superior Court of California in and for the County of Solano, but also to submit its dispute with Cheng Shin to a foreign nation's judicial system. The unique burdens placed upon one who must defend oneself in a foreign legal system should have significant weight in assessing the reasonableness of stretching the long arm of personal jurisdiction over national borders.

When minimum contacts have been established, often the interests of the plaintiff and the forum in the exercise of jurisdiction will justify even the serious burdens placed on the alien defendant. In the present case, however, the interests of the plaintiff and the forum in California's assertion of jurisdiction over Asahi are slight. All that remains is a claim for indemnification asserted by Cheng Shin, a Taiwanese corporation, against Asahi. The transaction on which the indemnification claim is based took place in Taiwan; Asahi's components were shipped from Japan to Taiwan. Cheng Shin has not demonstrated that it is more convenient for it to litigate its indemnification claim against Asahi in California rather than in Taiwan or Japan.

Because the plaintiff is not a California resident, California's legitimate interests in the dispute have considerably diminished. The Supreme Court of California argued that the State had an interest in "protecting its consumers by ensuring that foreign manufacturers comply with the state's safety standards." 39 Cal.3d, at 49, 216 Cal.Rptr., at 392, 702 P.2d, at 550. The State Supreme Court's definition of California's interest, however, was overly broad. The dispute between Cheng Shin and Asahi is primarily about indemnification rather than safety standards. Moreover, it is not at all clear at this point that California law should govern the question whether a Japanese corporation should indemnify a Taiwanese corporation on the basis of a sale made in Taiwan and a shipment of goods from Japan to Taiwan. Phillips Petroleum v. Shutts, 472 U.S. 797, 821–822, 105 S.Ct. 2965, 2979, 86 L.Ed.2d 628 (1985); Allstate Insurance Co. v. Hague, 449 U.S.

302, 312–313, 101 S.Ct. 633, 639–640, 66 L.Ed.2d 521 (1981). The possibility of being haled into a California court as a result of an accident involving Asahi's components undoubtedly creates an additional deterrent to the manufacture of unsafe components; however, similar pressures will be placed on Asahi by the purchasers of its components as long as those who use Asahi components in their final products, and sell those products in California, are subject to the application of California tort law.

World–Wide Volkswagen also admonished courts to take into consideration the interests of the "several States," in addition to the forum state, in the efficient judicial resolution of the dispute and the advancement of substantive policies. In the present case, this advice calls for a court to consider the procedural and substantive policies of other *nations* whose interests are affected by the assertion of jurisdiction by the California court. The procedural and substantive interests of other nations in a state court's assertion of jurisdiction over an alien defendant will differ from case to case. In every case, however, those interests, as well as the Federal interest in its foreign relations policies, will be best served by a careful inquiry into the reasonableness of the assertion of jurisdiction in the particular case, and an unwillingness to find the serious burdens on an alien defendant outweighed by minimal interests on the part of the plaintiff or the forum State. "Great care and reserve should be exercised when extending our notions of personal jurisdiction into the international field." United States v. First National City Bank, 379 U.S. 378, 404, 85 S.Ct. 528, 542, 13 L.Ed.2d 365 (1965) (Harlan, J., dissenting). See Born, Reflections on Judicial Jurisdiction in International Cases, to be published in 17 Ga.J.Int'l & Comp.L. 1 (1987).

Considering the international context, the heavy burden on the alien defendant, and the slight interests of the plaintiff and the forum State, the exercise of personal jurisdiction by a California court over Asahi in this instance would be unreasonable and unfair.

III

Because the facts of this case do not establish minimum contacts such that the exercise of personal jurisdiction is consistent with fair play and substantial justice, the judgment of Supreme Court of California is reversed, and the case is remanded for further proceedings not inconsistent with this opinion.

It is so ordered.

JUSTICE BRENNAN, with whom JUSTICE WHITE, JUSTICE MARSHALL, and JUSTICE BLACKMUN join, concurring in part and in the judgment.

I do not agree with the interpretation in Part II–A of the stream-of-commerce theory, nor with the conclusion that Asahi did not "purposely avail itself of the California market." * * * I do agree, however, with the Court's conclusion in Part II–B that the exercise of personal jurisdiction over Asahi in this case would not comport with "fair play and substantial justice," International Shoe Co. v. Washington, 326 U.S. 310, 320, 66 S.Ct. 154, 160, 90 L.Ed. 95 (1945). This is one of those rare cases in which "minimum requirements inherent in the concept of 'fair play and substantial justice' . . . defeat the reasonableness of jurisdiction even [though] the defendant has purposefully engaged in forum activities." Burger King Corp. v. Rudzewicz, 471 U.S. 462, 477–478, 105 S.Ct. 2174, 2184–2185, 85 L.Ed.2d 528 (1985). I therefore join Parts I and II–B of the Court's opinion, and write separately to explain my disagreement with Part II–A.

Part II–A states that "a defendant's awareness that the stream of commerce may or will sweep the product into the forum State does not convert the mere act of placing the product into the stream into an act purposefully directed toward the forum State." * * * Under this view, a plaintiff would be required to show "[a]dditional conduct" directed toward the forum before finding the exercise of jurisdiction over the defendant to be consistent with the Due Process Clause. * * * I see no need for such a showing, however. The stream of commerce refers not to unpredictable currents or eddies, but to the regular and anticipated flow of products from manufacture to distribution to retail sale. As long as a participant in this process is aware that the final product is being marketed in the forum State, the possibility of a lawsuit there cannot come as a surprise. Nor will the litigation present a burden for which there is no corresponding benefit. A defendant who has placed goods in the stream of commerce benefits economically from the retail sale of the final product in the forum State, and indirectly benefits from the State's laws that regulate and facilitate commercial activity. These benefits accrue regardless of whether that participant directly conducts business in the forum State, or engages in additional conduct directed toward that State. Accordingly, most courts and commentators have found that jurisdiction premised on the placement of a product into the stream of commerce is consistent with the Due Process Clause, and have not required a showing of additional conduct.

The endorsement in Part II–A of what appears to be the minority view among Federal Courts of Appeals represents a marked retreat from the analysis in World–Wide Volkswagen v. Woodson, 444 U.S. 286, 100 S.Ct. 559, 62 L.Ed.2d 490 (1980). In that case, "respondents [sought] to base jurisdiction on one, isolated occurrence and whatever inferences can be drawn therefrom: the fortuitous circumstance that a single Audi automobile, sold in New York to New York residents, happened to suffer an accident while passing through Oklahoma." Id., at 295, 100 S.Ct., at 566. The Court held that the possibility of an accident in Oklahoma, while to some extent foreseeable in light of the inherent mobility of the automobile, was not enough to establish minimum contacts between the forum State and the retailer or distributor. Id., at 295–296, 100 S.Ct., at 566. The Court then carefully explained:

> "[T]his is not to say, of course, that foreseeability is wholly irrelevant. But the foreseeability that is critical to due process analysis

is not the mere likelihood that a product will find its way into the forum State. Rather, it is that the defendant's conduct and connection with the forum State are such that he should reasonably anticipate being haled into Court there." Id., at 297, 100 S.Ct. at 567.

The Court reasoned that when a corporation may reasonably anticipate litigation in a particular forum, it cannot claim that such litigation is unjust or unfair, because it "can act to alleviate the risk of burdensome litigation by procuring insurance, passing the expected costs on to consumers, or, if the risks are too great, severing its connection with the State." Ibid.

To illustrate the point, the Court contrasted the foreseeability of litigation in a State to which a consumer fortuitously transports a defendant's product (insufficient contacts) with the foreseeability of litigation in a State where the defendant's product was regularly *sold* (sufficient contacts). The Court stated:

> "Hence if the *sale* of a product of a manufacturer or distributor such as Audi or Volkswagen is not simply an isolated occurrence, but arises from the efforts of the manufacturer or distributor to serve, *directly or indirectly,* the market for its product in other States, it is not unreasonable to subject it to suit in one of those States if its allegedly defective merchandise has there been the source of injury to its owner or to others. The forum State does not exceed its powers under the Due Process Clause if it asserts personal jurisdiction over a corporation that delivers its products into the stream of commerce *with the expectation that they will be purchased by consumers* in the forum State." Id., at 297–298, 100 S.Ct., at 567 (emphasis added).

The Court concluded its illustration by referring to Gray v. American Radiator & Standard Sanitary Corp., 22 Ill.2d 432, 176 N.E.2d 761 (1961), a well-known stream-of-commerce case in which the Illinois Supreme Court applied the theory to assert jurisdiction over a component-parts manufacturer that sold no components directly in Illinois, but did sell them to a manufacturer who incorporated them into a final product that was sold in Illinois. 444 U.S., at 297–298.

The Court in *World–Wide Volkswagen* thus took great care to distinguish "between a case involving goods which reach a distant State through a chain of distribution and a case involving goods which reach the same State because a consumer . . . took them there." 444 U.S., at 306–307, 100 S.Ct., at 584 (BRENNAN, J., dissenting). The California Supreme Court took note of this distinction, and correctly concluded that our holding in *World–Wide Volkswagen* preserved the stream-of-commerce theory. See App. to Pet. for Cert. C–9, and n. 3, C–13–C–15; cf. Comment, Federalism, Due Process, and Minimum Contacts: World–Wide Volkswagen Corp. v. Woodson, 80 Colum.L.Rev. 1341, 1359–1361, and nn. 140–146 (1980).

In this case, the facts found by the California Supreme Court support its finding of minimum contacts. The court found that "[a]lthough Asahi did not design or control the system of distribution that carried its valve assemblies into California, Asahi was aware of the distribution system's operation, and it knew that it would benefit economically from the sale in California of products incorporating its components." App. to Pet. for Cert. C–11. Accordingly, I cannot join the plurality's determination that Asahi's regular and extensive sales of component parts to a manufacturer it knew was making regular sales of the final product in California is insufficient to establish minimum contacts with California.

JUSTICE STEVENS, with whom JUSTICE WHITE and JUSTICE BLACKMUN join, concurring in part and concurring in the judgment.

The judgment of the Supreme Court of California should be reversed for the reasons stated in Part II–B of the Court's opinion. While I join Parts I and II–B, I do not join Part II–A for two reasons. First, it is not necessary to the Court's decision. An examination of minimum contacts is not always necessary to determine whether a state court's assertion of personal jurisdiction is constitutional. See Burger King Corp. v. Rudzewicz, 471 U.S. 462, 476–478, 105 S.Ct. 2174, 2184–2185, 85 L.Ed.2d 528 (1985). Part II–B establishes, after considering the factors set forth in World–Wide Volkswagen Corp. v. Woodson, 444 U.S. 286, 292, 100 S.Ct. 559, 564, 62 L.Ed.2d 490 (1980), that California's exercise of jurisdiction over Asahi in this case would be "unreasonable and unfair." * * * This finding alone requires reversal; this case fits within the rule that "minimum requirements inherent in the concept of 'fair play and substantial justice' may defeat the reasonableness of jurisdiction even if the defendant has purposefully engaged in forum activities." Burger King, 471 U.S., at 477–478, 105 S.Ct., at 2184–2185 (quoting International Shoe Co. v. Washington, 326 U.S. 310, 320, 66 S.Ct. 154, 160, 90 L.Ed. 95 (1945)). Accordingly, I see no reason in this case for the Court to articulate "purposeful direction" or any other test as the nexus between an act of a defendant and the forum State that is necessary to establish minimum contacts.

Second, even assuming that the test ought to be formulated here, Part II–A misapplies it to the facts of this case. The Court seems to assume that an unwavering line can be drawn between "mere awareness" that a component will find its way into the forum State and "purposeful availment" of the forum's market. * * * Over the course of its dealings with Cheng Shin, Asahi has arguably engaged in a higher quantum of conduct than "[t]he placement of a product into the stream of commerce, without more. . . ." * * * Whether or not this conduct rises to the level of purposeful availment requires a constitutional determination that is affected by the volume, the value, and the hazardous character of the components. In most circumstances I would be inclined to conclude that a regular course of dealing that results in deliveries of over 100,000 units annually over a period of several years would constitute "purposeful availment" even though the item delivered to the forum State was a standard product marketed throughout the world.

FURTHER NOTE ON INTERNATIONAL LITIGATION

1. Considerations Affecting Jurisdiction

Intersecting with, and often covertly influencing, the determination of whether a foreign defendant has the requisite contacts with an American forum are a number of other factors, including: (1) whether the action is brought in state or federal court; (2) whether the action is governed by state or federal law; (3) whether there are applicable international treaties; (4) the nature of the transaction, such as whether it involves international commerce, product liability, or personal status; and (5) the substantive law to be applied. For example, many cases against foreign defendants involving disputes over territorial jurisdiction are product liability claims premised on state law, where the plaintiff is trying to take advantage of the comparatively generous American rules governing such claims. Both *Asahi* and *Helicopteros* are examples. Is it reasonable to speculate that the Court in these cases was reluctant to permit jurisdiction because it was reluctant to subject the defendants to the substantive American law governing the actions, or, alternatively, to fashion a separate body of substantive law to be applied in product liability actions against foreign defendants? On the latter point, it is important to note that the Supreme Court has held choice of substantive law to be a state matter obligatory on federal courts. See Klaxon Co. v. Stentor Elec. Mfg. Co., infra p. 572; Day & Zimmermann, Inc. v. Challoner, 423 U.S. 3, 96 S.Ct. 167, 46 L.Ed.2d 3 (1975). Would it make more sense in cases like these to change the rules such that jurisdiction is permitted, but only if the forum court applies international commercial law? See Cox, The Interrelationship of Personal Jurisdiction and Choice of Law: Forging New Theory Through Asahi Metal Industry Co. v. Superior Court, 49 U.Pitt.L.Rev. 189 (1987). How is the Court in these cases using the competing concepts of convenience and sovereignty?

The doctrine of *forum non conveniens* is a supplement to the existing rules governing territorial jurisdiction in the international setting. The sovereignty theory can lead to jurisdiction based on the "presence" of the defendant. *Forum non conveniens* allows the court nonetheless to dismiss the action if another country would be a more appropriate forum, thereby preventing exploitation of generous United States choice of law and damages rules. See Piper Aircraft Co. v. Reyno, infra p. 427, and the Note following.

2. Comity and Due Process

International rules normally are based on considerations of comity. In the cases dealing with territorial jurisdiction in international litigation the Court has used due process language in a comity setting. Paradoxically, comity has come to permit less outreach than due process. In the interstate context, the strategic position of the Court is as a superior judicial body in the federal system having power as a matter of domestic law to delineate rules for the constituent members of the polity, i.e., the states. The states, of course, have a duty to obey pronouncements of the Court, having no recourse to measures such as diplomatic protest or other countermeasures. In the international setting, foreign nations can retaliate if American courts are too aggressive in asserting jurisdiction. Nevertheless, the Court seems to want to impose a kind of good citizenship on the states vis a vis the international community, riding herd on

[handwritten margin note: rule courtesy where one ct defers jursd. to another]

the assertiveness of private litigants in order to prevent "international incidents," so to speak. The issue thus is the difference between the constitutional structure of comity, in the international realm, as opposed to the constitutional structure of federal authority, in the interstate realm.

3. Aggregating Contacts

Where an alien corporation has scattered contacts with several states in the United States, some courts have held that the contacts may be aggregated in determining whether there are "minimum contacts," and that the question is one of federal law. See Lilly, Jurisdiction Over Domestic and Alien Defendants, 69 Va.L.Rev. 85 (1983); Note, Alien Corporations and Aggregate Contacts: A Genuinely Federal Jurisdictional Standard, 95 Harv.L.Rev. 470 (1981). The issue can be compared to the distinction made between "specific" and "general" jurisdiction, here in the context of a foreign defendant's contacts vis a vis the United States as a whole. Consider in this regard the Court's opinion in *Asahi,* especially the footnote at the end of section II A. Is the Court saying that *state* courts may not aggregate contacts in this manner, at least where the action is premised on state law, but that *federal* courts might be able to, at least if authorized by Congress to do so? What about a suit based on state law filed in federal court? Is this issue similar to the question whether Congress could constitutionally provide for nationwide service of process in federal court? See Further Note on Long Arm Statutes, infra p. 414. Why shouldn't the territorial jurisdiction of a state court in a case with international dimensions be measured by the standards determining the exercise of such jurisdiction by the United States as a country in the international community, i.e., by international law? Does the decision whether or not to aggregate contacts provide courts with another means for declining jurisdiction in cases where the defendant would be subject to comparatively liberal American standards for recovery?

5. STATUTORY REQUIREMENTS

INTRODUCTORY NOTE ON STATUTORY REQUIREMENTS

Long before *International Shoe,* most states had enacted statutes making foreign corporations that were "doing business" in the state subject to service of process. Generally speaking, these statutes had been construed as extending only to situations where the foreign corporation had local offices or employees, telephone book listings, bank accounts, etc., or some combination thereof sufficient in the view of the courts to justify the conclusion that the corporation was "present." See, e.g., Frene v. Louisville Cement Co., 134 F.2d 511 (D.C.Cir. 1943); Anno., 146 A.L.R. 941. Even though *International Shoe* extended the states' permissible reach against foreign corporations, it did not of its own force extend the range of state "doing business" or "long arm" statutes. Accordingly, a two-step inquiry was required: did the state statute reach the defendant in the case presented and, if so, was the application of the statute constitutional under *International Shoe* and its progeny? Usually, the statutes were regarded as requiring more in the way of contacts than the *International Shoe* minimum. See, e.g., Bomze v. Nardis Sportswear, Inc., 165 F.2d 33 (2d Cir.1948).

Bolder steps to implement the expanded jurisdictional authority conferred by *International Shoe* have been taken in most states, following the lead of Illinois, which in 1956 enacted the following statute, now codified at Ill.C.C.P. § 2–209:

"(a) Any person, whether or not a citizen or resident of this State, who in person or through an agent does any of the acts hereinafter enumerated, thereby submits such person, and, if an individual, his personal representative, to the jurisdiction of the courts of this State as to any cause of action arising from the doing of any of said acts:

"(1) The transaction of any business within this State;

"(2) The commission of a tortious act within this State;

"(3) The ownership, use, or possession of any real estate situated in this State;

"(4) Contracting to insure any person, property or risk located within this State at the time of contracting;

* * *

"(b) Service of process upon any person who is subject to the jurisdiction of the courts of this State, as provided in this Section, may be made by personally serving the summons upon the defendant outside this State, as provided in this Act, with the same force and effect as though summons had been personally served within this State.

* * *

"(d) Only causes of action arising from acts enumerated herein may be asserted against a defendant in an action in which jurisdiction over him is based upon this Section.

"(e) Nothing herein contained limits or affects the right to serve any process in any other manner now or hereafter provided by law."

The validity of the Illinois statute was sustained in Nelson v. Miller, 11 Ill.2d 378, 143 N.E.2d 673 (1957).

The boldest, and shortest, of the "long arm" statutes is of the type found in C.C.P. 410.10:

"A court of this state may exercise jurisdiction on any basis not inconsistent with the Constitution of this state or of the United States."

Statutes of the California type pose only the question whether permitting aggressive assertion of territorial jurisdiction exceeds the constitutional limit in a given case. For an interpretation that seems pretty expansive, see Cornelison v. Chaney, 16 Cal.3d 143, 127 Cal.Rptr. 352, 545 P.2d 264 (1976), with which compare Sibley v. Superior Court, 16 Cal.3d 442, 128 Cal.Rptr. 34, 546 P.2d 322 (1976).

Statutes that do not simply incorporate the constitutional test, such as the Illinois and New York statutes, pose a somewhat different problem. Consider the following cases.

AMERICAN EUTECTIC WELDING ALLOYS SALES CO. v. DYTRON ALLOYS CORP.

United States Court of Appeals for the Second Circuit, 1971.
439 F.2d 428.

FEINBERG, CIRCUIT JUDGE.

Once again we have the problem of predicting whether the courts of the State of New York would find jurisdiction over non-resident defendants under its "long-arm" statute, N.Y. CPLR § 302(a). The United States District Court for the Eastern District of New York,

Walter Bruchhausen, J., held that they would not, quashing service of process and dismissing an action against defendant Dytron Alloys Corporation (Dytron) and two of its employees, Ralph O. Karsner, Jr., and William N. Price.[1] Plaintiffs American Eutectic Welding Alloys Sales Co., Inc. (American Eutectic) and Eutectic Corporation, Inc. (Eutectic) appeal from that order. For reasons set forth below, we reverse as to the individual defendants and affirm as to the corporate defendant.

I

American Eutectic is the sales subsidiary of Eutectic; both are New York corporations. Eutectic manufactures metal welding rods and electrode alloys, grossing over $25 million in sales annually. American Eutectic employs over 350 sales personnel throughout the United States, including what the company calls Technical Representatives. The following is alleged in the complaint or supporting affidavits and therefore must be accepted as true for the purpose of this appeal from dismissal of the complaint. The individual defendants received an intensive three-month training course in New York, where plaintiffs' main offices are located. During that period, plaintiffs paid the salaries and living expenses of these defendants, who attended classes, received instruction in metallurgy and plaintiffs' specific welding techniques, and attended laboratory sessions. Each individual defendant signed an employment contract with American Eutectic, which provided that it would become binding upon American Eutectic "only after countersignature at our Home Office in Flushing, New York. . . . This agreement shall be deemed to be made under, and shall be governed by, the laws of the State of New York in all respects." They were then given various customer control cards, which contained the names of customers and their needs. This information was confidential and the individual defendants promised in the employment contract to keep it so. The contract assigned a particular territory outside of New York to the employee, who agreed that, if his employment ended, he would not work for two years thereafter for a competitor in the same territory. During their period of employment with plaintiffs, which was five and 13 years respectively, the individual defendants had continuous contact with New York by telephone with respect to orders and business problems. In addition, according to the affidavit of Eutectic's vice president, they "may have visited the home offices of the company many times."

The two individual defendants left plaintiffs' employ in the recent past and now work for defendant Dytron, a competitor of plaintiffs. Dytron, a Michigan corporation, is based in Detroit, and has sales in a number of states. The theory of the complaint is that Dytron induced plaintiffs' experienced sales employees to leave plaintiffs, come to

---

1. Plaintiffs also sued a third defendant, Kenneth R. Youngblood, who took no action in the district court. There was no dismissal as to him.

Dytron, and use confidential information to woo away plaintiffs' customers. The complaint alleges that the two individual defendants are soliciting plaintiffs' customers in Kentucky and Pennsylvania. Dytron is also accused of competing unfairly in other respects. Against all defendants, plaintiffs seek equitable relief, including an injunction against the use or disclosure of the confidential information imparted to the individual defendants.

In the district court, defendants moved to quash the service of summons and to dismiss the action for lack of jurisdiction.[2] In support of the motion, the individual defendants allege that they live outside of New York State in the area where they work, that they were served in their state of residence, that they are not assigned any New York State territory, and that they have not been within New York State since beginning employment with Dytron. Their carefully drawn affidavits state that they have not committed any tortious act "within the State of New York," or any act "outside the State of New York that could be deemed to constitute a tortious act causing injury . . . within the State of New York," but do not otherwise deny the wrongdoings alleged. The corporate defendant submitted an affidavit from its president, which similarly emphasizes the jurisdictional facts; e.g., Dytron was served in Michigan; within New York there have been no sales (nor are any planned) and no advertising, although "on rare occasions" Dytron has advertised in one of the three national magazines that serve the welding industry; Dytron has no office, telephone listing, bank account "or any contact of any nature with or within the State of New York."

With the case in this posture, the district court granted the motions to quash service of process and to dismiss, holding that the execution of employment contracts in New York was insufficient to bestow jurisdiction and that there was no "substantial contact" with New York justifying invoking its long-arm statute.

II

Plaintiffs' claim that there is jurisdiction over the individual defendants is based upon New York's long-arm statute, which provides in relevant part, N.Y. CPLR § 302(a)1:

> (a) *Acts which are the basis of jurisdiction.* As to a cause of action arising from any of the acts enumerated in this section, a court may exercise personal jurisdiction over any non-domiciliary, . . . who in person or through an agent:
>
> 1. transacts any business within the state . . . .

The statute was an attempt to clarify and expand the situations in which the New York courts would take personal jurisdiction over nonresident defendants. See United States v. Montreal Trust Co., 358 F.2d

2. Plaintiffs moved for summary judgment or a preliminary injunction and for leave to take depositions.

239, 242 (2d Cir.), cert. denied 384 U.S. 919, 86 S.Ct. 1366, 16 L.Ed.2d 440 (1966). While the statute has been liberally interpreted, whether jurisdiction exists under section 302(a)1 can be a close question for the New York Court of Appeals. See McKee Electric Co. v. Rauland-Borg Corp., 20 N.Y.2d 377, 283 N.Y.S.2d 34 (1967) (4–3 decision). A federal court has the added difficulty of predicting what the New York courts would do on particular facts. However, in this case the answer seems fairly clear, at least as to the action against the individual defendants. The key question is whether they "transact[ed] any business within the state" within the meaning of section 302(a)1, and the New York cases indicate that they did.

In Parke-Bernet Galleries, Inc. v. Franklyn, 26 N.Y.2d 13, 308 N.Y.S.2d 337, 340, 256 N.E.2d 506, 508 (1970), the New York Court of Appeals unanimously characterized "the situation where a defendant was physically present at the time the contract was made" as "the clearest sort of case in which our courts would have 302 jurisdiction." While it is not absolutely clear from the record before us that the employment contracts were signed by the individual defendants while they were present in New York, that apparently was the case. Indeed, the district judge seems to have made that assumption. Moreover, the evaluation leading up to the handing over of the control cards, the instructions regarding them, and the entire three-month training period for Technical Representatives all took place in New York. These were all "purposeful acts" participated in by the individual defendants "in this State in relation to the contract, albeit preliminary or subsequent to its execution." Longines-Wittnauer Watch Co. v. Barnes & Reinecke, Inc., 15 N.Y.2d 443, 261 N.Y.S.2d 8, 18, 209 N.E.2d 68, 75 (1965). Cf. Patrick Ellam, Inc. v. Nieves, 41 Misc.2d 186, 245 N.Y.S.2d 545 (Sup.Ct.1963); Iroquois Gas Corp. v. Collins, 42 Misc.2d 632, 248 N.Y.S.2d 494 (Sup.Ct.1964), aff'd, 23 A.D.2d 823, 258 N.Y.S.2d 376 (App. Div. 4th Dep't 1965).

Indeed, were we disposed to find no jurisdiction over these individual defendants, we would be hard put to distinguish adequately our own opinion in Liquid Carriers Corp. v. American Marine Corp., 375 F.2d 951 (2d Cir. 1967). In that case we relied on the negotiation in New York of a contract with a non-resident corporation in holding that New York had jurisdiction over that corporation in a breach of contract action against it, even though defendant had actually signed the contract in New Orleans and there was no contact at all thereafter between defendant and New York. Obviously, we cannot create binding law for New York, so that if our prior interpretation of New York law were shown to be incorrect, we would not have to follow it. But *Parke-Bernet* indicates that our approach in *Liquid Carriers* was sound.

The individual defendants quote from eminent authority [3] for the proposition that the mere formal execution of a contract in New York

---

3. J. McLaughlin, Supplementary Practice Commentary, CPLR § 302, at 137 (McKinney Supp.1970); 1 J. Weinstein, H. Korn & A. Miller, New York Civil Practice § 302.060, at 3–70 (1970).

should not be controlling, but that is not our case. The level of activity in New York by these defendants far exceeded the bare execution of employment contracts in New York. Defendants also cite McKee Electric Co. v. Rauland-Borg Corp., supra, and Lamarr v. Klein, 315 N.Y.S.2d 695 (App.Div. 1st Dep't 1970), a decision relied on by the district court. But in *McKee,* defendant's agent "spent, *in total,* less than a full working day in the State in connection with" the disputed contract. 283 N.Y.S.2d at 38 (emphasis in the original). And *Lamarr* bears only on the plaintiffs' burden of proof, which was met here.

We hold that by their conduct the individual defendants transacted business within the meaning of section 302(a)1. There remains the requirement that plaintiffs' cause of action be one "arising from" that activity, cf. Fontanetta v. American Board of Internal Medicine, 421 F.2d 355 (2d Cir. 1970), but there is little doubt about that. The claims against these defendants are based directly upon the employment contracts and the promises in them to keep certain material confidential and not to compete. We add in a possible excess of caution that we express no view as to the validity of those covenants, questions which have not yet been considered by the trial court.

III

The alleged basis of jurisdiction over defendant Dytron is another section of the long-arm statute, N.Y. CPLR § 302(a)3(ii), which provides for jurisdiction over a non-resident defendant who:

> 3. commits a tortious act without the state causing injury to person or property within the state, . . . if he
>
> . . .
>
> (ii) expects or should reasonably expect the act to have consequences in the state and derives substantial revenue from interstate or international commerce.

Thus, under this section, there would be jurisdiction over Dytron in New York if (1) Dytron committed a "tortious act" outside of New York, (2) causing "injury" to plaintiffs "within" New York and, (3) Dytron "expects or should reasonably expect" the tortious act to have consequences in New York; and (4) Dytron "derives substantial revenue from interstate . . . commerce." For purposes of appeal after a dismissal of the complaint, we think that on this record we must assume (1) and (4). But we do not believe that (2) is satisfied.

Plaintiffs, both New York corporations, claim that Dytron is, or will be, damaging their business by stealing customers in two states outside of New York, thereby injuring plaintiffs in New York. Without express guidance from the New York Court of Appeals, we must decide whether such damage is, under section 302(a)3, "injury . . . within the state." Resolution of that issue is complicated by the fact that the alleged tort here is not the type which that section was primarily designed to cover, since the tortious activity and its resulting damage are of a commercial rather than a physical nature.[4] Nevertheless we must locate the situs of injury, albeit only for the purpose of jurisdiction.

In Spectacular Promotions, Inc. v. Radio Station WING, 272 F.Supp. 734, 737 (E.D.N.Y.1967), on similar facts Judge Weinstein saw the problem as follows:

> In determining the situs of an injury resulting from an act of unfair competition for jurisdictional purposes—and here the relevant consideration is fairness of the trial forum—there are three possibilities worth considering: (1) any place where plaintiff does business; (2) the principal place of business of the plaintiff; and (3) the place where plaintiff lost business. For purposes of a jurisdictional statute such as New York's, the first can be rejected almost out of hand; the second has slight merit, and the third seems most apt. Where the plaintiff is a large national corporation, permitting it to sue in any of the fifty states in which it does business would obviously be unfair to the defendant. The main place of business of the plaintiff would have no predictable relationship with the tortious activities of the defendant. The place where the plaintiff lost business would normally be a forum reasonably foreseeable by a tortfeasor and it would usually be the place where the critical events associated with the dispute took place.

Under that analysis, there would be no jurisdiction over Dytron here because the places where plaintiffs "lost business" were all out of New York.[5]

Of course, there is no question that plaintiffs suffered some harm in New York in the sense that any sale lost anywhere in the United States affects their profits. But that sort of derivative commercial injury in the state is only the result of plaintiffs' domicile here. In

---

4. In 1966, the New York legislature amended § 302 in response to the interpretation given § 302(a)2 by the New York Court of Appeals in Feathers v. McLucas, 15 N.Y.2d 443, 261 N.Y.S.2d 8, 209 N.E.2d 68 (1965). In *Feathers,* plaintiff alleged that an out-of-state defendant had negligently constructed a propane gas tank in Kansas, which exploded in New York. The court denied jurisdiction, holding that defendant had not "commit[ted] a tortious act within the state" under § 302(a)2, and that the section could not be judicially construed to mean "commits a tortious act *without* the state which causes injury within the state." Id. at 21 (emphasis in the original). See Memorandum of the Judicial Conference on Ch. 590, Laws of 1966; Reese, "A Study of CPLR 302 in Light of Recent Judicial Decisions," in N.Y. Judicial Conference, Eleventh Annual Report 132 (1966); General Motors Acceptance Corp. v. Richardson, 59 Misc.2d 744, 300 N.Y.S.2d 757, 762 (Sup.Ct.1969).

5. Cf. the court's further observation in *Spectacular Promotions,* supra, 272 F.Supp. at 737:

Choice of law rules for conflicts purposes offers a weak analogy. The place of injury is only one of the contacts considered in choosing the law to be applied in tort actions. See American Law Institute, Restatement of the Law, Second, Conflict of Laws, § 379(2)(a) (Tentative Draft No. 9, 1964). In unfair competition actions the choice has been made on the basis of "place of the wrong" defined as the place "where the last event necessary to make an actor liable takes place." Vanity Fair Mills, [Inc.] v. T. Eaton Co., 234 F.2d 633, 639 (2d Cir. 1956). . . . Cf. Shoppers Fair of Arkansas, Inc. v. Sanders Co., 207 F.Supp. 718, 725 (W.D.Ark.1962) (place where customers deceived). See Restatement, Conflict of Laws, § 377.

Friedr. Zoellner (New York) Corp. v. Tex Metals Co., 396 F.2d 300, 303 (2d Cir. 1968), we stated:

> Zoellner lost its scrap metal in New Orleans. The process of reasoning by which Zoellner seeks to convert this New Orleans injury into an injury within New York defies restatement. However, even if it is assumed that some injury in New York flowed from the New Orleans injury, jurisdiction would be lacking. Section 302(a)(3) is not satisfied by remote or consequential injuries which occur in New York only because the plaintiff is domiciled, incorporated or doing business in the state. See Black v. Oberle Rentals, Inc., 55 Misc.2d 398, 285 N.Y.S.2d 226 (1967).

Oberle Rentals, cited by the court, involved an accident to New York domiciled plaintiffs, allegedly caused by defects in part of a trailer unit manufactured by the third-party defendant, an out-of-state corporation not doing business in New York. Although the accident occurred in Massachusetts, the "injury to person or property within" New York was alleged to be "permanent visible injuries [and] permanent loss of income." The court held that such "injury" did not confer jurisdiction under the statute:

> Certainly every person injured in an accident has resultant damage as well as the personal injury. He may suffer lost earnings, diminution of earning capacity, long periods of convalescence and all such attendant damages. Conceptually it is difficult for this Court to hold that a personal or property injury in another state by virtue of a tortious act committed in that state can be said to have suffered some injury within the State of New York simply because he is domiciled here. In other words, Section 302(a)(3) CPLR looks to the imparting of the original injury within the State of New York and not resultant damage, in order that jurisdiction might be effectuated. To hold otherwise would open a veritable Pandora's Box of litigation subjecting every conceivable prospective defendant involved in an accident with a New York domiciliary to defend actions brought against them in the State of New York. This is hardly the minimal contact with the State prerequisite to the exercise of its power over a prospective defendant.

285 N.Y.S.2d at 229. While the tort in *Oberle Rentals* was noncommercial and involved physical impact that occurred in Massachusetts, the court did cite *Spectacular Promotions* and characterized its "rationale" as "cogent." Id.

In arguing for jurisdiction here, plaintiffs cite Path Instruments International Corp. v. Asahi Optical Co., 312 F.Supp. 805 (S.D.N.Y. 1970), and General Motors Acceptance Corp. v. Richardson, 59 Misc.2d 744, 300 N.Y.S.2d 757 (Sup.Ct.1969). While not indicating an opinion on the merits of *Path Instruments,* we note that neither decision focussed on the precise issue before us, i.e., whether there was "injury" for jurisdictional purposes "within the state." In *General Motors Acceptance Corp.,* a Pennsylvania auctioneer sold an automobile in which plaintiff corporation had a security interest, and the court apparently assumed that conversion of the vehicle in Pennsylvania caused injury for jurisdictional purposes to the plaintiff in New York merely because it was domiciled or doing business here. In criticism of that decision, it has been pointed out that such an assumption would be

> that if the plaintiff is in New York when the injury occurs, the injury must occur in this state. The potential of so sweeping a doctrine is enormous, and it is suggested, in many cases would violate due process.

J. McLaughlin, Supplementary Practice Commentary, CPLR § 302, at 123 (McKinney Supp.1970).

Plaintiffs, however, contend that no similar assumption need be made here because Dytron must have expected its tortious acts to have consequences in New York. But this misses the point. We are concerned with whether there was "injury" within New York not with whether the corporate defendant could have "reasonabl[y] expect[ed] the act to have consequences" here. It is true that the foreseeability requirement in this respect cuts down the scope of the statute, but we do not reach it unless we first conclude that there was injury in New York. As to that, plaintiffs may be arguing that a loss of profits in plaintiffs' home office must be a "consequence," and that "injury" caused by a tortious act and "consequences" of that act are identical. Ordinarily the second proposition would be accurate, but we are not sure that it must always be so. E.g., in *Oberle Rentals,* supra, it may be that there were "consequences" in New York although legal "injury" clearly occurred in Massachusetts. Similarly, it may be that there were financial "consequences" to plaintiffs here in New York, although the legal "injury" occurred elsewhere. We mention such possibilities not to so decide or even to indicate a view, but to emphasize that the precise issue before us is whether Dytron's acts caused "injury" to plaintiffs "within" New York. A finding that it did would at least raise a serious constitutional question whether "the twin tests of fairness-reasonableness to the defendant on the one side and territorial respect for sister states' due spheres on the other" [6] were met. The former test was the focus of the quotation above from *Spectacular Promotions* and the latter, in view of Hanson v. Denckla, 357 U.S. 235, 78 S.Ct. 1228, 2 L.Ed.2d 1283 (1958), can hardly be completely disregarded. It is clear, in any event, that the legislature did not intend to extend the jurisdiction of the New York courts to the outer reaches of constitutional power.[7] This legislative restraint sheds some light on whether "injury . . . within the state" should be interpreted to press judicial jurisdiction to its fullest limits.

6. Rosenberg, "Proposed Direct Action Statute," in N.Y. Judicial Conference, Sixteenth Annual Report 264, 265 (1971).

the Civil Practice Law and Rules 12–24 (1966).

7. New York Judicial Conference, Report to the 1966 Legislature in Relation to

Based upon the limited guidance available to us, we believe that the New York courts would refuse to sustain jurisdiction over Dytron on these facts under section 302(a)3(ii). Perhaps the case would be different if the discernible local impact of the commercial injury to plaintiffs were greater, e.g., destruction of plaintiffs' business in New York by the loss of out-of-state customers, although we express no view as to that. But the injury here does not even approach that extreme. Accordingly we hold that Dytron's alleged tortious activity in Kentucky and Pennsylvania did not cause plaintiffs "injury . . . within the state," and we affirm dismissal of the complaint against Dytron.

In affirming as to Dytron but reversing as to the individual defendants, we recognize that we reach apparently inconsistent results. However, the relevant activities of the corporate and individual defendants were simply not the same. The difference in result flows directly from that. We agree that it makes little sense as a practical matter to have the suit against the individual defendants in New York and the suit against the corporate defendant elsewhere, but we cannot solve plaintiffs' tactical problems by making exceptions to what we believe the New York courts would regard as proper jurisdictional principles. However, if the plaintiffs commence suit against Dytron in another jurisdiction, a possible solution might be to seek to transfer the New York action against the individual defendants under 28 U.S.C.A. § 1404(a).

Affirmed in part and reversed in part.

BANCO AMBROSIANO, S.P.A. v. ARTOC BANK & TRUST LTD.

Court of Appeals of New York, 1984.
62 N.Y.2d 65, 476 N.Y.S.2d 64, 464 N.E.2d 432.

WACHTLER, JUDGE.

Plaintiff commenced this action by the attachment of approximately $8 million, representing the balance of defendant's account with its New York correspondent bank. Defendant's appeal, taken pursuant to leave granted by the Appellate Division, 97 A.D.2d 990, 469 N.Y.S.2d 832, focuses primarily on the question of whether this attempted assertion of quasi-in-rem jurisdiction over defendant's property is consistent with due process. We agree with the lower courts that the contacts among defendant, the forum and the litigation are sufficient to render this limited exercise of jurisdiction inoffensive to principles of due process.

Plaintiff Banco Ambrosiano (Ambrosiano) is an Italian banking corporation, the principal office of which is in Milan. Prior to being placed in liquidation, Ambrosiano was involved in the international banking business and, in this connection, maintained a representative office in New York City. Defendant Artoc Bank and Trust Limited (Artoc), also a banking corporation, is organized under the laws of Nassau, Bahamas, and regularly engages in international transactions.

Many of these transactions involve the borrowing and lending of United States dollars, which requires that the transfers be handled through a United States bank. For this purpose, Artoc utilizes an account with its New York correspondent bank, Brown Brothers Harriman and Co. (Brown Brothers). Neither Ambrosiano nor Artoc is authorized to engage in the banking business in this State.

Ambrosiano brought this action to recover $15 million which it allegedly loaned to Artoc, and which has not been repaid. Three transactions, each involving $5 million, were entered into by the parties. The memoranda drawn by Artoc indicate that Ambrosiano was to deposit these sums in Artoc's account with Brown Brothers, and that repayment was to be made to Ambrosiano's account with its New York correspondent bank. Artoc contends, in its defense, that the purpose of the transaction was to reloan the funds to Ambrosiano's controlled subsidiary in Peru and that it was understood that Artoc was to repay these sums only if and when the ultimate recipient repaid them.

With respect to the jurisdictional issue, it appears that all negotiations concerning this agreement were made outside of New York and all communications took place among the Bahamas, Italy, and Peru. The only connection with New York is that the funds were deposited to a New York bank account, were to be repaid to another New York bank account, and apparently were transferred to a New York account on behalf of the ultimate recipient. Artoc argues that the sole reason New York banks were utilized is that the transaction was to be in United States dollars and therefore had to be handled through such clearing accounts. In any event, it is clear that Artoc's sole contact with this State was its maintenance of the correspondent bank account with Brown Brothers.

Ambrosiano commenced this action by obtaining an ex parte restraining order, enjoining Brown Brothers from transferring the funds in Artoc's account. Ambrosiano's motion to confirm the attachment was granted over Artoc's challenge to the exercise of jurisdiction over its property. Special Term, noting that Ambrosiano conceded the lack of in personam jurisdiction, found that the property bore a reasonable relationship to the cause of action and that this relationship was sufficient to form the basis for quasi-in-rem jurisdiction. The Appellate Division unanimously affirmed.

Prior to the Supreme Court's expansion of the recognized bases for extraterritorial jurisdiction over a nondomiciliary, those who wished to sue in this State often resorted to the doctrine of quasi-in-rem jurisdiction to force a nondomiciliary defendant to litigate a claim in a forum where the defendant happened to own property. The conceptual basis for the State's power to adjudicate the claim was defendant's property, which was brought before the court by virtue of its seizure or attachment. Any resulting judgment was viewed as a judgment against the property only.

With the holding in International Shoe Co. v. Washington, 326 U.S. 310, 66 S.Ct. 154, 90 L.Ed. 95, the approach to jurisdictional analysis was greatly altered. While jurisdictional power had been a function of the defendant's presence, actual or constructive, in the forum State, *International Shoe* shifts the focus of the inquiry to the nature and quality of the defendant's contacts with the State. Those contacts must be such as to "make it reasonable and just, according to our traditional conception of fair play and substantial justice" to require the defendant to litigate the claim in the particular forum (id., at p. 320, 66 S.Ct. at p. 160). Where the cause of action arises out of the defendant's activities in or contacts with the State, the extraterritorial exercise of jurisdiction is deemed reasonable.

The long-arm jurisdiction legitimized by the *International Shoe* court was implemented in this State by statute. When the CPLR took effect in 1963, it contained two relevant sections. CPLR 301 preserves all previously existing jurisdictional bases, providing that the courts "may exercise such jurisdiction over persons, property, or status as might have been exercised heretofore". The long-arm statute, CPLR 302, provides that when a cause of action arises out of certain activities either occurring within the State or having an impact within the State, jurisdiction may be exercised over a nondomiciliary. Importantly, in setting forth certain categories of bases for long-arm jurisdiction, CPLR 302 does not go as far as is constitutionally permissible. Thus, a situation can occur in which the necessary contacts to satisfy due process are present, but in personam jurisdiction will not be obtained in this State because the statute does not authorize it (Siegel, N.Y.Prac., § 84, p. 95; Note, Minimum Contacts and Jurisdictional Theory in New York: The Effect of Shaffer v. Heitner, 42 Alb.L.Rev. 294, 306).

Even with the adoption of the long-arm statute, quasi-in-rem jurisdiction, which had been carried forward by virtue of CPLR 301, remained a viable method for subjecting a nondomiciliary to suit in this State. The use of this doctrine was drastically limited, however, by the Supreme Court's decision in Shaffer v. Heitner, 433 U.S. 186, 97 S.Ct. 2569, 53 L.Ed.2d 683. There, the court held that the minimum contacts analysis set forth in *International Shoe* is applicable to actions involving quasi-in-rem as well as in personam jurisdiction (id., at p. 207, 97 S.Ct. at p. 2581). Thus, when the property serving as the jurisdictional basis has no relationship to the cause of action and there are no other ties among the defendant, the forum and the litigation, quasi-in-rem jurisdiction will be lacking (id., at pp. 208–209, 97 S.Ct. at pp. 2581– 2582).

Although it may appear, at first blush, that the usefulness of quasi-in-rem jurisdiction has been eliminated by *Shaffer,* inasmuch as the minimum contacts necessary to support it will also generally provide in personam jurisdiction, that is not the case, at least in New York. As noted above CPLR 302 does not provide for in personam jurisdiction in every case in which due process would permit it. Thus, a "gap" exists in which the necessary minimum contacts, including the presence of

defendant's property within the State, are present, but personal jurisdiction is not authorized by CPLR 302. It is appropriate, in such a case,
to fill that gap utilizing quasi-in-rem principles (Siegel, N.Y.Prac.,
§ 104, p. 124; Note, Minimum Contacts and Jurisdictional Theory in
New York: The Effect of Shaffer v. Heitner, 42 Alb.L.Rev. 294, 306).

Whether quasi-in-rem jurisdiction exists in a given case involves an
inquiry into the presence or absence of the constitutionally mandated
minimum contacts * * *.

* * * This is not a case in which property is coincidentally
located within the State's borders and forms the only relevant link to
defendant; rather, Artoc's account with Brown Brothers is closely
related to plaintiff's claim. It is the very account through which Artoc
effectuated the transaction at issue, directing Ambrosiano to pay funds
to the account and presumably directing Brown Brothers to transfer
the funds out of this account to their ultimate recipient. Nor is this
transaction an isolated one, for it appears that Artoc utilizes this
account regularly to accomplish its international banking business,
communicating with Brown Brothers for disbursements of funds on its
behalf and directing others to deposit funds there. Finally, with
respect to performance of the agreement which forms the basis for
Ambrosiano's claim, Artoc not only directed that the funds be deposited
in its New York account, but it also agreed to repay these amounts
(according to Artoc, only if Ambrosiano's Peruvian subsidiary repaid
them) to Ambrosiano's New York account. * * *

* * *

FURTHER NOTE ON LONG ARM STATUTES

1. Constitutional and Statutory Standards

If New York had a "long arm" statute like California's—i.e., one that
authorized the broadest territorial jurisdiction permitted by the Constitution—
would the results have been different in *American Eutectic?* See Note, "Doing
Business": Defining State Control Over Foreign Corporations, 32 Vand.L.Rev.
1105 (1979); Anno., 27 A.L.R.3d 397. For a more expansive application of the
New York statutory provisions, see, e.g., Sybron Corp. v. Wetzel, 46 N.Y.2d 197,
413 N.Y.S.2d 127, 385 N.E.2d 1055 (1978), sustaining jurisdiction to issue an
injunction against piracy of trade secrets in circumstances similar to those in
American Eutectic. Note that the court in *American Eutectic* interpreted the
New York "long arm" statute as permitting jurisdiction over two defendants
but not a third. Might the statute permit jurisdiction over some causes of
action against a single defendant but not others? See Interface Biomedical
Laboratories Corp. v. Axiom Medical, Inc., 600 F.Supp. 731 (E.D.N.Y.1985),
where the court, relying on *American Eutectic,* replied in the affirmative.

Can a state expand its jurisdiction beyond its territorial boundaries by an
interstate compact with a neighboring state so that a defendant's contacts with
the adjacent state are also contacts with the forum state? See Intermeat, Inc.
v. American Poultry, Inc., 575 F.2d 1017 (2d Cir.1978); Note, Interstate Jurisdictional Compacts: A New Theory of Personal Jurisdiction, 49 Fordham L.Rev.
1097 (1981).

As *Banco Ambrosiano* shows, there can be situations where a restrictive "long arm" statute will preclude *in personam* jurisdiction even though constitutional "minimum contacts" are present, but where some kind of *in rem* basis of jurisdiction is arguably present. Is the court in *Banco Ambrosiano* correct to say that, in such cases, *in rem* jurisdiction can be used to "fill the gap"? Is this consistent with Shaffer v. Heitner, as the court asserts? If it is consistent, is the court's resolution of the problem a matter better left to the legislature to decide? Or is the court merely vindicating legislative intent in light of the decision in *Shaffer?*

2. Federal Adoption of State Territorial Limits

Congress has provided for nationwide service of process in certain types of actions in federal court. See, e.g., 28 U.S.C.A. § 2361, permitting nationwide service in any action under the Federal Interpleader Act, 28 U.S.C.A. § 1335. Compare F.R.C.P. 4(f), authorizing service outside the state where the District Court is located, up to 100 miles from the courthouse, against a party joined under F.R.C.P. 14 or 19. See also Note, Bulge Service Amenability: A Federal Standard, 41 U.Pitt.L.Rev. 801 (1980).

Aside from such special provisions, the territorial jurisdiction of the federal District Courts is governed by the general provisions of F.R.C.P. 4(e) and (f), which provide that a District Court may exercise jurisdiction over a defendant located outside the state where the court sits if the defendant can be reached under the state's "long arm" statute. As *American Eutectic* demonstrates, this limitation applies even if the statute does not reach as far as due process would permit. See also Mallard v. Aluminum Co. of Canada, Ltd., 634 F.2d 236 (5th Cir.1981). In addition, the limitation applies in federal question suits in the same way that it does in diversity suits, absent special provisions to the contrary in the statute in question. See Omni Capital International v. Rudolf Wolff & Co., Ltd., 484 U.S. 97, 108 S.Ct. 404, 98 L.Ed.2d 415 (1987).

If Congress decided to permit nationwide service of process in all actions brought in federal court, would this comport with due process standards—here, of the Fifth rather than the Fourteenth Amendment? Would it matter if such a statute applied to federal question suits but not to diversity suits? In passing on such a statute, how seriously do you think the Supreme Court would take its precedents focusing on convenience considerations? Convenience can be seen either as an independent requirement or as a measure of state sovereignty. See Further Note on Personal Liberty and Sovereignty, supra p. 369. If it is the former, presumably it would apply via the Fifth Amendment to the federal courts. But see Stafford v. Briggs, 444 U.S. 527, 100 S.Ct. 774, 63 L.Ed.2d 1 (1980), where the Court seems to imply that the Fifth Amendment does not impose a limitation on the federal courts similar to that imposed on the states by the Fourteenth Amendment. See also Note, Fifth Amendment Due Process Limitations on Nationwide Federal Jurisdiction, 61 B.U.L.Rev. 403 (1981); Fullerton, Constitutional Limits on Nationwide Personal Jurisdiction in the Federal Courts, 79 Nw.U.L.Rev. 1 (1984); Lusardi, Nationwide Service of Process: Due Process Limitations on the Power of the Sovereign, 33 Villa.L. Rev. 1 (1988).

6. CHALLENGING TERRITORIAL JURISDICTION

a. APPEARANCE

CUELLAR v. CUELLAR

Court of Civil Appeals of Texas, 1966.
406 S.W.2d 510.

GREEN, CHIEF JUSTICE.

*   *   *

Appellee-defendant and appellant-plaintiff, formerly husband and wife, were divorced in the district court of Cameron County, Texas, in April, 1948. Plaintiff, the former wife, was granted custody of Lidia Cuellar, a child of this marriage, who at the time of the hearing in November, 1965, was 23 years of age. This suit involved a motion to amend the divorce judgment rendered in said cause to provide for custodial support payments for Lidia, pursuant to Article 4639a–1, Vernon's Ann.Tex.Civ.St., as enacted in 1961. Defendant, a resident of Porter County, Indiana, was served with non-resident citation on October 11, 1965, giving him 20 days notice of the hearing on the motion which was set for November 1, 1965. On this latter date, defendant, thru his attorney, filed a written answer containing certain special exceptions to plaintiff's pleading, and a general denial. None of these exceptions in any way attacked the jurisdiction of the court over the person of the defendant. Counsel for both parties and the trial court agreed, in open court on November 1, 1965, that the plaintiff would proceed to put on her testimony at that time, and that counsel for the defendant would be given three weeks, until November 22, 1965, to study the law and prepare his case, and amend his pleadings if he considered that necessary, before proceeding further. Under such agreement, plaintiff did introduce her evidence, after which the court recessed the trial until November 22nd.

On November 22, 1965, defendant filed what he denominated "Defendant's First Amended Answer," in which he for the first time plead, under oath of his attorney, that he "objects to the jurisdiction of the Court over his person on the ground that he is not amenable to process issued by the Courts of this State." The trial court considered this as a proper plea to the jurisdiction of the court, and since the plaintiff's pleadings and the undisputed evidence showed that defendant was in fact a nonresident of Texas, and was served outside of the state, held that it had no jurisdiction of this case. This appeal is from such holding of no jurisdiction.

Art. 4639a–1, V.A.T.S., reads as follows:

"In addition to all other requirements, each petition for divorce shall further set out, if such is a fact, that (1) an unmarried child, born of the marriage sought to be dissolved, is physically or mentally unsound and requires custodial care, and (2) that such child cannot adequately take care of or provide for himself, and (3) that such child has no personal estate or income sufficient to provide for his reasonable and necessary care. If the Court shall find all of such has been proven by full and satisfactory evidence the Court may require and enforce support payments for such child, whether a minor or not, subject to the power and authority of the Court to alter, change, suspend, or otherwise revise its judgments as the facts and circumstances may require and in the manner required by law. Added Acts 1961, 57th Leg., 1st C.S., p. 135, ch. 31, § 1."

* * *

The trial court had jurisdiction of the subject matter of this motion, under the provisions of Art. 4639a–1, supra. The last sentence of said Article authorizes the trial court to alter, change, suspend or otherwise revise its judgments as the facts and circumstances may require and in the manner required by law. The motion of plaintiff conformed to the provisions of the statute. Matters of child support and enforcement of divorce decree are within the continuing jurisdiction of the court which rendered the original divorce decree, and the motion was properly filed in the original divorce suit. Livingston v. Nealy, Tex.Civ.App., 382 S.W.2d 511, writ ref. n.r.e. The plea which the court passed on was directed to the point that the court had no jurisdiction over the person of the defendant on the ground that he is not amenable to process issued by the courts of this State, being a non-resident, and having been served by non-resident notice outside of the State.

Since plaintiff is seeking a money judgment from defendant, this plea would have been good had defendant timely filed his jurisdictional plea. York v. State, 73 Tex. 651, 11 S.W. 869, affd., 137 U.S. 15, 11 S.Ct. 9, 34 L.Ed. 604; August Kern Barber Shop v. Freeze, 96 Tex. 513, 74 S.W. 303; Bonanza Inc. v. Lee, Tex.Civ.App., 337 S.W.2d 437.

However, the defendant did not timely file his plea to the jurisdiction of the court over his person. He voluntarily submitted himself to the court's jurisdiction when, on November 1, 1965, he filed a written answer to plaintiff's motion which did not raise any jurisdictional point. Rule 120a, T.R.C.P.; York v. State, supra; State v. Standard Oil Co., 130 Tex. 313, 107 S.W.2d 550; 42 Tex.Law Review 279 at page 315 et seq., Article by Professor E. Wayne Thode of University of Texas Law School.

Prior to the adoption of Rule 120a, T.R.C.P., in 1962, special appearance was unknown to Texas practice, and the filing by a defendant of any defensive pleading, including one to challenge the court's jurisdiction over the person of the defendant, constituted an appearance and submission to the jurisdiction of the forum. York v. State, supra. See author's comments to Rule 120a, Vernon's Anno.Tex. Rules and authorities cited; Professor Thode's article in 42 Tex.Law Review, page 279 et seq. Rule 120a was adopted and promulgated by our State

Supreme Court, so that now a defendant may make a special appearance in the cause to attack the court's jurisdiction over his person or property without subjecting himself to the jurisdiction of the court generally. However, such rule expressly provides that *"Such special appearance shall be made by sworn motion filed prior to plea of privilege or any other plea, pleading or motion. . . . Every appearance, prior to judgment, not in compliance with this rule is a general appearance."* See discussion of this portion of Rule 120a by Professor Thode in 42 Tex.Law Review on pages 315–317.

We hold that when the defendant filed his written answer in this cause on November 1, 1965, this constituted a general appearance, and he submitted himself to the jurisdiction of the court. The trial court erred in considering the subsequent plea attempting to raise the jurisdictional issue, filed three weeks later in an amended answer, and in holding that it has no jurisdiction in this cause.

* * *

Accordingly, the judgment of the trial court is reversed. That court upon remand is directed to take jurisdiction of this cause, and to require and enforce support payments by defendant Luis L. Cuellar to plaintiff as custodian for the benefit of such child in such amount as the court, in its sound discretion, feels proper from the evidence, such order of the court to be subject to the power and authority of the court to alter, change, suspend, or otherwise revise its judgment as the facts and circumstances may require and in the manner required by law. Art. 4639a–1, V.A.T.S.

Reversed and remanded with instructions.*

BALDWIN v. IOWA STATE TRAVELING MEN'S ASS'N

Supreme Court of the United States, 1931.
283 U.S. 522, 51 S.Ct. 517, 75 L.Ed. 1244.

Mr. Justice Roberts delivered the opinion of the Court.

A writ of certiorari was granted herein to review the affirmance by the Circuit Court of Appeals of a judgment for respondent rendered by the District Court for Southern Iowa. The action was upon the record of a judgment rendered in favor of the petitioner against the respondent in the United States District Court for Western Missouri.

The defense was lack of jurisdiction of the person of the respondent in the court which entered the judgment. After hearing, in which a jury was waived, this defense was sustained and the action dismissed. The first suit was begun in a Missouri state court and removed to the District Court. Respondent appeared specially and moved to quash and dismiss for want of service. The court quashed the service, but refused

* [Subject matter jurisdiction under Art.
4639a–1 was limited in Ex parte Hatch,
410 S.W.2d 773, 777 (Tex.1967)—Ed.]

to dismiss. An alias summons was issued and returned served, whereupon it again appeared specially, moved to set aside the service, quash the return, and dismiss the case for want of jurisdiction of its person. After a hearing on affidavits and briefs, the motion was overruled, with leave to plead within thirty days. No plea having been filed within that period, the cause proceeded, and judgment was entered for the amount claimed. Respondent did not move to set aside the judgment nor sue out a writ of error.

The ground of the motion made in the first suit is the same as that relied on as a defense to this one, namely, that the respondent is an Iowa corporation, that it never was present in Missouri, and that the person served with process in the latter state was not such an agent that service on him constituted a service on the corporation. The petitioner objected to proof of these matters, asserting that the defense constituted a collateral attack and a retrial of an issue settled in the first suit. The overruling of this objection and the resulting judgment for respondent are assigned as error.

The petitioner suggests that article 4, section 1, of the Constitution, forbade the retrial of the question determined on respondent's motion in the Missouri District Court; but the full faith and credit required by that clause is not involved, since neither of the courts concerned was a state court. Compare Cooper v. Newell, 173 U.S. 555, 567, 19 S.Ct. 506, 43 L.Ed. 808; Supreme Lodge, Knights of Pythias v. Meyer, 265 U.S. 30, 33, 44 S.Ct. 432, 68 L.Ed. 885. The respondent, on the other hand, insists that to deprive it of the defense which it made in the court below, of lack of jurisdiction over it by the Missouri District Court, would be to deny the due process guaranteed by the Fourteenth Amendment; but there is involved in that doctrine no right to litigate the same question twice. Chicago Life Ins. Co. v. Cherry, 244 U.S. 25, 37 S.Ct. 492, 61 L.Ed. 966; compare York v. Texas, 137 U.S. 15, 11 S.Ct. 9, 34 L.Ed. 604.

The substantial matter for determination is whether the judgment amounts to res judicata on the question of the jurisdiction of the court which rendered it over the person of the respondent. It is of no moment that the appearance was a special one expressly saving any submission to such jurisdiction. That fact would be important upon appeal from the judgment, and would save the question of the propriety of the court's decision on the matter, even though, after the motion had been overruled, the respondent had proceeded, subject to a reserved objection and exception, to a trial on the merits. Harkness v. Hyde, 98 U.S. 476, 25 L.Ed. 237 [citations omitted]. The special appearance gives point to the fact that the respondent entered the Missouri court for the very purpose of litigating the question of jurisdiction over its person. It had the election not to appear at all. If, in the absence of appearance, the court had proceeded to judgment, and the present suit had been brought thereon, respondent could have raised and tried out the issue in the present action, because it would never have had its day in court with respect to jurisdiction. Thompson v. Whitman, 18 Wall. (85 U.S.)

457, 21 L.Ed. 897; Pennoyer v. Neff, 95 U.S. 714, 24 L.Ed. 565; [citations omitted]. It had also the right to appeal from the decision of the Missouri District Court, as is shown by Harkness v. Hyde, supra, and the other authorities cited. It elected to follow neither of those courses, but, after having been defeated upon full hearing in its contention as to jurisdiction, it took no further steps, and the judgment in question resulted.

Public policy dictates that there be an end of litigation; that those who have contested an issue shall be bound by the result of the contest; and that matters once tried shall be considered forever settled as between the parties. We see no reason why this doctrine should not apply in every case where one voluntarily appears, presents his case and is fully heard, and why he should not, in the absence of fraud, be thereafter concluded by the judgment of the tribunal to which he has submitted his cause.

* * *

The judgment is reversed and the cause remanded for further proceedings in conformity with this opinion.

Reversed.

NOTE ON SPECIAL APPEARANCE AND ITS CONSEQUENCES

1. The Special Appearance Rule

Restatement Second of Conflict of Laws § 81:

> "A state will not exercise judicial jurisdiction over an individual who appears in the action for the sole purpose of objecting that there is no jurisdiction over him."

For an analysis of the policy underlying this rule, see Mladinich v. Kohn, 250 Miss. 138, 164 So.2d 785 (1964); Tigges v. City of Ames, 356 N.W.2d 503 (Iowa 1984); Thode, In Personam Jurisdiction; Article 2031B, the Texas "Long Arm" Jurisdiction Statute; and the Appearance to Challenge Jurisdiction in Texas and Elsewhere, 42 Tex.L.Rev. 279 (1964); Newton and Wicker, Personal Jurisdiction and the Appearance to Challenge Jurisdiction in Texas, 38 Baylor L.Rev. 491 (1986).

Under Texas Rule 120a, cited in *Cuellar*, would defendant have made a general appearance if he had interposed objection to jurisdiction over his person along with—rather than after—his exceptions to the plaintiff's pleading and his denial of its allegations? Would doing so be deemed a general appearance in California? See C.C.P. 418.10. Under F.R.C.P. 12? Under F.R.C.P. 12, what disposition would have been made on the facts in Cuellar v. Cuellar? See Neifeld v. Steinberg, 438 F.2d 423 (3d Cir. 1971). See also California Dental Ass'n v. American Dental Ass'n, 23 Cal.3d 346, 352, 152 Cal.Rptr. 546, 549, 590 P.2d 401, 404 (1979), reciting that "although a defendant may make a special appearance to challenge the jurisdiction of the court over his person * * * when he simultaneously answers to the merits he is no longer entitled to make this challenge." Cf. Islamic Republic of Iran v. Pahlavi, 160 Cal.App.3d 620, 206 Cal.Rptr. 752 (1984).

Compare Restatement Second of Judgments § 10, Comment b:

"While all states now provide at least for a special appearance, most go further in liberalizing the opportunity to make preliminary objection to notice and territorial jurisdiction. The most widely adopted procedural scheme is that prescribed in Federal Rules of Civil Procedure Rule 12(b). Under this procedure, a defendant may make an objection to process in a preliminary motion before asserting any other objections or defenses. Such a motion is in effect a special appearance, although it need not be designated as such in order to avoid submission to the court's jurisdiction. However, the scheme of Rule 12(b) is broader, for it permits a defendant to make an objection to process in a motion that also raises other objections such as improper venue, lack of subject matter jurisdiction, or failure of the complaint to state a claim. He may also assert the objection in his answer. The only requirement is that the motion or answer be his first appearance in the action."

C.C.P. 418.10 allows a defendant to contest jurisdiction by simultaneously filing a motion to quash service and a motion to stay or dismiss on grounds of an inconvenient forum. C.C.P. 418.11 specifies that an appearance at a hearing to seek ex parte relief or a provisional remedy by ex parte application does not constitute a general appearance or a waiver of defects in jurisdiction.

In some states that require a special appearance to challenge process, there has been an attempt to define what conduct by a defendant will constitute a general appearance. Compare Ill.C.C.P. § 2–301 with C.C.P. 1014. As pointed out in the discussion in Note, Special Appearance in California, 10 Stan.L.Rev. 711 (1958), C.C.P. 1014 gives an inaccurate picture of the California rules. On the one hand, certain types of appearances literally within the terms of C.C.P. 1014 are nevertheless treated as special appearances. On the other hand, certain types of appearances not mentioned in C.C.P. 1014 are nevertheless treated as general appearances. For further discussion and illustration, see Gorfinkel, Special Appearance in California—The Need for Reform, 5 Univ.San. Fran.L.Rev. 25 (1970); Annos., 31 A.L.R.2d 262; 25 A.L.R.2d 833; 77 A.L.R.3d 841. Cf. Goodwine v. Superior Court, 63 Cal.2d 481, 47 Cal.Rptr. 201, 407 P.2d 1 (1965), holding that a motion to quash based on want of jurisdiction over the person was not converted into a general appearance by reason of the fact that the motion was also based on an objection to the court's jurisdiction over the subject matter of the action. Would the same be true if the companion objection was that the complaint failed to state a cause of action? Why the difference? See also Creed v. Schultz, 148 Cal.App.3d 733, 196 Cal.Rptr. 252 (1983).

2. Availability of Appellate Review

The rules governing the availability of appellate review of a trial court's determination of a challenge to jurisdiction vary from jurisdiction to jurisdiction, but fall into three categories:

a. After the defendant has challenged the jurisdiction of the court over his person by special appearance, he must choose between (1) permitting a default judgment to be entered against him, appealing from that judgment and hoping to obtain reversal on the jurisdictional ruling, at the risk that if he fails to obtain reversal then he loses the opportunity to contest the merits; and (2) making his defenses on the merits but thereby making a general appearance and waiving his jurisdictional defense.

b. Upon the trial court's decision of the challenge to jurisdiction, the defendant may obtain immediate appellate review of that decision, by interlocutory appeal in some states and by extraordinary writ in others. If defendant fails to avail herself of this opportunity, she may not be able to raise the objection in an appeal from the judgment ultimately entered.

c. After the defendant has challenged jurisdiction, he may make his defense on the merits without waiver of his jurisdictional objection and may obtain appellate review of the jurisdictional issue in an appeal from the judgment ultimately rendered. If in such an appeal the appellate court concludes that the jurisdictional ruling was wrong, then the judgment is reversed and the action dismissed.

Which of these rules obtains in the Federal courts? In California? Compare C.C.P. 418.10; Ill.C.C.P. § 2–301. See also Anno., 62 A.L.R.2d 937.

3. Res Judicata

The *Baldwin* rule applies to decisions on jurisdiction rendered upon special appearance in a state court. See Davis v. Davis, 305 U.S. 32, 59 S.Ct. 3, 83 L.Ed. 26 (1938). See also Somportex Ltd. v. Philadelphia Chewing Gum Corp., 453 F.2d 435 (3d Cir. 1971) (enforcing English default judgment entered after defendant refused to proceed following a special appearance in which defendant unsuccessfully challenged jurisdiction). In Cuellar v. Cuellar, if on remand the trial court entered judgment against defendant, and plaintiff later sought to enforce the judgment in Indiana, could defendant contend in Indiana that the Texas court had not had personal jurisdiction over him?

4. Procedure for Enforcement of a Judgment Outside the State Where Rendered

What was the procedural means by which the plaintiff in *Baldwin* sought to collect in Iowa the judgment he obtained in Missouri? See Paulsen, Enforcing the Money Judgment in a Sister State, 42 Iowa L.Rev. 202 (1957), also discussing the Uniform Enforcement of Foreign Judgments Act, 9A U.L.A. 287 (1957) (latest edition, 13 U.L.A. 152 [Master ed. 1986]), which provides for an expedited proceeding for enforcing out-of-state judgments. See also Note on Full Faith and Credit, infra p. 683. A number of states have now adopted the Uniform Foreign Money–Judgments Recognition Act, 13 U.L.A. 261 (Master ed. 1986), which governs the recognition and enforcement of judgments of foreign nations. See Note on Federal–State and International Recognition of Judgments, infra p. 698. In the federal court system a judgment rendered in one federal District Court may be registered in any other federal District Court and upon registration will have the same effect as if rendered in the court in which it is registered. See Note on Federal–State and International Recognition of Judgments, infra p. 698.

b. LIMITED APPEARANCE

CHESHIRE NATIONAL BANK v. JAYNES

Supreme Judicial Court of Massachusetts, 1916.
224 Mass. 14, 112 N.E. 500.

RUGG, C. J. This is an action of contract brought by a national banking corporation domiciled in the state of New Hampshire against a resident of the state of Connecticut, upon whom no personal service has been made, but whose property has been attached by trustee process under the statute making provision for reaching the property of a non-resident. R.L. c. 170. The defendant filed a special appearance, whereby he has undertaken by apt words not to submit himself generally to the jurisdiction of the court, but only so far as is necessary in order to protect his interest in the goods, effects and credits in the hands of the alleged trustees. In proceedings, which need not be narrated in detail, the superior court has ruled that a non-resident defendant could not "appear, answer to the merits and defend the case for the purpose of protecting his rights in property trusteed or attached and at the same time by 'special appearance' repudiate the jurisdiction of the court. If he is in court claiming its protection upon the merits of the case, he must submit to the obligations which the court places upon every litigant before it." The correctness of this ruling is challenged.

This precise question does not appear to have been decided. It has been determined that a valid personal judgment cannot be rendered against a non-resident defendant who is not served with process within the state and who does not appear. When property of a non-resident defendant is attached within the state, valid judgment may be entered, enforceable against such property but possessing no further validity unless such non-resident defendant is served personally with process within the state or appears. Lowrie v. Castle, 198 Mass. 82, 89, 83 N.E. 1118; Eliot v. McCormick, 144 Mass. 10, 10 N.E. 705; Pennoyer v. Neff, 95 U.S. 714, 24 L.Ed. 565; Freeman v. Alderson, 119 U.S. 185, 7 S.Ct. 165, 30 L.Ed. 372. A non-resident defendant may ignore the proceedings in the courts of another jurisdiction when not served with process in that other jurisdiction and when no valid attachment of his property is made. When attempt is made to affect his rights by judgment obtained in the absence of service of process or attachment of property, he may show its invalidity in the courts of any forum, either under the "full faith and credit" clause of the federal Constitution or under general principles of international comity. Old Dominion Copper Mining & Smelting Co. v. Bigelow, 203 Mass. 159, 206–214, 89 N.E. 193, 40 L.R.A.,N.S., 314; Brown v. Fletcher's Estate, 210 U.S. 82, 28 S.Ct. 702, 52 L.Ed. 966. Perhaps it would be competent for the Legislature to enact, without violating any provision of the federal Constitution, that no one may voluntarily appear in our courts to contest any question there pending, even when some of the property is held under attachment, without at the same time submitting himself wholly to the jurisdiction of our courts for all purposes of the proceeding. York v. Texas, 137 U.S. 15, 11 S.Ct. 9, 34 L.Ed. 604; Western Indemnity Co. v. Rupp, 235 U.S. 261, 272, 35 S.Ct. 37, 59 L.Ed. 220; Coe v. Armour Fertilizer Works, 237 U.S. 413, 426, 35 S.Ct. 625, 59 L.Ed. 1027.

But that question is not now presented and expressly is left open. R.L. c. 170, § 1, which governs this matter, makes no such provision.[1]

1. Section 1. A personal action shall not be maintained against a person who is not an inhabitant of this commonwealth unless he has been served with process within this commonwealth or unless an effectual attachment of his property within

This section has been construed with some strictness. Roberts v. Anheuser Busch Brewing Ass'n, 215 Mass. 341, 102 N.E. 316. Its final clause does not deny full effect to a judgment rendered after a general appearance, even without service. Gahm v. Wallace, 206 Mass. 39, 91 N.E. 1002. But it does not disclose a purpose to impose upon a non-resident defendant the burden of entering a general appearance in order to protect his property rights so far as they are put in peril by effectual attachment of his property upon the original writ. It does not by apt words cover a situation like that now presented. So far as there is implication from the words used, it seems to be that the action shall not be maintained without service with process within this commonwealth (unless there is voluntary general appearance) except so far as it may affect property held under effectual attachment. The provisions for notice to a non-resident defendant in sections 6 and 9 of the same chapter, do not manifest a purpose to compel him to appear generally if he appears at all. Indeed, reading sections 1, 6 and 9 together, and giving them all appropriate force, they are quite satisfied by interpreting them to mean that when effectual attachment of property of a non-resident is made, the best kind of notice which can be given under the circumstances shall issue in order to afford him opportunity to come into court and be heard on the question whether the property so attached ought to be held to satisfy a judgment in accordance with the terms of section 1.

"The fundamental requisite of due process of law is the opportunity to be heard." Grannis v. Ordean, 234 U.S. 385, 394, 34 S.Ct. 779, 58 L.Ed. 1363.

"That to condemn without a hearing is repugnant to the due process clause of the Fourteenth Amendment needs nothing but statement." Riverside Mills v. Menefee, 237 U.S. 189–193, 35 S.Ct. 579, 59 L.Ed. 910.

Treating the question as one of general law, quite uncontrolled by statute, the same result is reached. It was said by Chief Justice Parsons in Bissell v. Briggs, 9 Mass. 462, at 468, 6 Am.Dec. 88:

"In order to entitle the judgment rendered in any court of the United States to the full faith and credit mentioned in the federal Constitution, the court must have had jurisdiction not only of the cause, but of the parties. To illustrate this position, it may be remarked that a debtor living in Massachusetts may have goods, effects, or credits in New Hampshire, where the creditor lives. The creditor there may lawfully attach these, pursuant to the laws of that state, in the hands of the bailiff, factor, trustee, or garnishee, of his debtor; and on recovering judgment, those goods, effects, and credits, may lawfully be applied to satisfy the judgment; and the bailiff, factor, trustee, or garnishee, if sued in this state for those

this commonwealth has been made upon the original writ, and in case of such attachment without such service, the judgment shall be valid to secure the application of the property so attached to the satisfaction of the judgment, and not otherwise.

goods, effects, or credits, shall in our courts be protected by that judgment, the court in New Hampshire having jurisdiction of the cause for the purpose of rendering that judgment, and the bailiff, factor, trustee, or garnishee, producing it, not to obtain execution of it here, but for his own justification. If, however, those goods, effects, and credits, are insufficient to satisfy the judgment, and the creditor should sue an action on that judgment in this state to obtain satisfaction, he must fail, because the defendant was not personally amenable to the jurisdiction of the court rendering the judgment. And if the defendant after the service of the process of foreign attachment, should either in person have gone into the state of New Hampshire, or constituted an attorney to defend the suit, so as to protect his goods, effects, or credits, from the effect of the attachment, he would not thereby have given the court jurisdiction of his person; since this jurisdiction must result from the service of the foreign attachment. It would be unreasonable to oblige any man living in one state, and having effects in another state, to make himself amenable to the courts of the last state, that he might defend his property there attached."

This decision was one of the earliest upon that subject in this country. It always has been recognized a leading authority. See Pennoyer v. Neff, 95 U.S. 714, 731, 24 L.Ed. 565. While the allusion to the injustice of requiring a nonresident to surrender himself wholly to the jurisdiction of the courts of a foreign state, in order to defend his property there attached, was by way of illustration rather than exact adjudication, it was employed to illuminate an essential step in the reasoning by which the decision was reached, and therefore was something more than a mere obiter dictum. It states a sound principle. It is decisive of the question at bar.

It may be urged that to reach this conclusion is to impair the doctrine of res judicata, in that it compels a plaintiff to try the merits of his case and be barred by his failure, while no such decisive result inheres in defeat to the defendant. But this consequence does not follow. It is elementary law that the doctrine of res judicata does not operate as an estoppel unless it is mutual and affects both parties alike. Old Dominion Copper Mining & Smelting Co. v. Bigelow, 203 Mass. 159, 217, 89 N.E. 193, 40 L.R.A.,N.S., 314; Id., 225 U.S. 111, 127, 32 S.Ct. 641, 56 L.Ed. 1009, Ann.Cas.1913E, 875. In a situation like that at bar, the plaintiff put his cause in issue no further than does the defendant. The bar of whatever judgment may be rendered, where a non-resident defendant appears specially merely for the purpose of protecting his interest in attached property, extends no further against the plaintiff than it does against the defendant. It relates only to the property of the defendant held under effectual attachment. The record of the judgment and the form of the execution when rendered against the defendant, explicitly show this. It runs only against the property so attached, and not otherwise. The record of the judgment when against the plaintiff should be equally categorical in showing that the plaintiff has failed to establish his case only against the property attached, and not that he has failed generally to establish a cause of action against the defendant. In such case the question of the general liability of the defendant to the plaintiff has not been put in issue, because the defendant has chosen to rely on his strict right by confining his appearance to the protection of the property alone and not to submit himself to the general jurisdiction of the court. When a defendant pursues this course he cannot at the same time claim the boon of general judgment if he wins, and the shelter of his special appearance if he loses. He cannot gamble with jurisdiction and invoke its benefit if favorable and repudiate its force if adverse. He must select his ground in advance and abide by the issue. If he stands only upon the special ground, he is entitled upon success only to a judgment which protects that property but which goes no further and will afford no shield against further prosecution of the plaintiff's claim against other property or against him personally, provided effectual attachment or personal service may be made.

The plaintiff, by instituting his action and making the effectual attachment of property, offers to the defendant the alternative, first, of coming into court generally and settling all issues by submitting to the jurisdiction of the court with the attendant advantage of ending that cause of action by a final judgment, or second, of appearing specially and protecting only the property attached and settling only that question and nothing else. The adjudication will be exactly commensurate with the alternative accepted by the defendant. This result is one of fairness and justice to both parties.

It is contended that because the defendant, after the entry of the order of the superior court to the effect that he could not appear specially but must submit to the jurisdiction generally if he desired to make any contest, answered generally attempting to continue his special appearance and also filed cross interrogatories for the taking of a deposition without questioning the jurisdiction, he has waived his special appearance and has in fact submitted himself generally to the jurisdiction of the court. But this contention cannot be supported. After having raised the point seasonably, he did not waive it by proceeding in accordance with the rulings of the court, which until reversed were the law of the trial. Walling v. Beers, 120 Mass. 548; Harkness v. Hyde, 98 U.S. 476, 25 L.Ed. 237. * * *

Exceptions sustained.

NOTE ON LIMITED APPEARANCE

1. Challenging the Legitimacy of Jurisdiction Over Property

Is there doubt that defendant can specially appear to contest whether an exercise of "in rem" or "quasi in rem" jurisdiction over his property is valid, in the same way that he can challenge an exercise of jurisdiction in personam? See Restatement Second of Judgments § 10, Comment c. If he does challenge such an exercise of jurisdiction and loses, is the determination binding under the Full Faith and Credit Clause if title to the property is later contested in the courts of another state? Compare Baldwin v. Iowa State Traveling Men's Ass'n, supra p. 418. See also Durfee v. Duke, 375 U.S. 106, 84 S.Ct. 242, 11 L.Ed.2d 186 (1963); Comment, Collateral Attack for Lack of Subject Matter Jurisdiction, 52 Calif.L.Rev. 623 (1964).

2. Limited Appearance

The "limited special appearance," of the type in Cheshire Nat. Bank v. Jaynes, has been rejected in most states in which the question has come up, sometimes by express provision, e.g., Minn.R.Civ.Proc. 4.04. See 1 Weinstein, Korn & Miller ¶ 320.16–320.19; U. S. v. Balanovski, 236 F.2d 298 (2d Cir. 1956). But see River Farms, Inc. v. Superior Court, 252 Cal.App.2d 604, 611, 60 Cal. Rptr. 665, 670 (1967); Dry Clime Lamp Corp. v. Edwards, 389 F.2d 590 (5th Cir. 1968). See also Restatement Second of Judgments § 8, Comment g.

7. REFUSALS TO TAKE JURISDICTION

PIPER AIRCRAFT CO. v. REYNO

Supreme Court of the United States, 1981.
454 U.S. 235, 102 S.Ct. 252, 70 L.Ed.2d 419.*

JUSTICE MARSHALL delivered the opinion of the Court.

These cases arise out of an air crash that took place in Scotland. Respondent, acting as representative of the estates of several Scottish citizens killed in the accident, brought wrongful death actions against petitioners in the United States District Court for the Middle District of Pennsylvania. Petitioners moved to dismiss on the ground of *forum non conveniens.* After noting that an alternative forum existed in Scotland, the District Court granted their motions. 479 F.Supp. 727 (1979). The United States Court of Appeals for the Third Circuit reversed. 630 F.2d 149 (1980). The Court of Appeals based its decision, at least in part, on the ground that dismissal is automatically barred where the law of the alternative forum is less favorable to the plaintiff than the law of the forum chosen by the plaintiff. Because we conclude that the possibility of an unfavorable change in law should not, by itself, bar dismissal, and because we conclude that the District Court did not otherwise abuse its discretion, we reverse.

I

A

In July 1976, a small commercial aircraft crashed in the Scottish highlands during the course of a charter flight from Blackpool to Perth. The pilot and five passengers were killed instantly. The decedents were all Scottish subjects and residents, as are their heirs and next of kin. There were no eyewitnesses to the accident. At the time of the crash the plane was subject to Scottish air traffic control.

---

* Some of the Court's footnotes are omitted.

The aircraft, a twin engine Piper Aztec, was manufactured in Pennsylvania by petitioner Piper Aircraft Company (Piper). The propellers were manufactured in Ohio by petitioner Hartzell Propeller, Inc. (Hartzell). At the time of the crash the aircraft was registered in Great Britain and was owned and maintained by Air Navigation and Trading Co., Ltd. (Air Navigation). It was operated by McDonald Aviation, Ltd. (McDonald), a Scottish air taxi service. Both Air Navigation and McDonald were organized in the United Kingdom. The wreckage of the plane is now in a hangar in Farnsborough, England.

The British Department of Trade investigated the accident several months after it occurred. A preliminary report found that the plane crashed after developing a spin, and suggested that mechanical failure in the plane or the propeller was responsible. At Hartzell's request, this report was reviewed by a three-member Review Board, which held a nine-day adversary hearing attended by all interested parties. The Review Board found no evidence of defective equipment and indicated that pilot error may have contributed to the accident. The pilot, who had obtained his commercial pilot's license only three months earlier, was flying over high ground at an altitude considerably lower than the minimum height required by his company's operations manual.

In July 1977, a California probate court appointed respondent Gaynell Reyno administratrix of the estates of the five passengers. Reyno is not related to and does not know any of the decedents or their survivors; she was a legal secretary to the attorney who filed this lawsuit. Several days after her appointment, Reyno commenced separate wrongful death actions against Piper and Hartzell in the Superior Court of California, claiming negligence and strict liability. Air Navigation, McDonald, and the estate of the pilot are not parties to this litigation. The survivors of the five passengers whose estates are represented by Reyno filed a separate action in the United Kingdom against Air Navigation, McDonald, and the pilot's estate. Reyno candidly admits that the action against Piper and Hartzell was filed in the United States because its laws regarding liability, capacity to sue, and damages are more favorable to her position than are those of Scotland. Scottish law does not recognize strict liability in tort. Moreover, it permits wrongful death actions only when brought by a decedent's relatives. The relatives may sue only for "loss of support and society."

On petitioners' motion, the suit was removed to the United States District Court for the Central District of California. Piper then moved for transfer to the United States District Court for the Middle District of Pennsylvania, pursuant to 28 U.S.C. § 1404(a).[4] Hartzell moved to dismiss for lack of personal jurisdiction, or in the alternative, to transfer.[5] In December 1977, the District Court quashed service on

---

4. Section 1404(a) provides: "For the convenience of parties and witnesses, in the interest of justice, a district court may transfer any civil action to any other district or division where it might have been brought."

5. The District Court concluded that it could not assert personal jurisdiction over

Hartzell and transferred the case to the Middle District of Pennsylvania. Respondent then properly served process on Hartzell.

B

In May 1978, after the suit had been transferred, both Hartzell and Piper moved to dismiss the action on the ground of *forum non conveniens.* The District Court granted these motions in October 1979. It relied on the balancing test set forth by this Court in Gulf Oil Corp. v. Gilbert, 330 U.S. 501, 67 S.Ct. 839, 91 L.Ed. 1055 (1947), and its companion case, Koster v. Lumbermens Mut. Cas. Co., 330 U.S. 518, 67 S.Ct. 828, 91 L.Ed. 1067 (1947). In those decisions, the Court stated that a plaintiff's choice of forum should rarely be disturbed. However, when an alternative forum has jurisdiction to hear the case, and when trial in the chosen forum would "establish . . . oppressiveness and vexation to a defendant out of all proportion to plaintiff's convenience," or when the "chosen forum [is] inappropriate because of considerations affecting the court's own administrative and legal problems," the court may, in the exercise of its sound discretion, dismiss the case. *Koster,* supra, at 524, 67 S.Ct., at 831–32. To guide trial court discretion, the Court provided a list of "private interest factors" affecting the convenience of the litigants, and a list of "public interest factors" affecting the convenience of the forum. *Gilbert,* supra, 330 U.S. at 508–509, 67 S.Ct., at 843.[6]

After describing our decisions in *Gilbert* and *Koster,* the District Court analyzed the facts of this case. It began by observing that an alternative forum existed in Scotland; Piper and Hartzell had agreed to submit to the jurisdiction of the Scottish courts and to waive any statute of limitations defense that might be available. It then stated that plaintiff's choice of forum was entitled to little weight. The court recognized that a plaintiff's choice ordinarily deserves substantial deference. It noted, however, that Reyno "is a representative of foreign citizens and residents seeking a forum in the United States because of the more liberal rules concerning products liability law," and that "the courts have been less solicitous when the plaintiff is not an American citizen or resident, and particularly, when the foreign citizens seek to

Hartzell consistent with due process. However, it decided not to dismiss Hartzell because the corporation would be amenable to process in Pennsylvania.

6. The factors pertaining to the private interests of the litigants included the "relative ease of access to sources of proof; availability of compulsory process for attendance of unwilling, and the cost of obtaining attendance of willing, witnesses; possibility of view of premises, if view would be appropriate to the action; and all other practical problems that make trial of a case easy, expeditious, and inexpensive."

Gilbert, 330 U.S. at 508, 67 S.Ct., at 843. The public factors bearing on the question included the administrative difficulties flowing from court congestion; the "local interest in having localized controversies decided at home"; the interest in having the trial of a diversity case in a forum that is at home with the law that must govern the action; the avoidance of unnecessary problems in conflicts of law, or in the application of foreign law; and the unfairness of burdening citizens in an unrelated forum with jury duty. Id., at 509, 67 S.Ct., at 843.

benefit from the more liberal tort rules provided for the protection of citizens and residents of the United States." 479 F.Supp. at 731.

The District Court next examined several factors relating to the private interests of the litigants, and determined that these factors strongly pointed towards Scotland as the appropriate forum. Although evidence concerning the design, manufacture, and testing of the plane and propeller is located in the United States, the connections with Scotland are otherwise "overwhelming." Id., at 732. The real parties in interest are citizens of Scotland, as were all the decedents. Witnesses who could testify regarding the maintenance of the aircraft, the training of the pilot, and the investigation of the accident—all essential to the defense—are in Great Britain. Moreover, all witnesses to damages are located in Scotland. Trial would be aided by familiarity with Scottish topography, and by easy access to the wreckage.

The District Court reasoned that because crucial witnesses and evidence were beyond the reach of compulsory process, and because the defendants would not be able to implead potential Scottish third-party defendants, it would be "unfair to make Piper and Hartzell proceed to trial in this forum." Id., at 733. The survivors had brought separate actions in Scotland against the pilot, McDonald, and Air Navigation. "[I]t would be fairer to all parties and less costly if the entire case was presented to one jury with available testimony from all relevant witnesses." Ibid. Although the court recognized that if trial were held in the United States, Piper and Hartzell could file indemnity or contribution actions against the Scottish defendants, it believed that there was a significant risk of inconsistent verdicts.[7]

The District Court concluded that the relevant public interests also pointed strongly towards dismissal. The court determined that Pennsylvania law would apply to Piper and Scottish law to Hartzell if the case were tried in the Middle District of Pennsylvania.[8] As a result, "trial in this forum would be hopelessly complex and confusing for a jury." Id., at 734. In addition, the court noted that it was unfamiliar with Scottish law and thus would have to rely upon experts from that country. The court also found that the trial would be enormously

---

7. The District Court explained that inconsistent verdicts might result if petitioners were held liable on the basis of strict liability here, and then required to prove negligence in an indemnity action in Scotland. Moreover, even if the same standard of liability applied, there was a danger that different juries would find different facts and produce inconsistent results.

8. Under Klaxon v. Stentor Electric Manufacturing Co., 313 U.S. 487, 61 S.Ct. 1020, 85 L.Ed. 1477 (1941), a court ordinarily must apply the choice-of-law rules of the state in which it sits. However, where a case is transferred pursuant to 28 U.S.C. § 1404(a), it must apply the choice-of-law rules of the state from which the case was

transferred. Van Dusen v. Barrack, 376 U.S. 612, 84 S.Ct. 805, 11 L.Ed.2d 945 (1946). Relying on these two cases, the District Court concluded that California choice-of-law rules would apply to Piper, and Pennsylvania choice-of-law rules would apply to Hartzell. It further concluded that California applied a "governmental interests" analysis in resolving choice-of-law problems, and that Pennsylvania employed a "significant contacts" analysis. The court used the "governmental interests" analysis to determine that Pennsylvania liability rules would apply to Piper, and the "significant contacts" analysis to determine that Scottish liability rules would apply to Hartzell.

costly and time-consuming; that it would be unfair to burden citizens with jury duty when the Middle District of Pennsylvania has little connection with the controversy; and that Scotland has a substantial interest in the outcome of the litigation.

In opposing the motions to dismiss, respondent contended that dismissal would be unfair because Scottish law was less favorable. The District Court explicitly rejected this claim. It reasoned that the possibility that dismissal might lead to an unfavorable change in the law did not deserve significant weight; any deficiency in the foreign law was a "matter to be dealt with in the foreign forum." Id., at 738.

On appeal, the United States Court of Appeals for the Third Circuit reversed and remanded for trial. The decision to reverse appears to be based on two alternative grounds. First, the Court held that the District Court abused its discretion in conducting the *Gilbert* analysis. Second, the Court held that dismissal is never appropriate where the law of the alternative forum is less favorable to the plaintiff.

* * *

II

The Court of Appeals erred in holding that plaintiffs may defeat a motion to dismiss on the ground of *forum non conveniens* merely by showing that the substantive law that would be applied in the alternative forum is less favorable to the plaintiffs than that of the present forum. The possibility of a change in substantive law should ordinarily not be given conclusive or even substantial weight in the *forum non conveniens* inquiry.

We expressly rejected the position adopted by the Court of Appeals in our decision in Canada Malting Co. v. Paterson Steamships, Ltd., 285 U.S. 413, 52 S.Ct. 413, 76 L.Ed. 837 (1932). That case arose out of a collision between two vessels in American waters. The Canadian owners of cargo lost in the accident sued the Canadian owners of one of the vessels in Federal District Court. The cargo owners chose an American court in large part because the relevant American liability rules were more favorable than the Canadian rules. The District Court dismissed on grounds of *forum non conveniens*. The plaintiffs argued that dismissal was inappropriate because Canadian laws were less favorable to them. This Court nonetheless affirmed:

> "We have no occasion to enquire by what law the rights of the parties are governed, as we are of the opinion that, under any view of that question, it lay within the discretion of the District Court to decline jurisdiction over the controversy. . . . '[T]he court will not take cognizance of the case if justice would be as well done by remitting the parties to their home forum.'" Id., at 419–420, 52 S.Ct., at 414, quoting Charter Shipping Co. v. Bowring, Jones & Tidy, 281 U.S. 515, 517, 50 S.Ct. 400, 414, 74 L.Ed. 1008 (1930).

The Court further stated that "there was no basis for the contention that the District Court abused its discretion." 285 U.S., at 423, 52 S.Ct., at 415–16.

It is true that *Canada Malting* was decided before *Gilbert,* and that the doctrine of *forum non conveniens* was not fully crystallized until our decision in that case.[13] However, *Gilbert* in no way affects the validity of *Canada Malting.* Indeed, by holding that the central focus of the *forum non conveniens* inquiry is convenience, *Gilbert* implicitly recognized that dismissal may not be barred solely because of the possibility of an unfavorable change in law.[14] Under *Gilbert,* dismissal will ordinarily be appropriate where trial in the plaintiff's chosen forum imposes a heavy burden on the defendant or the court, and where the plaintiff is unable to offer any specific reasons of convenience supporting his choice.[15] If substantial weight were given to the possibility of an unfavorable change in law, however, dismissal might be barred even where trial in the chosen forum was plainly inconvenient.

The Court of Appeals' decision is inconsistent with this Court's earlier *forum non conveniens* decisions in another respect. Those decisions have repeatedly emphasized the need to retain flexibility. * * * If central emphasis were placed on any one factor, the *forum non conveniens* doctrine would lose much of the very flexibility that makes it so valuable.

13. The doctrine of *forum non conveniens* has a long history. It originated in Scotland, see Braucher, The Inconvenient Federal Forum, 60 Harv.L.Rev. 908, 909–911 (1947), and became part of the common law of many states, see id., at 911–912; Blair, The Doctrine of Forum Non Conveniens in Anglo-American Law, 29 Colum. L.Rev. 1 (1929). The doctrine was also frequently applied in federal admiralty actions. See, e.g., Canada Malting Co. v. Paterson Steamships, Ltd., 285 U.S. 413, 52 S.Ct. 413, 76 L.Ed. 837 (1932); see also Bickel, The Doctrine of Forum Non Conveniens As Applied in the Federal Courts in Matters of Admiralty, 35 Cornell L.Q. 12 (1949). In Williams v. Green Bay & Western R., 326 U.S. 549, 66 S.Ct. 284, 90 L.Ed. 311 (1946), the Court first indicated that motions to dismiss on grounds of *forum non conveniens* could be made in federal diversity actions. The doctrine became firmly established when *Gilbert* and *Koster* were decided one year later.

In previous *forum non conveniens* decisions, the Court has left unresolved the question whether under Erie R. v. Tompkins, 304 U.S. 64, 58 S.Ct. 817, 82 L.Ed. 1188 (1938), state or federal law of *forum non conveniens* applies in a diversity case. *Gilbert,* supra, 330 U.S. at 509, 67 S.Ct., at 843; *Koster,* supra, 330 U.S. at 529, 67 S.Ct., at 834; Williams v. Green Bay & Western R., supra, 326 U.S. at 551, 558–559, 66 S.Ct., at 288–89 (1946). The Court did not decide this issue because the same result would have been reached in each case under federal or state law. The lower courts in this case reached the same conclusion: Pennsylvania and California law on *forum non conveniens* dismissals are virtually identical to federal law. See Reyno v. Piper Aircraft Co., 630 F.2d 149, 158 (CA3 1980). Thus, here, also, we need not resolve the *Erie* question.

14. See also Williams v. Green Bay & Western R., supra, 326 U.S. at 555 n. 4, 66 S.Ct., at 287 n. 4 (1946) (citing with approval a Scottish case that dismissed an action on the ground of *forum non conveniens* despite the possibility of an unfavorable change in law).

15. In other words, *Gilbert* held that dismissal may be warranted where a plaintiff chooses a particular forum, not because it is convenient, but solely in order to harass the defendant or take advantage of favorable law. This is precisely the situation in which the Court of Appeals' rule would bar dismissal.

In fact, if conclusive or substantial weight were given to the possibility of a change in law, the *forum non conveniens* doctrine would become virtually useless. Jurisdiction and venue requirements are often easily satisfied. As a result, many plaintiffs are able to choose from among several forums. Ordinarily, these plaintiffs will select that forum whose choice of law rules are most advantageous. Thus, if the possibility of an unfavorable change in substantive law is given substantial weight in the *forum non conveniens* inquiry, dismissal would rarely be proper.

* * *

* * * The flow of litigation into the United States would increase and further congest already crowded courts.[19]

The Court of Appeals based its decision, at least in part, on an analogy between dismissals on grounds of *forum non conveniens* and transfers between federal courts pursuant to § 1404(a). In Van Dusen v. Barrack, 376 U.S. 612, 84 S.Ct. 805, 11 L.Ed.2d 945 (1964), this Court ruled that a § 1404(a) transfer should not result in a change in the applicable law. * * *

* * *

The reasoning employed in Van Dusen v. Barrack is simply inapplicable to dismissals on grounds of *forum non conveniens*. That case did not discuss the common-law doctrine. Rather, it focused on "the construction and application" of § 1404(a). 376 U.S., at 613, 84 S.Ct., at 807–08. Emphasizing the remedial purpose of the statute, *Barrack* concluded that Congress could not have intended a transfer to be accompanied by a change in law. Id., at 622, 84 S.Ct., at 812. The statute was designed as a "federal housekeeping measure," allowing easy change of venue within a unified federal system. Id., at 613, 84 S.Ct., at 807–08. The Court feared that if a change in venue were accompanied by a change in law, forum-shopping parties would take unfair advantage of the relaxed standards for transfer. The rule was necessary to ensure the just and efficient operation of the statute.

We do not hold that the possibility of an unfavorable change in law should *never* be a relevant consideration in a *forum non conveniens*

19. In holding that the possibility of a change in law unfavorable to the plaintiff should not be given substantial weight, we also necessarily hold that the possibility of a change in law favorable to defendant should not be considered. Respondent suggests that Piper and Hartzell filed the motion to dismiss, not simply because trial in the United States would be inconvenient, but also because they believe the laws of Scotland are more favorable. She argues that this should be taken into account in the analysis of the private interests. We recognize, of course, that Piper and Hartzell may be engaged in reverse forum-shopping. However, this possibility ordinarily should not enter into a trial court's analysis of the private interests. If the defendant is able to overcome the presumption in favor of plaintiff by showing that trial in the chosen forum would be unnecessarily burdensome, dismissal is appropriate—regardless of the fact that defendant may also be motivated by a desire to obtain a more favorable forum. Cf. Kloeckener Reederei und Kohlenhandel v. A/S Hakedal, 210 F.2d 754, 757 (CA2) (defendant not entitled to dismissal on grounds of *forum non conveniens* solely because the law of the original forum is less favorable to him than the law of the alternative forum), cert. dismissed by stipulation, 348 U.S. 801, 75 S.Ct. 17, 99 L.Ed. 633 (1954).

inquiry. Of course, if the remedy provided by the alternative forum is so clearly inadequate or unsatisfactory that it is no remedy at all, the unfavorable change in law may be given substantial weight; the district court may conclude that dismissal would not be in the interests of justice.[22] In this case, however, the remedies that would be provided by the Scottish courts do not fall within this category. Although the relatives of the decedents may not be able to rely on a strict liability theory, and although their potential damage award may be smaller, there is no danger that they will be deprived of any remedy or treated unfairly.

III

* * * Furthermore, we do not believe that the District Court abused its discretion in weighing the private and public interests.

A

The District Court acknowledged that there is ordinarily a strong presumption in favor of the plaintiff's choice of forum, which may be overcome only when the private and public interest factors clearly point towards trial in the alternative forum. It held, however, that the presumption applies with less force when the plaintiff or real parties in interest are foreign.

The District Court's distinction between resident or citizen plaintiffs and foreign plaintiffs is fully justified. In *Koster,* the Court indicated that a plaintiff's choice of forum is entitled to greater deference when the plaintiff has chosen the home forum. *Koster,* supra, 330 U.S., at 524, 67 S.Ct., at 831–32. When the home forum has been chosen, it is reasonable to assume that this choice is convenient. When the plaintiff is foreign, however, this assumption is much less reasonable. Because the central purpose of any *forum non conveniens* inquiry is to ensure that the trial is convenient, a foreign plaintiff's choice deserves less deference.[24]

22. At the outset of any *forum non conveniens* inquiry, the court must determine whether there exists an alternative forum. Ordinarily, this requirement will be satisfied when the defendant is "amenable to process" in the other jurisdiction. *Gilbert,* supra, 330 U.S. at 506–507, 67 S.Ct., at 842. In rare circumstances, however, where the remedy offered by the other forum is clearly unsatisfactory, the other forum may not be an adequate alternative, and the initial requirement may not be satisfied. Thus, for example, dismissal would not be appropriate where the alternative forum does not permit litigation of the subject matter of the dispute. Cf. Phoenix Canada Oil Co. Ltd. v. Texaco, Inc., 78 F.R.D. 445 (DC Del. 1978) (court refuses to dismiss, where alternative forum is Ecuador, it is unclear whether Ecuadorian tribunal will hear the case, and there is no generally codified Ecuadorian legal remedy for the unjust enrichment and tort claims asserted).

24. See Pain v. United Technologies Corp., supra, 205 U.S.App.D.C. at 253, 637 F.2d, at 797 (citizenship and residence are proxies for convenience); see also Note, Forum Non Conveniens and American Plaintiffs in the Federal Courts, 47 U.Chi. L.Rev. 373, 382–383 (1980). * * *

B

The *forum non conveniens* determination is committed to the sound discretion of the trial court. It may be reversed only when there has been a clear abuse of discretion; where the court has considered all relevant public and private interest factors, and where its balancing of these factors is reasonable, its decision deserves substantial deference. * * * In examining the District Court's analysis of the public and private interests, however, the Court of Appeals seems to have lost sight of this rule, and substituted its own judgment for that of the District Court.

     * * *

Reversed.*

NOTE ON FORUM NON CONVENIENS AND OTHER REFUSALS TO TAKE JURISDICTION

1. Forum Non Conveniens and Territorial Jurisdiction

As discussed in *Piper Aircraft*, the doctrine of *forum non conveniens* refers to the discretionary power of a court to dismiss an action whenever it appears that the cause may be more appropriately tried elsewhere. The doctrine of territorial jurisdiction often involves similar kinds of considerations, but there are the following differences between the two:

     (1) The *forum non conveniens* doctrine explicitly involves an exercise of discretion by the court, whereas the "minimum contacts" concept of territorial jurisdiction takes the form of a more definite imperative once the court has weighed the relevant factors.

     (2) *Forum non conveniens* applies only if the court has jurisdiction over the action If the requisite "minimum contacts" are lacking, the court must dismiss the action on that basis, even if an alternative forum would be less convenient.

     (3) If the court dismisses the action on *forum non conveniens* grounds, it may condition the dismissal on the defendant's agreement to submit to jurisdiction in a more convenient forum, as discussed below. A court lacking territorial jurisdiction has no authority to impose such conditions.

See James & Hazard § 2.31.

2. Forum Non Conveniens in the State Courts

a. In General. The principle of *forum non conveniens* was not unknown to the state courts prior to Gulf Oil Corp. v. Gilbert, 330 U.S. 501, 67 S.Ct. 839, 91 L.Ed. 1055 (1947), but the doctrine was not popular prior to that decision. Many courts adhered to the notion that a court had a duty to exercise jurisdiction where it existed. Others held to the proposition, now discredited, that the Privileges and Immunities Clause, U.S. Const., Art. IV, Sec. 2, forbade a state to deny a forum to plaintiffs who were citizens of another state. See generally Barrett, The Doctrine of Forum Non Conveniens, 35 Calif.L.Rev. 380 (1947). While discrimination against non-"citizens" is barred by the Privileges

---

* The opinion of White, J., concurring in part and dissenting in part, and the opinion of Stevens, J., dissenting, are omitted.

and Immunities Clause, the Court has held that discrimination against non-"residents" is not. See Missouri ex rel. Southern Ry. Co. v. Mayfield, 340 U.S. 1, 71 S.Ct. 1, 95 L.Ed. 3 (1950). It is thus not unconstitutional to decline jurisdiction over cases which have no reasonable connection with the forum state. Moreover, the fact that a party to the action is a resident of the forum state does not preclude the court from dismissing or staying the action on *forum non conveniens* grounds. See, e.g., C.C.P. 410.30(a). For the application of the doctrine in the special context of F.E.L.A. actions, see *Mayfield,* supra. See generally Stewart, Forum Non Conveniens: A Doctrine in Search of a Role, 74 Calif.L.Rev. 1259 (1986).

The *Gilbert* decision was historically concurrent with the expansion of jurisdiction under the "minimum contacts" doctrine, the increase in "transient litigation" resulting from a more mobile population and other factors which awakened interest in discretionary refusals to take jurisdiction. In Price v. Atchison, T. & S.F. Ry. Co., 42 Cal.2d 577, 268 P.2d 457 (1954), the California Supreme Court recognized the *forum non conveniens* doctrine, which has since been codified at C.C.P. 410.30. Most other states now recognize the doctrine. See, e.g., Silver v. Great American Ins. Co., 29 N.Y.2d 356, 328 N.Y.S.2d 398, 278 N.E.2d 619 (1972).

In a novel approach to *forum non conveniens,* a New Jersey trial court bifurcated a trial, ruling New Jersey was an inconvenient forum to try the liability issues of a Florida accident, but retaining the damage issues for the New Jersey plaintiffs. The Appellate Division reversed. Radigan v. Innisbrook Resort and Golf Club, 150 N.J.Super. 427, 375 A.2d 1229 (1977).

b. Conditional Dismissal. The consequence of applying *forum non conveniens* in state courts is dismissal: there is no mechanism for transferring a case from the courts of one state to another akin to the power of transfer among federal district courts available under 28 U.S.C.A. § 1404(a). To ameliorate the consequences of dismissal the device of stay can be used, as in Archibald v. Cinerama Hotels, 15 Cal.3d 853, 126 Cal.Rptr. 811, 544 P.2d 947 (1976), whereby the forum stays the action before it in deference to a parallel action in a sister state. Dismissal can also be conditioned on submission to jurisdiction in a more convenient forum. See, e.g., MacLeod v. MacLeod, 383 A.2d 39 (Me.1978). See also Swift & Co. Packers v. Compania Colombiana Del Caribe, 339 U.S. 684, 70 S.Ct. 861, 94 L.Ed. 1206 (1950) (conditioning dismissal of action founded on attachment by requiring defendant to post equivalent security). But cf. Hill v. Upper Mississippi Towing Corp., 252 Minn. 165, 89 N.W.2d 654 (1958), taking literally the premise of *forum non conveniens,* that it "presupposes at least two forums in which defendant is amenable to process," and refusing to dismiss upon defendant's offer to submit to jurisdiction in the more convenient forum because defendant was not subject to involuntary process there. See also Note, Forum Non Conveniens in the Absence of an Alternative Forum, 86 Colum.L.Rev. 1000 (1986); Stein, Forum Non Conveniens and the Redundancy of Court–Access Doctrine, 133 U.Pa.L.Rev. 781 (1985).

3. Forum Non Conveniens in Federal Court

The year after the Supreme Court's decision in Gulf Oil Corp. v. Gilbert, supra, Congress enacted a statutory counterpart, 28 U.S.C.A. § 1404(a), that governs transfers "for convenience" from one federal District Court to another. This effectively transformed the *forum non conveniens* doctrine of *Gilbert* into a venue provision determining the proper court for trial in the federal system. See Van Dusen v. Barrack, 376 U.S. 612, 84 S.Ct. 805, 11 L.Ed.2d 945 (1964), and the discussion of it in *Piper Aircraft*, supra, and In re Korean Air Lines Disaster, infra p. 618.

4. Forum Non Conveniens in Actions Involving Foreign Parties

For application of *forum non conveniens* to transactions occurring in a foreign country, see, in addition to *Piper Aircraft*, Macedo v. Boeing Co., 693 F.2d 683 (7th Cir.1982) (reversing dismissal that would require resort to foreign forum). See also In re Union Carbide Corp. Gas Plant Disaster at Bhopal, India in December 1984, 809 F.2d 195 (2d Cir.1987), where the court held that the District Court properly dismissed the complaint on *forum non conveniens* grounds, but improperly conditioned the dismissal on defendant's consent (1) to be subject to discovery under the Federal Rules of Civil Procedure, and (2) to satisfy any judgment of an Indian court, provided the judgment did not violate due process.

Courts are divided on the question whether a greater showing of inconvenience should be required in order to deprive an American plaintiff, as opposed to a foreign plaintiff, of an American forum. See Comment, Forum Non Conveniens and American Plaintiffs in the Federal Courts, 47 U.Chi.L.Rev. 373 (1980), and the discussion in *Piper Aircraft*.

Piper Aircraft was not governed by § 1404(a) because it involved an application of *forum non conveniens* in an international as opposed to federal context, and so the Court relied on the older *Gilbert* standards. After *Piper Aircraft*, would a similar action brought in state court be governed by *Gilbert*, or by the state's own *forum non conveniens* rules?

5. Injunctions Against Prosecution of Action Elsewhere

Paralleling the application of *forum non conveniens* is the question of the propriety and efficacy of one forum enjoining the litigants before it from suing elsewhere. See James v. Grand Trunk Western R.R., 14 Ill.2d 356, 152 N.E.2d 858 (1958); Noto, Injunctions and Counterinjunctions as Means of Preserving Jurisdiction, 43 Minn.L.Rev. 1249 (1959); Comment, Forum Non Conveniens, Injunctions Against Suit and Full Faith and Credit, 29 U.Chi.L.Rev. 740 (1962); Annos., 6 A.L.R.2d 896, 74 A.L.R.2d 828. Note the injunctions issued in M/S Bremen and Unterweser Reederei v. Zapata Off–Shore Co., supra p. 370. Compare General Atomic Co. v. Felter, 436 U.S. 493, 98 S.Ct. 1939, 56 L.Ed.2d 480 (1978) (state court may not enjoin parties from suing in federal court). See also Note on Dismissal or Stay When Another Action is Pending, infra p. 703.

6. Immunity From Service of Process

a. The General Doctrine. The traditional doctrine of immunity from service of process holds that a nonresident witness or litigant, whether plaintiff or defendant, is immune from service of process while present to attend litigation, whether for the trial itself, e.g., Hammons v. Superior Court, 63 Cal. App. 700, 219 P. 1037 (1923), for such preliminary purposes as deposition, e.g., Russell v. Landau, 127 Cal.App.2d 682, 274 P.2d 681 (1954), or for appeal, e.g., Chase Nat. Bank v. Turner, 269 N.Y. 397, 199 N.E. 636 (1936). In addition, the witness or litigant is allowed a "reasonable time" to go to and fro. As may be surmised, the doctrine, where recognized, operates primarily to protect nonresidents who cannot be reached because "minimum contacts" with the forum state are lacking or because of limitations on the reach of the forum state's "long arm" statute. As such, the immunity doctrine is an exception to the old transitory presence rule of territorial jurisdiction.

The immunity rule was traditionally justified on two grounds: (1) courts must protect those who come to court for access to justice; and (2) judicial administration must be free from the interruptions which might be caused by service. The rule thus assertedly upholds the dignity of the court and encourages attendance of persons whose presence is needed for the exercise of the judicial function. See Halsey v. Stewart, 4 N.J.L. 366 (Sup.Ct.1817).

[handwritten: policy reasons]

The immunity is generally also applied where the nonresident has entered the jurisdiction as the result of fraud or force by the opposing party. See, e.g., Wyman v. Newhouse, 93 F.2d 313 (2d Cir.1937); Restatement Second of Conflict of Laws § 82. The farthest extension in this direction appears to be Western States Refining Co. v. Berry, 6 Utah 2d 336, 313 P.2d 480 (1957), where an Idaho resident who had come to Utah to confer with plaintiff regarding a dispute over a service station leasehold in Idaho was held immune from Utah process issued at plaintiff's instance immediately after the conference broke down in disagreement. The court said that "equity and good conscience will not permit plaintiff to take sharp advantage of defendant's presence * * * so long as defendant is in the jurisdiction for the purpose for which plaintiff invited him." The immunity is held not to extend to instances where service itself is effected by strategem on a person who has come into the jurisdiction of his own accord without fraud. See, e.g., Gumperz v. Hofmann, 245 App.Div. 622, 283 N.Y.S. 823 (1st Dept.1935), aff'd, 271 N.Y. 544, 2 N.E.2d 687 (1936). The cases dealing with service of process on a nonresident criminal defendant go in all directions. See Anno., 20 A.L.R.2d 163.

b. Limitations on the Doctrine. The doctrine of immunity has been criticized in its entirety, see, e.g., Keeffe and Roscia, Immunity and Sentimentality, 32 Cornell L.Q. 471 (1947), and many jurisdictions no longer recognize it. Those which do still recognize the doctrine now tend to restrict its application. The most important restriction is that immunity is usually denied to persons who are plaintiffs in litigation related in subject matter to that in which the immunity is claimed. See, e.g., Velkov v. Superior Court, 40 Cal.2d 289, 253 P.2d 25 (1953); cf. Threlkeld v. Tucker, 496 F.2d 1101 (9th Cir.1974). This qualification has been extended so as to deny immunity to any party in the first action, plaintiff or defendant, where the second action is related to it. See, e.g., St. John v. Superior Court, 178 Cal.App.2d 794, 3 Cal.Rptr. 535 (1960); Note, Immunity From Service of Civil Process: Aberration or Transition in the California Approach to Immunity?—St. John v. Superior Court, 48 Calif.L.Rev. 867 (1960); Anno., 84 A.L.R.2d 421. As a practical matter this qualification virtually swallows the rule. See Restatement Second of Judgments § 9, Comment a.

Some courts have integrated the concepts of immunity and *forum non conveniens,* holding that service of process is valid if the person served has "minimum contacts" with the forum and the forum is not an inconvenient place for trying the action. See Wangler v. Harvey, 41 N.J. 277, 196 A.2d 513 (1963), where service was upheld on this basis even though the person served was otherwise unreachable due to limitations in the state's "long arm" statute. Cf. Severn v. Adidas Sportschuhfabriken, 33 Cal.App.3d 754, 109 Cal.Rptr. 328 (1973), denying immunity to a nonresident who was subject to "long arm" jurisdiction.

c. Sovereign Immunity. The principle that a sovereign may be sued only with its consent is expressed procedurally in the rule that, in the absence of such consent, a sovereign is immune from service of process. See Jaffe, Suits Against Governments and Officers: Sovereign Immunity, 77 Harv.L.Rev. 1

(1963); Cramton, Nonstatutory Review of Federal Administrative Action, 68 Mich.L.Rev. 387 (1970), with which compare 28 U.S.C.A. §§ 1346, 1361 and 1391, and Comment, Sovereign Immunity: A Modern Rationale in Light of the 1976 Amendments to the Administrative Procedure Act, 1981 Duke L.J. 116. See also the Foreign Sovereign Immunities Act, 28 U.S.C.A. §§ 1330 and 1602 et seq.; Nevada v. Hall, 440 U.S. 410, 99 S.Ct. 1182, 59 L.Ed.2d 416 (1979), discussed in Stewart, The State as an Unwilling Defendant, 59 Neb.L.Rev. 246 (1980); Wolcher, Sovereign Immunity and the Supremacy Clause, 69 Calif.L. Rev. 189 (1981), and the references therein.

7. The Local Action Rule

a. The Traditional Doctrine. The local action rule is rooted in ancient English common law doctrine. It states that a court may not take jurisdiction over an action affecting real property located in another jurisdiction. The rule can be traced to the traditional distinction in English law between "transitory" actions, which might have arisen anywhere and could be brought wherever defendant was subject to service of process, and "local" actions, which involved real property and could be brought only in the county where the land was located. See Blume, Place of Trial of Civil Cases, 48 Mich.L.Rev. 1 (1949). By the nineteenth century, the rule was applied not only to actions concerning title to property, but also to those involving damages for injury to real property, and applied even where its application denied plaintiff a remedy. It was first invoked in the United States in the celebrated case of Livingston v. Jefferson, 15 F.Cas. 660 (C.C.Va.1811) (No. 8411), and was later adopted by most states. Three rationales were commonly used to justify or explain the rule: (1) courts are not in a good position to rule on title to land outside the jurisdiction; (2) since a tort concerning real property must take place where the land is located, plaintiff should sue before defendant leaves the jurisdiction; and (3) a traditional reluctance to subject citizens to suits by nonresidents.

b. The Modern Doctrine. The local action rule has been severely criticized in modern times, especially as it relates to actions for injury to land located in another jurisdiction. In the influential case of Reasor–Hill Corp. v. Harrison, 220 Ark. 521, 249 S.W.2d 994 (1952), the Arkansas Supreme Court disapproved the rule, arguing that the traditional rationales did not apply in the interstate, as opposed to international, setting. The court reasoned that: (1) courts constantly apply the laws of other states in "transitory" actions and can do so just as easily in "local" actions; (2) a plaintiff may not detect damage to his property before the tortfeasor leaves the jurisdiction and, unlike the power of a sovereign nation to prevent persons from leaving its jurisdiction, citizens of the various states have a constitutional right to pass freely from one jurisdiction to another; and (3) states should not provide sanctuary to one of its residents who has committed a tort elsewhere.

Reasor–Hill represents the better view. See also Restatement Second of Conflict of Laws § 87, which takes the position that a state may entertain an action for injury to land located in another state but that it should not entertain an action that would determine title. The court's reasoning in *Reasor–Hill* is bolstered further by the fact that there is apparently no question that a court has authority to give an equitable remedy, as distinct from a damages remedy, for redress of a wrong concerning real property in another state. See id., §§ 53, 55; cf. Rozan v. Rozan, 49 Cal.2d 322, 317 P.2d 11 (1957).

The local action rule, however, may be regarded simply as the application of *forum non conveniens* principles to actions concerning real property and, when applied consistently with the precepts of fairness embodied in that doctrine, can be given a coherent modern form. Under this view, a court should normally refuse to entertain an action, even for money damages, that concerns use or ownership of land located elsewhere—not because the court lacks power to adjudicate the controversy, but because it is an inappropriate forum for such litigation. On the other hand, if applying the doctrine would deny plaintiff a forum anywhere (e.g., because his home state's "long arm" statute cannot reach the defendant), then the court should sustain its jurisdiction. See James & Hazard § 2.30. This was the basis upon which the court sustained its jurisdiction in *Reasor–Hill.*

    c. The Internal Affairs Doctrine. Somewhat akin to the local action rule and *forum non conveniens* is the "internal affairs doctrine," under which courts of one state generally will refuse to resolve conflicts over the internal management of a corporation chartered in another jurisdiction. See, e.g., Prescott v. Plant Industries, Inc., 88 F.R.D. 257 (S.D.N.Y.1980) (presence of records or principal office in forum state is irrelevant).

B. COMMENCING THE ACTION: NOTICE

INTRODUCTORY NOTE ON NOTICE

    Mullane v. Central Hanover Bank & Trust, supra p. 303, is the starting point for understanding the modern doctrine on the requirements of constitutionally adequate notice. *Mullane* declared that notice must be "reasonably calculated, under all the circumstances, to apprise interested parties of the pendency of the action" and that the means employed "must be such as one desirous of actually informing the absentee might reasonably adopt." Recall further that *Mullane* made the "reasonable notice" requirement applicable to all actions, whether classified as *in rem* or *in personam.* The questions for the future included: (1) what kinds of notice would withstand scrutiny under this general standard, and (2) what kinds of persons or entities have sufficient interests at stake in an action such that they are entitled to notice. The first of these issues is addressed in the cases which follow. The second issue presents the question of a person's substantive legal interest in the transaction or subject matter involved in the litigation. Such an interest may be conferred by state law or federal law, including the Constitution. See the discussion of persons entitled to notice in Note on the Summons and Other Forms of Service, infra p. 458.

GREENE v. LINDSEY

Supreme Court of the United States, 1982.
456 U.S. 444, 102 S.Ct. 1874, 72 L.Ed.2d 249.*

    JUSTICE BRENNAN delivered the opinion of the Court.

    A Kentucky statute provides that in forcible entry or detainer actions, service of process may be made under certain circumstances by posting a summons on the door of a tenant's apartment. The question presented is whether this statute, as applied to tenants in a public housing project, fails to afford those tenants the notice of proceedings

  * Some of the Court's footnotes are omitted.

initiated against them required by the Due Process Clause of the Fourteenth Amendment.

I

Appellees Linnie Lindsey, Barbara Hodgens, and Pamela Ray are tenants in a Louisville, Ky., housing project. Appellants are the Sheriff of Jefferson County, Ky., and certain unnamed Deputy Sheriffs charged with responsibility for serving process in forcible entry and detainer actions. In 1975, the Housing Authority of Louisville initiated detainer actions against each of appellees, seeking repossession of their apartments. Service of process was made pursuant to Ky.Rev.Stat. § 454.030 (1975), which states:

> "If the officer directed to serve notice on the defendant in forcible entry or detainer proceedings cannot find the defendant on the premises mentioned in the writ, he may explain and leave a copy of the notice with any member of the defendant's family thereon over sixteen (16) years of age, and if no such person is found he may serve the notice by posting a copy thereof in a conspicuous place on the premises. The notice shall state the time and place of meeting of the court."

In each instance, notice took the form of posting a copy of the writ of forcible entry and detainer on the door of the tenant's apartment.[1] Appellees claim never to have seen these posted summonses; they state that they did not learn of the eviction proceedings until they were served with writs of possession, executed after default judgments had been entered against them, and after their opportunity for appeal had lapsed.

Thus without recourse in the state courts, appellees filed this suit as a class action in the United States District Court for the Western District of Kentucky, seeking declaratory and injunctive relief under 42 U.S.C. § 1983. They claimed that the notice procedure employed as a predicate to these eviction proceedings did not satisfy the minimum standards of constitutionally adequate notice described in Mullane v. Central Hanover Bank & Trust Co., 339 U.S. 306, 70 S.Ct. 652, 94 L.Ed. 865 (1950), and that the Commonwealth of Kentucky had thus failed to afford them the due process of law guaranteed by the Fourteenth Amendment. Named as defendants were the Housing Authority of Louisville, several public officials charged with responsibility over par-

---

1. "Posting" refers to the practice of placing the writ on the property by use of a thumbtack, adhesive tape, or other means. App. 74, 77 (deposition of process servers). Appellants describe the usual method of effecting service pursuant to § 454.030 in the following terms:

> "The officer of the court who is charged with serving notice in a forcible entry and detainer action, usually a Jefferson County Deputy Sheriff, takes the

following steps in notifying a tenant. First, the officer goes to the apartment in an effort to effectuate personal in-hand service. Second, if the named tenant is absent or will not appear at the door, personal in-hand service is made on any member of the tenant's family over sixteen years of age. Finally, if no one answers the door, a copy of the notice is posted on the premises, usually the door." Brief for Appellants 3.

ticular Louisville public housing projects, Joseph Greene, the Jefferson County Sheriff, and certain known and unknown Deputy Sheriffs.

* * *

II

A

"The fundamental requisite of due process of law is the opportunity to be heard." Grannis v. Ordean, 234 U.S. 385, 394, 34 S.Ct. 779, 783, 58 L.Ed. 1363 (1914). And the "right to be heard has little reality or worth unless one is informed that the matter is pending and can choose for himself whether to appear or default, acquiesce or contest," *Mullane,* supra, at 314, 70 S.Ct., at 657. Personal service guarantees actual notice of the pendency of a legal action; it thus presents the ideal circumstance under which to commence legal proceedings against a person, and has traditionally been deemed necessary in actions styled *in personam.* McDonald v. Mabee, 243 U.S. 90, 92, 37 S.Ct. 343, 344, 61 L.Ed. 608 (1917). Nevertheless, certain less rigorous notice procedures have enjoyed substantial acceptance throughout our legal history; in light of this history and the practical obstacles to providing personal service in every instance, we have allowed judicial proceedings to be prosecuted in some situations on the basis of procedures that do not carry with them the same certainty of actual notice that inheres in personal service. But we have also clearly recognized that the Due Process Clause does prescribe a constitutional minimum: "An elementary and fundamental requirement of due process in any proceeding which is to be accorded finality is *notice reasonably calculated, under all the circumstances, to apprise interested parties of the pendency of the action* and afford them an opportunity to present their objections." *Mullane,* 339 U.S., at 314, 70 S.Ct. at 657 (emphasis added). It is against this standard that we evaluate the procedures employed in this case.

B

Appellants argue that because a forcible entry and detainer action is an action *in rem,* notice by posting is *ipso facto* constitutionally adequate. * * *

As in *Mullane,* we decline to resolve the constitutional question based upon the determination whether the particular action is more properly characterized as one *in rem* or *in personam.* 339 U.S., at 312, 70 S.Ct., at 656. See Shaffer v. Heitner, supra, at 206, 97 S.Ct., at 2580. That is not to say that the nature of the action has no bearing on a constitutional assessment of the reasonableness of the procedures employed. The character of the action reflects the extent to which the court purports to extend its power, and thus may roughly describe the scope of potential adverse consequences to the person claiming a right to more effective notice. But " '[a]ll proceedings, like all rights, are really against persons.' " [3] In this case, appellees have been deprived of a significant interest in property: indeed, of the right to continued residence in their homes.[4] In light of this deprivation, it will not suffice to recite that because the action is *in rem,* it is only necessary to serve notice "upon the thing itself." [5] The sufficiency of notice must be tested with reference to its ability to inform people of the pendency of proceedings that affect their interests. In arriving at the constitutional assessment, we look to the realities of the case before us: In determining the constitutionality of a procedure established by the State to provide notice in a particular class of cases, "its effect must be judged in the light of its practical application to the affairs of men as they are ordinarily conducted." North Laramie Land Co. v. Hoffman, 268 U.S. 276, 283, 45 S.Ct. 491, 494, 69 L.Ed. 953 (1925).

It is, of course, reasonable to assume that a property owner will maintain superintendence of his property, and to presume that actions physically disturbing his holdings will come to his attention. See *Mullane,* supra, at 316, 70 S.Ct., at 658.[6] The frequent restatement of this rule impresses upon the property owner the fact that a failure to maintain watch over his property may have significant legal consequences for him, providing a spur to his attentiveness, and a consequent reinforcement to the empirical foundation of the principle. Upon this understanding, a State may in turn conclude that in most cases, the

3. Shaffer v. Heitner, 433 U.S. 186, 207, n. 22, 97 S.Ct., at 2581, n. 22 (1977), quoting Tyler v. Court of Registration, 175 Mass. 71, 76, 55 N.E. 812, 814 (Holmes, C.J.), writ of error dism'd, 179 U.S. 405, 21 S.Ct. 206, 45 L.Ed. 252 (1900).

4. The dissent directs our attention to the "nature and purpose" of Kentucky's forcible entry and detainer action. * * * Such proceedings are designed to offer an expeditious means of determining who is entitled to retain possession of an apartment. But that hardly explains why we may dispense with the constitutional requirement of adequate notice. After all, detainer proceedings, while in some sense "summary," are *proceedings* in which issues of fact and law are to be resolved, and important interests in property determined. We can agree with the dissent's observation that the "means chosen for making service of process . . . must be prompt and certain." * * * But it is difficult to see how, from the perspective of the landlord, any of the likely supplements to the form of service currently provided under § 454.030 will render the procedure markedly less prompt or certain. More significantly, *from the perspective of the tenant,* it is difficult to see how a means of serving process that fails to afford actual notice in a "not insubstantial" number of cases can be deemed *either* prompt or certain.

5. The Mary, 9 Cranch 126, 144 (1815).

6. As we noted in *Mullane:*

"The ways of an owner with tangible property are such that he usually arranges means to learn of any direct attack upon his possessory or proprietary rights. Hence, . . . entry upon real estate in the name of law may reasonably be expected to come promptly to the owner's attention. . . . A state may indulge the assumption that one who has left tangible property in the state either has abandoned it, in which case proceedings against it deprive him of nothing, . . . or that he has left some caretaker under a duty to let him know that it is being jeopardized." 339 U.S., at 316, 70 S.Ct., at 658.

Of course, the *Mullane* discussion of the special notice rules with respect to proceedings affecting property ownership focused on the forms of notice that might be appropriate as a supplement to the direct disturbance of the property itself. But where the State has reason to believe the premises to be occupied or under the charge of a caretaker, notice posted on the premises, if sufficiently apparent, is itself a form of disturbance, likely to come to the attention of the occupants or the caretaker.

secure posting of a notice on the property of a person is likely to offer that property owner sufficient warning of the pendency of proceedings possibly affecting his interests.

The empirical basis of the presumption that notice posted upon property is adequate to alert the owner or occupant of property of the pendency of legal proceedings would appear to make the presumption particularly well founded where notice is posted at a residence. With respect to claims affecting the continued possession of that residence, the application of this presumption seems particularly apt: If the tenant has a continuing interest in maintaining possession of the property for his use and occupancy, he might reasonably be expected to frequent the premises; if he no longer occupies the premises, then the injury that might result from his not having received actual notice as a consequence of the posted notice is reduced. Short of providing personal service, then, posting notice on the door of a person's home would, in many or perhaps most instances, constitute not only a constitutionally acceptable means of service, but indeed a singularly appropriate and effective way of ensuring that a person who cannot conveniently be served personally is actually apprised of proceedings against him.

 But whatever the efficacy of posting in many cases, it is clear that, in the circumstances of this case, merely posting notice on an apartment door does not satisfy minimum standards of due process. In a significant number of instances, reliance on posting pursuant to the provisions of § 454.030 results in a failure to provide actual notice to the tenant concerned. Indeed, appellees claim to have suffered precisely such a failure of actual notice. As the process servers were well aware, notices posted on apartment doors in the area where these tenants lived were "not infrequently" removed by children or other tenants before they could have their intended effect. Under these conditions, notice by posting on the apartment door cannot be considered a "reliable means of acquainting interested parties of the fact that their rights are before the courts." *Mullane*, 339 U.S., at 315, 70 S.Ct., at 657.

Of course, the reasonableness of the notice provided must be tested with reference to the existence of "feasible and customary" alternatives and supplements to the form of notice chosen. Ibid. In this connection, we reject appellants' characterization of the procedure contemplated by § 454.030 as one in which " 'posting' is used as a method of service only as a last resort." Brief for Appellants 7. To be sure, the statute requires the officer serving notice to make a visit to the tenant's home and to attempt to serve the writ personally on the tenant or some member of his family. But if no one is at home at the time of that visit, as is apparently true in a "good percentage" of cases, posting follows forthwith. Neither the statute, nor the practice of the process servers, makes provision for even a second attempt at personal service, perhaps at some time of day when the tenant is more likely to be at home. The failure to effect personal service on the first visit hardly suggests that the tenant has abandoned his interest in the apartment such that mere *pro forma* notice might be held constitutionally adequate. Cf. *Mullane*, 339 U.S., at 317–318, 70 S.Ct., at 658.

As noted by the Court of Appeals, and as we noted in *Mullane*, the mails provide an "efficient and inexpensive means of communication," id., at 319, 70 S.Ct., at 659, upon which prudent men will ordinarily rely in the conduct of important affairs, id., at 319–320, 70 S.Ct., at 659. Notice by mail in the circumstances of this case would surely go a long way toward providing the constitutionally required assurance that the State has not allowed its power to be invoked against a person who has had no opportunity to present a defense despite a continuing interest in the resolution of the controversy. Particularly where the subject matter of the action also happens to be the mailing address of the defendant, and where personal service is ineffectual, notice by mail may reasonably be relied upon to provide interested persons with actual notice of judicial proceedings. We need not go so far as to insist that in order to "dispense with personal service the substitute that is most likely to reach the defendant is the least that ought to be required," McDonald v. Mabee, 243 U.S., at 92, 37 S.Ct., at 344, in order to recognize that where an inexpensive and efficient mechanism such as mail service is available to enhance the reliability of an otherwise unreliable notice procedure, the State's continued exclusive reliance on an ineffective means of service is not notice "reasonably calculated to reach those who could easily be informed by other means at hand." *Mullane*, supra, at 319, 70 S.Ct., at 659.

* * *

JUSTICE O'CONNOR, with whom THE CHIEF JUSTICE and JUSTICE REHN-QUIST join, dissenting.

Today, the Court holds that the Constitution prefers the use of the Postal Service to posted notice. The Court reaches this conclusion despite the total absence of any evidence in the record regarding the speed and reliability of the mails. The sole ground for the Court's result is the scant and conflicting testimony of a handful of process servers in Kentucky. On this flimsy basis, the Court confidently overturns the work of the Kentucky Legislature and, by implication, that of at least 10 other States. I must respectfully dissent.

* * *

The Court * * * holds that notice via the mails is so far superior to posted notice that the difference is of constitutional dimension. How the Court reaches this judgment remains a mystery, especially since the Court is unable, on the present record, to evaluate the risks that notice mailed to public housing projects might fail due to loss, misdelivery, lengthy delay, or theft. Furthermore, the advantages of the mails over posting, if any, are far from obvious. It is no secret, after all, that unattended mailboxes are subject to plunder by thieves. Moreover, unlike the use of the mails, posting notice at least gives assurance that the notice has gotten as far as the tenant's door.

* * *

MENNONITE BOARD OF MISSIONS v. ADAMS

Supreme Court of the United States, 1983.
462 U.S. 791, 103 S.Ct. 2706, 77 L.Ed.2d 180.*

JUSTICE MARSHALL delivered the opinion of the Court.

This appeal raises the question whether notice by publication and posting provides a mortgagee of real property with adequate notice of a proceeding to sell the mortgaged property for nonpayment of taxes.

I

To secure an obligation to pay $14,000, Alfred Jean Moore executed a mortgage in favor of appellant Mennonite Board of Missions (MBM) on property in Elkhart, Indiana, that Moore had purchased from MBM. The mortgage was recorded in the Elkhart County Recorder's Office on March 1, 1973. Under the terms of the agreement, Moore was responsible for paying all of the property taxes. Without MBM's knowledge, however, she failed to pay taxes on the property.

Indiana law provides for the annual sale of real property on which payments of property taxes have been delinquent for 15 months or longer. Ind.Code § 6–1.1–24–1 et seq. (1982). Prior to the sale, the county auditor must post notice in the county courthouse and publish notice once each week for three consecutive weeks. § 6–1.1–24–3. The owner of the property is entitled to notice by certified mail to his last known address. § 6–1.1–24–4.[1] Until 1980, however, Indiana law did not provide for notice by mail or personal service to mortgagees of property that was to be sold for nonpayment of taxes.[2]

After the required notice is provided, the county treasurer holds a public auction at which the real property is sold to the highest bidder. § 6–1.1–24–5. The purchaser acquires a certificate of sale which constitutes a lien against the real property for the entire amount paid. § 6–1.1–24–9. This lien is superior to all other liens against the property which existed at the time the certificate was issued. Ibid.

The tax sale is followed by a 2-year redemption period during which the "owner, occupant, lienholder, or other person who has an interest in" the property may redeem the property. § 6–1.1–25–1. To redeem the property an individual must pay the county treasurer a sum sufficient to cover the purchase price of the property at the tax

---

* Some of the Court's footnotes are omitted.

1. Because a mortgagee has no title to the mortgaged property under Indiana law, the mortgagee is not considered an "owner" for purposes of § 6–1.1–24–4. First Savings & Loan Assn. of Central Indiana v. Furnish, 174 Ind.App. 265, 272 n. 14, 367 N.E.2d 596, 600 n. 14 (Ind.App.1977).

2. Ind.Code § 6–1.1–24–4.2, added in 1980, provides for notice by certified mail to any mortgagee of real property which is subject to tax sale proceedings, if the mortgagee has annually requested such notice and has agreed to pay a fee, not to exceed $10, to cover the cost of sending notice. Because the events in question in this case occurred before the 1980 amendment, the constitutionality of the amendment is not before us.

sale, the amount of taxes and special assessments paid by the purchaser following the sale, plus an additional percentage specified in the statute. § 6–1.1–25–2. The county in turn remits the payment to the purchaser of the property at the tax sale. § 6–1.1–25–3.

If no one redeems the property during the statutory redemption period, the purchaser may apply to the county auditor for a deed to the property. Before executing and delivering the deed, the county auditor must notify the former owner that he is still entitled to redeem the property. § 6–1.1–25–6. No notice to the mortgagee is required. If the property is not redeemed within thirty days, the county auditor may then execute and deliver a deed for the property to the purchaser, § 6–1.1–25–4, who thereby acquires "an estate in fee simple absolute, free and clear of all liens and encumbrances." § 6–1.1–25–4(d).

After obtaining a deed, the purchaser may initiate an action to quiet his title to the property. § 6–1.1–25–14. The previous owner, lienholders, and others who claim to have an interest in the property may no longer redeem the property. They may defeat the title conveyed by the tax deed only by proving, *inter alia,* that the property had not been subject to, or assessed for, the taxes for which it was sold, that the taxes had been paid before the sale, or that the property was properly redeemed before the deed was executed. § 6–1.1–25–16.

In 1977 Elkhart County initiated proceedings to sell Moore's property for nonpayment of taxes. The County provided notice as required under the statute: it posted and published an announcement of the tax sale and mailed notice to Moore by certified mail. MBM was not informed of the pending tax sale either by the county auditor or by Moore. The property was sold for $1,167.75 to appellee Richard Adams on August 8, 1977. Neither Moore nor MBM appeared at the sale or took steps thereafter to redeem the property. Following the sale of her property, Moore continued to make payments each month to MBM, and as a result MBM did not realize that the property had been sold. On August 16, 1979, MBM first learned of the tax sale. By then the redemption period had run and Moore still owed appellant $8,237.19.

In November 1979, Adams filed a suit in state court seeking to quiet title to the property. In opposition to Adams' motion for summary judgment, MBM contended that it had not received constitutionally adequate notice of the pending tax sale and of the opportunity to redeem the property following the tax sale. The trial court upheld the Indiana tax sale statute against this constitutional challenge. The Indiana Court of Appeals affirmed. 427 N.E.2d 686 (1981). We noted probable jurisdiction, 459 U.S. 903, 103 S.Ct. 204, 74 L.Ed.2d 164 (1982), and we now reverse.

II

In Mullane v. Central Hanover Bank & Trust Co., 339 U.S. 306, 314, 70 S.Ct. 652, 657, 94 L.Ed. 865 (1950), this Court recognized that prior to an action which will affect an interest in life, liberty, or property protected by the Due Process Clause of the Fourteenth Amendment, a State must provide "notice reasonably calculated, under all circumstances, to apprise interested parties of the pendency of the action and afford them an opportunity to present their objections." Invoking this "elementary and fundamental requirement of due process," ibid., the Court held that published notice of an action to settle the accounts of a common trust fund was not sufficient to inform beneficiaries of the trust whose names and addresses were known. The Court explained that notice by publication was not reasonably calculated to provide actual notice of the pending proceeding and was therefore inadequate to inform those who could be notified by more effective means such as personal service or mailed notice * * *.[3]

3. The decision in *Mullane* rejected one of the premises underlying this Court's previous decisions concerning the requirements of notice in judicial proceedings: that due process rights may vary depending on whether actions are *in rem* or *in personam*. 339 U.S., at 312, 70 S.Ct., at 656. See Shaffer v. Heitner, 433 U.S. 186, 206, 97 S.Ct. 2569, 2580, 53 L.Ed.2d 683 (1977). Traditionally, when a state court based its jurisdiction upon its authority over the defendant's person, personal service was considered essential for the court to bind individuals who did not submit to its jurisdiction. See, e.g., Hamilton v. Brown, 161 U.S. 256, 275, 16 S.Ct. 585, 592, 40 L.Ed. 691 (1896); Arndt v. Griggs, 134 U.S. 316, 320, 10 S.Ct. 557, 558, 33 L.Ed. 918 (1890); Pennoyer v. Neff, 95 U.S. 714, 726, 733–734, 24 L.Ed. 565 (1878) ("Due process of law would require appearance or personal service before the defendant could be personally bound by any judgment rendered."). In Hess v. Pawloski, 274 U.S. 352, 47 S.Ct. 632, 71 L.Ed. 1091 (1927), the Court recognized for the first time that service by registered mail, in place of personal service, may satisfy the requirements of due process. Constructive notice was never deemed sufficient to bind an individual in an action *in personam.*

In contrast, in *in rem* or *quasi in rem* proceedings in which jurisdiction was based on the court's power over property within its territory, see generally Shaffer v. Heitner, supra, 433 U.S., at 196–205, 97 S.Ct., at 2575–2580, constructive notice to nonresidents was traditionally understood to satisfy the requirements of due process. In order to settle questions of title to property within its territory, a state court was generally required to proceed by an *in rem* action since the court could not otherwise bind nonresidents. At one time constructive service was considered the only means of notifying nonresidents since it was believed that "[p]rocess from the tribunals of

one State cannot run into another State." Pennoyer v. Neff, supra, at 727. See Ballard v. Hunter, 204 U.S. 241, 255, 27 S.Ct. 261, 266, 51 L.Ed. 461 (1907). As a result, the nonresident acquired the duty "to take measures that in some way he shall be represented when his property is called into requisition." Id., at 262, 27 S.Ct., at 269. If he "fail[ed] to get notice by the ordinary publications which have been usually required in such cases, it [was] his misfortune." Ibid.

Rarely was a corresponding duty imposed on interested parties who resided within the State and whose identities were reasonably ascertainable. Even in actions *in rem,* such individuals were generally provided personal service. See, e.g., Arndt v. Griggs, supra, 134 U.S., at 326–327, 10 S.Ct., at 560–561. Where the identity of interested residents could not be ascertained after a reasonably diligent inquiry, however, their interests in property could be affected by a proceeding *in rem* as long as constructive notice was provided. See Hamilton v. Brown, supra, 161 U.S., at 275, 16 S.Ct., at 592; American Land Co. v. Zeiss, 219 U.S. 47, 61–62, 65–66, 31 S.Ct. 200, 206–207, 55 L.Ed. 82 (1911).

Beginning with *Mullane,* this Court has recognized, contrary to the earlier line of cases, "that an adverse judgment *in rem* directly affects the property owner by divesting him of his rights in the property before the court." Shaffer v. Heitner, supra, 433 U.S., at 206, 97 S.Ct., at 2580. In rejecting the traditional justification for distinguishing between residents and nonresidents and between *in rem* and *in personam* actions, the Court has not left all interested claimants to the vagaries of indirect notice. Our cases have required the State to make efforts to provide actual notice to all interested parties comparable to the efforts that were previously required only in *in personam* actions. * * *

In subsequent cases, this Court has adhered unwaiveringly to the principle announced in *Mullane*. In Walker v. City of Hutchinson, 352 U.S. 112, 77 S.Ct. 200, 1 L.Ed.2d 178 (1956), for example, the Court held that notice of condemnation proceedings published in a local newspaper was an inadequate means of informing a landowner whose name was known to the city and was on the official records. Similarly, in Schroeder v. City of New York, 371 U.S. 208, 83 S.Ct. 279, 9 L.Ed.2d 255 (1962), the Court concluded that publication in a newspaper and posted notices were inadequate to apprise a property owner of condemnation proceedings when his name and address were readily ascertainable from both deed records and tax rolls. Most recently, in Greene v. Lindsey, 456 U.S. 444, 102 S.Ct. 1874, 72 L.Ed.2d 249 (1982), we held that posting a summons on the door of a tenant's apartment was an inadequate means of providing notice of forcible entry and detainer actions. See also Memphis Light, Gas & Water Div. v. Craft, 436 U.S. 1, 13–15, 98 S.Ct. 1554, 1562–1563, 56 L.Ed.2d 30 (1978); Eisen v. Carlisle & Jacquelin, 417 U.S. 156, 174–175, 94 S.Ct. 2140, 2150–2151, 40 L.Ed.2d 732 (1974); Bank of Marin v. England, 385 U.S. 99, 102, 87 S.Ct. 274, 276, 17 L.Ed.2d 197 (1966); Covey v. Town of Somers, 351 U.S. 141, 146–147, 76 S.Ct. 724, 727, 100 L.Ed. 1021 (1956); City of New York v. New York, N.H. & H.R. Co., 344 U.S. 293, 296–297, 73 S.Ct. 299, 301, 97 L.Ed. 333 (1953).

This case is controlled by the analysis in *Mullane*. To begin with, a mortgagee possesses a substantial property interest that is significantly affected by a tax sale. Under Indiana law, a mortgagee acquires a lien on the owner's property which may be conveyed together with the mortgagor's personal obligation to repay the debt secured by the mortgage. Ind. Code § 32–8–11–7 (1982). A mortgagee's security interest generally has priority over subsequent claims or liens attaching to the property, and a purchase money mortgage takes precedence over virtually all other claims or liens including those which antedate the execution of the mortgage. § 32–8–11–4. The tax sale immediately and drastically diminishes the value of this security interest by granting the tax-sale purchaser a lien with priority over that of all other creditors. Ultimately, the tax sale may result in the complete nullification of the mortgagee's interest, since the purchaser acquires title free of all liens and other encumbrances at the conclusion of the redemption period.

Since a mortgagee clearly has a legally protected property interest, he is entitled to notice reasonably calculated to apprise him of a pending tax sale. Cf. Wiswall v. Sampson, 14 How. 52, 67, 14 L.Ed. 322 (1853). When the mortgagee is identified in a mortgage that is publicly recorded, constructive notice by publication must be supplemented by notice mailed to the mortgagee's last known available address, or by personal service. But unless the mortgagee is not reasonably identifiable, constructive notice alone does not satisfy the mandate of *Mullane*.[4]

4. In this case, the mortgage on file with the county recorder identified the mortgagee only as "MENNONITE BOARD OF MISSIONS a corporation, of Wayne County, in the State of Ohio." We assume that the mortgagee's address could have been ascertained by reasonably diligent efforts. See Mullane and Central Hanover Bank & Trust

Neither notice by publication and posting, nor mailed notice to the property owner, are means "such as one desirous of actually informing the [mortgagee] might reasonably adopt to accomplish it." *Mullane,* supra, 339 U.S., at 315, 70 S.Ct., at 657. Because they are designed primarily to attract prospective purchasers to the tax sale, publication and posting are unlikely to reach those who, although they have an interest in the property, do not make special efforts to keep abreast of such notices. * * * Notice to the property owner, who is not in privity with his creditor and who has failed to take steps necessary to preserve his own property interest, also cannot be expected to lead to actual notice to the mortgagee. Cf. Nelson v. New York City, 352 U.S. 103, 107–109, 77 S.Ct. 195, 197–199, 1 L.Ed.2d 171 (1956). The county's use of these less reliable forms of notice is not reasonable where, as here, "an inexpensive and efficient mechanism such as mail service is available." Greene v. Lindsey, supra, 456 U.S., at 455, 102 S.Ct., at 1881.

Personal service or mailed notice is required even though sophisticated creditors have means at their disposal to discover whether property taxes have not been paid and whether tax sale proceedings are therefore likely to be initiated. In the first place, a mortgage need not involve a complex commercial transaction among knowledgeable parties, and it may well be the least sophisticated creditor whose security interest is threatened by a tax sale. More importantly, a party's ability to take steps to safeguard its interests does not relieve the State of its constitutional obligation. It is true that particularly extensive efforts to provide notice may often be required when the State is aware of a party's inexperience or incompetence. See, e.g., Memphis Light, Gas & Water Div. v. Craft, supra, 436 U.S., at 13–15, 98 S.Ct., at 1562–1564; Covey v. Somers, supra. But it does not follow that the State may forego even the relatively modest administrative burden of providing notice by mail to parties who are particularly resourceful. Cf. New York v. New York, N.H. & H.R. Co., supra, 344 U.S., at 297, 73 S.Ct., at 301. Notice by mail or other means as certain to ensure actual notice is a minimum constitutional precondition to a proceeding which will adversely affect the liberty or property interests of *any* party, whether unlettered or well versed in commercial practice, if its name and address are reasonably ascertainable. Furthermore, a mortgagee's knowledge of delinquency in the payment of taxes is not equivalent to notice that a tax sale is pending. * * *

JUSTICE O'CONNOR, with whom JUSTICE POWELL and JUSTICE REHNQUIST join, dissenting.

* * *

Co., 339 U.S. 306, 317, 70 S.Ct. 652, 658–659, 94 L.Ed. 865 (1950). Simply mailing a letter to "Mennonite Board of Missions, Wayne County, Ohio," quite likely would have provided actual notice, given "the well-known skill of postal officials and employees in making proper delivery of letters defectively addressed." Grannis v. Ordean, 234 U.S. 385, 397–398, 34 S.Ct. 779, 784, 58 L.Ed. 1363 (1914). We do not suggest, however, that a governmental body is required to undertake extraordinary efforts to discover the identity and whereabouts of a mortgagee whose identity is not in the public record.

* * * Whether a particular method of notice is reasonable depends on the outcome of the balance between the "interest of the State" and "the individual interest sought to be protected by the Fourteenth Amendment." [*Mullane*], at 314, 70 S.Ct., at 657. Of course, "[i]t is not our responsibility to prescribe the form of service that the [State] . . . should adopt." *Greene, supra,* 456 U.S., at 455, n. 9, 102 S.Ct., at 1880, n. 9. It is the primary responsibility of the State to strike this balance, and we will upset this process only when the State strikes the balance in an irrational manner.

* * *

* * * Without knowing what state and individual interests will be at stake in future cases, the Court espouses a general principle ostensibly applicable whenever any legally protected property interest may be adversely affected. This is a flat rejection of the view that no "formula" can be devised that adequately evaluates the constitutionality of a procedure created by a State to provide notice in a certain class of cases. Despite the fact that *Mullane* itself accepted that constructive notice satisfied the dictates of due process in certain circumstances, the Court, citing *Mullane,* now holds that constructive notice can never suffice whenever there is a legally protected property interest at stake.

* * *

The Court also holds that the condition for receiving notice under its new approach is that the name and address of the party must be "reasonably ascertainable." In applying this requirement to the mortgagee in this case, the Court holds that the State must exercise "reasonably diligent efforts" in determining the address of the mortgagee * * * and suggests that the State is required to make some effort "to discover the identity and the whereabouts of a mortgagee whose identity is not in the public record." * * * Again, the Court departs from our prior cases. In *all* of the cases relied on by the Court in its analysis, the State either actually knew the identity or incapacity of the party seeking notice, or that identity was "very easily ascertainable." *Schroeder, supra,* 371 U.S., at 212–213, 83 S.Ct., at 282. * * * Under the Court's decision today, it is not clear how far the State must go in providing for reasonable efforts to ascertain the name and address of an affected party. * * *

It cannot be doubted that the State has a vital interest in the collection of its tax revenues in whatever reasonable manner that it chooses * * *.

Chief Justice Marshall wrote long ago that "it is part of common prudence for all those who have any interest in [property], to guard that interest by persons who are in a situation to protect it." The Mary, 13 U.S. (9 Cranch) 126, 144, 3 L.Ed. 678 (1815). * * *

* * * Unlike condemnation or an unexpected accounting, the assessment of taxes occurs with regularity and predictability, and the state action in this case cannot reasonably be characterized as unexpected in any sense. Unlike the parties in our other cases, the

Mennonite Board had a regular event, the assessment of taxes, upon which to focus, in its effort to protect its interest. Further, approximately 95% of the mortgage debt outstanding in the United States is held by private institutional lenders and federally-supported agencies. U.S. Dept. of Commerce, Statistical Abstract of the United States: 1982–83, p. 511 (103d ed.). It is highly unlikely, if likely at all, that a significant number of mortgagees are unaware of the consequences that ensue when their mortgagors fail to pay taxes assessed on the mortgaged property. Indeed, in this case, the Board itself required that Moore pay all property taxes.

There is no doubt that the Board could have safeguarded its interest with a minimum amount of effort. The county auctions of property commence by statute on the second Monday of each year. Ind.Code § 6–1.1–24–2(5). The county auditor is required to post notice in the county courthouse at least three weeks before the date of sale. § 6–1.1–24–3(a). The auditor is also required to publish notice in two different newspapers once each week for three weeks before the sale. §§ 6–1.1–24–3(a), 6–1.1–22–4(b). The Board could have supplemented the protection offered by the State with the additional measures suggested by the court below: The Board could have required that Moore provide it with copies of paid tax assessments, or could have required that Moore deposit the tax monies in an escrow account, or could have itself checked the public records to determine whether the tax assessment had been paid. Ind.App., 427 N.E.2d 686, 690, n. 9 (1981).

When a party is unreasonable in failing to protect its interest despite its ability to do so, due process does not require that the State save the party from its own lack of care. The balance required by *Mullane* clearly weighs in favor of finding that the Indiana statutes satisfied the requirements of due process. Accordingly, I dissent.

SCHIAVONE v. FORTUNE

Supreme Court of the United States, 1986.
477 U.S. 21, 106 S.Ct. 2379, 91 L.Ed.2d 18.*

JUSTICE BLACKMUN delivered the opinion of the Court.

* * *

The three petitioners instituted this diversity litigation on May 9, 1983, by filing their respective complaints in the United States District Court for the District of New Jersey. Each complaint alleged that the plaintiff was libeled in a cover story entitled "The Charges Against Reagan's Labor Secretary," which appeared in the May 31, 1982, issue of Fortune magazine. The caption of each complaint named "Fortune," without embellishment, as the defendant. See App. 8a. In its paragraph 2, each complaint described Fortune as "a foreign corporation having its principal offices at Time and Life Building, Sixth Avenue and 50th Street, New York, New York 10020." Id., at 9a. "Fortune,"

---

* Some of the Court's footnotes are omitted.

however, is only a trademark and the name of an internal division of Time, Incorporated (Time), a New York corporation.

On May 20, petitioners' counsel mailed the complaints to Time's registered agent in New Jersey. They were received on May 23. The agent refused service because Time was not named as a defendant.

On July 18, 1983, each petitioner amended his complaint to name as the captioned defendant "Fortune, also known as Time, Incorporated," and, in the body of the complaint, to refer to "Fortune, also known as Time, Incorporated," as a New York corporation with a specified registered New Jersey agent. See App. 25a, 26a. The amended complaints were served on Time by certified mail on July 21.

Time moved to dismiss the amended complaints. The District Court granted those motions. Id., at 96a, 98a, 100a. * * * Under New Jersey law, * * * see N.J.Stat.Ann. 2A:14–3 (West 1952), a libel action must be commenced within one year of the publication of the alleged libel. Supp.App. to Pet. for Cert. 18a. State law also provides that the " 'date upon which a substantial distribution occurs triggers the statute of limitations for any and all actions arising out of that publication,' " id., at 19a, quoting MacDonald v. Time, Inc., Civil No. 81–479 (DNJ Aug. 25, 1981). Supp.App. to Pet. for Cert. 19a.[4] The court found it unnecessary, for purposes of the motion, to determine the precise date the statute of limitations had begun to run.

Although Time acknowledged that the original filings were within the limitations period, it took the position that it could not be named as a party after the period had expired. Time contended that a party must be substituted within the limitations period in order for the amendment to relate back to the original filing date pursuant to Rule 15(c).[5]

* * *

A

The defendant named in the caption of each of the original complaints was "Fortune," and Fortune was described in the body of the

---

4. The court noted that, despite the magazine's cover date of May 31, 1982, the record "indicate[d]" that, for purposes of determining the limitations period, publication "occurred substantially before" May 31; that subscription copies were mailed May 12 and received by subscribers May 13–19; that newsstand copies went on sale May 17; that a press release was issued May 11; and that copies of the magazine were mailed to representatives of the press on that date. Supp.App. to Pet. for Cert. 19a.

5. Rule 15(c) provides in pertinent part:

"Whenever the claim or defense asserted in the amended pleading arose out of the conduct, transaction, or occur-

rence set forth or attempted to be set forth in the original pleading, the amendment relates back to the date of the original pleading. An amendment changing the party against whom a claim is asserted relates back if the foregoing provision is satisfied and, within the period provided by law for commencing the action against him, the party to be brought in by amendment (1) has received such notice of the institution of the action that he will not be prejudiced in maintaining his defense on the merits, and (2) knew or should have known that, but for a mistake concerning the identity of the proper party, the action would have been brought against him."

complaint as "a foreign corporation" having principal offices in the Time and Life Building in New York City. It also was alleged that Fortune was engaged in the publication of a magazine of that name. Attached to the complaint were a copy of the magazine's cover for its issue of May 31, 1982, an artist's depiction of an alleged payoff, and the text of parts of the article about which petitioners complained. The focus, as pleaded, was on Fortune.

We cannot understand why, in litigation of this asserted magnitude, Time was not named specifically as the defendant in the caption and in the body of each complaint. This was not a situation where the ascertainment of the defendant's identity was difficult for the plaintiffs. An examination of the magazine's masthead clearly would have revealed the corporate entity responsible for the publication.[6]

Petitioners nonetheless rely on Fortune's status as a division of Time to argue that institution of an action purportedly against the former constituted notice of the action to the latter, as a related entity. Some Courts of Appeals have recognized an "identity-of-interest" exception under which an amendment that substitutes a party in a complaint after the limitations period has expired will relate back to the date of the filing of the original complaint.[7] The Court of Appeals in this case rejected that approach. The object of the exception is to avoid the application of the statute of limitations when no prejudice would result to the party sought to be added.

Even if we were to adopt the identity-of-interest exception, and even if Fortune properly could be named as a defendant, we would be compelled to reject petitioners' contention that the facts of this case fall within the exception. Timely filing of a complaint, and notice within the limitations period to the party named in the complaint, permits imputation of notice to a subsequently named and sufficiently related party. In this case, however, neither Fortune nor Time received notice of the filing after the period of limitations had run. Thus, there was no proper notice to Fortune that could be imputed to Time. See Hernandez Jimenez v. Calero Toledo, 604 F.2d 99, 102–103 (CA1 1979); Norton v. International Harvester Co., 627 F.2d 18, 20–21 (CA7 1980).

---

6. The magazine's very issue in question, that of May 31, 1982, p. 2, recites:

"FORTUNE (ISSN 0015–8259), May 31, 1982, Vol. 105, No. 11. Issued biweekly by Time Inc., 3435 Wilshire Blvd., Los Angeles, Cal. 90010. . . . Principal offices: Time & Life Building, Rockefeller Center, New York, N.Y. 10020. . . . FORTUNE is a registered mark of Time Incorporated."

The parallel information set forth in current issues of Fortune magazine reads:

"FORTUNE (ISSN 0015–8259). Published biweekly, with three issues in October, by Time Inc., 10880 Wilshire Blvd., Los Angeles, CA 90024–4193. Time Inc., principal office: Time & Life Building, Rockefeller Center, New York, NY 10020–1393. . . . FORTUNE is a registered mark of Time Inc."

See issue of June 9, 1986, p. 2; issue of May 26, 1986, p. 4; issue of May 12, 1986, p. 4.

7. See, e.g., Travelers Indemnity Co. v. United States, ex rel. Construction Specialties Co., 382 F.2d 103 (CA10 1967); Montalvo v. Tower Life Building, 426 F.2d 1135 (CA5 1970); Korn v. Royal Carribean Cruise Line, Inc., 724 F.2d 1397 (CA9 1984).

B

The complaints as they were amended, of course, meet the identification standard. While the statement, "Fortune, also known as Time, Incorporated, was and is a corporation of the state of New York," is not a model of accuracy, it does focus on Time and sufficiently describes Time as the targeted defendant. The next question, then, is whether the amendment, made in July 1983, related back to the filing on May 9, a date concededly within the period of the applicable New Jersey statute of limitations.

Central to the resolution of this issue is the language of Rule 15(c). See n. 5, supra. Relation back is dependent upon four factors, all of which must be satisfied: (1) the basic claim must have arisen out of the conduct set forth in the original pleading; (2) the party to be brought in must have received such notice that it will not be prejudiced in maintaining its defense; (3) that party must or should have known that, but for a mistake concerning identity, the action would have been brought against it; and (4) the second and third requirements must have been fulfilled within the prescribed limitations period. We are not concerned here with the first factor, but we are concerned with the satisfaction of the remaining three.

The first intimation that Time had of the institution and maintenance of the three suits took place after May 19, 1983, the date the Court of Appeals said the statute ran "at the latest." 750 F.2d, at 16. Only on May 20 did petitioners' counsel mail the complaints to Time's registered agent in New Jersey. Only on May 23 were those complaints received by the registered agent, and then refused. Only on July 19 did each petitioner amend his complaint. And only on July 21 were the amended complaints served on Time.

It seems to us inevitably to follow that notice to Time and the necessary knowledge did not come into being "within the period provided by law for commencing the action against" Time, as is so clearly required by Rule 15(c). That occurred only after the expiration of the applicable 1–year period. This is fatal, then, to petitioners' litigation.

We do not have before us a choice between a "liberal" approach toward Rule 15(c), on the one hand, and a "technical" interpretation of the Rule, on the other hand. The choice, instead, is between recognizing or ignoring what the Rule provides in plain language. We accept the Rule as meaning what it says.

We are not inclined, either, to temper the plain meaning of the language by engrafting upon it an extension of the limitations period equal to the asserted reasonable time, inferred from Rule 4, for the service of a timely filed complaint. Rule 4 deals only with process. Rule 3 concerns the "commencement" of a civil action. Under Rule 15(c), the emphasis is upon "the period provided by law for commencing the action against" the defendant. An action is commenced by the filing of a complaint and, so far as Time is concerned, no complaint against it was filed on or prior to May 19, 1983.

Any possible doubt about this should have been dispelled 20 years ago by the Advisory Committee's 1966 Note about Rule 15(c). The Note specifically states that the Rule's phrase "within the period provided by law for commencing the action" means "within the applicable limitations period":

> "An amendment changing the party against whom a claim is asserted relates back if the amendment satisfies the usual condition of Rule 15(c) of 'arising out of the conduct . . . set forth . . . in the original pleading,' and if, *within the applicable limitations period,* the party brought in by amendment, first, received such notice of the institution of the action—the notice need not be formal—that he would not be prejudiced in defending the action, and, second, knew or should have known that the action would have been brought against him initially had there not been a mistake concerning the identity of the proper party" (emphasis supplied). Advisory Committee's Notes on Fed.Rule Civ.Proc. 15, 28 U.S.C.App., p. 551; 39 F.R.D. 83.

Although the Advisory Committee's comments do not foreclose judicial consideration of the Rule's validity and meaning, the construction given by the Committee is "of weight." Mississippi Publishing Corp. v. Murphree, 326 U.S. 438, 444, 66 S.Ct. 242, 245, 90 L.Ed. 185 (1946).

The commentators have accepted the literal meaning of the significant phrase in Rule 15(c) and have agreed with the Advisory Committee's Note. See 3 J. Moore, Federal Practice, § 15.15[4.–2], p. 15–225 (2nd ed. 1985) ("the Rule demands a showing that, within the period of limitations, the new party. . . ."); 6 C. Wright & A. Miller, Federal Practice and Procedure § 1498, p. 250 (Supp.1986) ("in order for an amendment adding a party to relate back under Rule 15(c) the party to be added must have received notice of the action before the statute of limitations has run").

The linchpin is notice, and notice within the limitations period. Of course, there is an element of arbitrariness here, but that is a characteristic of any limitations period. And it is an arbitrariness imposed by the legislature and not by the judicial process. See Note, Federal Rule of Civil Procedure 15(c): Relation Back of Amendments, 57 Minn.L.Rev. 83, 85, n. 8 (1972).

      *   *   *

JUSTICE STEVENS, with whom THE CHIEF JUSTICE and JUSTICE WHITE join, dissenting.

      *   *   *

According to the majority, petitioners' complaints are barred because they did not satisfy a four-pronged test articulated in Rule 15(c). *   *   * The majority ignores, however, a rather critical antecedent point. The four-pronged test is utterly irrelevant unless the amendment is one "changing the party against whom a claim is asserted." In this case, the technical correction filed in July added absolutely nothing to any party's understanding of "the party against whom" the claims were asserted—not to the plaintiffs' understanding, of course, and certainly not to Time, Incorporated's understanding, as its agent's letter in May made clear.

The plain language of Rule 15(c) discloses an obvious purpose to protect parties who are not named in the original complaint from prejudice that may arise when they are subsequently "brought in by amendment." If an original complaint names Smith as the tortfeasor and the plaintiff does not decide to sue Jones until after the statute of limitations has run, there would be obvious prejudice in allowing "an amendment changing the party against whom a claim is asserted" unless Jones had actual notice of the claim before the statute ran. There is also a risk of prejudice whenever the identification of the defendant is so inaccurate or ambiguous that a reading of the complaint itself would not enable the defendant himself to realize that he was the party being sued.

The misdescription in this case, however, is not remotely of the kind that the Rule's "plain language" addresses. By any standard of fair notice, the difference between the description of the publisher of Fortune in the original complaints and the description of the publisher of Fortune in the amended complaints is no more significant than a misspelling, or perhaps a reference to "Time, Inc." instead of "Time, Incorporated."

In short, I would not construe this amendment as one "changing the party" against whom petitioner's claim is asserted. Although the words "Time, Incorporated" were first added to the complaints by the amendment, that entity cannot, in my judgment, fairly be described as a party "brought in by amendment" within the meaning of Rule 15(c).

* * *

The heart of the majority's analysis is that petitioners failed to satisfy the fourth factor of the test it discerns in Rule 15(c)—that "the second and third requirements must have been fulfilled within the prescribed limitations period." * * * The majority thus finds petitioners' "fatal" mistake in the failure to amend within the statute of limitations period.

The language in the Rule imposing the deadline for amendments that relate back does not, however, refer to the statute of limitations. Rather, it describes "the period provided by law for commencing the action *against him* " (emphasis added). As I have noted, that period includes two components, the time for commencing the action by the filing of a complaint and the time in which the action "against him" must be implemented by the service of process. If the party is sufficiently described in the original complaint to avoid any possibility of prejudice to the defendant, I see no reason for not construing the Rule to embrace both components of the period provided by law for bringing a timely action against a particular defendant.

This construction is confirmed by a reference to the content of the notice requirement—what the majority labels the second prong of the four-part test. * * * The Rule requires that the party affected by the amendment must have "received such notice of the institution of the action that he will not be prejudiced in maintaining his defense on the merits." This language surely indicates that if the notice that the defendant actually receives is just as timely and just as informative as that which would have been received if no mistake had occurred, the purpose of the requirement has been satisfied. In this case, Time, Incorporated would have known nothing different on May 23, 1983, if the complaints sent to its agent referred to "Fortune, also known as Time Incorporated" than it knew from the complaints as sent, with their reference to "Fortune." Respondent has not even contended otherwise. Yet, for the Court, the first complaints would have been completely timely, and the second are completely barred.

* * *

NOTE ON THE SUMMONS AND OTHER FORMS OF SERVICE

1. Form and Service of the Summons

Notice in civil actions conventionally is given by service of summons. The protocol in making service in most jurisdictions is to exhibit the original of the summons to the person served and simultaneously hand him a copy thereof together with a copy of the complaint. Thereafter, the form for proof of service (which is typically printed on the summons itself) is filled out, executed, and filed with the court by the person making the service. For the form of summons used in the federal courts, see F.R.C.P. Appendix of Forms, Form 1. For the California form, see Calif.Rules of Court, Rule 982. See also Abbott and Medina, A Proposal to Revise the Forms of California Summons, 33 Hastings L.J. 313 (1981). In some states, civil process is ordinarily served by the sheriff or a deputy; in many states, including California and New York, private process-serving organizations customarily are employed to do so. In federal court, a United States marshall formerly was required to serve the summons and complaint. F.R.C.P. 4(c)(2)(A) now provides that they may be served by "any person who is not a party and is not less than 18 years of age," except in a limited number of situations specified in F.R.C.P. 4(c)(2)(B) and (C). All process other than summonses and complaints must still be served by a marshall, his deputy, or a person specially appointed by the court. F.R.C.P. 4(c)(1).

a. Personal Service. Under common law, process had to be served by physical delivery of the summons to the defendant. Delivery to the defendant's home or to someone on his behalf was regarded as insufficient.

b. Service Other Than Personal Service. Statutes and rules now typically provide for a variety of means of service other than personal service, as defined above. "Substituted" service usually refers to delivery of process to someone at defendant's place of abode or delivery by mail. See, e.g., C.C.P. 415.20 and C.C.P. 415.30; Note, Service of Process by Mail, 74 Mich.L.Rev. 381 (1975); Anno., 91 A.L.R.3d 827. F.R.C.P. 4 provides that service of process may be made by mail in most circumstances and requires the person served to complete and return within 20 days an acknowledgment of receipt under oath on forms provided, or to pay the costs of personal service. F.R.C.P. 4(c)(2)(C), (D) and (E).

See also Mullenix, The New Federal Express: Mail Service of Process Under Amended Rule 4, 4 Rev. of Litigation 299 (1985). This method of service, however, does not provide a default judgment sanction if the person served refuses to complete the acknowledgment. Hence, its use can be a procedural trap when the statute of limitations looms, as it often does. See Sinclair, Service of Process: Rethinking the Theory and Procedure of Serving Process Under Federal Rule 4(c), 73 Va.L.Rev. 1183 (1987).

Service by "publication" means service effected by publishing the summons in a newspaper. See C.C.P. 415.50. Most statutes require that publication be supplemented by mailing a copy of the summons and complaint to defendant's last known address. It is now clear that this much additional effort to give actual notice is constitutionally required. The old cases discussing service by publication frequently were silent on the question whether there was a mailing in addition to publication.

"Constructive" service means service by publication or by posting summons in a designated place. A classic place is the local courthouse. This method of notice is typical in actions seeking to notify and bar all potential claimants to a fund, such as a decedent's estate. However, the statutes often permit this device in situations not involving such necessity to notify unknown claimants. The statutes in Greene v. Lindsey and Mennonite Bd. of Missions v. Adams are examples. As these cases show, if diligent efforts are not made to personally serve a known (or reasonably ascertainable) defendant, or to otherwise ensure actual notice, the service is subject to constitutional attack. See also Tulsa Professional Collection Services, Inc. v. Pope, ___ U.S. ___, 108 S.Ct. 1340, 99 L.Ed.2d 565 (1988), holding that due process requires actual mail notice, rather than mere publication notice, to "known or reasonably ascertainable" creditors of an estate, advising them that the statute governing the period for filing claims has started to run. The Court distinguished such statutes from the normal "self-executing" statutes of limitations, which do not require notice of the impending expiration of the period.

At times, all of the aforementioned types of service are referred to without differentiation as "substituted" or "constructive" service.

c. Procedure for Service by Publication. The mechanics of service by publication are provided by statute and traditionally must be strictly followed. A modern statutory scheme is C.C.P. 415.50. The sequence there provided is the filing of the complaint and issuance of summons by the clerk; the filing of an affidavit stating the facts which show the case to come within one of the statutory classes of cases in which service by publication is proper; issuance of the court's order; publication of the summons; and the filing of affidavits establishing the fact of publication and mailing. If the party's address becomes known before the expiration of the time prescribed for publication, the summons and complaint must be mailed to her.

d. Time Limits for Service. In federal court service of the summons and complaint on the defendant must be made within 120 days after the complaint is filed, failing which the action is subject to dismissal without prejudice. F.R. C.P. 4(j). Compare C.C.P. 583.210, providing a three-year period for service and mandating dismissal if service is not made within that time, and C.C.P. 583.310, further mandating dismissal if the action is not brought to trial within five years from the date of filing. See also Johnson & Johnson v. Superior Court, 38 Cal.3d 243, 211 Cal.Rptr. 517, 695 P.2d 1058 (1985) (substituted mail service under C.C.P. 415.40 on foreign corporation is effected on date of mailing, not on date of receipt by defendant, for purposes of satisfying three-year time limit on serving process).

e. *Service on Corporations*. Service of process on a corporation is necessarily made upon an agent of the corporation. See F.R.C.P. 4(d)(3), which also applies to service on partnerships and associations. Strict compliance is usually required. See, e.g., Gottlieb v. Sandia American Corp., 452 F.2d 510 (3d Cir. 1971) (construing the requirement of F.R.C.P. 4(d)(3) that service be made on "an officer" or a "managing or general agent"). See also Anno., 17 A.L.R.3d 625.

f. *Process–Servers*. The ingenuity and determination of process-servers and evaders of process apparently knows no bounds. See, e.g., International Controls Corp. v. Vesco, 593 F.2d 166 (2d Cir.1979); Wyman v. Newhouse, 93 F.2d 313 (2d Cir.1937); Nowell v. Nowell, 24 Conn.Supp. 314, 190 A.2d 233 (1963); F.I. duPont, Glore Forgan & Co. v. Chen, 41 N.Y.2d 794, 396 N.Y.S.2d 343, 364 N.E.2d 1115 (1977), on remand 58 A.D.2d 789, 396 N.Y.S.2d 660 (1977). See also C.C.P. 1033.5, allowing recovery of reasonable costs of summoning where a registered process-server is employed.

2. Return

The process-server's endorsement on the reverse side of the original summons, showing proof of service, is the "return." The facts recited in the return are prima facie true, but their falsity, if proved, is a basis for setting aside a default judgment. In New York City, and possibly elsewhere, falsified service— "sewer service"—has been a common practice. See Tuerkheimer, Service of Process in New York City: A Proposed End to Unregulated Criminality, 72 Colum.L.Rev. 847 (1972). In many jurisdictions, to set aside service and a default judgment defendant also had to make a showing that he had a meritorious defense. In Peralta v. Heights Medical Center, Inc., ___ U.S. ___, 108 S.Ct. 896, 99 L.Ed.2d 75 (1988), the Supreme Court held that it was a denial of due process to require such a showing.

3. Persons Entitled to Notice

The general principle is that due process requires notice to a person before her rights may be determined in court. The problem is how far this principle should reach, given that even the most simple case often has externality effects on persons far removed from the core litigation. In Mennonite Bd. of Missions v. Adams, supra, the Court held that failure to provide adequate notice to the mortgagee violated due process because the mortgagee had a "substantial property interest" that was "significantly affected" by the tax sale. This seems reasonable enough, as far as it goes, but how should other, more attenuated property interests be handled? Compare Tulsa Professional Collection Services, Inc. v. Pope, discussed supra. What about other kinds of interests? In Lehr v. Robertson, 463 U.S. 248, 103 S.Ct. 2985, 77 L.Ed.2d 614 (1983), the Court held that an unwed father was not entitled to notice of a pending adoption proceeding where he had failed to establish any substantial parental relationship with the child and had not taken advantage of a statutory procedure for receiving notice. The Court stated that neither the court nor a litigant is required to give notice to nonparties "who are presumptively capable of asserting and protecting their own rights." Was the father's interest in the fate of his child any more attenuated than the mortgagee's interest in the property in *Mennonite Board*? Was the mortgagee any less capable of protecting its rights? Or is the point that the father had a statutory avenue available that would have ensured notice, while the mortgagee did not?

4. Notice and the Statute of Limitations

In most jurisdictions, the service of summons or other notice serves a function beyond that of giving notice. It also is the event by which an action is commenced for purposes of the statute of limitations. See Walker v. Armco Steel Corp., infra p. 597. The question therefore arises whether the service of summons in particular circumstances is sufficiently regular to toll the running of the statute.

If plaintiff mistakenly brings an action against a person who was not in fact the wrongdoer and the action goes to judgment, the judgment is valid, for it is up to the defendant to assert his defense and avoid a default judgment. More typically, such an error by the plaintiff will be discovered at some point prior to trial and the "wrong" defendant will be dismissed out of the action. If the statute of limitations has not run, plaintiff may amend his complaint and serve process on the "true" defendant. The difficulty arises if the statute of limitations has run at this point. If it has run, plaintiff cannot maintain the action against the new defendant unless saved by the "misnomer" or "fictitious name" devices described below. Thus, if plaintiff is struck down by a hit-and-run driver, it will avail him nothing to sue some other motorist.

In the more common case, however, plaintiff has some basis on which to identify the wrongdoer and undertakes to make service on that person or organization but does not correctly give the name of the party he is attempting to serve. This brings into play the misnomer doctrine and the fictitious name statutes.

a. Misnomer. If plaintiff sues a natural person and serves summons on the person who in fact committed the wrong, the courts typically allow a corrective amendment after the statute of limitations has run, regardless of the breadth of discrepancy between defendant's true name and the name given by plaintiff, because the "real" defendant has received timely notice, even if under a wrong name.

When the plaintiff sues a corporation, partnership, or other organization, the courts have more difficulty, as demonstrated by Schiavone v. Fortune. Traditionally the issue is framed in terms of whether, on the one hand, the "true" entity defendant has been a party all along, although identified by the wrong name (in which case an amendment will cure the "mere misnomer"), or, on the other hand, some entity other than the "true" defendant has been a party and plaintiff now proposes to "add a new party" by amendment. Was this the fundamental issue dividing the majority and dissenters in Schiavone v. Fortune? An organization legally treated as an entity is not in material fact an entity at all, but a legal idea. Precisely speaking, therefore, it is fatuous to ask whether the "true" organizational defendant is in court. All that should be asked is whether there is a person who is a representative of a legal construct entitled "X organization," and whether that person had notice of the suit within the applicable period.

F.R.C.P. 15(c) was adopted in an attempt to eliminate such conceptual difficulties. On the basis of *Schiavone,* do you think it succeeded? See Brussack, Outrageous Fortune: The Case for Amending Rule 15(c) Again, 61 So. Calif.L.Rev. 671 (1988), where the author proposes amending the rule to require notice "within the period provided by law for service of the original pleading" rather than requiring service within the limitations period for filing the complaint. See also Lewis, The Excessive History of Federal Rule 15(c) and Its Lessons for Civil Rules Revision, 85 Mich.L.Rev. 1507 (1987). In Hafferman v. Westinghouse Elec. Corp., 653 F.Supp. 423 (D.D.C.1986), *Schiavone* was held not controlling where defendant was responsible for the confusion over defendant's identity.

In the background of the Court's opinion in *Schiavone* is another problem, namely, whether the Federal Rules or state law should be applied in determining when an action has been commenced and in determining the applicable period for service of process for purposes of the statute of limitations in a diversity action. Compare Hanna v. Plumer, infra p. 586, with Walker v. Armco Steel Corp., infra p. 597. See also Lindley v. General Electric Co., discussed below.

A more run-of-the-mill application of Rule 15(c) is exemplified by Varlack v. SWC Caribbean, Inc., 550 F.2d 171 (3d Cir.1977). There it was held that a person could be added as a defendant after the statute of limitations had run where he knew that he had been identified as the co-defendant's "unknown employee" charged with the wrongful death in question, and had seen a copy of the complaint. Cf. Cory v. Crocker Nat. Bank, 123 Cal.App.3d 665, 177 Cal. Rptr. 150 (1981), sustaining the validity of process even though the summons omitted the corporate defendant's name, where the documents adequately indicated the identity of the party served.

On Rule 15(c), see also Amendment and the Statute of Limitations, supra p. 130.

  b. "John Doe" Defendants. Many jurisdictions have provisions allowing a plaintiff to sue a person described but not named in the complaint and, upon discovering the true name of the person sued, to amend the complaint to state her real name. See C.C.P. 474; N.Y.C.P.L.R. § 1024. In most states this simply paves the way for the later amendment allowed by rules such as F.R. C.P. 15(c).

In California, however, the statute has become a device by which a plaintiff can hedge against the possibility that, as his action progresses, it will appear that there is a more attractive person to sue than the person against whom the action was originally commenced. This use of the "John Doe" device appears to be unique to California and stems from two peculiarities of California procedural law. In the first place, in California the plaintiff is not required, as he is in most states with fictitious name statutes, to describe the fictitious defendant with such particularity as to indicate that plaintiff truly supposes there to be such a person. This anticipation would not be effective, however, were it not for another peculiarity of California law, namely, the rules by which it is determined when an action is commenced for purposes of the statute of limitations. In most jurisdictions, an action is deemed commenced for limitations purposes by service of process on a particular defendant either within a specified time or as soon as possible in the exercise of reasonable diligence. In California, by contrast, the action is deemed commenced by the filing of the complaint, see C.C.P. 350, subject only to the rather liberal requirement that, as described above, process be issued and service made within three years of the filing of the action and that return of service be made within 60 days thereafter. See C.C.P. 583.210. Accordingly, a plaintiff may serve process on the Doe defendant at any time within three years after the action is filed without concern that dilatory service will result in the action being barred by the statute of limitations.

Illustrating the effect of these provisions is Barrington v. A.H. Robins Co., 39 Cal.3d 146, 216 Cal.Rptr. 405, 702 P.2d 563 (1985): Plaintiff filed suit against a doctor, a drug manufacturer, and certain fictitious defendants for alleged medical malpractice and negligent failure to warn of the dangers of taking a drug. Plaintiff subsequently substituted A.H. Robins Co. for one of the fictitious defendants and, at a later date, filed an amended complaint adding a new cause of action against Robins only. Service and return of summons were made within three years of filing the amended complaint, but not within three years of filing the original complaint. It was held that, for purposes of complying with C.C.P. 583.210, a complaint which is amended to charge a fictitious defendant with a new cause of action arising from different operative facts is effective so long as summons is served within three years of the date on which the amended complaint was filed. See also Hogan, California's Unique Doe Defendant Practice, 30 Stan.L.Rev. 51 (1977). Compare McIntire v. Superior Court, 52 Cal.App.3d 717, 125 Cal.Rptr. 379 (1975) (amendment not permitted after action against other parties had gone to judgment).

Designation of John Doe defendants is disfavored in federal court but is permissible where the true identity is not known at the time of filing. Use of discovery to determine the actual name is permitted. See Gillespie v. Civiletti, 629 F.2d 637 (9th Cir.1980); Munz v. Parr, 758 F.2d 1254 (8th Cir.1985). The subsequent amendment to the complaint is not subject to bar by the statute of limitations if actual notice has prevented prejudice to the real defendant. See Swartz v. Gold Dust Casino, Inc., 91 F.R.D. 543 (D.Nev.1981). Diversity actions have posed the problem of determining the citizenship of a Doe defendant for purposes of the "complete diversity" requirement. As to this requirement, see Introductory Note on Jurisdiction of the Federal Courts, infra p. 523. The Judicial Improvements and Access to Justice Act of 1988 solved this problem by providing that, at least in an action removed from state to federal court, "the citizenship of defendants sued under fictitious names shall be disregarded." California's Doe defendant rules have been held effectively to extend the length of the statute of limitations period for purposes of applying F.R.C.P. 15(c), as where a Doe defendant is served after the applicable statute of limitations has run but within three years of the commencement of the action. Lindley v. General Electric Co., 780 F.2d 797 (9th Cir.1986), cert. denied, 476 U.S. 1186, 106 S.Ct. 2926, 91 L.Ed.2d 554 (1986). Is this consistent with *Schiavone*? With Hanna v. Plumer, infra p. 586, and Walker v. Armco Steel Corp., infra p. 597?

5. Adequacy of Notice

Whether notice is provided through personal service or by other means, it must reasonably inform the defendant of the pending matter. See Restatement Second of Judgments § 2; compare Memphis Light, Gas & Water Div. v. Craft, 436 U.S. 1, 98 S.Ct. 1554, 56 L.Ed.2d 30 (1978). F.R.C.P. 4(d) requires that the complaint be served along with the summons, thus giving notice of the claim asserted. Compare C.C.P. 415.10 et seq.; N.Y.C.P.L.R. 305(b). See also Aversano v. Town of Brookhaven, 77 A.D.2d 641, 430 N.Y.S.2d 133 (2d Dept.1980), construing the New York statute where defendant responded after having been served with summons alone.

Notice, to be adequate, must inform the defendant when he must appear and warn him that, in default of appearance, judgment may be entered against him. Should notice also inform the defendant of how to defend the action?

That was the conclusion reached in Aguchak v. Montgomery Ward Co., Inc., 520 P.2d 1352 (Alaska 1974), where the court, construing the due process clause of the Alaska Constitution (identical to the language in the United States Constitution), held that summons must inform a defendant that he may respond by mail. The court seemed moved by the fact that defendants in the instant case were a poor couple living in the bush, had been sued in a distant forum, and had failed to appear because they could not afford the trip to the court. The court, citing *Mullane,* held the summons inadequate because it was not "reasonably calculated to afford [them] an opportunity to be heard at a meaningful time and in a meaningful manner." In the absence of a meaningful commitment to aiding the poor in obtaining legal services, do decisions like this do more than provide "symbolic justice"? Or do they merely add further expense to a system which already prices many of the poor out of the legal system?

6. Formal Defects in Notice

Apart from problems connected with the tolling of the statute of limitations, under modern decisions irregularities in the form and mode of giving notice do not affect its effectiveness. See Restatement Second of Judgments § 3. But see, e.g., Feinstein v. Bergner, 48 N.Y.2d 234, 422 N.Y.S.2d 356, 397 N.E.2d 1161 (1979), where plaintiff mailed process to defendant and also affixed it to his former residence—so-called "nail and mail" service—after unsuccessful attempts to serve process personally. The process was held ineffective because it had not been affixed to defendant's present residence, even though the mailed copy was received.

7. Waiver of Notice

Contracts sometimes provide that one of the parties (the dominant one) may bring an action and obtain a judgment without notice to the other. When the contract is a promissory note to pay money, it is called a cognovit ("he has confessed") note. Such waivers are now valid only if knowingly made. See D.H. Overmyer Co., Inc. v. Frick Co., 405 U.S. 174, 92 S.Ct. 775, 31 L.Ed.2d 124 (1972); Note, Cognovit Revisited: Due Process and Confession of Judgment, 24 Hastings L.J. 1045 (1973). This requirement is often so strictly construed as to render the waiver provisions practically ineffective. See Isbell v. County of Sonoma, 21 Cal.3d 61, 145 Cal.Rptr. 368, 577 P.2d 188 (1978); Restatement Second of Judgments § 2, Comment i.

C. CHOICE OF LAW

ALLSTATE INSURANCE CO. v. HAGUE

Supreme Court of the United States, 1981.
449 U.S. 302, 101 S.Ct. 633, 66 L.Ed.2d 521.*

JUSTICE BRENNAN announced the judgment of the Court and delivered an opinion in which JUSTICE WHITE, JUSTICE MARSHALL, and JUSTICE BLACKMUN joined.

This Court granted certiorari to determine whether the Due Process Clause of the Fourteenth Amendment [1] or the Full Faith and

---

* Some of the Court's footnotes are omitted.

1. The Due Process Clause of the Fourteenth Amendment provides that no State

Credit Clause of Art. IV, § 1,[2] of the United States Constitution bars the Minnesota Supreme Court's choice of substantive Minnesota law to govern the effect of a provision in an insurance policy issued to respondent's decedent. 444 U.S. 1070, 100 S.Ct. 1012, 62 L.Ed.2d 750 (1980).

I

Respondent's late husband, Ralph Hague, died of injuries suffered when a motorcycle on which he was a passenger was struck from behind by an automobile. The accident occurred in Pierce County, Wis., which is immediately across the Minnesota border from Red Wing, Minn. The operators of both vehicles were Wisconsin residents, as was the decedent who, at the time of the accident, resided with respondent in Hager City, Wis., which is one and one-half miles from Red Wing. Mr. Hague had been employed in Red Wing for the 15 years immediately preceding his death and had commuted daily from Wisconsin to his place of employment.

Neither the operator of the motorcycle nor the operator of the automobile carried valid insurance. However, the decedent held a policy issued by petitioner Allstate Insurance Co. covering three automobiles owned by him and containing an uninsured motorist clause insuring him against loss incurred from accidents with uninsured motorists. The uninsured motorist coverage was limited to $15,000 for each automobile.[3]

After the accident, but prior to the initiation of this lawsuit, respondent moved to Red Wing. Subsequently, she married a Minnesota resident and established residence with her new husband in Savage, Minn. At approximately the same time, a Minnesota Registrar of Probate appointed respondent personal representative of her deceased husband's estate. Following her appointment, she brought this action in Minnesota District Court seeking a declaration under Minnesota law that the $15,000 uninsured motorist coverage on each of her late husband's three automobiles could be "stacked" to provide total coverage of $45,000. Petitioner defended on the ground that whether the three uninsured motorist coverages could be stacked should be determined by Wisconsin law, since the insurance policy was delivered in Wisconsin, the accident occurred in Wisconsin, and all persons involved were Wisconsin residents at the time of the accident.

The Minnesota District Court disagreed. Interpreting Wisconsin law to disallow stacking, the court concluded that Minnesota's choice-of-

unfriendly/hostile

P.C.

law rules required the application of Minnesota law permitting stacking. The court refused to apply Wisconsin law as "inimical to the public policy of Minnesota" and granted summary judgment for respondent.[4]

The Minnesota Supreme Court, sitting en banc, affirmed the District Court.[5] The court, also interpreting Wisconsin law to prohibit stacking,[6] applied Minnesota law after analyzing the relevant Minnesota contacts and interests within the analytical framework developed by Professor Leflar.[7] See Leflar, Choice-Influencing Considerations in Conflicts Law, 41 N.Y.U.L.Rev. 267 (1966). The state court, therefore, examined the conflict-of-laws issue in terms of (1) predictability of result, (2) maintenance of interstate order, (3) simplification of the judicial task, (4) advancement of the forum's governmental interests, and (5) application of the better rule of law. Although stating that the Minnesota contacts might not be, "in themselves, sufficient to mandate application of [Minnesota] law,"[8] 289 N.W.2d 43, 49 (1978), under the first four factors, the court concluded that the fifth factor—application of the better rule of law—favored selection of Minnesota law. The court emphasized that a majority of States allow stacking and that legal decisions allowing stacking "are fairly recent and well considered in light of current uses of automobiles." Id., at 49. In addition, the court found the Minnesota rule superior to Wisconsin's "because it requires the cost of accidents with uninsured motorists to be spread more broadly through insurance premiums than does the Wisconsin rule." Ibid. Finally, after rehearing en banc,[9] the court buttressed its initial opinion by indicating "that contracts of insurance on motor vehicles are in a class by themselves" since an insurance company "knows the automobile is a movable item which will be driven from state to state." 289 N.W.2d 49, 50 (1979). From this premise the court concluded that application of Minnesota law was "not so arbitrary and unreasonable as to violate due process." Ibid.

MN Sct

II

It is not for this Court to say whether the choice-of-law analysis suggested by Professor Leflar is to be preferred or whether we would make the same choice-of-law decision if sitting as the Minnesota Supreme Court. Our sole function is to determine whether the Minnesota Supreme Court's choice of its own substantive law in this case exceeded

4. App. C to Pet. for Cert. A–29.

5. 289 N.W.2d 43 (1978).

6. Respondent has suggested that this case presents a "false conflict." The court below rejected this contention and applied Minnesota law. Even though the Minnesota Supreme Court's choice of Minnesota law followed a discussion of whether this case presents a false conflict, the fact is that the court chose to apply Minnesota law. Thus, the only question before this

Court is whether that choice was constitutional.

7. Minnesota had previously adopted the conceptual model developed by Professor Leflar in Milkovich v. Saari, 295 Minn. 155, 203 N.W.2d 408 (1973).

8. The court apparently was referring to sufficiency as a matter of choice-of-law and not as a matter of constitutional limitation on its choice-of-law decision.

9. 289 N.W.2d, at 50 (1979).

federal constitutional limitations. Implicit in this inquiry is the recognition, long accepted by this Court, that a set of facts giving rise to a lawsuit, or a particular issue within a lawsuit, may justify, in constitutional terms, application of the law of more than one jurisdiction. See, e.g., Watson v. Employers Liability Assurance Corp., 348 U.S. 66, 72–73, 75 S.Ct. 166, 169–170, 99 L.Ed. 74 (1954); n. 11, infra. See generally Clay v. Sun Insurance Office, Ltd., 377 U.S. 179, 181–182, 84 S.Ct. 1197, 1198, 12 L.Ed. 229 (1964) (hereinafter cited as *Clay II*). As a result, the forum State may have to select one law from among the laws of several jurisdictions having some contact with the controversy.

In deciding constitutional choice-of-law questions, whether under the Due Process Clause or the Full Faith and Credit Clause,[10] this Court has traditionally examined the contacts of the State, whose law was applied, with the parties and with the occurrence or transaction giving rise to the litigation. See *Clay II*, supra, at 183, 84 S.Ct., at 1199. In order to ensure that the choice of law is neither arbitrary nor fundamentally unfair, see Alaska Packers Assn. v. Industrial Accident Commission, 294 U.S. 532, 542, 55 S.Ct. 518, 521, 79 L.Ed. 1044 (1935), the Court has invalidated the choice of law of a State which has had no significant contact or significant aggregation of contacts, creating state interests, with the parties and the occurrence or transaction.[11]

10. This Court has taken a similar approach in deciding choice-of-law cases under both the Due Process Clause and the Full Faith and Credit Clause. In each instance, the Court has examined the relevant contacts and resulting interests of the State whose law was applied. See, e.g., Nevada v. Hall, 440 U.S. 410, 424, 99 S.Ct. 1182, 1190, 59 L.Ed.2d 416 (1979). Although at one time the Court required a more exacting standard under the Full Faith and Credit Clause than under the Due Process Clause for evaluating the constitutionality of choice-of-law decisions, see Alaska Packers Assn. v. Industrial Accident Comm'n, 294 U.S. 532, 549–550, 55 S.Ct. 518, 524–525, 79 L.Ed. 1044 (1935) (interest of State whose law was applied was no less than interest of State whose law was rejected), the Court has since abandoned the weighing of interests requirement. Carroll v. Lanza, 349 U.S. 408 (1955); see Nevada v. Hall, supra; Weintraub, Due Process and Full Faith and Credit Limitations on a State's Choice of Law, 44 Iowa L.Rev. 449 (1959). Different considerations are of course at issue when full faith and credit is to be accorded to acts, records and proceedings outside the choice-of-law area, such as in the case of sister state court judgments.

11. Prior to the advent of interest analysis in the state courts as the "dominant mode of analysis in modern choice of law theory," Silberman, Shaffer v. Heitner:

The End of an Era, 53 N.Y.U.L.Rev. 33, 80, n. 259 (1978); cf. Richards v. United States, 369 U.S. 1, 11–13, and nn. 26–27, 82 S.Ct. 585, 591–593, 7 L.Ed.2d 492 (1962) (discussing trend toward interest analysis in state courts), the prevailing choice of law methodology focused on the jurisdiction where a particular event occurred. See, e.g., Restatement of the Law, Conflict of Laws (1934) (hereinafter cited as "Restatement First"). For example, in cases characterized as contract cases, the law of the place of contracting controlled the determination of such issues as capacity, fraud, consideration, duty, performance, and the like. Id., § 332; see Beale, What Law Governs the Validity of a Contract, 23 Harv.L.Rev. 260, 270–271 (1910). In the tort context, the law of the place of the wrong usually governed traditional choice-of-law analysis. Restatement First, supra, § 378; See Richards v. United States, supra, 369 U.S. at 11–12, 82 S.Ct., at 591–592.

Hartford Accident and Indemnity Co. v. Delta & Pine Land Co., 292 U.S. 143, 54 S.Ct. 634, 78 L.Ed. 1178 (1934), can, perhaps, best be explained as an example of that period. In that case, the Court struck down application by the Mississippi courts of Mississippi law which voided the limitations provision in a fidelity bond written in Tennessee between a Connecticut insurer and Delta, both of which were doing business in Tennessee and Mississippi. By its terms, the bond covered misapplication of

Two instructive examples of such invalidation are Home Ins. Co. v. Dick, 281 U.S. 397, 50 S.Ct. 338, 74 L.Ed. 926 (1930), and John Hancock Mutual Life Ins. Co. v. Yates, 299 U.S. 178, 57 S.Ct. 129, 81 L.Ed. 106 (1936). In both cases, the selection of forum law rested exclusively on the presence of one nonsignificant forum contact.

Home Ins. Co. v. Dick involved interpretation of an insurance policy which had been issued in Mexico, by a Mexican insurer, to a Mexican citizen, covering a Mexican risk. The policy was subsequently assigned to Mr. Dick, who was domiciled in Mexico and "physically present and acting in Mexico," 281 U.S., at 408, 50 S.Ct., at 341, although he remained a nominal, permanent resident of Texas. The policy restricted coverage to losses occurring in certain Mexican waters and, indeed the loss occurred in those waters. Dick brought suit in Texas against a New York reinsurer. Neither the Mexican insurer nor the New York reinsurer had any connection to Texas.[12] The Court held that application of Texas law to void the insurance contract's limitation-of-actions clause violated due process.[13]

The relationship of the forum State to the parties and the transaction was similarly attenuated in John Hancock Mutual Life Ins. Co. v. Yates. There, the insurer, a Massachusetts corporation, issued a contract of insurance on the life of a New York resident. The contract was applied for, issued and delivered in New York where the insured and his spouse resided. After the insured died in New York, his spouse moved to Georgia and brought suit on the policy in Georgia. Under Georgia law, the jury was permitted to take into account oral modifications when deciding whether an insurance policy application contained material misrepresentations. Under New York law, however, such misrepresentations were to be evaluated solely on the basis of the written application. The Georgia court applied Georgia law. This

funds "by any employee 'in any position, anywhere. . . .' " Id., at 145, 54 S.Ct., at 634. After Delta discovered defalcations by one of its Mississippi-based employees, a lawsuit was commenced in Mississippi.

That case, however, has scant relevance for today. It implied a choice-of-law analysis which, for all intents and purposes, gave an isolated event—the writing of the bond in Tennessee—controlling constitutional significance, even though there might have been contacts with another State (there Mississippi) which would make application of its law neither unfair nor unexpected. See Martin, Personal Jurisdiction and Choice of Law, 78 Mich.L.Rev. 872, 874, and n. 11 (1980).

12. Dick sought to obtain *quasi-in-rem* jurisdiction by garnishing the reinsurance obligation of the New York reinsurer. The reinsurer had never transacted business in Texas, but it "was cited by publication, in accordance with a Texas statute; attorneys were appointed for it by the trial court; and they filed on its behalf an answer which denied liability." Home Insurance Company v. Dick, 281 U.S. 397, 402, 50 S.Ct. 338, 339, 74 L.Ed. 926 (1930). There would be no jurisdiction in the Texas Courts to entertain such a lawsuit today. See Rush v. Savchuk, 444 U.S. 320, 100 S.Ct. 571, 62 L.Ed.2d 516 (1980); Shaffer v. Heitner, 433 U.S. 186, 97 S.Ct. 2569, 53 L.Ed.2d 683 (1977); Silberman, supra, 53 N.Y.U.L.Rev., at 62–65.

13. The Court noted that the result might have been different if there had been some connection to Texas upon "which the State could properly lay hold as the basis of the regulations there imposed." Home Insurance Co. v. Dick, supra, 281 U.S., at 408, n. 5, 50 S.Ct., at 341, n. 5; see Watson v. Employers Liability Corp,. supra, 348 U.S., at 71, 75 S.Ct., at 169.

Court reversed, finding application of Georgia law to be unconstitutional.

Dick and *Yates* stand for the proposition that if a State has only an insignificant contact with the parties and the occurrence or transaction, application of its law is unconstitutional.[14] *Dick* concluded that nominal residence—standing alone—was inadequate; *Yates* held that a postoccurrence change of residence to the forum State—standing alone—was insufficient to justify application of forum law. Although instructive as extreme examples of selection of forum law, neither *Dick* nor *Yates* governs this case. For in contrast to those decisions, here the Minnesota contacts with the parties and the occurrence are obviously significant. Thus, this case is like *Alaska Packers*, Cardillo v. Liberty Mutual Ins. Co., 330 U.S. 469, 67 S.Ct. 801, 91 L.Ed. 1028 (1947), and *Clay II*—cases where this Court sustained choice-of-law decisions based on the contacts of the State, whose law was applied, with the parties and occurrence.

In *Alaska Packers*, the Court upheld California's application of its Workmen's Compensation Act, where the most significant contact of the worker with California was his execution of an employment contract in California. The worker, a nonresident alien from Mexico, was hired in California for seasonal work in a salmon canning factory in Alaska. As part of the employment contract, the employer, who was doing business in California, agreed to transport the worker to Alaska and to return him to California when the work was completed. Even though the employee contracted to be bound by the Alaska Workmen's Compensation Law and was injured in Alaska, he sought an award under the California Workmen's Compensation Act. The Court held that the choice of California law was not "so arbitrary or unreasonable as to amount to a denial of due process," 294 U.S., at 542, because "[w]ithout a remedy in California, [he] would be remediless," ibid., and because of California's interest that the worker not become a public charge, ibid.

In Cardillo v. Liberty Mutual Ins. Co., supra, a District of Columbia resident, employed by a District of Columbia employer and assigned by the employer for the three years prior to his death to work in Virginia, was killed in an automobile crash in Virginia in the course of his daily commute home from work. The Court found the District's contacts with the parties and the occurrence sufficient to satisfy constitutional requirements, based on the employee's residence in the District, his commute between home and the Virginia workplace, and his status as an employee of a company "engaged in electrical construction work in the District of Columbia and surrounding areas." Id., at 471, 67 S.Ct., at 803.

Similarly, *Clay II* upheld the constitutionality of the application of forum law. There, a policy of insurance had issued in Illinois to an

14. See generally, Weintraub, supra, note 10, at 455–457.

Illinois resident. Subsequently the insured moved to Florida and suffered a property loss in Florida. Relying explicitly on the nation-wide coverage of the policy and the presence of the insurance company in Florida and implicitly on the plaintiff's Florida residence and the occurrence of the property loss in Florida, the Court sustained the Florida court's choice of Florida law.

The lesson from *Dick* and *Yates*, which found insufficient forum contacts to apply forum law, and from *Alaska Packers, Cardillo*, and *Clay II*, which found adequate contacts to sustain the choice of forum law, is that for a State's substantive law to be selected in a constitutionally permissible manner, that State must have a significant contact or significant aggregation of contacts, creating state interests, such that choice of its law is neither arbitrary nor fundamentally unfair. Application of this principle to the facts of this case persuades us that the Minnesota Supreme Court's choice of its own law did not offend the Federal Constitution.

III

Minnesota has three contacts with the parties and the occurrence giving rise to the litigation. In the aggregate, these contacts permit selection by the Minnesota Supreme Court of Minnesota law allowing the stacking of Mr. Hague's uninsured motorist coverages.

First, and for our purposes a very important contact, Mr. Hague was a member of Minnesota's workforce, having been employed by a Red Wing, Minn., enterprise for the 15 years preceding his death. While employment status may implicate a state interest less substantial than does resident status, that interest is nevertheless important. The State of employment has police power responsibilities towards the nonresident employee that are analogous, if somewhat less profound, than towards residents. Thus, such employees use state services and amenities and may call upon state facilities in appropriate circumstances.

In addition, Mr. Hague commuted to work in Minnesota, a contact which was important in Cardillo v. Liberty Mutual Ins. Co., supra, 330 U.S., at 475–476, 67 S.Ct., at 805–806 (daily commute between residence in District of Columbia and workplace in Virginia), and was presumably covered by his uninsured motorist coverage during the commute. The State's interest in its commuting nonresident employees reflects a state concern for the safety and well-being of its workforce and the concomitant effect on Minnesota employers.

That Mr. Hague was not killed while commuting to work or while in Minnesota does not dictate a different result. To hold that the Minnesota Supreme Court's choice of Minnesota law violated the Constitution for that reason would require too narrow a view of Minnesota's relationship with the parties and the occurrence giving rise to the litigation. An automobile accident need not occur within a particular jurisdiction for that jurisdiction to be connected to the occurrence.

Similarly, the occurrence of a crash fatal to a Minnesota employee in another State is a Minnesota contact. If Mr. Hague had only been injured and missed work for a few weeks the effect on the Minnesota employer would have been palpable and Minnesota's interest in having its employee made whole would be evident. Mr. Hague's death affects Minnesota's interest still more acutely, even though Mr. Hague will not return to the Minnesota work force. Minnesota's work force is surely affected by the level of protection the State extends to it, either directly or indirectly. Vindication of the rights of the estate of a Minnesota employee, therefore, is an important state concern.

Mr. Hague's residence in Wisconsin does not—as Allstate seems to argue—constitutionally mandate application of Wisconsin law to the exclusion of forum law.[21] If, in the instant case, the accident had occurred in Minnesota between Mr. Hague and an uninsured Minnesota motorist, if the insurance contract had been executed in Minnesota covering a Minnesota registered company automobile which Mr. Hague was permitted to drive, and if a Wisconsin court sought to apply Wisconsin law, certainly Mr. Hague's residence in Wisconsin, his commute between Wisconsin and Minnesota, and the insurer's presence in Wisconsin should be adequate to apply Wisconsin's law.[22] See general-

21. Petitioner's statement that the instant dispute involves the interpretation of insurance contracts which were "underwritten, applied for, and paid for by Wisconsin residents and issued covering cars garaged in Wisconsin," Brief for Petitioner 6, is simply another way of stating that Mr. Hague was a Wisconsin resident. Respondent could have replied that the insurance contract was underwritten, applied for and paid for by a Minnesota worker and issued covering cars that were driven to work in Minnesota and garaged there for a substantial portion of the day. The former statement is hardly more significant than the latter since the accident in any event did not involve any of the automobiles which were covered under Mr. Hague's policy. Recovery is sought pursuant to the uninsured motorist coverage.

In addition, petitioner's statement that the contracts were "underwritten . . . by Wisconsin residents" is not supported by the stipulated facts if petitioner means to include Allstate within that phrase. Indeed, the policy, which is part of the record, recites that Allstate signed the policy in Northbrook, Ill. Under some versions of the hoary rule of *lex loci contractus*, and depending on the precise sequence of events, a sequence which is unclear from the record before us, the law of Illinois arguably might apply to govern contract construction, even though Illinois would have less contact with the parties and the occurrence than either Wisconsin or Min-

nesota. No party sought application of Illinois law on that basis in the court below.

22. Of course Allstate could not be certain that Wisconsin law would necessarily govern any accident which occurred in Wisconsin, whether brought in the Wisconsin courts or elsewhere. Such an expectation would give controlling significance to the wooden *lex loci delicti* doctrine. While the place of the accident is a factor to be considered in choice-of-law analysis, to apply blindly the traditional, but now largely abandoned, doctrine, Silberman, supra, note 11, at 80, n. 259; see n. 11, supra, would fail to distinguish between the relative importance of various legal issues involved in a lawsuit as well as the relationship of other jurisdictions to the parties and the occurrence or transaction. If, for example, Mr. Hague had been a Wisconsin resident and employee who was injured in Wisconsin and was then taken by ambulance to a hospital in Red Wing, Minn., where he languished for several weeks before dying, Minnesota's interest in ensuring that its medical creditors were paid would be obvious. Moreover, under such circumstances, the accident itself might be reasonably characterized as a bi-state occurrence beginning in Wisconsin and ending in Minnesota. Thus, reliance by the insurer that Wisconsin law would necessarily govern any accident that occurred in Wisconsin, or that the law of another jurisdiction would necessarily govern any acci-

ly Cardillo v. Liberty Mutual Ins. Co., supra; Alaska Packers Assn. v. Industrial Accident Commission, supra; Home Insurance Company v. Dick, 281 U.S., at 408, n. 5, 50 S.Ct., at 341. Employment status is not a sufficiently less important status than residence, see generally Carroll v. Lanza, 349 U.S. 408, 75 S.Ct. 804, 99 L.Ed. 1183 (1955); Alaska Packers Assn. v. Industrial Accident Commission, supra, when combined with Mr. Hague's daily commute across state lines and the other Minnesota contacts present, to prohibit the choice-of-law result in this case on constitutional grounds.

Second, Allstate was at all times present and doing business in Minnesota.[23] By virtue of its presence, Allstate can hardly claim unfamiliarity with the laws of the host jurisdiction and surprise that the state courts might apply forum law to litigation in which the company is involved. "Particularly since the company was licensed to do business in [the forum], it must have known it might be sued there, and that [the forum] courts would feel bound by [forum] law." [24] Clay

dent that did not occur in Wisconsin, would be unwarranted. See n. 11, supra, cf. Rosenthal v. Warren, 475 F.2d 438 (CA2), cert. denied, 414 U.S. 856, 94 S.Ct. 159, 38 L.Ed.2d 106 (1973) (Massachusetts hospital could not have purchased insurance with expectation that Massachusetts law would govern damage recovery as to New York patient who died in hospital and whose widow brought suit in New York).

If the law of a jurisdiction other than Wisconsin did govern, there was a substantial likelihood, with respect to uninsured motorist coverage, that stacking would be allowed. Stacking was the rule in most States at the time the policy was issued. Indeed, the Wisconsin Supreme Court, in Nelson v. Employers Mutual Casualty Co., 63 Wis.2d 558, 563–566, and nn. 2–3, 217 N.W.2d 670, 672–674, and nn. 2–3 (1974), identified 29 States, including Minnesota, whose law it interpreted to allow stacking, and only 9 States whose law it interpreted to prohibit stacking. Clearly then, Allstate could not have expected that an anti-stacking rule would govern any particular accident in which the insured might be involved and thus cannot claim unfair surprise from the Minnesota Supreme Court's choice of forum law.

23. The court has recognized that examination of a State's contacts may result in divergent conclusions for jurisdiction and choice-of-law purposes. See Kulko v. Superior Court, 436 U.S. 84, 98, 98 S.Ct. 1690, 1700, 56 L.Ed.2d 132 (1978) (no jurisdiction in California but California law "arguably might" apply); Shaffer v. Heitner, supra, 433 U.S., at 215, 97 S.Ct., at 2585 (no jurisdiction in Delaware, although Delaware interest "may support the appli-

cation of Delaware law"); cf. Hanson v. Denckla, 357 U.S. 235, 254, and n. 27, 78 S.Ct. 1228, 1240, n.27, 2 L.Ed.2d 1283 (1958) (no jurisdiction in Florida; the "issue is personal jurisdiction, not choice of law," an issue which the Court found no need to decide). Nevertheless, "both inquiries 'are often closely related and to a substantial degree depend upon similar considerations.'" Shaffer, 433 U.S., at 224–225, 97 S.Ct., at 2590 (Brennan, J., concurring in part and dissenting in part). Here, of course, jurisdiction in the Minnesota courts is unquestioned, a factor not without significance in assessing the constitutionality of Minnesota's choice of its own substantive law. Cf. id., at 225, 97 S.Ct., at 2590 ("the decision that it is fair to bind a defendant by a State's laws and rules should prove to be highly relevant to the fairness of permitting that same State to accept jurisdiction for adjudicating the controversy").

24. There is no element of unfair surprise or frustration of legitimate expectations as a result of Minnesota's choice of its law. Because Allstate was doing business in Minnesota and was undoubtedly aware that Mr. Hague was a Minnesota employee, it had to have anticipated that Minnesota law might apply to an accident in which Mr. Hague was involved. See Clay II, supra, 377 U.S., at 182, 84 S.Ct., at 1198; Watson v. Employers Liability Assurance Corp., supra, 348 U.S., at 72–73, 75 S.Ct., at 169; Alaska Packers Assn. v. Industrial Accident Commission, supra, 294 U.S., at 538–543, 55 S.Ct., at 519–522; cf. Home Insurance Co. v. Dick, supra, 281 U.S., at 404, 50 S.Ct., at 340 (neither insurer nor reinsurer present in forum State). Indeed,

v. Sun Insurance Office Ltd., 363 U.S. 207, 221, 80 S.Ct. 1222, 1230, 4 L.Ed.2d 1170 (1960) (Black, J., dissenting).[25] Moreover, Allstate's presence in Minnesota gave Minnesota an interest in regulating the company's insurance obligations insofar as they affected both a Minnesota resident and court appointed representative—respondent—and a longstanding member of Minnesota's workforce—Mr. Hague. See Hoopeston Canning Co. v. Cullen, 318 U.S. 313, 316, 63 S.Ct. 602, 604, 87 L.Ed. 777 (1943).

Third, respondent became a Minnesota resident prior to institution of this litigation. The stipulated facts reveal that she first settled in Red Wing, Minn., the town in which her late husband had worked.[26] She subsequently moved to Savage, Minn., after marrying a Minnesota resident who operated an automobile service station in Bloomington, Minn. Her move to Savage occurred "almost concurrently," 289 N.W.2d, at 45, with the initiation of the instant case.[27] There is no suggestion that Mrs. Hague moved to Minnesota in anticipation of this litigation or for the purpose of finding a legal climate especially hospitable to her claim.[28] The stipulated facts, sparse as they are, negate any such inference.

While John Hancock Mutual Life Ins. Co. v. Yates, supra, held that a postoccurrence change of residence to the forum State was insufficient in and of itself to confer power on the forum State to choose its law, that case did not hold that such a change of residence was irrelevant. Here, of course, respondent's bona fide residence in Minnesota was not the sole contact Minnesota had with this litigation. And in connection with her residence in Minnesota, respondent was appointed personal representative of Mr. Hague's estate by the Registrar of Probate for the County of Goodhue, Minn. Respondent's residence and subsequent appointment in Minnesota as personal representative of her late husband's estate constitute a Minnesota contact which gives Minnesota an interest in respondent's recovery, an interest which the court below identified as full compensation for "resident accident vic-

---

Allstate specifically anticipated that Mr. Hague might suffer an accident either in Minnesota or elsewhere in the United States, outside of Wisconsin, since the policy it issued offered continental coverage. Cf. id., at 403, 50 S.Ct., at 339 (coverage limited to losses occurring in certain Mexican waters which were outside of jurisdiction whose law was applied). At the same time, Allstate did not seek to control construction of the contract since the policy contained no choice-of-law clause dictating application of Wisconsin law. See *Clay II*, supra, 377 U.S., at 182, 84 S.Ct., at 1198 (nationwide coverage of policy and lack of choice-of-law clause).

25. Justice Black's dissent in the first *Clay* decision, a decision which vacated and remanded a lower court determination to obtain an authoritative construction of

state law that might moot the constitutional question, subsequently commanded majority support in the second *Clay* decision. *Clay II*, supra, 377 U.S., at 180–183, 84 S.Ct., at 1197–1199.

26. The stipulated facts do not reveal the date on which Mrs. Hague first moved to Red Wing.

27. These proceedings began on May 28, 1976. Mrs. Hague was remarried on June 19, 1976.

28. The dissent suggests that considering respondent's postoccurrence change of residence as one of the Minnesota contacts will encourage forum shopping. * * * This overlooks the fact that her change of residence was bona fide and not motivated by litigation considerations.

tims" to keep them "off welfare rolls" and able "to meet financial obligations." 289 N.W.2d, at 49.

In sum, Minnesota had a significant aggregation [29] of contacts with the parties and the occurrence, creating state interests, such that application of its law was neither arbitrary nor fundamentally unfair. Accordingly, the choice of Minnesota law by the Minnesota Supreme Court did not violate the Due Process Clause or the Full Faith and Credit Clause.

Affirmed.

JUSTICE STEWART took no part in the consideration or decision of this case.

JUSTICE STEVENS, concurring in the judgment.

As I view this unusual case—in which neither precedent nor constitutional language provides sure guidance—two separate questions must be answered. First, does the Full Faith and Credit Clause [1] *require* Minnesota, the forum State, to apply Wisconsin law? Second, does the Due Process Clause [2] of the Fourteenth Amendment *prevent* Minnesota from applying its own law? The first inquiry implicates the federal interest in ensuring that Minnesota respect the sovereignty of the State of Wisconsin; the second implicates the litigants' interests in a fair adjudication of their rights. [3]

29. We express no view whether the first two contacts, either together or separately, would have sufficed to sustain the choice of Minnesota law made by the Minnesota Supreme Court.

1. Article IV, § 1 provides:

"Full Faith and Credit shall be given in each State to the public Acts, Records, and Judicial Proceedings of every other State. And the Congress may by general Laws prescribe the Manner in which such Acts, Records and Proceedings shall be proved, and the Effect thereof."

2. Section 1 of the Fourteenth Amendment provides, in part:

"No State shall . . . deprive any person of life, liberty, or property, without due process of law. . . ."

3. The two questions presented by the choice-of-law issue arise only after it is assumed or established that the defendant's contacts with the forum State are sufficient to support personal jurisdiction. Although the choice-of-law concerns—respect for another sovereign and fairness to the litigants—are similar to the two functions performed by the jurisdictional inquiry, they are not identical. In World-Wide Volkswagen Corp. v. Woodson, 444 U.S. 286, 291–292, 100 S.Ct. 559, 564, 62 L.Ed.2d 490 (1980), we stated:

"The concept of minimum contacts, in turn, can be seen to perform two related, but distinguishable, functions. It protects the defendant against the burdens of litigating in a distant or inconvenient forum. And it acts to ensure that the States, through their courts, do not reach out beyond the limits imposed on them by their status as coequal sovereigns in a federal system."

See also Reese, Legislative Jurisdiction, 78 Colum.L.Rev. 1587, 1589–1590 (1978). While it has been suggested that this same minimum contacts analysis be used to define the constitutional limitations on choice-of-law, see e.g., Martin, Personal Jurisdiction and Choice of Law, 78 Mich.L. Rev. 872 (1980), the Court has made it clear over the years that the personal jurisdiction and choice-of-law inquiries are not the same. See Kulko v. California Superior Court, 436 U.S. 84, 98, 98 S.Ct. 1690, 1700, 56 L.Ed.2d 132 (1978); Shaffer v. Heitner, 433 U.S. 186, 215, 97 S.Ct. 2569, 2585, 53 L.Ed.2d 683 (1977); id., 433 U.S., at 224–226, 97 S.Ct., at 2590–2591 (Brennan, J., dissenting in part); Hanson v. Denckla, 357 U.S. 235, 253–254, 78 S.Ct. 1228, 1239, 2 L.Ed.2d 1283 (1958); id., 357 U.S. at 258, 78 S.Ct. at 1241 (Black, J., dissenting).

I realize that both this Court's analysis of choice-of-law questions [4] and scholarly criticism of those decisions [5] have treated these two inquiries as though they were indistinguishable. Nevertheless, I am persuaded that the two constitutional provisions protect different interests and that proper analysis requires separate consideration of each.

* * *

JUSTICE POWELL, with whom THE CHIEF JUSTICE and JUSTICE REHNQUIST join, dissenting.

My disagreement with the plurality is narrow. I accept with few reservations Part II of the plurality opinion, which sets forth the basic principles that guide us in reviewing state choice-of-law decisions under the Constitution. The Court should invalidate a forum State's decision to apply its own law only when there are no significant contacts between the State and the litigation. This modest check on state power is mandated by the Due Process Clause of the Fourteenth Amendment and the Full Faith and Credit Clause of Art. IV, § 1. I do not believe, however, that the plurality adequately analyzes the policies such review must serve. In consequence, it has found significant what appear to me to be trivial contacts between the forum State and the litigation.

* * *

First, the post-accident residence of the plaintiff-beneficiary is constitutionally irrelevant to the choice-of-law question. John Hancock Mut. Life Ins. Co. v. Yates, supra. * * *

* * *

Second, the plurality finds it significant that the insurer does business in the forum State. * * * The State does have a legitimate interest in regulating the practices of such an insurer. But this argument proves too much. The insurer here does business in all 50 States. The forum State has no interest in regulating that conduct of the insurer unrelated to property, persons or contracts executed within

---

4. Although the Court has struck down a state court's choice of forum law on both due process, see, e.g., Home Insurance Co. v. Dick, 281 U.S. 397, 50 S.Ct. 338, 74 L.Ed. 926 (1930), and full faith and credit grounds, see, e.g., John Hancock Insurance Co. v. Yates, 299 U.S. 178, 57 S.Ct. 129, 81 L.Ed. 106 (1936), no clear analytical distinction between the two constitutional provisions has emerged. The Full Faith and Credit Clause, of course, was inapplicable in *Home Insurance* because the law of a foreign nation, rather than of a sister State, was at issue; a similarly clear explanation for the Court's reliance upon the Full Faith and Credit Clause in *John Hancock Insurance* cannot be found. Indeed, *John Hancock Insurance* is probably best understood as a due process case. See Reese, supra, 78 Colum.L.Rev., at 1589, and n. 17; Weintraub, Due Process and Full Faith and Credit Limitations on a State's Choice of Law, 44 Iowa L.Rev. 449, 457–458 (1959).

5. See R. Leflar, American Conflicts Law § 5, at 7, § 55, at 106–107 (3d ed. 1977). The Court's frequent failure to distinguish between the two clauses in the choice-of-law context may underlie the suggestions of various commentators that either the Full Faith and Credit Clause or the Due Process Clause be recognized as the single appropriate source for constitutional limitations on choice of law. Compare Martin, Constitutional Limitations on Choice of Law, 61 Corn.L.Rev. 185 (1976) (Full Faith and Credit), with Reese, Legislative Jurisdiction, 78 Colum.L.Rev. 1587 (1978) (Due Process); see also Kirgis, The Roles of Due Process and Full Faith and Credit in Choice of Law, 62 Corn.L.Rev. 94 (1976).

the forum State. See Hoopeston Canning Co. v. Cullen, 318 U.S. 313, 319, 63 S.Ct. 602, 606, 87 L.Ed. 777 (1943). The Court recognizes this flaw and attempts to bolster the significance of the local presence of the insurer by combining it with the other factors deemed significant: the presence of the plaintiff and the fact that the deceased worked in the forum State. This merely restates the basic question in the case.

Third, the plurality emphasizes particularly that the insured worked in the forum State. * * * The fact that the insured was a nonresident employee in the forum State provides a significant contact for the furtherance of some local policies. See, e.g., Pacific Ins. Co. v. Industrial Accident Comm'n, supra (forum State's interest in compensating workers for employment related injuries occurring within the State); Alaska Packers Assn. v. Industrial Accident Comm'n, 294 U.S. 532, 549, 55 S.Ct. 518, 524, 79 L.Ed. 1044 (1935) (forum State's interest in compensating the employment-related injuries of a worker hired in the State). The insured's place of employment is not, however, significant in this case. Neither the nature of the insurance policy, the events related to the accident, nor the immediate question of stacking coverage are in any way affected or implicated by the insured's employment status. The plurality's opinion is understandably vague in explaining how trebling the benefits to be paid to the estate of a nonresident employee furthers any substantial state interest relating to employment. Minnesota does not wish its workers to die in automobile accidents, but permitting stacking will not further this interest. The substantive issue here is solely one of compensation, and whether the compensation provided by this policy is increased or not will have no relation to the State's employment policies or police power. * * *

PHILLIPS PETROLEUM CO. v. SHUTTS

Supreme Court of the United States, 1985.
472 U.S. 797, 105 S.Ct. 2965, 86 L.Ed.2d 628.*

JUSTICE REHNQUIST delivered the opinion of the Court.

Petitioner is a Delaware corporation which has its principal place of business in Oklahoma. During the 1970's it produced or purchased natural gas from leased land located in 11 different States, and sold most of the gas in interstate commerce. Respondents are some 28,000 of the royalty owners possessing rights to the leases from which petitioner produced the gas; they reside in all 50 States, the District of Columbia, and several foreign countries. Respondents brought a class action against petitioner in the Kansas state court, seeking to recover interest on royalty payments which had been delayed by petitioner. They recovered judgment in the trial court, and the Supreme Court of Kansas affirmed the judgment over petitioner's contentions that the Due Process Clause of the Fourteenth Amendment prevented Kansas from adjudicating the claims of all the respondents, and that the Due

* Some of the Court's footnotes are omitted.

Process Clause and the Full Faith and Credit Clause of Article IV of the Constitution prohibited the application of Kansas law to all of the transactions between petitioner and respondents. 235 Kan. 195, 679 P.2d 1159 (1984). * * * We reject petitioner's jurisdictional claim, but sustain its claim regarding the choice of law.

Because petitioner sold the gas to its customers in interstate commerce, it was required to secure approval for price increases from what was then the Federal Power Commission, and is now the Federal Energy Regulatory Commission. Under its regulations the Federal Power Commission permitted petitioner to propose and collect tentative higher gas prices, subject to final approval by the Commission. If the Commission eventually denied petitioner's proposed price increase or reduced the proposed increase, petitioner would have to refund to its customers the difference between the approved price and the higher price charged, plus interest at a rate set by statute. See 18 CFR § 154.102 (1984).

Although petitioner received higher gas prices pending review by the Commission, petitioner suspended any increase in royalties paid to the royalty owners because the higher price could be subject to recoupment by petitioner's customers. Petitioner agreed to pay the higher royalty only if the royalty owners would provide petitioner with a bond or indemnity for the increase, plus interest, in case the price increase was not ultimately approved and a refund was due to the customers. Petitioner set the interest rate on the indemnity agreements at the same interest rate the Commission would have required petitioner to refund to its customers. A small percentage of the royalty owners provided this indemnity and received royalties immediately from the interim price increases; these royalty owners are unimportant to this case.

The remaining royalty owners received no royalty on the unapproved portion of the prices until the Federal Power Commission approval of those prices became final. Royalties on the unapproved portion of the gas price were suspended three times by petitioner, corresponding to its three proposed price increases in the mid–1970's. In three written opinions the Commission approved all of petitioner's tentative price increases, so petitioner paid to its royalty owners the suspended royalties of $3.7 million in 1976, $4.7 million in 1977, and $2.9 million in 1978. Petitioner paid no interest to the royalty owners although it had the use of the suspended royalty money for a number of years.

Respondents Irl Shutts, Robert Anderson, and Betty Anderson filed suit against petitioner in Kansas state court, seeking interest payments on their suspended royalties which petitioner had possessed pending the Commission's approval of the price increases. Shutts is a resident of Kansas and the Andersons live in Oklahoma. Shutts and the Andersons own gas leases in Oklahoma and Texas. Over petitioner's objection the Kansas trial court granted respondents' motion to certify the suit as a class action under Kansas law. Kan.Stat.Ann. § 60–223 et seq. (1983). The class as certified was comprised of 33,000 royalty owners who had royalties suspended by petitioner. The average claim of each royalty owner for interest on the suspended royalties was $100.

After the class was certified respondents provided each class member with notice through first-class mail. The notice described the action and informed each class member that he could appear in person or by counsel; otherwise each member would be represented by Shutts and the Andersons, the named plaintiffs. The notices also stated that class members would be included in the class and bound by the judgment unless they "opted out" of the lawsuit by executing and returning a "request for exclusion" that was included with the notice. The final class as certified contained 28,100 members; 3,400 had "opted out" of the class by returning the request for exclusion, and notice could not be delivered to another 1,500 members, who were also excluded. Less than 1,000 of the class members resided in Kansas. Only a miniscule amount, approximately one quarter of one percent, of the gas leases involved in the lawsuit were on Kansas land.

After petitioner's mandamus petition to decertify the class was denied, Phillips Petroleum v. Duckworth, No. 82–54608 (Kan., June 28, 1982), cert. denied, 459 U.S. 1103, 103 S.Ct. 725, 74 L.Ed.2d 951 (1983) the case was tried to the court. The court found petitioner liable under Kansas law for interest on the suspended royalties to all class members. The trial court relied heavily on an earlier, unrelated class action involving the same nominal plaintiff and the same defendant, Shutts, Executor v. Phillips Petroleum Co., 222 Kan. 527, 567 P.2d 1292 (1977), cert. denied, 434 U.S. 1068, 98 S.Ct. 1246, 55 L.Ed.2d 769 (1978). The Kansas Supreme Court had held in *Shutts, Executor* that a gas company owed interest to royalty owners for royalties suspended pending final Commission approval of a price increase. No federal statutes touched on the liability for suspended royalties, and the court in *Shutts, Executor* held as a matter of Kansas equity law that the applicable interest rates for computation of interest on suspended royalties were the interest rates at which the gas company would have had to reimburse its customers had its interim price increase been rejected by the Commission. The court in *Shutts, Executor* viewed these as the fairest interest rates because they were also the rates that petitioner required the royalty owners to meet in their indemnity agreements in order to avoid suspended royalties.

The trial court in the present case applied the rule from *Shutts, Executor,* and held petitioner liable for prejudgment and postjudgment interest on the suspended royalties, computed at the Commission rates governing petitioner's three price increases. See 18 CFR § 154.102 (1984). The applicable interest rates were: 7% for royalties retained until October 1974; 9% for royalties retained between October 1974 and September 1979; and thereafter at the average prime rate. The trial court did not determine whether any difference existed between the laws of Kansas and other States, or whether another State's laws should be applied to non-Kansas plaintiffs or to royalties from leases in states other than Kansas. 235 Kan., at 221, 679 P.2d, at 1180.

Petitioner raised two principal claims in its appeal to the Supreme Court of Kansas. It first asserted that the Kansas trial court did not possess personal jurisdiction over absent plaintiff class members as required by International Shoe Co. v. Washington, 326 U.S. 310, 66 S.Ct. 154, 90 L.Ed. 95 (1945), and similar cases. Related to this first claim was petitioner's contention that the "opt-out" notice to absent class members, which forced them to return the request for exclusion in order to avoid the suit, was insufficient to bind class members who were not residents of Kansas or who did not possess "minimum contacts" with Kansas. Second, petitioner claimed that Kansas courts could not apply Kansas law to every claim in the dispute. The trial court should have looked to the laws of each State where the leases were located to determine, on the basis of conflict of laws principles, whether interest on the suspended royalties was recoverable, and at what rate.

The Supreme Court of Kansas held that the entire cause of action was maintainable under the Kansas class-action statute and the court rejected both of petitioner's claims. 235 Kan. 195, 679 P.2d 1159 (1984). First, it held that the absent class members were plaintiffs, not defendants, and thus the traditional minimum contacts test of *International Shoe* did not apply. The court held that nonresident class action plaintiffs were only entitled to adequate notice, an opportunity to be heard, an opportunity to opt out of the case, and adequate representation by the named plaintiffs. If these procedural due process minima were met, according to the court, Kansas could assert jurisdiction over the plaintiff class and bind each class member with a judgment on his claim. The court surveyed the course of the litigation and concluded that all of these minima had been met.

The court also rejected petitioner's contention that Kansas law could not be applied to plaintiffs and royalty arrangements having no connection with Kansas. The court stated that generally the law of the forum controlled all claims unless "compelling reasons" existed to apply a different law. The court found no compelling reasons, and noted that "[t]he plaintiff class members have indicated their desire to have this action determined under the laws of Kansas." 235 Kan., at 222, 679 P.2d, at 1181. The court affirmed as a matter of Kansas equity law the award of interest on the suspended royalties, at the rates imposed by the trial court. The court set the postjudgment interest rate on all claims at the Kansas statutory rate of 15%. Id., at 224, 679 P.2d, at 1183.

I

As a threshold matter we must determine whether petitioner has standing to assert the claim that Kansas did not possess proper jurisdiction over the many plaintiffs in the class who were not Kansas residents and had no connection to Kansas. Respondents claim that a party generally may assert only his own rights, and that petitioner has no standing to assert the rights of its adversary, the plaintiff class, in order to defeat the judgment in favor of the class.

Standing to sue in any Article III court is, of course, a federal question which does not depend on the party's prior standing in state court. * * * Generally stated, federal standing requires an allegation of a present or immediate injury in fact, where the party requesting standing has "alleged such a personal stake in the outcome of the controversy as to assure that concrete adverseness which sharpens the presentation of issues." * * * There must be some causal connection between the asserted injury and the challenged action, and the injury must be of the type "likely to be redressed by a favorable decision." * * *

Additional prudential limitations on standing may exist even though the Article III requirements are met because "the judiciary seeks to avoid deciding questions of broad social import where no individual rights would be vindicated and to limit access to the federal courts to those litigants best suited to assert a particular claim." * * * One of these prudential limits on standing is that a litigant must normally assert his own legal interests rather than those of third parties. * * *

Respondents claim that petitioner is barred by the rule requiring that a party assert only his own rights; they point out that respondents and petitioner are adversaries and do not have allied interests such that petitioner would be a good proponent of class members' interests. They further urge that petitioner's interference is unneeded because the class members have had opportunity to complain about Kansas' assertion of jurisdiction over their claim, but none have done so. * * *

Respondents may be correct that petitioner does not possess standing *jus tertii,* but this is not the issue. Petitioner seeks to vindicate its own interests. As a class-action defendant petitioner is in a unique predicament. If Kansas does not possess jurisdiction over this plaintiff class, petitioner will be bound to 28,100 judgment holders scattered across the globe, but none of these will be bound by the Kansas decree. Petitioner could be subject to numerous later individual suits by these class members because a judgment issued without proper personal jurisdiction over an absent party is not entitled to full faith and credit elsewhere and thus has no res judicata effect as to that party. Whether it wins or loses on the merits, petitioner has a distinct and personal interest in seeing the entire plaintiff class bound by res judicata just as petitioner is bound. The only way a class action defendant like petitioner can assure itself of this binding effect of the judgment is to ascertain that the forum court has jurisdiction over every plaintiff whose claim it seeks to adjudicate, sufficient to support a defense of res judicata in a later suit for damages by class members.

While it is true that a court adjudicating a dispute may not be able to predetermine the res judicata effect of its own judgment, petitioner has alleged that it would be obviously and immediately injured if this class-action judgment against it became final without binding the plaintiff class. We think that such an injury is sufficient to give petitioner standing on its own right to raise the jurisdiction claim in this Court.

Petitioner's posture is somewhat similar to the trust settlor defendant in Hanson v. Denckla, 357 U.S. 235, 78 S.Ct. 1228, 2 L.Ed.2d 1283 (1958), who we found to have standing to challenge the forum's personal jurisdiction over an out-of-state trust company which was an indispensable party under the forum State's law. Because the court could not proceed with the action without jurisdiction over the trust company, we observed that, "any defendant affected by the court's judgment ha[d] that 'direct and substantial personal interest in the outcome' that is necessary to challenge whether that jurisdiction was in fact acquired." Id., at 245, 78 S.Ct., at 1235, quoting Chicago v. Atchison, T. & S.F.R. Co., 357 U.S. 77, 78 S.Ct. 1063, 2 L.Ed.2d 1174 (1958).

II

Reduced to its essentials, petitioner's argument is that unless out-of-state plaintiffs affirmatively consent, the Kansas courts may not exert jurisdiction over their claims. Petitioner claims that failure to execute and return the "request for exclusion" provided with the class notice cannot constitute consent of the out-of-state plaintiffs; thus Kansas courts may exercise jurisdiction over these plaintiffs only if the plaintiffs possess the sufficient "minimum contacts" with Kansas as that term is used in cases involving personal jurisdiction over out-of-state defendants. E.g., International Shoe Co. v. Washington, 326 U.S. 310, 66 S.Ct. 154, 90 L.Ed. 95 (1945); Shaffer v. Heitner, 433 U.S. 186, 97 S.Ct. 2569, 53 L.Ed.2d 683 (1977); World-Wide Volkswagen Corp. v. Woodson, 444 U.S. 286, 100 S.Ct. 559, 62 L.Ed.2d 490 (1980). Since Kansas had no prelitigation contact with many of the plaintiffs and leases involved, petitioner claims that Kansas has exceeded its jurisdictional reach and thereby violated the due process rights of the absent plaintiffs.

In *International Shoe* we were faced with an out-of-state corporation which sought to avoid the exercise of personal jurisdiction over it as a defendant by Washington state court. We held that the extent of the defendant's due process protection would depend "upon the quality and nature of the activity in relation to the fair and orderly administration of the laws. . . ." 326 U.S., at 319, 66 S.Ct., at 159. We noted that the Due Process Clause did not permit a State to make a binding judgment against a person with whom the State had no contacts, ties, or relations. Ibid. If the defendant possessed certain minimum contacts with the State, so that it was "reasonable and just, according to our traditional conception of fair play and substantial justice" for a

State to exercise personal jurisdiction, the State could force the defendant to defend himself in the forum, upon pain of default, and could bind him to a judgment. Id., at 320, 66 S.Ct., at 160.

The purpose of this test, of course, is to protect a defendant from the travail of defending in a distant forum, unless the defendant's contacts with the forum make it just to force him to defend there. As we explained in *Woodson,* supra, the defendant's contacts should be such that "he should reasonably anticipate being haled" into the forum. 444 U.S., at 297, 100 S.Ct., at 567. In Insurance Corp. of Ireland v. Compagnie des Bauxites de Guinee, 456 U.S. 694, 702–703, and n. 10, 102 S.Ct. 2099, 2104–2105, and n. 10, 72 L.Ed.2d 492 (1982) we explained that the requirement that a court have personal jurisdiction comes from the Due Process Clause's protection of the defendant's personal liberty interest, and said that the requirement "represents a restriction on judicial power not as a matter of sovereignty, but as a matter of individual liberty." (Footnote omitted).

Although the cases like *Shaffer* and *Woodson* which petitioner relies on for a minimum contacts requirement all dealt with out-of-state defendants or parties in the procedural posture of a defendant, cf. New York Life Ins. Co. v. Dunlevy, 241 U.S. 518, 36 S.Ct. 613, 60 L.Ed. 1140 (1916); Estin v. Estin, 334 U.S. 541, 68 S.Ct. 1213, 92 L.Ed. 1561 (1948), petitioner claims that the same analysis must apply to absent class-action plaintiffs. In this regard petitioner correctly points out that a chose in action is a constitutionally recognized property interest possessed by each of the plaintiffs. Mullane v. Central Hanover Bank & Trust Co., 339 U.S. 306, 70 S.Ct. 652, 94 L.Ed. 865 (1950). An adverse judgment by Kansas courts in this case may extinguish the chose in action forever through res judicata. Such an adverse judgment, petitioner claims, would be every bit as onerous to an absent plaintiff as an adverse judgment on the merits would be to a defendant. Thus, the same due process protections should apply to absent plaintiffs: Kansas should not be able to exert jurisdiction over the plaintiff's claims unless the plaintiffs have sufficient minimum contacts with Kansas.

We think petitioner's premise is in error. The burdens placed by a State upon an absent class-action plaintiff are not of the same order or magnitude as those it places upon an absent defendant. An out-of-state defendant summoned by a plaintiff is faced with the full powers of the forum State to render judgment *against* it. The defendant must generally hire counsel and travel to the forum to defend itself from the plaintiff's claim, or suffer a default judgment. The defendant may be forced to participate in extended and often costly discovery, and will be forced to respond in damages or to comply with some other form of remedy imposed by the court should it lose the suit. The defendant may also face liability for court costs and attorney's fees. These burdens are substantial, and the minimum contacts requirement of the Due Process Clause prevents the forum State from unfairly imposing them upon the defendant.

A class-action plaintiff, however, is in quite a different posture. The Court noted this difference in Hansberry v. Lee, 311 U.S. 32, 40–41, 61 S.Ct. 115, 117–118, 85 L.Ed. 22 (1940), which explained that a "class" or "representative" suit was an exception to the rule that one could not be bound by judgment *in personam* unless one was made fully a party in the traditional sense. Ibid., citing Pennoyer v. Neff, 95 U.S. (5 Otto) 714, 24 L.Ed. 565 (1878). As the Court pointed out in *Hansberry*, the class action was an invention of equity to enable it to proceed to a decree in suits where the number of those interested in the litigation was too great to permit joinder. The absent parties would be bound by the decree so long as the named parties adequately represented the absent class and the prosecution of the litigation was within the common interest.[1] 311 U.S., at 41, 61 S.Ct., at 117.

Modern plaintiff class actions follow the same goals, permitting litigation of a suit involving common questions when there are too many plaintiffs for proper joinder. Class actions also may permit the plaintiffs to pool claims which would be uneconomical to litigate individually. For example, this lawsuit involves claims averaging about $100 per plaintiff; most of the plaintiffs would have no realistic day in court if a class action were not available.

In sharp contrast to the predicament of a defendant haled into an out-of-state forum, the plaintiffs in this suit were not haled anywhere to defend themselves upon pain of a default judgment. As commentators have noted, from the plaintiffs' point of view a class action resembles a "quasi-administrative proceeding, conducted by the judge." 3B J. Moore & J. Kennedy, Moore's Federal Practice ¶ 23.45[4.–5] (1984); Kaplan, Continuing Work of the Civil Committee: 1966 Amendments to the Federal Rules of Civil Procedure (I), 81 Harv.L.Rev. 356, 398 (1967).

A plaintiff class in Kansas and numerous other jurisdictions cannot first be certified unless the judge, with the aid of the named plaintiffs and defendant, conducts an inquiry into the common nature of the named plaintiff's and the absent plaintiffs' claims, the adequacy of representation, the jurisdiction possessed over the class, and any other matters that will bear upon proper representation of the absent plaintiffs' interest. See, e.g., Kan.Stat.Ann. § 60–223 (1983); Fed.Rule Civ. Proc. 23. Unlike a defendant in a civil suit, a class-action plaintiff is not required to fend for himself. See Kan.Stat.Ann. § 60–223(d) (1983). The court and named plaintiffs protect his interests. Indeed, the class-action defendant itself has a great interest in ensuring that the absent plaintiffs' claims are properly before the forum. In this case, for example, the defendant sought to avoid class certification by alleging that the absent plaintiffs would not be adequately represented and

---

1. The holding in *Hansberry*, of course, was that petitioners in that case had not a sufficient common interest with the parties to a prior lawsuit such that a decree against those parties in the prior suit would bind the petitioners. But in the present case there is no question that the named plaintiffs adequately represent the class, and that all members of the class have the same interest in enforcing their claims against the defendant.

were not amenable to jurisdiction. See Phillips Petroleum v. Duckworth, No. 82–54608 (Kan., June 28, 1982).

The concern of the typical class-action rules for the absent plaintiffs is manifested in other ways. Most jurisdictions, including Kansas, require that a class action, once certified, may not be dismissed or compromised without the approval of the court. In many jurisdictions such as Kansas the court may amend the pleadings to ensure that all sections of the class are represented adequately. Kan.Stat.Ann. § 60–223(d) (1983); see also, e.g., Fed.Rule Civ.Proc. 23(d).

Besides this continuing solicitude for their rights, absent plaintiff class members are not subject to other burdens imposed upon defendants. They need not hire counsel or appear. They are almost never subject to counterclaims or cross-claims, or liability for fees or costs.[2] Absent plaintiff class members are not subject to coercive or punitive remedies. Nor will an adverse judgment typically bind an absent plaintiff for any damages, although a valid adverse judgment may extinguish any of the plaintiff's claims which were litigated.

Unlike a defendant in a normal civil suit, an absent class-action plaintiff is not required to do anything. He may sit back and allow the litigation to run its course, content in knowing that there are safeguards provided for his protection. In most class actions an absent plaintiff is provided at least with an opportunity to "opt out" of the class, and if he takes advantage of that opportunity he is removed from the litigation entirely. This was true of the Kansas proceedings in this case. The Kansas procedure provided for the mailing of a notice to each class member by first-class mail. The notice, as we have previously indicated, described the action and informed the class member that he could appear in person or by counsel, in default of which he would be represented by the named plaintiffs and their attorneys. The notice further stated that class members would be included in the class and bound by the judgment unless they "opted out" by executing and returning a "request for exclusion" that was included in the notice.

Petitioner contends, however, that the "opt out" procedure provided by Kansas is not good enough, and that an "opt in" procedure is required to satisfy the Due Process Clause of the Fourteenth Amendment. Insofar as plaintiffs who have no minimum contacts with the forum State are concerned, an "opt in" provision would require that each class member affirmatively consent to his inclusion within the class.

Because States place fewer burdens upon absent class plaintiffs than they do upon absent defendants in nonclass suits, the Due Process Clause need not and does not afford the former as much protection

---

2. Petitioner places emphasis on the fact that absent class members might be subject to discovery, counterclaims, cross-claims or court costs. Petitioner cites no cases involving any such imposition upon plaintiffs, however. We are convinced that such burdens are rarely imposed upon plaintiff class members, and that the disposition of these issues is best left to a case which presents them in a more concrete way.

from state-court jurisdiction as it does the latter. The Fourteenth Amendment does protect "persons," not "defendants," however, so absent plaintiffs as well as absent defendants are entitled to some protection from the jurisdiction of a forum State which seeks to adjudicate their claims. In this case we hold that a forum State may exercise jurisdiction over the claim of an absent class-action plaintiff, even though that plaintiff may not possess the minimum contacts with the forum which would support personal jurisdiction over a defendant. If the forum State wishes to bind an absent plaintiff concerning a claim for money damages or similar relief at law,[3] it must provide minimal procedural due process protection. The plaintiff must receive notice plus an opportunity to be heard and participate in the litigation, whether in person or through counsel. The notice must be the best practicable, "reasonably calculated, under all the circumstances, to apprise interested parties of the pendency of the action and afford them an opportunity to present their objections." *Mullane*, 399 U.S., at 314–315, 70 S.Ct. at 657; cf. Eisen v. Carlisle & Jacquelin, 417 U.S. 156, 174–175, 94 S.Ct. 2140, 2151, 40 L.Ed.2d 732 (1974). The notice should describe the action and the plaintiffs' rights in it. Additionally, we hold that due process requires at a minimum that an absent plaintiff be provided with an opportunity to remove himself from the class by executing and returning an "opt out" or "request for exclusion" form to the court. Finally, the Due Process Clause of course requires that the named plaintiff at all times adequately represent the interests of the absent class members. *Hansberry*, 311 U.S., at 42–43, 45, 61 S.Ct., at 118–119, 120.

We reject petitioner's contention that the Due Process Clause of the Fourteenth Amendment requires that absent plaintiffs affirmatively "opt in" to the class, rather than be deemed members of the class if they do not "opt out." We think that such a contention is supported by little, if any, precedent, and that it ignores the differences between class action plaintiffs, on the one hand, and defendants in non-class civil suits on the other. Any plaintiff may consent to jurisdiction. Keeton v. Hustler Magazine, Inc., 465 U.S. 770, 104 S.Ct. 1473, 79 L.Ed. 2d 790 (1984). The essential question, then, is how stringent the requirement for a showing of consent will be.

We think that the procedure followed by Kansas, where a fully descriptive notice is sent first-class mail to each class member, with an explanation of the right to "opt out," satisfies due process. Requiring a plaintiff to affirmatively request inclusion would probably impede the prosecution of those class actions involving an aggregation of small individual claims, where a large number of claims are required to make it economical to bring suit. See, e.g., *Eisen, supra*, 417 U.S., at 161, 94

---

3. Our holding today is limited to those class actions which seek to bind known plaintiffs concerning claims wholly or predominately for money judgments. We intimate no view concerning other types of class action lawsuits, such as those seeking equitable relief. Nor, of course, does our discussion of personal jurisdiction address class actions where the jurisdiction is asserted against a *defendant* class.

S.Ct., at 2144. The plaintiff's claim may be so small, or the plaintiff so unfamiliar with the law, that he would not file suit individually, nor would he affirmatively request inclusion in the class if such a request were required by the Constitution.[4] If, on the other hand, the plaintiff's claim is sufficiently large or important that he wishes to litigate it on his own, he will likely have retained an attorney or have thought about filing suit, and should be fully capable of exercising his right to "opt out."

In this case over 3,400 members of the potential class did "opt out," which belies the contention that "opt out" procedures result in guaranteed jurisdiction by inertia. Another 1,500 were excluded because the notice and "opt out" form was undeliverable. We think that such results show that the "opt out" procedure provided by Kansas is by no means *pro forma,* and that the Constitution does not require more to protect what must be the somewhat rare species of class member who is unwilling to execute an "opt out" form, but whose claim is nonetheless so important that he cannot be presumed to consent to being a member of the class by his failure to do so. Petitioner's "opt in" requirement would require the invalidation of scores of state statutes and of the class-action provision of the Federal Rules of Civil Procedure,[5] and for the reasons stated we do not think that the Constitution requires the State to sacrifice the obvious advantages in judicial efficiency resulting from the "opt out" approach for the protection of the *rara avis* portrayed by petitioner.

We therefore hold that the protection afforded the plaintiff class members by the Kansas statute satisfies the Due Process Clause. The interests of the absent plaintiffs are sufficiently protected by the forum State when those plaintiffs are provided with a request for exclusion that can be returned within a reasonable time to the court. See *Insurance Corp. of Ireland,* 456 U.S., at 702–703, and n. 10, 102 S.Ct., at 2104–2105, and n. 10. Both the Kansas trial court and the Supreme

---

4. In this regard the Reporter for the 1966 amendments to the Federal Rules of Civil Procedure stated:

"[R]equiring the individuals affirmatively to request inclusion in the lawsuit would result in freezing out the claims of people—especially small claims held by small people—who for one reason or another, ignorance, timidity, unfamiliarity with business or legal matters, will simply not take the affirmative step." Kaplan, Continuing Work of the Civil Committee: 1966 Amendments of the Federal Rules of Civil Procedure (I), 81 Harv.L.Rev. 356, 397–398 (1967).

5. The following statutes permit "opt out" notice in some types of class actions.

Fed.Rule Civ.Proc. 23(c)(2)(A); Ala.Rule Civ.Proc. 23(c)(2)(A); Alaska Rule Civ.Proc. 23(c)(2)(A); Ariz.Rule Civ.Proc. 23(c)(2)(A); Cal.Civ.Code Ann. § 1781(e)(1) (West 1973) (consumer class action); Colo.Rule Civ. Proc. 23(c)(2)(A); Del.Ch.Ct.Rule 23(c)(2)(A); D.C.Super.Ct.Rule Civ.Proc. 23(c)(2)(A); Fla.Rule Civ.Proc. 1.220(d)(2)(A); Idaho Rule Civ.Proc. 23(c)(2)(A); Ind.Rule Trial Proc. 23(C)(2)(a); Iowa Rule Civ.Proc. 42.8(b); Kan.Stat.Ann. § 60–223(c)(2) (1983); Ky.Rule Civ.Proc. 23.03(2)(a); Me. Rule Civ.Proc. 23(c)(2)(A); Md.Rule Civ. Proc. 2–231(e)(1); Mich.Ct.Rule 3.501(C)(5) (b); Minn.Rule Civ.Proc. 23.03(2)(A); Mo. Rule Civ.Proc. 52.08; Mont.Rule Civ.Proc. 23(c)(2)(A); Nev.Rule Civ.Proc. 23(c)(2)(A); N.J.Civ.Prac.Rule 4:32–2; N.Y.Civ.Prac. Law § 904 (McKinney 1976); N.D.Rule Civ.Proc. 23(g)(2)(B); Ohio Rule Civ.Proc. 23(C)(2)(a); Okla.Stat., Tit. 12, § 2023(C)(2) (a) (Supp.1984–1985); Ore.Rule Civ.Proc. 32F(1)(b)(ii); Pa.Rule Civ.Proc. 1711(a); Tenn.Rule Civ.Proc. 23.03(2)(a); Vt.Rule Civ.Proc. 23(c)(2)(A); Wash.Ct.Rule 23(c)(2) (i); Wyo.Rule Civ.Proc. 23(c)(2)(A).

Court of Kansas held that the class received adequate representation, and no party disputes that conclusion here. We conclude that the Kansas court properly asserted personal jurisdiction over the absent plaintiffs and their claims against petitioner.

III

The Kansas courts applied Kansas contract and Kansas equity law to every claim in this case, notwithstanding that over 99% of the gas leases and some 97% of the plaintiffs in the case had no apparent connection to the State of Kansas except for this lawsuit. Petitioner protested that the Kansas courts should apply the laws of the States where the leases were located, or at least apply Texas and Oklahoma law because so many of the leases came from those States. The Kansas courts disregarded this contention and found petitioner liable for interest on the suspended royalties as a matter of Kansas law, and set the interest rates under Kansas equity principles.

Petitioner contends that total application of Kansas substantive law violated the constitutional limitations on choice of law mandated by the Due Process Clause of the Fourteenth Amendment and the Full Faith and Credit Clause of Article IV, § 1. We must first determine whether Kansas law conflicts in any material way with any other law which could apply. There can be no injury in applying Kansas law if it is not in conflict with that of any other jurisdiction connected to this suit.

Petitioner claims that Kansas law conflicts with that of a number of States connected to this litigation, especially Texas and Oklahoma. These putative conflicts range from the direct to the tangential, and may be addressed by the Supreme Court of Kansas on remand under the correct constitutional standard. For example, there is no recorded Oklahoma decision dealing with interest liability for suspended royalties: whether Oklahoma is likely to impose liability would require a survey of Oklahoma oil and gas law. Even if Oklahoma found such liability, petitioner shows that Oklahoma would most likely apply its constitutional and statutory 6% interest rate rather than the much higher Kansas rates applied in this litigation.   *   *   *

Additionally, petitioner points to an Oklahoma statute which excuses liability for interest if a creditor accepts payment of the full principal without a claim for interest.   *   *   * Petitioner contends that by ignoring this statute the Kansas courts created liability that does not exist in Oklahoma.

Petitioner also points out several conflicts between Kansas and Texas law. Although Texas recognizes interest liability for suspended royalties, Texas has never awarded any such interest at a rate greater than 6%, which corresponds with the Texas constitutional and statutory rate.   *   *   * Moreover, at least one court interpreting Texas law appears to have held that Texas excuses interest liability once the gas company offers to take an indemnity from the royalty owner and pay him the suspended royalty while the price increase is still tentative. * * * Such a rule is contrary to Kansas law as applied below, but if applied to the Texas plaintiffs or leases in this case, would vastly reduce petitioner's liability.

The conflicts on the applicable interest rates, alone—which we do not think can be labeled "false conflicts" without a more thorough-going treatment than was accorded them by the Supreme Court of Kansas—certainly amounted to millions of dollars in liability. We think that the Supreme Court of Kansas erred in deciding on the basis that it did that the application of its laws to all claims would be constitutional.

Four Terms ago we addressed a similar situation in Allstate Ins. Co. v. Hague, 449 U.S. 302, 101 S.Ct. 633, 66 L.Ed.2d 521 (1981). In that case we were confronted with two conflicting rules of state insurance law. Minnesota permitted the "stacking" of separate uninsured motorist policies while Wisconsin did not. Although the decedent lived in Wisconsin, took out insurance policies and was killed there, he was employed in Minnesota and after his death his widow moved to Minnesota for reasons unrelated to the litigation, and was appointed personal representative of his estate. She filed suit in Minnesota courts, which applied the Minnesota stacking rule.

The plurality in *Allstate* noted that a particular set of facts giving rise to litigation could justify, constitutionally, the application of more than one jurisdiction's laws. The plurality recognized, however, that the Due Process Clause and the Full Faith and Credit Clause provided modest restrictions on the application of forum law. These restrictions required "that for a State's substantive law to be selected in a constitutionally permissible manner, that State must have a significant contact or significant aggregation of contacts, creating state interests, such that choice of its law is neither arbitrary nor fundamentally unfair." Id., at 312–313, 101 S.Ct., at 639–640. The dissenting Justices were in substantial agreement with this principle. Id., at 332, 101 S.Ct., at 650 (opinion of POWELL, J.). The dissent stressed that the Due Process Clause prohibited the application of law which was only casually or slightly related to the litigation, while the Full Faith and Credit Clause required the forum to respect the laws and judgments of other States, subject to the forum's own interests in furthering its public policy. Id., at 335–336, 101 S.Ct., at 651–652.

The plurality in *Allstate* affirmed the application of Minnesota law because of the forum's significant contacts to the litigation which supported the State's interest in applying its law. See id., at 313–329, 101 S.Ct., at 640–648. Kansas' contacts to this litigation, as explained by the Kansas Supreme Court, can be gleaned from the opinion below.

Petitioner owns property and conducts substantial business in the State, so Kansas certainly has an interest in regulating petitioner's conduct in Kansas. 235 Kan., at 210, 679 P.2d, at 1174. Moreover, oil and gas extraction is an important business to Kansas, and although only a few leases in issue are located in Kansas, hundreds of Kansas plaintiffs were affected by petitioner's suspension of royalties; thus the court held that the State has a real interest in protecting "the rights of these royalty owners both as individual residents of [Kansas] and as members of this particular class of plaintiffs." Id., at 211–212, 679 P.2d, at 1174. The Kansas Supreme Court pointed out that Kansas courts are quite familiar with this type of lawsuit, and "[t]he plaintiff class members have indicated their desire to have this action determined under the laws of Kansas." Id., at 211, 222, 679 P.2d, at 1174, 1181. Finally, the Kansas court buttressed its use of Kansas law by stating that this lawsuit was analogous to a suit against a "common fund" located in Kansas. Id., at 201, 211–212, 679 P.2d, at 1168, 1174.

We do not lightly discount this description of Kansas' contacts with this litigation and its interest in applying its law. There is, however, no "common fund" located in Kansas that would require or support the application of only Kansas law to all these claims. See, e.g., Hartford Life Ins. Co. v. Ibs, 237 U.S. 662, 35 S.Ct. 692, 59 L.Ed. 1165 (1915). As the Kansas court noted, petitioner commingled the suspended royalties with its general corporate accounts. 235 Kan., at 201, 679 P.2d, at 1168. There is no specific identifiable res in Kansas, nor is there any limited amount which may be depleted before every plaintiff is compensated. Only by somehow aggregating all the separate claims in this case could a "common fund" in any sense be created, and the term becomes all but meaningless when used in such an expansive sense.

We also give little credence to the idea that Kansas law should apply to all claims because the plaintiffs, by failing to opt out, evinced their desire to be bound by Kansas law. Even if one could say that the plaintiffs "consented" to the application of Kansas law by not opting out, plaintiff's desire for forum law is rarely, if ever controlling. In most cases the plaintiff shows his obvious wish for forum law by filing there. "If a plaintiff could choose the substantive rules to be applied to an action . . . the invitation to forum shopping would be irresistable." *Allstate,* 449 U.S., at 337, 101 S.Ct., at 652 (opinion of POWELL, J.). Even if a plaintiff evidences his desire for forum law by moving to the forum, we have generally accorded such a move little or no significance. John Hancock Mut. Life Ins. Co. v. Yates, 299 U.S. 178, 182, 57 S.Ct. 129, 131, 81 L.Ed. 106 (1936); Home Ins. Co. v. Dick, 281 U.S. 397, 408, 50 S.Ct. 338, 341, 74 L.Ed. 926 (1930). In *Allstate* the plaintiff's move to the forum was only relevant because it was unrelated and prior to the litigation. 449 U.S., at 318–319, 101 S.Ct., at 643. Thus the plaintiffs' desire for Kansas law, manifested by their participation in this Kansas lawsuit, bears little relevance.

The Supreme Court of Kansas in its opinion in this case expressed the view that by reason of the fact that it was adjudicating a nation-wide class action, it had much greater latitude in applying its own law to the transactions in question than might otherwise be the case:

"The general rule is that the law of the forum applies unless it is expressly shown that a different law governs, and in case of doubt, the law of the forum is preferred. . . . Where a state court determines it has jurisdiction over a nationwide class action and procedural due process guarantees of notice and adequate representation are present, we believe the law of the forum should be applied unless compelling reasons exist for applying a different law. . . . Compelling reasons do not exist to require this court to look to other state laws to determine the rights of the parties involved in this lawsuit." 235 Kan., at 221–222, 679 P.2d, at 1181.

We think that this is something of a "bootstrap" argument. The Kansas class-action statute, like those of most other jurisdictions, requires that there be "common issues of law or fact." But while a state may, for the reasons we have previously stated, assume jurisdiction over the claims of plaintiffs whose principal contacts are with other States, it may not use this assumption of jurisdiction as an added weight in the scale when considering the permissible constitutional limits on choice of substantive law. It may not take a transaction with little or no relationship to the forum and apply the law of the forum in order to satisfy the procedural requirement that there be a "common question of law." The issue of personal jurisdiction over plaintiffs in a class action is entirely distinct from the question of the constitutional limitations on choice of law; the latter calculus is not altered by the fact that it may be more difficult or more burdensome to comply with the constitutional limitations because of the large number of transactions which the State proposes to adjudicate and which have little connection with the forum.

Kansas must have a "significant contact or aggregation of contacts" to the claims asserted by each member of the plaintiff class, contacts "creating state interests," in order to ensure that the choice of Kansas law is not arbitrary or unfair. *Allstate,* supra, 449 U.S., at 312–313, 101 S.Ct., at 639–640. Given Kansas' lack of "interest" in claims unrelated to that State, and the substantive conflict with jurisdictions such as Texas, we conclude that application of Kansas law to every claim in this case is sufficiently arbitrary and unfair as to exceed constitutional limits.[8]

8. In this case the Kansas Supreme Court held that "[t]he trial court did not determine whether any difference existed between the laws of Kansas and other states or whether another state's law should be applied." 235 Kan. 195, 221, 679 P.2d 1159, 1180 (1984). Respondents contend that the trial court and the supreme court actually incorporated by reference the *Shutts, Executor* opinion, supra, where the court looked to the Texas and Oklahoma interest rate statutes and found them inapplicable. We do not think that the Kansas Supreme Court fully adopted the choice of law discussion in *Shutts, Executor* as its holding in this case. But even if we agreed that *Shutts, Executor* was somehow incorporated below, that would be insufficient. *Shutts, Executor* was a pre-*Allstate* case involving only two other states, rather than the 10 present here. Moreover, the gas region involved in *Shutts, Executor* was primarily within Kansas borders. *Shutts, Executor* only considered the conflict involving interest rate liability and state statutes, and in finding the 6% Texas rate inapplicable it cited but did not follow contrary Texas precedent. 222 Kan., at 562–565, 567 P.2d, at 1317–1319.

When considering fairness in this context, an important element is the expectation of the parties. See *Allstate,* supra, 449 U.S., at 333, 101 S.Ct., at 650 (opinion of POWELL, J.). There is no indication that when the leases involving land and royalty owners outside of Kansas were executed, the parties had any idea that Kansas law would control. Neither the Due Process Clause nor the Full Faith and Credit Clause requires Kansas "to substitute for its own [laws], applicable to persons and events within it, the conflicting statute of another state," Pacific Employees Insurance Co. v. Industrial Accident Comm'n, 306 U.S. 493, 502, 59 S.Ct. 629, 633, 83 L.Ed. 940 (1939), but Kansas "may not abrogate the rights of parties beyond its borders having no relation to anything done or to be done within them." Home Insurance Co. v. Dick, supra, 281 U.S., at 410, 50 S.Ct., at 342.

Here the Supreme Court of Kansas took the view that in a nationwide class action where procedural due process guarantees of notice and adequate representation were met, "the laws of the forum should be applied unless compelling reasons exist for applying a different law." 235 Kan. at 221, 679 P.2d at 1181. Whatever practical reasons may have commended this rule to the Supreme Court of Kansas, for the reasons already stated we do not believe that it is consistent with the decisions of this Court. We make no effort to determine for ourselves which law must apply to the various transactions involved in this lawsuit, and we reaffirm our observation in *Allstate* that in many situations a state court may be free to apply one of several choices of law. But the constitutional limitations laid down in cases such as *Allstate* and Home Insurance Co. v. Dick, supra, must be respected even in a nationwide class action.

We therefore affirm the judgment of the Supreme Court of Kansas insofar as it upheld the jurisdiction of the Kansas courts over the plaintiff class members in this case, and reverse its judgment insofar as it held that Kansas law was applicable to all of the transactions which it sought to adjudicate. We remand the case to that Court for further proceedings not inconsistent with this opinion.

It is so ordered.

* * *

JUSTICE STEVENS, concurring in part and dissenting in part.

For the reasons stated in Parts I and II of the Court's opinion, I agree that the Kansas courts properly exercised jurisdiction over this class action. I also recognize that the use of the word "compelling" in a portion of the Kansas Supreme Court's opinion, when read out of context, may create an inaccurate impression of that court's choice of law holding. * * * Our job, however, is to review judgments, not to edit opinions, and I am firmly convinced that there is no constitutional defect in the judgment under review.

As the Court recognizes, there "can be no [constitutional] injury in applying Kansas law if it is not in conflict with that of any other jurisdiction connected to this suit." * * * A fair reading of the

Kansas Supreme Court's opinion in light of its earlier opinion in Shutts v. Phillips Petroleum Co., 222 Kan. 527, 567 P.2d 1292 (1977), cert. denied, 434 U.S. 1068, 98 S.Ct. 1246, 55 L.Ed.2d 769 (1978) (hereinafter *Shutts I*), reveals that the Kansas court has examined the laws of connected jurisdictions and has correctly concluded that there is no "direct" or "substantive" conflict between the law applied by Kansas and the laws of those other States. * * * Kansas has merely developed general common law principles to accommodate the novel facts of this litigation—other State courts either agree with Kansas or have not yet addressed precisely similar claims. Consequently, I conclude that the Full Faith and Credit Clause of the Constitution [1] did not require Kansas to apply the law of any other State, and the Fourteenth Amendment's Due Process Clause [2] did not prevent Kansas from applying its own law in this case.

The Court errs today because it applies a loose definition of the sort of "conflict" of laws required to state a *constitutional* claim, allowing Phillips a tactical victory here merely on allegations of "putative" or "likely" conflicts. * * * The Court's choice of law analysis also treats the two relevant constitutional provisions as though they imposed the same constraints on the forum court. In my view, however, the potential impact of the Kansas choice on the interests of other sovereign States and the fairness of its decision to the litigants should be separately considered. See Allstate Insurance Co. v. Hague, 449 U.S., 302, 320, 101 S.Ct. 633, 644, 66 L.Ed.2d 521 (1981) (STEVENS, J., concurring in judgment). * * *

* * *

II

This Court, of course, can have no concern with the substantive merits of common law decisions reached by state courts faithfully applying their own law or the law of another state. When application of purely state law is at issue, "[t]he power delegated to us is for the restraint of unconstitutional [actions] by the States, and not for the correction of alleged errors committed by their judiciary." * * * The Constitution does not expressly mandate particular or correct choices of law. Rather, a State court's choice of law can invoke constitutional protections, and hence our jurisdiction, only if it contravenes some explicit constitutional limitation.[14]

1. "Full Faith and Credit shall be given in each State to the public Acts, Records, and judicial Proceedings of every other State. And the Congress may by general Laws prescribe the Manner in which such Acts, Records and Proceedings shall be proved, and the Effect thereof." U.S. Const., Art. IV, § 1. See also 28 U.S.C. § 1738.

2. "No State shall . . . deprive any person of life, liberty, or property, without due process of law. . . ." U.S. Const., Amdt. 14, § 1.

14. See 28 U.S.C. § 1257: "Final judgments or decrees rendered by the highest court of a State . . . may be reviewed by the Supreme Court . . . (3) [b]y writ of certiorari . . . where any title, right, privilege or immunity is specially set up or claimed *under the Constitution* " (emphasis added).

Thus it has long been settled that "a mere misconstruction by the forum of the laws of a sister State is not a violation of the Full Faith and Credit Clause." * * * That clause requires only that States accord "full faith and credit" to other States' laws—that is, acknowledge the validity and finality of such laws and attempt in good faith to apply them when necessary as they would be applied by home state courts. But as Justice Holmes explained, when there is "nothing to suggest that [one State's court] was not candidly construing [another State's law] to the best of its ability, . . . even if it was wrong something more than an error of construction is necessary" to invoke the Constitution. * * *

Merely to state these general principles is to refute any argument that Kansas' decision below violated the Full Faith and Credit Clause. As the opinion in *Shutts I* indicates, the Kansas court made a careful survey of the relevant laws of Oklahoma and Texas, the only other states whose law is proffered as relevant to this litigation. But, as the Court acknowledges, * * * no other State's laws or judicial decisions were precisely on point, and, in the Kansas court's judgment roughly analogous Texas and Oklahoma cases supported the results the Kansas court reached. The Kansas court expressly declared that, in a multistate action, a "court should also give careful consideration, as we have attempted to do, to any possible conflict of law problems." 222 Kan., at 557, 567 P.2d at 1314.[17] While a common law judge might disagree with the substantive legal determinations made by the Kansas court (although nothing in its opinion seems erroneous to me), that court's approach to the possible choices of law evinces precisely the "full faith and credit" that the Constitution requires.

It is imaginable that even a good faith review of another State's law might still "unjustifiably infring[e] upon the legitimate interests of another State" so as to violate the Full Faith and Credit Clause. *Allstate*, 449 U.S., at 323, 101 S.Ct., at 645 (STEVENS, J., concurring in judgment). If, for example, a Texas oil company or a Texas royalty owner with an interest in a Texas lease were treated directly contrary to a stated policy of the State of Texas by a Kansas court through some honest blunder, the Constitution might bar such "parochial entrenchment" on Texas' interests. Thomas v. Washington Gas Light Co., 448 U.S. 261, 272, 100 S.Ct. 2647, 2656, 65 L.Ed.2d 757 (1980) (plurality opinion).[18] But this case is so distant from such a situation that I need not pursue this theoretical possibility. Even Phillips does not contend

---

17. The Kansas court also stated that Kansas' statutory class action requirements would "not be fulfilled" if "liability is to be determined according to varying and inconsistent state laws." 222 Kan., at 557, 567 P.2d, at 1314. This belies any notion that the Kansas court plans to "bootstrap" * * * its choice of law decisions onto its assertion of jurisdiction over multistate actions; precisely the opposite is suggested.

18. As I noted in *Allstate*, however, the litigant challenging a court's choice of law clearly "bears the burden of establishing" a constitutional infringement. 449 U.S., at 325, n. 13, 101 S.Ct., at 647, n. 13. "*Prima facie* every state is entitled to enforce in its own courts its own statutes. . . . One who challenges that right . . . assumes the burden of showing, upon some rational basis, that of the conflicting interests involved those of the foreign state are superi-

that any stated policies of other States have been plainly contravened, and the Court's discussion is founded merely on an *absence* of reported decisions and the Court's speculation of what Oklahoma or Texas courts might "most likely" do in a case like this. * * * There is simply no demonstration here that the Kansas Supreme Court's decision has impaired the legitimate interests of any other States or infringed on their sovereignty in the slightest.

III

It is nevertheless possible for a State's choice of law to violate the Constitution because it is so "totally arbitrary or . . . fundamentally unfair" to a litigant that it violates the Due Process Clause. *Allstate,* 449 U.S., at 326, 101 S.Ct., at 647 (STEVENS, J., concurring in judgment). If the forum court has no connection to the lawsuit other than its jurisdiction over the parties, a decision to apply the forum State's law might so "frustrat[e] the justifiable expectations of the parties" as to be unconstitutional. Id., at 327, 101 S.Ct., at 647.[19]

Again, however, a constitutional claim of "unfair surprise" cannot be based merely upon an unexpected choice of a particular State's law—it must rest on a persuasive showing of an unexpected *result* arrived at by application of that law. Thus, absent any *conflict* of laws, in terms of the results they produce, the Due Process Clause simply has not been violated. This is because the underlying theory of a choice-of-law due process claim must be that parties plan their conduct and contractual relations based upon their legitimate expectations concerning the subsequent legal consequences of their actions. For example, they might base a decision on the belief that the law of a particular State will govern. But a change in that State's law in the interim between the execution and the performance of the contract would not

or to those of the forum." Alaska Packers Assn. v. Industrial Accident Comm'n, 294 U.S. 532, 547, 55 S.Ct. 518, 523, 79 L.Ed. 1044 (1935). See Western Life Indemnity Co. v. Rupp, 235 U.S. at 275, 35 S.Ct. at 41 ("It does not appear that the court's attention was called to any decision by the courts of Illinois placing a different construction, or indeed any construction, upon the section in question. If such decision existed, it was incumbent upon defendant to prove it"). Thus, if a litigant has failed to call a state court's attention to relevant law in other jurisdictions, it cannot raise that law here to create a constitutional issue.

19. I noted in *Allstate* that choice of forum law might also violate the Due Process Clause in other ways, such as by irrationally favoring residents over nonresidents or representing a "dramatic departure from the rule that obtains in most American jurisdictions." 449 U.S., at 327, 101 S.Ct., at 647. The first possibility

is not applicable here; all royalty owners were treated exactly alike in the Kansas court's analysis. As for the second possibility, a "dramatic departure" must be distinguished from the application of general equitable principles to address new situations. Phillips may criticize Kansas' allegedly "unique notions of contract and oil and gas law," Brief for Petitioner 33, but such is not a *constitutional* objection. State courts, like this Court, constantly must apply and develop general legal principles to accommodate novel factual circumstances with the overarching goal of achieving a just result. Today's decision, for example, newly establishes lawful jurisdiction over a multistate plaintiffs' class action that Phillips likely could not have anticipated 15 years ago. Absent some demonstration of a *departure* from some clear *rule* obtaining in other States, an argument merely that "[n]o other state ever has hinted" at Kansas' result, id., at 32, is unavailing.

violate the Due Process Clause. Nor would the Constitution be violated simply because a state court made an unanticipated ruling on a previously unanswered question of law—perhaps a choice of law question.

In this case it is perfectly clear that there has been no due process violation because this is a classic "false conflicts" case.[20] Phillips has not demonstrated that any significant conflicts exist merely because Oklahoma and Texas state case law is *silent* concerning the equitable theories developed by the Kansas courts in this litigation, or even because the language of some Oklahoma and Texas statutes suggests that those States would "most likely" reach different results. * * * The Court's heavy reliance on the characterization of the law provided by Phillips is not an adequate substitute for a neutral review. Ante * * * ("Petitioner claims," "petitioner shows," "petitioner points to," "Petitioner also points out . . . ."). As is unmistakable from a review of *Shutts I*, the Kansas Supreme Court has examined the same laws cited by the Court today as indicative of "direct" conflicts, and construed them as supportive of the Kansas result.[21] Our precedents, to say nothing of the Constitution and our statutory jurisdiction to review State court judgments, do not permit the Court to second guess these substantive judgments. Moreover, an independent examination demonstrates solid support for the Kansas court's conclusions.[22]

20. " '[F]alse conflict' really means 'no conflict of laws.' If the laws of both states relevant to the set of facts are the same, or would produce the same decision in the lawsuit, there is no real conflict between them." R. Leflar, American Conflicts Law § 93, p. 188 (3d ed. 1977). See also E. Scoles & P. Hay, Conflict of Laws § 2.6, p. 17 (1982) ("A 'false conflict' exists when the potentially applicable laws do not differ"). The absence of any direct conflicts here distinguishes this case from decisions such as Home Ins. Co. v. Dick, 281 U.S. 397, 50 S.Ct. 338, 74 L.Ed. 926 (1930) and John Hancock Mutual Life Ins. Co. v. Yates, 299 U.S. 178, 57 S.Ct. 129, 81 L.Ed. 106 (1936), where the interstate legal conflicts were clear, conceded, and dispositive.

21. In *Shutts II* the Kansas Supreme Court noted that "the legal issues presented are substantially the same" as in *Shutts I*, and that "[w]hile these issues are complex they were thoroughly reviewed in *Shutts I*." 235 Kan., at 211, 679 P.2d, at 1174. The Court then addressed the award and rate of interest as "damages to compensate the plaintiffs for the unjust enrichment derived by Phillips from the use of the plaintiffs' money," and concluded that "[i]n the instant case Phillips has not satisfactorily established why this court should not apply the rule enunciated in *Shutts I*"

respecting this claim. Id., at 221, 679 P.2d, at 1181. Two sentences later in the same paragraph, the Court made the broad statement that its forum law should apply absent "compelling reason." The only fair reading of this statement in context is that the Kansas court in *Shutts II* adopted its multi-state choice-of-law survey performed in *Shutts I*, and properly placed the burden on Phillips, see n. 18, supra, to show why the *Shutts I* conclusions should be reexamined. Even if this were ambiguous, this Court should give the Kansas Supreme Court the benefit of the doubt when reviewing its judgment. Thus, I frankly do not understand the Court's summary rejection of that court's attempt to incorporate *Shutts I*. Ante, * * * n. 8. As for the implication in that same footnote that the choice-of-law discussion in *Shutts I* may have been erroneous on the merits, the statement that the Kansas court "did not follow *contrary* Texas precedent" (emphasis added), is simply wrong. See n. 22, infra.

22. The Court provides a list of "putative conflicts" * * *. The errors and omissions apparent in the Court's discussion demonstrate the dangers of relying on characterizations of state law provided by an interested party.

* * *

The crux of my disagreement with the Court is over the standard applied to evaluate the sufficiency of allegations of choice-of-law conflicts necessary to support a constitutional claim. Rather than potential, "putative," or even "likely" conflicts, I would require demonstration of an *unambiguous* conflict with the *established* law of another State as an essential element of a constitutional choice-of-law claim. Arguments that a State court has merely applied general common law principles in a novel manner, or reconciled arguably conflicting laws erroneously in the face of unprecedented factual circumstances should not suffice to make out a constitutional issue.

In this case, the Kansas Supreme Court's application of general principles of equity, its interpretation of the agreements, its reliance on the Commission's regulations, and its construction of general statutory terms contravened no established legal principles of other States and consequently cannot be characterized as either arbitrary or fundamentally unfair to Phillips. I therefore can find no due process violation in the Kansas court's decision.[24]

IV

In final analysis, the Court today may merely be expressing its disagreement with the Kansas Supreme Court's statement that in a "nationwide class action . . . the law of the forum should be applied unless compelling reasons exist for applying a different law." 235 Kan., at 221, 679 P.2d at 1181. Considering this statement against the background of the Kansas Supreme Court's careful analysis in *Shutts I*, however, I am confident that court would agree that every State court has an obligation under the Full Faith and Credit Clause to "respect the legitimate interests of other States and avoid infringement upon their sovereignty." *Allstate*, 449 U.S., at 322, 101 S.Ct., at 645 (STE-

---

24. Neither Phillips nor the Court contends that Kansas cannot constitutionally apply its own laws to the claims of Kansas residents, even though the leased land may lie in other states and no other apparent connection to Kansas may exist. Phillips has done business in Kansas throughout the years relevant to this litigation and it seems unarguable that application of Kansas law, or indeed the law of any of the 50 states where royalty owners reside, to the claims of at least some of the plaintiff class members was thus "perceived as possible" by Phillips "at the time of contracting." *Allstate*, 449 U.S., at 331, n. 24, 101 S.Ct., at 649, n. 24 (Stevens, J., concurring in judgment); see id., at 316–318, and n. 22, 101 S.Ct., at 642–643, and n. 22. It was also possible, of course, that any number of royalty owners might have moved to Kansas in the years Phillips held their suspense royalties, and that Kansas has a substantial interest in seeing its residents treated fairly when they invoke the jurisdiction of its courts. See Weinberg, Conflicts Cases and the Problem of Relevant Time, 10 Hofstra L.Rev. 1023, 1040–1043 (1982). Because Phillips must have anticipated application of Kansas law to some claims, the eventual geographic distribution of royalty owners' residences goes only to "likelihood" and not to fairness of the application of Kansas law. *Allstate*, supra, 449 U.S., at 331, n. 24, 101 S.Ct., at 649, n. 24 (Stevens, J., concurring in judgment). Additionally, it is easy enough for national firms like Phillips to make clear their expectations by placing express choice-of-law clauses in their contracts. See *Allstate*, supra, at 318, n. 24, 101 S.Ct., at 643, n. 24; id., at 324, 328, 101 S.Ct., at 646, 648 (Stevens, J., concurring in judgment); Clay v. Sun Ins. Office, Ltd., 377 U.S. 179, 182, 84 S.Ct. 1197, 1199, 12 L.Ed.2d 229 (1964). No such clauses are present here, however.

VENS, J., concurring in judgment); see Nevada v. Hall, 440 U.S. 410, 421, 424, n. 24, 99 S.Ct. 1182, 1188, 1190, n. 24, 59 L.Ed.2d 416 (1979).

It is also agreed that "the fact that a choice-of-law decision may be unsound . . . does not necessarily implicate the federal concerns embodied in the Full Faith and Credit Clause." *Allstate*, 449 U.S., at 323, 101 S.Ct., at 645 (STEVENS, J., concurring); see ante * * * ("in many situations a state court may be free to apply one of several choices of law"); *Allstate*, 449 U.S., at 307, 101 S.Ct., at 637 (plurality opinion). When a suit involves claims connected to States other than the forum State, the Constitution requires only that the relevant laws of other States that are brought to the attention of the forum court be examined fairly prior to making a choice of law.[25] Because this Court "reviews judgments, not opinions," Chevron U.S.A., Inc. v. Natural Resources Defense Council, Inc., 467 U.S. 837, 842, 104 S.Ct. 2778, 2781, 81 L.Ed.2d 694 (1984), criticism of a portion of the Kansas court's opinion taken out of context provides an insufficient basis for reversing its judgment. Unless the actual *choice* of Kansas law violated substantial constitutional rights of the parties, see 28 U.S.C. § 2111, our power to review judgments of state law—including the state law of choice of law—does not extend to reversal based on disagreement with the law's application. A review of the record and the underlying litigation here convincingly demonstrates that, despite Phillips' protestations regarding Kansas' development of common law principles, no disregard for the laws of other States nor unfair application of Kansas law to the litigants has occurred. Phillips has no constitutional right to avoid judgment in Kansas because it might have convinced a court in another State to develop its law differently.

I do not believe the Court should engage in detailed evaluations of various States' laws. To the contrary, I believe our limited jurisdiction to review state court judgments should foreclose such review.[27] Accord-

25. See *Allstate*, supra, 449 U.S., at 326, 101 S.Ct., at 647 (Stevens, J., concurring in judgment) (footnote omitted): "I question whether a judge's decision to apply the law of his own State could ever be described as wholly irrational. For judges are presumably familiar with their own state law and may find it difficult and time consuming to discover and apply correctly the law of another State. The forum State's interest in fair and efficient administration of justice is therefore sufficient, in my judgment, to attach a presumption of validity to a forum State's decision to apply its own law to a dispute over which it has jurisdiction."

27. The Court's decision in *Allstate* has been criticized on the ground that there may well have been no true conflict of laws present, and, therefore, no need for extended constitutional discussion. See Weintraub, Who's Afraid of Constitutional Limitations on Choice of Law?, 10 Hofstra L.Rev. 17, 18–24 (1981). As I have demon-

strated, the Court is once again open to this criticism.

Indeed, unless our review is restricted to cases in which conflicts are unambiguous, the Court will constantly run the risk of misconstruing the common law of any number of States. For example the Kansas Supreme Court has already decided that Oklahoma would not apply its statutory interest rates where there is evidence of a contractual agreement to a different rate, and that such an agreement is present here. 235 Kan., at 220, 679 P.2d, at 1180; 222 Kan., at 562–565, 567 P.2d, at 1318–1319. Yet today the Court speculates that Oklahoma "would most likely apply" its statutory rates in this lawsuit. * * * Since this Court has no more authority to resolve such issues of Oklahoma law than does the Kansas Supreme Court, however, the latter court remains free to abide by its former judgment.

ingly, I trust that today's decision is no more than a momentary aberration, and that the Court's opinion will not be read as a decision to constitutionalize novel state court developments in the common law whenever a litigant can claim that another State connected to the litigation "most likely" would reach a different result. The Court long ago decided that State court choices of law are unreviewable here absent demonstration of an unambiguous conflict in the established laws of connected States. * * * "To hold otherwise would render it possible to bring to this court every case wherein the defeated party claimed that the statute of another State had been construed to his detriment." Johnson v. New York Life Ins. Co., 187 U.S. 491, 496, 23 S.Ct. 194, 195, 47 L.Ed. 273 (1903). Having ignored this admonition today, the Court may be forced to renew its turn-of-the-century efforts to convince the bar that State court judgments based on fair evaluations of other States' laws are final.

Accordingly, while I join Parts I and II of the Court's opinion, I respectfully dissent from Part III and from the judgment.

NOTE ON CHOICE OF LAW

1. Substantive vs. Procedural Law

Any multistate case may present choice of law questions, most of which usually are easily answered. Conventional analysis divides the issues into ones of procedural law and those of substantive law. Questions of choice of procedural law seldom arise because there is near universal agreement that the forum court should apply its own rules of "procedure," although at times a strong federal policy may dictate use of federal procedure in a federal claim tried in a state court. See Dice v. Akron, C. & Y.R.R., infra p. 603. However, the question frequently arises whether a particular rule is procedural or substantive for choice of law purposes. For example, is the burden of proof procedural or substantive for choice of law purposes? See Cities Service Oil Co. v. Dunlap, noted infra p. 569. How should the statute of limitations be classified? See Note on Statutes of Limitations and Laches, supra p. 234; see also Guaranty Trust Co. v. York, infra p. 573; Restatement Second of Conflict of Laws § 142.

Choice of law problems can be especially disconcerting in mass tort litigation, where various claimants and defendants may be subject to different statutes of limitations, standards of liability, rules of punitive damages, and discovery privileges. For a suggested resolution by statute, see Note, Mass Tort Litigation: A Statutory Solution to the Choice of Law Impasse, 96 Yale L.J. 1077 (1987).

Questions about choice of substantive law are rare in ordinary civil litigation because most claims are local in origin, arising within a single state where it is clear that the local state law should apply. Where a claim has multi-jurisdictional aspects, however, as in the cases reprinted above, the forum court must decide which jurisdiction's law is to determine the rights of the parties. Our dual federal-state court system generates similar issues as between federal and state law. Thus, if a non-federal claim is tried in federal court under its diversity jurisdiction, should state or federal law apply? This issue is addressed in the section on the so-called "Erie problem," infra p. 558.

2. Constitutional Considerations

Constitutional limitations on the choice of substantive law, sometimes called legislative jurisdiction, are discussed in *Allstate* and *Phillips Petroleum*. The generally accepted theories and limits used to select controlling state law are addressed in the subject called Conflict of Laws and are beyond the scope of this book. For extended treatments of choice of law principles, see Scoles and Hay, Conflict of Laws (Lawyers Ed.1984); Leflar, McDougal and Felix, American Conflicts Law (4th ed. 1986); Restatement Second of Conflict of Laws (1971).

As recognized in *Phillips Petroleum,* since more than one state often will have territorial jurisdiction over the parties, there must be some limits on choice of law by the forum chosen by plaintiff. Otherwise, forum shopping would be rampant because a plaintiff could vary his rights according to the state where he filed suit. See Black & White Taxi & Transfer Co. v. Brown & Yellow Taxi & Transfer Co., noted infra p. 562. On this score, are *Allstate* and *Phillips Petroleum* consistent with one another? Was the plaintiff in *Allstate* doing anything other than forum shopping?

A state's choice of its own law over that of another state is measured against two constitutional limits, due process and full faith and credit. Although the Supreme Court has applied these two concepts as if they were one and the same, Justice Stevens' comments in *Allstate* and *Phillips Petroleum,* that they are analytically different, would seem to have merit. Why was the Full Faith and Credit Clause included in the Constitution? See Nevada v. Hall, 440 U.S. 410, 424, 99 S.Ct. 1182, 59 L.Ed.2d 416 (1979) (threats to constitutional system of cooperative federalism); Carroll v. Lanza, 349 U.S. 408, 413, 75 S.Ct. 804, 99 L.Ed. 1183 (1955) (policy of hostility to the public acts of another state); Thomas v. Washington Gas Light Co., 448 U.S. 261, 272, 100 S.Ct. 2647, 65 L.Ed. 2d 757 (1980) (parochial encroachment on the interests of other states). Were such interests threatened in *Allstate?* In *Phillips Petroleum?*

Consider Justice Stevens' contention that *Phillips Petroleum* involved merely "false conflicts" raising no full faith and credit issues, then consider the very real and admitted conflict presented in *Allstate.* In which case would the interests of the other state be more invaded by application of forum law?

Nevada v. Hall, supra, involved a motor vehicle accident damages action in California against the State of Nevada, the owner of the motor vehicle involved. The California court refused to apply a Nevada statute limiting damages against the State of Nevada because the Nevada limit was "obnoxious" to California policy, and the Supreme Court affirmed. In Ehrlich-Bober & Co., Inc. v. University of Houston, 49 N.Y.2d 574, 427 N.Y.S.2d 604, 404 N.E.2d 726 (1980), New York took jurisdiction against an agency of the State of Texas despite a Texas statute that limited venue of such suits to Texas. New York relied on Nevada v. Hall to find that New York's strong policy interest in maintaining and encouraging its position as a financial and commercial center outweighted Texas's venue limitation, notwithstanding that New York had a similar venue limitation for its own state university. The forum's contacts with the parties and with the transaction involved in the litigation obviously have significance in the choice of the substantive law to be applied. But what degree and relative weight should be given to these factors? Were Kansas's interests and contacts with the transaction in *Phillips Petroleum* any more attenuated than Minnesota's interests and contacts in *Allstate?* Can public policy justify application of the forum's own law on the ground that the state's interest in the fair and efficient administration of justice is thereby promoted because local judges are familiar with their own state law, whereas application of foreign law may be time-consuming and subject to error? See Justice Brennan's partial dissent in Shaffer v. Heitner, 433 U.S. at 225–226.

Due process protects litigants from arbitrary or fundamentally unfair decision procedures. How important to the Court's decision in *Allstate* was the fact that the defendant was doing business in Minnesota and could not claim unfair surprise at Minnesota's choice of its own law? Compare Rush v. Savchuk, discussed supra p. 335, where the mere fact that a corporation was doing business in the forum state was held an insufficient contact for purposes of territorial jurisdiction. If the reasonable expectations of the parties are relevant, of what relevance are post-accident changes such as the residence of the plaintiff in *Allstate?* Further, if post-accident changes are not irrelevant, as *Allstate* says, doesn't this provide an incentive for a plaintiff to create contacts with a state that has the most favorable law, thus encouraging forum shopping? The *Allstate* opinion says that Mrs. Hague did not move to Minnesota for such a tactical purpose. If she had, would the Minnesota contacts have been any less real so long as her residence was genuine? At bottom, would this be any different from the "consent" argument for application of forum law rejected in *Phillips Petroleum?* Given the expansive treatment of the expectations issue in *Allstate,* was there any greater "unfair surprise" involved in *Phillips Petroleum?*

The full faith and credit clause applies not only to choice of law but also to recognition of judgments of sister states and federal courts. See Note on Full Faith and Credit, infra p. 683. In footnote 10 in *Allstate,* the opinion states that "[d]ifferent considerations are of course at issue when full faith and credit is to be accorded to acts, records and proceedings outside the choice-of-law area, such as in the case of sister state court judgment." Why is this so clear?

3. Choice of Law and Territorial Jurisdiction

As indicated in the *Allstate* opinion, choice of law used to be conceptualized in territorial terms paralleling those of the "presence" standard for territorial jurisdiction pronounced in Pennoyer v. Neff and its progeny. See fns. 11, 21–22. Concurrently as the rules governing territorial jurisdiction broadened to the "minimum contacts" approach of International Shoe v. State of Washington, a similar evolution took place in the rules governing choice of law. Although the Supreme Court has tried to keep the two analyses distinct, it is far from clear that it has succeeded in doing so or that it is consistent in its treatment of the relationship between the two. Nor is it clear that the two analyses should be distinct.

In several cases the Court has rejected the argument that because a state may apply its own law, it also has jurisdiction over the parties. See Hanson v. Denckla, noted supra p. 313; Shaffer v. Heitner, supra p. 315; Kulko v. Superior Court, 436 U.S. 84, 98 S.Ct. 1690, 56 L.Ed.2d 132 (1978). Should it be relevant in determining what substantive law to apply that the forum has territorial jurisdiction? *Phillips Petroleum* seems to say that it should not, but the Court has not always seen things this way. Consider first Justice Brennan's statement in his partial dissent in Shaffer v. Heitner:

" * * * I believe that practical considerations argue in favor of seeking to bridge the distance between the choice-of-law and jurisdictional inquiries. * * * [W]e could wisely act to minimize conflicts, confusion, and uncertainty by adopting a liberal view of jurisdiction, unless considerations of fairness or efficiency strongly point in the opposite direction." 433 U.S. at 225–226.

Next consider the statement in the *Allstate* plurality opinion, also written by Justice Brennan, that Minnesota's unquestioned jurisdiction over the parties was a "factor not without significance in assessing the constitutionality of Minnesota's choice of its own substantive law." Fn. 23. Does this mean that where territorial jurisdiction is at issue, choice of law should be irrelevant, but that where choice of law is disputed, territorial jurisdiction should be relevant? Is this coherent? Is this desirable?

Consider the forum shopping implications of being able to sue a defendant under a geographically expansive concept of territorial jurisdiction combined with a permissive view of legislative jurisdiction, so that a court could constitutionally apply its own law to actions reachable by long arm statutes such as California's. Would forum shopping also result from using legislative jurisdiction as a basis for finding territorial jurisdiction? See Hay, The Interrelation of Jurisdiction and Choice-of-Law in United States Conflicts Law, 28 Int'l & Comp. L.Q. 161 (1979).

These kinds of considerations presumably underlay the Court's pronouncement in *Phillips Petroleum* that, at least in a class action, a court "may not use [an] assumption of jurisdiction as added weight in the scale when considering the permissible constitutional limits on choice of substantive law" and its criticism of contrary arguments as "bootstrapping." Compare Ferens v. Deere & Co., 819 F.2d 423 (3d Cir.1987). See also Miller and Crump, Jurisdiction and Choice of Law in Multistate Class Actions After Phillips Petroleum Co. v. Shutts, 96 Yale L.J. 1 (1986).

Another approach is to apply the same analysis to both the territorial and choice of law questions, resolving both issues together. Compare the constitutional standards for territorial jurisdiction with those for choice of law. *International Shoe* requires sufficient "minimum contacts" such that the exercise of jurisdiction "does not offend traditional notions of fair play and substantial justice." *Allstate* requires "significant contact or significant aggregation of contacts, creating state interests, with the parties and the occurrence or transaction" to assure that the choice of law is "neither arbitrary nor fundamentally unfair." Do these standards differ? Do convenience and sovereignty considerations play themselves out differently under the two formulations? Consider Justice Black's statement in his dissent in Hanson v. Denckla:

> "True, the question whether the law of a State can be applied to a transaction is different from the question whether the courts of that State have jurisdiction to enter a judgment, but the two are often closely related and to a substantial degree depend upon similar considerations." 357 U.S. at 258.

Based on such relationship and common considerations, is it possible to integrate the two questions so that a single inquiry will give a common answer, viz., that a state that has territorial jurisdiction may apply its own law, and conversely, that a state which cannot apply its own law, because another state has a greater contact or interest in the action, cannot assume jurisdiction over the parties? Would this collapse due process and full faith and credit considerations? Should it? See Kogan, Toward a Jurisprudence of Choice of Law: The Priority of Fairness Over Comity, 62 N.Y.U.L.Rev. 651 (1987); Brilmayer and Lee, State Sovereignty and the Two Faces of Federalism: A Comparative Study of Federal Jurisdiction and the Conflict of Laws, 60 Notre Dame L.Rev. 833 (1985); Weinberg, Choice of Law and Minimal Scrutiny, 49 U.Chi.L.Rev. 440 (1982); Martin, Personal Jurisdiction and Choice of Law, 78 Mich.L.Rev. 872 (1980); Peterson, Proposals of Marriage Between Jurisdiction and Choice of Law, 14 U.C.Davis L.Rev. 869 (1981); Hill, The Judicial Function in Choice of Law, 85 Colum.L.Rev. 1585 (1985).

Which is more important to the defendant, choice of law or jurisdiction? One author left no doubt as to her answer to this question: "To believe that a defendant's contacts with the forum state should be stronger under the due process clause for jurisdictional purposes than for choice of law is to believe that an accused is more concerned with where he will be hanged than whether." Silberman, Shaffer v. Heitner: The End of an Era, 53 N.Y.U.L.Rev. 33, 88 (1978). If this is so, in a federal system of justice should there be more than one constitutionally proper substantive law? Is it more reasonable to have a doctrine of "choice of jurisdiction" than one of "choice of law"? See Kozyris, Reflections on Allstate: The Lessening of Due Process in Choice of Law, 14 U.C. Davis L.Rev. 889 (1981). Is *Allstate*'s assertion that the law of more than one state may be constitutionally proper consistent with Erie Railroad Co. v. Tompkins, infra p. 562, in which the Court sought to eliminate the application of different substantive laws in areas of overlapping federal-state jurisdiction on grounds of due process and the need to eliminate forum shopping?

D. ALLOCATION OF JUDICIAL AUTHORITY AMONG THE COURTS OF A STATE

1. SUBJECT MATTER JURISDICTION

INTRODUCTORY NOTE ON DISTRIBUTION OF JURISDICTION AMONG STATE TRIBUNALS

1. The Problem of Multiple Tribunals

If all controversies arising within a single jurisdiction were cognizable in one tribunal the problems of "jurisdiction of the subject matter" would be largely obviated. But nowhere are all controversies so cognizable. Many states have made progress toward a single system of judicial tribunals, and a few have succeeded in achieving this result. Administrative tribunals, however, have not been so consolidated in this country and probably never will be.

a. Causes of Multiplicity. The causes of a multiplicity of tribunals are practical and historical. A tribunal is typically created in response to the felt necessity for providing a convenient forum in which to hear a type of case demanding resolution. Justice courts were scattered into the rural areas because farmers' disputes could not await the journey to town; county courts, having a somewhat larger but still limited jurisdiction (typically including "probate"), were similarly created and for similar reasons; city courts were provided to save local citizens the inconvenience of traveling to the county seat. Specialized courts, such as probate courts, juvenile courts and, more modernly, "family" courts, were created partly to achieve real or imagined advantages of specialization and partly in an effort to "get away" from the "rigid technicalities" of existing tribunals. Similar pressures are at work in respect to administrative agencies.

Once established, specialized tribunals tend to perpetuate themselves. Incumbents like their jobs; practitioners before them prefer the accustomed ways of procedure; continuous minor adjustment to the familiar is thought easier than sudden major adjustment to the novel. In consequence, in many states today, notably New York, there is a handful of different courts, despite persistent reform efforts. See, e.g., Karlen and Miller, A New Judicial Article for New York, 39 N.Y.S.B.J. 9 (1967). Compare ABA Standards Relating to Court Organization §§ 1.10–1.12 (1974) (recommending a single trial court with specialized operating divisions). In all states there are literally dozens of administrative agencies.

b. The Language of Jurisdictional Statutes. When there is more than one trial court, the language used to define their jurisdiction is usually in the following terms:

"Actions at law." In many states, even though there has been a "merger" of law and equity insofar as the courts of general jurisdiction are concerned, courts of limited jurisdiction are granted jurisdiction only of actions "at law," with or without the addition of designated types of "equity" suits. See, e.g., C.C.P. 86 (municipal and justice courts).

"Probate." The jurisdiction of the ecclesiastical courts, which are the historical ancestors of the probate court, was not only confused but also was in large measure concurrent with equity and, to some extent, the common law courts. Early American statutory provisions for probate courts not only varied in their terms but were generally vague. Decisions in one jurisdiction were often relied on elsewhere without reference to the language of the statutes. The result is a confusion about the scope of "probate" jurisdiction which few states have been able to avoid and which no study of history can rectify. Compare Simes and Basye, The Organization of the Probate Court in America, 42 Mich.L.Rev. 965, 43 Mich.L.Rev. 113 (1944).

"Title to real property." The jurisdiction of inferior courts is typically defined in terms of a monetary amount, excluding, however, cases involving "title" to land. It is difficult to classify some types of complaints in these terms. See, e.g., Anno., 115 A.L.R. 504.

"Amount in controversy." The most common basis for defining the jurisdiction of courts of limited jurisdiction is in terms of the amount in controversy. When, as in California, the jurisdiction of inferior courts is made exclusive, then the ceiling on the inferior court is also the floor of the court of general jurisdiction. Several problems are presented:

(1) Whether the jurisdictional minimum amount is satisfied when a single plaintiff sues a single defendant on a multiplicity of unrelated claims which in aggregate exceed the minimum. The prevailing view is that it is so satisfied, and this is true even if some or all of the claims have been assigned to plaintiff for collection only. Hammell v. Superior Court, 217 Cal. 5, 17 P.2d 101 (1932); Anno., 93 A.L.R. 147; Depretto v. Superior Court, 116 Cal.App.3d 36, 171 Cal.Rptr. 810 (1981).

(2) Whether the amount is satisfied when several plaintiffs join in suing one defendant. Generally, the minimum is regarded as not satisfied in such instances, e.g., Colla v. Carmichael U-Drive Autos, Inc., 111 Cal.App.Supp. 784, 294 Pac. 378 (1930); Dix v. American

Bankers Life Assur. Co., 141 Mich.App. 650, 367 N.W.2d 896 (1985), but an "exception" has been recognized where the claims are factually related (as they must be for the plaintiffs to join in the first place) and one of the claims is in excess of the jurisdictional minimum. Emery v. Pacific Employers Ins. Co., 8 Cal.2d 663, 67 P.2d 1046 (1937); cf. Carvalho v. Coletta, ___ R.I. ___, 457 A.2d 614 (1983). An exception is also recognized when several claims are made against property or a fund the value of which exceeds the jurisdictional minimum. See Annos., 72 A.L.R. 193, 109 A.L.R. 1185.

(3) Whether there is aggregation of claims when the action is a class suit. See Daar v. Yellow Cab Co., 67 Cal.2d 695, 63 Cal.Rptr. 724, 433 P.2d 732 (1967).

(4) When the remedy sought is a declaratory judgment or an injunction, what is the "thing" to be evaluated? Thus, if a taxpayer seeks an injunction restraining enforcement of a tax, is the "amount in controversy" to be measured by the amount of the tax in a given year, the present value of the amount of the tax to be collected over some period of the future, the value of the property to be taxed, or some other measure? See Annos., 115 A.L.R. 1489, 30 A.L.R.2d 602; cf. Annos., 118 A.L.R. 715, 109 A.L.R. 300.

(5) The effect of a counterclaim or cross-complaint by the defendant. It is generally held that when plaintiff's claim satisfies the jurisdictional minimum of a superior court, defendant may assert a counterclaim for less than the minimum. Cf. Electra Ad Sign Co., Inc. v. Cedar Rapids Truck Center, 316 N.W.2d 876 (Iowa 1982). Anno., 58 A.L.R.2d 84. When plaintiff's claim is brought in an inferior court because less than the jurisdictional minimum of the superior court, defendant ordinarily cannot assert a counterclaim in excess of the jurisdictional maximum. In some states, however, it is provided that such claims may be asserted and that the whole action shall thereupon be transferred to the superior tribunal. See C.C.P. 396.

In determining the amount in controversy, the amount of *alleged* damages governs, unless on the facts pleaded there is no possibility that such an amount could be awarded. Bell v. Preferred Life Assur. Soc., 320 U.S. 238, 64 S.Ct. 5, 88 L.Ed. 15 (1943); Muller v. Reagh, 150 Cal.App.2d 99, 309 P.2d 826 (1957); Neumann v. Brigman, 475 So.2d 1247 (Fla.App.1985). In consequence, plaintiff may sometimes choose her court by selecting the size of her prayer. This is regularly done in personal injury litigation. See Anno., 47 A.L.R.2d 651.

2. Criteria for Channeling in Jurisdictional Statutes

Many of the problems suggested above could be avoided by more precise legislative draftsmanship. But there appear to be some unavoidable problems. The statutes have to be drafted with principal reference to the typical cases that the tribunals are supposed to entertain. However careful is the drafting, the variousness of private conduct giving rise to disputes will almost certainly outrun the foresight of the draftsman. Hence, there will be the unanticipated atypical case and with it jurisdictional problems. Consider the following two cases.

NELSON v. IOWA–ILLINOIS GAS & ELEC. CO.
Supreme Court of Iowa, 1966.
259 Iowa 101, 143 N.W.2d 289.

GARFIELD, CHIEF JUSTICE.

This appeal involves the jurisdiction of the district court to hear and determine an action for damages against an employer for death of its employee from an injury sustained in the course of his employment. The court held it was without jurisdiction. We agree.

Plaintiff, as administratrix of the estate of Raymond Nelson, deceased, brought this law action in district court against City Service Oil Company, Inc. (herein called defendant) and another to recover damages for his death. Defendant appeared specially for the sole purpose of attacking the court's jurisdiction on the ground it appears from the petition decedent was injured "while in the employment of defendant" and in the course thereof; by reason of chapters 85, 86 and 87, Code, 1962, the only forum for the trial of issues arising from such injuries as between employer and employee is the Iowa Industrial Commissioner; the court is therefore without jurisdiction to determine such issues.

* * *

After defendant's special appearance was filed but before it was sustained the petition was amended to allege decedent, while in the employment of defendant "either as an employee or as an independent contractor" was electrocuted. Except for the insertion in the petition of these quoted words following "while in the employment of defendant" it was not changed.

Upon this appeal plaintiff contends her decedent was excluded from coverage under the Workmen's Compensation Act because he was an independent contractor; the court had jurisdiction of the part of the amended petition which alleges decedent was an independent contractor; defendant was estopped to contend otherwise because it asserted before the industrial commissioner decedent was an independent contractor; and the allegation of the petition that decedent was such a contractor must be taken as true.

* * *

Unquestionably, as defendant concedes, an independent contractor is excluded from coverage under the workmen's compensation act. Section 85.61, 3, b so provides and a great many of our decisions recognize this. Thus if the petition had alleged decedent was injured while acting as an independent contractor the district court would have jurisdiction of the action. But, as stated, the allegation merely is decedent was either an employee or an independent contractor, one or the other. As we shall point out, under our decisions if he was an employee not excluded from coverage by the compensation act the court was without jurisdiction to hear such an action as this. This is the legal effect of the amended petition.

71 C.J.S. Pleading § 41, says in black type: "In the absence of a statute or rule of procedure providing otherwise, material facts should not be alleged in the alternative; alternative allegations may be permitted under certain circumstances, although they will be construed against the pleader and will be treated as no stronger than the weakest alternative."   *   *   *

*   *   *

Considering plaintiff's amended petition in the light of the authorities above referred to, it is apparent the claim decedent was injured while acting as an employee of defendant, in the course of his employment, is weaker than the alternative claim he was then an independent contractor.   As before explained   *   *   *   the district court was without jurisdiction to hear the former claim, but not the latter—if it had been pleaded directly.   Since the alleged alternative adds nothing in legal effect to the claim made in the original petition we must hold the special appearance was properly sustained.

*   *   *

Plaintiff's third assigned error, that defendant is estopped to contend decedent was not an independent contractor by asserting before the industrial commissioner he was such, is without merit.

Basis for the assignment is a copy of the deputy industrial commissioner's ruling decedent was an independent contractor which is attached to plaintiff's resistance to the special appearance.   The resistance does not assert an estoppel against defendant but it is argued here it is estopped to take a position inconsistent with that taken before the commissioner.   The petition contains nothing concerning this matter.

We have held the district court was without jurisdiction of the subject matter of the action pleaded in the amended petition.

Jurisdiction of a court over the subject matter is conferred by law and cannot be based on the estoppel of a party to deny its existence. Latta v. Utterback, 202 Iowa 1116, 1118, 211 N.W. 503, and citations; Grubb v. Public Utilities Comm., 281 U.S. 470, 475, 50 S.Ct. 374, 377, 74 L.Ed. 972, 977; Ford v. Industrial Commission of Ohio, 145 Ohio St. 1, 60 N.E.2d 471, 473; 20 Am.Jur.2d, Courts, section 95; 21 C.J.S. Courts § 109.   See also Chicago & N. W. R. Co. v. Fachman, 255 Iowa 989, 993, 125 N.W.2d 210, 212, and citations; Industrial Comm. of Ohio v. Weigand, 128 Ohio St. 463, 191 N.E. 696 (nor on waiver).

Grubb v. Public Utilities Comm., supra, states: "But the appellant does question that it had jurisdiction of the subject-matter; and this although at the outset he treated that jurisdiction as subsisting and invoked its exercise.   Of course, he is entitled to raise this question notwithstanding his prior inconsistent attitude, for jurisdiction of the subject-matter must arise by law and not by mere consent."

*   *   *

We find no reversible error assigned and argued.

Affirmed.

NUERNBERGER v. STATE

Court of Appeals of New York, 1976.
41 N.Y.2d 111, 390 N.Y.S.2d 904, 359 N.E.2d 412.

BREITEL, CHIEF JUDGE.

*   *   *

In April of 1966, claimant Nuernberger was indicted for three crimes committed on his 11-year-old daughter: incest, assault with intent to commit incest, and impairing the morals of a minor. Following a jury trial in Erie County Court, Nuernberger was convicted of both the assault and the impairment charges. The sentence imposed for the assault conviction was from three to six years; on the impairment count a suspended maximum sentence of one year was imposed. Unanimous affirmance of the conviction by the Appellate Division followed (People v. Nuernberger, 31 A.D.2d 718, 297 N.Y.S.2d 525). Undisputed is that claimant was imprisoned pursuant to the County Court commitment from April 14, 1967 until July 17, 1969, when his conviction for assault was reversed by this court and the proceedings transferred to the Family Court (People v. Nuernberger, 25 N.Y.2d 179, 183, 303 N.Y.S.2d 74, 76, 250 N.E.2d 352, 353).

In the prior appeal this court noted that the record sustained claimant's conviction for assault (25 N.Y.2d, at p. 183, 303 N.Y.S.2d, at p. 76, 250 N.E.2d, at p. 353). Reversal, however, was required by the Family Court Act which reposes initially in the Family Court "exclusive original jurisdiction" over "acts which would constitute . . . an assault . . . between parent and child." (Family Ct. Act, § 812; see N.Y.Const., art. VI, § 13, subd. b.) Of course, the Family Court may elect to transfer jurisdiction to an appropriate criminal court (Family Ct. Act, §§ 811, 816, subd. [a]; People v. Johnson, 20 N.Y.2d 220, 223, 282 N.Y.S.2d 481, 483, 229 N.E.2d 180, 181).

Not more than three months after his release by the Family Court, on one year's probation on consent, claimant sued in the Court of Claims. His argument was simple. Since initial exclusive original jurisdiction over the assault charge was in Family Court, the County Court in which he had been convicted and sentenced lacked jurisdiction over both the person of the claimant and the subject matter of the proceeding. Hence, he argues, any mandates issued by the County Court were null and void, affording no protection to the custodial authorities who acted in reliance on their validity.

To be sure, it has long been said and to some extent established, without examination evidently since the common-law reports in this State, that process or mandate is void and hence cannot be relied upon where on its face it is apparent that the issuing court was without jurisdiction over the subject matter, that is, without competence to adjudicate the kind of cause before it (Savacool v. Boughton, 5 Wend. 170, 172; cf. Harty v. State of New York, 29 A.D.2d 243, 244, 287 N.Y.S. 2d 306, 307, affd. 27 N.Y.2d 698, 314 N.Y.S.2d 14, 262 N.E.2d 220;

Douglas v. State of New York, 269 App.Div. 521, 525, 56 N.Y.S.2d 245, 248, affd. 296 N.Y. 530, 68 N.E.2d 605; see, also, Troutman v. State of New York, 273 App.Div. 619, 621–622, 79 N.Y.S.2d 709, 711, 712, pertaining to jurisdiction over the person). In general, the statement is true, except that it does not account for the power of a court to determine that it has no kind of jurisdiction over the category of cause before it (Family Ct. Act, § 813; see Restatement, Judgments, § 10, Comment a; see, also, Dobbs, Validation of Void Judgments: Bootstrap Principle, 53 Va.L.Rev. 1003, 1005–1006, 1009–1014).

This case, however, does not yield to the facile classification suggested by the traditional statement of the rule. To begin with, not every crime between members of a family is cognizable as a Family Court offense (Family Ct. Act, § 812; People v. Lewis, 29 N.Y.2d 923, 924, 329 N.Y.S.2d 100, 101, 279 N.E.2d 856, 857 [incest not within Family Court's exclusive original jurisdiction]). Illustrative is the impairment charge for which claimant was convicted (People v. Nuernberger, 25 N.Y.2d 179, 182, 303 N.Y.S.2d 74, 76, 250 N.E.2d 352, 353, supra). Had the sentence imposed for impairing the morals of a minor not been suspended, there would be no question but that claimant could have been committed to prison by order of County Court. And even were the instant conviction so clearly one to be initially resolved only in Family Court, the custodial authorities criticized by claimant may have assumed, reasonably, that the County Court proceeding took place only after the Family Court determined, as it could under the statute, that the matter should be criminally tried (Family Ct. Act, § 816). Not until this court reversed was it "clear" that the commitment issued pursuant to the judgment of conviction suffered from a "facial" invalidity, if that it was.

It is an encyclopedia commonplace that "[w]here a court is without jurisdiction in the particular case, its acts and proceedings can be of no force or validity, and are a mere nullity and void" (21 C.J.S. Courts § 116). However deceptively attractive and convenient, this commonplace is both too simple and too broad. Definitions of "jurisdiction" are too varied and the consequences flowing from defective "jurisdiction" too diverse. (See Lacks v. Lacks, 41 N.Y.2d 71, 74, 390 N.Y.S.2d 875, 877, 359 N.E.2d 386, decided herewith; Ehrenzweig, Conflict of Laws, § 25, pp. 72–73; Leflar, American Conflicts Law, § 3, pp. 4–6.) In fact discerning analysis would reveal that the absence of power of adjudication in a particular cause does not, in and of itself, automatically deprive a court's acts and proceedings of their validity.

Indeed, this court has recognized that a defect in a court's "jurisdiction", because a defendant had not been sentenced for a six-year period after verdict, may be the basis for habeas corpus relief, but no ground on which to recover damages for false imprisonment. Thus, in People ex rel. Harty v. Fay, 10 N.Y.2d 374, 223 N.Y.S.2d 468, 179 N.E.2d 483, defendant was successful in procuring his release from prison but his subsequent claim for false imprisonment was rejected (Harty v. State of

New York, 27 N.Y.2d 698, 314 N.Y.S.2d 14, 262 N.E.2d 220, affg., 29 A.D.2d 243, 287 N.Y.S.2d 306, supra).

In rejecting the damage claim, this court evidently accepted the Appellate Division interpretation of the prior Court of Appeals holding of lack of jurisdiction as really only illegality of sentence. Whether this reassessment was calculated to avoid the unfortunate consequences routinely associated with defective "jurisdiction" or to recast the prior holding in the light of the versatile use of the term "jurisdiction" is not important. What is important is that from a comparison of the results in the two litigations, one must conclude that notwithstanding the absence of "jurisdiction" for purposes of sustaining the sentence involved, power remained with the sentencing court sufficient to protect officials who carried out its mandates. In short, the *Harty* cases are an ideal example that "jurisdiction" is not a term of a single meaning and none of its uses has an invulnerable definition.

* * *

Conclusive in demonstrating that the voidness rule is not absolute is the exception that, in some circumstances, a court's erroneous determination that it has "subject matter jurisdiction" is subject to the doctrine of *res judicata* and, hence, is not vulnerable to collateral attack (O'Donoghue v. Boies, 159 N.Y. 87, 99, 103, 105–106, 53 N.E. 537, 540, 541, 542 [opns. per O'Brien, J., and Parker, Ch. J.]; Bolton v. Schriever, 135 N.Y. 65, 74, 31 N.E. 1001, 1003; Restatement, Conflicts 2d, § 97, and Comments *b*, *c*; Restatement, Judgments, § 10, subd. 1; Goodrich, Conflict of Laws [4th ed.], § 23, p. 38; Ehrenzweig, Conflict of Laws, § 57, subd. a, pp. 207–208; see Matter of Doey v. Howland Co., 224 N.Y. 30, 38–39, 120 N.E. 53, 54–55; cf. Vander v. Casperson, 12 N.Y.2d 56, 59, 236 N.Y.S.2d 33, 34, 187 N.E.2d 109, 110 [jurisdiction over defendants]). While the scope of this exception is no clearer than the rule to which it is an exception, key is that courts without so-called "subject matter jurisdiction" nonetheless issued binding orders. (See, generally, Dobbs, 53 Va.L.Rev. 1003, 1009–1014.)

By now, it should be evident that the competence of a court to entertain matters in categories over which it has power to adjudicate may be quite different from its power to adjudicate particular causes which arise in the categories (see Bullymore v. Cooper, 46 N.Y. 236, 241–242; cf. O'Donoghue v. Boies, 159 N.Y. 87, 103, 107–108, 53 N.E. 537, 540, 543 [opn. per Parker, Ch. J.], supra). As early as 1884, general "jurisdiction over the subject matter" was distinguished from jurisdiction in particular causes: "a ministerial officer is protected in the execution of process regular on its face, issued by a court, officer or body having general jurisdiction of the subject-matter, or jurisdiction to issue it under special circumstances, although in fact jurisdiction of the person or subject-matter did not exist in the particular case." (Woolsey v. Morris, 96 N.Y. 311, 315). But even this distinction does not solve all the problems.

The voidness rule is applied sketchily. The exceptions to the rule are applied equally sketchily. The rule and its exceptions were engendered by independent and different purposes. By encouraging self-help with impunity, the rule preserves an effective safeguard against judicial usurpation of power. The exceptions protect administrative officials from the consequences of doing what they are required to do by law (Woolsey v. Morris, 96 N.Y. 311, 315, supra).

And, of course, the troubles and the tensions between the rule and exceptions are both caused by and sheltered by the elastic and versatile definition and use of the term "jurisdiction". Sometimes the word means power to adjudicate (e.g., Hunt v. Hunt, 72 N.Y. 217, 228; Cooper v. Davis, 231 App.Div. 527, 529, 248 N.Y.S. 227). Sometimes it means power to enforce orders against a person (e.g., People ex rel. Harty v. Fay, 10 N.Y.2d 374, 379, 223 N.Y.S.2d 468, 471, 179 N.E.2d 483, 485, supra). Sometimes it means power to execute commitments against particular property (e.g., Woolsey v. Morris, 96 N.Y. 311, 315–316, supra). Sometimes it means power to adjudicate over a category of cases and another time it means power to adjudicate a particular case (compare O'Donoghue v. Boies, 159 N.Y. 87, 103, 107–108, 53 N.E. 537, 540, 543 [Parker, Ch. J.], with id., at pp. 97–99, 53 N.E. at pp. 539–540 [O'Brien, J.], supra). Sometimes this lack is fatal to the validity of any act of the tribunal. And sometimes it results in valid process or mandate because the issuing court, as in this case, was not wholly without competence to adjudicate something in the action before it.

With respect to Nuernberger's claim the result should be evident. It may be sustained only if the confusion in the term and concept of "jurisdiction" is allowed to generate still another anomaly in law and justice. The fact is that the County Court had general jurisdiction over criminal actions of the very categories for which claimant was tried and convicted. It also had at least the initial power to adjudicate whether the fact complex required transfer to the Family Court because of its initial exclusive original jurisdiction. Hence, the court was not without some power to adjudicate and its fault was no greater than that of error which remains uncorrected until the appeal was finally resolved in the State's highest court. To say that in such circumstances the mandates of the County Court were void is to deny the reality of the legally constituted courts which issued those mandates and the recognition which would be accorded those mandates in other actions and proceedings until reversal on direct appeal.

Accordingly the order of the Appellate Division should be reversed, without costs, and the claim dismissed.

NOTE ON CHALLENGING SUBJECT MATTER JURISDICTION

1. Threshold Objection to Subject Matter Jurisdiction

The defendant may challenge the court's jurisdiction of the subject matter of the action at the outset by motion, F.R.C.P. 12(h)(3), under code provisions by demurrer, see C.C.P. 430.10(a), or by answer. Does it have to be a special appearance, as in Nelson v. Iowa-Illinois Gas & Elec. Co.? Where reference to evidentiary matter outside the complaint is necessary to determine the jurisdictional question, it may be supplied by affidavit or by proof presented in open court, in which case the motion assumes the form of one for summary judgment. Moreover, the court may raise the question of subject matter jurisdiction on its own initiative, see, e.g., Goodwine v. Superior Court, 63 Cal.2d 481, 47 Cal.Rptr. 201, 407 P.2d 1 (1965), and has a duty—of vaguely defined rigor—to do so. The propriety of such a rule seems unquestionable if the jurisdictional question is raised at the preliminary stages of litigation and where dismissal for want of jurisdiction does not result in barring plaintiff from obtaining any remedy at all, as it may if the challenge to jurisdiction is made after the statute of limitations has run.

It is also doctrine, however, that the question of subject matter jurisdiction may be raised at any time, even after judgment. See F.R.C.P. 12(h)(3), 60(b)(4). This is because, it is said, a court lacking subject matter jurisdiction is equivalent to no court at all. Consideration of the problem revolves around the proposition that jurisdiction may not be conferred by consent.

2. "Jurisdiction May Not be Conferred by Consent"

a. Historical Background. The notion that the judgment of a court not having jurisdiction of the subject matter is void goes back at least into the middle ages. In that period the central common law courts, in the interest of preserving the authority of the Crown, maintained careful scrutiny of the doings of local courts. The doctrine ripened into high authority in the constitutional struggles under James I between the common lawyers, chiefly Coke, and the beneficiaries of the Jacobean royal dispensation. See the excellent historical analysis in Dobbs, The Decline of Jurisdiction by Consent, 40 N.C.L.Rev. 49 (1961).

The leading case was The Case of the Marshalsea, 10 Co.Rep. 68b, 77 E.R. 1027 (K.B.1613). That was an action in King's Bench for false imprisonment brought by a plaintiff who had been imprisoned in the jail of the Marshalsea court, a court of special and limited jurisdiction attached to the Royal Household. Defendants were the marshal of the prison and those acting under him, who justified the imprisonment on the ground that plaintiff was taken pursuant to process of the court. Plaintiff contended, however, that the Marshalsea court had no jurisdiction of the action in respect of which the process issued, that the process was therefore void and that defendant accordingly acted without justification. In King's Bench it was concluded that the Marshalsea court did not have jurisdiction. The next question was whether action taken in good faith under its process was nevertheless justified. It was held not, 10 Co. Rep. at 76a–76b, 77 E.R. at 1038–39:

> "[A] difference was taken when a Court has jurisdiction of the cause, and proceeds * * * erroneously, there * * * the officer or minister of the Court who executes the precept or process of the Court, no action lies against him. But when the Court has not jurisdiction of the cause, there the whole proceeding is *coram non judice*, and actions will lie against them without any regard of the precept or process * * * [for] it is not of necessity to obey him who is not Judge of the cause, no more than it is a mere stranger."

The rule of the *Marshalsea's Case* proved burdensome and troublesome in England and was seriously eroded by the counter-rule that "mere error" in the exercise of jurisdiction, even though that error was committed in respect to a fact on which jurisdiction depended, did not vitiate a judgment of a court of limited jurisdiction. See Papillon v. Buckner, Hardres 478, 145 E.R. 556 (1669). By the end of the period of England's constitutional troubles, the rule had been almost buried. See Brittain v. Kinnaird, 1 Brod. & Bing. 432, 129 E.R. 789 (C.P. 1819).

It was nevertheless transplanted to this country, appearing as a holding in a handful of cases, e.g., Coffin v. Tracy, 3 Caines 128 (N.Y.1805) (justice court judgment); Blin v. Campbell, 14 Johns. 432 (N.Y.1817) (same), and as dictum in many more, e.g., Wm. Overstreet & Co. v. J. Brown & Co., 4 McCord 79 (S.C.1826). See also Anno. 1 Smith's Leading Cases 816 (5th Am.Ed. 1848).

In matters relating to the jurisdiction of the federal courts, the rule was more rigorously applied, the constitutional implications being clearly recognized. Thus in Davis v. Packard, 32 U.S. (7 Pet.) 276, 8 L.Ed. 684 (1833), it was held that a consul of a foreign government did not waive his objection to state court jurisdiction by failure to assert it promptly. The Supreme Court observed that the jurisdictional grant in Art. III, Sec. 2, exercised by Congress as exclusive jurisdiction (cf. 28 U.S.C.A. § 1351), rested on "higher considerations of public policy" than mere personal privilege. Similarly, the exclusive jurisdiction of the federal courts in matters arising under the patent laws was recognized, despite defendant's initial stipulation to jurisdiction in state court, in Dudley v. Mayhew, 3 N.Y. 2 (1849). Conversely, the federal courts early and ever since have rigorously insisted that the existence of their jurisdiction be shown. If such jurisdiction does not appear the point may be raised for the first time on appeal, and may be raised by the court itself or even by the party who had invoked the court's jurisdiction. See Capron v. Van Noorden, 6 U.S. (2 Cranch) 126, 2 L.Ed. 229 (1804).

b. Cooley's Formulation. On the basis of what may charitably be described as a loose reading of the precedents, the principal ones being those cited above, Judge Cooley was moved to erect a formidable edifice of doctrine, Cooley, Constitutional Limitations *398 (4th ed. 1878):

"A court has jurisdiction of any subject-matter, if, by the law of its organization, it has authority to take cognizance of, try, and determine cases of that description. If it assumes to act in a case over which the law does not give it authority, the proceeding and judgment will be altogether void, and rights of property cannot be devested by means of them.

"It is a maxim in the law that consent can never confer jurisdiction: by which is meant that the consent of parties cannot empower a court to act upon subjects which are not submitted to its determination and judgment by the law. The law creates courts, and upon considerations of general public policy defines and limits their jurisdiction; and this can neither be enlarged nor restricted by the act of the parties."

3. Collateral Attack

The broadest implication of Cooley's formula was that an erroneous assumption of jurisdiction could be attacked not only at any time directly but also at any time collaterally. Observe that in Nuernberger v. State, the appeal in the criminal case was a "direct" attack on the judgment of conviction, while the damages suit was a "collateral" attack on it. This view has now been largely abandoned. See United States v. United Mine Workers, 330 U.S. 258, 67 S.Ct. 677, 91 L.Ed. 884 (1947). In Stoll v. Gottlieb, 305 U.S. 165, 59 S.Ct. 134, 83

L.Ed. 104 (1938), the Supreme Court held that where the issue of the court's jurisdiction had been litigated in the first action, it was res judicata and could not thereafter be challenged by collateral attack. See also Durfee v. Duke, 375 U.S. 106, 84 S.Ct. 242, 11 L.Ed.2d 186 (1963). This rule was extended in Chicot County Drainage District v. Baxter State Bank, 308 U.S. 371, 60 S.Ct. 317, 84 L.Ed. 329 (1940), to the case where the loser in the prior action had appeared and contested on the merits without expressly raising the jurisdictional point. This, too, was held res judicata, because the issue was one which was implicitly passed on and which might have been expressly litigated.

Compare Restatement Second of Judgments § 12, stating that a judgment in a contested action may be subsequently avoided only if:

"(1) The subject matter of the action was so plainly beyond the court's jurisdiction that its entertaining the action was a manifest abuse of authority; or

"(2) Allowing the judgment to stand would substantially infringe the authority of another tribunal or agency of government; or

"(3) The judgment was rendered by a court lacking capability to make an adequately informed determination of a question concerning its own jurisdiction and as a matter of procedural fairness the party seeking to avoid the judgment should have opportunity belatedly to attack the court's subject matter jurisdiction."

Compare Moore, Collateral Attack on Subject Matter Jurisdiction: A Critique of the Restatement (Second) of Judgments, 66 Cornell L.Rev. 534 (1981). See also Moffat v. Moffat, 27 Cal.3d 645, 165 Cal.Rptr. 877, 612 P.2d 967 (1980), holding that a judgment is res judicata and effective for issue preclusion even though in excess of the "jurisdiction" of the rendering court.

In Nelson v. Iowa-Illinois Gas & Elec. Co., suppose plaintiff had filed the action in district court first, alleging that her decedent was an independent contractor, and defendant failed to assert the defense of the workmen's compensation statute. If plaintiff had then won on the merits, would the judgment have been "void" because the defendant's failure to raise the defense amounted to an implied consent to the district court's jurisdiction? Compare Doney v. Tambouratgis, 23 Cal.3d 91, 151 Cal.Rptr. 347, 587 P.2d 1160 (1979) (defense may not be raised for the first time on appeal); Martineau, Subject Matter Jurisdiction as a New Issue on Appeal: Reining in an Unruly Horse, 1988 B.Y.U.L.Rev. 1. See also Owen Equip. and Erect. Co. v. Kroger, 437 U.S. 365, 98 S.Ct. 2396, 57 L.Ed.2d 274 (1978), at fn. 21, holding it irrelevant that the defendant concealed its objection to jurisdiction in federal court until after the state statute of limitations had run, because "[f]ederal judicial power does not depend upon 'prior action or consent of the parties.'"

Can the latter statement be fully reconciled with the holding in Chicot County Drainage District v. Baxter State Bank, supra, which was approved in Durfee v. Duke, supra?

See generally Note, Filling the Void: Judicial Power and Jurisdictional Attacks on Judgments, 87 Yale L.J. 164 (1977).

2. VENUE

INTRODUCTORY NOTE ON VENUE

The rules of venue determine the place of trial within a jurisdiction. Attention here is directed to venue problems in state court systems; problems of venue in the federal court system are treated infra p. 615.

1. Historical Background

Anglo-American concepts of venue derived partly from the peculiarities of the early rules governing process and judgment and partly from the fact that jurors were originally summoned to give the facts of the case, i.e., to act as witnesses, rather than to decide the case on the basis of evidence submitted to them.

Process in "real" actions, that is, actions for the recovery of land, could be served by giving notice to defendant at his house, or, if he could not be found, by proclaiming it at the church of the parish where the land lay. If defendant failed to appear, default judgment could be entered. Hence, the requirements of service of process plus the inviting prospect of a default judgment dictated that real actions be commenced in the county where the property was located. In contrast, process in personal actions, or at least most of them, was effected by the arrest of the defendant. Until 1725 no judgment could be entered in a personal action without the actual appearance of the defendant, so that it was essential to successful prosecution of the action to get hold of him. This required process directed to the sheriff of the county where defendant resided. From this root derives the tradition that personal actions are properly commenced in the county where defendant resides.

The problem of the place of trial, as distinct from the place of summons, was somewhat different but its resolution led to the same general result. Actions in the central common law courts were pleaded to issue at Westminster. They were then to be tried before jurors of the county where the events took place, for only such jurors would know the facts of the matter. In "real" actions the jurors would be from the county where the land in dispute was located; in personal actions, the jurors would be from the county where the disputed transaction took place, which in those days of limited travel was typically though not invariably the county where defendant (and usually plaintiff also) resided. The case might actually be tried at Westminster, the jurors being brought there for the purpose. But the cases were ordinarily set for trial in Westminster *nisi prius* ("unless first") the judges should come on circuit to the county where the jurors were. In time, the bulk of the cases were tried at *nisi prius*. The tradition was thus established that the proper place of trial in real actions was the county where the land was situated and in personal actions (usually) where defendant resided. On this see generally the valuable discussion in Blume, Place of Trial in Civil Cases, 48 Mich.L.Rev. 1 (1949).

2. Modern Statutory Provisions

a. In General. The essential features of early English venue law have been carried down to the present day. See generally Stevens, Venue Statutes: Diagnosis and Proposed Cure, 49 Mich.L.Rev. 307 (1951). As there set forth, practically all the states provide that actions concerning real property shall be brought in the county wherein the land is situated. But whether a particular action concerns the property in such a way as to come within the real property venue statute varies according to local statutory language and interpretive decisions. For example, actions for damages for injury to land are regarded as concerning real property in some states but not in others. Cf. Annos., 63 A.L.R.2d 456, 65 A.L.R.2d 1268, 77 A.L.R.2d 1014. A few states apply a like "situs" rule in actions for the recovery of personal property.

In actions other than those concerning property, all statutes permit and many require the action to be brought in the county where defendant resides, subject to exceptions and options in certain types of cases. Thus, the residence of the defendant is regarded as the "residual" basis of venue for "transitory" actions in practically all jurisdictions: venue is properly laid there except as otherwise specifically provided.

Special provisions are usually made for probate and domestic relations cases, actions against nonresidents, governmental agencies, insurance companies and, in many states, corporations generally. Special options frequently allow suit in the county where a "contract" is "made" or "to be performed" and where a tort "occurs." Cf. Annos., 69 A.L.R.2d 1324, 84 A.L.R.2d 994, 97 A.L.R. 2d 934. Compare Comment, Venue in Civil Actions in Wisconsin, 1960 Wis.L. Rev. 663; Fraser, Venue Oklahoma Style, 23 Okla.L.Rev. 182 (1970); Clermont, Restating Territorial Jurisdiction and Venue for State and Federal Courts, 66 Corn.L.Rev. 411 (1981); Clark, Venue in Civil Actions, 36 Okla.L.Rev. 643 (1983).

   b. Statutory Criteria for Determining Venue. As pointed out in Stevens, supra, the criteria for determining the place of trial under typical state statutes are both numerous and intersecting. The principal criteria are:

   (1) The situs of the "subject matter" of the litigation. This is the classifying principle of the rule for venue of actions involving real property.

   (2) The residence of one or the other of the parties. This is the classifying principle of the "residual" rule of venue in personal actions. It is also the principle, for example, for the rule regarding actions against nonresidents (which in many states may be brought in the county where plaintiff resides) and actions against an executor or administrator (which in most states must be brought in the county in which is located the court by which the executor or administrator has been appointed).

   (3) Where the "cause of action" "arose." This is the classifying principle, for example, of venue rules that authorize or require "tort" actions to be brought in the county where the tort "occurred" and that "contract" actions may be brought in the county where the contract is "made" or "to be performed." This principle is similar to the one regarding real property actions, if it is assumed (as is often but not always the case) that the disputed transaction between the parties concerning land took place in the county where the land is situated.

   (4) Where the defendant has a place of business or may be "found." This is an attenuated application of the residence principle. But the attenuation amounts to almost complete dilution when the action is brought against a state-wide business organization or a defendant who is served while traveling outside the county of his residence.

   (5) Plaintiff's choice. In some states some actions may be brought in any county. This is the typical rule regarding actions against nonresidents.

c. Plaintiff's Choice and its Consequences. Plaintiff has the initial power to lay the action in a particular county. This initiative has several implications. In the first place, it may make crucial which party first files an action concerning a dispute. The general rule is that the action first filed, if brought in a proper county, is the one in which the dispute will actually be fought out. A person in a strategically defensive position (i.e., interested in resisting a change in the status quo) sometimes has available remedies by which he can take the litigating initiative. Notable among these remedies are the declaratory judgment and equitable *quia timet* devices such as quiet title. See Note on Injunctions and Declaratory Relief, supra p. 198. By taking the litigating initiative a party to a dispute who is in a strategically defensive position may be able to lay venue to his advantage.

In the second place, proper venue is usually determined by the claim stated in the complaint. Within the range of the possible ways of framing a complaint regarding a particular dispute, plaintiff may frame his complaint on the basis, inter alia, of his venue preference. For example, he may treat a defendant's taking of property as the "tort" of conversion or, "waiving the tort and suing in implied contract," he may treat it as giving rise to the "contract" to pay the reasonable value of the property. If his framing of the complaint wildly distorts the transaction—if he fails to "state a cause of action" on the attempted theory or if the theory adopted is so unusual that the court will not sanction it as a basis for laying venue—then the complaint will not be regarded as determinative. Short of this, however, plaintiff may determine venue by framing his complaint in calculated response to the venue options available to him.

Defendant's remedies against plaintiff's choice vary from state to state. The traditional rule is that she may obtain dismissal, by special demurrer, motion or analogous device if, but only if, the action as framed is brought in the wrong county. The modern and more prevalent rule is that she may move for a transfer of the case to the county of proper venue. See, e.g., C.C.P. 396b, 397; N.Y.C.P.L.R. §§ 510, 511. In most states defendant's failure so to move at the threshold of the litigation is a waiver of her venue objection. But two difficulties are encountered. First, in some states the objection is not waived, so that the venue objection is assimilated to the objection of want of jurisdiction over the "subject matter." Second, in many states the trial court's ruling on a venue objection is not immediately reviewable in an appellate court but may be so reviewed only on an appeal from a judgment. See People ex rel. Norwegian-American Hospital v. Sandusky, 21 Ill.2d 296, 171 N.E.2d 640 (1961) (appellate review by mandamus available only in case of clear error). In these states if a venue objection is erroneously overruled, the subsequent proceedings may be completely vitiated by later reversal on the venue point. This is a check on undue stretching of the venue statutes by the plaintiff, but one that operates ex post facto and therefore expensively. Compare Barquis v. Merchants Collection Ass'n, 7 Cal.3d 94, 101 Cal.Rptr. 745, 496 P.2d 817 (1972), holding the place-of-trial provisions in justice courts to be mandatory and not waived by default, and allowing a class action for damages for defendants' systematic filing of collection suits in improper places of venue. See also the defendant's remedies for venue objections in California, discussed below.

3. The California Venue Rules

The California venue rules are fairly typical of those in most states.

a. The Basic Rule. The basic venue rule in California is that the action must be brought in the county where the defendant, or one of several defendants, resides. C.C.P. 395. Qualifying this basic rule are special provisions regarding real property actions, C.C.P. 392; actions involving public officials and state and local governmental agencies, C.C.P. 393, 394, 401, Cal.Govt.Code, 955, 955.2; dissolution of marriage, C.C.P. 395; most types of claims against executors and administrators, C.C.P. 395.1; nonresidents, C.C.P. 395, and others. Regarding actions against a state agency, see, e.g., Tharp v. Superior Court, 32 Cal.3d 496, 186 Cal.Rptr. 335, 651 P.2d 1141 (1982), construing Cal.Govt.Code 955, which permits the Attorney General to demand change of venue to Sacramento County in certain actions against the state. See also Brown v. Superior Court, 37 Cal.3d 477, 208 Cal.Rptr. 724, 691 P.2d 272 (1984): An action for damages for violation of the California Fair Employment and Housing Act (FEHA), Calif.Gov't Code 12900 et seq., and for intentional infliction of emotional distress and wrongful discharge, was brought in the county in which the alleged discriminatory practices took place, as provided by the special venue provision of the FEHA (Gov't Code 12965(b)). This venue was held proper even though three individual defendants resided elsewhere and the principal places of business of the corporate defendants also were located elsewhere. The court stated that in order to vindicate the policies of the FEHA, its special venue provisions must control in cases involving FEHA claims joined with non-FEHA claims where the various claims arise from the same set of facts.

The basic rule is further qualified by three other important exceptions:

(1) Actions for death, personal injury or property damage may at plaintiff's option be brought in the county "where the injury occurs." C.C.P. 395.

(2) "When a defendant has contracted to perform an obligation in a particular county," an action "founded" on the contract may be brought in the county where it "is to be performed, or in which the contract in fact was entered into." C.C.P. 395. This provision has given rise to much litigation, principally concerning whether a particular action is "founded" on the contract or on some duty arising outside the contract, and further legislative specification, C.C.P. 395(b). See, e.g., Mitchell v. Superior Court, 186 Cal.App.3d 1040, 231 Cal.Rptr. 176 (1986).

(3) Corporate and association defendants may be sued not only in a county as determined by the foregoing rules but also in a county "where the contract is made or is to be performed, or where the obligation or liability arises, or the breach occurs * * *." C.C.P. 395.5. This provision gives a plaintiff a somewhat wider range of choice in laying venue against corporations. See Hale v. Bohannon, 38 Cal.2d 458, 241 P.2d 4 (1952); Anaheim Extrusion Co., Inc. v. Superior Court, 170 Cal.App.3d 1201, 216 Cal.Rptr. 815 (1985).

b. The Local Action Rule. Venue for actions involving real property lies in a county where all, or some part, of the property is located. C.C.P. 392. This rule is subject to the waivability and transfer provisions that affect other venue statutes. See, e.g., C.C.P. 396a, 396b. Cal.Const. Art. VI, Sec. 5 formerly contained a similar provision (whose constitutional status gave rise to problems over whether it could be waived), but this provision was eliminated in the general revision of the Judicial Article in 1966.

c. Multiple Claims and Multiple Parties. Difficulties in the application of the venue rules in California, as elsewhere, are encountered when multiple claims or multiple parties are involved. In an excellent study on the subject, Venue of Mixed Actions in California, 44 Calif.L.Rev. 685 (1956), Professor Van Alstyne concludes that the applicable rule in such circumstances is as follows:

"If an action is commenced upon two or more causes of action or against two or more defendants, or both, in a county other than one designated [by the venue rules] as a proper court for the trial thereof with respect to each count and each defendant, considered separately, it must be transferred on proper and timely motion to any such proper court, agreed to, designated, or determined in the manner provided in [C.C.P. 398]. If there is no county which is proper for trial with respect to each count and each defendant, considered separately, the action must be transferred for trial to a county in which the defendants, or some of them, resided at the commencement of the action."

d. Contractual Stipulation of Venue. Contracts, particularly "adhesion" contracts, sometimes specify venue for actions arising out of them. The validity of such provisions poses questions comparable to those in National Equipment Rental Ltd. v. Szukhent, noted supra p. 382. See Anno., 31 A.L.R.4th 404; Mosby v. Superior Court, 43 Cal.App.3d 219, 117 Cal.Rptr. 588 (1974).

e. Change of Venue. The remedy to rectify improper venue is transfer and transfer may be made on timely motion from an admittedly proper county to some other county for the "convenience of witnesses and the ends of justice." C.C.P. 397; Annos., 74 A.L.R.2d 16, 10 A.L.R.4th 1046; Hamilton v. Superior Court, 37 Cal.App.3d 418, 112 Cal.Rptr. 450 (1974). The device for applying for venue change is a motion supported by affidavit establishing the facts showing the ground for the change, and, if the movant is a defendant, showing that defendant has a meritorious defense.

f. Appellate Review. An order granting or denying a venue change motion was formerly an appealable order in California. It is now reviewable, and apparently reviewable only, by means of writ of mandate applied for within 30 days of service of notice of the ruling on the motion. See C.C.P. 400. This method of appellate review is cheaper and faster than the former mode of ordinary appeal. It also helps explain why California has so much more appellate law concerning venue than most other states.

For a thorough treatment of California venue, see C.E.B., 1 Calif.Civ.Pro. Before Trial, c. 3 (1977); 3 Witkin 572–725.

CARRUTH v. SUPERIOR COURT

Court of Appeal of California, 1978.
80 Cal.App.3d 215, 145 Cal.Rptr. 344.

Brown, P. J.

Lowell T. Carruth and the law partnership of which he is a member, McCormick, Barstow, Sheppard, Coyle & Wayte (MBSC&W), seek a writ of mandate to compel the San Diego County Superior Court to grant their motion for change of venue (Code Civ.Proc. § 400).

In the underlying action, Roger D. Stoike, real party in interest, seeks damages from petitioners for malicious prosecution. The complaint alleges petitioners maliciously, and without probable cause, sued Stoike in San Diego County Superior Court for medical malpractice. The complaint further alleges: "As a direct and proximate result of the [petitioners] bringing the . . . action against [Stoike], [he] has been injured in his good name and reputation and . . . has been caused grievous mental and emotional suffering and distress. . . ."

Claiming the action was not commenced in a proper court (Code Civ.Proc., § 396b[1]), petitioners moved for a change of venue to Fresno County based upon Code of Civil Procedure section 395. Subdivision (a) of that section provides in pertinent part: "Except as otherwise provided by law and subject to the power of the court to transfer actions or proceedings as provided in this title, the county in which the defendants or some of them reside at the commencement of the action is the proper county for the trial of the action. If the action is for *injury to person* or personal property or for death from wrongful act or negligence, either the county where the injury occurs or the injury causing death occurs or the county in which the defendants, or some of them reside at the commencement of the action, shall be a proper county for the trial of the action." Stoike opposed the motion, contending (1) the action is one for "injury to person" within the meaning of that phrase in section 395; (2) pursuant to section 395.5, an unincorporated association such as MBSC&W "may be sued in the County where . . . the . . . liability arises," in this case San Diego County, where the malpractice action against Stoike was filed; and (3) petitioners had failed to rebut a legal presumption that MBSC&W was a resident of the county in which the action was filed.

The trial court, for reasons undisclosed by the record, denied petitioners' motion, and this proceeding followed. On petitioners' request, we stayed proceedings below. Although we view the evidence under the well-settled rules governing review of an order based on affidavits (see Kulko v. Superior Court, 19 Cal.3d 514, 519, fn. 1, 138 Cal.Rptr. 586, 564 P.2d 353), denial of the motion cannot be sustained.

The first issue is whether an action for malicious prosecution is one for "injury to person" as that phrase is used in section 395. If it is, the county "where the injury occurs" is a proper county for the commence-

---

1. "Except as otherwise provided in Section 396a, if an action or proceeding is commenced in a court having jurisdiction of the subject matter thereof, other than the court designated as the proper court for the trial thereof, under the provisions of this title, the action may, notwithstanding, be tried in the court where commenced, unless the defendant, at the time he answers or demurs, or, at his option, without answering or demurring and within the time otherwise limited to plead, files with the clerk, or with the judge if there be no clerk, an affidavit of merits and notice of motion for an order transferring the action or proceeding to the proper court, together with proof of service, upon the adverse party, of a copy of such papers. Upon the hearing of such motion the court shall, if it appears that the action or proceeding was not commenced in the proper court, order the same transferred to the proper court; . . . ." Unless otherwise noted, statutory references are to sections of the Code of Civil Procedure.

ment of the action. If it is not, only a county in which a defendant resides is a proper county (§ 395).

Monk v. Ehret, 192 Cal. 186, 219 P. 452, and Graham v. Mixon, 177 Cal. 88, 169 P. 1003, counsel that the Legislature used the phrase "injury to person" in section 395 to refer only to injuries of a physical or bodily nature, and not to injuries to character or reputation. Accordingly, it has been held malicious prosecution is not such an injury (Plum v. Newhart, 118 Cal.App. 73, 4 P.2d 805; Plum v. Forgay Lumber Co., 118 Cal.App. 76, 4 P.2d 804; see 6 Cal.Jur.3d, Assault with Other Wilful Torts, § 345, p. 577; 2 Witkin, Cal.Procedure (2d Ed. 1970) Actions, §§ 448, 459).

We are mindful in Plum v. Newhart, supra, 118 Cal.App. 73, 75 and Plum v. Forgay Lumber Co., supra, 118 Cal.App. 76, 79, no physical or personal injuries were alleged to have been inflicted; the complaints merely charged that the plaintiff was injured socially and financially, and suffered great loss and injury to his business, his good name, his credit and his reputation. Here, on the other hand, Stoike alleges, in addition to such injury, he has been caused grievous mental and emotional suffering and distress. The measure of compensatory damages for the malicious prosecution of a civil action includes compensation for such suffering and distress (Bertero v. National General Corp., 13 Cal.3d 43, 59, 118 Cal.Rptr. 184, 529 P.2d 608, 65 A.L.R.3d 878).

However, Lucas v. Lucas Ranching Co., 18 Cal.App.2d 453, 64 P.2d 160 holds such allegation of mental harm does not necessarily affect venue. In that case plaintiff claimed her estranged husband and other defendants conspired to place community property beyond her reach, causing her to suffer, in addition to monetary loss, "deep and grievous mental pain, anguish and suffering, great embarrassment, humiliation, worry and loss of sleep, and impairment of her nervous and physical condition." (Id., p. 455.)

The court reasoned: "From Monk v. Ehret, supra, as interpreted in Coley v. Hecker, . . . 206 Cal. 22, 28 . . ., we learn that the inspiration for the language we are considering was the 'situation brought about by the increasing use of motor vehicles.' In motor vehicle accidents, as in other cases where physical injury is directly caused by what has happened, the injury occurs at the place where the happening occurs, and there is logic in having that place a proper one for the trial. In an action such as plaintiff's, however, the place where the injury occurs is not the locale of the events which, ultimately, cause the injury. She is injured not at the site of the events, but, brooding over the wrongs done her, at the place or places where worry and loss of sleep finally take their toll. No reason appears why an injury which has no definite situs should be given potency in determining the place of trial." (Id., at p. 456.) The court concluded the cause of action was not one for "injury to person" within the purview of section 395 (id., at p. 455).

In an action for malicious prosecution, as in the action in *Lucas*, the place where the personal injury occurs is not necessarily the locale of the events which ultimately cause the injury. Such personal injury, with no definite situs, should not in reason determine the place of trial. A construction of "injury to person" permitting such a result would be in clear derogation of the right of a defendant to have an action brought against him tried in the county of his residence, "an ancient and valuable right, safe-guarded by statute and supported by a long line of decisions" (Kaluzok v. Brisson, 27 Cal.2d 760, 763, 167 P.2d 481, 163 A.L.R. 1308). We conclude this action is not one for "injury to person" within the meaning of section 395.

Stoike advances a second and distinct theory for sustaining the decision of the trial court. Section 395.5 of the Code of Civil Procedure provides: "A corporation or association may be sued in the county where . . . liability arises. . . ." Petitioners concede if the action were filed only against MBSC&W, San Diego County could be a proper place for suit under this statute; however, they assert where an individual and a corporation or association are joined as defendants, and plaintiff sues in a county in which neither defendant resides, but which is one of the other places in which a corporation or association may be sued pursuant to section 395.5, the individual defendant may obtain a change of venue. The rule asserted is well-recognized (see 2 Witkin, Cal.Procedure (2d Ed. 1970) Actions, § 513, pp. 1335–1336).

In Mosby v. Superior Court, 43 Cal.App.3d 219, 117 Cal.Rptr. 588, the court explained:

> ". . . two conflicting venue provisions are concurrently applicable to this case. The venue provisions applicable to individual defendants (§ 395) when applied to the circumstances of this case provide that only one county, that of [a] defendant's residence, is the proper county for trial. On the other hand, the venue provisions applicable to actions against unincorporated associations (§ 395.5) when applied to the facts of this case support the place of performance as a proper county for trial. As between these two conflicting venue provisions it has long been settled that preference will be accorded to the right of an individual defendant to trial in the county of his residence. When a plaintiff brings an action against several defendants, both individual and corporate, in a county which is neither the residence nor the principal place of business of any defendant, an individual defendant has a right upon proper showing to a change of venue to the county of his residence even though venue as initially laid may otherwise be justifiable upon one of the four alternative grounds provided by section 395.5 in actions against corporations. [Citations.] The foregoing rule applies with equal force where, as here, the business entity defendant is not a corporation but an unincorporated association. [Citation.]

"However, where individuals are properly joined as defendants with an unincorporated association and venue is laid in the county of residence of the association, the preference for residence venue is satisfied and an individual defendant may not of right secure a change of venue to the county of his residence. [Citation.]" (Id., at p. 226.)

Stoike contends the joinder rule should not apply as a matter of law where, as here, the individual sued is derivatively liable for the acts of his codefendant law partnership. (See Corp.Code §§ 15013, 15015, subd. (a).)

We find no merit to the contention. Where a plaintiff has not been satisfied to sue the members of an association under a common name, but has also sought to make an individual member of an association party to the action, and has sought a personal judgment against the individual, irrespective of the liability of the association, the action must be transferred to a county of residence of one of the defendants (see Mosby v. Superior Court, supra, 43 Cal.App.3d 219, 226; Nelson v. East Side Grocery Co., 26 Cal.App. 344, 146 P. 1055; The G. & S. Co. v. The M. & H. F. C. Co., 107 Cal. 378, 40 P. 495; McClung v. Watt, 190 Cal. 155, 157–159, 211 P. 17), if the individual defendant so insists (see Strassburger v. Santa Fe L. I. Co., 54 Cal.App. 7, 200 P. 1065). Thus, if neither Carruth nor MBSC&W resides in San Diego County, Carruth's demand for change of venue should have been granted. * * * [The court held the defendant's affidavit showed he was not a resident of San Diego County.]

FURTHER NOTE ON PROBLEMS OF VENUE

Could plaintiff in Carruth v. Superior Court have framed his complaint in such a way as to have established venue in San Diego County?

What advantages would have accrued to plaintiff if he had been able to sustain venue as he attempted?

In New York, plaintiff may choose any county as venue of the action. See N.Y.C.P.L.R. § 509. This option is subject to the right of the defendant to move for change of venue to a county determined by venue rules substantially similar to those prevailing in most states. Both plaintiff's privilege of initial choice and defendant's power of veto are subject to a discretionary power in the court to order venue elsewhere. 2 Weinstein, Korn & Miller ¶ 501 et seq. Is this approach an improvement over the approach in California?

E. BIFURCATED JUSTICE: SOME JUDICIAL PROBLEMS OF AMERICAN FEDERALISM

1. JURISDICTION OF THE FEDERAL DISTRICT COURTS

INTRODUCTORY NOTE ON JURISDICTION OF THE FEDERAL COURTS

The subject of federal jurisdiction is immensely complex when considered in all its refinements. The standard treatment is Bator, Meltzer, Mishkin and Shapiro, The Federal Courts and the Federal System (3d ed. 1988). An excellent introductory text is Wright, The Law of Federal Courts (4th ed. 1983). For a more abbreviated introduction, see James & Hazard c. 2.

Nevertheless, it is possible to suggest the principal features of federal court jurisdiction in a reasonably concise way. An understanding of these basic concepts is essential to understanding modern procedure, for contemporary litigation in federal courts includes much if not most of that which has general social significance—civil rights litigation, environmental litigation, antitrust litigation, etc. And in most all federal court litigation, adjudication of the merits is complicated by the fact that the procedural law consists of three interacting bodies of doctrine: rules of procedure as such, notably the Federal Rules of Civil Procedure and the federal statutory provisions on such matters as venue; the law of federal jurisdiction; and state law.

The beginning point in the law of federal jurisdiction is that the federal courts do not have general authority to hear all types of litigation. The Constitution conferred limited powers on the Federal Government as a whole and, in Article III, on the judicial branch of government. In the background of every case in federal court, and sometimes in the foreground, there is accordingly the question whether the court has authority to hear a particular claim.

1. The Limited Jurisdiction of the Federal Courts

The Judicial Power of the United States, defined in Article III of the Constitution, extends to specified classes of cases, among them:

"Cases, in Law and Equity, arising under this Constitution, the Laws of the United States, and Treaties made, or which shall be made, under their Authority; * * *

"Cases of admiralty and maritime Jurisdiction;

"Controversies to which the United States shall be a Party; * * *

"[Controversies] between Citizens of different States."

The federal district courts have authority to hear only those cases that fall within the categories prescribed in the Constitution and then only to the extent that Congress by implementing legislation has authorized exercise of such jurisdiction. The principal statutory provisions are 28 U.S.C.A. § 1331 ("civil actions arising under the Constitution, laws, or treaties of the United States"), § 1332 ("civil actions where the matter in controversy exceeds the sum or value of $50,000 * * * and is between * * * citizens of different States * * * "), and § 1333 ("[a]ny civil case of admiralty or maritime jurisdiction").

2. Admiralty Jurisdiction

On admiralty, see generally Gilmore and Black, The Law of Admiralty (2d ed. 1975). See also the valuable analysis in Robertson, Admiralty Procedure and Jurisdiction after the 1966 Unification, 74 Mich.L.Rev. 1627 (1976); cf. Watson, The Suits in Admiralty Act, 17 J.Mar.L. & Comm. 175 (1986); Olsen, Jurisdiction in Admiralty: Pennoyer v. Neff in Ship's Clothing?, 84 Dick.L.Rev. 395 (1980).

3. Diversity Jurisdiction

a. Corporations. For diversity jurisdiction purposes, a corporation, though not a citizen at all, is treated as a "citizen" of the state of its incorporation and also of the state in which it has its principal place of business. As to the location of a corporation's "principal place of business" for the purpose of 28 U.S.C.A. § 1332(c), see, e.g., Riggs v. Island Creek Coal Co., 542 F.2d 339 (6th Cir.1976); J.A. Olson Co. v. City of Winona, Miss., 818 F.2d 401 (5th Cir.1987). On the problem of a corporation incorporated in more than one state, see Comment, Corporate Diversity Jurisdiction: Voluntary Multiple Incorporation and the Forum Doctrine, 12 Gonzaga L.Rev. 347 (1977). On the problem of exercising jurisdiction over an alien corporation, see Comment, Diversity Jurisdiction Over Alien Corporations, 50 U.Chi.L.Rev. 1458 (1983).

b. Individuals and Associations. The "citizenship" of an individual for federal jurisdictional purposes is determined by substantially the same criteria as are used to determine "domicile" and "residence." It should be noted, however, that for certain purposes, including that of federal diversity jurisdiction, formal differentiation is made between "residence" and "citizenship," however coextensive the two concepts may be as applied. Thus, federal jurisdiction is not adequately founded on allegation and proof of "residence": "citizenship" is what must be shown, even though permanent residence, i.e., domicile, is equivalent to "citizenship." Regarding the relevant citizenship in a suit by a trustee, see Navarro Savings Ass'n v. Lee, 446 U.S. 458, 100 S.Ct. 1779, 64 L.Ed.2d 425 (1980). On the citizenship problems of associations, see Note on Capacity to Sue and Be Sued, infra p. 817. On the citizenship problems of partnerships, especially concerning the complete diversity requirement, see Molasky v. Garfinkle, supra p. 61. A resident alien is considered a citizen of the state where she is domiciled for diversity purposes. 28 U.S.C.A. § 1332(a). Generally speaking, a person appearing in a representative capacity, e.g., as an executor or guardian, is deemed to be a citizen of the same state as the represented party. 28 U.S.C.A. § 1332(c)(2).

c. The "Complete Diversity" Requirement. When litigation founded on diversity of citizenship under 28 U.S.C.A. § 1332 involves a multiplicity of parties, for example one plaintiff against two defendants, there must be "complete" diversity, e.g., there is no jurisdiction if one of the defendants is a co-citizen of the plaintiff. Strawbridge v. Curtiss, 7 U.S. (3 Cranch) 267, 2 L.Ed. 435 (1806). In such instances, the action against the nondiverse defendant must be dismissed. Furthermore, if the litigants attempt to rearrange the alignment of parties so as to create complete diversity, as by having one of the persons who would ordinarily be a defendant instead join as a plaintiff, the court will "realign" the parties according to the real axis of dispute. If upon realignment diversity is incomplete, dismissal follows. See, e.g., Indianapolis v. Chase National Bank, 314 U.S. 63, 62 S.Ct. 15, 86 L.Ed. 47 (1941). The requirement of "complete" diversity is, however, statutory rather than constitutional. Congress therefore can relax it as it has, e.g., for federal statutory interpleader. See State Farm Fire & Cas. Co. v. Tashire, infra p. 770.

d. Abolition of Diversity Jurisdiction. Many analysts have urged abolition of diversity jurisdiction on the ground that it is a low-priority use of federal judicial resources. See, e.g., Wright § 23. Others have advocated curtailing diversity jurisdiction by, e.g., raising the minimum amount which must be in controversy, a proposal which was adopted in the Judicial Improvements and Access to Justice Act of 1988, which increased the amount from $10,000 to $50,000.

4. Federal Claim Jurisdiction

The jurisdiction of the federal courts to entertain actions which "aris[e] under the Constitution, laws, or treaties of the United States," as provided in 28 U.S.C.A. § 1331, is generally referred to as the "general" "federal question" jurisdiction. Similar but limited grants of jurisdiction, referred to collectively as "special" "federal question" jurisdiction, are made by, e.g., 28 U.S.C.A. §§ 1337, 1338 and 1343. Moreover, acts of Congress regulating various activities often include special grants of jurisdiction for enforcement of the rights and duties created, grants of jurisdiction that do not appear in the Judicial Code, Title 28. Such, for example, is the grant of jurisdiction in F.E.L.A. actions, which is found in the F.E.L.A. itself, see 45 U.S.C.A. § 56. For a partial catalogue, see Wright § 32. Although all these grants of jurisdiction are commonly referred to as "federal question" jurisdiction, they are more accurately described as instances of "federal claim" jurisdiction.

What constitutes an action "arising under" a federal law is often a difficult question. On the one hand, it is clear that if an act of Congress prescribes a duty and also expressly provides a right of action for breach of that duty, as it has done in the F.E.L.A., then the action "arises under" federal law and may be entertained in the federal district courts. On the other hand, it is clear that if the federal law governs some incident of a *defense* to an action otherwise maintainable by the common law or statutory law of a state, the action does not "arise under" federal law. And this is true even if it is known in advance that the hard-fought issue in the case will be the interpretation and application of the supposed federal defense. And this is still true even if the plaintiff attempts to "anticipate" the defense by pleading it in his complaint and then explaining why it should not be available. The federal question, the rule goes, must appear from the facts of the complaint "well pleaded." On the difficulties of the "well pleaded" complaint rule, see Doernberg, There's No Reason for It; It's Just Our Policy: Why the Well-Pleaded Complaint Rule Sabotages the Purposes of Federal Question Jurisdiction, 38 Hastings L.J. 597 (1987). In between these limits, there may be wide variation in the extent to which federal law has displaced state law in determining the incidents of a "cause of action." See Wright & Miller §§ 3562–3564.

In addition, a federal claim may arise from the decisional law of the federal courts, as distinct from congressional legislation. Such decisional law rests ultimately on provisions either of federal statutes or of the Constitution. On implied causes of action premised on federal statutory law, see, e.g., Cort v. Ash, 422 U.S. 66, 95 S.Ct. 2080, 45 L.Ed.2d 26 (1975); cf. Thompson v. Thompson, 484 U.S. 174, 108 S.Ct. 513, 98 L.Ed.2d 512 (1988) (Federal Parental Kidnapping Prevention Act did not create an implied federal cause of action, but merely extended full faith and credit requirements to state custody determinations). See also Note, State Incorporation of Federal Law: A Response to the Demise of

Implied Federal Rights of Action, 94 Yale L.J. 1144 (1985), arguing that federal law can be considered as creating standards of conduct for violation of which state common law can provide rights of action. Federal claims premised on the Constitution include claims based on the provisions that subordinate the states to the Federal Government, see, e.g., Illinois v. City of Milwaukee, 406 U.S. 91, 92 S.Ct. 1385, 31 L.Ed.2d 712 (1972), and those guaranteeing rights of persons against federal interference, see, e.g., Bivens v. Six Unknown Named Agents of Federal Bureau of Narcotics, 403 U.S. 388, 91 S.Ct. 1999, 29 L.Ed.2d 619 (1971). See Katz, The Jurisprudence of Remedies: Constitutional Legality and the Law of Torts in Bell v. Hood, 117 U.Pa.L.Rev. 1 (1968); Mowe, Federal Statutes and Implied Private Actions, 55 Ore.L.Rev. 3 (1976); cf. Santa Clara Pueblo v. Martinez, 436 U.S. 49, 98 S.Ct. 1670, 56 L.Ed.2d 106 (1978).

In these materials, the question will have to be left at that point. See generally Mishkin, The Federal "Question" in the District Courts, 53 Colum.L. Rev. 157 (1953); Hart & Wechsler 960–1089; Comment, The Outer Limits of "Arising Under," 54 N.Y.U.L.Rev. 978 (1979). Note, however, that except where otherwise provided by law, the federal court's jurisdiction over federal claims is *not* exclusive: the states may and do exercise jurisdiction in such cases. See Gulf Offshore Co. v. Mobil Oil Corp., 453 U.S. 473, 101 S.Ct. 2870, 69 L.Ed.2d 784 (1981). An illustration of exclusive federal jurisdiction is 28 U.S. C.A. § 1338, providing for exclusive federal jurisdiction in actions "arising under" the patent and copyright laws. See generally Redish and Muench, Adjudication of Federal Causes of Action in State Court, 75 Mich.L.Rev. 311 (1976). On some aspects of the peculiar jurisdiction of the United States Court of Appeals for the Federal Circuit, see United States v. Hohri, 482 U.S. 64, 107 S.Ct. 2246, 96 L.Ed.2d 51 (1987).

5. Removal Jurisdiction

In addition to the jurisdiction granted to the federal courts in respect of actions originally commenced therein, i.e., at the instance of the plaintiff, there is "removal" jurisdiction. At the instance of a defendant who is sued in state court in an action "of which the district courts of the United States have original jurisdiction," the action may be removed from the state court to the federal district court of the district in which the state court is located. See 28 U.S.C.A. § 1441. The privilege of removal is, however, limited in two important respects. First, no removal is allowed if an act of Congress so provides, as it does, e.g., in the case of F.E.L.A. actions. Second, removal is allowed in diversity suits only where the defendants are noncitizens of the state in which the action is brought. Thus, if an out-of-state plaintiff chooses to sue in state court, the local defendant may not remove. Moreover, under present law, removal of a federal question case is permitted only where the federal question appears from plaintiff's complaint, and not where defendant has a federal defense. Upon removal the state court action is terminated and the state court has no authority to proceed further, unless the action is remanded. See, e.g., Carnegie-Mellon Univ. v. Cohill, infra p. 538; Allstate Ins. Co. v. Superior Court, 132 Cal.App.3d 670, 183 Cal.Rptr. 330 (1982). On removal generally see Hart & Wechsler 1767–88. See also Comment, Artful Pleading and Removal Jurisdiction: Ferreting Out the True Nature of a Claim, 35 U.C.L.A.L.Rev. 315 (1987).

The American Law Institute has proposed enlarging "federal claim" jurisdiction, principally by permitting removal on the basis of a federal defense or counterclaim. A.L.I., Study of the Division of Jurisdiction between State and Federal Courts 24–28 (1968).

6. Federal Government Litigation

General and special provisions grant jurisdiction to the federal courts where the United States or one of its agencies is plaintiff and, subject to the rule of sovereign immunity, where it is a defendant. See, e.g., 28 U.S.C.A. §§ 1345, 1346. Federal Government litigation is an important study all in itself. See generally Hart & Wechsler c. IX.

7. Amount in Controversy

The "general" federal claim grant of jurisdiction, 28 U.S.C.A. § 1331, was amended in 1980 to eliminate a $10,000 amount in controversy requirement, but, as noted above, diversity jurisdiction, 28 U.S.C.A. § 1332, is limited to cases where the matter in controversy exceeds $50,000, increased from $10,000 in 1988 in response to criticisms that diversity cases comprised a disproportionate amount of the federal judicial workload. Some special grants of federal jurisdiction have a minimum amount in controversy requirement, e.g., 28 U.S. C.A. § 1335 (the Federal Interpleader Act), but most do not, e.g., 28 U.S.C.A. § 1343 (civil rights and elective franchise) and § 1345 (United States as plaintiff).

When the action is for damages and the demand for relief is not patently absurd, the "amount in controversy" is the amount demanded in the prayer. Beyond this, as where an injunction is sought to restrain interference with some interest of plaintiff, difficult problems of valuation are presented, chiefly (1) what is the "matter" that is "in controversy," and (2) how a monetary evaluation of the "matter" is to be made. These and other questions regarding valuation of a claim for purposes of applying a statute defining jurisdiction in terms of the amount in controversy are substantially the same, though the answers may differ, in the federal courts and in state courts having monetary jurisdictional limits. Discussion of the problems of valuation under the Federal Judicial Code is therefore subordinated to the discussion of similar valuation problems in state courts. See Introductory Note on Distribution of Jurisdiction Among State Tribunals, supra p. 502. On valuation in federal courts, see generally Comment, The Jurisdictional Amount in Controversy in Suits to Enforce Federal Rights, 54 Tex.L.Rev. 545 (1976); e.g., McCarty v. Amoco Pipeline Co., 595 F.2d 389 (7th Cir. 1979); Wright & Miller §§ 3701 et seq.

8. Transfer Jurisdiction

The Federal Court Improvement Act of 1982 amended Title 28, United States Code, to add the following section:

"§ 1631. Transfer to cure want of jurisdiction

"Whenever a civil action is filed in a court as defined in section 610 of this title or an appeal, including a petition for review of administrative action, is noticed for or filed with such a court and that court finds that there is a want of jurisdiction, the court shall, if it is in the interest of justice, transfer such action or appeal to any other such court in which the action or appeal could have been brought at the time it was filed or noticed, and the action or appeal shall proceed as if it had been filed in or noticed for the court to which it is transferred on the date upon which it was actually filed in or noticed for the court from which it is transferred."

While the language of the act is not so limited, the Senate Report restricts its discussion to subject matter jurisdiction, leaving an inference that it does not apply to personal jurisdiction. Senate Rept. No. 97–275, 97th Cong., 2d Sess., 1982 U.S.Code Cong. & Admin.News 11. As to transfers for lack of personal jurisdiction under case law, see Note on Federal Venue Transfers, infra p. 625.

9. Foreign Government Litigation

Under the Foreign Sovereign Immunities Act of 1976, the federal courts have exclusive jurisdiction of all nonjury civil actions against foreign sovereigns as defined in the act and of all claims for relief in persons where the foreign state is not entitled to immunity. 28 U.S.C.A. § 1330(a). For an exposition of the Act see Kane, Suing Foreign Sovereigns: A Procedural Compass, 34 Stan.L.Rev. 385 (1982). See also Note, Resolving the Confusion Over Head of State Immunity: The Defined Rights of Kings, 86 Colum.L.Rev. 169 (1986).

ALDINGER v. HOWARD

Supreme Court of the United States, 1976.
427 U.S. 1, 96 S.Ct. 2413, 49 L.Ed.2d 276.

Mr. Justice Rehnquist delivered the opinion of the Court.

This case presents the "subtle and complex question with far-reaching implications," alluded to but not answered in Moor v. County of Alameda, 411 U.S. 693, 715, 93 S.Ct. 1785, 1799, 36 L.Ed.2d 596 (1973), and Philbrook v. Glodgett, 421 U.S. 707, 720, 95 S.Ct. 1893, 1901, 44 L.Ed.2d 525 (1975): whether the doctrine of pendent jurisdiction extends to confer jurisdiction over a party as to whom no independent basis of federal jurisdiction exists. In this action, where jurisdiction over the main, federal claim against various officials of Spokane County, Wash., was grounded in 28 U.S.C.A. § 1343(3), the Court of Appeals for the Ninth Circuit held that pendent jurisdiction was not available to adjudicate petitioner's state law claims against Spokane County, over which party federal jurisdiction was otherwise nonexistent. While noting that its previous holdings to this effect were left undisturbed by *Moor*, which arose from that circuit, the Court of Appeals was "not unaware of the widespread rejection" of its position in almost all other federal circuits. 513 F.2d 1257, 1261 (1975). We granted certiorari to resolve the conflict on this important question. 423 U.S. 823, 96 S.Ct. 36, 46 L.Ed.2d 39 (1975). We affirm.

I

This case arises at the pleading stage, and the allegations in petitioner's complaint are straightforward. Petitioner was hired in 1971 by respondent Howard, the Spokane County treasurer, for clerical work in that office. Two months later Howard informed petitioner by letter that although her job performance was "excellent," she would be dismissed, effective two weeks hence, because she was allegedly "living with [her] boy friend." Howard's action, petitioner alleged, was taken pursuant to a state statute which provides that the appointing county officer "may revoke each appointment at pleasure." [1] Though a hearing was requested, none was held before or after the effective date of the discharge.

Petitioner's action in the United States District Court for the Eastern District of Washington, as embodied in her second amended complaint, claimed principally under the Civil Rights Act of 1871, 42 U.S.C.A. § 1983,[2] that the discharge violated her substantive constitutional rights under the First, Ninth, and Fourteenth Amendments, and was procedurally defective under the latter's Due Process Clause. An injunction restraining the dismissal and damages for salary loss were [sic] sought against Howard, his wife, the named county commissioners, and the county. Jurisdiction over the federal claim was asserted under 28 U.S.C.A. § 1343(3),[3] and pendent jurisdiction was alleged to lie over the "state law claims against the parties." As to the county, the state law claim was said to rest on state statutes waiving the county's sovereign immunity and providing for vicarious liability arising out of tortious conduct of its officials. 513 F.2d, at 1358. The District Court dismissed the action as to the county on the ground that since it was not suable as a "person" under § 1983, there was no independent basis of jurisdiction over the county, and thus "this court [has no] power to exercise pendent jurisdiction over the claims against Spokane County." From this final judgment, see Fed.Rules Civ.Proc. 54(b), petitioner appealed.

The Court of Appeals first rejected petitioner's claim that her § 1983 action against the county fell within the District Court's § 1343(3) jurisdiction, as obviously foreclosed by this Court's decisions in *Moor* and City of Kenosha v. Bruno, 412 U.S. 507, 93 S.Ct.2222, 37 L.Ed.2d 109 (1973). Turning to petitioner's pendent jurisdiction argument, the Court of Appeals noted, 513 F.2d, at 1260, that the District

---

1. Wash.Rev.Code § 36.16.070 (1973).

2. "Every person who, under color of any statute, ordinance, regulation, custom, or usage, of any State or Territory, subjects, or causes to be subjected, any citizen of the United States or other person within the jurisdiction thereof to the deprivation of any rights, privileges, or immunities secured by the Constitution and laws, shall be liable to the party injured in an action at law, suit in equity, or other proper proceeding for redress."

3. "The district courts shall have original jurisdiction of any civil action authorized by law to be commenced by any person:
. . .

"(3) To redress the deprivation, under color of any State law, statute, ordinance, regulation, custom or usage, of any right, privilege or immunity secured by the Constitution of the United States or by any Act of Congress providing for equal rights of citizens or of all persons

within the jurisdiction of the United States. . . ."

The Court of Appeals also noted that petitioner's complaint alleged that jurisdiction lay under 28 U.S.C.A. § 1331, and that the amount in controversy exceeded $10,000. This was apparently an attempt to plead a cause of action directly under the Fourteenth Amendment, irrespective of the implementing civil rights legislation. The Court of Appeals, however, stated that petitioner had "consistently chosen to rely upon" § 1983, together with 28 U.S.C. § 1343(3), and pendent jurisdiction as the bases for her action against Spokane County. Thus, neither the District Court nor the Court of Appeals reached the question whether the complaint stated a cause of action over which § 1331 jurisdiction would lie. Petitioner did not raise the question in her petition for certiorari, and it is therefore not before us.

Court had made no alternative ruling on the "suitability of this case for the discretionary exercise of pendent jurisdiction" under the second part of the rule enunciated in United Mine Workers v. Gibbs, 383 U.S. 715, 726–727, 86 S.Ct. 1130, 1139, 16 L.Ed.2d 218 (1966). But since this Court in *Moor* had expressly left undisturbed the Ninth Circuit's refusal to apply pendent jurisdiction over a non-federal party, the instant panel felt free to apply that rule as set out in Hymer v. Chai, 407 F.2d 136 (CA9 1969), and Moor v. Madigan, 458 F.2d 1217 (CA9 1972), aff'd in part, rev'd in part, 411 U.S. 693, 93 S.Ct. 1785, 36 L.Ed.2d 596 (1973). This kind of case, the Court of Appeals reasoned, presented the "weakest rationale" for extension of *Gibbs* to pendent parties: (1) the state claims are pressed against a party who would otherwise not be in federal court;[4] (2) diversity cases generally present more attractive opportunities for exercise of pendent party jurisdiction, since all claims therein by definition arise from state law; (3) federal courts should be wary of extending court-created doctrines of jurisdiction to reach parties who are expressly excluded by Congress from liability, and hence federal jurisdiction, in the federal statute sought to be applied to the defendant in the main claim; (4) pendent state law claims arising in a civil rights context will "almost inevitably" involve the federal court in difficult and unsettled questions of state law, with the accompanying potential for jury confusion. 513 F.2d, at 1261–1262.

II

The question whether "pendent" federal jurisdiction encompasses not merely the litigation of additional *claims* between parties with respect to whom there is federal jurisdiction, but also the joining of additional *parties* with respect to whom there is no independent basis of federal jurisdiction, has been much litigated in other federal courts[5] and much discussed by commentators[6] since this Court's decision in *Gibbs*. *Gibbs*, in turn, is the most recent in a long line of our cases dealing with the relationship between the judicial power of the United States and the actual contours of the cases and controversies to which that power is extended by Art. III.

In Osborn v. Bank of the United States, 9 Wheat. 738, 6 L.Ed. 204 (1824), Chief Justice Marshall in his opinion for the Court addressed the argument that the presence in a federal lawsuit of questions which were not dependent on the construction of a law of the United States prevented the federal court from exercising Art. III jurisdiction, even in a case in which the plaintiff had been authorized by Congress to sue in

---

4. There is no diversity of citizenship under 28 U.S.C.A. § 1332 among the parties here, since all are citizens of the State of Washington.

5. See, e.g., cases cited in Moor, 411 U.S., at 713–714, nn. 29–30, 93 S.Ct., at 1797–1798.

6. See, e.g., 3A. J. Moore, Federal Practice ¶ 18.07[1.–4] (2d ed. 1974); P. Bator, P.

Mishkin, D. Shapiro & H. Wechsler, Hart and Wechsler's The Federal Courts and the Federal System 921–926 (2d ed. 1973); C. Wright, Law of Federal Courts § 19 (2d ed. 1970); Fortune, Pendent Jurisdiction—The Problem of "Pendenting Parties," 34 U.Pitt.L.Rev. 1 (1972); Shakman, The New Pendent Jurisdiction of the Federal Courts, 20 Stan.L.Rev. 262 (1968).

federal court. Noting that "[t]here is scarcely any case, every part of which depends" upon federal law, id., at 820, the Chief Justice rejected the contention:

"If it be a sufficient foundation for jurisdiction, that the title or right set up by the party, may be defeated by one construction of the constitution or law of the United States, and sustained by the opposite construction, provided the facts necessary to support the action be made out, then all the other questions must be decided as incidental to this, which gives that jurisdiction. Those other questions cannot arrest the proceedings. . . .

"We think, then, that when a question to which the judicial power of the Union is extended by the constitution, forms an ingredient of the original cause, it is in the power of Congress to give the Circuit Courts jurisdiction of that cause, although other questions of fact or of law may be involved in it." Id., at 822–823.

This doctrine was later applied in Siler v. Louisville & Nashville R. Co., 213 U.S. 175, 29 S.Ct. 451, 53 L.Ed. 753 (1909), to hold that where federal jurisdiction is properly based on a colorable federal claim, the court has the "right to decide all the questions in the case, even though it decided the Federal questions adversely to the party raising them, or even if it omitted to decide them at all, but decided the case on local or state questions only." Id., at 191. In Moore v. N.Y. Cotton Exchange, 270 U.S. 593, 609–610, 46 S.Ct. 367, 370–371, 70 L.Ed. 750 (1926), the Court in similar fashion sustained jurisdiction over a defendant's compulsory counterclaim arising out of the same transaction upon which the plaintiff's federal antitrust claim was grounded, although the latter had been dismissed for failure to state a claim, and the former had no independent federal jurisdictional basis. A few years later, in Hurn v. Oursler, 289 U.S. 238, 53 S.Ct. 586, 77 L.Ed. 1148 (1933), the Court drew upon the foregoing cases to establish federal jurisdiction to decide a state law claim joined with a federal copyright infringement claim, where both were considered "two distinct grounds in support of a single cause of action," although the federal ground had proved unsuccessful. Id., at 246, 53 S.Ct., at 589.

In *Gibbs*, the respondent brought an action in federal court against petitioner UMW, asserting parallel claims—a federal statutory claim and a claim under the common law of Tennessee—arising out of alleged concerted union efforts to deprive him of contractual and employment relationships with the coal mine's owners. Though the federal claim was ultimately dismissed after trial, and though diversity was absent, the lower courts sustained jurisdiction over the state law claim, and affirmed the damage award based thereon. Before reaching the merits (on which the lower courts were reversed), this Court addressed the argument that under the rule of pendent jurisdiction as set out in Hurn v. Oursler, supra, at 245–246, 53 S.Ct., at 589, Gibbs had merely stated "two separate and distinct causes of action" as opposed to "two distinct grounds in support of a single cause of action," in which former case the federal court lacked the power to "retain and dispose" of the "non-federal *cause of action*." The Court stated that since the *Hurn* test was formulated before the unification of law and equity by the Federal Rules of Civil Procedure, it was therefore unnecessarily tied to the outmoded concept of a "cause of action" developed under Code pleading rules. Recognizing that the Federal Rules themselves cannot expand federal court jurisdiction, the Court nevertheless found in them a sufficient basis to go beyond *Hurn's* "unnecessarily grudging" approach to parallel claims, and to adopt a more flexible treatment within the contours of Art. III, § 2. Thus, in a federal question case, where the federal claim is of sufficient substance, and the factual relationship between "that claim and the state claim permits the conclusion that the entire action before the court comprises but one constitutional 'case,'" pendent jurisdiction extends to the state claim. 383 U.S., at 725, 86 S.Ct., at 1138. The Court, in the second aspect of the *Gibbs* formulation, went on to enumerate the various factors bearing on a district court's discretionary decision whether the power should be exercised in a given parallel-claims case, emphasizing that "pendent jurisdiction is a doctrine of discretion, not of plaintiff's right." Id., at 726, 86 S.Ct., at 1139.

These cases, from *Osborn* to *Gibbs*, show that in treating litigation where nonfederal questions or claims were bound up with the federal claim upon which the parties were already in federal court, this Court has found nothing in Art. III's grant of judicial power which prevented adjudication of the nonfederal portions of the parties' dispute. None of them, however, adverted to the separate question, involved in the instant case, of whether a nonfederal claim could *in turn* be the basis for joining a party over whom no independent federal jurisdiction exists, simply because that claim could be derived from the "common nucleus of operative fact" giving rise to the dispute between the parties to the federal claim.

But while none of the foregoing line of cases discussed the joining of additional parties, other decisions of this Court have developed a doctrine of "ancillary jurisdiction," and it is in part upon this develop-ment—and its relationship to *Gibbs*—that petitioner relies to support "pendent party" jurisdiction here. Under this doctrine, the Court has identified certain considerations which justified the joining of parties with respect to whom there was no independent basis of federal jurisdiction. In Freeman v. Howe, 24 How. 450, 16 L.Ed. 749 (1860), the Court held that the state court had no jurisdiction over a replevin action brought by creditor claimants to property that had already been attached by the federal marshal in a federal diversity action. The claimants argued that a want of state court jurisdiction would leave them without a remedy, since diversity between them and the marshal was lacking. This Court stated that an equitable action in federal court by those claimants, seeking to prevent injustice in the diversity suit, would not have been "an original suit but ancillary and dependent, and supplementary merely to the original suit," and thus maintainable irrespective of diversity of citizenship. Id., at 460. A similar approach was taken in Stewart v. Dunham, 115 U.S. 61, 5 S.Ct. 1163, 29 L.Ed. 329 (1885), where, after a creditors' suit to set aside an allegedly fraudulent conveyance was removed to federal court on grounds of diversity, other nondiverse creditors were permitted to intervene to assert an identical interest. Since it was merely a matter of form whether the latter appeared as parties or came in later under a final decree to prove their claims before a master, the federal court "could incidentally decree in favor of [the non-diverse] creditors [, and] [s]uch a proceeding would be ancillary to the jurisdiction acquired between the original parties. . . ." Id., at 64, 5 S.Ct., at 1164. *Dunham* was in turn held controlling in Supreme Tribe of Ben-Hur v. Cauble, 255 U.S. 356, 41 S.Ct. 338, 65 L.Ed. 673 (1921). There, suing in diversity, out-of-state "Class A" members of an Indiana fraternal benefit society had sought a decree adjudicating their common interests in the control and disposition of the society's funds. After successfully defending that action, the society brought a second suit in federal court seeking to protect that judgment as against an identical state court action brought by members of "Class A" who were of Indiana citizenship. Since under *Dunham* "intervention of the Indiana citizens in the [original] suit would not have defeated the jurisdiction already acquired," 255 U.S., at 366, 41 S.Ct., at 342, the earlier judgment was binding against them, and the federal court had ancillary jurisdiction over the association's suit to enjoin the later state action, irrespective of diversity.

The doctrine of ancillary jurisdiction developed in the foregoing cases is bottomed on the notion that since federal jurisdiction in the principal suit effectively controls the property or fund under dispute, other claimants thereto should be allowed to intervene in order to protect their interests, without regard to jurisdiction.[7] As this Court stated in Fulton Bank v. Hozier, 267 U.S. 276, 280, 45 S.Ct. 261, 262, 69 L.Ed. 609 (1925):

> "The general rule is that when a federal court has properly acquired jurisdiction over a cause, it may entertain, by intervention, dependent or ancillary controversies; but no controversy can be regarded as dependent or ancillary unless it has direct relation to property or assets actually or constructively drawn into the court's possession or control by the principal suit."

The decisional bridge between these two relatively discrete lines of cases appears to be this Court's decision in *Moore*. Since the defen-

---

7. As one commentator has stated:

"Once it is agreed that a state court cannot interfere with property in the control of the federal court, the notion of ancillary jurisdiction put forward in Freeman v. Howe cannot be avoided. Unless the federal court has ancillary jurisdiction to hear the claims of all persons to the property, regardless of their citizenship, some persons, with a valid claim to the property would be deprived of any forum in which to press that claim." C. Wright, Law of Federal Courts § 9 (2d ed. 1970).

Ben-Hur sets out a corollary to *Howe*: ancillary jurisdiction extends to subsequent suits brought to effectuate a federal court's judgment determining the rights to such property.

dant's nonfederal counterclaim in *Moore* arose out of the same transaction giving rise to the antitrust dispute between the parties, and federal jurisdiction was sustained over the former, the Court in *Hurn*, though faced with a plaintiff's assertion of pendent jurisdiction over an additional nonfederal claim, thought the two cases, "in principle, cannot be distinguished." Hurn, 289 U.S., at 242, 53 S.Ct., at 588. It was *Hurn's* "unnecessarily grudging" test of pendent jurisdiction, of course, which the Court expanded in *Gibbs*. On the other hand because *Moore* was a suit in equity, the jurisdiction sustained there has been rationalized as falling under the umbrella of ancillary jurisdiction,[8] though *Moore* neither used that term nor cited to *Fulton Bank*, supra. Petitioner thus suggests that since *Moore*, read as an "ancillary" case, adopted a "transactional" test of jurisdiction quite similar to that set out in *Gibbs*, there is presently no "principled" distinction between the two doctrines. Since under the Federal Rules "joinder of claims, parties and remedies is strongly encouraged," G*ibbs*, 383 U.S., at 724, 86 S.Ct., at 1138, her use of the Rules here is as a matter of jurisdictional power assertedly limited only by whether the claim against the county "derive[s] from a common nucleus of operative fact." Id., at 725, 86 S.Ct., at 1138. Hence, petitioner concludes, based on *Gibbs'* treatment of pendent claims, and the use of ancillary jurisdiction to bring in additional parties, that her nonfederal claim against a nonfederal defendant falls within pendent jurisdiction since it satisfies *Gibbs'* test on its face.

For purposes of addressing the jurisdictional question in this case, however, we think it quite unnecessary to formulate any general, all-encompassing jurisdictional rule. Given the complexities of the many manifestations of federal jurisdiction, together with the countless factual permutations possible under the Federal Rules, there is little profit in attempting to decide, for example, whether there are any "principled" differences between pendent and ancillary jurisdiction, or, if there were, what effect *Gibbs* had on such differences. Since it is upon *Gibbs'* language that the lower federal courts have relied in extending the kind of pendent party jurisdiction urged by petitioner here, we think the better approach is to determine what *Gibbs* did and did not decide, and to identify what we deem are important differences between the jurisdiction sustained in *Gibbs* and that asserted here.

Gibbs and its lineal ancestor, *Osborn*, were couched in terms of Art. III's grant of judicial power in "Cases . . . arising under this Constitution, the Laws of the United States, and [its] Treaties," since they (and implicitly the cases which linked them) represented inquiries into the scope of Art. III jurisdiction in litigation where the "common nucleus of operative fact" gave rise to non-federal questions or claims between the parties. None of them posed the need for a further inquiry into the underlying statutory grant of federal jurisdiction insofar as a flexible analysis of concepts such as "question," "claim," and "cause of action,"

---

8. See Shulman & Jaegerman, Some Jurisdictional Limitations on Federal Procedure, 45 Yale L.J. 393, 413 (1936); 3 J. Moore, Federal Practice ¶ 13.15 (2d ed. 1974); C. Wright, Law of Federal Courts § 9 (2d ed. 1970).

because Congress had not addressed itself by statute to this matter. In short, Congress had said nothing about the scope of the word "Cases" in Art. III which would offer guidance on the kind of elusive question addressed in *Osborn* and *Gibbs*: whether and to what extent jurisdiction extended to a parallel state claim against the existing federal defendant.

Thus, it was perfectly consistent with Art. III, and the particular grant of subject-matter jurisdiction upon which the federal claim against the defendant in those cases was grounded, to require that defendant to answer as well to a second claim deriving from the "common nucleus" of fact, though it be of state law vintage. This would not be an "unfair" use of federal power by the suing party, he already having placed the defendant properly in federal court for a substantial federal cause of action. Judicial economy would also be served because the plaintiff's claims were "such that he would ordinarily be expected to try them all in one judicial proceeding. . . ." *Gibbs*, 383 U.S., at 725, 86 S.Ct., at 1138.

The situation with respect to the joining of a new party, however, strikes us as being both factually and legally different from the situation facing the Court in *Gibbs* and its predecessors. From a purely factual point of view, it is one thing to authorize two parties, already present in federal court by virtue of a case over which the court has jurisdiction, to litigate in addition to their federal claim a state law claim over which there is no independent basis of federal jurisdiction. But it is quite another thing to permit a plaintiff, who has asserted a claim against one defendant with respect to which there is federal jurisdiction, to join an entirely different defendant on the basis of a state law claim over which there is no independent basis of federal jurisdiction, simply because his claim against the first defendant and his claim against the second defendant "derive from a common nucleus of operative fact." Ibid. True, the same considerations of judicial economy would be served insofar as plaintiff's claims "are such that he would ordinarily be expected to try them all in one judicial proceeding. . . ." Ibid. But the addition of a completely new party would run counter to the well-established principle that federal courts, as opposed to state trial courts of general jurisdiction, are courts of limited jurisdiction marked out by Congress. We think there is much sense in the observation of Judge Sobeloff, writing for the Court of Appeals in Kenrose Mfg. Co. v. Fred Whitaker Co., 512 F.2d 890, 894 (CA4 1972):

> "The value of efficiency in the disposition of lawsuits by avoiding multiplicity may be readily conceded, but that is not the only consideration a federal court should take into account in assessing the presence or absence of jurisdiction. Especially is this true where, as here, the efficiency plaintiff seeks so avidly is available without question in the state courts."

There is also a significant legal difference. In *Osborn* and *Gibbs* Congress was silent on the extent to which the defendant, already properly in federal court under a statute, might be called upon to answer nonfederal questions or claims; the way was thus left open for the Court to fashion its own rules under the general language of Art. III. But the extension of *Gibbs* to this kind of "pendent party" jurisdiction—bringing in an additional defendant at the behest of the plaintiff—presents rather different statutory jurisdictional considerations. Petitioner's contention that she should be entitled to sue Spokane County as a new third party, and then to try a wholly state law claim against the county, all of which would be "pendent" to her federal claim against respondent county treasurer, must be decided not in the context of congressional silence or tacit encouragement, but in quite the opposite context. The question here, which was not necessary to address in *Gibbs* or *Osborn*, is whether by virtue of the statutory grant of subject-matter jurisdiction, upon which petitioner's principal claim against the treasurer rests, Congress has addressed itself to the *party* as to whom jurisdiction pendent to the principal claim is sought. And it undoubtedly has done so.

III

Congress has in specific terms conferred Art. III jurisdiction on the district courts to decide actions brought to redress deprivations of civil rights. Under the opening language of § 1343,[9] those courts "shall have original jurisdiction of any *civil action authorized by law* to be commenced by any person . . ." (emphasis added). The civil rights action set out in § 1983 [10] is of course included within the jurisdictional grant of subsection (3) of § 1343. Yet petitioner does not, and indeed could not, contest the fact that as to § 1983, counties are excluded from the "person[s]" answerable to the plaintiff "in an action at law [or] suit in equity" to redress the enumerated deprivations.[11] Petitioner must necessarily argue that in spite of the language emphasized above Congress left it open for the federal courts to fashion a jurisdictional doctrine under the general language of Art. III enabling them to circumvent this exclusion, as long as the civil rights action and the state law claim arise from a "common nucleus of operative fact." But the question whether jurisdiction over the instant lawsuit extends not only to a related state law claim, but to the defendant against whom that claim is made, turns initially not on the general contours of the language in Art. III, i.e., "Cases . . . arising under," but upon the deductions which may be drawn from congressional statutes as to whether Congress wanted to grant this sort of jurisdiction to federal courts. Parties such as counties, whom Congress *excluded* from liability in § 1983, and therefore by reference in the grant of jurisdiction under § 1343(3), can argue with a great deal of force that the scope of that "civil action" over which the district courts have been given

---

9. See n. 3, supra.

10. See n. 2, supra.

11. Monroe v. Pape, 365 U.S. 167, 187–191, 81 S.Ct. 473, 484–486, 5 L.Ed.2d 492

(1961); City of Kenosha v. Bruno, 412 U.S. 507, 511–513, 93 S.Ct. 2222, 2225–2226, 37 L.Ed.2d 109 (1973).

statutory jurisdiction should not be so broadly read as to bring them *back* within that power merely because the facts also give rise to an ordinary civil action against them under state law. In short, as against a plaintiff's claim of *additional* power over a "pendent party," the reach of the statute conferring jurisdiction should be construed in light of the scope of the cause of action as to which federal judicial power *has* been extended by Congress.

Resolution of a claim of pendent party jurisdiction, therefore, calls for careful attention to the relevant statutory language. As we have indicated, we think a fair reading of the language used in § 1343, together with the scope of § 1983, requires a holding that the joinder of a municipal corporation, like the county here, for purposes of asserting a state law claim not within federal diversity jurisdiction, is without the statutory jurisdiction of the district court.[12]

There are, of course, many variations in the language which Congress has employed to confer jurisdiction upon the federal courts, and we decide here only the issue of so-called "pendent party" jurisdiction with respect to a claim brought under § 1343(3) and § 1983. Other statutory grants and other alignments of parties and claims might call for a different result. When the grant of jurisdiction to a federal court is exclusive, for example, as in the prosecution of tort claims against the United States under 28 U.S.C.A. § 1346, the argument of judicial economy and convenience can be coupled with the additional argument that *only* in a federal court may all of the claims be tried together.[13] As we indicated at the outset of this opinion, the question of pendent party jurisdiction is "subtle and complex," and we believe that it would be as unwise as it would be unnecessary to lay down any sweeping pronouncement upon the existence or exercise of such jurisdiction. Two observations suffice for the disposition of the type of case before us. If the new party sought to be joined is not otherwise subject to federal jurisdiction, there is a more serious obstacle to the exercise of pendent jurisdiction than if parties already before the court are required to litigate a state law claim. Before it can be concluded that such jurisdiction exists, a federal court must satisfy itself not only that Art. III permits it, but that Congress in the statutes

---

12. The floor debates on the statute which became § 1983, relied upon by our Brother Brennan, insofar as any common understanding may be distilled from their diverse strains, indicate a recognition of the authority of United States courts to entertain suits against municipal corporations under their then-existing diversity jurisdiction. It is of course a fair inference from this theme that nothing in § 1983 or § 1343 was intended to disturb such jurisdiction, and it seems scarcely necessary to add that nothing we say in this opinion disturbs it in the slightest. All that we hold is that where the asserted basis of federal jurisdiction over a municipal corporation is not diversity of citizenship, but is a claim of jurisdiction pendent to a suit brought against a municipal officer within § 1343, the refusal of Congress to authorize suits against municipal corporations under the cognate provisions of § 1983 is sufficient to defeat the asserted claim of pendent party jurisdiction.

13. See, e.g., Hipp v. United States, 313 F.Supp. 1152 (E.D.N.Y.1970). Contra, Williams v. United States, 405 F.2d 951 (CA9 1969).

conferring jurisdiction has not expressly or by implication negated its existence.

We conclude that in this case Congress has by implication declined to extend federal jurisdiction over a party such as Spokane County. The judgment of the Court of Appeals for the Ninth Circuit is therefore

Affirmed.

MR. JUSTICE BRENNAN, with whom MR. JUSTICE MARSHALL and MR. JUSTICE BLACKMUN join, dissenting.*

CARNEGIE–MELLON UNIVERSITY v. COHILL

Supreme Court of the United States, 1988.
484 U.S. 343, 108 S.Ct. 614, 98 L.Ed.2d 720.†

JUSTICE MARSHALL delivered the opinion of the Court.

The question before us is whether a federal district court has discretion under the doctrine of pendent jurisdiction to remand a properly removed case to state court when all federal-law claims in the action have been eliminated and only pendent state-law claims remain.

I

Respondents, William and Carrie Boyle, commenced this action by filing a complaint against petitioners, Carnegie–Mellon University (CMU) and John Kordesich, in the Court of Common Pleas of Allegheny County, Pennsylvania. CMU is William Boyle's former employer; Kordesich is William Boyle's former supervisor. In the complaint, William Boyle charged CMU with violation of federal and state age-discrimination laws, wrongful discharge, breach of contract, intentional infliction of emotional distress, defamation, and misrepresentation. He stated many of the same claims, as well as tortious interference with a contractual relationship, against Kordesich. Carrie Boyle claimed that these alleged wrongs had caused her to suffer a loss of consortium, loss of companionship, and loss of her husband's household services. All of respondents' claims arose from CMU's discharge of William Boyle.

Petitioners removed the case from state court to the United States District Court for the Western District of Pennsylvania under 28 U.S.C. § 1441(a), which allows a defendant to remove an action that falls within the original jurisdiction of the federal district courts.[1] Petitioners stated that the entire lawsuit fell within the original jurisdiction, and hence within the removal jurisdiction, of the District Court because the complaint stated a claim arising under the Age Discrimination in Employment Act of 1967, 81 Stat. 602, as amended, 29 U.S.C. §§ 621–

---

* The dissenting opinion is omitted.

† Some of the Court's footnotes are omitted.

1. Section 1441(a) provides:

"Except as otherwise expressly provided by Act of Congress, any civil action brought in a State court of which the district courts of the United States have original jurisdiction, may be removed by the defendant or the defendants, to the district court of the United States for the district and division embracing the place where such action is pending."

634, and the state-law claims in the complaint were pendent to this federal-law claim. Respondents did not contest the removal.

Six months later, respondents moved to amend their complaint to delete the allegations of age discrimination and defamation and the request for damages for loss of consortium. In this motion, respondents stated that they now believed these claims were not tenable. At the same time, respondents filed a motion, conditional upon amendment of the complaint, to remand the suit to state court. Respondents noted that the amendment would eliminate their sole federal-law claim, which had provided the basis for removal of the case, and argued that a remand to state court was appropriate in these circumstances.

After granting the motion to amend, the District Court remanded the remaining claims to the state court in which respondents initially had filed the action. * * * The court noted that two sections of the statute authorize district courts to remand after removal. Under 28 U.S.C. § 1447(c), a court shall remand any case that "was removed improvidently and without jurisdiction";[2] under 28 U.S.C. § 1441(c), a court may remand any claim that is both independently nonremovable and "separate and independent" of the claim providing the basis for removal of the case.[3] The court held that § 1447(c) did not apply because the removal was jurisdictionally proper and that § 1441(c) did not apply because the remaining state-law claims in the case, although independently nonremovable, were pendent to, rather than separate and independent of, the federal-law claim that had provided the basis for removal. The District Court then stated that in Thermtron Products, Inc. v. Hermansdorfer, 423 U.S. 336, 96 S.Ct. 584, 46 L.Ed.2d 542 (1976), this Court had suggested that a district court could not remand a removed case or claim without specific statutory authorization. The District Court noted, however, that a number of appellate decisions since *Thermtron* had approved the remand of removed pendent state-law claims when the federal-law claim providing the basis for removal had been eliminated from the suit. The court found these later decisions persuasive and consequently opted to remand respondents' remaining state-law claims.

Petitioners filed a petition for writ of mandamus with the United States Court of Appeals for the Third Circuit, and a divided panel granted the petition.[4] * * *

2. Section 1447(c) provides, in pertinent part:

"If at any time before final judgment it appears that the case was removed improvidently and without jurisdiction, the district court shall remand the case, and may order the payment of just costs."

3. Section 1441(c) provides:

"Whenever a separate and independent claim or cause of action, which would be removable if sued upon alone, is joined with one or more otherwise non-removable claims or causes of action, the entire case may be removed and the district court may determine all issues therein, or, in its discretion, may remand all matters not otherwise within its original jurisdiction."

4. Petitioners also appealed the District Court's decision. The Court of Appeals, however, dismissed the appeal on the ground that 28 U.S.C. § 1447(d) of the removal statute bars appeals from remands

The Court of Appeals granted respondents' petition for rehearing *en banc* and * * * issued an order denying petitioners' application for a writ of mandamus. This order effectively left undisturbed the remand of respondents' case.

We granted certiorari, 479 U.S. 1083, 107 S.Ct. 1283, 94 L.Ed.2d 141 (1987), to resolve the split among the Circuits as to whether a district court has discretion to remand a removed case to state court when all federal-law claims have dropped out of the action and only pendent state-law claims remain. We now affirm.

II

The modern doctrine of pendent jurisdiction stems from this Court's decision in Mine Workers v. Gibbs, 383 U.S. 715, 86 S.Ct. 1130, 16 L.Ed.2d 218 (1966). Prior to *Gibbs*, this Court had recognized that considerations of judicial economy and procedural convenience justified the recognition of power in the federal courts to decide certain state-law claims involved in cases raising federal questions. See Hurn v. Oursler, 289 U.S. 238, 243–247, 53 S.Ct. 586, 588–90, 77 L.Ed. 1148 (1933). The test for determining when a federal court had jurisdiction over such state-law claims was murky, however, and the lower courts experienced considerable difficulty in applying it.[6] In *Gibbs*, the Court responded to this confusion, and the resulting hesitancy of federal courts to recognize jurisdiction over state-law claims, by establishing a new yardstick for deciding whether a federal court has jurisdiction over a state-law claim brought in a case that also involves a federal question. The Court stated that a federal court has jurisdiction over an entire action, including state-law claims, whenever the federal-law claims and state-law claims in the case "derive from a common nucleus of operative fact" and are "such that [a plaintiff] would ordinarily be expected to try them all in one judicial proceeding." Mine Workers v. Gibbs, 383 U.S., at 725, 86 S.Ct., at 1138. The Court intended this standard not only to clarify, but also to broaden, the scope of federal pendent jurisdiction. See ibid. (stating that the prior approach, at least as applied by lower courts, was "unnecessarily grudging"). According to *Gibbs*, "considerations of judicial economy, convenience and fairness to litigants" support a wide-ranging power in the federal courts to decide state-law claims in cases that also present federal questions. Id., at 726, 86 S.Ct., at 1139.

At the same time, however, *Gibbs* drew a distinction between the power of a federal court to hear state-law claims and the discretionary

---

to state courts with a single exception not applicable to this case.

6. The test established in Hurn v. Oursler provided that if a plaintiff presented "two distinct grounds," one state and one federal, "in support of a single cause of action," the federal court had jurisdiction over the entire action, but that if the plaintiff's assertions amounted to "two separate and distinct causes of action," the federal

court had jurisdiction only over the federal "cause of action." 289 U.S., at 246, 53 S.Ct., at 590. The difficulty with this test, as many commentators noted, was that it centered on the inherently elusive concept of a "cause of action." See, e.g., Shulman & Jaegerman, Some Jurisdictional Limitations on Federal Procedure, 45 Yale L.J. 393, 397–410 (1936).

exercise of that power. The *Gibbs* Court recognized that a federal court's determination of state-law claims could conflict with the principle of comity to the States and with the promotion of justice between the litigating parties. For this reason, *Gibbs* emphasized that "pendent jurisdiction is a doctrine of discretion, not of plaintiff's right." Ibid. Under *Gibbs,* a federal court should consider and weigh in each case, and at every stage of the litigation, the values of judicial economy, convenience, fairness, and comity in order to decide whether to exercise jurisdiction over a case brought in that court involving pendent state-law claims. When the balance of these factors indicates that a case properly belongs in state court, as when the federal-law claims have dropped out of the lawsuit in its early stages and only state-law claims remain, the federal court should decline the exercise of jurisdiction by dismissing the case without prejudice. Id., at 726–727, 86 S.Ct., at 1139. As articulated by *Gibbs,* the doctrine of pendent jurisdiction thus is a doctrine of flexibility, designed to allow courts to deal with cases involving pendent claims in the manner that most sensibly accommodates a range of concerns and values.

In the case before us, respondents' complaint stated a single federal-law claim and a number of state-law claims. The state-law claims fell within the jurisdiction of the District Court to which the action was removed because they derived from the same nucleus of operative fact as the federal-law claim: CMU's dismissal of William Boyle. Under the pendent jurisdiction doctrine set forth in *Gibbs,* however, the District Court had to consider throughout the litigation whether to exercise its jurisdiction over the case. When the single federal-law claim in the action was eliminated at an early stage of the litigation, the District Court had a powerful reason to choose not to continue to exercise jurisdiction. The question that this case presents is whether the District Court could relinquish jurisdiction over the case only by dismissing it without prejudice or whether the District Court could relinquish jurisdiction over the case by remanding it to state court as well.

*   *   *

As many lower courts have noted, a remand generally will be preferable to a dismissal when the statute of limitations on the plaintiff's state-law claims has expired before the federal court has determined that it should relinquish jurisdiction over the case. In such a case, a dismissal will foreclose the plaintiff from litigating his claims. This consequence may work injustice to the plaintiff: although he has brought his suit in timely manner, he is time-barred from pressing his case.[9] Equally important, and more easily overlooked, the foreclosure

---

9. Moreover, if a plaintiff bringing suit in state court knows that, notwithstanding the expiration of a statute of limitations, a federal court to which a case is removed must dismiss the case upon deciding that the exercise of pendent jurisdiction would be inappropriate, the plaintiff may well decline to allege any federal-law claims. By forgoing all federal-law claims, the plaintiff can insulate himself from the risk that the combination of removal, dismissal under the pendent jurisdiction doctrine, and the expiration of a statute of limitations will foreclose him from litigating his

of the state-law claims may conflict with the principle of comity to States. The preclusion of valid state-law claims initially brought in timely manner in state court undermines the State's interest in enforcing its law. The operation of state statutes of limitations thus provides a potent reason for giving federal district courts discretion to remand, as well as to dismiss, removed pendent claims.[10]

Even when the applicable statute of limitations has not expired, a remand may best promote the values of economy, convenience, fairness, and comity. Both litigants and States have an interest in the prompt and efficient resolution of controversies based on state law. Any time a district court dismisses, rather than remands, a removed case involving pendent claims, the parties will have to refile their papers in state court, at some expense of time and money. Moreover, the state court will have to reprocess the case, and this procedure will involve similar costs. Dismissal of the claim therefore will increase both the expense and the time involved in enforcing state law. Under the analysis set forth in *Gibbs,* this consequence, even taken alone, provides good reason to grant federal courts wide discretion to remand cases involving pendent claims when the exercise of pendent jurisdiction over such cases would be inappropriate.

Petitioners argue that the federal removal statute prohibits a district court from remanding properly removed cases involving pendent claims. This argument is based not on the language of Congress, but on its silence. Petitioners note that the removal statute explicitly authorizes remands in two situations. By failing similarly to provide for remands of removed cases involving pendent claims, petitioners assert, Congress intended to preclude district courts from remanding such cases.

state-law claims. Such protection will appear especially attractive to a plaintiff who has any doubt about the validity of his federal-law claims, because he will know that if the district court dismisses these claims on the merits prior to trial, the court may well decide that the rest of the case is unsuitable for resolution in a federal court and therefore dismiss the remaining claims. Thus, a rule that would require federal courts to dismiss a removed case that is not suitable for resolution in a federal court would operate not only to foreclose some plaintiffs from litigating their state-law claims, but also to chill other plaintiffs from bringing their federal-law claims.

10. Petitioners argue that the federal courts do not need discretion to remand because they can retain jurisdiction over any case in which the statute of limitations has expired. See Brief for Petitioners 20. At least one Court of Appeals has made the identical argument. See Cook v. Weber, 698 F.2d, at 909. This solution to the problem of an expired statute of limitations, however, is far from satisfying. Under petitioners' suggested approach, district courts would retain jurisdiction over cases that apart from the statute-of-limitations concern properly belong in state courts. There is no reason to compel or encourage district courts to retain jurisdiction over such cases when the alternative of a remand is readily available.

In similar vein, the dissent argues that federal courts do not need discretion to remand because some States have savings clauses that alleviate the statute-of-limitations problem arising from the dismissal of cases. But the existence of such clauses in some States, while diminishing the reason for remand in particular cases, hardly reverses our general conclusion that the balance of factors to be weighed under *Gibbs,* considered in light of the range of state statutes of limitations, supports giving federal district courts the authority to remand cases involving pendent claims.

We cannot accept petitioners' reasoning. We do not dispute that Congress could set a limitation of this kind on the federal courts' administration of the doctrine of pendent jurisdiction. But Congress has not done so, expressly or otherwise, in the removal statute.
* * *

As petitioners point out, this Court's opinion in Thermtron Products Inc. v. Hermansdorfer, 423 U.S. 336, 96 S.Ct. 584, 46 L.Ed.2d 542 (1976), contains some language that could be read to support the opposite conclusion. In *Thermtron,* a District Court remanded a properly removed case to state court on the ground that the federal docket was overcrowded. This Court held that the remand was improper. In so doing, the Court stated several times that a district court may not remand a case to a state court on a ground not specified in the removal statute. See id., at 345, 96 S.Ct., at 590. See also id., at 345, n. 9, 96 S.Ct., at 590, n. 9 ("Lower federal courts have uniformly held that cases properly removed from state to federal court within the federal court's jurisdiction may not be remanded for discretionary reasons not authorized by the controlling statute"). * * *

The language from *Thermtron* that petitioners cite, viewed in isolation, is admittedly far-reaching, but it loses controlling force when read against the circumstances of that case. The *Thermtron* decision was a response to a clearly impermissible remand, of a kind very different from that at issue here. In *Thermtron,* the District Court had no authority to decline to hear the removed case. The court had diversity jurisdiction over the case, which is not discretionary. Thus, the District Court could not properly have eliminated the case from its docket, whether by a remand or by a dismissal. In contrast, when a removed case involves pendent state-law claims, a district court has undoubted discretion to decline to hear the case. * * *

Petitioners also argue that giving district courts discretion to remand cases involving pendent state-law claims will allow plaintiffs to secure a state forum through the use of manipulative tactics. Petitioners' concern appears to be that a plaintiff whose suit has been removed to federal court will be able to regain a state forum simply by deleting all federal-law claims from the complaint and requesting that the district court remand the case. Brief for Petitioners 18–20. This concern, however, hardly justifies a categorical prohibition on the remand of cases involving state-law claims regardless of whether the plaintiff has attempted to manipulate the forum and regardless of the other circumstances in the case. A district court can consider whether the plaintiff has engaged in any manipulative tactics when it decides whether to remand a case. If the plaintiff has attempted to manipulate the forum, the court should take this behavior into account in determining whether the balance of factors to be considered under the pendent jurisdiction doctrine support a remand in the case. The district courts thus can guard against forum manipulation without a blanket rule that would prohibit the remand of all cases involving pendent state-law claims.

* * *

JUSTICE WHITE, with whom CHIEF JUSTICE REHNQUIST and JUSTICE SCALIA join, dissenting.

* * *

The Court's decision has the peculiar result of treating plaintiffs who bring suit in federal court less favorably than plaintiffs who bring suit in state court. If the Boyles had commenced this suit in federal court and their federal claims were later dismissed, the Federal District Judge could only have dismissed the remaining pendent claims or decided those claims himself. Because the Boyles instead commenced this suit in state court, however, the District Judge had the additional option of ordering a remand. The principal advantage to plaintiffs of this third option is that their state claims are less likely to be dismissed as time-barred. Accordingly, plaintiffs with claims arising under both federal and state law now will be encouraged to bring suit in state court, even when the state courts are as overburdened as those in Allegheny County are alleged to be, rather than in the federal courts that have been described as the "primary guardians" of federal rights. Steffel v. Thompson, 415 U.S. 452, 463, 94 S.Ct. 1209, 1218, 39 L.Ed.2d 505 (1974). In addition, defendants who are able to afford the costs and delays associated with a one-way trip to federal court but not the additional costs and delays associated with a round trip may now be discouraged from exercising their statutory right to removal in cases involving both federal and state claims.[2]

There is some incongruity in the Court's invocation of federal-state "comity" in support of a holding whose principal effect will be to relieve plaintiffs from state statutes of limitations. * * * It seems unnecessary for this Court to protect plaintiffs whose federal claims prove "not tenable" from the operation of state statutes of limitations when the States have shown themselves capable of achieving the same result through savings clauses similar to that enacted by Pennsylvania. See 42 Pa.Cons.Stat. § 5535(a) (1982).[3] Neither the parties nor the courts below have suggested that the Boyles would not have been protected by the Pennsylvania savings clause had their federal claims been dismissed involuntarily rather than at their own behest.

* * *

2. While the majority contends that the use of remands rather than dismissals will save time and money for the state courts, the record contains no support for this assertion. I would think that the costs to the state courts of processing a new case are not appreciably different from the costs of processing a remanded case. Furthermore, to the extent that the federal courts will now remand pendent claims that they previously would have retained, today's holding may result in increased costs for the state courts.

3. Section 5535(a) provides, in pertinent part, that "[i]f a civil action or proceeding is timely commenced and is terminated, a party . . . may . . . commence a new action or proceeding upon the same cause of action within one year after the termination." This provision is inapplicable to proceedings terminated by "a voluntary nonsuit, a discontinuance, a dismissal for neglect to prosecute the action or proceeding, or a final judgment upon the merits."

NOTE ON PENDENT JURISDICTION

1. Pendent claim jurisdiction, as opposed to pendent party or ancillary jurisdiction, is relatively uncontroversial. However, *Cohill* demonstrates that it can present problems. The effect of both pendent claim and ancillary jurisdiction is to expand the jurisdiction of federal courts: a claim that otherwise could be brought only in a state court can be maintained in federal court by virtue of its relation to a claim which falls within the jurisdiction of the federal courts. As indicated by the discussion in Aldinger v. Howard, both concepts are the product of decisional law rather than statute and have evolved into configurations that are inconsistent. For example, is it consistent to permit intervention and impleader of third parties without a requirement of complete diversity, but not to permit joinder of additional parties under the necessary parties rule in like situations? To permit pendent claim jurisdiction over state law counterclaims where plaintiff's complaint is premised on federal law, but not to permit removal of suits to federal court where the complaint is based on state law and the federal claim appears in the counterclaim? On intervention, see F.R.C.P. 24 and Historical Note on Intervention, infra p. 751. On impleader and counterclaims, see F.R.C.P. 14(a) and Note on Impleader and Cross–Claims, infra p. 748. On necessary parties, see F.R.C.P. 19 and Note on Compulsory Joinder of Parties, infra p. 737.

2. As discussed in Aldinger v. Howard and *Cohill,* where plaintiff asserts a federal claim, pendent claim jurisdiction allows a federal court also to adjudicate state law claims asserted by either plaintiff or defendant so long as they arise from the same transaction that provides the basis for the federal claim. What if a party fails to join a related state law claim and then attempts to assert it in a subsequent action? See Note on Res Judicata Between the Same Parties, infra p. 648, and F.R.C.P. 13. United Mine Workers v. Gibbs makes it clear that the authority of a federal court to hear pendent claims is discretionary, not a matter of plaintiff's right. Why should this be so? Should federal courts be more concerned with ensuring that their limited jurisdiction is not exceeded or with doing a complete job of adjudicating controversies that come before them?

3. Most jurisdictions have "savings" statutes of the sort discussed in *Cohill.* See Note on Statutes of Limitations and Laches, supra p. 234. Does this reduce the force of the majority's comity argument in *Cohill?* If a state chooses not to enact such a statute, why should a federal court seek to avoid the effects of state policy by remanding a case to state court after the statute of limitations has expired on the state claims? Considerations of justice may well support such a remand, but is the federal court really vindicating "the State's interest in enforcing its law," as the majority asserts, or is it infringing on that interest, as the dissenters imply? The dissenters also note that the effect of the Court's decision may be to encourage the filing of suits with both federal and state claims in state court. Might the majority have intended just such a result? Is such an incentive desirable?

On appellate review of orders remanding a removed case, see Herrmann, Thermtron Revisited: When and How Federal Trial Court Remand Orders Are Reviewable, 19 Ariz.St.L.J. 395 (1987).

4. The Supreme Court's refusal to apply the concept of pendent party or ancillary jurisdiction in Aldinger v. Howard elicited a good deal of critical comment that illuminates the history and contours of the concept itself. See

especially Comment, Aldinger v. Howard and Pendent Jurisdiction, 77 Colum.L. Rev. 127 (1977); Comment, The Impact of Aldinger v. Howard on Pendent Party Jurisdiction, 125 U.Pa.L.Rev. 1357 (1977). The specific holding in Aldinger v. Howard was undercut in Monell v. New York City Dept. of Social Services, 436 U.S. 658, 98 S.Ct. 2018, 56 L.Ed.2d 611 (1978), which overruled Monroe v. Pape and City of Kenosha v. Bruno, cited in *Aldinger* fn. 11. Hence, under *Monell* the county of Spokane would be a "person" within the meaning of 42 U.S.C.A. § 1983 and hence one against whom a federal claim would lie; the question of pendent party jurisdiction would disappear. If the federal claim could validly be asserted against the county, would the federal court also have jurisdiction of a claim against the county that the plaintiff's discharge violated her rights under state law?

Although the specific problem of pendent party jurisdiction in *Aldinger* is thus now moot, the more general question of the validity of pendent party jurisdiction in other contexts clearly is not. On this question, Justice Rehnquist's analysis of the Supreme Court precedents is very precise. The concept of pendent party jurisdiction was expounded in Astor-Honor, Inc. v. Grosset & Dunlap, Inc., 441 F.2d 627 (2d Cir. 1971), and Leather's Best, Inc. v. S. S. Mormaclynx, 451 F.2d 800 (2d Cir. 1971), two opinions by Judge Friendly. Most other circuits followed the assertion in these cases that pendent party jurisdiction is fairly implied by United Mine Workers v. Gibbs, see, e.g., Bowers v. Moreno, 520 F.2d 843 (1st Cir. 1975), but, as Justice Rehnquist indicated in *Aldinger*, others did not.

5. The concept of pendent party or ancillary jurisdiction has potential application in a variety of contexts. One, such as Aldinger v. Howard, is where foundational jurisdiction rests on a federal claim and the pendent party is charged with essentially the same wrongful act, under principles of respondeat superior or the like. Compare Leather's Best, Inc. v. S. S. Mormaclynx, supra; e.g., Tomkins v. Public Serv. Electric & Gas Co., 422 F.Supp. 553 (D.N.J.1976) (in federal sex discrimination action against employer, employee's supervisor sued on state law claim for assault). A second is where the pendent party has a claim or liability that may be adversely affected by the adjudication of the claim on which foundational jurisdiction rests. Illustrative are the intervention and counterclaim situations mentioned in Aldinger v. Howard. A third is where pendent party jurisdiction would be the only basis upon which the joinder of all interested parties could be effectuated, because one or more of them cannot be brought into state court. Such is the case when the Government is sued under the Tort Claims Act and other persons also allegedly liable are named as additional defendants. See Aldinger v. Howard, fn. 13; e.g., Ayala v. United States, 550 F.2d 1196 (9th Cir. 1977) (holding that pendent party jurisdiction is improper in such a case). A fourth situation is where a claimant in a diversity action seeks to assert a claim against a co-citizen that could be litigated without affecting the diversity claim itself.

6. In Owen Equipment & Erection Co. v. Kroger, 437 U.S. 365, 98 S.Ct. 2396, 57 L.Ed.2d 274 (1978), the situation was this: Plaintiff, a citizen of state N, sued a citizen of state I, who in turn impleaded a citizen of state N as a third-party defendant. Plaintiff then amended her complaint to assert a claim against the third-party defendant. The Court held, 437 U.S. at 375–377, that there was no jurisdiction of the amended claim:

> "It is true, as the Court of Appeals noted, that the exercise of ancillary jurisdiction over nonfederal claims has often been upheld in situations involving impleader, cross-claims or counterclaims. But in determining

whether jurisdiction over a nonfederal claim exists, the context in which the nonfederal claim is asserted is crucial. See Aldinger v. Howard * * *. And the claim here arises in a setting quite different from the kinds * * * falling within the ancillary jurisdiction of the federal courts.

"First, * * * the [plaintiff's] claim against the [third-party defendant] * * * was entirely separate from her original claim against [the original defendant], since the [third-party defendant's] liability to her depended not at all upon whether [the original defendant] was also liable. Far from being an ancillary and dependent claim, it was a new and independent one.

"Second, the nonfederal claim here was asserted by the plaintiff, who voluntarily chose to bring suit upon a state-law claim in a federal court. By contrast, ancillary jurisdiction typically involves claims by a defending party haled into court against his will, or by another person whose rights might be irretrievably lost unless he could assert them in an ongoing action in a federal court. * * *

" * * * [N]either the convenience of litigants nor considerations of judicial economy can suffice to justify extension of the doctrine of ancillary jurisdiction to a plaintiff's cause of action against a citizen of the same State in a diversity case."

7. Still another situation is where many claimants having small claims seek to aggregate their claims in a class suit so as to meet the minimum amount in controversy requirement that is applicable in diversity suits and in some federal question suits. The aggregation could be justified on the proposition that the claims are ancillary to each other, so to speak. The Supreme Court has held, however, that such aggregation would result in an unwarranted expansion of the statutory limits on the federal courts' jurisdiction. See Zahn v. International Paper Co., 414 U.S. 291, 94 S.Ct. 505, 38 L.Ed.2d 511 (1973).

8. A question of personal jurisdiction can arise where the principal claim, but not the pendent claim, enjoys a special statutory provision for "long arm" service of process. See Note, Removing the Cloak of Personal Jurisdiction From Choice of Law Analysis: Pendent Jurisdiction and Nationwide Service of Process, 51 Ford.L.Rev. 127 (1982).

See also Garvey, The Limits of Ancillary Jurisdiction, 57 Tex.L.Rev. 697 (1979); Shapiro, Jurisdiction and Discretion, 60 N.Y.U.L.Rev. 543 (1985); Miller, Ancillary and Pendent Jurisdiction, 26 S.Tex.L.J. 1 (1985); Dwyer, Pendent Jurisdiction and the Eleventh Amendment, 75 Calif.L.Rev. 129 (1987) (impact on pendent state claims of the Supreme Court's decision in Pennhurst State School and Hosp. v. Halderman, holding that Eleventh Amendment bars a federal court from basing relief against state officials on pendent state claims).

2. ABSTENTION

MIDDLESEX COUNTY ETHICS COMMITTEE v. GARDEN STATE BAR ASSOCIATION

Supreme Court of the United States, 1982.
457 U.S. 423, 102 S.Ct. 2515, 73 L.Ed.2d 116.*

CHIEF JUSTICE BURGER delivered the opinion of the Court.

We granted certiorari to determine whether a federal court should abstain from considering a challenge to the constitutionality of disciplinary rules that are the subject of a pending state disciplinary proceeding within the jurisdiction of the New Jersey Supreme Court. 454 U.S. 962, 102 S.Ct. 500, 70 L.Ed.2d 377 (1981). The Court of Appeals held that it need not abstain under Younger v. Harris, 401 U.S. 37, 91 S.Ct. 746, 27 L.Ed.2d 669 (1971). We reverse.

I

A

The Constitution of New Jersey charges the State Supreme Court with the responsibility for licensing and disciplining attorneys admitted to practice in the State. Art. 6, § 2, ¶ 3. Under the rules established by the New Jersey Supreme Court, enacted pursuant to its constitutional authority, a complaint moves through a three-tier procedure. First, local District Ethics Committees appointed by the State Supreme Court are authorized to receive complaints relating to claimed unethical conduct by an attorney. New Jersey Court Rule 1:20–2(d). At least two of the minimum of eight members of the District Ethics Committee must be nonattorneys. Complaints are assigned to an attorney member of the Committee to report and make a recommendation. Rule 1:20–2(h). The decision whether to proceed with the complaint is made by the person who chairs the Ethics Committee. If a complaint is issued by the Ethics Committee it must state the name of the complainant, describe the claimed improper conduct, cite the relevant rules, and state, if known, whether the same or a similar complaint has been considered by any other Ethics Committee. The attorney whose conduct is challenged is served with the complaint and has 10 days to answer.

Unless good cause appears for referring the complaint to another Committee member, each complaint is referred to the member of the Committee who conducted the initial investigation for review and further investigation, if necessary. The Committee member submits a written report stating whether a prima facie indication of unethical or unprofessional conduct has been demonstrated. The report is then evaluated by the chairman of the Ethics Committee to determine whether a prima facie case exists. Absent a prima facie showing, the

---

* Some of the Court's footnotes are omitted.

complaint is summarily dismissed. If a prima facie case is found, a formal hearing on the complaint is held before three or more members of the Ethics Committee, a majority of whom must be attorneys. The lawyer who is charged with unethical conduct may have counsel, discovery is available, and all witnesses are sworn. The panel is required to prepare a written report with its findings of fact and conclusions. The full Committee, following the decision of the panel, has three alternatives. The Committee may dismiss the complaint, prepare a private letter of reprimand, or prepare a presentment to be forwarded to the Disciplinary Review Board. Rule 1:20–2(o).

3 choices

The Disciplinary Review Board, a statewide board which is also appointed by the Supreme Court, consists of nine members, at least five of whom must be attorneys and at least three of whom must be nonattorneys. The Board makes a *de novo* review. Rule 1:20–3(d)(3).[4] The Board is required to make formal findings and recommendations to the New Jersey Supreme Court.

new/ 2nd time

All decisions of the Disciplinary Review Board beyond a private reprimand are reviewed by the New Jersey Supreme Court. Briefing and oral argument are available in the Supreme Court for cases involving disbarment or suspension for more than one year. Rule 1:20–4.

B

Respondent Lennox Hinds, a member of the New Jersey bar, served as executive director of the National Conference of Black Lawyers at the time of his challenged conduct. Hinds represented Joanne Chesimard in a civil proceeding challenging her conditions of confinement in jail. In 1977 Chesimard went to trial in state court for the murder of a policeman. Respondent Hinds was not a counsel of record for Chesimard in the murder case. However, at the outset of the criminal trial Hinds took part in a press conference, making statements critical of the trial and of the trial judge's judicial temperament and racial insensitivity. In particular, Hinds referred to the criminal trial as "a travesty," a "legalized lynching," and "a kangaroo court."

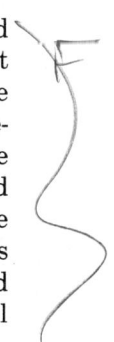

One member of the Middlesex County Ethics Committee read news accounts of Hinds' comments and brought the matter to the attention of the Committee. In February of 1977 the Committee directed one of its members to conduct an investigation. A letter was written to Hinds, who released the contents of the letter to the press. The Ethics Committee on its own motion then suspended the investigation until the conclusion of the Chesimard criminal trial.

4. Subsequent to the initiation of the disciplinary hearing involved in this case, Rule 1:20–3(e) was amended to provide:

"Constitutional challenges to the proceedings not raised before the District Committee shall be preserved, without Board action, for Supreme Court consideration as part of its review of the matter on the merits. Interlocutory relief may be sought only in accordance with Rule 1:20–4(d)(i)."

After the trial was completed the Committee investigated the complaint and concluded that there was probable cause to believe that Hinds had violated DR 1–102(A)(5) of the Disciplinary Rules of the Code of Professional Responsibility.[5] That section provides that "[a] lawyer shall not . . . [e]ngage in conduct that is prejudicial to the administration of justice." Respondent Hinds also was charged with violating DR 7–107(D), which prohibits extrajudicial statements by lawyers associated with the prosecution or defense of a criminal matter.[6] The Committee then served a formal statement of charges on Hinds.

Instead of filing an answer to the charges in accordance with the New Jersey bar disciplinary procedures, Hinds and the three respondent organizations filed suit in the United States District Court for the District of New Jersey contending that the disciplinary rules violated respondents' First Amendment rights. In addition, respondents charged that the disciplinary rules were facially vague and overbroad. The District Court granted petitioner's motion to dismiss based on *Younger v. Harris*, 401 U.S. 37, 91 S.Ct. 746, 27 L.Ed.2d 669 (1971), concluding that "[t]he principles of comity and federalism dictate that the federal court abstain so that the state is afforded the opportunity to interpret its rules in the face of a constitutional challenge." App. to Pet. for Cert. 53a–54a. At respondents' request the District Court reopened the case to allow respondents an opportunity to establish bad faith, harassment or other extraordinary circumstance which would constitute an exception to *Younger* abstention. *Dombrowski v. Pfister*, 380 U.S. 479, 85 S.Ct. 1116, 14 L.Ed.2d 22 (1965). After two days of hearings the District Court found no evidence to justify an exception to the *Younger* abstention doctrine and dismissed the federal court complaint.

A divided panel of the United States Court of Appeals for the Third Circuit reversed on the ground that the state bar disciplinary proceedings did not provide a meaningful opportunity to adjudicate constitutional claims. 643 F.2d 119 (1981). The court reasoned that the disciplinary proceedings in this case are unlike the state judicial proceedings to which the federal courts usually defer. The Court of Appeals majority viewed the proceedings in this case as administrative, "nonadjudicative" proceedings analogous to the preindictment stage of a criminal proceeding.[7]

---

5. The Disciplinary Rules of the Code of Professional Responsibility and Code of Judicial Conduct of the American Bar Association, with amendment and supplementation, have been adopted by the New Jersey Supreme Court as the applicable standard of conduct for members of the bar and the judges of New Jersey. New Jersey Court Rule 1:14.

6. DR 7–107 deals with "Trial Publicity" and states:

"(D) During the selection of a jury or the trial of a criminal matter, a lawyer or law firm associated with the prosecution or defense of a criminal matter shall not make or participate in making an extrajudicial statement that he expects to be disseminated by means of public communication and that relates to the trial, parties, or issues in the trial or other matters that are reasonably likely to interfere with a fair trial. . . ."

7. The majority concluded that the hearings are designed to elicit facts, not legal arguments, as indicated by the presence of nonlawyers. The court also found

On petition for rehearing petitioners attached an affidavit from the Clerk of the New Jersey Supreme Court which stated that the New Jersey Supreme Court would directly consider Hinds' constitutional challenges and that the court would consider whether such a procedure should be made explicit in the Supreme Court rules. On reconsideration a divided panel of the Third Circuit declined to alter its original decision, stating that the relevant facts concerning abstention are those that existed at the time of the District Court's decision. 651 F.2d 154 (1981).[8]

Pending review in this Court, the New Jersey Supreme Court has heard oral arguments on the constitutional challenges presented by respondent Hinds and has adopted a rule allowing for an aggrieved party in a disciplinary hearing to seek interlocutory review of a constitutional challenge to the proceedings.[9]

II

A

Younger v. Harris, supra, and its progeny espouse a strong federal policy against federal court interference with pending state judicial proceedings absent extraordinary circumstances. The policies underly-

that the ability to raise constitutional claims before the Ethics Committee does not constitute a meaningful opportunity to have constitutional questions adjudicated. No formal opinion is filed by the District Ethics Committee. The Third Circuit distinguished Gipson v. New Jersey Supreme Ct., 558 F.2d 701 (CA3 1977), on the ground that in *Gipson* the attorney being disciplined was already subject to the state court action at the time the federal proceeding had been initiated.

Judge Adams, concurring, emphasized that state courts have the primary responsibility to discipline their bar and, in general, the federal judiciary is to exercise no supervisory powers. Judge Weis, dissenting, argued that respondents have full opportunity in the New Jersey proceeding to raise constitutional issues, concluding that the disciplinary proceedings are not a series of separate segments before independent bodies but are part of a whole. Judge Weis also concluded that there was nothing to prevent the Ethics Committee from considering constitutional claims.

8. The panel majority noted that no rule existed at the time of the District Court's decision to assure the Court of Appeals that the New Jersey Supreme Court would consider the constitutional claims. The court also concluded that the possibility of a formal procedure of the New Jersey Court for consideration of constitutional claims does not moot this case because the

underlying dispute as to the validity of the rules still remains. Judge Weis, again dissenting, concluded that no justiciable controversy remained as to the issue in the Court of Appeals and recommended that the case be remanded and dismissed as moot.

9. Rule 1:20–4(d) states:

"(i) Interlocutory Review. An aggrieved party may file a motion for leave to appeal with the Supreme Court to seek interlocutory review of a constitutional challenge to proceedings pending before the District Ethics Committee or the Disciplinary Review Board. The motion papers shall conform to R. 2:8–1. Leave to appeal may be granted only when necessary to prevent irreparable injury. If leave to appeal is granted, the record below may, in the discretion of the Court, be supplemented by the filing of briefs and oral argument.

"(ii) Final Review. In any case in which a constitutional challenge to the proceedings has been properly raised below and preserved pending review of the merits of the disciplinary matter by the Supreme Court, the aggrieved party may, within 10 days of the filing of the report and recommendation of the Disciplinary Review Board, seek the review of the Court by proceeding in accordance with the applicable provisions of R. 1:19–8."

ing *Younger* abstention have been frequently reiterated by this Court. The notion of "comity" includes "a proper respect for state functions, a recognition of the fact that the entire country is made up of a Union of separate state governments, and a continuance of the belief that the National Government will fare best if the States and their institutions are left free to perform their separate functions in their separate ways." Id., at 44, 91 S.Ct., at 750.[10] Minimal respect for the state processes, of course, precludes any *presumption* that the state courts will not safeguard federal constitutional rights.

The policies underlying *Younger* are fully applicable to noncriminal judicial proceedings when important state interests are involved. Moore v. Sims, 442 U.S. 415, 423, 99 S.Ct. 2371, 2377, 60 L.Ed.2d 994 (1979); Huffman v. Pursue, Ltd., 420 U.S. 592, 604–605, 95 S.Ct. 1200, 1208, 43 L.Ed.2d 482 (1975). The importance of the state interest may be demonstrated by the fact that the noncriminal proceedings bear a close relationship to proceedings criminal in nature, as in *Huffman*, supra. Proceedings necessary for the vindication of important state policies or for the functioning of the state judicial system also evidence the state's substantial interest in the litigation. Trainor v. Hernandez, 431 U.S. 434, 97 S.Ct. 1911, 52 L.Ed.2d 486 (1977); Juidice v. Vail, 430 U.S. 327, 97 S.Ct. 1211, 51 L.Ed.2d 376 (1977). Where vital state interests are involved, a federal court should abstain "unless state law clearly bars the interposition of the constitutional claims." *Moore*, 442 U.S., at 426, 99 S.Ct., at 2379. "[T]he . . . pertinent inquiry is whether the state proceedings afford an adequate opportunity to raise the constitutional claims. . . ." Id., at 430, 99 S.Ct., at 2380. See also Gibson v. Berryhill, 411 U.S. 564, 93 S.Ct. 1689, 36 L.Ed.2d 488 (1973).

The question in this case is threefold: *first*, do state bar disciplinary hearings within the constitutionally prescribed jurisdiction of the State Supreme Court constitute an ongoing state judicial proceeding; *second*, do the proceedings implicate important state interests; and *third*, is there an adequate opportunity in the state proceedings to raise constitutional challenges.

B

The State of New Jersey, in common with most States,[11] recognizes the important state obligation to regulate persons who are authorized

---

10. Samuels v. Mackell, 401 U.S. 66, 91 S.Ct. 764, 27 L.Ed.2d 688 (1971), concluded that the same comity and federalism principles govern the issuance of federal court declaratory judgments concerning the state statute that is the subject of the ongoing state criminal proceeding.

11. See Shoaf, State Disciplinary Enforcement Systems Structural Survey (ABA National Center for Professional Responsibility 1980).

The New Jersey allocation of responsibility is consistent with § 2.1 of the ABA Standards for Lawyer Discipline and Disability Proceedings (Proposed Draft 1978), which states that the "[u]ltimate and exclusive responsibility within a state for the structure and administration of the lawyer discipline and disability system and the disposition of individual cases is within the inherent power of the highest court of the state."

to practice law. New Jersey expresses this in a state constitutional provision vesting in the New Jersey Supreme Court the authority to fix standards, regulate admission to the bar, and enforce professional discipline among members of the bar. New Jersey Const. Art. 6, § 2, ¶ 3. The Supreme Court of New Jersey has recognized that the local District Ethics Committees act as the arm of the court in performing the function of receiving and investigating complaints and holding hearings. Rule 1:20–2; In re Logan, 70 N.J. 222, 358 A.2d 787 (1976). The New Jersey Court has made clear that filing a complaint with the local ethics and grievance committee "is in effect a filing with the Supreme Court. . . ." Toft v. Ketchum, 18 N.J. 280, 284, 113 A.2d 671, 674, cert. denied, 350 U.S. 887 (1955). "From the very beginning a disciplinary proceeding is judicial in nature, initiated by filing a complaint with an ethics and grievance committee." [12] Ibid. It is clear beyond doubt that the New Jersey Supreme Court considers its bar disciplinary proceedings as "judicial in nature." [13] As such, the proceedings are of a character to warrant federal court deference. The remaining inquiries are whether important state interests are implicated so as to warrant federal court abstention and whether the federal plaintiff has an adequate opportunity to present the federal challenge.

C

The State of New Jersey has an extremely important interest in maintaining and assuring the professional conduct of the attorneys it licenses. States traditionally have exercised extensive control over the professional conduct of attorneys. See supra, n. 11. The ultimate objective of such control is "the protection of the public, the purification of the bar and the prevention of a reoccurrence." In re Baron, 25 N.J.

The rationale for vesting responsibility with the judiciary is that the practice of law "is so directly connected and bound up with the exercise of judicial power and the administration of justice that the right to define and regulate it naturally and logically belongs to the judicial department." Id., commentary at § 2.1.

12. The New Jersey Supreme Court has concluded that bar disciplinary proceedings are neither criminal nor civil in nature but rather are *sui generis*. In re Logan, 70 N.J. 222, 358 A.2d 787 (1976). See also, Standards for Lawyer Discipline and Disability Proceedings § 1.2 (Proposed Draft 1978). As recognized in Juidice v. Vail, supra, however, whether the proceeding "is labeled civil, quasi-criminal, or criminal in nature," the salient fact is whether federal court interference would unduly interfere with the legitimate activities of the state. 430 U.S., at 335–336, 97 S.Ct., at 1217.

The instant case arose before the 1978 rule change. In 1978 the New Jersey Su-

preme Court established a Disciplinary Review Board charged with review of findings of District Ethics Committees. Nothing in this rule change, however, altered the nature of such proceedings. The responsibility under Art. 6, § 2, ¶ 3 remains with the New Jersey Supreme Court.

13. The role of local ethics or bar association committees may be analogized to the function of a special master. Anonymous v. Assn. of the Bar of City of New York, 515 F.2d 427 (CA2), cert. denied, 423 U.S. 863, 96 S.Ct. 122, 46 L.Ed.2d 92 (1975). The essentially judicial nature of disciplinary actions in New Jersey has been recognized previously by the federal courts. In Gipson v. New Jersey Supreme Court, 558 F.2d 701 (CA3 1977), the United States Court of Appeals for the Third Circuit agreed that "incursions by federal courts into ongoing [New Jersey] disciplinary proceedings would be particularly disruptive of notions of comity." Id., at 704.

Judicial interest

445, 449, 136 A.2d 873, 875 (1957). The judiciary as well as the public is dependent upon professionally ethical conduct of attorneys and thus has a significant interest in assuring and maintaining high standards of conduct of attorneys engaged in practice. See In re Stein, 1 N.J. 228, 237, 62 A.2d 801, 805 (1949), quoting In re Cahill, 66 N.J.L. 527, 50 A. 119 (Sup.Ct. 1901). The State's interest in the professional conduct of attorneys involved in the administration of criminal justice is of special importance. Finally, the State's interest in the present litigation is demonstrated by the fact that the Middlesex County Ethics Committee, an agency of the Supreme Court of New Jersey, is the named defendant in the present suit and was the body which initiated the state proceedings against respondent Hinds.

The importance of the state interest in the pending state judicial proceeding and in the federal case calls *Younger* abstention into play. So long as the constitutional claims of respondents can be determined in the state proceedings and so long as there is no showing of bad faith, harassment or some other extraordinary circumstance that would make abstention inappropriate, the federal courts should abstain.

D

Respondent Hinds contends that there was no opportunity in the state disciplinary proceeding to raise his federal constitutional challenge to the disciplinary rules. Yet Hinds failed to respond to the complaint filed by the local Ethics Committee and failed even to *attempt* to raise any federal constitutional challenge in the state proceeding. Under the New Jersey procedure, its Ethics Committees constantly are called upon to interpret the state disciplinary rules. Respondent Hinds points to nothing existing at the time the complaint was brought by the local Committee to indicate that the members of the Ethics Committee, the majority of whom are lawyers, would have refused to consider a claim that the rules which they were enforcing violated federal constitutional guarantees. Abstention is based upon the theory that " '[t]he accused should first set up and rely upon his defense in the state courts, even though this involves a challenge of the validity of some statute, unless it plainly appears that this course would not afford adequate protection.' " Younger v. Harris, 401 U.S., at 45, 91 S.Ct., at 750, quoting Fenner v. Boykin, 271 U.S. 240, 244, 46 S.Ct. 492, 493, 70 L.Ed. 927 (1926).

In light of the unique relationship between the New Jersey Supreme Court and the local Ethics Committee, and in view of the nature of the proceedings, it is difficult to conclude that there was no "adequate opportunity" for respondent Hinds to raise his constitutional claims. *Moore*, 442 U.S., at 430, 99 S.Ct., at 2380.

Whatever doubt, if any, that may have existed about respondent Hinds' ability to have constitutional challenges heard in the bar disciplinary hearings was laid to rest by the subsequent actions of the New Jersey Supreme Court. Prior to the filing of the petition for certiorari

on its own volition

in this Court the New Jersey Supreme Court <u>*sua sponte*</u> entertained the constitutional issues raised by respondent Hinds. Respondent Hinds therefore has had abundant opportunity to present his constitutional challenges to the state disciplinary proceedings.[15]

There is no reason for the federal courts to ignore this subsequent development. In Hicks v. Miranda, 422 U.S. 332, 95 S.Ct. 2281, 45 L.Ed.2d 223 (1975), we held that "where state criminal proceedings are begun against the federal plaintiffs after the federal complaint is filed but before any proceedings of substance on the merits have taken place in federal court, the principles of Younger v. Harris should apply in full force." Id., at 349, 95 S.Ct., at 2291. An analogous situation is presented here; the principles of comity and federalism which call for abstention remain in full force. Thus far in the federal court litigation the sole issue has been whether abstention is appropriate. No proceedings have occurred on the merits and therefore no federal proceedings on the merits will be terminated by application of *Younger* principles. It would trivialize the principles of comity and federalism if federal courts failed to take into account that an adequate state forum for all relevant issues has clearly been demonstrated to be available prior to any proceedings on the merits in federal court. 422 U.S., at 350, 95 S.Ct., at 2292.[16]

Respondents have not challenged the findings of the District Court that there was no bad faith or harassment on the part of petitioners and that the state rules were not " 'flagrantly and patently' " unconstitutional. *Younger*, supra, 401 U.S., at 53, 91 S.Ct., at 754, quoting Watson v. Buck, 313 U.S. 387, 402, 61 S.Ct. 962, 967, 85 L.Ed. 1416 (1941). App. to Pet. for Cert. 50a–52a. We see no reason to disturb these findings, and no other extraordinary circumstances have been presented to indicate that abstention would not be appropriate.[17]

III

Because respondent Hinds had an "opportunity to raise and have timely decided by a competent state tribunal the federal issues in-

---

15. In addition, after the filing of the writ of certiorari the New Jersey Supreme Court amended the State bar disciplinary rules to expressly permit a motion directly to the New Jersey Supreme Court for interlocutory adjudication of constitutional issues. Rule 1:20–4(d)(i). See note 9 supra. Even if interlocutory review is not granted, constitutional issues are preserved for consideration by the New Jersey Supreme Court. Rule 1:20–2(j).

The New Jersey Supreme Court reviews all disciplinary actions except the issuance of private letters of reprimand. Rule 1:20–4. Rule 1:20–2(j), however, requires that all constitutional issues be withheld for consideration by the Supreme Court as part of its review of the decision of the Disciplinary Review Board. This appears to provide for Supreme Court review of constitutional challenges even when a private reprimand is made.

16. Indeed, the decision of the New Jersey Supreme Court to consider respondent Hinds' constitutional challenges indicates that the state court desired to give Hinds a swift judicial resolution of his constitutional claims.

17. It is not clear whether the Court of Appeals decided whether abstention would be proper as to the respondent organizations who are not parties to the state disciplinary proceedings. We leave this issue to the Court of Appeals on remand.

volved," Gibson v. Berryhill, 411 U.S., at 577, 93 S.Ct., at 1697, and because no bad faith, harassment or other exceptional circumstances dictate to the contrary, federal courts should abstain from interfering with the ongoing proceedings. Accordingly the judgment of the United States Court of Appeals for the Third Circuit is reversed, and the case remanded for further proceedings consistent with this opinion.

Reversed and remanded.

JUSTICE BRENNAN, concurring in the judgment.

For the reasons stated by Justice Marshall, I join the judgment in this case. I agree that federal courts should show particular restraint before intruding into an ongoing disciplinary proceeding by a state court against a member of the State's bar, where there is an adequate opportunity to raise federal issues in that proceeding. The traditional and primary responsibility of state courts for establishing and enforcing standards for members of their bars and the quasi-criminal nature of bar disciplinary proceedings, In re Ruffalo, 390 U.S. 544, 551, 88 S.Ct. 1222, 1226, 20 L.Ed.2d 117 (1968), call for exceptional deference by the federal courts. See Gipson v. New Jersey Supreme Court, 558 F.2d 701, 703–704 (CA3 1977); Erdmann v. Stevens, 458 F.2d 1205, 1209–1210 (CA2 1972). I continue to adhere to my view, however, that Younger v. Harris, 401 U.S. 37, 91 S.Ct. 746, 27 L.Ed.2d 669 (1971), is in general inapplicable to civil proceedings. See Huffman v. Pursue, Ltd., 420 U.S. 592, 613, 95 S.Ct. 1200, 1212, 43 L.Ed.2d 482 (1975) (Brennan, J., dissenting).

JUSTICE MARSHALL, with whom JUSTICE BRENNAN, JUSTICE BLACKMUN and JUSTICE STEVENS join, concurring in the judgment.

I agree with much of the general language in the Court's opinion discussing the importance of the State's interest in regulating the professional conduct of its attorneys. However, I believe that the question whether *Younger* abstention would have been appropriate at the time that the District Court or the Court of Appeals considered this issue is not as simple as the Court's opinion might be read to imply. As the Court acknowledges, absent an ongoing judicial proceeding in which there is an adequate opportunity for a party to raise federal constitutional challenges, *Younger* is inapplicable. * * * See also Gibson v. Berryhill, 411 U.S. 564, 577, 93 S.Ct. 1689, 1697, 36 L.Ed.2d 488 (1973). Here, it is unclear whether, at the time the lower courts addressed this issue, there was an adequate opportunity in the state disciplinary proceedings to raise a constitutional challenge to the disciplinary rules. Furthermore, it is unclear whether proceedings before the Ethics Committee are more accurately viewed as prosecutorial rather than judicial in nature.

I agree with the Court that we may consider events subsequent to the decisions of the courts below because the federal litigation has addressed only the question whether abstention is appropriate. Thus far, there have been no proceedings on the merits in federal court. * * * After the Court of Appeals rendered its decision and denied petitioner's petition for rehearing, the New Jersey Supreme Court certified the complaint against respondent Hinds to itself. App. to Pet. for Cert. 62a. Now, there are ongoing judicial proceedings in the New Jersey Supreme Court in which Hinds has been given the opportunity to raise his constitutional challenges. As a result, *Younger* abstention, at least with respect to Hinds, is appropriate at this time. For this reason only, I join the judgment of the Court.

NOTE ON FEDERAL COURT ABSTENTION

There are both statutory and decisional limitations on the authority of federal courts to exercise jurisdiction that, but for the limitations, would be within their authority. The complexity of the subject and the intensity of the debate over it are suggested, but certainly not exhausted, by the *Middlesex County* case. See generally Hart & Wechsler 1346–1454. See also Redish, Abstention, Separaton of Powers, and the Limits of Judicial Function, 94 Yale L.J. 71 (1984); Wells, Why Professor Redish is Wrong About Abstention, 19 Ga.L.Rev. 1097 (1985); Comment, Restriction of Access to Federal Courts: The Growing Role of Equity, Comity and Federalism, 50 Temple L.Q. 320 (1977); Comment, Abstention by Federal Courts in Suits Challenging State Administrative Decisions: The Scope of the Burford Doctrine, 46 U.Chi.L.Rev. 971 (1979). In litigation that does not involve the conduct of state officials or the validity of state procedures, there is division of opinion about abstention but not of such depth. See Colorado River Water Conservation District v. United States, 424 U.S. 800, 96 S.Ct. 1236, 47 L.Ed.2d 483 (1976), and the excellent Comment, Federal Court Stays and Dismissals in Deference to Parallel State Court Proceedings: The Impact of Colorado River, 44 U.Chi.L.Rev. 641 (1977). See also Will v. Calvert Fire Ins. Co., 437 U.S. 655, 98 S.Ct. 2552, 57 L.Ed.2d 504 (1978); Moses H. Cone Memorial Hosp. v. Mercury Constr. Corp., 460 U.S. 1, 103 S.Ct. 927, 74 L.Ed.2d 765 (1983); United Books, Inc. v. Conte, 739 F.2d 30 (1st Cir. 1984); Eli Lilly & Co. v. Home Ins. Co., 764 F.2d 876 (D.C.Cir. 1985). The federal courts have routinely abstained from taking jurisdiction over divorce and probate proceedings even though the requisites for diversity jurisdiction are otherwise met. See, e.g., Firestone v. Cleveland Trust Co., 654 F.2d 1212 (6th Cir. 1981) (domestic relations); Dragan v. Miller, 679 F.2d 712 (7th Cir. 1982) (probate); Hart & Wechsler 1454–1464.

One device by which to sustain federal judicial authority while giving deference to state determinations of state law is for the federal court to retain jurisdiction of the action but certify the contested state law questions to the state court. See Elkins v. Moreno, 435 U.S. 647, 98 S.Ct. 1338, 55 L.Ed.2d 614 (1978); Hall, Federal Courts, State Law and Certification, 23 Ga.St.B.J. 120 (1987).

For general discussions of the position of federal jurisdiction in the administration of civil justice, see A.L.I., Study of the Division of Jurisdiction Between State and Federal Courts (1968); Currie, The Federal Courts and the American Law Institute, 36 U.Chi.L.Rev. 1 (1968), 36 U.Chi.L.Rev. 268 (1969); Friendly, Federal Jurisdiction: A General View (1973).

3. THE ERIE PROBLEM

INTRODUCTORY NOTE ON THE LAW TO
BE APPLIED IN FEDERAL COURTS

Determining that a federal district court has jurisdiction to hear a case does not necessarily determine what law it should look to in deciding the case. This problem is conventionally referred to as the *Erie* problem, after Erie Railroad Co. v. Tompkins, 304 U.S. 64, 58 S.Ct. 817, 82 L.Ed. 1188 (1938), infra p. 562.

1. State Law as the Prima Facie Applicable Law

The starting place in the consideration of the question whether state law or federal law is to be applied to a legal controversy is the organization of our federal system. In a subtle and masterful treatment of the problem, Hart, The Relations Between State and Federal Law, 54 Colum.L.Rev. 489 (1954),* Professor Hart says, in small part, 54 Colum.L.Rev. at 489–497:

> "The law which governs daily living in the United States is a single system of law: it speaks in relation to any particular question with only one ultimately authoritative voice, however difficult it may be on occasion to discern in advance which of two or more conflicting voices really carries authority. In the long run and in the large, this must be so. People repeatedly subjected, like Pavlov's dogs, to two or more inconsistent sets of directions, without means of resolving the inconsistencies, could not fail in the end to react as the dogs did. The society, collectively, would suffer a nervous breakdown.

> "Yet the sources of the laws which say what Americans can, may or must do or not do and what happens if they act differently, or which seek to influence by official action what they are able or choose to do on their own account in the infinity of situations in which they have to decide whether to do or not do something, are exceedingly diverse. The problems of developing the necessary mechanisms for evoking or enforcing harmony are correspondingly complex.

> *   *   *

> "In any system of government, responsibility for doing these things is divided among the government's various branches. In a federal system, it is further divided between the federal government and the governments of the states and their political subdivisions.

> *   *   *

> "Nowhere is the theory and practice of American federalism more significantly revealed than in the constitutions of the states. These constitutions assume responsibility for dealing, and claim authority to deal, with the whole gamut of problems cast up out of the flux of every day life in the state, save only in the particular respects in which the Federal Constitution or statutes deprive the states of any competence whatever or provide for an overriding or displacing federal law. They announce clearly, in Madison's words, that whereas the powers of the federal government 'consist of special grants taken from the general mass of power [we, the state governments] possess the general mass with special exceptions only.'

* Copyright 1954 by the Columbia Law Review Association.

* * *

"At the cost of perhaps dangerous oversimplification it can be said broadly that federal substantive law operates in relation to state law in two principal ways. As to certain matters, federal law assumes and accepts the basic responsibility of the states, and seeks simply to regulate the exercise of state authority, [e.g., by the Due Process Clause of the Fourteenth Amendment]. As to other matters, federal law displaces state law, in whole or in part, and itself takes over, pro tanto, the basic task of governance of private activity.   ⤷ to such extent

* * *

"In a few of the spheres of affirmative federal governance the federal courts, like their state counterparts, have assumed a responsibility for the initial development of law, prompted only by a grant of jurisdiction. Maritime law is the most conspicuous example, although there are others which will be noticed hereafter. In such cases Congress has been left in the position characteristic of the state legislatures, reviewing and supplementing, by the techniques of enactment, the underlying body of federal decisional law. But the body of federal law directly governing private activity springs mainly from a statutory base.

"The predominantly statutory character of this body of law is not a reflection simply of preference, within the federal regime, for legislative rather than judicial initiative. It reflects, instead, an essential aspect of the relation between the federal and state governments. In some important but relatively few respects the constitutional grants of power to the United States have been treated as a federal occupation of the field, neutralizing further attempts to exercise state power. For the most part, however, the Constitution has been read as proceeding upon precisely the opposite principle. Broadly speaking, the legal systems of the states have been competent, historically, to handle most of the immediate exigencies of government, even in spheres which were subject to a power of control by the United States. In most of these spheres, accordingly, the plan of the Constitution has permitted the state systems to continue to operate until such time as the United States chose to intervene."

2. The Statutory Structure

In the past the relation between state and federal law set forth by Professor Hart was neither as well understood nor as scrupulously observed as it is today. Congress had spoken on the subject in its first session. In the Judiciary Act of 1789, in which the federal courts were created, it was provided, Section 34:

"That the laws of the several states, except where the constitution, treaties, or statutes of the United States shall otherwise require or provide, shall be regarded as the rules of decision in trials at common law in the courts of the United States in cases where they apply."

This provision, known as the Rules of Decision Act, has remained in force ever since and was addressed in both Swift v. Tyson, discussed just below, and Erie v. Tompkins. In 1948 it was revised in phraseology and made applicable to "civil actions" (not merely "trials at common law"). See 28 U.S.C.A. § 1652.

But the Rules of Decision Act was not and never has been the only provision of federal law concerning the law to be applied in federal courts, though many of the cases following Erie paid no attention to this fact. First, the Judiciary Act of 1789, in addition to creating the federal court system and specifying the "rules of decision" for federal courts, also included provisions dealing with such matters as: reserving the common law remedy in cases that might also be brought in admiralty (Section 9); limiting the range of civil process to the district in which the federal court sat (Section 11); fixing the procedure for removal of actions from state to federal court (Section 12); regulating the procedure for attachment (Section 13); authorizing *scire facias, habeas corpus,* "and other writs" (Section 14); etc. Furthermore, less than a week later, the first Congress enacted "An Act to regulate Processes in the Courts of the United States," 1 Stat. 93, which provided:

> "[E]xcept where by this act or other statutes of the United States is otherwise provided, the forms of writs and executions * * * and modes of process and rates of fees * * * in the circuit and district courts, in suits at common law, shall be the same in each state respectively as are now used or allowed in the supreme courts of the same. * * * And the forms and modes of proceedings in causes of equity, and of admiralty and maritime jurisdiction, * * * shall be according to the course of the civil law."

This statute, known as the Process Act, was amended in 1792 by 1 Stat. 275, Sec. 2, to provide that:

> "[T]he forms and modes of proceedings in suits in * * * equity * * * [shall be] according to the principles, rules and usages which belong to courts of equity * * * subject however to such alterations and additions as the said courts respectively shall in their discretion deem expedient, or to such regulations as the supreme court of the United States shall think proper from time to time by rule to prescribe * * *."

The Process Act was followed by the Conformity Act of 1872, 17 Stat. 196, which provided:

> "The practice, pleadings, and forms and modes of proceeding, in other than equity and admiralty cases * * * shall conform, as near as may be, to the practice, pleadings and forms and modes of proceedings existing at the time in like causes in the courts of record of the State within which such * * * district courts are held * * *."

The Conformity Act was in turn followed by the Enabling Act of 1934, 28 U.S.C.A. § 2072, which provided that:

> "The Supreme Court * * * shall have the power to prescribe, by general rules, for the district courts * * * the forms of process, writs, pleadings, and motions, and the practice and procedure in civil actions * * *."

See also Hart & Wechsler 749–765.

Thus, at least until the Enabling Act of 1934, the directives as to applicable law in the federal courts always included directions to follow state law on the law side and equity usage on the equity side with respect to "forms of writs" and "modes of process" and "proceeding." They also included the statutory procedural rules in the Judiciary Act of 1789 and other procedural provisions subsequently enacted by Congress from time to time. They further included constitutional provisions, specifically the Seventh Amendment. And they included decisions to the effect that federal law, though perhaps not constitutional law, displaced *both* the Conformity Act and the Rules of Decision Act. See Herron v. Southern Pac. Co., 283 U.S. 91, 94, 51 S.Ct. 383, 384, 75 L.Ed. 857, 860 (1931), concerning the power of a federal judge to direct a verdict:

"The function of the trial judge in a federal court is not in any sense a local matter, and state statutes which would interfere with the appropriate performance of that function are not binding upon the federal court under either the Conformity Act or the 'Rules of Decision' Act."

3. Swift v. Tyson

The question in the 19th century was whether the term "laws" in the Rules of Decision Act had some meaning less than a comprehensive one. The Supreme Court in that period decided that it did. The leading case was Swift v. Tyson, 41 U.S. (16 Pet.) 1, 10 L.Ed. 865 (1842). In an action commenced in federal court in New York in which jurisdiction was founded on the diverse citizenship of the parties, plaintiff sued to collect on a bill of exchange (a written promise to pay money) which had been executed by defendant in New York. The bill of exchange was in favor of Norton and Keith and had been indorsed over to plaintiff Swift. Defendant offered evidence that he had executed the bill of exchange in payment for the purchase of land from Norton and Keith, that Norton and Keith did not in fact have title to the land, and that accordingly, there was a failure of consideration which excused Tyson's duty to pay. Tyson contended, further, that by New York law this defense was equally good against Swift as transferee of the bill. When this contention was presented to the Supreme Court, Justice Story expressed doubt whether such was the New York law, but then said, 41 U.S. (16 Pet.) at 18–19:

"But, admitting the doctrine to be fully settled in New York, it remains to be considered, whether it is obligatory upon this court, if it differs from the principles established in the general commercial law. It is observable that the courts of New York do not found their decision upon this point upon any local statute, or positive, fixed, or ancient local usage; but they deduce the doctrine from the general principles of commercial law. It is, however, contended, that the [Rules of Decision Act] furnishes a rule obligatory upon this Court to follow the decisions of the state tribunals in all cases to which they apply. * * * In order to maintain the argument, it is essential, therefore, to hold, that the word 'laws,' in this section, includes within the scope of its meaning the decisions of the local tribunals. In the ordinary use of language it will be hardly contended that the decisions of courts constitute laws. They are, at most, only evidence of what the laws are, and are not of themselves laws. * * * The laws of a state are more usually understood to mean the rules and enactments promulgated by the legislative authority thereof, or long-established local customs having the force of laws. In all the various cases which have hitherto come before us for decision, this Court have uniformly supposed, that the true interpretation of [the Act] limited its application to State laws strictly local, that is to say, to the positive statutes of the State, and the construction thereof adopted by the local tribunals, and to rights and titles to things having a permanent locality, such as the rights and titles to real estate, and other matters immovable and intraterritorial in their nature and character. It never has been supposed by us, that the section did apply, or was designed to apply, to questions of a more general nature, not at all dependent upon local statutes or local usages of a fixed and permanent operation, as, for example, to the construction of ordinary contracts or other written instruments, and especially to questions of general commercial law, where the State tribunals are called upon to perform the like functions as ourselves, that is, to ascertain upon general reasoning and legal analogies, what is the true exposition of the contract or instrument, or what is the just rule furnished by the principles of commercial law to govern the case."

The correctness of Justice Story's reading of the Rules of Decision Act was often questioned but never reversed in the century following. The line of demarcation between "general law" and "local law" was never clearly fixed, as it could not be, but over the years it was so drawn as to admit of radical differences in approach to particular controversies between state courts, on the one hand, and federal courts sitting in diversity cases in the same state, on the other. Perhaps the most dramatic instance was Black & White Taxicab & Transfer Co. v. Brown & Yellow Taxicab & Transfer Co., 276 U.S. 518, 48 S.Ct. 404, 72 L.Ed. 681 (1928): A Kentucky corporation was engaged in the taxi and transfer business at Bowling Green, Kentucky, and desired to obtain exclusive rights to haul passengers and baggage to and from the depot of the Louisville & Nashville Railroad. Such arrangements were clearly regarded as illegal restraints of trade under Kentucky decisional law. Accordingly, a Tennessee corporation was organized to which all the assets of the Kentucky corporation were transferred. The Tennessee corporation thereupon obtained from the railroad a contract giving it the desired exclusive rights. A diversity suit was then brought in federal court against the defendant rival taxicab company, a Kentucky corporation, seeking an injunction restraining interference with the exclusive contract. The court sustained the granting of the injunction, holding that the question of the validity of the contract was "one of general law" and that under "general law" the contract was not invalid. In dissent, Justice Holmes protested that there was no "transcendental body of law outside of any particular State but obligatory within it."

It was against this background that the *Erie* case came before the Supreme Court. For a fuller consideration of the antecedents of *Erie* see Hart & Wechsler 749–783; 1A Moore ¶¶ 0.301–0.328.

ERIE RAILROAD CO. v. TOMPKINS

Supreme Court of the United States, 1938.
304 U.S. 64, 58 S.Ct. 817, 82 L.Ed. 1188.*

Mr. Justice Brandeis delivered the opinion of the Court.

The question for decision is whether the oft-challenged doctrine of Swift v. Tyson shall now be disapproved.

Tompkins, a citizen of Pennsylvania, was injured on a dark night by a passing freight train of the Erie Railroad Company while walking along its right of way at Hughestown in that state. He claimed that the accident occurred through negligence in the operation, or maintenance, of the train; that he was rightfully on the premises as licensee because on a commonly used beaten footpath which ran for a short distance alongside the tracks; and that he was struck by something which looked like a door projecting from one of the moving cars. To enforce that claim he brought an action in the federal court for Southern New York, which had jurisdiction because the company is a

* Some of the Court's footnotes are omitted.

corporation of that state. It denied liability; and the case was tried by a jury.

The Erie insisted that its duty to Tompkins was no greater than that owed to a trespasser. It contended, among other things, that its duty to Tompkins, and hence its liability, should be determined in accordance with Pennsylvania law; that under the law of Pennsylvania, as declared by its highest court, persons who use pathways along the railroad right of way—that is, a longitudinal pathway as distinguished from a crossing—are to be deemed trespassers; and that the railroad is not liable for injuries to undiscovered trespassers resulting from its negligence unless it be wanton or willful. Tompkins denied that any such rule had been established by the decisions of the Pennsylvania courts; and contended that, since there was no statute of the state on the subject, the railroad's duty and liability is to be determined in federal courts as a matter of general law.

The trial judge refused to rule that the applicable law precluded recovery. The jury brought in a verdict of $30,000; and the judgment entered thereon was affirmed by the Circuit Court of Appeals, which held (2 Cir., 90 F.2d 603, 604), that it was unnecessary to consider whether the law of Pennsylvania was as contended, because the question was one not of local, but of general, law, and that "upon questions of general law the federal courts are free, in absence of a local statute, to exercise their independent judgment as to what the law is; and it is well settled that the question of the responsibility of a railroad for injuries caused by its servants is one of general law. . . . Where the public has made open and notorious use of a railroad right of way for a long period of time and without objection, the company owes to persons on such permissive pathway a duty of care in the operation of its trains. . . . It is likewise generally recognized law that a jury may find that negligence exists toward a pedestrian using a permissive path on the railroad right of way if he is hit by some object projecting from the side of the train."

The Erie had contended that application of the Pennsylvania rule was required, among other things, by section 34 of the Federal Judiciary Act of September 24, 1789, c. 20, 28 U.S.C. § 725, 28 U.S.C.A. § 725, which provides: "The laws of the several States, except where the Constitution, treaties, or statutes of the United States otherwise require or provide, shall be regarded as rules of decision in trials at common law, in the courts of the United States, in cases where they apply." *

Because of the importance of the question whether the federal court was free to disregard the alleged rule of the Pennsylvania common law, we granted certiorari. 302 U.S. 671, 58 S.Ct. 50, 82 L.Ed. 518.

First. Swift v. Tyson, 16 Pet. 1, 18, 10 L.Ed. 865, held that federal courts exercising jurisdiction on the ground of diversity of citizenship

---

* [Now 28 U.S.C.A. § 1652, applying to "civil actions" rather than merely to "tri- als at common law" by reason of the 1948 revision of the Judicial Code.]

need not, in matters of general jurisprudence, apply the unwritten law of the state as declared by its highest court; that they are free to exercise an independent judgment as to what the common law of the state is—or should be; and that, as there stated by Mr. Justice Story, "the true interpretation of the 34th section limited its application to state laws, strictly local, that is to say, to the positive statutes of the state, and the construction thereof adopted by the local tribunals, and to rights and titles to things having a permanent locality such as the rights and titles to real estate, and other matters immovable and intra-territorial in their nature and character. It never has been supposed by us, that the section did apply, or was designed to apply, to questions of a more general nature, not at all dependent upon local statutes or local usages of a fixed and permanent operation, as, for example, to the construction of ordinary contracts or other written instruments, and especially to questions of general commercial law, where the state tribunals are called upon to perform the like functions as ourselves, that is, to ascertain, upon general reasoning and legal analogies, what is the true exposition of the contract or instrument, or what is the just rule furnished by the principles of commercial law to govern the case."

The Court in applying the rule of section 34 to equity cases, in Mason v. United States, 260 U.S. 545, 559, 43 S.Ct. 200, 204, 67 L.Ed. 396, said: "The statute, however, is merely declarative of the rule which would exist in the absence of the statute." The federal courts assumed, in the broad field of "general law," the power to declare rules of decision which Congress was confessedly without power to enact as statutes. Doubt was repeatedly expressed as to the correctness of the construction given section 34, and as to the soundness of the rule which it introduced. But it was the more recent research of a competent scholar, who examined the original document, which established that the construction given to it by the Court was erroneous; and that the purpose of the section was merely to make certain that, in all matters except those in which some federal law is controlling, the federal courts exercising jurisdiction in diversity of citizenship cases would apply as their rules of decision the law of the state, unwritten as well as written.[5]

Criticism of the doctrine became widespread after the decision of Black & White Taxicab & Transfer Co. v. Brown & Yellow Taxicab & Transfer Co., 276 U.S. 518, 48 S.Ct. 404, 72 L.Ed. 681, 57 A.L.R. 426. There, Brown & Yellow, a Kentucky corporation owned by Kentuckians, and the Louisville & Nashville Railroad, also a Kentucky corporation, wished that the former should have the exclusive privilege of soliciting passenger and baggage transportation at the Bowling Green, Ky., railroad station; and that the Black & White, a competing Kentucky corporation, should be prevented from interfering with that privilege. Knowing that such a contract would be void under the common law of Kentucky, it was arranged that the Brown & Yellow

5. Charles Warren, New Light on the History of the Federal Judiciary Act of 1789 (1923) 37 Harv.L.Rev. 49, 51–52, 81–88, 108.

reincorporate under the law of Tennessee, and that the contract with the railroad should be executed there. The suit was then brought by the Tennessee corporation in the federal court for Western Kentucky to enjoin competition by the Black & White; an injunction issued by the District Court was sustained by the Court of Appeals; and this Court, citing many decisions in which the doctrine of Swift v. Tyson had been applied, affirmed the decree.

Second. Experience in applying the doctrine of Swift v. Tyson, had revealed its defects, political and social; and the benefits expected to flow from the rule did not accrue. Persistence of state courts in their own opinions on questions of common law prevented uniformity; and the impossibility of discovering a satisfactory line of demarcation between the province of general law and that of local law developed a new well of uncertainties.

On the other hand, the mischievous results of the doctrine had become apparent. Diversity of citizenship jurisdiction was conferred in order to prevent apprehended discrimination in state courts against those not citizens of the state. Swift v. Tyson introduced grave discrimination by noncitizens against citizens. It made rights enjoyed under the unwritten "general law" vary according to whether enforcement was sought in the state or in the federal court; and the privilege of selecting the court in which the right should be determined was conferred upon the noncitizen. Thus, the doctrine rendered impossible equal protection of the law. In attempting to promote uniformity of law throughout the United States, the doctrine had prevented uniformity in the administration of the law of the state.

The discrimination resulting became in practice far-reaching. This resulted in part from the broad province accorded to the so-called "general law" as to which federal courts exercised an independent judgment. In addition to questions of purely commercial law, "general law" was held to include the obligations under contracts entered into and to be performed within the state; the extent to which a carrier operating within a state may stipulate for exemption from liability for his own negligence or that of his employee; the liability for torts committed within the state upon persons resident or property located there, even where the question of liability depended upon the scope of a property right conferred by the state; and the right to exemplary or punitive damages. Furthermore, state decisions construing local deeds, mineral conveyances, and even devises of real estate, were disregarded.

In part the discrimination resulted from the wide range of persons held entitled to avail themselves of the federal rule by resort to the diversity of citizenship jurisdiction. Through this jurisdiction individual citizens willing to remove from their own state and become citizens of another might avail themselves of the federal rule. And, without even change of residence, a corporate citizen of the state could avail itself of the federal rule by reincorporating under the laws of another state, as was done in the Taxicab Case.

The injustice and confusion incident to the doctrine of Swift v. Tyson have been repeatedly urged as reasons for abolishing or limiting diversity of citizenship jurisdiction. Other legislative relief has been proposed.[21] If only a question of statutory construction were involved, we should not be prepared to abandon a doctrine so widely applied throughout nearly a century.[22] But the unconstitutionality of the course pursued has now been made clear, and compels us to do so.

Third. Except in matters governed by the Federal Constitution or by acts of Congress, the law to be applied in any case is the law of the state. And whether the law of the state shall be declared by its Legislature in a statute or by its highest court in a decision is not a matter of federal concern. There is no federal general common law. Congress has no power to declare substantive rules of common law applicable in a state whether they be local in their nature or "general," be they commercial law or a part of the law of torts. And no clause in the Constitution purports to confer such a power upon the federal courts. As stated by Mr. Justice Field when protesting in Baltimore & Ohio R. R. Co. v. Baugh, 149 U.S. 368, 401, 13 S.Ct. 914, 927, 37 L.Ed. 772, against ignoring the Ohio common law of fellow-servant liability: "I am aware that what has been termed the general law of the country—which is often little less than what the judge advancing the doctrine thinks at the time should be the general law on a particular subject—has been often advanced in judicial opinions of this court to control a conflicting law of a state. I admit that learned judges have fallen into the habit of repeating this doctrine as a convenient mode of brushing aside the law of a state in conflict with their views. And I confess, that, moved and governed by the authority of the great names of those judges, I have, myself, in many instances, unhesitatingly and confidently, but I think now erroneously, repeated the same doctrine. But, notwithstanding the great names which may be cited in favor of the doctrine, and notwithstanding the frequency with which the doctrine has been reiterated, there stands, as a perpetual protest against its repetition, the constitution of the United States, which recognizes and preserves the autonomy and independence of the states,—indepen-

---

21. Thus, bills which would abrogate the doctrine of Swift v. Tyson have been introduced. S. 4333, 70th Cong., 1st Sess.; S. 96, 71st Cong., 1st Sess.; H.R. 8094, 72d Cong., 1st Sess. See, also, Mills, supra, note 4 at 68, 69; Dobie, supra, note 6, at 241; Frankfurter, supra, note 6, at 530; Campbell, supra, note 6, at 811. State statutes on conflicting questions of "general law" have also been suggested. See Heiskell, supra, note 4, at 760; Dawson, supra, note 6; Dobie, supra, note 6, at 241.

22. The doctrine has not been without defenders. See Eliot, The Common Law of the Federal Courts (1902) 36 Am.L.Rev. 498, 523–525; A. B. Parker, The Common Law Jurisdiction of the United States Courts (1907) 17 Yale L.J. 1; Schofield, Swift v. Tyson: Uniformity of Judge-Made State Law in State and Federal Courts (1910) 4 Ill.L.Rev. 533; Brown, The Jurisdiction of the Federal Courts Based on Diversity of Citizenship (1929) 78 U. of Pa. L.Rev. 179, 189–191; J. J. Parker, The Federal Jurisdiction and Recent Attacks Upon It (1932) 18 A.B.A.J. 433, 438; Yntema, The Jurisdiction of the Federal Courts in Controversies Between Citizens of Different States (1933) 19 A.B.A.J. 71, 74, 75; Beutel, Common Law Judicial Technique and the Law of Negotiable Instruments— Two Unfortunate Decisions (1934) 9 Tulane L.Rev. 64.

dence in their legislative and independence in their judicial departments. Supervision over either the legislative or the judicial action of the states is in no case permissible except as to matters by the constitution specifically authorized or delegated to the United States. Any interference with either, except as thus permitted, is an invasion of the authority of the state, and, to that extent, a denial of its independence."

The fallacy underlying the rule declared in Swift v. Tyson is made clear by Mr. Justice Holmes.[23] The doctrine rests upon the assumption that there is "a transcendental body of law outside of any particular State but obligatory within it unless and until changed by statute," that federal courts have the power to use their judgment as to what the rules of common law are; and that in the federal courts "the parties are entitled to an independent judgment on matters of general law":

"But the law in the sense in which courts speak of it today does not exist without some definite authority behind it. The common law so far as it is enforced in a State, whether called common law or not, is not the common law generally but the law of that State existing by the authority of that State without regard to what it may have been in England or anywhere else . . . .

"The authority and only authority is the State, and if that be so, the voice adopted by the State as its own [whether it be of its Legislature or of its Supreme Court] should utter the last word."

Thus the doctrine of Swift v. Tyson is, as Mr. Justice Holmes said, "an unconstitutional assumption of powers by the Courts of the United States which no lapse of time or respectable array of opinion should make us hesitate to correct." In disapproving that doctrine we do not hold unconstitutional section 34 of the Federal Judiciary Act of 1789 or any other act of Congress. We merely declare that in applying the doctrine this Court and the lower courts have invaded rights which in our opinion are reserved by the Constitution to the several states.

Fourth. The defendant contended that by the common law of Pennsylvania as declared by its highest court in Falchetti v. Pennsylvania R. Co., 307 Pa. 203, 160 A. 859, the only duty owed to the plaintiff was to refrain from willful or wanton injury. The plaintiff denied that such is the Pennsylvania law. In support of their respective contentions the parties discussed and cited many decisions of the Supreme Court of the state. The Circuit Court of Appeals ruled that the question of liability is one of general law; and on that ground declined to decide the issue of state law. As we hold this was error, the judgment is reversed and the case remanded to it for further proceedings in conformity with our opinion.

Reversed.*

---

23. Kuhn v. Fairmont Coal Co., 215 U.S. 349, 370–372, 30 S.Ct. 140, 54 L.Ed. 228; Black & White Taxicab, etc., Co. v. Brown & Yellow Taxicab, etc., Co., 276 U.S. 518, 532–536, 48 S.Ct. 404, 408, 409, 72 L.Ed. 681, 57 A.L.R. 426.

* The dissenting opinion of Butler, J., is omitted.

MR. JUSTICE CARDOZO took no part in the consideration or decision of this case.

MR. JUSTICE REED (concurring in part).

I concur in the conclusion reached in this case, in the disapproval of the doctrine of Swift v. Tyson, and in the reasoning of the majority opinion, except in so far as it relies upon the unconstitutionality of the "course pursued" by the federal courts.

The "doctrine of Swift v. Tyson," as I understand it, is that the words "the laws," as used in section 34, line 1, of the Federal Judiciary Act of September 24, 1789, 28 U.S.C.A. § 725, do not include in their meaning "the decisions of the local tribunals." Mr. Justice Story, in deciding that point, said, 16 Pet. 1, 19, 10 L.Ed. 865: "Undoubtedly, the decisions of the local tribunals upon such subjects are entitled to, and will receive, the most deliberate attention and respect of this court; but they cannot furnish positive rules, or conclusive authority, by which our own judgments are to be bound up and governed."

To decide the case now before us and to "disapprove" the doctrine of Swift v. Tyson requires only that we say that the words "the laws" include in their meaning the decisions of the local tribunals. As the majority opinion shows, by its reference to Mr. Warren's researches and the first quotation from Mr. Justice Holmes, that this Court is now of the view that "laws" includes "decisions," it is unnecessary to go further and declare that the "course pursued" was "unconstitutional," instead of merely erroneous.

The "unconstitutional" course referred to in the majority opinion is apparently the ruling in Swift v. Tyson that the supposed omission of Congress to legislate as to the effect of decisions leaves federal courts free to interpret general law for themselves. I am not at all sure whether, in the absence of federal statutory direction, federal courts would be compelled to follow state decisions. There was sufficient doubt about the matter in 1789 to induce the first Congress to legislate. No former opinions of this Court have passed upon it. Mr. Justice Holmes evidently saw nothing "unconstitutional" which required the overruling of Swift v. Tyson, for he said in the very opinion quoted by the majority, "I should leave Swift v. Tyson undisturbed, as I indicated in Kuhn v. Fairmont Coal Co., but I would not allow it to spread the assumed dominion into new fields." Black & White Taxicab Co. v. Brown & Yellow Taxicab Co., 276 U.S. 518, 535, 48 S.Ct. 404, 409, 72 L.Ed. 681, 57 A.L.R. 426. If the opinion commits this Court to the position that the Congress is without power to declare what rules of substantive law shall govern the federal courts, that conclusion also seems questionable. The line between procedural and substantive law is hazy, but no one doubts federal power over procedure. Wayman v. Southard, 10 Wheat. 1, 6 L.Ed. 253. The Judiciary Article, 3, and the "necessary and proper" clause of article 1, § 8, may fully authorize legislation, such as this section of the Judiciary Act.

stand by that which was decided

In this Court, stare decisis, in statutory construction, is a useful rule, not an inexorable command. Burnet v. Coronado Oil & Gas Co., 285 U.S. 393, dissent, page 406, note 1, 52 S.Ct. 443, 446, 76 L.Ed. 815. Compare Read v. Bishop of Lincoln, [1892] A.C. 644, 655; London Street Tramways v. London County Council, [1898] A.C. 375, 379. It seems preferable to overturn an established construction of an act of Congress, rather than, in the circumstances of this case, to interpret the Constitution. Cf. United States v. Delaware & Hudson Co., 213 U.S. 366, 29 S.Ct. 527, 53 L.Ed. 836.

There is no occasion to discuss further the range or soundness of these few phrases of the opinion. It is sufficient now to call attention to them and express my own nonacquiescence.

 NOTE ON *ERIE* AND THE SUBSTANCE/PROCEDURE DISTINCTION

One way of stating what *Erie* did is this: It withdrew the federal courts from law-making in areas in which they had no authority to make law. These areas were within the domain of state law because (1) they were clearly "substantive" *and* (2) within the category of substantive law, they were areas left to the states to regulate—either because they were in the exclusive domain of the states under the Constitution, or because they were in a domain that Congress could occupy with legislation but had not. This statement might be tested by asking, in light of the *Erie* facts, whether Congress could have legislated the rule governing liability of interstate railroads to pedestrians on the railroad right of way. If Congress could have done so, is the objection to applying federal decisional law that the federal *Government* could not provide the governing rule? Or that the federal *courts* could not provide the governing rule, especially in the light of the Rules of Decision Act?

Another way of stating what *Erie* did is that it reorganized the categories of law that the federal courts might apply. Under Swift v. Tyson, within the category of "substantive" law there were two sub-categories: "general law" (which the federal courts could formulate and apply notwithstanding contrary state law) and "local law" (in which the federal courts followed state law). Under *Erie,* these two categories were collapsed, so that all "substantive" law was "local" law (i.e., state law), except where the Constitution or federal statutes governed the situation.

But what about "procedure"? Did the *Erie* decision or the Rules of Decision Act apply to matters of "procedure"? This question vexed federal law for the next thirty years, centering in the decision in Guaranty Trust Co. v. York, reprinted infra p. 573. Prior to that case the Supreme Court decided the following cases:

Cities Service Oil Co. v. Dunlap, 308 U.S. 208, 60 S.Ct. 201, 84 L.Ed. 196 (1939): Plaintiff filed a quiet title suit in Texas federal district court, seeking to quiet its legal title against defendant's claim to a superior equitable title. Jurisdiction was based on diversity of citizenship. Under Texas law, the burden of proof of a superior equity was on him who attacked a legal title. The trial judge, following federal equity practice, nevertheless put that burden on plaintiff and on the merits found for defendant. In reversing the court of appeal's affirmance, the Supreme Court said, 308 U.S. at 212, 60 S.Ct. at 203, 84 L.Ed. at 198:

> "We cannot accept the view that the question presented was only one of practice in courts of equity. Rather we think it relates to a substantial right upon which the holder of recorded legal title to Texas land may confidently rely."

Sibbach v. Wilson & Co., 312 U.S. 1, 61 S.Ct. 422, 85 L.Ed. 479 (1941): Plaintiff brought an action in Illinois federal district court for personal injuries occurring in Indiana, jurisdiction being founded on diversity. On defendant's request, the trial court pursuant to F.R.C.P. 35(a) ordered plaintiff to submit to a physical examination by a doctor appointed by the court. Compulsory physical examination of a party was authorized in Indiana state courts but not in those of Illinois. Plaintiff refused to submit to examination, was held in contempt of court, and appealed, challenging the validity of the Rule on the ground of its conflict with the Federal Rules Enabling Act's provision that "[s]aid rules shall neither abridge, enlarge, nor modify the substantive rights of any litigant." See 28 U.S.C.A. § 2072. The Supreme Court rejected this contention, saying *inter alia*:

> "Congress has undoubted power to regulate the practice and procedure of federal courts, and may exercise that power by delegating to this or other federal courts authority to make rules not inconsistent with the statutes or Constitution of the United States; but it has never essayed to declare the substantive state law, or to abolish or nullify a right recognized by the substantive law of the state where the cause of action arose, save where a right or duty is imposed in a field committed to Congress by the Constitution. On the contrary it has enacted that the state law shall be the rule of decision in the federal courts.

> * * *

> "Whatever may be said as to the effect of the Conformity Act while it remained in force, the rules, if they are within the authority granted by Congress, repeal that statute, and the District Court was not bound to follow the Illinois practice respecting an order for physical examination. On the other hand if the right to be exempt from such an order is one of substantive law, the Rules of Decision Act required the District Court, though sitting in Illinois, to apply the law of Indiana, the state where the cause of action arose, and to order the examination. To avoid this dilemma the petitioner admits, and we think, correctly, that Rules 35 and 37 are rules of procedure. She insists, nevertheless, that by the prohibition against abridging substantive rights, Congress has banned the rules here challenged. In order to reach this result she translates 'substantive' into 'important' or 'substantial' rights. And she urges that if a rule affects such a right, albeit the rule is one of procedure merely, its prescription is not within the statutory grant of power embodied in the Act of June 19, 1934.
> * * *

>   * * *

> " * * * Is the phrase 'substantive rights' confined to rights conferred by law to be protected and enforced in accordance with the adjective law of judicial procedure? It certainly embraces such rights. One of them is the right not to be injured in one's person by another's negligence, to redress infraction of which the present action was brought. The petitioner says the phrase connotes more; that by its use Congress intended that in regulating procedure this court should not deal with important and sub-

stantial rights theretofore recognized. Recognized where and by whom? The state courts are divided as to the power in the absence of statute to order a physical examination. In a number such an order is authorized by statute or rule. The rules in question accord with the procedure now in force in Canada and England.

"The asserted right, moreover, is no more important than many others enjoyed by litigants in District Courts sitting in the several states, before the Federal Rules of Civil Procedure altered and abolished old rights or privileges and created new ones in connection with the conduct of litigation. The suggestion that the rule offends the important right to freedom from invasion of the person ignores the fact that as we hold, no invasion of freedom from personal restraint attaches to refusal so to comply with its provisions. If we were to adopt the suggested criterion of the importance of the alleged right we should invite endless litigation and confusion worse confounded. The test must be whether a rule really regulates procedure,— the judicial process for enforcing rights and duties recognized by substantive law and for justly administering remedy and redress for disregard or infraction of them. That the rules in question are such is admitted.

"Finally, it is urged that Rules 35 and 37 work a major change of policy and that this was not intended by Congress. Apart from the fact already stated, that the policy of the states in this respect has not been uniform, it is to be noted that the authorization of a comprehensive system of court rules was a departure in policy, and that the new policy envisaged in the enabling act of 1934 was that the whole field of court procedure be regulated in the interest of speedy, fair and exact determination of the truth. The challenged rules comport with this policy. Moreover, in accordance with the Act, the rules were submitted to the Congress so that that body might examine them and veto their going into effect if contrary to the policy of the legislature."

FRANKFURTER, J., speaking for four dissenters, said:

"* * * [I]t does not seem to me that the answer to our question is to be found by an analytic determination whether the power of examination here claimed is a matter of procedure or a matter of substance, even assuming that the two are mutually exclusive categories with easily ascertainable contents. * * *

"So far as national law is concerned, a drastic change in public policy in a matter deeply touching the sensibilities of people or even their prejudices as to privacy, ought not to be inferred from a general authorization to formulate rules for the more uniform and effective dispatch of business on the civil side of the federal courts. I deem a requirement as to the invasion of the person to stand on a very different footing from questions pertaining to the discovery of documents, pre-trial procedure and other devices for the expeditious, economic and fair conduct of litigation. * * *

"* * * Plainly the Rules are not acts of Congress and cannot be treated as such. Having due regard to the mechanics of legislation and the practical conditions surrounding the business of Congress when the Rules were submitted, to draw any inference of tacit approval from non-action by Congress is to appeal to unreality. And so I conclude that to make the drastic change that Rule 35 sought to introduce would require explicit legislation."

For Erie purposes, conflicts of law is subst. so uses state law including choice of law state picks

Klaxon Co. v. Stentor Elec. Mfg. Co., 313 U.S. 487, 61 S.Ct. 1020, 85 L.Ed. 1477 (1941): A diversity action for breach of a contract entered into in New York was brought in Delaware federal district court. After a verdict in its favor for $100,000, plaintiff moved to correct the judgment by adding interest from the date the action was commenced, pursuant to N.Y.C.P.A. § 480 so providing. The trial court granted the motion, its decision being affirmed by the court of appeals on the ground that under the "better view [in conflicts of law] * * * the rules for ascertaining the measure of damages are not a matter of procedure at all, but are matters of substance" and, as such, in the instant case called for reference to New York law, the place of performance of the contract. The Supreme Court reversed, without dissent, holding that whatever the "better view" might be, the federal courts in diversity cases were required by *Erie* to apply the conflicts of law rules of the states in which they sit, saying, 313 U.S. at 496, 61 S.Ct. at 1021, 85 L.Ed. at 1480:

> "We are of opinion that the prohibition declared in Erie Railroad v. Tompkins * * * against such independent determinations by the federal courts extends to the field of conflict of laws. The conflict of laws rules to be applied by the federal court in Delaware must conform to those prevailing in Delaware's state courts. Otherwise the accident of diversity of citizenship would constantly disturb equal administration of justice in coordinate state and federal courts sitting side by side."

Palmer v. Hoffman, 318 U.S. 109, 63 S.Ct. 477, 87 L.Ed. 645 (1943): An action for personal injuries was brought in New York federal district court, jurisdiction being founded on diversity. Defendant pleaded contributory negligence as a bar to recovery. At trial, the judge instructed the jury that defendant had the burden of proof on this issue, over defendant's objection that the applicable state rule, which was that plaintiff had the burden of proving freedom from contributory negligence, should have been applied. The Supreme Court in a unanimous opinion said that the instruction was wrong, 318 U.S. 117, 63 S.Ct. at 482, 87 L.Ed. at 651:

> "[Plaintiff] contends in the first place that the charge was correct because of the fact that Rule 8(c) of the Rules of Civil Procedure makes contributory negligence an affirmative defense. We do not agree. Rule 8(c) covers only the manner of pleading. The question of the burden of establishing contributory negligence is a question of local law which federal courts in diversity of citizenship cases (Erie R. Co. v. Tompkins * * *) must apply."

The Court made no reference to the fact that F.R.C.P. 8(c) was patterned after N.Y.C.P.A. § 242 and that the latter rule, though cast in the form of a rule governing only pleading, had been treated as also allocating the burden of proof. If it had so construed Rule 8(c), it seems pretty clear that it would have had to face squarely the question whether it was nevertheless displaced by *Erie*. The language of the opinion would imply that it would be so displaced.

It was against the background of these precedents that the Supreme Court decided Guaranty Trust Co. v. York, below.

———

GUARANTY TRUST CO. v. YORK

Supreme Court of the United States, 1945.
326 U.S. 99, 65 S.Ct. 1464, 89 L.Ed. 2079.*

[In 1942 plaintiff York filed in New York federal district court a diversity suit in equity for fraud in connection with certain transactions participated in by defendant in 1931. Defendant pleaded laches, invoking the New York rule that the statute of limitations period prescribed for the bringing of actions at law in that state applied alike to equity suits regardless of "equitable" considerations traditionally associated with the application of the laches defense. The Court of Appeals held that the federal trial court should have applied, not the New York "strict" time rule, but the more elastic federal laches doctrine, and accordingly reversed a summary judgment which had been entered for defendant. Defendant brought certiorari.]

MR. JUSTICE FRANKFURTER delivered the opinion of the Court.

* * *

And so this case reduces itself to the narrow question whether, when no recovery could be had in a State court because the action is barred by the statute of limitations, a federal court in equity can take cognizance of the suit because there is diversity of citizenship between the parties. Is the outlawry, according to State law, of a claim created by the States a matter of "substantive rights" to be respected by a federal court of equity when that court's jurisdiction is dependent on the fact that there is a State-created right, or is such statute of "a mere remedial character," Henrietta Mills v. Rutherford Co., supra, 281 U.S. at page 128, 50 S.Ct. at page 272, 74 L.Ed. 737, which a federal court may disregard?

Matters of "substance" and matters of "procedure" are much talked about in the books as though they defined a great divide cutting across the whole domain of law. But, of course, "substance" and "procedure" are the same key-words to very different problems. Neither "substance" nor "procedure" represents the same invariants. Each implies different variables depending upon the particular problem for which it is used. See Home Ins. Co. v. Dick, 281 U.S. 397, 409, 50 S.Ct. 338, 341, 74 L.Ed. 926, 74 A.L.R. 701. And the different problems are only distantly related at best, for the terms are in common use in connection with situations turning on such different considerations as those that are relevant to questions pertaining to ex post facto legislation, the impairment of the obligations of contract, the enforcement of federal rights in the State courts and the multitudinous phases of the conflict of laws. See, e.g., American Ry. Exp. Co. v. Levee, 263 U.S. 19, 21, 44 S.Ct. 11, 12, 68 L.Ed. 140; Davis v. Wechsler, 263 U.S. 22, 25, 44 S.Ct. 13, 14, 68 L.Ed. 143; Worthen Co. v. Kavanaugh, 295 U.S. 56, 60, 55 S.Ct. 555, 556, 79 L.Ed. 1298, 97 A.L.R. 905; Garrett v. Moore-McCormack Co., 317 U.S. 239, 248, 249, 63 S.Ct. 246, 252, 87 L.Ed. 239;

* The Court's footnotes are omitted.

and see Tunks, Categorization and Federalism: "Substance" and "Procedure" After Erie Railroad v. Tompkins (1939) 34 Ill.L.Rev. 271, 274–276; Cook, Logical and Legal Bases of Conflict of Laws (1942) 163–165.

Here we are dealing with a right to recover derived not from the United States but from one of the States. When, because the plaintiff happens to be a non-resident, such a right is enforceable in a federal as well as in a State court, the forms and mode of enforcing the right may at times, naturally enough, vary because the two judicial systems are not identical. But since a federal court adjudicating a state-created right solely because of the diversity of citizenship of the parties is for that purpose, in effect, only another court of the State, it cannot afford recovery if the right to recover is made unavailable by the State nor can it substantially affect the enforcement of the right as given by the State.

And so the question is not whether a statute of limitations is deemed a matter of "procedure" in some sense. The question is whether such a statute concerns merely the manner and the means by which a right to recover, as recognized by the State, is enforced, or whether such statutory limitation is a matter of substance in the aspect that alone is relevant to our problem, namely, does it significantly affect the result of a litigation for a federal court to disregard a law of a State that would be controlling in an action upon the same claim by the same parties in a State court?

It is therefore immaterial whether statutes of limitation are characterized either as "substantive" or "procedural" in State court opinions in any use of those terms unrelated to the specific issue before us. Erie R. Co. v. Tompkins was not an endeavor to formulate scientific legal terminology. It expressed a policy that touches vitally the proper distribution of judicial power between State and federal courts. In essence, the intent of that decision was to insure that, in all cases where a federal court is exercising jurisdiction solely because of the diversity of citizenship of the parties, the outcome of the litigation in the federal court should be substantially the same, so far as legal rules determine the outcome of a litigation, as it would be if tried in a State court. The nub of the policy that underlies Erie R. Co. v. Tompkins is that for the same transaction the accident of a suit by a non-resident litigant in a federal court instead of in a State court a block away, should not lead to a substantially different result. And so, putting to one side abstractions regarding "substance" and "procedure", we have held that in diversity cases the federal courts must follow the law of the State as to burden of proof, Cities Service Oil Co. v. Dunlap, 308 U.S. 208, 60 S.Ct. 201, 84 L.Ed. 196, as to conflict of laws, Klaxon Co. v. Stentor Co., 313 U.S. 487, 61 S.Ct. 1020, 85 L.Ed. 1477, as to contributory negligence, Palmer v. Hoffman, 318 U.S. 109, 117, 63 S.Ct. 477, 482, 87 L.Ed. 645, 144 A.L.R. 719. And see Sampson v. Channell, 1 Cir., 110 F.2d 754, 128 A.L.R. 394. Erie R. Co. v. Tompkins has been applied with an eye alert to essentials in avoiding disregard of State law in diversity cases in the federal courts. A policy so important to our federalism must be kept free from entanglements with analytical or terminological niceties.

Plainly enough, a statute that would completely bar recovery in a suit if brought in a State court bears on a State-created right vitally and not merely formally or negligibly. As to consequences that so intimately affect recovery or nonrecovery a federal court in a diversity case should follow State law. See Morgan, Choice of Law Governing Proof (1944) 58 Harv.L.Rev. 153, 155–158. The fact that under New York law a statute of limitations might be lengthened or shortened, that a security may be foreclosed though the debt be barred, that a barred debt may be used as a set-off, are all matters of local law properly to be respected by federal courts sitting in New York when their incidence comes into play there. Such particular rules of local law, however, do not in the slightest change the crucial consideration that if a plea of the statute of limitations would bar recovery in a State court, a federal court ought not to afford recovery.

* * *

To make an exception to Erie R. Co. v. Tompkins on the equity side of a federal court is to reject the considerations of policy which, after long travail, led to that decision. Judge Augustus N. Hand thus summarized below the fatal objection to such inroad upon Erie R. Co. v. Tompkins: "In my opinion it would be a mischievous practice to disregard state statutes of limitations whenever federal courts think that the result of the adopting them may be inequitable. Such procedure would promote the choice of United States rather than of state courts in order to gain the advantage of different laws. The main foundation for the criticism of Swift v. Tyson was that a litigant in cases where federal jurisdiction is based only on diverse citizenship may obtain a more favorable decision by suing in the United States courts." 2 Cir., 143 F.2d 503, 529, 531.

Diversity jurisdiction is founded on assurance to non-resident litigants of courts free from susceptibility to potential local bias. The Framers of the Constitution, according to Marshall, entertained "apprehensions" lest distant suitors be subjected to local bias in State courts, or, at least, viewed with "indulgence the possible fears and apprehensions" of such suitors. Bank of the United States v. Deveaux, 5 Cranch 61, 87, 3 L.Ed. 38. And so Congress afforded out-of-State litigants another tribunal, not another body of law. The operation of a double system of conflicting laws in the same State is plainly hostile to the reign of law. Certainly, the fortuitous circumstance of residence out of a State of one of the parties to a litigation ought not to give rise to a discrimination against others equally concerned but locally resident. The source of substantive rights enforced by a federal court under diversity jurisdiction, it cannot be said too often, is the law of the States. Whenever that law is authoritatively declared by a State, whether its voice be the legislature or its highest court, such law ought to govern in litigation founded on that law, whether the forum of application is a State or a federal court and whether the remedies be sought at law or may be had in equity.

Dicta may be cited characterizing equity as an independent body of law. To the extent that we have indicated, it is. But insofar as these general observations go beyond that, they merely reflect notions that have been replaced by a sharper analysis of what federal courts do when they enforce rights that have no federal origin. And so, before the true source of law that is applied by the federal courts under diversity jurisdiction was fully explored, some things were said that would not now be said. But nothing that was decided, unless it be the Kirby case, needs to be rejected.

The judgment is reversed and the case is remanded for proceedings not inconsistent with this opinion.

MR. JUSTICE ROBERTS and MR. JUSTICE DOUGLAS took no part in the consideration or decision of this case.

MR. JUSTICE RUTLEDGE.

I dissent. * * *

The words "substantive" and "procedural" or "remedial" are not talismanic. Merely calling a legal question by one or the other does not resolve it otherwise than as a purely authoritarian performance. But they have come to designate in a broad way large and distinctive legal domains within the greater one of the law and to mark, though often indistinctly or with overlapping limits, many divides between such regions.

One of these historically has been the divide between the substantive law and the procedural or remedial law to be applied by the federal courts in diversity cases, a division sharpened but not wiped out by Erie R. Co. v. Tompkins and subsequent decisions extending the scope of its ruling. The large division between adjective law and substantive law still remains, to divide the power of Congress from that of the states and consequently to determine the power of the federal courts to apply federal law or state law in diversity matters.

This division, like others drawn by the broad allocation of adjective or remedial and substantive, has areas of admixture of these two aspects of the law. In these areas whether a particular situation or issue presents one aspect or the other depends upon how one looks at the matter. As form cannot always be separated from substance in a work of art, so adjective or remedial aspects cannot be parted entirely from substantive ones in these borderland regions.

Whenever this integration or admixture prevails in a substantial measure, so that a clean break cannot be made, there is danger either of nullifying the power of Congress to control not only how the federal courts may act, but what they may do by way of affording remedies, or of usurping that function, if the Erie doctrine is to be expanded judicially to include such situations to the utmost extent.

* * *

Finally, this case arises from what are in fact if not in law interstate transactions. It involves the rights of security holders in relation to securities which were distributed not in New York or Ohio alone but widely throughout the country. They are the kind of rights which Congress acted to safeguard when it adopted the Securities and Exchange legislation. Specific provisions of that legislation are not involved in this litigation. The broad policies underlying it may be involved or affected, namely, by the existence of adequate federal remedies, whether judicial or legislative, for the protection of security holders against the misconduct of issuers or against the breach of rights by trustees. Even though the basic rights may be controlled by state law, in such situations the question is often a difficult one whether the law of one state or another applies; and this is true not only of rights clearly substantive but also of those variously characterized as procedural or remedial and substantive which involve the application of statutes of limitations.

Applicable statutes of limitations in state tribunals are not always the ones which would apply if suit were instituted in the courts of the state which creates the substantive rights for which enforcement is sought. The state of the forum is free to apply its own period of limitations, regardless of whether the state originating the right has barred suit upon it. Whether or not the action will be held to be barred depends therefore not upon the law of the state which creates the substantive right, but upon the law of the state where suit may be brought. This in turn will depend upon where it may be possible to secure service of process, and thus jurisdiction of the person of the defendant. It may be therefore that because of the plaintiff's inability to find the defendant in the jurisdiction which creates his substantive right, he will be foreclosed of remedy by the sheer necessity of going to the haven of refuge within which the defendant confines its "presence" for jurisdictional purposes. The law of the latter may bar the suit even though suit still would be allowed under the law of the state creating the substantive right.

* * *

MR. JUSTICE MURPHY joins in this opinion.

NOTE ON DEVELOPMENTS AFTER
GUARANTY TRUST CO. v. YORK

Between *Guaranty Trust* and Byrd v. Blue Ridge Rural Electric Cooperative, infra p. 581, the Supreme Court decided the following cases:

Angel v. Bullington, 330 U.S. 183, 67 S.Ct. 657, 91 L.Ed. 832 (1947): Plaintiff Bullington brought suit in a North Carolina court to recover the unpaid balance on a purchase money mortgage given by defendant on land in Virginia. Judgment on demurrer was given defendant on the strength of a North Carolina statute precluding deficiency judgments on purchase money mortgages, over Bullington's contention that the statute could not constitutionally be applied to bar recovery on a Virginia obligation. Bullington did not seek United States Supreme Court review but rather commenced a diversity suit in North Carolina federal district court. Angel's plea of res judicata was overruled and judgment rendered against him. In reversing, the Supreme Court said, 330 U.S. at 186–87, 67 S.Ct. at 659, 91 L.Ed. at 835: "The judgment of the Supreme Court of North Carolina would clearly bar this suit had it been brought anew in a state court. For purposes of diversity jurisdiction a federal court is 'in effect, only another court of the state.' Guaranty Trust Co. v. York * * * ."

Cohen v. Beneficial Industrial Loan Corp., 337 U.S. 541, 69 S.Ct. 1221, 93 L.Ed. 1528 (1949): Plaintiff, a holder of 100 of the two million shares of stock of defendant corporation (plaintiff's shares being worth $9,000), brought a stock-holder's derivative action to require the officers and directors of the corporation to return to it funds allegedly improperly diverted. The action was in New Jersey federal district court, jurisdiction being founded on diversity. After commencement of the action, defendant moved to compel plaintiff to post security for expenses, including attorneys' fees, pursuant to New Jersey statute.* The trial court denied the motion, the court of appeals reversed, and the Supreme Court on certiorari affirmed, 6–3. Jackson, J., speaking for the Court said, 337 U.S. at 555–56, 69 S.Ct. at 1230, 93 L.Ed. at 1541:

> " * * * Erie R. Co. v. Tompkins and its progeny have wrought a more far-reaching change in the relation of state and federal courts and the application of state law in the latter whereby in diversity cases the federal court administers the state system of law in all except details related to its own conduct of business. Guaranty Trust Co. of New York v. York, 326 U.S. 99, 65 S.Ct. 1464, 89 L.Ed. 2079, 160 A.L.R. 1231. The only substantial argument that this New Jersey statute is not applicable here is that its provisions are mere rules of procedure rather than rules of substantive law.

> "Even if we were to agree that the New Jersey statute is procedural, it would not determine that it is not applicable. Rules which lawyers call procedural do not always exhaust their effect by regulating procedure. But this statute is not merely a regulation of procedure. With it or without it the main action takes the same course. However, it creates a new liability where none existed before, for it makes a stockholder who institutes a derivative action liable for the expense to which he puts the corporation and other defendants, if he does not make good his claims. Such liability is not usual and it goes beyond payment of what we know as 'costs.' If all the Act did was to create this liability, it would clearly be substantive. But this new liability would be without meaning and value in many cases if it resulted in nothing but a judgment for expenses at or after the end of the case. Therefore, a procedure is prescribed by which the liability is insured by entitling the corporate defendant to a bond of indemnity before the outlay is incurred. We do not think a statute which so conditions the stockholder's action can be disregarded by the federal court as a mere procedural device.

* The statute, N.J.S.A. 14:3–15 to 17, provided: "In any action instituted or maintained in the right of any domestic or foreign corporation by the holder * * * of shares * * * having a total par value * * * of less than * * * 5% of the aggregate par value * * * unless the shares * * * held by such holder * * * have a market value in excess of * * * $50,000, the corporation * * * shall be entitled, at any stage of the proceeding before final judgment, to require the complainant * * * to give security for the reasonable expenses, including counsel fees, which may be incurred by it in connection with such action * * * to which the corporation shall have recourse in such amount as the court having jurisdiction shall determine upon the termination of such action. * * * "

"It is urged, however, that Federal Rule of Civil Procedure No. 23 deals with plaintiff's right to maintain such an action in federal court and that therefore the subject is recognized as procedural and the federal rule alone prevails. Rule 23 requires the stockholder's complaint to be verified by oath and to show that the plaintiff was a stockholder at the time of the transaction of which he complains or that his share thereafter devolved upon him by operation of law. In other words, the federal court will not permit itself to be used to litigate a purchased grievance or become a party to speculation in wrongs done to corporations. It also requires a showing that an action is not a collusive one to confer jurisdiction and to set forth the facts showing that the plaintiff has endeavored to obtain his remedy through the corporation itself. It further provides that the class action shall not be dismissed or compromised without approval of the court, with notice to the members of the class. These provisions neither create nor exempt from liabilities, but require complete disclosure to the court and notice to the parties in interest. None conflict with the statute in question and all may be observed by a federal court, even if not applicable in state court.

"We see no reason why the policy stated in Guaranty Trust Co. of New York v. York, 326 U.S. 99, 65 S.Ct. 1464, 89 L.Ed. 2079, 160 A.L.R. 1231, should not apply."

JUSTICES DOUGLAS, FRANKFURTER and RUTLEDGE dissented, saying:

"The measure of the cause of action is the claim which the corporation has against the alleged wrongdoers. This New Jersey statute does not add one iota to nor subtract one iota from that cause of action. It merely prescribes the method by which stockholders may enforce it. Each state has numerous regulations governing the institution of suits in its courts. They may favor the litigation or they may affect it adversely. But they do not fall under the principle of Erie R. Co. v. Tompkins, 304 U.S. 64, 58 S.Ct. 817, 82 L.Ed. 1188, 114 A.L.R. 1487, unless they define, qualify or delimit the cause of action or otherwise relate to it."

Ragan v. Merchants Transfer Co., 337 U.S. 530, 69 S.Ct. 1233, 93 L.Ed. 1520 (1949): Plaintiff commenced a diversity action, filing the complaint within the applicable state statute of limitation period but effectuating service of process only after the expiration of that period. Plaintiff, relying on F.R.C.P. 3 ("A civil action is commenced by filing a complaint with the court"), contended that the action was timely commenced; defendant, relying on a provision of the state limitations statute that "an action shall be deemed commenced, within the meaning of this article, as to each defendant, at the date of the summons which is served on him," contended that it was barred. In holding it barred, the Supreme Court, with only Justice Rutledge dissenting, said, 337 U.S. at 533–34, 69 S.Ct. at 1235, 93 L.Ed. at 1523:

"We can draw no distinction in this case because local law brought the cause of action to an end after, rather than before, suit was started in the federal court. In both cases local law created the right which the federal court was asked to enforce. In both cases local law undertook to determine the life of the cause of action. We cannot give it longer life in the federal court than it would have had in the state court without adding something to the cause of action. We may not do that consistently with Erie R. Co. v. Tompkins."

Woods v. Interstate Realty Co., 337 U.S. 535, 69 S.Ct. 1235, 93 L.Ed. 1524 (1949): A Tennessee corporation sued in Mississippi federal district court to collect a brokerage commission earned on the sale of Mississippi land. The district court dismissed the action because plaintiff had "done business" in the state but had not qualified as a foreign corporation, invoking a Mississippi statute providing that "Any foreign corporation failing to comply [with the qualification provision] shall not be permitted to bring or maintain any action or suit in any of the courts of this state." In holding the dismissal proper, the Supreme Court relied on Angel v. Bullington and Guaranty Trust Co. v. York, saying, 337 U.S. at 538, 69 S.Ct. at 1237, 93 L.Ed. at 1527:

> "The York case was premised on the theory that a right which local law creates but which it does not supply with a remedy is no right at all for purposes of enforcement in a federal court in a diversity case; that where in such cases one is barred from recovery in the state court, he should likewise be barred in the federal court. The contrary result would create discriminations against citizens of the State in favor of those authorized to invoke the diversity jurisdiction of the federal courts. It was that element of discrimination that Erie R. Co. v. Tompkins was designed to eliminate."

Bernhardt v. Polygraphic Co. of America, 350 U.S. 198, 76 S.Ct. 273, 100 L.Ed. 199 (1956): Plaintiff sued in Vermont state court for damages for discharge in breach of a contract of employment. The contract contained a provision calling for arbitration of any dispute. Defendant removed the action to federal district court and there moved for a stay pending arbitration. The trial judge denied the motion on the ground that under Vermont law an arbitration agreement was revocable at any time prior to award and therefore could not be enforced in federal court. On appeal, the Supreme Court held as an initial matter that § 2 of the United States Arbitration Act, 9 U.S.C.A. § 1 et seq., which makes enforceable arbitration agreements falling within its ambit, was not controlling since the transaction in question did not relate to interstate commerce or admiralty. The Court held further that § 2 restricted the reach of the stay provisions contained in § 3 of the Act, saying that this holding would allow the Court to avoid the "larger question presented here— that is, whether arbitration touche[s] on substantive rights, which Erie R. Co. v. Tompkins held were governed by local law, or [is] a mere form of procedure within the power of the federal courts or Congress to prescribe. Our view * * * is that § 3, so read, would invade the local law field. We therefore read § 3 narrowly to avoid the issue." The Court, upholding the disposition of the district court, then went on to consider "whether, apart from the Federal Act, a provision of a contract providing for arbitration is enforceable in a diversity case" in the face of contrary state law, saying, 350 U.S. at 202–204, 76 S.Ct. at 276–277, 100 L.Ed. at 205–206:

> "We deal here with a right to recover that owes its existence to one of the States, not to the United States. The federal court enforces the state-created right by rules of procedure which it has acquired from the Federal Government and which therefore are not identical with those of the state courts. Yet, in spite of that difference in procedure, the federal court enforcing a state-created right in a diversity case is, as we said in Guaranty Trust Co. of New York v. York, 326 U.S. 99, 108, 65 S.Ct. 1464, 1469, 89 L.Ed. 2079, in substance 'only another court of the State.' The federal court therefore may not 'substantially affect the enforcement of the right as given by the State.' Id., 326 U.S. 109, 65 S.Ct. 1470. If the federal court allows arbitration where the state court would disallow it, the outcome of

litigation might depend on the courthouse where suit is brought. For the remedy by arbitration, whatever its merits or shortcomings, substantially affects the cause of action created by the State. The nature of the tribunal where suits are tried is an important part of the parcel of rights behind a cause of action. The change from a court of law to an arbitration panel may make a radical difference in ultimate result. Arbitration carries no right to trial by jury that is guaranteed both by the Seventh Amendment and by Ch. 1, Art. 12th, of the Vermont Constitution. Arbitrators do not have the benefit of judicial instruction on the law; they need not give their reasons for their results; the record of their proceedings is not as complete as it is in a court trial; and judicial review of an award is more limited than judicial review of a trial—all as discussed in Wilko v. Swan, 346 U.S. 427, 435–438, 74 S.Ct. 182, 186, 188, 98 L.Ed. 168. We said in the York case that 'The nub of the policy that underlies Erie R. Co. v. Tompkins is that for the same transaction the accident of a suit by a nonresident litigant in a federal court instead of in a State court a block away, should not lead to a substantially different result.' 326 U.S. at 109, 65 S.Ct. 1470. There would in our judgment be a resultant discrimination if the parties suing on a Vermont cause of action in the federal court were remitted to arbitration, while those suing in the Vermont court could not be."

The source of the statement in *Bernhardt* that a federal court sitting in diversity is "only another court of the State" is Guaranty Trust Co. v. York. But the source of *that* premise in *Guaranty Trust* is not so clear. The Constitution? The Constitution authorized a separate federal court system whose jurisdiction included diversity cases, which doesn't sound like "another court of the State." The Rules of Decision Act? One of the curiosities of the decisions from Palmer v. Hoffman, supra p. 572, through *Bernhardt* is that they paid no attention to the fact that the Rules of Decision Act was only one of a number of statutes governing the federal court system and specifying the law to be applied in federal courts. Consider whether any of these other provisions, discussed supra pp. 559–560, should have been considered by the Court in these cases and, if so, how they should have affected the outcome.

There is also the matter brought into view in the following case.

BYRD v. BLUE RIDGE RURAL ELECTRIC COOPERATIVE

Supreme Court of the United States, 1958.
356 U.S. 525, 78 S.Ct. 893, 2 L.Ed.2d 953.*

MR. JUSTICE BRENNAN delivered the opinion of the Court.

This case was brought in the District Court for the Western District of South Carolina. Jurisdiction was based on diversity of citizenship. 28 U.S.C. § 1332, 28 U.S.C.A. § 1332. The petitioner, a resident of North Carolina, sued respondent, a South Carolina corporation, for damages for injuries allegedly caused by the respondent's negligence. He had judgment on a jury verdict. The Court of Appeals for the Fourth Circuit reversed and directed the entry of judgment for the respondent. 238 F.2d 346. We granted certiorari, 352 U.S. 999, 77 S.

* Some of the Court's footnotes are omitted.

Ct. 557, 1 L.Ed.2d 544, and subsequently ordered reargument, 355 U.S. 950, 78 S.Ct. 530, 2 L.Ed.2d 527.

The respondent is in the business of selling electric power to subscribers in rural sections of South Carolina. The petitioner was employed as a lineman in the construction crew of a construction contractor. The contractor, R. H. Bouligny, Inc., held a contract with the respondent in the amount of $334,300 for the building of some 24 miles of new power lines, the reconversion to higher capacities of about 88 miles of existing lines, and the construction of 2 new substations and a breaker station. The petitioner was injured while connecting power lines to one of the new substations.

One of respondent's affirmative defenses was that under the South Carolina Workmen's Compensation Act the petitioner—because the work contracted to be done by his employer was work of the kind also done by the respondent's own construction and maintenance crews—had the status of a statutory employee of the respondent and was therefore barred from suing the respondent at law because obliged to accept statutory compensation benefits as the exclusive remedy for his injuries. Two questions concerning this defense are before us: (1) whether the Court of Appeals erred in directing judgment for respondent without a remand to give petitioner an opportunity to introduce further evidence; and (2) whether petitioner, state practice notwithstanding, is entitled to a jury determination of the factual issues raised by this defense. * * * *†

A question is also presented as to whether on remand the factual issue is to be decided by the judge or by the jury. The respondent argues on the basis of the decision of the Supreme Court of South Carolina in Adams v. Davison-Paxon Co., 230 S.C. 532, 96 S.E.2d 566, that the issue of immunity should be decided by the judge and not by the jury. That was a negligence action brought in the state trial court against a store owner by an employee of an independent contractor who operated the store's millinery department. The trial judge denied the store owner's motion for a directed verdict made upon the ground that § 72–111 barred the plaintiff's action. The jury returned a verdict for the plaintiff. The South Carolina Supreme Court reversed, holding that it was for the judge and not the jury to decide on the evidence whether the owner was a statutory employer, and that the store owner had sustained his defense. The court rested its holding on decisions * * * involving judicial review of the Industrial Commission and said:

> "Thus the trial court should have in this case resolved the conflicts in the evidence and determined the fact of whether [the

† [The Court held that since the Court of Appeals differed from the trial court in the proper interpretation to be given the South Carolina statute, it should have remanded the case for new trial to allow plaintiff the opportunity to establish his case in the light of that interpretation.]

independent contractor] was performing a part of the 'trade, business or occupation' of the department store-appellant and, therefore, whether [the employee's] remedy is exclusively under the Workmen's Compensation Law." 230 S.C. at page 543, 96 S.E.2d at page 572.

The respondent argues that this state-court decision governs the present diversity case and "divests the jury of its normal function" to decide the disputed fact question of the respondent's immunity under § 72–111. This is to contend that the federal court is bound under Erie R. Co. v. Tompkins, 304 U.S. 64, 58 S.Ct. 817, 82 L.Ed. 1188, to follow the state court's holding to secure uniform enforcement of the immunity created by the State.[7]

First. It was decided in Erie R. Co. v. Tompkins that the federal courts in diversity cases must respect the definition of state-created rights and obligations by the state courts. We must, therefore, first examine the rule in Adams v. Davison-Paxon Co. to determine whether it is bound up with these rights and obligations in such a way that its application in the federal court is required. Cities Service Oil Co. v. Dunlap, 308 U.S. 208, 60 S.Ct. 201, 84 L.Ed. 196.

The Workmen's Compensation Act is administered in South Carolina by its Industrial Commission. The South Carolina courts hold that, on judicial review of actions of the Commission under § 72–111, the question whether the claim of an injured workman is within the Commission's jurisdiction is a matter of law for decision by the court, which makes its own findings of fact relating to that jurisdiction. The South Carolina Supreme Court states no reasons in Adams v. Davison-Paxon Co. why, although the jury decides all other factual issues raised by the cause of action and defenses, the jury is displaced as to the factual issue raised by the affirmative defense under § 72–111. The decisions cited to support the holding * * * are concerned solely with defining the scope and method of judicial review of the Industrial Commission. A State may, of course, distribute the functions of its judicial machinery as it sees fit. The decisions relied upon, however, furnish no reason for selecting the judge rather than the jury to decide this single affirmative defense in the negligence action. They simply reflect a policy, cf. Crowell v. Benson, 285 U.S. 22, 52 S.Ct. 285, 76 L.Ed. 598, that administrative determination of "jurisdictional facts" should not be final but subject to judicial review. The conclusion is inescapable that the _Adams_ holding is grounded in the practical consideration that the question had theretofore come before the South Carolina

---

7. See Cities Service Oil Co. v. Dunlap, 308 U.S. 208, 60 S.Ct. 201, 84 L.Ed. 196; West v. American Tel. & Tel. Co., 311 U.S. 223, 61 S.Ct. 179, 85 L.Ed. 139; Klaxon Co. v. Stentor Electric Mfg. Co., 313 U.S. 487, 61 S.Ct. 1020, 85 L.Ed. 1477; Guaranty Trust Co. of New York v. York, 326 U.S. 99, 65 S.Ct. 1464, 89 L.Ed. 2079; Angel v. Bullington, 330 U.S. 183, 67 S.Ct. 657, 91 L.Ed. 832; Ragan v. Merchants Transfer Co., 337 U.S. 530, 69 S.Ct. 1233, 93 L.Ed. 1520; Woods v. Interstate Realty Co., 337 U.S. 535, 69 S.Ct. 1235, 93 L.Ed. 1524; Cohen v. Beneficial Loan Corp., 337 U.S. 541, 69 S.Ct. 1221, 93 L.Ed. 1528; Bernhardt v. Polygraphic Co., 350 U.S. 198, 76 S.Ct. 273, 100 L.Ed. 199; Sampson v. Channell, 1 Cir., 110 F.2d 754, 128 A.L.R. 394.

courts from the Industrial Commission and the courts had become accustomed to deciding the factual issue of immunity without the aid of juries. We find nothing to suggest that this rule was announced as an integral part of the special relationship created by the statute. Thus the requirement appears to be merely a form and mode of enforcing the immunity, Guaranty Trust Co. of New York v. York, 326 U.S. 99, 108, 65 S.Ct. 1464, 1469, 89 L.Ed. 2079, and not a rule intended to be bound up with the definition of the rights and obligations of the parties. The situation is therefore not analogous to that in Dice v. Akron, C. & Y. R. Co., 342 U.S. 359, 72 S.Ct. 312, 96 L.Ed. 398, where this Court held that the right to trial by jury is so substantial a part of the cause of action created by the Federal Employers' Liability Act, 45 U.S.C.A. § 51 et seq., that the Ohio courts could not apply, in an action under that statute, the Ohio rule that the question of fraudulent release was for determination by a judge rather than by a jury.

Second. But cases following *Erie* have evinced a broader policy to the effect that the federal courts should conform as near as may be—in the absence of other considerations—to state rules even of form and mode where the state rules may bear substantially on the question whether the litigation would come out one way in the federal court and another way in the state court if the federal court failed to apply a particular local rule.[9] E.g., Guaranty Trust Co. of New York v. York, supra; Bernhardt v. Polygraphic Co., 350 U.S. 198, 76 S.Ct. 273, 100 L.Ed. 199. Concededly the nature of the tribunal which tries issues may be important in the enforcement of the parcel of rights making up a cause of action or defense, and bear significantly upon achievement of uniform enforcement of the right. It may well be that in the instant personal-injury case the outcome would be substantially affected by whether the issue of immunity is decided by a judge or a jury. Therefore, were "outcome" the only consideration, a strong case might appear for saying that the federal court should follow the state practice.

But there are affirmative countervailing considerations at work here. The federal system is an independent system for administering justice to litigants who properly invoke its jurisdiction. An essential characteristic of that system is the manner in which, in civil common-law actions, it distributes trial functions between judge and jury and, under the influence—if not the command [10]—of the Seventh Amendment, assigns the decisions of disputed questions of fact to the jury. Jacob v. City of New York, 315 U.S. 752, 62 S.Ct. 854, 86 L.Ed. 1166.[11]

9. Cf. Morgan, Choice of Law Governing Proof, 58 Harv.L.Rev. 153; 3 Beale, Conflict of Laws, § 594.1; Restatement of the Law, Conflict of Laws, pp. 699–701.

10. Our conclusion makes unnecessary the consideration of—and we intimate no view upon—the constitutional question whether the right of jury trial protected in federal courts by the Seventh Amendment embraces the factual issue of statutory immunity when asserted, as here, as an affirmative defense in a common-law negligence action.

11. The Courts of Appeals have expressed varying views about the effect of Erie R. Co. v. Tompkins on judge-jury problems in diversity cases. Federal practice was followed in Gorham v. Mutual Benefit Health & Accident Ass'n, 4 Cir. 1940, 114 F.2d 97; Diederich v. American News Co., 10 Cir., 1942, 128 F.2d 144; McSweeney v. Prudential Ins. Co., 4 Cir., 1942, 128 F.2d

The policy of uniform enforcement of state-created rights and obligations, see e.g., Guaranty Trust Co. of New York v. York, supra, cannot in every case exact compliance with a state rule [12]—not bound up with rights and obligations—which disrupts the federal system of allocating functions between judge and jury. Herron v. Southern Pacific Co., 283 U.S. 91, 51 S.Ct. 383, 75 L.Ed. 857. Thus the inquiry here is whether the federal policy favoring jury decisions of disputed fact questions should yield to the state rule in the interest of furthering the objective that the litigation should not come out one way in the federal court and another way in the state court.

We think that in the circumstances of this case the federal court should not follow the state rule. It cannot be gainsaid that there is a strong federal policy against allowing state rules to disrupt the judge-jury relationship in the federal courts. In Herron v. Southern Pacific Co., supra, the trial judge in a personal-injury negligence action brought in the District Court for Arizona on diversity grounds directed a verdict for the defendant when it appeared as a matter of law that the plaintiff was guilty of contributory negligence. The federal judge refused to be bound by a provision of the Arizona Constitution which made the jury the sole arbiter of the question of contributory negligence.[13] This Court sustained the action of the trial judge, holding that "state laws cannot alter the essential character or function of a federal court" because that function "is not in any sense a local matter, and state statutes which would interfere with the appropriate performance of that function are not binding upon the federal court under either the Conformity Act or the 'Rules of Decision' Act." Id., 283 U.S., at page 94, 51 S.Ct. at page 384. Perhaps even more clearly in light of the influence of the Seventh Amendment, the function assigned to the jury "is an essential factor in the process for which the Federal Constitution provides." Id., 283 U.S. at page 95, 51 S.Ct. at page 384. Concededly the *Herron* case was decided before Erie R. Co. v. Tompkins, but even when Swift v. Tyson, 16 Pet. 1, 10 L.Ed. 865, was governing law and allowed federal courts sitting in diversity cases to disregard state decisional law, it was never thought that state statutes or constitutions were similarly to be disregarded. Green v. Neal's Lessee, 6 Pet. 291, 8 L.Ed. 402. Yet *Herron* held that state statutes and constitutional provisions could not disrupt or alter the essential character or function of a federal court.[14]

660; Ettelson v. Metropolitan Life Ins. Co., 3 Cir., 1943, 137 F.2d 62; Order of United Commercial Travelers of America v. Duncan, 6 Cir., 1955, 221 F.2d 703. State practice was followed in Cooper v. Brown, 3 Cir., 1942, 126 F.2d 874; Gutierrez v. Public Service Interstate Transportation Co., 2 Cir., 1948, 168 F.2d 678; Prudential Ins. Co. of America v. Glasgow, 2 Cir., 1953, 208 F.2d 908; Pierce Consulting Engineering Co. v. City of Burlington, 2 Cir., 1955, 221 F.2d 607; Rowe v. Pennsylvania Greyhound Lines, 2 Cir., 1956, 231 F.2d 922.

12. This Court held in Sibbach v. Wilson & Co., 312 U.S. 1, 655, 61 S.Ct. 422, 85 L.Ed. 479, that Federal Rules of Civil Procedure 35 should prevail over a contrary state rule.

13. "The defense of contributory negligence or of assumption of risk shall, in all cases whatsoever, be a question of fact and shall, at all times, be left to the jury." § 5, Art. 18, A.R.S.

14. Diederich v. American News Co., 10 Cir., 128 F.2d 144, decided after Erie R. Co.

Third. We have discussed the problem upon the assumption that the outcome of the litigation may be substantially affected by whether the issue of immunity is decided by a judge or a jury. But clearly there is not present here the certainty that a different result would follow, cf. Guaranty Trust Co. of New York v. York, supra, or even the strong possibility that this would be the case, cf. Bernhardt v. Polygraphic Co., supra. There are factors present here which might reduce that possibility. The trial judge in the federal system has powers denied the judges of many States to comment on the weight of evidence and credibility of witnesses, and discretion to grant a new trial if the verdict appears to him to be against the weight of the evidence. We do not think the likelihood of a different result is so strong as to require the federal practice of jury determination of disputed factual issues to yield to the state rule in the interest of uniformity of outcome.[15]

The Court of Appeals did not consider other grounds of appeal raised by the respondent because the ground taken disposed of the case. We accordingly remand the case to the Court of Appeals for the decision of the other questions, with instructions that, if not made unnecessary by the decision of such questions, the Court of Appeals shall remand the case to the District Court for a new trial of such issues as the Court of Appeals may direct.

Reversed and remanded.*

HANNA v. PLUMER

Supreme Court of the United States, 1965.
380 U.S. 460, 85 S.Ct. 1136, 14 L.Ed.2d 8.

MR. CHIEF JUSTICE WARREN delivered the opinion of the Court.

The question to be decided is whether, in a civil action where the jurisdiction of the United States district court is based upon diversity of citizenship between the parties, service of process shall be made in the manner prescribed by state law or that set forth in Rule 4(d)(1) of the Federal Rules of Civil Procedure.

On February 6, 1963, petitioner, a citizen of Ohio, filed her complaint in the District Court for the District of Massachusetts, claiming damages in excess of $10,000 for personal injuries resulting from an

---

v. Tompkins, held that an almost identical provision of the Oklahoma Constitution, art. 23, § 6, O.S.1951, was not binding on a federal judge in a diversity case.

15. Stoner v. New York Life Ins. Co., 311 U.S. 464, 61 S.Ct. 336, 85 L.Ed. 284, is not contrary. It was there held that the federal court should follow the state rule defining the evidence sufficient to raise a jury question whether the state-created right was established. But the state rule did not have the effect of nullifying the function of the federal judge to control a

jury submission as did the Arizona constitutional provision which was denied effect in *Herron.* The South Carolina rule here involved affects the jury function as the Arizona provision affected the function of the judge: The rule entirely displaces the jury without regard to the sufficiency of the evidence to support a jury finding of immunity.

* The opinions of Justice Whittaker, concurring and dissenting, and Justice Frankfurter, with whom Justice Harlan joined in dissenting, are omitted.

automobile accident in South Carolina, allegedly caused by the negligence of one Louise Plumer Osgood, a Massachusetts citizen deceased at the time of the filing of the complaint. Respondent, Mrs. Osgood's executor and also a Massachusetts citizen, was named as defendant. On February 8, service was made by leaving copies of the summons and the complaint with respondent's wife at his residence, concededly in compliance with Rule 4(d)(1), which provides:

> "The summons and complaint shall be served together. The plaintiff shall furnish the person making service with such copies as are necessary. Service shall be made as follows:
>
> > "(1) Upon an individual other than an infant or an incompetent person, by delivering a copy of the summons and of the complaint to him personally or by leaving copies thereof at his dwelling house or usual place of abode with some person of suitable age and discretion then residing therein. . . ."

Respondent filed his answer on February 26, alleging, *inter alia*, that the action could not be maintained because it had been brought "contrary to and in violation of the provisions of Massachusetts General Laws (Ter.Ed.) Chapter 197, Section 9." That section provides:

> "Except as provided in this chapter, an executor or administrator shall not be held to answer to an action by a creditor of the deceased which is not commenced within one year from the time of his giving bond for the performance of his trust, or to such an action which is commenced within said year unless before the expiration thereof the writ in such action has been served by delivery in hand upon such executor or administrator or service thereof accepted by him or a notice stating the name of the estate, the name and address of the creditor, the amount of the claim and the court in which the action has been brought has been filed in the proper registry of probate. . . ." Mass.Gen.Laws Ann., c. 197, § 9 (1958).

On October 17, 1963, the District Court granted respondent's motion for summary judgment, citing Ragan v. Merchants Transfer & Warehouse Co., 337 U.S. 530, 69 S.Ct. 1233, and Guaranty Trust Co. v. York, 326 U.S. 99, 65 S.Ct. 1464, in support of its conclusion that the adequacy of the service was to be measured by § 9, with which, the court held, petitioner had not complied. On appeal, petitioner admitted noncompliance with § 9, but argued that Rule 4(d)(1) defines the method by which service of process is to be effected in diversity actions. The Court of Appeals for the First Circuit, finding that "[r]elatively recent amendments [to § 9] evince a clear legislative purpose to require personal notification within the year," [1] concluded that the conflict of

---

1. Section 9 is in part a statute of limitations, providing that an executor need not "answer to an action . . . which is not commenced within one year from the time of his giving bond. . . ." This part of the statute, the purpose of which is to speed the settlement of estates, Spaulding v. McConnell, 307 Mass. 144, 146, 29 N.E.2d 713, 715 (1940); Doyle v. Moylan, 141 F.Supp. 95 (D.C.D.Mass.1956), is not involved in this case, since the action clearly was timely commenced. (Respondent

state and federal rules was over "a substantive rather than a procedural matter," and unanimously affirmed. 331 F.2d 157. Because of the threat to the goal of uniformity of federal procedure posed by the decision below,[2] we granted certiorari, 379 U.S. 813, 85 S.Ct. 52.

We conclude that the adoption of Rule 4(d)(1), designed to control service of process in diversity actions,[3] neither exceeded the congressional mandate embodied in the Rules Enabling Act nor transgressed constitutional bounds, and that the Rule is therefore the standard against which the District Court should have measured the adequacy of the service. Accordingly, we reverse the decision of the Court of Appeals.

The Rules Enabling Act, 28 U.S.C.A. § 2072 provides, in pertinent part:

> "The Supreme Court shall have the power to prescribe, by general rules, the forms of process, writs, pleadings, and motions, and the practice and procedure of the district courts of the United States in civil actions.

> "Such rules shall not abridge, enlarge or modify any substantive right and shall preserve the right of trial by jury. . . ."

Under the cases construing the scope of the Enabling Act, Rule 4(d)(1) clearly passes muster. Prescribing the manner in which a defendant is to be notified that a suit has been instituted against him, it relates to the "practice and procedure of the district courts." Cf. Insurance Co. v. Bangs, 103 U.S. 435, 439.

> "The test must be whether a rule really regulates procedure,— the judicial process for enforcing rights and duties recognized by

filed bond on March 1, 1962; the complaint was filed February 6, 1963; and the service—the propriety of which is in dispute— was made on February 8, 1963.) 331 F.2d at 159. Cf. Guaranty Trust Co. v. York, supra; Ragan v. Merchants Transfer Co., supra.

Section 9 also provides for the manner of service. Generally, service of process must be made by "delivery in hand," although there are two alternatives: acceptance of service by the executor, or filing of a notice of claim, the components of which are set out in the statute, in the appropriate probate court. The purpose of this part of the statute, which *is* involved here, is, as the court below noted, to insure that executors will receive actual notice of claims. Parker v. Rich, 297 Mass. 111, 113–114, 8 N.E.2d 345, 347 (1937). Actual notice is of course also the goal of Rule 4(d)(1); however, the Federal Rule reflects a determination that this goal can be achieved by a method less cumbersome than that prescribed in § 9. In this case the goal seems to have been achieved; although the affi-

davit filed by respondent in the District Court asserts that he had not been served in hand nor had he accepted service, it does not allege lack of actual notice.

2. There are a number of state service requirements which would not necessarily be satisfied by compliance with Rule 4(d) (1). See, e.g., Cal.Civ.Proc.Code § 411(8); Idaho Code Ann. § 5–507(7) (1948); Ill.Rev. Stat., c. 110, § 13.2 (1963); Ky.Rev.Stat., Rules Civ.Proc., Rule 4.04 (1962); Md.Ann. Code, Rules Proc., Rule 104 b (1963); Mich. Rev.Jud.Act § 600.1912 (1961); N.C.Gen. Stat. § 1–94 (1953); S.D.Code § 33.0807(8) (Supp.1960); Tenn.Code Ann. § 20–214 (1955).

3. "These rules govern the procedure in the United States district courts in all suits of a civil nature whether cognizable as cases at law or in equity, with the exceptions stated in Rule 81. . . ." Fed.Rules Civ.Proc. 1.

This case does not come within any of the exceptions noted in Rule 81.

substantive law and for justly administering remedy and redress for disregard or infraction of them." Sibbach v. Wilson & Co., 312 U.S. 1, 14, 61 S.Ct. 422, 426.[4]

In Mississippi Pub. Corp. v. Murphree, 326 U.S. 438, 66 S.Ct. 242, this Court upheld Rule 4(f), which permits service of a summons anywhere within the State (and not merely the district) in which a district court sits:

> "We think that Rule 4(f) is in harmony with the Enabling Act. . . . Undoubtedly most alterations of the rules of practice and procedure may and often do affect the rights of litigants. Congress' prohibition of any alteration of substantive rights of litigants was obviously not addressed to such incidental effects as necessarily attend the adoption of the prescribed new rules of procedure upon the rights of litigants who, agreeably to rules of practice and procedure, have been brought before a court authorized to determine their rights. Sibbach v. Wilson & Co., 312 U.S. 1, 11–14, 61 S.Ct. 422, 425–427. The fact that the application of Rule 4(f) will operate to subject petitioner's rights to adjudication by the district court for northern Mississippi will undoubtedly affect those rights. But it does not operate to abridge, enlarge or modify the rules of decision by which that court will adjudicate its rights." Id., at 445–446, 66 S.Ct. at 246.

Thus were there no conflicting state procedure, Rule 4(d)(1) would clearly control. National Rental v. Szukhent, 375 U.S. 311, 316, 84 S.Ct. 411, 414. However, respondent, focusing on the contrary Massachusetts rule, calls to the Court's attention another line of cases, a line which—like the Federal Rules—had its birth in 1938. Erie R. Co. v. Tompkins, 304 U.S. 64, 58 S.Ct. 817, overruling Swift v. Tyson, 16 Pet. 1, held that federal courts sitting in diversity cases when deciding questions of "substantive" law, are bound by state court decisions as well as state statutes. The broad command of *Erie* was therefore identical to that of the Enabling Act: federal courts are to apply state substantive law and federal procedural law. However, as subsequent cases sharpened the distinction between substance and procedure, the line of cases following *Erie* diverged markedly from the line construing the Enabling Act. Guaranty Trust Co. v. York, 326 U.S. 99, 65 S.Ct. 1464, made it clear that *Erie*-type problems were not to be solved by reference to any traditional or common-sense substance-procedure distinction:

> "And so the question is not whether a statute of limitations is deemed a matter of 'procedure' in some sense. The question is . . . does it significantly affect the result of a litigation for a federal court to disregard a law of a State that would be controlling in an action upon the same claim by the same parties in a State court?" 326 U.S., at 109, 65 S.Ct., at 1470.[5]

---

4. See also Schlagenhauf v. Holder, 379 U.S. 104, 112–114, 85 S.Ct. 234, 239–241.

5. See also Ragan v. Merchants Transfer Co., supra; Woods v. Interstate Realty

Respondent, by placing primary reliance on *York* and *Ragan,* suggests that the *Erie* doctrine acts as a check on the Federal Rules of Civil Procedure, that despite the clear command of Rule 4(d)(1), *Erie* and its progeny demand the application of the Massachusetts rule. Reduced to essentials, the argument is: (1) *Erie,* as refined in *York,* demands that federal courts apply state law whenever application of federal law in its stead will alter the outcome of the case. (2) In this case, a determination that the Massachusetts service requirements obtain will result in immediate victory for respondent. If, on the other hand, it should be held that Rule 4(d)(1) is applicable, the litigation will continue, with possible victory for petitioner. (3) Therefore, *Erie* demands application of the Massachusetts rule. The syllogism possesses an appealing simplicity, but is for several reasons invalid.

In the first place, it is doubtful that, even if there were no Federal Rule making it clear that in-hand service is not required in diversity actions, the *Erie* rule would have obligated the District Court to follow the Massachusetts procedure. "Outcome-determination" analysis was never intended to serve as a talisman. Byrd v. Blue Ridge Rural Cooperative, 356 U.S. 525, 537, 78 S.Ct. 893, 900. Indeed, the message of *York* itself is that choices between state and federal law are to be made not by application of any automatic, "litmus paper" criterion, but rather by reference to the policies underlying the *Erie* rule. Guaranty Trust Co. v. York, supra, 326 U.S. at 108–112, 65 S.Ct. at 1469–1471.[6]

The *Erie* rule is rooted in part in a realization that it would be unfair for the character or result of a litigation materially to differ because the suit had been brought in a federal court.

> "Diversity of citizenship jurisdiction was conferred in order to prevent apprehended discrimination in state courts against those not citizens of the State. Swift v. Tyson introduced grave discrimination by non-citizens against citizens. It made rights enjoyed under the unwritten 'general law' vary according to whether enforcement was sought in the state or in the federal court; and the privilege of selecting the court in which the right should be determined was conferred upon the non-citizen. Thus, the doctrine rendered impossible equal protection of the law." Erie R. Co. v. Tompkins, supra, 304 U.S. at 74–75, 58 S.Ct. at 820–821.[7]

The decision was also in part a reaction to the practice of "forum-shopping" which had grown up in response to the rule of Swift v. Tyson, 304 U.S., at 73–74.[8] That the *York* test was an attempt to effectuate these policies is demonstrated by the fact that the opinion framed the

---

Co., 337 U.S. 535, 69 S.Ct. 1235; Bernhardt v. Polygraphic Co., 350 U.S. 198, 203–204, 207–208, 76 S.Ct. 273, 276–279; cf. Byrd v. Blue Ridge Cooperative, 356 U.S. 525, 78 S.Ct. 893.

6. See Iovino v. Waterson, 274 F.2d 41, 46–47 (C.A.2d Cir. 1959), cert. denied sub nom. Carlin v. Iovino, 362 U.S. 949, 80 S.Ct. 860.

7. See also Klaxon Co. v. Stentor Co., 313 U.S. 487, 496, 61 S.Ct. 1020, 1021; Woods v. Interstate Realty Co., supra, note 5, 337 U.S. at 538, 69 S.Ct. at 1237.

8. Cf. Black & White Taxicab Co. v. Brown & Yellow Taxicab Co., 276 U.S. 518, 48 S.Ct. 404.

inquiry in terms of "substantial" variations between state and federal litigation. 326 U.S., at 109. Not only are nonsubstantial or trivial variations not likely to raise the sort of equal protection problems which troubled the Court in *Erie;* they are also unlikely to influence the choice of a forum. The "outcome-determination" test therefore cannot be read without reference to the twin aims of the *Erie* rule: discouragement of forum-shopping and avoidance of inequitable administration of the laws.[9]

The difference between the conclusion that the Massachusetts rule is applicable, and the conclusion that it is not, is of course at this point "outcome-determinative" in the sense that if we hold the state rule to apply, respondent prevails, whereas if we hold that Rule 4(d)(1) governs, the litigation will continue. But in this sense *every* procedural variation is "outcome-determinative." For example, having brought suit in a federal court, a plaintiff cannot then insist on the right to file subsequent pleadings in accord with the time limits applicable in the state courts, even though enforcement of the federal timetable will, if he continues to insist that he must meet only the state time limit, result in determination of the controversy against him. So it is here. Though choice of the federal or state rule will at this point have a marked effect upon the outcome of the litigation, the difference between the two rules would be of scant, if any, relevance to the choice of a forum. Petitioner, in choosing her forum, was not presented with a situation where application of the state rule would wholly bar recovery;[10] rather, adherence to the state rule would have resulted only in altering the way in which process was served.[11] Moreover, it is difficult

---

9. The Court of Appeals seemed to frame the inquiry in terms of how "important" § 9 is to the State. In support of its suggestion that § 9 serves some interest the State regards as vital to its citizens, the court noted that something like § 9 has been on the books in Massachusetts a long time, that § 9 has been amended a number of times, and that § 9 is designed to make sure that executors receive actual notice. See note 1, supra. The apparent lack of relation among these three observations is not surprising, because it is not clear to what sort of question the Court of Appeals was addressing itself. One cannot meaningfully ask how important something is without first asking "important for what purpose?" *Erie* and its progeny make clear that when a federal court sitting in a diversity case is faced with a question of whether or not to apply state law, the importance of a state rule is indeed relevant, but only in the context of asking whether application of the rule would make so important a difference to the character or result of the litigation that failure to enforce it would unfairly discriminate against citizens of the forum State, or whether application of the rule would have so important an effect upon the fortunes of one or both of the litigants that failure to enforce it would be likely to cause a plaintiff to choose the federal court.

10. See Guaranty Trust Co. v. York, supra, at 326 U.S. 108–109, 65 S.Ct. at 1469; Ragan v. Merchants Transfer Co., supra, 337 U.S. at 532, 69 S.Ct. at 1234; Woods v. Interstate Realty Co., supra, note 5, 337 U.S. at 538, 69 S.Ct. at 1237.

Similarly, a federal court's refusal to enforce the New Jersey rule involved in Cohen v. Beneficial Loan Corp., 337 U.S. 541, 69 S.Ct. 1221, requiring the posting of security by plaintiffs in stockholders' derivative actions, might well impel a stockholder to choose to bring suit in the federal, rather than the state, court.

11. Cf. Monarch Insurance Co. of Ohio v. Spach, 281 F.2d 401, 412 (C.A.5th Cir. 1960). We cannot seriously entertain the thought that one suing an estate would be led to choose the federal court because of a belief that adherence to Rule 4(d)(1) is less likely to give the executor actual notice than § 9, and therefore more likely to produce a default judgment. Rule 4(d)(1) is

to argue that permitting service of defendant's wife to take the place of in-hand service of defendant himself alters the mode of enforcement of state-created rights in a fashion sufficiently "substantial" to raise the sort of equal protection problems to which the *Erie* opinion alluded.

There is, however, a more fundamental flaw in respondent's syllogism: the incorrect assumption that the rule of Erie R. Co. v. Tompkins constitutes the appropriate test of the validity and therefore the applicability of a Federal Rule of Civil Procedure. The *Erie* rule has never been invoked to void a Federal Rule. It is true that there have been cases where this Court has held applicable a state rule in the face of an argument that the situation was governed by one of the Federal Rules. But the holding of each such case was not that *Erie* commanded displacement of a Federal Rule by an inconsistent state rule, but rather that the scope of the Federal Rule was not as broad as the losing party urged, and therefore, there being no Federal Rule which covered the point in dispute, *Erie* commanded the enforcement of state law.

> "Respondent contends, in the first place, that the charge was correct because of the fact that Rule 8(c) of the Rules of Civil Procedure makes contributory negligence an affirmative defense. We do not agree. Rule 8(c) covers only the manner of pleading. The question of the burden of establishing contributory negligence is a question of local law which federal courts in diversity of citizenship cases (Erie R. Co. v. Tompkins, 304 U.S. 64, 58 S.Ct. 817) must apply." Palmer v. Hoffman, 318 U.S. 109, 117, 63 S.Ct. 477, 482.[12]

(Here, of course, the clash is unavoidable; Rule 4(d)(1) says—implicitly, but with unmistakable clarity—that in-hand service is not required in federal courts.) At the same time, in cases adjudicating the validity of Federal Rules, we have not applied the *York* rule or other refinements of *Erie*, but have to this day continued to decide questions concerning the scope of the Enabling Act and the constitutionality of specific Federal Rules in light of the distinction set forth in *Sibbach*. E.g., Schlagenhauf v. Holder, 379 U.S. 104, 85 S.Ct. 234.

Nor has the development of two separate lines of cases been inadvertent. The line between "substance" and "procedure" shifts as the legal context changes. "Each implies different variables depending upon the particular problem for which it is used." Guaranty Trust Co. v. York, supra, 326 U.S. at 108, 65 S.Ct. at 1469; Cook, The Logical and Legal Bases of the Conflict of Laws, pp. 154–183 (1942). It is true that both the Enabling Act and the *Erie* rule say, roughly, that federal courts are to apply state "substantive" law and federal "procedural" law, but from that it need not follow that the tests are identical. For

---

well designed to give actual notice, as it did in this case. See note 1, supra.

12. To the same effect, see Ragan v. Merchants Transfer Co., supra; Cohen v. Beneficial Loan Corp., supra, note 10, 337 U.S. at 556, 69 S.Ct. at 1230; Id., at 557, 69 S.Ct. at 1230 (Douglas, J., dissenting); cf. Bernhardt v. Polygraphic Co., supra, note 5, 350 U.S. at 201–202, 76 S.Ct. at 275; see generally Iovino v. Waterson, supra, note 6, at 47–48.

they were designed to control very different sorts of decisions. When a situation is covered by one of the Federal Rules, the question facing the court is a far cry from the typical, relatively unguided *Erie* choice: the court has been instructed to apply the Federal Rule, and can refuse to do so only if the Advisory Committee, this Court, and Congress erred in their prima facie judgment that the Rule in question transgresses neither the terms of the Enabling Act nor constitutional restrictions.[13]

We are reminded by the *Erie* opinion [14] that neither Congress nor the federal courts can, under the guise of formulating rules of decision for federal courts, fashion rules which are not supported by a grant of federal authority contained in Article I or some other section of the Constitution; in such areas state law must govern because there can be no other law. But the opinion in *Erie,* which involved no Federal Rule and dealt with a question which was "substantive" in every traditional sense (whether the railroad owed a duty of care to Tompkins as a trespasser or a licensee), surely neither said nor implied that measures like Rule 4(d)(1) are unconstitutional. For the constitutional provision for a federal court system (augmented by the Necessary and Proper Clause) carries with it congressional power to make rules governing the practice and pleading in those courts, which in turn includes a power to regulate matters which, though falling within the uncertain area between substance and procedure, are rationally capable of classification as either. Cf. M'Culloch v. Maryland, 4 Wheat. 316, 421. Neither *York* nor the cases following it ever suggested that the rule there laid down for coping with situations where no Federal Rule applies is coextensive with the limitation on Congress to which *Erie* had adverted. Although this Court has never before been confronted with a case where the applicable Federal Rule is in direct collision with the law of the relevant State,[15] courts of appeals faced with such clashes have rightly discerned the implications of our decisions.

"One of the shaping purposes of the Federal Rules is to bring about uniformity in the federal courts by getting away from local rules. This is especially true of matters which relate to the administration of legal proceedings, an area in which federal courts have traditionally exerted strong inherent power, completely aside from the powers Congress expressly conferred in the Rules. The

---

13. Sibbach v. Wilson & Co., supra, 312 U.S. at 13–15, 61 S.Ct. at 426–427; see Appointment of Committee to Draft Unified System of Equity and Law Rules, 295 U.S. 774; Orders re Rules of Procedure, 302 U.S. 783; Letter of Submittal, 308 U.S. 649; 1A Moore, Federal Practice ¶ 0.501[2], at 5027–5028 (2d ed. 1961).

14. Erie R. Co. v. Tompkins, supra, 304 U.S. at 77–79, 58 S.Ct. at 822–823; cf. Bernhardt v. Polygraphic Co., supra, note 5, 350 U.S. at 202, 76 S.Ct. at 275; Sibbach v. Wilson & Co., supra, 312 U.S. at 10, 61 S.Ct. at 424; Guaranty Trust Co. v. York, supra, 326 U.S. at 105, 65 S.Ct. at 1467.

15. In Sibbach v. Wilson & Co., supra, the law of the forum State (Illinois) forbade the sort of order authorized by Rule 35. However, *Sibbach* was decided before Klaxon Co. v. Stentor Co., supra, note 7, and the *Sibbach* opinion makes clear that the Court was proceeding on the assumption that if the law of any State was relevant, it was the law of the State where the tort occurred (Indiana), which, like Rule 35, made provision for such orders. 312 U.S. at 6–7, 10–11, 61 S.Ct. at 423, 424–425.

purpose of the Erie doctrine, even as extended in *York* and *Ragan,* was never to bottle up federal courts with 'outcome-determinative' and 'integral-relations' stoppers—when there are 'affirmative countervailing [federal] considerations' and when there is a Congressional mandate (the Rules) supported by constitutional authority." Lumbermen's Mutual Casualty Co. v. Wright, 322 F.2d 759, 764 (C.A.5th Cir. 1963).[16]

Erie and its offspring cast no doubt on the long-recognized power of Congress to prescribe housekeeping rules for federal courts even though some of those rules will inevitably differ from comparable state rules. Cf. Herron v. Southern Pacific Co., 283 U.S. 91, 51 S.Ct. 383. "When, because the plaintiff happens to be a non-resident, such a right is enforceable in a federal as well as in a State court, the forms and mode of enforcing the right may at times, naturally enough, vary because the two judicial systems are not identic." Guaranty Trust Co. v. York, supra, 326 U.S. at 108, 65 S.Ct. at 1469; Cohen v. Beneficial Indus. Loan Corp., 337 U.S. 541, 555, 69 S.Ct. 1221, 1229. Thus, though a court, in measuring a Federal Rule against the standards contained in the Enabling Act and the Constitution, need not wholly blind itself to the degree to which the Rule makes the character and result of the federal litigation stray from the course it would follow in state courts, Sibbach v. Wilson & Co., supra, 312 U.S. at 13–14, 61 S.Ct. at 426–427, it cannot be forgotten that the *Erie* rule, and the guidelines suggested in *York,* were created to serve another purpose altogether. To hold that a Federal Rule of Civil Procedure must cease to function whenever it alters the mode of enforcing state-created rights would be to disembowel either the Constitution's grant of power over federal procedure or Congress' attempt to exercise that power in the Enabling Act.[17] Rule 4(d)(1) is valid and controls the instant case.

Reversed.

MR. JUSTICE BLACK concurs in the result.

MR. JUSTICE HARLAN, concurring.

It is unquestionably true that up to now *Erie* and the cases following it have not succeeded in articulating a workable doctrine governing choice of law in diversity actions. I respect the Court's effort to clarify the situation in today's opinion. However, in doing so I think it has misconceived the constitutional premises of *Erie* and has failed to deal adequately with those past decisions upon which the courts below relied.

Erie was something more than an opinion which worried about "forum-shopping and avoidance of inequitable administration of the laws," * * * although to be sure these were important elements of the decision. I have always regarded that decision as one of the

---

16. To the same effect, see D'Onofrio Construction Co. v. Recon Co., 255 F.2d 904, 909–910 (C.A.1st Cir. 1958).

17. Mississippi Pub. Corp. v. Murphree, supra, 326 U.S. at 445–446, 66 S.Ct. at 246; Iovino v. Waterson, supra, note 6, at 46.

modern cornerstones of our federalism, expressing policies that profoundly touch the allocation of judicial power between the state and federal systems. *Erie* recognized that there should not be two conflicting systems of law controlling the primary activity of citizens, for such alternative governing authority must necessarily give rise to a debilitating uncertainty in the planning of everyday affairs.[1] And it recognized that the scheme of our Constitution envisions an allocation of lawmaking functions between state and federal legislative processes which is undercut if the federal judiciary can make substantive law affecting state affairs beyond the bounds of congressional legislative powers in this regard. Thus, in diversity cases *Erie* commands that it be the state law governing primary private activity which prevails.

The shorthand formulations which have appeared in some past decisions are prone to carry untoward results that frequently arise from oversimplification. The Court is quite right in stating that the "outcome-determinative" test of Guaranty Trust Co. v. York, 326 U.S. 99, 65 S.Ct. 1464, if taken literally, proves too much, for any rule, no matter how clearly "procedural," can affect the outcome of litigation if it is not obeyed. In turning from the "outcome" test of *York* back to the unadorned forum-shopping rationale of *Erie,* however, the Court falls prey to like oversimplification, for a simple forum-shopping rule also proves too much; litigants often choose a federal forum merely to obtain what they consider the advantages of the Federal Rules of Civil Procedure or to try their cases before a supposedly more favorable judge. To my mind the proper line of approach in determining whether to apply a state or a federal rule, whether "substantive" or "procedural," is to stay close to basic principles by inquiring if the choice of rule would substantially affect those primary decisions respecting human conduct which our constitutional system leaves to state regulation.[2] If so, *Erie* and the Constitution require that the state rule prevail, even in the face of a conflicting federal rule.

The Court weakens, if indeed it does not submerge, this basic principle by finding, in effect, a grant of substantive legislative power in the constitutional provision for a federal court system (compare Swift v. Tyson, 16 Pet. 1), and through it, setting up the Federal Rules as a body of law inviolate.

> "[T]he constitutional provision for a federal court system . . . carries with it congressional power . . . to regulate matters which, though falling within the uncertain area between substance and procedure, *are rationally capable of classification as either.*"
> * * * (Emphasis supplied.)

---

1. Since the rules involved in the present case are parallel rather than conflicting, this first rationale does not come into play here.

2. See Hart and Wechsler, The Federal Courts and the Federal System 678. Byrd v. Blue Ridge Coop., Inc., 356 U.S. 525, 536–540, 78 S.Ct. 893, 900–902, indicated that state procedures would apply if the state had manifested a particularly strong interest in their employment. Compare Dice v. Akron, C. & Y. R. Co., 342 U.S. 359, 72 S.Ct. 312. However, this approach may not be of constitutional proportions.

So long as a reasonable man could characterize any duly adopted federal rule as "procedural," the Court, unless I misapprehend what is said, would have it apply no matter how seriously it frustrated a State's substantive regulation of the primary conduct and affairs of its citizens. Since the members of the Advisory Committee, the Judicial Conference, and this Court who formulated the Federal Rules are presumably reasonable men, it follows that the integrity of the Federal Rules is absolute. Whereas the unadulterated outcome and forum-shopping tests may err too far toward honoring state rules, I submit that the Court's "arguably procedural, *ergo* constitutional" test moves too fast and far in the other direction.

The courts below relied upon this Court's decisions in Ragan v. Merchants Transfer & Warehouse Co., 337 U.S. 530, 69 S.Ct. 1233, and Cohen v. Beneficial Indus. Loan Corp., 337 U.S. 541, 69 S.Ct. 1221. Those cases deserve more attention than this Court has given them, particularly *Ragan* which, if still good law, would in my opinion call for affirmance of the result reached by the Court of Appeals. Further, a discussion of these two cases will serve to illuminate the "diversity" thesis I am advocating.

In *Ragan* a Kansas statute of limitations provided that an action was deemed commenced when service was made on the defendant. Despite Federal Rule 3 which provides that an action commences with the filing of the complaint, the Court held that for the purposes of the Kansas statute of limitations a diversity tort action commenced only when service was made upon the defendant. The effect of this holding was that although the plaintiff had filed his federal complaint within the state period of limitations, his action was barred because the federal marshal did not serve a summons on the defendant until after the limitations period had run. I think that the decision was wrong. At most, application of the Federal Rule would have meant that potential Kansas tort defendants would have to defer for a few days the satisfaction of knowing that they had not been sued within the limitations period. The choice of the Federal Rule would have had no effect on the primary stages of private activity from which torts arise, and only the most minimal effect on behavior following the commission of the tort. In such circumstances the interest of the federal system in proceeding under its own rules should have prevailed.

Cohen v. Beneficial Indus. Loan Corp. held that a federal diversity court must apply a state statute requiring a small stockholder in a stockholder derivative suit to post a bond securing payment of defense costs as a condition to prosecuting an action. Such a statute is not "outcome determinative"; the plaintiff can win with or without it. The Court now rationalizes the case on the ground that the statute might affect the plaintiff's choice of forum * * *, but as has been pointed out, a simple forum-shopping test proves too much. The proper view of *Cohen* is, in my opinion, that the statute was meant to inhibit small stockholders from instituting "strike suits," and thus it was designed and could be expected to have a substantial impact on private primary activity. Anyone who was at the trial bar during the period when *Cohen* arose can appreciate the strong state policy reflected in the statute. I think it wholly legitimate to view Federal Rule 23 as not purporting to deal with the problem. But even had the Federal Rules purported to do so, and in so doing provided a substantially less effective deterrent to strike suits, I think the state rule should still have prevailed. That is where I believe the Court's view differs from mine; for the Court attributes such overriding force to the Federal Rules that it is hard to think of a case where a conflicting state rule would be allowed to operate, even though the state rule reflected policy considerations which, under *Erie,* would lie within the realm of state legislative authority.

It remains to apply what has been said to the present case. The Massachusetts rule provides that an executor need not answer suits unless in-hand service was made upon him or notice of the action was filed in the proper registry of probate within one year of his giving bond. The evident intent of this statute is to permit an executor to distribute the estate which he is administering without fear that further liabilities may be outstanding for which he could be held personally liable. If the Federal District Court in Massachusetts applies Rule 4(d)(1) of the Federal Rules of Civil Procedure instead of the Massachusetts service rule, what effect would that have on the speed and assurance with which estates are distributed? As I see it, the effect would not be substantial. It would mean simply that an executor would have to check at his own house or the federal courthouse as well as the registry of probate before he could distribute the estate with impunity. As this does not seem enough to give rise to any real impingement on the vitality of the state policy which the Massachusetts rule is intended to serve, I concur in the judgment of the Court.

WALKER v. ARMCO STEEL CORP.

Supreme Court of the United States, 1980.
446 U.S. 740, 100 S.Ct. 1978, 64 L.Ed.2d 659.*

MR. JUSTICE MARSHALL delivered the opinion of the Court.

This case presents the issue whether in a diversity action the federal court should follow state law or, alternatively, Rule 3 of the Federal Rules of Civil Procedure in determining when an action is commenced for the purpose of tolling the state statute of limitations.

I

According to the allegations of the complaint, petitioner, a carpenter, was injured on August 22, 1975, in Oklahoma City, Okla., while pounding a sheffield nail into a cement wall. Respondent was the manufacturer of the nail. Petitioner claimed that the nail contained a defect which caused its head to shatter and strike him in the right eye,

* Some of the Court's footnotes are omitted.

resulting in permanent injuries. The defect was allegedly caused by respondent's negligence in manufacture and design.

Petitioner is a resident of Oklahoma, and respondent is a foreign corporation having its principal place of business in a State other than Oklahoma. Since there was diversity of citizenship, petitioner brought suit in the United States District Court for the Western District of Oklahoma. The complaint was filed on August 19, 1977. Although summons was issued that same day, service of process was not made on respondent's authorized service agent until December 1, 1977.[2] On January 5, 1978, respondent filed a motion to dismiss the complaint on the ground that the action was barred by the applicable Oklahoma statute of limitations. Although the complaint had been filed within the two-year statute of limitations, Okla.Stat., Tit. 12, § 95 (1971),[3] state law does not deem the action "commenced" for purposes of the statute of limitations until service of the summons on the defendant, Okla. Stat., Tit. 12, § 97 (1971).[4] If the complaint is filed within the limitations period, however, the action is deemed to have commenced from that date of filing if the plaintiff serves the defendant within 60 days, even though that service may occur outside the limitations period. Ibid. In this case service was not effectuated until long after this 60-day period had expired. Petitioner in his reply brief to the motion to dismiss admitted that his case would be foreclosed in state court, but he argued that Rule 3 of the Federal Rules of Civil Procedure governs the manner in which an action is commenced in federal court for all purposes, including the tolling of the state statute of limitations.

The District Court dismissed the complaint as barred by the Oklahoma statute of limitations. 452 F.Supp. 243 (1978). The court concluded that Okla.Stat., Tit. 12, § 97 (1971) was "an integral part of the Oklahoma statute of limitations," 452 F.Supp., at 245, and therefore,

---

2. The record does not indicate why this delay occurred. The face of the process record shows that the United States Marshal acknowledged receipt of the summons on December 1, 1977, and that service was effectuated that same day. App. A–5. At oral argument counsel for petitioner stated that the summons was found "in an unmarked folder in the filing cabinet" in counsel's office some 90 days after the complaint had been filed. Tr. of Oral Arg. 3. See also id., at 6. Counsel conceded that the summons was not delivered to the marshal until December 1. Id., at 3–4. It is unclear why the summons was placed in the filing cabinet. See id., at 17.

3. Under Oklahoma law, a suit for products liability, whether based on a negligence theory or a breach of implied warranty theory, is governed by the two-year statute of limitations period of Okla.Stat., Tit. 12, § 95 (1971). See Hester v. Purex Corp., 534 P.2d 1306, 1308 (Okl.1975); O'Neal v. Black & Decker Manufacturing

Co., 523 P.2d 614, 615 (Okl.1974); Kirkland v. General Motors Corp., 521 P.2d 1353, 1361 (Okl.1974). The period begins to run from the date of injury. O'Neal v. Black & Decker Manufacturing Co., supra, at 615; Kirkland v. General Motors Corp., supra, at 1361.

4. Okla.Stat., Tit. 12, § 97 (1971) provides in pertinent part: "An action shall be deemed commenced, within the meaning of this article [the statute of limitations], as to each defendant, at the date of the summons which is served on him, or on a codefendant, who is a joint contractor or otherwise united in interest with him. . . . An attempt to commence an action shall be deemed equivalent to the commencement thereof, within the meaning of this article, when the party faithfully, properly and diligently endeavors to procure a service; but such attempt must be followed by the first publication or service of the summons, . . . within sixty (60) days."

under Ragan v. Merchants Transfer & Warehouse Co., 337 U.S. 530, 69 S.Ct. 1233, 93 L.Ed. 1500 (1949), state law applied. The court rejected the argument that *Ragan* had been implicitly overruled in Hanna v. Plumer, 380 U.S. 460, 85 S.Ct. 1136, 14 L.Ed.2d 8 (1965).

The United States Court of Appeals for the Tenth Circuit affirmed. 592 F.2d 1133 (1979). That court concluded that Okla.Stat., Tit. 12, § 97 (1971) was in "direct conflict" with Rule 3. 592 F.2d, at 1135. However, the Oklahoma statute was "indistinguishable" from the statute involved in *Ragan,* and the court felt itself "constrained" to follow *Ragan.* 592 F.2d, at 1136.

We granted certiorari, 444 U.S. 823, 100 S.Ct. 43, 62 L.Ed.2d 29 (1979), because of a conflict among the Courts of Appeals. We now affirm.

II

The question whether state or federal law should apply on various issues arising in an action based on state law which has been brought in federal court under diversity of citizenship jurisdiction has troubled this Court for many years. In the landmark decision of Erie R. Co. v. Tompkins, 304 U.S. 64, 58 S.Ct. 817, 82 L.Ed. 1188 (1938), we overturned the rule expressed in Swift v. Tyson, 16 Pet. 1, 10 L.Ed. 865 (1842), that federal courts exercising diversity jurisdiction need not, in matters of "general jurisprudence," apply the nonstatutory law of the State. The Court noted that "[d]iversity of citizenship jurisdiction was conferred in order to prevent apprehended discrimination in state courts against those not citizens of the State," Erie R. Co. v. Tompkins, supra, 304 U.S., at 74, 58 S.Ct., at 820. The doctrine of Swift v. Tyson had led to the undesirable results of discrimination in favor of noncitizens, prevention of uniformity in the administration of state law, and forum shopping. 304 U.S., at 74–75, 58 S.Ct., at 820–821. In response, we established the rule that "[e]xcept in matters governed by the Federal Constitution or by Acts of Congress, the law to be applied in any [diversity] case is the law of the State," id., at 78, 58 S.Ct., at 822.

In Guaranty Trust Co. v. York, 326 U.S. 99, 65 S.Ct. 1464, 89 L.Ed. 2079 (1945), we addressed ourselves to "the narrow question whether, when no recovery could be had in a State court because the action is barred by the statute of limitations, a federal court in equity can take cognizance of the suit because there is diversity of citizenship between the parties," id., at 107, 65 S.Ct., at 1469. The Court held that the *Erie* doctrine applied to suits in equity as well as to actions at law. In construing *Erie* we noted that "[i]n essence, the intent of that decision was to insure that, in all cases where a federal court is exercising jurisdiction solely because of the diversity of citizenship of the parties, the outcome of the litigation in the federal court should be substantially the same, so far as legal rules determine the outcome of a litigation, as it would be if tried in a State Court." 326 U.S., at 109, 65 S.Ct., at 1470. We concluded that the state statute of limitations should be applied. "Plainly enough, a statute that would completely bar recovery in a suit if brought in a State court bears on a State-created right vitally and not merely formally or negligibly. As to consequences that so intimately affect recovery or non-recovery a federal court in a diversity case should follow State law." Id., at 110, 65 S.Ct. at 1470.

The decision in *York* led logically to our holding in Ragan v. Merchants Transfer & Warehouse Co., supra. In *Ragan*, the plaintiff had filed his complaint in federal court on September 4, 1945, pursuant to Rule 3 of the Federal Rules of Civil Procedure. The accident from which the claim arose had occurred on October 1, 1943. Service was made on the defendant on December 28, 1945. The applicable statute of limitations supplied by Kansas law was two years. Kansas had an additional statute which provided: "An action shall be deemed commenced within the meaning of [the statute of limitations], as to each defendant, at the date of the summons which is served on him. . . . An attempt to commence an action shall be deemed equivalent to the commencement thereof within the meaning of this article when the party faithfully, properly and diligently endeavors to procure a service; but such attempt must be followed by the first publication or service of the summons within sixty days." Kan.Gen.Stats.1935, § 60–308. The defendant moved for summary judgment on the ground that the Kansas statute of limitations barred the action since service had not been made within either the two-year period or the 60-day period. It was conceded that had the case been brought in Kansas state court it would have been barred. Nonetheless, the District Court held that the statute had been tolled by the filing of the complaint. The Court of Appeals reversed because "the requirement of service of summons within the statutory period was an integral part of that state's statute of limitations." *Ragan*, supra, 337 U.S., at 532, 69 S.Ct., at 1234.

We affirmed, relying on *Erie* and *York*. "We cannot give [the cause of action] longer life in the federal court than it would have had in the state court without adding something to the cause of action. We may not do that consistently with Erie R. Co. v. Tompkins." 337 U.S., at 533–534, 69 S.Ct., at 1235. We rejected the argument that Rule 3 of the Federal Rules of Civil Procedure governed the manner in which an action was commenced in federal court for purposes of tolling the state statute of limitations. Instead, we held that the service of summons statute controlled because it was an integral part of the state statute of limitations, and under *York* that statute of limitations was part of the state law cause of action.

Ragan was not our last pronouncement in this difficult area, however. In 1965 we decided Hanna v. Plumer, supra, holding that in a civil action where federal jurisdiction was based upon diversity of citizenship, Rule 4(d)(1) of the Federal Rules of Civil Procedure, rather than state law, governed the manner in which process was served.

* * *

* * * The Court concluded that the *Erie* doctrine was simply not the appropriate test of the validity and applicability of one of the Federal Rules of Civil Procedure:

"The *Erie* rule has never been invoked to void a Federal Rule. It is true that there have been cases where this Court had held applicable a state rule in the face of an argument that the situation was governed by one of the Federal Rules. But the holding of each such case was not that *Erie* commanded displacement of a Federal Rule by an inconsistent state rule, but rather that the scope of the Federal Rule was not as broad as the losing party urged, and therefore, there being no Federal Rule which governed the point in dispute, *Erie* commanded the enforcement of state law." 380 U.S., at 470, 85 S.Ct., at 1143.

The Court cited *Ragan* as one of the examples of this proposition, 380 U.S., at 470, n. 12, 85 S.Ct., at 1143, n. 12.[7] The Court explained that where the federal rule was clearly applicable, as in *Hanna,* the test was whether the rule was within the scope of the Rules Enabling Act, 28 U.S.C. § 2072, and if so, within a constitutional grant of power such as the Necessary and Proper Clause of Art. I. 380 U.S., at 470–472, 85 S.Ct., at 1143–1145.

III

The present case is indistinguishable from *Ragan.* * * *

Petitioner argues that the analysis and holding of *Ragan* did not survive our decision in *Hanna.*[8] Petitioner's position is that Okla.Stat., Tit. 12, § 97 (1971) is in direct conflict with the federal rule. Under *Hanna,* petitioner contends, the appropriate question is whether Rule 3 is within the scope of the Rules Enabling Act and, if so, within the constitutional power of Congress. In petitioner's view, the federal rule is to be applied unless it violates one of those two restrictions. This argument ignores both the force of *stare decisis* and the specific limitations that we carefully placed on the *Hanna* analysis.

We note at the outset that the doctrine of *stare decisis* weighs heavily against petitioner in this case. Petitioner seeks to have us overrule our decision in *Ragan.* *Stare decisis* does not mandate that earlier decisions be enshrined forever, of course, but it does counsel that we use caution in rejecting established law. In this case, the reasons petitioner asserts for overruling *Ragan* are the same factors which we concluded in *Hanna* did not undermine the validity of *Ragan.* A litigant who in effect asks us to reconsider not one but two prior decisions bears a heavy burden of supporting such a change in our jurisprudence. Petitioner here has not met that burden.

7. The Court in *Hanna* noted that "this Court has never before been confronted with a case where the applicable Federal Rule is in direct collision with the law of the relevant State." 380 U.S. 460, 472, 85 S.Ct. 1136, 1144, 14 L.Ed.2d 8 (1965).

8. Justice Harlan in his concurring opinion in *Hanna* concluded that *Ragan* was no longer good law. 380 U.S., at 474–478, 85 S.Ct., at 1145–1148. See also Sylvestri v. Warner & Swasey Co., 398 F.2d 598 (CA2 1968).

This Court in *Hanna* distinguished *Ragan* rather than overruled it, and for good reason. Application of the *Hanna* analysis is premised on a "direct collision" between the federal rule and the state law. 380 U.S., at 472, 85 S.Ct., at 1143. In *Hanna* itself the "clash" between Rule 4(d)(1) and the state in-hand service requirement was "unavoidable." Id., at 470, 85 S.Ct., at 1143. The first question must therefore be whether the scope of the federal rule in fact is sufficiently broad to control the issue before the Court. It is only if that question is answered affirmatively that the *Hanna* analysis applies.[9]

As has already been noted, we recognized in *Hanna* that the present case is an instance where "the scope of the Federal Rule [is] not as broad as the losing party urge[s], and therefore, there being no Federal Rule which cover[s] the point in dispute, *Erie* command[s] the enforcement of state law." Ibid. Rule 3 simply states that "[a] civil action is commenced by filing a complaint with the court." There is no indication that the Rule was intended to toll a state statute of limitations,[10] much less that it purported to displace state tolling rules for purposes of state statutes of limitations. In our view, in diversity actions [11] Rule 3 governs the date from which various timing requirements of the federal rules begin to run, but does not affect state

---

9. This is not to suggest that the Federal Rules of Civil Procedure are to be narrowly construed in order to avoid a "direct collision" with state law. The Federal Rules should be given their plain meaning. If a direct collision with state law arises from that plain meaning, then the analysis developed in Hanna v. Plumer applies.

10. "Rule 3 simply provides that an action is commenced by filing the complaint and has as its primary purpose the measuring of time periods that begin running from the date of commencement; the rule does not state that filing tolls the statute of limitations." 4 C. Wright & A. Miller, Federal Practice and Procedure, § 1057, at 191 (1969) (footnote omitted).

The Note of the Advisory Committee on the Rules states:

"[W]hen a Federal or State statute of limitations is pleaded as a defense, a question may arise under this rule whether the mere filing of the complaint stops the running of the statute, or whether any further step is required, such as, service of the summons and complaint or their delivery to the marshal for service. The answer to this question may depend on whether it is competent for the Supreme Court, exercising the power to make rules of procedure without affecting substantive rights, to vary the operation of statutes of limitations. The requirement of Rule

4(a) that the clerk shall forthwith issue the summons and deliver it to the marshal for service will reduce the chances of such a question arising." 28 U.S.C. App., pp. 394–395.

This Note establishes that the Advisory Committee predicted the problem which arose in *Ragan* and arises again in the instant case. It does not indicate, however, that Rule 3 was *intended* to serve as a tolling provision for statute of limitations purposes; it only suggests that the Advisory Committee thought the Rule *might* have that effect.

11. The Court suggested in *Ragan* that in suits to enforce rights under a federal statute Rule 3 means that filing of the complaint tolls the applicable statute of limitations. 337 U.S., at 533, 69 S.Ct., at 1234, distinguishing Bomar v. Keyes, 162 F.2d 136, 140–141 (CA2), cert. denied, 332 U.S. 825, 68 S.Ct. 166, 92 L.Ed. 400 (1947). See Ely, The Irrepressible Myth of Erie, 87 Harv.L.Rev. 693, 729 (1974). See also Walko Corp. v. Burger Chef Systems, Inc., 180 U.S.App.D.C. 306, 308, n. 19, 554 F.2d 1165, 1167, n. 19 (1977); 4 C. Wright & A. Miller, supra, § 1056, and authorities collected therein. We do not here address the role of Rule 3 as a tolling provision for a statute of limitations, whether set by federal law or borrowed from state law, if the cause of action is based on federal law.

statutes of limitations. Cf. 4 C. Wright & A. Miller, Federal Practice and Procedure, § 1057, at 190–191 (1969); id., § 1051, at 165–166.

In contrast to Rule 3, the Oklahoma statute is a statement of a substantive decision by that State that actual service on, and accordingly actual notice by, the defendant is an integral part of the several policies served by the statute of limitations.   *   *   *

*   *   * There is simply no reason why, in the absence of a controlling federal rule, an action based on state law which concededly would be barred in the state courts by the state statute of limitations should proceed through litigation to judgment in federal court solely because of the fortuity that there is diversity of citizenship between the litigants. The policies underlying diversity jurisdiction do not support such a distinction between state and federal plaintiffs, and *Erie* and its progeny do not permit it.

The judgment of the Court of Appeals is affirmed.

DICE v. AKRON, CANTON & YOUNGSTOWN RAILROAD CO.

Supreme Court of the United States, 1952.
342 U.S. 359, 72 S.Ct. 312, 96 L.Ed. 398.

Opinion of the Court by MR. JUSTICE BLACK, announced by MR. JUSTICE DOUGLAS.

Petitioner, a railroad fireman, was seriously injured when an engine in which he was riding jumped the track. Alleging that his injuries were due to respondent's negligence, he brought this action for damages under the Federal Employers' Liability Act, 35 Stat. 65, 45 U.S.C. § 51 et seq., 45 U.S.C.A. § 51 et seq., in an Ohio court of common pleas. Respondent's defenses were (1) a denial of negligence and (2) a written document signed by petitioner purporting to release respondent in full for $924.63. Petitioner admitted that he had signed several receipts for payments made him in connection with his injuries but denied that he had made a full and complete settlement of all his claims. He alleged that the purported release was void because he had signed it relying on respondent's deliberately false statement that the document was nothing more than a mere receipt for back wages.

After both parties had introduced considerable evidence the jury found in favor of petitioner and awarded him a $25,000 verdict. The trial judge later entered judgment notwithstanding the verdict. In doing so he reappraised the evidence as to fraud, found that petitioner had been "guilty of supine negligence" in failing to read the release, and accordingly held that the facts did not "sustain either in law or equity the allegations of fraud by clear, unequivocal and convincing evidence." [1] This judgment notwithstanding the verdict was reversed

1. The trial judge had charged the jury that petitioner's claim of fraud must be sustained "by clear and convincing evidence," but since the verdict was for petitioner, he does not here challenge this charge as imposing too heavy a burden under controlling federal law.

by the Court of Appeals of Summit County, Ohio, on the ground that under federal law, which controlled, the jury's verdict must stand because there was ample evidence to support its finding of fraud. The Ohio Supreme Court, one judge dissenting, reversed the Court of Appeals' judgment and sustained the trial court's action, holding that: (1) Ohio, not federal, law governed; (2) under that law petitioner, a man of ordinary intelligence who could read, was bound by the release even though he had been induced to sign it by the deliberately false statement that it was only a receipt for back wages; and (3) under controlling Ohio law factual issues as to fraud in the execution of this release were properly decided by the judge rather than by the jury. 155 Ohio St. 185, 98 N.E.2d 301. We granted certiorari because the decision of the Supreme Court of Ohio appeared to deviate from previous decisions of this Court that federal law governs cases arising under the Federal Employers' Liability Act. 342 U.S. 811, 72 S.Ct. 59.

First. We agree with the Court of Appeals of Summit County, Ohio, and the dissenting judge in the Ohio Supreme Court and hold that validity of releases under the Federal Employers' Liability Act raises a federal question to be determined by federal rather than state law. Congress in § 1 of the Act granted petitioner a right to recover against his employer for damages negligently inflicted. State laws are not controlling in determining what the incidents of this federal right shall be. Chesapeake & Ohio R. Co. v. Kuhn, 284 U.S. 44, 52 S.Ct. 45, 76 L.Ed. 157; Ricketts v. Pennsylvania R. Co., 2 Cir., 153 F.2d 757, 759, 164 A.L.R. 387. Manifestly the federal rights affording relief to injured railroad employees under a federally declared standard could be defeated if states were permitted to have the final say as to what defenses could and could not be properly interposed to suits under the Act. Moreover, only if federal law controls can the federal Act be given that uniform application throughout the country essential to effectuate its purposes. See Garrett v. Moore-McCormack Co., 317 U.S. 239, 244, 63 S.Ct. 246, 250, 87 L.Ed. 239, and cases there cited. Releases and other devices designed to liquidate or defeat injured employees' claims play an important part in the federal Act's administration. Compare Duncan v. Thompson, 315 U.S. 1, 62 S.Ct. 422, 86 L.Ed. 575. Their validity is but one of the many interrelated questions that must constantly be determined in these cases according to a uniform federal law.

Second. In effect the Supreme Court of Ohio held that an employee trusts his employer at his peril, and that the negligence of an innocent worker is sufficient to enable his employer to benefit by its deliberate fraud. Application of so harsh a rule to defeat a railroad employee's claim is wholly incongruous with the general policy of the Act to give railroad employees a right to recover just compensation for injuries negligently inflicted by their employers. And this Ohio rule is out of harmony with modern judicial and legislative practice to relieve injured persons from the effect of releases fraudulently obtained. [Citations omitted.] We hold that the correct federal rule is that announced by the Court of Appeals of Summit County, Ohio, and the dissenting judge in the Ohio Supreme Court—a release of rights under the Act is void when the employee is induced to sign it by the deliberately false and material statements of the railroad's authorized representatives made to deceive the employee as to the contents of the release. The trial court's charge to the jury correctly stated this rule of law.

Third. Ohio provides and has here accorded petitioner the usual jury trial of factual issues relating to negligence. But Ohio treats factual questions of fraudulent releases differently. It permits the judge trying a negligence case to resolve all factual questions of fraud "other than fraud in the factum." The factual issue of fraud is thus split into fragments, some to be determined by the judge, others by the jury.

It is contended that since a state may consistently with the Federal Constitution provide for trial of cases under the Act by a non-unanimous verdict, Minneapolis & St. Louis R. Co. v. Bombolis, 241 U.S. 211, 36 S.Ct. 595, 60 L.Ed. 961, Ohio may lawfully eliminate trial by jury as to one phase of fraud while allowing jury trial as to all other issues raised. The Bombolis case might be more in point had Ohio abolished trial by jury in all negligence cases including those arising under the federal Act. But Ohio has not done this. It has provided jury trials for cases arising under the federal Act but seeks to single out one phase of the question of fraudulent releases for determination by a judge rather than by a jury. Compare Testa v. Katt, 330 U.S. 386, 67 S.Ct. 810, 91 L.Ed. 967.

We have previously held that "The right to trial by jury is 'a basic and fundamental feature of our system of federal jurisprudence'" and that it is "part and parcel of the remedy afforded railroad workers under the Employers' Liability Act." Bailey v. Central Vermont R. Co., 319 U.S. 350, 354, 63 S.Ct. 1062, 1064, 87 L.Ed. 1444. We also recognized in that case that to deprive railroad workers of the benefit of a jury trial where there is evidence to support negligence "is to take away a goodly portion of the relief which Congress has afforded them." It follows that the right to trial by jury is too substantial a part of the rights accorded by the Act to permit it to be classified as a mere "local rule of procedure" for denial in the manner that Ohio has here used. Brown v. Western R. Co., 338 U.S. 294, 70 S.Ct. 105, 94 L.Ed. 100.

The trial judge and the Ohio Supreme Court erred in holding that petitioner's rights were to be determined by Ohio law and in taking away petitioner's verdict when the issues of fraud had been submitted to the jury on conflicting evidence and determined in petitioner's favor. The judgment of the Court of Appeals of Summit County, Ohio, was correct and should not have been reversed by the Supreme Court of Ohio. The cause is reversed and remanded to the Supreme Court of Ohio for further action not inconsistent with this opinion.

It is so ordered.

Reversed and remanded with directions.

MR. JUSTICE FRANKFURTER, whom MR. JUSTICE REED, MR. JUSTICE JACKSON and MR. JUSTICE BURTON join, concurring for reversal but dissenting from the Court's opinion.

Ohio, as do many other States,[1] maintains the old division between law and equity as to the mode of trying issues, even though the same judge administers both. The Ohio Supreme Court has told us what, on one issue, is the division of functions in all negligence actions brought in the Ohio courts: "Where it is claimed that a release was induced by fraud (other than fraud in the factum) or by mistake, it is . . . necessary, before seeking to enforce a cause of action which such release purports to bar, that equitable relief from the release be secured." 155 Ohio St. 185, 186, 98 N.E.2d 301, 304. Thus, in all cases in Ohio, the judge is the trier of fact on this issue of fraud, rather than the jury. It is contended that the Federal Employers' Liability Act requires that Ohio courts send the fraud issue to a jury in the cases founded on that Act. To require Ohio to try a particular issue before a different fact-finder in negligence actions brought under the Employers' Liability Act from the fact-finder on the identical issue in every other negligence case disregards the settled distribution of judicial power between Federal and State courts where Congress authorizes concurrent enforcement of federally-created rights.

It has been settled ever since the Second Employers' Liability Cases (Mondou v. New York, N. H. & H. R. Co.) 223 U.S. 1, 32 S.Ct. 169, 56 L.Ed. 327, that no State which gives its courts jurisdiction over common law actions for negligence may deny access to its courts for a negligence action founded on the Federal Employers' Liability Act. Nor may a State discriminate disadvantageously against actions for negligence under the Federal Act as compared with local causes of action in negligence. McKnett v. St. Louis & S. F. R. Co., 292 U.S. 230, 234, 54 S.Ct. 690, 692, 78 L.Ed. 1227; Missouri ex rel. Southern R. Co. v. Mayfield, 340 U.S. 1, 4, 71 S.Ct. 1, 3, 95 L.Ed. 3. Conversely, however, simply because there is concurrent jurisdiction in Federal and State courts over actions under the Employers' Liability Act, a State is under no duty to treat actions arising under that Act differently from the way it adjudicates local actions for negligence, so far as the mechanics of litigation, the forms in which law is administered, are concerned. This surely covers the distribution of functions as between judge and jury in the determination of the issues in a negligence case.

* * *

The judgment of the Ohio Supreme Court must be reversed for it applied the State rule as to validity of releases, 155 Ohio St. 185, 98 N.E.2d 301, and it is not for us to interpret Ohio decisions in order to be assured that on a matter of substance the State and Federal criteria coincide. Moreover, we cannot say with confidence that the Ohio trial judge applied the Federal standard correctly. He duly recognized that

---

1. Chafee, Simpson, and Maloney, Cases on Equity (1951 ed.) 12.

"the Federal law controls as to the validity of a release pleaded and proved in bar of the action, and the burden of showing that the alleged fraud vitiates the contract or compromise or release rests upon the party attacking the release." And he made an extended analysis of the relevant circumstances of the release, concluding, however, that there was no "clear, unequivocal and convincing evidence" of fraud. Since these elusive words fail to assure us that the trial judge followed the Federal test and did not require some larger quantum of proof, we would return the case for further proceedings on the sole question of fraud in the release.

CANNON v. KROGER CO.

United States Court of Appeals for the Fourth Circuit, 1987.
832 F.2d 303.*

K.K. HALL, CIRCUIT JUDGE:

Dorothy R. Cannon, plaintiff in a civil action alleging unfair labor practices by her former employer, The Kroger Company ("Kroger") and breach of the duty of fair representation by Locals 278, 305, and 400 of the United Food and Commercial Workers Union ("UFCW" or "the Unions") appeals an order of the district court dismissing her complaint as time barred, 647 F.Supp. 82. The district court held that the statute of limitations applicable to "hybrid" actions brought, in part, pursuant to § 301 of the Labor Management Relations Act, 29 U.S.C. § 185 was violated by Cannon's failure to file a complaint within six months of the allegedly wrongful act. We affirm.

I.

Cannon, a black female, was employed by Kroger from 1981 until 1985 as a meat clerk in a store located in Winston–Salem, North Carolina. During her tenure with Kroger, the terms and conditions of her employment were governed by two successive collective bargaining agreements executed between Kroger and Locals 305 and 278 of the UFCW. Cannon resigned her position with Kroger on September 7, 1985.

On March 7, 1986, six months to the day after she left her position, Cannon sought to initiate a "hybrid" civil action for unfair labor practices and breach of the duty of fair representation against Kroger and the Unions in the Superior Court of Forsyth County, North Carolina. In commencing her action, Cannon employed a mechanism available under the North Carolina Rules of Civil Procedure but which has no counterpart in the Federal Rules. North Carolina Rule 3 allows a plaintiff to postpone filing a complaint by first making application to the court stating the nature and purpose of the action and requesting

* Some of the court's footnotes are omitted.

permission to file a complaint within 20 days. Cannon sought and was granted the extended time. Pursuant to the North Carolina rule, a summons was issued to Kroger and the Unions.

In her complaint ultimately filed on March 27, 1986, Cannon alleged that during her period of employment, Kroger regularly granted wage increases to white, male employees in excess of the collective bargaining agreement while limiting her to the amount specified in the agreement. She further alleged that Kroger required her to perform additional duties in violation of safety rules and established company procedures. Finally, she maintained that the Unions' failure to defend her from Kroger's intolerable and discriminatory acts left her with no alternative but to resign her position.

Following receipt of the complaint, Kroger and the Unions removed the action to federal district court. The defendants then moved to dismiss Cannon's complaint on the ground that it was neither filed nor served within the six-month statute of limitations derived from § 10(b) of the National Labor Relations Act, 29 U.S.C. § 160(b).[2] The district court granted the motion for dismissal with prejudice pursuant to Fed. R.Civ.P. 12(b)(6), reasoning that Cannon's failure to file a complaint within six months of her resignation rendered her action untimely. The court further held that the statutory period could not be extended by the alternative means of commencing an action available under North Carolina law.

This appeal followed.

II.

The cause of action asserted by Cannon is popularly known as a "hybrid" § 301/fair representation claim. The gravamen of such an action is the assertion that an employer has breached its contractual obligations toward an employee under the collective bargaining agreement in violation of § 301 of the Labor Management Relations Act, 29 U.S.C. § 185 and that the employee's union, by failing to protect its member's rights, has failed to satisfy the duty of fair representation implied by the National Labor Relations Act, 29 U.S.C. § 151 et seq. Clearly, both components of this "hybrid" cause of action involve rights created by federal statute.

On appeal, Cannon contends that her action below did not violate the six-month statute of limitations applied by the Supreme Court to "hybrid" § 301/fair representation claims in DelCostello v. International Bro. of Teamsters, 462 U.S. 151, 103 S.Ct. 2281, 76 L.Ed.2d 476 (1983). She argues that *DelCostello* required only that a "hybrid" action be commenced within six months of the alleged wrongful act but did not specify commencement in accordance with the Federal Rules of Civil

---

2. Section 160(b) provides in pertinent part that: "No complaint shall issue based upon any unfair labor practice occurring more than six months prior to the filing of the charge with the Board and the service of a copy thereof upon the person against whom such charge is made. . . ."

Procedure. In Cannon's view, her timely compliance with the appropriate state procedures for initiating a civil action satisfied the dictates of *DelCostello*. Alternatively, appellant contends that the summons issued on March 7, 1986, pursuant to the North Carolina Rules, was the functional equivalent of a complaint under Fed.R.Civ.P. 8(a), thereby tolling the statutory limitation period on that date. We disagree with both of appellant's contentions.

A "hybrid" civil action in which an employee alleges wrongdoing by both his employer and his union necessarily intrudes into those "consensual processes that federal labor law is chiefly designed to promote—the formation of the . . . agreement and the private settlement of disputes under it." (citations omitted). *DelCostello,* 462 U.S., at 171, 103 S.Ct., at 2294, quoting United Parcel Service v. Mitchell, 451 U.S. 56, 70–71, 101 S.Ct. 1559, 1568, 67 L.Ed.2d 732 (1981). Striking a balance between the rights of an aggrieved employee and the substantial federal labor policies at stake demands the application of uniform national procedures. 462 U.S., at 171–72, 103 S.Ct., at 2294.

The Court in *DelCostello* admittedly did not expressly hold that a plaintiff in a "hybrid" action is required to commence an action by filing a complaint in accordance with Fed.R.Civ.P. 3 in order to toll the limitation period. The Court's announced goal of uniformity would be severely undercut, however, if alternative means of computing elapsed time were available. Moreover, in the recent decision in West v. Conrail, 481 U.S. 35, 107 S.Ct. 1538, 95 L.Ed.2d 32 (1987), the Supreme Court clearly relied upon the Federal Rules to resolve a dispute regarding the six-month limitation period [3]

After *West,* there can be no question that commencement of a "hybrid" claim brought in district court is to be assessed in accordance with the Federal Rules of Civil Procedure. Unlike appellant, we can perceive no justification for allowing a different result simply because the underlying action is initiated in a state court. The substantive rights involved remain purely federal in nature. Moreover, the choice of a forum in no way diminishes the subtle balance of interests noted in *DelCostello* as a justification for uniformity. The application of alternative state law procedures must inevitably intrude into the balance and threaten the goal of uniform adjudication. We conclude, therefore, that the statute of limitations applicable to "hybrid" actions runs until the action is properly commenced under the dictates of the Federal Rules of Civil Procedure.

3. The issue in *West* turned upon whether the adoption of the § 10(b) six-month limitation period in *DelCostello* also adopted the requirement in § 10(b) that the complaint be both filed and served within that time. The Court noted that it had borrowed only the time period and that for other procedural questions it "did not intend to replace any part of the Federal Rules of Civil Procedure. . . ." 107 S.Ct., at 1541. The Court, therefore, held that a complaint filed in conformity with Fed.R.Civ.P. 3 within the *DelCostello* six-month period was timely.

III.

Appellant's alternative contention that the state summons issued pursuant to North Carolina Rule 3 was somehow equivalent to a complaint under the Federal Rules is unpersuasive. A valid complaint under the Federal Rules must satisfy, *inter alia,* the demands of Rule 8(a)(2) by including a "plain statement of the claim showing that pleader is entitled to relief." The state summons issued to defendants below fell significantly short of this requirement.

Under the most liberal interpretation the summons stated nothing more than a conclusory allegation that defendant Kroger had forced Cannon to quit her job. There was absolutely no identification of any specific actions that allegedly violated appellant's rights and thus no basis on which relief could have been granted. Even under North Carolina state law, the summons is nothing more than a stopgap mechanism for delaying the filing of an actual complaint. We can see no reason for according it any greater dignity in a federal action.

IV.

For the foregoing reasons, we conclude that the district court did not err in dismissing appellant's hybrid action as untimely. The judgment of the district court is, accordingly, affirmed.

Affirmed.

SMALKIN, DISTRICT JUDGE, dissenting:

With great respect, I dissent from the majority's opinion. Although the majority's enforcement of the federal standard for case commencement provided by Fed.R.Civ.P. 8(a) certainly shows an admirable concern for uniformity of result in LMRA cases, I do not feel that this concern warrants supplanting a legitimate state procedural rule with a federal procedural rule.

In my judgment, whether the cause of action be derived from state or federal law in cases of concurrent jurisdiction, the law of the jurisdiction wherein the action was commenced ought to determine the question of when it was commenced. This is indisputably the general rule in removed cases, including removed cases on federal causes of action. Herb v. Pitcairn, 325 U.S. 77, 65 S.Ct. 954, 89 L.Ed. 1483 (1945). In such cases, procedural steps sufficient to initiate the case in state court, yet insufficient for the same purpose in federal court, have been recognized as establishing the date of case commencement. See, e.g., Dravo Corp. v. White Consol. Industries, 602 F.Supp. 1136, 1139 (W.D. Pa.1985) (applying Rule 1007 of the Pennsylvania Rules of Civil Procedure instead of Fed.R.Civ.P. 3, to determine the "commencement" issue). This approach is consistent with Fed.R.Civ.P. 81(c), which provides, in pertinent part, that "[t]hese rules apply to civil actions removed to the United States district courts from the state courts and govern procedure *after* removal." Fed.R.Civ.P. 81(c) (emphasis supplied). This Court recently has interpreted Rule 81(c) to prohibit the imposition of Rule 11 sanctions where a pleading is signed in state court, and the case subsequently is removed to federal court. Kirby v. Allegheny Beverage Corporation, 811 F.2d 253, 256–57 (4th Cir.1987). This Court there reasoned as follows: "By obvious implication [of Rule 81(c)], the rules, including Rule 11, do not apply to the filing of pleadings or motions prior to removal." Id., at 257. The majority's opinion is in direct conflict with the language of Rule 81(c) and with this Court's reasoning in the *Kirby* case.

I see nothing particularly unique about the cause of action involved in this case that justifies disregarding the general principle stated above. Certainly, nothing in *DelCostello* or in West v. Conrail compels us to disregard a valid state rule of procedure, substituting a federal rule for it, in the interests of achieving uniformity. Uniformity, important as it is, should not oust a plaintiff from a federal court with subject matter jurisdiction, where she in good faith commenced her action in a state court, also with subject matter jurisdiction, in accordance with all that was required of her under state law. Most respectfully, therefore, I dissent.

NOTE ON *DICE* AND *CANNON*

Is it accurate to regard the holdings of *Dice* (the validity of a release under the F.E.L.A. is to be determined by federal rather than state law) and *Cannon* (federal rules for determining when an action is commenced govern in a federal "hybrid" labor claim commenced in state court) as the reverse of the normal type of *Erie* problem? Are the holdings in these cases required by Art. VI, cl. 2 of the United States Constitution, providing that "This Constitution, and the laws of the United States which shall be made in pursuance thereof ∗ ∗ ∗ shall be the supreme law of the land ∗ ∗ ∗"? The rationale for the Court's decision in *Dice* was that the right to jury trial is "part and parcel" of the remedy provided by the F.E.L.A. Is this the same rationale as that in *Cannon*, which held that the federal rule had to be applied in order to vindicate the congressional intent that there be "uniform national procedures"?

With respect to the second question addressed in *Dice,* what were the sources by which it was determined what the uniform federal rule should be? Is the process by which a federal court determines the appropriate rule to be adopted as the uniform federal rule substantially similar to the process by which a state court determines the appropriate rule to be adopted in a case of first impression? See Mishkin, The Variousness of "Federal Law": Competence and Discretion in the Choice of National and State Rules for Decision, 105 U.Pa.L.Rev. 797 (1957).

On the problem of the mode of trial, is it fair to summarize *Byrd* and *Dice* as follows: Whereas *Byrd* insists on the federal forum's mode of trial in the teeth of the state's "substantive" law, which normally must control under *Erie* 's outcome test, *Dice* insists on the federal "substantive" law's primacy in the teeth of the state's procedural law, which normally would control as that of the forum? If stated accurately, is this proposition a function of federal supremacy? Or is it merely a function of the preferred status of jury trial? Preferred by whom? Observe that the Court in *Dice* said that Ohio may not "single out" the question of fraudulent releases for nonjury trial. This implies that Ohio was somehow discriminating in the way it handled F.E.L.A. releases, doesn't it? Was the discrimination with which Ohio was charged one of the two types mentioned by the Court in *Erie?* If so, which one? Is it relevant to *Dice* that an Ohio state court jury operated under different rules than a federal civil jury? The Ohio jury consisted of eight persons, not twelve, and Ohio Rev.Code § 2315.09 (Bald. ed. 1958) provided: "In all civil actions a jury shall render a verdict upon the concurrence of three fourths or more of their number."

"SUBSTANCE" AND "PROCEDURE" RECONSIDERED

1. The Scope of "Substantive" Law Under the Erie Doctrine

It is clear that *Erie* does not result in the application of state law to every substantive aspect of a diversity action. In diversity litigation in federal court, issues sometimes arise which are controlled by the Constitution, treaties or statutes of the United States. On such issues the federal court follows federal law, e.g., Francis v. Southern Pacific Co., 333 U.S. 445, 68 S.Ct. 611, 92 L.Ed. 798 (1948) (federal rule governing issuance of passes by interstate carriers supersedes state law in diversity suit for wrongful death).

Conversely, the *Erie* principle applies in respect to issues not governed by federal law arising in cases that are in federal court on some jurisdictional basis *other* than diversity (such as "federal question" cases). See, e.g., Commissioner v. Estate of Bosch, 387 U.S. 456, 87 S.Ct. 1776, 18 L.Ed.2d 886 (1967); De Sylva v. Ballentine, 351 U.S. 570, 76 S.Ct. 974, 100 L.Ed. 1415 (1956) (meaning of "children" under Copyright Act determined in accordance with state law); Westen and Lehman, Is There Life for Erie After the Death of Diversity?, 78 Mich.L.Rev. 311 (1980). Beyond these situations, state law is sometimes expressly adopted by federal statute, e.g., the Federal Tort Claims Act, 28 U.S.C.A. §§ 1346(b), 2674, 2680.

It should be repeated that not only the Constitution, treaties and Congress may supply a federal rule that supersedes otherwise applicable state law, but that the federal courts may also supply the rule where it appears to them that a uniform federal rule is required to supplement a federal legislative enactment. Textile Workers v. Lincoln Mills, 353 U.S. 448, 456, 77 S.Ct. 912, 917, 1 L.Ed.2d 972 (1957) ("We conclude that the substantive law to apply in suits under § 301(a) [of the Labor Management and Relations Act of 1947] is federal law, which the courts must fashion from the policy of our national labor laws."); Illinois v. City of Milwaukee, 406 U.S. 91, 92 S.Ct. 1385, 31 L.Ed.2d 712 (1972) (federal common law of interstate water pollution); Hill, The Law-Making Power of the Federal Courts: Constitutional Preemption, 67 Colum.L.Rev. 1024 (1967); Friendly, In Praise of Erie—And of the New Federal Common Law, 39 N.Y.U.L.Rev. 383 (1964). In some instances, having decided that the matter in question will be governed by a federal rule, the courts then decide that the "federal" rule is to incorporate applicable state law. See Comment, Adopting State Law as the Federal Rule of Decision: A Proposed Test, 43 U.Chi.L.Rev. 823 (1976). This is not entirely circular, because it leaves open the possibility of rejecting an aberrant state rule that would disrupt the federal legal scheme involved.

One other aspect of *Erie* is interesting. In Thomas, The Erosion of Erie in the Federal Courts: Is State Law Losing Ground?, 1977 Brigham Young L.Rev. 1, the author's study of lower court decisions purporting to adhere to *Erie* indicates that many of them in fact apply the courts' own idea of what "the law" of the state is, without strict attention to the applicable state precedents. Even with the best good faith effort it is sometimes very difficult for a federal court to discern what the state law is. See, e.g., McKenna v. Ortho Pharmaceutical Corp., 622 F.2d 657 (3d Cir. 1980). Further, the federal Courts of Appeals are not in agreement whether special deference should be given to the District Courts' presumed familiarity with local state law. Compare Saloomey v. Jeppesen & Co., 707 F.2d 671 (2d Cir. 1983) (yes) with Matter of McLinn, 739 F.2d 1395 (9th Cir. 1984) (no).

2. The Problem of Federal "Procedure"

In an illuminating analysis, Professor Ely points out that the "Erie" doctrine (as distinct from the *Erie* decision itself) attempts to resolve several distinct problems simultaneously. See Ely, The Irrepressible Myth of Erie, 87 Harv.L.Rev. 693 (1974). Perhaps they can be sorted out.

(a) To begin with, it is absurd to say that the relevant distinction is between rules that affect "outcome" and those that do not. Procedural rules are designed to affect outcome. This should be clear not only of rules prescribed by the Constitution, such as the right to jury trial, or by statute, but also of rules derived by the courts. Consider, for example, the rule about notice in connection with attachment that was laid down in Fuentes v. Shevin, noted supra p. 204. Does anyone think that rule didn't affect "outcome"?

(b) The Constitution prescribes rules that apply in federal courts, such as the right to jury trial, and they apply regardless of "outcome" effects—indeed, *because* of outcome effects. Suppose that in Byrd v. Blue Ridge the South Carolina statute had expressly provided that the question of "statutory employee" was for the judge to decide. Would that statute prevail over the Seventh Amendment?

(c) The Constitution also prescribes rules that apply in state courts, again *because* of outcome effects.

(d) Federal statute may prescribe rules that apply in federal courts, e.g., the Jones Act, 46 U.S.C.A. § 688 (jury trial in actions by seamen), and state courts, e.g., Bailey v. Central Vermont R.R., 319 U.S. 350, 63 S.Ct. 1062, 87 L.Ed. 1444 (1943) (jury trial under F.E.L.A. in state court).

(e) Federal decisional law may prescribe "procedural" rules that apply in federal court in diversity cases, if they go to an issue that affects the court's "appropriate performance." See Herron v. Southern Pac. Co., noted supra, and referred to in Byrd v. Blue Ridge Rural Elec. Coop. If this proposition is put together with the proposition that federal statutes may prescribe binding procedural rules, doesn't the correctness of the result in Bernhardt v. Polygraphic Co., supra p. 580, have to be reconsidered? Of course, as a matter of decisional law the federal courts may accept state law even if it does involve a question of "appropriate performance." Compare Day & Zimmerman, Inc. v. Challoner, 423 U.S. 3, 96 S.Ct. 167, 46 L.Ed.2d 3 (1975), refusing to develop federal rules as to choice of law and adhering to Klaxon v. Stentor Elec. Mfg. Co., noted supra p. 572.

(f) The Federal Rules are valid, even if inconsistent with state law, so long as they are within the terms of the Enabling Act. And the terms of the Enabling Act refer to "practice and procedure." 28 U.S.C.A. § 2072. See Burbank, The Rules Enabling Act of 1934, 130 U.Pa.L.Rev. 1015 (1982). Do these terms also impliedly define the boundaries of the Rules of Decision Act?

(g) State law governs whatever is left, and that is what is referred to by the Rules of Decision Act. Compare Note, The Law Applied in Diversity Cases: The Rules of Decision Act and the Erie Doctrine, 85 Yale L.J. 678 (1976); Redish and Phillips, Erie and the Rules of Decision Act: In Search of the Appropriate Dilemma, 91 Harv.L.Rev. 356 (1977). What does that include?

3. The Dimensions of the Problem

Erie is sometimes hard to keep in perspective.

(a) In a whole range of procedural matters there is no significant difference between state and federal practice. In the first place, a large number of the states have adopted rules of procedure that are substantially identical to the Federal Rules. Second, in many important respects the Federal Rules explicitly or implicitly incorporate by reference the applicable state rules. See, e.g., Rules 4(d) (mode of service of process on certain persons), 8(c) (affirmative defenses), 17(b) (capacity to sue of certain persons), 43(a) (admissibility of evidence), 64 (provisional remedies), and 69 (execution proceedings). Third, the directives to court or counsel under many of the Federal Rules, though cast in language different from their state counterparts, do not require different conduct. This may be so either because the effect of the directives is substantially the same (e.g., compare the Federal "counterclaim" with California's "cross-complaint"), or because the meaning of the directives is so vague (e.g., the allowable scope of amendments to pleadings, the allowable scope of departure from the issues framed by the pleadings or pre-trial order, and the limits placed on evidence by the relevancy rule) that they have little or no determinative value, let alone different determinative values, in the decision of a particular case. Fourth, the rules of procedure, whether federal or state, are infused with local shadings of meaning that derive from local traditions. The federal judges, by and large, have practiced in local state courts; counsel appearing in a federal court one day have appeared in local state court the day before. Viewpoint, habit and style survive change of forum so that differences among federal courts in different states may be more significant than differences between federal and state courts in the same state proceeding under different rules.

(b) As recognized in *Hanna,* all rules of procedure do or may affect "outcome." This is true because all procedural rules are designed mediately if not immediately to affect outcome: The difference between trial by ordeal and trial by human appraisal of proofs lies not in the substantive rules being applied (for they were the same) but in the "mode or manner" of applying those rules. So long as the federal courts have any rules at all that are different from state court rules, "outcome" will or may be affected.

(c) The dichotomy between "procedure" and "substance," though no doubt not "defining a great divide cutting across the whole domain of law," is not meaningless. To say that it does not resolve all cases is not to say that it resolves none. Every legal term, like every term of language, has a core of meaning manifested by the fact that it is usefully employed in the discourse of a community in which there is a large measure of shared values and purposes. Hence, as long as there is any important shared tradition among common lawyers—and our community will have approached the point of dissolution when there is not—the words "procedure" and "substance" will have some meaning and therefore serve to decode cases.

(d) Account must be taken of the relation between law as it operates as a guide to laymen's conduct in the out-of-court world and law as it operates as the medium of exchange in litigation. One may look at a particular legal rule as essentially nothing more than, in Holmes' phrase, a "prediction that if a man does or omits certain things he will be made to suffer in this or that way by judgment of the court." Holmes, The Path of the Law, 10 Harv.L.Rev. 61 (1897). If so, the "mode or manner" of enforcing that legal rule is not merely an incident of the rule but one of its basic terms. Cf. Bernhardt v. Polygraphic Co., supra p. 580. Accordingly, under this view it would be impossible fully to reconcile the existence of a diversity jurisdiction in the federal courts with the premises of *Erie.* Yet such a conception fails to account for the fact that most of the community most of the time recognizes the obligation of law without being told by a judge what it is. Cf. H.L.A. Hart, The Concept of Law (1961). If that is so, there is a hard core of meaning in a distinction between a non-litigious perspective of the law and the perspective that appears in litigation. That "substance" versus "procedure" may not well describe the distinction does not mean the distinction cannot be made.

(e) There are certain kinds of rules that simply cannot be classified clearly as procedural or substantive. Among them are statutes of limitation, the statute of frauds, and rules requiring a prior claim or exhaustion of remedies before bringing suit. See, for example, the statutes requiring that medical malpractice claims be submitted to a panel of arbitrators before suit may be brought. Do these create a condition precedent to a federal diversity suit? See Note, Medical Malpractice Panels and Federal Diversity Jurisdiction, 66 Corn. L.Rev. 337 (1981); e.g., Davison v. Sinai Hosp. of Baltimore, 617 F.2d 361 (4th Cir. 1980). Are we driven to conclude that the right to a hearing is always qualified by rules recognizing that the hearing may result in error, and therefore that under some conditions—such as the passage of time prescribed by a statute of limitations the possibility of a hearing will be foreclosed? Is this a second-order procedural proposition? And thus a "substantive" proposition about "procedure"?

4. FEDERAL VENUE AND TRANSFERS UNDER THE JUDICIAL CODE

INTRODUCTORY NOTE ON FEDERAL VENUE

1. Federal Venue Statutes

To assume authority to determine a case, a federal court must have subject-matter jurisdiction and, unless there is a waiver by the defendant, must also subject the defendant to proper service of process. On the limited subject-matter jurisdiction of the federal courts, see Introductory Note on Jurisdiction of the Federal Courts, supra p. 523. On the limited reach of process in federal courts, see Further Note on Long Arm Statutes, supra p. 414. In addition, unless there is waiver, the action must be commenced in the proper district as determined by the federal law of venue.

The principal provisions of federal venue law are in 28 U.S.C.A. § 1391, as amended in 1988, of which the first three subdivisions are of greatest practical importance:

"(a) A civil action wherein jurisdiction is founded only on diversity of citizenship may, except as otherwise provided by law, be brought only in the judicial district where all plaintiffs or all defendants reside, or in which the claim arose.

"(b) A civil action wherein jurisdiction is not founded solely on diversity of citizenship may be brought only in the judicial district where all defendants reside, or in which the claim arose, except as otherwise provided by law.

"(c) For purposes of venue under this chapter, a defendant that is a corporation shall be deemed to reside in any judicial district in which it is subject to personal jurisdiction at the time the action is commenced. In a State which has more than one judicial district and in which a defendant that is a corporation is subject to personal jurisdiction at the time an action is commenced, such corporation shall be deemed to reside in any district in that State within which its contacts would be sufficient to subject it to personal jurisdiction if that district were a separate State, and, if there is no such district, the corporation shall be deemed to reside in the district within which it has the most significant contacts."

If defendants reside in different districts in the same state, suit may be brought in any of such districts. 28 U.S.C.A. § 1392.

In addition to the general venue provisions, there are many special venue statutes governing the following types of actions, among others: actions against federal officials, 28 U.S.C.A. § 1391(e); actions against the United States, 28 U.S.C.A. § 1402; interpleader actions under the Interpleader Act, 28 U.S.C.A. § 1397; actions based on copyright or patent infringement, 28 U.S.C.A. § 1400; and stockholder derivative suits, 28 U.S.C.A. § 1401. For a resolution of conflicting provisions of two special venue statutes, see Radzanower v. Touche Ross & Co., 426 U.S. 148, 96 S.Ct. 1989, 48 L.Ed.2d 540 (1976).

2. Federal Venue in Original Actions and the Judicial Code of 1948

28 U.S.C.A. § 1391 was originally enacted as part of the 1948 revision of the Judicial Code. Of the many unsatisfactory aspects of that revision, perhaps none was more so than the treatment of venue. The Revisers explained that for the most part they were making only verbal changes and that such changes in substance as were made were explained in their Notes. But the Notes are obviously fragmentary. See generally Barrett, Venue and Service of Process in the Federal Courts—Suggestions for Reform, 7 Vand.L.Rev. 608 (1954).

In Fourco Glass Co. v. Transmirra Prod. Corp., 353 U.S. 222, 226–227, 77 S.Ct. 787, 790, 1 L.Ed.2d 786, 789 (1957), the court observed that "the reports of the Committee on the Judiciary of the Senate, and of the House, respecting the 1948 revision and recodification of the Judicial Code, make plain that every change made in the text is explained in detail in the Revisers' Notes. * * * Statements made by several of the persons having importantly to do with the 1948 revision are uniformly clear that no changes of law or policy are to be presumed from changes of language in the revision unless an intent to make such changes was clearly expressed." Thus, in the absence of an explanation by the Revisers that a change in meaning was intended, *Fourco* said that the language of the 1948 Judicial Code was to be read as though it meant the same as its predecessor. Yet in a number of instances where the Revisers' Notes disclose no purpose to effect a change in meaning, the new language had a literal meaning manifestly different from the old. The chief difficulties, though by no means the only ones, involved venue in cases in which a corporation is a litigant. The Judicial Improvements and Access to Justice Act of 1988 attempted to solve some of these problems by amending 28 U.S.C.A. § 1391(c), though with what success remains to be seen. Illustrative of these difficulties are:

a. Venue in respect of a corporate plaintiff. One problem that the 1988 amendment does not appear to resolve is venue where a corporation is the plaintiff. Section 1391(c) defines residence of a corporate *defendant* but does not address the problem of where a corporate *plaintiff* should be deemed to reside. In a diversity action, should a corporate plaintiff be permitted to sue wherever it could be sued if it were a defendant, i.e., wherever it could be reached for purposes of territorial jurisdiction? The better analysis is that a corporate plaintiff is a resident only of the state of its incorporation; if that state has more than one district, then of the district where its principal office is located.

b. Venue in respect of a corporate defendant. The 1988 amendment has resolved one formerly vexing problem, namely, the degree of contacts a corporate defendant must have with a district within a state for that district to be a proper one for venue purposes. Under the old language, a corporation could be sued where it was incorporated, licensed to do business, or actually "doing business," and courts were split as to whether the latter provision incorporated the expansive view of "doing business" developed in International Shoe Co. v. State of Washington and its progeny or the narrower view that had prevailed under state "doing business" statutes before *International Shoe.* The courts also were split as to whether a corporation doing business in a state with more than one federal district was a resident of all the districts in the state, or only of the district where it actually operated. As amended, § 1391(c) makes it clear that venue is proper wherever the corporation can be reached for purposes of territorial jurisdiction under the *International Shoe* line of cases and resolves the issue of venue in multidistrict states.

One issue which the amendment does not appear to resolve with respect to corporate defendants is the "residence" of such defendants for purposes of *special* venue statutes which require venue to be laid in the district where the defendant "resides." The *Fourco* case, supra, held that under the old § 1391(c) a corporate defendant was a resident only of its state of incorporation in patent actions under 28 U.S.C.A. § 1400(b), relying on a pre–1948 decision, Stonite Prod. Co. v. Melvin Lloyd Co., 315 U.S. 561, 62 S.Ct. 780, 86 L.Ed. 1026 (1942). However, § 1391(c) was held applicable to the special venue provision of the Jones Act in Pure Oil Co. v. Suarez, 384 U.S. 202, 86 S.Ct. 1394, 16 L.Ed.2d 474 (1966), where the Court implied that it was prima facie applicable to all venue statutes using residence as a criterion.

Where is the proper venue when the defendant is an unincorporated association? See Denver & R.G.W.R. Co. v. Brotherhood of Railroad Trainmen, 387 U.S. 556, 87 S.Ct. 1746, 18 L.Ed.2d 954 (1967).

c. Venue where claim arose. In 1966, 28 U.S.C.A. § 1391 was amended to add as a place of proper venue the district "in which the claim arose." On construction of this provision, see Comment, Federal Venue: Locating the Place Where the Claim Arose, 54 Tex.L.Rev. 392 (1976).

3. Venue in Removed Actions

In an action commenced in state court and thereafter removed to federal court, the proper venue is the district in which is located the state court from which removal is taken. See 28 U.S.C.A. § 1441(a); Polizzi v. Cowles Magazines, Inc., 345 U.S. 663, 73 S.Ct. 900, 97 L.Ed. 1331 (1953).

4. Appellate Review of Venue Determinations

A judgment of dismissal for improper venue in federal court is appealable, the same as any other final judgment. An order denying a motion to dismiss for improper venue is not appealable of right in the federal courts, but is reviewable on appeal from the final judgment rendered after trial. In view of the risks posed by denial of such a motion, shouldn't the provisions of 28 U.S.C.A. § 1292(b), permitting interlocutory appeals upon leave of the district and appellate courts, be liberally applied in such a situation? See, e.g., Ellicott Mach. Corp. v. Modern Welding Co., 502 F.2d 178 (4th Cir. 1974). See Wright & Miller § 3855.

IN RE KOREAN AIR LINES DISASTER OF SEPTEMBER 1, 1983

United States Court of Appeals for the District of Columbia, 1987.
829 F.2d 1171.*

RUTH BADER GINSBURG, CIRCUIT JUDGE:

This case arises out of an air disaster and raises turbulent federal questions. On September 1, 1983, Korean Air Lines (KAL) Flight 007, a commercial craft departing from Kennedy Airport in New York and bound for Seoul, South Korea, was destroyed over the Sea of Japan by Soviet Union military aircraft. Wrongful death actions were filed against KAL in several federal district courts; the Judicial Panel on Multidistrict Litigation transferred these actions to the District Court for the District of Columbia for pretrial proceedings pursuant to 28 U.S.C. § 1407 ("[C]ivil actions involving one or more common questions of fact . . . pending in different districts . . . may be transferred to any district for coordinated or consolidated pretrial proceedings.").

The nub of the controversy relates to the per passenger damage limitation of the Warsaw Convention,[1] raised to $75,000 by an accord among airlines known as the Montreal Agreement.[2] By motion for partial summary judgment, plaintiffs sought a declaration "that [KAL] is liable without fault for compensatory damages without any limitation of $75,000." Joint Appendix (J.A.) at 26. Plaintiffs grounded this motion on the inadequate type size of the liability limitation notice printed on KAL passenger tickets. The notice appeared in 8 point type; the Montreal Agreement specifies 10 point type. Denying plaintiffs' motion, the district court, on July 25, 1985, held that KAL could avail itself of the $75,000 per passenger limitation. In re Korean Air Lines

---

* Some of the court's footnotes are omitted. The Supreme Court affirmed this judgment on other grounds sub nom. Chan v. Korean Air Lines, ___ U.S. ___, ___ S.Ct. ___, ___ L.Ed.2d ___, 57 U.S.L.W. 4432 (1989).

1. Convention for the Unification of Certain Rules Relating to International Transportation by Air, October 12, 1929, 49 Stat. 3000, T.S. No. 876, 137 L.N.T.S. 11, reprinted in 49 U.S.C. § 1502 note (1982).

2. Agreement Relating to Liability Limitations of the Warsaw Convention and the Hague Protocol, CAB Agreement 18900, 31 Fed.Reg. 7302 (1966) (approved by CAB Order E-23680, May 13, 1966).

Disaster of September 1, 1983, 664 F.Supp. 1463, 19 Av.L.Rep. (CCH) 17,584 (D.D.C.1985). In so ruling, the district court considered and rejected contrary Second Circuit precedent: In re Air Crash Disaster at Warsaw, Poland, on March 14, 1980, 705 F.2d 85 (2d Cir.), cert. denied, 464 U.S. 845, 104 S.Ct. 147, 78 L.Ed.2d 138 (1983).

On September 24, 1985, the district court certified for interlocutory appeal under 28 U.S.C. § 1292(b) the question whether KAL "is entitled to avail itself of the limitation of damages provided by the Warsaw Convention and Montreal Agreement despite its defective tickets." We ruled that the requirements of section 1292(b) were met and that "wise exercise of our discretion dictates that the appeal be allowed." D.C.Cir. Order filed April 8, 1986.

On January 30, 1987, after argument of the appeal, we remanded the record for clarification of the scope of the district court's order denying plaintiffs' partial summary judgment motion. Specifically, we observed that the cases consolidated in this appeal

> can be grouped into three categories on the basis of the fora in which they were originally filed and to which they are to be remanded at or before the conclusion of pretrial proceedings, unless the actions are earlier terminated: (a) the Southern and Eastern Districts of New York; (b) the Eastern District of Michigan and the District of Massachusetts; and (c) the District of Columbia. The district judge, in his order denying plaintiffs' motion for partial summary judgment, did not expressly consider the contention that, by analogy to the principle set forth in Van Dusen v. Barrack, 376 U.S. 612, 84 S.Ct. 805, 11 L.Ed.2d 945 (1964), he was bound by Second Circuit precedent in resolving the claims of plaintiffs in the first category enumerated above.
>
> The extent of a transferee court's authority under 28 U.S.C. § 1407 independently to resolve issues of [federal] law already passed upon by the federal court of appeals for the circuit in which the transferor forum is located is apparently a question of first impression, and our consideration of this issue is hampered by uncertainty as to which plaintiffs were covered by the district court's July 1985 order.

D.C.Cir. Order filed January 30, 1987.

By Memorandum dated May 7, 1987, 664 F.Supp. 1488, the district court held that its July 25, 1985 decision denying plaintiffs' partial summary judgment motion applies to all three categories of cases described in this court's January 30, 1987 remand-for-clarification order. We now affirm the district court's dispositions. On the Warsaw Convention/Montreal Agreement $75,000 per passenger damage limitation issue, we adopt as our opinion the comprehensive July 25, 1985 decision of the district court, reported at 664 F.Supp. 1463. We set out below our reasons for concluding that the district court properly adhered to its own interpretation of the Warsaw Convention/Montreal

Agreement in all actions, including those transferred from district courts within the Second Circuit.

The Supreme Court, in Van Dusen v. Barrack, 376 U.S. 612, 84 S.Ct. 805, 11 L.Ed.2d 945 (1964), addressed and resolved this question: when a defendant in a diversity action moves for a venue transfer under 28 U.S.C. § 1404(a),[3] which state's law applies post-transfer? The state law that would have applied in the transfer court adheres to the case, the Supreme Court held; in the Court's words, "with respect to state law," the venue change will accomplish "but a change of courtrooms." Van Dusen, 376 U.S. at 639, 84 S.Ct. at 821.[4]

The Van Dusen interpretation of 28 U.S.C. § 1404(a), as the latter applies in diversity actions, rests on principles advanced in Erie R.R. v. Tompkins, 304 U.S. 64, 58 S.Ct. 817, 82 L.Ed. 1188 (1938), and cases in the Erie line. Van Dusen, 376 U.S. at 637–40, 84 S.Ct. at 819–21; see particularly Klaxon Co. v. Stentor Elec. Mfg. Co., 313 U.S. 487, 61 S.Ct. 1020, 85 L.Ed. 1477 (1941) (on issues of state law arising in diversity cases, federal courts must apply choice-of-law rules of states in which they sit). Justice Goldberg explained for the Court in Van Dusen:

> [O]ur interpretation [of § 1404(a)] . . . is supported by the policy underlying Erie [.] . . . [W]e should ensure that the "accident" of federal diversity jurisdiction does not enable a party to utilize a transfer to achieve a result in federal court which could not have been achieved in the courts of the State where the action was filed. . . . What Erie and the cases following it have sought was an identity or uniformity between federal and state courts; and the fact that in most instances this could be achieved by directing federal courts to apply the laws of the States "in which they sit" should not obscure that, in applying the same reasoning to § 1404(a), the critical identity to be maintained is between the federal district court which decides the case and the courts of the State in which the action was filed.

Van Dusen, 376 U.S. at 637–39, 84 S.Ct. at 820 (footnotes omitted).

Defendants in Van Dusen sought to transfer the case from the Eastern District of Pennsylvania to the District of Massachusetts. (Massachusetts, but not Pennsylvania, limited the damages plaintiffs could recover.) Were the transfer to be made, the Supreme Court

3. Under this change of venue prescription, "[f]or the convenience of parties and witnesses, in the interest of justice, a district court may transfer any civil action to any other district or division where it might have been brought."

4. The Van Dusen Court expressly did not decide whether the law of the state in which the transferor court sits would apply if plaintiff rather than defendant sought the transfer, or if a state court in the transferor court's state would dismiss the case on forum non conveniens grounds.

Van Dusen, 376 U.S. at 640, 84 S.Ct. at 821. Wright, Miller & Cooper indicate that several courts have applied the law of the transferor court even when plaintiff, rather than defendant, moves for a transfer. 15 C. Wright, A. Miller & E. Cooper, Federal Practice and Procedure § 3846, at 367 (2d ed. 1986). A strong argument, however, favors application of the law of the transferee state in such instances. See ALI, Study of Division of Jurisdiction Between State and Federal Courts, § 1306(c) & commentary (1969).

ruled, though all further proceedings would take place in the Massachusetts district court, Pennsylvania law, not Massachusetts law, would furnish the governing state prescriptions.

The question before us is whether the *Van Dusen* rule—that the law applicable in the transferor forum attends the transfer—should apply to transferred federal claims. It is a question meriting attention from Higher Authority. Congress, it appears, has not focused on the issue,[5] nor has the Supreme Court addressed it. * * * Recognizing that the question is perplexing, particularly in the context of 28 U.S.C. § 1407, a statute authorizing transfers only for pretrial purposes, we are persuaded by thoughtful commentary that "the transferee court [should] be free to decide a federal claim in the manner it views as correct without deferring to the interpretation of the transferor circuit." Marcus, Conflict Among Circuits and Transfers Within the Federal Judicial System, 93 Yale L.J. 677, 721 (1984); see also Steinman, Law of the Case: A Judicial Puzzle in Consolidated and Transferred Cases and in Multidistrict Litigation, 135 U.Pa.L.Rev. 595, 662–706 (1987).

As the district court stressed in response to our remand, the *Erie* policies served by the *Van Dusen* decision do not figure in the calculus when the law to be applied is federal, not state. Given the reality of conflict among the circuits on the proper interpretation of federal law, however, why deny to a plaintiff with a federal claim the "venue privilege" a diversity claimant enjoys? Plaintiffs in the *Van Dusen* situation could effectively pick Pennsylvania rather than Massachusetts law and retain the benefit of that choice after transfer. Why deny a similar right of selection and retention to plaintiffs who would fare better under the Second Circuit's interpretation of federal law than under the D.C. Circuit's interpretation?

The point has been cogently made that venue provisions are designed with geographical convenience in mind, and not to "guarantee that the plaintiff will be able to select the law that will govern the case." Piper Aircraft Co. v. Reyno, 454 U.S. 235, 257 n. 24, 102 S.Ct. 252, 266 n. 24, 70 L.Ed.2d 419 (1981); see Marcus, supra, 93 Yale L.J. at 696–701. In diversity cases, however, federal courts are governed by *Klaxon* and therefore may not compose federal choice-of-law principles; instead, they must look to state prescriptions in determining which state's law applies. With "no federal choice-of-law principles that favor the application of the law of one state over the law of another," the

---

5. In Senate hearings on the bill that eventually became the multidistrict litigation statute, two witnesses stated that *Van Dusen* would apply to choice-of-law issues under the measure. The experience of those witnesses related to federal claims for antitrust law violations and it may be that they intended their statements to cover such claims. See Multidistrict Litigation: Hearings on S. 3815 Before the Sub-comm. on Improvements in Judicial Machinery of the Senate Comm. on the Judiciary, 89th Cong., 2d Sess. 13, 25 (1966) (statements of Dean Phil Neal and Judge William Becker). The Supreme Court, however, in explicit and repeated qualifications, confined its *Van Dusen* opinion to questions of state law. See 376 U.S. at 625–26, 630, 633, 635, 639, 84 S.Ct. at 813–14, 816, 817, 818, 820. * * *

diversity plaintiff's opening move or "venue privilege" ordinarily fills the gap—it "prevails by default." Marcus, supra, 93 Yale L.J. at 700–01. For the adjudication of federal claims, on the other hand, "[t]he federal courts comprise a single system [in which each tribunal endeavors to apply] a single body of law," H.L. Green Co. v. MacMahon, 312 F.2d 650, 652 (2d Cir.1962), cert. denied, 372 U.S. 928, 83 S.Ct. 876, 9 L.Ed.2d 736 (1963); there is no compelling reason to allow plaintiff to capture the most favorable interpretation of that law simply and solely by virtue of his or her right to choose the place to open the fray.

As summarized in the commentary we find persuasive:

> The *Van Dusen* Court stressed the venue privilege because [under *Klaxon*] there is no federal principle by which to select the state law that should govern diversity cases. Where federal claims are transferred, however, the principle that the transferee federal court is competent to decide federal issues correctly indicates that the transferee's interpretation should apply.
>
>   . . .
>
> For federal courts, the most significant choice-of-law difference between issues of state law and issues of federal law is that they lack competence to [develop rules of decision for] the former and are presumptively competent to decide the latter. . . . [T]he federal courts have not only the power but the duty to decide [issues of federal law] correctly. There is no room in the federal system of review for rote acceptance of the decision of a court outside the chain of direct review. If a federal court simply accepts the interpretation of another circuit without [independently] addressing the merits, it is not doing its job.

Marcus, supra, 93 Yale L.J. at 679, 702; see also Friendly, The "Law of the Circuit" and All That, 46 St. John's L.Rev. 406, 412 (1972) ("I take [*Van Dusen*] to be limited to choices of *state* law.") (emphasis in original).

Application of *Van Dusen* in the matter before us, we emphasize, would not produce uniformity. There would be one interpretation of federal law for the cases initially filed in districts within the Second Circuit, and an opposing interpretation for cases filed elsewhere. Applying divergent interpretations of the governing federal law to plaintiffs, depending solely upon where they initially filed suit, would surely reduce the efficiencies achievable through consolidated preparatory proceedings. Indeed, because there is ultimately a single proper interpretation of federal law, the attempt to ascertain and apply diverse circuit interpretations simultaneously is inherently self-contradictory. Our system contemplates differences between different states' laws; thus a multidistrict judge asked to apply divergent state positions on a point of law would face a coherent, if sometimes difficult, task. But it is logically inconsistent to require one judge to apply simultaneously different and conflicting interpretations of what is supposed to be a unitary federal law.[8]

The district judge in the instant case observed that

> [i]f . . . more than one interpretation of federal law exists, the Supreme Court of the United States can finally determine the issue and restore uniformity in the federal system. The uniformity achieved in this [way] is an "informed uniformity" unlike the "blind uniformity" which would result from one court applying the interpretation of another by rote.

May 7, 1987 D.D.C. Memorandum 664 F.Supp. at 1489. We agree. The federal courts spread across the country owe respect to each other's efforts and should strive to avoid conflicts, but each has an obligation to engage independently in reasoned analysis. Binding precedent for all is set only by the Supreme Court, and for the district courts within a circuit, only by the court of appeals for that circuit.

We return, finally, to the most anomalous feature of this case. As earlier observed, we deal here not with an "all-purpose" transfer under 28 U.S.C. § 1404(a), but with a transfer under 28 U.S.C. § 1407 "for coordinated or consolidated pretrial proceedings." We have held, in accord with the district court, that the law of a transferor forum on a federal question—here, the law of the Second Circuit—merits close consideration, but does not have stare decisis effect in a transferee forum situated in another circuit. Should the several cases consolidated for pretrial preparation in the instant proceeding eventually return to transferor courts outside this circuit,[9] would our district court's Warsaw Convention/Montreal Agreement ruling, which we have affirmed, have binding force? We believe it should, as "law of the case," for if it did not, transfers under 28 U.S.C. § 1407 could be counterproductive, i.e., capable of generating rather than reducing the duplication and protraction Congress sought to check. See Steinman, supra, 135 U.Pa.L.Rev. at 664–67, 700–704. On this issue in the case at hand, however, our circuit is not positioned to speak the last word.

* * *

Affirmed.

D.H. GINSBURG, CIRCUIT JUDGE, concurring in which WILLIAMS, CIRCUIT JUDGE, joins:

---

8. Even if it appears plausible to legal minds to mete out in a consolidated case one version of federal law to plaintiffs whose counsel filed in the Southern or Eastern District of New York, another to plaintiffs whose counsel filed in the District Court for the District of Columbia, it would be difficult to explain the rationality of such divergencies to the lay persons served by the federal judicial system.

9. In practice, it has been reported, most cases transferred under § 1407 are not remanded. See 1986 Ann.Rep.Director

Admin.Off.U.S. Courts 128 (as of June 30, 1986, 15,026 actions had been subject to § 1407 proceedings; of those, 10,903 had been terminated by the transferee court); Steinman, Law of the Case: A Judicial Puzzle in Consolidated and Transferred Cases and In Multidistrict Litigation, 135 U.Pa.L.Rev. 595, 667 & n. 247, 700 & nn. 410, 411 (1987); Weigel, The Judicial Panel on Multidistrict Litigation, Transferor Courts, and Transferee Courts, 78 F.R.D. 575, 583 (1978).

* * *

When applied only to the District of Columbia and New York cases, adherence to the case law of the transferor circuit would be a fairly easy procedure for the transferee district court. It is almost a certainty, however, that the bifurcated ruling it produces would place the District of Columbia and New York cases on increasingly divergent courses. The District of Columbia plaintiffs, in conducting discovery, will have to pursue evidence of fault on the part of KAL, whereas the New York plaintiffs would be able to recover without such a showing. The entire course of discovery * * * would differ entirely between what would have become, in effect, two separate groups of consolidated cases. These differences would be further magnified by the vastly different incentives for settlement facing the two groups of plaintiffs. The District of Columbia plaintiffs, having to prove fault, will presumably be more amenable to settlement than would be the New York plaintiffs. All in all, therefore, it is unlikely that the bifurcated ruling would preserve, to any significant extent, either the efficiency or the consistency that section 1407(a) was intended to promote.

Under the New York plaintiffs' rule, therefore, the threat that the Second Circuit would reverse * * * and thereby unravel the New York cases is averted, in effect, by preemptively unraveling them in the transferee court. This seems to be a high price to pay—a virtual abandonment of the efficiency and consistency goals of section 1407(a)—to protect against a threat, i.e. unraveling in the transferor circuit courts, that could instead be avoided, at no cost to consistency and at a much lower cost in efficiency, through interlocutory appeal to the transferee circuit court and subsequent application by the transferor circuit of the law of the case doctrine.

The price that must be paid in abandoning the norm of independent judgment, however, looms even larger when one realizes that the New York plaintiffs have presented us with the deceptively easy alternative of applying [In re Air Crash Disaster at Warsaw, Poland, 705 F.2d 85 (2d Cir.1983)] to the New York cases, without suggesting to us how the district judge should have ruled with respect to the cases from districts in the First and Sixth Circuits, which have not decided this issue. In attempting to rule as would a district court in those circuits, he could have simply applied his own ruling to those cases, happy to believe that, if called upon, those circuits would see things his way. Or, taking to heart the New York plaintiffs' contention that, under *Van Dusen*, transfer should result in merely "a change of courtrooms" [20] he could have seriously attempted to divine how the First and Sixth Circuits might interpret the Convention if called upon to do so.

* * *

The conduct of multidistrict litigation, which is invariably time consuming as it is, will grind to a standstill while transferee judges

---

20. 376 U.S. at 639, 84 S.Ct. at 821.

read separate briefs, each based on the case law of a transferor circuit, on a single issue of federal law. Much of the advantage that transfer was intended to produce, and particularly the desiderata of furthering efficiency and preventing inconsistent rulings, will be lost by requiring transferee judges to wear a number of judicial hats. It is the prospect of this kind of quagmire that is likely to yield the result feared by the Court in *Van Dusen*—that courts would be "reluctant to grant transfers" and thereby "frustrate the remedial purposes of [section 1407]." [26] It may well be preferable to have multidistrict litigation remain dispersed in the courts of origin than to have transferee judges burdened with the hopelessly complex task of sitting as several federal judges at once.[27] Consequently, even though having transferee judges exercise independent judgment may in isolated instances result in an unraveling of a transferred case, I believe that this approach, although not a perfect solution, is by far the less problematic and the more consistent with the intent of Congress in enacting section 1407.

*   *   *

NOTE ON FEDERAL VENUE TRANSFERS

1. For further discussion of transfers under 28 U.S.C.A. § 1407, see Further Note on Case Management, infra p. 1234.

2. *Van Dusen v. Barrack,* 376 U.S. 612, 84 S.Ct. 805, 11 L.Ed.2d 945 (1964), held that the transferee court in a diversity case transferred under 28 U.S.C.A. § 1404(a) must apply the state law which would have been applied by the *tranferor* court. As indicated in *Korean Air Lines,* this result was held to be compelled by the underlying rationale of Erie R. Co. v. Tompkins and its progeny. Section 1404(a) is essentially a codification of the *forum non conveniens* doctrine as adopted by the Supreme Court in Gulf Oil Corp. v. Gilbert, 330 U.S. 501, 67 S.Ct. 839, 91 L.Ed. 1055 (1947), with the difference that transfer rather than dismissal is the consequence of a finding of inconvenience. See Piper Aircraft Co. v. Reyno, supra p. 427, and the Note following. This difference has possibly important consequences for the *Erie* questions involved, because the consequence of dismissal of a state court action on *forum non conveniens* grounds is that plaintiff, if she is to pursue her case at all, must refile it in another state, thus subjecting herself to that state's laws and other rules of decision. In deciding what state's law should apply following a § 1404(a) transfer, should fidelity to *Erie* require that the transferor court make a finding as to whether the action would have been dismissed on *forum non conveniens* grounds had it been filed in state court? Could a federal court ever decide such a question with any assurance of accuracy?

3. The Court in *Van Dusen* described § 1404(a) as a "federal judicial housekeeping measure" dealing with the place of litigation in cases where venue is proper, but where considerations of convenience and fairness call for "a change of courtrooms." By contrast, 28 U.S.C.A. § 1406(a) deals with the

---

26. *Van Dusen,* 376 U.S. at 636, 84 S.Ct. at 819.

27. This is particularly the case insofar as the rule applicable to transferee judges under section 1407(a) is applied as well in the analogous context of a transfer under section 1404(a). The prospect of a trial presided over by a judge expected to simulate different district courts throughout as many as twelve circuits is likely to discourage any court from ordering transfer under section 1404(a).

transfer of cases where venue is improper and authorizes a federal district court to transfer such a case "to any district or division in which it could have been brought." What are the requisites for a valid exercise by a transferor court of the power conferred by § 1406(a)? Must it have jurisdiction of the subject matter of the action? In personam jurisdiction over the defendant? In Goldlawr, Inc. v. Heiman, 369 U.S. 463, 82 S.Ct. 913, 8 L.Ed.2d 39 (1962), the Supreme Court held that personal jurisdiction over the defendant is not necessary in order for a court to transfer a case under § 1406(a). Should the same rule apply in cases where venue is properly laid? The circuits are split on this issue. See the discussion in Ellis v. Great Southwestern Corp., 646 F.2d 1099 (5th Cir.1981). If transfer under § 1404(a) is held unavailable where personal jurisdiction is lacking, can a court nonetheless transfer the case under § 1406(a), on the argument that it applies not merely where venue is improper, but also where there is an "obstacle [to] * * * an expeditious and orderly adjudication" on the merits? That was the conclusion of the court in Dubin v. United States, 380 F.2d 813 (5th Cir.1967). Compare Corke v. Sameiet M.S. Song of Norway, 572 F.2d 77 (2d Cir.1978), and *Ellis,* supra. The statute under which the case is transferred can be important because, under *Van Dusen,* the law of the transferor court applies in cases transferred under § 1404(a), while the law of the transferee court normally applies in cases transferred under § 1406(a). See, e.g., Martin v. Stokes, 623 F.2d 469 (6th Cir.1980). What state's choice of law rules should apply when a case is transferred under § 1404(a) on the ground of a lack of personal jurisdiction? When a case is transferred under § 1406(a)? See *Ellis,* supra.

The issue of the transferability of cases where the court lacks personal jurisdiction over the defendant may have been resolved by 28 U.S.C.A. § 1631, enacted in 1982, which authorizes transfers where there is a "want of jurisdiction." The Senate Report, by limiting its discussion to subject matter jurisdiction, leaves the inference that the section does not apply to personal jurisdiction, notwithstanding the unrestricted statutory language. See supra, pp. 527–528. Several courts have applied the statute to personal jurisdiction, though none has addressed the issue of the statute's ambiguity. See, e.g., Ross v. Colorado Outward Bound School, Inc., 822 F.2d 1524 (10th Cir.1987). Assuming that § 1631 does apply to personal jurisdiction and that it is now the proper mechanism for transferring cases where personal jurisdiction is lacking, regardless of whether venue is proper in the transferor court, then, under the terms of the statute, the law of the transferee court applies. See, e.g., Western Smelting & Metals, Inc. v. Slater Steel, Inc., 621 F.Supp. 578 (N.D.Ind.1985), and *Ross,* supra.

4. Conversely, under either § 1404(a) or § 1406(a), may a case be transferred to a district that lacks either subject matter or personal jurisdiction over the defendant? Generally speaking, such a case may not be transferred. See, e.g., Hoffman v. Blaski, 363 U.S. 335, 80 S.Ct. 1084, 4 L.Ed.2d 1254 (1960), where the Supreme Court held that a transfer under § 1404(a) was not permitted where the transferee court lacked both venue and personal jurisdiction, saying that such a forum was not a forum where the action "might have been brought" and that transfer is permitted only where plaintiff had "an unqualified right to bring suit" in the transferee court at the time the original action was filed. See also Van Dusen v. Barrack, supra; 15 Wright & Miller §§ 3827 and 3845.

5. In view of § 1404(a), what viability remains for the doctrine of *forum non conveniens* in a federal district court? See, e.g., Piper Aircraft Co. v. Reyno, supra p. 427; Fitzgerald v. Texaco, Inc., 521 F.2d 448 (2d Cir.1975).

"we command" / *higher ct tells lwr ct what to + not to do*

6.　A step toward localizing federal venue is evidenced by the Mandamus and Venue Act of 1962 (28 U.S.C.A. § 1391(e), which permits mandamus actions against federal officers and agencies to be brought in the district where the cause of action arose or where the plaintiff resides instead of exclusively in Washington, D.C.　See Stafford v. Briggs, 444 U.S. 527, 100 S.Ct. 774, 63 L.Ed. 2d 1 (1980).　Proponents of the "New Federalism" espouse amending the venue statutes to require that issues affecting particular localities be tried by local federal courts.　This "anti-Washington" feeling has focused most strongly on actions where the Federal Government is a party, and most particularly on environmental issues.　Under current venue statutes, such suits may be brought in Washington, D.C., and generally are brought there by national plaintiffs litigating national issues even though affecting a local area.　For example, motorboating on a western lake was enjoined by a federal judge sitting in the District of Columbia.　Defenders of Wildlife v. Andrus, 455 F.Supp. 446 (D.D.C.1978).　For an analysis of the problem and proposed solutions, see Currie, Venue and the Sagebrush Rebellion, in Venue at the Crossroads, p. 65 (National Legal Center for the Public Interest, 1982).　See also Sunstein, Participation, Public Law, and Venue Reform, 49 U.Chi.L.Rev. 976 (1982).

Part V

THE SIZE OF THE LITIGATION

INTRODUCTORY NOTE ON THE SIZE OF THE LITIGATION

1. The Legal Relationships Affected

A dispute serious enough to give rise to the possibility of litigation may be a relatively isolated or isolable occurrence of simple dimension. Such, for example, might be a punch in the nose at the corner tavern. More frequently, however, a dispute that results in legal controversy impinges on a whole complex of relationships which may have legal significance. A simple automobile accident involving a collision of a truck driven by a delivery boy thus may affect the following relationships:

(1) The relationship between the boy and his parents regarding authority and responsibility for providing him with medical and convalescent care and for the benefits and burdens of his personal and economic future;

(2) The relationship of the boy to insurers, if such there be, who have written insurance in favor of his parents for medical and surgical care for members of the family unit;

(3) The relationship of the boy and his parents to the boy's employer, and their respective insurers, if any, regarding the employer's liability for the boy's injuries and the liability of the boy and his parents to the employer for damage to the truck;

(4) The relationship of the boy and his parents and his employer to those who manufactured, sold and serviced the truck, if mechanical failure of the truck played any apparent part in the accident;

(5) The relationship of the boy and his parents and his employer and the manufacturer, seller and servicer of the truck, and their respective insurers, to the driver and the owner of the other car, and their respective insurers, in respect to liability for injuries and property damage that may have been sustained by the other owner and driver;

(6) The relationship inter sese of the driver and the owner of the other car in respect to liability for the injuries and property damage sustained respectively by them.

The effects of the controversy may be felt by others with more remote concerns. For example, if as a consequence of the reduction to judgment and execution of one or more claims that could arise out of the accident, one of the participants is rendered financially insolvent, then relationships between the insolvent and those with whom she has a financial interdependency may be involved. Furthermore, if as a consequence of the litigation regarding one or more of the affected relationships a new or unsettled point of law is established, it may have significance for many, perhaps countless others, who are similarly situated.

Of the potential ramifications of most litigated controversies, few are actually the subject of litigation in a particular case. Litigation may be avoided because the legal status of the relationship is sufficiently clear that all concerned acquiesce in a single view of it; because the amount involved is too little to justify the expense and delay of disputation; because the parties do not wish to press their claims to the fullest; because the parties strike a bargain in which mutually satisfactory concessions are made; or because no one thought about the particular matter and it went by default. Nevertheless, when the dispute concerns a transaction that is itself complex, the likelihood that there will be actual controversy over a number of relationships sharply increases.

It should be fairly obvious that a single court at a single time cannot effectively handle all the disputes that may arise out of a given sequence of events of even middling complexity. Presumably the outer boundary for the size of litigation is the biological limit of human capacity for sustained thought and attention. Limitations short of this boundary are established by the substantive law insofar as it declares that some consequences to some relationships are beyond the pale of legal protection. Within these limitations, should more circumscribed boundaries be prescribed? See McCoid, A Single Package for Multiparty Disputes, 28 Stan.L.Rev. 707 (1976), for a general view.

2. Plaintiff's Viewpoint

The person who has suffered adversity as the result of a change in the out-of-court status quo ordinarily has the strongest interest in seeing that official action is taken to rectify the situation. This interest may be paralleled or indeed exceeded by a public official interest. But in most judicial systems, the initiative for seeking private restitution ordinarily lies with the parties affected by the change in status quo, and in particular with the injured party. Hence, the initial decision about the size of the litigation is usually made by the injured party in framing his complaint as plaintiff. That decision must, of course, be made within the limits laid down by the procedural rules governing the size of litigation. And the decision may be modified, perhaps radically modified, at the instance of the defendant or at the instance of the court *sua sponte*. Nevertheless, the point holds that the plaintiff's decision is always influential and usually determinative of the shape that the litigation will take. What considerations go into the plaintiff's decision?

3. Defendant's Viewpoint

Depending on how the plaintiff frames his complaint and on other strategic and tactical considerations, the defendant may acquiesce in the boundaries of the litigation determined by the plaintiff. She may attempt to contract or expand them. What are the considerations that go into the defendant's decision?

4. The Judicial Viewpoint

The efforts of the parties to fix the size of the litigation will be passed upon by the court in response to objections from the opposing parties and, in some instances, on the court's own motion. The rules are cast in various terms: some are permissive, affording one party or the other the privilege of fixing the limits of the litigation within some designated boundaries; some are compulsory, requiring one party or the other to expand the limits of the litigation to designated boundaries; some are discretionary with the court, permitting the court to fix the limits of the litigation on an ad hoc basis.

A. COLLATERAL REGULATION OF THE SIZE OF THE LITIGATION

INTRODUCTORY NOTE ON COLLATERALLY REGULATING LITIGATION SIZE

The Federal Rules and rule systems patterned on them all deal expressly with the size of the litigation. Rules of "joinder" specify what claims and what parties a plaintiff may include in the suit he frames, and the circumstances under which additional parties may or must be brought in as participants. See F.R.C.P. 8(a), 8(e)(2), 13, 14, 17–25, 42; C.C.P. 367–390, 426.10–428.80; Ill.C.C.P. §§ 2–403 to 2–414, 2–608, 2–613, 2–614, 2–1006; N.Y.C.P.L.R. §§ 601–603, 1001–1026. We shall deal with these systems presently. There are, however, other sets of rules that also affect the size of the litigation, namely, the rules of res judicata and collateral estoppel, those governing recognition of judgments from other jurisdictions, and those that permit a court to stay one proceeding because a related one is pending. These are largely case-law rather than statute or statute-like rules, and traditionally have not been thought to regulate joinder. From the litigants' viewpoint, however, their practical consequence is the same as rules of joinder, for they specify consequences that flow from the adjudication of a case under particular conditions of claim or party joinder. Moreover, the rules of res judicata and collateral estoppel are taken into account in applying the joinder rules. Hence, we proceed to consider these rules prior to those of joinder.

1. RES JUDICATA AND COLLATERAL ESTOPPEL

a. PRECLUSION AS BETWEEN THE SAME PARTIES

INTRODUCTORY NOTE ON RES JUDICATA

1. The Doctrine

Restatement Second of Judgments § 17, Effects of Former Adjudication—General Rules:

"A valid and final personal judgment is conclusive between the parties, except on appeal or other direct review, to the following extent:

"(1) If the judgment is in favor of the plaintiff, the claim is extinguished and merged in the judgment and a new claim may arise on the judgment (see § 18);

"(2) If the judgment is in favor of the defendant, the claim is extinguished and the judgment bars a subsequent action on that claim (see § 19);

"(3) A judgment in favor of either the plaintiff or the defendant is conclusive, in a subsequent action between them on the same or a different claim, with respect to any issue actually litigated and determined if its determination was essential to that judgment (see § 27)."

These general rules are subject to exceptions: as to clauses (1) and (2), see §§ 20 and 26; as to clause (3), see § 28.

The effects of a judgment described above are collectively referred to as "res judicata." In traditional terminology this general category was subdivided into two: "res judicata" as to the "cause of action," which included the effects of merger and bar referred to in § 17(1) and (2), above; and "collateral estoppel," which included the effect on issues referred to in § 17(3), above. See, e.g., Note, Developments in the Law—Res Judicata, 65 Harv.L.Rev. 818 (1952). The modern terminology for these subcategories is that the effect on the "cause of action" or claim, i.e., merger and bar, is called "claim preclusion"; the effect on issues determined is called "issue preclusion."

2. The Critical Variables

(a) The scope of "claim" or "cause of action" for purposes of merger or bar (claim preclusion). The established doctrine is that preclusion operates even though plaintiff could present "evidence or grounds or theories of the case not presented in the first action" or seeks "remedies or forms of relief not demanded in the first action." Restatement Second of Judgments § 25. But there are lots of exceptions.

Restatement Second of Judgments § 26, Exceptions to the General Rule Concerning Splitting:

"(1) When any of the following circumstances exists, the general rule of § 24 does not apply to extinguish the claim, and part or all of the claim subsists as a possible basis for a second action by the plaintiff against the defendant:

"(a) The parties have agreed in terms or in effect that the plaintiff may split his claim, or the defendant has acquiesced therein; or

"(b) The court in the first action has expressly reserved the plaintiff's right to maintain the second action; or

"(c) The plaintiff was unable to rely on a certain theory of the case or to seek a certain remedy or form of relief in the first action because of the limitations on the subject matter jurisdiction of the courts or restrictions on their authority to entertain multiple theories or demands for multiple remedies or forms of relief in a single action, and the plaintiff desires in the second action to rely on that theory or to seek that remedy or form of relief; or

"(d) The judgment in the first action was plainly inconsistent with the fair and equitable implementation of a statutory or constitutional scheme, or it is the sense of the scheme that the plaintiff should be permitted to split his claim; or

"(e) For reasons of substantive policy in a case involving a continuing or recurrent wrong, the plaintiff is given an option to sue once for the total harm, both past and prospective, or to sue from time to time for the damages incurred to the date of suit, and chooses the later course; or

"(f) It is clearly and convincingly shown that the policies favoring preclusion of a second action are overcome for an extraordinary reason, such as the apparent invalidity of a continuing restraint or condition having a vital relation to personal liberty or the failure of the prior litigation to yield a coherent disposition of the controversy. * * *"

(b) The "issue," and whether it was decided, for purposes of issue preclusion.

Restatement Second of Judgments § 27, Comment c, on what is the "same" issue:

> "One of the most difficult problems in the application of the rule of this Section is to delineate the issue on which litigation is, or is not, foreclosed by the prior judgment. The problem involves a balancing of important interests: on the one hand, a desire not to deprive a litigant of an adequate day in court; on the other hand, a desire to prevent repetitious litigation of what is essentially the same dispute. When there is a lack of total identity between the particular matter presented in the second action and that presented in the first, there are several factors that should be considered in deciding whether for purposes of the rule of this Section the 'issue' in the two proceedings is the same, for example: Is there a substantial overlap between the evidence or argument to be advanced in the second proceeding and that advanced in the first? Does the new evidence or argument involve application of the same rule of law as that involved in the prior proceeding? Could pretrial preparation and discovery relating to the matter presented in the first action reasonably be expected to have embraced the matter sought to be presented in the second? How closely related are the claims involved in the two proceedings?"

3. Election of Remedies

The early common law had no doctrine of res judicata in the modern sense. Unless the statute of limitations prevented him, generally speaking a plaintiff could sue under one writ and, if unsuccessful, thereafter sue on another. While and to the extent that the writs were mutually exclusive, this privilege theoretically worked out fairly: if plaintiff failed in the first action because the wrong writ was chosen, in justice he should be able to try anew with the correct writ; if he failed in the first action on the merits, then that writ was the correct one and the record therein would estop him from maintaining the second action. But by the middle of the 18th century, the courts had so expanded the scope of many writs that there were large areas of overlap. Hence, a plaintiff often could bring successive actions on different writs, asserting substantially the same claim. To meet this evasion of the limits of the writ structure, the common law courts fashioned the doctrine of "election of remedies": a plaintiff who chose a writ on which he could recover, if the merits so disclosed, was deemed to have "elected" his remedy and was precluded from subsequently using another writ. The rule thus accomplished, and was intended to accomplish, much the same objectives as the present rule of merger and bar. See Hitchin v. Campbell, 2 W. Blackstone 827, 96 E.R. 487 (K.B. 1771).

In the 19th century in the United States, the "election of remedies" doctrine was extended to include equitable remedies: A plaintiff who had available to him a remedy at law (such as damages for deceit in the inducement of a contract) and a remedy in equity (such as rescission of the contract for fraud) and who sought one or the other was thereby deemed to have "elected" his remedy to the exclusion of the other. Insofar as the "election" doctrine was applied against a successful plaintiff seeking additional relief in a second action, it covered substantially the same ground as the modern rule of "merger." Insofar as it was applied against a plaintiff who had lost, e.g., for failure to prove fraud, it covered substantially the same ground as the modern rule of "bar." But in at least two respects it was sometimes applied with harsh consequences: First, a plaintiff having "elected" a remedy which he could not obtain for some reason idiosyncratic to that remedy (e.g., laches precluding a rescission) was in some jurisdictions nevertheless precluded by his "election" from pursuing his other remedy. Second, in those jurisdictions where law and equity remained separate a plaintiff could not assert his two potential remedies in the same suit, so that the statute of limitations would ordinarily have run by the time he had been authoritatively advised that his choice of remedy was wrong. See generally Note, Election of Remedies: A Delusion?, 38 Colum.L. Rev. 292 (1938).

Under modern codes and the Federal Rules, these results are avoided by allowing plaintiff to seek remedies in the alternative and to have both go to the trier of fact. In view of this privilege, is there any reason why pursuit of one remedy against a defendant should not preclude subsequent pursuit of a parallel remedy? See Restatement Second of Judgments § 25, supra; e.g., Anno., 38 A.L.R.3d 323 (decree of specific performance precludes subsequent damages action for same breach).

For a modern application of the "election of remedies" rule, see, e.g., Carter v. Superior Court, 142 Cal.App.2d 350, 298 P.2d 598 (1956) (employee, intentionally injured by his employer and thus having the option of claiming workmen's compensation or suing for civil damages, is precluded from seeking the latter by successfully prosecuting claim for the former); but cf. Unruh v. Truck Ins. Exchange, 7 Cal.3d 616, 102 Cal.Rptr. 815, 498 P.2d 1063 (1972). See also Thomas v. Washington Gas Light Co., 448 U.S. 261, 100 S.Ct. 2647, 65 L.Ed.2d 757 (1980). Related to but different from the rule of issue preclusion is the rule, or proposition, that a party may not assert a factual contention at variance with a contention she made in previous litigation. See, e.g., Scarano v. Central R. Co. of N.J., 203 F.2d 510 (3d Cir. 1953); cf. City of Kingsport v. Steel & Roof Structure, Inc., 500 F.2d 617 (6th Cir. 1974) (no preclusion from asserting contention at variance with one rejected in the first action). This proposition is usually referred to as an estoppel against taking inconsistent positions.

FEDERATED DEPARTMENT STORES, INC. v. MOITIE

Supreme Court of the United States, 1981.
452 U.S. 394, 101 S.Ct. 2424, 69 L.Ed.2d 103.*

JUSTICE REHNQUIST delivered the opinion of the Court.

The only question presented in this case is whether the Court of Appeals for the Ninth Circuit validly created an exception to the doctrine of res judicata.   * * *

I

In 1976 the United States brought an antitrust action against petitioners, owners of various department stores, alleging that they had violated § 1 of the Sherman Act, 15 U.S.C. § 1, by agreeing to fix the retail price of women's clothing sold in northern California. Seven parallel civil actions were subsequently filed by private plaintiffs seeking treble damages on behalf of proposed classes of retail purchasers, including that of respondent Moitie in state court (*Moitie I*) and

* Some of the Court's footnotes are omitted.

respondent Brown (*Brown I*) in the United States District Court for the Northern District of California. Each of these complaints tracked almost verbatim the allegations of the Government's complaint, though the *Moitie I* complaint referred solely to state law. All of the actions originally filed in the District Court were assigned to a single federal judge, and the *Moitie I* case was removed there on the basis of diversity of citizenship and federal question jurisdiction. The District Court dismissed all of the actions "in their entirety" on the ground that plaintiffs had not alleged an "injury" to their "business or property" within the meaning of § 4 of the Clayton Act, 15 U.S.C. § 15. Weinberg v. Federated Department Stores, 426 F.Supp. 880 (1977).

Plaintiffs in five of the suits appealed that judgment to the Court of Appeals for the Ninth Circuit. The single counsel representing Moitie and Brown, however, chose not to appeal and instead refiled the two actions in state court, *Moitie II* and *Brown II*. Although the complaints purported to raise only state-law claims, they made allegations similar to those made in the prior complaints, including that of the Government. Petitioners removed these new actions to the District Court for the Northern District of California and moved to have them dismissed on the ground of res judicata. In a decision rendered July 8, 1977, the District Court first denied respondents' motion to remand. It held that the complaints, though artfully couched in terms of state law, were "in many respects identical" with the prior complaints, and were thus properly removed to federal court because they raised "essentially federal law" claims. The court then concluded that because *Moitie II* and *Brown II* involved the "same parties, the same alleged offenses, and the same time periods" as *Moitie I* and *Brown I*, the doctrine of res judicata required that they be dismissed this time. Moitie and Brown appealed.

Pending that appeal, this Court on June 11, 1979 decided Reiter v. Sonotone Corp., 442 U.S. 330, 99 S.Ct. 2326, 60 L.Ed.2d 931, holding that retail purchasers can suffer an "injury" to their "business or property" as those terms are used in § 4 of the Clayton Act. On June 25, 1979, the Court of Appeals for the Ninth Circuit reversed and remanded the five cases which had been decided with *Moitie I* and *Brown I*, the cases that had been appealed, for further proceedings in light of *Reiter*.

When *Moitie II* and *Brown II* finally came before the Court of Appeals for the Ninth Circuit, the court reversed the decision of the District Court dismissing the cases. 611 F.2d 1267.[2] Though the court

---

2. The Court of Appeals also affirmed the District Court's conclusion that *Brown II* was properly removed to federal court, reasoning that the claims presented were "federal in nature." We agree that at least some of the claims had a sufficient federal character to support removal. As one treatise puts it, courts "will not permit plaintiff to use artful pleading to close off defendant's right to a federal forum . . . [and] occasionally the removal court will seek to determine whether the real nature of the claim is federal, regardless of plaintiff's characterization." 14 Wright, Miller & Cooper, Federal Practice and Procedure § 3722, pp. 565–566 (1976) (citing cases). The District Court applied that settled principle to the facts of this case. After

recognized that a "strict application of the doctrine of *res judicata* would preclude our review of the instant decision," id., at 1269, it refused to apply the doctrine to the facts of this case. It observed that the other five litigants in the *Weinberg* cases had successfully appealed the decision against them. It then asserted that "non-appealing parties may benefit from a reversal when their position is closely interwoven with that of appealing parties," and concluded that "because the instant dismissal rested on a case that has been effectively overruled," the doctrine of res judicata must give way to "public policy" and "simple justice." Id., at 1269–1270. * * *

9th circuit

II

There is little to be added to the doctrine of res judicata as developed in the case law of this Court. A final judgment on the merits of an action precludes the parties or their privies from relitigating issues that were or could have been raised in that action. Commissioner v. Sunnen, 333 U.S. 591, 597, 68 S.Ct. 715, 719, 92 L.Ed. 898 (1948); Cromwell v. County of Sac, 94 U.S. 351, 352–353, 24 L.Ed. 195 (1877). Nor are the res judicata consequences of a final, unappealed judgment on the merits altered by the fact that the judgment may have been wrong or rested on a legal principle subsequently overruled in another case. * * * As this Court explained in Baltimore Steamship S.S. Co. v. Phillips, 274 U.S. 316, 325, 47 S.Ct. 600, 604, 71 L.Ed. 1069 (1927), an "erroneous conclusion" reached by the court in the first suit does not deprive the defendants in the second action "of their right to rely upon the plea of *res judicata* . . . . A judgment merely voidable because based upon an erroneous view of the law is not open to collateral attack, but can be corrected only by a direct review and not by bringing another action upon the same cause [of action]." We have observed that "the indulgence of a contrary view would result in creating elements of uncertainty and confusion and in undermining the conclusive character of judgments, consequences which it was the very purpose of the doctrine of *res judicata* to avert." Reed v. Allen, 286 U.S. 191, 201, 52 S.Ct. 532, 534, 76 L.Ed. 1054 (1932).

In this case, the Court of Appeals conceded that the "strict application of the doctrine of *res judicata*" required that *Brown II* be dismissed. By that, the court presumably meant that the "technical elements" of res judicata had been satisfied, namely, that the decision in *Brown I* was a final judgment on the merits and involved the same

"an extensive review and analysis of the origins and substance of" the two *Brown* complaints, it found, and the Court of Appeals expressly agreed, that respondents had attempted to avoid removal jurisdiction by "artful[ly]" casting their "essentially federal law claims" as state-law claims. We will not question here that factual finding. See Prospect Dairy, Inc. v. Dellwood Dairy Co., 237 F.Supp. 176 (NDNY 1964); In re Wiring Device Antitrust Litigation, 498 F.Supp. 79 (EDNY 1980); Three J Farms, Inc. v. Alton Box Board Co., 1979–1 Trade Ca. (CCH) (DSC 1978), ¶ 62,423, rev'd on other grounds, 609 F.2d 112 (CA4 1979), cert. denied, 445 U.S. 911, 100 S.Ct. 1090, 63 L.Ed.2d 327 (1980).

claims and the same parties as *Brown II*.[3] The court, however, declined to dismiss *Brown II* because, in its view, it would be unfair to bar respondents from relitigating a claim so "closely interwoven" with that of the successfully appealing parties. We believe that such an unprecedented departure from accepted principles of res judicata is unwarranted. Indeed, the decision below is all but foreclosed by our prior case law.[4]

In Reed v. Allen, supra, this Court addressed the issue presented here. The case involved a dispute over the rights to property left in a will. *A* won an interpleader action for rents derived from the property and, while an appeal was pending, brought an ejectment action against the rival claimant *B*. On the basis of the decree in the interpleader suit *A* won the ejectment action. *B* did not appeal this judgment, but prevailed on his earlier appeal from the interpleader decree and was awarded the rents which had been collected. When *B* sought to bring an ejectment action against *A*, the latter pled res judicata, based on his previous successful ejectment action. This Court held that res judicata was available as a defense and that the property belonged to *A*:

> "The judgment in the ejectment action was final and not open to assault collaterally, but subject to impeachment only through some form of direct attack. The appellate court was limited to a review of the interpleader decree; and it is hardly necessary to say that jurisdiction to review one judgment gives an appellate court no power to reverse or modify another and independent judgment. If respondent, in addition to appealing from the [interpleader] decree, had appealed from the [ejectment] judgment, the appellate court, having both cases before it, might have afforded a remedy . . . . But this course respondent neglected to follow." Id., at 198, 52 S.Ct., at 533.

This Court's rigorous application of res judicata in *Reed*, to the point of leaving one party in possession and the other party entitled to the rents, makes clear that this Court recognizes no general equitable doctrine, such as that suggested by the Court of Appeals, which countenances an exception to the finality of a party's failure to appeal merely

3. The dismissal for failure to state a claim under Fed.Rule Civ.Proc. 12(b)(6) is a "judgment on the merits." See Angel v. Bullington, 330 U.S. 183, 190, 67 S.Ct. 657, 661, 91 L.Ed. 832 (1947); Bell v. Hood, 327 U.S. 678, 66 S.Ct. 773, 90 L.Ed. 939 (1946).

4. The decision below also conflicts with those of other Courts of Appeals holding that an adverse judgment from which no appeal has been taken is res judicata and bars any future action on the same claim, even if an authoritative contrary judicial decision on the legal issues involved is subsequently rendered in another case. E.g., National Association of Broad-casters v. FCC, 180 U.S.App.D.C. 259, 265, 554 F.2d 1118, 1124 (1976) ("It is the generally accepted rule in civil cases that where less than all of the several co-parties appeal from an adverse judgment, a reversal as to the parties appealing does not necessitate or justify a reversal as to the parties not appealing"); Clouatre v. Houston Fire & Cas. Co., 229 F.2d 596, 597–598 (CA5 1956); Appleton Toy & Furniture Co. v. Lehman Co., 165 F.2d 801, 802 (CA7 1948); Ripperger v. A. C. Allyn & Co., 113 F.2d 332, 333 (CA2), cert. denied, 311 U.S. 695, 61 S.Ct. 136, 85 L.Ed. 450 (1940).

because his rights are "closely interwoven" with those of another party.
* * *

The Court of Appeals also rested its opinion in part on what it viewed as "simple justice." But we do not see the grave injustice which would be done by the application of accepted principles of res judicata. "Simple justice" is achieved when a complex body of law developed over a period of years is evenhandedly applied. The doctrine of res judicata serves vital public interests beyond any individual judge's ad hoc determination of the equities in a particular case. There is simply "no principle of law or equity which sanctions the rejection by a federal court of the salutary principle of *res judicata*." Heiser v. Woodruff, 327 U.S. 726, 733, 66 S.Ct. 853, 856, 90 L.Ed. 970 (1946). The Court of Appeals' reliance on "public policy" is similarly misplaced. This Court has long recognized that "[p]ublic policy dictates that there be an end of litigation; that those who have contested an issue shall be bound by the result of the contest, and that matters once tried shall be considered forever settled as between the parties." Baldwin v. Traveling Men's Assn., 283 U.S. 522, 525, 51 S.Ct. 517, 518, 75 L.Ed. 1244 (1931). We have stressed that "[the] doctrine of *res judicata* is not a mere matter of practice or procedure inherited from a more technical time than ours. It is a rule of fundamental and substantial justice, 'of public policy and of private peace,' which should be cordially regarded and enforced by the courts . . . ." Hart Steel Co. v. Railroad Supply Co., 244 U.S. 294, 299, 37 S.Ct. 506, 507, 61 L.Ed. 1148 (1917). * * *

Respondents * * * argue that "the district court's dismissal on grounds of *res judicata* should be reversed, and the district court directed to grant respondent's motion to remand to the California state court." * * * In their view, *Brown I* cannot be considered res judicata as to their *state* law claims, since *Brown I* raised only federal-law claims and *Brown II* raised additional state-law claims not decided in *Brown I*, such as unfair competition, fraud and restitution.

It is unnecessary for this Court to reach that issue. It is enough for our decision here that *Brown I* is res judicata as to respondents' federal law claims. Accordingly, the judgment of the Court of Appeals is reversed, and the cause remanded for proceedings consistent with this opinion.

It is so ordered.

JUSTICE BLACKMUN, with whom JUSTICE MARSHALL joins, concurring in the judgment.

While I agree with the result reached in this case, I write separately to state my views on two points.

First, I, for one, would not close the door upon the possibility that there are cases in which the doctrine of res judicata must give way to what the Court of Appeals referred to as "overriding concerns of public policy and simple justice." 611 F.2d 1267, 1269 (CA9 1980). Professor Moore has noted: "Just as res judicata is occasionally qualified by an overriding, competing principle of public policy, so occasionally it needs an equitable tempering." 1B Moore's Federal Practice ¶ 0.405[12], p. 791 (1980) (footnote omitted). See also Reed v. Allen, 286 U.S. 191, 209, 52 S.Ct. 532, 537, 76 L.Ed. 1054 (1932) (Cardozo, J., joined by Brandeis and Stone, JJ., dissenting) ("A system of procedure is perverted from its proper function when it multiplies impediments to justice without the warrant of clear necessity"). But this case is clearly not one in which equity requires that the doctrine give way. Unlike the nonappealing party in *Reed*, respondents were not "caught in a mesh of procedural complexities." Ibid. Instead, they made a deliberate tactical decision not to appeal. Nor would public policy be served by making an exception to the doctrine in this case; to the contrary, there is a special need for strict application of res judicata in complex multiple party actions of this sort so as to discourage "break-away" litigation. Cf. Reiter v. Sonotone Corp., 442 U.S. 330, 345, 99 S.Ct. 2326, 2334, 60 L.Ed. 2d 931 (1979). Finally, this is not a case "where the rights of appealing and nonappealing parties are so interwoven or dependent upon each other as to require a reversal of the whole judgment when a part thereof is reversed." See Ford Motor Credit Co. v. Uresti, 581 S.W.2d 298, 300 (Tex.Civ.App. 1979).

Second, and in contrast, I would flatly hold that *Brown I* is res judicata as to respondents' state law claims. Like the District Court, the Court of Appeals found that those state law claims were simply disguised federal claims; since respondents have not cross-petitioned from that judgment, their argument that this case should be remanded to state court should be itself barred by res judicata. More important, even if the state and federal claims are distinct, respondents' failure to allege the state claims in *Brown I* manifestly bars their allegation in *Brown II*. The dismissal of *Brown I* is res judicata not only as to all claims respondents actually raised, but also as to all claims that could have been raised. See Commissioner v. Sunnen, 333 U.S. 591, 597, 68 S.Ct. 715, 719, 92 L.Ed. 898 (1948); Restatement (Second) of Judgments § 61.1 (Tent. Draft No. 5, Mar. 10, 1978). Since there is no reason to believe that it was clear at the outset of this litigation that the District Court would have declined to exercise pendent jurisdiction over state claims, respondents were obligated to plead those claims if they wished to preserve them. See id., § 61.1, Comment (e). Because they did not do so, I would hold the claims barred.

JUSTICE BRENNAN, dissenting.*

* The dissenting opinion is omitted.

SAWYER v. FIRST CITY FINANCIAL CORP.

District Court of Appeal of California, 1981.
124 Cal.App.3d 390, 177 Cal.Rptr. 398.

FROEHLICH, ASSOCIATE JUSTICE.

Plaintiffs appeal from adverse summary judgment rulings in favor of all defendants. An understanding of the litigation requires an analysis of two separate cases involving essentially the same parties, of which the present appeal relates specifically to the second. For reference purposes these two cases will be called "*Sawyer I*" and "*Sawyer II.*" Each case arises from the same general factual background.

Factual Background

The principal parties to both cases are the plaintiffs Sawyer, owners and sellers of land; the defendants First City Financial Corporation Ltd. and its subsidiaries, purchasers and encumbrancers of the land who sought to develop it; and Toronto Dominion Bank of California, the development lender to First City Financial's subsidiary. The broad brush of facts is that in May of 1974 the Sawyers sold 32 acres of land in La Jolla, California, to the subsidiary of First City—F.C. Financial Associates, Ltd.—for $1,180,000 consisting of $510,000 in cash and a note secured by deed of trust in the sum of $670,000. Concurrently with the sale, F.C. Financial Associates committed to borrow $1,800,000 in the form of a development loan from Toronto Dominion Bank. This loan was guaranteed by First City and was secured by a first deed of trust on the realty, the Sawyers specifically subordinating their deed of trust to the new encumbrance. The Sawyers as part of the sales documents specifically waived any deficiency judgment with respect to their note and deed of trust, with the result that after the sales and refinancing escrows closed their sole resource for collection of their $670,000 note was foreclosure on their deed of trust, now subordinate to a $1,800,000 first deed of trust to the Bank.

Early in 1975, F.C. Financial Associates discontinued payments on the note to Toronto Dominion Bank, asserting that it could not proceed further with development of the land because the construction bids it had received were excessively high. Total amounts owed on the note at that time approximated $900,000. Toronto Dominion Bank commenced non-judicial foreclosure proceedings on April 1, 1975, and purchased the land at foreclosure sale in September, 1975, for its bid of $650,000. The land was ultimately transferred in December 1976 to Lexington Properties, Inc., a corporation owned by one Richard Ehrlich, for a purchase price of some $800,000.

The Sawyers contend in pleadings and other documentation that at the time of the foreclosure sale Toronto Dominion Bank had agreed to resell the realty to First City for a price equal to the Bank's total investment in it, but that this transfer was delayed until the sale to Ehrlich and his corporation could be arranged, so that neither First

City nor its subsidiary again appeared as record titleholder. Ehrlich and his corporation obtained development funds for the property from a corporation called Lomitas Properties, Inc., which is a corporation owned and controlled by the majority stockholders, directors and officers of First City, and which derived its funds from First City.

Appellant's view of the facts, therefore, is that the Sawyers were induced to take a non-recourse note for more than half the consideration involved in the sale of their land, the security for which note was made subject to a large development loan. The development borrower then defaulted on the note and arranged with the development lender to foreclose, to buy in at the foreclosure sale, and to resell to the development borrower for the amount of the foreclosure sales price plus the balance of the loan guarantee. The practical effect of this transaction, it is alleged, was to wipe out the obligation to the Sawyers and permit First City to proceed with sale or development of the land without having to pay $650,000 of the purchase price. In order to avoid airing the mechanics of the transaction, the agreement between the Toronto Bank and First City was kept secret, and the resale to First City was not recorded, the ultimate purchaser being a puppet of First City set up in an apparently independent corporation, borrowing funds from a new and anonymous lending company, but actually deriving development funds indirectly from First City. We are alert to caution that the above construction of the facts from and after the foreclosure sale is that alleged by the plaintiffs, who seek the opportunity of proving same in a full-scale evidentiary trial.

Legal Proceedings

Sawyer I

Saywer I was commenced in July of 1975. The defendants were F.C. Financial Associates, its parent First City Financial Corporation, and, later, another subsidiary of First City (all sometimes called herein "Financial"); and Toronto Dominion Bank of California ("Bank"). The several causes of action all were based upon contractual theories. Reference was made to the Land Acquisition and Development Loan Agreement executed between Financial and Bank, which provided for the construction of a planned residential development in accordance with an existing permit. The Sawyers alleged that they were third party beneficiaries of that agreement and had been damaged by the failure of Financial to perform in accordance with it. The breach is alleged not only as a simple breach of contract, but as a breach by the defendants of "a contractual duty of good faith and fair dealing." A separate cause of action asks for declaratory relief with respect to the contractual commitments; and a final cause of action seeks judicial foreclosure of the Sawyer note. The monetary relief prayed for was the amount of the note ($674,500) plus attorney fees.

The case was tried in February of 1978. By stipulation the issues were severed for trial and dispositive issues were presented to a judge, sitting without jury. The judgment rendered in March of 1978, focused upon the issue of the validity of the waiver by Sawyers of their right to a deficiency judgment. This waiver was found to be effective and judgment was rendered in favor of all defendants on all causes of action. Following affirmance on appeal, the judgment became final in December of 1979.

Saywer II

Sawyer II was filed in January of 1978. Entitled "Complaint for Damages Based Upon Conspiracy and Fraud," it joined as defendants all of the parties named in *Sawyer I* and in addition the ultimate purchaser Ehrlich and his corporation, Lexington Properties; the new financier of the development, Lomitas Properties; and a number of officers and directors of the Financial Companies and the Toronto Bank. Three of the causes of action of this new lawsuit are based upon an alleged conspiracy among the defendants to cause a default in the Bank's note and trust deed, hold a sham sale, and take other action for the purpose of eliminating the obligation to the Sawyers. The only essential difference in the three causes of action is the date of commencement of the alleged conspiracy—one alleging the evil motives from the very start of the land acquisition transaction, a second alleging commencement of the conspiracy when Financial defaulted on its note payments, and a third alleging commencement of the conspiracy at the time of the foreclosure sale. The Fourth cause of action uses the same factual allegations as the basis for a claim of intentional interference with contractual relation (Financial's note obligation to the Sawyers). Damages alleged are the same as in *Sawyer I* except that additional punitive damages are sought.

The procedural history of *Sawyer II* is detailed as follows:

1. Promptly upon filing *Sawyer II*, counsel sought to consolidate with *Sawyer I*, and moved for a continuance of the trial of *Sawyer I*. This motion was opposed by the defendants, who objected because the issues and causes of action of *Sawyer II* were different from those of *Sawyer I*, and also because the case, then pending for two and one-half years, was scheduled for trial nine days later. The court denied a motion to continue the trial of *Sawyer I*, and it was tried without consolidation with *Sawyer II*.

2. In January of 1980, the Toronto Bank and its officers moved for summary judgment in *Sawyer II* upon the ground of the res judicata effect of *Sawyer I*, and also upon the basis of a written release which had been executed in favor of the Bank in *Sawyer I*—removing the Bank from the case before its trial. The Honorable Douglas Woodworth denied the motion based upon res judicata, but granted the motion as to the Bank only, upon the ground of the written waiver. The bank officers moved for reconsideration on the theory that the waiver should be construed to cover them as well as the Bank, and this motion was taken under submission by the judge in March of 1980. On

July 24, 1980, Judge Woodworth denied the motions by written minute order.

3. In May of 1980, a separate motion for summary judgment was filed by the Financial corporations on the ground that *Sawyer I* was res judicata to the issues of *Sawyer II*—that the plaintiffs had split their cause of action by attempting to relitigate the same issues in a second lawsuit. The bank officers (whose motion for reconsideration was then pending before Judge Woodworth) joined in this motion, and it was set for hearing before the Honorable Franklin B. Orfield. On July 25, 1980, Judge Orfield ruled in favor of all defendants on the ground of res judicata and the enforceability of the Bank's written release in *Sawyer I.*

The Appeal

Appellants appeal from the summary judgments of both Judge Woodworth (dismissing the Bank) and Judge Orfield (dismissing all parties), and also from a discovery ruling (described infra). Many bases of appeal are urged: The central and most important issue, however, is the question of res judicata. As reviewed in 3 Witkin, California Procedure (2d ed. 1971) Pleading, § 32 et seq., p. 1715, a single cause of action cannot be split and made the subject of several suits. If a primary right is so split, determination of the issues in the first suit will be res judicata to the attempt to relitigate them in the second suit. Where the plaintiff has several causes of action, however, even though they may arise from the same factual setting, and even though they might have been joined in one suit under permissive joinder provisions, the plaintiff is privileged to bring separate actions based upon each separate cause.

Res Judicata Issue

A valid final judgment on the merits in favor of a defendant serves as a complete bar to further litigation on the same cause of action. (Slater v. Blackwood (1975) 15 Cal.3d 791, 795, 126 Cal.Rptr. 225, 543 P.2d 593.) The question in this and similar cases, of course, is whether the attempted second litigation involves the "same cause of action." A "cause of action" is conceived as the remedial right in favor of a plaintiff for the violation of one "primary right." That several remedies may be available for violation of one "primary right" does not create additional "causes of action." However, it is also true that a given set of facts may give rise to the violation of more than one "primary right," thus giving a plaintiff the potential of two separate lawsuits against a single defendant. (See 3 Witkin, supra, pp. 1707 et seq.)

The theoretical discussion of what constitutes a "primary right" is complicated by historical precedent in several well-litigated areas establishing the question of "primary rights" in a manner perhaps contrary to the result that might be reached by a purely logical approach. For instance, the primary right to be free from personal injury has been construed as to embrace all theories of tort which might have given rise to the injury.   In Panos v. Great Western Packing Co. (1943) 21 Cal.2d 636, 134 P.2d 242 the plaintiff was injured in a meat packing house. His first cause of action was based upon alleged negligence of the packing house in permitting third parties to come upon the premises and operate equipment.   A defense judgment was then held to bar a second suit based upon an entirely different factual theory of negligence—that the defendant itself had negligently operated the equipment.   In Slater v. Blackwood, supra, 15 Cal.3d 791, 126 Cal.Rptr. 225, 543 P.2d 593, a defense judgment in a suit based upon violation of the guest statute (intoxication or willful misconduct) was held to bar a second suit (after the guest statute was held unconstitutional) based upon allegations of ordinary negligence.

Other examples of torts resulting in easily conceptualized types of damages have been settled, one way or the other, by precedent.   While one act of tortious conduct might well be deemed to violate only one "primary right"—the right to be free from the particular unlawful conduct—the resultant (1) injury to person and (2) damage to property have been deemed creative of separate causes of action.   On the other hand, one course of wrongful conduct which damages several pieces of property traditionally gives rise to only one cause of action.   (See 3 Witkin, supra, at pp. 1720–1721, and cases cited therein.)

Other classes of litigation, however, with perhaps less historical or precedential background, are not so well defined in terms of deciding how many "primary rights" derive from a single factual transaction. The tort in Agarwal v. Johnson (1979) 25 Cal.3d 932, 160 Cal.Rptr. 141, 603 P.2d 58, was unfair treatment of a minority race employee by an employer.   Plaintiff's first action was in federal court for back wages under the authority of the federal Civil Rights Act.   The state Supreme Court determined this was no bar to a second suit in superior court for general and punitive damages for defamation and intentional infliction of emotional distress.   Although the same set of facts is presented in each claim, one primary right is created by the federal statute prohibiting discriminatory employment practices; and the second primary right is grounded in state common law.   Also, the "harm suffered" was deemed separable—damages for lost wages in the federal action, and damages for injury to reputation and peace of mind in the state case. Compare Mattson v. City of Costa Mesa (1980) 106 Cal.App.3d 441, 164 Cal.Rptr. 913, where the actionable facts consisted of an unlawful arrest of the plaintiff and his abuse in confinement.   His first action in federal court under the authority of the Civil Rights Act was held to be a bar to a subsequent suit in state court for negligence, assault and battery.   The court found that the "primary rights" giving rise to the state common law tort action were the same as those reflected in the Civil Rights Act, and that the civil rights action was "simply a different way of expressing an invasion of the same primary rights or the assertion of a different legal theory for recovery."   (Id. at pp. 447–448,

164 Cal.Rptr. 913.) In City of Los Angeles v. Superior Court (1978) 85 Cal.App.3d 143, 153, 149 Cal.Rptr. 320, a federal civil rights action followed by a superior court common law tort action, both involving wrongful seizure of personal property, the appellate court reached the same conclusion and applied the bar of res judicata on the ground that "the civil rights action was designed to vindicate precisely the same interests in . . . personal property that . . . (the plaintiff) seeks to vindicate in the matter before us."

One would assume that the question of litigation of claims arising from one transaction first on the basis of contract, and then on alleged tort theories, would have received substantial appellate attention. The authorities, however, are surprisingly spar[s]e. The Restatement of the Law, Judgments (1942) chapter 3, section 63, page 261, provides several illustrations involving actions to cancel a deed. A failure to sustain the first action on contractual grounds (i.e., failure of execution or delivery of the deed) is held to bar a subsequent action based upon fraudulent procurement—thus suggesting that the "primary right" is the right to cancel the deed (as applied to our case, to validate the note) and that this gives rise to only one cause of action, whether it be framed in contract or tort.

Respondents rely upon two cases which purport to be illustrative of contract actions followed by separate tort actions, arising from the same transaction: Olwell v. Hopkins (1946) 28 Cal.2d 147, 168 P.2d 972; and Steiner v. Thomas (1949) 94 Cal.App.2d 655, 211 P.2d 321. The plaintiff's claim in *Olwell* resulted from farming operations carried on by a joint venture which included a Washington corporation. In the first suit the action was dismissed without a trial of the substantive issues on the ground that the corporation had never qualified to do business in California with the result that the contract upon which the suit was based was "void." A second suit based upon the same transaction alleged fraudulent concealment of facts and prayed that the defendants be declared constructive trustees of certain realty. While this scenario would seem to pose a problem similar to that of the case before us, it was resolved without addressing the issue of the existence of separate causes of action in contract and for fraud. The court assumed (and presumably counsel did not argue to the contrary) that there was only one cause of action, and that the second suit was merely an alternative statement of that one cause of action. (See Olwell v. Hopkins, supra, 28 Cal.2d at pp. 149, 150, 168 P.2d 972.) The question directly addressed by the court was the effect of dismissal of the first suit without a trial on the merits, and whether such dismissal on procedural grounds would operate as a bar to a second action, recognizing that in order to constitute a bar, the dismissal must have been following " 'an adjudication of the merits of the controversy, . . .' " (Id., at p. 149, 168 P.2d 972.)

In *Steiner*, two successive actions were brought against an administrator of a decedent's estate for the purpose of recovering a certain parcel of real property which had been transferred to the decedent by the plaintiff before the decedent's death. The first action was for rescission based upon fraud, alleging that the realty had been transferred so as to permit the decedent to collect rents and that the decedent had promised to reconvey the property at a later date. The second lawsuit was based upon an alleged breach of an agreement to devise the property to the plaintiff, as evidenced by two letters from the decedent to the plaintiff. The court resolved the question of res judicata against the plaintiff, focusing on the identity or similarity of facts litigated in the first suit as compared to those in issue at the second suit. The court stated:

> "The fact is that in the former action the merits of all the facts were determined and relief was denied . . . . Upon presentation of the special plea in the instant action the court had merely to decide whether the facts alleged in the first suit for rescission of the contract were substantially those alleged in the second action for breach of the same contract." (Steiner v. Thomas, supra, 94 Cal.App.2d at p. 658, 211 P.2d 321).

The court thus construed the situation as one in which alternative remedies in contract were successively brought—related to the same contract—rather than a case in which an action on contract was followed by an action for an intentional tort related to or as part of the transaction giving rise to the contract. Neither *Orwell* nor *Steiner* appears controlling.

The case before us is not one in which the same factual structure is characterized in one complaint as a breach of contract and in another as a tort. The first action is solely on contract and is based upon the note, deed of trust, and loan and development agreement. At the time of trial the principal issue litigated was the effectiveness of the waiver of deficiency judgment, and this issue was presented in the context of contractual theories. There was no contention and no evidence was presented relating to a possible invalidation of the waiver on grounds of fraud, misrepresentation or any other tort.

Sawyer II, of course, had as its object collection of the same promissory note which was the subject matter of *Sawyer I;* but the basis of the claim is completely different, and rests upon a completely separate set of facts. The complaint assumes and admits that the forms of the waiver of deficiency and the subordination are technically appropriate and enforceable. The pleading reaches beyond these documents, however, to highlight other conduct of the parties alleged to be tortious. The core of the alleged wrongful conduct is an agreement among the parties to conduct what is characterized as a sham foreclosure sale, the only substantive effect of which would be secretly to discharge the obligation to Sawyer, leaving all other parties in essentially the same position as prior to the sale. Surely one's breach of contract by failing to pay a note violates a "primary right" which is separate from the "primary right" not to have the note stolen. That the two causes of action might have been joined in one lawsuit under our permissive joinder provisions (see 3 Witkin, supra, at p. 1915) does not prevent the plaintiff from bringing them in separate suits if he elects to do so. While the monetary loss may be measurable by the same promissory note amount, and hence in a general sense the same "harm" has been done in both cases, theoretically the plaintiffs have been "harmed" differently by tortious conduct destroying the value of the note, than by the contractual breach of simply failing to pay it. We conclude, therefore, that *Sawyer II* is based upon a separate and severable cause of action from that litigated in *Sawyer I,* and that it was error to grant summary judgment on the ground of res judicata.

Estoppel

A second prong to appellant's argument about the summary judgment ruling as respects res judicata is that the moving parties were estopped to deny the separate nature of the two causes of action because they had earlier opposed a motion to consolidate the two cases. Appellants rely upon United Bank & Trust Co. v. Hunt (1934) 1 Cal.2d 340, 34 P.2d 1001, where the court at page 345 stated:

> " 'Where counsel by timely notice call to a court's attention the pendency of other proceedings covering kindred matters and strive to have the same embraced within the scope of the inquiry, and such attempt is successfully blocked by opposing counsel and the trial proceeds to the investigation of the specific issue before the court, counsel who were successful in preventing the consolidation of the issues cannot be heard later to object to a trial of the related matters upon the ground of *res judicata.* The course pursued by the court and counsel . . . was tantamount to an express determination on the part of the court with the consent of opposing counsel to reserve the issues involved for future adjudication. [Citation.] Litigants cannot successfully assume such inconsistent positions.' "

The inconsistent position asserted to have been taken by defense counsel was at the time of the hearing of a motion to continue the trial of *Sawyer I. Sawyer I* was filed in July of 1975. Plaintiffs filed a memorandum that the case was at issue in February 1976. On January 6, 1977, a trial setting conference was held, and a settlement conference was scheduled for September 13, 1977, with trial scheduled for September 29, 1977. On September 12, 1977, plaintiffs filed a motion to continue the trial date, which was heard on September 19, 1977, and resulted in a continuance to February 15, 1978. On February 5, 1978, nine days before the continued trial date, plaintiffs brought another motion for continuance of the trial, upon the ground that they had filed *Sawyer II* and wished to have time before the trial of *Sawyer I* to file and hear a motion for consolidation.

At the hearing of the motion for continuance on February 6, counsel for the defendants did argue that the case should not be continued to permit consideration of a consolidation motion because consolidation would be improper by virtue of the different theories and causes of action in *Sawyer II*.   However, no express argument was made about, nor consideration given, to the question of the res judicata effect of the prior trial of *Sawyer I*.   In light of the long period of preparation for trial and the then once-continued trial date impending only nine days hence, the trial court presumably considered further continuance to be prejudicial to the rights of the defendants.   A court is not required to grant a continuance of a trial when the pleadings have been completed, adequate time for discovery has been provided, the issues are joined, and one side is ready for trial, even though the moving party alleges newly discovered facts or newly found issues which suggest more discovery or an amendment to the pleadings.   (See County of San Bernardino v. Doria Mining & Engineering Corp. (1977) 72 Cal.App.3d 776, 783, 140 Cal.Rptr. 383.)

The reasonable interpretation to be derived from a review of the record in *Sawyer I* was that the court denied the motion for continuance because *Sawyer I* was ready for trial, had been delayed previously and should not be delayed further.   Therefore, while we have determined that the motion for summary judgment should not have been granted on the ground of res judicata, we must agree with the trial court that the moving parties were not estopped by their prior conduct from making the motion.

* * *

STANIFORTH, ACTING P. J., concurs.

WIENER, ASSOCIATE JUSTICE, concurring.

* * *

* * * I conclude defendants, except for the Toronto Dominion Bank and its officers, are estopped from raising the defense of res judicata.   Accordingly, I agree with the result reached by the majority.

* * *

Plaintiffs filed their first case (No. 369573) in July 1975; their second (No. 409803) on January 11, 1978.   On January 13, 1978, plaintiffs moved to consolidate both cases because some of the parties and certain of the issues were the same.   Unable to serve all defendants, plaintiffs' motion to consolidate was reset beyond February 15, 1978, the trial date in Case No. 369573.   Pending hearing on that motion, plaintiffs moved to continue the trial to allow the court to consider the motion for consolidation.   Counsel for First City defendants in *Sawyer I*, one of whom is appellate counsel here, opposed the motion for continuance by saying there was no basis for consolidation, arguing further that

> "[p]laintiffs are pursuing theories of action for conspiracy and fraud in Case No. 409803, whereas in the above-captioned action plaintiffs are pursuing theories for breach of contact, declaratory relief and judicial foreclosure.   *The issues raised in the two cases are necessarily and substantially different.*"   (Emphasis supplied.)
> * * *

* * * If defendants' counsel made the tactical decision to oppose the continuance on the assumption that if successful they would then be able to prevent litigation in the second case on the basis of res judicata, it would have been simple enough for them to tell the court that res judicata was involved. If they had done so the judge considering the motion would then have been able to evaluate all relevant factors affecting his decision before exercising discretion in making his ruling. In light of the language which defendants selected to oppose the motion for the continuance the ruling on which prevented the court from ever considering the merits of plaintiffs' request for consolidation, it was reasonable for both the court and plaintiffs' counsel to conclude defendants' opposition to the continuance would not prevent a trial of the second case in which the issues were represented to be "necessarily and substantially different." * * * Once having represented to the court there were two different actions with different issues, they may not now stop plaintiffs from having a full trial on those "different issues." * * *

NOTE ON RES JUDICATA BETWEEN THE SAME PARTIES

1. Claim Preclusion

(a) The rule of claim preclusion is that a judgment for or against a plaintiff on a "cause of action" or "claim" precludes reassertion of that cause of action or claim. Obviously a critical question in applying this rule is the scope of the "claim" involved. In this respect, is *Sawyer* consistent with *Moitie*? In *Sawyer*, does the court's rejection of a transactional definition of "claim" leave much left of the claim preclusion doctrine? Compare Justice Blackmun's concurrence in *Moitie*. See also Ferriell, Res Judicata in Ohio: Preclusion of Causes of Action or Claims?, 10 Ohio N.U.L.Rev. 241 (1983).

(b) On the scope of "cause of action" or "claim" see Restatement Second of Judgments § 24:

> *maj.*
>
> " * * * [T]he claim extinguished includes all rights of the plaintiff to remedies against the defendant with respect to all or any part of the transaction, or series of connected transactions, out of which the action arose."

Compare with *Sawyer* the approach in Gowan v. Tully, 45 N.Y.2d 32, 407 N.Y.S.2d 650, 379 N.E.2d 177 (1978). Compare with *Moitie* S.E.L. Maduro (Florida), Inc. v. M/V Antonio De Gastaneta, 833 F.2d 1477 (11th Cir. 1987) (plaintiff's prior unsuccessful admiralty in personam action for breach of contract not a bar to subsequent in rem action to enforce lien based on same obligation, because first "cause of action" was against the shipowner while the second involved a different cause against the ship).

(c) In ordinary tort litigation, a question that every jurisdiction has to answer is whether an automobile accident generates one cause of action for the driver-owner for his personal injuries and damage to his car, or two causes of action. See Holmes v. David H. Bricker, Inc., 70 Cal.2d 786, 76 Cal.Rptr. 431, 452 P.2d 647 (1969); Parrell v. Keenan, 389 Mass. 809, 452 N.E.2d 506 (1983); Restatement Second of Judgments § 24, Comment c and Illustration 1.

(d) A remedial scheme may qualify or abrogate the application of the rules of claim preclusion. See, e.g., Barrentine v. Arkansas-Best Freight System,

Inc., 450 U.S. 728, 101 S.Ct. 1437, 67 L.Ed.2d 641 (1981) (unfavorable determination of wage claim in collective bargaining arbitration does not preclude employee's assertion of Fair Labor Standards Act claim based on the same conduct); Vestal and Hill, Preclusion in Labor Controversies, 35 Okla.L.Rev. 281 (1982); Restatement Second of Judgments § 26(d). See the analysis in Jackson, Matheson and Piskorski, The Proper Role of Res Judicata and Collateral Estoppel in Title VII Suits, 79 Mich.L.Rev. 1485 (1981); cf. Note, Res Judicata in Title VII Actions, 27 B.C.L.Rev. 173 (1985).

(e) A court may raise the question of claim preclusion on its own motion, for the sake of judicial economy. See Alyeska Pipeline Serv. Co. v. United States, 688 F.2d 765 (Ct.Cl.1982).

(f) Preclusion in the context of class suits raises special issues and concerns. See Res Judicata in Class Suits, infra p. 825.

2. Issue Preclusion

(a) *Fact or Law.* Traditionally, the rule of preclusion was stated as applying only to issues of fact; stare decisis applied to issues of law. But the modern view applies preclusion to both. See Restatement Second of Judgments § 28, Comment b; see also Hazard, Preclusion as to Issues of Law: The Legal System's Interest, 70 Iowa L.Rev. 81 (1984); Buckley, Issue Preclusion and Issues of Law: A Doctrinal Framework Based on Rules of Recognition, Jurisdiction and Legal History, 24 Hous.L.Rev. 875 (1987). Is this in part because the rule of stare decisis itself is now weaker than it was?

(b) *"Ultimate" Fact.* A distinction was drawn between ultimate facts and mediate facts by Hand, J., in The Evergreens v. Nunan, 141 F.2d 927 (2d Cir. 1944). Most analysts have not been able to see the difference, or that it was relevant. It is now generally accepted that the question is not whether the issue was "ultimate" or "mediate," but whether it was treated as important and necessary to the decision in the first action, see Restatement Second of Judgments § 27, Comment j, applied in Synanon Church v. United States, 820 F.2d 421 (D.C.Cir. 1987), whether it was unforseeable that the issue might come up in a different context, and whether the party had an adequate incentive to litigate it the first time. Compare Yates v. United States, 354 U.S. 298, 77 S.Ct. 1064, 1 L.Ed.2d 1356 (1957), with Dobbins v. Title Guar. & Trust Co., 22 Cal.2d 64, 136 P.2d 572 (1943).

(c) *"Actually Litigated."* The difficult problem is presented by a consent judgment or a default judgment entered after defendant has made some kind of appearance. In both situations the issue has in some sense been litigated but it has not been resolved by the court on the basis of conflicting submissions. Such a judgment does result in claim preclusion. There is authority giving it issue preclusive effects, but the dominant view is to the contrary. See Restatement Second of Judgments § 27, Reporter's Note; Anno., 91 A.L.R.3d 1170. Compare Kaspar Wire Works, Inc. v. Leco Engineering & Mach. Co., 575 F.2d 530 (5th Cir. 1978), with Barber v. International Brotherhood of Boilermakers, 778 F.2d 750 (11th Cir. 1985). See also Kaufman v. Eli Lilly & Co., 65 N.Y.2d 449, 492 N.Y.S.2d 584, 482 N.E.2d 63 (1985) (issue preclusion denied as to issue of law which defendant did not contest in the prior litigation). What was "actually litigated" in such cases?

(d) *"Determined".* There is authority that refuses to apply preclusion where there is evidence that the issue was compromised by the finder of fact. See Taylor v. Hawkinson, 47 Cal.2d 893, 306 P.2d 797 (1957). Cf. Restatement

Second of Judgments § 29(5) (no use of issue preclusion as against third party). In Katz v. Eli Lilly & Co., 84 F.R.D. 378 (E.D.N.Y. 1979), interrogation of the jurors in the first action was permitted to determine whether they had compromised. See also Milks v. Eli Lilly & Co., 94 F.R.D. 674 (S.D.N.Y.1982); Note, Use of Juror Depositions to Bar Collateral Estoppel, 34 Vand.L.Rev. 143 (1981). Normally, however, the rule is stated to be that preclusion should be applied no matter how irregular or erroneous the prior judgment was. See, e.g., Shaid v. Consolidated Edison Co., 95 A.D.2d 610, 467 N.Y.S.2d 843 (1983); Eichman v. Fotomat Corp., 759 F.2d 1434 (9th Cir. 1985). Should an issue determined under the preponderance of evidence burden of proof be conclusive in a later proceeding where the burden of proof is higher, viz., clear and convincing evidence? Restatement Second of Judgments § 28(4) says it should not. But see In re C.M.H., 8 Family L.Rep. 1110 (Fla.App.1982).

(e) *"Essential to the Judgment."* The problem is whether an alternative determination is "essential." The competing ideas are that (1) a determination is no less such for being alternative, especially given the multi-issue, alternative theory modes of litigation we have in modern procedure, and (2) an alternative determination can be considered a "dictum." The Restatement Second of Judgments takes the position that an alternative determination is not conclusive unless both alternatives are reviewed and decided on appeal, which may be a strange compromise. See id., § 27, Comments i, j, and o. See also Note, Res Judicata Effects of Unappealed, Independently Sufficient Alternative Determinations, 70 Corn.L.Rev. 717 (1985).

(f) *Adversary Position of the Parties.* The rule used to be that an issue was never conclusive between parties on the same side of a litigation, for example between co-defendants. The modern rule is that the issue is conclusive if the parties were antagonistic to each other on the issue. See, e.g., Nevada v. United States, 463 U.S. 110, 103 S.Ct. 2906, 77 L.Ed.2d 509 (1983); McLellan v. Columbus I–70 West Auto-Truckstop, Inc., 525 F.Supp. 1233 (N.D.Ill.1981); Restatement Second of Judgments § 38.

(g) *"Fair Opportunity to Litigate."* An issue is not conclusive unless the proceeding in which it is determined has the characteristics of an adjudicative proceeding, including opportunity to offer direct and rebuttal evidence. See, e.g., Hooker v. Klein, 573 F.2d 1360 (9th Cir. 1978) (effect of finding in extradition proceeding); United States v. Utah Constr. & Mining Co., 384 U.S. 394, 86 S.Ct. 1545, 16 L.Ed.2d 642 (1966); Vella v. Hudgins, 20 Cal.3d 251, 142 Cal.Rptr. 414, 572 P.2d 28 (1977) (no preclusive effect to determination reached in summary proceedings where parties did not undertake intensive presentation of evidence on the issue). See also the discussion of administrative agency determinations, below. Where defendant has made a limited appearance in response to attachment jurisdiction, the question arises whether issue preclusion results from the judgment. Restatement Second of Judgments § 32(d) says that it does if the stakes offer sufficient inducement to litigate fully. But see Note, Limited Appearances and Issue Preclusion: Resetting the Trap?, 66 Corn. L.Rev. 595 (1981).

(h) *The "Parties."* For purposes both of issue and claim preclusion the general rule is that the party against whom preclusion is applied must have been the party to the prior litigation. Ordinarily, it is clear whether or not the parties are the same. However, a party may appear in different capacities in successive litigation, in which case he is regarded as two different parties. See Restatement Second of Judgments § 36. Cf. id., §§ 37, 39, 40. A variation of this problem arises when two different parties can enforce essentially the same claim, one acting on his own behalf, the other as representative or protector. See id., § 85. See also, e.g., Freeman v. Lester Coggins Trucking, Inc., 771 F.2d 860 (5th Cir. 1985) (plaintiff's suit in representative capacity for his wife and children in wrongful death action not precluded by prior judgment against plaintiff for his own injuries in same accident). Compare Williamson v. Bethlehem Steel Corp., 468 F.2d 1201 (2d Cir. 1972) (Government's suit to compel modification of employment practices does not preclude similar suit by employee affected by the practices).

Remedial policy may override the rule of issue preclusion, just as it may override that of claim preclusion. See Restatement Second of Judgments § 28. See also Allen v. McCurry, 449 U.S. 90, 101 S.Ct. 411, 66 L.Ed.2d 308 (1980), holding that a state court judgment should result in issue preclusion in a subsequent action based on 42 U.S.C.A. § 1983, and Migra v. Warren City School District, 465 U.S. 75, 104 S.Ct. 892, 79 L.Ed.2d 56 (1984), extending *Allen* to claim preclusion.

3. Law of the Case

Related to but distinct from the rules of res judicata is the "law of the case" doctrine, which is that a determination of an issue of law at one stage of a case becomes the "law of the case" and, absent a change in circumstances, will not be reexamined in a subsequent stage of the case. The most common application of the rule is where the issue has once been considered in an appeal and then, following remand and further proceedings in the lower court, comes up again in a subsequent appeal. See, e.g., Bray v. Cox, 38 N.Y.2d 350, 379 N.Y.S.2d 803, 342 N.E.2d 575 (1976); Jordan v. Jordan, 132 Ariz. 38, 643 P.2d 1008 (1982); Fine v. Bellefonte Underwriters Ins. Co., 758 F.2d 50 (2d Cir. 1985); Bigbee v. Pacific Telephone & Telegraph Co., 34 Cal.3d 49, 192 Cal.Rptr. 857, 665 P.2d 947 (1983); Steinman, Law of the Case: A Judicial Puzzle in Consolidated and Transferred Cases and in Multidistrict Litigation, 135 U.Pa.L.Rev. 595 (1987); Vestal, Law of the Case: Single-Suit Preclusion, 1967 Utah L.Rev. 1; Annos., 74 A.L.R.Fed. 878, 87 A.L.R.2d 271. See also Hayman Cash Register Co. v. Sarokin, 669 F.2d 162 (3d Cir. 1982). Compare United States v. Burns, 662 F.2d 1378 (11th Cir. 1981) (refusing to apply law of the case where manifest injustice would result).

4. Direct Estoppel

Similar to the law of the case doctrine is the rule that a factual finding in one stage of a case ordinarily precludes relitigation of the issue in another stage of the case, a consequence sometimes called "direct estoppel." Illustrative is Ritter v. Mount St. Mary's College, 814 F.2d 986 (4th Cir.1987): Plaintiff's action alleged three claims, one under Title VII (42 U.S.C.A. § 2000e et seq.); another under the Equal Pay Act (29 U.S.C.A. § 206(d)); and a third under the Age Discrimination in Employment Act (29 U.S.C.A. § 621 et seq.). The Title VII claim being "equitable," jury trial was not available of right as to that claim, but was as to the equal pay and age discrimination claims. See Right to Jury Trial, infra p. 997. The trial judge dismissed the latter two claims on the ground that the defendant, a religious college, was exempt from those Acts. The judge then tried the Title VII claim, determining for the defendant on the ground that the plaintiff lacked qualifications for the job she sought. The judge's decision as to the applicability of the Equal Pay and Age Discrimination Acts (claims two and three of the complaint) was appealed and reversed on the ground that religious colleges are covered by the statutes. However, the finding on the first claim, that the plaintiff lacked qualifications for the job, was held to be preclusive in her equal pay and age discrimination claims, even though those would have been tried to a jury had they not been dismissed at the outset. In Hussein v. Oshkosh Motor Truck Co., 816 F.2d 348 (7th Cir. 1987), it was held in similar circumstances that the prior decision should not preclude retrial of the common issue before a jury.

5. Governing Law

The binding effect of a state court judgment in subsequent litigation in that state is a matter of the state's law. See Restatement Second of Conflict of Laws §§ 94, 95. The effect of a judgment of one state in another state is determined primarily by the Full Faith and Credit Clause of the Constitution. See Interstate Recognition of Judgments, infra p. 679. The binding effect in federal court of a state court judgment is prescribed by 28 U.S.C.A. § 1738; the effect of a federal court judgment in subsequent state or federal proceedings is a matter of federal decisional law. See Federal–State Recognition of Judgments, infra p. 686. Was the latter principle essential to the result reached in *Moitie*?

6. The Compulsory Counterclaim

The Federal Rules, F.R.C.P. 13, and many codes, e.g., C.C.P. 426.10, 426.30, require a defendant to assert as counterclaims any claims she has arising out of the transaction sued on. See generally Kennedy, Counterclaims Under Federal Rule 13, 11 Hous.L.Rev. 255 (1974). The first general compulsory counterclaim rule was that adopted in the 1872 revision of the California Code of Civil Procedure, C.C.P. 439. Subsequently the Federal Equity Rules of 1912, Rule 30, adopted the antecedent of present F.R.C.P. 13(a), providing that a counterclaim arising out of the same transaction as that sued on is compulsory. Equity Rule 30 derived from the old cross-bill in equity, which permitted the assertion of claims by defendant "to bring every matter in dispute completely before the court * * * to procure a complete determination of a matter already in litigation in the court * * *." Mitford, Pleadings in the Court of Chancery 81*–82* (Jeremy, Smith, Moulton ed. 1849). Under the Chancery practice, however, the cross-bill was largely optional, at times could be asserted after the pleadings on the main bill had been closed or even after the case had come on for hearing, and occasionally could be directed to be filed by the court. Mitford, op. cit. at 81*–83.* In contrast, contemporary "transaction" compulsory counterclaim rules require that the counterclaim be asserted at the initial pleading stage.

While the sanction for failure to assert a compulsory counterclaim is not provided in F.R.C.P. 13(a), the general view is that the consequence is that explicitly provided in C.C.P. 426.30: an action may not thereafter be brought on the claim. See Restatement Second of Judgments § 22. Cf. Currie Medical Specialties, Inc. v. Brown, 136 Cal.App.3d 774, 186 Cal.Rptr. 543 (1982). But see Aeroquip Corp. v. Chunn, 526 F.Supp. 1259 (N.D.Ala.1981): Plaintiffs initially sued the defendant in federal court for corporate raiding and stealing trade secrets. No counterclaim was filed and the case was settled with an injunction issued. Defendant then sued plaintiff in state court alleging defamation. Plaintiff sought a federal injunction against the state action alleging the claim was a compulsory counterclaim under F.R.C.P. 13(a). The court held that a federal court could not impose Rule 13(a) on a state court.

What are the situations in which the compulsory counterclaim rule bars subsequent assertion of a claim that would not otherwise be barred by res judicata or collateral estoppel? The most difficult case is where the first action was settled before trial. That was the situation in, e.g., Datta v. Staab, 173 Cal. App.2d 613, 343 P.2d 977 (1959): Staab and Datta were in an automobile collision. Staab, retaining his own personal lawyer, sued Datta, whose defense was assumed by counsel retained on his behalf by his liability insurer. Datta then retained his own personal injury lawyer, sued Staab, whose defense was assumed by counsel retained by *his* insurer. Staab's insurer raised the objection that Datta's claim was a compulsory counterclaim in Staab's action. Thereafter, Staab's personal injury counsel settled Staab's claim with Datta's insurer and the first action was dismissed. Datta's present action was then dismissed for failure to assert the present claim as a counterclaim in Staab's action. This outcome is now qualified by C.C.P. 426.30(b), which makes the compulsory cross-complaint requirement inapplicable if defendant defaults. See also Martino v. McDonald's System, Inc., 598 F.2d 1079 (7th Cir. 1979) (F.R. C.P. 13(a) not applicable to consent judgment entered before a pleading filed); United States v. Snider, 779 F.2d 1151 (6th Cir. 1985) (F.R.C.P. 13(a) not applicable where action was dismissed before a pleading filed).

Courts have varied on the applicability of the compulsory counterclaim rule to the Truth-in-Lending Act. One view is that the lender's suit on the debt and the debtor's rights under the Act are related so that each is a compulsory counterclaim to the other with the result that ancillary jurisdiction applies to support the counterclaim. See Lacy v. General Finance Corp., 651 F.2d 1026 (5th Cir. 1981); Plant v. Blazer Financial Services, Inc., 598 F.2d 1357 (5th Cir. 1979). The other view is that neither is a compulsory counterclaim, with the result that independent jurisdiction is required for the counterclaim, see Agliam v. Ohio Sav. Ass'n, 99 F.R.D. 145 (N.D.Ohio 1983), and that the claim can be asserted as an independent action not barred by res judicata. See Stewart v. Dollar Federal Sav. & Loan Ass'n, 523 F.Supp. 218 (S.D.Ohio 1981); White v. World Finance of Meridian, Inc., 653 F.2d 147 (5th Cir. 1981).

7. Administrative Agency Determinations

Administrative agencies have jurisdiction to adjudicate many types of claims. These adjudications usually are subject to some kind of judicial review on the record. Such adjudications may involve issues or claims that coincide with or overlap those arising in court litigation. The old rule was that administrative adjudications were not real litigation and hence had no preclusive effects beyond the immediate proceeding. Administrative adjudication has gradually been formalized so that such a proceeding is hardly distinguishable from one in court: pleadings, discovery, adversarial evidentiary presentations, and legal argument before an administrative law judge are all features typically found in such proceedings today. Administrative proceedings that approximate court litigation in affording the parties a "full and fair" opportunity to litigate are generally treated as equivalent to court litigation for purposes of res judicata. See United States v. Utah Const. & Mining Co., 384 U.S. 394, 86 S.Ct. 1545, 16 L.Ed.2d 642 (1966). However, the assimilation is not complete, particularly where a statutory right is involved which the legislature apparently intended to be open to judicial determination. See generally Restatement Second of Judgments § 83; e.g., University of Tennessee v. Elliott, 478 U.S. 788, 106 S.Ct. 3220, 92 L.Ed.2d 635 (1986) (unreviewed state administrative proceeding did not have preclusive effect on employee's Title VII discrimination claims, but did have preclusive effect on employee's claims under 42 U.S.C.A. § 1983); Clemens v. Apple, 65 N.Y.2d 746, 492 N.Y.S.2d 20, 481 N.E.2d 560 (1985). See also Carlisle, Getting a Full Bite of the Apple: When Should the Doctrine of Issue Preclusion Make an Administrative or Arbitral Determination Binding in a Court of Law?, 55 Fordham L.Rev. 63 (1986); Note, Res Judicata Effects of State Agency Decisions in Title VII Actions, 70 Cornell L.Rev. 695 (1985). For the preclusive effects of an administrative proceeding in a later criminal action, see People v. Sims, 32 Cal.3d 468, 186 Cal.Rptr. 77, 651 P.2d 321 (1982).

Should preclusive effect be given to arbitration proceedings? What special considerations might apply? See Carlisle, supra, and Shell, Res Judicata and Collateral Estoppel Effects of Commercial Arbitration, 35 So.Calif.L.Rev. 623 (1988).

b. PRECLUSION AS AGAINST OTHER PARTIES

INTRODUCTORY NOTE ON PRECLUSION AS AGAINST OTHER PARTIES

A judgment may have preclusive effects not only between the parties to the original proceeding, but also between such a party and one who was *not* a party to the first action.

1. The Mutuality Rule

Suppose that A claims to be injured as the result of acts of B and C. A sues B, but loses on the ground that no injury was proven. Suppose A now sues C for the same injury. Should A be bound by the earlier finding that he suffered no injury?

As the law of res judicata stood until about 1940, the answer was that A would not be bound. This was by virtue of the "mutuality" rule, which went like this: Estoppel by judgment should apply only when it can apply "mutually"; one party should not be bound by a judgment unless, if the judgment had gone the other way, the opposing party would have been bound; hence, a party cannot invoke a judgment as binding in his favor unless it would have been binding on the other party had it gone the other way. Thus, in the hypothetical above, A would not be bound because C, having not been a party to the first action, would not have been bound if A won.

If this sounds like nonsense, it is, except for the historical explanation that the Anglo-American rule of res judicata originated in a rule having to do with estoppel against parties to a record. See Millar, The Historical Relation of Estoppel by Record to Res Judicata, 35 Ill.L.Rev. 41 (1940). But the mutuality rule was backed by good authority. See Bigelow v. Old Dominion Copper Mining & Smelting Co., 225 U.S. 111, 32 S.Ct. 641, 56 L.Ed. 1009 (1912).

The mutuality rule was always subject to exceptions. Most of the exceptions were subsumed under a category called "privity." There were two branches of "privity," one tied to a winning party and the other to a loser. If a person was in "privity" with a winner, he could take advantage of that winner's victory, despite the mutuality rule. See, e.g., Portland Gold Mining Co. v. Stratton's Independence, Ltd., 158 Fed. 63 (8th Cir. 1907). On the other hand, if a person was in "privity" with a loser, he was bound even though he never had his day in court.

The basic problems in the modern law of preclusion as against third persons have been (1) how far the mutuality rule should be abandoned, so that a person who litigates against one person is bound in subsequent litigation with another party, and (2) under what conditions an *absentee* should be bound, under the concept of "privity" or otherwise, by the judgment in an action to which he was not a party.

2. Preclusion in Favor of Third Parties

a. Issue Preclusion. The modern rule on issue preclusion derives from Bernhard v. Bank of America, 19 Cal.2d 807, 122 P.2d 892 (1942). There, the heirs of an old lady asserted that a man who acted as her financial advisor had transferred her money into his own bank account; they lost, on a finding that the money had been given to him as a gift. The beneficiaries then sued the bank that had made the transfer, contending that the transfer was improper and that the bank should have taken care to prevent it. The bank asserted that the prior judgment was conclusive against the beneficiaries on the question of the legitimacy of the transfer. The court applied preclusion, rejecting the mutuality rule and holding, 122 P.2d at 895, that the critical questions were: "Was the issue decided in the prior adjudication identical with the one presented in the action in question? Was there a final judgment on the merits? Was the party against whom the plea is asserted a party or in privity with a party to the prior adjudication?"

Bernhard v. Bank of America had a slow start in gaining adherents, but is now the accepted rule. See Restatement Second of Judgments § 29; e.g., Schwartz v. Public Adm'r, 24 N.Y.2d 65, 298 N.Y.S.2d 955, 246 N.E.2d 725 (1969); Anno., 31 A.L.R.3d 1044. And see Parklane Hosiery Co. v. Shore, which follows.

On the preclusive effects of a criminal conviction in a later civil action, see Further Note on Preclusion, infra p. 676.

b. Claim Preclusion. In a limited number of situations, a party who has lost in a suit against one defendant is precluded thereby not only as to issues actually litigated, but also as to all matters that might have been litigated—i.e., under the rule of claim preclusion. See Restatement Second of Judgments § 51. Indeed, the situation in Bernhard v. Bank of America could have been disposed of on that basis, because the bank's liability was derivative from that of the man who took the money.

3. Preclusion Against Third Parties

The concept of "privity" includes a variety of situations in which litigation between P and D results in concluding T, where T is related by privity to the loser of the litigation. Thus a person, T, is concluded as to her legal rights without a day in court. For this result to follow, the connection between T and the loser must be close enough that the loser can be treated as having represented T's interests. This question is considered further in the Note following Rynsburger v. Dairymen's Fertilizer Coop., infra p. 676.

PARKLANE HOSIERY CO. v. SHORE

Supreme Court of the United States, 1979.
439 U.S. 322, 99 S.Ct. 645, 58 L.Ed.2d 552.

MR. JUSTICE STEWART delivered the opinion of the Court.

This case presents the question whether a party who has had issues of fact adjudicated adversely to it in an equitable action may be collaterally estopped from relitigating the same issues before a jury in a subsequent legal action brought against it by a new party.

The respondent brought this stockholder's class action against the petitioners in a Federal District Court. The complaint alleged that the petitioners, Parklane Hosiery Company, Inc. (Parklane), and 13 of its officers, directors, and stockholders, had issued a materially false and misleading proxy statement in connection with a merger.[1] The proxy statement, according to the complaint, had violated §§ 14(a), 10(b), and 20(a) of the Securities Exchange Act of 1934, 48 Stat. 895, 891, 899, as amended, 15 U.S.C. §§ 78n(a), 78j(b), and 78t(a), as well as various rules and regulations promulgated by the Securities and Exchange Commission (SEC). The complaint sought damages, rescission of the merger, and recovery of costs.

Before this action came to trial, the SEC filed suit against the same defendants in the Federal District Court, alleging that the proxy statement that had been issued by Parklane was materially false and misleading in essentially the same respects as those that had been alleged in the respondent's complaint. Injunctive relief was requested. After a 4–day trial, the District Court found that the proxy statement was materially false and misleading in the respects alleged, and entered a declaratory judgment to that effect. SEC v. Parklane Hosiery Co., 422 F.Supp. 477. The Court of Appeals for the Second Circuit affirmed this judgment. 558 F.2d 1083.

The respondent in the present case then moved for partial summary judgment against the petitioners, asserting that the petitioners were collaterally estopped from relitigating the issues that had been resolved against them in the action brought by the SEC.[2] The District Court denied the motion on the ground that such an application of collateral estoppel would deny the petitioners their Seventh Amendment right to a jury trial. The Court of Appeals for the Second Circuit reversed, holding that a party who has had issues of fact determined against him after a full and fair opportunity to litigate in a nonjury trial is collaterally estopped from obtaining a subsequent jury trial of these same issues of fact. 565 F.2d 815. The appellate court concluded that "the Seventh Amendment preserves the right to jury trial only with

---

1. The amended complaint alleged that the proxy statement that had been issued to the stockholders was false and misleading because it failed to disclose: (1) that the president of Parklane would financially benefit as a result of the company going private; (2) certain ongoing negotiations that could have resulted in financial benefit to Parklane; and (3) that the appraisal of the fair value of Parklane stock was based on insufficient information to be accurate.

2. A private plaintiff in an action under the proxy rules is not entitled to relief simply by demonstrating that the proxy

solicitation was materially false and misleading. The plaintiff must also show that he was injured and prove damages. Mills v. Electric Auto-Lite, 396 U.S. 375, 386–390, 90 S.Ct. 616, 622–624, 24 L.Ed.2d 593. Since the SEC action was limited to a determination of whether the proxy statements contained materially false and misleading statements, the respondent conceded that he would still have to prove these other elements of his prima facie case in the private action. The petitioner's right to a jury trial on those remaining issues is not contested.

respect to issues of fact, [and] once those issues have been fully and fairly adjudicated in a prior proceeding, nothing remains for trial, either with or without a jury." Id., at 819. Because of an intercircuit conflict,[3] we granted certiorari. 435 U.S. 1006, 98 S.Ct. 1875, 56 L.Ed. 2d 387.

I

The threshold question to be considered is whether, quite apart from the right to a jury trial under the Seventh Amendment, the petitioners can be precluded from relitigating facts resolved adversely to them in a prior equitable proceeding with another party under the general law of collateral estoppel. Specifically, we must determine whether a litigant who was not a party to a prior judgment may nevertheless use that judgment "offensively" to prevent a defendant from relitigating issues resolved in the earlier proceeding.[4]

A

Collateral estoppel, like the related doctrine of res judicata,[5] has the dual purpose of protecting litigants from the burden of relitigating an identical issue with the same party or his privy and of promoting judicial economy by preventing needless litigation. Blonder-Tongue Laboratories, Inc. v. University of Illinois Foundation, 402 U.S. 313, 328–329, 91 S.Ct. 1434, 1442–1443, 28 L.Ed.2d 788. Until relatively recently, however, the scope of collateral estoppel was limited by the doctrine of mutuality of parties. Under this mutuality doctrine, neither party could use a prior judgment as an estoppel against the other unless both parties were bound by the judgment.[6] Based on the premise that it is somehow unfair to allow a party to use a prior judgment when he himself would not be so bound,[7] the mutuality

---

3. The position of the Court of Appeals for the Second Circuit is in conflict with that taken by the Court of Appeals for the Fifth Circuit in Rachal v. Hill, 435 F.2d 59.

4. In this context, offensive use of collateral estoppel occurs when the plaintiff seeks to foreclose the defendant from litigating an issue the defendant has previously litigated unsuccessfully in an action with another party. Defensive use occurs when a defendant seeks to prevent a plaintiff from asserting a claim the plaintiff has previously litigated and lost against another defendant.

5. Under the doctrine of res judicata, a judgment on the merits in a prior suit bars a second suit involving the same parties or their privies based on the same cause of action. Under the doctrine of collateral estoppel, on the other hand, the second action is upon a different cause of action and the judgment in the prior suit precludes relitigation of issues actually litigat-

ed and necessary to the outcome of the first action. 1B. J. Moore, Federal Practice ¶ 0.405[1], pp. 622–624 (2d ed. 1974); e.g., Lawlor v. National Screen Serv. Corp., 349 U.S. 322, 326, 75 S.Ct. 865, 867, 99 L.Ed. 1122 (1955); Commissioner of Internal Revenue v. Sunnen, 333 U.S. 591, 597, 68 S.Ct. 715, 719, 92 L.Ed. 898 (1948); Cromwell v. County of Sac, 94 U.S. 351, 352–353, 24 L.Ed. 681 (1876).

6. E.g., Bigelow v. Old Dominion Copper Co., 225 U.S. 111, 127, 32 S.Ct. 641, 642, 56 L.Ed. 1009 ("It is a principle of general elementary law that estoppel of a judgment must be mutual"); Buckeye Powder Co. v. E. I. du Pont de Nemours Powder Co., 248 U.S. 55, 63, 39 S.Ct. 38, 39, 63 L.Ed. 123; Restatement of Judgments § 93 (1942).

7. It is a violation of due process for a judgment to be binding on a litigant who was not a party nor a privy and therefore has never had an opportunity to be heard.

requirement provided a party who had litigated and lost in a previous action an opportunity to relitigate identical issues with new parties.

By failing to recognize the obvious difference in position between a party who has never litigated an issue and one who has fully litigated and lost, the mutuality requirement was criticized almost from its inception.[8] Recognizing the validity of this criticism, the Court in Blonder-Tongue Laboratories, Inc. v. University of Illinois Foundation, supra, abandoned the mutuality requirement, at least in cases where a patentee seeks to relitigate the validity of a patent after a federal court in a previous lawsuit has already declared it invalid.[9] The "broader question" before the Court, however, was "whether it is any longer tenable to afford a litigant more than one full and fair opportunity for judicial resolution of the same issue." 402 U.S., at 328, 91 S.Ct., at 1442. The Court strongly suggested a negative answer to that question:

"In any lawsuit where a defendant, because of the mutuality principle, is forced to present a complete defense on the merits to a claim which the plaintiff has fully litigated and lost in a prior action, there is an arguable misallocation of resources. To the extent the defendant in the second suit may not win by asserting, without contradiction, that the plaintiff had fully and fairly, but unsuccessfully, litigated the same claim in the prior suit, the defendant's time and money are diverted from alternative uses—productive or otherwise—to relitigation of a decided issue. And, still assuming that the issue was resolved correctly in the first suit, there is reason to be concerned about the plaintiff's allocation of resources. Permitting repeated litigation of the same issue as long as the supply of unrelated defendants holds out reflects either the aura of the gaming table or 'a lack of discipline and of disinterestedness on the part of the lower courts, hardly a worthy or wise basis for fashioning rules of procedure.' Kerotest Mfg. Co. v. C–O–Two Co., 342 U.S. 180, 185, 72 S.Ct. 219, 222, 96 L.Ed. 200 (1952). Although neither judges, the parties, nor the adversary system performs perfectly in all cases, the requirement of determining whether the party against whom an estoppel is asserted had a full

Blonder-Tongue Laboratories, Inc. v. University of Illinois Foundation, 402 U.S. 313, 329, 91 S.Ct. 1434, 1443, 28 L.Ed.2d 788; Hansberry v. Lee, 311 U.S. 32, 40, 61 S.Ct. 115, 117, 85 L.Ed. 22.

8. This criticism was summarized in the Court's opinion in Blonder-Tongue Laboratories, Inc. v. University of Illinois Foundation, 402 U.S. 313, 322–327, 91 S.Ct. 1434, 1439–1442, 28 L.Ed.2d 788. The opinion of Justice Traynor for a unanimous California Supreme Court in Bernhard v. Bank of America Nat. Trust & Savings Assn., 19 Cal.2d 807, 812, 122 P.2d 892, 895 (1942), made the point succinctly:

"No satisfactory rationalization has been advanced for a requirement of mutuali-

ty. Just why a party who was not bound by a previous action should be precluded from asserting it as res judicata against a party who was bound by it is difficult to comprehend."

9. In Triplett v. Lowell, 297 U.S. 638, 56 S.Ct. 645, 80 L.Ed. 949, the Court had held that a determination of patent invalidity in a prior action does not bar a plaintiff from relitigating the validity of a patent in a subsequent action against a different defendant. This holding of the *Triplett* case was explicitly overruled in the *Blonder-Tongue* case.

and fair opportunity to litigate is a most significant safeguard." Id., at 329, 91 S.Ct., at 1443.[10]

B

The *Blonder-Tongue* case involved defensive use of collateral estoppel—a plaintiff was estopped from asserting a claim that the plaintiff had previously litigated and lost against another defendant. The present case, by contrast, involves offensive use of collateral estoppel—a plaintiff is seeking to estop a defendant from relitigating the issues which the defendant previously litigated and lost against another plaintiff. In both the offensive and defensive use situations, the party against whom estoppel is asserted has litigated and lost in an earlier action. Nevertheless, several reasons have been advanced why the two situations should be treated differently.[11]

First, offensive use of collateral estoppel does not promote judicial economy in the same manner as defensive use does. Defensive use of collateral estoppel precludes a plaintiff from relitigating identical issues by merely "switching adversaries." Bernhard v. Bank of America Nat. Trust & Savings Assn., 19 Cal.2d, at 813, 122 P.2d, at 895.[12] Thus defensive collateral estoppel gives a plaintiff a strong incentive to join all potential defendants in the first action if possible. Offensive use of collateral estoppel, on the other hand, creates precisely the opposite incentive. Since a plaintiff will be able to rely on a previous judgment against a defendant but will not be bound by that judgment if the defendant wins, the plaintiff has every incentive to adopt a "wait and see" attitude, in the hope that the first action by another plaintiff will result in a favorable judgment. E.g., Nevarov v. Caldwell, 161 Cal.App. 2d 762, 767–768, 327 P.2d 111, 115 (1968); Reardon v. Allen, 88 N.J. Super. 560, 571–572, 213 A.2d 26, 32 (1965). Thus offensive use of collateral estoppel will likely increase rather than decrease the total amount of litigation, since potential plaintiffs will have everything to gain and nothing to lose by not intervening in the first action.[13]

---

10. The Court also emphasized that relitigation of issues previously adjudicated is particularly wasteful in patent cases because of their staggering expense and typical length. 402 U.S., at 334, 348, 91 S.Ct., at 1445, 1452. Under the doctrine of mutuality of parties an alleged infringer might find it cheaper to pay royalties than to challenge a patent that had been declared invalid in a prior suit, since the holder of the patent is entitled to a statutory presumption of validity. Id., at 338, 91 S.Ct., at 1447.

11. Various commentators have expressed reservations regarding the application of offensive collateral estoppel. Currie, Mutuality of Estoppel: Limits of the *Bernhard* Doctrine, 9 Stan.L.Rev. 281 (1957); Semmel, Collateral Estoppel, Mutuality and Joinder of Parties, 68 Colum.L.

Rev. 1457 (1968); Note, The Impacts of Defensive and Offensive Assertion of Collateral Estoppel by a Nonparty, 35 Geo. Wash.L.Rev. 1010 (1967). Professor Currie later tempered his reservations. Civil Procedure: The Tempest Brews, 53 Calif.L. Rev. 25 (1965).

12. Under the mutuality requirement, a plaintiff could accomplish this result since he would not have been bound by the judgment had the original defendant won.

13. The Restatement (Second) of Judgments (Tent. Draft No. 2, 1975) § 88(3), provides that application of collateral estoppel may be denied if the party asserting it "could have effected joinder in the first action between himself and his present adversary."

A second argument against offensive use of collateral estoppel is that it may be unfair to a defendant. If a defendant in the first action is sued for small or nominal damages, he may have little incentive to defend vigorously, particularly if future suits are not foreseeable. The Evergreens v. Nunan, 141 F.2d 927, 929 (CA 2); cf. Berner v. British Commonwealth Pac. Airlines, 346 F.2d 532 (CA 2) (application of offensive collateral estoppel denied where defendant did not appeal an adverse judgment awarding damages of $35,000 and defendant was later sued for over $7 million). Allowing offensive collateral estoppel may also be unfair to a defendant if the judgment relied upon as a basis for the estoppel is itself inconsistent with one or more previous judgments in favor of the defendant.[14] Still another situation where it might be unfair to apply offensive estoppel is where the second action affords the defendant procedural opportunities unavailable in the first action that could readily cause a different result.[15]

C

We have concluded that the preferable approach for dealing with these problems in the federal courts is not to preclude the use of offensive collateral estoppel, but to grant trial courts broad discretion to determine when it should be applied.[16] The general rule should be that in cases where a plaintiff could easily have joined in the earlier action or where, either for the reasons discussed above or for other reasons, the application of offensive estoppel would be unfair to a defendant, a trial judge should not allow the use of offensive collateral estoppel.

In the present case, however, none of the circumstances that might justify reluctance to allow the offensive use of collateral estoppel is present. The application of offensive collateral estoppel will not here reward a private plaintiff who could have joined in the previous action, since the respondent probably could not have joined in the injunctive

---

14. In Professor Currie's familiar example, a railroad collision injures 50 passengers all of whom bring separate actions against the railroad. After the railroad wins the first 25 suits, a plaintiff wins in suit 26. Professor Currie argues that offensive use of collateral estoppel should not be applied so as to allow plaintiffs 27 through 50 automatically to recover. Currie, Mutuality of Estoppel: Limits of the *Bernhard* Doctrine, 9 Stan.L.Rev. 281, 304 (1957). See Restatement (Second) of Judgments (Tentative Draft No. 2, 1975) § 88(4).

15. If, for example, the defendant in the first action was forced to defend in an inconvenient forum and therefore was unable to engage in full scale discovery or call witnesses, application of offensive collateral estoppel may be unwarranted. Indeed, differences in available procedures may sometimes justify not allowing a prior judgment to have estoppel effect in a subsequent action even between the same parties, or where defensive estoppel is asserted against a plaintiff who has litigated and lost. The problem of unfairness is particularly acute in cases of offensive estoppel, however, because the defendant against whom estoppel is asserted typically will not have chosen the forum in the first action. See id., § 88(2) and Comment d.

16. This is essentially the approach of id., § 88, which recognizes that "the distinct trend if not the clear weight of recent authority is to the effect that there is no intrinsic difference between 'offensive' as distinct from 'defensive' issue preclusion, although a stronger showing that the prior opportunity was adequate may be required in the former situation than the later." Id., Reporter's Note, at 99.

action brought by the SEC even had he so desired.[17]   Similarly, there is no unfairness to the petitioners in applying offensive collateral estoppel in this case. First, in light of the serious allegations made in the SEC's complaint against the petitioners, as well as the foreseeability of subsequent private suits that typically follow a successful government judgment, the petitioners had every incentive to litigate the SEC lawsuit fully and vigorously.[18]   Second, the judgment in the Commission action was not inconsistent with any previous decision. Finally, there will in the respondent's action be no procedural opportunities available to the petitioner that were unavailable in the first action of a kind that might be likely to cause a different result.[19]

We conclude, therefore, that none of the considerations that would justify a refusal to allow the use of offensive collateral estoppel is present in this case. Since the petitioners received a "full and fair" opportunity to litigate their claims in the SEC action, the contemporary law of collateral estoppel leads inescapably to the conclusion that the petitioners are collaterally estopped from relitigating the question of whether the proxy statements were materially false and misleading.

II

The question that remains is whether, notwithstanding the law of collateral estoppel, the use of offensive collateral estoppel in this case would violate the petitioners' Seventh Amendment right to a jury trial.[20]

A

"[T]he thrust of the [Seventh] Amendment was to preserve the right to jury trial as it existed in 1791." Curtis v. Loether, 415 U.S. 189, 193, 94 S.Ct. 1005, 1007, 39 L.Ed.2d 260. At common law, a litigant was not entitled to have a jury determine issues that had been previously adjudicated by a chancellor in equity. Hopkins v. Lee, 6 Wheat. 109; Smith v. Kernochen, 7 How. 198, 217–218, 12 L.Ed. 666; Brady v. Daly, 175 U.S. 148, 158–159, 20 S.Ct. 62, 66, 44 L.Ed. 109;

---

17. SEC v. Everest Management Corp., 2nd Cir., 475 F.2d 1236, 1240 ("the complicating effect of the additional issues and the additional parties outweighs any advantage of a single disposition of the common issues"). Moreover, consolidation of a private action with one brought by the SEC without its consent is prohibited by statute. 15 U.S.C. § 78u(g).

18. After a 4–day trial in which the petitioners had every opportunity to present evidence and call witnesses, the District Court held for the SEC. The petitioners then appealed to the Court of Appeals for the Second Circuit, which affirmed the judgment against them. Moreover, the petitioners were already aware of the action brought by the respondent, since it had commenced before the filing of the SEC action.

19. It is true, of course, that the petitioners in the present action would be entitled to a jury trial of the issues bearing on whether the proxy statement was materially false and misleading had the SEC action never been brought—a matter to be discussed in Part II of this opinion. But the presence or absence of a jury as fact-finder is basically neutral, quite unlike, for example, the necessity of defending the first lawsuit in an inconvenient forum.

20. The Seventh Amendment provides: "In suits at common law, where the value in controversy exceeds twenty dollars, the right to jury trial shall be preserved . . . ."

Shapiro & Coquillette, The Fetish of Jury Trials in Civil Cases: A Comment on Rachal v. Hill, 85 Harv.L.Rev. 442, 448–458 (1971).[21]

Recognition that an equitable determination could have collateral estoppel effect in a subsequent legal action was the major premise of this Court's decision in Beacon Theatres v. Westover, 359 U.S. 500, 79 S.Ct. 948, 3 L.Ed.2d 988. In that case the plaintiff sought a declaratory judgment that certain arrangements between it and the defendant were not in violation of the antitrust laws, and asked for an injunction to prevent the defendant from instituting an antitrust action to challenge the arrangements. The defendant denied the allegations and counterclaimed for treble damages under the antitrust laws, requesting a trial by jury of the issues common to both the legal and equitable claims. The Court of Appeals upheld denial of the request, but this Court reversed, stating that:

> "[T]he effect of the action of the District Court could be, as the Court of Appeals believed, 'to limit the petitioner's opportunity fully to try to a jury every issue which has a bearing upon its treble damage suit,' for determination of the issue of clearances by the judge might 'operate either by way of res judicata or collateral estoppel so as to conclude both parties with respect thereto at the subsequent trial of the treble damage claim.' " Id., at 504, 79 S.Ct., at 953.

It is thus clear that the Court in the *Beacon Theatres* case thought that if an issue common to both legal and equitable claims was first determined by a judge, relitigation of the issue before a jury might be foreclosed by res judicata or collateral estoppel. To avoid this result, the Court held that when legal and equitable claims are joined in the same action, the trial judge has only limited discretion in determining the sequence of trial and "that discretion . . . must, wherever possible, be exercised to preserve jury trial." Id., at 510, 79 S.Ct., at 956.[22]

Both the premise of *Beacon Theatres,* and the fact that it enunciated no more than a general prudential rule were confirmed by this Court's decision in Katchen v. Landy, 382 U.S. 323, 86 S.Ct. 467, 15 L.Ed.2d 391. In that case the Court held that a bankruptcy court, sitting as a statutory court of equity, is empowered to adjudicate equitable claims prior to legal claims, even though the factual issues decided in the equity action would have been triable by a jury under

---

21. The authors of this article conclude that the historical sources "indicates that in the late eighteenth century and early nineteenth centuries, determinations in equity were thought to have as much force as determinations at law and that the possible impact on jury trial rights was not viewed with concern . . . . If collateral estoppel is otherwise warranted, the jury trial question should not stand in the way." Id., at 455-456. This common-law rule is adopted in the Restatement of Judgments § 68, Comment j (1942).

22. Similarly, in both Dairy Queen, Inc. v. Wood, 369 U.S. 469, 82 S.Ct. 894, 8 L.Ed. 2d 44, and Meeker v. Ambassador Oil Corp., 375 U.S. 160, 84 S.Ct. 273, 11 L.Ed. 2d 261, the Court held that legal claims should ordinarily be tried before equitable claims to preserve the right to a jury trial.

the Seventh Amendment if the legal claims had been adjudicated first. The Court stated:

"Both *Beacon Theatres* and *Dairy Queen* recognized that there might be situations in which the Court would proceed to resolve the equitable claim first even though the results might be dispositive of the issues involved in the legal claim." Id., at 339, 86 S.Ct., at 478.

Thus the Court in Katchen v. Landy recognized that an equitable determination can have collateral estoppel effect in a subsequent legal action, and that this estoppel does not violate the Seventh Amendment.

B

Despite the strong support to be found both in history and in the recent decisional law of this Court for the proposition that an equitable determination can have collateral estoppel effect in a subsequent legal action, the petitioners argue that application of collateral estoppel in this case would nevertheless violate their Seventh Amendment right to a jury trial. The petitioners contend that since the scope of the Amendment must be determined by reference to the common law as it existed in 1791, and since the common law permitted collateral estoppel only where there was mutuality of parties, collateral estoppel cannot constitutionally be applied when such mutuality is absent.

The petitioners have advanced no persuasive reason, however, why the meaning of the Seventh Amendment should depend on whether or not mutuality of parties is present. A litigant who has lost because of adverse factual findings in an equity action is equally deprived of a jury trial whether he is estopped from relitigating the factual issues against the same party or a new party. In either case, the party against whom estoppel is asserted has litigated questions of fact, and has had the facts determined against him in an earlier proceeding. In either case there is no further factfinding function for the jury to perform, since the common factual issues have been resolved in the previous action. Cf. Ex parte Peterson, 253 U.S. 300, 310, 40 S.Ct. 543, 547, 64 L.Ed. 919 ("No one is entitled in a civil case to trial by jury, unless and except so far as there are issues of fact to be determined").

The Seventh Amendment has never been interpreted in the rigid manner advocated by the petitioners. On the contrary, many procedural devices developed since 1791 that have diminished the civil jury's historic domain have been found not to be inconsistent with the Seventh Amendment. See Galloway v. United States, 319 U.S. 372, 388–393, 63 S.Ct. 1077, 1086–1088, 87 L.Ed. 1458 (a directed verdict does not violate the Seventh Amendment); Gasoline Products Co. v. Champlin Refining Co., 283 U.S. 494, 497–498, 51 S.Ct. 513–514, 75 L.Ed. 1188 (retrial limited to question of damages does not violate the Seventh Amendment even though there was no practice at common law for setting aside a verdict in part); Fidelity & Deposit Co. v. United

States, 187 U.S. 315, 319–321, 23 S.Ct. 120, 121–122, 47 L.Ed. 194 (summary judgment does not violate the Seventh Amendment).[23]

The *Galloway* case is particularly instructive. There the party against whom a directed verdict had been entered argued that the procedure was unconstitutional under the Seventh Amendment. In rejecting this claim, the Court said:

> "The Amendment did not bind the federal courts to the exact procedural incidents or details of jury trial according to the common law in 1791, any more than it tied them to the common-law system of pleading or the specific rules of evidence then prevailing. Nor were 'the rules of the common law' then prevalent, including those relating to the procedure by which the judge regulated the jury's role on questions of fact, crystalized in a fixed and immutable system . . . .

> "The more logical conclusion, we think, and the one which both history and the previous decisions here support, is that the Amendment was designed to preserve the basic institution of jury trial in only its most fundamental elements, not the great mass of procedural forms and details varying even then so widely among common-law jurisdictions." 319 U.S., at 390, 392, 63 S.Ct., at 1087 (footnote omitted).

The law of collateral estoppel, like the law in other procedural areas defining the scope of the jury's function, has evolved since 1791. Under the rationale of the *Galloway* case, these developments are not repugnant to the Seventh Amendment simply for the reason that they did not exist in 1791. Thus if, as we have held, the law of collateral estoppel forecloses the petitioners from relitigating the factual issues determined against them in the SEC action, nothing in the Seventh Amendment dictates a different result, even though because of lack of mutuality there would have been no collateral estoppel in 1791.[24]

23. The petitioners' reliance on Dimick v. Schiedt, 293 U.S. 474, 55 S.Ct. 296, 79 L.Ed. 603, is misplaced. In the *Dimick* case the Court held that an increase by the trial judge of the amount of money damages awarded by the jury violated the *second* clause of the Seventh Amendment, which provides that "no fact tried by a jury, shall be otherwise reexamined in any Court of the United States, than according to the rules of the common law." Collateral estoppel does not involve the "re-examination" of any fact decided by a jury. On the contrary, the whole premise of collateral estoppel is that once an issue has been resolved in a prior proceeding, there is no further factfinding function to be performed.

24. In reaching this conclusion, the Court of Appeals went on to state:

"Were there any doubt about the [question whether the petitioners were enti-

tled to a jury redetermination of the issues otherwise subject to collateral estoppel] it should in any event be resolved against the defendants in this case for the reason that, although they were fully aware of the pendency of the present suit throughout the non-jury trial of the SEC case, they made no effort to protect their right to a jury trial of the damage claims asserted by plaintiffs, either by seeking to expedite trial of the present action or by requesting Judge Duffy, in the exercise of his discretion pursuant to Rule 39(b), (c) F.R.Civ.P., to order that the issues in the SEC case be tried by a jury or before an advisory jury." 565 F.2d, at 821–822. (Footnote omitted.)

The Court of Appeals was mistaken in these suggestions. The petitioners did not have a right to a jury trial in the equitable injunctive action brought by the SEC. Moreover, an advisory jury, which might

The judgment of the Court of Appeals is

Affirmed.

MR. JUSTICE REHNQUIST, dissenting.

*   *   *

I

The Seventh Amendment provides:

"In Suits at common law, where the value in controversy shall exceed twenty dollars, the right of trial by jury shall be preserved, and no fact tried by a jury, shall be otherwise reexamined in any Court of the United States, than according to the rules of common law."

The history of the Seventh Amendment has been amply documented by this Court and by legal scholars,[2] and it would serve no useful purpose to attempt here to repeat all that has been written on the subject. Nonetheless, the decision of this case turns on the scope and effect of the Seventh Amendment, which, perhaps more than with any other provision of the Constitution, are determined by reference to the historical setting in which the Amendment was adopted. See Colgrove v. Battin, 413 U.S. 149, 152, 93 S.Ct. 2448, 2450, 37 L.Ed.2d 522 (1973). It therefore is appropriate to pause to review, albeit briefly, the circumstances preceding and attending the adoption of the Seventh Amendment as a guide in ascertaining its application to the case at hand.

A

It is perhaps easy to forget, now more than 200 years removed from the events, that the right of trial by jury was held in such esteem by the colonists that its deprivation at the hands of the English was one of the important grievances leading to the break with England. See Sources and Documents Illustrating the American Revolution 1764–1788 and the Formation of the Federal Constitution 94 (S. Morison 2d ed. 1929); R. Pound, The Development of Constitutional Guarantees of Liberty 69–72 (1957); C. Ubbelohde, The Vice-Admiralty Courts and the American Revolution 208–211 (1960). The extensive use of vice-admiralty courts by colonial administrators to eliminate the colonists' right of jury trial was listed among the specific offensive English acts

have only delayed and complicated that proceeding, would not in any event have been a Seventh Amendment jury. And the petitioners were not in a position to expedite the private action and stay the SEC action. The Securities Act of 1934 provides for prompt enforcement actions by the SEC unhindered by parallel private actions. 15 U.S.C. § 78u(g).

2. See, e.g., Colgrove v. Battin, 413 U.S. 149, 93 S.Ct. 2448, 37 L.Ed.2d 522 (1973);

Capital Traction Co. v. Hof, 174 U.S. 1, 19 S.Ct. 580, 43 L.Ed. 873 (1899); Parsons v. Bedford, 3 Pet. 433, 7 L.Ed. 732 (1830); Henderson, The Background of the Seventh Amendment, 80 Harv.L.Rev. 289 (1966) (hereinafter Henderson); Wolfram, The Constitutional History of the Seventh Amendment, 57 Minn.L.Rev. 639 (1973) (hereinafter Wolfram). See also United States v. Wonson, 28 Fed.Cas. 745 (No. 16,750) (C.C.D.Mass.1812) (Story, C.J.).

denounced in the Declaration of Independence.[3] And after war had broken out, all of the 13 newly formed States restored the institution of civil jury trial to its prior prominence; 10 expressly guaranteed the right in their state constitutions and the 3 others recognized it by statute or by common practice.[4] Indeed, "[t]he right to trial by jury was probably the only one universally secured by the first American state constitutions . . . ." L. Levy, Legacy of Suppression: Freedom of Speech and Press in Early American History 281 (1960).[5]

* * *

B

The Seventh Amendment requires that the right of trial by jury be "preserved." Because the Seventh Amendment demands preservation of the jury trial right, our cases have uniformly held that the content of the right must be judged by historical standards. E.g., Curtis v. Loether, 415 U.S. 189, 193, 94 S.Ct. 1005, 1007, 39 L.Ed.2d 260 (1974); Colgrove v. Battin, 413 U.S. 149, 155–156, 93 S.Ct. 2448, 2451–2452, 37 L.Ed.2d 522 (1973); Ross v. Bernhard, 396 U.S. 531, 533, 90 S.Ct. 733, 735, 24 L.Ed.2d 729 (1970); Capital Traction Co. v. Hof, 174 U.S. 1, 8–9, 19 S.Ct. 580, 583, 43 L.Ed. 873 (1899); Parsons v. Bedford, 28 U.S. (3 Pet.) 433, 446, 7 L.Ed. 732 (1830). Thus, in Baltimore & Carolina Line, Inc. v. Redman, 295 U.S. 654, 657, 55 S.Ct. 890, 891, 79 L.Ed. 1636 (1935), the Court stated that "[t]he right of trial by jury thus preserved is the right which existed under the English common law when the amendment was adopted." And in Dimick v. Schiedt, 293 U.S. 474, 476, 55 S.Ct. 296, 297, 79 L.Ed. 603 (1935), the Court held: "In order to ascertain the scope and meaning of the Seventh Amendment, resort must be had to the appropriate rules of the common law established at

3. The Declaration of Independence states: "For depriving us in many cases, of the benefits of Trial by Jury." Just two years earlier, in the Declaration of Rights adopted October 14, 1774, the first Continental Congress had unanimously resolved that "the respective Colonies are entitled to the common law of England, and more especially to the great and inestimable privilege of being tried by their peers of the vicinage, according to the course of that law." 1 Journals of the Continental Congress 69 (1904).

Holdsworth has written that of all the new methods adopted to strengthen the administration of the British laws, "the most effective, and therefore the most disliked, was the extension given to the jurisdiction of the reorganized courts of admiralty and vice-admiralty. It was the most effective, because it deprived the defendant of the right to be tried by a jury which was almost certain to acquit him." XI Holdsworth, A History of English Law 110 (1966). While the vice-admiralty courts

dealt chiefly with criminal offenses, their jurisdiction also was extended to many areas of the civil law. Wolfram 654 n. 47.

4. Ga.Const. of 1777, Art. LXI, in 2 The Federal and State Constitutions, Colonial Charters, and Other Organic Laws 785 (F. Thorpe ed. 1909); Md.Const. of 1776, Art. III, in 3 id., at 1686–1687; Mass.Const. of 1780, Art. XV, in 3 id., at 1891–1892; N.H. Const. of 1784, Art. XX, in 4 id., at 2456; N.J.Const. of 1776, Art. XXII, in 5 id., at 2598; N.Y.Const. of 1777, Art. XLI, in 5 id., at 2637; N.C.Const. of 1776, Declaration of Rights, Art. XIV, in 5 id., at 2788; Pa. Const. of 1776, Declaration of Rights, Art. XI, in 5 id., at 3083; S.C.Const. of 1778, Art. XLI, in 6 id., at 3257; Va.Const. of 1776, Bill of Rights, § 11, in 7 id., at 3814. See Wolfram 655.

5. When Congress in 1787 adopted the Northwest Ordinance for governance of the territories west of the Appalachians, it included a guarantee of trial by jury in civil cases. 2 Thorpe 960–961.

the time of the adoption of that constitutional provision in 1791."[12] If a jury would have been impaneled in a particular kind of case in 1791, then the Seventh Amendment requires a jury trial today, if either party so desires.

To be sure, it is the substance of the right of jury trial that is preserved, not the incidental or collateral effects of common-law practice in 1791. Walker v. New Mexico & S. P. R. Co., 165 U.S. 593, 596, 17 S.Ct. 421, 422, 41 L.Ed. 837 (1897). "The aim of the amendment, as this Court has held, is to preserve the substance of the common-law right of trial by jury, as distinguished from mere matters of form or procedure, and particularly to retain the common-law distinction between the province of the court and that of the jury . . . ." Baltimore & Carolina Line, Inc. v. Redman, 295 U.S., at 657, 55 S.Ct., at 891. Accord, Colgrove v. Battin, 413 U.S., at 156–157, 93 S.Ct., at 2452–2453; Gasoline Products Co. v. Champlin Refining Co., 283 U.S. 494, 498, 51 S.Ct. 513, 514, 75 L.Ed. 1188 (1931); Ex parte Peterson, 253 U.S. 300, 309, 40 S.Ct. 543, 546, 64 L.Ed. 919 (1920). "The Amendment did not bind the federal courts to the exact procedural incidents or details of jury trial according to the common law of 1791, any more than it tied them to the common-law system of pleading or the specific rules of evidence then prevailing." Galloway v. United States, 319 U.S. 372, 390, 63 S.Ct. 1077, 1087, 87 L.Ed. 1458 (1943).

To say that the Seventh Amendment does not tie federal courts to the exact procedure of the common law in 1791 does not imply, however, that any nominally "procedural" change can be implemented, regardless of its impact on the functions of the jury. For to sanction creation of procedural devices which limit the province of the jury to a greater degree than permitted at common law in 1791 is in direct contravention of the Seventh Amendment. See Neely v. Martin K. Eby Constr. Co., 386 U.S. 317, 322, 87 S.Ct. 1072, 1076, 18 L.Ed.2d 75 (1967); Galloway v. United States, 319 U.S., at 395, 63 S.Ct., at 1089; Dimick v. Schiedt, 293 U.S., at 487, 55 S.Ct., at 301; Ex parte Peterson, 253 U.S., at 309–310, 40 S.Ct., at 546. And since we deal here not with the common law *qua* common law but with the Constitution, no amount of argument that the device provides for more efficiency or more accuracy or is fairer will save it if the degree of invasion of the jury's province is greater than allowed in 1791. To rule otherwise would effectively permit judicial repeal of the Seventh Amendment because nearly any change in the province of the jury, no matter how drastic the diminution of its functions, can always be denominated "procedural reform."

* * *

12. The majority suggests that Dimick v. Schiedt is not relevant to the decision in this case because it dealt with the second clause of the Seventh Amendment. * * * I disagree. There is no intimation in that opinion that the first clause should be treated any differently than the second. The *Dimick* Court's respect for the guarantees of the Seventh Amendment applies equally to the first clause as to the second.

C

Judged by the foregoing principles, I think it is clear that petitioners were denied their Seventh Amendment right to a jury trial in this case. Neither respondent nor the Court doubt that at common law as it existed in 1791, petitioners would have been entitled in the private action to have a jury determine whether the proxy statement was false and misleading in the respects alleged. The reason is that at common law in 1791, collateral estoppel was permitted only where the parties in the first action were identical to, or in privity with, the parties to the subsequent action.[13] It was not until 1971 that the doctrine of mutuality was abrogated by this Court in certain limited circumstances. Blonder-Tongue Laboratories, Inc. v. University of Illinois Foundation, 402 U.S. 313, 91 S.Ct. 1434, 28 L.Ed.2d 788.[14] But developments in the judge-made doctrine of collateral estoppel, however salutary, cannot, consistent with the Seventh Amendment, contract in any material fashion the right to a jury trial that a defendant would have enjoyed in 1791. In the instant case, resort to the doctrine of collateral estoppel does more than merely contract the right to a jury trial: It eliminates the right entirely and therefore contravenes the Seventh Amendment.

* * *

II

Even accepting, *arguendo*, the majority's position that there is no violation of the Seventh Amendment here, I nonetheless would not sanction the use of collateral estoppel in this case. The Court today holds:

> "The general rule should be that in cases where a plaintiff could easily have joined in the earlier action or where, either for the reasons discussed above or for other reasons, the application of offensive collateral estoppel would be unfair to a defendant, a trial judge should not allow the use of offensive collateral estoppel."

* * *

In my view, it is "unfair" to apply offensive collateral estoppel where the party who is sought to be estopped has not had an opportunity to have the facts of his case determined by a jury. Since in this case petitioners were not entitled to a jury trial in the Securities and Exchange Commission (SEC) lawsuit,[18] I would not estop them from

---

13. See Smith v. Kernochen, 7 How. 198, 218, 12 L.Ed. 666 (1849); Hopkins v. Lee, 6 Wheat. 109, 113–114, 5 L.Ed. 218 (1821); F. Buller, An Introduction to the Law Relative to Trials at Nisi Prius* 232; T. Peake, A Compendium of the Law of Evidence 38 (2d ed. 1806).

14. The Court's decision in Blonder-Tongue Laboratories, Inc. v. University of Illinois Foundation is, on its facts, limited to the defensive use of collateral estoppel

in patent cases. Abandonment of mutuality is a recent development. The case of Bernhard v. Bank of America Nat. Trust & Sav. Assn., 19 Cal.2d 807, 122 P.2d 892 (1942), generally considered the seminal case adopting the new approach, was not decided until 1942.

18. I agree with the Court that "petitioners did not have a right to a jury trial in the equitable injunctive action brought by the SEC." * * *

relitigating the issues determined in the SEC suit before a jury in the private action. I believe that several factors militate in favor of this result.

First, the use of offensive collateral estoppel in this case runs counter to the strong federal policy favoring jury trials, even if it does not, as the majority holds, violate the Seventh Amendment. The Court's decision in Beacon Theatres, Inc. v. Westover, 359 U.S. 500, 79 S.Ct. 948, 3 L.Ed.2d 988 (1959), exemplifies that policy. In *Beacon Theatres* the Court held that where both equitable and legal claims or defenses are presented in a single case, "only under the most imperative circumstances, circumstances which in view of the flexible procedures of the Federal Rules we cannot now anticipate, can the right to a jury trial of legal issues be lost through prior determination of equitable claims." Id., at 510–511, 79 S.Ct., at 957.[19] * * *

Second, I believe that the opportunity for a jury trial in the second action could easily lead to a different result from that obtained in the first action before the court and therefore that it is unfair to estop petitioners from relitigating the issues before a jury. This is the position adopted in the Restatement (Second) of Judgments, which disapproves of the application of offensive collateral estoppel where the defendant has an opportunity for a jury trial in the second lawsuit that was not available in the first action.[22] The Court accepts the proposition that it is unfair to apply offensive collateral estoppel "where the second action affords the defendant procedural opportunities unavailable in the first action that could readily cause a different result." * * * Differences in discovery opportunities between the two actions are cited as examples of situations where it would be unfair to permit offensive collateral estoppel. [Ante], n. 15. But in the Court's view, the fact that petitioners would have been entitled to a jury trial in the

19. Meeker v. Ambassador Oil Corp., 375 U.S. 160, 84 S.Ct. 273, 11 L.Ed.2d 261 (1963) (*per curiam*), is a case where the doctrine of collateral estoppel yielded to the right to a jury trial. In *Meeker*, plaintiffs asserted both equitable and legal claims, which presented common issues, and demanded a jury trial. The trial court tried the equitable claim first, and decided that claim, and the common issues, adversely to plaintiffs. As a result, it held that plaintiffs were precluded from relitigating those same issues before a jury on their legal claim. 308 F.2d 875, 884 (CA10 1962). Plaintiffs appealed, alleging a denial of their right to a jury trial, but the Tenth Circuit affirmed the trial court. This Court reversed the Court of Appeals on the basis of Beacon Theatres, Inc. v. Westover, 359 U.S. 500, 79 S.Ct. 948, 3 L.Ed.2d 988 (1959) and Dairy Queen, Inc. v. Wood, 369 U.S. 469, 82 S.Ct. 894, 8 L.Ed.2d 44 (1962), even though, unlike those cases, the equitable action in *Meeker* already had

been tried and the common issues determined by the court. Thus, even though the plaintiffs in *Meeker* had received a "full and fair" opportunity to try the common issues in the prior equitable action, they nonetheless were given the opportunity to retry those issues before a jury. Today's decision is totally inconsistent with *Meeker* and the Court fails to explain this inconsistency.

22. Restatement (Second) of Judgments § 88(2), Comment d, p. 92 (Tent. Draft No. 2 1975). Citing Rachal v. Hill, 435 F.2d 59 (CA5 1970), cert. denied, 403 U.S. 904, 91 S.Ct. 2203, 29 L.Ed.2d 680 (1971), the Reporter's Note states: "The differences between the procedures available in the first and second actions, while not sufficient to deny issue preclusion between the same parties, may warrant a refusal to carry over preclusion to an action involving another party." Id., at 100.

present action is not such a "procedural opportunit[y]" because "the presence or absence of a jury as factfinder is basically *neutral,* quite unlike, for example, the necessity of defending the first lawsuit in an inconvenient forum." ∗ ∗ ∗ (emphasis added).

As is evident from the prior brief discussion of the development of the civil jury trial guarantee in this country, those who drafted the Declaration of Independence and debated so passionately the proposed Constitution during the ratification period, would indeed be astounded to learn that the presence or absence of a jury is merely "neutral," whereas the availability of discovery, a device unmentioned in the Constitution, may be controlling. It is precisely because the Framers believed that they might receive a different result at the hands of a jury of their peers than at the mercy of the sovereign's judges, that the Seventh Amendment was adopted. And I suspect that anyone who litigates cases before juries in the 1970's would be equally amazed to hear of the supposed lack of distinction between trial by court and trial by jury. The Court can cite no authority in support of this curious proposition. The merits of civil juries have been long debated, but I suspect that juries have never been accused of being merely "neutral" factors.[23]

∗ ∗ ∗

RYNSBURGER v. DAIRYMEN'S FERTILIZER COOPERATIVE, INC.

Court of Appeal of California, 1968.
266 Cal.App.2d 269, 72 Cal.Rptr. 102.

KERRIGAN, ASSOCIATE JUSTICE.

In July 1965 appellants filed suit in the Orange County Superior Court for the purpose of obtaining an injunction to abate a nuisance against the Dairymen's Fertilizer Cooperative, Inc., and three officials thereof. Inasmuch as the officers and directors are only nominal parties, the corporate entity will be regarded herein as the sole adverse party and will be referred to as "Dairymen's" or "Respondent."

Respondent is a nonprofit cooperative corporation formed by a combination of dairymen for the purpose of removing manure from the numerous dairies in the area in and around the city of Dairy Valley [1] to the respondent's plant where it is stockpiled, composted, packaged and sold as commercial fertilizer. Appellants are eleven homeowners who reside in close proximity to the fertilizer plant. Their residences are

23. See, e.g., Hearings on Recording of Jury Deliberations before the Subcommittee to Investigate the Administration of the Internal Security Act of the Senate Committee on the Judiciary, 84th Cong., 1st Sess., 63–81 (1955) (thorough summary of arguments pro and con on jury trials and an extensive bibliography); H. Kalven & H. Zeisel, The American Jury 4, n. 2 (1966) (bibliography); Redish, Seventh Amendment Right to Jury Trial: A Study in the Irrationality of Rational Decision Making, 70 Nw.U.L.Rev. 486, 502–508 (1975) (discussion of arguments for and against juries).

1. The name of the city of Dairy Valley has been changed since the inception of this litigation and is now known as the city of Cerritos.

situated in different geographical areas: three live in the city of La Palma, in the county of Orange; two in the city of Lakewood, Los Angeles County; two in the city of Dairy Valley (Cerritos), in Los Angeles County; two in the city of Cypress in Orange County; and finally, two reside in an unincorporated area of Orange County.

Dairymen's had maintained a manure stockpile and fertilizer facility at 13155 183rd Street in the city of Dairy Valley for approximately eight years. In 1964 the State Division of Highways acquired the site for the development of the Artesia Freeway. It therefore became necessary for the respondent to acquire another location for the conduct of its business. Consequently, it purchased a 12-acre parcel of property located at 12801 Del Amo Boulevard in Dairy Valley for $360,000. Respondent was granted a "zone special use permit" in May 1965 for the construction of a fertilizer plant, subject to compliance with certain operating conditions imposed by the Dairy Valley City Council.

Dairymen's parcel is situated approximately 600 feet from the nearest residential property in La Palma, 500 feet from the nearest residential property in Cypress, and approximately 200 feet from the nearest residential property in Lakewood.

In July 1965 appellants filed the Orange County Superior Court action for an injunction to abate a nuisance, and secured an ex parte temporary restraining order prohibiting respondent from conducting fertilizer operations on the new site. However, the temporary restraining order was dissolved in October 1965, and Dairymen's was permitted to undertake operations on the subject property. In dissolving the temporary restraining order and denying a preliminary injunction, the court found that Dairymen's operations were necessary for health purposes, and that any harm to appellants was outweighed by the sanitary utility of Dairymen's function in removing the daily manure deposits of the thousands of cows maintained in the numerous dairies located in the city of Dairy Valley and the surrounding communities.

In February 1966 appellants' counsel appeared before the city councils of La Palma, Cypress and Lakewood and requested that an action be initiated by the municipalities to abate respondent's operations. In March 1966 the cities of La Palma and Cypress jointly filed a nuisance action in the Orange County Superior Court. The city of Lakewood filed a similar suit the following month in the Los Angeles Superior Court. After the issues were joined, it was stipulated that the municipalities' actions against Dairymen's be consolidated and that the venue be changed to the San Bernardino County Superior Court.

Trial of the consolidated suits commenced in the San Bernardino forum in May 1966 and ended a month later. Over sixty witnesses were called. Several of the appellants from the cities of La Palma, Cypress and Lakewood testified, but the court refused testimony of those appellants residing in Dairy Valley and those living in the unincorporated area of Orange County.

The San Bernardino County trial court found, *inter alia,* that: the respondent's operations had *not* created and did *not* constitute a public nuisance; a stockpiling and fertilizing operation on the Del Amo property would not create or constitute a public nuisance if the operations were conducted in conformity with the requirements imposed by the Dairy Valley City Council and the restrictions imposed by the court.

In granting the special use permit, the city had ordered Dairymen's: to develop the property in accordance with the plot plan approved by the council; * * * to restrict its operations to daylight hours; to limit the maximum height of the stockpile to 25 feet; and to furnish a bond to the city guaranteeing compliance with the conditions of the special use permit.

The court decreed that Dairymen's comply with the aforesaid conditions imposed by the Dairy Valley City Council, except that the maximum height of the stockpile was ordered not to exceed 20 feet. The court further ordered Dairymen's to comply with the following supplemental conditions: (1) Truck loading and packaging operations be conducted in a newly-constructed building equipped with dust control equipment sufficient to meet Air Pollution Control District Standards; * * * (5) fertilizer hauled in and out of the plant be fully covered with a tarpaulin or canvas; and (6) obtain Air Pollution Control District permits and clearances.

The judgment establishing the foregoing conditions governing Dairymen's operation became final in November 1966, and in the judgment, the court reserved continuing jurisdiction over Dairymen's future operations.

Thereafter, in January 1967, appellants took steps in the Orange County Superior Court to reactivate their original suit. Manifestly, appellants were disappointed with the result of the cities' actions against Dairymen's. When the Orange County Superior Court set the matter for trial for September 5, 1967, Dairymen's counsel countered by filing an order to show cause proceeding in the San Bernardino Superior Court to restrain appellants from taking any further proceedings in the Orange County Superior Court action. * * *

* * *

This appeal is taken from the two injunctions restraining the appellants from proceeding with the prosecution of the Orange County Superior Court nuisance action.

Appellants' attack on the injunctions is based on the premise that the judgment of the San Bernardino Superior Court determining that the respondent's operations did not constitute a *public nuisance* is not *res judicata* in a suit by private property owners for abatement of a *private nuisance.* In urging that the San Bernardino judgment is not a bar to the trial of the Orange County action, appellants present the following arguments: (1) The suits of the three municipalities initiated in the name of the People of the State of California were filed on the theory that Dairymen's maintenance and operation of a fertilizer plant constituted a *public nuisance,* whereas the existing Orange County suit filed by appellants was predicated on the concept that the defendant's activities constituted a *private nuisance;* (2) the San Bernardino Superior Court refused to permit certain appellants, who were not residents of the three cities, to testify at the trial and, therefore, the San Bernardino judgment may not be raised as a bar to the Orange County action charging a private nuisance.   *   *   *

While statutory and case authority exist reflecting that there is a clear distinction between private nuisances on the one hand and public nuisances on the other (Civ.Code, §§ 3479, 3480, 3481; Johnson v. V. D. Reduction Co., 175 Cal. 63, 65–67, 164 P. 1119, L.R.A.1917E 1007; County of Yuba v. Kate Haynes Min. Co., 141 Cal. 360, 74 P. 1049; Fisher v. Zumwalt, 128 Cal. 493, 494–497, 61 P. 82; Meek v. DeLatour, 2 Cal.App. 261, 83 P. 300), the critical issue is whether the San Bernardino Superior Court judgment determining that Dairymen's stockpile plant did not constitute a public nuisance bars appellant's suit for a private nuisance.

Under the doctrine of *res judicata,* an existing final judgment on the merits of a cause rendered by a court of competent jurisdiction is, in all subsequent actions, conclusive of the rights of the parties, and their privies, on all material issues that were or might have been determined. (French v. Rishell, 40 Cal.2d 477, 479, 254 P.2d 26; Dillard v. McKnight, 34 Cal.2d 209, 213, 209 P.2d 387, 11 A.L.R.2d 835; Wynn v. Treasure Co., 146 Cal.App.2d 69, 78, 303 P.2d 1067.) The doctrine rests upon the sound public policy that there must be an end of litigation and, accordingly, persons who have had one fair trial on the issue may not again have it adjudicated. (Dillard v. McKnight, supra, 34 Cal.2d p. 214, 209 P.2d 387.) The application of the doctrine in a given case depends on affirmative answers to these questions: "Was the issue decided in the prior adjudication identical with the one presented in the action in question? Was there a final judgment on the merits? Was the party against whom the plea [of *res judicata*] is asserted a party or in privity with a party to the prior adjudication?" (Bernhard v. Bank of America, 19 Cal.2d 807, 813, 122 P.2d 892, 895.)

With respect to the first question, appellants contend that they, as private individuals, have a separate and mutually exclusive cause of action for abatement of a private nuisance which is totally distinguishable, separate and independent of the municipalities' action for public nuisance. The record discloses, however, that the governing bodies of the three cities involved in the San Bernardino court trial were requested to take action by the attorneys who represent the appellants herein. The minutes of the city council meetings reflect that appellants' counsel advised the city officials that they represented the appellants in the Orange County action then pending, and that "90% of the work had been done and would be made available to the City Attorney." Many of the appellants testified in the San Bernardino trial. The cities'

action was filed for the purpose of benefiting all property owners located in proximity to the defendant's plant. The allegations contained in appellants' second amended complaint in the Orange County suit are substantially the same contentions set forth in the People's actions. There is a strong identity between the exhibits attached to the complaint in the appellants' Orange County action and those affixed to the cities' action. While appellants now assert that their Orange County action was instituted to enjoin a *private nuisance*, their second amended complaint alleges that the respondent's intended activity "resulted in a *public nuisance* to plaintiffs and others as defined by section 3479 of the Civil Code"; that said public nuisance would be abated by ". . . the complete enclosure by a dome superstructure of the entire operations . . . ." This allegation to the effect that Dairymen's operations constituted a public nuisance was repeated by reference in each of the six causes of action set forth in appellants' complaint. In the prayer, appellants also pray for "an injunction regulating defendants in a manner deemed appropriate by the court . . . so that the operation . . . will no longer constitute a public nuisance to plaintiffs and others residing in the vicinity . . . such as by requiring said defendant . . . to completely enclose by a building . . . its entire operation . . . ." It thus appears that appellants charge defendants in their Orange County action with the creation, operation and maintenance of the identical nuisance pleaded and tried in the San Bernardino action.

A public nuisance is one which affects at the same time an entire community or neighborhood, or any considerable number of persons, although the extent of the annoyance or damage inflicted upon individuals may be unequal. (Civ.Code, § 3480.) Clearly, the conditions complained of in both the San Bernardino and Orange County suits affect the entire neighborhood and amount to allegations of a public nuisance. (See Eaton v. Klimm, 217 Cal. 362, 368, 18 P.2d 678; Wade v. Campbell, 200 Cal.App.2d 54, 59, 19 Cal.Rptr. 173, 92 A.L.R.2d 966.) Consequently, appellants are precluded from converting what they formerly alleged to be a public nuisance into a series of private nuisances. (See Eaton v. Klimm, supra.)

Appellants next assert that the San Bernardino action is not *res judicata* inasmuch as appellants were not parties in the city suits, and for the further reason that the San Bernardino court excluded proffered testimony of certain of the appellants, thereby denying them their day in court. By the usual formulation of the rule, however, the effects of *res judicata* may also be applied to those in privity with parties to an action. (65 Harv.L.Rev. 885; 3 Witkin, Calif. Proc. 1956.) Privity involves a person so identified in interest with another that he represents the same legal right. (Zaragosa v. Craven, 33 Cal.2d 315, 318, 202 P.2d 73, 6 A.L.R.2d 461, quoting 30 Am.Jur., § 225, p. 957.) Where statutory authority to sue has been given specifically to a public entity by statute, a judgment rendered therein is *res judicata* as to *all* members of the class represented. (City of Chino v. Superior Court of

Orange County, 255 A.C.A. 873, 882, 63 Cal.Rptr. 532.) Therefore, citizens and residents, to the extent they are in privity with or represented by the city or state, are bound by judgments against the governmental body. (Price v. Sixth District Agricultural Assn., 201 Cal. 502, 513, 258 P. 387.) If it appears that a particular party, although not before the court in person, is so far represented by others that his interest received actual and efficient protection, the decree will be held to be binding upon him. (Graham v. Board of Supervisors, 25 A.D.2d 250, 269 N.Y.S.2d 477, 480; see King v. Internat. Union etc. Engineers, 114 Cal.App.2d 159, 164, 250 P.2d 11; Smith v. City of Los Angeles, 190 Cal.App.2d 112, 128, 11 Cal.Rptr. 898.) Since property owners similarly injured by a nuisance constitute a class (Rodman v. Rogers [6th Cir.] 109 F.2d 520, 521), and since that class was well represented in the San Bernardino action, the principle of *res judicata* applies. "The rule should not be defeated by minor differences of form, parties, or allegations, when these are contrived only to obscure the real purpose—a second trial on the same cause between the same parties . . . ." (Hochman v. Mortgage Finance Corporation, 289 Pa. 260, 137 A. 252, 253; see also Stearns v. Los Angeles City School Dist., 244 Cal.App.2d 696, 714–715, 53 Cal.Rptr. 482; Cade v. Superior Court, 191 Cal.App.2d 554, 558–559, 12 Cal.Rptr. 847; Myers v. Superior Court, 75 Cal.App.2d 925, 931, 172 P.2d 84.)

The San Bernardino judgment imposed numerous and complex regulations upon respondent respecting the operation of its fertilizer plant. The plant building was constructed and equipment installed in compliance with the conditions established by the San Bernardino tribunal. The record reflects that those improvements installed in compliance with the city of Dairy Valley restrictions alone amounted to some $19,000. In view of the fact that the San Bernardino court retained jurisdiction over Dairymen's operations, it obviously intended to enforce the conditions it imposed. Consequently, it would be intolerable for two or more courts to undertake the operations of the plant, for it is fairly deducible that two courts might impose different or conflicting regulations upon respondent's operations. The San Bernardino court's retention of jurisdiction is in accordance with the rule that a court of equity may retain continuing jurisdiction to meet future problems and changing conditions. (Ecker Bros. v. Jones, 186 Cal.App. 2d 775, 786, 9 Cal.Rptr. 335; Klinker v. Klinker, 132 Cal.App.2d 687, 694, 283 P.2d 83.) The San Bernardino court, having properly retained jurisdiction over Dairymen's operations, may therefore make such orders as are necessary to preserve its jurisdiction so as to prevent impairment of its judgment, to avoid conflicting regulations and vexatious litigation, and to make a complete adjudication of the controversy. (Hercules Glue Co. v. Littooy, 45 Cal.App.2d 42, 45, 113 P.2d 490; 18 Cal.Jur.2d, § 59, pp. 243–245.)

The propriety of injunctive relief to prevent conflicting or vexatious litigation has long been established in our law. (Civ.Code, § 3422; Code Civ.Proc., § 526(6).) Where there exists two or more actions involving the same subject matter or the same facts or principles, restraint is necessary to prevent a multiplicity of judicial proceedings. (Scott v. Industrial Acc. Comm., 46 Cal.2d 76, 81–82, 293 P.2d 18.) Restraint is also necessary to avoid unseemly conflict between courts that might arise if they were free to make contradictory decisions relating to the same controversy. (Scott v. Industrial Acc. Com., supra.)

In summary, the San Bernardino Superior Court's action in restraining the Orange County suit was fully justified since its judgment was *res judicata* on the nuisance issue, and since it was empowered to make such orders as necessary to prevent impairment of its judgment and to avoid conflicting regulations and vexatious litigation.

* * *

FURTHER NOTE ON PRECLUSION

1. Persons in "Privity"

There is a large and not easily summarized group of relationships, categorized as involving "privity," out of which a judgment binding a party is binding on a third person. See Restatement Second of Judgments §§ 37, 39–62. At least three could have been applied in *Rynsburger:* That the individual landowners were in a class represented by the cities, see Restatement, supra, § 41; that they were members of corporations that were parties to the suits, and hence bound in the same way that stockholders would be bound, see id. § 59; and that they stood by knowing that the litigation was intended to determine the proper use of the property, see id. § 62. What about a person who subsequently purchased land near the Dairymen's operation? Compare Restatement, supra, § 43; cf. Golden State Bottling Co. v. NLRB, 414 U.S. 168, 94 S.Ct. 414, 38 L.Ed.2d 388 (1973); Vulcan, Inc. v. Fordees Corp., 658 F.2d 1106 (6th Cir. 1981). For application of preclusion to members of a class who helped manage litigation, see Bolden v. Pennsylvania State Police, 578 F.2d 912 (3d Cir. 1978); cf. General Foods Corp. v. Massachusetts Dept. of Public Health, 648 F.2d 784 (1st Cir. 1981) (member of trade association who helped finance action by association); Crane v. Commissioner of Dept. of Agriculture, 602 F.Supp. 280 (D.Me.1985) (members of class who helped manage and finance action).

In Consumers Union of the United States, Inc. v. Consumer Product Safety Comm'n, 590 F.2d 1209 (D.C.Cir. 1978), the court held that the plaintiff was entitled to obtain TV test results and was not barred by the judgment in favor of the TV manufacturers in a prior reverse FOIA suit enjoining the Commission from releasing the tests. The court reasoned that the present plaintiff did not have its day in court and that the manufacturers should have joined persons like the plaintiff if they desired preclusive effect. The Supreme Court reversed on the ground that the Commission had not "improperly" withheld information under the Act when it denied the plaintiff's request because it had to obey the injunction out of respect for the judicial process. GTE Sylvania, Inc. v. Consumers Union of the United States, Inc., 445 U.S. 375, 100 S.Ct. 1194, 63 L.Ed.2d 467 (1980). Would the court have come to the same conclusion if the earlier judgment had been a declaratory judgment without injunctive relief? If so, does that mean declaratory and equitable relief are binding even against those who did not have notice of the proceedings or were not permitted to intervene? Should declaratory relief require notice to all interested persons?

See, e.g., Connecticut Practice Book, Superior Court Rules (Civil) § 390(d). Should such notice include an "opt out" provision as in class actions?

2. Settling to Avoid Future Preclusion

Because a judgment may have preclusive effects in favor of third persons, a losing party may be better off strategically if he settles the claim after judgment in return for the winner's vacating the judgment and thus wiping the determination off the books. This incentive gives additional bargaining power to one of several parties when all are adverse to another party, for example one of several plaintiffs. Allowing such a settlement may undercut the public interest in avoiding relitigation of the issues determined before the settlement erased them. See Note, Avoiding Issue Preclusion by Settlement Conditioned Upon the Vacatur of Entered Judgments, 96 Yale L.J. 860 (1987); Note, Collateral Estoppel Effects of Judgments Vacated Pursuant to Settlement, 1987 U.Ill.L.Rev. 731. See also Comment, The Impact of Collateral Estoppel on Postjudgment Settlements, 15 Sw.U.L.Rev. 343 (1985), discussing Sandoval v. Superior Court, 140 Cal.App.3d 932, 190 Cal.Rptr. 29 (1983), where the court held that a plaintiff who was not a party to the prior action could assert collateral estoppel against a defendant who had entered into a postjudgment settlement with a plaintiff in the prior action.

3. Defensive and Offensive Collateral Estoppel

The decision in Bernhard v. Bank of America, discussed supra p. 655, allowing defensive use of collateral estoppel by a non-party to the prior litigation, has met with general approbation. See Blonder–Tongue Laboratories, Inc. v. University of Illinois Foundation, 402 U.S. 313, 91 S.Ct. 1434, 28 L.Ed.2d 788 (1971), discussed in Parklane Hosiery Co. v. Shore, supra; Restatement Second of Judgments § 29. Offensive use of collateral estoppel by a non-party raises more difficult problems, as indicated by *Parklane.* See James & Hazard 635–637. In addition to the fairness concerns expressed by the Court in *Parklane,* critics have doubted the efficiency rationale of the doctrine. See Flanagan, Offensive Collateral Estoppel: Inefficiency and Foolish Consistency, 1982 Ariz.St.L.J. 45; Callen, Efficiency After All: A Reply to Professor Flanagan's Theory of Offensive Collateral Estoppel, 1983 Ariz.St.L.J. 799. See also Green, The Inability of Offensive Collateral Estoppel to Fulfill Its Promise: An Examination of Estoppel in Asbestos Litigation, 70 Iowa L.Rev. 141 (1984). Nevertheless, courts appear ready to apply collateral estoppel offensively, at least against private parties, where it would not be inequitable to do so. See Restatement Second of Judgments § 29. Different rules apply where the Government is a party, as discussed below.

4. Preclusion Effects of Criminal Convictions

A criminal conviction can be relied on for preclusive effect in a subsequent civil action in which the criminal defendant is a party. In Allen v. McCurry, 449 U.S. 90, 101 S.Ct. 411, 66 L.Ed.2d 308 (1980), the plaintiff (the accused in the previous criminal case) brought a civil rights action against police officers alleging an unconstitutional search and seizure in an arrest that was followed by a state court prosecution for possessing heroin and for assault. The court hearing the criminal case had denied the accused's pretrial motion to suppress made on the ground that the search and seizure was unconstitutional. In the accused's subsequent civil action against the police officers, the officers moved for summary judgment on the ground that the ruling on the motion to suppress precluded the accused from relitigating the constitutionality of the search and seizure. The Supreme Court affirmed the trial court's grant of summary judgment, finding that the plaintiff had a full and fair opportunity to litigate the issue in the state court criminal proceeding.

A criminal conviction can also have preclusive effect in a later civil action where the accused is not a party but where one of the parties was in privity with him. In Teitelbaum Furs, Inc. v. Dominion Ins. Co., 58 Cal.2d 601, 25 Cal. Rptr. 559, 375 P.2d 439 (1962), a corporation sued to recover on an insurance policy covering loss by theft. The defendant insurer pleaded that the prior conviction of the corporation's president for having taken the goods himself and having made a false insurance claim was preclusive in the present civil action. Held: for defendant. 25 Cal.Rptr. at 561–62: "Although plaintiffs' president did not have the initiative in his criminal trial, he was afforded a full opportunity to litigate the issue of his guilt with all the safeguards afforded the criminal defendant, and * * * he had every motive to make as vigorous and effective a defense as possible. * * * Teitelbaum's election not to testify in his own behalf in the criminal case was presumably made on the assumption that he would benefit thereby. His error, if any, in trial strategy would no more defeat the plea of collateral estoppel than the failure of a litigant to introduce relevant available evidence in any other situation." Is this analysis fully satisfying? Is the "trial strategy" problem of withholding a criminal defendant from the stand different from withholding evidence in a civil case? Are the interests at stake something more than conservation of judicial energy? Compare Priest v. American Smelting & Refining Co., 409 F.2d 1229 (9th Cir. 1969).

Convictions for major offenses are generally thought to be reliable and a proper subject for collateral estoppel, but there are some doubts about the reliability of convictions for minor offenses. For example, many states provide that a conviction for a motor vehicle violation may not be used to establish civil liability. There are similar reliability concerns about convictions based on guilty pleas, due to the harsh realities of the plea bargaining process. See Bower v. O'Hara, 759 F.2d 1117 (3d Cir.1985) (guilty plea not preclusive in later civil action). For a general discussion of the subject, see Thau, Collateral Estoppel and the Reliability of Criminal Determinations: Theoretical, Practical, and Strategic Implications for Criminal and Civil Litigation, 70 Geo.L.J. 1079 (1982); Shapiro, Should a Guilty Plea Have Preclusive Effect?, 70 Iowa L.Rev. 27 (1984).

In situations where the doctrine of collateral estoppel does not apply, a criminal conviction is admissible in evidence in certain jurisdictions as some proof of the fact in question. See Fed.R.Evid. 803(22) (felony conviction).

5. Preclusion Against the United States

The United States and other governments are generally subject to the usual rules of claim preclusion under the doctrine of res judicata. See United States v. Mendoza, 464 U.S. 154, 104 S.Ct. 568, 78 L.Ed.2d 379 (1984); Montana v. United States, 440 U.S. 147, 99 S.Ct. 970, 59 L.Ed.2d 210 (1979). The United States is also generally subject to issue preclusion where the party seeking to invoke collateral estoppel was a party to the prior litigation. Montana v. United States, supra. See also Levin and Leeson, Issue Preclusion Against the United States Government, 70 Iowa L.Rev. 113 (1984).

When faced with the issue of nonmutual offensive collateral estoppel against the United States, however, the Court distinguished public parties from private parties and held that nonmutual collateral estoppel should not be available against the United States. United States v. Mendoza, supra. The Court reasoned that the economy interests underlying the doctrine are outweighed by the doctrine's particular effect on the Government: (1) the Government is more likely than any private party to litigate with different parties over the same legal issue because of the breadth of its litigation relationships and because of the nature of the issues the Government litigates, particularly constitutional issues; (2) the Government would be forced to revise its strategic and tactical policies as to whether to appeal a case, and might have to appeal in every case to avoid foreclosing further review of the issue; and (3) the Supreme Court would be deprived of the benefit of multiple determinations by Courts of Appeals on difficult legal questions, because the development of such diverse judicial views would be frozen by the first final decision. See also Note, Collateral Estoppel and Nonacquiescence: Precluding Government Relitigation in the Pursuit of Litigant Equality, 99 Harv.L.Rev. 847 (1986).

2. RECOGNITION OF JUDGMENTS FROM OTHER JURISDICTIONS

---

a. INTERSTATE RECOGNITION OF JUDGMENTS

FAUNTLEROY v. LUM

Supreme Court of the United States, 1908.
210 U.S. 230, 28 S.Ct. 641, 52 L.Ed. 1039.

MR. JUSTICE HOLMES delivered the opinion of the Court:

This is an action upon a Missouri judgment, brought in a court of Mississippi. The declaration set forth the record of the judgment. The defendant pleaded that the original cause of action arose in Mississippi out of a gambling transaction in cotton futures; that he declined to pay the loss; that the controversy was submitted to arbitration, the question as to the illegality of the transaction, however, not being included in the submission; that an award was rendered against the defendant; that thereafter, finding the defendant temporarily in Missouri, the plaintiff brought suit there upon the award; that the trial court refused to allow the defendant to show the nature of the transaction, and that, by the laws of Mississippi, the same was illegal and void, but directed a verdict if the jury should find that the submission and award were made, and remained unpaid; and that a verdict was rendered and the judgment in suit entered upon the same. (The plaintiff in error is an assignee of the judgment, but nothing turns upon that.) The plea was demurred to on constitutional grounds, and the demurrer was overruled, subject to exception. Thereupon replications were filed, again setting up the Constitution of the United States (art. 4, § 1), and were demurred to. The supreme court of Mississippi held the plea good and the replications bad, and judgment was entered for the defendant. Thereupon the case was brought here.

The main argument urged by the defendant to sustain the judgment below is addressed to the jurisdiction of the Mississippi courts.

The laws of Mississippi make dealing in futures a misdemeanor, and provide that contracts of that sort, made without intent to deliver the commodity or to pay the price, "shall not be enforced by any court." Anotated Code of 1892, §§ 1120, 1121, 2117. The defendant contends that this language deprives the Mississippi courts of jurisdiction, and that the case is like Anglo–American Provision Co. v. Davis Provision Co., 191 U.S. 373, 48 L.ed. 225, 24 Sup.Ct.Rep. 92. There the New York statutes refused to provide a court into which a foreign corporation could come, except upon causes of action arising within the state, etc.; and it was held that the state of New York was under no constitutional obligation to give jurisdiction to its supreme court against its will. One question is whether that decision is in point.

No doubt it sometimes may be difficult to decide whether certain words in a statute are directed to jurisdiction or to merits; but the distinction between the two is plain. One goes to the power, the other only to the duty, of the court. Under the common law it is the duty of a court of general jurisdiction not to enter a judgment upon a parol promise made without consideration; but it has power to do it, and, if it does, the judgment is unimpeachable, unless reversed. Yet a statute could be framed that would make the power, that is, the jurisdiction, of the court, dependent upon whether there was a consideration or not. Whether a given statute is intended simply to establish a rule of substantive law, and thus to define the duty of the court, or is meant to limit its power, is a question of construction and common sense. When it affects a court of general jurisdiction, and deals with a matter upon which that court must pass, we naturally are slow to read ambiguous words as meaning to leave the judgment open to dispute, or as intended to do more than to fix the rule by which the court should decide.

The case quoted concerned a statute plainly dealing with the authority and jurisdiction of the New York court. The statute now before us seems to us only to lay down a rule of decision. The Mississippi court in which this action was brought is a court of general jurisdiction and would have to decide upon the validity of the bar, if the suit upon the award or upon the original cause of action had been brought there. The words "shall not be enforced by any court" are simply another, possibly less emphatic, way of saying that an action shall not be brought to enforce such contracts. As suggested by the counsel for the plaintiff in error, no one would say that the words of the Mississippi statute of frauds, "An action shall not be brought whereby to charge a defendant," Code 1892, § 4225, go to the jurisdiction of the court. Of course it could be argued that logically they had that scope, but common sense would revolt. See 191 U.S. 375, 48 L.ed. 227, 24 Sup. Ct.Rep. 92. A stronger case than the present is General Oil Co. v.

Crain, 209 U.S. 211, 216, ante, 475, 28 Sup.Ct.Rep. 475. We regard this question as open under the decisions below, and we have expressed our opinion upon it independent of the effect of the judgment, although it might be that, even if jurisdiction of the original cause of action was withdrawn, it remained with regard to a suit upon a judgment based upon an award, whether the judgment or award was conclusive or not. But it might be held that the law as to jurisdiction in one case followed the law in the other, and therefore we proceed at once to the further question, whether the illegality of the original cause of action in Mississippi can be relied upon there as a ground for denying a recovery upon a judgment of another state.

The doctrine laid down by Chief Justice Marshall was "that the judgment of a state court should have the same credit, validity, and effect in every other court in the United States which it had in the state where it was pronounced, and that whatever pleas would be good to a suit thereon in such state, and none others, could be pleaded in any other court in the United States." Hampton v. M'Connel, 3 Wheat. 234, 4 L.ed. 378. There is no doubt that this quotation was supposed to be an accurate statement of the law as late as Christmas v. Russell, 5 Wall. 290, 18 L.ed. 475, where an attempt of Mississippi, by statute, to go behind judgments recovered in other states, was declared void, and it was held that such judgments could not be impeached even for fraud.

But the law is supposed to have been changed by the decision in Wisconsin v. Pelican Ins. Co., 127 U.S. 265, 32 L.ed. 239, 8 Sup.Ct.Rep. 1370. That was a suit brought in this court by the state of Wisconsin upon a Wisconsin judgment against a foreign corporation. The judgment was for a fine or penalty imposed by the Wisconsin statutes upon such corporations doing business in the state and failing to make certain returns, and the ground of decision was that the jurisdiction given to this court by art. 3, § 2, as rightly interpreted by the judiciary act, now Rev.Stat. § 687, U.S.Comp.Stat. 1901, p. 565, was confined to "controversies of a civil nature," which the judgment in suit was not. The case was not within the words of art. 1, § 1, and, if it had been, still it would not have, and could not have, decided anything relevant to the question before us. It is true that language was used which has been treated as meaning that the original claim upon which a judgment is based may be looked into further than Chief Justice Marshall supposed. But evidently it meant only to justify the conclusion reached upon the specific point decided, for the proviso was inserted that a court "cannot go behind the judgment for the purpose of examining into the validity of the claim." 127 U.S. 293. However, the whole passage was only a *dictum* and it is not worth while to spend much time upon it.

We assume that the statement of Chief Justice Marshall is correct. It is confirmed by the act of May 26, 1790, chap. 11, 1 Stat. at L. 122 (Rev.Stat. § 905, U.S. Comp.Stat. 1901, p. 677), providing that the said records and judicial proceedings "shall have such faith and credit given to them in every court within the United States as they have by law or usage in the courts of the state from whence the said records are or

shall be taken." See further Tilt v. Kelsey, 207 U.S. 43, 57, ante, 1, 28 Sup.Ct.Rep. 1. Whether the award would or would not have been conclusive, and whether the ruling of the Missouri court upon that matter was right or wrong, there can be no question that the judgment was conclusive in Missouri on the validity of the cause of action. Pitts v. Fugate, 41 Mo. 405; State ex rel. Hudson v. Trammel, 106 Mo. 510, 17 S.W. 502; Re Copenhaver, 118 Mo. 377, 40 Am.St.Rep. 382, 24 S.W. 161. A judgment is conclusive as to all the *media concludendi* (United States v. California & O. Land Co., 192 U.S. 355, 48 L.ed. 476, 24 Sup.Ct. Rep. 266); and it needs no authority to show that it cannot be impeached either in or out of the state by showing that it was based upon a mistake of law. Of course, a want of jurisdiction over either the person or the subject-matter might be shown. Andrews v. Andrews, 188 U.S. 14, 47 L.ed. 366, 23 Sup.Ct.Rep. 237; Clarke v. Clarke, 178 U.S. 186, 44 L.ed. 1028, 20 Sup.Ct.Rep. 873. But, as the jurisdiction of the Missouri court is not open to dispute, the judgment cannot be impeached in Mississippi even if it went upon a misapprehension of the Mississippi law. See Godard v. Gray, L.R. 6 Q.B. 139; MacDonald v. Grand Trunk R. Co., 71 N.H. 448, 59 L.R.A. 448, 93 Am.St.Rep. 550, 52 Atl. 982; Peet v. Hatcher, 112 Ala. 514, 57 Am.St.Rep. 45, 21 So. 711.

We feel no apprehensions that painful or humiliating consequences will follow upon our decision. No court would give judgment for a plaintiff unless it believed that the facts were a cause of action by the law determining their effect. Mistakes will be rare. In this case the Missouri court no doubt supposed that the award was binding by the law of Mississippi. If it was mistaken, it made a natural mistake. The validity of its judgment, even in Mississippi, is, as we believe, the result of the Constitution as it always has been understood, and is not a matter to arouse the susceptibilities of the states, all of which are equally concerned in the question and equally on both sides.

Judgment reversed.

Mr. Justice White, with whom concurs Mr. Justice Harlan, Mr. Justice McKenna, and Mr. Justice Day, dissenting:

* * *

When the Constitution was adopted the principles of comity by which the decrees of the courts of one state were entitled to be enforced in another were generally known; but the enforcement of those principles by the several states had no absolute sanction, since they rested but in comity. Now, it cannot be denied that, under the rules of comity recognized at the time of the adoption of the Constitution, and which, at this time, universally prevail, no sovereignty was or is under the slightest moral obligation to give effect to a judgment of another sovereignty, when to do so would compel the state in which the judgment was sought to be executed to enforce an illegal and prohibited contract, when both the contract and all the acts done in connection with its performance had taken place in the latter state. This seems to me conclusive of this case, since, both in treatises of authoritative writers (Story, Confl.L. § 609), and by repeated adjudications of this court, it has been settled that the purpose of the due faith and credit clause was not to confer any new power, but simply to make obligatory that duty which, when the Constitution was adopted, rested, as has been said, in comity alone. Without citing the numerous decisions which so hold, reference is made to a few of the leading cases in which the prior rulings of this court were reviewed, the foregoing principle was stated, and the scope of the due faith and credit clause was fully expounded: Thompson v. Whitman, 18 Wall. 457, 21 L.ed. 897; Wisconsin v. Pelican Ins. Co., 127 U.S. 265, 32 L.ed. 239, 8 Sup.Ct.Rep. 1370; Cole v. Cunningham, 133 U.S. 107, 33 L.ed. 538, 10 Sup.Ct.Rep. 269; Andrews v. Andrews, 188 U.S. 14, 47 L.ed. 366, 23 Sup.Ct.Rep. 237. A more particular review of those cases will demonstrate why my conviction is that the decision in this case overrules the cases cited.

*   *   *

NOTE ON FULL FAITH AND CREDIT

1. Recognition of Judgments

Before the adoption of the Constitution, each state was considered a separate sovereign entity and recognition of judgments of sister states was governed by the doctrine of comity. Compare the discussion of international recognition of judgments, infra p. 699. To help forge one nation out of many, the framers of the Constitution included the Full Faith and Credit Clause. Article IV, section 1, provides:

> "Full Faith and Credit shall be given in each State to the public Acts, Records, and judicial Proceedings of every other State; And the Congress may by general Laws prescribe the Manner in which such Acts, Records and Proceedings shall be proved, and the Effect thereof."

The Clause covers "public acts" and "records" as well as judgments, but the history of its legal development and implementation has mainly concerned judgments. In general, courts have constitutionalized the common law principles of res judicata.

A judgment of one state must be recognized by other states, not only under the Full Faith and Credit Clause of the Constitution, but also by virtue of the Full Faith and Credit Act, 28 U.S.C.A. § 1738. See Restatement Second of Conflict of Laws § 93 et seq. The issue preclusive effects of such judgments are somewhat uncertain. See Scoles, Interstate Preclusion by Prior Litigation, 74 Nw.U.L.Rev. 742 (1979); Casad, Intersystem Preclusion and the Restatement (Second) of Judgments, 66 Cornell L.Rev. 510 (1981).

The Parental Kidnapping Prevention Act of 1980, 28 U.S.C.A. § 1738A, extended the requirement of full faith and credit to custody determinations, which some courts had found not sufficiently "final" so as to trigger full faith and credit requirements. See the discussion in Thompson v. Thompson, 484 U.S. 174, 108 S.Ct. 513, 98 L.Ed.2d 512 (1988).

Full faith and credit mandates that a state must give at least as much effect to the judgment of the rendering state as would the rendering state itself. But a state may give effect to another state's judgment even when not compelled to do so by full faith and credit. For example, if the rendering state adheres to the old mutuality rule, discussed supra p. 654, the enforcing state may disregard that rule and give a non-party the benefit of preclusion when a court of the rendering court would not. See Hart v. American Airlines, Inc., 61 Misc.2d 41, 304 N.Y.S.2d 810 (Sup.Ct.1969). See generally von Mehren and Trautman, Recognition of Foreign Adjudications: A Survey and a Suggested Approach, 81 Harv.L.Rev. 1601 (1968).

Not all judgments are entitled to full faith and credit. Judgments that are not final in the rendering state are not entitled to full faith and credit in other states. Judgments not "on the merits," i.e., judgments based on procedural faults rather than on substantive law, need not be given preclusive effect. Judgments based on faulty jurisdiction, venue, parties, pleading, or the statute of limitations thus generally are not subject to the Full Faith and Credit Clause. Moreover, where the rendering court has entered a substantive judgment, that judgment may be attacked in another state if the rendering state did not have jurisdiction over the subject matter or over the parties. See Hanson v. Denckla, supra p. 313. However, if the rendering court itself considered its own jurisdiction, its finding in favor of jurisdiction is entitled to res judicata effect on that issue and the only avenue of relief is an appeal from the judgment of the rendering court. See Baldwin v. Iowa State Traveling Men's Ass'n, supra p. 418.

Erroneous judgments are also entitled to full faith and credit. As exemplified by Fauntleroy v. Lum, if the rendering state had jurisdiction over the case, the only avenue of relief for the losing party is to appeal the erroneous judgment through the court system of the rendering state. See also Parsons Steel, Inc. v. First Alabama Bank, infra p. 694.

Where there are inconsistent judgments, the later judgment is entitled to full faith and credit, not the earlier one. The failure of the second judgment to give full faith and credit to the first judgment is res judicata on that issue and may be corrected only on appeal in the courts of the second state. See Treinies v. Sunshine Mining Co., 308 U.S. 66, 60 S.Ct. 44, 84 L.Ed. 85 (1939); see also Parsons Steel, Inc. v. First Alabama Bank, infra p. 694.

2. Enforcement of Judgments

A domestic judgment is enforced by a writ of execution issued by the courts of the state in which the judgment was rendered. See Further Note on the Judgment, infra p. 1200. A judgment of another state, however, traditionally could not be enforced directly by a domestic writ of execution; rather, the judgment creditor had to bring an independent action based on the foreign judgment in order to obtain a domestic judgment, which then could be enforced by a writ of execution. See Baldwin v. Iowa State Traveling Men's Ass'n, supra p. 418, and the Note following. To eliminate the delays and technicalities of this procedure, many states have adopted the Uniform Enforcement of Foreign Judgments Act, 13 U.L.A. 152 (Master ed. 1986), or a similar act. The pertinent sections of the Uniform Act provide:

§ 1. Definition.

In this Act "foreign judgment" means any judgment, decree, or order of a court of the United States or of any other court which is entitled to full faith and credit in this state.

§ 2. Filing and Status of Foreign Judgments.

A copy of any foreign judgment authenticated in accordance with the act of Congress or the statutes of this state may be filed in the office of the Clerk of any [District Court of any city or county] of this state. The Clerk shall treat the foreign judgment in the same manner as a judgment of the [District Court of any city or county] of this state. A judgment so filed has the same effect and is subject to the same procedures, defenses and proceedings for reopening, vacating, or staying as a judgment of a [District Court of any city or county] of this state and may be enforced or satisfied in like manner.

§ 3. Notice of Filing.

(a) At the time of the filing of the foreign judgment, the judgment creditor or his lawyer shall make and file with the Clerk of Court an affidavit setting forth the name and last known post office address of the judgment debtor, and the judgment creditor.

(b) Promptly upon the filing of the foreign judgment and the affidavit, the Clerk shall mail notice of the filing of the foreign judgment to the judgment debtor at the address given and shall make a note of the mailing in the docket. The notice shall include the name and post office address of the judgment creditor and the judgment creditor's lawyer, if any, in this state. In addition, the judgment creditor may mail a notice of the filing of the judgment to the judgment debtor and may file proof of mailing with the Clerk. Lack of mailing notice of filing by the Clerk shall not affect the enforcement proceedings if proof of mailing by the judgment creditor has been filed.

[(c) No execution or other process for enforcement of a foreign judgment filed hereunder shall issue until [   ] days after the date the judgment is filed.]

§ 4. Stay.

(a) If the judgment debtor shows the [District Court of any city or county] that an appeal from the foreign judgment is pending or will be taken, or that a stay of execution has been granted, the court shall stay enforcement of the foreign judgment until the appeal is concluded, the time for appeal expires, or the stay of execution expires or is vacated, upon proof that the judgment debtor has furnished the security for the satisfaction of the judgment required by the state in which it was rendered.

*   *   *

§ 6. Optional Procedure.

The right of a judgment creditor to bring an action to enforce his judgment instead of proceeding under this Act remains unimpaired.

On the general problems of enforcing a foreign judgment, see Scoles and Hay, Conflict of Laws § 24.12 et seq. (Lawyers Ed.1984).

b. FEDERAL–STATE RECOGNITION OF JUDGMENTS

MARRESE v. AMERICAN ACADEMY OF ORTHOPAEDIC SURGEONS

Supreme Court of the United States, 1985.
470 U.S. 373, 105 S.Ct. 1327, 84 L.Ed.2d 274.

JUSTICE O'CONNOR delivered the opinion of the Court.

This case concerns the preclusive effect of a state court judgment in a subsequent lawsuit involving federal antitrust claims within the exclusive jurisdiction of the federal courts. The Court of Appeals for the Seventh Circuit, sitting en banc, held as a matter of federal law that the earlier state court judgments barred the federal antitrust suit. 726 F.2d 1150 (1984). * * *

I

Petitioners are board-certified orthopaedic surgeons who applied for membership in respondent American Academy of Orthopaedic Surgeons (Academy). Respondent denied the membership applications without providing a hearing or a statement of reasons. In November 1976, petitioner Dr. Treister filed suit in the Circuit Court of Cook County, State of Illinois, alleging that the denial of membership in the Academy violated associational rights protected by Illinois common law. Petitioner Dr. Marrese separately filed a similar action in state court. Neither petitioner alleged a violation of state antitrust law in his state court action; nor did either petitioner contemporaneously file a federal antitrust suit. The Illinois Appellate Court ultimately held that Dr. Treister's complaint failed to state a cause of action, Treister v. American Academy of Orthopaedic Surgeons, 78 Ill.App.3d 746, 33 Ill. Dec. 501, 396 N.E.2d 1225 (1979), and the Illinois Supreme Court denied leave to appeal. 79 Ill.2d 630 (1980). After the Appellate Court ruled against Dr. Treister, the Circuit Court dismissed Dr. Marrese's complaint.

In March 1980, petitioners filed a federal antitrust suit in the United States District Court for the Northern District of Illinois based on the same events underlying their unsuccessful state court actions. As amended, the complaint alleged that respondent Academy possesses monopoly power, that petitioners were denied membership in order to discourage competition, and that their exclusion constituted a boycott in violation of § 1 of the Sherman Act, 15 U.S.C. § 1. App. 8, 26–30, 33. Respondent filed a motion to dismiss arguing that claim preclusion barred the federal antitrust claim because the earlier state court actions concerned the same facts and were dismissed with prejudice.[1]

---

1. In this opinion we use the term "claim preclusion" to refer to "res judicata" in a narrow sense, i.e., the preclusive effect of a judgment in foreclosing litigation of matters that should have been raised in an earlier suit. In contrast, we use the term "issue preclusion" to refer to the effect of a judgment in foreclosing relitigation of a matter that has been litigated and decided. See Migra v. Warren City

In denying this motion, the District Court reasoned that state courts lack jurisdiction over federal antitrust claims, and therefore a state court judgment cannot have claim preclusive effect in a subsequent federal antitrust suit. * * * In a divided vote, the Court of Appeals held that claim preclusion barred the federal antitrust suit * * *. 726 F.2d 1150 (CA 7 1984).

* * *

III

The issue presented by this case is whether a state court judgment may have preclusive effect on a federal antitrust claim that could not have been raised in the state proceeding. Although federal antitrust claims are within the exclusive jurisdiction of the federal courts, see, e.g., General Investment Co. v. Lake Shore & M.S.R. Co., 260 U.S. 261, 286–288, 43 S.Ct. 106, 116–117, 67 L.Ed. 244 (1922), the Court of Appeals ruled that the dismissal of petitioners' complaints in state court barred them from bringing a claim based on the same facts under the Sherman Act. The Court of Appeals erred by suggesting that in these circumstances a federal court should determine the preclusive effect of a state court judgment without regard to the law of the State in which judgment was rendered.

The preclusive effect of a state court judgment in a subsequent federal lawsuit generally is determined by the full faith and credit statute, which provides that state judicial proceedings "shall have the same full faith and credit in every court within the United States . . . as they have by law or usage in the courts of such State . . . from which they are taken." 28 U.S.C. § 1738. This statute directs a federal court to refer to the preclusion law of the State in which judgment was rendered. "It has long been established that § 1738 does not allow federal courts to employ their own rules of res judicata in determining the effect of state judgments. Rather, it goes beyond the common law and commands a federal court to accept the rules chosen by the State from which the judgment is taken." Kremer v. Chemical Construction Corp., 456 U.S. 461, 481–482, 102 S.Ct. 1883, 1897, 72 L.Ed.2d 262 (1982); see also Allen v. McCurry, 449 U.S. 90, 96, 101 S.Ct. 411, 415, 66 L.Ed.2d 308 (1980). Section 1738 embodies concerns of comity and federalism that allow the States to determine, subject to the requirements of the statute and the Due Process Clause, the preclusive effect of judgments in their own courts. See *Kremer,* supra, 456 U.S., at 478, 481–483, 102 S.Ct., at 1897–1898. Cf. Riley v. New York Trust Co., 315 U.S. 343, 349, 62 S.Ct. 608, 612, 86 L.Ed. 885 (1942) (discussing preclusive effect of state judgment in proceedings in another State).

The fact that petitioners' antitrust claim is within the exclusive jurisdiction of the federal courts does not necessarily make § 1738 inapplicable to this case. Our decisions indicate that a state court

School Dist. Bd. of Ed., 465 U.S. 75, 77, n. 1, 104 S.Ct. 892, 894, n. 1, 79 L.Ed.2d 56 (1984).

judgment may in some circumstances have preclusive effect in a subsequent action within the exclusive jurisdiction of the federal courts. Without discussing § 1738, this Court has held that the issue preclusive effect of a state court judgment barred a subsequent patent suit that could not have been brought in state court. Becher v. Contoure Laboratories, Inc., 279 U.S. 388, 49 S.Ct. 356, 73 L.Ed. 752 (1929). Moreover, *Kremer* held that § 1738 applies to a claim of employment discrimination under Title VII of the Civil Rights Act of 1964, 78 Stat. 253, as amended, 42 U.S.C. § 2000e et seq., although the Court expressly declined to decide whether Title VII claims can be brought only in federal courts. 456 U.S., at 479, n. 20, 102 S.Ct., at 1896, n. 20. *Kremer* implies that absent an exception to § 1738, state law determines at least the issue preclusive effect of a prior state judgment in a subsequent action involving a claim within the exclusive jurisdiction of the federal courts.

More generally, *Kremer* indicates that § 1738 requires a federal court to look first to state preclusion law in determining the preclusive effects of a state court judgment. Cf. Haring v. Prosise, 462 U.S. 306, 314, and n. 8, 103 S.Ct. 2368, 2373, and n. 8, 76 L.Ed.2d 595 (1983); Smith, Full Faith and Credit and Section 1983: A Reappraisal, 63 N.C.L.Rev. 59, 110–111 (1984). The Court's analysis in *Kremer* began with the finding that state law would in fact bar relitigation of the discrimination issue decided in the earlier state proceedings. 456 U.S., at 466–467, 102 S.Ct., at 1889–1890. That finding implied that the plaintiff could not relitigate the same issue in federal court unless some exception to § 1738 applied. Ibid. *Kremer* observed that "an exception to § 1738 will not be recognized unless a later statute contains an express or implied repeal." Id., at 468, 102 S.Ct., at 1890; see also Allen v. McCurry, supra, 449 U.S., at 99, 101 S.Ct., at 417. Title VII does not expressly repeal § 1738, and the Court concluded that the statutory provisions and legislative history do not support a finding of implied repeal. 456 U.S., at 476, 102 S.Ct., at 1894. We conclude that the basic approach adopted in *Kremer* applies in a lawsuit involving a claim within the exclusive jurisdiction of the federal courts.

To be sure, a state court will not have occasion to address the specific question whether a state judgment has issue or claim preclusive effect in a later action that can be brought only in federal court. Nevertheless, a federal court may rely in the first instance on state preclusion principles to determine the extent to which an earlier state judgment bars subsequent litigation. Cf. FDIC v. Eckhardt, 691 F.2d 245, 247–248 (CA6 1982) (applying state law to determine preclusive effect on claim within concurrent jurisdiction of state and federal courts). *Kremer* illustrates that a federal court can apply state rules of issue preclusion to determine if a matter actually litigated in state court may be relitigated in a subsequent federal proceeding. See 456 U.S., at 467, 102 S.Ct., at 1890.

With respect to matters that were not decided in the state proceedings, we note that claim preclusion generally does not apply where "[t]he plaintiff was unable to rely on a certain theory of the case or to seek a certain remedy because of the limitations on the subject matter jurisdiction of the courts. . . ." Restatement (Second) of Judgments § 26(1)(c)(1982). If state preclusion law includes this requirement of prior jurisdictional competency, which is generally true, a state judgment will *not* have claim preclusive effect on a cause of action within the exclusive jurisdiction of the federal courts. Even in the event that a party asserting the affirmative defense of claim preclusion can show that state preclusion rules in some circumstances bar a claim outside the jurisdiction of the court that rendered the initial judgment, the federal court should first consider whether application of the state rules would bar the particular federal claim.[2]

Reference to state preclusion law may make it unnecessary to determine if the federal court, as an exception to § 1738, should refuse to give preclusive effect to a state court judgment. The issue whether there is an exception to § 1738 arises only if state law indicates that litigation of a particular claim or issue should be barred in the subsequent federal proceeding. To the extent that state preclusion law indicates that a judgment normally does not have claim preclusive effect as to matters that the court lacked jurisdiction to entertain, lower courts and commentators have correctly concluded that a state court judgment does not bar a subsequent federal antitrust claim. See 726 F.2d, at 1174 (Cudahy, J., dissenting) (citing cases); 692 F.2d, at 1099 (Stewart, J., dissenting); Restatement, supra, § 25(1), Comment *e* ; id. § 26(1)(c), Illustration 2; 18 C. Wright, A. Miller, & F. Cooper, Federal Practice and Procedure § 4470, pp. 687–688 (1981). Unless application of Illinois preclusion law suggests, contrary to the usual view, that petitioners' federal antitrust claim is somehow barred, there will be no need to decide in this case if there is an exception to § 1738.[3]

---

2. Our analysis does not necessarily suggest that the Court of Appeals for the Fourth Circuit erred in its holding in Nash County Board of Education v. Biltmore Co., 640 F.2d 484, cert. denied, 454 U.S. 878, 102 S.Ct. 359, 70 L.Ed.2d 188 (1981). The Court of Appeals there applied federal preclusion principles to conclude that a state judgment approving settlement of state antitrust claims barred a subsequent federal antitrust claim. Although our decision today indicates that the Court of Appeals should have looked in the first instance to state law to determine the preclusive effect of the state judgment, the same holding would result if application of state preclusion law suggests that the settlement bars the subsequent federal claim and if there is no exception to § 1738 in these circumstances. Cf. 640 F.2d, at 487, n. 5 (noting that State law gives preclusive effect to consent judgment). We of course, do not address those issues here.

3. The Chief Justice notes that preclusion rules bar the splitting of a cause of action between a court of limited jurisdiction and one of general jurisdiction, and suggests that state requirements of jurisdictional competency may leave unclear whether a state court action precludes a subsequent federal antitrust claim. * * * The rule that the judgment of a court of limited jurisdiction concludes the entire claim assumes that the plaintiff might have commenced his action in a court *in the same system of courts* that was competent to give full relief. See Restatement (Second) of Judgments § 24, Comment *g* (1982). Moreover, the jurisdictional competency requirement generally is understood to imply that state court litigation based on a state statute analogous to a federal statute, e.g., a state antitrust law, does not bar subsequent attempts to secure relief in federal court if the state court lacked jurisdiction over the federal statuto-

The Court of Appeals did not apply the approach to § 1738 that we have outlined. Both the plurality opinion, see 726 F.2d, at 1154, and the concurring opinion, see id., at 1163–1164 (Flaum, J.), express the view that § 1738 allows a federal court to give a state court judgment greater preclusive effect than the state courts themselves would give to it. This proposition, however, was rejected by Migra v. Warren City School Dist. Bd. of Ed., 465 U.S. 75, 104 S.Ct. 892, 79 L.Ed.2d 56 (1984), a case decided shortly after the Court of Appeals announced its decision in the instant case. In *Migra,* a discharged schoolteacher filed suit under 42 U.S.C. § 1983 in federal court after she prevailed in state court on a contract claim involving the same underlying events. The Federal District Court dismissed the § 1983 action as barred by claim preclusion. The opinion of this Court emphasized that under § 1738, state law determined the preclusive effect of the state judgment. Id., at 81, 104 S.Ct., at 896. Because it was unclear from the record whether the District Court's ruling was based on state preclusion law, we remanded for clarification on this point. Id., at 87, 104 S.Ct., at 899. Such a remand obviously would have been unnecessary were a federal court free to give greater preclusive effect to a state court judgment than would the judgment-rendering State. See id., at 88, 104 S.Ct., at 900 (WHITE, J., concurring).

We are unwilling to create a special exception to § 1738 for federal antitrust claims that would give state court judgments greater preclusive effect than would the courts of the State rendering the judgment. Cf. Haring v. Prosise, 462 U.S., at 317–318, 103 S.Ct., at 2375 (refusing to create special preclusion rule for § 1983 claim subsequent to plaintiff's guilty plea). The plurality opinion for the Court of Appeals relied on Federated Department Stores, Inc. v. Moitie, 452 U.S. 394, 101 S.Ct. 2424, 69 L.Ed.2d 103 (1981), to observe that the doctrine of claim preclusion protects defendants from repetitive lawsuits based on the same conduct, 726 F.2d, at 1152, and that there is a practical need to require plaintiffs "to litigate their claims in an economical and parsimonious fashion." Id., at 1153. We agree that these are valid and important concerns, and we note that under § 1738 state issue preclusion law may promote the goals of repose and conservation of judicial resources by preventing the relitigation of certain issues in a subsequent federal proceeding. See *Kremer,* 456 U.S., at 485, 102 S.Ct., at 1899 (state judgment barred subsequent Title VII action in federal court).

If we had a single system of courts and our only concerns were efficiency and finality, it might be desirable to fashion claim preclusion rules that would require a plaintiff to bring suit initially in the forum of most general jurisdiction, thereby resolving as many issues as possi-

ry claim. Id. § 26(1)(c), Illustration 2. Although a particular State's preclusion principles conceivably could support a rule similar to that proposed by The Chief Justice, * * * where state preclusion rules do not indicate that a claim is barred, we do not believe that federal courts should fashion a federal rule to preclude a claim that could not have been raised in the state proceedings.

ble in one proceeding. See Restatement (Second) of Judgments § 24 Comment *g* (1982); C. Wright, A. Miller, & E. Cooper, supra, § 4407, p. 51; id. § 4412, p. 93. The decision of the Court of Appeals approximates such a rule inasmuch as it encourages plaintiffs to file suit initially in federal district court and to attempt to bring any state law claims pendent to their federal antitrust claims. Whether this result would reduce the overall burden of litigation is debatable, see 726 F.2d, at 1181–1182 (Cudahy, J., dissenting); C. Wright, A. Miller, & E. Cooper, supra, § 4407, pp. 51–52, and we decline to base our interpretation of § 1738 on our opinion on this question.

More importantly, we have parallel systems of state and federal courts, and the concerns of comity reflected in § 1738 generally allow States to determine the preclusive scope of their own courts' judgments. See *Kremer,* 456 U.S., at 481–482, 102 S.Ct., at 1897; Allen v. McCurry, 449 U.S., at 96, 101 S.Ct., at 415; cf. Currie, Res Judicata: The Neglected Defense, 45 U.Chi.L.Rev. 317, 327 (1978) (state policies may seek to limit preclusive effect of state court judgment). These concerns certainly are not made less compelling because state courts lack jurisdiction over federal antitrust claims. We therefore reject a judicially created exception to § 1738 that effectively holds as a matter of federal law that a plaintiff can bring state law claims initially in state court only at the cost of forgoing subsequent federal antitrust claims. Federated Department Stores, Inc. v. Moitie does not suggest a contrary conclusion. That case did not involve § 1738; rather it held that "accepted principles of res judicata" determine the preclusive effect of a federal court judgment. See 452 U.S., at 401, 101 S.Ct., at 2429.

In this case the Court of Appeals should have first referred to Illinois law to determine the preclusive effect of the state judgment. Only if state law indicates that a particular claim or issue would be barred, is it necessary to determine if an exception to § 1738 should apply. Although for purposes of this case, we need not decide if such an exception exists for federal antitrust claims, we observe that the more general question is whether the concerns underlying a particular grant of exclusive jurisdiction justify a finding of an implied partial repeal of § 1738. Resolution of this question will depend on the particular federal statute as well as the nature of the claim or issue involved in the subsequent federal action. Our previous decisions indicate that the primary consideration must be the intent of Congress. See *Kremer,* 456 U.S., at 470–476, 102 S.Ct., at 1891–1894 (finding no congressional intent to depart from § 1738 for purposes of Title VII); cf. Brown v. Felsen, 442 U.S. 127, 138, 99 S.Ct. 2205, 2212, 60 L.Ed.2d 767 (1979) (finding congressional intent that state judgments would not have claim preclusive effect on dischargeability issue in bankruptcy).

* * * Before this Court, the parties have continued to disagree about the content of Illinois preclusion law. We believe that this dispute is best resolved in the first instance by the District Court. Cf. Migra v. Warren City School Dist. Bd. of Ed., 465 U.S., at 87, 104 S.Ct., at 899.

* * *

The judgment of the Court of Appeals is reversed, and the case is remanded for further proceedings consistent with this opinion.

It is so ordered.

JUSTICE BLACKMUN and JUSTICE STEVENS took no part in the consideration or decision of this case.

CHIEF JUSTICE BURGER, concurring in the judgment.

I agree with the Court's implicit conclusion that the Court of Appeals approached 28 U.S.C. § 1738 too narrowly and technically by holding it irrelevant on the ground that Illinois law does not address the preclusive effect of a state court judgment on a federal antitrust suit, see 726 F.2d 1150, 1154 (CA7 1984). * * *

* * * The principles of Illinois res judicata doctrine appear to be indeterminate as to whether petitioners' ability to raise state antitrust claims in their prior state court suits should preclude their assertion of essentially the same claims in the present federal action. This indeterminancy arises from the fact that the Illinois courts have not addressed whether the notion of "questions which could have been raised" should be applied narrowly [1] or broadly.[2] No Illinois court has considered how the jurisdictional competency requirement should apply in the type of situation presented by this case, where the same theory of recovery may be asserted under different statutes. Nor has any Illinois court considered whether res judicata precludes splitting a cause of action between a court of limited jurisdiction and one of general jurisdiction.[3]

Hence it is likely that the principles of Illinois claim preclusion law do not speak to the preclusive effect that petitioners' state court

1. E.g., by inquiring whether the plaintiff could have raised the question whether the defendant violated a particular statute.

2. E.g., by inquiring whether the plaintiff could have raised the question whether the defendant engaged in a group boycott.

3. Compare Restatement (Second) of Judgments § 24, comment g, illus. 14:

"In an automobile collision, A is injured and his car damaged as a result of the negligence of B. Instead of suing in a court of general jurisdiction of the state, A brings his action for the damage to his car in a justice's court, which has jurisdiction in actions for damage to property but has no jurisdiction in actions for injury to the person. Judgment is rendered for A for the damage to the car. A cannot thereafter maintain an action against B to recover for the injury to his person arising out of the same collision."

See also 18 C. Wright, A. Miller, & E. Cooper, Federal Practice and Procedure § 4412, p. 95 (1981), stating that the "general rule" in state courts is that "[a] second action will not be permitted on parts of a single claim that could have been asserted in a court of broader jurisdiction simply because the plaintiff went first to a court of limited jurisdiction in the same state that could not hear them." The holding in Lucas v. Le Compte, 42 Ill. 303 (1866), is similar to this "general rule," but that holding was based on a construction of an Illinois statute, Ill.Rev.Stat., ch. 59, § 35 (1845), which (a) has been repealed, see Act of Apr. 15, 1965, 1965 Ill.Laws 331, and (b) had a broader preclusive effect than general Illinois res judicata doctrine has. Clancey v. McBride, 338 Ill. 35, 169 N.E. 729 (1929), involved the same circumstances as the above-quoted illustration from the Restatement. The court resolved the case, however, without reference to the limited jurisdiction of the justice's court, by concluding that injury to the person and injury to property are distinct legal wrongs that can be the subject of separate lawsuits.

judgments should have on the present action. In this situation, it may be consistent with § 1738 for a federal court to formulate a federal rule to resolve the matter. If state law is simply indeterminate, the concerns of comity and federalism underlying § 1738 do not come into play. At the same time, the federal courts have direct interests in ensuring that their resources are used efficiently and not as a means of harassing defendants with repetitive lawsuits, as well as in ensuring that parties asserting federal rights have an adequate opportunity to litigate those rights. Given the insubstantiality of the state interests and the weight of the federal interests, a strong argument could be made that a federal rule would be more appropriate than a creative interpretation of ambiguous state law.[4] When state law is indeterminate or ambiguous, a clear federal rule would promote substantive interests as well: "Uncertainty intrinsically works to defeat the opportunities for repose and reliance sought by the rules of preclusion, and confounds the desire for efficiency by inviting repetitious litigation to test the preclusive effects of the first effort." 18 C. Wright, A. Miller, & E. Cooper, supra, n. 3, § 4407, at 49.

A federal rule might be fashioned from the test, which this Court has applied in other contexts, that a party is precluded from asserting a claim that he had a "full and fair opportunity" to litigate in a prior action. See, e.g., Kremer v. Chemical Construction Corp., 456 U.S. 461, 485, 102 S.Ct. 1883, 1899, 72 L.Ed.2d 262 (1982); Allen v. McCurry, 449 U.S. 90, 95, 101 S.Ct. 411, 415, 66 L.Ed.2d 308 (1980); Montana v. United States, 440 U.S. 147, 153, 99 S.Ct. 970, 973, 59 L.Ed.2d 210 (1979); Blonder–Tongue Laboratories, Inc. v. University of Illinois Foundation, 402 U.S. 313, 328, 91 S.Ct. 1434, 1442, 28 L.Ed.2d 788 (1971). Thus, if a state statute is identical in all material respects with a federal statute within exclusive federal jurisdiction, a party's ability to assert a claim under the state statute in a prior state court action might be said to have provided, in effect, a "full and fair opportunity" to litigate his rights under the federal statute. Cf. Derish v. San Mateo–Burlingame Board of Realtors, 724 F.2d 1347 (CA9 1983); Nash County Board of Education v. Biltmore Co., 640 F.2d 484 (CA4), cert. denied, 454 U.S. 878, 102 S.Ct. 359, 70 L.Ed.2d 188 (1981).

The Court will eventually have to face these questions; I would resolve them now.

---

4. By contrast, when a federal court construes substantive rights and obligations under state law in the context of a diversity action, the federal interest is insignificant and the state's interest is much more direct than it is in the present situation, even if the relevant state law is ambiguous.

PARSONS STEEL, INC. v. FIRST ALABAMA BANK

Supreme Court of the United States, 1986.
474 U.S. 518, 106 S.Ct. 768, 88 L.Ed.2d 877.*

JUSTICE REHNQUIST delivered the opinion of the Court.

* * *

Petitioners Parsons Steel, Inc., and Jim and Melba Parsons sued respondents First Alabama Bank of Montgomery and Edward Herbert, a bank officer, in Alabama state court in February 1979, essentially alleging that the bank had fraudulently induced the Parsons to permit a third person to take control of a subsidiary of Parsons Steel and eventually to obtain complete ownership of the subsidiary. The subsidiary was adjudicated an involuntary bankrupt in April 1979, and the trustee in bankruptcy was added as a party plaintiff in the state action. In May 1979 Parsons Steel and the Parsons sued the bank in the United States District Court for the District of Alabama, alleging that the same conduct on the part of the bank that was the subject of the state-court suit also violated the Bank Holding Company Act (BHCA) amendments, 12 U.S.C. §§ 1971–1978. The trustee in bankruptcy chose not to participate in the federal action.

The parties conducted joint discovery in the federal and state actions. The federal action proceeded to trial on the issue of liability before the state action went to trial. A jury returned a verdict in favor of petitioners, but the District Court granted judgment n.o.v. to the bank. That judgment was affirmed on appeal. Parsons Steel, Inc. v. First Alabama Bank of Montgomery, 679 F.2d 242 (CA11 1982). After the federal judgment was entered, respondents pleaded in the state action the defenses of res judicata and collateral estoppel based on that judgment. The Alabama court, however, ruled that res judicata did not bar the state action. Almost a year after the federal judgment was entered, the state complaint was amended to include a Uniform Commercial Code (UCC) claim that the bank's foreclosure sale of the subsidiary's assets was commercially unreasonable. A jury returned a general verdict in favor of petitioners, awarding a total of four million and one dollars in damages.

Having lost in state court, respondents returned to the District Court that had previously entered judgment in the bank's favor and filed the present injunctive action against petitioners, the plaintiffs in the state action.[1] The District Court found that the federal BHCA suit and the state action were based on the same factual allegations and claimed substantially the same damages. The court held that the state claims should have been raised in the federal action as pendent to the BHCA claim and accordingly that the BHCA judgment barred the state claims under res judicata. Determining that the Alabama judgment in

---

* Some of the Court's footnotes are omitted.

1. Although the opinion of the Court of Appeals does not mention it, respondents

apparently also filed in state court a timely post-trial motion for new trial or judgment n.o.v.

effect nullified the earlier federal-court judgment in favor of the bank, the District Court enjoined petitioners from further prosecuting the state action.

A divided panel of the Court of Appeals affirmed in relevant part, holding that the issuance of the injunction was not "an abuse of discretion" by the District Court. 747 F.2d 1367, 1381 (1980). The majority first agreed with the District Court that the fraud and UCC claims presented issues of fact and law that could have been and should have been raised in the same action as the BHCA claim. Thus the parties to the BHCA action and their privies, including the trustee in bankruptcy, were barred by res judicata from raising these claims in state court after the entry of the federal judgment.

The majority then held that the injunction was proper under the so-called "relitigation exception" to the Anti–Injunction Act, 28 U.S.C. § 2283, which provides:

> "A court of the United States may not grant an injunction to stay proceedings in a State court except as expressly authorized by Act of Congress, or where necessary in aid of its jurisdiction, or *to protect or effectuate its judgments* " (emphasis added).

In reaching this holding, the majority explicitly declined to consider the possible preclusive effect, pursuant to the Full Faith and Credit Act, 28 U.S.C. § 1738,[2] of the state court's determination after full litigation by the parties that the earlier federal-court judgment did not bar the state action. According to the majority, "while a federal court is generally bound by other state court determinations, the relitigation exception empowers a federal court to be the final adjudicator as to the *res judicata* effects of its prior judgments on a subsequent state action." 747 F.2d, at 1376 (footnote omitted).

Finally, the majority ruled that respondents had not waived their right to an injunction by waiting until after the trial in the state action was completed. The majority concluded that the state-court pleadings were so vague that it was not clear until after trial that essentially the same cause of action was involved as the BHCA claim and that the earlier federal judgment was in danger of being nullified. According to the majority, the Anti–Injunction Act does not limit the power of a federal court to protect its judgment "to specific points in time in state court trials or appellate procedure." Id., at 1377.[3]

The dissenting judge rejected "the majority's conclusion that the Anti–Injunction Act . . . implicitly amended the Full Faith and Credit

2. The Full Faith and Credit Act provides, in pertinent part, that state judicial proceedings "shall have the same full faith and credit in every court within the United States . . . as they have by law or usage in the courts of such State . . . from which they are taken."

3. The Court of Appeals remanded the case to the District Court for a determina-

tion whether the trustee in bankruptcy should be allowed to litigate his UCC claim in state court because the trustee was not a party to the federal suit and the UCC claim might have been based on facts other than those that formed the basis for the federal action.

Act, 28 U.S.C. § 1738." Id., at 1381 (Hill, J., dissenting). He agreed with the majority that "section 2283 allows the district court to enter an injunction, perhaps grounded in the concept of res judicata, unless the state court has already addressed the res judicata issue on the merits," but would have held in cases where the state court has decided the res judicata issue that "section 1738 requires the federal court to afford full faith and credit to the state court's resolution of the issue." Ibid.

In our view, the majority of the Court of Appeals gave unwarrantedly short shrift to the important values of federalism and comity embodied in the Full Faith and Credit Act. As recently as last March, in Marrese v. American Academy of Orthopaedic Surgeons, 470 U.S. 373, 105 S.Ct. 1327, 84 L.Ed.2d 274 (1985), we reaffirmed our holding in Migra v. Warren City School Dist. Bd. of Education, 465 U.S. 75, 104 S.Ct. 892, 79 L.Ed.2d 56 (1984), that under the Full Faith and Credit Act a federal court must give the same preclusive effect to a state-court judgment as another court of that State would give. "It has long been established that § 1738 does not allow federal courts to employ their own rules of res judicata in determining the effect of state judgments. Rather, it goes beyond the common law and commands a federal court to accept the rules chosen by the State from which the judgment is taken." Kremer v. Chemical Construction Corp., 456 U.S. 461, 481–482, 102 S.Ct. 1883, 1898, 72 L.Ed.2d 262 (1982). The Full Faith and Credit Act thus "allow[s] the States to determine, subject to the requirements of the statute and the Due Process Clause, the preclusive effect of judgments in their own courts." Marrese, supra, at 380, 105 S.Ct. at 1332.

In the instant case, however, the Court of Appeals did not consider the possible preclusive effect under Alabama law of the state-court judgment, and particularly of the state court's resolution of the res judicata issue, concluding instead that the relitigation exception to the Anti–Injunction Act limits the Full Faith and Credit Act. We do not agree. "[A]n exception to § 1738 will not be recognized unless a later statute contains an express or implied partial repeal." Kremer, supra, at 468, 102 S.Ct., at 1890; Allen v. McCurry, 449 U.S. 90, 99, 101 S.Ct. 411, 417, 66 L.Ed.2d 308 (1980). Here, as in Kremer, there is no claim of an express repeal; rather, the Court of Appeals found an implied repeal. " 'It is, of course, a cardinal principle of statutory construction that repeals by implication are not favored,' Radzanower v. Touche Ross & Co., 426 U.S. 148, 154 [96 S.Ct. 1989, 1993, 48 L.Ed.2d 540] (1976); United States v. United Continental Tuna Corp., 425 U.S. 164, 168 [96 S.Ct. 1319, 1323, 47 L.Ed.2d 653] (1976), and whenever possible, statutes should be read consistently." 456 U.S., at 468, 102 S.Ct., at 1890. We believe that the Anti–Injunction Act and the Full Faith and Credit Act can be construed consistently, simply by limiting the relitigation exception of the Anti–Injunction Act to those situations in which the state court has not yet ruled on the merits of the res judicata issue. Once the state court has finally rejected a claim of res judicata, then the Full Faith and Credit Act becomes applicable and federal courts must turn to state law to determine the preclusive effect of the state court's decision.

The contrary holding of the Court of Appeals apparently was based on the fact that Congress in 1948 amended the Anti–Injunction Act to overrule this Court's decision in Toucey v. New York Life Insurance Co., 314 U.S. 118, 62 S.Ct. 139, 86 L.Ed. 100 (1941), in favor of the understanding of prior law expressed in Justice Reed's dissenting opinion. See Revisor's Note to 1948 Revision of Anti–Injunction Act, 28 U.S.C., p. 377. But the instant case is a far cry from *Toucey*, and one may fully accept the logic of Justice Reed's dissent without concluding that it sanctions the result reached by the Court of Appeals here. In each of the several cases involved in *Toucey*, the prevailing party in the federal action sought an injunction against relitigation in state court as soon as the opposing party commenced the state action, and before there was any resolution of the res judicata issue by the state court. In the instant case, on the other hand, respondents chose to fight out the res judicata issue in state court first, and only after losing there did they return to federal court for another try.

The Court of Appeals also felt that the District Court's injunction would discourage inefficient simultaneous litigation in state and federal courts on the same issue—that is, the res judicata effect of the prior federal judgment. But this is one of the costs of our dual court system:

> "In short, the state and federal courts had concurrent jurisdiction in this case, and neither court was free to prevent either party from simultaneously pursuing claims in both courts." Atlantic Coast Line R. Co. v. Locomotive Engineers, 398 U.S. 281, 295, 90 S.Ct. 1739, 1747, 26 L.Ed.2d 234 (1970).

Indeed, this case is similar to *Atlantic Coast Line*, in which we held that the various exceptions to the Anti–Injunction Act did not permit a federal court to enjoin state proceedings in circumstances more threatening to federal jurisdiction than the circumstances of this case. There we stated that the phrase "to protect or effectuate its judgments" authorized a federal injunction of state proceedings only "to prevent a state court from so interfering with a federal court's consideration or disposition of a case as to seriously impair the federal court's flexibility and authority to decide that case." Ibid.

We hold, therefore, that the Court of Appeals erred by refusing to consider the possible preclusive effect, under Alabama law, of the state-court judgment. Even if the state court mistakenly rejected respondents' claim of res judicata, this does not justify the highly intrusive remedy of a federal-court injunction against the enforcement of the state-court judgment. Rather, the Full Faith and Credit Act requires that federal courts give the state court judgment, and particularly the state court's resolution of the res judicata issue, the same preclusive effect it would have had in another court of the same State. Challenges to the correctness of a state court's determination as to the conclusive effect of a federal judgment must be pursued by way of appeal through the state-court system and certiorari from this Court. See Angel v. Bullington, 330 U.S. 183, 67 S.Ct. 657, 91 L.Ed. 832 (1947).

We think the District Court is best situated to determine and apply Alabama preclusion law in the first instance. See Marrese v. American Academy of Orthopaedic Surgeons, supra, at 386–387, 105 S.Ct. at 1335; Migra v. Warren City School Dist. Bd. of Education, 465 U.S., at 87, 104 S.Ct., at 899. Should the District Court conclude that the state-court judgment is not entitled to preclusive effect under Alabama law and the Full Faith and Credit Act, it would then be in the best position to decide the propriety of a federal-court injunction under the general principles of equity, comity, and federalism discussed in Mitchum v. Foster, 407 U.S. 225, 243, 92 S.Ct. 2151, 2162, 32 L.Ed.2d 705 (1972).

The judgment of the Court of Appeals is reversed, and the case is remanded for further proceedings consistent with this opinion.

NOTE ON FEDERAL–STATE AND INTERNATIONAL RECOGNITION OF JUDGMENTS

1. Federal–State Recognition

Since the Full Faith and Credit Clause of the Constitution applies only to the recognition of judgments by sister states, it is a federal statute, 28 U.S.C.A. § 1738 (the Full Faith and Credit Act), that prescribes the binding effect of state court judgments in federal court. The effect of a federal court judgment in subsequent state or federal proceedings was originally derived from § 1738 but seems better analyzed as a matter of federal decisional law. See Restatement Second of Judgments § 87; Degnan, Federalized Res Judicata, 85 Yale L.J. 741 (1976).

The *Marrese* and *Parsons Steel* cases show the strictness with which the federal courts cleave to the language of § 1738, holding that there are no implied exceptions (*Marrese*), not even for an erroneous failure to honor a prior federal judgment (*Parsons Steel*). On the remand in *Parsons Steel*, the District Court continued the injunction against further state court proceedings and the Court of Appeals affirmed, holding that (1) the state court's denial of the Bank's motion for judgment (seeking recognition of the prior federal judgment) was not final for preclusion purposes, and (2) the injunction was proper under the relitigation exception to the Anti–Injunction Act. First Alabama Bank v. Parsons Steel, Inc., 825 F.2d 1475 (11th Cir.1987), cert. denied sub nom. McGregor v. First Alabama Bank, ___ U.S. ___, 108 S.Ct. 1015, 98 L.Ed.2d 980 (1988).

A decision dismissing a federal action on forum non conveniens grounds does not resolve the question whether a state court in the state in which the federal court sits is also an inappropriate forum. Thus, a federal court injunction barring an identical suit in state court is not within the "relitigation" exception to the Anti–Injunction Act. Chick Kam Choo v. Exxon Corp., ___ U.S. ___, 108 S.Ct. 1684, 100 L.Ed.2d 127 (1988).

Federal judgments traditionally had to be enforced in substantially the same manner as state judgments. See Note on Full Faith and Credit, supra p. 683. Within the federal system, a judgment rendered in one federal district court now may be registered in any other federal district court and, upon registration, will have the same effect as though rendered in the court in which registered. 28 U.S.C.A. § 1963. See Note, Registration of Federal Judgments, 42 Iowa L.Rev. 285 (1957).

On federal-state recognition of judgments generally, see Lenich, The Collateral Estoppel Effect of State Court Judgments in Federal Antitrust Actions: Unmaking the Judge–Made Law, 38 Rutgers L.Rev. 241 (1986); Corr, Supreme Court Doctrine in the Trenches: The Case of Collateral Estoppel, 27 Wm. & Mary L.Rev. 35 (1986); Burbank, Interjurisdictional Preclusion, Full Faith and Credit and Federal Common Law: A General Approach, 71 Cornell L.Rev. 733 (1986); Symposium (on res judicata), 70 Iowa L.Rev. 13 (1984); Note, Erie and the Preclusive Effect of Federal Diversity Judgments, 85 Colum.L.Rev. 1505 (1985); Symposium, Preclusion in a Federal System, 70 Cornell L.Rev. 599 (1985).

2. International Recognition

Judgments of foreign countries are not within the mandates of the Full Faith and Credit Clause of the Constitution or the statutory provisions of the Full Faith and Credit Act. Absent a treaty, each state in the international community may decide for itself the extent to which it will recognize a judgment of a foreign nation. This voluntary process of giving recognition is known as "comity." In general, judgments of foreign countries will be recognized if the foreign judgment was obtained in accordance with American concepts of minimal due process, namely proper jurisdiction, adequate notice, and a fair hearing. See Restatement Third of the Foreign Relations Law of the United States § 481 et seq. In Hilton v. Guyot, 159 U.S. 113, 16 S.Ct. 139, 40 L.Ed. 95 (1895), the Supreme Court added a reciprocity requirement, namely, that a judgment of a United States court would be recognized by the country whose judgment was presented for recognition. The reciprocity doctrine is in disrepute today. See Scoles and Hay, Conflict of Laws § 24.33 et seq. (Lawyers Ed.1984).

The Uniform Money–Judgments Recognition Act, 13 U.L.A. 261 (Master ed. 1986), provides for the recognition and enforcement of money judgments of foreign nations, but lists the following grounds for non-recognition:

§ 4. [Grounds for Non-recognition]

(a) A foreign judgment is not conclusive if

(1) the judgment was rendered under a system which does not provide impartial tribunals or procedures compatible with the requirements of due process of law;

(2) the foreign court did not have personal jurisdiction over the defendant; or

(3) the foreign court did not have jurisdiction over the subject matter.

(b) A foreign judgment need not be recognized if

(1) the defendant in the proceedings in the foreign court did not receive notice of the proceedings in sufficient time to enable him to defend;

(2) the judgment was obtained by fraud;

(3) the [cause of action] [claim for relief] on which the judgment is based is repugnant to the public policy of this state;

(4) the judgment conflicts with another final and conclusive judgment;

(5) the proceeding in the foreign court was contrary to an agreement between the parties under which the dispute in question was to be settled otherwise than by proceedings in that court; or

(6) in the case of jurisdiction based only on personal service, the foreign court was a seriously inconvenient forum for the trial of the action.

The Restatement Third of the Foreign Relations Law of the United States, §§ 481, 482, provides for the recognition and enforcement of a money judgment of a foreign country under substantially the same circumstances, with the difference that the Restatement lists lack of subject matter jurisdiction of the foreign court as a ground for the discretionary denial of recognition, while the Uniform Law lists it as a mandatory ground for denial.

3. ANOTHER ACTION PENDING

CSOHAN v. UNITED BENEFIT LIFE INS. CO.

Court of Appeals of Ohio, Cuyahoga County, 1964.
200 N.E.2d 345, 33 Ohio Op.2d 36.

PER CURIAM.

This is an appeal on law and fact from an order issued by the Court of Common Pleas granting a temporary injunction. The facts developed in the record, about which there is no dispute, are that plaintiff, who is designated as the beneficiary in a life insurance policy issued by the defendant upon the life of her father, now deceased, filed an action in the Court of Common Pleas of Cuyahoga County on January 10, 1964, claiming $5,000.00, the face amount of the policy. It is conceded that the policy was in force, proof of death was filed and demand was made. Service was had upon the defendant. The plaintiff at the time of filing of the petition was a resident of San Diego, California.

On March 16, 1964, more than two months later, the defendant filed an action in interpleader in the Los Angeles Superior Court and at the same time asked a preliminary injunction to issue to restrain plaintiff herein from proceeding with her prior suit in Ohio. As an incident of the interpleader action, defendant prayed that a reasonable attorney fee be allowed its counsel and for recovery of its costs. The Superior Court of the State of California scheduled a hearing for March 30, 1964, requiring plaintiff to show cause why a California restraining order should not issue against her.

On March 27, 1964, on application of the plaintiff appellee, the Common Pleas Court of Cuyahoga County issued a temporary restraining order enjoining the defendant from proceeding with the California action, in the following language:

"On consideration of the pleadings, affidavits and exhibits, the court finds that it has prior jurisdiction of the within matter and that it would be oppressive to the plaintiff to be restrained by another court from proceeding with the within action, and accordingly,

"IT IS HEREBY ORDERED, ADJUDGED AND DECREED that the defendant be and hereby is enjoined from in any manner assisting, aiding, participating or engaging directly or indirectly in the prosecution or conduct of the action now pending in the Superior Court of California, for the County of Los Angeles, wherein United of Omaha is the plaintiff and Betty Csohan, etc., et al is defendant, being No. 835145 in said Court, or in any other action or suit in any court in any state other than the State of Ohio for determination of liability under Policy No. C–240727 on the life of John Csohan. Bond fixed in sum of $100.00.

> "DONALD F. LYBARGER,
> JUDGE."

* * *

On April 10, 1964, defendant filed in the Court of Common Pleas its application for a rehearing of the order granting the injunction. This was denied on April 15, 1964. Notice of appeal on law and fact was filed on April 16, 1964.

* * *

On the hearing before this court, plaintiff appellee moved that the appeal be dismissed for the reason that the granting of a temporary injunction is not a final order from which an appeal will lie. Considering the facts and circumstances in the record before us, to label the injunction temporary or permanent, is of no importance. The practical effect thereof, if it were to remain in full force and effect, would be to deprive this defendant of a valid legal or equitable remedy that might well protect it from having to pay the proceeds of this policy twice. Furthermore, such an order made in a special proceeding affects a substantial right. In view thereof the motion to dismiss the appeal is overruled.

The next question is the propriety of the granting of the injunction and specifically the premise upon which it was founded. The trial court stated that "the court finds that it has prior jurisdiction and . . . that it would be oppressive to the plaintiff to be restrained by another court from proceeding with the within action and accordingly" the court ordered the injunction.

There is no question that the action filed in Cuyahoga County, Ohio, had priority over the California proceeding in point of time, in jurisdiction of the subject matter and the parties plaintiff and the defendant. It is said in James v. Grand Trunk Western Railroad Company, Illinois Supreme Court, 14 Ill.2d 356, 152 N.E.2d 858, at page 865:

> "There is no quarrel with the basic principle that a court has a duty, as well as power, to protect its jurisdiction over a controversy in order to decree complete and final justice between the parties and may issue an injunction for that purpose, restraining proceedings in other courts." (Citing cases.)

However, in entertaining jurisdiction in the case at bar, is it within the power of the Court of Common Pleas of Cuyahoga County "to decree complete and final justice between the parties?"

When granting the injunction the court had before it the affidavit of the defendant wherein it is made to appear:

1. that defendant does not deny liability upon the policy in question;

2. that there are two claimants for the face value of the policy to the exclusion of each other;

3. that both claimants are residents of California, including the plaintiff herein;

4. that service upon both was had in California;

5. that the other claimant as a resident of California is not subject to the jurisdiction of the courts of Ohio;

6. documentary proof of presentation of claim and demand for payment by the other claimant, mother of this plaintiff, and proof of basis upon which mother's claim is founded;

7. that defendant is willing to pay the proceeds of the policy to the lawful beneficiary but that it does not know which beneficiary has the better claim at law;

8. that in the interpleader action the California court has jurisdiction of the subject matter as well as both claimants and has the power to decree complete and final justice to all persons interested in the subject matter.

Since the defendant is confronted with two claims for the proceeds of this insurance policy, it has resorted to the procedure known as interpleader in a court that has jurisdiction of the subject matter and jurisdiction of both claimants. The procedure of interpleader has been recognized as proper under such circumstances over the centuries. It is designed to protect a stakeholder when there are conflicting claims against the funds which are admittedly due to some one but the proper one is not known and a court of competent jurisdiction is asked to legally adjudicate the conflict.

It is apparent that the Cuyahoga County court cannot obtain jurisdiction over the person of the other claimant since she is a resident of California. If this is true, how then can the Court of Common Pleas of Cuyahoga County legally resolve the conflict? Since it is unable to do so, it does not have the power to decree complete and final justice in the proceedings.

The application of the Court of Common Pleas for an injunction invokes the equitable jurisdiction of the court and the application of equitable principles. If it were possible for the local court to obtain jurisdiction of the other claimant, it could and no doubt would entertain an interpleader by the defendant and then proceed to resolve the conflicting claims of the respective claimants. But to ignore its inability to do so and thus expose the defendant to the risk of being required to pay the proceeds twice is something which we cannot sanction. The defendant is also entitled to complete and final justice.

It must be borne in mind that it is not the defendant who is seeking a favorable court. The action here was instituted by the plaintiff. The defendant wants only to have the conflict determined where the court has the power to decide which of the claimants is the proper beneficiary and protect it from double exposure.

Counsel for the appellee has urged that the defendant could interplead in the local court and obtain service upon the other claimant by publication. That can only be done when a court obtains control over money or property belonging to such owner. Clearly, a prospective claim to such funds would not support the statutory requirement for service by publication.

Counsel for the appellee has also urged that the defendant in its interpleader procedure has prayed for allowance of a reasonable attorney fee and its costs. This is not only permissible and proper in California but also in Ohio if the interpleader were resorted to under the same circumstances.

We know of no reason why the merits of this action cannot be resolved by the California court where a final and complete adjudication of this matter can be had. We likewise cannot agree with the conclusion reached by the trial court that it would be oppressive to plaintiff to be restrained by another court from proceeding with the within action. While we agree that a court has the duty and power to protect its jurisdiction, we are of the opinion that the court seeking to do so should not overlook its inability to do complete and final justice where such fact becomes apparent to the court.

Decree for defendant appellant. Exceptions noted.

NOTE ON DISMISSAL OR STAY WHEN
ANOTHER ACTION IS PENDING

1. Abatement or Stay of Pending State Action

The rules of res judicata, collateral estoppel and compulsory counterclaim are retrospective regulation. A concurrently applied device is the plea to abate or the motion to stay a pending action on the ground that there is also pending another action between the same parties concerning the same subject matter. See, e.g., C.C.P. 430.10(c), 430.30 (abatement); C.C.P. 526(6) (stay). The consequence of sustaining a plea in abatement is ordinarily the dismissal of the second action, see, e.g., Wolfe Investments, Inc. v. Shroyer, 240 Or. 549, 402 P.2d 516 (1965); cf. Childs v. Eltinge, 29 Cal.App.3d 843, 105 Cal.Rptr. 864 (1973); but see Franchise Tax Board v. Firestone Tire & Rubber Co., 87 Cal.App.3d 878, 151 Cal.Rptr. 460 (1978). The granting of a motion to stay, as the name implies, simply suspends prosecution of the second action until the first is terminated. Accordingly, the criteria seemingly should differ for determining the propriety of the plea and the propriety of the motion.

The plea in abatement will be sustained, according to recognized doctrine, when it appears that the first action, were it to go to judgment, would be res judicata of the second, e.g., Moore v. State, 462 So.2d 1060 (Ala.Cr.App.1985); Lord v. Garland, 27 Cal.2d 840, 168 P.2d 5 (1946), and only when the first action is in the same jurisdiction and involves the same alignment of parties as the second, e.g., Weldon v. Hill, 678 S.W.2d 268 (Tex.App.1984). The formula "would be res judicata" is ambiguous in proportion to the uncertainty of res judicata doctrine, and to the uncertainty that the first action will go to judgment and, if it does, on what grounds; cf. Anno., 118 A.L.R. 1477. For this reason, and also because of the same-jurisdiction and same-alignment requirements, the plea in abatement is rare.

The motion to stay is not so strictly bounded. It may be granted when the prior action involves closely related issues even though it is not clear that res judicata will result, see Aldrich v. Transcontinental Land & Water Co., 131 Cal. App.2d 788, 281 P.2d 362 (1955), and even though the other action is in another jurisdiction, see Archibald v. Cinerama Hotels, Inc., 15 Cal.3d 853, 126 Cal.Rptr. 811, 544 P.2d 947 (1976); Sauter v. Sauter, 4 Conn.App. 581, 495 A.2d 1116 (1985). Cf. Anno., 18 A.L.R.3d 400 (appealability of stay order).

2.   Abatement or Stay in Federal Court

Should a federal court stay or dismiss an action in deference to a suit pending in a state court? In Colorado River Water Conservation Dist. v. United States, 424 U.S. 800, 96 S.Ct. 1236, 47 L.Ed.2d 483 (1976), the Supreme Court stated "only the clearest of justifications will warrant dismissal." In Moses H. Cone Memorial Hosp. v. Mercury Const. Corp., 460 U.S. 1, 103 S.Ct. 927, 74 L.Ed.2d 765 (1983), the Court distinguished Will v. Calvert Fire Ins. Co., 437 U.S. 655, 98 S.Ct. 2552, 57 L.Ed.2d 504 (1978) and strongly reaffirmed *Colorado River*, commenting, 460 U.S. at 16, 103 S.Ct. at 937: "[T]he decision whether to dismiss a federal action because of parallel state-court litigation does not rest on a mechanical checklist, but on a careful balancing of the important factors as they apply in a given case, with the balance heavily weighted in favor of the exercise of jurisdiction." See also Note, Staying Diversity Proceedings Pending the Outcome of Parallel Suits in State Court, 48 Mo.L.Rev. 1017 (1983); cf. Note on Federal Court Abstention, supra p. 557. *In rem* suits require dismissal, however, even in federal court, since the first court to obtain jurisdiction is deemed to have exclusive jurisdiction over the property. In re Washington, 623 F.2d 1169 (6th Cir. 1980). It has been held that jurisdiction under the Federal Interpleader Act should not be exercised where a pending state proceeding has all the involved parties before it. See Zellen v. Second New Haven Bank, 454 F.Supp. 1359 (D.Conn. 1978); Comment, Deference to State Courts in Federal Interpleader Actions, 47 U.Chi.L.Rev. 824 (1980). See also Note, The Appealability of Federal Court Orders Denying Stays in Deference to Concurrent State Court Proceedings, 59 Ind.L.J. 65 (1983).

The state decision will be res judicata if rendered before the federal decision. See Miller v. Miller, 423 F.2d 145 (10th Cir. 1970); Merrill Lynch, Pierce, Fenner & Smith, Inc. v. Haydu, 675 F.2d 1169 (11th Cir. 1982); Note, Preclusion Concerns as an Additional Factor When Staying a Federal Suit in Deference to a Concurrent State Proceeding, 53 Ford.L.Rev. 1183 (1985). The winner of the race to the federal or state courthouse may not prevail because the general rule of priority in time is not mechanically applied. See Brierwood Shoe Corp. v. Sears, Roebuck & Co., 479 F.Supp. 563 (S.D.N.Y.1979). Although abatement is not mentioned in the federal rules, the defense of pendency of another action should be raised by answer, not motion to dismiss, although a motion to stay is a proper motion independent of Rule 12(b). See Aetna State Bank v. Altheimer, 430 F.2d 750 (7th Cir. 1970); Blinder, Robinson & Co. v. S.E.C., 692 F.2d 102 (10th Cir. 1982).

3. Injunction Against Parallel Action

The converse, and at times the correlate, of a stay is an injunction issued in one proceeding against the prosecution of a parallel or related action in another proceeding, as in *Csohan*. See also Rynsburger v. Dairymen's Fertilizer Coop., supra p. 670. For the problems of injunctions issued by state courts against proceedings in the courts of a sister state, see Dumbauld, Judicial Interference with Litigation in Other Courts, 74 Dick.L.Rev. 369 (1970). For the invalidity of an injunction issued by a state court against proceedings in a federal court, see General Atomic Co. v. Felter, 434 U.S. 12, 98 S.Ct. 76, 54 L.Ed.2d 199 (1977); Harris v. Pernsley, 755 F.2d 338 (3d Cir. 1985). Injunctions by federal courts against proceedings in state courts are complicated by the provisions of the Anti-Injunction Act, 28 U.S.C.A. § 2283. See Parsons Steel, Inc. v. First Alabama Bank, supra p. 694. See also Mitchum v. Foster, 407 U.S. 225, 92 S.Ct. 2151, 32 L.Ed.2d 705 (1972) (§ 2283 does not bar injunctions under Civil Rights Act, 42 U.S.C.A. § 1983). Compare Trainor v. Hernandez, 431 U.S. 434, 97 S.Ct. 1911, 52 L.Ed.2d 486 (1977); Marshall v. Chase Manhattan Bank, 558 F.2d 680 (2d Cir. 1977); National City Lines, Inc. v. LLC Corp., 687 F.2d 1122 (8th Cir. 1982) (injunction to protect federal court's jurisdiction). See generally Redish, The Anti-Injunction Statute Reconsidered, 44 U.Chi.L.Rev. 717 (1977).

B. JOINDER OF CLAIMS

1. MULTIPLE CLAIMS IN THE COMPLAINT

NOTE ON HISTORICAL ATTITUDES TOWARD JOINDER

1. The Common Law

a. Joinder of Claims. The common law rules on joinder of claims, as all the common law procedural rules, began with the original writ. A writ conferred jurisdiction only to try a claim or claims subsumable under its terms. Hence, a plaintiff could join in one action only such claims as, considered separately, could be maintained under the form of writ he had chosen. Thus, multiple claims of trespass, whether factually related or not, could be asserted in a single action for trespass; conversely, claims arising out of contract and tort, for example, could not be asserted under the same writ even though the two claims arose out of a single out-of-court transaction. See generally Williams, Pleading Reform in Nineteenth Century America: The Joinder of Actions at Common Law and Under the Codes, 6 J.Legal Hist. 299 (1985).

b. Joinder of Parties. The common law rules on joinder of parties were simpler than those on joinder of claims, but even narrower. In actions involving a "joint" obligation, "joint" obligees were required to join as plaintiffs and "joint" obligors were required to be joined as defendants. In actions involving a "joint and several" obligation, any number of joint and several obligees were permitted to join as plaintiffs and any number of joint and several obligors were permitted to be joined as defendants. See Reed, Compulsory Joinder of Parties in Civil Actions, 55 Mich.L.Rev. 327, 356–74 (1957). For the purpose of applying this rule a "joint" obligation was one in which the parties stated their adhesion to the contract in the form, "we promise * * *"; a "joint and several" obligation was one in which adhesion was in the form "we, and each of us, promise * * *." See Restatement Second of Contracts § 112.

In common law tort actions, joinder of parties plaintiff was required where joint owners of property sued for injury to the property. Thus, for example, partners were required to join as plaintiffs in an action for injury to partnership property. See Shipman, Common Law Pleading 397 (3d ed. 1923). Joinder of parties defendant was permitted, though not required, where the defendants acted in prearranged concert. See Prosser, Joint Torts and Several Liability, 25 Calif.L.Rev. 413, 414–15 (1937). Except for these situations, and for the rule that a husband had to join with his wife in an action for injury to her or her property, joinder of parties was not permitted at common law.

2. Equity

The equity rules on joinder of claims and parties were amorphous. In part this was because the kinds of complex cases that came to Chancery were themselves often amorphous; in part, it was an aspect of the tradition that equity's function was to decide each case on its own peculiar facts without regard to "strict" legal right, a tradition that infused the procedural as well as the substantive rules of equity. Theoretically equity could take any case which could not be handled fairly in the law courts because of the narrow limitations of common law rules on the size of the action. But this theoretical scope of the equity suit was limited by rules developed gradually over the period from the 14th century to the 19th, rules which became increasingly formal and technical during the period of "modern" equity, that is, from about 1700 to about 1850. The rules of those days are set forth, e.g., in Story, Equity Pleadings 224–5 (2d ed. 1840):

> "[A] Bill should not be, what is technically termed, multifarious * * *. By multifariousness in a Bill is meant the improper joining in one Bill distinct and independent matters, and thereby confounding them; as for example, the uniting in one Bill of several matters, perfectly distinct and unconnected against one defendant, or the demand of several matters of a distinct and independent nature against several defendants in the same Bill."

The term "distinct and independent" had then no greater intelligibility than it has now. Some notion of its content can be gleaned from the illustrations that Story gives. Thus, in Story, supra:

> "[A]n author cannot file a joint Bill against several booksellers, for selling the same spurious edition of his work; for there is no privity between them; and his right against each of them is not joint, but is perfectly distinct."

Equity had, however, developed a series of devices by which the size of litigation could be significantly enlarged in certain situations. These were the rules regarding necessary parties, intervention, class suits and interpleader. These devices will be considered in more detail below.

3. The Codes

The Field Code rules on the size of the action were a strange mixture of the common law rules and those of equity.

a. Joinder of Claims. The Field Code scheme of allowable joinder of claims paralleled the common law limitation that several "counts" could be stated only if maintainable under the same writ. Thus, the Field Code originally provided, First Report of the Commissioners on Practice and Pleadings 157 (1848):

> "§ 143. The plaintiff may unite several causes of action in the same complaint, where they all arise out of:

> "1. Contract, express, or implied; or,

> "2. Injuries by force, to person or property; or,

> "3. Injuries without force to person or property; or,

> "4. Injuries to character; or,

> "5. Claims to recover real property, with or without damages, for the withholding thereof; or,

> "6. Claims to recover personal property, with or without damages, for the withholding thereof; or,

> "7. Claims against a trustee by virtue of a contract or by operation of law.

> "But the causes of action, so united, must all belong to one only of these classes, and must equally affect all the parties to the action, and not require different places of trial."

The first six situations of permissible joinder roughly corresponded respectively to the common law actions of assumpsit, trespass, trespass on the case, ejectment and trespass q.c.f., and replevin and detinue. But the term "unite" was taken from Chancery parlance, as was the formula that the several causes of action must "affect" all the parties to the action.

With some changes in phraseology, the Field Code formulation on joinder of claims was adopted in all the code states. Clark on Code Pleading 441 (2d ed. 1947). Over time, the code states adopted amendments which enlarged in varying measures the scope of allowable joinder of claims. In some code states, however, the Field Code restrictions still live. See, e.g., Conn. Practice Book, Superior Court Rules (Civil) § 133; Teris v. Dawson, 173 Conn. 206, 377 A.2d 288 (1977). See generally Williams, Pleading Reform in Nineteenth Century America, supra.

b. Joinder of Parties. The Field Code Commissioners gave rather more thought to the problem of joinder of parties, though they failed satisfactorily to integrate their rules on joinder of parties with their rules on joinder of claims. See First Report of the Commissioners on Practice and Pleadings 124 (1848):

> "The courts of law generally administer justice between those parties only who stand in the same relation to each other; while courts of equity bring before them various parties, standing in different relations, that the whole controversy may be settled, if possible, in one suit, and others avoided. This reasonable and just rule, we would adopt for all actions."

The Code Commissioners proposed the following rules, id. at 126–127:

"§ 97. All persons having an interest in the subject of the action, and in obtaining the relief demanded, may be joined as plaintiffs, except as otherwise provided in this title.

"§ 98. Any person may be made a party defendant, who has an interest in the controversy, adverse to the plaintiff.

"§ 99. Of the parties to the action, those who are united in interest must be joined as plaintiff or defendants * * *."

It will be seen that the terminology adopted was that of equity: "interest," "subject of the action," and "united in interest."

In the face of these statutory clouds, and in many instances motivated by a contempt for the reformed pleading system imposed on them, the courts of the code states tended to fall back on older rules of common law and equity.

4. The Federal Rules

The Federal Rules of Civil Procedure made sweeping changes in the rules regarding the scope of the action. They now allow plaintiff to join any claims he may wish against a single defendant, F.R.C.P. 18, and permit persons to join as plaintiffs and to be joined as defendants where the claims respectively for or against them arise out of "the same transaction, occurrence, or series of transactions or occurrences," F.R.C.P. 20(a). The California rules are essentially the same. See C.C.P. 378, 379, 427.10. Compare Ill.C.C.P. §§ 2–614, 2–404, 2–405; N.Y.C.P.L.R. §§ 601, 1002.

See generally James & Hazard cc. 9 and 10; Wright §§ 70–80; Kaplan, Continuing Work of the Civil Committee: 1966 Amendments to the Federal Rules of Civil Procedure (II), 81 Harv.L.Rev. 591 (1968).

2. COUNTERCLAIMS AND ANALOGOUS DEVICES

UNITED STATES EX REL. D'AGOSTINO EXCAVATORS, INC. v. HEYWARD–ROBINSON CO.

United States Court of Appeals for the Second Circuit, 1970.
430 F.2d 1077.*

FREDERICK VAN PELT BRYAN, DISTRICT JUDGE.

This is an appeal from a judgment for the plaintiff entered in the United States District Court for the District of Connecticut upon a jury verdict after trial before Chief Judge J. Edward Lumbard, of the Court of Appeals of this Circuit, sitting by designation.

The action involves two subcontracts for excavation work between D'Agostino Excavators, Inc. (D'Agostino) and The Heyward-Robinson Company, Inc. (Heyward) as prime contractor on two construction jobs in Connecticut. One of the prime contracts, for the construction of barracks at the Naval Submarine Base in New London, Groton, was with the federal government (the Navy job). The other, a non-federal

* Some of the court's footnotes are omitted.

job, was for the construction of a plant for Stelma, Inc. at Stamford (the Stelma job).

D'Agostino brought this action against Heyward and its surety, Maryland Casualty Company (Maryland) under the Miller Act, 40 U.S. C.A. §§ 270a and 270b, to recover payments alleged to be due on the Navy job. Heyward answered, denying liability on the Navy job and counterclaiming for alleged overpayments and extra costs of completing both the Navy job and the Stelma job. In reply, D'Agostino denied liability on the Heyward counterclaims and interposed a reply counterclaim to recover from Heyward monies alleged to be due on the Stelma job.

At the trial, the two subcontracts in suit were treated together. D'Agostino claimed that Heyward had breached both subcontracts by failing to make progress payments as required and that substantial sums were owing to it from Heyward on both jobs. Heyward claimed that D'Agostino had breached both subcontracts by permitting its compensation and employee liability insurance to lapse; that, as a result, Heyward on October 19, 1965 had terminated both; and that D'Agostino was liable for overpayments and costs of completion on both.

The issue as to whether Heyward had breached the subcontracts prior to October 19, 1965, when Heyward claimed to have terminated them, was submitted to the jury as a special question. The jury found that Heyward had breached the subcontracts prior to that date.

After amendment of the complaint by D'Agostino to allege a claim in quantum meruit for the work performed on both jobs, special questions then were submitted to the jury as to the reasonable value of the work performed by D'Agostino on each project and the net amount owed by Heyward to D'Agostino on both. The jury found, in answer to these questions, that the net amount owed by Heyward to D'Agostino on both jobs was $63,988.36. Judgment against Heyward was rendered accordingly. Under a formula agreed to by the parties, it was determined that the amount due to D'Agostino on the Navy job was $40,771.46 and judgment was entered against Maryland in that sum.

* * *

I.

Appellants' initial contention is that the District Court had no jurisdiction over the counterclaims on the Stelma job. They therefore contend that the Stelma claims must be dismissed and that since D'Agostino's claims on the Navy and Stelma jobs were presented to the jury as inseparable, the judgment below must be reversed.

Appellants urge that the Stelma counterclaims are not compulsory counterclaims over which the federal court acquired jurisdiction ancillary to the jurisdiction which it had over D'Agostino's Miller Act claim stated in the complaint. They say that these are permissive counterclaims over which the court had no ancillary jurisdiction and which lacked the required independent basis of federal jurisdiction.

This jurisdictional issue is raised for the first time in this Court. In the Court below appellants affirmatively urged that the Stelma counterclaims were compulsory. Nevertheless, it is well settled that lack of federal jurisdiction may be raised for the first time on appeal, even by a party who originally asserted that jurisdiction existed or by the Court sua sponte. E.g., American Fire & Casualty Co. v. Finn, 341 U.S. 6, 17–18, 71 S.Ct. 534, 95 L.Ed. 702 (1951) * * *.

It is apparent from the record that there is no independent basis of federal jurisdiction over the Stelma counterclaims. Both D'Agostino and Heyward are New York corporations with offices in New York. There is thus no diversity jurisdiction. Clearly there is no jurisdiction under the Miller Act over these counterclaims since the Stelma contract did not involve public work for the federal government.

The question is whether the Stelma counterclaims are compulsory or are permissive. Under the rule in this circuit, if they are permissive there is no Federal jurisdiction over them unless they rest on independent jurisdictional grounds. O'Connell v. Erie Lackawanna R. R. Co., 391 F.2d 156, 163 (2d Cir. 1968), vacated and ordered dismissed as moot, 395 U.S. 210, 89 S.Ct. 1767, 23 L.Ed.2d 213 (1969); * * * 3 J. Moore, Federal Practice ¶ 13.19[1] at 53–57 (2d ed. 1969). But see Revere Copper and Brass, Inc. v. Aetna Casualty and Surety Company, 426 F.2d 709 (5th Cir. May 8, 1970); G. Fraser, Ancillary Jurisdiction and the Joinder of Claims in the Federal Courts, 33 F.R.D. 27, 28–34 (1963); Green, Federal Jurisdiction over Counterclaims, 48 N.W.U.L.Rev. 271, 282–285 (1953).[1] On the other hand, if they are compulsory counterclaims, they are ancillary to the claim asserted in the complaint and no independent basis of Federal jurisdiction is required. E.g., United Artists Corp. v. Masterpiece Productions, Inc., 221 F.2d 213 (2d Cir. 1955). See, e.g., Moore v. New York Cotton Exchange, 270 U.S. 593, 46 S.Ct. 367, 70 L.Ed. 750 (1926); C. Wright, Law of Federal Courts, §§ 9, 79 (2d ed. 1970); 3 J. Moore, supra, ¶ 13.15 at 31–42.

Under Rule 13(a) Fed.R.Civ.P. a counterclaim is compulsory "if it arises out of the transaction or occurrence that is the subject matter of the opposing party's claim." In United Artists Corp. v. Masterpiece Productions, supra, Chief Judge Clark said:

> In practice this criterion has been broadly interpreted to require not an absolute identity of factual backgrounds for the two claims, but only a logical relationship between them. Lesnik v. Public

---

1. Apparently there is one limited exception to the rule that permissive counterclaims require an independent basis of Federal jurisdiction. Where the permissive counterclaim is in the nature of a set-off interposed merely to defeat or reduce the opposing party's claim and does not seek affirmative relief, no independent jurisdictional grounds are required. Fraser v. Astra Steamship Corp., supra; Marks v. Spitz, 4 F.R.D. 348 (D.Mass. 1945) (dictum); C. Wright, Law of Federal Courts § 79 at 351 (2d ed. 1970). See In re Monongahela Rye Liquors, Inc., 141 F.2d 864, 869–870 (3rd Cir. 1944); G. Fraser, supra, at pp. 31–34; 3 J. Moore, supra, ¶ 13.19[1].

Industrials Corp., 2 Cir., 144 F.2d 968, 975, citing and quoting, inter alia, Moore v. New York Cotton Exchange, 270 U.S. 593, 610, 46 S.Ct. 367, 371, 70 L.Ed. 750, thus: "'Transaction' is a word of flexible meaning. It may comprehend a series of many occurrences, depending not so much upon the immediateness of their connection as upon their logical relationship." See also Blair v. Cleveland Twist Drill Co., 7 Cir., 197 F.2d 842, 845; Wright, Estoppel by Rule: The Compulsory Counterclaim Under Modern Pleading, 38 Minn.L.Rev. 423, 440–445, 39 Iowa L.Rev. 255; 3 Moore's Federal Practice ¶ 13.13 (2d ed. 1948 and 1954 Supp.).

221 F.2d at 216. See United States for Use and Benefit of Pickard Engineering Co. v. Southern Construction Company, 293 F.2d 493, 500 (6th Cir. 1961), rev'd in part on other grounds, sub nom. Southern Construction Co. v. Pickard, 371 U.S. 57, 83 S.Ct. 108, 9 L.Ed.2d 31 (1962); United States v. Eastport Steamship Corporation, 255 F.2d 795 (2d Cir. 1958); C. Wright, supra, at 346–349.

Thus ". . . courts should give the phrase 'transaction or occurrence that is the subject matter' of the suit a broad realistic interpretation in the interest of avoiding a multiplicity of suits." 3 J. Moore, supra, ¶ 13.13 at 33–36 (2d ed. 1969). As the Supreme Court said in *Pickard:*

> The requirement that counterclaims arising out of the same transaction or occurrence as the opposing party's claim "shall" be stated in the pleadings was designed to prevent multiplicity of actions and to achieve resolution in a single lawsuit of all disputes arising out of common matters. 371 U.S. at 60, 83 S.Ct. at 110.

In the case at bar the counterclaims were compulsory within the meaning of Rule 13(a). There was such a close and logical relationship between the claims on the Navy and Stelma jobs that the Stelma counterclaims arose out of the same "transaction or occurrence" as those terms are now broadly defined. Both subcontracts were entered into by the same parties for the same type of work and carried on during substantially the same period. Heyward had the right to terminate both subcontracts in the event of a breach by D'Agostino of either. Heyward also had the right to withhold monies due on one to apply against any damages suffered on the other. Progress payments made by Heyward were not allocated as between jobs and were made on a lump sum basis for both as though for a single account.

A single insurance policy covered both jobs. The letters of Heyward to D'Agostino of October 8 and 19, 1965 threatening termination and terminating both jobs, allegedly because of the cancellation by D'Agostino of this joint insurance coverage and failure to properly man both projects, treated both jobs together. These letters formed the basis of one of Heyward's major claims at the trial.

The controversy between the parties which gave rise to this litigation was with respect to both jobs and arose from occurrences affecting both. Indeed, it would seem to have been impossible for Heyward to have fully litigated the claims against it on the Navy job without including the Stelma job, because the payments it made to D'Agostino could not be allocated between the two jobs.

As the appellants themselves point out in their brief, the "Stelma and Navy claims were so interwoven at the trial that they are now absolutely incapable of separation." The proof as to payments and alleged defaults in payments was made without any differentiation between the two claims and neither of the parties was able to offer any evidence of apportionment. Finally, the evidence as to the breaches of contract claimed by the respective parties related in the main to both contracts rather than to one or the other.

* * *

FRIENDLY, CIRCUIT JUDGE (concurring).

I cannot agree that, as maintained in Part I of the majority opinion, the counterclaim relating to the Stelma job was compulsory under F.R.Civ.P. 13(a). Of course, it is tempting to stretch a point when a jurisdictional objection is so belatedly raised by the very party who clamored for the exercise of jurisdiction until the decision went against it. But we must consider the question as if Heyward had not pleaded the Stelma counterclaim and proceeded to sue D'Agostino in some other court for failure to perform that subcontract, and D'Agostino then claimed that Heyward's failure to bring the Stelma transaction into this Miller Act suit barred the later action. Despite the desirability of requiring that all claims which in fact arise "out of the transaction or occurrence that is the subject matter of the opposing party's claim" be litigated in a single action, courts must be wary of extending these words in a way that could cause unexpectedly harsh results.

Even on a liberal notion of "logical relation," see C. Wright, Federal Courts, § 79 at 346–47 (2d ed. 1970), I am unable to perceive how Heyward's claim for breach of the Stelma subcontract arose "out of the transaction or occurrence" to wit, the Navy subcontract, that was the subject matter of D'Agostino's Miller Act claim. Whatever historical interest there may be in the circumstances that the two subcontracts were entered into between the same parties for the same type of work and were carried on during substantially the same period, these facts seem to me to be lacking in legal significance. So likewise do D'Agostino's having furnished a single insurance policy to cover both jobs and Heyward's having cancelled the subcontracts in one letter rather than two. * * *

* * *

Against all this appellee relied heavily on Southern Construction Co. v. Pickard, 371 U.S. 57, 83 S.Ct. 108, 9 L.Ed.2d 31 (1962). Since the counterclaim there at issue was held not compulsory, the decision can scarcely be authority that a claim like Heyward's on the Stelma subcontract was. I think it not only is not such authority but points just the other way. The Court there held that where a subcontractor on two federal projects was obliged to bring Miller Act suits in different districts because of venue requirements, the contractor was not obliged to counterclaim for an unallocated payment in the first suit. I do not see how the Court could have reached a different result if the subcontractor had one Miller Act subcontract and another in which he could sue only in a state or a different federal district court.

Nevertheless I think the court below had jurisdiction of the Stelma counterclaim. I would now reject the conventional learning, which I followed too readily in O'Connell v. Erie Lackawanna R. R., 391 F.2d 156, 163 (1968), that the permissive counterclaim "needs independent jurisdictional grounds to support it, with one exception," to wit, set-off, 3 Moore, Federal Practice ¶ 13.19 at 53–54 (2d ed. 1968). The Supreme Court left this question open in Moore v. New York Cotton Exchange, 270 U.S. 593, 609, 46 S.Ct. 367, 70 L.Ed. 750 (1926). I read Judge Clark's fine opinion for this court in Lesnick v. Public Industrial Corp., 144 F.2d 968, 976 n. 10 (2 Cir. 1944), as also doing this, although we cited it in *O'Connell* as upholding the conventional view, as do Professor Wright, Federal Courts 351 n. 56 (2d ed. 1970) and the majority here.

The reasons why the conventional view is wrong are set out in detail in an article by Professor Thomas F. Green, Jr., Federal Jurisdiction over Counterclaims, 48 N.W.U.L.Rev. 271 (1953), and nothing would be gained by repetition. I mention only two points. One is that for reasons there developed, id. at 277–81, Professor Moore's sound recognition—perhaps more accurately creation—of the exception that set-off requires no independent jurisdictional basis, see 3 Moore, Federal Practice, ¶ 13.19 at 54–55 n. 3; Marks v. Spitz, 4 F.R.D. 348 (D.Mass. 1945); Fraser v. Astra S. S. Corp., 18 F.R.D. 240 (S.D.N.Y.1955), carries the seeds of destruction of the supposed general rule. The other is that at least since United Mine Workers v. Gibbs, 383 U.S. 715, 86 S.Ct. 1130, 16 L.Ed.2d 218 (1966), it is no longer thought the heavens will fall if a federal court deals with a non-federal claim when it is convenient to do so. The only argument I see against Professor Green's position is the possibility of snowballing through a plaintiff's permissive counterclaim in reply to the defendant's permissive counterclaim etc. Id. at 289–90. But that is more theoretical than real. In a diversity case the plaintiff in all probability would already have pleaded this in his complaint; while the problem could arise in a federal question action, for example, if D'Agostino has a claim against Heyward on still another subcontract, such cases are extremely rare.

If the decision were mine, I would therefore ask that the court sit *in banc* and overrule the holding in *O'Connell,* supra, 391 F.2d at 163, that a permissive counterclaim requires independent jurisdictional grounds. Since my brothers find themselves able to affirm without doing this, I join in the result and leave the issue for another day. On all other points I concur in Judge Bryan's thorough opinion.

NOTE ON COUNTERCLAIMING DEVICES

1. Historical Development

The scope of affirmative relief available to a defendant against a plaintiff was rather narrowly confined at common law and in equity. At common law, the defendant was permitted "recoupment" in an action brought by a plaintiff. Recoupment was obtainable only in respect of the transaction sued on by the plaintiff and only to the extent of plaintiff's claim: no affirmative judgment could be entered in favor of defendant.

In equity, there were two strands of doctrine. First, there was the general principle that a cross-bill would lie in order that there be a "complete determination of the controversy." See Mitford, Pleadings in the Court of Chancery 81*–82* (Jeremy, Smith, Moulton ed. 1849). By definition this sort of claim for relief was available only in respect of the same transaction as that sued on by plaintiff: the purpose of the cross-bill was to do an entire job on that transaction. The second strand of doctrine was partly case-developed, deriving from the civil law doctrine of *compensatio* (compensation of mutual claims), and partly statutory. This was the rule that a defendant could raise as a "set off" any liquidated claim that he might have against the plaintiff. The "set off" was purely defensive, in that an affirmative judgment for defendant was not allowed. See generally Comment, Automatic Extinction of Cross-Demands: Compensatio from Rome to California, 53 Cal.L.Rev. 224 (1965).

The Field Code, as amended in 1851 to provide for a counterclaim, allowed a counterclaim if:

(1) It existed in favor of a defendant and against a plaintiff between whom a "several judgment" might be had; and

(2) Either:

(a) Arose out of the transaction sued on by plaintiff or was "connected with the subject of the action"; or

(b) When plaintiff's action was on contract, was a contract claim in favor of defendant.

2. Modern Counterclaim Rules

The English Judicature Act of 1873 had a liberal counterclaim provision, which was the model for F.R.C.P. 13(a) and (b). See also, e.g., Ill.C.C.P. § 2–608; N.Y.C.P.L.R. § 3019.

The California law concerning counterclaims was, until 1972, an historical and conceptual tangle involving two types of countersuits, a counterclaim and a cross-complaint. C.C.P. 425.10, 426.10–426.70, 428.10–428.80, adopted in that year, provide that the device available to defendant to assert relief against the plaintiff is a cross-complaint. A defendant may cross-complain with any cause of action he may have against a plaintiff, C.C.P. 428.10, and *must* assert as a cross-complaint any cause of action "which arises out of the same transaction, occurrence, or series of transactions or occurrences as the cause of action which the plaintiff alleges in his complaint." C.C.P. 426.10, 426.30. The California cross-complaint may also be used by a defendant to assert claims against a co-defendant or against a person who is not a party, but only if the claim thus asserted is one that arose out of the same transaction as the original action. C.C.P. 428.10. As employed in the latter fashion, the cross-complaint is like impleader under the Federal Rules, see F.R.C.P. 14 and the discussion infra p.

748. For the background of the 1972 changes in the California cross-complaint, see Friedenthal, Joinder of Claims, Counterclaims, and Cross-Complaints: Suggested Revision of the California Provisions, 23 Stan.L.Rev. 1 (1970).

Counterclaims and set-offs can create problems of fairness between the parties, particularly when insurance covers one or both claims. For example: In a jurisdiction adopting pure comparative negligence, P sues D for personal injuries and D counterclaims for her own injuries. The jury finds P is injured $10,000 and is 20% negligent, and that D is injured $100,000 but is 80% negligent. P is due 80% of $10,000 (i.e., $8,000) while D is due 20% of $100,000 (i.e., $20,000). If you were P, would you want to pay D $20,000 and receive $8,000 from D, or net it out and pay D $12,000? Why? If P and D are covered by insurance, is there any reason why the two insurers should not be allowed to set-off the two judgments? Compare Stuyvesant Ins. Co. v. Bournazian, 342 So. 2d 471 (Fla.1976), with Jess v. Herrmann, 26 Cal.3d 131, 161 Cal.Rptr. 87, 604 P.2d 208 (1979), the latter holding that set-off based on comparative negligence should take account of the parties' insurance coverages.

A plaintiff can only be sued by way of counterclaim in the capacity in which he brings suit, and a defendant can only counterclaim in the capacity in which he is sued. Banco Nacional de Cuba v. Chase Manhattan Bank, 658 F.2d 875 (2d Cir. 1981).

On the compulsory counterclaim, see also Note on Res Judicata Between the Same Parties, supra p. 648.

3. Ancillary Jurisdiction of Counterclaims in the Federal Courts

Ordinarily, no claim can be entertained in the federal courts unless there is a jurisdictional basis for it, either by reason of diversity of party citizenship or because the claim is based on federal law. The extension of federal jurisdiction to claims which, considered separately, are not cognizable in federal courts, but which arise in close connection with claims that are so cognizable, is generally referred to as "ancillary" or "pendent" jurisdiction. See Aldinger v. Howard, supra p. 528. Compulsory counterclaims under F.R.C.P. 13(a) may rest on ancillary jurisdiction, Curtis v. Sears, Roebuck & Co., 754 F.2d 781 (8th Cir. 1985), while permissive counterclaims under Rule 13(b) require independent jurisdictional grounds. Shelter Mutual Ins. Co. v. Public Water Supply Dist., 747 F.2d 1195 (8th Cir. 1984). The authority to assert a permissive counterclaim and the obligation to submit a compulsory counterclaim may be qualified by legal requirements external to F.R.C.P. 13. See, e.g., Baker v. Gold Seal Liquors, Inc., 417 U.S. 467, 94 S.Ct. 2504, 41 L.Ed.2d 243 (1974) (disturbing priority among creditors); Boynton v. United States, 566 F.2d 50 (9th Cir. 1977) (distribution of jurisdiction in tax cases).

3. CONSOLIDATION AND SEVERANCE

NOTE ON CONSOLIDATION AND SEVERANCE

Consolidation, i.e., simultaneous disposition of two separately filed actions, and severance, i.e., separate disposition of one or more claims or issues joined in a single action, are within the power of the trial court by historic usage or explicit statutory authorization. See, e.g., F.R.C.P. 42; C.C.P. 1048. Consolidation or severance may relate to all or only part of the phases of a lawsuit: consolidation may be ordered for trial alone, allowing pre-trial discovery and other procedures to go their separate courses, or it may be ordered for all phases of the litigation from threshold pleading problems through appeal. Use of consolidation and severance has increased under modern joinder devices: consolidation, because the courts, having become accustomed to handling the large-sized single actions presented to them by the parties, seem more willing to put together larger-sized actions on their own initiative; severance, because party exercise of the joinder privilege on occasion results in aggregations too large to handle in one sitting. But the "rule" that governs the exercise of choice is nothing more than that the trial judge must "exercise sound judicial discretion," and it seems that judges have very different predispositions on the problem. See, e.g., Arroyo v. Chardon, 90 F.R.D. 603 (D.P.R.1981) (refusing to consolidate nine actions by public employees who had been demoted for participation in a political party). The trial judge's choice, moreover, is ordinarily not reviewable in advance of appeal from final judgment in the action, when the appellate court has to decide not merely whether the trial judge made a bad choice, but whether he made one so bad as to justify retrial. See, e.g., Shump v. Balka, 574 F.2d 1341 (10th Cir. 1978). For a list of factors in severance, see Arnold v. Eastern Air Lines, 681 F.2d 186 (4th Cir. 1982).

See also F.R.C.P. 20(b) (separate trial provision in rule on permissive joinder of parties) and F.R.C.P. 21 (severance provision in rule on misjoinder and non-joinder of parties). See 5 Moore ¶ 42.03; 3A Id. ¶¶ 20.08, 21.05. Compare the authorization of consolidation and severance in C.C.P. 1048; see also C.C.P. 377 (consolidation of wrongful death actions and survivor actions for injuries, on motion of any interested party); C.C.P. 597 (court may order separate trial of defenses not involving merits, e.g., defenses of statute of limitations and prior judgment); C.C.P. 598 (court may order priority for trial of liability issue); C.C.P. 1250.240 (consolidation in condemnation suits). On consolidation and severance and separate trials generally in California, see 4 Witkin 351–381; C.E.B., 2 Calif.Civ.Pro.Before Trial, c. 27 (1978). See also C.C.P. 1281.2 and 1281.3 (concurrent arbitration proceedings).

When actions are pending in the same court that involve important issues in common, it is now routine that they be consolidated for trial. They also may be consolidated for pretrial purposes, especially if they involve extensive discovery. It is said that "consolidation * * * does not merge the suits into a single cause, or change the rights of the parties, or make those who are parties in one suit parties in another." Johnson v. Manhattan Ry. Co., 289 U.S. 479, 497, 53 S.Ct. 721, 728, 77 L.Ed. 1331 (1933); e.g., State Mut. Life Assur. Co. v. Deer Creek Park, 612 F.2d 259, 267 (6th Cir. 1979), although it is hard to see how this could be unqualifiedly true. On consolidation of cases filed in different federal districts for pretrial purposes, see Further Note on Case Management, infra p. 1234.

At one time the routine use of severance enjoyed enthusiastic support among some judges and commentators. In the Northern District of Illinois, for example, a practice was established that in negligence actions the issue of liability would be separately tried from the issue of damages, unless the trial judge ordered otherwise. See Hosie v. Chicago & Northwestern R. R. Co., 282 F.2d 639 (7th Cir. 1960). Doubts arose about whether court time was being saved, and also about the fairness to plaintiffs of keeping out the evidence of damage when considering the question of liability. See Weinstein, Routine Bifurcation of Jury Negligence Trials: An Example of the Questionable Use of Rule Making Power, 14 Vand.L.Rev. 831 (1961). The growing adoption of the rule of comparative negligence in any event requires simultaneous trial of liability and damages issues, see American Motorcycle Ass'n v. Superior Court, infra p. 740.

In mass accident cases there are obvious economies in determining the common liability or causation issues and separately trying damages. See, e.g., In re Beverly Hills Fire Litigation, 695 F.2d 207 (6th Cir. 1982).

MIDDLEBROOK, LIABILITY v. DAMAGES: A FAIR TRIAL OFTEN MEANS A SPLIT TRIAL

Wall St.J., June 13, 1988, at 16.*

Smart business people understand that large, complex problems become more manageable when broken into units and addressed one piece at a time. The technique has become a First Principle of executive success. Yet, in the big business of managing civil litigation (RAND Corp. estimates that between $27 billion and $34 billion was expended in 1985) we muddle along with an unnecessarily complex and inefficient trial process.

The norm for most trials is for the jury to hear in one unified process all the issues pertinent to the liability of the defendant and the value of the damages. This often results in a marathon of expert witnesses and exhibits on a diverse set of issues. The typical results: confused juries, courts congested with trials that last longer than necessary, and excessive transaction costs in the form of legal fees, expert witnesses and court costs.

A simple alternative is to bifurcate, or split, issues of liability from issues of damages and to try them separately. If the issue of liability is heard alone, and no liability is found, none of the evidence relating to the extent and value of the damages need be presented. The savings would be at least some of the time the lawyers would have spent developing their client's case on the damage issues, the time the court would have spent hearing the related evidence and arguments, and the costs of expert witnesses. Without liability, all the issues of damages become moot. If liability is found, experience teaches us that litigants are more likely to reach settlement, thus again avoiding the added expense and burden of a separate trial.

Juror effectiveness can also be improved. Narrowing the questions for immediate consideration sharpens the jury's focus and increases the likelihood that jurors will comprehend complex legal or technical issues. Presenting the issues in shorter phases also enhances juror recall (of particular value in courts where note-taking is prohibited).

The current process was carried to its most absurd extreme in a trial involving Monsanto Co., which concluded last fall. An award of $16.2 million in punitive damages was made to 65 plaintiffs exposed to one teaspoon of dioxin, despite the jury's conclusion that the plaintiffs suffered no ill effects. The verdict followed a complex trial of three years and eight months. The legal costs generated by this lengthy process, which included more than 200 witnesses and 6,000 exhibits, must have been staggering. Other litigants awaiting trial before the same court were denied access over this nearly four-year period—clearly a major disservice.

In the case that Texaco defended—and lost—against Pennzoil, Texaco chose not to enter any evidence regarding the value of potential damages out of fear that such evidence would undercut the credibility of its position on the liability issues. Had the case been split, Texaco would have presented the damage-related evidence it intentionally withheld. The damages—$10.5 billion—might well have been smaller, and Texaco might not have had to file for bankruptcy.

Other famous cases have been split. In a class-action suit in which Merrell Dow defended against charges that its drug Bendectin caused birth defects, the jury first heard the issues of scientific causation—whether the drug was capable of causing the harm alleged. The jury concluded it was not, obviating the need to hear any discussion of damages.

In a hazardous waste case tried in 1986 in Woburn, Mass., against W.R. Grace Co. and Beatrice Foods Co., the court split the trial into four phases. After the first phase was completed (in which the court found that Grace was, and Beatrice was not, responsible for the contamination of the wells in question) Grace settled with the plaintiffs. Although Grace maintained that it was not responsible for the contamination, the jury determination was a likely stimulus to settlement.

Judges strongly support the value of bifurcating trials, according to a Louis Harris poll released in April of 800 state and 200 federal trial court judges. Of those judges who had used bifurcation, an overwhelming majority—94% at the federal level and 82% at the state level—said its effects were positive. Most judges believe that it reduces transaction costs (79%, federal; 70%, state), that it speeds up the trial process (82%, federal; 77%, state), that it expedites settlements (85%, federal; 80%, state), and that it improves the fairness of the outcome (80%, federal; 77%, state).

Yet that same poll confirms that bifurcation is not used very often. More than half the polled judges who presided in jurisdictions where bifurcation is permitted and who have granted bifurcation have granted it less than five times over the past three years.

The explanations for this contradiction between opinion and action are largely a matter of conjecture. One possibility is that it just may not occur to overworked judges to split a trial without special prompting by the litigating parties.

A second possibility could be opposition from the plaintiffs' bar. Why? Some attorneys may seek to cloud the question of liability by emphasizing their clients' misfortunes. Experience suggests that juries may overlook weaknesses in the liability side of the case when sympathy is aroused by vivid evidence of damage.

The plaintiffs' bar recognizes this dynamic. For example, an article in the March issue of Trial magazine ("Bifurcated Trials, How to Avoid Them—and How to Win Them") discusses a 1963 study published in the Harvard Law Review. The study shows that split trials take less time and plaintiffs are less likely to win them. For the latter reason, the article recommends that plaintiffs' lawyers develop strategies opposing bifurcation.

There will always be cases, of course, that do not lend themselves to bifurcation. Issues such as liability and damage are not always separable. Also, issues may not be sufficiently complex to warrant this treatment. And, in eight states (including Illinois, the site of the Monsanto trial) there are no statutes or judicial rules permitting bifurcation. However, in those cases in which a split trial is appropriate, it is a sensible technique for streamlining civil litigation. A fair trial on liability, with any compensation delivered quickly and efficiently, advances the rights of all the litigating parties. Bifurcation should be one item on a broad agenda of reform of court procedures.

———

What is the counterargument against bifurcation? Is the case for or against bifurcation a matter of fairness and efficiency, or is it merely an economic battle between the plaintiffs' bar and the defense bar? See Zeisel and Callahan, Split Trials and Time Saving: A Statistical Analysis, 76 Harv.L.Rev. 1606 (1963) (bifurcation increases defense verdicts from 43% to 79%). Compare the Wall Street Journal editorial (by general counsel for an insurance company), supra, with Curry and Snider, Bifurcated Trials, 24 Trial 47 (March 1988). See also Report of the Action Committee to Improve the Tort Liability System, Recommendation 16, A.B.A. 1987 Midyear Meeting, New Orleans, Feb. 16–17, 1987.

C. JOINDER OF PARTIES

———

1. BASIC CONCEPTS OF PARTY JOINDER

———

a. PERMISSIVE JOINDER

LAMBERT v. SOUTHERN COUNTIES GAS CO.

Supreme Court of California, 1959.
52 Cal.2d 647, 340 P.2d 608.

SPENCE, JUSTICE.

Plaintiffs appeal from a judgment in favor of defendant Southern Counties Gas Company entered after said defendant's general demurrer to the first amended complaint had been sustained without leave to amend.

Plaintiffs sought damages for the loss of their "Caterpillar D8 tractor equipped with a Bulldozer 8S blade attachment and No. 29 Cable Control attachment; . . . hereinafter . . . referred to as plaintiffs' bulldozer." They had rented it to certain ranch owners and it was totally destroyed by fire after striking and puncturing a high-pressure gas pipeline less than 15 inches under the surface of the ranch property. The amended complaint is in two counts. Count one concerns only the alleged negligence of the ranch owners in the operation of the bulldozer over the pipeline when they should have known its location. Count two concerns only the alleged negligence of the gas company in permitting its pipeline to remain so near the surface of the ground.

The general demurrer of the gas company (the only defendant named in count two) was sustained on the ground that plaintiffs had affirmatively pleaded their own contributory negligence by alleging negligence on the part of the ranch overseer in count one, which negligence is imputed to plaintiffs, as owners of the bulldozer, under section 402 of the Vehicle Code. That section provides: "Every owner of a motor vehicle is liable and responsible for the . . . injury to . . . property resulting from negligence in the operation of such motor vehicle . . . by any person using or operating the same with the permission, express or implied, of such owner, and the negligence of such person shall be imputed to the owner for all purposes of civil damages."

Plaintiffs contend: (1) That their bulldozer may not properly be classified as a motor vehicle so as to permit the imputation of negligence as provided by said section 402; but (2) even if section 402 does apply so as to permit such imputation, the allegations of negligence of the ranch overseer in count one are not available to defeat plaintiffs' separately stated cause of action against the gas company in count two. On the other hand, the gas company claims: (1) That plaintiffs' bulldozer constitutes a motor vehicle within the meaning of the Vehicle Code so as to justify the imputation of negligence under section 402; and (2) that such negligence as shown in count one amounts to an affirmative pleading of plaintiffs' own contributory negligence so as to defeat plaintiffs' claim against the gas company though separately stated in count two. The gas company cites the general rule that a complaint which shows on its face contributory negligence is demurrable. Routh v. Quinn, 20 Cal.2d 488, 493, 127 P.2d 1, 149 A.L.R. 215; Nicolosi v. Clark, 169 Cal. 746, 747–748, 147 P. 971, L.R.A.1915F, 638; La Com v. Pacific Gas & Electric Co., 132 Cal.App.2d 114, 117, 281 P.2d 894, 48 A.L.R.2d 1455. By stipulation, defendant ranch owners are not required to answer the amended complaint until this appeal from the judgment sustaining the gas company's demurrer has been decided.

In Behling v. County of Los Angeles, 139 Cal.App.2d 684, 294 P.2d 534, 535, an "Allis-Chalmers tractor, crawler type with bulldozer," was held as a matter of law to be a "motor vehicle" within the meaning of sections 31 and 32 of the Vehicle Code. * * * The Vehicle Code comprehends those vehicles which may require special safeguard or special permit in order to be legally operated on the highways (Veh. Code, §§ 710, 710.5) as well as those vehicles which comply with existing statutory limitations. Plaintiffs' bulldozer therefore appears to be a "motor vehicle" as a matter of law, and the provisions of the Vehicle Code pertaining to the negligent operation thereof apply.

Count one of the amended complaint alleges the negligence of the ranch overseer, the agent of plaintiffs' bailees, in the operation of plaintiffs' bulldozer, and such negligence is imputable to plaintiffs as the "owner of a motor vehicle . . . for all purposes of civil damages." Veh.Code, § 402. Manifestly, the phrase "*all* purposes of civil damages" indicates application of the statute to "all cases where the rights and obligations of the owner are involved in civil action for damages" (Milgate v. Wraith, 19 Cal.2d 297, 300, 121 P.2d 10, 11), regardless of whether the owners be plaintiffs as here or whether the owner be the defendant as in Behling v. County of Los Angeles, supra. The gas company argues that since for the purpose of ruling on its demurrer, the allegations of the first amended complaint must be accepted as true (Carruth v. Fritch, 36 Cal.2d 426, 429, 224 P.2d 702, 24 A.L.R.2d 1403; Speegle v. Board of Fire Underwriters, 29 Cal.2d 34, 41, 172 P.2d 867), and it has demurred to the entire amended complaint rather than only to count two, it may avail itself of anything appearing "upon the face" of the amended complaint (Code Civ.Proc. § 430) to support its demurrer. Accordingly, it seeks to "dip into" count one of the amended complaint and avail itself of the allegations of negligence therein as imputed to plaintiffs to defeat plaintiffs' cause of action as separately stated in count two.

But a plaintiff may plead inconsistent causes of action in separate counts of a single complaint. Steiner v. Rowley, 35 Cal.2d 713, 719, 221 P.2d 9; Goldwater v. Oltman, 210 Cal. 408, 423, 292 P. 624, 71 A.L.R. 871; Turner v. Turner, 173 Cal. 782, 785–786, 161 P. 980; Tanforan v. Tanforan, 173 Cal. 270, 273, 159 P. 709; Western Title Insurance & Guaranty Co. v. Bartolacelli, 124 Cal.App.2d 690, 694, 269 P.2d 165; see also Stockton Combined Harvester & Agricultural Works v. Glens Falls Ins. Co., 121 Cal. 167, 171, 53 P. 565; Haskins v. Crumley, 157 Cal.App. 2d 524, 526, 321 P.2d 19. Each count or cause of action in a complaint must be complete in itself, and must either contain all the averments necessary to state a cause of action (Hopkins v. Contra Costa County, 106 Cal. 566, 570, 39 P. 933; Reading v. Reading, 96 Cal. 4, 6, 30 P. 803; Haskell v. Haskell, 54 Cal. 262, 264–265) or expressly refer therefor to other counts. Treweek v. Howard, 105 Cal. 434, 442, 39 P. 20; Green v. Clifford, 94 Cal. 49, 52, 29 P. 331. Similarly a count sufficient within itself may not ordinarily be defeated by importing, from another count, an allegation to which the sufficient count makes no reference. Lord v. Garland, 27 Cal.2d 840, 850, 168 P.2d 5; see also Steiner v. Rowley, supra, 35 Cal.2d 713, 719, 221 P.2d 9.

There are exceptional instances where the allegations of one count have been considered in connection with the allegations of another count in ruling on a demurrer. Thus a common count may be joined with a count wherein all of the facts are specially pleaded; and if the count containing the specific facts is demurrable, so is the common count which is obviously based on the same set of facts. Orloff v. Metropolitan Trust Co., 17 Cal.2d 484, 489, 110 P.2d 396; Neal v. Bank of America, 93 Cal.App.2d 678, 681, 209 P.2d 825; Rose v. Ames, 53 Cal. App.2d 583, 589, 128 P.2d 65; Hays v. Temple, 23 Cal.App.2d 690, 695, 73 P.2d 1248. This rule with respect to pleadings involving a common count apparently is based "on the anomalous nature of the common count in our system of pleading." Western Title Insurance & Guaranty Co. v. Bartolacelli, supra, 124 Cal.App.2d 690, 694, 269 P.2d 165, 168. Similarly in an extension of this rule, a count in a complaint premised on detailed factual allegations in another count must stand or fall with the other count. Ephraim v. Metropolitan Trust Co., 28 Cal.2d 824, 833, 172 P.2d 501; Ray v. Hanisch, 147 Cal.App.2d 742, 751, 306 P.2d 30; Stafford v. Russell, 117 Cal.App.2d 326, 327, 255 P.2d 814; Bos v. United States Rubber Co., 100 Cal.App.2d 565, 571, 224 P.2d 386. But in each of the last-cited cases, each count of the complaint rested basically on the same set of facts, and involved only a varying statement of the cause of action against the same defendant or defendants.

Here the gas company alone is named defendant in count two, and only its alleged negligence is involved in count two. Count two does not concern the alleged negligence of the ranch owners, which rests on a different premise for the recovery of damages as stated in count one. In short, the two counts in their respective separate statements of alleged negligence—that of the ranch owners, on the one hand, and that of the gas company, on the other—indicate that plaintiffs are in doubt as to which defendants should be held liable for the damages sustained, and for that reason plaintiffs have elected to set forth their two causes of action in the one complaint. Plaintiffs may do this under the right of joinder of defendants afforded by our system of code pleading (Code Civ.Proc. §§ 379a, 379b, and 379c; Kraft v. Smith, 24 Cal.2d 124, 130, 148 P.2d 23; Sareussen v. Lowe, 125 Cal.App.2d 288, 289–290, 270 P.2d 27). It would defeat the principles underlying our liberal system of pleading to permit the gas company, the only defendant named in count two, to import, from the separately stated count one, allegations against other defendants based on a different premise of liability. Rather, as plaintiffs' amended complaint is framed here, each count should be tested upon the basis of its own allegations. Lord v. Garland, supra, 27 Cal.2d 840, 850, 168 P.2d 5. So tested, we conclude that the allegations of count two are sufficient to state a cause of action against the gas company, and that its general demurrer should have been overruled.

The judgment is reversed, with directions to the trial court to overrule the general demurrer of defendant gas company to the amended complaint and to allow said defendant a reasonable time within which to answer.

GIBSON, C. J., and SHENK, TRAYNOR, SCHAUER, McCOMB, and PETERS, JJ., concur.

PAN AMERICAN WORLD AIRWAYS, INC. v. UNITED STATES DISTRICT COURT

United States Court of Appeals for the Ninth Circuit, 1975.
523 F.2d 1073.*

WALLACE, CIRCUIT JUDGE:

These petitions for writs of mandamus or prohibition consolidated in this case, arise from two lawsuits, each involving a separate airline crash. Nos. 74–2093 and 74–2240 are petitions respectively by the McDonnell Douglas Corporation (McDonnell Douglas) and by the United States in a case arising out of the crash of a jet airliner near Paris,

* Some of the court's footnotes are omitted.

France, on March 3, 1974. The airliner was manufactured by McDonnell Douglas, and operated by Turkish Airlines, not a party to the action below. The United States was implicated in the crash through the alleged failure of the Federal Aviation Administration properly to certify and inspect the aircraft involved in the crash. No. 74–1726 is a petition by Pan American World Airways, Inc. (Pan American) and The Boeing Company (Boeing) in a case arising out of the crash of a jet airliner at Pago Pago, American Samoa, on January 30, 1974. The airliner was operated by Pan American and manufactured by Boeing.

All three petitions for writs of mandamus or prohibition seek to prevent the district court from notifying potential plaintiffs of the actions before it. We grant the petitions.

I. *The Petitions in the Paris Action*

Between 346 and 360 persons died in the Paris crash. Only 23 were residents of the United States. At least ten actions arising from the crash have been filed in various federal district courts and, by order of the Panel on Multidistrict Litigation, these actions have all been consolidated in the Central District of California. At least one of these has been filed as a class action. Flanagan v. McDonnell Douglas Corp., CV No. 74–808–PH.

In the course of pretrial hearings in the *Flanagan* case, the district judge informed McDonnell Douglas that he intended to order production of a list of passengers and of the names and addresses of their next of kin. He further stated that he would use the list to notify potential plaintiffs of the actions pending before him. The following day, McDonnell Douglas moved that the district judge not seek a passenger list from any source and that he refrain from sending notice to nonlitigants. Both motions were denied. When certification of an interlocutory appeal pursuant to 28 U.S.C.A. § 1292(b) was denied, McDonnell Douglas filed the petition for mandamus in No. 74–2093. The petition seeks to prevent the district judge from notifying potential plaintiffs that actions arising from the crash are pending before him. The United States, a codefendant, subsequently filed a petition seeking identical relief in No. 74–2240. We have stayed all proceedings in the district court connected with notice to potential plaintiffs pending disposition of these petitions.

A. *Preliminary Questions*

Before we reach the merits of the petitions, we must discuss * * * whether the district court's order may be subjected to interlocutory review by means of a petition for mandamus. Several plaintiffs in actions arising out of the Paris crash (real parties in interest, hereinafter referred to as respondents) have opposed the petition claiming that this order does not involve the exceptional circumstances required for issuance of mandamus. We disagree. Mandamus is an appropriate remedy for actions in excess of the district court's power.

Will v. United States, 389 U.S. 90, 95–96, 88 S.Ct. 269, 19 L.Ed.2d 305 (1967); Schlagenhauf v. Holder, 379 U.S. 104, 110, 85 S.Ct. 234, 13 L.Ed. 2d 152 (1964). While the distinction between error subject to adequate review on appeal and "usurpation of power" sufficient for mandamus may not always be clear, cf. *Will*, supra, 389 U.S. at 95–96, 88 S.Ct. 269, the order in this case falls within the latter category. Notice from the court to potential plaintiffs not authorized explicitly by statute or rule is so extraordinary that review of such actions by mandamus will not frustrate the congressional policy permitting appeals only from final judgments. See Bankers Life & Cas. Co. v. Holland, 346 U.S. 379, 382–83, 74 S.Ct. 145, 98 L.Ed. 106 (1953). Furthermore, erroneous notice to potential plaintiffs cannot be remedied on appeal after final judgment. * * *

    * * *

B. *The Merits of the Case*

* * * [R]espondents contend * * * that several sources of judicial authority permit the district court to issue notice to potential plaintiffs; and * * * that such notice is required by the due process clause of the Fifth Amendment. * * *

Respondents' due process argument is that potential plaintiffs are constitutionally entitled to notice of pending actions in which they may join. Respondents cite no case reaching this conclusion, and understandably so. So long as the persons sought to be notified do not become parties to these actions, they will not be bound by the outcome. Hence they will not be adversely affected by these actions and need not be notified of them. As stated in Board of Regents v. Roth, 408 U.S. 564, 569, 92 S.Ct. 2701, 2705, 33 L.Ed.2d 548 (1972):

> The requirements of procedural due process apply only to the deprivation of interests encompassed by the Fourteenth Amendment's protection of liberty and property.

The requirements of the Fifth Amendment are the same. Arnett v. Kennedy, 416 U.S. 134, 151–52, 94 S.Ct. 1633, 40 L.Ed.2d 15 (1974) (plurality opinion); id. at 164–67, 94 S.Ct. 1633 (Powell, J., concurring and concurring in the result). When no interest is threatened, no notice is required.

Respondents' alternative argument is that the district court possesses discretion to issue the notice. They find several sources for such discretion: the equitable powers of the court; sections 0.21 and 1.10 of the Manual for Complex Litigation; and Federal Rules of Civil Procedure 1, 16, 19, 21, 23, 42 and 83.[3] Although most of these purported sources are plainly insufficient, a few require more extended treatment.

---

3. Judge Schnacke primarily argues in his dissent that authority to notify prospective plaintiffs rests upon a residual power of the district court that has yet to be limited by rule or statute. But he fails to specify the source of this residual power.

Traditionally in our judicial system, courts are powerless to act until litigants bring claims before them. Osborn v. Bank of the United States, 22 U.S. (9 Wheat.) 326, 361, 9 L.Ed. 905 (1824) (Marshall, C. J.) (dictum). The issuance of notice to po-

1. *Equitable Power*

Respondents rely upon Sprague v. Ticonic Nat'l Bank, 307 U.S. 161, 59 S.Ct. 777, 83 L.Ed. 1184 (1939), and Sprogis v. United Air Lines, Inc., 444 F.2d 1194, 1201–02 (7th Cir.), cert. denied, 404 U.S. 991, 92 S.Ct. 536, 30 L.Ed.2d 543 (1971), for the equitable power of a federal court to issue notice to potential plaintiffs. These cases are distinguishable. To the extent that *Sprague* permits notice to potential plaintiffs, it does so only because it held that the district court could assess attorney's fees against them for benefits already received. 307 U.S. at 166–67, 59 S.Ct. 777. *Sprogis* permitted the district court to retain jurisdiction to consider granting relief to persons with claims under the Civil Rights Act of 1964 similar to those of the named plaintiff but relied on policies embodied in the Act. 444 F.2d at 1201–02. Sending notice to prospective plaintiffs cannot be grounded in the general equitable powers of the district court.

2. *The Manual for Complex Litigation*

The Manual for Complex Litigation does not help respondents. Neither section 0.21 nor section 1.10 of the Manual concern notice, let alone notice to nonlitigants. But in any case, the Manual cannot serve as a source of judicial power because the committee that drafted it possessed authority only to issue recommendations. See Manual for Complex Litigation xiii–xiv (1973).

3. *Rules 16, 19 and 83*

Federal Rules of Civil Procedure 16, 19 and 83 likewise do not furnish the district court with authority to issue notice to potential plaintiffs. Rule 16 empowers the district court to conduct pretrial conferences concerning a broad range of subjects relevant to pending litigation but does not authorize such notice, at least absent stipulation by the parties. Rule 19 provides for joinder of necessary parties. The district court did not purport to order joinder of the persons sought to be notified, but even if it had, we fail to see how, in their absence, "complete relief cannot be accorded among those already parties." Fed.R.Civ.P. 19(a)(1). Rule 83 authorizes the various district courts to promulgate rules of court but notification from the court to potential plaintiffs is not authorized by any rule of the District Court for the Central District of California and a procedure that deviates so sharply from the traditional role of the judiciary cannot be justified as an ad hoc rule of practice. Compare Republic Int'l Corp. v. Amco Engineers, Inc., 516 F.2d 161, 166 (9th Cir. 1975). See note 3, supra. Finally, respondents argue that the preceding rules should be interpreted to

tential plaintiffs offends this principle in two ways: first, it permits a court to act upon a claim before it becomes the subject of a lawsuit; and second, it permits a court to acquire jurisdiction by encouraging law-suits. So sharp a deviation from the traditional role of the judiciary requires justification. Resort to a residual power of unspecified origin is insufficient.

authorize notice to potential plaintiffs because Rule 1 requires that the Federal Rules be construed "to secure the just, speedy, and inexpensive determination of every action." Fed.R.Civ.P. 1. Rule 1, however, concerns only construction of the rules. It does not allow the leap respondents would have us make to create, in effect, new rules far beyond the express language of the rules themselves.

Respondents' arguments from the provisions of Rules 21, 23 and 42, again as supplemented by Rule 1, are more forceful.

4. *Rule 23*

The district court did not find, and the respondents have not shown, that the action below meets the specific prerequisites of a class action. Fed.R.Civ.P. 23(a), (b). Respondents contend nevertheless that it falls within the notice provisions of Rule 23 because a case may be treated as a class action before it is found to be one. See City of Inglewood v. City of Los Angeles, 451 F.2d 948, 951 (9th Cir. 1971); Schy v. Susquehanna Corp., 419 F.2d 1112, 1116 (7th Cir.), cert. denied, 400 U.S. 826, 91 S.Ct. 51, 27 L.Ed.2d 55 (1970) (dictum); Philadelphia Elec. Co. v. Anaconda Am. Brass Co., 42 F.R.D. 324, 326–28 (E.D.Pa. 1967); 3B J. Moore, Federal Practice ¶ 23.50 (1974). However, none of the cited cases supports the notice sought in this case. In addition, although an Advisory Committee Note approves of discretionary notice to potential class members prior to the district court's determination whether the action should proceed as a class action, the notice proposed here serves no such limited purpose. See Fed.R.Civ.P. 23(d)(2); 3B J. Moore, supra, ¶ 23.01[11.–1], [12.–2] (1974), quoting Fed.R.Civ.P. 23, Advisory Committee Note (1966); Schy v. Susquehanna Corp., supra, 419 F.2d at 1116. Nor does the proposed notice provide only for notice of compromise or dismissal. See Fed.R.Civ.P. 23(e); Philadelphia Elec. Co. v. Anaconda Am. Brass Co., supra, 42 F.R.D. at 326–28. The admitted purpose of the notice in this case is to bring the claims of unnamed members of the plaintiff class before the court. Notice for this purpose usually has been thought to issue only after certification of a class action. American Pipe & Constr. Co. v. Utah, 414 U.S. 538, 547–49, 552, 94 S.Ct. 756, 38 L.Ed.2d 713 (1974) (dictum); Cherner v. Transitron Electronic Corp., 201 F.Supp. 934, 935–37 (D.Mass.1962) (Wyzanski, J.); Frankel, Some Preliminary Observations Concerning Civil Rule 23, 43 F.R.D. 39, 40–41 (1968). Otherwise, by notice and joinder of unnamed members of a possible plaintiff class, a district court could circumvent Rule 23 by creating a mass of joined claims that resembles a class action but fails to satisfy the requirements of the rule.[5] For that reason, notice for the purpose of bringing the claims of unnamed members of the plaintiff class before the court may not issue before a class action has been certified. This procedure, as outlined in

---

5. Indeed, this appears to be the theory of the district judge in an opinion supporting an identical ruling in an earlier case. Petition of Gabel, 350 F.Supp. 624, 627 (C.D.Cal.1972).

Petition of Gabel, 350 F.Supp. 624, 627 (C.D.Cal.1972), cannot be supported by Rule 23.[6]

5. *Rule 21*

Respondents' argument based upon Rule 21 must fail for the same reason. Rule 21 provides that "[p]arties may be dropped or added by order of the court on motion of any party or of its own initiative at any stage of the action and on such terms as are just." Respondents contend that since this rule authorizes the district court to order joinder of potential plaintiffs on its own motion, it also authorizes notice to such persons. The premise of this argument is untenable, again because it would effectively permit class actions that do not satisfy the requirements of Rule 23. The reasons, however, require some elaboration.

By itself, Rule 21 cannot furnish standards for the propriety of joinder, for it contains none. Hence it must incorporate standards to be found elsewhere.[7] The only standards for proper joinder relevant to this case are Rules 19 and 20 but, as earlier demonstrated, Rule 19 is inapplicable. This leaves Rule 20, which allows persons to join as plaintiffs in a single action if they assert claims arising out of the same occurrence and if those claims share a common question of law or fact. The claims of potential plaintiffs here presumably would meet this test.

Rule 21 has been used to join potential plaintiffs who meet the requirements of Rule 20 and who subsequently consent to be joined. Kincade v. Mikles, 144 F.2d 784, 787 (8th Cir. 1944); Gilbert v. General Elec. Co., 347 F.Supp. 1058, 1059–61 (E.D.Va.1972); * * *. But even if we were to follow these cases, they would not support the notice that would be issued in this case. With two exceptions not relevant here,[8]

6. My Sister Hufstedler takes no position on the question of pre-certification notice pursuant to Rule 23. But since our order prevents the district court from issuing any notice before certification of a class action, I believe it is necessary to address the question whether this case falls within any provision of Rule 23 arguably authorizing such notice. Since the record reveals no need for pre-certification notice for either of the purposes arguably permitted by Rule 23, this court may fairly conclude that such notice should not issue. I do not pass upon the district court's power to issue pre-certification notice beyond stating that if available, it does not extend to this case.

7. Rule 21 has been used to join potential plaintiffs who are necessary parties, see Rule 19(a), or real parties in interest, see Rule 17(a). See United States v. Aetna Cas. & Surety Co., 338 U.S. 366, 381–82, 70 S.Ct. 207, 94 L.Ed. 171 (1949) (dictum); Independent Wireless Tel. Co. v. Radio Corp. of Am., 269 U.S. 459, 468–73, 46 S.Ct. 166, 70 L.Ed. 357 (1926). However, a potential plaintiff is rarely joined as an involuntary plaintiff but usually is joined as a party defendant. Caprio v. Wilson, 513 F.2d 837, 839 (9th Cir. 1975); Eikel v. States Marine Lines, Inc., 473 F.2d 959, 961–62 (5th Cir. 1973); Coast v. Hunt Oil Co., 195 F.2d 870, 872 (5th Cir.), cert denied, 344 U.S. 836, 73 S.Ct. 46, 97 L.Ed. 651 (1952); 3A J. Moore, Federal Practice ¶ 19.06 (1974); 7 C. Wright & A. Miller, Federal Practice and Procedure §§ 1605, 1606, 1683 (1972).

8. Gilbert v. General Elec. Co., 347 F.Supp. 1058 (E.D.Va.1972), permitted joinder of an unspecified number of plaintiffs for jurisdictional and venue purposes. Id. at 1058–61. Adams v. Bell Aircraft Corp., 7 F.R.D. 48 (W.D.N.Y.1947), relied on Rule 21 to join plaintiffs in a class action authorized by statute. Id. at 48-49.

these cases all involve joinder of four persons or fewer.[9] In the present case, the district court has decided to send notice to the next of kin of several hundred passengers and crew. The effect of notice of this magnitude is the same as notice to an entire class. Such notice will effectively transform the present action into an unwieldly pseudo-class-action not authorized by Rule 23. Rules 20 and 21 cannot be read to circumvent the requirements of that rule.

6. *Rule 42*

Rule 42 is also deficient as a source of the district court's authority to issue notice. It provides in part:

> When actions involving a common question of law or fact are pending before the court, it may order a joint hearing or trial of any or all the matters in issue in the actions; it may order all the actions consolidated; and it may make such orders concerning proceedings therein as may tend to avoid unnecessary costs or delay.

Fed.R.Civ.P. 42(a). Respondents rely on the last clause quoted above, arguing that the notice contemplated by the district court is an order "concerning proceedings therein as may tend to avoid unnecessary costs or delay." But notice to potential plaintiffs does not further consolidation of actions already pending. At most, it expedites consolidation of pending actions with actions yet to be filed. * * *
* * *

HUFSTEDLER, CIRCUIT JUDGE (concurring specially):

I agree with Judge Wallace's Opinion, except in respect of his including some dicta in the discussion of Rules 21 and 23, upon which I decline to express any premature views. Accordingly, I would conclude the Rule 23 segment of the Opinion with Judge Wallace's observation that "none of the cited cases supports the notice sought in this case." I would limit the Rule 21 discussion to the simple points that Rule 21 furnishes no standards for joinder and hence supplies no foundation for determining who can be joined and notified of joinder. The persons that the district court sought to notify are outside the purview of Rules 19 and 20. Rule 19 is manifestly inapposite. Rule 20 is inapplicable because none of these nonparties is presently asserting any right to relief.

SCHNACKE, DISTRICT JUDGE (dissenting):

I dissent. Judge Peirson Hall has had almost unique experience in the handling of airline crash cases involving multiple deaths. He has found, as the record below indicates, that the disposition of such cases is

---

9. It is unnecessary to adopt the theory of joinder suggested by these cases. Because they permit at most limited, not mass, joinder, they are distinguishable from the present case. We need neither approve nor disapprove them. Other cases may arise that present reasons for notice to potential plaintiffs more compelling than the alleged need to foster pseudo-class-actions. Accordingly, as the issue need not be decided in this case, it is left open.

likely to be much complicated, long delayed, and far more costly if the disposition of actions pending before him must await the last of such cases which may reasonably be expected to come before him, either from this district or, as is often the case, from assignment by the Multidistrict Panel [28 U.S.C.A. § 1407]. It is implicit that he has found that discovery, use and deposing of experts, appraisal of total amount of damage, settlement, and other matters of concern to the Court may be handled faster and better if all potential parties be assembled at the earliest possible time.

In order to insure the expeditious handling of the cases before him, Judge Hall has required that the Court be advised of the names and next of kin of all victims of the disasters, with the intention of notifying each potential plaintiff that these actions are pending.

The majority, in my view, reaches the wrong result because it contemplates the wrong question. The question is not whether some rule permits the action proposed, but whether any rule, statute, or logical concept forbids it.

* * *

It may be conceded that the potential plaintiffs have no *right* to be notified, but they are certainly not injured if they are. The actual plaintiffs agree that the notice is desirable. Defendants object to it, but fail to show how any right of theirs is prejudiced. True, they may be precluded from settling cases with potential plaintiffs who are insufficiently advised of their rights, or unaware of a convenient forum in which their rights may be expeditiously adjudicated, but I can't believe the court should extend itself to preserve that opportunity.

* * *

NOTE ON PERMISSIVE JOINDER OF PARTIES

1. The Scope of Permissive Joinder

On the history of permissive joinder of parties, see Note on Historical Attitudes Toward Joinder, supra p. 705. The history of the New York joinder provisions is given in 15 N.Y.Jud.Council Rep. 209 (1949). New York, following Federal Rule 20, now has free joinder of plaintiffs and of defendants in respect of claims arising out of the same transaction or series of transactions where there is presented a common question of law or fact. See N.Y.C.P.L.R. § 1002. For the California history, see Comment, Joinder of Parties in California, 23 Calif.L.Rev. 320 (1935). For a helpful review of Illinois law, see Tone and Stifler, Joinder of Parties and Consolidation of Multiparty Actions, 1967 U.Ill. L.F. 209.

a. Joinder of Plaintiffs. The potentially dramatic sweep of F.R.C.P. 20 in joinder of plaintiffs in federal litigation is sharply restricted by the requirement that each plaintiff joined must be of diverse citizenship from all defendants and must satisfy the applicable venue requirements. In state courts, where such embarrassments are not encountered, permissive joinder has resulted in some hefty lawsuits. See, e.g., Akely v. Kinnicutt, 238 N.Y. 466, 144 N.E. 682 (1924): The defendants were alleged to have floated an issue of stock in a corporation at a grossly inflated price and to have sold it on the strength of a prospectus containing fraudulent misrepresentations. The action was brought by 193 plaintiffs each of whom alleged that he had been induced to buy by the representations. See also Adams v. Albany, 124 Cal.App.2d 639, 269 P.2d 142 (1954).

Compare City of Nokomis v. Sullivan, 14 Ill.2d 417, 153 N.E.2d 48 (1958): The plaintiff city brought suit against 29 separate property owners for an injunction restraining them from maintaining privy out-houses in violation of a city ordinance requiring all sewage to be disposed of through the city sewer system. Defendants' objection to the joinder was overruled on the strength of Ill.C.P.A. § 24 (now Ill.C.C.P. § 2–405), substantially similar to F.R.C.P. 20(a).

On the venue problems arising in actions with multiple claims and parties in California, see Carruth v. Superior Court, supra p. 518.

In applying F.R.C.P. 20(a) to joinder of defendants in federal court, as in joinder of plaintiffs, the venue requirements must be met for each defendant, e.g., Suttle v. Reich Bros. Const. Co., 333 U.S. 163, 68 S.Ct. 587, 92 L.Ed. 614 (1948). Ordinarily, the requirement concerning the minimum amount in controversy must also be met; e.g., Pearce v. Pennsylvania R. R., 162 F.2d 524 (3d Cir. 1947). See Wright § 36.

b. Class Actions. The use of class actions for mass torts has generally been rejected by the courts. See, e.g., In re Northern Dist. of California Dalkon Shield IUD Products Liability Litigation, infra p. 854, and the Note following.

2. Effect of Joinder on Problems of Proof

Isn't it clear that each plaintiff in the situations involved in Akely v. Kinnicutt and Adams v. Albany will have a better looking case by reason of its simultaneous presentation with other similar claims? Would it be just as advisable to join many plaintiffs when their claims are for personal injury? Or would the recovery by each plaintiff be likely to be greater if the claims were tried separately?

Observe that the permissive joinder of defendants in cases like Lambert v. Southern Counties Gas Co. eliminates the risk inherent in separate actions against the defendants that there might be inconsistent findings of fact, both adverse to the plaintiff. Observe also that plaintiff may be materially assisted in the proof of his case by the efforts of each defendant to implicate the other. Plaintiff may nevertheless face problems which no joinder rule can solve, such as that in Summers v. Tice, 33 Cal.2d 80, 199 P.2d 1 (1948): On a hunting trip with the two defendants, plaintiff was injured when defendants both negligently and simultaneously fired their shotguns in plaintiff's direction. It was clear that plaintiff had been hit by one of the two discharges, but which one could not be determined. In affirming a judgment against both defendants, the court said, 199 P.2d at 4: "When we consider the relative position of the parties and the results that would flow if plaintiff was required to pin the injury on one of the defendants only, a requirement that the burden of proof on that subject be shifted to defendants becomes manifest. * * * They brought about a situation where the negligence of one of them injured the plaintiff, hence it should rest with them each to absolve himself if he can."

b. **COMPULSORY JOINDER**

HAAS v. JEFFERSON NATIONAL BANK
United States Court of Appeals for the Fifth Circuit, 1971.
442 F.2d 394.

ALDISERT, CIRCUIT JUDGE:

Following a pre-trial conference, the district court entered an order finding that Charles H. Glueck was an "indispensable party" under Fed.R.Civ.Pro. 19, and dismissing the action on the ground that Glueck's presence in the case "violates the requirements of complete diversity." We must determine whether the court's action was appropriate at a pre-trial stage, and, if so, whether it abused its discretion in dismissing the action instead of proceeding without Glueck.

Invoking jurisdiction on the basis of diversity of citizenship, 28 U.S.C.A. § 1332, Haas, a citizen of Ohio, sought a mandatory injunction from the district court directing the Jefferson National Bank, a citizen of Florida, to issue to him 169½ shares of its common stock. Alternatively, he asked for damages reflecting the stock's value. He alleged a 1963 agreement with Glueck, also an Ohio citizen, under which they were to jointly purchase 250 shares of the bank's stock; the certificates were to issue in the name of Glueck but Haas was to have a one-half ownership of the shares. He also pleaded a similar 1966 agreement with Glueck to purchase 34 additional shares. According to Haas, he paid Glueck amounts representing one-half ownership, the bank had knowledge of his ownership interest, and the certificates and subsequent dividends were issued to Glueck.

Haas contends, however, that in 1967 he requested Glueck to order the bank to issue certificates in Haas' name, reflecting his ownership of 169½ shares, and that pursuant to this request Glueck presented to the bank properly endorsed certificates for 250 shares with instructions to reissue 170 shares to Haas and the balance to Glueck.

In its answer, the Bank explained that it had refused to make the assignment because at the time of the transfer request Glueck was indebted to it under the terms of a promissory note which required that Glueck pledge, assign, and transfer to the bank property of any kind owned by Glueck and coming into the possession of the Bank. The Bank averred that Glueck withdrew the transfer request and instead pledged the stock certificates with a second bank as collateral for a loan there.

With these contentions forming the backdrop of the pre-trial conference, the parties stipulated to the questions of fact which remained to be litigated at trial:

> (a) Did the Bank have knowledge of Haas' claimed ownership of the stock prior to Glueck's 1967 transfer request?

> (b) Did Glueck withdraw the 1967 transfer request?

(c) What was the status of Glueck's obligation to the bank as represented by the promissory note?

(d) Did the second bank have possession of the stock in controversy at the time Haas filed the action?

(e) Did Haas in fact own 169½ shares of the bank stock?

Following the pre-trial conference and the entry of these stipulations, the district court entered an order directing Haas to amend his complaint to join Glueck as a party. The court then denied his motion to dismiss Glueck as a party, and granted the Bank's motion to dismiss the amended complaint on the jurisdictional ground of incomplete diversity.[1]

We have no difficulty in concluding that the district court did not enter its joinder order prematurely. It was entirely appropriate to resolve Glueck's status on the basis of the pleadings and stipulations of the parties which posed the trial issues with completeness and precision. The vital factual issues having been joined, there was no reason to postpone the resolution of the indispensability problem until after the commencement of trial.[2]

Moreover, if the district court did not err in ordering the joinder of Glueck, it was obviously correct in finding a jurisdictional defect. It is clear beyond any doubt that the diversity statute requires complete diversity of citizenship. Indianapolis v. Chase Nat'l Bank, 314 U.S. 63, 62 S.Ct. 15, 86 L.Ed. 47 (1941); Treinies v. Sunshine Min. Co., 308 U.S. 66, 60 S.Ct. 44, 84 L.Ed. 85 (1939); Strawbridge v. Curtiss, 7 U.S. (3 Cranch) 267, 2 L.Ed. 435 (1806). "The policy of the statute calls for its strict construction." Healy v. Ratta, 292 U.S. 263, 270, 54 S.Ct. 700, 703, 78 L.Ed. 1248 (1934). It is of course immaterial that the nondiverse party has been required to be joined as an indispensable party. Provident Tradesmens Bank & Trust Co. v. Patterson, 390 U.S. 102, 88 S.Ct. 733, 19 L.Ed.2d 936 (1968). "It is settled that failure of the district court to acquire jurisdiction over indispensable parties to an action deprives the court of jurisdiction to proceed in the matter and

1. Service of process was not properly effectuated because the attempted service in Ohio was beyond the territorial limits of the district court in Florida. Fed.R.Civ. Pro. 4(f).

2. The Advisory Committee commented in part upon Rule 19 as follows:

A person may be added as a party at any stage of action on motion or on the court's initiative (see Rule 21); and a motion to dismiss, on the ground that a person has not been joined and justice requires that the action should not proceed in his absence, may be made as late as the trial on the merits (see Rule 12(h) (2), as amended; cf. Rule 12(b)(7), as amended). However, when the moving party is seeking dismissal in order to protect himself against a later suit by

the absent person (subdivision (a)(2)(ii)), and is not seeking vicariously to protect the absent person against a prejudicial judgment (subdivision (a)(2)(i)), his undue delay in making the motion can properly be counted against him as a reason for denying the motion. A joinder question should be decided with reasonable promptness, but decision may properly be deferred if adequate information is not available at the time. Thus the relationship of an absent person to the action, and the practical effects of an adjudication upon him and others, may not be sufficiently revealed at the pleading stage; in such a case it would be appropriate to defer decision until the action was further advanced, Cf. Rule 12(d).

render a judgment." Schuckman v. Rubenstein, 164 F.2d 952, 957 (6 Cir. 1947).[3]

In approaching the dispositive question whether Rule 19 required the joinder of Glueck, we begin with the formulation of Shields v. Barrow, 58 U.S. (17 How.) 130, 139, 15 L.Ed. 158 (1854). Indispensable parties were defined as

> [p]ersons who not only have an interest in the controversy, but an interest of such a nature that a final decree cannot be made without either affecting that interest, or leaving the controversy in such a condition that its final termination may be wholly inconsistent with equity and good conscience.

As Mr. Justice Harlan declared in Provident Tradesmens Bank & Trust Co. v. Patterson, supra, 390 U.S. 102, 124, 88 S.Ct. 733, 746, 19 L.Ed.2d 936, the generalizations of *Shields* "are still valid today, and they are consistent with the requirements of Rule 19. . . . Indeed, the . . . *Shields* definition states, in rather different fashion, the criteria for decision announced in Rule 19(b)." It is essential, however, to bear in mind that the broad statements in *Shields* "are not a substitute for the analysis required by that Rule." Id.

Fed.R.Civ.Pro. 19, as amended in 1966, provides:

(a) *Persons to be Joined if Feasible.* A person who is subject to service of process and whose joinder will not deprive the court of jurisdiction over the subject matter of the action shall be joined as a party in the action if (1) in his absence complete relief cannot be accorded among those already parties, or (2) he claims an interest relating to the subject of the action and is so situated that the disposition of the action in his absence may (i) as a practical matter impair or impede his ability to protect that interest or (ii) leave any of the persons already parties subject to a substantial risk of incurring double, multiple, or otherwise inconsistent obligations by reason of his claimed interest. . . .

(b) *Determination by Court Whenever Joinder not Feasible.* If a person as described in subdivision (a) (1)–(2) hereof cannot be made a party, the court shall determine whether in equity and good conscience the action should proceed among the parties before it, or should be dismissed, the absent person being thus regarded as indispensable. The factors to be considered by the court include: first, to what extent a judgment rendered in the person's absence might be prejudicial to him or those already parties; second, the extent to which, by protective provisions in the judgment, by the shaping of relief, or other measures, the prejudice can be lessened or avoided; third, whether a judgment rendered in the person's

---

3. See generally Note, Indispensable Parties in the Federal Courts, 65 Harv.L. Rev. 1050 (1952); Note, Indispensable Parties Under the Federal Rules of Civil Procedure, 56 Yale L.J. 1088 (1947).

absence will be adequate; fourth, whether the plaintiff will have an adequate remedy if the action is dismissed for nonjoinder.[4]

The Rule thus commands that we address ourselves to two broad questions: (1) Was Glueck a party "to be joined if feasible" under section (a)? If so, (2) was the court correct, under section (b), in dismissing the action or should it have proceeded without the additional party?

It is readily apparent that Glueck "falls within the category of persons who, under § (a), should be 'joined if feasible,'" Provident Tradesmens Bank & Trust Co. v. Patterson, supra, 390 U.S. at 108, 88 S.Ct. at 737, 19 L.Ed.2d 936, for his presence is critical to the disposition of the important issues in the litigation. His evidence will either support the complaint or bolster the defense: it will affirm or refute Haas' claim to half ownership of the stock; it will substantiate or undercut Haas' contention that the Bank had knowledge of his alleged ownership interest; it will corroborate or compromise the Bank's contention that Glueck rescinded the transfer order; and it will be crucial to the determination of Glueck's obligation to the Bank under the promissory note. The essence of Haas' action against the Bank is that it "unlawfully and recklessly seized, detained, [and] exercised improper dominion" over his shares in transferring and delivering them to the second bank as collateral for Glueck's loan. Thus, Glueck becomes more than a key witness whose testimony would be of inestimable

---

4. Rule 19, as amended, has not received uniform endorsement by commentators. See, e.g., Fink, Indispensable Parties and the Proposed Amendment to Federal Rule 19, 74 Yale L.J. 403 (1965). In arguing against the adoption of the new rule, the author concluded:

Undeniably the indispensable parties rule sometimes puts the federal courts to a cruel choice: whether to proceed without absent persons whose interests might be affected by any decree entered or whose presence is required for the entry of a complete, just, and viable decree, or to dismiss the action and thereby perhaps deny the present plaintiff any forum in which his action may be heard. This problem can best be attacked, not by seeking ways to proceed without interested persons, which inevitably has the effect of fragmenting law suits, but by searching for the means of bringing all interested persons before a single forum so that whole controversies may be expeditiously settled.

For this reason, the more desirable answers would seem to be an extension of service of process in the federal courts to bring in absent indispensable and conditionally necessary parties; a relaxation of venue requirements as to such parties,

and a relaxation of complete diversity requirements in regard to such absent parties. These changes, which may be made readily by the Court and by Congress, would meet the real problem involving joinder requirements—the largely artificial barriers which today prevent complete and expeditious adjudications of entire controversies in the federal courts.

Id., at 448. In this connection, see Cound, Friedenthal, Miller, Civil Procedure 489 (1968):

Notice that a federal court can acquire jurisdiction over an absentee not within the state pursuant to any long arm statute, Rule 4(e), and that it can also serve persons brought in under Rule 19 if they are within 100 miles from the place where the action is commenced, whether or not the place of service is within the state in which the action is pending, Rule 4(f). Should the remaining territorial barriers be broken down?

See also American Law Institute Study of the Division of Jurisdiction between State and Federal Courts, §§ 2341 et seq. (official draft 1968); Carrington, Civil Procedure, 896–899 (1969).

value. Instead he emerges as an active participant in the alleged conversion of Haas' stock.

Applying the criterion of Rule 19(a)(2)(ii), we believe that Glueck's absence would expose the defendant Bank "to a substantial risk of incurring double, multiple, or otherwise inconsistent obligations by reason of his claimed interest." If Haas prevailed in this litigation in the absence of Glueck and were adjudicated owner of half of the stock, Glueck, not being bound by *res adjudicata,* could theoretically succeed in later litigation against the Bank in asserting ownership of the whole. In addition, a favorable resolution of Haas' claim against the Bank could, under (a)(2)(i), "as a practical matter impair or impede [the absent party's] ability to protect [his] interest" in all of the shares—an interest that is at least apparent since all of the stock was issued in Glueck's name.

Because Glueck cannot be made a party without destroying diversity, however, it remains to be decided whether, under Rule 19(b), his presence is so vital that "in equity and good conscience the action . . . should be dismissed, the absent person being thus regarded as indispensable." This decision is always a matter of judgment and must be exercised with sufficient knowledge of the facts in order to evaluate the exact role of the absentees. As the Supreme Court has said:

> The decision whether to dismiss (i.e., the decision whether the person missing is "indispensable") must be based on factors varying with the different cases, some such factors being substantive, some procedural, some compelling by themselves, and some subject to balancing against opposing interests. Rule 19 does not prevent the assertion of compelling substantive interests; it merely commands the courts to examine each controversy to make certain that the interests really exist.

Provident Tradesmens Bank & Trust Co. v. Patterson, supra, 390 U.S. at 118, 119, 88 S.Ct. at 743, 19 L.Ed.2d 936. The spirit of the Rule is to depart from the tyranny of the old labels of "necessary" and "indispensable," and to solve each problem "in the context of particular litigation." Id. at 118, 88 S.Ct. at 742, 19 L.Ed.2d 936.[5]

We turn now to the specific factors enumerated in Rule 19(b), as applied to the facts before us. In our view the first factor tracks the considerations of 19(a)(2)(ii) discussed above: "to what extent a judgment rendered in the person's absence might be prejudicial to him or those already parties." And based on the reasoning previously set

---

5. See Wright, Law of Federal Courts, § 70, at 296–302 (2d ed. 1970). Prior to the amendment of the Rule in 1966, Professor James observed:

Moreover, in many cases a factual inquiry is needed before a realistic appraisal can be made of the weight properly to be attached to one or more of the factors.

Because of all this, the problem does not readily lend itself to solution by fixed and rigid rules. What is called for, rather, is flexibility and a case-by-case appraisal of the relevant factors.

James, Civil Procedure § 9.20, at 425 (1965).

forth, we believe this factor supplies weighty reason for a finding of indispensability.[6]

The second factor directs the court to consider the extent to which the shaping of relief might avoid or lessen the prejudice to existing or absent parties.[7] Because the title to the stock certificates, although not the immediate issue in this litigation, assumes such commanding importance, it is difficult to conceptualize a form of relief or protective provisions which would not require as a preliminary matter the determination of the question of title with all the resulting potential for prejudice.

In analyzing the third factor, "whether a judgment rendered in the person's absence will be adequate," Mr. Justice Harlan cautioned:

> [T]here remains the interest of the courts and the public in complete, consistent, and efficient settlement of controversies. We read the Rule's third criterion, whether the judgment issued in the absence of the nonjoined person will be "adequate," to refer to this public stake in settling disputes by wholes, whenever possible, for clearly the plaintiff, who himself chose both the forum and the parties defendant, will not be heard to complain about the sufficiency of the relief obtainable against them. . . .

Provident Tradesmens Bank & Trust Co. v. Patterson, supra, 390 U.S. at 111, 88 S.Ct. at 739, 19 L.Ed.2d 936. It seems evident to us that the absence of Glueck in this litigation would, of necessity, result in less than a complete settlement of this controversy. For reasons already discussed, there is no semblance of a guarantee that a judgment on Haas' terms would settle the whole dispute generated by the facts here.

Finally Rule 19(b) requires us to consider whether the plaintiff will have an avenue for relief if the district court's dismissal for nonjoinder is affirmed.[8] Clearly, the state courts of Ohio afford plaintiff Haas an

---

6. [T]he defendant may properly wish to avoid multiple litigation, or inconsistent relief, or sole responsibility for a liability he shares with another. . . . [T]here is [also] the interest of the outsider. . . . Of course, since the outsider is not before the court, he cannot be bound by the judgment rendered. This means, however, only that a judgment is not *res judicata* as to, or legally enforceable against, a nonparty. . . . Instead, as Rule 19(a) expresses it, the court must consider the extent to which the judgment may "as a practical matter impair or impede his ability to protect" his interest in the subject matter. . . .

Provident Tradesmens Bank & Trust Co. v. Patterson, supra, 390 U.S. at 110, 88 S.Ct. at 738, 19 L.Ed.2d 936.

7. Rule 19(b) also directs a district court to consider the possibility of shaping relief to accommodate these four interests. Commentators had argued that greater atten-

tion should be paid to this potential solution to a joinder stymie, and the Rule now makes it explicit that a court should consider modification of a judgment as an alternative to dismissal.

Id. at 111–112, 88 S.Ct. at 739, 19 L.Ed.2d 936.

8. [T]he plaintiff has an interest in having a forum. Before the trial, the strength of this interest obviously depends upon whether a satisfactory alternative forum exists. . . .

Id. at 109, 88 S.Ct. at 738, 19 L.Ed.2d 936. See James, Civil Procedure, § 9.20 at 432 (1965):

> [T]he availability of the state court is a factor properly to be considered by the federal court in weighing the relative interests which will be affected by a ruling of indispensability. Even if the plaintiff's preference for the federal forum deserves the court's enthusiastic

opportunity to adjudicate his rights against Glueck.[9] They provide a ready forum to settle the question of title to the stock. Moreover, assuming the disposition of the preliminary question of title in the Ohio courts, it is not difficult to conceptualize circumstances permitting the possibility of a second action against the Bank in which the problem of nonjoinder will not be so acute.

Accordingly, applying Rule 19(b)'s "equity and good conscience test," we hold that the district court did not abuse its discretion in concluding that Glueck was an indispensable party and in dismissing this action.

Affirmed.

NOTE ON COMPULSORY JOINDER OF PARTIES

1. The Necessary Parties Rule

The necessary parties rule derived from equity, which took the position that when a multi-faceted controversy was presented the court would require that all persons "interested" in the controversy be made parties. As stated in Mitford, Pleadings in the Court of Chancery 163*–164* (4th ed. Jeremy 1833):

> "It is the constant aim of a court of equity to do complete justice by deciding upon and settling the rights of all persons interested in the subject of the suit, to make the performance of the order of the court perfectly safe to those who are compelled to obey it, and to prevent future litigation. For this purpose all persons materially interested in the subject ought generally to be parties to the suit, plaintiffs or defendants, however numerous they may be * * *."

The content of the term "interest" was vague, but the objectives of the rule were, and still are, simple enough: from the viewpoint of the court, to do a complete job on the controversy in one sitting; from the viewpoint of those already parties, to protect them against the consequences of subsequent litigation reaching inconsistent results; from the viewpoint of those not made parties but by the rule required to be brought in, to assure that their practical out-of-court situation would not be adversely affected by changes in the status quo wrought in consequence of the judgment. Judged by these standards, was the right result reached in Haas v. Jefferson Nat'l Bank?

Compare, e.g., Kroese v. General Steel Castings Corp., 179 F.2d 760 (3d Cir.), cert. denied 339 U.S. 983, 70 S.Ct. 1026, 94 L.Ed. 1386 (1950): Plaintiff was a holder of preferred stock in defendant, a Delaware corporation with its principal office and plant in Pennsylvania. Plaintiff brought suit in Federal District Court in Pennsylvania to compel the directors of the corporation to declare the 6% dividend which was due and allegedly payable out of earnings. Plaintiff alleged that the directors were refusing to pay dividends on the preferred stock in subservience to the four principal common stockholders, who were empowered to and did elect the directors, and that the refusal was in arbitrary disregard of plaintiff's interests. The corporation was made a defendant. Also named as defendants and served were three of the 12 directors,

protection, the disappointment of that choice is not so great a hardship on the plaintiff as the foreclosing of all courts to him.

9. In response to the court's inquiry at oral argument, Haas' counsel reported that a state action between Haas and Glueck is now pending.

plaintiff alleging that the other nine were not amenable to process and that in no single state could a majority of the directors be served. Defendants objected that in a suit such as this, seeking to compel the directors as a group to take action, a majority of the directors had to be made parties. The court rejected this contention, saying, 179 F.2d at 763–765:

> "In such a case, even though individual directors are joined as parties, they are not called upon to exercise any business discretion. The case has passed that point. * * * [T]he court is declaring rights protected by a rule of law, not calling upon the directors to exercise judgment. If formal action is to be recorded, following a court decree, on a minute book of a directors' meeting, that formal action is nothing but a ministerial act. * * * If the formal act by the board of directors is necessary under the Delaware General Corporation Law to regularize the dividends to which shareholders are entitled, we cannot think that a receivership or sequestration of a foreign corporation's property will not produce the result."

Carey v. Klutznick, 653 F.2d 732 (2d Cir. 1981): The suit was by Governor Carey and other New Yorkers against the Director of the Census Bureau to compel upward adjustment of the census figures for New York on the ground that there had been an undercount. Defendant objected that the other 50 states should be made parties. The court observed, 653 F.2d at 736–737:

> "Although the census * * * serves as a convenient measuring stick for the dispensing of federal funds * * * its purpose under the Constitution was to determine the apportionment of Representatives among the States. * * * In effect, House membership is a fund in which fifty States have an interest. No State's share can be increased without adversely affecting at least one other State. * * * We think it clear beyond cavil that a statistically formulated increase in the population of only one State, such as New York, will have an adverse effect on other States * * *. The adversely affected States therefore fall within the category of parties who should be joined in the instant litigation if feasible. Because compulsory joinder of all fifty States was not feasible in the district court, pragmatic equitable alternatives should have been considered * * * [such as] notice of suit * * * to all of the States, with permission to intervene, [and] * * * multidistrict coordinated or consolidated pretrial proceedings * * *. It appears that thirty-one * * * actions have been transferred to the District of Maryland for coordinated or consolidated proceedings."

Union Carbide Corp. v. Superior Court, 36 Cal.3d 15, 201 Cal.Rptr. 580, 679 P.2d 14 (1984): In a class action on behalf of all California indirect purchasers of industrial gas from defendant Union Carbide, plaintiffs alleged they had been injured when price-fixing overcharges were passed on to them through the chain of distribution. Defendant demanded joinder of persons in the chain of distribution as indispensible parties. The California Supreme Court refused, holding that defendant had failed to demonstrate a "substantial risk" of "multiple liability" as required by C.C.P. 389(a)(2). Defendant had shown no more than a "theoretical possibility" that an absent party might also assert a claim for the same loss.

Compare Western Union Telegraph Co. v. Pennsylvania, 368 U.S. 71, 82 S.Ct. 199, 7 L.Ed.2d 139 (1961).

2. The Relation Between Necessary Party and Federal Diversity Jurisdiction

When, as in *Haas*, there is a third person who ought to be joined under Rule 19, but whose joinder would result in incomplete diversity, the necessary party rule can have the effect of requiring the court to dismiss the action for lack of jurisdiction. In this sense, the joinder of a necessary party has jurisdictional implications. See Freer, Rethinking Compulsory Joinder: A Proposal to Restructure Federal Rule 19, 60 N.Y.U.L.Rev. 1061 (1985). On the other hand, there are situations where adding the necessary party will not destroy diversity. See, e.g., Eikel v. States Marine Lines, Inc., 473 F.2d 959 (5th Cir. 1973), where the third party was held properly aligned as a plaintiff. Compare Wimes v. Eaton Corp., 573 F.Supp. 331 (E.D.Wis.1983). Why couldn't that have been done in *Haas*? Suppose the defendant bank had counterclaimed in interpleader under Rule 22, joining Glueck as an additional defendant in the counterclaim under F.R.C.P. 13(h)?

3. The Relation Between Necessary Party and Territorial Jurisdiction

There can be situations in which a state court will determine that a third party is necessary to the adjudication but that he is beyond the reach of process. See, e.g., Atlantic Richfield Co. v. Superior Court, 51 Cal.App.3d 168, 124 Cal.Rptr. 63 (1975), dismissing an action in California that concerned Texas land in which some non-Californians claimed interests that conflicted with those of the plaintiffs.

4. "Indispensability"

Beyond these impediments to bringing in a necessary party there developed the idea that a court could not enter judgment between the parties before it in the absence of the third party—as though, in *Haas*, the court could not enter judgment between Haas and the bank if Glueck were not a party. That strange idea plagued the federal necessary party doctrine for years, until purged by the 1966 amendments, which were based on the analyses in Reed, Compulsory Joinder of Parties in Civil Actions, 55 Mich.L.Rev. 327, 483 (1957), and Hazard, Indispensable Party: The Historical Origin of a Procedural Phantom, 61 Colum.L.Rev. 1254 (1961). See also Anderson v. Anderson, 109 R.I. 204, 283 A.2d 265 (1971). But the idea has not died that a court lacks power to proceed in the absence of a party who should be joined. See, e.g., Safeway Ins. Co. v. Harvey, 36 Ill.App.3d 388, 343 N.E.2d 679 (1976); Note, Application of "Indispensable Party" Provision of Colo.R.Civ.P. 19: The "Procedural Phantom" Still Stalks in Colorado, 46 U.Colo.L.Rev. 609 (1975); cf. Vitale v. City of Kansas City, 701 S.W.2d 213 (Mo.App.1985); Bank of the Orient v. Superior Court, 67 Cal.App.3d 588, 136 Cal.Rptr. 741 (1977). See also Tobias, Rule 19 and the Public Rights Exception to Party Joinder, 65 N.C.L.Rev. 745 (1987) (application of necessary parties rule where rights affect large number of members of public).

2. DEVICES FOR ADDING PARTIES

a. IMPLEADING, CROSS–CLAIMS AND RELATED DEVICES

AMERICAN MOTORCYCLE ASSOCIATION v. SUPERIOR COURT

Supreme Court of California, 1978.
20 Cal.3d 578, 146 Cal.Rptr. 182, 578 P.2d 899.*

TOBRINER, J.

Three years ago, in Li v. Yellow Cab Co. (1975) 13 Cal.3d 804, 119 Cal.Rptr. 858, 532 P.2d 1226, 78 A.L.R.3d 393, we concluded that the harsh and much criticized contributory negligence doctrine, which totally barred an injured person from recovering damages whenever his own negligence had contributed in any degree to the injury, should be replaced in this state by rule of comparative negligence, under which an injured individual's recovery is simply proportionately diminished, rather than completely eliminated, when he is partially responsible for the injury. In reaching the conclusion to adopt comparative negligence in *Li,* we explicitly recognized that our innovation inevitably raised numerous collateral issues, "[t]he most serious [of which] are those attendant upon the administration of a rule of comparative negligence in cases involving multiple parties." (13 Cal.3d at p. 823.) * * *

For the reasons explained below, we have reached the following conclusions with respect to the multiple party issues presented by this case. First we conclude that our adoption of comparative negligence to ameliorate the inequitable consequences of the contributory negligence rule does not warrant the abolition or contraction of the established "joint and several liability" doctrine; each tortfeasor whose negligence is a proximate cause of an indivisible injury remains individually liable for all compensable damages attributable to that injury. * * *

Second, although we have determined that *Li* does not mandate a diminution of the rights of injured persons through the elimination of the joint and several liability rule, we conclude that the general principles embodied in *Li* do warrant a reevaluation of the common law equitable indemnity doctrine, which relates to the allocation of loss *among* multiple tortfeasors. As we explain, California decisions have long invoked the equitable indemnity doctrine in numerous situations to permit a "passively" or "secondarily" negligent tortfeasor to shift his liability completely to a more directly culpable party. While the doctrine has frequently prevented a more culpable tortfeasor from completely escaping liability, the rule has fallen short of its equitable heritage because, like the discarded contributory negligence doctrine, it

* Some of the court's footnotes are omitted.

has worked in an "all-or-nothing" fashion, imposing liability on the more culpable tortfeasor only at the price of removing liability altogether from another responsible, albeit less culpable party.

Prior to *Li,* of course, the notion of apportioning liability on the basis of comparative fault was completely alien to California common law. In light of *Li,* however, we think that the long-recognized common law equitable indemnity doctrine should be modified to permit, in appropriate cases, a right of partial indemnity, under which liability among multiple tortfeasors may be apportioned on a comparative negligence basis. * * *

Third, we conclude that California's current contribution statutes do not preclude our court from evolving this common law right of comparative indemnity. In Dole v. Dow Chemical Company (1972) 30 N.Y.2d 143, 331 N.Y.S.2d 382, 282 N.E.2d 288, 53 A.L.R.3d 175, the New York Court of Appeals recognized a similar, common law partial indemnity doctrine at a time when New York had a contribution statute which paralleled California's present legislation. * * *

Fourth, and finally, we explain that under the governing provisions of the Code of Civil Procedure, a named defendant is authorized to file a cross-complaint against any person, whether already a party to the action or not, from whom the named defendant seeks to obtain total or partial indemnity. Although the trial court retains the authority to postpone the trial of the indemnity question if it believes such action is appropriate to avoid unduly complicating the plaintiff's suit, the court may not preclude the filing of such a cross-complaint altogether.

In light of these determinations, we conclude that a writ of mandate should issue, directing the trial court to permit petitioner-defendant to file a cross-complaint for partial indemnity against previously unjoined alleged concurrent tortfeasors.

In the underlying action in this case, plaintiff Glen Gregos, a teenage boy, seeks to recover damages for serious injuries which he incurred while participating in a cross-country motorcycle race for novices. Glen's second amended complaint alleges, in relevant part, that defendants American Motorcycle Association (AMA) and the Viking Motorcycle Club (Viking)—the organizations that sponsored and collected the entry fee for the race—negligently designed, managed, supervised and administered the race, and negligently solicited the entrants for the race. The second amended complaint further alleges that as a direct and proximate cause of such negligence, Glen suffered a crushing of his spine, resulting in the permanent loss of the use of his legs and his permanent inability to perform sexual functions. Although the negligence count of the complaint does not identify the specific acts or omissions of which plaintiff complains, additional allegations in the complaint assert, inter alia, that defendants failed to give the novice participants reasonable instructions that were necessary for their safety, failed to segregate the entrants into reasonable classes of equivalently skilled participants, and failed to limit the entry of participants to prevent the racecourse from becoming overcrowded and hazardous.

AMA filed an answer to the complaint, denying the charging allegations and asserting a number of affirmative defenses, including a claim that Glen's own negligence was a proximate cause of his injuries. Thereafter, AMA sought leave of court to file a cross-complaint, which purported to state two causes of action against Glen's parents. The first cause of action alleges that at all relevant times Glen's parents (1) knew that motorcycle racing is a dangerous sport, (2) were "knowledgeable and fully cognizant" of the training and instruction which Glen had received on the handling and operation of his motorcycle, and (3) directly participated in Glen's decision to enter the race by signing a parental consent form. This initial cause of action asserts that in permitting Glen's entry into the race, his parents negligently failed to exercise their power of supervision over their minor child; moreover, the cross-complaint asserts that while AMA's negligence, if any, was "passive," that of Glen's parents was "active." On the basis of these allegations, the first cause of action seeks indemnity from Glen's parents if AMA is found liable to Glen.

In the second cause of action of its proposed cross-complaint, AMA seeks declaratory relief. It reasserts Glen's parents' negligence, declares that Glen has failed to join his parents in the action, and asks for a declaration of the "allocable negligence" of Glen's parents so that "the damages awarded [against AMA], if any, [may] be reduced by the percentage of damages allocable to cross-defendants' negligence."
* * *

The trial court * * * concluded that existing legal doctrines did not support AMA's proposed cross-complaint, and accordingly denied AMA's motion for leave to file the cross-complaint. AMA petitioned the Court of Appeal for a writ of mandate to compel the trial court to grant its motion, and the Court of Appeal, recognizing the recurrent nature of the issues presented and the need for a speedy resolution of these multiple party questions, issued an alternative writ; ultimately, the court granted a peremptory writ of mandate. In view of the obvious statewide importance of the questions at issue, we ordered a hearing in this case on our own motion. All parties concede that the case is properly before us.
* * *

* * * Taking our cue from a recent decision of the highest court of one of our sister states, we conclude—in line with *Li's* objectives—that the California common law equitable indemnity doctrine should be modified to permit a concurrent tortfeasor to obtain partial indemnity from other concurrent tortfeasors on a comparative fault basis.
* * *

* * * [T]he New York Court of Appeals, in the celebrated decision of Dole v. Dow Chemical Company, supra, 30 N.Y.2d 143, 331 N.Y.S.2d 382, 282 N.E.2d 288, modified that state's traditional all-or-

nothing indemnity doctrine to permit a tortfeasor to obtain "partial indemnification" from another tortfeasor on the basis of comparative fault. * * *

Concluding that the all-or-nothing common law indemnity doctrine did not, in many situations, produce the equitable allocation of loss to which it aimed, the *Dole* court proceeded to modify the doctrine, holding that the "[r]ight to apportionment of liability or to full indemnity, . . . as among parties involved together in causing damage by negligence, should rest on relative responsibility. . . ." (331 N.Y.S.2d at pp. 391–392, 282 N.E.2d at p. 295.) The *Dole* court was undeterred from undertaking this modification of the prior common law indemnity doctrine either by the existence of a contribution statute which, like that currently in force in California, provided joint tortfeasors with a right of pro rata contribution in limited circumstances, or by the fact that at that time New York still adhered to the all-or-nothing contributory negligence doctrine.

* * *

Having concluded that a concurrent tortfeasor enjoys a common law right to obtain partial indemnification from other concurrent tortfeasors on a comparative fault basis, we must finally determine whether, in the instant case, AMA may properly assert that right by cross-complaint against Glen's parents, who were not named as codefendants in Glen's amended complaint. As we explain, the governing provisions of the Code of Civil Procedure clearly authorize AMA to seek indemnification from a previously unnamed party through such a cross-complaint. Accordingly, we conclude that the trial court erred in denying AMA leave to file its pleading.

As early as 1962, our court concluded that under the then governing provisions of the Code of Civil Procedure, a defendant could file a cross-complaint against a previously unnamed party when the defendant properly alleged that he would be entitled to indemnity from such party should the plaintiff prevail on the original complaint. (Roylance v. Doelger (1962) 57 Cal.2d 255, 19 Cal.Rptr. 7, 368 P.2d 535.) Although one commentator has suggested that our *Roylance* decision extended the then existing cross-complaint provision beyond its legislatively intended scope (see Friedenthal, Joinder of Claims, Counterclaims and Cross-Complaints: Suggested Revision of the California Provisions (1970) 23 Stan.L.Rev. 1, 31–32), when the cross-complaint statutes were completely revised in 1972, the Legislature specifically codified the *Roylance* rule in section 428.10 et seq. of the Code of Civil Procedure.

Section 428.10 provides in relevant part: "A party against whom a cause of action has been asserted . . . may file a cross-complaint setting forth . . . (b) Any cause of action he has against a person alleged to be liable thereon, *whether or not such person is already a party to the action,* if the cause of action asserted in his cross-complaint (1) arises out of the same transaction [or] occurrence . . . as the cause brought against him or (2) asserts a claim, right or interest in the . . .

controversy which is the subject of the cause brought against him." (Emphasis added.)

Section 428.20 reiterates the propriety of filing such a cross-complaint against a previously unnamed party, and section 428.70 explicitly confirms the fact that a cross-complaint may be founded on a claim of total or partial indemnity by defining a "third-party plaintiff" as one who files a cross-complaint claiming "the right to recover all *or part* of any amount for which he may be held liable" on the original complaint. (Emphasis added.) [8] The history of the legislation leaves no doubt but that these provisions authorize a defendant to file a cross-complaint against a person not named in the original complaint, from whom he claims he is entitled to indemnity. (See Recommendation and Study Relating to Counterclaims and Cross Complaints, Joinder of Causes of Action and Related Provisions (1970) 10 Cal.Law.Revision Com.Rep. pp. 551–555.)

Although real parties in interest claim that the effect of permitting a defendant to bring in parties whom the plaintiff has declined to join will have the undesirable effect of greatly complicating personal injury litigation and will deprive the plaintiff of the asserted "right" to control the size and scope of the proceeding (see, e.g., Thornton v. Luce (1962) 209 Cal.App.2d 542, 551–552 [26 Cal.Rptr. 393]), as our court observed in *Roylance*, 57 Cal.2d at pp. 261–262, 19 Cal.Rptr. 7, 11, 368 P.2d 535, to the extent that such claims are legitimate the problem may be partially obviated by the trial court's judicious use of the authority afforded by Code of Civil Procedure section 1048. Section 1048, subdivision (b) currently provides: "The court, in furtherance of convenience or to avoid prejudice, or when separate trials will be conducive to expedition and economy, may order a separate trial of any cause of action, *including a cause of action asserted in a cross-complaint,* or of any separate issue or any number of causes of action or issues, preserv-

---

8. Section 428.20 provides in full:

"When a person files a cross-complaint as authorized by Section 428.10, he may join any person as a cross-complainant or cross-defendant, whether or not such person is already a party to the action, if, had the cross-complaint been filed as an independent action, the joinder of that party would have been permitted by the statutes governing joinder of parties."

Section 428.70 provides in full:

"(a) As used in this section:

"(1) 'Third-party plaintiff' means a person against whom a cause of action has been asserted in a complaint or cross-complaint, who claims the right to recover all or part of any amounts for which he may be held liable on such cause of action from a third person, and who files a cross-complaint stating such claim as a cause of action against the third person.

"(2) 'Third-party defendant' means the person who is alleged in a cross-complaint filed by a third-party plaintiff to be liable to the third-party plaintiff if the third-party plaintiff is held liable on the claim against him.

"(b) In addition to the other rights and duties a third-party defendant has under this article, he may, at the time he files his answer to the cross-complaint, file as a separate document a special answer alleging against the third-party plaintiff any defenses which the third-party plaintiff has to such cause of action. The special answer shall be served on the third-party plaintiff and on the person who asserted the cause of action against the third-party plaintiff."

ing the right of trial by jury required by the Constitution or a statute of this state or of the United States."

In this context, of course, a trial court, in determining whether to sever a comparative indemnity claim, will have to take into consideration the fact that when the plaintiff is alleged to have been partially at fault for the injury, each of the third party defendants will have the right to litigate the question of the plaintiff's proportionate fault for the accident; as a consequence, we recognize that in this context severance may at times not be an attractive alternative.   Nonetheless, having already noted that under the comparative negligence doctrine a plaintiff's recovery should be diminished only by that proportion which the plaintiff's negligence bears to that of all tortfeasors, we think it only fair that a defendant who may be jointly and severally liable for all of the plaintiff's damages be permitted to bring other concurrent tortfeasors into the suit.   Thus, we conclude that the interaction of the partial indemnity doctrine with California's existing cross-complaint procedures works no undue prejudice to the rights of plaintiffs.

Accordingly, we conclude that under the governing statutory provisions a defendant is generally authorized to file a cross-complaint against a concurrent tortfeasor for partial indemnity on a comparative fault basis, even when such concurrent tortfeasor has not been named a defendant in the original complaint.[9]   *   *   * †

FAIRVIEW PARK EXCAVATING CO. v. AL MONZO CONSTRUCTION CO.

United States Court of Appeals for the Third Circuit, 1977.
560 F.2d 1122.*

GARTH, CIRCUIT JUDGE.

This appeal initially presented a jurisdictional question arising out of an action brought by the plaintiff subcontractor (Fairview) against its general contractor (Monzo) and a Pennsylvania municipal authority (Robinson Township) for which the construction work in issue was being performed.   After Fairview's claim against the Township had been dismissed on state law grounds, the district court then dismissed Monzo's cross-claim against the Township for lack of an independent

---

9. There are, of course, a number of significant exceptions to this general rule. For example, when an employee is injured in the scope of his employment, Labor Code section 3864 would normally preclude a third party tortfeasor from obtaining indemnification from the employer, even if the employer's negligence was a concurrent cause of the injury.   (See E. B. Wills Co. v. Superior Court (1976) 56 Cal.App.3d 650, 653–655, 128 Cal.Rptr. 541; cf. Mize v. Atchison, T. & S. F. Ry. Co. (1975) 46 Cal. App.3d 436, 458–460, 120 Cal.Rptr. 787.)

Similarly, as we have noted above such a partial indemnification claim cannot properly be brought against a concurrent tortfeasor who has entered a good faith settlement with the plaintiff, because permitting such a cross-complaint would obviously undermine the explicit statutory policy to encourage settlements reflected by the provisions of section 877 of the Code of Civil Procedure.   *   *   *

† The dissenting opinion of Clark, J., is omitted.

* Some of the court's footnotes are omitted.

(diversity) basis for federal subject matter jurisdiction. Monzo contends in this appeal that the dismissal of its cross-claim against the Township was erroneous. We agree. * * *

I

Fairview Park Excavating Co., Inc., the plaintiff/appellee, is an Ohio corporation which as a subcontractor provided labor and materials under certain construction contracts for Robinson Township. Al Monzo Construction Company, Inc., a defendant and the appellant in this Court, is a Pennsylvania corporation, which acted as general contractor to Robinson Township. Robinson Township Municipal Authority, the defendant/appellee, is a "citizen" of Pennsylvania. Maryland Casualty Co., a defendant/appellant, is a Maryland corporation which became a surety on Monzo's bond guaranteeing payment to subcontractors, laborers and materialmen.

Fairview completed its work as subcontractor but did not receive payment. Fairview then filed a diversity action in the United States District Court for the Western District of Pennsylvania—joining Monzo, Maryland Casualty and the Township as defendants.

The Township denied any liability to Fairview, claiming that Fairview was not in contractual privity with it. The Township asserted that it had contracted only with Monzo as its contractor, and that any monies still owing to Monzo were being withheld by the Township only until Monzo completed certain restoration work.

Monzo and Maryland Casualty, replying together, denied liability, counterclaimed against Fairview, and cross-claimed against the Township. The Township counterclaimed against Monzo for damages caused by defective work. Trial without a jury was set for March 16, 1976.

On the first day of trial, however, the district court granted the Township's motion that Fairview's complaint against it be dismissed. The district court subsequently explained the basis for its dismissal of the Township as a defendant as follows:

> * * * [U]nder the law of Pennsylvania a municipal corporation is liable to a contractor but not to a subcontractor, materialman or laborer. * * *

With the Township no longer a "defendant" in Fairview's suit, its only remaining connection to the case was provided by Monzo's cross-claim. However, even this connection was short-lived. On the same date, March 16, 1976, the district court dismissed Monzo's cross-claim because of an absence of diversity between the two parties. In its Memorandum Opinion of June 1, 1976, the district court stated: "The various disputes between Monzo and Robinson were not properly before us and are, in fact, matters for state court jurisdiction, there being no diversity of citizenship between these parties."

At this juncture, only Fairview's claim against Monzo was left. After trial, judgment was entered for Fairview. *   *   *

II

The primary complaint voiced by Monzo on this appeal is that the district court erred in dismissing its cross-claim against the Township on jurisdictional grounds. Monzo contends that, having once acquired jurisdiction over the Township as a defendant to its cross-claim, it could not be divested of jurisdiction by the Township's dismissal as a primary defendant to the plaintiff Fairview's claim if that dismissal was predicated (as it was) on nonjurisdictional grounds.

The Township's argument, in our view, is not to the contrary. In its brief, the Township quotes Professor Moore as follows:

> If the original bill or claim in connection with which the cross-claim arises is dismissed *for lack of jurisdiction,* it would seem, on analogy to cases concerning counterclaims, that the dismissal carries with it the cross-claim unless the latter is supported by independent jurisdictional grounds.[8]

However, reliance on that proposition affords little comfort to the Township, for here the original claim was dismissed on nonjurisdictional rather than jurisdictional grounds. As indicated earlier, the district court judge properly held that under Pennsylvania law an absence of contractual privity between the plaintiff and the Township was fatal to Fairview's cause of action. City of Philadelphia v. National Surety Corp., 140 F.2d 805, 807 (3d Cir. 1944).

The basis for the distinction between jurisdictional and nonjurisdictional dismissals is readily apparent. If a federal court dismisses a plaintiff's claim for lack of subject matter jurisdiction, any cross-claims dependent upon ancillary jurisdiction must necessarily fall as well, because it is the plaintiff's claim—to which the cross-claim is ancillary—that provides the derivative source of jurisdiction for the cross-claim. Deviation from this rule would work an impermissible expansion of federal subject matter jurisdiction. Yet by the same token, once a district court judge has properly permitted a cross-claim under F.R. Civ.P. 13(g), as was the case here, the ancillary jurisdiction that results should not be defeated by a decision on the merits adverse to the plaintiff on the plaintiff's primary claim. As Judge Aldrich has stated:

> [i]f [a defendant] had a proper cross-claim against its codefendants this gave the court ancillary jurisdiction even though all the parties to the cross-claim were citizens of the same state. The termination of the original claim would not affect this. This is but one illustration of the elementary principle that jurisdiction which has once attached is not lost by subsequent events.

8. 3 J. Moore, Federal Practice § 13.36, at 927–28 (1975) (emphasis added; footnotes deleted); see also 6 J. Wright & A. Miller, Federal Practice and Procedure § 1433, at 180 (1971) (hereinafter "Wright & Miller").

Atlantic Corp. v. United States, 311 F.2d 907, 910 (1st Cir. 1963) (citations omitted); see Parris v. St. Johnsbury Trucking Co., 395 F.2d 543, 544 (2d Cir. 1968) (reviewing decision on cross-claim between co-citizen defendants although plaintiff's diversity claim had been settled during trial); Barker v. Louisiana & Arkansas Ry. Co., 57 F.R.D. 489, 491 (W.D.La.1972). The contrary rule, which the Township urges here, would operate to make subject matter jurisdiction over every ancillary cross-claim dependent upon that claim's being resolved *prior to* the plaintiff's primary action. (Otherwise a judgment on the merits adverse to the plaintiff would drain the cross-claim of jurisdiction in every instance, a completely indefensible result.) Given that cross-claims necessarily involve co-defendants, Danner v. Anskis, 256 F.2d 123, 124 (3d Cir. 1958), a rule which would restrict the duration of federal court jurisdiction over cross-claims to the pendency of plaintiff's primary claim would be untenable: in many cases, cross-claims need not be heard until plaintiff has obtained a judgment on the merits. To permit the raising of a threat of a dismissal for want of jurisdiction at that point would destroy cross-claims otherwise properly maintainable by virtue of ancillary jurisdiction.

    *   *   *

NOTE ON IMPLEADER AND CROSS–CLAIMS

1. Substantive Right to Indemnity

The decision in Dole v. Dow Chem. Co., 30 N.Y.2d 143, 331 N.Y.S.2d 382, 282 N.E.2d 288 (1972), discussed in *American Motorcycle,* has had substantial impact in various other states and seems on its way to becoming the prevailing rule. Compare Northwest Airlines, Inc. v. Transport Workers Union, 451 U.S. 77, 101 S.Ct. 1571, 67 L.Ed.2d 750 (1981) (Equal Pay Act and Title VII), and Texas Indus., Inc. v. Radcliff Materials, Inc., 451 U.S. 630, 101 S.Ct. 2061, 68 L.Ed.2d 500 (1981) (federal antitrust laws), refusing to adopt the contribution rule as to liability under federal statutes. On the right to indemnity from a settling joint tortfeasor, see Comment, Total Equitable Indemnity Under Comparative Negligence: Anomaly or Necessity?, 74 Calif.L.Rev. 1057 (1986).

A simple accident involving a spouse as a guest passenger can generate intricacies in apportionment. See, e.g., Baget v. Shepard, 128 Cal.App.3d 433, 180 Cal.Rptr. 396 (1982). See also Rizzo and Arnold, Causal Apportionment in the Law of Torts: An Economic Theory, 80 Colum.L.Rev. 1399 (1980).

2. Procedure for Indemnity or Contribution

On the procedural aspects of impleader, see Davis, Comparative Negligence, Comparative Contribution, and Equal Protection in the Trial and Settlement of Multiple Defendant Product Cases, 10 Ind.L.Rev. 831 (1977); Comment, Comparative Negligence, Multiple Parties, and Settlements, 65 Calif.L.Rev. 1264 (1977). For the New York impleader procedure, see Jackson v. Long Island Lighting Co., 59 A.D.2d 523, 397 N.Y.S.2d 104 (1977). If an injured party sued two persons he contended were concurrently liable for his injuries, what would be the proper procedural device by which one defendant could seek contribution from the other under the Federal Rules? Under California procedure?

A related procedure is that of "vouching": A defendant against whom a claim is made but who believes another is liable therefore under commercial law may demand that her supplier step in and defend. The demand is made by private-party communication rather than a third-party complaint in litigation. See Restatement Second of Judgments § 57; Degnan and Barton, Vouching to Quality Warranty: Case Law and Commercial Code, 51 Calif.L.Rev. 471 (1963); Comment, Due Process Constraints on Vouching as a Device to Bind Non-Parties, 14 Colum.J.L. & Soc.Probs. 189 (1978).

With the evolution of comparative fault and contribution among joint tortfeasors has come a requirement of "good faith" for a defendant's settlement to confer immunity against liability for contribution. See, e.g., Tech–Bilt, Inc. v. Woodward–Clyde & Associates, 38 Cal.3d 488, 213 Cal.Rptr. 256, 698 P.2d 159 (1985). See also Note on Settlement Agreements, infra p. 995.

3. Mechanics of a Cross–Complaint

Under California law, the party against whom a complaint or cross-complaint is filed must obtain leave of the court to file a cross-complaint, unless the cross-complaint is filed before or with the party's answer. Cross-complaints by other parties may be filed at any time before trial. Leave of court is required for all parties in order to file a cross-complaint during trial. See C.C.P. 428.50. See also Note on Counterclaiming Devices, supra p. 714.

4. Federal Jurisdiction

There is division in the federal decisions as to whether ancillary jurisdiction supports a cross-claim based on the claimant's own loss, the situation in *Fairview Park*. It is well settled, however, that a claim in impleader bringing in a third party for indemnity or contribution is within ancillary jurisdiction. See 6 Wright & Miller §§ 1432, 1444. See also the discussion in Owen Equipment & Erection Co. v. Kroger, 437 U.S. 365, 98 S.Ct. 2396, 57 L.Ed.2d 274 (1978). The facts in *Owen Equipment* were as follows:

P, a citizen of Iowa, sued D, a citizen of Nebraska, in diversity on a tort claim. D, seeking contribution for the liability to P, impleaded T, a corporation incorporated in Iowa but having its principal place of business in Nebraska, and therefore deemed a citizen of both states. P amended her complaint to name T as an additional defendant in her action. Later, P's claim against D was dismissed on the merits; over T's objection that the court lacked jurisdiction because there was no diversity between P and T, the court entered judgment for P after a trial on the merits. The Eighth Circuit affirmed on the theory that the trial court had ancillary jurisdiction of the claim by P against T. The Supreme Court reversed, saying, 437 U.S. at 374–376:

> "It is a fundamental precept that federal courts are courts of limited jurisdiction. The limits upon federal jurisdiction, whether imposed by the Constitution or by Congress, must be neither disregarded nor evaded. Yet under the reasoning of the Court of Appeals in this case, a plaintiff could defeat the statutory requirement of complete diversity by the simple expedient of suing only those defendants who were of diverse citizenship and waiting for them to implead nondiverse defendants. If, as the Court of Appeals thought, a 'common nucleus of operative fact' were the only requirement for ancillary jurisdiction in a diversity case, there would be no principled reason why the respondent in this case could not have joined her cause of action against [petitioner] in her original complaint as ancillary to

her claim against [the original defendant]. Congress' requirement of complete diversity would thus have been evaded completely.

"It is true, as the Court of Appeals noted, that the exercise of ancillary jurisdiction over nonfederal claims has often been upheld in situations involving impleader, cross-claims or counterclaims.[18] But in determining whether jurisdiction over a nonfederal claim exists, the context in which the nonfederal claim is asserted is crucial. See Aldinger v. Howard, 427 U.S., at 14, 96 S.Ct., at 2420. And the claim here arises in a setting quite different from the kinds of nonfederal claims that have been viewed in other cases as falling within the ancillary jurisdiction of the federal courts.

"First, the nonfederal claim in this case was simply not ancillary to the federal one in the same sense that, for example, the impleader by a defendant of a third-party defendant always is. A third-party complaint depends at least in part upon the resolution of the primary lawsuit. * * * Its relation to the original complaint is thus not mere factual similarity but logical dependence. Cf. Moore v. New York Cotton Exchange, 270 U.S. 593, 610, 46 S.Ct. 367, 371, 70 L.Ed. 750. The respondent's claim against the petitioner, however, was entirely separate from her original claim against [the original defendant], since the petitioner's liability to her depended not at all upon whether or not [the original defendant] was also liable. Far from being an ancillary and dependent claim, it was a new and independent one.

"Second, the nonfederal claim here was asserted by the plaintiff, who voluntarily chose to bring suit upon a state-law claim in a federal court. By contrast, ancillary jurisdiction typically involves claims by a defendant party haled into court against his will, or by another person whose rights might be irretrievably lost unless he could assert them in an ongoing action in a federal court. A plaintiff cannot complain if ancillary jurisdiction does not encompass all of his possible claims in a case such as this one, since it is he who has chosen the federal rather than the state forum and must thus accept its limitations. '[T]he efficiency plaintiff seeks so avidly is available without question in the state courts.' Kenrose Mfg. Co. v. Fred Whitaker Co., 512 F.2d 890, 894 (CA4)."

See also Aldinger v. Howard, supra p. 528, and Note on Pendent Jurisdiction, supra p. 545.

"**18.** The ancillary jurisdiction of the federal courts derives originally from cases such as Freeman v. Howe, 24 How. 450, 16 L.Ed. 749, which held that when federal jurisdiction 'effectively controls the property or fund under dispute, other claimants thereto should be allowed to intervene in order to protect their interests, without regard to jurisdiction.' Aldinger v. Howard, 427 U.S., at 11, 96 S.Ct. at 2419. More recently, it has been said to include cases that involve multiparty practice, such as compulsory counterclaims, e.g., Moore v. New York Cotton Exchange, 270 U.S. 593, 46 S.Ct. 367, 70 L.Ed. 750; impleader, e.g., H. L. Peterson Co. v. Applewhite, 383 F.2d 430, 433 (CA5); Dery v. Wyer, 265 F.2d 804 (CA2); cross-claims, e.g., LASA Per L'Industria Del Marmo Soc. Per Azioni v. Alexander, 414 F.2d 143 (CA6); Scott v. Fancher, 369 F.2d 842, 844 (CA5); Glen Falls Indemnity Co. v. United States ex rel. Westinghouse Electric Supply Co., 229 F.2d 370, 373–374 (CA9); or intervention as of right, e.g., Phelps v. Oaks, 117 U.S. 236, 241, 6 S.Ct. 714, 716, 29 L.Ed. 888; Smith Petroleum Service, Inc. v. Monsanto Chemical Co., 420 F.2d 1103, 1113–1115 (CA5)."

b. INTERVENTION

HISTORICAL NOTE ON INTERVENTION

Intervention under modern statutes and rules derives from two traditions. The first is the tradition of equity, specifically the motion or petition *pro interesse suo.* This was an application by a nonparty, holding a superior claim in interest, to obtain property or the profits of property in the hands of a sequestrator or receiver. Thus, where sequestration had been ordered in Chancery and the property was subject to a prior claim such as that of a mortgagee or landlord entitled to the rents and profits of real property, the mortgagee or landlord was allowed to appear "for his own interest" to claim those profits in priority over the claim being enforced by sequestration. See Fawcett v. Fothergill, Dick. 19, 21 E.R. 173 (Ch.1703) (mortgagee); Dixon v. Smith, 1 Swans. 457, 36 E.R. 464 (Ch.1818) (landlord). See generally 2 Daniel, Pleading and Practice in Chancery 1268–73 (Perkins Am.ed. 1846).

[handwritten margin note: 3rd party can intervene in suit to the extent of her interest]

The doctrine might well have been confined to its limited historical role were it not for the fact that it was absorbed by the federal courts as a solution to the problem of doing tolerably complete justice in a multiparty dispute where complete diversity of citizenship was lacking. See Freeman v. Howe, 65 U.S. (24 How.) 450, 16 L.Ed. 749 (1861), relying on a *pro interesse suo* type of case, Pennock v. Coe, 64 U.S. (23 How.) 117, 16 L.Ed. 436 (1860), to establish the jurisdiction of a federal court to determine adverse claims to property seized by a federal marshal pursuant to a writ of attachment. From that point by degrees the concept was expanded until it today supports a welter of instances embraced in federal ancillary jurisdiction. See Hart & Wechsler 1044–1052. As said in Note, Intervention in Federal Equity Cases, 31 Colum.L.Rev. 1312 (1931), "The practice has been justified by * * * injustice." Is the "injustice" referred to that of making a determination which would be res judicata on an absentee, or is it that the decree might work a change in the out-of-court situation which would make it harder as a practical matter for the claimant to pursue his remedies?

The second root of the modern rules lies in the Field Code. The New York provision, adopted in N.Y.Laws 1851, c. 479, § 122, was that "when, in an action for the recovery of real or personal property, a person not a party to the action, but having an interest in the subject thereof, makes application to the court to be made a party, it may order him to be brought in by the proper amendment." This provision was narrowly construed and little used and was replaced by a provision modeled on F.R.C.P. 24. See N.Y.Temp.Comm'n, First Prelim.Rep. 46–47 (1957).

The broader intervention provision was framed in terms of the intervenor's "interest" in the controversy. It was drawn from the civil law rule in Louisiana, see Horn v. Volcano Water Co., 13 Cal. 62 (1859); Millar, Civil Procedure of the Trial Court in Historical Perspective 146–48 (1952), and now appears as C.C.P. 387 and provisions patterned after it. Although the term "interests" could be given wide scope, in general it was interpreted to mean "direct" interest in property. See, e.g., Allen v. California Water & Tele. Co., 31 Cal.2d 104, 187 P.2d 393 (1947). For modern California intervention procedure, see 4 Witkin 294–321; C.E.B., 2 Calif.Civ.Pro. Before Trial, c. 25 (1978).

Federal Rule 24 was drawn with a view to enlarging the opportunity for intervention. See Moore and Levi, Federal Intervention, 45 Yale L.J. 565 (1936). A distinction was drawn between permissive intervention, F.R.C.P. 24(b), and intervention of right, F.R.C.P. 24(a). Permissive intervention was permitted under the minimal constraint that the intervenor need only show that his claim in intervention involved "a question of law or fact in common" with the main action. However, permissive intervention depends on the discretion of the trial court and, in federal court, requires an independent basis of jurisdiction. Permissive intervention in federal court can also harm the plaintiff's ability to join another party later if the intervenor is opposed to and is non-diverse in citizenship from the new party sought to be joined. See Note, When a Permissive Intervenor Impairs the Plaintiff's Control, 35 Hastings L.J. 707 (1984). Intervention of right, on the other hand, does not depend on the trial court's permission and, being supported by ancillary jurisdiction, in federal court does not require an independent jurisdictional basis. See Note, Ancillary Jurisdiction and Intervention Under Federal Rule 24, 58 Ind.L.J. 111 (1982). The distinction between permissive intervention and intervention as of right is analytically tenuous and functionally dubious. See Shreve, Questioning Intervention of Right: Toward a New Methodology of Decisionmaking, 74 Nw.U.L.Rev. 894 (1980). Until amended in 1966, F.R.C.P. 24(a) was so construed that, except where statute independently gave a right of intervention, the proposed intervenor had to show that she would be "bound" by the judgment. This resulted in a "Catch-22" situation, because ordinarily she would be bound only if she became a party by being allowed to intervene. See Wright § 75, and the following case.

ATLANTIS DEVELOPMENT CORP. v. UNITED STATES

United States Court of Appeals for the Fifth Circuit, 1967.
379 F.2d 818.*

JOHN R. BROWN, CIRCUIT JUDGE.

* * * The District Court declined to permit mandatory intervention as a matter of right or to allow intervention as permissive. As is so often true, a ruling made to avoid delay, complications, or expense turns out to have generated more of its own. With the main case being stayed by the District Court pending this appeal, it is pretty safe to assume that the case would long have been decided on its merits (or lack of them) had intervention of either kind been allowed. And this seems especially unfortunate since it is difficult to believe that the presence of the attempted intervenor would have added much to the litigation. All of this becomes the more ironic, if not unfortunate, since the intervenor [1] and the Government sparring over why intervention ought or ought not to have been allowed, each try to persuade us the one was bound to win, the other lose on the merits which each proceeds to argue as though the parties were before or in the court. Adding to the problem, or perhaps more accurately, aiding in the solution of it, are the mid-1966 amendments to the Federal Rules of Civil Procedure including specifically those relating to intervention. We reverse.

---

* Some of the court's footnotes are omitted.

1. Atlantis Development Corporation, Ltd., a Bahamian corporation, will be referred to interchangeably as either Atlantis or Intervenor.

What the jousting [2] is all about is the ownership in, or right to control the use, development of and building on a number of coral reefs or islands comprising Pacific Reef, Ajax Reef, Long Reef, an unnamed reef and Triumph Reef which the intervenor has called the "Atlantis Group" because of the name given them by Anderson, its predecessor in interest and the supposed discoverer. Discovery in the usual sense of finding a land area, continent or island heretofore unknown could hardly fit this case. For these reefs are, and have been for years, shown on Coast and Geodetic Charts [3] and, more important, they are scarcely 4½ miles off Elliott Key and 10 miles off the Coast off the Florida Mainland. Although the depth of water washing over them at mean low water is likely one of the factual controversies having some possible significance, it seems undisputed that frequently and periodically the bodies of these reefs become very apparent especially in rough seas when the rock or the top surface of the rock becomes plainly visible in the troughs of the seas.

* * * Subsequently, Atlantis spent approximately $50,000 for surveys and the construction of four prefabricated buildings, three of which were destroyed by a hurricane in September 1963. Thereafter upon learning that the United States Corps of Engineers was asserting that permission was needed to erect certain structures on two of the reefs, Triumph and Long Reef, Atlantis commenced its long, but unrewarding, efforts either to convince the Corps of Engineers, the United States Attorney General, or both, that the island reefs were beyond the jurisdiction of United States control or to initiate litigation which would allow a judicial, peaceful resolution. The Engineers ultimately reaffirmed the earlier decision to require permits. In December 1964 on learning that the defendants in the main case had formally sought a permit from the Engineers, Atlantis notified the Government of its claim to ownership of the islands and the threatened unauthorized actions by the defendants. This precipitated further communications with the Department of Justice with Atlantis importuning, apparently successfully, the Government to initiate the present action.

It was against this background that the litigation commenced. The suit is brought by the United States against the main defendants.[5] The complaint was in two counts seeking injunctive relief. In the first the Government asserted that Triumph and Long Reefs are part of the bed

---

2. The "facts" are as yet unknown since no trial of either the main or the intervention case has been had. They are revealed in this record solely in the complaint, the answer, the proposed intervention, and supporting affidavit which in turn incorporated a detailed 32-page memorandum previously filed by the intervenor's counsel with the Office of Chief of Engineers, Department of Defense. This opinion must begin and end therefore with the caveat that nothing said or unsaid, expressed or implied, is even a remote, possible whisper of a suggestion as to what the merits (or demerits) might ultimately be. Cf. J. M.

Huber Corp. v. Denman, 5 Cir., 1966, 367 F.2d 104, 120–121. Discussion of such asserted facts and the legal theories is merely to illumine the factors bearing upon intervention, as of right or permissive.

3. They first appeared on U. S. Coast & Geodetic Survey Chart No. 166, issued in 1878. More recently, see Coast & Geodetic Survey Chart No. 1249, as corrected through June 1, 1963.

5. Acme General Contractors, Inc, and J. H. Coppedge Company, each Florida corporations, and Louis M. Ray, a resident of Dade County, Florida.

of the Atlantic Ocean included in the Outer Continental Shelf subject to the jurisdiction, control and power of disposition of the United States. The action of the defendants (note 5, supra) in the erection of caissons on the reefs, the dredging of material from the sea bed, and the depositing of the dredged material within the caissons without authorization was charged as constituting a trespass on government property. In the second count the Government alleged that the defendants were engaged in the erection of an artificial island or fixed structure on the Outer Continental Shelf in the vicinity of the reefs without a permit from the Secretary of the Army in violation of the Outer Continental Shelf Lands Act, 43 U.S.C.A. § 1333(f) and 33 U.S.C.A. § 403. Denying that the complaint stated a claim, F.R.Civ.P. 12(b), the defendants besides interposing general denial asserted that the Secretary of the Army lacks jurisdiction to require a permit for construction on the Outer Continental Shelf and that the District Court lacks jurisdiction since the reefs and the defendants' actions thereon are outside the territorial limits of the United States. As thus framed, the issues in the main case are whether (1) the District Court has jurisdiction of subject matter, (2) the defendants are engaged in acts which constitute a trespass against government property, and (3) the defendants' construction activities without a permit violate 43 U.S.C.A. § 1333(f) and 33 U.S.C.A. § 403.[6]

Atlantis seeking intervention by proposed answer and cross-claim against the defendants admitted the jurisdiction of the District Court. It asserted that the United States has no territorial jurisdiction, dominion or ownership in or over the reefs and cannot therefore maintain the action for an injunction, and that conversely Atlantis has title to the property by discovery and occupation. In the cross-claim, Atlantis charged the defendants as trespassers against it. Appropriate relief was sought by the prayer.[7]

The District Court without opinion declared in the order that intervenor "does not have such an interest in this cause as will justify its intervention, either as a matter of right or permissively." Leave was granted to appear amicus curiae.

We think without a doubt that under former F.R.Civ.P. 24(a), intervention as a matter of right was not compelled under (a)(2).[8] The

---

6. Issues (2) and (3) comprehend items (a), (b) and (c) in the prayer of intervenor's proposed answer. See note 7, infra.

7. It sought judgment adjudicating and determining (a) the rights of the parties to this action and those of the intervenor; (b) that the Government has no territorial jurisdiction over or ownership in Triumph Reef; (c) that the Secretary of Defense has no power to require application and permit for construction on the reefs; (d) that Atlantis has the paramount right, title and interest in the reefs; and that (e) the defendants have none.

8. F.R.Civ.P. 24. Intervention

"(a) Intervention of Right. Upon timely application anyone shall be permitted to intervene in an action: (1) when a statute of the United States confers an unconditional right to intervene; or (2) when the representation of the applicant's interest by existing parties is or may be inadequate and the applicant is or may be bound by a judgment in the action; or (3) when the applicant is so situated as to be adversely affected by a distribution or other disposition of property which is in the custody or subject to

situation did not present one in which the intervenor "is or may be bound" by a decree rendered in his absence in the sense articulated most recently in *Sam Fox*[9] in terms of res judicata. Although not quite so clear, we also think it did not measure up to the notions loosely reflected in a case-by-case development under which, although res judicata was technically lacking, the decree is considered "binding" since in a very practical sense it would have an immediate operative effect upon the intervenor.[10] In none of these cases was it suggested that if the only effect of the decree in intervenor's absence would be to raise the hurdle of stare decisis, this would amount to the absentee being bound as a practical matter.[11]

This brings us squarely to the effect of the 1966 Amendments and the new F.R.Civ.P. 24(a).[12] * * *

* * *

In assaying the new Rule, several things stand out. The first, as the Government acknowledges, is that this amounts to a legislative repeal of the rigid *Sam Fox* (note 9, supra)[15] res judicata rule. But

the control or disposition of the court or an officer thereof.

"(b) Permissive Intervention. Upon timely application anyone may be permitted to intervene in an action: (1) when a statute of the United States confers a conditional right to intervene; or (2) when an applicant's claim or defense and the main action have a question of law or fact in common. . . . In exercising its discretion the court shall consider whether the intervention will unduly delay or prejudice the adjudication of the rights of the original parties."

9. Sam Fox Publishing Co. v. United States, 1961, 366 U.S. 683, 81 S.Ct. 1309, 6 L.Ed.2d 604.

10. Ford Motor Co. v. Bisanz Bros., Inc., 8 Cir., 1957, 249 F.2d 22; Kozak v. Wells, 8 Cir., 1960, 278 F.2d 104, 84 A.L.R.2d 1400; Atlantic Ref. Co. v. Standard Oil Co., 1962, 113 U.S.App.D.C. 20, 304 F.2d 387, 393; International Mortgage & Inv. Corp. v. Von Clemm, 2 Cir., 1962, 301 F.2d 857; Textile Workers Union v. Allendale Co., 1955, 96 U.S.App.D.C. 401, 226 F.2d 765, 767, cert. denied, 1956, 351 U.S. 909, 76 S.Ct. 699, 100 L.Ed. 1444, expressly approved in International Union, UAW v. Scofield, 1965, 382 U.S. 205, 86 S.Ct. 373, 15 L.Ed.2d 272 at 280, n. 10; Wolpe v. Poretsky, 1944, 79 U.S.App.D.C. 141, 144 F.2d 505, cert. denied 323 U.S. 777, 65 S.Ct. 188, 89 L.Ed. 621.

11. See, e.g., Stadin v. Union Electric Co., 8 Cir., 1962, 309 F.2d 912, 918, cert. denied, 1963, 373 U.S. 915, 83 S.Ct. 1298, 10 L.Ed.2d 415, distinguishing its prior *Kozak* and *Ford Motor* cases (note 10, supra):

"Liberality, however, does not equate with rights of indiscriminate intervention. The applicant must still meet the requirement that he 'is or may be bound' by the judgments. . . . The presence or possibility of difficulty, even great difficulty, is not enough."

12.

"(a) *Intervention of Right.* Upon timely application anyone shall be permitted to intervene in any action: (1) when a statute of the United States confers an unconditional right to intervene; or (2) when the applicant claims an *interest relating to the property or transaction which is the subject of the action* and he is so situated that the *disposition of the action may as a practical matter impair or impede his ability to protect that interest,* unless the applicant's interest is adequately represented by existing parties." [Emphasis added.]

Rule 24(a), F.R.Civ.P., as amended July 1, 1966 (U.S.Code Cong. & Adm.News, 89th Cong., 2d sess., No. 3, Apr. 5, 1966, 799). See also 39 F.R.D. 69, 109–111; Cohn, The New Federal Rules of Civil Procedure, Essays reprinted from Geo.L.J. 7, 32–35 (1966).

15. 39 F.R.D. 69, 110: Advisory Committee Notes.

"Original Rule 24(a)(2), however, made it a condition of intervention that 'the applicant is or may be bound by a judgment in the action,' and this created difficulties with intervention in class actions. . . . See Sam Fox Publishing Co. v. United States, 366 U.S. 683 [81

more important, the revision was a coordinated one to tie more closely together the related situations of joinder, F.R.Civ.P. 19,[16] and class actions, F.R.Civ.P. 23.[17]

As the Advisory Committee's notes reflect, there are competing interests at work in this area. On the one hand, there is the private suitor's interests in having his own lawsuit subject to no one else's direction or meddling. On the other hand, however, is the great public interest, especially in these explosive days of ever-increasing dockets, of

S.Ct. 1309, 6 L.Ed.2d 604] (1961). . . . This reasoning might be linguistically justified by original Rule 24(a)(2); but it could lead to poor results. Compare the discussion in International M. & I. Corp. v. Von Clemm, 301 F.2d 857 (2d Cir. 1962); Atlantic Refining Co. v. Standard Oil Co., 113 U.S.App.D.C. 20, 304 F.2d 387 (D.C.Cir.1962). [See note 10, supra]. . . .

"The amendment provides that an applicant is entitled to intervene in an action when his position is comparable to that of a person under Rule 19(a)(2)(i), as amended, unless his interest is already adequately represented in the action by existing parties. The Rule 19(a)(2)(i) criterion imports practical considerations, and the deletion of the 'bound' language similarly frees the rule from undue preoccupation with strict consideration of *res judicata.*"

See also Stewart, J., dissenting, *El Paso II,* supra, note 14: "The purpose of the revision was to remedy certain logical shortcomings in the construction of the former 24(a)(2), see Sam Fox Publishing Co. v. United States, ..." 386 U.S. at 153, 87 S.Ct. at 946, 17 L.Ed.2d at 829.

16. F.R.Civ.P. 19 was completely rewritten:

"Joinder of Persons Needed for Just Adjudication

"(a) Persons to be Joined if Feasible. A person who is subject to service of process and whose joinder will not deprive the court of jurisdiction over the subject matter of the action shall be joined as a party in the action if (1) in his absence complete relief cannot be accorded among those already parties, or (2) *he claims an interest relating to the subject of the action* and is so situated that the *disposition of the action in his absence may (i) as a practical matter impair or impede his ability to protect that interest* or (ii) leave any of the persons already parties subject to a substantial risk of incurring double, multiple, or otherwise

inconsistent obligations by reason of his claimed interest. If he has not been so joined, the court shall order that he be made a party. If he should join as a plaintiff but refuses to do so, he may be made a defendant, or, in a proper case, an involuntary plaintiff. If the joined party objects to venue and his joinder would render the venue of the action improper, he shall be dismissed from the action.

"(b) Determination by Court Whenever Joinder not Feasible. * * *

"(c) Pleading Reasons for Nonjoinder. A pleading asserting a claim for relief shall state the names, if known to the pleader, of any persons as described in subdivision (a)(1)–(2) hereof who are not joined, and the reasons why they are not joined.

"(d) Exception of Class Actions. This rule is subject to the provisions of Rule 23." [Emphasis added.]

39 F.R.D. 69, 88–89. See discussion by Cohn, supra, note 12, at pp. 7–14.

17. Likewise Rule 23 was completely rewritten. See Alvarez v. Pan American Life Ins. Co., 5 Cir., 1967, 375 F.2d 992 at 995 & n. 3 [No. 22761, Mar. 27, 1967]. After specifying that for actions meeting the prerequisites of a class action set forth in 23(a), subpar. (b) provides that a class action may be maintained if in addition:

"(1) [T]he prosecution of separate actions by or against individual members of the class would create a risk of

". . .

"(B) adjudications with respect to individual members of the class which would *as a practical matter* be dispositive of the interests of the other members not parties to the adjudications or *substantially impair or impede their ability to protect their interests;* . . . ." [Emphasis added.]

39 F.R.D. 69, 96. See Cohn, supra note 12, at pp. 16–19.

having a disposition at a single time of as much of the controversy to as many of the parties as is fairly possible consistent with due process.[18]

In these three Rules the Advisory Committee, unsatisfied with the former Rules which too frequently defined application in terms of rigid legal concepts such as joint, common ownership, res judicata, or the like, as well as court efforts in applying them, deliberately set out on a more pragmatic course.[19] For the purposes of our problem, this course is reflected in the almost, if not quite, uniform language concerning a party who claims an interest relating to the subject of the action and is so situated that the disposition of the action may as a practical matter impair or impede his ability to protect that interest (see the italicized portions of Rules 19(a)(2)(i), 24 and 23(b)(1)(B), notes 16, 12 and 17, supra).

Although this is question-begging and is therefore not a real test, this approach shows that the question of whether an intervention as a matter of right exists often turns on the unstated question of whether joinder of the intervenor was called for under new Rule 19. Were this the controlling inquiry, we find ample basis here to answer it in the affirmative. Atlantis—having formally informed the Government in detail of its claim of ownership to the very reefs in suit, that the defendants were trespassing against it, and having successfully urged the Government to institute suit against the defendants—seems clearly to occupy the position of a party who ought to have been joined as a defendant under new Rule 19(a)(2)(i) [see the italicized portion of note 16, supra].

* * *

18. See, e.g., notes to F.R.Civ.P. 19. "New *subdivision (a)* defines the persons whose joinder in the action is desirable. . . . The interests that are being furthered here are not only those of the parties, but also that of the public in avoiding repeated lawsuits on the same essential subject matter. . . ." 39 F.R.D. 69, 91.

This Court has recently voiced the same objectives:

"The Rules allow joinder in such a case as the present; indeed in order to prevent costly, slow, multiplicitous litigation (with the danger of inconsistent results), they demand it. The Supreme Court has recently held that 'Under the Rules, the impulse is toward entertaining the broadest possible scope of action consistent with fairness to the parties; joinder of claims, parties and remedies is strongly encouraged.' United Mine Workers of America v. Gibbs, 1966, 383 U.S. 715, 724, 86 S.Ct. 1130, 1138, 16 L.Ed.2d 218, 227."

Har-Pen Truck Lines, Inc. v. Mills, 5 Cir., 1967, 378 F.2d 705, 709.

19. See, e.g., Advisory Committee Notes to Rule 19: "Clause (2)(i) recognizes the importance of protecting the person whose joinder is in question against the practical prejudice to him which may arise through a disposition of the action in his absence." 39 F.R.D. 69, 91.

See similar comments as to F.R.Civ.P. 24, note 15, supra, especially the following which warrants repeating: "The amendment provides that an applicant is entitled to intervene in an action when his position is comparable to that of a person under Rule 19(a)(2)(i), as amended, unless his interest is already adequately represented in the action by existing parties."

As to Rule 23(b)(1)(B) "[t]his clause takes in situations where the judgment in a non-class action by or against an individual member of the class, while not technically concluding the other members, might do so as a practical matter. The vice of an individual action would lie in the fact that the other members of the class, thus practically concluded, would have had no representation in the lawsuit." 39 F.R.D. 69, 100–101.

When approached in this light, we think that both from the terms of new Rule 24(a) and its adoption of 19(a)(2)(i) intervention of right is called for here.   Of course F.R.Civ.P. 24(a)(2) requires both the existence of an interest which may be impaired as a practical matter and an absence of adequate representation of the intervenor's interest by existing parties.   There can be no difficulty here about the lack of representation.   On the basis of the pleadings, see Kozak v. Wells, 8 Cir., 1960, 278 F.2d 104, 109, 84 A.L.R.2d 1400; cf. Stadin v. Union Electric Co., 8 Cir., 1962, 309 F.2d 912, 917, cert. denied, 1963, 373 U.S. 915, 83 S.Ct. 1298, 10 L.Ed.2d 415, Atlantis is without a friend in this litigation.   The Government turns on the defendants and takes the same view both administratively and in its brief here toward Atlantis. The defendants, on the other hand, are claiming ownership in and the right to develop the very islands claimed by Atlantis.

Nor can there be any doubt that Atlantis "claims an interest relating to the property or transaction which is the subject of the action."[20]   The object of the suit is to assert the sovereign's exclusive dominion and control over two out of a group of islands publicly claimed by Atlantis.   This identity with the very property at stake in the main case and with the particular transaction therein involved (the right to build structures with or without permission of the Corps of Engineers) is of exceptional importance.   For 24(a)(2) is in the conjunctive requiring both an interest relating to the property or transaction and the practical harm if the party is absent.   This sharply reduces the area in which stare decisis may, as we later discuss, supply the element of practical harm.

This brings us then to the question whether these papers reflect that in the absence of Atlantis, a disposition of the main suit may as a practical matter impair or impede its ability to protect that interest— its claim to ownership and the right to control, use and develop without hindrance from the Government, the Department of Defense or other agencies.   Certain things are clear.   Foremost, of course, is the plain proposition that the judgment itself as between Government and defendants cannot have any direct, immediate effect upon the rights of Atlantis, not a party to it.

But in a very real and practical sense is not the trial of this lawsuit the trial of Atlantis' suit as well?   Quite apart from the contest of Atlantis' claim of sovereignty vis-a-vis the Government resulting from its "discovery" and occupation of the reefs, there are at least two basic substantial legal questions directly at issue, but not yet resolved in any Court at any time between the Government and the defendants which are inescapably present in the claim of Atlantis against the Government.   One is whether these coral reefs built up by accretion of marine biology are "submerged lands" under the Outer Continental Shelf Lands Act, 43 U.S.C.A. § 1331 et seq.   The second basic question is whether, assuming both from the standpoint of geographical location

---

20.   24(a)(2), note 12, supra.

and their nature they constitute "lands," does the sovereignty of the United States extend to them with respect to any purposes not included in or done for the protection of the "exploring for, developing, removing, and transporting . . ." natural resources therefrom, 43 U.S.C.A. § 1333(a)(1). Another, closely related, is whether the authority of the Secretary of the Army to prevent obstruction of navigation extended by § 1333(f) to "artificial islands and fixed structures," includes structures other than those "erected thereon for the purpose of exploring for, developing, removing, and transporting" mineral resources therefrom (§ 1333(a)(1) * * *).

The Government would avoid all of these problems by urging us to rule as a matter of law on the face of the moving papers that the intervenors could not possibly win on the trial of the intervention and consequently intervention should be denied. In support it asserts that the claim that the reefs are beyond the jurisdiction of the United States is self-defeating, and under the plain meaning of the Outer Continental Shelf Lands Act and the facts revealed from the Coast and Geodetic Chart [25] of which we must take judicial knowledge as proof of all facts shown.[26]

The first is at least contingently answered by § 1333(b) which invests jurisdiction in the United States District Court of the nearest adjacent state. As to the others, it is, of course, conceivable that there will be some instances in which the total lack of merit is so evident from the face of the moving papers that denial of the right of intervention rests upon a complete lack of a substantial claim. But it hardly comports with good administration, if not due process, to determine the merits of a claim asserted in a pleading seeking an adjudication through an adversary hearing by denying access to the court at all. This seems especially important when dealing with interests in the Outer Continental Shelf in view of the legislative history which reflected domestically the purpose of asserting a limited "horizontal jurisdiction" [27] extending only to the seabed and subsoil, the limited

---

25. The Geodetic Chart shows the 100-fathom (600-foot) line—the seaward limit to the Outer Continental Shelf—is about three miles seaward of these reefs.

26. The Government urges Pfeifer Oil Transp. Co. v. The Ira S. Bushey, 2 Cir., 1942, 129 F.2d 606, 607; Krench v. United States, 6 Cir., 1930, 42 F.2d 354, 355. They cite also United States v. Romaine, 9 Cir., 1919, 255 F. 253, where the Court states that "We think the [United States Coast and Geodetic Survey Charts] should be given full credence, and should be taken as absolutely establishing the truth of all that they purport to show." 255 F. at 254.

27. See § 1332(b). "This subchapter shall be construed in such manner that the character as high seas of the waters above the outer Continental Shelf and the right to navigation and fishing therein shall not

be affected." Guess v. Read, 5 Cir., 1961, 290 F.2d 622, cert. denied, 1962, 368 U.S. 957, 82 S.Ct. 394, 7 L.Ed.2d 388, cf. Pure Oil Co. v. Snipes, 5 Cir., 1961, 293 F.2d 60, 63. See S.Rep.No. 411, 83rd Cong., 1st Sess.: "In §§ 3(a) and 4(a)(1), the jurisdiction and plenary control of the United States is extended to the seabed and subsoil of entire outer Continental Shelf adjacent to the shores of the United States instead of merely to the natural resources of the subsoil and seabed and to structures for their development. . . . At the same time, an amendment to the wording of Section 3(b) makes abundantly clear the unequivocal legislative intent of the committee that the jurisdiction asserted is a 'horizontal jurisdiction', extending only to the seabed and subsoil, and does not in any wise affect the character as high seas of

nature of which was formally recognized by the International Convention on the Continental Shelf.[28]   See United States v. States of Louisiana, Texas, Mississippi, Alabama and Florida, 1960, 363 U.S. 1, 30–31, 80 S.Ct. 961, 979, 4 L.Ed.2d 1025, 1046.

If in its claim against the defendants in the main suit these questions are answered favorably to the Government's position, the claim of Atlantis for all practical purposes is worthless. That statement assumes, of course, that such holding is either approved or made by this Court after an appeal to it and thereafter it is either affirmed, or not taken for review, on certiorari. It also assumes that in the subsequent separate trial of the claim of Atlantis against the Government [29] the prior decision would be followed as a matter of stare decisis. Do these assumptions have a realistic basis? Anyone familiar with the history of the Fifth Circuit could have but a single answer to that query. This Court, unlike some of our sister Circuit Courts who occasionally follow a different course, has long tried earnestly to follow the practice in which a decision announced by one panel of the Court is followed by all others until such time as it is reversed, either outright or by intervening decisions of the Supreme Court, or by the Court itself en banc.[30] That means that if the defendants in the main action do not prevail upon these basic contentions which are part and parcel of the claim of Atlantis, the only way by which Atlantis can win is to secure a rehearing en banc with a successful overruling of the prior decision or, failing in either one or both of those efforts, a reversal of the earlier decision by the Supreme Court on certiorari. With the necessarily limited number of en banc hearings in this Circuit [31] and with the small percentage of cases meriting certiorari,[32] it is an understatement to characterize these prospects as formidable.

the waters above that seabed and subsoil nor their use with respect to navigation and fishing."

28. Treaties and Other International Acts Series No. 5578 (1964), adopted at Geneva April 29, 1958, signed on behalf of the United States September 15, 1958, approved by the Senate on May 26, 1960 (106 Cong.Rec. 11182–83) ratified by the President on March 24, 1961 (44 State Dep't Bull. 609) and entered into force June 10, 1964 (50 State Dep't Bull. 946).

The Convention provides:

"Article 2.

"1. The coastal State exercises the continental shelf sovereign rights for the purpose of exploring it and exploiting its natural resources."

Par. 4 defines "natural resources,"
* * *.

29. Whatever difficulty there might be about a suit by Atlantis to challenge the Government's title to the reefs, there is none as to the controversy over whether these are outer Continental Shelf lands and whether the Corps of Engineers' permit is required. Both the Secretary of the Army and the Secretary of the Defense are amenable to suit everywhere including the Southern District of Florida, 28 U.S.C.A. §§ 1361, 1391(e), and see notes to Rule 19, 39 F.R.D. 69, 96.

30. As to the related problem of the law of the case, see Lincoln Nat. Life Ins. Co. v. Roosth, 5 Cir., 1962, 306 F.2d 110 (en banc), cert. denied, 372 U.S. 912, 83 S.Ct. 726, 9 L.Ed.2d 720.

31. See Alexander, En Banc Hearings in the Federal Courts of Appeals: Accommodating Institutional Responsibilities, 40 N.Y.U.L.Rev. 563 & 726 (1965).

32. Of the 1,164 petitions for certiorari (not in forma pauperis) on the appellate docket of the Supreme Court for the 1965–1966 term, only 124 or approximately 12% were granted with 140 petitions left on the docket at the end of the term. For the past decade, the percentage of petitions granted has varied between 12 and 17%

That is but a way of saying in a very graphic way that the failure to allow Atlantis an opportunity to advance its own theories both of law and fact in the trial (and appeal) of the pending case will if the disposition is favorable to the Government "as a practical matter impair or impede [its] ability to protect [its] interest." That is, to be sure, a determination by us that in the new language of 24(a)(2) stare decisis may now—unlike the former days under 24(a)(2)—supply that practical disadvantage which warrants intervention of right. It bears repeating,[33] however, that this holding does not presage one requiring intervention of right in every conceivable circumstance where under the operation of the Circuit's stare decisis practice, the formidable nature of an en banc rehearing or the successful grant of a writ of certiorari, an earlier decision might afford a substantial obstacle. We are dealing here with a conjunction of a claim to and interest in the very property and the very transaction which is the subject of the main action. When those coincide, the Court before whom the potential parties in the second suit must come must itself take the intellectually straight forward, realistic view that the first decision will in all likelihood be the second and the third and the last one. Even the possibility that the decision might be overturned by en banc ruling or reversal on certiorari does not overcome its practical effect, not just as an obstacle, but as the forerunner of the actual outcome. In the face of that, it is "as a practical matter" a certainty that an absent party seeking a right to enter the fray to advance his interest against all or some of the parties as to matters upon which he is for all practical purposes shortly to be foreclosed knows the disposition in his absence will "impair or impede his ability to protect that interest, . . ." F.R.Civ.P. 24(a)(2).[34]

Reversed.

but the trend is clearly a declining percentage since, while the number of petitions filed is increasing, those granted is relatively constant and presumably limited by the work-capacity of the Court. 1966 Annual Report of the Director of the Administrative Office of the United States Courts Table A–1 at 147. See also Statistics for 1965–1966 term in 35 L.W. 3028.

33. See note 20, supra, and related text.

34. Ending, as we began, with the caveat, see note 2, supra, that in outlining what may be at stake we have decided nothing except the right to intervene, we must take note also of the Government's contention that intervention should be denied because this is an unconsented suit against the United States. It relies particularly on United States v. Dry Dock Savings Ins., 2 Cir., 1945, 149 F.2d 917; United States v. Great Northern Ry., D.C.Mont., 1940, 32 F.Supp. 651, affirmed sub nom. MacDonald v. United States, 9 Cir., 1941, 119 F.2d 821, modified on other matters and affirmed, Great Northern Ry. v. United States, 1942, 315 U.S. 262, 62 S.Ct. 529, 86 L.Ed. 836; see also United States v. Sherwood, 1941, 312 U.S. 584, 589–590, 61 S.Ct. 767, 85 L.Ed. 1058; Humble Oil & Ref. Co. v. Sun Oil Co., 5 Cir., 1951, 190 F.2d 191, 197, rehearing denied, 1951, 191 F.2d 705, cert. denied, 1952, 342 U.S. 920, 72 S.Ct. 367, 96 L.Ed. 687. This is a matter for determination on the merits on remand. Intervention to be available does not have to be against every party. There is ample diversity jurisdiction as between Atlantis and the main defendants (see notes 1 and 5, supra), and lack of consent, sovereignty immunity, or related problems may wash out by the addition of new parties who are now amenable. See note 29, supra.

FURTHER NOTE ON INTERVENTION

1. Atlantis Development

Observe that Atlantis had been stymied in its effort to litigate the question of domain over the island with the Government. The Government refused to sue Atlantis; Atlantis apparently was unwilling to provoke a suit by making a major development investment in the face of uncertainty as to the domain; and Atlantis could not sue the Government without the latter's consent, under the doctrine of sovereign immunity. Should that doctrine have been considered in connection with the intervention? (Today, Atlantis presumably could sue the Government by virtue of 28 U.S.C.A. § 2409a, enacted in 1972, which limits the Government's immunity in suits over title to land.)

Observe that the "practical" impairment of the proposed intervenor's interest in *Atlantis* would be the precedent effect of the decision. Taken literally, this would mean that anyone concerned about the precedent to be established in a case could intervene in it. The court tries to narrow its holding by suggesting that it applies only in extraordinary circumstances. Compare Alaska Excursion Cruises, Inc. v. United States, 603 F.Supp. 541 (D.D.C. 1984). See also Comment, Intervention, Joinder, and Issue Preclusion, 6 Wm. Mitchell L.Rev. 361 (1980).

2. Intervention in Non-Damages Cases

In the Historical Note on Intervention, supra p. 751, it was noted that the origin of intervention was in cases involving property. Was the key fact about these cases that they involved property, or that they involved relief that would govern future action—of which disposition of property is simply one illustration? If the latter is a better analysis, then one would expect that the right of intervention would be more readily recognized as the courts have gotten more widely into the business of giving relief that governs future action. Consider the *Bustop* case which follows.

3. Timeliness

The opportunity to intervene may be lost if the proposed intervenor unduly delays in moving. On the problem of timeliness, see United Airlines, Inc. v. McDonald, 432 U.S. 385, 97 S.Ct. 2464, 53 L.Ed.2d 423 (1977); cf. Walker v. Jim Dandy Co., 747 F.2d 1360 (11th Cir. 1984); Note, The Timeliness Threat to Intervention of Right, 89 Yale L.J. 586 (1980); Note, Timeliness of a Motion to Intervene, 1984 B.Y.U.L.Rev. 219 (1984). Consider whether the intervenors should have been barred by delay in *Bustop*. Does the timeliness depend on the nature of the claim and the relief that the intervenor seeks? Should intervention be required at the outset of the litigation? C.C.P. 387, at issue in *Bustop*, used to provide that intervention was permitted "at any time before trial," but now provides, as does F.R.C.P. 24, for intervention "upon timely application." Restatement Second of Judgments § 62 states that under certain conditions "A person not a party to an action who has a claim arising out of the transaction that was the subject of the action, and who knew about the action prior to the rendition of judgment therein, may not thereafter maintain an action on his claim * * *." See, e.g., Aerojet General Corp. v. Askew, 511 F.2d 710 (5th Cir. 1975); Note, Preclusion of Absent Disputants to Compel Intervention, 79 Colum.L.Rev. 1551 (1979).

4. Judicial Efficiency

The court may refuse intervention even if there is no objection by the original parties. Wade v. Goldschmidt, 673 F.2d 182 (7th Cir. 1982). In ruling on a motion to intervene should a court consider the waste of judicial time if intervention is denied and the intervenor is forced to sue again? See Smith v. Pangilinan, 651 F.2d 1320 (9th Cir. 1981); cf. Garrity v. Gallen, 697 F.2d 452 (1st Cir. 1983).

5. Interlocutory Appeals

An important consequential difference between intervention of right and permissive intervention is that denial of the former, but not the latter, is an appealable order. That in turn makes the classification problem more crucial. See United States v. Jefferson County, 720 F.2d 1511 (11th Cir.1983).

BUSTOP v. SUPERIOR COURT

Court of Appeal of California, 1977.
69 Cal.App.3d 66, 137 Cal.Rptr. 793.

THE COURT:

In August of 1963, the case of "Mary Ellen Crawford, a minor, by Ellen Crawford, her guardian ad litem, et al., Plaintiffs, vs. Board of Education of the City of Los Angeles,[1] Defendant," (No. C 822 854) was instituted in the Superior Court of Los Angeles County. That action was aimed at correcting the alleged existence of racial segregation in the defendant school district.

In 1976, the California Supreme Court filed its opinion in that case (Crawford v. Board of Education, 17 Cal.3d 280, 130 Cal.Rptr. 724, 551 P.2d 28) affirming the trial court's determination that the defendant District was in fact segregated. The court also affirmed the trial court's order directing the defendant to prepare and implement "a reasonably feasible desegregation plan."

Subsequently defendant District undertook the political process of developing a "PLAN FOR THE INTEGRATION OF PUPILS IN THE LOS ANGELES UNIFIED SCHOOL DISTRICT" (the Plan). The record before us does not delineate in detail the procedural steps in that process but we are informed by the parties that citizen as well as staff participation was involved and that divergent recommendations were received and considered.

The ultimate responsibility for promulgating the Plan was that of the elected members of the school board and the wisdom of their proposal is, of course, in the political process subject to the scrutiny and reactions of their constituents. The adequacy of the Plan vis-a-vis the mandate of the court is subject to the scrutiny of the court.

The Plan was submitted to the Superior Court of Los Angeles County on March 18, 1977, and the issue of its adequacy is currently

---

1. The defendant later became the Los Angeles Unified School District.

being litigated.   Again we are not provided with the details of the Plan except to the extent that the parties concede that the Plan contemplates a certain amount of mandatory reassignment of students to schools other than their so-called "neighborhood schools," i.e., schools in the area in which they reside.

Prior to the presentation of the Plan petitioner Bustop, a non-profit corporation, petitioned for leave to intervene in the action pursuant to section 387 of the Code of Civil Procedure.   That section provides in part that "At any time before trial, any person, who has an interest in the matter in litigation, or in the success of either of the parties, *or an interest against both,* may intervene in the action or proceeding." (Emphasis added.)

Bustop is an organization with a membership of 65,000 parents, predominately white, residing within the Los Angeles Unified School District.   The organization's prime objective is the prevention of mandatory reassignment of students to schools other than those which they now attend or choose to attend.

The trial court by minute order entered March 14, 1977, denied Bustop's petition.   Bustop petitioned this court for a writ of mandate to compel the trial court to permit intervention.   We granted an alternative writ.

Bustop's proposed complaint in intervention alleges, and correctly so, that the Supreme Court in its opinion in *Crawford,* supra, did not require mandatory reassignment of students as a necessary element of any plan.

For that matter the court did not set forth any specific requirements but did state at page 306, 130 Cal.Rptr. at page 741, 551 P.2d at page 45: "In our view, reliance on the judgment of local school boards in choosing between alternative desegregation strategies holds society's best hope for the formulation and implementation of desegregation plans which will actually achieve the ultimate constitutional objective. . . ."

Plaintiffs and the defendant District both oppose intervention by Bustop.   They concede, and we agree, that Bustop represents a point of view which is entitled to and which should be heard and considered. The point of departure is the forum in which that hearing and consideration should take place.

The District's contention is that that point of view was considered in the political process of formulating the Plan but that now the issue is whether the Plan will satisfy the court and not whether the Plan is acceptable to the various elements that make up the District's constituency.

The trial court's order denying intervention followed the position of the District.   That order recites as follows:

"This case is now on remand to this Court with the specific direction that it first look to the plans that were to be formulated by the Board to insure that the plans presented and filed with this Court by the respondent have met the constitutional standards in response to the mandate.

"Therefore, within that frame of reference, the stated function of this Court in this portion of the proceedings is limited. There is not, at the present time, the necessity or requirement that the broad equity powers inherent in this Court for the enforcement of injunction or mandate decrees should be called into play. . . ."

The trial court's order further says that it is entered "without prejudice to renew the motions if at a later stage the function of the Court should be radically changed, ..."

The District's objection to intervention is further based on the arguments that (1) the District represents all of the residents of the District, and (2) that to permit Bustop to intervene would open the way for a multitude of other individuals and groups to also intervene.

For their part plaintiffs argue that the requirements of Code of Civil Procedure section 387 are not met by Bustop in that that organization has no "direct interest" in the outcome since no student has a "right" to remain assigned to any particular school and that any reassignment as a result of this litigation would only be an indirect consequence of an order designed to protect the interest of the minority students. We are of the opinion that facially Bustop satisfied the requirements of Code of Civil Procedure section 387 in its petition to intervene. Its members and the persons whom it purports to represent do have an interest in the litigation.

As was stated in Johnson v. San Francisco Unified School District, 9 Cir., 500 F.2d 349, at 353, "[A]ll students and parents, whatever their race, have an interest in a sound educational system and in the operation of that system in accordance with the law. That interest is surely no less significant where, as here, it is entangled with the constitutional claims of a racially defined class."

Certainly the reassignment of students to schools distant from their residences would have a direct social, educational and economic impact on the students so reassigned and their parents.

This interest of those persons represented by Bustop is not presently represented by the parties to the action. The plaintiffs admittedly represent only the interests of specific minority students. Counsel for the District frankly admitted on oral argument that the District opposes intervention because Bustop's interpretation of the *Crawford* decision is contrary to that of the District's interpretation and in effect the position of the two are opposing. While conceding that *Crawford* does not mandate reassignment or "busing" of students the District contends as a practical matter that compliance with the court mandate requires it. Bustop disagrees.

In Johnson v. San Francisco Unified School District, supra, parents of elementary school children of Chinese ancestry sought to intervene in an action involving the compulsory reassignment of students in San Francisco to schools outside the area of their residences in order to achieve integration of black students into predominantly white schools. They claimed that such reassignment would impinge on the cultural and educational interests of the Chinese community and that they should be entitled to participate in fashioning any "desegregation" decree. The United States Circuit Court of Appeals agreed. We find that case on principle to be indistinguishable from the case before us.

In answer to the argument that the school board represented all of the District, the court there said at page 354: "[W]e cannot agree . . . that the school district, which is charged with the representation of all parents within the district and which authored the very plan which appellants claim impairs their interest, adequately represents appellants."

The District's fear that Bustop's intervention may lead to a proliferation of intervenors is unfounded. Further intervention can easily be limited by permitting additional intervention only by persons or groups whose interest is presently unrepresented in the action.

Nor would the intervention of Bustop necessitate any duplication of evidence or repetition of proceedings heretofore conducted. While Bustop may recall witnesses for cross-examination or present its own evidence, it must take the proceedings as it finds them at the time of intervention. This includes the qualification of the trial judge and precludes any right to disqualify him pursuant to Code of Civil Procedure section 170.6.[2]

Bustop does not and has not challenged the original finding in this case that the schools of the District are "segregated." Nor does it seek to challenge the principle that the District has a legal responsibility to take action to alleviate that condition. Hence the "trial" of the matter for all practical purposes began with the proceedings aimed at obtaining court approval of the Plan. Bustop's petition to intervene was filed prior to that time and was therefore timely.

Finally we reach the issue of the trial court's discretion in refusing to permit intervention. We agree with the trial court's statements in its minute order which delineates a limited role for the court in these proceedings and which opines that the input of various constituencies should be confined to the political process. As we view it the single issue before the trial court at this time is whether the Plan satisfies the requirements of the decision of the *California Supreme Court ruling in Crawford.*

Apropos of that concept is the Supreme Court's language in Crawford v. Board of Education, supra, 17 Cal.3d 280, at pages 305 and 306, 130 Cal.Rptr. 724, at page 741, 551 P.2d 28, at page 45: "[S]o long as a local school board initiates and implements reasonably feasible steps to

2. Bustop has stipulated to waive the provisions of Code of Civil Procedure section 170.6 as a condition of intervention.

alleviate school segregation in its district, and so long as such steps produce meaningful progress in the alleviation of such segregation, and its harmful consequences, we do not believe the judiciary should intervene in the desegregation process. Under such circumstances, a court thus should not step in even if it believes that alternative desegregation techniques may produce more rapid desegregation in the school district."

So long as the litigation remains in the posture envisioned by the trial judge the role of Bustop as an intervenor may be limited by rulings on the admissibility of proffered evidence.

However, lurking in the background is the language of *Crawford,* at page 307, 130 Cal.Rptr. at page 741, 551 P.2d at page 45: "If, however, a court finds that a local school board has not implemented such a course of action, the court is left with no alternative but to intervene. . . . Faced with a recalcitrant or intractable school board, a trial court may exercise broad equitable powers in formulating and supervising a plan. . . ."

The history of performance of trial and appellate courts in this country in involvement with the operation of schools and school districts unfortunately has too often been one of over-involvement rather than restraint. We have no way of predicting what turn the present litigation may take and while the trial court's order is a model of judicial restraint, it suggests the possibility that down stream the picture may change.

In the interest of fairness and to insure the maximum involvement by all responsible interested and affected persons, we believe that the proper exercise of discretion would have been to permit Bustop, representing as it does a proper and legitimate interest, to participate in the fashioning of any decree which may result in the mandatory reassignment and busing of students.

Let a peremptory writ of mandate issue directing the trial court to grant Bustop's petition to intervene. The alternative writ is discharged.

Hearing denied; MOSK, J., dissenting.

NOTE ON INTERVENTION IN "PUBLIC QUESTION" SUITS

The *Bustop* case is one of many in which intervention has been allowed in cases involving injunctive or other future-directed relief affecting large numbers of people. Some but not all of these are class suits. Whether or not they are class suits seems less important, however, than the questions they involve and the relief that is sought. Consider the following:

Cascade Natural Gas Corp. v. El Paso Natural Gas Co., 386 U.S. 129, 87 S.Ct. 932, 17 L.Ed.2d 814 (1967): This was an antitrust proceeding by the Justice Department to compel dissolution of a merger of two gas pipeline companies supplying natural gas to communities in several western states. A controversy developed over the terms and conditions of the decree ordering the dissolution. The State of California sought to intervene, contending that the position of the Department of Justice was not demanding enough in relation to the interests of California users of gas. The Court sustained intervention under F.R.C.P. 24(a)(2) as amended in 1966, over a dissent by Justice Stewart to the effect that "[I]ntervention is improper when a private party appears in order to vindicate his theory of the *public* interest in an action brought by the Government. For as the Court has consistently recognized, it is the 'United States which must alone speak for the public interest' in antitrust litigation." Cf. Note, Intervention in Government Enforcement Actions, 89 Harv.L.Rev. 1174 (1976).

Smuck v. Hobson, 408 F.2d 175 (D.C.Cir.1969): The lawsuit challenged various policies and practices of the Board of Education of the District of Columbia and resulted, in Hobson v. Hansen, 269 F.Supp. 401 (D.D.C.1967), in a decree that the Court of Appeals thus summarized: "(1) *General:* The defendants were 'permanently enjoined from discriminating on the basis of racial or economic status in the operation of the District of Columbia school system;' (2) *Optional Zones:* The defendants were directed to abolish specified optional zones in which pupils could choose which of two schools they wished to attend; (3) *Faculty Integration:* The defendants were directed (a) to provide for substantial faculty integration in all District schools immediately, and (b) to file with the court a plan of full faculty integration in the future; (4) *Pupil Assignment:* The defendants were directed (a) to provide transportation for volunteering pupils from overcrowded schools east of Rock Creek Park to schools with excess capacity west of the park, and (b) to submit to the court a long-range plan of pupil assignment to alleviate racial imbalance among District schools; and (5) *Ability Grouping:* The defendants were directed to abolish the 'track system.' " The school board, which had been the defendant, decided not to appeal the decree. A member of the school board and several parents sought to intervene so that as parties they could then prosecute an appeal. The District Court's order permitting the intervention was sustained as to the parents under F.R. C.P. 24(a)(2), over a dissent by Judge McGowan that: "Congress has explicitly vested in the Board of Education the 'control of the public schools of the District of Columbia,' and has directed that that body 'shall determine all questions of general policy relating to the schools.' * * * Among such 'questions of general policy' was surely the one of whether the Board would appeal the decision of the District Court in this case. * * * The Board decided by a vote of 6 to 2 not to appeal. That action, in my view, ended this litigation for appellate purposes, except for such appeals as the Board may elect to take in the future from any further orders of the District Court."

See also Trbovich v. United Mine Workers, 404 U.S. 528, 92 S.Ct. 630, 30 L.Ed.2d 686 (1972) (union member given limited right of intervention in suit by Secretary of Labor seeking to invalidate election of union officers); Sagebrush Rebellion, Inc. v. Watt, 713 F.2d 525 (9th Cir. 1983) (conservation group allowed to intervene in suit challenging actions of Secretary of the Interior); State of Texas v. United States Dept. of Energy, 754 F.2d 550 (5th Cir. 1985) (utilities not permitted to intervene in state's appeal of Dept. of Energy's designation of long-term nuclear waste depository sites); County of Alameda v. Carleson, 5 Cal.3d 730, 97 Cal.Rptr. 385, 488 P.2d 953 (1971) (welfare recipients and their organization permitted to intervene in suit by county against state Director of Department of Social Welfare involving the validity of regulations governing entitlement to welfare benefits); People v. Superior Court, 17 Cal.3d 732, 131 Cal.Rptr. 800, 552 P.2d 760 (1976) (in public civil prosecution against false advertising, private victims allowed to intervene to recover losses); Planned

Parenthood of Minnesota, Inc. v. Citizens for Community Action, 558 F.2d 861 (8th Cir. 1977) (neighboring property owners allowed to intervene in suit by pro-abortion group to obtain zoning variance in order to establish abortion clinic); United States v. Allegheny-Ludlum Industries, Inc., 517 F.2d 826 (5th Cir. 1975) (NOW sought intervention in Government suit regarding discriminatory employment practices); Auerbach v. Bennett, 47 N.Y.2d 619, 419 N.Y.S.2d 920, 393 N.E.2d 994 (1979) (stockholder allowed to intervene to prosecute appeal from dismissal of derivative suit brought by another stockholder); United States v. Hooker Chemicals & Plastics Corp., 749 F.2d 968 (2d Cir. 1984) (citizen suit provisions of Safe Drinking Water Act, Resource Conservation and Recovery Act, and Clean Water Act do not authorize party intervention in Government injunctive water quality suit). See also Note, Institutional Reform Litigation: Representation in the Remedial Process, 91 Yale L.J. 1474 (1982).

Many cases uphold an effort by the government to intervene in private litigation that may have general public consequences. See, e.g., Merrill v. Town of Addison, 763 F.2d 80 (2d Cir. 1985) (state attorney general permitted to intervene in suit challenging constitutionality of state statute); Ameron, Inc. v. United States Army Corps of Engineers, 787 F.2d 875 (3d Cir. 1986) (Congress allowed to intervene when executive declines to defend statute or argues it is unconstitutional); County of San Bernardino v. Harsh California Corp., 52 Cal. 2d 341, 340 P.2d 617 (1959), Note, 12 Stan.L.Rev. 472 (1960) (United States allowed to intervene in state court action involving interpretation of a federal statute); People v. Ryerson, 241 Cal.App.2d 115, 50 Cal.Rptr. 246 (1966) (state public utilities commission allowed to intervene in suit over rates between shipper and carrier); New Orleans Public Serv., Inc. v. United Gas Pipe Line Co., 690 F.2d 1203 (5th Cir. 1982) (city officials but not consumers allowed to intervene in case involving gas contract). But see Mumford Cove Ass'n v. Town of Groton, 786 F.2d 530 (2d Cir. 1986) (nearby cities not allowed to intervene in federal action to compel town's compliance with state sewage abatement order); Blake v. Pallan, 554 F.2d 947 (9th Cir. 1977) (state corporation commissioner not permitted to intervene in federal securities act case to assert parallel state securities claim).

Would it follow that an environmental protection group, or a citizen interested in preserving natural oceanic features, could also intervene in the *Atlantis* case? When consideration is given to the *stare decisis* effects of a determination, as distinct from its res judicata effects, are there any limits that can be established on the opportunity to intervene? Would it really be unmanageable to allow everyone to intervene who wanted to invest the time and effort in doing so? Does the form of intervention—right to present written argument, right to present oral argument, right to present evidence, right to tender issues—have to be the same under all circumstances for all participants? Is the problem essentially the same as the problem of standing to sue, considered infra p. 779? Doesn't Rule 24 need to be reconsidered in this light? Cf. Trbovich v. United Mine Workers, supra; Shapiro, Some Thoughts on Intervention Before Courts, Agencies, and Arbitrators, 81 Harv.L.Rev. 721 (1968); Kennedy, Let's All Join In: Intervention Under Federal Rule 24, 57 Ky.L.J. 329 (1969); Symposium, Problems of Intervention in Public Law Litigation, 13 U.C. D.L.Rev. 211 (1980).

For a criticism of the decision in *Bustop*, see Yeazell, Intervention and the Idea of Litigation: A Commentary on the Los Angeles School Case, 25 U.C. L.A.L.Rev. 244 (1977). Professor Yeazell should not be understood as saying that only "good guys" ought to be able to intervene. If he is saying that allowing intervention by political action groups will turn public question cases into political caucuses, he is undoubtedly right. However, once one accepts that courts can give the kinds of remedies involved in *Bustop,* at the behest of private parties and despite the position of the government agency in charge (such as the school district), where can participation in the debate be justly cut off? Compare Valley Forge Christian College v. Americans United for Separation of Church and State, Inc., infra p. 781.

An alternative to intervention is to appear *amicus curiae.* However, an *amicus* ordinarily lacks the procedural rights of a party, particularly the right to offer direct and rebuttal evidence and the right to take an appeal. See generally Comment, The Amicus Curiae, 55 Nw.U.L.Rev. 469 (1960).

c. INTERPLEADER

STATE FARM FIRE & CASUALTY CO. v. TASHIRE

Supreme Court of the United States, 1967.
386 U.S. 523, 87 S.Ct. 1199, 18 L.Ed.2d 270.

Mr. Justice Fortas delivered the opinion of the Court.

Early one September morning in 1964, a Greyhound bus proceeding northward through Shasta County, California, collided with a southbound pickup truck. Two of the passengers aboard the bus were killed. Thirty-three others were injured, as were the bus driver, the driver of the truck and its lone passenger. One of the dead and 10 of the injured passengers were Canadians; the rest of the individuals involved were citizens of five American States. The ensuing litigation led to the present case, which raises important questions concerning administration of the interpleader remedy in the federal courts.

The litigation began when four of the injured passengers filed suit in California state courts, seeking damages in excess of $1,000,000. Named as defendants were Greyhound Lines, Inc., a California corporation; Theron Nauta, the bus driver; Ellis Clark, who drove the truck; and Kenneth Glasgow, the passenger in the truck who was apparently its owner as well. Each of the individual defendants was a citizen and resident of Oregon. Before these cases could come to trial and before other suits were filed in California or elsewhere, petitioner, State Farm Fire & Casualty Company, an Illinois corporation, brought this action in the nature of interpleader in the United States District Court for the District of Oregon.

In its complaint State Farm asserted that at the time of the Shasta County collision it had in force an insurance policy with respect to Ellis Clark, driver of the truck, providing for bodily injury liability up to $10,000 per person and $20,000 per occurrence and for legal representation of Clark in actions covered by the policy. It asserted that actions already filed in California and others which it anticipated would be filed far exceeded in aggregate damages sought the amount of its maximum liability under the policy. Accordingly, it paid into court the sum of $20,000 and asked the court (1) to require all claimants to establish their claims against Clark and his insurer in this single proceeding and in no other, and (2) to discharge State Farm from all further obligations under its policy—including its duty to defend Clark in lawsuits arising from the accident. Alternatively, State Farm expressed its conviction that the policy issued to Clark excluded from coverage accidents resulting from his operation of a truck which belonged to another and was being used in the business of another. The complaint, therefore, requested that the court decree that the insurer owed no duty to Clark and was not liable on the policy, and it asked the court to refund the $20,000 deposit.

Joined as defendants were Clark, Glasgow, Nauta, Greyhound Lines, and each of the prospective claimants. Jurisdiction was predicated upon 28 U.S.C.A. § 1335, the federal interpleader statute,[1] and upon general diversity of citizenship, there being diversity between two or more of the claimants to the fund and between State Farm and all of the named defendants.

An order issued, requiring each of the defendants to show cause why it should not be restrained from filing or prosecuting "any proceeding in any state or United States Court affecting the property or obligation involved in this interpleader action, and specifically against the plaintiff and the defendant Ellis D. Clark." Personal service was effected on each of the American defendants, and registered mail was employed to reach the 11 Canadian claimants. Defendants Nauta, Greyhound, and several of the injured passengers responded, contending that the policy did cover this accident and advancing various arguments for the position that interpleader was either impermissible or inappropriate in the present circumstances. Greyhound, however, soon switched sides and moved that the court broaden any injunction to include Nauta and Greyhound among those who could not be sued except within the confines of the interpleader proceeding.

When a temporary injunction along the lines sought by State Farm was issued by the United States District Court for the District of Oregon, the present respondents moved to dismiss the action and, in the alternative, for a change of venue—to the Northern District of California, in which district the collision had occurred. After a hearing, the court declined to dissolve the temporary injunction, but continued the motion for a change of venue. The injunction was later broadened to include the protection sought by Greyhound, but modified to permit the filing—although not the prosecution—of suits. The

---

1. 28 U.S.C.A. § 1335(a) provides: "The district courts shall have original jurisdiction of any civil action of interpleader or in the nature of interpleader filed by any person, firm, or corporation, association, or society having in his or its custody or possession money or property of the value of $500 or more, or having issued a . . . policy of insurance . . . of value or amount of $500 or more . . . if

"(1) Two or more adverse claimants, of diverse citizenship as defined in section 1332 of this title, are claiming or may claim to be entitled to such money or property, or to any one or more of the benefits arising by virtue of any . . . policy . . .; and if (2) the plaintiff has . . . paid . . . the amount due under such obligation into the registry of the court, there to abide the judgment of the court. . . ."

[See also 28 U.S.C.A. §§ 1397, 2361.— Ed.]

injunction, therefore, provided that all suits against Clark, State Farm, Greyhound, and Nauta be prosecuted in the interpleader proceeding.

On interlocutory appeal,[2] the Court of Appeals for the Ninth Circuit reversed. 363 F.2d 7. The court found it unnecessary to reach respondents' contentions relating to service of process and the scope of the injunction, for it concluded that interpleader was not available in the circumstances of this case. It held that in States like Oregon which do not permit "direct action" suits against the insurance company until judgments are obtained against the insured, the insurance company may not invoke federal interpleader until the claims against the insured, the alleged tortfeasor, have been reduced to judgment. Until that is done, said the court, claimants with unliquidated tort claims are not "claimants" within the meaning of § 1335, nor are they "[p]ersons having claims against the plaintiff" within the meaning of Rule 22 of the Federal Rules of Civil Procedure.[3] Id., at 10. In accord with that view, it directed dissolution of the temporary injunction and dismissal of the action. Because the Court of Appeals' decision on this point conflicts with those of other federal courts,[4] and concerns a matter of significance to the administration of federal interpleader, we granted certiorari. 385 U.S. 811, 87 S.Ct. 90, 17 L.Ed.2d 52 (1966). Although we reverse the decision of the Court of Appeals upon the jurisdictional

2. 28 U.S.C.A. § 1292(a)(1).

3. We need not pass upon the Court of Appeals' conclusions with respect to the interpretation of interpleader under Rule 22, which provides that "(1) Persons having claims against the plaintiff may be joined as defendants and required to interplead when their claims are such that the plaintiff is or may be exposed to double or multiple liability. . . ." First, as we indicate today, this action was properly brought under § 1335. Second, State Farm did not purport to invoke Rule 22. Third, State Farm could not have invoked it in light of venue and service of process limitations. Whereas statutory interpleader may be brought in the district where any claimant resides (28 U.S.C. § 1397), Rule interpleader based upon diversity of citizenship may be brought only in the district where all plaintiffs or all defendants reside (28 U.S.C. § 1391(a)). And whereas statutory interpleader enables a plaintiff to employ nationwide service of process (28 U.S.C. § 2361), service of process under Rule 22 is confined to that provided in Rule 4. See generally, 3 Moore, Fed.Prac. ¶ 22.04.

With respect to the Court of Appeals' views on Rule 22, which seem to be shared by our Brother Douglas, compare Underwriters at Lloyd's v. Nichols, 363 F.2d 357 (C.A.8th Cir. 1966), and A/S Krediit Bank v. Chase Manhattan Bank, 155 F.Supp. 30

(D.C.S.D.N.Y.1957), aff'd, 303 F.2d 648 (C.A.2d Cir. 1962), with National Cas. Co. v. Insurance Co. of North America, 230 F.Supp. 617 (D.C.N.D.Ohio 1964), and American Indem. Co. v. Hale, 71 F.Supp. 529 (D.C.W.D.Mo.1947). See also 3 Moore, Fed.Prac. ¶ 22.04, at 3008 and n. 4.

4. See, e.g., Travelers Indem. Co. v. Greyhound Lines, Inc., 260 F.Supp. 530 (D.C.W.D.La.1966); Commercial Union Ins. Co. of New York v. Adams, 231 F.Supp. 860 (D.C.S.D.Ind.1964); Pan American Fire & Cas. Co. v. Revere, 188 F.Supp. 474 (D.C. E.D.La.1960); Onyx Ref. Co. v. Evans Prod. Corp., 182 F.Supp. 253 (D.C.N.D.Tex.1959). Although *Travelers* and *Revere* were brought in Louisiana, a State which authorizes "direct action" suits against insurance companies, the statute was not relied upon in *Travelers* (see 260 F.Supp., at 533, n. 3), and furnished only an alternative ground in *Revere* (see 188 F.Supp., at 482–483).

The only post-1948 case relied upon by the Court of Appeals and respondents, National Cas. Co. v. Insurance Co. of North America, 230 F.Supp. 617 (D.C.N.D.Ohio 1964), turns out to be of little assistance with respect to statutory interpleader since that court denied statutory interpleader solely on the ground that all claimants were citizens of Ohio and hence lacked the required diversity of citizenship. Id., at 619.

question, we direct a substantial modification of the District Court's injunction for reasons which shall appear.

I

Before considering the issues presented by the petition for certiorari, we find it necessary to dispose of a question neither raised by the parties nor passed upon by the courts below. Since the matter concerns our jurisdiction, we raise it on our own motion. Treinies v. Sunshine Mining Co., 308 U.S. 66, 70, 60 S.Ct. 44, 47, 84 L.Ed. 85 (1939). The interpleader statute, 28 U.S.C.A. § 1335, applies where there are "Two or more adverse claimants, of diverse citizenship. . . ." This provision has been uniformly construed to require only "minimal diversity," that is, diversity of citizenship between two or more claimants, without regard to the circumstance that other rival claimants may be co-citizens.[5] The language of the statute, the legislative purpose broadly to remedy the problems posed by multiple claimants to a single fund, and the consistent judicial interpretation tacitly accepted by Congress, persuade us that the statute requires no more. There remains, however, the question whether such a statutory construction is consistent with Article III of our Constitution, which extends the federal judicial power to "Controversies . . . between citizens of different States . . . and between a State, or the Citizens thereof, and foreign States, Citizens or Subjects." In Strawbridge v. Curtiss, 3 Cranch 267, 2 L.Ed. 435 (1806), this Court held that the diversity of citizenship statute required "complete diversity": where co-citizens appeared on both sides of a dispute, jurisdiction was lost. But Chief Justice Marshall there purported to construe only "The words of the act of Congress," not the Constitution itself.[6] And in a variety of contexts this Court and the lower courts have concluded that Article III poses no obstacle to the legislative extension of federal jurisdiction, founded on diversity, so long as any two adverse parties are not co-citizens.[7]

5. See, e.g., Haynes v. Felder, 239 F.2d 868, 872–875 (C.A.5th Cir. 1957); Holcomb v. Aetna Life Ins. Co., 255 F.2d 577, 582 (C.A.10th Cir.), cert. denied, Fleming v. Aetna Life Ins. Co., 358 U.S. 879, 79 S.Ct. 118, 3 L.Ed.2d 110 (1958); Cramer v. Phoenix Mut. Life Ins. Co., 91 F.2d 141, 146–147 (C.A.8th Cir.), cert. denied, 302 U.S. 739, 58 S.Ct. 141, 82 L.Ed. 571 (1937); Commercial Union Ins. Co. of New York v. Adams, 231 F.Supp. 860, 863 (D.C.S.D.Ind.1964); 3 Moore, Fed.Prac. ¶ 22.09, at 3033.

6. Subsequent decisions of this Court indicate that *Strawbridge* is not to be given an expansive reading. See, e.g., Louisville C. & C. Railroad Co. v. Letson, 2 How. 497, 544–556, 11 L.Ed. 353 (1844), expressing the view that in 1839 Congress had in fact acted to "rid the courts of the decision in the case of Strawbridge and Curtiss." Id., at 556.

7. See, e.g., American Fire & Cas. Co. v. Finn, 341 U.S. 6, 10, n. 3, 71 S.Ct. 534, 538, 95 L.Ed. 702 (1951), and Barney v. Latham, 103 U.S. 205, 213, 26 L.Ed. 514 (1881), construing the removal statute, now 28 U.S.C. § 1441(c); Supreme Tribe of Ben-Hur v. Cauble, 255 U.S. 356, 41 S.Ct. 338, 65 L.Ed. 673 (1921), concerning class actions; Wichita R. R. & Light Co. v. Public Util. Comm., 260 U.S. 48, 43 S.Ct. 51, 67 L.Ed. 124 (1922), dealing with intervention by co-citizens. Full-dress arguments for the constitutionality of "minimal diversity" in situations like interpleader, which arguments need not be rehearsed here, are set out in Judge Tuttle's opinion in Haynes v. Felder, 239 F.2d, at 875–876; in Judge Weinfeld's opinion in Twentieth Century-Fox Film Corp. v. Taylor, 239 F.Supp. 913, 918–921 (D.C.S.D.N.Y.1965); and in ALI, Study of the Division of Jurisdiction Between State and Federal Courts, 176–186

Accordingly, we conclude that the present case is properly in the federal courts.

II

We do not agree with the Court of Appeals that, in the absence of a state law or contractual provision for "direct action" suits against the insurance company, the company must wait until persons asserting claims against its insured have reduced those claims to judgment before seeking to invoke the benefits of federal interpleader. That may have been a tenable position under the 1926[8] and 1936 interpleader statutes.[9] These statutes did not carry forward the language in the 1917 Act authorizing interpleader where adverse claimants "may claim" benefits as well as where they "are claiming" them.[10] In 1948, however, in the revision of the Judicial Code, the "may claim" language was restored.[11] Until the decision below, every court confronted by the question has concluded that the 1948 revision removed whatever requirement there might previously have been that the insurance company wait until at least two claimants reduced their claims to judgments.[12] The commentators are in accord.[13]

Considerations of judicial administration demonstrate the soundness of this view which, in any event, seems compelled by the language of the present statute, which is remedial and to be liberally construed. Were an insurance company required to await reduction of claims to judgment, the first claimants to obtain such a judgment or to negotiate a settlement might appropriate all or a disproportionate slice of the

(Official Draft, Pt. 1, 1965); 3 Moore, Fed. Prac. ¶ 22.09, at 3033–3037; Chafee, Federal Interpleader Since the Act of 1936, 49 Yale L.J. 377, 393–406 (1940); Chafee, Interpleader in the United States Courts, 41 Yale L.J. 1134, 1165–1169 (1932). We note that the American Law Institute's proposals for revision of the Judicial Code to deal with the problem of multiparty, multijurisdiction litigation are predicated upon the permissibility of "minimal diversity" as a jurisdictional basis.

8.   44 Stat. 416 (1926), which added casualty companies to the enumerated categories of plaintiffs able to bring interpleader, and provided for the enjoining of proceedings in other courts.

9.   49 Stat. 1096 (1936), which authorized "bill[s] in the nature of interpleader," meaning those in which the plaintiff is not wholly disinterested with respect to the fund he has deposited in court. See Chafee, The Federal Interpleader Act of 1936: I, 45 Yale L.J. 936 (1936).

10.   39 Stat. 929 (1917). See Klaber v. Maryland Cas. Co., 69 F.2d 934, 938–939, 106 A.L.R. 617 (C.A.8th Cir. 1934), which held that the omission in the 1926 Act of

the earlier statute's "may claim" language required the denial of interpleader in the face of unliquidated claims (alternative holding).

11.   Although the Reviser's Note did not refer to the statutory change or its purpose, we have it on good authority that it was the omission in the Note rather than the statutory change which was inadvertent. See 3 Moore, Fed.Prac. ¶ 22.08, 3025–3026, n. 13. And it was widely assumed that restoration of the "may claim" language would have the effect of overruling the holding in *Klaber* supra, that one may not invoke interpleader to protect against unliquidated claims. See, e.g., Chafee, 45 Yale L.J., at 1163–1167; Chafee, Federal Interpleader Since the Act of 1936, 49 Yale L.J. 377, 418–420 (1940). In circumstances like these, the 1948 revision of the Judicial Code worked substantive changes. Ex parte Collett, 337 U.S. 55, 69 S.Ct. 944, 93 L.Ed. 1207 (1949).

12.   See cases listed in n. 4.

13.   3 Moore, Fed.Prac. ¶ 22.08, at 3024–3025; Keeton, Preferential Settlement of Liability-Insurance Claims, 70 Harv.L.Rev. 27, 41–42 (1956).

fund before his fellow claimants were able to establish their claims. The difficulties such a race to judgment pose for the insurer,[14] and the unfairness which may result to some claimants, were among the principal evils the interpleader device was intended to remedy.[15]

III

The fact that State Farm had properly invoked the interpleader jurisdiction under § 1335 did not, however, entitle it to an order both enjoining prosecution of suits against it outside the confines of the interpleader proceeding and also extending such protection to its insured, the alleged tortfeasor. Still less was Greyhound Lines entitled to have that order expanded so as to protect itself and its driver, also alleged to be tortfeasors, from suits brought by its passengers in various state or federal courts. Here, the scope of the litigation, in terms of parties and claims, was vastly more extensive than the confines of the "fund," the deposited proceeds of the insurance policy. In these circumstances, the mere existence of such a fund cannot, by use of interpleader, be employed to accomplish purposes that exceed the needs of orderly contest with respect to the fund.

There are situations, of a type not present here, where the effect of interpleader is to confine the total litigation to a single forum and proceeding. One such case is where a stakeholder, faced with rival claims to the fund itself, acknowledges—or denies—his liability to one or the other of the claimants.[16] In this situation, the fund itself is the target of the claimants. It marks the outer limits of the controversy. It is, therefore, reasonable and sensible that interpleader, in discharge of its office to protect the fund, should also protect the stakeholder from vexatious and multiple litigation. In this context, the suits sought to be enjoined are squarely within the language of 28 U.S.C.A. § 2361, which provides in part:

> "In any civil action of interpleader or in the nature of interpleader under section 1335 of this title, a district court may issue its process for all claimants and enter its order restraining them from instituting or prosecuting *any proceeding* in any State or United States court *affecting the property, instrument or obligation involved in the interpleader action. . . .*" (Emphasis added.)

But the present case is another matter. Here, an accident has happened. Thirty-five passengers or their representatives have claims which they wish to press against a variety of defendants: the bus company, its driver, the owner of the truck, and the truck driver. The

---

14. See Keeton, op. cit. supra, n. 13.

15. The insurance problem envisioned at the time was that of an insurer faced with conflicting but mutually exclusive claims to a policy, rather than an insurer confronted with the problem of allocating a fund among various claimants whose independent claims may exceed the amount of the fund. S.Rep. No. 558, 74th Cong., 1st Sess., 2–3, 7, 8 (1935); Chafee, Modernizing Interpleader, 30 Yale L.J. 814, 818–819 (1921).

16. This was the classic situation envisioned by the sponsors of interpleader. See n. 15, supra.

circumstance that one of the prospective defendants happens to have an insurance policy is a fortuitous event which should not of itself shape the nature of the ensuing litigation. For example, a resident of California, injured in California aboard a bus owned by a California corporation should not be forced to sue that corporation anywhere but in California simply because another prospective defendant carried an insurance policy. And an insurance company whose maximum interest in the case cannot exceed $20,000 and who in fact asserts that it has no interest at all, should not be allowed to determine that dozens of tort plaintiffs must be compelled to press their claims—even those claims which are not against the insured and which in no event could be satisfied out of the meager insurance fund—in a single forum of the insurance company's choosing. There is nothing in the statutory scheme, and very little in the judicial and academic commentary upon that scheme, which requires that the tail be allowed to wag the dog in this fashion.

State Farm's interest in this case, which is the fulcrum of the interpleader procedure, is confined to its $20,000 fund. That interest receives full vindication when the court restrains claimants from seeking to enforce against the insurance company any judgment obtained against its insured, except in the interpleader proceeding itself. To the extent that the District Court sought to control claimants' lawsuits against the insured and other alleged tortfeasors, it exceeded the powers granted to it by the statutory scheme.

We recognize, of course, that our view of interpleader means that it cannot be used to solve all the vexing problems of multiparty litigation arising out of a mass tort. But interpleader was never intended to perform such a function, to be an all-purpose "bill of peace."[17] Had it been so intended, careful provision would necessarily have been made to insure that a party with little or no interest in the outcome of a complex controversy should not strip truly interested parties of substantial rights—such as the right to choose the forum in which to establish their claims, subject to generally applicable rules of jurisdiction, venue, service of process, removal, and change of venue. None of the legislative and academic sponsors of a modern federal interpleader device viewed their accomplishment as a "bill of peace," capable of sweeping dozens of lawsuits out of the various state and federal courts

---

17. There is not a word in the legislative history suggesting such a purpose. See S.Rep. No. 558, 74th Cong., 1st Sess. (1935). And Professor Chafee, upon whose work the Congress heavily depended, has written that little thought was given to the scope of the "second stage" of interpleader, to just what would be adjudicated by the interpleader court. See Chafee, Broadening the Second Stage of Federal Interpleader, 56 Harv.L.Rev. 929, 944–945 (1943). We note that in Professor Chafee's own study of the bill of peace as a device for

dealing with the problem of multiparty litigation, he fails even to mention interpleader. See Chafee, Some Problems of Equity 149–198 (1950). In his writing on interpleader, Chafee assumed that the interpleader court would allocate the fund "among all the claimants who get judgment within a reasonable time. . . ." Chafee, The Federal Interpleader Act of 1936: II, 45 Yale L.J. 1161, 1165–1166 (1936). See also Chafee, 49 Yale L.J., at 420–421.

in which they were brought and into a single interpleader proceeding. And only in two reported instances has a federal interpleader court sought to control the underlying litigation against alleged tortfeasors as opposed to the allocation of a fund among successful tort plaintiffs. See Commercial Union Ins. Co. of New York v. Adams, 231 F.Supp. 860 (D.C.S.D.Ind.1964) (where there was virtually no objection and where all of the basic tort suits would in any event have been prosecuted in the forum state), and Pan American Fire & Cas. Co. v. Revere, 188 F.Supp. 474 (D.C.E.D.La.1960). Another district court, on the other hand, has recently held that it lacked statutory authority to enjoin suits against the alleged tortfeasor as opposed to proceedings against the fund itself. Travelers Indem. Co. v. Greyhound Lines, Inc., 260 F.Supp. 530 (D.C.W.D.La.1966).

In light of the evidence that federal interpleader was not intended to serve the function of a "bill of peace" in the context of multiparty litigation arising out of a mass tort, of the anomalous power which such a construction of the statute would give the stakeholder, and of the thrust of the statute and the purpose it was intended to serve, we hold that the interpleader statute did not authorize the injunction entered in the present case. Upon remand, the injunction is to be modified consistently with this opinion.[18]

IV

The judgment of the Court of Appeals is reversed, and the case is remanded to the United States District Court for proceedings consistent with this opinion.

It is so ordered.

MR. JUSTICE DOUGLAS, dissenting.*

---

18. We find it unnecessary to pass upon respondents' contention, raised in the courts below but not passed upon by the Court of Appeals, that interpleader should have been dismissed on the ground that the 11 Canadian claimants are "indispensable parties" who have not been properly served. The argument is that 28 U.S.C.A. § 2361 provides the exclusive mode of effecting service of process in statutory interpleader and that § 2361—which authorizes a district court to "issue its process for all claimants" but subsequently refers to service of "such process" by marshals "for the respective districts where the claimants reside or may be found"—does not permit service of process beyond the Nation's borders. Since our decision will require basic reconsideration of the litigation by the parties as well as the lower courts, there appears neither need nor necessity to determine this question at this time. We intimate no view as to the exclusivity of § 2361, whether it authorizes service of process in foreign lands, whether in light of the limitations we have imposed on the interpleader court's injunctive powers the Canadian claimants are in fact "indispensable parties" to the interpleader proceeding itself, or whether they render themselves amenable to service of process under § 2361 when they come into an American jurisdiction to establish their rights with respect either to the alleged tortfeasors or to the insurance fund. See 2 Moore, Fed. Prac. ¶ 4.20, at 1091–1105.

* The dissenting opinion is omitted.

NOTE ON INTERPLEADER

1. Federal Interpleader

Pan American Fire & Casualty Co. v. Revere, 188 F.Supp. 474 (E.D.La. 1960), cited several times in *Tashire,* has an excellent analysis of several recurrent problems of federal interpleader. How should the question left open in footnote 18 of the *Tashire* opinion have been decided on its merits?

For an interesting attempt at interpleader to resolve a fight over the relocation of a professional football franchise, see Indianapolis Colts v. Mayor and City Council of Baltimore, 733 F.2d 484 (7th Cir.1984); 741 F.2d 954 (7th Cir.1984); 775 F.2d 177 (7th Cir.1985).

2. State Court Interpleader

a. The Problem of Jurisdiction. The chief impetus for the enactment of the Federal Interpleader Act was the decision in New York Life Ins. Co. v. Dunlevy, 241 U.S. 518, 36 S.Ct. 613, 60 L.Ed. 1140 (1916), apparently holding that a state in which the "fund" was located could not determine the claims to the fund of a claimant not amenable to personal service of process. Whether *Dunlevy* is still good law, and indeed whether it ever was, is subject to serious question. See Atkinson v. Superior Court, 49 Cal.2d 338, 316 P.2d 960 (1957). Cf. Harris v. Balk, 198 U.S. 215, 25 S.Ct. 625, 49 L.Ed. 1023 (1905), noted supra p. 292. Be that as it may, when interpleader is available under the Federal Interpleader Act, a stakeholder is probably better advised to use it rather than to invite jurisdictional challenges to state court interpleader involving absent claimants.

Could the insurer in Csohan v. United Benefit Life Ins. Co., supra p. 700, have sued under the Federal Interpleader Act? Under the general diversity statute, 28 U.S.C.A. § 1332, and plead under Rule 22? If not, why not?

b. The Restrictions on Interpleader. The modern provisions for interpleader constitute abrogations, in varying degrees, of the so-called traditional limitations on interpleader. As stated in the heyday of American procedural baroque in 4 Pomeroy, Equity Jurisprudence § 1322 (3d ed. 1905), the requirements were these:

> "1. The same thing, debt, or duty must be claimed by both or all the parties against whom the relief is demanded; 2. All their adverse titles or claims must be dependent, or be derived from a common source; 3. The person asking the relief—the plaintiff—must not have nor claim any interest in the subject-matter; 4. He must have incurred no independent liability to either of the claimants; that is, he must stand perfectly indifferent between them, in the position merely of a stake-holder."

Those jurisdictions which have adopted an interpleader rule patterned on F.R.C.P. 22 have abrogated all four of these requirements. See, e.g., C.C.P. 386, as amended in 1975; Note, 7 Pac.L.J. 316 (1976).

For a critique of the "traditional" limitations on interpleader, see Hazard and Moskovitz, An Historical and Critical Analysis of Interpleader, 52 Calif.L. Rev. 706 (1964). Compare the criticism in Chafee, Modernizing Interpleader, 30 Yale L.J. 814, 832–38 (1921).

The classic treatments of interpleader generally are the series of articles by Chafee: 30 Yale L.J. 814 (1921); 41 Yale L.J. 1134 (1932); 42 Yale L.J. 41 (1932); 45 Yale L.J. 963 (1936); 49 Yale L.J. 377 (1940); 56 Harv.L.Rev. 541

(1943); and 56 Harv.L.Rev. 929 (1943). An excellent treatment of the early but obsolete common law interpleader proceeding is Rogers, Historical Origins of Interpleader, 51 Yale L.J. 924 (1942). See also Clark on Code Pleading 427–433 (2d ed. 1947). For the New York provisions, see N.Y.C.P.L.R. §§ 1006, 2701, 2702. See also 7 Wright & Miller §§ 1701 et seq.

d. SUBSTITUTION OF PARTIES

NOTE ON SUBSTITUTION OF PARTIES

A substitution of parties is appropriate where a party to the action becomes incapacitated to participate in the action, in the case of a natural person by death or incompetency, in the case of a corporation by dissolution or other termination of corporate existence, or in the case of a person sued in an official capacity, such as an executor or a public official, by reason of termination of his status as such. When such incapacity occurs, it may also carry with it the substantive legal consequence of the termination of the right of action, as in the case of the death of a plaintiff having a cause of action for personal injuries at common law. The substantive problem is now widely regulated by statute and is beyond the province of these materials. See, e.g., Prosser and Keeton, Torts c. 23 (5th ed. 1984); Robertson v. Wegmann, 436 U.S. 584, 98 S.Ct. 1991, 56 L.Ed.2d 554 (1978); cf. Restatement Second of Judgments §§ 45–47. If the substantive consequence is that the right of action survives, the procedural problem arises of taking appropriate note of the change in parties.

The procedure at common law and in equity was complex, involving at common law scire facias proceedings, see, e.g., Graham, Practice of the Supreme Court of the State of New York c. VI (1832), and in equity the bill of revivor, see, e.g., Story, Equity Pleadings §§ 354 et seq. (2d ed. 1840). Under the provisions of most codes, e.g., C.C.P. 385, substitution may be made by simple motion, and the failure to do so is regarded as formal error. See 4 Witkin 338–345; cf. Collison v. Thomas, 55 Cal.2d 490, 11 Cal.Rptr. 555, 360 P.2d 51 (1961); Estate of Edwards, 82 Cal.App.3d 885, 147 Cal.Rptr. 458 (1978). C.C.P. 385(b) has a special provision for continuation of a suit against a defendant who is insured against liability but who dies after the suit has been commenced.

The federal procedural system suffered for many years, and continues to suffer, from the failure of Congress adequately to erase the anachronisms of the common law. See, e.g., Anderson v. Yungkau, 329 U.S. 482, 67 S.Ct. 428, 91 L.Ed. 436 (1947) (death of a party); Snyder v. Buck, 340 U.S. 15, 71 S.Ct. 93, 95 L.Ed. 15 (1950) (termination of tenure of public officer). Amendments to F.R. C.P. 25 have eliminated most but not all of the problems regarding substitution in actions against public officials, but do not overcome all the formal difficulties that ensue upon death of individual litigants. See generally 7C Wright & Miller §§ 1951–62; Comment, Substitution Under Amended Rule 25(a)(1), 1963 Duke L.J. 733.

3. STANDING TO SUE

INTRODUCTORY NOTE ON STANDING TO SUE

The concept of standing to sue is associated with the federal courts and particularly relates to whether a lawsuit can be maintained by a person who seeks to challenge the legality of the action of a government official, federal, state, or local. The problem arises at the intersection of two ideas. One is that government officials ought to obey the law and ought in some instances to be called to account in the courts if they do not. Whenever this happens, the court decides what the law is—or makes new law—and thereby determines the permissible course of government action, at least if its judgment is obeyed. As Chief Justice Marshall said in Marbury v. Madison, "[i]t is, emphatically, the province and duty of the judicial department to say what the law is." 5 U.S. (1 Cranch) 137, 177, 2 L.Ed. 60, 73 (1803). The other idea is that courts should not be legal ombudsbureaus, ready to pass on the legality of any government action that anyone might want to dispute. Rather, courts should decide what the law is only when obliged to do so, in connection with granting or denying relief to someone injured by the government action in question. As said in Massachusetts v. Mellon, 262 U.S. 447, 43 S.Ct. 597, 67 L.Ed. 1078 (1923), at 488–489: A suit by a person who has not suffered "direct" injury invites the court to "assume a position of authority over the governmental acts of another and co-equal department, an authority which plainly we do not possess."

Now this last statement is simply incompatible with Marbury v. Madison if and to the extent that the question of legality can be posed by one who has suffered "direct" injury. The important problem, then, is which injuries will be deemed "direct" and which ones not, as discussed in the *Valley Forge* case, reprinted just below. For a long time the Court held to the idea that an injury had to be economic, but that was abandoned. See, e.g., Baker v. Carr, 369 U.S. 186, 82 S.Ct. 691, 7 L.Ed.2d 663 (1962) (right to vote). For a long time it also adhered to the idea that the injury had to be imminent, but that too was abandoned, particularly in the free speech cases, where even a threat of government action might invade First Amendment rights by "chilling." Cf. Jenkins v. McKeithen, 395 U.S. 411, 89 S.Ct. 1843, 23 L.Ed.2d 404 (1969). In connection with suits involving government licenses, it held that a competitor of a proposed licensee could sue to prevent issuance of the license. See FCC v. Sanders Bros. Radio Station, 309 U.S. 470, 60 S.Ct. 693, 84 L.Ed. 869 (1940). This was extended to potential competitors in Association of Data Processing Service Organizations v. Camp, 397 U.S. 150, 90 S.Ct. 827, 25 L.Ed.2d 184 (1970). Add to this that suit may be brought on behalf of a class defined in terms of persons threatened by the government action and the "direct" requirement is further attenuated. See, e.g., Sosna v. Iowa, 419 U.S. 393, 95 S.Ct. 553, 42 L.Ed.2d 532 (1975).

If all these are put together, then a person claiming to be one of a group potentially subject to injury by contemplated conduct of a government official has suffered sufficient injury to bring suit to restrain that conduct. Awarding judicial redress at the behest of any person who could make such a claim would surely put the courts in the position of "assuming authority over the governmental acts of another and co-equal department" not only occasionally but systematically. Cf. Note, Judicial Resolution of Inter-Agency Legal Disputes, 89 Yale L.J. 1595 (1980). Apart from everything else, this might involve the courts in more policy-making than they would like to assume. Might standing doctrine, then, be better understood as a conceptual vehicle for courts to decline to recognize asserted rights that they consider should more properly be created by Congress? But where to draw the line? Are the considerations that underlie standing doctrine the same as those which govern the decision whether to permit a party to intervene? If not, should they be?

The attempt is persistently made to define "standing" as a requirement independent of the particular combination of government action and impact involved in a specific controversy. See Sierra Club v. Morton, 405 U.S. 727, 92 S.Ct. 1361, 31 L.Ed.2d 636 (1972). Does that necessarily involve trying to define the role of the courts in American government under the rubric of a procedural rule? In any event, procedurally it is difficult to administer the standing rule, which requires an inquiry at the threshold of the litigation, under a pleading system that allows vacuous statements of claim. See Roberts, Fact Pleading, Notice Pleading, and Standing, 65 Corn.L.Rev. 390 (1980). See also Fletcher, The Structure of Standing, 98 Yale L.J. 221 (1988); Note, "More Than an Intuition, Less Than a Theory": Toward a Coherent Doctrine of Standing, 86 Colum.L.Rev. 564 (1986).

VALLEY FORGE CHRISTIAN COLLEGE v. AMERICANS UNITED FOR SEPARATION OF CHURCH AND STATE, INC.

Supreme Court of the United States, 1982.
454 U.S. 464, 102 S.Ct. 752, 70 L.Ed.2d 700.*

JUSTICE REHNQUIST delivered the opinion of the Court.

I

Article IV, § 3, cl. 2, of the Constitution vests Congress with the "Power to dispose of and make all needful Rules and Regulations respecting the . . . Property belonging to the United States." Shortly after the termination of hostilities in the Second World War, Congress enacted the Federal Property and Administrative Services Act of 1949, 63 Stat. 377, as amended, 40 U.S.C. § 471 et seq. (1976 ed. and Supp. III). * * * Property that has outlived its usefulness to the Federal Government is declared "surplus" and may be transferred to private or other public entities. * * *

* * *

The property which spawned this litigation was acquired by the Department of the Army in 1942, as part of a larger tract of approximately 181 acres of land northwest of Philadelphia. The Army built on that land the Valley Forge General Hospital, and for 30 years thereafter, that hospital provided medical care for members of the Armed Forces. In April 1973, as part of a plan to reduce the number of military installations in the United States, the Secretary of Defense proposed to close the hospital, and the General Services Administration declared it to be "surplus property."

The Department of Health, Education, and Welfare (HEW) eventually assumed responsibility for disposing of portions of the property, and in August 1976, it conveyed a 77–acre tract to petitioner, the Valley Forge Christian College. The appraised value of the property at the time of conveyance was $577,500. This appraised value was discounted, however, by the Secretary's computation of a 100% public

---

* Some of the Court's footnotes are omitted.

benefit allowance, which permitted petitioner to acquire the property without making any financial payment for it. The deed from HEW conveyed the land in fee simple with certain conditions subsequent, which required petitioner to use the property for 30 years solely for the educational purposes described in petitioner's application. In that description, petitioner stated its intention to conduct "a program of education . . . meeting the accrediting standards of the State of Pennsylvania, The American Association of Bible Colleges, the Division of Education of the General Council of the Assemblies of God and the Veterans Administration."

Petitioner is a nonprofit educational institution operating under the supervision of a religious order known as the Assemblies of God. * * *

In September 1976, respondents Americans United for Separation of Church and State, Inc. (Americans United), and four of its employees, learned of the conveyance through a news release. Two months later, they brought suit in the United States District Court for the District of Columbia, later transferred to the Eastern District of Pennsylvania, to challenge the conveyance on the ground that it violated the Establishment Clause of the First Amendment.[8] * * * In its amended complaint, Americans United described itself as a nonprofit organization composed of 90,000 "taxpayer members." The complaint asserted that each member "would be deprived of the fair and constitutional use of his (her) tax dollar for constitutional purposes in violation of his (her) rights under the First Amendment of the United States Constitution." * * * Respondents sought a declaration that the conveyance was null and void, and an order compelling petitioner to transfer the property back to the United States. * * *

On petitioner's motion, the District Court granted summary judgment and dismissed the complaint. * * * The court found that respondents lacked standing to sue as taxpayers under Flast v. Cohen, 392 U.S. 83, 88 S.Ct. 1942, 20 L.Ed.2d 947 (1968), and had "failed to allege that they have suffered any actual or concrete injury beyond a generalized grievance common to all taxpayers." * * *

Respondents appealed to the Court of Appeals for the Third Circuit, which reversed the judgment of the District Court by a divided vote. * * * [W]e granted certiorari, 450 U.S. 909, 101 S.Ct. 1345, 67 L.Ed.2d 332 (1981), and we now reverse.

II

Article III of the Constitution limits the "judicial power" of the United States to the resolution of "cases" and "controversies." The constitutional power of federal courts cannot be defined, and indeed has no substance, without reference to the necessity "to adjudge the legal rights of litigants in actual controversies." Liverpool S.S. Co. v. Com-

---

8. "Congress shall make no law respecting an establishment of religion. . . ."

missioners of Emigration, 113 U.S. 33, 39, 5 S.Ct. 352, 355, 28 L.Ed. 899 (1885). The requirements of Art. III are not satisfied merely because a party requests a court of the United States to declare its legal rights, and has couched that request for forms of relief historically associated with courts of law in terms that have a familiar ring to those trained in the legal process. The judicial power of the United States defined by Art. III is not an unconditioned authority to determine the constitutionality of legislative or executive acts. The power to declare the rights of individuals and to measure the authority of governments, this Court said 90 years ago, "is legitimate only in the last resort, and as a necessity in the determination of real, earnest and vital controversy." Chicago & Grand Trunk R. Co. v. Wellman, 143 U.S. 339, 345, 12 S.Ct. 400, 402, 36 L.Ed. 176 (1892). Otherwise, the power "is not judicial . . . in the sense in which judicial power is granted by the Constitution to the courts of the United States." United States v. Ferreira, 13 How. 40, 48, 14 L.Ed. 42 (1852).

As an incident to the elaboration of this bedrock requirement, this Court has always required that a litigant have "standing" to challenge the action sought to be adjudicated in the lawsuit. The term "standing" subsumes a blend of constitutional requirements and prudential considerations, see Warth v. Seldin, 422 U.S. 490, 498, 95 S.Ct. 2197, 2204, 45 L.Ed.2d 343 (1975), and it has not always been clear in the opinions of this Court whether particular features of the "standing" requirement have been required by Art. III *ex proprio vigore,* or whether they are requirements that the Court itself has erected and which were not compelled by the language of the Constitution. See Flast v. Cohen, supra, at 97, 88 S.Ct., at 1951.

A recent line of decisions, however, has resolved that ambiguity, at least to the following extent: at an irreducible minimum, Art. III requires the party who invokes the court's authority to "show that he personally has suffered some actual or threatened injury as a result of the putatively illegal conduct of the defendant," Gladstone, Realtors v. Village of Bellwood, 441 U.S. 91, 99, 99 S.Ct. 1601, 1608, 60 L.Ed.2d 66 (1979), and that the injury "fairly can be traced to the challenged action" and "is likely to be redressed by a favorable decision," Simon v. Eastern Kentucky Welfare Rights Org., 426 U.S. 26, 38, 41, 96 S.Ct. 1917, 1924, 1925, 48 L.Ed.2d 450 (1976).[9] In this manner does Art. III limit the federal judicial power "to those disputes which confine federal courts to a role consistent with a system of separated powers and which

9. See Watt v. Energy Action Educational Foundation, 454 U.S. 151, 161, 102 S.Ct. 205, 212, 70 L.Ed.2d 309 (1981); Duke Power Co. v. Carolina Environmental Study Group, Inc., 438 U.S. 59, 72, 98 S.Ct. 2620, 2629, 57 L.Ed.2d 595 (1978); Arlington Heights v. Metropolitan Housing Dev. Corp., 429 U.S. 252, 261, 262, 97 S.Ct. 555, 561, 50 L.Ed.2d 450 (1977); Warth v. Seldin, 422 U.S. 490, 499, 95 S.Ct. 2197, 2205, 45 L.Ed.2d 343 (1975); Schlesinger v. Reservists Committee to Stop the War, 418 U.S. 208, 218, 220–221, 94 S.Ct. 2925, 2930, 2931–2932, 41 L.Ed.2d 706 (1974); United States v. Richardson, 418 U.S. 166, 179–180, 94 S.Ct. 2940, 2947–2948, 41 L.Ed.2d 678 (1974); O'Shea v. Littleton, 414 U.S. 488, 493, 94 S.Ct. 669, 674, 38 L.Ed.2d 674 (1974); Linda R.S. v. Richard D., 410 U.S. 614, 617–618, 93 S.Ct. 1146, 1148–1149, 35 L.Ed.2d 536 (1973).

are traditionally thought to be capable of resolution through the judicial process." Flast v. Cohen, 392 U.S., at 97, 88 S.Ct., at 1951.

The requirement of "actual injury redressable by the court," *Simon*, supra, 426 U.S., at 39, 96 S.Ct., at 1924, serves several of the "implicit policies embodied in Article III," *Flast*, supra, 392 U.S., at 96, 88 S.Ct., at 1950. It tends to assure that the legal questions presented to the court will be resolved, not in the rarified atmosphere of a debating society, but in a concrete factual context conducive to a realistic appreciation of the consequences of judicial action. The "standing" requirement serves other purposes. Because it assures an actual factual setting in which the litigant asserts a claim of injury in fact, a court may decide the case with some confidence that its decision will not pave the way for lawsuits which have some, but not all, of the facts of the case actually decided by the court.

The Art. III aspect of standing also reflects a due regard for the autonomy of those persons likely to be most directly affected by a judicial order. The federal courts have abjured appeals to their authority which would convert the judicial process into "no more than a vehicle for the vindication of the value interests of concerned bystanders." United States v. SCRAP, 412 U.S. 669, 687, 93 S.Ct. 2405, 2416, 37 L.Ed.2d 254 (1973). Were the federal courts merely publicly funded forums for the ventilation of public grievances or the refinement of jurisprudential understanding, the concept of "standing" would be quite unnecessary. But the "cases and controversies" language of Art. III forecloses the conversion of courts of the United States into judicial versions of college debating forums. As we said in Sierra Club v. Morton, 405 U.S. 727, 740, 92 S.Ct. 1361, 1368, 31 L.Ed.2d 636 (1972):

> "The requirement that a party seeking review must allege facts showing that he is himself adversely affected . . . does serve as at least a rough attempt to put the decision as to whether review will be sought in the hands of those who have a direct stake in the outcome."

The exercise of judicial power, which can so profoundly affect the lives, liberty, and property of those to whom it extends, is therefore restricted to litigants who can show "injury in fact" resulting from the action which they seek to have the court adjudicate.

The exercise of the judicial power also affects relationships between the coequal arms of the National Government. The effect is, of course, most vivid when a federal court declares unconstitutional an act of the Legislative or Executive Branch. While the exercise of that "ultimate and supreme function," Chicago & Grand Trunk R. Co. v. Wellman, supra at 345, 12 S.Ct., at 402, is a formidable means of vindicating individual rights, when employed unwisely or unnecessarily it is also the ultimate threat to the continued effectiveness of the federal courts in performing that role. While the propriety of such action by a federal court has been recognized since Marbury v. Madison, 1 Cranch 137, 2 L.Ed. 60 (1803), it has been recognized as a tool of last resort on the part of the federal judiciary throughout its nearly 200 years of existence:

"[R]epeated and essentially head-on confrontations between the life-tenured branch and the representative branches of government will not, in the long run, be beneficial to either. The public confidence essential to the former and the vitality critical to the latter may well erode if we do not exercise self-restraint in the utilization of our power to negative the actions of the other branches." United States v. Richardson, 418 U.S., at 188, 94 S.Ct., at 2952 (POWELL, J., concurring).

* * *

Beyond the constitutional requirements, the federal judiciary has also adhered to a set of prudential principles that bear on the question of standing. Thus, this Court has held that "the plaintiff generally must assert his own legal rights and interests, and cannot rest his claim to relief on the legal rights or interests of third parties." Warth v. Seldin, 422 U.S., at 499, 95 S.Ct., at 2205.[10] In addition, even when the plaintiff has alleged redressable injury sufficient to meet the requirements of Art. III, the Court has refrained from adjudicating "abstract questions of wide public significance" which amount to "generalized grievances," pervasively shared and most appropriately addressed in the representative branches. Id., at 499–500, 95 S.Ct., at 2205–2206. Finally, the Court has required that the plaintiff's complaint fall within "the zone of interests to be protected or regulated by the statute or constitutional guarantee in question." Association of Data Processing Service Orgs. v. Camp, 397 U.S. 150, 153, 90 S.Ct. 827, 830, 25 L.Ed.2d 184 (1970).

Merely to articulate these principles is to demonstrate their close relationship to the policies reflected in the Art. III requirement of actual or threatened injury amenable to judicial remedy. But neither the counsels of prudence nor the policies implicit in the "case or controversy" requirement should be mistaken for the rigorous Art. III requirements themselves. Satisfaction of the former cannot substitute for a demonstration of " 'distinct and palpable injury' . . . that is likely to be redressed if the requested relief is granted." Gladstone, Realtors v. Village of Bellwood, 441 U.S., at 100, 99 S.Ct., at 1608 (quoting Warth v. Seldin, supra, 422 U.S., at 501, 95 S.Ct., at 2206). That requirement states a limitation on judicial power, not merely a factor to be balanced in the weighing of so-called "prudential" considerations.

* * *

10. See Gladstone, Realtors v. Village of Bellwood, 441 U.S. 91, 100, 99 S.Ct. 1601, 1608, 60 L.Ed.2d 66 (1979); Duke Power Co. v. Carolina Environmental Study Group, Inc., supra, at 80, 98 S.Ct., at 2634; Singleton v. Wulff, 428 U.S. 106, 113–114, 96 S.Ct. 2868, 49 L.Ed.2d 826 (1976).

III

The injury alleged by respondents in their amended complaint is the "depriv[ation] of the fair and constitutional use of [their] tax dollar." App. 10. As a result, our discussion must begin with Frothingham v. Mellon, 262 U.S. 447, 43 S.Ct. 597, 67 L.Ed. 1078 (1923) (decided with Massachusetts v. Mellon). In that action a taxpayer brought suit challenging the constitutionality of the Maternity Act of 1921, which provided federal funding to the States for the purpose of improving maternal and infant health. The injury she alleged consisted of the burden of taxation in support of an unconstitutional regime, which she characterized as a deprivation of property without due process. "Looking through forms of words to the substance of [the] complaint," the Court concluded that the only "injury" was the fact "that officials of the executive department of the government are executing and will execute an act of Congress asserted to be unconstitutional." Id., at 488, 43 S.Ct., at 601. Any tangible effect of the challenged statute on the plaintiff's tax burden was "remote, fluctuating and uncertain." Id., at 487, 43 S.Ct., at 601. In rejecting this as a cognizable injury sufficient to establish standing, the Court admonished:

> "The party who invokes the power [of judicial review] must be able to show not only that the statute is invalid but that he has sustained or is immediately in danger of sustaining some direct injury as the result of its enforcement, and not merely that he suffers in some indefinite way in common with people generally. . . . Here the parties plaintiff have no such case." Id., at 488, 43 S.Ct., at 601.

Following the decision in *Frothingham*, the Court confirmed that the expenditure of public funds in an allegedly unconstitutional manner is not an injury sufficient to confer standing, even though the plaintiff contributes to the public coffers as a taxpayer. * * *

The Court again visited the problem of taxpayer standing in Flast v. Cohen, 392 U.S. 83, 88 S.Ct. 1942, 20 L.Ed.2d 947 (1968). The taxpayer plaintiffs in *Flast* sought to enjoin the expenditure of federal funds under the Elementary and Secondary Education Act of 1965, which they alleged were being used to support religious schools in violation of the Establishment Clause. The Court developed a two-part test to determine whether the plaintiffs had standing to sue. First, because a taxpayer alleges injury only by virtue of his liability for taxes, the Court held that "a taxpayer will be a proper party to allege the unconstitutionality only of exercises of congressional power under the taxing and spending clause of Art. I, § 8, of the Constitution." Id., at 102, 88 S.Ct., at 1954. Second, the Court required the taxpayer to "show that the challenged enactment exceeds specific constitutional limitations upon the exercise of the taxing and spending power and not simply that the enactment is generally beyond the powers delegated to Congress by Art. I, § 8." Id., at 102–103, 88 S.Ct., at 1954.

The plaintiffs in *Flast* satisfied this test because "[t]heir constitutional challenge [was] made to an exercise by Congress of its power under Art. I, § 8, to spend for the general welfare," id., at 103, 88 S.Ct., at 1954, and because the Establishment Clause, on which plaintiffs' complaint rested, "operates as a specific constitutional limitation upon the exercise by Congress of the taxing and spending power conferred by Art. I, § 8," id., at 104, 88 S.Ct., at 1954. The Court distinguished Frothingham v. Mellon, supra, on the ground that Mrs. Frothingham had relied, not on a specific limitation on the power to tax and spend, but on a more general claim based on the Due Process Clause. 392 U.S., at 105, 88 S.Ct., at 1955. Thus, the Court reaffirmed that the "case or controversy" aspect of standing is unsatisfied "where a taxpayer seeks to employ a federal court as a forum in which to air his generalized grievances about the conduct of government or the allocation of power in the Federal System." Id., at 106, 88 S.Ct., at 1956.

Unlike the plaintiffs in *Flast*, respondents fail the first prong of the test for taxpayer standing. Their claim is deficient in two respects. First, the source of their complaint is not a congressional action, but a decision by HEW to transfer a parcel of federal property.[15] *Flast* limited taxpayer standing to challenges directed "only [at] exercises of congressional power." Id., at 102, 88 S.Ct., at 1954. See Schlesinger v. Reservists Committee to Stop the War, 418 U.S., at 228, 94 S.Ct., at 2935 (denying standing because the taxpayer plaintiffs "did not challenge an enactment under Art. I, § 8, but rather the action of the Executive Branch").

Second, and perhaps redundantly, the property transfer about which respondents complain was not an exercise of authority conferred by the Taxing and Spending Clause of Art. I, § 8. The authorizing legislation, the Federal Property and Administrative Services Act of 1949, was an evident exercise of Congress' power under the Property Clause, Art. IV, § 3, cl. 2. Respondents do not dispute this conclusion, see Brief for Respondents Americans United et al. 10, and it is decisive of any claim of taxpayer standing under the *Flast* precedent.

Any doubt that once might have existed concerning the rigor with which the *Flast* exception to the *Frothingham* principle ought to be applied should have been erased by this Court's recent decisions in United States v. Richardson, 418 U.S. 166, 94 S.Ct. 2940, 41 L.Ed.2d 678 (1974), and Schlesinger v. Reservists Committee to Stop the War, supra. In *Richardson*, the question was whether the plaintiff had standing as a federal taxpayer to argue that legislation which permitted the Central Intelligence Agency to withhold from the public detailed information about its expenditures violated the Accounts Clause of the Constitu-

---

15. Respondents do not challenge the constitutionality of the Federal Property and Administrative Services Act itself, but rather a particular Executive Branch action arguably authorized by the Act.

tion.[18] We rejected plaintiff's claim of standing because "his challenge [was] not addressed to the taxing or spending power, but to the statutes regulating the CIA." 418 U.S., at 175, 94 S.Ct., at 2945. The "mere recital" of those claims "demonstrate[d] how far he [fell] short of the standing criteria of *Flast* and how neatly he [fell] within the *Frothingham* holding left undisturbed." Id., at 174–175, 94 S.Ct., at 2945.

The claim in *Schlesinger* was marred by the same deficiency. Plaintiffs in that case argued that the Incompatibility Clause of Art. I [19] prevented certain Members of Congress from holding commissions in the Armed Forces Reserve. We summarily rejected their assertion of standing as taxpayers because they "did not challenge an enactment under Art. I, § 8, but rather the action of the Executive Branch in permitting Members of Congress to maintain their Reserve status." 418 U.S., at 228, 94 S.Ct., at 2935 (footnote omitted).

* * *

IV

* * *

The complaint in this case shares a common deficiency with those in *Schlesinger* and *Richardson*. Although respondents claim that the Constitution has been violated, they claim nothing else. They fail to identify any personal injury suffered by them *as a consequence* of the alleged constitutional error, other than the psychological consequence presumably produced by observation of conduct with which one disagrees. That is not an injury sufficient to confer standing under Art. III, even though the disagreement is phrased in constitutional terms. It is evident that respondents are firmly committed to the constitutional principle of separation of church and State, but standing is not measured by the intensity of the litigant's interest or the fervor of his advocacy. "[T]hat concrete adverseness which sharpens the presentation of issues," Baker v. Carr, 369 U.S., at 204, 82 S.Ct., at 703, is the anticipated consequence of proceedings commenced by one who has been injured in fact; it is not a permissible substitute for the showing of injury itself.[21]

In reaching this conclusion, we do not retreat from our earlier holdings that standing may be predicated on noneconomic injury. See, e.g., United States v. SCRAP, 412 U.S., at 686–688, 93 S.Ct., at 2415–

---

18. U.S. Const., Art. I, § 9, cl. 7 ("[A]nd a regular Statement and Account of the Receipts and Expenditures of all public Money shall be published from time to time").

19. U.S. Const., Art. I, § 6, cl. 2 ("[N]o Person holding any Office under the United States, shall be a Member of either House during his Continuance in Office").

21. In *Schlesinger*, we rejected the argument that standing should be recognized because "the adverse parties sharply conflicted in their interests and views and

were supported by able briefs and arguments." 418 U.S., at 225, 94 S.Ct., at 2934:

"We have no doubt about the sincerity of respondents' stated objectives and the depth of their commitment to them. But the essence of standing 'is not a question of motivation but of possession of the requisite . . . interest that is, or is threatened to be, injured by the unconstitutional conduct.' Doremus v. Board of Education, 342 U.S. 429, 435 [72 S.Ct. 394, 397, 96 L.Ed. 475] (1952)." Id., at 225–226, 94 S.Ct., at 2934.

2416; Association of Data Processing Service Orgs. v. Camp, 397 U.S., at 153–154, 90 S.Ct., at 829–830. We simply cannot see that respondents have alleged an *injury* of *any* kind, economic or otherwise, sufficient to confer standing.[22] Respondents complain of a transfer of property located in Chester County, Pa. The named plaintiffs reside in Maryland and Virginia;[23] their organizational headquarters are located in Washington, D.C. They learned of the transfer through a news release. Their claim that the Government has violated the Establishment Clause does not provide a special license to roam the country in search of governmental wrongdoing and to reveal their discoveries in federal court.[24] The federal courts were simply not constituted as ombudsmen of the general welfare.

22. Respondents rely on our statement in Association of Data Processing Service Orgs. v. Camp, 397 U.S., at 154, 90 S.Ct., at 830, that "[a] person or family may have a spiritual stake in First Amendment values sufficient to give standing to raise issues concerning the Establishment Clause and the Free Exercise Clause. Abington School District v. Schempp, 374 U.S. 203 [83 S.Ct. 1560, 10 L.Ed.2d 844] [1963]." Respondents apparently construe this language to mean that any person asserting an Establishment Clause violation possesses a "spiritual stake" sufficient to confer standing. The language will not bear that weight. First, the language cannot be read apart from the context of its accompanying reference to Abington School District v. Schempp, 374 U.S. 203, 83 S.Ct. 1560, 10 L.Ed.2d 844 (1963). In *Schempp,* the Court invalidated laws that required Bible reading in the public schools. Plaintiffs were children who attended the schools in question, and their parents. The Court noted:

"It goes without saying that the laws and practices involved here can be challenged only by persons having standing to complain. . . . The parties here are school children and their parents, who are directly affected by the laws and practices against which their complaints are directed. These interests surely suffice to give the parties standing to complain." Id., at 224, n. 9, 83 S.Ct., at 1572, n. 9.

The Court also drew a comparison with Doremus v. Board of Education, 342 U.S. 429, 72 S.Ct. 394, 96 L.Ed. 475 (1952), in which the identical substantive issues were raised, but in which the appeal was "dismissed upon the graduation of the school child involved and because of the appellants' failure to establish standing as taxpayers." 374 U.S., at 224, n. 9, 83 S.Ct., at 1573, n. 9. The Court's discussion of the standing issue is not extensive, but it is sufficient to show the error in respondents' broad reading of the phrase "spiritual stake." The plaintiffs in *Schempp* had standing, not because their complaint rested on the Establishment Clause—for as *Doremus* demonstrated, that is insufficient—but because impressionable schoolchildren were subjected to unwelcome religious exercises or were forced to assume special burdens to avoid them. Respondents have alleged no comparable injury.

23. Respondent Americans United claims that it has certain unidentified members who reside in Pennsylvania. It does not explain, however, how this fact establishes a cognizable injury where none existed before. Respondent is still obligated to allege facts sufficient to establish that one or more of its members has suffered, or is threatened with, an injury other than their belief that the transfer violated the Constitution.

24. Respondents also claim standing by reference to the Administrative Procedure Act, 5 U.S.C. § 702, which authorizes judicial review at the instance of any person who has been "adversely affected or aggrieved by agency action within the meaning of a relevant statute." Neither the Administrative Procedure Act, nor any other congressional enactment, can lower the threshold requirements of standing under Art. III. See, e.g., Gladstone, Realtors v. Village of Bellwood, 441 U.S., at 100, 99 S.Ct., at 1608; Warth v. Seldin, 422 U.S., at 501, 95 S.Ct., at 2206. Respondents do not allege that the Act creates a legal right, "the invasion of which creates standing," Linda R.S. v. Richard D., 410 U.S., at 617, n. 3, 93 S.Ct., at 1148, n. 3, and there is no other basis for arguing that its existence alters the rules of standing otherwise applicable to this case.

V

The Court of Appeals in this case ignored unambiguous limitations on taxpayer and citizen standing. It appears to have done so out of the conviction that enforcement of the Establishment Clause demands special exceptions from the requirement that a plaintiff allege " 'distinct and palpable injury to himself,' . . . that is likely to be redressed if the requested relief is granted." Gladstone, Realtors v. Village of Bellwood, 441 U.S., at 100, 99 S.Ct., at 1608 (quoting Warth v. Seldin, 422 U.S., at 501, 95 S.Ct., at 2206). * * *

* * * Respondents' claim of standing implicitly rests on the presumption that violations of the Establishment Clause typically will not cause injury sufficient to confer standing under the "traditional" view of Art. III. But "[t]he assumption that if respondents have no standing to sue, no one would have standing, is not a reason to find standing." Schlesinger v. Reservists Committee to Stop the War, 418 U.S., at 227, 94 S.Ct., at 2935. This view would convert standing into a requirement that must be observed only when satisfied. * * *

JUSTICE BRENNAN, with whom JUSTICE MARSHALL and JUSTICE BLACKMUN join, dissenting.

A plaintiff's standing is a jurisdictional matter for Art. III courts, and thus a "threshold question" to be resolved before turning attention to more "substantive" issues. See Linda R.S. v. Richard D., 410 U.S. 614, 616, 93 S.Ct. 1146, 1148, 35 L.Ed.2d 536 (1973). But in consequence there is an impulse to decide difficult questions of substantive law obliquely in the course of opinions purporting to do nothing more than determine what the Court labels "standing" * * *.

The opinion of the Court is a stark example of this unfortunate trend of resolving cases at the "threshold" while obscuring the nature of the underlying rights and interests at stake. The Court waxes eloquent on the blend of prudential and constitutional considerations that combine to create our misguided "standing" jurisprudence. *But not one word is said about the Establishment Clause right that the plaintiff seeks to enforce.* * * *

* * *

Frothingham's reasoning remains obscure. The principal interpretive difficulty lies in the manner in which *Frothingham* chose to blend the language of policy with seemingly absolute statements about jurisdiction. For example, the Court commented with significance on the sheer number of taxpayers who might have raised a claim similar to that of Mrs. Frothingham. Id., at 487, 43 S.Ct., at 601. Yet it can hardly be argued that the Constitution bars from federal court a plaintiff who has suffered injury merely because others are similarly aggrieved. "[S]tanding is not to be denied simply because many people suffer the same injury." United States v. SCRAP, 412 U.S. 669, 687, 93 S.Ct. 2405, 2416, 37 L.Ed.2d 254 (1973). And it is equally clear that the Constitution draws no distinction between injuries that are large, and those that are comparatively small. The line between more dollars and less is no valid constitutional measure. Cf. Everson v. Board of Education, 330 U.S. 1, 48–49, 67 S.Ct. 504, 527, 91 L.Ed. 711 (1947) (Rutledge, J., dissenting). The only distinction that a Constitution guaranteeing justice to all can recognize is one between some injury and none at all.

Frothingham also stressed the indirectness of the taxpayer's injury. But, *as a matter of Art. III standing,* if the causal relationship is sufficiently certain, the length of the causal chain is irrelevant. See Warth v. Seldin, 422 U.S., at 505, 95 S.Ct., at 2208. The financial stake of a federal taxpayer in the outcome of a lawsuit challenging an allegedly unlawful federal expenditure is not qualitatively different from that of a state or a municipal taxpayer attacking a local expenditure. More importantly, the injury suffered by a taxpayer is not dependent on the extent of his tax payment. The concept of taxpayer injury necessarily recognizes the continuing stake of the taxpayer in the disposition of the Treasury to which he has contributed his taxes, and his right to have those funds put to lawful uses. Until *Frothingham* there was nothing in our precedents to indicate that this concept, so comfortably applied to municipal taxpayers, was inconsistent with the framework of rights and remedies established by the Federal Constitution.

The explanation for the limit on federal taxpayer "standing" imposed by *Frothingham* must be sought in more substantive realms. Justice Harlan, dissenting in *Flast,* came close to identifying what I consider the unstated premise of the *Frothingham* rule:

> "[The] taxpayer's complaint can consist only of an allegation that public funds have been, or shortly will be, expended for purposes inconsistent with the Constitution. The taxpayer cannot ask the return of any portion of his previous tax payments, cannot prevent the collection of any existing tax debt, and cannot demand an adjudication of the propriety of any particular level of taxation. His tax payments are received for the general purposes of the United States, and are, upon proper receipt, lost in the general revenues." 392 U.S., at 128, 88 S.Ct., at 1967.

* * *

In 1947, nine Justices of this Court recognized that the Establishment Clause does impose a very definite restriction on the power to tax. The Court held in Everson v. Board of Education, 330 U.S., at 15, 67 S.Ct., at 511, that the " 'establishment of religion' clause of the First Amendment means at least this:"

> "No tax in any amount, large or small, can be levied to support any religious activities or institutions, whatever they may be called, or whatever form they may adopt, to teach or practice religion." Id., at 16, 67 S.Ct., at 511.

* * *

Many of the early settlers of this Nation came here to escape the tyranny of laws that compelled the support of government-sponsored churches and that inflicted punishments for the failure to pay establishment taxes and tithes. Id., at 8–9, 67 S.Ct., at 507–508. But the inhabitants of the various Colonies soon displayed a capacity to recreate the oppressive practices of the countries that they had fled. Once again persons of minority faiths were persecuted, and again such persons were subjected—this time by the colonial governments—to tithes and taxes for support of religion. Id., at 10, and n. 8, 67 S.Ct., at 509, and n. 8; Reynolds v. United States, 98 U.S. 145, 162–163, 25 L.Ed. 244 (1879).

> "These practices became so commonplace as to shock the freedom-loving colonials into a feeling of abhorrence. The imposition of taxes to pay ministers' salaries and to build and maintain churches and church property aroused their indignation. It was these feelings which found expression in the First Amendment." *Everson,* supra, at 11, 67 S.Ct., at 509 (footnotes omitted).

In 1784–1785, before the adoption of the Constitution, the continuing conflict between those who saw state aid to religion as but the natural expression of "commonly shared" religious sentiments, and those who saw such support as a threat to the very notion of civil government, culminated in the battle fought in the Virginia House of Delegates over "a bill establishing provision for teachers of the Christian religion." [13] *Reynolds,* supra, 98 U.S., at 162–163. The introduction of that bill in the state assembly prompted James Madison to prepare and circulate his famous "Memorial and Remonstrance Against Religious Assessments," imploring the legislature to establish and maintain the complete separation of religion and civil authority, and thus to reject the bill. In the end, the bill was rejected by the Virginia Legislature, and in its place Madison succeeded in securing the enactment of "A Bill for Establishing Religious Freedom," first introduced in the Virginia General Assembly seven years earlier by Thomas Jefferson. 98 U.S., at 163; *Everson,* 330 U.S., at 11–13, 67 S.Ct., at 509–510 (majority opinion); id., at 35–40, 67 S.Ct., at 521–523 (Rutledge, J., dissenting). Because Madison and Jefferson played such leading roles in the events leading to the adoption of the First Amendment, the *Everson* opinions did not hesitate to reproduce the partial text of their Virginia bill as a primary source for understanding the objectives, and protections, afforded by the more concise phrasing of the Establishment Clause. *Everson,* supra, at 12–13, 28, 67 S.Ct., at 509–510, 517; see *Reynolds,* supra, 98 U.S., at 163–164. Extracts from that bill also bear repeating in the present context. The preamble provided, in part:

> "[T]o compel a man to furnish contributions of money for the propagation of opinions which he disbelieves, is sinful and tyrannical; that even the forcing him to support this or that teacher of his own religious persuasion, is depriving him of the comfortable liberty of giving his contributions to the particular pastor, whose morals he would make his pattern." 12 Hening's Stat. 85.

---

13. The bill, and Madison's Remonstrance, are both appended to the dissenting opinion of Justice Rutledge in *Everson.* Id., at 63–74, 67 S.Ct., at 534–539.

Its operative language emphatically stated:

"That no man shall be compelled to frequent or support any religious worship, place, or ministry whatsoever, nor shall be enforced, restrained, molested, or burthened in his body or goods, nor shall otherwise suffer on account of his religious opinions or belief. . . ." Id., at 86.

* * *

It is clear * * * that one of the primary purposes of the Establishment Clause was to prevent the use of tax moneys for religious purposes. *The taxpayer was the direct and intended beneficiary of the prohibition on financial aid to religion.* This basic understanding of the meaning of the Establishment Clause explains why the Court in *Everson,* while rejecting appellant's claim on the merits, perceived the issue presented there as it did. The appellant sued "in his capacity as a district taxpayer," 330 U.S., at 3, 67 S.Ct., at 505, challenging the actions of the Board of Education in passing a resolution providing reimbursement to parents for the cost of transporting their children to parochial schools, and seeking to have that resolution "set aside." Appellant's Establishment Clause claim was precisely that the "statute . . . forced inhabitants to pay taxes to help support and maintain" church schools. Id., at 5, 67 S.Ct., at 506. * * *

* * *

It may be that Congress can tax for *almost* any reason, or for no reason at all. There is, so far as I have been able to discern, but one constitutionally imposed limit on that authority. Congress cannot use tax money to support a church, or to encourage religion. That is "*the* forbidden exaction." Everson v. Board of Education, 330 U.S., at 45, 67 S.Ct., at 526 (Rutledge, J., dissenting) (emphasis added). See *Flast,* supra, 392 U.S., at 115–116, 88 S.Ct., at 1960 (Fortas, J., concurring). In absolute terms the history of the Establishment Clause of the First Amendment makes this clear. History also makes it clear that the federal taxpayer is a singularly "proper and appropriate party to invoke a federal court's jurisdiction" to challenge a federal bestowal of largesse as a violation of the Establishment Clause. Each, and indeed every, federal taxpayer suffers precisely the injury that the Establishment Clause guards against when the Federal Government directs that funds be taken from the pocketbooks of the citizenry and placed into the coffers of the ministry.

* * *

JUSTICE STEVENS, dissenting.*

* Justice Stevens' opinion is omitted.

FURTHER NOTE ON STANDING TO SUE

Simon v. Eastern Kentucky Welfare Rights Organization, 426 U.S. 26, 96 S.Ct. 1917, 48 L.Ed.2d 450 (1976): A welfare rights organization, suing for various indigents as a class, sought to compel revocation by the Government of the tax-exempt status of hospitals that refused to offer indigents treatment without charge. In holding that the action could not be maintained the Court referred to the question as one of standing and then said, 426 U.S. at 40–42:

"The complaint alleges specific occasions on which each of the individual respondents sought but was denied hospital services solely due to his indigency * * *. But injury at the hands of a hospital is insufficient by itself to establish a case or controversy in the context of this suit, for no hospital is a defendant. The only defendants are officials of the Department of the Treasury, and the only claims of illegal action * * * are charged to those officials. * * * In other words, the 'case or controversy' limitation * * * still requires that a federal court act only to redress injury that fairly can be traced to the challenged action of the defendant, and not injury that results from the independent action of some third party not before the court."

Duke Power Co. v. Carolina Environmental Study Group, Inc., 438 U.S. 59, 98 S.Ct. 2620, 57 L.Ed.2d 595 (1978): Property owners adjacent to a nuclear power plant sued for an adjudication of the constitutionality of an Act of Congress limiting liability of power companies in nuclear plant disasters. Their claim was that the limitation was an incentive to build the plant and a deprivation of their property because it left them partially remediless if a disaster were to occur. The Court said, 438 U.S. at 78–79, 98 S.Ct. at 2633, that it is not necessary, except in taxpayer suits, that the injuries claimed be

"directly related to the constitutional attack * * *. No cases have been cited outside the context of taxpayer suits where we have demanded this type of subject-matter nexus between the right asserted and the injury alleged * * *."

But consider Warth v. Seldin, 422 U.S. 490, 95 S.Ct. 2197, 45 L.Ed.2d 343 (1975): A non-profit organization, several construction contractors, and several low-income persons filed a class action alleging that the zoning ordinances of a New York town unconstitutionally prevented the construction of adequate low- and middle-income housing. The contractors claimed injury by denial of potential profits, and the low-income plaintiffs asserted injury in the form of higher housing costs and higher taxes. In upholding the denial of standing to all plaintiffs, the Court said, 422 U.S. at 499–500, 95 S.Ct. at 2205:

"First, the Court has held that when the asserted harm is a 'generalized grievance' shared in substantially equal measure by all or a large class of citizens, that harm alone normally does not warrant exercise of jurisdiction. * * * Second, even when the plaintiff has alleged injury sufficient to meet the 'case or controversy' requirement, this Court has held that the plaintiff generally must assert his own legal rights and interests, and cannot rest his claim to relief on the legal rights or interests of third parties. * * * Essentially, the standing question in such cases is whether the constitutional or statutory provision on which the claim rests properly can be understood as granting persons in the plaintiff's position a right to judicial relief."

Harman v. City and County of San Francisco, 7 Cal.3d 150, 101 Cal.Rptr. 880, 496 P.2d 1248 (1972): The city had a procedure whereby landowners could petition for the vacating of unused streets adjoining their property and then buy the land from the city. In administering the procedure, the city charged only 50% of the full market value of the land. A taxpayer sued to restrain the city from charging the reduced price. The plaintiff's standing was sustained, the court saying, 7 Cal.3d at 159:

> "The propriety of a private person's judicial challenge to legislative or executive acts depends upon the fitness of the person to raise an issue ('standing') and the amenability of the issue raised to judicial redress ('justiciability'). * * * A party enjoys standing to bring his complaint into court if his stake in the resolution of that complaint assumes the proportions necessary to ensure that he will vigorously present his case. * * * Plaintiff, as a municipal taxpayer seeking to avoid the waste of municipal assets, falls into the category of a type of claimant long recognized to possess a sufficiently intense interest in his claim to establish his 'standing' to enter the courtroom."

See also Hawaii v. Standard Oil Co. of California, noted infra p. 808.

Standing can be simply a matter of alleging the requisite injury and naming the right plaintiffs. Compare Sierra Club v. Morton, 405 U.S. 727, 92 S.Ct. 1361, 31 L.Ed.2d 636 (1972), where the complaint was dismissed because it did not allege injury to the plaintiff organization itself, with United States v. Students Challenging Regulatory Agency Procedures (SCRAP), 412 U.S. 669, 93 S.Ct. 2405, 37 L.Ed.2d 254 (1973), where the complaint was upheld because it included members of the organization as named plaintiffs.

For an imaginative and thoughtful discussion of the standing of non-humans to protect "themselves," see Stone, Should Trees Have Standing? Toward Legal Rights for Natural Objects, 45 So.Calif.L.Rev. 450 (1972); Stone, Should Trees Have Standing? Revisited: How Far Will Law and Morals Reach? A Pluralist Perspective, 59 So.Calif.L.Rev. 1 (1985). Stone's theory was embraced in Justice Douglas' dissent in Sierra Club v. Morton, 405 U.S. at 734–35, 92 S.Ct. at 1365–66.

On standing see also 13 Wright & Miller § 3531; Albert, Standing to Challenge Administrative Action, 83 Yale L.J. 425 (1974); Allen v. Wright, 468 U.S. 737, 104 S.Ct. 3315, 82 L.Ed.2d 556 (1984) (parents of black children lack standing to challenge standards adopted by Internal Revenue Service for determining tax-exempt status of private schools that have admissions policies with racially discriminatory effect). If the problem of standing involves (partly, if not exclusively) the question whether the courts should resolve the particular legal issue at stake, and if there are some legal questions the courts should not resolve, is it possible to frame any generalizations about standing?

4. NOMINAL PARTIES

VIRGINIA ELECTRIC & POWER CO. v. WESTINGHOUSE ELECTRIC CORP.

United States Court of Appeals for the Fourth Circuit, 1973.
485 F.2d 78.

CRAVEN, CIRCUIT JUDGE. Virginia Electric and Power Company (VEPCO) brought this action on April 16, 1969, on its own behalf and on behalf of its insurer and partial subrogee, Insurance Company of North America (INA), to recover damages resulting from the failure of one of VEPCO's power generating stations. The defendants are Westinghouse Electric Corporation, builder of the station, and Stone and Webster Engineering Corporation, the engineers. Jurisdiction was founded on diversity of citizenship under 28 U.S.C. § 1332.

The defendants moved to dismiss the action urging that INA, by virtue of the subrogation, was the real party in interest under Fed.R. Civ.P. 17 and must prosecute the action as plaintiff. Since INA is a Pennsylvania corporation, its joinder as party plaintiff would destroy diversity jurisdiction and require dismissal because defendant Westinghouse is also a Pennsylvania corporation. Alternatively, the defendants urged that INA was an indispensable person who could not be made a party (because to do so would destroy diversity jurisdiction) and that under Fed.R.Civ.P. 19(b) the action should be dismissed. The district court denied the motion to dismiss and certified, under 28 U.S. C.A. § 1292(b), that a controlling question of law was involved as to which there existed a substantial ground for difference of opinion and that an immediate appeal would materially advance the litigation. We granted an interlocutory appeal to determine whether the district court properly concluded VEPCO could pursue this action for the entire loss and that the action could continue without joinder of INA. We think so, and affirm.

I

On January 22, 1967, a failure occurred at VEPCO's Mount Storm Generating Station, resulting in alleged losses of approximately $2,200,000. There was in effect an insurance policy issued by INA securing VEPCO against the risk of additional operating costs due to physical damage or loss to facilities. The policy contained a $100,000 deductible clause. Pursuant to the policy, INA originally paid VEPCO $1,900,000.

VEPCO then brought this action on its own behalf for $200,000 (the $100,000 loss uninsured under the deductible provision of the insurance policy plus $100,000 alleged expediting expenses) and for $1,900,000 for its insurer, INA. VEPCO also instituted a separate action against INA for an alleged balance owing under the insurance policy of approximately $200,000. VEPCO and INA settled that action, and VEPCO received an additional $50,000 from INA, leaving VEPCO with an unreimbursed loss of $150,000. In consideration of the settlement, VEPCO and INA agreed that INA would furnish counsel and have exclusive control over the present action and that INA would prosecute VEPCO's claims for the remaining uninsured loss.[1] Additionally,

---

1. VEPCO executed a cooperation agreement which provided in part:

 Vepco also agrees that the conduct of the continuing action to recover against Westinghouse and/or S. & W. for such claims shall be under the exclusive direction and control of the Insurer. . . .

 (7) Vepco and I.N.A. further agree that counsel for I.N.A. shall represent its claims, if any, against Westinghouse

VEPCO executed a subrogation agreement whereby INA was subrogated to the rights of VEPCO against Westinghouse and Stone and Webster.[2]

The district court, construing the agreement of cooperation and the instrument of subrogation, found "that VEPCO has retained a pecuniary interest and that standing is retained by virtue of its intent to recover the uninsured loss." This finding is not contested on appeal. The district court then held that VEPCO as a real party in interest could proceed in the action to attempt to recover the full loss. The court concluded that INA was also a real party in interest and that the question of INA's joinder was to be determined under Rule 19. The district court found: (1) that nonjoinder would not prejudice the parties, (2) any danger of double claims against the defendants could be protected against by appropriate decrees;[3] (3) no other adequate form existed for the resolution of the dispute in view of the interstate character of the dispute and the problems involved in obtaining personal jurisdiction in a state court. The court determined that in equity and good conscience the action should proceed among the parties before it without joinder of INA.

II

About the best that can be said for Fed.R.Civ.P. 17[4] is that it conveys a certain amount of correct information about naming plaintiffs. C. Wright, Law of Federal Courts § 70, at 293–94 (2d ed. 1970). Originally intended to incorporate the more permissive practice of equity to permit persons having an equitable or beneficial interest to sue in their own names, it is now thought by some commentators to

and/or S. & W. for uninsured loss, claim for which is in the sum of $150,000.00, but it shall be under no obligation for costs and expenses incurred in the prosecution of such claims conjunctively with those to which I.N.A. is subrogated.

2. The subrogation instrument provided in relevant part:

. . . Vepco subrogates the Insurer to all of its remaining rights of recovery against Westinghouse Electric Corporation and/or Stone & Webster Engineering Corporation . . . for the losses and claims and damages resulting from an occurrence on January 22, 1967, at its Mount Storm Power Station, Mt. Storm, West Virginia. . . .

3. Counsel for INA has now represented to the court that INA is willing to execute an agreement binding it to any final judgment in this action. Brief for appellee at 22.

4. Fed.R.Civ.P. 17(a) provides:

(a) Real Party in Interest. Every action shall be prosecuted in the name of the real party in interest. An executor, administrator, guardian, bailee, trustee of an express trust, a party with whom or in whose name a contract has been made for the benefit of another, or a party authorized by statute may sue in his own name without joining with him the party for whose benefit the action is brought; and when a statute of the United States so provides, an action for the use or benefit of another shall be brought in the name of the United States. No action shall be dismissed on the ground that it is not prosecuted in the name of the real party in interest until a reasonable time has been allowed after objection for ratification of commencement of the action by, or joinder or substitution of, the real party in interest; and such ratification, joinder, or substitution shall have the same effect as if the action had been commenced in the name of the real party in interest.

serve only to confuse the already complex problems of determining whether diversity of citizenship exists. 6 C. Wright & A. Miller, Federal Practice & Procedure: Civil § 1541. Intended to expand the class of those who may sue to include persons having an equitable or beneficial interest, the rule is unfortunately susceptible to efforts to prevent prosecution of claims as illustrated by this appeal. Ingenious counsel are enabled to present yet another "decision point" resulting in extravagant expenditures of time and effort before ever reaching the merits. See J. Frank, American Law, The Case for Radical Reform 65 (1969).

"Rule 17(a) is a barnacle on the federal practice ship. It ought to be scraped away. . . . Rules 19, 17(b) and substantive rules as to stating a claim for relief are adequate without interjecting the meaningless, logically inconsistent commands of the real party in interest rule. . . ." Kennedy, Federal Rule 17(a): Will the Real Party in Interest Please Stand?, 51 Minn.L.Rev. 675, 724 (1967).

The meaning and object of the real party in interest principle embodied in Rule 17 is that the action must be brought by a person who possesses the right to enforce the claim and who has a significant interest in the litigation.[5] Whether a plaintiff is entitled to enforce the asserted right is determined according to the substantive law. In a diversity action such as this one, the governing substantive law is the law of the state.[6] While the question of in whose name the action must be prosecuted is procedural, and thus governed by federal law, its resolution depends on the underlying substantive law of the state.[7]

In the present case it appears that VEPCO has both a sufficient interest in the litigation and is entitled under the substantive law to recover for the entire loss resulting from the failure of its generating station. VEPCO retained a significant pecuniary interest in the litigation. Thus this is not a case where an insurer-subrogee has paid an *entire* loss suffered by the insured and is the only real party in interest who must sue in his own name. United States v. Aetna Casualty & Surety Co., 338 U.S. 366, 380–381, 70 S.Ct. 207, 94 L.Ed. 171 (1949).[8] In addition to having a sufficient interest in the litigation, VEPCO, as

5. 6 C. Wright & A. Miller, Federal Practice & Procedure: Civil § 1542, at 639, § 1543 at 643–44 (1971) [hereinafter cited as Wright & Miller]; 3A J. Moore, Federal Practice ¶ 17.02 at 53 (2d ed. 1970) [hereinafter cited as Moore].

6. United States v. 936.71 Acres of Land, 418 F.2d 551 (5th Cir. 1969); Hoeppner Constr. Co. v. United States ex rel. Mangum, 287 F.2d 108 (10th Cir. 1960); Moore, ¶ 17.07 at 224–25. See also Travelers Indem. Co. v. Westinghouse Elec. Corp., 429 F.2d 77 (5th Cir. 1970); Standard Accident Ins. Co. v. Lohman, 295 F.2d 261 (7th Cir. 1961).

7. Cf. Gas Serv. Co. v. Hunt, 183 F.2d 417 (10th Cir. 1950).

8. See also City Stores Co. v. Lerner Shops, 133 U.S.App.D.C. 311, 410 F.2d 1010 (1969). Where an insured has been fully recompensed but appears as a party, the insured is a nominal party only. The insured's citizenship is not considered for purposes of diversity of citizenship, and upon timely motion the insurer-subrogee must be substituted as the party plaintiff. Link Aviation, Inc. v. Downs, 117 U.S.App. D.C. 40, 325 F.2d 613 (1963). In the present case, the subrogation is only partial, and it is only the citizenship of the plaintiff, VEPCO, which is considered in determining diversity. C. Wright, Law of Federal Courts §§ 28–29 (2d ed. 1970).

subrogor, is entitled under the substantive law to bring suit for its entire loss.[9] VEPCO, being entitled to enforce the right, may bring this action even though INA will ultimately receive the major portion of any recovery.[10]

To allow VEPCO to maintain this action for the entire loss accords with the purposes of Rule 17. Under the common–law practice, a subrogee or assignee could enforce his rights only in the name of his subrogor or assignor. The original purpose of Rule 17 was to liberalize party rules, i.e., to allow an assignee or subrogee to enforce his rights in his own name.[11] The permissive function of Rule 17 has been accomplished, and Rule 17 now serves primarily a negative function. It is to enable a defendant to present defenses he has against the real party in interest, to protect the defendant against a subsequent action by the party actually entitled to relief, and to ensure that the judgment will have proper res judicata effect.[12] In view of its current purpose, to protect defendants against subsequent suits, Rule 17 will not bar a suit by a real party in interest which will have the effect of preventing a multiplicity of suits.[13]

Where there is partial subrogation, there are two real parties in interest under Rule 17. Either party may bring suit—the insurer-subrogee to the extent it has reimbursed the subrogor, or the subrogor for either the entire loss or only its unreimbursed loss. If either the subrogor or subrogee brings suit, joinder is often appropriate upon proper motion by the defendant.[14] But joinder is not appropriate, and certainly not required by Rule 17, for the purpose of destroying diversity jurisdiction and requiring dismissal. Even without joinder the partial subrogee is generally precluded from bringing a subsequent action against the defendants where a judgment has been rendered in a suit by the subrogor for the entire loss.[15] Multiplicity of suits, one by

9. Miller v. Tomlinson, 194 Va. 367, 73 S.E.2d 378 (1952); Glens Falls Ins. Co. v. Sherritt, 95 F.2d 823 (4th Cir. 1938); Carozza v. Boxley, 203 F. 673 (4th Cir. 1913). Va.Code Ann. § 38.1–31.2 (Supp.1970) provides that an insurer-subrogee may bring suit in its own name, but this is permissive and does not prevent the subrogor from suing for the entire loss.

10. Wright & Miller, § 1543, at 643–44. See Interstate Fire Ins. Co. v. Sayers, 468 F.2d 1361 (5th Cir. 1972); Jackson Mfg. Co. v. United States, 434 F.2d 1027 (5th Cir. 1970).

11. Notes of Advisory Committee on Rules, Fed.R.Civ.P. 17, 28 U.S.C.A. at 16.

12. Celanese Corp. v. John Clark Indus., Inc., 214 F.2d 551 (5th Cir. 1954). See generally United Fed'n of Postal Clerks, AFL–CIO v. Watson, 133 U.S.App.D.C. 176, 409 F.2d 462, 470–471 n. 34, cert. denied, 396 U.S. 902, 90 S.Ct. 212, 24 L.Ed.2d 178 (1969).

13. United Fed'n of Postal Clerks, AFL–CIO v. Watson, 133 U.S.App.D.C. 176, 409 F.2d 462, 470, cert. denied, 396 U.S. 902, 90 S.Ct. 212, 24 L.Ed.2d 178 (1969). It is urged that INA is already a party to the litigation by virtue of its being named a use plaintiff and because of the presence of its counsel. We think neither factor makes INA a party and that VEPCO may properly represent INA. See cases cited note 9 supra.

14. *Aetna,* 338 U.S. at 381–382, 70 S.Ct. 207; Kansas Elec. Power Co. v. Janis, 194 F.2d 942, 944 (10th Cir. 1952); National Garment Co. v. New York, C. & St. L. R.R., 173 F.2d 32 (8th Cir. 1949).

15. Joyner v. F & B Enterprises, Inc., 145 U.S.App.D.C. 262, 448 F.2d 1185 (1971). Under substantive law the partial subrogee may be collaterally estopped from bringing a subsequent action and any recovery by the subrogor is impressed with a trust in favor of the subrogee. See Braniff Airways, Inc. v. Falkingham, 20 F.R.D. 141

the subrogor for his loss and one by the subrogee for the reimbursed loss, is thus prevented as fully as if joinder were compelled.

In the present case INA will clearly be precluded from subjecting Westinghouse and Stone and Webster to further suits. Under the cooperation agreement between VEPCO and INA filed with the court, INA has full and exclusive control of the litigation. It is settled under the applicable substantive law that any judgment will have full res judicata effect as to INA in these circumstances.[16]

Thus we conclude that the district court properly allowed the suit to continue with VEPCO as the party plaintiff. "It would result in unnecessary hardship and confusion to hold that such a company [as INA], entitled to partial subrogation, . . . must go into a state court and try over again issues that [will be] settled in the federal court. There is nothing in modern practice which sanctions any such absurdity." Virginia Electric & Power Co. v. Carolina Peanut Co., 186 F.2d 816, 821 (4th Cir. 1951).

As noted, the modern function of Rule 17 is to prevent the defendant from being subjected to subsequent suits. In Provident Tradesmens Bank & Trust Co. v. Patterson, 390 U.S. 102, 88 S.Ct. 733, 19 L.Ed.2d 936 (1968), the Court stated that one of the primary considerations under Rule 19 in whether to allow a suit to continue where a party cannot be joined is the protection of a defendant from multiple litigation, or inconsistent relief. 390 U.S. at 10, 88 S.Ct. 733. In view of this overlap between Rule 17 and Rule 19, we think the emphasis in a case such as this should be on whether under Rule 19 the action should be allowed to continue without joinder of the absent party.[17] That an absent person who cannot be joined is a real party in interest does not conclude the matter—the court must determine whether, in equity and good conscience, the action should proceed without the person.[18]

III

It is clear that a partial subrogee is a person to be joined if feasible under Fed.R.Civ.P. 19(a).[19] United States v. Aetna Casualty & Surety

(D.Minn.1957). Also, as here, the subrogee may agree to be bound by the judgment. Urrutia Aviation Enterprises, Inc. v. B. B. Burson & Assoc., 406 F.2d 769 (5th Cir. 1969).

16. Patterson v. Saunders, 194 Va. 607, 74 S.E.2d 204, cert. denied, 345 U.S. 998, 73 S.Ct. 1132, 97 L.Ed. 1405 (1953).

17. See Gargis v. B. F. Goodrich Co., 386 F.2d 534 (3d Cir. 1967); Hoeppner Constr. Co. v. United States for use of Mangum, 287 F.2d 108 (10th Cir. 1960); Peoples Loan & Finance Corp. v. Lawson, 271 F.2d 529 (5th Cir. 1959), cert. denied, 362 U.S. 903, 80 S.Ct. 613, 4 L.Ed.2d 555 (1960); Celanese Corp. v. John Clark Indus., Inc.,

214 F.2d 551 (5th Cir. 1954); Potomac Elec. Power Co. for use of Royal Indem. Co. v. Babcock & Wilcox Co., 54 F.R.D. 486 (D.Md.1972); Maryland for use of Geils v. Baltimore Transit Co., 37 F.R.D. 34 (D.Md. 1965).

18. C. Wright, Law of Federal Courts § 70, at 296 (2d ed. 1970).

19. Fed.R.Civ.P. 19(a) provides:

(a) Persons to be Joined if Feasible. A person who is subject to service of process and whose joinder will not deprive the court of jurisdiction over the subject matter of the action shall be joined as a party in the action if (1) in his absence

Co., 338 U.S. 366, 381–382, 70 S.Ct. 207, 94 L.Ed. 171 (1949). However, here the partial subrogee, INA, cannot be joined without destroying diversity jurisdiction, and Rule 19 by its own terms exhibits concern that the courts not be deprived of jurisdiction by unnecessary joinder. Fed.R.Civ.P. 19(a). In such a case the court must consider the four factors enumerated in Rule 19(b) [20] to determine whether in equity and good conscience the action should proceed, or should be dismissed, the absent person being regarded as indispensable. "Whether a person is 'indispensable,' that is, whether a particular lawsuit must be dismissed in the absence of that person, can only be determined in the context of particular litigation." Provident Tradesmens Bank & Trust Co. v. Patterson, 390 U.S. 102, 118, 88 S.Ct. 733, 742, 19 L.Ed.2d 936 (1968).

A review of the four interests which must be considered by the district court in its discretion demonstrates that the court below properly allowed the action to continue without joinder of INA. First, it is difficult to see how a judgment in this action might be prejudicial to either INA or the parties before the court. INA has control of the litigation and the opportunity to fully litigate its derivative rights arising out of subrogation. The defendants have failed to show how they would be prejudiced on the merits by nonjoinder of INA. Second, if any prejudice were shown, it can be avoided by the shaping of relief. Third, it is clear that a judgment rendered in INA's absence will be fully adequate to protect both INA and the parties and the public interest in the termination of disputes on the merits. The defendants have not sought any affirmative relief against VEPCO and do not suggest they would seek affirmative relief against INA if it were joined. Also because of INA's control of the suit, it will be bound by any judgment in favor of the defendants.[21] Fourth, it is not clear that plaintiff would have an adequate remedy in the courts of either Virgin-

complete relief cannot be accorded among those already parties, or (2) he claims an interest relating to the subject of the action and is so situated that the disposition of the action in his absence may (i) as a practical matter impair or impede his ability to protect that interest or (ii) leave any of the persons already parties subject to a substantial risk of incurring double, multiple, or otherwise inconsistent obligations by reason of his claimed interest. If he has not been so joined, the court shall order that he be made a party. If he should join as a plaintiff but refuses to do so, he may be made a defendant, or, in a proper case, an involuntary plaintiff. If the joined party objects to venue and his joinder would render the venue of the action improper, he shall be dismissed from the action.

20. Fed.R.Civ.P. 19(b) provides:

(b) Determination by Court Whenever Joinder not Feasible. If a person as de-

scribed in subdivision (a)(1)–(2) hereof cannot be made a party, the court shall determine whether in equity and good conscience the action should proceed among the parties before it, or should be dismissed, the absent person being thus regarded as indispensable. The factors to be considered by the court include: first, to what extent a judgment rendered in the person's absence might be prejudicial to him or those already parties; second, the extent to which, by protective provisions in the judgment, by the shaping of relief, or other measures, the prejudice can be lessened or avoided; third, whether a judgment rendered in the person's absence will be adequate; fourth, whether the plaintiff will have an adequate remedy if the action is dismissed for nonjoinder.

21. Patterson v. Saunders, 194 Va. 607, 74 S.E.2d 204, cert. denied, 345 U.S. 998, 73 S.Ct. 1132, 97 L.Ed. 1405 (1953).

ia or another state against both Stone and Webster and Westinghouse.[22] INA, the partial subrogee, is thus clearly not an "indispensable" party to this litigation. See United States v. Aetna Casualty & Surety Co., 338 U.S. 366, 382 n. 19, 70 S.Ct. 207 (1949); Peoples Loan & Finance Corp. v. Lawson, 271 F.2d 529, 532 (5th Cir. 1959), cert. denied, 362 U.S. 903, 80 S.Ct. 613, 4 L.Ed.2d 555 (1960). The district court below correctly allowed the action to continue without joinder of INA.[23] Accordingly, for the reasons stated, the decision of the district court is

Affirmed.

NOTE ON THE REAL PARTY IN INTEREST RULE

1. Historical Background

The rule that an action must be brought "in the name of the real party in interest" originated in the Field Code, §§ 91, 92, 93. Apparently, the Field Code draftsmen were running together two ideas. One was that a person who had a protectable legal interest ought to be able himself to bring suit to protect that interest, without having to rely on someone else to do so. The other was that the plaintiff in an action ought to be identified by his own name and not a fictitious name. Both ideas responded to a now obsolete procedural peculiarity having to do with assigned claims. See Cook, The Alienability of Choses in Action, 29 Harv.L.Rev. 816 (1916); Atkinson, The Real Party in Interest Rule: A Plea for Its Abolition, 32 N.Y.U.L.Rev. 926 (1957); James & Hazard § 10.3.

The Field Code's aim to confirm the right of the assignee to sue was wholly unnecessary. Further, it led to confusion because the question inevitably arose whether the real party in interest rule also had application to situations (other than assignments) where there was doubt about whether a person had an interest he could sue to enforce. For example, the real party in interest rule was invoked in disputes over whether a third party beneficiary of a contract could sue, and whether a private citizen could sue to enforce a public nuisance. That is, the Code's attempt to deal with the right-to-sue problem in one context was argued to be an implied rejection of the right-to-sue in other contexts. The rule thus got interjected into substantive legal questions in the guise of some kind of general procedural principle. Compare the problem of standing to sue in this respect.

The Field Code's second aim—to eliminate fictitious denomination of parties—was laudable if relatively trivial. Compare N.Y.Rev.Stat.1828, Pt. 3, ch. v. § 6, which did the same job much more simply: "The use of fictitious names of plaintiffs or defendants and the names of any other than the real claimants and the real defendants * * * are hereby abolished." Even so, this objective was frustrated. In the 1850's the New York courts permitted use of fictitiously denominated suits in order to achieve a perfectly understandable procedural goal. At the time, "parties in interest" were not allowed to testify as witnesses, a restriction that was coming to be regarded as an anachronism. The courts got around the restriction by allowing a nominal assignment of the claim to be made, so that the assignee became a fictional plaintiff acting on

22. It further appears that commencement of suit in another court may now be barred by the statute of limitations. 7 C. Wright & A. Miller, Federal Practice & Procedure: Civil § 1608, at 80 (1972).

23. See Moore, ¶ 19.14[1]; 7 C. Wright & A. Miller, Federal Practice & Procedure: Civil § 1608 (1972).

behalf of the assignor (who, because the claim had been assigned, was nominally no longer the "party in interest" and therefore could testify). See Freeman v. Spalding, 12 N.Y. 373 (1855); Allen v. Smith, 16 N.Y. 415 (1857). Hence, so far as fictional designation of parties was concerned, it was back to square one.

2. Use of a Nominal Plaintiff

There are several variations of the problem posed in Virginia Electric & Power Co. v. Westinghouse Electric Corp. They begin with the fact that an insurer that pays a casualty loss is subrogated to the rights of the insured against the person who caused the loss. If the insurance company pays the loss, by virtue of subrogation it becomes owner of the claim and the proper person to sue for the loss. But this presents a suit by an insurance company against some "ordinary" person (herself usually also insured), and among other things that looks bad to a jury. The insurance companies hit upon the device of "lending" the money due under the policy to the insured, under an agreement whereby the insured permits suit to be brought in her name against the tortfeasor and also whereby the insured must repay the loan only out of the proceeds of that suit. The plaintiff insurer thus is disguised by its insured, while the defendant insurer is disguised by its insured. Is that fair enough? See generally Comment, The Loan Receipt and Insurers' Subrogation, 50 Tul.L. Rev. 115 (1975); Anno., 13 A.L.R.3d 42. Compare Anheuser-Busch, Inc. v. Starley, 28 Cal.2d 347, 170 P.2d 448 (1946), involving a somewhat different kind of a disguise, and Bank of the Orient v. Superior Court, 67 Cal.App.3d 588, 136 Cal.Rptr. 741 (1977), holding on facts much like *Virginia Electric* that the insurer was a necessary party plaintiff.

Assuming that it is appropriate to permit the disguise of the insurance company for purposes of jury trial, is that relevant to the problem in Virginia Electric Power v. Westinghouse? Bear in mind that if the power company and the insurance company were joint owners of the claim from the beginning—or had been joint owners of the power plant itself—they both would have had to join as plaintiffs and complete diversity would have been lacking.

In a few states there is no real party in interest rule, and no one seems to miss it. See Ill.C.C.P. § 2–403. See also Kennedy, Federal Rule 17(a): Will the Real Party in Interest Please Stand?, 51 Minn.L.Rev. 675 (1967).

3. Res Judicata Consequences

Sometimes the real party in interest rule is justified as a means of assuring that an obligor will not be sued twice on the same claim by different parties. The rule does not guarantee against this consequence and other means, such as the necessary party rule, provide adequate protection against it. Compare Restatement Second of Judgments § 37.

4. Suits "For the Use of"

In certain situations a government may sue as the nominal plaintiff "for the use of," or *ex relatione* (ex rel.), a private person. Suit is brought in the name of the state but on the information and at the instigation of an individual who has a private interest in the matter. For example, in United States ex rel. D'Agostino Excavators, Inc. v. Heyward–Robinson Co., supra p. 708, the injured subcontractor on a federal project had to sue in the name of the government because of the contractual arrangements involved. See 6 Wright & Miller § 1551.

5. FIDUCIARY PARTIES

a. FIDUCIARY CLAIMANTS

CZAPLICKI v. THE S.S. HOEGH SILVERCLOUD

Supreme Court of the United States, 1956.
351 U.S. 525, 76 S.Ct. 946, 100 L.Ed. 1387.*

Opinion of the Court by MR. JUSTICE HARLAN, announced by MR. JUSTICE BURTON.

Czaplicki was injured in 1945 while working as a longshoreman on the "SS Hoegh Silvercloud," a vessel owned by the Norwegian Shipping and Trade Mission and operated by the Kerr Steamship Company. The injury occurred when some steps, constructed by the Hamilton Marine Contracting Company, gave way, causing Czaplicki to fall about five feet. At the time, Czaplicki was employed by the Northern Dock Company, which was insured for purposes of the Longshoremen's and Harbor Workers' Compensation Act [1] by the Travelers Insurance Company. Travelers, which was also the insurer of the Hamilton Company, filed notice with the Compensation Commission that any compensation claim by Czaplicki would be controverted.[2] Three weeks after the accident, Czaplicki elected to accept compensation rather than proceed against any third parties, and, one day later, a formal compensation award was entered by a Deputy Commissioner. Payments under the award were made by Travelers.

In 1952, Czaplicki filed a libel against the vessel, her owners and operators, and the Hamilton Company, claiming damages for his injuries on grounds of unseaworthiness and negligence. After various proceedings in the District Court for the Southern District of New York, the libel was dismissed as to all respondents, on the ground that Czaplicki was not the proper party libelant, since his election to accept compensation under the award had operated, under §§ 33(b) and 33(i),[5] as an assignment to Northern and its insurer, Travelers, of his rights of action against third parties. The District Court also overruled Czaplicki's contention that the compensation award was invalid because of alleged procedural defects, and denied his motion to add

* Some of the Court's footnotes are omitted.

1. 44 Stat. 1424, as amended, 52 Stat. 1167, 33 U.S.C.A. § 901 et seq.

2. The only reason given for controverting the claim was: "Injured is undecided whether or not to sue the 3rd party and reserves the right to controvert for such other reasons as may later appear."

5. 33 U.S.C. § 933(b), 33 U.S.C.A. § 933(b): "Acceptance of such compensation under an award in a compensation

order filed by the deputy commissioner shall operate as an assignment to the employer of all right of the person entitled to compensation to recover damages against such third person."

33 U.S.C. § 933(i), 33 U.S.C.A. § 933(i): "Where the employer is insured and the insurance carrier has assumed the payment of the compensation, the insurance carrier shall be subrogated to all the rights of the employer under this section."

Travelers "as party libelant to sue in its behalf and as trustee for libelant," or simply to add Travelers as a party. The District Court found it unnecessary, in light of this disposition of the case, to consider the defense of laches, which had been interposed by each respondent. The Court of Appeals, affirming the District Court, held the compensation award valid and the libel barred by laches; although it indicated some doubt as to the correctness of the District Court's decision on Czaplicki's right to maintain the suit, it did not pass on that question. We granted certiorari, 350 U.S. 872, 76 S.Ct. 118, because of the importance of these questions in the administration of the Longshoremen's and Harbor Workers' Compensation Act.

*   *   *

Under § 33(b) of the Compensation Act, Czaplicki's acceptance of the compensation award had the effect of assigning his rights of action against third parties to his employer, Northern. Travelers, as Northern's insurer, was in turn subrogated to all Northern's rights by § 33(i). Travelers, therefore, was the proper party to sue on those rights of action.[12] Travelers was also the insurer of Hamilton, one of the third parties subject to suit. Hamilton had constructed the steps on which the accident occurred, and might be held liable if its negligence was the cause of Czaplicki's injuries; it might also be subject to a claim over by Kerr or the Norwegian Trade Mission if either of them should be held liable. Cf. Ryan Stevedoring Co. v. Pan-Atlantic S.S. Corp., 350 U.S. 124, 76 S.Ct. 232. The result is that Czaplicki's rights of action were held by the party most likely to suffer were the rights of action to be successfully enforced. In these circumstances, we cannot agree that Czaplicki is precluded by the assignment of his rights of action from enforcing those rights in an action brought by himself.

Although § 33(b) assigns to the employer "all right of the person entitled to compensation to recover damages" against third parties when there has been acceptance of compensation under an award, this does not mean that the assignee is entitled to retain all damages in the event of a recovery against a third party. Instead, § 33(e) specifically apportions any such recovery between the assignee and the employee whose right of action it was originally, giving to the former an amount

---

12. Aetna Life Ins. Co. v. Moses, 287 U.S. 530, 53 S.Ct. 231, 77 L.Ed. 477, was an action at law brought under this Act, which had been made applicable as a workmen's compensation law in the District of Columbia. It was held that the employer was the proper party to bring the action. Since that case was decided, § 33(i) has been added to the Compensation Act, providing that "the insurance carrier shall be subrogated to all the rights of the employer under this section." 52 Stat. 1168, 33 U.S.C. § 933(i), 33 U.S.C.A. § 933(i). As noted in the Moses case, 287 U.S. at page 542, 53 S.Ct. at page 233, note 3, it has long been the admiralty rule that the insurer subrogated to the rights of the insured can sue in his own name. See, e.g., Liverpool & Great Western Steam Co. v. Phenix Ins. Co., 129 U.S. 397, 462, 9 S.Ct. 469, 479, 32 L.Ed. 788; The Potomac, 105 U.S. 630, 634, 26 L.Ed. 1194. Travelers was, therefore, the proper party libelant had it chosen to sue in this case. Cf. United States v. Aetna Cas. & Surety Co., 338 U.S. 366, 380–381, 70 S.Ct. 207, 215, 94 L.Ed. 171. Doleman v. Levine, 295 U.S. 221, 55 S.Ct. 741, 79 L.Ed. 1402, again an action at law, is not in point, since in that case unlike the case at bar, there was no complete assignment of the employee's right of action.

equal to the expenses incurred in enforcing the right, expenses of medical care for the employee, and any amounts paid and payable as compensation, and to the latter any balance remaining. In a very real sense, therefore, the injured employee has an interest in his right of action even after it has been assigned. Normally, this interest will not be inconsistent with that of the assignee, for presumably the assignee will want to recoup the payments made to the employee. Since the assignee's right to recoup comes before the employee's interest, and because the assignee is likely to be in a better position to prosecute any claims against a third party, control over the right of action is given to the assignee, who can either institute proceedings for the recovery of damages against a third person, "or may compromise with such third person either without or after instituting such proceeding." § 33(d), 33 U.S.C. § 933(d), 33 U.S.C.A. § 933(d). In giving the assignee exclusive control over the right of action, however, we think that the statute presupposes that the assignee's interests will not be in conflict with those of the employee, and that through action of the assignee the employee will obtain his share of the proceeds of the right of action, if there is a recovery. Here, where there is such a conflict of interests, the inaction of the assignee operates to defeat the employee's interest in any possible recovery. Since an action by Travelers would, in effect, be an action against itself, Czaplicki is the only person with sufficient adverse interest to bring suit. In this circumstance, we think the statute should be construed to allow Czaplicki to enforce, in his own name, the rights of action that were his originally.

We need not go so far as to say that by giving the employee an interest in the proceeds of a third-party action the statute places the assignee in the position of a fiduciary, cf. United States Fidelity & Guaranty Co. v. United States, 2 Cir., 152 F.2d 46, 48; all we hold is that, given the conflict of interests and inaction by the assignee, the employee should not be relegated to any rights he may have against the assignee, but can maintain the third-party action himself. In so holding, we recognize that one Court of Appeals has held otherwise under this same statute, see Hunt v. Bank Line, 4 Cir., 35 F.2d 136, as have certain state courts under similar statutes, see Taylor v. New York Central R. Co., 294 N.Y. 397, 62 N.E.2d 777; cf. Whalen v. Athol Mfg. Co., 242 Mass. 547, 136 N.E. 600. We think, however, that allowing suit by the employee in these circumstances is the proper way to ensure him the rights given by the Compensation Act.

Travelers is, of course, a proper party to this suit, since any recovery must first go to reimburse it for amounts already paid out. If Travelers is subject to the court's jurisdiction it should therefore be made a party, pursuant to Czaplicki's motion, assuming that there has been proper service of process.

* * *

Reversed and remanded.

Mr. Justice Frankfurter, concurring.

The disposition of a case is of prime importance to the parties. How a result is reached concerns the rational development of law. I agree with the Court's disposition of this case, but I would dispose of the main issue—the nature of Czaplicki's interest that survives his acceptance of compensation under the Longshoremen's and Harbor Workers' Compensation Act, 44 Stat. 1424, as amended, 52 Stat. 1164, 33 U.S.C. § 901 et seq., 33 U.S.C.A. § 901 et seq.—on the basis of the analysis made in United States Fidelity & Guaranty Co. v. United States, 2 Cir., 152 F.2d 46, 48. The reasoning of that case seems to me to carry out the scheme of the legislation with appropriate consistency.

> "So far as concerns the tortfeasor's liability to the employee beyond the amount of workmen's compensation, no agreement between the tortfeasor and the employer can prejudice the employee, because although it is true that, by accepting compensation, the employee assigns his claim against the tortfeasor to the employer or insurer, the assignee holds it for the benefit of the employee, so far as it is not necessary for his own recoupment. The assignee is in effect a trustee, and, although it is true that the statute gives him power to compromise the whole claim, he must not, in doing so, entirely disregard the employee's interest." 152 F.2d 46, 48.

Although the suit was brought directly against the tortfeasor, the Court directs that Travelers, the subrogee insurer, should be made a party. Since I deem the proper theory on which Czaplicki may recover despite his compensation award to be Travelers' fiduciary responsibility, I would direct reconstruction of this proceeding so that it should be against Travelers, while the vessel would be retained as a party.

NOTE ON FIDUCIARY CLAIMANTS

1. Real Party in Interest

How should the court have dealt with an argument by defendant that plaintiff in *Czaplicki* was not the "real party in interest," if the argument had been made? Compare Landis v. First National Bank, 20 Cal.App.2d 198, 66 P.2d 730 (1937): One Flatt died leaving an estate including certain shares of stock. Grimes was executor of Flatt's estate and sold the stock through a straw man to the defendant bank, of which Grimes was president, the sale at a price far below the stock's worth. Plaintiffs were the legatees under Flatt's will and brought an action against the bank and Grimes for an accounting for the stock and its return to the estate. Defendants objected that the executor and not the estate beneficiary was the proper party to bring the suit, relying on C.C.P. 369. Held: For plaintiffs. "[T]he general rule is that beneficiaries may not prosecute actions for the recovery of property belonging to the estate, and that it is the duty of the executor or personal representative to do so. This rule has its exceptions. * * * '[T]he beneficiary may prosecute claims where the personal representative himself, by collusion with the debtor, or otherwise, obstructs the natural course which the law establishes for the transmission of the estate to the heirs.'" Accord, Restatement Second of Trusts § 282; cf. id., §§ 294, 295.

2. Res Judicata Effects

A party who sues or is sued in a representative capacity is, generally speaking, not bound in his individual capacity. The theory is that two different legal personalities are involved. Restatement Second of Judgments § 36.

3. Diversity Jurisdiction

When a fiduciary is the proper party, in federal diversity litigation it is the citizenship of the fiduciary and not that of the beneficiaries that is determinative of jurisdiction, Navarro Sav. Ass'n v. Lee, 446 U.S. 458, 100 S.Ct. 1779, 64 L.Ed.2d 425 (1980), except where the fiduciary was appointed solely to establish federal jurisdiction. See 6 Wright & Miller § 1548.

4. Suits by Sovereigns as Parens Patriae

A sovereign may not enter a case to present the claims of an individual citizen, but it may act as a representative of its citizens where the injury "affects the general population of a State in a substantial way." Maryland v. Louisiana, 451 U.S. 725, 737, 101 S.Ct. 2114, 2124, 68 L.Ed.2d 576 (1981). This right of a sovereign to sue as *parens patriae* derives from the state's interest in protecting its inhabitants from serious threats to their welfare. See Pennsylvania v. West Virginia, 262 U.S. 553, 592, 43 S.Ct. 658, 67 L.Ed. 1117 (1923).

In Hawaii v. Standard Oil Co. of California, 405 U.S. 251, 92 S.Ct. 885, 31 L.Ed.2d 184 (1972), the State of Hawaii sued four defendants, charging them with conspiring to restrain trade in the marketing of petroleum products in violation of the Sherman Act. It sued in three capacities: (1) in its own proprietary capacity for excessive prices paid for petroleum products by the State itself; (2) as *parens patriae* for all its citizens who had paid such prices; and (3) as a representative of a class defined as all purchasers of petroleum products in Hawaii. The suit in the first capacity was acknowledged by the defendant to be maintainable; the class suit was held by the district court to be "unmanageable"; the propriety of the suit as *parens patriae* was taken on appeal under 28 U.S.C.A. § 1292(b) to the Court of Appeals and then to the Supreme Court. Holding that the State could not maintain such a suit, the Supreme Court said, 405 U.S. at 259–64:

> "[I]n Georgia v. Pennsylvania Railroad Co., 324 U.S. 439, 65 S.Ct. 716 (1945) * * * Georgia sought to invoke the original jurisdiction of this Court * * * alleging, in essence, that the railroads had conspired to restrain trade and to fix prices in a manner that would favor shippers in other States (particularly Northern States) to the detriment of Georgia shippers. * * *

> "The Court upheld Georgia's claim as *parens patriae* with respect to injunctive relief, but had no occasion to consider whether the antitrust laws also authorized damages for an injury to the State's economy * * *.

> "[Section] 4 of the Clayton Act * * * reads: 'Any person who shall be injured in his business or property by reason of anything forbidden in the antitrust laws may sue therefor * * * and shall recover threefold the damages by him sustained * * *.' * * *

> "Thus, § 4 permits Hawaii to sue in its proprietary capacity for three times the damages it has suffered from respondents' alleged antitrust violations. The section gives the same right to every citizen of Hawaii with respect to any damage to business or property. Were we, in addition, to

hold that Congress authorized the State to recover damages for injury to its general economy, we would open the door to duplicate recoveries."

See also Anno., 42 A.L.R.Fed. 23.

b. THE PROBLEM OF THE INSURED DEFENDANT

CRISCI v. SECURITY INSURANCE CO.

Supreme Court of California, 1967.
66 Cal.2d 425, 58 Cal.Rptr. 13, 426 P.2d 173.

PETERS, J.

In an action against The Security Insurance Company of New Haven, Connecticut, the trial court awarded Rosina Crisci $91,000 (plus interest) because she suffered a judgment in a personal injury action after Security, her insurer, refused to settle the claim. Mrs. Crisci was also awarded $25,000 for mental suffering. Security has appealed.

June DiMare and her husband were tenants in an apartment building owned by Rosina Crisci. Mrs. DiMare was descending the apartment's outside wooden staircase when a tread gave way. She fell through the resulting opening up to her waist and was left hanging 15 feet above the ground. Mrs. DiMare suffered physical injuries and developed a very severe psychosis. In a suit brought against Mrs. Crisci the DiMares alleged that the step broke because Mrs. Crisci was negligent in inspecting and maintaining the stairs. They contended that Mrs. DiMare's mental condition was caused by the accident, and they asked for $400,000 as compensation for physical and mental injuries and medical expenses.

Mrs. Crisci had $10,000 of insurance coverage under a general liability policy issued by Security. The policy obligated Security to defend the suit against Mrs. Crisci and authorized the company to make any settlement it deemed expedient.[1] Security hired an experienced lawyer, Mr. Healy, to handle the case. Both he and defendant's claims manager believed that unless evidence was discovered showing that Mrs. DiMare had a prior mental illness, a jury would probably find that the accident precipitated Mrs. DiMare's psychosis. And both men believed that if the jury felt that the fall triggered the psychosis, a verdict of not less than $100,000 would be returned.

An extensive search turned up no evidence that Mrs. DiMare had any prior mental abnormality. As a teenager Mrs. DiMare had been in a Washington mental hospital, but only to have an abortion. Both Mrs. DiMare and Mrs. Crisci found psychiatrists who would testify that the accident caused Mrs. DiMare's illness, and the insurance company knew of this testimony. Among those who felt the psychosis was not related to the accident were the doctors at the state mental hospital where Mrs. DiMare had been committed following the accident. All

---

1. Mrs. Crisci's own attorney, Mr. Pardini, was consulted by the counsel for the insurance company, but Mr. Pardini did not direct or control either settlement negotiations or the defense of Mrs. DiMare's suit.

the psychiatrists agreed, however, that a psychosis could be triggered by a sudden fear of falling to one's death.

The exact chronology of settlement offers is not established by the record. However, by the time the DiMares' attorney reduced his settlement demands to $10,000, Security had doctors prepared to support its position and was only willing to pay $3,000 for Mrs. DiMare's physical injuries. Security was unwilling to pay one cent for the possibility of a plaintiff's verdict on the mental illness issue. This conclusion was based on the assumption that the jury would believe all of the defendant's psychiatric evidence and none of the plaintiff's. Security also rejected a $9,000 settlement demand at a time when Mrs. Crisci offered to pay $2,500 of the settlement.

A jury awarded Mrs. DiMare $100,000 and her husband $1,000. After an appeal (DiMare v. Cresci,[2] 58 Cal.2d 292, 23 Cal.Rptr. 772, 373 P.2d 860) the insurance company paid $10,000 of this amount, the amount of its policy. The DiMares then sought to collect the balance from Mrs. Crisci. A settlement was arranged by which the DiMares received $22,000, a 40 percent interest in Mrs. Crisci's claim to a particular piece of property, and an assignment of Mrs. Crisci's cause of action against Security. Mrs. Crisci, an immigrant widow of 70, became indigent. She worked as a babysitter, and her grandchildren paid her rent. The change in her financial condition was accompanied by a decline in physical health, hysteria, and suicide attempts. Mrs. Crisci then brought this action.

The liability of an insurer in excess of its policy limits for failure to accept a settlement offer within those limits was considered by this court in Comunale v. Traders & General Ins. Co., 50 Cal.2d 654, 328 P.2d 198. It was there reasoned that in every contract, including policies of insurance, there is an implied covenant of good faith and fair dealing that neither party will do anything which will injure the right of the other to receive the benefits of the agreement; that it is common knowledge that one of the usual methods by which an insured receives protection under a liability insurance policy is by settlement of claims without litigation; that the implied obligation of good faith and fair dealing requires the insurer to settle in an appropriate case although the express terms of the policy do not impose the duty; that in determining whether to settle the insurer must give the interests of the insured at least as much consideration as it gives to its own interests; and that when "there is great risk of a recovery beyond the policy limits so that the most reasonable manner of disposing of the claim is a settlement which can be made within those limits, a consideration in good faith of the insured's interest requires the insurer to settle the claim." (50 Cal.2d at p. 659.)

In determining whether an insurer has given consideration to the interests of the insured, the test is whether a prudent insurer without

2. In the prior litigation plaintiff was sued as "Rosina Cresci."

policy limits would have accepted the settlement offer. (Kinder v. Western Pioneer Ins. Co., 231 Cal.App.2d 894, 900, 42 Cal.Rptr. 394; Critz v. Farmers Ins. Group, 230 Cal.App.2d 788, 798, 41 Cal.Rptr. 401; Martin v. Hartford Acc. & Indem. Co., 228 Cal.App.2d 178, 183, 41 Cal. Rptr. 401; Davy v. Public National Ins. Co., 181 Cal.App.2d 387, 400, 5 Cal.Rptr. 488; see Hodges v. Standard Accident Ins. Co., 198 Cal.App.2d 564, 579, 18 Cal.Rptr. 17.)

Several cases, in considering the liability of the insurer, contain language to the effect that bad faith is the equivalent of dishonesty, fraud, and concealment. (See Critz v. Farmers Ins. Group, supra, 230 Cal.App.2d 788, 796; Palmer v. Financial Indem. Co., 215 Cal.App.2d 419, 429, 30 Cal.Rptr. 204; Davy v. Public National Ins. Co., supra, 181 Cal.App.2d 387, 396.) Obviously a showing that the insurer has been guilty of actual dishonesty, fraud, or concealment is relevant to the determination whether it has given consideration to the insured's interest in considering a settlement offer within the policy limits. The language used in the cases, however, should not be understood as meaning that in the absence of evidence establishing actual dishonesty, fraud, or concealment no recovery may be had for a judgment in excess of the policy limits. Comunale v. Traders & General Ins. Co., supra, 50 Cal.2d 654, 658–659, makes it clear that liability based on an implied covenant exists whenever the insurer refuses to settle in an appropriate case and that liability may exist when the insurer unwarrantedly refuses an offered settlement where the most reasonable manner of disposing of the claim is by accepting the settlement. Liability is imposed not for a bad faith breach of the contract but for failure to meet the duty to accept reasonable settlements, a duty included within the implied covenant of good faith and fair dealing. Moreover, examination of the balance of the *Palmer, Critz,* and *Davy* opinions makes it abundantly clear that recovery may be based on unwarranted rejection of a reasonable settlement offer and that the absence of evidence, circumstantial or direct, showing actual dishonesty, fraud, or concealment is not fatal to the cause of action.

Amicus curiae argues that, whenever an insurer receives an offer to settle within the policy limits and rejects it, the insurer should be liable in every case for the amount of any final judgment whether or not within the policy limits. As we have seen, the duty of the insurer to consider the insured's interest in settlement offers within the policy limits arises from an implied covenant in the contract, and ordinarily contract duties are strictly enforced and not subject to a standard of reasonableness. Obviously, it will always be in the insured's interest to settle within the policy limits when there is any danger, however slight, of a judgment in excess of those limits. Accordingly the rejection of a settlement within the limits where there is any danger of a judgment in excess of the limits can be justified, if at all, only on the basis of interests of the insurer, and, in light of the common knowledge that settlement is one of the usual methods by which an insured receives protection under a liability policy, it may not be unreasonable for an insured who purchases a policy with limits to believe that a sum of money equal to the limits is available and will be used so as to avoid liability on his part with regard to any covered accident. In view of such expectation an insurer should not be permitted to further its own interests by rejecting opportunities to settle within the policy limits unless it is also willing to absorb losses which may result from its failure to settle.

The proposed rule is a simple one to apply and avoids the burdens of a determination whether a settlement offer within the policy limits was reasonable. The proposed rule would also eliminate the danger that an insurer, faced with a settlement offer at or near the policy limits, will reject it and gamble with the insured's money to further its own interests. Moreover, it is not entirely clear that the proposed rule would place a burden on insurers substantially greater than that which is present under existing law. The size of the judgment recovered in the personal injury action when it exceeds the policy limits, although not conclusive, furnishes an inference that the value of the claim is the equivalent of the amount of the judgment and that acceptance of an offer within those limits was the most reasonable method of dealing with the claim.

Finally, and most importantly, there is more than a small amount of elementary justice in a rule that would require that, in this situation where the insurer's and insured's interests necessarily conflict, the insurer, which may reap the benefits of its determination not to settle, should also suffer the detriments of its decision. On the basis of these and other considerations, a number of commentators have urged that the insurer should be liable for any resulting judgment where it refuses to settle within the policy limits. (Note (1966) 18 Stan.L.Rev. 475, 482–485; Note (1951) 60 Yale L.J. 1037, 1041–1042; Comment (1949) 48 Mich.L.Rev. 95, 102; Note (1945) 13 U.Chi.L.Rev. 105, 109.)

We need not, however, here determine whether there might be some countervailing considerations precluding adoption of the proposed rule because, under Comunale v. Traders & General Ins. Co., supra, 50 Cal.2d 654, and the cases following it, the evidence is clearly sufficient to support the determination that Security breached its duty to consider the interests of Mrs. Crisci in proposed settlements. Both Security's attorney and its claims manager agreed that if Mrs. DiMare won an award for her psychosis, that award would be at least $100,000. Security attempts to justify its rejection of a settlement by contending that it believed Mrs. DiMare had no chance of winning on the mental suffering issue. That belief in the circumstances present could be found to be unreasonable. Security was putting blind faith in the power of its psychiatrists to convince the jury when it knew that the accident could have caused the psychosis, that its agents had told it that without evidence of prior mental defects a jury was likely to believe the fall precipitated the psychosis, and that Mrs. DiMare had reputable psychiatrists on her side. Further, the company had been told by a psychiatrist that in a group of 24 psychiatrists, 12 could be found to support each side.

The trial court found that defendant "knew that there was a considerable risk of substantial recovery beyond said policy limits" and that "the defendant did not give as much consideration to the financial interests of its said insured as it gave to its own interests." That is all that was required. The award of $91,000 must therefore be affirmed.

We must next determine the propriety of the award to Mrs. Crisci of $25,000 for her mental suffering. In Comunale v. Traders & General Ins. Co., supra, 50 Cal.2d 654, 663, it was held that an action of the type involved here sounds in both contract and tort and that "where a case sounds both in contract and tort the plaintiff will ordinarily have freedom of election between an action of tort and one of contract. (Eads v. Marks, 39 Cal.2d 807, 811, 249 P.2d 257.) An exception to this rule is made in suits for personal injury caused by negligence, where the tort character of the action is considered to prevail [citations], but no such exception is applied in cases, like the present one, which relate to financial damage [citations]." [3] Although this rule was applied in *Comunale* with regard to a statute of limitations, the rule is also applicable in determining liability. (Weaver v. Bank of America, 59 Cal.2d 428, 432, 30 Cal.Rptr. 4, 380 P.2d 644; Lucas v. Hamm, 56 Cal.2d 583, 589, fn. 2, 15 Cal.Rptr. 821, 364 P.2d 685; Acadia, California, Ltd. v. Herbert, 54 Cal.2d 328, 336, 5 Cal.Rptr. 686, 353 P.2d 294.) Insofar as language in Critz v. Farmers Ins. Group, supra, 230 Cal.App.2d 788, 799, might be interpreted as providing that the action for wrongful refusal to settle sounds solely in contract, it is disapproved.

Fundamental in our jurisprudence is the principle that for every wrong there is a remedy and that an injured party should be compensated for all damage proximately caused by the wrongdoer. Although we recognize exceptions from these fundamental principles, no departure should be sanctioned unless there is a strong necessity therefor.

The general rule of damages in tort is that the injured party may recover for all detriment caused whether it could have been anticipated or not. (Civ.Code, § 3333; see Hunt Bros. Co. v. San Lorenzo etc. Co., 150 Cal. 51, 56, 87 P. 1093, 7 L.R.A.,N.S., 913.) In accordance with the general rule, it is settled in this state that mental suffering constitutes an aggravation of damages when it naturally ensues from the act complained of, and in this connection mental suffering includes nervousness, grief, anxiety, worry, shock, humiliation and indignity as well as physical pain. The commonest example of the award of damages for mental suffering in addition to other damages is probably where the plaintiff suffers personal injuries in addition to mental distress as a result of either negligent or intentional misconduct by the defendant.

---

3. Comunale v. Traders & General Ins. Co., supra, 50 Cal.2d 654, was mainly concerned with the contract aspect of the action. This may be due to the facts that the tort duty is ordinarily based on the insurer's assumption of the defense and of settlement negotiations (see Keeton, Liability Insurance and Responsibility for Settlement (1954) 67 Harv.L.Rev. 1136, 1138– 1139; Note (1966), supra, 18 Stan.L.Rev. 475), and that in *Comunale* the insurer did not undertake defense or settlement but denied coverage. In any event *Comunale* expressly recognizes that "wrongful refusal to settle has generally been treated as a tort." (50 Cal.2d at p. 663, 328 P.2d at p. 203.)

(DiMare v. Cresci, supra, 58 Cal.2d 292, 300–301; Deevy v. Tassi, 21 Cal. 2d 109, 120, 130 P.2d 389; Dryden v. Continental Banking Co., 11 Cal. 2d 33, 39–40, 77 P.2d 833.) Such awards are not confined to cases where the mental suffering award was in addition to an award for personal injuries; damages for mental distress have also been awarded in cases where the tortious conduct was an interference with property rights without any personal injuries apart from the mental distress. (Acadia, California, Ltd. v. Herbert, supra, 51 Cal.2d 328, 337; Kornoff v. Kingsburg Cotton Oil Co., 45 Cal.2d 265, 271 et seq., 288 P.2d 507; Herzog v. Grosso, 41 Cal.2d 219, 225, 259 P.2d 429; Emden v. Vitz, 88 Cal.App.2d 313, 316 et seq., 198 P.2d 696.)

We are satisfied that a plaintiff who as a result of a defendant's tortious conduct loses his property and suffers mental distress may recover not only for the pecuniary loss but also for his mental distress. No substantial reason exists to distinguish the cases which have permitted recovery for mental distress in actions for invasion of property rights. The principal reason for limiting recovery of damages for mental distress is that to permit recovery of such damages would open the door to fictitious claims, to recovery for mere bad manners, and to litigation in the field of trivialities. (Prosser, Torts (3d ed. 1964) § 11, p. 43.) Obviously, where, as here, the claim is actionable and has resulted in substantial damages apart from those due to mental distress, the danger of fictitious claims is reduced, and we are not here concerned with mere bad manners or trivialities but tortious conduct resulting in substantial invasions of clearly protected interests.[4]

Recovery of damages for mental suffering in the instant case does not mean that in every case of breach of contract the injured party may recover such damages. Here the breach also constitutes a tort. Moreover, plaintiff did not seek by the contract involved here to obtain a commercial advantage but to protect herself against the risks of accidental losses, including the mental distress which might follow from the losses. Among the considerations in purchasing liability insurance, as insurers are well aware, is the peace of mind and security it will provide in the event of an accidental loss, and recovery of damages for mental suffering has been permitted for breach of contracts which directly concern the comfort, happiness or personal esteem of one of the parties. (Chelini v. Nieri, 32 Cal.2d 480, 482, 196 P.2d 915.)

It is not claimed that plaintiff's mental distress was not caused by defendant's refusal to settle or that the damages awarded were excessive in the light of plaintiff's substantial suffering.

The judgment is affirmed.

TRAYNOR, C. J., McCOMB, J., TOBRINER, J., MOSK, J., and BURKE, J., concur.

---

4. Nor are we here concerned with the problem whether invasion of the plaintiff's right to be free from emotional disturbance is actionable where there is no injury to person or property rights in addition to the inflicted mental distress. (Cf. Amaya v. Home Ice, Fuel & Supply Co., 59 Cal.2d 295, 29 Cal.Rptr. 33, 379 P.2d 513.)

NOTE ON THE INSURED DEFENDANT

1. Whether *Crisci* is still good law in California is uncertain. Following *Crisci*, the California legislature amended Cal.Ins.Code § 790.03 to make it an unlawful act for any insurance company to engage in "unfair claims settlement practices," including "[n]ot attempting in good faith to effectuate prompt, fair, and equitable settlements of claims in which liability has become reasonably clear." Cal.Ins.Code § 790.03(h). The California Supreme Court in 1979 held that the amended statute created a private cause of action against an insurer by either an insured or a third party claimant injured by the insured's wrongful actions. Royal Globe Ins. Co. v. Superior Court, 23 Cal.3d 880, 153 Cal.Rptr. 842, 592 P.2d 329 (1979). *Royal Globe* was overruled in 1988, however, with the California Supreme Court holding that the statute created no private cause of action for either the insured or third party claimants, but merely authorized the state Insurance Commissioner to institute actions against insurers. Moradi–Shalal v. Fireman's Fund Ins. Co., 46 Cal.3d 287, 250 Cal.Rptr. 116, 758 P.2d 58 (1988). Although the majority was careful to state that California courts would still retain jurisdiction "to impose civil damages or other remedies against insurers in appropriate common law actions, based on such traditional theories as fraud, infliction of emotional distress, and (as to the insured) either breach of contract or breach of the implied covenant of good faith and fair dealing," the dissent was not so sanguine, commenting that the majority's interpretation of the statute "would overturn by implication the rule of Crisci v. Security Ins. Co.," presumably because of legislative preemption of the prior common law. A California initiative which would have revived the *Royal Globe* ruling was defeated in 1988.

2. The starting place for the problem of the insured defendant is the general rule that the liability insurer of a tortfeasor, typically the insured motorist, may not be directly sued by the injured party until after a judgment has been obtained against the insured. See Leigh, Direct Actions Against Liability Insurers, 1949 Ins.L.J. 633; Prosser and Keeton, Torts § 82 (5th ed. 1984). In some jurisdictions, so-called "direct action" statutes have been enacted which allow the injured party to proceed directly against the insurer in the first instance, see Note, Direct-Action Statutes: Their Operational and Conflict-of-Laws Problems, 74 Harv.L.Rev. 357 (1960); cf. Note, The Liability Insurer as a Real Party in Interest, 41 Minn.L.Rev. 784 (1957), and an exception is usually recognized in situations where, as is ordinarily the case with respect to common carriers, statute or ordinance requires the insurance. See Anno., 20 A.L.R.2d 1097. Generally speaking, however, the insurer may not be made a party either singly or as a co-defendant. See, e.g., Roberts v. Sparks, 99 N.M. 152, 655 P.2d 539 (App.1982); Taylor v. Federal Kemper Ins. Co., 534 F.Supp. 196 (W.D.Ark.1982). Rather, the insurance company, acting under terms of the policy empowering it to do so, assumes the defense of the action brought against the insured—employing counsel, bearing the expenses of the defense, conducting the settlement negotiations and, within the limits of liability fixed by the policy, paying any settlement and any judgment. Within the limits of the policy it is in every sense the "real" defendant. The litigation, nevertheless, proceeds as though the insured were the defendant.

The insurance companies have been generally successful in resisting efforts to adopt "direct action" legislation, their resistance grounded on the fear that jury verdicts will be higher if the fact of insurance is fully disclosed. Whether this fear is well-founded has been much mooted, see Note, Direct-Action Statutes, supra, at 358, but there seems little question that the "indirect action" against the insurance company poses serious difficulties, including the following:

a. The problem of settlement when the policy limits are lower than the plaintiff's claim, as in the *Crisci* case. On this see, e.g., Samson v. Transamerica Ins. Co., 30 Cal.3d 220, 178 Cal.Rptr. 343, 636 P.2d 32 (1981). While most states have adopted the so-called "good faith" test for determining the extent of the insurer's duty to settle, a few have applied a "negligence" criterion. To reduce the risk of liability for wrongful refusal to settle, most insurers have made a practice to call to the insured's attention the fact that the claim exceeds the policy limits and to invite him to retain his own counsel to assist in the defense. See, e.g., Murach v. Massachusetts Bonding & Ins. Co., 339 Mass. 184, 158 N.E.2d 338 (1959). See also C.C. 2860, codifying San Diego Navy Fed. Credit Union v. Cumis Ins. Soc'y, 162 Cal.App.3d 358, 208 Cal.Rptr. 494 (1984), which held that an insurance company is required not only to provide a defense but also to pay for independent counsel when there is a potential conflict of interest between the insurer and insured. See Note, The Cumis Decision— What Has It Done to Insurance Policies?, 23 Cal.West.L.Rev. 125 (1986); Comment, Reexamining Conflicts of Interest: When is Private Counsel Necessary?, 17 Pacific L.J. 1421 (1986). Would this serve any purpose under the *Crisci* rule? Did the court in *Crisci* in effect adopt the rule suggested by the amicus curiae that it said it found unnecessary to adopt? How could an insurer establish that in rejecting a settlement offer within the policy limits, it had nevertheless given "as much consideration" to the insured's financial interest as its own?

b. The problem of pre-trial discovery by the plaintiff of the liability limits of the defendant's policy. Plaintiffs want this information in order to make their position in settlement negotiations better informed and hence more effective; insurers do not want to disclose the information for the converse reason. On this see Introductory Note on Discovery, infra p. 901.

c. The problem of the attempt of a subrogated insurer who is the "real" plaintiff to hide behind its insured, by means of a "loan receipt" or otherwise. See Note on the Real Party in Interest Rule, supra 802. This problem is aggravated when the defense insurer is concealing itself behind the defendant.

d. The problem of representation of the insured defendant in the prosecution of her claims against the plaintiff. This presents perhaps the most difficult problem, in view of the rules of collateral estoppel and particularly in jurisdictions having the compulsory counterclaim rule. Are there serious objections on ethical grounds to the representation by insurance counsel of the insured in respect to her claims against the plaintiff? If the insured defendant does counterclaim against plaintiff, then plaintiff's insurance company is empowered to employ counsel to participate with plaintiff's personal injury attorney in the trial of the case. Does this, too, present serious practical and ethical problems in the strategy and tactics to be employed on behalf of plaintiff? Is there any escape from these problems?

3. Is the approach in *Crisci* applicable to any person who undertakes to defend litigation on behalf of another? Would it apply as well to a person who assumes to prosecute litigation on behalf of another?

c. CAPACITY TO SUE AND BE SUED

NOTE ON CAPACITY TO SUE AND BE SUED

The problem regarding "capacity" to sue and be sued is two-fold: first, whether the name used in the litigation documents refers to an individual or group which is for legal purposes treated as a "person"; second, if there be such a "person," whether there are any peculiar circumstances which preclude her from participating in the litigation. See generally Kennedy, Federal Civil Rule 17(b) and (c): Qualifying to Litigate in Federal Court, 43 Notre Dame L.Rev. 273 (1968); 3A Moore ¶¶ 17.16 et seq.; 4 Witkin 97–137.

Problems of "capacity" arise with relative infrequency but they can be difficult. Some of these difficulties will be suggested in the following materials.

1. Natural Persons

The archetype of litigating capacity is the adult who is a citizen of the jurisdiction in which the court sits and who suffers from no mental or legally imposed disability. Questions of capacity may arise when the party litigant differs in some respect from this model.

a. Minors. A suit by or against a minor may be maintained in the name of the minor but must be managed by a guardian, either his general guardian if he has one or a guardian ad litem appointed for the particular suit. See C.C.P. 372; F.R.C.P. 17(c); Ill.C.C.P. § 2–1008. Failure to make the appointment may be corrected by motion at any stage of the proceedings, if the protection of the minor's interests has not been impaired by the failure, see, e.g., Bereuter v. Bereuter, 655 S.W.2d 789 (Mo.App.1983); Ritzler v. Eckleberry, 167 Ohio St. 439, 149 N.E.2d 728 (1958). If judgment is rendered in absence of a guardian, the minor traditionally was accorded the privilege of disaffirming the judgment, a privilege which, however, may be lost by the failure promptly to invoke it. See, e.g., McDowell v. McDowell, 670 S.W.2d 518 (Mo.App.1984). Shouldn't even this privilege be withheld if the minor is adequately represented by counsel, e.g., in the case of an insured minor defendant defended by his insurer? See Restatement Second of Judgments § 35; e.g., Johnson v. Superior Court, 31 Cal.App.3d 143, 107 Cal.Rptr. 83 (1973).

b. Incompetents. The rules applicable to infants, and the qualifications thereto, apply as well to incompetents. See, e.g., C.C.P. 372; Matter of Chicago, Rock Island & Pacific R.R., 788 F.2d 1280 (7th Cir. 1986).

c. Aliens. Aliens are accorded the same right of access to courts as citizens. See, e.g., Janusis v. Long, 284 Mass. 403, 188 N.E. 228 (1933); Alvarez v. Sanchez, 105 A.D.2d 1114, 482 N.Y.S.2d 184 (1984). The right is said to rest on comity among nations, e.g., Sliosberg v. New York Life Ins. Co., 244 N.Y. 482, 155 N.E. 749 (1927), though it would appear at least arguable that it rests on the more secure footing of the equal protection clause of the 14th Amendment, U.S. Constitution. Cf. Kwong Hai Chew v. Colding, 344 U.S. 590, 73 S.Ct. 472, 97 L.Ed.2d 576 (1953); Examining Board of Engineers v. Flores de Otero, 426 U.S. 572, 96 S.Ct. 2264, 49 L.Ed.2d 65 (1976). For diversity purposes, a resident alien is considered a citizen of the state where she is domiciled. 28 U.S.C.A. § 1332(a).

d. Citizens of Sister States. The privileges and immunities clause of Art. IV, Sec. 2, U.S. Constitution, confers on the citizens of every state the same right of access to the courts of another state as the citizens of the latter. See

Barrell v. Benjamin, supra p. 281. The privilege does not extend to corporations, which are not "citizens," Paul v. Virginia, 75 U.S. (8 Wall.) 168, 19 L.Ed. 357 (1869), and may be limited by conditions discriminating between local "residents" and nonresidents, so long as the discrimination is not drawn on the line of local state citizenship as such. See Missouri ex rel. Southern Ry. Co. v. Mayfield, 340 U.S. 1, 71 S.Ct. 1, 95 L.Ed. 3 (1950) (application of forum non conveniens against nonresident's cause of action arising outside of the state).

   e. *Individuals Appearing in a Representative Capacity.* When the individual appears not to represent an interest of his own but as a representative empowered by law to act for others, such as an administrator, executor or receiver, his capacity is determined qua representative and not according to the rules applicable were he suing in his own behalf. See Restatement Second of Judgments § 36. Speaking generally, a locally appointed representative has the same capacity, in his representative functions, as an adult individual. On the capacity to sue and be sued locally of representatives appointed in another jurisdiction see Currie, The Multiple Personality of the Dead: Executors, Administrators, and the Conflict of Laws, 33 U.Chi.L.Rev. 429 (1966). For diversity purposes, the legal representative of an estate is deemed a citizen of the same state as the decedent, and the legal representative of a minor or incompetent is deemed a citizen of the same state as the minor or incompetent. 28 U.S.C.A. § 1332(c)(2).

2. Corporations

   a. *Historical Development.* The essence of the modern corporation is that for legal purposes it is treated as a person, i.e., it is regarded as having a capacity to act, including a capacity to sue and be sued, distinct from that of the individuals who manage it and who may own interests in it. The evolution of the notion of corporateness at common law was a long and tortuous process. See generally Goebel, The Development of Legal Institutions 328–414, esp. 367–8 (1946). There lingered on for many years the idea that a group could attain corporate capacity by the mere act of association (coupled, probably, with continued functioning as such for a period "time out of mind"). But in the aftermath of the collapse of the great speculative joint stock ventures of the early 18th century, notably the South Sea Company, the enactment of the Bubble Act made it clear, so far as England was concerned, that corporate character depended on charter: "The Act succeeded in quenching any remaining vestiges of the notion once prevalent that corporate capacity could be acquired by voluntary association." Goebel, supra, at 413. See also Dodd, Dogma and Practice in the Law of Associations, 42 Harv.L.Rev. 977, 980–86 (1929). An association was therefore an aggregate of individuals and not an entity distinct from its members. See Lloyd v. Loaring, 6 Ves.Jr. 773, 31 E.R. 1302 (Ch.1802). See also, e.g., Duvergier v. Fellows, 5 Bing. 248, 267, 130 E.R. 1056, 1063 (C.P.1828).

   While it was thus clearly recognized that an unchartered association could not be treated as a corporation, the concept of the chartered corporate body as a separate legal personality remained as yet uncertain in some respects. The strongest impetus to complete acceptance in this country of the notion of corporate legal personality came from Chief Justice Marshall's dictum in Dartmouth College v. Woodward, 17 U.S. (4 Wheat.) 518, 636, 4 L.Ed. 629, 659 (1819):

   "A corporation is an artificial being, invisible, intangible, and existing only in contemplation of law. Being the mere creature of law, it possesses only those properties which the charter of its creation confers upon it, either expressly or as incidental to its very existence. These are such as are supposed best calculated to effect the object for which it was created. Among the most important are immortality, and, if the expression may be allowed, individuality; properties by which a perpetual succession of many persons are considered as the same, and may act as a single individual."

Paralleling the uncertainty about the nature of the corporate entity was an uncertainty as to how it should be treated for procedural purposes—denomination as a party, service of process, mesne process such as attachment, appearance and the effect of a judgment. The story is a long one. Cf. Dodd, American Business Corporations Until 1860, esp. 36–44 (1954); Laski, The Personality of Associations, 29 Harv.L.Rev. 404, 408–415 (1916). Suffice it to say that by the end of the 19th century a corporation was a legal entity separate from its managers and owners and by virtue thereof had the capacity to sue and be sued, and to be subjected to liability enforceable against assets held in its name, in the same manner as a natural person. See Restatement Second of Judgments § 59.

One vestige of the older view of a corporation as an association of individuals remains of contemporary importance. This is the rule that for the purposes of the diversity jurisdiction of the federal courts (1) a corporation is regarded as having the citizenship of its shareholders, and (2) the citizenship of the shareholders is conclusively presumed to be that of the state of incorporation. Observe that without the first of these two steps a corporation could not sue or be sued on diversity jurisdiction at all and that without the second step frequently there would not be the "complete" diversity of citizenship required for jurisdiction under 28 U.S.C.A. § 1332. See generally McGovney, A Supreme Court Fiction, 56 Harv.L.Rev. 853, 1090, 1225 (1943); cf. Green, Corporations as Persons, Citizens, and Possessors of Liberty, 94 U.Pa.L.Rev. 202 (1946); Hart & Wechsler 1670–1674.

b. Foreign Corporations. The conceptual problems of the capacity of corporations were multiplied in the case of foreign corporations. The conclusion, arrived at in the *Dartmouth College* case, that a corporation was a "person" did not avoid the fact that it was "the mere creature of the law." The question then put was this: If the corporation "exists" as a creature of law, how can it "exist" outside of the sovereign creating it so as to sue or be sued, contract or hold property or otherwise function outside the territorial limits of the state of its incorporation?

This question was put most searchingly in Bank of Augusta v. Earle, 38 U.S. (13 Pet.) 519, 10 L.Ed. 274 (1839), an action in the federal court in Alabama by a Georgia corporation. Webster for the bank urged that the corporation be treated for this purpose, as it was for purposes of the diversity jurisdiction of the federal courts, as composed of its individual owners, so that under the privileges and immunities clause of Art. IV, Sec. 2, U.S. Constitution, it should be held to have a right to sue in Alabama quite apart from Alabama's attitude toward it. The court avoided this suggestion, later rejected in Paul v. Virginia, 75 U.S. (8 Wall.) 168, 19 L.Ed. 357 (1869), supra, Taney, C.J., pointing out, 13 Pet. at 586–587, 10 L.Ed. at 307, that such a view "would deprive every state of all control over the extent of corporate franchises proper to be granted in the state," and rested the decision in favor of the bank on the ground of comity, 13 Pet. at 592, 10 L.Ed. at 309–310:

"We think it well settled, that by the law of comity among nations, a corporation created by one sovereign is permitted to make contracts in another, and to sue in its courts; and that the same law of comity prevails among the several sovereignties of this Union."

But because the corporation's capacity outside the state of its creation depended upon comity, 13 Pet. at 589, 10 L.Ed. at 308:

"Every power, however, of the description of which we are speaking, which a corporation exercises in another state, depends for its validity upon the laws of the sovereignty in which it is exercised * * *."

The thesis of Bank of Augusta v. Earle remains the premise for problems of the capacity of the foreign corporation. The most commonly encountered present application of its rule is the statutory refusal of access to local courts of foreign corporations which are "doing business" locally without having obtained a permit to do so from the appropriate state authority. See, e.g., Calif. Corp.Code § 2203. For application of such a statute, see, e.g., Eli Lilly & Co. v. Sav-on-Drugs, Inc., 366 U.S. 276, 81 S.Ct. 1316, 6 L.Ed.2d 288 (1961). But a state lacks authority to deny access to its courts to foreign corporations doing exclusively interstate business, which are protected therein by the Commerce Clause. See Allenberg Cotton Co. v. Pittman, 419 U.S. 20, 95 S.Ct. 260, 42 L.Ed. 2d 195 (1974). See generally Henderson, The Position of Foreign Corporations in American Constitutional Law (1918); Note, The Legal Consequences of Failure to Comply with Domestication Statutes, 110 U.Pa.L.Rev. 241 (1961).

   c. *Contemporary Conceptual Problems.* Having with much effort arrived at the concept of the corporation as a person, the courts have on occasion proceeded to apply it literally. See, e.g., MacAffer v. Boston & Maine R.R., 268 N.Y. 400, 197 N.E. 328 (1935); J.C. Peacock, Inc. v. Hasko, 184 Cal.App.2d 142, 7 Cal.Rptr. 490 (1960), treating as nonexistent a merged corporation. See also Note, Survival of Rights of Action After Corporate Merger, 78 Mich.L.Rev. 250 (1979).

   By statute in most states a dissolved corporation continues to "exist" for purposes of winding up the business and, incidental thereto, suing and being sued. See, e.g., Calif.Corp.Code § 2010. See also Marcus, Suability of Dissolved Corporations—A Study in Interstate and Federal-State Relationships, 58 Harv. L.Rev. 675 (1945); Henn and Alexander, Laws of Corporations 990–997 (3d ed. 1983).

3. Unincorporated Associations

   a. *In General.* If an association is not in the form of a corporation, the attitude of the law was, and generally still is, that expressed in Lloyd v. Loaring, 6 Ves.Jr. 773, 31 E.R. 1302 (Ch.1802), supra: the court would treat the associated persons "not with reference to them as a voluntary society, but as individuals." As summarized in Puerto Rico v. Russell & Co., 288 U.S. 476, 480, 53 S.Ct. 447, 448, 77 L.Ed. 903, 907 (1933), "The tradition of the common law is to treat as legal persons only incorporated groups and to assimilate all others to partners."

   The treatment of association members as individuals with partner-like legal characteristics can be sorted out into three problems:

   1. Is an association member chargeable (i.e., fully liable personally) for acts done by officers or other members of the association, and if so under what conditions?

   2. In addition, or as an alternative, to individual member liability as above, may the assets of the association be reached to pay a liability based on

acts of an officer or member of the association, and if so, under what conditions?

3. In what procedural form and upon whose participation may a suit involving an association be maintained?

Each of these questions involves a problem of representation of one person's interest by someone else. That the issues cannot be analyzed in isolation from each other is clear enough. See Witmer, Trade Union Liability: The Problem of the Unincorporated Association, 51 Yale L.J. 40, 47 (1941); cf. Sturges, Unincorporated Associations as Parties to Action, 33 Yale L.J. 383 (1924). Yet one of the chief obstacles to their satisfying analysis is the procedural accident that the last of the questions stated above is the one that ordinarily comes up first, in the form of an objection to designation or joinder of parties. Is it possible to deal sensibly with such an objection without first having arrived at conclusions concerning the other questions? For an example of the kinds of problems that can arise, see Oskoian v. Canuel, 269 F.2d 311 (1st Cir. 1959).

b. The Substantive Questions. Treating the relationship of association members as similar to partnership, as the common law traditionally did, implies that:

(a) Each individual member seeks to assert a claim on her own behalf, or to resist a claim that can be fastened on her personally;

(b) A member is entitled to recovery only by showing a cause of action in her individual favor, and can be held liable only if it is shown that she herself acted wrongfully or that she authorized or ratified another's wrongful act;

(c) There are no assets of the association as such (since there is no association "as such"), but only a pool of assets in which the individual members have fractional undivided interests.

These legal relationships have proved manageable for enterprises with a small number of members, where the activities and personalities of the partners merge, or at least mesh, with one another. See Restatement Second of Judgments § 60. But as extended to large unincorporated associations, such as unions or trade associations, the partnership analogy becomes unreal and its constituent rules unworkable. Consider, for example, that where an association complains of defamation, unless it is given entity treatment each member must be shown to have been defamed. Cf. Daniels v. Sanitarium Ass'n, 59 Cal. 2d 602, 30 Cal.Rptr. 828, 381 P.2d 652 (1963). By the same token, when an association is sued, the assets of the association can be reached only in proportion as it is shown that the individual members are liable. Moreover, if such individual liability is established, it is not limited to the member's interest in the association assets but extends to his whole personal estate. It is this latter consequence in particular that has always caused anxiety, especially among labor unions, and not without reason. Cf. Lawlor v. Loewe, 235 U.S. 522, 35 S.Ct. 170, 59 L.Ed. 341 (1915) (Danbury Hatters case, imposing liability on union members participating in a boycott).

The most obvious alternative to treating an association as a partnership is to treat it as a corporation—a legal entity distinct from its members, capable of owning property, doing acts through its officers and members, and suing and being sued. Congress has provided entity treatment for unions subject to the National Labor Relations Act insofar as their relations to employers are concerned. See the Labor Management Relations Act of 1947 (the Taft–Hartley

Act) § 301(b), 29 U.S.C.A. § 185(b); International Longshoremen's & Warehousemen's Union v. Juneau Spruce Corp., 342 U.S. 237, 72 S.Ct. 235, 96 L.Ed. 275 (1952); Atkinson v. Sinclair Refining Co., 370 U.S. 238, 82 S.Ct. 1318, 8 L.Ed.2d 462 (1962). Most states, it now appears, treat unions as entities, either by statute or by judicial decision, and a growing number accord the same treatment to other associations. See Restatement Second of Judgments § 61.

c. *Associations in Federal Court.* The problems in federal court of unincorporated associations begin with the fact that a distinction has to be drawn between diversity cases involving associations and those where jurisdiction is based on federal question or some other basis (e.g., admiralty). In diversity cases, it seems clear that entity treatment *versus* partnership treatment, so far as liability questions go, is a matter of state law under Erie v. Tompkins, supra p. 562. If state law accords an association entity treatment, then so do the federal courts, and the association's capacity is likened to that of a corporation. See F.R.C.P. 17(b). If state law does not accord an association entity treatment, or does so only in part, then the following questions arise:

(a) Does plaintiff have to show that each member of the associaton is individually liable?

(b) If that is so, isn't the suit—however it is entitled—a class suit in which the named defendants are treated as representatives of the individuals comprising the association? Cf. Anno., 92 A.L.R.2d 499.

(c) And if that is so, isn't the important question whether such a representative proceeding is appropriate? Compare F.R.C.P. 23.2.

The problems of associations involved in federal question litigation stem largely from the obscurities of the leading Supreme Court case on the problem, United Mine Workers v. Coronado Coal Co., 259 U.S. 344, 42 S.Ct. 570, 66 L.Ed. 975 (1922), where the Court, after noting that a union by name and function is a collectivity, said, 259 U.S. at 387–90, 42 S.Ct. at 575–76, 66 L.Ed. at 986–87:

> "[O]ut of the very necessities of the existing conditions and the utter impossibility of doing justice otherwise, the suable character of such an organization as this has come to be recognized in some jurisdictions, and many suits for and against labor unions are reported, in which no question has been raised as to the right to treat them in their closely united action and functions as artificial persons capable of suing and being sued. * * *
>
> "Though such a conclusion as to the suability of trades unions is of primary importance in the working out of justice * * * it is after all in essence and principles merely a procedural matter. As a matter of substantive law, all the members of the union engaged in a combination doing unlawful injury are liable in suit and recovery * * * *."

How Chief Justice Taft, writing for the Court, could suggest that the problem was "merely a procedural matter" is impossible to understand. The Taft-Hartley Act, as noted earlier, provided explicitly for entity treatment of unions for transactions within its scope. F.R.C.P. 17(b), interpreting *Coronado* broadly, provides that an unincorporated association may sue or be sued in its common name in federal court in "enforcing for or against it a substantive right existing under the Constitution or laws of the United States." F.R.C.P. 17(b) does not, and presumably cannot, deal with the question of entity treatment of an association on the question of *liability* of its members, nor on the question of entity treatment where a federal substantive right is enforced by or against an association in *state* court.

In Denver & Rio Grande Western R.R. v. Brotherhood of Railroad Train-men, 387 U.S. 556, 87 S.Ct. 1746, 18 L.Ed.2d 954 (1967), a union not covered by the Taft-Hartley Act was said to be an entity by virtue of *Coronado,* a rule that the Court's language indicates applies as well to other types of unincorporated associations. *Denver & Rio Grande* also settled that for venue purposes, at least in federal question cases, an unincorporated association can be sued in any district where it does business, 28 U.S.C.A. § 1391(b), (c). If unincorporated associations are treated as entities for purposes of determining citizenship in diversity cases, few national unions can sue or be sued under diversity jurisdiction. This is because the citizenship of their members is determinative in applying the "complete diversity" rule of 28 U.S.C.A. § 1332(a). See United Steelworkers v. R.H. Bouligny, Inc., 382 U.S. 145, 86 S.Ct. 272, 15 L.Ed.2d 217 (1965).

6. CLASS SUITS

HISTORICAL NOTE ON CLASS SUITS

The class suit, often called a representative suit, is provided for in such contemporary formulations as F.R.C.P. 23, 23.1 and 23.2; C.C.P. 382; and N.Y. C.P.L.R. §§ 901–909. The class suit was devised in 18th and 19th century equity practice to deal with the following problems:

a. As a means of applying the principle of compulsory joinder of all interested parties in circumstances where the number of parties was so large as to make their joinder difficult or impractical. See, e.g., Brown v. Vermuden, 1 Ch.Cas. 272, 22 E.R. 796 (Ch. 1676) (suit to determine terms and applicability of a "modus," i.e., a charge for support of a parish in lieu of a tithe, asserted against a group of miners); Mayor of York v. Pilkington, 1 Atk. 282, 26 E.R. 180 (Ch. 1737) (suit by mayor on behalf of town citizens to establish exclusive right of fishery in river, as against rival claim of riparian landowner). See the interesting analysis in Yeazell, Group Litigation and Social Context: Toward A History of the Class Action, 77 Colum.L.Rev. 866 (1977).

b. As a means of achieving the fairness of consistent determinations of a question affecting persons having a similar legal situation, but who were too numerous to be joined practicably. See, e.g., City of London v. Perkins, 3 Bro. P.C. 157, 1 E.R. 1524 (1734) (suit by city against masters of vessels to establish validity of a duty imposed on cheese landed in port of London).

c. As means of providing procedural capacity for unincorporated associations and other groups. See the valuable analysis in Yeazell, From Group Litigation to Class Action, 27 UCLA L.Rev. 514, 1067 (1980); e.g., Chancey v. May, Prec.Ch. 592, 24 E.R. 265 (Ch. 1722) (suit by managers of a brass works owned by unincorporated proprietors). See also Note on Capacity to Sue and Be Sued, supra p. 817.

Though these early cases were generally cryptic in their analysis, several themes ran through them. First, there were no doctrinal or doctrinaire formulations of the types of legal situations or relationships in which the class suit might be used. Second, there was little effort to set boundaries concerning circumstances where a class suit might *not* be used in any case having a common question involving numerous people. Indeed, we have seen no case before 1800 refusing to permit use of the class suit where the questions were common and the parties many; the inference may be that the practical inhibitions to the litigants were adequate restraint on inappropriate use of the class suit. Third, the courts were very much concerned that the representatives of the class indeed be representative of its members' interest. See Chafee, Some Problems of Equity, cc. 6, 7 (1950); cf. Hazard, Indispensable Party: The Historical Origin of a Procedural Phantom, 61 Colum.L.Rev. 1254 (1961). The law of class suits down to about 1760 thus was, like the annals of the poor, short and simple.

The law of class suits from the mid-18th century to the end of the 19th changed very little. The courts were concerned chiefly with whether absentees had to be joined through the class suit device in order to satisfy the necessary parties rule, and secondarily with whether the class members would be bound by the judgment. It is in this period that there appeared such phrases as "well defined community of interest" to describe what made up a class, and "common or general" to describe the legal problem its members had in common. Compare Smith v. Swormstedt, 57 U.S. (16 How.) 288, 14 L.Ed. 942 (1853), with, e.g., Weaver v. Pasadena Tournament of Roses Ass'n, 32 Cal.2d 833, 198 P.2d 514 (1948), and Brenner v. Title Guarantee & Trust Co., 276 N.Y. 230, 11 N.E.2d 890 (1937).

On the critical question of whether the determination of the representative suit was conclusive on persons within the class, but who were not parties, there was confusion and anxiety. Consider Pomeroy, Remedies and Remedial Rights § 400 (1876):

"If * * * the prior suit has been terminated, and the question arises in a subsequent controversy, and involves the conclusive effect of the former adjudication upon the class of persons represented by the actual parties, in order that such judgment should be conclusive upon any particular person of the class either in his favor or against him, there must have been the previous formal act on his part of * * * making him a party to the action * * * or it must be shown that he had notice of the proceedings, and an opportunity to unite in them of which he neglected or refused to avail himself."

In the Fourth Edition of Pomeroy's treatise, by Professor Thomas Bogle in 1904, this passage was unchanged, as it was in the Fifth Edition appearing in 1929.

If the cases went no further than Pomeroy said they did, the class suit was little more than a joinder device: Members of the class were bound only if they became parties, or had notice that approximated summons. Cf. Mullane v. Central Hanover Bank & Trust Co., supra p. 303. A number of important cases had held that a class suit could bind persons in the class who were not only unjoined in but unaware of the litigation. See, e.g., Supreme Tribe of Ben Hur v. Cauble, 255 U.S. 356, 41 S.Ct. 338, 65 L.Ed. 673 (1921). And, of particular note, in the revision of the Federal Equity Rules in 1912, the rule was amended so as to delete the bracketed phrase:

"When the question is one of common or general interest to many persons constituting a class so numerous as to make it impracticable to bring them all before the court, one or more may sue or defend for the whole [, but in such cases the decree shall be without prejudice to the rights and claims of the absent parties]."

Thus some of the cases and text-writers had said that members of a class were bound only if joined or at least notified. Other cases said they could be bound if their representation had been adequate. Cf. Keeffe, Levy and Donovan, Lee Defeats Ben Hur, 33 Cornell L.Rev. 327 (1948).

It was in this confused state that the draftsmen of the Federal Rules undertook the analysis and formulation of the original version of Rule 23. Shortly thereafter came Hansberry v. Lee.

a. RES JUDICATA IN CLASS SUITS

HANSBERRY v. LEE

Supreme Court of the United States, 1940.
311 U.S. 32, 61 S.Ct. 115, 85 L.Ed. 22.

MR. JUSTICE STONE delivered the opinion of the Court.

The question is whether the Supreme Court of Illinois, by its adjudication that petitioners in this case are bound by a judgment rendered in an earlier litigation to which they were not parties, has deprived them of the due process of law guaranteed by the Fourteenth Amendment.

Respondents brought this suit in the Circuit Court of Cook County, Illinois, to enjoin the breach by petitioners of an agreement restricting the use of land within a described area of the City of Chicago, which was alleged to have been entered into by some five hundred of the landowners. The agreement stipulated that for a specified period no part of the land should be "sold, leased to or permitted to be occupied by any person of the colored race," and provided that it should not be effective unless signed by the "owners of 95 per centum of the frontage" within the described area. The bill of complaint set up that the owners of 95 per cent of the frontage had signed; that respondents are owners of land within the restricted area who have either signed the agreement or acquired their land from others who did sign and that petitioners Hansberry, who are Negroes, have, with the alleged aid of the other petitioners and with knowledge of the agreement, acquired and are occupying land in the restricted area formerly belonging to an owner who had signed the agreement.

To the defense that the agreement had never become effective because owners of 95 per cent of the frontage had not signed it, respondents pleaded that that issue was res judicata by the decree in an earlier suit. Burke v. Kleiman, 277 Ill.App. 519. To this petitioners pleaded, by way of rejoinder, that they were not parties to that suit or bound by its decree, and that denial of their right to litigate, in the present suit, the issue of performance of the condition precedent to the validity of the agreement would be a denial of due process of law guaranteed by the Fourteenth Amendment. It does not appear, nor is it contended that any of petitioners is the successor in interest to or in privity with any of the parties in the earlier suit.

The circuit court, after a trial on the merits, found that owners of only about 54 per cent of the frontage had signed the agreement and that the only support of the judgment in the Burke case was a false and fraudulent stipulation of the parties that 95 per cent had signed. But it ruled that the issue of performance of the condition precedent to the validity of the agreement was res judicata as alleged and entered a decree for respondents. The Supreme Court of Illinois affirmed. 372 Ill. 369, 24 N.E.2d 37. We granted certiorari to resolve the constitutional question. 309 U.S. 652, 60 S.Ct. 889, 84 L.Ed. 1002.

The Supreme Court of Illinois, upon an examination of the record in Burke v. Kleiman, supra, found that that suit, in the Superior Court of Cook County, was brought by a landowner in the restricted area to enforce the agreement which had been signed by her predecessor in title, in behalf of herself and other property owners in like situation, against four named individuals who had acquired or asserted an interest in a plot of land formerly owned by another signer of the agreement; that upon stipulation of the parties in that suit that the agreement had been signed by owners of 95 per cent of all the frontage, the court had adjudged that the agreement was in force, that it was a covenant running with the land and binding all the land within the described area in the hands of the parties to the agreement and those claiming under them including defendants, and had entered its decree restraining the breach of the agreement by the defendants and those claiming under them, and that the appellate court had affirmed the decree. It found that the stipulation was untrue but held, contrary to the trial court, that it was not fraudulent or collusive. It also appears from the record in Burke v. Kleiman that the case was tried on an agreed statement of facts which raised only a single issue, whether by reason of changes in the restricted area, the agreement had ceased to be enforcible in equity.

From this the Supreme Court of Illinois concluded in the present case that Burke v. Kleiman was a "class" or "representative" suit and that in such a suit "where the remedy is pursued by a plaintiff who has the right to represent the class to which he belongs, other members of the class are bound by the results in the case unless it is reversed or set aside on direct proceedings"; [372 Ill. 369, 24 N.E.2d 39], that petitioners in the present suit were members of the class represented by the plaintiffs in the earlier suit and consequently were bound by its decree which had rendered the issue of performance of the condition precedent to the restrictive agreement res judicata, so far as petitioners are concerned. The court thought that the circumstance that the stipulation in the earlier suit that owners of 95 per cent of the frontage had signed the agreement was contrary to the fact as found in the present suit did not militate against this conclusion since the court in the earlier suit had jurisdiction to determine the fact as between the parties before it and that its determination, because of the representative character of the suit, even though erroneous, was binding on petitioners until set aside by a direct attack on the first judgment.

State courts are free to attach such descriptive labels to litigations before them as they may choose and to attribute to them such consequences as they think appropriate under state constitutions and laws, subject only to the requirements of the Constitution of the United States. But when the judgment of a state court, ascribing to the judgment of another court the binding force and effect of res judicata, is challenged for want of due process it becomes the duty of this Court to examine the course of procedure in both litigations to ascertain whether the litigant whose rights have thus been adjudicated has been afforded such notice and opportunity to be heard as are requisite to the due process which the Constitution prescribes. Western Life Indemnity Co. v. Rupp, 235 U.S. 261, 273, 35 S.Ct. 37, 40, 59 L.Ed. 220.

It is a principle of general application in Anglo-American jurisprudence that one is not bound by a judgment in personam in a litigation in which he is not designated as a party or to which he has not been made a party by service of process. Pennoyer v. Neff, 95 U.S. 714, 24 L.Ed. 565; 1 Freeman on Judgments, 5th Ed., § 407. A judgment rendered in such circumstances is not entitled to the full faith and credit which the Constitution and statute of the United States, R.S. § 905, 28 U.S.C. § 687, 28 U.S.C.A. § 687, prescribe, Pennoyer v. Neff, supra; Lafayette Ins. Co. v. French, 18 How. 404, 15 L.Ed. 451; Hall v. Lanning, 91 U.S. 160, 23 L.Ed. 271; Baker v. Baker, E. & Co., 242 U.S. 394, 37 S.Ct. 152, 61 L.Ed. 386, and judicial action enforcing it against the person or property of the absent party is not that due process which the Fifth and Fourteenth Amendments require. Postal Telegraph-Cable Co. v. Newport, 247 U.S. 464, 38 S.Ct. 566, 62 L.Ed. 1215; Old Wayne Mut. L. Ass'n v. McDonough, 204 U.S. 8, 27 S.Ct. 236, 51 L.Ed. 345.

To these general rules there is a recognized exception that, to an extent not precisely defined by judicial opinion, the judgment in a "class" or "representative" suit, to which some members of the class are parties, may bind members of the class or those represented who were not made parties to it. Smith v. Swormstedt, 16 How. 288, 14 L.Ed. 942; Royal Arcanum v. Green, 237 U.S. 531, 35 S.Ct. 724, 59 L.Ed. 1089, L.R.A.1916A, 771; Hartford L. Ins. Co. v. Ibs, 237 U.S. 662, 35 S.Ct. 692, 59 L.Ed. 1165, L.R.A.1916A, 765; Hartford Life Ins. Co. v. Barber, 245 U.S. 146, 38 S.Ct. 54, 62 L.Ed. 208; Supreme Tribe of Ben-Hur v. Cauble, 255 U.S. 356, 41 S.Ct. 338, 65 L.Ed. 673; cf. Christopher v. Brusselback, 302 U.S. 500, 58 S.Ct. 350, 82 L.Ed. 388.

The class suit was an invention of equity to enable it to proceed to a decree in suits where the number of those interested in the subject of the litigation is so great that their joinder as parties in conformity to the usual rules of procedure is impracticable. Courts are not infrequently called upon to proceed with causes in which the number of those interested in the litigation is so great as to make difficult or impossible the joinder of all because some are not within the jurisdiction or because their whereabouts is unknown or where if all were made parties to the suit its continued abatement by the death of some would prevent or unduly delay a decree. In such cases where the interests of those not joined are of the same class as the interests of those who are, and where it is considered that the latter fairly represent the former in the prosecution of the litigation of the issues in which all have a common interest, the court will proceed to a decree.

Brown v. Vermuden, 1 Ch.Cas. 272; City of London v. Richmond, 2 Vern. 421; Cockburn v. Thompson, 16 Ves.Jr. 321; West v. Randall, Fed.Cas. No. 17,424, 2 Mason 181; Beatty v. Kurtz, 2 Pet. 566, 7 L.Ed. 521; Smith v. Swormstedt, supra; Supreme Tribe of Ben-Hur v. Cauble, supra; Story, Equity Pleading (2d Ed.) § 98.

It is evident that the considerations which may induce a court thus to proceed, despite a technical defect of parties, may differ from those which must be taken into account in determining whether the absent parties are bound by the decree or, if it is adjudged that they are, in ascertaining whether such an adjudication satisfies the requirement of due process and of full faith and credit. Nevertheless there is scope within the framework of the Constitution for holding in appropriate cases that a judgment rendered in a class suit is res judicata as to members of the class who are not formal parties to the suit. Here, as elsewhere, the Fourteenth Amendment does not compel state courts or legislatures to adopt any particular rule for establishing the conclusiveness of judgments in class suits [citations omitted], nor does it compel the adoption of the particular rules thought by this court to be appropriate for the federal courts. With a proper regard for divergent local institutions and interests, cf. Jackson County v. United States, 308 U.S. 343, 351, 60 S.Ct. 285, 288, 84 L.Ed. 313, this Court is justified in saying that there has been a failure of due process only in those cases where it cannot be said that the procedure adopted, fairly insures the protection of the interests of absent parties who are to be bound by it. Chicago, B. & Q. R. Co. v. Chicago, 166 U.S. 226, 235, 17 S.Ct. 581, 584, 41 L.Ed. 979.

It is familiar doctrine of the federal courts that members of a class not present as parties to the litigation may be bound by the judgment where they are in fact adequately represented by parties who are present, or where they actually participate in the conduct of the litigation in which members of the class are present as parties [citations omitted], or where the interest of the members of the class, some of whom are present as parties, is joint, or where for any other reason the relationship between the parties present and those who are absent is such as legally to entitle the former to stand in judgment for the latter. Smith v. Swormstedt, supra; cf. Christopher v. Brusselback, supra, 302 U.S. at pages 503, 504, 58 S.Ct. at page 352, 82 L.Ed. 388, and cases cited.

In all such cases, so far as it can be said that the members of the class who are present are, by generally recognized rules of law, entitled to stand in judgment for those who are not, we may assume for present purposes that such procedure affords a protection to the parties who are represented though absent, which would satisfy the requirements of due process and full faith and credit. See Bernheimer v. Converse, 206 U.S. 516, 27 S.Ct. 755, 51 L.Ed. 1163; Marin v. Augedahl, 247 U.S. 142, 38 S.Ct. 452, 62 L.Ed. 1038; Chandler v. Peketz, 297 U.S. 609, 56 S.Ct. 602, 80 L.Ed. 881. Nor do we find it necessary for the decision of this case to say that, when the only circumstance defining the class is that the determination of the rights of its members turns upon a single issue of fact or law, a state could not constitutionally adopt a procedure whereby some of the members of the class could stand in judgment for all, provided that the procedure were so devised and applied as to insure that those present are of the same class as those absent and that the litigation is so conducted as to insure the full and fair consideration of the common issue. Compare New England Divisions Case, 261 U.S. 184, 197, 43 S.Ct. 270, 275, 67 L.Ed. 605; Taggart v. Bremner, 7 Cir., 236 F. 544. We decide only that the procedure and the course of litigation sustained here by the plea of res judicata do not satisfy these requirements.

The restrictive agreement did not purport to create a joint obligation or liability. If valid and effective its promises were the several obligations of the signers and those claiming under them. The promises ran severally to every other signer. It is plain that in such circumstances all those alleged to be bound by the agreement would not constitute a single class in any litigation brought to enforce it. Those who sought to secure its benefits by enforcing it could not be said to be in the same class with or represent those whose interest was in resisting performance, for the agreement by its terms imposes obligations and confers rights on the owner of each plot of land who signs it. If those who thus seek to secure the benefits of the agreement were rightly regarded by the state Supreme Court as constituting a class, it is evident that those signers or their successors who are interested in challenging the validity of the agreement and resisting its performance are not of the same class in the sense that their interests are identical so that any group who had elected to enforce rights conferred by the agreement could be said to be acting in the interest of any others who were free to deny its obligation.

Because of the dual and potentially conflicting interests of those who are putative parties to the agreement in compelling or resisting its performance, it is impossible to say, solely because they are parties to it, that any two of them are of the same class. Nor without more, and with the due regard for the protection of the rights of absent parties which due process exacts, can some be permitted to stand in judgment for all.

It is one thing to say that some members of a class may represent other members in a litigation where the sole and common interest of the class in the litigation, is either to assert a common right or to challenge an asserted obligation. Smith v. Swormstedt, supra; Supreme Tribe of Ben-Hur v. Cauble, supra; Groves v. Farmers State Bank, 368 Ill. 35, 12 N.E.2d 618. It is quite another to hold that all those who are free alternatively either to assert rights or to challenge them are of a single class, so that any group merely because it is of the class so constituted, may be deemed adequately to represent any others of the class in litigating their interests in either alternative. Such a selection of representatives for purposes of litigation, whose substantial interests are not necessarily or even probably the same as those whom they are deemed to represent, does not afford that protection to absent parties which due process requires. The doctrine of representation of absent parties in a class suit has not hitherto been thought to go so far. See Terry v. Bank of Cape Fear, C.C., 20 F. 777, 781; Weidenfeld v. Northern Pac. Ry. Co., 8 Cir., 129 F. 305, 310; McQuillen v. National Cash Register Co., D.C., 22 F.Supp. 867, 873, affirmed, 4 Cir., 112 F.2d 877, 882; Brenner v. Title Guarantee & Trust Co., 276 N.Y. 230, 11 N.E. 2d 890, 114 A.L.R. 1010; cf. Wabash R. R. Co. v. Adelbert College, 208 U.S. 38, 28 S.Ct. 182, 52 L.Ed. 379; Coe v. Armour Fertilizer Works, 237 U.S. 413, 35 S.Ct. 625, 59 L.Ed. 1027. Apart from the opportunities it would afford for the fraudulent and collusive sacrifice of the rights of absent parties, we think that the representation in this case no more satisfies the requirements of due process than a trial by a judicial officer who is in such situation that he may have an interest in the outcome of the litigation in conflict with that of the litigants. Tumey v. Ohio, 273 U.S. 510, 47 S.Ct. 437, 71 L.Ed. 749, 50 A.L.R. 1243.

The plaintiffs in the Burke case sought to compel performance of the agreement in behalf of themselves and all others similarly situated. They did not designate the defendants in the suit as a class or seek any injunction or other relief against others than the named defendants, and the decree which was entered did not purport to bind others. In seeking to enforce the agreement the plaintiffs in that suit were not representing the petitioners here whose substantial interest is in resisting performance. The defendants in the first suit were not treated by the pleadings or decree as representing others or as foreclosing by their defense the rights of others, and even though nominal defendants, it does not appear that their interest in defeating the contract outweighed their interest in establishing its validity. For a court in this situation to ascribe to either the plaintiffs or defendants the performance of such functions on behalf of petitioners here, is to attribute to them a power that it cannot be said that they had assumed to exercise, and a responsibility which, in view of their dual interests it does not appear that they could rightly discharge.

Reversed.

MR. JUSTICE MCREYNOLDS, MR. JUSTICE ROBERTS and MR. JUSTICE REED concur in the result.

COOPER v. FEDERAL RESERVE BANK OF RICHMOND

Supreme Court of the United States, 1984.
467 U.S. 867, 104 S.Ct. 2794, 81 L.Ed.2d 718.*

JUSTICE STEVENS delivered the opinion of the Court.

The question to be decided is whether a judgment in a class action determining that an employer did not engage in a general pattern or practice of racial discrimination against the certified class of employees precludes a class member from maintaining a subsequent civil action

* Some of the Court's footnotes are omitted.

alleging an individual claim of racial discrimination against the employer.

I

On March 22, 1977, the Equal Employment Opportunity Commission commenced a civil action against respondent, the Federal Reserve Bank of Richmond. Respondent operates a branch in Charlotte, N.C. (the Bank), where during the years 1974–1978 it employed about 350–450 employees in several departments. The EEOC complaint alleged that the Bank was violating § 703(a) of Title VII of the Civil Rights Act of 1964 by engaging in "policies and practices" that included "failing and refusing to promote *blacks* because of race." App. 9a.

Six months after the EEOC filed its complaint, four individual employees [2] were allowed to intervene as plaintiffs. In their "complaint in intervention," these plaintiffs alleged that the Bank's employment practices violated 42 U.S.C. § 1981, as well as Title VII; that each of them was the victim of employment discrimination based on race; and that they could adequately represent a class of black employees against whom the Bank had discriminated because of their race. In due course, the District Court entered an order conditionally certifying the following class pursuant to Federal Rules of Civil Procedure 23(b)(2) and (3):

> "All black persons who have been employed by the defendant at its Charlotte Branch Office at any time since January 3, 1974 [6 months prior to the first charge filed by the intervenors with EEOC], who have been discriminated against in promotion, wages, job assignments and terms and conditions of employment because of their race."

After certifying the class, the District Court ordered that notice be published in the Charlotte newspapers and mailed to each individual member of the class. The notice described the status of the litigation, and plainly stated that members of the class "will be bound by the judgment or other determination" if they did not exclude themselves by sending a written notice to the clerk.[4] Among the recipients of the

---

2. Sylvia Cooper, Constance Russell, Helen Moore, and Elmore Hannah, Jr., sometimes referred to by the District Court as the "intervening plaintiffs" and by the parties as the "Cooper petitioners."

* * *

4. The actual text of the critical paragraphs of the notice read as follows:

"3. The class of persons who are entitled to participate in this action as members of the class represented by the plaintiff-intervenors, for whom relief may be sought in this action by the plaintiff-intervenors and who will be bound by the determination in this action is defined to include: all black per-

sons who were employed by the Federal Reserve Bank of Richmond at its Charlotte Branch Office at any time since January 3, 1974.

"4. If you fit in the definition of the class in paragraph 3 you are a class member. As a class member, you are entitled to pursue in this action any claim of racial discrimination in employment that you may have against the defendant. You need to do nothing further at this time to remain a member of the class. However, if you so desire, you may exclude yourself from the class by notifying the Clerk, United States Dis-

notice were Phyllis Baxter and five other individuals employed by the Bank.[5] It is undisputed that these individuals—the Baxter petitioners—are members of the class represented by the intervening plaintiffs and that they made no attempt to exclude themselves from the class.

At the trial the intervening plaintiffs, as well as the Baxter petitioners, testified. The District Court found that the Bank had engaged in a pattern and practice of discrimination from 1974 through 1978 by failing to afford black employees opportunities for advancement and assignment equal to opportunities afforded white employees in pay grades 4 and 5. Except as so specified, however, the District Court found that "there does not appear to be a pattern and practice of discrimination pervasive enough for the court to order relief." App. to Pet. for Cert. 193a–194a. With respect to the claims of the four intervening plaintiffs, the court found that the Bank had discriminated against Cooper and Russell, but not against Moore and Hannah. Finally, the court somewhat cryptically stated that although it had an opinion about "the entitlement to relief of some of the class members who testified at trial," it would defer decision of such matters to a further proceeding. Id., at 194a.

Thereafter, on March 24, 1981, the Baxter petitioners moved to intervene, alleging that each had been denied a promotion for discriminatory reasons. With respect to Emma Ruffin, the court denied the motion because she was a member of the class for which relief had been ordered and therefore her rights would be protected in the Stage II proceedings to be held on the question of relief. With respect to the other five Baxter petitioners, the court also denied the motion, but for a different reason. It held that because all of them were employed in jobs above the grade 5 category, they were not entitled to any benefit from the court's ruling with respect to discrimination in grades 4 and 5. The District Court stated: "The court has found no proof of any classwide discrimination above grade 5 and, therefore, they are not entitled to participate in any Stage II proceedings in this case." Id., at

trict Court, as provided in paragraph 6 below.

"5. If you decide to remain in this action, you should be advised that: the court will include you in the class in this action unless you request to be excluded from the class in writing; the judgment in this case, whether favorable or unfavorable to the plaintiff and the plaintiff-intervenors, will include all members of the class; all class members will be bound by the judgment or other determination of this action; and if you do not request exclusion, you may appear at the hearings and trial of this action through the attorney of your choice.

"6. If you desire to exclude yourself from this action, you will not be bound by any judgment or other determination

in this action and you will not be able to depend on this action to toll any statutes of limitations on any individual claims you may have against the defendant. You may exclude yourself from this action by notifying the Clerk in writing that you do not desire to participate in this action. The Clerks' address is: Clerk, United States District Court, Post Office Box 1266, Charlotte, North Carolina 28232." App. 35a–37a.

5. In addition to Baxter, they were Brenda Gilliam, Glenda Knott, Emma Ruffin, Alfred Harrison, and Sherri McCorkle. All of these individuals, sometimes referred to as the "Baxter petitioners," stipulated that they received the notice. See Id., at 95a.

287a. The court added that it could "see no reason why, if any of the would be intervenors are actively interested in pursuing their claims, they cannot file a Section 1981 suit next week. . . ." Id., at 288a.

A few days later the Baxter petitioners filed a separate action against the Bank alleging that each of them had been denied a promotion because of their race in violation of 42 U.S.C. § 1981. The Bank moved to dismiss the complaint on the ground that each of them was a member of the class that had been certified in the Cooper litigation, that each was employed in a grade other than 4 or 5, and that they were bound by the determination that there was no proof of any classwide discrimination above grade 5. The District Court denied the motion to dismiss, but certified its order for interlocutory appeal under 28 U.S.C. § 1292(b). The Bank's interlocutory appeal from the order was then consolidated with the Bank's pending appeal in the Cooper litigation.

The United States Court of Appeals for the Fourth Circuit reversed the District Court's judgment on the merits in the Cooper litigation, concluding that (1) there was insufficient evidence to establish a pattern or practice of racial discrimination in grades 4 and 5, and (2) two of the intervening plaintiffs had not been discriminated against on account of race. EEOC v. Federal Reserve Bank of Richmond, 698 F.2d 633 (4th Cir.1983). The court further held that under the doctrine of res judicata, the judgment in the Cooper class action precluded the Baxter petitioners from maintaining their individual race discrimination claims against the Bank. * * *

II

Claims of two types were adjudicated in the Cooper litigation. First, the individual claims of each of the four intervening plaintiffs have been finally decided in the Bank's favor. Those individual decisions do not, of course, foreclose any other individual claims. Second, the class claim that the Bank followed "policies and practices" of discriminating against its employees has also been decided. It is that decision on which the Court of Appeals based its res judicata analysis.

There is of course no dispute that under elementary principles of prior adjudication a judgment in a properly entertained class action is binding on class members in any subsequent litigation. See, e.g., Supreme Tribe of Ben–Hur v. Cauble, 255 U.S. 356, 41 S.Ct. 338, 65 L.Ed. 673 (1921); Restatement of Judgments § 86 (1942); Restatement (Second) of Judgments § 41(1)(e) (1982); see also Fed.Rule Civ.Proc. 23(c)(3); see generally Moore & Cohn, Federal Class Actions—Jurisdiction and Effect of Judgments, 32 Ill.L.Rev. 555 (1938). Basic principles of res judicata (merger and bar or claim preclusion) and collateral estoppel (issue preclusion) apply. A judgment in favor of the plaintiff class extinguishes their claim, which merges into the judgment granting relief. A judgment in favor of the defendant extinguishes the claim, barring a subsequent action on that claim. A judgment in favor of either side is conclusive in a subsequent action between them on any issue actually litigated and determined, if its determination was essential to that judgment.

III

A plaintiff bringing a civil action for a violation of § 703(a) of Title VII of the Civil Rights Act of 1964, 78 Stat. 255, as amended, 42 U.S.C. § 2000e–2(a), has the initial burden of establishing a prima facie case that his employer discriminated against him on account of his race, color, religion, sex, or national origin. A plaintiff meets this initial burden by offering evidence adequate to create an inference that he was denied an employment opportunity on the basis of a discriminatory criterion enumerated in Title VII.

A plaintiff alleging one instance of discrimination establishes a prima facie case justifying an inference of individual racial discrimination by showing that he (1) belongs to a racial minority, (2) applied and was qualified for a vacant position the employer was attempting to fill, (3) was rejected for the position, and (4) after his rejection, the position remained open and the employer continued to seek applicants of the plaintiff's qualifications. McDonnell Douglas Corp. v. Green, 411 U.S. 792, 802, 93 S.Ct. 1817, 1824, 36 L.Ed.2d 668 (1973). Once these facts are established, the employer must produce "evidence that the plaintiff was rejected, or someone else was preferred, for a legitimate, nondiscriminatory reason." Texas Dept. of Community Affairs v. Burdine, 450 U.S. 248, 254, 101 S.Ct. 1089, 1094, 67 L.Ed.2d 207 (1981). At that point, the presumption of discrimination "drops from the case," id., at 255, n. 10, 101 S.Ct., at 1095, n. 10, and the district court is in a position to decide the ultimate question in such a suit: whether the particular employment decision at issue was made on the basis of race. United States Postal Service Board of Governors v. Aikens, 460 U.S. 711, 714– 715, 103 S.Ct. 1478, 1481–1482, 75 L.Ed.2d 403 (1983); Texas Dept. of Community Affairs v. Burdine, 450 U.S., at 253, 101 S.Ct., at 1093. The ultimate burden of persuading the trier of fact that the defendant intentionally discriminated against the plaintiff regarding the particular employment decision "remains at all times with the plaintiff," ibid., and in the final analysis the trier of fact "must decide which party's explanation of the employer's motivation it believes." United States Postal Service Board of Governors v. Aikens, 460 U.S., at 716, 103 S.Ct., at 1482.

In Franks v. Bowman Transportation Co., 424 U.S. 747, 96 S.Ct. 1251, 47 L.Ed.2d 444 (1976), the plaintiff, on behalf of himself and all others similarly situated, alleged that the employer had engaged in a pervasive pattern of racial discrimination in various company policies, including the hiring, transfer, and discharge of employees. In that class action we held that demonstrating the existence of a discriminatory pattern or practice established a presumption that the individual class members had been discriminated against on account of race. Id., at 772, 96 S.Ct., at 1268. Proving isolated or sporadic discriminatory acts by the employer is insufficient to establish a prima facie case of a pattern or practice of discrimination; rather it must be established by a preponderance of the evidence that "racial discrimination was the company's standard operating procedure—the regular rather than the unusual practice." Teamsters v. United States, 431 U.S. 324, 336, 97 S.Ct. 1843, 1855, 52 L.Ed.2d 396 (1977) (footnote omitted). While a finding of a pattern or practice of discrimination itself justifies an award of prospective relief to the class, additional proceedings are ordinarily required to determine the scope of individual relief for the members of the class. Id., at 361, 97 S.Ct., at 1867.

The crucial difference between an individual's claim of discrimination and a class action alleging a general pattern or practice of discrimination is manifest. The inquiry regarding an individual's claim is the reason for a particular employment decision, while "at the liability stage of a pattern-or-practice trial the focus often will not be on individual hiring decisions, but on a pattern of discriminatory decision-making." Id., at 360, n. 46, 97 S.Ct., at 1867, n. 46. See generally, Furnco Construction Corp. v. Waters, 438 U.S. 567, 575, n. 7, 98 S.Ct. 2943, 2948 n. 7, 57 L.Ed.2d 957 (1978).

This distinction was critical to our holding in General Telephone Co. of Southwest v. Falcon, 457 U.S. 147, 102 S.Ct. 2364, 72 L.Ed.2d 740 (1982), that an individual employee's claim that he was denied a promotion on racial grounds did not necessarily make him an adequate representative of a class composed of persons who had allegedly been refused employment for discriminatory reasons. We explained:

> "Conceptually, there is a wide gap between (a) an individual's claim that he has been denied a promotion on discriminatory grounds, and his otherwise unsupported allegation that the company has a policy of discrimination, and (b) the existence of a class of persons who have suffered the same injury as that individual, such that the individual's claim and the class claims will share common questions of law or fact and that the individual's claim will be typical of the class claims. For respondent to bridge that gap, he must prove much more than the validity of his own claim. Even though evidence that he was passed over for promotion when several less deserving whites were advanced may support the conclusion that respondent was denied the promotion because of his national origin, such evidence would not necessarily justify the additional inferences (1) that this discriminatory treatment is typical of petitioner's promotion practices, (2) that petitioner's promotion practices are motivated by a policy of ethnic discrimination that pervades petitioner's Irving division, or (3) that this policy of ethnic discrimination is reflected in petitioner's other employment practices, such as hiring, in the same way it is manifested in the promotion practices." Id., at 157–158, 102 S.Ct., at 2371.

After analyzing the particulars of the plaintiff's claim in that case, we pointed out that if "one allegation of specific discriminatory treatment were sufficient to support an across-the-board attack, every Title VII case would be a potential companywide class action." Id., at 159, 102 S.Ct., at 2371. We further observed:

"In this regard it is noteworthy that Title VII prohibits discriminatory employment *practices,* not an abstract policy of discrimination. The mere fact that an aggrieved private plaintiff is a member of an identifiable class of persons of the same race or national origin is insufficient to establish his standing to litigate on their behalf all possible claims of discrimination against a common employer." Id., at 159, n. 15, 102 S.Ct., at 2372, n. 15.

Falcon thus holds that the existence of a valid individual claim does not necessarily warrant the conclusion that the individual plaintiff may successfully maintain a class action. It is equally clear that a class plaintiff's attempt to prove the existence of a companywide policy, or even a consistent practice within a given department, may fail even though discrimination against one or two individuals has been proved. The facts of this case illustrate the point.

The District Court found that two of the intervening plaintiffs, Cooper and Russell, had both established that they were the victims of racial discrimination but, as the Court of Appeals noted, they were employed in grades higher than grade 5 and therefore their testimony provided no support for the conclusion that there was a practice of discrimination in grades 4 and 5.[10] Given the burden of establishing a prima facie case of a pattern or practice of discrimination, it was entirely consistent for the District Court simultaneously to conclude that Cooper and Russell had valid individual claims even though it had expressly found no proof of any classwide discrimination above grade 5. It could not be more plain that the rejection of a claim of classwide discrimination does not warrant the conclusion that no member of the class could have a valid individual claim. "A racially balanced work force cannot immunize an employer from liability for specific acts of discrimination." Furnco Construction Corp. v. Waters, 438 U.S., at 579, 98 S.Ct., at 2950–2951.

The analysis of the merits of the Cooper litigation by the Court of Appeals is entirely consistent with this conclusion. In essence, the Court of Appeals held that the statistical evidence, buttressed by expert testimony and anecdotal evidence by three individual employees in

---

10. The Court of Appeals wrote:

"In denying the motion the District Court stated that all intervenors 'in grades higher than grade 5' were not members of the class in whose favor the District Court had found 'classwide discrimination.' By this test, Cooper, Moore, Russell, Baxter, Gilliam, Knott and McCorckle were not members of the class in which discrimination was found

and their testimony could not have been included within the District Court's term 'oral testimony of class members,' complaining of promotion out of either pay grade 4 or pay grade 5; only the testimony of Ruffin and Harrison met that qualifying standard." EEOC v. Federal Reserve Bank of Richmond, 698 F.2d 633, 644 (1983).

grades 4 and 5, was not sufficient to support the finding of a pattern of bankwide discrimination within those grades. It is true that the Court of Appeals was unpersuaded by the anecdotal evidence; it is equally clear, however, that it did not regard two or three instances of discrimination as sufficient to establish a general policy. It quite properly recognized that a "court must be wary of a claim that the true color of a forest is better revealed by reptiles hidden in the weeds than by the foliage of countless freestanding trees." NAACP v. Claiborne Hardware Co., 458 U.S. 886, 934, 102 S.Ct. 3409, 3437, 73 L.Ed.2d 1215 (1982). Conversely, a piece of fruit may well be bruised without being rotten to the core.

The Court of Appeals was correct in generally concluding that the Baxter petitioners, as members of the class represented by the intervening plaintiffs in the Cooper litigation, are bound by the adverse judgment in that case. The court erred, however, in the preclusive effect it attached to that prior adjudication. That judgment (1) bars the class members from bringing another class action against the Bank alleging a pattern or practice of discrimination for the relevant time period and (2) precludes the class members in any other litigation with the Bank from relitigating the question whether the Bank engaged in a pattern and practice of discrimination against black employees during the relevant time period. The judgment is not, however, dispositive of the individual claims the Baxter petitioners have alleged in their separate action. Assuming they establish a prima facie case of discrimination under *McDonnell Douglas,* the Bank will be required to articulate a legitimate reason for each of the challenged decisions, and if it meets that burden, the ultimate questions regarding motivation in their individual cases will be resolved by the District Court. Moreover, the prior adjudication may well prove beneficial to the Bank in the Baxter action: the determination in the Cooper action that the Bank had not engaged in a general pattern or practice of discrimination would be relevant on the issue of pretext. See McDonnell Douglas, 411 U.S., at 804–805, 93 S.Ct., at 1825–1826.

The Bank argues that permitting the Baxter petitioners to bring separate actions would frustrate the purposes of Rule 23. We think the converse is true. The class-action device was intended to establish a procedure for the adjudication of common questions of law or fact. If the Bank's theory were adopted, it would be tantamount to requiring that every member of the class be permitted to intervene to litigate the merits of his individual claim.

It is also suggested that the District Court had a duty to decide the merits of the individual claims of class members, at least insofar as the individual claimants became witnesses in the joint proceeding and subjected their individual employment histories to scrutiny at trial.[12] Unless these claims are decided in the main proceeding, the Bank

---

12. We find the Bank's contention that the District Court actually found against the Baxter petitioners on the basis of the testimony in the Cooper action wholly without merit.

argues that the duplicative litigation that Rule 23 was designed to avoid will be encouraged, and that defendants will be subjected to the risks of liability without the offsetting benefit of a favorable termination of exposure through a final judgment.

This argument fails to differentiate between what the District Court might have done and what it actually did. The District Court did actually adjudicate the individual claims of Cooper and the other intervening plaintiffs, as well as the class claims, but it pointedly refused to decide the individual claims of the Baxter petitioners. Whether the issues framed by the named parties before the court should be expanded to encompass the individual claims of additional class members is a matter of judicial administration that should be decided in the first instance by the District Court. Nothing in Rule 23 requires as a matter of law that the District Court make a finding with respect to each and every matter on which there is testimony in the class action. Indeed, Rule 23 is carefully drafted to provide a mechanism for the expeditious decision of *common* questions. Its purposes might well be defeated by an attempt to decide a host of individual claims before any common question relating to liability has been resolved adversely to the defendant. We do not find the District Court's denial of the Baxter petitioners' motion for leave to intervene in the Cooper litigation, or its decision not to make findings regarding the Baxter petitioners' testimony in the Cooper litigation, to be inconsistent with Rule 23.

The judgment of the Court of Appeals is reversed, and the case is remanded for further proceedings consistent with this opinion.

It is so ordered.

NOTE ON RES JUDICATA IN CLASS SUITS

The unique characteristic of a class action is that a determination made in respect of self-constituted representatives of a group is, or at least purports to be, binding for or against the absent members of the group. In other forms of representative actions, such as a suit by an executor on behalf of a decedent's estate or by a trustee on behalf of the trust estate, representation results from appointment on notice and hearing (as in the case of an executor) or at the instance of one presumably interested in the welfare of those to be represented (as in the case of a trust settlor's designation of a trustee). In the class suit, on the other hand, those represented ordinarily have neither of right nor in fact an advance opportunity to challenge the qualifications of those who undertake to speak on their behalf. See Restatement Second of Judgments §§ 41 and 42.

The notion that a person is deemed to have had his day in court by virtue of the appearance of a stranger who purported to speak for him is, to say the least, in Professor Chafee's phrase, "an incongruity." Chafee, Some Problems of Equity 203 (1950). In an otherwise illustrious treatment, Kalven and Rosenfield, The Contemporary Function of the Class Suit, 8 U.Chi.L.Rev. 684, 710–714 (1941), it is argued that the problem of the res judicata effect of a judgment in a class action is irrelevant to a consideration of the propriety of a class suit. They assume the injustice of applying res judicata *against* a member of a class of the type to which they refer (i.e., a class suit founded on the convenience of asserting in one action a multitude of substantially similar claims), but contend that this is no reason why res judicata should not operate in *favor* of the members of such a class. As to this they say, 8 U.Chi.L.Rev. at 713–14:

> "The second and perhaps most fundamental reason [for the objection to allowing absentees to take advantage of a favorable decree but not binding them to an unfavorable one] is simply that—legal technicalities aside—it is unfair to afford the absentees all the benefits of winning but to impose upon them none of the burdens of losing. This, it seems, just isn't cricket. But * * * the defendant has been afforded his day in court; he has had the opportunity to present his case fully in his own right, and he has lost.
> * * *
>
> "It is probably true that the unfairness argument also derives some plausibility from the not unpopular assimilation of litigation to gambling. The absentees are permitted, it might be contended, in effect to place their bets after the race is over. This probably does violate the better gambling etiquette, but that is not an altogether relevant consideration * * *.
>
> "* * * It is an extraordinary thing to bar a man who has not had an actual day in court, and the policy of assuring to each a day in court certainly competes with whatever policy there is in favor of putting an end to litigation. The difficulties of reconciling these policies are undeniably real. But the solution of the simple question of participation after decree should not be compelled to await the ultimate resolution of the res judicata question, which is at once more difficult and less significant."

There seem to be at least three things wrong with this approach. In the first place, Hansberry v. Lee had affirmed that the members of a class could under certain circumstances be bound by a representative. On reflection, the circumstances that justify binding the class seem to have less to do with the type of claim involved than the type of representation. Hence, the authors' initial assumption, that a class *cannot* be bound by an unsuccessful result, seems unwarranted. Second, it is difficult to see why res judicata should not be two-way. Third, it is in principle impossible to distinguish between a victory for the class litigant, and a defeat. A favorable judgment at the same time confers benefits and circumscribes them. If finality is not to be accorded to defeat of a class, on what basis can it be accorded to limited victory, the only kind the law awards?

There are problems in applying res judicata against members of an unsuccessful class, but they stem more from failure to precisely delineate the scope of the action at the outset than from any inherent difficulties or injustices. Was this the problem in Cooper v. Federal Reserve Bank? Consider two possibilities: (1) the intervenors in *Cooper* were class representatives only, with the individual evidence presented by them relevant only to the claim that there had been a "pattern or practice" of discrimination; or (2) the intervenors were both class representatives and individual claimants, with the evidence presented by them probative of both the class and individual claims. How would the claim preclusion effects differ under each of these possibilities, both for the intervenors and the non-intervening class members? Was the Court right in its reading of the scope of the claims?

As observed in the Historical Note on Class Suits, supra p. 823, the question of the binding effect of representative proceedings was in sharp dispute prior to Hansberry v. Lee. Some authorities held out that there could be no res judicata effect on absentees. Others ignored the question. The draftsmen of the original version of Federal Rule 23 conceived that the matter was not in dispute at all, but that the res judicata effects of a class suit turned on the type of legal relationship that the class members had vis-a-vis their adversary. Accordingly, class suits were classified into three types—"true," where the class members' rights were "joint, or common," Rule 23(a)(1); "hybrid," where the class members' rights were several but affected specific property, Rule 23(a)(2); or "spurious," where their rights were "several," Rule 23(a)(3).

The draftsmen found that the precedents fell into these categories, res judicata being dependent on the conceptual characterization of the legal claims involved. It seems not to have occurred to them that the conceptual characterizations were not distinguishable from each other and that variation in res judicata effects found in the cases was explained, rather, by different judicial attitudes toward res judicata in representative suits. The trifurcation of the original F.R.C.P. 23 evoked acid criticism among the commentators. See Chafee, supra, c. 7; Note, Federal Class Actions: A Suggested Revision of Rule 23, 46 Colum.L.Rev. 818 (1946).

Perhaps inspired by these criticisms, some courts undertook to confront the res judicata problem in terms of the adequacy of the representation of the class and the practical usefulness of the class suit device. In Dickinson v. Burnham, 197 F.2d 973 (2d Cir. 1952), the court was able to find that a class action for damages for fraud resulted in a fund of liability money, and that the members of the class consisting of those who had been defrauded each had an "interest" in the fund. This conceptualization of the problem, far from ineluctable and perhaps barely plausible, permitted the court to say that the members of the class were bound by the award and that the judgment therefore liquidated and determined the measure of defendant's liability. In Union Carbide and Carbon Corp. v. Nisley, 300 F.2d 561 (10th Cir. 1961), the problem of the binding effect of a class suit was presented in unambiguous form. In that case, a small group of miners of vanadium and uranium ore sued two large metals processing companies under the antitrust laws, complaining that the defendants by agreement between themselves had held down the price they would pay for ores produced by miners in the Colorado area. The plaintiffs sued in their individual capacities and as representatives of a class defined as all miners supplying ore to the defendants. Plaintiffs won a jury verdict and then sought to invite the other members of the class to join in to prove their individual damages. The court sustained the intervention, observing, 300 F.2d at 588–589:

> "One line of authority is to the effect that a 23(a)(3) class action [under Rule 23 as it was before the 1966 revision] is merely another joinder device, placed in the Federal Rules in order to obviate the jurisdictional requirements of complete diversity 'where there are numerous persons who have claims or defenses that involve a common question of law or fact.' * * * From this it has been reasoned that * * * only those persons who are actually parties to the litigation are bound by or can share in a money judgment. * * *

> "Other courts, in cases where there has been an identifiable class, have allowed unnamed plaintiffs to intervene and share in the judgment obtained by their representatives, insofar as each is able to prove both membership in the class and damages. * * *

"Undoubtedly this latter solution results in more expeditious and efficient disposition of litigation and ought therefore to be favored."

Judge Picket in dissent expressed worry: "I am convinced that the adoption of this concept of the rule will not only lead to its unfair use, but will be conducive to the undesirable solicitation of claims in tort cases in which there are multiple injuries."

The decision in Union Carbide v. Nisley was in turn importantly relied on in the 1966 revision of Rule 23. The 1966 revision undertook three tasks: First, it sought to eliminate the confusing, and in our view unsound, classification system of the original Rule 23. Second, it sought to make absolutely clear the availability of a class suit in cases where joinder of a large number of people was indicated under the necessary parties principle of Rule 19. Third, it provided encouragement and machinery for new uses of the class suit, specifically in cases like Union Carbide v. Nisley. See Advisory Committee's Note; Kaplan, Continuing Work of the Civil Committee: 1966 Amendments of the Federal Rules of Civil Procedure (I), 81 Harv.L.Rev. 356, 375 et seq. (1967). Moreover, the revision assumed that a class suit judgment would bind all class members, except those who "opted out" from a damages class suit under revised Rule 23(b)(3). See Note, Collateral Attack on the Binding Effect of Class Action Judgments, 87 Harv.L.Rev. 589 (1974).

The 1966 revision of Rule 23 is not only in effect in the federal courts but also in most state courts having the Federal Rules, for they have generally adopted the revisions as they have been made. By fresh judicial interpretation in Daar v. Yellow Cab Co., 67 Cal.2d 695, 63 Cal.Rptr. 724, 433 P.2d 732 (1967), the long-standing California provision on class actions, C.C.P. 382, was infused with Revised Rule 23. In that case, plaintiff brought suit on behalf of himself and all persons who had used defendant's cabs, seeking recovery of an alleged $100,000 of overcharges collected by defendant's setting its taxi meters to operate at rates higher than an ordinance authorized. Defendant's objections to the suit were rejected, 63 Cal.Rptr. at 733–737:

"We have said that it is not essential to the establishment of a class action that a common fund exist. * * * We have also said that it is not essential that the represented parties be so united in interest with the plaintiff as to make them necessary parties. * * * Nor is a common recovery required in order to establish a community of interest. * * * A determination of the interest of each member of the class in any damages recovered does not seem to us dissimilar to a determination of each member's interest in a common trust fund, such determination sometimes being required after the common issues have been resolved in a class action. * * * The fact that each individual ultimately must prove his separate claim to a portion of any recovery by the class is only one factor to be considered in determining whether a class action is proper. As we are not unmindful that substantial benefits * * * should be found before the imposition of a judgment binding on absent parties can be justified, our determination depends upon whether the common questions are sufficiently important to permit adjudication in a class action rather than in a multiplicity of separate suits.

* * *

"We also find of interest the additional criteria prescribed by rule 23 which * * * are in substantial coincidence with our views * * * as to the applicable criteria under section 382."

Aside from the res judicata question, the difficult problem in class suits used to be whether the rules could be construed to permit them—whether specific situations fitted within the definitions in the rules. Since the 1966 revision of Rule 23, this is no longer a serious problem because the Rule's language is broad enough to include virtually any "group" litigation. The difficult problems now are whether particular types of group litigation *should* be permitted. Generally, judicial conservatives have applied the rules narrowly, and suggested that a broader scope for class suits should come from the legislature; judicial activists have thought otherwise. In this conflict, the question of res judicata is reopened.

b. USES AND ADMINISTRATION OF CLASS SUITS

VASQUEZ v. SUPERIOR COURT

Supreme Court of California, 1971.
4 Cal.3d 800, 94 Cal.Rptr. 796, 484 P.2d 964. *

MOSK, J.

We consider whether a group of consumers who have bought merchandise under installment contracts may maintain a class action seeking rescission of the contracts for fraudulent misrepresentation on behalf of themselves and others similarly situated, against both the seller of a product and the finance company to which the installment contracts were assigned. We conclude that such an action will lie against the seller under the principles set forth in Daar v. Yellow Cab Co. (1967) 67 Cal.2d 695, 63 Cal.Rptr. 724, 433 P.2d 732, and that the assignee of the contract is a proper party to such an action under the circumstances presented here.

The action was brought by 37 named plaintiffs on behalf of themselves as well as others who are residents of San Joaquin and Stanislaus Counties and who purchased frozen food and freezers from Bay Area Meat Company. They each executed two retail installment sales contracts to finance the purchases, one in payment of the food, and the other for the freezer, and a binder contract. These contracts were assigned by Bay Area to three finance companies, Avco Thrift, Sterling Finance Corporation, and Beneficial Finance Company of Turlock, which were also named as defendants. Defendants demurred to the complaint on the ground that it did not state a cause of action, and the demurrers were sustained without leave to amend insofar as the complaint alleged a class action for fraud but were overruled on the fraud count as to the named plaintiffs. A second cause of action, also alleged as a class action, charged violations of the Unruh Act (Civ.Code, § 1801 et seq.) in that the installment contracts failed to meet the requirements of that act. The demurrers of all defendants were overruled as to the second cause of action.

* Some of the court's footnotes are omitted.

In upholding the demurrers to the class action aspect of the fraud count, the trial court made it clear that it was not concerned with the sufficiency of the particular allegations to assert a class action but, rather, that in its view a class action for fraud may not be maintained by consumers.

Plaintiffs seek a writ of mandate to compel the trial court to vacate its order sustaining the demurrers to the first cause of action as a class action and to order the court to allow them to proceed to try the cause of action for fraud as a class action.

I

We are met at the threshold with a contention of defendants that mandate is an inappropriate remedy because plaintiffs have an adequate remedy by appeal. It seems clear, however, that plaintiffs may not appeal from the trial court's judgment dismissing their first cause of action as a class action because such a course would violate the rule that an appeal may be taken only from a final judgment. (Code Civ. Proc. § 963, subd. 1.) Under this principle an appeal may not be taken from a judgment which disposes of less than all the causes of action between the parties. (See, e.g., Bank of America v. Superior Court (1942) 20 Cal.2d 697, 701, 128 P.2d 357; Mather v. Mather (1936) 5 Cal. 2d 617, 618, 55 P.2d 1174.)

The complaint here seeks rescission of the contracts on the theory of fraud in the first cause of action and on the theory of a violation of the Unruh Act in the second cause of action. *Mather* refused to allow piecemeal disposition of a cause, and determines that where, as here, all the causes of action set forth in the complaint have a single object, an appeal will not be permitted from a judgment disposing of only one count of the complaint.[4]

We conclude, therefore, that since plaintiffs cannot appeal from the order which bars a substantial portion of their cause from being heard on the merits, their petition for a writ of mandate deserves consideration.

II

Thirty years ago commentators, in urging the utility of the class suit to vindicate the rights of stockholders, made this incisive observa-

---

4. Neither our holding in *Daar* nor the provisions of section 581, subdivision 3, of the Code of Civil Procedure are contrary to this conclusion. We held in *Daar* that an order of the trial court sustaining a demurrer to a complaint as a class action was appealable even though it was not embodied in a formal judgment, but the order appealed from there sustained a demurrer as to both causes of action alleged in the complaint. Here the trial court has sustained demurrers to the class action allega- tions of the first cause of action but overruled demurrers to the second cause alleging a class action for rescission because of the violation of the Unruh Act. Section 581, subdivision 3, merely states that the trial court may dismiss an action after sustaining a demurrer without leave to amend. It does not purport to affect the question whether the order of dismissal is appealable if it does not dispose of all the issues between the parties.

tion: "Modern society seems increasingly to expose men to . . . group injuries for which individually they are in a poor position to seek legal redress, either because they do not know enough or because such redress is disproportionately expensive. If each is left to assert his rights alone if and when he can, there will at best be a random and fragmentary enforcement, if there is any at all. This result is not only unfortunate in the particular case, but it will operate seriously to impair the deterrent effect of the sanctions which underlie much contemporary law. The problem of fashioning an effective and inclusive group remedy is thus a major one." (Kalven and Rosenfield, Function of Class Suit (1941) 8 U.Chi.L.Rev. 684, 686.)

What was noteworthy in the milieu three decades ago for stockholders is of far greater significance today for consumers. Not only have the means of communication improved and the sophistication of promotional and selling techniques sharpened in the intervening years, but consumers as a category are generally in a less favorable position than stockholders to secure legal redress for wrongs committed against them. For these reasons, the desirability of consumers suing as a class for fraud or other improper conduct of predatory sellers has been the topic of much thoughtful analysis in recent years. Numerous commentators have urged adaptation of class proceedings to consumer frauds. (See, e.g., Starrs, The Consumer Class Action (1969) 49 B.U.L.Rev. 211–250, 407–513; Eckhardt, Consumer Class Actions (1970) 45 Notre Dame Law. 663; Goldhammer, The Consumer Class Action in California (1970) 45 L.A.Bar Bull. 235.)

* * *

Frequently numerous consumers are exposed to the same dubious practice by the same seller so that proof of the prevalence of the practice as to one consumer would provide proof for all. Individual actions by each of the defrauded consumers is often impracticable because the amount of individual recovery would be insufficient to justify bringing a separate action; thus an unscrupulous seller retains the benefits of its wrongful conduct. A class action by consumers produces several salutary by-products, including a therapeutic effect upon those sellers who indulge in fraudulent practices, aid to legitimate business enterprises by curtailing illegitimate competition, and avoidance to the judicial process of the burden of multiple litigation involving identical claims. The benefit to the parties and the courts would, in many circumstances, be substantial.

In California, we do not lack authority on the subject of the amenability of consumer claims to class action litigation. Section 382 of the Code of Civil Procedure provides, " * * * when the question is one of a common or general interest, of many persons, or when the parties are numerous, and it is impracticable to bring them all before the court, one or more may sue or defend for the benefit of all." In the leading case of Daar v. Yellow Cab Co., supra, 67 Cal.2d 695, we * * * concluded that two requirements must be met to sustain a class action. The first is existence of an ascertainable class, and the second is a well-defined community of interest in the questions of law and fact involved.

As to the necessity for an ascertainable class, the right of each individual to recover may not be based on a separate set of facts applicable only to him.[5]

The requirement of a community of interest does not depend upon an identical recovery, and the fact that each member of the class must prove his separate claim to a portion of any recovery by the class is only one factor to be considered in determining whether a class action is proper. The mere fact that separate transactions are involved does not of itself preclude a finding of the requisite community of interest so long as every member of the alleged class would not be required to litigate numerous and substantial questions to determine his individual right to recover subsequent to the rendering of any class judgment which determined in plaintiffs' favor whatever questions were common to the class.

Substantial benefits both to the litigants and to the court should be found before the imposition of a judgment binding on absent parties can be justified, and the determination of the question whether a class action is appropriate will depend upon whether the common questions are sufficiently pervasive to permit adjudication in a class action rather than in a multiplicity of suits.

* * *

III

Sufficiency of the Allegations to State a Class Action

With these principles in mind, we turn to the allegations of the complaint which seeks to rescind the contracts on the ground that plaintiffs were induced to execute the instruments by the fraudulent representations of Bay Area. The complaint alleges that the same representations regarding the food and the freezers were made to each plaintiff, that Bay Area knew the representations were false, that they were made with intent to defraud, and that plaintiffs signed the agreements in reliance thereon. It is further alleged that plaintiffs are united in interest in that, inter alia, they have all signed contracts to purchase food and a freezer in reliance upon the misrepresentations, which in turn were based upon recitations by salesmen of a standard sales monologue contained in a training book and sales manual. Proof

---

5. *Daar* involved the question of identification of class members, an issue which, as we shall see, presents no serious obstacle to the maintenance of a class action here. In *Daar* it was held that the fact that individual taxicab riders could not be identified at the time the action was brought was not significant because a complete determination of the issues affecting the class (i.e., such as whether there was an overcharge and the total amount there-

of) could be made without identification and without the appearance of the individual class members. An accounting could determine the total of the overcharges, we stated, and after the questions relating to the alleged impropriety of the charge and the total amount of the overcharge had been determined, each class member could come forward to prove his own separate damages.

of a common state of facts, it is alleged, will establish the right of each class member to rescind his contract.

1. *Ascertainability of the Class*

The first requisite for maintenance of a class action, ascertainability of the class, presents no serious obstacle in this case. The complaint alleges that the members of the class are all those who have signed installment contracts with Bay Area for the purchase of meat and a freezer after January 1, 1966, who reside in Stanislaus or San Joaquin Counties, and who have paid or are obligated to pay money on the contracts to one of the defendants. It appears that there are approximately 200 persons in the class. Furthermore, it is alleged, the names and addresses of the class members may be ascertained from defendants' books.

2. *Community of Interest*

We next ascertain whether there are issues common to the class as a whole sufficient in importance so that their adjudication on a class basis will benefit both the litigants and the court. In this evaluation the mere fact that the transaction between Bay Area and each plaintiff was separately consummated is not determinative so long as each class member will not be required to litigate numerous and substantial issues to establish his individual right to recover.

In order to prevail plaintiffs must show that Bay Area made false representations with knowledge of their falsity, that these representations were made with intent to and did induce reasonable reliance by plaintiffs, and that plaintiffs suffered damages as a result. (Ach v. Finkelstein (1968) 264 Cal.App.2d 667, 674, 70 Cal.Rptr. 472.) Defendants assert that none of these elements may be proved by the device of a class action because each plaintiff entered into a separate transaction at a different time and proof of the fact of representation, its falsity, and reliance as to the named plaintiffs will not supply proof of these elements as to the absent members of the class. Thus, it is asserted, each member of the class must establish his right to recover on the basis of facts peculiar to his own circumstances, because of which the action may not be tried as a class suit.

a. *The Representations*

The representations conveniently fall into two categories: those concerning the contract for the purchase of the freezer and those relating to the frozen food contract. We examine them separately.

Plaintiffs allege that Bay Area's salesmen represented to each member of the class that the freezers were of high quality and guaranteed for a lifetime, and that they were sold at a reasonable retail price. It is asserted by plaintiffs that they can demonstrate these representations were in fact made to each class member without individual testimony because the salesmen employed by Bay Area memorized a standard statement containing the representations (which in turn were based on a printed narrative and sales manual) and that this statement was recited by rote to every member of the class. The demurrers must be deemed to admit these facts. If plaintiffs can prove their allegations at the trial, an inference that the representations were made to each class member would arise, in which case it would be unnecessary to elicit the testimony of each plaintiff as to whether the representations were in fact made to him.

It is also alleged that the representations regarding the freezers were false, and that the prices charged for them were exorbitant, excessive and unconscionable, amounting to not less than twice the reasonable retail price. The falsity of these representations could be shown on a common basis since proof of the allegations regarding the quality and price of the freezers purchased by the named plaintiffs would provide proof as to all. Although it appears that not every member of the class purchased the same brand and model of freezer, it is likely that all the brands and models are represented among the 37 named plaintiffs and to the extent that this is not so evidence may be introduced to cure the omission.

We turn next to the alleged misrepresentations regarding the frozen food purchased by plaintiffs. It is averred that Bay Area salesmen represented to each class member that the food orders were sold at a wholesale rate, that each order would last a minimum of seven months, and that the total cost of a "seven-month" food order and a freezer would be less than the amount plaintiffs were spending each month for similar food at retail stores.

① *allegatio*

According to the allegations, a common sales recitation was also employed in the sale of the frozen food and, for the reasons discussed above regarding the freezer contracts, we assume for the present that these representations were in fact made to each plaintiff.

As to the falsity of the representations, we perceive no singular difficulty in proving on a common basis whether the food supplied by Bay Area was sold at wholesale rates. Defendants insist, however, that it would be impossible without the individual testimony of each plaintiff to demonstrate the falsity of the alleged representations that the supply of food would last for seven months. It is argued that each plaintiff must have given an estimate of his consumption to the salesman, that the accuracy of this estimate as well as the salesman's calculation of the amount of food required for a seven-month supply would vary in each case, and that individual proof of consumption of each plaintiff's family during the period would be required.

Δ's args

This contention is unpersuasive at the pleading stage of the proceedings because we cannot assume that plaintiffs will be unable to establish their allegations without the separate testimony of each class member; at least they must be afforded the opportunity to show that they can prove their allegations on a common basis. An examination of the contracts attached to the complaint indicates that Bay Area sold varying quantities of food to the several plaintiffs, but that each order was of a standard type. Thus, for example, customers who purchased

Pack F received 119 pounds of beef and 123 pounds of assorted variety meats, vegetables, and fruit juices. Each type of food pack had a standard price.

The existence of these standard orders raises at least a rebuttable implication that the salesmen utilized a defined formula to determine the amount of food a particular family would need for a specified period of time. Whether this formula related to the size of the family, the amount the family spent for food each month [8] or a combination of factors, is not clear. If a formula was in fact utilized the alleged falsity of the representation regarding the length of time a food order would suffice can be demonstrated by proof of such factors as the average monthly consumption of food for a family of a particular size.

The final allegation of misrepresentation with regard to the frozen food is that Bay Area salesmen told plaintiffs the total cost of a "seven-month" food order and a freezer would be less than the amount each plaintiff was spending every month on food at retail stores. The thrust of this allegation is that it was represented the price differential between the cost of the food purchased from Bay Area and its retail value elsewhere would be adequate to pay for the freezers purchased by plaintiffs. It appears from what has been said above that this allegation, too, may be amenable to proof on a common basis.

There may be other methods by which plaintiffs can establish the alleged falsity of the representations regarding the food orders for the class as a whole. For the purpose of determining if the demurrers should have been overruled, it is sufficient that there is a reasonable possibility plaintiffs can establish a prima facie community of interest among the class members on the false representation issue. Plaintiffs' inability to do so, if that be the ultimate result, can be determined at a later stage of the proceeding.

b. *Reliance*

The next element which plaintiffs must prove in order to prevail is reliance upon the alleged misrepresentations. If they can establish without individual testimony that the representations were made to each plaintiff and that they were false, it should not be unduly complicated to sustain their burden of proving reliance thereon as a common element.

The rule in this state and elsewhere is that it is not necessary to show reliance upon false representations by direct evidence. "The fact of reliance upon alleged false representations may be inferred from the circumstances attending the transaction which oftentimes afford much stronger and more satisfactory evidence of the inducement which prompted the party defrauded to enter into the contract than his direct testimony to the same effect." (Hunter v. McKenzie (1925) 197 Cal. 176, 185, 239 P. 1090; Gormly v. Dickinson (1960) 178 Cal.App.2d 92,

8. There is some indication in the record that salesmen asked prospective customers the amounts they spent on food each month and that this amount was written down in the course of the sale.

105, 2 Cal.Rptr. 650; Thomas v. Hawkins (1950) 96 Cal.App.2d 377, 380, 215 P.2d 495; Mathewson v. Naylor (1937) 18 Cal.App.2d 741, 744, 64 P.2d 979; see Bank of St. Helena v. Lilienthal-Brayton Co. (1928) 89 Cal.App. 258, 262, 264 P. 546; 12 Williston on Contracts (3d ed. 1970) p. 480.)

Williston speaks in terms of a presumption: "Where representations have been made in regard to a material matter and action has been taken, in the absence of evidence showing the contrary, it will be presumed that the representations were relied on." (12 Williston on Contracts (3d ed. 1970) 480.) This rule is in accord with the Restatement. (Rest., Contracts, § 479, illus. 1.) Whether an inference (as held in Hunter v. McKenzie, supra, 197 Cal. 176, 185) or a presumption (as described by Williston and the Restatement) of reliance arises upon proof of a material false representation we need not determine in this case. It is sufficient for our present purposes to hold that if the trial court finds material misrepresentations were made to the class members, at least an inference of reliance would arise as to the entire class.[9] Defendants may, of course, introduce evidence in rebuttal.

Some federal class action cases in which stockholders have alleged fraud on the basis of printed misrepresentations in a corporation prospectus hold that individual proof may not be required to establish reliance by each stockholder. (See, e.g., Green v. Wolf Corporation (2d Cir. 1968) 406 F.2d 291, 301; Dolgow v. Anderson, supra, 43 F.R.D. 472, 491.)[10]

c. *Damages*

The final element of plaintiffs' cause of action is damages. *Daar* makes it clear that although ultimately each class member will be required in some manner to establish his individual damages this circumstance does not preclude the maintenance of the suit as a class action.[11]

* * *

9. The requirement that reliance must be justified in order to support recovery may also be shown on a class basis. If the court finds that a reasonable man would have relied upon the alleged misrepresentations, an inference of justifiable reliance by each class member would arise. It should be noted in this connection that a misrepresentation may be the basis of fraud if it was a substantial factor in inducing the plaintiff to act and that it need not be the sole cause of damage. (Wennerholm v. Stanford Univ. Sch. of Med. (1942) 20 Cal.2d 713, 717, 128 P.2d 522, 141 A.L.R. 1358.) Plaintiffs suggest that individual proof of reliance may be dispensed with if, as they assert, fraud may be presumed from the alleged unconscionable price of the freezers. We need not discuss the merit of this theory since we conclude that if the trial court finds that the alleged misrepresentations were material, it could find an inference or rebuttable presumption of reliance by each class member without his direct testimony.

10. Beneficial cites Morris v. Burchard (S.D.N.Y.1971) 51 F.R.D. 530, in support of its position that individual proof of reliance is required. In *Morris* it was held that the fact of reliance could not be proved on a collective basis because the alleged misrepresentations to the class members were not similar. The present case is distinguishable, because here plaintiffs have alleged a community of interest as to the representations.

11. Plaintiffs pray for return of the amounts they paid on the contracts, less the value of the food they consumed, a sum of $1,300 or less for most plaintiffs, and not more than $1,700 for any of them. In

IV

Defendant's Contentions

Defendants insist that a class action is inappropriate under these circumstances. It is argued that the present case is distinguishable from *Daar* because there separate suits would have been impractical since the recovery of the individual class members would have been very small whereas in the present case each plaintiff's claim is sufficiently large to justify separate actions.

The complaint alleges that the total obligation of most class members on their contracts is less than $1,300. While the impracticability of bringing an individual action for comparatively small potential recovery is a consideration in favor of allowing a class action it cannot be said that a potential recovery for each class member larger than a nominal sum necessarily militates against maintenance of such a suit. In a recent case we allowed an individual stockholder to sue on behalf of a class although the damages alleged for each member were substantially more than those prayed for in the present case. (See Jones v. H. F. Ahmanson & Co. (1969) 1 Cal.3d 93, 81 Cal.Rptr. 592, 460 P.2d 464.) We cannot conclude as a matter of law that consumers are entitled to less protection as a class than stockholders.[13]

Several other contentions raised by defendants are based upon policy considerations applicable to consumer class actions generally. It is asserted that a far more effective and efficient remedy for consumers than the class action is the intervention of a governmental body to protect the interests of consumers,[14] that class actions are invitations to litigation, that they are an unsuitable vehicle in a situation where, as here, the parties have mutual obligations toward one another, and that the real motivation behind such suits is not to benefit the consumer but to punish the wrong-doing seller. Defendants claim judicial efficiency will not be promoted by permitting consumer class actions because no defendant will abide by preliminary determinations of such questions as the composition of the class without prosecuting an appeal since the

addition, they seek damages for injury to their credit standing in the community as a result of the outstanding obligation on the contracts and compensation for storing the unused freezers in their homes. These damages are alleged to amount to no more than $1,000 for any one plaintiff. Finally, they ask punitive damages of $5,000 each, alleging that defendants were guilty of oppression, fraud and malice.

13. The United States Supreme Court has interpreted rule 23 of the Federal Rules of Civil Procedure (28 U.S.C.A.) as prohibiting the aggregation of separate and distinct claims to fulfill the $10,000 requirement for federal district court jurisdiction. (Snyder v. Harris (1969) 394 U.S. 332, 89 S.Ct. 1053, 22 L.Ed.2d 319.) Thus, a class action in the federal courts is not appropriate where the claim of each plaintiff is separate and distinct unless a class member has a claim of $10,000 or more.

14. The Attorney General has filed an amicus curiae brief on behalf of plaintiffs in which he asserts that class actions by private litigants are necessary to vindicate the rights of consumers. His office receives 10,000 consumer complaints a year and the Consumer Frauds Division has fewer personnel than the average small law firm engaged in the representation of the sellers of goods. Furthermore, he states, although his office may take legal action in cases of major significance, it cannot undertake to represent private citizens seeking vindication of personal rights.

consequences will be serious in view of the size of the potential judgment. Finally, argue defendants, considerations of practicality and fairness require that a more exacting proceeding than the class action be fashioned to vindicate consumer rights and that the Legislature rather than the courts should devise the remedy.

A two-prong response to the foregoing contentions is manifest. First, *Daar* makes it clear that a consumer class action is an appropriate remedy under section 382 of the Code of Civil Procedure. Second, the Legislature has recently indicated in unmistakable terms that consumers may bring suit as a class to seek redress for damages sustained as a result of false representations by sellers.

While the present case was pending before this court the Legislature enacted the Consumers Legal Remedies Act. (Civ.Code, § 1750 et seq.) The act specifies certain unfair or deceptive practices (§ 1770) and provides that a class action to recover damages may be filed if such practices have caused damage to a number of consumers similarly situated (§ 1781, subd. (a)). The circumstances under which the court may allow the suit to proceed as a class action and the procedure to be followed are also set forth in the act (§ 1781, subds. (b),[15] (c), (d), (e), (f), (g)). Finally, the act requires that before filing suit the consumer shall afford the person alleged to have committed the wrong an opportunity for rectification (§ 1782, subds. (a), (b)). If a correction is made or will be made within a reasonable time no action for damages will lie (§ 1782, subd. (c)).

Significantly, the act provides in section 1752 that its provisions are not exclusive, that the remedies provided therein shall be in addition to any other procedures or remedies provided for in any other law, and that nothing in the act shall limit any other statutory or any common law rights to bring class actions. However, class actions by consumers brought under section 1770 of the act (which lists certain unlawful deceptive practices) must be brought under the provisions of the act. The statute applies to suits filed on or after January 1, 1971. (§ 1756.)

The Legislature thus made it abundantly clear that consumer class actions allowable under any other provisions of law are not affected by the act. (See Reed, Consumer Legislation (1971) 2 Pacific L.J. 1, 9.)

* * *

* * *

15. Section 1781, subdivision (b), provides, "The court shall permit the suit to be maintained on behalf of all members of the represented class if all of the following conditions exist:

"(1) It is impracticable to bring all members of the class before the court.

"(2) The questions of law or fact common to the class are substantially similar and predominate over the questions affecting the individual members.

"(3) The claims or defenses of the representative plaintiffs are typical of the claims or defenses of the class.

"(4) The representative plaintiffs will fairly and adequately protect the interests of the class."

V

Procedure

If the class action is to prove a useful tool to the litigants and the court, pragmatic procedural devices will be required to simplify the potentially complex litigation while at the same time protecting the rights of all the parties. Although we have concluded that the provisions of the Consumers Legal Remedies Act do not apply retroactively to this case, no valid reason exists to prevent the trial court from utilizing many of the procedural provisions of the act in the interests of efficiency.

Section 1781, subdivision (c), of the Civil Code provides for a hearing, upon notice and motion, supported by affidavits, to determine if a class action is proper, whether published notice to the class members is necessary, and whether the action is without merit or whether there is a defense to the action. Subdivision (d) of that section provides that if the cause is to be permitted as a class action the court may direct either party to notify each class member and subdivision (e) sets forth the requirements of such notice, including a statement that the court will exclude the member notified from the class if he so requests by a specified date. Subdivision (f) prohibits settlement of a class action without approval of the court and notice to the class members, and subdivision (g) specifies the manner in which notice of the judgment must be given and provides that the judgment must state the names of the class members.

Although we have determined that the trial court acted improperly in sustaining the demurrers to the first cause of action as a class action because plaintiffs may be able to demonstrate a community of interest as to the elements of their claims of fraud, plaintiffs must nevertheless demonstrate that the questions which they will be required to litigate separately are not numerous or substantial and that the action meets the other requirements for a class action set forth in detail above. It would be appropriate for the trial court to utilize the hearing procedure specified in subdivision (c) of section 1781 in making such a determination.

The technique described in the act may not adequately encompass all the procedural problems facing a court in the trial of a class action. In the event of a hiatus, rule 23 of the Federal Rules of Civil Procedure prescribes procedural devices which a trial court may find useful. (Cf. Daar v. Yellow Cab Co., supra, 67 Cal.2d 695, 709.) It is desirable for the trial court to retain some measure of flexibility in the pretrial and trial of a class action, for conceivably even after an initial determination of the propriety of such an action the trial court may discover subsequently that it is not appropriate. For example, it is possible that, after notice to the class members, the court might find that an insufficient number of the class desires to participate in the suit to justify its maintenance as a class action and may determine that joinder of some other procedural device would be a more suitable method of proceeding. Subdivision (c)(1) of rule 23 provides that the trial court's initial determination may be conditional and may be altered or amended before a decision on the merits. As another example, it is possible that the court will find that efficiency would be promoted if the class were divided into subclasses. Subdivision (4)(B) of rule 23 contemplates such a procedure.

The foregoing examples are intended to be illustrative and not exhaustive. As pointed out in the preface to California Retail Installment Sales (Cont.Ed.Bar 1969) page vii, "Much of the law in this field is in the formative stage. . . ." Therefore we must rely upon the ability of trial courts to adopt innovative procedures which will be fair to the litigants and expedient in serving the judicial process.

VI

Liability of Finance Company Defendants

The final question is whether the finance company defendants to which the sales contracts were assigned are proper parties defendant in the action.[18] In the instant case, as in many situations in which consumers have been defrauded by a seller, a judgment against the seller alone would represent a Pyrrhic victory because the defrauding seller is insolvent and the victorious consumers remain liable to the finance companies, which as the assignees of the installment contracts claim that they are entitled to payment even if the seller acted fraudulently. Bay Area merely filed a demurrer and answer in the trial court and has indicated no inclination to oppose the action further. Obviously, if plaintiffs are to be made whole for the wrongs allegedly done to them, the finance company defendants must be held liable as assignees if Bay Area is culpable.

The lenders contend, however, that even if plaintiffs prove that Bay Area was guilty of fraud they are nevertheless entitled as assignees to payment under the contracts because they enjoy the privileges of a holder in due course and take free of plaintiffs' defenses against Bay Area. Although it is not entirely clear from the record, this claim apparently rests on a clause in the contracts signed by plaintiffs waiving all defenses against assignees.[19]

It seems clear under both statute and established legal principles that the finance company defendants would not be deemed holders in

---

18. Strictly speaking, it is not necessary to decide the question at this time. The trial court has concluded, at least for the purpose of ruling on the demurrers, that the finance companies are proper parties defendant since it overruled their demurrers to the fraud cause of action insofar as the individual plaintiffs are concerned. However, the issue has been briefed extensively, the question of the finance company defendants' liability will undoubtedly arise at the trial, and we discuss the matter here in order to guide the trial court in its conduct of the action.

19. The Unruh Act prohibits the execution of a note by a buyer which will when separately negotiated cut off as to third parties any right of action or defense which the buyer may have against the seller. (Civ.Code, § 1810.9).

due course under the allegations of the complaint, even if they were holding an ordinary promissory note. The complaint alleges that Avco, Sterling and Beneficial had actual or constructive knowledge of Bay Area's fraudulent practices. Under section 3302, subdivision (1)(c), of the Commercial Code, one who takes with notice of a defense against an instrument is not a holder in due course. (See Norman v. World Wide Distributors, Inc. (1963) 202 Pa.Super. 53, 195 A.2d 115, 118.)

Moreover, it has long been settled in California that a financial institution may be denied the status of a holder in due course because of its close connection with the seller. (Commercial Credit Corp. v. Orange Co. Mach. Works (1950) 34 Cal.2d 766, 214 P.2d 819; see Morgan v. Reasor Corp. (1968) 69 Cal.2d 881, 895, 73 Cal.Rptr. 398, 447 P.2d 638.) * * *

* * *

WRIGHT, C. J., PETERS, J., TOBRINER, J., BURKE, J., and SULLIVAN, J., concur.

IN RE NORTHERN DISTRICT OF CALIFORNIA DALKON SHIELD IUD PRODUCTS LIABILITY LITIGATION

United States Court of Appeals for the Ninth Circuit, 1982.
693 F.2d 847.[*]

GOODWIN, CIRCUIT JUDGE.

Plaintiffs appeal from a district court order conditionally certifying their claims as: (1) a nationwide class action on the issue of punitive damages pursuant to Federal Rule of Civil Procedure 23(b)(1)(B); and (2) a statewide (California) class action on the issue of liability pursuant to Rule 23(b)(3). In re Northern District of California "Dalkon Shield" IUD Products Liability Litigation, 521 F.Supp. 1188 (N.D.Calif.1981); 526 F.Supp. 887 (N.D.Calif.1981).

All plaintiffs claim to have been injured by the Dalkon Shield intrauterine device. All of those plaintiffs who have joined in this appeal challenge class certification. Defendant A.H. Robins also opposes certification of the California 23(b)(3) class. Defendant Hugh J. Davis opposes certification of both classes.

Between June 1970 and June 1974, approximately 2.2 million Dalkon Shields were inserted in women in the United States. Many users sustained injuries. Complaints include uterine perforations, infections, ectopic and uterine pregnancies, spontaneous abortions, fetal injuries and birth defects, sterility, and hysterectomies. Several deaths also were reported. On June 28, 1974, Robins withdrew the Dalkon Shield from the market.

By May 31, 1981, approximately 3,258 actions relating to the Dalkon Shield had been filed, and 1,573 claims were pending. The

[*] Cert. denied, 459 U.S. 1171, 103 S.Ct. 817, 74 L.Ed.2d 1015 (1983).

claims are based on various theories: negligence and negligent design, strict products liability, breach of express and implied warranty, wanton and reckless conduct, conspiracy, and fraud. Most plaintiffs seek both compensatory and punitive damages.

Some plaintiffs joined Robins, Davis, and Irwin W. Lerner as defendants, as well as their own doctors or medical practitioners who recommended and inserted the Dalkon Shield, and local suppliers. Many plaintiffs sued fewer defendants.

In 1975 all actions then pending in federal district courts alleging damages from the use of the Dalkon Shield were transferred by the Judicial Panel on Multidistrict Litigation to the District of Kansas for consolidated pretrial proceedings. In re A.H. Robins Co. Inc., "Dalkon Shield" Liability Litigation, 406 F.Supp. 540 (Jud.Pan.Mult.Lit.1975), 419 F.Supp. 710 (Jud.Pan.Mult.Lit.1976), 438 F.Supp. 942 (Jud.Pan. Mult.Lit.1977). After four years of consolidated discovery, the Judicial Panel began vacating its conditional transfer orders and remanding the cases to their respective transferor courts. In re A.H. Robins Co. Inc., "Dalkon Shield" IUD Products Liability Litigation, 453 F.Supp. 108 (Jud.Pan.Mult.Lit.1978), 505 F.Supp. 221 (Jud.Pan.Mult.Lit.1981).

State courts have also received a number of Dalkon Shield cases. The results have been mixed. Some plaintiffs have recovered substantial verdicts. Others have recovered nothing. Many cases have been settled.

Approximately 166 Dalkon Shield cases were pending in the Northern District of California. After one jury trial that lasted nine weeks, Judge Williams consolidated all Dalkon Shield cases pending in that district and ordered briefing on the feasibility of a class action. All but one of California plaintiffs' counsel opposed class certification. Out-of-state plaintiffs were not notified of the briefing request and did not participate in the status conferences held to discuss the class action proposal. All defendants at that time opposed class certification.

On June 25, 1981, Judge Williams entered an order conditionally certifying a nationwide class, under Fed.R.Civ.P. 23(b)(1)(B),[1] consisting

---

1. Fed.R.Civ.P. 23(b)(1)(B) provides:

"(b) Class Actions Maintainable. An action may be maintained as a class action if the prerequisites of subdivision (a) are satisfied, and in addition:

"(1) the prosecution of separate actions by or against individual members of the class would create a risk of

. . .

"(B) adjudications with respect to individual members of the class which would as a practical matter be dispositive of the interests of the other members not parties to the adjudications or substantially impair or impede their ability to protect their interests; . . ."

The prerequisites of subdivision (a) are:

"(a) Prerequisites to a Class Action. One or more members of a class may sue or be sued as representative parties on behalf of all only if (1) the class is so numerous that joinder of members is impracticable, (2) there are questions of law or fact common to the class, (3) the claims or defenses of the representative parties are typical of the claims or defenses of the class, and (4) the representative parties will fairly and adequately protect the interests of the class."

of all persons who filed actions for punitive damages against Robins.[2] The court asserted jurisdiction on the basis of diversity of citizenship, 28 U.S.C. § 1332. One stated purpose of certification was to insure the rights of all plaintiffs to a proportionate share of any punitive damages recovery from the "limited fund" of Robins' assets. Judge Williams stated:

> "At the present time, some 1,573 suits involving claims for compensatory damages well over $500 million and claimed punitive damages in excess of $2.3 billion, are pending against A.H. Robins. The potential for the constructive bankruptcy of A.H. Robins, a company whose net worth is $280,394,000.00, raises the unconscionable possibility that large numbers of plaintiffs who are not first in line at the courthouse door will be deprived of a practical means of redress."

No testimony was taken and the way in which the "fund" was limited was not specified.

Judge Williams also conditionally certified a California statewide subclass under Rule 23(b)(3) consisting of plaintiffs who have filed actions against Robins in California.[3] This California class is limited to the question of Robins' liability arising from the manufacture and sale of the Dalkon Shield. Any plaintiff may opt out of this class, whereas all plaintiffs in the nation would be bound by the determination on punitive damages.

Plaintiffs from California, Oregon, Ohio, Florida, and Kansas moved to decertify the punitive damages class. The district court denied the motion and certified the issues for an interlocutory appeal, pursuant to 28 U.S.C. § 1292(b). This court granted the interlocutory appeals and ordered them expedited.

2. On the following day, June 26, Robins moved for certification of a plaintiff punitive damages class under Rule 23(b)(1)(B).

3. Fed.R.Civ.P. 23(b)(3) provides:

"(b) Class Actions Maintainable. An action may be maintained as a class action if the prerequisites of subdivision (a) are satisfied, and in addition:

"(3) the court finds that the questions of law or fact common to the members of the class predominate over any questions affecting only individual members, and that a class action is superior to other available methods for the fair and efficient adjudication of the controversy. The matters pertinent to the findings include: (A) the interest of members of the class in individually controlling the prosecution or defense of separate actions; (B) the extent and nature of any litigation concerning the controversy already commenced by or against members of the class; (C) the desirability or undesirability of concentrating the litigation of the claims in the particular forum; (D) the difficulties likely to be encountered in the management of a class action."

I

The Rule 23(b)(1)(B) Nationwide Punitive Damages Class

A. *Rule 23(a) Prerequisites*

1. *Commonality.*

The district court held that the punitive damages class presented common questions about Robins' knowledge of the safety of its product at material times while the Shield was on the market. What Davis, Lerner and Robins knew about the Dalkon Shield, when they knew it, what information they withheld from the public, and what they stated in their advertising to doctors and in their product instructions during various time periods may all be common questions. These questions are not entirely common, however, to all plaintiffs.

Moreover, as the plaintiffs correctly argue, the 50 jurisdictions in which these cases arise do not apply the same punitive damages standards. Punitive damages standards can range from gross negligence to reckless disregard to various levels of wilfullness and wantonness. If commonality were the only problem in this case, it might be possible to sustain some kind of a punitive damage class. But difficulties remain with other certification requirements.

2. *Typicality.*

Typicality, while it may not be insurmountable, remains a significant problem. The district court order recites that representative parties have been selected. In Re Northern District of California "Dalkon Shield" IUD Products Liability Litigation, 526 F.Supp. at 919. However, all of the appealing plaintiffs assert that no plaintiff has accepted the role, and that no single plaintiff or group of plaintiffs could be typical of the numerous persons who might have claims. No plaintiff has appeared in this appeal in support of class certification. Again, while typicality alone might not be an insurmountable problem, it helps make the overall situation difficult to rationalize as proper for class treatment.

3. *Adequacy of representation.*

The court designated lead counsel for the nationwide class, but he has resigned. New counsel has been designated but has not yet started to represent the class. Apparently none of the attorneys already involved in the case is willing to serve as class counsel. The district judge may well be better able to choose a good lawyer than some of the plaintiffs may be, but the right of litigants to choose their own counsel is a right not lightly to be brushed aside.

The plaintiffs argue that newly appointed, even if expert counsel, may not litigate the action as vigorously as counsel selected by plaintiffs. This court is hesitant to force unwanted counsel upon plaintiffs on the assumption that appointed counsel will be adequate. Even if the class were otherwise acceptable, it would have to be decertified if adequate lead counsel turned out to be unavailable.

We are not necessarily ruling out the class action tool as a means for expediting multi-party product liability actions in appropriate cases, but the combined difficulties overlapping from each of the elements of Rule 23(a) preclude certification in this case.

B. *The Rule 23(b)(1)(B) Requirements*

1. *Applicability of McDonnell Douglas.*

The Ninth Circuit has expressly barred class certification under 23(b)(1)(B) for independent tort claims seeking compensatory damages, unless separate actions "inescapably will alter the substance of the rights of others having similar claims." McDonnell Douglas Corp. v. U.S. Dist. Ct., C.D. of Cal., 523 F.2d 1083, 1086 (9th Cir.1975), cert. denied, 425 U.S. 911, 96 S.Ct. 1506, 47 L.Ed.2d 761 (1976), quoting LaMar v. H & B Novelty & Loan Company, 489 F.2d 461, 467 (9th Cir. 1973). In *McDonnell Douglas,* this court found that "[a]t worst, individual actions (for air crash damages) would leave unnamed members of the class with the same complexity and expense as if no prior actions had been brought." 523 F.2d at 1086.

Robins argues that *McDonnell Douglas* does not preclude the 23(b) (1)(B) certification of a nationwide punitive damage class because that case treated only individual compensatory damage claims, and punitive damages were not at issue. The district judge did not discuss *McDonnell Douglas* but stated that certification under 23(b)(1)(B) is appropriate if individual actions "may" affect the claims of parties not before the court. Because total claims, if successful, might exceed Robins' current assets, the judge noted that the earliest individual actions tried could exhaust Robins' assets and thus adversely affect the claims of plaintiffs who sued later and who might not be able to collect on their judgments. The judge cited Green v. Occidental Petroleum Corp., 541 F.2d 1335, 1340 n. 9 (9th Cir.1976), in which the court stated that Rule 23(b)(1)(B) applied "where the claims of all plaintiffs exceeded the assets of the defendant and hence to allow any group of individuals to be fully compensated would impair the rights of those not in court." *Green,* however, was a 10b–5 action and did not involve mass personal injury claims. The quoted dictum did not discuss whether Rule 23(b)(1)(B) would apply in a tort case. One reason for certification obviously was to avoid any detrimental effect of earlier individual claims upon later claims.

McDonnell Douglas, however, appears to prohibit Rule 23(b)(1)(B) certification of mass tort actions for compensatory or punitive damages unless the record establishes that separate punitive awards inescapably will affect later awards. The detrimental effect of earlier claims upon later claims commends itself to this court as worthy of future judicial and legislative consideration. As plaintiffs in this case correctly argue, though, not every plaintiff will prevail and not every plaintiff will receive a jury award in the amount requested. Thus on the present state of the record, the detrimental effect of separate punitive damages awards is not clearly inescapable.

2. *The limited fund concept.*

The drafters of Rule 23 intended 23(b)(1)(B) to apply to "limited fund" cases where numerous plaintiffs claim "against a fund insufficient to satisfy all claims." Advisory Committee Note to the 1966 Revision of Rule 23, 39 F.R.D. 69, 101 (1966).

The district court certified the "limited fund" punitive damage class before requesting or receiving adequate evidence of Robins' net worth, earnings or available insurance coverage. The judge received Robins' attorney's affidavit showing the total claims against Robins and Robins' fund of assets but did not reopen discovery to permit plaintiffs to challenge these affidavits. The record does not show how many cases have been settled.

Similarly, the court in In re Agent Orange Product Liability Litigation, 506 F.Supp. 762, 789–90 (E.D.N.Y.1980), refused to certify "Agent Orange" claims under Rule 23(b)(1)(B) because the plaintiffs offered no evidence of the likely insolvency of defendants. See also Payton v. Abbott Labs, 83 F.R.D. 382, 389 (D.Mass.1979) (class certification granted under Rule 23(b)(3) but denied under 23(b)(1)(B) because the plaintiffs offered no evidence of the likely insolvency of the defendants and, "without more, numerous plaintiffs and a large *ad damnum* clause should [not] guarantee (b)(1)(B) certification.").

Rule 23(b)(1)(B) certification is proper only when separate punitive damage claims necessarily will affect later claims. The district court erred by ordering certification without sufficient evidence of, or even a preliminary fact-finding inquiry concerning Robins' actual assets, insurance, settlement experience and continuing exposure.

The court's other consideration for certifying the punitive damage issue as a nationwide class action was to ensure that Robins would be punished only once. The court correctly notes, and appellants agree, that no rule of law limits the amount of punitive damages a jury may award. A class action, however, is not the only way to protect a defendant from unreasonable punitive damages. Given the difficulties in complying with the requirements of Rule 23(b)(1)(B) in this case, it was error to certify a nationwide class of punitive damages claimants.

II

The Rule 23(b)(3) California Liability Class

A. *Suitability of Class Action Litigation of Mass Products Liability Cases*

The Advisory Committee Note to the 1966 Revision of Rule 23(b)(3) (39 F.R.D. 69, 103) states:

"A 'mass accident' resulting in injuries to numerous persons is ordinarily not appropriate for a class action because of the likelihood that significant questions, not only of damages but of liability and defenses to liability, would be present, affecting the individuals in different ways. In these circumstances an action conducted nominally as a class action would degenerate in practice into multiple lawsuits separately tried. . . . ."

Relying in part on that note and on the inherent obstacles to personal injury class actions, many courts have denied plaintiffs' motions for class certification in mass tort or personal injury actions, especially those alleging negligence by one or more defendants over extended periods. See Ryan v. Eli Lilly and Co., 84 F.R.D. 230 (D.S.C.1979) ("DES" action); Mink v. University of Chicago, 460 F.Supp. 713 (N.D.Ill.1978) ("DES" action); Harrigan v. United States, 63 F.R.D. 402 (E.D.Penn.1974) (action for negligent surgery in veterans' hospital); Snyder v. Hooker Chemicals & Plastics Corp., 104 Misc.2d 735, 429 N.Y.S.2d 153 (1980) (Love Canal toxic waste action); Rosenfeld v. A.H. Robins Co., 63 A.D.2d 11, 407 N.Y.S.2d 196 (1978) (Dalkon Shield case) (discussed below); Hobbs v. Northeast Airlines, Inc., 50 F.R.D. 76 (E.D. Penn.1970) (Rule 23(b)(3) certification of airplane crash cases denied because individual plaintiffs in tort actions have an interest in controlling their own lawsuits; many other suits already were pending in other states; and Pennsylvania causes of action, under which prospective named plaintiffs were suing, might not be available to out-of-state claimants); Daye v. Commonwealth of Pennsylvania, 344 F.Supp. 1337, 1342–43 (E.D.Penn.1972), cert. denied, 416 U.S. 946, 94 S.Ct. 1956, 40 L.Ed.2d 298 (1974) (Rule 23(b)(3) certification of school bus accident cases denied because some plaintiffs would bring personal injury claims while other plaintiffs would bring wrongful death claims); Marchesi v. Eastern Airlines, Inc., 68 F.R.D. 500, 501 (E.D.N.Y.1975) (class certification under any Rule 23 subsection denied).

In Causey v. Pan American World Airways, Inc., 66 F.R.D. 392 (E.D.Va.1975), the court denied the plaintiffs' motion for class certification of airplane crash cases under Rule 23(b)(1)(A) and (B) and under Rule 23(b)(2) or (3) because most prospective plaintiffs were not United States citizens. The court noted, however, that mass accident litigation "may and probably ought to be maintained as a class action" where: (1) the class action is limited to the issue of liability; (2) class members support the action; (3) choice of law problems are minimized because the accident occurred or substantially all plaintiffs reside in the same jurisdiction; and (4) the 23(b)(3) requirement of "superiority" also is met. Id. at 397. But see Petition of Gabel, 350 F.Supp. 624 (C.D.Cal. 1972) (fifty deaths in airplane crash) (overruled by McDonnell Douglas); Hernandez v. Motor Vessel Skyward, 61 F.R.D. 558 (S.D.Fla.1973), affirmed, 507 F.2d 1279 (5th Cir.1975) (disapproved in McDonnell Douglas) (Rule 23(b)(1)(A) certification on issue of defendants' negligence in preparing or making available contaminated food in suits for food poisoning on cruise ship); Bentkowski v. Marfuerza Compania Maritima, S.A., 70 F.R.D. 401 (E.D.Penn.1976) (Rule 23(b)(3) class certification in cruise ship food poisoning cases on negligence issue); Ouellette v. International Paper Co., 86 F.R.D. 476 (D.Vt.1980) (class certification in lake pollution cases); American Trading and Pro. Corp. v. Fischbach & Moore, Inc., 47 F.R.D. 155 (N.D.Ill.1969) (fire at Chicago trade center).

In the typical mass tort situation, such as an airplane crash or a cruise ship food poisoning, proximate cause can be determined on a class-wide basis because the cause of the common disaster is the same for each of the plaintiffs.

In products liability actions, however, individual issues may outnumber common issues. No single happening or accident occurs to cause similar types of physical harm or property damage. No one set of operative facts establishes liability. No single proximate cause applies equally to each potential class member and each defendant. Furthermore, the alleged tortfeasor's affirmative defenses (such as failure to follow directions, assumption of the risk, contributory negligence, and the statute of limitations) may depend on facts peculiar to each plaintiff's case. See Rosenfeld v. A.H. Robins Co., 104 Misc.2d 735, 407 N.Y.S.2d 196, (1978) (class certification denied under New York statute patterned after Rule 23(b)(3)).

A federal district court also denied Rule 23(b)(3) class certification of asbestosis cases for these reasons. Yandle v. PPG Industries Inc., 65 F.R.D. 566, 569 (E.D.Tex.1974). The *Yandle* court also suggested that when personal injuries are involved, each plaintiff should have the right to prosecute his own claim and to be represented by the lawyer of his choice.

Federal district courts recently have conditionally certified two "mass tort" class actions that involve products liability and numerous injuries caused by individual products over a long period of time. In re Agent Orange Product Liability Litigation, supra, 506 F.Supp. 762, and Payton v. Abbott Labs, supra, 83 F.R.D. 382 ("DES" case). In both cases, the plaintiffs sought class status. Both cases were certified under Rule 23(b)(3).

The *Agent Orange* court found that Rule 23(b)(3) requirements were met because: (1) the litigation was at such an early stage that resolution of preliminary issues concerning the relationship between the government and the Agent Orange manufacturer would affect every plaintiff's claim; (2) discovery and proof in such "untested areas of law" would be so expensive and complicated that no single attorney would be likely to succeed; (3) all cases currently pending already were before that same court under multidistrict litigation procedures; and (4) facts and issues in all pending and future cases were identical or parallel. 506 F.Supp. at 790–91.

The *Payton* court, without distinguishing the cases prohibiting class action litigation of mass torts, certified a plaintiff class of all women who were exposed to DES *in utero* in Massachusetts. The court found that "over 90% of the trial time" in two individual DES suits had been devoted to "whether and when defendants knew or should have known of the dangers of DES exposure." 83 F.R.D. at 391–92. The class action was limited to resolving those issues and issues of what injuries Massachusetts law would recognize. Id. at 386–87. The *Payton* court partially relied upon the nonavailability in Massachusetts of offensive collateral estoppel, which in some states would prevent relitigation of decided issues. Id. at 392. Both the *Payton* and *Agent Orange* courts have recognized that neither causation nor damages may be determined in class proceedings. 83 F.R.D. at 394, 506 F.Supp. at 790.

B. *Rule 23(a) Prerequisites*

*   *   *

From the large California class the court may be able to find plaintiffs whose claims are fairly representative of the varying injuries. In proving liability under a negligence theory, however, the plaintiffs have to prove not only their injuries, but that Robins and each defendant owed them a duty of care and also what those different standards of care were, if they were breached, and—most important—if the breaches proximately caused the plaintiffs' varying injuries. See generally, W. Prosser, Law of Torts, §§ 41–42 (4th ed. 1971); Restatement (Second) of Torts, ch. 16, §§ 430–461 (1965). To prove liability under a breach of warranty theory, representative plaintiffs must exist for each type of warranty, assurance, or medical advice each plaintiff received. The difficulty of meeting the typicality requirement seems obvious.

*   *   *

C. *Rule 23(b)(3) Requirements*

*   *   *

1. *Predominance.*

*   *   *

Although [there] are common factual questions, the court should have balanced these concerns with the greater number of questions affecting individual class members. The 23(b)(3) class is limited to the issue of liability, but Robins' overall liability, under some of the theories, cannot be proved unless each plaintiff also proves that Robins' breach of its duty proximately caused her particular injury.

For those plaintiffs who assert a breach of warranty claim, additional individual factual issues will have to be argued and determined. Robins' warranties consisted mainly of various medical journal and medical trade-show advertisements over a four-year period. Different types of advertisements were printed on different dates in different journals. Different doctors read various periodicals. The advertisements were made to and read not by plaintiffs but by their doctors.

While facts about what warranties or representations Robins made and whether Robins breached them could be determined on a class basis, these facts can also be reached in consolidated discovery proceedings, and can be expected to become standardized after a few trials.

2. *Superiority.*

*   *   *

A trial court can sever and try only certain issues on a class basis under Rule 23(c)(4)(A). The few issues that might be tried on a class basis in this case, balanced against issues that must be tried individually, indicate that the time saved by a class action may be relatively insignificant. A few verdicts followed by settlements might be equally efficacious.

3. *Considerations of Rule 23(b)(3)(A–D).*

In determining if common issues predominate and a class action is superior, the court should consider the factors provided in 23(b)(3)(A–D).

A. The California liability class members have a strong interest in controlling the prosecution of separate actions. Counsel for plaintiffs who have appealed have stated they will recommend that their clients opt out of the class. If a large number do so, the class will be unable to proceed.

B. Several Dalkon Shield cases already have been completed in California, and over 300 are pending.

C. The majority of California Dalkon Shield cases were not filed in the Northern District of California, although most plaintiffs' counsel are from the Northern or Central Districts.

D. Management is made difficult by the complexity and multiplicity of issues and by plaintiffs' hostility to the class action.

In addition, in this case, many plaintiffs have sued other defendants, such as their individual doctors, and the presence of these separate defendants creates additional problems of management.

CONCLUSION

The California liability class does not satisfy the typicality requirement of Rule 23(a)(3) or the Rule 23(b)(3) requirement that the class action be superior to other available means of adjudication. We do not preclude further consideration by the district court of motions to certify a more limited class or subclasses under Rule 23(b)(3).

*   *   *

NOTE ON CLASS SUITS IN PRODUCT LIABILITY AND MASS TORT LITIGATION

Attempts to use class actions in nationwide product liability and mass accident cases have generally been rejected. In addition to *In re Dalkon Shield*, see In re Federal Skywalk Cases, 93 F.R.D. 415 (W.D.Mo.1982), vacated 680 F.2d 1175 (8th Cir.1982), cert. denied 459 U.S. 988, 103 S.Ct. 342, 74 L.Ed.2d 383 (1982); In re School Asbestos Litigation, 104 F.R.D. 422 (E.D.Pa.1984), affirmed in part, vacated in part 789 F.2d 996 (3d Cir.1986), cert. denied sub nom. Celotex Corp. v. School Dist. of Lancaster, 479 U.S. 852, 107 S.Ct. 182, 93 L.Ed. 2d 117 (1986), cert. denied sub nom. National Gypsum Co. v. School Dist. of Lancaster, 479 U.S. 915, 107 S.Ct. 318, 93 L.Ed.2d 291 (1986), vacated 791 F.2d

920 (3d Cir.1986); In re "Bendectin" Products Liability Litigation, 102 F.R.D. 239 (S.D.Ohio 1984), vacated 749 F.2d 300 (6th Cir.1984).

For a successful attempt to use a class action claiming personal injuries as a result of veterans' exposure to herbicides during the Vietnam War, see In re "Agent Orange" Product Liability Litigation, 100 F.R.D. 718 (E.D.N.Y.1983), petition for writ of mandamus denied sub nom. In re Diamond Shamrock Chemicals Co., 725 F.2d 858 (2d Cir.1984); cert. denied 465 U.S. 1067, 104 S.Ct. 1417, 79 L.Ed.2d 743 (1984).

For a discussion of these cases, see Miller and Crump, Jurisdiction and Choice of Law in Multistate Class Actions After Phillips Petroleum Co. v. Shutts, 96 Yale L.J. 1 (1986). See also Mullenix, Class Resolution of the Mass– Tort Case: A Proposed Federal Procedure Act, 64 Tex.L.Rev. 1039 (1986); Note, Strategic Bankruptcies: Class Actions, Classification and the Dalkon Shield Cases, 7 Cardozo L.Rev. 817 (1986).

EISEN v. CARLISLE & JACQUELIN

Supreme Court of the United States, 1974.
417 U.S. 156, 94 S.Ct. 2140, 40 L.Ed.2d 732.

MR. JUSTICE POWELL delivered the opinion of the Court.

On May 2, 1966, petitioner filed a class action on behalf of himself and all other odd-lot [1] traders on the New York Stock Exchange (the Exchange). The complaint charged respondents with violations of the antitrust and securities laws and demanded damages for petitioner and his class. Eight years have elapsed, but there has been no trial on the merits of these claims. Both the parties and the courts are still wrestling with the complex questions surrounding petitioner's attempt to maintain his suit as a class action under Fed.Rule Civ.Proc. 23. We granted certiorari to resolve some of these difficulties. 414 U.S. 908, 94 S.Ct. 235, 38 L.Ed.2d 146 (1973).

I

* * * Respondent brokerage firms Carlisle & Jacquelin and DeCoppet & Doremus together handled 99% of the Exchange's odd-lot business. S.E.C., Report of Special Study of Securities Markets, H.R.Doc. No. 95, pt. 2, 88th Cong., 1st Sess., 172 (1963). They were compensated by the odd-lot differential, a surcharge imposed on the odd-lot investor in addition to the standard brokerage commission applicable to round-lot transactions. For the period in question the differential was ⅛ of a point (12½¢) per share on stocks trading below $40 per share and ¼ of a point (25¢) per share on stocks trading at or above $40 per share.[2]

Petitioner charged that respondent brokerage firms had monopolized odd-lot trading and set the differential at an excessive level in violation of §§ 1 and 2 of the Sherman Act, 15 U.S.C.A. §§ 1 and 2, and

---

1. Odd lots are shares traded in lots of fewer than a hundred. Shares traded in units of a hundred or multiples thereof are round-lots.

2. On July 1, 1966, the $40 "breakpoint" was raised to $55.

he demanded treble damages for the amount of the overcharge. Petitioner also demanded unspecified money damages from the Exchange for its alleged failure to regulate the differential for the protection of investors in violation of §§ 6 and 19 of the Securities Exchange Act of 1934, 15 U.S.C.A. §§ 78f and 78s. Finally, he requested attorneys' fees and injunctive prohibition of future excessive charges.

A critical fact in this litigation is that petitioner's individual stake in the damages award he seeks is only $70. No competent attorney would undertake this complex antitrust action to recover so inconsequential an amount. Economic reality dictates that petitioner's suit proceed as a class action or not at all. Opposing counsel have therefore engaged in prolonged combat over the various requirements of Rule 23. The result has been an exceedingly complicated series of decisions by both the District Court and the Court of Appeals for the Second Circuit. To understand the labyrinthian history of this litigation, a preliminary overview of the decisions may prove useful.

In the beginning, the District Court determined that petitioner's suit was not maintainable as a class action. On appeal, the Court of Appeals issued two decisions known popularly as *Eisen I* and *Eisen II*. The first held that the District Court's decision was a final order and thus appealable. * * *

*   *   *

Nearly 18 months later the Court of Appeals reversed the dismissal of the class action in a decision known as *Eisen II.* 391 F.2d 555 (1968). In reaching this result the court undertook an exhaustive but ultimately inconclusive analysis of Rule 23. Subdivision (a) of the Rule sets forth four prerequisites to the maintenance of any suit as a class action: "(1) the class is so numerous that joinder of all members is impracticable, (2) there are questions of law or fact common to the class, (3) the claims or defenses of the representative parties are typical of the claims or defenses of the class, and (4) the representative parties will fairly and adequately protect the interests of the class." The District Court had experienced little difficulty in finding that petitioner satisfied the first three prerequisites but had concluded that petitioner might not "fairly and adequately protect the interests of the class" as required by Rule 23(a)(4). The Court of Appeals indicated its disagreement with the reasoning behind the latter conclusion and directed the District Court to reconsider the point.

In addition to meeting the four conjunctive requirements of 23(a), a class action must also qualify under one of the three subdivisions of 23(b).[3] Petitioner argued that the suit was maintainable as a class

---

3. "(b) Class Actions Maintainable.

"An action may be maintained as a class action if the prerequisites of subdivision (a) are satisfied, and in addition:

"(1) the prosecution of separate actions by or against individual members of the class would create a risk of

"(A) inconsistent or varying adjudications with respect to individual members of the class which would establish incompatible standards of conduct for the party opposing the class, or

"(B) adjudications with respect to individual members of the class which would as a practical matter be dispositive of the

action under all three subdivisions. The Court of Appeals held the first two subdivisions inapplicable to this suit [4] and therefore turned its attention to the third subdivision, (b)(3). That subdivision requires a court to determine whether "questions of law or fact common to the members of the class predominate over any questions affecting only individual members" and whether "a class action is superior to other available methods for the fair and efficient adjudication of the controversy." More specifically, it identifies four factors relevant to these inquiries. After a detailed review of these provisions, the Court of Appeals concluded that the only potential barrier to maintenance of this suit as a class action was the Rule 23(b)(3)(D) directive that a court evaluate "the difficulties likely to be encountered in the management of a class action." Commonly referred to as "manageability," this consideration encompasses the whole range of practical problems that may render the class action format inappropriate for a particular suit. With reference to this litigation, the Court of Appeals noted that the difficulties of distributing any ultimate recovery to the class members would be formidable, though not necessarily insuperable, and commented that it was "reluctant to permit actions to proceed where they are not likely to benefit anyone but the lawyers who bring them." 391 F.2d, at 567. The Court therefore directed the District Court to conduct "a further inquiry . . . in order to consider the mechanics involved in the administration of the present action." Ibid.

* * *

After it held the evidentiary hearing on remand, which together with affidavits and stipulations provided the basis for extensive findings of fact, the District Court issued an opinion and order holding the suit maintainable as a class action. 52 F.R.D. 253 (1971). The court first

interests of the other members not parties to the adjudications or substantially impair or impede their ability to protect their interests; or

"(2) the party opposing the class has acted or refused to act on grounds generally applicable to the class, thereby making appropriate final injunctive relief or corresponding declaratory relief with respect to the class as a whole; or

"(3) the court finds that the questions of law or fact common to the members of the class predominate over any questions affecting only individual members, and that a class action is superior to other available methods for the fair and efficient adjudication of the controversy. The matters pertinent to the findings include: (A) the interest of members of the class in individually controlling the prosecution or defense of separate actions; (B) the extent and nature of any litigation concerning the controversy already commenced by or against members of the class; (C) the desirability or unde-

sirability of concentrating the litigation of the claims in the particular forum; (D) the difficulties likely to be encountered in the management of a class action."

4. Before the Court of Appeals, petitioner dropped the contention that the suit qualified under subdivision (b)(1)(B). The court held subdivision (b)(1)(A) inapplicable on the ground that the prospective class consisted entirely of small claimants, none of whom could afford to litigate this action in order to recover his individual claim and that consequently there was little chance of "inconsistent or varying adjudications with respect to individual members of the class which would establish incompatible standards of conduct for the party opposing the class. . . ." Subdivision (b)(2) was held to apply only to actions exclusively or predominantly for injunctive or declaratory relief. Advisory Committee's Note, Proposed Rules of Civil Procedure, 28 U.S.C.A. App., p. 7766.

noted that petitioner satisfied the criteria identified by the Court of Appeals for determining adequacy of representation under Rule 23(a)(4). Then it turned to the more difficult question of manageability. Under this general rubric the court dealt with problems of the computation of damages, the mechanics of administering this suit as a class action, and the distribution of any eventual recovery. The last-named problem had most troubled the Court of Appeals, prompting its remark that if "class members are not likely ever to share in an eventual judgment, we would probably not permit the class action to continue." 391 F.2d, at 567. The District Court attempted to resolve this difficulty by embracing the idea of a "fluid class" recovery whereby damages would be distributed to future odd-lot traders rather than to the specific class members who were actually injured. The court suggested that "a fund equivalent to the amount of unclaimed damages might be established and the odd-lot differential reduced in an amount determined reasonable by the court until such time as the fund is depleted." 52 F.R.D., at 265. The need to resort to this expedient of recovery by the "next best class" arose from the prohibitively high cost of computing and awarding multitudinous small damages claims on an individual basis.

Finally, the District Court took up the problem of notice. The court found that the prospective class included some six million individuals, institutions, and intermediaries of various sorts; that with reasonable effort some two million of these odd-lot investors could be identified by name and address;[5] and that the names and addresses of an additional 250,000 persons who had participated in special investment programs involving odd-lot trading[6] could also be identified with reasonable effort. Using the then current first-class postage rate of six cents, the court determined that stuffing and mailing each individual notice form would cost 10 cents. Thus individual notice to all identifiable class members would cost $225,000,[7] and additional expense would be incurred for suitable publication notice designed to reach the other four million class members.

The District Court concluded, however, that neither Rule 23(c)(2) nor the Due Process Clause required so substantial an expenditure at the outset of this litigation. Instead, it proposed a notification scheme consisting of four elements: (1) individual notice to all member firms of the Exchange and to commercial banks with large trust departments; (2) individual notice to the approximately 2,000 identifiable class mem-

---

5. These two million traders dealt with brokerage firms who transmitted their odd-lot transactions to respondents Carlisle & Jacquelin and DeCoppet & Doremus via teletype. By comparing the odd-lot firms' computerized records of these teletype transactions and the general-services brokerage firms' computerized records of all customer names and addresses, the names and addresses of these two million odd-lot traders can be obtained.

6. In the period from May 1962 through June 1968, 100,000 individuals had odd lot transactions through participation in the Monthly Investment Plan operated by the Exchange and 150,000 persons traded in odd-lots through participation in a number of payroll deduction plans operated by Merrill Lynch, Pierce, Fenner & Smith.

7. Adjusting this figure to reflect the subsequent 4¢ increase in first-class postage would yield a figure of $315,000.

bers with 10 or more odd-lot transactions during the relevant period; (3) individual notice to an additional 5,000 class members selected at random; and (4) prominent publication notice in the Wall Street Journal and in other newspapers in New York and California. The court calculated that this package would cost approximately $21,720.

The only issue not resolved by the District Court in its first opinion on remand from *Eisen II* was who should bear the cost of notice. Because petitioner understandably declined to pay $21,720 in order to litigate an action involving an individual stake of only $70, this question presented something of a dilemma:

> "If the expense of notice is placed upon [petitioner], it would be the end of a possibly meritorious suit, frustrating both the policy behind private antitrust actions and the admonition that the new Rule 23 is to be given a liberal rather than a restrictive interpretation, *Eisen II* at 563. On the other hand, if costs were arbitrarily placed upon [respondents] at this point, the result might be the imposition of an unfair burden founded upon a groundless claim. In addition to the probability of encouraging frivolous class actions, such a step might also result in [respondents'] passing on to their customers, including many of the class members in this case, the expenses of defending these actions." 52 F.R.D., at 269.

Analogizing to the laws of preliminary injunctions, the court decided to impose the notice cost on respondents if petitioner could show a strong likelihood of success on the merits, and it scheduled a preliminary hearing on the merits to facilitate this determination. After this hearing the District Court issued an opinion and order ruling that petitioner was "more than likely" to prevail at trial and that respondents should bear 90% of the cost of notice, or $19,548. 54 F.R.D. 565, 567 (1972).

* * *

On May 1, 1973, the Court of Appeals issued *Eisen III*. 479 F.2d 1005. The majority disapproved the District Court's partial reliance on publication notice, holding that Rule 23(c)(2) required individual notice to all identifiable class members. The majority further ruled that the District Court had no authority to conduct a preliminary hearing on the merits for the purpose of allocating costs and that the entire expense of notice necessarily fell on petitioner as representative plaintiff. Finally, the Court of Appeals rejected the expedient of a fluid-class recovery and concluded that the proposed class action was unmanageable under Rule 23(b)(3)(D). For all of these reasons the Court of Appeals ordered the suit dismissed as a class action. One judge concurred in the result solely on the ground that the District Court had erred in imposing 90% of the notice costs on respondents. Petitioner's requests for rehearing and rehearing en banc were denied. 479 F.2d, at 1020.

Thus, after six and one-half years and three published decisions, the Court of Appeals endorsed the conclusion reached by the District

Court in its original order in 1966—that petitioner's suit could not proceed as a class action. In its procedural history, at least, this litigation has lived up to Judge Lumbard's characterization of it as a "Frankenstein monster posing as a class action." *Eisen II*, 391 F.2d, at 572.

II

At the outset we must decide whether the Court of Appeals in *Eisen III* had jurisdiction to review the District Court's orders permitting the suit to proceed as a class action and allocating the cost of notice. Petitioner contends that it did not. Respondents counter by asserting two independent bases for appellate jurisdiction: first, that the orders in question constituted a "final" decision within the meaning of 28 U.S.C.A. § 1291 [8] and were therefore appealable as of right under that section; and, second, that the Court of Appeals in *Eisen II* expressly retained jurisdiction pending further development of a factual record on remand and that consequently no new jurisdictional basis was required for the decision in *Eisen III*. Because we agree with the first ground asserted by respondents, we have no occasion to consider the second.

Restricting appellate review to "final decisions" prevents the debilitating effect on judicial administration caused by piecemeal appellate disposition of what is, in practical consequence, but a single controversy. While the application of § 1291 in most cases is plain enough, determining the finality of a particular judicial order may pose a close question. No verbal formula yet devised can explain prior finality decisions with unerring accuracy or provide an utterly reliable guide for the future.[9] We know, of course, that § 1291 does not limit appellate review to "those final judgments which terminate an action . . .," Cohen v. Beneficial Indus. Loan Corp., 337 U.S., at 545, 69 S.Ct., at 1225, but rather that the requirement of finality is to be given a "practical rather than a technical construction." Id., at 546, 69 S.Ct., at 1226. The inquiry requires some evaluation of the competing considerations underlying all questions of finality—"the inconvenience

---

8. Section 1291 provides:

"The courts of appeals shall have jurisdiction of appeals from all final decisions of the district courts of the United States, the United States District Court for the District of the Canal Zone, the District Court of Guam, and the District Court of the Virgin Islands, except where a direct review may be had in the Supreme Court."

9. As long ago as 1892 the Court complained:

"Probably no question of equity practice has been the subject of more frequent discussion in this court than the finality of decrees. . . . The cases, it must be

conceded, are not altogether harmonious." McGourkey v. Toledo & Ohio C.R. Co., 146 U.S. 536, 544–545, 13 S.Ct. 170, 172, 36 L.Ed. 1079. In the intervening years the difficulty of resolving such questions has not abated. As Mr. Justice Black commented in Gillespie v. U.S. Steel Corp., 379 U.S. 148, 152, 85 S.Ct. 308, 311, 13 L.Ed.2d 199 (1964), "whether a ruling is 'final' within the meaning of § 1291 is frequently so close a question that decision of that issue either way can be supported with equally forceful arguments, and . . . it is impossible to devise a formula to resolve all marginal cases coming within what might well be called the 'twilight zone' of finality."

and costs of piecemeal review on the one hand and the danger of denying justice by delay on the other." Dickinson v. Petroleum Conversion Corp., 338 U.S. 507, 511, 70 S.Ct. 322, 324, 94 L.Ed. 299 (1950) (footnote omitted).

We find the instant case controlled by our decision in Cohen v. Beneficial Indus. Loan Corp., supra. There the Court considered the applicability in a federal diversity action of a forum state statute making the plaintiff in a stockholder's derivative action liable for litigation expenses, if ultimately unsuccessful, and entitling the corporation to demand security in advance for their payment. The trial court ruled the statute inapplicable, and the corporation sought immediate appellate review over the stockholder's objection that the order appealed from was not final. This Court held the order appealable on two grounds. First, the District Court's finding was not "tentative, informal or incomplete." 337 U.S., at 546, 69 S.Ct., at 1225, but settled conclusively the corporation's claim that it was entitled by state law to require the shareholder to post security for costs. Second, the decision did not constitute merely a "step toward final disposition of the merits of the case. . . . ." Ibid. Rather, it concerned a collateral matter that could not be reviewed effectively on appeal from the final judgment. The Court summarized its conclusion in this way:

> "This decision appears to fall in that small class which finally determine claims of right separable from, and collateral to, rights asserted in the action, too important to be denied review and too independent of the cause itself to require that appellate consideration be deferred until the whole case is adjudicated." Ibid.

Analysis of the instant case reveals that the District Court's order imposing 90% of the notice costs on respondents likewise falls within "that small class." It conclusively rejected respondents' contention that they could not lawfully be required to bear the expense of notice to the members of petitioner's proposed class. Moreover, it involved a collateral matter unrelated to the merits of petitioner's claims. Like the order in *Cohen*, the District Court's judgment on the allocation of notice costs was "a final disposition of a claimed right which is not an ingredient of the cause of action and does not require consideration with it," id., at 546–547, 69 S.Ct., at 1226, and it was similarly appealable as a "final decision" under § 1291. In our view the Court of Appeals therefore had jurisdiction to review fully the District Court's resolution of the class action notice problems in this case, for that court's allocation of 90% of the notice costs to respondents was but one aspect of its effort to construe the requirements of Rule 23(c)(2) in a way that would permit petitioner's suit to proceed as a class action.[10]

---

10. As explained in Part III of this opinion, we find the notice requirements of Rule 23 to be dispositive of petitioner's attempt to maintain the class action as presently defined. We therefore have no occasion to consider whether the Court of Appeals correctly resolved the issues of manageability and fluid-class recovery, or indeed, whether those issues were properly before the Court of Appeals under the theory of retained jurisdiction.

III

Turning to the merits of the case, we find that the District Court's resolution of the notice problems was erroneous in two respects. First, it failed to comply with the notice requirements of Rule 23(c)(2), and second, it imposed part of the cost of notice on respondents.

A

Rule 23(c)(2) provides that, in any class action maintained under subdivision (b)(3), each class member shall be advised that he has the right to exclude himself from the action on request or to enter an appearance through counsel, and further that the judgment, whether favorable or not, will bind all class members not requesting exclusion. To this end, the court is required to direct to class members "the best notice practicable under the circumstances *including individual notice to all members who can be identified through reasonable effort.*"[11] We think the import of this language is unmistakable. Individual notice must be sent to all class members whose names and addresses may be ascertained through reasonable effort.

The Advisory Committee's Note to Rule 23 reinforces this conclusion. See 28 U.S.C.A.App., p. 7765. The Advisory Committee described subdivision (c)(2) as "not merely discretionary" and added that the "mandatory notice pursuant to subdivision (c)(2) . . . is designed to fulfill requirements of due process to which the class action procedure is of course subject." Id., at 7768. The Committee explicated its incorporation of due process standards by citation to Mullane v. Central Hanover Bank & Trust Co., 339 U.S. 306, 70 S.Ct. 652, 94 L.Ed. 865 (1950), and like cases.

In *Mullane* the Court addressed the constitutional sufficiency of publication notice rather than mailed individual notice to known beneficiaries of a common trust fund as part of a judicial settlement of accounts. The Court observed that notice and an opportunity to be heard were fundamental requisites of the constitutional guarantee of procedural due process. It further stated that notice must be "reasonably calculated, under all the circumstances, to apprise interested parties of the pendency of the action and afford them an opportunity to

---

11. Emphasis added. Subdivision (c)(2) provides in full:

"(2) In any class action maintained under subdivision (b)(3), the court shall direct to the members of the class the best notice practicable under the circumstances, including individual notice to all members who can be identified through reasonable effort. The notice shall advise each member that (A) the court will exclude him from the class if he so requests by a specified date; (B) the judgment, whether favorable or not, will include all members who do not request exclusion; and (C) any member who does not request exclusion may, if he desires, enter an appearance through his counsel."

present their objections." Id., at 314, 70 S.Ct., at 657. The Court continued:

"But when notice is a person's due, process which is a mere gesture is not due process. The means employed must be such as one desirous of actually informing the absentee might reasonably adopt to accomplish it. The reasonableness and hence the constitutional validity of any chosen method may be defended on the ground that it is in itself reasonably certain to inform those affected." Id., at 315, 70 S.Ct., at 657.

The Court then held that publication notice could not satisfy due process where the names and addresses of the beneficiaries were known.[12] In such cases, "the reasons disappear for resort to means less likely than the mails to apprise them of [an action's] pendency." Id., at 318, 70 S.Ct., at 659.

* * *

Viewed in this context, the express language and intent of Rule 23(c)(2) leave no doubt that individual notice must be provided to those class members who are identifiable through reasonable effort. In the present case, the names and addresses of 2,250,000 class members are easily ascertainable, and there is nothing to show that individual notice cannot be mailed to each. For these class members, individual notice is clearly the "best notice practicable" within the meaning of Rule 23(c)(2) and our prior decisions.

Petitioner contends, however, that we should dispense with the requirement of individual notice in this case, and he advances two reasons for our doing so. First, the prohibitively high cost of providing individual notice to 2,250,000 class members would end this suit as a class action and effectively frustrate petitioner's attempt to vindicate the policies underlying the antitrust and securities laws. Second petitioner contends that individual notice is unnecessary in this case, because no prospective class member has a large enough stake in the matter to justify separate litigation of his individual claim. Hence, class members lack any incentive to opt out of the class action even if notified.

The short answer to these arguments is that individual notice to identifiable class members is not a discretionary consideration to be waived in a particular case. It is, rather, an unambiguous requirement of Rule 23. As the Advisory Committee's Note explained, the Rule was

---

12. The Court's discussion of the inadequacies of published notice bears attention:

"It would be idle to pretend that publication alone, as prescribed here, is a reliable means of acquainting interested parties of the fact that their rights are before the courts. . . . Chance alone brings to the attention of even a local resident an advertisement in small type inserted in the back pages of a newspaper, and if he makes his home outside the area of the newspaper's normal circulation the odds that the information will never reach him are large indeed. The chance of actual notice is further reduced when, as here, the notice required does not even name those whose attention it is supposed to attract, and does not inform acquaintances who might call it to attention." 339 U.S., at 315, 70 S.Ct., at 658.

intended to insure that the judgment, whether favorable or not, would bind all class members who did not request exclusion from the suit. 28 U.S.C.A.App., pp. 7765, 7768. Accordingly, each class member who can be identified through reasonable effort must be notified that he may request exclusion from the action and thereby preserve his opportunity to press his claim separately or that he may remain in the class and perhaps participate in the management of the action. There is nothing in Rule 23 to suggest that the notice requirements can be tailored to fit the pocketbooks of particular plaintiffs.[13]

Petitioner further contends that adequate representation, rather than notice, is the touchstone of due process in a class action and therefore satisfies Rule 23. We think this view has little to commend it. To begin with, Rule 23 speaks to notice as well as to adequacy of representation and requires that both be provided. Moreover, petitioner's argument proves too much, for it quickly leads to the conclusion that no notice at all, published or otherwise, would be required in the present case. This cannot be so, for quite apart from what due process may require, the command of Rule 23 is clearly to the contrary. We therefore conclude that Rule 23(c)(2) requires that individual notice be sent to all class members who can be identified with reasonable effort.[14]

B

We also agree with the Court of Appeals that petitioner must bear the cost of notice to the members of his class. * * *

We find nothing in either the language or history of Rule 23 that gives a court any authority to conduct a preliminary inquiry into the merits of a suit in order to determine whether it may be maintained as a class action. Indeed, such a procedure contravenes the Rule by allowing a representative plaintiff to secure the benefits of a class action without first satisfying the requirements for it. He is thereby allowed to obtain a determination on the merits of the claims advanced on behalf of the class without any assurance that a class action may be maintained. This procedure is directly contrary to the command of subdivision (c)(1) that the court determine whether a suit denominated a class action may be maintained as such "[a]s soon as practicable after the commencement of [the] action. . . ." In short, we agree with Judge Wisdom's conclusion in Miller v. Mackey International, 452 F.2d

13. Petitioner also argues that class members will not opt out because the statute of limitations has long since run out on the claims of all class members other than petitioner. This contention is disposed of by our recent decision in American Pipe & Construction Co. v. Utah, 414 U.S. 538, 94 S.Ct. 756, 38 L.Ed.2d 713 (1974), which established that commencement of a class action tolls the applicable statute of limitations as to all members of the class.

14. We are concerned here only with the notice requirements of subdivision (c)(2), which are applicable to class actions maintained under subdivision (b)(3). By its terms subdivision (c)(2) is inapplicable to class actions for injunctive or declaratory relief maintained under subdivision (b)(2). Petitioner's effort to qualify his suit as a class action under subdivisions (b)(1) and (b)(2) was rejected by the Court of Appeals. See n. 4, supra.

424 (CA5 1971), where the court rejected a preliminary inquiry into the merits of a proposed class action:

> "In determining the propriety of a class action, the question is not whether the plaintiff or plaintiffs have stated a cause of action or will prevail on the merits, but rather whether the requirements of Rule 23 are met." Id., at 427.

Additionally, we might note that a preliminary determination of the merits may result in substantial prejudice to a defendant, since of necessity it is not accompanied by the traditional rules and procedures applicable to civil trials. The court's tentative findings, made in the absence of established safeguards, may color the subsequent proceedings and place an unfair burden on the defendant.

In the absence of any support under Rule 23, petitioner's effort to impose the cost of notice on respondents must fail. The usual rule is that a plaintiff must initially bear the cost of notice to the class. The exceptions cited by the District Court related to situations where a fiduciary duty pre-existed between the plaintiff and defendant, as in a shareholder derivative suit.[15] Where, as here, the relationship between the parties is truly adversary, the plaintiff must pay for the cost of notice as part of the ordinary burden of financing his own suit.

Petitioner has consistently maintained, however, that he will not bear the cost of notice under subdivision (c)(2) to members of the class as defined in his original complaint. See 479 F.2d, at 1008; 52 F.R.D., at 269. We therefore remand the cause with instructions to dismiss the class action as so defined.[16]

The judgment of the Court of Appeals is vacated and the cause remanded for proceedings consistent with this opinion.

It is so ordered.

MR. JUSTICE DOUGLAS, with whom MR. JUSTICE BRENNAN and MR. JUSTICE MARSHALL, concur, dissenting in part.*

15. See, e.g., Dolgow v. Anderson, 43 F.R.D. 472, 498–500 (EDNY 1968). We, of course, express no opinion on the proper allocation of the cost of notice in such cases.

16. The record does not reveal whether a small class of odd-lot traders could be defined, and if so, whether petitioner would be willing to pay the cost of notice to members of such a class. We intimate no view on whether any such subclass would satisfy the requirements of Rule 23. We do note, however, that our dismissal of the class action as originally defined is without prejudice to any efforts petitioner may make to redefine his class either under Rule 23(c)(4) or Fed.Rule Civ.Proc. 15.

* Justice Douglas's opinion is omitted.

HENSON v. EAST LINCOLN TOWNSHIP

United States Court of Appeals for the Seventh Circuit, 1987.
814 F.2d 410.*

POSNER, CIRCUIT JUDGE.

The question for decision is whether classes of defendants are permissible in actions governed by Rule 23(b)(2) of the Federal Rules of Civil Procedure. The district judge said "no," 108 F.R.D. 107 (C.D.Ill. 1985), and we must decide whether he was right.

Following Goldberg v. Kelly, 397 U.S. 254, 90 S.Ct. 1011, 25 L.Ed.2d 287 (1970), this court, in White v. Roughton, 530 F.2d 750 (7th Cir.1976) (per curiam), held that the due process clause of the Fourteenth Amendment requires local welfare departments in Illinois to establish written standards for welfare ("general assistance") eligibility, and notice-and-hearing procedures for the grant or denial of applications for welfare. The *White* case involved the welfare department of the township of Champaign, and the consent decree that was entered in the wake of our decision (and that we revisited in White v. Roughton, 689 F.2d 118 (7th Cir.1982)) provided no state-wide relief. A downstate legal-aid bureau, the Land of Lincoln Legal Assistance Foundation, filed the present suit in 1980. The purpose of the suit is to make other welfare departments in Illinois comply with the principles laid down in our 1976 decision. The suit is on behalf of one named plaintiff, Henson, a resident of East Lincoln Township, and every other person in 65 downstate Illinois counties (the counties served by the Foundation) who has been denied due process of law in connection with an application for welfare. The suit is against East Lincoln Township and its welfare supervisor—they are the named defendants—plus every other local welfare department (and its supervisor) in the 65 counties that does not receive any state aid. The defendant departments are all what are called "non-receiving" departments; welfare departments that receive state aid are bound by state procedural regulations that comply with the principles of White v. Roughton. Henson believes there are 770 "non-receiving" departments in the 65 counties, and they and their supervisors are the members of the defendant class. The suit seeks only injunctive relief, and the Foundation asked for certification of the defendant class only under subsection (b)(2) of Rule 23.

The Foundation notified each of the 770 departments of the suit, and the district judge allowed it to serve each of them with a deposition on written questions (Fed.R.Civ.P. 30). Most of the 525 departments that answered at least some of the Foundation's questions acknowledged that they were not complying with one or more of the principles announced in White v. Roughton—at least that is the construction that

---

* The Supreme Court has granted certiorari in this case, ___ U.S. ___, 108 S.Ct. 283, 98 L.Ed.2d 244 (1987).

the Foundation places on their answers and for purposes of this appeal we shall assume it is correct.

The district judge denied the plaintiff's motion under Fed.R.Civ.P. 23(c)(1) to certify the defendant class, on the ground that Rule 23(b)(2) does not permit defendant classes. He certified his ruling for an immediate appeal under 28 U.S.C. § 1292(b), see 108 F.R.D. at 113, and we agreed to hear it. He has stayed all proceedings in the case until we decide the appeal.

Rule 23 provides, so far as is pertinent to this appeal:

(a) Prerequisites to a Class Action. One or more members of a class may sue or be sued as representative parties on behalf of all only if (1) the class is so numerous that joinder of all members is impracticable, (2) there are questions of law or fact common to the class, (3) the claims or defenses of the representative parties are typical of the claims or defenses of the class, and (4) the representative parties will fairly and adequately protect the interests of the class.

(b) Class Actions Maintainable. An action may be maintained as a class action if the prerequisites of subdivision (a) are satisfied, and in addition:

(1) the prosecution of separate actions by or against individual members of the class would create a risk of

(A) inconsistent or varying adjudications with respect to individual members of the class which would establish incompatible standards of conduct for the party opposing the class, or

(B) adjudications with respect to individual members of the class which would as a practical matter be dispositive of the interests of the other members not parties to the adjudications or substantially impair or impede their ability to protect their interests; or

(2) the party opposing the class has acted or refused to act on grounds generally applicable to the class, thereby making appropriate final injunctive relief or corresponding declaratory relief with respect to the class as a whole; or

(3) the court finds that the questions of law or fact common to the members of the class predominate over any questions affecting only individual members, and that a class action is superior to other available methods for the fair and efficient adjudication of the controversy. . . .

It is apparent from the words of Rule 23(a) ("sue or be sued as representative parties") that suits against a defendant class are permitted. But it does not follow that they are permitted under all three subsections of Rule 23(b). They plainly are permitted under (b)(1), which speaks of "separate actions by or against individual members of the class." Nor is there anything to preclude them under (b)(3). Henson (realistically, the Foundation) cannot fit his case under (b)(1), however, because that subsection contemplates a joint right or obligation. An example would be a suit against members of an unincorporated association naming the officers of the association as the representatives of the defendant class. See Advisory Committee's Notes to 1966 Amendment of Rule 23. And Henson is not interested in bringing the action under (b)(3). Any member of a defendant (as of a plaintiff) class in a (b)(3) suit can "opt out" and thus not be bound by the judgment. See Rule 23(c)(3). Henson fears that every member of the defendant class would do just that. It is (b)(2) or nothing.

The question whether there can be a defendant class in a Rule 23(b)(2) suit cannot be answered by reference to authority. Although the question was declared "settled" in favor of permitting a defendant class in Marcera v. Chinlund, 595 F.2d 1231, 1238 (2d Cir.), vacated on other grounds under the name of Lombard v. Marcera, 442 U.S. 915, 99 S.Ct. 2833, 61 L.Ed.2d 281 (1979), in neither of the cases that the court in *Marcera* cited for this proposition—Washington v. Lee, 263 F.Supp. 327 (M.D.Ala.1966) (3–judge court), aff'd without opinion, 390 U.S. 333, 88 S.Ct. 994, 19 L.Ed.2d 1212 (1968), and Lynch v. Household Finance Corp., 360 F.Supp. 720, 722 n. 3 (D.Conn.1973) (3–judge court)—had the issue been discussed. *Lee* had been filed before the 1966 amendments to Rule 23 that added (b)(2) (though it was decided after); the opinion does not even mention (b)(2). According to a count by the defendants in this case that Henson does not suggest is inaccurate, district courts have certified a defendant class in 45 cases under (b)(2) since 1966. (Many of these are discussed in 1 Newberg on Class Actions § 4.64 (2d ed.1985).) But the only courts of appeals to discuss the permissibility of such actions (there is decision but no discussion in *Marcera*) have held that they are not permissible. * * *

　　　* * *

Henson's main argument is that to interpret Rule 23(b)(2) as excluding defendant class actions would create a remedial gap so large that the draftsmen's failure to provide for such actions must be ascribed to oversight. The premise of this argument is not persuasive. The ease and speed with which the Federal Rules of Civil Procedure can be amended by those whom Congress entrusted with the responsibility for doing so should make federal judges hesitate to create new forms of judicial proceeding in the teeth of the existing rules. Neither the rules committee nor any of its advisors has ever considered whether actions such as the present should be maintainable and if so under what conditions and with what limitations; and the fact that in 45 out of almost two million civil lawsuits filed in federal district courts since 1966 a defendant class has been certified under (b)(2) does not prove that the (b)(2) defendant class action fills an essential need. Such an action creates as we shall see severe problems of manageability and due process, and if the need for such actions is nonetheless an urgent one, the problems they create should be addressed by the persons charged with primary responsibility for formulating the rules of procedure for the federal courts.

The Foundation points out that if this suit cannot be maintained against a class of defendants, the plaintiff class will shrink to welfare applicants in East Lincoln Township—for they alone have a quarrel with the named defendants. To get all the relief this suit seeks the Foundation will have to find a plaintiff in each of the other 770 townships (or in however many actually are violating the Fourteenth Amendment)—and one suit will become several hundred and clog the overcrowded dockets of the federal district courts in central and southern Illinois. The Foundation paints with too vivid a palette. Any township that is violating the principles of White v. Roughton has strong incentives to bring itself voluntarily into prompt and full compliance (and all or most of them may, for all we know, have done so during the five-year course of this litigation). By virtue of 42 U.S.C. § 1988, the plaintiff in a federal civil rights suit is normally entitled to the award of a reasonable attorney's fees if he prevails, so townships that prove obdurate in defending the indefensible will pay not only their own legal expenses but those of their adversaries. Furthermore, it may be that in many of these townships either there are no denials of due process or the denials aren't hurting anyone who cares to step forward and be a class representative, in which event the number of separate suits that would replace this two-sided class action might be many fewer than the Foundation predicts. (Indeed, it acknowledged at argument that the difficulty of lining up plaintiffs in the other townships was one of its motivations for seeking to certify a defendant class.) Even if several hundred cases are filed, they can be consolidated for pretrial discovery and for trial in one court, before one judge, and all but the lead case stayed until that case is resolved, and then the others resolved summarily. See 28 U.S.C. § 1407. The practical difference between class treatment and individual-case treatment, so far as securing the constitutional rights of welfare recipients in Illinois is concerned, could turn out to be small.

It is relevant to our consideration to note that a double class action would be unwieldy, or worse, in the circumstances disclosed by this case, and probably generally. The law firm retained by one Illinois township of modest size is being asked to shoulder responsibility for defending the interests of hundreds of others, which by the same token are being asked to place the responsibility for a litigation vital to the discharge of their essential and financially burdensome public functions in lawyers they may never have heard of. Indeed, "told" rather than "asked"; for not only is there no provision in (b)(2) for a class member to opt out of the suit, but there is no requirement of notifying the members of the class, though such notice was provided here. It would be odd if the rule permitted a defendant class without requiring notice; this is one more bit of evidence against Henson's reading of the statute.

And because the defendant class consists of local governments and their officials, in effect the federal district court is being asked to override the state's allocation of powers among local governmental bodies and treat the welfare system as if it were a state system rather than a local system—though it really is local, except for those townships that receive state aid, and they are not involved in this case. It is only an accident, moreover, that this litigation is limited to 65 counties in Illinois. On the Foundation's reading of (b)(2), as it acknowledged at argument, this suit could have been brought as a nationwide class action pitting all welfare applicants in the United States who are being denied due process of law against all the welfare departments in the United States that are thought to be denying those benefits. The welfare department of Eugene, Oregon might find itself an unnamed defendant in the Central District of Illinois, represented by the law firm retained by the township of East Lincoln, Illinois. True, it might be able to interpose objections based on lack of personal jurisdiction. See 3B Moore's Federal Practice ¶ 23.40[6], at p. 23–313 n. 8 (2d ed. 1985). But this would not solve the deeper problems of such a suit. By the very definition of a double class action there is no controversy between most plaintiffs and most defendants. Residents of East Lincoln have no quarrel with any defendant except East Lincoln; East Lincoln has no quarrel with any plaintiff except Henson. And so it goes for all the members of the plaintiff and defendant classes. The double class action is a legislative or regulatory device for bringing about general compliance with law (the injunction issued at the end of the action corresponding to a statute or regulation that binds all persons within its scope, whether or not they have been guilty of any wrongdoing in the past), rather than an adjudicative device for resolving a dispute. Indeed, as we have said, the Foundation's fear of not being able to enlist a plaintiff against each and every one of the allegedly noncomplying townships was one of the motivations behind seeking the certification of a defendant class. It is possible that in a double class action with thousands of parties only two would have a dispute—Hensen and East Lincoln Township. Without having to decide whether Article III permits a federal court to assert jurisdiction over a mass of parties that may not be engaged in an actual controversy with anyone, we believe that a federal court should not claim such jurisdiction on the basis of a rule of procedure not intended by its draftsmen to confer it.

An influential current in contemporary legal thought believes that the old-fashioned bipolar model of adjudication is hopelessly outmoded and that the federal courts should embrace with enthusiasm a newer model of adjudication, in which federal district courts carry out ambitious restructurings of public institutions, such as state and local welfare systems, in the manner of a regulatory agency. See, e.g., Chayes, The Role of the Judge in Public Law Litigation, 89 Harv.L.Rev. 1281 (1976). Whatever the abstract merits of this approach (and maybe it should not be evaluated in the abstract), we do not find it embodied in Rule 23(b)(2), and we have no authority to amend the rule.

* * * Nothing in the structure or history of the rule suggests that it was intended as a broad delegation to the courts of a power that judges would domesticate by bringing to bear limiting principles found elsewhere in Rule 23, or in the Constitution, or in the Judicial Code.

Granted, such limiting principles abound. We have mentioned one already—the limitations on a court's personal jurisdiction. There are others, so that even if (b)(2) double class actions were possible in principle, the present class action or our hypothetical nationwide class action might be precluded—whether by Rule 11, which requires that counsel inquire before rather than after bringing suit whether his client has a claim against the defendant (including we suppose members of a defendant class), or by Rule 23(a)(4), which requires that "the representative parties will fairly and adequately protect the interests of the class," see La Mar v. H & B Novelty & Loan Co., 489 F.2d 461, 466 (9th Cir.1973). At the very least, such actions might be trimmed down to manageability by orders issued under Rule 23(d), such as an order permitting the district court to allow each member of the defendant class to intervene in the suit with the full rights of a named party. But the managerial burdens placed on the district court would be great, and the potential for litigation over rulings under these provisions considerable. We are loath to embark on these uncharted and, as it seems to us, perilous seas without some indication that the framers of Rule 23 would have wanted us to do so; there is no such indication. * * *

Our conclusion is supported not only by the cases cited earlier but by the Wright and Miller treatise, see 7A Wright, Miller & Kane, Federal Practice and Procedure § 1775, at pp. 461–62 (2d ed. 1986), and by the thorough discussion in Comment, Defendant Class Actions and Federal Civil Rights Litigation, 33 UCLA L.Rev. 283, 316–25 (1985). Professor Moore, though sympathetic to allowing (b)(2) suits against classes, admits that it would require stretching the language of the rule and would create a variety of problems; why he nevertheless favors the device is unclear. See 3B Moore's Federal Practice, supra, ¶ 23.40[6]. The case for the (b)(2) defendant class is well argued in Note, Certification of Defendant Classes Under Rule 23(b)(2), 84 Colum.L.Rev. 1371 (1984), stressing the utility of the device in a case such as the present where local officials are alleged to be unwilling to comply with decisional law; but for reasons explained earlier we are less impressed than the note's author is by the practical arguments for the device. We note, finally, that double class actions remain possible under (b)(3), as in Appleton Electric Co. v. Advance–United Expressways, 494 F.2d 126, 137 and n. 22 (7th Cir.1974).

The district court's order declining to certify a defendant class is

Affirmed.

WILLIAM J. CAMPBELL, SENIOR DISTRICT JUDGE, concurring in part and dissenting in part:

I concur in the result reached in this case by the majority, however, I have no desire to join in the majority's issuance of an absolute prohibition against Rule 23(b)(2) defendant class actions. * * *

* * * In *Marcera,* Chief Judge Irving Kaufman of the Second Circuit astutely—and neatly—put the sheriffs' departments of New York's 62 counties in their place. The issue was what kind of "contact

visits" should be allowed pretrial detainees in New York state jails. Five years earlier, in 1974, in Rhem v. Malcolm, 371 F.Supp. 594 (S.D. N.Y.), aff'd 507 F.2d 333 (2d Cir.1974), the Second Circuit held that due process mandated that pretrial detainees have the right "to shake hands with a friend, to kiss a wife, or to fondle a child." 371 F.Supp. at 626. The rationale was that pretrial detainees should be considered innocent until proven guilty and that a kiss, handshake or fondle was not too much to ask.

Two years later, in 1976, the issue was still being litigated one penal institution (or county) at a time, each case culminating with the issuance of a decree mandating to that particular county or sheriff what was already known—contact visits must be made available. Also in 1976, the New York State Corrections Commission took the pains to promulgate regulations requiring each corrections facility to implement a contact visitation program. The sheriffs still refused to cooperate, claiming the Commission had infringed on their turf as administrators of the jails.

In November of 1976, two state prison inmates, Joseph Marcera and John Dillon, brought an action in federal district court to enforce their right to contact visitations.   *   *   *

  *   *   * Chief Judge Kaufman explained the group of 47 sheriffs was large enough to meet the numerosity requirement of Rule 23(a)(1). Questions of law common to the class were also presented to satisfy 23(b)(2). Chief Judge Kaufman emphasized Sheriff Lombard's defenses were typical of those of the class. Typical defenses were that contact visits would threaten security and increase contraband smuggling within the system. Lombard could not cite a case where the defenses were different. While Lombard contended the court's expectation of similar defenses was unrealistic since variations in architecture, staffing and inmate population at different detention facilities would lead to different defenses, Chief Judge Kaufman found this reasoning unacceptable. He rebutted that these considerations would be relevant in fashioning various decrees, yet it was settled law that the prospect of minor variations of decrees covering these areas did not justify a blanket refusal of contact visitations.   *   *   *

Marcera is not a case without its administrative complexities and constitutional soft spots. Chief among them, as Judge Van Graafeiland stated in his thoughtful dissent, is what are the parameters of the term "contact visit" and how can such a visit be effectuated at different jails under different architectural and managerial circumstances? The cost could be high and federal courts could be caught in the "minutiae of jail administration." 595 F.2d at 1246. Yet as Judge Kaufman implicitly recognized, before *Marcera*, by having to handle pretrial detainee suits on a case by case basis, the federal courts were already caught in the "minutiae of jail administration." Is a protracted battle more desirable? Certainly the interests of justice point toward the 23(b)(2) defendant class certification in this situation.   *   *   *

* * *

In the instant case, I concur in the result because I view the suit as too unmanageable and the remedies too unfocused. It is true that, in some respects, the difference between *Marcera* and the case at bar is one of degree. But matters of degree are often at the heart of rulings addressing whether to certify a class. In the action at bar there are 770 defendants. All 770 defendants presumably would have to formulate notice and hearing procedures subject to court approval. Various defendants undoubtedly represent populations of various sizes in locales with varied resources. In *Marcera* the court was concerned with physical visits in rooms. In the case at bar, the concern is the creation of a great number of administrative or quasi-judicial approval boards— arguably 770 bureaucratic systems. Again, with 23(b)(2) defendant class actions, it's best that when in doubt, don't. In the instant case there is no inference of a willful defiance of well-recognized law or statewide administrative policy as witnessed in *Marcera*. I agree with the majority that defendant class certification here is too problematical.

* * *

PHILLIPS PETROLEUM CO. v. SHUTTS

Supreme Court of the United States, 1985.
472 U.S. 797, 105 S.Ct. 2965, 86 L.Ed.2d 628.

[This case appears, supra, p. 476]

NOTE ON THE USES AND ADMINISTRATION OF CLASS SUITS

No procedural change since the discovery provisions of the Federal Rules has elicited as much heated discussion as the 1966 revision of Rule 23, particularly since the impetus of "consumerism" felt since the late 1960's. Compare, e.g., Handler, The Shift from Substantive to Procedural Innovations in Antitrust Suits, 71 Colum.L.Rev. 1 (1971) (characterizing class suits in antitrust actions as "legalized blackmail"); Landers, Of Legalized Blackmail and Legalized Theft: Consumer Class Actions and the Substance-Procedure Dilemma, 47 S.Cal.L.Rev. 842 (1974); Homburger, State Class Actions and the Federal Rule, 71 Colum.L.Rev. 609 (1971); Note, Developments in the Law— Class Actions, 89 Harv.L.Rev. 1318 (1976); Newberg, Class Actions (5 vols.) (2d ed. 1985); Symposium (on class suits), 62 Ind.L.J. 497 (1987). For a viewpoint from abroad, see Australia Law Reform Comm'n, Access of Courts—II: Class Actions, Discussion Paper No. 11, June 1979.

There seems to be little open controversy over 23(b)(1) and 23(b)(2) suits, though there can be very difficult procedural problems in them. At least in Title VII suits many of these difficulties have been overcome, sometimes by overriding the terms of Rule 23. See Rutherglen, Title VII Class Actions, 47 U.Chi.L.Rev. 688 (1980). Compare Bell, Serving Two Masters: Integration Ideals and Client Interests in School Desegregation Litigation, 85 Yale L.J. 470 (1976). As *Henson* shows, one important controversy is whether 23(b)(2) permits suits against a defendant class. As indicated in the introductory note to *Henson*, the Supreme Court has granted certiorari in the case, presumably to resolve the conflict over this issue.

The controversy has centered in damages class suits, of which *Vasquez, Eisen, In re Dalkon Shield,* and *Phillips* are illustrations. See also, e.g., Fletcher v. Security Pac. Nat. Bank, 23 Cal.3d 442, 153 Cal.Rptr. 28, 591 P.2d 51 (1979); King v. Club Med, Inc., 76 A.D.2d 123, 430 N.Y.S.2d 65 (1st Dept. 1980). Particularly controversial is the "fluid recovery" class suit, i.e., where damages are measured by the injuries inflicted even though all the individual claimants cannot be identified or located and the residue of the recovery is distributed to persons similarly situated. See, e.g., Bruno v. Superior Court, 127 Cal.App.3d 120, 179 Cal.Rptr. 342 (1981); State of California v. Levi Strauss & Co., 41 Cal.3d 460, 224 Cal.Rptr. 605, 715 P.2d 564 (1986) (requirements in implementing fluid recovery plan). See also Note, An Economic Analysis of Fluid Class Recovery Mechanisms, 34 Stan.L.Rev. 173 (1981); Note, The Consumer Trust Fund: A Cy Pres Solution to Undistributed Funds in Consumer Class Actions, 38 Hastings L.J. 729 (1987). It has been persuasively argued that the damages class suit is a heavy claimants' weapon only because the "American rule" as to attorney's fees gives the plaintiff high incentive and low risk in prosecuting such a suit. See Dewees, Prichard and Trebilcock, An Economic Analysis of Cost and Fee Rules for Class Actions, 10 J. Legal Stud. 155 (1981).

Quite plainly, there are differences of opinion as to whether these kinds of suits should be maintainable at all. Are the differences ones of "substantive" policy? Whatever they are, they manifest themselves in the resolution of various specific problems arising in 23(b)(3) class suits. These problems arise in connection with whether the suit should be certified as a class suit or should proceed merely as an action by the plaintiff individually. See, e.g., *In re Dalkon Shield,* supra p. 854; see also East Texas Motor Freight System, Inc. v. Rodriguez, 431 U.S. 395, 97 S.Ct. 1891, 52 L.Ed.2d 453 (1977); United States Parole Comm'n v. Geraghty, 445 U.S. 388, 100 S.Ct. 1202, 63 L.Ed.2d 479 (1980); Miller, An Overview of Class Actions, Past, Present and Future (Federal Judicial Center 1977).

Among the important problems with damages class suits are:

1. Timeliness of Certification

Rule 23(c)(1) requires that an action's status as a class suit be determined "as soon as practicable after the commencement" of the action. The prevailing rule is that the maintainability of the class suit must be determined prior to proceeding to the merits of the class claim, see, e.g., People v. Pacific Land Research Co., 20 Cal.3d 10, 141 Cal.Rptr. 20, 569 P.2d 125 (1977); Eggleston v. Chicago Journeymen Plumbers' Union, 657 F.2d 890 (7th Cir. 1981); Sembach v. McMahon College, Inc., 94 F.R.D. 260 (S.D.Tex.1982); Peritz v. Liberty Loan Corp., 523 F.2d 349 (7th Cir. 1975); cf. California Employment Development Dept. v. Superior Court, 30 Cal.3d 256, 178 Cal.Rptr. 612, 636 P.2d 575 (1981), but certification at the point of entering judgment has also been permitted, e.g., Larionoff v. United States, 533 F.2d 1167 (D.C.Cir. 1976). See 7B Wright & Miller § 1785. Compare Green v. Obledo, 29 Cal.3d 126, 172 Cal.Rptr. 206, 624 P.2d 256 (1981) (decertification after judgment for plaintiff). See Note, Reopening the Debate: Postjudgment Certification in Rule 23(b)(3) Class Actions, 66 Cornell L.Rev. 1218 (1981).

2. "Predominance" of Common Questions

A 23(b)(3) suit may be maintained only if the court finds that the common questions "predominate" over the questions peculiar to each individual member of the class. Whether they do so is partly a matter of focus, and hence a matter of discretion, and in any case can be manipulated by reformulating the law to be applied on the merits. Observe how this was done in *Vasquez* with regard to the issue of reliance and in *In re Dalkon Shield* with regard to the issue of duty of care. Contrast, e.g., City of San Jose v. Superior Court, 12 Cal.3d 447, 115 Cal.Rptr. 797, 525 P.2d 701 (1974) (valuation of separate land parcels involves individual questions precluding class suit by landowners near airport for damage from overflights); McDonnell Douglas Corp. v. United States District Court, 523 F.2d 1083 (9th Cir. 1975) (no class action for wrongful death of 335 airplane crash victims); Ross v. Amrep Corp., 57 A.D.2d 99, 393 N.Y.S.2d 410 (1977) (no class suit for fraudulent land sales scheme carried out much like that in *Vasquez*). Cf. Note, Class Action in a Products Liability Context: The Predomination Requirement and Cause-in-Fact, 7 Hofstra L.Rev. 859 (1979). Did the common questions predominate in Cooper v. Federal Reserve Bank, supra p. 830? If not, what alternative action might the trial judge in the initial suit have taken?

One obvious way to assure "predominance" of the common questions among a group is to subdivide the group into subclasses within which common interests clearly predominate. See, e.g., Officers for Justice v. Civil Service Comm'n, 688 F.2d 615 (9th Cir. 1982). But this reduces the scope of the claim by each such class. Cf. General Tel. Co. v. Falcon, 457 U.S. 147, 102 S.Ct. 2364, 72 L.Ed.2d 740 (1982). See also Comment, The Use of Subclasses in Class Action Suits Under Title VII, 9 Indus.Rel.L.J. 116 (1987). Correlatively, if the class is defined in general terms, the class claim is broader but the commonality of interests among its members is reduced. See generally Rhode, Class Conflicts in Class Actions, 34 Stan.L.Rev. 1183 (1982).

3. "Adequacy" of Representation

There are decisions saying that the plaintiff must herself have been injured in the way that she complains members of the class were injured, as a guaranty of her interest in vindicating the class claim and hence of the vigor of her representation. See General Tel. Co. v. Falcon, supra; East Texas Motor Freight System, Inc. v. Rodriguez, 431 U.S. 395, 97 S.Ct. 1891, 52 L.Ed.2d 453 (1977). But there are others that have not enforced this requirement. See United States Parole Comm'n v. Geraghty, 445 U.S. 388, 100 S.Ct. 1202, 63 L.Ed.2d 479 (1980) (plaintiff no longer in class but may continue as representative for purposes of obtaining certification of class suit); Kagan v. Gibraltar Sav. & Loan Ass'n, 35 Cal.3d 582, 200 Cal.Rptr. 38, 676 P.2d 1060 (1984) (plaintiff filed class suit under the California Consumers Legal Remedies Act, C.C. 1750 et seq., alleging damages from defendant's falsely advertising that customers would not be charged management fees in connection with individual retirement accounts; held: the fact that plaintiff previously received individual restitution is not sufficient to disqualify plaintiff as a class representative since the legislature intended to avoid such "picking off" of prospective class plaintiffs); Sosna v. Iowa, 419 U.S. 393, 95 S.Ct. 553, 42 L.Ed.2d 532 (1975); Haas v. Pittsburgh Nat. Bank, 526 F.2d 1083 (3d Cir. 1975); cf. EEOC v. D.H. Holmes Co., 556 F.2d 787 (5th Cir. 1977) (class suit brought by government agency). See also Note, Article III Justiciability and Class Actions: Standing and Mootness, 59 Tex.L.Rev. 297 (1981). Is membership in the class really related to adequacy of representation? See Note, The Binding Effect of EEOC-Initiated Actions, 80 Colum.L.Rev. 395 (1980), as to whether the protective government agency will be deemed to represent the private party for purposes of preclusion. See also Restatement Second of Judgments § 4. The requirement does restrict the eligible volunteers who can represent the class. See Gen. Tel. Co. v. Falcon, supra. It is in the discretion of the court whether an attorney may represent a class of which he is a named representative. McGhee v. Bank of America Nat'l Trust & Sav. Ass'n, 60 Cal.App.3d 442, 131 Cal.Rptr. 482 (1976); cf. Reich v. Club Universe, 125 Cal.App.3d 965, 178 Cal.Rptr. 473 (1981). Some cases suggest that in any event the plaintiff must show technical prowess and financial resources sufficient to carry the action forward. See, e.g., Chevalier v. Baird Sav. Ass'n, 72 F.R.D. 140 (E.D. Pa.1976); Kaye and Sinex, The Financial Aspect of Adequate Representation under Rule 23(a)(4), 31 U.Miami L.Rev. 651 (1977); Comment, The Importance of Being Adequate: Due Process Requirements in Class Actions Under Federal Rule 23, 123 U.Pa.L.Rev. 1217 (1975); Note, Class Standing and the Class Representative, 94 Harv.L.Rev. 1637 (1981). See also Richmond v. Dart Indus., Inc., 29 Cal.3d 462, 174 Cal. Rptr. 515, 629 P.2d 23 (1981) (some conflict within class does not preclude certification); Note, Conflicts in Class Actions and Protection of Absent Class Members, 91 Yale L.J. 590 (1982).

Generally the real question is not the adequacy of the named representative plaintiff but the adequacy of plaintiff's counsel. See, e.g., McGowan v. Faulkner Concrete Pipe Co., 659 F.2d 554 (5th Cir. 1981). But plaintiff's counsel can go too far in assuming responsibility for the suit. See In re Mid-Atlantic Toyota Antitrust Litigation, 93 F.R.D. 485 (D.Md.1982) (counsel's agreement to bear costs of suit is unethical).

4. "Manageability"

Really dreamy class suits do seem unmanageable, e.g., City of Philadelphia v. American Oil Co., 53 F.R.D. 45 (D.N.J.1971) (no class treatment for retail gasoline buyers in area including Pennsylvania, New Jersey and Delaware). But, certainly if "fluid recovery" is permitted, some very large classes can be accommodated if the court seriously wants to do so. Should a trial court have discretion to decide whether a plaintiff has a great big lawsuit, possibly worth millions and at any rate thousands in settlement, or only a little lawsuit? The legislature may provide guidance by sanctioning certain types of class suits, e.g., C.C. 1781 (consumer claims), or by indicating that class suits are to be permitted unless plainly unmanageable. See, e.g., N.Y.C.P.L.R. § 902, adopted in 1973:

> "Among the matters which the court shall consider in determining whether the action may proceed as a class action are:
>
> "1. the interest of members of the class in individually controlling the prosecution or defense of separate actions;
>
> "2. the impracticability or inefficiency of prosecuting or defending separate actions * * *."

See also Uniform Class Actions Act (1976), which lists thirteen factors. Compare Berry, Ending Substance's Indenture to Procedure: The Imperative for Comprehensive Revision of the Class Damage Action, 80 Colum.L.Rev. 299 (1980); Kennedy, Federal Class Actions: A Need for Legislative Reform, 32 Sw. L.J. 1209 (1979); and Mickum and Rhees, Federal Class Action Reform: A Response to the Proposed Legislation, 69 Kentucky L.J. 799 (1981), discussing proposed federal statutory class actions of two types—small-sized claims and others—with somewhat different procedures for each.

5. Notice

(a) Many analysts think the Supreme Court's holding in *Eisen,* that individual notice is required in 23(b)(3) class suits, was not compelled by the terms of the rule and is incompatible with the concept of a class suit. (If individual notice is given, why not call it a "summons" and simply make the class members parties to the suit?) See Dam, Class Action Notice: Who Needs It?, 1974 Sup.Ct.Rev. 97. Compare Cartt v. Superior Court, 50 Cal.App.3d 960, 124 Cal.Rptr. 376 (1975) (individual notice not required in consumer class actions); N.Y.C.P.L.R. § 904(c) ("In determining the method by which notice is to be given, the court shall consider * * * the cost * * * the resources of the parties and * * * the stake of each represented member of the class, and the likelihood that significant numbers of represented members would desire to exclude themselves from the class or to appear individually, which may be determined, in the court's discretion, by sending notice to a random sample of the class."); Uniform Class Actions Act § 7(c).

As for the burden of cost, *Eisen* may be on sound ground in suggesting that the cost should not be imposed on the opposing party in the absence of statute. See Oppenheimer Fund, Inc. v. Sanders, 437 U.S. 340, 98 S.Ct. 2380, 57 L.Ed.2d 253 (1978); Cartt v. Superior Court, supra. Compare N.Y.C.P.L.R. § 904(d), giving the court discretion to impose the cost on the opposing party, with Uniform Class Actions Act § 7(f), requiring plaintiff to pay the cost. See also Comment, Cost Allocation in California Class Actions, 13 Cal.W.L.Rev. 65 (1976); cf. Comment, Allocation of Identification Costs in Class Actions, 91 Harv.L.Rev. 703 (1978).

(b) In Johnson v. General Motors Corp., 598 F.2d 432 (5th Cir. 1979), the court held that the judgment in a class suit for both injunctive and monetary relief was not res judicata against the money claim of a member of the class who had not received 23(b)(3) notice at the beginning of the class suit proceeding. It said, 598 F.2d at 437: "Although under the text of Rule 23 and the cases interpreting it notice is not required in all representative suits in order to bind absent class members, due process requires that it be provided before individual monetary claims may be barred." And further: "In light of these developments, we have previously suggested that when both monetary and injunctive relief are sought in an action certified under Rule 23(b)(2), notice may be mandatory if absent class members are to be bound." Can this be squared with Hansberry v. Lee and Mullane v. Central Hanover Bank? Compare Hallman v. Pennsylvania Life Ins. Co., 536 F.Supp. 745 (N.D.Ala.1982) (preclusion applied on similar facts where notice was "reasonably calculated" to reach class members).

(c) A related issue is communication by plaintiff with members of the class. Some lower courts had imposed severe limitations on such communication, essentially on the ground they amounted to champerty. Gulf Oil Co. v. Bernard, 452 U.S. 89, 101 S.Ct. 2193, 68 L.Ed.2d 693 (1981), reserving First Amendment issues, held that Rule 23(d) permits such restrictions only "on a clear record and specific findings that reflect a weighing of the need for a limitation and the potential interference with the rights of the parties." See also Domingo v. New England Fish Co., 727 F.2d 1429 (9th Cir. 1984), modified 742 F.2d 520 (9th Cir. 1984).

(d) Another notice issue arises in settlement of class suits, whether before or after certification. See Handschu v. Special Services Div., 787 F.2d 828 (2d Cir. 1986); Weinberger v. Kendrick, 698 F.2d 61 (2d Cir. 1982); Almond,

Settling Rule 23 Class Actions at the Precertification Stage, 56 N.C.L.Rev. 303 (1978).

6. Statute of Limitations

In American Pipe & Const. Co. v. Utah, 414 U.S. 538, 94 S.Ct. 756, 38 L.Ed. 2d 713 (1974), the court observed that "the filing of a timely class action complaint commences the action for all members of the class as subsequently determined," 414 U.S. at 550, 94 S.Ct. at 764, even for those members of the class who were unaware of the suit, 414 U.S. at 552, 94 S.Ct. at 765. It held that, where certification was denied because the numerosity requirement was not met, the action nevertheless tolled the statute of limitations until "timely" motion to intervene by the excluded members, and said, 414 U.S. at 554, 94 S.Ct. at 766, that "the commencement of a class action suspends the applicable statute of limitations as to all asserted members of the class who would have been parties had the suit been permitted to continue as a class action." Presumably the latter dictum would permit tolling regardless of the reason for denying class treatment. See also Crown, Cork & Seal Co. v. Parker, 462 U.S. 345, 103 S.Ct. 2392, 76 L.Ed.2d 628 (1983); Chardon v. Fumero Soto, 462 U.S. 650, 103 S.Ct. 2611, 77 L.Ed.2d 74 (1983); Note, Limitation Tolling When Class Status Denied, 60 Notre Dame L.Rev. 686 (1985); Comment, Class Actions and Statutes of Limitations, 48 U.Chi.L.Rev. 106 (1981). Suppose the class is certified, but in more narrowly drawn terms than claimed by the plaintiff—is the statute tolled for the excluded subclass, and if so for how long? The tolling applies to claimants who become class members, not to those who seek to bring separate actions. See Korwek v. Hunt, 827 F.2d 874 (2d Cir. 1987).

In Jolly v. Eli Lilly & Co., 44 Cal.3d 1103, 245 Cal.Rptr. 658, 751 P.2d 923 (1988), the California Supreme Court rejected the rule in *American Pipe,* holding that the filing of a class action suit did not toll the statute of limitations for members of the putative class, including plaintiff, until the time class certification was denied.

7. Appellate Review of Certification

Observe how in *Vasquez* appellate review was obtained of whether the action could be maintained as a class action. *Eisen* held that the order imposing costs of notice is an appealable order, on the ground that it was a "collateral order," but in Coopers & Lybrand v. Livesay, infra p. 1296, the Court held that an order denying class treatment was not appealable of right, and said that an order granting such treatment was likewise not appealable. However, an order granting or denying class treatment may be reviewed under 28 U.S.C.A. § 1292(b), which allows a District Court judge to certify a question for interlocutory review and grants the Court of Appeals discretion whether to take the appeal. This was the route used in *In re Dalkon Shield,* supra p. 854, and *Henson,* supra p. 875. Deposit Guar. Nat. Bank v. Roper, 445 U.S. 326, 100 S.Ct. 1166, 63 L.Ed.2d 427 (1980), held that the class representative could appeal denial of certification following judgment even though his individual claim was mooted by defendant's tender of the amount thereof. In Chief Justice Burger's opinion for the Court, he observed:

"Where it is not economically feasible to obtain relief within the traditional framework of a multiplicity of small individual suits for damages, aggrieved persons may be without any effective redress unless they may employ the class action device. That there is a potential for abuse of the class action mechanism is obvious * * * [b]ut the remedy for abuses does not lie in denying the relief sought here, but with re-examination of Rule 23 * * *.

"A district court's ruling on the certification issue is often the most significant decision rendered in these class action proceedings. To deny the right to appeal simply because the defendant has sought to 'buy off' the individual private claims of the named plaintiffs would * * * frustrate the objectives of class actions * * *." 445 U.S. at 339, 100 S.Ct. at 1174.

Uniform Class Actions Act § 4(c) makes the order of certification appealable.

8. Discovery Against the Class Members

While discovery is available against the members of the class individually, special limitations are imposed to prevent discovery being used for delay or harassment. Brennan v. Midwestern United Life Ins. Co., 450 F.2d 999 (7th Cir. 1971), followed in Dellums v. Powell, 566 F.2d 167 (D.C.Cir. 1977), represents the clear weight of authority. See Note, Obtaining Discovery From Absent Class Members, 30 Drake L.Rev. 347 (1981). See also Southern California Edison Co. v. Superior Court, 7 Cal.3d 832, 103 Cal.Rptr. 709, 500 P.2d 621 (1972); Spoon v. Superior Court, 130 Cal.App.3d 735, 182 Cal.Rptr. 44 (1982), establishing a similar approach.

9. Jurisdiction Over Class Members Outside the Territory

Before Phillips Petroleum Co. v. Shutts, supra, it was controverted whether members of a class who were not subject to in personam jurisdiction were nevertheless bound by reason of the court's jurisdiction over their representative. *Shutts* seems to have answered that question with regard to absentee members of a plaintiff class, at least where there is an opportunity to opt out of the class, but the Court strongly hinted that different standards would apply to absentee members of a defendant class. See Note on Consent, supra p. 381.

10. Dismissal or Compromise of Class Suits

Rule 23(e) requires court approval of the dismissal or compromise of a class action suit. For a similar state rule, see California Rules of Court, Civil Law and Motion Rule 365.

Of all the problems in class suits, none has proved more troublesome than settlement, where the plaintiff's attorney and the defendant often find themselves standing shoulder to shoulder against the class.

---

c. SETTLEMENT OF CLASS SUITS

SAYLOR v. LINDSLEY

United States Court of Appeals for the Second Circuit, 1972.
456 F.2d 896. *

FRIENDLY, CHIEF JUDGE.

This appeal raises questions about the settlement of a stockholder's derivative action over the objection of the plaintiff. While we decline

---

* Some of the court's footnotes are omitted.

to lay down a rule that this may never be done, we hold that the procedures here followed did not adequately protect the right of plaintiff, and of other objecting stockholders, to develop a record which might show that the settlement was improvident.

The transaction here at issue, the two-step sale to Mines Incorporated, in 1951 and 1953, by the Tonopah Mining Company of Nevada (Tonopah) of the stock of Tonopah Nicaragua Company (Tonopah Nicaragua), owner of the Rosita copper mine, is no stranger to the courts of this circuit. The history of an earlier action attacking the sale, Hawkins v. Lindsley, brought in 1957, in the District Court for the Southern District of New York, is recounted in Judge Swan's opinion for this court, 327 F.2d 356 (2 Cir. 1964). It suffices here to say that a second amended complaint in that action charged that the sale violated both state law of fiduciary obligations and the Investment Company Act of 1940; that in September, 1958, Judge Noonan dismissed the claim under the Investment Company Act and required the furnishing of $50,000 of security pursuant to § 61–b of the New York General Corporation Law (McKinney's Consol.Laws, c. 23 Supp. 1971–72); and that when plaintiff failed to post security, Judge Ryan, on July 27, 1961, ordered dismissal with prejudice. Plaintiff failed to take a timely appeal, and other efforts to vacate Judge Ryan's order of dismissal were rejected in the opinion cited.

In February, 1965, plaintiff Saylor began this action, also in the District Court for the Southern District of New York. Federal jurisdiction was based on violations of the federal securities laws, and state claims were alleged merely as pendent. Defendants responded by way of a motion for summary judgment on the basis that this new action was barred by *res judicata* and by the applicable statute of limitations. Judge Cooper granted the motion and dismissed the complaint on the ground of *res judicata;* in addition, while not purporting to decide the defense of limitations, he suggested that this presented a question which, if plaintiff appropriately amended his complaint, would create a triable issue of fact, 274 F.Supp. 253 (S.D.N.Y.1967). We reversed on the ground that the dismissal of the *Hawkins* action for failure to post security was not "on the merits" for purposes of *res judicata;* we indicated agreement with Judge Cooper's statement as to the defense of limitations and remanded for further proceedings with respect to that issue. 391 F.2d 965 (2 Cir. 1968). In an opinion on remand, Judge Cooper determined that with respect to the federal claims there were indeed factual questions whether the applicable statute of limitations had run, and therefore denied summary judgment on that ground; however, with regard to the pendent state claims, he granted summary judgment on the basis of the running of the applicable limitations period unless within thirty days of the court's order plaintiff amended his complaint in certain material respects, 302 F.Supp. 1174 (S.D. N.Y.1969). The defendants filed their answer on January 9, 1970, denying most of the allegations in the complaint and setting up a number of affirmative defenses.

On September 24, 1970, Mr. Markowitz, "attorney for plaintiff," entered into a stipulation of settlement with the attorneys for the various individual and corporate defendants and the attorneys for Tonopah, which had previously been dissolved. This provided for the payment to Wilmington Trust Company, which a Delaware court had appointed to receive and distribute any assets of Tonopah that could not be distributed in liquidation before March 31, 1965, of $250,000 less the costs of notice of the settlement hearing and the fees and disbursements of plaintiff's counsel. Although there is a dispute when agreement on the settlement was actually reached, it is not asserted that plaintiff Saylor at any time authorized it or that Markowitz or anyone else advised him of its terms until November 4, 1970.

On that date Judge Ryan had signed an order setting a hearing on the settlement for December 1, 1970. The notice approved for transmission to stockholders contained no intelligible reference to the most important allegation of the complaint, namely, that defendants had intended the sales to Mines Incorporated to constitute only a step in an ultimate transfer to defendant La Luz Mines, Limited. The notice informed stockholders that transcripts of depositions could be read at the office of the clerk of the district court, and that exhibits could be inspected at the offices of the attorneys. The notice indicated that Mr. Markowitz would apply for an allowance of $83,000 and expenses of $1,313.73. After deduction of these sums, which were subsequently allowed, distribution to Tonopah stockholders would be something less than $166,000, or about 19 cents a share, as against the many millions of dollars in damages alleged to have been suffered. Of this amount, over $109,000 would be paid to the unserved defendant, Falconbridge Nickel Mines, Limited, which held some 74% of Tonopah's shares at the time of the latter's dissolution; the balance, some $57,000, would go to the independent stockholders.

At the hearing on December 1, 1970, Mr. Markowitz announced that he appeared "on behalf of the plaintiff." This elicited a response by Lillian Eichman, who had been of counsel in the *Hawkins* action, that she appeared on behalf of Mr. Saylor in opposition to the settlement. Avrom S. Fischer announced he represented another opposing stockholder, Roseanne Horn, and was of counsel to Mrs. Eichman. Gerard J. O'Brien appeared on behalf of another objecting stockholder, Michael J. McLaughlin. McLaughlin, Saylor, and Fischer, on Miss Horn's behalf, filed affidavits in opposition. Mr. Markowitz made an extended statement in support of the settlement, which was seconded by Mr. Jacobi, counsel for the defendants, and Mr. Singer, counsel for Tonopah, who reported approval of the settlement by Wilmington Trust Company. After briefly hearing Mr. Fischer and Mr. O'Brien, the judge gave them two weeks in which to submit further papers. McLaughlin and Fischer filed extensive affidavits; Markowitz submitted a reply affidavit. On January 14, 1971, the court issued an opinion approving the settlement, [1970–71 Transfer Binder] CCH Fed.Sec.L.

Rep. ¶ 92,222, at 90,410 (S.D.N.Y.1971); this was followed by the order here under appeal.

As earlier stated, there is a dispute about the time when the settlement was actually reached. McLaughlin's second affidavit stated that Markowitz informed him on June 4, 1969, of a meeting to be held the next day to discuss settlement; that "on Aug. 20, 1969, [Markowitz] informed me of the present offer, which I refused. Mr. Saylor soon thereafter advised me that he had similarly told Mr. Markowitz that he does not agree to any settlement, such as the present proposal." Fischer's second affidavit pointed to a letter to Miss Horn, dated October 29, 1969, from a member of the firm representing defendants, which states in part:

> Without going into details as to all the procedural matters that have taken place in the meantime, I can tell you that we have been in active negotiations with counsel for the plaintiff and today agreed on a settlement of the case. It will be necessary to have examinations of several people because the entire settlement will be subject to approval of the court and the court will have to be convinced that it is in the best interest of the stockholders.

Fischer also relied on the nature of the three depositions taken by Markowitz and filed with the District Court, which, we must say, impress us as designed to justify a settlement rather than as an aggressive effort to ferret out facts helpful to prosecution of the suit, as evidence that a settlement had been agreed upon by the time they were taken. In contrast, Markowitz asserted in his reply affidavit that on August 20, 1969, he did not inform McLaughlin of defendants' offer but essentially of the prospects of negotiations; that on September 27, 1969, he called Saylor to advise him of the negotiations and the weakness of plaintiff's case; that he and counsel for Lindsley did believe on October 28, 1969, they had agreed on a settlement, but this subsequently fell through because there was in fact no agreement on the extent to which Falconbridge as a stockholder of Tonopah should share in the proceeds; that subsequent negotiations foundered; and that on January 15, 1970, he sent McLaughlin a letter which he claims informed McLaughlin that settlement negotiations were halted.[4] We find it unnecessary to resolve this dispute or to direct the district court to do so, for even on the basis of Markowitz' version of the relevant events we cannot conclude that enough was done here to protect the rights of the stockholder plaintiff.

We are willing to go along with appellees and hold, despite the seeming incongruity, that the assent of the plaintiff (or plaintiffs) who

---

4. The pertinent part of the letter read:

I have concluded all discussions of settlement and am proceeding with pretrial proceedings. In that connection, the defendants are supplying me with documents that I have requested and depositions of defendants and others are being scheduled.

Everything turns on the meaning of "concluded." Plaintiff says it means "finished." Markowitz, relying on the reference to "pre-trial proceedings", contends it means "broken off". Plaintiff counters that the October 29 letter of defendants' counsel quoted in the text contemplated the taking of depositions prior to a hearing on a settlement.

brought a derivative stockholder's action is not essential to a settlement;[5] a contrary view would put too much power in a wishful thinker or a spite monger to thwart a result that is in the best interests of the corporation and its stockholders. On the other hand, despite the fact that the usual plaintiff in a derivative stockholder's action does not give his attorney the help normally furnished by a client, we are not willing to go to the other extreme and accept the view that the attorney for the plaintiff is the *dominus litis* and the plaintiff only a key to the courthouse door dispensable once entry has been effected. The attorney remains bound to keep his client fully informed of settlement negotiations, to advise the client before signing a stipulation of settlement on his behalf, and, if the client has objected, to inform the court of this when presenting the settlement so that it may devise procedures whereby the plaintiff, with a new attorney, may himself conduct further inquiry if so advised.[6] We find the record before us inadequate to sustain the conclusion that this obligation was met here—whatever the timing of the initial agreement in principle on the settlement. As has been said in an article much relied upon by appellee Markowitz, "As a practical matter, derivative settlements concluded over the head of the complaining stockholders are extremely rare and should be so." Haudek, The Settlement and Dismissal of Stockholders' Actions—Part II: The Settlement, 23 Sw.L.J. 765, 771 (1969).

There can be no blinking at the fact that the interests of the plaintiff in a stockholder's derivative suit and of his attorney are by no means congruent. While, in a general sense, both are interested in maximizing the recovery this is only a half-truth. Even apart from special considerations which, as has been noted, may cause special

---

5. See 3B Moore, Federal Practice ¶ 23.1.24[2], at 23.1–407 (1969); 2 Barron & Holtzoff, Federal Practice and Procedure § 570, at 335. (Wright ed. 1961). Denicke v. Anglo California Nat'l Bank, 141 F.2d 285 (9 Cir.), cert. denied, 323 U.S. 739, 65 S.Ct. 44, 89 L.Ed. 592 (1944), the case usually cited for this proposition, supports it only to a limited extent. There the corporation, the real party in interest, had come under new management, which made a settlement with the defendants and secured court approval of it over the objection of the stockholder plaintiff. Settlement of a derivative action by the real party in interest over the plaintiff's objection is quite different from settlement by the plaintiff's own attorney over the plaintiff's objection. Moreover, it appears that in *Denicke* the corporation attempted to keep the stockholder plaintiff informed of the settlement negotiations. 141 F.2d at 286. Although in this case the Wilmington Trust Company could arguably be cast in the role of the settling real party in interest, we are not inclined to do that here since the statements made at the

hearing and the affidavit submitted by its attorney in support of the settlement do not convey the impression that it either actively participated in the negotiations or reviewed the settlement in depth.

6. In this connection we find it rather significant that although the stipulation of settlement was signed on September 24, 1970, Mr. Markowitz did not formally advise his client of the settlement until November 4, after Judge Ryan had signed the order directing a hearing and approving the form of notice. It was thus largely his own fault that, as claimed in his affidavit of December 17, 1970, "[he] had no knowledge of Mr. Saylor's objection to the settlement until the Hearing before the Court." What is more important, prompt advice of the signature of the stipulation to Mr. Saylor would have allowed the latter to communicate his opposition to Mr. Markowitz and the Court before the notice of the hearing was approved; if he had done so, the notice should have stated this and a greater amount of opposition might have developed.

divergence of interest in cases where extremely large amounts are at stake, see Haudek, supra, 23 Sw.L.J. at 768 & n. 166, there is a difference in every case. The plaintiff's financial interest is in his share of the total recovery less what may be awarded to counsel, *simpliciter;* counsel's financial interest is in the amount of the award to him less the time and effort needed to produce it. A relatively small settlement may well produce an allowance bearing a higher ratio to the cost of the work than a much larger recovery obtained only after extensive discovery, a long trial and an appeal. The risks in proceeding to trial vary even more essentially. For the plaintiff, a defendant's judgment may mean simply the defeat of an expectation, often of relatively small amount; for his lawyer it can mean the loss of years of costly effort by himself and his staff. In this respect a derivative action is in a quite different posture from a personal injury action conducted on a contingent basis. We say this not in criticism but in simple recognition of the facts of class action life. While recognition of this conflict of interest should not mandate rejection of a settlement opposed by the plaintiff but represented by the attorney to be in the best interest of all stockholders, it does require the court to exercise particular care to see to it that the nonassenting plaintiff has had a full opportunity to develop the basis for his objection.

In many suits which have been prepared almost to the point of trial, the pretrial discovery, conducted when the objectives of plaintiff's attorney was still to develop the strongest possible basis for a recovery, may be entirely adequate to that end. But that is not the case here. Two of the defendants, La Luz and Falconbridge, had not even been served. The only depositions taken were those of defendants Zeckhausen and McWilliams and of H. S. McGowan, president of La Luz. Naturally these gentlemen were not disposed to assist plaintiff in sustaining his theories of recovery; helpful testimony from them could be obtained only by confronting them with documents they would find difficult to explain. Yet there had been little discovery of documentary evidence save of such generally self-serving instruments as minutes and annual reports, although even these proved valuable to plaintiff as we shall see; there had been no attempt to find the kind of inculpatory correspondence that so often reposes in corporate files even for the long time here involved, and refutes, or at least casts doubt upon, exculpatory testimony by the defendants of the sort here given.[8]

Despite all this, we ought not to take up the time of the district court and the parties with a remand if, on the basis of undisputed facts, a substantial recovery here was hopeless or nearly so. We do not think, however, this can fairly be said on the record before us. We shall limit our discussion to what we consider plaintiff's most promising theory—that the defendants, or at least some of them, in obtaining the SEC exemptions from § 17(a) of the Investment Company Act of 1940 which were required for the sale of the stock of Tonopah Nicaragua to

---

8. The annals of antitrust litigation and, indeed, of stockholder's derivative ac- tions include many such instances, includ- ing the "destroy all copies" sort.

Mines Incorporated, had concealed that the true beneficiary of the transfers was always intended to be La Luz,[9] which was in a peculiarly advantageous position to develop the mine economically, and thus the consideration was unfairly low.

In order to understand the problem, some knowledge of the intricate intercorporate relations is needed. * * *

* * * If in its applications [to the SEC] Tonopah made "any untrue statement of a material fact" or omitted "to state therein any fact necessary in order to prevent the statements made therein, in the light of the circumstances under which they were made, from being materially misleading," this would be "unlawful" under § 34(b) of the Investment Company Act and would provide a basis for imposing civil liability on those who were responsible for the statements or omissions or who profited therefrom with knowledge of the falsity. See Brown v. Bullock, 194 F.Supp. 207, 231 (S.D.N.Y.), aff'd, 294 F.2d 415 (2 Cir. 1961) (en banc); J. I. Case Co. v. Borak, 377 U.S. 426, 84 S.Ct. 1555, 12 L.Ed.2d 423 (1964); Mills v. Electric Auto-Lite Co., 396 U.S. 375, 90 S.Ct. 616, 24 L.Ed.2d 593 (1970).

We do not mean any of this to be taken either as indicating that plaintiff in fact has a winning case on the theory here discussed or that others of his theories may not have promise, at least as against some of the defendants. We have felt compelled to go this far into the merits only to show that the settlement should not have been approved over his opposition when there is such doubt whether there had been truly adversary discovery prior to the stipulation of settlement and he was afforded no opportunity for any thereafter.

We recognize that since "[t]he very purpose of a compromise is to avoid the trial of sharply disputed issues and to dispense with wasteful litigation," the court must not turn the settlement hearing "into a trial or a rehearsal of the trial"; and that the court "is concerned with the likelihood of success or failure and ought, therefore, to avoid any actual determination of the merits." See Haudek, supra, 23 Sw.L.J. at 795 (footnotes omitted). Still, in passing on the settlement of a derivative suit, as on a compromise in a proceeding under Ch. X of the Bankruptcy Act, the judge must have "apprised himself of all facts necessary for an intelligent and objective opinion of the probabilities of ultimate success should the claim be litigated." Protective Committee for Independent Stockholders of TMT Trailer Ferry, Inc. v. Anderson, 390 U.S. 414, 424–425, 88 S.Ct. 1157, 1163, 20 L.Ed.2d 1 (1968). We cannot say that, particularly in light of the reasoned objections of the plaintiff, as well as of other stockholders, the court did that here. No one would think of applying to the presentation of plaintiff's former attorney at the hearing in this case the characterization of "thoroughness, thoughtfulness and disinterested judgment," which Judge Wyzanski used in approving the settlement in Cherner v. Transitron Electronic Corp., 221

---

9. La Luz, like Mines Incorporated, was an "affiliated person" of Tonopah within § 2(a)(3) of the Investment Company Act, see infra.

F.Supp. 48, 51 (D.Mass.1963).[11] The plaintiff, through his new counsel, and the other objectors should be allowed to delve somewhat more deeply into the merits of this action; whether this should be done by further discovery, or by taking evidence in open court, or by both, is for the district court to determine in the exercise of sound discretion. While a remand may well result in renewed approval of the settlement, this should come only after thorough consideration of what the parties will present although "less than a trial." See Isaacs v. Forer, 39 Del. Ch. 105, 159 A.2d 295, 296 (1960).

The order is reversed and the cause remanded for further consistent proceedings.

FURTHER NOTE ON CLASS SUITS

See also Dunn v. H.K. Porter Co., 602 F.2d 1105 (3d Cir. 1979), holding that the court has inherent authority to review the reasonableness of the fee for the class attorney, notwithstanding a written fee agreement with representatives of the class. An attorney fee from a class suit judgment fund is chargeable against the unclaimed portion of the fund as well as that claimed by class members. See Boeing Co. v. Van Gemert, 444 U.S. 472, 100 S.Ct. 745, 62 L.Ed. 2d 676 (1980).

For a discussion of the issues arising in class action settlements, including the problem addressed in Saylor v. Lindsley, see Note, Abuse in Plaintiff Class Action Settlements: The Need for a Guardian During Pretrial Settlement Negotiations, 84 Mich.L.Rev. 308 (1985). On the incentives behind the rise of "professional plaintiff's attorneys," see Coffee, Understanding the Plaintiff's Attorney: The Implications of Economic Theory for Private Enforcement of Law Through Class and Derivative Actions, 86 Colum.L.Rev. 669 (1986). See also Garth, Nagel, and Plager, The Institution of the Private Attorney General: Perspectives From an Empirical Study of Class Action Litigation, 61 So.Calif.L. Rev. 353 (1988) (distinguishing between the "mercenary law enforcer" and the "social advocate").

Whether class suits are a "good thing" can be answered categorically only if the question is grossly oversimplified. More light and less heat has emerged from careful studies of the class suit in operation. See Kennedy, Securities Class and Derivative Actions in the United States District Court for the Northern District of Texas: An Empirical Study, 14 Hous.L.Rev. 769 (1977); DuVal, The Class Action as an Antitrust Enforcement Device: The Chicago

---

11. We are not overly impressed with the observation, [1970–71 Transfer Binder] CCH Fed.Sec.L.Rep. ¶ 92,922, at 90,415, that plaintiff would face serious difficulties of proof because the only living members of the Tonopah board involved in the transaction at suit are defendants McWilliams and Lindsley; that the latter is old, ill and almost deaf; and that because of Tonopah's dissolution in 1965 many of its documents cannot be located. Our recital shows that plaintiff was not far from making a *prima facie* case solely on the basis of the few documents that were discovered; if the distance should be narrowed, for example, by further discovery of documents or by testimony of mining engineers that the process ultimately adopted was known all along, and that, particularly with the power resources of La Luz available, the Rosita mine had much better possibilities than were represented to the SEC, the handicaps arising from unavailability of Tonopah's directors would weigh more heavily on the defendants than on the plaintiff. Furthermore, whatever the state of Tonopah's files, there is no indication that those of Frobisher, Mines, La Luz, and the now merged Falconbridge and Ventures are not available.

Experience, 1976 A.B.F.Res.J. 1021, 1273, where the author concludes, id. at 1327:

> "Judged by results, the class action has proved a rather feeble engine of antitrust enforcement. No litigated judgment has been entered in favor of a class. Of 27 terminated cases defendants won a total victory in 9. Ten other cases resulted in settlements with the named plaintiffs, in a majority of cases for a relatively small amount. In only 8 of the terminated cases * * * was any relief entered in favor of the class, and in only 3 of these cases were the settlements sizable."

Part VI

THE PRETRIAL STAGE

A. FORMULATION OF THE ISSUES

LASKY, MEMORANDUM FOR THE COMMITTEE ON RULE 8

13 F.R.D. 275 (1952).*

There is nothing wrong with Rule 8(a) as it was written in 1938. What is wrong is the construction and gloss courts have chosen to place upon it.

Rule 8(a) does not state that a complaint need only set forth a "claim for relief"; i.e., it does not say that it is sufficient merely to assert a claim. What it says is that a "pleading which sets forth a claim for relief . . . shall contain . . . a short and plain statement of the claim *showing that the pleader is entitled to relief.*"

C.C.P. § 426 (typical of code pleading) requires a "statement of the facts constituting the cause of action, in ordinary and concise language." C.C.P., Sec. 22 defines an "action" as a proceeding by which one "prosecutes another for the declaration, enforcement, or protection of a right . . . or prevention of a wrong." A *cause* of action consists of the grounds on which one is *entitled* to the declaration, enforcement or protection of a right or prevention of a wrong. In short, it consists of the grounds on which one is entitled to "relief."

There is thus no real difference between Rule 8 and C.C.P. § 426 and no sound justification for construing Rule 8 as creating "notice pleading." Rule 8 and C.C.P. § 426 both require more than a mere assertion, or notice of assertion, of a claim. Both require the assertion, plus *enough* to establish the right to the relief, if proved.

Enough of what? Obviously, enough of whatever it is that the law deals with in deciding cases. Those who support what has happened to Rule 8 shy away from terms such as "fact" in pleadings. But any legal problem consists of law and fact. Presumably the courts know the law. But they have to be told the facts. The complaint should tell them and the adversary enough facts.

Opponents of a change in Rule 8 as presently construed stress the difficulty of distinguishing between "ultimate fact" and "evidentiary facts" and between "ultimate fact" and "conclusions of law." They assume that by adopting a new name, "claim for relief," in place of the old, "cause of action," these difficulties vanish. It may be granted that the difficulties sometimes exist. But they are

---

* In recent years, the focus of controversy about the function of pleading has been F.R.C.P. 8. Rule 8 has generally been interpreted to permit vague statements of position in pleadings. It thus contemplates that the tasks previously performed by pleadings will be postponed until some post-pleading stage of the litigation and will be performed by some procedural device, written or oral, other than the pleadings. Whether such postponement is desirable has been questioned, e.g., in Mr. Lasky's paper, presented to the Judicial Conference of the Judges of the Ninth Circuit, 1952, see Claim or Cause of Action, 13 F.R.D. 253 (1952).

inherent in the materials with which the law must deal. Supplanting "cause of action" by "claim [for] relief" and then construing "claim for relief" as no more than a notice of disaffection on the part of the plaintiff do not spirit the difficulties away. They merely defer the difficulties to a later point in the litigation.

Supplanting the term "cause of action" by "claim for relief" merely indulged a professorial foible and a common fallacy that changing labels achieves reform. The "new" pleader points to the many decisions that grappled with the concept of a cause of action as a reason for abandoning the term. And so we now have many cases dealing with "claim for relief." Nor have we thereby escaped the basic question which arises in many contexts, such as in the application of res judicata, statute of limitations, and the like.

But, while there was no reason for the change of terms, similarly there would be no particular magic in changing back. What is needed is to end the improper application of Rule 8. Since the books are now full of decisions reading out of that rule what is there, something may well be added to assure that it is read correctly. Perhaps the following addition would do:

"A statement of a claim shall not be deemed sufficient to show that the pleader is entitled to relief unless its allegations of fact, if established, would support a judgment in favor of the pleader. Mere assertion of a claim or of bare legal conclusion shall not be sufficient."

However, correction of Rule 8 is only the starting point, for what the courts have done to that rule is only an aspect of a wider concern. Courts have fallen into a tendency of deferring the accent in litigation to the last possible syllable. The cure is to move the accent back to the earliest, just as an Englishman tends to pronounce his words.

Every controversy starts as an undigested, unorganized and diffused mass of facts. The human mind is not capable of reaching judgments on such a mass. It must first reduce the bulk. To do so it must first determine what principles are relevant, organize the facts into categories, and discard those that are irrelevant. We often hear the plea that a piece of evidence should be received "to complete the picture," and judges often let the evidence in for that purpose. But the job of judge and lawyer is the reverse of completing pictures. A photograph is full of detail. But before a controversy can be resolved, details must be washed out and the photograph reduced to a line drawing, a schematic outline.

From the moment a client drags a case into the office, the lawyer must start the task of refining, defining and eliminating. Until he does so, he can know neither what is pertinent nor how to present his case. From the moment the case comes into court, the judge must start on the same job. Until he does so, he cannot decide the case, except by way of an emotional response to some stray fact that may bubble to the surface or attract his eye by its glitter.

The sooner the job of refining, defining and eliminating begins, the better. There are those who belittle "issue pleading." But one cannot decide a case unless he knows what he has to decide. It is not enough to know that he has to decide whether or not the plaintiff gets what he wants. The undigested mass must be broken down into specific questions that can be tested against specific facts and matched against specific legal principles. When this is done, the case has been reduced to issues. This job cannot be avoided. It can only be deferred. In the end the deferment merely gives us new names for old jobs.

For example, those who insist on "notice pleading" and the use of the pre-trial conference to "simplify," i.e., to discover the issues—particularly those who formalize the pre-trial procedure and the pre-trial order—have discovered nothing new and are repeating an old experience. At early common law, a suit started with the issuance of one of a number of formal writs, which were in effect notices of disaffection stating in a vague way the general area of the law in which the grievance was set. Then the parties came before judge or clerk and engaged in a dialogue to determine what the contorversy was about and what issue the court was to decide. The results of the dialogue were reduced to writing by the clerk. Call it what you will, this was a pre-trial order. Later, the waste of time involved in this process was obviated by requiring the parties to reduce their dialogue to a series of pleadings, done at greater leisure in the lawyer's office. This development went to seed in later common law pleading and in equity practice. But I make so bold as to say that code pleading as practiced in the metropolitan areas of California has been a better system than federal practice under the Clark version of Rule 8.

The conversion of Rule 8 to notice pleading is part of a broader tendency of deferring the inevitable necessity of thinking through a case. The pleadings are reduced to nothing. If the opponent's pleading is bare and sparse, like an OPA or OPS complaint—replete with recitals of what the statute says but empty of fact—one is told that he may not have a more definite statement. If the complaint is loaded with innuendoes and historical irrelevances like an anti-trust complaint, one is denied a motion to strike. In each instance the necessary job of coming to grips with the issues is deferred, with the consoling assurance to counsel that the issues can be found and framed by discovery procedures and the pre-trial conference.

Consider these two. Discovery practice does not define issues. It simply throws into the hopper the whole undigested mass of facts. Anything goes. Attorneys must inquire into everything and prepare for everything, because no court will tell them where to stop or permit them to stop an adversary. The waste of time and money is immense. Discovery is simply not an instrument to find issues. It is a process for finding facts or proving one's case. And it ought not to be required until some preliminary definition of issues has occurred.

Consider next the pre-trial conference. If the issues are simple, a simple pre-trial order can be prepared. But the job could be equally done by proper pleading. If the issues are complicated, as much effort is involved in framing a pre-trial order as would be involved in framing pleadings. And, to boot, the judge is under foot, instead of sitting back and cutting Gordian knots when counsel find themselves at loggerheads.

By having the court rule at a pre-trial conference on whether an issue is relevant, instead of doing the same thing on a demurrer or a motion to strike, names are changed, and the task has been deferred.

As likely as not, the essential job of defining the issues and cutting out the irrelevant is once again deferred at the pre-trial conference, with the excuse that the court can better tell the significance of things after the whole picture has been completed at a trial. The attorney who sought the pre-trial conference goes away frustrated.

Having failed to induce the court to come to grips with the case on the pleadings, counsel may try again, by a motion for summary judgment, hoping in this way to strike at the jugular vein before time and money are squandered. As Judge Chase remarked in Arnstein v. Porter, 2 Cir., 154 F.2d 464, 479, there must be some procedure to avoid useless trials, and if courts will not use pleadings for the purpose, they ought to use the summary judgment procedure. But once again courts defer the inevitable. Instead of exercising their powers of acumen to pierce to the core of the case, they frequently exercise powers of imagination to turn up lurking issues of fact.

And so the parties come to the trial. But objections to evidence will not be sustained. Everything goes in, either to "complete the picture" or "subject to a motion to strike." If a motion to strike is made, counsel are told, as likely as not, that it will be ruled on when the case is decided.

The parties come down the home stretch, still entangled in an undigested mass of fact. Everything has to be discussed in the closing briefs and argument. At the very end the court must do what it should have been doing steadily throughout the litigation. No one would think of trying to refine gold from the base rock without having first subjected it to the several steps of crushing, concentrating and smelting. The refinery would break down if the ore were dumped into it directly. Yet courts reach final judgments in much this way.

Nor is that all. If an attempt is made by counsel, whether victor or vanquished, to define and refine the case by adequate findings, so that he may have a clear issue for the appeal, he is likely to be eluded entirely. The court writes an opinion, intermingling fact, law and argument as opinions ought to do. And then it adopts its opinion as its findings, often more to the satisfaction of appellant than appellee.

And thus the case goes up on appeal. The record is huge, for nothing has been winnowed out. Everything has to be briefed—albeit in 80 pages—because nothing has been defined. And when the Court of Appeals writes its opinion, it may find its own facts. And no one recognizes the case as the same one tried below.

The starting point is Rule 8. Good lawyers can adapt themselves to any kind of procedure. If loose and easy pleading is tolerated—indeed, required— good lawyers will take advantage of it. Why not? But they would prefer to present a clean case.

Rule 8 as now construed makes litigation expensive, ponderous and amorphous. The alternative is not over-refined and technical pleading. It is the intelligent effort to use all the machinery available, to the end of defining and confining the case, beginning at the earliest possible moment and keeping at it at every stage. Stricter pleading, plus the motion for summary judgment, plus the pre-trial conference would make an excellent system.

Rule 8 should be amended. But this Committee or another should be continued to consider and report on the whole problem of judicial deferment of the task of coming to grips with cases.

B. DISCLOSURE OF THE EVIDENCE

1. MECHANICS OF DISCOVERY

INTRODUCTORY NOTE ON DISCOVERY

1. The Functions of Discovery

The nominal purpose and perhaps the principal justification for discovery procedure is to enable the parties to obtain a more informed picture of the facts of the case than they could by reliance on their own unaided initiative. The premise is that fuller disclosure, which ultimately entails enforced disclosure, will permit each party to present at trial the fullest and most favorable case that can be made on his behalf and will minimize the possibility that ignorance of relevant facts or the opponent's sudden presentation at trial of unanticipated evidence will obscure the true state of affairs out of which the controversy arose. It must not be overlooked, however, that comprehensive discovery devices also may serve other functions, some clearly proper, others not so.

The chief additional function that may safely be regarded as legitimate is the promotion of settlement. Settlement is typically reached when the parties' respective appraisals of the value of the case are identical or substantially so. That appraisal is the party's calculation of the maximum worth of the case in the event of victory, discounted by the likelihood of defeat, and of intermediate possibilities. The accuracy of estimates of maximum worth and the likelihood of defeat are obviously affected by the extent to which there is made available before trial the information on which decision will be made in the event of trial (i.e., the evidence) providing, of course, that the information is intelligently and realistically appraised. Hence, the discovery process is assumed to aid in some degree the settlement process, though to what degree may be debatable. Compare Glaser, Pretrial Discovery and the Adversary System 91–101, 200 (1968).

Another function of discovery is to make available prior to plenary trial data which reveal that the case may be disposed of, in whole or in part, without the necessity of plenary trial. That is, the material produced by discovery may serve as the foundation for a motion for summary judgment.

A further function of discovery may be the harassment of an opponent. To be sure, this is not accounted a legitimate function of discovery, but between the limits of the clearly acceptable scope of discovery and the clearly abusive there is a range in which the litigant may maneuver to the greater or lesser annoyance and expense of her opponent. And the existence of that range of maneuver is a fact of life under modern procedure. See, e.g., Eggleston v. Chicago Journeymen Plumbers Union, 657 F.2d 890 (7th Cir. 1981).

A final function of discovery may be to facilitate the "reconstruction" of a litigant's evidence in anticipation of the line of an opponent's proof at trial. Any such reconstruction by a litigant is, of course, improper; if done with the knowledge of counsel is a breach of ethics by the latter and, at the extreme, is subornation of perjury. But between the lines of perjury and refreshed memory is an area in which some litigants have made substantial travels, at times with the acquiescence of their attorneys. This, too, is a fact of life.

The question concerning the proper scope of discovery has been, and will continue to be, whether the advantages gained from comprehensive disclosure outweigh the risks of its abuse. To that question various answers have been given. Although discovery is much criticized for being abused, abuse seems not to be a serious problem in mine run litigation. See Brazil, Civil Discovery: Lawyers' Views of Its Effectiveness, Its Principal Problems and Abuses, 1980 Am.B.Found.Res.J. 787; Connolly, Holleman, and Kuhlman, Judicial Controls and the Civil Litigative Process: Discovery (Federal Judicial Center, 1978). See also Haydock and Herr, Discovery: Theory, Practice, and Problems (1983). Discovery problems in complex litigation are, however, formidable. See Complex Litigation, infra p. 1203.

2. Modern Discovery Practice

The federal discovery rules as promulgated in 1938 remained substantially unchanged until 1970, when extensive changes were made. See Advisory Committee Report, 48 F.R.D. 485 (1970). Minor changes have been made on several occasions since then. See, e.g., Friedenthal, A Divided Supreme Court Adopts Discovery Amendments to the Federal Rules of Civil Procedure, 69 Calif.L.Rev. 806 (1981). The federal discovery rules incorporate the five principal devices of modern discovery: depositions of parties and witnesses; interrogatories to other parties; production of documents and things; physical examinations; and demand for admissons. These Rules have given impetus to the adoption by many states of substantially identical or similar provisions, sometimes by rules, sometimes by statutes. Thus there is increasing correspondence between federal and state discovery practice. See generally 6 Wigmore on Evidence §§ 1856 et seq. (Chadbourn ed. 1976); James & Hazard c. 5. For an historical analysis and description of the limited range of discovery prior to the Federal Rules, see Ragland, Discovery Before Trial (1932).

We consider first the techniques of modern discovery in an ordinary lawsuit. Then we turn to some of the basic and apparently persistent problems of discovery. The references are to the Federal Rules, whose California analogues are approximately as follows:

F.R.C.P.	C.C.P.
26	2017, 2018, 2023, 2025(i), 2034
27	2035, 2036
28	2025(k), 2026(c)
29	2021
30	2025
31	2028
32	2025(u)
33	2030
34	2031
35	2032
36	2033
37	2017, 2023

LOUISELL, DISCOVERY TODAY *

Consideration of the possible uses of the various discovery devices in a hypothetical case enhances comprehension of modern discovery as a unified system of rules. Therefore, we shall consider the illustrative use of the devices in a representative diversity suit for personal injuries. This discussion should demonstrate

(1) the breadth, inclusiveness and thoroughness of the discovery procedures;

(2) the close integration of the various devices into a unitary mechanism; and

(3) the potential overlap between the various devices, sometimes inviting or necessitating choice among them.

The Facts. Let us assume that plaintiff, while driving alone on a country road at night, encounters a car speeding in the opposite direction. It suddenly swerves over the center line and collides with his car, knocking it into a ditch and rendering him unconscious. It then flees the scene. Plaintiff's attorney interviews Plaintiff, the good Samaritan who extricated Plaintiff from his demolished car and took him to a hospital, a not overly cooperative sheriff, and police officials, but other than the information already stated, he learns only the name of the registered owner of the offending car—its out-of-state license plate apparently having been dislodged by the collision and dropped near the scene. Let us assume that Plaintiff commences a diversity suit against the registered owner in an appropriate district court. How can modern federal discovery techniques be used to best advantage by Plaintiff?

Scope of Discovery. The whole range of discovery devices is governed by a very broad rule as to scope, i.e., "any matter, not privileged, which is relevant to the subject matter involved in the pending action." F.R.C.P. 26(b)(1). Relevance is largely a matter of logic and probability, and the concept can be pushed to the limits of plausibility. In any event, material is clearly relevant that would be used only for cross-examination. The paradigm of such material is movies of a claimant's physical movements taken surreptitiously. See Note, 33 Univ.Fla.L.Rev. 448 (1981); cf. Delvaux v. Ford Motor Co., 518 F.Supp. 1249 (E.D.Wis.1981) (movie made by plaintiff to show her limited daily routine). Discovery may be had of facts relevant to jurisdiction as well as those relevant to the merits. Insurance Corp. of Ireland, Ltd. v. Compagnie des Bauxites de Guinee, 456 U.S. 694, 102 S.Ct. 2099, 72 L.Ed.2d 492 (1982).

Interrogatories. Once the summons and complaint are served upon Owner, interrogatories may be served upon him. No court order is necessary to authorize the questions. Plaintiff serves written interrogatories on Owner under Rule 33, asking him for the name and address of the person driving his automobile on the night involved. Of course, instead of serving such interrogatories, Plaintiff might have elected to take Owner's deposition. But in the first 30 days after commencement of the action leave of court would be required (unless the special notice provisions of Rule 30 are utilized). And note the relative ease, convenience, and economy of merely serving the interrogatories; unlike a deposition, they involve no expense other than that entailed in the time for dictating the questions. They involve none of the details of the

---

* The original version appears in 45 Calif.L.Rev. 486 (1957).

deposition mechanism, such as arranging for the notary-stenographer and fixing the time and place for the deposition.

Owner's answers to the interrogatories, like testimony given at a deposition, must be under the sanction of an oath. And, if the answer to the interrogatory should prove unsatisfactory to Plaintiff, the fact that an interrogatory was first propounded is no barrier whatever to later taking Owner's deposition.

Oral Depositions. Let us suppose that Owner answers the written interrogatories by stating that on the occasion involved, John Driver, a resident of Nevada, was driving Owner's car. Plaintiff now has Driver's name and address. More than 30 days now having passed since the commencement of the action, Plaintiff promptly serves on Owner, without having to obtain prior court permission, notice of taking Driver's deposition at the office of Plaintiff's attorney at a specified date and hour a reasonable time in the future. To avoid the possibility that costs will be assessed against him if Driver should fail to appear at the examination, Plaintiff is careful to subpoena Driver to appear for the taking of the deposition.

In his notice, Plaintiff does not, because he need not, indicate whether the deposition is taken for discovery purposes, for use at the trial, or both. As noted earlier, Rule 26 permits a broad scope of discovery into "any matter, not privileged, which is relevant to the subject matter involved in the pending action." And Plaintiff's attorney of course realizes that by taking Driver's deposition Plaintiff has not made Driver his own witness for any purpose.

If during the course of the deposition Plaintiff becomes abusive of the witness, or insists upon answers to confidential matters, protective orders are available. The Rules are quite specific on the mechanical procedures governing the taking of the deposition.

After the deposition is completed, Plaintiff names Driver as an additional defendant.

Discovery of Inadmissible Testimony. Let us assume that by careful interrogation of Driver, Plaintiff among other facts has compelled the admission that on the night involved Driver's car had two other occupants, Rider and Passenger, both residents of the forum state. Plaintiff serves notice on Owner and Driver that Plaintiff at a specified date, hour and place will take Rider's deposition, and subpoenas Rider accordingly. At the taking of this deposition Rider testifies that prior to the collision Passenger told Rider that Driver had said that Driver intended to deliver some cartons of cigarettes to a country store on behalf of Driver's employer, a cigarette company. This testimony is proper discovery even though at trial it would be objectionable as hearsay. A chronic relevance question under the Federal Rules had been whether insurance coverage was discoverable. See Anno., 13 A.L.R.3d 822. The 1970 amendment in Rule 26(b)(2) expressly provides that it is.

Deposition by Written Questions. To make further discovery concerning the mentioned conversation between Rider and Passenger, Plaintiff decides to take Passenger's deposition. Normally, this deposition too would be taken orally, so that Plaintiff would have the advantage of on-the-spot examination of Passenger. However, for some reason of policy, tactics, or economy, Plaintiff takes this deposition on written questions purusuant to Rule 31. The written questions and cross questions from the opponents are served, and then submitted to the officer designated in the notice of the deposition. The designated officer places the deponent under oath, reads the questions to him, and records the answers given. The presiding officer then prepares a copy of the deposition, certifies it, and mails or files it with the court. Of course, this entire procedure is distinct from the submission of interrogatories. In a deposition upon written questions the deponent must answer fairly quickly, and he does not have time to peruse the questions before the examination.

Additional Depositions. Plaintiff now decides that he has discovered enough to justify naming the cigarette company as an additional defendant. (Let us assume that diversity jurisdiction would still exist.) After doing so Plaintiff serves notice on Owner, Driver and the company that he will take a second deposition of Driver. The number of depositions of any party or witness is not arbitrarily limited, and a second or even a third deposition may be taken, subject only to the right of an adverse party or the deponent to obtain a protective order against annoyance, embarrassment or oppression. At this deposition Plaintiff discovers from Driver that the company probably is in possession of a set of written regulations governing working conditions, use of noncompany vehicles, and the hours of employment of its employees.

Choosing the Proper Device. Plaintiff now considers it important to see the company's regulations. How should he proceed? There would seem to be three overlapping possibilities: (1) Submitting interrogatories to the company under Rule 33, asking whether it is in possession of such regulations and, if so, requesting it to attach a copy thereof to its answers; (2) taking the deposition of an appropriate company agent under Rule 30(b)(6) and in connection therewith serving him with a subpoena duces tecum requiring him to produce the regulations at the taking of his deposition; (3) submitting a request under Rule 34 for the production and inspection, including copying, of the regulations. Cf. Note, Limiting the Scope of Litigation: Bills of Particulars, Interrogatories, and Requests for Admission in Illinois and Federal Courts, 1979 U.Ill.L.F. 211.

Requests for Inspection. Let us suppose that Plaintiff elects to request production and inspection of the company regulations, and thereby views and copies those of interest to him. Thereafter, Plaintiff serves notice on all defendants that he will take the deposition of an appropriate company agent, and at this deposition testimony is adduced that correspondence has passed between company officials pertaining to the company regulations already inspected by Plaintiff. Plaintiff thereupon requests inspection of this correspondence under Rule 34. The company, raising no question of privilege, nevertheless opposes the motion. It files a written objection within 30 days stating as its ground that such correspondence cannot possibly constitute admissible evidence. It is clear under modern discovery principles that this objection is improper. Inadmissibility is not grounds for objection to discovery if the information sought appears reasonably calculated to lead to the discovery of admissible evidence. Plaintiff therefore moves for and obtains an order under Rule 37(a) compelling production. To avoid the sanctions of the latter Rule, the company permits inspection of the correspondence. The company may be required to pay Plaintiff the costs incurred in obtaining the court order, however, unless the court finds that its opposition to the motion was substantially justified or that an award of expenses would be unjust.

Subpoena Duces Tecum. Suppose Plaintiff, rather than requesting inspection of the company's correspondence under Rule 34, seeks discovery thereof by taking the deposition of a company agent and in connection therewith serves a subpoena duces tecum. The permissible scope of discovery under such a procedure has been the subject of considerable confusion and remains complicated in some jurisdictions. See 9 Wright & Miller § 2452.

Requests for Admissions. Let us assume that by one technique or another Plaintiff examines the company correspondence. He now feels that he is in a position to make requests for admission on the company. He therefore serves pursuant to Rule 36 requests that the company admit (1) the genuineness of one of the letters purportedly written by a company executive, which Plaintiff discovered as part of the mentioned correspondence, and (2) the truth of the fact that on the occasion involved, Driver was making a delivery for the company. Rule 36 contains closely knit provisions calculated to compel admission as to all things that cannot reasonably be controverted. Thus if the company takes no action on the request, the matters are deemed admitted. The initiative is on the party served to deny, or state why he cannot truthfully admit or deny, or object if the requests for admission are improper. The requested material in question here is clearly within the broad scope of Rule 36, which permits requests as to "the truth of any matters within the scope of Rule 26(b)."

Physical Examination. While we have been considering discovery by Plaintiff, it is obvious that the shoe might well have been on the other foot; defendants might have been doing many of the same things in an attempt to establish, for instance, Plaintiff's contributory negligence. As the Supreme Court said in Hickman v. Taylor, 329 U.S. 495, 507 (1947):

> "[F]raming the problem in terms of assisting individual plaintiffs in their suits against corporate defendants is unsatisfactory. * * * Discovery, in other words, is not a one-way proposition. It is available in all types of cases at the behest of any party, individual or corporate, plaintiff or defendant. The problem thus far transcends the situation confronting this petitioner. And we must view that problem in the light of the limitless situations where the particular kind of discovery * * * might be used."

One discovery device especially significant for the defendant is provided by Rule 35, governing physical and mental examinations (including blood tests). If defendant makes such an examination, Rule 35(b) requires that a report thereof be given to plaintiff, and it has been held that the party taking the examination has a duty to have the examining physician prepare such a report. Salvatore v. American Cyanamid Co., 94 F.R.D. 156 (D.R.I.1982). However, it should not be overlooked that Plaintiff may also have Driver examined if he is able to make the required showing of "good cause" for the examination and provided the condition to be examined is "in controversy." See Schlagenhauf v. Holder, 379 U.S. 104, 85 S.Ct. 234, 13 L.Ed.2d 152 (1964).

Supplementation of Responses. F.R.C.P. 26(e) prescribes a limited duty to supplement discovery responses on the basis of subsequently acquired information. See Slomanson, Supplementation of Discovery Responses in Federal Civil Procedure, 17 San Diego L.Rev. 233 (1980).

The Sanctions of Discovery. The sanctions available to the court under F.R.C.P. 37 range the gamut from drawing an unfavorable conclusion against a disobedient party in the matters which his disobedience involves, to rendering judgment by default against him or even issuing an order treating as contempt of court the failure to obey a discovery order, except an order to submit to a F.R.C.P. 35 examination.

FURTHER NOTE ON THE MECHANICS OF DISCOVERY

1. The California Civil Discovery Act of 1986

In 1986, the California legislature enacted a comprehensive revision of the Code of Civil Procedure's discovery provisions, the first major overhaul since 1957. The Civil Discovery Act of 1986, codified at C.C.P. 2016 et seq., reorganized and clarified prior law, codified a number of judicial decisions on discovery procedure, and generally conformed California procedure more closely with the Federal Rules of Civil Procedure. There are still important differences, however, the principal ones of which are discussed below. See generally State Bar–Judicial Council Joint Commission on Discovery, Proposed California Civil Discovery Act of 1986 (Proposed Act and Reporter's Notes, January 1986); Selected 1986 California Legislation (Civil Procedure), 18 Pacific L.J. 500 (1987). The legislature followed up the next year with further revisions of more modest scope. See Selected 1987 California Legislation (Civil Procedure), 19 Pacific L.J. 514 (1988).

2. Depositions

a. Place of Deposition. Under federal practice, a deposition may be taken on notice anywhere within the United States, F.R.C.P. 28(a). But the reach of the federal subpoena for compulsory attendance of deponents is strictly limited. See F.R.C.P. 45(d)(2). And although state lines do not provide arbitrary barriers in federal deposition practice, notices of depositions requiring travel distances that are unreasonable under the circumstances are subject to protective orders under F.R.C.P. 26(c). See 4 Moore ¶ 26.70.

Depositions taken under state discovery practice normally are taken within the state for use in actions pending in that state. By party agreement a deposition can be taken out of state, and such agreements are routine. However, in the absence of agreement, detailed limitations on the place for deposition, both within and without the state, may govern. Consider, e.g., the provisions of C.C.P. 2025(e)(1): "The deposition of a natural person, whether or not a party to the action, shall be taken at a place that is, at the option of the party giving notice of the deposition, either within 75 miles of the deponent's residence, or within the county where the action is pending and within 150 miles of the deponent's residence, unless the court orders otherwise * * *." See also C.C.P. 2025(e)(2) (similar restrictions on deposing businesses and other organizations); C.C.P. 2025(e)(3) (permitting the court, on motion, to compel deposition of a natural person at a place more distant than otherwise provided); C.C.P. 2034(i)(1) (restrictions on place of deposition of an expert). State statutes generally provide for a local deposition under a commission issued by another state or foreign jurisdiction, e.g., C.C.P. 2029, and for taking a deposition out of the state in connection with an action pending in the state, e.g., C.C.P. 2026, 2027.

b. Limits on the Number of Depositions. Under federal practice, there is no fixed limit on the number of times a party or other person may be deposed, although a deponent can ask the court for a protective order under F.R.C.P. 26(c). In practice, good cause normally must be shown to subject a person to a subsequent deposition. Some states have specific restrictions to this effect. C.C.P. 2025(t), enacted as part of the 1986 revisions to California's discovery laws, provides that once a party has taken the deposition of any person, neither the deposing party nor any other party who received notice of the deposition may take a subsequent deposition of that person unless good cause is shown.

c. Videotaping Depositions. The basic recording procedure for an oral deposition is a stenographic record taken by a court reporter that is then transcribed into a written text. The rules now generally acknowledge the use of audio or video taping, but in most jurisdictions such an alternative may be used only by stipulation of the parties or court order, e.g., F.R.C.P. 30(b)(4). Some jurisdictions also provide for audio or video taping at a party's option so long as it is specified in the deposition notice, e.g., C.C.P. 2025(*l*). As a practical matter a written transcript will usually be necessary if the deposition is to be used for cross-examination. A videotape can be very effective when the deposition has to be used in lieu of live testimony by the witness. See F.R.C.P. 32(a)(3). C.C.P. 2025(u) provides that a videotaped deposition of any expert may be used at trial even if the expert is available to testify in person, so long as the deposition notice states the intention to use the deposition at trial. Under C.C.P. 2025(*l*), the operator of the recording equipment must be authorized to administer an oath if the videotape is to be used at trial.

d. Depositions of Nonparties and Organizations. Discovery from nonparties is normally accomplished by means of a deposition subpoena, which may be used to compel the taking of an oral or a written deposition, and for a deposition for production of records. See F.R.C.P. 45(d); C.C.P. 2020. In practice, nonparty depositions are usually arranged by stipulation. A subpoena for the deposition of a corporation, partnership, or other organization, whether or not a party, typically must describe with "reasonable particularity" the matters upon which examination is sought, and the organization must designate and produce those officers, directors, or other agents or employees who are most qualified to testify on the matters. See F.R.C.P. 30(b)(6); C.C.P. 2025(d).

3. Interrogatories

a. Limits on the Number of Interrogatories. As with depositions, the Federal Rules place no limits on the number of interrogatories that a party may be required to answer, although many district courts have local rules limiting their number. See, e.g., *Local 472 v. Georgia Power Co.,* 684 F.2d 721 (11th Cir.1982). Many states have enacted such limits either by rule or statute. Under C.C.P. 2030(c), no party may propound more than 35 specially prepared interrogatories (as opposed to official form interrogatories, on which there are no limits) except by stipulation or court order. A greater number is permitted if warranted by "(A) The complexity or the quantity of the existing and potential issues in the particular case; (B) The financial burden on a party entailed in conducting the discovery by oral deposition; [or] (C) The expedience of using this method of discovery to provide to the responding party the opportunity to conduct an inquiry, investigation, or search of files or records to supply the information sought." A party taking advantage of these provisos must attach to its interrogatories a Declaration for Additional Discovery and has the burden of justifying its need for the additional interrogatories if challenged by the opposing party. C.C.P. 2030(c)(2), (3).

b. Supplementation of Responses. Responses to interrogatories, like responses to deposition questions, are based on the knowledge then available to the responding person. Under California law, the party receiving interrogatories has no duty to voluntarily supplement its answers by later acquired information, but the propounding party may serve a limited number of supplemental interrogatories designed to elicit such information. C.C.P. 2030(c)(8).

Compare F.R.C.P. 26(e), which imposes a duty of supplementation on the answering party.

4. Requests for Admission

a. Responses to Requests for Admission. Failure to serve a timely response to a request for admission may result in the request being deemed admitted, a consequence that can severely damage a litigant's case. See F.R. C.P. 36(a); C.C.P. 2033(k). Further, if an answer is given that fails to admit the genuineness of a document or the truth of a matter, and the requesting party later proves that the answer was incorrect, the court may impose sanctions on the responding party. F.R.C.P. 37(c); C.C.P. 2033(*o*). An answer to a request for admission is conclusive only against the responding party and only in the pending action, i.e., it may not be used against the party in any other proceeding. F.R.C.P. 36(b); C.C.P. 2033(n). A party may not refuse to answer a request for admission on the ground that the request calls for the application of law to fact. F.R.C.P. 36(a); C.C.P. 2033(a).

b. Limits on the Number of Requests for Admission. F.R.C.P. 36 places no limit on the number of requests a party may serve. Compare C.C.P. 2033(c), which provides that no party may request that any other party admit to more than 35 matters except by stipulation or court order, but provides further that there is no limit on the number of requests for admission of the genuineness of documents and that the limit of 35 requests may be exceeded if the requesting party attaches a Declaration for Additional Discovery.

5. Physical and Mental Examinations

In recognition of the privacy considerations involved, physical and mental examinations typically may be had only on court order "for good cause shown" absent agreement among the parties, and only where the mental or physical condition of a party is in controversy. F.R.C.P. 35; C.C.P. 2032(d). C.C.P. 2032(b)(2) allows a defendant in a personal injury action to demand one physical examination without court order provided that the proposed examination does not include any procedure which is "painful, protracted, or intrusive." Under C.C.P. 2032(d), a mental examination of a personal injury plaintiff is not permitted if plaintiff stipulates that no claim is being made for emotional distress beyond that usually associated with the claimed physical injuries and that no psychiatric testimony will be presented at trial in support of the claim for damages for such emotional distress.

The party examined has a right to a copy of the examination report. F.R. C.P. 35(b)(1); C.C.P. 2032(h). A party who exercises this right, or who deposes the examiner, thereby waives all privileges regarding any other examinations made of the party, e.g., examinations by the party's own physician. F.R.C.P. 35(b)(2); C.C.P. 2032(i). On the privileges that normally apply, see, e.g., F.R. C.P. 26(b)(4), construed in Ager v. Jane C. Stormont Hospital, infra p. 929.

On the difficult privacy issues raised by mental examinations, see Vinson v. Superior Court, infra p. 943.

6. Discovery from Sources Abroad

Obtaining discovery from foreign parties subject to United States jurisdiction poses special problems. The Hague Convention on the Taking of Evidence Abroad contains elaborate procedural provisions and specifications of the permitted scope of discovery. See Restatement Third of the Foreign Relations Law of the United States §§ 442, 473. Although the terms of the Hague Convention appear to preempt national law that is inconsistent, the Supreme Court has held that it is not preempted. However, the Court refused to delineate between use of the Federal Rules and use of the Hague Convention. The Court has left the line to be drawn by the trial court "based on its knowledge of the case and of the claims and interests of the parties and the governments whose statutes and policies they invoke." Societe Nationale Industrielle Aerospatiale v. United States District Court, 482 U.S. 522, 107 S.Ct. 2542, 96 L.Ed.2d 461 (1987). See Note, The Role of the Hague Convention for Gathering Evidence Abroad, 24 Stan.J.Int'l L. 309 (1987).

Particularly vexing is the issue of obtaining discovery of documents located in a foreign country. Many countries have enacted laws barring the production of documents in their jurisdiction for any proceeding in another country. Under these laws, the enforcement of a court order compelling discovery may open the producing party to criminal liability in the country where the documents are housed. These statutes are aimed directly at American discovery, which is regarded as extraterritorial and invasive. See Restatement Third of the Foreign Relations Law of the United States, supra. However, permitting the foreign source to withhold the documents may cause substantial harm to the requesting party. See Note, Strict Enforcement of Extraterritorial Discovery, 38 Stan.L.Rev. 841 (1986). The Supreme Court's nondecision in the *Aerospatiale* case has resulted in widely divergent lower court decisions. See, e.g., Hudson v. Hermann Pfauter GmbH & Co., 117 F.R.D. 33 (N.D.N.Y.1987) (applying the Hague Convention); Benton Graphics v. Uddeholm Corp., 118 F.R.D. 386 (D.N.J.1987) (applying presumption in favor of the Federal Rules).

7. Limiting Discovery

Apart from specific discovery limitations provided in statutes and rules, courts have discretion to limit discovery. F.R.C.P. 26(b)(1) and 26(c) give the trial court broad discretion, including the power to order that "the discovery not be had." Cf. C.C.P. 2017(c). However, the power to limit has its own limits. Thus, it has been held that oral deposition is so superior a method of inquiring of a witness, as compared with interrogatories, that it is ordinarily an abuse of discretion to limit the discovering party to interrogatories. See Meritplan Ins. Co. v. Superior Court, 124 Cal.App.3d 237, 177 Cal.Rptr. 236 (1981). See also the discussion of provisions and proposals for curtailing discovery as a means of controlling abuse, infra p. 967.

8. Expanding Discovery

Courts have interpolated *limitations* on discovery that are not expressly provided for, e.g., the "work product" rule recognized in Hickman v. Taylor, infra p. 913. What about expansions? While California law now authorizes the court to order that a deposition be videotaped, for example, that provision was not in effect when Bailey v. Superior Court, 19 Cal.3d 970, 140 Cal.Rptr. 669, 568 P.2d 394 (1977), was decided. This was a suit by the purchaser of a power saw who suffered severance of four fingers, against the manufacturer of the saw, which was alleged to have been of unsafe design. Defendant sought to compel plaintiff prior to trial to reenact the injury before a videotape camera. The trial court's order directing plaintiff to do so was reversed on the ground that the deposition statute, as it then read, provided for *written* recordation of "testimony." 19 Cal.3d at 978: "Whether other methods of recording and reporting depositions should now be authorized is a matter for the Legislature to determine." Why did the court define the issue as the mode of recording testimony rather than whether a party might be required to undergo special discovery adapted to the circumstances of the case? Or was the court's major premise that there is no discovery except as statute permits? The court refused to follow Blumberg v. Dornbusch, 139 N.J.Super. 433, 354 A.2d 351 (1976), which sanctioned videotaped depositions absent statutory authority.

Compare Shepherd v. Superior Court, 17 Cal.3d 107, 130 Cal.Rptr. 257, 550 P.2d 161 (1976), holding that a defendant could be ordered to put on the clothing he wore on the day of the incident and be photographed in that attire, although C.C.P. 2031 speaks only of photographing "things." See also Vinson v. Superior Court, infra p. 943, declining to permit the presence of plaintiff's attorney during an examination by defendant's psychologist in the absence of statutory authority, and distinguishing Sharff v. Superior Court, 44 Cal.2d 508, 282 P.2d 896 (1955), which held that in a *physical* examination counsel had a right to be present. The latter holding was later codified at C.C.P. 2032(g).

9. Discovery From the Government

Litigation involving the Federal Government as a party entails special problems. See Note, Preferential Treatment of the United States Under Federal Civil Discovery Procedures, 13 Ga.L.Rev. 550 (1979); Note, The Civil Investigative Demand: A Constitutional Analysis and Model Proposal, 33 Vand. L.Rev. 1451 (1980). Different issues arise where information is sought from the Government in litigation where the Government is not a party. See Tomlinson, Use of the Freedom of Information Act for Discovery Purposes, 43 Md.L. Rev. 119 (1984). On disclosure and discovery of information relevant to a civil action that has been obtained in a grand jury investigation, see United States v. John Doe, Inc. I, 481 U.S. 102, 107 S.Ct. 1656, 95 L.Ed.2d 94 (1987).

10. Discovery in Criminal Cases

Discovery in criminal cases is something else again. The prosecution has a broad obligation to produce evidence favorable to the defendant, but the defendant has a much more limited obligation. See generally LaFave and Israel, Criminal Procedure §§ 19.3 et seq. (1984).

11. Appellate Review of Discovery Orders

Discovery orders are not final judgments and hence ordinarily are not appealable. However, by various means immediate appellate review may be obtained under some circumstances. See, e.g., Marrese v. American Academy of Orthopaedic Surgeons, 706 F.2d 1488 (7th Cir.1983) (contempt ruling for refusal to produce is appealable); In re Intern. Systems & Controls Corp. Securities Litigation, 693 F.2d 1235 (5th Cir.1982) (third party in possession of documents); Comment, Appellate Review of Discovery Orders in the Federal Courts, 1980 So.Ill.L.J. 339.

2. TRIAL PREPARATION PRIVILEGES

a. THE ATTORNEY–CLIENT AND WORK PRODUCT PRIVILEGES

INTRODUCTORY NOTE ON THE ATTORNEY–CLIENT PRIVILEGE

The privilege granted to communications between attorney and client is the oldest and most frequently invoked of the traditional privileges given to communications made in confidence. See generally Cleary et al., McCormick on Evidence c. 10 (3d ed. 1984). The purpose of the privilege is, as the Supreme Court noted in Upjohn Co. v. United States, infra p. 920, "to encourage full and frank communication between attorneys and their clients and thereby promote broader public interests in the observance of law and administration of justice." But the privilege has not always enjoyed the expansive interpretation given it in modern jurisprudence, partly because of the legitimate concern that it is not only a principle of privacy, but also a device for cover-ups. The privilege originated in the common law of England in the context of a division of function between barrister and solicitor. Originally, it appears to have been a narrow privilege protecting communications only between a client and his barrister, the lawyer who actually presented the evidence and argued the law in court. It did not necessarily extend to communications between the client and his attorney or solicitor, the lawyer who bore responsibility for preparing the case for trial. See Hazard, An Historical Perspective on the Attorney–Client Privilege, 66 Calif.L.Rev. 1061 (1978). During the course of the nineteenth century, the privilege was expanded to include communications with attorneys and solicitors and to protect communications by the client concerning transactions other than preparation for litigation. Consider the oft-quoted language of Judge Wyzanski in United States v. United Shoe Machinery Corp., 89 F.Supp. 357, 358–59 (D.Mass.1950):

> "The privilege applies only if (1) the asserted holder of the privilege is or sought to become a client; (2) the person to whom the communication was made (a) is a member of the bar of a court, or his subordinate and (b) in connection with this communication is acting as a lawyer; (3) the communication relates to a fact of which the attorney was informed (a) by his client (b) without the presence of strangers (c) for the purpose of securing primarily either (i) an opinion on law or (ii) legal services or (iii) assistance in some legal proceeding, and not (d) for the purpose of committing a crime or tort; and (4) the privilege has been (a) claimed and (b) not waived by the client."

This formulation draws in part from Dean Wigmore's equally classic eight-part test. See 8 Wigmore on Evidence § 2292 (McNaughton ed. 1961).

By 1947, when Hickman v. Taylor was decided, two issues were awaiting resolution: (1) whether a privilege should be recognized for aspects of the attorney's trial preparation other than communications from the client, e.g., the attorney's "work product"; and (2) whether a privilege should exist for communications or other facts about the transaction received by the attorney from persons other than the client and, if so, how far into the transaction such a privilege should reach.

HICKMAN v. TAYLOR

Supreme Court of the United States, 1947.
329 U.S. 495, 67 S.Ct. 385, 91 L.Ed. 451.*

Mr. Justice Murphy delivered the opinion of the Court.

This case presents an important problem under the Federal Rules of Civil Procedure * * * as to the extent to which a party may inquire into oral and written statements of witnesses, or other information, secured by an adverse party's counsel in the course of preparation for possible litigation after a claim has arisen. Examination into a person's files and records, including those resulting from the professional activities of an attorney, must be judged with care. It is not without reason that various safeguards have been established to preclude unwarranted excursions into the privacy of a man's work. At the same time, public policy supports reasonable and necessary inquiries. Properly to balance these competing interests is a delicate and difficult task.

On February 7, 1943, the tug "J. M. Taylor" sank while engaged in helping to tow a car float of the Baltimore & Ohio Railroad across the Delaware River at Philadelphia. The accident was apparently unusual in nature, the cause of it still being unknown. Five of the nine crew members were drowned. Three days later the tug owners and the underwriters employed a law firm, of which respondent Fortenbaugh is a member, to defend them against potential suits by representatives of the deceased crew members and to sue the railroad for damages to the tug.

A public hearing was held on March 4, 1943, before the United States Steamboat Inspectors, at which the four survivors were examined. This testimony was recorded and made available to all interested parties. Shortly thereafter, Fortenbaugh privately interviewed the survivors and took statements from them with an eye toward the anticipated litigation; the survivors signed these statements on March 29. Fortenbaugh also interviewed other persons believed to have some information relating to the accident and in some cases he made memoranda of what they told him. At the time when Fortenbaugh secured the statements of the survivors, representatives of two of the deceased crew members had been in communication with him. Ultimately claims were presented by representatives of all five of the deceased; four of the claims, however, were settled without litigation. The fifth claimant, petitioner herein, brought suit in a federal court under the Jones Act on November 26, 1943, naming as defendants the two tug owners, individually and as partners, and the railroad.

One year later, petitioner filed 39 interrogatories directed to the tug owners. The 38th interrogatory read: "State whether any statements of the members of the crews of the Tugs 'J. M. Taylor' and 'Philadelphia' or of any other vessel were taken in connection with the towing of the car float and the sinking of the Tug 'John M. Taylor.'

---

* Some of the Court's footnotes are omitted.

Attach hereto exact copies of all such statements if in writing, and if oral, set forth in detail the exact provisions of any such oral statements or reports."

Supplemental interrogatories asked whether any oral or written statements, records, reports or other memoranda had been made concerning any matter relative to the towing operation, the sinking of the tug, the salvaging and repair of the tug, and the death of the deceased. If the answer was in the affirmative, the tug owners were then requested to set forth the nature of all such records, reports, statements or other memoranda.

The tug owners, through Fortenbaugh, answered all of the interrogatories except No. 38 and the supplemental ones just described. While admitting that statements of the survivors had been taken they declined to summarize or set forth the contents. They did so on the ground that such requests called "for privileged matter obtained in preparation for litigation" and constituted "an attempt to obtain indirectly counsel's private files." It was claimed that answering these requests "would involve practically turning over not only the complete files, but also the telephone records and, almost, the thoughts of counsel."

In connection with the hearing on these objections, Fortenbaugh made a written statement and gave an informal oral deposition explaining the circumstances under which he had taken the statements. But he was not expressly asked in the deposition to produce the statements. The District Court for the Eastern District of Pennsylvania, sitting en banc, held that the requested matters were not privileged. 4 F.R.D. 479. The court then decreed that the tug owners and Fortenbaugh, as counsel and agent for the tug owners, forthwith "Answer Plaintiff's 38th interrogatory and supplementary interrogatories; produce all written statements of witnesses obtained by Mr. Fortenbaugh, as counsel and agent for Defendants; state in substance any fact concerning this case which Defendants learned through oral statements made by witnesses to Mr. Fortenbaugh whether or not included in his private memoranda and produce Mr. Fortenbaugh's memoranda containing statements of fact by witnesses or to submit these memoranda to the Court for determination of those portions which should be revealed to Plaintiff." Upon their refusal, the court adjudged them in contempt and ordered them imprisoned until they complied.

The Third Circuit Court of Appeals, also sitting en banc, reversed the judgment of the District Court. 153 F.2d 212. It held that the information here sought was part of the "work product of the lawyer" and hence privileged from discovery under the Federal Rules of Civil Procedure. The importance of the problem, which has engendered a great divergence of views among district courts, led us to grant certiorari. 328 U.S. 876, 66 S.Ct. 1337.

The pre-trial deposition-discovery mechanism established by Rules 26 to 37 is one of the most significant innovations of the Federal Rules of Civil Procedure. Under the prior federal practice, the pre-trial functions of notice-giving, issue-formulation and fact-revelation were performed primarily and inadequately by the pleadings.[2] Inquiry into the issues and the facts before trial was narrowly confined and was often cumbersome in method. The new rules, however, restrict the pleadings to the task of general notice-giving and invest the deposition-discovery process with a vital role in the preparation for trial. The various instruments of discovery now serve (1) as a device, along with the pre-trial hearing under Rule 16, to narrow and clarify the basic issues between the parties, and (2) as a device for ascertaining the facts, or information as to the existence or whereabouts of facts, relative to those issues. Thus civil trials in the federal courts no longer need be carried on in the dark. The way is now clear, consistent with recognized privileges, for the parties to obtain the fullest possible knowledge of the issues and facts before trial.[4]

Discovery Functions

There is an initial question as to which of the desposition-discovery rules is involved in this case. Petitioner, in filing his interrogatories, thought that he was proceeding under Rule 33. That rule provides that a party may serve upon any adverse party written interrogatories to be answered by the party served. The District Court proceeded on the same assumption in its opinion, although its order to produce and its contempt order stated that both Rules 33 and 34 were involved. * * *

* * * *

But under the circumstances we deem it unnecessary and unwise to rest our decision upon this procedural irregularity, an irregularity which is not strongly urged upon us and which was disregarded in the two courts below. It matters little at this late stage whether Fortenbaugh fails to answer interrogatories filed under Rule 26 or under Rule 33 or whether he refuses to produce the memoranda and statements pursuant to a subpoena under Rule 45 or a court order under Rule 34. The deposition-discovery rules created integrated procedural devices. And the basic question at stake is whether any of those devices may be used to inquire into materials collected by an adverse party's counsel in the course of preparation for possible litigation. The fact that the petitioner may have used the wrong method does not destroy the main thrust of his attempt. Nor does it relieve us of the responsibility of dealing with the problem raised by that attempt. It would be inconsistent with the liberal atmosphere surrounding these rules to insist that petitioner now go through the empty formality of pursuing the right procedural device only to reestablish precisely the same basic problem now confronting us. We do not mean to say, however, that there may not be situations in which the failure to

Sub - I

---

2. "The great weakness of pleading as a means for developing and presenting issues of fact for trial lay in its total lack of any means for testing the factual basis for the pleader's allegations and denials." Sunderland, "The Theory and Practice of Pre-Trial Procedure," 36 Mich.L.Rev. 215, 216.

See also Ragland, Discovery Before Trial (1932), ch. I.

4. Pike and Willis, "The New Federal Deposition-Discovery Procedure," 38 Col.L. Rev. 1179, 1436; Pike, "The New Federal Deposition-Discovery Procedure and the Rules of Evidence," 34 Ill.L.Rev. 1.

proceed in accordance with a specific rule would be important or decisive. But in the present circumstances, for the purposes of this decision, the procedural irregularity is not material. Having noted the proper procedure, we may accordingly turn our attention to the substance of the underlying problem.

In urging that he has a right to inquire into the materials secured and prepared by Fortenbaugh, petitioner emphasizes that the deposition-discovery portions of the Federal Rules of Civil Procedure are designed to enable the parties to discover the true facts and to compel their disclosure wherever they may be found. It is said that inquiry may be made under these rules, epitomized by Rule 26, as to any relevant matter which is not privileged; and since the discovery provisions are to be applied as broadly and liberally as possible, the privilege limitation must be restricted to its narrowest bounds. On the premise that the attorney-client privilege is the one involved in this case, petitioner argues that it must be strictly confined to confidential communications made by a client to his attorney. And since the materials here in issue were secured by Fortenbaugh from third persons rather than from his clients, the tug owners, the conclusion is reached that these materials are proper subjects for discovery under Rule 26.

As additional support for this result, petitioner claims that to prohibit discovery under these circumstances would give a corporate defendant a tremendous advantage in a suit by an individual plaintiff. Thus in a suit by an injured employee against a railroad or in a suit by an insured person against an insurance company the corporate defendant could pull a dark veil of secrecy over all the pertinent facts it can collect after the claim arises merely on the assertion that such facts were gathered by its large staff of attorneys and claim agents. At the same time, the individual plaintiff, who often has direct knowledge of the matter in issue and has no counsel until some time after his claim arises could be compelled to disclose all the intimate details of his case. By endowing with immunity from disclosure all that a lawyer discovers in the course of his duties, it is said, the rights of individual litigants in such cases are drained of vitality and the lawsuit becomes more of a battle of deception than a search for truth.

But framing the problem in terms of assisting individual plaintiffs in their suits aginst corporate defendants is unsatisfactory. Discovery concededly may work to the disadvantage as well as to the advantage of individual plaintiffs. Discovery, in other words, is not a one-way proposition. It is available in all types of cases at the behest of any party, individual or corporate, plaintiff or defendant. The problem thus far transcends the situation confronting this petitioner. And we must view that problem in light of the limitless situations where the particular kind of discovery sought by petitioner might be used.

We agree, of course, that the deposition-discovery rules are to be accorded a broad and liberal treatment. No longer can the time-honored cry of "fishing expedition" serve to preclude a party from inquiring into the facts underlying his opponent's case. Mutual knowledge of all the relevant facts gathered by both parties is essential to proper litigation. To that end, either party may compel the other to disgorge whatever facts he has in his possession. The deposition-discovery procedure simply advances the stage at which the disclosure can be compelled from the time of trial to the period preceding it, thus reducing the possibility of surprise. But discovery, like all maters of procedure, has ultimate and necessary boundaries. As indicated by Rules 30(b) and (d) and 31(d), limitations inevitably arise when it can be shown that the examination is being conducted in bad faith or in such a manner as to annoy, embarrass or oppress the person subject to the inquiry. And as Rule 26(b) provides, further limitations come into existence when the inquiry touches upon the irrelevant or encroaches upon the recognized domains of privilege.

We also agree that the memoranda, statements and mental impressions in issue in this case fall outside the scope of the attorney-client privilege and hence are not protected from discovery on that basis. It is unnecessary here to delineate the content and scope of that privilege as recognized in the federal courts. For present purposes, it suffices to note that the protective cloak of this privilege does not extend to information which an attorney secures from a witness while acting for his client in anticipation of litigation. Nor does this privilege concern the memoranda, briefs, communications and other writings prepared by counsel for his own use in prosecuting his client's case; and it is equally unrelated to writings which reflect an attorney's mental impressions, conclusions, opinions or legal theories.

But the impropriety of invoking that privilege does not provide an answer to the problem before us. Petitioner has made more than an ordinary request for relevant, non-privileged facts in the possession of his adversaries or their counsel. He has sought discovery as of right of oral and written statements of witnesses whose identity is well known and whose availability to petitioner appears unimpaired. He has sought production of these matters after making the most searching inquiries of his opponents as to the circumstances surrounding the fatal accident, which inquiries were sworn to have been answered to the best of their information and belief. Interrogatories were directed toward all the events prior to, during and subsequent to the sinking of the tug. Full and honest answers to such broad inquiries would necessarily have included all pertinent information gleaned by Fortenbaugh through his interviews with the witnesses. Petitioner makes no suggestion, and we cannot assume, that the tug owners or Fortenbaugh were incomplete or dishonest in the framing of their answers. In addition, petitioner was free to examine the public testimony of the witnesses taken before the United States Steamboat Inspectors. We are thus dealing with an attempt to secure the production of written statements and mental impressions contained in the files and the mind of the attorney Fortenbaugh without any showing of necessity or any indication or claim that denial of such production would unduly prejudice the preparation of petitioner's case or cause him any hardship or injustice. For aught that appears, the essence of what petitioner seeks either has been revealed to him already through the interrogatories or is readily available to him direct from the witnesses for the asking.

* * *

In our opinion, neither Rule 26 nor any other rule dealing with discovery contemplates production under such circumstances. That is not because the subject matter is privileged or irrelevant, as those concepts are used in these rules.[9] Here is simply an attempt, without purported necessity or justification, to secure written statements, private memoranda and personal recollections prepared or formed by an adverse party's counsel in the course of his legal duties. As such, it falls outside the arena of discovery and contravenes the public policy underlying the orderly prosecution and defense of legal claims. Not even the most liberal of discovery theories can justify unwarranted inquiries into the files and the mental impressions of an attorney.

Historically, a lawyer is an officer of the court and is bound to work for the advancement of justice while faithfully protecting the rightful interests of his clients. In performing his various duties, however, it is essential that a lawyer work with a certain degree of privacy, free from unnecessary intrusion by opposing parties and their counsel. Proper preparation of a client's case demands that he assemble information, sift what he considers to be the relevant from the irrelevant facts, prepare his legal theories and plan his strategy without undue and needless interference. That is the historical and the necessary way in which lawyers act within the framework of our system of jurisprudence to promote justice and to protect their clients' interests. This work is reflected, of course, in interviews, statements, memoranda, correspondence, briefs, mental impressions, personal beliefs, and countless other tangible and intangible ways—aptly though roughly termed by the Circuit Court of Appeals in this case as the "work product of the lawyer." Were such materials open to opposing

---

9. The English courts have developed the concept of privilege to include all documents prepared by or for counsel with a view to litigation. "All documents which are called into existence for the purpose— but not necessarily the sole purpose—of assisting the deponent or his legal advisers in any actual or anticipated litigation are privileged from production. . . . Thus all proofs, briefs, draft pleadings, etc., are privileged; but not counsel's indorsement on the outside of his brief, . . . nor any deposition or notes of evidence given publicly in open Court. . . . So are all papers prepared by any agent of the party *bona fide* for the use of his solicitor for the purposes of the action, whether in fact so used or not. . . . Reports by a company's servant, if made in the ordinary course of routine, are not privileged, even though it is desirable that the solicitor should have them and they are subsequently sent to him; but if the solicitor has requested that such documents shall always be prepared for his use and this was one of the reasons why they were prepared, they need not be disclosed." Odgers on Pleading and Practice (12th ed., 1939), p. 264.

See Order 31, rule 1, of the Rules of the Supreme Court, 1883, set forth in The Annual Practice, 1945, p. 519, and the discussion following that rule. For a compilation of the English cases on the matter see 8 Wigmore on Evidence (3d ed., 1940), § 2319, pp. 618–622, notes.

counsel on mere demand, much of what is now put down in writing would remain unwritten. An attorney's thoughts, heretofore inviolate, would not be his own. Inefficiency, unfairness and sharp practices would inevitably develop in the giving of legal advice and in the preparation of cases for trial. The effect on the legal profession would be demoralizing. And the interests of the clients and the cause of justice would be poorly served.

We do not mean to say that all written materials obtained or prepared by an adversary's counsel with an eye toward litigation are necessarily free from discovery in all cases. Where relevant and non-privileged facts remain hidden in an attorney's file and where production of those facts is essential to the preparation of one's case, discovery may properly be had. Such written statements and documents might, under certain circumstances, be admissible in evidence or give clues as to the existence or location of relevant facts. Or they might be useful for purposes of impeachment or corroboration. And production might be justified where the witnesses are no longer available or can be reached only with difficulty. Were production of written statements and documents to be precluded under such circumstances, the liberal ideals of the deposition-discovery portions of the Federal Rules of Civil Procedure would be stripped of much of their meaning. But the general policy against invading the privacy of an attorney's course of preparation is so well recognized and so essential to an orderly working of our system of legal procedure that a burden rests on the one who would invade that privacy to establish adequate reasons to justify production through a subpoena or court order. That burden, we believe, is necessarily implicit in the rules as now constituted.

* * * No attempt was made to establish any reason why Fortenbaugh should be forced to produce the written statements. There was only a naked, general demand for these materials as of right and a finding by the District Court that no recognizable privilege was involved. That was insufficient to justify discovery under these circumstances and the court should have sustained the refusal of the tug owners and Fortenbaugh to produce.

* * *

* * * Petitioner's counsel frankly admits that he wants the oral statements only to help prepare himself to examine witnesses and to make sure that he has overlooked nothing. That is insufficient under the circumstances to permit him an exception to the policy underlying the privacy of Fortenbaugh's professional activities. If there should be a rare situation justifying production of these matters, petitioner's case is not of that type.

* * *

Affirmed.

UPJOHN CO. v. UNITED STATES

Supreme Court of the United States, 1981.
449 U.S. 383, 101 S.Ct. 677, 66 L.Ed.2d 584.*

JUSTICE REHNQUIST delivered the opinion of the Court.

We granted certiorari in this case to address important questions concerning the scope of the attorney-client privilege in the corporate context and the applicability of the work-product doctrine in proceedings to enforce tax summonses. * * *

I

Petitioner Upjohn Co. manufactures and sells pharmaceuticals here and abroad. In January 1976 independent accountants conducting an audit of one of petitioner's foreign subsidiaries discovered that the subsidiary made payments to or for the benefit of foreign government officials in order to secure government business. The accountants so informed petitioner, Mr. Gerard Thomas, Upjohn's Vice-President, Secretary, and General Counsel. Thomas is a member of the Michigan and New York bars, and has been Upjohn's General Counsel for 20 years. He consulted with outside counsel and R. T. Parfet, Jr., Upjohn's Chairman of the Board. It was decided that the company would conduct an internal investigation of what were termed "questionable payments." As part of this investigation the attorneys prepared a letter containing a questionnaire which was sent to "All Foreign General and Area Managers" over the Chairman's signature. The letter began by noting recent disclosures that several American companies made "possibly illegal" payments to foreign government officals and emphasized that the management needed full information concerning any such payments made by Upjohn. The letter indicated that the Chairman had asked Thomas, identified as "the company's General Counsel," "to conduct an investigation for the purpose of determining the nature and magnitude of any payments made by the Upjohn Company or any of its subsidiaries to any employee or official of a foreign government." The questionnaire sought detailed information concerning such payments. Managers were instructed to treat the investigation as "highly confidential" and not to discuss it with anyone other than Upjohn employees who might be helpful in providing the requested information. Responses were to be sent directly to Thomas. Thomas and outside counsel also interviewed the recipients of the questionnaire and some 33 other Upjohn officers or employees as part of the investigation.

On March 26, 1976, the company voluntarily submitted a preliminary report to the Securities and Exchange Commission on Form 8–K disclosing certain questionable payments. A copy of the report was simultaneously submitted to the Internal Revenue Service, which im-

---

* Some of the Court's footnotes are omitted.

mediately began an investigation to determine the tax consequences of the payments. Special agents conducting the investigation were given lists by Upjohn of all those interviewed and all who had responded to the questionnaire. On November 23, 1976, the Service issued a summons pursuant to 26 U.S.C. § 7602 demanding production of:

> "All files relative to the investigation conducted under the supervision of Gerard Thomas to identify payments to employees of foreign governments and any political contributions made by the Upjohn Company or any of its affiliates since January 1, 1971 and to determine whether any funds of the Upjohn Company had been improperly accounted for on the corporate books during the same period.
>
> "The records should include but not be limited to written questionnaires sent to managers of the Upjohn Company's foreign affiliates, and memoranda or notes of the interviews conducted in the United States and abroad with officers and employees of the Upjohn Company and its subsidiaries." App. 17a–18a.

The company declined to produce the documents specified in the second paragraph on the grounds that they were protected from disclosure by the attorney-client privilege and constituted the work product of attorneys prepared in anticipation of litigation. On August 31, 1977, the United States filed a petition seeking enforcement of the summons under 26 U.S.C. §§ 7402(b) and 7604(a) in the United States District Court for the Western District of Michigan. * * *

II

Federal Rule of Evidence 501 provides that "the privilege of a witness . . . shall be governed by the principles of the common law as they may be interpreted by the courts of the United States in light of reason and experience." The attorney-client privilege is the oldest of the privileges for confidential communications known to the common law. 8 J. Wigmore, Evidence § 2290 (McNaughton rev.1961). Its purpose is to encourage full and frank communication between attorneys and their clients and thereby promote broader public interests in the observance of law and administration of justice. The privilege recognizes that sound legal advice or advocacy serves public ends and that such advice or advocacy depends upon the lawyer being fully informed by the client. As we stated last Term in Trammel v. United States, 445 U.S. 40, 51, 100 S.Ct. 906, 913, 63 L.Ed.2d 186 (1980): "The lawyer-client privilege rests on the need for the advocate and counselor to know all that relates to the client's reasons for seeking representation if the professional mission is to be carried out." And in Fisher v. United States, 425 U.S. 391, 403, 96 S.Ct. 1569, 1577, 48 L.Ed.2d 39 (1976), we recognized the purpose of the privilege to be "to encourage clients to make full disclosures to their attorneys." This rationale for the privilege has long been recognized by the Court, see Hunt v. Blackburn, 128 U.S. 464, 470, 9 S.Ct. 125, 127, 32 L.Ed. 488 (1888)

(privilege "is founded upon the necessity, in the interest and administration of justice, of the aid of persons having knowledge of the law and
skilled in its practice, which assistance can only be safely and readily
availed of when free from the consequences or the apprehension of
disclosure"). Admittedly complications in the application of the privilege arise when the client is a corporation, which in theory is an
artifical creature of the law, and not an individual; but this Court has
assumed that the privilege applies when the client is a corporation.
United States v. Louisville & Nashville R. Co., 236 U.S. 318, 336, 35
S.Ct. 363, 369, 59 L.Ed. 598 (1915), and the Government does not contest
the general proposition.

The Court of Appeals, however, considered the application of the
privilege in the corporate context to present a "different problem,"
since the client was an inanimate entity and "only the senior management, guiding and integrating the several operations, . . . can be said
to possess an identity analogous to the corporation as a whole." 600
F.2d at 1226. The first case to articulate the so-called "control group
test" adopted by the court below, Philadelphia v. Westinghouse Electric
Corp., 210 F.Supp. 483, 485 (ED Pa.), petition for mandamus and
prohibition denied sub nom. General Electric Co. v. Kirkpatrick, 312
F.2d 742 (CA3 1962), cert. denied, 372 U.S. 943, 83 S.Ct. 937, 9 L.Ed.2d
969 (1963), reflected a similar conceptual approach:

> "Keeping in mind that the question is, Is it the corporation which
> is seeking the lawyer's advice when the asserted privileged commu-
> nication is made?, the most satisfactory solution, I think, is that if
> the employee making the communication, of whatever rank he may
> be, is in a position to control or even to take a substantial part in a
> decision about any action which the corporation may take upon the
> advice of the attorney, . . . then, in effect, *he is (or personifies) the
> corporation* when he makes his disclosure to the lawyer and the
> privilege would apply." (Emphasis supplied.)

Such a view, we think, overlooks the fact that the privilege exists to
protect not only the giving of professional advice to those who can act
on it but also the giving of information to the lawyer to enable him to
give sound and informed advice. See *Trammel*, supra, at 51, 100 S.Ct.,
at 913; *Fisher*, supra, at 403, 96 S.Ct. at 1577. The first step in the
resolution of any legal problem is ascertaining the factual background
and sifting through the facts with an eye to the legally relevant. See
ABA Code of Professional Responsibility, Ethical Consideration 4–1:

> "A lawyer should be fully informed of all the facts of the matter he
> is handling in order for his client to obtain the full advantage of
> our legal system. It is for the lawyer in the exercise of his
> independent professional judgment to separate the relevant and
> important from the irrelevant and unimportant. The observance
> of the ethical obligation of a lawyer to hold inviolate the confi-
> dences and secrets of his client not only facilitates the full develop-

ment of facts essential to proper representation of the client but also encourages laymen to seek early legal assistance."

See also Hickman v. Taylor, 329 U.S. 495, 511, 67 S.Ct. 385, 393–394, 91 L.Ed. 451 (1947).

In the case of the individual client the provider of information and the person who acts on the lawyer's advice are one and the same. In the corporate context, however, it will frequently be employees beyond the control group as defined by the court below—"officers and agents . . . responsible for directing [the company's] actions in response to legal advice"—who will possess the information needed by the corporation's lawyers. Middle-level—and indeed lower-level—employees can, by actions within the scope of their employment, embroil the corporation in serious legal difficulties, and it is only natural that these employees would have the relevant information needed by corporate counsel if he is adequately to advise the client with respect to such actual or potential difficulties. This fact was noted in Diversified Industries, Inc. v. Meredith, 572 F.2d 596 (CA8 1978) (en banc):

> "In a corporation, it may be necessary to glean information relevant to a legal problem from middle management or non-management personnel as well as from top executives. The attorney dealing with a complex legal problem 'is thus faced with a "Hobson's choice." If he interviews employees not having "the very highest authority," their communications to him will not be privileged. If, on the other hand, he interviews *only* those employees with the "very highest authority," he may find it extremely difficult, if not impossible, to determine what happened.'" Id., at 608–609 (quoting Weinschel, Corporate Employee Interviews and the Attorney-Client Privilege, 12 B.C.Ind. & Comm.L.Rev. 873, 876 (1971)).

The control group test adopted by the court below thus frustrates the very purpose of the privilege by discouraging the communication of relevant information by employees of the client to attorneys seeking to render legal advice to the client corporation. The attorney's advice will also frequently be more significant to noncontrol group members than to those who officially sanction the advice, and the control group test makes it more difficult to convey full and frank legal advice to the employees who will put into effect the client corporation's policy. See, e.g., Duplan Corp. v. Deering Milliken, Inc., 397 F.Supp. 1146, 1164 (DSC 1974) ("After the lawyer forms his or her opinion, it is of no immediate benefit to the Chairman of the Board or the President. It must be given to the corporate personnel who will apply it").

The narrow scope given the attorney-client privilege by the court below not only makes it difficult for corporate attorneys to formulate sound advice when their client is faced with a specific legal problem but also threatens to limit the valuable efforts of corporate counsel to ensure their client's compliance with the law. In light of the vast and complicated array of regulatory legislation confronting the modern corporation, corporations, unlike most individuals, "constantly go to lawyers to find out how to obey the law," Burnham, The Attorney-Client Privilege in the Corporate Arena, 24 Bus.Law. 901, 913 (1969), particularly since compliance with the law in this area is hardly an instinctive matter, see, e.g., United States v. United States Gypsum Co., 438 U.S. 422, 440–441, 98 S.Ct. 2864, 2875–2876, 57 L.Ed.2d 854 (1978) ("the behavior proscribed by the [Sherman] Act is often difficult to distinguish from the gray zone of socially acceptable and economically justifiable business conduct"). The test adopted by the court below is difficult to apply in practice, though no abstractly formulated and unvarying "test" will necessarily enable courts to decide questions such as this with mathematical precision. But if the purpose of the attorney-client privilege is to be served, the attorney and client must be able to predict with some degree of certainty whether particular discussions will be protected. An uncertain privilege, or one which purports to be certain but results in widely varying applications by the courts, is little better than no privilege at all. The very terms of the test adopted by the court below suggest the unpredictability of its application. The test restricts the availability of the privilege to those officers who play a "substantial role" in deciding and directing a corporation's legal response. Disparate decisions in cases applying this test illustrate its unpredictability. Compare, e.g., Hogan v. Zletz, 43 F.R.D. 308, 315–316 (ND Okl.1967), aff'd in part sub nom. Natta v. Hogan, 392 F.2d 686 (CA10 1968) (control group includes managers and assistant managers of patent division and research and development department) with Congoleum Industries, Inc. v. GAF Corp., 49 F.R.D. 82, 83–85 (ED Pa. 1969), aff'd, 478 F.2d 1398 (CA3 1973) (control group includes only division and corporate vice-presidents, and not two directors of research and vice-president for production and research).

　　　*　*　*

The Court of Appeals declined to extend the attorney-client privilege beyond the limits of the control group test for fear that doing so would entail severe burdens on discovery and create a broad "zone of silence" over corporate affairs. Application of the attorney-client privilege to communications such as those involved here, however, puts the adversary in no worse position than if the communications had never taken place. The privilege only protects disclosure of communications; it does not protect disclosure of the underlying facts by those who communicated with the attorney:

> "[T]he protection of the privilege extends only to *communications* and not to facts. A fact is one thing and a communication concerning that fact is an entirely different thing. The client cannot be compelled to answer the question, 'What did you say or write to the attorney?' but may not refuse to disclose any relevant fact within his knowledge merely because he incorporated a statement of such fact into his communication to his attorney." Philadelphia v. Westinghouse Electric Corp., 205 F.Supp. 830, 831 (ED Pa.1962).

See also *Diversified Industries,* 572 F.2d, at 611; State ex rel. Dudek v. Circuit Court, 34 Wis.2d 559, 580, 150 N.W.2d 387, 399 (1967) ("the courts have noted that a party cannot conceal a fact merely by revealing it to his lawyer"). Here the Government was free to question the employees who communicated with Thomas and outside counsel. Upjohn has provided the IRS with a list of such employees, and the IRS has already interviewed some 25 of them. While it would probably be more convenient for the Government to secure the results of petitioner's internal investigation by simply subpoenaing the questionnaires and notes taken by petitioner's attorneys, such considerations of convenience do not overcome the policies served by the attorney-client privilege. As Justice Jackson noted in his concurring opinion in *Hickman* v. *Taylor,* 329 U.S., at 516, 67 S.Ct., at 396: "Discovery was hardly intended to enable a learned profession to perform its functions . . . on wits borrowed from the adversary."

* * *

III

Our decision that the communications by Upjohn employees to counsel are covered by the attorney-client privilege disposes of the case so far as the responses to the questionnaires and any notes reflecting responses to interview questions are concerned. The summons reaches further, however, and Thomas has testified that his notes and memoranda of interviews go beyond recording responses to his questions. App. 27a–28a, 91a–93a. To the extent that the material subject to the summons is not protected by the attorney-client privilege as disclosing communications between an employee and counsel, we must reach the ruling by the Court of Appeals that the work-product doctrine does not apply to summonses issued under 26 U.S.C. § 7602.

The Government concedes, wisely, that the Court of Appeals erred and that the work-product doctrine does apply to IRS summonses. * * *

As we stated last Term, the obligation imposed by a tax summons remains "subject to the traditional privileges and limitations." United States v. Euge, 444 U.S. 707, 714, 100 S.Ct. 874, 879–880, 63 L.Ed.2d 741 (1980). Nothing in the language of the IRS summons provisions or their legislative history suggests an intent on the part of Congress to preclude application of the work-product doctrine. Rule 26(b)(3) codifies the work-product doctrine, and the Federal Rules of Civil Procedure are made applicable to summons enforcement proceedings by Rule 81(a)(3). See Donaldson v. United States, 400 U.S. 517, 528, 91 S.Ct. 534, 541, 27 L.Ed.2d 580 (1971). While conceding the applicability of the work-product doctrine, the Government asserts that it has made a sufficient showing of necessity to overcome its protections. The Magistrate apparently so found, 78–1 USTC ¶ 9277, p. 83,605. The Government relies on the following language in *Hickman*:

"We do not mean to say that all written materials obtained or prepared by an adversary's counsel with an eye toward litigation are necessarily free from discovery in all cases. Where relevant and nonprivileged facts remain hidden in an attorney's file and where production of those facts is essential to the preparation of one's case, discovery may properly be had. . . . And production might be justified where the witnesses are no longer available or may be reached only with difficulty." 329 U.S., at 511, 67 S.Ct., at 394.

The Government stresses that interviewees are scattered across the globe and that Upjohn has forbidden its employees to answer questions it considers irrelevant. The above-quoted language from *Hickman,* however, did not apply to "oral statements made by witnesses . . . whether presently in the form of [the attorney's] mental impressions or memoranda." Id., at 512, 67 S.Ct., at 394. As to such material the Court did "not believe that any showing of necessity can be made under the circumstances of this case so as to justify production. . . . If there should be a rare situation justifying production of these matters petitioner's case is not of that type." Id., at 512–513, 67 S.Ct., at 394–395. See also *Nobles,* supra, 422 U.S., at 252–253, 95 S.Ct., at 2177 (White, J., concurring). Forcing an attorney to disclose notes and memoranda of witnesses' oral statements is particularly disfavored because it tends to reveal the attorney's mental processes, 329 U.S., at 513, 67 S.Ct., at 394–395 ("what he saw fit to write down regarding witnesses' remarks"); id., at 516–517, 67 S.Ct., at 396 ("the statement would be his [the attorney's] language, permeated with his inferences") (Jackson, J., concurring).[8]

Rule 26 accords special protection to work product revealing the attorney's mental processes. The Rule permits disclosure of documents and tangible things constituting attorney work product upon a showing of substantial need and inability to obtain the equivalent without undue hardship. This was the standard applied by the Magistrate, 78–1 USTC ¶ 9277, p. 83,604. Rule 26 goes on, however, to state that "[i]n ordering discovery of such materials when the required showing has been made, the court shall protect against disclosure of the mental impressions, conclusions, opinions or legal theories of an attorney or other representative of a party concerning the litigation." Although this language does not specifically refer to memoranda based on oral statements of witnesses, the *Hickman* court stressed the danger that compelled disclosure of such memoranda would reveal the attorney's mental processes. It is clear that this is the sort of material the draftsmen of the Rule had in mind as deserving special protection. See

---

8. Thomas described his notes of the interviews as containing "what I consider to be the important questions, the substance of the responses to them, my beliefs as to the importance of these, my beliefs as to how they related to the inquiry, my thoughts as to how they related to other questions. In some instances they might even suggest other questions that I would have to ask or things that I needed to find elsewhere." 78–1 USTC ¶ 9277, p. 83,599.

Notes of Advisory Committee on 1970 Amendment to Rules, 28 U.S.C.App., p. 442 ✶ ✶ ✶.

Based on the foregoing, some courts have concluded that *no* showing of necessity can overcome protection of work product which is based on oral statements from witnesses. See, e.g., In re Grand Jury Proceedings, 473 F.2d 840, 848 (CA8 1973) (personal recollections, notes and memoranda pertaining to conversation with witnesses); In re Grand Jury Investigation, 412 F.Supp. 943, 949 (ED Pa.1976) (notes of conversation with witness "are so much a product of the lawyer's thinking and so little probative of the witness's actual words that they are absolutely protected from dislcosure"). Those courts declining to adopt an absolute rule have nonetheless recognized that such material is entitled to special protection. See, e.g., In re Grand Jury Investigation, 599 F.2d 1224, 1231 (CA3 1979) ("special considerations . . . must shape any ruling on the discoverability of interview memoranda . . .; such documents will be discoverable only in a 'rare situation' "); Cf. In re Grand Jury Subpoena, 599 F.2d, at 511–512.

We do not decide the issue at this time. It is clear that the Magistrate applied the wrong standard when he concluded that the Government had made a sufficient showing of necessity to overcome the protections of the work-product doctrine. The Magistrate applied the "substantial need" and "without undue hardship" standard articulated in the first part of Rule 26(b)(3). The notes and memoranda sought by the Government here, however, are work product based on oral statements. If they reveal communications, they are, in this case, protected by the attorney-client privilege To the extent they do not reveal communications, they reveal the attorneys' mental processes in evaluating the communications. As Rule 26 and *Hickman* make clear, such work product cannot be disclosed simply on a showing of substantial need and inability to obtain the equivalent without undue hardship.

While we are not prepared at this juncture to say that such material is always protected by the work-product rule, we think a far stronger showing of necessity and unavailability by other means than was made by the Government or applied by the magistrate in this case would be necessary to compel disclosure. ✶ ✶ ✶†

NOTE ON THE WORK PRODUCT PRIVILEGE

In *Upjohn*, the Court seems to assume that the investigation by the company's counsel was conducted "in anticipation of litigation." Would it be more realistic to say that it was prepared to forefend litigation? If the latter is a fair characterization, isn't that also true of most of a lawyer's office work? Does *Upjohn* therefore make all lawyer work qualifiedly privileged? For a study suggesting that lawyers actually look at the work product rule this way, see Shapiro, Some Problems of Discovery in an Adversary System, 63 Minn.L. Rev. 1055 (1979). For a discussion of one type of problem caused by giving an absolute privilege to opinion work product, see Comment, Legal Malpractice

† The concurring opinion of Burger, C.J., is omitted.

and Discovery of Opinion Work Product in California: The Dilemma Created by Absolute Protection, 17 Pacific L.J. 1393 (1986).

Compare Bank of the Orient v. Superior Court, 67 Cal.App.3d 588, 136 Cal. Rptr. 741 (1977): Two days after a bank's branch manager was discovered to have embezzled a large sum of money, the bank's directors sought a report by a certified public accounting firm concerning the bank's financial controls, which the accounting firm thereafter submitted to the board under the title, "Suggestions for Improvement to Our System of Internal Control." This report was held not privileged, 67 Cal.App.3d at 598: "[T]he report was commissioned not by an attorney but by the board of directors, some four months prior to the time the complaint was filed. A report which is not the product of an attorney or of his agents or employees is not an attorney work product, and an attorney 'cannot, by retroactive adoption, convert the independent work of another, already performed, into his own.'" See also United States v. American Telephone & Telegraph Co., 86 F.R.D. 603, 627–631 (D.D.C.1979). In Simon v. G.D. Searle & Co., 816 F.2d 397 (8th Cir.1987), a system for compiling and analyzing documents relating to multiple products liability claims against a company was held not covered by the work product privilege where the system was operated by a "risk management" group rather than under direction of counsel working on the litigation.

One strategem to take advantage of the work product doctrine has been questioned by courts. In Mission National Insurance Co. v. Lilly, 112 F.R.D. 160 (D.Minn.1986), a property insurer hired attorneys to investigate a fire loss claim and, in a later action against the insured, contended that all of its files relating to the investigation were privileged. The court ordered the insurer to produce the files, excluding material that revealed mental processes and opinions directly related to litigation preparation, and permitted depositions to be taken of the investigating attorneys. To the same effect is National Farmers Union Property & Casualty Co. v. District Court, 718 P.2d 1044 (Colo. 1986). But in Heidebrink v. Moriwaki, 104 Wn.2d 392, 706 P.2d 212 (1985), statements by an insured to the insured's liability insurer investigator were held privileged under the work product doctrine, as being in anticipation of litigation.

When the matter sought to be discovered concededly is the work of the opposing party's attorney prepared in anticipation of litigation, it may nevertheless be discoverable. In Berkey Photo, Inc. v. Eastman Kodak Co., 74 F.R.D. 613 (S.D.N.Y.1977), the court held that notebooks prepared by counsel outlining the defense version of the facts may be discoverable for use in plaintiff's cross-examination of a defense expert witness, where it is shown that the expert used the notebooks in organizing his own testimony. This goes pretty far. But see Bogosian v. Gulf Oil Corp., 738 F.2d 587 (3d Cir.1984); see also Note, Discovery Under the Federal Rules of Civil Procedure of Attorney Opinion Work Product Provided to an Expert Witness, 53 Fordham L.Rev. 1159 (1985). Equally far in the other direction perhaps is City of Long Beach v. Superior Court, 64 Cal.App. 3d 65, 134 Cal.Rptr. 468 (1976), holding that while a party can be compelled to disclose the names of persons who may have knowledge relating to the matter in litigation, it is improper to require a party to list the non-expert witnesses intended to be called at trial, for it reveals his attorney's work product. 64 Cal. App.3d at 73: "The forced revelation of this list would violate the work product doctrine because counsel's decision in this respect is strategic; it necessarily reflects his evaluation of the strengths and weaknesses of his case." Would it also be an invasion of the work product privilege if such a list were required by the court in an order issuing from a pretrial conference? C.C.P. 2034 permits either party to demand that both sides exchange lists of expert witnesses to be called at trial. Most federal courts require each party to disclose their orders of proof, including the names of the witnesses to be called and the identity of documents and other exhibits to be offered. Compare the discussion of the pretrial conference, infra p. 969.

As the discussion of F.R.C.P. 26 in *Upjohn* indicates, attorney work product may be discoverable if the information is relevant, nonprivileged, and essential to the preparation of the opponent's case and if no other reasonable means exist to obtain the information. Cf. C.C.P. 2018. Exactly what this standard means has vexed the federal courts. It is clear that discovery will be permitted only under unusual and compelling circumstances. However, at least one court has said that in certain situations the standard means not only that the work product may be discovered, but that deposition may be had of opposing counsel, although deposition was denied in the instant case. See Shelton v. American Motors Corp., 805 F.2d 1323 (8th Cir.1986).

Failure to claim privilege as to a privileged document generally constitutes a waiver of the privilege not only as to that document but as to the subject as well. This makes "implied waiver" a continuous risk. See Marcus, The Perils of Privilege: Waiver and the Litigator, 84 Mich.L.Rev. 1605 (1986); Davidson and Voth, Waiver of the Attorney–Client Privilege, 64 Or.L.Rev. 637 (1986). See also C.C.P. 2025(m)(1). On the controversial issue of attorney disclosure to prevent harm to third parties, see Subin, The Lawyer as Superego: Disclosure of Client Confidences to Prevent Harm, 70 Iowa L.Rev. 1091 (1985).

On the work product privilege generally, see 8 Wright & Miller §§ 2021 et seq.; Note, Discovery of an Attorney's Work Product in Subsequent Litigation, 1974 Duke L.J. 799; Special Project, The Work Product Doctrine, 68 Cornell L.Rev. 760 (1983). See also Note, Applying the Attorney–Client and Work Product Privilege to Allied Party Exchange of Information in California, 36 U.C.L.A.L.Rev. 151 (1988).

b. EXPERTS AND EXAMINATIONS

AGER v. JANE C. STORMONT HOSPITAL & TRAINING SCHOOL FOR NURSES

United States Court of Appeals for the Tenth Circuit, 1980.
622 F.2d 496.*

Barrett, Circuit Judge.

Lynn R. Johnson, counsel for plaintiff Emily Ager, appeals from an order of the District Court adjudging him guilty of civil contempt. Jurisdiction vests by reason of 28 U.S.C.A. § 1826(b).

Emily was born April 4, 1955, at Stormont-Vail Hospital in Topeka, Kansas. During the second stage of labor, Emily's mother suffered a massive rupture of the uterine wall. The ensuing loss of blood led to Mrs. Ager's death. Premature separation of the placenta from the uterine wall also occurred, resulting in fetal asphyxia. Following Emily's delivery, it was discovered that she evidenced signs of severe

---

* Some of the court's footnotes are omitted.

neurological dysfunction. Today, she is mentally impaired and a permanently disabled quadraplegic with essentially no control over her body functions.

In March, 1977, Emily's father filed, on her behalf, a complaint for the damages sustained at her birth. The complaint alleges, in essence, that "the hemorrhaging and resultant death of her mother and the brain damage and other injuries which she sustained . . . while still in her mother's womb and/or during her delivery, were directly and proximately caused by the negligence and carelessness of the defendants [Stormont-Vail Hospital and Dr. Dan L. Tappen, the attending physician] which joined and concurred in causing plaintiff's mother's death and plaintiff's bodily injuries and damages and resultant disability." [R., Vol. I, p. 4]. After joining the issues, Dr. Tappen propounded a series of interrogatories to the plaintiff. The specific interrogatories at issue here are:

1. Have you contacted any person or persons, whether they are going to testify or not, in regard to the care and treatment rendered by Dr. Dan Tappen involved herein?

2. If the answer to the question immediately above is in the affirmative, please set forth the name of said person or persons and their present residential and/or business address.

3. If the answer to question #1 is in the affirmative, do you have any statements or written reports from said person or persons?

[R., Vol. I, p. 1].

In response, plaintiff filed written objections, accompanied by a lengthy brief. Dr. Tappen answered the plaintiff's objections. The answer brief was treated by the United States Magistrate as a motion for an order compelling discovery pursuant to Fed.Rules Civ.Proc., rule 37(a), 28 U.S.C.A. Following his review, the Magistrate ordered the plaintiff to answer the interrogatories * * *.

Plaintiff's counsel answered the interrogatories in part, but failed to provide any information concerning consultative experts not expected to testify at trial. Plaintiff apparently based the refusal to answer on her contention that an expert who advises a party that his opinion will not aid the party in the trial of the case falls within the definition of experts informally consulted but not retained or specially employed. * * *

Rather than complying with the Magistrate's order, Ager sought review by the District Court pursuant to 28 U.S.C.A. § 636(b)(1)(A). The District Court denied plaintiff's motion for review as untimely. On reconsideration, the Court affirmed the Magistrate's order:

In the context of this malpractice case the question is whether plaintiff must identify each and every doctor, physician or medical expert plaintiff's counsel retained or specially employed during pretrial investigation and preparation. The courts have been divided on the issue. Compare Weiner v. Bache Halsey Stuart, Inc.,

76 F.R.D. 624 (S.D.Fla.1977), Baki v. B.F. Diamond Const. Co., 71 F.R.D. 179 (D.Md.1976), Sea Colony, Inc. v. Continental Ins. Co., 63 F.R.D. 113 (D.Del.1974) and Nemetz v. Aye, 63 F.R.D. 66 (W.D.Penn.1974) with Guilloz v. Falmouth Hospital Ass'n, Inc., 21 F.R.Serv.2d 1367 (D.Mass.1976) and Perry v. W.S. Darley & Co., 54 F.R.D. 278 (E.D.Wis.1971). The Magistrate relied upon *Baki* and *Nemetz,* supra, and held the identities of persons retained or specially employed for an opinion (i.e. to whom some consideration had been paid) to be discoverable. We have again read the Magistrate's Order and the suggestions of counsel. We find plaintiff's argument based upon the Advisory Committee Notes to be unpersuasive. After reviewing the cases and the suggestions of counsel we cannot find the Magistrate's Order to be "contrary to law." [Supp.R., Vol.I, pp. 4–5]. [Parenthetical remark in original text].

Plaintiff's counsel filed a formal response to the Court's order and refused to comply. The Court thereafter entered a civil contempt order against Johnson.[1] Johnson was committed to the custody of the United States Marshal until his compliance with the Court's order. Execution of the custody order was stayed pending appeal, after Johnson posted a recognizance bond. The Court specifically found that the appeal was not frivolous or taken for purposes of delay.

The issues on appeal are whether: (1) the District Court erred in adjudging Johnson guilty of civil contempt; and (2) a party may routinely discover the names of retained or specially employed consultative non-witness experts, pursuant to Fed.Rules Civ.Proc., rule 26(b)(4)(B), 28 U.S.C.A., absent a showing of exceptional circumstances justifying disclosure.

The Contempt Power

When a recalcitrant witness fails to obey the duly issued orders of a court, he may be cited for contempt, either criminal, civil or both. Whether the adjudication of contempt "survives the avoidance of [the] underlying order depends on the nature of the contempt decree. If the contempt is criminal it stands; if it is civil it falls." Latrobe Steel Co. v. United Steelworkers, 545 F.2d 1336, 1342 (3d Cir. 1976). [Footnote omitted]. See also: United States v. United Mine Workers, 330 U.S. 258, 67 S.Ct. 677, 91 L.Ed. 884 (1947); Burkett v. Chandler, 505 F.2d 217 (10th Cir. 1974), cert. denied, 423 U.S. 876, 96 S.Ct. 149, 46 L.Ed.2d 110 (1975); Hyde Construction Co. v. Koehing Co., 348 F.2d 643 (10th Cir. 1965), rev'd on other grounds, 382 U.S. 362, 86 S.Ct. 522, 15 L.Ed.2d 416 (1966).

The primary purpose of a criminal contempt is to punish defiance of a court's judicial authority. Accordingly, the normal beneficiaries of such an order are the courts and the public interest. Norman Bridge Drug Co. v. Banner, 529 F.2d 822 (5th Cir. 1976). On the other hand,

1. At the contempt hearing, Johnson agreed to accept any sanctions on behalf of plaintiff for failing to disclose the identities of plaintiff's consultative witnesses.

civil contempt is characterized by the court's desire "to *compel* obedience of the court order or to compensate the litigant for injuries sustained from the disobedience." Id. at p. 827. The remedial aspects outweigh the punitive considerations. Thus, the primary beneficiaries of such an order are the individual litigants. The judicial system benefits to a lesser extent. United States v. Wendy, 575 F.2d 1025 (2d Cir. 1978).

Our review of the order, and the proceedings held in connection therewith, convinces us that the citation was framed in the nature of a coercive civil contempt. We recognize that coercive, as opposed to compensatory, civil contempt approaches the criminal arena. Thus, it can be argued that the contempt judgment should survive the invalidity of an underlying order. It is our view, however, that the "civil nature of the contempt is not turned criminal by the court's efforts at vindicating its authority, an interest which may be implicated in either civil or criminal proceedings. . . . [W]e are giving . . . weight to the punitive-remedial dichotomy." United States v. Wendy, supra, at p. 1029 n. 13. See United States v. Work Wear Corp., 602 F.2d 110 (6th Cir. 1979). We find the reasoning of Latrobe Steel Co. v. United Steelworkers, supra, particularly persuasive under the facts presented in this case:

> [T]he reasoning implicit in *United Mine Workers* requires that coercive contempt be treated in the same fashion as compensatory contempt. In coercive contempt, as with remedial contempt, the reversal of the underlying injunction indicates that the complainant never had a valid right which was enforceable against the defendant. Just as a person is not entitled to reap a monetary benefit in such circumstances, so, too, should he be unable to insist upon the exaction of coercive sanctions to finalize a process initiated by himself for his own benefit.

545 F.2d at p. 1347. [Footnotes omitted].

Validity of the Underlying Order

Having held that the viability of the contempt citation depends upon the validity of the underlying order, we now turn to the issue of whether a party may routinely discover the identities of non-witness expert consultants absent a showing of exceptional circumstances justifying disclosure.[3]

Fed.Rules Civ.Proc., rule 26, 28 U.S.C.A., governs the scope of discovery concerning experts or consultants. Subdivision (b)(4) separates these experts into four categories, applying different discovery limitations to each:

3. While any "factual findings of the magistrate adopted by the district court [are] subject to the clearly erroneous standard of Rule 53(a), . . . the legal decision of the magistrate [is] subject to the full review of this court." Small v. Olympic Prefabricators, Inc., 588 F.2d 287, 291 (9th Cir. 1978), quoting DeCosta v. Columbia Broadcasting System, Inc., 520 F.2d 499, 509 (1st Cir. 1975), cert. denied, 423 U.S. 1073, 96 S.Ct. 856, 47 L.Ed.2d 83 (1976).

(1) Experts a party expects to use at trial. The opponent may learn by interrogatories the names of these trial witnesses and the substance of their testimony but further discovery concerning them can be had only on motion and court order.

(2) Experts retained or specially employed in anticipation of litigation or preparation for trial but not expected to be used at trial. Except as provided in rule 35 for an examining physician, the facts and opinions of experts in this category can be discovered only on a showing of exceptional circumstances.

(3) Experts informally consulted in preparation for trial but not retained. No discovery may be had of the names or views of experts in this category.

(4) Experts whose information was not acquired in preparation for trial. This class, which includes both regular employees of a party not specially employed on the case and also experts who were actors or viewers of the occurrences that gave rise to suit, is not included within Rule 26(b)(4) at all and facts and opinions they have are freely discoverable as with any ordinary witness. [Footnotes omitted].

Wright & Miller, Federal Practice and Procedure: Civil § 2029, [hereinafter cited as Wright & Miller].

We are here concerned *only* with the second and third category of experts.

A. *Discovery of Experts Informally Consulted, But Not Retained or Specially Employed*

No provision in Fed.Rules Civ.Proc., rule 26 (b)(4), 28 U.S.C.A., expressly deals with non-witness experts who are informally consulted by a party in preparation for trial, but not retained or specially employed in anticipation of litigation. The advisory committee notes to the rule indicate, however, that subdivision (b)(4)(B) "precludes discovery against experts who [are] informally consulted in preparation for trial, but not retained or specially employed." We agree with the District Court that this preclusion not only encompasses information and opinions developed in anticipation of litigation, but also insulates discovery of the identity and other collateral information concerning experts consulted informally. * * * Wright & Miller, Civil § 2033; 4 Moore's Federal Practice para. 26.66[4]; Graham, Discovery of Experts Under Rule 26(b)(4) of the Federal Rules of Civil Procedure: Part One, an Analytical Study, 1976 U.Ill.L.F. 895, 938–939 [hereinafter cited as Graham, Part One].

Relying on Professor Graham's article, Ager urges that "an expert 'would be considered informally consulted if, for any reason, the consulting party did not consider the expert of any assistance', and that '[a] consulting party may consider the expert of no assistance because of his insufficient credentials, his unattractive demeanor, or his excessive fees.' " Brief of appellant at p. 37, quoting, Graham, Part One at pp. 939–940 n. 182. This view is, of course, at odds with the Trial Court's ruling that:

> The commonly accepted meaning of the term "informally consulted" necessarily implies a consultation without formality. If one makes an appointment with a medical expert to discuss a case or examine records and give advice or opinion for which a charge is made and the charge is paid or promised—what is informal about such consultation? On the other hand, an attorney meets a doctor friend at a social occasion or on the golf course and a discussion occurs concerning the case—no charge is made or contemplated— no written report rendered—such could clearly be an "informal consultation."

[R., Vol. I, p. 25.]

See also, Nemetz v. Aye, supra.

We decline to embrace either approach in its entirety. In our view, the status of each expert must be determined on an *ad hoc* basis. Several factors should be considered: (1) the manner in which the consultation was initiated; (2) the nature, type and extent of information or material provided to, or determined by, the expert in connection with his review; (3) the duration and intensity of the consultative relationship; and, (4) the terms of the consultation, if any (e.g., payment, confidentiality of test data or opinions, etc.). Of course, additional factors bearing on this determination may be examined if relevant.

Thus, while we recognize that an expert witness' lack of qualifications, unattractive demeanor, excessive fees, or adverse opinions may result in a party's decision not to use the expert at trial, nonetheless, there are situations where a witness is retained or specifically employed in anticipation of litigation prior to the discovery of such undesirable information or characteristics. On the other hand, a telephonic inquiry to an expert's office in which only general information is provided may result in informal consultation, even if a fee is charged, provided there is no follow-up consultation.

The determination of the status of the expert rests, in the first instance, with the party resisting discovery. Should the expert be considered informally consulted, that categorization should be provided in response. The propounding party should then be provided the opportunity of requesting a determination of the expert's status based on an *in camera* review by the court. Inasmuch as the District Court failed to express its views on this question, we deem it appropriate to remand rather than attempt to deal with the merits of this issue on appeal. Dandridge v. Williams, 397 U.S. 471, 476 n. 6, 90 S.Ct. 1153, 1157 n. 6, 25 L.Ed.2d 491 (1970). If the expert is considered to have been only informally consulted in anticipation of litigation, discovery is barred.

B. Discovery of the Identities of Experts Retained or Specially Employed

Subdivision (b)(4)(B) of rule 26 specifically deals with non-witness experts who have been retained or specially employed by a party in anticipation of litigation. The text of that subdivision provides that "facts or opinions" of non-witness experts retained or specially employed may only be discovered upon a showing of "exceptional circumstances under which it is impracticable for the party seeking discovery to obtain facts or opinions on the same subject by other means." Inasmuch as discovery of the identities of these experts, absent a showing of exceptional circumstances, was not expressly precluded by the text of subdivision (b)(4)(B), the District Court found the general provisions of rule 26(b)(1) controlling. Subdivision (b)(1) provides:

> (b) Scope of Discovery. Unless otherwise limited by order of the court in accordance with these rules, the scope of discovery is as follows:
>
> (1) *In General.* Parties may obtain discovery regarding any matter, not privileged, which is relevant to the subject matter involved in the pending action, . . . including the . . . identity and location of persons having knowledge of any discoverable matter. . . .

The District Court's ruling on this issue follows Arco Pipeline Co. v. S/S Trade Star, supra; Weiner v. Bache Halsey Stuart, Inc., supra; Baki v. B.F. Diamond Const. Co., supra; and Sea Colony, Inc. v. Continental Ins. Co., supra. Several decisions, however, have held that rule 26(b)(4)(B) requires a showing of exceptional circumstances before names of retained or specially employed consultants may be discovered. Guilloz v. Falmouth Hospital Association, Inc., 21 F.R.Serv.2d 1367 (D.Mass.1976) * * *.

The advisory committee notes indicate that the structure of rule 26 was largely developed around the doctrine of unfairness—designed to prevent a party from building his own case by means of his opponent's financial resources, superior diligence and more aggressive preparation. Dr. Tappen contends that "[d]iscoverability of the identity of an expert retained or specially employed by the other party but who is not to be called to testify hardly gives the discovering party a material advantage or benefit at the expense of the opposing party's preparation. Once those identities are disclosed, the discovering party is left to his own diligence and resourcefulness in contacting such experts and seeking to enlist whatever assistance they may be both able and willing to offer." Brief of appellee at pp. 12–13. The drafters of rule 26 did not contemplate such a result:

> Subdivision (b)(4)(B) is concerned only with experts retained or specially consulted in relation to trial preparation. Thus the subdivision precludes discovery against experts who were informally consulted in preparation for trial, but not retained or specially

employed. As an ancillary procedure, a party may *on a proper showing* require the other party to *name* experts retained or specially employed, but not those informally consulted. [Emphasis supplied].

We hold that the "proper showing" required to compel discovery of a non-witness expert retained or specially employed in anticipation of litigation[5] corresponds to a showing of "exceptional circumstances under which it is impracticable for the party seeking discovery to obtain facts or opinions on the same subject by other means." Fed.Rules Civ.Proc., rule 26(b)(4)(B), 28 U.S.C.A.

There are several policy considerations supporting our view. Contrary to Dr. Tappen's view, once the identities of retained or specially employed experts are disclosed, the protective provisions of the rule concerning facts known or opinions held by such experts are subverted. The expert may be contacted or his records obtained and information normally non-discoverable, under rule 26(b)(4)(B), revealed. Similarly, although perhaps rarer, the opponent may attempt to compel an expert retained or specially employed by an adverse party in anticipation of trial, but whom the adverse party does not intend to call, to testify at trial. Kaufman v. Edelstein, 539 F.2d 811 (2d Cir. 1976).[6] The possibility also exists, although we do not suggest it would occur in this case, or that it would be proper, that a party may call his opponent to the stand and ask if certain experts were retained in anticipation of trial, but not called as a witness, thereby leaving with the jury an inference that the retaining party is attempting to suppress adverse facts or opinions. Finally, we agree with Ager's view that "[d]isclosure of the identities of [medical] consultative experts would inevitably lessen the number of candid opinions available as well as the number of consultants willing to even discuss a potential medical malpractice claim with counsel. . . . [I]n medical malpractice actions [perhaps] more than any other type of litigation, the limited availability of consultative experts and the widespread aversion of many health care providers to assist plaintiff's counsel require that, absent special circumstances, discovery of the identity of evaluative consultants be denied. If one assumes that access to informed opinions is desirable in both prosecuting valid claims and eliminating groundless ones, a discovery practice that would do harm to these objectives should not be condoned." Brief of appellant at pp. 27–28, 29–30.

In sum, we hold that the identity, and other collateral information concerning an expert who is retained or specially employed in anticipation of litigation, but not expected to be called as a witness at trial, is not discoverable except as "provided in Rule 35(b)[7] or upon a showing of

---

5. The distinction between experts who are retained or specially employed in anticipation of litigation is somewhat unclear. Virginia Elec. & Power Co. v. Sun Shipbuilding & D.D. Co., 68 F.R.D. 397 (E.D.Va. 1975); compare, Seiffer v. Topsy's International Inc., 69 F.R.D. 69, 72 (D.Kan.1975).

See also: Harasimowitz v. McAllister, 78 F.R.D. 319 (E.D.Pa.1978).

6. We do no here decide the propriety of this action.

7. Rule 35(b), Fed.Rules Civ.Proc., 28 U.S.C.A., deals with the exchange of infor-

exceptional circumstances under which it is impracticable for the party seeking discovery to obtain facts or opinions on the same subject by other means."[8]   Fed.Rules Civ.Proc., rule 26(b)(4)(B), 28 U.S.C.A.   The party "seeking disclosure under Rule 26(b)(4)(B) carries a heavy burden" in demonstrating the existence of exceptional circumstances. Hoover v. United States Dept. of Interior, 611 F.2d 1132, 1142 n. 13 (5th Cir. 1980).

Disposition

The order of the District Court adjudging Lynn R. Johnson guilty of civil contempt is vacated.   The cause is remanded.   On remand, the status of the non-witness experts against whom discovery is sought should be undertaken as a two-step process.   First, was the expert informally consulted in anticipation of litigation but not retained or specially employed?   If so, no discovery may be had as to the identity or opinions of the expert.   Second, if the expert *was not* informally consulted, but rather retained or specially employed in anticipation of litigation, but not expected to testify at trial, do exceptional circumstances exist justifying disclosure of the expert's identity, opinions or other collateral information?

Vacated and remanded.

NOTE ON DISCOVERY OF EXPERTS

Before the 1970 revision of the Federal Rules the federal decisions were widely split on whether and in what circumstances an opposing party's expert could be subjected to discovery.   Many cases assimilated expert opinion to attorney work product and hence accorded it a qualified privilege.   This approach was adopted in the 1970 revision of Rule 26.   The compromise on subjecting an expert to discovery by deposition was probably ill-conceived.   See Graham, Discovery of Experts Under Rule 26(b)(4) of the Federal Rules of Civil Procedure, 1976 U.Ill.L.F. 895, 1977 U.Ill.L.F. 169, including both legal analysis and empirical inquiry, concluding, 1977 U.Ill.L.F. at 172, that the procedure for discovering an expert's opinion by means of written interrogatory "is recognized as a totally unsatisfactory method of providing adequate preparation for cross-examination and rebuttal.   In practice, full discovery is the rule, and practitioners use all available means of disclosure including both the discovery of expert's reports and depositions."   Professor Graham recommends that

mation concerning physical or mental examinations of persons.   These provisions are not at issue here.

8. Professor Albert Sacks, reporter to the advisory committee, listed two examples of exceptional circumstances at a Practising Law Institute Seminar on Discovery held in Atlanta, Georgia, September 25–26, 1970:

(a) Circumstances in which an expert employed by the party seeking discovery could not conduct important experiments and test[s] because an item of equipment, etc., needed for the test[s]

has been destroyed or is otherwise no longer available.   If the party from whom discovery is sought had been able to have its experts test the item before its destruction or nonavailability, then information obtained from those tests might be discoverable.

(b) Circumstances in which it might be impossible for a party to obtain its own expert.   Such circumstances would occur when the number of experts in a field is small and their time is already fully retained by others.

See: ALI–ABA, Civil Trial Manual p. 189.

discovery of an expert be permitted through deposition as well as interrogatory. See also Comment, Compelling Experts to Testify: A Proposal, 44 U.Chi.L.Rev. 851 (1977); Anno., 33 A.L.R.Fed. 403; Note, Discovery of the Nontestifying Expert Witness' Identity Under the Federal Rules of Civil Procedure, 37 Hastings L.J. 201 (1985); Note, Discovery and Testimony of Unretained Experts: Creating a Clear and Equitable Standard to Govern Compliance with Subpoenas, 1987 Duke L.J. 140.

C.C.P. 2034 has a provision essentially similar to F.R.C.P. 26(b)(4). C.C.P. 2034(i) allows a testifying expert's deposition to be taken upon payment of a reasonable hourly or daily rate for the expert's time. See also C.C.P. 2034(a)(3), permitting a party to demand exchange of "discoverable reports and writings, if any, made by any expert * * * in the course of preparing that expert's opinion." C.C.P. 2034(f)(2)(B) provides for the exchange of brief narrative statements of the general substance of the testimony experts are expected to give.

DIAMOND,* THE FALLACY OF THE IMPARTIAL EXPERT†

3 Archives of Crim. Psychodynamics 221 (1959).

It is quite generally assumed that the battle of the experts, that always disconcerting and often sensational disagreement of psychiatrists in testifying on issues of legal insanity and criminal responsibility, could be eliminated through the device of the neutral or impartial expert.

Such a neutral expert witness is supposedly entirely outside the traditional adversary system of the courts. Not in the employment of either the defense or the prosecution, but acting in the name of the court, such a witness presumedly can remain detached and objective. Disagreement between expert witnesses is supposed to be greatly reduced; thereby aiding the court in reaching a higher level of fair, just and impartial decisions.

* * *

I would guess that, today, nine-tenths of the psychiatrists in this country would unhesitatingly agree to the desirability of removing the psychiatric expert from the legal adversary system. It is the purpose of this editorial to challenge this widespread agreement. It is proper that this discussion take the form of an editorial, rather than that of a scientific paper. For opinion pro and con this matter can hardly be considered as objective facts to be solemnly presented as a scientific advance. Quite properly they are to be considered as personal opinions of the author and nothing more.

It is a fiction of the law that only the immediate parties to a legal action— the defendant and the plaintiff or prosecutor and their counsel—are adversaries. All else: the judge, the jury, and the witnesses, are not to be partisans. All witnesses, both expert and lay witnesses, of fact, are sworn to tell the truth, the whole truth, and nothing but the truth. This truth, as revealed in the testimony of the witness, may favor one or the other side, but the witness may not. That this is a fiction, not a reality is evidenced by the customary manner of labeling witnesses as *for* the defendant or *for* the prosecution.

* Bernard L. Diamond, M.D., Ass't Chief of Psychiatry, Mt. Zion Hospital, San Francisco. [Now Professor Emeritus of Law and Criminology, University of California, Berkeley.]

† Copyright © 1959.

I will thus concede at the outset that the expert witness called by either adversary is likely to be biased to some degree, that his opinions are not truly impartial, and that he, himself, as a party to the adversary system, becomes to a certain degree an advocate. I concede this with full awareness that both legal and medical codes of ethics demand the impartiality of the expert witness, irrespective of the side that calls him. The desirability of such an ethical ideal must not blind us to the reality that the ideal is seldom, if ever, achieved.

The crude charge is sometimes asserted that under the adversary system the expert witness sells his opinion. Because he is paid by one or the other side, he is accused of prostituting his medical knowledge in providing truthful testimony in return for the money he is paid. This charge is too base to defend by more that just a simple statement: I do not believe that this happens.

Undoubtedly what does happen is that the expert witness, through his close operational identification with one side of the conflict, does become an advocate. Because his testimony does in fact support one side of the legal battle, he, if he is at all human, must necessarily identify himself with his own opinion, and subjectively desire that "his side" win. This can vary all the way from a deliberate, conscious participation in the planning of the legal strategy with the lawyers who call upon him for expert advice and opinion, to a more aloof, detached, facsimile of impartiality that masks his secret hope for victory of his own opinion. Such a detached witness may be totally unconscious of the innumerable subtle distortions and biases in his testimony that spring from this wish to triumph.

This is well recognized by our courts of law. It is the duty of the counsel for the opposing side to cross examine the witness, revealing these distortions and biases, attempting to impeach his testimony. It is wholly legitimate to impeach the testimony through an attack upon the witness himself. That is, by eliciting evidence to show that the witness is not the expert he proclaims himself to be, that the clinical facts upon which the expert bases his opinions are not complete or may not even be true, that the skill and knowledge of the expert in his professional field are deficient, and that his expert opinions are faulty and unwarranted. Under such cross examination or through redirect examination by the counsel who engaged him, the expert is expected to defend his expert status, his clinical facts, his professional knowledge, and to justify his opinions. It is absurd to pretend that the psychiatric expert remains neutral under such a legal procedure. For the sake of his own ego integrity, he must identify himself with his own opinions and become the advocate of those opinions. But in proportion as those opinions favor one side or the other, the witness loses his hypothetical impartiality.

Because both the impartial, court appointed, independent witness as well as the adversary witness are required to submit to cross examination and defend their opinions it is here asserted that there is no such thing as a truly impartial expert; that all witnesses, regardless of who engaged them, identify closely with their own opinions, and unintentionally introduce, as a result, a certain degree of bias and deviation from their oath to tell the truth, the whole truth, and nothing but the truth.

Certain other factors also contribute to the lack of impartiality of the court appointed expert. However, let us first place these issues within the framework of a specific case. I deliberately choose a trial in which all elements are greatly exaggerated. I do not mean that the description of the trial to be given below is exaggerated, for the description is entirely accurate of what actually occurred. But the facts of the case, itself, and the circumstances of the expert examinations and testimony are far more extreme than is usual.

A certain California multi-millionaire was charged with perverse sexual acts on two adolescent boys. It was a matter of common public knowledge that the defendant had overtly and unashamedly practiced homosexuality for many years, but he had never previously been accused of seducing children. He pleaded not guilty by reason of insanity. The defendant had no insight into his mental illness, nor did he consider himself insane in any sense of the word. However, he consented to the plea on the insistence of his attorneys and his family. Practically unlimited sums of money were available for purposes of his defense. An exceptionally high powered battery of attorneys, headed by the most outstanding criminal lawyer in the area, represented him. He was quickly convicted of the acts charged in the indictment, for the evidence was conclusive. Then he was tried on the question of his insanity, as is required by the peculiar split-trial system used in California. A jury trial had been waived.

Two court appointed psychiatrists had examined him, and submitted reports to the court stating that he was sane under the M'Naghten rules; that he was a sociopath, manifesting a sexual deviation which made him a menace to society; hence he came under the California sexual psychopathy law permitting indefinite confinement.

Two other psychiatrists, who had been engaged by the defense, testified that they had examined the defendant, and found him to be suffering from a major psychosis; that he was insane under the M'Naghten rules; that his long standing homosexuality as well as the specific perverse sexual acts with the children were symptoms of his psychosis; and that he was not a sociopath or a sexual psychopath.

The court appointed psychiatrists received the usual fee for their examinations and time spent in court, probably not over fifty or one hundred dollars each. The two defense psychiatrists each were paid several thousand dollars for their examinations and time in court.

Here we have an extreme instance of the battle of the experts. How to explain the disparate testimony of the experts? Would the verdict of the judge have been more just if all four psychiatrists had been neutral? What role did the sharp discrepancy in fees paid to the witnesses play?

The differences in the diagnoses reached by the court appointed witnesses and the defense witnesses hinged largely upon the question as to whether certain statements asserted by the defendant were actually delusions or whether they were either true, or possible exaggerations or perhaps even deliberate lies. The neutral experts had only the usual hour or so of examination time, and no sources of information outside the defendant's statements, to formulate their opinion on this very difficult question. The defendant had no intention of admitting even the possibility that he might be suffering from a psychotic thinking disorder. He went to great lengths to rationalize his peculiar thoughts and to justify his conduct, both past and present, as the actions of a sane person who chose voluntarily to lead an eccentric life. He concealed from the court appointed psychiatrists the details of his past history, which included hospitalization in private sanitariums in England and in France on nine previous occasions.

It was certainly no reflection upon the clinical abilities of the two neutral experts that they reached the conclusions they did. Under the limited circumstances of their examination and with the restricted information that they had access to, it is difficult to imagine how they could have reached any other conclusions.

On the other hand, the defense psychiatrists were paid to spend practically unlimited time and to use all possible clinical facilities in their study of the defendant. Batteries of psychological tests were administered. An exhaustive neurological investigation was done, including spinal puncture and an EEG (certain symptoms suggested general paresis). An attorney was dispatched to Europe to obtain copies of the previous hospital records and to take depositions from all of the European physicians who had previously treated him over a period of some thirty years. The aged mother of the defendant was brought to California from her home in Europe and made available for a social history. When the clinical evidence was all in, the conclusion was inescapable that this man was psychotic and not responsible for his actions. The judge agreed and found him not guilty by reason of insanity, and he was committed to a state hospital.

Beyond doubt the verdict was just. The great wealth of the defendant was not used to purchase biased and untruthful testimony from dubious experts. Rather it was used to make certain that every scrap of evidence, every clinical possibility was exhaustively investigated, and that nothing was overlooked. The injustice inherent in this extreme example is, of course, the fact that if this defendant had been a poor man he would have probably been found to be sane, and would have been imprisoned.

The assumption is often made that the elimination of the adversary expert witness will lead to testimony of greater objectivity, thoroughness, and accuracy. Corollary to this assumption is the implication that examinations performed by adversary witnesses are neither objective, thorough, nor accurate. In our case of the millionaire sex offender, just the opposite was true. But how about in ordinary cases? It is very difficult to give a definite answer to this question without having some basis of statistical information. However, I believe there are logical reasons to infer that quite generally psychiatric investigations done for the defense are likely to be more thorough than those done by the ordinary court appointed psychiatrist. The latter is apt to approach the examination situation in a routine manner, a job to be done, so to speak, and to restrict his time, energy, and thought on the case to a level determined by the habitual fees paid for this work. The public funds available to the court appointed psychiatrist are very limited, the courts taking it for granted that he should be able to perform an adequate examination and reach a conclusion in one or two hours. Rarely is money available for auxiliary examinations, such as projective techniques. The fact that there are a few notable exceptions to this situation does not alter the general inference.

* * *

I think it is possible to make the generalization that court appointments tend to be handled by psychiatrists as a kind of routine job, in which, despite totally unreasonable time restrictions, there nevertheless results a fairly medium level of clinical competence. The psychiatrist called by the defense, on the other hand, is much more apt to regard the examination situation as a highly challenging task, to which he devotes considerable time and effort, with or without adequate remuneration. If for his own personal reasons he cannot enter into the case on this superior level, he is likely to turn it down altogether, rather than handle it as just routine.

Does the fact that a psychiatrist is called as a witness for the court, that he is neither directly involved with the prosecution nor the defense make it more likely that his opinion is less biased and more truthful and objective than that of the adversary witness? I concede that the defense psychiatrist is apt to be biased in favor of the side which has engaged him. It is my editorial opinion that court appointed experts are consistently biased in favor of the prosecution. The selection of court appointed psychiatrists is seldom made from the random universe of the psychiatric population. Certain psychiatrists tend to be appointed over and over again. These are generally men who have an active interest in forensic psychiatry. More than not they tend to be Kraepelinian and less dynamic in their approach to their cases. They are often drawn from the ranks of administrative psychiatry, an area deficient in psychoanalytically oriented therapists. They are less inclined to probe deeply, more inclined to uncritically accept surface manifestations, and are prone to interpret the legal criteria for insanity in a narrowly restricted way. (Many of my forensic psychiatrist friends will take me to task for making these assertions—I will merely tell them that they are the exceptions who prove the rule.)

* * *

So I claim that there is no such thing as a neutral, impartial witness. No matter whether a psychiatrist is engaged by the defense or by the prosecution or is allowed to remain completely outside of the system of adversary conflict, he is bound to be biased and partial, and strongly motivated towards advocacy of his particular prejudiced point of view.

This lack of impartiality of the expert witness need not be a serious obstacle to the administration of justice. It is inherent in our traditional system of adversary procedure that both sides be presented to the jury and the jury is to choose within the conflict of evidence that side which is most credible. However, serious injustice may occur when an adversary witness is disguised as a neutral witness. When actual partiality is masked as impartiality, the judge and jury are deceived and misled. The response is less to the credibility of the witness and the logic of his testimony and more to his status as a so-called neutral. In Massachusetts, where the Briggs law has been in operation for a good many years, it is still permissible for the defense to call its own expert witnesses. But advocates of the neutral system of expert testimony use as one of their chief arguments the fact that the jury almost invariably accepts the opinion of the neutral experts. They consider it progress that under such circumstances it is hardly worth while for the defense to call in its own experts. Thus the battle of the experts is eliminated. But does this provide a better brand of justice than does the adversary method? I doubt it. In a legal situation where impartiality is impossible, let us frankly label the witness for what he is, and let the jury choose. To be sure there will be instances of bad choice, of incorrect, illogical and unjust verdicts. But to disguise the partisan character of the expert through status labels of neutrality and court appointment will not contribute to more rational jury decision.

* * *

The traditional adversary system of calling witnesses for each side and then examining the witness by direct and cross examination has been evolved for just the purpose of exposing these shortcomings and biases. The court and jury are then free to take them into consideration in allotting the weight which it will attach to the testimony of each witness. To utilize a system in which the expert witness is labeled as "impartial" in no way eliminates the shortcomings; it merely conceals them from the jury and creates the illusion of psychiatric omniscience. Such illusions may be good for the public relations of psychiatry, but they are not good for the administration of justice.*

VINSON v. SUPERIOR COURT

Supreme Court of California, 1987.
43 Cal.3d 833, 239 Cal.Rptr. 292, 740 P.2d 404.

Mosk, Justice.

The plaintiff in a suit for sexual harassment and intentional infliction of severe emotional distress petitions for a writ of mandate and/or prohibition to direct respondent court to forbid her pending psychiatric examination, or in the alternative to protect her from any inquiry into her sexual history, habits, or practices. She also requests that her attorney be allowed to attend the examination if it is held. We conclude that the examination should be permitted but that a writ should issue to restrict its scope. We further conclude that her counsel should not be present.

Plaintiff is a 59–year–old widow who in 1979 applied for a job in Oakland with a federally funded program, administered at the time by defendant Peralta Community College District, under the direction of co-defendant Grant. Plaintiff alleges that Grant, during an interview with her in a private cubicle, commented on how attractive she appeared for a woman of her age. He assertedly made some salacious observations regarding her anatomy and expressed his desires with regard thereto. He allegedly concluded the interview by intimating that acquiring the position was subject to a condition precedent: her acquiescence to his sexual yearnings. Plaintiff claims she declined his advances as unconscionable and left greatly distraught.

Unknown to Grant, plaintiff was later hired by defendant college district as a certification technician. She asserts that once he discovered she was working for the program, he had her transferred to the payroll unit, a position for which he apparently knew she had no training. Soon thereafter he terminated her employment.

Plaintiff filed suit on several causes of action, among them sexual harassment, wrongful discharge, and intentional infliction of emotional distress. Defendants' actions are said to have caused her to suffer continuing emotional distress, loss of sleep, anxiety, mental anguish, humiliation, reduced self-esteem, and other consequences.

Defendants moved for an order compelling her to undergo a medical and a psychological examination.[1] The examinations were meant to test the true extent of her injuries and to measure her ability to function in the workplace. Plaintiff opposed the motion as a violation

---

* Compare the lawyer's viewpoint of the so-called impartial expert, as expressed in Louisell, Book Review, 45 Calif.L.Rev. 572 (1957) (reviewing Report of the Special Committee, Association of the Bar of the City of New York, Impartial Medical Testimony (1956)).

1. We use the terms "psychiatric," "psychological" and "mental" examination interchangeably for the purposes of this issue.

of her right to privacy. In the alternative, if the court were to permit the examination she requested a protective order shielding her from any probing into her sexual history or practices, and asked that her attorney be allowed to attend in order to assure compliance with the order. The court granted the motion without imposing any of these limitations. Plaintiff petitioned the Court of Appeal for a writ of prohibition and/or mandate to direct the trial court to forbid the examination or to issue appropriate protective orders. The Court of Appeal denied the petition.

We use prerogative writs in discovery matters only to review questions that are of general importance to the trial courts and the profession, and when broad principles can be enunciated to guide the courts in future cases. (Oceanside Union School Dist. v. Superior Court (1962) 58 Cal.2d 180, 185–186, fn. 4, 23 Cal.Rptr. 375, 373 P.2d 439; Pacific Tel. & Tel. Co. v. Superior Court (1970) 2 Cal.3d 161, 169, 84 Cal. Rptr. 718, 465 P.2d 854.) As we shall see, intervening legislative enactments have partially resolved some of the issues raised by this petition. Nonetheless, important questions remain regarding the right of a defendant in a case alleging sexual harassment and emotional distress to conduct discovery and a plaintiff's countervailing right to privacy.

I. *The Appropriateness of a Mental Examination*

Plaintiff first contends the psychiatric examination should not be permitted because it infringes on her right to privacy. Before we can entertain this constitutional question, we must determine the statutory scope of the discovery laws.[2]

Code of Civil Procedure section 2032, subdivision (a),[3] permits the mental examination of a party in any action in which the mental condition of that party is in controversy. Plaintiff disputes that her mental condition is in controversy. She points to Cody v. Marriott Corp. (D.Mass.1984) 103 F.R.D. 421, 422, a case interpreting rule 35(a) of the Federal Rules of Civil Procedure. Like the California rule that was patterned on it, rule 35 requires that physical or mental condition be "in controversy" before an examination is appropriate.[4] *Cody* was

---

2. Part 4, title 3, chapter 3, article 3, of the Code of Civil Procedure (§§ 2016–2036.5), the applicable legislation on depositions and discovery at the time this action began, has been repealed. (Stats.1986, ch. 1334, § 1.) The repeal was operative July 1, 1987, on which date a new article 3 (entitled the Civil Discovery Act of 1986) came into effect. The act provides, however, that the use of a discovery method initiated before July 1, 1987, will be governed by the law regulating that method at the time it was initiated. (Stats.1987, ch. 86, § 20). We must therefore apply the superseded discovery procedures to this case. But as we shall show by appropriate references to the new act, many of its relevant provisions are substantially similar.

3. Unless otherwise noted, all further statutory references are to the Code of Civil Procedure, and this and all further references to sections 2016 to 2036 refer to the version of those sections operative until July 1, 1987.

4. Because section 2032 was based on federal rule 35, judicial construction of the federal rule may be useful in construing section 2032. (Reuter v. Superior Court (1979) 93 Cal.App.3d 332, 337, 155 Cal. Rptr. 525.)

an employment discrimination case in which the plaintiffs alleged mental and emotional distress. The court held that the claim of emotional distress did not ipso facto place the plaintiff's mental state in controversy.

The reasoning of *Cody* rested in large part on Schlagenhauf v. Holder (1964) 379 U.S. 104, 85 S.Ct. 234, 13 L.Ed.2d 152, in which the United States Supreme Court examined the "in controversy" requirement. In *Schlagenhauf* the plaintiffs were passengers injured when their bus collided with the rear of a truck. The defendant truck company, in answer to a cross-claim by the codefendant bus company, charged that the bus driver had been unfit to drive and moved to have him undergo a mental and physical examination. The Supreme Court recognized that at times the pleadings may be sufficient to put mental or physical condition in controversy, as when a plaintiff in a negligence action alleges mental or physical injury. (Id. at p. 119, 85 S.Ct. at p. 243.) But it determined that the driver had not asserted his mental condition in support of or in a defense of a claim, nor did the general charge of negligence put his mental state in controversy. (Id. at pp. 119–122, 85 S.Ct. at pp. 243–245.) *Schlagenhauf* thus stands for the proposition that one party's unsubstantiated allegation cannot put the mental state of another in controversy.

It is another matter entirely, however, when a party places his *own* mental state in controversy by alleging mental and emotional distress. Unlike the bus driver in *Schlagenhauf,* who had a controversy thrust upon him, a party who chooses to allege that he has mental and emotional difficulties can hardly deny his mental state is in controversy. To the extent the decision in *Cody,* supra, 103 F.R.D. 421, is inconsistent with this conclusion, we decline to follow it. (See also Reuter v. Superior Court, supra, 93 Cal.App.3d at p. 340, 155 Cal.Rptr. 525.)

In the case at bar, plaintiff haled defendants into court and accused them of causing her various mental and emotional ailments. Defendants deny her charges. As a result, the existence and extent of her mental injuries is indubitably in dispute. In addition, by asserting a causal link between her mental distress and defendants' conduct, plaintiff implicitly claims it was not caused by a preexisting mental condition, thereby raising the question of alternative sources for the distress. We thus conclude that her mental state is in controversy.

We emphasize that our conclusion is based solely on the allegations of emotional and mental damages in this case. A simple sexual harassment claim asking compensation for having to endure an oppressive work environment or for wages lost following an unjust dismissal would not normally create a controversy regarding the plaintiff's mental state. To hold otherwise would mean that every person who brings such a suit implicitly asserts he or she is mentally unstable, obviously an untenable proposition.

Determining that the mental or physical condition of a party is in controversy is but the first step in our analysis. In contrast to more pedestrian discovery procedures, a mental or physical examination requires the discovering party to obtain a court order. The court may grant the motion only for good cause shown. (§ 2032, subd. (a).) [5]

Section 2036 defines a showing of "good cause" as requiring that the party produce specific facts justifying discovery and that the inquiry be relevant to the subject matter of the action or reasonably calculated to lead to the discovery of admissible evidence.[6] The requirement of a court order following a showing of good cause is doubtless designed to protect an examinee's privacy interest by preventing an examination from becoming an annoying fishing expedition. While a plaintiff may place his mental state in controversy by a general allegation of severe emotional distress, the opposing party may not require him to undergo psychiatric testing solely on the basis of speculation that something of interest may surface. (Schlagenhauf v. Holder, supra, 379 U.S. at pp. 116–122, 85 S.Ct. at pp. 241–245.)

Plaintiff in the case at bar asserts that she continues to suffer diminished self-esteem, reduced motivation, sleeplessness, loss of appetite, fear, lessened ability to help others, loss of social contacts, anxiety, mental anguish, loss of reputation, and severe emotional distress. In their motion defendants pointed to these allegations. Because the truth of these claims is relevant to plaintiff's cause of action and justifying facts have been shown with specificity, good cause as to these assertions has been demonstrated. Subject to limitations necessitated by plaintiff's right to privacy, defendants must be allowed to investigate the continued existence and severity of plaintiff's alleged damages.

II. *Privacy Limitations on the Scope of a Mental Examination*

If we find, as we do, that an examination may be ordered, plaintiff urges us to circumscribe its scope to exclude any probing into her sexual history, habits, or practices. Such probing, she asserts, would intrude impermissibly into her protected sphere of privacy. Furthermore, it would tend to contravene the state's strong interest in eradicating sexual harassment by means of private suits for damages. An examination into a plaintiff's past and present sexual practices would inhibit the bringing of meritorious sexual harassment actions by compelling the plaintiff—whose privacy has already been invaded by the harassment—to suffer another intrusion into her private life.

A right to privacy was recognized in the seminal case of Griswold v. Connecticut (1965) 381 U.S. 479, 85 S.Ct. 1678, 14 L.Ed.2d 510. It protects both the marital relationship (ibid.) and the sexual lives of the unmarried (Eisenstadt v. Baird (1972) 405 U.S. 438, 92 S.Ct. 1029, 31

---

5. After July 1, 1987, this requirement is contained in section 2032, subdivision (d).

6. This section has been repealed and has apparently not been replaced by equiv- alent language. There is no indication, however, that the Legislature intended repeal of former section 2036 to change the requirements for good cause in regard to mental examinations.

L.Ed.2d 349). More significantly, California accords privacy the constitutional status of an "inalienable right," on a par with defending life and possessing property. (Cal.Const., art. I, § 1; White v. Davis (1975) 13 Cal.3d 757, 120 Cal.Rptr. 94, 533 P.2d 222.) California's privacy protection similarly embraces sexual relations. (See Fults v. Superior Court (1979) 88 Cal.App.3d 899, 152 Cal.Rptr. 210; Morales v. Superior Court (1979) 99 Cal.App.3d 283, 160 Cal.Rptr. 194.)

Defendants acknowledge plaintiff's right to privacy *in abstracto* but maintain she has waived it for purposes of the present suit. In addition, they urge us to take heed of their right to a fair trial, which they claim depends on a "meaningful" examination of plaintiff. Defendants contend they would not have requested a mental examination if plaintiff had simply brought a sexual harassment suit; but because she claims emotional and mental damage, they should be entitled to present expert testimony on the extent of the injury. Preparing such testimony, they suggest, requires not simply a mental examination, but one without substantial restrictions on its scope.

We cannot agree that the mere initiation of a sexual harassment suit, even with the rather extreme mental and emotional damage plaintiff claims to have suffered, functions to waive all her privacy interests, exposing her persona to the unfettered mental probing of defendants' expert. Plaintiff is not compelled, as a condition to entering the courtroom, to discard entirely her mantle of privacy. At the same time, plaintiff cannot be allowed to make her very serious allegations without affording defendants an opportunity to put their truth to the test.

In Britt v. Superior Court (1978) 20 Cal.3d 844, 143 Cal.Rptr. 695, 574 P.2d 766, we faced a similar conflict between discovery procedures and the parties' constitutional rights. The plaintiffs were property owners near an airport operated by the local port district. They sued the district for diminution of property values, personal injuries, and emotional disturbance brought about by the airport's activities. The defendant sought to discover the plaintiffs' entire medical history, including all illnesses, injuries, and mental or emotional disturbances for which they had sought treatment at any time in their lives. Furthermore, it asked for information regarding their membership in various community organizations.

Responding to the assertion that the plaintiffs had waived their right to privacy by bringing suit, we stated that "while the filing of a lawsuit may implicitly bring about a partial waiver of one's constitutional right of associational privacy, the scope of such 'waiver' must be narrowly rather than expansively construed, so that plaintiffs will not be unduly deterred from instituting lawsuits by the fear of exposure of their private associational affiliations and activities." (Id. at p. 859, 143 Cal.Rptr. 695, 574 P.2d 766.) Therefore, we noted, an implicit waiver of a party's constitutional rights encompasses only discovery directly relevant to the plaintiff's claim and essential to the fair resolution of the lawsuit. (Id. at p. 859, 143 Cal.Rptr. 695, 574 P.2d 766; see also In re Lifschutz (1970) 2 Cal.3d 415, 431, 85 Cal.Rptr. 829, 467 P.2d 557.)

Plaintiff's present mental and emotional condition is directly relevant to her claim and essential to a fair resolution of her suit; she has waived her right to privacy in this respect by alleging continuing mental ailments. But she has not, merely by initiating this suit for sexual harassment and emotional distress, implicitly waived her right to privacy in respect to her sexual history and practices. Defendants fail to explain why probing into this area is directly relevant to her claim and essential to its fair resolution. Plaintiff does not contend the alleged acts were detrimental to her present sexuality. Her sexual history is even less relevant to her claim. We conclude that she has not waived her right to sexual privacy.

But even though plaintiff retains certain unwaived privacy rights, these rights are not necessarily absolute. On occasion her privacy interests may have to give way to her opponent's right to a fair trial. Thus courts must balance the right of civil litigants to discover relevant facts against the privacy interests of persons subject to discovery. (Valley Bank of Nevada v. Superior Court (1975) 15 Cal.3d 652, 657, 125 Cal.Rptr. 553, 542 P.2d 977.)

Before proceeding, we note the Legislature recently enacted a measure designed to protect the privacy of plaintiffs in cases such as these. Section 2036.1 (operative until July 1, 1987; presently, substantially the same provision is contained in § 2017, subdivision (d)), provides that in a civil suit alleging conduct that constitutes sexual harassment, sexual assault, or sexual battery, any party seeking discovery concerning the plaintiff's sexual conduct with individuals other than the alleged perpetrator must establish specific facts showing good cause for that discovery, and that the inquiry is relevant to the subject matter and reasonably calculated to lead to the discovery of admissible evidence.[7] (See also Priest v. Rotary (N.D.Cal.1983) 98 F.R.D. 755.) We must determine whether the general balancing of interests embodied in this new legislation has obviated the need for us to engage in an individualized balancing of privacy with discovery in the case at bar.

In enacting the measure, the Legislature took pains to declare that "The discovery of sexual aspects of complainant's [sic] lives, as well as those of their past and current friends and acquaintances, has the clear potential to discourage complaints and to annoy and harass litigants. . . . without protection against it, individuals whose intimate lives are unjustifiably and offensively intruded upon might face the 'Catch–22' of invoking their remedy only at the risk of enduring further

---

7. Although the motion to order an examination was made before this provision went into effect, we apply the section to the case at bar because procedural changes generally govern pending as well as future cases. (Woodland Hills Residents Assn., Inc. v. City Council (1979) 23 Cal.3d 917, 930–932, 154 Cal.Rptr. 503, 593 P.2d 200; Pacific Vegetable Oil Corp. v. C.S.T., Ltd. (1946) 29 Cal.2d 228, 232–233, 174 P.2d 441; Sour v. Superior Court (1934) 1 Cal.2d 542, 545, 36 P.2d 373.)

intrusions into the details of their personal lives in discovery. . . . [¶] . . . Absent extraordinary circumstances, inquiry into those areas should not be permitted, either in discovery or at trial." (Stats. 1985, ch. 1328, § 1.)[8]

Nowhere do defendants establish specific facts justifying inquiry into plaintiff's zone of sexual privacy or show how such discovery would be relevant. Rather they make only the most sweeping assertions regarding the need for wide latitude in the examination. Because good cause has not been shown, discovery into this area of plaintiff's life must be denied.

Section 2036.1, thus amply protects plaintiff's privacy interests. We anticipate that in the majority of sexual harassment suits, a separate weighing of privacy against discovery will not be necessary. It should normally suffice for the court, in ruling on whether good cause exists for probing into the intimate life of a victim of sexual harassment, sexual battery, or sexual assault, to evaluate the showing of good cause in light of the legislative purpose in enacting this section and the plaintiff's constitutional right to privacy.

III. *Presence of Counsel*

In the event a limited psychiatric examination is proper, plaintiff urges us to authorize the attendance of her attorney. She fears that the examiner will stray beyond the permitted area of inquiry. Counsel would monitor the interview and shield her from inappropriate interrogation. And depicting the examination as an "alien and frankly hostile environment," she asserts that she needs her lawyer to provide her with aid and comfort.

Defendants, joined by amici California Psychiatric Association and Northern California Psychiatric Association, counter that a meaningful mental examination cannot be conducted with an attorney interposing objections. And if plaintiff's counsel is present, defense counsel would also seek to attend. Defendants maintain these adversaries would likely convert the examination into a chaotic deposition.

We contemplated whether counsel must be allowed to attend the psychiatric examination of a client in Edwards v. Superior Court (1976) 16 Cal.3d 905, 130 Cal.Rptr. 14, 549 P.2d 846. The plaintiff in *Edwards* alleged that because of the defendant school district's failure to properly instruct and supervise users of school equipment, she sustained

---

8. Plaintiff suggests that section 2036.1 does not adequately protect her privacy interests because section 2032 already requires "good cause" for a mental examination, and nothing is added by again requiring good cause for inquiry into a plaintiff's sexual history and practices. But the above-quoted legislative declaration accompanying section 2036.1, i.e., that inquiry into sexuality should not be permitted absent "extraordinary circumstances," suggests that a stronger showing of good cause must be made to justify inquiry into this topic than is needed for a general examination. Furthermore, section 2032 merely requires good cause for the examination as a whole; in emotional distress cases that will often be present. By contrast, a defendant in a sexual harassment case desiring to ask sex-related questions must show specific facts justifying that particular inquiry.

physical and emotional injuries. The trial court granted a motion compelling her to undergo a psychiatric examination alone. Holding that the plaintiff could not insist on the presence of her counsel, a majority of this court denied her petition for a peremptory writ.

The plaintiff in *Edwards* raised many of the points urged upon us here. She asserted that her attorney should be present to protect her from improper inquiries. We were skeptical that a lawyer, unschooled in the ways of the mental health profession, would be able to discern the psychiatric relevance of the questions. And the examiner should have the freedom to probe deeply into the plaintiff's psyche without interference by a third party. (Id. at p. 911, 130 Cal.Rptr. 14, 549 P.2d 846.) The plaintiff further suggested counsel should be present to lend her comfort and support in an inimical setting. We responded that an examinee could view almost any examination of this sort, even by her own expert, as somewhat hostile. Whatever comfort her attorney's handholding might afford was substantially outweighed by the distraction and potential disruption caused by the presence of a third person. (Ibid.) Finally, we concluded counsel's presence was not necessary to ensure accurate reporting. Verbatim transcription might inhibit the examinee, preventing an effective examination. Furthermore, other procedural devices—pretrial discovery of the examiner's notes or cross-examination, for example—were available for the plaintiff's protection. (Id. at pp. 911–912, 130 Cal.Rptr. 14, 549 P.2d 846.)

A number of federal courts have since pondered this question. The court in Zabkowicz v. West Bend Co. (E.D.Wis.1984) 585 F.Supp. 635, agreed that the plaintiff in an action charging sexual harassment and extreme emotional distress was entitled to have her attorney or a recording device present to ensure that the defendant's expert did not overstep his bounds. But in another federal case, Lowe v. Philadelphia Newspapers (E.D.Pa.1983) 101 F.R.D. 296, the court ruled the plaintiff could not have counsel present at the psychiatric examination, although she could have a psychiatrist or other medical expert as an observer. In *Lowe* there were indications the defense had engaged in offensive tactics during discovery, which may explain the court's willingness to allow third parties into the examination. In contrast, in Brandenberg v. El Al Israel Airlines (S.D.N.Y.1978) 79 F.R.D. 543, there were no signs portending abuse, and the court denied the plaintiff's request for the presence of her counsel. These cases suggest that in the federal courts a mental examinee has no absolute right to the presence of an attorney; but when the circumstances warrant it, the courts may fashion some means of protecting an examinee from intrusive or offensive probing.

Despite the dissent in *Edwards,* 16 Cal.3d 905, 914, 130 Cal.Rptr. 14, 549 P.2d 846 (dis. opn. by Sullivan, J. and Mosk, J.), we conclude that a reconsideration of that decision—which is barely 10 years old—is not justified.[9] We emphasize, however, that *Edwards* should be viewed

---

9. Section 2032, subdivision (g) (operative July 1, 1987), now specifically provides for the attendance of an attorney at a *physical* examination. (See Sharff v. Superior Court (1955) 44 Cal.2d 508, 282 P.2d 896.) Subdivision (g)(2) states, however,

as standing for the proposition that the presence of an attorney is not *required* during a mental examination. In light of their broad discretion in discovery matters (see generally Greyhound Corp. v. Superior Court (1961) 56 Cal.2d 355, 15 Cal.Rptr. 90, 364 P.2d 266), trial courts retain the power to permit the presence of counsel or to take other prophylactic measures when needed.

Plaintiff makes no showing that the court abused its discretion in excluding her counsel from the examination. Her fears are wholly unfounded at this point; not a shred of evidence has been produced to show that defendants' expert will not respect her legitimate rights to privacy or might disobey any court-imposed restrictions. Plaintiff's apprehension appears to derive less from the reality of the proposed analysis than from the popular image of mental examinations.

Plaintiff's interests can be adequately protected without having her attorney present. In the first place, section 2032 requires the court granting a physical or mental examination to specify its conditions and scope. We must assume, absent evidence to the contrary, that the examiner will proceed in an ethical manner, adhering to these constraints. And if plaintiff truly fears that the examiner will probe into impermissible areas, she may record the examination on audio tape. This is an unobtrusive measure that will permit evidence of abuse to be presented to the court in any motion for sanctions.[10]

Plaintiff refers us to the history of psychiatric examinations for victims of sexual assault. Such examinations were widely viewed as inhibiting prosecutions for rape by implicitly placing the victim on trial, leading to a legislative prohibition of examinations to assess credibility. (Pen.Code, § 1112; see also Note, Psychiatric Examinations of Sexual Assault Victims: A Reevaluation (1982) 15 U.C. Davis L.Rev. 973.) The victim of sexual harassment is analogous to the prosecutrix in a rape case, plaintiff asserts, and she points to legislative findings that discovery of sexual aspects of complainants' lives "has the clear potential to discourage complaints." (Stats.1985, ch. 1328, § 1.) If we conclude on the basis of general considerations that a mental examination is appropriate and that it should occur without the presence of counsel, plaintiff urges us to adopt a special rule exempting those who bring harassment charges from either or both of these requirements.

We believe that in these circumstances such a special rule is unwarranted. In the first place, we should be guided by the maxim

that nothing in the discovery statutes shall be construed to alter, amend, or affect existing case law with respect to the presence of counsel or other persons during a mental examination by agreement or court order. Had the Legislature felt it desirable to have counsel present at psychiatric examinations, it would certainly have provided for this in its thorough revision of the section. Indeed, in the course of that revision the Legislature considered and rejected a provision that would have annulled our decision in *Edwards* by permitting counsel to attend a mental examination.

10. We note that the new discovery act explicitly provides both examiners and examinees the opportunity to perpetuate the interview on audio tape. (§ 2032, subd. (g) (2) (operative July 1, 1987).)

that *entia non sunt multiplicanda praeter necessitatem:* we should carve out exceptions from general rules only when the facts require it. The state admittedly has a strong interest in eradicating the evil of sexual harassment, and the threat of a mental examination could conceivably dampen a plaintiff's resolve to bring suit. But we have seen that those who allege harassment have substantial protection under existing procedural rules. In general it is unlikely that a simple sexual harassment suit will justify a mental examination. Such examinations may ordinarily be considered only in cases in which the alleged mental or emotional distress is said to be ongoing. When an examination is permitted, investigation by a psychiatrist into the private life of a plaintiff is severely constrained, and sanctions are available to guarantee those restrictions are respected.

Finally, the mental examination in this case largely grows out of plaintiff's emotional distress claim. We do not believe the state has a greater interest in preventing emotional distress in sexual harassment victims than it has in preventing such distress in the victims of any other tort.

* * *

3. OTHER PRIVILEGES

HERBERT v. LANDO

Supreme Court of the United States, 1979.
441 U.S. 153, 99 S.Ct. 1635, 60 L.Ed.2d 115.*

MR. JUSTICE WHITE delivered the opinion of the Court.

By virtue of the First and Fourteenth Amendments, neither the Federal nor a State Government may make any law "abridging the freedom of speech, or of the press. . . ." The question here is whether those Amendments should be construed to provide further protection for the press when sued for defamation than has hitherto been recognized. More specifically, we are urged to hold for the first time that when a member of the press is alleged to have circulated damaging falsehoods and is sued for injury to the plaintiff's reputation, the plaintiff is barred from inquiring into the editorial processes of those responsible for the publication, even though the inquiry would produce evidence material to the proof of a critical element of his cause of action.

I

Petitioner, Anthony Herbert, is a retired Army officer who had extended wartime service in Vietnam and who received widespread media attention in 1969–1970 when he accused his superior officers of covering up reports of atrocities and other war crimes. Three years later, on February 4, 1973, respondent Columbia Broadcasting System,

---

* Some of the Court's footnotes are omitted.

Inc. (CBS), broadcast a report on petitioner and his accusations. The program was produced and edited by respondent Barry Lando and was narrated by respondent Mike Wallace. Lando later published a related article in Atlantic Monthly magazine. Herbert then sued Lando, Wallace, CBS, and Atlantic Monthly for defamation in Federal District Court, basing jurisdiction on diversity of citizenship. In his complaint, Herbert alleged that the program and article falsely and maliciously portrayed him as a liar and a person who had made war-crimes charges to explain his relief from command, and he requested substantial damages for injury to his reputation and to the literary value of a book he had just published recounting his experiences.

Although his cause of action arose under New York State defamation law, Herbert conceded that because he was a "public figure" the First and Fourteenth Amendments precluded recovery absent proof that respondents had published a damaging falsehood "with 'actual malice'—that is, with knowledge that it was false or with reckless disregard of whether it was false or not." This was the holding of New York Times v. Sullivan, 376 U.S. 254, 280, 84 S.Ct. 710, 726, 11 L.Ed.2d 686 (1964), with respect to alleged libels of public officials, and extended to "public figures" by Curtis Publishing Co. v. Butts, 388 U.S. 130, 87 S.Ct. 1975, 18 L.Ed.2d 1094 (1967). Under this rule, absent knowing falsehood, liability requires proof of reckless disregard for truth, that is, that the defendant "in fact entertained serious doubts as to the truth of his publication." St. Amant v. Thompson, 390 U.S. 727, 731, 88 S.Ct. 1323, 1325, 20 L.Ed.2d 262 (1968). Such "subjective awareness of probable falsity," Gertz v. Robert Welch, Inc., 418 U.S. 323, 335 n. 6, 94 S.Ct. 2997, 3004, 41 L.Ed.2d 789 (1974), may be found if "there are obvious reasons to doubt the veracity of the informant or the accuracy of his reports." St. Amant v. Thompson, supra, 390 U.S., at 732, 88 S.Ct., at 1326.

In preparing to prove his case in light of these requirements, Herbert deposed Lando at length and sought an order to compel answers to a variety of questions to which response was refused on the ground that the First Amendment protected against inquiry into the state of mind of those who edit, produce or publish, and into the editorial process.[2] Applying the standard of Fed.Rule Civ.Proc. 26(b), which permits discovery of any matter "relevant to the subject matter

2. The Court of Appeals summarized the inquiries to which Lando objected as follows:

"1. Lando's conclusions during his research and investigations regarding people or leads to be pursued, or not to be pursued, in connection with the '60 Minutes' segment and the Atlantic Monthly article;

"2. Lando's conclusions about facts imparted by interviewees and his state of mind with respect to the veracity of persons interviewed;

"3. The basis for conclusions where Lando testified that he did reach a conclusion concerning the veracity of persons, information or events;

"4. Conversations between Lando and Wallace about matter to be included or excluded from the broadcast publication; and

"5. Lando's intentions as manifested by his decision to include or exclude certain material." 568 F.2d 974, 983 (CA2 1977).

involved in the pending action" if it would either be admissible in evidence or "appears reasonably calculated to lead to the discovery of admissible evidence," the District Court ruled that because the defendant's state of mind was of "central importance" to the issue of malice in the case, it was obvious that the questions were relevant and "entirely appropriate to Herbert's efforts to discover whether Lando had any reason to doubt the veracity of certain of his sources, or, equally significant, to prefer the veracity of one source over another." 73 F.R.D. 387, 395, 396 (S.D.N.Y.1977). The District Court rejected the claim of constitutional privilege * * *.

* * *

II

Civil and criminal liability for defamation was well established in the common law when the First Amendment was adopted, and there is no indication that the Framers intended to abolish such liability. Until *New York Times* the prevailing jurisprudence was that "[l]ibelous utterances [are not] within the area of constitutionally protected speech. . . ." Beauharnais v. Illinois, 343 U.S. 250, 266, 72 S.Ct. 725, 735, 96 L.Ed. 919 (1952); * * *. The accepted view was that neither civil nor criminal liability for defamatory publications abridge freedom of speech or freedom of the press, and a majority of jurisdictions made publishers liable civilly for their defamatory publications regardless of their intent.[4] *New York Times* and *Butts* effected major changes in the standards applicable to civil libel actions. Under these cases public officials and public figures who sue for defamation must prove knowing or reckless falsehood in order to establish liability. Later, in Gertz v. Robert Welch, Inc., [supra,] the Court held that nonpublic figures must demonstrate some fault on the defendant's part and, at least where knowing or reckless untruth is not shown, some proof of actual injury to the plaintiff before liability may be imposed and damages awarded.

These cases rested primarily on the conviction that the common law of libel gave insufficient protection to the First Amendment guarantees of freedom of speech and freedom of press and that to avoid self-

---

4. See, e.g., Restatement of Torts § 580 (1938); Pedrick, Freedom of the Press and the Law of Libel: The Modern Revised Translation, 49 Corn.L.Q. 581, 583–584 (1964); Developments in the Law—Defamation, 69 Harv.L.Rev. 875, 902–910 (1956). In Peck v. Tribune Co., 214 U.S. 185, 189, 29 S.Ct. 554, 555, 53 L.Ed. 960 (1909), Mr. Justice Holmes summarized the prevailing view of strict liability in the course of reviewing a libel judgment rendered in a federal diversity of citizenship action:

"There was some suggestion that the defendant published the portrait by mistake, and without knowledge that it was the plaintiff's portrait or was not what it purported to be. But the fact, if it was one, was no excuse. If the publication was libellous the defendant took the risk. As was said of such matters by Lord Mansfield, 'Whatever a man publishes he publishes at his peril.' The King v. Woodfall, Lofft 776, 781. . . . The reason is plain. A libel is harmful on its face. If a man sees fit to publish manifestly hurtful statements concerning an individual, without other justification than exists for an advertisement or a piece of news, the usual principles of tort will make him liable, if the statements are false or are true only of some one else."

censorship it was essential that liability for damages be conditioned on the specified showing of culpable conduct by those who publish damaging falsehood. Given the required proof, however, damages liability for defamation abridges neither freedom of speech nor freedom of the press.

Nor did these cases suggest any First Amendment restriction on the sources from which the plaintiff could obtain the necessary evidence to prove the critical elements of his cause of action. On the contrary, *New York Times* and its progeny made it essential to proving liability that plaintiffs focus on the conduct and state of mind of the defendant. To be liable, the alleged defamer of public officials or of public figures must know or have reason to suspect that his publication is false. In other cases proof of some kind of fault, negligence perhaps,[5] is essential to recovery. Inevitably, unless liability is to be completely foreclosed, the thoughts and editorial processes of the alleged defamer would be open to examination.

It is also untenable to conclude from our cases that, although proof of the necessary state of mind could be in the form of objective circumstances from which the ultimate fact could be inferred, plaintiffs may not inquire directly from the defendants whether they knew or had reason to suspect that their damaging publication was in error. In *Butts*, for example, it is evident from the record that the editorial process had been subjected to close examination and that direct as well as indirect evidence was relied on to prove that the defendant magazine had acted with actual malice. The damages verdict was sustained without any suggestion that plaintiff's proof had trenched upon forbidden areas.

Reliance upon such state-of-mind evidence is by no means a recent development arising from *New York Times* and similar cases. Rather, it is deeply rooted in the common-law rule, predating the First Amendment, that a showing of malice on the part of the defendant permitted plaintiffs to recover punitive or enhanced damages.[7] In *Butts*, the Court affirmed the substantial award of punitive damages which in

---

5. The definition of fault was to be the responsibility of state laws. Gertz v. Robert Welch, Inc., 418 U.S. 323, 347, 94 S.Ct. 2997, 3010, 41 L.Ed.2d 789 (1974).

7. A. Hanson, Libel and Related Torts ¶ 163 (1969); Developments in the Law—Defamation, supra n. 4, at 938; 50 Am.Jur. 2d, Libel and Slander § 352 (1970); 53 C.J.S. Libel and Slander § 260 (1955).

The Restatement originally provided in a separate section for the award of punitive damages for malicious defamations. Restatement of Torts § 1068 (Tent. Draft 13, 1936):

"One who is liable for harm to another's reputation caused by the publication of a libel or slander is also liable for punitive damages if the defamatory matter was published with knowledge of its falsity or if it was published in reckless indifference to its truth or falsity or solely for the purpose of causing harm to the plaintiff's reputation or other legally protected interest."

The provision was later omitted with the explanation that recovery of punitive damages would be determined by the rules in the Restatement with respect to damages in general. Restatement of Torts § 1068 (Proposed Final Draft 3, 1937).

Gertz v. Robert Welch, Inc., supra, 418 U.S., at 350, 94 S.Ct., at 3012, limited the entitlement to punitive damages, but such damages are still awardable upon a showing of knowing or reckless falsehood.

Georgia were conditioned upon a showing of "wanton or reckless indifference or culpable negligence" or " 'ill will, spite, hatred and an intent to injure. . . .' " 388 U.S., at 165–166, 87 S.Ct., at 1997.

* * *

Furthermore, long before *New York Times* was decided, certain qualified privileges had developed to protect a publisher from liability for libel unless the publication was made with malice. Malice was defined in numerous ways, but in general depended upon a showing that the defendant acted with improper motive. This showing in turn hinged upon the intent or purpose with which the publication was made, the belief of the defendant in the truth of his statement, or upon the ill will which the defendant might have borne toward the defendant.

* * *

In the face of this history, old and new, the Court of Appeals nevertheless declared that two of this Court's cases had announced unequivocal protection for the editorial process. In each of these cases, Miami Herald Publishing Co. v. Tornillo, 418 U.S. 241, 94 S.Ct. 2831, 41 L.Ed.2d 730 (1974), and Columbia Broadcasting System v. Democratic National Committee, 412 U.S. 94, 93 S.Ct. 2080, 36 L.Ed.2d 772 (1973), we invalidated governmental efforts to preempt editorial decision by requiring the publication of specified material. In *Columbia Broadcasting System*, it was the requirement that a television network air paid political advertisements and in *Tornillo*, a newspaper's obligation to print a political candidate's reply to press criticism. Insofar as the laws at issue in *Tornillo* and *Columbia Broadcasting System* sought to control in advance the content of the publication, they were deemed as invalid as were prior efforts to enjoin publication of specified materials. But holdings that neither a State nor the Federal Government may dictate what must or must not be printed neither expressly nor impliedly suggest that the editorial process is immune from any inquiry whatsoever.

* * *

III

It is nevertheless urged by respondents that the balance struck in *New York Times* should now be modified to provide further protections for the press when sued for circulating erroneous information damaging to individual reputation. * * *

We are thus being asked to modify firmly established constitutional doctrine by placing beyond the plaintiff's reach a range of direct evidence relevant to proving knowing or reckless falsehood by the publisher of an alleged libel, elements that are critical to plaintiffs such as Herbert. The case for making this modification is by no means clear and convincing, and we decline to accept it.

In the first place, it is plain enough that the suggested privilege for the editorial process would constitute a substantial interference with the ability of a defamation plaintiff to establish the ingredients of malice as required by *New York Times*. As respondents would have it, the defendant's reckless disregard of the truth, a critical element, could not be shown by direct evidence through inquiry into the thoughts, opinions, and conclusions of the publisher, but could be proved only by objective evidence from which the ultimate fact could be inferred. It may be that plaintiffs will rarely be successful in proving awareness of falsehood from the mouth of the defendant himself, but the relevance of answers to such inquiries, which the District Court recognized and the Court of Appeals did not deny, can hardly be doubted. To erect an impenetrable barrier to the plaintiff's use of such evidence on his side of the case is a matter of some substance, particularly when defendants themselves are prone to assert their good-faith belief in the truth of their publications, and libel plaintiffs are required to prove knowing or reckless falsehood with "convincing clarity." New York Times Co. v. Sullivan, 376 U.S., at 285–286, 84 S.Ct., at 729.

Furthermore, the outer boundaries of the editorial privilege now urged are difficult to perceive. The opinions below did not state, and respondents do not explain, precisely when the editorial process begins and when it ends. Moreover, although we are told that respondent Lando was willing to testify as to what he "knew" and what he had "learned" from his interviews, as opposed to what he "believed," it is not at all clear why the suggested editorial privilege would not cover knowledge as well as belief about the veracity of published reports. It is worth noting here that the privilege as asserted by respondents would also immunize from inquiry the internal communications occur ring during the editorial process and thus place beyond reach what the defendant participants learned or knew as the result of such collegiate conversations or exchanges. If damaging admissions to colleagues are to be barred from evidence, would a reporter's admissions made to third parties not participating in the editorial process also be immune from inquiry? We thus have little doubt that Herbert and other defamation plaintiffs have important interests at stake in opposing the creation of the asserted privilege.

Nevertheless, we are urged by respondents to override these important interests because requiring disclosure of editorial conversations and of a reporter's conclusions about the veracity of the material he has gathered will have an intolerable chilling effect on the editorial process and editorial decisionmaking. But if the claimed inhibition flows from the fear of damages liability for publishing knowing or reckless falsehoods, those effects are precisely what *New York Times* and other cases have held to be consistent with the First Amendment. Spreading false information in and of itself carries no First Amendment credentials. "[T]here is no constitutional value in false statements of fact." Gertz v. Robert Welch, Inc., supra, 418 U.S., at 340, 94 S.Ct., at 3007.

Realistically, however, some error is inevitable; and the difficulties of separating fact from fiction convinced the Court in *New York Times*, *Butts, Gertz,* and similar cases to limit liability to instances where some degree of culpability is present in order to eliminate the risk of undue self-censorship and the suppression of truthful material. Those who publish defamatory falsehoods with the requisite culpability, however, are subject to liability, the aim being not only to compensate for injury but also to deter publication of unprotected material threatening injury to individual reputation. Permitting plaintiffs such as Herbert to prove their cases by direct as well as indirect evidence is consistent with the balance struck by our prior decisions. If such proof results in liability for damages which in turn discourages the publication of erroneous information known to be false or probably false, this is no more than what our cases contemplate and does not abridge either freedom of speech or of the press.

Of course, if inquiry into editorial conclusions threatens the suppression not only of information known or strongly suspected to be unreliable but also of truthful information, the issue would be quite different. But as we have said, our cases necessarily contemplate examination of the editorial process to prove the necessary awareness of probable falsehood, and if indirect proof of this element does not stifle truthful publication and is consistent with the First Amendment, as respondents seem to concede, we do not understand how direct inquiry with respect to the ultimate issue would be substantially more suspect.[20] Perhaps such examination will lead to liability that would not have been found without it, but this does not suggest that the determinations in these instances will be inaccurate and will lead to the suppression of protected information. On the contrary, direct inquiry from the actors, which affords the opportunity to refute inferences that might otherwise be drawn from circumstantial evidence, suggests that more accurate results will be obtained by placing all, rather than part, of the evidence before the decisionmaker. Suppose, for example, that a reporter has two contradictory reports about the plaintiff, one of which is false and damaging, and only the false one is published. In resolving the issue whether the publication was known or suspected to be false, it is only common sense to believe that inquiry from the author, with an opportunity to explain, will contribute to accuracy. If the publication is false but there is an exonerating explanation, the defendant will surely testify to this effect.[21] Why should not the plaintiff be permitted to inquire before trial? On the other hand, if the publisher in fact had serious doubts about accuracy, but published nevertheless, no undue self-censorship will result from permitting the relevant inquiry. Only knowing or reckless error will be discouraged; and unless there is to be an absolute First Amendment

20. The kind of question respondents seek to avoid answering is, by their own admission, the easiest to answer. See Tr. of Oral Arg. 31:

"[T]hey are set-up questions for our side. . . . [T]hese are not difficult questions to answer."

21. Often it is the libel defendant who first presents at trial direct evidence about the editorial process in order to establish good faith and lack of malice. That was true in New York Times v. Sullivan, see, e.g., Record, O.T.1963, No. 39, p. 762 * * *.

privilege to inflict injury by knowing or reckless conduct, which respondents do not suggest, constitutional values will not be threatened.

It is also urged that frank discussion among reporters and editors will be dampened and sound editorial judgment endangered if such exchanges, oral or written, are subject to inquiry by defamation plaintiffs.[22] We do not doubt the direct relationship between consultation and discussion on the one hand and sound decisions on the other; but whether or not there is liability for the injury, the press has an obvious interest in avoiding the infliction of harm by the publication of false information, and it is not unreasonable to expect the media to invoke whatever procedures that may be practicable and useful to that end. Moreover, given exposure to liability when there is knowing or reckless error, there is even more reason to resort to prepublication precautions, such as a frank interchange of fact and opinion. Accordingly, we find it difficult to believe that error-avoiding procedures will be terminated or stifled simply because there is liability for culpable error and because the editorial process will itself be examined in the tiny percentage of instances in which error is claimed and litigation ensues. Nor is there sound reason to believe that editorial exchanges and the editorial process are so subject to distortion and to such recurring misunderstanding that they should be immune from examination in order to avoid erroeneous judgments in defamation suits. The evidentiary burden Herbert must carry to prove at least reckless disregard for the truth is substantial indeed, and we are unconvinced that his chances of winning an undeserved verdict are such that an inquiry into what Lando learned or said during the editorial process must be foreclosed.

This is not to say that the editorial discussions or exchanges have no constitutional protection from casual inquiry. There is no law that subjects the editorial process to private or official examination merely to satisfy curiosity or to serve some general end such as the public interest; and if there were, it would not survive constitutional scrutiny as the First Amendment is presently construed. No such problem exists here, however, where there is a specific claim of injury arising from a publication that is alleged to have been knowing or recklessly false.

Evidentiary privileges in litigation are not favored,[24] and even those rooted in the Constitution must give way in proper circumstances. The President, for example, does not have an absolute privilege against

---

22. They invoke our observation in United States v. Nixon, 418 U.S. 683, 705, 94 S.Ct. 3090, 3106, 41 L.Ed.2d 1039 (1974): "[T]hose who expect public dissemination of their remarks may well temper candor with a concern for appearances and for their own interests to the detriment of the decisionmaking process."

24. See Elkins v. United States, 364 U.S. 206, 234, 80 S.Ct. 1437, 1454, 4 L.Ed. 2d 1669 (1960) (Frankfurter, J., dissenting):

"Limitations are properly placed upon the operation of this general principle [of no testimonial privilege] only to the very limited extent that permitting a refusal to testify or excluding relevant evidence has a public good transcending the normally predominant principle of utilizing all rational means for ascertaining truth." See also 8 J. Wigmore, Evidence § 2192 (McNaughton rev. 1961); 4 The Works of Jeremy Bentham 321 (J. Bowring ed. 1843).

disclosure of materials subpoenaed for a judicial proceeding. United States v. Nixon, 418 U.S. 683, 94 S.Ct. 3090, 41 L.Ed.2d 1039 (1974). In so holding, we found that although the President has a powerful interest in confidentiality of communications between himself and his advisers, that interest must yield to a demonstrated specific need for evidence. As we stated, in referring to existing limited privileges against disclosure, "[w]hatever their origins, these exceptions to the demand for every man's evidence are not lightly created nor expansively construed, for they are in derogation of the search for truth." Id., at 710, 94 S.Ct., at 3108.

With these considerations in mind, we conclude that the present construction of the First Amendment should not be modified by creating the evidentiary privilege which the respondents now urge.

IV

Although defamation litigation, including suits against the press, is an ancient phenomenon, it is true that our cases from *New York Times* to *Gertz* have considerably changed the profile of such cases. In years gone by, plaintiffs made out a prima facie case by proving the damaging publication. Truth and privilege were defenses. Intent, motive and malice were not necessarily involved except to counter qualified privilege or to prove exemplary damages. The plaintiff's burden is now considerably expanded. In every or almost every case, the plaintiff must focus on the editorial process and prove a false publication attended by some degree of culpability on the part of the publisher. If plaintiffs in consequence now resort to more discovery, it would not be surprising; and it would follow that the cost and other burdens of this kind of litigation would escalate and become much more troublesome for both plaintiffs and defendants. It is suggested that the press needs constitutional protection from these burdens if it is to perform its task,[25] which is indispensable in a system such as ours.

Creating a constitutional privilege foreclosing direct inquiry into the editorial process, however, would not cure this problem for the press. Only complete immunity from liability from defamation would effect this result, and the Court has regularly found this to be an untenable construction of the First Amendment. Furthermore, mushrooming litigation costs, much of it due to pretrial discovery, are not peculiar to the libel and slander area. There have been repeated expressions of concern about undue and uncontrolled discovery, and voices from this Court have joined the chorus.[26] But until and unless

25. It is urged that the large costs of defending lawsuits will intimidate the press and lead to self-censorship, particularly where smaller newspapers and broadcasters are involved. It is noted that Lando's deposition alone continued intermittently for over a year and filled 26 volumes containing nearly 3,000 pages and 240 exhibits. As well as out-of-pocket expenses of the deposition, there were substantial legal fees, and Lando and his associates were diverted from news gathering and reporting for a significant amount of time.

26. Blue Chip Stamps v. Manor Drug Stores, 421 U.S. 723, 740–741, 95 S.Ct. 1917, 1928, 44 L.Ed.2d 539 (1975); ACF

there are major changes in the present Rules of Civil Procedure, reliance must be had on what in fact and in law are ample powers of the district judge to prevent abuse.

The Court has more than once declared that the deposition-discovery rules are to be accorded a broad and liberal treatment to effect their purpose of adequately informing the litigants in civil trials. Schlagenhauf v. Holder, 379 U.S. 104, 114–115, 85 S.Ct. 234, 241, 13 L.Ed.2d 152 (1964); Hickman v. Taylor, 329 U.S. 495, 501, 507, 67 S.Ct. 385, 388, 391, 91 L.Ed. 451 (1947). But the discovery provisions, like all of the Federal Rules of Civil Procedure, are subject to the injunction of Rule 1 that they "be construed to secure the just, *speedy,* and *inexpensive* determination of every action." (Emphasis added.) To this end, the requirement of Rule 26(b)(1) that the material sought in discovery be "relevant" should be firmly applied, and the district courts should not neglect their power to restrict discovery where "justice requires [protection for] a party or person from annoyance, embarrassment, oppression, or undue burden or expense. . . ." Rule 26(c). With this authority at hand, judges should not hesitate to exercise appropriate control over the discovery process.

Whether, as a constitutional matter, however, the trial judge properly applied the rules of discovery was not within the boundaries of the question certified under 28 U.S.C. § 1292(b) and accordingly is not before us. The judgment of the Court of Appeals is reversed.[*]

FURTHER NOTE ON PRIVILEGED MATTER

1. Other Privileges

For the rules defining the traditional privileges such as attorney-client, see Cleary et al., McCormick on Evidence cc. 8–12 (3d ed. 1984). There are various additional privileges, some created by statute and others by decision. See, e.g., Black Panther Party v. Smith, 661 F.2d 1243 (D.C.Cir.1981) (First Amendment refusal to disclose party officers effective in "balancing" against defendant's discovery needs; similar approach to plaintiff's Fifth Amendment claim); Britt v. Superior Court, 20 Cal.3d 844, 143 Cal.Rptr. 695, 574 P.2d 766 (1978) (similar approach to freedom of association claim under state constitution); Carey v. Klutznick, 653 F.2d 732 (2d Cir. 1981) (privilege of Census Bureau as to census returns); Roseville Community Hospital v. Superior Court, 70 Cal.App.3d 809, 139 Cal.Rptr. 170 (1977) (statute making immune from discovery the proceedings of hospital committees "having the responsibility of evaluation and improvement of the quality of care rendered in the hospital," i.e., "tissue committees"); Sav–On Drugs, Inc. v. Superior Court, 15 Cal.3d 1, 123 Cal.Rptr. 283, 538 P.2d 739 (1975) (case-law developed privilege against disclosing tax return);

Industries, Inc. v. EEOC, 439 U.S. 1081, 99 S.Ct. 865, 59 L.Ed.2d 52 (1979) (Powell, Stewart and Rehnquist, JJ., dissenting from denial of certiorari); Burger: Agenda for 2000 A.D.: A Need for Systematic Anticipation, Address at the Pound Conference, 70 F.R.D. 83, 95–96 (1976). The Committee on Rules of Practice and Procedure of the Judicial Conference of the United States has proposed amendments to the Federal Rules of Civil Procedure designed to ameliorate this problem. Preliminary Draft of Proposed Amendments to the Federal Rules of Civil Procedure (1978).

[*] The concurring opinion of Powell, J., and the dissenting opinions of Brennan, J., Stewart, J., and Marshall, J., are omitted.

People v. Superior Court, 60 Cal.App.3d 352, 131 Cal.Rptr. 476 (1976) (privilege against disclosure of report of vehicle accident other than disclosure to persons involved in or incurring liability for the accident); Richards of Rockford, Inc. v. Pacific Gas & Elec. Co., 71 F.R.D. 388 (N.D.Calif.1976), Note, 9 Conn.L.Rev. 326 (1977) (information gathered by social scientists); Welfare Rights Org. v. Crisan, 33 Cal.3d 766, 190 Cal.Rptr. 919, 661 P.2d 1073 (1983) (privilege as to communications between welfare claimants and lay representatives authorized to represent them in administrative hearings); Note, Discovery of Government Documents and the Official Information Privilege, 76 Colum.L.Rev. 142 (1976). See also the formidable list of privileges in C.E.B., California Trial Objections (1967), and Supplement (1978), and in United States v. American Tel. & Tel. Co., 86 F.R.D. 603 (D.D.C.1979).

There are, however, limits to how far courts are willing to go in recognizing privileges, as Herbert v. Lando demonstrates. Other situations where courts have refused to recognize privileges include communications with and papers of an accountant, United States v. Arthur Young & Co., 465 U.S. 805, 104 S.Ct. 1495, 79 L.Ed.2d 826 (1984). As indicated in a number of the cases reprinted and noted above, whether a court will recognize a non-statutory privilege ultimately depends on the court's view of the competing rights and interests involved. See also Mitchell v. Superior Court, 37 Cal.3d 268, 208 Cal.Rptr. 152, 690 P.2d 625 (1984), recognizing a qualified privilege against compelled disclosure of confidential sources by media defendants in libel actions.

2. Third Party Privileges

Information in the hands of third persons ordinarily can be obtained only by deposition upon subpoena, or subpoena duces tecum in the case of documents. Cf. Note, Rule 34(c) and Discovery of Nonparty Land, 85 Yale L.J. 112 (1975). But information obtainable from a party often may concern the interests of third persons. To protect these interests, a kind of privilege has been developing. See, e.g., Rudnick v. Superior Court, 11 Cal.3d 924, 114 Cal.Rptr. 603, 523 P.2d 643 (1974) (defendant drug company, sued in products liability case, allowed to raise doctor-patient privilege concerning communications to it by doctors whose patients suffered similar effects of product); Valley Bank of Nevada v. Superior Court, 15 Cal.3d 652, 125 Cal.Rptr. 553, 542 P.2d 977 (1975) (bank claiming qualified privilege against disclosure of information concerning its customers). See also C.C.P. 1985.3, requiring notice to an individual who is the subject of such records in the hands of banks, insurance companies, attorneys, accountants, pharmacists, psychotherapists, private or public schools, and other specified classes.

3. Self–Incrimination

The cases are divided, but it is argued that a plaintiff's invocation of the Fifth Amendment is not a basis for dismissing her suit, see Comment, Plaintiff as Deponent: Invoking the Fifth Amendment, 48 U.Chi.L.Rev. 158 (1981), e.g., Campbell v. Gerrans, 592 F.2d 1054 (9th Cir. 1979), although the refusal to testify permits an adverse inference as to the matter inquired into, see Baxter v. Palmigiano, 425 U.S. 308, 96 S.Ct. 1551, 47 L.Ed.2d 810 (1976). Compare Daly v. Superior Court, 19 Cal.3d 132, 137 Cal.Rptr. 14, 560 P.2d 1193 (1977): In a private party action for wrongful death resulting from an intentional beating inflicted by defendants, the defendants refused to answer deposition questions on the ground that the answers might incriminate them. The court held that the trial court could compel the defendants to answer if they were given "use" immunity, i.e., immunity from the statements they might give being used against them; that such immunity could be conferred notwithstanding that the suit was by a private party; but that it should not be given unless the trial court was satisfied that doing so would not interfere with possible criminal prosecution of the defendants. To determine the latter, 19 Cal.3d at 148, "the absence of any unduly detrimental effect of a proposed immunity order upon future criminal proceedings to be brought by a prosecuting official against the witness can be sufficiently established by that official's *failure to object* to the granting of the order after being given adequate notice and opportunity to do so." Cf. Pillsbury Co. v. Conboy, 459 U.S. 248, 103 S.Ct. 608, 74 L.Ed.2d 430 (1983). With regard to self-incrimination in supplying records, see United States v. Doe, 465 U.S. 605, 104 S.Ct. 1237, 79 L.Ed.2d 552 (1984). See generally Heidt, The Conjurer's Circle: The Fifth Amendment Privilege in Civil Cases, 91 Yale L.J. 1062 (1982); Wolfson, Civil Discovery and the Privilege Against Self-Incrimination, 15 Pacific L.J. 785 (1984).

Asserting privilege during discovery may preclude introducing at trial evidence covered by the privilege. See Anno., 36 A.L.R.3d 1367.

4. Protective Orders

Similar to privilege, but qualified and ad hoc, is the protective order requiring that discoverable material be held in some degree of confidence, for example, that the material be examined only by counsel and not be copied, e.g., Jepsen v. Florida Bd. of Regents, 610 F.2d 1379 (5th Cir. 1980); that material produced not be made available to other litigants in parallel litigation, e.g., American Tel. & Tel. Co. v. Grady, 594 F.2d 594 (7th Cir. 1979); Martindell v. International Tel. & Tel. Corp., 594 F.2d 291 (2d Cir. 1979); or that names of individual members of a class not be disclosed, e.g., Akron Center for Reproductive Health, Inc. v. City of Akron, 651 F.2d 1198 (6th Cir. 1981), see Note, Anonymity in Civil Litigation: The "Doe" Plaintiff, 57 Notre Dame Lawyer 580 (1982); but cf. Halkin v. Helms, 090 F.2d 977 (D.C.Cir. 1982). Compare In re Halkin, 598 F.2d 176 (D.C.Cir. 1979), holding that protective orders are governed by First Amendment rights to access to information. See Note, Nonparty Access to Discovery Materials in the Federal Courts, 94 Harv.L.Rev. 1085 (1981); Note, Rule 26(c) Protective Orders and the First Amendment, 80 Colum.L.Rev. 1645 (1980); Comment, The First Amendment Right to Disseminate Discovery Materials, 92 Harv.L.Rev. 1550 (1979). For enforcement of such an order against a nonparty, see Quinter v. Volkswagen of America, 676 F.2d 969 (3d Cir. 1982). Protective orders may also be used to limit the scope of permissible discovery, as in Vinson v. Superior Court, supra. See F.R.C.P. 26(c) for the federal rules governing protective orders.

4. DISCOVERY ABUSES

NATIONAL HOCKEY LEAGUE v. METROPOLITAN HOCKEY CLUB, INC.

Supreme Court of the United States, 1976.
427 U.S. 639, 96 S.Ct. 2778, 49 L.Ed.2d 747.

Per Curiam.

This case arises out of the dismissal, under Fed.Rule Civ.P. 37, of respondent's antitrust action against petitioners for failure to timely answer written interrogatories as ordered by the District Court, 63

F.R.D. 641. The Court of Appeals for the Third Circuit reversed the judgment of dismissal, finding that the District Court had abused its discretion, 531 F.2d 1188. The question presented is whether the Court of Appeals was correct in so concluding. Rule 37 provides in pertinent part as follows:

> "If a party . . . fails to obey an order to provide or permit discovery . . . the court in which the action is pending may make such orders in regard to the failure as are just, and among others the following: . . . (C) An order striking out pleadings or parts thereof, or staying further proceedings until the order is obeyed, or dismissing the action or proceeding or any part thereof, or rendering a judgment by default against the disobedient party."

This Court held in Societe Internationale v. Rogers, 357 U.S. 197, 212, 78 S.Ct. 1087, 1096, 2 L.Ed.2d 1255 (1958), that Rule 37

> "should not be construed to authorize dismissal of [a] complaint because of petitioner's noncompliance with a pretrial production order when it has been established that failure to comply has been due to inability, and not to willfulness, bad faith, or any fault of petitioner."

While there have been amendments to the Rule since the decision in *Rogers*, neither the parties, the District Court, nor the Court of Appeals suggested that the changes would affect the teachings of the quoted language from that decision.

The District Court, in its memorandum opinion directing that respondents' complaint be dismissed, summarized the factual history of the discovery proceeding in these words:

> "After seventeen months where crucial interrogatories remained substantially unanswered despite numerous extensions granted at the eleventh hour and, in many instances, beyond the eleventh hour, and notwithstanding several admonitions by the Court and promises and commitments by the plaintiffs, the Court must and does conclude that the conduct of the plaintiffs demonstrates the callous disregard of responsibilities counsel owe to the Court and to their opponents. The practices of the plaintiffs exemplify flagrant bad faith when after being expressly directed to perform an act by a date certain, viz., June 14, 1974, they failed to perform and compounded that noncompliance by waiting until five days afterwards before they filed any motions. Moreover, this action was taken in the face of warnings that their failure to provide certain information could result in the imposition of sanctions under Fed.R.Civ.P. 37. If the sanction of dismissal is not warranted by the circumstances of this case, then the Court can envisage no set of facts whereby that sanction should ever be applied." 63 F.R.D. 641, 656 (1974).

The Court of Appeals, in reversing the order of the District Court by a divided vote, concluded that:

"After carefully reviewing the record, we conclude that there is insufficient evidence to support a finding that M–GB's failure to file supplemental answers by June 14, 1974 was in flagrant bad faith, willful or intentional." 531 F.2d 1188, 1195 (1976).

The Court of Appeals did not question any of the findings of historical fact which had been made by the District Court, but simply concluded that there was in the record evidence of "extenuating factors." The Court of Appeals emphasized that none of the parties had really pressed discovery until after a consent decree was entered between petitioners and all of the other original plaintiffs except the respondents approximately one year after the commencement of the litigation. It also noted that respondents' counsel took over the litigation, which previously had been managed by another attorney, after the entry of the consent decree, and that respondents' counsel encountered difficulties in obtaining some of the requested information. The Court of Appeals also referred to a colloquy during the oral argument on petitioners' motion to dismiss in which respondents' counsel assured the District Court that he would not knowingly and willingly disregard the final deadline.

While the Court of Appeals stated that the District Court was required to consider the full record in determining whether to dismiss for failure to comply with discovery orders, see Link v. Wabash Railway Co., 370 U.S. 626, 633–634, 82 S.Ct. 1386, 1390, 8 L.Ed.2d 734 (1962), we think that the comprehensive memorandum of the District Court supporting its order of dismissal indicates that the court did just that. That record shows that the District Court was extremely patient in its efforts to allow the respondents ample time to comply with its discovery orders. Not only did respondents fail to file their responses on time, but the responses which they ultimately did file were found by the District Court to be grossly inadequate.

The question, of course, is not whether this Court, or whether the Court of Appeals, would as an original matter have dismissed the action; it is whether the District Court abused its discretion in so doing. E.g., Wright & Miller, Federal Practice and Procedure: Civil § 2284, p. 765 (1970); General Dynamics Corp. v. Selb Mfg. Co., 481 F.2d 1204, 1211 (CA8 1973); Baker v. F & F Investment, 470 F.2d 778, 781 (CA2 1972). Certainly the findings contained in the memorandum opinion of the District Court quoted earlier in this opinion are fully supported by the record. We think that the lenity evidenced in the opinion of the Court of Appeals, while certainly a significant factor in considering the imposition of sanctions under Rule 37, cannot be allowed to wholly supplant other and equally necessary considerations embodied in that Rule.

There is a natural tendency on the part of reviewing courts, properly employing the benefit of hindsight, to be heavily influenced by the severity of outright dsmissal as a sanction for failure to comply with a discovery order. It is quite reasonable to conclude that a party who has been subjected to such an order will feel duly chastened, so that even though he succeeds in having the order reversed on appeal he will nonetheless comply promptly with future discovery orders of the district court.

But here, as in other areas of the law, the most severe in the spectrum of sanctions provided by statute or rule must be available to the district court in appropriate cases, not merely to penalize those whose conduct may be deemed to warrant such a sanction, but to deter those who might be tempted to such conduct in the absence of such a deterrent. If the decision of the Court of Appeals remained undisturbed in this case, it might well be that *these* respondents would faithfully comply with all future discovery orders entered by the District Court in this case. But other parties to other lawsuits would feel freer than we think Rule 37 contemplates they should feel to flout other discovery orders of other district courts. Under the circumstances of this case, we hold that the District Judge did not abuse his discretion in finding bad faith on the part of these respondents, and concluding that the extreme sanction of dismissal was appropriate in this case by reason of respondents' "flagrant bad faith" and their counsel's "callous disregard" of their responsibilities. Therefore, the petition for a writ of certiorari is granted and the judgment of the Court of Appeals is reversed.

So ordered.*

NOTE ON ABUSE OF DISCOVERY: SANCTIONS AND CONTROLS

1. Providing Effective Sanctions

The discovery rules provide sanctions that seem formidable indeed, as the *National Hockey League* case suggests. See, e.g., Note, The Emerging Deterrence Orientation in the Imposition of Discovery Sanctions, 91 Harv.L.Rev. 1033 (1978); Sherwood, Curbing Discovery Abuse: Sanctions Under the Federal Rules of Civil Procedure and the California Code of Civil Procedure, 21 Santa Clara L.Rev. 567 (1981); California Practicum, The Sanction Provision of the New California Civil Discovery Act, Section 2023: Will It Make a Difference or Is It Just Another Paper Tiger?, 15 Pepperdine L.Rev. 401 (1988) (background and terms of the California Civil Discovery Act of 1986, revising the 1957 California discovery rules); Anno., 56 A.L.R.3d 1109 (dismissal of plaintiff's action for failure to comply with discovery); Anno., 6 A.L.R.3d 713 (default judgment against defendant for failure to comply with discovery); Anno., 86 A.L.R.3d 1089 (answers in discovery limit proof that party may offer at trial); e.g., Sig M. Glukstad, Inc. v. Lineas Aereas Nacional—Chile, 656 F.2d 976 (5th Cir. 1981) (dismissal of plaintiff's action); Telectron, Inc. v. Overhead Door Corp., 116 F.R.D. 107 (S.D.Fla.1987) (default judgment where defendant destroyed documents covered by discovery demand); Kelly v. GAF Corp., 115 F.R.D. 257 (E.D.Pa.1987) (new trial ordered due to pervasive attorney misconduct at deposition); Pesaplastic, C.A. v. Cincinnati Milacron Co., 799 F.2d 1510 (11th Cir. 1986) (sanctions imposed for failure to produce adequately prepared

* Brennan, J., and White, J., dissented without opinion. Stevens, J., took no part in the case.

Rule 30(b)(6) witness); Smith v. Ford Motor Co., 626 F.2d 784 (10th Cir. 1980) (reversible error to pemit doctor to testify on matter as to which discovery was obstructed); Carroll v. Abbott Laboratories, 32 Cal.3d 892, 187 Cal.Rptr. 592, 654 P.2d 775 (1982) (reversible error to refuse to dismiss for flagrant noncompliance by plaintiff's attorney). See also Roadway Express, Inc. v. Piper, 447 U.S. 752, 100 S.Ct. 2455, 65 L.Ed.2d 488 (1980) (costs imposed on attorney); Kahn v. Kahn, 68 Cal.App.3d 372, 137 Cal.Rptr. 332 (1977) (dismissal for failure to comply with discovery rule is "on the merits" so as to preclude refiling of action). But see Greenup v. Rodman, 42 Cal.3d 822, 231 Cal.Rptr. 220, 726 P.2d 1295 (1986) (default judgment as a discovery sanction upheld, but reversible error to award damages in excess of the demand in the complaint).

The control and sanction system in Rule 37 as it stands is based on the notion of "abuse." The concept was formerly construed to require virtually intentional refusal to comply. See Societe Internationale v. Rogers, 357 U.S. 197, 78 S.Ct. 1087, 2 L.Ed.2d 1255 (1958). This interpretation was superseded by the 1970 revision of Rule 37, where the word "failure" was adopted. However, this term has generally been construed to require gross neglect or conscious non-compliance, e.g., Affanato v. Merrill Brothers, 547 F.2d 138 (1st Cir. 1977). See Note, Federal Rules of Civil Procedure: Defining a Feasible Culpability Threshold for the Imposition of Severe Discovery Sanctions, 65 Minn.L.Rev. 137 (1980); cf. C.C.P. 2017, 2023.

See also Renfrew, Discovery Sanctions: A Judicial Perspective, 67 Calif.L.Rev. 264, 278 (1979), observing that "Perhaps the most important reason why the judicial process is abused is because the stakes of litigation are so high that they create an occasionally irrepressible temptation to cheat." "Cheating" by a nonparty who refuses to comply with discovery is virtually immune from effective sanction if the recalcitrant holds out long enough. See, e.g., Soobzokov v. CBS, Inc., 642 F.2d 28 (2d Cir. 1981). The sanction of dismissal or default is too heavy for routine use against the litigants. What other incentives might be established against cheating?

2. Curtailing Discovery

One solution to abuse of discovery and "cheating" is to curtail or abolish discovery. Alternatives include (1) "better" judicial control over discovery; (2) limiting discovery in certain types of cases or limiting the use of certain discovery devices; and (3) changing the rules as to costs of discovery. With regard to judicial control, compare Schwarzer, Managing Antitrust and Other Complex Litigation: A Handbook for Lawyers (1982), with Resnik, Managerial Judges, 96 Harv.L.Rev. 376 (1982). But tight judicial control by a judge who lacks good practical judgment can simply create an even bigger mess. See, e.g., International Business Machines Corp. v. United States, 493 F.2d 112 (2d Cir. 1973). F.R.C.P. 26(f) attempts to place the burden of control on both the court and counsel by requiring the court, on motion of counsel, to hold a conference for the purpose of devising a discovery plan and by imposing a duty of good faith on counsel to cooperate in devising a reasonable plan at the request of opposing counsel. See also F.R.C.P. 16.

One serious experiment in limiting discovery was conducted in certain municipal and superior courts in California from 1978 to 1983 as part of a Pilot Project in Economical Litigation. Discovery was substantially abolished except for the demand for admission of the genuineness of documents. For an account of the experiment, see Note, California's Pilot Project in Economical Litigation, 53 So.Calif.L.Rev. 1497 (1980). The experiment seemed to be reasonably successful, but perhaps only because the special rules were limited to cases involving relatively small claims, and other evidence indicates that discovery abuse is uncommon in such cases anyway. See Brazil, Civil Discovery: Lawyers' Views of Its Effectiveness, Its Principal Problems and Abuses, 1980 Am.B. Found.Res.J. 787; Trubek, Sarat, Felstiner, Kritzer and Grossman, The Costs of Ordinary Litigation, 31 U.C.L.A.L.Rev. 72 (1983). If the problem of controlling abuse arises mainly in the relatively big cases, it is surely anomalous to concentrate reform on the relatively little cases. The obvious explanation for this anomaly is that proposals for seriously curtailing discovery in big cases would meet intense resistance by spokespeople for the "have nots," who not only have less money than others, but also have less information about matters affecting them. Discovery is vital to them in obtaining information in litigation over their rights. For statutory provisions imposing modest limits on the use of specific discovery devices, see, e.g., California's limitations on the use of depositions, interrogatories, and requests for admission, discussed in Further Note on the Mechanics of Discovery, supra p. 907.

Perhaps a more important objection to curtailing discovery is that it is either unnecessary or unworkable as a means for controlling abuse, at least in the absence of some concept of "normal" discovery. Consider, for example, the 1983 revisions to Rule 26, which supplemented the sanctions in Rule 37 with particular regard for the problem of excessive discovery. The revisions permit the court to limit discovery in the interest of relieving parties from duplicative, burdensome, or abusive discovery requests, taking into account the nature of the case and other factors, Rule 26(b)(1), and impose an affirmative duty on attorneys to engage in discovery in good faith, Rule 26(g). Compare C.C.P. 2017, 2023. The standards are obligatory on attorneys in formulating discovery requests, and failure to comply with the standards can be the basis for imposing sanctions. These revisions do little more than add emphasis to the court's preexisting authority under Rule 26(c), and they assume that there is such a thing as "normal" discovery and that cost sanctions are the appropriate remedy for anything going beyond that. This assumption likewise underlies the cost provisions of Rule 37 for motions to compel discovery.

These types of provisions require both court and counsel to draw a line between discovery probes that are aggressive, detailed, penetrating and in "good faith," and discovery probes that are aggressive, detailed, penetrating but in "bad faith." And this in turn involves relatively subjective judgments by judges who differ from one another in their attitudes toward the "discovery problem" and the merits of the big-discovery cases, applying them to attorneys who differ from one another even more so in these respects. It may well be that, except at the margin, the variety and uncertainty of litigation is so great as to preclude the formulation of any intelligible norm.

In addition to the question whether such norms are workable is the issue of whether they are truly necessary. It should be noted that Rule 11, discussed supra p. 135, now attaches sanctions with bite to the requirement that plaintiff have a nonfrivolous case at the time of filing. This in effect means that plaintiff must have evidence indicating probable cause that the action has merit. If plaintiff's action fails to meet this standard, Rule 11 and not discovery rules should deal with it. If plaintiff's action does have probable merit, the question then becomes whether there is any basis for allowing less than full discovery, at least until the discovery process in a case has been so productive that any further discovery clearly would be redundant. The revisions to Rule 26, then, may be a dead letter. Experience suggests that courts do not much rely on them.

One possibility that has received little attention is making a party pay for the discovery costs imposed on the opposing party. On the one hand, this would avoid the problem of trying to give content to concepts such as "abuse," "normal" discovery, "bad faith" and the like. It also would force parties to consider what discovery is truly essential to their case. On the other hand, "have nots" would clearly be at a disadvantage, not only because they have less money, but because, as discussed above, they are more likely than are the "haves" to lack information that is in the hands of the opposing party. Is there any way of devising a system that would not overly burden impecunious litigants but would still provide incentives to limit discovery?

C. THE PRETRIAL CONFERENCE

LOUISELL, DISCOVERY AND PRE-TRIAL UNDER THE MINNESOTA RULES

36 Minn.L.Rev. 633, 660–667 (1952).*

*   *   *

It is natural to follow discussion of discovery with discussion of pre-trial because often the latter may properly be conceived of as the fulfillment of the former. Pre-trial often offers the chance of bringing discovery measures to fruition.[88]

The author's observation that the discovery rules do not negate the common law's conception of litigation as adversary and competitive, is equally true of pre-trial. Pre-trial is not an attempt to obviate the struggle that is common law litigation, but to guarantee that the struggle will be real, not sham, and that the battles will be fought out in the heartland of the controversy, not on the fringes.

Minnesota Rule 16 on pre-trial is almost identical with the corresponding federal rule. Both refrain from requiring pre-trial; both provide that "the court may in its discretion" order pre-trial. This constitutes acknowledgement that the necessity for and the utility of pre-trial are in large part dependent on local conditions of legal practice and judicial administration. Thus, whereas by

---

* Copyright 1952 by the Minnesota Law Review. The original version of the article from which the following excerpt is adapted was written in connection with Minnesota's adoption of F.R.C.P. 16 on pre-trial, along with the substance of the other Federal Rules, effective in 1952. The excerpt is believed to reflect the permanent problems of pre-trial and to be as relevant to the state experience as to that under F.R.C.P. 16.

88. Of course, discovery measures may have come to such full fruition as to obviate pre-trial, by laying the foundation for a successful motion for summary judgment under Rule 56. "The judgment sought shall be rendered forthwith if the pleadings, *depositions,* and *admissions* on file, together with the affidavits, if any, show that there is no genuine issue as to any material fact and that the moving party is entitled to a judgment as a matter of law." Rule 56.03 [Italics added. This Rule was revised in 1963 to include "answers to interrogatories"]. This is another illustration of the close integration of the rules. The party taking a deposition need not specify in his notice whether he wants it for discovery purposes, or use at the trial, or as a basis for a motion for summary judgment.

Pre-trial sometimes can be at least a partial substitute for discovery measures. The pre-trial judge's quest for simplification of the issues and admissions of facts and documents not genuinely disputed, is essentially "discovery."

rule of court pre-trial is compulsory in some federal districts in most types of cases, in others, including the Minnesota federal district, it is had only on motion of one of the parties. The need for pre-trial is one thing in judicial districts with trial calendars that are current and quite another in districts as much as fifteen or eighteen months behind. And the possibilities for sound judicial administration of pre-trial are one thing in judicial districts embracing large geographical areas with only one or two judges, and quite another in metropolitan centers with numerous judges who could in rotation handle the pre-trial calendar.

* * *

With the philosophy and objectives of pre-trial in mind, what are the best means of achieving them? While opinion differs as to the period that should intervene between pre-trial and trial the consensus seems to be that the period ought to be two to six weeks. From the lawyer's viewpoint of avoiding unnecessary duplication of preparation, the shorter the period the better. Still, obviously the interval must be enough to permit counsel to achieve the stipulations of pre-trial. Another relevant consideration is the desirability of giving enough time for the lawyers and parties to think over dispassionately possible opinions from the judge about settlement. Further, while ordinarily discovery measures should be completed by pre-trial, if the pre-trial conference develops the utility of further discovery measures and the circumstances are such that a party should be afforded the opportunity to undertake them, the interval before trial may have to be substantially increased. Conditions of the trial calendar may impose supervening practical considerations. But it seems to the writer that, ideally, at least from the lawyers' viewpoint, trial ought ordinarily to follow pre-trial by about two weeks. Another question is whether the pre-trial judge ought to be one other than the judge who is to preside at the trial. Despite some opinion that it is immaterial whether the pre-trial judge is the same as the trial judge, it seems to the writer that except before judges of unusual ability and tact, pretrial is apt to suffer if the lawyers know that the judge who hears them at pre-trial will preside at the trial. Psychologically this knowledge is likely to repress the frankness by counsel essential to the best results at pre-trial. In metropolitan districts with a large staff of judges, the practice sometimes is for each in rotation to take the pre-trial calendar for several months at a time.

Some judges prefer to hold the pre-trial conference in chambers, thinking this best conduces to the informality productive of full and frank discussion. Others prefer the formality of the courtroom, possibly thinking it conduces to efficiency and dispatch of business. One experienced pre-trial judge has been observed to use the courtroom but leave the bench and occupy the clerk's seat, possibly effecting a compromise between the extremes of formality and informality! Some prefer that a transcript of the pre-trial conference be, and others that it not be, made.

The pre-trial conference normally opens with a statement of the facts by plaintiff's lawyer from plaintiff's viewpoint, and of plaintiff's basic claims. This is often followed by questions from the judge to plaintiff's lawyer to fill in hiatuses. Then the defendant's lawyer makes a similar statement, also often followed by questions. From the two statements and answers to the questions, the basic contentions of facts and legal theories of the parties should emerge. Next it is natural to consider whether the pleadings should be amended to reflect the present claims of the parties. Often discovery procedures, or revelations made at pre-trial, will point up the necessity or at least the desirability of amending the pleadings. Then counsel will be asked for stipulations respecting the admissibility of exhibits such as charts, x-rays, and other documentary items. If agreement of counsel waiving formal proof of such items is reached, as it customarily is in most lawsuits, the exhibits will be stamped with the pre-trial court's stamp indicating that they are to be admitted subject only to objections pertaining to relevancy, or to competency other than objections on matters of formal proof. In other words, the necessity of formal proof of the authenticity of the exhibit at the trial is obviated. Often counsel, knowing that there is no genuine issue about the reasonableness of doctors' and hospitals' bills, will stipulate thereto, resulting in such bills being similarly stamped. The pre-trial judge may then suggest further admission in an attempt to eliminate issues as to which there is no bona fide dispute, obtain a stipulation for limiting the number of expert witnesses on each side, and possibly set a day certain for trial. He may the inquire of counsel whether there have been attempts to settle the case, and suggest his opinion about the reasonableness of the offers and counter-offers. The philosophy of pre-trial judges differs widely as to how far the judge should intrude into the matter of settlement. Some experienced judges and lawyers feel that pre-trial suffers substantially if lawyers get the idea that it is primarily a device to coerce settlements in order to relieve congested dockets. But where the judge approaches settlement with restraint and objectivity, listening mostly, and making it abundantly clear that he is not trying to dictate to counsel, most experienced lawyers welcome his thoughts on what the case is worth. They are often valuable in the lawyer's later conferences with an unreasonable or indecisive client.

It is important that the pre-trial order required by Rule 16 be prepared promptly by the judge. Some experienced pre-trial judges prefer to dictate the order at the close of the conference in the presence of the attorneys to a typist who then and there types the original and copies, so that the judge can sign the order and the attorneys receive their copies before they leave the conference. This has the obvious advantage of producing a pre-trial order formulated while the facts and issues are fresh in the judge's mind, and subject to immediate correction by the attorneys if the judge falls into some inaccuracy. * * *

    * * *

RIGBY v. BEECH AIRCRAFT CO.

United States Court of Appeals for the Tenth Circuit, 1977.
548 F.2d 288.*

ARTHUR J. STANLEY, JR., SENIOR DISTRICT JUDGE.

The plaintiffs-appellants appeal from a judgment entered on a jury verdict for the defendant in an action for damages resulting from the crash of a private airplane manufactured by Beech. The aircraft, a Beech Baron twin engine plane manufactured in 1961, was purchased by Dr. Elmer C. Rigby and Sterling G. Pollock in October 1968, from its third successive owner. On the afternoon of November 27, 1968, Dr. Rigby as pilot commenced a flight from Van Nuys, California with his wife, Penelope A. Rigby and two of their children, William and Nikila, as passengers. His intended destination was Salt Lake City. The

* The court's footnotes are omitted.

plane crashed en route and the pilot and passengers were injured, Mrs. Rigby fatally. In the ensuing action Dr. Rigby and his children sought damages for the wrongful death of Mrs. Rigby; Dr. Rigby, William and Nikila sued to recover damages for their personal injuries; and Dr. Rigby, Mr. Pollock, and the United Pacific Insurance Company (insurer of the aircraft) claimed damages for the destruction of the plane.

The plaintiffs claim that the crash was caused by defects in the design and construction of the auxiliary fuel tanks of the aircraft; that the Flight Manual, Owner's Handbook, service letters, and bulletins provided by Beech were defective and misleading in that they failed to describe a possible fuel starvation phenomenon in the auxiliary tanks and failed to advise users of the nature and extent of a problem that might confront operators of the plane. It was further contended that Beech did not properly perform or adequately conduct the required unusable fuel tests for the auxiliary fuel cells. It was claimed that Beech misrepresented the air-worthiness of the airplane to the Federal Aviation Administration and failed to meet the minimum standards prescribed by the F.A.A.; that Beech was well aware of the deficiencies in the auxiliary fuel cells and nevertheless concealed their dangerous propensities.

Beech denied that the auxiliary fuel cells were defective and alleged that the crash occurred as a result of pilot error or by misuse of the aircraft. Beech denied any fraudulent, malicious or negligent conduct.

The issues presented on appeal are that the trial court erred:

* * *

(2) in excluding evidence on the following items:

(a) "testimony of witnesses concerning fuel starvation in 40 gallon main fuel cells or any fuel cells other than the 31 gallon fuel cell;

(b) "any notice to Beech in connection with any fuel cell other than the 31 gallon fuel cell;

(c) "correspondence between Beech and others concerning possibility of fuel starvation in any fuel cell other than the 31 gallon fuel cell."

* * *

The trial court excluded testimony offered by the plaintiffs-appellants with respect to claimed defects in design or manufacture of the 40-gallon main fuel cells comprising a part of the aircraft's fuel system. That system included two 40-gallon main fuel cells and two 31-gallon auxiliary fuel cells.

The plaintiffs-appellants, in support of their claim of error in the exclusion of evidence with reference to the 40-gallon main fuel cells, point out that in their complaint they alleged defective design and construction of the aircraft's *fuel system* and argue that the fuel system was an integrated system including both the main (40-gallon) and the auxiliary (31-gallon) cells so that evidence as to claimed deficiencies in the 40-gallon cells sould have been admitted. This argument is undercut by the fact that by their answers to interrogatories calling for a particularized statement "of every part of the aircraft in question alleged to have been defective in design" the plaintiffs-appellants responded:

"ANSWER

"13. The auxiliary fuel cells failed to contain any bladder sumps, baffles or other restraining devices to prevent displacement of the fuel away from the exit port in the tank, which would allow air to enter the fuel system and cause a loss of power.

"QUESTION

"14. List separately each part of the aircraft in question that is alleged to have been negligently constructed, stating what was defective or improper in respect to such construction, what was the negligent act of construction as to each part, and the facts establishing such conclusions.

"ANSWER

"14. See answer to interrogatory No. 13 above."

Further, in the Pre-Trial Order (R.817) the plaintiffs' claims were set forth at length and reference is made consistently and repeatedly to alleged defects in the 31-gallon auxiliary fuel cells. No mention is made of any claim based upon any defect in the 40-gallon main fuel cells, either separately or as part of an integrated system. Listed in the Order as uncontroverted facts are the statements:

"9. The fuel system for the aircraft consisted of two 40 gallon main fuel cells and two 31 gallon auxiliary fuel cells. At the time of the accident and sometime prior thereto, the aircraft was being operated by the pilot on the auxiliary fuel cells."

and

"15. The 31 gallon auxiliary fuel cells are installed to increase the aircraft's operational range, however, the design and construction of the cells require that their use is restricted to level flight only and this limitation is expressly prescribed by the manufacturer."

The contested issues of fact specified in the Pre-Trial Order deal only with claimed defects in the 31-gallon auxiliary fuel cells. Consistent with Rule 16, Federal Rules of Civil Procedure, the Pre-Trial Order contained a provision that the order should control the course of the trial and that all pleadings were deemed merged therein.

There was evidence that the 40-gallon and the 31-gallon fuel cells differed in shape, size and position in the airplane, so that experience with the one could not be transposed to the other. We are convinced, as was the trial court, that the proffered evidence with respect to the design and characteristics of the 40-gallon fuel cells was not relevant.

Evidence which is not relevant is not admissible. Rule 402, Federal Rules of Evidence.

* * *

NOTE ON THE PRETRIAL CONFERENCE

1. If the pretrial conference consistently performed the functions outlined in Louisell, Discovery and Pre-Trial Under the Minnesota Rules, supra, it would no doubt be a useful thing. In routine cases, however, the lawyers regard it as mostly a waste of time because the realized saving in trial time is marginal and is contingent on the case actually going to trial, whereas attending the conference is expensive in time. Correlatively, the judge's interest can be perfunctory. In any event, lawyers are reluctant to be fully open about their positions. See City of Long Beach v. Superior Court, 64 Cal.App.3d 65, 134 Cal.Rptr. 468 (1976), holding that discovery cannot be used to ascertain the identity of non-expert witnesses an opposing party intends to call at trial. In many states, the pretrial conference is optional rather than mandatory. See California Rules of Court, Superior Court Rule 212. Compare F.R.C.P. 16. Hence, the pretrial conference remains an institution of doubtful significance in mine run litigation. See Rosenberg, The Pretrial Conference and Effective Justice (1964); Note, Pretrial Conference Procedures, 26 S.C.L.Rev. 481 (1974). On mandatory settlement conferences before trial, see Menkel-Meadow, For and Against Settlement: Uses and Abuses of the Mandatory Settlement Conference, 33 U.C.L.A.L.Rev. 485 (1985).

F.R.C.P. 16 was extensively revised in 1983 to encourage federal district court judges to take a more active role in pretrial management. These revisions have been criticized by some as prescribing rigid rules that may actually hinder effective management. See Further Note on Case Management, infra p. 1234.

2. Despite criticisms of the significance and effectiveness of the pretrial conference, it is nevertheless crucial for the lawyer to take the pretrial order seriously, as demonstrated by Rigby v. Beech Aircraft Co. However, judicial attitudes vary (over time, from judge to judge, and from court system to court system) about the proper rigor in enforcing the specification of issues in the pretrial order. Compare, e.g., De Castro & Co. v. Liberty Steamship of Panama, S.A., 186 Cal.App.2d 628, 9 Cal.Rptr. 107 (1960) (refusing to allow a party to offer a perfectly valid and easily proved defense because it was not listed among the issues in the pretrial order) and Lane v. Geiger–Berger Associates, 608 F.2d 1148 (8th Cir.1979) (statement of claim in pretrial order supersedes complaint), with Rangel v. Graybar Elec. Co., 70 Cal.App.3d 943, 139 Cal.Rptr. 191 (1977) (allowing witness to be called who was not listed in pretrial order, where opposing counsel was informally forewarned and no prejudice was shown). See also Withrow and Larm, The "Big" Antitrust Case: 25 Years of Sisyphean Labor, 62 Cornell L.Rev. 1, 5 (1976):

> "[W]e maintain that the crux of truly fair and efficient management of large cases is still 'iron-hearted' control by the judge. * * * Second, we believe that large antitrust litigations would be better controlled and certainly more fairly adjudicated if it were frankly recognized that pretrial, and not trial, is where the merits of such cases are revealed. Trial, if it occurs at all, is but the final denouement of pretrial adjudication, save in the case where pretrial responsibilities have been neglected by the presiding judge."

3. In complex litigation, pretrial conferences are virtually indispensable. In such cases there is not one conference but a series, whose purposes include control of discovery and development of issues as well as fixing the trial scenario when the trial becomes imminent. See Pointer and Tigar, Complex Litigation: Demonstration of Pretrial Conference, 6 Rev. of Litigation 285 (1987); see also Complex Litigation, infra p. 1203. Such a procedure begins to resemble the normal procedure in litigation under the civil law system as described by Professor Kaplan in the following article. However, Gottwald, Simplified Civil Procedure in West Germany, 31 Am.J.Comp.Law 687 (1983), suggests that Professor Kaplan's account of German civil procedure portrays it as more efficient, and as involving more energy on the part of the judge, than is in fact ordinarily the case. See also Langbein, The German Advantage in Civil Procedure, 52 U.Chi.L.Rev. 823 (1985).

KAPLAN, CIVIL PROCEDURE—REFLECTIONS ON THE COMPARISON OF SYSTEMS*

9 Buff.L.Rev. 409 (1960).

* * * I shall abandon the local scene altogether and talk about procedure in a Continental civil-law system, that of Western Germany. I shall try to pack that procedure into a medium-sized nutshell. I shall then speak of certain of the forces that shaped the German system, and reach out for various contrasts between the German and American procedure. I shall attempt a few observations about comparative procedure and procedure in general, veering back occasionally to our particular domestic concerns.

I

To begin, the rules governing civil procedure in Germany today are laid down by legislative enactment stemming from the famous code of 1877; judicial rule-making plays virtually no part. There is no jury. The courts, at least those concerned in the regular proceedings for cases of consequence, are collegial in structure, acting through benches of three or—in the court of final review—five judges. To some extent, however, the plural bench may use a single judge as a representative or helper.

One of the leitmotifs of the German process is sounded by the Siegfried horn of the summons in the action. This invites appearance at a *Termin zur mündlichen Verhandlung,* a court-session for oral-argument, or rather for conference, since the ideal style of proceeding is less that of a contentious confrontation than a cooperative discussion. The conference is set perhaps three to four weeks after initial service of the papers—which by the way is usually accomplished by mail—and it is commonly attended by the parties as well as counsel. Now the point to be made is that the whole procedure up to judgment may be viewed as being essentially a series of such conferences, the rest of the process having a sort of dependent status. Prooftaking occurs to the extent necessary in the spaces, as it were, between conferences. Intermediate decisions are made along the way. But the conferences are the heart of the matter. Very promptly, then, the litigants are brought under the eye of the court and the case begins to be shaped; and this treatment is applied to the action at intervals until it is fully opened and finally broken. "Conference" betokens informality and this characterizes the entire German procedure.

* Copyright © 1960.

"Conference" also suggests what is the fact, that possibilities of settlement are openly, vigorously, and continually exploited.

I must relate German pleadings to the conference method—I shall use the word "pleadings" although these writings are quite different from the American variety. The action starts with a complaint served together with the summons, but beyond this there is no prescribed number or sequence of pleadings. Pleadings are to be put in in such numbers and at such times as to prepare for, strengthen, and expedite the conferences and thereby the general movement of the case. They have no position independent of the conferences. Indeed the framers of the code of 1877 looked to a free, oral restatement of the pleadings at conference. Such oral recapitulation no longer occurs: the court reads the pleadings in advance and the lawyers are assumed to adopt the pleadings except as they speak up to the contrary. Still no question arises as to the sufficiency of the pleadings as such, nor is there any motion practice directed to the pleadings themselves. In short, pleadings merge into, and are an ingredient of the conferences. What is wanted from the pleadings as adopted and perhaps revised at conference is a narrative of the facts as the parties see them at the time, with offers of proof—mainly designated witnesses and documents—and demands for relief. There is no insistence on niceties of form, and legal argumentation, though strictly out of place, is common in today's pleadings. Amendments, even drastic amendments, of the statements can be made until the end of the case, normally without any penalty for late change. This malleability of the pleadings flows from the realization and expectation that a case may change its content and color as it is repeatedly discussed and as proof is from time to time adduced.

Returning to the conduct of the conferences, we find the presiding judge highly vocal and dominant, the parties themselves often voluble, the lawyers relatively subdued. To understand the judicial attitude and contribution at conference, we must take account of two related concepts. First, there is the principle jura novit curia, the court knows and applies the law without relying on the parties to bring it forward. Second, article 139 of the code, as strengthened in recent years, imposes a duty on all courts to clarify the cause and lead the parties toward full development of their respective positions. Thus with awareness of the law implicit in the case, the court is obliged to discuss it freely with the litigants, and in that light to indicate what will be material to decision. By discussion with counsel and the parties the court completes the picture of the controversy as presented by the litigants, throwing light upon obscurities, correcting misunderstandings, marking out areas of agreement and disagreement. It spurs and guides the parties to any necessary further exploration of facts and theories, and may suggest appropriate allegations, proof offers, and demands. The court, however, is not bound to take over and commandeer the litigation, nor does it have the power to do so in an ultimate sense. To some degree—the power is greater in "family" matters than in ordinary cases— the court may call up evidence and background information and disregard parties' admissions. The calling of experts is basically a matter for the court. But, in general, allegations, proof offers, and demands can be made only by the parties and so in the last analysis major control of the case-materials remains with them. Nevertheless, as the parties are likely to follow the court's suggestions, we have here a significant potential in the court which imparts a special quality to the procedure; and this is so despite the fact that clarification and leading are hardly noticeable in simpler cases where the lawyers seem to be providing competent representation. The role of the court not only at conference but throughout the proceedings is envisioned as being both directive and protective. The court as vigorous chairman is to move the case along at a good pace, stirring the parties to action on their own behalf, exercising its limited sua sponte powers where necessary, conscious of a duty to strive for the right solution of the controversy regardless of faults of advocacy.

Conferences propel the lawsuit. Most dates are set by the court in open session. It acts in discretion with due regard to the convenience of the parties: few "iron" time provisions are laid down in the code, and the parties cannot control the pace by stipulation. When discussions disclose ripe questions of law, a time will be set for decision. If they show up disputed issues of fact, there will be an order and a time set for prooftaking.

To understand German prooftaking, we have first to ask what investigation of the facts a German lawyer customarily makes. He consults his client and his client's papers. But he has substantially no coercive means of "discovering" material for the purpose of preparing his proof offers or readying himself for prooftaking. Moreover he is by no means at liberty to go out and talk informally with prospective witnesses. He is hobbled by the principle that he is to avoid all suspicion of influencing those who may be later called to give evidence in court. I shall not attempt to mark the exact boundaries of this inhibition or to dredge up the possible evasive contrivances. I shall simply say that German lawyers are not prime movers with respect to the facts. The régime just described does make for unrehearsed witnesses. It begins to explain why a party in German litigation is not charged with any "proprietorship" over the witnesses whom he has nominated and neither "vouches" for them nor is "bound" by their testimony.

The court draws up the order for prooftaking, the *Beweisbeschluss,* from the nominations set out in the pleadings as they may have been revised at conference. Prooftaking need not be concentrated at a single session, and is in fact not often so concentrated. Accordingly the court may pick and choose what it wants to hear at particular sessions. It can take proof in any order—evidence on a defense ahead of evidence on the main case, even evidence on the negative of an issue ahead of the affirmative.

Witnesses are sequestered, kept out of the courtroom until called. The court asks the witness to state what he knows about the proof theme on which he has been summoned. When the witness has done that in narrative without undue interruption, the court interrogates him, and this is the principal interrogation. Counsel put supplemental questions. Lawyers' participation is likely to be meager. If a lawyer puts too many questions he is implying that the court does not know its business, and that is a dubious tactic. A full stenographic transcript is not kept. Instead the court dictates a summary of the witness' testimony for the minutes which is then read back and perhaps corrected.

German law has few rules excluding relevant evidence. In general relevant evidence is admissible and when admitted is freely evaluated: thus there is no bar to the admission of hearsay. But a few qualifications must be made. German law recognizes a series of privileges. It is somewhat irresolute in compelling production in court of various kinds of documentary proof. Testimony will be received from the parties themselves only in particular circumstances defined by law, and in no event may a party be compelled to testify. Party-testimony is viewed as a kind of last resort. This raises a quiddity, for parties are regularly heard in conference, nominally for purposes of clarification, not proof. I say "nominally" because German law tends to blur the line between evidence stricto sensu and other happenings in the courtroom.

Prooftaking is succeeded by conference, conference by prooftaking, and so on to the end of the regular proceedings in the first-instance court; and now we naturally ask, are there any shortcuts, any special devices for closing a case out promptly when it appears that there is overwhelming strength on one side and corresponding weakness on the other? The answer is no. The German system relies on the succession of conferences and prooftakings to show up strength or weakness with reasonable dispatch. Nor is there much in the way of stage-preclusion, that is, rules intended to discourage delaying afterthoughts by requiring that particular offers or objections be made at fixed points in the proceeding on pain of being otherwise lost to the party. The German action is not segmented into clear-cut stages—recall how pleadings may be thrown in late in the day—and it has in general a quality of "wholeness" or unity. But we do need to say here that the German system makes interestingly brisk provision for handling defaults; and we should also call attention to certain special speed-up devices: "dunning" proceedings, *Mahnverfahren,* available for "collection" cases and carried on regardless of amount in the inferior one-judge court; and "documentary-process," *Urkundenprozess,* used chiefly in suits on commercial paper, with proof initially limited to documents and party-testimony.

We come now to appellate review. The most notable fact about it is that on appeal to the court of second instance from final judgment, or from the important type of intermediate judgment which determines liability but leaves damages to be ascertained, the parties are entitled to a redoing of the case. The record made below, so far as it is thought to be free of error, stands as part of the proceedings, but the parties may add new proofs and invoke new legal theories, and the conduct of the cause is quite similar to that in the court below. Remember that article 139 on clarification and leading, with related duties and powers, continues to apply. The final court of review hears "revisions" on questions of law. As to matters of substance as distinguished from procedure, the court is not confined to the grounds urged by counsel. It seems a mark of the reality of the principle jura novit curia that this national court, dealing with a very large number of revisions coming up from the lower courts administered by the states, the *Länder,* is served by a bar limited by law to less than a score of lawyers.

The German court system is manned by a quite sizeable number of judges. They are career men, appointed on the basis of government examinations, modestly paid, of good but not exalted social prestige, looking primarily to ministerial departments of justice for advancement. In normal times men customarily enter into judicial service at an early age, generally without substantial experience in practice. Judges have traditionally been chided for *Lebensfremdheit,* undue detachment from the rough-and-tumble of life. We have caught a hint of their paternalistic role in the court procedure. This is not far distant from, indeed it comprises, an element of the bureaucratic. Working, many of them, in collegial courts whose judgments, stiffly authoritative in style, disclose neither individual authorship nor individual dissent, German judges live rather anonymous lives. And they are desk-bound through a large part of their working time, for files must be read in preparation for court sessions, and most decisions in actions large and small must be compendiously written up.

As to the German lawyers, I must avoid leaving the impression that their contribution to litigation is unimportant, or that their attitude is flaccid. Despite the court's capacity for active interpositions, the frame of the case is made by the lawyers and there is room for contentious striving. Still the procedural system we have outlined does not make for notably vigorous performance by counsel. Moreover the education of lawyers tends against their full identification with clients as combatants: a significant part of their post-University required training is as apprentice-judges. Most important, we must notice some economic facts. Lawyers' fees for litigation, generally corresponding with statutory scales fixed in relation to the amount in controversy, are low.

Court costs are also fixed by statute in relation to the amount in suit, so that a litigant is on the one hand prompted to moderate his demand for judgment, and can on the other hand make a reasonably accurate advance estimate of the expense of litigation. Taking all elements of expense into consideration, German litigation is cheap by comparison with the American brand. But on the threshold a German litigant must conjure with the fact that if as plaintiff or defendant he turns out loser in the lawsuit, he will have to reimburse his opponent's expenses—counsel fees and court costs at the statutory rates together with ordinary disbursements. Let us note here that contingent-fee arrangements—agreements for quota litis—are proscribed in German practice. A comprehensive system of state-provided legal aid aims to enable not only downright paupers but any citizen of insufficient means to prosecute or defend civil cases upon a plausible showing of a prospect of success.

Lastly, I must respond to the nervous question which any American laywer would surely want to ask: Does the German system get over its court business without undue delay? German court statistics—at least those publicly available and not held in subterranean tunnels by the ministries—are curiously sparse; but these figures combine with the opinion of German lawyers familiar with the scene to indicate that the courts, although handling a very considerable volume of cases, are disposing of their calendars with fair speed. However, the court of final review—the *Bundesgerichtshof* sitting in Karlsruhe, successor to the famous *Reichsgericht* which used to reside in Leipzig—has had a hard time in recent years overcoming a serious backlog.

II

* * * Let your mind range backward over my account of German procedure and contrast for the two systems the modes of determining and allocating expenses of litigation; the character and functions of the lawyers and of the judges; the concept of appeal; the approach to facts and proof; the pleadings; the central motor power of the process as a whole. Our short journey through the German system may well make us wary of joining hands with those amiable scholars who like to conclude, even over great apparent odds, that legal institutions in the Western world are in essence really the same.

* * *

Now see how this feature [of orality of proceedings] determines and intermeshes with others. Staggered prooftaking, which allows for afterthoughts, relieves the pressure to articulate fixed and precise issues in advance of receiving proof in order to prevent "surprise." There is little anxiety about the pleadings and small room for devices to trim and correct them. So also "discovery" mechanisms ahead of the display of proof in court, again directed to preventing surprise, can hardly be felt as an urgent need in the German system. Lawyers can get along with limited informal access to prospective witnesses. Incidentally, expense of investigation is not a large figure on the litigation budget. These are a few obvious examples of how episodic prooftaking ramifies its effects further and still further through the German procedure.

With us in this country jury trial must be carried out as a single continuous drama, for a jury cannot be assembled, dismissed and reconvened over a period of time. We tend toward concentrated trial even when the judge sits alone, perhaps by magnetic attraction to jury trial as the historic centerpiece of civil procedure, perhaps because the system puts a high value on the trier's fresh impression of live proof, perhaps for other reasons. Hence, the opposing sides must appear in court knowing the precise issues and fully armed and prepared to meet them. To these ends we have our pleadings and amendments and motions, our discovery devices, our pretrial conference. Concentrated trial forces accommodations in many rules and practices and has no doubt profoundly affected the character and role of the American lawyer and judge.

                    *   *   *

Probing further into attitudes towards facts and proof, do we not find on the American side a striking concern with exhausting sources of evidence and squeezing the last drop of advantage out of the pulp of multitudinous details? Facts are today often thrice canvassed at heavy expense: by informal methods, again by official discovery devices, and again at the trial proper. Pretrial sifting of the facts may improve the chance for settlement or other disposition without trial; it minimizes surprise at some risk of taking the fresh bloom off the testimony if the matter should reach trial. Although pretrial investigation is loose and far-ranging, the trial itself, faithful to its tough adversary spirit, perhaps responsive to the supposed needs of the jury as inexperienced, once-in-a-life-time triers, proceeds according to a code duello of exclusionary rules of evidence, with litigants "bound" by "their" witnesses. Examination and cross-examination, minutely recorded, pursue detail and test credibility with relentless assiduity.

In many respects German practice turns the tables. Prooftaking in court is notably untrammeled by tight rules of evidence: the triers are professionals, the adversary spirit is muffled. To be sure a restrictive attitude persists toward party-testimony. On a superficial view this attitude seems to be traceable to a cynical estimate of the amount of truth-telling that can be expected from those interested in the stakes. Continental writers sometimes relate it to a desire to preserve the individual's dignity. As we have seen, the restriction is in practice substantially overcome by interrogation of parties at conference; and I should perhaps add that it does not go so far as to prevent blood tests of the parties. The rules as to party-testimony thus hardly confound the generalization that prooftaking is "free." On the other hand the search for facts is neither broad nor vigorous. We have spoken of the limited access of lawyers to prospective witnesses out-of-court. It is true that the episodic movement of the case affords opportunity to the litigant—led by the court or stirred by hints in the testimony—to search for and offer additional proof whose existence or pertinence was unknown to him at the start; and there is still a further chance to enlarge the proofs on appeal. But episodic prooftaking, while providing room for something on the order of American discovery, is not thought of in that way. So the tendency is to bar "fishing" exercises at prooftakings, that is, to disallow questions to witnesses designed merely to uncover possible sources of proof. We may surely conclude that fact investigation in the German system does not in practice attain anywhere near the strength of the American.

The German method of taking testimony itself strikes an American lawyer as lamentably imprecise. Remember that the initial and principal interrogation of witnesses is conducted by the court which at least in the early stages of litigation will not have a comprehensive idea of the facts. Recording testimony in paraphrase is well calculated to bleach out color and blur detail. Some evidence may be received by the deciding plural bench only at relay from the single-judge acting as representative of the court. Impressions of the evidence are dulled by the very process of receiving it in installments over a period of time.

If the Germans are more casual than we are about the facts, if they are content to get a kind of generalized or synoptic rather than meticulous perception of the events in suit, if, as I believe, prooftaking as a whole has a subsidiary place in the German system, then we are led to speculations about the relation of procedural forms to the style of the substantive law. Is a fully codified substantive-law system of the civil-law type congenial to a pattern of fact-finding which would be felt to be inadequate to the needs of a common-law system? Is it significant for procedural development that primary reference in the one system is to the generalizations of the substantive code, not the case decisions, while the other system grows by matching case with case? Or are we in this country simply paying too much in time, effort, and money to pursue the finer lineaments of truth which must in any event elude us? * * *

* * *

Part VII

TRIAL

A. JUDGMENT WITHOUT TRIAL

1. DEVICES TO OBVIATE PLENARY TRIAL

NOTE ON MOTIONS FOR JUDGMENT BEFORE TRIAL

1. Judgment on the Pleadings

The motion for judgment on the pleadings has been considered previously. See Note on Challenging and Amending Pleadings After the Pleading Stage, supra p. 128. This device is mentioned here to suggest that functionally it is an additional means of avoiding a plenary trial. See James & Hazard § 5.18; F.R. C.P. 12(c). Although there is no express statutory authority in California for a motion for judgment on the pleadings, its use is well-recognized; there is no express time limitation governing this motion, which may be made prior to trial or presented for the first time at trial. The court on such a motion will look only to the face of the pleadings, not to supporting facts set forth in affidavits or otherwise. 6 Witkin 563–571. Cf. Fitzsimmons v. Jones, 179 Cal.App.2d 5, 3 Cal.Rptr. 373 (1960) (error to grant judgment for plaintiff on the pleadings in supersession of pretrial order which defined issues for trial: "We conclude * * * that the pre-trial order must control; that it precludes the rendered judgment on the pleadings, premised, as it is, on a resurrected, defective answer."). See also Godfrey v. Steinpress, 128 Cal.App.3d 154, 180 Cal.Rptr. 95 (1982).

2. Summary Judgment

See the section on summary judgment, supra p. 143. Compare the motion for summary judgment with the motion for judgment on the pleadings in light of F.R.C.P. 12(c). Can a motion for judgment on the pleadings ever be appropriate after discovery has been completed? See also N.Y. Temp. Comm'n, First Prelim.Rep. 315 (1957) (Statutes and Rules Regulating Summary Judgment, Judgment on the Pleadings and Related Procedures Prior to Trial).

3. Voluntary and Involuntary Dismissal

In addition to general demurrers (and their equivalent, i.e., motions to dismiss for failure to state a claim) and motions for judgment on the pleadings and summary judgment, there are other pre-trial procedural devices which may obviate the necessity of a plenary trial. Thus, there are motions to dismiss, both voluntary and involuntary. As to voluntary dismissals by plaintiff, compare C.C.P. 581(b)(1) with F.R.C.P. 41(a), noting that under the former plaintiff may voluntarily dismiss "at any time before the actual commencement of trial * * *," see 6 Witkin 378–379, whereas under the Federal Rule plaintiff's right to unilateral voluntary dismissal must be exercised "at any time before service by the adverse party of an answer or of a motion for summary judgment, whichever first occurs * * *." See 5 Moore ¶ 41.02. In both California and Federal practice, plaintiff's right of voluntary dismissal is curtailed where defendant has set up a counterclaim or otherwise sought affirmative relief. Compare C.C.P. 581(h), see 6 Witkin 381, with F.R.C.P. 41(a) (2), see 5 Moore ¶ 41.09. On some of the other difficulties that may arise in seeking to voluntarily dismiss a claim, see Unioil, Inc. v. E.F. Hutton & Co., supra p. 135. As to involuntary dismissals before trial, e.g., for abandonment or failure to prosecute the action, compare the general provisions of Rule 41(b) with the detailed California scheme discussed just below. See 5 Moore ¶ 41.11[2]; Colokathis v. Wentworth-Douglass Hospital, 693 F.2d 7 (1st Cir. 1982).

4. California Dismissal for Lack of Prosecution

California has an elaborate set of rules governing the involuntary dismissal of cases for want of prosecution. C.C.P. 583.110 et seq. The statutory scheme declares that a plaintiff must proceed with reasonable diligence in the prosecution of an action and that all parties must cooperate in bringing the action to trial or other disposition, although C.C.P. 583.130 states that trial on the merits is to be preferred over dismissal for lack of prosecution except in clear cases of statutory violation. C.C.P. 583.210 requires that service of process be effected within three years from the date of filing the action and that return of service be filed within 60 days thereafter. See Mannesmann Demag, Ltd. v. Superior Court, 172 Cal.App.3d 1118, 218 Cal.Rptr. 632 (1985). These provisions are mandatory and require the court to dismiss the action if they are not met, C.C.P. 583.250, unless the parties stipulate to a longer time, C.C.P. 583.230, or the three-year period is for some reason tolled, C.C.P. 583.240. Further, C.C.P. 583.310 requires dismissal of an action if it is not brought to trial within five years after it is commenced, though again the parties may stipulate otherwise, C.C.P. 583.330, and the period may be tolled in certain circumstances, C.C.P. 583.340. See Gorman v. Holte, 164 Cal.App.3d 984, 211 Cal.Rptr. 34 (1985).

5. Offer of Judgment

F.R.C.P. 68 provides for an offer of judgment by a defendant, and that "If the judgment finally obtained by the offeree is not more favorable than the offer, the offeree must pay the costs incurred after the making of the offer." In Delta Air Lines, Inc. v. August, 450 U.S. 346, 101 S.Ct. 1146, 67 L.Ed.2d 287 (1981), this provision was held inapplicable where a plaintiff rejected an offer and then lost altogether at trial, because there was no "judgment obtained by the offeree." Many states have provisions for offers both ways, e.g., Conn.Prac.Book, Superior Court Rules (Civil) §§ 341–350. See Burbank, Proposals to Amend Rule 68—Time to Abandon Ship, 19 U.Mich.J.L.Ref. 425 (1986); Miller, An Economic Analysis of Rule 68, 15 J.Legal Stud. 93 (1986).

In Marek v. Chesny, 473 U.S. 1, 105 S.Ct. 3012, 87 L.Ed.2d 1 (1985), the Supreme Court held that the term "costs" in Rule 68 includes attorneys fees recoverable under the Civil Rights Attorney's Fees Awards Act of 1976 (42 U.S. C.A. § 1988), so that a civil rights plaintiff who rejected a settlement offer and later recovered an amount less than the offer could not recover attorneys fees incurred subsequent to the rejection. The Court reasoned that all costs properly awardable in an action, including statutory attorneys fees, fall within the scope of Rule 68 and rejected the argument that denying recovery of such fees violated congressional intent and created a disincentive to the filing of civil rights actions. The Court also held that binding settlement offers under Rule 68 may include amounts for both substantive relief and attorneys fees.

2. DEFAULT JUDGMENTS

UNITED STATES v. CIRAMI

United States Court of Appeals for the Second Circuit, 1976.
535 F.2d 736.*

MULLIGAN, CIRCUIT JUDGE:

This is an appeal from an order of the United States District Court for the Eastern District of New York, Hon. Walter Bruchhausen, J., filed on October 6, 1975, denying the motion of defendants, pursuant to Fed.R.Civ.P. 60(b)(6), to vacate a summary judgment against them in favor of the United States in an action arising out of an alleged tax deficiency. We affirm.

I. FACTS

The tax deficiency imposed here arose out of Salvatore Cirami's operation in the early 1960's of Air Freight Haulage Co., which was engaged in the business of supplying truck transportation service. Since Cirami operated the company as a sole proprietorship, the income and expenses of the business were reflected on his personal federal income tax returns, which he filed jointly with his then-wife. The returns for the years 1961–1963 inclusive were audited by the Internal Revenue Service, resulting in wholesale disallowances of claimed business expenses and deductions which allegedly were not substantiated. Accordingly, on September 14, 1966 a statutory notice of deficiency reflecting the disallowances was sent by IRS to the Ciramis; the total tax deficiency assessed was $153,087.34, plus a penalty of $19,578.91. * * *

On February 28, 1973, almost six years later, IRS instituted an action in the Eastern District of New York against appellants and their son, James, in order to reduce the stated tax assessments to judgment, to set aside allegedly fraudulent conveyances of property made by Salvatore Cirami to his son, and for other ancillary relief. To defend the action the Ciramis retained the services of Peter R. Newman, Esq., of Syosset, New York, who was recommended by the Ciramis' accountant DeStefano and who himself (according to the government's attorney at oral argument of the appeal) was a former IRS agent. On March 20 Newman filed an answer on behalf of his clients; essentially the answer consisted of a general denial and a counterclaim for taxes "illegally and erroneously collected."

---

* Some of the court's footnotes are omitted. See also 563 F.2d 26 (2d Cir. 1977), setting aside the default in further proceedings upon a fuller showing of facts by the defendant.

On December 28, 1973, the government moved for partial summary judgment against the Ciramis, pursuant to Fed.R.Civ.P. 56; the motion was supported by an affidavit from the IRS district director, setting forth the amounts assessed, and by a memorandum of law which attempted to demonstrate that the defendants' general denial contained in their answer did not overcome the presumptive correctness of the assessments made against them. No opposition to the motion was ever filed on defendants' behalf. As a result, Judge Bruchhausen granted partial summary judgment "in all respects" by order dated March 18, 1974; the order also stated that "[c]opies hereof are being forwarded to the attorneys for the respective parties." Judgment was entered on June 12, 1974 against Salvatore and Margaret Cirami in the total amount of $270,792.43, plus interest from the date of entry. The judgment itself again noted that no opposition was filed to the government's motion for partial summary judgment. Notice of entry of judgment was filed on July 5.

Thereafter, appellants retained new counsel. According to his brief on this appeal, Salvatore Cirami substituted Carl Mione, Esq. as his counsel on August 28, 1974.[4] A notice of appearance for Margaret Cirami was filed on December 23, 1974 by the firm of Wagman, Cannon & Musoff; however, according to the government, that firm advised IRS on October 4, 1974 that it was representing Margaret Cirami.

On May 1, 1975, appellants, through their new attorneys, filed a motion pursuant to Fed.R.Civ.P. 60(b)(6) to vacate the partial summary judgment entered for the government. In support of the motion, on July 1 appellants introduced records and papers of Air Freight Haulage Co., plus affidavits from two accountants (Bernard Zipern and Seymour Unterberg) who had audited the company's books during the years in question. These affidavits sought to explain some of the company's record-keeping procedures, and in one of them, accountant Unterberg said that his findings "indicate that, with minor exception, all of the business deductions claimed by Salvatore and Margaret Cirami on their joint 1961, 1962 and 1963 income tax returns are fully substantiated by the available books and records of Air Freight Haulage Co." In addition the notice of motion itself was accompanied by an affidavit of Salvatore Cirami, dated April 28, 1975, in which Cirami claimed that "[i]t was not until my present attorney, Mr. Mione took possession of Mr. Newman's files in this matter did I know that the United States had taken summary judgment against my former wife Margaret and myself."

The government filed memoranda in opposition to appellants' motion to vacate the earlier judgment. On October 6, 1975, Judge Bruchhausen entered an order denying the motion, essentially on the grounds that appellants failed to meet the requirement of extraordinary circumstances necessary for relief under Rule 60(b)(6), and that appellants did

---

4. It appears, however, that Cirami and Mione were acquainted before that, since on June 6, 1973 Mione notarized Cirami's affidavit in opposition to the government's motion to dismiss the Ciramis' counterclaim * * *.

not make their motion within a reasonable time, as is also required by the Rule.[6] This appeal followed.

II. DISCUSSION

Rule 60(b) of the Federal Rules of Civil Procedure permits a party to be relieved from a final judgment basically for the following reasons (corresponding to the subdivisions of the Rule): (1) "mistake, inadvertence, surprise, or excusable neglect"; (2) "newly discovered evidence which by due diligence could not have been discovered in time to move for a new trial under Rule 59(b)"; (3) "fraud . . . misrepresentation, or other misconduct of an adverse party"; (4) "the judgment is void"; (5) "the judgment has been satisfied, released, or discharged . . ." or (6) "any other reason justifying relief from the operation of the judgment." The motion made below was pursuant to subdivision 6 of Rule 60(b) which while general in terms is properly applicable only upon a showing of "exceptional circumstances." Rinieri v. News Syndicate Co., 385 F.2d 818, 822 (2d Cir. 1967); Ackermann v. United States, 340 U.S. 193, 202, 71 S.Ct. 209, 213, 95 L.Ed. 207, 212 (1950).

The motion made below was based upon a three-page affidavit of Salvatore Cirami * * *.

The last four paragraphs of the Cirami affidavit which are here pertinent follow:

> 9. When the summons was served upon me in the instant action, I went to Mr. DeStefano who referred me to Peter Newman, Esq.

> 10. Mr. Newman agreed to represent my former wife, Margaret, my son, James and myself in this proceeding.

> 11. Mr. Newman and I met on some three occasions including the initial conference at which time we only discussed personal background information.

> 12. It was not until my present attorney, Mr. Mione took possession of Mr. Newman's files in this matter did I know that the United States had taken summary judgment against my former wife Margaret and myself.

The exceptional circumstances relied upon by the appellants here is the fact that their then-counsel, Newman, permitted the United States to take summary judgment for more than $270,000 by default for reasons described by appellants as "unknown." We have been provided with no affidavit of Newman which would cast any light on the

---

6. The opinion below also took notice of the earlier conviction of Salvatore and James Cirami for attempted evasion of social security and unemployment taxes and for aiding in the preparation of false returns. In that action, another trucking corporation run by the Ciramis (Air Package Distribution Service Ltd.) sought to classify its truck drivers not as employees but rather as independent contractors, so as to avoid paying social security and unemployment taxes. The convictions were affirmed by this court, United States v. Cirami, 2 Cir., 510 F.2d 69, and certiorari was denied, 421 U.S. 964, 95 S.Ct. 1952, 44 L.Ed.2d 451 (1975).

circumstances of his failure to contest the government's motion for partial summary judgment. Neither have we received any affidavits from present counsel of appellants which would indicate what efforts, if any, have been made to elicit Newman's testimony, either voluntarily or under subpoena. * * *

The question of the extent to which the error of counsel may constitute a basis for Rule 60(b) relief is somewhat vexing. Normally, the motion would be made pursuant to Rule 60(b)(1) on the theory that counsel's error constitutes a mistake or excusable neglect. This Circuit has rather consistently refused to relieve a client of the burdens of a final judgment entered against him due to the mistake or omission of his attorney by reason of the latter's ignorance of the law or of the rules of the court, or his inability to efficiently manage his caseload. * * * This approach is supported by the opinion of Mr. Justice Harlan for the Court in Link v. Wabash R. R., 370 U.S. 626, 633–34, 82 S.Ct. 1386, 1390, 8 L.Ed.2d 734, 740 (1962) where he commented:

> There is certainly no merit to the contention that dismissal of petitioner's claim because of his counsel's unexcused conduct imposes an unjust penalty on the client. Petitioner voluntarily chose this attorney as his representative in the action, and he cannot now avoid the consequences of the acts or omissions of this freely selected agent. Any other notion would be wholly inconsistent with our system of representative litigation, in which each party is deemed bound by the acts of his lawyer-agent and is considered to have "notice of all facts, notice of which can be charged upon the attorney." (Citation omitted).
>
> * * *

At the same time there is authority for the proposition that where the conduct of counsel is grossly negligent, there may be a basis for relief under Rule 60(b)(6). The leading case for this proposition is L. P. Steuart, Inc. v. Matthews, 117 U.S.App.D.C. 279, 329 F.2d 234, cert. denied, 379 U.S. 824, 85 S.Ct. 50, 13 L.Ed.2d 35 (1964). * * *

The appellants here rely upon subdivision 6 of Rule 60(b) and not subdivision 1. Since subdivision 1 requires that the motion be made within one year after the judgment and a subdivision 6 motion must be made only "within a reasonable time," the distinction becomes crucial in some cases. Here, the motion was made within a year so that the choice of appellant was obviously not dictated by time considerations. The question then becomes: should we follow *Steuart* and hold that gross negligence of counsel warrants the relief sought. * * *

* * *

* * * L. P. Steuart, Inc. v. Matthews, supra, is * * * inapposite. In that case former counsel's affidavit revealed that at the time of his default he had been beset by personal problems, including the death of his parents and the serious illness of his wife. Moreover, his client's affidavit noted that he had made numerous inquiries of his former counsel who had either refused to answer or had assured him that the

case was proceeding and would soon be settled. Judge Edgerton found that Rule 60(b)(6) was broad enough to permit relief when "personal problems of counsel cause him grossly to neglect a diligent client's case and mislead the client." 329 F.2d at 235.[8] In sum, even if gross negligence provides a basis for Rule 60(b)(6) relief, the record before us fails to establish any gross negligence or misleading of the appellants by counsel and is bereft of any indication of client diligence.

* * *

NOTE ON DEFAULTS AND DEFAULT JUDGMENTS

1. Note the distinction, explicit in both F.R.C.P. 55 and C.C.P. 585, between entry of "default" and entry of "*judgment* by default." In California the clerk, if there is a clerk, always enters the default (except where service is by publication); but whether he also enters the judgment by default without court order, or whether the court must order entry of judgment, depends on the kind of case involved. Respecting the types of situations in which the clerk may enter judgment by default, contrast F.R.C.P. 55(b)(1) and N.Y.C.P.L.R. § 3215 with C.C.P. 585; see also C.C.P. 579, 586. See Ford v. Superior Court, 34 Cal.App.3d 338, 109 Cal.Rptr. 844 (1973); 6 Witkin 536–538; Reynolds Securities, Inc. v. Underwriters Bank & Trust Co., 44 N.Y.2d 568, 406 N.Y.S.2d 743, 378 N.E.2d 106 (1978). On the California procedure generally, see C.E.B., 2 Calif.Civ.Pro. Before Trial c. 30 (1978); Note, California's Default and Default Judgment: A Procedural and Substantive Review, 15 W.St.U.L.Rev. 679 (1988).

2. Under F.R.C.P. 54(c) and C.C.P. 580 the relief granted to the plaintiff by default judgment, in contrast to other judgments, cannot exceed that demanded in her complaint. See Becker v. S. P. V. Constr. Co., 27 Cal.3d 489, 165 Cal. Rptr. 825, 612 P.2d 915 (1980), applying the C.C.P. 580 limitation that a default judgment may not exceed the prayer but sustaining the judgment up to the amount of the prayer. Compare N.Y.C.P.L.R. § 3215(b); see 4 Weinstein, Korn & Miller ¶ 3215.11. See also Greenup v. Rodman, 42 Cal.3d 822, 231 Cal.Rptr. 220, 726 P.2d 1295 (1986), holding C.C.P. 580 applicable to a default judgment entered as a discovery sanction.

3. Where defendant has "appeared in the action," F.R.C.P. 55(b)(2) requires notice of the application for judgment. See Anno., 73 A.L.R.3d 1250 (what constitutes "appearance" for this purpose). In some types of actions, judgment by default is not permitted at all, e.g., in California, actions for dissolution of marriage, C.C. 4511; adverse possessor's suits, C.C.P. 764.010, see also C.C.P. 585(c); actions to reestablish destroyed land records, C.C.P. 751.14; applications for writs of mandamus, C.C.P. 1088. What philosophy or philosophies underly these sections? Compare F.R.C.P. 55(e) (no judgment by default against the United States unless the claimant establishes his right to relief by satisfactory evidence); see 6 Moore ¶ 55.12.

4. Where, after default of defendant, the plaintiff applies to the court for entry of default judgment, note that under F.R.C.P. 55(b)(2) the court, when

---

8. In his dissent in *Steuart*, Judge Miller followed the reasoning of Link v. Wabash R. R., supra, and its holding that the client is bound by the acts and omissions of his attorney. He suggested that the proper remedy was a malpractice action by the client against his negligent attorney, 329 F.2d at 238. A similar suggestion was made by Judge Smith in Schwarz v. United States, supra, 384 F.2d at 835–36. We do not imply at all that such a remedy is feasible here in view of the record, or more accurately, lack of any record, before us.

necessary, "may conduct such hearings or order such references as it deems necessary and proper and shall accord a right of trial by jury to the parties when and as required by any statute of the United States." Compare C.C.P. 585(b).

The Soldiers' and Sailors' Civil Relief Act, 50 U.S.C.A.App. § 501 et seq., is a comprehensive measure for the protection of the rights of those in military service and the suspension in certain circumstances of the enforcement of their civil liabilities. Section 520 provides a detailed scheme to safeguard persons in the military service against entry of default judgments without protection of their rights, including provision for appointment of an attorney to represent such persons. See 6 Moore ¶ 55.13; 6 Witkin 218–219; Douglas, Heilbroner and DeGrandpre, The Soldiers' and Sailors' Act: A Guide for the Practitioner, 25 N.H.B.J. 193, 211 (1984). Clerks' offices commonly provide forms of affidavit so that plaintiff's attorney conveniently can effect compliance with the provisions of § 520.

5. On setting aside default judgments, see also C.C.P. 473; N.Y.C.P.L.R. 5015; 6 Moore ¶ 55.10 and 7 Moore ¶ 60.22[2]; 10 Wright & Miller §§ 2692–2700 and 11 id. § 2858; 8 Witkin 545–593. Compare C.C.P. 473.5, giving a defendant not personally served (i.e., served only by publication or mailing) a right to have a broader right of relief from default than a defendant who has been personally served. See also Restatement Second of Judgments § 67.

In Shamblin v. Brattain, 44 Cal.3d 474, 243 Cal.Rptr. 902, 749 P.2d 339 (1988), defendant's name had been removed inadvertently from the court's mailing list and he therefore failed to receive notice of a new trial. Default judgment was entered. After discovering the default judgment, defendant moved to set it aside pursuant to C.C.P. 473. Defendant's failure to appear was held excusable.

In a similar vein, the Supreme Court, in Peralta v. Heights Medical Center, Inc., __ U.S. __, 108 S.Ct. 896, 99 L.Ed.2d 75 (1988), held that it is a denial of due process to require that a party who was not properly served must, as a condition to having a default judgment set aside, show that he has a nonfrivolous defense on the merits.

3. SETTLEMENT

1 BELLI, MODERN TRIALS § 109 (1954)*
Technique of Settlement From the Plaintiff's Viewpoint

I believe it can be said that in every case there is a figure which it would be to the plaintiff's advantage to accept and which it would also be the defendant's advantage to pay. Therefore, speaking theoretically, every damage case should be settled and no case should go through trial.

For illustration, let us take a case that has a true settlement value of $10,000.00. To try that case would probably cost the defendant about $1,000.00 in attorney fees, jury fees, expert and lay witness fees. So, it would be to the defendant's advantage to settle the case for any figure under $11,000.00.

On the other hand, if we placed a fair value on the plaintiff attorney's time, it would also cost the plaintiff and his attorney about $1,000.00 in similar time and expense to try the case. So, it would be to the plaintiff's advantage to settle for any figure above $9,000.00.

In other words, on this theoretical case which has a true settlement value of $10,000.00, there is a zone between $9,000.00 and $11,000.00 within which it would be to the advantage of both the plaintiff and the defendant to settle. The most equitable settlement figure, of course, would be $10,000.00.

Now, if it be true that theoretically every damage case should be settled, why is it that our trial Courts are constantly busy? Why do I try some of my cases? We all recognize that a jury trial is the most expensive way there is to settle the rights of litigants. The time and expense of lawyers, litigants, the witnesses, Courts and juries all add up to an enormous cost.

Obviously, the answer is that the plaintiff thinks he has more to gain by trial than by acceptance of the defendant's offer; and also that the defendant thinks he has more to gain by trial than by payment of the plaintiff's demand. In other words, we go through trial because we can't agree on the settlement value of the case.

Therefore, whenever a case goes through trial it means that someone has missed on his settlement evaluation. Either the plaintiff has valued it too high or the defendant too low. If the settlement figures are quite far apart, it may be that both parties missed the right figure.

EDWARDS v. BORN, INC.
United States District Court, Virgin Islands, 1985.
608 F.Supp. 580.

DAVID V. O'BRIEN, DISTRICT JUDGE.

On behalf of their respective clients, the attorneys in this personal injury case reached a settlement during a pre-trial conference on December 12, 1984. The plaintiffs' attorney accepted an offer made jointly by the defendants' counsel of $150,000 in full settlement of all plaintiffs' claims. Each attorney stated that he had the authority to act on behalf of his client.

Shortly thereafter, plaintiffs repudiated the settlement and asserted that their attorney had no authority to enter into it. * * *

I. FACTS

Keithley Edwards was employed at Hess Virgin Islands Corporation on September 24, 1982 when he was injured while working on a boiler supplied by Born, Inc., installed by Fluor Engineers & Constructors, Inc., and owned by St. Croix Petrochemical Corporation. He filed this action against all three companies, and later his wife was added as party plaintiff with a loss of consortium claim. Both were represented by the same attorney.

Full discovery took place among the parties. Mr. Edwards' essential claim of injuries concerned his back, a partial loss of the sense of taste and complete loss of the sense of smell. Since he did not lose a great deal of time from work, the issue of lost wages past, or future earning capacity, was not a major consideration in the monetary calculation of his claim.

A trial date was set for the period commencing January 8, 1985, and several weeks prior to that time, the Court scheduled an informal pre-trial conference among the attorneys to inquire into the possibility of settlement. * * *

* * * The purpose was to seek a narrowing of the differences to a point where a settlement offer could be made which would be mutually acceptable.

In the instant situation, the narrowing of positions resulted in an offer by defendants' counsel to plaintiffs' counsel within the range of what the latter had informed the Court was necessary to settle all of plaintiffs' claims. After the offer was made and accepted in chambers, a court reporter was called in and the offer and acceptance was repeated. The transcript was made a part of this record.

One of the defendants' counsel, speaking for all three of them, when asked by the Court whether he had an offer of settlement, responded:

"The offer is $150,000 in full settlement of all claims."

To which the Court inquired:

"And that is all claims of all plaintiffs? Plaintiff will pay his own compensation claim out of the proceeds; is that correct?"

The attorney responded:

"That is correct."

All defendants' counsel placed on the record their authority to make this combined offer. The Court then turned to plaintiffs' counsel who stated:

"I accept that offer. I am authorized to accept it on behalf of the plaintiffs."

Defense counsel then ordered settlement drafts totaling $150,000 which were delivered to plaintiffs' attorney. At that point, the plaintiffs rejected the checks, claiming that they had not given their attorney authority to settle their claims for $150,000. The attorney moved to withdraw and plaintiffs retained their present counsel.

At the hearing, plaintiffs' original attorney testified under oath that plaintiffs told him they would rely on his good judgment and experience as to the amount of the settlement. No figures were discussed. The plaintiffs filed affidavits indicating that at no time, orally or in writing, did they authorize the attorney to settle their claims and that the question of a settlement demand was never discussed. Both plaintiffs indicated that they had no idea a settlement conference was to take place. Mr. Edwards asserted that he was in Antigua at the time it was scheduled. The plaintiffs further swore that the first they learned of any settlement was after the conference when they were notified by the attorney.

II. DISCUSSION

A. *Public Policy Behind Settlements*

The Third Circuit Court of Appeals has consistently held that "[a]n agreement to settle a law suit is binding upon the parties, whether or not made in the presence of the court, and even in the absence of a writing." Green v. John H. Lewis & Co., 436 F.2d 389, 390 (3d Cir. 1970). * * *

B. *Express Authority to Settle*

It is a well accepted principle that an attorney has no power to settle his client's case nor to consent to a dismissal upon the merits without express authority. United States v. Beebe, 180 U.S. 343, 21 S.Ct. 371, 45 L.Ed. 563 (1901); Bradford Exchange v. The Treins Exchange, 600 F.2d 99 (7th Cir.1979); Associates Discount Co. v. Goldman, 524 F.2d 1051 (3d Cir.1975); Thomas v. Colorado Trust Deed Funds, Inc., 366 F.2d 136 (10th Cir.1966); In re Gsand, 153 F.2d 1001 (3d Cir.1946); Griego v. Kokkeler, 543 P.2d 729 (Colo.Ct.App.1975). Express authority is the authority that the principal, the client, expressly or explicitly gives to the agent, the attorney. United States v. Martinez, 613 F.2d 473, 481 (3d Cir.1980); Downing v. Fortuna Bay Estates, Inc., 17 V.I. 20, 26 (D.V.I.1980); see also Restatement (Second) of Agency § 7 comment c (1958).

It is clear from the plaintiffs' affidavits as well as the testimony of their original attorney that by no acts of theirs was express authority conferred on the attorney to settle plaintiffs' claims. When an attorney is told by his or her client that the client relies on the attorney's judgment and experience in these matters, the attorney is not relieved from further consultation with the client when settlement negotiations reach specific dollar amounts.

According to the ABA Code of Professional Responsibility a lawyer is entitled to make decisions of his or her own only in those areas "not affecting the merits of the cause or substantially prejudicing the rights of a client." It is for the client to decide whether or not to accept a settlement offer. Model Code of Professional Responsibility EC 7–7 (1983).

C. *Apparent Authority*

Notwithstanding the lack of express settlement authority, we must discern whether plaintiffs' attorney had apparent authority to settle the action. In order to determine whether the settlement should be set aside, we must also decide whether apparent authority is sufficient to bind the client.

Under the law of agency, apparent authority is defined as "the power to affect the legal relations of another person by transactions with third persons, professedly as agent for the other, arising from and in accordance with the other's manifestations to such third persons." Restatement (Second) of Agency § 8 (1958) (applicable to the Virgin Islands by virtue of 1 V.I.C. § 4 (1967)).

Certain courts hold that apparent authority is sufficient to bind a client to a settlement entered into by his or her attorney. In Glazer v. J.C. Bradford & Co., 616 F.2d 167 (5th Cir.1980), the court found that "a client is bound by his attorney's agreement to settle a lawsuit, even though the attorney may not have had express authority to settle, if the opposing party was unaware of any limitation on the attorney's apparent authority." Id. at 168 (Georgia law).

Similarly, in International Telemeter Corp. v. Teleprompter Corp., 592 F.2d 49, 55 (2d Cir.1979), the court held that as long as there was no reason to believe the attorney was exceeding the scope of his apparent authority in settlement negotiations, the opposing party was entitled to rely on it.

The reasoning behind these rulings was stated in Bergstrom v. Sears, Roebuck & Co., 532 F.Supp. 923 (D.Minn.1982). The court found that "where one of two innocent parties must suffer from the wrongful act of another, the loss should fall upon the one who, by his conduct, created the circumstances which enabled the third party to perpetrate the wrong and cause the loss." Id. at 933 (citing 3 Am.Jur.2d Agency § 76 (1962)).

Thus, although the settlement should not be set aside, the client would have a remedy against his or her attorney. See, e.g. Parker v. Board of Trustees of Southern Illinois Univ., 74 Ill.App. 467, 220 N.E.2d 258, 260 (1966); Cohen v. Goldman, 85 R.I. 434, 132 A.2d 414, 417 (1957); Hallock v. State of New York, 64 N.Y.2d 224, 485 N.Y.S.2d 510, 474 N.E.2d 1178 (Dec. 27, 1984); see generally R. Mallen & V. Levit, Legal Malpractice § 580 at 727 (2d ed. 1981).

There is, however, a distinct minority view, relied on by the plaintiffs, which states that an attorney has no authority to settle or compromise an action without express permission from his or her client. See Harrop v. Western Airlines, Inc., 550 F.2d 1143 (9th Cir. 1977) (California law); United States v. State of Texas, 523 F.Supp. 703 (E.D.Tex.1981); Daley v. Bright, 413 F.Supp. 28, 29 (E.D.Pa.1975) (Pennsylvania law); Rothman v. Fillette, 305 Pa.Super. 28, 451 A.2d 225 (1982).

We believe that the majority position instructs us, public policy compels us, and the special circumstances of legal practice in the Virgin Islands requires us to uphold settlements entered into by an attorney clothed with apparent authority. Of course, if the settlement is so unfair as to put the third party on notice of fraud, collusion, mistake or accident, it will be set aside.

* * *

The dispositive question, then, is whether plaintiffs' original attorney had apparent authority to settle the plaintiffs' claim. The mere retention of an attorney does not bestow apparent authority to settle or compromise a client's cause of action. See, e.g., Luis C. Forteza e Hijos, Inc. v. Mills, 534 F.2d 415, 418 (1st Cir.1976); Hayes v. Eagle–Picher Industries, Inc., 513 F.2d 892, 893 (10th Cir.1975); Sockolof v. Eden Point North Condominium, 421 So.2d 716, 719 (Fla.Dist.Ct.App.1982); Rothman v. Fillette, 305 Pa.Super. 28, 451 A.2d 225, 227–28 (1982); Annot., 30 A.L.R.2d 944 (1953).

According to the Restatement (Second) of Agency § 27 (1958):

> apparent authority to do an act is created as to a third person by written or spoken words or any other conduct of the principal which, reasonably interpreted, causes the third person to believe that the principal consents to have the act done on his behalf by the person purporting to act for him.

See Amritt v. Paragon Homes, Inc., 9 V.I. 570, 573, 474 F.2d 1251, 1252 (3d Cir.1973); Leader v. Merchant's Market, Inc., 1985 St.T.Supp. ___, (D.V.I. Feb. 7, 1985); Downing v. Fortuna Bay Estates, 17 V.I. 20, 26 (Terr.Ct.1980).

Because the agent, in this instance the attorney, cannot clothe himself with apparent authority, we must examine the representations made by the principal, the plaintiffs, to the third party, the defendants' counsel. These representations may be made directly, or through authorized statements of the agent, from documents or other indicia of authority given by the principal to the agent, or from third persons who have heard of the agent's authority through authorized channels. Restatement (Second) of Agency § 27 comment a (1958).

It is justifiable for third persons to rely on an agent's apparent authority when the principal puts an agent into, or knowingly permits him or her to occupy, a position in which, according to the ordinary habits of persons in the locality or profession, it is usual for the agent to have such authority, unless there is a reason to know otherwise. Restatement (Second) of Agency § 49 comment c (1958).

In this case the complaint was filed on December 10, 1982. Plaintiffs were represented from the outset by the same attorney. When interrogatories were sent from the defense to plaintiffs' counsel requiring the personal signature of Keithley Edwards on the answers, such signed answers were returned via the plaintiffs' attorney as a matter of course. When other documents and medical data of Keithley Edwards were requested, they were produced via the plaintiffs' attorney. When a deposition of the plaintiff was noticed to his attorney, Keithley Edwards promptly appeared. Two separate pre-trial orders were entered requiring counsel to appear with settlement authority, or to have the client actually present at the pre-trial conference. Plaintiffs' attorney appeared at all conferences of this nature without his clients. Under such a situation, there is an understanding that the attorney arrives with authority to settle unless restrictions are expressly stated.

In sum, then, whenever the performance of the client was personally necessary, he acted through the attorney. Whether it was in answering interrogatories or producing documents, or showing up at his own deposition, he either answered, produced, or appeared through or with his attorney.

The manifestation by plaintiff Keithley Edwards of the extent of the authority he granted to his attorney was strikingly indicated when defense counsel took his deposition. He revealed that his attorney had recommended, and he had accepted without question, the very physicians who would diagnose his injuries and treat them. These are injuries which he considered serious and possibly permanent or disabling. He also accepted without question the recommendation of his attorney as to a psychiatrist who would probe each recess of his mind, and to whom he would reveal the most personal of data. If a client would unhesitatingly place himself in the hands of his attorney to provide medical and psychiatric assistance of the most vital and personal nature, and defendants' counsel have been made aware of this form of apparent authority, can there be any doubt that the same defense counsel would consider that the client extended this authority in his attorney to matters monetary?

This Court conducted the pre-trial settlement conference. All information on potential damages was reviewed, as well as possible contributory negligence and other defenses. We believe that the settlement was within the acceptable range, and cannot be set aside for fraud, collusion or overreaching. It was no easy task for the Court to move defense counsel up from the original offer to the amount finally agreed upon.

Given all that has been pointed out herein, the reliance by defendants' counsel on the appearance of authority in the hands of plaintiffs' counsel was entirely reasonable. We therefore conclude that plaintiffs' counsel was clothed with apparent authority to settle their claims.

* * *

NOTE ON SETTLEMENT AGREEMENTS

1. As the Belli excerpt, supra, indicates, litigation can be considered simply a failure of the settlement process. The literature on settlement is enormous. See, e.g., Priest and Klein, The Selection of Disputes for Litigation, 13 J.Legal Stud. 1 (1984); Nalebuff, Credible Pretrial Negotiation, 18 RAND J. Econ. 198 (1987); Galanter, Reading the Landscape of Disputes: What We Know and Don't Know (And Think We Know) About Our Allegedly Contentious and Litigious Society, 31 U.C.L.A.L.Rev. 4 (1983) (arguing that there has not been an explosion of litigation and that most disputes are abandoned or settled).

2. For a general discussion of the contractual aspects of settlements, see Havighurst, Problems Concerning Settlement Agreements, 53 Nw.U.L.Rev. 283 (1958). For discussion and criticism of the distinction between "release" and "covenant not to sue," see Havighurst, The Effect of a Settlement with One Co-Obligor Upon the Obligations of the Others, 45 Corn.L.Q. 1 (1959). For discussions of the California cases involving attempts by plaintiffs to avoid releases, see Comment, Effect of the Personal Injury Release on Further Recovery in California, 42 Calif.L.Rev. 161 (1954); Note, New Proposal for an Old Problem: Protect Victims of Unfair Releases, 1 Stan.L.Rev. 298 (1949). See

also Dice v. Akron, C. & Y.R.R., supra p. 603. On the special problems of settlement in dissolution of marriage litigation, see C.E.B., California Marital Termination Settlements (1971).

Because there are significant differences in the laws of various states on releases, covenants and similar contracts, complications sometimes arise when a settlement contract is made in one state relating to a dispute that arose in another state. On this, see Note, Releases in the Conflict of Laws, 60 Colum.L. Rev. 522 (1960).

3. A "release" or a "covenant not to sue" may be entered into either before or after suit has been commenced. When a settlement has been reached after suit has been commenced, it usually takes the form of a release together with a stipulated entry of judgment of dismissal. It may, however, take the form of entry of judgment against defendant in the amount agreed upon. For a discussion of settlements involving judgments, see Note, The Consent Judgment as an Instrument of Compromise and Settlement, 72 Harv.L.Rev. 1314 (1959). On consent decrees, see the analysis and review of authorities in Mengler, Consent Decree Paradigms: Models Without Meaning, 29 B.C.L.Rev. 291 (1988); Symposium, Consent Decrees: Practical Problems and Legal Dilemmas, 1987 U.Chi.Legal Forum 1. For forms of release and consent judgment see C.E.B., California Civil Procedure During Trial c. 24 (1960). Settlement agreements are enforcible like other contracts, see, e.g., Harman v. Pauley, 678 F.2d 479 (4th Cir. 1982).

4. An attorney has no power to settle a case without his client's authority, see 1 Witkin 213–216, although some courts, as Edwards v. Born indicates, will approve settlements over a client's objection if the attorney had "apparent" authority to enter into the agreement. And once a settlement has been agreed upon, whether by express or apparent authority of the attorney, it seems clear that the client cannot disavow it. See Reid v. Prentice–Hall, Inc., 261 F.2d 700 (6th Cir.1958) (trial judge properly dismissed complaint when plaintiff refused to accept defendant's tender of the amount agreed upon in settlement); Beirne v. Fitch Sanitarium, Inc., 167 F.Supp. 652 (S.D.N.Y.1958) (entry of summary judgment against defendant in the amount of the settlement). Would the plaintiffs in Edwards v. Born have a remedy against their attorney for acting in excess of authority? What would be the proof of damage?

5. Federal Rule 68 provides that a defending party may make an offer of settlement which, if rejected by the claimant, entitles the defending party to costs incurred after the offer was made "[i]f the judgment finally obtained by the offeree is not more favorable than the offer." In Delta Air Lines, Inc. v. August, 450 U.S. 346, 101 S.Ct. 1146, 67 L.Ed.2d 287 (1981), defendant in a Title VII action offered $450 to settle plaintiff's $20,000 claim; after the offer was rejected, the case was tried and defendant won. The Supreme Court held that the quoted language did not apply because the judgment was not "obtained by the offeree." Hence, the judge retained discretion under Rule 54(d) to require each party to bear its own costs. Compare C.C.P. 998, construed in T.M. Cobb Co. v. Superior Court, 36 Cal.3d 273, 204 Cal.Rptr. 143, 682 P.2d 338 (1984).

6. As a rule settlements do not require court approval, but there are exceptions. Compromises of class actions require court consent, as do dismissals. F.R.C.P. 23(e). See Saylor v. Lindsley, supra p. 888. The Antitrust Procedures and Penalties Act (Tunney Act), 15 U.S.C.A. § 16(b–h), requires public disclosure and judicial scrutiny of consent decrees in antitrust cases. But this act is not applicable to a stipulation of outright dismissal under

F.R.C.P. 41(a)(1). In re International Business Mach. Corp., 687 F.2d 591 (2d Cir. 1982). Consent decrees containing provisions analogous to injunctions are modifiable by the court for changed conditions under its equitable powers. Delaware Valley Citizens' Council v. Commonwealth of Pennsylvania, 674 F.2d 976 (3d Cir. 1982).

7. When one of several defendants settles before trial, the settlement not only terminates the plaintiff's claim as to that defendant but also generally insulates the defendant from liability for contributing to any amount that the other defendants will have to pay. However, this insulation is effective only if the terms of the settlement meet a "good faith" requirement. See, e.g., C.C.P. 877 et seq.; Tech–Bilt, Inc. v. Woodward–Clyde & Associates, 38 Cal.3d 488, 213 Cal.Rptr. 256, 698 P.2d 159 (1985); Note, California Code of Civil Procedure Sections 877, 877.5 and 877.6: The Settlement Game in the Ballpark that Tech–Bilt, 13 Pepperdine L.Rev. 823 (1986). See also Abbott Ford, Inc. v. Superior Court, 43 Cal.3d 858, 239 Cal.Rptr. 626, 741 P.2d 124 (1987) (sliding scale recovery agreement can be a good faith settlement if it represents "reasonable value"); Comment, California's Sliding Scale Settlement Agreements—Finality Instead of Fairness, 23 San Diego L.Rev. 227 (1986). Under C.C.P. 877.6(e), an aggrieved party may seek immediate review of a good-faith determination by filing a petition for writ of mandate within 20 days after receiving notice of the determination; the trial court, at its discretion, may extend this period by another 20 days.

B. THE RIGHT TO JURY TRIAL

1. INTRODUCTION

NOTE ON THE STRUCTURE OF A TRIAL

The best way for the student to get a realistic grasp of an adversary trial— short of participating in one herself—is to witness a well conducted one from beginning to end. But the following brief description of the structure of a trial may help. In it we write of trial by jury as the mode more formal and complete than trial by judge alone. The latter by definition lacks such devices as selecting and instructing the jury, and may also differ in the degree of adherence to evidence rules, formality or orderliness of proceeding, and psychological overtones. But essentially the two modes are similar in basic structure, and an explanation of the more formal one roughly serves for both. We take as the norm the typical case of one plaintiff against one defendant respecting one principal transaction. Multi-party causes obviously may present additional complexities. See also Note on the Structure of a Law Suit, supra p. 1.

After the pleadings, discovery proceedings and pretrial motions have been completed or otherwise disposed of, prescribed machinery is available to move the case along. In some places the machinery is very simple: the clerk is instructed by standing rule on his own initiative to calendar the case for trial when the pleadings are closed, and to notify the parties accordingly. More typically, however, as in California, it is incumbent on one of the parties to take some initiative to put the case on the trial calendar. The mechanics of the various jurisdictions differ in detail but essentially the problem is one of requiring the clerk to calendar the case and notifying the adversary.

When the time for trial arrives the parties find assembled a group of prospective jurors selected under a system more or less elaborate, depending on the community involved. The prospective jurors are put on oath truthfully to answer the questions asked them on their voir dire examination, which is the inquiry conducted by the judge, counsel, or both, to find out whether they are suitable jurors. When the required number of jurors is selected (usually 12 or 6), the jury is sworn to try the case according to the law and the evidence. The tribunal is now complete.

The party with the burden of proof on the principal issues, usually of course the plaintiff, then commences to present his case by first making an opening statement to the jury. The purpose of this statement is to outline plaintiff's evidence so as to help the jury follow it intelligently. Usually defendant may make her opening statement immediately after plaintiff completes his, or defendant may wait until plaintiff's evidence has been presented.

After completing his opening statement (and after defendant makes hers, unless she defers it) plaintiff proceeds to present his evidence, oral, documentary, and "real," i.e., actual objects such as a gun, clothing, or whatever may have evidentiary value on the case. This part of the proceeding is called plaintiff's "case in chief." Usually plaintiff's lawyer may exercise his own judgment as to the best order in which to call witnesses and present documents, and often the order is quite significant tactically. Sometimes by local rule a particular order may be prescribed in part, as where plaintiff himself, in the absence of good reason to the contrary, is required to take the stand first if he is to testify in his case in chief.

As each witness for plaintiff takes the stand and is sworn he is first directly examined by plaintiff's lawyer. To begin, the lawyer will ask preliminary questions designed to introduce the witness to the tribunal, and to show his acquaintance with the facts involved: questions as to his name, address, family status, occupation, and his connection with the case on trial. Our law has elaborate rules governing the method of getting information from witnesses. Some of these rules are essentially forensic in nature, i.e., primarily geared to assuring orderliness and discipline in procedure. These concern, e.g., the format of testimony, whether in the witness's own narrative or question-and-answer style; the phraseology of questions, the general rule being against leading questions on direct examination; the extent of the judge's questioning; the manner of objecting to improper questions; the authentication of documents or other items of real evidence; the manner of attacking witnesses' credibility; and many like matters. As to the forensic rules, the trial judge often has a large measure of discretion to permit for good reason departure from the norm; e.g., she may permit leading questions to be asked of a child or other inarticulate person because of the necessities of the situation. Other rules governing evidence are more substantive in their nature and cannot be departed from except, sometimes, by waiver of the party entitled to their benefit, e.g., the exclusionary hearsay rule. All of these rules, the forensic and substantive ones, constitute the subject matter of an elaborate course in Evidence; here only brief reference can be made to most of them.

After plaintiff's lawyer has completed his direct examination of the witness, defendant's lawyer may cross examine him. Generally the purposes of cross examination are (i) to draw out whatever in the witness's knowledge potentially is favorable to the cross examiner, for in an adversary system the direct examiner will have focused on facets favorable to his side; (ii) to expose deficiencies of observation or narration (whether deliberate or unintentional) respecting the parts of the witness's direct testimony favorable to the party who called him; (iii) to establish bias, self-interest, or any other characteristic of the witness which in normal human experience might indicate distortion of the facts by the witness (this is a form of "impeachment" of the witness). Various rules of evidence circumscribe cross examination, e.g., in most jurisdictions, including California, cross examination relative to the merits of the case (as distinguished from impeachment of the witness) is limited to the scope of the direct examination. Cross examination, sometimes described as the greatest engine for discovery of the truth ever devised, plays a more significant role in Anglo-American adjudication than in that of most other systems. After the cross examination is completed, plaintiff may conduct re-direct examination of the witness. Normally this is limited to matters gone into on cross examination, but the judge may exercise discretion to relieve plaintiff's lawyer from oversight during the direct examination and thus permit new matters to be presented on re-direct. Then there may come re-cross examination, normally limited to the re-direct, and the process may be continued back and forth, like a tennis ball over the net, until the witness's knowledge is exhausted.

When the plaintiff has presented all of his witnesses and documentary and real evidence, he "rests." This means he turns the forum over to the defendant. Various devices are then customarily available to the defendant with which to attempt to take the case away from the jury, i.e., have a result favorable to defendant immediately proclaimed by the judge "as a matter of law." These devices include motions for nonsuits and directed verdicts. Assuming that defendant does not attempt to use any such device because she is confident none would be successful, or having made the attempt fails therein, she then proceeds to present her "case in chief" to the jury. Each witness she calls is, in turn, subject to cross examination by plaintiff. After defendant rests plaintiff may move for a directed verdict in his favor, which would be granted only if the defense as a matter of law was inadequate to controvert plaintiff's established claim.

If plaintiff does not make a motion for a directed verdict or does not prevail on one, he may then present rebuttal evidence. Normally he is limited to rebutting defendant's case in chief although, again, the trial court may grant plaintiff an opportunity to supply inadvertent omissions in his case in chief. Then the defendant may present her "surrebuttal," normally limited to meeting plaintiff's rebuttal, and the process may go on, much as with the individual witness, until both sides have exhausted all they wish and are able to present. After both sides have rested, either or both may move for a directed verdict, a condition precedent in some jurisdictions to a motion after the trial for a judgment notwithstanding the verdict.

If the judge decides to let the case go to the jury, the next step usually is the argument of counsel. Typically plaintiff opens with his principal argument; then defendant argues; then plaintiff has a short time to conclude. Then come the judge's instructions to the jury on the controlling legal principles. (In a few jurisdictions, the instructions may be before argument. And in most all jurisdictions the judge may give some instructions at appropriate times earlier in the trial. This is most likely to be done when the case is particularly complicated.) In some places the judge may comment on the evidence, frankly giving her opinion as to which witnesses were, and which were not, likely telling the truth. Elsewhere, she may marshall the evidence, that is summarize it, for the jury. But in many places her instructions may consist only of the applicable principles of law. Sometimes they are given orally only; sometimes they are reduced to writing and taken by the jury to the deliberation room. After the instructions the case is submitted to the jury for deliberation and rendition of its verdict, either general, special, or general with answers to interrogatories. Various post trial motions, including those for judgment notwithstanding the verdict or a new trial, are then available to the loser.

NOTE ON BRINGING THE CASE TO TRIAL

1. Machinery to process cases and bring them to trial must be established for every court system. In the past, initiative in this respect lay chiefly with counsel and the procedure was relatively simple, usually notice to opposing counsel that the case would be tried at a designated term, and notice to the clerk to calendar accordingly. Today, often the machinery is an intricate composite of statutes and court rules. The terminology for the various steps differs from place to place; compare N.Y.C.P.L.R. 3402's "note of issue" with the "at-issue memorandum" of California's Rules of Court, Superior Court Rule 209. Almost everywhere, however, the pressures of modern litigation have increasingly called for intelligent calendar management, and in turn attention to the intrinsic problems of fair administrative process: (i) adequate notice to officials and to all interested parties of the movement of the case to trial; (ii) avoidance of "busy work," such as dispensable "calls of the calendar"; (iii) regard for the differences in local situations, e.g., between crowded metropolitan calendars and leisurely rural ones; (iv) squeezing out the "water," i.e., the cases that really will never be tried, from the calendar; (v) saving time and patience for the cases that are important, i.e., those that will be tried.

The student is advised to trace through in detail the procedures of a particular jurisdiction. For California, see C.C.P. 594; the Superior Court Rules governing caseflow and calendar management, Rules 209–226; C.E.B., 2 Calif.Civ.Pro. Before Trial, c. 26 (1978); 7 Witkin 47–84. For New York, see N.Y.C.P.L.R. 3401, 3402; 4 Weinstein, Korn & Miller ¶¶ 3402.01–3402.17. The student should also be cautioned that local rules, including unwritten practices, are often critical in the calendaring processes.

2. Some causes are by statute entitled to calendar preference, e.g., declaratory judgment actions, C.C.P. 1062.3, and suits for injunctions, C.C.P. 527. New York includes actions by or against the state or political subdivisions within the preferred category. N.Y.C.P.L.R. 3403. For actions not entitled to statutory preference, occasionally preference is achieved by a motion to advance the cause on the calendar showing compelling reasons for the request.

3. "For more than three centuries it has now been recognized as a fundamental maxim that the public (in the words sanctioned by Lord Hardwicke) has a right to every man's evidence." 8 Wigmore on Evidence § 2192 (McNaughton ed. 1961). But because every person will not come forward voluntarily to testify, compulsory process to compel attendance of non-party witnesses is essential unless a witness agrees to attend voluntarily and can be counted on to fulfill his agreement. When the attendance of an individual to give oral testimony only is called for, the compulsory process is known as a *subpoena ad testificandum* or simply, *subpoena*; when the production of documents or other tangible things is called for, the process is called a *subpoena duces tecum*. Customarily, the clerk of court will issue to an attorney subpoena forms in blank, to be filled in by the attorney with the appropriate names of witnesses and other data.

The two most basic California statutory provisions on subpoenas are C.C.P. 1985 and 2064. For comprehensive discussions of the California provisions on subpoenas and subpoenas duces tecum, see C.E.B., California Civil Procedure During Trial c. 3 (1960); Witkin, California Evidence §§ 761–764A, 1012, 1015. For New York, see N.Y.C.P.L.R. 2301; 2A Weinstein, Korn & Miller ¶¶ 2301.01– 2301.11. Compare with the state provisions, F.R.C.P. 45; see 5A Moore c. 45.

2. THE SEVENTH AMENDMENT

NOTE ON THE RIGHT TO JURY TRIAL UNDER THE UNITED STATES CONSTITUTION

1. The United States Constitution, Art. III, Sec. 2, Clause 3 provides, *inter alia*: "The trial of all crimes, except in cases of impeachment, shall be by jury * * * ." The Constitution itself, however, says nothing about jury trial in civil cases. But Amendment VII, proposed by the first Congress along with the other first ten amendments popularly known as "A Bill of Rights" and effective in 1791, provides:

> "In suits at common law, where the value in controversy shall exceed twenty dollars, the right of trial by jury shall be preserved, and no fact tried by a jury, shall be otherwise re-examined in any court of the United States, than according to the rules of the common law."

Amendment V provides *inter alia* for indictment by grand jury, and Amendment VI contains further specifications respecting jury trial in criminal cases.

The first ten amendments were intended as checks only on the federal government, not on the states. The story of the assimilation, after the Civil War, of certain of their guarantees by the Due Process Clause of the Fourteenth Amendment is one of the most important chapters of American constitutional history, and is pursued in detail in Constitutional Law. The varying philosophies according to which specific provisions of the first ten amendments have either been incorporated into or excluded from the scope of Due Process, and hence rendered applicable or inapplicable to the states and their various subgovernments, are exemplified in, e.g., Tumey v. Ohio, 273 U.S. 510, 47 S.Ct. 437, 71 L.Ed. 749 (1927) (right to impartial tribunal); Mapp v. Ohio, 367 U.S. 643, 81 S.Ct. 1684, 6 L.Ed.2d 1081 (1961) (privilege against unreasonable searches and seizures); Malloy v. Hogan, 378 U.S. 1, 84 S.Ct. 1489, 12 L.Ed.2d 653 (1964) and Griffin v. California, 380 U.S. 609, 85 S.Ct. 1229, 14 L.Ed.2d 106 (1965) (privilege against self-incrimination).

In 1968 the Supreme Court, noting that trial by jury in criminal cases is fundamental to the American scheme of justice, held that the Fourteenth Amendment guarantees a right of jury trial in all criminal cases which—were they to be tried in federal court—would come within the Sixth Amendment's guarantee. Duncan v. Louisiana, 391 U.S. 145, 88 S.Ct. 1444, 20 L.Ed.2d 491 (1968). But the federal constitutional guarantee of jury trial in civil cases has not been incorporated into the Fourteenth Amendment. So far as the federal constitution is concerned a state is free to modify or wholly abolish trial by jury in civil cases, see Walker v. Sauvinet, 92 U.S. (2 Otto) 90, 23 L.Ed. 678 (1876). At least, such a generalization may still be taken as the starting point. But what of cases wherein a state court enforces a federal cause of action? See Dice v. Akron, C. & Y.R.R., supra p. 603. And, conversely, where a federal court in a diversity case enforces a state cause of action, what is the extent of the obligation, if any, to abide by the state's mode of trial, whether by jury or otherwise, under Erie R. Co. v. Tompkins, supra p. 562? See Byrd v. Blue Ridge Rural Electric Cooperative, supra p. 581. Even more difficult, perhaps, is the problem of distinguishing those cases, or issues, which fall within the ambit of "suits at common law" and hence within the Seventh Amendment's guarantee of jury trial, from those that are equitable and thus without the guarantee's scope. Has the "merger" of law and equity in one form of civil action, F.R.C.P. 2, simplified or complicated this problem? And what of new remedies, such as administrative proceedings, unknown in 1791, to enforce today rights also recognized then?

2. The point of beginning is that in order to ascertain the scope and meaning of the Seventh Amendment, "resort must be had to the appropriate rules of the common law established at the time of the adoption of that constitutional provision in 1791." Dimick v. Schiedt, 293 U.S. 474, 476, 55 S.Ct. 296, 79 L.Ed. 603 (1935). "The right of trial by jury thus preserved is the right which existed under the English common law when the [Seventh] Amendment was adopted." Baltimore & Carolina Line v. Redman, 295 U.S. 654, 657, 55 S.Ct. 890, 79 L.Ed. 1636 (1935). And what was trial by jury at the English common law in 1791? Capital Traction Co. v. Hof, 174 U.S. 1, 13–14, 19 S.Ct. 580, 43 L.Ed. 873 (1899) says:

> " 'Trial by jury,' in the primary and usual sense of the term at the common law and in the American constitutions, is not merely a trial by a jury of twelve men before an officer vested with authority to cause them to be summoned and impanelled, to administer oaths to them and to the constable in charge, and to enter judgment and issue execution on their verdict; but it is a trial by a jury of twelve men, in the presence and under the superintendence of a judge empowered to instruct them on the law and to advise them on the facts, and (except on acquittal of a criminal charge) to set aside their verdict if in his opinion it is against the law or the evidence. This proposition has been so generally admitted, and so seldom contested, that there has been little occasion for its distinct assertion. Yet there are unequivocal statements of it to be found in the books."

Compare Patton v. United States, 281 U.S. 276, 288, 50 S.Ct. 253, 74 L.Ed. 854 (1930), a felony prosecution, where the Court, after quoting Art. III, Sec. 2, Clause 3 and the Sixth Amendment of the Constitution, said:

> " * * * we first inquire what is embraced by the phrase 'trial by jury.' That it means a trial by jury as understood and applied at common law, and includes all the essential elements as they were recognized in this country and England when the Constitution was adopted, is not open to question. Those elements were: (1) That the jury should consist of twelve men, neither more nor less; (2) that the trial should be in the presence and under the superintendence of a judge having power to instruct them as to the law and advise them in respect of the facts; and (3) that the verdict should be unanimous."

See generally Henderson, The Background of the Seventh Amendment, 80 Harv.L.Rev. 289 (1966); Wolfram, The Constitutional History of the Seventh Amendment, 57 Minn.L.Rev. 639 (1973).

3. The scope of the Seventh Amendment guaranty has always been a problem that is both technically intricate and laden with connotations about the role of the ordinary citizen in the administration of justice. See, e.g., Parsons v. Bedford, 28 U.S. (3 Pet.) 433, 7 L.Ed. 732 (1830) (right of jury trial in action removed from Louisiana state court, where jury trial would not have

been available). Cf. Chesnin and Hazard, Chancery Procedure and the Seventh Amendment: Jury Trial of Issues in Equity Cases Before 1791, 83 Yale L.J. 999 (1974), with which compare Langbein, Fact Finding in the English Court of Chancery: A Rebuttal, 83 Yale L.J. 1620 (1974). The boundary between law and equity was neither sharp nor complete in 1791, so that some matters could come before either a law court or an equity court at that time. But in establishing the federal court system, Congress did not perpetuate the system of separate equity courts. Hence, the classification of a case as "legal" or "equitable" for purposes of jury trial (as well as for other purposes) could not depend on the court in which it was brought. Other criteria of classification had to be evolved.

Furthermore, federal procedure was gradually modified so that "legal" and "equitable" claims under various circumstances could be tried in the same action. Full "merger" of law and equity did not occur in the federal courts until adoption of the Federal Rules in 1938. But long before that situations had arisen in which both legal and equitable claims were presented in the same action, and the problem was whether the issues were triable to a jury. The distinct tendency of the cases was toward non-jury trial, perhaps because jury trial was not regarded with favor by the federal judiciary, perhaps for other reasons. See American Life Ins. Co. v. Stewart, reprinted just below.

4. A different difficulty in applying the historical approach to determining the right of jury trial arises from the fact that Congress has created many rights and remedies, including administrative agency remedies, that did not exist at common law. This problem was presented in N.L.R.B. v. Jones & Laughlin Steel Corp., 301 U.S. 1, 57 S.Ct. 615, 81 L.Ed. 893 (1937), and in Atlas Roofing Co. v. Occupational Safety & Health Review Comm'n, infra p. 1027, and Tull v. United States, infra p. 1034.

A somewhat similar problem arose in Katchen v. Landy, 382 U.S. 323, 86 S.Ct. 467, 15 L.Ed.2d 391 (1966). There, an Act of Congress provided for a procedure in a court—not an administrative agency—whereby claims concerning a bankrupt would be determined by summary procedure, i.e., at a hearing without jury and without the elaborate discovery of an ordinary civil action. Congress could validly do this, said the Court, without very clearly saying why, except that "The Bankruptcy Act * * * converts the creditor's legal claim into an equitable claim * * * and * * * the proceedings of bankruptcy courts are inherently proceedings in equity * * *." 382 U.S. at 336. But cf. Northern Pipeline Constr. Co. v. Marathon Pipe Line Co., 458 U.S. 50, 102 S.Ct. 2858, 73 L.Ed.2d 598 (1982) (Article III limits Congress's power regarding remedial systems). See also Gibson, Jury Trials in Bankruptcy: Obeying the Commands of Article III and the Seventh Amendment, 72 Minn.L.Rev. 967 (1988).

See generally James & Hazard c. 8.

AMERICAN LIFE INS. CO. v. STEWART

Supreme Court of the United States, 1937.
300 U.S. 203, 57 S.Ct. 377, 81 L.Ed. 605.

Mr. Justice Cardozo delivered the opinion of the Court.

In these cases suits have been brought for the cancellation of policies of life insurance on the ground of fraud in their procurement, the policies providing that they shall cease to be contestable unless contest shall be begun within a stated time. The question to be determined is the existence, in the circumstances, of a remedy in equity.

On February 23, 1932, petitioner, a Colorado corporation, issued to Reese Smith Stewart, a citizen of Kansas, two policies of life insurance, each for $5,000, one payable to his son, who is a respondent in No. 440, and the other payable to his wife, who is a respondent in No. 441. Each policy contains a provision that it "shall be incontestable, except for non-payment of the premium, after one year from its date of issue if the Insured be then living, otherwise after two years from its date of issue." On May 31, 1932, three months and eight days after obtaining the insurance, the insured died, having made in his application fraudulent misstatements, or so the insurer charges, as to his health and other matters material to the risk. On September 3, 1932, the insurer brought suit to cancel the insurance, a separate suit for each policy, the executrix of the insured being joined as a defendant with the respective beneficiaries. The complaint in each suit refers in a paragraph numbered 8 to the provision that the policy shall be incontestable after the lapse of two years. In the same paragraph it states in substance that the beneficiary may delay the commencement of the action at law till the time for contest has gone by, or, beginning such an action within the period, may afterwards dismiss it and then begin anew. The insurer asks the court to act while yet the barrier is down.

On September 26, 1932, the defendants moved in each suit to dismiss the bill for want of equity. On October 11, 1932, the beneficiaries began actions at law in the same court to recover the insurance. On October 29, the insurer filed its supplemental bills setting forth the pendency of the actions at law, and praying an injunction against their continued prosecution. On July 28, 1933, the District Court denied the motions to dismiss, without passing, however, on motions made by the insurer to enjoin the actions at law. On August 29, a stipulation was signed and filed in each case that "the suit in equity shall be tried" by the court "before said law action is tried, Provided, however, that the issues in said law action shall in the meantime be made up in order that said law issues thus joined shall stand ready for trial, with the understanding that said law issues, if any remain for trial, shall be tried as soon after the trial of the suit in equity as the court shall determine," and this stipulation was approved by the court and an order made accordingly. On October 10, 1933, the defendants in each of the equity suits filed their answers to the bills, denying the fraud, admitting the making of the "incontestability clause" as stated in paragraph 8, and as to the other allegations of that paragraph denying any knowledge or information sufficient to form a belief. The answers did not state that the remedy at law was adequate.

Upon the trial of the suits in equity, the District Court found the fraudulent representations charged in the complaints, and decreed the cancellation and surrender of the policies. There was an appeal to the Circuit Court of Appeals for the Tenth Circuit, where the decree was reversed, one judge dissenting, the court holding that the insurer had an adequate remedy at law. 80 F.2d 600; 85 F.2d 791. We granted certiorari to settle an important question, and one likely to recur, as to the scope of equitable remedies.

No doubt it is the rule, and one recently applied in decisions of this court, that fraud in the procurement of insurance is provable as a defense in an action at law upon the policy, resort to equity being unnecessary to render that defense available. Enelow v. New York Life Ins. Co., 293 U.S. 379, 385, 55 S.Ct. 310, 312, 79 L.Ed. 440; Adamos v. New York Life Ins. Co., 293 U.S. 386, 55 S.Ct. 315, 79 L.Ed. 444; Insurance Co. v. Bailey, 13 Wall. 616, 20 L.Ed. 501; Cable v. United States Life Ins. Co., 191 U.S. 288, 306, 24 S.Ct. 74, 48 L.Ed. 188. That being so, an insurer, though the victim of a fraud, may commonly stand aside and await the hour of attack. But this attitude of aloofness may at times be fraught with peril. If the policy is to become incontestable soon after the death of the insured, the insurer becomes helpless if he must wait for a move by some one else, who may prefer to remain motionless till the time for contest has gone by. A "contest" within the purview of such a contract has generally been held to mean a present contest in a court, not a notice of repudiation or of a contest to be waged thereafter. See, e.g., Killian v. Metropolitan Life Ins. Co., 251 N.Y. 44, 48, 166 N.E. 798; New York Life Ins. Co. v. Hurt, C.C.A., 35 F.2d 92, 95; Harnischfeger Sales Corp. v. National Life Ins. Co., C.C.A., 72 F.2d 921, 922. Accordingly, an insurer, who might otherwise be condemned to loss through the mere inaction of an adversary, may assume the offensive by going into equity and there praying cancellation. This exception to the general rule has been allowed by the lower federal courts with impressive uniformity.[1] It has had acceptance in the state courts.[2] It was

1. From the fourth circuit: Jefferson Standard Life Ins. Co. v. Keeton, 292 Fed. 53, 54–56; Jones v. Reliance Life Ins. Co., 11 F.2d 69, 70; Brown v. Pacific Mutual Life Ins. Co., 62 F.2d 711, 712; New York Life Ins. Co. v. Truesdale, 79 F.2d 481, 485; Pacific Mutual Life Ins. Co. v. Parker, 71 F.2d 872, 874. From the fifth circuit: Jefferson Standard Life Ins. Co. v. McIntyre, 294 Fed. 886, 888. From the sixth circuit: New York Life Ins. Co. v. Seymour, 45 F.2d 47, 48, 49; Rose v. Mutual Life Ins. Co. of New York, 19 F.2d 280, 282. From the seventh circuit: Harnischfeger Sales Corp. v. National Life Ins. Co., 72 F.2d 921, 922, 923. From the eighth circuit: Peake v. Lincoln National Life Ins. Co., 15 F.2d 303, 305, 306; Lincoln National Life Ins. Co. v. Hammer, 41 F.2d 12, 17. From the ninth circuit: Massachusetts Bonding & Ins. Co. v. Anderegg, 83 F.2d 622, 625. From the tenth circuit: New York Life Ins. Co. v. Thompson, 78 F.2d 946, 947 (semble). From the District of Columbia: Densby v. Acacia Mutual Life Assn., 64 App.D.C. 319, 78 F.2d 203, 206.

2. New York Life Ins. Co. v. Rigas, 117 Conn. 437, 168 A. 22; Ebner v. Ohio State Life Ins. Co., 69 Ind.App. 32, 121 N.E. 315; Aetna Life Ins. Co. v. Daniel, 328 Mo. 876, 42 S.W.2d 584; New York Life Ins. Co. v. Cobb, 219 Mo.App. 609, 282 S.W. 494; New York Life Ins. Co. v. Steinman, 103 N.J.Eq. 403, 143 A. 529; Ameri-

recognized only recently in an opinion of this court, though the facts were not such as to call for its allowance. Enelow v. New York Life Ins. Co., supra, 293 U.S. 379 at p. 384, 55 S.Ct. 310, 312, 79 L.Ed. 440.[3]

The argument is made, however, that the insurer, even if privileged to sue in equity, should not have gone there quite so quickly. Six months and ten days had gone by since the policies were issued. There would be nearly a year and a half more before the bar would become absolute. But how long was the insurer to wait before assuming the offensive, and how was it to know where the beneficiaries would be if it omitted to strike swiftly? Often a family breaks up and changes its abode after the going of its head. The like might happen to this family. To say that the insurer shall keep watch of the coming and going of the survivors is to charge it with a heavy burden. The task would be hard enough if beneficiaries were always honest. The possibility of bad faith, perhaps concealed and hardly provable, accentuates the difficulty. There are statements by judges of repute which suggest a possibility that the contest barrier may stand though the holder of the policy has gone to foreign lands. New York Life Ins. Co. v. Panagiotopoulos, C.C.A., 80 F.2d 136, 139. There are statements that it will stand though an action at law, brought within the period, had been dismissed or discontinued later. See New York Life Ins. Co. v. Seymour, C.C.A., 45 F.2d 47, 48; Harnischfeger Sales Corp. v. National Life Ins. Co., C.C.A., 72 F.2d 921, 925; New York Life Ins. Co. v. Truesdale, C.C.A., 79 F.2d 481, 485, with which contrast New York Life Ins. Co. v. Miller, C.C.A., 73 F.2d 350, 355; Thomas v. Metropolitan Life Ins. Co., 135 Kan. 381, 387, 10 P.2d 864, and Powell v. Mutual Life Ins. Co., 313 Ill. 161, 170, 144 N.E. 825. Whether such statements go too far we are not required to determine, for a slight variance in the facts, as, e.g., in the rule prevailing in the jurisdiction where the final suit is brought, may have a bearing on the conclusion. At least in such warnings there are possibilities of danger which a cautious insurer would not put aside as visionary. "Where equity can give relief plaintiff ought not to be compelled to speculate upon the chance of his obtaining relief at law." Davis v. Wakelee, 156 U.S. 680, 688, 15 S.Ct. 555, 558, 39 L.Ed. 578. To this must be added the danger that witnesses may disappear and evidence be lost. A remedy at law does not exclude one in equity unless it is equally prompt and certain and in other ways efficient. Boyce's Executors v. Grundy, 3 Pet. 210, 7 L.Ed. 655; Drexel v. Berney, 122 U.S. 241, 7 S.Ct. 1200, 30 L.Ed. 1219; Walla Walla v. Walla Walla Water Co., 172 U.S. 1, 19 S.Ct. 77, 43 L.Ed. 341; Union Pacific R. Co. v. Weld County, 247 U.S. 282, 287, 38 S.Ct. 510, 62 L.Ed. 1110. "It must

can Trust Co. v. Life Ins. Co. of Virginia, 173 N.C. 558, 92 S.E. 706; Prudential Ins. Co. v. Tanenbaum, 53 R.I. 355, 167 A. 147.

3. "The instant case is not one in which there is resort to equity for cancellation of the policy during the life of the insured and no opportunity exists to contest liability at law. Nor is it a case where, although death may have occurred, action has not been brought to recover upon the policy, and equitable relief is sought to protect the insurer against loss of its defense by the expiration of the period after which the policy by its terms is to become incontestable."

be a remedy which may be resorted to without impediment created otherwise than by the act of the party." Cable v. United States Life Ins. Co., supra, 191 U.S. 288 at p. 303, 24 S.Ct. 74, 76, 48 L.Ed. 188. Here the insurer had no remedy at law at all except at the pleasure of an adversary. There was neither equality in efficiency nor equality in certainty nor equality in promptness. "The remedy at law cannot be adequate if its adequacy depends upon the will of the opposing party." Bank of Kentucky v. Stone, C.C., 88 Fed. 383, 391; cf. Lincoln National Life Ins. Co. v. Hammer, C.C.A., 41 F.2d 12, 16. To make a contract incontestable after the lapse of a brief time is to confer upon its holder extraordinary privileges. We must be on our guard against turning them into weapons of oppression.

The argument is made that the suits in equity should have been dismissed when it appeared upon the trial that after the filing of the bills, and in October, 1932, the beneficiaries of the policies had sued on them at law. But the settled rule is that equitable jurisdiction existing *Rule* at the filing of a bill is not destroyed because an adequate legal remedy may have become available thereafter. Dawson v. Kentucky Distilleries Co., 255 U.S. 288, 296, 41 S.Ct. 272, 275, 65 L.Ed. 638; Lincoln National Life Ins. Co. v. Hammer, supra; New York Life Ins. Co. v. Seymour, supra. There is indeed, a possibility that the bringing of actions at law might have been used by the respondents to their advantage if they had not chosen by a stipulation to throw the possibility away. A court has control over its own docket. Landis v. North American Co., 299 U.S. 248, 57 S.Ct. 163, 81 L.Ed. 153. In the exercise of a sound discretion it may hold one lawsuit in abeyance to abide the outcome of another, especially where the parties and the issues are the same. Ibid. If request had been made by the respondents to suspend the suits in equity till the other causes were disposed of, the District Court could have considered whether justice would not be done by pursuing such a course, the remedy in equity being exceptional and the outcome of necessity. Cf. Harnischfeger Sales Corp. v. National Life Ins. Co., C.C.A., 72 F.2d 921, 922, 923. There would be many circumstances to be weighed, as, for instance, the condition of the court calendar, whether the insurer had been precipitate or its adversaries dilatory, as well as other factors. In the end, benefit and hardship would have to be set off, the one against the other, and a balance ascertained. Landis v. North American Co., supra. But respondents, as already indicated, gave that possibility away. They stipulated that the issues in equity should be tried in advance of those at law, and that only such issues, if any, as were left should be disposed of later on. The cases were allowed to stand as if challenge to the suits had been made by a demurrer only. So challenged, they prevail.

The decree should be reversed, and the cause remanded to the Court of Appeals for a consideration of the merits and for other proceedings in accord with this opinion.

Reversed.

———

BEACON THEATRES, INC. v. WESTOVER

Supreme Court of the United States, 1959.
359 U.S. 500, 79 S.Ct. 948, 3 L.Ed.2d 988. *

Mr. Justice Black delivered the opinion of the Court.

Petitioner, Beacon Theatres, Inc., sought by mandamus to require a district judge in the Southern District of California to vacate certain orders alleged to deprive it of a jury trial of issues arising in a suit brought against it by Fox West Coast Theatres, Inc. The Court of Appeals for the Ninth Circuit refused the writ, holding that the trial judge had acted within his proper discretion in denying petitioner's request for a jury. 252 F.2d 864. We granted certiorari, 356 U.S. 956, 78 S.Ct. 996, 2 L.Ed.2d 1064, because "Maintenance of the jury as a fact-finding body is of such importance and occupies so firm a place in our history and jurisprudence that any seeming curtailment of the right to a jury trial should be scrutinized with the utmost care." Dimick v. Schiedt, 293 U.S. 474, 486, 55 S.Ct. 296, 301, 79 L.Ed. 603.

Fox had asked for declaratory relief against Beacon alleging a controversy arising under the Sherman Antitrust Act, 26 Stat. 209, as amended, 15 U.S.C. §§ 1, 2, 15 U.S.C.A. §§ 1, 2, and under the Clayton Act, 38 Stat. 731, 15 U.S.C. § 15, 15 U.S.C.A. § 15, which authorizes suits for treble damages against Sherman Act violators. According to the complaint Fox operates a movie theatre in San Bernardino, California, and has long been exhibiting films under contracts with movie distributors. These contracts grant it the exclusive right to show "first run" pictures in the "San Bernardino competitive area" and provide for "clearance"—a period of time during which no other theatre can exhibit the same pictures. After building a drive-in theatre about 11 miles from San Bernardino, Beacon notified Fox that it considered contracts barring simultaneous exhibitions of first-run films in the two theatres to be overt acts in violation of the antitrust laws.[1] Fox's complaint alleged that this notification, together with threats of treble damage suits against Fox and its distributors, gave rise to "duress and coercion" which deprived Fox of a valuable property right, the right to negotiate for exclusive first-run contracts. Unless Beacon was restrained, the complaint continued, irreparable harm would result. Accordingly, while its pleading was styled a "Complaint for Declaratory Relief," Fox prayed both for a declaration that a grant of clearance between the Fox and Beacon theatres is reasonable and not in violation

---

* Some of the Court's footnotes are omitted.

1. Beacon allegedly stated that the clearances granted violated both the antitrust laws and the decrees issued in United States v. Paramount Pictures, Inc., D.C., 66 F.Supp. 323; 70 F.Supp. 53, affirmed in part and reversed in part, 334 U.S. 131, 68 S.Ct. 915, 92 L.Ed. 1260, subsequent proceedings in the District Court, 85 F.Supp.

881. The decrees in that case set limits on what clearances could be given when theatres were in competition with each other and held that there should be no clearances between theatres not in substantial competition. Neither Beacon nor Fox, however, appears to have been a party to those decrees. Their relevance, therefore, seems to be only that of significant precedents.

of the antitrust laws, and for an injunction, pending final resolution of the litigation, to prevent Beacon from instituting any action under the antitrust laws against Fox and its distributors arising out of the controversy alleged in the complaint.[2] Beacon filed an answer, a counterclaim against Fox, and a cross-claim against an exhibitor who had intervened. These denied the threats and asserted that there was no substantial competition between the two theatres, that the clearances granted were therefore unreasonable, and that a conspiracy existed between Fox and its distributors to manipulate contracts and clearances so as to restrain trade and monopolize first-run pictures in violation of the antitrust laws. Treble damages were asked.

Beacon demanded a jury trial of the factual issues in the case as provided by Federal Rule of Civil Procedure 38(b), 28 U.S.C.A. The District Court, however, viewed the issues raised by the "Complaint for Declaratory Relief," including the question of competition between the two theatres, as essentially equitable. Acting under the purported authority of Rules 42(b) and 57, it directed that these issues be tried to the court before jury determination of the validity of the charges of antitrust violations made in the counterclaim and cross-claim.[3] A common issue of the "Complaint for Declaratory Relief," the counterclaim, and the cross-claim was the reasonableness of the clearances granted to Fox, which depended, in part, on the existence of competition between the two theatres. Thus the effect of the action of the District Court could be, as the Court of Appeals believed, "to limit the petitioner's opportunity fully to try to a jury every issue which has a bearing upon its treble damage suit," for determination of the issue of clearances by the judge might "operate either by way of res judicata or collateral estoppel so as to conclude both parties with respect thereto at the subsequent trial of the treble damage claim." 252 F.2d at page 874.

The District Court's finding that the Complaint for Declaratory Relief presented basically equitable issues draws no support from the Declaratory Judgment Act, 28 U.S.C. §§ 2201, 2202, 28 U.S.C.A. §§ 2201, 2202; Fed.Rules Civ.Proc. 57. See also 48 Stat. 955, 28 U.S.C. (1940 ed.) § 400. That statute, while allowing prospective defendants to sue to establish their nonliability, specifically preserves the right to jury trial for both parties.[4] It follows that if Beacon would have been entitled to a jury trial in a treble damage suit against Fox it cannot be deprived of that right merely because Fox took advantage of the availability of declaratory relief to sue Beacon first. Since the right to

---

2. Other prayers aside from the general equitable plea for "such further relief as the court deems proper" added nothing material to those set out.

3. Fed.Rules Civ.Proc., 42(b) reads: "The court in furtherance of convenience or to avoid prejudice may order a separate trial of any claim, cross-claim, counter-claim, or third-party claim, or of any separate issue or of any number of claims, cross-claims, counterclaims, third-party

claims, or issues." Rule 57 reads in part: "The court may order a speedy hearing of an action for a declaratory judgment and may advance it on the calendar."

4. See, e.g., (American) Lumbermens Mut. Cas. Co. of Illinois v. Timms & Howard, Inc., 2 Cir., 108 F.2d 497; Hargrove v. American Cent. Ins. Co., 10 Cir., 125 F.2d 225; Johnson v. Fidelity & Casualty Co., 8 Cir., 238 F.2d 322. See Fed.Rules Civ. Proc., 57, 38, 39.

trial by jury applies to treble damage suits under the antitrust laws, and is, in fact, an essential part of the congressional plan for making competition rather than monopoly the rule of trade, see Fleitmann v. Welsbach Street Lighting Co., 240 U.S. 27, 29, 36 S.Ct. 233, 234, 60 L.Ed. 505, the Sherman and Clayton Act issues on which Fox sought a declaration were essentially jury questions.

Nevertheless the Court of Appeals refused to upset the order of the district judge. It held that the question of whether a right to jury trial existed was to be judged by Fox's complaint read as a whole. In addition to seeking a declaratory judgment, the court said, Fox's complaint can be read as making out a valid plea for injunctive relief, thus stating a claim traditionally cognizable in equity. A party who is entitled to maintain a suit in equity for an injunction, said the court, may have all the issues in his suit determined by the judge without a jury regardless of whether legal rights are involved. The court then rejected the argument that equitable relief, traditionally available only when legal remedies are inadequate, was rendered unnecessary in this case by the filing of the counterclaim and cross-claim which presented all the issues necessary to a determination of the right to injunctive relief. Relying on American Life Ins. Co. v. Stewart, 300 U.S. 203, 215, 57 S.Ct. 377, 380, 81 L.Ed. 605, decided before the enactment of the Federal Rules of Civil Procedure, it invoked the principle that a court sitting in equity could retain jurisdiction even though later a legal remedy became available. In such instances the equity court had discretion to enjoin the later lawsuit in order to allow the whole dispute to be determined in one case in one court.[5] Reasoning by analogy, the Court of Appeals held it was not an abuse of discretion for the district judge, acting under Federal Rule of Civil Procedure 42(b), to try the equitable cause first even though this might, through collateral estoppel, prevent a full jury trial of the counterclaim and cross-claim which were as effectively stopped as by an equity injunction.[6]

Beacon takes issue with the holding of the Court of Appeals that the complaint stated a claim upon which equitable relief could be granted. As initially filed the complaint alleged that threats of lawsuits by petitioner against Fox and its distributors were causing irreparable harm to Fox's business relationships. The prayer for relief, however, made no mention of the threats but asked only that pending litigation of the claim for declaratory judgment, Beacon be enjoined

---

5. Compare Enelow v. New York Life Ins. Co., 293 U.S. 379, 55 S.Ct. 310, 79 L.Ed. 440, with American Life Ins. Co. v. Stewart, 300 U.S. 203, 57 S.Ct. 377, 81 L.Ed. 605. See also City of Morgantown, W. Va. v. Royal Ins. Co., 337 U.S. 254, 69 S.Ct. 1067, 93 L.Ed. 1347; Peake v. Lincoln Nat. Life Ins. Co., 8 Cir., 15 F.2d 303.

6. 252 F.2d at page 874. In Ettelson v. Metropolitan Life Ins. Co., 317 U.S. 188, 192, 63 S.Ct. 163, 164, 87 L.Ed. 176, this Court recognized that orders enabling equi-table causes to be tried before legal ones had the same effect as injunctions. In City of Morgantown, W. Va. v. Royal Ins. Co., 337 U.S. 254, 69 S.Ct. 1067, 93 L.Ed. 1347, the Court denied at least some such orders the status of injunctions for the purposes of appealability. It did not, of course, imply that when the orders came to be reviewed they would be examined any less strictly than injunctions. 337 U.S. at page 258, 69 S.Ct. at page 1069.

from beginning any lawsuits under the antitrust laws against Fox and its distributors arising out of the controversy alleged in the complaint. Evidently of the opinion that this prayer did not state a good claim for equitable relief, the Court of Appeals construed it to include a request for an injunction against threats of lawsuits. This liberal construction of a pleading is in line with Rule 8 of the Federal Rules of Civil Procedure. See Conley v. Gibson, 355 U.S. 41, 47–48, 78 S.Ct. 99, 102–103, 2 L.Ed.2d 80. But this fact does not solve our problem. Assuming that the pleadings can be construed to support such a request and assuming additionally that the complaint can be read as alleging the kind of harassment by a multiplicity of lawsuits which would *traditionally* have justified equity to take jurisdiction and settle the case in one suit, we are nevertheless of the opinion that, under the Declaratory Judgment Act and the Federal Rules of Civil Procedure, neither claim can justify denying Beacon a trial by jury of all the issues in the antitrust controversy.

The basis of injunctive relief in the federal courts has always been irreparable harm and inadequacy of legal remedies. At least as much is required to justify a trial court in using its discretion under the Federal Rules to allow claims of equitable origins to be tried ahead of legal ones, since this has the same effect as an equitable injunction of the legal claims. And it is immaterial in judging if that discretion is properly employed, that before the Federal Rules and the Declaratory Judgment Act were passed, courts of equity, exercising a jurisdiction separate from courts of law, were, in some cases, allowed to enjoin subsequent legal actions between the same parties involving the same controversy. This was because the subsequent legal action, though providing an opportunity to try the case to a jury, might not protect the right of the equity plaintiff to a fair and orderly adjudication of the controversy. See, e.g., New York Life Ins. Co. v. Seymour, 6 Cir., 45 F.2d 47, 73 A.L.R. 1523. Under such circumstances the legal remedy could quite naturally be deemed inadequate. Inadequacy of remedy and irreparable harm are practical terms, however. As such their existence today must be determined, not by precedents decided under discarded procedures, but in the light of the remedies now made available by the Declaratory Judgment Act and the Federal Rules.[9]

Viewed in this manner, the use of discretion by the trial court under Rule 42(b) to deprive Beacon of a full jury trial on its counterclaim and cross-claim, as well as on Fox's plea for declaratory relief, cannot be justified. Under the Federal Rules the same court may try

---

9. See, e.g., Cook, Cases on Equity (4th ed.), 18; 4 Pomeroy, Equity Jurisprudence (5th ed.), § 1370; 5 Moore, Federal Practice, 154–158; Morris, Jury Trial Under the Federal Fusion of Law and Equity, 20 Tex.L.Rev. 427, 441–443. Cf. Maryland Theater Corp. v. Brennan, 180 Md. 377, 389, 24 A.2d 911; Hasselbring v. Koepke, 263 Mich. 466, 248 N.W. 869, 93 A.L.R. 1170. But cf. 1 Pomeroy, Equity Jurispru-dence (5th ed.), §§ 182, 183. Significantly the Court of Appeals itself relied on the procedural changes brought about by the Federal Rules when it found the plea for equitable relief valid, for it did so by relying on Conley v. Gibson, 355 U.S. 41, 78 S.Ct. 99, 2 L.Ed.2d 80, which emphasized the liberal construction policies of the Rules.

both legal and equitable causes in the same action. Fed.Rules Civ.Proc. 1, 2, 18. Thus any defenses, equitable or legal, Fox may have to charges of antitrust violations can be raised either in its suit for declaratory relief or in answer to Beacon's counterclaim. On proper showing, harassment by threats of other suits, or other suits actually brought, involving the issues being tried in this case, could be temporarily enjoined pending the outcome of this litigation. Whatever permanent injunctive relief Fox might be entitled to on the basis of the decision in this case could, of course, be given by the court after the jury renders its verdict. In this way the issues between these parties could be settled in one suit giving Beacon a full jury trial of every antitrust issue. Cf. Ring v. Spina, 2 Cir., 166 F.2d 546. By contrast, the holding of the court below while granting Fox no additional protection unless the avoidance of jury trial be considered as such, would compel Beacon to split his antitrust case, trying part to a judge and part to a jury.[10] Such a result, which involves the postponement and subordination of Fox's own legal claim for declaratory relief as well as of the counterclaim which Beacon was compelled by the Federal Rules to bring,[11] is not permissible.

Our decision is consistent with the plan of the Federal Rules and the Declaratory Judgment Act to effect substantial procedural reform while retaining a distinction between jury and nonjury issues and leaving substantive rights unchanged.[12] Since in the federal courts equity has always acted only when legal remedies were inadequate,[13] the expansion of adequate legal remedies provided by the Declaratory Judgment Act and the Federal Rules necessarily affects the scope of equity. Thus, the justification for equity's deciding legal issues once it obtains jurisdiction, and refusing to dismiss a case, merely because subsequently a legal remedy becomes available, must be re-evaluated in the light of the liberal joinder provisions of the Federal Rules which allow legal and equitable causes to be brought and resolved in one civil action.[14] Similarly the need for, and therefore, the availability of such equitable remedies as Bills of Peace, *Quia Timet* and Injunction must be reconsidered in view of the existence of the Declaratory Judgment Act as well as the liberal joinder provision of the Rules.[15] This is not only

---

10. Since the issue of violation of the antitrust laws often turns on the reasonableness of a restraint on trade in the light of all the facts, see, e.g., Standard Oil Co. of New Jersey v. United States, 221 U.S. 1, 60, 31 S.Ct. 502, 515, 55 L.Ed. 619, it is particularly undesirable to have some of the relevant considerations tried by one factfinder and some by another.

11. Fed.Rules Civ.Proc., 13(a).

12. See 28 U.S.C. § 2072, 28 U.S.C.A. § 2072; Fed.Rules Civ.Proc., 39(a), 57. * * *

13. See 36 Stat. 1163, derived from Act of Sept. 24, 1789, § 16, 1 Stat. 82. This provision, which antedates the Seventh

Amendment, is discussed in 5 Moore, Federal Practice, 32. * * *

14. See Fed.Rules Civ.Proc., 1, 2, 18. Cf. Prudential Ins. Co. of America v. Saxe, 77 U.S.App.D.C. 144, 134 F.2d 16, 31–34; Morris, Jury Trial Under the Federal Fusion of Law and Equity, 20 Tex.L.Rev. 427, 441–443.

15. See 1 Pomeroy, Equity Jurisprudence (5th ed.) §§ 251¾, 254, 264(b); 5 Moore, Federal Practice, 32; but cf. id., 209–211. See also, Note, The Joinder Rules and Equity Jurisdiction in the Avoidance of a Multiplicity of Suits, 12 Md.L. Rev. 88. Of course, unless there is an issue of a right to jury trial or of other rights

in accord with the spirit of the Rules and the Act but is required by the provision in the Rules that "[t]he right of trial by jury as declared by the Seventh Amendment to the Constitution or as given by a statute of the United States shall be preserved . . . inviolate." [16]

If there should be cases where the availability of declaratory judgment or joinder in one suit of legal and equitable causes would not in all respects protect the plaintiff seeking equitable relief from irreparable harm while affording a jury trial in the legal cause, the trial court will necessarily have to use its discretion in deciding whether the legal or equitable cause should be tried first. Since the right to jury trial is a constitutional one, however, while no similar requirement protects trials by the court,[17] that discretion is very narrowly limited and must, wherever possible, be exercised to preserve jury trial. As this Court said in Scott v. Neely, 140 U.S. 106, 109–110, 11 S.Ct. 712, 714, 35 L.Ed. 358: "In the Federal courts this [jury] right cannot be dispensed with, except by the assent of the parties entitled to it; nor can it be impaired by any blending with a claim, properly cognizable at law, of a demand for equitable relief in aid of the legal action, or during its pendency." [18] This long-standing principle of equity dictates that only under the most imperative circumstances, circumstances which in view of the flexible procedures of the Federal Rules we cannot now anticipate, [19] can the right to a jury trial of legal issues be lost through prior determination of equitable claims. See Leimer v. Woods, 8 Cir., 196 F.2d 828, 833–836. As we have shown, this is far from being such a case.

Respondent claims mandamus is not available under the All Writs Act, 28 U.S.C. § 1651, 28 U.S.C.A. § 1651. Whatever differences of opinion there may be in other types of cases, we think the right to grant mandamus to require jury trial where it has been improperly denied is settled.

The judgment of the Court of Appeals is reversed.

Reversed.

---

which depend on whether the cause is a "legal" or "equitable" one, the question of adequacy of legal remedies is purely academic and need not arise.

16. Fed.Rules Civ.Proc., 38(a). In delegating to the Supreme Court responsibility for drawing up rules, Congress declared that: "Such rules shall not abridge, enlarge or modify any substantive right and shall preserve the right of trial by jury as at common law and as declared by the Seventh Amendment to the Constitution." 28 U.S.C. § 2072, 28 U.S.C.A. § 2072. The Seventh Amendment reads: "In Suits at common law, where the value in controversy shall exceed twenty dollars, the right of trial by jury shall be preserved, and no fact tried by a jury, shall be otherwise reexam-

ined in any Court of the United States, than according to the rules of the common law."

17. See Hurwitz v. Hurwitz, 78 U.S. App.D.C. 66, 136 F.2d 796, 798–799, 148 A.L.R. 226; cf. The Genesee Chief v. Fitzhugh, 12 How. 443, 459–460, 13 L.Ed. 1058.

18. This Court has long emphasized the importance of the jury trial. See Parsons v. Bedford, 3 Pet. 433, 446, 7 L.Ed. 732. See also Galloway v. United States, 319 U.S. 372, 63 S.Ct. 1077, 87 L.Ed. 1458. Id., 319 U.S. at page 396, 63 S.Ct. at page 1090 (dissenting opinion).

19. For an example of the flexible procedures available under the Federal Rules, see Ring v. Spina, 2 Cir., 166 F.2d 546, 550.

MR. JUSTICE FRANKFURTER took no part in the consideration or decision of this case.

MR. JUSTICE STEWART, with whom MR. JUSTICE HARLAN and MR. JUSTICE WHITTAKER concur, dissenting.

* * *

The complaint filed by Fox stated a claim traditionally cognizable in equity. That claim, in brief, was that Beacon had wrongfully interfered with the right of Fox to compete freely with Beacon and other distributors for the licensing of films for first-run exhibition in the San Bernardino area. The complaint alleged that the plaintiff was without an adequate remedy at law and would be irreparably harmed unless the defendant were restrained from continuing to interfere—by coercion and threats of litigation—with the plaintiff's lawful business relationships.

The Court of Appeals found that the complaint, although inartistically drawn, contained allegations entitling the petitioner to equitable relief. That finding is accepted in the prevailing opinion today. If the complaint had been answered simply by a general denial, therefore, the issues would under traditional principles have been triable as a proceeding in equity. Instead of just putting in issue the allegations of the complaint, however, Beacon filed pleadings which affirmatively alleged the existence of a broad conspiracy among the plaintiff and other theatre owners to monopolize the first-run exhibition of films in the San Bernardino area to refrain from competing among themselves, and to discriminate against Beacon in granting film licenses. Based upon these allegations, Beacon asked damages in the amount of $300,000. Clearly these conspiracy allegations stated a cause of action triable as of right by a jury. What was demanded by Beacon, however, was a jury trial not only of this cause of action, but also of the issues presented by the original complaint.

Upon motion of Fox the trial judge ordered the original action for declaratory and equitable relief to be tried separately to the court and in advance of the trial of the defendant's counterclaim and cross-claim for damages. The court's order, which carefully preserved the right to trial by jury upon the conspiracy and damage issues raised by the counterclaim and cross-claim, was in conformity with the specific provisions of the Federal Rules of Civil Procedure.[3] Yet it is decided today that the Court of Appeals must compel the district judge to rescind it.

Assuming the existence of a factual issue common both to the plaintiff's original action and the defendant's counterclaim for damages, I cannot agree that the District Court must be compelled to try

---

3. Rule 42(b) provides: "(b) Separate Trials. The court in furtherance of convenience or to avoid prejudice may order a separate trial of any claim, cross-claim, counterclaim, or third-party claim, or of any separate issue or of any number of claims, cross-claims, counterclaims, third-party claims, or issues." * * *

the counterclaim first.[4] It is, of course, a matter of no great moment in what order the issues between the parties in the present litigation are tried. What is disturbing is the process by which the Court arrives at its decision—a process which appears to disregard the historic relationship between equity and law.

I.

The Court suggests that "the expression of adequate legal remedies provided by the Declaratory Judgment Act . . . necessarily affects the scope of equity." Does the Court mean to say that the mere availability of an action for a declaratory judgment operates to furnish "an adequate remedy at law" so as to deprive a court of equity of the power to act? That novel line of reasoning is at least implied in the Court's opinion. But the Declaratory Judgment Act did not "expand" the substantive law. That Act merely provided a new statutory remedy, neither legal nor equitable, but available in the areas of both equity and law. When declaratory relief is sought, the right to trial by jury depends upon the basic context in which the issues are presented. See Moore's Federal Practice (2d ed.) §§ 38.29, 57.30; Borchard, Declaratory Judgments (2d ed.), 399–404. If the basic issues in an action for declaratory relief are of a kind traditionally cognizable in equity, e.g., a suit for cancellation of a written instrument, the declaratory judgment is not a "remedy at law."[5] If, on the other hand, the issues arise in a context traditionally cognizable at common law, the right to a jury trial of course remains unimpaired, even though the only relief demanded is a declaratory judgment.[6]

4. It is not altogether clear at this stage of the proceedings whether the existence of substantial competition between Fox and Beacon is actually a material issue of fact common to both the equitable claim and the counterclaim for damages. The respondent ingeniously argues that determination in the equitable suit of the issue of competition between the theatres would be determinative of little or nothing in the counterclaim for damages. "The fact issue in the action for equitable and declaratory relief is whether the Fox West Coast California Theatre and the Petitioner's drive-in are substantially competitive with each other. The fact issue in the counterclaim is whether the cross-defendants and co-conspirators therein named conspired together in restraint of trade and to monopolize in the manner alleged in the counterclaim. Absent conspiracy, whether or not the distributors licensed a single first run picture to Petitioner's drive-in, be it in substantial competition or not in substantial competition with other first run theatres in the San Bernardino area, Petitioner will not have made out a case on its counterclaim. . . . If Petitioner on its counterclaim should fail to prove conspiracy the issue of competition between the theatres is meaningless. If petitioner on the other hand succeeds in proving the allegations of its counterclaim, the conspiracy to monopolize first run and to discriminate against the new drive-in, the existence or non-existence of competition between the theatres would exculpate none of the alleged wrongdoers, although if there was an absence of competition between the drive-in and the other first run theatres, as Petitioner contended in its answer to the complaint, it might have some difficulty proving injury to its business."

5. State Farm Mut. Auto. Ins. Co. v. Mossey, 7 Cir., 195 F.2d 56, 60; Connecticut General Life Ins. Co. v. Candimat Co., D.C., 83 F.Supp. 1.

6. Dickinson v. General Accident F. & L. Assur. Corp., 9 Cir., 147 F.2d 396; Hargrove v. American Cent. Ins. Co., 10 Cir., 125 F.2d 225; Pacific Indemnity Co. v. McDonald, 9 Cir., 107 F.2d 446, 131 A.L.R. 208.

Thus, if in this case the complaint had asked merely for a judgment declaring that the plaintiff's specified manner of business dealings with distributors and other exhibitors did not render it liable to Beacon under the antitrust laws, this would have been simply a "juxtaposition of parties" case in which Beacon could have demanded a jury trial.[7] But the complaint in the present case, as the Court recognizes, presented issues of exclusively equitable cognizance, going well beyond a mere defense to any subsequent action at law. Fox sought from the court protection against Beacon's allegedly unlawful interference with its business relationships—protection which this Court seems to recognize might not have been afforded by a declaratory judgment, unsupplemented by equitable relief. The availability of a declaratory judgment did not, therefore, operate to confer upon Beacon the right to trial by jury with respect to the issues raised by the complaint.

II.

The Court's opinion does not, of course, hold or even suggest that a court of equity may never determine "legal rights." For indeed it is precisely such rights which the Chancellor, when his jurisdiction has been properly invoked, has often been called upon to decide. Issues of fact are rarely either "legal" or "equitable." All depends upon the context in which they arise. The examples cited by Chief Judge Pope in his thorough opinion in the Court of Appeals in this case are illustrative: ". . . [I]n a suit by one in possession of real property to quiet title, or to remove a cloud on title, the court of equity may determine the legal title. In a suit for specific performance of a contract, the court may determine the making, validity and the terms of the contract involved. In a suit for an injunction against trespass to real property the court may determine the legal right of the plaintiff to the possession of that property. Cf. Pomeroy, Equity Jurisprudence, 5th ed., §§ 138–221, 221a, 221b, 221d, 250." 252 F.2d 864, 874.

Though apparently not disputing these principles, the Court holds, quite apart from its reliance upon the Declaratory Judgment Act, that Beacon by filing its counterclaim and cross-claim acquired a right to trial by jury of issues which otherwise would have been properly triable to the court. Support for this position is found in the principle that, "in the federal courts equity has always acted only when legal remedies were inadequate. . . ." Yet that principle is not employed in its traditional sense as a limitation upon the exercise of power by a court of equity. This is apparent in the Court's recognition that the allegations of the complaint entitled Fox to equitable relief—relief to which Fox would not have been entitled if it had had an adequate remedy at law. Instead, the principle is employed today to mean that because it is

7. Moore's Federal Practice (2d ed.) § 57.31[2]. "Transposition of parties" would perhaps be a more accurate description. A typical such case is one in which a plaintiff uses the declaratory judgment procedures to seek a determination of non-liability to a legal claim asserted by the defendant. The defendant in such a case is, of course, entitled to a jury trial.

possible under the counterclaim to have a jury trial of the factual issue of substantial competition, that issue must be tried by a jury, even though the issue was primarily presented in the original claim for equitable relief. This is a marked departure from long-settled principles.

It has been an established rule "that equitable jurisdiction existing at the filing of a bill is not destroyed because an adequate legal remedy may have become available thereafter."[8] American Life Ins. Co. v. Stewart, 300 U.S. 203, 215, 57 S.Ct. 377, 380, 81 L.Ed. 605. See Dawson v. Kentucky Distilleries & Warehouse Co., 255 U.S. 288, 296, 41 S.Ct. 272, 275, 65 L.Ed. 638. It has also been long settled that the District Court in its discretion may order the trial of a suit in equity in advance of an action at law between the same parties, even if there is a factual issue common to both. In the words of Mr. Justice Cardozo, writing for a unanimous Court in American Life Ins. Co. v. Stewart, supra:

> "A court has control over its own docket. . . . In the exercise of a sound discretion it may hold one lawsuit in abeyance to abide the outcome of another, especially where the parties and the issues are the same. . . . If request had been made by the respondents to suspend the suits in equity till the other causes were disposed of, the District Court could have considered whether justice would not be done by pursuing such a course, the remedy in equity being exceptional and the outcome of necessity. . . . There would be many circumstances to be weighed, as, for instance, the condition of the court calendar, whether the insurer had been precipitate or its adversaries dilatory, as well as other factors. In the end, benefit and hardship would have to be set off, the one against the other, and a balance ascertained." 300 U.S. 203, 215–216, 57 S.Ct. 377, 380.[9]

III.

The Court today sweeps away these basic principles as "precedents decided under discarded procedures." It suggests that the Federal Rules of Civil Procedure have somehow worked an "expansion of adequate legal remedies" so as to oust the District Courts of equitable jurisdiction, as well as to deprive them of their traditional power to control their own dockets. But obviously the Federal Rules could not and did not "expand" the substantive law one whit.[10]

---

8. The suggestion by the Court that "This was because the subsequent legal action, though providing an opportunity to try the case to a jury, might not protect the right of the equity plaintiff to a fair and orderly adjudication of the controversy" is plainly inconsistent with many of the cases in which the rule has been applied. See, e.g., Beedle v. Bennett, 122 U.S. 71, 7 S.Ct. 1090, 30 L.Ed. 1074; Clark v. Wooster, 119 U.S. 322, 7 S.Ct. 217, 30 L.Ed. 392.

9. It is arguable that if a case factually similar to American Life Ins. Co. v. Stewart were to arise under the Declaratory Judgment Act, the defendant would be entitled to a jury trial. See footnote 7. But cf. 5 Moore's Federal Practice (2d ed.), p. 158.

10. Congressional authorization of the Rules expressly provided that "Said rules shall neither abridge, enlarge, nor modify the substantive rights of any litigant." 48

Like the Declaratory Judgment Act, the Federal Rules preserve inviolate the right to trial by jury in actions historically cognizable at common law, as under the Constitution they must. They do not create a right of trial by jury where that right "does not exist under the Constitution or statutes of the United States." Rule 39(a). Since Beacon's counterclaim was compulsory under the Rules, see Rule 13(a), it is apparent that by filing it Beacon could not be held to have waived its jury rights.[12] Compare American Mills Co. v. American Surety Co., 260 U.S. 360, 43 S.Ct. 149, 67 L.Ed. 306. But neither can the counterclaim be held to have transformed Fox's original complaint into an action at law.[13] See Bendix Aviation Corp. v. Glass, D.C., 81 F.Supp. 645.

The Rules make possible the trial of legal and equitable claims in the same proceeding, but they expressly affirm the power of a trial judge to determine the order in which claims shall be heard. Rule 42(b). Certainly the Federal Rules were not intended to undermine the basic structure of equity jurisprudence, developed over the centuries and explicitly recognized in the United States Constitution.[14]

For these reasons I think the petition for a writ of mandamus should have been dismissed.

ROSS v. BERNHARD

Supreme Court of the United States, 1970.
396 U.S. 531, 90 S.Ct. 733, 24 L.Ed.2d 729.

MR. JUSTICE WHITE delivered the opinion of the Court.

The Seventh Amendment to the Constitution provides that in "[s]uits at common law, where the value in controversy shall exceed twenty dollars, the right of trial by jury shall be preserved." Whether the Amendment guarantees the right to a jury trial in stockholders' derivative actions is the issue now before us.

Petitioners brought this derivative suit in federal court against the directors of their closed-end investment company, the Lehman Corporation and the corporation's brokers, Lehman Brothers. They contended that Lehman Brothers controlled the corporation through an illegally large representation on the corporation's board of directors, in violation

---

Stat. 1064. See 28 U.S.C. § 2072, 28 U.S.C.A. § 2072.

12. This is not, of course, to suggest that the filing of a permissive "legal" counterclaim to an "equitable" complaint would amount to a waiver of jury rights on the issues raised by the counterclaim.

13. Determination of whether a claim stated by the complaint is triable by the court or by a jury will normally not be dependent upon the "legal" or "equitable" character of the counterclaim. See

Borchard, Declaratory Judgments (2d ed.), p. 404. There are situations, however, such as a case in which the plaintiff seeks a declaration of invalidity or noninfringement of a patent, in which the relief sought by the counterclaim will determine the nature of the entire case. See Moore's Federal Practice (2d ed.) § 38.29.

14. "The Judicial Power shall extend to all cases, in Law and Equity. . . ." Art. III, § 2.

of the Investment Company Act of 1940, 54 Stat. 789, 15 U.S.C.A. § 80a–1 et seq., and used this control to extract excessive brokerage fees from the corporation. The directors of the corporation were accused of converting corporate assets and of "gross abuse of trust, gross misconduct, willful misfeasance, bad faith, [and] gross negligence." Both the individual defendants and Lehman Brothers were accused of breaches of fiduciary duty. It was alleged that the payments to Lehman Brothers constituted waste and spoliation, and that the contract between the corporation and Lehman Brothers had been violated. Petitioners requested that the defendants "account for and pay to the Corporation for their profits and gains and its losses." Petitioners also demanded a jury trial on the corporation's claims.

On motion to strike petitioners' jury trial demand, the District Court held that a shareholder's right to a jury on his corporation's cause of action was to be judged as if the corporation were itself the plaintiff. Only the shareholder's initial claim to speak for the corporation had to be tried to the judge. 275 F.Supp. 569. Convinced that "there are substantial grounds for difference of opinion as to this question and . . . an immediate appeal would materially advance the ultimate termination of this litigation," the District Court permitted an interlocutory appeal. 28 U.S.C.A. § 1292(b). The Court of Appeals reversed, holding that a derivative action was entirely equitable in nature, and no jury was available to try any part of it. 403 F.2d 909. It specifically disagreed with DePinto v. Provident Security Life Ins. Co., 323 F.2d 826 (C.A. 9th Cir. 1963), cert. denied Garsuch v. De P, 376 U.S. 950, 84 S.Ct. 965, 11 L.Ed.2d 969 (1964), on which the District Court had relied. Because of this conflict, we granted certiorari 394 U.S. 917, 89 S.Ct. 1190, 22 L.Ed.2d 450 (1969).

We reverse the holding of the Court of Appeals that in no event does the right to a jury trial preserved by the Seventh Amendment extend to derivative actions brought by the stockholders of a corporation. We hold that the right to jury trial attaches to those issues in derivative actions as to which the corporation, if it had been suing in its own right, would have been entitled to a jury.

The Seventh Amendment preserves to litigants the right to jury trial in suits at common law—

"not merely suits, which the *common* law recognized among its old and settled proceedings, but suits in which *legal* rights were to be ascertained and determined, in contradistinction to those where equitable rights alone were recognized, and equitable remedies were administered. . . . In a just sense, the amendment then may well be construed to embrace all suits, which are not of equity and admiralty jurisdiction, whatever may be the peculiar form which they may assume to settle legal rights." Parsons v. Bedford, Breedlove & Robeson, 3 Pet. 433, 447, 7 L.Ed. 732 (1830).

However difficult it may have been to define with precision the line between actions at law dealing with legal rights and suits in equity dealing with equitable matters, Whitehead v. Shattuck, 138 U.S. 146, 151, 11 S.Ct. 276, 277, 34 L.Ed. 873 (1891), some proceedings were unmistakably actions at law triable to a jury. The Seventh Amendment, for example, entitled the parties to a jury trial in actions for damages to a person or property, for libel and slander, for recovery of land, and for conversion of personal property.[1] Just as clearly, a corporation, although an artificial being, was commonly entitled to sue and be sued in the usual forms of action, at least in its own State. See Paul v. Virginia, 8 Wall. 168, 19 L.Ed. 357 (1869). Whether the corporation was viewed as an entity separate from its stockholders or as a device permitting its stockholders to carry on their business and to sue and be sued, a corporation's suit to enforce a legal right was an action at common law carrying the right to jury trial at the time the Seventh Amendment was adopted.[2]

The common law refused, however, to permit stockholders to call corporate managers to account in actions at law. The possibilities for abuse, thus presented, were not ignored by corporate officers and directors. Early in the 19th century, equity provided relief both in this country and in England. Without detailing these developments,[3] it suffices to say that the remedy in this country, first dealt with by this Court in Dodge v. Woolsey, 18 How. 331, 15 L.Ed. 401 (1856), provided redress not only against faithless officers and directors but also against third parties who had damaged or threatened the corporate properties and whom the corporation through its managers refused to pursue. The remedy made available in equity was the derivative suit, viewed in this country as a suit to enforce a *corporate* cause of action against officers, directors, and third parties. As elaborated in the cases, one precondition for the suit was a valid claim on which the corporation could have sued; another was that the corporation itself had refused to proceed after suitable demand, unless excused by extraordinary conditions.[4] Thus the dual nature of the stockholder's action: first, the plaintiff's right to sue on behalf of the corporation and, second, the merits of the corporation claim itself.[5]

1. See, e.g., Curriden v. Middleton, 232 U.S. 633, 34 S.Ct. 458, 58 L.Ed. 765 (1914); Whitehead v. Shattuck, 138 U.S. 146, 11 S.Ct. 276, 34 L.Ed. 873 (1891); 5 J. Moore, Federal Practice ¶ 38.11[5] (2d ed. 1969).

2. 1 W. Blackstone, Commentaries *475; cf. Bank of Columbia v. Patterson's Adm'r, 7 Cranch 299, 3 L.Ed. 351 (1813); President and Directors of Bank of Commonwealth of Kentucky v. Wister, 2 Pet. 318, 7 L.Ed. 437 (1829).

3. Prunty, The Shareholders' Derivative Suit: Notes on Its Derivation, 32 N.Y. U.L.Rev. 980 (1957), treats the development of the equitable remedy.

4. Delaware & Hudson Co. v. Albany & S. R. Co., 213 U.S. 435, 29 S.Ct. 540, 53 L.Ed. 862 (1909); Doctor v. Harrington, 196 U.S. 579, 25 S.Ct. 355, 49 L.Ed. 606 (1905); City of Quincy v. Steel, 120 U.S. 241, 7 S.Ct. 520, 30 L.Ed. 624 (1887); Hawes v. City of Oakland, 104 U.S. 450, 26 L.Ed. 827 (1882). Soon after Hawes v. Oakland, supra, the pre-conditions to a shareholder's suit were promulgated as Equity Rule 94, 104 U.S. IX, which became Equity Rule 27, 226 U.S. 656 (1912), then Fed.Rule Civ. Proc. 23(b), 308 U.S. 690 (1938), and is now Fed.Rule Civ.Proc. 23.1, 383 U.S. 1050 (1966).

5. See Koster v. Lumbermens Mut. Cas. Co., 330 U.S. 518, 522–523, 67 S.Ct. 828, 830–831, 91 L.Ed. 1067 (1947); Ashwander v. TVA, 297 U.S. 288, 56 S.Ct. 466, 80 L.Ed. 688 (1936). See also 13 W. Fletcher, Cyclopedia of the Law of Private Corpora-

Derivative suits posed no Seventh Amendment problems where the action against the directors and third parties would have been by a bill in equity had the corporation brought the suit. Our concern is with cases based upon a legal claim of the corporation against directors or third parties. Does the trial of such claims at the suit of a stockholder and without a jury violate the Seventh Amendment?

The question arose in this Court in the context of a derivative suit for treble damages under the antitrust laws. Fleitmann v. Welsbach Street Lighting Co., 240 U.S. 27, 36 S.Ct. 233, 60 L.Ed. 505 (1916). Noting that the bill in equity set up a claim of the corporation alone, Mr. Justice Holmes observed that if the corporation were the plaintiff, "no one can doubt that its only remedy would be at law," and inquired "why the defendants' right to a jury trial should be taken away because the present plaintiff cannot persuade the only party having a cause of action to sue,—how the liability which is the principal matter can be converted into an incident of the plaintiff's domestic difficulties with the company that has been wronged"? Id., at 28, 36 S.Ct., at 234. His answer was that the bill did not state a good cause of action in equity. Agreeing that there were "cases in which the nature of the right asserted for the company, or the failure of the defendants concerned to insist upon their rights, or a different state system, has led to the whole matter being disposed of in equity," he concluded that when the penalty of triple damages is sought, the antitrust statute plainly anticipated a jury trial and should not be read as "attempting to authorize liability to be enforced otherwise than through the verdict of a jury in a court of common law." Id., at 28–29, 36 S.Ct., at 234. Although the decision had obvious Seventh Amendment overtones, its ultimate rationale was grounded in the antitrust laws.[6]

Where penal damages were not involved, however, there was no authoritative parallel to *Fleitmann* in the federal system squarely passing on the applicability of the Seventh Amendment to the trial of a legal claim presented in a pre-merger derivative suit. What can be gleaned from this Court's opinions [7] is not inconsistent with the general

tions § 5941.1 (1961 ed.); 2 G. Hornstein, Corporation Law and Practice § 716 (1959); 4 J. Pomeroy, Equity Jurisprudence § 1095, p. 278 (5th ed. 1941). Insofar as the stockholders may have been asserting their own direct interest, they closely resemble other class action plaintiffs who could proceed, before merger, only in equity.

6. The dilemma of the stockholder seeking treble damages for the corporation became real and complete in United Copper Co. v. Amalgamated Copper Co., 244 U.S. 261, 37 S.Ct. 509, 61 L.Ed. 1119 (1917), where the stockholder-plaintiff sought treble damages in an action at law. The Court rejected the claim by reiterating the traditional view that a shareholder was without standing to sue at law on a corpo-

rate cause. The treble-damage action was a legal proceeding and only the corporation could bring it. The Court of Appeals for the Second Circuit has held that the federal rules have resolved the dilemma and that derivative actions for treble damages under the antitrust laws are now proper. Fanchon & Marco, Inc. v. Paramount Pictures, Inc., 202 F.2d 731 (C.A. 2d Cir. 1953). Cf. Ramsburg v. American Inv. Co. of Ill., 231 F.2d 333 (C.A. 7th Cir. 1956). See generally Comment, Federal Antitrust Law—Stockholders' Remedies For Corporate Injury Resulting From Antitrust Violations: Derivative Antitrust Suit and Fiduciary Duty Action, 59 Mich.L.Rev. 904 (1961).

7. For example, in *Amalgamated Copper* the Court noted that in City of Quincy

understanding, reflected by the state court decisions and secondary sources, that equity could properly resolve corporate claims of any kind without a jury when properly pleaded in derivative suits complying with the equity rules.[8]

Such was the prevailing opinion when the Federal Rules of Civil Procedure were adopted in 1938. It continued until 1963 when the Court of Appeals for the Ninth Circuit, relying on the Federal Rules as construed and applied in Beacon Theatres, Inc. v. Westover, 359 U.S. 500, 79 S.Ct. 948, 3 L.Ed.2d 988 (1959), and Dairy Queen, Inc. v. Wood, 369 U.S. 469, 82 S.Ct. 894, 8 L.Ed.2d 44 (1962), required the legal issues in a derivative suit to be tried to a jury.[9] DePinto v. Provident Security Life Ins. Co., 323 F.2d 826. It was this decision that the District Court followed in the case before us and that the Court of Appeals rejected.

Beacon and *Dairy Queen* presaged *DePinto*. Under those cases, where equitable and legal claims are joined in the same action, there is a right to jury trial on the legal claims which must not be infringed either by trying the legal issues as incidental to the equitable ones or by a court trial of a common issue existing between the claims. The Seventh Amendment question depends on the nature of the issue to be tried rather than the character of the overall action.[10] See Simler v. Conner, 372 U.S. 221, 83 S.Ct. 609, 9 L.Ed.2d 691 (1963). The principle of these cases bears heavily on derivative actions.

We have noted that the derivative suit has dual aspects: first, the stockholder's right to sue on behalf of the corporation, historically an equitable matter; second, the claim of the corporation against directors or third parties on which, if the corporation had sued and the claim presented legal issues, the company could demand a jury trial. As

v. Steel, 120 U.S. 241, 7 S.Ct. 520, 30 L.Ed. 624 (1887), a shareholder's bill in equity that sought to enforce "a purely legal claim of the corporation,—damages for breach of contract" was dismissed, "not because the suit should have been at law, but because the bill failed to show that complainant had made sufficient effort to induce the directors to enter suit." 244 U.S., at 264–265, n. 3, 37 S.Ct., at 511. Delaware & Hudson Co. v. Albany & S. R. Co., supra, n. 4, involved a derivative suit for money damages due under a lease. The stockholders' right to sue was sustained; no jury trial issue appears to have been raised.

8. See, e.g., Goetz v. Manufacturers' & Traders' Trust Co., 154 Misc. 733, 277 N.Y.S. 802 (Sup.Ct.1935); Isaac v. Marcus, 258 N.Y. 257, 179 N.E. 487 (1932); Morton v. Morton Realty Co., 41 Idaho 729, 241 P. 1014 (1925); Neff v. Barber, 165 Wis. 503, 162 N.W. 667 (1917); Robinson v. Smith, 3 Paige Ch. 222, 231, 233 (N.Y.1832); 4 W. Cook, Corporations § 734 (8th ed. 1923); S. Thompson & J. Thompson, Law of Corpora-

tions § 4661 (Supp.1931); 6 Id., § 4653 (3d ed. 1927).

9. The possibility that the merged federal practice altered the procedures in derivative suits was early recognized, Fanchon & Marco, Inc. v. Paramount Pictures, Inc., supra, n. 6, but until the action of the District Court below *DePinto* was alone in holding that a right to a jury trial existed in derivative actions. Cf. Richiand v. Crandall, 259 F.Supp. 274 (D.C.S.D.N.Y. 1966). See also Metcalf v. Shamel, 166 Cal.App.2d 789, 333 P.2d 857 (1959); Steinway v. Griffith Consol. Theatres, 273 P.2d 872 (Okla.1954).

10. As our cases indicate, the "legal" nature of an issue is determined by considering, first, the pre-merger custom with reference to such questions; second, the remedy sought; and third, the practical abilities and limitations of juries. Of these factors, the first, requiring extensive and possibly abstruse historical inquiry, is obviously the most difficult to apply. See James, Right to a Jury Trial in Civil Actions, 72 Yale L.J. 655 (1963).

implied by Mr. Justice Holmes in *Fleitmann*, legal claims are not magically converted into equitable issues by their presentation to a court of equity in a derivative suit. The claim pressed by the stockholder against directors or third parties "is not his own but the corporation's." Koster v. Lumbermens Mut. Cas. Co., 330 U.S. 518, 522, 67 S.Ct. 828, 831 (1947). The corporation is a necessary party to the action; without it the case cannot proceed. Although named a defendant, it is the real party in interest, the stockholder being at best the nominal plaintiff. The proceeds of the action belong to the corporation and it is bound by the result of the suit.[11] The heart of the action is the corporate claim. If it presents a legal issue, one entitling the corporation to a jury trial under the Seventh Amendment, the right to a jury is not forfeited merely because the stockholder's right to sue must first be adjudicated as an equitable issue triable to the court. *Beacon* and *Dairy Queen* require no less.

If under older procedures, now discarded, a court of equity could properly try the legal claims of the corporation presented in a derivative suit, it was because irreparable injury was threatened and no remedy at law existed as long as the stockholder was without standing to sue and the corporation itself refused to pursue its own remedies. Indeed, from 1789 until 1938, the judicial code expressly forbade courts of equity from entertaining any suit for which there was an adequate remedy at law.[12] This provision served "to guard the right of trial by jury preserved by the Seventh Amendment and to that end it should be liberally construed." Schoenthal v. Irving Trust Co., 287 U.S. 92, 94, 53 S.Ct. 50, 51, 77 L.Ed. 185 (1932). If, before 1938, the law had borrowed from equity, as it borrowed other things, the idea that stockholders could litigate for their recalcitrant corporation, the corporate claim, if legal, would undoubtedly have been tried to a jury.

Of course, this did not occur, but the Federal Rules had a similar impact. Actions are no longer brought as actions at law or suits in equity. Under the Rules there is only one action—a "civil action"—in which all claims may be joined and all remedies are available. Purely procedural impediments to the presentation of any issue by any party, based on the difference between law and equity, were destroyed. In a civil action presenting a stockholder's derivative claim, the court after passing upon the plaintiff's right to sue on behalf of the corporation is now able to try the corporate claim for damages with the aid of a jury.[13] Separable claims may be tried separately, Fed.Rule Civ.Proc. 42(b), or

---

11. See Koster v. Lumbermens Mut. Cas. Co., 330 U.S. 518, 67 S.Ct. 828, 91 L.Ed. 1067 (1947); Meyer v. Fleming, 327 U.S. 161, 167, 66 S.Ct. 382, 386, 90 L.Ed. 595 (1946); Davenport v. Dows, 18 Wall. 626, 21 L.Ed. 938 (1874).

12. The Judicial Code of 1911, § 267, 36 Stat. 1163, re-enacting the Act of Sept. 24, 1789, § 16, 1 Stat. 82, provided: "Suits in equity shall not be sustained in any court of the United States in any case where a plain, adequate, and complete remedy may be had at law."

13. It would appear that the same conclusions could have been reached under Equity Rule 23 and the Law and Equity Act of 1915, Act of March 3, 1915, 38 Stat. 956. See Southern R. Co. v. City of Greenwood, 40 F.2d 679 (D.C.W.D.S.C.1928); 2 J.

legal and equitable issues may be handled in the same trial. Fanchon & Marco, Inc. v. Paramount Pictures, Inc., 202 F.2d 731 (C.A.2d Cir. 1953). The historical rule preventing a court of law from entertaining a shareholder's suit on behalf of the corporation is obsolete; it is no longer tenable for a district court, administering both law and equity in the same action, to deny legal remedies to a corporation, merely because the corporation's spokesmen are its shareholders rather than its directors. Under the rules, law and equity are procedurally combined; nothing turns now upon the form of the action or the procedural devices by which the parties happen to come before the court. The "expansion of adequate legal remedies provided by . . . the Federal Rules necessarily affects the scope of equity." Beacon Theatres, Inc. v. Westover, 359 U.S., at 509, 79 S.Ct., at 956.

Thus, for example, before-merger class actions were largely a device of equity, and there was no right to a jury even on issues that might, under other circumstances, have been tried to a jury. 5 J. Moore, Federal Practice ¶ 38.38[2] (2d ed. 1969); 3B id., ¶ 23.02[1]. Although at least one post-merger court held that the device was not available to try legal issues,[14] it now seems settled in the lower federal courts that class action plaintiffs may obtain a jury trial on any legal issues they present. Montgomery Ward & Co. v. Langer, 168 F.2d 182 (C.A.8th Cir. 1948); see Oskoian v. Canuel, 269 F.2d 311 (C.A.1st Cir. 1959), aff'g 23 F.R.D. 307; Syres v. Oil Workers Int'l Union, Local 23, 257 F.2d 479 (C.A.5th Cir. 1958), cert. denied, 358 U.S. 929, 79 S.Ct. 315, 3 L.Ed.2d 302 (1959). 2 W. Barron & A. Holtzoff, Federal Practice and Procedure § 571 (Wright ed. 1961).

Derivative suits have been described as one kind of "true" class action. Id., § 562.1. We are inclined to agree with the description, at least to the extent it recognizes that the derivative suit and the class action were both ways of allowing parties to be heard in equity who could not speak at law.[15] 3B J. Moore, Federal Practice ¶¶ 23.02[1],

Moore, Federal Practice ¶ 2.05 (2d ed. 1967). Rule 23 provided:

"If in a suit in equity a matter ordinarily determinable at law arises, such matters shall be determined in that suit according to the principles applicable, without sending the case or question to the law side of the court."

14. Farmers Co-operative Oil Co. v. Socony-Vacuum Oil Co., 43 F.Supp. 735 (D.C. N.D.Iowa 1942).

15. Other equitable devices are used under the rules without depriving the parties employing them of the right to a jury trial on legal issues. For example, although the right to intervene may in some cases be limited, United States for Use and Benefit of Browne & Bryan Lumber Co. v. Massachusetts Bonding & Ins. Co., 303 F.2d 823 (C.A.2d Cir. 1962); Dickinson v. Burnham, 197 F.2d 973 (C.A.2d Cir.), cert. de-

nied 344 U.S. 875, 73 S.Ct. 169, 97 L.Ed. 678 (1952), when intervention is permitted generally, the intervenor has a right to a jury trial on any legal issues he presents. See 3B J. Moore, Federal Practice ¶ 24.16[7] (2d ed. 1969); 5 id., ¶ 38.38[3]. A similar development seems to be taking place in the lower courts in interpleader actions. Before merger interpleader actions lay only in equity, and there was no right to a jury even on issues that might, under other circumstances, have been tried to a jury. Liberty Oil Co. v. Condon Nat. Bank, 260 U.S. 235, 43 S.Ct. 118, 67 L.Ed. 232 (1922). This view continued for some time after merger, see Bynum v. Prudential Life Ins. Co., 7 F.R.D. 585 (D.C.E.D.S.C. 1947), but numerous courts and commentators have now come to the conclusion that the right to a jury should not turn on how the parties happen to be brought into court. See Pan American Fire & Cas. Co.

23.1.16[1] (2d ed. 1969). After adoption of the rules there is no longer any procedural obstacle to the assertion of legal rights before juries, however the party may have acquired standing to assert those rights. Given the availability in a derivative action of both legal and equitable remedies, we think the Seventh Amendment preserves to the parties in a stockholder's suit the same right to a jury trial that historically belonged to the corporation and to those against whom the corporation pressed its legal claims.

In the instant case we have no doubt that the corporation's claim is, at least in part, a legal one. The relief sought is money damages. There are allegations in the complaint of a breach of fiduciary duty, but there are also allegations of ordinary breach of contract and gross negligence. The corporation, had it sued on its own behalf, would have been entitled to a jury's determination, at a minimum, of its damages against its broker under the brokerage contract and of its rights against its own directors because of their negligence. Under these circumstances it is unnecessary to decide whether the corporation's other claims are also properly triable to a jury. Dairy Queen, Inc. v. Wood, 369 U.S. 469, 82 S.Ct. 894, 8 L.Ed.2d 44 (1962). The decision of the Court of Appeals is reversed.

It is so ordered.

Decision of Court of Appeals reversed.

MR. JUSTICE STEWART, with whom THE CHIEF JUSTICE and MR. JUSTICE HARLAN join, dissenting.

In holding as it does that the plaintiff in a shareholder's derivative suit is constitutionally entitled to a jury trial, the Court today seems to rely upon some sort of ill-defined combination of the Seventh Amendment and the Federal Rules of Civil Procedure. Somehow the Amendment and the Rules magically interact to do what each separately was expressly intended not to do, namely, to enlarge the right to a jury trial in civil actions brought in the courts of the United States.

The Seventh Amendment, by its terms, does not extend, but merely *preserves* the right to a jury trial "[i]n Suits at common law." All agree that this means the reach of the Amendment is limited to those actions that were tried to the jury in 1791 when the Amendment was adopted.[1] Suits in equity, which were historically tried to the court, were there-

v. Revere, 188 F.Supp. 474 (D.C.E.D.La. 1960); Savannah Bank & Trust Co. v. Block, 175 F.Supp. 798 (D.C.S.D.Ga.1959); Westinghouse Elec. Corp. v. United Elec. Radio & Mach. Workers of America, 99 F.Supp. 597 (D.C.W.D.Pa.1951); John Hancock Mut. Life Ins. Co. v. Yarrow, 95 F.Supp. 185 (D.C.E.D.Pa.1951); 2 W. Barron & A. Holtzoff, Federal Practice and Procedure § 556 (Wright ed. 1961); 3A J. Moore, Federal Practice ¶ 22.14[4] (2d ed. 1969). But see Pennsylvania Fire Ins. Co. v. American Airlines, Inc., 180 F.Supp. 239 (D.C.E.D.N.Y.1960); Liberty Nat. Life Ins. Co. v. Brown, 119 F.Supp. 920 (D.C.M.D. Ala.1954).

1. Where a new cause of action is created by Congress, and nothing is said about how it is to be tried, the jury trial issue is determined by fitting the cause into its nearest historical analogy. Luria v. United States, 231 U.S. 9, 34 S.Ct. 10, 58 L.Ed. 101; see James, Right to a Jury Trial in Civil Actions, 72 Yale L.J. 655.

fore unaffected by it. Similarly, Rule 38 of the Federal Rules has no bearing on the right to a jury trial in suits in equity, for it simply preserves inviolate "[t]he right of trial by jury as declared by the Seventh Amendment." Thus this Rule, like the Amendment itself, neither restricts nor enlarges the right to jury trial.[2] Indeed nothing in the Federal Rules can rightly be construed to enlarge the right of jury trial, for in the legislation authorizing the Rules, Congress expressly provided that they "shall neither abridge, enlarge, nor modify the substantive rights of any litigant." 48 Stat. 1064. See 28 U.S.C.A. § 2072. I take this plain, simple, and straightforward language to mean that after the promulgation of the Federal Rules, as before, the constitutional right to a jury trial attaches only to suits at common law. So, apparently, has every federal court that has discussed the issue.[3] Since, as the Court concedes, a shareholder's derivative suit could be brought only in equity, it would seem to me to follow by the most elementary logic that in such suits there is no constitutional right to a trial by jury.[4] Today the Court tosses aside history, logic and over 100 years of firm precedent to hold that the plaintiff in a shareholder's derivative suit does indeed have a constitutional right to a trial by jury. This holding has a questionable basis in policy[5] and no basis whatever in the Constitution.

* * *

---

2. See, e.g., Ettelson v. Metropolitan Life Ins. Co., 3 Cir., 137 F.2d 62, 65; 5 J. Moore, Federal Practice ¶ 38.07[1] and cases cited therein.

3. The principle that the Rules effected no enlargement or restriction of the right of jury trial has "received complete judicial approbation." 5 J. Moore, Federal Practice ¶ 38.07[1] and cases cited therein.

4. Virtually every state and federal court that has faced this issue has similarly reasoned to the same conclusion. See, e.g., Goetz v. Manufacturers' & Traders' Trust Co., 154 Misc. 733, 277 N.Y.S. 802 (Sup.Ct.); Metcalf v. Shamel, 166 Cal.App. 2d 789, 333 P.2d 857; Liken v. Shaffer, D.C., 64 F.Supp. 432; Miller v. Weiant, D.C., 42 F.Supp. 760. The equitable nature of the derivative suit has been recognized in several decisions of this Court. See, e.g., Cohen v. Beneficial Industrial Loan Corp., 337 U.S. 541, 547–548, 69 S.Ct. 1221, 1226,

93 L.Ed. 1528. It was also reflected in the adoption of Equity Rule 94 in 1882, and Rule 27 of the Equity Rules of 1912 which established the preconditions to bringing shareholders' derivative suits in the federal courts. These rules are the forerunners of Rule 23(b) of Fed.Rule Civ.Proc. of 1938, and of Fed.Rule Civ.Proc. 23.1 (1966), which now controls the initiation of such suits. See 3B J. Moore, Federal Practice ¶ 23.1.15[1].

5. See, e.g., Frank, Courts on Trial 110–111 (1949). Certainly there is no consensus among commentators on the desirability of jury trials in civil actions generally. Particularly where the issues in the case are complex—as they are likely to be in a derivative suit—much can be said for allowing the court discretion to try the case itself. See discussion in 5 J. Moore, Federal Practice ¶ 38.02[1].

ATLAS ROOFING CO. v. OCCUPATIONAL SAFETY AND HEALTH REVIEW COMMISSION

Supreme Court of the United States, 1977.
430 U.S. 442, 97 S.Ct. 1261, 51 L.Ed.2d 464.*

MR. JUSTICE WHITE delivered the opinion of the Court.

The issue in this case is whether, consistent with the Seventh Amendment, Congress may create a new cause of action in the Government for civil penalties enforceable in an administrative agency where there is no jury trial.

I

After extensive investigation, Congress concluded, in 1970, that work-related deaths and injuries had become a "drastic" national problem. Finding the existing state statutory remedies as well as state common law actions for negligence and wrongful death to be inadequate to protect the employee population from death and injury due to unsafe working conditions, Congress enacted the Occupational Safety and Health Act of 1970 (OSHA or Act), 84 Stat. 1590, 29 U.S.C.A. § 651 et seq. The Act created a new statutory duty to avoid maintaining unsafe or unhealthy working conditions, and empowers the Secretary of Labor to promulgate health and safety standards. Two new remedies were provided—permitting the Federal Government, proceeding before an administrative agency, (1) to obtain abatement orders requiring employers to correct unsafe working conditions and (2) to impose civil penalties on any employer maintaining any unsafe working condition. Each remedy exists whether or not an employee is actually injured or killed as a result of the condition, and existing state statutory and common law remedies for actual injury and death remain unaffected.

Under the Act, inspectors, representing the Secretary of Labor, are authorized to conduct reasonable safety and health inspections. 29 U.S.C.A. § 657(a). If a violation is discovered, the inspector, on behalf of the Secretary, issues a citation to the employer fixing a reasonable time for its abatement and, in his discretion, proposing a civil penalty. §§ 658, 659. Such proposed penalties may range from nothing for *de minimis* and nonserious violations, to not more than $1,000 for serious violations, to a maximum of $10,000 for willful or repeated violations, §§ 658(a), 659(a), 666(a)–(c) and (j).

If the employer wishes to contest the penalty or the abatement order, he may do so by notifying the Secretary of Labor within 15 days, in which event the abatement order is automatically stayed. §§ 659(a), (b), 666(d). An evidentiary hearing is then held before an administrative law judge of the Occupational Safety and Health Review Commission. The Commission consists of three members, appointed for six-year terms, each of whom is qualified "by reason of training, education

* Some of the Court's footnotes are omitted.

or experience" to adjudicate contested citations and assess penalties. §§ 651(b)(3), 659(c), 661, 666(i). At this hearing the burden is on the Secretary to establish the elements of the alleged violation and the propriety of his proposed abatement order and proposed penalty; and the judge is empowered to affirm, modify, or vacate any or all of these items, giving due consideration in his penalty assessment to "the size of the business of the employer . . . , the gravity of the violation, the good faith of the employer, and the history of previous violations." § 666(i). The judge's decision becomes the Commission's final and appealable order unless within 30 days a Commissioner directs that it be reviewed by the full Commission. §§ 659(c), 661(i); see 29 CFR §§ 2200.90 and 2200.91 (1976).

If review is granted, the Commission's subsequent order directing abatement and the payment of any assessed penalty becomes final unless the employer timely petitions for judicial review in the appropriate court of appeals. 29 U.S.C.A. § 660(a). The Secretary similarly may seek review of Commission orders, § 660(b), but, in either case, "[t]he findings of the Commission with respect to questions of fact, if supported by substantial evidence on the record considered as a whole, shall be conclusive." § 660(a). * * *

    * * *

* * * We granted the petitions for writs of certiorari limited to the important question whether the Seventh Amendment prevents Congress from assigning to an administrative agency, under these circumstances the task of adjudicating violations of OSHA. 424 U.S. 964, 96 S.Ct. 1458, 47 L.Ed.2d 731.

III

The Seventh Amendment provides that "in Suits at common law, where the value in controversy shall exceed twenty dollars, the right of trial by jury shall be preserved . . . ." The phrase "Suits at common law" has been construed to refer to cases tried prior to the adoption of the Seventh Amendment in courts of law in which jury trial was customary as distinguished from courts of equity or admiralty in which jury trial was not. Parsons v. Bedford, 3 Pet. 433, 7 L.Ed. 732 (1830). Petitioners claim that a suit in a federal court by the Government for civil penalties for violation of a statute is a suit for a money judgment which is classically a suit at common law, Whitehead v. Shattuck, 138 U.S. 146, 151, 11 S.Ct. 276, 34 L.Ed. 873 (1891); and that the defendant therefore has a Seventh Amendment right to a jury determination of all issues of fact in such a case, see Hepner v. United States, 213 U.S. 103, 115, 29 S.Ct. 474, 479, 53 L.Ed. 720 (1909) (dictum); United States v. Regan, 232 U.S. 37, 47, 34 S.Ct. 213, 216, 58 L.Ed. 494 (1914) (dictum). Petitioners then claim that to permit Congress to assign the function of adjudicating the Government's rights to civil penalties for violation of the statute to a different forum—an administrative agency in which no jury is available—would be to permit Congress to deprive a defendant of his Seventh Amendment jury right. We disagree. At least in cases in which "public rights" are being litigated—e.g., cases in which the Government sues in its sovereign capacity to enforce public rights created by statutes within the power of Congress to enact—the Seventh Amendment does not prohibit Congress from assigning the factfinding function and initial adjudication to an administrative forum with which the jury would be incompatible.[7]

Congress has often created new statutory obligations, provided for civil penalties for their violation, and committed exclusively to an administrative agency the function of deciding whether a violation has in fact occurred. These statutory schemes have been sustained by this Court, albeit often without express reference to the Seventh Amendment. Thus taxes may constitutionally be assessed and collected together with penalties, with the relevant facts in some instances being adjudicated only by an administrative agency. Phillips v. Commissioner, 283 U.S. 589, 599–600, 51 S.Ct. 608, 612, 75 L.Ed. 1289 (1931); Murray's Lessee v. Hoboken Land Co., 18 How. 272, 284, 15 L.Ed. 372 (1856).[8] Neither of these cases expressly discussed the question whether the taxation scheme violated the Seventh Amendment. However, in Helvering v. Mitchell, 303 U.S. 391, 58 S.Ct. 630, 82 L.Ed. 917 (1938), the Court said, in rejecting a claim under the Sixth Amendment that the assessment and adjudication of tax penalties could not be made without a jury, that "the determination of the facts upon which liability is based may be by an administrative agency instead of a jury," id., at 402, 58 S.Ct. at 635. Similarly, Congress has entrusted to an administrative agency the task of adjudicating violations of the customs and immigration laws and assessing penalties based thereon. Lloyd Sabaudo Societa v. Elting, 287 U.S. 329, 335, 53 S.Ct. 167, 170, 77 L.Ed. 341 (1932) ("[D]ue process of law does not require that the courts, rather than administrative officers, be charged with determining the facts upon which the imposition of [fines] depends"); Oceanic Nav. Co. v. Stranahan, 214 U.S. 320, 29 S.Ct. 671, 53 L.Ed. 1013 (1909).[9] See also

7. These cases do not involve purely "private rights." In cases which do involve only "private rights," this Court has accepted factfinding by an administrative agency, without intervention by a jury, only as an adjunct to an Art. III court, analogizing the agency to a jury or a special master and permitting it in admiralty cases to perform the function of the special master. Crowell v. Benson, 285 U.S. 22, 51–65, 52 S.Ct. 285, 292–298, 76 L.Ed. 598 (1932). The Court there said: "On the common-law side of the federal courts, the aid of juries is not only deemed appropriate but is required by the Constitution itself." Id., at 51, 52 S.Ct. at 292.

8. In *Murray's Lessee*, the Court stated:

"[T]here are matters, *involving public rights*, which may be presented in such form that the judicial power is capable of acting on them, and which are susceptible of judicial determination, but *which congress may or may not bring within the cognizance of the courts of the United States, as it may deem proper.*" 18 How., at 284. (Emphasis added.)

9. In *Oceanic*, the Court stated:

"In accord with this settled judicial construction the legislation of Congress from the beginning, not only as to tariff, but as to internal revenue, taxation, *and other subjects*, has proceeded on the conception that *it was within the competency of Congress, when legislating as to matters exclusively within its control,* to impose appropriate obligations, and sanction their enforcement by reasonable money penalties, *giving to executive officers the power to enforce such penalties without the necessity of involving the judicial power.*" 214 U.S., at 339, 29 S.Ct. at 676. (Emphasis added.)

Ex parte Bakelite Corp., 279 U.S. 438, 451, 458, 49 S.Ct. 411, 416, 73 L.Ed. 789 (1929).

In Block v. Hirsh, 256 U.S. 135, 41 S.Ct. 458, 65 L.Ed. 865 (1921), the Court sustained Congress' power to pass a statute, applicable to the District of Columbia, temporarily suspending landlords' legal remedy of ejectment and relegating them to an administrative factfinding forum charged with determining fair rents at which tenants could hold over despite the expiration of their leases. In that case the Court squarely rejected a challenge to the statute based on the Seventh Amendment, stating:

> "The statute is objected to on the further ground that land-lords and tenants are deprived by it of a trial by jury on the right to possession of the land. *If the power of the Commission established by the statute to regulate the relation is established*, as we think it is, by what we have said, *this objection amounts to little. To regulate the relation and to decide the facts affecting it are hardly separable*." Id., at 158, 41 S.Ct. at 460. (Emphasis added.)

In Crowell v. Benson, 285 U.S. 22, 52 S.Ct. 285, 76 L.Ed. 598 (1932), apparently referring to the above-cited line of authority, the Court stated:

> "[T]he distinction is at once apparent between cases of private right and those which arise *between the Government and persons subject to its authority in connection with the performance of the constitutional functions of the executive or legislative departments*. . . . [T]he Congress, in exercising the powers confided to it may establish 'legislative' courts . . . to serve as special tribunals 'to examine and determine various matters, arising between the government and others, which from their nature do not require judicial determination and yet are susceptible of it.' But '*the mode of determining matters of this class is completely within congressional control*. Congress may reserve to itself the power to decide, *may delegate that power to executive officers*, or may commit it to judicial tribunals.' . . . Familiar illustrations of *administrative agencies created for the determination of such matters are found in connection with the exercise of the congressional power as to interstate* and foreign *commerce*, taxation, immigration, the public lands, public health, the facilities of the post office, pensions, and payments to veterans." Id., at 50–51, 52 S.Ct. at 292. (Emphasis added.)

In NLRB v. Jones & Laughlin Steel Corp., 301 U.S. 1, 57 S.Ct. 615, 81 L.Ed. 893 (1937), the Court squarely addressed the Seventh Amendment issue involved when Congress commits the factfinding function under a new statute to an administrative tribunal. Under the National Labor Relations Act, Congress had committed to the National Labor Relations Board, in a proceeding brought by its litigating arm, the task of deciding whether an unfair labor practice had been committed and of ordering back pay where appropriate. The Court stated:

> "The instant case is not a suit at common law or in the nature of such a suit. The proceeding is one unknown to the common law. *It is a statutory proceeding.* Reinstatement of the employee and payment for time lost *are requirements [administratively] imposed for violation of the statute and are remedies appropriate to its enforcement.* The contention under the Seventh Amendment is without merit." Id., at 48–49, 57 S.Ct. at 629. (Emphasis added.) [10]

This passage from *Jones & Laughlin* has recently been explained in Curtis v. Loether, 415 U.S. 189, 94 S.Ct. 1005, 39 L.Ed.2d 260 (1974), in which the Court held the Seventh Amendment applicable to private damage suits in federal courts brought under the housing discrimination provisions of the Civil Rights Act of 1968. The Court rejected the argument that *Jones & Laughlin* held the Seventh Amendment inapplicable to any action based on a statutorily created right even if the action was brought before a tribunal which customarily utilizes a jury as its factfinding arm. Instead, we concluded that *Jones & Laughlin* upheld

> "congressional power to entrust enforcement of statutory rights to *an administrative process or specialized court of equity* [11] free from the strictures of the Seventh Amendment." 415 U.S., at 194–195, 94 S.Ct. at 1009. (Emphasis added.)

Finally, in Pernell v. Southall Realty, 416 U.S. 363, 94 S.Ct. 1723, 40 L.Ed.2d 198 (1974),[12] in discussing Block v. Hirsh, [supra], and *Jones & Laughlin*, we stated:

> "Block v. Hirsh merely stands for the principle that *the Seventh Amendment is generally inapplicable in administrative proceedings,*

---

10. The Court also rejected the Seventh Amendment claim in *Jones & Laughlin* on the separate ground that that Amendment is inapplicable where "recovery of money damages is an incident to [non-legal] relief even though damages might have been recovered in an action at law," 301 U.S., at 48–49, 57 S.Ct. at 629, since in such cases courts of equity would historically have granted monetary relief. In *Jones & Laughlin*, the NLRB ordered reinstatement of a dismissed employee, an order analogous to injunctive relief historically obtainable only in a court of equity, and consequently this alternate ground was an adequate one to decide *Jones & Laughlin*. However, this alternate ground would have been insufficient to decide the more general question of the NLRB's power to order backpay where, for one reason or another, no such equitable order was sought. See Radio Officers Union of Commercial Telegrapher's Union v. NLRB, 347 U.S. 17, 54, 74 S.Ct. 323, 343, 98 L.Ed. 455 (1954); NLRB v. National Garment Co., 166 F.2d 233 (CA8 1948); NLRB v. Brookside Industries, Inc., 308 F.2d 224 (CA4 1962); Bon Hennings Log-

ging Co. v. NLRB, 308 F.2d 548 (CA9 1962); NLRB v. West Coast Casket Co., Inc., 205 F.2d 902 (CA9 1953); Reliance Mfg. Co. v. NLRB, 125 F.2d 311 (CA7 1941); NLRB v. Local 1423, Etc., 238 F.2d 832 (CA5 1956); Indianapolis Power & Light Co. v. NLRB, 122 F.2d 757 (CA7 1941).

11. The Court had reference to Katchen v. Landy, 382 U.S. 323, 86 S.Ct. 467, 15 L.Ed. 2d 391 (1966), in which this Court sustained the power of a bankruptcy court, exercising summary jurisdiction without a jury, to adjudicate the otherwise legal issues of voidable preferences. The Court did so on the ground that a bankruptcy court, exercising its summary jurisdiction, was a specialized court of equity and constituted a forum before which a jury would be out of place and would go far to dismantle the statutory scheme.

12. The holding in *Pernell* was that the Seventh Amendment applies to resolution of disputes of a "legal" nature—those regarding right to possession of real property when the resolution is entrusted to a forum which customarily employs a jury.

where jury trials would be incompatible with the whole concept of administrative adjudication. . . . We may assume that the Seventh Amendment would not be a bar to a congressional effort to entrust landlord-tenant disputes, including those over the right to possession, to an administrative agency. Congress has not seen fit to do so, however, but rather has provided that actions under § 16–1501 be brought as ordinary civil actions in the District of Columbia's court of general jurisdiction. Where it has done so, and where the action involves rights and remedies recognized at common law, it must preserve to parties their right to a jury trial." 416 U.S., at 383, 94 S.Ct. at 1733. (Emphasis added.)

In sum, the cases discussed above stand clearly for the proposition that when Congress creates new statutory "public rights," it may assign their adjudication to an administrative agency with which a jury trial would be incompatible, without violating the Seventh Amendment's injunction that jury trial is to be "preserved" in "suits at common law." [13] Congress is not required by the Seventh Amendment to choke the already crowded federal courts with new types of litigation or prevented from committing some new types of litigation to administrative agencies with special competence in the relevant field. This is the case even if the Seventh Amendment would have required a jury where the adjudication of those rights is assigned to a federal court of law instead of an administrative agency.   *   *   *

    *   *   *

    *   *   * [I]t is said, Congress could utterly destroy the right to a jury trial by always providing for administrative rather than judicial resolution of the vast range of cases that now arise in the courts. The argument is well put, but it overstates the holdings of our prior cases and is in any event unpersuasive. Our prior cases support administrative factfinding in only those situations involving "public rights," e.g., where the Government is involved in its sovereign capacity under an otherwise valid statute creating enforceable public rights. Wholly private tort, contract, and property cases, as well as a vast range of other cases are not at all implicated.

More to the point, it is apparent from the history of jury trial in civil matters that factfinding, which is the essential function of the jury in civil cases, Colgrove v. Battin, 413 U.S. 149, 157, 93 S.Ct. 2448, 2452, 37 L.Ed.2d 522 (1973), was never the exclusive province of the jury under either the English or American legal systems at the time of the adoption of the Seventh Amendment; and the question whether a fact would be found by a jury turned to a considerable degree on the nature of the forum in which a litigant found himself. Critical factfinding was

---

13. We note that the decision of the administrative tribunal in these cases on the law is subject to review in the federal courts of appeals, and on the facts is subject to review by such courts of appeals under a substantial evidence test. Thus, this case does not present the question whether Congress may commit the adjudication of public rights and the imposition of fines for their violation to an administrative agency without any sort of intervention by a court at any stage of the proceedings.

performed without juries in suits in equity, and there were no juries in admiralty, Parsons v. Bedford, 3 Pet. 433, 7 L.Ed. 732 (1830); nor were there juries in the military justice system. The jury was the factfinding mode in most suits in the common law courts, but it was not exclusively so: Condemnation was a suit at common law but constitutionally could be tried without a jury, Kohl v. United States, 91 U.S. 367, 375–376, 23 L.Ed. 449 (1876); Bauman v. Ross, 167 U.S. 548, 593, 42 L.Ed. 270 (1897); United States v. Reynolds, 397 U.S. 14, 18, 90 S.Ct. 803, 806, 25 L.Ed.2d 12 (1970). "[M]any civil as well as criminal proceedings at common law were without a jury." Kohl v. United States, supra, at 376, 23 L.Ed. 449. The question whether a particular case was to be tried in a court of equity—without a jury—or a court of law—with a jury—did not depend on whether the suit involved factfinding or on the nature of the facts to be found. Factfinding could be a critical matter either at law or in equity. Rather, as a general rule, the decision turned on whether courts of law supplied a cause of action and an adequate remedy to the litigant.[14] If it did, then the case would be tried in a court of law before a jury. Otherwise the case would be tried to a court of equity sitting without a jury. Thus, suits for damages for breach of contract, for example, were suits at common law with the issues of the making of the contract and its breach to be decided by a jury; but specific performance was a remedy unavailable in a court of law and where such relief was sought the case would be tried in a court of equity with the facts as to making and breach to be ascertained by the court.

The Seventh Amendment was declaratory of the existing law, for it required only that jury trial in suits at common law was to be "preserved." It thus did not purport to require a jury trial where none was required before. Moreover, it did not seek to change the factfinding mode in equity or admiralty nor to freeze equity jurisdiction as it existed in 1789, preventing it from developing new remedies where those available in courts of law were inadequate. Ross v. Bernhard, 396 U.S. 531, 90 S.Ct. 733, 24 L.Ed.2d 729 (1970), is instructive in this respect. We there held that a jury trial is required in stockholder derivative suits where, if the corporation had itself sued, a jury trial would have been available to the corporation. It is apparent, however, that prior to the 1938 Federal Rules of Civil Procedure merging the law and equity functions of the federal courts, the very suit involved in *Bernhard* would have been in a court of equity sitting without a jury, not because the underlying issue was any different at all from the issue the corporation would have presented had it sued, but because the stockholder plaintiff who was denied standing in a court of law to sue

---

14. The Judiciary Act of 1789, 1 Stat. 82, which was in this respect declaratory of existing law, provided:

"Sec. 16. *And be it further enacted,* That suits in equity shall not be sustained in either of the courts of the United States, in any case where plain, adequate and complete remedy may be had at law."

on the issue was enabled in proper circumstances, starting in the early part of the 19th century, to sue in equity on behalf of the company.

The point is that the Seventh Amendment was never intended to establish the jury as the exclusive mechanism for factfinding in civil cases. It took the existing legal order as it found it, and there is little or no basis for concluding that the Amendment should now be interpreted to provide an impenetrable barrier to administrative factfinding under otherwise valid federal regulatory statutes. We cannot conclude that the Amendment rendered Congress powerless—when it concluded that remedies available in courts of law were inadequate to cope with a problem within Congress' power to regulate—to create new public rights and remedies by statute and commit their enforcement, if it chose, to a tribunal other than a court of law—such as an administrative agency—in which facts are not found by juries. * * * [15]

* * *

TULL v. UNITED STATES

Supreme Court of the United States, 1987.
481 U.S. 412, 107 S.Ct. 1831, 95 L.Ed.2d 365.*

JUSTICE BRENNAN delivered the opinion of the Court.

The question for decision is whether the Seventh Amendment guaranteed petitioner a right to a jury trial on both liability and amount of penalty in an action instituted by the Federal Government seeking civil penalties and injunctive relief under the Clean Water Act, 62 Stat. 1155, as amended, 33 U.S.C. § 1251 et seq.

I

The Clean Water Act prohibits discharging, without a permit, dredged or fill material into "navigable waters," including the wetlands adjacent to the waters. 33 U.S.C. §§ 1311, 1344 and 1362(7); 33 CFR §§ 323.2(a)(1)–(7) (1986). "Wetlands" are "swamps, marshes, bogs and similar areas." 33 CFR § 323.2(c) (1986). The Government sued petitioner, a real estate developer, for dumping fill on wetlands on the island of Chincoteague, Virginia. The Government alleged in the original complaint that petitioner dumped fill on three sites: Ocean Breeze Mobile Homes Sites, Mire Pond Properties, and Eel Creek. The Government later amended the complaint to allege that petitioner also placed fill in a manmade waterway, named Fowling Gut Extended, on the Ocean Breeze property.[1]

---

15. Finally, it should be noted that, if the fines involved in this case were made criminal fines instead of civil fines, the Seventh Amendment would be inapplicable by its terms. The Sixth Amendment would then govern the employer's right to a jury and under our prior cases no jury trial would be required. Muniz v. Hoffman, 422 U.S. 454, 95 S.Ct. 2178, 45 L.Ed. 2d 319 (1975). It would be odd to hold that Congress could avoid the jury trial requirement by labeling the civil penalties criminal fines but not by assigning their adjudication to an administrative agency.

* Some of the Court's footnotes are omitted.

1. Additionally, the Government alleged that petitioner's dumping of fill in Fowling Gut Extended violated another

Section 1319 enumerates the remedies available under the Clean Water Act. Subsection (b) authorizes relief in the form of temporary or permanent injunctions. Subsection (d) provides that violators of certain sections of the Act "shall be subject to a civil penalty not to exceed $10,000 per day" during the period of the violation. The Government sought in this case both injunctive relief and civil penalties. When the complaint was filed, however, almost all of the property at issue had been sold by petitioner to third parties. Injunctive relief was therefore impractical except with regard to a small portion of the land.[2] App. 110, 119. The Government's complaint demanded the imposition of the maximum civil penalty of $22,890,000 under subsection (d). App. 31–34.

Petitioner's timely demand for a trial by jury was denied by the District Court. During the 15–day bench trial, petitioner did not dispute that he had placed fill at the locations alleged and did not deny his failure to obtain a permit. Petitioner contended, however, that the property in question did not constitute "wetlands." 615 F.Supp. 610, 615–618 (ED Va.1983). The Government concedes that triable issues of fact were presented by disputes between experts involving the composition and nature of the fillings. Tr. of Oral Arg. 44.

The District Court concluded that petitioner had illegally filled in wetland areas on all properties in question, but drastically reduced the amount of civil penalties sought by the Government. With respect to the Ocean Breeze Mobile Homes Sites, the court imposed a civil fine of $35,000, noting that petitioner had sold seven lots at a profit of $5000 per lot. 615 F.Supp., at 626. The court fined the petitioner another $35,000 for illegal fillings on the Mire Pond Properties, ibid., and $5000 for filling that affected a single lot in Eel Creek, ibid., although petitioner had realized no profit from filling in these properties. In addition, the court imposed on petitioner a $250,000 fine to be suspended, however, "on the specific condition that he restore the extension of Fowling Gut to its former navigable condition. . . ." Id. at 627. Although petitioner argued that such restoration required purchasing the land from third parties at a cost of over $700,000, thus leaving him no choice but to pay the fine, the court refused to alter this order. App. 107a–108a. The court also granted separate injunctive relief: it ordered the restoration of wetlands on the portions of Mire Pond and Eel Creek still owned by petitioner, 615 F.Supp., at 627, and further ordered the removal of fillings on five lots of the Ocean Breeze Mobile Homes Sites unless petitioner were granted an "after-the-fact permit" validating the fillings. Id., at 626.

statute, the Rivers and Harbors Act, which prohibits the placement of fill in navigable waters without the authorization of the Secretary of the Army. 33 U.S.C. § 403. Petitioner does not base his Seventh Amendment claim on the Government's prosecution under this statute, which provides for injunctive relief but not for civil penalties.

2. The Government's complaint alleged violations involving over 1 million square feet of land. The Government obtained injunctive relief, however, relating to only 6,000 square feet. Brief for Petitioner 5.

[handwritten margin note: Ct Appeals affm'd no jury]

The Court of Appeals affirmed over a dissent, rejecting petitioner's argument that, under the Seventh Amendment, he was entitled to a jury trial. 769 F.2d 182 (CA4 1985). The court expressly declined to follow the decision of the Court of Appeals for the Second Circuit in United States v. J.B. Williams Co., 498 F.2d 414 (1974), which held that there was a Seventh Amendment " 'right of jury trial when the United States sues . . . to collect a [statutory civil] penalty, even though the statute is silent on the right of jury trial.' " 498 F.2d, at 422–423 (quoting 5 J. Moore, Federal Practice ¶ 38.–31[1], p. 232–233 (2d ed. 1971)). The Court of Appeals in this case also found unpersuasive the dictum in Hepner v. United States, 213 U.S. 103, 115, 29 S.Ct. 474, 479, 53 L.Ed. 720 (1909), and in United States v. Regan, 232 U.S. 37, 46–47, 34 S.Ct. 213, 216–217, 58 L.Ed. 494 (1914), that the Seventh Amendment's guarantee applies to civil actions to collect a civil penalty. The court concluded that, while in *Hepner* and *Regan* the civil penalties were statutorily prescribed fixed amounts, the District Court in the present case exercised "statutorily conferred equitable power in determining the amount of the fine." 769 F.2d, at 187. The Court of Appeals also noted that the District Court fashioned a " 'package' of remedies" containing both equitable and legal relief with "one part of the package affecting assessment of the others." Ibid.

In Atlas Roofing Co. v. Occupational Safety and Health Review Comm'n, 430 U.S. 442, 449, n. 6, 97 S.Ct. 1261, 1266, n. 6, 51 L.Ed.2d 464 (1977), we explicitly declined to decide whether the dictum of *Hepner* and *Regan* "correctly divines the intent of the Seventh Amendment." To resolve this question and the conflict between circuits, we granted certiorari. 476 U.S. 1139, 106 S.Ct. 2244, 90 L.Ed.2d 691 (1986). We reverse.

II

The Seventh Amendment provides that, "[i]n Suits at common law, where the value in controversy shall exceed twenty dollars, the right of trial by jury shall be preserved. . . ."[3] The Court has construed this language to require a jury trial on the merits in those actions that are analogous to "Suits at common law." Prior to the Amendment's adoption, a jury trial was customary in suits brought in the English *law* courts. In contrast, those actions that are analogous to 18th–century cases tried in courts of equity or admiralty do not require a jury trial. See Parsons v. Bedford, 3 Pet. 433 (1830). This analysis applies not

---

3. Before initiating the inquiry into the applicability of the Seventh Amendment, "[w]e recognize, of course, the 'cardinal principle that this Court will first ascertain whether a construction of the statute is fairly possible by which the [constitutional] question may be avoided.' " Curtis v. Loether, 415 U.S. 189, 192 n. 6, 94 S.Ct. 1005, 1007, n. 6, 39 L.Ed.2d 260 (1974) (citation omitted); see also Pernell v. Southall Realty, 416 U.S. 363, 365, 94 S.Ct. 1723, 1724, 40 L.Ed.2d 198 (1974). Nothing in the language of the Clean Water Act or its legislative history implies any congressional intent to grant defendants the right of a jury trial during the liability or penalty phase of the civil suit proceedings. Given this statutory silence, we must answer the constitutional question presented.

only to common law forms of action, but also to causes of action created by congressional enactment. See Curtis v. Loether, 415 U.S. 189, 193, 94 S.Ct. 1005, 1007, 39 L.Ed.2d 260 (1974).

To determine whether a statutory action is more similar to cases that were tried in courts of law than to suits tried in courts of equity or admiralty, the Court must examine both the nature of the action and of the remedy sought. First, we compare the statutory action to 18th-century actions brought in the courts of England prior to the merger of the courts of law and equity. See, e.g., Pernell v. Southall Realty, 416 U.S. 363, 378, 94 S.Ct. 1723, 1731, 40 L.Ed.2d 198 (1974); Dairy Queen, Inc., v. Wood, 369 U.S. 469, 477, 82 S.Ct. 894, 899, 8 L.Ed.2d 44 (1962). Second, we examine the remedy sought and determine whether it is legal or equitable in nature. See, e.g., Curtis v. Loether, supra, at 196, 94 S.Ct., at 1009; Ross v. Bernhard, 396 U.S. 531, 542, 90 S.Ct. 733, 740, 24 L.Ed.2d 729 (1970).[4]

A

Petitioner analogizes this Government suit under § 1319(d) to an action in debt within the jurisdiction of English courts of law. Prior to the enactment of the Seventh Amendment, English courts had held that a civil penalty suit was a particular species of an action in debt that was within the jurisdiction of the courts of law. See, e.g., Atcheson v. Everitt, 1 Cowper 382, 98 Eng.Rep. 1142 (K.B.1776) (characterizing civil penalty suit as a type of action in debt); Calcraft v. Gibbs, 5 T.R. 19, 101 Eng.Rep. 11 (K.B.1792) (granting new jury trial in an action in debt for a civil penalty).

After the adoption of the Seventh Amendment, federal courts followed this English common law in treating the civil penalty suit as a particular type of an action in debt, requiring a jury trial. See, e.g., United States v. Mundell, 27 F.Cas. 23 (No. 15,834) (CC Va.1795) (bail not required in a civil penalty case tried by a jury because it was an action in debt); Jacob v. United States, 13 F.Cas. 267 (No. 7,157) (CC Va.1821) (action in debt by United States to recover civil penalty of $500 and costs of violation of an Act of Congress); Lees v. United States, 150 U.S. 476, 479, 14 S.Ct. 163, 164, 37 L.Ed. 1150 (1893) ("[A]lthough the recovery of a penalty is a proceeding criminal in nature, yet in this class of cases it may be enforced in a civil action, and in the same manner that debts are recovered in the ordinary civil courts"). Actions by the Government to recover civil penalties under statutory provisions therefore historically have been viewed as one type of action in debt requiring trial by jury.

---

4. The Court has also considered the practical limitations of a jury trial and its functional compatibility with proceedings outside of traditional courts of law in holding that the Seventh Amendment is not applicable to administrative proceedings. See, e.g., Atlas Roofing Co. v. Occupational Safety and Health Review Comm'n, 430 U.S. 442, 454, 97 S.Ct. 1261, 1268, 51 L.Ed. 2d 464 (1977); Pernell v. Southall Realty, supra, at 383, 94 S.Ct., at 1733. But the Court has not used these considerations as an independent basis for extending the right to a jury trial under the Seventh Amendment.

It was against this historical background that the Court in Hepner v. United States, 213 U.S. 103, 29 S.Ct. 474, 53 L.Ed. 720 (1909), considered the propriety of a directed verdict by a District Court Judge in favor of the Government where there was undisputed evidence that a defendant had committed an offense under § 8 of the Alien Immigration Act of 1903, which provided for a $1,000 civil penalty. The Court held that a directed verdict was permissible and did not violate the defendant's right to a jury trial under the Seventh Amendment. The Court said:

> "The objection made in behalf of the defendant, that an affirmative answer to the question certified could be used so as to destroy the constitutional right of trial by jury, is without merit and need not be discussed. *The defendant was, of course, entitled to have a jury summoned in this case,* but that right was subject to the condition, fundamental in the conduct of civil actions, that the court may withdraw a case from the jury and direct a verdict, according to the law if the evidence is uncontradicted and raises only a question of law." 213 U.S., at 115, 29 S.Ct., at 479 (emphasis added).

In United States v. Regan, 232 U.S. 37, 34 S.Ct. 213, 58 L.Ed. 494 (1914), the Court assumed that a jury trial was required in civil penalty actions. In that case, the Court upheld the validity of a jury instruction in an action brought by the Government under the Alien Immigration Act of 1907. The Court stated that the instruction requiring proof beyond a reasonable doubt was incorrect because:

> "While the defendant was entitled to have the issues tried before a jury, this right did not arise from Article III of the Constitution or from the Sixth Amendment, for both relate to prosecutions which are strictly criminal in their nature, but it derives out of the fact that in a civil action of debt involving more than twenty dollars a jury trial is demandable." 232 U.S., at 47, 34 S.Ct., at 216 (citation omitted).

In the instant case, the Government sought penalties of over $22 million for violation of the Clean Water Act and obtained a judgment in the sum of $325,000. This action is clearly analogous to the 18th-century action in debt, and federal courts have rightly assumed that the Seventh Amendment required a jury trial.

The Government argues, however, that—rather than an action in debt—the closer historical analogue is an action to abate a public nuisance. In 18th-century English law, a public nuisance was "an act or omission 'which obstructs or causes inconvenience or damage to the public in the exercise of rights common to all Her Majesty's subjects.'" W. Prosser, Law of Torts 583 (4th ed.1971) (hereinafter Prosser) (footnote omitted). The Government argues that the present suit is analogous to two species of public nuisances. One is the suit of the sovereign in the English courts of equity for a "purpresture" to enjoin or order the repair of an enclosure or obstruction of public waterways; the other is the suit of the sovereign to enjoin "offensive trades and manufactures" that polluted the environment. 4 W. Blackstone, Commentaries *167.

It is true that the subject matter of this Clean Water Act suit—the placement of fill into navigable waters—resembles these two species of public nuisance. Whether, as the Government argues, a public nuisance action is a better analogy than an action in debt is debatable. But we need not decide the question. As Pernell v. Southall Realty, 416 U.S., at 375, 94 S.Ct., at 1729, cautioned, the fact that the subject matter of a modern statutory action and an 18th-century English action are close equivalents "is irrelevant for Seventh Amendment purposes," because "that Amendment requires trial by jury in actions unheard of at common law." It suffices that we conclude that both the public nuisance action and the action in debt are appropriate analogies to the instant statutory action.

The essential function of an action to abate a public nuisance was to provide a civil means to redress "a miscellaneous and diversified group of minor criminal offenses, based on some interference with the interests of the community, or the comfort or convenience of the general public." Prosser 583. Similarly, the essential function of an action in debt was to recover money owed under a variety of statutes or under the common law. Both of these 18th-century actions, then, could be asserted by the sovereign to seek relief for an injury to the public in numerous contexts.

We need not rest our conclusion on what has been called an "abstruse historical" search for the nearest 18th-century analogue. See Ross v. Bernhard, 390 U.S., at 538, n. 10, 90 S.Ct., at 738, n. 10. We reiterate our previously expressed view that characterizing the relief sought is "[m]ore important" than finding a precisely analogous common law cause of action in determining whether the Seventh Amendment guarantees a jury trial. Curtis v. Loether, 415 U.S., at 196, 94 S.Ct., at 1009.[6]

B

A civil penalty was a type of remedy at common law that could only be enforced in courts of law. Remedies intended to punish culpable individuals, as opposed to those intended simply to extract compensation or restore the status quo, were issued by courts of law, not courts of equity. See, e.g., Curtis v. Loether, supra, at 197, 94 S.Ct. at 1009 (punitive damages remedy is legal, not equitable, relief); Ross v.

---

6. The Government contends that both the cause of action and the remedy must be legal in nature before the Seventh Amendment right to a jury trial attaches. It divides the Clean Water Act action for civil penalties into a cause of action and a remedy, and analyzes each component as if the other were irrelevant. Thus, the Government proposes that a public nuisance action is the better historical analogue for the cause of action, and that an action for disgorgement is the proper analogy for the remedy. We reject this novel approach. Our search is for a single historical analogue, taking into consideration the nature of the cause of action and the remedy as two important factors. See Pernell v. Southall Realty, 416 U.S., at 375, 94 S.Ct., at 1729; Curtis v. Loether, 415 U.S., at 195–196, 94 S.Ct., at 1008–1009.

Bernhard, supra, at 536, 90 S.Ct., at 737 (treble-damages remedy for securities violation is a penalty, which constitutes legal relief).[7] The action authorized by § 1319(d) is of this character. Subsection (d) does not direct that the "civil penalty" imposed be calculated solely on the basis of equitable determinations, such as the profits gained from violations of the statute, but simply imposes a maximum penalty of $10,000 per day of violation. The legislative history of the Act reveals that Congress wanted the district court to consider the need for retribution and deterrence, in addition to restitution, when it imposed civil penalties. 123 Cong.Rec. 39191 (1977) (remark of Sen. Muskie citing EPA memorandum outlining enforcement policy). A court can require retribution for wrongful conduct based on the seriousness of the violations, the number of prior violations, and the lack of good-faith efforts to comply with the relevant requirements. Ibid. It may also seek to deter future violations by basing the penalty on its economic impact. Ibid. Subsection 1319(d)'s authorization of punishment to further retribution and deterrence clearly evidences that this subsection reflects more than a concern to provide equitable relief. In the present case, for instance, the District Court acknowledged that petitioner received no profits from filling in properties in Mire Pond and Eel Creek, but still imposed a $35,000 fine. App. to Pet. for Cert. 60a. Thus, the District Court intended not simply to disgorge profits but also to impose punishment. Because the nature of the relief authorized by § 1319(d) was traditionally available only in a court of law, the petitioner in this present action is entitled to a jury trial on demand.

The punitive nature of the relief sought in this present case is made apparent by a comparison with the relief sought in an action to abate a public nuisance. A public nuisance action was a classic example of the kind of suit that relied on the injunctive relief provided by courts in equity. Prosser 603. "Injunctive relief [for enjoining a public nuisance at the request of the Government] is traditionally given by equity upon a showing of [peril to health and safety]." Steelworkers v. United States, 361 U.S. 39, 61, 80 S.Ct. 1, 186, 4 L.Ed.2d 12 (1959) (Frankfurter, J., concurring). The Government, in fact, concedes that public nuisance cases brought in equity sought injunctive relief, not monetary penalties. Brief for United States 24, n. 17. Indeed, courts in equity refused to enforce such penalties. See James, Right to a Jury Trial in Civil Actions, 72 Yale L.J. 655, 672 (1963).

The Government contends, however, that a suit enforcing civil penalties under the Clean Water Act is similar to an action for

---

7. The Government distinguishes this suit from other actions to collect a statutory penalty on the basis that the statutory penalty here is not fixed or readily calculable from a fixed formula. We do not find this distinction to be significant. The more important characteristic of the remedy of civil penalties is that it exacts punishment—a kind of remedy available only in courts of law. Thus, the remedy of civil penalties is similar to the remedy of punitive damages, another legal remedy that is not a fixed fine. See, e.g., Curtis v. Loether, supra, at 189–190, 94 S.Ct., at 1005–1006 (defendant entitled to jury trial in an action based on a statute authorizing actual damages and punitive damages of not more than $1000).

disgorgement of improper profits, traditionally considered an equitable remedy. It bases this characterization upon evidence that the District Court determined the amount of the penalties by multiplying the number of lots sold by petitioner by the profit earned per lot. Tr. of Oral Arg. 27. An action for disgorgement of improper profits is, however, a poor analogy. Such an action is a remedy only for restitution—a more limited form of penalty than a civil fine. Restitution is limited to "restoring the status quo and ordering the return of that which rightfully belongs to the purchaser or tenant." Porter v. Warner Holding Co., 328 U.S. 395, 402, 66 S.Ct. 1086, 1091, 90 L.Ed. 1332 (1946). As the above discussion indicates, however, § 1319(d)'s concerns are by no means limited to restoration of the status quo.

The Government next contends that, even if the civil penalties under § 1319(d) are deemed legal in character, a jury trial is not required. A court in equity was empowered to provide monetary awards that were incidental to or intertwined with injunctive relief. The Government therefore argues that its claim under § 1319(b), which authorizes injunctive relief, provides jurisdiction for monetary relief in equity. Brief for United States 38. This argument has at least three flaws. First, while a court in equity may award monetary restitution as an adjunct to injunctive relief, it may not enforce civil penalties. See Porter v. Warner Holding Co., supra, at 399, 66 S.Ct., at 1089. Second, the Government was aware when it filed suit that relief would be limited primarily to civil penalties, since petitioner had already sold most of the properties at issue. App. 110, 119. A potential penalty of $22 million hardly can be considered incidental to the modest equitable relief sought in this case.

Finally, the Government was free to seek an equitable remedy in addition to, or independent of, legal relief. Section 1319 does not intertwine equitable relief with the imposition of civil penalties. Instead each kind of relief is separably authorized in a separate and distinct statutory provision. Subsection (b), providing injunctive relief, is independent of subsection (d), which provides only for civil penalties. In such a situation, if a "legal claim is joined with an equitable claim, the right to jury trial on the legal claim, including all issues common to both claims, remains intact. The right cannot be abridged by characterizing the legal claim as 'incidental' to the equitable relief sought." Curtis v. Loether, 415 U.S., at 196, n. 11, 94 S.Ct., at 1009, n. 11. Thus, the petitioner has a constitutional right to a jury trial to determine his liability on the legal claims.

III

The remaining issue is whether the petitioner additionally has a Seventh Amendment right to a jury assessment of the civil penalties. At the time this case was tried, § 1319(d) did not explicitly state whether juries or trial judges were to fix the civil penalties. The legislative history of the 1977 Amendments to the Clean Water Act shows, however, that Congress intended that trial judges perform the highly discretionary calculations necessary to award civil penalties after liability is found. 123 Cong.Rec. 39190–39191 (1977) (remarks of Sen. Muskie citing letter from EPA Assistant Administrators of Enforcement of Dec. 14, 1977) ("[P]enalties assessed by judges should be sufficiently higher than penalties to which the Agency would have agreed in settlement to encourage violators to settle"). We must decide therefore whether Congress can, consistent with the Seventh Amendment, authorize judges to assess civil penalties.

The Seventh Amendment is silent on the question whether a jury must determine the remedy in a trial in which it must determine liability.[9] The answer must depend on whether the jury must shoulder this responsibility as necessary to preserve the "substance of the common-law right of trial by jury." Colgrove v. Battin, 413 U.S. 149, 157, 93 S.Ct. 2448, 2452, 37 L.Ed.2d 522 (1973). Is a jury role necessary for that purpose? We do not think so. " 'Only those incidents which are regarded as fundamental, as inherent in and of the essence of the system of trial by jury, are placed beyond the reach of the legislature.' " Id., at 156, n. 11, 93 S.Ct., at 2452, n. 11 (quoting Scott, Trial by Jury and the Reform of Civil Procedure, 31 Harv.L.Rev. 669, 671 (1918)). See also Galloway v. United States, 319 U.S. 372, 392, 63 S.Ct. 1077, 1088, 87 L.Ed. 1458 (1943) ("[T]he Amendment was designed to preserve the basic institution of jury trial in only its most fundamental elements"). The assessment of a civil penalty is not one of the "most fundamental elements." Congress' authority to fix the penalty by statute has not been questioned, and it was also the British practice, see, e.g., Atcheson v. Everitt, 1 Cowper 382, 98 Eng.Rep. 1142 (K.B. 1776). In the United States, the action to recover civil penalties usually seeks the amount fixed by the Congress. See, e.g., United States v. Regan, 232 U.S., at 40, 34 S.Ct., at 213; Hepner v. United States, 213 U.S., at 109, 29 S.Ct., at 477. The assessment of civil penalties thus cannot be said to involve the "substance of a common-law right to a trial by jury," nor a "fundamental element of a jury trial."

Congress' assignment of the determination of the amount of civil penalties to trial judges therefore does not infringe on the constitutional right to a jury trial. Since Congress itself may fix the civil penalties, it may delegate that determination to trial judges. In this case, highly discretionary calculations that take into account multiple factors are necessary in order to set civil penalties under the Clean Water Act.

---

9. Nothing in the Amendment's language suggests that the right to a jury trial extends to the remedy phase of a civil trial. Instead, the language "defines the kind of cases for which jury trial is preserved, namely 'suits at common law.' " Colgrove v. Battin, 413 U.S. 149, 152, 93 S.Ct. 2448, 2450, 37 L.Ed.2d 522 (1973). Although " '[w]e have almost no direct evidence concerning the intention of the framers of the seventh amendment itself,' the historical setting in which the Seventh Amendment was adopted highlighted a controversy that was generated . . . by fear that the civil jury itself would be abolished." Ibid. (footnote and citation omitted). We have been presented with no evidence that the Framers meant to extend the right to a jury to the remedy phase of a civil trial.

These are the kinds of calculations traditionally performed by judges. See Albemarle Paper Co. v. Moody, 422 U.S. 405, 442–443, 95 S.Ct. 2362, 2384–2385, 45 L.Ed.2d 280 (1975) (Rehnquist, J., concurring). We therefore hold that a determination of a civil penalty is not an essential function of a jury trial, and that the Seventh Amendment does not require a jury trial for that purpose in a civil action.

IV

We conclude that the Seventh Amendment required that petitioner's demand for a jury trial be granted to determine his liability, but that the trial court and not the jury should determine the amount of penalty, if any. The judgment of the Court of Appeals is therefore reversed, and the case is remanded for further proceedings consistent with this opinion.

It is so ordered.

JUSTICE SCALIA, with whom JUSTICE STEVENS joins, concurring in part and dissenting in part.

I join the Court's disposition, and Parts I and II of its opinion. I do not join Part III because in my view the right to trial by jury on whether a civil penalty of unspecified amount is assessable also involves a right to trial by jury on what the amount should be. The fact that the Legislature could elect to fix the amount of penalty has nothing to do with whether, if it chooses not to do so, that element comes within the jury-trial guarantee. Congress could, I suppose, create a private cause of action by one individual against another for a fixed amount of damages, but it surely does not follow that if it creates such a cause of action *without* prescribing the amount of damages, that issue could be taken from the jury.

While purporting to base its determination (quite correctly) upon historical practice, the Court creates a form of civil adjudication I have never encountered. I can recall no precedent for judgment of civil liability by jury but assessment of amount by the court. Even punitive damages are assessed by the jury when liability is determined in that fashion. One is of course tempted to make an exception in a case like this, where the Government is imposing a non-compensatory remedy to enforce direct exercise of its regulatory authority, because there comes immediately to mind the role of the sentencing judge in a criminal proceeding. If criminal trials are to be the model, however, determination of liability by the jury should be on a standard of proof requiring guilt beyond a reasonable doubt. Having chosen to proceed in civil fashion, with the advantages which that mode entails, it seems to me the Government must take the bitter with the sweet. Since, as the Court correctly reasons, the proper analogue to a civil-fine action is the common-law action for debt, the government need only prove liability by a preponderance of the evidence; but must, as in any action for debt, accept the amount of award determined not by its own officials but by 12 private citizens. If that tends to discourage the Government from proceeding in this fashion, I doubt that the Founding Fathers would be upset.

I would reverse and remand for jury determination of both issues.

IN RE JAPANESE ELECTRONIC PRODUCTS ANTITRUST LITIGATION

United States Court of Appeals for the Third Circuit, 1980.
631 F.2d 1069.*

SEITZ, CHIEF JUDGE.

This certified interlocutory appeal from a pretrial order of the district court raises an issue that currently is the subject of much debate: In an action for treble damages under the antitrust and antidumping laws, do the parties have a right to trial by jury without regard to the practical ability of a jury to decide the case properly?

I.

This litigation began in the District of New Jersey with the complaint of National Union Electric Corp. (NUE). A corporate successor to the Emerson Radio Co., NUE was a major domestic producer of television receivers until February 1970. The following December, it filed the first complaint of this litigation, charging several of its Japanese competitors with violations of the antitrust laws and the laws governing competition in international trade. * * *

* * *

Zenith Radio Corp., a major domestic producer of consumer electronic products, filed the second complaint of this litigation in 1974 in the Eastern District of Pennsylvania. The Zenith complaint named all of the defendants of the NUE action, a few additional subsidiaries, and two American companies: Motorola, Inc., and Sears, Roebuck, and Co. Two of the common defendants, Sony Corp. and its American sales subsidiary, Sony Corp. of America, subsequently reached a complete settlement with Zenith. They are now defendants only in the NUE action.

The Zenith complaint repeats NUE's allegations of dumping, conspiracy, and intent to destroy domestic competition in the American market, but Zenith's allegations are broader in two respects. First, Zenith seeks damages for injuries sustained over a longer period, from 1968 through 1977, as opposed to a period of 1966 through 1970 in NUE's complaint. Second, Zenith's allegations cover not only televisions but also radios, phonographs, tape and audio equipment, and electronic components. In addition, Zenith charges defendants with discriminating in price among American purchasers, in violation of the Robinson–Patman Act, 15 U.S.C. § 13(a) (1976). Finally, Zenith asserts that the Matsushita and Sanyo defendants have violated § 7 of the

* Some of the court's footnotes are omitted.

Clayton Act, 15 U.S.C. § 18 (1976), by acquiring interests in domestic producers of consumer electronic products previously held by Motorola and Sears. Like NUE, Zenith prays for treble damages and injunctive relief.

A group of the Japanese defendants in the Zenith action filed two counterclaims. The first charges Zenith and its distributors throughout the United States with territorial allocations, horizontal and vertical price-fixing schemes, "key dealer preferences," and price discrimination, in violation of §§ 1 and 2 of the Sherman Act and the Robinson-Patman Act, 15 U.S.C. §§ 1, 2, 13(a) (1976). The second counterclaim charges Zenith and about 30 coconspirators with maintaining a program of sham litigation against Zenith's competitors. See Otter Tail Power Co. v. United States, 410 U.S. 366, 379–80, 93 S.Ct. 1022, 35 L.Ed. 2d 359 (1973).

Sears filed a separate counterclaim challenging Zenith's advertising claims that Zenith color televisions are manufactured in the United States. Sears claims that the advertisements create an impression that all components of Zenith's color televisions and other consumer electronic products are of American origin, when some components are manufactured abroad. Sears asserts a violation of § 43 of the Lanham Act, 15 U.S.C. § 1125 (1976), which prohibits false designations of origin, and prays for damages and injunctive relief.

Shortly after the filing of the Zenith action, the two suits were consolidated for pretrial proceedings in the Eastern District of Pennsylvania. *   *   *

Both NUE and Zenith made timely demands for jury trial. Fourteen of the defendants moved to strike the demands, arguing that the case is too large and complex for a jury. *   *   *

II.

Appellants argue that the proof of the foregoing claims will be too burdensome and complicated for a jury. They have cited several dimensions of complexity.

The district court accepted one of the appellants' basic contentions: the trial will be protracted. The court predicted that the trial would last a full year. It noted that the parties are nearing the end of discovery, which after nine years has produced millions of documents and over 100,000 pages of depositions. The court did not estimate how much of this evidence will be introduced at trial.

Beyond these observations of the district court, we have only the parties' divergent predictions of the proof that appellees' claims call for. We understand their primary disagreements to concern four general sources of complexity: proof of the Antidumping Act claims, proof of the alleged conspiracy, resolution of a number of financial issues, and understanding of several conceptually difficult legal and factual issues.

Under the Antidumping Act, appellees must prove that the defendants made sales of articles in the United States at a price lower than the price of "such articles" in Japan. 15 U.S.C. § 72 (1976). Appellants read the Act to permit price comparisons only for identical products sold in the two countries. During the relevant periods, defendants produced thousands of technically distinct models of the products covered by this litigation. They contend that to identify the products appropriate for price comparisons, the jury will have to review the technical features of thousands of different models and understand how differences between the models relate to cost of manufacture, product performance, and marketability. Appellees construe the Antidumping Act to permit price comparisons between functionally equivalent products, such as all portable color televisions with particular screen size and VHF–UHF channel selection. They contend that a jury could identify such functionally equivalent products without massive or highly technical proof.

The conspiracy charged in this suit is massive. Appellees allege that it has lasted for at least 30 years, involved almost 100 firms around the world, and affected international trade in several consumer electronic products.   *   *   *

Some parts of the case will require the jury to resolve a series of financial issues. Appellants have highlighted three such parts. First, for the Antidumping Act claims, the jury will have to decide whether the price of an article sold in the United States is "substantially less than the actual market value or wholesale price" in Japan and whether a defendant has maintained differential pricing "commonly and systematically." 15 U.S.C. § 72 (1976). This inquiry may be complicated by several influences on prices that might have to be factored out before comparing prices, such as currency fluctuations and different marketing techniques in the two countries. Second, appellees allege that the conspirators disguised their artificially low prices in the United States by a series of complicated rebate schemes. Appellants say that the jury will be able to test this allegation only by reviewing the circumstances surrounding thousands of separate transactions. Third, appellees intend to show injury by proving that they lowered their own prices in response to defendants' artificially low prices and that they lost sales to defendants. These allegations will require evidence of appellees' transactions and may raise issues regarding appellees' pricing policies and marketing techniques and the quality of appellees' products.

Appellants contend that litigation of these three parts of the case will produce an enormous mass of financial documentation for the jury to work through. They also contend that the jury will need the assistance of substantial amounts of expert testimony on accounting, marketing, and other technical matters. Appellees reject this prediction, arguing that all the relevant financial evidence can be submitted neatly in computer printouts with accompanying summaries. They do not foresee great problems in the jury's understanding of the evidence.
   *   *   *

III.

Appellees offer a statutory ground for affirming the district court. They assert that the Clayton Act grants a right to jury trial even if the extraordinary complexity of the suit renders the seventh amendment guarantee inapplicable.   *   *   *

*   *   *

In short, the legislative history indicates nothing more than the expectation of several congressmen that the seventh amendment generally would guarantee a right to jury trial in treble damage actions under the antitrust laws. We are unable to translate their expectations of the ordinary application of the seventh amendment into an intention to require jury trial by statute.

*   *   *

IV.

The seventh amendment provides in relevant part: "In Suits at common law . . . the right of trial by jury shall be preserved." The Supreme Court's basic tool of construction in interpreting the amendment has been history: "The right of trial by jury thus preserved is the right which existed under the English common law when the Amendment was adopted." Baltimore & Carolina Line, Inc. v. Redman, 295 U.S. 654, 657, 55 S.Ct. 890, 891, 79 L.Ed. 1636 (1935).[9]   At times, the Court has determined that some aspects of the seventh amendment right, such as the validity of certain jury control techniques, should reflect the specific historical dimensions of the common law of 1791, the year of the amendment's adoption. See, e.g., Dimick v. Schiedt, 293 U.S. 474, 55 S.Ct. 296, 79 L.Ed. 603 (1935) (the seventh amendment does not permit a court to increase amount of a jury verdict).

However, the Court has never relied on this static view of history to confine the seventh amendment guarantee to causes of action recognized by the common law of 1791. Beginning with an 1830 decision, Parsons v. Bedford, 28 U.S. (3 Pet.) 433, 446–47, 7 L.Ed. 732 (1830), the Court has held the guarantee applicable to almost any suit, including a suit based on a statutorily created cause of action, that falls within the federal courts' jurisdiction over suits at law as opposed to suits in equity or admiralty. See Curtis v. Loether, 415 U.S. 189, 193–94, 94 S.Ct. 1005, 1007–08, 39 L.Ed.2d 260 (1974).

Usually, courts have categorized suits among law, equity, and admiralty on the basis of the presence of a subject matter or a remedy peculiarly associated with one of the three jurisdictional categories. Thus, a suit to establish title to real property is normally considered legal because of the special competence that courts of law have exercised in these matters. See Whitehead v. Shattuck, 138 U.S. 146, 11

---

9. In some cases, the Court has referred to the common law of American states as well as of England. Continental Ill. Nat'l Bank v. Chicago, R. I. & P. Ry., 294 U.S. 648, 669, 55 S.Ct. 595, 603, 79 L.Ed. 1110 (1935).

S.Ct. 276, 34 L.Ed. 873 (1891). Where such common indicia of law, equity, or admiralty have not been present, courts have classified a suit by comparing it with the particular actions that the courts of common law, chancery, or admiralty historically recognized as within their respective jurisdictions. See Pernell v. Southall Realty, 416 U.S. 363, 94 S.Ct. 1723, 40 L.Ed.2d 198 (1974); Damsky v. Zavatt, 289 F.2d 46 (2d Cir. 1961).

Suits for treble damages under the antitrust and antidumping laws, as a class, are plainly legal in nature. They seek relief in a form traditionally associated with courts of law: compensatory and punitive damages for injuries caused by legal wrongs. See Curtis v. Loether, 415 U.S. 189, 195–96, 94 S.Ct. 1005, 1008–09, 39 L.Ed.2d 260 (1974). Indeed, prior cases have always assumed that the seventh amendment guarantees a jury trial in antitrust suits. See Beacon Theatres, Inc. v. Westover, 359 U.S. 500, 504, 79 S.Ct. 948, 953, 3 L.Ed.2d 988 (1959); Columbia Metal Culvert Co. v. Kaiser Aluminum & Chemical Corp., 579 F.2d 20, 23 (3d Cir.), cert. denied, 439 U.S. 876, 99 S.Ct. 214, 58 L.Ed.2d 190 (1978).

Appellants dispute none of the foregoing and concede that a right to jury trial normally exists in suits for treble damages under the antitrust and antidumping laws. They argue that the seventh amendment does not guarantee a right to jury trial when any particular lawsuit, because of its extraordinary complexity, is beyond the ability of a jury to decide.

* * *

V.

Appellants' first argument relies on historical analysis to advance the proposition that the fact of extraordinary complexity renders a suit equitable in nature. Although complexity is not commonly recognized as a defining feature of equity, appellants argue that by the time of the adoption of the seventh amendment the chancellor's jurisdiction had extended to any suit that he found too complex for a jury. They have submitted a large body of historical authorities to support this proposition. The brief of International Business Machines Corporation, amicus curiae in this case, provides some additional historical authorities to support several of appellants' arguments.

A.

Most of these authorities are suits seeking relief in the form of an accounting between the parties.[11] The chancellor's jurisdiction over

11. Kirby v. Lake Shore & M. S. R. R., 120 U.S. 130, 7 S.Ct. 430, 30 L.Ed. 569 (1887); Fowle v. Lawrason's Executor, 30 U.S. (5 Pet.) 494, 8 L.Ed. 204 (1831); Farmer's & Mechanic's Bank v. Polk, 1 Del.Ch. 167, 175–76 (1821); Cranford Twp. v. Watters, 48 A. 316 (N.J.Ch.1901); Ludlow v. Simond, 2 Cai.Cas. 1, 2 N.Y. Common Law Rep. 747 (1805); Duke of Bridgewater v. Edwards, 6 Bro.P.C. 368, 2 Eng.Rep. 1139 (H.L.1733); Duke of Marlborough v. Strong, 1 Bros.P.C. 175, 1 Eng.Rep. 496 (H.L.1721); South Eastern Ry. v. Brogden, 3 Mac. & G. 8, 42 Eng.Rep. 163 (Ch.1850);

accounting actions consisted of two general categories. First, he had exclusive jurisdiction over any suit in which the substantive rules of equity imposed a duty to render an account. Second, he had jurisdiction when the accounts between the parties were too numerous and complicated for a common-law jury to unravel. Part of the rationale for equitable relief in this latter group of cases was that the difficulty of the jury's task made relief at law inadequate. See generally H. McClintock, Handbook of the Principles of Equity §§ 200–202 (1948). Appellants analogize complex antitrust and antidumping suits to actions for equitable accountings in this second group.

This analogy rests upon an incomplete statement of the chancellor's jurisdiction over complex accountings. Not every form of monetary liability at law could be characterized as a set of accounts for purposes of this jurisdiction. The chancellor typically ordered an accounting for money owing between persons with a particular legal relationship, like partnership or agency. In some cases, the chancellor ordered an accounting where no such relationship existed but money was owed as a result of contractual liability or fraud. See generally 2 J. Story, Commentaries on Equity Jurisprudence §§ 598–697 (14th ed. 1948); Langdell, A Brief Survey of Equity Jurisdiction IV, 2 Harv.L. Rev. 241 (1889). We are aware of no case, however, in which a chancellor ordered an accounting in a suit involving nothing more than liability for money damages in trespass or tort. Several American courts have held that an equitable accounting is not available in these circumstances. See United States v. Bitter Root Development Co., 200 U.S. 451, 470–71, 478–79, 26 S.Ct. 318, 324–327, 50 L.Ed. 550 (1906); Conklin v. Bush, 8 Pa.St. 514, 516–17 (1848); see Annot., Accounting in Equity in Case of Tort, 53 A.L.R. 815 (1928).

Suits for treble damages under the antitrust and antidumping laws are similar in form to suits for damages in tort. See Northwestern Oil Co. v. Socony-Vacuum Oil Co., 138 F.2d 967, 970 (7th Cir. 1943), cert. denied, 321 U.S. 792, 64 S.Ct. 790, 88 L.Ed. 1081 (1944). They impose liability for money damages without requiring any legal or contractual relationship between the parties or a showing of fraud. Hence, the present lawsuit is most similar to actions in which an equitable accounting was unavailable. Appellants' analogy, therefore, fails.

B.

Appellants also cite a variety of cases that do not involve accountings. They claim that in each of these cases the chancellor took jurisdiction because extraordinary complexity made the suit too complex for a common-law jury.

Many of the appellants' cases arose under England's merged system of law and equity created by the Supreme Court of Judicature Acts,

Frowd v. Lawrence, 1 Jac. & W. 655, 37 Eng.Rep. 518 (Ch.1820); M'Intosh v. Great Western Ry., 3 Sm. & Giff. 146, 68 Eng. Rep. 600 (V.C.1855); O'Connor v. Spaight, 1 Sch. & Lef. 305 (Ire.Ch.1804).

36 & 37 Vict., ch. 66 (1873), 38 & 39 Vict., ch. 77 (1875). The procedural rules adopted in conjunction with the 1875 Act made jury trials generally available upon timely notice by either party. Order XXXVI, Rules 2, 3. This right was subject to the exception that a court without a jury could try an issue "arising in any cause or matter which previously to the passing of the Act could, without any consent of the parties, be tried without a jury." Id. Rule 26.

Appellants look for support in cases applying this exception. They first cite a passage from Clarke v. Cookson, 2 Ch.D. 746, 747–48 (V.C. 1876), which they say is a restatement of premerger equity:

> This rule was framed expressly to meet cases which would under the old system have been tried in the Chancery Division, and which might be considered, by reason of involving a mixture of law and fact, or from great complexity, or otherwise, not capable of being conveniently tried before a jury.

See also Bordier v. Burrell, 5 Ch.D. 512, 514 (M.R.1877). This passage gives no support to appellants' argument. It identifies two separate prerequisites to a denial of a jury trial demand: trial of the matter in the court of chancery prior to the merger and complexity or other grounds for believing that a jury would be unsuitable. Its use of the conjunction "and" implies the opposite of appellants' argument: complexity alone was not grounds for relief in equity.

Appellants cite two postmerger cases that rely on the passage quoted from Clarke v. Cookson. Wedderburn v. Pickering, 13 Ch.D. 769 (M.R.1879); Garling v. Royds, 25 W.R. 123 (V.C.1876). These cases confirm our reading of the passage. In each, a clear ground for equitable jurisdiction other than complexity was present. In Wedderburn v. Pickering, supra, the plaintiffs prayed for an injunction. The relief sought in Garling v. Royds, supra, was cancellation of a note allegedly obtained by fraud and misrepresentation.

IBM's brief cites premerger cases involving a limitation on the use of advisory juries in chancery. The chancellor had the discretion to submit to common-law jury issues of fact arising in an equity case. However, the use of advisory juries remained subject to his discretion, and he declined to direct an issue when he considered it too difficult for a jury. Gartside v. Isherwood, 1 Bro.C.C. 558, 28 Eng.Rep. 1297 (Ch. 1783); Gyles v. Wilcox, 2 Atk. 141, 26 Eng.Rep. 489 (Ch.1740). The advisory jury cases are irrelevant to our inquiry. The Chancellor's authority to direct an issue to a jury derived from his control over the method of finding facts in suits already within his jurisdiction. See generally Langbein, Fact Finding in the English Court of Chancery: A Rebuttal, 83 Yale L.J. 1620 (1974). These cases say nothing about the chancellor's authority to provide for nonjury trials in suits at common law.

* * *

VI.

Both appellants and IBM offer a second constitutional argument. They contend that the due process clause of the fifth amendment prohibits trial by jury of a suit that is too complex for a jury. They further contend that this due process limitation prevails over the seventh amendment's preservation of the right to jury trial.

Although no specific precedent exists for finding a due process violation in the trial of any case to a jury, the principles that define the procedural requirements of due process would seem to impose some limitations on the range of cases that may be submitted to a jury. The primary value promoted by due process in factfinding procedures is "to minimize the risk of erroneous decisions." Greenholtz v. Inmates of the Nebraska Penal and Correctional Complex, 442 U.S. 1, 13, 99 S.Ct. 2100, 2107, 60 L.Ed.2d 668 (1979). See also Mathews v. Eldridge, 424 U.S. 319, 335, 96 S.Ct. 893, 903, 47 L.Ed.2d 18 (1976). A jury that cannot understand the evidence and the legal rules to be applied provides no reliable safeguard against erroneous decisions. Moreover, in the context of a completely adversary proceeding, like a civil trial, due process requires that "the decisionmaker's conclusion . . . rest solely on the legal rules and evidence adduced at the hearing." Goldberg v. Kelly, 397 U.S. 254, 271, 90 S.Ct. 1011, 1022, 25 L.Ed.2d 287 (1970). Unless the jury can understand the legal rules and evidence, we cannot realistically expect that the jury will rest its decision on them.

* * * We conclude that due process precludes trial by jury when a jury is unable to perform this task with a reasonable understanding of the evidence and the legal rules.

If a particular lawsuit is so complex that a jury cannot satisfy this requirement of due process but is nonetheless an action at law, we face a conflict between the requirements of the fifth and seventh amendments. In this situation, we must balance the constitutionally protected interest[s], as they are implicated in this particular context, and reach the most reasonable accommodation between the two constitutional provisions. See Gannett Co. v. DePasquale, 443 U.S. 368, 99 S.Ct. 2898, 2911–12, 61 L.Ed.2d 608 (1979); Nebraska Press Ass'n v. Stuart, 427 U.S. 539, 96 S.Ct. 2791, 49 L.Ed.2d 683 (1976).

The due process objections to jury trial of a complex case implicate values of fundamental importance. If judicial decisions are not based on factual determinations bearing some reliable degree of accuracy, legal remedies will not be applied consistently with the purposes of the laws. There is a danger that jury verdicts will be erratic and completely unpredictable, which would be inconsistent with evenhanded justice. Finally, unless the jury can understand the evidence and the legal rules sufficiently to rest its decision on them, the objective of most rules of evidence and procedure in promoting a fair trial will be lost entirely. We believe that when a jury is unable to perform its decisionmaking task with a resonable understanding of the evidence and legal rules, it undermines the ability of a district court to render basic justice.

The loss of the right to jury trial in a suit found too complex for a jury does not implicate the same fundamental concerns. The absence of a jury trial requirement in equitable and maritime actions indicates that federal courts can provide fair trials and can grant relief in accordance with the principles of basic justice without the aid of a jury. Moreover, the Supreme Court has consistently refused to rule that preservation of civil jury trial is an essential element of ordered liberty required of the states by the due process clause of the fourteenth amendment. Palko v. Connecticut, 302 U.S. 319, 324–25, 58 S.Ct. 149, 151, 82 L.Ed. 288 (1937); Hardware Dealers Mutual Fire Ins. Co. v. Glidden Co., 284 U.S. 151, 158, 52 S.Ct. 69, 71, 76 L.Ed. 214 (1931); Melancon v. McKeithen, 345 F.Supp. 1025 (E.D.La.) (three-judge court), aff'd mem. 409 U.S. 943, 93 S.Ct. 289, 34 L.Ed.2d 214 (1972), 409 U.S. 1098, 93 S.Ct. 908, 24 L.Ed.2d 679 (1972).

* * *

The district court asserted that the due process argument fails to account for the special benefits that juries bring to civil litigation. Because the jury is a representative of the community and can call upon the community's wisdom and values, the legal system has relied on it to perform two important functions. The first is "black box" decisionmaking. The jury issues a verdict without an opinion to explain or justify its decision. This feature allows juries to perform a type of "jury equity," modifying harsh results of law to conform to community values in cases where a judge would have to apply the law rigidly. The second function is to accord a greater measure of legitimacy to decisions that depend upon determinations of degree rather than of absolutes, such as whether particular conduct constitutes negligence. Certain decisions of this "line-drawing" nature seem less arbitrary when made by a representative body like the jury. 478 F.Supp. at 938–42.

In the context of a lawsuit of the complexity that we have posited, however, these features do not produce real benefits of substantial value. The function of "jury equity" may be legitimate when the jury actually modifies the law to conform to community values. However, when the jury is unable to determine the normal application of the law to the facts of a case and reaches a verdict on the basis of nothing more than its own determination of community wisdom and values, its operation is indistinguishable from arbitrary and unprincipled decision-making. Similarly, the "line-drawing" function is difficult to justify when the jury cannot understand the evidence or legal rules relevant to the issue of where to draw a line.

The district court also noted that preservation of the right to jury trial is important because the jury "provides a needed check on judicial power." 478 F.Supp. at 942. See also Higginbotham, Continuing the Dialogue: Civil Juries and the Allocation of Judicial Power, 56 Tex.L.

Rev. 47, 58–60 (1977). A jury unable to understand the evidence and legal rules is hardly a reliable and effective check on judicial power. Our liberties are more secure when judicial decisionmakers proceed rationally, consistently with the law, and on the basis of evidence produced at trial. If the jury is unable to function in this manner, it has the capacity of becoming itself a tool of arbitrary and erratic judicial power.

*   *   *

VII.

The district court devoted most of its discussions of appellants' due process argument not to factors relevant to the balancing of interests set out in the foregoing section but to a number of practical objections to the argument. We shall consider those objections in this section.

First, the district court challenged the premise that a case could exceed a jury's ability to decide rationally [15] and asserted that a jury was at least as able as a judge, the only alternative factfinder, to decide complex cases. 478 F.Supp. at 935–36. The court noted that a jury possesses the wisdom, experience, and common sense of twelve persons. It has a greater effect than a judge in disciplining attorneys to present their cases clearly and concisely. Furthermore, its capabilities can be enhanced by special trial techniques like the preliminary charge and interim charges on the law contemplated by the district court in this case. Id. at 935. See generally Higginbotham, Continuing the Dialogue: Civil Juries and the Allocation of Judicial Power, 56 Tex.L.Rev. 47, 53–55 (1977); Kalven, The Dignity of the Civil Jury, 50 Va.L.Rev. 1055, 1066–67 (1964). On the basis of these observations, the court concluded that a jury "is brighter, more astute, and more perceptive than a single judge, even in a complex or technical case; at least it is not less so." 478 F.Supp. at 935.

Any assessment of a jury's ability to decide complex cases should include consideration not only of a jury's particular strengths and the possible enhancement of its capabilities but also of the particular constraints that operate on a jury in complex cases. The long time periods required for most complex cases are especially disabling for a jury. A long trial can interrupt the career and personal life of a jury member and thereby strain his commitment to the jury's task. The prospect of a long trial can also weed out many veniremen whose professional backgrounds qualify them for deciding a complex case but also prohibits them from lengthy jury service. See Note, The Right to an Incompetent Jury: Protracted Commercial Litigation and the Seventh Amendment, 10 Conn.L.Rev. 775, 776–83 (1978). Furthermore, a jury is likely to be unfamiliar with both the technical subject matter of a complex case and the process of civil litigation. The probability is not

---

15. The Ninth Circuit rejected a due-process argument with a similar expression of doubt. In re U. S. Financial Securities Litigation, 609 F.2d 411, 427–31 (9th Cir. 1979), cert. denied sub nom., Gant v. Union Bank, 446 U.S. 929, 100 S.Ct. 1866, 64 L.Ed.2d 281 (1980).

remote that a jury will become overwhelmed and confused by a mass of evidence and issues and will reach erroneous decisions. The reality of these difficulties that juries encounter in complex cases is underscored by the experience of some federal district judges who have found particular suits to have exceeded the practical abilities of a jury. See, e.g., ILC Peripherals Leasing Corp. v. IBM, 458 F.Supp. 423, 447–48 (N.D.Cal.1978), appeal docketed, Nos. 78–3050, 78–3236 (9th Cir. Sept. 12 and Oct. 6, 1978).

Given that a jury has both particular strengths and weaknesses in deciding complex cases, we cannot conclude *a priori* that a jury is capable of deciding a suit of any degree of complexity. A litigant might prove that a particular suit is too complex for a jury. Because of the important due process rights implicated, a litigant should have the opportunity to make that showing.

A general presumption that a judge is capable of deciding an extraordinarily complex case, by contrast, is reasonable. A long trial would not greatly disrupt the professional and personal life of a judge and should not be significantly disabling. In fact, the judge's greater ability to allocate time to the task of deciding a complex case can be a major advantage in surmounting the difficulties posed by the suit. Although we cannot presume that a judge will be more intelligent than a jury or more familiar with technical subject matters, a judge will almost surely have substantial familiarity with the process of civil litigation, as a result of experience on the bench or in practice. This experience can enable him to digest a large amount of evidence and legal argument, segregate distinct issues and the portions of evidence relevant to each issue, assess the opinions of expert witnesses, and apply highly complex legal standards to the facts of the case. The judge's experience also can enable him to make better use of special trial techniques designed to help the factfinder in complex cases, like colloquies with expert witnesses. The requirement that a judge issue findings of fact and conclusions of law offsets the substantial tendency to overlook issues in order that a verdict might be reached in these difficult cases. Fed.R.Civ.P. 52(a). Finally, if after trial and during deliberation a judge finds himself confused on certain matters or unable to decide certain issues, he can reopen the trial for the purpose of obtaining clarification or additional evidence. Fed.R.Civ.P. 59(a).

A judge's abilities are, of course, not unbounded. It is conceivable that a case might be so complex that a judge could not decide it rationally and competently. However, the possibility of such a case cannot justify trial by jury, because the presence of a jury does not relieve the judge of the need to understand the issues disputed in a case and the relevance and strength of the evidence. Such an understanding is necessary for the court to rule on most of the important matters committed to its decision in a jury trial, including motions for summary judgment, directed verdict, and new trial and exclusions of evidence as irrelevant, cumulative, or prejudicial.

*   *   *

The district court's second objection to appellants' due process argument was that the court can prevent an "irrational" verdict with its power to direct a verdict or to grant judgment n.o.v.   *   *   *

*   *   *   The district court's review of evidence on motions for directed verdict and judgment n.o.v. will not serve this purpose adequately. The court may not grant one of these motions if the evidence might reasonably support a verdict for either side.   *   *   *   Thus, the court can only ensure that the jury will return one of a range of possible verdicts that the court finds reasonably but minimally supported by the evidence. Given that substantial property rights often are at stake in actions at law, we believe that due process requires a greater measure of reliability in the decisionmaking process. It requires some fair assurance that the jury's findings of fact and applications of legal rules are reasonably correct. When a jury is unable to understand the evidence and the legal rules, it cannot provide this measure of assurance.

*   *   *

*   *   *   Because preservation of the right to jury trial remains a constitutionally protected interest, denials of jury trial on grounds of complexity should be confined to suits in which due process clearly requires a nonjury trial. This implies a high standard. It is not enough that trial to the court would be preferable. The complexity of a suit must be so great that it renders the suit beyond the ability of a jury to decide by rational means with a reasonable understanding of the evidence and applicable legal rules. Moreover, the district court should not deny a jury trial if by severance of multiple claims, thoughtful use of the procedures suggested in the Manual for Complex Litigation, or other methods the court can enhance a jury's capabilities or can reduce the complexity of a suit sufficiently to bring it within the ability of a jury to decide. Due process should allow denials of jury trials only in exceptional cases.

*   *   *

*   *   *   We shall vacate the court's order on the basis of our previous discussion and shall leave for consideration on remand the issue of the complexity of this lawsuit.

*   *   *

GIBBONS, CIRCUIT JUDGE, dissenting.

*   *   *

*   *   *   The trial court never determined whether after the case is broken down into the separate components in which it would be presented at common law it would or would not be too complex. Therefore, I would vacate the order granting leave to take an interlocutory appeal and wait for a case which actually presents the seventh amendment complexity issue in what I believe to be its actual rather than its hypothetical dimensions.

*   *   *

* * * If the issue were properly ripe for decision I would be prepared to hold that I cannot conceive of a case in which what would be a separate claim for relief at common law, sufficiently comprehensible to a trial judge to satisfy due process, would be too complex for trial to a jury. There may be such a case, but it is inconceivable to me that it could be recognized as such in the absence of a trial record.

I have, however, a more serious disagreement with the majority. * * * The majority opinion attempts to objectify the factors that bear upon complexity, but in the end the factors which are identified will permit the exercise of trial court discretion. I fear that the exercise of that discretion will sometimes be influenced by unarticulated sympathies for or hostilities toward the underlying policies sought to be advanced in the lawsuit. Trial court discretion, moreover, in any practical sense will be completely unreviewable. The majority suggests that an erroneous denial of jury trial can be remedied before trial by a writ of mandamus. * * * That remedy is hardly adequate, since formalistic application of the factors mentioned by the majority will result in a holding that the trial court acted within the bounds of its permissible discretion. In the event of a post-trial appeal on the ground that a demand for jury trial was erroneously denied, the pressure on an appellate tribunal not to order retrial of an otherwise error-free trial in a complex case will, I suspect, inevitably be irresistible. I would be less uncomfortable with the majority's rule if interlocutory review were available as a matter of right.

Part of my difficulty with the majority's position probably results from a perception of the nature of the judicial process and the role of juries in that process. It is often said that the judicial process involves the search for objective truth. We have no real assurance, however, of objective truth whether the trial is to the court or to a jury. The judicial process can do no more than legitimize the imposition of sanctions by requiring that some minimum standards of fair play, which we call due process, are adhered to. In this legitimizing process, the seventh amendment is not a useless appendage to the Bill of Rights, but an important resource in maintaining the authority of the rule of law. In the process of gaining public acceptance for the imposition of sanctions, the role of the jury is highly significant. The jury is a sort of ad hoc parliament convened from the citizenry at large to lend respectability and authority to the process. Judges are often prone to believe that they, alone, can bear the full weight of this legitimizing function. I doubt that they can. Any erosion of citizen participation in the sanctioning system is in the long run likely, in my view, to result in a reduction in the moral authority that supports the process.

In light, therefore, of the important functions served by the seventh amendment's protection of the right to a trial by jury, I would hold that there is no case in which properly separated claims for relief cognizable at common law would be so complex that trial by jury would amount to a violation of due process.

FURTHER NOTE ON THE FEDERAL RIGHT OF JURY TRIAL

1. Just what implications are to be drawn from the Supreme Court's decisions on the right of jury trial has not been entirely clear to the lower courts. In SEC v. Commonwealth Chemical Securities, Inc., 574 F.2d 90 (2d Cir. 1978), the action was one in federal district court by the SEC for an injunction to require a company that had sold stock to rescind the sale and return the proceeds to the buyers. Defendants' demand for jury trial was denied, the court, per Friendly, J., saying, 574 F.2d at 95–96:

> "On the other hand, not all money claims are triable to a jury. A historic equitable remedy was the grant of restitution 'by which defendant is made to disgorge ill-gotten gains or to restore the status quo, or to accomplish both objectives.' See 5 Moore, supra, ¶ 38.24[2] at 190.5, and Porter v. Warner Holding Co., supra, 328 U.S. at 400–02, 66 S.Ct. 1086. And '[w]hen restitution is sought in the form and in the situations allowed in equity prior to the rules or authorized by valid statutes there is no right to jury trial.' 5 Moore, supra, ¶ 38.24[2] at 190.6. Disgorgement of profits in an action brought by the SEC to enjoin violations of the securities laws appears to fit this description; the court is not awarding damages to which plaintiff is legally entitled but is exercising the chancellor's discretion to prevent unjust enrichment.

> "This view is consistent with recent judicial pronouncements. In Curtis v. Loether, supra, 415 U.S. 189, 94 S.Ct. 1005, 39 L.Ed.2d 260, while sustaining the right to a jury trial in an action for damages for discrimination in housing under § 812 of the Civil Rights Act of 1968, 42 U.S.C.A. § 3612, the Court said it was not predicting that it would reach the same result in discriminatory employment cases under Title VII of the Civil Rights Act of 1964 where courts are authorized, 42 U.S.C.A. § 2000e–5(g), not only to enjoin but to 'order such affirmative action as may be appropriate, which may include, but is not limited to, reinstatement or hiring of employees, with or without back pay,' 415 U.S. at 196–97, 94 S.Ct. at 1010. And the Court was at further pains to say:

> > Nor is there any sense in which the award here can be viewed as requiring the defendant to disgorge funds wrongfully withheld from the plaintiff.

415 U.S. at 197, 94 S.Ct. at 1010. In Albemarle Paper Co. v. Moody, 422 U.S. 405, 416–18, 95 S.Ct. 2362, 45 L.Ed.2d 280 (1975), the Court characterized the power to order back pay under Title VII as 'equitable in nature.' See also Pearson v. Western Electric Co., 542 F.2d 1150, 1152 (10 Cir. 1976). Further, lower courts have continued in the wake of *Curtis* to hold that back pay may be awarded without a jury trial in Title VII cases, see, e.g., EEOC v. Detroit Edison Co., 515 F.2d 301, 308 (6 Cir. 1975), vacated on other grounds, 431 U.S. 951, 97 S.Ct. 2669, 53 L.Ed.2d 267 (1977); Slack v. Havens, 522 F.2d 1091, 1094 (9 Cir. 1975). However, the Court has recently held that Congress intended that there be a right to a jury trial in a private action for lost wages under the Age Discrimination in Employment Act (ADEA). Lorillard v. Pons, 434 U.S. 575, 98 S.Ct. 866, 55 L.Ed.2d 40 (1978). This decision went largely on the basis that Congress had directed that the ADEA should be enforced in accordance with the 'powers, remedies, and procedures' of the Fair Labor Standards Act, where the right to a jury trial in private actions had long been recognized. Without deciding the jury

trial issue with respect to Title VII actions, the Court did distinguish the ADEA from Title VII on the basis that under the latter, but not the former, 'the availability of back pay is a matter of equitable discretion.' 434 U.S. at 584, 98 S.Ct. at 872.

"While from the standpoint of a defendant in an action for violation of the securities laws there may be no great difference between paying money in response to a private suit for damages and in a SEC action for injunction and disgorgement wherein the SEC makes the proceeds of disgorgement available to injured parties, the suit by the SEC is decidedly more analogous to the traditional jurisdiction of equity to award restitution. Its availability is entrusted to the discretion of the court, a factor that has been considered significant in the resolution of the question whether back pay awards in discrimination cases are equitable or legal in nature. See Curtis v. Loether, supra, 415 U.S. at 197, 94 S.Ct. 1005, 1010; Albemarle Paper Co. v. Moody, supra, 422 U.S. at 443, 95 S.Ct. 2362 (Rehnquist, J., concurring) * * * ."

Does the Court's discussion of the issue of disgorgement in *Tull* require a rethinking of Judge Friendly's analysis? Also, observe that Judge Friendly did not cite *Atlas Roofing*. One wonders why. Consider that Judge Friendly had written for the Second Circuit in United States v. J. B. Williams Co., 498 F.2d 414 (2d Cir. 1974), holding that in an action in federal district court for a civil penalty not unlike that involved in *Atlas Roofing*, defendant was entitled to a jury trial. The decision was based partly on historical analysis, partly on interpretation of congressional intent.

2. The Court's decisions on the scope of the Seventh Amendment admit of interpretations ranging from (a) every money remedy is jury triable of right, e.g., *Dairy Queen*, supra, to (b) no statutory remedy is jury triable of right, *Atlas Roofing*. The *Tull* decision read in the light of *Atlas Roofing* seems to imply that where Congress entrusts enforcement of a statute to an Article III tribunal, a jury may be available of right, at least where Congress was silent on the question, depending on the closest historical analogy to the statutory remedy. If this interpretation is accurate, should the question of the right to a jury depend on whether enforcement of a statutory remedy is entrusted to an administrative or a judicial tribunal? Do the Court's comments in *Atlas Roofing* concerning the difference between "public" and "private" rights provide a workable standard for determining whether enforcement of a statutory remedy can be entrusted to an administrative forum without a jury? Or could the very fact that the remedy is statutory convert what might otherwise be viewed as a "private" right into a "public" one?

Several of the decisions involved statutes creating money remedies enforcible in the federal district courts but not unequivocally specifying whether jury trial was available. The Court has treated these cases as involving statutory interpretation and historical analogy, as in *Tull*. Implicitly if not explicitly, this approach establishes that the Seventh Amendment does not require jury trial in all such instances. See, e.g., Albemarle Paper Co., supra; Lorillard v. Pons, supra. In Lehman v. Nakshian, 453 U.S. 156, 101 S.Ct. 2698, 69 L.Ed.2d 548 (1981), the Court held that extension of the Age Discrimination in Employment Act (ADEA), involved in Lorillard v. Pons, to employment by the Government did not carry with it the right of jury trial. The court said that a remedy against the Government does not entail jury trial unless "Congress clearly and unequivocally" so provides. Cf. Ruggiero v. Compania Peruana de Vapores, 639 F.2d 872 (2d Cir. 1981) (Foreign Sovereign Immunities

Act, 28 U.S.C.A. § 1330(a), validly excludes jury trial in actions against foreign sovereigns).

3. Does *Atlas Roofing* mean, however, that if Congress expressly so provided, an action in federal district court by the Government for a penalty could be tried without a jury? Does *Tull* answer this question, or provide guidance in answering it? Compare Note, Congressional Provision for Nonjury Trial Under the Seventh Amendment, 83 Yale L.J. 401 (1973); Note, Article III Implications for the Applicability of the Seventh Amendment to Federal Statutory Actions, 95 Yale L.J. 1459 (1986). The issues in a private diversity damages suit concededly must be tried by jury, e.g., Byrd v. Blue Ridge Rural Elec. Coop., supra p. 581. Given the political concerns that induced adoption of the Seventh Amendment, see Wolfram, The Constitutional History of the Seventh Amendment, 57 Minn.L.Rev. 639 (1973), does this configuration of decisions make any sense? Compare Rendleman, Chapters of the Civil Jury, 65 Ky.L.J. 769 (1977). See also Kirst, Finding a Role for the Civil Jury in Modern Litigation, 69 Judicature 333 (1986).

4. A recurrent argument against jury trial is that it is expensive to the parties, burdensome to the jurors, and entails poor decision-making, especially in complex cases. In re Japanese Electronic Products Antitrust Litigation is an example of how courts have tried to deal with the latter problem given the seemingly categorical terms of the Seventh Amendment. For an historical analysis arguing that the Seventh Amendment does not exempt complex cases, see Arnold, A Historical Inquiry Into the Right to Trial by Jury in Complex Civil Litigation, 128 U.Pa.L.Rev. 829 (1980), with which compare Campbell and Le Poidevin, Complex Cases and Jury Trials: A Reply to Professor Arnold, id. at 965, and Devlin, Jury Trial of Complex Cases: English Practice at the Time of the Seventh Amendment, 80 Colum.L.Rev. 43 (1980). See also Comment, Complex Civil Litigation and the Seventh Amendment Right to a Jury Trial, 51 U.Chi.L.Rev. 581 (1984); Lempert, Civil Juries and Complex Cases: Let's Not Rush to Judgment, 80 Mich.L.Rev. 68 (1981); Jorde, The Seventh Amendment Right to Jury Trial of Antitrust Issues, 69 Calif.L.Rev. 1 (1981); Note, The Case for Special Juries in Complex Cases, 89 Yale L.J. 1155 (1980). Compare In re U.S. Financial Securities Litigation, 609 F.2d 411, 432 (9th Cir.1979): "[I]n view of the mandate of the Seventh Amendment, time might be better spent in searching for ways to improve rather than erode the jury system."

For practical techniques in the jury trial of complex cases, see Symposium, The Jury in Complex Litigation, 65 Judicature 393 (1982). In Pittsburgh Corning Corp. v. Bradley, 499 Pa. 291, 453 A.2d 314 (1982), a local court rule assigning over 1,850 asbestos-related suits for non-jury trial, with a right to jury trial de novo, was held not to unconstitutionally burden the right to a jury trial. See also Carlstrom v. United States, infra p. 1238.

5. Whatever Congress's power to determine the scope of the jury trial right in federal tribunals, judicial and administrative, it is clear that Congress can require the use of juries in state courts when a federal right is being adjudicated. Whether Congress has so ordained in any specific situation is a matter of statutory interpretation, which has at times been strained. See Dice v. Akron, C. & Y.R.R., supra p. 603; Note, State Enforcement of Federally Created Rights, 73 Harv.L.Rev. 1551 (1960).

6. Even where a jury is not available of right, advisory juries may sometimes be used as an aid to settlement. See Note, Practice and Potential of the Advisory Jury, 100 Harv.L.Rev. 1363 (1987).

NOTE ON THE RIGHT TO JURY TRIAL UNDER STATE LAW

1. The constitutions of all of the states guarantee jury trial in at least the serious criminal cases, and most of them guarantee it in those civil cases which, prior to merger, were "actions at law." Louisiana has no constitutional right to jury trial in civil cases, see Deutsch, Jury Trials Under the Federal Rules and the Louisiana Practice, 3 La.L.Rev. 422 (1941), and the constitutions of Colorado, Art. II, Sec. 23, and Wyoming, Art. 1, Sec. 9, have only indirect provisions respecting civil jury trial. In the other states the constitutional guarantees of jury trial in civil cases usually are phrased in strong but not very detailed language. The constitutional authors generally were content to provide that trial by jury "shall remain inviolate forever," "shall remain inviolate," "shall be secured," "shall remain as heretofore," etc. See Blume, American Civil Procedure 370 (1955). At least implicitly the purport is that the right shall remain in substance as it was when the state constitutional provision was adopted. "It is the right to trial by jury as it existed at common law which is preserved; and what that right is, is a purely historical question, a fact which is to be ascertained like any other social, political or legal fact. The right is the historical right enjoyed at the time it was guaranteed by the Constitution. It is necessary, therefore, to ascertain what was the rule of the English common law upon this subject in 1850." People v. One 1941 Chevrolet Coupe, 37 Cal.2d 283, 287, 231 P.2d 832, 835 (1951); see Comment, 2 U.C.L.A.L.Rev. 370 (1955). Some scholars argue that under this historical test a jury is not constitutionally mandated in many states for small monetary claims. See, e.g., Barrett, The Constitutional Right to Jury Trial: A Historical Exception for Small Monetary Claims, 39 Hastings L.J. 125 (1987). In California the jury trial guarantee originally was in the Constitution of 1849, Art. I, Sec. 3, but California was not formally admitted to the Union until 1850. 1 Cal.Jur.2d xix, xxxii (1952).

2. Thus the state courts have not escaped, any more than have the federal courts, the difficult questions of right to jury trial in the one civil action consequent upon merger of law and equity. Merger in California was first accomplished by the California Civil Practice Act of 1849, cf. Gray v. Dougherty, 25 Cal. 266 (1864); see C.C.P. 307. The California constitutional provision is perhaps as typical as any, and an exploration of the law thereunder is as revealing—and, it might be added, as inconclusive—as one in any other state. California Constitution, Art. I, Sec. 16, as amended, provides:

> "Trial by jury is an inviolate right and shall be secured to all, but in a civil cause three-fourths of the jury may render a verdict. A jury may be waived in a criminal cause by the consent of both parties expressed in open court by the defendant and the defendant's counsel. In a civil cause a jury may be waived by the consent of the parties expressed as prescribed by statute.

> "In a civil cause the jury shall consist of 12 persons or a lesser number agreed on by the parties in open court. In civil causes in municipal or justice court the Legislature may provide that the jury shall consist of eight persons or a lesser number agreed on by the parties in open court."

See also C.C.P. 592, the Code's attempted elucidation of the constitutional right to jury trial in the light of the merger of law and equity; Ripling v. Superior Court, 112 Cal.App.2d 399, 247 P.2d 117 (1952). Contrary to the federal rule, *Beacon*, supra p. 1008, California apparently has a preference for prior trial of equitable issues. Connell v. Bowes, 19 Cal.2d 870, 872, 123 P.2d 456 (1942);

Raedeke v. Gibraltar Sav. and Loan Ass'n, 10 Cal.3d 665, 111 Cal.Rptr. 693, 517 P.2d 1157 (1974).

New York's statutory attempt to give specificity to the constitutional guarantee of jury trial, N.Y.C.P.L.R. § 4101, is as follows:

"In the following actions, the issues of fact shall be tried by a jury unless a jury trial is waived or a reference is directed under section 4317, except that equitable defenses and equitable counterclaims shall be tried by the court:

"1. an action in which a party demands and sets forth facts which would permit a judgment for a sum of money only;

"2. an action of ejectment; for dower; for waste; for abatement of and damages for a nuisance; to recover a chattel; or for determination of a claim to real property under article fifteen of the real property actions and proceedings law; and

"3. any other action in which a party is entitled by the constitution or by express provision of law to a trial by jury."

See also 4 Weinstein, Korn & Miller §§ 4101–4103.

3. Although the Seventh Amendment has never been "incorporated" into the Fourteenth Amendment and thus made binding on the states, see supra p. 1001, the Supreme Court's decisions in this area might be expected to influence state courts in construing state constitutional provisions protecting the right to jury trial in civil actions, particularly since the states have followed the federal pattern of merging equity and law into one procedure. In fact, however, the *Beacon Theatres* line of decisions has not been well received in the states. Intermediate appellate courts in California and Indiana have referred to Supreme Court Seventh Amendment decisions only to reject them. In Rankin v. Frebank Co., 47 Cal.App.3d 75, 121 Cal.Rptr. 348 (1975), where minority shareholders sued to dissolve a corporation and recover secret profits allegedly diverted from it, the court considered plaintiffs' invitation to be guided by Ross v. Bernhard, but held that California's constitutional guarantee of a jury trial merely preserved the right as it existed at common law in 1850. In Hiatt v. Yergin, 152 Ind.App. 497, 284 N.E.2d 834 (1972), plaintiffs sued for damages and specific enforcement of agreements for sale and repurchase of corporate stock. The court upheld the denial of plaintiffs' request for a jury trial on the ground that the suit was "equitable." The court adopted the dissent's view in *Beacon Theatres* that the Federal Rules were not intended to undermine the basic structure of equity, holding that the right to a jury trial "is determined by reference to the essential character and nature of the claim for relief * * * ." 284 N.E.2d at 850.

See also Lanman Lithotech, Inc. v. Gurwitz, 478 So.2d 425 (Fla.App.1985), taking a similar approach. Compare Pernell v. Southall Realty, 416 U.S. 363, 94 S.Ct. 1723, 40 L.Ed.2d 198 (1974) (jury trial of right in landlord's summary eviction proceeding) and Dept. of Transportation v. Kerrigan, 153 Cal.App.3d Supp. 41, 200 Cal.Rptr. 865 (1984) (same, under state constitution), with Kredi v. Benson, 1 Conn.App. 511, 473 A.2d 333 (1984) (no right to jury). In C & K Engineering Contractors v. Amber Steel Co., 23 Cal.3d 1, 151 Cal.Rptr. 323, 587 P.2d 1136 (1978), it was held that no jury trial right existed in a claim based on "the equitable doctrine of promissory estoppel," even though the relief sought was monetary compensation.

On the other hand, the Alabama Supreme Court relied on federal decisions in upholding a right to jury trial in a statutory action to enforce a mechanic's lien. Cumens v. Garrett, 294 Ala. 535, 319 So.2d 665 (1975). See also State v. Credit Bureau of Laredo, Inc., 530 S.W.2d 288 (Tex.1975) (suit for penalty for violating injunction); Loomis Electronic Protection, Inc. v. Schaefer, 549 P.2d 1341 (Alaska 1976) (action arising under state employment discrimination statute). Cf. Anno., 17 A.L.R.3d 1321.

NOTE ON DEMANDING AND WAIVING JURY TRIAL

1. Note that under the scheme of F.R.C.P. 38 a party waives her right to jury trial if she does not seasonably demand it. See F.R.C.P. 38(b), 38(d). This differs from the pre-Rules philosophy whereby, in the absence of an express waiver, jury trial followed as a matter of course in actions at law. 5 Moore ¶ 38.39. Experienced practitioners under the Federal Rules who desire jury trial guard against inadvertent waiver by following the wise custom authorized by F.R.C.P. 38(b) of endorsing the demand for a jury on the complaint when they represent the plaintiff, and on the answer when they represent the defendant and plaintiff has not demanded a jury. Under F.R.C.P. 39(b) the court in its discretion on motion may relieve a party from the consequences of his waiver by ordering a jury trial. See 5 Moore ¶ 39.08. Rule 39(c) permits impanelling an advisory jury where the issues are not jury triable of right. Cf. Anno., 9 A.L.R.4th 1041 (authority under state practice).

2. The California waiver procedure is more complicated, so that a more deliberate act is required to result in waiver. See C.C.P. 631, construed in Taylor v. Union Pacific R. R., 16 Cal.3d 893, 130 Cal.Rptr. 23, 549 P.2d 855 (1976). Compare N.Y.C.P.L.R. § 4102; 4 Weinstein, Korn & Miller ¶¶ 4102.10–4102.16.

3. Suppose an action commenced in state court is duly removed to federal court under 28 U.S.C.A. § 1441. Must the party desiring a jury make a demand in federal court and if so, when? See F.R.C.P. 81(c).

4. In California and many other states, a party demanding jury must post the cost of the jurors' fees, see C.C.P. 631(5), or pay a flat fee. See Robertson v. Apuzzo, 170 Conn. 367, 365 A.2d 824 (1976), holding that such a requirement is not constitutionally invalid; Matter of G.P., 679 P.2d 976 (Wyo.1984) (same); cf. County of Portage v. Steinpreis, 104 Wis.2d 466, 312 N.W.2d 731 (1981) (jury fees in small claims court).

C. SELECTION OF THE TRIER OF FACT

1. THE JURY

a. THE JURY PANEL

INTRODUCTORY NOTE ON THE JURY PANEL

1. Most cases dealing with jury panels are criminal cases. Beginning with Smith v. Texas, 311 U.S. 128, 61 S.Ct. 164, 85 L.Ed. 84 (1940), the Supreme Court has established that systematic exclusion of potential jurors on the basis of race is constitutionally impermissible. See also Peters v. Kiff, 407 U.S. 493,

92 S.Ct. 2163, 33 L.Ed.2d 83 (1972), holding that a white person has standing to object to the exclusion of blacks from juries; People v. Navarette, 54 Cal.App.3d 1064, 127 Cal.Rptr. 55 (1976) (underrepresentation of women). In Thiel v. Southern Pacific Co., 328 U.S. 217, 66 S.Ct. 984, 90 L.Ed. 1181 (1946), the Supreme Court had one of its rare occasions for considering discriminatory selection of a civil jury. In that case, the clerk of court and jury commissioner in selecting jurors for the federal district court had used a city directory as the source for names and, in using this source, had systematically excluded all persons who worked for a daily wage. The explanation was that such persons were always excused on grounds of economic hardship and hence it was a waste of time to summon them. It also appeared that "business men and their wives constituted at least 50% of the jury lists, although both the clerk and the commissioner denied that they consciously chose according to wealth or occupation." The Court held the procedure could not be justified by "federal or state law" or "general principles underlying proper jury selection." Federal law at the time provided that federal jurors should meet the qualifications prescribed for jurors in the state where the federal court sat; the relevant state law, California's, required only that a juror be 21, a citizen of the United States, resident in the state and county for one year, and conversant in English. Although excuse for hardship might be given, that did not justify allowing the selection "to discriminate against persons of low economic and social status." 328 U.S. at 223.

2. As a practical matter, however, the cases governing selection of criminal petit and grand juries are very significant in determining the selection of civil juries. That is because in almost all jurisdictions civil and criminal jurors are drawn from the same lists and by the same procedure; grand jurors are sometimes specially selected, but usually from the same master list that is used for petit juries.

STATE v. PORRO

Superior Court of New Jersey, 1977.
152 N.J.Super. 259, 377 A.2d 950.

SCHIAFFO, J. S. C.

This motion challenges the array of the grand jury and seeks dismissal of the indictment.

*   *   *

Under-Representation

The thrust of the defendants' challenge is that because of certain alleged defects in the jury selection process they have been denied their constitutional right to a grand jury which represents a fair cross-section of the community.

Although the Fifth Amendment right to indictment has not been deemed one of those essential rights applicable to the states through the Fourteenth Amendment, where, however, the individual states elect to grant this right, it is axiomatic that the principles of due process and equal protection must adhere. Hurtado v. California, 110 U.S. 516, 4 S.Ct. 111, 28 L.Ed. 232 (1884); Alexander v. Louisiana, 405 U.S. 625, 92

S.Ct. 1221, 31 L.Ed.2d 536 (1972) (Douglas, J. concurring). The State of New Jersey has extended this right to individuals. N.J.Const. (1947), Art. I, par. 8. One need not dwell on the recognition that a necessary extension of both the Fifth and Sixth Amendments of the Federal Constitution is that the defendants be indicted and tried by juries of integrity representative of a valid cross-section of the community. Neal v. Delaware, 103 U.S. 370, 26 L.Ed. 567 (1881); Peters v. Kiff, 407 U.S. 493, 92 S.Ct. 2163, 33 L.Ed.2d 83 (1972). However, the scope of this right does not entitle defendants to personally select to their satisfaction the grand jury which will consider the charges brought against them. Thiel v. Southern Pacific Co., 328 U.S. 217, 66 S.Ct. 984, 90 L.Ed. 1181 (1946); Virginia v. Rives, 100 U.S. 313, 25 L.Ed. 667 (1880); Hoyt v. Florida, 368 U.S. 57, 82 S.Ct. 159, 7 L.Ed.2d 118 (1961). The Constitution protects them from consideration by a grand jury selected as a result of systematic exclusion, intentional design or scheme which excludes any identifiable class of persons solely because of that classification. This rationale extends to the situation where a grand jury will be absent or proportionately lacking members of a cognizable class. Virginia v. Rives, supra; State v. Smith, 55 N.J. 476, 262 A.2d 868 (1970). There is no constitutional tolerance for the systematic and deliberate exclusion of members of any cognizable class, notwithstanding the underlying motive of good faith of those entrusted with the selection process. Dow v. Carnegie-Illinois Steel Corp., 224 F.2d 414 (3 Cir. 1955), cert. den. 350 U.S. 971, 76 S.Ct. 442, 100 L.Ed. 842 (1956); Crawford v. Bounds, 395 F.2d 297 (4 Cir. 1968).

In arguing the under-representation of certain classes, the defense introduced the testimony of a qualified expert in the field of policy sciences and psychology, Dr. John B. McConahay, presently associated with Duke University. Dr. McConahay testified as to the alleged under-representation of women, young people between 18–34 years of age, blue collar workers and blacks, and provided the court with a statistical evaluation of these groups in relation to their presence in the county and in the grand jury pool. He further pointed out that the use of voter registration lists as the source of names in jury selection could, as here, foreseeably result in a situation where the master list would end with prospective jurors having surnames beginning with the letters M–W. This, he argued, allegedly creates the risk of a disproportionate number of jurors not being representative of certain ethnic groups, although no specific proof was offered in this regard.

These arguments are without merit. The use of voter registration lists as the sole source of names for prospective jurors has been consistently upheld by the federal courts and the courts of this State despite the inevitable result of some statistical disparity and disproportionate representation of certain groups. Federal Jury Selection and Service Act of 1968, 28 U.S.C.A. § 1861 et seq.; State v. Rochester, 54 N.J. 85, 253 A.2d 474 (1969); * * *. Precedent therefore recognizes that disproportionate representation may result. This may be attributable to those citizens who elect not to register to vote or there may be a disparity in the demographic characteristics of the population between any two municipalities in a given county. The jury need not be the mirror image of the community. Clones, need not, nor can be produced.

Systematic Exclusion of Students

Defendants have the burden of proof as to a prima facie case of systematic exclusion. See, e.g., Akins v. Texas, 325 U.S. 398, 65 S.Ct. 1276, 89 L.Ed. 1692 (1945), reh. den. 326 U.S. 806, 66 S.Ct. 86, 90 L.Ed. 491 (1945). To sustain this burden they must demonstrate that (1) an identifiable class does in fact exist and (2) purposeful exclusion of this class has occurred. Hernandez v. Texas, 347 U.S. 475, 74 S.Ct. 667, 98 L.Ed. 866 (1954). Cognizability may be determined by considering three factors: (1) the presence of some quality or attribute which defines and limits the group; (2) a cohesiveness of attitudes and experience which distinguishes the group from society in general, and (3) a "community of interest" which may not be adequately represented by other societal groups. United States v. Guzman, 337 F.Supp. 140, 143 (S.D.N.Y.), aff'd 468 F.2d 1245 (2 Cir. 1972), cert. den. 410 U.S. 937, 93 S.Ct. 1397, 35 L.Ed.2d 602 (1973).

In the present case defendants have effectively demonstrated that at the time of the subject indictment the grand jury selection process in Bergen County was such that full-time students were automatically excluded from service. Hence, the second criterion enunciated in *Hernandez*, supra, has been satisfied. The more perplexing issue is whether students constitute a cognizable class so as to satisfy the first criterion. Before reaching that determination, it is necessary to place the entire analysis within the context of the Bergen County grand jury selection process affecting the 1975 term.

Pursuant to R. 1:33–2 and In re Supervision and Assignment of the Petit Jury Panels in Essex Cty., 60 N.J. 554, 292 A.2d 4 (1972), the assignment judge of the county is vested with the primary responsibility for the supervision of jury selection mechanics. This responsibility is further delegated and shared in conjunction with the jury commissioners and associated personnel. During the period of time in question the selection process of both grand and petit jurors was in substantial accord with the Manual on the Selection of Grand and Petit Jurors prepared by the Administrative Office of the Courts (March 1973). Pursuant to the *Manual*, which cites as its authority a State Supreme Court directive, voter registration lists were and presently are the sole source of prospective jurors. The initial ratio is the total number of registered voters in each municipality over the total number of registered voters in the county. The resultant percentage represents the total number of persons desirable from each municipality to be considered prospective jurors. Once the list of prospective jurors is formed, questionnaires are sent, and upon their return the jury commissioners apply the certain statutory qualifications and exemptions based upon the content of the questionnaire. The final compilation is the master list. The theory of random selection prevails throughout the process and the ultimate panel is so drawn.

Defendants produced the depositions of the assignment judge and the jury commissioners which confirm the fact that at the time of this indictment students were systematically and purposely excluded from the list from which the prospective jurors were ultimately drawn. There is not presently, nor was there at that time, any existing statutory or administrative authority permitting the blanket exclusion of students from jury service in the State of New Jersey or Bergen County. These depositions disclose no malevolent intent or rationale underlying this process. In fact it appears that the motivation was the good faith belief that students should not be disturbed in their academic pursuits, particularly when jury service would require their return to Bergen County from learning institutions quite some distance away. However, the fact of this benign or neutral motivation is irrelevant as deliberation and intention need not be shown where a cognizable class has been systematically excluded from the array. Crawford v. Bounds, supra; Dow v. Carnegie-Illinois Steel Corp., supra. The procedure under attack has since been altered in Bergen County to include students and others on the list of prospective jurors and to consider excuses on a case by case basis commencing January 1, 1977.

Thus having shown the systematic exclusion of students, the defendants' obligation at this juncture is to demonstrate that "students" do in fact constitute an existing identifiable class of constitutional import, the systematic exclusion of which, irrespective of motive, would taint the composition of the master list rendering the ensuing indictment invalid.

The threshold inquiry is the definition of a student. A student is a person formally engaged in learning; one enrolled in a school or college; any person who studies, investigates or examines thoughtfully. The Random House Dictionary of the English Language (unabridged ed. 1966). A student is a learner or a scholar; one who attends school. Webster's Seventh New Collegiate Dictionary (1972 ed.).

Students are therefore persons who are engaged in a course of study. Given this definition, the three factors suggested by the *Guzman* case must be applied to determine their status as cognizable or noncognizable. First, is there within the concept of students the presence of some quality or attribute which defines and limits the parameters of this group? Second, do they demonstrate a cohesiveness of attitudes and experience which distinguish them from society in general? Third, is there a "community of interests" which may not be adequately represented by other societal groups? This court finds that students do not constitute a cognizable class when assessed in light of these factors.

There are certain groups in society which have classically constituted identifiable classes for the purpose of constitutional protection and definition. Race, sex and economic status are examples of these classifications. Carter v. Jury Comm'n of Greene Cty., 396 U.S. 320, 90 S.Ct. 518, 24 L.Ed.2d 549 (1970) (blacks); Taylor v. Louisiana, 419 U.S. 522, 95 S.Ct. 692, 42 L.Ed.2d 690 (1975) (women); Thiel v. Southern Pacific Co., supra (daily wage earners). Our own statutes governing juries recognize these same classifications specifically and prohibit the disqualification of any juror falling within any of these enumerated classes where he otherwise meets those qualifications prescribed by law. N.J.S.A. 2A:72–7. Students per se have not been so isolated by statute or case law for special constitutional treatment.

This court further notes that there exist portions of our statutes dealing with juries which in fact result in the systematic exclusion of certain groups, primarily on the basis of employment. N.J.S.A. 2A:69–2 provides for the exemption from service a number of groups: school teachers during the school year; regularly licensed and practicing physicians and dentists; members of the police force and State Legislature, etc. Systematic exclusion also results with respect to those disqualified for service under the provisions of N.J.S.A. 2A:69–1 for reasons of residency, age, literacy and ability to comprehend English. These and similar exemptions or preconditions to service have been upheld as necessary and reasonable providing no valid basis for challenge. See, e.g., Government of the Canal Zone v. Scott, 502 F.2d 566 (5 Cir. 1974) (military personnel); United States v. Catena, 500 F.2d 1319 (3 Cir. 1974), cert. den. 419 U.S. 1047, 95 S.Ct. 621, 42 L.Ed.2d 641 (1974) (physicians in active practice); Rawlins v. Georgia, 201 U.S. 638, 26 S.Ct. 560, 50 L.Ed. 899 (1906) (lawyers, doctors, firemen); State v. Anderson, 132 N.J.Super. 231, 333 A 2d 201 (App.Div.1975) (residence requirements).

Students do not conform to our traditional concepts of constitutionally defined identifiable classes. Their motivations and goals are diverse. In this court's opinion this so-called group is best analogized to an occupational status. This conclusion is mindful of the guidelines set forth in United States v. Guzman, supra. A student is basically not different from a doctor, lawyer or teacher. Each of these professions possesses certain affinities and collective sensibilities among its members which sets it apart from the others. However, none of these professions retains a uniqueness so predominate as to raise it to a level of constitutional recognition as an identifiable class.

The more probing question involves the parameters of this group. There is a tendency in society to harbor a stereotypical image of the student. The vivid events of the 1960s have left us with the general impression that all students are young, perhaps within the age range of 18–34 years. This court rejects such an image as a fallacy in the 1970s.[1] Institutions of learning have opened their doors to persons from every societal strata. Today, persons engaged in a course of study

---

1. It is worthy of note that the statistical disparities testified to by Dr. McConahay show no gross disparity in relation to other groups studied with respect to the number of those 18–34 years of age in the jury wheel studied.

are not confined to the liberal arts campus. Instead, we presently offer courses of study on a part-time basis, vocational training, correspondence study, schools devoted entirely to the study of theater arts, *ad infinitum*. Each individual enrolled in one of these curriculums falls within the accepted dictionary definition of a student. The contemporary student profile may be of a mother returning to school to either commence or complete her formal education.

Even more compelling is the realization that the age range of students is expansive. There is a very definite trend toward the enrollment of persons over 30 at both the graduate and undergraduate levels. *   *   *

*   *   * This court sees no common bond existing between a student of nuclear physics and a student of the arts, a student of modern languages and a student of air-conditioning and refrigeration, and a student of theology and a student of the ballet—other than the pursuit of study. It is for these reasons that the court must find that students do not constitute a cognizable class of constitutional dimensions whereby their exclusion would deprive defendants of indictment by a grand jury of integrity, representative of a valid cross-section of the community. Neal v. Delaware, supra.

 *   *   *

FURTHER NOTE ON THE JURY PANEL

1. The question of the source lists for drawing jurors has been much vexed. Most court systems use the voter list, a base that has been challenged, as in State v. Porro, on the ground that it is unrepresentative of the general population. Reversing decades of practice, the California Supreme Court in 1984 accepted this argument and held that exclusive reliance on voter lists was unconstitutional. People v. Harris, 36 Cal.3d 36, 201 Cal.Rptr. 782, 679 P.2d 433 (1984). While the court's ruling was limited to source lists for criminal juries, presumably it would apply to civil trials as well. See also Kairys, Kadane, and Lehoczky, Jury Representativeness: A Mandate for Multiple Source Lists, 65 Calif.L.Rev. 776 (1977). The latter analysis indicates just how great the discrepancy in representativeness can be. It also shows how modern computer techniques vitiate the traditional argument that use of voter lists is justified because multiple lists are inconvenient. Compare Comment, Underrepresentation of Economic Groups on Federal Juries, 57 B.U.L.Rev. 198 (1977). The courts have said that statistical analysis may be used to prove systematic discrimination, see Castaneda v. Partida, 430 U.S. 482, 97 S.Ct. 1272, 51 L.Ed.2d 498 (1977), but, with the notable exception of the California high court, generally have not held master lists invalid simply because they do not substantially mirror the adult population. On types of statistical evidence regarding underrepresentation of blacks, see State v. Ramseur, 106 N.J. 123, 524 A.2d 188 (1987). Do the courts thus endorse the legitimacy of a selection system that overrepresents the "civic minded," i.e., voters, so long as it does not otherwise discriminate against "identifiable classes"? C.C.P. 197 now requires selection "at random from a fair cross section of the population," and C.C.P. 204.7 facilitates use of lists of licensed drivers to augment registered voter lists as sources for master lists. Another issue in compiling source lists concerns the geographic area from which the lists are drawn. See, e.g., O'Hare v.

Superior Court, 43 Cal.3d 86, 233 Cal.Rptr. 332, 729 P.2d 766 (1987), holding that the jury may be drawn from an administrative subdivision of a county despite evidence of underrepresentation of blacks.

2. The first step in the procurement of twelve jurors for the trial of a case is the selection of a group of citizens from the source lists and screening them for entry on to the master list. Every jurisdiction has elaborate statutory provisions governing this process: Selection of individuals from the body of available citizens, qualifications and exemptions, special venires when sufficient numbers fail to appear, and like matters. The most important California provisions are contained in C.C.P. 190 et seq., 600 et seq.; see 7 Witkin 111–152. For the basic provisions governing selection of federal juries, see 28 U.S.C.A. §§ 1861–1871; 5A Moore ¶¶ 47.02–47.05. For comparable New York provisions, see Judic.Law, §§ 500–523; N.Y.C.P.L.R. §§ 4104–4106. Compare Keilitz and Caviness, Evaluating Jury Selection, Utilization, and Management, 4 State Court Journal 9 (Winter 1980).

Typical statutory provisions governing selection of jurors concern, most broadly, two kinds of challenges: to the panel, or "array" as it is sometimes called, and to individual jurors. However, in California it has been said that "[a] challenge leveled at the panel is not contemplated by the statute in civil cases." Livesey v. Stock, 208 Cal. 315, 321, 281 P. 70, 72 (1929); see C.C.P. 601. Cf. Anno., 76 A.L.R.2d 678. Challenges to individual jurors may be either for cause, or peremptory. Those for cause may be either general, i.e., applicable in all cases, e.g., incompetency as a result of conviction of a felony, C.C.P. 199, 602(1); or particular, i.e., applicable only to the instant case, e.g., bias to a party, C.C.P. 602(8). Bias may be implied, e.g., as in the case of consanguinity or affinity within the fourth degree to any party, or as in the case of certain relationships such as master-servant, guardian-ward, etc., C.C.P. 602(3), 602(4); or bias may be actual, C.C.P. 602(8). All challenges for cause are decided by the court in civil cases, C.C.P. 603; in some states in serious criminal cases, provision is made for a special panel of triers of challenges. A challenge for cause must be made at the earliest opportunity; the challenged juror and others may be examined as witnesses. The trial court's determination ordinarily controls; and even though the judge erroneously denies a challenge the error is not reversible unless it is shown that the challenger used up all his peremptory challenges and was still not satisfied with the jury. 7 Witkin 148–150.

3. Many classes of people traditionally were exempted from jury duty. C.C.P. 200 formerly exempted military and government officers, attorneys and their clerks and secretaries, ministers, teachers, physicians, mail carriers, railroad personnel, and many others. The modern tendency has been to eliminate exemptions and to provide for hardship by individual excuse. See C.C.P. 202.5, which exempts only judges and peace officers. See also McKusick and Boxer, Uniform Jury Selection and Service Act, 8 Harv.J.Legis. 280 (1971); ABA, Standards of Judicial Administration § 2.11. Compare 28 U.S.C.A. § 1863(b), which exempts members of the armed forces, fire fighters and police officers, and state and federal officials. See also United States v. Benmuhar, 658 F.2d 14 (1st Cir. 1981), sustaining a requirement that jurors be proficient in English, even if the requirement would affect the representativeness of the jury.

4. The jury traditionally consisted of twelve persons, although in many states a lesser number was authorized, sometimes only in civil cases, sometimes only in courts of limited jurisdiction. In Colgrove v. Battin, 413 U.S. 149, 93

S.Ct. 2448, 37 L.Ed.2d 522 (1973), it was held that a jury of six satisfied the Seventh Amendment requirement, even though as a matter of history that seems plainly insupportable and the lesser size of the jury can make a difference in outcome. On the latter point, see Lempert, Uncovering "Nondiscernible" Differences: Empirical Research and the Jury-Size Cases, 73 Mich.L. Rev. 643 (1975). C.C.P. 194.5 provides for experimental eight person juries. Cf. Williams v. Florida, 399 U.S. 78, 90 S.Ct. 1893, 26 L.Ed.2d 446 (1970) (six person jury held sufficient for state court criminal jury). See also Anno., 47 A.L.R.3d 895 (validity of statutory provisions requiring jury of less than twelve persons). Compare Ballew v. Georgia, 435 U.S. 223, 98 S.Ct. 1029, 55 L.Ed.2d 234 (1978) (five person criminal jury too small).

F.R.C.P. 47(b) authorizes impanelling alternate jurors but states explicitly that the replacement of a regular juror must be made before the jury retires. Compare Griesel v. Dart Indus., Inc., 23 Cal.3d 578, 153 Cal.Rptr. 213, 591 P.2d 503 (1979), holding it error to interject an alternate juror after deliberations are under way.

5. Traditionally also, the jury verdict had to be unanimous. That requirement has been modified in many states. See Comment, The Case for Retention of the Unanimous Civil Jury, 15 De Paul L.Rev. 403 (1966); C.C.P. 613, 618 (nine out of twelve); N.Y.C.P.L.R. § 4113(a) (ten out of twelve). In Masino v. Outboard Marine Corp., 652 F.2d 330 (3d Cir. 1981), the requirement of unanimity in an eight person federal jury was upheld against the claim that the state rule, of ⁵⁄₆ concurrence, should apply. See Zeisel, The Verdict of Five out of Six Civil Jurors: Constitutional Problems, 1982 Am.B.F.Res.J. 141.

b. VOIR DIRE

McDONOUGH POWER EQUIPMENT, INC. v. GREENWOOD

Supreme Court of the United States, 1984.
464 U.S. 548, 104 S.Ct. 845, 78 L.Ed.2d 663.

JUSTICE REHNQUIST delivered the opinion of the Court.

Respondents, Billy Greenwood and his parents, sued petitioner McDonough Power Equipment, Inc., to recover damages sustained by Billy when his feet came in contact with the blades of a riding lawn mower manufactured by petitioner. The United States District Court for the District of Kansas entered judgment for petitioner upon a jury verdict and denied respondents' motion for new trial. On appeal, however, the Court of Appeals for the Tenth Circuit reversed the judgment of the District Court and ordered a new trial. It held that the failure of a juror to respond affirmatively to a question on *voir dire* seeking to elicit information about previous injuries to members of the juror's immediate family had "prejudiced the Greenwoods' right of peremptory challenge," 687 F.2d 338, 342 (1982), and that a new trial was necessary to cure this error. We granted certiorari, 462 U.S. 1130, 103 S.Ct. 3109, 77 L.Ed.2d 1365 (1983), and now hold that respondents are not entitled to a new trial unless the juror's failure to disclose denied respondents their right to an impartial jury.

During the *voir dire* prior to the empaneling of the six-member jury, respondents' attorney asked prospective jurors the following question:

"Now, how many of you have yourself or any members of your immediate family sustained any severe injury, not necessarily as severe as Billy, but sustained any injuries whether it was an accident at home, or on the farm or at work that resulted in any disability or prolonged pain and suffering, that is you or any members of your immediate family?" App. 19.

Ronald Payton, who eventually became a juror, did not respond to this question, which was addressed to the panel as a whole. After a trial which extended over a 3-week period, the jury found for petitioner McDonough.[1] Four days after judgment was entered for petitioner, respondents moved under local Rule 23A for permission to approach the members of the jury. In support of their motion respondents asserted that they were of "information and belief" that juror Payton's son may have been injured at one time, a fact which had not been revealed during *voir dire*. Id., at 68. The District Court ruled that respondents had failed to show just cause to approach the jury. Id., at 73.

Undeterred, the next day respondents filed a second motion for permission to approach the jury, attaching an affidavit from respondent John Greenwood,[2] who asserted that in the course of his employment as a Navy recruiter, he had reviewed the enlistment application of juror Payton's son. In that application Payton's son stated that he had been injured in the explosion of a truck tire. The District Court granted respondents permission to approach juror Payton regarding the injuries allegedly sustained by his son. The District Court directed that the inquiry should be brief and polite and made in a manner convenient to the juror. The District Court noted that it was not "overly impressed with the significance of this particular situation." Id., at 89. No provision was made to record the inquiry of juror Payton.

On the same day that the District Court granted respondents permission to approach juror Payton, respondents moved for a new trial, asserting 18 grounds in justification, including the District Court's alleged error in denying respondents' motion to approach the jury.

---

1. Although respondents sued only petitioner McDonough, under Kansas law, which applied in this diversity action, the jury was permitted to consider the relative fault of three nondefendants: Jeff Morris, a next-door neighbor who was operating the lawn mower involved in the accident, Jeff's father, and Billy's mother. The jury assessed Billy's damages in the amount of $375,000, and found Jeff Morris 20% at fault, Jeff's father 45% at fault, and Billy's mother 35% at fault. The jury determined that petitioner McDonough's percentage of fault was zero.

2. It is not clear from the opinion of the Court of Appeals whether the information stated in Greenwood's affidavit was known to respondents or their counsel at the time of the *voir dire* examination. If it were, of course, respondents would be barred from later challenging the composition of the jury when they had chosen not to interrogate juror Payton further upon receiving an answer which they thought to be factually incorrect. See Johnson v. Hill, 274 F.2d 110, 115–116 (CA8 1960).

This was the only instance when respondents even tangentially referred the District Court to the juror's failure to respond as a ground for a new trial. Shortly after the parties placed a telephone conference call to juror Payton, the District Court denied respondents' motion for a new trial, finding that the "matter was fairly and thoroughly tried and that the jury's verdict was a just one, well-supported by the evidence." Id., at 106. The District Court was never informed of the results of the examination of juror Payton, nor did respondents ever directly assert before the District Court that juror Payton's nondisclosure warranted a new trial.

On appeal, the Court of Appeals proceeded directly to the merits of respondents' claim that juror Payton's silence had prejudiced their right to exercise peremptory challenges, rather than remanding the case back to the District Court for a hearing.[3] The Court of Appeals simply recited the recollections of counsel for each party of their conference telephone call with juror Payton contained in their appellate briefs, stating that the "unrevealed information" indicated probable bias "because it revealed a particularly narrow concept of what constitutes a serious injury." 687 F.2d, at 343. The Court of Appeals assumed that juror Payton had answered in good faith, but stated:

> "Good faith, however, is irrelevant to our inquiry. If an average prospective juror would have disclosed the information, and that information would have been significant and cogent evidence of the juror's probable bias, a new trial is required to rectify the failure to disclose it." Ibid. (citation omitted).

This Court has long held that " '[a litigant] is entitled to a fair trial but not a perfect one,' for there are no perfect trials." Brown v. United

---

3. Although neither party challenges the propriety of the Court of Appeals having disposed of the question on the merits, we believe that the proper resolution of the legal issue should be made by the District Court. * * * Nevertheless, we address the issue in order to correct the legal standard the District Court should apply upon remand.

Both parties apparently agree that during the telephone conversation with juror Payton, he related that his son had received a broken leg as the result of an exploding tire. Counsel for respondents in their brief to the Court of Appeals recalled Payton saying that "it did not make any difference whether his son had been in an accident and was seriously injured," "that having accidents are a part of life," and that "all his children have been involved in accidents." Brief for Appellants in No. 80–1698 (CA10), p. 7. Counsel for petitioners recall Payton as saying that he "did not regard [his son's broken leg] as a 'severe' injury and as he understood the question [the injury] did not result in any 'disability

or prolonged pain and suffering.' As far as Mr. Payton is concerned he answered counsel's question honestly, and correctly, by remaining silent." Brief for Appellee in No. 80–1698 (CA10), p. 18.

Nevertheless, the manner in which the parties presented the issue of juror Payton's failure to respond on *voir dire* was highly unorthodox. While considerations of judicial economy might have motivated the Court of Appeals in this case to proceed directly to the issue of the effect of juror Payton's nondisclosure, in cases in which a party is asserting a ground for new trial, the normal procedure is to remand such issues to the district court for resolution. Although petitioner does not dispute respondents' version of the telephone call to juror Payton, it is foreseeable that in another such case, the parties could present the appellate court with a continuing, difficult factual dispute. Appellate tribunals are poor substitutes for trial courts for developing a record or resolving factual controversies.

States, 411 U.S. 223, 231–232, 93 S.Ct. 1565, 1570–1571, 36 L.Ed.2d 208 (1973), quoting Bruton v. United States, 391 U.S. 123, 135, 88 S.Ct. 1620, 1627, 20 L.Ed.2d 476 (1968), and Lutwak v. United States, 344 U.S. 604, 619, 73 S.Ct. 481, 490, 97 L.Ed. 593 (1953). Trials are costly, not only for the parties, but also for the jurors performing their civic duty and for society which pays the judges and support personnel who manage the trials. It seems doubtful that our judicial system would have the resources to provide litigants with perfect trials, were they possible, and still keep abreast of its constantly increasing case load. Even this straightforward products liability suit extended over a 3-week period.

We have also come a long way from the time when all trial error was presumed prejudicial and reviewing courts were considered " 'citadels of technicality.' " Kotteakos v. United States, 328 U.S. 750, 759, 66 S.Ct. 1239, 1245, 90 L.Ed. 1557 (1946), quoting Kavanagh, Improvement of Administration of Criminal Justice by Exercise of Judicial Power, 11 A.B.A.J. 217, 222 (1925). The harmless error rules adopted by this Court and Congress embody the principle that courts should exercise judgment in preference to the automatic reversal for "error" and ignore errors that do not affect the essential fairness of the trial. See Kotteakos, supra, at 759–760, 66 S.Ct., at 1245–1246. For example, the general rule governing motions for a new trial in the district courts is contained in Federal Rule of Civil Procedure 61, which provides:

> "No error . . . or defect in any ruling or order or in anything done or omitted by the court or by any of the parties is ground for granting a new trial or for setting aside a verdict . . . unless refusal to take such action appears to the court inconsistent with substantial justice. The court at every stage of the proceeding *must* disregard any error or defect in the proceeding which does not affect the substantial rights of the parties." (Emphasis added)

While in a narrow sense Rule 61 applies only to the district courts, see Fed.Rule Civ.Proc. 1, it is well-settled that the appellate courts should act in accordance with the salutary policy embodied in Rule 61. See, e.g., Keaton v. Atchison, T.&S.F. R. Co., 321 F.2d 317, 319 (CA7 1963); Box v. Swindle, 306 F.2d 882, 887 (CA5 1962); De Santa v. Nehi Corp., 171 F.2d 696, 698 (CA2 1948). Congress has further reinforced the application of Rule 61 by enacting the harmless error statute, 28 U.S.C. § 2111, which applies directly to appellate courts and which incorporates the same principle as that found in Rule 61. See Tipton v. Socony Mobil Oil Co., 375 U.S. 34, 37, 84 S.Ct. 1, 3, 11 L.Ed.2d 4 (1963); United States v. Borden Co., 347 U.S. 514, 516 and n. 5, 74 S.Ct. 703, 705 and n. 5, 98 L.Ed. 903 (1954).[4]

4. The text of 28 U.S.C. § 2111 reads in full:

"On the hearing of any appeal or writ of certiorari in any case, the court shall give judgment after an examination of the record without regard to errors or defects which do not affect the substantial rights of the parties."

This provision traces its lineage to the harmless error provision of § 269 of the former Judicial Code, which was enacted in 1919. Act of February 26, 1919, c. 48, 40 Stat. 1181; see Kotteakos v. United States, 328 U.S. 750, 758–762, 66 S.Ct. 1239, 1244–1247, 90 L.Ed. 1557 (1946); C. Wright & A.

The ruling of the Court of Appeals in this case must be assessed against this background. One touchstone of a fair trial is an impartial trier of fact—"a jury capable and willing to decide the case solely on the evidence before it." Smith v. Phillips, 455 U.S. 209, 217, 102 S.Ct. 940, 946, 71 L.Ed.2d 78 (1982). *Voir dire* examination serves to protect that right by exposing possible biases, both known and unknown, on the part of potential jurors. Demonstrated bias in the responses to questions on *voir dire* may result in a juror's being excused for cause; hints of bias not sufficient to warrant challenge for cause may assist parties in exercising their peremptory challenges. The necessity of truthful answers by prospective jurors if this process is to serve its purpose is obvious.

The critical question posed to juror Payton in this case asked about "injuries . . . that resulted in any disability or prolonged pain or suffering." App. 19. Juror Payton apparently believed that his son's broken leg sustained as a result of an exploding tire was not such an injury. In response to a similar question from petitioner's counsel, however, another juror related such a minor incident as the fact that his 6-year-old son once caught his finger in a bike chain. Id., at 52. Yet another juror failed to respond to the question posed to juror Payton, and only the subsequent questioning of petitioner's counsel brought out that her husband had been injured in a machinery accident. Id., at 19, 53–54.

The varied responses to respondents' question on *voir dire* testify to the fact that jurors are not necessarily experts in English usage. Called as they are from all walks of life, many may be uncertain as to the meaning of terms which are relatively easily understood by lawyers and judges. Moreover, the statutory qualifications for jurors require only a minimal competency in the English language. 28 U.S.C. § 1865 (1976 ed. and Supp. V). Thus, we cannot say, and we doubt that the Court of Appeals could say, which of these three jurors was closer to the "average juror" in his or her response to the question, but it is evident that such a standard is difficult to apply and productive of uncertainties.

To invalidate the result of a 3-week trial because of a juror's mistaken, though honest, response to a question, is to insist on something closer to perfection than our judicial system can be expected to give. A trial represents an important investment of private and social resources, and it ill serves the important end of finality to wipe the slate clean simply to recreate the peremptory challenge process because counsel lacked an item of information which objectively he should have obtained from a juror on *voir dire* examination. Whatever the merits of the Court of Appeals' standard in a world which would redo and reconstruct what had gone before upon any evidence of abstract imperfection, we think it is contrary to the practical necessities of judicial

Miller, Federal Practice and Procedure
§ 2881 (1973).

managment reflected in Rule 61 and § 2111. We hold that to obtain a new trial in such a situation, a party must first demonstrate that a juror failed to answer honestly a material question on *voir dire*, and then further show that a correct response would have provided a valid basis for a challenge for cause. The motives for concealing information may vary, but only those reasons that affect a juror's impartiality can truly be said to affect the fairness of a trial.

Generally, motions for a new trial are committed to the discretion of the district court. Montgomery Ward & Co. v. Duncan, 311 U.S. 243, 251, 61 S.Ct. 189, 194, 85 L.Ed. 147 (1940). The Court of Appeals was mistaken in deciding as it did that respondents were entitled to a new trial. In the event that the issue remains relevant after the Court of Appeals has disposed of respondents' other contentions on appeal, the District Court may hold a hearing to determine whether respondents are entitled to a new trial under the principles we state here. The judgment of the Court of Appeals is

Reversed.

JUSTICE BLACKMUN, with whom JUSTICE STEVENS and JUSTICE O'CONNOR join, concurring.

I agree with the Court that the proper inquiry in this case is whether the defendant had the benefit of an impartial trier of fact. I also agree that, in most cases, the honesty or dishonesty of a juror's response is the best initial indicator of whether the juror in fact was impartial. I therefore join the Court's opinion, but I write separately to state that I understand the Court's holding not to foreclose the normal avenue of relief available to a party who is asserting that he did not have the benefit of an impartial jury. Thus, regardless of whether a juror's answer is honest or dishonest, it remains within a trial court's option, in determining whether a jury was biased, to order a post-trial hearing at which the movant has the opportunity to demonstrate actual bias or, in exceptional circumstances, that the facts are such that bias is to be inferred. See Smith v. Phillips, 455 U.S. 209, 215–216, 102 S.Ct. 940, 944–945, 71 L.Ed.2d 78 (1982); id., at 221–224, 102 S.Ct., at 948–949 (O'Connor, J., concurring).

JUSTICE BRENNAN, with whom JUSTICE MARSHALL joins, concurring in the judgment.

*   *   *

I agree with the Court that a finding that less than complete information was available to counsel conducting *voir dire* does not by itself require a new trial. I cannot join, however, in the legal standard asserted by the Court's opinion. In my view, the proper focus when ruling on a motion for new trial in this situation should be on the bias of the juror and the resulting prejudice to the litigant. More specifically, to be awarded a new trial, a litigant should be required to demonstrate that the juror incorrectly responded to a material question on *voir dire,* and that, under the facts and circumstances surrounding the particular case, the juror was biased against the moving litigant. See, e.g., McCoy v. Goldston, 652 F.2d 654, 659–660 (CA6 1981).

When applying this standard, a court should recognize that "[t]he bias of a prospective juror may be actual or implied; that is, it may be bias in fact or bias conclusively presumed as [a] matter of law." United States v. Wood, 299 U.S. 123, 133, 57 S.Ct. 177, 179, 81 L.Ed. 78 (1936). See also Smith v. Phillips, 455 U.S. 209, 221–224, 102 S.Ct. 940, 948–949, 71 L.Ed.2d 78 (1982) (O'Connor, J., concurring). * * * Whether the juror answered a particular question on *voir dire* honestly or dishonestly, or whether an inaccurate answer was inadvertent or intentional, are simply factors to be considered in this latter determination of actual bias.* I therefore cannot agree with the Court when it asserts that a new trial is not warranted whenever a prospective juror provides an honest answer to the question posed. * * * One easily can imagine cases in which a prospective juror provides what he subjectively believes to be an honest answer, yet that same answer is objectively incorrect and therefore suggests that the individual would be a biased juror in the particular case.

* * *

PEOPLE OF CALIFORNIA v. HUEY P. NEWTON

Alameda County, California, 1972.
44 So.Cal.L.Rev. 951.†

Interrogation in part of prospective juror Mr. S. by Charles R. Garry, counsel of defendant; Mr. Lowell Jensen, District Attorney.

* * *

BY MR. GARRY: Well, let me ask you this, Mr. S: You know what we are trying to arrive at, do you, sir?

A. I beg your pardon?

Q. I say, you know what * * * we are trying to ask, these questions, both Mr. Jensen and myself?

A. Yes.

Q. We are trying to give you an opportunity to speak so that we will be able to tell whether there is some hidden crevices in your mind

---

* The Court of Appeals recognized several other factors in this case, not completely acknowledged by the Court's opinion, which might suggest that juror Payton was biased or that his potential bias resulted in prejudice to the Greenwoods. For example, by claiming during his informal examination after trial that "having accidents are a part of life," Payton may have displayed insufficient sensitivity to the Greenwoods' claims in this product liability action. This potential bias could only have been exacerbated by the fact that Payton served as foreman of the jury. Moreover, the jury initially returned a verdict assessing $0.00 in damages despite the fact that

Billy Greenwood lost both his feet in the lawn mower accident; only upon reconvening after being admonished by the trial judge did the jury assess damages totaling $375,000. These factors should be considered along with any other relevant facts and circumstances by the District Court on remand.

† For more extensive voir dire transcripts and a complete discussion of this case, see Minimizing Racism in Jury Trials: The Voir Dire Conducted by Charles R. Garry in People of California v. Huey P. Newton (A. Ginger ed. 1969).

that may be an interference in the proper evaluation of that case as the evidence unfolds. You understand that?

A. Yes.

Q. Now, it's a fact, is it not, that you already had an opinion before you came here about this case?

A. Well, to a certain extent, yes.

Q. All right. Now, is your opinion that you had about this case before you got here such that it would take the tremendous amount of evidence to overcome that opinion?

A. No. It wouldn't. If—what evidence will show, that I will evaluate and see who is right and who is wrong.

Q. It's not a question so much as to who is right and who is wrong. As you sit there, Mr. S, in your opinion, right now while you are sitting there this minute, is Huey P. Newton guilty or not guilty?

A. Well, I don't know for sure whether he shot the officer or not, but the officer is dead.

Q. And by that same standard, just because the officer is dead, you are going to say that Huey Newton did it; is that right?

A. Well, that's got to be proven.

Q. Well, my question is: As you sit there right now, do you believe that Huey Newton shot and killed, stabbed, whatever it was, Officer Frey?

A. I don't know whether he shot him or not. That I can't say.

THE COURT: Mr. S, you see, under our law there is a presumption of innocence to start with. When you start the case the defendant is presumed to be innocent, and it is up to the People, the prosecution to prove to you beyond a reasonable doubt that the defendant is guilty. Do you understand that?

THE JUROR: Yes.

THE COURT: So, now, not having heard any evidence, you must start with a presumption of innocence. Do you know what I mean by presumption? You must say, "As far as I know the man is innocent." Do you understand that?

THE JUROR: Yes.

THE COURT: "And it is up to the prosecution to prove to me that he is guilty." Do you understand that?

THE JUROR: Yes.

THE COURT: So, therefore, as it stands right now, do you believe he is guilty before you hear any evidence? * * *

THE JUROR: No.

* * *

MR. GARRY: Well, do you really believe that as Huey Newton sits here right now next to me, that he is innocent of any wrongdoing of any kind?

A. No. That I don't believe.

MR. GARRY: See? There you are, Judge. I challenge this juror for cause.

THE COURT: Well, you see, I will have to explain to you again and see if you understand it, Mr. S.

The fact that the Grand Jury has indicted under our law, from that mere fact that he has been indicted by the Grand Jury, you are not to infer or presume in any way that the defendant is or must be guilty. Do you understand that?

THE JUROR: Yes.

THE COURT: Do you accept that rule of law? If you don't accept that rule of law, you don't understand it. Do you accept it? Do you understand what I am saying?

THE JUROR: (Juror nods head affirmatively.)

THE COURT: Now, under the rule of law, different places in the world have different rules of law, but it is the law of the United States and of the State of California that a defendant charged with a crime is presumed to be innocent until his guilt is established beyond and to the exclusion of every reasonable doubt. Do you understand what that means?

THE JUROR: (Juror nods head affirmatively.)

THE COURT: Now, if that is the case, you must—before you hear any evidence at all—you must start on the theory and believe that this man is innocent. But as soon as they produce proof which satisfies you beyond a reasonable doubt that he is guilty, then you can feel otherwise. Do you understand that?

THE JUROR: Yes.

THE COURT: Are you willing to start out with that theory? Are you willing to start out on that basis?

THE JUROR: Yes.

THE COURT: You may examine further.

MR. GARRY: But you are not willing, Mr. S, as you have already stated, to accept the fact that Huey Newton is absolutely innocent as he sits right now, are you, sir?

A. Well, that's a question I can't answer before I hear the evidence.

MR. GARRY: I submit the challenge, Your Honor.

THE COURT: No. I don't think that's sufficient. I think that it is a matter of semantics. Before you hear any evidence, have you got an idea that he must be guilty or else he wouldn't be here? Is that your idea?

THE JUROR: Yes.

THE COURT: Well, that is not our law, Mr. S. Under our law the fact that he is here is not any evidence at all of his guilt. You may examine further, Mr. Jensen, if you wish, but otherwise—

MR. GARRY: I submit the challenge, Your Honor.

MR. JENSEN: Let me ask you this, Mr. S: If you walked out of this courtroom right now with this jury and you went upstairs and they gave you two verdicts to vote on, guilty or not guilty, and all you know about the case is what you know right now, would you find him not guilty?

A. No, not alone on that, what I have heard here.

Q. So that there is no evidence at all for you to make a verdict; is that right?

A. That's correct.

Q. So there is no evidence that would justify you in finding the man guilty; is that correct?

A. (Juror nods head affirmatively.)

Q. In other words, as Mr. Newton sits there, you, as a juror, have no evidence about any of the charges in this case; is that correct?

A. Right.

Q. Now, the District Attorney, the prosecution has the burden of bringing some evidence in before you before anything can happen. Do you understand that?

A. Yes.

Q. Now, if the District Attorney does not produce any evidence at all, the man is not guilty. Isn't that correct?

A. That's right.

Q. So that if you are to deliberate right now you have no evidence; isn't that right?

A. That's right.

Q. So you would find him not guilty; isn't that right?

Q. Is there any evidence as far as you are concerned right now that Mr. Newton is guilty of anything?

A. No.

Q. The fact that there has been a charge here, that is that he is charged with murder, assault, and kidnapping, is that, as far as you are concerned, evidence that he is guilty of anything?

A. No. That isn't evidence, no.

Q. As far as you are concerned, what is evidence?

A. What I am going to hear here in Court.

Q. Is that going to come from witnesses, as far as you are concerned?

A. From witnesses, yes.

Q. It is not going to be newspapers or anything like that?

A. No.

Q. Will you decide the case, just on what the witnesses say?

A. Yes.

MR. JENSEN: As Your Honor said, I think this is a semantic problem.

THE COURT: You may examine further, Mr. Garry.

BY MR. GARRY: Mr. S, again I ask you that same question which you have answered three times to me now * * * . As Huey Newton sits here next to me now, in your opinion is he absolutely innocent?

A. Yes.

Q. But you don't believe it, do you?

A. No.

THE COURT: Challenge is allowed.

NOTE ON VOIR DIRE

1. Voir Dire Procedure

In Levitt, Nelson, Ball and Chernick, Expediting Voir Dire: An Empirical Study, 44 So.Cal.L.Rev. 916, 928–30 (1971) (footnotes omitted), three voir dire methods are set forth:

"The first, denominated the federal method because of its codification in the federal rules, is characterized by complete judge control of the examination. The initial questioning is done by the judge; residuary examination in areas not covered, or more detailed questioning about matters already discussed, may be suggested by the attorney and posed to the jury by the court. * * *

"The second general sort of voir dire technique is for convenience denominated the 'state method.' The hallmark of a state method voir dire is the combined questioning of a venire by court and counsel. It should not be forgotten, however, that there are as many degrees of court-counsel control in a state method voir dire as there are judges. But typical state impanelment is one in which both judge and counsel conduct some portion of the questioning. Usually the more obvious and perfunctory questions are asked of the venire by the court; then the questioning is turned over to the attorneys who have ample opportunity to delve deeply into the matters unique to that particular case. The only limitation on the sorts of questions that may be put to the prospective juror is the judge's interpretation of the case law on what sorts of questions are impermissible.

"Finally, there is a relatively new method of jury impanelment, tried in only a few jurisdictions, the touchstone of which is the examination of prospective jurors by counsel out of the presence of the court. The method was first used in New York, and it was adapted for use in the Los Angeles Superior Court initially for testing purposes during the early months of 1970. Under the 'New York' method, sometimes referred to as the Bench and Bar Cooperative Jury Selection Plan, a judge is only present for a short time to administer an oath and explain the procedures to the venire. On his departure, counsel conduct the entire examination themselves, and the judge is only summoned when problems or disagreements arise. When the jury is impaneled, they are transferred to an available courtroom for the commencement of trial."

Compare Federal Judicial Center, Conduct of the Voir Dire Examination: Practices and Opinions of Federal District Judges (1977) (most federal judges conduct the entire examination, asking additional questions propounded by counsel; only about 20% allow counsel to put questions directly to the jury). See also Babcock, Voir Dire: Preserving "Its Wonderful Power," 27 Stan.L.Rev. 545 (1975); Suggs and Sales, Juror Self-Disclosure in the Voir Dire, 56 Ind.L.J. 245 (1981); Note, Juror Bias: A Practical Screening Device and the Case for Permitting its Use, 64 Minn.L.Rev. 987 (1980) (attitude questionnaire in criminal cases).

California Rules of Court, Superior Court Rule 228 provides:

" * * * [T]he trial judge shall examine the prospective jurors and upon completion of the initial examination * * * shall permit counsel for each party * * * to submit additional questions which the judge shall put to the jurors. Upon request of counsel, the trial judge shall permit counsel to supplement the judge's examination by oral and direct questioning of any of the prospective jurors. * * * In civil cases, the court may, upon stipulation by * * * all parties * * * permit counsel to examine the prospective jurors outside a judge's presence."

Commercial enterprises often make available to counsel "jury books," containing for each juror on the panel for a particular term of court the juror's name, address and occupation, how she voted in other cases, the amount of verdicts rendered by juries on which she sat, and like information. Is their use unethical? See Baugh v. Beatty, 91 Cal.App.2d 786, 205 P.2d 071 (1949), holding that it is not. Compare Zeisel and Diamond, The Jury Selection in the Mitchell-Stans Conspiracy Trial, 1976 A.B.F.Res.J. 151.

For an empirical appraisal of voir dire, see Penrod and Linz, Voir Dire: Uses and Abuses, in Kaplan, ed., The Impact of Social Psychology on Procedural Justice (1986).

2. Challenge for Cause

Was the successful challenge of juror Mr. S in People v. Newton, supra, vindication of voir dire interrogation by counsel compared to that by court? Or a mere triumph of semantic trickery? For some of the complications that can arise if a juror's bias is discovered during the course of the trial, see People v. Compton, 6 Cal.3d 55, 98 Cal.Rptr. 217, 490 P.2d 537 (1971). See also Tapia v. Barker, 160 Cal.App.3d 761, 206 Cal.Rptr. 803 (1984) (holding that failure of jury member to reveal racial bias in voir dire was prejudicial concealment warranting a new trial).

How far the court is required to go in probing for cause, particularly in cases where race is a factor, is far from clear. See Rosales-Lopez v. United States, 451 U.S. 182, 101 S.Ct. 1629, 68 L.Ed.2d 22 (1981). While questioning of jurors should not only probe for cause but also provide some foundation for peremptory challenge, the court also has to consider protecting prospective jurors from harassment or retribution, particularly in criminal cases. The balance is uneasy. See, e.g., United States v. Gibbons, 602 F.2d 1044 (2d Cir. 1979).

3. Peremptory Challenge

Peremptory challenges are those for which no reason need be assigned; they are arbitrary choices by counsel for any reason, or for no reason at all. Traditionally, this description of peremptory challenges applied with no qualifications, but in recent years the courts have, somewhat reluctantly, agreed to scrutinize their exercise more closely in certain circumstances.

In Swain v. Alabama, 380 U.S. 202, 85 S.Ct. 824, 13 L.Ed.2d 759 (1965), the Supreme Court held that it was not a prima facie denial of due process for a prosecutor to use peremptory challenges to strike all members of an accused's race from a jury, and the Court set up a formidable evidentiary burden for defendants wishing to prove a due process violation. See Comment, Peremptory Challenges and the Meaning of Jury Representation, 89 Yale L.J. 1177 (1980). Some state courts reached a contrary result by applying their own constitutional provisions, see, e.g., People v. Wheeler, 22 Cal.3d 258, 148 Cal. Rptr. 890, 583 P.2d 748 (1978); Commonwealth v. Soares, 377 Mass. 461, 387 N.E.2d 499 (1979). The Supreme Court itself significantly eased the evidentiary burden placed on the defendant by *Swain* in Batson v. Kentucky, 476 U.S. 79, 106 S.Ct. 1712, 90 L.Ed.2d 69 (1986), where it held that it is unconstitutional to systematically strike all members of an accused's race from a jury if (1) the accused can establish a prima facie case that the prosecutor used that practice in his trial, and (2) the prosecutor fails to rebut that case with a neutral explanation for peremptorily challenging jurors of the accused's race. See also People v. Snow, 44 Cal.3d 216, 242 Cal.Rptr. 477, 746 P.2d 452 (1987); People v. Trevino, 39 Cal.3d 667, 217 Cal.Rptr. 652, 704 P.2d 719 (1985) (conviction overturned where prosecutor exercised peremptory challenges to exclude all Spanish-surnamed veniremen).

The applicability of Batson v. Kentucky to civil cases is not clear. Compare Esposito v. Buonome, 642 F.Supp. 760 (D.Conn.1986) (*Batson* not applicable to civil case) with Edmonson v. Leesville Concrete Co., 860 F.2d 1308 (5th Cir. 1988) (*Batson* applicable to civil case); Fludd v. Dykes, 863 F.2d 822 (11th Cir. 1989) (same). See also Note, Rethinking Limitations on the Peremptory Challenge, 85 Colum.L.Rev. 1357 (1985); Comment, Vitiation of Peremptory Challenge in Civil Actions, 61 St. John's L.Rev. 155 (1986).

The peremptory challenge reflects tactical decisions to get rid of persons considered likely to be undesirable from the viewpoint of the challenger. In California in Superior Court civil cases, each party is ordinarily entitled to six peremptory challenges. If there are more than two parties on a "side," each "side" has eight peremptories. C.C.P. 601. In most jurisdictions a more modest number of peremptories, usually three, is permitted. See, e.g., 28 U.S.C.A. § 1870; cf. Anno., 32 A.L.R.3d 747.

It is now widely recognized that voir dire examination may include questions designed to elicit information helpful to the intelligent exercise of peremptory challenges. The Supreme Court discussed this principle in *Swain*, supra, and it was the basis for reversal of a jury verdict in Kiernan v. Van Schaik, 347 F.2d 775 (3d Cir. 1965), where the trial judge severely restricted the scope of voir dire examination. See also Art Press, Ltd. v. Western Printing Mach. Co., 791 F.2d 616 (7th Cir. 1986); People v. Williams, 29 Cal.3d 392, 174 Cal.Rptr. 317, 628 P.2d 869 (1981); Note, Voir Dire for California's Civil Trials: Applying the Williams Standard, 39 Hastings L.J. 517 (1988); Note, Voir Dire: Establishing Minimum Standards to Facilitate the Exercise of Peremptory Challenges, 27 Stan.L.Rev. 1493 (1975). But, as shown by McDonough Power Equipment,

Inc. v. Greenwood, supra p. 1070, a complaining party may have to meet a burden of proving actual prejudice where the fault lies not with the court's restriction of questioning but with a juror's failure to disclose possibly relevant information.

While the Federal Jury Selection and Service Act of 1968, 28 U.S.C.A. § 1862, prohibits exclusion from jury service based on race, color, religion, sex, national origin, or economic status, trial lawyers believe these factors are relevant in selecting a jury. See Picking a Jury, The New Yorker, February 26, 1972, p. 70. A variant method of exercising peremptory challenges is the "struck jury," in which a group of prospective jurors is cleared for cause and then peremptories are exercised alternately by the parties. See United States v. Morris, 623 F.2d 145 (10th Cir. 1980); Ter Keurst v. Miami Elevator Co., 453 So.2d 501 (Fla.App.1984).

2. THE JUDGE

LILJEBERG v. HEALTH SERVICES ACQUISITION CORP.

Supreme Court of the United States, 1988.
___ U.S. ___, 108 S.Ct. 2194, 100 L.Ed.2d 855.*

JUSTICE STEVENS delivered the opinion of the Court.

* * *

I

In November 1981, respondent Health Services Acquisition Corp. brought an action against petitioner John Liljeberg, Jr., seeking a declaration of ownership of a corporation known as St. Jude Hospital of Kenner, Louisiana (St. Jude). The case was tried by Judge Robert Collins, sitting without a jury. Judge Collins found for Liljeberg and, over a strong dissent, the Court of Appeals affirmed. Approximately 10 months later, respondent learned that Judge Collins had been a member of the Board of Trustees of Loyola University while Liljeberg was negotiating with Loyola to purchase a parcel of land on which to construct a hospital. The success and benefit to Loyola of these negotiations turned, in large part, on Liljeberg prevailing in the litigation before Judge Collins.

Based on this information, respondent moved pursuant to Federal Rule of Civil Procedure 60(b)(6) to vacate the judgment on the ground that Judge Collins was disqualified under [28 U.S.C.A.] § 455 at the time he heard the action and entered judgment in favor of Liljeberg. Judge Collins denied the motion and respondent appealed. The Court of Appeals determined that resolution of the motion required factual findings concerning the extent and timing of Judge Collins' knowledge of Loyola's interest in the declaratory relief litigation. Accordingly, the panel reversed and remanded the matter to a different judge for such findings. App. to Pet. for Cert. 40a. On remand, the District Court found that based on his attendance at Board meetings Judge Collins

---

* Some of the Court's footnotes are omitted.

had actual knowledge of Loyola's interest in St. Jude in 1980 and 1981. The court further concluded, however, that Judge Collins had forgotten about Loyola's interest by the time the declaratory judgment suit came to trial in January 1982. On March 24, 1982, Judge Collins reviewed materials sent to him by the Board to prepare for an upcoming meeting. At that time—just a few days after he had filed his opinion finding for Liljeberg and still within the 10–day period allowed for filing a motion for a new trial—Judge Collins once again obtained actual knowledge of Loyola's interest in St. Jude. Finally, the District Court found that although Judge Collins thus lacked actual knowledge during trial and prior to the filing of his opinion, the evidence nonetheless gave rise to an appearance of impropriety. However, reading the Court of Appeals' mandate as limited to the issue of actual knowledge, the District Court concluded that it was compelled to deny respondent's Rule 60(b) motion. App. to Pet. for Cert. 14a.

The Court of Appeals again reversed. The court first noted that Judge Collins should have immediately disqualified himself when his actual knowledge of Loyola's interest was renewed. The court also found that regardless of Judge Collins' actual knowledge, "a reasonable observer would expect that Judge Collins would remember that Loyola had some dealings with Liljeberg and St. Jude and seek to ascertain the nature of these dealings." 796 F.2d 796, 803 (1986). Such an appearance of impropriety, in the view of the Court of Appeals, was sufficient ground for disqualification under § 455(a). Although recognizing that caution is required in determining whether a judgment should be vacated after becoming final, the court concluded that since the appearance of partiality was convincingly established and since the motion to vacate was filed as promptly as possible, the appropriate remedy was to vacate the declaratory relief judgment. Because the issues presented largely turn on the facts as they give rise to an appearance of impropriety, it is necessary to relate the sequence and substance of these events in some detail.

II

Petitioner, John Liljeberg, Jr., is a pharmacist, a promoter, and a half-owner of Axel Realty, Inc., a real estate brokerage firm. In 1976, he became interested in a project to construct and operate a hospital in Kenner, Louisiana, a suburb of New Orleans. * * * The successful operation of such a hospital depended upon the acquisition of a "certificate of need" from the State of Louisiana; without such a certificate the hospital would not qualify for health care reimbursement payments under the federal medicare and medicaid programs. * * *

During the next two years Liljeberg engaged in serious negotiations with at least two major parties. One set of negotiations involved a proposal to purchase a large tract of land from Loyola University for use as a hospital site, coupled with a plan to rezone adjoining University property. The proposed benefits to the University included not only the proceeds of the real estate sale itself, amounting to several million dollars, but also a substantial increase in the value to the University of the rezoned adjoining property. The progress of these negotiations was regularly reported to the University's Board of Trustees by its Real Estate Committee and discussed at Board meetings. The minutes of those meetings indicate that the University's interest in the project was dependent on the issuance of the certificate of need.[3]

Liljeberg was also conducting serious negotiations with respondent's corporate predecessor, Hospital Affiliates International (HAI), a national health management company. In the summer of 1980, Liljeberg and HAI reached an agreement in principle, outlining their respective roles in developing the hospital. The agreement contemplated that HAI would purchase a tract of land in Kenner (not owned by the University) and construct the hospital on that land; prepare and file the certificate of need; and retain Liljeberg as a consultant to the hospital in various capacities. In turn, it was understood that Liljeberg would transfer St. Jude to HAI. Pursuant to this preliminary agreement, various documents were executed, including an agreement by HAI to purchase the tract of land from its owner for five million dollars and a further agreement by HAI to place $500,000 in escrow. In addition, it was agreed that Axel Realty, Inc., would receive a $250,000 commission for locating the property. Eventually, Liljeberg signed a "warranty and indemnity agreement," which HAI understood to transfer ownership of St. Jude to HAI. After the warranty and indemnity agreement was signed, HAI filed an application for the certificate of need.

On August 26, 1981, the certificate of need was issued and delivered to Liljeberg. He promptly advised HAI and HAI paid the real estate commission to Axel Realty. A dispute arose, however, over whether the warranty and indemnity agreement did in fact transfer ownership of St. Jude to HAI. Liljeberg contended that the transfer of ownership of St. Jude—and hence, the certificate of need—was conditioned upon reaching a final agreement concerning his continued

3. The District Court found:

"Discussions of the St. Jude Hospital project are reflected in the minutes of the next meeting of the Board of Trustees on January 24, 1980, which Judge Collins attended. See Plaintiff's Exhibit 22. Liljeberg's first offer on behalf of St. Jude Properties to purchase approximately 75 acres of Loyola's Kenner property was presented in a Real Estate Committee report, which was summarized in the Board minutes. The minutes also include the response of Loyola University to Liljeberg, including the Committee's expression of interest in continuing negotiations with St. Jude Properties. The minutes further reflect the Real Estate Committee's communication to Liljeberg that 'until a certificate of need were forthcoming, Loyola would more than likely not be interested in the project.' The minutes outline the terms of a second offer received by Loyola University from St. Jude Properties raising the purchase price by $7,000.00 per acre, 'with no financing necessary and no commitments of any kind except the dedication of 110 feet for roadway purposes, with the improvement cost paid totally by the Liljeberg group.' The minutes elaborate on the details of the offer, including St. Jude Properties' desire for a sixty day period to secure financing to finalize the sale." App. to Pet. for Cert. 19a–20a.

participation in the hospital project. This contention was not supported by any written instrument. HAI denied that there was any such unwritten understanding and insisted that, by virtue of the warranty and indemnity agreement, it had been sole owner of St. Jude for over a year. The dispute gave rise to this litigation.

Respondent filed its complaint for declaratory judgment on November 30, 1981. The case was tried by Judge Collins, sitting without a jury, on January 21 and January 22, 1982. At the close of the evidence, he announced his intended ruling, and on March 16, 1982, he filed a judgment (dated Mar. 12, 1982) and his findings of fact and conclusions of law. He credited Liljeberg's version of oral conversations that were disputed and of critical importance in his ruling.[5]

During the period between November 30, 1981, and March 16, 1982, Judge Collins was a trustee of Loyola University, but was not conscious of the fact that the University and Liljeberg were then engaged in serious negotiations concerning the Kenner hospital project, or of the further fact that the success of those negotiations depended upon his conclusion that Liljeberg controlled the certificate of need. To determine whether Judge Collins' impartiality in the Liljeberg litigation "might reasonably be questioned," it is appropriate to consider the state of his knowledge immediately before the lawsuit was filed, what happened while the case was pending before him, and what he did when he learned of the University's interest in the litigation.

After the certificate of need was issued, and Liljeberg and HAI became embroiled in their dispute, Liljeberg reopened his negotiations with the University. On October 29, 1981, the Real Estate Committee sent a written report to each of the trustees, including Judge Collins, advising them of "a significant change" concerning the proposed hospital in Kenner and stating specifically that Loyola's property had "again

---

5. For example, Liljeberg's attorney testified that before returning the signed copy of the warranty and indemnity agreement to HAI, he told HAI's associate corporate counsel that Liljeberg would not transfer ownership of St. Jude until they reached a binding agreement concerning Liljeberg's continued participation in the hospital project. HAI's associate corporate counsel testified that no such conversation occurred. App. to Pet. for Cert. 61a, n. 3.

Although noting this conflicting testimony, the Fifth Circuit held on appeal that Judge Collins did not abuse his discretion in awarding the certificate to Liljeberg. Judge Rubin, in dissent, pointed to another example of where Liljeberg received the benefit of the doubt on a critical disputed fact. Liljeberg's attorney received the proposed warranty and indemnity agreement from HAI under cover of a letter which stated: ". . . I believe this is the only document . . . that would be needed in effecting the transfer." Id., at 60a, n. 2.

Liljeberg's attorney testified, however, that he did not read the letter of transmittal. Yet, as Judge Rubin observed:

"It is curious that a lawyer would fail to read a letter that comes to him attached to an important document. It is curiouser, as Alice said, after she had passed through the looking glass into Wonderland, that Liljeberg, who repeatedly testified that he distrusted HAI although he had contemplated entering into a complex and potentially lucrative relationship with the corporation, designed to operate over a seven-year period, did not respond to the cover letter. . . .

"It is curiouser still that [Liljeberg's attorney], who testified that he did not read the cover letter, nevertheless knew that HAI believed that the Warranty and Indemnity Agreement was sufficient to transfer 'ownership.'" Id., at 75a, n. 4.

become a prime location." App. 72. The Committee submitted a draft of a resolution authorizing a University vice-president "to continue negotiations with the developers of the St. Jude Hospital." Id., at 73. At the Board meeting on November 12, 1981, which Judge Collins attended, the trustees discussed the connection between the rezoning of Loyola's land in Kenner and the St. Jude project and adopted the Real Estate Committee's proposed resolution. Thus, Judge Collins had actual knowledge of the University's potential interest in the St. Jude hospital project in Kenner just a few days before the complaint was filed.

While the case was pending before Judge Collins, the University agreed to sell 80 acres of its land in Kenner to Liljeberg for $6,694,000. The progress of negotiations was discussed at a Board meeting on January 28, 1982. Judge Collins did not attend that meeting, but the Real Estate Committee advised the trustees that "the federal courts have determined that the certificate of need will be awarded to the St. Jude Corporation." Id., at 37. Presumably this advice was based on Judge Collins' comment at the close of the hearing a week earlier, when he announced his intended ruling because he thought "it would be unfair to keep the parties in doubt as to how I feel about the case." App. to Pet. for Cert. 41a.

The formal agreement between Liljeberg and the University was apparently executed on March 19th. App. 50–58. The agreement stated that it was not in any way conditioned on Liljeberg's prevailing in the litigation "pending in the U.S. District Court for the Eastern District of Louisiana . . . involving the obtaining by [Liljeberg] of a Certificate of Need," id., at 55, but it also gave the University the right to repurchase the property for the contract price if Liljeberg had not executed a satisfactory construction contract within one year and further provided for nullification of the contract in the event the rezoning of the University's adjoining land was not accomplished. Thus, the University continued to have an active interest in the outcome of the litigation because it was unlikely that Liljeberg could build the hospital if he lost control of the certificate of need; moreover, the rezoning was in turn dependent on the hospital project.[6]

---

6. As the Court of Appeals pointed out:

"The district court's determination that Loyola's interest in the litigation terminated as of March 19, 1982 is clearly erroneous. Although the agreement between Loyola and Liljeberg was not contingent on the outcome of the lawsuit, as a practical matter Loyola still had a substantial interest in Liljeberg's obtaining the certificate of approval. Without the certificate, it is very likely that Liljeberg would not have been able to build the hospital on the Monroe Tract. The construction of a hospital on its property was extremely important to Loyola as shown by the fact that Loyola was allowed under its agreement with Liljeberg to repurchase the land if a hospital was not built. Furthermore, the construction of a hospital on the Monroe Tract was critical to the effort to rezone the surrounding property owned by Loyola; the rezoning was also of vital interest to Loyola. Therefore, Loyola's interest in the litigation did not terminate as of March 19, 1982 and Judge Collins should have recused himself when he obtained actual knowledge of that interest on March 24." 796 F.2d, at 800–801.

The details of the transaction were discussed in three letters to the trustees dated March 12, March 15, and March 19, 1982, but Judge Collins did not examine any of those letters until shortly before the Board meeting on March 25, 1982. Thus, he acquired actual knowledge of Loyola's interest in the litigation on March 24, 1982. As the Court of Appeals correctly held, "Judge Collins should have recused himself when he obtained actual knowledge of that interest on March 24." 796 F.2d, at 801.

In considering whether the Court of Appeals properly vacated the declaratory relief judgment, we are required to address two questions. We must first determine whether § 455(a) can be violated based on an appearance of partiality, even though the judge was not conscious of the circumstances creating the appearance of impropriety, and second, whether relief is available under Rule 60(b) when such a violation is not discovered until after the judgment has become final.

III

Title 28 U.S.C. § 455 provides in relevant part: [7]

"(a) Any justice, judge, or magistrate of the United States shall disqualify himself in any proceeding in which his impartiality might reasonably be questioned.

"(b) He shall also disqualify himself in the following circumstances:

. . .

"(4) He knows that he, individually or as a fiduciary, or his spouse or minor child residing in his household, has a financial interest in the subject matter in controversy or in a party to the proceeding, or any other interest that could be substantially affected by the outcome of the proceeding.

. . .

"(c) A judge should inform himself about his personal and fiduciary financial interests, and make a reasonable effort to inform himself about the personal financial interests of his spouse and minor children residing in his household."

---

7. Prior to the 1974 amendments, § 455 simply provided:

"Any justice or judge of the United States shall disqualify himself in any case in which he has a substantial interest, has been of counsel, is or has been a material witness, or is so related to or connected with any party or his attorney as to render it improper, in his opinion, for him to sit on the trial, appeal, or other proceeding therein." 62 Stat. 908.

The statute was amended in 1974 to clarify and broaden the grounds for judicial disqualification and to conform with the recently adopted ABA Code of Judicial Conduct, Canon 3C (1984). See S.Rep. No. 93–419, p. 1 (1973); H.R.Rep. No. 93–1453, pp. 1–2 (1974), U.S.Code Cong. & Admin. News 1974, p. 6351. The general language of subsection (a) was designed to promote public confidence in the integrity of judicial process by replacing the subjective "in his opinion" standard with an objective test. See S.Rep. No. 93–419, at 5 (1973); H.R.Rep. No. 93–1453, at 5, U.S.Code Cong. & Admin.News 1974, p. 6355.

Scienter is not an element of a violation of § 455(a). The judge's lack of knowledge of a disqualifying circumstance may bear on the question of remedy, but it does not eliminate the risk that "his impartiality might reasonably be questioned" by other persons. To read § 455(a) to provide that the judge must know of the disqualifying facts, requires not simply ignoring the language of the provision—which makes no mention of knowledge—but further requires concluding that the language in subsection (b)(4)—which expressly provides that the judge must *know* of his or her interest—is extraneous. A careful reading of the respective subsections makes clear that Congress intended to require knowledge under subsection (b)(4) and not to require knowledge under subsection (a).[8] Moreover, advancement of the purpose of the provision—to promote public confidence in the integrity of the judicial process, see S.Rep. No. 93–419, p. 5 (1973); H.R.Rep. No. 93–1453, p. 5 (1974)—does not depend upon whether or not the judge actually knew of facts creating an appearance of impropriety, so long as the public might reasonably believe that he or she knew. As Chief Judge Clark of the Court of Appeals explained:

> "The goal of section 455(a) is to avoid even the appearance of partiality. If it would appear to a reasonable person that a judge has knowledge of facts that would give him an interest in the litigation then an appearance of partiality is created even though no actual partiality exists because the judge does not recall the facts, because the judge actually has no interest in the case or because the judge is pure in heart and incorruptible. The judge's forgetfulness, however, is not the sort of objectively ascertainable fact that can avoid the appearance of partiality. Hall v. Small Business Administration, 695 F.2d 175, 179 (5th Cir.1983). Under section 455(a), therefore, recusal is required even when a judge lacks actual knowledge of the facts indicating his interest or bias in the case if a reasonable person, knowing all the circumstances,

---

8. Petitioner contends that § 455(a) must be construed in light of § 455(b)(4). He argues that the reference to knowledge in § 455(b)(4) indicates that Congress must have intended that scienter be an element under § 455(a) as well. Petitioner reasons that § 455(a) is a catchall provision, encompassing all of the specifically enumerated grounds for disqualification under § 455(b), as well as other grounds not specified. Not requiring knowledge under § 455(a), in petitioner's view, would thus render meaningless the knowledge requirement under § 455(b)(4). The requirement could always be circumvented by simply moving for disqualification under § 455(a), rather than § 455(b).

Petitioner's argument ignores important differences between subsections (a) and (b) (4). Most importantly, § 455(b)(4) requires

disqualification no matter how insubstantial the financial interest and regardless of whether or not the interest actually creates an appearance of impropriety. See § 455(d)(4); In re Cement and Concrete Litigation, 515 F.Supp. 1076 (Ariz.1981), mandamus denied, 688 F.2d 1297 (CA9 1982), aff'd by the absence of quorum, 459 U.S. 1191, 103 S.Ct. 1173, 75 L.Ed.2d 425 (1983). In addition, § 455(e) specifies that a judge may not accept a waiver of any ground for disqualification under § 455(b), but may accept such a waiver under § 455(a) after "a full disclosure on the record of the basis for disqualification." Section 455(b) is therefore a somewhat stricter provision, and thus is not simply redundant with the broader coverage of § 455(a) as petitioner's argument posits.

would expect that the judge would have actual knowledge." 796 F.2d, at 802.

Contrary to petitioner's contentions, this reading of the statute does not call upon judges to perform the impossible—to disqualify themselves based on facts they do not know. If, as petitioner argues, § 455(a) should only be applied prospectively, then requiring disqualification based on facts the judge does not know would of course be absurd; a judge could never be expected to disqualify himself based on some fact he does not know, even though the fact is one that perhaps he should know or one that people might reasonably suspect that he does know. But to the extent the provision can also, in proper cases, be applied retroactively, the judge is not called upon to perform an impossible feat. Rather, he is called upon to rectify an oversight and to take the steps necessary to maintain public confidence in the impartiality of the judiciary. If he concludes that "his impartiality might reasonably be questioned," then he should also find that the statute has been violated. This is certainly not an impossible task. No one questions that Judge Collins could have disqualified himself and vacated his judgment when he finally realized that Loyola had an interest in the litigation. The initial appeal was taken from his failure to disqualify himself and vacate the judgment *after* he became aware of the appearance of impropriety, not from his failure to disqualify himself when he first became involved in the litigation and lacked the requisite knowledge.

In this case both the District Court and the Court of Appeals found an ample basis in the record for concluding that an objective observer would have questioned Judge Collins' impartiality. Accordingly, even though his failure to disqualify himself was the product of a temporary lapse of memory, it was nevertheless a plain violation of the terms of the statute.

A conclusion that a statutory violation occurred does not, however, end our inquiry. As in other areas of the law, there is surely room for harmless error committed by busy judges who inadvertently overlook a disqualifying circumstance.[9] There need not be a draconian remedy for every violation of § 455(a). It would be equally wrong, however, to adopt an absolute prohibition against any relief in cases involving forgetful judges.

---

9. Large, multidistrict class actions, for example, often present judges with unique difficulties in monitoring any potential interest they may have in the litigation. In such cases, the judge is required to familiarize him or herself with the named parties and all the members of the class, which in an extreme case may number in the hundreds or even thousands. This already difficult task is confounded by the fact that the precise contours of the class are often not defined until well into the litigation. See Union Carbide Corp. v. U.S. Cutting Service, Inc., 782 F.2d 710, 714 (CA7 1986); In re Cement and Concrete Antitrust Litigation, 515 F.Supp., at 1080.

Of course, notwithstanding the size and complexity of the litigation, judges remain under a duty to stay informed of any personal or fiduciary financial interest they may have in cases over which they preside. See 28 U.S.C. § 455(c). The complexity of determining the conflict, however, may have a bearing on the Rule 60(b)(6) extraordinary circumstance analysis.

IV

Although § 455 defines the circumstances that mandate disqualification of federal judges, it neither prescribes nor prohibits any particular remedy for a violation of that duty. Congress has wisely delegated to the judiciary the task of fashioning the remedies that will best serve the purpose of the legislation. In considering whether a remedy is appropriate, we do well to bear in mind that in many cases—and this is such an example—the Court of Appeals is in a better position to evaluate the significance of a violation than is this Court. Its judgment as to the proper remedy should thus be afforded our due consideration. A review of the facts demonstrates that the Court of Appeals' determination that a new trial is in order is well supported.

Section 455 does not, on its own, authorize the reopening of closed litigation. However, as respondent and the Court of Appeals recognized, Federal Rules of Civil Procedure 60(b) provides a procedure whereby, in appropriate cases, a party may be relieved of a final judgment.[10] In particular, Rule 60(b)(6), upon which respondent relies, grants federal courts broad authority to relieve a party from a final judgment "upon such terms as are just," provided that the motion is made within a reasonable time and is not premised on one of the grounds for relief enumerated in clauses (b)(1) through (b)(5).[11] The

10. Federal Rule Civil Procedure 60(b) provides in relevant part:

"On motion and upon such terms as are just, the court may relieve a party or a party's legal representative from a final judgment, order, or proceeding for the following reasons: (1) mistake, inadvertence, surprise, or excusable neglect; (2) newly discovered evidence which by due diligence could not have been discovered in time to move for a new trial under Rule 59(b); (3) fraud . . ., misrepresentation, or other misconduct of an adverse party; . . . or (6) any other reason justifying relief from the operation of the judgment. The motion shall be made within a reasonable time, and for reasons (1), (2), and (3) not more than one year after the judgment, order, or proceeding was entered or taken."

11. In Klapprott v. United States, 335 U.S. 601, 613 (1949), we held that a party may "not avail himself of the broad 'any other reason' clause of 60(b)" if his motion is based on grounds specified in clause (1)— "mistake, inadvertence, surprise or excusable neglect." Rather, "extraordinary circumstances" are required to bring the motion within the "other reason" language and to prevent clause (6) from being used to circumvent the 1–year limitations period that applies to clause (1). This logic, of course, extends beyond clause (1) and sug-

gests that clause (6) and clauses (1) through (5) are mutually exclusive. See 11 C. Wright & A. Miller, Federal Practice and Procedure § 2864 (1973). We conclude that the basis for relief in this case is extraordinary and that the motion was thus proper under clause (6). * * * Of particular importance, this is not a case involving neglect or lack of due diligence by respondent. Any such neglect is rather chargeable to Judge Collins. Had he informed the parties of his association with Loyola and of Loyola's interest in the litigation on March 24, 1982, when his knowledge of the University's interest was renewed, respondent could have raised the issue in a motion for a new trial or on appeal without requiring that the case be reopened. Moreover, even if respondent had taken the unusual step of reviewing the Judge's financial disclosure forms— which reveal that he was a member of the Board of Trustees—the conflict would not have been brought to its attention. The conflict arose not simply from the Judge's service on the Board of Trustees, but from his service on the Board while the University was involved in its dealings with Liljeberg. This latter fact would not have been made apparent through examination of the disclosure reports and, according to respondent, was not a matter of public

rule does not particularize the factors that justify relief, but we have previously noted that it provides courts with authority "adequate to enable them to vacate judgments whenever such action is appropriate to accomplish justice," Klapprott v. United States, 335 U.S. 601, 614–615, 69 S.Ct. 384, 390, 93 L.Ed. 266 (1949), while also cautioning that it should only be applied in "extraordinary circumstances," Ackermann v. United States, 340 U.S. 193, 71 S.Ct. 209, 95 L.Ed. 207 (1950). Rule 60(b)(6) relief is accordingly neither categorically available nor categorically unavailable for all § 455 violations. We conclude that in determining whether a judgment should be vacated for a violation of § 455, it is appropriate to consider the risk of injustice to the parties in the particular case, the risk that the denial of relief will produce injustice in other cases, and the risk of undermining the public's confidence in the judicial process. We must continuously bear in mind that "to perform its high function in the best way 'justice must satisfy the appearance of justice.' " In re Murchison, 349 U.S. 133, 136, 75 S.Ct. 623, 625, 99 L.Ed. 942 (1955) (citation omitted).

Like the Court of Appeals, we accept the District Court's finding that while the case was actually being tried Judge Collins did not have actual knowledge of Loyola's interest in the dispute over the ownership of St. Jude and its precious certificate of need. When a busy federal judge concentrates his or her full attention on a pending case, personal concerns are easily forgotten. The problem, however, is that people who have not served on the bench are often all too willing to indulge suspicions and doubts concerning the integrity of judges.[12] The very purpose of § 455(a) is to promote confidence in the judiciary by avoiding even the appearance of impropriety whenever possible. See S.Rep. No. 93–419, at 5; H.R.Rep. No. 93–1453, at 5. Thus, it is critically important in a case of this kind to identify the facts that might reasonably cause an objective observer to question Judge Collins' impartiality. There are at least four such facts.

First, it is remarkable that the judge, who had regularly attended the meetings of the Board of Trustees since 1977, completely forgot

record at the time the case was tried and decided.

12. As we held in Aetna Life Ins. Co. v. Lavoie, 475 U.S. 813, 106 S.Ct. 1580, 89 L.Ed.2d 823 (1986), this concern has constitutional dimensions. In that case we wrote:

"We conclude that Justice Embry's participation in this case violated appellant's due process rights as explicated in Tumey [v. Ohio, 273 U.S. 510, 47 S.Ct. 437, 71 L.Ed. 749 (1927)], Murchison, and Ward [v. Village of Monroeville, 409 U.S. 57, 93 S.Ct. 80, 34 L.Ed.2d 267 (1972)]. We make clear that we are not required to decide whether in fact Justice Embry was influenced, but only whether sitting on the case then before the Supreme Court of Alabama ' "would

offer a possible temptation to the average [judge] . . . [to] lead him not to hold the balance nice, clear and true." ' The Due Process Clause 'may sometimes bar trial by judges who have no actual bias and who would do their very best to weigh the scales of justice equally between contending parties. But to perform its high function in the best way, "justice must satisfy the appearance of justice." ' " Id., at 825, 106 S.Ct. at 1587. (citations omitted).

A finding by another judge—faced with the difficult task of passing upon the integrity of a fellow member of the bench—that his or her colleague merely possessed *constructive* knowledge, and not *actual* knowledge, is unlikely to significantly quell the concerns of the skeptic.

about the University's interest in having a hospital constructed on its property in Kenner. The importance of the project to the University is indicated by the fact that the 80–acre parcel, which represented only about 40% of the entire tract owned by the University, was sold for $6,694,000 and that the rezoning would substantially increase the value of the remaining 60%. The "negotiations with the developers of the St. Jude Hospital" were the subject of discussion and formal action by the trustees at a meeting attended by Judge Collins only a few days before the lawsuit was filed. App. 35.

Second, it is an unfortunate coincidence that although the judge regularly attended the meetings of the Board of Trustees, he was not present at the January 28, 1982, meeting, a week after the 2–day trial and while the case was still under advisement. The minutes of that meeting record that representatives of the University monitored the progress of the trial, but did not see fit to call to the judge's attention the obvious conflict of interest that resulted from having a University trustee preside over that trial. These minutes were mailed to Judge Collins on March 12, 1982. If the Judge had opened that envelope when he received it on March 14th or 15th, he would have been under a duty to recuse himself *before* he entered judgment on March 16.[13]

Third, it is remarkable—and quite inexcusable—that Judge Collins failed to recuse himself on March 24, 1982. A full disclosure at that time would have completely removed any basis for questioning the Judge's impartiality and would have made it possible for a different judge to decide whether the interests—and appearance –of justice would have been served by a retrial. Another 2–day evidentiary hearing would surely have been less burdensome and less embarrassing than the protracted proceedings that resulted from Judge Collins' nonrecusal and nondisclosure. Moreover, as the Court of Appeals correctly noted, Judge Collins' failure to disqualify himself on March 24, 1982, also constituted a violation of § 455(b)(4), which disqualifies a judge if he "knows that he, individually or as a fiduciary, . . . has a financial interest in the subject matter in controversy or in a party to the proceeding, or any other interest that could be substantially affected by the outcome of the proceeding." This separate violation of § 455 further compels the conclusion that vacatur was an appropriate remedy; by his silence, Judge Collins deprived respondent of a basis for

---

13. One of the provisions of the contract between Loyola and Liljeberg is also remarkable. Despite the fact that earlier minutes of the Board make it clear that the University's interest in serious negotiations with Liljeberg was conditioned upon the certificate of need, the contract expressly recites that control of the certificate was the subject of pending litigation and then provides "that this sale shall not be in any way conditioned upon" the outcome of that litigation. App. 55. The University, however, retained the right to re-purchase the property if Liljeberg was unable to go forward with the hospital project. If Liljeberg was found not to control the certificate of need, he, at least arguably, would have been precluded from going forward with the hospital. Moreover, if the parties simply wanted to make the transaction unconditional, they could have omitted any reference to the litigation. An objective observer might reasonably question why the parties felt a need to include this clause.

making a timely motion for a new trial and also deprived it of an issue on direct appeal.[14]

Fourth, when respondent filed its motion to vacate, Judge Collins gave three reasons for denying the motion,[15] but still did not acknowledge that he had known about the University's interest both shortly before and shortly after the trial. Nor did he indicate any awareness of a duty to recuse himself in March of 1982.

These facts create precisely the kind of appearance of impropriety that § 455(a) was intended to prevent. The violation is neither insubstantial nor excusable. Although Judge Collins did not know of his fiduciary interest in the litigation, he certainly should have known. In fact, his failure to stay informed of this fiduciary interest, may well constitute a separate violation of § 455. See § 455(c). Moreover, providing relief in cases such as this will not produce injustice in other cases; to the contrary, the Court of Appeals' willingness to enforce § 455 may prevent a substantive injustice in some future case by encouraging a judge or litigant to more carefully examine possible grounds for disqualification and to promptly disclose them when discovered. It is therefore appropriate to vacate the judgment unless it can be said that respondent did not make a timely request for relief, or that it would otherwise be unfair to deprive the prevailing party of its judgment.

If we focus on fairness to the particular litigants, a careful study of Judge Rubin's analysis of the merits of the underlying litigation suggests that there is a greater risk of unfairness in upholding the judgment in favor of Liljeberg than there is in allowing a new judge to take a fresh look at the issues.[16] Moreover, neither Liljeberg nor

---

14. We note that the Court of Appeals affirmed by a divided panel. The majority opinion relied extensively on the deference due a trial court as to its findings of fact. Although it is now too late to determine what effect this additional argument might have had on the decision, it is certainly within the realm of the possible that the court's decision would have been swayed.

15. These were his three reasons:

"First, Loyola University was not and is not a party to this litigation, nor was any of its real estate the subject matter of this controversy. Second, Loyola University is a non-profit, educational institution, and any benefits inuring to that institution would not benefit any individual personally. Finally, and most significantly, this Judge never served on either the Real Estate or Executive Committees of the Loyola University Board of Trustees. Thus, this Judge had no participation of any kind in negotiating Loyola University's real estate transactions and, in fact, had no knowledge of

such transactions." App. to Pet. for Cert. 50a.

16. In an unpublished opinion a majority of the Court of Appeals concluded that Judge Collins' findings of fact were not clearly erroneous. In dissent, Judge Rubin expressed the opinion that "Liljeberg's chicanery," id., at 78a, gave rise to an estoppel as a matter of law. He wrote:

"Whether Liljeberg consciously intended to mislead HAI we need not decide. His decision to sign and return the agreement knowing that HAI believed it to be sufficient to transfer 'ownership' makes it clear that he was willing to mislead HAI. . . .

"HAI was misled by Liljeberg's silence into doing what it would not otherwise have done: filing the application for a certificate of need. The HAI witnesses all testified that the company never filed an application unless it wholly controlled the filing corporation; Liljeberg testified that he was aware of that policy.[8]" Id., at 76a–77a.

Loyola University has made a showing of special hardship by reason of their reliance on the original judgment.[17] Finally, although a delay of 10 months after the affirmance by the Court of Appeals would normally foreclose relief based on a violation of § 455(a), in this case the entire delay is attributable to Judge Collins' inexcusable failure to disqualify himself on March 24, 1982; had he recused himself on March 24, or even disclosed Loyola's interest in the case at that time, the motion could have been made less than 10 days after the entry of judgment. "The guiding consideration is that the administration of justice should reasonably appear to be disinterested as well as be so in fact." Public Utilities Comm'n v. Pollak, 343 U.S. 451, 466–467, 72 S.Ct. 813, 822–823, 96 L.Ed. 1068 (1952) (Frankfurter, J., in chambers). In sum, we conclude that Chief Judge Clark's opinion of the Court of Appeals reflects an eminently sound and wise disposition of this case.

The judgment of the Court of Appeals is accordingly

Affirmed.

CHIEF JUSTICE REHNQUIST, with whom JUSTICE WHITE and JUSTICE SCALIA join, dissenting.

The Court's decision in this case is long on ethics in the abstract, but short on workable rules of law. The Court first finds that 28 U.S.C. § 455(a) can be used to disqualify a judge on the basis of facts not known to the judge himself. It then broadens the standard for over-

---

At this point, Judge Rubin inserted the following footnote:

"[8] That HAI was misled is clear from the face of the application. HAI there described St. Jude as a 'wholly-owned subsidiary.' Indeed, the entire 407–page application is devoted to describing HAI, its hospitals, its management experience, and its assets. Liljeberg's name appears only in three letters of intent to file an application for a certificate of need dated before July, 1980, and on a copy of the Warranty and Indemnity Agreement. HAI also changed the name of St. Jude's registered agent, further demonstrating its belief that it controlled St. Jude." Id., at 77a, n. 8.

Judge Rubin then continued:

"Therefore, Liljeberg's silence at the time he signed the warranty agreement should estop him from claiming that the agreement, read in conjunction with the HAI cover letter and Douglas' letter enclosing corporate documents, did not transfer control of St. Jude to HAI. However, because Liljeberg's deception did not end there, the estoppel need not rest on that alone.

"Liljeberg signed the March 16, 1981 commission agreement which stated that he was to receive $250,000 (plus interest) only if HAI received final section 1122

approval. After the certificate of need was issued, Liljeberg requested and received the commission, which, when paid, amounted to $271,000. In relieving Hospital Corporation of America (HCA), HAI's successor, of $271,000, Liljeberg never mentioned his contention that he still 'owned' St. Jude, and that St. Jude, not HAI, had received the certificate. . . .

"HAI relied on Liljeberg's agreement that it owned St. Jude in buying the property on which the hospital was to be built. HCA justifiably relied on Liljeberg's agreement that it owned St. Jude in paying the commission." Id., at 77a–78a.

17. In fact, Liljeberg's ownership of the certificate of need has never been entirely settled. On January 31, 1983, just two weeks after the Fifth Circuit's judgment affirming Judge Collins on the merits became final, respondent filed suit against St. Jude and various federal and state agencies. The new action alleges that the certificate was improperly issued in the name of St. Jude and that respondent is instead entitled to the certificate. See Health Services Acquisition Corporation v. Guissinger, Civil Action No. 83–3031, Sec. C (ED La.). This litigation is still pending.

turning final judgments under Federal Rule of Civil Procedure 60(b). Because these results are at odds with the intended scope of § 455 and Rule 60(b), and are likely to cause considerable mischief when courts attempt to apply them, I dissent.

I

* * * Section 455 was substantially revised by Congress in 1974 to conform with the recently adopted Canon 3C of the American Bar Association's Code of Judicial Conduct (1974). * * * Congress hoped that this objective standard would promote public confidence in the impartiality of the judicial process by instructing a judge, when confronted with circumstances in which his impartiality could reasonably be doubted, to disqualify himself and allow another judge to preside over the case.[2] The amended statute also had the effect of removing the so-called "duty to sit," which had become an accepted gloss on the existing statute.[3]

* * *

The purpose of § 455 is obviously to inform judges of what matters they must consider in deciding whether to recuse themselves in a given case. The Court here holds, as did the Court of Appeals below, that a judge must recuse himself under § 455(a) if he *should have known* of the circumstances requiring disqualification, even though in fact he did not know of them. I do not believe this is a tenable construction of subsection (a). A judge considering whether or not to recuse himself is necessarily limited to those facts bearing on the question of which he has knowledge. To hold that disqualification is required by reason of facts which the judge does *not* know, even though he should have known of them, is to posit a conundrum which is not decipherable by ordinary mortals. While the concept of "constructive knowledge" is useful in other areas of the law, I do not think it should be imported into § 455(a).

At the direction of the Court of Appeals, Judge Schwartz of the District Court for the Eastern District of Louisiana made factual findings concerning the extent and timing of Judge Collins' knowledge of Loyola's interest in the underlying lawsuit. Judge Schwartz determined that Judge Collins had no actual knowledge of Loyola's involvement when he tried the case. Not until March 24, 1982, when he reviewed materials in preparation for a Board meeting, did Judge

---

2. See H.R.Rep. No. 93–1453, p. 5 (1974). See also Bloom, Judicial Bias and Financial Interest as Grounds for Disqualification of Federal Judges, 35 Case W.Res. L.Rev. 662, 670–676 (1985); Comment, Disqualification of Federal Judges for Bias or Prejudice, 46 U.Chi.L.Rev. 236, 238–242 (1978).

3. While § 455 provides guidance to a judge when he is considering recusing him-

self, 28 U.S.C. § 144 supplies a litigant with the opportunity to file an affidavit that the judge before whom the matter is pending has a personal bias or prejudice sufficient to mandate disqualification. Respondent filed no affidavit or motion under § 144 in this case.

Collins obtain actual knowledge of the negotiations between petitioners and Loyola.

* * * In short, as is unquestionably the case with subsection (b), I would adhere to a standard of actual knowledge in § 455(a), and not slide off into the very speculative ground of "constructive" knowledge.

* * *

JUSTICE O'CONNOR, dissenting.*

NOTE ON THE RECUSAL OF THE JUDGE

1. The Judicial Improvements and Access to Justice Act of 1988 amended 28 U.S.C.A. § 455 to provide that a judge who would otherwise be required to recuse himself by reason of holding a financial interest in a party is not required to recuse himself if "substantial judicial time has been devoted to the matter" and he divests himself "of the interest that provides the grounds for the disqualification" after its discovery, unless the interest is one that could be "substantially affected by the outcome." 28 U.S.C.A. § 455(f). What affect, if any, would this provision have had on the outcome in *Liljeberg* if it had been in effect when that case was decided?

2. Observe that under 28 U.S.C.A. § 455 the judge against whom the motion for recusal is made hears and decides any factual issues presented, including the question of his actual bias. See 13A Wright & Miller § 3551; e.g., Bradley v. Milliken, 426 F.Supp. 929 (E.D.Mich.1977); Commonwealth v. Local Union 542, Intern. Union of Operating Engineers, 388 F.Supp. 155 (E.D.Pa.1974). Compare ABA Standards of Judicial Administration § 2.–32(a), recommending that "factual issues raised by the motion should be heard and resolved by another judge." The federal procedure is arguably justified on the ground that it prevents the disruption of referring the recusal question to another judge, but it is also a deterrent against moving for recusal. The motion of necessity is taken personally and the opinions sometimes have a special quality of protestation. See, e.g., Duplan Corp. v. Deering Milliken, Inc., 400 F.Supp. 497 (D.S.C.1975). For a case of plainly excessive punctillio, see In re Virginia Elec. & Power Co., 539 F.2d 357 (4th Cir. 1976). See generally Comment, Meeting the Challenge: Rethinking Judicial Disqualification, 69 Calif.L.Rev. 1445 (1981); Garn and Oliphant, Disqualification of Judges Under 28 U.S.C.A. § 455(a), 4 Harv.J.L. & Pub. Pol. 1 (1981); Anno., 23 A.L.R.3d 1416; Anno., 56 A.L.R.Fed. 494 (mandamus to compel disqualification); Leubsdorf, Theories of Judging and Judge Disqualification, 62 N.Y.U.L.Rev. 237 (1987); Stempel, Rehnquist, Recusal, and Reform, 53 Brooklyn L.Rev. 589 (1987).

3. The recusal procedure in some states amounts to a peremptory challenge of the judge, i.e., one that need not be based on an actual showing of bias. Sometimes an expressly peremptory challenge is allowed. See Note, Disqualification of Judges for Prejudice or Bias, 48 Or.L.Rev. 311 (1969). In California, the same result is reached by permitting a party to support the motion for disqualification with an affidavit which states in conclusory form that the judge is biased and which may not be controverted. C.C.P. 170.6, upheld and applied in Solberg v. Superior Court, 19 Cal.3d 182, 137 Cal.Rptr. 460, 561 P.2d 1148 (1977). Contrast Johnson v. Goldman, 94 Nev. 6, 575 P.2d 929 (1978), holding a peremptory challenge procedure constitutionally invalid as an invasion of the judicial power. On the procedure for recusal in California, see C.C.P. 170–

* Justice O'Connor's opinion is omitted.

170.5. See also ABCNY Committee on Federal Courts, A Proposal for Peremptory Challenges of Federal Judges in Civil and Criminal Cases, 36 The Record 231 (1981), and the criticism of the proposal in Bartels, Peremptory Challenges to Federal Judges, 68 A.B.A.J. 449 (1982). A quite different method of controlling judicial misconduct is investigation, censure, and possibly removal. See Braithwaite, Who Judges the Judges? (1971); ABA Standards of Judicial Administration § 1.22; Neisser, The New Federal Judicial Discipline Act, 65 Judicature 142 (1981). For application of the power of removal for judicial misconduct see, e.g., Wenger v. Commission on Judicial Performance, 29 Cal.3d 615, 175 Cal.Rptr. 420, 630 P.2d 954 (1981).

The Supreme Court has held that the issue of recusal by state court judges is generally a nonconstitutional matter, but that failure to recuse may raise constitutional issues in certain cases. See Tumey v. Ohio, 273 U.S. 510, 47 S.Ct. 437, 71 L.Ed. 749 (1927). This principle received strong reaffirmation in Aetna Life Ins. Co. v. Lavoie, 475 U.S. 813, 106 S.Ct. 1580, 89 L.Ed.2d 823 (1986), discussed in *Liljeberg,* where the Court held it a violation of due process when an Alabama Supreme Court justice refused to disqualify himself where he had participated as a party in a parallel suit.

D. RESPONSIBILITIES OF COURT AND COUNSEL

NOTE ON PROCEDURE DURING TRIAL

The presentation of proof and argument at trial is simultaneously a task requiring theatrical skill by the protagonists and a process closely governed by rules. The skills of trial advocacy can be developed only through exercise—in trial moot court, trial advocacy courses, clinical legal training and trial work itself. At one time it was thought they could be learned only first hand in court, but there has now emerged an array of trial advocacy training programs both in law schools and at the continuing legal education level. There are supporting teaching materials, of which Keeton, Trial Tactics and Methods (2d ed. 1973), and Jeans, Trial Advocacy (1975) are the best general introductions. The production of proof at trial is regulated partly by rules governing order of presentation, see Note on the Structure of a Trial, supra p. 997, and also by the law of Evidence. Cleary et al., McCormick on Evidence (3d ed. 1984) is an excellent introduction to the latter. The coverage of this book does not extend to either the skills of trial advocacy or the law of evidence and hence deals only in a limited way with the trial itself. This coverage is designed to convey a flavor of trial and to deal with certain salient problems concerning the role of judge and counsel.

PEOPLE v. RIGNEY
Supreme Court of California, 1961.
55 Cal.2d 236, 10 Cal.Rptr. 625, 359 P.2d 23.

TRAYNOR, JUSTICE.

Defendant appeals from a judgment entered on a jury verdict convicting him of two counts of assault with a deadly weapon and one count of assault with a deadly weapon with intent to commit murder.

[The assault was a shooting of defendant's wife and a man named Brown at the wife's apartment in San Diego.]

Defendant testified that his memory was impaired as to all events after his return to San Diego. He remembered drinking one single and one double martini and upon reaching his wife's apartment the second time seeing Brown suddenly appear at the screen door, jump to the side of the door and reach for his hip pocket. He did not remember going to his room and getting his gun. He did remember, however, that he had no intent to kill anyone and that he armed himself to prevent a fight with Brown. He testified that he remembered only isolated events after seeing Brown reach for his hip pocket and that he did not remember firing the gun.

Defendant contended throughout the trial that he did not form the specific intent to commit murder. His description of his state of mind during the period between his first departure from his wife's apartment and the moment he ceased firing as well as the conclusions of his medical expert, Dr. Robert F. Brandmeyer, a member of the psychiatric staff of the United States Naval Hospital in San Diego, as to his state of mind during those critical moments were therefore vital to his defense. He contends that the trial judge erroneously questioned him and his medical expert in such an extensive, repetitious, and argumentative manner as to indicate to the jury the judge's disbelief that defendant could not remember what had happened and that the judge compounded his error by failing adequately to charge the jury that they were the sole judges of the facts.

A trial judge may examine witnesses to elicit or clarify testimony (People v. Corrigan, 48 Cal.2d 551, 555, 310 P.2d 953; People v. Ottey, 5 Cal.2d 714, 721, 56 P.2d 193; People v. Carlin, 178 Cal.App.2d 705, 714–715, 3 Cal.Rptr. 301; People v. Montgomery, 47 Cal.App.2d 1, 18, 117 P.2d 437). Indeed, "it is the right and duty of a judge to conduct a trial in such a manner that the truth will be established in accordance with the rules of evidence." People v. Corrigan, supra, 48 Cal.2d at page 559, 310 P.2d at page 958. The trial judge, however, must not become an advocate for either party or under the guise of examining witnesses comment on the evidence or cast aspersions or ridicule on a witness. People v. Campbell, 162 Cal.App.2d 776, 787, 329 P.2d 82; People v. Lancellotti, 147 Cal.App.2d 723, 731, 305 P.2d 926; People v. Huff, 134 Cal.App.2d 182, 187–188, 285 P.2d 17; People v. Deacon, 117 Cal.App.2d 206, 209, 255 P.2d 98.

Both Penal Code, § 1122 and Code of Civil Procedure, § 611 provide that the judge must admonish the jury not to form or express any opinions on any subject connected with the trial until the case is finally submitted to them. A judge must not defeat the purpose of these provisions by comment on the evidence during the trial but must also keep an open mind until he has had an opportunity to hear all the evidence. Moreover, comment should be expressly labeled as the judge's opinion, and the jury advised that it may be disregarded;

questions are not so labeled, and when they convey the judge's opinion of the credibility of a witness, there is grave danger not only that they may induce the jury to form an opinion before the case is finally submitted to them, but that the jury will substitute the judge's opinion for its own. The judge, therefore, may not ask questions to convey to the jury his opinion of the credibility of a witness. People v. Huff, 134 Cal.App.2d 182, 188, 285 P.2d 17. Nor should he intervene so extensively in behalf of the prosecutor as to align himself with the prosecutor in the minds of the jury. People v. Robinson, 179 Cal.App.2d 624, 633–637.

In the present case the trial judge, over defendant's objection, examined him extensively as to events immediately preceding the shooting, interrupting the deputy district attorney's cross-examination to do so. The judge questioned defendant closely to clarify inconsistencies between his testimony on the stand and statements he had previously made. After defendant was excused as a witness and Doctor Brandmeyer was about to take the stand, the judge recalled defendant and once again questioned him as to his memory of the shooting. After defendant had been excused a second time and before Doctor Brandmeyer's examination began, the parties retired to chambers for a conference.

During the conference the judge stated that he did not believe defendant's testimony about his lapse of memory and that he believed that defendant went to his wife's apartment the second time, not to discuss visitation rights, but to fight with Brown. The court said: "He didn't think there was going to be any discussion. . . . I'm not going to swallow that at all. . . . I'm not going to let the jury swallow it." The judge, however, had stated earlier:

"It seems to me rather strange that this young man can remember up to the point where he not only sees a man reach for his hip pocket, but after that he reasons in his mind, 'I'm about to be killed unless I can act,' and before he can act, he forgets everything. It seems to me that was a very convenient time to start suffering from amnesia. I am frank to say I don't believe it. I'm not trying the facts in this case. The defendant under the constitution is entitled to a jury by twelve people, and they might believe it, and if they do believe it, he is entitled to that, and I would a whole lot rather one guilty man go free, whether he be guilty or not, than I would rather ten guilty men go free and one innocent man be convicted, in my book.

"Now my view is simply this, gentlemen. I will tell you that very frankly. I don't think a courtroom is a place to play a checker game. I don't think a courtroom is a football contest or boxing contest. I don't think the courtroom is a contest for the purpose of seeing who is the smarter lawyer, or who can persuade the jury best, at all. I think the courtroom is a place to see that justice is done, and I think a courtroom is a place to bring out all the facts that bear upon the subject, and to bring them out fairly and impartially to the end that justice may be approximated as closely as may be by the jury. That is why I asked this young man some questions to find out just at what point he claims he started suffering this loss of memory and as I have said, in the absence of the jury and on this record, I can't quite accept all of his story, but I don't know what the jury's going to think about it, and I'm not going to tell the jury what they ought to think about it. I'm going to ask questions as I see fit, to give the jury all the light that they can have in order that they may derive,—arrive at their own opinions. . . ."

These statements were made out of the presence of the jury and did not induce defendant to abandon any of his defenses.

Following the conference in chambers the judge examined Doctor Brandmeyer at great length concerning petitioner's alleged retrograde amnesia. Defendant's motion for a mistrial and a new trial based partly on the judge's questioning defendant and Doctor Brandmeyer were denied.

Although the judge questioned defendant and Doctor Brandmeyer at great length "the mere fact that the judge examined . . . at some length does not establish misconduct." People v. Corrigan, supra, 48 Cal.2d 551, 559, 310 P.2d 953, 958; People v. Montgomery, supra, 47 Cal.App.2d 1, 18, 117 P.2d 437.

It is ordinarily better practice for a trial judge to let counsel develop the case and to undertake the examination of witnesses only when it appears that relevant and material testimony will not be elicited by counsel. See People v. Campbell, 162 Cal.App.2d 776, 787, 329 P.2d 82. Even if the testimony elicited by the judge's questions, however, would probably have been elicited by counsel, that fact alone does not render the judge's questions improper.

Defendant contends that the judge's comments in the conference in chambers disclosed his purpose to invade the province of the jury by inducing it to disbelieve defendant's evidence about his lapse of memory and that the judge accomplished that purpose by improper questioning of defendant and Doctor Brandmeyer.

It is immaterial that the judge did not believe defendant's evidence or even that his purpose was to induce the jury not to believe it so long as he sought to accomplish that purpose by getting the truth established according to the governing rules of law. Certainly there is nothing improper in the judge's candidly advising counsel in chambers of his disbelief in defendant's evidence. Nor is there anything improper in his questioning witnesses to induce the jury to share that disbelief, if his questions are designed, as the judge stated in the conference in chambers, "to bring out all the facts that bear upon the subject, and to bring them out fairly and impartially to the end that justice may be approximated as closely as may be by the jury."

The questions the judge asked defendant were designed to distinguish clearly the facts that defendant remembered and the facts that he did not remember and to clarify the inconsistencies between his testimony and his previous statement to his naval superiors. The questions the judge asked Doctor Brandmeyer were designed to get a full explanation of the nature and causes of retrograde amnesia. A careful examination of the record convinces us that the judge's questions were not a guise for conveying to the jury the court's disbelief in defendant's evidence but were asked to get the truth established, and that they fairly and impartially brought out relevant and material testimony. Moreover, the judge instructed the jury that any intimation in his questions or the questions of counsel that certain facts were or were not true must be disregarded, and he adequately instructed them that they were the exclusive judges of the effect and value of the evidence.

* * *

GIBSON, C.J., and McCOMB, WHITE and DOOLING, JJ., concur.

SCHAUER, J., concurs in the judgment.

PETERS, JUSTICE.

I dissent. In my opinion the record in this case demonstrates that the trial judge aligned himself with the prosecution by assuming the role of prosecutor, and clearly indicated to the jury his disbelief in the main defense of the defendant. The two witnesses were constantly interrupted by the trial judge, who then exhaustively, argumentatively and repetitiously examined them almost to the complete exclusion of the district attorney. Such examination was officious and unnecessary. It necessarily deprived the defendant of that fair and impartial trial guaranteed to him by the Constitution of this state and of the United States. Const. art. 1, § 13; U.S.Const. Amend. 14.

The majority opinion correctly and fairly states the facts. It also sets forth the general principles applicable to the examination of witnesses by the trial judge, and briefly mentions the limitations on that power. * * *

In my opinion the record demonstrates that all of these rules were violated. The record shows that defendant's defense was that he acted in self-defense up to a point, and that he then suffered a loss of memory. After the defendant testified as to the claimed loss of memory, and while the prosecutor was cross-examining, the judge simply took over that cross-examination. His questions covered the pertinent periods time and time again, and embraced much of the material already brought out by the prosecution. After the prosecutor had concluded his examination, the judge took over again, and again covered the same field that he had already covered at great length. After the defendant had been removed from the stand the judge recalled him and again subjected him to a grueling cross-examination. All objections by defense counsel to these tactics were overruled. The questions were partisan, repetitive and argumentative, and some of them ridiculed the witness.

*   *   *

Undoubtedly the trial judge tried to be fair, and undoubtedly his motives were of the best, but his examination of these witnesses was such that it ridiculed the defendant's defense, and obviously was aimed at inducing the jury to disbelieve that testimony. This was prejudicial. These errors clearly denied defendant the fair trial to which he was entitled. I would reverse the judgment.

SITRIN BROS., INC. v. DELUXE LINES, INC.

County Court, Oneida County, New York, 1962.
35 Misc.2d 1041, 231 N.Y.S.2d 943.

EDMUND A. McCARTHY, JUDGE.

This was action 194 on the Oneida County Court June Term, 1962. It was tried before a jury and a verdict rendered in the sum of $550.50 (five hundred and fifty dollars and fifty cents) for the plaintiff. After the entry of the jury's verdict, a Motion was made to set the verdict aside as being contrary to the law and contrary to the evidence under Section 549 of the Civil Practice Act.

The sharpest question of fact in this case that the jury was called upon to decide and determine was whether or not the driver, Mr. Thorpe, of the Deluxe Lines hit this door and damaged it and its respective parts. Three witnesses, at least, for the plaintiff testified as to the collision and the accident. Mr. Thorpe testified to a general denial of accident liability or collision. The witnesses for the plaintiff testifying after a lapse of two years or more, presented evidence that the door and its sections were damaged and that they assisted in the repair of this door. Mr. Bankert who finally furnished the sections and made the repairs to the door of a permanent nature, testified that he saw damage marks on eleven feet of the door. Now this was all evidence on the part of the plaintiff. Whether it was two feet, four feet, six feet or eleven feet was a question for the jury to determine as a matter of fact after evaluating all of the evidence.

There was evidence that during the period subsequent to the accident there was electrical trouble with this door which was demonstrated by the blowing of fuses, and Mr. Diehl was called to make certain inspections of the electrical equipment and in the course of these inspections he recommended that the motor be opened up and its interior examined. These check-ups were six and nine months after the accident as alleged and his recommendation was not followed and the only evidence that was submitted to the jury was his estimate as to the cost of such recommended dismantlement of the motor. The jury found as a matter of fact that there was no worth to this proof as to damage and they disregarded this testimony entirely.

We always have a divergence of testimony and alleged facts in all jury cases and this one was no exception, because we were dealing with the ordinary laboring class of intellect who are not too keenly interested in the Sitrin Brothers repairs and probably knew that the door had been damaged but how far or where the damage went was no concern of theirs and consequently, their recollection was rather hazy.

Part of the evidence indicated that this truck was backing up a grade in front of this door and if the grade was of sufficient plane, some part of the van of the truck could have hit the door without damaging the protruding warning lights on the top edge of the van and apparently the jury so found.

What it amounted to, was the question of integrity which was submitted to the jury and they believed the plaintiff's witnesses and did not believe Mr. Thorpe.

During the trial several of the jurors who probably had some knowledge of electrical equipment propounded one or two questions with reference to electric motors and their operation. These questions were directed to Mr. Diehl, an expert witness. Objection was taken by counsel to this procedure after the jury retired.

This point does not seem to have been covered by any New York State precedent, although we do find in 53 American Jurisprudence, page 623, under the heading, "Trials," a reference to the effect that, "ordinarily there is no occasion for a juryman to interrogate a witness. The fact that inquiries are propounded by a juror does not obviate the necessity of interposing objection to save the question for review.

"But in some cases more orderly practice would require the trial court in its discretion to ask the juror to indicate the point of his inquiry, and then to see that the question is properly formulated, as by directing counsel to put it so as to afford the usual opportunity for objection and exception."

The type of questions asked by these various jurors would have been difficult to formulate in the lawyer's language and perhaps the purpose of the inquiry would have been completely lost.

* * *

Our Courts have taken the position that whether a juror should be permitted to interrogate witnesses is one within the sound discretion of the trial court. People v. Knapper, 230 App.Div. 487, 245 N.Y.S. 245.

The questions asked in this case by the jury apparently were in an endeavor to get them to better understand the trouble with electric circuits controlling motors, and their inquiry covered a field in which apparently counsel was not too interested or too well advised and as a result of their inquiry and the answers of the witness, they made no award for alleged damage to electrical equipment. Consequently, their inquiry was in search of knowledge which the evidence had not disclosed to them and which enabled them to throw out the claim for electrical damage.

Under the circumstances of this case, it cannot be said that the questions asked by the jurymen were prejudicial to the defendant, rather these questions were helpful to the defense.

*   *   *

COMMITTEE ON PROFESSIONAL ETHICS v. CRARY

Supreme Court of Iowa, 1976.
245 N.W.2d 298.

UHLENHOPP, JUSTICE.

This proceeding involves a determination of charges of unethical conduct on the part of an attorney, respondent William R. Crary. The record establishes the following by a convincing preponderance of the facts and circumstances in evidence. See Committee on Professional Ethics and Conduct v. Wright, 178 N.W.2d 749 (Iowa).

Respondent, who was himself involved in litigation with his former wife over their children, became enamoured with Sue Evans Curtis, the wife of and mother of three children by Maury Wetzel Curtis. Respondent and Mrs. Curtis spent nights, weekends, and longer periods together, and engaged in sexual intercourse. Mr. Curtis and sitters attended the Curtis children during Mrs. Curtis' absences. At the time, respondent and the Curtis family resided in Cedar Rapids, Iowa, about four blocks apart.

Unknown to respondent and Mrs. Curtis, Mr. Curtis employed private investigators to observe Mrs. Curtis.

About March 13, 1970, Mrs. Curtis told her husband she was going to Vail, Colorado to stay at Tivoli Lodge. Instead, she went to respondent's home on that date and stayed with him until March 22.

On April 29, 1970, Mrs. Curtis commenced a suit against her husband, seeking a divorce, custody of their children, alimony, and child support. She alleged that she had conducted herself as a dutiful and loving wife. Her attorney was Mr. William O. Gray, assisted by respondent who was then Mr. Gray's associate. Mr. Gray was unaware at the time of the relationship between respondent and Mrs. Curtis.

About May 15, 1970, Mrs. Curtis told a sitter that she was going to Chicago, Illinois. Instead, that day she went to Minneapolis, Minnesota, where she stayed with respondent until May 17.

On Wednesday, June 3, 1970, Mr. Justin W. Albright, attorney for Mr. Curtis in the divorce suit, commenced taking the discovery deposition of Mrs. Curtis at the office of Mr. Gray and respondent. In the course of this deposition in respondent's presence, Mrs. Curtis testified falsely regarding the period between March 13 and 22, 1970, when she was in respondent's home. Mrs. Curtis, respondent, and Mr. Albright knew the testimony was false, but Mrs. Curtis and respondent did not realize that Mr. Albright knew of the falsity. Mrs. Curtis did not assert the privilege against self-incrimination, but testified in part concerning the March 13 to 22 period:

Q. [by Mr. Albright] And as I understand it, you told Mr. Curtis that you were going to Vail, Colorado on this trip and that you were going to stay at the Tivoli Lodge, is that correct? A. That's correct. . . .

Q. Well, where did you go? A. I went to Chicago . . . .

Q. And well, where did you stay in Chicago? A. With a friend.

Q. Who is that? A. Mrs. Richard Needham . . . .

Q. And what's her address? A. Just a minute; I will look it up: 537 Rose Mary Road, Lake Forest, Illinois . . . .

Q. Well, did you stay with her all during the time that you were there? A. Uh-huh, yes.

Q. And who all did you see while you were there in Chicago? A. Friends of hers . . . .

Q. And as I understand it then, you stayed all that period of time, from March 13th until March 22nd when you returned home, with Mrs. Richard Needham in Chicago, is that correct? A. I did.

Q. Is that correct? A. Yes.

Q. And well, did you see anyone at all from Cedar Rapids while you were on this trip? A. No. Why would I see anyone from Cedar Rapids? . . .

Q. Well, hadn't you previously arranged that Mary Becker would drive you to the airport there on Friday morning, March 13th? A. Yes . . . .

Q. Who did you leave with from Mary Becker's place, from 212 Twelfth Street, S.E., on the morning of Friday of March 13th? A. Mr. Crary . . . .

Q. And where did you go? A. Downtown . . . .

Q. You went to the Roosevelt Hotel to get a cab? A. Uh-huh, or a limousine, whichever one showed up first.

Q. And then he did not take you to the airport, is that correct? A. Oh, no; heavens no.

Q. Well, what airport did you land at in Chicago? A. O'Hare . . . .

Q. Well, how did you get from O'Hare Airport out to Mrs. Richard Needham's? A. I took a limousine into town.

Q. You went downtown then. How did you get to her place from downtown? A. I drove out with her later in the day . . . .

Q. Well now, on Sunday, March 15th, the Sunday after you left, you called home about 9:30 in the morning and talked with Mr. Curtis, did you not? A. Could be . . . .

Q. And you gave the impression that you were at Vail, Colorado?
A. Why, of course . . . .

Q. Well now, on Sunday March 22nd, about 9:30 in the morning, you called your home and talked to Mr. Curtis didn't you? That's the day you came back . . . . A. Yeah, it was the day I returned, yes.

Q. And didn't he ask you where you were, and you said you were still in Vail? A. Yup-yes . . . .

Q. And then he offered to meet the plane, did he not, and you said absolutely not? A. That's right . . . .

Q. Well on all these calls, I take it they were made from Lake Forest, Illinois? A. They were.

At no time during this portion of the deposition did respondent request a recess or interrupt the perjury.

At 3:00 p.m. on June 3, 1970, the parties recessed the deposition until 1:00 p.m. on Friday, June 5, 1970. During that interim, respondent, knowing that Mrs. Curtis' Wednesday testimony was false, took no measure to correct it, to withdraw from the case as an attorney, to warn Mrs. Curtis she should lie no further, to inform Mr. Gray of the perjury, or to reveal the true situation to anyone.

The deposition resumed on June 5 with the same individuals present. At that time Mrs. Curtis testified falsely regarding the weekend of May 15 to 17, 1970, which she actually spent in Minneapolis with respondent. Again Mrs. Curtis, respondent, and Mr. Albright knew the testimony was false, but again Mrs. Curtis and respondent did not realize that Mr. Albright knew it was false—until later in the deposition. Mrs. Curtis testified in part:

Q. [by Mr. Albright] Well, did you go with anyone? A. No.

Q. Well, just tell us where you went. A. I went to Chicago to see Mrs. Needham . . . .

Q. Well now, the second passenger who was right behind you was Mr. William R. Crary, was that correct, getting off this flight? A. I have no idea who was getting off behind me. . . .

Q. Did you happen to see him on the plane on Ozark Flight No. 917? A. Not that I recall. . . .

Q. And then at the bottom of the steps after you got off the plane, you were observed to meet with Mr. William R. Crary and walked together with him into the terminal, is that correct? A. I don't remember. . . .

Q. Well, now, where did you board this Ozark plane on Flight No. 917 on May 17, 1970? . . . A. I told you I went to Chicago to see Mrs. Needham, and I came home.

Respondent did not seek to recess the deposition during this perjury or to halt Mrs. Curtis from falsely testifying.

As the deposition progressed, Mr. Albright's questions made evident that investigators had followed Mrs. Curtis and that Mr. Albright knew the truth. Respondent's testimony in later proceedings revealed what then happened at the Friday session of the deposition:

> It became obvious, from the questions and the answers that I— or the questions that were being asked, that she had been followed by private detectives and that her former husband and her husband at that time [Mr. Curtis] knew everything that she had done and where she had been and who she had seen.

> Q. Was the deposition then adjourned? A. Yes, it was. Actually what happened is that she became very shaken about the whole thing and asked to go to the ladies' room, and Bill Gray said, come on, let's go and find out about this. And he and I went into an office, and he said is she lying about these things with you and with her? And I said, yeah, she is and I was. And he said, we can't go on with this. She can't sit there and tell this story. And he said, what do you think we ought to do? And I said, I think we ought to recess the deposition, and we can't go on. I know we can't go on with it, no way. And so he went back into the office—or into the library, where we had been taking the deposition, and I gather adjourned it or recessed it or whatever.

> *　*　*

II. *The Deposition Perjury.* *　*　* Count I of the complaint sets forth in considerable detail the facts relating to the perjury and respondent's connection with it. A person of ordinary intelligence would readily perceive the gravamen of that count. As a conclusion, the Committee alleges that complainant violated specified statutes in the Iowa Code and also specified clauses of the Iowa Code of Professional Responsibility for Lawyers.

Section 610.14(3) of the Iowa Code prescribes as one of the duties of an attorney:

> It is the duty of an attorney and counselor: . . .

> 3. To employ, for the purpose of maintaining the causes confided to him, such means only as are consistent with truth, and never to seek to mislead the judges by any artifice or false statement of fact or law.

Then § 610.24(3), which is one of the statutes specified by the Committee, provides:

> The following are sufficient causes for revocation or suspension [of an attorney's license]: . . .

> 3. A willful violation of any of the duties of an attorney or counselor as hereinbefore prescribed.

Respondent contends that Count I of the complaint must fail because the Committee founded it on the Code of Professional Responsibility, which was not in effect when the perjury occurred.

We would doubt the soundness of respondent's contention that Count I must fail even if § 610.24(3) of the Iowa statutes were not alleged by the Committee. But we need not go that far. The statute is alleged. We therefore place the Code of Professional Responsibility aside as a basis for decision and proceed under the statute.

*   *   *

Respondent contends, however, that the record contains no express testimony by him or Mrs. Curtis that he put her up to the false stories she related in the deposition. Yet those stories did not come out of thin air; they took some contriving. We doubt that Mrs. Curtis simply developed those stories about Mrs. Needham as the deposition progressed or that she developed them alone.

We think respondent was involved in the whole shameful episode, but we will accept arguendo his contention that he did not contrive the perjury with Mrs. Curtis. Then we have a situation in which respondent as an attorney at a deposition listened, his client started to lie under oath, he knew she was lying, and he just "sat there" and let her lie. More than that, the deposition recessed over Thursday, and respondent did nothing to stop Mrs. Curtis from lying some more. She resumed her lying on Friday and respondent still just sat there.

What is the *law* of this matter? We are not disposed to read §§ 610.14(3) and 610.24(3) of the Iowa Code in a narrow, technical, or legalistic manner. Assuming respondent did not know in advance that Mrs. Curtis was going to lie, his guilt was in failing to stop her or otherwise to call a halt when she started to lie.

Central to the administration of justice is the fact-finding process. Legislatures and courts can devise the finest rules of law, but if those rules are applied to false "facts," justice miscarries.

The attorney functions at the heart of the fact-finding process, both in trial and in pre- and post-trial proceedings. If he knowingly suffers a witness to lie, he undermines the integrity of the fact-finding system of which he himself is an integral part. Thus the fundamental rule is unquestioned that *an attorney must not knowingly permit a witness to lie.* In re Hardenbrook, 135 App.Div. 634, 121 N.Y.S. 250, affd. 199 N.Y. 539, 92 N.E. 1086, app. den. 144 App.Div. 928, 129 N.Y.S. 1126 (disbarment where attorney learned after first day of trial that client lied, but nevertheless recalled client to testify on second day); In re Crary, 223 App.Div. 277, 228 N.Y.S. 340; In re Barach, 279 Pa. 89, 123 A. 727 (disbarment where attorney permitted witnesses to testify they were present at injury when he knew they were not present); C.J.S. Attorney & Client § 23 at 753–754 ("There is no recognized rule of law or ethics which justifies the conduct of counsel in any case, civil or criminal, in endeavoring by dishonest means to mislead the court or jury, even if to do so might work to the advantage of his cient, and such conduct will constitute a ground for suspension or disbarment. . . . An attorney may be suspended or disbarred for perverting, or attempting to pervert, a decision of a cause on its merits, by . . . introducing evidence or *allowing evidence to be given* which he knows to be false or forged"—italics added).

But respondent contends he was not required to volunteer to opposing counsel or the court that Mrs. Curtis' testimony was false, since this could have provided evidence for building an adultery case against him. He cites authority that an attorney like others is privileged not to produce evidence which will incriminate him. Spevack v. Klein, 385 U.S. 511, 87 S.Ct. 625, 17 L.Ed.2d 574.

Respondent does not seem to grasp the point here. We do not place the decision on respondent's failure to inform opposing counsel or the court of the truth. In the present case no need really existed for this. Opposing counsel was not misled. His subsequent questions revealed he knew the facts; he made Mrs. Curtis' perjury patent. The vice of respondent's conduct was not in failing to reveal the truth but in participating in the corruption of the fact-finding system by knowingly permitting Mrs. Curtis to lie. Indeed if Mr. Curtis had not had private investigators, the falsity of this testimony might never have come to light; Mrs. Curtis' perjury, countenanced by respondent, might have subsequently carried the day in court. Contrast with respondent's conduct the acts of Mr. Gray. When that attorney suspected on Friday that Mrs. Curtis was lying he confronted respondent and upon learning the truth said, "She can't sit there and tell this story." He thereupon recessed the deposition.

Apart from self-incrimination, respondent contends that his duty to protect his client, Mrs. Curtis, conflicted with his duty to the justice system to divulge the falsity, and that he properly placed his duty to his client first. He bases this contention on the attorney-client privilege.

Respondent confuses the duty to divulge the truth after perjury is committed with the duty not to permit a witness to give false testimony in the first place. We will proceed on this contention, however, on respondent's basis, as though respondent's breach was in not divulging the truth to opposing counsel or the court after the false testimony was given. We address respondent's contention as he does under the attorney-client privilege and without reference to any other privilege.

The difficulty with respondent's contention is that it proceeds from a false premise. He cites the article entitled Perjury, The Lawyer's Trilemma, in Litigation (Winter 1975 Journ. of A.B.A. Litigation Section). From this article, he concludes that a conflict between two duties exists: one to the client, the other to the justice system.

The flaw in respondent's reasoning is that no duty exists to the client when the client perjures himself to the knowledge of the attorney. Such conduct by the client falls outside the attorney-client relationship. When a prospective client approaches an attorney, he may expect that the attorney will assist him to the best of the attorney's ability. He may not expect, however, that the attorney will tolerate lying or any other species of fraud in the process. Prior to the present Code of Professional Responsibility, Canon 15 stated:

> Nothing operates more certainly to create or to foster popular prejudice against lawyers as a class and to deprive the profession of

that full measure of public esteem and confidence which belongs to the proper discharge of its duties than does the false claim, often set up by the unscrupulous in defense of questionable transactions, that it is the duty of the lawyer to do whatever will enable him to succeed in winning a client's cause . . . .

The office of attorney does not permit, much less does it demand of him for any client, violation of law or any manner of fraud or chicane. He must obey his own conscience and not that of his client. Canons of Professional Ethics (A.B.A.1957).

Correspondingly, the present rules state that "A lawyer shall not . . . [e]ngage in conduct involving dishonesty, fraud, deceit, or misrepresentation," "[e]ngage in conduct that is prejudicial to the administration of justice," "[p]articipate in the creation or preservation of evidence when he knows or it is obvious that the evidence is false," or "[c]ounsel or assist his client in conduct that the lawyer knows to be illegal or fraudulent." Iowa Code of Professional Responsibility for Lawyers (1971) DR1–102(A)(4) and (5), DR7–102(A)(6) and (7).

We hold that respondent acted unethically in knowingly permitting Mrs. Curtis to commit perjury on the first day of the deposition and to resume the perjury two days later, and that in so doing, he violated §§ 610.14(3) and 610.24(3) of the Iowa Code.

III. *Frustration of Decree.* The issue under the second count of the complaint, dealing with the child custody order in the Curtis divorce decree, is largely factual. * * *

⁎ ⁎ ⁎

An attorney may of course challenge a decree of a court by motion, appeal, or other legal means, but as long as the decree stands he must abide by it. Fisher v. Pace, 336 U.S. 155, 69 S.Ct. 425, 93 L.Ed. 569; see Maness v. Meyers, 419 U.S. 449, 94 S.Ct. 584, 42 L.Ed.2d 574; In re Daly, 291 Minn. 488, 189 N.W.2d 176. In like manner he must not counsel others to disobey decrees or be a party with them to disobedience. Territory v. Clancy, 7 N.M. 580, 37 P. 1108; In re Apfel, 202 App. Div. 76, 195 N.Y.S. 325; Ex Parte Miller, 37 Or. 304, 60 P. 999. Respondent violated the latter principle here.

We hold that respondent acted unethically in proceeding in concert with Mrs. Curtis to nullify the custody decree, and that in so doing he violated §§ 610.14(1) and 610.24(3) of the Iowa Code.

IV. *Discipline.* Reprimand is wholly inadequate discipline in this case. Respondent participated in the debasement of the fact-finding process and he took part in the overthrow of a decree of a court. His conduct was diametrically opposed to the fundamental duties of attorneys to bring truth rather than untruth to light and to uphold rather than bring down the judgments of courts.

The first requisite of an attorney is basic character. Uppermost in our minds is the question whether respondent possesses the character necessary to qualify him as an attorney.

We have placed in the balance all of the factors shown in evidence. After doing so, we conclude that respondent's license should be revoked, and we so order.

LICENSE REVOKED.

NOTE ON THE RESPONSIBILITIES OF COURT
AND COUNSEL AT TRIAL

1. On the trial judge's authority to examine witnesses, see also Schonberg v. Perry, 247 Cal.App.2d 436, 55 Cal.Rptr. 579 (1967), a civil case; 3 Wigmore on Evidence § 784 (Chadbourn ed. 1970); Cleary et al., McCormick on Evidence § 8 (3d ed. 1984). See also Schwarzer, Dealing with Incompetent Counsel: The Trial Judge's Role, 93 Harv.L.Rev. 633 (1980). At one time there was much enthusiasm for having the court call "impartial" expert witnesses in cases where technical issues were in controversy, but this has subsided. See ABCNY, Report of Special Committee on Impartial Medical Testimony (1956), reviewed in Louisell, 45 Calif.L.Rev. 572 (1957); see also Diamond, The Fallacy of the Impartial Expert, supra p. 938. On questions by jurors, see Anno., 31 A.L.R.3d 872. Juror questions are generally regarded with horror by bench and bar, because they sometimes are as in O'Nellion v. Haynes, 122 Cal.App. 329, 9 P.2d 853 (1932), where a juror asked defendant, "You carry liability insurance, don't you?" See also Prather v. Nashville Bridge Co., 286 Ala. 3, 236 So.2d 322 (1970), where jurors asked over 100 questions, but without objection from counsel.

2. On counsel's responsibility for the truthfulness of evidence offered in behalf of his case, see the excellent treatment in Wolfram, Client Perjury, 50 So.Calif.L.Rev. 809 (1977). For a proposal and debate concerning the responsibility of counsel to disclose information relevant to factual matters in issue, see Frankel, The Search for Truth: An Umpirial View, 123 U.Pa.L.Rev. 1031 (1975), and the succeeding articles by Professors Freedman and Uviller, 123 U.Pa.L.Rev. at 1060, 1067. Compare F.R.C.P. 26(e).

3. When a judge sustains an objection to testimony offered by a party, and the lawyer believes the testimony to be admissible and wants to preserve the point for a possible motion for a new trial and appeal, she should protect her record by making an offer of proof, i.e., by reciting on the record, but out of the presence of the jury, the substance of the testimony the witness would give if permitted to answer. See Cleary et al., McCormick on Evidence § 51 (3d ed. 1984); Witkin, California Evidence §§ 1310–1314. Cf. Reynolds v. Bank of America, supra p. 50. Contrast in federal practice offers of proof in a jury trial with the proceedings on offer of proof in a trial to the judge alone, F.R.C.P. 43(e); see 10 Moore ¶ 103.21.

4. At common law the party aggrieved by a ruling of the trial judge sustaining or overruling an objection to evidence had to take an "exception" to the ruling in order to preserve the point for a post-trial motion or appeal. The word "exception," formally signifying non-acquiescence in the ruling, acquired almost magical significance, and if it was not pronounced, the point was lost. In modern procedure formal exceptions are unnecessary, but the party must make his position clear. F.R.C.P. 46; C.C.P. 646, 647; see 5A Moore ¶ 46.02; 8 Witkin 442–443.

5. Although there is a right to have assistance of counsel in civil cases, there is no generally recognized right to be provided assistance of counsel in the

case of a person unable to afford to hire such assistance, as there is in criminal cases. See Further Note on Litigation Expenses, supra p. 274. Also see Anno., 67 A.L.R.2d 1102; cf. Note, Developments in the Law—Civil Commitment of the Mentally Ill, 87 Harv.L.Rev. 1190, 1271 (1974). Compare ABA Standards of Judicial Administration § 2.20:

> "The following litigants should be provided with counsel if they cannot afford to retain counsel themselves:
>
> * * *
>
> "(3) Persons subject to civil proceedings in which the result may be detention for a period longer than 72 hours;
>
> "(4) Parents of a minor, or persons having custody of a minor *in loco parentis*, and the minor, in any civil proceeding in which the parent or such other person may be deprived of custody;
>
> "(5) A litigant in any other case having potentially serious consequences when, in the opinion of the court, assistance of counsel is needed to prevent a miscarriage of justice."

6. A problem of increasing recurrence is that of the disqualification of an attorney from participating in litigation against a party who was formerly his client. It is settled that an attorney may not do so when the matter in litigation is that in which he was previously involved, but beyond this the law is quite unsettled. Cf. Comment, The Appealability of Orders Denying Motions for Disqualification of Counsel in the Federal Courts, 45 U.Chi.L.Rev. 450 (1978).

E. THE PROVINCE OF THE JURY

---

1. TAKING THE CASE FROM THE JURY

INTRODUCTORY NOTE ON TAKING THE CASE FROM THE JURY

The strongest control of jury functioning by the judge is taking the case away from the jury. This can be done at trial, e.g., by a directed verdict, or after trial, by judgment notwithstanding the verdict (judgment n.o.v.). The problem of exercise of this control is two-fold: (i) What cases should be taken from the jury? (ii) By what device should they be withdrawn from the jury? The first problem is essentially the same whether the withdrawal be at or after trial, and we consider it at the outset. Then we shall examine the mechanics of withdrawal, and the determinations of timing and strategy which aid in selecting among the various alternatives available. See Note on Devices for Taking a Case From the Jury, infra p. 1134. Finally, we shall examine the post-trial device of judgment notwithstanding the verdict, along with a less severe post-trial method of jury control, the grant of a new trial because the verdict is not supported by the evidence. See Motions After Verdict, infra p. 1159.

SIOUX CITY & PACIFIC RAILROAD CO. v. STOUT

Supreme Court of the United States, 1873.
84 U.S. (17 Wall.) 657, 21 L.Ed. 745.

Henry Stout, a child six years of age and living with his parents, sued, by his next friend, the Sioux City and Pacific Railroad Company, in the court below, to recover damages for an injury sustained upon a turntable belonging to the said company. The turntable was in an open space, about eighty rods from the company's depot, in a hamlet or settlement of one hundred to one hundred and fifty persons. Near the turntable was a travelled road passing through the depot grounds, and another travelled road near by. On the railroad ground, which was not inclosed or visibly separated from the adjoining property, was situated the company's station-house, and about a quarter of a mile distant from this was the turntable on which the plaintiff was injured. There were but few houses in the neighborhood of the turntable, and the child's parents lived in another part of the town, and about three-fourths of a mile distant. The child, without the knowledge of his parents, set off with two other boys, the one nine and the other ten years of age, to go to the depot, with no definite purpose in view. When the boys arrived there, it was proposed by some of them to go to the turntable to play. The turntable was not attended or guarded by any servant of the company, was not fastened or locked, and revolved easily on its axis. Two of the boys began to turn it, and in attempting to get upon it, the foot of the child (he being at the time upon the railroad track) was caught between the end of the rail on the turntable as it was revolving, and the end of the iron rail on the main track of the road, and was crushed.

One witness, then a servant of the company, testified that he had previously seen boys playing at the turntable, and had forbidden them from playing there. But the witness had no charge of the table, and did not communicate the fact of having seen boys playing there, to any of the officers or servants of the company having the table in charge.

One of the boys, who was with the child when injured, had previously played upon the turntable when the railroad men were working on the track, in sight, and not far distant.

It appeared from the testimony that the child had not, before the day on which he was now injured, played at the turntable, or had, indeed, ever been there.

The table was constructed on the railroad company's own land, and, the testimony tended to show, in the ordinary way. It was a skeleton turntable, that is to say, it was not planked between the rails, though it had one or two loose boards upon the ties. There was an iron latch fastened to it which turned on a hinge, and, when in order, dropped into an iron socket on the track, and held the table in position while using. The catch of this latch was broken at the time of the accident. The latch, which weighed eight or ten pounds, could be easily lifted out of the catch and thrown back on the table, and the table was allowed to be moved about. This latch was not locked, or in any way fastened down before it was broken, and all the testimony on that subject tended to show that it was not usual for railroad companies to lock or guard turntables, but that it was usual to have a latch with a catch, or draw-bolt, to keep them in position when used.

The record stated that "the counsel for the defendant disclaimed resting their defence on the ground that the plaintiff's parents were negligent, or that the plaintiff (considering his tender age) was negligent, but rested their defence on the ground that the company was not negligent, and asserted that the injury to the plaintiff was accidental or brought upon himself."

On the question whether there was negligence on the part of the railway company in the management or condition of its turntable, the judge charged the jury—"that to maintain the action it must appear by the evidence that the turntable, in the condition, situation, and place where it then was, was a dangerous machine, one which, if unguarded or unlocked, would be likely to cause injury to children; that if in its construction and the manner in which it was left it was not dangerous in its nature, the defendants were not liable for negligence; that they were further to consider whether, situated as it was as the defendants' property in a small town, somewhat remote from habitations, there was negligence in not anticipating that injury might occur if it was left unlocked or unguarded; that if they did not have reason to anticipate that children would be likely to resort to it, or that they would be likely to be injured if they did resort to it, then there was no negligence."

The jury found a verdict of $7500 for the plaintiff, from the judgment upon which this writ of error was brought.

Mr. Justice Hunt delivered the opinion of the court.

* * *

2d. Was there negligence on the part of the railway company in the management or condition of its turntable?

The charge on this point * * * was an impartial and intelligent one. Unless the defendant was entitled to an order that the plaintiff be nonsuited, or, as it is expressed in the practice of the United States courts, to an order directing a verdict in its favor, the submission was right. If, upon any construction which the jury was authorized to put upon the evidence, or by any inferences they were authorized to draw from it, the conclusion of negligence can be justified, the defendant was not entitled to this order, and the judgment cannot be disturbed. To express it affirmatively, if from the evidence given it might justly be inferred by the jury that the defendant, in the construction, location, management, or condition of its machine had omitted that care and attention to prevent the occurrence of accidents which prudent and careful men ordinarily bestow, the jury was at liberty to find for the plaintiff.

That the turntable was a dangerous machine, which would be likely to cause injury to children who resorted to it, might fairly be inferred from the injury which actually occurred to the plaintiff. There was the same liability to injury to him, and no greater, that existed with reference to all children. When the jury learned from the evidence that he had suffered a serious injury, by his foot being caught between the fixed rail of the road-bed and the turning rail of the table they were justified in believing that there was a probability of the occurrence of such accidents.

So, in looking at the remoteness of the machine from inhabited dwellings, when it was proved to the jury that several boys from the hamlet were at play there on this occasion, and that they had been at play upon the turntable on other occasions, and within the observation and to the knowledge of the employees of the defendant, the jury were justified in believing that children would probably resort to it, and that the defendant should have anticipated that such would be the case.

As it was in fact, on this occasion, so it was to be expected that the amusement of the boys would have been found in turning this table while they were on it or about it. This could certainly have been prevented by locking the turntable when not in use by the company. It was not shown that this would cause any considerable expense or inconvenience to the defendant. It could probably have been prevented by the repair of the broken latch. This was a heavy catch which, by dropping into a socket, prevented the revolution of the table. There had been one on this table weighing some eight or ten pounds, but it had been broken off and had not been replaced. It was proved to have been usual with railroad companies to have upon their turntables a latch or bolt, or some similar instrument. The jury may well have believed that if the defendant had incurred the trifling expense of replacing this latch, and had taken the slight trouble of putting it in its place, these very small boys would not have taken the pains to lift it out, and thus the whole difficulty have been avoided. Thus reasoning, the jury would have reached the conclusion that the defendant had omitted the care and attention it ought to have given, that it was negligent, and that its negligence caused the injury to the plaintiff. The evidence is not strong and the negligence is slight, but we are not able to say that there is not evidence sufficient to justify the verdict. We are not called upon to weigh, to measure, to balance the evidence, or to ascertain how we should have decided if acting as jurors. The charge was in all respects sound and judicious, and there being sufficient evidence to justify the finding, we are not authorized to disturb it.

3d. It is true, in many cases, that where the facts are undisputed the effect of them is for the judgment of the court, and not for the decision of the jury. This is true in that class of cases where the existence of such facts come in question rather than where deductions or inferences are to be made from the facts. If a deed be given in evidence, a contract proven, or its breach testified to, the existence of such deed, contract or breach, there being nothing in derogation of the evidence, is no doubt to be ruled as a question of law. In some cases, too, the necessary inference from the proof is so certain that it may be ruled as a question of law. If a sane man voluntarily throws himself in contact with a passing engine, there being nothing to counteract the effect of this action, it may be ruled as a matter of law that the injury to him resulted from his own fault, and that no action can be sustained by him or his representatives. So if a coach-driver intentionally drives within a few inches of a precipice, and an accident happens, negligence may be ruled as a question of law. On the other hand, if he had placed a suitable distance between his coach and the precipice, but by the breaking of a rein or an axle, which could not have been anticipated, an injury occurred, it might be ruled as a question of law that there was no negligence and no liability. But these are extreme cases. The range between them is almost infinite in variety and extent. It is in relation to these intermediate cases that the opposite rule prevails. Upon the facts proven in such cases, it is a matter of judgment and discretion, of sound inference, what is the deduction to be drawn from the undisputed facts. Certain facts we may suppose to be clearly established from which one sensible, impartial man would infer that proper care had not been used, and that negligence existed; another man equally sensible and equally impartial would infer that proper care had been used, and that there was no negligence. It is this class of cases and those akin to it that the law commits to the decision of a jury. Twelve men of the average of the community, comprising men of education and men of little education, men of learning and men whose learning consists only in what they have themselves seen and heard, the merchant, the mechanic, the farmer, the laborer; these sit together, consult, apply their separate experience of the affairs of life to the facts proven, and draw a unanimous conclusion. This average judgment thus given it is the great effort of the law to obtain. It is assumed that twelve men know more of the common affairs of life than does one man, that they can draw wiser and safer conclusions from admitted facts thus occurring than can a single judge.

In no class of cases can this practical experience be more wisely applied than in that we are considering. We find, accordingly, although not uniform or harmonious, that the authorities justify us in holding in the case before us, that although the facts are undisputed it is for the jury and not for the judge to determine whether proper care was given, or whether they establish negligence.

In Redfield on the Law of Railways, [vol. 2, p. 231] it is said: "And what is proper care will be often a question of law, where there is no controversy about the facts. But ordinarily, we apprehend, where there is any testimony tending to show negligence, it is a question for the jury." * * *

In Patterson v. Wallace, [1 McQueen's House of Lords Cases, 748] there was no controversy about the facts, but only a question whether certain facts proved established negligence on the one side, or rashness on the other. The judge at the trial withdrew the case from the jury, but it was held in the House of Lords to be a pure question of fact for the jury, and the judgment was reversed.

In Mangam v. Brooklyn Railroad, [1868, 38 N.Y. 455, 11 Tiffany 455, 98 Am.Dec. 66] the facts in relation to the conduct of the child injured, the manner in which it was guarded, and how it escaped from those having it in charge, were undisputed. The judge at the trial ordered a nonsuit, holding that these facts established negligence in those having the custody of the child. The Court of Appeals of the State of New York held that the case should have been submitted to the jury, and set aside the nonsuit.

In Detroit & W.R.R. Co. v. Van Steinburg, [1868, 17 Mich. 99] the cases are largely examined, and the rule laid down, that when the facts are disputed, or when they are not disputed, but different minds might honestly draw different conclusions from them, the case must be left to the jury for their determination.

It has been already shown that the facts proved justified the jury in finding that the defendant was guilty of negligence, and we are of the opinion that it was properly left to the jury to determine that point.

Upon the whole case, the judgment must be affirmed.

SIMBLEST v. MAYNARD
United States Court of Appeals for the Second Circuit, 1970.
427 F.2d 1.

TIMBERS, DISTRICT JUDGE.*

We have before us another instance of Vermont justice—this time at the hands of a federal trial judge who, correctly applying the law, set aside a $17,125 plaintiff's verdict and entered judgment n.o.v. for defendant, Rule 50(b), Fed.R.Civ.P., in a diversity negligence action arising out of an intersection collision between a passenger vehicle driven by plaintiff and a fire engine driven by defendant in Burlington, Vermont, during the electric power blackout which left most of New England in darkness on the night of November 9, 1965. We affirm.

I

Plaintiff, a citizen and resident of New Hampshire, was 66 years of age at the time of the accident. He was a distributor of reference books and had been in Burlington on business for three days prior to the accident. He was an experienced driver, having driven an average of some 54,000 miles per year since 1922. He was thoroughly familiar with the intersection in question. His eyesight was excellent and his hearing was very good.

* Chief Judge of the District of Connecticut, sitting by designation.

Defendant, a citizen of Vermont, had resided in Burlington for 44 years. He had been a full time fireman with the Burlington Fire Department for 17 years. He was assigned to and regularly drove the 500 gallon pumper which he was driving at the time of the accident. He was thoroughly familiar with the intersection in question.

The accident occurred at the intersection of Main Street (U.S. Route 2), which runs generally east and west, and South Willard Street (U.S. Routes 2 and 7), which runs generally north and south. The neighborhood is partly business, partly residential. At approximately the center of the intersection there was an overhead electrical traffic control signal designed to exhibit the usual red and green lights.

At the time of the accident, approximately 5:27 P.M., it was dark, traffic was light and the weather was clear. Plaintiff was driving his 1964 Chrysler station wagon in a westerly direction on Main Street, approaching the intersection. Defendant was driving the fire engine, in response to a fire alarm, in a southerly direction on South Willard Street, also approaching the intersection.

Plaintiff testified that the traffic light was green in his favor as he approached and entered the intersection; but that when he had driven part way through the intersection the power failure extinguished all lights within his range of view, including the traffic light. All other witnesses, for both plaintiff and defendant, testified that the power failure occurred at least 10 to 15 minutes prior to the accident; and there was no evidence, except plaintiff's testimony, that the traffic light was operating at the time of the accident.

Plaintiff also testified that his speed was 12 to 15 miles per hour as he approached the intersection. He did not look to his right *before* he entered the intersection; [1] after looking to his left, to the front and to the rear (presumably through a rear view mirror), he looked to his right

---

1. Plaintiff has stated in his brief in this Court that "as he approached the intersection, he *did* look to his right" (Appellant's Brief, 5); and he emphasizes "the only direct evidence on this point . . . from the plaintiff who testified as follows:

'Q. You did look to the right? A. Oh yes, sir. I sure did.'" (Appellant's Brief, 12–13.)

We find this testimony, lifted out of context, unfortunately to have created a mistaken impression on a critical issue in the case.

Plaintiff's complete direct testimony as to when he looked to his right, and in the sequence given, is as follows:

"*Direct Examination* (By Mr. Grussing)
. . .

Q. Now, tell us, Mr. Simblest, in your own words, just what occurred when you entered that intersection. A. Well, I will repeat. I had the 'green' light with me, proceeded through, was talf (sic) to ¾ through the street, looked to my right, and within 12 feet of me, here is a big, massive fire truck. . . . . (Tr. 17)

. . .

Q. Did you, as you approached this intersection, did you look to your right at all to see what was coming out of the intersection? A. Coming into an intersection with people ready to go across, with fairly decent eyesight I could see from the left to the right to the front, and I had already watched in the rear before they got to that angle.

Q. You did look to the right? A. Oh, yes, sir. I sure did.

Q. Were you able, or did you see this truck approaching? A. Within '12' feet. It was too late.

Q. The first time you saw it, it was within 12 feet of you? A. That is right." (Tr. 19)

for the first time *when he was one-half to three-quarters of the way through the intersection* and then for the first time saw the fire engine within 12 feet of him. He testified that he did not hear the fire engine's siren or see the flashing lights or any other lights on the fire engine.

Plaintiff further testified that his view to the north (his right) as he entered the intersection was obstructed by various objects, including traffic signs, trees on Main Street and a Chamber of Commerce information booth on Main Street east of the intersection. All of the evidence, including the photographs of the intersection, demonstrates that, despite some obstruction of plaintiff's view to the north, he could have seen the approaching fire engine if he had looked between the obstructions and if he had looked to the north after he passed the information booth. One of plaintiff's own witnesses, Kathleen Burgess, testified that "maybe five to ten seconds previous to when he was struck he might have seen the fire truck," referring to the interval of time after plaintiff passed the information booth until the collision.

Defendant testified that, accompanied by Captain Fortin in the front seat, he drove the fire engine from the Mansfield Avenue Fire Station, seven and one-half blocks away from the scene of the accident, in the direction of the fire on Maple Street. While driving in a southerly direction on South Willard Street and approaching the intersection with Main Street, the following warning devices were in operation on the fire engine: the penetrator making a wailing sound; the usual fire siren; a flashing red light attached to the dome of the fire engine; two red lights on either side of the cab; and the usual headlights. Defendant saw plaintiff's car east of the information booth and next saw it as it entered the intersection. Defendant testified that he was traveling 20 to 25 miles per hour as he approached the intersection;[2] he slowed down, applied his brakes and turned the fire engine to his right, in a westerly direction, in an attempt to avoid the collision. He estimated that he was traveling 15 to 20 miles per hour at the time of impact. A police investigation found a 15 foot skid mark made by the fire engine but no skid marks made by plaintiff's car.

The fire engine struck plaintiff's car on the right side, in the area of the fender and front door. Plaintiff's head struck the post on the left side of his car, causing him to lose consciousness for about a minute. He claims that this injury aggravated a chronic pre-existing degenerative arthritic condition of the spine.

Other witnesses who virtually bracketed the intersection from different vantage points were called. Frank Valz, called by plaintiff, was looking out a window in a building on the northeast corner of the intersection; he saw the fire engine when it was a block north of the intersection; he heard its siren and saw its flashing red lights. Kathleen Burgess, another of plaintiff's witnesses (referred to above), was

2. The maximum speed attributed to the fire engine as it approached the inter- section was 30 to 35 miles per hour (testimony of Captain Fortin).

driving in a northerly direction on South Willard Street, just south of the intersection; seeing the fire engine when it was a block north of the intersection, she pulled over to the curb and stopped; she saw its flashing lights, but did not hear its siren.   Holland Smith and Irene Longe, both called by defendant, were in the building at the southwest corner of the intersection; as the fire engine approached the intersection, they each heard its warning signals and saw its flashing lights in operation.

Defendant's motions for a directed verdict at the close of plaintiff's case and at the close of all the evidence having been denied and the jury having returned a plaintiff's verdict, defendant moved to set aside the verdict and the judgment entered thereon and for entry of judgment n.o.v. in accordance with his motion for a directed verdict.   Chief Judge Leddy filed a written opinion granting defendant's motion.

On appeal plaintiff urges that the district court erred in granting defendant's motion for judgment n.o.v. or, in the alternative, in declining to charge the jury on the doctrine of last clear chance.   We affirm both rulings of the district court.

II

In determining whether the motion for judgment n.o.v. should have been granted, a threshold question is presented as to the correct standard to be applied.   This standard has been expressed in various ways.   Simply stated, it is whether the evidence is such that, without weighing the credibility of the witnesses or otherwise considering the weight of the evidence, there can be but one conclusion as to the verdict that reasonable men could have reached.   See, e.g., Brady v. Southern Railway Company, 320 U.S. 476, 479–80 (1943); O'Connor v. Pennsylvania Railroad Company, 308 F.2d 911, 914–15 (2 Cir. 1962).   See also 5 Moore's Federal Practice ¶ 50.02[1], at 2320–23 (2d ed. 1968); Wright, Law of Federal Courts § 95, at 425 (2d ed. 1970).   On a motion for judgment n.o.v., the evidence must be viewed in the light most favorable to the party against whom the motion is made and he must be given the benefit of all reasonable inferences which may be drawn in his favor from that evidence.   O'Connor v. Pennsylvania Railroad Company, supra, at 914–15;   5 Moore, supra, at 2325;   Wright, supra, at 425.

We acknowledge that it has not been settled in a diversity action whether, in considering the evidence in the light most favorable to the party against whom the motion is made, the court may consider all the evidence or only the evidence favorable to such party and the uncontradicted, unimpeached evidence unfavorable to him.   Under Vermont law, all the evidence may be considered.   Kremer v. Fortin, 119 Vt. 1, 117 A.2d 245 (1955) (intersection collision between fire engine and passenger car).   Plaintiff here urges that under the federal standard only evidence favorable to him should have been considered, citing Wilkerson v. McCarthy, 336 U.S. 53, 57 (1949).   As plaintiff reads that case, the court below should not have considered anything else, not even the uncontradicted, unimpeached evidence unfavorable to him. However, we are committed to a contrary view in a diversity case. O'Connor v. Pennsylvania Railroad Company, supra.

The Supreme Court at least twice has declined to decide whether the state or federal standard as to the sufficiency of the evidence is controlling on such motions in diversity cases. Mercer v. Theriot, 377 U.S. 152, 156 (1964) (per curiam); Dick v. New York Life Insurance Company, 359 U.S. 437, 444–45 (1959). Our Court likewise has declined to decide this issue in recent cases. Mull v. Ford Motor Company, 368 F.2d 713, 716 n. 4 (2 Cir. 1966); Hooks v. New York Central Railroad Company, 327 F.2d 259, 261 n. 2 (2 Cir. 1964); Jacobs v. Great Atlantic & Pacific Tea Company, 324 F.2d 50, 51 n. 1 (2 Cir. 1963); Evans v. S. J. Groves & Sons Company, 315 F.2d 335, 342 n. 2 (2 Cir. 1963). See 5 Moore, supra, at 2347–50.[3]

Our careful review of the record in the instant case leaves us with the firm conviction that, under either the Vermont standard or the more restrictive federal standard, plaintiff was contributorily negligent as a matter of law; and that Chief Judge Leddy correctly set aside the verdict and entered judgment for defendant n.o.v. O'Connor v. Pennsylvania Railroad Company, supra, at 914; Presser Royalty Company v. Chase Manhattan Bank, 272 F.2d 838, 840 (2 Cir. 1959).

Under the Vermont standard which permits all the evidence to be considered, Kremer v. Fortin, supra, plaintiff was so clearly guilty of contributory negligence that no further dilation is required.

Under the more restrictive federal standard—i.e., considering only the evidence favorable to plaintiff and the uncontradicted, unimpeached evidence unfavorable to him—while a closer question is presented than under the Vermont standard, we nevertheless hold that plaintiff was guilty of contributory negligence as a matter of law.[4]

In our view, applying the federal standard, the critical issue in the case is whether the fire engine was sounding a siren or displaying a red

3. Assuming that the federal standard were controlling, plaintiff's contention that under that standard evidence introduced by the moving party may not be considered is open to question. Plaintiff relies on Wilkerson v. McCarthy, 336 U.S. 53, 57 (1949). But most Courts of Appeals have held that evidence introduced by the moving party may be considered, distinguishing Wilkerson on the ground that FELA cases are sui generis. 5 Moore, supra, at 2329.

See especially the comprehensive opinion of the Fifth Circuit in Boeing Company v. Shipman, 411 F.2d 365 (5 Cir. 1969) (en banc), holding (1) that in diversity cases a federal rather than state standard should be applied in testing the sufficiency of the evidence in connection with motions for a

directed verdict and for judgment n.o.v.; (2) that the FELA standard for testing the sufficiency of the evidence on such motions is not applicable in diversity cases; and (3) that the federal standard to be applied in diversity cases requires the court to consider "all of the evidence—not just that evidence which supports the nonmover's case—but in the light and with all reasonable inferences most favorable to the party opposed to the motion." 411 F.2d at 374.

4. We emphasize that, solely for the purpose of testing the validity of plaintiff's claim under the federal standard, we assume without deciding that the federal standard is as stated. But compare, e.g., Boeing Company v. Shipman, supra note 3, at 373–75.

light as it approached the intersection immediately before the collision. Upon this critical issue, Chief Judge Leddy accurately and succinctly summarized the evidence as follows:

> "All witnesses to the accident, except the plaintiff, testified that the fire truck was sounding a siren or displaying a flashing red light. All of the witnesses except Miss Burgess and the plaintiff testified that the fire truck was sounding its siren and displaying a flashing red light."

The reason such evidence is critical is that under Vermont law, 23 V.S.A. § 1033, upon the approach of a fire department vehicle which is sounding a siren or displaying a red light, or both, all other vehicles are required to pull over to the right lane of traffic and come to a complete stop until the emergency vehicle has passed.[5] Since the emergency provision of this statute supersedes the general right of way statute regarding intersections controlled by traffic lights, 23 V.S.A. § 1054, the lone testimony of plaintiff that the traffic light was green in his favor as he approached and entered the intersection is of no moment. And since the emergency provision of 23 V.S.A. § 1033 becomes operative if *either* the siren is sounding *or* a red light is displayed on an approaching fire engine, we focus upon plaintiff's own testimony that he did not see the fire engine's flashing light, all other witnesses having testified that the red light was flashing.

As stated above, plaintiff testified that he first saw the fire engine when he was one-half to three-quarters of the way through the intersection and when the fire engine was within 12 feet of his car. At the speed at which the fire engine was traveling, plaintiff had approximately one-third of a second[6] in which to observe the fire engine prior to the collision. Accepting plaintiff's testimony that his eyesight was excellent, and assuming that the fire engine's flashing red light was revolving as rapidly as 60 revolutions per minute, plaintiff's one-third of a second observation does not support an inference that the light was not operating, much less does it constitute competent direct evidence to that effect. Opportunity to observe is a necessary ingredient of the competency of eyewitness evidence. Plaintiff's opportunity to observe,

---

5. 23 V.S.A. § 1033, in relevant part, provides:

"Except as hereinafter provided, all vehicles shall give the right of way to other vehicles approaching at intersecting highways from the right; and shall have the right of way over those approaching from the left; provided that upon the approach of an ambulance, police or fire department vehicle which is sounding a siren or displaying a red light or both, all other vehicles shall pull to the right of the lane of traffic and come to a complete stop until such emergency vehicle has passed. . . ."

Violation of this statute under Vermont law constitutes prima facie evidence of negligence. Dashnow v. Myers, 121 Vt. 273, 155 A.2d 859 (1959).

6. This is the arthimetical mean (.322 seconds) between the maximum and minimum time intervals, according to the evidence, within which plaintiff could have observed the fire engine travel 12 feet. The minimum interval (.230 seconds) is based on Captain Fortin's testimony that the fire engine was traveling 35 miles per hour as it approached the intersection (supra note 2); the maximum interval (.414 seconds) is based on defendant's testimony that he was traveling 20 miles per hour (supra pages 3 and 4).

accepting his own testimony, simply was too short for his testimony on the operation of the light to be of any probative value whatsoever.

Plaintiff's testimony that he did not see the fire engine's flashing red light, in the teeth of the proven physical facts, we hold is tantamount to no proof at all on that issue. O'Connor v. Pennsylvania Railroad Company, supra, at 915. As one commentator has put it, ". . . the question of the total absence of proof quickly merges into the question whether the proof adduced is so insignificant as to be treated as the equivalent of the absence of proof." 5 Moore, supra, at 2320. If plaintiff had testified that he had not looked to his right at all, he of course would have been guilty of contributory negligence as a matter of law. We hold that his testimony in fact was the equivalent of his saying that he did not look at all.

Chief Judge Leddy concluded that plaintiff was guilty of contributory negligence as a matter of law; accordingly, he set aside the verdict and entered judgment n.o.v. for defendant. We agree.

III

Plaintiff urges in the alternative the claim that the district court erred in declining to charge the jury on the doctrine of last clear chance; of course this doctrine is relevant only if plaintiff was guilty of contributory negligence. Since we hold, as did Chief Judge Leddy, that plaintiff was contributorily negligent, his last clear chance claim is properly before us.

Moreover, we reject defendant's contentions that plaintiff failed properly to plead the doctrine of last clear chance (the complaint was amended to reflect such claim); and that plaintiff's requests to charge on the doctrine consisted of mere abstract propositions of law (the trial judge denied plaintiff's request to charge on last clear chance on the ground that "I do not think there is any evidence to support it").

We turn directly to whether there was evidence sufficient to warrant charging the jury on the issue of last clear chance. In addition to the usual essential elements of last clear chance, Vermont law requires the existence of a period of time during which *plaintiff*, in the exercise of due care, *could not* have avoided the accident *and* during which *defendant*, in the exercise of due care, *could* have avoided the accident. Spencer v. Fondry, 122 Vt. 149, 152, 167 A.2d 372 (1960).

Plaintiff's claim regarding last clear chance is pegged entirely on the theory that, there being no traffic behind his car, defendant should have seen such absence of traffic and should have had sufficient time to turn the fire engine to his left, rather than to his right, and thus to maneuver it into the space to the rear of plaintiff's car.

We agree with Chief Judge Leddy's ruling, directed precisely to plaintiff's claim in this respect, in refusing to charge on the doctrine of last clear chance:

> "The evidence is that, as I recall it, that while there was sufficient space behind the rear of the plaintiff's car and the easterly line of Willard Street, all of the testimony is that at the rate of speed the truck was going and because of the closeness of the two vehicles, it was impossible for the truck to make a maneuvering to go through that space, and that was testified to by the driver and also Miss Burgess who was parked on the opposite side of the intersection."

We hold, assuming *arguendo* there was an interval of time during which plaintiff in the exercise of due care could not have avoided the accident, that—based on the proven physical facts regarding the speed of the fire engine and the proximity of the two vehicles referred to above—the overwhelming, uncontroverted evidence demonstrates that defendant in the exercise of due care simply could not have avoided the accident. Spencer v. Fondry, supra, at 152.

Affirmed.

NEWING v. CHEATHAM

Supreme Court of California, 1975.
15 Cal.3d 351, 124 Cal.Rptr. 193, 540 P.2d 33.*

SULLIVAN, JUSTICE.

In this action for damages for wrongful death arising out of the crash of a private airplane, defendant Steven Eugene Cheatham as administrator of the estate of Harold Cheatham (hereafter Cheatham) deceased appeals from a judgment entered upon a jury verdict in favor of plaintiffs and against decedent's estate in the sum of $125,000. Plaintiffs are the surviving wife and children of Richard Newing, an occupant of the plane who died in the crash. Defendant's decedent who also died in the crash was the owner and pilot of the plane.

About 1 p.m. on Sunday, October 25, 1970, Richard Newing, Harold Cheatham, and Ronald Bird departed from Brown Field at Chula Vista, California, aboard a single-engine Cessna 172 aircraft owned and piloted by Cheatham. Neither Newing nor Bird was a licensed pilot. At the time of take-off the weather was clear and the visibility unrestricted. There was no evidence that the plane landed at any other field that afternoon, or that it sent any radio messages. When it failed to return, a search was commenced. On the following day the plane's wreckage was located by a search aircraft in mountainous terrain about 13 miles east of Tijuana, Mexico, and an equal distance southeast of Brown Field. A rescue party found all occupants of the airplane dead. The clock on the instrument panel was stopped at 5:18.

* Some of the court's footnotes are omitted.

Plaintiffs brought this action for wrongful death alleging that the crash had been caused by Cheatham's negligence. At trial, three theories were advanced in support of plaintiffs' case. The first was that Cheatham had negligently permitted the airplane to run out of fuel while in flight. The second was that he had been negligent as a matter of law in that he had violated applicable federal air regulations. Finally, Cheatham's negligence was said to be established by the doctrine of res ipsa loquitur.

In support of the first of these theories, plaintiffs offered the testimony of Jorge Areizaga Rojo, then Commandante of the Tijuana Airport, and of Jesus Leon an airport mechanic. Rojo, who testified as an expert witness, had been a member of the rescue party that first reached the wreckage of the aircraft. Accompanied by Leon, he returned to the site on the second day after the crash in order to gather information for a report to the Mexican authorities. Rojo testified that he visually inspected the fuel tanks of the aircraft, which were carried on its wings, but saw no fuel. He also attempted, but without success, to drain fuel from the bottom of each tank by removing drain plugs.

Leon testified that he had inspected the aircraft's fuel system, although he had not dismantled it, but had found no trace of fuel. Both men visually inspected the ground beneath the aircraft, but saw no indication of fuel spillage. They also attempted to measure the fuel in one of the wing tanks; Leon estimated the level of the fuel to be $3/16$ of an inch. Rojo indicated that whatever fuel remained in the tanks was probably "unusable," in the sense that it was not a sufficient quantity to reach the engine. Rojo also testified concerning the general structural condition of the aircraft, the appearance of the propeller and control surfaces, the upright position in which the plane had come to rest, and the general description of the accident site. All of these factors, he said, indicated that the crash had been caused by fuel exhaustion.

On cross-examination, however, Rojo conceded that the appearance and condition of the plane would have been the same if the crash had been caused by engine failure or some similar mechanical malfunction resulting in loss of power. He also indicated that since the aircraft had not been brought to a level position before he had attempted to drain fuel from the tanks, a usable amount of fuel might have remained within. He admitted that there had been no very thorough investigation of other potential causes of the crash. Despite the foregoing, however, he remained of the opinion that the plane had crashed because it had run out of fuel.

Plaintiffs also called as an expert witness Michael Potter, an airline pilot who had logged some 1,200 hours of flight time in small aircraft, including 200 hours in a Cessna 172. Potter testified at length concerning the training received by student pilots with respect to fuel management and emergencies in flight. He stated that a prudent pilot maintains at the minimum a 45-minute reserve of fuel, and ordinarily flies high enough above surrounding terrain to permit his aircraft to glide to a safe landing in the event of a power failure. Potter also testified that, according to the operator's manual, a Cessna 172 has sufficient fuel capacity to fly for 4.3 hours when operated at the usual power settings and with a "lean" fuel mixture. Thus, he said, the Cheatham plane, if operated in the usual manner with respect to power settings, fuel mixture, and altitude, should have run out of fuel at just the time indicated on its damaged clock.[2] However, he indicated on cross-examination that the endurance of a Cessna 172 can be greater or less than 4.3 hours depending upon the manner in which it is operated. Despite this, Potter said that the crash had probably been caused by fuel exhaustion and the pilot's failure to maintain proper terrain clearance. This opinion was based upon his examination of photographs of the wreckage, his observations made during overflights of the crash site, the testimony of Rojo and Leon, and an experiment in which he ran the engine of a stationary Cessna 172 until its fuel supply was exhausted. From such experiment Potter found that $5/16$ of an inch of fuel remained in the tanks after the engine had stopped.

Defendant called as an expert witness Robert Rudich, an experienced air traffic controller who had written widely on the subject of air crash investigations and had participated in many such investigations, though chiefly as an analyst of cockpit recording devices and as an editor of final reports. Rudich expressed no opinion as to the cause of the crash, but testified instead about the procedures that must be employed in a sound air crash investigation. * * * The court did not permit Rudich to express an opinion as to the quality of the investigation conducted by Rojo and Leon, although the implication of his testimony was that their investigation had been rudimentary at best. However, Rudich was allowed to testify about an experiment he performed on a detached Cessna 172 wing arranged at an angle approximating that of the wing of the downed plane as shown in photographs of the wreckage. Rudich found that it required 7.5 gallons of gasoline to raise the fuel level in the wing tank to $3/16$ of an inch. This was said to constitute a usable amount of fuel.

In addition to this expert testimony, defendant introduced evidence that the three dead men had been drinking beer together on the day of the crash. The owner of a National City tavern testified that Newing, a man named "Harold," and another man had drunk draft beer in his establishment for about an hour that morning, although he was unable to say how much beer they had consumed. A member of the rescue party testified that eight or nine empty beer cans had been found in the wreckage of the Cheatham plane. Evidence was also produced that the Mexican physicians who had performed autopsies on the bodies of the

---

2. According to Rojo, the clock probably had been stopped by the impact of the crash. Thus, a crash at 5:18, the time at which the clock stopped, would have occurred just 4.3 hours after the take-off at 1 p.m. However, there was no evidence that the clock had been properly set. Nor was there any evidence as to the altitude, power settings, or fuel mixture at which the plane had been operated.

three men, had noted a strong odor of alcohol emanating from the remains of Cheatham and Bird, but not from Newing's.

After the close of the evidence, the trial judge * * * granted plaintiffs' motion for a directed verdict on the issue of liability, concluding that the elements of res ipsa loquitur had been established as a matter of law and that the inference of negligence arising from the doctrine had not been rebutted as required by Evidence Code section 646. The jury returned a verdict in favor of plaintiffs in the amount of $125,000. Judgment was entered accordingly. This appeal followed.
* * *

We proceed * * * mindful of the familiar rules governing the granting of a motion for a directed verdict. Adverting to them in the context of a directed verdict in favor of the plaintiff, we had this to say in Walters v. Bank of America (1937) 9 Cal.2d 46, 49, 69 P.2d 839, 840: "The trial court, in a proper case, may direct a verdict in favor of a party upon whom rests the burden of proof, in this case the plaintiff. Substantially the same rules apply to directed verdicts in favor of plaintiffs as apply to such verdicts in favor of defendants. [Citations.] A directed verdict may be granted, when, disregarding conflicting evidence, and indulging every legitimate inference which may be drawn from the evidence in favor of the party against whom the verdict is directed, it can be said that there is no evidence of sufficient substantiality to support a verdict in favor of such party, if such a verdict has been rendered. [Citations.] In passing on the propriety of the trial court's action in directing a verdict, the doctrine of scintilla of evidence has been rejected in this state. [Citation.] A motion for a directed verdict may be granted upon the motion of the plaintiff, where, upon the whole evidence, the cause of action alleged in the complaint is supported and no substantial support is given to the defense alleged by the defendant. [Citations.]" * * *

It is settled law in this state that the "doctrine of res ipsa loquitur is applicable where the accident is of such a nature that it can be said, in the light of past experience, that it probably was the result of negligence by someone and that the defendant is probably the one responsible. [Citations.]" (Di Mare v. Cresci (1962) 58 Cal.2d 292, 298–299, 23 Cal.Rptr. 772, 776, 373 P.2d 860, 864.) According to the classic and oft-repeated statement, there are three conditions for the application of the doctrine: "(1) the accident must be of a kind which ordinarily does not occur in the absence of someone's negligence; (2) it must be caused by an agency or instrumentality within the exclusive control of the defendant; (3) it must not have been due to any voluntary action or contribution on the part of the plaintiff." * * *
* * *

Whether aircraft accidents are more often than not the result of negligence is a question that has vexed the courts of many jurisdictions for decades. (See cases collected in Annot., 6 A.L.R.2d 528 (1949), and Speiser, Res Ipsa Loquitur (1972) § 10:1 et seq.) According to Prosser, many early cases took the position that not enough was known about the hazards of flight to permit an inference of negligence to arise from the mere fact of a plane crash. (Prosser, Law of Torts (4th ed. 1971) p. 216.) Advances in the safety and frequency of air travel, however, have led to a trend in the opposite direction. Thus, while judicial opinion on the subject is by no means unanimous, res ipsa loquitur, over the years, has been applied to an increasing variety of aircraft mishaps. * * *

It is not fatal to the ruling here under review that the above cited cases dealt with the application of the doctrine of res ipsa loquitur as a question of fact to be determined by the jury whereas in the case at bench, it was applied by the trial judge to the air crash here involved as a matter of law. Essentially any differences in the manner of establishing the doctrine lies in the state of the evidence and the posture of the case. * * *

* * * In the instant case, it seems reasonably clear in light of the circumstances surrounding the crash that the accident ordinarily would not have taken place in the absence of negligence. The evidence is uncontradicted that the airplane took off from Chula Vista in clear weather with no restrictions on visibility. There is no evidence that weather conditions contributed in any way to the crash of the plane. Nor was there any evidence that the plane had collided with other aircraft while in flight. Indeed the condition of the plane after the crash was such as to eliminate an air collision. It thus fell to the ground, apparently unaffected by external factors, only a few miles from the airport whence it had departed some hours earlier. Under the circumstances of the present case, "it seems reasonably clear that the accident probably would not have occurred without negligence by someone." (Zentz v. Coca Cola Bottling Co., supra, 39 Cal.2d 436, 447, 247 P.2d 344, 350.) The evidence bearing on these circumstances is not only uncontradicted but of such a nature that no issue of fact is raised as to the existence of the first condition for the application of the doctrine of res ipsa loquitur. (Roddiscraft, Inc. v. Skelton Logging Co., supra, 212 Cal.App.2d 784, 794, 28 Cal.Rptr. 277.) We conclude that the first condition is established as a matter of law.

The doctrine's second condition, as traditionally formulated, is that the agency or instrumentality causing the accident must have been within the exclusive control or management of the defendant. The purpose of this requirement is to link the defendant with the probability, already established, that the accident was negligently caused. (Zentz v. Coca Cola Bottling Co., supra, 39 Cal.2d 436, 443, 247 P.2d 344.)

The facts of this case are such as to satisfy this condition, like the first, as a matter of law. Cheatham was the owner of the aircraft, and there is no dispute that he was at the controls when the plane took off on its final flight. Since neither of his passengers seems to have been a licensed pilot, there is no reason to suppose that anyone other than he operated the plane at any time before the crash. Moreover, Cheatham's ultimate responsibility for all decisions concerning the aircraft's operation was established by an applicable federal air regulation.[5] * * *

* * *

The third of the traditional conditions for the application of res ipsa loquitur is that the accident must not have been caused by any voluntary action or contribution on the part of the plaintiff. * * *

* * * [T]he uncontradicted evidence shows that the body of plaintiffs' decedent was found by the rescue party in one of the rear seats of the four-seater aircraft. From that position, it is difficult to imagine how he could have interfered physically with the operation of the aircraft in any way. (Cf. Guerra v. Handlery Hotels, Inc. (1959) 53 Cal.2d 266, 271, 1 Cal.Rptr. 330, 347 P.2d 674.) * * *

A separate question in this respect, however, is said to arise from the evidence that the three men drank beer together on the day of the crash. Defendant argues that Newing's conduct in drinking with Cheatham may have contributed to the happening of the accident, and that plaintiffs have not carried their burden with respect to negating this possibility. For reasons which will be more fully discussed in connection with the defenses of contributory negligence and assumption of risk, the evidence concerning the beer drinking was too vague to support a finding that Newing contributed by means of it to the happening of the crash. Plaintiffs are not obligated to eliminate entirely speculative causal possibilities involving the conduct of their decedent. It is enough if they rebut those inferences of their decedent's responsibility which are reasonably supported by the evidence. Plaintiffs discharged this burden by introducing evidence from which it must be inferred that Newing did not interfere with Cheatham's operation or command of the aircraft.

The evidence presented in the trial court, therefore, was such as to satisfy all three conditions for the applicability of res ipsa loquitur as a matter of law. * * * This gave rise to a presumption affecting the burden of producing evidence pursuant to Evidence Code section 646.[6]

---

5. 14 Code of Federal Regulations, section 91.3(a) provides: "The pilot in command of an aircraft is directly responsible for, and is the final authority as to, the operation of that aircraft."

6. Evidence Code section 646 provides:

"(a) As used in this section, 'defendant' includes any party against whom the res ipsa loquitur presumption operates.

"(b) The judicial doctrine of res ipsa loquitur is a presumption affecting the burden of producing evidence.

"(c) If the evidence, or facts otherwise established, would support a res ipsa loquitur presumption and the defendant has introduced evidence which would support a finding that he was not negligent or that any negligence on his part was not a proximate cause of the occurrence, the court may, and upon request shall, instruct the jury to the effect that:

"(1) If the facts which would give rise to a res ipsa loquitur presumption are found or otherwise established, the jury may draw the inference from such facts that a proximate cause of the occurrence was some negligent conduct on the part of the defendant; and

"(2) The jury shall not find that a proximate cause of the occurrence was some negligent conduct on the part of the defendant unless the jury believes, after weighing all the evidence in the

It then became defendant's obligation to introduce sufficient evidence to sustain a finding either that the accident resulted from some cause other than Cheatham's negligence, or, else, that Cheatham exercised due care in all possible respects wherein he might have been negligent. (See Cal.Law Revision Com. comment to Evid.Code, § 646.) Defendant introduced no such evidence. He has at most argued that the crash *could* have resulted from causes other than the negligence of his decedent. Mere speculation of this sort is insufficient to discharge defendant's burden of explanation. (Dierman v. Providence Hospital (1947) 31 Cal.2d 290, 295–296, 188 P.2d 12; Roberts v. Trans World Airlines, supra, 225 Cal.App.2d 344, 354–355, 37 Cal.Rptr. 291.) Consequently, the trial court was correct in concluding that res ipsa loquitur established Cheatham's negligence as a matter of law.

*   *   *

DOBSON v. MASONITE CORP.

United States Court of Appeals for the Fifth Circuit, 1966.
359 F.2d 921.

HUTCHESON, CIRCUIT JUDGE.

By this suit Clyde Dobson seeks to recover from Masonite Corporation for breach of an oral contract. The jury returned a verdict favorable to Dobson and assessed damages against Masonite. The district court, of the opinion that only a legal question was involved, and that the law favored Masonite, entered judgment notwithstanding the verdict absolving Masonite of liability. We conclude that the case as presented to the district court made necessary a factual determination; that in entering judgment notwithstanding the verdict, the district court undertook to find the facts itself, and thereby invaded the fact-finding province of the jury; and that the entry of judgment notwithstanding the verdict was thus manifestly improper. Accordingly, we reverse the judgment and remand the case with instructions to reinstate the jury's verdict.

Masonite desired to rid its Mississippi lands, consisting of some 9,200 acres, of all oak timber and undesirable and unwanted species of tree. In March, 1963, Dobson orally agreed to undertake cutting operations on Masonite's lands. Neither party disputes the existence of the oral agreement; nor is there any real quarrel regarding the basic terms of the agreement. Under the contract Dobson was (1) to cut all oak, whether dead, diseased, defective, or merchantable; (2) to have complete control over the entire cutting operation and the timber cut; (3) to sell so much of the cut timber as he could; and (4) to pay Masonite initially twelve dollars, and subsequently ten dollars, per thousand log feet of oak actually sold, and to retain all amounts

case and drawing such inferences therefrom as the jury believes are warranted, that [it] is more probable than not that the occurrence was caused by some negligent conduct on the part of the defendant."

received in excess thereof as compensation for his services. Dobson incurred rather heavy expenditures in preparing for operations, found buyers for much of the oak to be cut, and commenced clearing the lands.

During the period in question the stumpage value of oak was approximately twenty dollars per thousand log feet; thus by selecting and selling the merchantable oak from that which he cut, Dobson was able to realize profits from his operations. Dobson continued clearing operations from March, 1963, to December, 1963, at which time Masonite unilaterally terminated the agreement and ordered Dobson to discontinue his operations. Dobson during this time cleared 4,000 acres of land, and realized a net profit, after all expenses, including payments to Masonite, of $9,383.02.

This suit was initiated by Dobson to recover the amount of net profits he would have realized had he been permitted to complete the clearing of Masonite's lands. Dobson interpreted the contract as one for services; he argued that the agreement was for clearing the land of unwanted oak trees. Masonite denied liability, interpreting the contract as one for the sale of standing timber, and invoking the Mississippi Statute of Frauds[1] to bar Dobson's claim. At the close of the evidence Masonite moved for a directed verdict. The court denied this motion and submitted the case to the jury on special interrogatories inquiring (1) whether the contract was for services or for the sale of timber; and (2) whether the agreement could have been completed within the permissible period under the Statute of Frauds.[2] The jury answered the interrogatories in favor of Dobson and assessed damages at $26,500.

Masonite then moved for judgment notwithstanding the verdict under Fed.R.Civ.P. 50(b). The district court sustained this motion, stating that only "the legal analysis and legal effect of that done" was in question, ruling that as a matter of law Dobson by virtue of the

---

1. Mississippi Code of 1942 Sec. 264 provides in pertinent part:

"An action shall not be brought whereby to charge a defendant or other party:. . .

(c) Upon any contract for the sale of lands, tenements, or hereditaments . . .;

(d) Upon any agreement which is not to be performed within the space of fifteen months from the making thereof; . . .

Unless, in each of said cases, the promise or agreement upon which such action may be brought, or some memorandum or note thereof, shall be in writing, and signed by the party to be charged therewith. . . ."

2. The special interrogatories and the jury's answers thereto read as follows:

(1) Was the agreement of March 1, 1963, between Dobson and West for Masonite one:

(a) Solely and alone for a service to be performed by Dobson to lands of Masonite by his salvage cuttings on its lands?

Answer: (Yes or No) <u>Yes</u>

OR

(b) In whole or in part for the sale by Masonite to Dobson of felled or standing timber on its lands?

Answer: (Yes or No) <u>No</u>

(2) Could the plaintiff (Dobson) have completed the performance of the entire contract which he said was made with defendant (Masonite) on or before June 1, 1964?

Answer: (Yes or No) <u>Yes</u>

contract acquired an interest in standing timber, and holding that recovery under the contract was therefore barred by the Statute of Frauds.

The district court quite properly observed that under the Mississippi Statute of Frauds, an oral contract for the sale of standing timber is unenforceable. See, e.g., Towles v. Hodges, 235 Miss. 258, 108 So.2d 884 (1959); Rowan v. Rosenblatt, 206 Miss. 259, 39 So.2d 873, (1949) (en banc). Counsel for Dobson is also correct in his statement of Mississippi law; an agreement for services in cutting and clearing land of timber is not within the Statute. See, e.g., Herring v. Edwards, 29 So. 787 (Miss.1901).

But this is of little assistance in determining *which type* of contract—sales or service—was here involved. This calls for an interpretation of the agreement between the parties to determine what they meant by the terms of that agreement. Interpretation is always a question of fact. Aetna Ins. Co. v. Neville G. Penrose, Inc., 304 F.2d 612, 616 (5th Cir. 1962); 3 Corbin, Contracts, Section 554, p. 219 (1960); 17A C.J.S. Contracts §§ 616, 618, p. 1240 et seq. (1963). As a question of fact, this issue was properly presented to, and determined by, the jury; and unless there was no evidence which, if believed, would authorize the jury's conclusions, they must stand. See Marsh v. Illinois C. R. R., 175 F.2d 498 (5th Cir. 1949); Howard v. Louisiana & A. Ry., 49 F.2d 571 (5th Cir. 1931).

Plainly what the parties meant by the language of the contract was uncertain and at the heart of this controversy; just as plainly, this was the very issue presented to the jury through special interrogatories. On the record before us, there is certainly ample evidence from which the jury could conclude that the contract between Dobson and Masonite was for the rendition of services, rather than for the sale of standing timber. In drawing the ultimate conclusion as to the meaning of the parties, we believe the jury was fulfilling its traditional function as the finder of the facts. See Byrd v. Blue Ridge Rural Elec. Co-op., 356 U.S. 525, 537, 78 S.Ct. 893, 2 L.Ed.2d 953 (1958); Wright v. Paramount-Richards Theatres, Inc., 198 F.2d 303 (5th Cir. 1952); Howard v. Louisiana & A. Ry., supra.

The district court, apparently because there was no dispute regarding the existence of the oral contract or its terms, felt that only a legal question, what was the legal effect of the contract, was involved.[3] But "legal effect" is the result of applying rules of law to the facts; necessarily this determination must await a determination of all the facts. And, as we have stated, deciding what is the meaning of the contract is a question of fact.

We are of the firm opinion that a factual question regarding what type of contract existed between the parties was presented to, and decided by, the jury. The record clearly contains substantial evidence

---

3. Corbin points out the importance of the distinction between "legal effect" and "interpretation" at 3 Corbin, Contracts Section 554 (1960).

in support of the jury's verdict. Therefore the district court erroneously entered judgment notwithstanding the verdict. We reverse that judgment and remand for reinstatement of the jury's verdict.

Reversed and remanded with directions.

NOTE ON DEVICES FOR TAKING A CASE FROM THE JURY

1. At common law there was a device for taking a case from the jury, in addition to nonsuit and directed verdict, known as the demurrer to the evidence. Gibson v. Hunter, 2 H.Blackst. 187, 126 E.R. 499 (House of Lords, 1793). See Galloway v. United States, 319 U.S. 372, 391 n. 23, 63 S.Ct. 1077, 1087, 87 L.Ed. 1458 (1943); 5A Moore ¶ 50.03 [3]. Directing a verdict for the party having the burden of proof may involve different institutional considerations, if not analytical ones, from directing a verdict against such a party. See 9 Wright & Miller § 2535; Note, Directing a Verdict in Favor of the Party with the Burden of Proof, 16 Wake Forest L.Rev. 607 (1980).

2. Compare F.R.C.P. 50(a)'s provisions for a directed verdict with F.R.C.P. 41(a)(2)'s provisions for dismissal. What is the difference between a directed verdict for defendant at the end of plaintiff's case, and a dismissal? Observe that in federal practice a motion for a directed verdict may be made by defendant (1) upon completion of plaintiff's opening statement; (2) at the close of plaintiff's case in chief; and (3) at the close of all the evidence. See F.R.C.P. 50; 5A Moore ¶ 50.04. When may a plaintiff move for a directed verdict in federal court? Note that under F.R.C.P. 50(b) "Whenever a motion for a directed verdict made at the close of all the evidence is denied or for any reason is not granted, the court is deemed to have submitted the action to the jury subject to a later determination of the legal questions raised by the motion." Why is a motion for a directed verdict at the close of all the evidence a condition precedent of a motion for judgment notwithstanding the verdict? See Motions after Verdict, infra p. 1159.

3. Observe that C.C.P. 581c expressly authorizes defendants to move for judgments of nonsuit, whereas C.C.P. 629 and C.C.P. 630 assume the availability of, but do not expressly authorize, motions for directed verdicts for both parties. As stated in Estate of Lances, 216 Cal. 397, 400, 14 P.2d 768 (1932):

"It has become the established law of this state that the power of the court to direct a verdict is absolutely the same as the power of the court to grant a nonsuit. A nonsuit or a directed verdict may be granted 'only when, disregarding conflicting evidence and giving to the plaintiff's evidence all the value to which it is legally entitled, herein indulging in every legitimate inference which may be drawn from that evidence, the result is a determination that there is no evidence of sufficient substantiality to support a verdict in favor of the plaintiff if such a verdict were given.' "

See also Dailey v. Los Angeles Unified School Dist., 2 Cal.3d 741, 745, 87 Cal.Rptr. 376, 470 P.2d 360 (1970) (reaffirming Lances' definition of a directed verdict).

In California a motion for a directed verdict is not a condition precedent of a motion for judgment notwithstanding the verdict. C.C.P. 629; see also C.C.P. 630.

Is there good reason for the overlapping functions in California of motions for nonsuit and directed verdict? Could not the California law in regard to both of these motions be more succinctly and clearly codified? See Note, 48

Calif.L.Rev. 816 (1960). Compare the simplicity resulting from New York's consolidation of the various motions into one Rule, 4401, governing motions for judgment during trial; see 4 Weinstein, Korn & Miller ¶¶ 4401.01–4401.18. Until the law is further clarified it is recommended that the practitioner in a California court who believes he is entitled to prevail as a matter of law and who therefore wishes to attempt to take the case away from the jury at trial proceed as follows:

> (a) If he represents the defendant, move for a nonsuit at the close of plaintiff's case in chief, or in the rare situation which justifies it, at the conclusion of plaintiff's opening statement.

> (b) If he represents the defendant, move for a directed verdict at the conclusion of all of the evidence.

> (c) If he represents the plaintiff, move for a directed verdict at the conclusion of defendant's case in chief, and again at the conclusion of all of the evidence.

4. Instructions to the jury are of course another device for control of the jury. See James, Sufficiency of the Evidence and Jury-Control Devices Available Before Verdict, 47 Va.L.Rev. 218, 235 (1961); James & Hazard § 7.14; Mansfield, Jury Notice, 74 Georgetown L.J. 395 (1985). By instructions the outcome as to certain issues, rather than the whole case, may be judge-controlled at least in theory, and depending in part on the type of verdict used, whether general, special, or general with answers to interrogatories. See Note on Instructions to the Jury, infra p. 1149. On the general problem of functions of court and jury in negligence cases, see Prosser and Keeton, Torts 235 et seq. (5th ed. 1984); James, Functions of Judge and Jury in Negligence Cases, 58 Yale L.J. 667 (1949); cf. 9 Wigmore on Evidence § 2494 (Chadbourn ed. 1981).

5. Professor Jerome Michael, in speaking of the jury's functions, once said that the court

> "is supposed to submit an issue to the jury if, as the judges say, the jury can decide reasonably either way. But to say that I can decide an issue of fact reasonably either way is to say, I submit, that I cannot, by the exercise of reason, decide the question. That means that the issue we typically submit to juries is an issue which the jury cannot decide by the exercise of its reason.

> "The decision of an issue of fact in cases of closely balanced probabilities, therefore, must, in the nature of things, be an emotional rather than a rational act * * *." Michael, The Basic Rules of Pleading, 5 The Record 175, 199–200 (1950).

See generally Cooper, Directions for Directed Verdicts: A Compass for Federal Courts, 55 Minn.L.Rev. 903 (1971).

2. PUTTING THE CASE TO THE JURY

SABELLA v. SOUTHERN PACIFIC CO.

Supreme Court of California, 1969.
70 Cal.2d 311, 74 Cal.Rptr. 534, 449 P.2d 750.*

MOSK, JUSTICE.

Defendant appeals from a judgment in favor of plaintiff under the Federal Employers' Liability Act. The jury brought in a verdict of $115,500, but by remittitur to which plaintiff consented the award was reduced to $80,000. Defendant cites as error the trial court's refusal to admit evidence of a disability pension, and purported misconduct by plaintiff's counsel. We conclude that the judgment must be affirmed.

Plaintiff Mike Sabella was injured while working as a "carman cutter" for defendant railroad. Among other duties, it was his task to cut damaged freight cars into scrap. While doing so, plaintiff fell from the roof of a car he was cutting and sustained severe back injuries. He alleged that his fall was caused by the negligence of defendant's crane operator in moving the roof section, which had been attached to the crane preparatory to lifting the section off, while plaintiff was still walking on it; and by the failure of defendant to provide a reasonably safe place in which to work. The defense was based on a denial of negligence and an allegation of contributory negligence, which may reduce an F.E.L.A. award.

At the conclusion of the trial, and following the verdict in favor of plaintiff, defendant moved for a new trial on multiple grounds: (1) insufficiency of the evidence; (2) excessive damages; (3) disregard by the jury of the court's instructions as to contributory negligence; (4) error in law in excluding evidence of a disability pension received by plaintiff; and (5) misconduct by plaintiff's counsel. The court made an order finding "That the evidence is insufficient to sustain the verdict of the jury; and [that there] was error in law, occurring at the trial and excepted to by defendant, and that such error was prejudicial. . . ." A new trial was denied, however, on the condition that plaintiff consent to a reduction of the verdict from $115,500 to $80,000. Plaintiff agreed and does not now challenge the propriety of the reduction.

*   *   *

We turn now to defendant's second major contention, i.e., that plaintiff's counsel was guilty of prejudicial misconduct. The alleged misconduct consisted, among other things, of repeated references, both direct and indirect, to defendant as "inhuman" and heartless, sending plaintiff "down the tubes" and casting him on the "human trash pile"; as "cheapskates" attempting to put up a "smokescreen" by perjury and deceit so as to deprive plaintiff of his just due and put the money instead into defendant's "coffers." Reference was also made to the

---

* Some of the court's footnotes are omitted.

disparity in wealth between plaintiff and defendant, combined with an appeal to the jurors' personal sympathies.[4] It is unnecessary to detail any further the precise language used or to make a phrase-by-phrase comparison between this and other exemplars of misconduct since it is only the record as a whole, and not specific phrases out of context, that can reveal the nature and effect of such tactics. Upon review of the entire record we conclude that plaintiff's counsel was guilty of deplorable misconduct which might well have been prejudicial. However, in view of defendant's failure to take proper steps to preserve the latter issue of prejudice on appeal, we find it unnecessary to reach it on the merits.[5]

Assuming counsel's conduct was both improper and prejudicial, and further assuming for purposes of discussion that such misconduct went to the issue of liability and so could not be cured by remittitur * * *, we examine the record before us in light of the applicable legal principles.

"Generally a claim of misconduct is entitled to no consideration on appeal unless the record shows a timely and proper objection and a request that the jury be admonished." (Horn v. Atchison, T. & S. F. Ry. Co. (1964) 61 Cal.2d 602, 610, 39 Cal.Rptr. 721, 725, 394 P.2d 561, 565.) "As the effect of misconduct can ordinarily be removed by an instruction to the jury to disregard it, it is generally essential, in order that such act be reviewed on appeal, that it shall first be called to the attention of the trial court at the time, to give the court an opportunity to so act in the premises, if possible, as to correct the error and avoid a mistrial. Where the action of the court is not thus invoked, the alleged misconduct will not be considered on appeal, if an admonition to the jury would remove the effect." (Cope v. Davison (1940) supra, 30 Cal.2d at 202, 180 P.2d at 879.) " 'It is only in extreme cases that the court, when acting promptly and speaking clearly and directly on the subject, cannot, by instructing the jury to disregard such matters, correct the impropriety of the act of counsel and remove any effect his conduct or remarks would otherwise have.' (Tingley v. Times-Mirror, 151 Cal. 1, 23, 89 P. 1097, 1106) . . . [W]e are aware of no California case wherein a plaintiff's verdict was reversed for misconduct during his counsel's argument in the lack of timely objections and a request that the jury be admonished where such admonition could be effective."

---

4. In recent years a number of personal injury lawyers have written books suggesting a variety of somewhat deceptive means of eliciting sympathy for litigants appearing before a jury. (See Prosser, 43 Cal.L.Rev. 556 (1955), reviewing Belli, Modern Trials (1954); R. M. Mosk, 16 U.C. L.A.L.Rev. 216 (1969), reviewing Appleman, Preparation and Trial (1967).) Such tactics are not part of the repertoire of the ethical professional man.

5. In any event, the trial court impliedly found no misconduct, or at least no prejudice, when ruling on the motion for new trial. "A trial judge is in a better position than an appellate court to determine whether a verdict resulted wholly, or in part, from the asserted misconduct of counsel and his conclusion in the matter will not be disturbed unless, under all the circumstances, it is plainly wrong." (Cope v. Davison (1947) 30 Cal.2d 193, 203, 180 P.2d 873, 879, 171 A.L.R. 667.)

(Horn v. Atchison, T. & S. F. Ry. Co. (1964) supra, 61 Cal.2d at pp. 610–611, 39 Cal.Rptr. at p. 725, 394 P.2d at p. 565.)

This case is neither precisely like *Horn,* supra, in which no objection or request for admonition was made until after conclusion of the closing argument (and relief was thus denied); nor like Hoffman v. Brandt (1966) 65 Cal.2d 549, 55 Cal.Rptr. 417, 421 P.2d 425, in which an admonition, especially as there given by the trial court, could not have been effective under the circumstances; nor like Love v. Wolf (1964) 226 Cal.App.2d 378, 38 Cal.Rptr. 183, in which admonition of the jury was requested several times but disregarded by the trial court. Here defendant remained silent as to all but one line of argument, and as to the latter he objected but failed at any time to request an admonition of the jury to disregard the remarks. Under the circumstances we conclude that defendant must be denied relief. (See Estate of Hart (1951) 107 Cal.App.2d 60, 70, 236 P.2d 884.)

The record indicates that while plaintiff's counsel accused witnesses of perjury, made reference to defendant's wealth and plaintiff's lack of resources, and appealed, though indirectly, to the jurors to place themselves in plaintiff's position, all of which tactics are improper and to be condemned (see e.g., Hoffman v. Brandt (1966) supra, 65 Cal.2d 549, 55 Cal.Rptr. 417, 421 P.2d 425; Horn v. Atchison, T. & S. F. Ry. Co. (1964) supra, 61 Cal.2d 602, 39 Cal.Rptr. 721, 394 P.2d 561; Love v. Wolf (1964) supra, 226 Cal.App.2d 378, 38 Cal.Rptr. 183), defendant did not once object to such remarks, much less request an admonition to the jury. "In the absence of a timely objection the offended party is deemed to have waived the claim of error through his participation in the atmosphere which produced the claim of prejudice." (Horn v. Atchison, T. & S. F. Ry. Co. (1964) supra, 61 Cal.2d at p. 610, 39 Cal. Rptr. at p. 726, 394 P.2d at p. 566.)

Defendant did object, however, to one distinct line of argument by his adversary. As discussed earlier, defendant challenged references to turning its back on plaintiff and refusing to help him or to give him a job and generally being out to defeat his claim. This was, in fact, perhaps the mildest and least prejudicial of the alleged instances of misconduct. Although counsel used improper language, the question of defendant's treatment of plaintiff appears to have been put in issue, at least in part, by defendant when it asserted during opening statement that there was work plaintiff could do on the railroad. However, even assuming that the entire line of argument was misconduct, defendant remained silent when during opening argument plaintiff's counsel at least twice alluded to defendant's denial of a job and of hospitalization to plaintiff, and when during the trial he used such terms as "cheapskates" in referring to defendant. It was not until closing argument, after defendant had attempted to counter the "unfairness" argument with evidence of plaintiff's disability pension * * * , rather than by means of the long established procedure of admonishing the jury,[6] that defendant finally objected, but even at that tardy point counsel did not request an admonition. Certainly as to this particular line of argument an admonition would have been effective, especially if requested at the outset. One of the primary purposes of admonition at the beginning of an improper course of argument is to avoid repetition of the remarks and thus obviate the necessity of a new trial. (Horn v. Atchison, T. & S. F. Ry. Co. (1964) supra, 61 Cal.2d at p. 610, 39 Cal.Rptr. 721, 394 P.2d 561.) Except perhaps in cases of highly emotional or inflammatory language or reference to extremely prejudicial circumstances not in evidence, a jury must be deemed capable, if so instructed, of ignoring references to a litigant's personal or corporate virtues and confining itself to the merits of the case. (Compare Deevy v. Tassi (1942) supra, 21 Cal.2d 109, 123, 130 P.2d 389, with People v. Kirkes (1952) 39 Cal.2d 719, 726, 249 P.2d 1.)[7]

Defendant urges us to ignore the rules of procedure relating to the "magic words" of proper objection and admonition. But the procedure outlined above is not a meaningless ritual; it has been designed through judicial experience to prevent by timely words of caution the very problem with which we are here concerned.

We emphasize again that the particular language used by counsel and the form or lack of objection by defendant in this case are not meant to serve as invariable guidelines for future reference. Each case must ultimately rest upon a court's view of the overall record, taking into account such factors, inter alia, as the nature and seriousness of the remarks and misconduct, the general atmosphere, including the judge's control,[8] of the trial, the likelihood of prejudicing the jury, and the efficacy of objection or admonition under all the circumstances.

Our conclusions should in no way be interpreted as condoning the deplorable conduct of plaintiff's counsel.[9] However, punishment of

---

6. Defendant asserts that it did not know at the outset how heavily this line of argument would be emphasized, although during one objection defendant claimed that it had been "anticipating" such an argument and meant to counter it by evidence of the disability pension. Obviously, the fact that this counterevidence was subsequently excluded cannot alone excuse the failure to object if in fact the argument was improper. It was not the exclusion of the pension evidence that determined the propriety of the language and allusions employed by plaintiff's counsel.

7. Defendant was apparently not unaware of the tactical availability and desirability of an admonition to the jury. When plaintiff attempted to argue damages on a "per diem" basis, defendant objected strenuously and asked for and received an admonition that the jury disregard this line of argument. (As to the propriety of that

ruling, see Beagle v. Vasold (1966) 65 Cal. 2d 166, 53 Cal.Rptr. 129, 417 P.2d 673.) It is significant that far more questionable statements made at the same time, which defendant now cites as misconduct, were not alluded to in the "per diem" objection.

8. While it cannot be said that the trial court here "lost control" of the proceedings (cf. Love v. Wolf (1964) supra, 226 Cal.App. 2d 378, 391, 38 Cal.Rptr. 183), a court should on its own initiative intercede to prevent potentially prejudicial conduct of counsel. Such action here, directed either at counsel or to the jury, not only might have mitigated the prejudice here alleged, but it would have enhanced the dignity and demeanor of the proceedings.

9. Counsel's law firm has been the subject of judicial condemnation in at least two other recent instances of comparable misconduct. (Horn v. Atchison, T. & S.F.

counsel to the detriment of his client is not the function of the court. (See Shaff v. Baldwin (1951) 107 Cal.App.2d 81, 87, 236 P.2d 634.) Intemperate and unprofessional conduct by counsel as is here involved runs a grave and unjustifiable risk of sacrificing an otherwise sound case for recovery, and as such is a disservice to a litigant. These same tactics, in another context, would likely result in a reversal. However, under the facts and circumstances of this case, we conclude that the award to plaintiff, as modified by the remittitur, is justified.

The judgment is affirmed.

McComb, Peters, Tobriner, Burke, and Sullivan, JJ., concur.

Traynor, Chief Justice (dissenting).

I dissent.

I would reverse the judgment on the ground that the misconduct of counsel for plaintiff deprived defendant of its right to a fair trial.

In his opening statement, counsel for plaintiff made a preliminary appeal to the sympathy of the jury by stressing that plaintiff had left school after the seventh grade to go to work and had worked for defendant for 36 years. Thereafter in the course of the trial, counsel deliberately sought to implant prejudice in the jury against defendant. He insinuated, without offering any evidence to prove it, that defense counsel had withheld photographs favorable to plaintiff. He referred to defendant and its attorneys as "cheapskates." He asked rhetorical questions calculated to convey the impression that defense witnesses were not honest in their testimony. Nor was that all. After several days of trial, when a trial court is normally reluctant to grant a mistrial, he used his closing argument to intensify his appeal to the passion and prejudice of the jury. The appeal was the more insidious because it followed upon a fulsome declaration of his great trust in the jury system. His trust was such that he urged a verdict on issues extraneous to the merits. Approximately a third of his argument consisted of emotional attacks on defendant, its counsel, and its witnesses for defendant. He called upon the jury to "tell the Southern Pacific in that verdict it is high time to quit treating their employees that way."

There is no question that his conduct was on its face prejudicial. The question to be resolved is whether or not defendant waived its right to complain even though it repeatedly made objections at the trial.[1]

Ry. Co., supra, 61 Cal.2d 602, 39 Cal.Rptr. 721, 394 P.2d 561; Love v. Wolf, supra, 226 Cal.App.2d 378, 38 Cal.Rptr. 183.)

1. Counsel for defendant objected ten times during the closing argument for plaintiff. The appeals to prejudice and the corresponding objections are tallied below:

First: "Now, ladies and gentlemen, I know that before you folks sat here, that you came here on January 25th, 1964, and I know in your hearts, as in my heart, after you saw the presentation of this case, that I'll bet you are amazed and stunned beyond belief. This isn't really 1964 at all. This goes back to the early stages of man's inhumanity to man long before they were savages, because I submit, and I will discuss with you folks this afternoon, never in the history of man could anyone have been taken down the tubes or down the drain like one Mike Sabella was.

The objections were more than enough to alert the trial court. The court itself sought to call a halt to the objectionable conduct by

"And I say to you, ladies and gentlemen, that the conduct of his employer, the Southern Pacific Company in this case, is about as reprehensible in 1956 [sic]—

"MR. PHELPS: [counsel for defendant]: Your Honor, I am going to object to this line of argument and assign it as misconduct, particularly in view of Your Honor's ruling that is keeping out of evidence the matter that I wanted to introduce, the matter that I—the argument is along the lines I was anticipating and I could have met and did want to meet by evidence, and I will object and cite it as misconduct and ask for a mistrial.

"THE COURT: Well, the motion for a mistrial will be denied; and I suggest, Mr. Teerlink, that you confine yourself to the evidence and such reasonable implications as you may draw therefrom.

"MR. TEERLINK: Yes, Your Honor."

Second: "Did they even agree to pick up $11.50 a month to see that the poor guy got his hospitalization? No."

"MR. PHELPS: If Your Honor please, I am going to object in view of the offer of proof I made in chambers as to what this man's actual situation was and the election he made, and I think it is misconduct to encroach in the manner that has been done.

"MR. TEERLINK: The stipulation, as I understand, Your Honor, was that the railroad company tendered the right to pick up his hospital benefits, and they declined; that was the stipulation that you entered.

"MR. PHELPS: I understand that, but you are arguing something that prevents me from answering.

"THE COURT: Let's not go beyond the stipulation."

Third: "They cut off—no more hospital benefits, no more out-patient, by the time of December—

"MR. PHELPS: I make the same objection, Your Honor please, in view of the situation, my hands having been tied—

"MR. TEERLINK: I say there are no benefits payable after December. That is the evidence.

"MR. PHELPS: 'What did the Southern Pacific Company do when you'—

"THE COURT: Let's—

"MR. PHELPS:—I object to that and assign it as misconduct.

"MR. TEERLINK: That is the evidence, Your Honor. He had no benefits after December.

"THE COURT: I know, but you are going beyond that.

"MR. PHELPS: You foreclosed me.

"THE COURT: Let's stay within the confines."

Fourth: "Do you think that was strategy? This is the way they play the ball game. They don't know how to play it fair. The last witness, ladies and gentlemen, is, lo and behold, McLaughlin—

"MR. PHELPS: I object and assign that as misconduct: 'They don't know how to play it fair.' There is a case that this very firm has been reversed for, argument of a similar nature, and I assign it as misconduct and ask for a mistrial.

"THE COURT: Motion denied."

Fifth: "They employ 45,000 people, and they couldn't make room for him to do anything—maybe even delivering the messages down at 65 Market Street; you mean to tell me, ladies and gentlemen, if you have got the good will of your employee at stake that you won't at least call him up and say—

"MR. PHELPS: I am going to object to this on the same ground and cite it as misconduct. Your Honor knows what the situation is. Your Honor knows what I was foreclosed from, and I think that this is improper argument.

"THE COURT: Just a moment.

"MR. PHELPS: Your Honor knows what the situation was.

"THE COURT: Let's keep it within the confines of the evidence."

Sixth: "Now, ladies and gentlemen, isn't it interesting to you, when they've got all these pictures, where is that claims man with the rest of the pictures they didn't show? He has been around here for two weeks, and we haven't seen or heard from him.

"MR. PHELPS: Just a moment. He is implying—you told me you didn't want him his [sic] morning.

"MR. TEERLINK: Only—

"MR. PHELPS: You told me you didn't want him. I had him here at your request.

admonishing counsel for plaintiff to "confine yourself to the evidence and such reasonable implications as you may draw therefrom." When counsel for plaintiff nevertheless made fresh appeals to the passion and prejudice of the jury, and defense counsel continued to object, the court once again admonished counsel for plaintiff to "stay within the confines." When counsel for plaintiff persisted in his misconduct, in the face not only of defendant's objections and motions for mistrial but also of the admonitions of the court, he evinced a studied determination to ride roughshod over any and all objections or admonitions.

Though he threw one caution after another to the wind, he now contends that defendant waived objection to any misconduct by not supplementing his repeated objections with a request that the trial court admonish the jury to disregard the misconduct.[2] No admonition, howev-

"MR. TEERLINK: Sit down and let me finish my argument.

"THE COURT: All right, gentlemen; we have a time limit. Please."

Seventh: "Does it seem ironical to you, ladies and gentlemen, that they can take aerial photographs—

"MR. PHELPS: I—

"MR. TEERLINK: Will you keep out of my argument—that they can take aerial photographs within a few hours or less than that? Imagine getting an airplane and camera equipment and start shooting photographs to defeat a claim— and rulers, when all they would have had to do—"

(The photographs were not taken from an airplane.)

Eighth: "Mike Sabella was lying on his back with a busted back thinking maybe they were going to do something decent for him, maybe once in a life the friendly Southern Pacific could be friendly. No, sir. All we get is a second best, a lousy evidence that they decide to bring in.

"You see, all the pictures that may show it to his advantage, you don't see them.

"MR. PHELPS: Now—

"MR. TEERLINK: They are not here.

"MR. PHELPS: I will object to that and assign it as misconduct. This is, again, characteristic of the defense, and without any evidence, without justification, and the type of thing that the courts have said is not proper, and I object to it.

"THE COURT: Go ahead."

Ninth: "Now, what about poor Mr. Medina [a witness for defendant]? What do you think poor Mr. Medina must

think when he sees and he knows what they are doing to Mike? What would happen to poor Medina if he didn't go along with it? Ever think about that?

"When they see how they threw him on the human trash pile, how quick would they give it to Medina if he didn't go along—

"MR. PHELPS: I object again and cite this as misconduct in view of the fact I was foreclosed from proving that isn't the fact as to what we did or what was done for this man, and I cannot stand still and listen to this, knowing what the facts are."

Tenth: "[Y]ou can look at the sorrowful look in a man's eyes when you are taking his deposition, and they cry out to you. 'I would like to help you, Mr. Teerlink, but I can't; I've got to send him down the tubes; it is him or me,' and that is the way you see it.

"MR. PHELPS: If Your Honor please, 'down the tubes,' when this man is down—the situation is such. Your Honor please, I am foreclosed from saying it—

"MR. TEERLINK: You've said that about 14 times.

"MR. PHELPS: The ruling—

"MR. TEERLINK: You haven't given him a job; that is for sure.

"MR. PHELPS: That is just—Now, there we go again.

"If Your Honor please, instruct Mr. Teerlink to desist from that. I assign it again as misconduct and move for a mistrial in view of the offers that I made of proof.

"THE COURT: Denied. Proceed."

2. It is at least debatable that implicit in any objection to misconduct is a request

er, could cure the prejudicial effect of such misconduct as prevailed throughout this case. Accordingly, defendant's failure to request admonitions to the jury does not preclude it from challenging the misconduct on appeal. (Hoffman v. Brandt (1966) 65 Cal.2d 549, 553, 55 Cal.Rptr. 417, 421 P.2d 425; Horn v. Atchison, T. & S. F. Ry. Co. (1964) 61 Cal.2d 602, 611, 39 Cal.Rptr. 721, 394 P.2d 561; Love v. Wolf (1964) 226 Cal.App.2d 378, 392, 38 Cal.Rptr. 183.) Plaintiff's counsel can hardly claim that his repeated appeals to passion and prejudice were of such little appeal that they could have been simply erased by admonitions.

*   *   *

We take great care to excuse prospective jurors who may be subject to emotional appeals. We take great care to instruct jurors not to discuss the case with outsiders or to read about it, so that they will remain beyond the reach of influence outside the courtroom. It is a minimum propriety to guard against calculated attempts to prejudice the jury inside the courtroom, for they do violence to the substantial rights of a litigant. Still worse, they would in the long run so debase the judicial process that no one could enter a courtroom confident of a fair trial.

NOTE ON ARGUMENT

1. New York Central Railroad Co. v. Johnson, 279 U.S. 310, 49 S.Ct. 300, 73 L.Ed. 706 (1929), also involving a demagogic argument, is one of the classics on improper argument to the jury. See also City of Cleveland v. Peter Kiewit Sons' Co., 624 F.2d 749 (6th Cir. 1980).

2. Each party has a right to argue the cause to the jury, King v. Kaplan, 94 Cal.App.2d 697, 211 P.2d 578 (1949), and "the denial or serious curtailment of that right, directly or by pressure to force an unwilling consent to submit [the cause] without argument, may constitute prejudicial error." 7 Witkin 164; cf. 4 Weinstein, Korn & Miller ¶ 4016.02. Thus in Shippy v. Peninsula Rapid Transit Co., 197 Cal. 290, 240 P. 785 (1925), it was held that a new trial was properly granted where the trial judge had left it up to the jury to decide whether or not they wanted to hear argument.

California follows the normal American practice, state and federal, whereby arguments to the jury precede the court's instructions, but in some states the instructions precede the arguments. California also follows the usual practice respecting the order of argument: "When the evidence is concluded, unless the case is submitted to the jury on either side or on both sides without argument, the plaintiff must commence and may conclude the argument." C.C.P. 607, subd. 7; see also N.Y.C.P.L.R. 4016. Does this simply recognize a basic rule of orderly forensic procedure, namely, that the right to open and close should be with the party who has the initiative respecting production of evidence? Compare Walker, Thibaut, and Andreoli, Order of Presentation at Trial, 82 Yale L.J. 216 (1972); Lawson, Order of Presentation as a Factor in Jury Persuasion, 56 Ky.L.J. 523 (1968). And if the defendant has the burden of proof, should he not be allowed to open and close the argument? Observe that C.C.P. 607 itself provides that the

that the jury be admonished to disregard it. Thus, in Hoffman v. Brandt (1966) 65 Cal.2d 549, 553, 55 Cal.Rptr. 417, 421 P.2d 425, counsel objected but did not request an admonition. The trial court, however, admonished the jury on its own motion. We nevertheless held that the admonition did not cure the error.

court for special reasons may direct an order of procedure different from that specified in § 607.

3. Code of Professional Responsibility, American Bar Association, Ethical Consideration 7–24 provides in part:

> "The expression by a lawyer of his personal opinion as to the justness of a cause, as to the credibility of a witness, as to the culpability of a civil litigant, or as to the guilt or innocence of an accused is not a proper subject for argument to the trier of fact."

What is the philosophy of this restriction? Compare People v. Bain, 5 Cal.3d 839, 97 Cal.Rptr. 684, 489 P.2d 564 (1971); Anno., 88 A.L.R.3d 449 (prosecutor in criminal cases); cf. Anno., 45 A.L.R. 4th 602 (counsel's vouching for credibility of witness improper). Only a few civil cases have involved the problem. See, e.g., McCormick v. Malecha, 266 Minn. 33, 122 N.W.2d 446 (1963). Is the violation of this rule more serious in a criminal case than in a civil one? Compare Ethical Consideration 5–10, providing in substance that a lawyer should leave the trial of a case to other counsel if he has appeared as a witness except as to merely formal matters. Is there anything about argument to the jury that tends to justify such a restriction?

For a thoughtful analysis of the cogency of the rule that permits counsel in argument to " 'violate all logical rules, and do violence to all the laws of legitimate inference,' " see Levin and Levy, Persuading the Jury with Facts Not in Evidence, 105 U.Pa.L.Rev. 139 (1956).

Much emphasis is placed on avoidance of improper argument. However, it seems not amiss to recall the lawyer's duty of effective representation of her client in an adversary system. As put by Traynor, J., in Gallagher v. Municipal Court, 31 Cal.2d 784, 796, 192 P.2d 905, 913 (1948):

> "An attorney has the duty to protect the interests of his client. He has a right to press legitimate argument and to protest an erroneous ruling. It is reported in Oswald on Contempt of Court that the following interchange occurred between Erskine and Buller, J.: 'At length Erskine said, "I stand here as an advocate for a brother citizen, and I desire that the word 'only' be recorded;" whereupon Buller, J., said, "Sit down, sir! remember your duty or I shall be obliged to proceed in another manner,"—to which Erskine retorted, "Your Lordship may proceed in whatever manner you think fit. I know my duty as well as your Lordship knows yours. I shall not alter my conduct." The Judge took no notice of this reply. Lord Campbell speaks of the conduct of Erskine as "a noble stand for the independence of the Bar." ' (Oswald, (3d ed.), pp. 51–52.) The foregoing quotation is illustrative of the rule in the Platnauer and Curran cases, that an attorney may assert that which he believes to be correct in a forthright manner, if he is acting in the due course of a judicial proceeding. (Matter of Rotwein, 291 N.Y. 116, 122–123 [51 N.E.2d 669].)"

JAMES AND HAZARD, PREVERDICT DEVICES FOR CONTROLLING THE JURY: INSTRUCTIONS TO THE JURY

Civil Procedure, § 7.14 (3d ed. 1985).*

It is the common law tradition that in all civil jury trials the judge has the right and duty to instruct the jury upon the substantive law applicable to all the ultimate issues made by the pleadings and the proof.[1] This duty was not dependent on the making of any requests to charge by parties [2]—to this extent it represents a departure from notions of party presentation and prosecution and is an instance of judicial responsibility for seeing that certain steps in the litigation process are taken, and properly taken. Judges often sum up the evidence in the course of their charges and indicate just how the legal rules should be applied to the various factual findings permissible under the evidence.[3] Moreover, they may also *comment* on the weight of the evidence and indicate their own opinion concerning the credibility of witnesses and the relative strength of competing permissible inferences, provided always that they make it clear to the jury that it is the jury's province to decide such questions of weight and credibility.[4]

Because of the judge's position of prestige and respect in the trial, the charge can be used to exert a good deal of psychological influence on the jurors, who are laypersons and sometimes inexperienced and impressionable. This influence is enhanced by the timing of the charge—it occurs after arguments of counsel and is the last significant event at the trial before the jury's deliberation. All this was not regarded as a disadvantage of the procedure but rather as an essential safeguard against the jury's possible ignorance and undue susceptibility to appeals to the "passional elements" in their nature. "It is not too much to say of any period, in all English history," says Thayer, "that it is impossible to conceive of trial by jury as existing there in a form which would withhold from the jury the assistance of the court in dealing with the facts." [5]

The basic features of instructions to the jury which have just been described are found today in the federal courts and those of several of the states.[6] But the nineteenth century witnessed a popular political movement which led to, among other things, an aggrandizement of the importance and stature of the jury (as the popular branch of the tribunal) and to a corresponding diminution of the importance and stature of the judge.[7] Among the results of this movement, several are pertinent to the present subject matter: (1) statutes and even constitutional provisions forbidding judges to comment upon the evidence; [8] (2) rules and statutes

---

1. Thayer, Evidence 112–114 (1898); Farley, Instructions to Juries—Their Role in the Judicial Process, 42 Yale L.J. 194 (1932); Herron v. Southern Pac. Co., 283 U.S. 91, 51 S.Ct. 383, 75 L.Ed. 857 (1931).

2. For modern cases which follow the common law in this respect, see Investors Syndicate v. Thompson, 172 Ga. 203, 158 S.E. 20 (1931); Cipollone v. D'Alessandro–Crognale, Inc., 333 Mass. 469, 131 N.E.2d 754 (1956); Shiers v. Cowgill, 157 Neb. 265, 59 N.W.2d 407 (1953); Perlman v. Haigh, 90 N.H. 404, 10 A.2d 228 (1939); McNeill v. McDougald, 242 N.C. 255, 87 S.E.2d 502 (1955); Reithof v. Pittsburg Rys., 361 Pa. 489, 65 A.2d 346 (1949). Compare Robinson, Proposal for Limiting the Duty of the Trial Judge to Instruct the Jury Sua Sponte, 11 San Diego L.Rev. 325 (1974).

3. See 9 Wigmore, Evidence § 2551 (Chadbourn rev. 1981); Wright, Instructions to the Jury: Summary Without Comment, [1954] Wash.U.L.Q. 177.

4. See Quercia v. United States, 289 U.S. 466, 53 S.Ct. 698, 77 L.Ed. 1321 (1933); Evans v. Wright, 505 F.2d 287 (4th Cir.1974); Sheahan v. Barry, 27 Mich. 217, 226–227 (1873); 9 Wigmore, supra note 3, § 2551; Sunderland, The Inefficiency of the American Jury, 13 Mich.L.Rev. 302, 305 (1915). See generally Wright, The Invasion of Jury: Temperature of the War, 27 Temp.L.Q. 137 (1953).

5. Thayer, Evidence 188 n. 2 (1898).

6. See Wright, Adequacy of Instructions to the Jury, 53 Mich.L.Rev. 505, 813 (1955). See also, e.g., Devitt and Blackman, Federal Jury Practice and Instructions (2d ed. 1970).

7. See Sunderland, The Inefficiency of the American Jury, 13 Mich.L.Rev. 302, 307–309 (1915).

8. Ibid. See Wright, Adequacy of Instructions to the Jury, 53 Mich.L.Rev. 505, 813 (1955) (pts. 1 and 2); Wright, Instructions to the Jury: Summary Without Comment, [1954] Wash.U.L.Q. 177; Wright, The Invasion of Jury: Temperature of the War, 27 Temp.L.Q. 137 (1953).

relieving the court of its traditional duty to take the initiative in covering the whole law of the case in its charge, and requiring the court to charge only upon points expressly covered by specific requests to charge; [9] and (3) rules requiring the charge to be given *before* final arguments of counsel.[10] These steps toward diminution of judicial responsibility and control have been widely condemned by commentators, and the tide has turned the other way. But, because of the differences in practice just described, it is difficult to make valid generalizations about what a charge should and should not contain. The rules that follow are, however, widely applied.

The charge should tell the jury which questions are for them to decide and which are not. Usually this means that the judge tells the jury what the issues are and what rule or rules of substantive law they should apply to the various possible findings of fact they might make under the evidence. And the judge should explain to the jury which party has the burden of proof (persuasion burden) on each issue and the measure to which they must be persuaded before that burden is met. The court usually tells the jury that questions of the credibility of witnesses are for them to decide. It may also give them some guide for drawing rational inferences of fact.

If the proponent has failed to meet her production burden on the whole case or on some element necessary for recovery, the court will, as we have seen, take the case from the jury by nonsuit, directed verdict, or dismissal. But it often happens that proponents who are entitled to go to the jury on some issues fail to meet their production burden on an issue that is not necessarily dispositive of the whole case. It then becomes the judge's duty to withdraw that issue from the jury's consideration.

The court may determine that on one permissible version of the facts there would be no question of evaluation properly for the jury, while on another permissible version there would be such a question for them. Suppose, for example, one witness puts the speed of defendant's automobile at twenty miles an hour, another at forty. If the judge believes that the former speed could not reasonably be found negligent under the circumstances, while the latter might, a conditionally binding instruction should be given on the point. He or she should tell them that if they find the speed to have been twenty miles an hour, they must find the driver free from negligence in this particular, but that if they find the speed to have been forty miles an hour, they should then go on to determine whether that was a reasonable speed under all the circumstances.[11]

Where it is a question for the court what the construction of a writing is, or whether given facts constitute probable cause in malicious prosecution, the court will—if the case is for the jury at all—tell them that the written words have such and such meaning,[12] or that such and such facts do (or do not) constitute probable cause.[13]

9. Wright, Instructions to the Jury: Summary Without Comment, supra note 8, at 180–182; Wright, Adequacy of Instructions to the Jury: II, supra note 8, at 821–822 (1955).

10. See Wright, Instructions to the Jury: Summary Without Comment, supra note 8, at 183–189. Compare Blatt, Judge's Charge to Jury Should Precede Arguments of Counsel, 33 J.Am.Jud.Socy. 56 (1949), with Hartshorne, The Timing of the Charge to the Jury, 33 J.Am.Jud.Socy. 90 (1949).

11. 2 Harper and James, Torts § 15.4 (1956).

12. De Shields v. Insurance Company of North America, 125 S.C. 457, 118 S.E. 817 (1923); see I Reid's Branson, Instructions to Juries § 13. Compare Dobson v. Masonite Corp., 359 F.2d 921 (5th Cir.1966).

13. Carson v. Doggett, 231 N.C. 629, 58 S.E.2d 609 (1950); Patrick v. Wigley, 206 Okla. 194, 242 P.2d 423 (1952); Byers v. Ward, 368 Pa. 416, 84 A.2d 307 (1951). See Thayer, Evidence 221–232 (1898).

If the case is one in which parol evidence is admissible as an aid in construing a contract, it is up to the jury to resolve any conflicts revealed by the parol evidence and also to resolve any question of construction "if, when all the evidence is in, both written and oral, fair-minded men might reasonably arrive at different conclusions" upon it.[14]

The charge must not assume the existence or the nonexistence of a fact in issue.[15]

All jurisdictions allow for the filing by the parties of requests to charge. A rule or statute usually prescribes a time for filing such requests (e.g., at the close of the evidence) and requires them to be in writing.[16] Other requirements, such as separately numbered paragraphs, citation of supporting authority, and so on, may also be imposed.

The court gives the instructions at the end of the case. In most jurisdictions, instructions follow summations by counsel but in a few the instructions are given first and then counsels' argument follows. The court has discretion to give interim instructions during the course of the trial, which can be especially useful in long, complicated cases.[17]

The importance of requests to charge varies among the different jurisdictions, inversely with the duty of the court to instruct fully upon the ultimate issues. As one court has put it, even where there are no requests a federal court must nevertheless charge "on the broad general fundamental rules of law applicable to the principal issues of fact in the case."[18] And if there is a failure in this regard, an objection made according to the rule will preserve the rights of the objecting party. Moreover, there is a "plain error" doctrine. This is that an erroneous charge is reversible error even in the absence of objection by counsel where the instruction was "plain error" and resulted in a miscarriage of justice. Obviously, counsel cannot rely on being rescued by this rule, but it does sometimes provide rescue.[19]

If, however, counsel wants the jury instructed specifically on a particular matter, requests for such instructions must be filed as a condition to putting the trial court in error for a failure to cover the "particular matter."[20] Thus in a negligence case the trial judge will be bound to give the general formula for negligence as being conduct involving a foreseeable and unreasonable risk of harm to others under the circumstances. And judges on their own initiative may, and often will, mention the circumstances which they think significant. But if a party wishes to compel the judge to mention any particular circumstance (on pain of being in error for an omission to do so), then it should file a request to charge the jury upon that circumstance.

Even under this rule it will often be desirable, though perhaps not necessary, to file requests to charge for the purposes of: (1) getting before the judge a party's

14. Geoghegan Sons & Co. v. Arbuckle Bros., 139 Va. 92, 101, 123 S.E. 387, 389 (1924). See also MacIntyre v. Angel, 109 Cal. App.2d 425, 240 P.2d 1047 (1952); Terminal Construction Corp. v. Bergen County, 18 N.J. 294, 113 A.2d 787 (1955); Swift v. McMurray, 133 Okla. 104, 271 P. 635 (1927).

15. Barnett v. H.L. Green Co., 233 Ala. 453, 171 So. 911 (1936).

16. See Fed.R.Civ.P. 51. Compare Cal. Code Civ.P. §§ 607 et seq.; N.Y.C.P.L.R. 4017, 5501. See also Annot. 91 A.L.R.2d 836.

17. Comment, Memory, Magic, and Myth: The Timing of Jury Instructions, 59 Ore.L. Rev. 451 (1981).

18. Turner Construction Co. v. Houlihan, 240 F.2d 435, 439 (1st Cir.1957).

19. See, e.g., Mazer v. Lipschutz, 327 F.2d 42 (3d Cir.1963).

20. Turner Construction Co. v. Houlihan, 240 F.2d 435 (1st Cir.1957).

legal theory of the case (especially where the theory is unusual or unfamiliar); (2) clarifying legal points in advance of argument of counsel, so that the argument may be shaped in accordance with the law as the judge will declare it.[21]

Under procedural systems that condition the judge's duty to charge upon the filing of a proper request on the point in question, the importance of filing such requests is obviously greater than under the common law rule.

Under either system the framing of proper requests to charge is something of an art. Clearly the request must embody a correct statement of substantive law and avoid all the pitfalls which the charge itself must avoid, such as the assumption of a fact in issue. On the other hand, the charge should be expressed in language the jury can understand. In a former day courts were preoccupied with the technical legal accuracy of instructions (or at least often used technical inaccuracy as a ground for reversing verdicts), and instructions were often put in language that made them nearly incomprehensible. Today, greater emphasis is given to clarity. In many jurisdictions "pattern" instructions have been developed for use in commonly recurring types of cases and these tend to be cast in simple if relatively general language.[22]

If a request clearly identifies a point upon which the party filing it is entitled to a charge, but is improper in form or substance, the question arises whether the trial court will be in error if it fails to give a proper instruction on the point. There is certainly authority that where the meaning of a request is reasonably apparent, and its subject matter is significant and not sufficiently covered by the general charge, a court would be unjustified in ignoring the request merely because it is susceptible of such an interpretation as to make its proposition not absolutely accurate.[23] Yet the instances are legion where the appellate court finds no error on the ground that the request is inaccurate or not in conformity with the rules.[24] So complete is appellate discretion to choose one or the other of these attitudes in any specific case, and so reluctant are such courts to reverse except where error is clear or a clear miscarriage of justice is sensed, that counsel is well advised to frame important requests with precision and care.

Most jurisdictions require a party to make specific objections to the charge as a condition to appellate review of statements or omissions in the charge.[25] Such objections are generally made at the close of the charge before the jury retires. The provision to this effect in Rule 51 of the Federal Rules of Civil Procedure is to be read in connection with Rule 46, which dispenses with the need for formal exceptions wherever a party makes known to the court what he wants the court to do and why, or "his objection to the action of the court and his grounds therefor." Taking these two rules together, courts of appeals have held that points clearly

21. See, e.g., Keeton, Trial Tactics, c. 6 (2d ed. 1973). See also Blackman, Problems of Court and Counsel in Requests and Exceptions, 62 F.R.D. 251 (1974).

22. See Am.Jud.Socy., Pattern Jury Instructions (1972); Annot. 49 A.L.R.3d 128 (statutes requiring use of pattern instructions). Even pattern instructions may be difficult for a jury to follow, because of the use of elaborate legal language. See Charrow and Charrow, Making Legal Language Understandable; A Psycholinguistic Study of Jury Instructions, 79 Colum.L.Rev. 1306 (1979). See also Schwarzer, Communicating

with Juries: Problems and Remedies, 69 Calif.L.Rev. 731 (1981).

23. Montgomery v. Virginia Stage Lines, Inc., 191 F.2d 770, 772 (D.C.Cir.1951) (request embodying applicable regulations of I.C.C. "not entirely correct"). See also Annes v. Connecticut Co., 107 Conn. 126, 129, 139 A. 511, 512 (1927) (request embodying applicable last-chance doctrine "of somewhat doubtful accuracy").

24. See 1 Reid's Branson Instructions to Juries § 180.

25. See 1 Reid's Branson, id. §§ 170–175.

raised in proper requests to charge need not be repeated by objection at the close of a charge that failed to give such a request.[26]

NOTE ON INSTRUCTIONS TO THE JURY

1. In Kalven and Zeisel, The American Jury c. 11 (1966), the authors lead off their discussion of jury comprehension of the case with the following two paragraphs:

"The hypothesis that the jury does *not* understand the case has loomed large in the debate over the jury. It has not infrequently been charged that the modern jury is asked to perform heroic feats of attention and recall well beyond the capacities of ordinary men. A trial, it has been argued, presents to the jury a mass of material which it cannot possibly absorb, and presents it in an artificial sequence which aggravates the jury's intellectual problem. The upshot is said to be that the jury often does not get the case straight and, therefore, is deciding a case different from the one actually before it.

"We begin our inquiry into what the jury makes of the evidence by establishing two basic propositions. The first is simply that * * * the jury does by and large understand the facts and get the case straight. The second proposition is that the jury's decision by and large moves with the weight and direction of the evidence."

Hastie, Penrod and Pennington, Inside the Jury (1983), report carefully constructed simulation research on jury deliberations, concluding, among other things, that:

"In their task of factfinding, juries perform efficiently and accurately. * * * Because jury performance of the factfinding task is so remarkably competent, few innovations are needed to improve performance. * * * The major conceptual obstacles to reaching a proper verdict arise from jurors' inability to keep the verdict categories and their elements in order. * * * Providing the jury with a written transcript, written summary, or audiotaped recording of the final charge can effectively remedy these confusions."

Id. at 230–231.

See also Forston, Sense and Non-Sense: Jury Trial Communication, 1975 B.Y.U.L.Rev. 601, and the extensive bibliography in footnotes 2–14 therein. For a thoughtful summary of the psychology of jury instructions, see Elwork and Sales, Jury Instructions, in Kassin and Wrightsman, The Psychology of Evidence and Trial Procedure (1985).

The problems of instructing the jury fall into several groups: (i) those of accuracy, i.e., correctly stating the controlling substantive law and the governing procedural principles that concern the jury, e.g., who has the burden of proof; (ii) those of clarity, i.e., intelligently communicating with the jury so that its members comprehend what they are told; (iii) those of marshalling the evidence and commenting on it.

Does intelligibility of instructions to jurors decrease as the complexity necessitated by appellate insistence on precision increases? In 7 Witkin 253–254 it is stated: "The ideal instruction should be clear, concise and understandable to a layman. * * * The ideal is seldom attainable, for two reasons: First, because each party has a right to instructions on any tenable theory of his case * * *,

---

26. E.g., Montgomery v. Virginia Stage Lines, Inc., 191 F.2d 770 (D.C.Cir.1951); Wright v. Farm Journal, Inc., 158 F.2d 976 (2d Cir.1947); Williams v. Powers, 135 F.2d 153 (6th Cir.1943).

and second, because in stating an instruction on the law in approved legal language, simplicity and understandability may often be sacrificed to achieve accuracy and comprehensiveness."

An aspect of intelligibility is whether the jurors should be so instructed that they can understand the legal consequences of a particular finding, such as the extent of a plaintiff's contributory negligence. This problem arises where a special verdict is used, see Note on the General and Special Verdicts, infra p. 1158, but can arise in other situations. See, e.g., Roman v. Mitchell, 82 N.J. 336, 413 A.2d 322 (1980); Comment, 12 Rutgers L.J. 365 (1981).

On the right of a party to instructions on every issue in the case, even when he has taken inconsistent positions on different issues, see Mathews v. United States, 485 U.S. 58, 108 S.Ct. 883, 99 L.Ed.2d 54 (1988).

2. The principal jury instruction provisions of the Federal Rules are in Rule 51; see also F.R.C.P. 46. Observe that Rule 51 provides inter alia: "No party may assign as error the giving or the failure to give an instruction unless that party objects thereto before the jury retires to consider its verdict, stating distinctly the matter objected to and the grounds of the objection." Compare the similar provision in F.R.Crim.Proc. 30, but note that the latter is affected by F.R.Crim. Proc. 52(b) which provides: "Plain errors or defects affecting substantial rights may be noticed although they were not brought to the attention of the court." Should there be a similar modification of F.R.C.P. 51? New York requires, as a condition precedent to reversal on grounds of error in jury instruction, that the moving party raise objection first at the trial level. N.Y.C.P.L.R. 4017, 5501.

3. The most important California provisions on instructing the jury in civil cases are contained in C.C.P. §§ 607–614 and California Rules of Court, Superior Court Rule 229. See also C.C.P. 475 (disregard of nonprejudicial error, including that in instructions); C.C.P. 647 (certain errors in instructions and comments on evidence deemed excepted to); C.C.P. 657 subd. 7 (errors of law as grounds for a new trial). The rules on instructing the jury exemplify adherence to the principle of party-prosecution of the case, i.e., that the primary burden is on each party, not on the court, to invoke and insist upon the rights of each. "Although the court, in charging the jury, may, of its own motion, instruct them on all matters which it thinks necessary for their information in reaching a verdict, Alwood v. City of Los Angeles, 139 Cal.App.2d 49, 293 P.2d 69 (1956), a party is entitled to an instruction, generally, only if he requests it. The trial court has no duty, in civil cases, to give on its own motion instructions on issues not covered by the instructions offered by the attorneys. Gould v. Samuels, 132 Cal.App.2d 459, 282 P.2d 566 (1955)." C.E.B., California Civil Procedure During Trial 413 (1960). See also, e.g., Merlo v. Standard Life & Acc. Ins. Co., 59 Cal.App.3d 5, 130 Cal.Rptr. 416 (1976). If a requested instruction is erroneous the judge may simply reject it; she has no duty to correct it and give it to the jury. E.g., Ernest W. Hahn, Inc. v. Sunshield Insulation Co., 68 Cal.App.3d 1018, 137 Cal.Rptr. 732 (1977). On the other hand, the cases also say that "Even if the instruction [defendants] requested and the court rejected was inaccurate, it was the duty of the court to instruct the jury correctly * * * and if necessary request counsel to prepare an accurate, or *more* accurate instruction for that purpose." Pepper v. Underwood, 48 Cal.App.3d 698, 122 Cal.Rptr. 343 (1975). See also 7 Witkin 250, saying that "the complete failure to instruct properly on a basic issue may be reversible error." Can these propositions be reconciled? Compare N.Y.C.P.L.R. 4511; 4 Weinstein, Korn & Miller ¶ 4404.–17.

Note the following characteristics of California jury-instructing procedures:

(a) The proper time for submission of jury instructions to the court and opposing counsel is "before the first witness is sworn." C.C.P. 607a. But that section permits the submission of additional instructions before the argument is begun if they concern "questions of law developed by the evidence and not disclosed by the pleadings." And if argument of counsel raises matters not covered in instructions previously submitted, undoubtedly counsel may request additional instructions pertinent to such matters. The enforcement of the timing of requests for instructions varies according to the practices of individual judges. Compare F.R.C.P. 51.

(b) California policy favors reduction of instructions to writing and the reading of them to the jury, rather than oral delivery. California Rules of Court, Superior Court Rule 229.

(c) In civil cases the jury may take the instructions to the deliberation room if it so requests. C.C.P. 612.5; see also Cal.Pen.Code § 1093(f).

The rules contemplate instructions at the end of the case. It has long been recognized that preliminary and intermediate instructions, particularly in a complex case, help. See Comment, Memory, Magic, and Myth: The Timing of Jury Instructions, 59 Or.L.Rev. 451 (1981). In federal court, the judge may now instruct the jury "before or after argument, or both," under a 1987 amendment to F.R.C.P. 51. Comprehensive consideration of jury-instructing in California appears in 7 Witkin 245 et seq. The California practice has been much affected by the availability of the Book of Approved Jury Instructions, popularly known as BAJI, originated in Los Angeles Superior Court. BAJI has been supplemented by CALJIC, a counterpart for criminal cases. Both are used state-wide. These manuals contain hundreds of model jury instructions covering the issues recurring in jury cases. Similar pattern instructions are in use in many jurisdictions. See Anno., 49 A.L.R.3d 128. Cf. Devitt, Blackmar and Wolff, Federal Jury Practice and Instructions (4th ed. 1987). Pattern instructions may sacrifice intelligibility for convenience and doctrinal purity. See Schwarzer, Communicating with Juries: Problems and Remedies, 69 Calif.L.Rev. 731 (1981). Charrow and Charrow, Making Legal Language Understandable: A Psycholinguistic Study of Jury Instructions, 79 Colum.L.Rev. 1306 (1979), suggests that many of the problems result from orotund grammar.

EVANS v. WRIGHT

United States Court of Appeals for the Fourth Circuit, 1974.
505 F.2d 287.

CRAVEN, CIRCUIT JUDGE:

Primarily this appeal questions the extent of the power of a federal trial judge to comment on the evidence in the course of his charge to the jury. In order to understand what we hold it will be necessary to paraphrase much of the evidence. For just as jury instructions must always "be drawn with reference to the particular facts of the case on trial," Collazo v. United States, 90 U.S.App.D.C. 241, 196 F.2d 573, 578, cert. denied, 343 U.S. 968, 72 S.Ct. 1065, 96 L.Ed. 1364 (1952), so also we cannot intelligently review an instruction in the abstract. Although exercising his power to perhaps its outer limit, we think, the able trial judge below did not invade the province of the jury as understood in the federal system, and we therefore affirm.

I

Appellant George Wright and appellee Sil Evans engaged in the coal mining business in the corporate form of Kentucky Mason Coal Company. Evans was front man and apparently chief operator, and Wright put up most if not all of the corporate capital. When things did not go well, Wright resorted to self-help by writing a check on the corporation in the amount of $115,000 to get part of his investment out. Not surprisingly this led to a lawsuit (with which we are concerned only as background), which resulted in a settlement agreement entered into on April 24, 1971, that divided the assets of Kentucky Mason between the two parties. One of the provisions of the agreement provided that Wright and Evans would divide equally any corporate tax refund that might be received by Kentucky Mason subsequent to the date of the agreement. Early in 1972 Wright received $13,607.01 in refund of 1971 federal and state taxes paid by Kentucky Mason. Although agreeing that he owed Evans half of this amount ($6,803.51), Wright nevertheless refused to divide the funds on the ground that he was entitled to deduct from Evans' one-half share the sum of $2,575 that Evans had received from Kentucky Mason some nine days prior to the April 24 settlement agreement. Wright admitted that he had learned of Evans' receiving the $2,575 early in May 1971, shortly after the settlement agreement, and thus had known of it for at least 13 months without ever mentioning it, much less protesting it, to anybody. Evans' excuse for paying himself the $2,575 was that he had previously turned over to the corporation by depositing it to a corporate account known as "Kentucky Mason No. 2," $5,000 of his dividend income and $215 additional personal funds.[1] That he had done so was apparently not in dispute and is supported by corporate records. Indeed, Evans added to his tax refund claim a second claim for the $5,215 he had given the company.

The case thus went to the jury in this posture: George Wright unquestionably owed Sil Evans one-half of the tax refund ($6,803.51) unless (1) Wright was entitled to set off against Evans' share the sum of $2,575 that Evans had paid himself out of corporate funds, or unless (2) Wright owed Evans not only one half of the tax refund but also the $5,215 contributed by Evans for corporate purposes. The jury returned a verdict in Evans' favor for one-half the tax refund, but denied both Evans' additional claim for $5,215 and Wright's setoff. Wright claims on appeal that the trial judge unfairly prejudiced his claim to a setoff by impermissible commentary on the evidence during his charge to the jury.

---

1. Evans used the $2,575 received from Kentucky Mason to pay his personal taxes. He testified at trial that he felt justified in doing so because his personal taxes had increased as a result of the $5,000 dividend, *all* of which he had plowed back into Kentucky Mason.

II

We begin our consideration of Wright's contention with the premise that a United States district judge is not a bump on a log. Nor is he a referee at a prize fight. He is, instead, the governor of the trial with the power of the common law judge to implement justice. And this power extends to his charge to the jury. As stated in the leading case Quercia v. United States, 289 U.S. 466, 469, 53 S.Ct. 698, 77 L.Ed. 1321 (1933):

> In charging the jury, the trial judge is not limited to instructions of an abstract sort. It is within his province, whenever he thinks it necessary, *to assist the jury in arriving at a just conclusion* by explaining and commenting upon the evidence, by drawing their attention to the parts of it which he thinks important, *and he may express his opinion upon the facts,* provided he makes it clear to the jury that all matters of fact are submitted to their determination. [Emphasis added]

See also Capital Traction Co. v. Hof, 174 U.S. 1, 13–14, 19 S.Ct. 580, 43 L.Ed. 873 (1899). In this tradition Rule 105 of the Proposed Rules of Evidence for United States Courts and Magistrates states the prerogative in clear terms:

> After the close of the evidence and arguments of counsel, the judge may fairly and impartially sum up the evidence and *comment to the jury upon the weight of the evidence and the credibility of the witnesses,* if he also instructs the jury that they are to determine for themselves the weight of the evidence and the credit to be given to the witnesses and that they are not bound by the judge's summation or comment. [Emphasis added] * * *[2]

Of course, the district judge's power of summary and comment is not unbounded. As stated in *Quercia,* 289 U.S. at 470, 53 S.Ct. at 699 (citations omitted):

> This privilege of the judge to comment on the facts has its inherent limitations. His discretion is not arbitrary and uncontrolled, but judicial, to be exercised in conformity with the standards governing the judicial office. In commenting upon testimony he may not assume the role of a witness. He may analyze and dissect the evidence, but he may not either distort it or add to it. . . . This Court has accordingly emphasized the duty of the trial judge to use great care that an expression of opinion upon the evidence "should be so given as not to mislead, and especially that it should not be one-sided;" that "deductions and theories not warranted by the evidence should be studiously avoided."

2. Unlike the United States district judge, the trial judges in many of our states are forbidden, often by statute, from all summary of and comment on the evidence. The federal judge's power is more akin to that of an English judge in the common law courts, who often undertook to condense all evidence presented into a manageable package for the jury, and even to give them his strong opinions on parts of it. See Myers v. George, 271 F.2d 168, 172 (8th Cir. 1959). Wright, The Invasion of Jury: Temperature of the War, 27 Temple L.Q. 137 (1953).

And the judge below conformed to these constraints. In a charge remarkably free of confusing "boilerplate abstractions," United States v. Lozaw, 427 F.2d 911, 916 (2d Cir. 1970), the able trial judge in this case began by saying that the members of the jury were the triers of fact, that the jury should not infer from rulings on the evidence or any admonishment given to attorneys that the court was "for or against any party to this suit," that the jury were "the sole judges of the credibility of the witnesses and the weight of the evidence," and that it was within their province to give "the testimony of each witness such credibility as you may think it deserves."

Then the trial judge got "to the cause of action" and very clearly and concisely applied the law to the facts as the jury should find them to be. See United States v. Holley, 502 F.2d 273 (4th Cir. 1974). Helpfully, he directed their attention to what he termed "essentially three matters to be considered by you in this case." He noted that the contract called for a division of any tax refund, and that Wright had admitted that he owed Evans $6,803.51 as his one-half share. He then took up Evans' contention that he was entitled not only to his one-half of the tax refund but also to $5,215 which he had deposited to the account of Kentucky Mason Mine No. 2 for corporate purposes. The judge noted that the settlement agreement provided that the obligations of Mine No. 2 were to be expressly assumed by Evans. It was then that he "commented upon the evidence," and exactly what he said is quoted in the margin.[3]

The trial judge thereupon directed the attention of the jury to Wright's claim for a setoff of the $2,575 which Evans had paid himself out of corporate funds. He noted that Wright knew of the check soon after the execution of the settlement agreement and certainly by May 1971, and yet never mentioned the claimed setoff until a year later and several months after the books of the company were closed out by a certified public accountant.[4]

Then the judge again commented on the evidence as fully set out in the margin.[5] It is to this commentary that Wright takes exception.

---

3. Since this money was deposited to the account of Mine No. 2 by the plaintiff, it seems more likely that this was in contemplation of the parties, and especially of the plaintiff, at the time the agreement of April 24th was entered into, and I comment on the evidence in this matter to say that I think you should find that the plaintiff should not receive any judgment against the defendant for the extra sum of $5,215, although the weight and sufficiency of the evidence and the intent of the parties when they signed the agreement are being submitted to the jury for your consideration, including this question. I do not direct a verdict on this point; I suggest what I think you should do. You are not bound by my suggestion.

4. The judge said to the jury on the matter of the closeout:

I particularly note that neither party objected to the debits and credits in closing out of the books by Mr. Maness [the CPA] and neither item of $5,215 nor $2,575 was testified about by Mr. Maness, or even brought to his attention when he made the distribution so far as we know.

Neither counsel objected to or requested any modification of this narration of the evidence, although they were afforded the opportunity to do so under Rule 51.

5. I recite this evidence to show you why I consider the claim of Mr. Wright for the $2,575 credit with almost the same degree of doubt I consider the $5,215 extra claim of Mr. Evans. I charge you that in my opinion the weight of the evidence does not support the allowance of the $2,575 credit, but, as I have told you concerning the $5,215 claim, the weight and sufficiency of the evidence and the credibility of the witnesses are for the jury, and I leave this matter to you and do not direct a verdict on it, although in my

There can be no reasonable contention on this charge that the trial judge was biased in favor of one party or prejudiced against the other. With fair indifference he expressed his opinion against the validity of *both* Wright's setoff *and* Evans' $5,215 claim. Nor did he comment on credibility. He did not suggest to the jury that Wright was lying and Evans telling the truth or vice versa. Indeed, the facts were really not in dispute. Everyone agreed that the settlement agreement had been executed by the parties, that not long before execution of that agreement Evans had first contributed $5,215 to the corporation for corporate purposes and then paid himself $2,575 out of corporate funds, and that Wright had learned of Evans' receiving corporate funds not long after the agreement was signed yet had remained silent about it for a year. Thus the credibility of witnesses could not have been an issue.

Although there is substantial authority that is even more permissive, we are inclined to think that ordinarily a district judge should not express an opinion on an *ultimate issue* in a jury trial, e.g., instruct that negligence has been proved, Travelers Ins. Co. v. Ryan, 416 F.2d 362 (5th Cir. 1969); Trezza v. Dame, 370 F.2d 1006 (5th Cir. 1967), and that his doing so may amount to a directed verdict, Nunley v. Pettway Oil Co., 346 F.2d 95, 99 (6th Cir. 1965). But cf. Doyle v. Union Pac. Ry., 147 U.S. 413, 422–430, 13 S.Ct. 333, 37 L.Ed. 223 (1893); United States v. Philadelphia & Reading R.R., 123 U.S. 113, 8 S.Ct. 77, 31 L.Ed. 138 (1887); Tipton v. Socony Mobil Oil Co., 315 F.2d 660, 661–662 (5th Cir.), rev'd per curiam on other grounds, 375 U.S. 34, 84 S.Ct. 1, 11 L.Ed.2d 4 (1963). But that is not what we have here. In this case the district judge's comments amounted, we think, to no more than fairly assisting the jury in interpreting the April 24, 1971, settlement agreement. The basic question was whether that agreement took into account and wiped out both Evans' additional claim for $5,215 and Wright's setoff claim.[6] The judge simply instructed that in his opinion the settlement agreement embraced these two claims as well

---

opinion the $2,575 setoff ought not to be allowed.

To sum it up, it seems to me that both the $5,215 additional claim of the plaintiff Evans and the $2,575 setoff claim of the defendant Wright are afterthoughts and have been brought up to bolster their respective sides in this litigation.

I say to you that is my opinion, that you should give a verdict for half of the tax, which is $6,803.51 and should not allow the additional claim of Mr. Wright in the amount of $5,215 of Mr. Evans (sic) and should not allow the $2,575 setoff of Mr. Wright. But other than the tax, which I tell you you must return, the two other claims I am leaving to your consideration. You would not have to follow my suggestions or my recommendations to you.

6. The settlement agreement included the following clause:

Also heretofore in the past each of the parties have (sic) had numerous dealings with each other and with the corporation and the corporation had numerous dealings with the parties and in consideration of these premises it is hereby expressly agreed that this agreement is a complete settlement among Sil Evans, George Wright and Kentucky Mason Coal Company, Inc. and that by the execution of the terms hereinabove stated that a complete accord and satisfaction will have been perfected and neither of the parties shall be indebted to the other in any way whatsoever.

On its face, this clause would appear to bar both Evans' $5,215 claim and Wright's setoff claim, since the transactions giving rise to both occurred before the date of the settlement agreement.

as all others. Ordinarily the interpretation of a contract is for the court and not for the jury, see 75 Am.Jur.2d Trial §§ 408, 410 (1974), and here any questions for the jury were inseparable from the terms of the settlement contract itself.[7] In this context we hold that the judge's commentary, if error at all, was harmless, and that substantial justice does not require a reversal and remand for a new trial. See Trezza v. Dame, supra, 370 F.2d at 1008–1009; Employers Liab. Assur. Corp. v. Freeman, 229 F.2d 547 (10th Cir. 1955).

III

Wright also challenges the trial judge's sending the jury back to reconsider what Wright claims was a perfectly good verdict. The jury first returned a verdict for Evans for one half of the federal tax refund "plus interest from May 1972," the month Wright received the refund. Because the jury had by oversight failed to consider the *state* tax refund, the judge sent it back with instructions to add Evans' share of that refund to its verdict. No one questions the propriety of that action. On its return, however, the jury's verdict—though correctly including Evans' shares of both federal and state refunds—contained the phrase "plus interest until paid." The judge noted to the jury the discrepancy between its two verdicts on the matter of interest, and the fact that under its second verdict interest would start from the date of judgment, i.e., September 21, 1973. Stating that "I don't know what you intend," the judge sent the jury out again to consider whether they wanted to state a date for interest to start. He also told the jurors they could leave the verdict as it was if they wished, that it was entirely up to them. The jury retired, and four minutes later returned a verdict stating that interest was to begin May 1, 1972.

Wright objects to the judge's sending the jury out to consider the interest point, because the jury's addition of a date cost him over a year's additional interest. He argues that the judge exceeded his authority in sending the jury out again, since its second verdict, silent as to the date for the start of interest, was unambiguous and perfectly proper.

We see no merit in this argument. While the jury's second verdict was on its face unambiguous, we agree with the trial judge that it was rather puzzling. There was no explanation for dropping the starting date for interest which had been in the first verdict. In this context it was natural for the trial judge to wonder whether the jury had intended to omit reference to a starting date, or whether instead the jurors had simply overlooked that matter in revising their verdict. His comments did no more than express his puzzlement and offer them an opportunity to correct their oversight if indeed that was what it was. He did not in any

7. This case did not involve the possibility of fraud or duress in the execution of the settlement agreement, or circumstances in which one party to the agreement had no opportunity to learn the true facts before entering into the agreement. Had either of those possibilities been an issue, resolution would have been for the jury alone, and the judge's comments would give us considerably more difficulty. See 15 Am.Jur.2d Compromise and Settlement §§ 30–33 (1964).

way suggest to them what to do. Furthermore, it took the jury only four minutes to add the starting date for interest; this strongly suggests that its omission had indeed been an oversight. We hold that sending the jury out again, while not required for a valid verdict, was within the sound discretion of the district judge. Cf. 53 Am.Jur. Trial § 1099.

Affirmed.

NOTE ON COMMENTING ON THE EVIDENCE

In most state courts the power of the judge to comment on the evidence is nominally similar to that of federal judges. For example, Calif. Const. Art. VI § 10 states:

> "The court may make such comment on the evidence and the testimony and credibility of any witness as in its opinion is necessary for the proper determination of the cause."

Contrast, however, e.g., Ariz. Const. Art. 6, § 27:

> "Judges shall not charge juries with respect to matters of fact, nor comment thereon, but shall declare the law."

Whatever the governing constitutional and statutory provisions, the fact is that state court judges generally do not exercise the authority to comment as often or as intensively as do federal judges. Compare the following statements of the law. People v. Brock, 66 Cal.2d 645, 58 Cal.Rptr. 321, 426 P.2d 889 (1967):

> "The vice of a general comment on guilt without discussion of the evidence is that it does not aid the jury in applying the instructions on the law to the evidence in the case but to the contrary provides for the jury a means to avoid the preliminary determinations called for by the instructions on the law and instead to rely on the words of the judge in returning a conviction. This is not the kind of comment contemplated by the constitutional provision. * * * The jury is ordinarily aware that the judge has participated in numerous trials * * * and that numerous matters regarding the case have taken place in the presence of the judge but outside the presence of the jury. In these circumstances there is a great danger that a jury which may wish to escape its responsibility to determine the facts will give weight to the comment of the judge without considering the evidence and the instructions." 66 Cal.2d at 651–652.

People v. Rincon-Pineda, 14 Cal.3d 864, 123 Cal.Rptr. 119, 538 P.2d 247 (1975):

> "This power is to be exercised with great care, lest the province of the jury be invaded * * *. But it is the fitting instrument to be employed when a jury needs to be made aware, in the particular circumstances of a given case, that it must give credence to certain evidence as the cornerstone of a certain verdict. * * * We recognize that trial courts have grown wary of commenting upon the evidence. * * * Trial courts should realize, however, that this constraint should not inhibit appropriate comments solicited by defendants themselves or which otherwise appear necessary to protect *defendants'* interests." 14 Cal.3d at 886 (emphasis in original).

3. JURY VERDICTS

NOTE ON THE GENERAL AND SPECIAL VERDICTS

The form of verdict usually employed in a jury trial is a "general" verdict. The jury is given two forms (unless the case involves multiple parties). One form, for plaintiff, is essentially, "We find for plaintiff in the amount of $_____." The other is "We find for defendant." The general verdict obviously conceals the reasoning process by which the jury reached its conclusion, and this is one of its great practical and perhaps theoretical virtues. It would be impractical to require the jury to agree on a narrative statement of the basis of its verdict in all cases. Still, if the jury were required to indicate its basic findings, this would (a) perhaps improve the jury's deliberative process, (b) reduce the need for retrials when part of the jury's conclusions were based on insufficient evidence or erroneous instructions or were otherwise contaminated, and (c) provide a more illuminating basis for determining whether the verdict was contaminated, in connection with a post-trial motion in the trial court or on appeal. Hence, there are attractions to requiring the jury to explain itself.

At common law, there was a device with this effect known as the special verdict, whereby the jury had to find specifically on all the issues essential to the plaintiff's case. The device was very tricky, owing to ambiguities in the term "issue" and to inevitable errors in drafting statements of issues. See James & Hazard § 7.15. A few states, notably Texas, used such verdicts for a long time notwithstanding that their virtue was fully offset by their complexity and vulnerability to error. The Federal Rules and most state procedures therefore have variations, which include a general verdict accompanied by special findings or by answers to special interrogatories. See Dobson v. Masonite Corp., supra p. 1131. See F.R.C.P. 49; C.C.P. 624, 625; N.Y.C.P.L.R. 4111; Anno., 6 A.L.R.3d 438.

A number of commentators and a few judges have strongly urged wider use of the special verdict or interrogatory, especially in complex cases. The classic, tendentious statement of this view is by Frank, J., in Skidmore v. Baltimore & Ohio R.R. Co., 167 F.2d 54 (2d Cir. 1948). See also Comment, Special Verdicts: Rule 49 of the Federal Rules of Civil Procedure, 74 Yale L.J. 483 (1965); Wright, The Use of Special Verdicts in Federal Court, 38 F.R.D. 199 (1965); Brown, Federal Special Verdicts: The Doubt Eliminator, 44 F.R.D. 338 (1967). But the device is not much used. Its use is normally discretionary with the trial court, see 9 Wright & Miller §§ 2505, 2511; e.g., Masonite Corp. v. Pacific Gas & Electric Co., 65 Cal. App.3d 1, 135 Cal.Rptr. 170 (1976), although California enacted a law in 1983 requiring courts, in actions involving punitive damages, to direct the jury to render a special verdict that distinguishes punitive damages from compensatory damages; see C.C.P. 625. No case has been found in which a trial judge has been reversed for refusing to submit a special verdict or interrogatory. The effect of a special finding is diminished by rules that minimize the significance of a discrepancy between such a finding and the general verdict. See, e.g., Hasson v. Ford Motor Co., 19 Cal.3d 530, 138 Cal.Rptr. 705, 564 P.2d 857 (1977), 19 Cal.3d at 540:

> " 'A special finding is inconsistent with the general verdict only when, as a matter of law, the special finding when taken by itself would authorize a judgment different from that which the general verdict will permit.' * * *
> The general and special verdicts must be beyond possibility of reconciliation under any possible application of the evidence and instructions."

See also Julien J. Studley, Inc. v. Gulf Oil Corp., 407 F.2d 521 (2d Cir. 1969), to much the same effect. But if the finding cannot be reconciled with the verdict the verdict cannot stand, which makes the procedure vulnerable. See, e.g., Guidry v. Kem Mfg. Co., 598 F.2d 402 (5th Cir. 1979). Given the limited "control" that the special finding thus has on a general verdict, and the possibility for contradiction if the special findings are not posed and answered clearly, why should a trial judge bother with them? See also Note, Resolving Inconsistencies in Federal Special Verdicts, 53 Ford.L.Rev. 1089 (1985); Comment, Informing the Jury of the Legal Effect of Special Verdict Answers in Comparative Negligence Actions, 1981 Duke L.J. 824.

Resch v. Volkswagen of America, Inc., 36 Cal.3d 676, 205 Cal.Rptr. 827, 685 P.2d 1178 (1984), was a personal injury action against an automobile manufacturer in which the questions of defect and causation were submitted to the jury for special verdicts. Nine of the twelve found a manufacturing defect, but ten of the twelve found that the defect was not a substantial factor in causing plaintiff's injuries. Three of the ten jurors voting on the substantiality issue had concluded there was no defect in the automobile at all. Plaintiff moved for a mistrial, arguing that the verdict was improper unless the identical nine jurors who found a manufacturing defect also found a lack of causation. The California Supreme Court affirmed the trial court's denial of the motion, holding that where a case is submitted to a jury for special verdicts, all jurors may participate in each special verdict regardless of any asserted inconsistencies that might result. The court relied on Juarez v. Superior Court, 31 Cal.3d 759, 183 Cal.Rptr. 852, 647 P.2d 128 (1982), where it had abandoned the "identical nine" rule.

4. MOTIONS AFTER VERDICT

INTRODUCTORY NOTE ON POST-TRIAL MOTIONS

1. After the verdict in a case tried to a jury, or after the decision by the judge in a nonjury case, judgment should be entered forthwith. See F.R.C.P. 58; C.C.P. 664; California Rules of Court, Superior Court Rule 232. Entry of judgment has significance for a variety of purposes, e.g., computation of time to appeal. Moreover, the date of entry of judgment ordinarily determines the time within which post-trial motions may be made. See F.R.C.P. 59(b) (motion for new trial must be "served not later than 10 days after the entry of judgment"), 59(d) (same period allowed for trial court to order new trial on its own initiative), 50(b) (motion for judgment notwithstanding the verdict must be made within identically defined period); C.C.P. 659 (new trial motion must be made within 15 days of "mailing notice of entry of judgment by the clerk" or "service * * * of written notice of entry"), C.C.P. 629 (motion for judgment notwithstanding the verdict must be made "within the period specified by Section 659"). For the technicalities in the timing of a new trial motion under C.C.P. 659, see Ehrler v. Ehrler, 126 Cal.App.3d 147, 178 Cal.Rptr. 642 (1981).

There are essentially two things that can be done through a motion after a jury trial, other than allowing the verdict and judgment to stand. One is to order a new trial; the other is to enter judgment against the verdict-winner, i.e., judgment notwithstanding the verdict. Judgment notwithstanding the verdict (or judgment n.o.v.) is based on a determination that the evidence is so weak that a verdict may not justly be based on it. A new trial can be appropriate either because the evidence is weak in this sense or because procedural errors contaminated the proceeding, e.g., there was improperly admitted evidence, improper conduct or argument during trial, or error in instructions. When the question is the weakness of the evidence, rather than procedural error, it is a nice question whether the trial judge should grant a new trial or judgment n.o.v. Resolution of that question may be determined according to different procedural and substantive criteria in different jurisdictions. Thus, under the Federal Rules if the verdict-loser had not made a motion for directed verdict at the close of all the evidence at trial, judgment n.o.v. is not authorized; the only post-trial remedy would be a new trial. F.R.C.P. 50(b). On the other hand, in California practice the trial judge may grant judgment n.o.v. on his own motion but may grant a new trial only if a party has moved for a new trial. Further, the substantive standards—determining how strong the evidence must be to support a verdict—are variously formulated. See Note on Setting Aside a Verdict, infra p. 1168.

2. The forms of contamination that might justify a new trial are practically infinite. See C.C.P. 657, enumerating several; cf. Note, Written Specification of Reasons for New Trial Orders, 64 Calif.L.Rev. 286 (1976). Perhaps in recognition of the difficulty of enumeration, F.R.C.P. 59(a) provides that a new trial may be awarded "for any of the reasons for which new trials have heretofore been granted in actions at law in the courts of the United States." See 6A Moore ¶ 59.02; 11 Wright & Miller § 2805. See also N.Y.C.P.L.R. 4404. All the cases considered up to this point in this section are illustrative. In addition, a new trial may be granted on the ground of "newly discovered" evidence. To obtain relief on this ground, the applicant must show that she used due diligence before and during trial to ferret out the evidence belatedly discovered. This requirement is rather rigidly applied in most federal courts, see 11 Wright & Miller § 2808; e.g., Owens v. International Paper Co., 528 F.2d 606 (5th Cir. 1976), but more liberally in California, e.g., Lostritto v. Southern Pacific Transportation Co., 73 Cal.App.3d 737, 140 Cal.Rptr. 905 (1977); Andersen v. Howland, 3 Cal.App.3d 380, 83 Cal.Rptr. 308 (1970).

In jury trials there are also many mishaps that can occur in the jury room. The rule used to be that a juror could not be heard to impeach his verdict, i.e., testimony of a juror would not be received to show that some mishap had occurred in the jury's performance of its functions. This rule had the effect, as intended, that it was difficult to show that jury misconduct had occurred and hence to have a verdict set aside on the ground of such misconduct. See James & Hazard § 7.19; Comment, Impeachment of Jury Verdicts by Jurors: A Proposal, 1969 U.Ill.L.F. 388. See also Anno., 32 A.L.R.3d 1356. In recent years, this rule has been much relaxed. For example, proof by some jurors that others were doing crossword puzzles and reading during trial was admitted by the court, although it was held insufficient misconduct for a new trial, following a personal injury verdict for $11.5 million in Hasson v. Ford Motor Co., 32 Cal.3d 388, 185 Cal.Rptr. 654, 650 P.2d 1171 (1982). Federal Rules of Evidence Rule 606(b) provides:

> "(b) Inquiry Into Validity of Verdict or Indictment. Upon any inquiry into the validity of a verdict or indictment, a juror may not testify as to any matter or statement occurring during the course of the jury's deliberations or to the effect of anything upon his or any other juror's mind or emotions as influencing him to assent to or dissent from the verdict or indictment or concerning his mental processes in connection therewith, except that a juror may testify on the question whether extraneous prejudicial information was improperly brought to the jury's attention or whether any outside infuence was improperly brought to bear upon any juror. Nor may his affidavit or evidence of any statement by him concerning a matter about which he would be precluded from testifying be received for these purposes."

[handwritten margin note: what juror may testify to:]

Despite some relaxation, the traditional standard embodied in Rule 606(b) still has bite, as evidenced by the following case.

TANNER v. UNITED STATES

Supreme Court of the United States, 1987.
483 U.S. 107, 107 S.Ct. 2739, 97 L.Ed.2d 90.*

JUSTICE O'CONNOR delivered the opinion of the Court.

Petitioners William Conover and Anthony Tanner were convicted of conspiring to defraud the United States in violation of 18 U.S.C. § 371, and of committing mail fraud in violation of 18 U.S.C. § 1341. The United States Court of Appeals for the Eleventh Circuit affirmed the convictions. 772 F.2d 765 (1985). Petitioners argue that the District Court erred in refusing to admit juror testimony at a post-verdict hearing on juror intoxication during the trial * * *.

I

* * *

The day before petitioners were scheduled to be sentenced, Tanner filed a motion, in which Conover subsequently joined, seeking continuance of the sentencing date, permission to interview jurors, an evidentiary hearing, and a new trial. According to an affidavit accompanying the motion, Tanner's attorney had received an unsolicited telephone call from one of the trial jurors, Vera Asbul. App. 246. Juror Asbul informed Tanner's attorney that several of the jurors consumed alcohol during the lunch breaks at various times throughout the trial, causing them to sleep through the afternoons. Id., at 247. The District Court continued the sentencing date, ordered the parties to file memoranda, and heard argument on the motion to interview jurors. The District Court concluded that juror testimony on intoxication was inadmissible under Federal Rule of Evidence 606(b) to impeach the jury's verdict. The District Court invited petitioners to call any nonjuror witnesses, such as courtroom personnel, in support of the motion for new trial. Tanner's counsel took the stand and testified that he had observed one of the jurors "in a sort of giggly mood" at one point during the trial but did not bring this to anyone's attention at the time. Id., at 170.

* * *

Following the hearing the District Court filed an order stating that "[o]n the basis of the admissible evidence offered I specifically find that the motions for leave to interview jurors or for an evidentiary hearing at which jurors would be witnesses is not required or appropriate." The District Court also denied the motion for new trial. Id., at 181–182.

While the appeal of this case was pending before the Eleventh Circuit, petitioners filed another new trial motion based on additional evidence of jury misconduct. In another affidavit, Tanner's attorney stated that he

---

* Some of the Court's footnotes are omitted.

received an unsolicited visit at his residence from a second juror, Daniel Hardy. Id., at 241. Despite the fact that the District Court had denied petitioners' motion for leave to interview jurors, two days after Hardy's visit Tanner's attorney arranged for Hardy to be interviewed by two private investigators. Id., at 242. The interview was transcribed, sworn to by the juror, and attached to the new trial motion. In the interview Hardy stated that he "felt like . . . the jury was on one big party." Id., at 209. Hardy indicated that seven of the jurors drank alcohol during the noon recess. Four jurors, including Hardy, consumed between them "a pitcher to three pitchers" of beer during various recesses. Id., at 212. Of the three other jurors who were alleged to have consumed alcohol, Hardy stated that on several occasions he observed two jurors having one or two mixed drinks during the lunch recess, and one other juror, who was also the foreperson, having a liter of wine on each of three occasions. Id., at 213–215. Juror Hardy also stated that he and three other jurors smoked marijuana quite regularly during the trial. Id., at 216–223. Moreover, Hardy stated that during the trial he observed one juror ingest cocaine five times and another juror ingest cocaine two or three times. Id., at 227. One juror sold a quarter pound of marijuana to another juror during the trial, and took marijuana, cocaine and drug paraphernalia into the courthouse. Id., at 234–235. Hardy noted that some of the jurors were falling asleep during the trial, and that one of the jurors described himself to Hardy as "flying." Id., at 229. Hardy stated that before he visited Tanner's attorney at his residence no one had contacted him concerning the jury's conduct, and Hardy had not been offered anything in return for his statement. Id., at 232. Hardy said that he came forward "to clear my conscience" and "[b]ecause I felt . . . that the people on the jury didn't have no business being on the jury. I felt . . . that Mr. Tanner should have a better opportunity to get somebody that would review the facts right." Id., at 231–232.

The District Court, stating that the motions "contain supplemental allegations which differ quantitatively but not qualitatively from those in the April motions," id., at 256, denied petitioners' motion for a new trial.

* * *

II

* * *

By the beginning of this century, if not earlier, the near-universal and firmly established common-law rule in the United States flatly prohibited the admission of juror testimony to impeach a jury verdict. See 8 J. Wigmore, Evidence § 2352, pp. 696–697 (McNaughton rev. ed. 1961) (common-law rule, originating from 1785 opinion of Lord Mansfield, "came to receive in the United States an adherence almost unquestioned").

Exceptions to the common-law rule were recognized only in situations in which an "extraneous influence," Mattox v. United States, 146 U.S. 140, 149, 13 S.Ct. 50, 53, 36 L.Ed. 917 (1892), was alleged to have affected the jury. In *Mattox,* this Court held admissible the testimony of jurors describing how they heard and read prejudicial information not admitted into evidence. The Court allowed juror testimony on influence by outsiders in Parker v. Gladden, 385 U.S. 363, 365, 87 S.Ct. 468, 470, 17 L.Ed.2d 420 (1966) (bailiff's comments on defendant), and Remmer v. United States, 347 U.S. 227, 228–230, 74 S.Ct. 450, 450–452, 98 L.Ed. 654 (1954) (bribe offered to juror). See also Smith v. Phillips, 455 U.S. 209, 102 S.Ct. 940, 71 L.Ed.2d 78 (1982) (juror in criminal trial had submitted an application for employment at the District Attorney's office). In situations that did not fall into this exception for external influence, however, the Court adhered to the common-law rule against admitting juror testimony to impeach a verdict. McDonald v. Pless, 238 U.S. 264, 35 S.Ct. 783, 59 L.Ed. 1300 (1915); Hyde v. United States, 225 U.S. 347, 384, 32 S.Ct. 793, 808, 56 L.Ed. 1114 (1912).

Lower courts used this external/internal distinction to identify those instances in which juror testimony impeaching a verdict would be admissible. The distinction was not based on whether the juror was literally inside or outside the jury room when the alleged irregularity took place; rather, the distinction was based on the nature of the allegation. * * *

Most significant for the present case, however, is the fact that lower federal courts treated allegations of the physical or mental incompetence of a juror as "internal" rather than "external" matters. * * * See also Sullivan v. Fogg, 613 F.2d 465, 467 (CA2 1980) (allegation of juror insanity is internal consideration); United States v. Allen, 588 F.2d 1100, 1106, n. 12 (CA5 1979) (noting "specific reluctance to probe the minds of jurors once they have deliberated their verdict"); United States v. Pellegrini, 441 F.Supp. 1367 (ED Pa.1977), aff'd, 586 F.2d 836 (CA3), cert. denied, 439 U.S. 1050, 99 S.Ct. 731, 58 L.Ed.2d 711 (1978) (whether juror sufficiently understood English language was not a question of "extraneous influence"). This line of federal decisions was reviewed in Government of the Virgin Islands v. Nicholas, supra, in which the Court of Appeals concluded that a juror's allegation that a hearing impairment interfered with his understanding of the evidence at trial was not a matter of "external influence." Id., at 1079.

Substantial policy considerations support the common-law rule against the admission of jury testimony to impeach a verdict. As early as 1915 this Court explained the necessity of shielding jury deliberations from public scrutiny:

"[L]et it once be established that verdicts solemnly made and publicly returned into court can be attacked and set aside on the testimony of those who took part in their publication and all verdicts could be, and many would be, followed by an inquiry in the hope of discovering something which might invalidate the finding. Jurors would be harassed and beset by the defeated party in an effort to secure from them evidence of facts which might establish misconduct sufficient to set aside a verdict. If evidence thus secured could be thus used, the result would be to make what was intended to be a private deliberation, the constant subject of public investigation—to the destruction of all frankness and freedom of discussion and conference." McDonald v. Pless, 238 U.S., at 267–268, 35 S.Ct., at 784.

See also Mattox v. United States, 146 U.S. 140, 13 S.Ct. 50, 36 L.Ed. 917 (1892).

The Court's holdings requiring an evidentiary hearing where extrinsic influence or relationships have tainted the deliberations do not detract from, but rather harmonize with, the weighty government interest in insulating the jury's deliberative process. See Smith v. Phillips, 455 U.S. 209, 102 S.Ct. 940, 71 L.Ed.2d 78 (1982) (juror in criminal trial had submitted an application for employment at the District Attorney's office); Remmer v. United States, 347 U.S. 227, 74 S.Ct. 450, 98 L.Ed. 654 (1954) (juror reported attempted bribe during trial and was subjected to investigation). The Court's statement in *Remmer* that "[t]he integrity of jury proceedings must not be jeopardized by unauthorized invasions," id., at 229, 74 S.Ct., at 451, could also be applied to the inquiry petitioners seek to make into the internal processes of the jury.

There is little doubt that post-verdict investigation into juror misconduct would in some instances lead to the invalidation of verdicts reached after irresponsible or improper juror behavior. It is not at all clear, however, that the jury system could survive such efforts to perfect it. Allegations of juror misconduct, incompetency, or inattentiveness, raised for the first time days, weeks, or months after the verdict seriously disrupt the finality of the process. See, e.g., Government of Virgin Islands v. Nicholas, 759 F.2d, at 1081 (one year and eight months after verdict rendered, juror alleged that hearing difficulties affected his understanding of the evidence). Moreover, full and frank discussion in the jury room, jurors' willingness to return an unpopular verdict, and the community's trust in a system that relies on the decisions of laypeople would all be undermined by a barrage of post verdict scrutiny of juror conduct. See Note, Public Disclosures of Jury Deliberations, 96 Harv.L.Rev. 886, 888–892 (1983).

Federal Rule of Evidence 606(b) is grounded in the common-law rule against admission of jury testimony to impeach a verdict and the exception for juror testimony relating to extraneous influences. * * *

Petitioners have presented no argument that Rule 606(b) is inapplicable to the juror affidavits and the further inquiry they sought in this case, and, in fact, there appears to be virtually no support for such a proposition. See 3 D. Louisell & C. Mueller, Federal Evidence § 287, pp. 121–125 (1979) (under Rule 606(b), "proof to the following effects is excludable . . . that one or more jurors was inattentive during trial or deliberations, sleeping or thinking about other matters"); cf. Note, Impeachment of Verdicts by Jurors—Rule of Evidence 606(b), 4 Wm. Mitchell L.Rev. 417, 430–431 and n. 88 (1978) (observing that under Rule 606(b), "juror testimony as to . . . juror intoxication probably will be inadmissible"; note author suggests that "[o]ne possibility is for the courts to determine that certain acts, such as a juror becoming intoxicated outside the jury room, simply are not within the rule," but cites no authority in support of the suggestion). Rather, petitioners argue that substance abuse constitutes an improper "outside influence" about which jurors may testify under Federal Rule of Evidence 606(b). In our view the language of the Rule cannot easily be stretched to cover this circumstance. However severe their effect and improper their use, drugs or alcohol voluntarily ingested by a juror seems no more an "outside influence" than a virus, poorly prepared food, or a lack of sleep.

In any case, whatever ambiguity might linger in the language of Rule 606(b) as applied to juror intoxication is resolved by the legislative history of the Rule. In 1972, following criticism of a proposed rule that would have allowed considerably broader use of juror testimony to impeach verdicts, the Advisory Committee drafted the present version of Rule 606(b). Compare 51 F.R.D. 315, 387 (1971) with 56 F.R.D. 183, 265 (1972) * * *.

　　* * *

The Conference Committee Report reaffirms Congress' understanding of the differences between the House and Senate versions of Rule 606(b): "[T]he House bill allows a juror to testify about objective matters occurring during the jury's deliberation, such as the misconduct of another juror or the reaching of a quotient verdict. The Senate bill does not permit juror testimony about any matter or statement occurring during the course of the jury's deliberations." H.R.Conf.Rep. No. 93–1597, p. 8 (1974), U.S.Code Cong. & Admin.News 1974, p. 7102. The Conference Committee adopted, and Congress enacted, the Senate version of Rule 606(b).

Thus, the legislative history demonstrates with uncommon clarity that Congress specifically understood, considered, and rejected a version of Rule 606(b) that would have allowed jurors to testify on juror conduct during deliberations, including juror intoxication. This legislative history provides strong support for the most reasonable reading of the language of Rule 606(b)—that juror intoxication is not an "outside influence" about which jurors may testify to impeach their verdict.

　　* * *

Petitioners also argue that the refusal to hold an additional evidentiary hearing at which jurors would testify as to their conduct "violates the sixth amendment's guarantee to a fair trial before an impartial and *competent* jury." Brief for Petitioners 34 (emphasis in original).

This Court has recognized that a defendant has a right to "a tribunal both impartial and mentally competent to afford a hearing." Jordan v. Massachusetts, 225 U.S. 167, 176, 32 S.Ct. 651, 652, 56 L.Ed. 1038 (1912). In this case the District Court held an evidentiary hearing in response to petitioners' first new trial motion at which the judge invited petitioners to introduce any admissible evidence in support of their allegations. At issue in this case is whether the Constitution compelled the District Court to hold an additional evidentiary hearing including one particular kind of evidence inadmissible under the Federal Rules.

　　* * *

In light of these other sources of protection of the petitioners' right to a competent jury, we conclude that the District Court did not err in deciding, based on the inadmissibility of juror testimony and the clear insufficiency of the nonjuror evidence offered by petitioners, that an additional post verdict evidentiary hearing was unnecessary.

* * *

JUSTICE MARSHALL, with whom JUSTICE BRENNAN, JUSTICE BLACKMUN, and JUSTICE STEVENS join, concurring in part and dissenting in part.

Every criminal defendant has a constitutional right to be tried by competent jurors. * * *

* * *

* * * Rule 606(b) is not applicable to juror testimony on matters *unrelated* to the jury's deliberations. By its terms, Rule 606(b) renders jurors incompetent to testify only as to three subjects: (i) any "matter or statement" occurring during deliberations; (ii) the "effect" of anything upon the "mind or emotions" of any juror as it relates to his or her "assent to or dissent from the verdict"; and (iii) the "mental processes" of the juror in connection with his "assent to or dissent from the verdict." [5] Even as to matters involving deliberations, the bar is not absolute.[6]

It is undisputed that Rule 606(b) does not exclude juror testimony as to matters occurring before or after deliberations. See 3 D. Louisell & C. Mueller, Federal Evidence § 290, p. 151 (1979); cf. Note, Impeachment of Verdicts by Jurors—Rule of Evidence 606(b), 4 Wm. Mitchell L.Rev. 417, 431, n. 88 (1978). But, more particularly, the Rule only "operates to prohibit testimony as to *certain* conduct by the jurors which has no verifiable manifestations," 3 J. Weinstein & M. Berger, Weinstein's Evidence ¶ 606[04], p. 606–28 (1985) (emphasis added); as to other matters, jurors remain competent to testify. See Fed.Rule Evid. 601. Because petitioners' claim of juror misconduct and incompetency involves objectively verifiable conduct occurring prior to deliberations, juror testimony in support of the claims is admissible under Rule 606(b).

* * * As the Court emphasizes, the debate over two proposed versions of the Rule—the more restrictive Senate version ultimately adopted and the permissive House version * * * focused on the extent to which jurors would be permitted to testify as to what transpired *during the course of the deliberations themselves*.[7] Similarly, the Conference

---

5. Rule 606(b) provides, in relevant part:

"[A] juror may not testify as to any matter or statement occurring during the course of the jury's deliberations or to the effect of anything upon his or any other juror's mind or emotions as influencing him to assent to or dissent from the verdict or indictment or concerning his mental processes in connection therewith, except that a juror may testify on the question whether extraneous prejudicial information was improperly brought to the jury's attention or whether any outside influence

was improperly brought to bear upon any juror."

6. Rule 606(b) expressly authorizes jurors to testify as to "extraneous prejudicial information" or "outside influence." * * *

7. Proponents of the more restrictive Senate version were reluctant to allow juror testimony as to irregularities in the process by which a verdict was reached, such as the resort to a "quotient verdict." See, e.g., 120 Cong.Rec. 2374–2375 (1974) (statement of Rep. Wiggins); 117 Cong.Rec. 33642, 33645 (1971) (letter from Sen. McClellan); id., at

Committee Report, quoted by the Court, * * * compares the two versions solely in terms of the admissibility of testimony as to matters occurring during, or relating to, the jury's deliberations: "[T]he House bill allows a juror to testify about objective matters occurring during the jury's deliberation, such as the misconduct of another juror or the reaching of a quotient verdict. The Senate bill does not permit juror testimony about any matter or statement occurring *during the course of the jury's deliberations.*" H.R.Conf.Rep. No. 93–1597, p. 8 (1974), U.S. Code Cong. & Admin.News 1974, p. 7102 (emphasis added). The obvious conclusion, and the one compelled by Rule 601, is that *both* versions of Rule 606(b) would have permitted jurors to testify as to matters not involving deliberations. The House Report's passing reference to juror intoxication during deliberations * * * is not to the contrary. Reflecting Congress' consistent focus on the deliberative process, it suggests only that the authors of the House Report believed that the Senate version of Rule 606(b) did not allow testimony as to juror intoxication during deliberations.[8]

In this case, no invasion of the jury deliberations is contemplated. Permitting a limited postverdict inquiry into juror consumption of alcohol and drugs *during trial* would not "make what was intended to be a private deliberation, the constant subject of public investigation—to the destruction of all frankness and freedom of discussion and conference." McDonald v. Pless, 238 U.S., at 267–268, 35 S.Ct., at 784. "Allowing [jurors] to testify as to matters other than their own inner reactions involves no particular hazard to the values sought to be protected." Advisory Committee's Notes of Fed.Rule Evid. 606(b), 28 U.S.C.App., p. 701.

Even if I agreed with the Court's expansive construction of Rule 606(b), I would nonetheless find the testimony of juror intoxication admissible under the Rule's "outside influence" exception. As a common sense matter, drugs and alcohol *are* outside influences on jury members. * * *

 * * *

33649, 33655 (Dept. of Justice Analysis and Recommendations Regarding Revised Draft of Proposed Rules of Evidence for the U.S. Courts and Magistrates).

As the Court explains, * * * the Senate rejected the House version because it "would have the effect of opening verdicts up to challenge on the basis of what happened during the jury's *internal deliberations,* for example, where a juror alleged that the jury refused to follow the trial judge's instructions or that some of the jurors did not take part in deliberations." S.Rep. No. 93–1277, p. 13 (1974), U.S.Code Cong. & Admin.News 1974, p. 7060 (emphasis added). See also id., at 14, U.S.Code Cong. & Admin.News 1974, p. 7060 ("[R]ule 606 should not permit any inquiry into the internal deliberations of the jurors").

8. H.R.Rep. No. 93–650, p. 10 (1973), U.S.Code Cong. & Admin.News 1974, p. 7083 ("Under this formulation a quotient verdict could not be attacked through the testimony of a juror, nor could a juror testify to the drunken condition of a fellow juror which so disabled him that he could not participate in the jury's deliberations").

NOTE ON SETTING ASIDE A VERDICT

With *Tanner* compare Krouse v. Graham, 19 Cal.3d 59, 137 Cal.Rptr. 863, 562 P.2d 1022 (1977), applying a similar California rule but reaching a contrary result. See also Attridge v. Cencorp Division, 836 F.2d 113 (2d Cir.1987) (Rule 606(b) did not preclude inquiry after jurors were discharged to determine whether verdict they designated as "Total Verdict Amount" incorporated twenty percent reduction for plaintiff's negligence); United States v. Bailey, 834 F.2d 218 (1st Cir.1987) (interrogation of former jurors in defense to criminal charge of bribing jury).

In addition to procedural errors at trial, a post-trial motion may aim at setting aside the verdict as a matter of substance. The available motions are those for new trial on the ground of insufficiency of the evidence, which results in the case being tried again before another jury, and for judgment notwithstanding the verdict, which as its name implies results in the immediate entry of judgment against the verdict-winner. Obviously the remedy of judgment n.o.v. is the more drastic. When judgment n.o.v. is granted the verdict-winner has no chance to supplement the proofs offered in the first trial, a possibility that may sometimes exist. On the other hand, if judgment n.o.v. is granted, the verdict-winner has an immediate appeal which may result in reinstatement of the verdict whereas when a new trial is granted, the verdict-winner cannot appeal until after the new trial has gone to judgment; if she has lost in the second trial, she has the heavy burden on appeal of showing that the original verdict should displace the second one. See Evers v. Equifax, Inc., 650 F.2d 793 (5th Cir. 1981).

In considering the motion for judgment n.o.v. and a motion for new trial based on the insufficiency of the evidence, two distinct problems arise. The first is the procedure required in making the respective motions; the second is the degree of insufficiency of evidence that justifies granting one or the other of the motions. The following chart undertakes to compare the Federal Rules and the California provisions in these respects. California imposes additional requirements that the judge rule on a new trial motion within 60 days and specify the insufficiency of evidence when that is the ground for granting the new trial. See Sanchez-Corea v. Bank of America, 38 Cal.3d 892, 215 Cal.Rptr. 679, 701 P.2d 826 (1985). For the substantive criteria under the Federal Rules, see 9 Wright & Miller §§ 2524 and 2536, 11 id. § 2819. For the California criteria, see 7 Witkin 425–438. For the New York rules, see N.Y.C.P.L.R. 4404; 4 Weinstein, Korn & Miller ¶ 4404.04, 4404.09; Gillman v. Liberty Airport Authority, 32 A.D.2d 296, 302 N.Y.S.2d 203 (1969).

	F.R.C.P 50(b), 59	C.C.P. 629, 657
Time for Party Motion	10 days after judgment	15 days after notice of judgment
Condition Precedent	J.n.o.v.: Motion for directed verdict at close of all evidence New Trial: None	J.n.o.v.: None New Trial: None

	F.R.C.P 50(b), 59	C.C.P. 629, 657
Post-Trial Motion by Party Required?	J.n.o.v. Yes New Trial: No	J.n.o.v.: No New Trial: Yes
Standard	J.n.o.v.: "one conclusion . . . that reasonable men could have reached" New Trial: against "great weight" of evidence	J.n.o.v.: "no other reasonable conclusion is legally deductible from the evidence" New Trial: "clearly should have reached a different verdict"
Appellate Review Standard	J.n.o.v.: Was verdict insufficient as "matter of law"? New Trial: "clear abuse of discretion"	J.n.o.v.: Was verdict insufficient as "matter of law"? New Trial: "manifest abuse of discretion"

See generally Louis, Post-Verdict Rulings on the Sufficiency of the Evidence, 1975 Wis.L.Rev. 503; James & Hazard §§ 7.20–7.22. The federal courts are divided as to how rigidly to apply the requirement in F.R.C.P. 50(b) that there have been a prior motion for directed verdict at the close of all the evidence as distinct from a motion at the close of plaintiff's case. See, e.g., Bonner v. Coughlin, 657 F.2d 931 (7th Cir. 1981). On the difference in the trial judge's scope of authority in granting a new trial as compared with judgment n.o.v., see, e.g., Bevevino v. Saydjari, 574 F.2d 676 (2d Cir. 1978). See also Stafford v. Neurological Medicine, Inc., 811 F.2d 470 (8th Cir. 1987), where the court held that a trial judge may not grant a new trial unless the jury's verdict was a "plain injustice" or a "monstrous" or "shocking" result.

A jury verdict acquitting a criminal defendant of one charge while convicting him of another, where the two verdicts are inherently inconsistent, has been held not to invalidate the conviction, on the theory that the jury could have been lenient in the acquittal, which was within its prerogative. United States v. Powell, 469 U.S. 57, 105 S.Ct. 471, 83 L.Ed.2d 461 (1984). Would the same approach to inconsistent verdicts be justified in a civil case?

SPURLIN v. GENERAL MOTORS CORP.

United States Court of Appeals for the Fifth Circuit, 1976.
528 F.2d 612.*

TUTTLE, CIRCUIT JUDGE:

This diversity suit arises out of a school bus crash which occurred in Morgan County, Alabama, on April 23, 1968, when the bus's brakes failed. Two wrongful death suits and twenty-two personal injury actions were filed, on behalf of the children who were in the bus at the time, against the manufacturer of the school bus chassis, General

---

* Some of the court's footnotes are omitted.

Motors Corporation. Following consolidation of the cases for trial by the district court,[1] a six-person jury heard evidence for approximately two weeks. The court then submitted the cases on the theory of alleged negligent design of the braking system, and the jury returned a verdict for the plaintiffs, awarding damages in the amount of $70,000 each in the wrongful death cases. The district court, however, granted defendant's post-trial motions for judgment notwithstanding the verdict and, in the alternative, a new trial, on the ground that the verdict was not supported by the evidence. This appeal followed. We consider the district court's two post-trial rulings in turn, beginning with its grant of General Motors' motion for judgment notwithstanding the verdict.

I. CORRECTNESS OF THE DISTRICT COURT'S GRANT OF JUDGMENT NOTWITHSTANDING THE VERDICT

A. *The Standard of Review.*

The applicable standard of review for judging the correctness of a district court's grant or denial of a motion for judgment notwithstanding the verdict was carefully delineated by this court in Boeing Co. v. Shipman, 411 F.2d 365 (5th Cir. 1969) (en banc):

> "On motions for directed verdict and for judgment notwithstanding the verdict the Court should consider all of the evidence—not just that evidence which supports the nonmover's case—but in the light and with all reasonable inferences most favorable to the party opposed to the motion. . . . [I]f there is substantial evidence opposed to the motions, that is, evidence of such quality and weight that reasonable and fair-minded men in the exercise of impartial judgment might reach different conclusions, the motions shall be denied, and the case submitted to the jury. . . . There must be a conflict on substantial evidence to create a jury question. However, it is the function of the jury as the traditional finder of the facts, and not the Court, to weigh conflicting evidence and inferences, and determine the credibility of witnesses." 411 F.2d at 374–375 (footnotes omitted).

* * * It is important to note * * * that defendant General Motors has not assigned, as separate grounds for cross-appeal, the commission of any errors by the district court in admitting into evidence any particular items or testimony given by any of the witnesses. This Court, therefore, is not required to consider the issue of the scope of the evidence which was properly before the jury in reaching its verdict, but is free to examine and rely upon all the evidence which the district court charged the jury it could consider in deciding the case.

---

1. Over defendant's objection, the district court consolidated all of the cases for trial on the issue of liability, and additionally consolidated the two wrongful death actions for trial on the issue of damages. The latter were brought under the Alabama Homicide Act, Title 7, § 119, under which a successful plaintiff is awarded punitive rather than compensatory damages.

B. *Plaintiffs' Theory of Recovery.*

Briefly stated, the theory upon which the cases were submitted to the jury was one of alleged negligent design of the bus's braking system by General Motors, coupled with a failure to warn of the unique problems and need for frequent servicing and maintenance associated with operating school buses. Specifically, the plaintiffs contended that the braking system with which the 1965 66-passenger school bus at issue was equipped was not reasonably safe for the use for which it was intended in that: (1) the single hydraulic braking system on the bus was a dangerous system because of the inevitability of total failure of braking power in the event of a loss of brake fluid through undetected leakage; (2) there was no effective emergency brake on the bus, only a parking brake which was not intended to stop a loaded, moving vehicle such as this one; and (3) there was no warning device of any sort, such as a gauge or warning light, to indicate when the brake fluid in the reservoir was running low. Furthermore, the plaintiffs alleged, the owner's manual which came with the bus suggested brake fluid level checks only every 6,000 miles, which on a school bus would be only once a year, whereas safe maintenance practices would actually require checking the brake fluid in such a vehicle every two weeks to a month.

C. *Sufficiency of the Evidence Under the Boeing Co. Test.*

* * *

* * * While it is unnecessary to catalogue in detail the evidence presented on these issues at trial, a brief summary of the mechanics involved in the braking system in use on this particular bus, and the testimony offered by witnesses on both sides regarding its safety will serve to support our holding that there was sufficient "substantial evidence" as required by Boeing Co. v. Shipman, supra, for the jury to have found that the braking system on the bus was not reasonably safe and consequently that GM had breached its duty as a manufacturer.

The bus which crashed was a 1965 66-passenger school bus, the chassis portion of which was designed and built by General Motors. It was equipped with a single hydraulic braking system, containing a single reservoir in the master cylinder supplying all of the brake fluid which transmits pressure to the brake cylinders on each wheel. In such a system, a leak which exhausts the brake fluid in the reservoir causes a sudden and total failure of braking ability, as happened in this case. A dual hydraulic braking system, on the other hand, is equipped with two brake fluid reservoirs, each of which services the brake cylinders on two separate wheels, so that in the event of loss of fluid from one of the reservoirs, whether from leakage or some other cause, the vehicle continues to have braking power on the wheels serviced by the other reservoir. The only other braking mechanism with which the bus in this case was equipped was a parking brake, which by the admission of all those who testified at the trial was never intended to function as an emergency brake.

We find that the evidence offered at trial on the safety of the braking system as described above was more than sufficient to withstand a motion for judgment n.o.v. under the test set out in *Boeing*. Although a GM Senior Design Engineer, Paul Fisher, testified that he considered a dual hydraulic braking system to be less reliable than a single system (because of the existence of more parts and consequently a greater possibility that one of them could malfunction), the plaintiffs put on expert testimony that the single hydraulic braking system in use on the bus at issue was not reasonably safe for the purpose for which it was intended. Both of plaintiffs' expert witnesses, Professor Milton Koenig, a professor of mechanical engineering at Wayne State University in Detroit, and Dr. Leslie W. Ball, Director of Safety at Marshall Space Flight Center in Huntsville, Alabama, were found by the district court to be qualified to give expert opinions on the braking design issues on which they testified. Both Professor Koenig and Dr. Ball stated several times during their testimony that they considered a single hydraulic braking system such as was used on the bus in this case to be "inherently unsafe" or "not reasonably safe." Certainly the jury could have found, from this expert testimony admitted by the district court, that the braking system on the bus was not a sufficiently safe one.

* * *

Plaintiffs introduced into evidence copies of the 1965 GM owner's and shop maintenance manuals, both of which stated the fluid in the brake fluid reservoir should be checked every 6,000 miles. In addition, the owner's manual stated that "[t]he Chevrolet braking system requires very little care. The braking system should be checked occasionally for indications of fluid leaks. If leaks are found necessary repairs should be made at once. Keep the brakes properly adjusted, check all vacuum hose connections for leaks." The 1965 truck shop manual contained only the following additional warning: "Sustained heavy duty and high speed operation, or operation under adverse conditions may require more frequent servicing."

Plaintiffs alleged, and sought to prove, that these statements in the manuals were inadequate and grossly misleading in that checking the brake fluid level on a school bus every 6,000 miles would mean inspecting it only once a year, whereas GM engineers who testified at trial admitted that it would be necessary to check the fluid level on a school bus several times a month in order to conform with good maintenance practices. Plaintiffs' experts, Professor Koenig and Dr. Ball, testified that in their opinions the manuals were misleading and inaccurate with respect to the frequency of servicing which should have been stated as required for school bus operations. GM's Field Maintenance Supervisor also testified that the fluid level on a school bus should be checked once a week, but insisted that at yearly seminars held by him and attended by school bus maintenance personnel, (including some from Morgan County) verbal instructions were given that school bus braking systems required at least weekly checks of the level of the brake fluid. Such supplemental verbal instructions, it was urged, were certainly sufficient to cure any deficiency in the written ones in the manuals.

Given the existence of all this conflicting evidence bearing on the issue of the adequacy of the warnings in the two GM manuals that came with the bus chassis purchased by Morgan County in 1964, this Court is of the opinion that sufficient evidence was adduced at trial to create a jury issue on the negligence *vel non* of the Morgan County officials and whether such negligence, if it occurred, was foreseeable by GM. With respect to the possibility of intervening negligence in the form of the bus driver's failure to notice operational signs indicating possible loss of brake fluid, we note that the driver denied noticing either any signs of leakage or the gradual development of any significant "give" in his brake pedal prior to the accident, thus creating a jury question on this issue also.

From the above analysis, then, it appears that there was ample evidence introduced at trial under the Boeing Co. v. Shipman test to warrant submitting the issue of proximate cause to the jury. Since we have already determined that there was sufficient evidence to go to the jury on the breach of duty issue, it follows that the plaintiffs put on the kind and quantity of evidence which this Court had held is required to withstand a defense motion for judgment n.o.v., and the district court's grant of that motion by GM must therefore be reversed.

II. THE ALTERNATIVE ORDER GRANTING THE MOTION FOR NEW TRIAL

We now turn to a consideration of the propriety of the district court's alternative grant of a new trial on the ground that the evidence was insufficient to support the jury verdict. We think it critical that the case law on this point be read against the background of the Seventh Amendment, which provides that

"[i]n Suits at common law, where the value in controversy shall exceed twenty dollars, the right of trial by jury shall be preserved, and no fact tried by a jury, shall be otherwise reexamined in any Court of the United States, than according to the rules of the common law." U.S.Const. Amend. VII.

While this constitutional provision obviously cannot be applied so as to foreclose any scrutiny of a jury's fact-findings, it expresses in clear terms the principle that facts once found by a jury in the context of a civil trial are not to be reweighed and a new trial granted lightly.

The general rule, as uniformly stated by the commentators and applied by the courts, is that a district court's grant of a new trial is within the discretion of the court, and is ordinarily nonreviewable save for an abuse of that discretion. Montgomery Ward & Co. v. Duncan, 311 U.S. 243, 61 S.Ct. 189, 85 L.Ed. 147 (1940); see generally 6A Moore's Federal Practice, ¶ 59.08[5]. Several jurisdictions, however, have carefully distinguished the situation where the trial court has granted a new trial on the grounds of insufficiency of the evidence, since by so doing the court is in a sense intruding upon the jury's function and affecting a litigant's Seventh Amendment rights. Appellate courts in these jurisdictions are more exacting in reviewing such a new trial grant. See, e.g., Lind v. Schenley Industries, Inc., 278 F.2d 79 (3d Cir.), cert. denied, 364 U.S. 835, 81 S.Ct. 58, 5 L.Ed.2d 60 (1960); Cities Service Oil Co. v. Launey, 403 F.2d 537 (5th Cir. 1968); Duncan v. Duncan, 377 F.2d 49, 52–55 (6th Cir.), cert. denied, 389 U.S. 913, 88 S.Ct. 239, 19 L.Ed.2d 260 (1967); Fireman's Fund Ins. Co. v. AALCO Wrecking Co., Inc., 466 F.2d 179 (8th Cir. 1972), cert. denied, 410 U.S. 930, 93 S.Ct. 1371, 35 L.Ed.2d 592 (1973).

The standard adopted by this Court is that the district court should not grant a new trial motion unless the jury verdict is "at least . . . against the *great* weight of the evidence." Cities Service Oil Co. v. Launey, supra, at 540 (emphasis in the original). A rule which would permit a court to grant a new trial when the verdict was merely against the "greater weight" of the evidence, this Court said, "would destroy the role of the jury as the principal trier of the facts, and would enable the trial judge to disregard the jury's verdict at will." Id.

Applying the test enunciated in *Cities Service,* we conclude after careful examination of the record, that the district court erred in granting a new trial in the alternative. Without reiterating in detail any of the evidence previously discussed, it should be clear from the preceding section of this opinion that the evidence was at most conflicting on the issues of negligent design and proximate cause. In such a situation, as the Supreme Court has stated,

> "[c]ourts are not free to reweigh the evidence and set aside the jury verdict merely because the jury could have drawn different inferences or conclusions or because judges feel that other results are more reasonable." Tennant v. Peoria & Pekin Union Ry., 321 U.S. 29, 35, 64 S.Ct. 409, 412, 88 L.Ed. 520 (1944).

Factors this Court has previously considered in reviewing a district court's alternative grant of a new trial include, among others, the simplicity or complexity of the issues, the degree to which the evidence presented was in dispute, and whether any "undesirable or pernicious element" occurred or was introduced into the trial. O'Neil v. W. R. Grace & Co., 410 F.2d 908, 913, 915 (5th Cir. 1969). Examining this case in light of those factors, we find that both the issue as to the reasonable safety of the single hydraulic braking system without an emergency brake backup, and the issue as to the "state of the art" in the automotive industry in 1964 were sufficiently simple so as not to form a basis for granting a new trial. Juries are constantly being called upon to pass upon negligent design issues in the products liability area, and the sometimes confusing amount and type of technical testimony that was elicited on the design issue at the trial of this case should not as a matter of law have precluded the jury that heard the case from being able fully to comprehend and assess the basic safety and technological feasibility issues involved.

Furthermore, there have been no allegations that the case was improperly tried, or that counsel on either side made prejudicial statements; this appeal has been argued, by counsel for both parties, solely on the issue of the sufficiency of the evidence to support the jury verdict. Finally, the fact that the evidence, as we have observed, was conflicting on certain elements of appellants' case, is not enough in itself to justify the district court's decision to grant a new trial. Tennant v. Peoria & Pekin Union Ry. Co., supra.

* * *

MANN v. HUNT

New York Supreme Court, Appellate Division, Third Department, 1953.
283 A.D. 140, 126 N.Y.S.2d 823.

BERGAN, JUSTICE.

The jury's verdict in this negligence case was for the defendant; but the judge was of opinion the verdict was against the weight of evidence and set it aside. The semantic problem that adheres to the expression "against the weight of evidence" has never been given an entirely successful solution. It involves essentially a matter of judgment and appraisal with the standards stemming back deep in the soil of the experience of the profession.

Every one would admit that there are circumstances in which a trial judge's duty may require him to set aside a verdict which is too high, too low, or so wrong that it will not stand. The judge, indeed, has the active and continuous burden of supervising the work of the juries which report to him. But he will not interfere just because he dislikes the verdict; or feels quite strongly he would have done something else; or even because he may think the verdict is unjust.

The point of interference is not fixed on the caprice of judicial individualism; it is rather arrived at by a synthesis of all the experience that the judge has had; in the beginning as a law student, in the later controversies of law practice, in the hearing of cases and the writing of decisions, in the sum of all that he has absorbed in the court room and in the library.

In the end it is an informed professional judgment; and although lawyers might differ greatly about how the components of the judgment are arranged and added up, there would be a very considerable agreement about the result to be reached in any case once the facts were thoroughly understood.

The problem presented by the term "against the weight of evidence", indeed, is very similar in its implications to the problem of what the profession has meant by the word "reasonable" applied to private conduct or official act. Therefore, while the rule is not easily, or at all, capable of being laid down in plain words as an infallible guide to decision and can be illustrated only imperfectly by opinions in

past cases, it is a rule which the profession understands as the cumulative product of its own experience.

A court which reviews the weight of evidence as well as the law, as does an Appellate Division, must approach an appeal from a decision by a trial judge setting aside a verdict in the light of the nature of the duty and the subtle and not easily definable measure of responsibility which the judge exercises in decision.

The duty of the judge to supervise the reasonableness of the verdicts returned to him ought to be viewed liberally on appeal because the independence of mind with which that duty is exercised is ingredient to the sound health of the judicial process. Lipschitz v. Sloan, 1952, 280 App.Div. 855, 113 N.Y.S.2d 333.

Even if the judges who look at the case on appeal would not themselves have set the verdict aside had they acted in the first instance, they should not find in this alone a ground for reversal. If the case comes within the area within which judicial interference would not be regarded by the profession as unreasonable, the exercise of the power thus to deal with the verdict ought to be upheld.

In the case now before us the question is whether the plaintiff was physically in a parked automobile when it was struck by the car standing in front which in turn was forced back by the impact of defendant's car coming diagonally across the street and striking it. Defendant said he had "lost control of the car". The defendant's negligence in striking the first parked car is not in dispute and on appeal he admits that the sole issue was plaintiff's presence in the car.

Defendant himself testified that immediately after the accident there was no one in the car in which plaintiff claims to have been injured and that he "first saw" her coming across the street seven minutes after the accident. This testimony was quite fully substantiated by one witness and in some material respects by two other witnesses, but plaintiff testified unequivocally she was sitting in the car and injured by the impact.

There were two witnesses who substantiated her. One was a storekeeper who had placed a bundle of groceries in the car and who said plaintiff was then sitting in the car and who heard the crash when he was a short distance away from the car. Another witness testified that he was in actual conversation with plaintiff while she was sitting in the car and that she was in the car at the time of collision.

A physician who examined plaintiff on the day of the accident found her suffering from abrasions and contusions of the right upper arm, the appearance of which, he said, was "discolored and contused". This was consistent with plaintiff's own description of her injury.

It is our view that the case lies well within the area of the judge's power to set the verdict aside in the supervision of the jury's work before him. Having himself heard the facts developed from the witnesses and sensed the atmosphere and texture of the trial, he had the duty of maintaining reasonable consistency between the weight of evidence and the verdict reached. Appellant has not demonstrated, as he is bound to do to have a reversal, that the order for a new trial was not reasonably grounded.

App. hasn't shown OtCJ P reg'd

There is "no standard by which to determine" when a verdict should be set aside as against the weight of evidence. The decision "depends upon the discretion of the court." McDonald v. Metropolitan St.Ry.Co., 167 N.Y. 66, 69, 60 N.E. 282, 283.

The order should be affirmed with costs to appellant to abide the event.

C

Order affirmed, on the law and facts, with costs to the appellant to abide the event.

FOSTER, P.J., and COON, HALPERN and IMRIE, JJ., concur.

NOTE ON EXCESSIVE OR INADEQUATE VERDICTS

1. Among the jury determinations that must satisfy the standard of having sufficient support in the evidence is determination of the amount of damages. In cases where the measure of damages is relatively definite, there is little difficulty determining whether an award by the jury is supported by sufficient evidence. Cf. Reynolds v. Bank of America, supra p. 50. It is rare in such cases that a jury makes a wildly inappropriate award, although sometimes the jury may compromise the question of liability and return a verdict for half of the plaintiff's clearly proven damages. In personal injury and other cases where the measure of damages is imprecise, however, the question whether the damages are excessive or inadequate yields correspondingly indeterminate answers. Nevertheless, the law is that the trial judge must set aside a verdict when its amount is not supported by the evidence. See Dagnello v. Long Island R.R., 289 F.2d 797 (2d Cir. 1961), which has a comprehensive citation of authority. But what amount of damages is within the limits of reasonableness for a given set of injuries can be the subject of profound disagreement among judges. See, e.g., O'Gee v. Dobbs Houses, Inc., 570 F.2d 1084 (2d Cir. 1978): The jury returned a verdict for $170,000. The trial judge denied a motion to set it aside on the ground of excessiveness, stating that he believed any verdict up to $200,000 would have been reasonable. On appeal, the Court of Appeals ordered reduction to $85,000 over an "emphatically" dissenting judge who thought the verdict entirely reasonable. See also, e.g., Fruit v. Shreiner, 502 P.2d 133 (Alaska 1972); Pistorius v. Prudential Ins. Co., 123 Cal.App.3d 541, 176 Cal. Rptr. 660 (1981), sustaining a verdict of $1 million in punitive damages against an insurance company for discontinuing payments under a disability insurance policy. On the issue of whether constitutional limits should be placed on the size of punitive damages awards, see Note on Damages, supra p. 186.

2. If the trial judge thinks the verdict is excessive or inadequate, it makes sense that she be able to adjust the judgment to bring it within the limits of reasonableness without having to require a new trial. But this involves directly substituting her appraisal of damages for that of the jury's, thus "invading the province" of the jury and to that extent denying the parties the right of jury trial on the damages issue. Many years ago a way around this difficulty was evolved to deal with the problem of an excessive verdict: At the hearing on the defendant's motion for a new trial, the judge would indicate

what he thought was the upper limit of a reasonable verdict; he then conditionally granted the motion, the order for new trial being ineffective if the plaintiff consented to accept a judgment in the reduced amount. The justifying theory was that the defendant was not being denied jury trial, because he already had a run before a jury on the question of damages, and that plaintiff was not being denied jury trial because she was consenting to the reduced verdict rather than putting the question of damages to another jury. This procedure is called remittitur. See Dimick v. Schiedt, 293 U.S. 474, 55 S.Ct. 296, 79 L.Ed. 603 (1935). See also Donovan v. Penn Shipping Co., 429 U.S. 648, 97 S.Ct. 835, 51 L.Ed.2d 112 (1977), holding that a plaintiff who has accepted the denial of defendant's motion for new trial cannot then appeal "to seek reinstatement of the original verdict." Cf. Schelbauer v. Butler Mfg. Co., 35 Cal.3d 442, 198 Cal.Rptr. 155, 673 P.2d 743 (1984), holding that remittitur is improper when used to reapportion damages on the basis of the trial judge's redetermination of comparative fault between plaintiff and defendant. See also Note, Remittitur Practice in the Federal Courts, 76 Colum.L.Rev. 299 (1976). Remittitur as an alternative to a new trial is particularly appropriate in complex cases. See United States v. 47.14 Acres of Land, 674 F.2d 722 (8th Cir. 1982). The use of remittitur is not uncontroversial, however. For example, its use has been entirely abolished in Missouri because the court viewed it as an unnecessary practice leading to inconsistent results. Firestone v. Crown Center Redevelopment Corp., 693 S.W.2d 99 (Mo.1985).

A corresponding device, called additur, can be used to deal with an inadequate verdict: The trial judge denies plaintiff's motion for a new trial, on the condition that defendant agree to increase the award to an amount specified by the judge. This procedure has not been adopted in the federal courts; it was thought to invade the jury's province inasmuch as the amount fixed by the judge was outside the range of the amount pronounced by the jury. Dimick v. Schiedt, supra. But many state courts sanction additur. See Jehl v. Southern Pacific Co., 66 Cal.2d 821, 59 Cal.Rptr. 276, 427 P.2d 988 (1967), codified at C.C.P. 662.5, which provides that the trial court may increase or decrease a verdict to that amount which "the court in its independent judgment determines from the evidence to be fair and reasonable." See Note, California Restores Additur, 8 Santa Clara Lawyer 123 (1967). See generally James & Hazard § 7.21.

F.   DECISIONS IN JUDGE–TRIED CASES

NOTE ON THE STRUCTURE OF A NON–JURY TRIAL

The trial of a case to the court sitting without a jury proceeds substantially in the same way as a trial to a jury. See Note on the Structure of a Trial, supra p. 997. The only formal differences in federal practice concern the reception of offers of proof under Federal Rules of Evidence 103(c) and the requirement of findings of fact and conclusions of law under F.R.C.P. 52 and the related provision therein as to the scope of appellate review of the trial judge's findings of fact, considered infra p. 1194. Compare California Rules of Court, Superior Court Rule 232. However, the style of presentation of a case to a judge may be considerably different from a jury case. Thus:

— many judges indicate they do not want an opening statement (because they have read the pleadings or pretrial order and believe they know what the case is about); if such a statement is made, its content is usually somewhat different from an opening to a jury;

— the rules of evidence, particularly the hearsay rule, are applied in more relaxed fashion and the reception of inadmissible evidence is very unlikely to be regarded as reversible error;

— the judge may intervene in examination of witnesses more readily, uninhibited by concern for prejudicing the jury;

— examination of witnesses and admission of real evidence (documents, etc.) usually is more expedited;

— the judge may ask that final argument take the form of written submissions rather than an oral presentation;

— the judge is not obliged to render a decision before adjourning, and may take the case under submission for a prolonged period.

For an interesting comparison between trial procedure in civil law systems, where trials are ordinarily to the court without a jury, see Damaska, Presentation of Evidence and Factfinding Precision, 123 U.Pa.L.Rev. 1083 (1975).

Above all, a case tried to a judge is different from a jury trial because there is one finder of fact, whose predispositions may be crucial. The question, then, is under what circumstances a party may disqualify a judge who might be adversely predisposed.

PULLMAN–STANDARD v. SWINT

Supreme Court of the United States, 1982.
456 U.S. 273, 102 S.Ct. 1781, 72 L.Ed.2d 66.*

JUSTICE WHITE delivered the opinion of the Court.

Respondents were black employees at the Bessemer, Ala., plant of petitioner, Pullman-Standard (the Company), a manufacturer of railway freight cars and parts. They brought suit against the Company and the union petitioners—the United Steelworkers of America, AFL–CIO–CLC, and its Local 1466 (collectively USW)—alleging violations of Title VII of the Civil Rights Act of 1964, as amended, 78 Stat. 253, 42 U.S.C. § 2000e et seq. and 42 U.S.C. § 1981. As they come here, these cases involve only the validity, under Title VII, of a seniority system maintained by the Company and USW. The District Court found "that the differences in terms, conditions or privileges of employment resulting [from the seniority system] are 'not the result of an intention to discriminate' because of race or color," App. to Pet. for Cert. in No. 80–1190, p. A–147 (hereinafter App.), and held, therefore, that the system satisfied the requirements of § 703(h) of the Act. The Court of Appeals for the Fifth Circuit reversed:

"Because we find that the differences in the terms, conditions and standards of employment for black workers and white workers at Pullman-Standard resulted from an intent to discriminate because of race, we hold that the system is not legally valid under section

* Some of the Court's footnotes are omitted.

703(h) of Title VII, 42 U.S.C. 2000e–2(h)."   624 F.2d 525, 533–534 (1980).

We granted the petitions for certiorari filed by USW and by the Company, 451 U.S. 906, 101 S.Ct. 1972, 68 L.Ed.2d 293 (1981), limited to the first question presented in each petition: whether a court of appeals is bound by the "clearly erroneous" rule of Fed.Rules Civ.Proc. 52(a) in reviewing a district court's findings of fact, arrived at after a lengthy trial, as to the motivation of the parties who negotiated a seniority system; and whether the court below applied wrong legal criteria in determining the bona fides of the seniority system. We conclude that the Court of Appeals erred in the course of its review and accordingly reverse its judgment and remand for further proceedings.

I

Title VII is a broad remedial measure, designed "to assure equality of employment opportunities."   McDonnell Douglas Corp. v. Green, 411 U.S. 792, 800, 93 S.Ct. 1817, 1823, 36 L.Ed.2d 668 (1973).   The Act was designed to bar not only overt employment discrimination, "but also practices that are fair in form, but discriminatory in operation."   Griggs v. Duke Power Co., 401 U.S. 424, 431, 91 S.Ct. 849, 853, 28 L.Ed. 2d 158 (1971).   "Thus, the Court has repeatedly held that a prima facie Title VII violation may be established by policies or practices that are neutral on their face and in intent but that nonetheless discriminate in effect against a particular group."   Teamsters v. United States, 431 U.S. 324, 349, 97 S.Ct. 1843, 1861, 52 L.Ed.2d 396 (1977) (hereinafter *Teamsters*).   The Act's treatment of seniority systems, however, establishes an exception to these general principles.   Section 703(h) * * * provides in pertinent part:

> "Notwithstanding any other provision of this subchapter, it shall not be an unlawful employment practice for an employer to apply different standards of compensation, or different terms, conditions or privileges of employment pursuant to a bona fide seniority . . . system . . . provided that such differences are not the result of an intention to discriminate because of race."

Under this action, a showing of disparate impact is insufficient to invalidate a seniority system, even though the result may be to perpetuate pre-Act discrimination.   In Trans World Airlines, Inc. v. Hardison, 432 U.S. 63, 82, 97 S.Ct. 2264, 2275, 53 L.Ed.2d 113 (1977), we summarized the effect of § 703(h) as follows: "[A]bsent a discriminatory purpose, the operation of a seniority system cannot be an unlawful employment practice even if the system has some discriminatory consequences."   Thus, any challenge to a seniority system under Title VII will require a trial on the issue of discriminatory intent: Was the system adopted because of its racially discriminatory impact?

* * *

II

Petitioners submit that the Court of Appeals failed to comply with the command of Rule 52(a) that the findings of fact of a district court may not be set aside unless clearly erroneous. We first describe the findings of the District Court and the Court of Appeals.

Certain facts are common ground for both the District Court and the Court of Appeals. The Company's Bessemer plant was unionized in the early 1940's. Both before and after unionization, the plant was divided into a number of different operational departments.[3] USW sought to represent all production and maintenance employees at the plant and was elected in 1941 as the bargaining representative of a bargaining unit consisting of most of these employees. At that same time, [the International Association of Machinists and Aerospace Workers (IAM)] became the bargaining representative of a unit consisting of five departments. Between 1941 and 1944, IAM ceded certain workers in its bargaining unit to USW. As a result of this transfer, the IAM bargaining unit became all white.

Throughout the period of representation by USW, the plant was approximately half black. Prior to 1965, the Company openly pursued a racially discriminatory policy of job assignments. Most departments contained more than one job category and as a result most departments were racially mixed. There were no lines of progression or promotion within departments.

The seniority system at issue here was adopted in 1954. Under that agreement, seniority was measured by length of continuous service in a particular department. Seniority was originally exercised only for purposes of layoffs and hirings within particular departments. In 1956, seniority was formally recognized for promotional purposes as well. Again, however, seniority, with limited exceptions, was only exercised within departments; employees transfering to new departments forfeited their seniority. This seniority system remained virtually unchanged until after this suit was brought in 1971.

The District Court approached the question of discriminatory intent in the manner suggested by the Fifth Circuit in James v. Stockham Valves & Fittings Co., 559 F.2d 310 (1977). There, the Court of Appeals stated that under *Teamsters* "the totality of the circumstances in the development and maintenance of the system is relevant to examining that issue." 559 F.2d, at 352. There were, in its view, however, four particular factors that a court should focus on.[8]

---

3. In 1941, prior to unionization, the Bessemer plant was divided into 20 departments. By 1954, there were 28 departments—26 USW units and 2 IAM units. The departments remained essentially unchanged after 1954.

8. The Fifth Circuit relied upon the following passage in *Teamsters*, 431 U.S. 324,

355–356, 97 S.Ct. 1843, 1864–1865, 52 L.Ed. 2d 396 (1977):

"The seniority system in this litigation is entirely bona fide. It applies equally to all races and ethnic groups. To the extent that it 'locks' employees into non-line-driver jobs, it does so for all. . . . The placing of line drivers in a separate

First, a court must determine whether the system "operates to discourage all employees equally from transferring between seniority units." Ibid. The District Court held that the system here "was facially neutral and . . . was applied equally to all races and ethnic groups." App. A–132. Although there were charges of racial discrimination in its application, the court held that these were "not substantiated by the evidence." Id., at A–133. It concluded that the system "applied equally and uniformly to all employees, black and white, and that given the approximately equal number of employees of the two groups, it was quantitatively neutral as well." Id., at A–134.⁹

Second, a court must examine the rationality of the departmental structure, upon which the seniority system relies, in light of the general industry practice. *James,* supra, at 352. The District Court found that linking seniority to "departmental age" was "the modal form of agreements generally, as well as with manufacturers of railroad equipment in particular." App. A–137. Furthermore, it found the basic arrangement of departments at the plant to be rationally related to the nature of the work and to be "consistent with practices which were . . . generally followed at other unionized plants throughout the country." Id., at A–136—A–137. While questions could be raised about the necessity of certain departmental divisions, it found that all of the challenged lines of division grew out of historical circumstances at the plant that were unrelated to racial discrimination.¹⁰ Although unionization did produce an all-white IAM bargaining unit, it found that USW "cannot be charged with racial bias in its response to the IAM situation. [USW] sought to represent all workers, black and white, in the plant." Id., at A–145. Nor could the Company be charged with any racial discrimination that may have existed in IAM:

> "The company properly took a 'hands-off' approach towards the establishment of the election units. . . . It bargained with those unions which were afforded representational status by the NLRB and did so without any discriminatory animus." Id., at A–146.

Third, a court had to consider "whether the seniority system had its genesis in racial discrimination," *James,* supra, at 352, by which it meant the relationship between the system and other racially discrimi-

bargaining unit from other employees is rational, in accord with the industry practice, and consistent with National Labor Relation Board precedents. It is conceded that that seniority system did not have its genesis in racial discrimination, and that it was negotiated and has been maintained free from any illegal purpose."

This passage was of course not meant to be an exhaustive list of all the factors that a district court might or should consider in making a finding of discriminatory intent.

9. The court specifically declined to make any finding on whether the no-trans-

fer provision of the seniority system had a greater relative effect on blacks than on whites, because of qualitative differences in the departments in which they were concentrated. It believed that such an inquiry would have been inconsistent with the earlier Fifth Circuit opinion in this case.

10. In particular, the court focused on the history of the unionization process at the plant and found certain of the departmental divisions to be based on the evolving relationship between USW and IAM.

natory practices. Athough finding ample discrimination by the company in its employment practices and some discriminatory practices by the union,[11] the District Court concluded that the seniority system was in no way related to the discriminatory practices:

> "The seniority system . . . had its genesis . . . at a period when racial segregation was certainly being practiced; but this system was not itself the product of this bias. The system rather came about as a result of colorblind objectives of a union which—unlike most structures and institutions of the era—was not an arm of a segregated society. Nor did it foster the discrimination . . . which was being practiced by custom in the plant." App. A–144.

Finally, a court must consider "whether the system was negotiated and has been maintained free from any illegal purpose." *James,* supra, at 352. Stating that it had "carefully considered the detailed record of negotiation sessions and contracts which span a period of some thirty-five years," App. A–146, the court found that the system was untainted by any discriminatory purpose. Thus, although the District Court focused on particular factors in carrying out the analysis required by § 703(h), it also looked to the entire record and to the "totality of the system under attack." Id., at A–147.

The Court of Appeals addressed each of the four factors of the *James* test and reached the opposite conclusion. First, it held that the District Court erred in putting aside qualitative differences between the departments in which blacks were concentrated and those dominated by whites, in considering whether the system applied "equally" to whites and blacks.[12] This is a purported correction of a legal standard under which the evidence is to be evaluated.

Second, it rejected the District Court's conclusion that the structure of departments was rational, in line with industry practice, and did not reflect any discriminatory intent. Its discussion is brief but focuses on the role of IAM and certain characteristics unique to the Bessemer plant. The court concluded:

> "The record evidence, generally, indicates arbitrary creation of the departments by the company since unionization and an attendant adverse affect [sic] on black workers. The individual differences

11. With respect to USW, the District Court found that "[u]nion meetings were conducted with different sides of the hall for white and black members, and social functions of the union were also segregated." App. A–142. It also found, however, that "[w]hile possessing some of the trappings taken from an otherwise segregated society, the USW local was one of the few institutions in the area which did not function in fact to foster and maintain segregation; rather, it served a joint interest of white and black workers which had a higher priority than racial considerations." Id., at A–143.

12. It does not appear to us that the District Court actually found a qualitative difference but held it to be irrelevant. The relevant passage of the District Court opinion read as follows: "By ranking the twenty-eight USW and IAM departments according to some perceived order of desirability, one could . . . attempt to measure the relative effect of the no-transfer rule on white and black employees . . . . It may well be that a somewhat greater impact was felt by blacks than whites although . . . this conclusion is by no means certain." Id., at A–134.

between the departmental structure at Pullman-Standard and that of other plants, and as compared with industry practice, are indicative of attempts to maintain one-race departments." 624 F.2d, at 532.

In reaching this conclusion, the Court of Appeals did not purport to be correcting a legal error, nor did it refer to or expressly apply the clearly-erroneous standard.

Third, in considering the "genesis" of the system, the Court of Appeals held that the District Court erred in holding that the motives of IAM were not relevant.[13] This was the correction of a legal error on the part of the District Court in excluding relevant evidence. The court did not stop there, however. It went on to hold that IAM was acting out of discriminatory intent—an issue specifically not reached by the District Court—and that "considerations of race permeated the negotiation and adoption of the seniority system in 1941 and subsequent negotiations thereafter." Ibid.

Fourth, despite this conclusion under the third *James* factor the Court of Appeals then recited, but did not expressly set aside or find clearly erroneous, the District Court's findings with respect to the negotiation and maintenance of the seniority system.

The court then announced that "[h]aving carefully reviewed the evidence offered to show whether the departmental seniority system in the present case is 'bona fide' within the meaning of § 703(h) of Title VII, we reject the district court's finding." 624 F.2d, at 533. Elaborating on its disagreement, the Court of Appeals stated:

"An analysis of the totality of the facts and circumstances surrounding the creation and continuance of the departmental system at Pullman-Standard leaves us with the definite and firm conviction that a mistake has been made. There is no doubt, based upon the record in this case, about the existence of a discriminatory purpose. The obvious principal aim of the I.A.M. in 1941 was to exclude black workers from its bargaining unit. That goal was ultimately reached when maneuvers by the I.A.M. and U.S.W. resulted in an all-white I.A.M. unit. The U.S.W., in the interest of increased membership, acquiesced in the discrimination while succeeding in significantly segregating the departments within its own unit.

"The district court might have reached a different conclusion had it given the I.A.M.'s role in the creation and establishment of the seniority system its due consideration." Ibid. (footnote omitted).

* * *

13. The original complaint in this case did not mention IAM. Prior to the first trial, respondents sought and received leave to amend their complaint to add IAM as a Rule 19 defendant, "insofar as the relief requested may involve or infringe upon the provisions of such Union's collective bargaining agreement with the Company." Order of the District Court, June 4, 1974 (App. 29).

In connection with its assertion that it was convinced that a mistake had been made, the Court of Appeals, in a footnote, referred to the clearly-erroneous standard of Rule 52(a). Id., at 533, n. 6.[14] It pointed out, however, that if findings "are made under an erroneous view of controlling legal principles, the clearly-erroneous rule does not apply, and the findings may not stand." Ibid. Finally, quoting from East v. Romine, Inc., 518 F.2d 332, 339 (CA5 1975), the Court of Appeals repeated the following view of its appellate function in Title VII cases where purposeful discrimination is at issue:

" 'Although discrimination *vel non* is essentially a question of fact it is, at the same time, the ultimate issue for resolution in this case, being expressly proscribed by 42 U.S.C.A. § 2000e–2(a). As such, a finding of discrimination or nondiscrimination is a finding of ultimate fact. [Cites omitted.] In reviewing the district court's findings, therefore, we will proceed to make an independent determination of appellant's allegations of discrimination, though bound by findings of subsidiary fact which are themselves not clearly erroneous.' " 624 F.2d, at 533, n. 6.

III

Pointing to the above statement of the Court of Appeals and to similar statements in other Title VII cases coming from that court, petitioners submit that the Court of Appeals made an independent determination of discriminatory purpose, the "ultimate fact" in this case, and that this was error under Rule 52(a). We agree with petitioners that if the Court of Appeals followed what seems to be the accepted rule in that Circuit, its judgment must be reversed.[16]

14. In United States v. United States Gypsum Co., 333 U.S. 364, 395, 68 S.Ct. 525, 541, 92 L.Ed. 746 (1948), this Court characterized the clearly-erroneous standard as follows:

"A finding is 'clearly erroneous' when although there is evidence to support it, the reviewing court on the entire evidence is left with the definite and firm conviction that a mistake has been committed."

We note that the Court of Appeals quoted this passage at the conclusion of its analysis of the District Court opinion. Supra, at 1787.

16. There is some indication in the opinions of the Court of Appeals for the Fifth Circuit * * * that the Circuit rule with respect to "ultimate facts" is only another way of stating a standard of review with respect to mixed questions of law and fact—the ultimate "fact" is the statutory, legally determinative consideration (here, intentional discrimination) which is or is not satisfied by subsidiary facts admitted or found by the trier of fact. As indi-

cated in the text, however, the question of intentional discrimination under § 703(h) is a pure question of fact. Furthermore, the Court of Appeals' opinion in this case appears to address the issue as a question of fact unmixed with legal considerations.

At the same time, this Court has on occasion itself indicated that findings on "ultimate facts" are independently reviewable. In Baumgartner v. United States, 322 U.S. 665, 64 S.Ct. 1240, 88 L.Ed. 1525 (1944), the issue was whether or not the findings of the two lower courts satisfied the clear and convincing standard of proof necessary to sustain a denaturalization decree. The Court held that the conclusion of the two lower courts that the exacting standard of proof had been satisfied was not an unreviewable finding of fact but one that a reviewing court could independently assess. The Court referred to the finding as one of "ultimate" fact, which in that case involved an appraisal of the strength of the entire body of evidence. The Court said that the significance of the clear and convincing proof standard "would be lost"

Rule 52(a) broadly requires that findings of fact not be set aside unless clearly erroneous. It does not make exceptions or purport to exclude certain categories of factual findings from the obligation of a court of appeals to accept a district court's findings unless clearly erroneous. It does not divide facts into categories; in particular, it does not divide findings of fact into those that deal with "ultimate" and those that deal with "subsidiary" facts.

The Rule does not apply to conclusions of law. The Court of Appeals, therefore, was quite right in saying that if a district court's findings rest on an erroneous view of the law, they may be set aside on that basis. But here the District Court was not faulted for misunderstanding or applying an erroneous definition of intentional discrimination.[17] It was reversed for arriving at what the Court of Appeals thought was an erroneous finding as to whether the differential impact of the seniority system reflected an intent to discriminate on account of race. That question, as we see it, is a pure question of fact, subject to Rule 52(a)'s clearly-erroneous standard. It is not a question of law and not a mixed question of law and fact.

The Court has previously noted the vexing nature of the distinction between questions of fact and questions of law. See Baumgartner v. United States, 322 U.S. 665, 671, 64 S.Ct. 1240, 1243, 88 L.Ed. 1525 (1944). Rule 52(a) does not furnish particular guidance with respect to distinguishing law from fact. Nor do we yet know of any other rule or principle that will unerringly distinguish a factual finding from a legal conclusion. For the reasons that follow, however, we have little doubt about the factual nature of § 703(h)'s requirement that a seniority system be free of an intent to discriminate.

if the ascertainment by the lower courts whether that exacting standard of proof had been satisfied on the whole record were to be deemed a "fact" of the same order as all other "facts not open to review here." Id., at 671, 64 S.Ct., at 1243.

The Fifth Circuit's rule on appellate consideration of "ultimate facts" has its roots in this discussion in *Baumgartner.* In Galena Oaks Corp. v. Scofield, 218 F.2d 217 (CA5 1954), in which the question was whether the gain derived from the sale of a number of houses was to be treated as capital gain or ordinary income, the Court of Appeals relied directly on *Baumgartner* in holding that this was an issue of "ultimate fact" that an appellate court may review free of the clearly-erroneous rule. Causey v. Ford Motor Co., supra, at 421, relying on Galena Oaks Corp. v. Scofield, supra, said that "although discrimination *vel non* is essentially a question of fact, it is, at the same time, the ultimate issue for resolution in this case" and as such, was deemed to be independently reviewable.

The passage from East v. Romine, Inc., supra, at 339, which was repeated in the cases before us now, supra, at 1788, rested on the opinion in Causey v. Ford Motor Co.

Whatever *Baumgartner* may have meant by its discussion of "ultimate facts," it surely did not mean that whenever the result in a case turns on a factual finding, an appellate court need not remain within the constraints of Rule 52(a). *Baumgartner's* discussion of "ultimate facts" referred not to pure findings of fact—as we find discriminatory intent to be in this context—but to findings that "clearly impl[y] the application of standards of law." 322 U.S., at 671, 64 S.Ct., at 1243.

17. As we noted above, the Court of Appeals did at certain points purport to correct what it viewed as legal errors on the part of the District Court. The presence of such legal errors may justify a remand by the Court of Appeals to the District Court for additional fact finding under the correct legal standard. * * *

Treating issues of intent as factual matters for the trier of fact is commonplace. In Dayton Board of Education v. Brinkman, 443 U.S. 526, 534, 99 S.Ct. 2971, 2977, 61 L.Ed.2d 720 (1979), the principal question was whether the defendants had intentionally maintained a racially segregated school system at a specified time in the past. We recognized that issue as essentially factual, subject to the clearly-erroneous rule. In Commissioner v. Duberstein, 363 U.S. 278, 80 S.Ct. 1190, 4 L.Ed.2d 1218 (1960), the Court held that the principal criterion for identifying a gift under the applicable provision of the Internal Revenue Code was the intent or motive of the donor—"one that inquires what the basic reason for his conduct was in fact." Id., at 286, 80 S.Ct., at 1197. Resolution of that issue determined the ultimate issue of whether a gift had been made. Both issues were held to be questions of fact subject to the clearly-erroneous rule. In United States v. Yellow Cab, 338 U.S. 338, 341, 70 S.Ct. 177, 179, 94 L.Ed. 150 (1949), an antitrust case, the Court referred to "[f]indings as to the design, motive and intent with which men act" as peculiarly factual issues for the trier of fact and therefore subject to appellate review under Rule 52.

Justice Black's dissent in *Yellow Cab* suggested a contrary approach. Relying on United States v. Griffith, 334 U.S. 100, 68 S.Ct. 941, 92 L.Ed. 1236 (1948) he argued that it is not always necessary to prove "specific intent" to restrain trade; it is enough if a restraint is the result or consequence of a defendant's conduct or business arrangements. Such an approach, however, is specifically precluded by § 703(h) in Title VII cases challenging seniority systems. Differentials among employees that result from a seniority system are not unlawful employment practices unless the product of an intent to discriminate. It would make no sense, therefore, to say that the intent to discriminate required by § 703(h) may be presumed from such an impact. As § 703(h) was construed in *Teamsters*, there must be a finding of actual intent to discriminate on racial grounds on the part of those who negotiated or maintained the system. That finding appears to us to be a pure question of fact.

This is not to say that discriminatory impact is not part of the evidence to be considered by the trial court in reaching a finding on whether there was such a discriminatory intent as a factual matter.[18] We do assert, however, that under § 703(h) discriminatory intent is a finding of fact to be made by the trial court; it is not a question of law and not a mixed question of law and fact of the kind that in some cases may allow an appellate court to review the facts to see if they satisfy some legal concept of discriminatory intent.[19] Discriminatory intent

---

18. See, e.g., Furnco Construction Corp. v. Waters, 438 U.S. 567, 580, 98 S.Ct. 2943, 2951, 57 L.Ed.2d 957 (1978): "Proof that [an employer's] work force was racially balanced or that it contained a disproportionately high percentage of minority employees is not wholly irrelevant on the issue of intent when that issue is yet to be decided."

19. We need not, therefore, address the much-mooted issue of the applicability of the Rule 52(a) standard to mixed questions of law and fact—i.e., questions in which the historical facts are admitted or estab-

here means actual motive; it is not a legal presumption to be drawn from a factual showing of something less than actual motive. Thus, a court of appeals may only reverse a district court's finding on discriminatory intent if it concludes that the finding is clearly erroneous under Rule 52(a). Insofar as the Fifth Circuit assumed otherwise, it erred.

IV

Respondents do not directly defend the Fifth Circuit rule that a trial court's finding on discriminatory intent is not subject to the clearly-erroneous standard of Rule 52(a).[20] Rather, among other things, they submit that the Court of Appeals recognized and, where appropriate, properly applied Rule 52(a) in setting aside the findings of the District Court. This position has force, but for two reasons it is not persuasive.

First, although the Court of Appeals acknowledged and correctly stated the controlling standard of Rule 52(a), the acknowledgement came late in the court's opinion. The court had not expressly referred to or applied Rule 52(a) in the course of disagreeing with the District Court's resolution of the factual issues deemed relevant under James v. Stockham Valves & Fittings, 559 F.2d 310 (1977).[21] Furthermore, the paragraph in which the court finally concludes that the USW seniority system is unprotected by § 703(h) strongly suggests that the outcome was the product of the court's independent consideration of the totality of the circumstances it found in the record.

Second and more fundamentally, when the court stated that it was convinced that a mistake had been made, it then not only identified the

lished, the rule of law is undisputed, and the issue is whether the facts satisfy the statutory standard, or to put it another way, whether the rule of law as applied to the established facts is or is not violated. There is substantial authority in the Circuits on both sides of this question. Compare Johnson v. Johnson, 531 F.2d 169, 174 n. 12 (CA3 1976); Stafos v. Jarvis, 477 F.2d 369, 372 (CA10 1973); and Johnson v. Salisbury, 448 F.2d 374, 377 (CA6 1971), with Rogers v. Bates, 431 F.2d 16, 18 (CA8 1970); and Pennsylvania Cas. Co. v. McCoy, 167 F.2d 132 (CA5 1948). There is also support in decisions of this Court for the proposition that conclusions on mixed questions of law and fact are independently reviewable by an appellate court, e.g., Bogardus v. Comm'r, 302 U.S. 34, 39, 58 S.Ct. 61, 64, 82 L.Ed. 32 (1937); Helvering v. Tex-Penn Oil Co., 300 U.S. 481, 491, 57 S.Ct. 569, 573, 81 L.Ed. 755 (1937); Helvering v. Rankin, 295 U.S. 123, 131, 55 S.Ct. 732, 736, 79 L.Ed. 1343 (1935). But cf., Comm'r v. Duberstein, 363 U.S. 278, 289, 80 S.Ct. 1190, 1198, 4 L.Ed.2d 1218 (1960); Comm'r v. Heininger, 320 U.S. 467, 475, 64 S.Ct. 249, 254, 88 L.Ed. 171 (1943).

20. Neither does the dissent contend that Rule 52(a) is inapplicable to findings of discriminatory intent. Rather, it contends, that the Rule was properly applied by the Court of Appeals.

21. In particular, in regard to the second *James* factor—whether the departmental structure was rational or in line with industry practice—the Court of Appeals did not focus on the evidentiary basis for any particular finding of the District Court. It appeared to make an independent examination of the record and arrive at its own conclusion contrary to that of the District Court. Likewise, in dealing with the genesis of the seniority system and whether or not the negotiation or maintenance of the system was tainted with racial discrimination, the Court of Appeals, while identifying what it thought was legal error in failing to consider the racial practices and intentions of IAM, did not otherwise overturn any of the District Court's findings as clearly erroneous.

mistake but also the source of that mistake. The mistake of the District Court was that on the record there could be no doubt about the existence of a discriminatory purpose. The source of the mistake was the District Court's failure to recognize the relevance of the racial purposes of IAM. Had the District Court "given the IAM's role in the creation and establishment of the seniority system its due consideration," it "might have reached a different conclusion." * * *

When an appellate court discerns that a district court has failed to make a finding because of an erroneous view of the law, the usual rule is that there should be a remand for further proceedings to permit the trial court to make the missing findings:

> "[F]actfinding is the basic responsibility of district courts, rather than appellate courts, and . . . the Court of Appeals should not have resolved in the first instance this factual dispute which had not been considered by the District Court." DeMarco v. United States, 415 U.S. 449, 450, n., 94 S.Ct. 1185, 1186, n., 39 L.Ed.2d 501 (1974).[22]

Likewise, where findings are infirm because of an erroneous view of the law, a remand is the proper course unless the record permits only one resolution of the factual issue. Kelley v. Southern Pacific Co., 419 U.S. 318, 331–332, 95 S.Ct. 472, 479–480, 42 L.Ed.2d 498 (1974). * * *

Accordingly, the judgment of the Court of Appeals is reversed and the case remanded to that court for further proceedings consistent with this opinion.

So ordered. *

JUSTICE MARSHALL, with whom JUSTICE BLACKMUN joins * * * dissenting.

* * *

The majority rejects the Court of Appeals' clear articulation and implementation of the clearly-erroneous rule on the apparent ground that in the course of correctly setting forth the requirements of Rule 52(a), the court also included the following quotation from its prior decision in East v. Romine, Inc., 518 F.2d 332, 339 (1975):

> " 'Although discrimination *vel non* is essentially a question of fact it is, at the same time, the ultimate issue for resolution in this case, being expressly proscribed by 42 U.S.C.A. § 2000e–2(a). As such, a finding of discrimination or nondiscrimination is a finding of ultimate fact. [Cites omitted]. In reviewing the district court's findings, therefore, we will proceed to make an independent determination of appellant's allegations of discrimination, though bound by

---

22. See 5A J. Moore & J. Lucas, Moore's Federal Practice § 52.06[2] (1982) ("Where the trial court fails to make findings, or to find on a material issue, and an appeal is taken, the appellate court will normally vacate the judgment and remand the action for appropriate findings to be made"); * * *.

* The concerning opinion of Justice Stevens is omitted.

findings of subsidiary fact which are themselves not clearly errone-ous.'" 624 F.2d, at 533 n. 6.

The only question presented by this case, therefore, is whether this reference to East v. Romine should be read as negating the Court of Appeals' unambiguous acknowledgment of the "controlling standard of Rule 52." * * * The majority bases its affirmative answer to that question on two factors. First, the majority contends that the Court of Appeals must not have properly respected the clearly-erroneous rule because its acknowledgment that Rule 52(a) supplied the controlling standard "came late in the court's opinion." * * * Second, the Court of Appeals "identified not only the mistake" that it felt had been made, "but also the source of that mistake." * * * If the Court of Appeals had really been applying the clearly-erroneous rule, it should have abided by the "usual requirement of remanding for further proceedings to the tribunal charged with the task of fact-finding in the first instance." * * *

Neither of these arguments justifies the majority's conclusion that this case must be remanded for a fourth trial on the merits. I am aware of no rule of decision embraced by this or any other court that places dispositive weight on whether an accurate statement of control-ling principle appears "early" or late in a court's opinion. * * * The heart of the majority's argument, therefore, is that the failure to remand the case to the District Court after rejecting its conclusion that the seniority system was "bona fide" within the meaning of § 703(h) indicates that the Court of Appeals did not properly follow the clearly-erroneous rule. Before addressing this issue, however, it is necessary to examine the nature of the finding of "intent" required by this Court in *Teamsters,* the procedure that courts of appeals should follow in review-ing a district court's finding on intent, and the extent to which the court below adhered to that procedure in this case.

The District Court examined the four factors approved by the Fifth Circuit in James v. Stockham Valves & Fittings Co., 559 F.2d 310 (1977), cert. denied, 434 U.S. 1034, 98 S.Ct. 767, 54 L.Ed.2d 781 (1978), to determine whether the departmental seniority system at Pullman-Standard was adopted or maintained for a discriminatory purpose. Although indicating that these four factors are not the only way to demonstrate the existence of discriminatory intent,[2] the Court today implicitly acknowledges that proof of these factors satisfies the require-ments of *Teamsters.*[3] In particular, the majority agrees that a finding of discriminatory intent sufficient to satisfy *Teamsters* can be based on circumstantial evidence, including evidence of discriminatory impact. * * *

2. Contrary to the majority's sugges-tion, *ante,* * * * n. 8, I find nothing in the Fifth Circuit's decision in James v. Stockham Valves & Fittings Co. to imply that these factors constitute the only rele-vant criteria for determining discriminato-ry intent.

3. This conclusion would seem to be compelled since, as the majority notes, the *James* factors are nothing more than a summary of the criteria examined by this Court in Teamsters v. United States, 431 U.S. 324, 355–356, 97 S.Ct. 1843, 1864–65, 52 L.Ed.2d 396 (1977).

Given the nature of this factual inquiry, the court of appeals must first determine whether the district court applied correct legal principles and therefore *considered* all of the legally relevant evidence presented by the parties. This, as the majority acknowledges, is a "legal" function that the court of appeals must perform in the first instance. * * * Second, the court of appeals must determine whether the district court's finding with respect to intent is *supported* by all of the legally relevant evidence. This, the Court holds today, is generally a factual determination limited by the dictates of Rule 52(a). Finally, if the court of appeals sets aside the district court's finding with respect to intent, either because that finding is clearly erroneous or because it is based on an erroneous legal standard, it may determine, in the interest of judicial economy, whether the legally relevant evidence presented to the district court "permits only one resolution of the factual issue." * * * If only one conclusion is possible, the reviewing court is free to find the existence of the fact in question as a matter of law. See Bigelow v. Virginia, 421 U.S. 809, 826–827, 95 S.Ct. 2222, 2234–35, 44 L.Ed.2d 600 (1972); Levin v. Mississippi River Fuel Corp., 386 U.S. 162, 170, 87 S.Ct. 927, 932, 17 L.Ed.2d 834 (1967).

A common-sense reading of the opinion below demonstrates that the Court of Appeals followed precisely this course in examining the issue of discriminatory intent. Even the majority concedes that the Court of Appeals determined that the District Court committed "legal error" by failing to consider all of the relevant evidence in resolving the first and the third *James* factors. * * * With respect to the first *James* factor—whether the system inhibits all employees equally from transferring between seniority units—the District Court found that the departmental system "locked" both Negro and white workers into departments by discouraging transfers. The District Court acknowledged that Negroes might suffer a greater impact because the company's previous discriminatory policy of openly maintaining "Negro" jobs and "white" jobs had caused Negroes to be concentrated in less desirable positions. The District Court concluded, however, that this differential impact was irrelevant in determining whether the seniority system operated neutrally. The Court of Appeals properly held that the District Court erred in failing to consider the fact that the departmental system locked Negroes into less desirable jobs.

Similarly, as for the third *James* factor—whether the seniority system had its genesis in racial discrimination—the District Court rejected respondents' argument that the motives of the IAM were relevant. It concluded that the USW could not be charged with the racial bias of the IAM. The Court of Appeals held that this conclusion was erroneous because the "motives and intent of the I.A.M. in 1941 and 1942 are significant in consideration of whether the seniority system has its genesis in racial discrimination." 624 F.2d, at 532.[4]

4. As the majority indicates in a footnote, * * * the discriminatory motive of the IAM is "relevant . . . to the extent that it may shed light on the purpose of USW or the Company in creating and maintaining the separate seniority system

* * * Having found that the District Court's findings as to the first and third *James* factors were made under an erroneous view of controlling legal principles, the Court of Appeals was *compelled* to set aside those findings free of the requirements of the clearly-erroneous rule.[5] But once these two findings were set aside, the District Court's conclusion that the departmental system was bona fide within the meaning of § 703(h) also had to be rejected, since that conclusion was based at least in part on its erroneous determinations concerning the first and the third *James* factors.

At the very least, therefore, the Court of Appeals was entitled to remand this case to the District Court for the purpose of reexamining the bona fides of the seniority system under proper legal standards. However, as we have often noted, in some cases a remand is inappropriate where the facts on the record are susceptible to only one reasonable interpretation. See Dayton Board of Education v. Brinkman, 443 U.S. 526, 534–537, 99 S.Ct. 2971, 2977–78, 61 L.Ed.2d 720 (CA6 1979); Bigelow v. Virginia, supra, at 826–827, 95 S.Ct., at 2234–2235. In such cases, "[e]ffective judicial administration" requires that the court of appeals draw the inescapable factual conclusion itself, rather than remand the case to the district court for further needless proceedings. Levin v. Mississippi River Fuel Corp., supra, 386 U.S., at 170, 87 S.Ct., at 932. Such action is particularly appropriate where the court of appeals is in as good a position to evalute the record evidence as the district court. The major premise behind the deference to trial courts expressed in Rule 52(a) is that findings of fact "depend peculiarly upon the credit given to witnesses by those who see and hear them." United States v. Yellow Cab Co., 338 U.S. 338, 341, 70 S.Ct. 177, 179, 94 L.Ed. 150 (1949); see also United States v. Oregon State Medical Society, 343 U.S. 326, 332, 72 S.Ct. 690, 695, 96 L.Ed. 978 (1952). Indeed Rule 52(a) expressly acknowledges the importance of this factor by stating that "due regard shall be given to the opportunity of the trial court to judge the credibility of the witnesses." Consequently, this Court has been especially reluctant to resolve factual issues which depend on the credibility of witnesses. See generally United States v. Oregon State Medical Society, supra, at 332, 72 S.Ct., at 179.

In the case before the Court today this usual deference is not required because the District Court's findings of fact were entirely based on documentary evidence.[6] As we noted in United States v. General Motors Corp., supra, at 141 n. 16, 86 S.Ct., at 1328 n. 16, "the

at issue in this case." I do not read the Court of Appeals opinion in this case as holding anything more than that if the USW participated in establishing a system that was designed for the purpose of perpetuating past discrimination, the third *James* factor would be satisfied. Given that the IAM is a party to this litigation, its participation in the creation of the seniority system can hardly be deemed irrelevant.

5. It is therefore irrelevant that the Court of Appeals did not specifically hold that the District Court's other factual findings were clearly erroneous.

6. Only two witnesses testified during the brief hearing that the District Court conducted on the question whether the seniority system at Pullman-Standard was immune under § 703(h). Both of these witnesses were long time Negro employees of Pullman-Standard who testified on be-

trial court's customary opportunity to evaluate the demeanor and thus the credibility of the witnesses, which is the rationale behind Rule 52(a) . . . plays only a restricted role . . . [in] a 'paper case.' " See also Jennings v. General Medical Corp., 604 F.2d 1300, 1305 (CA10 1979) ("When the findings of a trial court are based on documentary, rather than oral evidence, they do not carry the same weight on appellate review"); Orvis v. Higgins, 180 F.2d 537, 539 (CA2 1950).[7]

I believe that the Court of Appeals correctly determined that a finding of discriminatory intent was compelled by the documentary record presented to the District Court. With respect to three of the four *James* factors, the Court of Appeals found overwhelming evidence of discriminatory intent. First, in ruling that the District Court erred by not acknowledging the legal significance of the fact that the seniority system locked Negroes into the least remunerative jobs in the company, the Court of Appeals determined that such disproportionate impact demonstrated that the system did not " 'operat[e] to discourage all employees equally from transferring between seniority units.' " 624 F.2d, at 530, quoting James v. Stockham Valves & Fittings Co., 559 F.2d, at 352. Second, noting that "[n]o credible explanation ha[d] been advanced to sufficiently justify" the existence of two separate Die and Tool Departments and two separate Maintenance Departments, a condition not found at any other Pullman-Standard plant, or the creation of all-white and all-Negro departments at the time of unionization and in subsequent years, the Court of Appeals concluded that the second *James* factor had not been satisfied.[8] 624 F.2d, at 533. Finally, with respect to the third *James* factor the Court of Appeals found that once the role of the IAM was properly recognized, it was "crystal clear that considerations of race permeated the negotiation and the adoption of

half of *respondents* concerning racial segregation at the plant and by the USW. There is no indication in the District Court's opinion that it relied upon the testimony of these two witnesses in concluding that the system was bona fide within the meaning of § 703(h). The remainder of the record before the District Court consisted entirely of 139 exhibits submitted by respondents, the company, and the unions concerning the development and maintenance of the seniority system from 1940 through the 1970's.

7. This is not to say that the clearly-erroneous rule does not apply to "document" cases. See United States v. Singer Manufacturing Co., 374 U.S. 174, 194 n. 9, 83 S.Ct. 1773, 1783 n. 9, 10 L.Ed.2d 823 (1963). However, "when the decision of the court below rests upon an incorrect reading of an undisputed document, [the appellate] court is free to substitute its own reading of the document." Eutectic Corporation v. Metco, Inc., 579 F.2d 1, 5 (CA2 1978). See also McKensie v. Sea Land

Service, 551 F.2d 91 (CA5 1977); Best Medium Pub. Co. v. National Insider, Inc., 385 F.2d 384 (CA7 1967), cert denied, 390 U.S. 955, 88 S.Ct. 1052, 19 L.Ed.2d 1150 (1968); United States ex rel. Binion v. O'Brien, 273 F.2d 495 (CA3 1959), cert. denied, 363 U.S. 812, 80 S.Ct. 1249, 4 L.Ed.2d 1154 (1960).

8. * * * "The record evidence indicates that a significant number of one-race departments were established upon unionization at Pullman-Standard, and during the next twenty five years, one-race departments were carved out of previously mixed departments. The establishment and maintenance of the segregated departments appear to be based on *no other considerations than the objective to separate the races.*" 624 F.2d, at 531 (emphasis added). In my opinion, this statement is sufficient to satisfy the requirements of Rule 52(a), particularly in light of the Court of Appeals' general acknowledgement that it was bound by the clearly-erroneous rule. * * *

the seniority system in 1941 and subsequent negotiations thereafter."
624 F.2d, at 532.

After reviewing all of the relevant record evidence presented to the
District Court, the Court of Appeals concluded: "There is no doubt,
based upon the record in this case, about the existence of a discriminatory purpose." Id., at 533. Because I fail to see how the Court of
Appeals erred in carrying out its appellate function, I respectfully
dissent from the majority's decision to prolong respondents' 11-year
quest for the vindication of their rights by requiring yet another trial.

NOTE ON FINDINGS OF FACT AND CONCLUSIONS OF LAW

1. The conflict between majority and minority in the *Pullman-Standard*
decision mirrors conflicts in lower courts in other cases and earlier conflicts in
the Supreme Court. See especially Commissioner v. Duberstein, 363 U.S. 278,
80 S.Ct. 1190, 4 L.Ed.2d 1218 (1960), involving inferences of intent from
undisputed facts with regard to whether a transfer was a gift or an emolument.

A decade after *Duberstein's* guidance to the lower federal courts, the
Alaska Supreme Court gave this resumé of the confused state of federal
decisions applying F.R.C.P. 52(a) to review of findings based on documentary
evidence, Alaska Foods, Inc. v. American Mfg's Mutual Ins. Co., 482 P.2d 842,
844–45 (Alaska 1971):

> "The portion of Civil Rule 52(a) involved here is identical with a
> procedural rule in the federal judiciary relating to findings of fact made by
> the United States District Courts.[8] In interpreting that rule, where find-
> ings are based upon documentary evidence or undisputed facts, it is said
> that the federal courts of appeals are 'indescribably confused,' and that
> '[e]ven within a single circuit, decisions vacillate inexplicably from one test
> to another.'[9]

> "Some federal courts have taken the position that where the trial
> judge did not see the witnesses, the appellate court is in as good a position
> as the trial court to interpret the evidence, and will 'more readily' declare
> the trial judge's findings to be clearly erroneous.[10] This is what has been
> referred to as placing a 'gloss' on the rule.[11]

> "Other federal appellate courts have gone further and held flatly that
> they are not bound at all by the clearly erroneous standard where the
> evidence was not oral, and that they are free to completely disregard the
> trial judge's findings and make for themselves a de novo review of the

---

8. Rule 52(a), Federal Rules of Civil
Procedure, provides in part:

Findings of fact shall not be set aside
unless clearly erroneous, and due regard
shall be given to the opportunity of the
trial court to judge of the credibility of
the witnesses.

9. 2B W. Barron & A. Holtzoff, Federal
Practice and Procedure § 1132, at 516 (C.
Wright ed. 1961).

10. See Best Medium Publishing Co. v.
National Insider, Inc., 385 F.2d 384, 386
(7th Cir.1967), cert. denied, 390 U.S. 955,
88 S.Ct. 1052, 19 L.Ed.2d 1150 (1968); Ad-

ler v. Nicholas, 381 F.2d 168, 170–171 (5th
Cir.1967); Hicks v. United States, 368 F.2d
626, 630–631 (4th Cir.1966); International
Minerals & Chem. Corp. v. Moore, 361 F.2d
849, 851 (5th Cir.1966).

11. See Clark, Special Problems in
Drafting and Interpreting Procedural
Codes and Rules, 3 Vand.L.Rev. 493, 505–
06 (1950); Wright, The Doubtful Omniscience of Appellate Courts, 41 Minn.L.Rev.
751, 764 (1957); Note, Rule 52(a): Appellate Review of Findings of Fact Based on
Documentary or Undisputed Evidence, 49
Va.L.Rev. 506, 517 (1963).

evidence.[12] The decision most frequently cited in support of this approach is that of Judge Jerome Frank in Orvis v. Higgins.[13] Judge Frank stated that if the trial judge decides a fact issue on written evidence alone, the appellate court is as able as he to determine credibility, and could disregard the trial judge's finding. Judge Frank then went on to formulate different degrees of freedom of review depending upon the proportion of the evidence that was oral and the proportion that was written, including the effect that the written testimony may have had upon the crediblity of the oral testimony.[14] This so-called 'Frank' position on standard of review has been recommended as proper by Professor Moore in his work on federal practice and procedure.[15]

"Then there are the courts that take the position that the words 'findings of fact shall not be set aside unless clearly erroneous' mean what they say, and that the clearly erroneous test applies to all non-jury cases, regardless of the nature of the evidence involved, whether oral, written, or both.[16] The writers principally espousing this view are Judge Clark, one of the draftsmen of the Federal Rules of Civil Procedure,[17] and Professor Charles Alan Wright in his revision of Barron and Holtzoff's work on federal practice and procedure.[18] It is pointed out by Professor Wright in 2B W. Barron and A. Holtzoff, Federal Practice and Procedure, section 1132, at 522–23, that the United States Supreme Court took this view of Rule 52(a) in its 1948 decision in United States v. United States Gypsum Co.,[19] and has reiterated that position in later decisions.[20] "

The Supreme Court has tried to clear up some of this confusion, holding that under the "clearly erroneous" standard an appellate court may not reverse a trial court merely because it is convinced that it would have decided the case differently, so long as the trial court's determination is "plausible" in light of

---

12. See Borden Co. v. Clearfield Cheese Co., 369 F.2d 96, 101 (3d Cir.1966); Harris v. United States, 370 F.2d 887, 894 (4th Cir. 1966); Ellison v. Frank, 245 F.2d 837, 839 (9th Cir.1957). See also Note, Rule 52(a): Appellate Review of Findings of Fact Based on Documentary or Undisputed Evidence, 49 Va.L.Rev. 506, 517 & n. 62 (1963).

13. 180 F.2d 537 (2d Cir.), cert. denied, 340 U.S. 810, 71 S.Ct. 37, 95 L.Ed. 595 (1950).

14. 180 F.2d at 539–540. For a discussion of Judge Frank's views see 2B W. Barron & A. Holtzoff, Federal Practice and Procedure § 1132, at 520–21 (C. Wright ed. 1961); Note, Rule 52(a): Appellate Review of Findings of Fact Based on Documentary or Undisputed Evidence, 49 Va.L.Rev. 506, 520–24 (1963); Comment, Scope of Appellate Fact Review Widened, 2 Stan.L.Rev. 784 (1950).

15. 5 J. Moore, Federal Practice ¶ 52.04, at 2688 (2d ed. 1969).

16. United States Steel Corp. v. Fuhrman, 407 F.2d 1143, 1145–1146 (6th Cir. 1969); Snider v. England, 374 F.2d 717, 720 (9th Cir.1967); Cole v. Neaf, 334 F.2d 326, 329–330 (8th Cir.1964); United States v. Allinger, 275 F.2d 421, 423 (6th Cir.1960);

Texas Co. v. R. O'Brien & Co., 242 F.2d 526, 529 (1st Cir.1957).

17. Clark & Stone, Review of Findings of Fact, 4 U.Chi.L.Rev. 190 (1937); Clark, Review of Facts Under Proposed Federal Rules, 20 J.Am.Jud.Soc'y 129 (1936). See 5 J. Moore, Federal Practice ¶ 52.04, at 2687–88 (1969); Wright, The Doubtful Omniscience of Appellate Courts, 41 Minn.L.Rev. 751, 768–69 (1957); Note, Rule 52(a): Appellate Review of Findings of Fact Based on Documentary or Undisputed Evidence, 49 Va.L.Rev. 506, 518 (1963).

18. 2B W. Barron & A. Holtzoff, Federal Practice and Procedure § 1132, at 521–24 (C. Wright ed. 1961); Wright, The Doubtful Omniscience of Appellate Courts, 41 Minn.L.Rev. 751 (1957).

19. 333 U.S. 364, 394, 68 S.Ct. 525, 541, 92 L.Ed. 746, 765 (1948).

20. United States v. Singer Mfg. Co., 374 U.S. 174, 194 n. 9, 83 S.Ct. 1773, 1784 n. 9, 10 L.Ed.2d 823, 838 n. 9 (1963); Commissioner of Internal Revenue v. Duberstein, 363 U.S. 278, 291, 80 S.Ct. 1190, 1200, 4 L.Ed.2d 1218, 1228 (1960). See 2B W. Barron & A. Holtzoff, Federal Practice and Procedure § 1132, at 522–23 (C. Wright ed. 1961).

the record; that this standard applies even when the trial court's findings do not rest on the credibility of witnesses but rather on physical or documentary evidence; and that when findings are based on credibility, Rule 52(a) demands even greater deference to the trial court's findings. Anderson v. City of Bessemer, 470 U.S. 564, 105 S.Ct. 1504, 84 L.Ed.2d 518 (1985). Shortly after the *Anderson* decision, F.R.C.P. 52(a) was amended to make it clear that it applies to reviews of findings based on documentary evidence. Whether this revision, coupled with the *Anderson* decision, will significantly aid lower courts in applying Rule 52(a) remains to be seen. See also Icicle Seafoods, Inc. v. Worthington, 475 U.S. 709, 106 S.Ct. 1527, 89 L.Ed.2d 739 (1986) ("clearly erroneous" standard applies in Fair Labor Standards Act cases).

The scope of appellate review is more extensive in certain types of cases, such as those involving free speech. See Bose Corp. v. Consumers Union, 466 U.S. 485, 104 S.Ct. 1949, 80 L.Ed.2d 502 (1984). Review of federal district court decisions involving interpretations of state law traditionally had been said to require deference to the trial judge's special knowledge of state law, but this view has been rejected by some courts; see, e.g., Matter of McLinn, 739 F.2d 1395 (9th Cir.1984).

2. It should not be understood that these difficulties arise only in the federal system. Findings of fact and conclusions of law are not mandatory in California but a statement of decision may be demanded by a party. C.C.P. 632. See also California Rules of Court, Superior Court Rule 232, Municipal Court Rule 520. See generally 7 Witkin 373 et seq. But when findings are made in California, the question arises as to their conclusiveness on appeal:

Primm v. Primm, 46 Cal.2d 690, 693, 299 P.2d 231 (1956): "When a finding of fact is attacked on the ground that there is not any substantial evidence to sustain it, the power of an appellate court *begins* and *ends* with the determination as to whether there is any substantial evidence contradicted or uncontradicted which will support the finding of fact. * * * When two or more inferences can reasonably be deduced from the facts, a reviewing court is without power to substitute its deductions for those of the trial court."

Earl v. Saks & Co., 36 Cal.2d 602, 610, 226 P.2d 340 (1951): "Although 'actual fraud is always a question of fact,' * * * and although findings of ultimate fact ordinarily cannot be controlled by findings of probative facts * * * here the finding that Saks was not guilty of fraud is not controlling, for it was drawn as a conclusion from the findings of probative facts which not only do not support it but which establish the contrary * * *."

Tahoe Nat. Bank v. Phillips, 4 Cal.3d 11, 92 Cal.Rptr. 704, 480 P.2d 320 (1971): This was an action upon a written agreement that was entitled "assignment" but which the plaintiff claimed was intended as an equitable mortgage. The majority held that as a matter of law the agreement was an assignment, notwithstanding the trial court's "finding of fact" that it was intended as a mortgage and the dissenter's contention that "the sole issue before us * * * is whether the evidence is sufficient to support the trial court's finding * * *."

Consider also the synthesis in 5 Am.Jur.2d, Appeal and Error § 829: "Since the determination as to whether the issue is in fact one of law or one of fact clearly presents an issue of law for appellate decision, it is apparent that the reviewing court has considerable discretion in classifying a particular matter as one of fact or law, and consequently in determining whether it is or is not reviewable * * *."

See also Comment, The Fact–Opinion Distinction: An Analysis of the Subjectivity of Language and Law, 70 Marq.L.Rev. 673 (1987); Zuckerman, Law, Fact or Justice?, 66 B.U.L.Rev. 487 (1986).

3. Note that under F.R.C.P. 52(a) findings are required not only after trials without a jury or with an advisory jury but also when the judge grants or refuses an interlocutory injunction under F.R.C.P. 65; and they are also required under F.R.C.P. 41(b) when the judge in a court-tried case dismisses plaintiff's case on the merits at the conclusion of plaintiff's evidence.

4. Is the trial court justified in asking the prevailing counsel to prepare the findings? It is not improper to do so, Citizens for Balanced Environment & Transportation, Inc. v. Volpe, 650 F.2d 455 (2d Cir.1981), although appellate courts swallow hard and losing litigants choke where, as noted in Monroe County Conservation Council, Inc. v. Adams, 566 F.2d 419, 425 n. 7 (2d Cir. 1977), "the district judge adopted the [prevailing party's] proposed findings of fact and conclusions of law in their entirety, omitting the formality of retyping, on the day following oral argument, during the course of which he indicated that he had not yet read the voluminous documents upon which his decision hinged." See also 5A Moore ¶ 52.06[3]; 7 Witkin 381–382; California Rules of Court, Superior Court Rule 232.

5. There is greater flexibility respecting post-trial motions and judicial action thereon in judge-tried as contrasted with jury-tried cases. Thus, a motion for amended findings under F.R.C.P. 52(b) may be blended with one for a new trial under F.R.C.P. 59, and Rule 59(a) contains the provision: "On a motion for a new trial in an action tried without a jury, the court may open the judgment if one has been entered, take additional testimony, amend findings of fact and conclusions of law or make new findings and conclusions, and direct the entry of a new judgment." In effect a motion for a new trial in a court-tried case may result essentially in a *continuation* of the original trial, rather than in a *new* trial in whole or part. See 6A Moore ¶ 59.07. See also F.R.C.P. 58 on entry of judgment.

G. THE JUDGMENT

INTRODUCTORY NOTE ON JUDGMENTS

Many principles of widely differing scope, significance and function are subsumed under "Judgments," e.g.: (1) the constituents of a judgment, the difference between its *rendition* and *entry,* and its effective date for such important purposes as terminating the power of the trial court over the case, commencement of the time to appeal, and issuance of a writ of execution; see Jackson v. Sears, Roebuck & Co., just below, and the Note following; (2) the res judicata effect of judgments, already considered supra p. 630, and the recognition and enforcement of judgments in other states and countries, considered supra p. 679; (3) defaults and default judgments, considered supra p. 984; (4) the levying of execution on judgments and the rights and remedies of creditors and debtors; (5) extraordinary relief from judgments, considered infra p. 1329.

A careful reading of F.R.C.P. 54, 58 and 79 is a good start for those judgment problems appropriate for study here.

JACKSON v. SEARS, ROEBUCK & CO.

Supreme Court of Arizona, 1957.
83 Ariz. 20, 315 P.2d 871.

STRUCKMEYER, JUSTICE.

Appellee, as plaintiff in the court below, sued Clarence O. Jackson, appellant herein, on the balance due on an account. Trial was duly had before the Court sitting without a jury and on the 18th day of May, 1955, the trial judge wrote a letter to the Clerk of Court of Maricopa County stating in part as follows: "You will please let the record show that judgment be entered for the plaintiff . . . from date . . . ." This letter was received by the Clerk on the following day, but no order was entered on the civil docket until May 31, 1955. The notation in the civil docket provides:

> "May 31, 1955 Judgment entered from minutes of May 19, 1955—Div. 2—'It is Ordered that plaintiff have Judgment against the defendant for the sum of $625.59 with interest at a rate of 6% per annum from date each party to bear their own costs.'"

Five days prior to the above entry of judgment, that is, on May 26, 1955, appellee caused an execution to issue against real property owned by appellant, and subsequently the sheriff of Maricopa County levied upon and sold it to appellee for the amount of the judgment, together with interest and costs. It is appellant's position that on the 26th day of May, 1955, there was no valid judgment upon which execution could issue; that accordingly, all subsequent proceedings, including execution, sale, and delivery of sheriff's deed were void and a nullity.

It is the general rule that an execution issued without a judgment to support it is void, no authority is conferred upon the officer to whom it is directed, and even if a judgment is subsequently obtained, it will not have a retroactive effect so as to validate the execution. Evans v. City of American Falls, 52 Idaho 7, 11 P.2d 363, 368; Bovard v. Bovard, 233 Mo.App. 1019, 128 S.W.2d 274. The foregoing general rule must be distinguished from those situations where the matters are merely irregularities which can, or have been, removed. There the execution is voidable and if the matter causing the irregularity has been removed, a motion to quash will be denied and the execution and levy thereunder will stand. Mosher v. Ganz, 42 Ariz. 314, 25 P.2d 555. There is by no means a unanimity of opinion as to whether this present case presents a curable irregularity.

At the common law, an execution might issue as soon as the final judgment was signed, before its entry of record, nor was the docketing of the judgment deemed essential to execution. Stevens v. Manson, 87 Me. 436, 32 Atl. 1002. Most of the early cases held that the execution, if issued after pronouncement or rendition of judgment, could not be voided by a showing that the judgment had not, in fact, been entered at the time of issuance, Los Angeles Bank v. Raynor, 61 Cal. 145; Weigley v. Matson, 125 Ill. 64, 16 N.E. 881, 8 Am.St.Rep. 333, although there is authority to the contrary. Knights v. Martin, 155 Ill. 486, 40 N.E. 358, affirmed 56 Ill.App. 65; Lowther v. Davis, 33 W.Va. 132, 10 S.E. 20. The holding in these latter cases has been both distinguished and criticized. 1 Freeman on Executions (3rd Ed.), section 24.

In recent cases, it has been held that a judgment is operative from the date of its rendition, and that the failure of the clerk to perform the ministerial act of entering the judgment of record does not delay its operation. State v. Haney, Mo., 277 S.W.2d 632; Cinebar Coal & Coke Co. v. Robinson, 1 Wash.2d 620, 97 P.2d 128; and a judgment after its entry relates back to the time of its pronouncement. Wickiser v. Powers, 324 Ill.App. 130, 57 N.E.2d 522. In some states, by virtue of statute, execution may issue after judgment has been rendered; e.g. Ex Parte Lewis, 335 Mich. 640, 56 N.W.2d 211. At the present time, both the clear weight of authority and statutory trend do not require a formal entry after pronouncement or rendition of judgment in order for a valid execution to issue. 21 Am.Jur., Executions, section 21, p. 26.

However, in this state, both by statute and rule of procedure, the formal entry by the clerk is an indispensable prerequisite to valid execution. Rule 79(a), Rules of Civil Procedure, 16 A.R.S., requires the clerk of the court to keep a book known as the "civil docket" in which shall be entered all judgments. Rule 58(a) provides that the notation in the civil docket constitutes entry of judgment and the judgment "*is not effective before such entry.*" These rules of civil procedure have been several times construed, the most recent being Harbel Oil Co. v. Steele, 81 Ariz. 104, 301 P.2d 757, 758, reversing 80 Ariz. 368, 298 P.2d 789. There we said, "For our purpose here it is immaterial when the order or judgment was announced or ordered—it was not effective until it was entered in the docket."

Not only is a judgment ineffective until entry thereof in the civil docket, but the legislature has provided that "the party in whose favor a judgment is given may, at any time within five years *after entry of the judgment,* have a writ of execution issued for its enforcement." A.R.S. § 12–1551, subd. A. The time of entry is the day when the clerk makes the notation in the civil docket. By the specific language of the statute, execution may not issue prior to such entry. Where the statute requires that a judgment be entered before execution, there can be no valid or lawful execution without such an entry. Tanner v. Wilson, 184 Ga. 628, 192 S.E. 425. Since the execution was issued five days prior to the entry of judgment, it was issued without authority of law and was a legal nullity. The subsequent acts and matters dependent thereon, including levy, sale, and the sheriff's deed are void.

Without the determination of further questions raised which need not be discussed in the light of our conclusions here, the judgment of the court below is reversed with directions that the execution be quashed and all proceedings had thereunder be vacated and set aside.

UDALL, C.J., and WINDES, PHELPS and JOHNSON, JJ., concur.

FURTHER NOTE ON THE JUDGMENT

1. Entry of the Judgment

    a. Form of the Judgment. A suggested form for Judgment on a Jury Verdict (F.R.C.P. Appendix of Forms, Form 31) follows:

United States District Court for the Southern
District of New York

Civil Action, File Number _____

A.B., Plaintiff
       v.   } Judgment
C.D., Defendant

    This action came on for trial before the Court and a jury, Honorable John Marshall, District Judge, presiding, and the issues having been duly tried and the jury having rendered its verdict,

    It is Ordered and Adjudged

    [that the plaintiff A.B. recover of the defendant C.D. the sum of _____, with interest thereon at the rate of _____ per cent as provided by law, and his costs of action.]

    [that the plaintiff take nothing, that the action be dismissed on the merits, and that the defendant C.D. recover of the plaintiff A.B. his costs of action.]

    Dated at New York, New York, this _____ day of _____, 19__.

_____
Clerk of Court

    b. Content of the Judgment. With what precision and certainty must a judgment be phrased? In Kittle v. Lang, 107 Cal.App.2d 604, 237 P.2d 673 (1951), an action for a money judgment and for other relief with respect to an alleged partnership agreement, the trial court concluded that (1) plaintiff was entitled to a judgment against defendant in the sum of $1,452; (2) plaintiff was entitled to judgment for the immediate delivery and return "of all the machinery, equipment, tools and supplies listed in plaintiff's Exhibit I, which are now in the possession of the defendant"; and (3) plaintiff was entitled to judgment for the immediate delivery "of any and all sums of money collected by defendant, and by him held for and on behalf of plaintiff." Judgment was entered in the same language. In affirming in part and reversing in part the appellate court said, 107 Cal.App.2d at 612–13, 237 P.2d at 678:

    "It is true that findings, as well as the judgment based thereon, should be definite and certain. At least they should be sufficiently clear and definite to enable a party to comply with their requirements. * * * The judgment here involved is merely an order to the defendant to turn over to plaintiff such part of the personal property assets of the partnership now in defendant's possession as are described in Exhibit I, which exhibit is made a part of the findings and judgment by reference. Defendant admitted he still had in his possession much of this equipment but claimed title to it under the terms of the quitclaim deed, which deed the court found was ineffective as to this particular personal property.

"As between the parties to this action, we believe the findings and judgment, in this respect, are sufficiently clear and definite to enable defendant to comply with its requirements. * * *

"As to the finding and judgment for the payment of money, a stricter rule seems to prevail, i.e., that a judgment for money must be stated with certainty and should specify the amount. * * * The portion of the finding reciting that 'Defendant has collected certain sums of money on behalf of plaintiff, as more particularly appears from defendant's testimony herein, and that plaintiff is entitled to any and all of said sums of money so collected by defendant,' and the judgment entered thereon that plaintiff 'is entitled to judgment for the immediate delivery of any and all sums of money collected by defendant, and by him held for and on behalf of plaintiff' is quite uncertain as to the amount, to say the least. It refers to the testimony of defendant on this subject. We have examined the record * * *. It may have been clear to the scrivener of the findings and judgment how much was due plaintiff under that testimony, but it certainly is not clear to this court what amount was intended by the judgment. This portion of the judgment is too indefinite and uncertain to be enforced."

c. Provisions of the Federal Rules. F.R.C.P. 58 requires that the judgment be contained in a separate document, the filing of which triggers the time to appeal. The Rule was intended to forfend uncertainty as to when the time to appeal starts to run, as in United States v. F. & M. Schaefer Brewing Co., 356 U.S. 227, 78 S.Ct. 674, 2 L.Ed.2d 721 (1958), and has been said to require application "mechanically." United States v. Indrelunas, 411 U.S. 216, 93 S.Ct. 1562, 36 L.Ed.2d 202 (1973). But see Bankers Trust Co. v. Mallis, 435 U.S. 381, 98 S.Ct. 1117, 55 L.Ed.2d 357 (1978), which said that the record could be searched for something that looked like a judgment.

F.R.C.P. 54(b) permits the court to direct the entry of a final judgment "as to one or more but fewer than all of the claims or parties." Being final, such partial judgments are appealable. See Kallay, A Study in Rule–Making by Decision: California Courts Adopt Federal Rule of Civil Procedure 54(b), 13 Sw. U.L.Rev. 87 (1982).

d. California and New York Provisions. The most important California provisions on entry of judgments are C.C.P. 664, 664.5, 664.6, 669; California Rules of Court, Appellate Rule 2 (time of filing notice of appeal). See generally 7 Witkin 483 et seq. For the New York provisions, see N.Y.C.P.L.R. 5011–5019, 5230, 9702. See generally Weinstein, Korn & Miller ¶¶ 5011.01 et seq.

In addition to the general provisions governing entry of judgments, the California Rules of Court permit a court to announce a tentative decision not constituting a judgment, which is subject to later modification on the judge's own motion or upon motion of any party. Superior Court Rule 232.

2. Enforcement of Money Judgments

a. Procedure for Enforcement. Judgments for the payment of money are enforced by a writ of execution, issued by the court and addressed to the sheriff, directing the seizure of the judgment debtor's non-exempt property and the public sale of that property. From the sale proceeds are deducted the costs of the sale, prior encumbrances, and the judgment debt, with the balance, if any, returned to the judgment debtor. See Green, Basic Civil Procedure 222–23 (2d ed. 1979). See also C.C.P. 695.010 et seq.; N.Y.C.P.L.R. 5201 et seq. In federal court, money judgments are enforced in accordance with the practice and procedure of the state in which the federal court sits, unless there is a preempting federal statute. F.R.C.P. 69(a). When a judgment has been paid, the judgment creditor is generally required to sign and file a form entitled "Satisfaction of Judgment." See C.C.P. 724.020; N.Y.C.P.L.R. 5020, 5021.

Procedures are available to judgment creditors "in aid" of their judgments, such as the discovery of assets belonging to the judgment debtor and the recording and enforcement of judgment liens. Body execution, the seizure of the judgment debtor's person until payment is made, generally is no longer available, but a jail sentence remains a possibility by way of contempt should the debtor refuse to disclose assets or comply with a court's remedial order. See Green, Basic Civil Procedure 223–24 (2d ed. 1979).

    b. Due Process Considerations. Postjudgment execution has been found to raise due process concerns where exempt property is seized. See, e.g., Finberg v. Sullivan, 634 F.2d 50 (3d Cir.1980). Concerns center on notice to the owner of his exemption, and notice and hearing on the exemption before the property is turned over to the judgment creditor. See Note, Due Process, Postjudgment Garnishment, and "Brutal Need" Exemptions, 1982 Duke L.J. 192; Note, Postjudgment Garnishment Procedures in Connecticut: A Due Process Analysis and Practical Guide, 14 Conn.L.Rev. 883 (1982).

    c. Enforcement of Judgments From Other Jurisdictions. Judgments rendered in other jurisdictions cannot be enforced in the same manner as domestic money judgments. Traditionally, execution was possible only after the foreign judgment had been "domesticated" by a suit on the foreign judgment and the rendition of a domestic judgment for the amount of the foreign judgment. Because of the delay and red tape involved in this procedure, many jurisdictions have adopted a "registration" procedure instead. The enforcement of foreign judgments is discussed more fully in Note on Full Faith and Credit, supra p. 683, and Note on Federal–State and International Recognition of Judgments, supra p. 698.

3. Enforcement of Judgments Ordering Specific Acts

When a judgment orders a party to perform a specific act, such as the execution or delivery of a deed or other document, and the party fails to perform within the time ordered, the court generally will direct that the act be done by some other person authorized by the court to act for the recalcitrant party, and at his expense. In a proper case the court may hold the disobedient party in contempt and issue a writ of attachment, garnishment, or execution. If the property is within its jurisdiction, the court, rather than ordering conveyance of the property, may simply enter a judgment divesting the party of title to the property and vesting title in others. See F.R.C.P. 70; C.C.P. 712.010 et seq.; N.Y.C.P.L.R. 5201 et seq. Such is the nature of a suit to quiet title.

Part VIII

SPECIAL PROBLEMS OF
MODERN LITIGATION

A. COMPLEX LITIGATION

---

1. INTRODUCTION

CHAYES, THE ROLE OF THE JUDGE IN PUBLIC LAW LITIGATION

89 Harv.L.Rev. 1281, 1282–1302 (1976).[*]

* * * We are witnessing the emergence of a new model of civil litigation and, I believe, our traditional conception of adjudication and the assumptions upon which it is based provide an increasingly unhelpful, indeed misleading framework for assessing either the workability or the legitimacy of the roles of judge and court within this model.

In our received tradition, the lawsuit is a vehicle for settling disputes between private parties about private rights. The defining features of this conception of civil adjudication are:

(1) The lawsuit is *bipolar*. Litigation is organized as a contest between two individuals or at least two unitary interests, diametrically opposed, to be decided on a winner-takes-all basis.

(2) Litigation is *retrospective*. The controversy is about an identified set of completed events: whether they occurred, and if so, with what consequences for the legal relations of the parties.

(3) *Right and remedy are interdependent.* The scope of the relief is derived more or less logically from the substantive violation under the general theory that the plaintiff will get compensation measured by the harm caused by the defendant's breach of duty—in contract by giving plaintiff the money he would have had absent the breach; in tort by paying the value of the damage caused.

(4) The lawsuit is a *self-contained* episode. The impact of the judgment is confined to the parties. If plaintiff prevails there is a simple compensatory transfer, usually of money, but occasionally the return of a thing or the performance of a definite act. If defendant prevails, a loss lies where it has fallen. In either case, entry of judgment ends the court's involvement.

(5) The process is *party-initiated* and *party-controlled*. The case is organized and the issues defined by exchanges between the parties. Re-

sponsibility for fact development is theirs. The trial judge is a neutral arbiter of their interactions who decides questions of law only if they are put in issue by an appropriate move of a party.

* * * Although I do not contend that the traditional conception ever conformed fully to what judges were doing in fact, I believe it has been central to our understanding and our analysis of the legal system.

Whatever is historical validity, the traditional model is clearly invalid as a description of much current civil litigation in the federal district courts. Perhaps the dominating characteristic of modern federal litigation is that lawsuits do not arise out of disputes between private parties about private rights. Instead the object of litigation is the vindication of constitutional or statutory policies. The shift in the legal basis of the lawsuit explains many, but not all, facets of what is going on "in fact" in federal trial courts. For this reason, although the label is not wholly satisfactory, I shall call the emerging model "public law litigation."

The characteristic features of the public law model are very different from those of the traditional model. The party structure is sprawling and amorphous, subject to change over the course of the litigation. The traditional adversary relationship is suffused and intermixed with negotiating and mediating processes at every point. The judge is the dominant figure in organizing and guiding the case, and he draws for support not only on the parties and their counsel, but on a wide range of outsiders—masters, experts, and oversight personnel. Most important, the trial judge has increasingly become the creator and manager of complex forms of ongoing relief, which have widespread effects on persons not before the court and require the judge's continuing involvement in administration and implementation. School desegregation, employment discrimination, and prisoners' or inmates' rights cases come readily to mind as avatars of this new form of litigation. But it would be mistaken to suppose that it is confined to these areas. Antitrust, securities fraud and other aspects of the conduct of corporate business, bankruptcy and reorganizations, union governance, consumer fraud, housing discrimination, electoral reapportionment, environmental management—cases in all these fields display in varying degrees the features of public law litigation.

The object of this Article is first to describe somewhat more fully the public law model and its departures from the traditional conception, and second, to suggest some of its consequences for the place of law and courts in the American political and legal system.

I. THE RECEIVED TRADITION

The traditional conception of adjudication reflected the late nineteenth century vision of society, which assumed that the major social and economic arrangements would result from the activities of autonomous individuals. In such a setting, the courts could be seen as an adjunct to private ordering, whose primary function was a resolution of disputes about the fair implications of individual interactions. The basic conceptions governing legal liability were "intention" and "fault." Intentional arrangements, not in conflict with more or less universal attitudes like opposition to force or fraud, were entitled to be respected, and other private activities to be protected unless culpable. Government regulatory action was presumptively suspect, and was tested by what was in form a common law action against the offending official in his private person. The predominating influence of the private law model can be seen even in constitutional litigation, which, from its first appearance in Marbury v. Madison, was understood as an outgrowth of the judicial duty to decide otherwise-existing private disputes.

Litigation also performed another important function—clarification of the law to guide future private actions. This understanding of the legal system, together with the common law doctrine of stare decisis, focused professional and scholarly concern on adjudication at the appellate level, for only there did the process reach beyond the immediate parties to achieve a wider import through the elaboration of generally applicable legal rules. * * *

In contrast to the appellate court, to which the motive power in the system was allocated, the functions of the trial judge were curiously neglected in the traditional model. Presumably, the trial judge, like the multitude of private persons who were supposed to order their affairs with reference to appellate pronouncements, would be governed by those decisions in disposing smoothly and expeditiously of the mine-run of cases. But if only by negative implication, the traditional conception of adjudication carried with it a set of strong notions about the role of the trial judge. In general he was passive. He was to decide only those issues identified by the parties, in accordance with the rules established by the appellate courts, or, infrequently, the legislature.

Passivity was not limited to the law aspects of the case. It was strikingly manifested in the limited involvement of the judge in factfinding. Indeed, the sharp distinction that Anglo-American law draws between factfinding and law declaration is itself remarkable. In the developed common law system, these were not only regarded as analytically distinct processes, but each was assigned to a different tribunal for performance. The jury found the facts. The judge was a neutral umpire, charged with little or no responsibility for the factual aspects of the case or for shaping and organizing the litigation for trial.

* * *

The emphasis on systematic statement of liability rules involved a corresponding disregard of the problems of relief. There was, to be sure, a good deal of discussion of measure of damages, as a corollary to the analysis of substantive rights and duties. Similarly, the question of the availability of specific performance and other equitable remedies came in for a share of attention. But the discussion was carried forward within the accepted framework that compensatory money damages was the usual form of relief. Prospective relief was highly exceptional in the traditional model and was largely remitted to the discretion of the trial judge.

* * *

II. The Public Law Litigation Model

* * *

A. The Demise of the Bipolar Structure

* * * The standing issue could hardly arise at common law or under early code pleading rules, that is, under the traditional model. There the question of plaintiff's standing merged with the legal merits: On the facts pleaded, does this particular plaintiff have a right to the particular relief sought from the particular defendant from whom he is seeking it? With the erosion of the tight structural integration of the lawsuit, the pressure to expand the circle of potential plaintiffs has been inexorable. Today, the Supreme Court is struggling manfully, but with questionable success, to establish a

formula for delimiting who may sue that stops short of "anybody who might be significantly affected by the situation he seeks to litigate."

"Anybody"—even "almost anybody"—can be a lot of people, particularly where the matters in issue are not relatively individualized private transactions or encounters. Thus, the stage is set for the class action * * *. Whatever the resolution of the current controversies surrounding class actions, I think it unlikely that the class action will ever be taught to behave in accordance with the precepts of the traditional model of adjudication. The class suit is a reflection of our growing awareness that a host of important public and private interactions—perhaps the most important in defining the conditions and opportunities of life for most people—are conducted on a routine or bureaucratized basis and can no longer be visualized as bilateral transactions between private individuals. From another angle, the class action responds to the proliferation of more or less well-organized groups in our society and the tendency to perceive interests as group interests, at least in very important aspects.

The emergence of the group as the real subject or object of the litigation not only transforms the party problem, but raises far-reaching new questions. How far can the group be extended and homogenized? To what extent and by what methods will we permit the presentation of views diverging from that of the group representative? When the judgment treads on numerous—perhaps innumerable—absentees, can the traditional doctrines of finality and preclusion hold? And in the absence of a particular client, capable of concretely defining his own interest, can we rely on the assumptions of the adversary system as a guide to the conduct and duty of the lawyer?

These questions are brought into sharp focus by the class action device. But it would be a mistake to think that they are confined to that procedural setting. The class action is only one mechanism for presenting group interests for adjudication, and the same basic questions will arise in a number of more familiar litigating contexts. Indeed, it may not be too much to say that they are pervasive in the new model.

B. The Triumph of Equity

One of the most striking procedural developments of this century is the increasing importance of equitable relief. It is perhaps too soon to reverse the traditional maxim to read that money damages will be awarded only when no suitable form of specific relief can be devised. But surely, the old sense of equitable remedies as "extraordinary" has faded.

I am not concerned here with specific performance—the compelled transfer of a piece of land or a unique thing. This remedy is structurally little different from traditional money-damages. It is a one-time, one-way transfer requiring for its enforcement no continuing involvement of the court. Injunctive relief, however, is different in kind, even when it takes the form of a simple negative order. Such an order is a presently operative prohibition, enforceable by contempt, and it is a much greater constraint on activity than the risk of future liability implicit in the damage remedy. Moreover, the injunction is continuing. Over time, the parties may resort to the court for enforcement or modification of the original order in light of changing circumstances. Finally, by issuing the injunction, the court takes public responsibility for any consequences of its decree that may adversely affect strangers to the action.

Beyond these differences, the prospective character of the relief introduces large elements of contingency and prediction into the proceedings. Instead of a dispute retrospectively oriented toward the consequences of a closed set of events, the court has a controversy about future probabilities. Equitable doctrine, naturally enough, given the intrusiveness of the injunction and the contingent nature of the harm, calls for a balancing of the interests of the parties. And if the immediate parties' interests were to be weighed and evaluated, it was not too difficult to proceed to a consideration of other interests that might be affected by the order.

* * *

C. The Changing Character of Factfinding

The traditional model of adjudication was primarily concerned with assessing the consequences for the parties of specific past instances of conduct. This retrospective orientation is often inapposite in public law litigation, where the lawsuit generally seeks to enjoin future or threatened action, or to modify a course of conduct presently in train or a condition presently existing. * * *

In the remedial phases of public law litigation, factfinding is even more clearly prospective. As emphasized above, the contours of relief are not derived logically from the substantive wrong adjudged, as in the traditional model. The elaboration of a decree is largely a discretionary process within which the trial judge is called upon to assess and appraise the consequences of alternative programs that might correct the substantive fault. In both the liability and remedial phases, the relevant inquiry is largely the same: How can the policies of a public law best be served in a concrete case?

In public law litigation, then, factfinding is principally concerned with "legislative" rather than "adjudicative" fact. And "fact evaluation" is perhaps a more accurate term than "factfinding." The whole process begins to look like the traditional description of legislation: Attention is drawn to a "mischief," existing or threatened, and the activity of the parties and court is directed to the development of on-going measures designed to cure that mischief. Indeed, if, as is often the case, the decree sets up an affirmative regime governing the activities in controversy for the indefinite future and having binding force for persons within its ambit, then it is not very much of a stretch to see it as, *pro tanto,* a legislative act.

* * *

The courts, it seems, continue to rely primarily on the litigants to produce and develop factual materials, but a number of factors make it impossible to leave the organization of the trial exclusively in their hands. With the diffusion of the party structure, fact issues are no longer sharply drawn in a confrontation between two adversaries, one asserting the affirmative and the other the negative. The litigation is often extraordinarily complex and extended in time, with a continuous and intricate interplay between factual and legal elements. It is hardly feasible and, absent a jury, unnecessary to set aside a contiguous block of time for a "trial stage" at which all significant factual issues will be presented. The scope of the fact investigation and the sheer volume of factual material that can be exhumed by the discovery process pose enormous problems of organization and assimilation. All these factors thrust the trial judge into an active role in shaping, organizing and facilitating the litigation. We may not yet have reached the investigative judge of the continental systems, but we have left the passive arbiter of the traditional model a long way behind.

D. The Decree

The centerpiece of the emerging public law model is the decree. It differs in almost every relevant characteristic from relief in the traditional model of adjudication, not the least in that it *is* the centerpiece. The decree seeks to adjust future behavior, not to compensate for past wrong. It is deliberately fashioned rather than logically deduced from the nature of the legal harm suffered. It provides for a complex, on-going regime of performance rather than a simple, one-shot, one-way transfer. Finally, it prolongs and deepens, rather than terminates, the court's involvement with the dispute.

The decree is also an order of the court, signed by the judge and issued under his responsibility (itself a shift from the classical money judgment). But it cannot be supposed that the judge, at least in a case of any complexity, composes it out of his own head. How then is the relief formulated?

The reports provide little guidance on this question. Let me nonetheless suggest a prototype that I think finds some support in the available materials. The court will ask the parties to agree on an order or it will ask one party to prepare a draft. In the first case, a negotiation is stipulated. In the second, the dynamic leads almost inevitably in that direction. The draftsman understands that his proposed decree will be subject to comment and objection by the other side and that it must be approved by the court. He is therefore likely to submit it to his opponents in advance to see whether differences cannot be resolved. Even if the court itself should prepare the initial draft of the order, some form of negotiation will almost inevitably ensue upon submission of the draft to the parties for comment.

* * *

For these reasons, the judge will often find himself a personal participant in the negotiations on relief. But this course has obvious disadvantages, not least in its inroads on the judge's time and his pretentions to disinterestedness. To avoid these problems, judges have increasingly resorted to outside help— masters, amici, experts, panels, advisory committees—for information and evaluation of proposals for relief. These outside sources commonly find themselves exercising mediating and even adjudicatory functions among the parties. They may put forward their own remedial suggestions, whether at the request of the judge or otherwise.

* * *

I suggested above that a judicial decree establishing an ongoing affirmative regime of conduct is *pro tanto* a legislative act. But in actively shaping and monitoring the decree, mediating between the parties, developing his own sources of expertise and information, the trial judge has passed beyond even the role of legislator and has become a policy planner and manager.

LEVI, THE BUSINESS OF THE COURTS: A SUMMARY AND A SENSE OF PERSPECTIVE
70 F.R.D. 212 (1976).*

* * * The topic itself suggests that courts, or some courts, may be engaged in the resolution of disputes they are not well equipped to resolve, or

---

* This address by Attorney General Edward Levi was given at the Roscoe Pound Conference, 1976, and reviews the comments of several panelists on the subject,

that other institutions could resolve these kinds of disputes more efficiently and effectively. But the immediate phenomenon of concern is that the number of suits submitted for judicial resolution has increased dramatically. In addition, it is said litigation has become increasingly complex. Taken together all panelists agreed that at some point the torrent and complexity of litigation may prevent courts from devoting to those matters, as to which their exercise of judgment is critical, the necessary attention and care. Indeed it is suggested that increasingly courts are finding it difficult to act in their best tradition. For example, they are not allowing oral argument; they are deciding frequently without opinions. I believe all would agree that the courts exemplify the reasoning tradition of the application of standards to particular situations and do this in a way, as the Solicitor General said, that there is an accountability which comes at least from explanation.

Because of the volume of suits and their complexity, delays in the administration of justice have occurred. Judge Rifkind said that for some plaintiffs in some kinds of cases, the delaying effect of litigation may be the primary, perhaps the sole, reason for filing suit—simply to delay and impose expense on the other party. As Judge Higginbotham emphasizes in his paper, delay in litigation adversely affects not only the litigants, but also others—witnesses and jurors—who become involved in the system. Delay may allow the commission of further crimes or illegal actions by the defendant. Another consequence of delay and of the expense of complex litigation, Professor Sander wrote, is that potential litigants may be driven to avoidance; that is, to withdraw from situations likely to create disputes that can be resolved only by resort to the courts. Such avoidance may entail heavy social or individual costs. Several speakers emphasized that costs and delays discourage potential plaintiffs from attempting to get redress for legal wrongs.

Contributing to the number and complexity of suits is the change in the use of the courts. It was suggested the traditional model of the judicial process—a dispute between two parties resolved through the adversary system with an allocation of the burden of proof and with the judgment directly affecting only the immediate parties—has, in substantial measure, collapsed. Courts now often are engaged, not in dispute resolution in this traditional sense, but in what Judge Rifkind termed "problem solving." * * *

The "problem solving" model of the judicial process was related not only to the mass-parties, mass-remedies phenomenon, but also to the kinds of issues courts are called on to resolve. Courts have become, Judge Rifkind said, "jacks of all trades," dealing with extended variants of what Professor Sander termed "polycentric problems," which can implicate wide-ranging social and economic interests not fully or, conceivably, at all represented by the adversaries in court.

Procedural and substantive changes may be essential if the courts are to be effective and efficient. But the question then is the cost of what has been given up and whether other remedies are available. This is of course true of all the remedies suggested.

The vast growth in the dimensions and subjects of governmental concerns is undoubtedly among the chief causes of the increase in the volume of judicial business. * * *

"The Business of Courts: What Types of Disputes are Best Resolved by Judicial Action and What Kinds are Better Assigned to Another, More Appropriate Forum?"

There has been an increasing turning to the courts by the legislature. Not only have new categories of legal obligations been confided to the courts for enforcement, but obligations come surrounded with legislative indefiniteness. The turning to the courts is evidenced in the legislative use of the courts as a means of monitoring the activities of the executive by insisting on judicial review, and through the device of private litigation against government, encouraged by both the courts and the legislature, to attempt to ensure conformity with a vague legislative will or to give new substance to individual rights.

* * *

* * * Several speakers emphasized the growth in the use of the courts as mediators between the government and individuals or groups, and observed that the courts now have moved to fill voids created by the default or failure of other governmental institutions—particularly the failure to respond to the demands of individual rights or to take positive steps to achieve social justice. At this point one must recognize that concepts are slippery—one agency's determinations may be viewed by another as defaults. The question cuts deep. It raises the issue of ultimate responsibility.

* * *

In short, the speakers described a spreading judicialization of relationships, the enlargement of the use of governmental power to control and channel private activity, the concomitant increase in the necessity of creating and enforcing limitations on that power, and the increased use of the courts as the instruments to those ends. * * *

* * * The courts can be compelled or at least are willing to decide complex issues as a matter of law or right, in circumstances in which the legislature or executive has avoided or deferred decision, perhaps because the legislature or executive has determined that the data for decision are unavailable, or has decided governmental action should not reach that far.

At the same time the judicial remedy may raise expectations and generate dissatisfaction when the expectation is not fulfilled. Indeed dissatisfaction may result even when the expectation is fulfilled in this way. If we move from a consideration of the most effective administration of justice to an inquiry into the sources of dissatisfaction, then I think we have to admit we are in an area where the creation of some remedies, or the way they are created, may spread feelings of dissatisfaction. It is one thing to improve by legislation the social organization of the state; it is another thing to accomplish reform by a court-created constitutional condemnation of prior behavior as violative of the fundamental rights of man. This does not mean the condemnation has not been properly given. It does mean that a powerful weapon has to be used with care.

* * *

There is tension among the criteria presented for judicial reform. There is doubt about the courts' competence or authority to become a problem-solver for society and a desire that courts confine themselves to their traditional role. At the same time, there is great reluctance to deny access to the courts, or to deny protection of rights when, as it is said, other institutions have defaulted. The tension is understandable. But the dilemma of what happens when the theory meets an actual situation seems to point to a defect in our governmental structure.

* * *

Procedural reforms were proposed, including the way the issues in a case might be sorted out and priority given. The increased use of alternate dispute-resolving mechanisms was emphasized. Mediation and conciliation were thought by Professor Sander to be especially appropriate for disputes that arise in long term relationships. He also suggested the use of ombudsmen. Special emphasis was given to arbitration—a form of adjudication, but more informal. Indeed, there was a suggestion that arbitration clauses in contracts be required. Screening devices were discussed as means to filter out frivolous cases or to encourage settlement at the start of the court process. Some of these devices involve the allocation of litigation costs. Judge Rifkind, for example, mentioned the English practice of imposing the expense of attorneys' fees on the losing party, but noted that our history is opposed to such a rule. Other devices involve the requirement of posting a bond for defendant's costs. Professor Sander described the Massachusetts system for medical malpractice cases under which a plaintiff, before being allowed to proceed further in the court process, must convince a three-man board, composed of a doctor, lawyer and trial judge, that his claim has "prima facie" merit or, failing that, post bond for the defendant's costs. Professor Sander also described the Michigan Mediation System, under which a panel of a judge and two lawyers determines damages in tort cases in which liability is acknowledged. If the plaintiff or defendant refuses to settle for that figure determined by the panel, he is taxed for costs and attorney's fees, unless the judgment is substantially more favorable to him than the panel's estimate. Judge Rifkind suggests that a civil litigant be required initially to show "probable merit" in his claim before the case proceeds to lengthy discovery and trial. He also mentioned the variety of gates, traditionally used, although perhaps somewhat battered, to exclude some would-be litigants from the courthouse.

It was recognized that these screening devices are in tension with the notion of free access by aggrieved citizens to the courts. Care must be taken to ensure that a screening device does not work to exclude individuals for adventitious reasons. The importance of judicial resolution, to society as well as the litigant, may have no relationship whatever to the size of the claim. Professor Sander added the further point: The creation of alternative dispute resolution mechanisms may result in an actual increase in the number of disputes to be resolved governmentally. * * *

    * * *

The present reality, as described by the panelists, is that the courts are now deluged with business. It may well be that courts are no longer able to discharge their traditional function but will be required instead to assume a new role. If so, the loss will be great. Courts are like other important institutions in American life; they share the commitment to attempt to achieve appropriate excellence. There are times, however, when the nature and processes of institutions must change because their responsibilities must change. This has been the case with other institutions in American life and it may also be the case with the courts. It is possible, after all, to conceive of courts as mini-legislatures. But if courts are to function as mini-legislatures, then they must adapt to the requirements of the political process. Public opinion and political responsibility inevitably become important factors in the decision-making process. This is always the case, but the change will make the courts more vulnerable, and their service to the country will be of a different kind. One has to weigh the costs.

    * * *

COFFIN, THE FRONTIER OF REMEDIES:
A CALL FOR EXPLORATION
67 Calif.L.Rev. 983, 989 (1979).

*   *   *

Here is my catalogue of differences: [11]

	Conventional Adjudication	*New Model*
The Issue	Likely to be of private rights and duties. If public body involved, issue likely to be procedural.	Likely to involve substantive rights and means of compelling a public body to effectuate those rights.
Parties	Likely to be one "person" suing another.	Likely to be a class of individuals suing a class of officials, public institutions, and political entities.
Critical facts	Historical (what has happened) and adjudicative (relevant to rights and liabilities of the two parties).	Predictive (situation as it is likely to exist during life of decree) and legislative (relevant to continuing decree).
Governing Principle	Legal precedents.	Strategy, tactics, and potential outcomes not informed by legal precedent.
Taking of evidence	Adversary hearing and rules of evidence.	Wide participation, relaxed standards, more expert opinions.
Relief sought	Declaration, negative injunction, damages; normally narrow, closely tied to legal injury.	Affirmative injunction, affecting many beyond parties; potentially broad.
Framing of decree	Imposed by court after hearing evidence.	Large amount of negotiation.
Impact	Confined to parties.	Affects a large segment of society.
Duration of court involvement	One-time judgment.	Continuing decree; subject to reopening and amendment.
Role of Judge	Passive: adjudicative in resolving dispute between two parties in a one time, normally self-executing, judgment.	Active: legislative in framing criteria; executive in implementing decree.
Review	Abuse of discretion and error of law; sufficiency of evidence and legal precedents important.	Contribution of appellate court to policy, strategy, and tactics more important than monitoring fact findings or legal principles.

*   *   *

11. For a number of these perceptions, I am indebted to Abram Chayes and his article, The Role of the Judge in Public Law Litigation, 89 Harv.L.Rev. 1281, 1302 (1976).

2. PARTICIPATION

VINCENT v. HUGHES AIR WEST, INC.

United States Court of Appeals for the Ninth Circuit, 1977.
557 F.2d 759.*

WALLACE, CIRCUIT JUDGE.

* * *

I

On June 6, 1971, a Marine Corps jet fighter and a Hughes Air West DC–9 collided in mid-air over Duarte, California. All 49 occupants of the commercial airliner were killed, as was the pilot of the military jet. The radar man, or navigator, of the military jet parachuted to safety. Ten days later the family of Keith A. Gabel, one of the Air West passengers, filed a petition in the Central District of California to perpetuate testimony. In this petition, which contained some "class" allegations, the Gabel family (Gabel) was represented by the law firm of Miller, Bronn, Brummett & Porter (Miller firm).

On the same day that the Gabel family filed its petition, and in the following weeks, the next-of-kin of various crash victims commenced actions against Hughes and other defendants.[1] These actions, eventually to total more than 60, were brought in state and federal courts in Washington, Utah and California. More than 30 of these actions were filed in the Central District of California, all of which were assigned to the same district judge.

On June 18, 1971, the district judge ordered Hughes to file *in camera* a sealed list containing the names and addresses of all crash victims and their survivors. On July 8 Hughes complied and on July 30 the district court sent notice to next-of-kin advising them, among other things, that various actions involving the air crash had already been commenced in that court, that all actions arising out of the crash might involve common questions of law and fact on the issue of liability, that "common discovery proceedings" would be beneficial, and that the recipient of the notice should contact counsel. Also in July, the court granted the Gabel petition to perpetuate testimony. Thereafter, the Miller firm and different law firms representing various other plaintiffs commenced discovery against both Hughes and the United States.

In January 1972, the Miller firm filed a complaint on behalf of Gabel against the United States. This complaint, in addition to the individual claims, contained class allegations and sought on behalf of the entire class a declaratory judgment on the issue of liability. The

---

* Some of the court's footnotes are omitted.

1. Under the Federal Tort Claims Act, suits against the United States could not be filed until six months after claims seeking administrative relief were lodged. 28 U.S.C.A. § 2675.

complaint was accompanied by a request that this newly-commenced action be consolidated with an earlier Gabel action against Hughes and the initial petition to perpetuate testimony. After the district court granted the consolidation request, Gabel moved for an order certifying the class. Both the United States and various plaintiffs—including the plaintiffs represented on this appeal by Magana & Cathcart (Cathcart), Oliver, Sloan, Shaffer & Lindvig (Oliver), Ned Good and Floyd Demanes—opposed the motion.

The district court did not act on this motion immediately. It did, however, in April 1972, send notice to all survivors on the *in camera* list that Hughes and the United States had reached an agreement regarding their respective contribution to any eventual settlement or adverse judgment.

In July 1972, the Judicial Panel on Multidistrict Litigation, pursuant to 28 U.S.C. § 1407, transferred to the Central District of California 11 cases arising out of the crash and then pending in other districts. Nine came from the District of Utah; two from the Western District of Washington. In re Air Crash Disaster at Duarte, California, 346 F.Supp. 529 (Jud.Pan.Mult.Lit.1972); see also In re Duarte, California Air Crash Disaster, 354 F.Supp. 278 (Jud.Pan.Mult.Lit.1973). Soon thereafter, the district judge ordered all of the air crash cases consolidated for the sole purpose of determining liability. On the same day, August 30,[2] he appointed John D. Miller of the Miller firm "liaison counsel between plaintiffs' counsel" and directed Miller to call a meeting of plaintiffs' counsel

> for the purpose of agreeing upon lead counsel or a committee of lead counsel, with Mr. Miller as Chairman, for all plaintiffs, to conduct all further discovery on liability and to try the case on liability, if that becomes necessary, and to voluntarily agree upon the contribution by non-members of such committee to a fund to be deposited with the Clerk from moneys paid by defendants resulting from the above-numbered lawsuits, to reimburse said committee members for such additional work as may result from the activities of said committee, and for compensation of fees to the members of said committee for work performed for the benefit of all plaintiffs. The members of the committee will keep accurate account of their time and expenditures as members of and for said committee.

At the ordered meeting of plaintiffs' counsel, a majority of those present selected four law firms to serve as a committee of lead counsel: the Miller firm; Ray, Quinney & Nebeker of Salt Lake City; Margolis, McTernan, Scope & Sacks of Los Angeles; and Prince, Yeates, Ward, Miller & Geldzahler of Salt Lake City. (These firms are the real appellees as they have the total stake in the present appeal.) A majority of those present also agreed to let the district court determine

---

2. All dates referring to materials in the Clerk's Record are taken from the clerk's file stamp.

the method and amount of payment to lead counsel for their work. Some objected to this plan.

The proceedings of this meeting were presented to the district judge and on December 11, 1972, he confirmed the appointment of the committee of lead counsel. In support of his action, the judge noted that "there has been some unnecessary duplication of effort among plaintiffs' counsel" regarding pretrial motions and discovery and pointed to his authority under Rule 43, Fed.R.Civ.P., to "make such orders . . . as may tend to avoid unnecessary costs and delay." The court then outlined both the responsibilities of lead counsel—"to conduct all further pre-trial proceedings, to bring or oppose all motions, and to prepare and conduct the trial on the issue of liability"—and the concurrent restrictions on plaintiffs' counsel not so designated (nonlead counsel), constituting generally a prohibition against initiating either further discovery proceedings or pretrial motions without first securing approval of lead counsel. The court did not grant lead counsel an absolute veto, however. Nonlead counsel disappointed with a decision of lead counsel could "apply to the Court for an order authorizing him to file [his proposed] motion or initiate [his proposed] discovery proceeding." Regarding attorney fees, the court stated:

> Reasonable compensation for the services of the committee members and reimbursement of their costs shall be provided in such amounts as shall be fixed by the Court and shall be payable by the class members in such proportions as the Court shall determine after appropriate hearing on notice.

In this order, the court referred to "class members" because it had, two months prior to that date, granted Gabel's motion and certified the consolidated Gabel actions as a class action. Petition of Gabel, 350 F.Supp. 624 (C.D.Cal.1972). Although Gabel had moved for certification under all three subsections of Rule 23(b), Fed.R.Civ.P., the court certified the class under only the first two, Rule 23(b)(1) and (2). Accordingly, class members were extended no opportunity to opt-out, and the vigorous efforts of many plaintiffs, some of whom are present here as appellants, to exclude themselves from the class were denied.

On March 2, 1973, the Miller firm moved for an order requiring class members to deposit five percent of any judgment or settlement with the clerk of the court and prohibiting Hughes and the United States from settling any class member's claim without prior court approval. The motion also requested that Hughes and the United States be required to disclose all prior settlements with class members and to deposit with the clerk an amount equal to five percent of those settlements. In addition, the motion sought clarification from the court on the amount and source of attorneys' fees for lead counsel. The United States opposed the motion, as did many nonlead attorneys. Indeed, even a member of the committee of lead counsel, the firm of Ray, Quinney & Nebeker, opposed the motion, arguing that the five percent requirement should not extend to settlements involving class members represented by lead counsel.

After a hearing, the district judge entered an order granting substantial portions of the Miller firm's motion. Only that portion of the motion dealing with settlements already completely concluded was not incorporated in the court's order. To clarify the source of the five percent payment, the court directed that it come from the contingent fee of the claimant's attorney to the extent that that fee exceeded 20 percent of the total recovery. The balance, if any, was to be paid from the claimant's portion of the recovery.

On March 19, 1973, the district judge, sua sponte, ordered "that all of the cases not originating in this District [but transferred here] . . . are transferred to the Central District of California on all issues for all purposes." In re Aircrash Near Duarte, California, 357 F.Supp. 1013, 1016 (C.D.Cal.1973). Soon thereafter, on April 5, 1973, Hughes and the United States agreed not to contest the issue of liability, and the court immediately sent notice of this agreement to all survivors appearing on the *in camera* list. Settlement efforts then proceeded and by the end of the year most of the claimants had agreed on a settlement figure with the defendants.

As settlements were finalized and approved by the court and five percent of the recoveries deposited, the amount in the depository, generally referred to as the Special Class Fund, grew to over $450,000. In December 1973, the district court gave notice of a hearing to consider disbursement of the fund. The Miller firm and others commenced filing affidavits and other materials as proof of the time and costs they had expended on the liability issue. Some of the firms also filed pleadings and affidavits opposing the claims of various attorneys.

During four days in April 1974, the court conducted a hearing on the disbursement issue. The committee of lead counsel called two experts, as did the court. The court-appointed experts were attorneys, not involved in any of the Duarte air crash cases, with extensive experience in aviation litigation. On the basis of their testimony and the entire record of the consolidated actions, the district judge, in final orders issued in August 1974, found that the work of lead counsel was competent and benefitted all claimants by removing the liability issue, that any services of nonlead counsel were not "for and on behalf of the entire Class," and that the value of lead counsel's services was between five and ten percent of the gross recoveries. Accordingly, the district judge awarded the entire Special Class Fund, minus the costs incurred by individual attorneys on the liability issue, to the committee of lead counsel. He further directed members of that committee to reach an agreement among themselves regarding division of the fund or, in the event of a failure to do so, to submit the matter to arbitration.

Most attorneys not on the committee and their clients acquiesced in the orders. Five groups of claimants and attorneys, however, have appealed: Jewel Vincent, who "appeared" in the district court pro se but who is represented on this appeal, the claimants represented by Mr. Demanes, those represented by Mr. Good, and those represented by the Oliver and Cathcart firms in a jointly-prosecuted appeal. We have consolidated these appeals on our own motion.

II

The position of Jewel Vincent in these consolidated appeals is unique. Soon after receiving word of her husband's death in the air crash, she determined, first, that because liability was (to her) clear, she had no need to and would not file a lawsuit against any person in any court but rather would use nonjudicial means to secure recovery, and, second, that no outsider would "profit" from her husband's death. Accordingly, she directed the law firm that previously had assisted her and her husband in their business activities to commence negotiations with Hughes and the United States without filing suit. Also at her direction, her attorneys undertook this task on a per hour, rather than on a contingent fee, basis.

* * *

The only plausible basis for valid district court jurisdiction over Vincent or her settlement is the class action. But as is discussed in detail in IV, A infra, the class certification order of October 12, 1972, was erroneous. No valid class action including Vincent among its unnamed plaintiffs ever existed. Accordingly, we reverse the order of August 29, 1974, and direct that Vincent's contribution to the Special Class Fund, plus accrued interest, be returned to her.

III

Our disposition of the appeal brought by Mr. Demanes turns on a question of fact. Demanes contends that his clients concluded their settlement negotiations with Hughes and the United States in July 1972. Lead counsel were not designated until the end of August 1972 and the class was not certified until October 1972. Accordingly, Demanes contends, the district court had no basis for requiring him to contribute to the Special Class Fund; lead counsel could not possibly have conferred any benefit on his clients through their discovery efforts undertaken after their appointment. Lead counsel dispute the July settlement date and point to certain activities of Demanes as late as December 1972 that are inconsistent with a finding of a July settlement.

The evidence in the record establishes that Demanes' clients settled in July 1972. Most crucial is a pleading filed by Hughes and the United States on April 15, 1974, entitled "Compliance with Court Order of April 9, 1974" in which Hughes and the United States produced "copies of all letter offers to settle cases and copies of all letters confirming settlements in cases arising out of the mid-air collision at Duarte, California. . . . " One of those letters, from the United States to Demanes, confirms their settlement agreement; it is dated

July 11, 1972. * * * As to this issue, the final order is reversed. Demanes is entitled to a return of his deposit, plus interest.

IV

The remaining appellants (hereafter referred to jointly as "nonlead counsel" because all of the money at issue here came from the attorneys' portion of the settlements) can be treated as one for the purposes of this appeal; their cases cannot be distinguished on the basis of any material fact. To respond to the arguments of nonlead counsel, we turn first to one of the two asserted bases for the district court's orders in the present case: the federal courts' historic equity powers in class actions.

A

The propriety of a Rule 23 class action covering a mass accident, such as the crash of a commercial airliner, has generated considerable scholarly debate, e.g., 3B J. Moore, Federal Practice ¶ 23.45[3], at p. 23–811 n. 35; 7A Wright & Miller, Federal Practice & Procedure § 1783; Note, Mass Accident Class Actions, 60 Cal.L.Rev. 1615 (1972); Annot., 28 A.L.R.Fed. 719 (1976), and to a more limited extent analysis by the federal courts, e.g., McDonnell Douglas Corp. v. United States District Court, 523 F.2d 1083 (9th Cir. 1975), cert. denied, 425 U.S. 911, 96 S.Ct. 1506, 47 L.Ed.2d 761 (1976); Causey v. Pan American World Airways, Inc., 66 F.R.D. 392 (E.D.Va.1975); Petition of Gabel, supra, 350 F.Supp. 624. It is now settled in this circuit, however, that a class action brought on behalf of the next-of-kin of aircrash victims and certified under Rule 23(b)(1) or (2) is not proper. McDonnell Douglas Corp. v. United States District Court, supra, 523 F.2d 1083. * * *

* * *

Because the class was certified only under 23(b)(1) and 23(b)(2), we must conclude, on authority of McDonnell Douglas Corp. v. United States District Court, supra, 523 F.2d 1083, that no valid class action ever existed and that the district court's equitable authority over attorneys and attorneys' fees under Rule 23 [5] cannot serve in the present case, where nonlead counsel objected to the class, to sustain the court's orders. We turn, therefore, to a related theory upon which lead counsel primarily rely: the "common benefit" doctrine.

B

In its traditional form, and as originally developed, the common benefit rule was limited to the reimbursement or award of attorneys' fees from an identifiable fund under the court's control and was referred to as the "common fund" doctrine. More recently, within approximately the last 20 years, a significant variation on the common

---

5. See generally 7A Wright & Miller, Federal Practice & Procedure § 1803; Dawson, Lawyers and Involuntary Clients in Public Interest Litigation, 88 Harv.L. Rev. 849, 915–29 (1975); Annot., 38 A.L.R.3d 1384 (1971).

fund approach has appeared, generally referred to as the "substantial benefit" doctrine.[6] See generally Dawson, Lawyers and Involuntary Clients: Attorney Fees from Funds, 87 Harv.L.Rev. 1597 (1974) (hereafter cited as I Dawson); Dawson, Lawyers and Involuntary Clients in Public Interest Litigation, 88 Harv.L.Rev. 849 (1975) (hereafter cited as II Dawson); Note, Reimbursement for Attorneys' Fees from the Beneficiaries of Representative Litigation, 58 Minn.L.Rev. 933 (1974). * * *
          * * *

Certain elements of the common fund doctrine, either as developed in these two cases or as fashioned in the many cases applying the doctrine since, are relevant to the present case. First, the original client's attorney's fees are not shifted to—or the attorney's personal claim for an extra fee is not lodged against—the adversary-losing party; rather, fees are shifted to third parties, people viewed as beneficiaries of the fund in some way. Second, no contractual relationship exists between the original attorney and the third parties. Rather, the common fund doctrine is rooted in concepts of quasi-contract and restitution. Third, the beneficiaries are expected to pay litigation costs in proportion to the benefits that the litigation produced for them. See [I Dawson] at 1633. Fourth, as a general rule, if the third parties hire their own attorneys and appear in the litigation, the original claimant cannot shift to them his attorney's fees. See id. at 1647–51. Some cases stand as an exception to this element, however. E.g., Doherty v. Bress, 104 U.S.App.D.C. 308, 262 F.2d 20 (1958), cert. denied, 359 U.S. 934, 79 S.Ct. 649, 3 L.Ed.2d 636 (1959). Fifth, the third parties are not personally liable for the litigation costs. Any claim must be satisfied out of the fund. Note, supra, 58 Minn.L.Rev. at 944. A concomitant element of the doctrine, indeed one of its foundation stones, is that there must exist some identifiable assets on which a court can impose a charge. See I Dawson 1618. Nevertheless, the concept of "fund" is flexible, and it is now settled that a money judgment or even a settlement can serve as a fund. Id. at 1620; Doherty v. Bress, supra, 262 F.2d 20. What is crucial is that the court can legitimately exercise authority or control over the asset. I Dawson 1618.

Some of these elements are clearly satisfied in this case. For example, the extra fee awarded to lead counsel came from beneficiaries of the litigation (or, more accurately in most cases, from their attorneys) in proportion to the benefits that the litigation produced for them.[9] No fee was awarded against Hughes or the United States. Further, although the participation of most counsel in the "selection"

---

6. The variation is sufficiently extensive that some commentators have categorized the substantial benefit doctrine as a separate exception to the general rule that the prevailing party is not entitled to collect a reasonable attorney's fee from the loser. E.g., Case Note, 1975 B.Y.U.L.Rev. 777, 780–81; cf. Note, Attorney Fees: Exceptions to the American Rule, 25 Drake L.Rev. 717, 729–33 (1976).

9. In his findings of fact, the district judge stated that "the reasonable value of the legal services of Class Counsel of Benefit to all Class Members on the issue of liability is not less than 5% of the total recoveries of Class Members." The clear implication of this statement is that the efforts of lead counsel had benefitted each member of the class at least to the extent

of lead counsel has somewhat the flavor of a consensual agreement, it is clear that the district court, in granting the award, proceeded on concepts of quasi-contract and restitution and not on any theory of contract enforcement. Finally, lead counsel were given a charge on the Special Class Fund, not a personal judgment against any claimant or nonlead counsel.

> * * *

The general rule that third parties can "purchase immunity"[12] by hiring their own attorneys and participating in the litigation poses greater problems. * * *

Nevertheless, the courts have created an exception to this general rule where the contributions of the original or lead attorneys and the attorneys hired by the "stranger" beneficiaries are unequal. See I Dawson 1648–51; but cf. Estate of Korthe, 9 Cal.App.3d 572, 576–77, 88 Cal.Rptr. 465 (1970). The purpose of this exception is of course identical to the purpose of the broader common fund doctrine itself: avoidance of unjust enrichment, or as it has been referred to in this litigation, "coattailing." The leading decision demonstrating this exception, Doherty v. Bress, supra, 262 F.2d 20, is also, of all the cases we have discovered, the case most factually similar to the present case. * * *

> * * *

C

As noted above, the disparity in the efforts of lead and nonlead counsel was effectively compelled by provisions in the district court's order confirming the appointment of lead counsel. On this appeal, nonlead counsel make a frontal attack on the power of the district court to promulgate such an order, specifically to appoint lead counsel in multiparty litigation and to restrict the activities of nonlead counsel. We believe that the district court has such power and that the district court properly exercised it in these consolidated cases.

In recent decades, complex multiparty litigation has become an increasingly frequent occurrence in the federal district courts. The causes are many and include, in addition to the substantive laws underlying much of this litigation, the liberal joinder and intervention rules of the Federal Rules of Civil Procedure, Rules 19–20, 24, the provisions of Rule 42(a) permitting consolidation of actions, the provisions of 28 U.S.C.A. § 1404 permitting transfer by a single district judge, and the significant transfer authority granted to the Judicial Panel on Multidistrict Litigation by 28 U.S.C.A. § 1407. With this advent of complex multiparty litigation have come serious administrative problems, and the federal courts have found it necessary to develop innovative procedures to meet the problems. One of the earlier-devised procedures was the appointment of a "liaison counsel." The liaison

of five percent of the amount recovered by the class member.

12. See Dawson, Lawyers and Involuntary Clients: Attorney Fees from Funds, 87 Harv.L.Rev. 1597, 1649 (1974).

counsel serves all parties on one side of the dispute. He is selected either by his colleagues or by the court, and his duties are generally ministerial. For example, he may receive and distribute to the parties on his side notices and other documents from the court or adverse parties, or he may call meetings where joint action is considered. The concept of liaison counsel was incorporated in an early edition of the Manual for Complex Litigation. See Manual for Complex and Multidistrict Litigation § 1.9 (1970).

The limited scope of both liaison counsel's authority and his duties, however, sometimes created new problems, especially for plaintiffs in multidistrict aircrash cases. See Beatty, The Impact of Consolidated Multidistrict Proceedings on Plaintiffs in Mass-Disaster Litigation, 38 J.Air L. & Comm. 183, 185–91 (1972). Accordingly, proposals were advanced calling for creation of the role of "lead counsel," an attorney or group of attorneys with significant authority and a concomitant responsibility to conduct pretrial discovery and, if necessary, to litigate the liability issue. See id. at 189–91. In 1972, the editors of the Manual for Complex Litigation incorporated many of these proposals in section 1.92 of the Manual.[14]

Although some courts at an earlier time apparently doubted their power to create the role of lead counsel and oversee its filling, Beatty, supra, 38 J.Air L. & Comm. at 191, by the time section 1.92 was added to the Manual for Complex Litigation the authority of the district courts regarding lead counsel was well-established. MacAlister v. Gu-

---

14. Section 1.92 reads in part:

In complex and multidistrict litigation involving multiple opposing parties, lead counsel and steering committees have proved to be unusually efficient in pretrial proceedings. Lead counsel are the counsel chosen by the groups of parties having a common interest to brief and argue motions, file opposing briefs in pretrial proceedings initiated by other parties, to prepare proposed written interrogatories, to initiate and conduct proceedings and motions for production and inspection of documents, and to conduct the examination of witnesses in depositions on oral interrogatories, among other things. While the court should not, in the absence of exceptional circumstances, select and appoint lead counsel, the court can request the parties to select such counsel and encourage the use of lead counsel. Liaison counsel may also act as lead counsel generally or in particular proceedings. In massive litigation where depositions are scheduled simultaneously in several different locations, it will be necessary that there be more than one lead counsel for the groups or parties interested in the depositions. Similarly, it is the court which must make a final determination of any

question of whether lead counsel is able to continue as lead counsel. It is also the court which must grant permission to withdraw, as lead counsel. See Part I, § 1.44, p. 46, supra.

At trial of cases involving a large number of parties represented by different counsel, the court should encourage the opposing parties to select lead counsel to conduct the initial examinations of witnesses, permitting supplemental and non-repetitive questioning by counsel for other parties. And where the parties fail to agree upon a selection, it may be necessary for the court to select and designate the lead counsel who will conduct the initial examination for the opposing parties and groups of parties.

In order to provide leadership for large groups of parties and to coordinate the actions of groups of parties having common interests, the use of steering committees has been beneficial. A steering committee may consist of a number of counsel chosen by the group having a common interest to meet, confer, and to take coordinated action on behalf of the group. The court should encourage the use of steering committees in appropriate cases.

terma, 263 F.2d 65 (2d Cir. 1958), represented "the first time that the power of the courts to order consolidation for the pre-trial stages and the appointment of general [lead] counsel to supervise and coordinate the prosecution of plaintiffs' case [was] presented to a federal appellate court." Id. at 67. Defendants in a stockholders' derivative suit moved the district court for an order consolidating various related actions and appointing lead counsel for the consolidated plaintiffs. The district court refused. On appeal, the Second Circuit held that the district court had the "inherent powers" to consolidate and appoint lead counsel but that in that case, the district judge had not abused his discretion in refusing to do so. In support of its decision regarding the district court's authority to appoint lead counsel, the Second Circuit noted:

> The benefits achieved by consolidation and the appointment of general counsel, i.e. elimination of duplication and repetition and in effect the creation of a coordinator of diffuse plaintiffs through whom motions and discovery proceedings will be channeled, will most certainly redound to the benefit of all parties to the litigation. The advantages of this procedure should not be denied litigants in the federal courts because of misapplied notions concerning interference with a party's right to his own counsel.

Id. at 69 (citation omitted).

The authority recognized in *MacAlister* has never been seriously disputed. Indeed, many courts since that decision have explicitly reaffirmed their authority to appoint lead counsel and have exercised that authority. See, e.g., Katz v. Realty Equities Corp., 521 F.2d 1354, 1356 (2d Cir. 1975); Farber v. Riker-Maxson Corp., 442 F.2d 457 (2d Cir. 1971); Feldman v. Hanley, 49 F.R.D. 48 (S.D.N.Y.1969); Abrams v. Occidental Petroleum Corp., 44 F.R.D. 543 (S.D.N.Y.1968). In *Abrams,* for example, the district court took action similar to that taken by the district judge in this case. The court appointed lead counsel but limited his authority to discovery and other pretrial proceedings. Nonlead counsel's activities were restricted but they were permitted, in the event of a dispute with lead counsel, to seek special permission from the court to take independent action. The court also indicated that it would fix reasonable compensation for lead counsel after a hearing on the matter.

We likewise hold that the district court had the authority to direct the appointment of a committee of lead counsel.[15] * * *

  *   *   *

15. It is conceivable that the district court's authority to appoint lead counsel could serve as an independent basis for an order awarding lead or liaison counsel an extra fee for their services. We need not finally decide that question in this case, however. Regarding all the appellants but Vincent and Demanes, the traditional common fund doctrine is available to sustain the district court's orders. Regarding Vin- cent and Demanes, we are convinced that any attorneys' fees doctrine based on the district court's power to appoint lead counsel would require, as does the common fund doctrine, control over a fund or jurisdiction over the parties and a finding of benefit-in-fact. Accordingly, we deem it unnecessary to resolve at this time the question raised here.

NOTE ON PARTICIPATION IN COMPLEX SUITS

All the rules on joinder of parties have special relevance in complex suits. See particularly Fairview Park Excavating Co. v. Al Monzo Construction Co., supra p. 745; Atlantis Development Corp. v. United States, supra p. 752; Bustop v. Superior Court, supra p. 763; and Saylor v. Lindsley, supra p. 888. See also Trangsrud, Joinder Alternatives in Mass Tort Litigation, 70 Cornell L.Rev. 779 (1985).

3. CASE MANAGEMENT

INTRODUCTORY NOTE ON PRETRIAL MANAGEMENT
OF BIG CASES

1. Complex cases can be identified by the fact that they involve large stakes, broad-ranging discovery, and sometimes multiple parties. The pretrial stage of such cases is critical. As observed in Withrow and Larm, The "Big" Antitrust Case: 25 Years of Sisyphean Labor, 62 Corn.L.Rev. 1, 5 (1976):

> "[W]e maintain that the crux of truly fair and efficient management of large cases is still 'iron-hearted' control by the judge. * * * Second, we believe that large antitrust litigations would be better controlled and certainly more fairly adjudicated if it were frankly recognized that pretrial, and not trial, is where the merits of such cases are revealed. Trial, if it occurs at all, is but the final denouement of pretrial adjudication, save in the case where pretrial responsibilities have been neglected by the presiding judge."

For doctrine on management of the big case, see Federal Judicial Center, Manual for Complex Litigation (5th rev. 1980). Compare Kendig, Procedures for Management of Non-Routine Cases, 3 Hofstra L.Rev. 701 (1975); Kaminsky, Proposed Federal Discovery Rules for Complex Civil Litigation, 48 Ford.L.Rev. 907 (1980); Brazil, Improving Judicial Controls Over the Pretrial Development of Civil Actions, 1981 Am.Bar.Found.Res.J. 873; Peckham, The Federal Judge as a Case Manager: The New Role in Guiding a Case from Filing to Disposition, 69 Calif.L.Rev. 770 (1981); Am. College of Trial Lawyers, Recommendations on Major Issues Affecting Complex Litigation, 90 F.R.D. 207 (1981); Symposium, Litigation Management, 53 U.Chi.L.Rev. 305 (1986). But see Resnik, Managerial Judges, 96 Harv.L.Rev. 374 (1982). Compare Hazard and Rice, infra p. 1224. See also McGovern, Toward a Functional Approach for Managing Complex Litigation, 53 U.Chi.L.Rev. 440 (1986), discussing the resolution of three complex cases (an environmental case in Michigan, a utilities rate case in Alabama, and an asbestos case in Ohio) and pointing out the importance of effective participation by the effective "players." The effective players are not limited to the formal parties but may include political action groups and attorneys for the parties.

2. Chief among the special pretrial problems in big cases is the handling of masses of documents in discovery. See, e.g., Sherman and Kinnard, Development, Discovery, and Use of Computer Support Systems in Achieving Efficiency in Litigation, 79 Colum.L.Rev. 267 (1979), summarizing techniques and making suggestions for more efficiency. The techniques used by litigants for this purpose are themselves important lawyer work product. Compare Note, Work Product Protection for Compilations of Nonparty Documents, 66 Va.L.Rev. 1323 (1980). A nonparty who incurs substantial cost in complying with a subpoena

to produce documents may be able to recover the cost involved from the party demanding the documents. See United States v. Columbia Broadcasting System, Inc., 666 F.2d 364 (9th Cir. 1982); Calif.Evid.Code § 1563.

3. As so often is the case, cases of novel dimensions invite substantive or quasi-substantive innovation as well as "procedural" and "administrative" adaptation. See, e.g., Vasquez v. Superior Court, supra p. 842, and In re Northern District of California Dalkon Shield IUD Products Liability Litigation, supra p. 854.

HAZARD AND RICE, JUDICIAL MANAGEMENT OF THE PRETRIAL PROCESS IN MASSIVE LITIGATION: SPECIAL MASTERS AS CASE MANAGERS
1982 A.B.F.Res.J. 375.*

INTRODUCTION

Management of the pretrial and trial processes in massive complex litigation has received considerable attention over the past few decades. The most recent general study is the 1979 report of the National Commission for the Review of Antitrust Laws and Procedures. * * *

To achieve more effective judicial control, a variety of proposals have been made for management of the pretrial processes. Aside from the 1979 Commission report, proposals have been made in the Manual for Complex Litigation, in the Report of the Judicial Conference of the United States on Procedure in Antitrust and Other Protracted Cases (the Prettyman Report), and in the Handbook of Recommended Procedures for the Trial of Protracted Cases. * * *

Although it acknowledges that effective judicial control will lead to cooperative efforts between counsel and decrease the need for sanctions, the Commission strongly supports strengthening the sanction provisions and using them more frequently to deter dilatory and abusive conduct.

Although many of these proposals are essential to effective management of litigation, we believe that they are only initial steps in the process of management. To varying degrees in each set of proposals the recommendations are incomplete and in some instances misdirected both in concept and in technique. All of the proposals consider the litigation almost exclusively in terms of the goals and viewpoints of the judge. They do not differentiate various functions that a judge performs in a case. They rely almost exclusively on management by directive: the judge issues orders, the litigants obey. Some tend to equate rigidity with firmness. Finally, the proposals are almost entirely procedural: they deal with the techniques for initiating and terminating issues without any attention to the content of decisions. Usually they call for additional or alternate procedures without taking into account the novel problems of specific litigation.

These limitations are cumulative: taken together they amount to a system in which the judge should control the case by making decisions and issuing orders, which the litigants will obey and thus move the case forward. This convention for managing massive cases seems to us wooden and literally uneconomical. * * *

* * * Our vantage point was that of special masters—lawyers appointed by a United States district judge as quasi-judicial officers to supervise certain aspects of these large cases. * * *

Limited in scope and purpose, our article is essentially a "debriefing" of our experience in supervising a complex case. Its aim is to suggest a concept of management of complex cases somewhat different from what now generally prevails. At this time we inquire rather than demonstrate, simply because we have not done the extensive comparative studies required to sustain a more powerful argument.

I. History of the Action

The complaint in United States v. American Telephone & Telegraph Co. was filed on November 20, 1974. In broad, sweeping, and typically vague language, it alleged that section 2 of the Sherman Act was violated by the American Telephone and Telegraph Company (AT&T), which owns all or part of the stock in 23 Bell Operating Companies; Western Electric Company, Inc. (Western Electric), which is wholly owned by AT&T; and Bell Telephone Laboratories, Inc., which is owned in equal parts by Western Electric and AT&T. It was contended that an unlawful combination and conspiracy existed between AT&T, the 23 Bell Operating Companies, and the other defendants to restrict competition from purveyors of other telecommunications services and from other manufacturers and suppliers of telecommunications equipment. It was alleged that the defendants achieved and were maintaining their monopoly over the telecommunications industry through illegal practices. The primary relief sought by the government was divestiture of various parts of the AT&T system.

* * *

II. The Pretrial Program—Generally

As originally filed, the action was assigned to Judge Waddy. * * *

We were appointed special masters to adjudicate claims of privilege. Our appointment, upon nomination by the parties, came about through recognition by the parties that the volume of anticipated privilege claims was so great that neither the judge nor the magistrate could fairly adjudicate them within a reasonable period of time because of the other responsibilities they had to assume.

Immediately after our appointment Judge Waddy had to resign the case because of ill health, whereupon the case was assigned to Judge Harold H. Greene. * * *

Judge Greene and the two of us thus came into the case late, after discovery had been going on in a desultory way for 3 years and in an intensive way for about 6 months. Judge Waddy's orders had established a division of responsibility between us and Magistrate Lawrence S. Margolis, but the division boundary was unclear. Judge Greene undertook to redesign the pretrial process in a way that was generally consistent with the orders previously issued by Judge Waddy but also more purposive and urgent.

Although we all did the best we could, in retrospect this arrangement suggests at least three serious mistakes in handling a big case. First, it is a mistake to have a horizontal division of responsibility between judge and magistrate or magistrate and special master. By horizontal division, we mean a coordinate division of responsibility over subject matter. In United States v. AT&T this division had discovery go to the magistrate, privilege claims to the special masters, and everything else to the judge. In this arrangement coordination theoretically is defined in orders and policed through appeals to the judge from the magistrate or special master. But the swirl of pretrial does not categorize so easily, and coordination by these means is slow and rigid. As things evolved, there emerged a vertical division of responsibility. We as special masters became responsible for almost all of the pretrial under the judicial authority and administrative superintendence of the judge. This allowed a division of labor between the judge and the subordinate judicial officers but put both the judge and us in a position to see and guide the case as a whole. The result was much closer coordination of the court responses to various parts of the case.

A second mistake, an unavoidable one, was the reassignment of the case from one judge to another. This turned out well in this particular case because of Judge Greene's unusual ability. However, the change in administration took a long time to become fully effective. It is generally recognized that a big case should be handled by one judge from start to finish, if possible. Our experience validates that proposition.

A third mistake was trying to fix the timetable for the case once and for all at the beginning. Judge Waddy had aimed at this objective, as called for in standard doctrine on management of big cases. At the time of our entry in the case it was evident that the schedule had become unrealistic. Judge Greene sought to remedy this and did so to the extent of rescheduling several stages of the process. However, we believe that he also may have sought to forecast too rigidly the conduct of a very complex and inherently unknowable course of events. We recognize the need for firm schedules and for a trial date target. We recognize also that in some sense the lawyers will never be fully ready for trial and hence have to be prodded and perhaps ultimately bludgeoned into going to the mark. On the other hand, we think that good planning anticipates flexibility and requires, to some extent, the capacity for feeling one's way along. Fortunately, neither of these was missing in Judge Greene's supervision of our management of his pretrial program. An unpleasant but intractable feature of a schedule for any complex unpracticed event is that it declines rapidly in its reliability the farther it projects into the future. A big trial is quintessentially a complex unpracticed event.

* * *

Judge Greene's role in supervising the case was three-fold. First, he prescribed the basic rules—the constitution of the litigation, as it were. These rules established the general timetable, the events to be accomplished within the timetable, and our responsibility and authority. By implication they defined his residual authority over matters not delegated to us. Second, Judge Greene was the appellate judicial authority for all adjudicative decisions we might make. We had no unreviewable discretion, although as it turned out our decisions and exercises of discretion were appealed on relatively few occasions. Third, Judge Greene monitored our administration. We kept him generally advised on the status, progress, and prospects of the case. On certain matters, particularly as the trial date approached, we gave him detailed written reports.

* * *

Three techniques of control were thus used—rules, adjudication, and administration. Different procedures were used in each technique, including party proposals with regard to rules, formal argument in adjudication, and informal discussion and negotiation in administration. Both rules (i.e., general orders governing the case) and adjudication were conducted by the conventional legal procedure of briefing, hearing, and ruling. In general, when administration was involved we worked with the parties or with the judge, and often as a go-between; rarely did Judge Greene become involved with the parties in give-and-take discussions over management of the case. This distance protected the court's detachment. It also reduced the amount of "gaming" between the judge and the parties. Much of the "gaming" that was inevitably necessary was carried out through us as brokers.

III. Approaching the Management Task

    *   *   *

We believe that the judicial participation necessary for coping effectively with these other problems of delay can be accomplished only through the drastic alteration of the way the court is apprised of and responds to the needs of the litigation. The court must be able to act quickly on every issue that threatens to delay the process. This can be accomplished only through (1) altering the formal procedures for bringing matters to the court for resolution, (2) expanding the flow of information (through an increase in quantity, quality, and the speed with which it is conveyed) between the litigants and the court through informal lines of communication, and (3) tailoring the procedures to accommodate the needs of each case.

IV. The Supervision Process

A. Procedural Rules

The discovery process, specifically Federal Rules 26–37, offers an excellent example of the need for changes. Under present law, the court's involvement in the discovery process after establishing the schedule is limited to the resolution of disputes brought to it by formal motion. If, for example, a request for documents is made under Rule 34, there is no judicial screening of the reasonableness of the demand. Indeed, the court is not even notified of its service on the opposing party. The party upon whom the request has been served has 30 days to respond or to object. If either the documents requested or the proposed schedule for production is contested, the parties are expected to attempt to negotiate an acceptable compromise. To this point the court has received neither the Rule 34 request nor notification of the pending dispute. It is only when compromise efforts have failed that the court is brought into the affray by the demanding party's filing a Motion to Compel Discovery under Rule 37. The dispute will not be ripe for judicial resolution, however, for at least two more weeks and often longer depending on the time allowed in the local rules of practice for response and reply briefs. Thereafter the matter will be placed on the motion calendar for oral presentation to the court. This often causes another week of delay. As a consequence, at least 2 months will have elapsed from the time the dispute arose until judicial action is possible, and in the normal course of litigation, more than 3 months would not be uncommon. Even then, owing to demands on the time of the presiding judicial officer, there will usually be additional delays before the matter is resolved.

Depending on the nature of the disputes that have arisen, the entire document discovery process may have lain dormant for this period of time. Yet legally no delay has occurred, because the parties have complied with all applicable procedural details. This scenario must be repeated each time a dispute arises in the numerous discovery requests in large cases. The resulting impact on the pretrial schedule is disastrous. Either the overall schedule collapses, or the recalcitrant party wins by attrition, or both. The standard discovery procedures, which may be justified in run-of-the-mill litigation, ill serve the ends of justice in the big case.

Our solution to this problem has been to require that all discovery demands be filed with us. This is done, not for our screening and approval, but to keep us apprised of developments in the action. If the responding party objects to a demand for any reason, he must file a written objection within 10 days. Hearings on objections are set within 7 days of their filing. This practice shifts the burden of seeking court assistance from the demanding party to the responding party and establishes a specific time period within which to do so. Briefs are accepted either at the hearing or within a short period of time thereafter. All discovery must be completed under each demand within 30 days of the request or of the court order. Failure to do so must be justified in writing. We have found that this practice ensures that developing problems are addressed from their inception. In fact, our experience has been that all discovery disputes can be resolved in a shorter period than is allowed under existing discovery rules for making objections to the demanding party. And production under this procedure is usually completed before those disputes would have been presented to the court under the existing practice.

*   *   *

This brings out another point about administering a big case: the court, whether by itself or through a magistrate or special master, should insist on promptness in the subsidiary adjudications and other transactions within the case. Every issue requiring adjudication should be briefed and argued expeditiously, and it should also be decided expeditiously. *   *   * Decision time for the court is often down time for the parties, bringing the progress of the case to a temporary halt. If there is a series of such halts, the whole train of motion slows or stops. We surmise that many judges do not understand the dynamics of this movement, which becomes crucial in big litigation where there are so many tasks so complexly interlinked.

*   *   *

B. Informality

*   *   *

To maximize our management potential and minimize any delay that might arise in the various processes, we encouraged the parties to communicate informally with us on matters they felt required or would benefit from our immediate action. We met regularly with the parties on an informal basis— usually once a month, but during periods of intense activity we often met on a weekly basis. We were in daily telephone contact with them. Often we initiated these contacts to stay abreast of developing issues and to check on the parties' compliance with informal commitments they had made. Through this informality the lines of communication between the parties and the court were kept open. This maximized their use and efficiency and, as a consequence, our knowledge and understanding of the dynamics of each process and the problems being encountered by each party. It enabled us to resolve disputes more quickly and sensitively because of a better understanding of their origins, details, and implications. In many instances we were able to avoid or resolve problems before they caused delay. In all instances we were able to resolve problems before they reached their full delaying potential under the standard procedures.

* * *

Critical to the success of efficient pretrial is thus the ability of the court to respond promptly and authoritatively to the myriad questions that arise in that stage. The court must appreciate that parties are constantly having to make important tactical decisions, both substantive and procedural, that are freighted with enormous economic and legal consequences. The court must be willing and able to respond clearly, decisively, and with the same speed that is expected of the parties.

The same general point can be seen from a somewhat different angle. It has long since been observed that in modern complex litigation, pretrial and trial merge into each other. Certainly, in a big case, pretrial is as unrehearsed, spontaneous, and risk laden as a trial ever was. Taking the point one step further, pretrial *is* a trial: it is a close, contentious interaction between contending legal forces for procedural dominance and control of the instruments of legal victory. If a fair and orderly trial at trial requires the continuous presence of a judicial officer—observing, administering, admonishing, guiding, and ruling—the same is true for the trial at pretrial.

C. Tailoring of Procedures to the Litigation at Hand

1. *The Privilege Claim Process*

a) The scope of the problem ☐☐ As indicated, our initial responsibilities were limited to the resolution of privilege claims. At the time of our appointment it was estimated that the documents being withheld on privilege grounds by the litigants and third parties numbered in the tens of thousands. The sheer volume of materials to be read and evaluated was overwhelming. The diverse statutory privileges that potentially could be asserted, particularly by the government agencies, made a further complication. Also, the law was unclear on several vital points, particularly whether the "control group" test limited the attorney-client privilege.

* * *

One of the significant steps taken to expedite the production process and to reduce potential privilege claims was the issuance of protective orders by Judge Greene. In substance, these orders shielded all documents produced from inspection by third parties and precluded use of the documents for purposes other than the instant litigation. * * *

A second aspect of the protective order was also important. The court ordered that a waiver of privilege would not result when a document was produced inadvertently to the opposing side. By eliminating the risk of inadvertent waiver through the production of documents, the order eliminated the necessity of hypercareful scrutiny of each document prior to its disclosure. The waiver doctrine entails the result of waiver not only of the claim for the particular document, but for any other document relating to the same subject matter. For this reason, the risk it poses is enormous. This permitted relatively free exchange of the exceptionally large mass of demanded and subpoenaed materials. As things worked out in practice, in many instances an adequate level of protection was achieved merely by the designation "protected"—a procedure that avoided the time, trouble, and expense required to make formal privilege assertions.

To guide the parties in asserting privilege claims and to minimize the number of inappropriate claims, we promulgated substantive guidelines for resolving those claims. We tried to make these guidelines specific enough that marginal claims, as well as the clearly inappropriate ones, could more readily be distinguished. We hoped that as a result the parties would examine each document more carefully and critically before asserting a privilege claim. We also realized that making a claim could be initially "cheap" unless a party was required to support the claim factually. And we realized that if claims could be made cheaply, it would be expensive for everyone to hear and determine them. Hence, we wanted a procedure in which successfully asserting a claim necessitated submitting written evidence sufficient to substantiate each element of the claim. * * * However, the material supplied in support of an initial claim under our system also was prima facie sufficient to sustain the claim. It was also a sufficient description of the document to constitute fair notice to the opposing party to make informed objection. Hence, the first cost in the procedure was also most of the total cost. That cost was laid on the party seeking the benefit of the privilege. A less technical procedure with a lower initial cost would probably have entailed a greater total cost for each claim, would have shifted more of the cost to the objecting party, and therefore probably would have resulted in more claims.

b) Substantive and procedural guidelines □□ The substantive and procedural guidelines for claiming privilege were promulgated by order of the special masters and submitted to the presiding judge for his approval. This was done to establish the substantive and procedural law of the case so that there could be no appeals of individual privilege decisions on any basis other than the application of the established standards. This approval process resulted in a reduction in both the number and scope of appeals and in the inherent uncertainty of the process.

A note is appropriate as to how the substantive guidelines were drafted. In essence, we held a rule-making proceeding. Each party was asked to tender substantive proposals in the form of rules or a restatement of the law of privilege, together with supporting analysis and authorities. We revised and integrated these submissions into a draft, which we circulated to the parties for comment. We revised the draft in light of the comments and then submitted the product to Judge Greene for review. The parties were given the opportunity to object. The rules were then settled by Judge Greene and promulgated by him through a declaratory order establishing the rules as guidelines.

    * * *

2. Isolating the Contested Issues

a) Statements of contention and proof □□ In the normal course of litigation, particularly in complex actions, the litigants draft their pleadings with sufficient ambiguity to "leave their options open." Broad allegations compel each party to develop evidence supporting or responding to all factual contentions the other party might conceivably advance under the pleadings. If uncontrolled, this situation not only inflates discovery but makes trial a dumping ground for every piece of evidence that either side believes might have some relevance to any factual contention or legal theory in the case. Such is the modern system of simplified pleadings as it works in big cases.

The pleadings in United States v. AT&T were of this kind. Discovery was correspondingly broad and expensive. To identify the issues as discovery was completed, the court required the parties to file a series of Statements of

Contentions and Proof. In these Statements the parties were required to describe with particularity each factual contention it was advancing in support of its claims or defense and to list the witnesses and documentary evidence to be used to prove each factual contention. There were to be three iterations of these statements as discovery progressed. Theoretically coordinated with completion of phases of discovery, the successive statements were to be progressively more focused in substance, nonconclusory in form, and preclusory in effect.

* * *

The Supreme Court has construed the pleading rules to permit a party to go forward with very general allegations until after discovery. So long as this view obtains, it would seem impermissible to require parties to make, through Statements of Contention, binding positional commitments in advance of discovery. * * *

Limiting discovery is one thing, guiding it is something else. It seems to us that the early iterations of Statements of Contentions should be used not to limit discovery but to provide an agenda for discovery. * * *

Requiring detailed Statements of Contention and Proof *after* discovery is substantially completed is also something else. Here the purpose is not to limit discovery but to pull together the sprawling evidence, to find out what is in dispute, and to arrange an order of proof for trial. The Second Statements of Contention and Proof in United States v. AT&T did not quite do this. They had been filed before discovery was complete, when the parties were not ready to "close the books" on available evidence. Also, they were not explicitly intended as an order of proof. Indeed, the pretrial order anticipated that there would be a Third Statement of Contention and Proof after discovery completion and before trial.

As things worked out, however, the Second Statement of Contentions became the basis of something like a massive pretrial conference that did isolate the issues in dispute and establish, tentatively at least, an order of proof. * * *

b) The stipulation process □□ * * * The Statements were important because they required the parties to organize their cases. The Statements could be used in the negotiation of stipulations, however, only if their corresponding contentions were aligned. Through such alignment there is a specific joining of the factual issues upon which negotiations had to focus. Thereafter, the process of weaving the contentions into one narrative statement of the issues of the case would be a relatively simple matter of language modification.

It was agreed by the parties that the case would be divided into 82 episodes. Each episode constituted a distinct transaction or set of related transactions, and its narrative contained both parties' contentions. The word processor printouts displayed the integrated Statements in a two-column format. The right column was for Contentions, and the left was for Stipulations. At the beginning of negotiations all contentions were, of course, displayed on the right side. The source of each contention was indicated by the prefix "Plaintiff contends" or "Defendants contend." As factual allegations were agreed to, after the parties examined the supporting evidence and negotiated changes in the language, those allegations became tentative stipulations and were moved from the right to the left column. When a statement was moved to the left, all indications of source (whether plaintiff or defendant) and citations to supporting evidentiary materials were deleted. The contentions upon which agreement could not be reached remained in the right column along with the identification of source and of their evidentiary support. Following each contention the opposing party would indicate why it refused to stipulate. This indication served to join the factual issues.

Stipulation/Contention printouts served three general purposes. First, in advance of trial, a vast mass of factual data was organized into manageable, understandable segments or "episodes." Second, the undisputed factual matters were set forth in narrative, and the disputed ones were catalogued. Third, with regard to the contested allegations, the parties were required to organize their evidence and present a firm list of the witnesses and documentary evidence upon which they intended to rely. The end product was a combined narrative stipulation, pretrial order of issues in dispute, and a tentative order of proof. The printout focused all legal and factual issues in dispute and provided the judge with a tool for managing the trial and a format for the ultimate findings of fact.

c) *Supervising the negotiations* □□ * * * In the large majority of instances, negotiations proceeded smoothly. It was the consensus of the participants, however, that even these negotiations would have gone better with closer supervision. Discussions could have been more focused, and disputes could have been resolved before giving rise to delay. In most instances the disputes that arose, even though intractable without intervention, were not perceived to be important enough to solicit special intervention by the special masters. Their cumulative effect, however, was significant.

d) *The product of stipulation negotiations* □□ About 80 to 85 percent of the factual contentions in the episodes were agreed to. Also, the inadequacy of several portions of the government's case was revealed. As a consequence, the government ultimately dropped 14 episodes from the case. The process compelled the litigants to examine, in a way that may not have occurred otherwise, the merits of the contentions in light of the available evidentiary support. As a consequence, the testimony at trial was more focused and more efficiently presented. Since the substance of each witness's testimony was set forth in the Contention column, abbreviated testimonial presentations were possible. The direct testimony of most witnesses was submitted in writing. Background and preliminary questioning of witnesses was entirely eliminated. The primary purpose of oral testimony on direct examination was not to convey information but to establish the credibility of the source. Such testimony was usually limited to a summary of the written submission. The cross-examinations at trial were correspondingly short. The effect on trial was substantial, perhaps radical. Presentations that normally would be estimated to require a half day took an hour or less. In fact, ordinary estimates of time for testimony were so disconcerted at the early stages of the trial that midweek adjournments were necessary to keep pace with the original schedule of presentations.

* * *

V. CONCLUDING REFLECTIONS

The litigants do not perceive the case the way the judge does, nor do they have the same interest in it. The judge knows little about the case, especially at the beginning, and in any event does not want to reach a firm view of its merits until the end of trial. But information about the merits of the case is also information that is necessary for administration of the case. In this respect the litigants have a great comparative advantage over the judge. The judge has great authority in administration of the case, however, and the parties comparatively little. From a management perspective, therefore, a massive case is an anomaly: the person with administrative authority has relatively little information about the matter and is severely inhibited from getting such information, while the people who have the information have no authority to act on it. Indeed, the litigants often have incentives to use their superior information to offset or to subvert the judge's efforts at administration.

A key to expediting massive cases is to develop *incentives* for the *lawyers* to advance rather than retard the case. Of course, both sanctions and directives can and should be used. However, we do not believe sanctions have worked well or can work well in managing large cases, nor do we believe that directives will work without either sanctions or incentives. That leaves incentives as a largely unexplored possibility. Factoring out the incentive system is tricky, but there seem to be at least two principles: reciprocity and reduction of risk and waste. Reciprocity simply means that as many transactions as possible should be set up so that the litigants are benefited and burdened in equal degree. For example, the procedure for producing documents should distribute burden approximately equally. Reduction of risk and waste takes account of what seems to be a fact, that most of what the lawyers do in preparing a big case is to protect against eventualities that never happen. This wasted preparation is costly to the client. Probably more important as a practical matter, it is boring and exasperating to lawyers who have been in the trenches for months and years. Measures that advance the case by reducing this kind of waste benefit both court and litigants, except where one party has the primary aim of not getting to trial. We were not involved in such a case. * * *

* * *

Where the parties were required to take a position on a matter of consequence, as a general rule we allowed them to take an interim position before having to commit finally. For example, in making privilege claims a party had a "second shot," after our draft ruling, in which to correct technical error or supply additional documentation. Again, in the stipulation process all stipulations were tentative until confirmed after a period for review and retraction. Again, in many other transactions, we would say, "Why don't you try it this way and see how it goes? If you don't like it, come back and we will hear argument and make a formal decision."

Such tentativeness and irresolution violates all the conventions of legal procedure, which entail binding court dispositions based on binding party dispositions. Yet we found this "trial run" technique more productive and firmer than "tough" technique. We have pondered why this is so, and suggest the following explanations. In the first place, a big case is a series of small, unrehearsed transactions in which there is no assurance that a particular technique will work. Why compel the lawyers to fight a proposal they have doubts about without letting them see whether their doubts are justified? In the second place, lawyers are trained to be sensitive to risk and hence are very averse to an unproven technique. Why subject their risk aversion to maximum stress? Third, a trial run can lead to modifications, or to abandonment. Lawyers are practical people, why not capitalize on their practical judgment?

Underlying this point is a very important proposition about the pretrial transactions in big litigation as compared with routine litigation. In routine litigation, most pretrial transactions happen only once or a few times. There are a few depositions, a few documents, a few motions, one pretrial conference, and so on. In a big case every type of event occurs dozens or even hundreds of times. A big case is a stream of "repeat business" and not a "one shot" transaction. Hence, it is important to establish techniques that will work when put to repeated use between parties who have incentives to cooperate but also incentives to commit sabotage or engage in opportunism. This makes it worthwhile to invest in evolving such techniques through little experiments rather than regarding the transactions as singular and isolated. In a sense, the big case should be regarded as its own universe with its own evolving practice and "common law" and its own self-critical and adaptive processes.

We have described the aspects in which the procedures we used were *legally* informal. But that does not mean that they lacked form in political, psychological, or managerial terms. This is a hard point to get across to lawyers. To most lawyers "formal" means a court-like happening, and "informal" means every other kind of happening. However, a parliament has form, a partnership has form, a board of directors has form. All transactions can be analyzed into elements of goals, incentives and constraints, participants and powers, and information systems. The particular management form that evolved differed from that in conventional use, as we understand current conventions in pretrial management. The point is only that it had form, though not the form of adjudication.

We do not say that the form was "democratic," for it certainly was not, or that exercise of authority was not necessary, for it certainly was. What we say is simply that the form was relatively open rather than closed, experimental rather than presuming a priori knowledge, and propelled by party initiative rather than judicial directive. It gave relatively greater scope to the lawyers' instinct for creative craftsmanship as against their impulse to obstruct. Considered all in all, it could be described, in the current jargon, as management by participation.

FURTHER NOTE ON CASE MANAGEMENT

1. Flexibility in Pretrial Management

Extensive revisions to F.R.C.P. 16 were adopted in 1983 to encourage a more active judicial role in pretrial management of complex cases. After reading the following comments on the revisions, consider whether Rule 16 as it now reads would have permitted or facilitated the use of the various management techniques described by Hazard and Rice, supra.

"Letter from Geoffrey C. Hazard, Jr. to

"The Honorable Edward T. Gignoux

"Committee on Rules of Practice and Procedure, July 14, 1981

  * * *

"Third, I am troubled by the tone of some parts of the proposed revision of Rule 16. This has to do with the relation between the process of case management in the pretrial stage and rules governing that process. I believe there is general agreement that there needs to be much closer, continuous, and active involvement by the court in the discovery stage, particularly in complex cases. Professor Brazil's work in particular demonstrates this very clearly. From this premise, all of us who are trained as lawyers are inclined to move toward rules that mandate the particulars in which this more active stance is to be manifested. Thus, proposed Rule 16(b) requires a scheduling order except in cases that are categorically excluded. Putting the problem of scheduling in this dichotomous system immediately introduces distortion of the process of effective management.

That is, some cases are categorically exempted from scrutiny as to whether they should be intensely managed, whereas other cases are to be 'brought under management' by a scheduling order. Management is simply not this kind of ordinal activity. Treating it as such results in formalistic active management, which is often worse than no active management at all.

"In particular, I believe it is a mistake in complex cases to specify that there must be an order 'that limits the time' in which the parties are allowed 'to complete' discovery. At the beginning of a complex case, one simply cannot foresee accurately when discovery ought to be 'completed.' At most one can set goals, establish intermediate targets for approximation, and anticipate the possibility of fixing a firm target only after the process has gone forward in extent and degree sufficient to permit a realistic appraisal of a completion date. This may seem like a cavil over words, but it is not. It is a very important proposition about the nature of management, in contrast to the nature of rule-making or adjudication. I realize that we cannot educate judges and lawyers in the art of management through the mechanism of our choice of words in Rule 16. On the other hand, we can avoid in the Rule a selection of terminology that invites misunderstanding.

"The same point presents itself in the proposal concerning modification of scheduling orders. The proposal is that a schedule shall not be modified except upon a 'showing of good cause.' The concept of 'good cause' is surely to be preferred, as the explanatory note indicates, to the concept of modification only on the basis of manifest injustice. However, the 'good cause' formula still uses the notion of 'showing' and 'good cause' which taken together imply an evidentiary establishment of the fact that something has occurred which was not anticipated at the time the scheduling order was adopted. This in turn presupposes that a scheduling order can be based and should be based on an accurate forecast of the way in which events in the pretrial stage will unfold. I believe such forecasts are impossible, unless the case is so cut and dried that the schedule is merely a formality or the estimate of the required time is made so conservatively that it serves no effective controlling function."

2. Multidistrict Litigation

28 U.S.C.A. § 1407 provides for transfer to a single district and consolidation there for "coordinated or consolidated *pretrial* proceedings." See, e.g., In re Korean Air Lines Disaster, supra p. 618. An action therefore cannot be transferred for trial, In re Liquid Carbonic Truck Drivers' Chemical Poisoning Litigation, 423 F.Supp. 937 (Jud.Panel Mult.Lit.1976), although once the pretrial stage has been completed the parties may and often do stipulate for consolidated trial before the judge who has presided over the pretrial stage. In 1976, a proviso was added, 28 U.S.C.A. § 1407(h), permitting transfer for purposes of trial actions under Section 4C of the Clayton Act, 15 U.S.C.A. § 15c. Hence, it may be expected in years to come that 1407 will be enlarged by other, similar exceptions. Useful as § 1407 is, the provision would be much more useful if it permitted transfer for trial of any type of action. It should be recognized that some of the powers exercised by the trial judge in Vincent v. Hughes Air West, supra p. 1213, may be of doubtful validity. See In re Air Crash Disaster at Tenerife, Canary Islands, 435 F.Supp. 927 (Jud.Panel Mult. Lit.1977) (no power to compel airline to disclose list of names of claimants); cf. Hartland v. Alaska Airlines, Inc., 544 F.2d 992 (9th Cir. 1976) (no power to

require claimant who has not yet filed suit to contribute to costs of discovery). The law is evidently not yet ready to treat the large multi-claimant action, such as the air crash case, as similar to a necessary parties case or an interpleader in which all the potential claimants are summoned and joined. Compare Pan American World Airways, Inc. v. United States District Court, supra p. 722. What is the basis of this reluctance? Cf. McCoid, A Single Package for Multiparty Disputes, 28 Stan.L.Rev. 707 (1976); Rowe and Sibley, Beyond Diversity: Federal Multiparty, Multiforum Jurisdiction, 135 U.Pa.L.Rev. 7 (1986).

On the multidistrict panel, see Manual for Complex Litigation (2d ed. 1977); Comment, A Survey of Federal Multidistrict Litigation—28 U.S.C.A. § 1407, 15 Vill.L.Rev. 916 (1970) (giving the legislative history); Note, The Judicial Panel and the Conduct of Multidistrict Litigation, 87 Harv.L.Rev. 1001 (1974) (reviewing experience in use of the procedure). On the scope of the panel's powers, see Stavro v. Upjohn Co., 664 F.2d 114 (6th Cir. 1982). See also Symposium, The Multidistrict Panel: One Decade, 47 ABA Antitrust L.J. 1233 (1979).

Occasionally, situations of a similar sort can arise in a state court system. That is, a number of actions arising out of a single occurrence are filed in different counties in the same state and the question is whether they can be transferred with the aim of consolidation. Typical state provisions dealing with change of venue speak in terms of change of the place of *trial*, e.g., C.C.P. 397: "The court may, on motion, change the place of trial * * * when the convenience of witnesses and the ends of justice would be promoted by the change." Such provisions do not contemplate the facilitation of discovery and, as an historical matter, were adopted before discovery had come to be such a substantial part of the adjudication of a complex lawsuit. Still, the provisions of C.C.P. 397 do not exclude the use of transfer for the purpose of facilitating discovery as well as trial. Compare N.Y.C.P.L.R. § 510, essentially similar to C.C.P. 397; see also 2 Weinstein, Korn & Miller ¶ 510.10. In Linton v. Lehigh Valley R. R. Co., 32 A.D.2d 148, 300 N.Y.S.2d 468 (1969), the fact that actions arising out of the same occurrence had been consolidated was given decisive effect in refusing to change venue of one of the actions. See also C.E.B., 2 Calif. Civ.Pro. Before Trial c. 28 (1978); Rosenfield, Class Actions: Engrafting Federal "Complex and Multi-District Litigation" Procedures in Appropriate California Cases, 47 L.A.Bar Bull. 445 (1972).

On the possibilities for consolidating multiforum litigation into a single state court, see Note, The Consolidation of Multistate Litigation in State Courts, 96 Yale L.J. 1099 (1987).

3. Para–Judicial Officers

In addition to juries and judges, decision in court may be made by para-judicial officials. In the federal courts, these include magistrates and masters. Magistrates are now full time assistant judges appointed under 28 U.S.C.A. §§ 631–639; originally they were part time officials who could act only in criminal cases. See Note, Masters and Magistrates in the Federal Courts, 88 Harv.L.Rev. 779 (1975); Note, United States Magistrates: Additional Duties in Civil Proceedings, 27 Case W.Res.L.Rev. 542 (1977). Generally speaking, the magistrates are assigned pretrial motions, discovery matters, and various ancillary criminal matters, and may sit as judge at trial upon stipulation of the parties. See, e.g., Kerr v. United States District Court, infra p. 1305. The counterpart of the magistrate in the California system is the court commissioner. See Calif.Const.Art. 6, § 22; Calif. Gov't Code §§ 70141 et seq.; C.C.P. 259; Christensen, Private Justice: California's General Reference Procedure, 1982 Am.Bar Found.Res.J. 79.

Masters are specially appointed persons, usually lawyers, appointed for the purpose of hearing evidence or determining specified issues, such as those arising in discovery, or complicated financial questions, e.g., Zegers v. Zegers, Inc., 458 F.2d 726 (7th Cir.1972). See Brazil, Special Masters in the Pretrial Development of Big Cases, 1982 Am.B.Found.Res.J. 287; cf. LaBuy v. Howes Leather Co., 352 U.S. 249, 77 S.Ct. 309, 1 L.Ed.2d 290 (1957) (holding it improper to refer trial of an antitrust action to a master). See C.C.P. 638–645.1 for California counterparts. However, masters have also been appointed as essentially administrative officers in cases involving "institutional" decrees. See Silberman, Masters and Magistrates Part II: The American Analogue, 50 N.Y.U.L.Rev. 1297 (1975); Comment, Equitable Remedies: An Analysis of Judicial Utilization of Neo-Receiverships to Implement Large-Scale Institutional Change, 1976 Wis.L.Rev. 1161; cf. Nagel, Separation of Powers and the Scope of Federal Equitable Remedies, 30 Stan.L.Rev. 661 (1978); Levine, The Authority for the Appointment of Remedial Special Masters in Federal Institutional Reform Litigation: The History Reconsidered, 17 U.C.Davis L.Rev. 753 (1984).

Significant changes in F.R.C.P. 53 and 72–76 were adopted in 1983 to define and regulate the powers of magistrates and masters. Rule 53 was made applicable to a magistrate who is appointed as a master under 28 U.S.C.A. § 636(b)(2). Rule 72 distinguishes between "a pretrial matter not dispositive of a claim or defense" and matters that are dispositive. This distinction parallels the provision in 28 U.S.C.A. § 636(b)(1)(A) which allows a district judge to assign any matter to a magistrate "except a motion for injunctive relief, for judgment on the pleadings, for summary judgment, to dismiss or quash an indictment or information made by the defendant, to suppress evidence in a criminal case, to dismiss or to permit maintenance of a class action, to dismiss for failure to state a claim upon which relief can be granted, and to involuntarily dismiss an action." A magistrate's ruling on a "pretrial matter not dispositive of a claim or defense" is an adjudication that may be set aside by the judge if "clearly erroneous or contrary to law." Rule 72(a). A magistrate's ruling on a "dispositive matter" is a "recommendation for disposition of the matter" with respect to which the judge is to make "a de novo determination upon the record, or after additional evidence." Rule 72(b).

Rule 73 implements the provisions of 28 U.S.C.A. § 636(c) concerning assignment of magistrates to sit in lieu of judges in civil matters by consent of the parties and addresses the problem of appeal to the court of appeals. Rules 74 and 75 deal with appeals to the district judge under the option provided in 28 U.S.C.A. § 636(c)(4) in actions tried to a magistrate by consent. Rule 76 deals with appeals to the court of appeals from a district judge's decision following an appeal from the magistrate to the district judge.

4. JURY TRIAL

CARLSTROM v. UNITED STATES

United States Court of Appeals for the Ninth Circuit, 1960.
275 F.2d 802.*

BARNES, CIRCUIT JUDGE.

This is an appeal from a final judgment of the district court in a condemnation proceeding, after a jury trial. The government action condemned *first*, on May 1, 1953, an estate for years, and *secondly*, on June 16, 1955 (by an amended complaint), fee title, both in a portion of an aircraft plant (Plancor #20) at San Diego, California.

This plant, declared surplus after World War II, was purchased by Carlstrom from the government in May 1948 at a surplus property sale. He thereafter transferred title of various portions to the other plaintiffs and appellants herein.

Seventy acres were condemned, but by time of trial the just compensation for only forty-six and nine-tenths acres remained to be determined. For convenience, the property included in the *term taking* was described in "parcels"; the property in the *fee taking* described in "tracts."

The verdict the jury returned covered the fair market value of nine tracts, six fourteen month term parcels, and six options to renew—a total of twenty-one valuations.[1] In addition, by the answer to special interrogatories, the jury determined the fair market value by which each parcel and tract was enhanced because of parking facilities appurtenant thereto, which values had been included in their larger general verdicts. This called for fifteen additional valuations. There were also three interrogatories as to the reasonable probability of unitization. Based on the jury's award for the fourteen month term, the court made a prorated and adjusted award for the second or twelve month extended term. Other awards had been made by agreement (United States v. 70.39 Acres of Land, D.C., 164 F.Supp. 451, 460) between the parties.

---

* Some of the court's footnotes are omitted.

1. | "Parcel No. | Fair Market Value of 14-Month Term | | Fair Market Value of Option to Renew |
|---|---|---|---|
| 5 | $ 62,000.00 | | $ 17,712.00 |
| 6 | $ 185,000.00 | | $ 52,856.00 |
| 7 | $ 202,000.00 | | $ 57,684.00 |
| 9–A | $ 315,000.00 | | $ 90,000.00 |
| 9–B | $ 700.00 | | $ 200.00 |
| X | $ 12,000.00 | | $ 3,428.00 |

Tract No.	Fair Market Value	Tract No.	Fair Market Value
A–100	$ 275,000.00	A–108	$122,000.00
A–101	$1,146,000.00	A–109	$195,000.00
A–102	$2,830,000.00	A–120	$ 22,000.00
A–106	$ 30,000.00	A–121	$208,000.00"
A–107	$ 49,000.00		

Error is alleged as follows:

(1) In permitting condemnation of the term and fee in one action; (2) in permitting condemnation of the term and fee before one jury at one time; (3) in rejecting or admitting certain evidence; and (4) by rejecting appellants' instructions with respect to the evidence so admitted or rejected.

Appellants' first two alleged errors are really one: that the case was too big for any one jury to swallow and digest. "Of course, appellants' basic grievance is that they did not receive sufficient compensation for the interests and title which the government took from them." (Appellants' Opening Brief, p. 3.)[3]

We would not deny that a difficult task was presented to the jury in this case. That would not render this case unique in legal history. But as the trial was handled by the trial judge; as he carefully and patiently explained in layman's language (as much as it was possible) the intricacies of condemnation to the jury, we felt an admirable task had been ably accomplished. And we also thought the jury indicated by its conclusions it had arrived at a rather sound understanding of the law suit and of the issues submitted to the jurors.

Here, say appellants, "the only figures available were supplied by hired experts, one group seeking to inflate values to the benefit of the

---

3. The average values each side's appraisers testified to (in round figures) and the amounts awarded by the jury are as follows:

Use and Occupancy:

Parcel No.	Government	Landowner	Jury
5	$ 45,000.00	$ 120,000.00	$ 62,000.00
6	$ 133,000.00	$ 371,000.00	$ 185,000.00
7	$ 147,000.00	$ 398,000.00	$ 202,000.00
9–A	$ 282,000.00	$ 580,000.00	$ 315,000.00
9–B	$ 750.00	$ 1,000.00	$ 700.00
X	$ 14,700.00	$ 17,000.00	$ 12,000.00

Option:

Parcel No.	Government	Landowner	Jury
5	$ 6,000.00	$ 32,000.00	$ 18,000.00
6	$ 18,000.00	$ 110,000.00	$ 53,000.00
7	$ 17,000.00	$ 118,000.00	$ 58,000.00
9–A	$ 38,000.00	$ 160,000.00	$ 90,000.00
9–B	$ 100.00	$ 238.00	$ 200.00
X	$ 2,000.00	$ 5,000.00	$ 3,400.00

Fee:

Tract No.	Government	Landowner	Jury
A–100	$ 205,000.00	$ 480,000.00	$ 275,000.00
A–101	$ 565,000.00	$2,530,000.00	$1,146,000.00
A–102	$1,650,000.00	$6,000,000.00	$2,830,000.00
A–106	$ 7,000.00	$ 9,100.00	$ 30,000.00
A–107	$ 50,000.00	$ 77,000.00	$ 49,000.00
A–108	$ 105,000.00	$ 175,000.00	$ 122,000.00
A–109	$ 150,000.00	$ 350,000.00	$ 195,000.00
A–120	$ 17,000.00	$ 42,000.00	$ 22,000.00
A–121	$ 150,000.00	$ 380,000.00	$ 208,000.00

owners, and the other seeking to deflate them to the benefit of the sovereign." If this be true, it is a truth applicable to all condemnation cases, and in fact, to all lawsuits involving partisan expert testimony. It would be ideal, of course, if experts were just experts, and not partisans nor advocates. Perhaps there are better ways to determine values of condemned land, or other factual disputes as to which experts give their opinions, but the adversary procedure—each side with its experts and occasionally aided by experts of the court's choosing—is as yet the best our law has found. It is practical, and acceptable to most litigants.

Whether the taking of the fee should be added to a lawsuit originally containing merely the taking of a term estate is a matter peculiarly within the discretion of the trial court, judicially exercised. Eagle Lake Improvement Co. v. United States, 5 Cir., 1947, 160 F.2d 182; Silberman v. United States, 1 Cir., 1942, 131 F.2d 715.

We find no abuse of discretion in permitting such an amendment. No case is cited by appellants as holding that it was.

Once the issues are framed by the pleadings, it again is a part of the judicial discretion of the trial judge as to how the several issues are to be tried. It might well be that one jury could more accurately pass on one parcel of realty, and another on a second. Or, one jury better pass on five parcels, or ten, rather than one, and another on the next five or ten. The converse may be true. Here there were thirty-six valuations determined by the jury involving ten buildings on nine "tracts" of land—actually nine subdivisions of one contiguous piece of industrial property being used fundamentally for its one undisputed best purpose, but capable of several uses. We cannot find as a matter of law that one jury is incapable of deciding thirty-six property valuations in four differing types of estates (nine in ordinary fee title, six in value of leaseholds, six in value of options, and fifteen in value of parking facilities appurtenant to leasehold and fee). None of these four concepts of property ownership is bizarre or occult concepts of rights in real property. The average lay person during his life time has some dealing with leaseholds, options, title in fee, and, in Southern California at least, a great deal of experience with parking facilities. Under careful supervision, explanation and instruction (and no specific instruction given below is here criticized), there seems no reason why an ordinary jury could not ascertain the values herein required of this jury. As a matter of law, there was no abuse of the district court's discretion in permitting it to do so.

Appellants urge that the case here is so complicated that to require one jury to find the answer deprives them of due process of law. They rely on Gwathmey v. United States, 5 Cir., 1954, 215 F.2d 148. This is the only case on the subject cited by appellants in either their opening or closing briefs. For that reason we consider it at some length.

Gwathmey, supra, involved the condemnation of the Cape Canaveral area in Florida. Appellant points out that in the instant case, the trial took seventeen weeks as compared to three in Gwathmey; that the jury deliberated fifteen days in this case and three days in Gwathmey; that here there were seven forms of verdicts while in Gwathmey but one. In Gwathmey the appellate court believed

"the very size of the case as tried, without the additional complexities [added by a "value zone system" used by government appraisers], was such that the jury must have been overwhelmed. In fact, during the trial there were so many tracts and so much evidence that the witnesses, the attorneys and even the judge himself seemed to be confused at times."

215 F.2d 148, at pages 155–156. Therefore, say appellants here, if Gwathmey was a denial of due process in a condemnation case, then the instant case was doubly so.

We do not find the Gwathmey case controlling. We say this for several reasons.

(1) As the court says in Gwathmey, "Whether or not there has been an abuse of discretion, whether or not there has been a denial of due process, are questions which turn on the circumstances of each case." Id., at page 157.

(2) Here there were at the most thirty-six "tracts;" in Gwathmey there were originally nine hundred and thirty-three separate tracts and ultimately two hundred and thirty-eight separate tracts and verdicts.

(3) In Gwathmey the government appraisers developed a theory of arbitrarily assigning tracts to certain "value zones," which "added greatly to the confusion and to the mass of evidence with which the jury was burdened." Id., at page 154.

(4) In Gwathmey attorneys and owners of property were excused from attendance at the trial, yet evidence as to value of their property was introduced during their absence. "Cross-examination [was] either not allowed at all or allowed so long after direct examination that it was totally ineffective." Id., at page 154.

(5) In Gwathmey the appellate court conceded that inasmuch as but fifty separate tracts remained in the case after appeal, "It may well be that . . . this case can be fairly tried in one proceeding before one jury." Id., at page 158.

(6) We note not only that Gwathmey is a decision of the fifth circuit, not binding on this circuit, but that the opinion was the product of agreement between one circuit judge and one district judge, and that the third member of the panel, before his death, "felt very strongly and insisted this case should be affirmed."

(7) But one case is cited in the entire Gwathmey opinion. It is Atlantic Coast Line R. Co. v. United States, 5 Cir., 1943, 132 F.2d 959, where the fifth circuit found no confusion or prejudice in *seriatim* trials of different tracts before one jury.

But the primary reason we do not find the Gwathmey case controlling is that we find no abuse of the court's discretion in supervising the introduction of the evidence. To the contrary, we think it was a difficult job well done. We adopt the language used in appellee's brief as pertinent.[4]

Appellant urges that the obvious mistake made by the jury as to Tract A–106 invalidates their conclusions as to all other values. The jury rendered a verdict of $30,000 for this parcel. The highest value testified to was $10,000; the lowest $6,500. The court ordered $22,000 remitted to fix the figure of $8,000. This was agreed to.

The significance of this one error is subject to debate. Does proof of but one mistake prove the jury did a remarkably efficient job on the other thirty-five valuations that did not need correction? It was, as appellee points out, with respect to a valuation that was one-tenth of one per cent of the total alleged value of the condemned property. We should not gloss over an error, no matter how small. It was an error. The jury made it. It was corrected. In our opinion, in view of the correction, it was not a prejudicial error, or one that colors the entire result of the jury's deliberations so as to make it suspect. Far less would it invalidate it as a matter of law. We find no failure of due process.

* * *

Finding no error, the judgment is affirmed.

4. "The handling of this case by the district court, far from being an abuse of discretion, showed great competence, skill and ability. The jury was given more assistance than a jury normally receives even in long and complicated cases. From time to time during the trial, the jury was told the purpose of the introduction of particular classes of evidence, the law applicable thereto and the facts it would have to decide. When it retired to the jury room to deliberate it had before it, summarized in exhibits, practically all of the really determinative factors in the case. It had all comparable sales and leases in Exhibits 25–S, 33, 57 and 57–1. All of the pertinent data about these sales and leases were compiled in easily comprehensible tabular form, size, location, description of improvements, dates, terms, rents, rents averaged per square foot per month, and sales price averaged per square foot of building and open space. The jury had before it the summary of each expert's testimony on both the fee and the term takings. Again, all these exhibits illustrating the expert's

opinion were clearly tabulated by parcel or tract to explain the basis of the opinion.

"The capitalization of income approach was summarized for the jury. The income was capitalized for the property as a whole, and each major building of the fee taking was listed separately on an exhibit illustrating how to arrive at fair market value by capitalization of income. The trend of prices of real estate in the San Diego area was also illustrated for the jury by an exhibit. There were other exhibits, maps, photographs, and mathematical illustrations, to refresh the jury's recollection of this property with which it had become intimately familiar through the several months of testimony. The jury had seen the property. It heard detailed descriptions of its condition. It had heard the preparations, the factors, the reasons, the highest and best uses, and the fair market values repeated 14 times. . . . ."

Appellee's Brief, pp. 83–85 (References to transcript omitted).

IN RE JAPANESE ELECTRONIC PRODUCTS ANTITRUST LITIGATION

United States Court of Appeals for the Third Circuit, 1980.
631 F.2d 1069.

[This case appears, supra, p. 1044]

5. DECREE

STURM, THE RHODE ISLAND PRISON DECREE *

1. The Situation

The study focuses on the Rhode Island prison known as the Adult Correctional Institution (hereafter called the ACI). The author based her analysis primarily on information obtained in the course of employment as law clerk to the Special Master appointed to monitor compliance with the decree issued by the United States District Court of Rhode Island in Palmigiano v. Garrahy, 443 F.Supp. 956 (D.R.I.1977), concerning the conditions of confinement in the ACI. This information was supplemented by the case histories prepared in the ABA study, Harris and Spiller, After Decision: Implementation of Judicial Decrees in Correctional Settings (1977), and secondary literature describing and analyzing the dynamics of prison systems.

2. Historical Background: The Evolution of Chaos

The prison system in Rhode Island was not always in turmoil. While it never bordered on the rehabilitative, the prison system during the 1950's functioned as a relatively stable community. Rules were enforced and visible violence was at a minimum. The warden (who held that position for fifteen years) lived on the grounds and was accessible to and respected by inmates and staff alike. Generally, the inmates, guards, and wardens had settled expectations of each other and the prison functioned relatively smoothly.

In 1968 the political situation in Rhode Island shifted. For reasons that remain unclear to the author the warden was fired. The Department of Corrections was reorganized and the position of director was created. From that point on, no individual occupied the position of director for longer than two years. The Governor treated the appointment as political. The first two directors were strangers to the world of corrections. Both lacked a coherent philosophy of corrections and both chose not to live on the grounds. They preferred not to deal personally with inmates. Both saw within a relatively short period of time that they were in the wrong business and left.

Their successor rode in on a wave of prison reform. He viewed himself as a humanist and was determined to bring the "treatment" approach to Rhode Island. He inherited a system in which power struggles among inmates and guards had developed and the inmates were harder to control. The director's response was to bargain with the most powerful inmates, conceding demands for increased privileges in return for the inmates' agreement to "keep the lid on" the prison. This informal bargaining arrangement excluded guards, fostering their resentment over loss of control.

* By Susan Sturm, Yale Law School, 1979, with additions.

The bargain subjected the rest of the prison population to the will of a powerful minority. The inmate control group organized the National Prisoners Reform Association, Rhode Island chapter, which came to wield tremendous power in the prison, that was often used to the personal advantage of the members. Some inmates were given permission to set up workshops and sell their products. In addition to giving some inmates control over hammers, saws, and other potentially dangerous instruments, this arrangement enabled the "proprietors" of the workshops to force other inmates to work without pay, by threatening them with force or reduction of privileges. Money earned through these and other undertakings (there was a lucrative drug business within the prison) was used for such luxuries as catered dinners within the prison. Select inmates were allowed conjugal visits within the prison, while others were not allowed even contact visits.

The new director accompanied his reliance on informal bargaining with a "treatment-oriented approach" to corrections. He instituted a number of programs separate from the daily operational functions of the prison and employed a separate staff of counselors to carry them out. Guards were excluded from participation since they were viewed as "custody oriented." They reacted by refusing to cooperate in the programs and sabotaging them where possible. Treatment personnel reacted to guards' lack of cooperation with anger and hostility and blamed the failure of any of the new programs on "custody." They escalated the conflict by refusing to even address security considerations in their plans and programs. The situation developed into a battle of philosophies—treatment and custody—with personnel lining up on either side according to job function.

In the meantime, inmates continued to increase their demands for privileges to compensate for maintaining order within the prison. When the director refused to bargain further with the inmates, they ceased policing the prison and stirred up inmate hostility. (The situation may have been exacerbated by the outside political atmosphere of the early seventies.) There were several riots, one culminating in a fire that destroyed the industrial arts building. The director, probably recognizing the seriousness of the situation, his inability to deal with it, and the vulnerability of his professional reputation, resigned.

The position of Director of Corrections remained vacant for almost a year, during which time a former Assistant to the Director served as Acting Director. This individual perceived himself as powerless, largely because of his temporary status and affiliation with a now disfavored administration, and conducted himself accordingly. The guards capitalized on the leadership vacuum and formed the Brotherhood of Correctional Officers, a union whose power quickly grew in the absence of any direction from the administration.

Eleven months later, the Governor appointed as the new director a young ambitious Rhode Islander with no prior experience in corrections. He and his immediate assistants had little understanding of the problems they were about to confront and took no positive action for several months. Staff members were reluctant to act because of uncertainty concerning the direction of the new administration and the allocation of power and responsibility. (But inmates continued to use force and informal power to control many aspects of prison life.)

As the situation deteriorated, the administration increasingly relied on the guards' use of force to re-establish order. "Custody" re-established its dominance over "rehabilitation." Minor incidents were treated as harshly as major disturbances, inmates were locked in their cells for long periods of time, and there was retaliation against disfavored inmates. Treatment people were openly challenged and their access restricted by security staff. The prison's internal atmosphere rapidly changed from relative anarchy to a repressive, tightly closed system.

In the midst of this turmoil, the federal district court issued a decision in a class action suit, Palmigiano v. Garrahy, challenging the constitutionality of the conditions of confinement at the ACI. The inmates were represented by the ACLU National Prisoners' Rights Project and by a local attorney who was familiar with inmates and prison conditions through his extensive criminal practice. The plaintiffs claimed that the levels of fear and violence, the unsanitary conditions of confinement, and the unequal treatment of inmates violated the Eighth and Fourteenth Amendments. The trial extended over two weeks and included extensive testimony of expert witnesses. On August 10, 1977, Judge Pettine issued an opinion documenting the conditions of the ACI and declaring them to be a violation of inmates' constitutional rights. The accompanying order required the defendants in effect to clean up the physical environment and reduce the level of violence in the prison, through an elaborate program of reform subject to strict deadlines.

At the time the decree was entered, there had been no strong direction from the administration for almost ten years. All inmates, from misdemeanants to "lifers," were placed directly in maximum security. Medium security had been abolished; informers and informants, rapers and rapees, were housed in close proximity. There was virtually no information available to the staff describing either the number or characteristics of the inmate population and no established rules and regulations. The prison was filthy and unsanitary; prisoners milled around in the halls all day; outbreaks of violence were frequent.

Five days after the court order was issued there was a minor disturbance involving about ten inmates. In response the administration instituted a prison-wide lock-up. Inmates were kept in the cells twenty-four hours a day; visits, programs, and furloughs were suspended; and meals were served in the cells. The lock-up continued in full effect for seven months. In the midst of this confusion, the Director of Corrections resigned, the warden was fired, and a new director from out of state was hired.

3. Prison Politics: Opposition from Within

The sequence of events in Rhode Island approximated that in prisons across the country. During the late 50's, prison reformers embraced the concept of rehabilitation through treatment, a policy accompanied by an influx of outsider professionals. Reform administrations relied on the philosophy of openness and treatment to replace discipline and force. These changes threatened the power of existing interests, primarily guards, wardens, and the inmate elite.

Inmates. The inmates at ACI might be supposed to support the court-ordered reforms. They are the plaintiffs in the litigation and live in the atrocious conditions. Yet inmates continue to contribute to the persistence of the dirt and the violence. Inmate leaders have on several occasions organized massive protests consisting of throwing food onto the tiers and refusing to perform routine cleaning duties. In addition inmates aid guards in setting up other prisoners (for example, by placing a home-made weapon or drugs under another inmate's mattress prior to a search), thereby precipitating a disturbance.

There is a small but powerful group of inmates whose interests are furthered by maintaining the existing conditions—the long-term inmates who have previously wielded authority over the general population and the administration. (Ironically, several of these inmates are named plaintiffs in the lawsuit against the prison administration.) They are familiar with the unwritten rules of prison life and have on-going relationships with various guards. They mediate disputes and prevent major disruptions. In return, they are relatively free from interference from institutional officials, although they are also more vulnerable to administrative retribution because their future in prison is a long one. Furthermore, they obtain prison jobs in strategic positions, which gives them mobility and access to information.

The balance between inmates and guards was disrupted by the intervention of outsiders. The reform administration by-passed the organizational hierarchy and dealt directly and covertly with inmate leaders, reducing the guards' ability and incentive to control the inmates. When the guards' power was reasserted inmate leaders incited violence and kept the prison in a state of turmoil in order to maintain an atmosphere beyond the control of the guards.

The leadership of the National Prisoners Reform Association within the prison, consisting mainly of heavies and jailhouse lawyers, only maintains power through the court-ordered reforms, by maintaining the administration's dependence on them for compliance with the decree. Inmates may try to maintain conditions requiring court intervention for less grandiose reasons as well. They derive personal satisfaction and status from participation in the suit. By occupying the status of plaintiff in a law suit against the very people who are keeping them locked up, inmates achieve moral equality with their jailors; in the courtroom, they sit in the same witness stand as the director. Newspaper coverage also enhances their status in the eyes of other inmates. On the other hand this "clout" is a perishable commodity that loses value to the extent beneficial change is not generated by the court.

The inmates who want to "do their time and get out" have the least control over the current situation. They do not work their way up the inmate hierarchy and are most vulnerable in a system which formally treats all inmates as equally powerless. There is no mechanism for communicating the needs of passive or non-disruptive inmates to the administration, so the administration and sometimes the court have based their policies on the behavior exhibited by the most volatile and disruptive. Thus, passive inmates become embittered and suspicious of outside intervention and refuse to participate in new programs.

The power structure among inmates often divides along racial lines. In many prisons, black inmates do not get the jobs that provide freedom of movement and access to prison information. One study of the Eastern Correctional Institution in Pennsylvania documented this systematic exclusion of black inmates from positions of influence and attributed it in part to the racial prejudice of guards, the overwhelming majority of whom were white. Another factor seemed to be black inmates' unwillingness to enter into a cooperative relationship with guards, which the blacks regarded as "Tomism." Both factors contributed to their non-involvement in the corruption of authority and accompanying influence in the prison. This collective exclusion, even though in part involuntary, created resentment among blacks and increased the potential for their collective identification and action. In the context of a prison, this usually means actual or threatened violence.

Guards. Guards are at the bottom of the organizational hierarchy. In some systems, the administration subjects them to such scrutiny and discipline that their position is analagous to that of the inmates. They are held accountable for maintaining control and order in the prison. They are expected to accomplish this function through enforcement of regulations and imposition of force if necessary. However, the effectiveness of physical force is limited by the high inmate-guard ratio and the ever-present potential of precipitating uncontrollable violence.

Consequently, guards have relied on a system of reward and punishment to maintain order. They overlook various rule infractions to gain favor and control over inmates. They sometimes participate in illicit marketing. They selectively distribute rewards, such as desirable jobs and extra food, to make deals or trades with the captives. This system of maintaining control places guards in a precarious position, however, for it is unstable and there are many inmates outside of the bargaining structure. Reform administration and the courts have imposed new constraints on guards' power to use force legitimately. The treatment staff has introduced a new conception of inmate as patient or client and attempted to control the reward structure by distributing privileges on the basis of successful completion of rehabilitative programs. Inmates have direct contact with counsellors and sometimes administrators and so in some respects have greater access to information than the guards. Thus, guards perceive that they will lose their status and control if change is successful.

There are, of course, guards who oppose the arbitrariness and brutality of the current system. However, influential guards strongly discourage their peers from speaking out, through tactics such as ostracism and threats of violence. Furthermore, some of those who are unwilling to conform to the protocol of the current system are black and/or young. The white career guards sometimes hold these individuals responsible for the infractions and contraband in the prison, and the turnover of these individuals is very high.

The career guards also control the Brotherhood of Correctional Officers. The union's power over the administration derives largely from management's fear of work stoppages and accompanying likelihood of violence in the prison. The Director has conceded important areas of decisionmaking to the union, in the hope of preserving order. Currently, the union controls policies relating to job assignment, job rotation, and overtime.

Counselling Staff. The counselling staff originally perceived the intervention of the court as a great victory for "treatment." However, counsellors were never given any line authority and the guards have maintained control over the movement of inmates through the system. The failure of the reform administration to obtain its goals reduced the credibility of counsellors in the system. Counsellors' roles evolved into performing ministerial functions and preparing appearances before various committees, such as the Classification Board and the Parole Board. The administration contracted out some of the programmatic functions and hired new staff for others. Consequently, counsellors are frozen in a position that dooms them to powerlessness and perhaps obsolescence.

Wardens. The three wardens at the ACI rose through the ranks of the correctional officers union. They have been schooled in the tradition of security and evaluate a prison by the power of its guards. Having experienced the chaos of the "treatment" orientation, they are suspicious of any new programs. They are especially resentful of control by inexperienced newcomers. Thus, proposed changes are likely to meet their resistance.

Middle Management. In addition to the wardens and the senior correctional officers, there is a contingent of middle management working outside the institution. Middle management personnel have virtually no control over the day-to-day operation of the prison and rarely visit the prison. Most of them prefer to think of themselves as professional managers rather than correctional professionals. Furthermore, it is much easier to perform the function for which they are held accountable—constructing a well-run system on paper—if they are not personally aware of the incongruence between description and action. They have little contact with either the inmates or the legislature and yet are responsible for developing programs to satisfy both groups. In sum, middle management has responsibility without authority or knowledge.

The Director. To an outsider, the solution to the problem of dirt and violence may seem clear: The Director must order inmates to clean and guards to follow clearly established rules. But the director of corrections is in a precarious position. He is held responsible for the current problems at the prison and is expected by both his staff and his superiors (the Governor and the legislature) to solve them. At the same time, some of the same groups who criticize the Director's inability to "clean up the mess" are protecting their own interests by making that job as difficult as possible. Finally, those who keep the Director in office have different and sometimes competing expectations than those for whom he is responsible on a day-to-day basis.

The Court. The Federal Court, then, finds itself in the midst of a complex set of relationships. To a large extent, the issues discussed above are outside the scope of the Court's inquiry. The Court must determine whether the conditions in the ACI today violate the Constitution. If liability is established, the Court must attempt to frame a remedy. The Court thus uses different criteria in defining the problem and a different vocabulary in formulating a resolution.

The power struggle continues beneath the surface, hidden in Court by disputes over specifics of the decree. The judge, unaware of or aloof to these underlying tensions, is frustrated at the administration's inability to accomplish seemingly simple tasks. He continues to view the federal court as an institution above the political struggles of other competing interest groups.

The Governor. The Governor has no personal commitment to corrections and sees court intervention and the recent disturbances as a thorn in his side. He is primarily concerned with minimizing the prison's drain on his political and economic resources. Early in the suit, he attempted to use it to establish a national reputation as an innovator. He appointed a three-man committee, called the Governor's Implementation Team, and gave it full responsibility for implementation of the Court's order. The corrections staff was to continue in its day-to-day operations, turning its planning operations over to the Team. The Governor was convinced he had an unprecedented example of cooperation between the judiciary and the legislature that would warrant national attention, but overlooked several drawbacks. Several Team members had been public critics of the director. They came across as self-righteous reformers moving in to clean up Corrections' mess. The Department responded by giving the Team only the information specifically requested, and as little cooperation as possible. After several months, the Team was disbanded and responsibility for implementing the decree returned to the Department.

The Governor's scheme had a long term negative impact on the court's effectiveness because it predisposed the staff to disclaim responsibility for integrating the changes ordered by the decree. No one within the Department was given specific responsibility for instituting court-ordered reforms until the Department was found in contempt of court six months later.

The Legislature. The federal court is viewed by the legislature as an illegitimate intruder. The battle between Judge Pettine and the state legislature began long before the current suit was filed and the legislature has taken the opportunity to "put the Court in its place." Also, the Governor has fallen out of favor with the dominant party and the legislature has refused to support the Governor's requested appropriations. So far, the legislature has had the last word.

See Eisenberg and Yeazell, The Ordinary and the Extraordinary in Institutional Litigation, 93 Harv.L.Rev. 465 (1980). For a survey and references on the subject see Brakel, Special Masters in Institutional Litigation, 1979 Am.Bar Found.Res.J. 543. Compare Note, Judicial Intervention and Organization Theory: Changing Bureaucratic Behavior and Policy, 89 Yale L.J. 513 (1980).

----

6. APPELLATE REVIEW

NOTE ON APPELLATE REVIEW

The general rule is that appellate review is available only from a final judgment. This rule is subjected to special strain in complex litigation, for every issue in such a case is "heavier" than in ordinary litigation. An error early in such a case can make the rest of the trial court proceedings an expensive nullity if eventual appeal results in reversal. Compare Coopers & Lybrand v. Livesay, infra p. 1296, and Note on Appealability of Non-Final Orders in Federal Courts, infra p. 1317.

B. SMALL CASES

STEELE, THE HISTORICAL CONTEXT OF SMALL CLAIMS COURTS

1981 A.B.F. Res. J. 295.*

Small claims, the ordinary day-to-day grievances and disputes involving the common man, have during most eras been seen as a distinct class of cases, and often they have been handled by a distinct set of courts. While the small claims court forms only a small portion of the system of civil courts, it has through its long and varied history acquired a special symbolic importance, inspiring vigorous debate and voluminous documentation. An examination of the development of the small claims court can thus illuminate issues central to the entire system of civil justice in this country and help us to understand some of the dominant and recurring themes associated with American legal institutions generally during the past 100 years.

Civil litigation in the Anglo-American legal system has at most times been perceived as two broad categories of cases: small claims and "regular" cases. Small claims have been viewed very differently in different eras, and they have frequently been viewed with some ambivalence. In some periods they have been seen as low-status, "petty" cases and have been all but ridiculed for a variety of reasons, including the small dollar amounts involved, the perceived unimportance of the issues at stake, their purely private relevance, and the perceived lack of social stature of at least one of the parties involved. At other times small claims have been granted very high priority and importance, perhaps because they generally are so numerous and because they involve and potentially affect all people and all phases of life. These characterizations have generally held true both for grievances of the common man (e.g., money, wages, or rent due, defective goods or services) and for grievances against the common man (particularly the collection of past due accounts arising from consumer purchases). Similarly the courts that handle small claims have been viewed sometimes as the vanguard of the legal system at its point of contact with the life of the ordinary citizen and sometimes as "lower" courts that must, as quickly and efficiently as possible, dispose of huge numbers of petty private quarrels that are without relevance to the important events of the day or to the development of the law. At some times small claims courts have been seen as the vanguard of procedural reform and even as the crucible in which reform experiments will be tested and refined for later use in all courts, while at other times they have been largely ignored or viewed as judicial backwaters characterized by stultifying routines of little consequence.

* * *

The first central issue is the mode of characterizing small claims—one's view of the "problem" to which the small claims court is the solution. We will discuss two contrasting and complementary views of small claims: the "conserving view" and the "reforming view." These two views are based on divergent characterizations or perceptions of what small claims actually are and thus lead to differing views of the "problem" of small claims and the appropriate responses to it.

The conserving view typically sees small claims as expressions of somewhat arbitrary intractability, as "petty" claims asserted by people who are not prominent social actors, as isolated differences of opinion with no significance for the broader society in terms of either the issues or the resources at stake. Perceived in this way, small claims have little just claim on scarce collective resources for adjudication. According to the reforming view, on the other hand, small claims are perceived as the particularized consequences of general widespread socioeconomic injustices which therefore have a strong claim on collective resources available to redress collective wrongs. These two polar views of the nature of small claims have led to fundamentally different notions of appropriate response and reform.

The conserving view defines the problem in such a way that the appropriate response is to adjust the system of adjudication to dispose of small claims with a minimal expenditure of public resources. It accepts as appropriate the high entry costs that serve as barriers to the pressing of small claims in courts of law. In this view the process of adjudication is an important social resource that should be rationed and saved only for those cases deemed important or for those cases in which the potential societal rewards of litigation are thought to justify its costs. The reforming view of small claims, on the other hand, emphasizes the collective social significance of small cases. This view has produced a very different response to the small claims problem—the radical expansion of the sphere of adjudication so that every meritorious civil case can be fully and fairly adjudicated before a judge. The catchword of this reform direction is "accessibility": every man deserves his day in court.

* * *

The fourth central issue involves the mode of institutional response to particular disputes of the small claims type. * * * Many human situations can be approached on both an individual and an aggregate level. We might draw an analogy to the field of medicine, for instance, which has conceived of treatment primarily on an individual scale, whereas public health has taken a more aggregate approach. The ambivalent experiences of neighborhood legal service offices in trying both to solve individual client problems and to achieve aggregate social reform through such means as "public interest" litigation is another example. * * *

* * *

By the late 1960s and early 1970s, the small claims court became once again an object of intense professional and public concern and reform activity. * * *

* * * The new critics tacitly admitted that the specific reforms urged during the Progressive period had been largely achieved. The small claims courts were available, inexpensive, and fairly speedy. But it was perceived that the courts were being used, not by the poor, but against them and that the justice dispensed was hurried, routinized, biased, and mechanical—unlike the ideal of wise, compassionate, individualized justice. The new criticism centered on the heavy use of the small claims courts by business plaintiffs, on the high proportion of individual and poor defendants, the high number of default judgments, often uncollectible, and the huge transaction costs in lost wages, time, and energy relative to the size of the claims. It was less that the early reformers had failed than that they had been naive in their understanding of the complex social entanglements of the poor. The systemic nature of consumer grievances—exploitation, deception, shabby merchandise, and so forth—which peculiarly (but not exclusively) affect the poor was at the center of public attention aroused by the urgings of the "consumer movement" and social reformers attuned to the war on poverty and civil rights movements.

* * *

* * * The remedies suggested did not differ much from those suggested earlier. Some consensus seemed to have developed on the problems of small claims courts. The need included the reduction of expense and delay through lowered filing fees; service of process by ordinary mail; simplification of pleadings; evening and weekend hours to eliminate the need to lose wages through taking time off from work; neighborhood court room locations; assistance from law students, paralegals, and court clerks to diminish the need for counsel; and simplification of collection and enforcement procedures to make the judgment of the court collectable and at the same time increase procedural protections in the process of wage garnishment to make creditors' judgments harder to collect. Courts were to be overhauled and new courts created. The monetary limits of jurisdiction were to be increased and the courts increasingly publicized and promoted, sometimes in minority languages where appropriate.

Increasing use of the courts by consumers as plaintiffs accompanied the general trend toward increased assertiveness by consumers.

* * *

By the mid-1970s the attention of legal reformers appears to have shifted toward collective or macrosocial issues and away from the processing of small claims. * * *

During the latter part of the 1970s attention returned to the mechanisms of justice in individual small disputes. This third wave of reform activity began to look beyond the small claims courts to other "informal dispute resolution mechanisms." The old dream of informal understandable justice without lawyers reemerged. Growing out of the burgeoning literature analyzing existing nonjudicial dispute resolution systems, new noncourt mechanisms were advocated.

No longer was the emphasis on redressing the balance between rich and poor. Small claims and minor disputes came to be seen as general social problems. Everyone, rich or poor, is a consumer and a neighbor, and may be a spouse or a tenant, and thus is entitled to means of effective redress. Much of the attention to small disputes arose too from a desire to ease the growing caseloads of courts by "diverting" cases to other forums as well as to make the means of providing justice simpler and more available. The consensus seemed to be that courts, even small claims courts, were not appropriate to all types of matters and ought properly to be last resorts after less formal, less adversarial remedies had been tried. Experimentation with mediation, conciliation, arbitration, counseling, ombudsmen, specialized programs, neighborhood centers, and other variations has become increasingly visible both to reformers and to users (Neighborhood Justice Centers are the most prominent example). The all-things-to-all-people tenor of earlier small claims court reform rhetoric has given way to a more differentiated and complex advocacy of specialized tribunals and of screening and sequential procedures that try first one and then another procedure to resolve a dispute until something works. * * *

* * *

The second central thematic issue is the perception of the social function of processing small claims. One of the partially hidden sources of tension in our judicial system since colonial times has been the dual roles assigned to courts—both dispensing justice and making policy. * * *

* * * Gradually the concept of the judicial role evolved toward that of policy making. Important cases that brought lawyers and judges prestige came to be those that affected social policy. Cases that raised no novel legal or policy issues came to be seen by many as less important. The complex trial procedures that had been built up were seen as necessary for the fine tuning of legal policy in important cases but as less appropriate in the "private disputes" not involving social policy. In such cases, complex procedures simply served to render litigation so slow and expensive as to deny access to most citizens with disputes. * * *

As a result of this divergence in role concept, certain large classes of cases were carved out as not involving important issues of policy and therefore being appropriate for less formal resolution, for example, industrial accident commission and worker's compensation cases before the boards, administrative agencies, juvenile courts, and especially "petty" small claims. Small claims came to be seen as a separable class, somehow ineffably different, simpler, really less important to policy. * * *

The third central thematic issue is the perception of breadth of impact of dispute processing. A macrosocial dispute is one that is generally viewed as important to a broad segment of society as a whole in terms of either the potential impact of the outcome of the dispute upon general social policy (such as, e.g., by direct rule making or legislation, the precedential value of a case, collective bargaining settlement for a leading industry), or the direct aggregate impact of the outcome of the dispute upon the society as a whole (such as disputes involving large amounts of money, single, publicly important transactions, or large aggregate institutions such as corporations, government, universities, churches, and so forth, which in turn affect many people directly). A microsocial dispute, on the other hand, is one whose likely impact and relevance is generally perceived to be limited to the individuals directly involved in the dispute and which in itself has little potential for making general policy or affecting numerous individuals by means of aggregating institutions. * * *

* * *

The implications of this distinction between macrosocial and microsocial disputes is clear. Disputes seen as macrosocial would logically require the most perfect possible process of ascertaining the true state of affairs and the appropriate decisional outcome because that particular outcome will profoundly affect society as a whole. * * *

* * *

* * * [M]icrosocial disputes are to be put to rest as efficiently as possible since their outcome has no major macrosocial or policy impact. * * * Arbitration, mediation, conciliation, counseling, and other "more efficient alternatives" have been suggested as suitable remedies for microsocial disputes since they may require a lower expenditure of scarce resources to terminate a dispute. There is, of course, a continuum between formal and informal processing. Negotiation itself has a norm-creating impact on the parties to the negotiation and their future relationship, and such norms may extend beyond the parties themselves to a small group. This phenomenon has been demonstrated, for example, in contract negotiations between businessmen; it also clearly occurs in labor negotiation and marriage counseling, where ongoing long-term relationships are involved. Many small claims involve disputes between strangers arising out of isolated, single transactions such as automobile accidents, the purchase of consumer goods or services, evictions, and landlord/tenant security deposit disputes, not stable, ongoing relationships. This duality or ambiguity concerning the nature of small claims themselves has given rise to a shifting conception of the proper role to be played by those established and ongoing means of governmental intervention which continue to operate—the courts. Thus the perceived breadth of impact of dispute processing is closely linked to the mode of institutional response.

* * *

* * * When particular types of disputes are perceived as involving macrosocial policy issues and as having broad macrosocial collective impact— that is, when they tend to be perceived from the reforming point of view—they are often shifted out of the context of individual adjudication characteristic of a dispute-oriented perspective and into an aggregate mode characteristic of the criminal and the regulatory responses. What might have been viewed as individual, rather small complaints are thereby combined and approached as aggregate problems in such regulatory contexts. What remains is a residue of unrelated individual claims.

In the 1960s and 1970s the reforming perspective again emerged into prominence, and the process of skimming off certain normatively important classes of cases from the mass of small claims and other civil cases continued. False and deceptive advertising, food and drug adulteration, consumer fraud, product safety, automobile safety, civil rights, discrimination, environmental pollution, and occupational health and safety, for example, were specifically addressed by the creation of aggregate and criminal response mechanisms. What remains after the skimming off of such macrosocially important matters for aggregate response is a residue of individual claims that have not been defined or perceived as aggregate, macrosocially important problems. Thus the residue of individual claims tends to lose its luster and its normative significance, and the perception of such civil matters swings back toward the conserving view, or dispute-oriented perspective, that now seems more appropriate to the cases that remain.

* * *

NOTE ON SMALL CLAIMS COURTS

Mr. Steele's article cites extensive bibliography.

Areas frequently singled out for reform and improvement in the small claims court system include limits on the amount in controversy, available remedies, and attorney representation. See Note, Small Claims Courts: An Overview and Recommendation, 9 U. Mich. J. of Law Reform 590 (1976). How should the jurisdictional limit be determined? What are the advantages of a high amount or a low amount? How can the amount be made responsive to current economic conditions? Small claims courts are usually limited to money damages. Should they be granted equitable powers such as reformation, rescission, and promissory estoppel? A common source of complaint is that lawyers not only increase the formality, complexity and cost of small cases, but also create an unfair advantage in favor of wealthier represented plaintiffs suing poorer unrepresented defendants. Should attorneys be barred from small claims courts? Statistics from Florida seem to indicate that lawyers, at least in Florida, do not significantly affect the outcome of cases. Stauber, Small Claims Courts in Florida: An Empirical Study, 54 Fla.B.J. 130 (1980); see also Steadman and Rosenstein, "Small Claims" Consumer Plaintiffs in the Philadelphia Municipal Court: An Empirical Study, 121 U.Pa.L.Rev. 1309 (1973); O'Barr and Conley, Lay Expectations of the Civil Justice System, 22 Law & Soc'y Rev. 137 (1988), excerpted supra p. 31. If attorneys were barred, would paraprofessionals and business agents take their place? Would they be better or worse than lawyers? If attorneys are deemed necessary to a fair small claims proceeding, is it feasible to provide representation given the multitude of claimants and the economics of the situation? What can be said for limiting access to small claims courts to individuals and barring corporations?

All studies indicate that the vast majority of cases are brought by "professional" plaintiffs, i.e., collection agencies, merchants and utilities, against buyers of consumer goods and services, and result in a large number of default judgments. See, e.g., Kosmin, The Small Claims Court Dilemna, 13 Houston L.Rev. 934 (1976). Note that in such a context the very attributes of the small claims system intended to provide efficient and inexpensive justice to the public can be viewed, depending on one's perspective, as either devices to railroad disadvantaged debtors or as necessary procedures for an economically viable consumer credit based society. For California reforms see C.C.P. 116 et seq.

A continuing problem for successful plaintiffs, whether consumers with valid complaints or creditors with valid debts, is the difficulty of collecting on their judgments. Not only are small claims defendants normally recalcitrant, hard to find, and impecunious, but sheriffs and other officials who collect or enforce judgments may be unwilling to help small claims plaintiffs or may charge disproportionately high fees. See Purdum, Examining the Claims of a Small Claims Court, 65 Judicature 25 (1981). Should the small claims system subsidize the collection function of small claims as well as the adjudication function? For a proposal for a Department of Economic Justice to dispense relief in cash or kind to consumers unable to obtain satisfaction from a manufacturer or seller of a defective product, see Rosenberg, Devising Procedures That Are Civil to Provide Justice That is Civilized, 69 Mich.L.Rev. 797 (1971).

Are streamlined procedures necessary to combat costs and delays in "small" claims in the range of $10,000 to $25,000? The California Civil Procedure Code has provisions for cases under $25,000 which simplify pleadings, limit pretrial motions and severely restrict discovery. C.C.P. 1823–1833.2. See Note, California's Pilot Project in Economical Litigation, 53 So.Calif.L.Rev. 1497 (1980); Weller, Ruhnka and Martin, What Happened When Interrogatories Were Eliminated, 21 Judges' J. 8 (1982).

C. ARBITRATION

MENTSCHIKOFF, THE SIGNIFICANCE OF ARBITRATION— A PRELIMINARY INQUIRY

17 Law & Contemp.Probs. 698 (1952).*

Dispute settlement is a fundamental aspect of any legal system and one of the prime requisites of a peaceful society or group is that the settlement of trouble cases be by processes which are non-violent in character. Although the courts are our official organs for that purpose, we have long known that many of the trouble cases of our society are settled by methods other than the formal legal process. These methods can be methods either of compromise or of decision.[1] Every lawyer is conscious of the extent of settlement negotiated directly between the disputants and is to some extent also cognizant of the amount of negotiated settlement achieved through the aid and intervention of an agreed or volunteer third party (mediation or conciliation). These two methods of settling disputes are our most informal and their essence lies in the fact that the solution achieved is acceptable to the immediate parties to the dispute and that it typically gives each party less than he originally desired or felt was his due. Mediation or conciliation or negotiation are means of compromising disputes on a give-and-take basis and as informal compromises combine to constitute a distinct and well recognized phase of trouble shooting.

---

* Some of the author's footnotes are omitted.

1. The importance of determining whether a particular method is essentially one of compromise or of decision lies in the psychological attitude which accompanies resort to it. In the one context, "bargain" and the emotive connotations of that word are evoked; in the other, "judgment" and the emotive connotations of that come into play. This distinction is of peculiar significance in evaluating the arbitration process and in attempting to place it in the general machinery of our legal institutions.

But when the method of settling a dispute shifts from one of compromise to one of decision, we tend to think primarily of the court process and to overlook or discount the importance of the arbitration process or else to dismiss it as another type of compromise machinery. The thesis of this paper is that in so doing we fail to perceive the importance and generative power of the arbitration process.

I have not been able to find complete or even semi-complete figures on the extent of arbitration in this country, but preliminary inquiry suggests that if we lay aside first the cases in which the government is a party and second the accident cases, then the matters going to arbitration rather than to the courts represent 70 per cent or more of our total civil litigation. This suggests that the major decisional process of dispute settlement may be the arbitration and not the formal legal process. If, as further appears to be the case, the trend to arbitration seems to be increasing, then we are now living through a more violent change of judicial machinery than was present when equity emerged into conflict with the common law courts. It is not impossible to envisage a future in which the adjudicatory work of the formal legal system will be limited to the regulatory type of litigation while the resolution of private disputes becomes almost entirely a matter of consensual tribunals.

What then are the major characteristics of this growing system of resolving disputes? Why is the system being used to the extent it is? What effect on life in general do the decisions of its judges have? How do the errors of such a system get cured? Who is handling the trial of issues in the arbitration process? Is legal education preparing * * * [students] for the handling of matters in such a tribunal and is our working substantive law in fact the law of the legislatures and courts or is it being made all unknowingly in the privacy of the arbitration chamber?

* * *

The four essential aspects of arbitration are (1) it is resorted to only by agreement of the parties; (2) it is a method not of compromising disputes but of deciding them; (3) the person making the decision has no formal connection with our system of courts; but (4) before the award is known it is agreed to be "final and binding."[2]

Inherent in the consensual character of the arbitration process is the fact that its procedure can be adjusted to fit the particular needs of the particular case or disputants. This * * * does not mean that there are no rules of evidence or of procedure or of presentation. It only means that these may and frequently do vary from those used in our formal legal system.

---

2. Some of the federal courts in construing the Federal Arbitration Act as inapplicable to labor controversies have been motivated, at least in part, by the fear of "compulsory arbitration." See, e.g., International Union United Furniture Workers v. Colonial Hardwood Flooring Co., 168 F.2d 33 (4th Cir. 1948).

This is a misuse of terms. The only semi-compulsive element in arbitration is that the award is final and binding, but this results only from the agreement of the parties. Arbitration is an essentially consensual process, even though the agreement may have been made prior to the existence of the dispute. I suggest that in discussion of "compulsory arbitration" what is really involved is a process of compelling parties by law to resort to a peaceful method of settlement in which the decider is a person having no formal connection with our system of courts. The basic question is one of peaceful or violent settlement of labor controversy, not at the option of the parties, but by legislative decree. No such issue is involved in the application of the Federal Arbitration Act to an agreement to submit labor disputes to arbitration.

The decisional nature of arbitration is what distinguishes it from the more informal types of settlement with which we are all familiar and makes it true kin to our court process. This aspect of arbitration has been the most frequently misunderstood and this misunderstanding has in turn led to a general lack of perception of the importance and significance of the process itself. The misunderstanding stems, I think, from the fact that most present reactions to arbitration are conditioned by the dramatic publicity about labor arbitration. Labor arbitration still, though decreasingly, tends to be thought about as a means of compromising the differences between labor and management.[4] "Compromise" in this sense is a correct word only if we should think of our courts as "compromising" the differences between buyers and sellers, pedestrians and automobilists, and the like. In that sense decision of any matter which does not turn wholly on an attempt to determine what happened in fact would be classified as an attempt at compromise. But such a classification destroys the usefulness of differentiating the concept of compromise from the concept of judgment. The formal legal system and arbitration are alike in the sense that both are essentially decisional procedures. They can indeed be distinguished on the method of decision, but not by saying that in the courts the decisions are foreshadowed and limited by the tradition of authority and its use. For I find a like limitation to exist in fact on arbitrators and the parties before them. The difference lies rather in the explicit criteria of decision.

The essential thing to note at this stage is that although there are indeed standards or criteria for decision in arbitration, they are as in matters of procedure and evidence more flexible and more dependent on the requirements of the particular case or particular disputants than we normally find in the formal legal system. Whether those arbitration standards are as live to the needs of all-of-us as are our formal legal criteria is, however, open to question.[5]

The fact that the person chosen to make the decision in the arbitration process is not connected with the formal legal system bears an important relation (1) to the type of proof necessary in a proceeding, (2) to the explicit

---

4. I do not mean to suggest by this that all arbitrators realize that their function is to judge rather than to make a bargain for the parties. In the labor field, in particular, a nonjusticiable issue tends to be frequently arbitrated. It is the kind of issue which can be stated simply as "what should the clause about X be in the new contract between the parties?" Since the context of the issue is necessarily one of bargain, the attitude of the arbitrator and the result can and often is one of bargain, a placing of himself into the position of the parties and the working out of a reasonable provision which represents a compromise between the two positions urged upon him by the parties. Some of the excitement about the wage aspects of the steel decision seems to center on the fact that the Stabilization Board failed to adopt this attitude. Whether fact finding boards should operate as arbitration boards is beyond the scope of this paper. * * *

The vital thing is that with the exception of this one type of issue, the issues going to arbitration are identical with those going to the courts. In other words, in only a single area is the scope of arbitration greater than the scope of the justiciable.

5. One of the curses of modern civilization is our dependence upon experts and the unnecessary but unfortunate fact that expert training, whether it be in law or medicine or engineering or anything else, seldom is accompanied with training in the function and needs of the totality of the civilization. Similarly business experience or training, as it approaches expert status, tends to become narrowed to the needs of the particular business group being served. We are familiar with the fact that judges, although they acquire more breadth by assumption of the robe, still tend to bring with them much of the attitudes and values of their prior practice. The safeguard lies in the fact that our highest courts sit as benches. There are, of course, individual exceptions; but the net picture is not changed by them.

criteria involved in decision, and (3) to the growth and extent of the doctrine of precedent in arbitration.

One obvious illustration of the difference in the proof necessary is the use made of experts. If the arbitrator is himself an expert the concept of "judicial notice" is automatically enlarged to cover the area of his expertness and the proof tends to become limited to the particulars of the dispute before him. This expert quality of the arbitrator may also influence the type of hearing. There is something to be said for showing an expert how a piece of machinery or a particular operation actually runs. There may even sometimes be some justification for using that showing in lieu of testimony and for limiting the hearing to argument.[6] There clearly is no such justification in the case of a non-expert tribunal, be it judge, jury, or arbitrator.

On the question of explicit criteria for decision, the fact that the arbitrator need not be a member of any craft connected with the formal legal institution is of peculiar importance. Who would think of arguing to a lay arbitrator in a commercial case the rules of formal law alone? Obviously he is as much if not more interested, and explicitly so, in the conflict of interest which exists, the practices which are normal, the allocation of risks which parties in the business normally make, and any factor which makes the particular case materially different from the normal.

The question of criteria for decision is intimately linked with the value and use of precedent and of course conditions that use. The doctrine of precedent is not an institution peculiar to our common law. It is in essence a response to the human need in any group for reckonability and predictability of result. Who has not heard a small child say "But one time you let me," and been thereby forced into meticulous and careful distinction (if that is possible) of the prior case? It is strange to me, therefore, to hear the drums beat for arbitration on the ground that it is an "ad hoc" process without precedent value. What is really meant is that formal legal precedent formally used is not the only controlling criterion for decision. But this is no real point of departure from the formal legal system. The decided law itself has never, even in the short wooden period from about 1880 to 1910, been applied as by a slot machine. The felt drive for the just result, even when hidden below the manipulation of prior cases and statutes, has always been present. The trouble has been that too many of the bar have been fooled by their law school educations into believing that rules, especially as built out of the narrow holdings, are necessarily definitive of the outcome of cases[8] and that argument of the policy involved is somehow non-respectable and must be done in an undercover or even underhanded manner. No really successful appellate lawyer has ever labored under this illusion and no court sitting as a bench has

---

6. I, personally, would never, as a matter of tactics, permit the proof to rest on any such survey. Unless matters which a party believes are significant are specifically called to the attention of the arbitrator, he may overlook them. The opening statement in arbitration may supply this lack, but undirected view of anything can seldom, if ever, be counted on to yield an adequate factual base on which to rest the burden of persuasion. This is twice as true if the decider is a layman and the process or machine to be observed has the slightest technical implications.

8. I am not saying by this that there is no certainty in our law or that courts are constantly shifting decisions. What I am saying is that there is constant growth by expansion or limitation and that the fundamental drive of the courts is to achieve justice. One safeguard against constant shift is that in much larger areas than is commonly recognized, the law does approximate justice for long stretches of time. Another is that slow small shifts to meet need are of the essence of true stability. It is only the *absence* of such shifting that comes to any person's notice.

ever really believed it. The proponents of "ad hoc" arbitration are only urging that in arbitration the policy factors can be brought out into the open and made the explicit bases for decision, *and that arbitration knows no convention against that being done;* and, further, that the error of a prior decision should not control the determination of future cases. They do not mean that an interpretation of a clause in a contract used nationally or covering many departments in a single plant should be (or is) totally disregarded except for the particular case or department involved in the case which led to the interpretation. Such a result would really lead to the chaos which the bar keeps unsuccessfully but direly predicting whenever the courts of the formal legal system adapt prior decisions by open shift or overruling to present need.

But here again in trying to give a definitive picture we are faced with a dearth of information. We do not really know what the precedent value of arbitrators' awards is, still less how that precedent value may differ as among different areas of industry or problem. All we know is that there is some precedent value; that there must be more than is recognized since a precedent system is an inherent part of the nature of man living in a group; and that in the labor field dramatic new patterns of relation have been set in particular cases and followed thereafter in other cases. * * * [We need to know:] Is there a significant correlation between the use of a professional arbitrator (a phenomenon of the labor field) and the extent of precedent value? Is precedent of greater importance in arbitrations held within an industry or within a commodity or other exchange than in those held under the auspices of the American Arbitration Association? Are there variations in precedent value based on personnel similar to those which we find in the formal legal system to be based on particular lower court judges or particular appellate benches? We would expect the answers to these questions to be yes. We would further expect to find that in the industry and exchange type of arbitration there is a fairly close interaction between rules or practices and awards; that this interaction more closely approximates the ideal of interrelation of legislature and judiciary than has ever been existent in our formal machinery of government and judiciary. Finally, we * * * [need] to find out definitively how formal legal precedent is used in arbitrations.

* * *

SHEARSON/AMERICAN EXPRESS, INC. v. McMAHON

Supreme Court of the United States, 1987.
482 U.S. 220, 107 S.Ct. 2332, 96 L.Ed.2d 185.*

JUSTICE O'CONNOR delivered the opinion of the Court.

This case presents two questions regarding the enforceability of predispute arbitration agreements between brokerage firms and their customers. The first is whether a claim brought under § 10(b) of the Securities Exchange Act of 1934 (Exchange Act), 48 Stat. 891, 15 U.S.C. § 78j(b), must be sent to arbitration in accordance with the terms of an arbitration agreement. The second is whether a claim brought under the Racketeer Influenced and Corrupt Organizations Act (RICO), 18 U.S.C. § 1961 et seq., must be arbitrated in accordance with the terms of such an agreement.

---

* Some of the Court's footnotes are omitted.

I

Between 1980 and 1982, respondents Eugene and Julia McMahon, individually and as trustees for various pension and profit-sharing plans, were customers of petitioner Shearson/American Express Inc. (Shearson), a brokerage firm registered with the Securities and Exchange Commission (SEC or Commission). Two customer agreements signed by Julia McMahon provided for arbitration of any controversy relating to the accounts the McMahons maintained with Shearson. The arbitration provision provided in relevant part as follows:

> "Unless unenforceable due to federal or state law, any controversy arising out of or relating to my accounts, to transactions with you for me or to this agreement or the breach thereof, shall be settled by arbitration in accordance with the rules, then in effect, of the National Association of Securities Dealers, Inc. or the Boards of Directors of the New York Stock Exchange, Inc. and/or the American Stock Exchange, Inc. as I may elect." 618 F.Supp. 384, 385 (1985).

In October 1984, the McMahons filed an amended complaint against Shearson and petitioner Mary Ann McNulty, the registered representative who handled their accounts, in the United States District Court for the Southern District of New York. The complaint alleged that McNulty, with Shearson's knowledge, had violated § 10(b) of the Exchange Act and Rule 10b–5, 17 CFR § 240.10b–5 (1986), by engaging in fraudulent, excessive trading on respondents' accounts and by making false statements and omitting material facts from the advice given to respondents. The complaint also alleged a RICO claim, 18 U.S.C. § 1962(c), and state law claims for fraud and breach of fiduciary duties.

Relying on the customer agreements, petitioners moved to compel arbitration of the McMahons' claims pursuant to § 3 of the Federal Arbitration Act, 9 U.S.C. § 3. The District Court granted the motion in part. 618 F.Supp. 384 (1985). The court first rejected the McMahons' contention that the arbitration agreements were unenforceable as contracts of adhesion. It then found that the McMahons' § 10(b) claims were arbitrable under the terms of the agreement, concluding that such a result followed from this Court's decision in Dean Witter Reynolds Inc. v. Byrd, 470 U.S. 213, 105 S.Ct. 1238, 84 L.Ed.2d 158 (1985), and the "strong national policy favoring the enforcement of arbitration agreements." 618 F.Supp., at 388. The District Court also held that the McMahons' state law claims were arbitrable under Dean Witter Reynolds Inc. v. Byrd, supra. It concluded, however, that the McMahons' RICO claim was not arbitrable "because of the important federal policies inherent in the enforcement of RICO by the federal courts." 618 F.Supp., at 387.

The Court of Appeals affirmed the District Court on the state law and RICO claims, but it reversed on the Exchange Act claims. 788 F.2d

94 (CA2 1986). With respect to the RICO claim, the Court of Appeals concluded that "public policy" considerations made it "inappropriat[e]" to apply the provisions of the Arbitration Act to RICO suits. Id., at 98. The court reasoned that RICO claims are "not merely a private matter." Ibid. Because a RICO plaintiff may be likened to a "private attorney general" protecting the public interest, ibid., the Court of Appeals concluded that such claims should be adjudicated only in a judicial forum. It distinguished this Court's reasoning in Mitsubishi Motors Corp. v. Soler Chrysler–Plymouth, Inc., 473 U.S. 614, 105 S.Ct. 3346, 87 L.Ed.2d 444 (1985), concerning the arbitrability of antitrust claims, on the ground that it involved international business transactions and did not affect the law "as applied to agreements to arbitrate arising from domestic transactions." 788 F.2d, at 98.

With respect to respondents' Exchange Act claims, the Court of Appeals noted that under Wilko v. Swan, 346 U.S. 427, 74 S.Ct. 182, 98 L.Ed. 168 (1953), claims arising under § 12(2) of the Securities Act of 1933 (Securities Act), 48 Stat. 84, 15 U.S.C. § 77l(2), are not subject to compulsory arbitration. The Court of Appeals observed that it previously had extended the *Wilko* rule to claims arising under § 10(b) of the Exchange Act and Rule 10b–5. See, e.g., Allegaert v. Perot, 548 F.2d 432 (CA2), cert. denied, 432 U.S. 910, 97 S.Ct. 2959, 53 L.Ed.2d 1084 (1977); Greater Continental Corp. v. Schechter, 422 F.2d 1100 (CA2 1970). The court acknowledged that Scherk v. Alberto–Culver Co., 417 U.S. 506, 94 S.Ct. 2449, 41 L.Ed.2d 270 (1974), and Dean Witter Reynolds Inc. v. Byrd, supra, had "cast some doubt on the applicability of *Wilko* to claims under § 10(b)." 788 F.2d, at 97. The Court of Appeals nevertheless concluded that it was bound by the "clear judicial precedent in this Circuit," and held that *Wilko* must be applied to Exchange Act claims. 788 F.2d, at 98.

We granted certiorari, 479 U.S. 812, 107 S.Ct. 60, 93 L.Ed.2d 20 (1986), to resolve the conflict among the Courts of Appeals regarding the arbitrability of § 10(b) and RICO claims.

II

The Federal Arbitration Act, 9 U.S.C. § 1 et seq., provides the starting point for answering the questions raised in this case. The Act was intended to "revers[e] centuries of judicial hostility to arbitration agreements," Scherk v. Alberto–Culver Co., supra, at 510, 94 S.Ct., at 2453, by "plac[ing] arbitration agreements 'upon the same footing as other contracts.'" 417 U.S., at 511, 94 S.Ct., at 2453, quoting H.R.Rep. 96, 68th Cong., 1st Sess. 1, 2 (1924). The Arbitration Act accomplishes this purpose by providing that arbitration agreements "shall be valid, irrevocable, and enforceable, save upon such grounds as exist at law or in equity for the revocation of any contract." 9 U.S.C. § 2. The Act also provides that a court must stay its proceedings if it is satisfied that an issue before it is arbitrable under the agreement, § 3; and it authorizes a federal district court to issue an order compelling arbitration if there has been a "failure, neglect, or refusal" to comply with the arbitration agreement, § 4.

The Arbitration Act thus establishes a "federal policy favoring arbitration," Moses H. Cone Memorial Hospital v. Mercury Construction Corp., 460 U.S. 1, 24, 103 S.Ct. 927, 941, 74 L.Ed.2d 765 (1983), requiring that "we rigorously enforce agreements to arbitrate." Dean Witter Reynolds Inc. v. Byrd, supra, at 221, 105 S.Ct., at 1243. This duty to enforce arbitration agreements is not diminished when a party bound by an agreement raises a claim founded on statutory rights. As we observed in Mitsubishi Motors Corp. v. Soler Chrysler–Plymouth, Inc., "we are well past the time when judicial suspicion of the desirability of arbitration and of the competence of arbitral tribunals" should inhibit enforcement of the Act " 'in controversies based on statutes.' " 473 U.S., at 626–627, 105 S.Ct., at 3354, quoting Wilko v. Swan, supra, at 432, 74 S.Ct. at 185. Absent a well-founded claim that an arbitration agreement resulted from the sort of fraud or excessive economic power that "would provide grounds 'for the revocation of any contract,' " 473 U.S., at 627, the Arbitration Act "provides no basis for disfavoring agreements to arbitrate statutory claims by skewing the otherwise hospitable inquiry into arbitrability." Ibid.

The Arbitration Act, standing alone, therefore mandates enforcement of agreements to arbitrate statutory claims. Like any statutory directive, the Arbitration Act's mandate may be overridden by a contrary congressional command. The burden is on the party opposing arbitration, however, to show that Congress intended to preclude a waiver of judicial remedies for the statutory rights at issue. See id., at 628, 105 S.Ct., at 3354. If Congress did intend to limit or prohibit waiver of a judicial forum for a particular claim, such an intent "will be deducible from [the statute's] text or legislative history," ibid., or from an inherent conflict between arbitration and the statute's underlying purposes. See id., at 632–637, 105 S.Ct., at 3356–3359; Dean Witter Reynolds Inc. v. Byrd, 470 U.S., at 217, 105 S.Ct., at 1240.

To defeat application of the Arbitration Act in this case, therefore, the McMahons must demonstrate that Congress intended to make an exception to the Arbitration Act for claims arising under RICO and the Exchange Act, an intention discernible from the text, history, or purposes of the statute. We examine the McMahons' arguments regarding the Exchange Act and RICO in turn.

III

When Congress enacted the Exchange Act in 1934, it did not specifically address the question of the arbitrability of § 10(b) claims. The McMahons contend, however, that congressional intent to require a judicial forum for the resolution of § 10(b) claims can be deduced from § 29(a) of the Exchange Act, 15 U.S.C. § 78cc(a), which declares void "[a]ny condition, stipulation, or provision binding any person to waive compliance with any provision of [the Act]."

First, we reject the McMahons' argument that § 29(a) forbids waiver of § 27 of the Exchange Act, 15 U.S.C. § 78aa. Section 27 provides in relevant part:

"The district courts of the United States . . . shall have exclusive jurisdiction of violations of this title or the rules and regulations thereunder, and of all suits in equity and actions at law brought to enforce any liability or duty created by this title or the rules and regulations thereunder."

The McMahons contend that an agreement to waive this jurisdictional provision is unenforceable because § 29(a) voids the waiver of "any provision" of the Exchange Act. The language of § 29(a), however, does not reach so far. What the antiwaiver provision of § 29(a) forbids is enforcement of agreements to waive "compliance" with the provisions of the statute. But § 27 itself does not impose any duty with which persons trading in securities must "comply." By its terms, § 29(a) only prohibits waiver of the substantive obligations imposed by the Exchange Act. Because § 27 does not impose any statutory duties, its waiver does not constitute a waiver of "compliance with any provision" of the Exchange Act under § 29(a).

We do not read Wilko v. Swan, 346 U.S. 427, 74 S.Ct. 182, 98 L.Ed. 168 (1953), as compelling a different result. In *Wilko,* the Court held that a predispute agreement could not be enforced to compel arbitration of a claim arising under § 12(2) of the Securities Act, 15 U.S.C. § 77*l* (2). The basis for the ruling was § 14 of the Securities Act, which, like § 29(a) of the Exchange Act, declares void any stipulation "to waive compliance with any provision" of the statute. At the beginning of its analysis, the *Wilko* Court stated that the Securities Act's jurisdictional provision was "the kind of 'provision' that cannot be waived under § 14 of the Securities Act." 346 U.S., at 435, 74 S.Ct., at 186. This statement, however, can only be understood in the context of the Court's ensuing discussion explaining why arbitration was inadequate as a means of enforcing "the provisions of the Securities Act, advantageous to the buyer." Ibid. The conclusion in *Wilko* was expressly based on the Court's belief that a judicial forum was needed to protect the substantive rights created by the Securities Act: "As the protective provisions of the Securities Act require the exercise of judicial direction to fairly assure their effectiveness, it seems to us that Congress must have intended § 14 . . . to apply to waiver of judicial trial and review." Id., at 437, 74 S.Ct., at 188. *Wilko* must be understood, therefore, as holding that the plaintiff's waiver of the "right to select the judicial forum," id., at 435, 74 S.Ct., at 186, was unenforceable only because arbitration was judged inadequate to enforce the statutory rights created by § 12(2).

Indeed, any different reading of *Wilko* would be inconsistent with this Court's decision in Scherk v. Alberto–Culver Co., 417 U.S. 506, 94 S.Ct. 2449, 41 L.Ed.2d 270 (1974). In *Scherk,* the Court upheld enforcement of a predispute agreement to arbitrate Exchange Act claims by parties to an international contract. The *Scherk* Court assumed for purposes of its opinion that *Wilko* applied to the Exchange Act, but it determined that an international contract "involve[d] considerations and policies significantly different from those found controlling in *Wilko.*" 417 U.S., at 515, 94 S.Ct., at 2455. The Court reasoned that arbitration reduced the uncertainty of international contracts and obviated the danger that a dispute might be submitted to a hostile or unfamiliar forum. At the same time, the Court noted that the advantages of judicial resolution were diminished by the possibility that the opposing party would make "speedy resort to a foreign court." Id., at 518, 94 S.Ct., at 2456. The decision in *Scherk* thus turned on the Court's judgment that under the circumstances of that case, arbitration was an adequate substitute for adjudication as a means of enforcing the parties' statutory rights. *Scherk* supports our understanding that *Wilko* must be read as barring waiver of a judicial forum only where arbitration is inadequate to protect the substantive rights at issue. At the same time, it confirms that where arbitration does provide an adequate means of enforcing the provisions of the Exchange Act, § 29(a) does not void a predispute waiver of § 27—*Scherk* upheld enforcement of just such a waiver.

The second argument offered by the McMahons is that the arbitration agreement effects an impermissible waiver of the substantive protections of the Exchange Act. Ordinarily, "[b]y agreeing to arbitrate a statutory claim, a party does not forego the substantive rights afforded by the statute; it only submits to their resolution in an arbitral, rather than a judicial, forum." Mitsubishi Motors Corp. v. Soler Chrysler–Plymouth, Inc., 473 U.S., at 628, 105 S.Ct., at 3355. The McMahons argue, however, that § 29(a) compels a different conclusion. Initially, they contend that predispute agreements are void under § 29(a) because they tend to result from broker overreaching. They reason, as do some commentators, that *Wilko* is premised on the belief "that arbitration clauses in securities sales agreements generally are not freely negotiated." See, e.g., Sterk, Enforceability of Agreements to Arbitrate: An Examination of the Public Policy Defense, 2 Cardozo L.Rev. 481, 519 (1981). According to this view, *Wilko* barred enforcement of predispute agreements because of this frequent inequality of bargaining power, reasoning that Congress intended for § 14 generally to ensure that sellers did not "maneuver buyers into a position that might weaken their ability to recover under the Securities Act." 346 U.S., at 432, 74 S.Ct., at 185. The McMahons urge that we should interpret § 29(a) in the same fashion.

We decline to give *Wilko* a reading so far at odds with the plain language of § 14, or to adopt such an unlikely interpretation of § 29(a). The concern that § 29(a) is directed against is evident from the statute's plain language: it is a concern with whether an agreement "waive[s] compliance with [a] provision" of the Exchange Act. The voluntariness of the agreement is irrelevant to this inquiry: if a stipulation waives compliance with a statutory duty, it is void under

§ 29(a), whether voluntary or not. Thus, a customer cannot negotiate a reduction in commissions in exchange for a waiver of compliance with the requirements of the Exchange Act, even if the customer knowingly and voluntarily agreed to the bargain. Section 29(a) is concerned, not with whether brokers "maneuver[ed customers] into" an agreement, but with whether the agreement "weaken[s] their ability to recover under the [Exchange] Act." 346 U.S., at 432, 74 S.Ct., at 185. The former is grounds for revoking the contract under ordinary principles of contract law; the latter is grounds for voiding the agreement under § 29(a).

The other reason advanced by the McMahons for finding a waiver of their § 10(b) rights is that arbitration does "weaken their ability to recover under the [Exchange] Act." Ibid. That is the heart of the Court's decision in *Wilko*, and respondents urge that we should follow its reasoning. *Wilko* listed several grounds why, in the Court's view, the "effectiveness [of the Act's provisions] in application is lessened in arbitration." 346 U.S., at 435, 74 S.Ct., at 185. First, the *Wilko* Court believed that arbitration proceedings were not suited to cases requiring "subjective findings on the purpose and knowledge of an alleged violator." Id., at 435–436, 74 S.Ct., at 186–187. *Wilko* also was concerned that arbitrators must make legal determinations "without judicial instruction on the law," and that an arbitration award "may be made without explanation of [the arbitrator's] reasons and without a complete record of their proceedings." Id., at 436, 74 S.Ct., at 187. Finally, *Wilko* noted that the "[p]ower to vacate an award is limited," and that "interpretations of the law by the arbitrators in contrast to manifest disregard are not subject, in the federal courts, to judicial review for error in interpretation." Id., at 436–437, 74 S.Ct., at 187–188. *Wilko* concluded that in view of these drawbacks to arbitration, § 12(2) claims "require[d] the exercise of judicial direction to fairly assure their effectiveness." Id., at 437, 74 S.Ct., at 187.

As Justice Frankfurter noted in his dissent in *Wilko*, the Court's opinion did not rest on any evidence, either "in the record . . . [or] in the facts of which [it could] take judicial notice," that "the arbitral system . . . would not afford the plaintiff the rights to which he is entitled." Id., at 439, 74 S.Ct., at 189. Instead, the reasons given in *Wilko* reflect a general suspicion of the desirability of arbitration and the competence of arbitral tribunals—most apply with no greater force to the arbitration of securities disputes than to the arbitration of legal disputes generally. It is difficult to reconcile *Wilko*'s mistrust of the arbitral process with this Court's subsequent decisions involving the Arbitration Act. See, e.g., Mitsubishi Motors Corp. v. Soler Chrysler–Plymouth Inc., supra; Dean Witter Reynolds Inc. v. Byrd, 470 U.S. 213, 105 S.Ct. 1238, 84 L.Ed.2d 158 (1985); Southland Corp. v. Keating, 465 U.S. 1, 104 S.Ct. 852, 79 L.Ed.2d 1 (1984); Moses H. Cone Memorial Hospital v. Mercury Construction Corp., 460 U.S. 1, 103 S.Ct. 927, 74 L.Ed.2d 765 (1983); Scherk v. Alberto–Culver Co., 417 U.S. 506, 94 S.Ct. 2449, 41 L.Ed.2d 270 (1974).

Indeed, most of the reasons given in *Wilko* have been rejected subsequently by the Court as a basis for holding claims to be nonarbitrable. In *Mitsubishi*, for example, we recognized that arbitral tribunals are readily capable of handling the factual and legal complexities of antitrust claims, notwithstanding the absence of judicial instruction and supervision. See 473 U.S., at 633–634, 105 S.Ct. at 3357–3358. Likewise, we have concluded that the streamlined procedures of arbitration do not entail any consequential restriction on substantive rights. Id., at 628, 105 S.Ct., at 3354–3355. Finally, we have indicated that there is no reason to assume at the outset that arbitrators will not follow the law; although judicial scrutiny of arbitration awards necessarily is limited, such review is sufficient to ensure that arbitrators comply with the requirements of the statute. See id., at 636–637, and n. 19, 105 S.Ct. at 3358–3359, and n. 19 (declining to assume that arbitration will not be resolved in accordance with statutory law, but reserving consideration of "effect of an arbitral tribunal's failure to take cognizance of the statutory cause of action on the claimant's capacity to reinstate suit in federal court").

The suitability of arbitration as a means of enforcing Exchange Act rights is evident from our decision in *Scherk*. Although the holding in that case was limited to international agreements, the competence of arbitral tribunals to resolve § 10(b) claims is the same in both settings. Courts likewise have routinely enforced agreements to arbitrate § 10(b) claims where both parties are members of a securities exchange or the National Association of Securities Dealers (NASD), suggesting that arbitral tribunals are fully capable of handling such matters. See, e.g., Axelrod & Co. v. Kordich, Victor & Neufeld, 320 F.Supp. 193 (SDNY 1970), aff'd, 451 F.2d 838 (CA2 1971); Brown v. Gilligan, Will & Co., 287 F.Supp. 766 (SDNY 1968). And courts uniformly have concluded that *Wilko* does not apply to the submission to arbitration of existing disputes, see, e.g., Gardner v. Shearson, Hammill & Co., 433 F.2d 367 (CA5 1970); Moran v. Paine, Webber, Jackson & Curtis, 389 F.2d 242 (CA3 1968), even though the inherent suitability of arbitration as a means of resolving § 10(b) claims remains unchanged. Cf. *Mitsubishi*, 473 U.S., at 633, 105 S.Ct., at 3357.

Thus, the mistrust of arbitration that formed the basis for the *Wilko* opinion in 1953 is difficult to square with the assessment of arbitration that has prevailed since that time. This is especially so in light of the intervening changes in the regulatory structure of the securities laws. Even if *Wilko*'s assumptions regarding arbitration were valid at the time *Wilko* was decided, most certainly they do not hold true today for arbitration procedures subject to the SEC's oversight authority.

In 1953, when *Wilko* was decided, the Commission had only limited authority over the rules governing self-regulatory organizations (SROs)—the national securities exchanges and registered securities associations—and this authority appears not to have included any authority at all over their arbitration rules. See Brief for the Securities and Exchange Commission as Amicus Curiae 14–15. Since the 1975 amendments to § 19 of the Exchange Act, however, the Commission has had expansive power to ensure the adequacy of the arbitration procedures employed by the SROs. No proposed rule change may take effect unless the SEC finds that the proposed rule is consistent with the requirements of the Exchange Act, 15 U.S.C. § 78s(b)(2); and the Commission has the power, on its own initiative, to "abrogate, add to, and delete from" any SRO rule if it finds such changes necessary or appropriate to further the objectives of the Act, 15 U.S.C. § 78s(c). In short, the Commission has broad authority to oversee and to regulate the rules adopted by the SROs relating to customer disputes, including the power to mandate the adoption of any rules it deems necessary to ensure that arbitration procedures adequately protect statutory rights.

In the exercise of its regulatory authority, the SEC has specifically approved the arbitration procedures of the New York Stock Exchange, the American Stock Exchange, and the National Association of Securities Dealers, the organizations mentioned in the arbitration agreement at issue in this case. We conclude that where, as in this case, the prescribed procedures are subject to the Commission's § 19 authority, an arbitration agreement does not effect a waiver of the protections of the Act. While *stare decisis* concerns may counsel against upsetting *Wilko*'s contrary conclusion under the Securities Act, we refuse to extend *Wilko*'s reasoning to the Exchange Act in light of these intervening regulatory developments. The McMahons' agreement to submit to arbitration therefore is not tantamount to an impermissible waiver of the McMahons' rights under § 10(b), and the agreement is not void on that basis under § 29(a).

The final argument offered by the McMahons is that even if § 29(a) as enacted does not void predispute arbitration agreements, Congress subsequently has indicated that it desires for § 29(a) to be so interpreted. According to the McMahons, Congress expressed this intent when it failed to make more extensive changes to § 28(b), 15 U.S.C. 78bb(b), in the 1975 amendments to the Exchange Act. Before its amendment, § 28(b) provided in relevant part:

> "Nothing in this chapter shall be construed to modify existing law (1) with regard to the binding effect on any member of any exchange of any action taken by the authorities of such exchange to settle disputes between its members, or (2) with regard to the binding effect of such action on any person who has agreed to be bound thereby, or (3) with regard to the binding effect on any such member of any disciplinary action taken by the authorities of the exchange." 48 Stat. 903.

The chief aim of this provision was to preserve the self-regulatory role of the securities exchanges, by giving the exchanges a means of enforcing their rules against their members. See, e.g., Tullis v. Kohlmeyer & Co., 551 F.2d 632, 638 (CA5 1977) ("[P]reserv[ing] for the stock exchanges a major self-regulatory role . . . is the basis of § 28(b)");

Axelrod & Co. v. Kordich, Victor & Neufeld, 451 F.2d, at 840–841. In 1975, Congress made extensive revisions to the Exchange Act intended to "clarify the scope of the self-regulatory responsibilities of national securities exchanges and registered securities associations . . . and the manner in which they are to exercise those responsibilities." S.Rep. No. 94–75, p. 22 (1975). In making these changes, the Senate Report observed: "The self-regulatory organizations must exercise governmental-type powers if they are to carry out their responsibilities under the Exchange Act. When a member violates the Act or a self-regulatory organization's rules, the organization must be in a position to impose appropriate penalties or to revoke relevant privileges." Id., at 24.

The amendments to § 28 reflect this objective. Paragraph (3) of § 28(b) was deleted and replaced with new § 28(c), which provided that the validity of any disciplinary action taken by an SRO would not be affected by a subsequent decision by the SEC to stay or modify the sanction. See 15 U.S.C. § 78bb(c). At the same time, § 28(b) was expanded to ensure that all SROs as well as the Municipal Securities Rulemaking Board had the power to enforce their substantive rules against their members. Section 28(b), as amended, provides:

> "Nothing in this chapter shall be construed to modify existing law with regard to the binding effect (1) on any member of or participant in any self-regulatory organization of any action taken by the authorities of such organization to settle disputes between its members or participants, (2) on any municipal securities dealer or municipal securities broker of any action taken pursuant to a procedure established by the Municipal Securities Rulemaking Board to settle disputes between municipal securities dealers and municipal securities brokers, or (3) of any action described in paragraph (1) or (2) on any person who has agreed to be bound thereby."

Thus, the amended version of § 28(b), like the original, mentions neither customers nor arbitration. It is directed at an entirely different problem: enhancing the self-regulatory function of the SROs under the Exchange Act.

The McMahons nonetheless argue that we should find it significant that Congress did *not* take this opportunity to address the general question of the arbitrability of Exchange Act claims. Their argument is based entirely on a sentence from the Conference Report, which they contend amounts to a ratification of *Wilko* 's extension to Exchange Act claims. The Conference Report states:

> "The Senate bill amended section 28 of the Securities Exchange Act of 1934 with respect to arbitration proceedings between self-regulatory organizations and their participants, members, or persons dealing with members or participants. The House amendment contained no comparable provision. The House receded to the Senate. It was the clear understanding of the conferees that

this amendment did not change existing law, as articulated in Wilko v. Swan, 346 U.S. 427 [74 S.Ct. 182, 98 L.Ed. 168] (1953), concerning the effect of arbitration proceedings provisions in agreements entered into by persons dealing with members and participants of self-regulatory organizations." H.R.Conf.Rep. No. 94–229, p. 111 (1975).

The McMahons contend that the conferees would not have acknowledged *Wilko* in a revision of the Exchange Act unless they were aware of lower court decisions extending *Wilko* to § 10(b) claims and intended to approve them. We find this argument fraught with difficulties. We cannot see how Congress could extend *Wilko* to the Exchange Act without enacting into law any provision remotely addressing that subject. See Train v. City of New York, 420 U.S. 35, 45, 95 S.Ct. 839, 845, 43 L.Ed.2d 1 (1975). And even if it could, there is little reason to interpret the Report as the McMahons suggest. At the outset, the committee may well have mentioned *Wilko* for a reason entirely different from the one postulated by the McMahons—lower courts had applied § 28(b) to the Securities Act, see, e.g., Axelrod & Co. v. Kordich, Victor & Neufeld, supra, at 843, and the committee may simply have wished to make clear that the amendment to § 28(b) was not otherwise intended to affect *Wilko*'s construction of the Securities Act. Moreover, even if the committee were referring to the arbitrability of § 10(b) claims, the quoted sentence does not disclose what committee members thought "existing law" provided. The conference members might have had in mind the two Court of Appeals decisions extending *Wilko* to the Exchange Act, as the McMahons contend. See Greater Continental Corp. v. Schechter, 422 F.2d 1100 (CA2 1970); Moran v. Paine, Webber, Jackson & Curtis, 389 F.2d 242 (CA3 1968). It is equally likely, however, that the committee had in mind this Court's decision the year before expressing doubts as to whether *Wilko* should be extended to § 10(b) claims. See Scherk v. Alberto–Culver Co., 417 U.S., at 513, 94 S.Ct., at 2454 ("[A] colorable argument could be made that even the semantic reasoning of the *Wilko* opinion does not control [a case based on § 10(b)]"). Finally, even assuming the conferees had an understanding of existing law that all agreed upon, they specifically disclaimed any intent to change it. Hence, the *Wilko* issue was left to the courts: it was unaffected by the amendment to § 28(b). This statement of congressional inaction simply does not support the proposition that the 1975 Congress intended to engraft onto unamended § 29(a) a meaning different from that of the enacting Congress.

We conclude, therefore, that Congress did not intend for § 29(a) to bar enforcement of all predispute arbitration agreements. In this case, where the SEC has sufficient statutory authority to ensure that arbitration is adequate to vindicate Exchange Act rights, enforcement does not effect a waiver of "compliance with any provision" of the Exchange Act under § 29(a). Accordingly, we hold the McMahons' agreements to arbitrate Exchange Act claims "enforce[able] . . . in accord with the explicit provisions of the Arbitration Act." Scherk v. Alberto–Culver Co., supra, at 520, 94 S.Ct., at 2457.

IV

Unlike the Exchange Act, there is nothing in the text of the RICO statute that even arguably evinces congressional intent to exclude civil RICO claims from the dictates of the Arbitration Act. This silence in the text is matched by silence in the statute's legislative history. The private treble-damages provision codified as 18 U.S.C. § 1964(c) was added to the House version of the bill after the bill had been passed by the Senate, and it received only abbreviated discussion in either House. See Sedima, S.P.R.L. v. Imrex Co., 473 U.S. 479, 486–488, 105 S.Ct. 3275, 3280–3281, 87 L.Ed.2d 346 (1985). There is no hint in these legislative debates that Congress intended for RICO treble-damages claims to be excluded from the ambit of the Arbitration Act. See Genesco, Inc. v. T. Kakiuchi & Co., Ltd., 815 F.2d 840, 850–851 (CA2 1987); Mayaja, Inc. v. Bodkin, 803 F.2d 157, 164 (CA5 1986).

Because RICO's text and legislative history fail to reveal any intent to override the provisions of the Arbitration Act, the McMahons must argue that there is an irreconcilable conflict between arbitration and RICO's underlying purposes. Our decision in Mitsubishi Motors Corp. v. Soler Chrysler–Plymouth, Inc., 473 U.S. 614, 105 S.Ct. 3346, 87 L.Ed. 2d 444 (1985), however, already has addressed many of the grounds given by the McMahons to support this claim. In *Mitsubishi,* we held that nothing in the nature of the federal antitrust laws prohibits parties from agreeing to arbitrate antitrust claims arising out of international commercial transactions. Although the holding in *Mitsubishi* was limited to the international context, see id., at 629, 105 S.Ct., at 3355, much of its reasoning is equally applicable here. Thus, for example, the McMahons have argued that RICO claims are too complex to be subject to arbitration. We determined in *Mitsubishi,* however, that "potential complexity should not suffice to ward off arbitration." Id., at 633, 105 S.Ct., at 3357. Antitrust matters are every bit as complex as RICO claims, but we found that the "adaptability and access to expertise" characteristic of arbitration rebutted the view "that an arbitral tribunal could not properly handle an antitrust matter." Id., at 633–634, 105 S.Ct., at 3358.

Likewise, the McMahons contend that the "overlap" between RICO's civil and criminal provisions renders § 1964(c) claims nonarbitrable. See Page v. Mosley, Hallgarten, Estabrook & Weeden, Inc., 806 F.2d 291, 299, n. 13 (CA1 1986) ("[T]he makings of a 'pattern of racketeering' are not yet clear, but the fact remains that a 'pattern' for civil purposes is a 'pattern' for criminal purposes"). Yet § 1964(c) is no different in this respect from the federal antitrust laws. In Sedima, S.P.R.L. v. Imrex Co., supra, we rejected the view that § 1964(c) "provide[s] civil remedies for offenses criminal in nature." See 473 U.S., at 492, 105 S.Ct., at 3283. In doing so, this Court observed: "[T]he fact that conduct can result in both criminal liability and treble damages does not mean that there is not a bona fide civil action. The familiar provisions for both criminal liability and treble damages under the antitrust laws indicate as much." Ibid. *Mitsubishi* recognized that treble-damages suits for claims arising under § 1 of the Sherman Act may be subject to arbitration, even though such conduct may also give rise to claims of criminal liability. See Mitsubishi Motors Corp. v. Soler Chrysler–Plymouth, Inc., supra. We similarly find that the criminal provisions of RICO do not preclude arbitration of bona fide civil actions brought under § 1964(c).

The McMahons' final argument is that the public interest in the enforcement of RICO precludes its submission to arbitration. *Mitsubishi* again is relevant to the question. In that case we thoroughly examined the legislative intent behind § 4 of the Clayton Act in assaying whether the importance of the private treble-damages remedy in enforcing the antitrust laws precluded arbitration of § 4 claims. We found that "[n]otwithstanding its important incidental policing function, the treble-damages cause of action . . . seeks primarily to enable an injured competitor to gain compensation for that injury." 473 U.S., at 635, 105 S.Ct., at 3359. Emphasizing the priority of the compensatory function of § 4 over its deterrent function, *Mitsubishi* concluded that "so long as the prospective litigant effectively may vindicate its statutory cause of action in the arbitral forum, the statute will continue to serve both its remedial and deterrent function." Id., at 637, 105 S.Ct., at 3360.

The legislative history of § 1964(c) reveals the same emphasis on the remedial role of the treble-damages provision. In introducing the treble-damages provision to the House Judiciary Committee, Representative Steiger stressed that "those who have been wronged by organized crime should at least be given access to a legal remedy." Hearings on S. 30 and related proposals before Subcommittee No. 5 of the House Committee on the Judiciary, 91st Cong., 2d Sess., 520 (1970). The policing function of § 1964(c), although important, was a secondary concern. See ibid. ("In addition, the availability of such a remedy would enhance the effectiveness of title IX's prohibitions"). During the congressional debates on § 1964(c), Representative Steiger again emphasized the remedial purpose of the provision: "It is the intent of this body, I am certain, to see that innocent parties who are the victims of organized crime have a right to obtain proper redress . . . . It represents the one opportunity for those of us who have been seriously affected by organized crime activity to recover." 116 Cong.Rec. 35346–35347 (1970). This focus on the remedial function of § 1964(c) is reinforced by the recurrent references in the legislative debates to § 4 of the Clayton Act as the model for the RICO treble-damages provision. See, e.g., 116 Cong.Rec. 35346 (statement of Rep. Poff) (RICO provision "has its counterpart almost in haec verba in the antitrust statutes"); id., at 25190 (statement of Sen. McClellan) (proposed amendment would "authorize private civil damage suits based upon the concept of section

4 of the Clayton Antitrust Act"). See generally Sedima, S.P.R.L. v. Imrex Co., 473 U.S., at 489, 105 S.Ct., at 3282 ("The clearest current in [RICO's] history is the reliance on the Clayton Act model").

Not only does *Mitsubishi* support the arbitrability of RICO claims, but there is even more reason to suppose that arbitration will adequately serve the purposes of RICO than that it will adequately protect private enforcement of the antitrust laws. Antitrust violations generally have a widespread impact on national markets as a whole, and the antitrust treble-damages provision gives private parties an incentive to bring civil suits that serve to advance the national interest in a competitive economy. See Lindsay, "Public" Rights and Private Forums: Predispute Arbitration Agreements and Securities Litigation, 20 Loyola (LA) L.Rev. 643, 691–692 (1987). RICO's drafters likewise sought to provide vigorous incentives for plaintiffs to pursue RICO claims that would advance society's fight against organized crime. See Sedima, S.P.R.L. v. Imrex Co., supra, at 498, 105 S.Ct., at 3286. But in fact RICO actions are seldom asserted "against the archetypal, intimidating mobster." Id., at 499, 105 S.Ct., at 3287; see also id., at 506, 105 S.Ct., at 3295 (Marshall, J., dissenting) ("[O]nly 9% of all civil RICO cases have involved allegations of criminal activity normally associated with professional criminals"). The special incentives necessary to encourage civil enforcement actions against organized crime do not support nonarbitrability or run-of-the-mill civil RICO claims brought against legitimate enterprises. The private attorney general role for the typical RICO plaintiff is simply less plausible than it is for the typical antitrust plaintiff, and does not support a finding that there is an irreconcilable conflict between arbitration and enforcement of the RICO statute.

In sum, we find no basis for concluding that Congress intended to prevent enforcement of agreements to arbitrate RICO claims. The McMahons may effectively vindicate their RICO claim in an arbitral forum, and therefore there is no inherent conflict between arbitration and the purposes underlying § 1964(c). Moreover, nothing in RICO's text or legislative history otherwise demonstrates congressional intent to make an exception to the Arbitration Act for RICO claims. Accordingly, the McMahons, "having made the bargain to arbitrate," will be held to their bargain. Their RICO claim is arbitrable under the terms of the Arbitration Act.

V

Accordingly, the judgment of the Court of Appeals for the Second Circuit is reversed, and the case is remanded for further proceedings consistent with this opinion.

It is so ordered.

JUSTICE BLACKMUN, with whom JUSTICE BRENNAN and JUSTICE MARSHALL join, concurring in part and dissenting in part.

I concur in the Court's decision to enforce the arbitration agreement with respect to respondents' RICO claims and thus join Parts I, II, and IV of the Court's opinion. I disagree, however, with the Court's conclusion that respondents' § 10(b) claims also are subject to arbitration.

Both the Securities Act of 1933 and the Securities Exchange Act of 1934 were enacted to protect investors from predatory behavior of securities industry personnel. In Wilko v. Swan, 346 U.S. 427, 74 S.Ct. 182, 98 L.Ed. 168 (1953), the Court recognized this basic purpose when it declined to enforce a predispute agreement to compel arbitration of claims under the Securities Act. Following that decision, lower courts extended *Wilko*'s reasoning to claims brought under § 10(b) of the Exchange Act, and Congress approved of this extension. In today's decision, however, the Court effectively overrules *Wilko* by accepting the Securities and Exchange Commission's newly adopted position that arbitration procedures in the securities industry and the Commission's oversight of the self-regulatory organizations (SROs) have improved greatly since *Wilko* was decided. The Court thus approves the abandonment of the judiciary's role in the resolution of claims under the Exchange Act and leaves such claims to the arbitral forum of the securities industry at a time when the industry's abuses towards investors are more apparent than ever.

　*　　*　　*

II

There are essentially two problems with the Court's conclusion that predispute agreements to arbitrate § 10(b) claims may be enforced. First, the Court gives *Wilko* an overly narrow reading so that it can fit into the syllogism offered by the Commission and accepted by the Court, namely, (1) *Wilko* was really a case concerning whether arbitration was adequate for the enforcement of the substantive provisions of the securities laws; (2) all of the *Wilko* Court's doubts as to arbitration's adequacy are outdated; (3) thus *Wilko* is no longer good law. *　*　* Brief for Securities and Exchange Commission as Amicus Curiae 10. Second, the Court accepts uncritically petitioners' and the Commission's argument that the problems with arbitration, highlighted by the *Wilko* Court, either no longer exist or are not now viewed as problems by the Court. This acceptance primarily is based upon the Court's belief in the Commission's representations that its oversight of the SROs ensures the adequacy of arbitration.

　*　　*　　*

B

Even if I were to accept the Court's narrow reading of *Wilko,* as a case dealing only with the inadequacies of arbitration in 1953, I do not think that this case should be resolved differently today so long as the policy of investor protection is given proper consideration in the analysis. Despite improvements in the process of arbitration and changes in the judicial attitude towards it, several aspects of arbitration that were seen by the *Wilko* court to be inimical to the policy of investor protection still remain. Moreover, I have serious reservations about the Commission's contention that its oversight of the SROs' arbitration procedures will ensure that the process is adequate to protect an investor's rights under the securities Acts.

As the Court observes, * * * in *Wilko* the Court was disturbed by several characteristics of arbitration that made such a process inadequate to safeguard the special position in which the Securities Act had placed the investor. The Court concluded that judicial review of the arbitrators' application of the securities laws would be difficult because arbitrators were required neither to give the reasons for their decisions nor to make a complete record of their proceedings. See 346 U.S., at 436, 74 S.Ct., at 187. The Court also observed that the grounds for vacating an arbitration award were limited. The Court noted that, under the Arbitration Act, there were only four grounds for vacation of an award: fraud in procuring the award, partiality on the part of arbitrators, gross misconduct by arbitrators, and the failure of arbitrators to render a final decision. Id., at 436, n. 22, 74 S.Ct., at 187, n. 22, quoting 9 U.S.C. § 10 (1952 ed., Supp. V). The arbitrators' interpretation of the law would be subject to judicial review only under the "manifest disregard" standard. 346 U.S., at 436, 74 S.Ct., at 187.

The Court today appears to argue that the *Wilko* Court's assessment of arbitration's inadequacy is outdated, first, because arbitration has improved since 1953 and, second, because the Court no longer considers the criticisms of arbitration made in *Wilko* to be valid reasons why statutory claims, such as those under § 10(b), should not be sent to arbitration. It is true that arbitration procedures in the securities industry have improved since *Wilko's* day. Of particular importance has been the development of a code of arbitration by the Commission with the assistance of representatives of the securities industry and the public. See Uniform Code of Arbitration, Exh. C., Fifth Report of the Securities Industry Conference on Arbitration 29 (Apr.1986) (Fifth SICA Report).[16]

Even those who favor the arbitration of securities claims do not contend, however, that arbitration has changed so significantly as to

---

16. This Code has been used to harmonize the arbitration procedures among the SROs. See Katsoris, The Arbitration of a Public Securities Dispute, 53 Ford.L.Rev. 279, 283–284 (1984) (Katsoris). As the Commission explained: "[T]his [Code] marks a substantial improvement over the various arbitration procedures currently being utilized by the securities industry and represents an important step towards establishing a uniform system for resolving investor complaints through arbitration." SEC Exchange Act Rel. No. 16390 (Nov. 30, 1979), 44 Fed.Reg. 70616, 70617.

The rules of the Uniform Code provide for the selection of arbitrators and the manner in which the proceedings are conducted. See Fifth SICA Report; see also Code of Arbitration Procedure, CCH NASD Manual ¶¶ 3701–3744 (July 1986); Arbitration Rules 600–620, CCH American Stock Exchange Guide ¶¶ 9540–9551J (May 1986); Arbitration Rules 600–634, CCH New York Stock Exchange Guide, ¶¶ 2600–2634 (Mar. 1985). Some arbitration agreements permit arbitration before the American Arbitration Association, whose rules are similar to those in the above Codes. Brief for American Arbitration Association as Amicus Curiae 12–13 and App. B.; see also Fletcher 451.

eliminate the essential characteristics noted by the *Wilko* Court. Indeed, proponents of arbitration would not see these characteristics as "problems," because, in their view, the characteristics permit the unique "streamlined" nature of the arbitral process. As at the time of *Wilko,* preparation of a record of arbitration proceedings is not invariably required today.[17] Moreover, arbitrators are not bound by precedent and are actually discouraged by their associations from giving reasons for a decision. See R. Coulson, Business Arbitrations—What You Need to Know 29 (3d ed.1986) ("Written opinions can be dangerous because they identify targets for the losing party to attack"); see also Duke Note 553; Fletcher 456–457. Judicial review is still substantially limited to the four grounds listed in § 10 of the Arbitration Act and to the concept of "manifest disregard" of the law. See, e.g., French v. Merrill Lynch, Pierce, Fenner & Smith, Inc., 784 F.2d 902, 906 (CA9 1986), citing Swift Industries, Inc. v. Botany Industries, Inc., 466 F.2d 1125, 1131 (CA3 1972) (an arbitrator's decision must be upheld unless it is " 'completely irrational' ").[18]

The Court's "mistrust" of arbitration may have given way recently to an acceptance of this process, not only because of the improvements in arbitration, but also because of the Court's present assumption that the distinctive features of arbitration, its more quick and economical resolution of claims, do not render it inherently inadequate for the resolution of statutory claims. See Mitsubishi Motors Corp. v. Soler Chrysler–Plymouth, Inc., 473 U.S., at 633, 105 S.Ct., at 3357. Such reasoning, however, should prevail only in the absence of the congressional policy that places the statutory claimant in a special position with respect to possible violators of his statutory rights. As even the most ardent supporter of arbitration would recognize, the arbitral process *at best* places the investor on an equal footing with the securities-industry personnel against whom the claims are brought.

Furthermore, there remains the danger that, *at worst,* compelling an investor to arbitrate securities claims puts him in a forum controlled by the securities industry. This result directly contradicts the goal of both securities Acts to free the investor from the control of the market professional. The Uniform Code provides some safeguards [19] but de-

---

17. Under the Uniform Code of Arbitration:

"Unless requested by the arbitrators or a party or parties to a dispute, no record of an arbitration proceeding shall be kept. If a record is kept, it shall be a verbatim record. If a party or parties to a dispute elect to have the record transcribed, the cost of such transcription shall be borne by the party or parties making the request." Fifth SICA Report § 25, p. 36.

18. The Uniform Code of Arbitration and the SRO codes modeled upon it do provide for limited discovery, see Brief for Securities Industry Association, Inc., et al., as Amici Curiae 9, and the ability to sub-poena witnesses, see Brief for American Arbitration Association as Amicus Curiae 13. Yet, by arbitrating their disputes, investors lose the wide choice of venue and the extensive discovery provided by the courts. See Katsoris 287, n. 52.

19. The Uniform Code mandates that a majority of an arbitration panel, usually composed of between three to five arbitrators, be drawn from outside the industry. Fifth SICA Report § 8(a). Each arbitrator, moreover, is directed to disclose "any circumstances which might preclude such arbitrator from rendering an objective and impartial determination." § 11. In addition, the parties are informed of the business associations of the arbitrators, § 9,

spite them, and indeed because of the background of the arbitrators, the investor has the impression, frequently justified, that his claims are being judged by a forum composed of individuals sympathetic to the securities industry and not drawn from the public. It is generally recognized that the codes do not define who falls into the category "not from the securities industry." Brown, Shell, & Tyson 35, and n. 94; Katsoris 309–312. Accordingly, it is often possible for the "public" arbitrators to be attorneys or consultants whose clients have been exchange members or SROs. See Panel of Arbitrators 1987–1988, CCH American Stock Exchange Guide 158–160 (1987) (71 out of 116 "public" arbitrators are lawyers). The uniform opposition of investors to compelled arbitration and the overwhelming support of the securities industry for the process suggest that there must be *some* truth to the investors' belief that the securities industry has an advantage in a forum under its own control. See N.Y. Times, Mar. 29, 1987, section 3, p. 8, col. 1 (statement of Sheldon H. Elsen, Chairman, American Bar Association Task Force on Securities Arbitration: "The houses basically like the present system because they own the stacked deck").[20]

* * *

Moreover, the Commission's own description of its enforcement capabilities contradicts its position that its general overview of SRO rules and procedures can make arbitration adequate for resolving securities claims. The Commission does not pretend that its oversight consists of anything other than a general review of SRO rules and the ability to require that an SRO adopt or delete a particular rule. It does not contend that its "sweeping authority," Brief for Securities and Exchange Commission as Amicus Curiae 16, includes a review of specific arbitration proceedings. It thus neither polices nor monitors the results of these arbitrations for possible misapplications of securities laws or for indications of how investors fare in these proceedings. Given, in fact, the present constraints on the Commission's resources in this time of market expansion, see General Accounting Office, Report to the Chairman, Subcommittee on Telecommunications, Consumer Protection, and Finance of the House Committee on Energy and Commerce: Securities Regulations—Securities and Exchange Commission

and each party has the right to one peremptory challenge and to unlimited challenges for cause, § 10. The arbitrators are usually individuals familiar with the federal securities laws. See Brener v. Becker Paribas Inc., 628 F.Supp. 442, 448 (SDNY 1985).

20. Commentators have argued that more public participation in the SRO arbitration procedures is needed to give investors the impression that they are not in a forum biased in favor of the securities industry. See, e.g., Katsoris 313. The *amici* in support of petitioners and some commentators argue that the statistics concerning the results of arbitration show that the process is not weighted in favor of the securities industry. See Brief for Securities Industry Association, Inc., et al., as Amici Curiae 9; Brief for American Arbitration Association as Amicus Curiae 17; Fletcher 452. Such statistics, however, do not indicate the damages received by customers in relation to the damages to which they believed they were entitled. It is possible for an investor to "prevail" in arbitration while recovering a sum considerably less than the damages he actually incurred.

Oversight of Self–Regulation 60 (1986) (Report), it is doubtful whether the Commission could undertake to conduct any such review.[25]

Finally, the Court's complacent acceptance of the Commission's oversight is alarming when almost every day brings another example of illegality on Wall Street. See, e.g., N.Y. Times, Jan. 2, 1987, p. B6, col. 3. Many of the abuses recently brought to light, it is true, do not deal with the question of the adequacy of SRO arbitration. They, however, do suggest that the industry's self-regulation, of which the SRO arbitration is a part, is not functioning acceptably. See Report 63. Moreover, these abuses have highlighted the difficulty experienced by the Commission, at a time of growth in the securities market and a decrease in the Commission's staff, see id., at 60–61, to carry out its oversight task. Such inadequacies on the part of the Commission strike at the very heart of the reasoning of the Court, which is content to accept the soothing assurances of the Commission without examining the reality behind them. Indeed, while the *amici* cite the number of arbitrations of securities disputes as a sign of the success of this process in the industry, see Brief for Securities Industry Association, Inc., et al. as Amici Curiae 10–11, these statistics have a more portentous meaning. In this era of deregulation, the growth in complaints about the securities industry, many of which find their way to arbitration, parallels the increase in securities violations and suggests a market not adequately controlled by the SROs. See General Accounting Office, Report to the Chairman, Subcommittee on Oversight and Investigation of the House Committee on Energy and Commerce: Statistics on SEC's Enforcement Program 3–4 (1985). In such a time, one would expect more, not less, judicial involvement in resolution of securities disputes.

III

There is, fortunately, a remedy for investors. In part as a result of the Commission's position in this case, Congress has begun to look into the adequacy of the self-regulatory arbitration and the Commission's oversight of the SROs. In a letter dated February 11, 1987, Representative Dingell, Chairman of the House Subcommittee on Oversight and Investigations, notified the Chairman of the Commission that the Subcommittee is "conducting an inquiry into the adequacy of the current self-regulatory system and the Commission's oversight thereof in connection with complaints against broker-dealers for securities-law violations." Letter, p. 1, enclosed with Letter from Theodore G. Eppen-

---

25. Even those who would agree with the Commission that its general oversight of SRO arbitration procedures has bettered the adequacy of arbitration recognize that improvements in this oversight still are needed. For example, commentators have suggested that the Commission should revise the Uniform Code of Arbitration in order to ensure that predispute arbitration agreements are displayed prominently, that the reference to a person drawn from "outside the securities industry" be more specifically defined, and that arbitrators be required to give a more detailed statement of their reasoning. See Brown, Shell, & Tyson 34–36. Congress could give to the Commission specific rule-making authority in the area of arbitration with the goal of preventing abuses in the process that have surfaced in recent years. Id., at 34.

stein, counsel for respondents, to Joseph F. Spaniol, Jr., Clerk of this Court (Mar. 2, 1987). Representative Dingell noted that his Subcommittee was "particularly concerned about increasing numbers of complaints in connection with churning and violations of suitability requirements, as well as complaints that arbitration procedures are rife with conflicts of interest (since the arbitrators are peers of the brokerage firm being sued) and are inadequate to enforce the statutory rights of customers against broker-dealers." Ibid. To justify this inquiry, he cited several well-publicized examples of abuse of investors by securities-industry personnel and a General Accounting Office report on the increase in securities-law violations by brokers that went undetected by the SROs. In concluding the letter, Representative Dingell expressed his surprise at the Commission's position in the present case. In his view, that position was at odds with the one the Commission consistently had taken before the Subcommittee, which stressed the limitations on the Commission's authority over the SROs in general, and over arbitrations in particular. Id., at 3. Thus, there is hope that Congress will give investors the relief that the Court denies them today.

In the meantime, the Court leaves lower courts with some authority, albeit limited, to protect investors before Congress acts. Courts should take seriously their duty to review the results of arbitration to the extent possible under the Arbitration Act. As we explained in Mitsubishi Motors Corp. v. Soler Chrysler–Plymouth, Inc., "courts should remain attuned to well-supported claims that the agreement to arbitrate resulted from the sort of fraud or overwhelming economic power that would provide grounds 'for the revocation of any contract.' " 473 U.S., at 627, 105 S.Ct., at 3354, quoting 9 U.S.C. § 2. Indeed, in light of today's decision compelling the enforcement of predispute arbitration agreements, it is likely that investors will be inclined, more than ever, to bring complaints to federal courts that arbitrators were partial or acted in "manifest disregard" of the securities laws. See Brown, Shell, & Tyson 36. It is thus ironic that the Court's decision, no doubt animated by its desire to rid the federal courts of these suits, actually may *increase* litigation about arbitration.

I therefore respectfully dissent in part.

JUSTICE STEVENS, concurring in part and dissenting in part.[*]

NOTE ON ARBITRATION

1. Commercial Arbitration

Arbitration of disputes over commercial relationships has a long history of development hampered until recently by judicial hostility. Courts were especially reluctant to enforce agreements to arbitrate future disputes because the parties were bypassing the jurisdiction of the court. Beginning in the 1920's, various state legislatures and the Congress began to see the utility of giving explicit legislative sanction to arbitration and Federal law and the laws of most states now recognize the legitimacy of the arbitration process and provide the

---

[*] Justice Stevens' opinion is omitted.

legal foundation for its enforcement. Passage of these laws also resulted, whether wisely or not, in a greater degree of uniformity in arbitral practice. See, for example, the United States Arbitration Act, 9 U.S.C.A. §§ 1–15; C.C.P. 1280–1294.2; Uniform Arbitration Act, 7 U.L.A. 1 (Master ed. 1985). See also Bernstein, Private Dispute Settlement (1968), cc. 2, 3, 7; N.Y. Judicial Conference, 23d Annual Report, c. 7 (1978).

The waning of the traditional hostility toward arbitration can be traced in the cases where the issue is whether a given statutory scheme overrides the federal policy favoring arbitration as embodied in the United States Arbitration Act. As Shearson/American Express, Inc. v. McMahon describes, Wilko v. Swan represented a high point of judicial hostility to arbitration. It was followed by decisions that eroded both the holding of that case and its underlying policy. Although *Wilko* was not expressly overruled in *McMahon*, does it continue to have any force? Did the Court in *McMahon* provide adequate guidelines for determining when a statutory scheme will be deemed to override a commercial arbitration agreement? Not all courts are as eager as the Supreme Court to enforce arbitration clauses. See, e.g., Keating v. Superior Court, 31 Cal.3d 584, 183 Cal.Rptr. 360, 645 P.2d 1192 (1982), rev'd in part, appeal dismissed in part sub nom. Southland Corp. v. Keating, 465 U.S. 1, 104 S.Ct. 852, 79 L.Ed.2d 1 (1984). Compare McDonald v. City of West Branch, 466 U.S. 284, 104 S.Ct. 1799, 80 L.Ed.2d 302 (1984) (labor arbitration is not a "judicial proceeding" within the meaning of federal full faith and credit statute, and so federal courts are not required to give preclusive effect to unappealed labor arbitration awards in subsequent civil rights suits). On the enforceability of nonbinding arbitration agreements under the United States Arbitration Act, see AMF Inc. v. Brunswick Corp., 621 F.Supp. 456 (E.D.N.Y.1985). See also Fletcher, Privatizing Securities Disputes Through the Enforcement of Arbitration Agreements, 71 Minn.L.Rev. 393 (1987).

Businessmen's disputes can be resolved by trade associations, by an arbitrator provided by an uninterested professional group like the American Arbitration Association, or by an arrangement specifically designed for the particular parties involved. For a model code of procedure, see American Arbitration Association, Commercial Arbitration Rules (1964). Arbitration intends to be an informal system of settling disputes based more closely on common business practices and the relationships of the particular parties involved; however, the losing party often contests the process through litigation, and, inevitably, a body of law has developed around the arbitration mechanism. In general, see Wilmer, Domke on Commercial Arbitration (rev. ed. 1984); Levin and Golash, Alternative Dispute Resolution in Federal District Courts, 37 U.Fla.L.Rev. 29 (1985); Note, Commercial Arbitration in Federal Courts, 20 Vand.L.Rev. 607 (1967).

Special problems can arise where an international commercial agreement contains an arbitration clause; see generally Scherk v. Alberto–Culver Co., 417 U.S. 506, 94 S.Ct. 2449, 41 L.Ed.2d 270 (1974), discussed in *McMahon*. In 1988, California adopted a comprehensive statute to facilitate arbitration and conciliation of international commercial disputes connected with California; see C.C.P. 1297.11 et seq. The statute mandates judicial enforcement of arbitration, conciliation, and choice of law clauses in international agreements and specifies procedures to be followed in conducting arbitration and conciliation proceedings. See also Craig, Park and Paulsson, International Commercial Arbitration: International Chamber of Commerce Arbitration (1984); Paulsson, International Commercial Arbitrations (1987).

2. Labor Arbitration

Arbitration agreements are quite prevalent in labor-management contracts. They often prescribe very detailed systems for handling grievances that involve several levels of attempts at discussion and conciliation before the issue is submitted for arbitration. Often, a contract clause providing for compulsory arbitration of all grievances is combined with a clause prohibiting strikes by the employees. As with commercial arbitration, labor arbitration agreements were prevalent prior to statutes making them enforceable in court. See Bernstein, supra, cc. 9–13; Fleming, The Labor Arbitration Process (1965); Updegraff, Arbitration and Labor Relations (3d ed. 1970). See also DeTomaso v. Pan American World Airways, Inc., 43 Cal.3d 517, 235 Cal.Rptr. 292, 733 P.2d 614 (1987) (employee's tort claim preempted by Federal Railway Labor Act requirement that an employment grievance be resolved by arbitration).

3. Arbitration in Other Areas

Arbitration can obviously be an advantageous method of resolving conflicts in areas outside of labor relations and the commercial areas to which it has been traditionally limited. Resolution of consumer grievances would seem to be one such area. See Cal.Bus. & Prof.Code § 6200 et seq. (arbitration of attorney fee disputes); Cal.Vehicle Code § 3050 (New Motor Vehicle Board to "arbitrate or otherwise resolve any honest difference of opinion or viewpoint" between a new car dealer and "any member of the public"); Cal.Insurance Code § 11580.2 (arbitration of disputes over the extent of insurance against collisions with uninsured motorists); McGonagle, Arbitration of Consumer Disputes, 27 Arb.J. 65 (1972). Specific statutory schemes should be scrutinized carefully, however, for they may unconstitutionally deprive consumers of a right to a jury trial. See Stanley, The Resolution of Minor Disputes and the Seventh Amendment, 60 Marq.L.Rev. 963 (1977). Compare C.C.P. 1141.10 et seq., providing for arbitration of civil actions that have reached issue in which the court determines that recovery is unlikely to exceed $50,000. The procedure is enforced by the sanction of paying for the cost of the trial that may be had after arbitration, if a more advantageous verdict is not obtained at trial. For the rules governing arbitration under these provisions, see California Rules of Court, Judicial Arbitration Rules for Civil Cases, Rule 1600 et seq. On California's experience with alternative dispute resolution generally, see Comment, Institutionalization of Alternative Dispute Resolution by the State of California, 14 Pepperdine L.Rev. 943 (1987). On New York's arbitration procedures, see A.B.C.N.Y., Committee on Arbitration, An Outline of Procedure Under Arbitration Law in New York (April 1984).

Resolving disputes between different governmental agencies is another area amenable to arbitration. For example, see the Uniform Act on Interstate Arbitration of Death Taxes, 8A U.L.A. 521 (Master ed. 1983), adopted in California, Cal.Revenue and Taxation Code §§ 13820 et seq.

Problems relating to land and natural resources have also been the subject of legislative submission to arbitration. See C.C. 845 (disputes between co-owners over maintenance of easements); Cal.Public Resources Code § 6357 (establishment of high-water or low-water mark of submerged state lands); Cal. Water Code § 1246 (damage claims against municipal corporations for the taking of lands or water for their water supply). Mediation has proven successful in settling seemingly intractable environmental disputes. See Calm After The Storm: Grandmother of Environmental Lawsuits Settled By Mediation, 11 Env.L.Rep. 10074 (1981).

There will no doubt be more and more attempts at extending the domain of arbitration in order both to provide relief for congested court dockets and to find more flexible approaches to the resolution of complicated disputes. See Symposium, Arbitration, 6 Litigation 8 (1980); Comment, Judicial Deference to Arbitral Determinations: Continuing Problems of Power and Finality, 23 U.C. L.A.L.Rev. 936 (1976). The Judicial Improvements and Access to Justice Act of 1988, for example, instituted an experimental court-annexed arbitration program in a limited number of federal districts. See 28 U.S.C.A. § 651 et seq. The provisions allow any case to be referred to arbitration on consent of the parties and authorize the judge to require arbitration in any case where the damages sought do not exceed $100,000, except in cases alleging the violation of a constitutional right or of Federal civil rights statutes. Within 30 days after an arbitration award is filed with the court, any party may demand trial de novo in the district court. Absent such demand, the arbitrator's decision becomes the final judgment of the court and may not be appealed. An assessment of an earlier, more limited experimental program noted only "modest benefits" and "mild" endorsement by participants. See Lind and Shapard, Evaluation of Court-Annexed Arbitration in Three Federal District Courts (Federal Judicial Center, 1981). For a somewhat more optimistic assessment of arbitration, court-annexed and otherwise, see Kanowitz, Alternative Dispute Resolution and the Public Interest: The Arbitration Experience, 38 Hastings L.J. 239 (1987). See also Delgado, Dunn, Brown, Lee and Hubbert, Fairness and Formality: Minimizing the Risk of Prejudice in Alternative Dispute Resolution, 1985 Wis.L.Rev. 1359; Walker, Court-Ordered Arbitration Comes to North Carolina and the Nation, 21 Wake Forest L.Rev. 901 (1986).

4. Mediation, Ombudsmen, Community Justice Centers and Other Possibilities

In recent years there has been great interest in developing alternatives to adjudication, especially in "small" controversies (i.e., those involving small monetary stakes) and "neighborhood" disputes, whatever that might include. See generally Johnson, Kantor and Schwartz, Outside the Courts—A Survey of Diversion Alternatives in Civil Cases (Nat'l Center for State Courts, 1977). See also ABA, Report on the National Conference on Minor Disputes Resolution (1977) (prepared by Professor Frank Sander). On California's so-called "rent-a-judge" phenomenon, see Note, California Rent-a-Judge Experiment: Constitutional and Policy Considerations of Pay-as-You-Go Courts, 94 Harv.L.Rev. 1592 (1981); Comment, Private Means to Public Ends: Implications of the Private Judging Phenomenon in California, 17 U.C.Davis L.Rev. 611 (1984). Other possibilities include the expanded use of advisory juries as an aid to settlement in cases where a jury is not available of right; see Note, Practice and Potential of the Advisory Jury, 100 Harv.L.Rev. 1363 (1987).

For a general review of alternative dispute resolution techniques, see Goldberg, Green and Sander, Dispute Resolution (1985); ADR and the Courts: A Manual for Judges and Lawyers (Center for Public Resources 1987). See also Note on Alternatives to Formal Adjudication, supra p. 37.

Part IX

REVIEW OF THE DISPOSITION

INTRODUCTORY NOTE ON APPELLATE REVIEW

It is recognized in American law that a person against whom a final judgment has been rendered in an action involving substantial stakes should have the right to bring the decision before an appellate court to consider the loser's assertions that (1) the court below failed to adhere to proper procedure in reaching the decision or (2) the decision was based on misapplication of the substantive law or gross misapprehension of the facts. But this proposition leaves out many possibilities:

1. What about a judgment that does not involve substantial stakes, for example a judgment in a small claims court or a judgment for a small amount of damages? In many jurisdictions there used to be a minimum amount in controversy requirement for appellate jurisdiction. Today in some jurisdictions the right of appeal in small claims cases is limited. See C.C.P. 117.8, providing that a *defendant* may appeal a small claims judgment, but that a plaintiff may not except on a showing of good cause (on the theory that plaintiff chose the special small claims procedure), and 117.10, providing that upon appeal the case "shall be tried anew" in the superior court. Compare ABA Standards of Judicial Administration § 2.75(g), recommending that a decision in small claims court "should be final except that appellate review should be allowed of questions of law certified by the trial judge as being of general significance." The tradition of right to appeal is so strong, however, that except for such minor exceptions there is a right to appellate review of virtually every kind of civil final judgment. Cf. Friedman v. State of New York, 24 N.Y.2d 528, 301 N.Y.S.2d 484, 249 N.E.2d 369 (1969), allowing a collateral attack on a judgment from which no appeal was allowed, precisely because review would not otherwise have been available to the losing party.

2. What about a person who has *won* a judgment? If the person has won less than that which he sought in the way of relief, he is an "aggrieved party" who can seek appellate relief. But if he obtained the relief he sought, he cannot pursue an appeal to secure vindication of a legal theory the lower court declined to adopt or to obtain an appellate imprimatur on the judgment. See, e.g., DeKorwin v. First Nat. Bank of Chicago, 235 F.2d 156 (7th Cir.1956); Moore v. Younger, 54 Cal.App.3d 1122, 127 Cal.Rptr. 171 (1976); Anno., 69 A.L.R.2d 701. However, this limitation should be considered in light of the fact that appellate courts frequently decide mooted cases when the question of law is of general and recurring interest. See, e.g., SEC v. Sloan, 436 U.S. 103, 98 S.Ct. 1702, 56 L.Ed.2d 148 (1978).

3. What about a person who was not a party to the action but was substantially affected by the judgment? Since the rule is that only a "party" to the action may appeal, such a person may not seek appellate review. See, e.g., Marino v. Ortiz, 484 U.S. 301, 108 S.Ct. 586, 98 L.Ed.2d 629 (1988). A way around this obstacle is intervention so that the affected person becomes a party. See, e.g., Smuck v. Hobson, 408 F.2d 175 (D.C.Cir.1969) (parents intervening in school desegregation case to pursue appeal from decree); County of Alameda v.

Carleson, 5 Cal.3d 730, 97 Cal.Rptr. 385, 488 P.2d 953 (1971) (welfare rights claimants intervening in suit concerning regulations governing welfare eligibility); cf. Saylor v. Lindsley, supra p. 888. But allowing intervention is discretionary and it may be denied. See Spangler v. Pasadena City Bd. of Educ., 427 F.2d 1352 (9th Cir.1970) (sustaining denial of intervention in circumstances much like Smuck v. Hobson, supra).

4. The general rule is that orders entered during the course of the trial proceeding, called "interlocutory" orders, may be reviewed in connection with an appeal from a final judgment, but may not be reviewed prior to that time by means of an interlocutory appeal. See James & Hazard § 12.4. At first blush, the "final judgment rule" seems only to govern timing, for if an order cannot be directly appealed it can be complained of in the appeal from the final judgment. But there are many situations where if interlocutory appeal is not allowed, appellate review will be of little practical value. It is this problem that generates especially intense pressure against the final judgment rule. See Coopers & Lybrand v. Livesay, infra p. 1296. A related problem is when the extraordinary remedy of mandamus may be used to correct asserted mistakes in lower courts. See Kerr v. United States District Court, infra, p. 1305.

5. The scope of appellate review is confined by rules that govern the procedure for asserting complaints about what was done in the trial court and that limit the matters that may be considered in the appellate court. James & Hazard § 12.8. Ordinarily, therefore:

(a) A matter cannot be complained of on appeal unless objection concerning it was intelligibly made in the trial court at the time the mishap occurred, or promptly thereafter. Cf. F.R.C.P. 46. See, however, Martineau, Considering New Issues on Appeal: The General Rule and the Gorilla Rule, 40 Vand.L.Rev. 1023 (1987) (appellate courts occasionally do consider issues not argued in the trial court); Martineau, Subject Matter Jurisdiction as a New Issue on Appeal: Reining in an Unruly Horse, 1988 B.Y.U.L.Rev. 1. A variation on this rule is that the Supreme Court will not decide issues not adequately raised in state court. See Bankers Life & Casualty Co. v. Crenshaw, infra p. 1320.

(b) A matter will not be considered by the appellate court unless it is properly cited in the appellant's papers on appeal. In some procedures, this requires an elaborate specification of grounds of error; in modern appellate procedure it is sufficient if the complaint is made in the brief, supported by the record.

(c) An appellate court will not receive new evidence, see Louisell and Degnan, Rehearing in American Appellate Courts, 44 Calif.L.Rev. 627 (1956), and will reverse a determination of fact only when it is "unsupported by evidence" or in accordance with similar formulas that limit the scope of appellate review of factual issues.

(d) An appellate court will not disturb rulings that are within the "sound discretion" of the trial court, unless there was an "abuse" of that discretion. See Rosenberg, Judicial Discretion of the Trial Court, A View from Above, 22 Syr.L.Rev. 635 (1971).

(e) Even if there have been errors in the trial proceeding, reversal will not be granted if those errors were "harmless" or "nonprejudicial." See Traynor, The Riddle of Harmless Error (1970); Note, Courting Reversal: The Supervisory Role of State Supreme Courts, 87 Yale L.J. 1191 (1978); cf.

Note, Principles for Application of the Harmless Error Standard, 41 U.Chi. L.Rev. 616 (1974).

(f) The scope of review of injunctive relief traditionally has been limited to "abuse of discretion," although this may now be changing. See Hinkle, Appellate Supervision of Remedies in Public Law Adjudication, 4 Fla.State U.L.Rev. 411 (1976).

For an excellent summary of the procedure and jurisdiction of appeals in the federal court system, see Wright cc. 11, 12; see also Symposium, Civil Appellate Jurisdiction (pts. 1 & 2), 47 Law & Contemp. Probs. (Spring 1984) 1, 47 Law & Contemp. Probs. (Summer 1984) 1. For a comparative analysis, see Karlen, Civil Appeals: American and English Approaches Compared, 21 W. & M.L.Rev. 121 (1979).

A. MECHANICS OF APPEAL

NOTE ON THE MECHANICS OF APPEAL

The following are synopses of the procedure in two appellate procedure systems.

1. Federal Appellate Procedure

Wright, Federal Courts 718–724 (4th ed. 1983): *

Under the rules the timely filing of a simple notice of appeal is the only step required to take an appeal. Such former devices as writs of errors, bills of exceptions, summons and severance, petitions for allowance of appeal, citations, assignments of errors, and similar vestiges of procedural antiquity have been "consigned, without mourners, to the legal limbo." [2]

It is true that an appellant who has filed a notice of appeal cannot then sit back and do nothing until his case is called for argument. He must file a cost bond (in a civil case),[3] file the record on appeal,[4] docket the appeal,[5] and file his brief and appendix,[6] but none of these steps is jurisdictional.[7] The appeal may be dismissed for failure to take these further steps at the proper time, but the matter is within the discretion of the court of appeals. It need not dismiss the appeal and ordinarily will not do so in the absence of prejudice to the appellee.[8]

The only exceptions to this general pattern are interlocutory appeals under 28 U.S.C.A. § 1292(b) and certain bankruptcy appeals. In these instances the party seeking to appeal must petition the appellate court and his petition must be allowed before the appeal may proceed further.[9]

---

* Copyright 1983, West Pub. Co. Reprinted with permission.

2. Cf. Wiener, The Supreme Court's New Rules, 1954, 68 Harv.L.Rev. 20, 59.

3. Appellate Rule 7.

4. Appellate Rules 10, 11, 12(b).

5. Appellate Rule 12(a).

6. Appellate Rules 28, 30–32.

7. Appellate Rule 3(a).

8. Compare Savard v. Marine Contracting, Inc., 471 F.2d 536, 543 (2d Cir. 1972), certiorari denied 412 U.S. 943, 93 S.Ct. 2778, 37 L.Ed.2d 404 (1973), and Mik-

kelson v. Young Men's Christian Assn. of Chicago, 317 F.2d 78 (7th Cir.1963), with Paac v. Rizzo, 502 F.2d 306, 309 n. 3 (3d Cir.1974), certiorari denied 419 U.S. 1108, 95 S.Ct. 780, 42 L.Ed.2d 804 (1975) and Johnson v. Danielson, 295 F.2d 12 (9th Cir. 1961).

9. 28 U.S.C.A. § 1292(b). The procedure for petitioning is set out in Appellate Rules 5 and 6.

The rule on bankruptcy appeals is obsolete since the drastic changes made by the 1978 Bankruptcy Act. See § 102 n. 6.

The notice of appeal, as described in Appellate Rule 3(c), is an extremely simple document.[10] Some notice of appeal, regarded as sufficient by the appellate court, must be filed, for the notice of appeal is the one jurisdictional prerequisite to an appeal.[11] The courts are very liberal, however, in entertaining an appeal even where the notice fails to comply with the rule. The notice should not be used as a technical trap for the unwary draftsman, and a defective notice of appeal should not warrant dismissal for want of jurisdiction if the intention to appeal from a specific judgment may be reasonably inferred from the text of the notice and the defect has not materially misled the appellee.[12] This has been fully understood by the courts. As noted by the Ninth Circuit, "there is a considerable body of authority indicating that in determining whether an attempted appeal has been accomplished, most informally drawn papers and improperly labeled documents have been held sufficient to accomplish the apparent objective of taking an appeal. . . . The rationale of the cases relating to informal or irregular appeals is that notwithstanding the papers filed were inaptly worded, or labeled, or even failed to use the word 'appeal,' or were filed in the wrong court, yet they sufficed to show the party intended to appeal."[13] The Supreme Court has endorsed this liberality in passing on the sufficiency of a notice of appeal.[14]

In civil cases the notice of appeal must be filed within 30 days after entry of judgment except where the United States is a party to the suit, in which case 60 days is allowed.[15] In a criminal case the notice must be filed within ten days.[16] Prior to 1966 the time could be extended for 30 days in a civil case only because the party, through excusable neglect, had failed to learn of the entry of the judgment.[17] In criminal cases there could be no extension for any reason.[18] These provisions were changed in 1966 and in both civil and criminal cases the time for noticing the appeal may now be extended an additional 30 days for "excusable neglect" of any kind.[19] If the trial court finds excusable neglect, and grants an extension, the appellate court should not second-guess this determination and thus defeat the appeal, though some courts have done so.[20]

10. See Official Form 1 of the Appellate Rules.

11. United States v. Robinson, 361 U.S. 220, 224, 80 S.Ct. 282, 285, 4 L.Ed.2d 259 (1960); Federal Deposit Ins. Corp. v. Congregation Poiley Tzedeck, 159 F.2d 163, 166 (2d Cir.1946).

12. Williams v. General Motors Corp., 656 F.2d 120, 125–126 (5th Cir.1981); Vargas v. McNamara, 608 F.2d 15, 21 (1st Cir. 1979); Scherer v. Kelley, 584 F.2d 170, 174–175 (7th Cir.1978), certiorari denied 440 U.S. 964, 99 S.Ct. 1511, 59 L.Ed.2d 778 (1979); Donovan v. Esso Shipping Co., 259 F.2d 65, 68 (3d Cir.1958), certiorari denied 359 U.S. 907, 79 S.Ct. 583, 3 L.Ed.2d 572 (1959); Crump v. Hill, 104 F.2d 36, 38 (5th Cir.1939).

13. Yanow v. Weyerhaeuser S.S. Co., 274 F.2d 274, 282–283 (9th Cir.1959), certiorari denied 362 U.S. 919, 80 S.Ct. 671, 4 L.Ed.2d 739 (1960).

14. Foman v. Davis, 371 U.S. 178, 83 S.Ct. 227, 9 L.Ed.2d 222 (1962). See also Sanabria v. U.S., 437 U.S. 54, 67 n. 21, 98 S.Ct. 2170, 2180 n. 21, 57 L.Ed.2d 43 (1978). But see Griggs v. Provident Consumer Discount Co., 459 U.S. 56, 103 S.Ct. 400, 74 L.Ed.2d 225 (1982).

15. Appellate Rule 4(a)(1).

16. Appellate Rule 4(b).

17. E.g., Watson v. Providence Washington Ins. Co., 201 F.2d 736 (4th Cir.1953).

18. Berman v. U.S., 378 U.S. 530, 84 S.Ct. 1895, 12 L.Ed.2d 1012 (1964); U.S. v. Robinson, 361 U.S. 220, 80 S.Ct. 282, 4 L.Ed.2d 259 (1960).

19. As further amended in 1979, the rule now allows extension of time in a civil case for either excusable neglect or good cause. Appellate Rule 4(a)(5). Only excusable neglect will suffice in a criminal case. Appellate Rule 4(b). See 16 Wright, Miller & Cooper, Jurisdiction § 3950.

20. Pellegrino v. Marathon Bank, 640 F.2d 696 (5th Cir.1981); Fase v. Seafarers Welfare & Pension Plan, 574 F.2d 72 (2d Cir.1978); and cases cited 16 Wright, Miller & Cooper, Jurisdiction § 3950 n. 15.

On the other hand, some courts have given a surprisingly permissive reading to the provision. This has come in cases in which the appellant never seeks an extension from the trial court but simply files his notice of appeal during the period to which the time could have been extended. Several courts in these circumstances have remanded the case, long after the time for extension has run, so that the trial court may determine whether there was excusable neglect and if so grant a nunc pro tunc extension.[21]

It is important to observe that it is the "filing" of the notice within the designated time that is required. Service on the opposing party will not do.[22] Neither will deposit in the mail if the notice is not actually received in the clerk's office within the designated time,[23] though an exception has been made in extreme cases.[24] If the clerk actually receives the notice, however, he cannot refuse to file it on the ground that his fee has not been paid.[25]

Certain post-trial motions suspend the finality of the judgment and the time for giving notice of appeal runs from the decision of the motions. In criminal cases a motion for a new trial, under Criminal Rule 33, or a motion for arrest of judgment, under Rule 34, has this effect,[26] though curiously a motion for judgment of acquittal under Rule 29(c) does not.[27] In civil cases the time is extended by: a motion for judgment notwithstanding the verdict, under Civil Rule 50(b); a motion to amend the findings, under Rule 52(b); a motion for a new trial, under Rule 59; a motion to alter or amend the judgment, under Rule 59(e).[28] A motion for relief from the judgment or order under Rule 60(b) does not affect the finality of the judgment and thus does not affect the time to appeal.[29] A post-trial motion must itself be timely if it is to extend the time for appeal.[30]

An appellee may defend a judgment on any ground consistent with the record, even if rejected in the lower court.[31] But he cannot attack the decree

21. United States v. McKnight, 593 F.2d 230 (3d Cir.1979); United States v. Umfress, 562 F.2d 359 (5th Cir.1977); Stirling v. Chem. Bank, 511 F.2d 1030 (2d Cir. 1975); Reed v. Michigan, 398 F.2d 800 (6th Cir.1968); Evans v. Jones, 366 F.2d 772 (4th Cir.1966).

22. Federal Deposit Ins. Corp. v. Congregation Poiley Tzedeck, 159 F.2d 163 (2d Cir.1946).

23. Allen v. Schnuckle, 253 F.2d 195 (9th Cir.1958); Kahler–Ellis Co. v. Ohio Turnpike Comm., 225 F.2d 922 (6th Cir. 1955); Lejeune v. Midwestern Ins. Co. of Oklahoma City, Okla., 197 F.2d 149 (5th Cir.1952).

24. Fallen v. United States, 378 U.S. 139, 84 S.Ct. 1689, 12 L.Ed.2d 760 (1964); Da'Ville v. Wise, 470 F.2d 1364 (5th Cir. 1973), certiorari denied 414 U.S. 818, 94 S.Ct. 40, 38 L.Ed.2d 50, and 414 U.S. 818, 94 S.Ct. 170, 38 L.Ed.2d 50; Hegler v. Board of Educ. of Bearden Sch. Dist., 447 F.2d 1078 (8th Cir.1971).

25. Parissi v. Telechron, Inc., 349 U.S. 46, 75 S.Ct. 577, 99 L.Ed. 867 (1955). But see Stirling v. Chem. Bank, 511 F.2d 1030 (2d Cir.1975).

See also Aldabe v. Aldabe, 616 F.2d 1089 (9th Cir.1980), holding the appeal timely where the notice was received by the clerk on the last day even though it was not "filed" for another two weeks.

26. Appellate Rule 4(b).

27. 2 Wright, Criminal 2d § 465.

28. Appellate Rule 4(a)(4).

29. Textile Banking Co., Inc. v. Rentschler, 657 F.2d 844, 848–850 (7th Cir. 1981); Hardy v. St. Paul Fire & Marine Ins. Co., 599 F.2d 628, 629 (5th Cir.1979); 11 Wright & Miller, Civil § 2871 n. 90.

30. Hulson v. Atchison, T. & S.F. Ry. Co., 289 F.2d 726 (7th Cir.1961), certiorari denied 368 U.S. 835, 82 S.Ct. 61, 7 L.Ed.2d 36; John E. Smith's Sons Co. v. Lattimer Foundry & Machine Co., 239 F.2d 815 (3d Cir.1956); Albers v. Gant, 435 F.2d 146 (5th Cir.1970).

31. Colautti v. Franklin, 439 U.S. 379, 397 n. 16, 99 S.Ct. 675, 686 n. 16, 58 L.Ed. 2d 596 (1979); Massachusetts Mut. Life Ins. Co. v. Ludwig, 426 U.S. 479, 96 S.Ct. 2158, 48 L.Ed.2d 784 (1976); Kennecott Copper Corp. v. Curtiss–Wright Corp., 584 F.2d 1195, 1206 (2d Cir.1978); In re Henderson, 577 F.2d 997 (5th Cir.1978).

with a view either to enlarging his own rights thereunder or to lessening the rights of his adversary unless he files a cross appeal, whether what he seeks is to correct an error or to supplement the decree with respect to a matter not dealt with below.[32] Until 1966 the appellee was given no additional time in which to file notice of his cross-appeal and might be trapped if he did not learn of his opponent's appeal until the time for appeal has elapsed. The rule now provides that if one party files a timely notice of appeal, any other party may file a notice of appeal within 14 days of the filing of the first notice or within the time in which he might otherwise have given notice of appeal, whichever period last expires.[33]

Ordinarily the appellant cannot seek reversal upon a ground not raised in the trial court, but this is only a rule of practice and may be relaxed if the public interest so requires.[34]

Appellate Rules 10 and 11 prescribe how the record on appeal is to be prepared and transmitted to the appellate court. The record on appeal is defined as being "the original papers and exhibits filed in the district court, the transcript of proceedings, if any, and a certified copy of the docket entries prepared by the clerk." [35] When the Civil Rules were originally adopted a certified copy of the record on file in the district court was made and sent to the appellate court. This was a wasteful burden and expense.[36] In 1948 the Civil Rules were amended to permit a court of appeals, if it wished, to provide by rule that the original district court record could be used as the record on appeal and by 1962 every circuit had exercised this sensible option.

In addition to the record, of which only a single copy is required, some provision must be made for putting into the hands of each of the judges who will hear the appeal those portions of the record that are of particular significance. This document, known as the appendix, "is exactly what its name implies: an addendum to the briefs for the convenience of the judges." [37] What is to go into it and how it is to be prepared is of great significance because it forms a large part of the cost of appellate review. Rule 32(a) makes an important contribution by permitting briefs and appendices to be produced "by standard typographic printing or by any duplicating or copying process which produces a clear black image on white paper." Thus modern copying methods may be used and the parties are no longer confined to printing or offset duplicating.[38]

---

32. Morley Const. Co. v. Maryland Cas. Co., 300 U.S. 185, 191–192, 57 S.Ct. 325, 327–328, 81 L.Ed. 593 (1937); Alexander v. Cosden Pipe Line Co., 290 U.S. 484, 487–488, 54 S.Ct. 292, 293–294, 78 L.Ed. 452 (1934); Third Nat. Bank of Nashville v. United States, 454 F.2d 689 (6th Cir.1972); Stern, When to Cross–Appeal or Cross–Petition—Certainty or Confusion?, 1974, 87 Harv.L.Rev. 763.

33. Appellate Rule 4(a)(3). The rule reaches "any other party" and is not limited to a cross-appeal. Kurdziel v. Pittsburgh Tube Co., 416 F.2d 882 (6th Cir. 1969).

34. Wratchford v. S.J. Groves & Sons Co., 405 F.2d 1061 (4th Cir.1969); Green v. Brown, 398 F.2d 1006 (2d Cir.1968); New York, N.H. & H.R. Co. v. Reconstruction Fin. Corp., 180 F.2d 241, 244 (2d Cir.1950).

35. Appellate Rule 10(a).

36. See Dean, Proposed Rule for Hearing of Appeals on Original Papers, 1948, 8 F.R.D. 143, 148.

37. Ward, note 1 above, at 108.

38. "In 1964 the cost of a single page of the brief or of the reproduction of the record by standard letterpress printing was approaching $4.00 per page; the cost of a page by offset duplicating, the only other method generally permitted by the circuits, was approximately $2.80 per page." Ward, note 1 above, at 108. See also Wilcox, Karlen & Roemer, Justice Lost—By

The question of the contents and preparation of the appendix was more controversial than any other question in the preparation of the Appellate Rules and at one point three different drafts were distributed for consideration by the profession.[39] The rule finally adopted contemplates that there will be filed with the appellant's brief a single appendix, prepared by the appellant, and containing all the portions of the record to which either the appellant or the appellee wishes "to direct the particular attention of the court."[40] The rule makes it very clear that the parties and the court may rely on portions of the record that are not included in the appendix[41] and it cautions that "in designating parts of the record for inclusion in the appendix, the parties shall have regard for the fact that the entire record is always available to the court for reference and examination and shall not engage in unnecessary designation."[42]

Rule 30(c) also provides that in some circumstances the appendix may be deferred until after the briefs have been prepared and filed 21 days after the brief of the appellee. The thought is that if the appendix is not prepared until after the briefs are completed the parties will be able to see precisely what the issues are, and what parts of the record need to be reproduced, and that this will encourage smaller appendices. In large cases the deferred appendix will be advantageous though the procedure for preparing it and referring to the appendix in the briefs is quite complicated. The rule was amended in 1970 to provide that the deferred appendix may be used only if the court has provided by rule for classes of cases or by order in the specific case.

Finally Rule 30(f) somewhat grudgingly provides that a court of appeals may dispense with the requirement of an appendix altogether and permit appeals to be heard on copies of the relevant parts of the original record. It has been estimated that such a procedure, taking advantage of inexpensive modern copying machines, can cut the cost of reproduction by two-thirds and also eliminate most of the lawyer time otherwise required for preparation of the record.[43] This has been standard procedure in the Ninth Circuit since 1962[44] and a number of other circuits now permit use of the original record and two copies of it in many kinds of cases.

As other circuits obtain experience with the Ninth Circuit practice in limited classes of cases, they are likely to become aware of its usefulness and to make it applicable in all cases. Just as in 14 years every circuit exercised the option given it and elected to adopt the original papers as the record on appeal, so too the option provided in Rule 30(f) is likely in a short time to have been exercised universally. Although a distinguished authority has said flatly of the

What Appellate Papers Cost, 1958, 33 N.Y. U.L.Rev. 934.

39. Drafts of Proposed Rule 30, Uniform Rules of Federal Appellate Procedure, December 1966, 41 F.R.D. 311.

40. Appellate Rule 30. See Alger v. Hayes, 452 F.2d 841 (8th Cir.1972); Slade, The Appendix to the Briefs: Rule 30 of the Federal Rules of Appellate Procedure, 1968, 28 Fed.B.J. 116.

41. Appellate Rule 30(a).

42. Appellate Rule 30(b). Rule 11(c), 1st Cir.Rules, provides:

"Notwithstanding the provisions of FRAP Rule 30 the court may decline to refer to portions of the record omitted from the Appendix, except by inadvertence, unless leave be granted prior to argument." The rule seems plainly invalid as inconsistent with Appellate Rule 30(b).

43. Joiner, Lawyer Attitudes Toward Law and Procedural Reform, 1966, 50 Judicature 23, 25.

44. Rule 4(b), 9th Cir.Rules.

Ninth Circuit practice that "it is not workable as a practical matter," [45] the Advisory Committee Note to Rule 30(f) states that "the judges of the Court of Appeals for the Ninth Circuit have expressed complete satisfaction with the practice there in use and have suggested that attention be called to the advantages which it offers in terms of reducing cost." [46]

The major change in appellate procedure in the last 15 years has been with regard to oral argument and publication of opinions. In the face of overwhelming caseloads, most courts of appeals have felt the need to institute screening procedures to decide which cases merit oral argument and how much time should be allowed for it. In addition, many cases are now disposed of by summary orders.[47] Even when an opinion is written, it is frequently designated as not for publication and frequently is regarded as without precedential effect.[48] If these drastic reforms had not been instituted, the federal courts of appeals would have collapsed under the pressure of docket congestion. Even so, there is concern for the implications these new devices may have for the quality of justice administered by the appellate courts.[49]

One additional point beyond those developed by Professor Wright: the question of to which appellate court to take appeal. Appeal from a federal district court is always taken to the Court of Appeals of the Circuit in which the District Court is located. But appeals from federal administrative agencies in many instances may be taken to more than one Court of Appeals, thus begetting races to favorable courthouses. See ABCNY Committee on Federal Court, Races to the Courthouse, 36 The Record 618 (1981); McGarity, Multi-Party Forum Shopping for Appellate Review of Administrative Action, 129 U.Pa.L.Rev. 302 (1980).

2. California Appellate Procedure

a. Time to Appeal. An appellate court does not obtain jurisdiction to review a case unless a notice of appeal is filed in the proper period. This is a

---

45. Prettyman, The New Federal Rules of Appellate Procedure, 1968, 28 Fed.B.J. 97, 99.

46. 1967, 43 F.R.D. 61, 150.

47. Appellate Rule 34(a); Commission on Revision of the Federal Court Appellate System, Structure and Internal Procedures: Recommendations for Change, 1975, 67 F.R.D. 195, 247–260; Wasby, Oral Argument in the Ninth Circuit: The View from Bench and Bar, 1981, 11 Golden Gate L.Rev. 21; Haworth, Screening and Summary Procedures in the United States Courts of Appeals, 1973 Wash.U.L.Q. 257.

48. Reynolds & Richman, An Evaluation of Limited Publication in the United States Courts of Appeals, 1981, 48 U.Chi.L. Rev. 573; Reynolds & Richman, The Non–Precedential Precedent—Limited Publication and No–Citation Rules in the United States Courts of Appeals, 1978, 78 Col.L. Rev. 1167; Newbern & Wilson, Rule 21: Unprecedent and the Disappearing Court, 1978, 32 Ark.L.Rev. 37; Stern, The Enigma of Unpublished Opinions, 1978, 64 A.B.A.J. 1191; Walther, The Noncitation Rule and the Concept of Stare Decisis, 1978, 61 Marq.L.Rev. 581; Gardner, Ninth Circuit's Unpublished Opinions: Denial of Equal Justice, 1975, 61 A.B.A.J. 1224; Note, Unreported Decisions in the United States Courts of Appeals, 1977, 63 Cornell L.Rev. 128.

49. Compare Carrington, Ceremony and Realism: Demise of Appellate Procedure, 1980, 66 A.B.A.J. 860, with Godbold, Improvements in Appellate Procedure: Better Use of Available Facilities, 1980, 66 A.B.A.J. 863.

The extent to which screening procedures and dispositions without published opinions are being used in each circuit is examined by the Senate Judiciary Committee in S.Rep. No. 94–404, 1975, and concern expressed that "our concept of due process imposes limits on the nature and on the extent of permissible short-cuts in the appellate process. . . . ." Id. at 25.

jurisdictional requirement; the time for filing cannot be extended, modified, excused, or overlooked. See California Rules of Court, Appellate Rule 45(c); Pressler v. Donald L. Bren Co., 32 Cal.3d 831, 187 Cal.Rptr. 449, 654 P.2d 219 (1982). Failure to file on time results in an inability to appeal, for the court of review does not have jurisdiction to hear the case. Even if neither party mentions the fact of late notice, the appellate court can examine the record and dismiss the appeal. Hollister Convalescent Hospital, Inc. v. Rico, 15 Cal.3d 660, 125 Cal.Rptr. 757, 542 P.2d 1349 (1975). Cf. Molien v. Kaiser Foundation Hospital, 27 Cal.3d 916, 167 Cal.Rptr. 831, 616 P.2d 813 (1980), treating a nonfinal order as a final judgment for the purpose of appeal where the defect was merely technical. If the remedy of appeal is lost, there may be no remedy other than the possibility of extraordinary trial court relief.

In application of the time requirements, some doubtful cases have been resolved in favor of the right to appeal, but these cases usually involve special circumstances not likely to occur with much regularity. For example, the appellant relied upon an erroneous date in an order denying a motion for a new trial that had been prepared by respondent's counsel. Slawinski v. Mocettini, 63 Cal.2d 70, 45 Cal.Rptr. 15, 403 P.2d 143 (1965). See 9 Witkin 404–408. While it is presently unclear if these cases can be categorized into a "quasi-estoppel" exception, Thompson, Curtis, Lawson & Parish v. Thorne, 21 Cal.App. 3d 797, 98 Cal.Rptr. 753 (1971), a wise practitioner would do well to file appeals on time and avoid relying on an uncertain and very limited modification of the general rule.

A notice of appeal must be filed with the clerk of the trial court within 60 days of the date of mailing of notice of the entry of judgment, or 180 days after date of entry, whichever is earliest, with some exceptions. California Rules of Court, Appellate Rule 2. The exceptions are: (1) If a party serves and files a valid notice of intention to move for a new trial within 60 days after entry of judgment, then (a) if the motion is denied, time for filing notice of appeal is extended until 30 days after denial of the motion, but in no event may notice be filed more than 180 days after entry of judgment, Rule 3(a), or (b) if the motion for new trial is granted and an appeal is taken from the order granting it, any other party may file notice of appeal from the judgment within 20 days after the mailing by the clerk of the notification of the appeal from the order. Rule 3(c). See also Wenzoski v. Central Banking Sys., Inc., 43 Cal.3d 539, 237 Cal.Rptr. 167, 736 P.2d 753 (1987) (timeliness of notice of appeal where motion for new trial was made prior to judgment). (2) If a party files a valid notice of intention to move to vacate a judgment within 60 days after entry of judgment, then (a) the time for filing notice of appeal from the judgment is extended until the earliest of 30 days after entry of the order denying the motion to vacate, *or* 90 days after filing the motion to vacate, *or* 180 days after entry of the judgment, Rule 3(b), or (b) if the motion is granted within 150 days after entry of judgment and an appeal is taken from the order granting it, any other party may appeal from the judgment as originally entered within 20 days after mailing of notification by the clerk of appeal from the order. Rule 3(c). (3) If the same party serves and files valid notices of intention to move for a new trial and to move for entry of a judgment notwithstanding the verdict, and both motions are denied or not decided within 60 days after the filing of the notice of intention to move for a new trial, the time for filing notice of appeal from the judgment or from denial of the motion for judgment notwithstanding the verdict is extended until the earlier of 30 days after entry of the order denying a new trial *or* 180 days after entry of the judgment. Rule 3(d). (4) If the law specifically provides for another period of time, that period prevails. Rule 2(a).

Note that the 180 day period runs from entry of the judgment.[1] The judgment is "entered" when it is entered in the judgment book. Rule 2(b). With some exceptions, an appealable order is "entered" when entered in the permanent minutes; if the appealable order is one which is not entered in the minutes, it is "entered" when the order signed by the court is filed. Rule 2(b).

Whenever a party files a notice of appeal, the clerk is directed to mail a notification thereof to the other parties. This notification by the clerk is not a jurisdictional requirement; if the clerk neglects his duty the appeal is still good. Rule 1(b).

Different rules apply to review of Courts of Appeal decisions by the Supreme Court. A party seeking review of a decision rendered by a Court of Appeal must file a petition with the Supreme Court within 10 days after the decision of the Court of Appeal becomes final. Rule 28(b). The Supreme Court then has 60 days to grant or reject the petition. Rule 28(a)(2). Alternatively, the Supreme Court may, if no petition for review is filed, order review of a Court of Appeal decision on its own motion within 30 days after the decision becomes final. Rule 28(a)(1).

b. Form. The notice of appeal must be signed by appellant or his attorney, and "shall be sufficient if it states in substance that the appellant appeals from a specified judgment or a particular part thereof." Rule 1(a). The notice should read "appeals" or "does appeal" rather than "intends to appeal" or "is thinking about appealing." The notice must "substantially state a present intention," and show that the party is appealing from some specific thing—the judgment or some appealable order. Kronsberg v. Wershow, 238 Cal.App.2d 170, 47 Cal.Rptr. 592 (1965). A notice describing only part of the judgment will not bring up the whole judgment. In re Fink's Marriage, 54 Cal. App.3d 357, 126 Cal.Rptr. 626 (1976).

Note that the notice of appeal is necessary to confer jurisdiction on the reviewing court. Once the notice is filed, the superior court loses jurisdiction except in those limited matters relating to the perfection of the record and in matters included in the action but which are not being appealed. See C.C.P. 916. The notice must be accompanied by the filing fee. Rule 10(a).

c. Preparation of the Record. Essentially there are five ways in which the necessary records from the trial court may be taken before the reviewing court: (1) By clerk's and reporter's transcripts, (2) by settled statement, (3) by agreed statement, (4) by an appendix, or (5) by proceeding on the judgment roll alone. The judgment roll is included in the discussion of the clerk's transcript below, and the clerk's and reporter's transcripts are discussed separately in an attempt at simplicity.

Certain combinations of the various methods of taking the record before the reviewing court may be used. Generally which method or combination of methods is used depends on the peculiar facts of the case and which method appellant prefers. Normally, "the appellant must affirmatively show error by

---

1. But a premature notice of appeal is valid. "A notice of appeal filed prior to entry of the judgment, but after its rendition, shall be valid and shall be deemed to have been filed immediately after entry. A notice of appeal filed prior to rendition of the judgment, but after the judge has announced his intended ruling, may, in the discretion of the reviewing court for good cause, be treated as filed immediately after entry of the judgment." Rule 2(c).

an adequate record." 9 Witkin 415. Appellant's failure to perform any act necessary in preparing the record is ground for dismissal of the appeal. Rule 10(c).

(1) Clerk's transcript and original papers: This includes most of the material that is not part of the reporter's transcript (oral proceedings, covered infra).

Always included in the clerk's transcript are: "(1) The notice of appeal; (2) the notices or stipulations to prepare the clerk's transcript and the reporter's transcript, if any, and the notices or stipulations for the preparation of a settled statement or agreed statement, if any; (3) the judgment appealed from, with an endorsement by the clerk showing the date notice of entry thereof was mailed by the clerk or served by a party; (4) the pretrial order, if any, whenever the judgment roll or any part thereof has been designated by the parties; (5) any notice of intention to move for a new trial or motion to vacate the judgment, and the ruling thereon, if any." Rule 5(d). These papers are essential to any appeal. 9 Witkin 422–435.

The following material is included only if designated by any of the parties: "(6) the judgment roll, or any part thereof; (7) any other papers, records or affidavits (other than exhibits admitted in evidence or rejected) on file or lodged with the clerk; (8) any written instructions given or refused; (9) exhibits admitted in evidence or rejected that the parties have directed to be copied." Rule 5(d). "Papers or records on file with the clerk" may include the clerk's minutes, any written opinion of the superior court, affidavits and written instructions given or refused, and exhibits. Rule 5(a). Generally, the originals of exhibits and affidavits are sent up. Rule 5(a), (b), (c), (e).

The appellant must serve on the respondent and file with the clerk of the superior court a notice designating which of these papers or records he wants incorporated in the record on appeal. Appellant's designation of papers or records must be served and filed within 10 days after filing the notice of appeal. Rule 5(a).

The respondent may want certain of these records sent up which the appellant did not request. If so, he has 10 days after being served with appellant's notice in which to designate additional papers or records. Rule 5(b).

The parties may stipulate what is to be included in the record on appeal, in which case the written stipulation is to be filed within 10 days after the filing of the notice of appeal. Rule 5(b).

The clerk will notify the parties of the estimated cost of preparing the transcript. The party requesting the material must make arrangements with the clerk for payment within 10 days or the notice of designation is ineffective for any purpose. Rule 5(b), (c).

The appeal may be taken solely on the clerk's transcript or on the judgment roll. See Rule 5(f). Note that appellant must so designate if she wants only the judgment roll. If the appellant requests only a clerk's transcript or the judgment roll, the respondent can designate only material properly included in the clerk's transcript or in the judgment roll. Rule 5(f). Of course, the reviewing court may allow the record to be augmented. Rule 5(f).

(2) Reporter's transcript: The reporter's transcript is a record of the oral proceedings of the court. To get this, appellant must file with the clerk of the trial court a notice to prepare a reporter's transcript. This notice should be made within 10 days after filing the notice of appeal, Rule 4(a); it may be included in the notice of appeal. Rule 5(a).

Even if a full transcript is requested, the reporter will not prepare the voir dire examination of jurors, the opening statements, arguments to the jury, or proceedings on a motion for a new trial unless that material is specifically designated in the notice for a reporter's transcript. Rule 4(a).

If only a partial transcript is desired, the parties may stipulate what is not wanted. Rule 4(b). An alternative method is for the appellant, in his notice to the clerk, to state the points he intends to raise on appeal and designate what parts of the oral proceedings he wants transcribed. Rule 4(b). Respondent can designate any parts he wants that appellant did not request, if he serves and files his notice within 10 days after appellant's notice. Rule 4(b).

The whole testimony of any one witness is included in the reporter's transcript unless the parties stipulate otherwise. The reporter includes nothing in his transcript which is properly part of the clerk's transcript. Rule 4(b).

The reporter will estimate the cost of the transcription, Rule 4(a), and the record will not be prepared until the estimated cost is deposited with the clerk, within 10 days of notification of the cost. Rule 4(c). Depositing clerk's or reporter's fees can be vital—no record, no appeal.

(3) Settled statement: Still another way of taking the record before the reviewing court is the settled statement. If the reporter fails, refuses, or becomes unable to transcribe the oral proceedings, the superior court may grant leave to prepare a settled statement and extend the time requirements. Rule 4(e). The settled statement is also an alternative method of taking the record before the reviewing court; the settled statement can be used in place of the reporter's transcript or the clerk's transcript. See Rule 7(a) and (b). If the clerk's transcript is not used, necessary parts of the judgment roll and other papers essential to all appeals must be included in the settled statement. Rule 7(b).

(4) Agreed statement: An agreed statement is little more than a stipulation in which the parties show the nature of the controversy, the basis on which it is claimed that the reviewing court has jurisdiction, and how the questions arose and were decided by the superior court. See Rule 6.

Only such facts as are necessary to a determination of the questions on appeal should be included in the agreed statement. Rule 6(a). As with all methods of taking the record to the reviewing court, the statement should include a copy of the judgment and a copy of the notice of appeal with its filing date, as well as any notice of intention to move for a new trial or motion to vacate the judgment. Rule 6(a).

The agreed statement may be used in conjunction with the other methods of taking the record before the appellate court, or it may be used as the only method. See Rule 6(a). Two copies of the agreed statement must be filed with the clerk of the superior court within 40 days after filing the notice of appeal. Rule 6(a).

"Within 10 days after filing the notice of appeal, the parties may file with the clerk of the superior court a preliminary stipulation stating that they are attempting to prepare an agreed statement." Rule 6(b). This will extend the time for service and filing of the notices for the other methods of taking up the record, in case the parties are unable to agree on a statement. In this event, the time is extended to 50 days from the date of filing the notice of appeal. Rule 6(b).

(5) Appendix: The appendix method is essentially the same as the appendix method in federal appellate procedure, described by Professor Wright, supra. See Rule 5.1.

d. *Transmission and Filing of the Record.* When the record on appeal has been completed, the clerk of the superior court forwards original transcripts or agreed or settled statements to the appellate court. Rule 10(b). Exhibits are not sent up unless then requested. Rule 10(d). A copy of the record is given the appellant, and then passed on to respondent, to aid in writing the briefs. Rule 10(e).

e. *Briefs.* Every appellant files an opening brief and each respondent files a respondent's brief. Rules 13, 14. Each party may adopt by reference any brief in the same or companion cases. Ibid.

"The opening brief shall contain a statement of the case, setting forth concisely, but as fully as necessary for a proper consideration of the case, in such order as the appellant may prefer, the nature of the action or proceeding and the relief sought, a summary of the material facts, and the judgment or ruling of the superior court. The statement shall be accurate and confined to matters in the record on appeal." Rule 13.

After the respondent's brief, the appellant may file an appellant's reply brief. Rule 14(a). The permission of the Chief Justice or Presiding Justice is required for additional or supplementary briefs. Ibid.

One copy of each brief must be deposited with the clerk of the superior court. Rule 16(b). When the state is a party, the brief must be served on the attorney general. Rule 16(c).

To file an *amicus curiae* brief, the applicant first files a signed request with the clerk of the reviewing court specifying the points to be argued in the amicus brief, stating that he is familiar with the questions involved and the scope of their presentation, and that he believes that there is a necessity for additional argument on the points. Rule 14(b). If the application is granted, the time within which the amicus brief may be filed is specified. The amicus brief must be served on all parties before it is filed. The parties may answer the amicus brief. Ibid.

Rule 15 contains the technical requirements for briefs.

Appellant's opening brief must be "served and filed within 30 days after the filing of the record (or the reporter's transcript if there was an election under rule 5.1) in the reviewing court." Rule 16(a). Respondent must serve and file his brief within 30 days after appellant's opening brief is filed. Appellant's reply brief must be served and filed within 20 days after the filing of respondent's brief. The parties may extend each of the periods up to 60 days by stipulation, as long as the stipulation is filed before the period has run. Further extensions must be obtained from the Chief Justice or the Presiding Justice. Ibid.

If the respondent cross-appeals, the cross-appeal brief may be included as part of his reply brief. Rule 14(c). Appellant then has 30 days to reply as cross-respondent, and respondent then has another 20 days to file a reply brief as cross-appellant. Rule 16(a).

A thirty day grace period is given for late briefs, and further extensions of time may be granted by the Chief Justice or Presiding Justice if good cause is shown. Rule 17. If appellant is nevertheless late in filing his brief, the appeal may be dismissed. Rule 17(a). If respondent is late, the case may be decided on the appellant's brief and the record. Rule 17(b).

In a case accepted for review by the Supreme Court, petitioner's brief must be served and filed within 15 days of the order granting review, if petitioner uses the brief filed in the Court of Appeal, or within 30 days if a new brief is used. Respondent must serve and file his brief within 15 days after petitioner's brief is filed, if respondent uses the brief filed in the Court of Appeal, or within 30 days if a new brief is used. Rule 29.3.

f. Court to which Appeal Taken. California appellate courts include the Supreme Court of California and the Courts of Appeal. Cal. Const. Art. 6, §§ 1, 3, 11; Cal.Gov't Code §§ 69100 et seq.

For the most part, the jurisdiction of the Supreme Court and the District Courts of Appeal is the same. However, only the Supreme Court has appellate jurisdiction over any death sentence, Cal.Const. Art. 6, § 11, if such sentence can be held constitutional.

There is no loss of right of appeal because of a misdirected appeal; the cause will be transferred to the proper court under the authority of Cal.Gov't Code § 68915. See also Rule 20, authorizing the Supreme Court to order the transfer of all causes.

After the Court of Appeal has decided a case, the Supreme Court will order a hearing if: (1) "[i]t appears necessary to secure uniformity of decision or the settlement of important questions of law; (2) * * * [t]he Court of Appeal was without jurisdiction of the cause; or (3) where, because of disqualification or other reason, the decision of the Court of Appeal lacks the concurrence of the required majority of qualified judges." Rule 29(a).

g. Disposition of the Appeal. Before the record is filed in the reviewing court, an appeal may be voluntarily abandoned with consequent dismissal. Rule 19(a). After the filing of the record in the reviewing court, that court may dismiss the appeal upon written request of the appellant or written stipulation of the parties. Rule 19(b).

The Supreme Court has authority to order the transfer of a cause from the Supreme Court to a Court of Appeal, from a Court of Appeal to the Supreme Court, from one Court of Appeal to another, or from one division thereof to another. Rule 20. The Supreme Court may also limit its decision to one or more issues and transfer the cause to a Court of Appeal for decision of the remaining issues. Rule 29.4.

The clerk of the reviewing court notifies the parties of the time and place of the hearing. Rule 21(c). At this time the parties must designate to the clerk of the superior court which of the previously designated exhibits or affidavits are to be sent up as originals to the reviewing court. Rules 21(c), 10(d).

A judge on a reviewing court who has not heard oral argument may not participate in the decision of the case. See Moles v. Regents of the Univ. of California, 32 Cal.3d 867, 187 Cal.Rptr. 557, 654 P.2d 740 (1982).

Decisions of appellate courts are filed with their clerks. Rule 24(a). Unless the court orders otherwise before the period expires, a decision of the Supreme Court becomes final 30 days after filing. Ibid. A Court of Appeal decision becomes final as to that court 30 days after filing. Ibid. When the appellate court affirms on the condition that the prevailing party consent to a remission of part of the judgment, or some such similar condition, the judgment is reversed unless the party consents to the remission within 30 days after the decision was filed. Rule 24(c). An ordinary, unqualified reversal vacates the judgment and ordinarily means a new trial when the case goes back to the lower court on remittitur. See Cowdery v. London & San Francisco Bank, 139 Cal. 298, 73 P. 196 (1903); Sloan v. Court Hotel, 72 Cal.App.2d 308, 164 P.2d 516 (1945).

The decision of the reviewing court is transmitted to the trial court by "remittitur," which is about the same thing as the "mandate" of the U.S. Supreme Court. Noel v. Smith, 2 Cal.App. 158, 162, 83 P. 167, 169 (1905). See C.C.P. 43, 912. Remittitur serves to re-invest the trial court with jurisdiction of the cause, "but only such jurisdiction as is defined by the terms of the remittitur." Hampton v. Superior Court, 38 C.2d 652, 655, 242 P.2d 1, 3 (1952). Remittitur normally issues when the judgment becomes final but can issue immediately. Rule 25(a) and (b). Similarly, the issuance of the remittitur can be stayed, and remittitur can be recalled. Rule 25(c) and (d). Grounds for recall are established by case law. Procedurally, a party seeking recall must do so by a noticed motion, supported by affidavits, or on stipulation. Rule 25(d).

Either the Supreme Court or a Court of Appeal "may grant a rehearing after its own decision in any cause except the denial by a Court of Appeal of a petition for a writ within its original jurisdiction without issuance of an alternative writ or order to show cause or the denial of a transfer to a Court of Appeal * * *." Rule 27(a). For a civil case, a petition for a rehearing must be served and filed within 15 days after the decision was filed. Rule 27(b).

h. Stay and Bond or Supersedeas. During the pendency of an appeal the judgment is in effect unless procedures are invoked to suspend its effectiveness. This means that a money judgment can be enforced through execution and that an injunction must be complied with even though an appeal is pending. In order to suspend these consequences, the appellant may seek a stay, in connection with which a bond may be required. See C.C.P. 916 et seq.; 9 Witkin 221 et seq. For the comparable federal provisions, see Fed.R.App.Pro. 7 and 8; 9 Moore ¶¶ 207.01 et seq., 208.01 et seq.

See generally Stern, Appellate Practice in the United States (1981). On California appellate practice, see C.E.B., Calif.Civil Appellate Practice (1966).

B. FEDERAL APPELLATE REVIEW

---

1. REVIEWABILITY OF DECISIONS

COOPERS & LYBRAND v. LIVESAY
Supreme Court of the United States, 1978.
437 U.S. 463, 98 S.Ct. 2454, 57 L.Ed.2d 351.

MR. JUSTICE STEVENS delivered the opinion of the Court.

The question in this case is whether a district court's determination that an action may not be maintained as a class action pursuant to Fed. Rule Civ.Proc. 23 is a "final decision" within the meaning of 28 U.S. C.A. § 1291 [1] and therefore appealable as a matter of right. Because

---

1. "The courts of appeals shall have jurisdiction of appeals from all final decisions of the district courts of the United States . . . except where a direct review may be had in the Supreme Court."

there is a conflict in the Circuits over this issue,[2] we granted certiorari and now hold that such an order is not appealable under § 1291.

Petitioner, Coopers & Lybrand, is an accounting firm that certified the financial statements in a prospectus issued in connection with a 1972 public offering of securities in Punta Gorda Isles for an aggregate price of over $18 million. Respondents purchased securities in reliance on that prospectus. In its next annual report to shareholders, Punta Gorda restated the earnings that had been reported in the prospectus for 1970 and 1971 by writing down its net income for each year by over $1 million. Thereafter, respondents sold their Punta Gorda securities and sustained a loss of $2,650 on their investment.

Respondents filed this action on behalf of themselves and a class of similarly situated purchasers. They alleged that petitioner and other defendants [3] had violated various sections of the Securities Act of 1933 and the Securities Exchange Act of 1934.[4] The District Court first certified, and then, after further proceedings, decertified the class.

Respondents did not request the District Court to certify its order for interlocutory review under 28 U.S.C.A. § 1292(b).[5] Rather, they filed a notice of appeal pursuant to § 1291.[6] The Court of Appeals regarded its appellate jurisdiction as depending on whether the decertification order had sounded the "death knell" of the action. After examining the amount of respondents' claims in relation to their financial resources and the probable cost of the litigation, the court

2. Compare Hackett v. General Host Corp., 455 F.2d 618 (CA3), cert. denied, 407 U.S. 925, 92 S.Ct. 2460, 32 L.Ed.2d 812 (1972); King v. Kansas City Southern Industries, Inc., 479 F.2d 1259 (CA7 1973) (holding that such an order is not immediately appealable under § 1291) with Hartmann v. Scott, 488 F.2d 1215 (CA8 1973); Ott v. Speedwriting Pub. Co., 518 F.2d 1143 (CA6 1975); Eisen v. Carlisle & Jacquelin, 370 F.2d 119 (CA2 1966), cert. denied, 386 U.S. 1035, 87 S.Ct. 1487, 18 L.Ed.2d 598 (1967) (holding that such an order is immediately appealable under § 1291).

3. The other defendants, Punta Gorda and several of its officers and directors, also filed a petition for writ of certiorari in this Court. Punta Gorda Isles, Inc. v. Livesay, 76–1837. After we granted certiorari in this case and 76–1837, 434 U.S. 954, 98 S.Ct. 478, 54 L.Ed.2d 312, the parties entered into a tentative settlement agreement. Respondents and petitioners in No. 76–1837 agreed to dismiss that petition; petitioner in this case, however, did not stipulate to dismissal of its petition. In view of the tentative nature of the settlement, this case is not moot.

4. Sections 11, 12(2) and 17(b) of the Securities Act of 1933, 15 U.S.C.A. §§ 77k, 77l (2) and 77q(a), and § 10(b) of the Securi-

ties Exchange Act of 1934, 15 U.S.C.A. § 78j(b).

5. Section 1292(b) provides:

"When a district judge, in making in a civil action an order not otherwise appealable under this section, shall be of the opinion that such order involves a controlling question of law as to which there is substantial ground for difference of opinion and that an immediate appeal from the order may materially advance the ultimate termination of the litigation he shall so state in writing in such order. The Court of Appeals may thereupon, in its discretion, permit an appeal to be taken from such order, if application is made to it within ten days after the entry of the order: *Provided, however,* That application for an appeal hereunder shall not stay proceedings in the district court unless the district judge or the Court of Appeals or a judge thereof shall so order."

6. Respondents also petitioned for a writ of mandamus directing the District Court to recertify the class. Since the Court of Appeals accepted appellate jurisdiction, it dismissed the petition for a writ of mandamus.

concluded that they would not pursue their claims individually.[7] The Court of Appeals therefore held that it had jurisdiction to hear the appeal and, on the merits, reversed the order decertifying the class. 550 F.2d 1106.

Federal appellate jurisdiction generally depends on the existence of a decision by the District Court that "ends the litigation on the merits and leaves nothing for the court to do but execute the judgment." Catlin v. United States, 324 U.S. 229, 233, 65 S.Ct. 631, 633, 89 L.Ed. 911.[8] An order refusing to cer ... , or decertifying, a class does not of its own force terminate the entire litigation because the plaintiff is free to proceed on his individual claim. Such an order is appealable, therefore, only if it comes within an appropriate exception to the final judgment rule. In this case respondents rely on the "collateral order" exception articulated by this Court in Cohen v. Beneficial Industrial Loan Corp., 337 U.S. 541, 69 S.Ct. 1221, 93 L.Ed. 1528, and on the "death knell" doctrine adopted by several circuits to determine the appealability of orders denying class certification.

I

In *Cohen*, the District Court refused to order the plaintiff in a stockholder's derivative action to post the security for costs required by a New Jersey statute. The defendant sought immediate review of the question whether the state statute applied to derivative suits in federal court. This Court noted that the purpose of the finality requirement "is to combine in one review all stages of the proceeding that effectively may be reviewed and corrected if and when final judgment results."

7. "Plaintiffs, both of whom are employed, have an aggregate yearly gross income of $26,000. Their total net worth is approximately $75,000, but only $4,000 of this sum is in cash. The remainder consists of equity in their home and investments.

"As of December 1974 plaintiffs had already incurred expenses in excess of $1,200 in connection with this lawsuit. Plaintiffs' new counsel has estimated expenses of this lawsuit to be $15,000. The nature of this case will require extensive discovery, much of which must take place in Florida, where most defendants reside. Moreover, the allegations regarding the prospectus and financial statements will likely require expert testimony at trial.

"After considering all the relevant information in the record, we are convinced that plaintiffs have sustained their burden of showing that they will not pursue their individual claim if the decertification order stands. Although plaintiffs' total net worth could absorb the cost of this litigation, 'it [takes] no great understanding of the mysteries of high finance to make obvious the futility of spending a thousand dollars to get a thousand dollars—or even

less.' Douglas, Protective Committees in Railroad Reorganizations, 47 Harv.L.Rev. 565, 567 (1934). We conclude we have jurisdiction to hear the appeal." 550 F.2d 1106, 1109–1110.

8. For a unanimous Court in Cobbledick v. United States, 309 U.S. 323, 325, 60 S.Ct. 540, 541, 84 L.Ed. 783, Mr. Justice Frankfurter wrote:

"Since the right to a judgment from more than one court is a matter of grace and not a necessary ingredient of justice, Congress from the very beginning has, by forbidding piecemeal disposition on appeal of what for practical purposes is a single controversy, set itself against enfeebling judicial administration. Thereby is avoided the obstruction to just claims that would come from permitting the harassment and cost of a succession of separate appeals from the various rulings to which a litigation may give rise, from its initiation to entry of judgment. To be effective, judicial administration must not be leaden-footed. Its momentum would be arrested by permitting separate reviews of the component elements in a unified cause."

Id., at 546, 69 S.Ct., at 1225. Because immediate review of the District Court's order was consistent with this purpose, the Court held it appealable as a "final decision" under § 1291. The ruling had "settled conclusively the corporation's claim that it was entitled by state law to require the shareholder to post security for costs . . . [and] concerned a collateral matter that could not be reviewed effectively on appeal from the final judgment."[9]

To come within the "small class" of decisions excepted from the final judgment rule by *Cohen*, the order must conclusively determine the disputed question, resolve an important issue completely separate from the merits of the action, and be effectively unreviewable on appeal from a final judgment.[10] Abney v. United States, 431 U.S. 651, 658, 97 S.Ct. 2034, 2039, 52 L.Ed.2d 651; United States v. MacDonald, 435 U.S. 850, 98 S.Ct. 1547, 1549, 56 L.Ed.2d 18. An order passing on a request for class certification does not fall in that category. First, such an order is subject to revision in the District Court. Fed.Rule Civ.Proc. 23(c)(1).[11] Second, the class determination generally involves considerations that are "enmeshed in the factual and legal issues comprising the plaintiff's cause of action." Mercantile Nat. Bank v. Langdeau, 371 U.S. 555, 558, 83 S.Ct. 520, 522, 9 L.Ed.2d 523.[12] Finally, an order denying class certification is subject to effective review after final judgment at the behest of the named plaintiff or intervening class members. United Air Lines v. McDonald, 432 U.S. 385, 97 S.Ct. 2464, 53 L.Ed.2d 423. For these reasons, as the Courts of Appeals have consistently recognized,[13] the collateral-order doctrine is not applicable to the kind of order involved in this case.

II

Several Circuits, including the Court of Appeals in this case, have held that an order denying class certification is appealable if it is likely to sound the "death knell" of the litigation.[14] The "death knell"

9. Eisen v. Carlisle & Jacquelin, 417 U.S. 156, 171, 94 S.Ct. 2140, 2149, 40 L.Ed. 2d 732.

10. As the Court summarized the rule in *Cohen:*

"This decision appears to fall in that small class which finally determine claims of right separable from, and collateral to, rights asserted in the action, too important to be denied review and too independent of the cause itself to require that appellate consideration be deferred until the whole case is adjudicated." 337 U.S., at 546, 69 S.Ct., at 1225.

11. The Rule provides that an order involving class status may be "altered or amended before the decision on the merits." Thus, a district court's order denying or granting class status is inherently tentative.

12. "Evaluation of many of the questions entering into determination of class action questions is intimately involved with the merits of the claims. The typicality of the representative's claims or defenses, the adequacy of the representative, and the presence of common questions of law or fact are obvious examples. The more complex determinations required in Rule 23(b)(3) class actions entail even greater entanglement with the merits. . . ." 15 C. Wright, A. Miller & E. Cooper, Federal Practice and Procedure § 3911, p. 485, n. 45 (1976).

13. See, e.g., King v. Kansas City Southern Industries, Inc., 479 F.2d 1259 (CA7 1973); Williams v. Mumford, 167 U.S.App. D.C. 125, 511 F.2d 363 (1975), cert. denied, 423 U.S. 828, 96 S.Ct. 47, 46 L.Ed.2d 46.

14. See n. 2, supra.

doctrine assumes that without the incentive of a possible group recovery the individual plaintiff may find it economically imprudent to pursue his lawsuit to a final judgment and then seek appellate review of an adverse class determination. Without questioning this assumption, we hold that orders relating to class certification are not independently appealable under § 1291 prior to judgment.

In addressing the question whether the "death knell" doctrine supports mandatory appellate jurisdiction of orders refusing to certify class actions, the parties have devoted a portion of their argument to the desirability of the small-claim class action. Petitioner's opposition to the doctrine is based in part on criticism of the class action as a vexatious kind of litigation. Respondent, on the other hand, argues that the class action serves a vital public interest and, therefore, special rules of appellate review are necessary to ensure that district judges are subject to adequate supervision and control. Such policy arguments, though proper for legislative consideration, are irrelevant to the issue we must decide.

There are special rules relating to class actions and, to that extent, they are a special kind of litigation. Those rules do not, however, contain any unique provisions governing appeals. The appealability of any order entered in a class action is determined by the same standards that govern appealability in other types of litigation. Thus, if the "death knell" doctrine has merit, it would apply equally to the many interlocutory orders in ordinary litigation—rulings on discovery, on venue, on summary judgment—that may have such tactical economic significance that a defeat is tantamount to a "death knell" for the entire case.

Though a refusal to certify a class is inherently interlocutory, it may induce a plaintiff to abandon his individual claim. On the other hand, the litigation will often survive an adverse class determination. What effect the economic disincentives created by an interlocutory order may have on the fate of any litigation will depend on a variety of factors.[15] Under the "death knell" doctrine, appealability turns on the court's perception of that impact in the individual case. Thus, if the court believes that the plaintiff has adequate incentive to continue, the order is considered interlocutory; but if the court concludes that the ruling, as a practical matter, makes further litigation improbable, it is considered an appealable final decision.

The finality requirement in § 1291 evinces a legislative judgment that "[r]estricting appellate review to 'final decisions' prevents the debilitating effect on judicial administration caused by piecemeal appeal disposition of what is, in practical consequence, but a single controversy." Eisen v. Carlisle & Jacquelin, 417 U.S. 156, 170, 94 S.Ct. 2140, 2149, 40 L.Ed.2d 732. Although a rigid insistence on technical

15. E.g., the plaintiff's resources; the size of his claim and his subjective willingness to finance prosecution of the claim; the probable cost of the litigation and the possibility of joining others who will share that cost; and the prospect of prevailing on the merits and reversing an order denying class certification.

finality would sometimes conflict with the purposes of the statute, Cohen v. Beneficial Industrial Loan Corp., [supra,] even adherents of the "death knell" doctrine acknowledge that a refusal to certify a class does not fall in that limited category of orders, which, though nonfinal, may be appealed without undermining the policies served by the general rule. It is undisputed that allowing an appeal from such an order in the ordinary case would run "directly contrary to the policy of the final judgment rule embodied in 28 U.S.C.A. § 1291 and the sound reasons for it. . . ." [16] Yet several Courts of Appeals have sought to identify on a case-by-case basis those few interlocutory orders which, when viewed from the standpoint of economic prudence, may induce a plaintiff to abandon the litigation. These orders, then, become appealable as a matter of right.

In administering the "death knell" rule, the courts have used two quite different methods of identifying an appealable class ruling. Some courts have determined their jurisdiction by simply comparing the claims of the named plaintiffs with an arbitrarily selected jurisdictional amount; [17] others have undertaken a thorough study of the possible impact of the class order on the fate of the litigation before determining their jurisdiction. Especially when consideration is given to the consequences of applying these tests to pretrial orders entered in nonclass action litigation, it becomes apparent that neither provides an acceptable basis for the exercise of appellate jurisdiction.

The formulation of an appealability rule that turns on the amount of the plaintiff's claim is plainly a legislative, not a judicial, function. While Congress could grant an appeal of right to those whose claims fall below a specific amount in controversy, it has not done so. Rather, it has made "finality" the test of appealability. Without a legislative prescription, an amount-in-controversy rule is necessarily an arbitrary measure of finality because it ignores the variables that inform a litigant's decision to proceed, or not to proceed, in the face of an adverse class ruling.[18] Moreover, if the jurisdictional amount is to be measured by the aggregated claims of the named plaintiffs, appellate jurisdiction

---

16. Korn v. Franchard Corp., 443 F.2d 1301, 1305 (CA2 1971).

17. Thus, orders denying class certification have been held nonappealable because the plaintiffs alleged damages in the $3,000–$8,000 range. Shayne v. Madison Square Garden, 491 F.2d 397 (CA2 1974); Milberg v. Western Pacific Railroad Co., 443 F.2d 1301 (CA2 1971); Gosa v. Securities Inv. Co., 449 F.2d 1330 (CA5 1971); Domaco Venture Capital Fund v. Teltronics Services, Inc., 551 F.2d 508 (CA2 1977). Smaller claims, however, have been held sufficient to support appellate jurisdiction in other cases. See, e.g., Green v. Wolf Corp., 406 F.2d 291 (CA2 1968), cert. denied, 395 U.S. 977, 89 S.Ct. 2131, 23 L.Ed. 2d 766 (1969).

18. See n. 15, supra. Thus, it is not at all clear that the prospect of recovering $3,000 would provide more incentive to sustain complex litigation against corporate defendants than the prospect of recovering $1,000. Yet the amount-in-controversy test allows an appeal in the latter case but not in the former. Compare Green v. Wolf Corp., 406 F.2d 291, 295 n. 6 (CA2 1968), cert. denied, 395 U.S. 977, 89 S.Ct. 2131, 23 L.Ed.2d 766 (1969) with Gosa v. Securities Inv. Co., 449 F.2d 1330 (CA5 1971). The arbitrariness of this approach is exacerbated by the fact that the Courts of Appeals have not settled on a specific jurisdictional amount; rather, they have simply determined on an *ad hoc* basis whether the plaintiff's claim is too small to warrant individual prosecution.

may turn on the joinder decisions of counsel rather than the finality of the order.[19]

While slightly less arbitrary, the alternative approach to the "death knell" rule would have a serious debilitating effect on the administration of justice. It requires class action plaintiffs to build a record in the trial court that contains evidence of those factors deemed relevant to the "death knell" issue and district judges to make appropriate findings.[20] And one Court of Appeals has even required that the factual inquiry be extended to all members of the class because the policy against interlocutory appeals can be easily circumvented by joining "only those whose individual claims would not warrant the cost of separate litigation"; [21] to avoid this possibility, the named plaintiff is required to prove that no member of the purported class has a claim that warrants individual litigation.

A threshold inquiry of this kind may, it is true, identify some orders that would truly end the litigation prior to final judgment; allowing an immediate appeal from those orders may enhance the quality of justice afforded a few litigants. But this incremental benefit is outweighed by the impact of such an individualized jurisdictional inquiry on the judicial system's overall capacity to administer justice.

The potential waste of judicial resources is plain. The district court must take evidence, entertain argument, and make findings; and the Court of Appeals must review that record and those findings simply to determine whether a discretionary class determination is subject to appellate review. And if the record provides an inadequate basis for this determination, a remand for further factual development may be required.[22] Moreover, even if the court makes a "death knell" finding and reviews the class designation order on the merits, there is no assurance that the trial process will not again be disrupted by interlocutory review. For even if a ruling that the plaintiff does not adequately represent the class is reversed on appeal, the district court may still refuse to certify the class on the ground that, for example, common questions of law or fact do not predominate. Under the "death knell" theory, plaintiff would again be entitled to an appeal as a matter of right pursuant to § 1291. And since other kinds of interlocutory orders may also create the risk of a premature demise, the potential for multiple appeals in every complex case is apparent and serious.

Perhaps the principal vice of the "death knell" doctrine is that it authorizes *indiscriminate* interlocutory review of decisions made by the trial judge. The Interlocutory Appeals Act of 1958, 28 U.S.C.A. § 1292(b),[23] was enacted to meet the recognized need for prompt review of certain nonfinal orders. However, Congress carefully confined the

---

19. Cf. Milberg v. Western Pacific Railroad, 443 F.2d 1301 (CA2 1971).

20. See, e.g., Hooley v. Red Carpet Corp., 549 F.2d 643 (CA9 1977); Ott v. Speedwriting Publishing Co., 518 F.2d 1143 (CA6 1975).

21. Hooley v. Red Carpet Corp., 549 F.2d 643, 645 (CA9 1977).

22. See, e.g., Jelfo v. Hickok Manufacturing Co., 531 F.2d 680, 681 (CA2 1976).

23. See n. 5, supra.

availability of such review. Nonfinal orders could never be appealed as a matter of right. Moreover, the discretionary power to permit an interlocutory appeal is not, in the first instance, vested in the courts of appeals.[24] A party seeking review of a nonfinal order must first obtain the consent of the trial judge. This screening procedure serves the dual purpose of ensuring that such review will be confined to appropriate cases and avoiding time-consuming jurisdictional determinations in the court of appeals.[25] Finally, even if the district judge certifies the order under § 1292(b), the appellant still "has the burden of persuading the court of appeals that exceptional circumstances justify a departure from the basic policy of postponing appellate review until after the entry of a final judgment." Fisons, Ltd. v. United States, 458 F.2d 1241, 1248 (CA7 1972). The appellate court may deny the appeal for any reason, including docket congestion.[26] By permitting appeals of right from class designation orders after jurisdictional determinations that turn on questions of fact, the "death knell" doctrine circumvents these restrictions.[27]

Additional considerations reinforce our conclusion that the "death knell" doctrine does not support appellate jurisdiction of prejudgment orders denying class certification. First, the doctrine operates only in

---

24. Thus, Congress rejected the notion that the courts of appeals should be free to entertain interlocutory appeals whenever, in their discretion, it appeared necessary to avoid unfairness in the particular case. H.R.Rep. No. 1667, 85th Cong., 2d Sess., 4–6 (1958); Note, Interlocutory Appeals in the Federal Courts under 28 U.S.C.A. § 1292(b), 88 Harv.L.Rev. 607, 610 (1975).

25. House Report, supra n. 24, at 5–6:

"We also recognize that such savings may be nullified in practice by indulgent extension of the amendment to inappropriate cases or by enforced consideration in Courts of Appeals of many ill-founded applications for review. The problem, therefore, is to provide a procedural screen through which only the desired cases may pass, and to avoid the wastage of a multitude of fruitless applications to invoke the amendment contrary to its purpose. . . .

". . . Requirement that the Trial Court certify the case as appropriate for appeal serves the double purpose of providing the Appellate Court with the best informed opinion that immediate review is of value, and at once protects appellate dockets against a flood of petitions in inappropriate cases. . . . [A]voidance of ill-founded applications in the Courts of Appeals for piecemeal review is of particular concern. If the consequence of change is to be crowded appellate dockets as well as any substan-

L., H. & T.–Cs.Plead. & Proc.6th Ed. UCB—30

tial number of unjustified delays in the Trial Court, the benefits to be expected from the amendment may well be outweighed by the lost motion of preparation, consideration, and rejection of unwarranted applications for its benefits."

26. Hearings on H.R. 6238 and H.R. 7260 before Subcommittee No. 3 of the House Committee on the Judiciary, 85th Cong., 2d Sess., ser. II, at 21 (1958).

27. Several Courts of Appeals have heard appeals from discretionary class determinations pursuant to § 1292(b). See, e.g., Lukenas v. Bryce's Mountain Resort Inc., 538 F.2d 594 (CA4 1976); Susman v. Lincoln American Corp., 561 F.2d 86 (CA7 1977). See also Samuel v. University of Pittsburgh, 506 F.2d 355 (CA3 1974). As Judge Friendly has noted:

"[T]he best solution is to hold that appeals from the grant or denial of class action designation can be taken only under the procedure for interlocutory appeals provided by 28 U.S.C. § 1292(b). . . . Since the need for review of class action orders turns on the facts of the particular case, this procedure is preferable to attempts to formulate standards which are necessarily so vague as to give rise to undesirable jurisdictional litigation with concomitant expense and delay." Parkinson v. April Industries, Inc., 520 F.2d 650, 660 (CA2 1975) (concurring opinion).

favor of plaintiffs even though the class issue—whether to certify, and if so, how large the class should be—will often be of critical importance to the defendant as well. Certification of a large class may so increase the defendant's potential damage liability and litigation costs that he may find it economically prudent to settle and to abandon a meritorious defense. Yet the Courts of Appeals have correctly concluded that orders granting class certification are interlocutory. Whatever similarities or differences there are between plaintiffs and defendants in this context involve questions of policy for Congress.[28] Moreover, allowing appeals of right from nonfinal orders that turn on the facts of a particular case thrusts appellate courts indiscriminately into the trial process and thus defeats one vital purpose of the final judgment rule— "that of maintaining the appropriate relationship between the respective courts. . . . This goal, in the absence of most compelling reasons to the contrary, is very much worth preserving." [29]

Accordingly, we hold that the fact that an interlocutory order may induce a party to abandon his claim before final judgment is not a sufficient reason for considering it a "final decision" within the meaning of § 1291.[30] The judgment of the Court of Appeals is reversed with directions to dismiss the appeal.

---

28. "The Congress is in a position to weigh the competing interests of the dockets of the trial and appellate courts, to consider the practicability of savings in time and expense, and to give proper weight to the effect on litigants. . . . This Court . . . is not authorized to approve or declare judicial modification. It is the responsibility of all courts to see that no unauthorized extension or reduction of jurisdiction, direct or indirect, occurs in the federal system. . . . Any such *ad hoc* decisions disorganize practice by encouraging attempts to secure or oppose appeals with a consequent waste of time and money. The choices fall in the legislative domain." Baltimore Contractors v. Bodinger, 348 U.S. 176, 181–182, 75 S.Ct. 249, 252–53, 99 L.Ed. 233.

29. Parkinson v. April Industries, Inc., 520 F.2d 650, 654 (CA2 1975).

30. Respondents also suggest that the Court's decision in Gillespie v. U.S. Steel Corp., 379 U.S. 148, 85 S.Ct. 308, 13 L.Ed. 2d 199, supports appealability of a class designation order as a matter of right. We disagree. In *Gillespie*, the Court upheld an exercise of appellate jurisdiction of what it considered a marginally final order that disposed of an unsettled issue of national significance because review of that issue unquestionably "implemented the same policy Congress sought to promote in § 1292(b)," id., at 154, 85 S.Ct. at 312, and the arguable finality issue had not been presented to this Court until argument on the merits, thereby ensuring that none of the policies of judicial economy served by the finality requirement would be achieved were the case sent back with the important issue undecided. In this case, in contrast, respondents sought review of an inherently nonfinal order that tentatively resolved a question that turns on the facts of the individual case; and, as noted above, the indiscriminate allowance of appeals from such discretionary orders is plainly inconsistent with the policies promoted by § 1292(b). If *Gillespie* were extended beyond the unique facts of that case, § 1291 would be stripped of all significance.

KERR v. UNITED STATES DISTRICT COURT

Supreme Court of the United States, 1976.
426 U.S. 394, 96 S.Ct. 2119, 48 L.Ed.2d 725.*

MR. JUSTICE MARSHALL delivered the opinion of the Court.

Petitioners, defendants in a class action, sought issuance of writs of mandamus from the United States Court of Appeals for the Ninth Circuit to compel the District Court to vacate two discovery orders. The Court of Appeals refused to issue the writs. We hold that in the circumstances of this case—and particularly in light of the availability of an alternative, less extreme, path to modification of the challenged discovery orders—issuance of the writ is inappropriate. We therefore affirm.

I

Seven prisoners in the custody of the Department of Corrections of the State of California filed a class action in the United States District Court for the Northern District of California on behalf of themselves and "on behalf of all adult male felons who now are, as well as all adult male felons who in the future will be, in the custody of the California Department of Corrections, whether confined in an institution operated by the Department or on parole." App. 370.[1] Among the defendants in the action are petitioners in this case: the individual members of the California Adult Authority, the Administrative Officer of the California Adult Authority, and the Director of Corrections of the State of California. Plaintiffs' complaint alleges substantial constitutional violations in the manner in which the California Adult Authority carries out its function of determining the length and conditions of punishment for convicted criminal offenders.

In the course of discovery, plaintiffs submitted requests for the production of a number of documents pursuant to Fed.Rule Civ.Proc. 34. Petitioners' subsequent two petitions for writs of mandamus were concerned with two classes of documents that were part of these requests. The first class, part of a series of requests first made in June 1973, and which will be referred to here as the "Adult Authority files," is generally comprised of the personnel files of all members and employees of the Adult Authority, all Adult Authority documents relating to its past, present or future operation, and all memoranda written by the Chairman of the Adult Authority within the preceding five years.[2] The second class of documents with which we are con-

---

* Some of the Court's footnotes are omitted.

1. The seven prisoners and the class they represent will be referred to here as "plaintiffs."

2. The documents were specifically described in plaintiffs' requests numbered 7, 14, 15, 18, 20, 21, and 22:

"7. All files, including all personnel files which are maintained by the Adult Authority or by the Department of Corrections, or by any officer or employee thereof with respect to each member, each hearing representative, and the Executive Officer of the Adult Authority. . . .

cerned was first requested by plaintiffs in November 1973, and will be referred to here as the "prisoners' files." Plaintiffs requested the opportunity to examine the files of every twentieth inmate at each California Department of Corrections institution, App. 234; the class of documents, therefore, is comprised of the correctional files of a sample of the prisoners in the custody of the California Department of Corrections.

When presented with the request for the Adult Authority files, petitioners objected, claiming that the files were irrelevant, confidential, and privileged, and suggesting that they should not be required to turn over the files to plaintiffs without prior *in camera* review by the District Court to evaluate the claims of privilege. Plaintiffs moved, pursuant to Fed.Rule Civ.Proc. 37, for an order compelling discovery. App. 76. The District Court referred the matter to a Magistrate for findings and recommendations, and the Magistrate recommended that the District Court order production of the Adult Authority files without undertaking an *in camera* inspection of the files. The District Court accepted the Magistrate's recommendations and ordered the production of the documents. Seeking to limit distribution of the personnel files of the Adult Authority members and their employees, however, the District Court issued a protective order limiting the number of people associated with the plaintiffs who could examine those documents:

> "[N]o personnel file of any member of the Adult Authority, hearing representative or executive officer, nor any copy of any of its contents, shall be shown to any person except counsel of record for the plaintiffs and no more than a total of two investigators designated by such counsel, and then only to the extent necessary to the conduct of this action." Petition for Cert. xvi.

"14. Each report submitted by any member, hearing representative, Executive Officer, or any other employee or official of the Adult Authority. . . .

"15. All written statements written or delivered by any member or hearing representative or the Executive Officer of the Adult Authority during the past 5 years favoring, opposing, or in any way commenting upon bills or other legislation or legislative proposals pending in the U.S. House of Representatives, the Senate of the United States, or the California Legislature . . . .

"18. All written proposals for any change whatsoever in the organization or operation of, qualifications for, or substantive criteria and procedures to be employed by the Adult Authority. . . .

"20. All memoranda written by the Chairman of the Adult Authority during the past 5 years, no matter to whom sent including without limitation memoranda sent to other government organizations, agencies or officials, or to other members, hearing representatives, officials or employees of the Adult Authority.

"21. All documents in effect on November 15, 1972 which pertain to any Policy Statement or Resolution issued by the Adult Authority, including without limitation any file maintained on any Resolution or Policy Statement and all such documents executed or issued subsequent to that date.

"22. All documents, however formal or informal, issued during the past calendar year, which concern the Adult Authority's adoption of new policies, procedures, criteria, and the like, to be followed by members, hearing representatives, officials and employees. . . ." App. 52–56.

Dissatisfied with the District Court's ruling, petitioners filed a petition for a writ of mandamus under 28 U.S.C.A. § 1651(a),[3] requesting the Court of Appeals for the Ninth Circuit to vacate the District Court's order granting plaintiffs' motion to compel discovery. The Court of Appeals denied the petition in an opinion filed on January 17, 1975. 511 F.2d 192. * * *

A similar course was followed with regard to the requests for the prisoners' files. When petitioners, asserting grounds of privilege, objected to the requests, plaintiffs filed a motion to compel production which the District Court referred for findings and recommendations to a Magistrate. The Magistrate recommended that petitioners be required to produce up to 200 prisoner files subject to a protective order "that would restrict examination and inspection of inmate files to attorneys for plaintiffs and for their use only in connection with this lawsuit." Pet. for Cert. xl. The District Court accepted the Magistrate's recommendation, but added to the recommended protective order a requirement that no prisoner's file be turned over for examination without the inmate's consent. Id., at xxxi, xxxiii. Petitioners then filed a petition for mandamus which the Court of Appeals denied by order and without opinion on December 18, 1974. Id., at xxiii.

Petitioners sought review in this Court of the denial of both petitions. We granted certiorari. 421 U.S. 987, 95 S.Ct. 1988, 44 L.Ed. 2d 476 (1975).

II

The remedy of mandamus is a drastic one, to be invoked only in extraordinary situations. Will v. United States, 389 U.S. 90, 95, 88 S.Ct. 269, 273, 19 L.Ed.2d 305 (1967); Bankers Life & Cas. Co. v. Holland, 346 U.S. 379, 382–385, 74 S.Ct. 145, 147–149, 98 L.Ed. 106 (1953); Ex parte Fahey, 332 U.S. 258, 259, 67 S.Ct. 1558, 1559, 91 L.Ed. 2041 (1947). As we have observed, the writ "has traditionally been used in the federal courts only 'to confine an inferior court to a lawful exercise of its prescribed jurisdiction or to compel it to exercise its authority when it is its duty to do so.'" Will v. United States, 389 U.S., at 95, 88 S.Ct., at 273, quoting Roche v. Evaporated Milk Assn., 319 U.S. 21, 26, 63 S.Ct. 938, 941, 87 L.Ed. 1185 (1943). And, while we have not limited the use of mandamus by an unduly narrow and technical understanding of what constitutes a matter of "jurisdiction," Will v. United States, 389 U.S., at 95, 88 S.Ct., at 273, the fact still remains that "only exceptional circumstances amounting to a judicial 'usurpation of power' will justify the invocation of this extraordinary remedy." Ibid.

Our treatment of mandamus within the federal court system as an extraordinary remedy is not without good reason. As we have recog-

---

3. Title 28 U.S.C.A. § 1651(a) provides: "The Supreme Court and all courts established by Act of Congress may issue all writs necessary or appropriate in aid of their respective jurisdictions and agreeable to the usages and principles of law."

nized before, mandamus actions such as the one involved in the instant case "have the unfortunate consequence of making the [district court] judge a litigant, obliged to obtain personal counsel or to leave his defense to one of the litigants [appearing] before him" in the underlying case. Bankers Life & Cas. Co. v. Holland, 346 U.S., at 384–385, 74 S.Ct., at 149, quoting Ex parte Fahey, 332 U.S., at 260, 67 S.Ct., at 1559. More importantly, particularly in an era of excessively crowded lower court dockets, it is in the interest of the fair and prompt administration of justice to discourage piecemeal litigation. It has been Congress' determination since the Judiciary Act of 1789 that as a general rule "appellate review should be postponed . . . until after final judgment has been rendered by the trial court." Will v. United States, 389 U.S., at 96, 88 S.Ct., at 274; Parr v. United States, 351 U.S. 513, 520–521, 76 S.Ct. 912, 917–918, 100 L.Ed. 1377 (1956).[6] A judicial readiness to issue the writ of mandamus in anything less than an extraordinary situation would run the real risk of defeating the very policies sought to be furthered by that judgment of Congress.

As a means of implementing the rule that the writ will issue only in extraordinary circumstances, we have set forth various conditions to its issuance. Among these are that the party seeking issuance of the writ have no other adequate means to attain the relief he desires, Roche v. Evaporated Milk Assn., 319 U.S., at 26, 63 S.Ct., at 941, and that he satisfy "the burden of showing that [his] right to issuance of the writ is 'clear and indisputable.'" Bankers Life & Cas. Co. v. Holland, 346 U.S., at 384, 74 S.Ct., at 148, quoting United States ex rel. Bernardin v. Duell, 172 U.S. 576, 582, 19 S.Ct. 286, 287, 43 L.Ed. 559 (1899); Will v. United States, 389 U.S., at 96, 88 S.Ct., at 274. Moreover, it is important to remember that issuance of the writ is in large part a matter of discretion with the court to which the petition is addressed. Schlagenhauf v. Holder, 379 U.S. 104, 112 n. 8, 85 S.Ct. 234, 239, 13 L.Ed.2d 152 (1964); Parr v. United States, 351 U.S., at 520, 76 S.Ct., at 917. See also Technitrol Inc. v. McManus, 405 F.2d 84 (CA8), cert. denied, 394 U.S. 997, 89 S.Ct. 1591, 22 L.Ed.2d 775 (1969); Pacific Car and Foundry Co. v. Pence, 403 F.2d 949 (CA9 1968).

When looked at in the framework of these factors, it would appear that the actions of the Court of Appeals in this case should be affirmed. What petitioners are seeking here is not a declaration that the documents in question are absolutely privileged and that plaintiffs can never have access to any of them. On the contrary, petitioners request only that "production of the confidential documents not be compelled without a prior informed determination by the district court that plaintiffs' need for them in the action below outweighs their confidentiality." Brief for Petitioners 77–78. Petitioners ask in essence only that the District Court review the challenged documents *in camera* before passing on whether each one individually should or should not be disclosed. But the Court of Appeals' opinion dealing with the Adult

---

6. The use of extraordinary writs aside, it is only in narrowly defined circumstances, see 28 U.S.C.A. § 1292, that the appellate jurisdiction of the courts of appeals extends to interlocutory orders.

Authority files did not foreclose the possible necessity of such *in camera* review. Its denial of the writ was based largely on the grounds that the governmental privilege had not been asserted personally by anyone eligible to assert it, and that it had not been asserted with the requisite specificity. The court apparently left open the opportunity for petitioners to return to the District Court, assert the privilege more specifically and through responsible officials, and then have their request for an *in camera* review of the materials by the District Court reconsidered in a different light:

> "Since there may be information in the requested documents which should be protected, the petitioners may assert a privilege to a particular document or class of documents, and perhaps seek *in camera* inspection, at the time the documents are discovered in the district court." 511 F.2d, at 198–199.

Petitioners contend that by denying the petition for mandamus the Court of Appeals has afforded them no remedy at all. To the contrary, we read the above quoted language of the opinion as providing petitioners an avenue far short of mandamus to achieve precisely the relief they seek.

To the extent that the opinion below might be regarded as ambiguous, we are fortified in our reading of it by a recognition of the serious consequences which could flow from an unwarranted failure to grant petitioners the opportunity to have the documents reviewed by the trial judge *in camera* before being compelled to turn them over. Petitioners' claims of privilege rest in large part on the notion that turning over the requested documents would result in substantial injury to the State's prison-parole system by unnecessarily chilling the free and uninhibited exchange of ideas between staff members within the system, by causing the unwarranted disclosure and consequent drying up of confidential sources,[7] and in general by unjustifiably compromising the confidentiality of the system's records and personnel files.[8] In light of the potential seriousness of these considerations and in light of the fact that the weight to be accorded them will inevitably vary with the nature of the specific documents in question, it would seem that an *in camera* review of the documents is a relatively costless and eminently worthwhile method to insure that the balance between petitioners' claims of irrelevance and privilege and plaintiffs' asserted need for the documents is correctly struck.[9] Indeed, this Court has long held the view that *in camera* review is a highly appropriate and useful means of dealing with

7. See Metros v. United States District Court for District of Colorado, 441 F.2d 313 (CA10 1971).

8. See United States Board of Parole v. Merhige, 487 F.2d 25 (CA4 1973), cert. denied, 417 U.S. 918, 94 S.Ct. 2625, 41 L.Ed. 2d 224 (1974).

9. Petitioners also assert, citing Ford Motor Co. v. Dept. of Treasury of Indiana, 323 U.S. 459, 65 S.Ct. 347, 89 L.Ed. 389 (1945), and Edelman v. Jordan, 415 U.S.

651, 94 S.Ct. 1347, 39 L.Ed.2d 662 (1974), that discovery of material which is actually the property of the State or its agencies is limited by the Eleventh Amendment. In view of our resolution of this case and the fact that petitioners did not raise this issue either in the discovery proceedings in the District Court or in their petition for mandamus to the Court of Appeals we need not reach this issue.

claims of governmental privilege. E.g., United States v. Nixon, 418 U.S. 683, 706, 94 S.Ct. 3090, 3106, 41 L.Ed.2d 1039 (1974); United States v. Reynolds, 345 U.S. 1, 73 S.Ct. 528, 97 L.Ed. 727 (1953).

Insofar as discovery of the prisoners' files is concerned, it is true that the Court of Appeals' order denying the petition for a writ of mandamus with regard to those files was issued without any statement of reasons for the denial. However, there is no reason to think that by its order the Court of Appeals meant to foreclose petitioners from following precisely the same avenue with regard to the prisoners' files as it gave them the opportunity to follow with regard to the Adult Authority files.

We are thus confident that the Court of Appeals did in fact intend to afford the petitioners the opportunity to apply for and, upon proper application, receive *in camera* review. Accordingly the orders of the Court of Appeals are affirmed.

So ordered.

MR. JUSTICE STEVENS took no part in the consideration or decision of this case.

COX BROADCASTING CORP. v. COHN

Supreme Court of the United States, 1975.
420 U.S. 469, 95 S.Ct. 1029, 43 L.Ed.2d 328.*

MR. JUSTICE WHITE delivered the opinion of the Court.

The issue before us in this case is whether, consistently with the First and Fourteenth Amendments, a State may extend a cause of action for damages for invasion of privacy caused by the publication of the name of a deceased rape victim which was publicly revealed in connection with the prosecution of the crime.

I

In August 1971, appellee's 17-year-old daughter was the victim of a rape and did not survive the incident. * * *

In May 1972, appellee brought an action for money damages against appellants, * * * claiming that his right to privacy had been invaded by the television broadcasts giving the name of his deceased daughter. Appellants admitted the broadcasts but claimed that they were privileged under both state law and the First and Fourteenth Amendments. The trial court, rejecting appellants' constitutional claims and holding that the Georgia statute gave a civil remedy to those injured by its violation, granted summary judgment to appellee as to liability, with the determination of damages to await trial by jury.

* Some of the Court's footnotes are omitted.

On appeal, the Georgia Supreme Court, in its initial opinion, held that * * * the complaint stated a cause of action "for the invasion of the appellee's right of privacy, or for the tort of public disclosure"—a "common law tort exist[ing] in this jurisdiction without the help of the statute that the trial judge in this case relied on." Id., at 62, 200 S.E.2d, at 130. Although the privacy invaded was not that of the deceased victim, the father was held to have stated a claim for invasion of his own privacy by reason of the publication of his daughter's name. The court explained, however, that liability did not follow as a matter of law and that summary judgment was improper; whether the public disclosure of the name actually invaded appellee's "zone of privacy," and if so, to what extent, were issues to be determined by the trier of fact. Also, "in formulating such an issue for determination by the fact-finder, it is reasonable to require the appellee to prove that the appellants invaded his privacy with wilful or negligent disregard for the fact that reasonable men would find the invasion highly offensive." Id., at 64, 200 S.E.2d, at 131. The Georgia Supreme Court did agree with the trial court, however, that the First and Fourteenth Amendments did not, as a matter of law, require judgment for appellants.

*   *   *

   *   *   *

II

Appellants invoke the appellate jurisdiction of this Court under 28 U.S.C.A. § 1257(2) and, if that jurisdictional basis is found to be absent, through a petition for certiorari under 28 U.S.C.A. § 2103.   *   *   *

   *   *   *

Since 1789, Congress has granted this Court appellate jurisdiction with respect to state litigation only after the highest state court in which judgment could be had has rendered a "[f]inal judgment or decree." Title 28 U.S.C.A. § 1257 retains this limitation on our power to review cases coming from state courts. The Court has noted that "[c]onsiderations of English usage as well as those of judicial policy" would justify an interpretation of the final-judgment rule to preclude review "where anything further remains to be determined by a State court, no matter how dissociated from the only federal issue that has finally been adjudicated by the highest court of the State." Radio Station WOW, Inc. v. Johnson, 326 U.S. 120, 124, 65 S.Ct. 1475, 1478, 89 L.Ed. 2092 (1945). But the Court there observed that the rule had not been administered in such a mechanical fashion and that there were circumstances in which there has been "a departure from this requirement of finality for federal appellate jurisdiction." Ibid.

These circumstances were said to be "very few," ibid.; but as the cases have unfolded, the Court has recurringly encountered situations in which the highest court of a State has finally determined the federal issue present in a particular case, but in which there are further proceedings in the lower state courts to come. There are now at least four categories of such cases in which the Court has treated the decision on the federal issue as a final judgment for the purposes of 28 U.S.C.A. § 1257 and has taken jurisdiction without awaiting the completion of the additional proceedings anticipated in the lower state courts. In most, if not all, of the cases in these categories, these additional proceedings would not require the decision of other federal questions that might also require review by the Court at a later date,[6] and immediate rather than delayed review would be the best way to avoid "the mischief of economic waste and of delayed justice," Radio Station WOW, Inc. v. Johnson, supra, at 124, 65 S.Ct., at 1478, as well as precipitate interference with state litigation.[7] In the cases in the first two categories considered below, the federal issue would not be mooted or otherwise affected by the proceedings yet to be had because those proceedings have little substance, their outcome is certain, or they are wholly unrelated to the federal question. In the other two categories, however, the federal issue would be mooted if the petitioner or appellant seeking to bring the action here prevailed on the merits in the later state-court proceedings, but there is nevertheless sufficient justification for immediate review of the federal question finally determined in the state courts.

In the first category are those cases in which there are further proceedings—even entire trials—yet to occur in the state courts but where for one reason or another the federal issue is conclusive or the outcome of further proceedings preordained. In these circumstances, because the case is for all practical purposes concluded, the judgment of

---

6. Eminent domain proceedings are of the type that may involve an interlocutory decision as to a federal question with another federal question to be decided later. "For in those cases the federal constitutional question embraces not only a taking but a taking on payment of just compensation. A state judgment is not final unless it covers both aspects of that integral problem." North Dakota State Board of Pharmacy v. Snyder's Drug Stores, Inc., 414 U.S. 156, 163, 94 S.Ct. 407, 412, 38 L.Ed.2d 379 (1973). See also Grays Harbor Logging Co. v. Coats-Fordney Logging Co., 243 U.S. 251, 256, 37 S.Ct. 295, 297, 61 L.Ed. 702 (1917); Radio Station WOW, Inc. v. Johnson, 326 U.S. 120, 127, 65 S.Ct. 1475, 1480, 89 L.Ed. 2092 (1945).

7. Gillespie v. United States Steel Corp., 379 U.S. 148, 85 S.Ct. 308, 13 L.Ed. 2d 199 (1964), arose in the federal courts and involved the requirement of 28 U.S. C.A. § 1291 that judgments of district courts be final if they are to be appealed to the courts of appeals. In the course of deciding that the judgment of the District Court in the case had been final, the Court indicated its approach to finality requirements:

"And our cases long have recognized that whether a ruling is 'final' within

the meaning of § 1291 is frequently so close a question that decision of that issue either way can be supported with equally forceful arguments, and that it is impossible to devise a formula to resolve all marginal cases coming within what might well be called the 'twilight zone' of finality. Because of this difficulty this Court has held that the requirement of finality is to be given a 'practical rather than a technical construction.' Cohen v. Beneficial Industrial Loan Corp. [337 U.S. 541, 546, 69 S.Ct. 1221, 1226, 93 L.Ed. 1528]. See also Brown Shoe Co. v. United States, 370 U.S. 294, 306, 82 S.Ct. 1502, 1503, 8 L.Ed.2d 510; Bronson v. Railroad Co., 2 Black 524, 531, 17 L.Ed. 347, 359; Forgay v. Conrad, 6 How. 201, 203, 12 L.Ed. 404. Dickinson v. Petroleum Conversion Corp., 338 U.S. 507, 511, 70 S.Ct. 322, 324, 94 L.Ed. 299, pointed out that in deciding the question of finality the most important competing considerations are 'the inconvenience and costs of piecemeal review on the one hand and the danger of denying justice by delay on the other.'" 379 U.S., at 152–153, 85 S.Ct., at 311.

the state court on the federal issue is deemed final. In Mills v. Alabama, 384 U.S. 214, 86 S.Ct. 1434, 16 L.Ed.2d 484 (1966), for example, a demurrer to a criminal complaint was sustained on federal constitutional grounds by a state trial court. The State Supreme Court reversed, remanding for jury trial. This Court took jurisdiction on the reasoning that the appellant had no defense other than his federal claim and could not prevail at trial on the facts or any nonfederal ground. To dismiss the appeal "would not only be an inexcusable delay of the benefits Congress intended to grant by providing for appeal to this Court, but it would also result in a completely unnecessary waste of time and energy in judicial systems already troubled by delays due to congested dockets." Id., at 217–218, 86 S.Ct., at 1436 (footnote omitted).[8]

Second, there are cases such as *Radio Station WOW*, supra, and Brady v. Maryland, 373 U.S. 83, 83 S.Ct. 1194, 10 L.Ed.2d 215 (1963), in which the federal issue, finally decided by the highest court in the State, will survive and require decision regardless of the outcome of future state-court proceedings. In *Radio Station WOW*, the Nebraska Supreme Court directed the transfer of the properties of a federally licensed radio station and ordered an accounting, rejecting the claim that the transfer order would interfere with the federal license. The federal issue was held reviewable here despite the pending accounting on the "presupposition . . . that the federal questions that could come here have been adjudicated by the State court, and that the accounting which remains to be taken could not remotely give rise to a federal question . . . that may later come here. . . ." 326 U.S., at 127, 65 S.Ct., at 1480. The judgment rejecting the federal claim and directing the transfer was deemed "dissociated from a provision for an accounting even though that is decreed in the same order." Id., at 126, 65 S.Ct., at 1479. Nothing that could happen in the course of the accounting, short of settlement of the case, would foreclose or make unnecessary decision on the federal question. Older cases in the Court had reached the same result on similar facts. Carondelet Canal & Nav. Co. v. Louisiana, 233 U.S. 362, 34 S.Ct. 627, 58 L.Ed. 1001 (1914); Forgay v.

---

8. Other cases from state courts where this Court's jurisdiction was sustained for similar reasons include: Organization for a Better Austin v. Keefe, 402 U.S. 415, 418 n., 91 S.Ct. 1575, 1577, 29 L.Ed.2d 1 (1971); Construction Laborers v. Curry, 371 U.S. 542, 550–551, 83 S.Ct. 531, 536–537, 9 L.Ed. 2d 514 (1963); Pope v. Atlantic C.L.R. Co., 345 U.S. 379, 382, 73 S.Ct. 749, 750, 97 L.Ed. 1094 (1953); Richfield Oil Corp. v. State Board, 329 U.S. 69, 73–74, 67 S.Ct. 156, 158–159, 91 L.Ed. 80 (1946). In the *Richfield* case the Court said with respect to finality:

"The designation given the judgment by state practice is not controlling. Department of Banking, State of Nebraska v. Pink, 317 U.S. 264, 268, 63 S.Ct. 233,

235, 87 L.Ed. 254. The question is whether it can be said that 'there is nothing more to be decided' (Clark v. Williard, 292 U.S. 112, 118, 54 S.Ct. 615, 618, 78 L.Ed. 1160), that there has been 'an effective determination of the litigation.' Market Street Ry. Co. v. Railroad Commission, 324 U.S. 548, 551, 65 S.Ct. 770, 773, 89 L.Ed. 1171; see Radio Station W.O.W. v. Johnson, 326 U.S. 120, 123–124, 65 S.Ct. 1475, 1477, 89 L.Ed. 2092. That question will be resolved not only by an examination of the entire record (Clark v. Williard, supra) but, where necessary, by resort to the local law to determine what effect the judgment has under the state rules of practice." Id., at 72, 67 S.Ct., at 158.

Conrad, 6 How. 201, 12 L.Ed. 404 (1848). In the latter case, the Court, in an opinion by Mr. Chief Justice Taney, stated that the Court had not understood the final-judgment rule "in this strict and technical sense, but has given [it] a more liberal, and, as we think, a more reasonable construction, and one more consonant to the intention of the legislature." Id., at 203.

In the third category are those situations where the federal claim has been finally decided, with further proceedings on the merits in the state courts to come, but in which later review of the federal issue cannot be had, whatever the ultimate outcome of the case. Thus, in these cases, if the party seeking interim review ultimately prevails on the merits, the federal issue will be mooted; if he were to lose on the merits, however, the governing state law would not permit him again to present his federal claims for review. The Court has taken jurisdiction in these circumstances prior to completion of the case in the state courts. California v. Stewart, 384 U.S. 436, 86 S.Ct. 1602, 16 L.Ed.2d 694 (1966) (decided with Miranda v. Arizona), epitomizes this category. There the state court reversed a conviction on federal constitutional grounds and remanded for a new trial. Although the State might have prevailed at trial, we granted its petition for certiorari and affirmed, explaining that the state judgment was "final" since an acquittal of the defendant at trial would preclude, under state law, an appeal by the State. Id., at 498 n. 71, 86 S.Ct., at 1640.

A recent decision in this category is North Dakota State Board of Pharmacy v. Snyder's Drug Stores, Inc., 414 U.S. 156, 94 S.Ct. 407, 38 L.Ed.2d 379 (1973), in which the Pharmacy Board rejected an application for a pharmacy operating permit relying on a state statute specifying ownership requirements which the applicant did not meet. The State Supreme Court held the statute unconstitutional and remanded the matter to the Board for further consideration of the application, freed from the constraints of the ownership statute. The Board brought the case here, claiming that the statute was constitutionally acceptable under modern cases. After reviewing the various circumstances under which the finality requirement has been deemed satisfied despite the fact that litigation had not terminated in the state courts, we entertained the case over claims that we had no jurisdiction. The federal issue would not survive the remand, whatever the result of the state administrative proceedings. The Board might deny the license on state-law grounds, thus foreclosing the federal issue, and the Court also ascertained that under state law the Board could not bring the federal issue here in the event the applicant satisfied the requirements of state law except for the invalidated ownership statute. Under these circumstances, the issue was ripe for review.[10]

---

10. Cohen v. Beneficial Industrial Loan Corp., 337 U.S. 541, 69 S.Ct. 1221, 93 L.Ed. 1528 (1949), was a diversity action in the federal courts in the course of which there arose the question of the validity of a state statute requiring plaintiffs in stockholder suits to post security for costs as a prerequisite to bringing the action. The District Court held the state law inapplicable, the Court of Appeals reversed, and this Court, after granting certiorari, held that the issue of security for costs was separable from and independent of the merits and that if review were to be postponed until the ter-

Lastly, there are those situations where the federal issue has been finally decided in the state courts with further proceedings pending in which the party seeking review here might prevail on the merits on nonfederal grounds, thus rendering unnecessary review of the federal issue by this Court, and where reversal of the state court on the federal issue would be preclusive of any further litigation on the relevant cause of action rather than merely controlling the nature and character of, or determining the admissibility of evidence in, the state proceedings still to come. In these circumstances, if a refusal immediately to review the state court decision might seriously erode federal policy, the Court has entertained and decided the federal issue, which itself has been finally determined by the state courts for purposes of the state litigation.

In Construction Laborers v. Curry, 371 U.S. 542, 83 S.Ct. 531, 9 L.Ed.2d 514 (1963), the state courts temporarily enjoined labor union picketing over claims that the National Labor Relations Board had exclusive jurisdiction of the controversy. The Court took jurisdiction for two independent reasons. First, the power of the state court to proceed in the face of the preemption claim was deemed an issue separable from the merits and ripe for review in this Court, particularly "when postponing review would seriously erode the national labor policy requiring the subject matter of respondents' cause to be heard by the . . . Board, not by the state courts." Id., at 550, 83 S.Ct., at 536. Second, the Court was convinced that in any event the union had no defense to the entry of a permanent injunction other than the preemption claim that had already been ruled on in the state courts. Hence the case was for all practical purposes concluded in the state tribunals.

In Mercantile National Bank v. Langdeau, 371 U.S. 555, 83 S.Ct. 520, 9 L.Ed.2d 523 (1963), two national banks were sued, along with others, in the courts of Travis County, Tex. The claim asserted was conspiracy to defraud an insurance company. The banks as a preliminary matter asserted that a special federal venue statute immunized them from suit in Travis County and that they could properly be sued only in another county. Although trial was still to be had and the banks might well prevail on the merits, the Court, relying on *Curry,* entertained the issue as a "separate and independent matter, anterior to the merits and not enmeshed in the factual and legal issues comprising the plaintiff's cause of action." Id., at 558, 83 S.Ct., at 522. Moreover, it would serve the policy of the federal statute "to determine now in which state court appellants may be tried rather than to subject them . . . to long and complex litigation which may all be for naught if consideration of the preliminary question of venue is postponed until the conclusion of the proceedings." Ibid.

Miami Herald Publishing Co. v. Tornillo, 418 U.S. 241, 94 S.Ct. 2831, 41 L.Ed.2d 730 (1974), is the latest case in this category.[11] There a candidate for public office sued a newspaper for refusing, allegedly

mination of the litigation, "it will be too late effectively to review the present order and the rights conferred by the statute, if it is applicable, will have been lost, proba-

bly irreparably." Id., at 546, 69 S.Ct., at 1225.

11. Meanwhile Hudson Distributors v. Eli Lilly, 377 U.S. 386, 84 S.Ct. 1273, 12

contrary to a state statute, to carry his reply to the paper's editorial critical of his qualifications. The trial court held the act unconstitutional, denying both injunctive relief and damages. The State Supreme Court reversed, sustaining the statute against the challenge based upon the First and Fourteenth Amendments and remanding the case for a trial and appropriate relief, including damages. The newspaper brought the case here. We sustained our jurisdiction, relying on the principles elaborated in the *North Dakota* case and observing:

> "Whichever way we were to decide on the merits, it would be intolerable to leave unanswered, under these circumstances, an important question of freedom of the press under the First Amendment; an uneasy and unsettled constitutional posture of § 104.38 could only further harm the operation of a free press. Mills v. Alabama, 384 U.S. 214, 221–222, 86 S.Ct. 1434, 1438, 16 L.Ed.2d 484 (1966) (Douglas, J., concurring). See also Organization for a Better Austin v. Keefe, 402 U.S. 415, 418 n., 91 S.Ct. 1575, 1577, 29 L.Ed. 2d 1 (1971)." 418 U.S., at 247 n. 6, 94 S.Ct., at 2834.[12]

In light of the prior cases, we conclude that we have jurisdiction to review the judgment of the Georgia Supreme Court rejecting the challenge under the First and Fourteenth Amendments to the state law authorizing damage suits against the press for publishing the name of a rape victim whose identity is revealed in the course of a public prosecution. The Georgia Supreme Court's judgment is plainly final on the federal issue and is not subject to further review in the state courts. Appellants will be liable for damages if the elements of the state cause of action are proved. They may prevail at trial on nonfederal grounds, it is true, but if the Georgia court erroneously upheld the statute, there should be no trial at all. Moreover, even if appellants prevailed at trial and made unnecessary further consideration of the constitutional question, there would remain in effect the unreviewed decision of the State Supreme Court that a civil action for publishing the name of a rape victim disclosed in a public judicial proceeding may go forward despite the First and Fourteenth Amendments. Delaying final decision of the First Amendment claim until after trial will "leave unanswered . . . an important question of freedom of the press under the First Amend-

L.Ed.2d 394 (1964), another case of this genre, had been decided. There a retailer sued to invalidate a state fair trade act as inconsistent with the federal antitrust laws and not saved by a federal statute authorizing state fair trade legislation under certain conditions. The defendant manufacturer cross-petitioned for enforcement of the state act against the plaintiff-retailer. The trial court struck down the statute, but a state appellate court reversed and remanded for trial on the cross-petition. The Ohio Supreme Court affirmed that decision. Relying on *Curry* and Mercantile National Bank v. Langdeau, 371 U.S. 555, 83 S.Ct. 520, 9 L.Ed.2d 523 (1963), this

Court found the state-court judgment to be ripe for review, although the retailer might prevail at the trial. 377 U.S., at 389 n. 4, 84 S.Ct., at 1276.

12. The import of the Court's holding in *Tornillo* is underlined by its citation of the concurring opinion in Mills v. Alabama. There, Mr. Justice Douglas, joined by Mr. Justice Brennan, stated that even if the appellant had a defense and might prevail at trial, jurisdiction was properly noted in order to foreclose unwarranted restrictions on the press should the state court's constitutional judgment prove to be in error.

ment," "an uneasy and unsettled constitutional posture [that] could only further harm the operation of a free press." *Tornillo,* supra, 418 U.S., at 247 n. 6, 94 S.Ct., at 2834. On the other hand, if we now hold that the First and Fourteenth Amendments bar civil liability for broadcasting the victim's name, this litigation ends. Given these factors—that the litigation could be terminated by our decision on the merits [13] and that a failure to decide the question now will leave the press in Georgia operating in the shadow of the civil and criminal sanctions of a rule of law and a statute the constitutionality of which is in serious doubt—we find that reaching the merits is consistent with the pragmatic approach that we have followed in the past in determining finality. See Gillespie v. United States Steel Corp., 379 U.S. 148, 85 S.Ct. 308, 13 L.Ed.2d 199 (1964); Radio Station WOW, Inc. v. Johnson, 326 U.S. at 124, 65 S.Ct., at 1478; Mills v. Alabama, 384 U.S., at 221–222, 86 S.Ct., at 1438–1439 (Douglas, J., concurring).

       *   *   * †

NOTE ON APPEALABILITY OF NON–FINAL ORDERS IN FEDERAL COURTS

1. Justice Stevens' opinion in Coopers & Lybrand v. Livesay does not fully indicate the extent to which the Courts of Appeals had built upon Cohen v. Beneficial Indust. Loan Corp. in permitting interlocutory appeals under the "collateral order" doctrine. See 15 Wright & Miller §§ 3911–3918, indicating the array of situations in which the doctrine has been invoked, successfully and otherwise. See also, e.g., André, The Final Judgment Rule and Party Appeals of Civil Contempt Orders, 55 N.Y.U.L.Rev. 1041 (1980); Note, Appealability of Abstention Orders, 10 Ind.L.Rev. 556 (1977). Indeed, until a few years ago the trend of the cases was sufficiently strong that it could be said the courts were applying a "pragmatic" test for appealability within the federal system as well as in appealability to the Supreme Court from state courts. Redish, The Pragmatic Approach to Appealability in the Federal Courts, 75 Colum.L.Rev. 89 (1975). But the Supreme Court's position has oscillated over time and *Coopers*

---

13. Mr. Justice Rehnquist * * * is correct in saying that this factor involves consideration of the merits in determining jurisdiction. But it does so only to the extent of determining that the issue is substantial and only in the context that if the state court's final decision on the federal issue is incorrect, federal law forecloses further proceedings in the state court. That the petitioner who protests against the state court's decision on the federal question might prevail on the merits on nonfederal grounds in the course of further proceedings anticipated in the state court and hence obviate later review of the federal issue here is not preclusive of our jurisdiction. Curry, Langdeau, North Dakota State Board of Pharmacy, California v. Stewart, 384 U.S. 436, 86 S.Ct. 1602, 16 L.Ed.2d 694 (1966) (decided with Miranda v. Arizona), and Miami Herald Publishing Co. v. Tornillo, 418 U.S. 241, 94 S.Ct. 2831,

41 L.Ed.2d 730 (1974), make this clear. In those cases, the federal issue having been decided, arguably wrongly, and being determinative of the litigation if decided the other way, the finality rule was satisfied.

The author of the dissent, a member of the majority in *Tornillo,* does not disavow that decision. He seeks only to distinguish it by indicating that the First Amendment issue at stake there was more important and pressing than the one here. This seems to embrace the thesis of that case and of this one as far as the approach to finality is concerned, even though the merits and the avoidance doctrine are to some extent involved.

† The concurring opinions of Justice Powell and Justice Douglas, and the dissenting opinion of Justice Rehnquist, are omitted.

& *Lybrand* surely signals present disapproval of expansion. As suggested in that opinion, the enactment of 28 U.S.C.A. § 1292(b) can be taken as a congressional indication that interlocutory review should be allowed only in three circumstances:

(a) Where a "separate" judgment has been entered with regard to one or more but less than all of the claims in a multi-claim or multi-party case, as provided for in F.R.C.P. 54(b). See Curtiss-Wright Corp. v. General Elec. Co., 446 U.S. 1, 100 S.Ct. 1460, 64 L.Ed.2d 1 (1980). Omitting to take an interlocutory appeal under § 1292(b) does not preclude the party from challenging the order in question in a subsequent appeal from the final judgment. See Drayer v. Krasner, 572 F.2d 348 (2d Cir. 1978).

(b) Where the trial judge has certified the order for interlocutory review and the appellate court accepts the appeal, as provided in § 1292(b). See generally Note, Interlocutory Appeals in the Federal Courts Under 28 U.S.C.A. § 1292(b), 88 Harv.L.Rev. 607 (1975).

(c) Where the case involves an extraordinary error warranting use of mandamus or prohibition.

Since the decision in *Coopers & Lybrand,* the Supreme Court has continued to resist expansion of the "collateral order" doctrine. The Court subsequently held, for example, that both orders granting and denying motions to disqualify counsel are not appealable. An order denying intervention as of right but granting permissive intervention subject to conditions does not fall within the "collateral order" exception, Stringfellow v. Concerned Neighbors in Action, 480 U.S. 370, 107 S.Ct. 1177, 94 L.Ed.2d 389 (1987), and neither does an order granting or denying a stay of a federal action when a similar action is pending in a state court, Gulfstream Aerospace Corp. v. Mayacamas Corp., ___ U.S. ___, 108 S.Ct. 1133, 99 L.Ed.2d 296 (1988). But in Sanko Steamship Co. v. Galin, 835 F.2d 51 (2d Cir.1987), the Second Circuit held that a Rule 11 cost sanction imposed before final judgment is an appealable "collateral order."

Budinich v. Becton Dickinson & Co., ___ U.S. ___, 108 S.Ct. 1717, 100 L.Ed. 2d 178 (1988), holds that federal rather than state law determines what constitutes an appealable final decision in a diversity action, and that a judgment for damages is final although an award of attorneys fees, provided by a state statute applicable to the cause of action, remains to be made.

While an order improperly remanding an action removed to federal court from state court is not reviewable by appeal, see 28 U.S.C.A. § 1447(d), the Supreme Court has held that under certain circumstances it may be reviewed by extraordinary writ. Thermtron Products, Inc. v. Hermansdorfer, 423 U.S. 336, 96 S.Ct. 584, 46 L.Ed.2d 542 (1976). See also Herrmann, Thermtron Revisited: When and How Federal Trial Court Remand Orders are Reviewable, 19 Ariz.St.L.J. 395 (1987).

2. Kerr v. United States District Court, supra p. 1305, illustrates how the effect of appellate review by extraordinary writ can be virtually achieved even when the writ is denied. Kerr appears to be an artfully written opinion that ostensibly limits use of extraordinary writs for interlocutory review while carefully "saving" the Court's earlier decisions that had enlarged their use, for example, Schlagenhauf v. Holder, 379 U.S. 104, 85 S.Ct. 234, 13 L.Ed.2d 152 (1964), where a writ was granted to review an order dealing with the scope of discovery. For a broad interpretation of the scope of the proper use of extraordinary writs, see Colonial Times, Inc. v. Gasch, 509 F.2d 517, 524 (D.C. Cir. 1975): "*Schlagenhauf* authorizes departure from the final judgment rule

when the appellate court is convinced that resolution of an important, undecided issue will forestall future error in trial courts, eliminate uncertainty, and add importantly to the efficient administration of justice." See also Berger, The Mandamus Power of the United States Courts of Appeal, 31 Buff.L.Rev. 37 (1982); and Bonner and Appler, Interlocutory Appeals and Mandamus, 4 Litigation 25 (1978), indicating that writs have been issued by federal appellate courts when a trial judge:

— Refuses to dismiss a case although jurisdiction is lacking or a meritorious preliminary defense exists;

— Stays trial proceedings pending arbitration, exhaustion of some administrative remedy or resolution of a related case in another forum;

— Quashes writs of attachment or garnishment filed before the trial to ensure any judgment can be satisfied;

— Denies permission to file a cross-claim or other pleading amendment, or refuses to permit intervention;

— Refuses to permit depositions of certain individuals, or grants permission to take inappropriate depositions or improperly limits or conditions depositions;

— Enters orders limiting or denying discovery, or requires the production of privileged material;

— Denies class action status, or consolidates or severs two trials, or refuses to do so;

— Refuses to recuse himself.

The authors add that seeking mandamus "has frequently been useful even where the writ does not issue. Often the court will review the merits of the request, state how it believes the trial judge should have decided the issue, but decline to issue the writ for technical reasons * * *. It is rare that the district court does not 'get the message' and grant the relief voluntarily."

The decision in *Kerr* nevertheless seems to have had a chilling effect on interlocutory review by extraordinary writ in the federal system. See also Allied Chem. Corp. v. Daiflon, Inc., 449 U.S. 33, 101 S.Ct. 188, 66 L.Ed.2d 193 (1980), reversing a circuit court's issuance of mandamus to prevent a new trial in a district court. The determination of the application for an extraordinary writ may be res judicata of the matter in issue. Anno., 21 A.L.R.3d 206.

3. The relevant statute considered in *Cox Broadcasting,* 28 U.S.C.A. § 1257, provides that "final judgments or decrees rendered by the highest court of a State * * * may be reviewed by the Supreme Court," while the relevant statute in *Coopers & Lybrand,* 28 U.S.C.A. § 1291, provides that the "courts of appeals * * * shall have jurisdiction of appeals from all final decisions of the district courts * * *." The term "final judgment" was not given the same meaning in the two cases, was it? Why? There is no counterpart of 28 U.S.C.A. § 1292(b) that applies to Supreme Court review of interlocutory orders rendered in state court proceedings, nor have extraordinary writs been used for interlocutory review by the Supreme Court of orders in state courts. Are there relevant differences in the procedural contexts of the use of the term "final judgment" in § 1257 and § 1291 respectively? See generally Note, The Finality Rule for Supreme Court Review of State Court Orders, 91 Harv.L.Rev. 1004 (1978).

4. There are several statutory exceptions to the "final judgment" rule. See 28 U.S.C.A. § 1292(a); 16 Wright & Miller § 3920 et seq.

For a fuller treatment of federal appellate jurisdiction, see Hart & Wechsler cc. 5, 15. For a concise discussion of the present jurisdiction of the United States Supreme Court, including an analysis of the statutory elimination in 1988 of virtually all mandatory appeals to the Court, see Boskey and Gressman, The Supreme Court Bids Farewell to Mandatory Appeals, 121 F.R.D. 81 (1988).

2. REVIEWABILITY OF CONTENTIONS

BANKERS LIFE & CASUALTY CO. v. CRENSHAW

Supreme Court of the United States, 1988.
__ U.S. __, 108 S.Ct. 1645, 100 L.Ed.2d 62.*

JUSTICE MARSHALL delivered the opinion of the Court.

* * *

I

This action grows out of allegations that appellant Bankers Life and Casualty Company refused in bad faith to pay appellee Lloyd Crenshaw's insurance claim for loss of a limb. According to testimony at trial, appellee was injured on January 6, 1979, when a car alternator he was repairing rolled off his workbench and landed on his foot. Three days later, after the injury had not responded to home treatment, appellee went to the emergency room of the local Air Force Base hospital. Hospital doctors prescribed a splint, crutches, and pain medication, and told appellee to return in a week. Appellee revisited the hospital three times over the next five days, each time complaining of continuing pain in his foot. By the last visit, appellee's foot had swollen and begun to turn blue, and the examining doctor recommended a surgery consultation. Appellee was admitted to the hospital, where, on January 17, an Air Force general surgeon determined that a surgical amputation was necessary. The following day, appellee's leg was amputated below the knee.

At the time of the amputation, appellee was insured under a group policy issued by appellant. The policy provided a $20,000 benefit for loss of limb due to accidental bodily injury. In April of 1979, appellee submitted a claim under the policy. Appellant denied the claim. The apparent basis for the denial was an opinion of appellant's Medical Director, Dr. Nathaniel McParland, that the cause of the amputation was not appellee's accident but a pre-existing condition of arteriosclerosis, a degenerative vascular disease. Appellee responded to the company's denial by furnishing a statement signed by three doctors who treated him at the hospital. They stated that appellee's arteriosclerosis was "an underlying condition and not the immediate cause of the gangrenous necrosis. The precipating [sic] event must be considered to be the trauma which initially brought him to the Emergency Room on 9

* Some of the Court's footnotes are omitted.

January." 483 So.2d 254, 261 (Miss.1985). Dr. McParland and a company analyst concluded that this statement was inconsequential, and appellant adhered to its position that the arteriosclerosis was responsible for the loss of limb.

Appellee persisted in his efforts to recover under the policy, eventually hiring an attorney, and appellant persisted in its intransigence. In its correspondence with appellee and his attorney, appellant repeatedly asserted that appellee had not suffered an injury as defined in the policy, that is, a " 'bodily injury, causing the loss while this policy is in force, directly and independently of all other causes and effected solely through an accidental bodily injury to the insured person.' " Id., at 262, quoting letter of Apr. 8, 1980, from Wm. Herzau to appellee. In contemporaneous internal memoranda, however, appellant noted that notwithstanding the policy language, appellee was entitled to recovery under Mississippi law if his injury had "aggravate[d], render[ed] active, or set in motion a latent or dormant pre-existing physical condition or disease." Id., at 262, 263. The memoranda also demonstrated that appellant knew its files were incomplete yet never attempted to obtain appellee's medical records, most notably his emergency room report, even though Mississippi law and internal company procedures required such efforts.

After appellant again denied the claim on the ground that there was no evidence that appellee's " 'injury caused this loss "directly and independently of all other causes," ' " see id., at 263, appellee brought this suit in Mississippi state court. His complaint requested $20,000 in actual damages, and, as amended, $1,635,000 in punitive damages for the tort of bad-faith refusal to pay an insurance claim. The jury awarded appellee the $20,000 provided by the policy and punitive damages of $1.6 million.

The Mississippi Supreme Court affirmed the jury verdict without modification. It concluded that the punitive damages award was not excessive in light of appellant's financial worth and the degree of its wrongdoing. See id., at 279. * * * In its appeal to the Mississippi Supreme Court, appellant did not raise a federal constitutional challenge to the size of the punitive damages award.[1] Following the affirmance of the jury verdict, appellant filed a petition for rehearing. Appellant argued in the petition that "[t]he punitive damage verdict was clearly excessive, not reasonably related to any legitimate purpose, constitutes excessive fine, and violates constitutional principles." App. to Juris. Statement 139a. An accompanying brief asserted that the punitive damage award violated "due process, equal protection, and other constitutional standards." Id., at 151a. * * *

---

1. Appellant did offer on appeal a federal due process challenge based on the alleged "chilling effect" of unrestricted punitive damages awards on the exercise of a litigant's right of access to the courts. See App. to Juris. Statement 135a. We read this attack on the alleged open-endedness of Mississippi's punitive damages awards to be distinct from the attack on the size of the particular award that appellant has waged before this Court.

II

Appellant focuses most of its efforts in this appeal to challenging the punitive damages award of $1.6 million. It contends foremost that the award violates the Eighth Amendment's guarantee that "excessive fines [shall not be] imposed." U.S. Const., Amdt. 8. Appellant argues first, that the Excessive Fines Clause applies to punitive damages awards rendered in civil cases, and second, that the particular award in this case was constitutionally excessive. In addition to its excessive fines claim, appellant challenges the punitive damage award in this case on the grounds that it violates the Due Process Clause and the Contract Clause. Although we noted probable jurisdiction as to all of the questions presented in appellant's jurisdictional statement, appellant's challenges to the size of the punitive damages award do not fall within our appellate jurisdiction. See 28 U.S.C. § 1257(2). We therefore treat them as if contained in a petition for a writ of certiorari, and our unrestricted notation of probable jurisdiction of the appeal is to be understood as a grant of the writ as to these claims. See Mishkin v. New York, 383 U.S. 502, 512, 86 S.Ct. 958, 965, 16 L.Ed.2d 56 (1966). We conclude, however, that these claims were not raised and passed upon in state court, and we decline to reach them here. See ibid. ("The issue thus remains within our certiorari jurisdiction, and we may, for good reason, even at this stage, decline to decide the merits of the issue, much as we would dismiss a writ of certiorari as improvidently granted").

Appellant maintains that it raised its various challenges to the size of the punitive damage award in its petition for rehearing before the Mississippi Supreme Court. In urging us to entertain the claims, appellant relies on our decision in Hathorn v. Lovorn, 457 U.S. 255, 262–265, 102 S.Ct. 2421, 2426–2428, 72 L.Ed.2d 824 (1982), in which we accepted certiorari jurisdiction of claims that were raised, but not passed upon, in the Mississippi Supreme Court on petition for rehearing. *Hathorn* would be apposite were we to conclude that appellant had adequately raised its claims on rehearing. But appellant's petition for rehearing alleged only that the punitive damage award "was clearly excessive, not reasonably related to any legitimate purpose, constitutes excessive fine, and violates constitutional principles." App. to Juris. Statement 139a. The vague appeal to constitutional principles does not preserve appellant's Contract Clause or due process claim. A party may not preserve a constitutional challenge by generally invoking the Constitution in state court and awaiting review in this Court to specify the constitutional provision it is relying upon. Cf. Taylor v. Illinois, 484 U.S. ___, ___ n. 9, 108 S.Ct. 646, 651 n. 9, 98 L.Ed.2d 798 (1988) ("A generic reference to the Fourteenth Amendment is not sufficient to preserve a constitutional claim based on an unidentified provision of the Bill of Rights . . .").

Appellant's reference to the excessiveness of the punitive damage award more colorably raises a cognizable constitutional challenge to the size of the award, one based on the Excessive Fines Clause of the Eighth Amendment. But this language as well is too oblique to allow us to conclude that appellant raised before the Mississippi Supreme Court the federal claim it now urges us to resolve. As this Court stated in Webb v. Webb, 451 U.S. 493, 501, 101 S.Ct. 1889, 1894, 68 L.Ed.2d 392 (1981), "[a]t the minimum . . . there should be no doubt from the record that a claim under a *federal* statute or the *Federal* Constitution was presented in the state courts and that those courts were apprised of the nature or substance of the federal claim at the time and in the manner required by the state law." Although the petition for rehearing alleges that the fine is excessive, it does not indicate that the fine is excessive as a constitutional matter, be it state or federal. It certainly does not identify the Excessive Fines Clause of the Eighth Amendment to the Federal Constitution as the source of appellant's claim. Indeed, the crucial language from appellant's petition contains no reference whatsoever to the Eighth Amendment, the Federal Constitution, or federal law. This failure to invoke the Federal Constitution is especially problematic in this case because the Mississippi Constitution contains its own Excessive Fines Clause. Miss. Const. Art. 3, § 28. Thus, even if the Mississippi Supreme Court understood appellant to be offering a constitutional challenge, it may very well have taken that challenge to be anchored in the state constitution. Cf. *Webb,* supra, at 496–498, 101 S.Ct., at 1891–1892 (finding that party's reference to "full faith and credit" in state court proceedings had failed to raise a federal constitutional claim even though the state constitution contained no full faith and credit clause); id., at 502–503, 101 S.Ct., at 1894–1895 (MARSHALL, J., dissenting). We therefore conclude that appellant's Eighth Amendment challenge, like its other challenges to the size of the punitive damage award, was not properly raised below.[2]

Whether appellant's failure to raise these claims in the Mississippi courts deprives us of all power to review them under our certiorari jurisdiction is an unsettled question. As Chief Justice Rehnquist wrote for the Court in Illinois v. Gates, 462 U.S. 213, 103 S.Ct. 2317, 76 L.Ed. 2d 527 (1983), the cases have been somewhat inconsistent in their characterization of the "not pressed or passed upon below" rule. Early opinions seemed to treat the requirement as jurisdictional, whereas more recent cases clearly view the rule as merely a prudential restriction that does not pose an insuperable bar to our review. See id., at 218–219, 103 S.Ct., at 2321–2322 (discussing cases). We are not called

---

2. Similarly, appellant's challenges in this Court to the size of the punitive damage award in no way qualify as "mere enlargements" of claims made before the Mississippi Supreme Court. Under the mere enlargement doctrine, "[p]arties are not confined here to the same arguments which were advanced in the courts below upon a Federal question there discussed." Dewey v. Des Moines, 173 U.S. 193, 198, 19 S.Ct. 379, 380, 43 L.Ed. 665 (1899). See also Stanley v. Illinois, 405 U.S. 645, 658, n. 10, 92 S.Ct. 1208, 1216, n. 10, 31 L.Ed.2d 551 (1972). *Dewey* makes clear, however, that the federal question must be brought to the attention of the court below in some manner. "A claim or right which has never been made or asserted cannot be said to have been denied by a judgment which does not refer to it." 173 U.S., at 200, 19 S.Ct., at 381.

on today to conclusively characterize the "not pressed or passed upon below" rule, however, because assuming that the rule is merely prudential, we believe that the more prudent course in this case is to decline to review appellant's claims.

In determining whether to exercise jurisdiction over questions not properly raised below, the Court has focused on the policies that animate the "not pressed or passed upon below" rule. These policies are first, comity to the States, and second, a constellation of practical considerations, chief among which is our own need for a properly developed record on appeal. See Webb v. Webb, supra, 451 U.S., at 500–501, 101 S.Ct., at 1893–1894. Because the chief issue appellant would have us resolve—whether the Eighth Amendment's Excessive Fines Clause serves to limit punitive damages in state civil cases—is a question of some moment and difficulty, these policies apply with special force. See Illinois v. Gates, supra, 462 U.S., at 224, 103 S.Ct., at 2325 ("Where difficult issues of great public importance are involved, there are strong reasons to adhere scrupulously to the customary limitations on our discretion"); Mishkin v. New York, 383 U.S., at 512–513, 86 S.Ct., at 965 ("The far-reaching and important questions tendered by this claim are not presented by the record with sufficient clarity to require or justify their decision"). Our review of appellant's claim now would short-circuit a number of less intrusive, and possibly more appropriate, resolutions: the Mississippi State Legislature might choose to enact legislation addressing punitive damage awards for bad-faith refusal to pay insurance claims;[3] failing that, the Mississippi state courts may choose to resolve the issue by relying on the state constitution or on some other adequate and independent nonfederal ground; and failing that, the Mississippi Supreme Court will have its opportunity to decide the question of federal law in the first instance, while any ultimate review of the question that we might undertake will gain the benefit of a well-developed record and a reasoned opinion on the merits. We think it unwise to foreclose these possibilities, and therefore decline to address appellant's challenges to the size of the punitive damage award.

*   *   *

JUSTICE STEVENS and JUSTICE KENNEDY took no part in the consideration or decision of this case.

JUSTICE WHITE, with whom JUSTICE SCALIA joins, concurring.

I join Parts I and III of the Court's opinion but not Part II. I continue to believe that "the statute which gives us jurisdiction in this cause, 28 U.S.C. § 1257(3), prevents us from deciding federal constitutional claims raised here for the first time on review of state-court decisions. Cardinale v. Louisiana, 394 U.S. 437, 438–439 [89 S.Ct. 1161, 1162–1163, 22 L.Ed.2d 398]." Illinois v. Gates, 462 U.S. 213, 247, 103

---

3. Several States have enacted limits on punitive damages in specified types of causes of action. See, e.g., Fla.Stat.Ann. § 713.31(2)(c) (1988) (fraudulent filing of mechanics' lien); Wash.Rev.Code § 9A.36.080 (1987) (malicious harassment); Cal.Civ.Code Ann. § 1787.3 (West 1985) (consumer credit denial).

S.Ct. 2317, 2337, 76 L.Ed.2d 527 (1983) (WHITE, J., concurring in the judgment). Thus, I disagree with the Court's analysis—under "prudential" standards—of appellant's preservation of its challenge to the punitive damage award here. * * * Ultimately, because the majority properly declines to address claims which I believe are not within this Court's jurisdiction, I concur in Part II's result, but not its reasoning.

JUSTICE O'CONNOR, with whom JUSTICE SCALIA joins, concurring in part and concurring in the judgment.

I do not agree with the Court's analysis of our jurisdiction over appellant's federal due process claim. I therefore do not join Part II or footnote 1 of the Court's opinion. I join the remainder of the opinion, and I agree with the analysis of Part II insofar as claims under the Excessive Fines Clause and Contract Clause are concerned. Moreover, for the reasons given below, I ultimately concur in the Court's judgment with respect to the due process claim as well.

In its brief on appeal to the Mississippi Supreme Court, appellant expressly invoked the Due Process Clause of the Fourteenth Amendment and argued that Mississippi law chilled its fundamental right of access to the courts by authorizing unlimited punitive damages. App. to Juris. Statement 135a. The Court does not acknowledge this argument in its discussion of why the due process claim was not raised and passed upon below, but only notes that appellant did not present a due process argument clearly in its petition for rehearing. * * * The Court suggests that it need not consider the due process argument raised in appellant's brief to the Mississippi Supreme Court because it is "distinct from the attack on the size of the particular award that appellant has waged before this Court." * * * Standing alone, this observation is insufficient to deprive this Court of jurisdiction over appellant's due process claim. "Parties are not confined here to the same arguments which were advanced in the courts below upon a Federal question there discussed." Dewey v. Des Moines, 173 U.S. 193, 197–198, 19 S.Ct. 379, 380–381, 43 L.Ed. 665 (1899). See Illinois v. Gates, 462 U.S. 213, 248, 103 S.Ct. 2317, 2337, 76 L.Ed.2d 527 (1983) (WHITE, J., concurring in judgment).

Accordingly, the Court should examine the federal due process argument that appellant makes in this Court to determine whether it is "only an enlargement" of the due process argument it raised below. See *Dewey,* supra, 173 U.S., at 197, 19 S.Ct., at 380. In its principal brief in this Court, appellant contends that the Mississippi Supreme Court changed its standard for judging when an insurer may be liable for punitive damages and applied the new standard retroactively to this case. Appellant explains that it therefore had no advance notice of what conduct could render it liable for punitive damages. Citing cases in which this Court has struck down criminal statutes as void for vagueness, e.g., Roberts v. United States Jaycees, 468 U.S. 609, 104 S.Ct. 3244, 82 L.Ed.2d 462 (1984); Giaccio v. Pennsylvania, 382 U.S. 399, 86 S.Ct. 518, 15 L.Ed.2d 447 (1966), appellant maintains that this violated the Due Process Clause. Brief for Appellant 40–43. Then, in a supplemental brief filed after argument with the Court's leave, appellant expands the due process argument pressed below and mounts a more general attack on permitting juries to impose unlimited punitive damages on an ad hoc basis. Post-argument Brief for Appellant 4–10.

Appellant has touched on a due process issue that I think is worthy of the Court's attention in an appropriate case. Mississippi law gives juries discretion to award any amount of punitive damages in any tort case in which a defendant acts with a certain mental state. In my view, because of the punitive character of such awards, there is reason to think that this may violate the Due Process Clause.

Punitive damages are awarded not to compensate for injury but, rather, "to punish reprehensible conduct and to deter its future occurrence." *Gertz v. Welch, Inc.*, 418 U.S. 323, 350, 94 S.Ct. 2997, 3012, 41 L.Ed.2d 789 (1974). Punitive damages are not measured against actual injury, so there is no objective standard that limits their amount. Hence, "the impact of these windfall recoveries is unpredictable and potentially substantial." *Electrical Workers v. Foust*, 442 U.S. 42, 50, 99 S.Ct. 2121, 2127, 60 L.Ed.2d 698 (1979). For these reasons, the Court has forbidden the award of punitive damages in defamation suits brought by private plaintiffs, *Gertz*, supra, 418 U.S., at 349–359, 94 S.Ct., at 3011–3012, and in unfair representation suits brought against unions under the Railway Labor Act, *Electrical Workers*, supra, 442 U.S., at 52, 99 S.Ct., at 2128. For similar reasons, the Court should scrutinize carefully the procedures under which punitive damages are awarded in civil lawsuits.

Under Mississippi law, the jury may award punitive damages for any common law tort committed with a certain mental state, that is, "for a willful and intentional wrong, or for such gross negligence and reckless negligence as is equivalent to such a wrong." 483 So.2d 254, 269 (Miss.1985) (opinion below). Although this standard may describe the required mental state with sufficient precision, the amount of the penalty that may ensue is left completely indeterminate. As the Mississippi Supreme Court said, "the determination of the amount of punitive damages is a matter committed solely to the authority and discretion of the jury." Id., at 278. This grant of wholly standardless discretion to determine the severity of punishment appears inconsistent with due process. The Court has recognized that "vague sentencing provisions may pose constitutional questions if they do not state with sufficient clarity the consequences of violating a given criminal statute." *United States v. Batchelder*, 442 U.S. 114, 123, 99 S.Ct. 2198, 2204, 60 L.Ed.2d 755 (1979). Nothing in Mississippi law warned appellant that by committing a tort that caused $20,000 of actual damages, it could expect to incur a $1.6 million punitive damage award.

This due process question, serious as it is, should not be decided today. The argument was not appellant's principal submission to this Court. The analysis in the briefs and the discussion at oral argument were correspondingly abbreviated. Although the Court could assert jurisdiction over the due process question on the theory that the argument made here was a "mere enlargement" of the due process argument raised below, it would not be prudent to do so. Accordingly, I concur in the Court's judgment on this question and would leave for another day the consideration of these issues.

JUSTICE SCALIA, concurring in part and concurring in the judgment.

I join Part I (except for footnote 1) and Part III of the opinion of the Court, and concur in its judgment. As to Part II, I agree with Justice White that the question of our entertaining the issues there discussed should be resolved as a matter of law, and not of discretion, and I therefore join his opinion. The Court having chosen not to follow that course, I agree with Justice O'Connor regarding the basis on which our discretion should be exercised concerning the due process claim, and therefore join her opinion.

JUSTICE BLACKMUN, concurring in part and dissenting in part.*

C. APPELLATE REVIEW IN STATE COURT

NOTE ON APPELLATE REVIEW IN STATE COURT

In many states appellate procedure is a highly parochial body of law, having twists and turns entirely peculiar to that state. Compare Korn, Civil Jurisdiction of the New York Court of Appeals and Appellate Divisions, 16 Buffalo L.Rev. 307 (1967). In this respect, appellate procedure is different from trial court procedure. Trial court procedure in most states today is based either on the Federal Rules or, as in California and New York, on a system that has a close family resemblance to the Federal Rules. But federal appellate procedure has not been a similar model for the states. One important reason for this was that until 1968 there was no uniform federal appellate procedure, for it was only in that year that the Federal Rules of Appellate Procedure were promulgated. See Ward, The Federal Rules of Appellate Procedure, 28 Fed.B.J. 100 (1968). Before 1968, federal appellate procedure was chiefly prescribed in rules of each Circuit and these rules varied widely from each other. Related to this was the fact that the rules of the Circuits were in many respects outmoded, for example in requiring printed briefs and an appendix. Hence, if a state was inspired to reform its appellate procedure there was no federal model to use as a reference.

Two state models have been influential, however. These are the California appellate rules of 1943, adopted under the leadership of Chief Justice Phil Gibson and with the technical direction of Bernard Witkin, and the New Jersey rules adopted in 1948 after the comprehensive reorganization of that state's court system, under the leadership of Chief Justice Arthur Vanderbilt. The essential features of these systems may be said to be as follows:

    1. The final judgment rule is a basic but flexible premise. Whereas in New York, for example, many kinds of trial court rulings (e.g., on a motion to dismiss) are appealable of right to the Appellate Division, under the California and New Jersey systems trial court rulings are not ordinari-

---

* Justice Blackmun's opinion is omitted.

ly reviewable of right prior to appeal from a final judgment. On the other hand, in these states, the final judgment rule is both defined and administered without the attempts at precision that have characterized federal appellate procedural law. See, e.g., In re Marriage of Skelley, 18 Cal.3d 365, 134 Cal.Rptr. 197, 556 P.2d 297 (1976); City of East Orange v. Palmer, 52 N.J. 329, 245 A.2d 327 (1968), with which compare Scheinkman, Civil Jurisdiction of the New York Court of Appeals: The Rule and Role of Finality, 54 St. John L.Rev. 443 (1980), indicating the impenetrable complexity of the New York definition of "final judgment"; see also Kallay, A Study in Rule-Making by Decision: California Courts Adopt Federal Rule of Civil Procedure 54(b), 13 Sw.U.L.Rev. 87 (1982).

2. Means exist whereby interlocutory orders involving important or novel questions, or representing a serious blunder by the trial judge, can be reviewed at the discretion of the appellate court. In California this is done by liberal use of the extraordinary writs, which in effect are applications for interlocutory review. Many illustrations are found in the California cases in this book. For use of mandamus to provide appellate review at the pleading stage, see, e.g., Taylor v. Superior Court, 24 Cal.3d 890, 157 Cal. Rptr. 693, 598 P.2d 854 (1979). See also C.E.B., California Civil Writs (1970). In New Jersey, the counterpart is a provision simply that "the Appellate Division may grant leave to appeal, in the interest of justice, from an interlocutory order ＊ ＊ ＊." Rules Governing Courts of New Jersey 2:2–4 (1978).

3. Virtually all appeals from final judgments and applications for interlocutory review go from the trial court of general jurisdiction to the intermediate appellate court (the Court of Appeal in California, the Appellate Division of the Superior Court in New Jersey). The Supreme Court of the state exercises a secondary, highly selective reviewing authority whose primary function is the clarification or redefinition of the law.

It is in the light of this experience that the ABA Standards of Judicial Administration § 3.12 makes the following recommendation:

"(a) Final Judgment. Appellate review ordinarily should be available only upon the rendition of final judgment in the court from which appeal or application for review is taken.

"(b) Interlocutory Review. Orders other than final judgments ordinarily should be subject to immediate appellate review only at the discretion of the reviewing court where it determines that resolution of the questions of law on which the order is based will:

"(1) Materially advance the termination of the litigation or clarify further proceedings therein;

"(2) Protect a party from substantial and irreparable injury; or

"(3) Clarify an issue of general importance in the administration of justice."

D. THE APPELLATE "CRUNCH"

NOTE ON THE APPELLATE "CRUNCH"

The volume of appellate litigation has increased by geometric proportions over the last two decades. In response, many states that previously had a single level appellate system (i.e., a supreme court) have created intermediate appellate courts; procedural rules have been revised with an eye to streamlining procedure, especially from the court's point of view; much greater use is being made of para-judicial officials (clerks, etc.) at the appellate level; and much more systematic attention is being given to management of the caseflow in appellate courts. On all this see ABA Standards of Judicial Administration, Appellate Courts (1976); Carrington, Meador and Rosenberg, Justice on Appeal (1976); Meador, Appellate Courts: Staff and Process in the Crisis of Volume (Nat'l Center for State Courts 1974). Legislatures often try to relieve some classes of litigants from delay by requiring that they be given scheduling priority. See ABCNY Committee on Federal Legislation, The Impact of Civil Expediting Provisions on the United States Courts of Appeals, 37 The Record 19 (1982). Worthwhile discussions of specific aspects of these problems include Stolz, Federal Review of State Court Decisions of Federal Questions: The Need for Additional Appellate Capacity, 64 Calif.L.Rev. 871 (1976); Note, Unreported Decisions in the United States Court of Appeals, 63 Corn.L.Rev. 128 (1977); Note, Securing Uniformity of National Law: A Proposal for National Stare Decisis in the Courts of Appeals, 87 Yale L.J. 1219 (1978); Comment, Minnesota Supreme Court Prehearing Conference: An Empirical Evaluation, 63 Minn.L. Rev. 1221 (1979); Hellman, Central Staff in Appellate Courts: The Experience of the Ninth Circuit, 68 Calif.L.Rev. 937 (1980); Janes, Paras and Shapiro, The Appellate Settlement Conference Program in Sacramento, 56 Calif.St.Bar.J. 110 (1981); Comment, The California Supreme Court and Selective Review, 72 Calif.L.Rev. 720 (1984).

One other method of controlling the explosion in appellate litigation is to impose penalties on litigants for frivolous appeals, see C.C.P. 907, interpreted in Coleman v. Gulf Ins. Group, 41 Cal.3d 782, 226 Cal.Rptr. 90, 718 P.2d 77 (1986), and In re Marriage of Flaherty, 31 Cal.3d 637, 183 Cal.Rptr. 508, 646 P.2d 179 (1982), or, more drastically, to impose penalties on all unsuccessful appellants. The Supreme Court upheld a penalty of the latter type in Bankers Life & Casualty Co. v. Crenshaw, supra p. 1320, in a section of the opinion not reprinted above, saying that the penalty was reasonably related to the state's objective of discouraging frivolous appeals. On federal provisions relating to frivolous appeals, see Martineau, Frivolous Appeals: The Uncertain Federal Response, 1984 Duke L.J. 845.

E. EXTRAORDINARY RELIEF FROM JUDGMENTS

ACKERMANN v. UNITED STATES

Supreme Court of the United States, 1950.
340 U.S. 193, 71 S.Ct. 209, 95 L.Ed. 207.*

MR. JUSTICE MINTON delivered the opinion of the Court.

Petitioner Hans Ackermann filed a motion in the District Court for the Western District of Texas to set aside a judgment entered December 7, 1943, in that court cancelling his certificate of naturalization. The motion was filed March 25, 1948, pursuant to amended Rule 60(b) of the Federal Rules of Civil Procedure, 28 U.S.C.A., which became effective March 19, 1948. The United States filed a motion to dismiss petitioner's motion. The District Court denied petitioner's motion and the

* The Court's footnotes are omitted.

Court of Appeals affirmed. 178 F.2d 983. We granted certiorari. 339 U.S. 962, 70 S.Ct. 997.

The question is whether the District Court erred in denying the motion for relief under Rule 60(b).

Petitioner and his wife Frieda were natives of Germany. They were naturalized in 1938. They resided, as now, at Taylor, Texas, where petitioner and Max Keilbar owned and operated a German language newspaper. Frieda Ackermann wrote for the paper. She was a sister of Keilbar, who was also a native of Germany and who had been naturalized in 1933.

In 1942 complaints were filed against all three to cancel their naturalization on grounds of fraud. Petitioner and Keilbar were represented by counsel and answered the complaints. After an order of consolidation, trial of the three cases began November 1, 1943, and separate judgments were entered December 7, 1943, cancelling and setting aside the orders admitting them to citizenship. Keilbar appealed to the Court of Appeals, and by stipulation with the United States Attorney his case in that court was reversed, and the complaint against him was ordered dismissed. The Ackermanns did not appeal.

Petitioner in his motion here under consideration alleges that his "failure to appeal from said judgment is excusable" for the reason that he had no money or property other than his home in Taylor, Texas, owned by him and his wife and worth $2,500, "and the costs of transcribing the evidence and printing the record and brief on appeal were estimated at not less than $5,000.00." On December 11, 1943, petitioner was detained in an Alien Detention Station at Seagoville, Texas. Before time for appeal had expired, petitioner was advised by his attorney that he and his wife could not appeal on affidavits of inability to pay costs until they had "appropriated said home to the payment of such costs to the full extent of the proceeds of a sale thereof;" that this information distressed them, and they sought advice from W.F. Kelley, "Assistant Commissioner for Alien Control, Immigration and Naturalization Department," in whose custody petitioner and his wife were being held, "and he being a person in whom they had great confidence"; that Kelley on being informed of their financial condition and the advice of their attorney that it would be necessary for them to dispose of their home in order to appeal, advised them in substance to "hang on to their home," and told them further that they had lost their American citizenship and were stateless, and that they would be released at the end of the war; that relying upon Kelley's advice, they refrained from appealing from said judgments; that on April 29, 1944, after time for appeal had expired, they were interned, and on January 25, 1946, the Attorney General ordered them to depart within thirty days or be deported. They did not depart, and they have not been deported, although the orders of deportation are still outstanding. Petitioner further alleged that he would show that the judgment of December 7, 1943, was unlawful and erroneous by producing the record in the Keilbar case [Keilbar v. United States, 5 Cir., 144 F.2d 866].

The District Court on September 28, 1948, denied petitioner's motion to vacate the judgment of denaturalization, the court stating in the order that "there is no merit to said motion."

It will be noted that petitioner alleged in his motion that his failure to appeal was *excusable.* A motion for relief because of excusable neglect as provided in Rule 60(b)(1) must, by the rule's terms, be made not more than one year after the judgment was entered. The judgment here sought to be relieved from was more than four years old. It is immediately apparent that no relief on account of "excusable neglect" was available to this petitioner on the motion under consideration.

But petitioner seeks to bring himself with Rule 60(b)(6), which applies if "any other reason justifying relief" is present, as construed and applied in Klapprott v. United States, 335 U.S. 601, 69 S.Ct. 384, 389, 93 L.Ed. 266. The circumstances alleged in the motion which petitioner asserts bring him within Rule 60(b)(6) are that the denaturalization judgment was erroneous; that he did not appeal and raise that question because his attorney advised him he would have to sell his home to pay costs, while Kelley, the Alien Control officer, in whom he alleges he had confidence and upon whose advice he relied, told him "to hang on to their home" and that he would be released at the end of the war; and that these circumstances justify failure to appeal the denaturalization judgment.

We cannot agree that petitioner has alleged circumstances showing that his failure to appeal was justifiable. It is not enough for petitioner to allege that he had confidence in Kelley. On the allegations of the motion before us, Kelley was a stranger to petitioner. In that state of the pleadings there are two reasons why petitioner cannot be heard to say his neglect to appeal brings him within the rule. First, anything said by Kelley could not be used to relieve petitioner of his duty to take legal steps to protect his interest in litigation in which the United States was a party adverse to him. Munro v. United States, 303 U.S. 36, 58 S.Ct. 421, 82 L.Ed. 633; Burnham Chemical Co. v. Krug, D.C., 81 F.Supp. 911, 913, affirmed per curiam sub nom. Burnham Chemical Co. v. Chapman, 86 U.S.App.D.C. 412, 181 F.2d 288. Secondly, petitioner had no right to repose confidence in Kelley, a stranger. There is no allegation of any fact or circumstance which shows that Kelley had any undue influence over petitioner or practiced any fraud, deceit, misrepresentation, or duress upon him. There are no allegations of privity or any fiduciary relations existing between them. Indeed, the allegations of the motion all show the contrary. However, petitioner had a confidential adviser in his own counsel. Instead of relying upon that confidential adviser, he freely accepted the advice of a stranger, a source upon which he had no right to rely. Petitioner made a considered choice not to appeal, apparently because he did not feel that an appeal would prove to be worth what he thought was a required sacrifice of his home. His choice was a risk, but calculated and deliberate and such as follows a free choice. Petitioner cannot be relieved of such a choice because hindsight seems to indicate to him that his decision not to appeal was probably wrong, considering the outcome of the Keilbar case. There must be an end to litigation someday, and free, calculated, deliberate choices are not to be relieved from.

As further evidence of the inadequacy of petitioner's motion to bring himself within any division of Rule 60(b) which would excuse him from not having taken an appeal, we call attention to the fact that Keilbar got the record before the Court of Appeals, and it contained all the evidence that was introduced as to petitioner and his wife, who were tried together with Keilbar. The Ackermanns and Keilbar were related, yet no effort was made to get into the Court of Appeals and use the same record as to the evidence that Keilbar used. It certainly would not have taken five thousand dollars or one-tenth thereof for petitioner and his wife to have supplemented the Keilbar record with that pertaining to themselves and to prepare a brief, even if all of it were printed. We are further aware of the practice of the Courts of Appeals permitting litigants who are poor but not paupers to file typewritten records and briefs at a very small cost to them. With the same counsel representing petitioner as represented his kinsman Keilbar, and with Frieda Ackermann having funds sufficient to employ separate counsel, failure to appeal because of the fear of losing his home in defraying the expenses of the brief and record, makes it further evident that Rule 60(b) has no application to petitioner in this setting.

The Klapprott case was a case of extraordinary circumstances. Mr. Justice Black stated in the following words why the allegations in the Klapprott case, there taken as true, brought it within Rule 60(b)(6): "But petitioner's allegations set up an extraordinary situation which cannot fairly or logically be classified as mere 'neglect' on his part. The undenied facts set out in the petition reveal far more than a failure to defend the denaturalization charges due to inadvertence, indifference, or careless disregard of consequences. For before, at the time, and after the default judgment was entered, petitioner was held in jail in New York, Michigan, and the District of Columbia by the United States, his adversary in the denaturalization proceedings. Without funds to hire a lawyer, petitioner was defended by appointed counsel in the criminal cases. Thus petitioner's prayer to set aside the default judgment did not rest on mere allegations of 'excusable neglect.' The foregoing allegations and others in the petition tend to support petitioner's argument that he was deprived of any reasonable opportunity to make a defense to the criminal charges instigated by officers of the very United States agency which supplied the secondhand information upon which his citizenship was taken away from him in his absence. The basis of his petition was not that he had neglected to act in his own defense, but that in jail as he was, weakened from illness, without a lawyer in the denaturalization proceedings or funds to hire one, disturbed and fully occupied in efforts to protect himself against the gravest criminal charges, he was no more able to defend himself in the New Jersey court than he would have been had he never received notice of the charges." Klapprott v. United States, 335 U.S. 601, 613–614, 69 S.Ct. 384, 389, 93 L.Ed. 266.

By no stretch of imagination can the voluntary, deliberate, free, untrammeled choice of petitioner not to appeal compare with the Klapprott situation. Mr. Justice Black set forth in order the extraordinary circumstances alleged by Klapprott. We paraphrase them and give the comparable situation of Ackermann.

In the spring of 1942 Klapprott was ill, and the illness left him financially poor and unable to work. On May 12, 1942, proceedings were commenced in a New Jersey District Court to cancel his citizenship. As for Ackermann, when he was sued he was well, and had a home worth $2,500, one-half interest in a newspaper, and the means to employ counsel.

When complaint was served upon Klapprott, he had no money to hire a lawyer, and he wrote an answer to the complaint filed against him and a letter to the American Civil Liberties Union asking it to represent him without fee. Ackermann had the means to hire and did hire able counsel of his own choice who prepared and filed an answer for him.

In less than two months after the complaint was served on the penniless, ill Klapprott, he was arrested for conspiracy to violate the Selective Service Act, 50 U.S.C.A.Appendix § 301 et seq., and taken to New York and jailed in default of bond. His letter to the American Civil Liberties Union was taken by the Federal Bureau of Investigation before time for him to answer had expired, and was not mailed by that Bureau. Ackermann was never indicted or in jail from the time complaint was filed against him until after judgment, during all of which time he had the benefit of counsel and freedom of movement and action.

Within ten days after his arrest, Klapprott was defaulted in the citizenship proceedings in New Jersey. He was still in jail in New York. No evidence was offered to prove the complaint in the denaturalization proceedings, which complaint was verified on information and belief only. In Ackermann's case, no default was entered. He appeared in person and by counsel and had a trial in open court with able counsel to defend him. Much evidence was introduced and a record was made of it.

Klapprott was convicted in New York and sent to a penitentiary in Michigan. He was later transferred to the District of Columbia, where he was lodged in jail and tried on another charge, later dismissed. The New York conviction was reversed, but he had been in jail for about two years. He was then lodged at Ellis Island for deportation because his citizenship had been cancelled in the New Jersey proceedings where he had been defaulted.   While at Ellis Island, the motion to relieve from the default judgment cancelling his citizenship was prepared and filed, denied by the District Court and the Court of Appeals and finally sustained by this Court.   Ackermann was never under criminal charges or detained while the suit for cancellation of his citizenship was pending.   During all of that time he was free, well, and able to defend himself, and in that regard had able counsel representing him in a trial in open court.   Even after the judgment cancelling his citizenship, he had counsel and free access to him, although detained by the United States Government.

From a comparison of the situations shown by the allegations of Klapprott and Ackermann, it is readily apparent that the situations of the parties bore only the slightest resemblance to each other.   The comparison strikingly points up the difference between no choice and choice;   imprisonment and freedom of action;   no trial and trial;   no counsel and counsel;   no chance for negligence and inexcusable negligence.   Subsection 6 of Rule 60(b) has no application to the situation of petitioner.   Neither the circumstances of petitioner nor his excuse for not appealing is so extraordinary as to bring him within Klapprott or Rule 60(b)(6).

The motion for relief was properly denied, and the judgment is affirmed.

Affirmed.

No. 36, Frieda Ackermann v. United States, is a companion case to No. 35, and it was stipulated that the decision in No. 36 should be the same as in No. 35.   The judgment in No. 36 therefore is also affirmed.

Affirmed.

MR. JUSTICE CLARK took no part in the consideration or decision of this case.

MR. JUSTICE BLACK, with whom MR. JUSTICE FRANKFURTER and MR. JUSTICE DOUGLAS concur, dissenting.

The Court's interpretation of amended Rule 60(b) of the Federal Rules of Civil Procedure neutralizes the humane spirit of the Rule and thereby frustrates its purpose.   The Rule empowers courts to set aside judgments under five traditional, specified types of circumstances in which it would be inequitable to permit a judgment to stand.   But the draftsmen of the Rule did not intend that these specified grounds should prevent the granting of similar relief in other situations where fairness might require it.   Accordingly, there was added a broad sixth ground: "any other reason justifying relief from the operation of the judgment."   The Court nevertheless holds that the allegations of the present motions were not sufficient to justify the District Court in hearing evidence to determine whether justice would best be served by granting relief from the judgments against petitioners. * * *

* * *

In holding that the allegations of these motions are not even sufficient to justify the District Court in hearing evidence, the Court relies heavily on its assertion that petitioners "had no right to repose confidence in Kelley" because Kelley was a "stranger" to them. In the first place, Rule 60(b)'s broad grant of power to the District Court should not be constricted by the importation of the concept of legal "rights." Moreover, far from being a stranger, Kelley was the United States official who held petitioners in custody. Any person held by the United States should be able to repose confidence in the Government official entrusted with his custody. There are obvious reasons why this should be true in the case of the foreign born, less familiar with our customs than are our native citizens.

The Court also relies on the fact that the motions to set aside the judgments contain "no allegations of privity or any fiduciary relations existing" between petitioners and Kelley. Surely the liberalizing provisions of 60(b) should not be emasculated by common-law ideas of "privity" or "fiduciary relations." If relevant, however, I should think that the phrase "fiduciary relations" given its best meaning encompasses the relationship between petitioners and the official who held them in custody.

Finally, since the Court holds that the allegations of petitioners' motions were insufficient to justify the hearing of evidence by the District Court, I think it inappropriate for the Court to consider what purports to be its judicial knowledge of the cost of transcripts and the ability of litigants to file typewritten records and briefs. The motions refute any such knowledge on the part of these petitioners and I am satisfied that no such knowledge would be established if the District Court were permitted to try these cases.

The result of the Court's illiberal construction of 60(b) is that these foreign-born people, dependent on our laws for their safety and protection, are denied the right to appeal to the very court that held (on the Government's admission) that the judgment against their co-defendant was unsupported by adequate evidence. It does no good to have liberalizing rules like 60(b) if, after they are written, their arteries are hardened by this Court's resort to ancient common-law concepts. I would reverse.

NOTE ON PROCEDURES FOR RELIEF FROM A JUDGMENT

Historically there were three methods of obtaining relief from a judgment: (1) making a motion or other procedural device in the action in which the judgment was rendered; (2) bringing a separate suit in equity to set aside the judgment; and (3) in the case of a "void" judgment, awaiting the time when the judgment was relied on (for example, when an attempt was made to enforce it through execution) and defensively asserting that the judgment was void. For an instance of the latter type of attack, see, e.g., Arndt v. Griggs, 134 U.S. 316, 10 S.Ct. 557, 33 L.Ed. 918 (1890), noted supra p. 292. For a modern illustration, see Friedman v. State of New York, 24 N.Y.2d 528, 301 N.Y.S.2d 484, 249 N.E.2d 369 (1969); cf. In re Berry, 68 Cal.2d 137, 65 Cal.Rptr. 273, 436 P.2d 273 (1968). The separate suit in equity still may be employed when it can be shown that the motion procedure will not afford an adequate remedy. See, e.g., Bennett v. Hibernia Bank, 47 Cal.2d 540, 305 P.2d 20 (1956). However, the procedure of relief by motion in the court where the judgment was rendered has been enlarged by statute to include all the grounds formerly available through the other mechanisms for seeking relief. F.R.C.P. 60(b); compare C.C.P. 473, from which F.R.C.P. 60(b) was adapted. See also N.Y. C.P.L.R. 5015. Accordingly, the motion is generally the preferred procedure. See, e.g., Allen v. Cole Realty, Inc., 325 A.2d 19 (Maine 1974); Estate of Sanders, 40 Cal.3d 607, 221 Cal.Rptr. 432, 710 P.2d 232 (1985) (timeliness of motion to set aside judgment allegedly procured by fraud); Restatement Second of Judgments § 78. On the history of F.R.C.P. 60(b), see Moore and Rogers, Federal Relief from Civil Judgments, 55 Yale L.J. 623 (1946). See also Note, Relief from Final Judgment Under Rule 60(b)(1) Due to Judicial Errors of Law, 83 Mich.L.Rev. 1571 (1985).

There is one serious technical difficulty with F.R.C.P. 60(b). It provides for six categories of relief, of which the first three are subject to a one-year limitation period while the last three are not. Yet the subdivisions that are free of the limitations period seem to overlap those that are subject to the limitation, certainly so if the historical origins of the categories are examined. In particular, it seems impossible to distinguish "mistake * * * or excusable neglect" referred to in 60(b)(1) from "any other reason justifying relief," referred to in 60(b)(6). Courts that are stingy about granting relief give a narrow reading to 60(b)(6), as Ackermann v. United States indicates. But other decisions give it a more generous interpretation. See United States v. Karahalias, 205 F.2d 331 (2d Cir.1953); Liljeberg v. Health Services Acquisition Corp., supra p. 1083. The result is a great deal of confusion. See generally Comment, Rule 60(b): Survey and Proposal for General Reform, 60 Calif.L.Rev. 531 (1972); Kane, Relief From Federal Judgments: A Morass Unrelieved by Rule, 30 Hast.L.J. 41 (1978). A somewhat similar problem arises under C.C.P. 473. This section requires that application for relief be made within six months, but does not preclude relief by motion or independent suit when the judgment from which relief is sought is "void" or was procured by "extrinsic" fraud. The distinctions are blurred. See 8 Witkin 550 et seq.

A number of other problems recur in administering the motion procedure. An important one is that the statutory provisions do not generally distinguish between relief from a default judgment and relief after a contest on the merits. See, however, the special provisions in C.C.P. 473 concerning default judgment after service by publication. Yet the cases show a strong tendency readily to grant relief from a default but to give relief after a contested action only in the case of plain fraud or mistake amounting to inadequacy of representation. See Restatement Second of Judgments §§ 65 et seq.; Comment, Relief from Default Judgments Under Rule 60(b), 49 Ford.L.Rev. 956 (1981). Another problem is whether the neglect or mistake of a party's attorney should be attributed to the party. See United States v. Cirami, 535 F.2d 736 (2d Cir.1976), supra p. 984. And there is the apparently intractable problem of distinguishing between that kind of fraud against which a party should be wary, and hence from which relief will not be permitted, and that kind of fraud upon which relief will be granted. The traditional statement of the distinction is between fraud that is "intrinsic" (no relief) and that which is "extrinsic."

Generally on the problem of relief from a judgment, see Restatement Second of Judgments, ch. 5; James & Hazard §§ 12.13 et seq.

KULCHAR v. KULCHAR

Supreme Court of California, 1969.
1 Cal.3d 467, 82 Cal.Rptr. 489, 462 P.2d 17.

TRAYNOR, CHIEF JUSTICE.

Plaintiff appeals from an order of the Superior Court of San Mateo County modifying an interlocutory decree of divorce to relieve defendant of liability to pay federal income taxes assessed against the parties on income accruing to plaintiff in New Zealand.

Plaintiff secured an interlocutory decree of divorce from defendant on July 3, 1964. The decree included the disposition of the community and separate property of the parties.[1] The decree provided, in part: "Defendant shall indemnify and hold plaintiff free and harmless in the matter of any monies due any taxing agency, whether Federal, State, or County, for the calendar years prior to 1964."

In 1966, following the divorce proceedings defendant received a tax assessment of approximately $22,000 for federal income taxes based on theretofore undisclosed income accumulated during the marriage by a New Zealand corporation in plaintiff's name. Defendant moved to modify the divorce decree to relieve him of any liability for taxes on the New Zealand income on the grounds of extrinsic fraud and extrinsic mistake. After a hearing on defendant's motion, the trial court concluded that the tax provision in the decree "was included and approved by the parties as a result of the mutual mistake of the parties and further, that there was no intent of the parties that defendant should pay United States Federal income tax resulting from income to plaintiff in New Zealand." The court struck the tax provision from the decree "because of the mutual mistake of the parties."

Under certain circumstances a court, sitting in equity, can set aside or modify a valid final judgment. (Olivera v. Grace (1942) 19 Cal.2d 570, 575–576, 122 P.2d 564, 140 A.L.R. 1328; Caldwell v. Taylor (1933) 218 Cal. 471, 475, 23 P.2d 758, 88 A.L.R. 1194.) This power, however, can only be exercised when the circumstances of the case are sufficient to overcome the strong policy favoring the finality of judgments. "A basic requirement of an action which can lead to a valid judgment is that a procedure should be adopted which in the normal case will give to the parties an opportunity for a fair trial which is reasonable in view of the requirements of public policy in the particular type of case. If this requirement is met, a judgment awarded in an action is not void merely because the particular individual against whom it was rendered did not in fact have an opportunity to present his claim or defense before an impartial tribunal. . . . [P]ublic policy requires that only in exceptional circumstances should the consequences of res judicata be denied to a valid judgment." (Rest., Judgments, § 118, com. a.)

---

1. There was no formal property settlement agreement. All provisions of the decree relating to the distribution of property were submitted to the court on the stipulation of the parties.

Interlocutory divorce decrees are res judicata as to all questions determined therein, including the property rights of the parties. (In re Williams' Estate (1950) 36 Cal.2d 289, 292, 223 P.2d 248, 22 A.L.R.2d 716; Adamson v. Adamson (1962) 209 Cal.App.2d 492, 501, 26 Cal.Rptr. 236.) If a property settlement is incorporated in the divorce decree, the settlement is merged with the decree and becomes the final judicial determination of the property rights of the parties. (Broome v. Broome (1951) 104 Cal.App.2d 148, 154–155, 231 P.2d 171.) Thus, the rules governing extrinsic fraud and mistake apply to alimony awards and property settlements incorporated in divorce decrees. (Jorgensen v. Jorgensen (1948) 32 Cal.2d 13, 18–23, 193 P.2d 728; Cameron v. Cameron (1948) 88 Cal.App.2d 585, 595–597, 199 P.2d 443; Hosner v. Skelly (1946) 72 Cal.App.2d 457, 461, 164 P.2d 573; Horton v. Horton (1941) 18 Cal.2d 579, 584–585, 116 P.2d 605; Hendricks v. Hendricks (1932) 216 Cal. 321, 323–324, 14 P.2d 83; Godfrey v. Godfrey (1939) 30 Cal.App.2d 370, 378–380, 86 P.2d 357; Smith v. Smith (1954) 125 Cal.App.2d 154, 161–164, 270 P.2d 613.)

Extrinsic fraud usually arises when a party is denied a fair adversary hearing because he has been "deliberately kept in ignorance of the action or proceeding, or in some other way fraudulently prevented from presenting his claim or defense." (3 Witkin, Cal. Procedure, p. 2124.) "Where the unsuccessful party has been prevented from exhibiting fully his case, by fraud or deception practiced on him by his opponent, as by keeping him away from court, a false promise of a compromise; or whether the defendant never had knowledge of the suit being kept in ignorance by the acts of the plaintiff; or where an attorney fraudulently or without authority assumes to represent a party and connives at his defeat; or where the attorney regularly employed corruptly sells out his client's interest to the other side,—these, and similar cases which show that there has never been a real contest in the trial or hearing of the case, are reasons for which a new suit may be sustained to set aside and annul the former judgment or decree, and open the case for a new and fair hearing." (United States v. Throckmorton (1878) 98 U.S. 61, 65–66, 25 L.Ed. 93.)

The right to relief has also been extended to cases involving extrinsic mistake. (Bacon v. Bacon (1907) 150 Cal. 477, 491–492, 89 P. 317; Olivera v. Grace, supra, 19 Cal.2d at p. 577, 122 P.2d 564.) "In some cases . . . the ground of relief is not so much the fraud or other misconduct of the defendant as it is the excusable neglect of the plaintiff to appear and present his claim or defense. If such neglect results in an unjust judgment, *without a fair adversary hearing*, the basis for equitable relief is present, and is often called 'extrinsic mistake.' " (3 Witkin, Cal. Procedure, p. 2128.)

Extrinsic mistake is found when a party becomes incompetent but no guardian ad litem is appointed (Olivera v. Grace, supra, 19 Cal.2d at p. 577, 122 P.2d 564; Dei Tos v. Dei Tos (1951) 105 Cal.App.2d 81, 84–85, 232 P.2d 873; Winslow v. McCarthy (1918) 39 Cal.App. 337, 340, 178 P. 720); when one party relies on another to defend (Weitz v. Yankosky (1966) 63 Cal.2d 849, 855–856, 48 Cal.Rptr. 620, 409 P.2d 700; Roussey

v. Ernest W. Hahn, Inc. (1967) 251 Cal.App.2d 251, 256, 59 Cal.Rptr. 399); when there is reliance on an attorney who becomes incapacitated to act (Jeffords v. Young (1929) 98 Cal.App. 400, 405–406, 277 P. 163; Smith v. Busniewski (1952) 115 Cal.App.2d 124, 127–128, 251 P.2d 697; Antonsen v. Pacific Container Co. (1941) 48 Cal.App.2d 535, 538, 120 P.2d 148); when a mistake led a court to do what it never intended (Sullivan v. Lumsden (1897) 118 Cal. 664, 669, 50 P. 777; Bacon v. Bacon, supra, 150 Cal. at pp. 492–493, 89 P. 317); when a mistaken belief of one party prevented proper notice of the action (Aldabe v. Aldabe (1962) 209 Cal.App.2d 453, 475, 26 Cal.Rptr. 208; Boyle v. Boyle (1929) 97 Cal.App. 703, 706, 276 P. 118); or when the complaining party was disabled at the time the judgment was entered (Watson v. Watson (1958) 161 Cal.App.2d 35, 39–40, 235 P.2d 1011; Saunders v. Saunders (1958) 157 Cal.App.2d 67, 72–73, 320 P.2d 131; Evry v. Tremble (1957) 154 Cal.App.2d 444, 447–449, 316 P.2d 49). Relief has also been extended to cases involving negligence of a party's attorney in not properly filing an answer (Hallett v. Slaughter (1943) 22 Cal.2d 552, 556–557, 140 P.2d 3; Turner v. Allen (1961) 189 Cal.App.2d 753, 757–760, 11 Cal.Rptr. 630); and mistaken belief as to immunity from suit (Bartell v. Johnson (1943) 60 Cal.App.2d 432, 436–437, 140 P.2d 878).[2]

Relief is denied, however, if a party has been given notice of an action and has not been prevented from participating therein. He has had an opportunity to present his case to the court and to protect himself from mistake or from any fraud attempted by his adversary. (Jorgensen v. Jorgensen, supra, 32 Cal.2d 13 at p. 18, 193 P.2d 728; Westphal v. Westphal (1942) 20 Cal.2d 393, 397, 126 P.2d 105; Gale v. Witt (1948) 31 Cal.2d 362, 367, 188 P.2d 755.) Moreover, a mutual mistake that might be sufficient to set aside a contract is not sufficient to set aside a final judgment. The principles of res judicata demand that the parties present their entire case in one proceeding. "Public policy requires that pressure be brought upon litigants to use great care in preparing cases for trial and in ascertaining all the facts. A rule which would permit the re-opening of cases previously decided because of error or ignorance during the progress of the trial would in a large measure vitiate the effects of the rules of res judicata." (Rest., Judgments, § 126, com. a.) Courts deny relief, therefore, when the fraud or mistake is "intrinsic"; that is, when it "goes to the merits of the prior proceedings, which should have been guarded against by the plaintiff at that time." (Comment, Equitable Relief From Judgments, Orders and Decrees Obtained by Fraud (1934) 23 Cal.L.Rev. 79, 83–84; see Pico v. Cohn (1891) 91 Cal. 129, 134, 25 P. 970, 27 P. 537, 13 L.R.A. 336; Hendricks v. Hendricks, supra, 216 Cal. at pp. 323–324, 14 P.2d 83.)

Relief is also denied when the complaining party has contributed to the fraud or mistake giving rise to the judgment thus obtained. (Ham-

---

2. The decisions in both *Hallett* and *Bartell* have been criticized. (See Comment (1943) 31 Cal.L.Rev. 600.) "The cases on *intrinsic fraud*, involving perjury, false documents and other reprehensible conduct by the adverse party, are far more compelling, yet relief is uniformly denied for good reason. . . . The *Hallett* and *Bartell* cases involved no true extrinsic factors in the accepted sense, and they raise serious questions as to the practical finality of any default judgment." (3 Witkin, Cal. Procedure, p. 2130.)

mell v. Britton (1941) 19 Cal.2d 72, 80, 119 P.2d 333; Rudy v. Slotwinsky (1925) 73 Cal.App. 459, 465, 238 P. 783; Rest., Judgments, § 129.) "If the complainant was guilty of negligence in permitting the fraud to be practiced or the mistake to occur equity will deny relief." (Wilson v. Wilson (1942) 55 Cal.App.2d 421, 427, 130 P.2d 782, 785.)

Whether the case involves intrinsic or extrinsic fraud or mistake is not determined abstractly. "It is necessary to examine the facts in the light of the policy that a party who failed to assemble all his evidence at the trial should not be privileged to relitigate a case, as well as the policy permitting a party to seek relief from a judgment entered in a proceeding in which he was deprived of a fair opportunity fully to present his case." (Jorgensen v. Jorgensen, supra, 32 Cal.2d 13 at p. 19, 193 P.2d 728, at p. 732.)

The evidence in the present case establishes that it is a case in which a party "failed to assemble all his evidence at the trial." Defendant testified that he knew of the New Zealand holdings prior to the divorce and that plaintiff was receiving $640 every four months from New Zealand. In defendant's divorce questionnaire, circulated to determine the extent of marital property holdings, expenses and income, he listed as plaintiff's separate property "50% stock interest in David Lloyd Co., Ltd.,—a New Zealand holding corporation for many subsidiary companies (cement, coal, paper)—exact worth unknown to defendant—estimated to run into millions of dollars." In a letter sent by defendant's attorney to plaintiff's attorney in which the principal points of the property settlement were summarized, defendant proposed to transfer to plaintiff "any interest he may have in her holdings in New Zealand." Plaintiff also knew of the holdings but did not know of their value or their tax consequences. In 1957 when preparing income tax returns, an attorney, who later represented defendant in the divorce action, made some inquiry into the nature of the New Zealand income at the request of defendant. The attorney abandoned further investigation after plaintiff stated that a law firm known to defendant's attorney had advised her that the New Zealand income was not taxable. The attorney knew that the New Zealand holdings were "sizable." Both parties testified that the tax provision was included in the decree because of an audit being conducted by the Internal Revenue Service with respect to an unrelated transaction by defendant.

Clearly the present case does not involve the failure of one spouse to disclose fully the assets to be divided upon separation. (See Taylor v. Taylor (1923) 192 Cal. 71, 218 P. 756, 51 A.L.R. 1074; Milekovich v. Quinn (1919) 40 Cal.App. 537, 181 P. 256.) The duty to disclose arises out of the fiduciary relationship between the husband and wife. (Vai v. Bank of America (1961) 56 Cal.2d 329, 337–340, 15 Cal.Rptr. 71, 364 P.2d 247; Jorgensen v. Jorgensen, supra, 32 Cal.2d 13 at pp. 19–21, 193 P.2d 728.) There is no evidence that the wife withheld any information relevant to the nature of her New Zealand income.

The factual situation in the present case is analogous to that in Jorgensen v. Jorgensen, supra. In *Jorgensen* the husband disclosed all known assets of the parties. The husband claimed certain assets as his separate property. The wife and her attorney accepted the husband's statements at face value without any independent investigation. Subsequent to the divorce decree, however, they learned that some of the assets the husband claimed as separate property were actually community property, in which the wife was entitled to a one-half interest. The wife was denied the right to set aside the property settlement agreement. "If the wife and her attorney are satisfied with the husband's classification of the property as separate or community, the wife cannot reasonably contend that fraud was committed or that there was such mistake as to allow her to overcome the finality of a judgment. . . . Plaintiff is barred from obtaining equitable relief by her admission that she and her attorney did not investigate the facts, choosing instead to rely on the statements of the husband as to what part of the disclosed property was community property." (Jorgensen v. Jorgensen, supra, 32 Cal.2d 13 at pp. 22–23, 193 P.2d 728, at p. 734; see also, Cameron v. Cameron, supra, 88 Cal.App.2d 585 at pp. 595–597, 199 P.2d 443 wherein the holding of *Jorgensen* was found controlling.)

In the present case both parties knew of the New Zealand assets, but the husband and his attorney chose not to investigate their taxability. The property settlement agreement expressly covered unknown tax liability. Having had full opportunity to consider all income of the wife and its concurrent tax consequences, the husband cannot now complain of the added tax burden.

The order is reversed.

———

NOTE ON FINAL FINALITY

A common law counterpart of Rule 60(b) as to a judgment that has been affirmed is to petition for recall of the appellate court's order of affirmation. See Comment, Recall of Appellate Mandates in Federal Civil Litigation, 64 Corn.L.Rev. 704 (1979).

*

INDEX

References are to Pages

FEDERAL COURTS—Cont'd
"Necessary" party and, 731–737, 739
Permissive joinder and, 729
Unincorporated associations and, 64–65, 822–823
Compulsory joinder and, 731–737, 739
Corporations, 524, 819
See also Capacity; Corporations
Cross-claims, 747–750
Erie doctrine, 558–615
See also *Erie* Doctrine
Fiduciary claimants, 808
Individuals, 524
Appearing in representative capacity, 818
Interpleader, 525, 773–774
"Necessary" party and, 731–737, 739
Permissive joinder and, 729
Unincorporated associations, 64–65, 524, 822–823
See also Capacity
Federal government litigation, 527
Federal question jurisdiction, 16, 65, 525–526
Federal defenses, 525, 526–527
Implied causes of action, 65, 525–526
Sufficiency of the complaint and, 65
"Well pleaded complaint" rule, 525
Foreign government litigation, 528
Limited nature of federal jurisdiction, 523
Pendent jurisdiction, 64–66, 528–547, 710–713, 715, 731–737, 739, 747–748, 749–750, 752
Counterclaims and, 531, 710–713, 715
Cross-claims and, 747–750
Intervention and, 752
"Necessary" party and, 731–737, 739
Pendent claim jurisdiction, 64, 66, 530–532, 538–547
Pendent party (ancillary) jurisdiction, 66, 528–538, 545–547
Removal from and remand to state court, 538–544
Removal jurisdiction, 526–527, 538–544
Statutory provisions, 523–528
Transfer jurisdiction, 527–528
See also Venue, Federal rules
Jury trial,
See Jury Trial
Law applied in federal courts,
See *Erie* Doctrine
Pendent jurisdiction,
See Jurisdiction, this topic
Removal jurisdiction,
See Jurisdiction, this topic
Rulemaking authority, 17–18
Transfer jurisdiction,
See Jurisdiction, this topic
Trial courts, 15–16
See also Jurisdiction, this topic
Venue,
See Venue, Federal rules

FEDERAL QUESTION JURISDICTION
See Federal Courts, Jurisdiction

FEDERAL RULES OF CIVIL PROCEDURE
Adoption by states, 28
Authority for adoption of, 17–18
Background, 27–28
Notice pleading under, 90, 94, 96–97, 102–104, 105, 897–900
Principal features, 28

FIDUCIARY PARTIES
See also Capacity; Nominal Parties; Real Party in Interest Rule
Fiduciary claimants, 804–809
Diversity jurisdiction, 808
Parens patriae, suits by sovereigns as, 808–809
Real party in interest rule, 797–800, 802–803, 807
Res judicata effects, 803, 808
Suits "for the use of" (ex rel.), 803
Insured defendant, 809–816
Conflicts of interest between insurer and insured, 816
Direct action statutes, 815–816
Discovery of insurance coverage, 816
Insurer's duty to settle, 809–816

FIELD CODE
Legislative reform of procedure, 27, 93

FINAL JUDGMENT RULE
See Appellate Review, Federal procedure

FORUM NON CONVENIENS
Generally, 427–437
Conditional dismissal, 436
Federal courts, 427–435, 436–437
See also Venue, Federal rules
Foreign nationals, actions against, 434, 437
Injunction against prosecution of action elsewhere, compared, 437
State courts, 435–436
Territorial jurisdiction doctrine compared, 435

FORUM SELECTION CLAUSES
See Jurisdiction

FULL FAITH AND CREDIT
See Recognition of Judgments

GARNISHMENT
See Attachment; Jurisdiction, Attachment, garnishment or sequestration

GENERAL APPEARANCE
See Appearance

GERMANY, WEST
Civil procedure, 975–981

GRAND JURY
See also Jury Trial, Selection of the jury

†